UK GAAP 2019

Application of FRS 100-104 in the UK

Rob Carrington

Larissa Connor

Diego Fernandez

Archibald Groenewald

Prahalad Halgeri

Jane Hurworth

Maria Kingston

Dean Lockhart

Sharon MacIntyre

Anna Malcolm

Amanda Marrion

Tina Patel

Anna Pickup

Michael Pratt

Timothy Rogerson

Claire Taylor

Michael Varila

EY
Building a better
working world

WILEY

About this book

UK GAAP 2019 is the third edition of the EY publication on UK GAAP following the replacement of all previous UK accounting standards with new financial reporting standards. The original publication, New UK GAAP 2015, was published in 2015 and a revised edition, UK GAAP 2017, was published in 2017. This publication has been fully revised and updated in order to:

- incorporate the amendments made to FRSs 100-104 in December 2016, May 2017, July 2017 and December 2017. This includes the *Amendments to FRS 102 – The Financial Reporting Standard applicable in the UK and Republic of Ireland – Triennial review 2017 and Incremental improvements and clarifications* (published in December 2017). (Triennial review 2017) The changes made by the Triennial review 2017 are discussed in each relevant chapter;

- include the changes to legal requirements for UK companies and LLPs introduced since the previous edition; and

- provide further insight on the many issues relating to the practical application of the new UK accounting standards, based on the extensive experience of the book's authors in dealing with recent day-to-day issues. In particular, additional guidance on accounting for group reconstructions, including hive-up, hive-down and hive-across transactions, has been included in Chapter 17.

This book comprises 34 chapters. Each chapter includes a detailed list of contents and list of illustrative examples. The book contains an index of references to standards and interpretations.

FRS 101 – *Reduced Disclosure Framework – Disclosure exemptions from EU-adopted IFRS for qualifying entities* – uses the recognition and measurement principles of International Financial Reporting Standards (IFRS). In certain circumstances, FRS 102 also refers entities to IFRS. Detailed guidance on applying IFRS can be found in EY's publication, EY International GAAP 2019®.

Preface

With effect from accounting periods beginning on or after 1 January 2015 (or, for small entities that choose to apply the small entities regime and micro entities that choose to apply the micro entities regime, accounting periods beginning on or after 1 January 2016), all previous UK GAAP was replaced with new Financial Reporting Standards (FRSs 100-105) along with the associated accounting requirements of the Companies Act 2006 (CA 2006).

Since the publication of UK GAAP 2017, further amendments have been made to FRSs 100-104. The most significant of these were as a result of the first triennial review of the new standards. When FRS 102 was issued originally in March 2013, the FRC indicated that it would be reviewed every three years. The first triennial review was completed in December 2017 and revised versions of FRSs 100-104 were issued in March 2018 reflecting those amendments as well as incorporating amendments issued subsequent to the previous versions of the standards. The Triennial review 2017 amendments are mandatory for accounting periods beginning on or after 1 January 2019. These amendments can be adopted early provided that all are applied at the same time although there are two exceptions to this general rule.

The Triennial review 2017 amendments were developed in response to stakeholder feedback and therefore address a number of implementation issues reported to the FRC, many of which were highlighted in the previous edition of this publication. In our view, the principal changes to FRS 102 which are likely to have the most impact relate to:

- the introduction of an accounting policy choice for entities that rent investment property to other group entities, to reclassify those properties as property, plant and equipment and measure those properties either at cost (less depreciation or impairment) or at fair value;

- the introduction of more guidance supporting the conditions for classifying a financial instrument as 'basic', including a principles-based approach for classification of a debt instrument as a 'basic' financial instrument. Other changes to financial instrument accounting include an amendment to allow loans with two way compensation clauses (common in social housing loans) to be classified as 'basic' financial instruments and guidance on debt-for-equity swaps;

- for small entities, the ability to initially measure a loan from a person within a directors' group of close family members that includes at least one shareholder at transaction price rather than present value;

- a revised definition of separable intangible assets acquired in a business combination, which is likely to result in fewer intangible assets being separated from goodwill. However, entities may choose to separately recognise additional intangible assets if this provides useful information to the entity and to the users of its financial statements;

- an amended definition of a financial institution, which removes references to 'generate wealth' and 'manage risk' as well as eliminating stockbrokers and retirement benefit plans from the definition. This is intended to reduce interpretational difficulties and the number of entities meeting the definition of a financial institution; and

- an amendment to allow the tax effect of gift aid payments by subsidiaries to their charitable parents to be taken into account at the reporting date when it is probable that the gift aid payment will be made in the following nine months.

Following consultation, the FRC did not introduce elements of IFRS 9 – *Financial Instruments*, IFRS 15 – *Revenue from Contracts with Customers* – and IFRS 16 – *Leases* – into FRS 102 in the Triennial review 2017. The FRC's current intention is to consider major changes to IFRS on a case-by-case basis and to monitor any implementation issues arising before any consultation process begins.

Going forward, the FRC now envisages that FRS 102 will be subject to periodic review every four to five years rather than the three year cycle originally envisaged. The reason for the change in time frame is to allow time for experience of the most recent edition of FRS 102 to emerge before seeking stakeholder feedback. However, the FRC will continue to assess emerging issues as they arise and therefore it is possible that there will be amendments issued outside the regular review cycle.

Since the publication of EY UK GAAP 2017, the FRC has issued amendments to FRS 101 with the main purpose of providing disclosure exemptions from IFRS 16 and to reflect the EU endorsement of IFRS 9. The amended definition of a financial institution discussed above also applies to FRS 101.

On 29 March 2017, the UK Government started the legal process of negotiating a withdrawal by the UK from the European Union (EU). Under the provisions of the relevant laws and treaties, the UK will leave the EU by 29 March 2019, unless either a deal is reached which results in a change to the date of departure, or the negotiation period is extended by unanimous consent of the European Council. On 14 November 2018 a *Draft Agreement on the Withdrawal of the United Kingdom from the European Union* was published. At the time of writing this publication, the draft agreement is subject to approval of the UK parliament. This approval is uncertain. Other scenarios remain a possibility.

After the EU referendum result, the FRC issued a press notice confirming that companies must continue to abide by the regulations under UK law, including those derived from EU law and continue with implementation plans for legislation that is still to come into effect. Many requirements that derive from EU legislation, treaties and directives have been directly incorporated into UK company law. As a result, even in the event of EU legislation ceasing to apply, UK financial and reporting regulations will not change until applicable company law and regulations are amended. In particular, the application of EU adopted IFRS is enshrined in the CA 2006 and nothing will change in that respect without a change to the CA 2006.

The Accounts and Reports (Amendment) (EU Exit) Regulations 2018 were laid in draft before Parliament on 31 October 2018. This draft Statutory Instrument amends certain provisions of the CA 2006 that refer to the EU, EEA or entities within these areas. The timing of the effective date of this proposed legislation depends on whether or not a transition period is agreed with the EU.

The UK will also need to establish its policy on the endorsement of future IFRSs. It appears likely, at the time of writing this publication, that a UK endorsement process will be established although any details are yet to be published.

Given the uncertain nature of the final terms of the UK's withdrawal from the EU, the final form of the draft legislation described above and the extent of further legislative and regulatory changes in the UK affecting the financial reporting framework, the matters referred to above are subject to change.

FRS 102 is much shorter in length than either IFRS or previous UK GAAP and, as a result, is less prescriptive on many issues. This publication includes our views on the judgemental areas we believe are likely to be most common in practice based on our experience of applying the new standards and similar issues encountered in applying IFRS. As experience of applying FRS 102 grows over time, we expect our views will continue to evolve. It is not possible for this publication to cover every aspect of company reporting. For some of the more complicated or less common areas which are not covered by FRS 102 and for which IFRSs provide relevant guidance, further explanations can be found in our publication International GAAP® 2019.

****

We are deeply indebted to many of our colleagues within the UK organisation of EY for their selfless assistance and support in the publication of this book.

Our thanks go particularly to those who reviewed, edited and assisted in the preparation of drafts, most notably: Mike Bonham, Tony Clifford, Tim Denton, Bernd Kremp, Richard Moore and Kirsty Smith.

Our thanks also go to everyone who directly or indirectly contributed to the book's creation, including the following members of the Financial Reporting Group in the UK: David Bradbery, Denise Brand, and Mqondisi Ndlovu.

We also thank Jeremy Gugenheim for his assistance with the production technology throughout the period of writing.

London, November 2018			
	Rob Carrington	*Maria Kingston*	*Anna Pickup*
	Larissa Connor	*Dean Lockhart*	*Michael Pratt*
	Diego Fernandez	*Sharon MacIntyre*	*Timothy Rogerson*
	Archibald Groenewald	*Anna Malcolm*	*Claire Taylor*
	Prahalad Halgeri	*Amanda Marrion*	*Michael Varila*
	Jane Hurworth	*Tina Patel*	

List of chapters

References and abbreviations

The following references and abbreviations are used in this book:

References in index of standards:

Foreword.19	Paragraph 19 of the Foreword to Accounting Standards issued by the FRC (March 2018)
FRS 100 Summary (i)	Paragraph i of the Summary of FRS 100
FRS 100.4	Paragraph 4 of FRS 100
FRS 100 Appendix I	Appendix I:Glossary to FRS 100
FRS 100.AG7	Paragraph 7 of the Application Guidance to FRS 100
FRS 101.10	Paragraph 10 of FRS 101
FRS 101 Appendix I Table 1	Table 1 of Appendix I to FRS 101
FRS 101 Appendix III.2	Paragraph 2 of Appendix III to FRS 101
FRS 101.BC15	Paragraph 15 of the Basis for Conclusions to FRS 101
FRS 102.1A.7	Paragraph 7 of Section 1A of FRS 102
FRS 102.23.9	Paragraph 9 of Section 23 of FRS 102
FRS 102.PBE34.89	Paragraph PBE34.89 of Section 34 of FRS 102
FRS 102 Appendix I	Appendix I of FRS 102: Glossary
FRS 102 Appendix II	Appendix II of FRS 102: Table of equivalence for company law terminology
FRS 102 Appendix III.5	Paragraph 5 of Appendix III of FRS 102: Note on legal requirements
FRS 102 Appendix IV.1	Paragraph 1 of Appendix IV to FRS 102: Republic of Ireland legal references
FRS 102.BC.B2.7	Paragraph B2.7 of the Basis for Conclusions to FRS 102
FRS 103.1	Paragraph 1 of FRS 103
FRS 103.IG2.15	Paragraph 15 of Section 2 of the Implementation Guidance to accompany FRS 103
FRS 103 Appendix II.5	Paragraph 5 of Appendix II to FRS 103: Definition of an insurance contract
FRS 103.BC18	Paragraph 18 of the Basis for Conclusions to FRS 103

FRS 104.1	Paragraph 1 of FRS 104
FRS 105.1	Paragraph 1 of FRS 105
FRS 11.9	Paragraph 9 of FRS 11
SSAP 19.11	Paragraph 11 of SSAP 19
FRSSE 6.51	Paragraph 6.51 of the Financial Reporting Standard for Smaller Entities
IFRS 1 Appendix A	Appendix A of IFRS 1
IFRS 3.29	Paragraph 29 of IFRS 3
IFRS 4.IG70	Paragraph 70 of the Implementation Guidance to IFRS 4
IFRS 10 Appendix B.98	Paragraph 98 of Appendix B to IFRS 10
IAS 1.12	Paragraph 12 of IAS 1
IAS 27.15 (2012)	Paragraph 15 of the version of IAS 27 effective in 2012
IFRIC 18.BC22	Paragraph 22 of the Basis for Conclusions to IFRIC 18
s395(2)	Section 395 subsection (2) of the Companies Act 2006
s408 (LLP)	Section 408 of The Limited Liability Partnerships (Accounts and Audit) (Application of Companies Act 2006) Regulations 2008 (SI 2008/1911)
Regulations 6(2)	Paragraph 6(2) of the Large and Medium-sized Companies and Groups (Accounts and Reports) Regulations 2008 (SI 2008/1910)
1 Sch 55	Paragraph 55 of Schedule 1 to the Large and Medium-sized Companies and Groups (Accounts and Reports) Regulations 2008 (SI 2008/1910)
Regulations (SC) 8	Paragraph 8 of the Small Companies and Groups (Accounts and Directors' Report) Regulations 2008 (SI 2008/409)
1 Sch 1C (SC)	Paragraph 1C of Schedule 1 to the Small Companies and Groups (Accounts and Directors' Report) Regulations 2008 (SI 2008/409)
LLP Regulations 3	Paragraph 3 of The Large and Medium-sized Limited Liability Partnerships (Accounts) Regulations 2008 (SI 2008/1913)
1 Sch 1 (LLP)	Paragraph 1 of Schedule 1 to The Large and Medium-sized Limited Liability Partnerships (Accounts) Regulations 2008 (SI 2008/1913)
LLP SC Regulations 6	Paragraph 6 of The Small Limited Liability Partnerships (Accounts) Regulations 2008 (SI 2008/1912)

1 Sch 10(2) (LLP SC)	Paragraph 10(2) of Schedule 1 to the Small Limited Liability Partnerships (Accounts) Regulations 2008 (SI 2008/1912)
TECH 02/17BL	Technical Release 02/17BL: *Guidance on Realised and Distributable Profits under the Companies Act 2006* issued by the ICAEW and ICAS (April 2017)
DTR 7.2	Paragraph 7.2 of the Disclosure and Transparency Rules
LR 11	Paragraph 11 to the LSE Listing Rules
LLP SORP Appendix 4	Appendix 4 to the Statement on Recommended Practice – Accounting by Limited Liability Partnerships - issued by the CCAB (January 2017)

Professional and regulatory bodies:

BEIS	Department for Business, Energy & Industrial Strategy
CCAB	Consultative Committee of Accountancy Bodies
CRC	Corporate Reporting Council (formally Accounting Council (AC))
FRC	Financial Reporting Council
IASB	International Accounting Standards Board
ICAEW	Institute of Chartered Accountants in England and Wales
ICAS	Institute of Chartered Accountants of Scotland
IFRIC	International Financial Reporting Interpretations Committee
PRA	Prudential Regulation Authority
TAG	UK GAAP Technical Advisory Group

Accounting related terms:

AIM	Alternative Investment Market
CA 2006	Companies Act 2006
CGU	Cash-generating unit
Code	The UK Corporate Governance Code (April 2016) issued by the FRC
E&E	Exploration and evaluation
EBIT	Earnings before interest and taxes
EBITDA	Earnings before interest, tax, depreciation and amortisation
EBT	Employee benefit trust
EIR	Effective interest rate
EPS	Earnings per share

FC	Foreign currency
FIFO	First-in, first-out basis of valuation
FRED	Financial Reporting Exposure Draft (issued by the FRC)
FRS	Financial Reporting Standard (issued by the FRC)
FRSSE	Financial Reporting Standard for Smaller Entities
FTA	First-time adoption
FVLCD	Fair value less costs of disposal
FVLCS	Fair value less costs to sell
GAAP	Generally Accepted Accounting Practice
IAS	International Accounting Standard (issued by the former board of the IASC)
IBOR	Interbank offer rate
IFRS	International Financial Reporting Standard (issued by the IASB)
IIR	Implicit interest rate (in a lease)
IRR	Internal rate of return
JA	Joint arrangement
JANE	Joint arrangement that is not an entity
JCA	Jointly controlled asset
JCE	Jointly controlled entity
JV	Joint venture
LIBOR	London Inter Bank Offered Rate
LIFO	Last-in, first-out basis of valuation
LLP	Limited liability partnership
LLP Regulations	The Large and Medium-sized Limited Liability Partnerships (Accounts) Regulations 2008 (SI 2008/1913)
NCI	Non-controlling interest
NBV	Net book value
NPV	Net present value
NRV	Net realisable value
OCI	Other comprehensive income
PP&E	Property, plant and equipment
R&D	Research and development
Regulations	The Large and Medium-sized Companies and Groups (Accounts and Reports) Regulations 2008 (SI 2008/410)
SCA	Service concession arrangement
SE	Structured entity

SI 2015/980	The Companies, Partnerships and Groups (Accounts and Reports) Regulations 2015 (SI 2015/980)
SI 2016/575	The Limited Liability Partnerships, Partnerships and Groups (Accounts and Audit) Regulations 2016 (SI 2016/575)
Small Companies Regulations	The Small Companies and Groups (Accounts and Directors' Report) Regulations 2008 (SI 2008/409)
Small LLP Regulations	The Small Limited Liability Partnerships (Accounts) Regulations 2008 (SI 2008/1912)
SME	Small or medium-sized entity
SORP	Statement of Recommended Practice
SPE	Special purpose entity
SSAP	Statement of Standard Accounting Practice
SV	Separate vehicle
TSR	Total shareholder return
Triennial review 2017	*Amendments to FRS 102 – The Financial Reporting Standard applicable in the UK and Republic of Ireland - Triennial review 2017 and Incremental improvements and clarifications* – issued in December 2017
2016 FRC Guidance	Guidance on the Going Concern Basis of Accounting and Reporting on Solvency and Liquidity Risks – Guidance for directors of companies that do not apply the UK Corporate Governance Code (April 2016) - issued by the FRC
UITF	Urgent Issues Task Force
UK	United Kingdom
VIU	Value in use
WACC	Weighted average cost of capital

Authoritative literature

The content of this book takes into account all UK accounting standards and exposure drafts extant as at November 2018.

References to the main text of each chapter to the pronouncements below for FRSs 100-105 are generally based on the version of the standard issued in March 2018 (which incorporate amendments made in December 2017 and earlier).

Accounting Standards

Foreword to Accounting Standards (March 2018)

FRS 100 – Application of Financial Reporting Requirements (March 2018)

FRS 101 – Reduced Disclosure Framework – Disclosure exemptions from EU-adopted IFRS for qualifying entities (March 2018)

Amendments to Basis for Conclusions FRS 101 – Reduced Disclosure Framework – 2017/2018 cycle (May 2018)

FRS 102 – The Financial Reporting Standard applicable in the UK and Republic of Ireland (March 2018)

FRS 103 – Insurance Contracts – Consolidated accounting and reporting requirements for entities in the UK and Republic of Ireland issuing insurance contracts (March 2018)

FRS 104 – Interim Financial Reporting (March 2018)

FRS 105 – The Financial Reporting Standard applicable to the Micro-entities Regime (March 2018)

Chapter 1   FRS 100 – Application of financial reporting requirements

Chapter 1

List of examples

List of examples

Chapter 1 FRS 100 – Application of financial reporting requirements

1 INTRODUCTION

In 2012, 2013 and 2014 the Financial Reporting Council (FRC), following a lengthy period of consultation (between 2002 and 2012), changed financial reporting standards in the United Kingdom and the Republic of Ireland. Evidence from consultation supported a move towards an international-based framework for financial reporting that was proportionate to the needs of preparers and users.

As a result of the changes, 'UK and Irish GAAP' now consists of the following Financial Reporting Standards:

- FRS 100 – *Application of Financial Reporting Requirements*;
- FRS 101 – *Reduced Disclosure Framework: Disclosure exemptions from EU-adopted IFRS for qualifying entities* (see Chapter 2);
- FRS 102 – *The Financial Reporting Standard applicable in the UK and Republic of Ireland*;
- FRS 103 – *Insurance Contracts – Consolidated accounting and reporting requirements for entities in the UK and Republic of Ireland issuing insurance contracts* (see Chapter 33);
- FRS 104 – *Interim Financial Reporting* (see Chapter 34); and
- FRS 105 – *The Financial Reporting Standard applicable to the Micro-entities Regime*.

This chapter deals only with the application of FRS 100. This standard, which was issued originally in November 2012, sets out the new financial reporting framework and applies to entities preparing financial statements in accordance with legislation, regulations or accounting standards applicable in the UK and the Republic of Ireland (i.e. FRSs 101 to 105). *[FRS 100.1]*.

This chapter deals only with the March 2018 version of FRS 100, which incorporates the changes made by *Amendments to FRS 102 The Financial Reporting Standard applicable in the UK and Ireland – Triennial review 2017 – incremental improvements and clarifications* (Triennial review 2017).

Under the Companies Act 2006 (CA 2006) the choice of financial reporting framework is closely related to the requirements of company law or other regulatory requirements. UK companies with transferable securities admitted to trading on a regulated market (at the financial year end) are required under the IAS Regulation to prepare their consolidated financial statements using EU-adopted IFRS. A list of regulated markets is available online.[1]

Entities that are not required by UK company law to prepare financial statements using EU-adopted IFRS may be required to do so by other regulatory requirements, such as the AIM Rules (see 4.4.1 below) or by other agreements (e.g. shareholders' or partnership agreements).

However, other UK companies are permitted to prepare their consolidated and/or individual financial statements as IAS accounts (using EU-adopted IFRS) or Companies Act accounts (using 'applicable accounting standards' – see 4.6.1 below), subject to company law restrictions concerning the 'consistency of financial reporting framework' used in the individual accounts of group undertakings and over changes in financial reporting framework from IAS accounts to Companies Act accounts. See 6.1.2 below.

The requirements for preparation of financial statements under the CA 2006 are addressed at 6 below. Except where otherwise stated, the rest of this chapter will refer to the requirements for UK companies, and therefore will refer to UK GAAP prior to implementation of FRS 100 to FRS 103 and FRS 105 as 'previous UK GAAP'. UK LLPs and other entities preparing financial statements in accordance with Part 15 of the CA 2006 are subject to similar requirements, modified as necessary by the regulations that govern the content of their financial statements.

2   SUMMARY OF FRS 100

The following is a summary of FRS 100:

- FRS 100 sets out the application of the financial reporting framework for UK and Republic of Ireland entities (see 4 below). The detailed accounting requirements are included in EU-adopted IFRS, FRS 101, FRS 102 and FRS 105, depending on the choice of GAAP made by the entity. FRS 103 applies to financial statements prepared in accordance with FRS 102. FRS 104 applies to interim financial statements and can be applied by entities preparing annual financial statements under FRS 101 or FRS 102.

- FRS 100 sets out the effective date of the new standards. FRS 100, FRS 101, FRS 102 and FRS 103 were mandatory, effective for accounting periods beginning on or after 1 January 2015. However, the Triennial review 2017 amendments to FRS 100 to FRS 105 (which are included in the March 2018 editions of these standards) are mandatory, effective for accounting periods beginning on or after 1 January 2019. Early application of the March 2018 edition of FRS 100 is permitted providing that all the Triennial review 2017 amendments to the standard are applied at the same time. *[FRS 100.10A]*.

- FRS 100 sets out the application of SORPs (see 4.7 below).

- FRS 100 sets out the transition arrangements to FRS 101, FRS 102, and FRS 105 (see 5 below).

- FRS 100 withdrew virtually all previous UK GAAP, with effect from its original application date of 1 January 2015. Some parts of previous UK GAAP have been retained by incorporation of their requirements into FRS 101, FRS 102 or FRS 103 (see 4.3 below).

- FRS 100 includes application guidance on the interpretation of 'equivalence' for the purposes of:

  (i) the exemption from preparation of consolidated financial statements in section 401 of the CA 2006. This is discussed in Chapter 2 at 2.3 (for FRS 101) and Chapter 8 at 3.1.1 (for FRS 102) but the same requirements apply to IAS accounts; and

  (ii) the reduced disclosure framework discussed in Chapter 2 (for FRS 101) and in Chapter 3 at 3 (for FRS 102) respectively.

3   DEFINITIONS

The following terms used in FRS 100 are as defined in the Glossary (included as Appendix I to FRS 100):

- *EU Accounting Directive* – Directive 2013/34/EU of the European Parliament and of the Council of 26 June 2013;

- *CA 2006* – the Companies Act 2006;

- *Date of transition* – the beginning of the earliest period for which an entity presents full comparative information under a given standard in its first financial statements that comply with that standard;

- *EU-adopted IFRS* – IFRSs adopted in the European Union in accordance with EU Regulation 1606/2002 ('IAS Regulation');

- *IAS Regulation* – EU Regulation 1606/2002;

- *IFRS (or IFRSs)* – standards and interpretations issued or (adopted) by the International Accounting Standards Board (IASB). They comprise International Financial Reporting Standards, International Accounting Standards, Interpretations developed by the IFRS Interpretations Committee (the Interpretations Committee) or the former Standing Interpretations Committee (SIC);

- *Individual financial statements* – accounts that are required to be prepared by an entity in accordance with the CA 2006 or relevant legislation.

  For example, this term includes 'individual accounts' as set out in section 394 of the CA 2006, a 'statement of accounts' as set out in section 132 of the Charities Act 2011, or 'individual accounts' as set out in section 72A of the Building Societies Act 1986.

  Separate financial statements are included in the meaning of the term 'individual financial statements':

- *Micro-entities Regulations* – The Small Companies (Micro Entities' Accounts) Regulations 2013 (SI 2013/3008);

- *Non-financial Reporting Directive* – Directive 2014/95/EU of the European Parliament and of the Council of 22 October 2014 amending Directive 2013/34/EU as regards disclosure of non-financial and diversity information by certain large undertakings and groups;

- *Non-financial Reporting Regulations* – The Companies, Partnerships and Groups (Accounts and Non-financial Reporting) Regulations 2016 (SI 2016/1245). This Statutory Instrument primarily implements the requirements of the Non-financial Reporting Directive in the UK;

- *Qualifying entity* – a member of a group where the parent of that group prepares publicly available consolidated financial statements, which are intended to give a true and fair view (of the assets, liabilities, financial position and profit or loss) and that member is included in the consolidation (as set out in section 474). For the purposes of FRS 101 only, a charity cannot be a qualifying entity. See Chapter 2 at 2.1 (for FRS 101) and Chapter 3 at 3.1 (for FRS 102);

- *Small entity* – (a) a company meeting the definition of a small company as set out in section 382 or 383 of the CA 2006[2] and not excluded from the small companies regime by section 384; (b) an LLP qualifying as small and not excluded from the small LLPs regime, as set out in the LLP Regulations; or (c) any other entity that would have met the criteria in (a) had it been a company incorporated under company law (see Chapter 5 at 4.1);

- *SI 2015/980* – The Companies, Partnerships and Groups (Accounts and Reports) Regulations 2015 (SI 2015/980). This Statutory Instrument implements the requirements of the EU Accounting Directive (Directive 2013/34/EU) in the UK; and

- *SORP* – an extant Statement of Recommended Practice (SORP) developed in accordance with the FRC's *Policy on Developing Statements of Recommended Practice (SORPs)*.[3] SORPs recommend accounting practices for specialised industries or sectors, and supplement accounting standards and other legal and regulatory requirements in light of the special factors prevailing or transactions undertaken in a particular industry or sector.

Consistent with the FRS 102 Glossary, this chapter refers to *The Small Companies and Groups (Accounts and Directors' Report) Regulations 2008* (SI 2008/409) as 'the Small Companies Regulations', and *The Large and Medium-sized Companies and Groups (Accounts and Reports) Regulations 2008* (SI 2008/410) as 'the Regulations'.

4   FRS 100 – APPLICATION OF FINANCIAL REPORTING REQUIREMENTS

The publication of FRS 100 to FRS 105 followed a lengthy period of consultation (from 2002 to 2012) on changes to financial reporting in the UK and Republic of Ireland (the 'Future of UK and Irish GAAP'). Further background on these consultations and the evolution of the FRC's approach leading up to the development of the new standards is included in Appendix III to the November 2012 version of FRS 100.

In developing the new standards, the FRC has set out an overriding objective to enable users of accounts to receive high-quality understandable financial reporting proportionate to the size and complexity of the entity and users' information needs. *[FRS 100.BC.1].*

In meeting this objective, the FRC has stated that it aims to provide succinct financial reporting standards that: *[FRS 100.BC2]*

- have consistency with global accounting standards through application of an IFRS-based solution unless an alternative clearly better meets the overriding objective;

- balance improvement, through reflecting up-to-date thinking and developments in the way businesses operate and the transactions they undertake, with stability;

- balance consistent principles for accounting by all UK and Republic of Ireland entities with proportionate and practical solutions based on size, complexity, public interest and users' information needs;

- promote efficiency within groups; and

- are cost-effective to apply.

The financial reporting framework set out in FRS 100 is summarised in the diagram below:

Figure 1.1 The UK Financial Reporting Framework

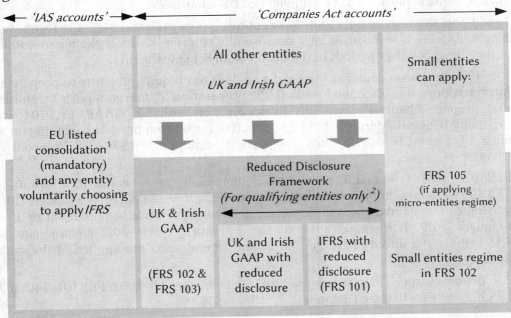

1: Consolidated financial statements of an entity with transferable securities admitted to trading on an EEA regulated market (See 4.4.1 below).

2: A qualifying entry (i.e. a parent or subsidiary undertaking) which is consolidated in publicly available consolidated financial statements that give a true and fair view can take advantage of the reduced disclosure framework. Applies to individual financial statements only and shareholders must be notified in writing about and not object to the disclosure exemptions. The IFRS 7, IFRS 13 and capital management disclosure exemptions (and in FRS 102, financial instruments-related disclosure exemptions) cannot be used by financial institutions.

4.1   Scope of FRS 100

The objective of FRS 100 is to set out the applicable financial reporting framework for entities presenting financial statements in accordance with legislation, regulations or accounting standards applicable in the UK and Republic of Ireland. *[FRS 100.1]*.

FRS 100 applies to financial statements intended to give a true and fair view of assets, liabilities, financial position and profit or loss for a period. *[FRS 100.2]*.

FRS 100 to FRS 105 can be applied by an entity that is not a UK or Irish company, preparing financial statements that are intended to give a true and fair view. However, Appendix II to FRS 100 states that the FRC sets accounting standards within the framework of the CA 2006 and therefore it is the company law requirements that the FRC primarily considered when developing FRS 102. See 4.4 below.

4.2   Effective date

FRS 100 to FRS 103 were mandatory for accounting periods beginning on or after 1 January 2015. In September 2015 new versions of FRS 100 to FRS 102 were issued reflecting various amendments made in July 2015 which were mandatory for accounting periods beginning on or after 1 January 2016. There were certain early application provisions (explained in Chapter 3 at 1.3.3 of EY UK GAAP 2017) that were intended to align with the application of SI 2015/980 (for UK companies).

In addition, a new standard, FRS 105, for entities applying the micro-entities regime was issued. FRS 105 is mandatory for a micro-entity choosing to apply the micro-entities regime for accounting periods beginning on or after 1 January 2016.

FRS 104 is not an accounting standard, and does not require an entity to prepare an interim report. It is intended for use in the preparation of interim reports by entities that prepare financial statements in accordance with UK GAAP. FRS 104 was originally issued in March 2015 and is effective for interim periods beginning on or after 1 January 2015, with early application permitted. FRS 104 is discussed in Chapter 34.

Following the Triennial review 2017, amendments were made to FRS 100 to FRS 105. The amendments to FRS 100, which are included in the March 2018 version of the standard, are effective for accounting periods beginning on or after 1 January 2019. Early application of the Triennial review 2017 amendments to FRS 100 are permitted provided that all the amendments are applied at the same time. *[FRS 100.10A]*.

For details of the Triennial review 2017 amendments affecting FRS 101, FRS 102, FRS 103 and FRS 104, see Chapters 2, 3, 5, 33 and 34.

4.3   Withdrawal of previous UK and Irish GAAP

FRS 100 withdrew all previous UK and Irish GAAP with effect from its application date. *[FRS 100.14]*. However, some parts of previous UK and Irish GAAP were retained by direct incorporation of their requirements into FRS 100 or FRS 102.

The following statements were also withdrawn when FRS 100 applied: *[FRS 100.15]*

- *Statement of Principles for Financial Reporting;*
- *Statement of Principles for Financial Reporting – Interpretation for public benefit entities;*
- *Reporting Statement: Retirement Benefits – Disclosures;*
- *Reporting Statement – Preliminary announcements;* and
- *Reporting Statement – Half-yearly financial reports* (replaced by FRS 104).

Separately, in June 2014, the FRC issued *Guidance on the Strategic Report* which superseded *Reporting Statement: Operating and Financial Review.* In July 2018, the FRC issued revised *Guidance on the Strategic Report* which supersedes the 2014 Guidance. The revised Guidance incorporates the new disclosure requirements introduced by the Non-financial Reporting Regulations which were effective for financial years beginning on or after 1 January 2017 and disclosures associated with the legislative requirements relating to the directors' section 172 duty to promote the success of the company, which are effective for financial years beginning on or after 1 January 2019.

The Financial Reporting Standard for Smaller Entities (effective January 2015) (FRSSE) was withdrawn for accounting periods beginning on or after 1 January 2016 (or on earlier application of SI 2015/980) and replaced by Section 1A of FRS 102. *[FRS 100.15A]*. See 4.4.5 below.

4.4 Basis of preparation of financial statements

FRS 100 does not address which entities must prepare financial statements, but sets out the applicable financial reporting framework for entities presenting financial statements in accordance with legislation, regulations or accounting standards applicable in the UK and Republic of Ireland. *[FRS 100.1]*.

The individual or consolidated financial statements of any entity within the scope of FRS 100 (that is not required by the IAS Regulation or other legislation or regulations to be prepared in accordance with EU-adopted IFRS) must be prepared in accordance with either: *[FRS 100.4]*

- FRS 105, if the entity is a micro entity eligible to apply that standard and chooses to do so – see 4.4.6 and 6.4 below; or
- if the financial statements are those of an entity that is not eligible to apply FRS 105:
  - EU-adopted IFRS (see 4.4.2 below); or
  - FRS 102 (see 4.4.3 below) and, where applicable, FRS 103 (see Chapter 33); or
  - FRS 101 (if the financial statements are individual financial statements of a qualifying entity) (see 4.4.4 below).

The above choices are also available for the individual financial statements of an entity that is required to prepare consolidated financial statements in accordance with EU-adopted IFRS. *[FRS 100.4, FRS 102.1.3]*.

An entity's choice of financial reporting framework must be permitted by the legal framework or other regulations or requirements that govern the preparation of the entity's financial statements. Other agreements or arrangements (such as shareholders' agreements, banking agreements) may also restrict the choice of financial reporting framework.

4.4.1   Company law and regulatory requirements governing financial reporting framework

As required by Article 4 of the IAS Regulation, a UK parent company with transferable securities admitted to trading on a regulated market at its financial year end must prepare its consolidated financial statements as IAS group accounts. *[s403(1)]*. The individual financial statements of such a parent company may be either Companies Act individual accounts or IAS individual accounts. *[s395(1)]*.

AIM is not a regulated market. An 'AIM company' (i.e. a company with a class of security admitted to AIM) incorporated in an EEA country (including, for this purpose, a company incorporated in the Channel Islands or the Isle of Man) must prepare and present its annual accounts in accordance with EU-adopted IFRS. However, an AIM company incorporated in an EEA country that is not a parent company at the end of the relevant financial period may prepare and present its annual accounts either in accordance with EU-adopted IFRS or in accordance with the accounting and company legislation and regulations that are applicable to that company due to its country of incorporation (which, under the new UK and Irish financial reporting framework, could include EU-adopted IFRS, FRS 101 – if a qualifying entity – and FRS 102). While the AIM Rules do not specifically differentiate between consolidated and individual financial statements, many AIM companies incorporated in the UK use EU-adopted IFRS in their consolidated financial statements but national GAAP in their individual financial statements. However, a parent company that only prepares individual financial statements, e.g. it is exempt from preparing consolidated financial statements, must prepare these in accordance with EU-adopted IFRS.[4]

For a UK company, the choice of framework, discussed at 4.4 above, is subject to the requirements in the CA 2006 on change in financial reporting framework (from IAS accounts to Companies Act accounts) (see 6.1.2 below) and consistency of financial reporting framework in individual accounts of group undertakings (see 6.1.3 below).

For the purposes of the CA 2006, only statutory accounts prepared in accordance with full EU-adopted IFRS are IAS accounts, whereas statutory accounts prepared in accordance with FRS 102, FRS 101, or FRS 105 are Companies Act accounts. *[s395(1), s403(2)]*.

UK charitable companies are not permitted to prepare IAS accounts under the CA 2006, *[s395(2), s403(3)]*, and charities are not permitted to apply FRS 101 (as excluded from its definition of a qualifying entity). *[FRS 100 Appendix I, FRS 101 Appendix I]*. UK charitable companies preparing financial statements under the CA 2006 must, therefore, apply FRS 102. Other charities in England and Wales and Scotland preparing financial statements under charities legislation must also apply FRS 102.

There is further detail on the requirements of the CA 2006 in relation to annual reports and accounts at 6 below.

FRS 101, FRS 102 and FRS 105 may also be used by entities preparing financial statements intended to give a true and fair view but that are not subject to the CA 2006 (or Irish law). Entities preparing such financial statements intended to give a true and fair view within other legal frameworks will need to satisfy themselves that the standard being applied does not conflict with any relevant legal obligations. *[FRS 100 Appendix II.20, FRS 102 Appendix III.41].* Appendix III to FRS 100 and Appendix IV to FRS 102 include observations on the requirements of specific UK and Northern Ireland legislation, although some of this legislation may subsequently have been amended or superseded. Where an entity is subject to a SORP, the relevant SORP will provide more details on the relevant legislation. *[FRS 100 Appendix II.2, 21, FRS 102 Appendix III.2, 42].*

4.4.2   EU-adopted IFRS

EU-adopted IFRS means IFRSs as adopted by the EU pursuant to the IAS Regulation. *[s474].*

4.4.3   FRS 102 – The Financial Reporting Standard applicable in the UK and Republic of Ireland

FRS 102 is a single, largely stand-alone, financial reporting standard based on a significantly modified version of the IFRS for SMEs issued by the IASB in 2009.

FRS 102 was originally issued in March 2013 but has had several subsequent amendments (see Chapter 3 at 1.2 and 1.3). A consolidated version of the standard issued in September 2015, incorporating the July 2015 amendments, was mandatory for periods beginning on or after 1 January 2016. Early application was permitted for accounting periods beginning on or after 1 January 2015 provided that the requirements of SI 2015/980 were applied from the same date.

A revised version of FRS 102 was issued in March 2018 (see Chapter 3 at 1.3 for details of the effective date) incorporating the following amendments made after the September 2015 version (which included the July 2015 and earlier amendments):

- *Amendments to FRS 102 The Financial Reporting Standard applicable in the UK and Ireland – Fair value hierarchy disclosures* issued in March 2016;
- *Amendments to FRS 101 Reduced Disclosure Framework and FRS 102 The Financial Reporting Standard applicable in the UK and Republic of Ireland – Notification of shareholders* issued in December 2016;
- *Triennial review 2017* issued in December 2017; and
- some minor typographical or presentational corrections.

Amendments to FRS 102 The Financial Reporting Standard applicable in the UK and Ireland – Directors' loans – optional interim relief for small entities issued in May 2017 provided an optional interim relief, with immediate effect, when accounting for loans made to a small entity by a director who is a natural person and a shareholder in the small entity (or a close member of the family of that person). These amendments were removed by the Triennial review 2017 (once applied) which include a more extensive relief. See Chapter 5 at 6.3.

FRS 102 is arranged into sections: Section 1 addresses scope, Sections 2 to 33 each address a separate accounting topic, Section 34 addresses specialised activities, and Section 35 – *Transition to this FRS* – addresses transition. There is a reduced disclosure framework available for qualifying entities (see 4.5 below) in their individual financial statements and also a separate disclosure framework for small entities introduced in July 2015 (see Chapter 5).

4.4.4   FRS 101 – Reduced Disclosure Framework

FRS 101 was issued originally on 22 November 2012. A consolidated version of the standard incorporating subsequent amendments was issued in September 2015 and was mandatory for accounting periods beginning on or after 1 January 2016, with certain early application provisions.

In March 2018, a revised edition of FRS 101 was issued which updates the September 2015 version for the following amendments (see Chapter 2 at 1.2):

- *Amendments to FRS 101 – Reduced Disclosure Framework 2015/16 cycle* issued in July 2016;
- Amendments to *FRS 101 Reduced Disclosure Framework and FRS 102 The Financial Reporting Standard applicable in the UK and Republic of Ireland – Notification of shareholders* issued in December 2016;
- *Amendments to FRS 101 – Reduced Disclosure Framework 2016/17 cycle* issued in July 2017;
- *Triennial review 2017 amendments* issued in December 2017; and
- some minor typographical or presentational corrections.

Amendments to Basis for Conclusions FRS 101 – Reduced Disclosure Framework – 2017/18 Cycle, issued in May 2018, made an amendment to the Basis for Conclusions in respect of IFRS 17 – *Insurance Contracts* – and updated Table 2 which sets out IFRS publications considered in the development of FRS 101. However, no changes were made to the standard itself.

See Chapter 2 at 1.2 for further details, including the circumstances in which the standard can be adopted early.

FRS 101 sets out a framework which addresses the financial reporting requirements and disclosure exemptions for the individual financial statements of qualifying entities (see 4.5 below) that otherwise apply the recognition, measurement and disclosure requirements of standards and interpretations issued by the International Accounting Standards Board (IASB) that have been adopted in the European Union (EU-adopted IFRS).

An entity reporting under FRS 101 complies with EU-adopted IFRS except as modified by the standard. FRS 101 contains various recognition and measurement modifications to EU-adopted IFRS, primarily to ensure compliance with UK company law.

The FRC will review FRS 101 annually to ensure that the reduced disclosure framework continues to be effective in providing disclosure reductions for qualifying entities when compared with EU-adopted IFRS. *[FRS 101.BC10].*

4.4.5 Section 1A of FRS 102

Small entities can apply Section 1A of FRS 102. Section 1A was introduced in the July 2015 amendments to FRS 102 and is effective for accounting periods beginning on or after 1 January 2016 (see Chapter 5 at 5 for further details of effective date and early application). Section 1A requires small entities to apply the recognition and measurement requirements of FRS 102 in full. However, the presentation and disclosure requirements required by Section 1A are based on those required by the CA 2006 and the Small Companies Regulations for companies subject to the small companies regime.

The application of the small entities regime in Section 1A is not mandatory and an entity can instead apply FRS 102 in full, FRS 101 (if the entity is a 'qualifying entity' preparing individual financial statements – see Chapter 2), EU-adopted IFRS, or FRS 105 if subject to the micro-entities regime (see 4.4.6 below).

The small entities regime of FRS 102 is discussed in Chapter 5.

4.4.6 FRS 105 – The Financial Reporting Standard applicable to the Micro-entities Regime

An entity that chooses to prepare its financial statements in accordance with the micro-entities regime (see 6.4 below) as set out in *The Small Companies (Micro-entities' Accounts) Regulations 2013 (SI 2013/3008)* is required to apply FRS 105 for periods beginning on or after 1 January 2016. Early application was permitted. FRS 105 was initially only available to UK companies, but was later extended to LLPs and Irish Companies. Amendments to FRS 105 were published in December 2017 as part of the Triennial Review 2017. The amendments mainly introduce new disclosure requirements and are effective for accounting periods beginning on or after 1 January 2019.

The recognition and measurement requirements of FRS 105 are based on those in FRS 102 (but with significant simplifications) and its presentation and disclosure requirements are consistent with the micro-entity provisions (in UK company and LLP law).

FRS 105 is outside the scope of this publication.

4.4.7 Considerations on choice of financial reporting framework

Entities will need to carefully consider their choice of financial reporting framework, based on their individual circumstances. In doing so, entities may need to consider the implications of a new financial reporting framework for other aspects of their business, such as covenants in loan agreements, employee remuneration (e.g. performance-related bonuses), the effect on key performance indicators, accounting systems, taxation and distributable profits.

Factors influencing the choice of financial reporting framework might include:

- whether the entity is a member of a group, and if so, what GAAP is used for group reporting. In particular, subsidiaries of groups reporting under IFRS or in multinational groups may prefer to apply IFRS or FRS 101 rather than FRS 102;

- the level of disclosures required in the financial statements.

  FRS 101 and FRS 102 financial statements prepared by a UK company are Companies Act accounts and therefore must comply with the requirements of the CA 2006 and all applicable schedules of the Regulations (as well as accounting standards). Financial statements prepared under EU-adopted IFRS do not need to comply with Schedules 1, 2 or 3 to the Regulations but must comply with the extensive disclosure requirements in IFRS (see 6.7 below).

  The level of disclosure also depends on whether the entity is a qualifying entity and can make use of a reduced disclosure framework (under FRS 101 or FRS 102) in its individual financial statements (see 4.5 below). While FRS 102 has fewer disclosures than IFRS, the level of disclosure required may sometimes not be significantly different from FRS 101, but this will depend on the entity's individual circumstances;

- stability of the financial reporting framework (in general, there are more frequent changes to IFRS than to FRS 102);

- the implications of new IFRSs (such as IFRS 9 – *Financial Instruments* – or IFRS 15 – *Revenue from Contracts with Customers* – or IFRS 16 – *Leases*) or expected changes to IFRS that will be implemented or expected to be finalised in future periods;

- IFRS provides detailed and sometimes complex guidance, whereas the requirements in FRS 102 are much shorter (but lack the same level of application guidance as in IFRS, and are likely to involve increased application of management judgement in applying the standard); and

- the implications of different GAAPs for distributable profits (see 5.5 below) and taxation, in particular cash tax. This will also depend on the interaction with tax legislation, and whether tax elections are made.

4.5   Reduced disclosure framework

Both FRS 101 and FRS 102 provide for a reduced disclosure framework for qualifying entities in individual financial statements.

A 'qualifying entity' is a member of a group (i.e. a parent or subsidiary) where the parent of that group prepares publicly available consolidated financial statements which are intended to give a true and fair view (of the assets, liabilities, financial position and profit or loss) and that member is included in the consolidation. *[FRS 100 Appendix I, FRS 101 Appendix I, FRS 102 Appendix I].* The term 'included in the consolidation' has the meaning set out in section 474(1) of the CA 2006, i.e. that the qualifying entity is consolidated in the financial statements by full (and not proportional) consolidation. Under FRS 101, a charity cannot be a qualifying entity. *[FRS 101 Appendix I].*

The disclosure exemptions available in FRS 102 are more limited than in FRS 101, which provides a reduced disclosure framework for qualifying entities under EU-adopted IFRS. This reflects the fact that FRS 102 (as a starting point) has much simpler disclosures than EU-adopted IFRS. Under the reduced disclosure framework in both standards, there are fewer disclosure exemptions available for the individual financial statements of financial institutions.

Certain disclosures require 'equivalent' disclosures to be included in the publicly available consolidated financial statements of the parent in which the qualifying entity is consolidated (i.e. of the parent referred to in the definition of qualifying entity). FRS 100 provides guidance on the concept of 'equivalence' for these purposes. *[FRS 100.AG8-10]*.

Chapter 2 has further discussion of the reduced disclosure framework under FRS 101 and Chapter 3 discusses further the reduced disclosure framework under FRS 102, including the detailed requirements for its use, the definitions of 'qualifying entity' and 'financial institution', the disclosure exemptions available, and guidance on 'equivalence' for the purpose of the reduced disclosure framework.

4.6   Statement of compliance

FRS 100 requires that an entity preparing its financial statements in accordance with FRS 101 or FRS 102 (and where applicable, FRS 103) includes a statement of compliance in the notes to the financial statements in accordance with the requirements of the relevant standard. This requirement is not mandatory for a small entity applying the small entities regime in FRS 102 (Section 1A), although including a statement of compliance in the notes to the accounts is encouraged. *[FRS 100.9, FRS 103.1.12, FRS 102.3.3, FRS 101.10]*. See Chapter 2 at 1.3 (for FRS 101 financial statements), Chapter 6 at 3.8 (for FRS 102 financial statements), and Chapter 5 at 11.2.5 and 11.3 (for small entities under FRS 102).

This requirement is similar to that in IAS 1 – *Presentation of Financial Statements* – for an entity preparing its financial statements using EU-adopted IFRS to give an explicit and unreserved statement of compliance with IFRSs.

In the same way as required for IFRS financial statements, financial statements should not be described as complying with FRS 101 or FRS 102, unless they comply with *all* of the requirements of the relevant standard. Indeed, FRS 102 includes an explicit requirement to this effect. *[FRS 102.3.3]*.

FRS 105 requires a statement, on the statement of financial position in a prominent position above the signature, that the financial statements are prepared in accordance with the micro-entity provisions. *[FRS 105.3.14, s414(3)]*.

4.6.1   Related Companies Act 2006 requirements

Where the directors of a large or medium-sized company (i.e. a company not subject to the micro-entity provisions or the small companies regime – see 6.4 and 6.5 below) prepare Companies Act individual or group accounts (such as those prepared under FRS 101 and FRS 102), the notes to the accounts must include a statement as to whether the accounts have been prepared in accordance with applicable accounting standards. Particulars of any material departure from those standards and the reasons for the departure must be given. This statement is not required in the individual accounts of medium-sized companies (see 6.6.2.A below). *[Regulations 4(2A), 1 Sch 45]*.

'Applicable accounting standards' means statements of standard accounting practice issued by the FRC (and SSAPs, FRSs issued by the Accounting Standard Board and UITF

Abstracts, until withdrawn).[5] Therefore, FRS 100 to FRS 103 (and FRS 105 for companies applying the micro-entity provisions only) are 'applicable accounting standards'.[6]

Where the directors of a company prepare IAS individual or IAS group accounts (see 6.1 below), the notes to the accounts must include a statement that the accounts have been prepared in accordance with international accounting standards (i.e. EU-adopted IFRS). *[s397, s406, s474].*

4.7   SORPs

References to a SORP are to an extant Statement of Recommended Practice developed in accordance with the FRC's *Policy on Developing Statements of Recommended Practice (SORPs)*. SORPs recommend accounting practices for specialised industries or sectors. They supplement accounting standards and other legal and regulatory requirements in the light of the special factors prevailing or transactions undertaken in a particular industry or sector. *[FRS 100 Appendix I].*

SORPs may only be developed and issued by 'SORP-making bodies', being bodies recognised by the FRC for the purpose of producing the SORP for a particular industry or sector. SORP-making bodies have a responsibility to act in the public interest when developing a SORP. To be recognised as a SORP-making body, a particular industry or sectoral body must meet criteria set by the FRC and must agree to develop SORPs in accordance with the FRC's Policy on Developing Statements of Recommended Practice (SORPs). SORPs recommend particular accounting treatments and disclosures with the aim of narrowing areas of difference and variety between comparable entities. Compliance with a SORP that has been generally accepted by an industry or sector leads to enhanced comparability between the financial statements of entities in that industry or sector. Comparability is further enhanced if users are made aware of the extent to which an entity complies with a SORP, and the reasons for any departures. *[FRS 100.7].*

FRS 100 states that if an entity's financial statements are prepared in accordance with FRS 102, SORPs apply in the circumstances set out in those SORPs. *[FRS 100.5].*

The application of SORPs under FRS 102 is discussed at Chapter 3 at 2.3.

When a SORP applies, an entity, other than a small entity applying the small entities regime in FRS 102 (i.e. Section 1A of FRS 102), must state in the financial statements the title of the SORP and whether the financial statements have been prepared in accordance with the SORP's provisions currently in effect. The provisions of a SORP cease to have effect, for example, to the extent they conflict with a more recent financial reporting standard. *[FRS 100.6].*

Paragraph 6 of the FRC's Policy on Developing Statements of Recommended Practice (SORPs) explains that SORPs should be developed in line with current accounting standards and best practice. A SORP's provisions cannot override provisions of the law, regulatory requirements or accounting standards. Therefore, where at the time of issue, the SORP's provisions conflict with accounting standards or legal or regulatory requirements, these take precedence over the SORP and the FRC's Statement on the SORP will usually be varied to refer to this. When a more recently issued accounting standard or change in legislation leads to conflict with the provisions of an existing SORP, the relevant provisions of the SORP cease to have effect. The SORP-making body is responsible for updating the relevant provisions of the SORP on a timely basis to bring them in line with new legislation or accounting standards, or to withdraw them, as appropriate.

Where an entity departs from the SORP's provisions, it must give a brief description of how the financial statements depart from the recommended practice set out in the SORP, which must include: *[FRS 100.6]*

- for any treatment that is not in accordance with the SORP, the reasons why the treatment adopted is judged more appropriate to the entity's particular circumstances; and

- brief details of any disclosures recommended by the SORP that have not been provided, together with the reasons why not.

A small entity applying the small entities regime in FRS 102 is encouraged to provide these disclosures. *[FRS 100.6]*.

The effect of a departure from a SORP need not be quantified, except in those rare cases where such quantification is necessary for the entity's financial statements to give a true and fair view. *[FRS 100.7]*.

Entities whose financial statements do not fall within the scope of a SORP may, if the SORP is otherwise relevant to them, nevertheless choose to comply with the SORP's recommendations when preparing financial statements, providing that the SORP does not conflict with the requirements of the framework adopted. Where this is the case, entities are encouraged to disclose this fact. *[FRS 100.8]*.

FRS 100, therefore, does not require an entity preparing its financial statements in accordance with FRS 101, or EU-adopted IFRS, to disclose whether it has applied the relevant SORP. However, FRS 100 does not preclude such an entity from following a SORP (provided its requirements do not conflict with EU-adopted IFRS) but encourages the entity to disclose that it has done so.

4.7.1 Status of SORPs

Certain SORPs were withdrawn on implementation of the new UK and Irish GAAP framework. Other SORPs have been updated to conform with FRS 102 (although two Charities SORPs have been issued, one for use with the FRSSE and one for use with FRS 102).

The following SORPs have been updated to conform with FRS 102:

- *Accounting for Further and Higher Education* (October 2018);
- *Financial Statements of UK Authorised Funds* (May 2014, as amended in June 2017);
- *Charities (FRS 102)* (July 2014, as updated Update Bulletin 1 in February 2016 and Update Bulletin 2 in October 2018);
- *Limited Liability Partnerships* (January 2017);
- *Registered Social Housing Providers* (September 2014);
- *Investment Trust Companies and Venture Capital Trusts* (November 2014, as updated in February 2018); and
- *Pension Schemes* (July 2018).

Refer to Chapter 3 at 2.3 for further details on the application of SORPs.

As a consequence of the December 2017 amendments to FRS 102 following the triennial review, all seven SORP-making bodies have either updated, or are in the process of updating, their respective SORPs to reflect the amendments. At the time of writing only the Pensions Scheme SORP has been updated. A draft version of the updated Limited Liability Partnerships SORP was published in August 2018 for consultation.

4.8   Brexit

On 29 March 2017, the UK Government started the legal process of negotiating a withdrawal by the UK from the European Union (EU). Under the provisions of the relevant laws and treaties, the UK will leave the EU by 29 March 2019, unless either a deal is reached at an earlier date, or the negotiation period is extended by unanimous consent of the European Council. Until that date, the UK remains a member of the EU and all laws and regulations continue to apply on that basis. On 14 November 2018 a *Draft Agreement on the Withdrawal of the United Kingdom from the European Union* was published. At the time of writing this publication, the draft agreement is subject to approval of the UK parliament. This approval is uncertain. Other scenarios remain a possibility.

Many requirements that derive from EU legislation, treaties and directives have been directly incorporated into UK company law. As a result, even in the event of EU legislation ceasing to apply, UK financial and reporting regulations will not change until applicable company law and regulations are amended. In particular, the application of EU adopted IFRS is enshrined in the CA 2006 and nothing will change in that respect without a change to the CA 2006.

The Accounts and Reports (Amendment) (EU Exit) Regulations 2018 were laid in draft before Parliament on 31 October 2018. This draft Statutory Instrument amends certain provisions of the CA 2006 that refer to the EU, EEA or entities within these areas. The timing of the effective date of this proposed legislation depends on whether or not a transition period is agreed with the EU.

The UK will also need to establish its policy on the endorsement of future IFRSs. It appears likely, at the time of writing this chapter, that a UK endorsement process will be established although any details have yet to be published.

Given the uncertain nature of the final terms of the UK's withdrawal from the EU, the final form of the draft legislation above and the extent of further legislative and regulatory changes in the UK affecting the financial reporting framework, are subject to change.

4.9   Future development of FRS 102

Any amendments to FRS 102 to reflect major changes in IFRS will be considered by the FRC on a case-by-case basis, including the appropriate timing. In addition, FRS 102 will be subject to periodic reviews reflecting stakeholder feedback, minor changes in IFRS and the IFRS for SMEs and other issues. These periodic reviews are likely to take place every four to five years, to allow time for experience of the most recent edition of FRS 102 to develop before seeking stakeholder feedback. However, the FRC will continue to assess emerging issues as they arise to determine whether action needs to be taken. When necessary this will include issuing amendments to standards outside regular review cycles. *[FRS 102.BC.A44-45]*.

5   TRANSITION

FRS 100 sets out the requirements for transition to FRS 101, FRS 102 and FRS 105. The requirements differ depending on the standard transitioned to and whether the entity previously reported under EU-adopted IFRS or other GAAP (e.g. another form of UK GAAP).

The date of transition is the beginning of the earliest period for which an entity presents full comparative information under a given standard in its first financial statements which comply with that standard. *[FRS 100 Appendix I]*. Therefore, 1 January 2018 is the date of transition for an entity with a 31 December year-end which prepares its first IFRS (or FRS 101 or FRS 102) financial statements for the financial year ended 31 December 2019.

Before deciding to transition to a particular standard in the new UK and Irish GAAP framework, entities should assess whether this is permitted by the statutory framework or other regulation that applies to them. See 6.1 and 6.2.1.D below for considerations applicable to the CA 2006.

On first-time application of FRS 100 or when an entity changes its basis of preparation of its financial statements within the requirements of FRS 100, it should apply the transitional arrangements relevant to its circumstances as explained at 5.1 to 5.3 below.

There is no requirement to change the GAAP applied by a UK parent and its UK subsidiaries at the same time. However, the CA 2006 sets out restrictions over changes in financial reporting framework (in both individual and group accounts) and over consistency of financial reporting framework in individual accounts of group undertakings (see 6.1.2 and 6.1.3 below).

5.1   Transition to EU-adopted IFRS

An entity transitioning to EU-adopted IFRS must apply the transitional requirements of IFRS 1 – *First-time Adoption of International Financial Reporting Standards*, as adopted by the EU. *[FRS 100.11(a)]*.

An entity's first IFRS financial statements (to which IFRS 1 must be applied) are the first annual financial statements in which the entity adopts EU-adopted IFRS, by an explicit and unreserved statement in those financial statements of compliance with EU-adopted IFRS. *[IFRS 1.2-3]*.

An entity that has applied EU-adopted IFRS in a previous reporting period, but whose most recent previous annual financial statements did not contain an explicit and unreserved statement of compliance with EU-adopted IFRS must either apply IFRS 1 or else apply EU-adopted IFRS retrospectively in accordance with IAS 8 – *Accounting Policies, Changes in Accounting Estimates and Errors* – as if the entity had never stopped applying IFRSs. *[IFRS 1.4A]*.

The requirements of IFRS 1 are discussed in Chapter 5 of EY International GAAP 2019.

5.2   Transition to FRS 101

A qualifying entity can transition to FRS 101 from either EU-adopted IFRS or another form of UK or Irish GAAP. In this context, another form of UK or Irish GAAP means FRS 102 or FRS 105. The transition requirements differ depending on whether the qualifying entity is applying EU-adopted IFRS or not prior to the date of transition. *[FRS 100.11(b), 12-13]*. The transition requirements to FRS 101 are explained in Chapter 2 at 3.

5.3   Transition to FRS 102

A first-time adopter of FRS 102 is an entity that presents its first annual financial statements that conform to FRS 102, regardless of whether its previous financial reporting framework was EU-adopted IFRS or another set of GAAP such as its national accounting standards, or another framework such as the local income tax basis. *[FRS 102.35.1, Appendix I]*. An entity transitioning to FRS 102 must apply the transitional arrangements set out in Section 35 of the standard. *[FRS 100.11(c), FRS 102.35.1]*.

FRS 102 also addresses the situation where an entity has previously applied FRS 102, and then applies a different GAAP for a period before re-applying FRS 102. An entity that adopted FRS 102 in a previous reporting period but whose most recent annual financial statements did not contain an explicit and unreserved statement of compliance with FRS 102 must either apply Section 35 or else apply FRS 102 retrospectively in accordance with Section 10 – *Accounting Policies, Changes in Estimates and Errors*, as if the entity had never stopped applying the standard. *[FRS 102.35.2]*.

An entity applying FRS 102 is required to apply FRS 103 to insurance contracts (including reinsurance contracts) that the entity issues and reinsurance contracts that the entity holds, and to financial instruments (other than insurance contracts) that the entity issues with a discretionary participation feature. *[FRS 103.1.2]*. An entity may, therefore, apply FRS 103 at the same time as it adopts FRS 102 or after it has adopted FRS 102, depending on whether it has transactions within scope of FRS 103 on adoption of FRS 102. It is not, however possible to apply FRS 103 without also applying FRS 102. *[FRS 103.1.11]*. See Chapter 33.

5.4   Transition to FRS 105

A first time adopter of FRS 105 is an entity that presents its first annual financial statements that conform to FRS 105, regardless of its previous financial reporting framework. *[FRS 105 Appendix I]*. In practice, most first time adopters of FRS 105 are likely to have previously applied Section 1A of FRS 102. An entity transitioning to FRS 105 must apply the transitional arrangements set out in Section 28 – *Transition to this FRS* – of FRS 105. *[FRS 100.11(d), FRS 105.28.3]*.

As noted in 4.4.6 above, the application of FRS 105 is outside the scope of this publication.

5.5   Impact of transition on distributable profits

There may be circumstances where a conversion to FRS 101, FRS 102, FRS 105 or EU-adopted IFRS eliminates an entity's realised profits or even turns those realised profits into a realised loss. TECH 02/17BL – *Guidance on realised and distributable profits under the Companies Act 2006*, issued by the ICAEW and ICAS, states that the change in the treatment of a retained profit or loss as realised (or unrealised) as a result of a change in the law or in accounting standards or interpretations would not render unlawful a distribution already made out of realised profits determined by reference to 'relevant accounts' which had been prepared in accordance with principles accepted at the time that the accounts are prepared (subject to the considerations below). This is because the CA 2006 defines realised profits and realised losses for determining the lawfulness of a distribution as 'such profits or losses of the company as fall to be treated as realised in accordance with principles generally accepted at the time when the accounts are prepared, with respect to the determination for accounting purposes of realised profits or losses'. *[s853(4), TECH 02/17BL.3.28-3.29]*.

The effects of the introduction of a new accounting standard or of the adoption of IFRSs (or FRS 101, FRS 102 or FRS 105) become relevant to the application of the common law capital maintenance rule only in relation to distributions accounted for in periods in which the change will first be recognised in the accounts. This means that a change in accounting policy known to be adopted in a financial year needs to be taken into account in determining the dividend to be approved by shareholders in that year. Therefore, for example, an entity converting to a new financial reporting framework (FRS 101, FRS 102, FRS 105, or EU-adopted IFRS) in 2019 must have regard to the effect of adoption of the new financial reporting framework in respect of all dividends payable in 2019, including any final dividends in respect of 2018, even though the 'relevant accounts' may still be those for 2018 prepared under another GAAP. These considerations apply to all dividends whether in respect of shares classified as equity or as debt (or partly equity or debt). *[TECH 02/17BL.3.30-3.33]*.

There is no requirement to prepare statutory 'interim accounts' under sections 836(2) and 838 of the CA 2006 (and delivered to the Registrar if the company is a public company) if a proposed distribution can be justified by reference to the relevant accounts. However, under common law, a company cannot lawfully make a distribution out of capital and the directors may therefore consider preparing non-statutory 'interim accounts' using the new financial framework to ascertain that there are sufficient distributable profits and, if the company is a public company, that the net asset restriction in section 831 of the CA 2006 is not breached. *[TECH 02/17BL.3.35]*. In some cases, however, the directors may be satisfied that no material adjustments arise from transition to the new financial framework (and therefore that there are sufficient distributable profits) without preparing such 'interim accounts'. Statutory 'interim accounts' would be required if transition to a new financial reporting framework increases distributable profits and the directors wish to make a distribution not justified by reference to the relevant accounts. *[TECH 02/17BL.3.34-35, 37]*. TECH 02/17BL states that if the directors have not yet decided whether to adopt EU-adopted IFRS, say, for the current financial year, the company's accounting policies are those that it has previously applied until a decision is made to change them. Therefore, in applying the above, it is not necessary to have regard to possible changes of policy that are being considered but have not yet been agreed. *[TECH 02/17BL.3.36]*.

Distributable profits are discussed more generally at 6.8 below.

6   COMPANIES ACT 2006

6.1   Basis of preparation of financial statements

The directors of every company (except certain dormant subsidiary undertakings that qualify for exemption from preparation of accounts – the criteria are set out in sections 394A to C) must prepare individual accounts for the company for each financial year (see 6.2 below). *[s394]*. The directors of a parent company must prepare group accounts, unless there is an exemption available from preparation of group accounts (see 6.3 below).

Directors must not approve accounts unless they are satisfied that they give a true and fair view of the assets, liabilities, financial position and profit or loss of the company and in the case of group accounts, of the undertakings included in the consolidation as a whole, so far as concerns members of the company. *[s393]*. See 7.2 below for a discussion of accounting standards and 'true and fair'.

6.1.1   *Choice of IAS accounts and Companies Act accounts under the CA 2006*

The CA 2006 distinguishes between IAS accounts and Companies Act accounts. Financial statements prepared in accordance with the CA 2006 using EU-adopted IFRS are IAS accounts. Financial statements prepared in accordance with the CA 2006 using FRS 101, FRS 102 or FRS 105 are Companies Act accounts.

See 6.2 below for the requirements for IAS accounts and Companies Act accounts.

A company's individual accounts may be prepared:

- in accordance with section 396 (Companies Act individual accounts); or
- in accordance with EU-adopted IFRS (IAS individual accounts). *[s395(1)]*.

This is subject to the restrictions on changes of financial reporting framework and the requirements for consistency of financial reporting framework within the individual accounts of group undertakings (see 6.1.2 and 6.1.3 below).

The group accounts of certain parent companies are required by Article 4 of the IAS Regulation to be prepared in accordance with EU-adopted IFRS. *[s403(1)]*. Article 4 of the IAS Regulation requires an EEA-incorporated company with securities admitted to trading on a regulated market (as at its financial year end) to prepare its consolidated financial statements in accordance with EU-adopted IFRS.

The group accounts of other companies may be prepared:

- in accordance with section 404 (Companies Act group accounts); or
- in accordance with EU-adopted IFRS (IAS group accounts). *[s403(2)]*.

This is subject to the restrictions on changes of financial reporting framework (see 6.1.2 below).

The individual and any group accounts of a company that is a charity must be Companies Act accounts. *[s395(2), s403(3)]*.

6.1.2   CA 2006 restrictions on changes of financial reporting framework

Under the CA 2006, a company which wishes to change from preparing IAS individual accounts to preparing Companies Act individual accounts (such as financial statements prepared under FRS 101, FRS 102 or FRS 105) may do so only:

- if there is a relevant change of circumstance (see below); or
- for financial years ending on or after 1 October 2012, for a reason other than a relevant change of circumstance, provided the company has not changed to Companies Act individual accounts in the period of five years preceding the first day of that financial year. In calculating the five year period, no account is taken of a change made due to a relevant change of circumstance. *[s395(3)-(5)]*.

The same requirements apply where a company wishes to change from preparing IAS group accounts to preparing Companies Act group accounts, except that the references to individual accounts above are to group accounts. *[s403(4)-(6)]*.

These requirements enable a group where the parent and subsidiary undertakings prepare IAS individual accounts to instead prepare FRS 101 financial statements or even FRS 102 financial statements (as these are both Companies Act individual accounts) where the above criteria are met.

A relevant change of circumstance in respect of individual accounts occurs if, at any time during or after the first financial year in which the directors of a company prepare IAS individual accounts:

- the company becomes a subsidiary undertaking of another undertaking that does not prepare IAS individual accounts;
- the company ceases to be a subsidiary undertaking;
- the company ceases to be a company with securities admitted to trading on a regulated market in an EEA State; or
- a parent undertaking of the company ceases to be an undertaking with securities admitted to trading on a regulated market in an EEA State. *[s395(4)]*.

A relevant change of circumstance for the purposes of group accounts occurs if, at any time during or after the first financial year in which the directors of a parent company prepare IAS group accounts:

- the company becomes a subsidiary undertaking of another undertaking that does not prepare IAS group accounts;
- the company ceases to be a company with securities admitted to trading on a regulated market in an EEA State; or
- a parent undertaking of the company ceases to be an undertaking with securities admitted to trading on a regulated market in an EEA State. *[s403(5)]*.

Section 395's requirements in respect of individual accounts and section 403's requirements in respect of group accounts operate independently of each other. Therefore, an IFRS reporter would be permitted to move from IAS accounts to Companies Act accounts in its individual accounts, while continuing to prepare IAS group accounts.

Paragraph 9.18 of the June 2008 BERR document *Guidance for UK Companies on Accounting and Reporting: Requirements under the Companies Act 2006 and the application of the IAS regulation* notes that the first example of a relevant change in circumstance in the lists above is 'intended to deal with situations where a subsidiary undertaking is sold by a group generally using IAS, to another group or entity not generally using IAS. It is not intended that companies switch between accounting regimes on the basis of an internal group restructuring.'

The restriction is 'one-way' only from IAS accounts to Companies Act accounts. There is no restriction on the number of times a company can move from Companies Act accounts to IAS accounts or *vice versa* so theoretically a company could 'flip' from IAS accounts to Companies Act accounts and back again several times without a relevant change of circumstance provided it reverted back to Companies Act accounts no more than once every five years.

The CA 2006 does not restrict changes made between FRS 101, FRS 102 or FRS 105 since these are all Companies Act accounts.

6.1.3   Consistency of financial reporting framework in individual accounts of group undertakings

The CA 2006 requires that the directors of a UK parent company must secure that the individual accounts of the parent company and of each of its subsidiary undertakings are prepared under the same financial reporting framework, be it IAS accounts or Companies Act accounts, except to the extent that in the directors' opinion there are 'good reasons' for not doing so. *[s407(1)]*. However, this requirement does not apply:

- where the UK parent company does not prepare group accounts under the CA 2006; *[s407(2)]*

- to accounts of subsidiary undertakings not required to be prepared under Part 15 of the CA 2006 (e.g. accounts of a foreign subsidiary undertaking); *[s407(3)]* or

- to accounts of any subsidiary undertakings that are charities, *[s407(4)]*, (so charities and non-charities within a group are not required to use the same financial reporting framework in their accounts). Charities are not permitted to prepare either IAS group or IAS individual accounts. *[s395(2), s403(3)]*.

Additionally, a parent company that prepares both consolidated and separate financial statements under EU-adopted IFRS (i.e. IAS group accounts and IAS individual accounts) is not required to ensure that its subsidiary undertakings all prepare IAS individual accounts. However, it must ensure that its subsidiary undertakings use the same financial reporting framework (i.e. all prepare IAS accounts or all prepare Companies Act accounts) in their individual accounts unless there are 'good reasons' for not doing so. *[s407(5)]*.

Although not explicitly stated by FRS 100, there appears to be no requirement that all subsidiary undertakings in a group must use the same GAAP for their Companies Act individual accounts. Some could use, for example, FRS 101, and others could use FRS 102 since all are Companies Act individual accounts and therefore part of the same financial reporting framework. This approach would comply with the statutory requirements of Section 407. However, groups that use a 'mix' of GAAP in the individual financial statements may be challenged by HMRC, particularly if this results in tax arbitrage. Examples of 'good reasons' for not preparing all individual accounts within a group using the same financial reporting framework are contained in the June 2008 BERR document *Guidance for UK Companies On Accounting and Reporting: Requirements under the Companies Act 2006 and the application of the IAS regulation*. Paragraph 9.17 of the Guidance notes that this provision is intended to provide a degree of flexibility where there are genuine (including cost/benefit) grounds for using different accounting frameworks within a group of companies and identifies the following examples:

- 'A group using IAS acquired a subsidiary undertaking that had not been using IAS; in the first year of acquisition, it might not be practical for the newly acquired company to switch to IAS straight away.

- The group contains subsidiary undertakings that are themselves publicly traded, in which case market pressures or regulatory requirements to use IAS might come into play, without necessarily justifying a switch to IAS by the non-publicly traded subsidiaries.

- A subsidiary undertaking or the parent were planning to apply for a listing and so might wish to convert to IAS in advance, but the rest of the group was not planning to apply for a listing.

- The group contains minor or dormant subsidiaries where the costs of switching accounting framework would outweigh the benefits.

The key point is that the directors of the parent company must be able to justify any inconsistency to shareholders, regulators or other interested parties'.

6.2   Companies Act requirements for the annual report and accounts

Part 15 of the CA 2006 sets out the requirements for the annual report and accounts for UK companies.

The company's 'annual accounts' are the company's individual accounts for that year and any group accounts prepared by the company for that year.

Section 408 permits a parent company preparing group accounts (whether as IAS group accounts or Companies Act group accounts) to omit the individual profit and loss account from the annual accounts, where the conditions for this exemption are met (see 6.3.2 below). *[s471(1)].*

References in Part 15 to the annual accounts (or to a balance sheet or profit and loss account) include notes to the accounts giving information required by any provision of the CA 2006 or EU-adopted IFRS, and that is required or allowed by any such provision to be given in a note to the company's accounts. *[s472].*

The principal CA 2006 requirements for annual accounts are set out at 6.2.1 below and for the annual report at 6.2.2 below. While this chapter focuses on the disclosure requirements for UK companies, LLPs and other types of entities other than companies are also subject to similar statutory requirements. Reference should be made to the legislation that applies to such entities.

The Listing Rules, Disclosure and Transparency Rules or rules of the relevant securities market may require additional information beyond that required by the CA 2006 (and related regulations) to be included in the annual reports. For example, premium listed companies must state how they apply the main principles of, and present a statement of compliance or otherwise with the provisions of the UK Corporate Governance Code.[7] It is beyond the scope of this publication to cover such regulatory requirements.

6.2.1   Companies Act requirements for annual accounts

6.2.1.A   Companies Act accounts

Companies Act individual accounts and Companies Act group accounts are prepared in accordance with sections 396 and 404 of the CA 2006 respectively. Companies Act accounts comprise:

- a balance sheet as at the last day of the financial year that gives a true and fair view of the state of affairs of the company (and in respect of group accounts, of the parent company and its subsidiary undertakings included in the consolidation as a whole, so far as concerns members of the company) as at the end of the financial year; and

- a profit and loss account that gives a true and fair view of the profit or loss of the company (and in respect of group accounts, of the parent company and its subsidiary undertakings included in the consolidation as a whole, so far as concerns members of the company) for the financial year. *[s396(1)-(2), s404(1)-(2)]*.

The accounts must comply with regulations as to the form and content of the company balance sheet and profit and loss account (and in respect of group accounts, of the consolidated balance sheet and consolidated profit and loss account) and additional information provided by way of notes to the accounts. *[s396(3), s404(3)]*.

These regulations are principally *The Large and Medium-sized Companies and Groups (Accounts and Reports) Regulations 2008* (Regulations), as amended. Companies subject to the small companies regime (see 6.5 below) are entitled to apply *The Small Companies and Groups (Accounts and Directors' Report) Regulations 2008* (Small Companies Regulations), as amended. Micro-entities (see 6.4 below) are entitled to apply *The Small Companies (Micro Entities' Accounts) Regulations 2013* (Micro-entities Regulations), as amended.

If compliance with the regulations and any other provisions made by or under the CA 2006 as to the matters to be included in the accounts or notes to those accounts would not be sufficient to give a true and fair view, the necessary additional information must be given in the accounts or notes to the accounts. *[s396(4), s404(4)]*. If in special circumstances, compliance with any of those provisions is inconsistent with the requirement to give a true and fair view, the directors must depart from that provision to the extent necessary to give a true and fair view. Particulars of any such departure, the reasons for it and its effect must be given in a note to the accounts. *[s396(5), s404(5)]*. See Chapter 6 at 9.2 for further discussion of the 'true and fair override' provided for in the CA 2006 and FRS 102's requirements for a true and fair view.

6.2.1.B   IAS accounts

Where the directors prepare IAS individual and/or IAS group accounts, they must state in the notes to those accounts that they have been prepared in accordance with EU-adopted IFRS. *[s397(2), s406(2), s474]*.

Where the section 408 exemption to omit the individual profit and loss account is taken where group accounts are prepared, the notes to IAS individual accounts must state that they have been prepared in accordance with EU-adopted IFRS as applied in accordance with the provisions of the CA 2006. See 6.3.2 below.

6.2.1.C   General – Companies Act accounts and IAS accounts

There are two types of CA 2006 disclosures required for a UK company:

(a)   those required by the Regulations (or other applicable regulations, as discussed below) for an entity preparing Companies Act accounts but not for an entity preparing IAS accounts (see 6.7.1 below); and

(b)   those required for both IAS accounts and Companies Act accounts (see 6.7.2 below).

The CA 2006 distinguishes between companies that are micro-entities (see 6.4 below), companies subject to the small companies regime (see 6.5 below), and medium-sized companies (see 6.6 below).

The above categories of company are all based on meeting certain size criteria and not being excluded from the applicable regime. These companies benefit from a lighter disclosure regime in their financial statements than for large companies, i.e. the default category of companies that are not medium-sized companies, subject to the small companies regime or the micro-entities regime. Certain disclosure exemptions are available to companies preparing IAS accounts or Companies Act accounts, whereas others are only available to companies preparing Companies Act accounts. Companies subject to the small companies regime are entitled to follow the Small Companies Regulations and companies subject to the micro-entities regime are entitled to follow the Micro-entities Regulations (rather than the Regulations).

The CA 2006 also distinguishes between quoted and unquoted companies. While there is no difference in the disclosures required in the financial statements by the CA 2006 and the Regulations for quoted and unquoted companies, there are significant additional disclosures for quoted companies in the annual report (see 6.2.2 below). There are also disclosures only required to be given by companies with securities admitted to trading on a regulated market (see 6.2.2. below).

The CA 2006 requires that both Companies Act and IAS accounts group and individual accounts must give disclosures to explain the status of a company. A company must state: *[s396(A1), s397(1), s404(A1), s406(1)]*

- the part of the United Kingdom in which the company is registered;
- the company's registered number;
- whether the company is a public or private company and whether it is limited by shares or by guarantee;
- the address of the company's registered office; and
- where appropriate, the fact that the company is being wound-up.

A company's annual accounts must be approved by the board of directors and signed on behalf of the board by a director of the company, with the signature included on the company's balance sheet. *[s414(1)]*.

6.2.1.D   Interaction of the Small Companies Regulations with FRS 101 and FRS 102

FRS 101 and FRS 102 (unless Section 1A is applied) do not permit use of the formats included in the Small Companies Regulations (see 6.5 below). *[FRS 101.5(b), AG1(h)-(i), FRS 102.4.2, 5.5, 5.7]*. However, a small entity that applies Section 1A of FRS 102 must present a statement of financial position and profit or loss in accordance with the requirements set out in Part 1 of Schedule 1 to the Small Companies Regulations or Part 1 of Schedule 1 to the Small LLP Regulations (except to the extent that these requirements are not permitted by any statutory framework under which such entities report). *[FRS 102.1A.4, 1A.12, 1A.14]*.

In our view, a company subject to the small companies regime which chooses to apply FRS 101, or which chooses to apply FRS 102 without applying Section 1A, is not precluded from taking advantage of other exemptions applicable to companies subject to the small companies regime. See Chapter 2 at 2.2 and Chapter 3 at 4.1.1.

Companies applying the micro-entity provisions (see 6.4 below) must apply FRS 105 (see 4.4.6 above).

6.2.2   Companies Act requirements for annual reports

The content of the annual report depends principally on whether the company is an unquoted company or a quoted company.

A quoted company means a company whose equity share capital:

- has been included in the Official List (as defined in section 103(1) of the Financial Services and Markets Act 2000) in accordance with the provisions of Part 6 of the Financial Services and Markets Act 2000; or
- is officially listed in an EEA State; or
- is admitted to dealing on either the New York Stock Exchange or the exchange known as Nasdaq.

A company is a quoted company in relation to a financial year if it is a quoted company immediately before the end of the accounting reference period (defined in section 391 of the CA 2006) by reference to which that financial year was determined. An unquoted company means a company that is not a quoted company. *[s385(1)-(3)]*.

The content of the annual reports and accounts of an unquoted and a quoted company are as follows:

- an unquoted company's annual accounts and reports comprise its annual accounts, strategic report (if required – see 6.2.2.B below), directors' report (unless a micro-entity – see 6.2.2.B below), any separate corporate governance statement and the auditor's report (unless the company is exempt from audit); and
- a quoted company's annual accounts and reports comprise its annual accounts, directors' remuneration report, strategic report, directors' report, any separate corporate governance statement, and the auditor's report.

Where the company is a parent company preparing group accounts, the directors' and strategic reports must be consolidated reports (i.e. a 'group directors' report' and 'group strategic report') relating to the undertakings included in the consolidation. These group reports may, when appropriate, give greater emphasis to the matters that are significant to the undertakings included in the consolidation. *[s414A-s414D, s415-s419]*.

In addition, companies with more than 500 employees that are traded companies, banking companies, authorised insurance companies and companies carrying on insurance market activity are required to comply with the Non-financial Reporting Regulations and must prepare a non-financial information statement within the strategic report. However, there are some scope exceptions (see 6.2.2.D below). The information should be provided on a consolidated basis for groups. *[s414CA-CB]*.

Entities are encouraged to meet the requirements of the non-financial information statement through a title and a series of cross-references, so as to maintain the coherence of the strategic report. Entities are discouraged from replicating information located elsewhere in the strategic report in the non-financial information statement.[8]

Small and medium-sized companies are entitled to certain exemptions (see 6.2.2.B below). Companies with securities admitted to a regulated market must make statutory corporate governance disclosures in the annual report and quoted companies have extended disclosures (see 6.2.2.C below). These include the Takeovers Directive disclosures required in the directors' report for companies with securities carrying voting rights admitted to trading on a regulated market at the financial year end. *[7 Sch 13]*. For large private companies, The Companies (Miscellaneous Reporting) Regulations 2018 (see 6.2.2.A) introduce a requirement to include disclosures of their corporate governance arrangements in the Directors' Report. AIM Rule 26 also requires that from 28 September 2018, AIM companies must provide details (on a website) explaining how they comply with, and where they depart from, a chosen 'recognised' corporate governance code.

A company's strategic report (if any), directors' report, directors' remuneration report (if any), and separate corporate governance statement (if any) must be approved by the board of directors and signed on behalf of the board by a director or the secretary of the company. *[s414D(1), s419(1), s419A, s422(1)]*.

It is beyond the scope of this publication to set out the content of the directors' report, strategic report, directors' remuneration report or corporate governance statement. In July 2018, the FRC published updated *Guidance on the Strategic Report*. The Guidance is intended to be persuasive rather than have mandatory force. In September 2016, the GC 100 and Investor Group published *Directors' Remuneration Report Guidance* which provides best practice guidance on the directors' remuneration report prepared by quoted companies.

In July 2018, Parliament approved the statutory instrument, The Companies (Miscellaneous Reporting) Regulations 2018 (SI 2018/860). The legislation introduces a wide range of disclosures, with varying applicability, discussed at 6.2.2.A below.

6.2.2.A   The Companies (Miscellaneous Reporting) Regulations 2018

The disclosures required by The Companies (Miscellaneous Reporting) Regulations 2018 (SI 2018/860) are applicable to accounting periods beginning on or after 1 January 2019.

The main disclosure requirements introduced are:

- a statement in the strategic report to set out how directors have had regard to the matters set out in Section 172 (1) (a)-(f). Section 172 covers the directors' duty to promote the success of the company for the benefit of its members as a whole and sets out certain matters to which the directors' must have regard in doing this. This statement is called a 'section 172(1) statement' (applies to all companies that prepare a strategic report unless they qualify as medium-sized);

- the directors' report must detail how directors have engaged with employees, and the effect of their regard for employee interests on principal decisions taken by the company (applies to all companies with more than 250 UK employees or for companies that are parents, more than 250 UK employees in the group);

- the directors' report must summarise how directors have had regard for suppliers, customers and others, and the effect of that regard on principal decisions taken by the company (applies to any company which meets two or more of the following size criteria – turnover above £36m, balance sheet total of over £18m, more than 250 employees);

- a statement of corporate governance arrangements must be made in the directors' report detailing which corporate governance code the company applies (and how the code is applied, including explanations for any departure from application), and if no code is applied, why and what governance arrangements are in place (applies to all UK companies with either (a) more than 2,000 employees globally, and / or (b) turnover above £200m and a balance sheet of over £2bn. There are a number of exemptions. For example, companies required to prepare a statutory corporate governance statement under section 472A of CA 2006 (see 6.2.2.C) are exempt; and

- a 'pay ratios table' of executive pay to the first quartile, median and third quartile of employee pay. Where a company is a parent, the ratio information must relate to the group (applies to quoted companies with more than 250 UK employees or for quoted companies that are parents, with more than 250 UK employees in the group).

In addition, for quoted companies, there are a number of other amendments to directors' remuneration report requirements, including enhanced reporting on the impact of a share price change on executive pay awards.

Many of the disclosure requirements above that are subject to size thresholds are only required in the second year in which the company exceeds the relevant thresholds, however the specific requirements vary in each case so careful consideration will be required to determine whether the disclosure requirements are applicable in respect of a particular financial year.

6.2.2.B   Exemptions for micro, small and medium-sized companies

The directors of a company must prepare a strategic report for the financial year unless the company is entitled to the small companies exemption (see 6.5 below). *[s414A(2), s414B]*.

There are certain disclosure exemptions available in respect of the strategic report for a medium-sized company (see 6.6 below).

All companies, except for micro entities, must prepare a directors' report for the financial year. *[s415]*. The exemption for micro entities was introduced following the implementation of the EU Accounting Directive. *[s415(1A)]*. A company subject to the small companies regime (see 6.5 below) is entitled to prepare the directors' report in accordance with the Small Companies Regulations which has significantly fewer disclosures than a directors' report prepared in accordance with the Regulations. *[s382-s384, 5 Sch (SC)]*. There are also certain disclosure exemptions available in respect of the directors' report for a company entitled to the small companies exemption. These exemptions are discussed in Chapter 5 at 12.2.

6.2.2.C   *Additional requirements for quoted companies and companies with transferable securities admitted to trading on a regulated market*

The directors of a quoted company must prepare a directors' remuneration report for the financial year. *[s420-s422, 8 Sch 1]*.

A quoted company must also include additional disclosures in the directors' report (greenhouse gas disclosures) and strategic report compared to those required for an unquoted company. Additional disclosures for quoted companies in the strategic report include:

- the company's strategy and business model;
- gender diversity disclosures; and
- to the extent necessary for an understanding of the development, performance or position of the company's business:
  - the main trends and factors likely to affect the future development, performance and position of the company's business; and
  - certain information about environmental matters (including the impact of the company's business on the environment), the company's employees and social, community and human rights issues). *[s414C(7)-(10)]*.

Where group accounts are prepared, the information required relates to the undertakings included in the consolidation (i.e. the consolidated group) rather than the company, except that there are detailed requirements on the gender diversity disclosures required. *[s414C(10), (13)]*.

UK companies with transferable securities admitted to trading on a regulated market are required to prepare a statutory corporate governance statement. *[s472A]*. The requirements for the statutory corporate governance statement are included in the FCA's Disclosure and Transparency Rules (DTR) for a UK company, although the DTR extend the requirement to prepare a corporate governance statement to certain overseas listed companies, *[DTR 1B.1.4-1.6, DTR 7.2]*, and there may be corresponding requirements in other EEA states.

UK and overseas premium listed companies are also required to state how they apply the main principles of, and present a statement of compliance or otherwise with the provisions of the UK Corporate Governance Code.[9] This UK Corporate Governance Code statement overlaps with certain of the content requirements in DTR 7.2 for the statutory corporate governance statement (and with the required statement on audit committees included in DTR 7.1 which applies to issuers with securities admitted to trading on a regulated market required to appoint a statutory auditor, unless exempted from the requirements). *[DTR 1B.1.1-1.3, DTR 7.1]*.

In addition, the disclosures in DTR 7.2.8AR (diversity policy) must be made in the corporate governance statement required by DTR 7.2. The disclosures must explain the diversity policy applied to the issuer's administrative, management and supervisory bodies with regard to aspects such as, for instance, age, gender, or educational and professional backgrounds. In addition, the following must also be disclosed:

- the objectives of the diversity policy;
- how the diversity policy has been implemented; and
- the result of applying the policy in the reporting period.

The disclosures in DTR 7.2.8AR do not apply to:

(a) a company which has not issued shares admitted to trading, unless it has issued shares which are traded on an MTF (multilateral trading facility); or

(b) a company that qualifies as a small company (as defined in sections 382-382 CA 2006) or a medium company (as defined in sections 465-466 CA 2006 in the financial year; or

(c) an overseas company that would qualify as a small or medium company if it were incorporated in the UK. *[DTR.1B.1.6R-8R]*.

The statutory corporate governance statement can be included as part of the directors' report or as a separate corporate governance statement published together with and in the same manner as its annual report or on a website. *[DTR 7.2.9-11]*. A 'separate corporate governance statement' is defined as one not included in the directors' report, and therefore has its own approval and publication requirements. *[s472A(3)]*.

The directors' report of a company with securities carrying voting rights admitted to trading on a regulated market at the financial year end must include certain disclosures concerning the company's capital and control (Takeovers Directive disclosures). *[7 Sch 13]*. These disclosures are also required by DTR 7.2 as part of the statutory corporate governance statement.

6.2.2.D   Additional requirements for Public Interest Entities ('PIEs')

PIEs are required to include a non-financial reporting information statement within the strategic report. A PIE is defined as an entity that, at any time in the financial year, is:

- a traded company (i.e. a company with transferable securities admitted to trading on a regulated market);
- a banking company;
- an authorised insurance company; or
- a company carrying on insurance market activity.

The non-financial information statement requirements were introduced in December 2016, by *The Companies, Partnerships and Groups (Accounts and Non-financial Reporting) Regulations 2016* (SI 2016/1245). This Statutory Instrument primarily implements the requirements of the Non-financial Reporting Directive in the UK. The requirement to prepare a non-financial reporting information statement are effective for companies (and qualifying partnerships) for financial years beginning on or after 1 January 2017.

The requirement applies where the company, or if the company is a parent company, the group, is not small (i.e. is not subject to the small companies regime in sections 382 to 384) or medium-sized (as set out in sections 465 to 467), and where the company or the group headed by the company has over 500 employees (average monthly total) in the financial year. However, subsidiary undertakings that are included in a group strategic report of its UK parent containing the non-financial information statement (or the consolidated management report /separate report of an EEA parent containing the information required by the Non-financial Reporting Directive) are exempt.

The non-financial information statement must contain information, to the extent necessary for an understanding of the company's development, performance and position and the impact of its activity, relating to, as a minimum:

- environmental matters (including the impact of the company's business on the environment);
- the company's employees;
- social matters;
- respect for human rights; and
- anti-corruption and anti-bribery matters.

The information disclosed must include:

(a) a brief description of the company's business model;

(b) a description of the policies pursued by the company in relation to the matters above and any due diligence process implemented by the company in pursuance of those policies;

(c) a description of the outcome of those policies;

(d) a description of the principal risks relating to the matters above arising in connection with the company's operations and, where relevant and proportionate:

    (i) a description of its business relationships, products and services which are likely to cause adverse impacts in those areas of risk, and

    (ii) a description of how it manages the principal risks; and

(e) a description of the non-financial key performance indicators relevant to the company's business.

6.3   Preparation of consolidated financial statements

The CA 2006 requires a UK company that is a parent company at its financial year end, to prepare group accounts (i.e. consolidated financial statements) unless otherwise exempt (see below). *[s399]*. A company that is exempt from the requirement to prepare group accounts may still do so. *[s399(4)]*.

A company that is subject to the small companies regime (or would be subject to the small companies regime except for it being a public company) is not required to prepare group accounts, but may do so. The exemption from preparing group accounts does not apply if the company is a member of a group which, at any time during the financial year, has an undertaking as a member which is established under the law of an EEA State, has to prepare its accounts in accordance with the EU Accounting Directive, and is an undertaking:

- which has been designated by an EEA State as a 'public-interest entity' under the EU Accounting Directive; or

- whose transferable securities are admitted to trading on a regulated market in an EEA State ('a traded company'); or

- which is a credit institution (as per Article 4(1)(1) of Regulation 575/2013 other than one listed in Article 2 of Directive 2013/36/EU); or

- which is an insurance undertaking (as per Article 2(1) of Directive 91/674/EEC). *[s399(2), s399(2A)-(2B)]*.

The other CA 2006 exemptions from preparation of group accounts comprise:

- Section 400 – parent company is a majority or wholly owned subsidiary undertaking whose immediate parent undertaking is established under the law of an EEA State, and is consolidated in group accounts of a larger group drawn up by an EEA parent undertaking (see Chapter 8 at 3.1.1.A);

- Section 401 – parent company is a majority or wholly owned subsidiary undertaking whose parent undertaking is not established under the law of an EEA State, and which is consolidated in group accounts of a larger group drawn up by a parent undertaking (see Chapter 8 at 3.1.1.B); and

- Section 402 – parent company, none of whose subsidiary undertakings need be included in the consolidation (see Chapter 8 at 3.1.1.E). *[s399(3)]*.

FRS 102 has been developed to be consistent with the requirements for group accounts (and exemptions) included in Part 15 of the CA 2006. Consequently, the detailed conditions for the above exemptions from preparing group accounts under the CA 2006 are discussed further in Chapter 8 at 3.1.1 and Chapter 5 at 6.2.

The application guidance to FRS 100 explains the use of equivalence in the context of the exemption from preparing consolidated financial statements under s401. This is discussed in Chapter 2 at 2.1.6 (FRS 101) and Chapter 8 at 3.1.1.C (FRS 102).

6.3.1   Requirements of accounting standards to prepare consolidated financial statements

FRS 100 does not address the requirements to prepare consolidated financial statements (nor do FRS 101 or FRS 105, since these standards only address individual financial statements).

EU-adopted IFRS and FRS 102 both include requirements on which entities should prepare consolidated financial statements, and how these should be prepared. Their requirements need to be read in conjunction with the requirements of the relevant statutory framework for preparation of the entity's financial statements.

FRS 102 requires an entity, that is a parent at its year end, to present consolidated financial statements in which it consolidates all its investments in subsidiaries in accordance with the standard (except those permitted or required to be excluded from consolidation) unless it is exempt from the requirement to prepare consolidated financial statements provided in the standard. *[FRS 102.9.2-9.3].* As noted above, FRS 102's requirements to prepare group accounts (and exemptions) are consistent with the requirements of the CA 2006. A small entity that is a parent entity is not required to prepare consolidated financial statements under Section 1A of FRS 102 (see Chapter 5 at 6.2). *[FRS 102.1A.21].* However, the CA 2006 is more restrictive than this, requiring a small entity that is a parent entity to prepare group accounts if the company is a member of a group which contains certain types of entities (see 6.3 above and Chapter 5 at 6.2).

6.3.2 Exemption from publishing the individual profit and loss account where group accounts are prepared

Where a company prepares group accounts in accordance with the CA 2006,

- the company's individual profit and loss account need not contain the information specified in paragraphs 65 to 69 of Schedule 1 to the Regulations (specified information supplementing the profit and loss account); and
- the company's individual profit and loss account must be approved by the directors in accordance with section 414(1) but may be omitted from the company's annual accounts.

This exemption is conditional on the company's individual balance sheet showing the company's profit or loss for the financial year (determined in accordance with the CA 2006) and use of the exemption conferred by section 408 being disclosed in the annual accounts. *[s408, Regulations 3(2)].*

Example 1.1: Example of a s408 exemption statement

Basis of preparation
The group accounts consolidate the financial statements of ABC Limited (the company) and all its subsidiary undertakings drawn up to 31 December each year. No individual profit and loss account is presented for ABC Limited as permitted by section 408 of the Companies Act 2006.
[...]
Parent company balance sheet
The profit for the financial year of the company is £130,000 (2018: £111,000).

The exemption is available for both Companies Act and IAS group accounts. Paragraph 9.24 of the June 2008 BERR document *Guidance for UK Companies on Accounting and Reporting: Requirements under the Companies Act 2006 and the application of the IAS regulation* clarifies that:

'The omission of the profit and loss account (referred to within IAS as the income statement) might be considered to be inconsistent with certain aspects of IAS, for example, the requirement in IAS 1 *Presentation of Financial Statements* in relation to a fair presentation. However, IAS does not in itself require the preparation of separate financial statements but permits the omission of certain elements. In other words, the separate financial statements required to be published under the 2006 Act are an extract of the full IAS separate financial statements. This exemption should not affect the ability of a parent company to be treated as a "first-time adopter" and hence to take advantage of exemptions for first time use under the provisions of IFRS 1. The company will need to provide the disclosure required by section 408(4) i.e. that advantage has been taken of the publication exemption in section 408(1). The auditor will also need to describe the accounting framework that has been used within its audit reports. In respect of individual accounts, the reference to the framework will need to make clear that its basis is IAS as adopted by the EU as applied in accordance with the provisions of the 2006 Act.'

Paragraph 9.25 of the BERR guidance further notes that:

'The exemption in the 2006 Act relates only to the profit and loss account. By virtue of section 472(2), the exemption also extends to the notes to the profit and loss account. The individual IAS accounts would, however, still need to include the other primary statements and note disclosures required by IAS, including a cash flow statement and a statement of changes in shareholders' equity.'

6.4   Micro-entities regime

The voluntary regime for companies that are micro-entities was introduced into UK companies legislation by *The Small Companies (Micro-Entities' Accounts) Regulations 2013* (SI 2013/3008) (Micro-entities Regulations), and was effective for financial years ending on or after 30 September 2013 for companies filing their accounts on or after 1 December 2013. These regulations implemented the provisions of the EU Accounting Directive, which sets out certain minimum requirements for micro-entities into UK company law.

The Limited Liability Partnerships, Partnerships and Groups (Accounts and Audit) Regulations 2016 (SI 2016/575), issued in May 2016, extended the scope of the micro-entities regime to LLPs and qualifying partnerships for accounting periods beginning on or after 1 January 2016 (early application was permitted for periods beginning on or after 1 January 2015).

In response to the introduction of the Micro-entities Regulations and the new financial reporting framework (see 1 above) the FRC issued FRS 105 (see 4.4.6 above). FRS 105 is outside the scope of this publication and 6.4.1 and 6.4.2 below only address the Companies Act requirements for micro-entities.

6.4.1   *Scope of the micro-entities regime*

A company or an LLP or qualifying partnership can only use the micro-entity provisions if it meets the size criteria and is not excluded from being treated as a micro-entity. The size criteria operate in the same way as for the small companies regime (see 6.5 below and Chapter 5 at 4.3).

The micro-entity provisions are not available to overseas companies and other entities. The Explanatory Note to the Micro-entities Regulations confirms that the regime is only available to companies formed and registered (or treated as formed and registered) under the CA 2006.

The qualifying conditions for UK entities are met in a year in which the entity satisfies two or more of the following requirements: *[s384A(4)-(7)]*

- turnover must not exceed £632,000;
- balance sheet total (gross assets) must not exceed £316,000; and
- the number of employees must not exceed 10.

In the case of an entity which is a parent entity, the entity qualifies as a micro-entity in relation to a financial year only if the entity qualifies as a micro-entity in relation to that year and the group headed by the entity qualifies as a small group. *[s384A(8)]*.

The micro-entity provisions do not apply to an entity's accounts for a particular financial year if the entity was at any time within that year: *[s384B(1)]*

- a company excluded from the small companies regime, or small LLPs regime, by section 384;
- an investment undertaking as defined in Article 2(14) of the EU Accounting Directive (Directive 2013/34/EU);
- a financial holding undertaking as defined in Article 2(15) of the EU Accounting Directive;
- a credit institution as defined in Article 4 of Directive 2006/48/EC (other than one referred to in Article 2 of that directive);
- an insurance undertaking as defined in Article 2(1) of Directive 91/674/EEC; or
- a charity.

The micro-entity provisions also do not apply in relation to an entity's accounts for a financial year if the entity is a parent company which prepares group accounts for that year as permitted by section 399(4), or is not a parent entity but its accounts are included in consolidated group accounts for that year. *[s384B(2)]*.

6.4.2 Companies Act requirements for micro-entities

The Micro-entities Regulations provide extensive presentation and disclosure exemptions for micro-entities (known as the micro-entity provisions). In summary, a micro-entity applies one of two abridged formats for the balance sheet and one abridged format for the profit and loss account, as set out in the Section C formats included in the Small Companies Regulations and presents limited prescribed notes which must be included at the foot of the balance sheet. *[s472(1A)]*. The formats and related notes disclosures are known as the 'micro-entity minimum accounting items'. *[s474(1)]*.

The prescribed notes comprise: information on directors' advances, credits and guarantees (required by s413); and on financial guarantees and commitments (required by 1 Sch 57 to the Small Companies Regulations). The micro-entity is not required to give any of the other information required by way of notes to the accounts set out in Schedules 1 to 3 to the Small Companies Regulations. This means there is no requirement to give the information on related undertakings set out in Schedule 2 or the disclosures on directors' remuneration set out in Schedule 3. *[Regulations (SC) 4, 5, 5A]*.

Micro-entities are not required to prepare a directors' report. *[s415(1A)]*.

The alternative accounting rules and fair value accounting rules (explained further in Chapter 6 at 10) do not apply where the micro-entity provisions are applied; therefore a micro-entity applying the micro-entity provisions is not permitted to revalue tangible fixed assets, investment properties or financial instruments.

In considering whether the individual accounts give a true and fair view, the directors apply the following provisions:

- where the accounts comprise only micro-entity minimum accounting items, the directors must disregard any provision of an accounting standard which would require the accounts to contain information additional to those items;

- in relation to a micro-entity minimum accounting item contained in the accounts, the directors must disregard any provision of an accounting standard which would require the accounts to contain further information in relation to that item; and

- where the accounts contain an item of information additional to the micro-entity minimum accounting items, the directors must have regard to any provision of an accounting standard which relates to that item. *[s393(1A)]*.

Even though the presentation and disclosure requirements are minimal, 'the micro-entity minimum accounting items' included in the company's accounts for the year are presumed to give the true and fair view required (the usual requirements to give additional information where the matters required to be included in the accounts are not sufficient to give a true and fair view and the provisions on 'true and fair override' do not apply in relation to the micro-entity minimum accounting items included in the company's accounts for the year).

The auditor of a company which qualifies as a micro-entity in relation to a financial year applies the same provisions above in considering whether the individual accounts of the company for that year give a true and fair view. *[s495(3A)]*.

If the accounts are prepared in accordance with the micro-entity provisions, the balance sheet must contain a statement to this effect in a prominent place above the signature(s) of the director(s). *[s414(3)(a)]*.

Companies using the micro-entity provisions must file a copy of their accounts at Companies House. *[s444(3)]*. Micro-entities can use the filing exemptions for companies subject to the small companies regime (subject to making the statement that the accounts (and reports) have been delivered in accordance with the provisions applicable to companies subject to the small companies regime). *[s444(1)-(2), (5)]*.

6.4.3   Micro-entities in the Republic of Ireland

Equivalent legislation to the Micro-entities Regulations (see 6.4 above) was signed into Irish law in May 2017 (with a commencement date of 9 June 2017) as part of the Companies (Accounting) Act 2017. The Companies (Accounting) Act 2017 is mandatory for accounting periods beginning on or after 1 January 2017, but the micro-entities provisions can be adopted by Irish companies for periods beginning on or after 1 January 2015.

The qualifying conditions for Irish entities are different to those for UK entities (see 6.4.1 above) and are met in a year in which the entity satisfied two or more of the following requirements: *[FRS 105 Appendix IV.4]*

- turnover must not exceed €700,000;

- balance sheet total (gross assets) must not exceed €350,000; and

- the number of employees must not exceed 10.

Certain companies are excluded from being treated as micro companies, including those excluded from the small companies regime, investment undertakings, financial holding undertakings, holding companies voluntarily preparing consolidated financial statements and subsidiaries included in consolidated financial statements. The Companies Act 2014 should be referred to for a full list of excluded companies. *[FRS 105 Appendix IV.4]*.

6.5   Small companies

There are two sets of exemptions available for small companies:

- the small companies regime – which applies to the preparation and/or filing of the financial statements; and
- the small companies exemption – which applies to the preparation and/or filing of the strategic report and directors' report.

The small companies regime and small companies exemption under the Companies Act are discussed in Chapter 5 at 12. This discussion is relevant to both companies preparing Companies Act accounts (such as those prepared in accordance with FRS 101 and FRS 102) and IAS accounts (in accordance with EU-adopted IFRS).

Chapter 5 also addresses the requirements in Section 1A of FRS 102 for entities subject to the small entities regime.

6.6   Medium-sized companies and groups

Medium-sized companies and groups must apply the Regulations in preparing their annual reports and accounts. A medium-sized company may take advantage of certain disclosure exemptions in its annual reports and accounts for a financial year in which the company qualifies as medium-sized and is not an excluded company. *[s465-467]*.

There is no requirement for the annual reports and accounts of a medium-sized company to state use of the disclosure exemptions.

6.6.1   *Qualification as medium-sized company*

The medium-sized companies regime works in the same way as the small companies regime (described in Chapter 3 at 4.1.2). The size criteria and excluded companies are detailed below.

6.6.1.A   *Size criteria for medium-sized companies and groups*

A company qualifies as medium-sized in relation to its first financial year if the qualifying conditions are met in that year. *[s465(1)]*.

A group qualifies as medium-sized in relation to a subsequent financial year if the qualifying conditions are met in that year. *[s465(2)]*. In relation to a subsequent financial year, where on its balance sheet date a company meets or cease to meet the qualifying conditions, then that will affect its qualification as a medium-sized company only if it occurs in two consecutive years. *[s465(3)]*.

Where the company itself is a parent undertaking, then it only qualifies as medium-sized if the group that it heads qualifies as a medium-sized group. This is the case whether or not group accounts are prepared. A group qualifies as medium-sized in relation to its first financial year if the qualifying conditions (as set out below) are met in that year. In relation to a subsequent financial year, where on its balance sheet date a group meets or ceases to meet the qualifying conditions, then that will affect its qualification as a medium-sized company only if it occurs in two consecutive years. *[s466]*.

The qualifying conditions for a medium-sized company are met in a year in which the company satisfies two or more of the following requirements: *[s465]*

- turnover must not exceed £36 million;
- balance sheet total (gross assets) must not exceed £18 million; and
- the number of employees must not exceed 250.

The qualifying conditions for a medium-sized group are met in a year in which the group headed by the company satisfies two or more of the following requirements: *[s466]*

- turnover must not exceed £36 million net (or £43.2 million gross);
- balance sheet total must not exceed £18 million (or £21.6 million gross); and
- the number of employees must not exceed 250.

The aggregate figures for the above limits are ascertained by aggregating the relevant figures determined in accordance with section 466 for each member of the group. The figures used for each subsidiary undertaking are those included in its individual accounts for the relevant financial year. That is, where its financial year is coterminous with that of the parent company, the financial year that ends at the same date as the parent company, or where its financial year is not coterminous, the financial year ending last before the end of the financial year of the parent company. If those figures are not obtainable without disproportionate expense or undue delay, the latest available figures are used.

The turnover and balance sheet total criteria may be satisfied on either the gross or net of consolidation adjustments basis. For Companies Act accounts (such as FRS 102 financial statements), the consolidation adjustments are determined in accordance with regulations made under section 404, i.e. the Regulations. For IAS accounts, the consolidation adjustments are determined in accordance with EU-adopted IFRS. It is permissible to satisfy one limit on the 'net' basis and the other on the 'gross' basis. *[s466(4)-(7)]*.

6.6.1.B   Companies excluded from medium-sized companies

A company is not entitled to take advantage of any of the provisions available for companies qualifying as medium-sized if it was at any time within the financial year to which the accounts relate:

- a public company;
- a company that has permission under Part 4 of the Financial Services and Markets Act 2000 to carry on a regulated activity;
- a company that carries on an insurance market activity;
- an e-money issuer; or
- a member of an ineligible group. *[s467(1)]*.

A group is ineligible if any of its members is:

- a traded company;
- a body corporate (other than a company) whose shares are admitted to trading on a regulated market in an EEA State (as defined in Directive 2004/39/EC);
- a person (other than a small company) who has permission under Part 4 of the Financial Services and Markets Act 2000 to carry on a regulated activity;
- an e-money issuer;
- a small company that is an authorised insurance company, banking company, a MiFID investment firm or a UCITS management company; or
- a person who carries on an insurance market activity. *[s467(2)]*.

A company is a small company for the purposes of section 467(2) if it qualified as small in relation to its last financial year ending on or before the end of the financial years to which the accounts relate. *[s467(3)]*.

The reference to a 'company' above is to a company formed and registered (or treated as formed and registered) under the CA 2006. This means a company formed and registered under the CA 2006, or prior to 1 October 2009 under the Companies Act 1985, Companies (Northern Ireland) Order 1986 or former Companies Acts (i.e. an 'existing company' for the purposes of that Act and Order). *[s1]*.

A public company means a company limited by shares or limited by guarantee and having a share capital (a) whose certificate of incorporation states that it is a public company and (b) in relation to which the requirements of the CA 2006 or former Companies Acts as to registration or re-registration as a public company have been complied with (on or after the relevant date, being 22 December 1980 in Great Britain and 1 July 1983 in Northern Ireland). *[s4]*. Therefore, a public company means a UK-incorporated company that is a 'plc' or 'PLC' rather than a publicly traded company.

A traded company means a company any of whose transferable securities are admitted to trading on a regulated market. *[s474]*.

An authorised insurance company is defined in section 1165(2), a banking company in section 1164(2)-(3) and insurance market activity in section 1165(7). See Chapter 6 at 4.2.2 and 4.2.3.

The terms e-money issuer, MiFID investment firm, regulated activity, and UCITS management company are defined in section 474 of the CA 2006. The term 'e-money issuer' means an electronic money institution within the meaning of *The Electronic Money Regulations 2011* (SI 2011/99) or a person who has permission under Part 4A of the Financial Services and Markets Act 2008 (c 8) to carry on the activity of issuing electronic money within the meaning of article 9B of the Financial Services and Markets Act 2000 (Regulated Activities) Order 2001 (SI 20101/544). *[s474]*.

A body corporate includes a body incorporated outside the UK but does not include (a) a corporation sole or (b) a partnership that, whether or not a legal person, is not regarded as a body corporate under the law by which it is governed. *[s1173(1)]*. Therefore, a body corporate would include an overseas company or a UK LLP.

6.6.2   *Disclosure exemptions available for medium-sized companies*

6.6.2.A   *Disclosure exemptions available in the accounts and reports prepared for members*

The disclosure exemptions for medium-sized companies include:

- no requirement to disclose non-financial key performance indicators, including information relating to environmental matters and employee matters, in the strategic report; *[s414C(6)]*

- no requirement for Companies Act individual accounts to disclose the information required by paragraph 45 (the statement that the accounts have been prepared in accordance with applicable accounting standards, giving particulars and reasons for any material departures from these standards) or paragraph 72 (related party disclosures) of Schedule 1 to the Regulations (see 4.6.1 above); *[Regulations 4(2A)-4(2B)]*

- no requirement to disclose auditor's remuneration in respect of non-audit services. Like companies subject to the small companies regime, only remuneration for the auditing of the annual accounts receivable by the company's auditor (but not the associates of the auditor) is required to be disclosed. *[s494]*.[10] TECH 14/13 FRF – *Disclosure of auditor information* – provides guidance on disclosure of auditor remuneration; and

- certain exemptions from disclosures required by The Companies (Miscellaneous Reporting) Regulations 2018 (see 6.2.2.A above).

Medium-sized entities preparing financial statements in accordance with FRS 101 or FRS 102 must still give the disclosures required by accounting standards, e.g. medium-sized companies still need to give the related party disclosures required by accounting standards.

6.6.2.B   *Abbreviated accounts*

There is no option for medium-sized companies to deliver abbreviated accounts to the Registrar. Refer to Chapter 5 at 13 for details of the filing requirements for small companies.

6.7   Disclosures

The CA 2006 (particularly Part 15), the Regulations and other statutory instruments include disclosure requirements which apply to Companies Act accounts and IAS accounts. As discussed at 6.7.1 below, only some parts of the Regulations apply to IAS accounts. See 6.7.2 for a list of Companies Act disclosures applicable to both IAS accounts and Companies Act accounts.

The disclosure exemptions for companies subject to the small companies regime in the CA 2006 and the Small Companies Regulations are addressed in Chapter 5.

6.7.1   *Disclosures required by the Regulations*

The Regulations contain the following schedules:

- Schedule 1 (Companies Act individual accounts – companies other than banking and insurance companies);
- Schedule 2 (Companies Act individual accounts: banking companies);
- Schedule 3 (Companies Act individual accounts: insurance companies);
- Schedule 4 (Information about related undertakings – Companies Act or IAS accounts);
- Schedule 5 (Information about directors' benefits: remuneration – Companies Act or IAS accounts);
- Schedule 6 (Companies Act group accounts);
- Schedule 7 (Matters to be dealt with in directors' report);
- Schedule 8 (Directors' remuneration report – quoted companies);
- Schedule 9 (Definition of 'provisions'); and
- Schedule 10 (General interpretation).

A company preparing IAS individual accounts in accordance with section 397 (or IAS group accounts in accordance with section 406) does not apply Schedules 1 to 3, or Schedule 6 to the Regulations.

A company preparing Companies Act accounts must comply with all the requirements of the Regulations, including Schedules 1 to 3 (as applicable) and, where group accounts are prepared, Schedule 6. Schedules 1 to 3 include the formats for the profit and loss account and balance sheet, recognition and measurement principles, and disclosure requirements. Schedule 1 applies to all companies (other than banking companies and insurance companies), Schedule 2 to banking companies and groups, and Schedule 3 to insurance companies and groups. See Chapter 6 at 4.2.2 and 4.2.3 for definitions of banking and insurance companies and groups respectively.

The Regulations require various disclosures to be given in the financial statements. In particular, Parts 3 of Schedules 1 to 3 for Companies Act accounts require certain disclosures to be made in the notes to the financial statements if not given in the primary statements. The relevant paragraphs are as follows:

- Schedule 1 paragraphs 42 to 72B;
- Schedule 2 paragraphs 52 to 92B;
- Schedule 3 paragraphs 60 to 90B; and
- Schedule 6 various paragraphs.

Although some of these disclosure requirements are replicated in EU-adopted IFRS, others are not. Entities that move to FRS 101 or FRS 102 from previous UK GAAP will have been required to provide the statutory disclosures required for Companies Act accounts previously and therefore these requirements will not increase their reporting burden. Entities that move to FRS 101 or FRS 102 from EU-adopted IFRS are required to provide the additional statutory disclosures for Companies Act accounts and should consider carefully the impact of these new requirements against the benefits of the reduced disclosures under those standards.

6.7.2   Existing Companies Act disclosures in the accounts and reports applicable to IAS accounts and Companies Act accounts

Companies preparing IAS accounts or Companies Act accounts are subject to the following disclosures:

- section 396(A1) and 397(1) – information about the status of the company where individual accounts are prepared. See 6.2.1.C above;
- section 404(A1) and 406(1) – information about the status of the company where group accounts are prepared See 6.2.1.C above; and
- section 409 (and Schedule 4 to the Regulations) – information about related undertakings;
- section 410A – off-balance sheet arrangements (unless subject to the small companies regime). See Chapter 6 at 8.7;
- section 411 – employee numbers and costs (unless subject to the small companies regime). See Chapter 6 at 8.6;
- section 412 (and Schedule 5 and paragraph 22A of Schedule 6 to the Regulations) – directors' benefits: remuneration;
- section 413 – directors' benefits: advances, credits and guarantees. See Chapter 6 at 8.8;
- section 414A-D – strategic report (including the non-financial information statement report disclosures required by section 414CA-CB for certain large public interest entities). The FRC's *Guidance on the Strategic Report* (June 2018) provides best practice guidance. This is intended to be persuasive rather than have mandatory force;
- section 236, sections 415 to 419 (and Schedule 7 to the Regulations) – directors' report;
- sections 420 to 421 (and Schedule 8 to the Regulations) – directors' remuneration report (quoted companies only). The GC 100 and Investor Group's *Directors' Remuneration Report Guidance 2016* (see 6.2.2 above), provides best practice guidance on the directors' remuneration report prepared by quoted companies; and
- section 494 (and *Companies (Disclosure of Auditor Remuneration and Liability Limitation Agreements) Regulations 2008*) – services provided by auditor and associates and related remuneration.

  Medium-sized companies are only required to disclose remuneration for the audit of the annual accounts receivable by the company's auditor (but not the associates of the auditor) and are not required to disclose remuneration for non-audit services. *[s494]*.[11]

TECH 14/13 FRF provides guidance on disclosure of auditor remuneration but does not reflect the amendments made by SI 2016/649[12]:

- to remove the requirement for companies subject to the small companies regime to disclose, in a note to the annual accounts, the amount of any remuneration receivable by the auditor for the auditing of those accounts.

  This disclosure remains for medium-sized companies; or

- to restrict the conditions for exemption for a subsidiary company, from disclosing information required by regulation (5)(1)(b) of SI 2008/489 (remuneration for services other than the auditing of the company's accounts) in the subsidiary's individual accounts, to situations where the statutory auditor of the subsidiary company is the same as the statutory auditor of the parent that is required to prepare and does prepare group accounts in accordance with the CA 2006 (which consolidate the subsidiary).

The other conditions for use of this exemption by a subsidiary company are unchanged. There is also no change to the conditions for the same exemption for the individual accounts of a parent company.

LLPs may also have specific disclosure requirements, which are outside the scope of this publication.

In addition, other CA 2006 or related disclosures may apply depending on individual circumstances such as the disclosures required for a parent taking advantage of the exemption from preparing consolidated accounts under either sections 400 or 401 of the CA 2006.

6.8 Distributable profits

The determination of realised profits and losses and of profits available for distribution is governed by UK common law and statutory provisions. *[TECH 02/17BL.2.1]*. The ICAEW issued TECH 02/17BL – *Guidance on realised and distributable profits under the Companies Act 2006* – in April 2017. The purpose of the guidance is to identify, interpret and apply the principles relating to the determination of realised profits and losses for the purposes of making distributions under the Companies Act. *[TECH 02/17BL.1.1]*.

TECH 02/17BL is based on the previous guidance issued by the ICAEW and ICAS, TECH 02/10 – *Guidance on the determination of realised profits and losses in the context of distributions under the Companies Act 2016.*

The main changes made by TECH 02/17 BL include:

- additional guidance on the definition of a distribution, highlighting that it is the purpose and substance of a transaction that matters in determining whether a distribution has been made, not the 'label' given to the transaction;
- new guidance on distributions in specie;
- new guidance on the impact of current and deferred tax on distributable profits;
- additional guidance on the impact on distributable profits of intra-group loans made at below market rates of interest;
- simplified guidance on the impact of retirement benefit schemes on distributable profits; and
- new guidance addressing distributable profits implications for long term insurance businesses.

A company may make a distribution only out of profits available for that purpose. A company's distributable profits are its accumulated realised profits (so far as not previously distributed or capitalised) less its accumulated realised losses (so far as not previously written off in a reduction or reorganisation of its share capital). Realised losses cannot be offset against unrealised profits. *[TECH 02/17BL.2.7]*. A further restriction is placed on public companies, which may only make a distribution if, after giving effect to such distribution, the amount of its net assets (as defined in section 831) is not less than the aggregate of its called up share capital and undistributable reserves (see section 831(4) for a list of undistributable reserves) as shown in the relevant accounts. *[s831]*.

Paragraph 13(a) of Schedule 1 to the Regulations (and its equivalents in Schedules 2 and 3 and the LLP Regulations) require that only profits realised at the balance sheet date are included in the profit or loss account. *[FRS 101 Appendix II.12, FRS 102 Appendix III.25]*. Consequently, profits that are not realised should normally be included in other comprehensive income rather than profit or loss in financial statements prepared under FRS 101 and FRS 102. However, paragraph 39 of Schedule 1 to the Regulations (and its equivalents in Schedules 2 and 3 and the LLP Regulations) allow stocks, investment property and living animals or plants to be held at fair value in Companies Act accounts. *[FRS 101 Appendix II.13, FRS 102 Appendix III.26]*. Paragraph 40(2) of Schedule 1 to the Regulations (and its equivalents in Schedules 2 and 3 and the LLP Regulations) require that movements in the fair value of financial instruments, investment properties or living animals and plants are recognised in the profit and loss account notwithstanding the usual restrictions allowing only realised profits and losses to be included in the profit and loss account. Therefore, paragraph 40 of Schedule 1 overrides paragraph 13(a) of Schedule 1 and such fair value gains can be recognised in profit and loss under FRS 101 and FRS 102. *[FRS 101 Appendix II.14, FRS 102 Appendix III.27]*.

The legal appendices to FRS 101 and FRS 102 both state that entities measuring investment properties, living animals or plants, or financial instruments at fair value may transfer such amounts to a separate non-distributable reserve instead of carrying them forward in retained earnings but are not required to do so. The FRC suggests that presenting fair value movements that are not distributable profits in a separate reserve may assist with the identification of profits available for that purpose. *[FRS 101 Appendix II.15, FRS 102 Appendix III.28]*.

Discussed below are some of the key terms and principles set out in TECH 02/17BL.

6.8.1   Realised profits

Profit is realised, as a matter of generally accepted accounting practice, where it arises from: *[TECH 02/17BL.3.9]*

(a)   a transaction where the consideration received by the company is 'qualifying consideration' (see 6.8.2 below); or

(b)   an event which results in 'qualifying consideration' being received by the company in circumstances where no consideration is given by the company; or

(c)   the recognition in the financial statements of a change in fair value, in those cases where fair value has been determined in accordance with measurement guidance in the relevant accounting standards or company law, and to the extent that the change recognised is readily convertible to cash; or

(d)   the translation of:

   (i)   a monetary asset which comprises qualifying consideration; or

   (ii)   a liability,

   denominated in a foreign currency; or

(e)   the reversal of a loss previously regarded as realised; or

(f)   a profit previously regarded as unrealised (such as amounts taken to a revaluation reserve, merger reserve, or other similar reserve) becoming realised as a result of:

   (i)   consideration previously received by the company becoming 'qualifying consideration'; or

   (ii)   the related asset being disposed of in a transaction where the consideration received by the company is 'qualifying consideration'; or

   (iii)   a realised loss being recognised on the scrapping or disposal of the related asset; or

   (iv)   a realised loss being recognised on the write-down for depreciation, amortisation, diminution in value or impairment of the related asset;

   (v)   the distribution in kind of the asset to which the unrealised profit relates; or

   (vi)   the receipt of a dividend in the form of qualifying consideration when no profit is recognised because the dividend is deducted from the book value of the investment to which the unrealised profit relates,

   in which case the appropriate proportion of the related unrealised profit becomes a realised profit; or

(g)   the remeasurement of a liability, to the extent that the change recognised is readily convertible to cash.

If the write down in (f)(iv) above is subsequently reversed, an equal amount of profit should be regarded as becoming unrealised. In other words, the amount of profit regarded as becoming realised is equal to the cumulative amount of any write down treated as a realised loss.

In addition to those instances of realised profit included in the definition of realised profit set out above, the following would also constitute a realised profit per the guidance in TECH 02/17BL: *[TECH 02/17BL.3.14]*

(a)   the receipt or accrual of investment or other income receivable in the form of qualifying consideration; or

(b)   a gain arising on a return of capital on an investment where the return is in the form of qualifying consideration; or

(c)   a gift (such as a 'capital contribution') received in the form of qualifying consideration. However, this does not apply when the legal form of the transaction is a loan even though it is accounted for as a capital contribution (see paragraph 6.20 of the TECH 02/17BL guidance regarding the proceeds of issue of convertible debt and paragraph 9.53 of the TECH 02/17BL guidance regarding intra-group off-market loans); or

(d)   the release of a provision for a liability or loss which was treated as a realised loss; or

(e)   the reversal of a write-down or provision for diminution in value or impairment of an asset which was treated as a realised loss.

6.8.2   *Qualifying consideration*

Qualifying consideration comprises: *[TECH 02/17BL.3.11]*

(a)   cash; or

(b)   an asset that is readily convertible to cash; or

(c)   the release, or the settlement or assumption by another party, of all or part of a liability of the company; or

(d)   an amount receivable in any of the above forms of consideration where:

    (i)   the debtor is capable of settling the receivable within a reasonable period of time; and

    (ii)   there is a reasonable certainty that the debtor will be capable of settling when called upon to do so; and

    (iii)   there is an expectation that the receivable will be settled; or

(e)   an amount receivable from a shareholder where and to the extent that:

    (i)   the company intends to make a distribution to the shareholder of an amount equal to or less than its receivable from that shareholder; and

    (ii)   the company intends to settle such distribution by off-setting against the amount receivable (in whole or in part); and

    (iii)   within the meaning of paragraph 3.5 and 3.5A of the TECH 02/17BL guidance, (i) and (ii) are linked.

6.8.3   *Realised losses*

Losses should be regarded as realised losses except to the extent that the law, accounting standards or the guidance in TECH 02/17BL provide otherwise. *[TECH 02/17BL.3.10]*.

Realised losses will include: *[TECH 02/17BL.3.15]*

(a)   a cost or an expense (other than one charged to the share premium account) which results in a reduction in recorded net assets;

(b)   a loss arising on the sale or other disposal or scrapping of an asset;

(c)   the writing down, or providing for the depreciation, amortisation, diminution in value or impairment, of an asset (except in the circumstances set out in paragraphs 2.33 and 2.36 of the TECH 02/17BL guidance);

(d)   the creation of, or increase in a provision for a liability or loss (other than deferred tax arising in the circumstances discussed in paragraph 3.17 of the TECH 02/17BL guidance) which results in an overall reduction in recorded net assets;

(e)   a gift made by the company (or the release of all or part of a debt due to that company or the assumption of a liability by the company) to the extent that it results in an overall reduction in recorded net assets; and

(f)   a loss arising from fair value accounting where profits on remeasurement of the same asset or liability would be treated as realised profits.

6.8.4   *Disclosure of distributable profits*

Except for companies authorised to carry on long-term insurance business (e.g. life insurers), there is no requirement under UK law or accounting standards for financial statements to distinguish between realised and unrealised profits or between distributable profits and non-distributable profits. However, companies should maintain sufficient records to enable them to distinguish between those profits that are available for distribution and those which are not. *[TECH 02/17BL.2.25]*.

For companies authorised to carry on long-term insurance business, Schedule 3 to the Regulations requires that every balance sheet of such a company must show separately as an additional item the aggregate of any capital and reserves which are not required to be treated as realised profits under section 843 of the CA 2006. *[3 Sch 11(1)]*.

For companies authorised to carry on long-term insurance business in accordance with Article 14 of the Solvency 2 Directive, the realised profit or loss of the company in respect of which its relevant accounts are prepared is the amount calculated by a given formula. *[s833A]*. In summary, this formula is the company's net assets as calculated by the Solvency 2 Directive less share capital, share premium, any capital redemption reserve and any other reserve that the company is prohibited from distributing.

For companies that are not required to comply with the Solvency 2 Directive, realised profits or losses are determined using the normal UK common law and statutory requirements (see 6.8 above).

6.8.5   Impact of transition on distributable profits

The potential impact on distributable profits on transition to FRS 101, FRS 102 or FRS 105 is discussed at 5.5 above.

7   FINANCIAL REPORTING COUNCIL (FRC) AND ACCOUNTING STANDARD SETTING

This section draws on information concerning the FRC structure that is included on the FRC website.

The FRC Board is now supported by three governance committees (the Audit Committee, the Nominations Committee and the Remuneration Committee), two business committees (the Codes & Standards Committee and the Conduct Committee) and three advisory councils (Corporate Reporting, Audit & Assurance and Actuarial).

This chapter discusses the role of the FRC in accounting standard setting.

7.1   Accounting standards setting

Accounting standards are statements of standard accounting practice issued by such body or bodies prescribed by regulations.[13] *[s464(1)]*. Prior to 2 July 2012, this body was the Accounting Standards Board and from 2 July 2012, the Financial Reporting Council. New accounting standards, or amendments to or withdrawal of existing accounting standards must be approved by the FRC Board, having received advice from the Corporate Reporting Council and/or the Codes & Standards Committee (see below).

The FRC's objective in setting accounting standards is to enable users of accounts to receive high quality, understandable financial reporting proportionate to the size and complexity of the entity and users' information needs. *[Foreword.8]*. The FRC collaborates with accounting standard setters from other countries and the IASB to influence the development of international accounting standards and to ensure that its standards are developed with due regard for international developments. The FRC works closely with the European Financial Reporting Advisory Group (EFRAG), which advises the European Commission on IFRSs in Europe and with the International Forum of Accounting Standard Setters (IFASS).

The Codes & Standards Committee, which contains both FRC Board members and others with particular technical expertise (including practising professionals) is responsible, *inter alia*, for advising the FRC Board on maintaining an effective framework of UK codes and standards for Corporate Governance, Stewardship, Accounting, Auditing and Assurance, and Actuarial technical standards. In relation to accounting standard setting, the FRC Board and the Codes & Standards Committee are advised by the Corporate Reporting Council (which is appointed by the Codes & Standards Committee). Its advice is put fully to the FRC Board, with the Board member chairing the Council responsible for submitting the Council's advice to the Board. The Corporate Reporting Council, which is appointed by the Codes & Standards Committee:

- provides strategic input and thought leadership, in the fields of accounting and financial reporting and in the work-plan of the FRC as a whole. This involves 'horizon-scanning' and consulting with practitioners or users;
- considers and advises the FRC Board upon draft codes and standards (or amendments thereto) to ensure that a high quality, effective and proportionate approach is taken;
- considers and comments on proposed developments in relation to international codes and standards and regulations; and
- considers and advises on research proposals and other initiatives undertaken to inform the FRC on matters material to its remit and any resultant publications.

In June 2013, the FRC established a UK GAAP Technical Advisory Group (TAG) to assist the Corporate Reporting Council. The TAG advises the Corporate Reporting Council on all issues relating to UK accounting standards, including areas where unsatisfactory or conflicting interpretations of accounting standards or Companies Act provisions have developed or seem likely to develop, as well as those relating to smaller entities.

The TAG also assists the Corporate Reporting Council in relation to the development of SORPs by SORP-making bodies by carrying out a limited review of a SORP (see 4.7 above). An Academic Panel also meets regularly to discuss issues relating to the FRC's work. The Corporate Reporting Council may also establish short-term advisory groups to provide input to specific projects.

The FRC's procedure for issuing accounting standards is set out in the *FRC Codes & Standards Committee: Procedures.*[14]

7.2   Scope and authority of accounting standards

The *Foreword to Accounting Standards*, last issued in March 2018, explains the authority, scope and application of accounting standards, known as Financial Reporting Standards (FRSs) issued by the FRC.

Accounting standards are applicable to the financial statements of a reporting entity that are required to give a true and fair view of its financial position at the reporting date; and of its profit or loss (or income and expenditure) for the reporting period. *[Foreword.4]*.

Accounting standards developed by the FRC are designated Financial Reporting Standards (FRSs). The FRC may issue FRSs that relate to other aspects of financial reporting, but which are not accounting standards. Each FRS will indicate its status, i.e. that it is an accounting standard or, if not, the circumstances in which it may be applied. *[Foreword.9-11]*. FRS 100 to FRS 103 and FRS 105 (but not FRS 104) are accounting standards for the purpose of company law.

Where exposure drafts are issued for comment and are subject to revision, until it is finalised as an accounting standard the requirements of any existing accounting standard that would be affected by proposals in the exposure draft remain in force. *[Foreword.13]*.

7.2.1   Accounting standards and true and fair

Section 393 of the CA 2006 requires that the directors of a company must not approve accounts unless they are satisfied that they give a true and fair view of the assets, liabilities, financial position and profit or loss. *[s393]*.

Predecessor bodies to the FRC obtained legal opinions that have confirmed the centrality of the true and fair concept to the preparation and audit of financial statements, whether prepared in accordance with UK accounting standards or international accounting standards. The latest Opinion written by Martin Moore QC (2008) followed the enactment of the CA 2006 and the introduction of international accounting standards and endorsed the analysis in the earlier Opinions of Leonard Hoffman QC (1983) and Mary Arden (1984) and Mary Arden QC (1993) as to the approach that Courts would take to accounting standards when considering whether accounts show a true and fair view.

In October 2013, the then Department of Business, Skills and Innovation (BIS) published a ministerial statement:

'The Department of Business has given serious consideration to concerns raised by some stakeholders that accounts prepared over the past 30 years, in accordance with UK or international financial reporting standards, have not been properly prepared under UK and EU law.

'However, it is entirely satisfied that the concerns expressed are misconceived and that the existing legal framework, including international financial reporting standards, is binding under European Law.

'In preparing financial statements, achieving a true and fair view is and remains the overriding objective (and legal requirement). In the vast majority of cases, compliance with accounting standards will result in a true and fair view. However, where compliance with an accounting standard may not achieve that objective, accounting standards expressly provide that that standard may be overridden. [...]'

The FRC published its independent legal advice, available on the FRC website. The Opinion written by Martin Moore QC (3 October 2013) – *International Accounting Standards and the true and fair view* – considered issues addressed in an Opinion written by George Bompas QC (8 April 2013), in particular the interaction of

International Accounting Standards and the legal requirement that directors must not approve accounts that do not show a true and fair view, and the place of prudence.

However, both the FRC (in its Press Notice of 3 October 2013) and the BIS ministerial statement noted scope for improvements in aspects of international financial reporting standards and the IASB's Conceptual Framework, for example:

- stewardship reporting (i.e. holding directors to account for their management of the company's property) should be regarded as a primary objective of financial reporting;

- prudence (i.e. the exercise of caution), should be explicitly acknowledged in the Conceptual Framework; and

- there should be clear principles to describe when specific measurement bases, such as fair value (which needs to be appropriately defined) should be used. Performance reporting should present movements in fair value clearly and appropriately.

The FRC noted that investors raised other concerns and that it looked forward to working with investors and other stakeholders to address the full range of issues.

In June 2014, the FRC issued updated guidance – *True and Fair*. This confirms the fundamental importance of the true and fair requirement in both IFRS and UK GAAP, whether applying FRS 100 to FRS 103 or previous UK GAAP. This guidance emphasises the application of objective professional judgement, which applies at all stages of preparation of the financial statements, to ensure the financial statements give a true and fair view. The guidance specifically addresses the concept of prudence and reflecting the substance of transactions under both IFRS and UK GAAP.

The FRC expects preparers, those charged with governance and auditors to stand back and ensure that the financial statements as a whole give a true and fair view, provide additional disclosures where compliance with an accounting standard is insufficient to present a true and fair view, to use the true and fair override where compliance with the standards does not result in the presentation of a true and fair view and to ensure that the consideration they give to these matters is evident in their deliberations and documentation. See Chapter 6 at 9.2.

7.3   UK GAAP

UK GAAP is a wider concept than accounting standards, as defined at 7.2 above. For example, UK GAAP can include:

- SORPs (where an entity is within the scope of a SORP – see 4.7 above);

- other pronouncements issued by the FRC or its predecessor bodies (such as FREDs or best practice Reporting Statements) – providing these do not conflict with an extant accounting standard;

- pronouncements by authoritative bodies, such as Technical Releases issued by the Institute of Chartered Accountants in England and Wales and/or the Institute of Chartered Accountants in Scotland (examples include TECH 02/17BL); and

- generally accepted accounting practice where areas are not covered by specific accounting standards. This could include reference to the requirements of other bodies of GAAP where it addresses an issue, but does not conflict with accounting standards. For example, FRS 102 permits but does not require management to refer to the requirements of EU-adopted IFRS dealing with similar and related issues in developing and applying a reliable and relevant accounting policy. *[FRS 102.10.6]*. Generally accepted accounting practice can also include established industry practice in accounting for transactions.

In addition, an entity must comply with any legal or regulatory requirements applicable to its annual report and financial statements, including the overall requirement for directors of a company to prepare accounts that give a true and fair view.

References

1 https://ec.europa.eu/info/node/7511
2 Irish small entities (including partnerships that are required to comply with Part 6 of the Companies Act 2014, by virtue of the European Communities (Accounts) Regulations 1993) should refer to sections 280A and 280B of the Companies Act 2014.
3 *Policy on Developing Statements of Recommended Practice (SORPs)*, Financial Reporting Council, October 2018.
4 AIM Rules, March 2018, para. 19, Glossary.
5 s464, *The Statutory Auditors (Amendment of Companies Act 2006 and Delegation of Functions etc.) Order 2012* (SI 2012/1741).
6 *The Accounting Standards (Prescribed Bodies) (United States of America and Japan) Regulations 2015* (SI 2015/1675) permits companies with securities registered with the SEC or publicly traded on specified Japanese exchanges (but that do not have securities admitted to trading on an (EEA) regulated market) to prepare consolidated financial statements (but not individual financial statements) using US GAAP or JGAAP. Therefore, in these circumstances, US GAAP and JGAAP are applicable accounting standards. Such consolidated financial statements would also be Companies Act accounts. The Regulations, which replace a similar Statutory Instrument, come into force on 1 October 2015 and apply for financial years beginning on or after 1 January 2015. However, the dispensation applies only in respect of the group financial statements of a parent company for the first 4 financial years following incorporation of that company. It ceases to have effect on 30 September 2022.
7 Listing Rules, FCA, paras. 9.8.6(5), (6).
8 *Guidance on the Strategic Report*, Financial Reporting Council, July 2018, para. 7B.84.
9 Listing Rules, FCA, paras. 9.8.6(5), (6).
10 *The Companies (Disclosure of Auditor Remuneration and Liability Limitation Agreements) Regulations 2008* (SI 2008/489), para. 4.
11 SI 2008/489, para. 4.
12 *The Statutory Auditors and Third Country Auditors Regulations 2016* (SI 2016/649), paras. 1(4), 18.
13 See footnote 4 above. *The Accounting Standards (Prescribed Bodies) (United States of America and Japan) Regulations 2015* extend the prescribed bodies for issuing accounting standards to include the FASB and the Accounting Standards Board of Japan for group accounts of parent companies with securities registered with the Securities Exchange Commission of the United States of America and specified Japanese exchanges respectively, with the restrictions set out in the statutory instrument.
14 https://www.frc.org.uk/About-the-FRC/Procedures/Regulatory-policies.aspx

Chapter 1

Chapter 2

FRS 101 – Reduced disclosure framework

Chapter 2

List of examples

Chapter 2

FRS 101 – Reduced disclosure framework

1   INTRODUCTION

This chapter deals only with the application of FRS 101 – *Reduced Disclosure Framework: Disclosure exemptions from EU-adopted IFRS for qualifying entities* – as issued in March 2018 and amended by *Amendments to Basis for Conclusions FRS 101 – Reduced Disclosure Framework 2017/18 cycle* issued in May 2018. References made to FRS 101 throughout this chapter are to the March 2018 edition of the standard unless otherwise indicated.

FRS 101 sets out a framework which addresses the financial reporting requirements and disclosure exemptions for the individual financial statements of subsidiaries and parents that otherwise apply the recognition, measurement and disclosure requirements of standards and interpretations issued by the International Accounting Standards Board (IASB) that have been adopted by the European Union (EU-adopted IFRS).

To use the framework in FRS 101, an entity needs to be a 'qualifying entity', i.e. a parent or subsidiary which is included in publicly available consolidated financial statements of its parent which are intended to give a true and fair view.

An entity preparing financial statements in accordance with FRS 101 ('FRS 101 financial statements') complies with EU-adopted IFRS except as modified in accordance with this FRS. This chapter does not discuss EU-adopted IFRS, which is covered in EY International GAAP 2019. The FRC's overriding objective is to enable users of accounts to receive high-quality, understandable financial reporting proportionate to the size and complexity of the entity and the users' information needs. In other words, the objective of FRS 101 is to enable the financial statements of subsidiaries and parents to be prepared under the recognition and measurement rules of EU-adopted IFRS, without the need for some of the copious disclosures which are perceived to act as a barrier to those entities preparing those financial statements under EU-adopted IFRS.

An entity using the reduced disclosure framework of FRS 101 is unable to make the explicit and unreserved statement that its financial statements comply with EU-adopted IFRS. This is because an accounting framework that allows such reduced disclosures cannot be described as EU-adopted IFRS. UK companies that prepare FRS 101 financial statements in accordance with Part 15 of the CA 2006 prepare Companies Act individual accounts as defined in s395(1)(a) of the CA 2006. This means that FRS 101 financial statements are subject to different Companies Act requirements from financial statements prepared under EU-adopted IFRS (which are IAS accounts prepared under s395(1)(b) of the CA 2006). In particular, FRS 101 financial statements prepared by a UK company must comply with Schedule 1, 2 (if a banking company) or 3 (if an insurance company) to *The Large and Medium-sized Companies and Groups (Accounts and Reports) Regulations 2008* (SI 2008/410), as amended ('the Regulations') – these schedules do not apply to IAS accounts. LLPs and certain other entities also prepare financial statements in accordance with Part 15 of the CA 2006 and are subject to similar requirements. Generally, this chapter refers to UK companies and the Regulations. The requirements for LLPs and *The Large and Medium-sized Limited Liability Partnerships (Accounts) Regulations 2008*, as amended ('the LLP Regulations') are similar, although there are some minor differences.

This chapter discusses FRS 101 only as it applies to UK companies, LLPs and other entities preparing financial statements under Part 15 of the Companies Act 2006 ('CA 2006'). However, FRS 101 may also be applied by non-UK entities currently applying IFRS as issued by the IASB, or another GAAP, although this may depend on local legislation (or regulatory or other requirements).

1.1   Summary of FRS 101

Application of FRS 101 can be summarised as follows:

- adoption of FRS 101 is voluntary, being one of a number of accounting standards available for financial reporting in the UK and Republic of Ireland (see Chapter 1);

- FRS 101 can only be applied in individual financial statements (see 2 below);

- FRS 101 can only be applied by a 'qualifying entity' (see 2.1 below);

- entities can transition to FRS 101 from IFRS or another GAAP (usually this will be from a form of UK GAAP) (see 3 below);

- entities using FRS 101 apply the recognition and measurement principles of EU-adopted IFRS, as amended by FRS 101 (see 4 below);

- entities using FRS 101 must prepare a balance sheet and profit and loss account (either as a separate income statement or as a section of the statement of comprehensive income) in accordance with the Regulations or, where applicable, the LLP Regulations. UK companies (other than banking or insurance companies) and LLPs may either apply statutory formats or adapted formats (which are based on IAS 1 – *Presentation of Financial Statements*) (see 5 below);

- entities using FRS 101 can take advantage of various disclosure exemptions from EU-adopted IFRS. Entities defined as 'financial institutions' have fewer exemptions than entities that are not financial institutions. Some of these disclosure exemptions are conditional on equivalent disclosures being included in the publicly available consolidated financial statements of the group in which the entity is consolidated and which are intended to give a true and fair view (see 6 below); and

- in addition to IFRS disclosures, entities using FRS 101 must comply with any legal requirements relating to financial statements, e.g. disclosures required by the CA 2006 and the Regulations, if subject to those requirements (see 7 below).

1.2 Effective date of FRS 101

FRS 101 was issued originally on 22 November 2012. Consolidated versions of the standard incorporating subsequent amendments were subsequently issued in August 2014, September 2015 and March 2018. The March 2018 version reflects the *Amendments to FRS 102 – The Financial Reporting Standard applicable in the UK and Republic of Ireland – Triennial review 2017 – Incremental improvements and clarifications* issued in December 2017 (Triennial review 2017) discussed at 1.2.1 below. Subsequent to the March 2018 version of the standard, minor changes to the Basis for Conclusions have been made by *Amendments to Basis for Conclusions FRS 101 – Reduced Disclosure Framework 2017/18 cycle* issued in May 2018 (discussed at 1.2.2 below).

FRS 101 has been available for use for accounting periods beginning on or after 1 January 2015. Early application was permitted but was required to be disclosed. *[FRS 101.11]*.

The March 2018 version of FRS 101 is effective for accounting periods beginning on or after 1 January 2019. Early application of the March 2018 version of FRS 101 for accounting periods beginning prior to 1 January 2019 is permitted provided that all amendments made by the Triennial review 2017 are made at the same time. If an entity applies the Triennial review 2017 for an accounting period beginning before 1 January 2019 it shall disclose that fact. *[FRS 101.14]*.

Since FRS 101 is based on EU-adopted IFRS, any disclosure exemptions referring to a specific requirement of IFRS are effective only once the IFRS has been EU-adopted and is first applied by the entity. *[FRS 101.1, 8]*.

The FRC reviews FRS 101 annually to ensure that the reduced disclosure framework maintains consistency with EU-adopted IFRS. In addition, limited amendments have been made to FRS 101 (compared to EU-adopted IFRS) for compliance with the CA 2006 and the Regulations.

1.2.1 Amendments to FRS 101 incorporated into the March 2018 edition

The March 2018 edition of FRS 101 updates the edition of FRS 101 issued in September 2015 for all amendments to the standard issued between those dates. The amendments are as follows:

- *Amendments to FRS 101 – Reduced Disclosure Framework – 2015/16 cycle*, issued in July 2016, which:
  - provided disclosure exemptions in relation to IFRS 15 – *Revenue from Contracts with Customers* – which are applicable when an entity first applies IFRS 15 (see 6.1.6 below); *[FRS 101.8(eA)]* and
  - clarified that a qualifying entity preparing financial statements in accordance with FRS 101 should have regard to the legal requirement to present the notes to the financial statements in the order in which, where relevant, the items to which they relate are presented in the statement of financial position and the income statement when determining a systematic manner for the presentation of its notes to the financial statements in accordance with IAS 1. *[FRS 101 Appendix II.11A]*.
- *Amendments to FRS 101 – Reduced Disclosure Framework and FRS 102 – The Financial Reporting Standard applicable in the UK and Republic of Ireland – Notification of Shareholders* issued in December 2016. These amendments

removed the requirement for a qualifying entity to notify its shareholders in writing of its intention to use the disclosure exemptions in FRS 101 (and under the reduced disclosure framework in FRS 102) and the ability of shareholders to object to the use of the disclosure objections. *[FRS 101.13]*.

- *Amendments to FRS 101 – Reduced Disclosure Framework – 2016/17 cycle* issued in July 2017, which:
  - provides disclosure exemptions in relation to IFRS 16 – *Leases* – which are applicable when an entity first applies IFRS 16 (see 6.1.7 below); *[FRS 101.8(eB)]* and
  - made amendments to reflect the EU endorsement of IFRS 9 – *Financial Instruments* – which are applicable from when an entity first applies IFRS 9 and the issue of *The Limited Liability Partnerships, Partnerships and Groups (Accounts and Audit) Regulations 2016* (SI 2016/575) (see 4.2 and 4.11 below).

- Amendments made by the Triennial review 2017 issued in December 2017. These amendments apply for accounting periods beginning on or after 1 January 2019. Early application is permitted (but this must be disclosed) for accounting periods beginning prior to 1 January 2019 provided all amendments made by the Triennial review 2017 are applied at the same time.

  The principal amendment made is a change in the definition of a financial institution (see 6.4 below). As fewer entities are likely to meet the revised definition of a financial institution, some entities may wish to early adopt FRS 101 for this reason.

  There are also some minor typographical or presentational corrections or clarifications. These include guidance on presentation of a disposal group (see 5.1.2.B below) and a requirement that when paragraphs D16 and D17 of IFRS 1 – *First-time Adoption of International Financial Reporting Standards* – are applied, that the qualifying entity must ensure its assets and liabilities are measured in accordance with company law (see 3.4.1 and 3.4.2 below).

1.2.2   Amendments to FRS 101 issued in May 2018

Amendments to Basis for Conclusions FRS 101 – Reduced Disclosure Framework – 2017/18 Cycle made an amendment to the Basis for Conclusions in respect of IFRS 17 – *Insurance Contracts* (see 8.1 below) and updated Table 2 which sets out IFRS publications considered in the development of FRS 101. However, no changes were made to the standard itself.

1.3   Statement of compliance with FRS 101

A set of financial statements prepared in accordance with FRS 101 must contain a statement in the notes to the financial statements that 'These financial statements were prepared in accordance with Financial Reporting Standard 101 Reduced Disclosure Framework'. Since the standard does not comply with all of the requirements of EU-adopted IFRS, financial statements prepared in accordance with FRS 101 should not contain the unreserved statement of compliance referred to in paragraph 3 of IFRS 1 and otherwise required by paragraph 16 of IAS 1. *[FRS 101.10]*.

The Regulations require a large and medium-sized UK company (except a medium-sized company preparing individual accounts) preparing Companies Act accounts to state in the notes to the accounts whether the accounts have been prepared in accordance with applicable accounting standards, giving particulars of any material departure from those standards and the reasons for it. *[1 Sch 45]*. Financial statements prepared in accordance with FRS 101 are prepared in accordance with applicable accounting standards (which are defined in section 464 of CA 2006), *[s464]*, and therefore this statement would be required. See Chapter 1 at 4.6.1.

2   SCOPE OF FRS 101

FRS 101 may be applied to the individual financial statements of a 'qualifying entity' (see 2.1 below), that are intended to give a true and fair view of the assets, liabilities, financial position and profit or loss for a period. *[FRS 101.2]*.

Individual financial statements to which FRS 101 applies are accounts that are required to be prepared by an entity in accordance with the CA 2006 or relevant legislation, for example: individual accounts as set out in section 394 of the CA 2006 or as set out in section 72A of the Building Societies Act 1986. Separate financial statements, as defined by IAS 27 – *Separate Financial Statements*, are included in the meaning of the term individual financial statements. *[FRS 101 Appendix I]*. A charity, however, cannot apply FRS 101 (see 2.1 below).

This means that FRS 101 can be used in:

- individual financial statements of subsidiaries;
- separate financial statements of an intermediate parent which does not prepare consolidated financial statements; and
- separate financial statements of a parent which does prepare consolidated financial statements.

However, the entity applying FRS 101 must be included in a set of publicly available consolidated financial statements intended to give a true and fair view (see 2.1.6 below).

A parent company that prepares consolidated financial statements but applies FRS 101 in its separate financial statements can also use the exemption in the CA 2006 from presenting a profit and loss account and related notes in its individual financial statements, as well as taking advantage of the reduced disclosures from EU-adopted IFRS. *[s408]*.

FRS 101 cannot be applied in consolidated financial statements even if the entity preparing consolidated financial statements is a qualifying entity. *[FRS 101.3]*.

FRS 101 financial statements are not prepared in accordance with EU-adopted IFRS. A qualifying entity must ensure it complies with any relevant legal requirements applicable to it. Individual financial statements prepared by UK companies in accordance with FRS 101 are Companies Act accounts rather than IAS accounts as set out in section 395(1) of the CA 2006. Accordingly, UK companies that apply FRS 101 must comply with the requirements of the CA 2006 and any relevant regulations such as the Regulations. *[FRS 101.4A]*. The presentation requirements of relevant regulations applying to UK entities, including the requirements of the Regulations (which cover rules on recognition and measurement, the formats for the balance sheet and profit and loss account, and notes disclosures) are discussed in Chapter 6.

Chapter 2

In order to ensure that FRS 101 financial statements comply with the CA 2006 and the Regulations, some limited recognition, measurement and presentational changes have been made in FRS 101 to EU-adopted IFRS. The amendments necessary to remove conflicts between EU-adopted IFRS, the CA 2006 and the Regulations are set out in paragraph AG1 of the Application Guidance to FRS 101. The standard emphasises that, for the avoidance of doubt, the Application Guidance is an integral part of the standard and is applicable to any qualifying entity applying FRS 101, not just to UK companies. *[FRS 101.5(b)]*. These amendments are discussed at 4 and 5 below.

FRS 101 does not permit use of the formats for the balance sheet and profit and loss account included in Part 1 'General Rules and Formats' of *The Small Companies and Groups (Accounts and Directors' Report) Regulations 2008* (SI 2008/409) ('the Small Companies Regulations'). However, our view is that companies subject to the small companies regime can still apply FRS 101, and, in doing so, are not prevented from taking advantage of other Companies Act exemptions applicable to companies subject to the small companies regime. Likewise, medium-sized entities applying FRS 101 can still take advantage of applicable Companies Act disclosure exemptions for medium-sized entities. This chapter does not generally refer to the Small Companies and Small LLP Regulations.

While the discussion above refers to UK companies, there are similar requirements for LLPs (see 4.11 below).

2.1   Definition of a qualifying entity

FRS 101 defines a qualifying entity as 'a member of a group where the parent of that group prepares publicly available consolidated financial statements, which are intended to give a true and fair view (of the assets, liabilities, financial position and profit or loss) and that member is included in the consolidation'. *[FRS 101 Appendix I]*.

A charity may not be a qualifying entity and therefore may not apply FRS 101. *[FRS 101 Appendix I]*.

There is no requirement that a qualifying entity is a member of the group in which it is consolidated for its entire reporting period. There is also no requirement that the financial statements of the qualifying entity and the consolidated financial statements of the parent of that group (which may be the reporting entity itself) must be coterminous or have reporting dates within a particular timeframe. The use of the present tense implies that the intention is only that the qualifying entity (where it does not prepare its own consolidated financial statements) is a subsidiary of the parent at its reporting date. This is consistent with UK company law which requires that an entity which is a parent at the end of a financial year must prepare group accounts unless it is exempted from the requirement. *[s399(2)]*.

The phrase 'included in the consolidation' is referenced to section 474(1) of the CA 2006 which states that this means that 'the undertaking is included in the accounts by the method of full (and not proportional) consolidation, and references to an undertaking excluded from consolidation shall be construed accordingly'. Therefore, entities that are not fully consolidated in the consolidated financial statements, such as subsidiaries of investment entities which are accounted for at fair value through profit or loss where required by IFRS 10 – *Consolidated Financial Statements*, cannot use FRS 101.

Associates and joint ventures are not qualifying entities since they are not members of a group (see 2.1.2 below).

There is no requirement for the consolidated financial statements in which the qualifying entity is included to be prepared under EU-adopted IFRS nor that the parent that prepares the consolidated financial statements is a UK entity. However, the consolidated financial statements must be intended to give a true and fair view (see 2.1.6 below).

2.1.1   Reporting date of the consolidated financial statements of the parent

The requirement for the qualifying entity to be included in the consolidation implies that the consolidated financial statements of the parent should be approved before, or at the same time as, the FRS 101 individual financial statements of the qualifying entity are approved. FRS 101 is silent on whether the reporting date and period of those consolidated financial statements has to be identical to that of the qualifying entity. In contrast, both sections 400 and 401 of the CA 2006 require that the exemption from preparing group accounts for a parent company that is a subsidiary undertaking is conditional on the inclusion of the company in the consolidated financial statements of a parent undertaking drawn up to the same date or to an earlier date in the same financial year. It would seem logical that the reporting date criteria in sections 400 and 401 should also be used for FRS 101.

However, when the consolidated financial statements are prepared as at an earlier date than the date of the qualifying entity's financial statements, some of the disclosure exemptions may not be available to the qualifying entity because the consolidated financial statements may not contain the 'equivalent' disclosures (see 6.2 below).

2.1.2   Definition of group and subsidiary

The definition of a qualifying entity contains a footnote that refers to section 474(1) of the CA 2006 which defines a 'group' as 'a parent undertaking and its subsidiary undertakings'. EU-adopted IFRS defines a group as 'a parent and its subsidiaries'. *[IFRS 10 Appendix A, s474(1)].*

EU-adopted IFRS defines a parent as 'an entity that controls one or more entities' and a subsidiary as 'an entity that is controlled by another entity'. *[IFRS 10 Appendix A].*

The CA 2006 states that an undertaking is a parent undertaking in relation to another undertaking, a subsidiary undertaking, if:

(a)   it holds a majority of the voting rights in the undertaking; or

(b)   it is a member of the undertaking and has the right to appoint or remove a majority of its board of directors; or

(c)   it has the right to exercise a dominant influence over the undertaking by virtue of provisions in the undertaking's articles or by virtue of a control contract; or

(d)   it is a member of the undertaking and controls alone, pursuant to an agreement with other shareholders or members, a majority of the voting rights in the undertaking.

An undertaking should also be treated as a member for the purposes above if any of its subsidiary undertakings is a member of that undertaking or if any shares in that other undertaking are held by a person acting on behalf of the undertaking or any of its subsidiary undertakings.

An undertaking is also a parent undertaking in relation to another undertaking, a subsidiary undertaking, if it has the power to exercise, or actually exercises, dominant influence or control over it; or it and the subsidiary undertaking are managed on a unified basis.

A parent undertaking is treated as the parent undertaking of undertakings in relation to which any of its subsidiary undertakings are, or are to be treated as, parent undertakings; and references to its subsidiary undertakings should be construed accordingly. *[s1162(1)-(5)].* Schedule 7 to the CA 2006 provides interpretation and references to 'shares' in section 1162 and in Schedule 7 are to 'allotted shares'. *[s1162(6)-(7)].*

These differences in definition make it possible for an entity to be a subsidiary undertaking under the CA 2006 but not under EU-adopted IFRS, for example an entity in which a parent owns a majority of the voting rights but does not have control over the subsidiary (as defined in EU-adopted IFRS). However, the key issue for the application of FRS 101 is whether the subsidiary is included in the consolidation of the parent's consolidated financial statements. A company that meets the definition of a subsidiary undertaking under the CA 2006 but is not included in the consolidation of the consolidated financial statements of its parent cannot apply FRS 101.

2.1.3   *Publicly available consolidated financial statements*

By 'publicly available', we believe that FRS 101 requires that the consolidated financial statements can be accessed by the public as the use of the disclosure exemptions set out in the standard is conditional on a disclosure by the qualifying entity indicating from where those consolidated financial statements can be obtained (see 2.2 below). This does not mandate that the consolidated financial statements must be filed with a regulator. Therefore, for example, consolidated financial statements of a UK company that have not been filed with the Registrar of Companies, at the date the subsidiary's FRS 101 financial statements are approved, must be publicly available via some other medium.

2.1.4   *Non-UK qualifying entities*

There is no requirement that a qualifying entity is a UK entity. Non-UK entities can apply FRS 101 in their individual or separate financial statements subject to meeting the criteria for the use of the standard (see 2.2 below) and provided FRS 101 is allowed for use in their own jurisdiction.

2.1.5   *Non-controlling interests*

There is no ownership threshold for a subsidiary to apply FRS 101. Therefore, a qualifying entity can apply FRS 101 even if its parent holds less than a majority of the voting rights.

As a result of amendments made in December 2016 (see 1.2.1 above), there is no requirement for a qualifying entity to notify its shareholders about the proposed use of the disclosure exemptions and the ability of minority shareholders holding a specified proportion of the voting rights to object to the disclosure exemptions has also been removed. The requirement to notify shareholders was removed because the FRC considered that it was no longer cost-effective in practice and sufficient information would continue to exist for minority shareholders to understand the effects of the reduced disclosure framework. *[FRS 101.BC27]*. The FRC further considered that it was unnecessary to retain the right to object for shareholders holding a specified proportion of the voting rights given the information available to shareholders and their existing rights. *[FRS 101.BC28]*.

2.1.6 Intended to give a true and fair view

In the definition of a qualifying entity (see 2.1 above), the consolidated financial statements in which the qualifying entity is included are not required to give an explicit true and fair view of the assets, liabilities, financial position and profit or loss. Rather, they are '*intended* to give a true and fair view' (our emphasis). This means that the consolidated financial statements in which the qualifying entity is consolidated need not contain an explicit opinion that they give a 'true and fair view' but, in substance, they should be intended to give such a view. The FRC guidance – *True and Fair* – issued in June 2014 states that 'Fair presentation under IFRS is equivalent to a true and fair view'.[1]

A UK parent company that wishes to claim an exemption from preparing group accounts under either section 400 or section 401 of the CA 2006 must be a subsidiary included in the consolidated accounts for a larger group. Those consolidated accounts (and where appropriate, the group's annual report) must be drawn up: *[s400(2)(b), s401(2)(b)]*

- in accordance with the provisions of Directive 2013/34/EU ('the Accounting Directive') (for sections 400 and 401); or

- in a manner equivalent to consolidated accounts and consolidated reports so drawn up (for section 401); or

- in accordance with international accounting standards adopted pursuant to the IAS Regulation, i.e. EU-adopted IFRS (for sections 400 and 401); or

- in accordance with accounting standards which are equivalent to such international accounting standards, as determined pursuant to Commission Regulation (EC) No. 1569/2007 (for section 401).

There are similar requirements for a parent LLP but for section 401, there is no reference to the basis on which the consolidated reports are drawn up. *[s400(2)(b) (LLP), s401(2)(b) (LLP)]*. We believe that references to 'in accordance with the Accounting Directive', in relation to a banking or insurance group in sections 400 and 401, mean as modified by the provisions of the Bank Accounts Directive or the Insurance Accounts Directive respectively. *[s400(2)(b), s401(2)(b), s400(2)(b) (LLP), s401(2)(b) (LLP)]*.

In our view, a set of consolidated financial statements that would meet the above criteria (i.e. the consolidated financial statements are drawn up in accordance with or in a manner equivalent to the Accounting Directive, or in accordance with EU-adopted IFRS or accounting standards which are equivalent to EU-adopted IFRS as determined by the mechanism established by the EU Commission) is intended to give a true and fair view.

Chapter 2

The Application Guidance to FRS 100 – *Application of Financial Reporting Requirements* – states that consolidated financial statements of a higher parent will meet the test of equivalence in the Accounting Directive if they are intended to give a true and fair view and:

- are prepared in accordance with FRS 102;
- are prepared in accordance with EU-adopted IFRS;
- are prepared in accordance with IFRS, subject to the consideration of the reasons for any failure by the European Commission to adopt a standard or interpretation; or
- are prepared using other GAAPs which are closely related to IFRS, subject to the consideration of the effect of any differences from EU-adopted IFRS.

Consolidated financial statements of the higher parent prepared using other GAAPs or the IFRS for SMEs should be assessed for equivalence with the Accounting Directive based on the particular facts, including the similarities to and differences from the Accounting Directive. *[FRS 100.AG6]*.

In accordance with Commission Regulation (EC) No. 1569/2007 of 21 December 2007 (see above), the EU Commission has identified the following GAAPs as equivalent to international accounting standards. This means that these GAAPs are equivalent to international accounting standards as a matter of UK law: *[FRS 100.AG7]*

Equivalent GAAP	Applicable from
GAAP of Japan	1 January 2009
GAAP of the United States of America	I January 2009
GAAP of the People's Republic of China	1 January 2012
GAAP of Canada	1 January 2012
GAAP of the Republic of Korea	1 January 2012

In addition, third country issuers were permitted to prepare their annual consolidated financial statements and half-yearly consolidated financial statements in accordance with the GAAP of the Republic of India for financial years starting before 1 April 2016. For reporting periods beginning on or after 1 April 2016, in relation to GAAP of the Republic of India, equivalence should be assessed on the basis of the particular facts.

The concept of equivalence for the purposes of section 401 is discussed further in Chapter 8 at 3.1.1.C.

In theory, there is no reason why consolidated financial statements of a parent prepared under a GAAP that is not 'equivalent' to the Accounting Directive cannot be used provided those consolidated financial statements in which the entity is included are publicly available and are intended to give a true and fair view.

In addition, as set out above, a number of the disclosure exemptions from EU-adopted IFRS in FRS 101 are conditional on 'equivalent' disclosures being made in those consolidated financial statements in which the qualifying entity is included. Where the equivalent disclosure is not made, the relevant disclosure exemptions cannot be applied in the qualifying entity's financial statements prepared under

FRS 101 (see 6.2 below). A GAAP that is not 'equivalent' to the Accounting Directive is less likely to have those 'equivalent' disclosures.

One issue not addressed by FRS 101 is the impact of a qualified audit opinion on the parent's consolidated financial statements on a qualifying entity's ability to use FRS 101. A Queen's Counsel's opinion obtained by the FRC in 2008 stated that 'the scope for arguing that financial statements which do not comply with relevant accounting standards nevertheless give a true and fair view, or a fair presentation, is very limited'.[2]

2.2   Use of the disclosure exemptions

The use of the disclosure exemptions in FRS 101 (see 6 below) is conditional on all of the following criteria being met: *[FRS 101.5]*

- the reporting entity applies, as its financial reporting framework, the recognition, measurement and disclosure requirements of EU-adopted IFRS but makes those amendments to EU-adopted IFRS as required by the Application Guidance to FRS 101 that are necessary in order to comply with the CA 2006 and the Regulations. This is because financial statements prepared under FRS 101 are Companies Act individual accounts as defined in section 395(1) of the CA 2006 but the Application Guidance applies to any qualifying entity applying FRS 101, including those that are not companies (see 4 and 5 below);

- the reporting entity discloses in the notes to its financial statements a brief narrative summary of the disclosure exemptions adopted; and

- the reporting entity discloses the name of the parent of the group in whose consolidated financial statements its financial statements are consolidated (i.e. the parent identified in the definition of a 'qualifying entity') and from where those financial statements may be obtained.

A qualifying entity which is a financial institution is entitled to more limited disclosure exemptions (see 6.4 below).

2.3   The impact of section 400 and section 401 of the CA 2006 on FRS 101

FRS 101 does not override either section 400 or section 401 of the CA 2006. Section 400 exempts a UK parent company from preparing consolidated accounts if it is a subsidiary undertaking (whose immediate parent undertaking is established under the law of an EEA State) and is included in the consolidated accounts of a larger group drawn up to the same date, or to an earlier date in the same financial year, by a parent undertaking established under the law of an EEA State. Section 401 exempts a UK parent company from preparing consolidated accounts if it is a subsidiary undertaking of a parent undertaking *not* established under the law of an EEA State and the company and all of its subsidiary undertakings are included in the consolidated accounts of a larger group drawn up to the same date, or to an earlier date in the same financial year, by a parent undertaking. The exemptions from preparing consolidated accounts in both sections 400 and 401 are subject to various conditions including 'equivalence' (in respect of section 401, which is discussed at 2.1.6 above). The detailed conditions for the above exemptions from preparing group accounts under the CA 2006 are discussed further in Chapter 8 at 3.1.1.

If a UK parent company does not meet all of the conditions set out in either section 400 or section 401 (and is not otherwise exempt under the CA 2006) then it must prepare consolidated financial statements. Such consolidated financial statements cannot be prepared under FRS 101. However, the parent entity could still prepare its individual financial statements under FRS 101.

At the time of writing this chapter, the company law requirements of sections 400-401 have not been altered as a result of Brexit. However, the government has published draft legislative proposals – *The Accounts and Reports (Amendment) (EU Exit) Regulations 2018*. See Chapter 8 at 3.1.1.G for discussion of these draft proposals.

2.4   Interim financial statements

FRS 101 does not address the preparation of interim financial statements. However, entities applying FRS 101 to annual financial statements may use FRS 104 – *Interim Financial Reporting* – as a basis for their interim financial reports. FRS 104 is discussed in Chapter 34.

3   TRANSITION TO FRS 101

An entity can transition to FRS 101 from either EU-adopted IFRS or another form of GAAP (e.g. another form of UK GAAP). In this context, another form of UK GAAP currently means either FRS 102 or FRS 105 – *The Financial Reporting Standard applicable to the Micro-entities Regime*.

FRS 101 is adopted in the first accounting period for which a reporting entity makes a statement of compliance with the standard (see 1.3 above). The date of transition is the beginning of the earliest period for which an entity presents full comparative information under a given standard in its first financial statements that comply with that standard. *[FRS 100 Appendix I]*. For example, the date of transition is 1 January 2018 for an entity with a 31 December year-end adopting FRS 101 for the first time in its 2019 financial statements. *[FRS 100 Appendix I]*.

3.1   Companies Act restrictions on changes to FRS 101

Under the CA 2006, a company that wishes to change from preparing IAS individual accounts to preparing individual accounts under FRS 101 may do so either:

- if there is a 'relevant change of circumstance' as defined in section 395(4) of the CA 2006; or
- for financial years ending on or after 1 October 2012, for a reason other than a relevant change of circumstance, once in a five year period. *[FRS 100 Appendix II.14]*.

There is no restriction on the number of times an entity can move from Companies Act accounts to IAS accounts or *vice versa*. Theoretically, an entity could 'flip' from IAS accounts to FRS 101 and back again several times without a 'relevant change in circumstance' provided such flips are done no more than once every five years and provided that the entity is also complying with the requirements of the CA 2006 such as those relating to consistency of financial reporting within groups (see 3.2 below).

There are no Companies Act restrictions on a change from FRS 102 or FRS 105 to FRS 101 and back again or *vice versa* since these are all Companies Act accounts.

3.2   Consistency of financial statements within the group

The CA 2006 requires that the directors of a UK parent company secure that the individual accounts of the parent company and of each of its subsidiary undertakings are prepared under the same financial reporting framework, be it IAS accounts or Companies Act accounts, except to the extent that in the directors' opinion there are good reasons for not doing so. *[s407(1)]*. However, this rule does not apply:

- if the parent company does not prepare group accounts; *[s407(2)]*

- if the accounts of the subsidiary undertaking are not required to be prepared under Part 15 of the CA 2006 (for example, foreign subsidiary undertakings); *[s407(3)]* or

- to any subsidiary undertakings that are charities (charities and non-charities within a group are not required to use the same accounting framework). *[s407(4)]*. This is because charities are not permitted to prepare either IAS group or individual accounts. *[s395(2), s403(3)]*.

Additionally, a UK parent company that prepares both consolidated and separate financial statements under EU-adopted IFRS (i.e. IAS group accounts and IAS individual accounts) is not required to ensure that its subsidiary undertakings all prepare IAS individual accounts. However, it must ensure that each of its subsidiary undertakings use the same accounting framework in their individual accounts unless there are good reasons for not doing so. *[s407(5)]*.

Therefore, a group that decides to use FRS 101 for any of its UK subsidiary undertakings, must ensure, unless there are good reasons for not doing so, that all its UK subsidiary undertakings prepare Companies Act individual accounts (i.e. the same financial reporting framework). This requirement only applies to subsidiary undertakings in scope of the section 407 consistency requirements.

Although not explicitly stated by FRS 100, there appears to be no requirement that all UK subsidiary undertakings in a group must use FRS 101 for their Companies Act individual accounts. Some subsidiary undertakings could also use FRS 102, since these are all Companies Act individual accounts and therefore they are all under the same financial reporting framework. However, while this approach would comply with the statutory requirements, groups that use a 'mix' of GAAP in the individual financial statements may be challenged by HMRC, particularly if this results in tax arbitrage.

Examples of 'good reasons' for not preparing all individual accounts within a group using the same reporting framework are contained in the document *Guidance for UK Companies on Accounting and Reporting: Requirements under the Companies Act 2006 and the application of the IAS Regulation* issued by the Department for Business Enterprise and Regulatory Reform (BERR) in June 2008.

3.3   Transition from EU-adopted IFRS to FRS 101

In substance, the transition requirements for entities that have been applying EU-adopted IFRS prior to conversion to FRS 101 treat the qualifying entity as not having changed its financial reporting framework. Disclosure is required only where changes are made on transition. *[FRS 100.12, FRS 101.7A]*. FRS 101 modifies EU-adopted IFRS in certain respects, in order to comply with the Companies Act and the Regulations.

A qualifying entity that is applying EU-adopted IFRS prior to the date of transition to FRS 101 will then be preparing Companies Act individual accounts in accordance with s395(1)(a) of the CA 2006 (rather than IAS individual accounts in accordance with s395(1)(b) of the CA 2006). It therefore must consider whether amendments are required to comply with paragraph 5(b) of FRS 101 – see 4 and 5 below – but it does not reapply the provisions of IFRS 1. Where amendments in accordance with paragraph 5(b) of FRS 101 are required, the entity should determine whether the amendments have a material effect on the first FRS 101 financial statements presented. *[FRS 100.12]*. Details of measurement differences between EU-adopted IFRS and FRS 101 which might result in a material effect on the financial statements are discussed at 4 below.

Where there is no material effect of such changes, the qualifying entity should disclose that it has undergone transition to FRS 101 and give a brief narrative of the disclosure exemptions taken for all periods presented in the financial statements. *[FRS 100.12(a)]*.

Where there is a material effect caused by such changes, the qualifying entity's first FRS 101 financial statements should include: *[FRS 100.12(b)]*

- a description of the nature of each material change in accounting policy;
- reconciliations of its equity determined in accordance with EU-adopted IFRS to its equity determined in accordance with FRS 101 for both the date of transition to FRS 101 and for the end of the latest period presented in the entity's most recent annual financial statements prepared in accordance with EU-adopted IFRS; and
- a reconciliation of the profit or loss determined in accordance with EU-adopted IFRS to its profit or loss determined in accordance with FRS 101 for the latest period presented in the entity's most recent annual financial statements prepared in accordance with EU-adopted IFRS.

This means that, for an entity adopting FRS 101 for the first time in its annual financial statements ending on 31 December 2019 (and presenting one comparative period), reconciliations will be required of:

- equity as at 1 January 2018 and 31 December 2018; and
- profit or loss for the year ended 31 December 2018.

There is no requirement for a transition balance sheet to be prepared. *[FRS 100.12, FRS 101.7A]*.

Amendments with a material effect must be applied retrospectively on transition unless impracticable. When it is impracticable to apply the amendments retrospectively, the qualifying entity should apply the amendment to the earliest period for which it is practicable to do so and it should identify the data presented for prior periods that are not comparable with the data for the period in which it prepares its first financial statements that conform to FRS 101. *[FRS 100.13]*. 'Impracticable' is defined in IAS 8 – *Accounting Policies, Changes in Accounting Estimates and Errors*.

Paragraph 5(b) of FRS 101 cross-refers to Application Guidance 1 to the standard (which forms an integral part of the standard) that includes presentational as well as recognition and measurement modifications to EU-adopted IFRS required when applying the standard. The transitional rules contain no explicit requirement to disclose material presentational changes such as the use of balance sheet and profit and loss formats in accordance with the Regulations (especially where statutory rather than adapted formats are used). However, we recommend that entities explain any material presentational changes compared to EU-adopted IFRS arising from adoption of FRS 101 in order to assist readers' understanding of the financial statements.

3.4   Transition from another version of UK GAAP or another GAAP to FRS 101

In substance, the transition requirements treat conversion to FRS 101 from another version of UK GAAP (currently FRS 102 or FRS 105) or another GAAP as a full first time conversion to EU-adopted IFRS (as modified by FRS 101).

A qualifying entity that transitions to FRS 101 should, unless it is applying EU-adopted IFRS prior to the date of transition (see 3.3 above), apply the requirements of paragraphs 6 to 33 of IFRS 1 (as adopted by the EU) including the relevant appendices, except for the requirement of paragraphs 6 and 21 to present an opening statement of financial position at the date of transition. References to IFRSs in IFRS 1 are interpreted to mean EU-adopted IFRS as amended in accordance with paragraph 5(b) of FRS 101. *[FRS 100.11(b)]*. This means that all of the recognition, measurement and disclosure rules for an IFRS first-time adopter apply (except for the requirement to present an opening statement of financial position) to the extent they do not conflict with EU-adopted IFRS as amended by paragraph 5(b) of FRS 101. First-time adoption of IFRS is discussed in Chapter 5 of EY International GAAP 2019.

IFRS 1 sets out specific requirements for where a subsidiary becomes a first-time adopter later than its parent ('the D16 election'). or where a parent becomes a first-time adopter later than its subsidiary or a parent becomes a first-time adopter in its separate financial statements earlier or later than in its consolidated financial statements ('the D17 requirements'). *[IFRS 1.Appendix D.16-17]*. These requirements are both amended by FRS 101 as described at 3.4.1 and 3.4.2 below.

3.4.1   The D16 election

FRS 101 amends the D16 election to: *[FRS 101.AG1(a)]*

- remove the sentence stating that the election to use the carrying amounts that would be included in the parent's consolidated financial statements, based on the parent's transition to IFRSs, is not available to a subsidiary of an investment entity that is required to be measured at fair value through profit or loss; and

- add a sentence stating that 'A qualifying entity that applies this provision must ensure that its assets and liabilities are measured in accordance with company law'.

The purpose of the second amendment is to restrict the application of the D16 election to situations where the measurement of assets and liabilities in the subsidiary's or parent's individual financial statements based on consolidated financial statements would comply with company law. FRS 101 financial statements must comply with the measurement requirements of the CA 2006 which may be inconsistent with those of EU-adopted IFRS applied in the consolidated financial statements. *[FRS 101 Appendix II.Table 1]*. The sentence was amended by the Triennial review 2017.

Previously, it stated that 'A qualifying entity that applies this provision must ensure that its assets and liabilities are measured in compliance with FRS 101.'

The FRC does not explain the first amendment although an entity which is not consolidated by its parent cannot apply FRS 101 (see 2.1 above).

3.4.2   The D17 requirements

FRS 101 amends the D17 requirements by adding a sentence stating that 'A qualifying entity that applies this provision must ensure that its assets and liabilities are measured in accordance with company law'. *[FRS 101.AG1(b)].*

This amendment (which was made by the Triennial review 2017 in the same way as for the D16 election) has the same purpose as described at 3.4.1 above. *[FRS 101 Appendix II.Table 1].*

FRS 101 also amends the D17 requirements to remove the sentence 'Notwithstanding this requirement, a non-investment entity parent shall not apply the exception to consolidation that is used by any investment entity subsidiaries'. However, this sentence is not relevant to FRS 101 financial statements, which are not consolidated financial statements.

3.5   The impact of transition on realised profits

There may be circumstances where a conversion to FRS 101 eliminates a qualifying entity's realised profits or turns those realised profits into a realised loss. TECH 02/17BL – *Guidance on Realised and Distributable Profits under the Companies Act 2006* – issued by the ICAEW and ICAS, (TECH 02/17BL) states that the change in the treatment of a retained profit or loss as realised (or unrealised) as a result of a change in the law or in accounting standards or interpretations would not render unlawful a distribution already made out of realised profits determined by reference to 'relevant accounts' which had been prepared in accordance with generally acceptable accounting principles applicable to those accounts. This is because the CA 2006 defines realised profits or losses for determining the lawfulness of a distribution as 'such profits and losses of the company as fall to be treated as realised in accordance with principles generally accepted at the time when the accounts are prepared, with respect to the determination for accounting purposes of realised profits or losses'. *[TECH 02/17BL.3.28-29].*

The effects of the introduction of a new accounting standard or of the adoption of IFRS become relevant to the application of the common law capital maintenance rule only in relation to distributions accounted for in periods in which the change will first be recognised in the accounts. This means that a change in accounting policy known to be adopted in a financial year needs to be taken into account in determining the dividend to be approved by shareholders in that year. Therefore, for example, an entity converting to FRS 101 in 2019 must have regard to the effect of adoption of FRS 101 in respect of all dividends payable in 2019 (including any final dividends in respect of 2018) even though the 'relevant accounts' may still be those for 2018 prepared under another GAAP. *[TECH 02/17BL.3.30-37].*

Statutory 'interim accounts' are required to be prepared under sections 836(2) and 838 of the CA 2006 (and delivered to the Registrar if the company is a public company) if a proposed distribution cannot be justified by reference to the relevant accounts. See Chapter 1 at 5.5 for further discussion.

4 MEASUREMENT DIFFERENCES BETWEEN FRS 101 AND EU-ADOPTED IFRS

As noted at 2 above, entities applying FRS 101 use EU-adopted IFRS as amended by the standard in order to comply with the CA 2006 and the Regulations. This is because financial statements prepared under FRS 101 are Companies Act individual accounts and not IAS individual accounts. There are several conflicts between the recognition and measurement rules of EU-adopted IFRS and those required by the Regulations. Consequently, entities applying FRS 101 apply a modified version of EU-adopted IFRS designed to eliminate these differences.

FRS 101 does not modify EU-adopted IFRS in respect of goodwill and indefinite-life intangible assets. However, non-amortisation of those assets conflicts with the Regulations necessitating use of a 'true and fair override' as explained at 4.1 below.

Similarly, FRS 101 does not modify IFRS 9's requirement to present changes in the fair value of a financial liability attributable to own credit risk in other comprehensive income. However, this presentation conflicts with the Regulations necessitating use of a 'true and fair override' as explained at 4.2 below.

In respect of the matters discussed at 4.3 to 4.11 below, FRS 101 specifically amends EU-adopted IFRS to remove conflicts identified between EU-adopted IFRS and the Regulations. Therefore, the issue of invoking a 'true and fair override' does not arise in respect of these other matters.

FRS 101 changes EU-adopted IFRS in respect of the following matters:

- negative goodwill (see 4.3 below);
- contingent consideration balances arising from business combinations (see 4.4 below);
- government grants deducted from the cost of fixed assets (see 4.5 below);
- provisions, contingent assets and contingent liabilities (see 4.6 below);
- realised profits (see 4.7 below);
- equalisation provisions (see 4.8 below);
- investments in subsidiaries, associates and joint ventures by banking and insurance entities (see 4.9 below); and
- investment entities (see 4.10 below).

The position as regards limited liability partnerships (LLPs) is discussed at 4.11 below.

4.1 Positive goodwill and indefinite-life intangible assets

No changes have been made to EU-adopted IFRS in respect of positive goodwill that is not amortised. Instead, FRS 101 states that paragraph B63(a) of IFRS 3 – *Business Combinations*, which requires that goodwill is measured at cost less impairment, should be read in accordance with paragraph A2.8 of FRS 101. *[FRS 101.AG1(f)]*. The non-amortisation of goodwill required by IFRS 3 conflicts with paragraph 22 of Schedule 1 to the Regulations (and its equivalents in Schedules 2 and 3) which require that an intangible asset (including goodwill) must be written off over its useful economic life.

FRS 101 notes that the non-amortisation of goodwill will usually be a departure, for the overriding purpose of giving a true and fair view, from the requirements of the Regulations.

FRS 101 goes on to state that this is not a new instance of the use of the 'true and fair override' and it would have been required for companies reporting under previous UK GAAP which used an indefinite life for goodwill as permitted by FRS 10 – *Goodwill and intangible assets*. *[FRS 101 Appendix II.8, 1 Sch 22]*.

This means that the FRC expects that entities with positive goodwill should not amortise that goodwill under FRS 101. Those entities should invoke a true and fair override as permitted by paragraph 10(2) of Schedule 1 to the Regulations (or its equivalents in Schedules 2 and 3) to overcome the requirement to write off goodwill over its useful economic life in paragraph 22 of Schedule 1 to the Regulations (or its equivalents in Schedules 2 and 3). The use of the true and fair override requires disclosure of the particulars of the departure from the Regulations, the reasons for it and its effect. *[FRS 101 Appendix II.8, 1 Sch 10(2)]*. Continuation of goodwill amortisation, if permitted under previous GAAP, is not allowed by FRS 101.

It is anticipated that the use of a true and fair override in respect of goodwill amortisation will be limited in application since, in individual financial statements, there will only be goodwill where a business that is not an entity has been acquired.

FRS 101 goes on to state that similar considerations (i.e. the need for a true and fair override) may apply to other intangible assets that are not amortised because they have an indefinite life and intangible assets that have a residual value that is not zero (i.e. intangible assets that are not written off over their useful economic life). *[FRS 101 Appendix II.8A, 1 Sch 22]*.

4.2   Presentation of fair value gains and losses attributable to changes in own credit risk on financial liabilities designated at fair value through profit or loss in other comprehensive income

IFRS 9 requires qualifying entities to present fair value gains or losses attributable to changes in own credit risk on financial liabilities designated at fair value through profit or loss in other comprehensive income. The Note on Legal Requirements to FRS 101 observes that this will usually be a departure from the requirement of paragraph 40 of Schedule 1 of the Regulations (and its equivalents in Schedules 2 and 3) for the overriding purpose of giving a true and fair view. As a result, when applicable, disclosure will need to be given in the notes to the accounts of 'particulars of the departure, the reasons for it and its effect'. *[FRS 101 Appendix II.7F]*.

FRS 101 is silent about the other two circumstances in IFRS 9 in which accounting for fair value gains and losses are required in other comprehensive income. In our view:

- accounting for changes in the fair value of an equity instrument through other comprehensive income (without recycling of fair value changes to profit and loss) makes use of the alternative accounting rules in the Regulations and does not therefore require the use of a true and fair override (see Chapter 6 at 10.2); and

- the model used for accounting for changes in the fair value of a debt instrument through other comprehensive income is similar, but not identical, to the available-for-sale asset model under IAS 39 – *Financial Instruments: Recognition and Measurement*. In our view, it is inferred from FRS 101's silence on the matter that this model is included within the fair value accounting rules in the Regulations (see Chapter 6 at 10.3) and does not therefore require the use of a true and fair override to apply.

4.3 Negative goodwill

FRS 101 changes paragraph 34 of IFRS 3 so that any gain arising from a bargain purchase (i.e. negative goodwill) is not recognised immediately in profit and loss. Instead, any amount of negative goodwill resulting from a business combination should be shown on the face of the statement of financial position on the acquisition date, immediately below goodwill, and followed by a subtotal of the net amount of positive and negative goodwill. Subsequently, the negative goodwill up to the fair value of the non-monetary assets acquired should be recognised in profit and loss in the periods in which the non-monetary assets are recovered. Any amount of the negative goodwill in excess of the fair values of the non-monetary assets acquired should be recognised in profit or loss in the periods expected to be benefited. *[FRS 101.AG1(c)].*

This change to EU-adopted IFRS was necessary because the Accounting Directive (on which the requirements in the Regulations are based) may be inconsistent with the recognition requirements for negative goodwill under EU-adopted IFRS. *[FRS 101 Appendix II Table 1].*

Monetary assets are defined in EU-adopted IFRS as 'money held and assets to be received in fixed or determinable amounts of money'. *[IAS 38.8].* Conversely, an essential feature of a non-monetary asset is the absence of a right to receive a fixed or determinable number of units of currency. IAS 21 – *The Effects of Changes in Foreign Exchange Rates* – gives examples of non-monetary assets as amounts prepaid for goods and services, goodwill, intangible assets, inventories and property, plant and equipment. *[IAS 21.16].* IFRS 9 states that investments in equity instruments are non-monetary items. *[IFRS 9.B5.7.3].* This suggests that equity investments in subsidiaries, associates or joint ventures are also non-monetary items.

4.4 Contingent consideration balances arising from business combinations

Contingent consideration balances arising from business combinations whose acquisition dates are on or after the date an entity first applied the amendments to company law, set out in *The Companies, Partnerships and Groups (Accounts and Reports) Regulations 2015* (SI 2015/980), i.e. generally the start of accounting periods beginning on or after 1 January 2016 when SI 2015/980 was not early adopted, should be accounted for in accordance with IFRS 3. *[FRS 101.AG1(d)].* This means that contingent consideration is initially recognised at fair value with subsequent changes in the fair value of contingent consideration not classified as equity recognised in profit or loss. *[IFRS 3.58].*

Contingent consideration balances arising from business combinations whose acquisition dates preceded the date when an entity first applied the amendments to company law set out in SI 2015/980 should not be adjusted as a result of the change in company law. Instead, the entity's previous accounting policies for contingent consideration should continue to apply. *[FRS 101.AG1(d)].* Prior to the July 2015 amendments which incorporate SI 2015/980, FRS 101 required that an adjustment to the cost of a business combination contingent on future events be recognised only if the estimated amount of the adjustment was probable and could be measured reliably. If the potential adjustment was not recognised at the acquisition date but subsequently became probable and could be measured reliably, the additional consideration was treated as an adjustment to the cost of the combination (i.e. goodwill).

FRS 101 is silent on accounting for contingent consideration on the acquisition of a subsidiary, associate or joint venture which is accounted for as an investment under IAS 27. However, in practice, if contingent consideration is included in the initial measurement of the asset, subsequent payments are either recognised in profit or loss or capitalised as part of the cost of the asset. We believe that, consistent with the view expressed in Chapter 8 at 2.1.1 of EY International GAAP 2019, until the IASB issues further guidance, differing views remain about the circumstances in which, and to what extent, variable payments, such as contingent consideration should be recognised when initially recognising the underlying asset. There are also differing views about the extent to which subsequent changes should be recognised through profit or loss or capitalised as part of the cost of the asset. Where entities have made an accounting policy choice regarding recognition of contingent consideration and subsequent changes in accounting for the cost of investments in subsidiaries, associates or joint ventures in separate financial statements, the policy should be disclosed and consistently applied.

4.5   Government grants deducted from the cost of fixed assets

FRS 101 has deleted paragraph 28 of IAS 16 – *Property, Plant and Equipment* – and has amended or deleted paragraphs 24 to 29 of IAS 20 – *Accounting for Government Grants and Disclosure of Government Assistance* – in order to eliminate the option in IFRS that permits a government grant relating to an asset to be deducted in arriving at the carrying amount of the asset. Consequently, all government grants related to assets should be presented in the financial statements by setting up the grant as deferred income that is recognised in profit or loss on a systematic basis over the useful life of the asset. In addition, the option in paragraph 29 of IAS 20 that permits grants related to income to be deducted in reporting the related expense has been deleted. Consequently, in profit or loss the grant must be reported either separately or under a general heading such as 'Other operating income'. *[FRS 101.AG1(l)-(r)]*.

These changes to EU-adopted IFRS were necessary because the Regulations prohibit off-setting of items that represent assets against items that represent liabilities unless specifically permitted or required. *[FRS 101 Appendix II Table 1]*.

4.6   Provisions, contingent assets and contingent liabilities

FRS 101 changes paragraph 92 of IAS 37 – *Provisions, Contingent Liabilities and Contingent Assets* – to state that when, in extremely rare cases, disclosure of some or all of the information required by paragraphs 84-89 of IAS 37 can be expected to prejudice seriously the position of the entity in a dispute with other parties, on the subject matter of the provision, contingent liability or contingent asset, the entity need not disclose all of the information required by those paragraphs insofar as it relates to the dispute, but should disclose at least the following: *[FRS 101.AG1(s)]*

- in relation to provisions:
  - a table showing the reconciliation required by paragraph 84 in aggregate, including the source and application of any amounts transferred to or from provisions during the reporting period;
  - particulars of each provision in any case where the amount of the provision is material; and
  - the fact that, and reason why, the information required by paragraphs 84 and 85 has not been disclosed.
- in relation to contingent liabilities:
  - particulars and the total amount of any contingent liabilities (excluding those which arise out of insurance contracts) that are not included in the statement of financial position;
  - the total amount of contingent liabilities which are undertaken on behalf of or for the benefit of:
    - any parent or fellow subsidiary of the entity;
    - any subsidiary of the entity; or
    - any entity in which the reporting entity has a participating interest,
    should each be stated separately; and
  - the fact that, and reason why, the information required by paragraph 86 has not been disclosed.
- In relation to contingent assets, the entity should disclose the general nature of the dispute, together with the fact that, and reason why, the information required by paragraph 89 has not been disclosed.

This amendment was made because the 'seriously prejudicial' exemption in IAS 37 does not apply to disclosures required by the Regulations. Although this matter is implicitly covered by paragraph 4A of FRS 101, which requires that the requirements of the Regulations must be complied with (see 2 above), the FRC decided to specifically highlight this constraint on the IAS 37 exemption. *[FRS 101.BC79]*.

These amended disclosures apply to all entities applying FRS 101, not just entities subject to the requirements of the Regulations.

4.7   Realised profits

FRS 101 has changed paragraph 88 of IAS 1 to clarify the precedence of the Regulations over IFRS in this matter by adding the words 'or unless prohibited by the Act' after 'an entity should recognise all items of income and expense arising in a period in profit or loss unless an IFRS requires or permits otherwise'. *[FRS 101.AG1(k)]*.

Paragraph 13(a) of Schedule 1 to the Regulations (and its equivalents in Schedules 2 and 3 (the related requirement in Schedule 3 is modified)) require that only profits realised at the balance sheet date are included in the profit or loss account. *[FRS 101 Appendix II.12]*. Paragraph 39 of Schedule 1 to the Regulations (and its equivalents in Schedules 2 and 3) allow stocks, investment property and living animals or plants to be held at fair value in Companies Act accounts. *[FRS 101 Appendix II.13]*. Paragraph 40(2) of Schedule 1 to the

Regulations (and its equivalents in Schedules 2 and 3) require that, in general, movements in the fair value of financial instruments, stocks, investment properties or living animals and plants are recognised in the profit and loss account notwithstanding the usual restrictions allowing only realised profits and losses to be included in the profit and loss account. Therefore, paragraph 40 of Schedule 1 overrides paragraph 13(a) of Schedule 1 and such fair value gains can be recognised in profit and loss under FRS 101. *[FRS 101 Appendix II.14]*.

The legal appendix to FRS 101 states that entities measuring investment properties, living animals or plants, or financial instruments at fair value may transfer such amounts to a separate non-distributable reserve instead of carrying them forward in retained earnings but are not required to do so. The FRC suggests that presenting fair value movements that are not distributable profits in a separate reserve may assist with the identification of profits available for that purpose. *[FRS 101 Appendix II.15]*.

Whether profits are available for distribution must be determined in accordance with applicable law. Entities may also refer to TECH 02/17BL to determine the profits available for distribution. *[FRS 101 Appendix II.16]*.

4.8   Equalisation provisions

FRS 101 has changed paragraph 14(a) of IFRS 4 – *Insurance Contracts* – to insert the words 'unless otherwise required by the regulatory framework that applies to the entity' at the beginning of the sentence which prohibits the recognition of catastrophe provisions and equalisation provisions. In addition, the following sentence has been added to the end of the paragraph. 'The presentation of any such liabilities should follow the requirements of the Regulations (or other legal framework that applies to that entity).' *[FRS 101.AG1(fA)]*.

The purpose of these amendments was to remove a conflict between IFRS 4 (which does not permit the recognition of equalisation and catastrophe provisions for claims that have not been incurred) and Schedule 3 to the Regulations (which requires the recognition of equalisation provisions as a liability).

However, following the implementation of the Solvency II regulatory regime, with effect from 1 January 2016, the UK regulatory framework no longer allows insurers to recognise catastrophe provisions and equalisation provisions (although Schedule 3 to the Regulations was not amended). However, insurers may recognise equalisation or catastrophe provisions if permitted under another legal framework.

4.9   Equity accounting for investments in subsidiaries, associates and joint ventures

IAS 27, Schedule 1 to the Regulations and the LLP Regulations permit the use of equity accounting for investments in subsidiaries, associates and joint ventures.

The use of equity accounting for these interests is conditional on the investment in subsidiary, associate or joint venture qualifying as a participating interest (see Chapter 6 at 5.3.4.D), which will usually be the case. If participating interests are accounted for using the equity method and the profit attributable to a participating interest recognised in profit and loss account exceeds the amount of any dividends (including dividends already paid and those whose payment can be claimed), the difference must be placed in a reserve which cannot be distributed to shareholders. *[1 Sch 29A(2)(b)]*.

However, Schedule 2 and Schedule 3 to the Regulations do not permit the use of equity accounting for participating interests. Therefore, entities applying either Schedule 2 or Schedule 3 to the Regulations (i.e. banking and insurance entities, respectively) may not take advantage of the option in paragraph 10(c) of IAS 27 to account for investments in subsidiaries, joint ventures and associates using the equity method. *[FRS 101 Appendix II.7E]*.

4.10   Investment entities

FRS 101 does not apply to consolidated financial statements. However, a parent that meets the definition of an investment entity under IFRS 10, and is therefore required (in most situations) to measure its investment in a subsidiary at fair value through profit or loss, must measure that investment in the same way in its separate financial statements, as required by paragraph 11A of IAS 27. In other words, a qualifying entity that meets the definition of an investment entity must measure its investment in subsidiaries at fair value through profit or loss in its individual financial statements. *[FRS 101 Appendix II.17]*.

An investment entity which measures its investments in subsidiaries at fair value through profit or loss will be required to make the additional disclosures required by paragraph 36(4) of Schedule 1 to the Regulations (see 6.3 below). *[FRS 101 Appendix II.20]*.

4.11   Limited liability partnerships (LLPs)

LLPs applying FRS 101 will be doing so in conjunction with *The Limited Liability Partnerships, (Accounts and Audit) (Application of Companies Act 2006) Regulations 2008 (SI 2008/1911)* and the LLP Regulations, both as amended. It is considered by the FRC that in many cases these regulations are similar to the Regulations, limiting the situations in which legal matters relevant to the financial statements of LLPs are not addressed in Appendix II to FRS 101. *[FRS 101 Appendix II.21]*.

Therefore, generally, the issues identified in relation to Schedule 1 to the Regulations at 4.1 to 4.10 above also apply to Schedule 1 to the LLP Regulations.

5   PRESENTATIONAL DIFFERENCES BETWEEN FRS 101 AND EU-ADOPTED IFRS

As noted at 2 above, UK companies applying FRS 101 must prepare their financial statements in accordance with the CA 2006 and the Regulations. This is because financial statements prepared under FRS 101 are Companies Act accounts and not IAS accounts. *[FRS 101 Appendix II.3]*. The presentation requirements of the CA 2006 and the Regulations are discussed in Chapter 6. While, generally, this chapter refers to companies and the Regulations, the requirements for LLPs are similar, although there are some minor differences.

The following presentational matters are discussed below:

- balance sheet and profit and loss account formats required by FRS 101 (see 5.1 below);
- order of presentation of the notes to the financial statements (see 5.2 below);
- presentation of extraordinary activities (see 5.3 below); and
- presentation of discontinued operations (see 5.4 below).

The Regulations address the balance sheet and profit and loss account formats and the notes required in the statutory accounts of UK companies. Accordingly, the presentation amendments made in Application Guidance 1 to FRS 101 (which apply to all qualifying entities, not just UK companies) relate to the balance sheet and profit and loss section of the statement of comprehensive income (whether in one or two statements). IAS 1's requirements for presentation of other comprehensive income still apply. FRS 101 makes no amendments to the requirement in IAS 1 to present a statement of changes in equity for the reporting period.

There is no requirement to present a statement of cash flows when the reduced disclosure exemption is taken and use of the disclosure exemption is disclosed in the financial statements (see 6.1.10 below).

A UK parent company presenting both consolidated financial statements (either IAS group accounts or Companies Act group accounts) and individual financial statements under FRS 101 can take advantage of the exemption in section 408 of the CA 2006 from presenting a profit and loss account and related notes in respect of its individual profit and loss account. *[s408]*.

5.1   Balance sheet and profit and loss formats required by FRS 101

Qualifying entities subject to Schedule 1 to the Regulations have a choice regarding the presentation of the balance sheet and the profit and loss account. These entities can either:

- comply with the balance sheet and profit and loss format requirements in Section B of Part 1 of Schedule 1 to the Regulations (i.e. use 'statutory formats'); or
- adapt one of the balance sheet or profit and loss account formats in Section B of Part 1 of Schedule 1 to the Regulations (i.e. use 'adapted formats') so as:
  - (in the case of the balance sheet) to distinguish between current and non-current items in a different way; and
  - provided that (for both the balance sheet and profit and loss account):
    - the information given is at least equivalent to that which would have been required by the use of such format had it not been thus adapted; and
    - the presentation is in accordance with generally accepted accounting principles or practice. *[1 Sch 1A]*.

The LLP Regulations allow the same choice for LLPs. *[1 Sch 1A (LLP)]*.

The choice to apply the adapted balance sheet and profit and loss formats (i.e. the presentation requirements of IAS 1) is available only for those entities applying Schedule 1 to the Regulations or the LLP Regulations. The choice is not available to entities applying Schedule 2 to the Regulations (banking companies) or Schedule 3 to the Regulations (insurance companies).

FRS 101 states that when a qualifying entity chooses to use the adapted formats as described above, it should apply the relevant presentation requirements of IAS 1 and, in addition, the profit and loss account (whether presented as a component of the statement of comprehensive income, or as a separate statement) should disclose 'profit or loss before taxation'. *[FRS 101.AG1(h)-(i)]*. The presentation requirements of IAS 1 are discussed in Chapter 3 at 3 of EY International GAAP 2019.

A qualifying entity not permitted or not choosing to apply the adapted formats, *[1 Sch 1A(1)-(2)]*, should comply with the balance sheet format requirements and present the components of profit or loss in the statement of comprehensive income (in either the single statement or two statement approach) in accordance with the profit and loss account formats of the CA 2006 (i.e. the statutory formats), instead of paragraphs 54 to 76, 82, and 85 to 86 of IAS 1.

A qualifying entity should apply, as required by company law, either Part 1 'General Rules and Formats' of Schedule 1 to the Regulations; Part 1 'General Rules and Formats' of Schedule 2 to the Regulations; Part 1 'General Rules and Formats' of Schedule 3 to the Regulations; or Part 1 'General Rules and Formats' of Schedule 1 to the LLP Regulations ('the General Rules to the formats'). *[FRS 101.AG1(h)-(i)]*.

The General Rules to the formats apply to statutory formats. So far as is practicable, the General Rules to the formats (set out in paragraphs 2 to 9A of Section A of Part 1 of Schedule 1 to the Regulations) also apply to the adapted formats. *[1 Sch 1A(3)]*. There are similar requirements in the LLP Regulations. The General Rules to the formats are discussed in Chapter 6 at 4.4.

When an asset or liability relates to more than one item in the balance sheet, the relationship of such asset or liability to the relevant items must be disclosed either under those items or in the notes to the accounts. *[1 Sch 9A]*. This requirement in the General Rules to the formats applies to both statutory and adapted formats.

Therefore, banking and insurance companies, as well as those entities applying Schedule 1 to the Regulations but choosing not to use the adapted formats, must use the statutory balance sheet and profit and loss account formats set out in Section B of Part 1 of the relevant schedule to the Regulations. The legal appendix to FRS 101 confirms that the requirements of paragraphs 54 to 76, 82 and 85 to 86 of IAS 1 do not apply unless the adapted formats in Schedule 1 to the Regulations (i.e. the option to use the IAS formats) are chosen. *[FRS 101 Appendix II Table 1]*.

FRS 101 can also be applied by qualifying entities not subject to the Regulations or the LLP Regulations. The requirements in the Application Guidance to FRS 101 apply to all entities not just companies. *[FRS 101.5(b)]*. A qualifying entity must also ensure it complies with any relevant legal requirements applicable to it. *[FRS 101.4A]*. FRS 102 is more specific and requires entities to apply the formats included in one of Schedules 1, 2 or 3 to the Regulations or the LLP Regulations (so allowing the choice of statutory or adapted formats where Schedule 1 to the Regulations or the LLP Regulations are applied), except to the extent that these requirements are not permitted by any statutory framework under which such entities report. *[FRS 102.4.1, 4.2, 5.1, 5.5, 5.7]*. It seems likely a similar approach is intended under FRS 101.

The required format to be used by a qualifying entity that is not a company or an LLP may be determined by the legal framework governing the financial statements of such entities (see discussion in Chapter 6 at 4.2 on which formats apply to different types of entities). In other cases, management of such entities must apply judgement in determining the most appropriate format in the Regulations or LLP Regulations to use for the circumstances of the entity concerned, where the statutory framework is not prescriptive.

Chapter 2

The General Rules to the formats to Schedule 1 to the Regulations state that once a particular format (in Section B of Part 1 to that schedule) for the balance sheet (or profit and loss account) has been adopted for any financial year, the company's directors must use the same format in preparing Companies Act accounts for subsequent financial years, unless in their opinion there are special reasons for a change. Particulars of any such change must be given in a note to the accounts in which the new format is first used, and the reasons for the change must be explained. *[1 Sch 2, 6 Sch 1]*. Schedule 1 to the Regulations provides a choice of two balance sheet and two profit and loss account statutory formats. There is a similar requirement in the LLP Regulations. There is, however, no choice of statutory formats available in Schedules 2 or 3 of the Regulations.

The above paragraph is discussing a change in the statutory format adopted but, as the paragraph is included in the General Rules to the formats, its requirements apply so far as is practicable where adapted formats are used.

FRS 101 is silent on how an entity would implement a change from a statutory balance sheet and profit and loss account format to an IAS 1 format (i.e. adapted format) (or *vice versa*) in an accounting period subsequent to adoption of FRS 101. In our view, this is a voluntary change in accounting policy to which IAS 8 applies. Consequently, the change should be applied retrospectively, prior periods should be restated and the disclosures required by paragraph 29 of IAS 8 must be made (as well as the disclosures required by the Regulations described above).

5.1.1   Additional presentation requirements where an entity is using the adapted (IAS 1) balance sheet and profit and loss account formats

The legal appendix to FRS 101 clarifies that an entity applying the adapted balance sheet and profit and loss account formats – see 5.1 above – should apply the relevant presentation requirements of IAS 1 subject to: *[FRS 101 Appendix II.9A]*

- the disclosure of profit or loss before taxation and the amendment to IFRS 5 – *Non-current Assets Held for Sale and Discontinued Operations* – included in paragraph AG1(g) of FRS 101, as set out at 5.4 below; and
- any further disaggregation of the statement of financial position, for example in relation to trade and other receivables and trade and other payables (which may be provided in the notes to the financial statements), that is necessary to meet the requirement to give the equivalent information.

The legal appendix does not elaborate what is meant by a 'further disaggregation of the statement of financial position' other than provide the examples above. It reiterates that the option to apply the presentation requirements of IAS 1 is not available to a qualifying entity applying Schedule 2 or Schedule 3 to the Regulations. *[FRS 101 Appendix II.9A]*.

The presentation requirements of IAS 1 are discussed in Chapter 3 of EY International GAAP 2019. IAS 1 permits an entity to present assets and liabilities in the statement of financial position in order of liquidity instead of a current/non-current basis if presentation in order of liquidity is reliable and more relevant. *[IAS 1.60]*. In our view, FRS 101 does not permit the use of a liquidity presentation for assets and liabilities. The use of the adapted formats is intended only to allow an entity to distinguish between current and non-current items in a different (i.e. IFRS) way from the current/non-current presentation required by the statutory formats in Schedule 1 to the Regulations (and the LLP Regulations). The adapted formats do not permit a basis of presentation other than current/non-current.

The Regulations (and LLP Regulations) require supplementary information to be given in the notes to the accounts. These disclosure requirements apply where statutory formats or adapted formats are used. One complexity is that the information required sometimes refers to items found in the statutory formats (which may differ to the line items identified where the adapted formats are used). For example, the adapted formats do not refer to fixed assets, creditors: amounts falling due within one year, creditors: amounts falling due after more than one year, investments, land or buildings, or turnover. Therefore, a UK company using adapted formats in Companies Act accounts will need to identify which of its assets, liabilities, revenue streams needs to be included in the required disclosures. While the classification of non-current assets and current assets used in adapted formats differs to the fixed assets and current assets classification required in statutory formats, the statutory definition of 'fixed assets' (see Chapter 6 at 5.2.2) is relevant for the purposes of disclosures in respect of fixed assets in the Regulations.

5.1.2   Additional presentation requirements needed to comply with IFRS by an entity using the Companies Act balance sheet and profit and loss account formats (statutory formats)

The legal appendix to FRS 101 clarifies that for a qualifying entity not permitted or not choosing to apply the adapted (i.e. IAS 1) balance sheet or profit and loss account formats – see 5.1 above – the format and presentation requirements of IAS 1 may conflict with those of company law because of the following: *[FRS 101 Appendix II.9B]*

- differences in the definition of 'fixed assets' (the term used in the Regulations meaning assets which are intended for use on a continuing basis in the entity's activities) and 'non-current assets' (the term used in EU-adopted IFRS). See Chapter 6 at 5.1.1 and 5.2.2;

- differences in the definition of 'current assets' as the term is used in the Regulations and EU-adopted IFRS. See Chapter 6 at 5.1.1 and 5.2.2;

- differences in the definition of 'creditors: amounts falling due within or after more than one year' (the terms used in the Regulations) and 'current and non-current liabilities' (the terms used in EU-adopted IFRS). See Chapter 6 at 5.1.2 and 5.2.3. Under the CA 2006, a loan is treated as due for repayment on the earliest date on which a lender could require repayment, whilst under EU adopted IFRS the due date is based on when the entity expects to settle the liability or has no unconditional right to defer payment; and

- the CA 2006 requires presentation of debtors falling due after more than one year within current assets. Under EU-adopted IFRS, these items will (usually) be presented in non-current assets. The legal appendix to FRS 101 provides further guidance on the presentation of debtors falling due after more than one year (which are shown in current assets) in the statutory formats – see 5.1.2.A below.

The statutory formats for the balance sheet and profit and loss account (and the related notes to the formats that should be followed) in Schedule 1 to the Regulations and the LLP Regulations are discussed in Chapter 6 at 5.2, 5.3 and 6.6.

5.1.2.A   Debtors due after more than one year

The statutory balance sheet formats require all debtors to be shown under 'current assets'. However, the Regulations require the amount falling due after more than one year to be shown separately for each item included under debtors. The Note on Legal Requirements to FRS 101 reproduces the consensus of UITF 4 – *Presentation of long-term debtors in current assets* – that 'in most cases it will be satisfactory to disclose the size of debtors due after more than one year in the notes to the accounts. There will be some instances, however, where the amount is so material in the context of the total net current assets that in the absence of disclosure of debtors due after more than one year on the face of the balance sheet readers may misinterpret the accounts. In such circumstances, the amount should be disclosed on the face of the balance sheet within current assets'. *[FRS 101 Appendix II.10].*

This disclosure is only relevant where statutory formats rather than adapted (i.e. IAS 1) formats are applied.

5.1.2.B   Non-current assets or disposal groups held for sale

IFRS 5 requires an entity to present: *[IFRS 5.38]*

- a non-current asset classified as held for sale and the assets of a disposal group classified as held for sale separately from other assets in the statement of financial position; and

- the liabilities of a disposal group classified as held for sale separately from other liabilities in the statement of financial position.

IAS 1 requires a single line approach in the balance sheet for 'the total of assets classified as held for sale and assets included in disposal groups classified as held for sale in accordance with IFRS 5' and for 'liabilities included in disposal groups classified as held for sale in accordance with IFRS 5'. Detailed analysis of the components of the assets and liabilities held for sale is required in the notes to the financial statements. *[IAS 1.54].*

However, a qualifying entity that has a disposal group classified as held for sale must ensure that its presentation of the disposal group, in accordance with IFRS 5, meets company law requirements. The Note on Legal Requirements to FRS 101 states that a single line presentation of non-current assets (or liabilities) held for sale will usually not meet company law requirements when the Company Law formats are applied. Therefore, additional aggregation should be provided either in the statement of financial position or in the notes. When the items are material, this should be on the face of the statement of financial position. *[FRS 101 Appendix II.10A].* This conflict arises because the statutory formats included in the Regulations (and LLP Regulations) do not otherwise permit the aggregation of different types of assets and liabilities in this way. One practical solution could be to present the disposal group aggregations as a memorandum on the statement of financial position cross-referenced to the detailed analysis in the notes.

5.2 Notes to the financial statements

Schedule 1 to the Regulations (and its equivalents in Schedule 2 and Schedule 3 and the LLP Regulations) require the notes to the financial statements to be presented in the order in which, where relevant, the items to which they relate are presented in the statement of financial position and the income statement. *[1 Sch 42(2)]*. A qualifying entity preparing financial statements in accordance with FRS 101 should have regard to this requirement when determining a systematic manner for the presentation of its notes to the financial statements in accordance with paragraphs 113 and 114 of IAS 1. *[FRS 101 Appendix II.11A]*.

5.2.1 Particulars of turnover

Schedule 1 to the Regulations (and its equivalents in Schedule 2 and Schedule 3 and the LLP Regulations) require particulars of turnover to be disclosed, including the amount of turnover attributable to each class of business carried on by the company. Where relevant, turnover attributable to different markets must also be disclosed. Although FRS 101 provides an exception from paragraph 114 of IFRS 15, the requirements of the Regulations should still be complied with. *[FRS 101 Appendix II.11B]*.

5.3 Extraordinary items

IFRS has no concept of 'extraordinary items'. The concept of extraordinary items has also been removed for entities applying Schedule 1 to the Regulations or the LLP Regulations.

Consequently, only entities applying Schedule 2 or Schedule 3 to the Regulations (i.e. banking companies and insurance companies) are still required to present extraordinary items separately in the profit and loss account. However, we would expect this requirement to have no practical impact as we would not expect to see any extraordinary items under FRS 101. The legal appendix to FRS 101 states that 'entities should note that extraordinary items are extremely rare as they relate to highly abnormal events or transactions'. *[FRS 101 Appendix II.11]*.

Ordinary activities (for entities reporting under Schedule 2 or Schedule 3 to the Regulations) are defined as 'any activities which are undertaken by a reporting entity as part of its business and such related activities in which the reporting entity engages in furtherance of, incidental to, or arising from, these activities. Ordinary activities include any effects on the reporting entity of any event in the various environments in which it operates, including the political, regulatory, economic and geographical environments, irrespective of the frequency or unusual nature of the events'. *[FRS 101.AG1(j)]*.

Extraordinary activities are 'material items possessing a high degree of abnormality which arise from events or transactions that fall outside the ordinary activities of the reporting entity and which are not expected to recur. They do not include items occurring within the entity's ordinary activities that are required to be disclosed by IAS 1.97, nor do they include prior period items merely because they relate to a prior period'. *[FRS 101.AG1(j)]*.

5.4   Presentation of discontinued operations

FRS 101 amends IFRS 5 to: [FRS 101.AG1(g)]

- remove the option to present the analysis of discontinued operations into its component parts (i.e. revenue, expenses, pre-tax profit, related income tax expense, gain or loss on remeasurement to fair value less costs to sell or on disposal of the discontinued operation and the related income tax expense) in the notes to the financial statements. This analysis must be presented on the face of the statement of comprehensive income;

- require the analysis above to be shown on the face of the statement of comprehensive income in a column identified as related to discontinued operations (i.e. separately from continuing operations);

- require a total column (i.e. the sum of continuing and discontinued operations) to be presented on the face of the statement of comprehensive income; and

- remove the option to present income from continuing operations and from discontinued operations attributable to owners of the parent in the notes to the financial statements. This analysis must be presented on the face of the statement of comprehensive income.

This amended presentation is required for all entities applying FRS 101, even those who have chosen to apply the adapted (i.e. IAS 1) balance sheet and profit and loss account presentation formats (see 5.1 above).

In substance, this means that the single line presentation of discontinued operations in IFRS is replaced by a three-column approach with the detailed analysis of the results from the discontinued operation shown on the face of the statement of comprehensive income. This is illustrated in the following example which uses the Schedule 1 statutory formats:

Example 2.1:   Example of presentation of discontinued operations (statutory format)

Statement of comprehensive income
For the year ended 31 December 2019

	Continuing operations 2019 £000	Dis-continued operations 2019 £000	Total 2019 £000	Continuing operations 2018 £000	Dis-continued operations 2018 £000	Total 2018 £000
Turnover	4,200	1,232	5,432	3,201	1,500	4,701
Cost of Sales	(2,591)	(1,104)	(3,695)	(2,281)	(1,430)	(3,711)
Gross profit	1,609	128	1,737	920	70	990
Administrative expenses	(452)	(110)	(562)	(418)	(120)	(538)
Other operating income	212	–	212	198	–	198
Operating profit	1,369	18	1,387	700	(50)	650
Profit on disposal of operations		301	301		-	-
Interest receivable and similar income	14	–	14	16	–	16
Interest payable and similar expenses	(208)	–	(208)	(208)	–	(208)
Profit before tax	1,175	319	1,494	508	(50)	458
Tax on profit or loss	(390)	(4)	(394)	(261)	3	(258)
Profit after taxation and profit for the financial year	785	315	1,100	247	(47)	200

Other comprehensive income

Remeasurement changes on defined benefit pension plans	(108)	(68)
Deferred tax movement relating to remeasurement changes	28	18
Total Comprehensive income for the year	1,020	150

6   DISCLOSURE EXEMPTIONS FOR QUALIFYING ENTITIES

Qualifying entities may take advantage in their financial statements of a number of disclosure exemptions from EU-adopted IFRS (see 6.1 below).

Qualifying entities that are financial institutions, as defined by FRS 101, are not entitled to some disclosure exemptions (see 6.4 below).

Some, but not all, of these exemptions are conditional on 'equivalent' disclosures in the consolidated financial statements of the group in which the entity is consolidated (see 6.2 below).

In addition, disclosures required by the Regulations (or the LLP Regulations) for certain financial instruments that are held at fair value must be made even if the qualifying entity takes advantage of the disclosure exemptions from the disclosure requirements of IFRS 7 – *Financial Instruments: Disclosures* – and/or IFRS 13 – *Fair Value Measurement* (see 6.3 below). *[FRS 101 Appendix II.5A].*

6.1   Disclosure exemptions

Qualifying entities are permitted the following disclosure exemptions from EU-adopted IFRS from when the relevant standard is applied: *[FRS 101.7-8]*

- the requirement of paragraphs 6 and 21 of IFRS 1 to present an opening statement of financial position at the date of transition and related notes on first-time adoption of FRS 101 (see 3.4 above);

- the requirements of paragraphs 45(b) and 46 to 52 of IFRS 2 – *Share-based Payment* – provided that for a qualifying entity that is:

  - a subsidiary, the share-based payment arrangement concerns equity instruments of another group entity;

  - an ultimate parent, the share-based payment arrangement concerns its own equity instruments and its separate financial statements are presented alongside the consolidated financial statements of the group;

  and, in both cases, provided that equivalent disclosures are included in the consolidated financial statements of the group in which the entity is consolidated (see 6.1.1 below);

- the requirements of paragraphs 62, B64(d), (e), (g), (h), (j) to (m), n(ii), (o)(ii), (p), (q)(ii), B66 and B67 of IFRS 3 provided that equivalent disclosures are included in the consolidated financial statements of the group in which the entity is consolidated (see 6.1.2 below);

- the requirements of paragraph 33(c) of IFRS 5 provided that equivalent disclosures are included in the consolidated financial statements of the group in which the entity is consolidated (see 6.1.3 below);

- the requirements of IFRS 7 provided that equivalent disclosures are included in the financial statements of the group in which the entity is consolidated (see 6.1.4 below). However, entities which are subject to the CA 2006 and the Regulations (or the LLP Regulations) are legally required to provide disclosures related to financial instruments including those measured at fair value (see 6.3 and 7.2 below). Qualifying entities that are financial institutions do not receive this exemption and must apply the disclosure requirements of IFRS 7 in full (see 6.4 below);

- the requirements of paragraphs 91 to 99 of IFRS 13 provided that equivalent disclosures are included in the consolidated financial statements of the group in which the entity is consolidated (see 6.1.5 below). However, entities which are subject to the CA 2006 and the Regulations (or the LLP Regulations) are legally required to provide disclosures related to financial instruments including those measured at fair value (see 6.3 and 7.2 below). Qualifying entities that are financial institutions can only take advantage of the exemptions to the extent that they apply to assets and liabilities other than financial instruments (see 6.4 below);

- the requirements of the second sentence of paragraph 110 and paragraphs 113(a), 114, 115, 118, 119(a) to (c), 120 to 127 and 129 of IFRS 15 (see 6.1.6 below).

- the requirements of paragraph 52, the second sentence of paragraph 89, and paragraphs 90, 91 and 93 of IFRS 16 as well as the requirements of paragraph 58 of IFRS 16, provided that the disclosure of details of indebtedness required by paragraph 61(1) of Schedule 1 to the Regulations is presented separately for lease liabilities and other liabilities, and in total (see 6.1.7 below);

- the requirement in paragraph 38 of IAS 1 to present comparative information in respect of:
  - paragraph 79(a)(iv) of IAS 1;
  - paragraph 73(e) of IAS 16;
  - paragraph 118(e) of IAS 38 – *Intangible Assets*;
  - paragraphs 76 and 79(d) of IAS 40 – *Investment Property*; and
  - paragraph 50 of IAS 41 – *Agriculture* (see 6.1.8 below);

- the requirements of paragraphs 10(d), 10(f), 16, 38A to 38D, 40A to 40D, 111 and 134 to 136 of IAS 1 (see 6.1.9 below). However, qualifying entities that are financial institutions are not permitted to take advantage of the exemptions in paragraphs 134 to 136 of IAS 1 (see 6.4 below);

- the requirements of IAS 7 – *Statement of Cash Flows* (see 6.1.10 below);

- the requirements of paragraphs 30 and 31 of IAS 8 (see 6.1.11 below);

- the requirements of paragraphs 17 and 18A of IAS 24 – *Related Party Disclosures* – and the requirements in IAS 24 to disclose related party transactions entered into between two or more members of a group, provided that any subsidiary which is a party to the transaction is wholly owned by such a member (see 6.1.12 below); and

- the requirements of paragraphs 130(f)(ii), 130(f)(iii), 134(d) to 134(f) and 135(c) to 135(e) of IAS 36 – *Impairment of Assets* – provided that equivalent disclosures are included in the consolidated financial statements of the group in which the entity is consolidated (see 6.1.13 below).

When a paragraph within a given standard cross-refers to the requirements of an exempted paragraph listed above, the qualifying entity is nevertheless permitted to take the exemption in the exempted paragraph. *[FRS 101.8A].*

Use of the disclosure exemptions is conditional on the following disclosures in the notes to the financial statements: *[FRS 101.5(c)]*

(a)   a brief narrative summary of the exemptions adopted; and

(b)   the name of the parent of the group in whose consolidated financial statements the reporting entity is consolidated and from where those financial statements may be obtained (i.e. the parent identified in the term 'qualifying entity').

There is no requirement to list all of the disclosure exemptions in detail. Reporting entities can also choose to apply the disclosure exemptions on a selective basis. This may be necessary, for example, where not all of the relevant 'equivalent' disclosures are made in the consolidated financial statements of the parent on the grounds of materiality (see 6.2 below).

Each of the disclosure exemptions listed above is discussed below.

6.1.1   Share-based payment (IFRS 2)

The disclosure exemption eliminates all IFRS 2 disclosures apart from those required by paragraphs 44 and 45(a), (c) and (d) of IFRS 2. In summary, this reduces the specific minimum disclosure requirements of IFRS 2 to:

- a description of each type of share-based payment arrangements that existed during the reporting period, including general terms and conditions, the maximum terms of options granted, and the method of settlement (e.g. whether in cash or equity);

- the weighted average share price at the date of exercise for share options exercised during the reporting period (or the weighted average share price during the period, if options were exercised on a regular basis throughout the period); and

- the range of exercise prices and weighted average remaining contractual life for share options outstanding at the end of the reporting period.

In addition, an entity is still subject to the general disclosure objective of IFRS 2 to disclose information that enables users of the financial statements to understand the nature and extent of share-based payment arrangements that existed during the period which may require additional disclosures beyond those specially required above.

6.1.2   Business combinations (IFRS 3)

In summary, this disclosure exemption eliminates the qualitative disclosures required for a business combination. However, a number of factual or quantitative disclosures are still required for each business combination including:

- the name and description of the acquiree, acquisition date and percentage of voting equity interests acquired;
- the acquisition-date fair value of total consideration transferred split by major class;
- the amount recognised at the acquisition date for each major class of assets acquired and liabilities assumed;
- the amount of any negative goodwill recognised and the line item in the statement of comprehensive income in which it is recognised;
- the amount of any non-controlling interest recognised and the measurement basis for the amount (although there should be no non-controlling interests for acquisitions in individual financial statements);
- the amounts of revenue and profit or loss of the acquiree since acquisition date included in comprehensive income for the period; and
- the information above (except for the information in the first bullet) in aggregate for individually immaterial business combinations that are collectively material.

In addition, an acquirer is still subject to the general requirements of paragraphs 59 to 61 of IFRS 3 which may require additional disclosures beyond those specially required. These require disclosure of information that enables users of the financial statements to evaluate the nature and effect of a business combination that occurs, either during the current reporting period or at the end of the financial reporting period but before the financial statements are authorised for issue. These paragraphs also require disclosure of information that enables users of the financial statements to evaluate the financial effects of adjustments recognised in the current reporting period relating to business combinations that occurred in the current or previous periods.

6.1.3   Discontinued operations (IFRS 5)

This exemption eliminates the requirement to disclose cash flows attributable to discontinued operations. This cash flow disclosure exemption is contingent on equivalent disclosures in the consolidated financial statements of the parent, although equivalent disclosures in the parent are not necessary to make use of the exemption not to prepare a cash flow statement.

6.1.4   Financial instruments (IFRS 7)

This exemption removes all of the disclosure requirements of IFRS 7. However, notwithstanding this exemption, some IFRS 7 disclosures are still required for certain financial instruments measured at fair value (see 6.3 below). In addition, some specific financial instruments disclosures are required by the Regulations or the LLP Regulations (see 7.2 below).

Financial institutions are not permitted to use this exemption (see 6.4 below).

6.1.5   Fair values (IFRS 13)

This exemption removes all of the disclosure requirements of IFRS 13. However, notwithstanding this exemption, some IFRS 13 disclosures are still required for certain financial instruments measured at fair value (see 6.3 below). In addition, specific disclosures in respect of the fair value of stocks, financial instruments, investment property and living animals and plants carried at fair value are required by the Regulations (see 6.3 and 7.2 below).

Financial institutions are not permitted to use this IFRS 13 disclosure exemption in respect of financial instruments. However, they can use this exemption in respect of fair value disclosures of non-financial assets and liabilities (see 6.4 below).

6.1.6   Revenue from contracts with customers (IFRS 15)

IFRS 15 is effective for accounting periods beginning on or after 1 January 2018 but can be applied early.

The intention of these disclosure exemptions is to confine the revenue disclosures to those that the FRC consider would be of relevance to a provider of credit to a qualifying entity (identified as being the likely external users of a qualifying entity's financial statements). That is, information supporting the statement of financial position rather than the income statement. *[FRS 101.BC48]*. Hence, exemptions are given from the following disclosures:

- the disclosure objectives (paragraph 110);
- revenue recognised from contracts with customers (paragraph 113(a));
- disaggregation of revenue (paragraph 114);
- disclosure of the relationship between disaggregated revenue and revenue information disclosed for each reportable segment, if IFRS 8 – *Operating Segments* – is applied (paragraph 115);
- a qualitative and quantitative explanation of significant changes in contract assets and contract liabilities during the reporting period (paragraph 118);
- information about satisfying performance obligations, significant payment terms and the nature of goods and services transferred (paragraphs 119(a)-(c));
- information about allocating the transaction price to performance obligations (paragraphs 120 to 122);
- significant judgements made in applying IFRS 15 (paragraph 123);
- the methods used to recognise revenue satisfied over time; and, for performance obligations satisfied at a point in time, the significant judgements in evaluating when a customer obtains control (paragraphs 124 and 125);
- information about the methods, inputs and assumptions used for determining the transaction price, assessing whether the estimate of variable consideration is constrained, allocating the transaction price, and measuring obligations for returns, refunds and other similar obligations (paragraph 126);
- judgements made in determining costs to obtain and fulfil a contract with a customer, and the method used to determine amortisation of those costs (paragraph 127); and
- the use of any practical expedients concerning the existence of significant financing components or the incremental costs of obtaining a contract (paragraph 129).

Chapter 2

Qualifying entities are still required to make the following specific disclosures:

- impairment losses on receivables or contract assets arising from an entity's contracts with customers, to be disclosed separately from impairment losses on other contracts (paragraph 113(b));

- the opening and closing balances of receivables, contract assets and contract liabilities from contracts with customers (paragraph 116(a));

- revenue recognised in the reporting period included in the contract liability at the beginning of the period (paragraph 116(b));

- revenue recognised in the reporting period from performance obligations satisfied or partially satisfied in prior periods (paragraph 116(c));

- an explanation (which may use qualitative information) as to how the timing of satisfaction of performance obligations relates to the typical timing of payment and the effect that those factors have on the contract asset and liability balances (paragraph 117);

- a description of obligations for return, refunds and other similar obligations; and types of warranties and related obligations (paragraph 119(d)-(e)); and

- the closing balances of assets recognised from the costs incurred to obtain or fulfil a contract by main category of asset; and the amount of amortisation and impairment in the reporting period (paragraph 128).

Qualifying entities are also still required to make the following disclosure requirements:

- company law requirements relating to disaggregation of turnover (see 5.2.1 above); and

- the requirements of IAS 1 related to judgements having a significant effect on the amounts recognised in the entity's financial statements. *[FRS 101.BC49]*.

The Basis for Conclusions also clarifies that, for the avoidance of doubt, although paragraph 117 of IFRS 15 (from which a qualifying entity is not exempt) cross-refers to paragraph 119, it is not necessary to comply with paragraph 119 in order to meet the requirements of paragraph 117. *[FRS 101.8A, BC50]*.

6.1.7   Leases (IFRS 16)

IFRS 16 is effective for accounting periods beginning on or after 1 January 2019 but can be applied early as long as IFRS 15 is also applied. *[IFRS 16 Appendix C.1]*.

The intention of the disclosure exemptions for lessors is to provide similar disclosure exemptions to those given from disclosures in IFRS 15. *[FRS 101.BC61]*. The disclosure exemptions are as follows:

- the requirement for a lessee to provide all lease disclosures in a single note or separate section in its financial statements (paragraph 52);

- a lessee's maturity analysis of lease liabilities, separately from that of other financial liabilities (paragraph 58) provided that the disclosure of details of indebtedness required by paragraph 61(1) of Schedule 1 to the Regulations is presented separately for lease liabilities and other liabilities, and in total;

- the sentence that states that paragraphs 90 to 97 specify requirements on how to meet the disclosure objective for lessors (second sentence of paragraph 89). Some of these disclosures are not required;

- a lessor's lease income, finance income and selling profit/loss disclosures (paragraphs 90 to 91); and
- a qualitative and quantitative explanation of the significant changes in the carrying amount of the net investment in finance leases (paragraph 93).

The exemption from the requirement of a lessee to provide all lease disclosures in a single note (or separate section in the financial statements) is provided because the FRC consider that it would result in unnecessary additional work that would provide minimal additional benefits to the users of the financial statements. This is because paragraph 42(2) of Schedule 1 to the Regulations (and its equivalents in Schedule 2 and Schedule 3 to the Regulations and the LLP Regulations) require entities to present the notes to the accounts in the order in which, where relevant, the items to which they relate are presented in the balance sheet and in the profit and loss account. *[FRS 101.BC52-54].*

The exemption from the requirement for lessees to disclose a maturity analysis of lease liabilities is provided because FRS 101 provides an exemption for non-financial institutions from the maturity analysis requirements of IFRS 7 for financial liabilities (provided that equivalent disclosures are included in the consolidated financial statements of the group in which the qualifying entity is included). However, this exemption is conditional on an entity providing the company law disclosures about details of indebtedness separately for lease liabilities and other liabilities, and in total. This is because it was considered that users would find separate disclosures of lease liabilities useful. *[FRS 101.BC55-59].*

An exemption from paragraphs 94 and 97 of IFRS 16 (which require lessors to provide a maturity analysis of finance and operating lease receivables) was not introduced as no equivalent requirements exist under company law and the FRC consider that these maturity analyses provide useful information to users about the lessor's liquidity and solvency. *[FRS 101.BC60].* Apart from the exemptions above, lessees and lessors are subject to the detailed disclosure requirements of IFRS 16.

6.1.8   Comparatives (IAS 1, IAS 16, IAS 38, IAS 40, IAS 41)

This exemption eliminates the requirement for comparatives to be presented for reconciliations of:

- outstanding shares at the beginning and end of the current period (IAS 1);
- the carrying amount of property, plant and equipment at the beginning and end of the current period (IAS 16);
- the carrying amount of intangible assets at the beginning and end of the current period (IAS 38);
- the carrying amount of investment property held at either fair value or cost at the beginning and end of the current period (IAS 40); and
- the carrying amount of biological assets at the beginning and end of the current period (IAS 41).

Chapter 2

6.1.9   *Presentation (IAS 1)*

This exemption removes:

- the requirement to present a cash flow statement (paragraphs 10(d) and 111 – see 6.1.10 below);

- the requirement to present a statement of financial position and related notes at the beginning of the earliest comparative period (or third balance sheet) whenever an entity applies an accounting policy retrospectively, makes a retrospective restatement, or when it reclassifies items in its financial statements (paragraph 10(f) and paragraphs 40A-40D);

- the requirement to make an explicit statement of compliance with IFRS. Indeed, FRS 101 prohibits such a statement of compliance and an FRS 101 statement of compliance is required instead (paragraph 16 – see 1.3 above);

- the requirements to present two primary statements as a minimum, information about narrative information in previous reporting periods relevant to understanding the current period's financial statements, and the suggestion that entities may present additional comparative information (paragraphs 38A-38D); and

- the requirement to disclose information about capital and how it is managed (paragraphs 134-136).

Financial institutions are not permitted to use the exemption in respect of the disclosure of information about capital and how it is managed. This is because financial institutions are usually subject to externally imposed capital requirements.

6.1.10   *Cash flows (IAS 7)*

The exemption removes the requirement for a cash flow statement for any qualifying entity.

6.1.11   *Standards issued but not effective (IAS 8)*

This exemption removes the requirement to provide information about the impact of IFRSs that have been issued but are not yet effective.

6.1.12   *Related party transactions (IAS 24)*

The exemptions in respect of IAS 24 remove:

- the requirement to disclose information about key management personnel compensation (paragraphs 17);

- the requirement to disclose amounts incurred for the provision of key management personnel services that are provided by a separate management entity (paragraph 18A); and

- the requirements to disclose related party *transactions* between two or more members of a group, provided that any subsidiary which is a party to the transaction is wholly owned by such a member.

The last disclosure exemption above refers to transactions only and not to outstanding balances. As explained in the Basis for Conclusions to FRS 102, this is because there is a separate legal requirement in relation to the format of the balance sheet which requires disclosure of outstanding balances in aggregate for group undertakings and, separately, for undertakings in which the company has a participating interest. As a result, it is not possible to provide an effective exemption from the disclosure of outstanding balances with group undertakings. *[FRS 102.BC.B33.2]*.

Although the requirement to disclose information about key management personnel compensation is eliminated, UK companies are required separately by Schedule 5 to the Regulations to disclose information in respect of directors' remuneration. Additionally, quoted companies must prepare a directors' remuneration report. There is no exemption from other IAS 24 disclosure requirements, so disclosure of other transactions with key management personnel (e.g. director loans) is still required.

The wording of the exemption from disclosure of transactions with other wholly owned subsidiaries has been taken directly from the Regulations. *[FRS 101.BC68]*. It is stated in the Basis for Conclusions that, in December 2017, amendments were made to Appendix II: *Note on legal requirements* to FRS 102 to clarify the FRC's view that: *[FRS 101.BC69]*

- the exemption may be applied to transactions between entities within a sub-group when the transacting subsidiary is wholly-owned by the intermediate parent of that sub-group, even if that intermediate parent is not wholly-owned by the ultimate controlling entity; and

- the exemption may not be applied to transactions between entities in an intermediate parent's sub-group (including the intermediate parent itself) and the entities in the larger group if the intermediate parent is not wholly-owned by the parent of that larger group.

This is illustrated by Example 2.2 below.

Example 2.2: *Application of the exemption from disclosure of transactions between wholly-owned subsidiary undertakings*

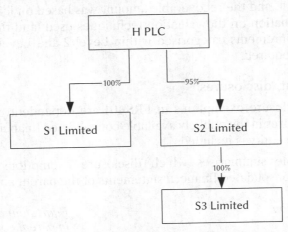

Because H PLC only owns 95% of S2 Limited, the wholly owned subsidiaries exemption cannot be used in (a) the separate financial statements of H PLC in respect of transactions with S2 Limited and S3 Limited, (b) the individual financial statements of S1 Limited in respect of transactions with S2 Limited and S3 Limited (c) the separate financial statements of S2 Limited in respect of any transactions with H PLC and S1 Limited or (d) the individual financial statements of S3 Limited in respect of any transactions with H PLC and S1 Limited.

The exemption can be used for any transactions in individual financial statements between H PLC and S1 Limited and between S2 Limited and S3 Limited.

However, if the remaining 5% of S2 Limited (not directly held by H PLC) was held by another wholly owned subsidiary undertaking of H PLC, then S2 Limited would be a wholly owned subsidiary undertaking of H PLC. In those circumstances, the exemption from disclosing transactions with the other entities in the group should be available in the individual financial statements of H PLC, S1 Limited, S2 Limited and S3 Limited (as S1 Limited, S2 Limited and S3 Limited would all be wholly owned subsidiary undertakings of the H PLC group).

The exemption has no other conditions: it can be applied, for example, to an entity with an overseas parent.

6.1.13   *Impairment of assets (IAS 36)*

This exemption eliminates all requirements to disclose information about estimates used to measure recoverable amounts of each cash-generating unit (or group of units) containing goodwill or intangible assets with indefinite useful lives, including details of fair value measurements where the recoverable amount is fair value less costs of disposal other than:

- the carrying amounts of goodwill and carrying amounts of indefinite life intangibles allocated to each such cash generating unit (or group of units) (paragraphs 134(a), 134(b), 135(a), 135(b)); and

- the basis on which the recoverable amount of those units has been determined (i.e. value in use or fair value less costs of disposal) (paragraph 134(c)).

Qualifying entities must still give the other disclosures required by paragraphs 126 to 135 of IAS 36 in respect of impairment losses (and reversal of impairment losses) recognised or reversed in the period. These include, *inter alia*, the recoverable amount of the asset (or cash generating unit) and whether the recoverable amount is its fair value less costs of disposal or its value in use. However, where an impairment loss has been recognised or reversed during the period in respect of an individual asset (including goodwill) or a cash-generating unit, and the recoverable amount was based on fair value less costs of disposal, the information on the valuation techniques used (and the key assumptions) for fair value measurements categorised within Level 2 and Level 3 of the fair value hierarchy are not required.

6.2   'Equivalent' disclosures

Certain of the disclosure exemptions in FRS 101 are dependent on the provision of 'equivalent' disclosures in the publicly available consolidated financial statements of the parent in which the entity is included.

The following table summarises which disclosure exemptions need 'equivalent' disclosures in the consolidated financial statements of the parent and which do not.

Disclosure exemption	*Equivalent disclosures required in parent consolidated financial statements*
First-time adoption exemption (see 6.1 above)	No
Share-based payment (see 6.1.1 above)	Yes
Business combinations (see 6.1.2 above)	Yes
Discontinued operations (see 6.1.3 above)	Yes
Financial instruments (see 6.1.4 above)	Yes
Fair values (see 6.1.5 above)	Yes

Revenue from Contracts with Customers (see 6.1.6 above)	No
Leases (see 6.1.7 above)	No
Comparatives (see 6.1.8 above)	No
Presentation (see 6.1.9 above)	No
Cash flows (see 6.1.10 above)	No
Standards issued but not effective (see 6.1.11 above)	No
Related party transactions (see 6.1.12 above)	No
Impairment of assets (see 6.1.13 above)	Yes

FRS 101 refers to the Application Guidance in FRS 100 in deciding whether the consolidated financial statements of the group in which the reporting entity is included provides disclosures that are 'equivalent' to the requirements of EU-adopted IFRS from which relief is provided. *[FRS 101.9]*.

The Application Guidance in FRS 100 states that:

- it is necessary to consider whether the publicly available consolidated financial statements of the parent provide disclosures that meet the basic disclosure requirements of the relevant standard or interpretation issued (or adopted) by the relevant standard setter without regarding strict conformity with each and every disclosure. This assessment should be based on the particular facts, including the similarities to and differences from the requirements of the relevant standard from which relief is provided. The concept of 'equivalence' is intended to be aligned to that described in section 401 of the CA 2006; *[FRS 100.AG8-9]* and

- disclosure exemptions for subsidiaries are permitted where the relevant disclosure requirements are met in the consolidated financial statements, even where the disclosures are made in aggregate or abbreviated form, or in relation to intra-group balances, those intra-group balances have been eliminated on consolidation. If, however, no disclosure is made in the consolidated financial statements on the grounds of materiality, the relevant disclosures should be made at the subsidiary level if material in those financial statements. *[FRS 100.AG10]*.

This means that a qualifying entity must review the consolidated financial statements of its parent to ensure that 'equivalent' disclosures have been made for each of the above exemptions that it intends to use. Where a particular 'equivalent' disclosure has not been made (unless the disclosure relates to an intra-group balance eliminated on consolidation) then the qualifying subsidiary cannot use the exemption in respect of that disclosure.

6.3   Disclosures required by the Regulations in the financial statements for certain financial instruments (and other assets) which may be held at fair value

Paragraph 36(4) of Schedule 1 to the Regulations (and its equivalents in Schedule 2 and Schedule 3 to the Regulations and the LLP Regulations) state that financial instruments which under international accounting standards may be included in accounts at fair value, may be so included, provided that the disclosures required by such accounting standards are made. *[FRS 101 Appendix II.6]*. The reference to 'international accounting standards' in this context means EU-adopted IFRS.

The legal appendix to FRS 101 confirms that a qualifying entity that has financial instruments measured at fair value in accordance with the requirements of paragraph 36(4) of Schedule 1 to the Regulations (or its equivalents) is legally required to provide the relevant disclosures set out in extant EU-adopted IFRS. *[FRS 101 Appendix II.7]*. The most logical interpretation of this is that an entity should make all material disclosures required by IFRS 7 and IFRS 13 in respect of such instruments.

The financial instruments referred to by paragraph 36(4) of Schedule 1 of the Regulations (and its equivalents) are those listed in paragraphs 36(2)(c) and 36(3) of Schedule 1 to the Regulations (and its equivalents). These are: *[1 Sch 36]*

- any financial liability which is not held for trading or a derivative, i.e. a financial liability measured or designated at fair value through profit or loss (FVPL) under paragraphs 4.2.2, 4.3.5 or 4.3.6 of IFRS 9;

- loans and receivables originated by the reporting entity, not held for trading purposes, and measured or designated at either fair value through other comprehensive income (FVOCI) or FVPL under paragraphs 4.1.2A, 4.1.4 or 4.1.5 of IFRS 9;

- interests in subsidiary undertakings, associated undertakings and joint ventures accounted at FVOCI or FVPL under IFRS 9 via paragraphs 10, 11 or 11A of IAS 27 or paragraph 18 of IAS 28 – *Investments in Associates and Joint Ventures*;

- contracts for contingent consideration in a business combination measured at FVPL; or

- other financial instruments with such special characteristics that the instruments according to generally accepted accounting principles or practice, should be accounted for differently from other financial instruments.

In addition, qualifying entities that are preparing Companies Act accounts must provide the disclosures required by paragraph 55 of Schedule 1 to the Regulations (and its equivalents in Schedules 2 and 3 to the Regulations and the LLP Regulations) which set out requirements relating to financial instruments at fair value. *[FRS 100 Appendix II.7D]*. These disclosures relate to financial instruments and other assets held at fair value generally and not just to those financial instruments measured at fair value in accordance with paragraph 36(4) as discussed above. Disclosures are required of: *[1 Sch 55]*

- the significant assumptions underlying the valuation models and techniques used when determining the fair value of the instruments or other assets;

- for each category of financial instrument or other asset, the fair value of the assets and the changes in value included directly in the profit and loss account or credited to or debited from the fair value reserve in respect of those assets;

- for each class of derivatives, the extent and nature of the instruments, including significant terms and conditions that may affect the amount, timing and certainty of future cash flows; and

- where any amount is transferred to or from the fair value reserve during the financial year, disclosure (in tabular form) of the opening and closing balance of the reserve, the amount transferred to or from the reserve during the year and the source and application respectively of the amounts so transferred.

6.4   Disclosure exemptions for financial institutions

Financial institutions are permitted to apply FRS 101 but receive fewer disclosure exemptions. A qualifying entity which is a financial institution may take advantage in its individual financial statements of the disclosure exemptions set out at 6.1 above except for: *[FRS 101.7]*

- the disclosure exemptions from IFRS 7;
- the disclosure exemptions from paragraphs 91 to 99 of IFRS 13 to the extent that they apply to financial instruments. Therefore, a financial institution can take advantage of the disclosure exemptions from paragraphs 91 to 99 of IFRS 13 for assets and liabilities other than financial instruments (e.g. property plant and equipment, intangible assets, and investment property); and
- the capital disclosures of paragraphs 134 to 136 of IAS 1.

Entities which are subject to the CA 2006 and the Regulations or the LLP Regulations are legally required to provide disclosures related to financial instruments and assets and liabilities including those measured at fair value (see 6.3 above and 7.2 below).

The FRC has opted not to provide a generic definition of a financial institution. Instead, it has provided a list of entities that are stated to be financial institutions. A 'financial institution' is stated to be any of the following: *[FRS 101 Appendix I]*

(a) a bank which is:

    (i) a firm with a Part 4A permission (as defined in section 55A of the Financial Services and Markets Act 2000 or references to equivalent provisions of any successor legislation) which includes accepting deposits and:

        (a) which is a credit institution; or

        (b) whose Part 4A permission includes a requirement that it complies with the rules in the General Prudential sourcebook and the Prudential sourcebook for Banks, Building Societies and Investment Firms relating to banks, but which is not a building society, a friendly society or a credit union;

    (ii) an EEA bank which is a full credit institution;

(b) a building society which is defined in section 119(1) of the Building Societies Act 1986 as a building society incorporated (or deemed to be incorporated) under that Act;

(c) a credit union, being a body corporate registered under the Co-operative and Community Benefit Societies Act 2014 as a credit union in accordance with the Credit Unions Act 1979, which is an authorised person;

(d) custodian bank or broker-dealer;

(e) an entity that undertakes the business of effecting or carrying out insurance contracts, including general and life assurance entities;

(f) an incorporated friendly society incorporated under the Friendly Societies Act 1992 or a registered friendly society registered under section 7(1)(a) of the Friendly Societies Act 1974 or any enactment which it replaced, including any registered branches;

(g) an investment trust, Irish investment company, venture capital trust, mutual fund, exchange traded fund, unit trust, open-ended investment company (OEIC); or

(h) [deleted]

(i) any other entity whose principal activity is similar to those listed above but is not specifically included in that list.

    A parent entity whose sole activity is to hold investments in other group entities is not a financial institution.

Chapter 2

The Triennial review 2017 removed stockbrokers (from item (d) above) and a retirement benefit plan (previously (h) above) from the list of entities considered to be a financial institution. In addition, (i) above was amended to remove the words highlighted in italics, 'any other entity whose principal activity is *to generate wealth or manage risk through financial instruments. This is intended to cover entities that have business activities* similar to those listed above but are not specifically included in the list above'. The purpose of this latter change was to help reduce interpretational difficulties and to reduce the number of entities meeting the definition of a financial institution. Accordingly, an entity which generated wealth or managed risk through financial instruments but which is not similar to those listed at (a) to (g) above is no longer to be a financial institution. *[FRS 101.BC19]*. These changes may be an incentive for some entities to early adopt the Triennial review 2017.

However, in some cases, judgement, based on the facts and circumstances, may be needed in assessing whether an entity's *principal activities* are similar to those listed at (a) to (g) above. For example, the Basis for Conclusions observes that judgement will need to be applied in determining whether a group treasury company is similar to the other entities listed in the definition of a financial institution. *[FRS 101.BC21]*.

7   ADDITIONAL COMPANIES ACT DISCLOSURES

FRS 101 individual financial statements (which are Companies Act accounts) are subject to disclosures required by the Regulations as well as other disclosures required by the Companies Act or other related regulations. These disclosures are in addition to those required by EU-adopted IFRS.

There are two types of Companies Act disclosures that are required for a UK entity applying FRS 101:

(a)   those required for both IAS accounts (prepared under EU-adopted IFRS) and Companies Act accounts (prepared under a form of UK GAAP) (see 7.1 below); and

(b)   those required by the Regulations for Companies Act accounts but not for IAS accounts (see 7.2 below).

This means that, in certain scenarios, a move from EU-adopted IFRS to FRS 101 would result in increased disclosures for an entity despite the use of the disclosure exemptions described at 6 above.

There may also be additional disclosures for an entity other than a company where that entity is subject to separate regulations.

7.1   Existing Companies Act disclosures in the financial statements for EU-adopted IFRS and UK GAAP reporters that also apply under FRS 101

FRS 100 identifies the following required disclosures: *[FRS 100 Appendix II.19]*

- section 410A – Off-balance sheet arrangements;
- section 411 – Employee numbers and costs;
- section 412 – Directors' benefits: remuneration;
- section 413 – Directors' benefits: advances, credit and guarantees;

- sections 414A to 414D – Strategic report;
- sections 415 to 419 – Directors' report;
- sections 420 to 421 – Directors' remuneration report; and
- section 494 – Services provided by auditor and associates and related remuneration.

The disclosures identified by FRS 100 above is incomplete and omits, for example, the information about related undertakings required by section 409. There are also certain disclosure exemptions for small companies and medium-sized companies (see Chapter 5 at 12 and Chapter 1 at 6.6.2).

LLPs are not subject to equivalent statutory requirements to those in sections 412 to 421 above although banking and insurance LLPs are required to prepare a strategic report for financial years beginning on or after 1 January 2017.

In addition, other Companies Act or related disclosures may apply depending on individual circumstances such as the disclosures required for a parent taking advantage of the exemption from preparing group accounts under either section 400 or section 401 of the CA 2006.

7.2   Disclosures required by the Regulations and the LLP Regulations in FRS 101 financial statements but not required under EU-adopted IFRS

The Regulations and the LLP Regulations require various disclosures in financial statements. In particular, Part 3 of Schedules 1 to 3 to the Regulations (and Part 3 of Schedule 1 to the LLP Regulations) require certain disclosures to be made in the notes to the financial statements if not given in the primary statements. The relevant paragraphs are as follows:

- Schedule 1 paragraphs 42 to 75;
- Schedule 2 paragraphs 52 to 92B;
- Schedule 3 paragraphs 60 to 90B; or
- the LLP Regulations paragraphs 42 to 70B.

Although some of these disclosure requirements are replicated in EU-adopted IFRS, others are not. Entities that move to FRS 101 from FRS 102 will have made these disclosures previously and therefore these requirements will not increase their reporting burden. Entities that move to FRS 101 from EU-adopted IFRS will not have made these disclosures previously or any other disclosures required by the applicable schedule above and should consider carefully the impact of these new requirements against the benefits of the reduced disclosures discussed at 6 above.

In addition, entities subject to the Regulations and LLP Regulations are required to present the notes to the financial statements in the order in which, where relevant, the items to which they relate are presented in the balance sheet and profit and loss accounts (see 5.2 above). The General Rules to the formats in the Regulations and LLP Regulations require that where an asset or liability relates to more than one item in the balance sheet, the relationship of such asset or liability to the relevant items must be disclosed either under those items or in the notes to the accounts (see 5.1 above). *[1 Sch 9A].*

Some examples of disclosures not required under EU-adopted IFRS in individual or separate financial statements are shown below. The disclosures illustrated below are not intended to be an exhaustive list of additional disclosures required by the Regulations and LLP Regulations for entities applying FRS 101 that have previously reported under EU-adopted IFRS.

(a)   Schedule 1 companies (i.e. companies other than banking and insurance companies):

- disclosures required for certain financial instruments which may be held at fair value (see 6.3 above); *[1 Sch 36]*

- a statement required by large companies that the accounts have been prepared in accordance with applicable accounting policies; *[1 Sch 45]*

- disclosures in respect of share capital and debentures including information about shares and debentures allotted and contingent rights to shares; *[1 Sch 47-50]*

- disclosure of the split of land between freehold and leasehold and the leasehold land between that held on a long lease and that held on a short lease; *[1 Sch 53]*

- disclosure of information about listed investments; *[1 Sch 54]*

- disclosure of information about the fair value of financial assets and liabilities, investment property, living animals and plant which, in substance, 'reinstates' some parts of IFRS 7 and IFRS 13. In particular, there are requirements to disclose significant assumptions underlying the valuation models and techniques used when determining fair value of the instruments, details of the fair value of financial instruments by category and details concerning significant terms and conditions of derivatives (see 6.3 above); *[1 Sch 55]*

- disclosure of information about creditors due after five years; *[1 Sch 61]*

- disclosure of information about guarantees and other financial commitments including charges on assets to secure liabilities, the particulars and total amount of any guarantees, contingencies and commitments not recorded in the balance sheet, the nature and form of valuable security given and separate disclosure of pension commitments and guarantees and commitments given to certain related entities; *[1 Sch 63]*

- disclosure of information about loans made in connection with the purchase of own shares; *[1 Sch 64]*

- disclosure of particulars of taxation; *[1 Sch 67]* and

- disclosure of information about turnover by class of business and geographical markets. IFRS 8 does not require segmental information if an entity's debt or equity instruments are not traded in a public market or the entity is not in the process of filing financial statements for that purpose. However, the disclosures in the Regulations are required even if the entity is out of scope of IFRS 8. See also 5.2.1 above. *[1 Sch 68]*.

The profit and loss account of a company that falls within section 408 of the CA 2006 (individual profit and loss account where group accounts prepared) need not contain the information specified in paragraphs 65 to 69 of Schedule 1. *[Regulations 3(2)].*

(b)   Schedule 2 companies (i.e. banking companies)

- a statement that the accounts have been prepared in accordance with applicable accounting policies; *[2 Sch 54]*

- disclosures in respect of share capital and debentures including information about shares and debentures allotted and contingent rights to shares; *[2 Sch 58-61]*

- disclosure of the split of land between freehold and leasehold and the leasehold land between that held on a long lease and that held on a short lease; *[2 Sch 64]*

- disclosure of a specific maturity analysis for loans and advances and liabilities; *[2 Sch 72]*

- disclosure of arrears of fixed cumulative dividends; *[2 Sch 75]*

- disclosure of information about guarantees and other financial commitments including charges on assets to secure liabilities, the particulars and total amount of any guarantees, contingencies and commitments not recorded in the balance sheet, the nature and form of valuable security given and separate disclosure of pension commitments and guarantees and commitments given to certain related entities; *[2 Sch 77]*

- disclosure of details of transferable securities; *[2 Sch 79]*

- disclosure of leasing transactions; *[2 Sch 80]*

- disclosure of assets and liabilities denominated in a currency other than the presentational currency; *[2 Sch 81]*

- disclosure of details of unmatured forward transactions; *[2 Sch 83]*

- disclosure of loans made in connection with the purchase of own shares; *[2 Sch 84]*

- disclosure of particulars of taxation; *[2 Sch 86]* and

- disclosure of certain profit and loss account information by geographical markets. IFRS 8 does not require segmental information if an entity's debt or equity instruments are not traded in a public market or the entity is not in the process of filing financial statements for that purpose. However, the disclosures in the Regulations are required even if the entity is out of scope of IFRS 8. *[2 Sch 87].*

The profit and loss account of a banking company that falls within section 408 of the CA 2006 (individual profit and loss account where group accounts prepared) need not contain the information specified in paragraphs 85 to 91 of Schedule 2. *[Regulations 5(2)].*

(c) Schedule 3 companies (i.e. insurance companies)

- a statement that the accounts have been prepared in accordance with applicable accounting policies; *[3 Sch 62]*
- disclosures in respect of share capital and debentures including information about shares and debentures allotted and contingent rights to shares; *[3 Sch 65-68]*
- disclosure of the split of land between freehold and leasehold and the leasehold land between that held on a long lease and that held on a short lease; *[3 Sch 71]*
- disclosure of information about listed investments; *[3 Sch 72]*
- disclosure of creditors due after five years; *[3 Sch 79]*
- disclosure of information about guarantees and other financial commitments including charges on assets to secure liabilities, the particulars and total amount of any guarantees, contingencies and commitments not recorded in the balance sheet, the nature and form of valuable security given and separate disclosure of pension commitments and guarantees and commitments given to certain related entities; *[3 Sch 81]*
- disclosure of loans made in connection with the purchase of own shares; *[3 Sch 82]*
- disclosure of particulars of taxation; *[3 Sch 84]*
- disclosure of certain profit and loss account information by type of business and by geographical area. IFRS 8 does not require segmental information if an entity's debt or equity instruments are not traded in a public market or the entity is not in the process of filing financial statements for that purpose. However, the disclosures in the Regulations are required even if the entity is out of scope of IFRS 8; *[3 Sch 85-87]* and
- disclosure of total commissions for direct insurance business. *[3 Sch 88]*.

The profit and loss account of an insurance company that falls within section 408 of the CA 2006 (individual profit and loss account where group accounts prepared) need not contain the information specified in paragraphs 83 to 89 of Schedule 3. *[Regulations 6(2)]*.

Banking and insurance companies are financial institutions (see 6.4 above) and therefore must comply with IFRS 7 disclosures in full and IFRS 13 disclosures in respect of financial instruments, including disclosures about the fair value of financial assets and liabilities.

(d) LLPs (i.e. entities subject to the LLP Regulations)

- a statement required by large companies that the accounts have been prepared in accordance with applicable accounting policies; *[1 Sch 45 (LLP)]*
- disclosures in respect of loans and debts due to members; *[1 Sch 47 (LLP)]*
- disclosures in respect of debentures; *[1 Sch 48 (LLP)]*
- disclosure of the split of land between freehold and leasehold and the leasehold land between that held on a long lease and that held on a short lease; *[1 Sch 51 (LLP)]*
- disclosure of information about listed investments; *[1 Sch 52 (LLP)]*

- disclosure of information about the fair value of financial assets and liabilities, stocks, investment property and living animals and plant where those assets and liabilities have been valued at fair value which, in substance, 'reinstates' some parts of IFRS 7 and IFRS 13. In particular, there are requirements to disclose information about significant assumptions where the fair value of a financial instrument results from generally accepted valuation models and techniques, details of the fair value of financial instruments by category and details concerning significant terms and conditions of derivatives (see 6.3 above); *[1 Sch 53 (LLP)]*

- disclosure of information about creditors due after five years; *[1 Sch 59 (LLP)]*

- disclosure of information about guarantees and other financial commitments including charges on assets to secure liabilities, the particulars and total amount of any guarantees, contingencies and commitments not recorded in the balance sheet, the nature and form of valuable security given and separate disclosure of pension commitments and guarantees and commitments given to certain related entities; *[1 Sch 60 (LLP)]*

- disclosure of particulars of taxation; *[1 Sch 64 (LLP)]*

- disclosure of information about turnover by class of business and geographical markets. IFRS 8 does not require segmental information if an entity's debt or equity instruments are not traded in a public market or the entity is not in the process of filing financial statements for that purpose; *[1 Sch 65 (LLP)]* and

- disclosure of particulars of members. *[1 Sch 66 (LLP)]*.

8. FUTURE CHANGES TO IFRS AND THEIR IMPACT ON FRS 101

Although not specifically addressed by FRS 101, future changes to EU-adopted IFRS would appear to be automatically incorporated into FRS 101 unless they are modified by the FRC.

The FRC reviews FRS 101 annually to ensure that the reduced disclosure framework continues to be effective in providing disclosure reductions for qualifying entities when compared with EU-adopted IFRS. *[FRS 101.BC10]*.

The principles established for FRS 101 is that the FRC aims to provide succinct financial reporting standards that: *[FRS 101.BC4]*

- have consistency with global accounting standards through the application of an IFRS-based solution unless an alternative clearly better meets the overriding objective;

- balance improvement, through reflecting up-to-date thinking and developments in the way businesses operate and the transactions they undertake, with stability;

- balance consistent principles for accounting by all UK and Republic of Ireland entities with proportionate and practical solutions, based on size, complexity, public interest and users' information needs;

- promote efficiency within groups; and

- are cost-effective to apply.

Whenever a new IFRS is issued or an amendment is made to an existing EU-adopted IFRS, the FRC has to consider the following on qualifying entities: *[FRS 101.BC7]*

- Relevance – does the disclosure requirement provide information that is capable of making a difference to the decisions made by users of the financial statements of a qualifying entity?

- Cost constraint on useful financial reporting – does the disclosure requirement impose costs on the preparers of the financial statements of a qualifying entity that are not justified by the benefits to the users of those financial statements?

- Avoid gold plating – Does the disclosure requirement override an existing exemption provide by company law in the UK?

8.1   IFRS 17 – *Insurance Contracts*

In May 2017, the IASB issued IFRS 17. As a result of the 2017/18 review cycle, it was concluded that a more detailed consideration of this standard is required but that this would be deferred until a clearer picture of the progress of the endorsement of the standard is known. Company law contains specific requirements for insurance companies, in terms of both the presentation and determination of provisions. IFRS 17 will need to be considered in more detail to determine whether there are any inconsistencies with company law, and if so what options might be available for addressing them. *[FRS 101.BC61A]*.

References

1 *True and Fair*, FRC, June 2014.

2 *The Financial Reporting Council: The True and Fair Requirement Revised – Opinion*, Martin Moore QC, May 2008, para. 4(F).

Chapter 3   Scope of FRS 102

Chapter 3   Scope of FRS 102

1   INTRODUCTION

Section 1 – *Scope* – of FRS 102 – *The Financial Reporting Standard applicable in the UK and Republic of Ireland* – sets out which entities can apply FRS 102. Its requirements are consistent with the general financial reporting framework set out in FRS 100 – *Application of Financial Reporting Requirements*, discussed further at 2.1 below. FRS 102 applies to financial statements intended to give a true and fair view. As its application is not restricted to UK and Irish companies, all entities should ensure that preparation of their financial statements in accordance with FRS 102 is permitted by the legal framework in which they operate. The legal framework for UK companies is discussed in more detail in Chapter 1 at 6.

This chapter covers the following topics:

- summary (see 1.1 below);
- development of FRS 102 and its ongoing review (see 1.2 below);
- effective date of FRS 102 (and FRS 103) (see 1.3 below);
- structure of FRS 102 (see 1.4 below);
- scope of FRS 102 (see 2 below);
- reduced disclosure framework (available to qualifying entities in their individual financial statements) (see 3 below); and
- Companies Act 2006 ('CA 2006') requirements including the exemptions available for small and medium-sized companies and LLPs (see 4 below).

Except where otherwise stated, the rest of this chapter will refer to the requirements for UK companies and LLPs, and refers to UK GAAP (prior to implementation of FRS 100 to FRS 103) as 'previous UK GAAP'.

FRS 103 – *Insurance Contracts – Consolidated accounting and reporting requirements for entities in the UK and Republic of Ireland issuing insurance contracts* (see 1.2.4 below and Chapter 33) applies to financial statements prepared in accordance with FRS 102 by entities that issue insurance contracts (including reinsurance contracts), hold reinsurance contracts or issue financial instruments (other than insurance contracts) with discretionary participation features. *[FRS 103.1.1-1.3, FRS 102.1.6].*

FRS 104 – *Interim Financial Reporting* – is a voluntary standard that FRS 102 reporters can apply in preparing interim financial statements. This is discussed at 1.2.5 below and Chapter 34.

1.1 Summary

This summary covers a number of areas relevant to the scope of FRS 102 and to its structure which are addressed more fully in the chapter, as indicated.

- Adoption of FRS 102 is voluntary – the standard applies to the financial statements of entities preparing financial statements in accordance with legislation, regulation or accounting standards applicable in the UK and the Republic of Ireland that are *not* prepared in accordance with EU-adopted IFRS, FRS 101 – *Reduced Disclosure Framework* – or FRS 105 – *The Financial Reporting Standard applicable to the Micro-entities Regime*. See 2.1 below.

- FRS 102 does not set out which entities must prepare financial statements; this is governed by the legal framework (or other regulation or requirements), if any, relating to the preparation of the entity's financial statements. For example, statutory accounts prepared in accordance with FRS 102 by a UK company are Companies Act accounts. While FRS 102 has been developed with the requirements for Companies Act accounts primarily in mind, the standard is available for adoption by entities other than UK companies, including non-UK entities. An entity applying FRS 102 must ensure that it complies with any applicable legal requirements. See 2.1 below.

- FRS 102 was originally issued in March 2013, and subsequently amended several times. All amendments are listed at 1.2 below and the effective date of the March 2018 version of the standard is addressed at 1.3 below.

- FRS 102 applies to general purpose financial statements of entities, including public benefit entities (see 2.5.2 below) that are intended to give a true and fair view. FRS 102 can be applied in consolidated and/or individual financial statements.

- FRS 102 is a single financial reporting standard based on the IFRS for SMEs, which itself generally includes simplified requirements and disclosures compared to full IFRSs. A number of modifications have been made to FRS 102 compared to the IFRS for SMEs (see 1.2 below). While largely based on IFRSs, FRS 102 is not just a simplified version of IFRSs. In certain cases, the standard includes direct references to IFRSs.

- Since FRS 102 includes less guidance than IFRSs, judgement is likely to be required in applying the standard. Section 10 – *Accounting Policies, Estimates and Errors* – sets out a 'GAAP hierarchy' that management should refer to in developing and applying relevant and reliable accounting policies where the standard does not specifically address the issue. This hierarchy includes references to applicable SORPs. Certain SORPs have been updated to comply with FRS 102, whereas others have been withdrawn on implementation of FRS 102. See 2.3 below. In addition, management may but is not required to refer to IFRSs addressing similar and related issues.

- FRS 102 requires certain types of entities to directly apply particular IFRSs, namely IAS 33 – *Earnings per Share*, IFRS 6 – *Exploration for and Evaluation of Mineral Resources* – and IFRS 8 – *Operating Segments*. These standards apply to FRS 102 reporters that would fall within the scope of these standards if applying IFRS. See 2.4 below.

- In addition, an entity applying FRS 102 has a choice of applying the recognition and measurement requirements for financial instruments in:

  - Section 11 – *Basic Financial Instruments* – and Section 12 – *Other Financial Instruments Issues* – of FRS 102;

  - IAS 39 – *Financial Instruments: Recognition and Measurement* (the version extant immediately prior to IFRS 9 – *Financial Instruments* – superseding IAS 39); or

  - IFRS 9 and IAS 39 (as amended by IFRS 9).

  Whatever policy choice for the recognition and measurement of financial instruments is followed, FRS 102 reporters must give the disclosures required by Sections 11 and 12 and follow the presentation requirements (on offset of financial assets and financial liabilities) in these sections, rather than those required by IFRSs. See Chapter 10 at 4.

- FRS 102 requires an entity to apply FRS 103 to insurance contracts (including reinsurance contracts) that it issues and reinsurance contracts that it holds, and financial instruments (other than insurance contracts) with a discretionary participation feature that it issues. See 1.2.4 below.

- Since statutory accounts prepared by UK companies in accordance with FRS 102 are Companies Act accounts, these must comply with the requirements of the CA 2006 and of *The Large and Medium-sized Companies and Groups (Accounts and Reports) Regulations 2008* (SI 2008/410) ('the Regulations') or *The Small Companies and Groups (Accounts and Directors' Report) Regulations 2008* (SI 2008/409) ('the Small Companies Regulations').

  Statutory accounts prepared by LLPs in accordance with FRS 102 are non-IAS accounts and must comply with similar requirements under LLP law.

  The CA 2006 and the relevant regulations set out the formats for the balance sheet and profit and loss account (see Chapter 6 at 4 to 6), recognition and measurement principles and further disclosures required in Companies Act accounts (or non-IAS accounts, for an LLP). Entities not subject to the Regulations (or LLP Regulations) must also use the statutory or, where permitted, adapted formats for the balance sheet and profit and loss account, set out in those regulations except to the extent that these requirements are not permitted by any statutory framework under which such entities report.

  While FRS 102 (and Appendix III – *Note on Legal Requirements* – to the standard) highlight certain issues relevant to Companies Act accounts, the discussion is not comprehensive. See 4 below, Chapter 1 at 6 and Chapter 6 at 9 and 10.

- Section 34 – *Specialised Activities* – sets out specific accounting and disclosure requirements for agriculture, extractive activities, service concession arrangements, financial institutions, retirement benefit plans, heritage assets, funding commitments, and certain issues specific to public benefit entities. Paragraphs marked PBE throughout the standard are specific to public benefit entities, and not for general application. See 2.5 below.

Section 34, in particular, sets out additional disclosure requirements for the financial statements of a financial institution (and for the consolidated financial statements of a group containing a financial institution) and for the financial statements of a retirement benefit plan. The definition of a 'financial institution' and the required disclosures are discussed at 2.5.1 below.

- FRS 102 includes a reduced disclosure framework for qualifying entities, available in their individual financial statements only, where the criteria are met. The FRC withdrew the requirement for shareholder notification in December 2016 with immediate effect.

A qualifying entity is a member of a group that is consolidated in publicly available consolidated financial statements of the parent of that group which are intended to give a true and fair view. Some of the disclosure exemptions available under the reduced disclosure framework are conditional on equivalent disclosures being included in the consolidated financial statements of the group in which the entity is consolidated. In addition, a financial institution has fewer exemptions than an entity that is not a financial institution. See 3 below.

- Section 35 – *Transition to this FRS* – addresses transition to FRS 102. Section 35 is based on a simplified version of IFRS 1 – *First-time Adoption of International Financial Reporting Standards*, but with significant modifications. See Chapter 32.

1.2   Development of FRS 102

FRED 44 – *Financial Reporting Standard for Medium-sized Entities*, published in 2010, proposed that the standard, based on the IFRS for SMEs, would apply to entities that did not have public accountability. Under the proposals, entities that did have public accountability would have been required to apply EU-adopted IFRS. However, respondents were not supportive of the extension of the application of EU-adopted IFRS, and the former ASB decided to amend the IFRS for SMEs so that it is relevant to a broader group of preparers and users. *[FRS 102 Overview (v)]*. See 1.2.1 below.

In developing the framework, the FRC set out an overriding objective to enable users of accounts to receive high-quality understandable financial reporting proportionate to the size and complexity of the entity and users' information needs. *[FRS 102 Overview (i)]*. See Chapter 1 at 4.

The Accounting Standards Board (replaced by the FRC in 2012) decided IFRS for SMEs would be used as a basis for the development of FRS 102, noting that it was a way of achieving a consistent accounting framework (as a simplification of IFRSs), reflected more up-to-date thinking and developments than previous UK GAAP, was a single standard setting out clear accounting requirements, and was a cost effective way of updating previous UK GAAP. *[FRS 102.BC.A.4]*.

To be consistent with objective of providing succinct financial reporting standards, certain UITF Abstracts were incorporated into FRS 102, namely UITF – Abstract 4 *Presentation of long-term debtors in current assets,* UITF Abstract 31 – *Exchange of businesses or other non-monetary assets for an interest in a subsidiary, joint venture or associate*, UITF Abstract 32 – *Employee benefit trusts and other intermediate payment arrangements* and UITF Abstract 43 – *The Interpretation of equivalence for the purposes of section 228A of the Companies Act 1985. [FRS 102.BC.A.9].*

Initially a three tier system, using public accountability as a differentiator, was mooted, but concerns were expressed about this and therefore public accountability was eliminated as a differentiator. As a result, FRS 102 is applicable to all entities which are not required to apply EU-adopted IFRS. Consequently various entities which are outside the scope of IFRS for SMEs are in the scope of FRS 102 and additional requirements have been developed for financial institutions, public benefit entities and entities whose debt or equity instruments are publicly traded, but not on a regulated market. *[FRS 102.BC.A.11-13].* Requirements which conflicted with company law were simultaneously removed from FRS 102 and it was concluded that all entities applying FRS 102 would be required to follow company law formats to promote consistency. *[FRS 102.BC.A.14-15].*

FRS 102 was published in March 2013. Subsequently, the following amendments to FRS 102 have been issued:

- Amendments to FRS 102 – *The Financial Reporting Standard applicable in the UK and Republic of Ireland – Basic Financial Instruments and Hedge Accounting* (July 2014);

- Amendments to FRS 102 – *The Financial Reporting Standard applicable in the UK and Republic of Ireland – Pension Obligations* (February 2015);

- Amendments to FRS 102 – *The Financial Reporting Standard applicable in the UK and Republic of Ireland – Small Entities and other minor amendments* (July 2015);

- Amendments to FRS 102 – *The Financial Reporting Standard applicable in the UK and Republic of Ireland – Fair value hierarchy disclosures* (March 2016);

- Amendments to FRS 101 – *Reduced Disclosure Framework* and FRS 102 – *The Financial Reporting Standard applicable in the UK and Republic of Ireland – Notification of shareholders* (December 2016) (see 1.2.3.A below);

- Amendments to FRS 102 – *The Financial Reporting Standard applicable in the UK and Republic of Ireland – Directors' loans – optional interim relief for small entities* (May 2017) (see 1.2.3.B below);

- Amendments to FRS 102 – *The Financial Reporting Standard applicable in the UK and Republic of Ireland – Triennial Review 2017 – Incremental Improvements and Clarifications* (December 2017). (Triennial review 2017) (see 1.2.3.C below).

All of the above amendments are now incorporated in the March 2018 version of the standard. The FRC has issued the following subsequent versions of the standard:

- 'the August 2014 version' of FRS 102, which includes the original standard and the July 2014 amendments (note that this version does not include all amendments effective for accounting periods beginning on or after 1 January 2015);

- 'the September 2015 version' of FRS 102, which incorporates the July 2015 and all earlier amendments made to the standard; and

- 'the March 2018 version' of FRS 102 (which is effective for accounting periods beginning on or after 1 January 2019) and includes all amendments from March 2016 onwards, including the amendments introduced in the Triennial review 2017.

Chapter 3

FRS 103 and FRS 104, which are applicable to certain entities applying FRS 102, are discussed respectively at 1.2.4 and 1.2.5 below.

See 1.3 below for the effective dates of the amendments to FRS 102 and FRS 103.

1.2.1   Amendments made in FRS 102 compared to the IFRS for SMEs

The Accounting Standards Board (replaced by the FRC in 2012), replying to concerns from respondents about the removal of certain accounting policy options and noting that some pragmatism was required in determining what amendments were to be made to the IFRS for SMEs, developed a set of guidelines for application in the UK and Republic of Ireland (ROI). *[FRS 102.BC.A.5-6]*.

The guidelines were as follows:

- Changes should be made to permit accounting treatments that existed in FRSs at the transition date which align with EU-adopted IFRS.

- Changes should be consistent with EU-adopted IFRS unless a non-IFRS based solution clearly better meets the objective of providing high-quality understandable financial reporting proportionate to the size and complexity of the entity and the users' information needs. In these cases, elements of an IFRS-based solution may nevertheless be retained.

- Use should be made, where possible, of existing exemptions in company law to avoid gold-plating.

- Changes should be made to provide clarification, by reference to EU-adopted IFRS, which would avoid unnecessary diversity in practice. *[FRS 102.BC.A.6]*.

As a result of applying the guidelines, FRS 102 now includes accounting options for the capitalisation of borrowing costs, the revaluation of property, plant and equipment and intangible assets and, in certain circumstances, the capitalisation of development costs. *[FRS 102.BC.A.7]*.

Further clarifications were also made, some by reference to EU-adopted IFRS and some to previous UK and Ireland accounting standards. Examples of these include: *[FRS 102.BC.A.8]*

- Amending the disclosure requirements for discontinued operations for compliance with company law.

- Providing an option to use cost or fair value for the measurement of investments by an investor which is not a parent, but has an investment in one or more associates and/or jointly controlled entities.

- Clarifying that the life of goodwill cannot exceed 10 years, where the entity is otherwise unable to make a reliable estimate – this also applies to intangible assets. Previously the time period was 5 years, but this was changed subsequent to the implementation of the EU Accounting Directive in 2015.

- Clarifying the accounting treatment of group share-based payments when the award is granted by the parent or another group entity.

Subsequent amendments made to FRS 102 have continued to follow the guidelines set out above. The Triennial review 2017 represents the most significant revision of FRS 102 to date and has been carried out in response to stakeholder feedback on the implementation of FRS 102 and after considering recent improvements in financial reporting.

Scope of FRS 102

1.2.2 Review of FRS 102

1.2.2.A Triennial review 2017

When FRS 102 was first issued, the FRC indicated that the standard would be reviewed every three years, in response to feedback from stakeholders on areas for improvement and to areas identified by the FRC. The review process was seen as an opportunity to look at the implementation of FRS 102 and whether it had achieved its aims, as well as an opportunity to make improvements. Sources of potential improvements used included feedback from stakeholders on possible areas of improvement, areas identified by the FRC for review, the IASB's 2015 *Amendments to the IFRS for SMEs* and changes in IFRS (both new IFRS, amendments to existing IFRS and new interpretations). Feedback from stakeholders was gathered through a request for information, a consultation document on the approach to changes in IFRS and exposure drafts setting out the proposed amendments. While amendments to IFRS for SMEs remained a useful source for considering the development of FRS 102, the wider scope of FRS 102 meant that the FRC also reviewed changes in IFRS, as it was seeking an overall IFRS-based solution. *[FRS 102.BC.A.33-35]*.

In December 2017, the FRC published the amendments resulting from the first of these triennial reviews as Triennial review 2017 and in March 2018 it issued the standard, incorporating all the amendments made in the Triennial review 2017. The main changes required by the Triennial review 2017 are set out below at 1.2.3.C below.

1.2.2.B Periodic review

In the Basis for Conclusions, it is noted that FRS 102 will continue to be subject to periodic review, likely every four to five years, rather than the three year cycle originally envisaged. The reason for the change in time frame is to allow time for experience of the most recent version to emerge before seeking stakeholder feedback. Such periodic reviews will consider stakeholder feedback, minor changes in IFRS, the IFRS for SMEs and other issues. However, the FRC will continue to assess emerging issues as they arise and therefore it is possible that there will be amendments issued outside the regular review cycle. *[FRS 102.BC.A.45]*.

At the time of writing, there is no timetable for bringing the requirements of IFRS 9, IFRS 15 – *Revenue from Contracts with Customers* – and IFRS 16 – *Leases* – into FRS 102. The FRC's current intention is to consider major changes to IFRS on a case-by-case basis and to monitor any implementation issues arising over an unspecified period of time: only at the end of that period would a consultation process begin. *[FRS 102.BC.A.44]*.

1.2.3 Amendments made to FRS 102 from December 2016

All amendments up to and including the Triennial review 2017 have been incorporated in the 2018 version of the standard. All amendments since December 2016 are discussed at 1.2.3.A to 1.2.3.C below.

1.2.3.A Amendments to FRS 101 Reduced Disclosure Framework and FRS 102 The Financial Reporting Standard applicable in the UK and Republic of Ireland – Notification of shareholders

The notification of shareholders amendment was issued in December 2016 and was applicable to both FRS 101 and FRS 102 reporters. *[FRS 102.BC.B1.3]*. The amendment removed the need to notify shareholders in writing about a qualifying entity's intention to use the disclosure exemptions; this requirement had originally been introduced to protect minority shareholders, by giving them an opportunity to object to the use of reduced disclosures. This opportunity has now been removed and it is considered by the FRC that sufficient information will continue to exist for minority shareholders to understand the effects of the reduced disclosure framework. *[FRS 102.BC.B1.4]*. The amendment was applicable to all accounting periods beginning or after 1 January 2016 and therefore had immediate effect on its publication. It was made after concerns were raised about the cost-effectiveness of requiring the notification of shareholders and uncertainty about how frequently such notification should be given. The lack of guidance on the latter point led to diversity in practice.

The FRC therefore concluded that a specific right to object to the use of the disclosure exemptions was not necessary given the information already available to shareholders and their existing rights. *[FRS 102.BC.B1.6]*.

1.2.3.B   Amendment to FRS 102 (May 2017): Directors' loans – optional interim relief for small entities

This amendment was issued with immediate effect in May 2017 and could be applied retrospectively. It inserted paragraph 1.15A into Section 1 to permit a small entity to measure a basic financial liability, which is a loan from a director (a natural person), who is also a shareholder in the small entity (or a close member of the family of that person) initially at the transaction price and subsequently to carry it at amortised cost, even if it is a financing transaction. This amendment was removed from Section 1 in the Triennial review 2017 and the same concession was inserted into paragraph 13A of Section 11 (see Chapter 10).

1.2.3.C   The Triennial review 2017

The Triennial review 2017 is the first comprehensive review of FRS 102 since its introduction in 2013. The amendments have been developed in response to stakeholder feedback and to recent developments in financial reporting; they therefore address many of the implementation issues reported by preparers to the FRC. The aim of the changes is to make the standard clearer and easier to use, by simplifying some accounting policies and introducing additional choices and exemptions, while maintaining cost effective financial reporting. The major changes introduced by the review are listed below, with references to where they are discussed in more detail in other chapters.

- Removal of the undue cost or effort exemptions from all sections.
- For an entity leasing an investment property to another group entity, an accounting policy choice has been introduced to permit the property to be treated as property, plant and equipment under Section 17, rather than being accounted for at fair value through profit or loss (see Chapter 14 at 3.1.2).
- The introduction of a description of a basic financial instrument to support the detailed conditions for classification as basic. If a financial instrument does not meet the conditions set out in paragraph 9 of Section 11, it may apply the general principle in paragraph 9A of Section 11, whereby a financial instrument may still be classified as basic if it gives rise to cash flows on specified dates that constitute the repayment of the principal advanced, together with reasonable compensation for

the time value of money, credit risk and other basic lending risks and costs. The intention of this amendment is to permit a small number of financial instruments, which previously breached the conditions to be classified as basic, to be now classified as basic. In particular, the FRC considered that this would assist with the classification of social housing loans with two-way compensation clauses as a basic financial instrument (see Chapter 10 at 6.1.2.E). *[FRS 102.BC.B11.16-18]*.

- For small entities, the ability to measure a loan from a director who is also a shareholder at its transaction price and subsequently at amortised cost, even if it is a financing transaction– see 1.2.3.B above.

- Entities will be required to recognise fewer intangible assets separately from goodwill in a business combination, thus reducing the cost of compliance. Entities may choose to recognise additional intangible assets meeting the recognition criteria if that would provide more useful information to the users of the financial statements. If the latter is adopted as an accounting policy, it must be consistently applied to the relevant class of intangible assets (see Chapter 16 at 2.1)

- The definition of a financial institution has been amended to remove references to 'generate wealth' and 'manage risk'. This change is intended both to reduce the number or entities meeting the definition of a financial institution and to assist with interpretational difficulties in applying the definition. Retirement benefit plans and stockbrokers have also been removed from the definition (see 2.5.1.A below).

1.2.4   FRS 103 – Insurance Contracts

FRS 103 (and its accompanying Implementation Guidance) consolidated existing financial reporting requirements for entities in the UK and Republic of Ireland issuing insurance contracts. It replaced the previous requirements in FRS 27 – *Life Assurance* – and the ABI SORP – *Statement of Recommended Practice on Accounting for Insurance Business*, which were withdrawn for accounting periods beginning on or after 1 January 2015. *[FRS 103.1.13]*. *Amendments to FRS 103 – Solvency II –* was issued in May 2016 and the standard was included in the scope of the Triennial review 2017. FRS 103 is discussed in Chapter 33.

1.2.5   FRS 104 – Interim Financial Reporting

FRS 102 does not address the presentation of interim financial reports. Entities preparing such reports must describe the basis for preparing and presenting such information. The original version of FRS 104 was issued by the FRC in November 2014 and set out a basis for the preparation and presentation of interim financial reports that an entity may apply. *[FRS 102.3.25]*. This standard was also included in the scope of the Triennial review 2017 and consequential amendments were made; the latest version of the standard was issued in March 2018. FRS 104 is discussed in Chapter 34.

1.3   Effective date of FRS 102 (and FRS 103)

For accounting periods beginning on or after 1 January 2019, there is one version of FRS 102 applicable to preparers. However, for accounting periods beginning before this date there are a number of amendments to the then extant September 2015 version and these are listed below at 1.3.2.

1.3.1   *Accounting periods beginning on or after 1 January 2019*

For accounting periods beginning on or after 1 January 2019, the following apply:

- the March 2018 version of FRS 102, containing the Triennial review 2017 amendments;
- the March 2018 version of FRS 103 (if an entity is in scope of FRS 103); and
- the March 2018 version of FRS 104 (if an entity is applying this standard to its interim reporting).

FRS 100 (March 2018) must be applied from the same date that the March 2018 version of FRS 102 is applied.

1.3.2   *Accounting periods beginning before 1 January 2019*

For accounting periods beginning before 1 January 2019, entities have a choice of (a) applying the March 2018 version of the standard early (see 1.3.1 above) or (b) applying the September 2015 version, in conjunction with the amendments issued in 2016 and 2017. If (b) is chosen, the following apply:

- the September 2015 version of FRS 102 (see 1.2 above);
- the February 2017 version of FRS 103 (if an entity is in scope of FRS 103) and the accompanying implementation guidance and clarification on Solvency II (see 1.2.4 above); *[FRS 103.1.11A]*
- the March 2015 version of FRS 104 (if an entity is applying this standard to its interim reporting);
- the March 2016 amendment to FRS 102; *[FRS 102.1.16]*
- the December 2016 amendment to FRS 102 (see 1.2.3.A above); and
- the May 2017 amendment to FRS 102 (see 1.2.3.B above).

Early application of the March 2018 version of FRS 102 is permitted, provided that all the amendments to the FRS are applied at the same time – in other words, cherry picking is not permitted. If an entity does early adopt the Triennial review 2017 amendments, it must disclose that fact. A small entity is not obliged to disclose that it has early adopted the amendments, but it is encouraged to make the disclosure. *[FRS 102.1.18]*.

There are three exceptions to the above, where amendments may be applied early without early application of the rest of the Triennial review 2017 amendments. The first relates to directors' loans (see 1.2.3.B above). The second relates to gift aid payments made within charitable groups; this early application was permitted following feedback from respondents.

The third exception relates to small entities in the Republic of Ireland only. For these entities, the Triennial review 2017 amendments to Section 1A are effective for accounting periods beginning on or after 1 January 2017, in order to align the effective date with the implementation of the Companies (Accounting) Act 2017. These amendments can also be early adopted and a small entity so adopting is encouraged, though not required, to disclose that fact. *[FRS 102.1.18]*. Such an entity must disclose that its financial statements have been prepared in accordance with Section 1A of FRS 102 and the effect of and reasons for any material departure from that section must also be disclosed. *[FRS 102.1AD.3]*.

1.3.3   Effective date – entities subject to SORP

Following the issuance of FRS 102, some SORPs have been updated for consistency with the original version of FRS 102 and others withdrawn. See Chapter 1 at 4.7.1 for a list of the extant SORPs. However, some SORPS have not been updated and there remains inconsistency in updating SORPS for subsequent amendments to FRS 102, leading to a lag between revisions to FRS 102 and the update of SORPs.

Amendments to the relevant SORPs are not necessary before any changes to FRS 102 take effect because a change in accounting standards after a SORP has been issued means any conflicting provisions of a SORP cease to have effect. *[FRS 100.6]*. However, where there is a lag between amendments made to FRS 102 and review of a SORP, there may be uncertainty as to which parts of a SORP are considered in conflict with the amended version of FRS 102 and over what, if any, changes to a SORP may subsequently be made. Consequently, an entity may be wary of early applying amendments to FRS 102 until the relevant SORP (which will generally include additional guidance and disclosures) has been reviewed. For example, it is generally understood that small charities may not adopt Section 1A of FRS 102. The *Charities SORP (FRS 102)* (as amended by Update Bulletin 2 in 2018) also includes additional disclosures for charities beyond those required by FRS 102, which would apply to small charities (unless specifically exempted by the SORP). See Chapter 5 at 4.2.

Certain entities may also be subject to legal requirements relating to the application of SORPs which may restrict the ability of an entity to early apply an amendment to FRS 102 (or related SORP). This issue may affect some charities but could also affect other entities not discussed below. It is therefore always important for entities to understand the legislative or other regulatory requirements governing the preparation of their financial statements.

1.3.3.A   Charities

The legal framework for charities differs in England and Wales, Scotland, Northern Ireland and the Republic of Ireland and differs for unincorporated charities and charitable companies. It is beyond the scope of this publication to address the requirements for annual accounts and reports of charities and therefore this section only contains a brief overview of SORPs which may be applicable.

For entities with an accounting period beginning on or after 1 January 2019, the *Charities SORP (FRS 102)* should be applied in conjunction with Update Bulletin 2, which brings into the Charities SORP the Triennial review 2017 amendments. Except where prohibited by regulations or charity or company law, early application of the amendments to the SORP are permitted, provided that all of the amendments are applied at the same time.

1.4   Structure of FRS 102

FRS 102 includes Section 1 which addresses the scope of FRS 102, Section 1A – *Small Entities*, Section 2 – *Concepts and Pervasive Principles*, Sections 3 to 33 each addressing a separate accounting topic, Section 34 on specialised activities (see 2.5 below) and Section 35 on transition to FRS 102.

Chapter 3

All paragraphs have equal authority. Some sections include appendices of implementation guidance or examples. Some of these are an integral part of FRS 102 whereas others provide guidance, but each specifies its status. Terms defined in the Glossary (included in Appendix I to FRS 102) are in bold type the first time they appear in each section of FRS 102 and in each sub-section of Section 34. *[FRS 102 Overview (vi)-(vii)]*.

Appendix II *Table of equivalence for company law terminology* compares company law terminology with that used in FRS 102 and Appendix III *Note on legal requirements* provides an overview of how the requirements in FRS 102 address the requirements of the CA 2006 (Appendix IV – *Republic of Ireland Legal References* – addresses Irish law).

The Basis for Conclusions summarises the main issues considered by the FRC in developing FRS 102.

Section 1 of FRS 102 is addressed in this chapter.

2   SCOPE OF FRS 102

FRS 102 applies to financial statements that are intended to give a true and fair view of a reporting entity's financial position and profit or loss (or income and expenditure) for a period. *[FRS 102.1.1]*.

FRS 102 is designed to apply to general purpose financial statements and to the financial reporting of entities including those that are not constituted as companies and those that are not profit-oriented, i.e. to financial statements which are intended to focus on the common information needs of a wide range of users (such as shareholders, lenders, other creditors, employees and members of the public). *[FRS 102 Overview (v)]*.

FRS 102 applies to public benefit entities (PBEs) and other entities, not just to companies. *[FRS 102.1.2]*. Paragraph numbers prefixed with a 'PBE' are applicable to public benefit entities, and are not applied directly or by analogy to entities that are not public benefit entities (other than, where specifically directed, entities within a public benefit entity group). *[FRS 102.1.2]*. A public benefit entity must apply all paragraphs prefixed with a 'PBE' to the extent that they are relevant, provided that any SORP relating to that public benefit entity permits it. These paragraphs are generally found in Section 34 but are not restricted to that section. See 2.5.2 below.

An entity applying FRS 102 must ensure it complies with any relevant legal requirements applicable to it. FRS 102 does not necessarily contain all legal disclosure requirements. Section 1A includes most legal disclosures for small companies but, for example, those only relevant when the financial statements have been audited are not included. *[FRS 102.1.2A]*. See Chapter 5 at 11 for disclosures required for small companies (and LLPs), including disclosures omitted by Section 1A.

2.1   Basis of preparation of financial statements

FRS 100 sets out the applicable financial reporting framework for entities preparing financial statements intended to give a true and fair view in accordance with legislation, regulations or accounting standards applicable in the UK and the Republic of Ireland. *[FRS 100.1-2]*.

As stated in FRS 100, an entity required by the IAS Regulation (or other legislation or regulation) to prepare consolidated financial statements in accordance with EU-adopted IFRS must do so.

The individual financial statements of such an entity, or the individual financial statements or consolidated financial statements of any other entity within the scope of FRS 100, must be prepared in accordance with the following requirements:

(a)   if the financial statements are the individual financial statements of an entity that is eligible to apply FRS 105 (and the entity chooses to do so), FRS 105; or

(b)   if the financial statements are those of an entity that is not eligible to (or is eligible to but chooses not to) apply FRS 105, the financial statements must be prepared in accordance with:

   (i)   FRS 102; or

   (ii)   EU-adopted IFRS; or

   (iii)   FRS 101 (if the financial statements are individual financial statements of a qualifying entity) (see Chapter 2). *[FRS 100.4, FRS 102.1.3]*.

The above requirements in Section 1 largely reinforce and are consistent with the general requirements on basis of preparation of financial statements in FRS 100. However, FRS 100 sets out the choices available slightly differently to Section 1 (see Chapter 1 at 4.4). FRS 100 states that the choice in (a) and (b) above relates to financial statements (whether consolidated financial statements *or* individual financial statements) that are not required by the IAS Regulation (or other legislation or regulation) to be prepared in accordance with EU-adopted IFRS. *[FRS 100.4]*. While the IAS Regulation does not require individual financial statements of UK companies with securities admitted to trading on a regulated market to be prepared in accordance with EU-adopted IFRS, some UK companies may be subject to other regulations that do require EU-adopted IFRS in individual financial statements.

FRS 105 can be applied by a UK company, qualifying partnership, or LLP that meets the eligibility conditions to apply the micro-entity provisions and is not excluded. See Chapter 1 at 4.4.6 and 6.2.2.B.

FRS 102 can also be used by entities that are not subject to the CA 2006 (or the Companies Act 2014 in the Republic of Ireland). An entity's choice of financial reporting framework must be permitted by the legal framework or other regulations or requirements that govern the preparation of the entity's financial statements. Other agreements or arrangements (such as shareholders' agreements or banking agreements) may restrict the choice of financial reporting framework.

The basis of preparation of financial statements in the UK is addressed in more detail in Chapter 1 at 4.4.

The requirements of the CA 2006 (and certain other regulatory rules) governing preparation of financial statements by UK companies are discussed in Chapter 1 at 6. The CA 2006 exemptions available to small companies, small LLPs and small qualifying partnerships are addressed in Chapter 5 at 13, which explains how FRS 102 interacts with the CA 2006 exemptions for small and medium-sized companies, LLPs and qualifying partnerships, where Section 1A is *not* applied.

2.2   Small entities

Small entities (as defined in Chapter 5 at 4.1) are entitled to apply Section 1A of FRS 102.

Small entities applying Section 1A follow the same recognition and measurement principles as full FRS 102 but the presentation and disclosure requirements in Section 1A, which are based on the statutory requirements applicable to companies subject to the small companies regime (and LLPs subject to the small LLPs regime) and are somewhat lighter than those that apply in full FRS 102. See Chapter 5 for a full discussion of the requirements of Section 1A.

A small entity, whether or not applying Section 1A, also benefits from:

*   exemption from the preparation of a cash flow statement (see Chapter 7 at 3.1); and

*   exemption from the preparation of consolidated financial statements (see Chapter 8 at 3.1.1.D).

2.3   Application of SORPs

SORPs recommend accounting practices for specialised industries or sectors, and supplement accounting standards and other legal and regulatory requirements in light of the special factors prevailing or transactions undertaken in a particular industry or sector. *[FRS 102 Appendix I].*

FRS 102 makes reference to current SORPs (to the extent the provisions are in effect) as part of the hierarchy for management to consider when developing and applying accounting policies. *[FRS 102.10.5].* See Chapter 9 at 3.2.

The provisions of a SORP cease to apply, for instance, where they conflict with a more recent financial reporting standard. *[FRS 100.6].* See 1.3.3 above.

Individual SORPs should be referred to in order to understand the circumstances in which they apply. If a SORP does apply, the entity should state in its financial statements the title of the SORP and whether the financial statements have been prepared in accordance with the SORP's provisions that are currently in effect.

If the provisions of the SORP have been departed from, the entity should give a description of how the financial statements depart from the practice recommended by the SORP. In particular, for any treatment not in accordance with the SORP, the entity should disclose why the chosen treatment is judged more appropriate to the entity's circumstances and in the case of any omitted disclosures recommended by the SORP, the reason for the omission. A small entity applying the small entities regime in FRS 102 is exempt from this requirement, but such an entity is encouraged to provide the disclosures. *[FRS 102.1.7A, FRS 100.6].*

2.4   Extension of specific IFRSs to certain types of entities

As FRS 102 is accessible to a wider scope of entities than the IFRS for SMEs, the FRC has extended its requirements (compared to the IFRS for SMEs) to address specific issues by way of direct references to IFRSs (as adopted by the EU). These IFRSs apply with the same scope as contained within the individual IFRS, as follows:

*   IAS 33 – this standard applies to an entity whose ordinary shares or potential ordinary shares are publicly traded or that files, or is in the process of filing, its

financial statements with a securities commission or other regulatory organisation for the purpose of issuing ordinary shares in a public market, or an entity that chooses to disclose earnings per share; *[FRS 102.1.4]*

- IFRS 6 – this standard applies to an entity that is engaged in the exploration for and/or evaluation of mineral resources (extractive activities); *[FRS 102.34.11]*
- IFRS 8 – this standard applies to an entity whose debt or equity instruments are publicly traded, or that files, or is in the process of filing, its financial statements with a securities commission or other regulatory organisation for the purpose of issuing any class of instruments in a public market, or an entity that chooses to provide information described as segment information. If an entity discloses disaggregated information, but that information does not comply with IFRS 8's requirements, the information shall not be described as segment information. *[FRS 102.1.5]*. See Chapter 6 at 3.3.2.

References to other IFRSs made in IAS 33, IFRS 6 or IFRS 8 shall be taken to be references to the relevant section or paragraph made in FRS 102 (except that when applying paragraph 21 of IFRS 6, a cash generating unit or group of cash generating units shall be no larger than an operating segment (as defined in FRS 102's Glossary) and the reference to IFRS 8 shall be ignored). *[FRS 102.1.7, 34.11A-B]*.

2.4.1   Application of FRS 103

FRS 102 is not applicable to insurance contracts (including reinsurance contracts) issued or held by an entity, nor to financial instruments with a discretionary participation feature that an entity issues. Instead an entity must apply FRS 103 to such contracts and instruments. *[FRS 102.1.6, FRS 103.1.2]*. This is the same scope as for IFRS 4 – *Insurance Contracts* – and may be wider than entities that are legally insurers for legal or supervisory purposes. See 1.2.4 above and Chapter 33 for information on FRS 103.

2.5   Specialised activities

Section 34 of FRS 102 is devoted to additional requirements specific to specialised activities. These address:

- financial institutions (disclosures) (see 2.5.1 below);
- agriculture;
- extractive activities;
- service concession arrangements;
- heritage assets;
- funding commitments;
- incoming resources from non-exchange transactions;
- retirement benefit plans (accounting for retirement benefit plans and disclosures for such plans are not within the scope of this publication); and
- public benefit entities (see 2.5.2 below).

Importantly, Section 34 sets out requirements on certain areas not addressed directly by previous UK accounting standards or IFRSs. FRS 102's requirements on specialised activities are addressed in Chapter 31.

Chapter 3

2.5.1   Financial institutions – disclosure requirements

A financial institution that is a qualifying entity is not entitled to make use of the disclosure exemptions from Sections 11 and 12 when applying the reduced disclosure framework in its individual financial statements (see 3 below). *[FRS 102.1.9]*.

Section 34 of FRS 102 includes additional disclosure requirements for financial institutions (see definition at 2.5.1.A below) in financial statements prepared in accordance with FRS 102.

These disclosure requirements set out in paragraphs 19 to 33 of Section 34 must be provided in: *[FRS 102.34.17]*

- the individual financial statements of a financial institution; and
- the consolidated financial statements of a group containing a financial institution where the financial institution's financial instruments are material to the group.

Disclosures are required in the consolidated financial statements of a group containing a financial institution even if the principal activities of the group itself are not being a financial institution. This has an implication for group accounts where a group company is identified as a financial institution (see 2.5.1.A below). Disclosures will be required in the group accounts in relation to financial instruments of the group company (to the extent the transactions have not eliminated on consolidation), where these are material to the group.

The additional disclosures required by financial institutions are set out in Chapter 10 at 11.2.4.

2.5.1.A   Definition of a financial institution

The FRC has opted not to provide a generic definition of a financial institution. Instead, it has provided a list of entities that are stated to be financial institutions. A 'financial institution' is stated to be any of the following: *[FRS 102 Appendix I]*

(a)   a bank which is:

    (i)   a firm with a Part 4A permission (as defined in section 55A of the Financial Services and Markets Act 2000 or the equivalent provisions of any successor legislation) which includes accepting deposits and:

        (a)   which is a credit institution; or

        (b)   whose Part 4A permission includes a requirement that it complies with the rules in the General Prudential sourcebook and the Prudential sourcebook for Banks, Building Societies and Investment Firms relating to banks, but which is not a building society, a friendly society or a credit union;

    (ii)   an EEA bank which is a full credit institution;

(b)   a building society which is defined in section 119(1) of the Building Societies Act 1986 as a building society incorporated (or deemed to be incorporated) under that act;

(c)   a credit union, being a body corporate registered under the Co-operative and Community Benefit Societies Act 2014 as a credit union in accordance with the Credit Unions Act 1979, which is an authorised person;

(d)   custodian bank or broker-dealer;

(e) an entity that undertakes the business of effecting or carrying out insurance contracts, including general and life assurance entities;

(f) an incorporated friendly society incorporated under the Friendly Societies Act 1992 or a registered friendly society registered under section 7(1)(a) of the Friendly Societies Act 1974 or any enactment which it replaced, including any registered branches;

(g) an investment trust, Irish Investment Company, venture capital trust, mutual fund, exchange traded fund, unit trust, open-ended investment company (OEIC);

(h) any other entity whose principal activity is similar to those listed above but is not specifically included in the list above.

A parent entity whose sole activity is to hold investments in other group entities is not a financial institution.

The final category ((h) above) has been amended since the 2015 version of the standard, following a number of queries about how the definition of a financial institution was applied in practice and perceived anomalies within the definition. The principle has therefore been amended to remove references to 'generate wealth' and 'manage risk'. It is believed that these changes will both reduce the number of entities meeting the definition of a financial institution and will reduce interpretational difficulties with regard to implementing the concept. *[FRS 102.BC.B34D.4-5]*. It has additionally removed references to retirement benefit plans, as they are not deemed to be similar to the other institutions in the list and also to stockbrokers, as they are considered to be generally dissimilar from other entities as they do not hold financial instruments on behalf of others. *[FRS 102.BC.B34D.6-7]*

The difficulties in applying the previous definition to group treasury companies are acknowledged and it is believed that some of the issues have been alleviated by the change in definition. Nonetheless, it highlights that an assessment of whether such an entity is a financial institution will depend on individual facts and circumstances. Whether a group entity is similar to the other entities listed in the definition of a financial institution will require judgement. *[FRS 102.BC.B34D.8]*.

Identifying a group entity as a financial institution impacts both the disclosures that need to be given in the individual financial statements of that entity (prepared in accordance with FRS 102) and, where the financial instruments of the financial institution are material to the group, in the consolidated financial statements including the entity (where prepared in accordance with FRS 102) (see 2.5.1 above). If the risks arising from financial instruments are particularly significant to a business, additional disclosure may be required to enable users to evaluate the significance of those instruments, regardless of whether the entity meets the definition of a financial institution. If a group entity ceases to meet the definition of a financial institution, the disclosures relating to both the individual financial statements and the consolidated financial statements will no longer be required. *[FRS 102.BC.B34D.9]*.

2.5.2 Public benefit entities

Paragraphs in FRS 102 that are prefixed by PBE are specific to public benefit entities (see definition in the Glossary to FRS 102, and discussed further in Chapter 31 at 6).

These paragraphs must not be applied directly, or by analogy, to entities that are not public benefit entities (other than, where specifically directed, entities within a public benefit entity group, i.e. a public benefit entity parent and all its wholly-owned subsidiaries). *[FRS 102.1.2, FRS 102 Appendix I]*.

Section 34 addresses incoming resources from non-exchange transactions, public benefit entity combinations, and public benefit entity concessionary loans. These parts of Section 34 include paragraphs prefixed by PBE and, therefore, apply only to public benefit entities. Other sections of FRS 102 also contain paragraphs prefixed by PBE. Section 34 also addresses other accounting topics such as heritage assets and funding commitments, which may be of particular relevance to some public benefit entities, but (as the paragraphs are not prefixed by PBE) apply to all entities. See Chapter 31 at 6 and Chapter 19 at 3.9.

Many public benefit entities may also be subject to the requirements of a SORP (see 1.3.4 and 2.3 above).

3   REDUCED DISCLOSURE FRAMEWORK

FRS 102 provides for a reduced disclosure framework available only in the individual financial statements of a 'qualifying entity' (see 3.1 below). *[FRS 102.1.8-13]*. A qualifying entity which is required to prepare consolidated financial statements (for example, it is a parent company required by section 399 of the CA 2006 to prepare group accounts and is not entitled to any of the exemptions in sections 400 to 402 of the CA 2006 or chooses not to take advantage of these exemptions) may not take advantage of the disclosure exemptions in its consolidated financial statements. *[FRS 102.1.10]*. This does not preclude the reduced disclosure framework being applied in the individual financial statements of a parent preparing consolidated financial statements.

Individual financial statements to which FRS 102 applies are the accounts that are required to be prepared by an entity in accordance with the CA 2006 or relevant legislation, for example: 'individual accounts' as set out in section 394 of the CA 2006, a 'statement of accounts' as set out in section 132 of the Charities Act 2011, or 'individual accounts' as set out in section 72A of the Building Societies Act 1986. Separate financial statements are included in the meaning of the term 'individual financial statements'. *[FRS 102 Appendix I]*.

It is worth noting that FRS 102 uses the term 'separate financial statements' to mean those presented by a parent in which the investments in subsidiaries, jointly controlled entities or associates are accounted for either at cost or fair value rather than on the basis of the reported results and net assets of the investees. *[FRS 102 Appendix I]*. This differs to the definition of 'separate financial statements' in IFRSs. *[IAS 27.4]*.

This means that FRS 102's reduced disclosure framework can be used in:

- individual financial statements of subsidiary undertakings;
- separate financial statements of an intermediate parent undertaking which does not prepare consolidated financial statements; and
- separate financial statements of a parent undertaking which does prepare consolidated financial statements.

However, the entity applying FRS 102's reduced disclosure framework must be included in a set of publicly available consolidated financial statements intended to give a true and fair view (see 3.1.6 below).

A parent company that prepares consolidated financial statements but applies FRS 102 in its individual financial statements can also use the exemption in section 408 of the CA 2006 from presenting a profit and loss account and related notes in the individual financial statements. This is the case whether or not it applies FRS 102's reduced disclosure framework.

3.1 Definition of a qualifying entity

FRS 102 defines a qualifying entity as 'a member of a group where the parent of that group prepares publicly available consolidated financial statements which are intended to give a true and fair view (of the assets, liabilities, financial position and profit or loss) and that member is included in the consolidation'. *[FRS 102 Appendix I].* A charity can be a qualifying entity under FRS 102 (unlike under FRS 101).

There is no requirement that a qualifying entity is a member of the group in which it is consolidated for its entire reporting period. There is also no requirement that the financial statements of the qualifying entity and the consolidated financial statements of the parent of that group (which may be the reporting entity itself) must be coterminous or have reporting dates within a particular timeframe. The use of the present tense implies that the intention is only that the qualifying entity (where it does not prepare its own consolidated financial statements) is a subsidiary of the parent at its reporting date. This is consistent with UK company law which requires that an entity which is a parent at the end of the financial year must prepare group accounts unless it is exempted from the requirement. *[s399(2), s399(2) (LLP)].*

The phrase 'included in the consolidation' is referenced to section 474(1) of the CA 2006 which states that this means that 'the undertaking is included in the accounts by the method of full (and not proportional) consolidation and references to an undertaking excluded from consolidation shall be construed accordingly'. Therefore, entities that are not fully consolidated in the consolidated financial statements, such as subsidiaries excluded from consolidation under FRS 102 *[FRS 102.9.9-9B]* or subsidiaries of investment entities that are accounted for at fair value through profit or loss under IFRS 10 – *Consolidated Financial Statements*, cannot use FRS 102's reduced disclosure framework. Associates and jointly controlled entities are not qualifying entities since they are not members of a group (see 3.1.2 below).

There is no requirement for the consolidated financial statements in which the qualifying entity is included to be prepared under FRS 102 nor that the parent that prepares the consolidated financial statements is a UK entity. However, the consolidated financial statements must be intended to give a true and fair view (see 3.1.6 below).

3.1.1 Reporting date of the consolidated financial statements of the parent

The requirement for the qualifying entity to be included in the consolidation implies that the consolidated financial statements of the parent should be approved before, or at the same time as, the FRS 102 individual financial statements of the qualifying entity are approved, where FRS 102's reduced disclosure framework is used in the individual financial statements of the qualifying entity. FRS 102 is silent on whether the reporting date and period of those consolidated financial statements has to be identical to that of the qualifying entity. In contrast, both sections 400 and 401 of the CA 2006 require that the exemption from preparing group accounts for a parent company that is a subsidiary undertaking is conditional on the inclusion of the company in consolidated financial statements of a parent undertaking drawn up to the same date or to an earlier date in the same financial year. It would seem logical that the reporting date criteria in sections 400 and 401 should also be used for FRS 102's reduced disclosure framework.

However, when the consolidated financial statements are prepared as at an earlier date than the date of the qualifying entity's financial statements, some of the disclosure exemptions may not be available to the qualifying entity because the consolidated financial statements may not contain the 'equivalent' disclosures (see 3.6 below).

3.1.2   Definition of 'group' and 'subsidiary'

The definition of a qualifying entity contains a footnote that refers to section 474(1) of the CA 2006 which defines a 'group' as a 'parent undertaking and its subsidiary undertakings'. *[s474(1)]*.

The CA 2006 states that an undertaking is a parent undertaking in relation to another undertaking, a subsidiary undertaking, if:

(a)   it holds a majority of the voting rights in the undertaking;

(b)   it is a member of the undertaking and has the right to appoint or remove a majority of its board of directors;

(c)   it has the right to exercise a dominant influence over the undertaking by virtue of provisions contained in the undertaking's articles or by virtue of a control contract; or

(d)   it is a member of the undertaking and controls alone, pursuant to an agreement with other shareholders or members, a majority of the voting rights in the undertaking.

An undertaking should be treated as a member for the purposes above if any of its subsidiary undertakings is a member of that undertaking or if any shares in that other undertaking are held by a person acting on behalf of the undertaking or any of its subsidiary undertakings.

An undertaking is also a parent undertaking in relation to another (subsidiary) undertaking if it has the power to exercise, or actually exercises, dominant influence or control over it, or it and the subsidiary undertaking are managed on a unified basis.

A parent undertaking should be treated as the parent undertaking of undertakings in relation to which any of its subsidiary undertakings are, or are to be treated as, parent undertakings, and references to its subsidiary undertakings should be construed accordingly. *[s1162(1)-(5)]*. Schedule 7 to the CA 2006 provides interpretation and references to 'shares' in section 1162 and in Schedule 7 are to 'allotted shares'. *[s1162(6)-(7)]*.

FRS 102 defines a subsidiary as an entity that is controlled by the parent. Control is the power to govern the financial and operating policies of an entity so as to obtain benefits from its activities. FRS 102 goes on to explain in what circumstances control exists or can exist. *[FRS 102.9.4-6A]*. These circumstances are similar but not identical to those included in the definition of a subsidiary undertaking under section 1162.

Although there are slight differences in wording emphasis between the definition of a subsidiary undertaking in section 1162 and the requirements of Section 9 – *Consolidated and Separate Financial Statements*, we would expect to see few conflicts arising in practice between Section 9 and the CA 2006 (see Chapter 8 at 3.2). The key issue for the application of FRS 102's reduced disclosure framework is whether the subsidiary is included in the consolidation of the parent's consolidated financial statements. A company that meets the definition of a subsidiary undertaking under the CA 2006 but is not included in the consolidation of the consolidated financial statements of its parent cannot apply FRS 102's reduced disclosure framework.

3.1.3   Publicly available consolidated financial statements

By 'publicly available', we believe that FRS 102 requires that the consolidated financial statements can be accessed by the public as the use of FRS 102's reduced disclosure framework is conditional on a disclosure by the qualifying entity indicating from where those consolidated financial statements can be obtained (see 3.2 below). This does not mandate that the consolidated financial statements must be filed with a regulator. Therefore, for example, UK consolidated financial statements that have not been filed with the Registrar of Companies, at the date that the subsidiary's financial statements prepared in accordance with FRS 102 are approved, must be publicly available via some other medium.

3.1.4   Non-UK qualifying entities

There is no requirement that a qualifying entity is a UK entity. Non-UK entities can apply FRS 102's reduced disclosure framework in their individual or separate financial statements subject to meeting the criteria for its use, and provided FRS 102 is allowed for use in their own jurisdiction.

3.1.5   Non-controlling interests

There is no ownership threshold for a subsidiary to apply FRS 102's reduced disclosure framework. Therefore, a qualifying entity can apply the reduced disclosure framework even if its parent holds less than a majority of the voting rights, provided that the parent has control via other means (see Chapter 8 at 3.2).

3.1.6   Intended to give a true and fair view

In the definition of a qualifying entity (see 3.1 above), the consolidated financial statements in which the qualifying entity is included are not required to give an explicit true and fair view of the assets, liabilities, financial position and profit or loss. Rather, they are '*intended* to give a true and fair view' [emphasis added]. This means that the consolidated financial statements in which the qualifying entity is consolidated need not contain an explicit opinion that they give a 'true and fair view' but, in substance, they should be intended to give such a view. The FRC guidance – *True and Fair* – issued in June 2014 states that 'Fair presentation under IFRS is equivalent to a true and fair view'.

3.1.7   Equivalence

A UK parent company that wishes to claim an exemption from preparing group accounts under either section 400 or section 401 of the CA 2006 must be a subsidiary included in the consolidated accounts for a larger group. Those consolidated accounts (and where appropriate, the group's annual report) must be drawn up: *[s400(2)(b), s401(2)(b)]*

- in accordance with the provisions of Directive 2013/34/EU ('the Accounting Directive') (for sections 400 and 401);
- in a manner equivalent to consolidated accounts and consolidated reports so drawn up (for section 401);
- in accordance with international accounting standards adopted pursuant to the IAS Regulation, i.e. EU-adopted IFRS (for sections 400 and 401); or
- in accordance with accounting standards which are equivalent to international accounting standards, as determined pursuant to Commission Regulation (EC) No. 1569/2007 (for section 401).

There are similar requirements for a parent LLP but for section 401, there is no reference to the basis on which the consolidated reports are drawn up. *[s400(2)(b) (LLP), s401(2)(b) (LLP)]*.

We believe that references to 'in accordance with the Accounting Directive' in relation to a banking or insurance group in section 400 or section 401, mean as modified by the provisions of the Bank Accounts Directive or the Insurance Accounts Directive respectively. *[s400(2)(b), s401(2)(b), s400(2)(b) (LLP), s401(2)(b) (LLP)]*.

In our view, a set of consolidated financial statements that would meet the above criteria (i.e. the consolidated financial statements are drawn up in accordance with or in a manner equivalent to the Accounting Directive, or in accordance with EU-adopted IFRS or accounting standards which are equivalent to EU-adopted IFRS as determined by the mechanism established by the EU Commission) is intended to give a true and fair view.

The Application Guidance to FRS 100 states that consolidated financial statements of the higher parent will meet the exemption or the test of equivalence in the Accounting Directive if they are intended to give a true and fair view and:

- are prepared in accordance with FRS 102;
- are prepared in accordance with EU-adopted IFRS;
- are prepared in accordance with IFRS, subject to the consideration of the reason for any failure by the European Commission to adopt a standard or interpretation; or
- are prepared using other GAAPs which are closely related to IFRS, subject to consideration of the effect of any differences from EU-adopted IFRS.

Consolidated financial statements of the higher parent prepared using other GAAPs or the IFRS for SMEs should be assessed for equivalence with the Accounting Directive based on the particular facts, including the similarities to and differences from the Accounting Directive. *[FRS 100.AG6]*.

In accordance with Commission Regulation (EC) No. 1569/2007(a) of 21 December 2007 (see above), the EU Commission has identified the following GAAPs as equivalent to international accounting standards. This means that these GAAPs are equivalent to international accounting standards as a matter of UK law: *[FRS 100.AG7]*

Equivalent GAAP	Applicable From
GAAP of Japan	1 January 2009
GAAP of the United States of America	1 January 2009
GAAP of the People's Republic of China	1 January 2012
GAAP of Canada	1 January 2012
GAAP of the Republic of Korea	1 January 2012

In addition, third country issuers were permitted to prepare their annual consolidated financial statements and half-yearly consolidated financial statements in accordance with the GAAP of the Republic of India for financial years starting before 1 April 2016. For reporting periods beginning on or after 1 April 2016, in relation to GAAP of the Republic of India, equivalence should be assessed on the basis of the particular facts. *[FRS 100.AG7]*.

The concept of equivalence for the purposes of section 401 is discussed further in Chapter 8 at 3.1.1.C.

In theory, there is no reason why consolidated financial statements of a parent prepared under a GAAP that is not 'equivalent' to the Accounting Directive cannot be used provided those consolidated financial statements in which the entity is included are publicly available and are intended to give a true and fair view.

In addition, a number of the disclosure exemptions under FRS 102's reduced disclosure framework are conditional on 'equivalent' disclosures being made in those publicly available consolidated financial statements in which the qualifying entity is included. *[FRS 102.1.13]*. Where the equivalent disclosure is not made, the relevant disclosure exemptions cannot be applied in the qualifying entity's individual financial statements prepared under FRS 102 (see 3.6 below). A GAAP that is not 'equivalent' to the Accounting Directive is less likely to have those 'equivalent' disclosures.

One issue not addressed by FRS 102 is the impact of a qualified audit opinion on the parent's consolidated financial statements. A Queen's Counsel's opinion, obtained by the FRC in 2008, stated that 'the scope for arguing that financial statements which do not comply with relevant accounting standards nevertheless give a true and fair view, or a fair presentation, is very limited'.[1]

3.2   Use of the disclosure exemptions

The use of the disclosure exemptions in FRS 102's reduced disclosure framework (see 3.3 to 3.5 below) is conditional on all of the following criteria being met:

- the reporting entity applies the recognition, measurement and disclosure requirements of FRS 102;
- the reporting entity discloses in the notes to its financial statements:
  - a brief narrative summary of the disclosure exemptions adopted; and
  - the name of the parent of the group in whose consolidated financial statements its financial statements are consolidated (i.e. the parent identified in the definition of 'qualifying entity') and from where those financial statements may be obtained. *[FRS 102.1.11]*.

There is no requirement to list all of the disclosure exemptions in detail. Reporting entities can also choose to apply the disclosure exemptions on a selective basis. This may be necessary, for example, where not all of the relevant 'equivalent disclosures' are made in the consolidated financial statements of the parent on the grounds of materiality (see 3.6 below).

3.3   Disclosure exemptions for qualifying entities

A qualifying entity may take advantage of the following disclosure exemptions in its individual financial statements: *[FRS 102.1.8, 1.9, 1.12]*

- the requirements of Section 7 – *Statement of Cash Flows* – and Section 3 – *Financial Statement Presentation*, paragraph 3.17(d) (see 3.3.1 below);
- the requirements of:
  - Section 11, paragraphs 11.42, 11.44, 11.45, 11.47, 11.48(a)(iii), 11.48(a)(iv), 11.48(b) and 11.48(c); and
  - Section 12, paragraphs 12.26 (in relation to those cross-referenced paragraphs from which a disclosure exemption is available), 12.27, 12.29(a), 12.29(b) and 12.29A.

  These disclosure exemptions are subject to certain conditions and exceptions. See 3.3.2 and 3.4 below;
- the requirements of Section 26 – *Share-based Payment,* paragraphs 26.18(b), 26.19 to 26.21 and 26.23, provided that for a qualifying entity that is:
  - a subsidiary, the share-based payment arrangement concerns equity instruments of another group entity;
  - an ultimate parent, the share-based payment arrangement concerns its own equity instruments and its separate financial statements are presented alongside the consolidated financial statements of the group;

  and, in both cases, provided that the equivalent disclosures required by FRS 102 are included in the consolidated financial statements of the group in which the entity is consolidated (see 3.3.3 below);
- the requirement of Section 33 – *Related Party Disclosures*, paragraph 33.7 (see 3.3.4 below).

Qualifying entities must still ensure that they comply with any relevant legal requirements. FRS 102 does not necessarily contain all legal disclosure requirements. *[FRS 102.1.2A]*.

3.3.1   Statement of cash flows

The exemption removes the requirement for a cash flow statement for any qualifying entity in its individual financial statements.

3.3.2   Financial instruments

The exemption removes certain of the disclosure requirements of Sections 11 and 12 (see 3.3 above). *[FRS 102.1.12(c)]*.

Financial institutions are not permitted to use this exemption (see 3.5 below).

The exemption depends on there being equivalent disclosures in the publicly available consolidated financial statements in which the qualifying entity is included. The guidance on 'equivalence' included in FRS 100 (see 3.6 below) is clear that the exemption can be taken in relation to intra-group balances that are eliminated on consolidation in these consolidated financial statements.

Notwithstanding this exemption, where a qualifying entity that is not a financial institution has financial instruments held at fair value subject to the requirements of paragraph 36(4) of Schedule 1 to the Regulations (or its equivalents in the Small Companies Regulations, LLP Regulations or Small LLP Regulations), it must give the disclosures required by 'international accounting standards' (see 3.4 below). *[1 Sch 36(4), 1 Sch 36(4) (LLP)]*.

The reduction in disclosure exemptions in relation to Sections 11 and 12 applies even if the qualifying entity is *not* subject to UK company and LLP law. See Chapter 10 at 11.2.1.

3.3.2.A   Other disclosures required by the Regulations for financial instruments

Qualifying entities must also ensure that they comply with any relevant legal requirements. The standard does not necessarily contain all legal disclosure requirements. *[FRS 102.1.2A]*.

FRS 102 financial statements prepared in accordance with Part 15 of the CA 2006 are Companies Act accounts. A UK company's statutory accounts prepared in accordance with FRS 102 should give the disclosures in respect of financial instruments required by the Regulations (or by the Small Companies Regulations) even if the company is a qualifying entity using the reduced disclosure framework. Similarly, a UK LLP should comply with the disclosure requirements of the LLP Regulations (or the Small LLP Regulations).

In particular, qualifying entities that are preparing Companies Act accounts must provide the disclosures required by paragraph 55 of Schedule 1 to the Regulations (and its equivalents in the Small Companies Regulations, LLP Regulations and Small LLP Regulations) which set out requirements relating to financial instruments at fair value. These disclosures relate to financial instruments held at fair value generally and not just to those financial instruments measured at fair value in accordance with paragraph 36(4) as discussed at 3.4 below. FRS 102 reporters applying IFRS 9 or IAS 39 to the recognition and measurement of financial instruments may have financial instruments measured at fair value, but with fair value changes outside profit and loss. Appendix III to FRS 102 states that most of these disclosures will be satisfied by equivalent requirements of FRS 102 but cautions that entities will need to take care to ensure appropriate disclosure of derivatives is provided. *[FRS 102 Appendix III.12D]*.

Chapter 3

Disclosures are required of: *[1 Sch 55, 1 Sch 53 (LLP)]*

- the significant assumptions underlying the valuation models and techniques used when determining the fair value of the instruments;
- for each category of financial instrument, the fair value of the [instruments] in that category and the changes in value:
  - included directly in the profit and loss account; or
  - credited to or (as the case may be) debited from the fair value reserve;
- for each class of derivatives, the extent and nature of the instruments, including significant terms and conditions that may affect the timing and certainty of future cash flows; and
- a tabular disclosure of amounts transferred to or from the fair value reserve reconciling the opening and closing balance of the reserve, showing the amount transferred to or from the reserve during the year and the source and application of the amounts so transferred.

While the Regulations refer to 'assets' rather than 'instruments' in the second bullet above, this appears to be a typographical error.

There are, however, other differences in the disclosures between FRS 102 and the Regulations. For example, the Regulations contain disclosures concerning investments and loans that have not been included in FRS 102. *[1 Sch 50, 1 Sch 54, 1 Sch 61, 1 Sch 48 (LLP), 1 Sch 52 (LLP), 1 Sch 59 (LLP)]*. Care is needed to ensure compliance with the statutory requirements in addition to the disclosures listed in the standard. See Chapter 10 at 11.2.5 for further statutory disclosures for financial instruments required in the accounts of a UK company.

In addition, the Regulations require that the directors' report of a UK company should contain, in relation to the use of financial instruments, an indication of the financial risk management objectives, policies (including the policy for hedging each major type of forecasted transaction for which hedge accounting is used) and the exposure of the company to price risk, credit risk, liquidity risk and cash flow risk, unless not material. In respect of a group directors' report, this information is required for the company and its consolidated subsidiary undertakings. *[7 Sch 6]*. These requirements do not apply to LLPs.

3.3.3   *Share-based payment*

This exemption removes all the disclosure requirements of Section 26 except for the following:

- a description of each type of share-based payment arrangements that existed at any time during the period, including the general terms and conditions of each arrangement, such as vesting requirements, the maximum term of options granted, and the method of settlement (e.g. whether in cash or equity). An entity with substantially similar types of share-based payment arrangement may aggregate this information; *[FRS 102.26.18(a)]* and
- if the entity is part of a group share-based payment plan, and it recognises and measures its share-based payment expense on the basis of a reasonable allocation of the expense recognised for the group, it shall disclose that fact and the basis for the allocation (addressed further in paragraph 26.16). *[FRS 102.26.22]*.

3.3.4   *Related party transactions*

This exemption removes the requirement to disclose key management personnel compensation in total. *[FRS 102.1.12(e)]*.

3.4   Disclosures required by the Regulations in the financial statements for certain financial instruments held at fair value

As set out in 3.3 above, a qualifying entity may take advantage of the following disclosure exemptions for financial instruments in its individual financial statements, the requirements of: *[FRS 102.1.8, 1.9, 1.12]*

- Section 11, paragraphs 11.42, 11.44, 11.45, 11.47, 11.48(a)(iii), 11.48(a)(iv), 11.48(b) and 11.48(c); and

- Section 12, paragraphs 12.26 (in relation to those cross-referenced paragraphs from which a disclosure exemption is available), 12.27, 12.29(a), 12.29(b) and 12.29A.

Financial institutions are in any event required to give the disclosures required by Section 11 and Section 12, although care may be required in order to comply with the statutory requirements (see 3.5 below for further discussion). All qualifying entities must now make the disclosures required by paragraph 41 of Section 11 (as amended by the Triennial review 2017), requiring an entity to show separately the carrying amounts at the reporting date of financial assets and liabilities measured at fair value through profit or loss.

The Triennial review 2017 has also removed a requirement for a qualifying entity that is not a financial institution to apply the disclosure requirements of Section 11 to those financial instruments held at fair value subject to the requirements of paragraph 36(4) of Schedule 1 to the Regulations (and its equivalents). However, the disclosures required by paragraph 36(4) of Schedule 1 to the Regulations (and its equivalents) will still need to be given.

See 3.4.1 below for a discussion of which financial instruments are held at fair value in accordance with paragraph 36(4) of Schedule 1 to the Regulations (and its equivalents).

See 3.4.2 below for a discussion of the disclosure requirements where financial instruments are held at fair value in accordance with paragraph 36(4) of Schedule 1 to the Regulations (and its equivalents).

3.4.1   *Which financial instruments may be included at fair value in accordance with paragraph 36(4) of Schedule 1 to the Regulations?*

Paragraph 36 of Schedule 1 to the Regulations (and its equivalents in Schedules 2 and 3 to the Regulations, the Small Companies Regulations, LLP Regulations and Small LLP Regulations) allow financial instruments to be included in the financial statements at fair value, where their fair value can be measured reliably, but paragraphs 36(2) and 36(3) exclude certain types of financial instruments, unless these are permitted to be held at fair value by paragraph 36(4). *[1 Sch 36, 2 Sch 44, 3 Sch 30, 1 Sch 36 (SC), 1 Sch 36 (LLP), 1 Sch 36 (LLP SC)]*.

Paragraph 36(4) of Schedule 1 to the Regulations (and its equivalents) state that 'financial instruments which under international accounting standards may be included in accounts at fair value, may be so included, provided that the disclosures required by such accounting standards are made.' *[1 Sch 36(4), 1 Sch 36(4) (LLP)]*.

The reference to 'international accounting standards' in this context would mean EU-adopted IFRS. *[s474, s 474(LLP)]*. Accordingly, reference is made to extant EU-adopted IFRS in determining whether certain financial instruments may be held at fair value and the required disclosures.

Financial instruments listed in paragraphs 36(2)(c) and 36(3) of Schedule 1 to the Regulations (and its equivalents) are as follows:

- financial liabilities, unless they are held as part of a trading portfolio or are derivatives;
- financial instruments (other than derivatives) held to maturity;
- loans and receivables originated by the company (or the LLP) and not held for trading purposes;
- interests in subsidiary undertakings, associated undertakings and joint ventures;
- equity instruments issued by the company (or the LLP);
- contracts for contingent consideration in a business combination; or
- other financial instruments with such special characteristics that the instruments according to generally accepted accounting principles or practice, should be accounted for differently from other financial instruments. *[1 Sch 36(2)-36(3), 1 Sch 36(2) (LLP)-36(3) (LLP)]*.

FRS 102 allows a choice of applying either IAS 39, IFRS 9, or Sections 11 and 12 in the recognition and measurement of financial instruments. The situations in which financial instruments are carried at fair value under FRS 102 will differ depending on the choice taken. Following the adoption by the EU of IFRS 9, this standard is now the principal point of reference for which financial instruments may be included in the accounts at fair value when referring to paragraph 36(4) of Schedule I to the Regulations.

Furthermore, the Regulations (and its equivalents) were written with the application of the previously extant IAS 39 in mind. Terms such as 'loans and receivables', 'held to maturity' and 'held for trading' are not defined in FRS 102. The Regulations indicate that these terms are defined in the Accounting Directive (Directive 2013/34/EU) and Directive 91/674/EEC (for insurance undertakings) and in paragraph 96 of Schedule 2 to the Regulations (for banking companies). *[10 Sch 3(1), 4 Sch 2(1) (LLP)]*. Some of these terms are no longer used in IFRS 9 and therefore it would be necessary to refer back to definitions under the version of IAS 39 extant immediately before the introduction of IFRS 9.

Sections 11 and 12, where applied to the recognition and measurement of financial instruments, distinguish between basic and other financial instruments. These requirements differ significantly to those of IAS 39 and IFRS 9. Most basic financial instruments (with certain exceptions) are carried at cost or amortised cost, whereas other financial instruments are carried at fair value through profit or loss. For other financial instruments, Section 12 does not permit measurement at fair value through profit or loss where this is not permitted by the Regulations (and its equivalents). *[FRS 102.12.8(c)]*. Hence the potential for conflict between Sections 11 and 12 and the Regulations (and its equivalents) over financial instruments permitted to be carried at fair value should be limited. See Chapter 10 at 6 for a discussion of the classification and measurement of financial instruments and which financial instruments may be held at fair value under Sections 11 and 12.

Financial instruments that are held at fair value subject to paragraph 36(4) of Schedule 1 to the Regulations (and its equivalents) in FRS 102 financial statements (under any of the accounting choices) therefore include:

(a) financial liabilities (which are not held as part of a trading portfolio nor derivatives) that are designated at fair value through profit or loss – because this eliminates or significantly reduces an 'accounting mismatch' or a group of financial assets and/or financial liabilities is managed and its performance evaluated on a fair value basis (IAS 39, IFRS 9 and Section 11 have similar but not identically worded provisions); *[IAS 39.9, IFRS 9.4.2.2, FRS 102.11.14(b)]*

(b) where Section 11 is applied, financial liabilities (which are not held as part of a trading portfolio nor derivatives) that do not qualify as basic financial instruments, but would meet the conditions to be measured or designated at fair value through profit or loss under EU-adopted IFRS (i.e. under paragraphs 4.3.5 and 4.3.6 of IFRS 9); *[IFRS 9.4.2.2, 4.3.5-6]*

(c) where IAS 39 or IFRS 9 are applied, financial liabilities (which are not held as part of a trading portfolio nor derivatives) that are not covered by (a), but are measured or designated at fair value through profit or loss; *[IAS 39.11A, 12, IFRS 9.4.3.5-6]*

(d) financial assets, which could have been designated as held to maturity (which are not derivatives) or loans and receivables originated by the reporting entity (and which are not held for trading purposes) that:

   (i) where IAS 39 is applied, are designated at either available-for-sale or are measured or designated at fair value through profit or loss (i.e. under paragraphs 9, 11A or 12 of IAS 39) – but would meet the conditions to be measured or designated at fair value under EU-adopted IFRS; *[IAS 39.9, 11A, 12, IFRS 9.4.1.2A, 4.1.4-5, IFRS 9.4.3.5-6]*

   (ii) where Section 11 is applied, are designated at fair value through profit or loss; *[FRS 102.11.14(b)]*

   (iii) where Section 11 is applied, do not qualify as basic financial instruments but would meet the conditions to be measured or designated at fair value through profit or loss under EU-adopted IFRS); *[FRS 102.11.14(b), 12.8(c), IFRS 9.4.1.4-5, IFRS 9.4.3.5-6]*

   (iv) are measured at fair value in accordance with IFRS 9 (which is extant EU-adopted IFRS); *[IFRS 9.4.1.2A, 4.1.4-5]* and

(e) investments in subsidiaries, associated undertakings and joint ventures measured at fair value through profit or loss in consolidated or individual financial statements. *[FRS 102.9.9-9B, 9.26(c), 14.4(d), 14.4B, 15.9(d), 15.9B]*. See Chapter 8 at 3.4, 4.1 and 4.2, Chapter 12 at 3.3.1 and Chapter 13 at 3.6.2 and 3.6.3.

FRS 102 permits or requires investments in subsidiaries, associates and joint ventures to be measured at fair value in consolidated and/or individual financial statements in certain circumstances. However, where such investments are held at fair value through profit and loss, these fall within the scope of paragraph 36(4) of Schedule 1 to the Regulations (and its equivalents). The interaction with company and LLP law is explained further in Chapter 6 at 10.3.1.C.

Chapter 3

Contingent consideration arising in a business combination is not permitted to be held at fair value (whatever accounting policy choice is applied to the recognition and measurement of financial instruments). *[FRS 102.19.12-13, FRS 102.BC.A.28]*. Equity instruments are not held at fair value under Section 22 – *Liabilities and Equity*.

3.4.2   What disclosures are required by paragraph 36(4) to Schedule 1 to the Regulations?

Appendix III to FRS 102 comments that an entity applying FRS 102 and holding financial instruments measured at fair value may be required to provide the disclosures required by paragraph 36(4) of Schedule 1 to the Regulations. *[FRS 102 Appendix III.13]*.

As noted at 3.4.1 above, the disclosures required by paragraph 36(4) of Schedule 1 to the Regulations (and its equivalents) are those in extant EU-adopted IFRS, as confirmed by Appendix II – *Note on legal requirements* – to FRS 101 which addresses the same paragraph. *[FRS 101 Appendix II.7]*. The most logical interpretation of this is that an entity should make all material disclosures required by IFRS 7 – *Financial Instruments: Disclosures* – and IFRS 13 – *Fair Value Measurement* – in respect of such financial instruments.

However, Appendix III to FRS 102 states that the disclosures required by paragraph 36(4) of Schedule 1 to the Regulations have been incorporated into Section 11. Some of the disclosure requirements of Section 11 apply to all financial instruments measured at fair value, whilst others (such as paragraph 11.48A) apply only to certain financial instruments (this does not include financial instruments held as part of a trading portfolio nor derivatives). The disclosure requirements of paragraph 11.48A will predominantly apply to certain financial liabilities, however, there may be instances where paragraph 36(3) of Schedule 1 to the Regulations requires that the disclosures must also be provided in relation to financial assets, e.g. investments in subsidiaries, associates or jointly controlled entities measured at fair value through profit or loss. *[FRS 102 Appendix III.13, FRS 102.9.27B]*.

While the guidance in Appendix III above (and the amendments made to the disclosures covered by the reduced disclosure framework), implies that FRS 102 reporters complying with the disclosures included in Sections 11 and 12 will meet the disclosure requirements of paragraph 36(4) of Schedule 1 to the Regulations (and its equivalents), we consider that care needs to be taken with both the scope of the disclosures and which disclosures are required. In any event, FRS 102 reminds entities that they must ensure that they comply with any relevant legal requirements applicable to them and that the standard does not necessarily contain all legal disclosure requirements. *[FRS 102.1.2A]*.

The disclosure requirements of Sections 11 and 12 apply to financial instruments within the scope of whichever accounting standard is applied for the recognition and measurement of financial instruments. *[FRS 102.11.1, 11.7, 12.1, 12.3, 12.26]*.

Paragraph 11.48A, which is excluded from the disclosure exemptions in the reduced disclosure framework, has a more restricted scope. It states that: 'An entity, *including an entity that is not a company*, shall provide the following disclosures only for financial instruments measured at *fair value through profit or loss in accordance with paragraph 36(4) of Schedule 1 to the Regulations*. This does not include financial liabilities held as part of a trading portfolio nor derivatives.' [emphasis added]. *[FRS 102.11.48A]*.

However, the reference to an 'entity, including an entity that is not a company' implies that the disclosures in paragraph 11.48A should be given by entities that are not subject to the statutory requirements in paragraph 36(4) of Schedule 1 to the Regulations (or its equivalents) if they hold financial instruments that would fall within that paragraph as if the entity had been a UK company.

FRS 102 also requires a parent adopting a policy of accounting for its investments in subsidiaries, associates or jointly controlled entities at fair value through profit or loss in its separate financial statements to comply with the requirements of paragraph 36(4) of Schedule 1 to the Regulations by applying the disclosure requirements of Section 11 to those investments. *[FRS 102.9.27B]*. This means that all applicable disclosures in Section 11 must be given in respect of those investments. In our view, the same requirement would also apply where investments in subsidiaries, associates or jointly controlled entities are held at fair value through profit or loss in the consolidated financial statements or in the individual financial statements of an investor or venturer (that is not a parent).

Care should also be taken where IAS 39 or IFRS 9 is applied to the recognition and measurement of financial instruments, as financial instruments held at fair value (but not through profit or loss) may in principle be held at fair value subject to paragraph 36(4) of Schedule 1 to the Regulations (or its equivalents). Examples might include an available-for-sale financial asset or debt instrument at fair value through other comprehensive income that falls within the financial instruments listed in paragraph 36(3). Section 11 and Section 12's disclosure requirements for financial instruments at fair value, including paragraph 11.48A, are generally framed in respect of financial instruments at fair value through profit or loss (and therefore may not capture all financial instruments for which disclosures are required – see Chapter 10 at 11.2).

3.5   Entities that are financial institutions

A qualifying entity that is a financial institution (see 2.5.1.A above) may take advantage in its individual financial statements of the disclosure exemptions set out in 3.3 above, except for the disclosure exemptions from Sections 11 and 12. *[FRS 102.1.9]*.

Where an entity has financial instruments held at fair value subject to the requirements of paragraph 36(4) of Schedule 1 to the Regulations (or its equivalents), it is required to give the disclosures required by extant IFRSs adopted by the EU. The FRC has identified these disclosures as being the disclosure requirements of Section 11. Since financial institutions do not benefit from disclosure exemptions in respect of Section 11, under the reduced disclosure framework, this implies that financial institutions will already be giving the required disclosures in respect of financial instruments. However, in our view, care needs to be taken with both the scope of the disclosures and which disclosures are required. This is particularly relevant where investments in subsidiaries, associates and joint ventures are measured at fair value through profit or loss or where IFRS 9 or IAS 39 is applied to the recognition and measurement of financial instruments. See 3.4 above.

An entity that is a financial institution must also give the disclosures set out in Section 34 for financial institutions (see 2.5.1 above).

Qualifying entities must also ensure that they comply with any relevant legal requirements. FRS 102 does not necessarily contain all legal disclosure requirements. *[FRS 102.1.2A]*.

Chapter 3

Therefore, an entity subject to these statutory requirements must also give the disclosures required by the CA 2006 and the Regulations (or the Small Companies Regulations, LLP Regulations or Small LLP Regulations). See 3.3.2.A above.

3.6   Equivalent disclosures

The disclosure exemptions in respect of financial instruments and share-based payments set out in paragraphs 1.12(c) and (d) respectively of FRS 102 are dependent on the provision of 'equivalent' disclosures in the publicly available consolidated financial statements of the parent in which the qualifying entity is included.

FRS 102 refers to the Application Guidance in FRS 100 in deciding whether the consolidated financial statements of the group in which the reporting entity is included provides disclosures that are 'equivalent' to the requirements of FRS 102 from which relief is provided. *[FRS 102.1.13]*.

The Application Guidance in FRS 100 states that:

- it is necessary to consider whether the consolidated financial statements of the parent provide disclosures that meet the basic disclosure requirements of the relevant standard or interpretation without regarding strict conformity with each and every disclosure. This assessment should be based on the particular facts, including the similarities to and differences from the requirements of the relevant standard from which relief is provided. 'Equivalence' is intended to be aligned to that described in section 401 of the CA 2006 (see Chapter 8 at 3.1.1.C and 3.1.6 above); *[FRS 100.AG8-9]* and

- disclosure exemptions for subsidiaries are permitted where the relevant disclosure requirements are met in the consolidated financial statements, even where the disclosures are made in aggregate or in an abbreviated form, or in relation to intra-group balances, those intra-group balances have been eliminated on consolidation. If, however, no disclosure is made in the consolidated financial statements on the grounds of materiality, the relevant disclosures should be made at the subsidiary level if material in those financial statements. *[FRS 100.AG10]*.

This means that a qualifying entity must review the consolidated financial statements of its parent to ensure that 'equivalent' disclosures have been made for each of the above exemptions that it intends to use. Where a particular 'equivalent' disclosure has not been made (unless the disclosure relates to an intra-group balance eliminated on consolidation) then the qualifying subsidiary cannot use the exemption in respect of that disclosure.

4   CA 2006 REQUIREMENTS

The requirements of the CA 2006 (and certain other regulatory rules) governing preparation of financial statements by UK companies are addressed in Chapter 1 at 6. See also 2.1 above for the requirements for which entities can apply FRS 102.

Qualifying entities must also ensure that they comply with any relevant legal requirements. FRS 102 does not necessarily contain all legal disclosure requirements. *[FRS 102.1.2A]*.

Statutory accounts prepared by a UK company in accordance with FRS 102 are Companies Act individual or group accounts, and are therefore required to comply with the applicable provisions of Parts 15 and 16 of the CA 2006 and with the Regulations. *[FRS 102 Appendix III.7]*. These requirements include the rules on recognition and measurement, the Companies Act accounts formats and note disclosures (see Chapter 6). While Appendix III to FRS 102, when discussing legal requirements relevant to FRS 102 financial statements, generally refers to specific provisions of Schedule 1 to the Regulations, entities applying Schedules 2, 3 or 6 to the Regulations should read such references as referring to the equivalent paragraph in those schedules. *[FRS 102 Appendix III.3]*.

Similar provisions (to those for UK companies) also apply to LLPs in Schedule 1 to the LLP Regulations or Schedule 1 to the Small LLP Regulations.

Appendix III states that it does not list every legal requirement but instead focuses on those areas where greater judgement might be required in determining compliance with the law. *[FRS 102 Appendix III.11]*. It notes that the standard 'is not intended to be a one-stop-shop for all accounting and legal requirements, and although the FRC believes the FRS 102 is not inconsistent with company law, compliance with FRS 102 alone will often be insufficient to ensure compliance with all the disclosure requirements set out in the Act and the Regulations. As a result preparers will continue to be required to have regard to the requirements of company law in addition to accounting standards.' *[FRS 102 Appendix III.10]*.

4.1 Small and medium-sized entities

This section is relevant to small and medium-sized companies and LLPs that do not apply Section 1A of FRS 102. The requirements for entities applying Section 1A are covered in Chapter 5.

While this section refers to companies and LLPs, there are equivalent provisions for a qualifying partnership preparing the 'like accounts and reports', as if a UK company, in accordance with the *Partnerships (Accounts) Regulations 2008*. See Chapter 6 at 4.2.4.

4.1.1 Small companies regime, small LLPs regime and small companies exemption

A UK company subject to the small companies regime (or an LLP subject to the small LLPs regime) can apply the Small Companies Regulations (or the Small LLP Regulations) and is exempt from the requirement to prepare group accounts and from giving certain disclosures required in the notes to the financial statements by Part 15 of the CA 2006. LLPs subject to the small LLPs regime are exempt from the requirement to prepare group accounts.

A UK company that takes advantage of the small companies exemption is not required to prepare a strategic report, *[s414A]*, and is entitled to certain disclosure exemptions in the directors' report. *[s415A]*. LLPs are not required to prepare a directors' report or strategic report and there is, therefore, no equivalent of the small companies exemption for LLPs. Some LLPs choose to prepare a separate members' report but this is not a statutory requirement; while the LLP SORP includes certain disclosures (such as principal activities, a list of designated members etc.) that could be included in such a report, the disclosures may be presented anywhere in the annual report. *[LLP SORP.30-31]*.

A UK company subject to the small companies regime or taking advantage of the small companies exemption is entitled to certain filing exemptions. An LLP subject to the small LLPs regime is also entitled to filing exemptions. The criteria for use of the small companies regime, small LLPs regime and the small companies exemption (which has a wider scope than the small companies regime), together with the exemptions available, are discussed in Chapter 5 at 4 and 12.

FRS 102 (where Section 1A is not applied) requires use of the profit and loss account and balance sheet formats included in Part 1 'General Rules and Formats' of Schedule 1 (or where applicable, Schedule 2 or Schedule 3) to the Regulations or Part 1 'General Rules and Formats' of Schedule 1 to the LLP Regulations. As explained in Chapter 6 at 4, there is a choice of adapted formats or statutory formats where Schedule 1 to the Regulations or the LLP Regulations are applied. Unless Section 1A is applied, a small company or small LLP is not permitted to use the formats included in Part 1 'General Rules and Formats' of Schedule 1 to the Small Companies Regulations or Part 1 'General Rules and Formats' of Schedule 1 to the Small LLP Regulations.

However, our view is that companies and LLPs applying FRS 102 (but not Section 1A) are not prevented from taking advantage of other exemptions applicable to companies subject to the small companies regime or LLPs subject to the small LLPs regime. This is because regulation 3(3) of the Small Companies Regulations specifically states that 'Accounts are treated as having complied with any provision of Schedule 1 to these Regulations if they comply instead with the corresponding provision of Schedule 1 to *The Large and Medium-sized Companies and Groups (Accounts and Reports) Regulations 2008*.' Regulation 8(2) of the Small Companies Regulations makes a similar statement in respect of the group accounts formats included in Schedule 6 to the Small Companies Regulations and Schedule 6 to the Regulations. *[Regulations SC 3(3), 8(2)]*. For LLPs, the corresponding statements are made in paragraphs 3(1) and 6(1) of the Small LLP Regulations. *[LLP SC Regulations 3(1), 6(1)]*.

4.1.2   Medium-sized companies and LLPs

A medium-sized company (or LLP) may take advantage of certain disclosure exemptions for a financial year in which the company (or the LLP) qualifies as medium-sized and is not an excluded company (or LLP) (see Chapter 1 at 6.6). *[s465-s467, s465 (LLP)-s467 (LLP)]*. The exemptions for medium-sized companies impacting the strategic report (not to disclose non-financial KPIs) are not relevant for LLPs.

Companies (or LLPs) applying FRS 102 can make use of these exemptions to the extent they do not conflict with accounting standards, e.g. medium-sized companies would need to give related party disclosures in individual financial statements because this is required by FRS 102 notwithstanding the exemption in the Regulations. *[Regulations 4(2B), LLP Regulations 4(2B)]*.

References

1 *The Financial Reporting Council: The True and Fair Requirement Revisited* – Opinion by Martin Moore QC, May 2008, para. 4(F).

Chapter 4

Concepts and pervasive principles

Chapter 4

Concepts and pervasive principles

1 INTRODUCTION

Section 2 – *Concepts and Pervasive Principles* – sets out the objectives of the financial statements of entities within the scope of FRS 102 and the qualities that make those financial statements useful. It also sets out the concepts and basic principles underlying the financial statements of entities within the scope of FRS 102. *[FRS 102.2.1]*.

Section 2 is FRS 102's equivalent of the IFRS Conceptual Framework for Financial Reporting. An updated IFRS Conceptual Framework was published in March 2018, replacing the 2010 version, and has been in use by the International Accounting Standards Board (IASB) from that date, though preparers are not required to use the updated framework until January 2020. Section 2 is not a statement or framework as such but a list of concepts and pervasive principles that underlie the Standard. The concepts and pervasive principles are largely derived from the equivalent concepts and pervasive principles section in the IFRS for SMEs. However, there are some differences in wording.

Section 2 affects recognition and measurement only when FRS 102 or a Statement of Recommended Practice (SORP) does not specifically address the accounting for a transaction, other event or condition. In the absence of such guidance, management has to refer to the definitions, recognition criteria and measurement concepts for assets, liabilities, income and expenses and the pervasive principles within Section 2 in using its judgment in developing and applying a relevant and reliable accounting policy for that transaction, other event or condition. *[FRS 102.10.4-5]*.

In recognition of this hierarchy of sources, it is reiterated that where there is an inconsistency between the concepts and principles in Section 2 and the specific requirements of another section of FRS 102, then the specific requirements of that other section take precedence. *[FRS 102.2.1A]*.

Section 2 introduces a number of definitions which are discussed separately below.

2 COMPARISON BETWEEN SECTION 2 AND IFRS

There are some differences between the concepts and pervasive principles of FRS 102 and the IFRS Conceptual Framework for Financial Reporting published in March 2018 (the IFRS Conceptual Framework). Furthermore, FRS 102 does not address all the concepts covered by the IFRS Conceptual Framework – for example the concepts of capital and capital maintenance. However, these differences and lacunae are unlikely to result in any recognition and measurement differences in practice since the definitions that actually affect amounts reported in the financial statements are virtually identical.

The main conceptual difference is that Section 2 does not identify any of its qualitative characteristics of information in financial statements as 'fundamental', 'enhancing' or otherwise assign priority. FRS 102 sets out ten qualitative characteristics, none of which are given precedence over the others. The IFRS Conceptual Framework identifies two fundamental qualitative characteristics, relevance, including materiality, and faithful representation as well as four enhancing qualitative characteristics, comparability, verifiability, timeliness and understandability.[1] Neither faithful representation, nor its related qualitative characteristic, verifiability, are qualitative characteristics of FRS 102. However, in terms of financial reporting, this difference of emphasis has little, if any, practical impact.

Section 2 defines stewardship as the 'accountability of management for the resources entrusted to it'. The 2010 version of the IFRS Conceptual Framework did not use the term 'stewardship' because of the difficulty in translating the concept. The term 'stewardship' has now been explicitly reintroduced into the IFRS Conceptual Framework, though a definition of the term is not provided. The framework instead contains a description of what stewardship encapsulates: 'Information about how efficiently and effectively the reporting entity's management has discharged its responsibilities to use the entity's economic resources...' The IFRS Conceptual Framework gives examples of management's responsibilities to use the entity's economic resources: protecting those resources from unfavourable effects of economic factors, such as price and technological changes and ensuring the entity complies with applicable laws, regulations and contractual provisions. Despite the longer exposition of the meaning of stewardship in the IFRS Conceptual framework, we do not believe that there is any conceptual difference between FRS 102 and the IFRS Conceptual Framework.[2]

3   THE CONCEPTS AND PERVASIVE PRINCIPLES OF SECTION 2

Section 2 explains the objective of financial statements, the qualitative characteristics of information in financial statements, the financial position of an entity, performance, and the recognition and measurement principles of assets, liabilities, income and expenses. Each of these is discussed below.

3.1   Objective of financial statements

There are two overriding objectives of financial statements:

- to provide information about the financial position, performance and cash flows of an entity that is useful for economic decision-making by a broad range of users who are not in a position to demand reports tailored to meet their particular information needs; and

- to show the results of the stewardship of management – the accountability of management for the resources entrusted to it. *[FRS 102.2.2-3]*.

These objectives are broader than the IFRS Conceptual Framework which limits users to potential investors, lenders and other creditors. In contrast, there is no limit put on the 'broad range of users' by Section 2.

The inclusion of stewardship as an objective of financial reporting in FRS 102 is consistent with past publications of the ASB (the predecessor body to the FRC). In June 2007, the ASB and others published a paper discussing the rationale for including stewardship, or directors' accountability to shareholders, as a separate objective of financial reporting.[3]

The inclusion of both of these objectives in FRS 102 is an attempt to reconcile two differing strands of thought regarding the purpose of financial statements; the view that financial statements are forward-looking, assisting a user in making economic decisions about future interactions with the entity and the view that financial statements are backward-looking, recording past performance, based on the effectiveness of management's stewardship of the economic resources entrusted to it.

3.2 Qualitative characteristics of information in financial statements

Section 2 identifies ten qualitative characteristics of information in financial statements. It does not describe any of these qualitative characteristics as 'fundamental', 'key' or otherwise assign priority. However, the language that describes the qualitative characteristics places emphasis on how those qualitative characteristics make financial statements relevant and reliable.

Going concern is not one of the qualitative characteristics identified by Section 2. The subject of going concern is addressed separately in Section 3 – *Financial Statement Presentation* (see Chapter 6 at 9.3).

Each of FRS 102's ten qualitative characteristics are discussed in sections 3.2.1 to 3.2.10 below.

3.2.1 Understandability

Understandability is described as the presentation of information in a way that makes it comprehensible by users who have a reasonable knowledge of business and economic activities and accounting and a willingness to study the information with reasonable diligence. However, the need for understandability does not allow relevant information to be omitted on the grounds that it may be too difficult for some. *[FRS 102.2.4]*.

3.2.2 Relevance

Relevance is described as the quality of information that allows it to influence the economic decisions of users by helping them evaluate past, present or future events or confirming, or correcting their past evaluations. Information provided in financial statements must be relevant to the decision-making needs of users. *[FRS 102.2.5]*.

Where FRS 102 does not specifically address a transaction, other event or condition, Section 10 – *Accounting Policies, Estimates and Errors* – requires an entity's management to use its judgement in developing and applying an accounting policy that results in information that is both relevant to the economic decision-making needs of users and reliable. *[FRS 102.10.4]*.

3.2.3   *Materiality*

Section 2 states that information is material – and therefore has relevance – if its omission or misstatement, individually or collectively, could influence the economic decisions of users taken on the basis of the financial statements. *Materiality* depends on the size and nature of the omission or misstatement judged in the surrounding circumstances. The size or nature of the item, or a combination of both, could be the determining factor. However, it is inappropriate to make, or leave uncorrected, immaterial departures from FRS 102 to achieve a particular presentation of an entity's financial position, financial performance or cash flows. *[FRS 102.2.6].*

The ICAEW issued a technical release in June 2008, TECH 03/08 – *Guidance on Materiality in Financial Reporting by UK Entities,* which considers the issue of materiality in financial reporting and is intended to help with the practical application of the definition and explanations of materiality. It describes the determinants of materiality as the size and nature of an item, judged in the particular circumstances of the case.

3.2.4   *Reliability*

Reliability is defined as the quality of information that makes it free from material error and bias and represents faithfully that which it either purports to represent or could reasonably be expected to represent. Information provided in financial statements must be reliable. Financial statements are not free from bias (i.e. not neutral) if, by the selection or presentation of information, they are intended to influence the making of a decision or judgement in order to achieve a predetermined result or outcome. *[FRS 102.2.7].*

Where FRS 102 does not specifically address a transaction, other event or condition, Section 10 of FRS 102 requires an entity's management to use its judgement in developing and applying an accounting policy that results in information that is both relevant and reliable. *[FRS 102.10.4].*

Section 10 of FRS 102 further states that for information to be reliable, financial statements should:

- represent faithfully the financial position, financial performance and cash flows of the entity;
- reflect the economic substance of transactions, other events and conditions and not merely their legal form;
- be neutral, i.e. free from bias;
- be prudent; and
- be complete in all material respects. *[FRS 102.10.4].*

There may sometimes be a tension between 'neutrality' and 'prudence'. On the one hand, financial statements must be free from bias, i.e. neutral. On the other hand, they must also be prudent, i.e. prepared with a degree of caution such that assets or income are not overstated and liabilities or expenses are not understated. See 3.2.6 below.

'Completeness' is discussed at 3.2.7 below.

3.2.5 *Substance over form*

Transactions and other events and conditions should be accounted for and presented in accordance with their substance and not merely their legal form. This enhances the reliability of financial statements. *[FRS 102.2.8]*.

Substance over form is also a requirement of UK company law and is required by both *The Large and Medium-sized Companies and Groups (Accounts and reports) Regulations 2008 (SI 2008/410)* (the Regulations) and *The Small Companies and Groups (Accounts and Directors' Report) Regulations 2008 (SI 2008/409)* (the Small Companies' Regulations). *[1 Sch 9, 2 Sch 10, 3 Sch 8, 1 Sch 9 (SC)]*.

3.2.6 *Prudence*

Prudence is the inclusion of a degree of caution in the exercise of the judgements needed in making the estimates required under conditions of uncertainty, such that assets or income are not overstated and liabilities or expenses are not understated. The uncertainties that will inevitably surround many events and circumstances are acknowledged by the disclosure of their nature and extent and by the exercise of prudence in the preparation of the financial statements. However, the exercise of prudence does not allow the deliberate understatement of assets or income, or the deliberate overstatement of liabilities or expenses. In short, prudence does not permit bias. *[FRS 102.2.9]*.

For UK companies, the Regulations also require that the amount of any item must be determined on a prudent basis. In particular, only profits realised at the balance sheet date are to be included in the profit and loss account and all liabilities which have arisen in respect of the financial year in which the accounts relate or a previous financial year must be taken into account including those which only become apparent between the balance sheet date and the date on which it is signed on behalf of the board of directors in accordance with section 414 of the Companies Act 2006 (CA 2006). *[1 Sch 13, 2 Sch 19, 3 Sch 18, 1 Sch 13 (SC)]*.

3.2.7 *Completeness*

To be reliable, the information in financial statements must be complete within the bounds of materiality and cost. An omission can cause information to be false or misleading and thus unreliable and deficient in terms of its relevance. *[FRS 102.2.10]*.

3.2.8 *Comparability*

Users must be able to compare the financial statements of an entity through time to identify trends in its financial position and performance. Users must also be able to compare the financial statements of different entities to evaluate their relative financial position, performance and cash flows. Hence, the measurement and display of the financial effects of like transactions and other events and conditions must be carried out in a consistent way throughout an entity and over time for that entity, and in a consistent way across entities. In addition, users must be informed of the accounting policies employed in the preparation of the financial statements, and of any changes in those policies and the effects of such changes. *[FRS 102.2.11]*.

There is more detailed guidance on comparability in Section 10 which requires an entity to select and apply its accounting policies consistently for similar transactions, other events or obligations unless an FRS or FRC Abstract specifically requires or permits

Chapter 4

categorisation of items for which different policies may be appropriate. *[FRS 102.10.7]*. Section 8 – *Notes to the Financial Statements* – requires an entity to disclose a summary of significant accounting policies, *[FRS 102.8.4(b)]*, and Section 10 requires disclosures where there are changes in accounting policies. *[FRS 102.10.13-14]*.

3.2.9   Timeliness

To be relevant, financial information must be able to influence the economic decisions of users. *Timeliness* means providing the information within the decision time frame. If there is undue delay in the reporting of information it may lose its relevance. Management may need to balance the relative merits of timely reporting and the provision of reliable information. In achieving a balance between relevance and reliability, the overriding consideration is how best to satisfy the needs of users in making economic decisions. *[FRS 102.2.12]*.

UK companies are required by law to file accounts within specified time limits. For a private company, the period allowed by the CA 2006 for filing financial statements is nine months after the end of the relevant accounting reference period and, for a public company, the period allowed for filing is six months after the end of the relevant accounting reference period. *[s442]*.

3.2.10   Balance between benefit and cost

Section 2 states that the benefits derived from information should exceed the cost of providing it. It is further stated that the evaluation of benefits and costs is substantially a judgemental process. Furthermore, the costs are not necessarily borne by those users who enjoy the benefits, and often the benefits of the information are enjoyed by a broad range of external users. *[FRS 102.2.13]*.

Section 2 also asserts that financial reporting information helps capital providers make better decisions, which results in more efficient functioning of capital markets and a lower cost of capital for the economy as a whole. In the FRC's view, individual entities also enjoy benefits, including improved access to capital markets, favourable effect on public relations, and perhaps lower costs of capital. The benefits may also include better management decisions because financial information used internally is often based at least partly on information prepared for general purpose financial reporting purposes. *[FRS 102.2.14]*.

3.3   Financial position

Section 2 defines the concepts behind the statement of financial position and the statement of comprehensive income. It does not define the concepts behind the other primary statements (the statement of changes in equity and the statement of cash flows).

The *statement of financial position* is a financial statement that presents the relationship of an entity's assets, liabilities and equity as of a specific date. The CA 2006 refers to this financial statement as a balance sheet. *[FRS 102 Appendix I]*.

Assets, liabilities and equity are defined as follows:

- an asset is a resource controlled by the entity as a result of past events and from which future economic benefits are expected to flow to the entity – see 3.3.1 below;

- a liability is a present obligation of the entity arising from past events, the settlement of which is expected to result in an outflow from the entity of resources embodying economic benefits – see 3.3.2 below; and

- equity is the residual interest in the assets of the entity after deducting all its liabilities – see 3.3.3 below. *[FRS 102.2.15]*.

Some items that meet the definition of an asset or a liability may not be recognised as assets or liabilities in the statement of financial position because they do not satisfy the criteria for recognition – see 3.5 below. In particular, the expectation that future economic benefits will flow to or from an entity must be sufficiently certain to meet the probability criterion before an asset or liability is recognised. *[FRS 102.2.16]*.

In addition, FRS 102 does not generally allow the recognition of items in the statement of financial position that do not meet the definition of assets or liabilities regardless of whether they result from applying the notion commonly referred to as the 'matching concept' for measuring profit or loss – see 3.9.5 below.

3.3.1   Assets

The future economic benefit of an asset is its potential to contribute, directly or indirectly, to the flow of cash and cash equivalents to the entity. Those cash flows may come from using the asset or from disposing of it. *[FRS 102.2.17]*.

Many assets, for example property, plant and equipment, have a physical form. However, physical form is not essential to the existence of an asset. Some assets are intangible. *[FRS 102.2.18]*.

In determining the existence of an asset, the right of ownership is not essential. Thus, for example, property held on a lease is an asset if the entity controls the benefits that are expected to flow from the property. *[FRS 102.2.19]*.

3.3.2   Liabilities

An essential characteristic of a liability is that the entity has a present obligation to act or perform in a particular way. The obligation may be either a legal obligation or a constructive obligation. A legal obligation is legally enforceable as a consequence of a binding contract or statutory requirement. A constructive obligation is an obligation that derives from an entity's actions when:

- by an established pattern of past practice, published policies or a sufficiently specific current statement, the entity has indicated to other parties that it will accept certain responsibilities; and

- as a result, the entity has created a valid expectation on the part of those other parties that it will discharge those responsibilities. *[FRS 102.2.20]*.

The settlement of a present obligation usually involves the payment of cash, transfer of other assets, provision of services, the replacement of that obligation with another obligation, or conversion of the obligation to equity. An obligation may also be extinguished by other means, such as a creditor waiving or forfeiting its rights. *[FRS 102.2.21]*.

Chapter 4

3.3.3   Equity

As equity is simply a residual figure, FRS 102 does not require that it be subdivided into any particular components although it is suggested that sub-classifications for a corporate entity may include funds contributed by shareholders, retained earnings and gains or losses recognised in other comprehensive income. *[FRS 102.2.22]*.

However, for a UK company, the balance sheet formats of the Regulations require separate disclosure of various elements of equity. These separate components are: called up share capital; share premium account; revaluation reserve; capital redemption reserve; reserve for own shares; reserves provided by articles of association; fair value reserve, other reserves and the profit and loss account (or retained earnings).

Section 6 – *Statement of Changes in Equity and Statement of Income and Retained Earnings* – requires a reconciliation of each component of equity separately disclosing changes resulting from profit or loss, other comprehensive income and other transactions. An analysis of other comprehensive income by item for each component of equity is also required. *[FRS 102.6.3-3A]*.

3.4   Performance

Performance is described as the relationship of the income and expenses of an entity during a reporting period. FRS 102 permits entities to present performance in a single financial statement (a statement of comprehensive income) or in two financial statements (an income statement and a statement of comprehensive income). *[FRS 102.2.23]*. Section 2 states that total comprehensive income and profit or loss are frequently used as measures of performance or as the basis for other measures, such as return on investment or earnings per share.

Income and expenses are defined as follows:

- income is increases in economic benefits during the reporting period in the form of inflows or enhancements of assets or decreases of liabilities that result in increases in equity, other than those relating to contributions from equity investors; and

- expenses are decreases in economic benefits during the reporting period in the form of outflows or depletions of assets or incurrences of liabilities that result in decreases in equity, other than those relating to distributions to equity investors. *[FRS 102.2.23]*.

The recognition of income and expenses results directly from the recognition and measurement of assets and liabilities. *[FRS 102.2.24]*. The definition means that any activity which does not increase or decrease an asset or liability cannot be regarded as income or expense unless specifically permitted by a section of FRS 102. Criteria for the recognition of income and expenses are discussed at 3.5 below.

3.4.1   Income

The definition of income (see 3.4 above) encompasses both revenue and gains.

Revenue is income that arises in the course of the ordinary activities of an entity and is referred to by a variety of names including sales, fees, interest, dividends, royalties and rent.

Gains are other items that meet the definition of income but are not revenue. When gains are recognised in the statement of comprehensive income, they are usually displayed separately because knowledge of them is useful for making economic decisions. *[FRS 102.2.25]*.

This split of income between revenue and gains has little meaning for accounting purposes since Section 5 – *Statement of Comprehensive Income and Income Statement* – requires that the format of the income statement should comply with the Regulations (or, where applicable, the LLP Regulations) except to the extent that these requirements are not permitted by any statutory framework under which an entity is required to report. In practice, this means that items of income which result from decreases in liabilities, for example a release of a provision, should be presented in the line item in which the cost was first recognised. *[FRS 102.5.1].*

3.4.2   Expenses

The definition of expenses encompasses losses as well as those expenses that arise in the course of the ordinary activities of the entity.

Expenses that arise in the course of the ordinary activities of the entity include, for example, cost of sales, wages and depreciation. They usually take the form of an outflow or depletion of assets such as cash and cash equivalents, inventory, or property, plant and equipment.

Losses are other items that meet the definition of expenses and may arise in the course of the ordinary activities of the entity. When losses are recognised in the statement of comprehensive income, they are usually presented separately because knowledge of them is useful for making economic decisions. *[FRS 102.2.26].*

As discussed at 3.4.1 above, this split of expenses between expenses and losses has little meaning for accounting purposes since the format of the income statement is prescribed by the Regulations.

3.5   Recognition of assets, liabilities, income and expenses

Recognition is described as the process of incorporating in the statement of financial position or statement of comprehensive income an item that meets the definition of an asset, liability, equity, income or expense (discussed at 3.9.1 to 3.9.4 below) and satisfies the following criteria:

- it is probable that any future economic benefit associated with the item will flow to or from the entity (see 3.5.1 below); and

- the item has a cost or value that can be measured reliably (see 3.5.2 below). *[FRS 102.2.27].*

The failure to recognise an item that satisfies these criteria is not rectified by disclosure of the accounting policies used or by notes or explanatory material. *[FRS 102.2.28].*

3.5.1   The probability of future economic benefit

The concept of probability is used in the first recognition criterion (see 3.5 above) to refer to the degree of uncertainty that the future economic benefits associated with the item will flow to or from the entity. Assessments of the degree of uncertainty attaching to the flow of future economic benefits are made on the basis of the evidence relating to conditions at the end of the reporting period available when the financial statements are prepared. Those assessments are made individually for individually significant items, and for a group for a large population of individually insignificant items. *[FRS 102.2.29].*

Probability as applicable to recognition in the financial statements is discussed at Section 3.9 below.

3.5.2 Reliability of measurement

The second criterion for the recognition of an item (see 3.5 above) is that it possesses a cost or value that can be measured with reliability. Reliability is discussed at 3.2.4 above.

In many cases, the cost or value of an item is known. In other cases it must be estimated. The use of reasonable estimates is an essential part of the preparation of financial statements and does not undermine their reliability. When a reasonable estimate cannot be made, the item is not recognised in the financial statements. *[FRS 102.2.30]*.

An item that fails to meet these recognition criteria may qualify for recognition at a later date as a result of subsequent circumstances or events. *[FRS 102.2.31]*.

Section 2 notes that an item that fails to meet the criteria for recognition may nonetheless warrant disclosure in the notes or explanatory material, or in supplementary schedules. This disclosure is considered appropriate when knowledge of the item is relevant to the evaluation of the financial position, performance and changes in financial position of an entity by the users of financial statements. *[FRS 102.2.32]*. It is not clear what is meant by 'explanatory material' or 'supplemental schedules' since a complete set of financial statements includes only the primary statements and the notes to the financial statements. The notes are described as comprising 'explanatory information', so it seems probable that the explanatory material referred to means explanations given in the notes to the financial statements. *[FRS 102.3.17]*.

3.6 Measurement of assets, liabilities, income and expenses

Measurement is the process of determining the monetary amounts at which an entity measures assets, liabilities, income and expenses in its financial statements. Measurement involves the selection of a basis of measurement. The various sections of FRS 102 specify (or, sometimes, allow a choice of) which measurement basis an entity shall use for many types of assets, liabilities, income and expenses. *[FRS 102.2.33]*.

Two common measurement bases used by FRS 102 are historical cost and fair value. For assets, historical cost is the amount of cash or cash equivalents paid or the fair value of the consideration given to acquire the asset at the time of its acquisition. For liabilities, historical cost is the amount of proceeds of cash or cash equivalents received or the fair value of non-cash assets received in exchange for the obligation at the time the obligation is incurred, or in some circumstances (for example, income tax) the amounts of cash or cash equivalents expected to be paid to settle the liability in the normal course of business. Amortised historical cost is the historical cost of an asset or liability plus or minus that portion of its historical cost previously recognised as an expense or income.

Fair value is the amount for which an asset could be exchanged, a liability settled, or an equity instrument granted could be exchanged, between knowledgeable, willing parties in an arm's length transaction. In the absence of any specific guidance provided in a relevant section of FRS 102, where fair value measurement is permitted or required, the guidance in the appendix to Section 2 shall be applied. *[FRS 102.2.34]*. Fair value guidance is discussed at 3.13 below.

Measurement at initial recognition is discussed at 3.10 below and subsequent measurement is discussed at 3.11 below. There is no overriding principle which determines whether historical cost or fair value is the more appropriate method of measurement.

3.7 Pervasive recognition and measurement principles

Section 2 refers to the hierarchy in Section 10 that applies for an entity to follow in deciding on the appropriate accounting policy in the absence of a requirement that applies specifically to a transaction or other event or condition. The third level of that hierarchy requires an entity to look to the definitions, recognition criteria and measurement concepts for assets, liabilities, income and expenses and the pervasive principles set out in Section 2. *[FRS 102.2.35]*. The hierarchy is discussed in Chapter 9 at 3.2.

This clarifies that guidance in Section 2 is subordinate to specific requirements in the other sections of FRS 102.

3.8 Accruals basis

Financial statements, except for cash flow information, should be prepared using the accrual basis of accounting. Under the accrual basis, items are recognised as assets, liabilities, equity, income or expenses when they satisfy the definitions and recognition criteria for those items (see 3.9 below). *[FRS 102.2.36]*.

The definition of the accrual basis is somewhat circular as it means that an item is, for example, recognised as income when it meets the definition and recognition criteria of income. The Regulations require that all income and charges relating to the financial year to which the accounts relate must be taken into account, without regard to the date or receipt of payment. *[1 Sch 14, 2 Sch 20, 3 Sch 19, 1 Sch 14 (SC)]*.

In practice, we do not expect these wording differences to have a material effect as the impact, where applicable, is likely to be similar.

3.9 Recognition in the financial statements

3.9.1 Assets

Section 2 states that an entity shall recognise an asset in the statement of financial position when it is probable that the future economic benefits will flow to the entity and the asset has a cost or value that can be measured reliably. Conversely, an asset is not recognised in the statement of financial position when expenditure has been incurred for which it is considered not probable that economic benefits will flow to the entity beyond the current reporting period. Instead such a transaction results in the recognition of an expense in the statement of comprehensive income (or in the income statement, if presented). *[FRS 102.2.37]*.

Section 2 repeats the requirements of Section 21 – *Provisions and Contingencies* – that an entity shall not recognise a contingent asset as an asset but, when the flow of future economic benefits to the entity is virtually certain, then the related asset is not a contingent asset, and its recognition is appropriate. *[FRS 102.2.38]*.

It is clear from the scope of Section 21 that the 'virtually certain' criteria applies only to contingent assets within the scope of that section. Assets arising from financial instruments and executory contracts which are not onerous are not within the scope of Section 21 and the 'probable' criterion applies to the recognition of those assets.

Chapter 4

3.9.2   Liabilities

An entity shall recognise a liability in the statement of financial position when:

- the entity has an obligation at the end of the reporting period as a result of a past event;
- it is probable that the entity will be required to transfer resources embodying economic benefits in settlement; and
- the settlement amount can be measured reliably. *[FRS 102.2.39]*.

A contingent liability is either a possible but uncertain obligation or a present obligation that is not recognised because it fails to meet one or both of the second or third conditions above. An entity should not generally recognise a contingent liability as a liability (see Chapter 19 at 3.4), except for contingent liabilities of an acquiree in a business combination (see Chapter 17 at 3.7). *[FRS 102.2.40]*.

3.9.3   Income

The recognition of income results directly from the recognition and measurement of assets and liabilities. An entity shall recognise income in the statement of comprehensive income (or in the income statement, if presented) when an increase in future economic benefits related to an increase in an asset or a decrease of a liability has arisen that can be measured reliably. *[FRS 102.2.41]*.

Although this states that the reduction of a liability is regarded as 'income', this does not mean that it should be presented as 'turnover' or 'revenue' in the statement of comprehensive income. The presentation of items in the statement of comprehensive income follows either the statutory formats required by the Regulations or LLP Regulations or the 'adapted formats'. See Chapter 6 at 6.

3.9.4   Expenses

The recognition of expenses results directly from the recognition and measurement of assets and liabilities. An entity shall recognise expenses in the statement of comprehensive income (or in the income statement, if presented) when a decrease in future economic benefits related to a decrease in an asset or an increase of a liability has arisen that can be measured reliably. *[FRS 102.2.42]*.

3.9.5   Total comprehensive income and profit or loss

Total comprehensive income is the arithmetical difference between income and expenses. It is not a separate element of financial statements, and a separate recognition principle is not needed for it. *[FRS 102.2.43]*.

Profit or loss is the arithmetical difference between income and expenses other than those items of income and expense that FRS 102 classifies as items of other comprehensive income. It is not a separate element of financial statements, and a separate recognition principle is not needed for it. *[FRS 102.2.44]*.

Generally, FRS 102 does not allow the recognition of items in the statement of financial position that do not meet the definition of assets or of liabilities regardless of whether they result from applying the notion commonly referred to as the 'matching concept' for measuring profit or loss. *[FRS 102.2.45]*.

3.10   Measurement at initial recognition

At initial recognition, an entity shall measure assets and liabilities at historical cost unless FRS 102 requires initial measurement on another basis such as fair value. *[FRS 102.2.46]*.

3.11   Subsequent measurement

3.11.1   Financial assets and financial liabilities

As discussed in Chapter 10 at 8 an entity measures basic financial assets and basic financial liabilities at amortised cost less impairment except for:

- investments in non-derivative instruments that are equity of the issuer (e.g. most ordinary shares and certain preference shares) that are publicly traded or whose fair value can otherwise be measured reliably, which are measured at fair value with changes in fair value recognised in profit or loss; and

- any financial instruments that upon their initial recognition were designated by the entity as at fair value through profit or loss. *[FRS 102.2.47]*.

An entity generally measures all other financial assets and financial liabilities at fair value, with changes in fair value recognised in profit or loss, unless FRS 102 requires or permits measurement on another basis such as cost or amortised cost. *[FRS 102.2.48]*.

3.11.2   Non-financial assets

Most non-financial assets that an entity initially recognised at historical cost are subsequently measured on other measurement bases. For example, as discussed in Chapter 15 at 3.5 and 3.6, an entity measures property, plant and equipment using either the cost model or the revaluation model and an entity measures inventories at the lower of cost and selling price less costs to complete and sell.

Measurement of assets at amounts lower than initial historical cost is intended to ensure that an asset is not measured at an amount greater than the entity expects to recover from the sale or use of that asset. *[FRS 102.2.49]*.

For certain types of non-financial assets, FRS 102 permits or requires measurement at fair value. For example:

- investments in associates and joint ventures that an entity measures at fair value (see Chapters 12 and 13);

- investment property that an entity measures at fair value (see Chapter 14);

- biological assets that an entity measures at fair value less estimated costs to sell in accordance with the fair value model and agricultural produce that an entity measures, at the point of harvest, at fair value less estimated costs to sell in accordance with either the fair value model or cost model (see Chapter 31);

- property, plant and equipment that an entity measures in accordance with the revaluation model (see Chapter 15); and

- intangible assets that an entity measures in accordance with the revaluation model (see Chapter 16). *[FRS 102.2.50]*.

Chapter 4

3.11.3   Liabilities other than financial liabilities

Most liabilities other than financial liabilities are measured at the best estimate of the amount that would be required to settle the obligation at the reporting date. *[FRS 102.2.51]*.

This wording is identical to that required for provisions by Section 21 which provides additional explanatory guidance. *[FRS 102.21.7]*. See Chapter 19.

3.12   Offsetting

An entity shall not offset assets and liabilities, or income and expenses, unless required or permitted by FRS 102. However, measuring assets net of valuation allowances (for example, allowances for inventory obsolescence and allowances for uncollectible receivables) is not offsetting. *[FRS 102.2.52]*.

If an entity's normal operating activities do not include buying and selling fixed assets, including investments and operating assets, then the entity reports gains and losses on disposal of such assets by deducting from the proceeds on disposal the carrying amount of the asset and related selling expenses. *[FRS 102.2.52]*.

This implies that no recycling of unrealised gains from a revaluation reserve within equity to profit and loss is generally permitted by FRS 102, though the gain becomes realised at the point of disposal. A reserves transfer from the revaluation reserve to retained earnings within the statement of changes in equity would be recorded. However, such recycling is permitted for the following:

- financial instruments held at available for sale, under the provisions of IAS 39 – *Financial Instruments: Recognition and Measurement* – that can be applied under Section 12 – *Other Financial Instruments Issues* – of FRS 102; *[FRS 102.12.2]*

- debt instruments carried at fair value through other comprehensive income, under the provisions of IFRS 9 – *Financial Instruments*, that can be applied under Section 12 – *Other Financial Instruments Issues* – of FRS 102; *[FRS 102.12.2]* and

- the effective portion of gains and losses on hedging instruments in a cash flow hedge. *[FRS 102.12.23, IFRS 9.6.5.11]*.

3.13   Fair value

FRS 102 defines fair value as the amount for which an asset could be exchanged, a liability settled, or an equity instrument granted could be exchanged, between knowledgeable, willing parties in an arm's length transaction. FRS 102 goes on to say that, in the absence of any specific guidance provided in the relevant section of this FRS, the guidance in the Appendix to Section 2 should be used in determining fair value. *[FRS 102 Appendix I]*.

This definition of fair value is similar to that found in the version of IAS 39 prior to issuance of IFRS 13 – *Fair Value Measurement* – and appears to be based on the notion of an 'entry price'. This is made explicit by the explanation that the best evidence is usually the current bid price. The definition differs from that in IFRS 13 which defines fair value as 'the price that would be received to sell an asset or paid to transfer a liability in an orderly transaction between market participants at the measurement date'. *[IFRS 13.9]*. The IFRS 13 definition is therefore based on an exit price. The difference in definitions could lead to different measurements of fair values, in particular for financial liabilities as the amount to settle a liability required by FRS 102 to determine fair value may differ from the amount paid to transfer the same liability, which is the definition of fair value under IFRS 13 (see Chapter 10 at 8.6).

3.13.1   *Hierarchy used to estimate fair value of shares*

As mentioned above, the key guidance on how to calculate fair values is contained in the appendix to Section 2. The guidance sets out a hierarchy to estimate fair value for which the best evidence of fair value is a quoted price for an identical asset (or similar asset) in an active market. *[FRS 102.2A.1]*. Figure 4.1 below shows the fair value hierarchy to be used.

Figure 4.1: Hierarchy

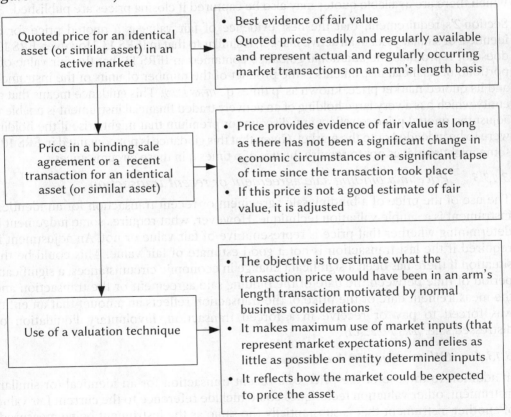

Reporting entities should measure fair value using the highest available level within the hierarchy. Section 2 is explicit that the best evidence of fair value is a quoted price for an identical (or similar) instrument in an active market and it is only when such quoted prices are unavailable, does an entity use the price in a binding sale agreement or a recent transaction for an identical (or similar) instrument and failing that, a valuation technique. *[FRS 102.2A.1, 29]*. However, the above guidance is somewhat theoretical and no examples are provided to illustrate its application, nor does the Basis for Conclusions shed any further light.

3.13.2   Quoted price in an active market

'Active market' is defined as 'a market in which all the following conditions exist:

(a)   the items traded in the market are homogeneous;

(b)   willing buyers and sellers can normally be found at any time; and

(c)   prices are available to the public.' *[FRS 102 Appendix I]*.

Based on the above definition, most equities and bonds that are listed on an exchange for which there is a liquid secondary market in terms of regular trading will be considered to be traded in an active market. In addition, instruments that are frequently traded in over-the-counter markets (i.e. instruments that are not listed on an exchange), such as interest rate swaps and options, foreign exchange derivatives and credit default swaps, and for which there are available quotes may also be captured if closing prices are published.

Section 2's requirement, that the best evidence of fair value is a quoted price for an identical or similar asset in an active market, is similar to that in IFRS 13. However, FRS 102 does not reproduce the additional guidance contained in IFRS 13 that the fair value of a portfolio of financial instruments is the product of the number of units of the instrument and its quoted market price, known as 'p times q'. *[IFRS 13.80]*. This guidance means that an entity which has a very large holding of an actively traded financial instrument is unable to adjust the quoted price to reflect any discount or premium that might arise if the holding were to be unloaded onto the market. Given that this guidance is not contained in FRS 102, some might read it as not to require the use of p times q in these circumstances.

3.13.3   Price in a binding sale agreement or recent transaction

The use of the price of a binding sale agreement or recent transaction for an identical instrument is a simple valuation technique. However, what requires some judgement is determining whether that price is representative of fair value or not. An adjustment is required if the last transaction is not a good estimate of fair value. This could be the situation if there has been a significant change in economic circumstances, a significant period of time between the date of the binding sale agreement or the transaction and the measurement date or the price of the transaction reflects an amount that an entity was forced to pay or receive in a forced transaction, involuntary liquidation or distressed sale. *[FRS 102.2.2A.1]*.

3.13.4   Other valuation techniques

In addition to the use of the price of a recent transaction for an identical (or similar) instrument, other valuation techniques could include reference to the current fair value of another instrument that is substantially the same as the instrument being measured, discounted cash flow analysis and option pricing models. If there is a valuation technique commonly used by market participants to price the asset and that technique has been demonstrated to provide reliable estimates of prices obtained in actual market transactions, the entity uses that technique. *[FRS 102.2.2A.2]*.

The objective of using a valuation technique is to determine what the transaction price would have been on the measurement date in an arm's length exchange motivated by normal business considerations. Fair value should be established using a valuation technique which makes maximum use of market inputs (i.e. inputs external to the entity) and relies as little as possible on entity-determined inputs. A reliable estimate would be achieved by a valuation technique which reasonably reflected how the market could be expected to price the asset and the inputs to the valuation should reasonably represent market expectations and measures of the risk return factors inherent in the asset. *[FRS 102.2A.3]*.

Many entities applying FRS 102 will not enter into instruments that are required to be recorded at fair value through profit or loss and for which a quoted price in active markets is not available. However if they do invest in, or issue complex instruments that must be fair valued but do not have quoted prices in active markets, they may have to draw upon the larger body of guidance within IFRS 13 in making judgements regarding how to measure fair value, especially regarding the use of valuation techniques. Further information regarding IFRS 13 can be found in Chapter 14 of EY International GAAP 2019.

3.13.4.A   Consideration of own credit risk

Although guidance in IFRS 13 on valuation techniques may be helpful in some circumstances, caution should be taken in applying the guidance. For instance, IFRS 13 is clear that entities must include in the fair value of financial liabilities such as derivatives any changes in fair value attributable to their own credit risk. *[IFRS 13.42]*. This has the unintuitive consequence that such entities will record profits on revaluation when their credit risk increases. FRS 102 contains no specific equivalent recognition or measurement requirement, unless the option has been chosen to apply IFRS 9, although entities are required to disclose the effect of own credit risk on liabilities recorded at fair value through profit or loss (see Chapter 10 at 11.2.2) for those financial liabilities that do not form part of a trading book and are not derivatives. This could be interpreted to imply that fair value for such liabilities should include the effects of changes in own credit risk; however, since FRS 102 determines that fair value of a liability should be measured on a settlement basis rather than at the amount paid to transfer it (see Chapter 10 at 8.6.4.A), the consideration of own credit risk would be an accounting policy choice.

3.13.5   Fair value not reliably measurable

For assets that do not have a quoted market price in an active market, fair value is considered reliably measurable when the range of reasonable fair value estimates is not significant or the probabilities of the various estimates within the range can be reasonably assessed and used in estimating fair value. *[FRS 102.2A.4]*. No further guidance is provided to assess significance or probabilities in this context, hence, entities will need to exercise judgement. However, we believe that the bar for determining that a fair value measurement is not reliably measurable is relatively high as there is an expectation that it is normally possible to estimate the fair value of an asset that an entity has acquired from an outside party. *[FRS 102.2A.5]*. Therefore situations in which the range of reasonable estimates is significant and the probabilities of those estimates cannot be reasonably be assessed will be limited to investments such as equity holdings in private companies, for which the investee has no comparable peers.

If a reliable measure of fair value is no longer available for an asset measured at fair value, it must use as its new cost the carrying amount at the last date when the fair value was reliably measurable as its new cost. The asset will then be carried at cost less impairment, until a reliable measure of fair value becomes available again. *[FRS 102.2A.6]*.

Chapter 4

3.13.6   *Financial liabilities due on demand*

The fair value of a financial liability that is due on demand is deemed to be not less than the amount payable on demand, discounted from the first date that the amount could be required to be paid. *[FRS 102.12.11]*. The logic is that a rational lender would demand repayment if the fair value were ever less than the net present value of the amount repayable, even though in practice many people do not withdraw their demand deposits in such circumstances. No guidance is provided in this context as to the appropriate discount rate, although the guidance on financing transactions would be appropriate (see Chapter 10 at 7.2). The requirement about the manner of measuring the fair value of a financial liability with a demand feature is identical to that in paragraph 47 of IFRS 13, hence, further information can be found in Chapter 14 of EY International GAAP 2019.

References

1 *The Conceptual Framework for Financial Reporting (Conceptual Framework)*, IASB, paras. 2.5-34.

2 *Conceptual Framework*, IASB, paras. 1.22-23.

3 *Stewardship/Accountability As An Objective of Financial Reporting: A Comment on the IASB/FASB Conceptual Framework Project*, ASB, EFRAG and others, June 2007.

Chapter 5   FRS 102 – Small entities

Chapter 5

List of examples

Chapter 5

Chapter 5   FRS 102 – Small entities

1   INTRODUCTION

1.1   Background

Company law changes implementing the Accounting Directive (Directive 2013/34/EU), which had mandatory effect for financial years beginning on or after 1 January 2016, necessitated changes to the accounting framework for small entities. UK company law changes implementing the Accounting Directive were principally made by *The Companies, Partnerships and Groups (Accounts and Reports) Regulations 2015* (SI 2015/980) (for UK companies and qualifying partnerships) and were extended to LLPs by *The Limited Liability Partnerships, Partnerships and Groups (Accounts and Audit) Regulations 2016* (SI 2016/575).

In July 2015, the FRC issued FRS 105 – *The Financial Reporting Standard applicable to the Micro-entities Regime* – and introduced a new small entities regime, Section 1A – *Small Entities* – into FRS 102 – *The Financial Reporting Standard applicable in the UK and Republic of Ireland*. FRS 105 and Section 1A of FRS 102 are effective for accounting periods beginning on or after 1 January 2016 (with certain early application provisions).

Section 1A of FRS 102 requires small entities to apply the recognition and measurement requirements of FRS 102 in full. However, the presentation and disclosure requirements of Section 1A are based on the requirements of the CA 2006 and *The Small Companies and Groups (Accounts and Directors' Report) Regulations 2008* (SI 2008/409), as amended ('the Small Companies Regulations'), for companies subject to the small companies regime. In particular, Appendix C to Section 1A of FRS 102 closely reflects the UK company law disclosure requirements for small companies.

Following changes made to Irish law to implement the Accounting Directive, the small entities regime in Section 1A also became available to entities in the Republic of Ireland. In December 2017, *Amendments to FRS 102 – The Financial Reporting Standard applicable in the UK and Republic of Ireland – Triennial Review 2017 – Incremental improvements and clarifications* (Triennial review 2017) – amended Section 1A of FRS 102, principally to reflect the changes made to Irish law. See 4.5 below.

FRS 100 – *Application of Financial Reporting Requirements* – and FRS 102 (see Chapter 1 at 4.4 and Chapter 3 at 2.1) set out the accounting framework for preparation of an entity's financial statements, as follows: *[FRS 100.4, FRS 102.1A.1-2, FRS 102.1.3]*

- entities that are eligible to apply the micro-entities regime may apply FRS 105;
- other entities (that are not required to apply EU-adopted IFRS) have a choice of applying EU-adopted IFRS, FRS 101 – *Reduced Disclosure Framework: Disclosure exemptions from EU-adopted IFRS for qualifying entities* (individual financial statements of a qualifying entity only), or FRS 102; and
- an entity qualifying for the small entities regime that adopts FRS 102 can choose to apply Section 1A or the full standard.

Micro-entities applying the micro-entities regime in the UK or Republic of Ireland must apply FRS 105. *[FRS 105.1.4-4A]*. See Chapter 1 at 6.4.

1.2   Scope of this chapter

This chapter principally addresses the requirements of Section 1A and the related company law requirements (for companies subject to the small companies regime) and the related LLP law requirements (for LLPs subject to the small LLPs regime).

While Section 1A can now be used by small entities in the Republic of Ireland ('Irish small entities'), this chapter does not discuss in detail the qualifying criteria for an Irish small entity, nor the presentation and disclosure requirements of Irish law and Section 1A specific to Irish small entities. However, an outline of the changes to Irish law made in 2017 to introduce a small companies regime is included at 4.5 below. The disclosure framework for Irish small entities (set out in a new Appendix D to Section 1A, which largely mirrors Appendix C for UK companies) is briefly discussed at 11.6 below.

References in this chapter to FRS 100 to FRS 102 are to those accounting standards, as amended by the Triennial review 2017, i.e. the compendium versions of those standards issued in March 2018. The changes made by the Triennial review 2017 relevant to small entities are summarised at 1.3 below.

A summary of Section 1A is included at 2 below, and its content is discussed at 6 to 11 below. Key definitions used in this chapter are included at 3 below. The effective dates of Section 1A (and the amendments made to this section by the Triennial review 2017) are discussed at 5 below.

A company subject to the small companies regime (in the UK or Republic of Ireland), an LLP subject to the small LLPs regime, and an entity that would have qualified for the small companies regime had it been a company, are permitted to use Section 1A. *[s382-s384, s382 (LLP)-s384 (LLP), FRS 102 Appendix I]*. See the definition of a 'small entity' at 3 below. The qualifying criteria for UK companies and LLPs are discussed at 4 below.

UK companies subject to the small companies regime apply the Small Companies Regulations and are eligible for certain disclosure exemptions in the CA 2006. Similarly, LLPs subject to the small LLPs regime apply the Small LLP Regulations (as amended) and are eligible for certain disclosure exemptions in the CA 2006 as applied to LLPs. In general, the Small Companies Regulations and Small LLP Regulations contain considerably fewer disclosures than the Regulations and LLP Regulations. Financial statements of a UK company prepared in accordance with FRS 102 are Companies Act accounts. The disclosures required in Companies Act accounts for companies subject to the small companies regime (which have been largely included in Appendix C of Section 1A) are set out at 11 below. Some differences for small LLPs are discussed at 11.5 below.

The presentation requirements of full FRS 102 that are mandatory for entities applying Section 1A are covered in 7 below. These include the overriding requirement for the financial statements to give a true and fair view. If a small entity chooses not to apply Section 1A (or presents additional primary statements), refer to Chapter 6 which addresses the presentation requirements of full FRS 102.

FRS 102 includes transition exemptions for small entities (see 6.4 below). However, these only apply for small entities adopting FRS 102 for accounting periods beginning before 1 January 2017. FRS 102 also exempts small entities from preparing a cash flow statement (see 7.1 below) and provides a concession in accounting for certain loans from a director or his / her close family member (see 6.3 below). These exemptions are available to a small entity, whether or not Section 1A is applied.

This chapter has been cross referred from Chapter 1 (which discusses FRS 100) because it includes the qualifying criteria for the small companies regime and the small LLPs regime. The qualifying criteria apply to companies and LLPs preparing Companies Act accounts (non-IAS accounts, for an LLP) or IAS accounts.

The statutory disclosure and filing exemptions for:

- the financial statements of UK companies and LLPs, prepared in accordance with the small companies regime and small LLPs regime respectively; and
- the reports of UK companies taking advantage of the small companies exemption

are discussed at 12 and 13 below.

The disclosure exemptions available in the financial statements of companies subject to the small companies regime differ for Companies Act accounts and IAS accounts. Companies Act accounts include financial statements prepared in accordance with FRS 101, FRS 102 and FRS 105. However, the micro-entity provisions (which apply to financial statements prepared in accordance with FRS 105 by a UK company or LLP) are addressed in Chapter 1 at 6.4 rather than this chapter.

1.3   Changes made by the Triennial review 2017

The main changes made by the Triennial review 2017 to Section 1A are to add Irish legal references and a new Appendix D, which sets out the disclosure requirements for Irish small entities and closely follows the statutory requirements in the Republic of Ireland.

Other changes are to refer to the small LLPs regime (which post-dated the July 2015 amendments to FRS 102 that introduced Section 1A) or are mainly clarifications.

In addition, Appendix III – *Note on legal requirements* – to FRS 102 has been updated to reflect the changes to LLP law made by SI 2016/575, *[FRS 102 Appendix III.43]*, and a new Appendix IV – *Republic of Ireland legal references* – has been added (reflecting the changes to Irish law in 2017). *[FRS 102 Appendix IV]*.

2   SUMMARY OF SECTION 1A (AND RELATED CA 2006 REQUIREMENTS)

- Section 1A sets out accounting requirements for entities subject to the small entities regime (see 4 below), whether or not they report under the CA 2006 (or for small entities in the Republic of Ireland, the Companies Act 2014).

- Section 1A can be applied by a company qualifying for the small companies regime in the UK (see 4.3 below) or in the Republic of Ireland (see 4.5 below), an LLP qualifying for the small LLPs regime (see 4.4 below), or an entity that would have qualified for the small companies regime had it been a company incorporated under company law. The effective date for when small entities in the UK and Republic of Ireland can apply Section 1A differs, as explained at 5 below.

- Section 1A is optional and small entities can choose to apply full FRS 102.

- SORPs may include more restrictive provisions. For instance, it is generally understood that the Charities SORP (FRS 102),[1] as amended by *Charities SORP – FRS 102 Update Bulletin 1 (February 2016)* ('Update Bulletin 1') and *Charities SORP – FRS 102 Update Bulletin 2 (October 2018)* ('Update Bulletin 2'), does not allow charities within its scope to apply Section 1A (see 4.2 below). The Statement of Recommended Practice – *Accounting by Limited Liability Partnerships (January 2017)* – also requires small LLPs to make some additional disclosures in their financial statements, as explained at 11.5 below.

- Section 1A requires that small entities apply the recognition and measurement requirements of FRS 102 in full (see 6 below) and exempts small entities from most of the existing presentation requirements of FRS 102 (although the general principles concerning the presentation of financial statements, such as the requirement for the financial statements to show a true and fair view, still apply – see 7 below).

- Where Section 1A is applied by a small entity, a complete set of financial statements comprises: a statement of financial position, an income statement, and notes. Small entities are encouraged to but are not required to present a statement of comprehensive income, or statement of changes in equity (or statement of income and retained earnings). See 8 below.

- Small entities applying FRS 102 are not required to prepare a cash flow statement (even if they do not apply Section 1A). However, small charities with gross income exceeding £500,000 (or €500,000 in the Republic of Ireland) are required by the Charities SORP (FRS 102) to prepare a cash flow statement. See 4.2 and 7.1 below.

- Section 1A requires the statement of financial position and income statement to be presented in accordance with Part 1 of Schedule 1 to the Small Companies Regulations or Part 1 of Schedule 1 to the Small LLP Regulations (which permit the use of abridged formats, adapted formats or statutory formats). Irish small entities refer instead to Part II of Schedule 3A to the Companies Act 2014. Irish law does not permit use of abridged formats. See 8 to 10 below.

- Small entities in the UK must provide the disclosures set out in Appendix C to Section 1A, which are based on the statutory disclosures in the CA 2006 and the Small Companies Regulations for companies subject to the small companies regime. Appendix C covers the vast majority of statutory disclosures applicable to individual accounts of companies subject to the small companies regime. In the small number of cases where the disclosures in Section 1A and the statutory disclosures for LLPs differ, LLPs should apply the equivalent disclosures required by the Small LLP Regulations rather than those in Appendix C of Section 1A. Irish small entities should instead provide the disclosures set out in Appendix D to Section 1A, which are based on the statutory disclosures in the Companies Act 2014. See 11 below.

- Financial statements prepared by small entities are required to give a true and fair view; consequently, additional disclosures beyond those specifically mandated may be required (see 7.2, 8 and 11 below). Appendix E to Section 1A sets out additional disclosures specifically encouraged for small entities. See 11.3 below.

- Section 1A does not require a small entity that is a parent entity to prepare consolidated financial statements. Section 1A sets out requirements for consolidated financial statements, where prepared. However, changes to UK company law, effective for financial years beginning on or after 1 January 2017, mean that some UK companies eligible for the small companies regime may be required to prepare consolidated financial statements. See 6.2 below.

3   KEY DEFINITIONS AND ABBREVIATIONS

See Chapter 6 at 3.1 for relevant definitions.

In addition, definitions relevant to qualification for the small companies regime (and the small LLPs regime) are included at 4 below.

The terms 'Irish small entities' and 'small entities in the Republic of Ireland' mean the same and are used interchangeably.

References to the 'General Rules to the formats' mean the 'General Rules', as included in Section A of Part 1 of Schedule 1 to the Small Companies Regulations or the equivalent requirements in the Small LLP Regulations.

The following statutory instruments are referred to by their statutory instrument number:

- *The Limited Liability Partnerships (Accounts and Audit) (Application of Companies Act 2006) Regulations 2008* (SI 2008/1911). This statutory instrument sets out how Parts 15 and 16 of the Companies Act 2006 apply to LLPs and is also referred to as 'the CA 2006 as applied to LLPs'.

- *The Companies, Partnerships and Groups (Accounts and Reports) Regulations 2015* (SI 2015/980). This statutory instrument implemented the Accounting Directive (Directive 2013/34/EU) and made significant amendments to the small companies regime.

- *The Limited Liability Partnerships, Partnerships and Groups (Accounts and Audit) Regulations 2016* (SI 2016/575). This statutory instrument made significant amendments to the small LLPs regime.

References to 'LLP SORP' are to The Statement of Recommended Practice – *Accounting by Limited Liability Partnerships* (January 2017) – issued by the Consultative Committee of Accountancy Bodies (CCAB).

References to the 'Charities SORP (FRS 102)' are to *Charities SORP (FRS 102): Accounting and Reporting by Charities: Statement of Recommended Practice applicable to charities preparing their accounts in accordance with the Financial Reporting Standard applicable in the UK and Republic of Ireland (FRS 102)* – issued by the Charity Commission and Office of the Scottish Charity Regulator in 2014.

References to 'Update Bulletin 1' and 'Update Bulletin 2' are to the *Charities SORP – FRS 102 Update Bulletin 1 (February 2016)* and the *Charities SORP – FRS 102 Update Bulletin 2 (October 2018)*.

4   SCOPE OF SMALL ENTITIES REGIME

This section defines a small entity and discusses the application of Section 1A. It also explains the conditions for the small companies regime (in the UK and Republic of Ireland) and the small LLPs regime (in the UK) which are relevant to determining which entities can apply Section 1A.

4.1   Definition of a small entity

A small entity is defined as: *[FRS 102 Appendix I]*

(a)   a company meeting the definition of a small company as set out in sections 382 or 383 of the CA 2006 and not excluded from the small companies regime by section 384 (see 4.3 below);

(b)   an LLP qualifying as small and not excluded from the small LLPs regime, as set out in LLP Regulations (meaning in this context, sections 382 to 384 of CA 2006, as applied to LLPs) (see 4.4 below); or

(c)   any other entity that would have met the criteria in (a) had it been a company incorporated under company law.

The Triennial review 2017 added a footnote to (a) above that explains that Irish small entities (including partnerships that are required to comply with Part 6 of the Companies Act 2014, by virtue of the European Communities (Accounts) Regulations 1993 (as amended)) shall refer to sections 280A and 280B of the Companies Act 2014.

4.2   Application of Section 1A

Section 1A sets out the information to be presented and disclosed in the financial statements of a small entity that chooses to apply the small entities regime. Unless specifically excluded (see 7.1 below), all of the requirements of FRS 102, including the recognition and measurement requirements, apply to a small entity applying Section 1A. *[FRS 102.1A.1]*. While Section 1A does not set out any exemptions from the recognition and measurement requirements, there are some limited reliefs available for small entities in other parts of the standard which are explained in 6.1, 6.3 and 6.4 below.

Unless a small entity chooses to apply EU-adopted IFRS (or, if eligible, FRS 101), a small entity that chooses not to apply the small entities regime shall apply FRS 102, excluding Section 1A. *[FRS 102.1A.2]*. Section 1A is therefore optional for small entities to apply.

However, as noted in Chapter 1 at 4.4, an entity's choice of financial reporting framework must be permitted by the legal framework or other regulations or requirements that govern the preparation of the entity's financial statements. Other agreements or arrangements (such as shareholders' agreements, banking agreements) may restrict the choice of financial reporting framework.

Entities that are subject to a SORP should confirm the applicability of Section 1A. Most extant SORPs are reviewed annually, and may have published update statements or revisions since original publication. SORPs may restrict entities within their scope from applying Section 1A or require additional disclosures in order to comply with the SORP.

For example, Update Bulletin 1 amended the requirements of the Charities SORP (FRS 102) (2014) (and withdrew *The Charities SORP (FRSSE)* (2014)), effective for accounting periods beginning on or after 1 January 2016. Update Bulletin 1 also introduced exemptions from preparing a cash flow statement for small charities with a gross income not exceeding £500,000 (or in the Republic of Ireland, €500,000). As Update Bulletin 1 did not amend the SORP to state that small charities can apply Section 1A, it is generally understood that this is not allowed. The LLP SORP also requires small LLPs to make some additional disclosures in their financial statements, as explained at 11.5 below.

References to a small entity in paragraphs 1A.4 to 1A.22 of Section 1A (and its appendices), i.e. in the rest of Section 1A, are to a small entity that chooses to apply the small entities regime. *[FRS 102.1A.3]*.

Section 1A applies to all small entities applying the small entities regime, whether or not they report under the CA 2006. Small entities that do not report under the CA 2006 must comply with Section 1A and with the CA 2006 and the Small Companies Regulations (or, where applicable, the CA 2006 as applied to LLPs and the Small LLP Regulations) where referred to by Section 1A, except to the extent that these requirements are not permitted by any statutory framework under which such entities report. For Irish small entities, references to the CA 2006 are instead references to the Companies Act 2014, and references to the Small Companies Regulations are instead references to Schedule 3A to the Companies Act 2014. *[FRS 102.1A.4]*.

One of the requirements of the CA 2006, included in Section 1A, is for the financial statements of a small entity to give a true and fair view. *[s393]*. Irish small entities should instead refer to section 289 of the Companies Act 2014. *[FRS 102.1A.5]*. The requirement for the financial statements of the small entity to give a true and fair view and, where applicable, comply with any statutory requirements may mean that additional disclosures to those listed in Section 1A may be required. *[FRS 102.1A.6]*. See 7.2 and 11 below for further guidance.

4.3   Small companies regime

The small companies regime applies to a company for a financial year in relation to which the company qualifies as small (see 4.3.1 and 4.3.2 below for the criteria for UK companies) and is not excluded from the regime (see 4.3.3 below for the types of excluded companies in the UK). *[s381]*.

4.3.1   Companies qualifying as small – company is not a parent undertaking (size criteria)

A company qualifies as small in relation to its first financial year if the qualifying conditions (as set out below) are met in that year. *[s382(1)]*.

A company qualifies as small in relation to a subsequent financial year if the qualifying conditions are met in that year except that in relation to a subsequent financial year, where on its balance sheet date a company meets or ceases to meet the qualifying conditions, then that will affect its qualification as a small company only if it occurs in two consecutive years. *[s382(1A), s382(2)]*.

This provision is designed to assist companies which fluctuate in and out of the qualifying conditions. However, if a company fails to meet the criteria in two consecutive years, it will cease to qualify, and then would need to meet the criteria in two later consecutive years to re-qualify for the exemptions.

The qualifying conditions are met in a year in which the company satisfies two or more of the following requirements: *[s382(3)]*

- turnover must not exceed £10.2 million;
- the balance sheet total must not exceed £5.1 million; and
- the number of employees must not exceed 50.

If the company's financial year is not in fact a full year, the maximum turnover figure should be adjusted proportionately. The 'balance sheet total' means the aggregate of the amounts shown as assets in the balance sheet, i.e. total assets. The number of employees means the average number of persons employed under contracts of service by the company in the year (determining for each month, the number of such persons – whether employed throughout the month or not, adding together the monthly totals and dividing by the number of months in the financial year). *[s382(4)-(6)]*.

Although the small size criteria increased, effective for financial years beginning on or after 1 January 2016 (or 1 January 2015, where SI 2015/980 was early adopted), the new size thresholds are applied to all preceding financial years in assessing whether a company is small in a particular financial year.[2] This is illustrated in Example 5.1 below.

Example 5.1:   Applying the new small size thresholds for UK companies and LLPs

Company A	2019	2018	2017	2016	2015
	£'000	£'000	£'000	£'000	£'000
Turnover	10,000	11,200	11,000	8,000	6,800
Balance sheet total	5,000	5,000	4,500	4,150	4,000
Number of employees	55	55	51	45	45
Are at least two of the small size criteria (as amended by SI 2015/980) met?	Yes	No	No	Yes	Yes

In this example, Company A, which is not a parent undertaking, prepares its financial statements for financial years that are calendar years and first applies SI 2015/980 in 2016. Company A was incorporated in 2015 and did not qualify as small for its 2015 financial statements (based on the then small size criteria). However, Company A did meet at least two of the three small size criteria set out in SI 2015/980 in 2016 and in the previous year and so would qualify as small for its 2016 financial statements. In 2017, Company A did not meet two of the small size criteria but still qualifies as small for its 2017 financial statements because two of the small size criteria (as amended by SI 2015/980) were met in the two preceding financial years, i.e. 2016 and 2015. However, Company A ceases to qualify as small for its 2018 financial statements (as it failed to meet two of the small size criteria for two financial years running). Although Company A again meets two of the small size criteria in 2019, it does not qualify as small for its 2019 financial statements. However, if Company A met two of the small size criteria again in 2020, it will requalify as small for its 2020 financial statements.

4.3.2   Companies qualifying as small – company is a parent undertaking (size criteria)

Where the company is itself a parent undertaking, then it only qualifies as small if the group that it heads qualifies as a small group. *[s382(7), s383(1)]*. This is the case whether or not group accounts are prepared.

A group qualifies as small in relation to the parent's first financial year if the qualifying conditions (as set out below) are met in that year. *[s383(2)]*.

A group qualifies as small in relation to a subsequent financial year if the qualifying conditions are met in that year except that in relation to a subsequent financial year, where on its balance sheet date the group meets or ceases to meet the qualifying conditions, then that will affect the group's qualification as small only if it occurs in two consecutive years. *[s383(2A), s383(3)]*.

The qualifying conditions for a small group are met in a year in which the group headed by the company satisfies two or more of the following requirements: *[s383(4)]*

- turnover must not exceed £10.2 million net (or £12.2 million gross);
- the balance sheet total must not exceed £5.1 million (or £6.1 million gross); and
- the number of employees must not exceed 50.

The aggregate figures for the above limits are ascertained by aggregating the relevant figures determined in accordance with section 382 for each member of the group. The figures used for each subsidiary undertaking are those included in its individual accounts for the relevant financial year, i.e. where its financial year is coterminous with that of the parent company, the financial year that ends at the same date as the parent company, or where its financial year is not coterminous, the financial year ending last before the end of the financial year of the parent company. If those figures are not obtainable without disproportionate expense or undue delay, the latest available figures are used. The turnover and balance sheet total criteria may be satisfied on either the gross or net of consolidation adjustments basis. For Companies Act accounts (such as FRS 102 financial statements), the consolidation adjustments are determined in accordance with regulations made under section 404, i.e. the Regulations or the Small Companies Regulations. For IAS accounts, the consolidation adjustments are determined in accordance with EU-adopted IFRS. It is permissible to satisfy one limit on the 'net' basis and the other on the 'gross' basis. *[s383(5)-(7)]*.

Chapter 5

4.3.3   Companies excluded from the small companies regime

A company is excluded from the small companies regime if it was at any time in the financial year to which the accounts relate: *[s384(1)]*

- a public company;
- a company that is an authorised insurance company, a banking company, an e-money issuer, a MiFID investment firm or a UCITS management company;
- a company that carries on an insurance market activity; or
- a member of an ineligible group.

A group is ineligible if any of its members is: *[s384(2)]*

- a traded company;
- a body corporate (other than a company) whose shares are admitted to trading on a regulated market in an EEA State;
- a person (other than a small company) who has permission under Part 4A of the Financial Services and Markets Act 2000 to carry on a regulated activity;
- an e-money issuer;
- a small company that is an authorised insurance company, banking company, a MiFID investment firm or a UCITS management company; or
- a person who carries on an insurance market activity.

A company is a small company for the purposes of section 384(2) if it qualified as small in relation to its last financial year ending on or before the end of the financial year to which the accounts relate. *[s384(3)]*.

A group means a parent undertaking and its subsidiary undertakings. *[s474(1)]*. Therefore, in determining whether a small company is excluded on the grounds that it is a member of an ineligible group, the term 'group' comprises the widest group of which the reporting company is a member. This differs from the scope of a 'group' used when evaluating whether the small size criteria are met, which is the group *headed* by the reporting company.

The definition of an ineligible group may change in the future as a result of draft legislation pursuant to Brexit (see 12.3 below).

4.3.3.A   Relevant definitions for small companies regime

The reference to a 'company' above is to a company formed and registered (or treated as formed and registered) under the CA 2006. This means a company formed and registered under the CA 2006, or prior to 1 October 2009 under the Companies Act 1985, Companies (Northern Ireland) Order 1986 or former Companies Acts (i.e. the company was an existing company for the purposes of that Act and Order). *[s1]*. In fact, sections 382 to 384 do also apply to unregistered companies via separate regulations[3] (but such companies are outside the scope of this publication).

A traded company is a company any of whose transferable securities are admitted to trading on a regulated market. *[s474(1)]*.

A regulated market is as defined in Directive 2014/65/EC (or in the case of an EEA State that has not implemented that Directive, is as defined in Directive 2004/39/EC). A list of regulated markets is obtainable from the ESMA website.[4] *[s1173(1)]*.

A public company means a company limited by shares or limited by guarantee and having a share capital (a) whose certificate of incorporation states that it is a public company and (b) in relation to which the requirements of the CA 2006 or the former Companies Acts as to registration or re-registration as a public company have been complied with (on or after the relevant date, being 22 December 1980 in Great Britain and 1 July 1983 in Northern Ireland). *[s4]*. Therefore, a public company means any UK-incorporated company that is a 'plc' or 'PLC' rather than a publicly traded company.

An authorised insurance company is defined in section 1165(2), a banking company in section 1164(2)-(3) and insurance market activity in section 1165(7). See Chapter 6 at 4.2.2 and 4.2.3.

The terms e-money issuer, MiFID investment firm, regulated activity, and UCITS management company are defined in section 474 of the CA 2006. *[s474]*.

A body corporate includes a body incorporated outside the UK but does not include (a) a corporation sole or (b) a partnership that, whether or not a legal person, is not regarded as a body corporate under the law by which it is governed. *[s1173(1)]*. Therefore, a body corporate would include an overseas company or a UK LLP.

4.4   Small LLPs regime

The small LLPs regime applies to an LLP for a financial year in relation to which the LLP qualifies as small (see 4.4.1 below for the size criteria for UK LLPs) and is not excluded from the regime (see 4.4.2 below for the types of excluded LLPs in the UK). *[s381 (LLP)]*.

4.4.1   *Size criteria*

The small size criteria for an LLP that is not a parent and for an LLP that is a parent are the same as the small size criteria applied for a company that is not a parent (see 4.3.1 above) and a company that is a parent (see 4.3.2 above). These size criteria operate in the same way as described for companies above. *[s382 (LLP), s383 (LLP)]*.

4.4.2   *Excluded LLPs*

An LLP is excluded from the small LLPs regime if it was at any time in the financial year to which the accounts relate: *[s384(1) (LLP)]*

- a traded LLP (meaning an LLP any of whose transferable securities are admitted to trading on a regulated market);
- an LLP that is an authorised insurance company, a banking LLP, an e-money issuer, a MiFID investment firm or a UCITS management company;
- an LLP that carries on an insurance market activity; or
- a member of an ineligible group.

A group is ineligible if any of its members is: *[s384(2) (LLP)]*

- a traded company;
- a body corporate (other than a company) whose shares are admitted to trading on a regulated market in an EEA State;
- a person (other than a small company or small LLP) who has permission under Part [4A] of the Financial Services and Markets Act 2000 to carry on a regulated activity;
- an e-money issuer;
- a small company or small LLP that is an authorised insurance company, banking company or banking LLP, a MiFID investment firm or a UCITS management company; or
- a person who carries on an insurance market activity.

A company or LLP is a small company or small LLP for the purposes of section 384(2) if it qualified as small in relation to its last financial year ending on or before the end of the financial year to which the accounts relate.

The definition of an ineligible group for small LLPs still refers to 'a person ... who has permission under Part 4 of the Financial Services and Markets Act...'. This appears to be an oversight (since this Part has been replaced) and should, in our view, refer to Part 4A, as in the definition of an ineligible group for companies.

The definitions are the same as discussed at 4.3.3.A above.

The definition of an ineligible group may change in the future as a result of draft legislation pursuant to Brexit (see 12.3 below).

4.5   Companies in the Republic of Ireland

In 2017, the Republic of Ireland transposed the Accounting Directive into Irish law. The Companies (Accounting) Act 2017 amended the Companies Act 2014 to introduce the small companies regime and a micro-companies regime (similar to but not identical to the UK small companies regime and micro-entities regime) into Irish law. These changes were effective for financial years beginning on or after 1 January 2017 (but could be early applied for financial years beginning on or after 1 January 2015, provided the financial statements had not yet been approved). *[FRS 102.BC.A53-A56, FRS 105 Appendix IV.4]*.

The qualifying conditions operate in a similar way to those for UK companies but the size thresholds, as set out in section 280A of the Companies Act 2014, are: turnover of €12 million, balance sheet total of €6 million and average number of employees of 50. As in the UK, a holding company can only qualify as a small company in relation to a financial year if the group that it heads qualified as small (as set out in section 280B of the Companies Act 2014). These sections also detail certain companies that are excluded from the small companies regime. *[FRS 102 Appendix IV.6]*.

The statutory disclosure requirements for companies subject to the small companies regime in the Republic of Ireland differ in certain respects from the UK. Therefore, the Triennial review 2017 introduced a new Appendix D into Section 1A of FRS 102 which sets out the disclosure requirements for small entities in the Republic of Ireland (whereas Appendix C relates to disclosure requirements for small entities in the UK).

There is no equivalent legislation to that for UK LLPs in the Republic of Ireland. However, certain Irish partnerships are required to comply with Part 6 of the Companies Act 2014 by virtue of the *European Communities (Accounts) Regulations 1993* (as amended). *[FRS 102 Appendix IV.11]*.

Appendix IV to FRS 102 – *Republic of Ireland legal references* – has been updated to refer to the Companies Act 2014 in the March 2018 compendium version of FRS 102.

5   EFFECTIVE DATE

FRS 102 (amended July 2015), which introduced Section 1A, was effective for accounting periods beginning on or after 1 January 2016. There were certain early application provisions (explained in Chapter 3 at 1.3 of EY UK GAAP 2017) that were intended to align with the application of SI 2015/980 (for UK companies). *[FRS 102.1.15]*.

The Triennial review 2017 subsequently made changes to Section 1A, principally to reflect the changes made to Irish law in 2017 and to update Section 1A for the small LLPs regime. However, there were a number of other amendments, mainly clarifications.

The Triennial review 2017 (other than the amendments for small entities in the Republic of Ireland – see 5.1 below) is effective for accounting periods beginning on or after 1 January 2019. Early application is permitted provided that all the amendments to FRS 102 are applied at the same time. However, certain amendments to FRS 102 can be early applied separately, as explained in Chapter 3 at 1.3. These include the relief available to a small entity when accounting for certain loans made by a director of the small entity or his / her close family member (see 6.3 below). A small entity applying Section 1A is encouraged to disclose early application. *[FRS 102.1.18]*.

5.1   Small entities in the Republic of Ireland

The amendments to Section 1A for small entities in the Republic of Ireland are effective for accounting periods beginning on or after 1 January 2017 (which aligns with the changes made to the Companies Act 2014). *[FRS 102.1.18]*.

A small entity in the Republic of Ireland may apply the amendments made to Section 1A for accounting periods beginning on or after 1 January 2017, with early application permitted provided the Companies (Accounting) Act 2017 is applied from the same date. If a small entity in the Republic of Ireland applies the amendments to Section 1A before 1 January 2017, it is encouraged to disclose that fact. This is in addition to the statement required in paragraph 1AD.3 as to whether the small entity's financial statements are prepared in accordance with Section 1A of FRS 102, giving the effect of any material departure from Section 1A, the effect of the departure and the reasons for it. *[FRS 102.1AD.3]*.

Otherwise, the Triennial review 2017 is effective for accounting periods beginning on or after 1 January 2019 (with early application available). A small entity applying Section 1A is encouraged to disclose early application. *[FRS 102.1.18]*.

6   RECOGNITION AND MEASUREMENT REQUIREMENTS

Section 1A does not set out a separate recognition and measurement regime for small entities, instead requiring that small entities follow the recognition and measurement requirements of full FRS 102 (although there are some limited reliefs available) – see 6.1 below. It also addresses the requirements where a small entity prepares consolidated financial statements (see 6.2 below).

6.1   Recognition and measurement requirements of FRS 102

All the recognition and measurement requirements of FRS 102 apply to a small entity applying Section 1A. The only exclusions from the remainder of FRS 102 that are set out in Section 1A relate to certain presentation and disclosure requirements. *[FRS 102.1A.1, 7]*. See 7.1 below.

Having said that, FRS 102 includes certain transition exemptions for small entities (adopting FRS 102 for accounting periods beginning prior to 1 January 2017) – see 6.4 below. In addition, there is a relief allowing small entities to measure certain loans from a director or his / her close family members at transaction price – see 6.3 below.

The LLP SORP reflects both the requirements of Section 1A and the changes to LLP law made by SI 2016/575. The SORP states that small LLPs applying Section 1A must follow the SORP's recognition and measurement requirements in full, but give certain additional disclosures. *[LLP SORP.27-28]*. See 11.5 below.

6.2   Preparation of consolidated financial statements under Section 1A

A small entity that is a parent entity is not required to prepare consolidated financial statements. *[FRS 102.1A.21]*. The qualifying criteria for a small parent company and LLP in the UK are set out in 4.3 and 4.4 above.

The exemption from preparing consolidated financial statements, as set out in Section 1A, differs from the current statutory requirements for small companies and small LLPs to prepare group accounts (which also need to be met where a small entity is subject to these requirements). This statutory exemption from preparing group accounts has been included in Section 9 – *Consolidated and Separate Financial Statements*. *[FRS 102.9.3(e)]*. See Chapter 8 at 3.1.1.D.

For financial years beginning on or after 1 January 2017, a company is exempt from the requirement to prepare group accounts if: *[s399(2A)]*

(a)   at the end of the financial year, the company is:

   (i)   subject to the small companies regime; or

   (ii)   would be subject to the small companies regime but for being a public company; and

(b)   is not a member of a group which, at any time during the financial year, has an undertaking falling within section 399(2B) as a member.

An undertaking falls within section 399(2B) if: *[s399(2A)-(2B)]*

(a)   it is established under the law of an EEA State;

(b)   it has to prepare accounts in accordance with the Accounting Directive; and

(c) it is:

  (i)   an undertaking which has been designated by an EEA State as a public-interest entity under the Accounting Directive;

  (ii)   an undertaking whose transferable securities are admitted to trading on a regulated market in an EEA State;

  (iii) a credit institution (within the meaning given by Article 4(1)(1) of Regulation (EU) No. 575/2013 of the European Parliament and of the Council, other than one listed in Article 2 of Directive 2013/36/EU of the European Parliament and of the Council); or

  (iv)   an insurance undertaking (within the meaning given by Article 2(1) of Council Directive 91/674/EEC of the European Parliament and of the Council).

A 'member of a group' means a parent undertaking or its subsidiary undertaking. *[s474]*. Other relevant definitions are at 4.3.3.A above. The list included in section 399(2B) identifies the types of undertakings treated as public interest entities in the UK. However, other EEA States may have designated other types of undertakings as public interest entities.

Similarly, for financial years beginning on or after 1 January 2017, an LLP is exempt from the requirement to prepare group accounts if: *[s399(2A) (LLP), (2B) (LLP)]*

(a)   at the end of the financial year, the LLP is subject to the small LLPs regime (see 4.4 above); and

(b)   is not a member of a group which, at any time in the financial year, has an undertaking falling within section 399(2B) (i.e. the same list as above) as a member.

Other statutory exemptions from preparing group accounts are discussed more generally in Chapter 8 at 3.1.1.

A UK company or LLP exempt from the requirement to prepare group accounts may still do so. *[s399(4), s399(4) (LLP)]*. Such group accounts could be prepared as statutory group accounts, or as non-statutory group accounts for the members.

The definition of the small companies regime and the list of undertakings falling within section 399(2B) may change in the future as a result of draft legislation pursuant to Brexit (see 12.3 below).

6.2.1   Voluntary preparation of consolidated financial statements

If a small entity that is a parent voluntarily chooses to prepare consolidated financial statements, it: *[FRS 102.1A.22]*

(a)   must apply the consolidation procedures set out in Section 9 (see Chapter 8 at 3.5);

(b)   is encouraged to provide the disclosures set out in paragraph 9.23 (see 11.4.1 below);

(c)   must comply so far as practicable with the requirements of Section 1A as if it were a single entity (Schedule 6 of the Small Companies Regulations, paragraph 1(1)), subject to any restrictions or exemptions set out in legislation; and

(d)   must provide any disclosures required by Schedule 6 of the Small Companies Regulations (see 11.4.3 and 11.4.4 below).

Chapter 5

6.2.2   *Interaction with statutory requirements (where consolidated financial statements are prepared)*

Group accounts are drawn up as at the same date as the accounts of the parent company or parent LLP. *[6 Sch 2(1A) (SC), 4 Sch 2(1A) (LLP SC)]*. Only the adapted formats or statutory formats can be applied in group accounts. The abridged formats are not available in group accounts. *[6 Sch 1(1A) (SC), 4 Sch 1(1A) (LLP SC)]*. See 8.1 below for further discussion of the formats.

Small companies must comply with Schedule 6 to the Small Companies Regulations (and small LLPs with Schedule 4 to the Small LLP Regulations) which set out further requirements over consolidation procedures, the acquisition method, the conditions for merger accounting and disclosures. The recognition and measurement requirements for consolidated financial statements in the Small Companies Regulations (and Small LLP Regulations) are the same as those in the Regulations (and LLP Regulations). These are discussed in Chapter 8 and Chapter 17.

The conditions for accounting for an acquisition as a merger are: *[6 Sch 10 (SC)]*

(a)   that the undertaking whose shares are acquired is ultimately controlled by the same party both before and after the acquisition;

(b)   that the control referred to in paragraph (a) is not transitory; and

(c)   that adoption of the merger method accords with generally accepted accounting principles or practice.

The conditions for merger accounting in LLP law are solely that adoption of the merger accounting method accords with generally accepted accounting principles or practice. *[4 Sch10 (LLP SC)]*. See Chapter 17 at 5.

6.3   Loans from a director or a close member of his / her family

6.3.1   *Background to the exemption*

Generally, FRS 102 requires that a financial asset or financial liability that is a financing transaction is measured at the present value of the future payments discounted at a market rate of interest for a similar debt instrument as determined at initial recognition adjusted for transaction costs. *[FRS 102.11.13]*.

The FRC received feedback in the triennial review from many stakeholders concerning the accounting for directors' loans (which were previously required to be measured at present value in accordance with paragraph 11.13). Such loans can often be interest free or at below market rates. The FRC considers that accounting at present value is appropriate since such transactions contain both an interest-bearing loan and a transfer of value.

However, concerns were raised about some of the practicalities of the accounting requirements, in particular that such loans are often made by directors, especially those of small companies, because commercial funding is unavailable and therefore it is difficult to determine an appropriate market rate for a similar debt instrument. Comments were also received concerning the nature of the transaction in the context of a small entity where the same individual is employee, director, shareholder and lender. It was also noted that FRS 102 already included an exemption from the financing transaction requirements for public benefit entity concessionary loans. Generally, the FRC considers that all entities within the scope of FRS 102 should be subject to consistent recognition and measurement requirements, although occasional specific exemptions may be granted in order to meet the principles of providing proportionate and practical solutions. The FRC therefore proposed an exemption that is intended to provide relief to small owner-managed businesses. The background to this exemption is further explained in the Basis of Conclusions to FRS 102. *[FRS 102.BC.B11.32-39]*.

6.3.2   Exemption for certain loans from a director or his/her close family members

The Triennial review 2017 included a relief for certain loans from a director or his / her close family members allowing them to be measured at transaction price. The FRC had previously granted interim relief (with immediate effect) in May 2017 – for loans from a director who is a natural person and a shareholder in the small entity (or a close member of the family of that person). *[FRS 102.1.15A]*.

The Triennial review 2017 removed the amendment made in May 2017 (by deleting paragraph 1.15A) but extended the scope of the exemption. *[FRS 102.11.13A(a), 11.13B-C, 11.14(a)(i)]*. These paragraphs setting out the exemption are available for separate early application without early application of the rest of the Triennial review 2017 (see Chapter 3 at 1.3) in order to extend the interim relief granted in May 2017 to all circumstances within the scope of the exemption. *[FRS 102.BC.A61(a)]*. An entity early applying the Triennial review 2017 must disclose this fact (unless it is a small entity applying Section 1A, in which case such disclosure is encouraged). *[FRS 102.1.18]*.

The amendments state that, as an exception to paragraph 11.13, a basic financial liability of a small entity that is a loan from a person who is within a director's group of close family members, when that group contains at least one shareholder in the entity, may be measured initially at transaction price. *[FRS 102.11.13A(a)]*. The effective interest rate used when subsequently measuring the loan at amortised cost is the interest rate implicit in the contract, which may be zero. *[FRS 102.11.14(a)(i)]*.

A director's group of close family members means, in this context, the director and the close members of the family of that director. This includes a person who is the sole director-shareholder of an entity. For an LLP, the reference to a 'shareholder' is read as 'a member who is a person'. *[FRS 102.11.13A(a)]*. We believe the exemption is intended to be limited to a director (or member of an LLP) who is a natural person (individual) and would exclude a corporate director-shareholder or corporate member of an LLP.

The close members of the director's family are those family members who may be expected to influence, or be influenced by, that director in their dealings with the entity including: *[FRS 102 Appendix I]*

- that director's children and spouse or domestic partner;
- children of that director's spouse or domestic partner; and
- dependants of that director or that director's spouse or domestic partner.

Therefore, relief is now available for loans to small entities from the director or close members of the director's family, providing that this group also includes a shareholder in the entity. A loan from a director, who is not a shareholder and has no close family members that are shareholders, will not qualify for the relief. *[FRS 102.BC.B11.38]*.

An example of a situation where the exemption would be available is where the spouse of a director of the small entity is a shareholder in the small entity. The director (or the spouse) makes an interest free loan to the small entity. The amount of the loan £200,000 is repayable after three years by the entity. Where the concession is used, the loan liability is recorded at its transaction price of £200,000 and no interest is charged to profit or loss. The loan is then repaid at £200,000 in three years' time, extinguishing the liability.

The FRC notes that loans from directors or shareholders with a participating interest to a small entity that are non-interest bearing or bear interest at a non-market rate fall within the disclosure requirements of paragraphs 1AC.35 or 1AD.51 (related party transactions) (see 11.1.8.A below). *[FRS 102.1AC.35, 1AD.51]*. Small entities are encouraged to consider whether disclosures about such loans from other parties is necessary for the purposes of a true and fair view. *[FRS 102.BC.B11.40]*.

6.3.3   Small entity becomes or ceases to be eligible for the exemption in measuring directors' loans at present value

An entity that was not a small entity when the transaction was entered into, but subsequently becomes eligible to take advantage of the above exemption, and chooses to do so, applies the exemption retrospectively. *[FRS 102.11.13C]*.

An entity that has taken advantage of the exemption but subsequently ceases to be a small entity is permitted, when remeasuring the financial liability to present value prospectively from the first reporting date after it ceases to be a small entity, to determine the present value on the basis of the facts and circumstances existing at that time or at the date the financing arrangement was entered into. *[FRS 102.11.13B]*.

This means that in the first reporting period in which the entity ceases to be a small entity, the financial liability is remeasured at its present value at the end of the reporting period – either at the present value required by paragraph 11.13 (using the market rates applicable to a similar transaction at the date the financing transaction was entered into) or on the basis of the facts and circumstances at the end of the reporting period. While the adjustment is to be reflected prospectively, it is not specified where any catch up for any remeasurement required should be reflected. However, in our view, the adjustment should most appropriately be reflected in equity (consistent with the accounting for any difference between the transaction price and the present value of such a loan on initial recognition, if the above exemption available for small entities had not been taken).

6.4   Transition

Section 35 – *Transition to this FRS* – of FRS 102 includes three transitional exemptions – relating to share-based payment transactions, fair value measurement of financial instruments and financing transactions involving related parties – that apply specifically to small entities (whether applying Section 1A or not). *[FRS 102.35.10(b), 10(u)-(v)]*.

The transition exemptions only applied where a small entity first adopted FRS 102 for an accounting period that commenced before 1 January 2017 and were intended to help with transition from the FRSSE to FRS 102. The transition exemptions are therefore not discussed in Chapter 32 of this publication. However, a full discussion is included in Chapter 32 at 5.4, 5.19 and 5.20 of EY UK GAAP 2017.

Where a small entity has taken a transition exemption relating to share-based payment transactions and / or financing transactions involving related parties, this may impact the accounting in subsequent financial statements of small entities. The transition exemption relating to fair value measurement of financial instruments allowed entities not to restate comparatives in the first FRS 102 financial statements.

Small entities who made use of the transition exemption relating to share-based payments are not required to apply Section 26 – *Share-based Payment* – to equity instruments granted before the start of the first FRS 102 reporting period. However, such small entities are required to make disclosures in respect of off-balance sheet arrangements in accordance with paragraph 1AC.31 (see 11.1.5.H below). *[FRS 102.35.10(b)]*.

The transition exemption relating to financing transactions involving related parties allowed a small entity applying the requirement in paragraph 11.13 to determine the present value of the financial asset or liability based on the facts and circumstances at the start of the first FRS 102 reporting period, rather than at the date of the original transaction. *[FRS 102.35.10(v)]*. The approach taken would impact the measurement of the financing transaction under the amortised cost method in later financial statements.

7   PRESENTATION REQUIREMENTS IN SECTION 3 THAT STILL APPLY WHERE SECTION 1A IS APPLIED

A small entity applying Section 1A must still comply with Section 3 – *Financial Statement Presentation*, except for certain specified paragraphs (see 7.1 below). *[FRS 102.1A.7, 3.1A]*.

This means such an entity must still comply with Section 3's requirements on:

- the financial statements giving a 'true and fair view' (including the provisions for a 'true and fair override') (see 7.2 below); *[FRS 102.3.2, 3.4-6]*

- assessment of the entity's ability to continue as a going concern (see 7.3 below); *[FRS 102.3.8]*

- frequency of reporting (see 7.4 below); *[FRS 102.3.10]*

- consistency of presentation, excluding the requirements on reclassification (see 7.5 below); *[FRS 102.3.11]*

- comparative information (see 7.5 below); *[FRS 102.1A.10, 3.14, 3.20]*

- materiality and aggregation (see 7.6 below); *[FRS 102.3.15-16B]*

- requirements to present each financial statement in a complete set of financial statements with equal prominence, and ability to use other titles for the financial statements as long as they are not misleading; *[FRS 102.1A.11, 3.21-22]*

- identification of the financial statements, except for paragraph 3.24(b) (see 7.7 below); *[FRS 102.3.23, 3.24(a)]* and

- interim financial reports (see 7.8 below). *[FRS 102.3.25]*.

7.1   Exemptions from certain presentation and disclosure requirements in FRS 102 for a small entity applying Section 1A

A small entity applying Section 1A is not required to comply with the following paragraphs of Section 3 (see also discussion below): *[FRS 102.1A.7, 3.1A]*

- paragraph 3.3 (statement of compliance with FRS 102 – see 7.1.1 below);
- paragraph PBE 3.3A (statement of compliance with FRS 102 by a public benefit entity – see 7.1.1 below);
- paragraph 3.9 (disclosure of material uncertainties over going concern and certain disclosures where the financial statements not prepared on a going concern basis – see 7.3 below);
- paragraph 3.12 (reclassification of comparatives where the presentation or classification of items in the financial statements has changed, unless impracticable to do so – see 7.5.2 below);
- paragraph 3.13 (disclosure of the reasons why it is impracticable to reclassify comparatives where the presentation or classification of items in the financial statements has changed);
- paragraph 3.17 (content of a complete set of financial statements – see 7.1.2 below);
- paragraph 3.18 (option to present a statement of income and retained earnings, where certain conditions are met);
- paragraph 3.19 (option to present only an income statement where there are no items of other comprehensive income, or to label the bottom line of the statement of comprehensive income as 'profit or loss'); and
- paragraph 3.24(b) (description of the nature of the entity's operations and its principal activities, unless disclosed in the business review (or similar statement) accompanying the financial statements).

In addition, a small entity applying Section 1A is not required to comply with Section 4 – *Statement of Financial Position*, Section 5 – *Statement of Comprehensive Income and Income Statement*, Section 6 – *Statement of Changes in Equity and Statement of Income and Retained Earnings*, Section 7 – *Statement of Cash Flows*, and the disclosure requirements in Sections 8 to 35. *[FRS 102.1A.7, 1A.17]*.

The above requirements have been disapplied because they relate to disclosures not required by the CA 2006, the Small Companies Regulations or the Small LLP Regulations and because UK company law (and LLP law) only requires presentation of a balance sheet and profit and loss account.

7.1.1   *Statement of compliance*

The Triennial review 2017 clarified that small entities must make the statement of compliance that the financial statements are prepared in accordance with the small companies regime or small LLPs regime, where required by legislation. Other entities may refer to the small entities regime. This statement is included on the statement of financial position, in a prominent position above the signature (see 9 below). *[FRS 102.1A.6A]*.

Notwithstanding the general exemption available to small entities applying Section 1A from complying with paragraph 3.3 (and making an explicit and unreserved statement of compliance that the financial statements are prepared in accordance with FRS 102), small entities in the Republic of Ireland are *required* to make a statement of whether the financial statements have been prepared in accordance with Section 1A, giving the effect of and reasons for any material departures from Section 1A (section 291(7) of the Companies Act 2014). *[FRS 102.1A.7, 1AD.3, 3.3]*. This reflects a disclosure required for Irish companies under Irish law. Appendix E, instead, *encourages* small entities in the UK to give a statement of compliance with FRS 102, adapted to refer to Section 1A. *[FRS 102.1AE.1(a)]*.

Both Irish and UK small entities are encouraged, where applicable, to make an explicit and unreserved statement that the small entity is a public benefit entity. *[FRS 102.1AE.1(b), 1AE.2]*.

7.1.2 Content of complete set of financial statements

As explained further at 8 below, Section 1A states that a complete set of financial statements includes a statement of financial position and income statement, prepared in accordance with the requirements of Part 1 of Schedule 1 to the Small Companies Regulations (or Part 1 of Schedule 1 to the Small LLP Regulations) – except to the extent that these requirements are not permitted by any statutory framework under which such entities report – together with the required notes. Irish small entities instead refer to Part II of Schedule 3A to the Companies Act 2014. *[FRS 102.1A.4, 1A.8, 1A.12, 1A.14]*.

However, a small entity is encouraged to present a statement of total comprehensive income, where it has items in other comprehensive income, and to present a statement of changes in equity (or statement of income and retained earnings) where it has transactions with equity holders. Such additional statements may be needed in order for the financial statements to give a true and fair view (see 7.2 below). *[FRS 102.1A.5, 1A.9]*.

The exemption from including a statement of cash flows is available to any small entity, whether or not applying Section 1A. *[FRS 102.7.1B]*. However, the Triennial review 2017 clarified that a small entity (regardless of the regime applied in the preparation of its financial statements) is not required to include a statement of cash flows in its financial statements unless it is required to do so by an applicable SORP or law or other relevant regulation. *[FRS 102.3.1B]*. See, for example, the discussion on Update Bulletin 1 to the Charities SORP (FRS 102) (2014) at 4.2 above.

Section 1A requires that a complete set of financial statements prepared by a small entity also includes notes in accordance with paragraphs 1A.16 to 1A.20. *[FRS 102.1A.8]*. In particular, additional disclosures may be required in order for the financial statements to give a true and fair view. See 7.2, 8 and 11 below. Consequently, the presentation sections of FRS 102, beyond the mandatory paragraphs of Section 3, remain relevant to small entities applying Section 1A that present additional primary statements or disclosures.

More generally, entities subject to SORPs may be subject to additional requirements. See, for example, the discussion on the Charities SORP (FRS 102) (2014) at 4.2 above) and in relation to small LLPs at 11.5 below.

Chapter 5

7.2   True and fair view

Section 1A requires that the financial statements of a small entity shall give a true and fair view of the assets, liabilities, financial position and profit or loss of the small entity for the reporting period. *[FRS 102.1A.5]*.

This is consistent with the statutory requirements for a company in the CA 2006 (or in the CA 2006, as applied to LLPs). The directors of a company (or members of an LLP) must not approve accounts unless they are satisfied that the accounts give a true and fair view of the assets, liabilities, financial position and profit or loss of the company (or LLP) (and in respect of any group accounts, the undertakings included in the consolidation as a whole, so far as concerns the members of the company (or LLP)). *[s393, s393 (LLP)]*. Irish small entities refer to section 289 of the Companies Act 2014,

Section 3 provides further guidance on the requirement that financial statements must give a true and fair view. *[FRS 102.3.1]*. Application of FRS 102, with additional disclosure when necessary, is presumed to result in financial statements that give a true and fair view of the financial position, financial performance and, when required to be presented, cash flows of entities. Additional disclosures are necessary when compliance with the specific requirements in FRS 102 is insufficient to enable users to understand the effect of particular transactions, other events and conditions on the entity's financial position and financial performance. *[FRS 102.3.2]*.

The 'true and fair view' requirement in paragraph 1A.5 refers to profit or loss (rather than financial performance, as in paragraph 3.2) and excludes reference to cash flows because small entities are not generally required to present a statement of comprehensive income or a cash flow statement (see 7.1.2 above). *[FRS 102.1A.5]*.

Section 1A's similar requirement (to Section 3) to present additional disclosures where necessary to meet the requirement for the financial statements to give a true and fair view *[FRS 102.1A.16]* is consistent with the statutory requirement that if compliance with the regulations, and any other provision made by or under the CA 2006 as to matters to be included in a company's (or LLP's) individual and / or group accounts or in notes to those accounts, would not be sufficient to give a true and fair view, the necessary additional information must be given in the accounts or in a note to the accounts. *[s396(4), s404(4), s396(4) (LLP), s404(4) (LLP)]*.

A particular issue for small entities relates to the fact that the statutory disclosures for companies subject to the small companies regime (and LLPs subject to the small LLPs regime) – which are the basis for the disclosures included in Section 1A – are considerably more limited than the disclosures required for entities applying full FRS 102. Consequently, a small entity may need to provide disclosures in addition to those set out in Section 1A in order to comply with the requirement in paragraph 1A.5 that the financial statements give a true and fair view of the assets, liabilities, financial position and profit or loss of the small entity. *[FRS 102.1A.5, 1A.6]*. See 11 below for further guidance.

The LLP SORP requires small LLPs to give certain additional disclosures and also notes that, depending on the individual facts and circumstances, some or all of the disclosures in FRS 102 and the SORP may be necessary in order for the LLP's financial statements to give a true and fair view (judgement will be needed) (see 11.5 below). *[LLP SORP.27A-28]*.

The general principles governing the preparation of financial statements – the going concern presumption, consistency (in applying accounting policies and measurement bases), use of prudence, use of the accruals basis, separate determination of individual assets and liabilities (no offsetting); and the requirement that the opening balance sheet for a financial year corresponds to the closing balance sheet for the previous financial year – are set out in the Small Companies Regulations (and Small LLP Regulations). These general principles are exactly the same as those set out in the Regulations (and LLP Regulations), as discussed in Chapter 6 at 9.1.1. *[1 Sch 11-15A (SC), 1 Sch 11-15A (LLP SC)].*

Similarly, the Small Companies Regulations (and Small LLP Regulations) set out the historical cost accounting rules, alternative accounting rules and fair value accounting rules. *[1 Sch 16-41 (SC), 1 Sch 16-41 (LLP SC)].* These contain the same recognition and measurement requirements as the Regulations (and LLP Regulations), as discussed in Chapter 6 at 10, but have simpler disclosures. Small companies, qualifying partnerships[5] and small LLPs that are micro entities preparing accounts in accordance with the micro-entity regime cannot apply the alternative accounting rules or fair value accounting rules (but would apply FRS 105 rather than Section 1A). *[Regulations (SC) 3(1A), LLP SC Regulations 3(1A)].*

There is further discussion on the true and fair view requirement (including its relationship with accounting standards) in Chapter 1 at 7.2.1 and Chapter 6 at 9.2.

7.2.1   True and fair override

In special circumstances when management concludes that compliance with any requirement of FRS 102 or applicable legislation (only when it allows for a true and fair override) is inconsistent with the requirement to give a true and fair view, the entity shall depart from that requirement in the manner set out in paragraph 3.5. *[FRS 102.3.4].* Paragraphs 3.5 and 3.6 set out the disclosures required where an entity departs from a requirement of the standard or from a requirement of applicable legislation (see 11.1.4 below). *[FRS 102.3.5-6].* In our view, for a small entity applying Section 1A, paragraphs 3.5 and 3.6 should be read with adaptations to refer to 'profit or loss' rather than 'financial performance', consistent with the concept of 'true and fair view' in Section 1A.

FRS 102's requirements for the disclosures in respect of departures from the standard or legislation (for the overriding purpose of the financial statements giving a true and fair view) are consistent with the requirements of the CA 2006 for companies (and the CA 2006 as applied to LLPs) to give the particulars of, reasons for and effect of any departure in a note to the financial statements. *[s396(5), s404(5), s396(5) (LLP), s404(5) (LLP)].*

Appendix III to FRS 102 highlights certain instances where the requirements of FRS 102 result in a departure from the requirements of the Regulations in order to give a 'true and fair view'. These examples, which are not exhaustive, are relevant to UK companies preparing Companies Act accounts (and similarly, LLPs preparing non-IAS accounts).

In addition, where it appears to the directors (or the members of the LLP) that there are special reasons for departing from any of the general principles (see 7.2 above) in preparing the accounts for the financial year, the particulars of the departure, the reasons for it and its effect should be disclosed in a note to the accounts. *[1 Sch 10(2) (SC), 1 Sch 10(2) (LLP SC)].*

There is further discussion of the true and fair override requirement in FRS 102 and company law in Chapter 6 at 9.2.2.

7.3   Going concern

FRS 102 requires management, when preparing financial statements, to make an assessment of an entity's ability to continue as a going concern. An entity is a going concern unless management either intends to liquidate the entity or to cease trading, or has no realistic alternative but to do so. In assessing whether the going concern assumption is appropriate, management takes into account all available information about the future, which is at least, but is not limited to, twelve months from the date when the financial statements are authorised for issue. *[FRS 102.3.8, FRS 102 Appendix I]*.

The FRC's *Guidance on the Going Concern Basis of Accounting and Reporting on Solvency and Liquidity Risks – Guidance for directors of companies that do not apply The UK Corporate Governance Code* (April 2016) ('2016 FRC Guidance') similarly requires directors of companies reporting under FRS 102 to consider a period of at least twelve months from the date of authorisation of the financial statements. This is longer than that required by IAS 1 – *Presentation of Financial Statements* – but the 2016 FRC Guidance, in any event, recommends directors of companies reporting under IFRS to consider a period of at least twelve months from the date of authorisation of the financial statements.[6] While small entities are not required to apply the 2016 FRC Guidance, its relevance to small entities is discussed at 7.3.1 below.

When management is aware, in making its assessment, of material uncertainties related to events or conditions that cast significant doubt upon the entity's ability to continue as a going concern, those uncertainties should be disclosed in the financial statements. *[FRS 102.3.9]*. While a small entity is not required to comply with paragraph 3.9 (see 7.1 above), Section 1A specifically encourages a small entity to make this disclosure by way of its inclusion in Appendix E to Section 1A which sets out disclosures 'which may nevertheless be necessary to give a true and fair view'. *[FRS 102.1A.7, 1A.20, 1AE.1(c), 1AE.2]*.

FRS 102 states that an entity shall not prepare its financial statements on a going concern basis if management determines after the reporting period either that it intends to liquidate the entity or to cease trading or that it has no realistic alternative but to do so. Deterioration in operating results and financial position after the reporting period may indicate a need to consider whether the going concern assumption is no longer appropriate. If the going concern assumption is no longer appropriate, the effect is so pervasive that a fundamental change in the basis of accounting rather than an adjustment to the amounts recognised within the original basis of accounting is required, and therefore the disclosures in paragraph 3.9 (as set out below) apply. *[FRS 102.32.7A-B]*.

When financial statements are not prepared on a going concern basis, that fact should be disclosed, together with the basis on which the financial statements are prepared and the reason why the entity is not regarded as a going concern. *[FRS 102.3.9]*.

Although a small entity applying Section 1A is not required to comply with paragraph 3.9, the Triennial review 2017 clarified that if a small entity departs from the principle that it is presumed to be carrying on business as a going concern, it must provide the disclosures required by paragraph 1AC.10 or paragraph 1AD.11, as relevant. *[FRS 102.1A.7]*. This is because preparation of the financial statements on a non-going concern basis would be a departure from one of the general principles (see 7.2 above). Particulars of the departure, the reasons for it and its effect are required to be disclosed by the Small Companies Regulations and Small LLP Regulations (see 11.1.4 below). *[1 Sch 10(2) (SC), 1 Sch 10(2) (LLP SC), FRS 102.1AC.10]*. In practice, this is likely to require similar disclosures to those set out in paragraph 3.9.

FRS 102 provides no further guidance concerning what impact there should be on the financial statements if it is determined that the going concern basis is not appropriate. Accordingly, entities will need to consider carefully their individual circumstances to arrive at an appropriate basis.

7.3.1 FRC Guidance on Going Concern

FRS 102's requirements are supplemented by the 2016 FRC guidance referred to at 7.3 above.

The 2016 FRC guidance is non-mandatory, best practice guidance which aims to provide a proportionate and practical guide for directors of companies not applying the *UK Corporate Governance Code*. The 2016 FRC guidance covers factors to consider when determining whether the going concern basis of accounting is appropriate; making an assessment of the solvency and liquidity risks that might constitute principal risks for a company requiring disclosure in the strategic report; guidance on the assessment periods for the going concern basis of accounting and those risks; and guidance on the assessment process. It also includes summaries of the related reporting requirements.

While the 2016 FRC Guidance refers to directors and companies for simplicity, the guidance notes that it is also likely to be relevant to other entities.

Small and micro-companies must assess whether the going concern basis of accounting is appropriate in preparing their financial statements. However, they are excluded from the scope of the 2016 FRC Guidance. For small companies applying Section 1A, this is on the basis that:

- such entities are not required to provide disclosures on the going concern basis of accounting, although their directors are encouraged to provide such disclosures, where appropriate, in meeting their responsibility to prepare financial statements that give a true and fair view; and
- they are not required to prepare a strategic report.

Chapter 5

The 2016 FRC Guidance includes a table of the requirements in the CA 2006 and accounting standards and highlights the relevant sections in the guidance that may assist directors in meeting the requirements. For completeness, this table includes small micro-entities and small companies. The relevant requirements for small companies are identified, as follows:

- Assessment of the appropriateness of the going concern basis of accounting *[FRS 102.3.8]* – addressed in the 2016 FRC Guidance, paragraphs 3.1 to 3.6.

- Disclosure when there are material uncertainties or when the company does not prepare financial statements on a going concern basis *[FRS 102.3.9]* – addressed in the 2016 FRC Guidance, paragraphs 3.7 to 3.8.

  The guidance notes that while there is no explicit requirement in the CA 2006 or FRS 102 for companies subject to the small companies regime to report on the going concern basis of accounting and material uncertainties, the directors are required to make such disclosures that are necessary for the financial statements to provide a true and fair view. Appendix E to Section 1A encourages the inclusion of disclosures on material uncertainties in order to meet this requirement (see 11.3 below).

  As discussed in 7.3 above, the disclosures set out in paragraphs 1AC.10 or 1AD.11 must be given where the financial statements are not prepared on a going concern basis (as this is a departure from one of the general principles for preparation of financial statements). *[FRS 102.1A.7, 1AC.10]*.

- Additional disclosures that may be required to give a true and fair view *[s393]* – addressed in the 2016 FRC Guidance, paragraphs 3.9 to 3.10.

The 2016 FRC Guidance is discussed further in Chapter 6 at 9.3.1.

7.4   Frequency of reporting

A small entity must present a complete set of financial statements (including comparative information) at least annually. When the end of an entity's reporting period changes and annual financial statements are presented for a period longer or shorter than one year, the entity shall disclose that fact, the reason for using a longer or shorter period, and the fact that comparative amounts presented in the financial statements (including the related notes) are not entirely comparable. *[FRS 102.3.10]*.

Normally, financial statements are consistently prepared covering a one year period. Some entities, particularly in the retail sector, present financial statements for a 52-week period. This practice is permitted by the CA 2006 which allows companies to prepare financial statements to a financial year end, not more than 7 days before or after the end of the accounting reference period (based on the accounting reference date notified to the Registrar). *[s390(2)(b), s391, s390(2)(b) (LLP), s391 (LLP)]*. While FRS 102 does not explicitly address this issue, we consider that financial statements prepared in accordance with FRS 102 can be made up to a financial year end, not more than 7 days from the end of the accounting reference period.

7.5   Comparative information (including consistency of presentation)

Except when FRS 102 permits or requires otherwise, a small entity presents comparative information in respect of the preceding period for all amounts presented in the current period's financial statements. *[FRS 102.1A.10, 3.14]*. This means that the requirement to present comparative information applies both to mandatory and voluntary information presented for the current period.

In certain cases, FRS 102 provides specific exemptions from presenting comparatives (as indicated in the disclosures listed at 11 below). The General Rules to the formats (as defined in 3 above) also contain requirements on comparatives (see 8.2 below).

7.5.1   *Comparative information for narrative and descriptive information*

An entity shall include comparative information for narrative and descriptive information when it is relevant to an understanding of the current period's financial statements. *[FRS 102.3.14]*. See Chapter 6 at 3.6.1.

7.5.2   *Consistency of comparative information*

The requirements on consistency of comparative information where Section 1A is applied are the same as under full FRS 102. *[FRS 102.3.11]*. See Chapter 6 at 3.6.2.

The Triennial review 2017 added paragraphs 3.12 and 3.13 (disclosures in relation to reclassification of comparatives) to the list of exemptions from presentation requirements. However, the General Rules to the formats (see 8.2 below) include disclosures concerning the non-comparability of and any adjustment made to corresponding amounts (i.e. comparatives), as set out in paragraph 1AC.8 for UK small entities and 1AD.10 for small entities in the Republic of Ireland (see 11.1.3 below). *[FRS 102.1AC.8, 1 Sch 7(2)]*.

7.6   Materiality and aggregation

Financial statements result from processing large numbers of transactions or other events that are aggregated into classes according to their nature or function. The final stage in the process of aggregation and classification is the presentation of condensed and classified data, which form line items in the financial statements. *[FRS 102.3.16]*. When applying FRS 102, an entity must decide, taking into consideration all relevant facts and circumstances, how it aggregates information in the financial statements (including the notes). The understandability of the entity's financial statements must not be reduced by obscuring material information with immaterial information or by aggregating material items that have different natures or functions. *[FRS 102.3.16A]*.

'Material' is defined as follows: 'Omissions or misstatements of items are material if they could, individually or collectively, influence the economic decisions of users taken on the basis of the financial statements. Materiality depends on the size and nature of the omission or misstatement judged in the surrounding circumstances. The size or nature of the item, or a combination of both, could be the determining factor.' However, it is inappropriate to make, or leave uncorrected, immaterial departures from the standard to achieve a particular presentation of an entity's financial position, financial performance or cash flows. *[FRS 102.2.6, Appendix I]*.

FRS 102 requires an entity to present each material class of similar items separately and to present separately items of a dissimilar nature or function unless they are immaterial. *[FRS 102.3.15]*. If a line item is not individually material, it is aggregated with other items either in those statements or in the notes. An item that may not warrant separate presentation in those financial statements may warrant separate presentation in the notes. *[FRS 102.3.16]*. The principle of materiality and level of aggregation is particularly relevant to small entities in determining whether additional information is required to be presented in the notes to the financial statements in order for the financial statements to give a true and fair view (see 7.2 above). *[FRS 102.1A.16-17]*.

A small company (or small LLP) reporting under FRS 102 must comply with the balance sheet and profit and loss account formats set out in the Small Companies Regulations (or Small LLP Regulations) respectively (see 8.1 below).

The General Rules to the formats (see 8.2 below) allow the directors (or members of the LLP) to combine items denoted with Arabic numbers in the statutory balance sheet and profit and loss account formats if:

- their individual amounts are not material to assessing the state of affairs, or profit or loss, of the company (or LLP) for the financial year in question; or

- the combination facilitates that assessment (in the latter case, the individual amounts of the line items combined must be disclosed in the notes). *[1 Sch 4(2) (SC), 1 Sch 4(2) (LLP SC)]*.

In respect of the abridged formats, certain line items are permitted to be combined on the face of the balance sheet and profit and loss account (see 9.2 and 10.2 below). Section 1A states that disaggregation of gross profit or loss, disclosure of turnover and disaggregation of information in the balance sheet may be necessary in the notes to the financial statements in order to give a true and fair view. *[FRS 102.1AA.2, 1AB.2]*.

The detailed content of the adapted formats is not set out in the Small Companies Regulations and therefore the adapted formats have no line items denoted with an Arabic number. However, the General Rules still apply 'so far as is practicable' – see 8.2.3 below for a discussion of how the above requirements apply to adapted formats.

FRS 102 states that an entity need not provide a specific disclosure required by the standard if the information resulting from that disclosure is not material, except when required by the CA 2006 (for Irish entities, the Companies Act 2014) regardless of materiality. This is the case even if FRS 102 contains a list of specific requirements or describes them as minimum requirements (including those set out in paragraph 1A.18 and Appendix C or Appendix D, as relevant). *[FRS 102.1A.17A, 18, 3.16B]*.

However, certain disclosures required by the CA 2006 must be given regardless of materiality. *[FRS 102.3.16B]*. Most of the disclosures listed in Appendix C derive from Schedule 1 to the Small Companies Regulations (and there are similar disclosures in Schedule 1 to the Small LLP Regulations). The Small Companies Regulations (and Small LLP Regulations), where applied, also permit that 'amounts which in the particular context of any provision of Schedule 1 to these Regulations are not material may be disregarded for the purposes of that provision.' *[8 Sch 7 (SC), 5 Sch 7 (LLP SC)]*. However, examples of disclosures to which materiality considerations do not apply are the average number of employees, analysed by category (see 11.1.7 below), *[s411, FRS 102.1AC.33]*, and details of directors' advances, credits and guarantees, *[s413, FRS 102.1AC.36]*, (see 11.1.8.C below). In addition, in group accounts, certain information on related undertakings in Part 2 of Schedule 6 to the Small Companies Regulations (and in Part 2 of Schedule 4 of the Small LLP Regulations) are required, even if not material.

7.7   Identification of the financial statements

It is commonly the case that financial statements will form only part of a larger annual report, regulatory filing or other document, but FRS 102 only applies to the financial statements (including the notes). The annual report and accounts for a small UK company, for example, comprise the directors' report and the annual accounts. An LLP is not required to prepare a members' report (with the exception described below). Although the LLP SORP requires certain information to be disclosed, which may be included in a separate members' report, these disclosures are not required to be given by a small LLP (see 11.5 below). *[LLP SORP.27A-28, 30-31]*.

For financial years beginning on or after 17 June 2016, a traded LLP or a banking LLP is required to prepare a strategic report. *[s414A(1), s414A(1) (LLP)]*. This change to LLP law was made in *The Statutory Auditors Regulations 2017* (SI 2017/1164)[7] and post-dates the publication of LLP SORP. As discussed in 4.4.2 above, such an LLP would not qualify for the small LLPs regime. *[s384(1) (LLP)]*.

Accordingly, FRS 102 requires that an entity clearly identifies the financial statements and the notes, and distinguishes them from other information in the same document. In addition, the entity must display the following information prominently, and repeat it, when necessary, for an understanding of the information presented: *[FRS 102.1A.7, 3.23]*

- the name of the reporting entity and any change in its name since the end of the preceding reporting period;
- whether the financial statements cover the individual entity or a group of entities;
- the date of the end of the reporting period and the period covered by the financial statements;
- the presentation currency, as defined in Section 30 – *Foreign Currency Translation* (discussed in Chapter 27 at 3.1 and 3.7); and
- the level of rounding, if any, used in presenting amounts in the financial statements.

In practice, these requirements can be met through the use of appropriate headings for pages, statements, notes and columns. This could include, for example: the inclusion of a basis of preparation note within the accounting policies, the use of appropriate titles for the primary financial statements, distinguishing group and company and the use of appropriate headings in the columns in the primary financial statements (and notes to the financial statements). Entities will need to consider how best to present the required information where financial statements are made available electronically.

Financial statements are usually presented to an appropriate level of rounding, such as thousands or millions of currency units. An appropriate level of rounding can avoid obscuring useful information but entities need to ensure that material information is not omitted. The level of rounding used must be clearly disclosed in the primary statements and notes to the financial statements. Entities are not precluded from using lower levels of rounding in certain notes to the financial statements. In all cases, it is important that the units used are clearly stated.

The legal form of the entity, its country of incorporation and the address of its registered office (or principal place of business, if different from the registered office) are required to be disclosed in a note to the financial statements. *[FRS 102.1A.7, 3.24(a)]*. See similar disclosures at 11.1.9 below.

7.8   Interim financial reports

FRS 102 does not address the presentation of interim financial reports. It is unlikely that many small entities will be preparing interim financial reports but, if they do, such reports must describe the basis for preparing and presenting such information. FRS 104 – *Interim Financial Reporting* – sets out a basis for the preparation and presentation of interim financial reports that an entity may apply. *[FRS 102.3.25]*.

See Chapter 34 if interim reporting is relevant for a small entity.

8   COMPLETE SET OF FINANCIAL STATEMENTS

A complete set of financial statements of a small entity must include all of the following (with comparatives – see 7.5 above): *[FRS 102.1A.7-8, 12, 14, 16-20, 3.20]*

- a statement of financial position as at the reporting date, in accordance with paragraph 1A.12 (see 9 below);

- an income statement for the reporting period in accordance with paragraph 1A.14 (see 10 below); and

- notes in accordance with paragraphs 1A.16 to 1A.20 (see 11 below).

Small entities (regardless of whether applying Section 1A or not) need not prepare a cash flow statement, unless required to do so by an applicable SORP or law or other relevant regulation. *[FRS 102.1A.7, 3.1B, 7.1B]*.

A small entity may use other titles for the financial statements as long as they are not misleading. *[FRS 102.1A.7, 11, 3.22]*. Consequently, the terms 'balance sheet' or 'profit and loss account' remain acceptable for use. In a complete set of financial statements, an entity should present each financial statement with equal prominence. *[FRS 102.1A.7, 3.21]*.

While paragraphs 3.17 to 3.19 (covering the content of a complete set of financial statements in full FRS 102) do not apply to entities applying Section 1A, a small entity is not prohibited from applying any or all of Sections 3 to 7. *[FRS 102.1A.7]*.

In addition to the statement of financial position and income statement (required by company and LLP law, and set out in paragraph 1A.8 above), a small entity is encouraged to present a statement of total comprehensive income when it recognises gains or losses in other comprehensive income, and to present a statement of changes in equity or a statement of changes in retained earnings when it has transactions with equity holders. This is in order to meet the requirements in 1A.5 (for the financial statements to give a true and fair view). *[FRS 102.1A.9]*.

The LLP SORP also encourages but does not require small LLPs applying Section 1A to present the reconciliation of the movement in members' other interests (i.e. the statement of changes in equity. *[LLP SORP.27D, 59]*. See 11.5 below.

Notes to the financial statements contain information in addition to those presented in the primary financial statements and provide narrative descriptions or disaggregations of items presented in those statements and information about items that do not qualify for recognition in those statements. *[FRS 102 Appendix I]*. Consistent with the Small Companies Regulations (and Small LLP Regulations), the notes must be presented in the order in which, where relevant, the items to which they relate are presented in the statement of financial position and in the income statement. *[FRS 102.1AC.2, 1 Sch 42(2) (SC), 1 Sch 42(2) (LLP SC)]*.

The notes must include sufficient information in order to meet the requirement for the financial statements of the small entity to give a true and fair view. Appendix C of Section 1A (for a small entity reporting in the UK) and Appendix D of Section 1A (for a small entity reporting in the Republic of Ireland) set out specific note disclosures to be given by a small entity that are based on the statutory requirements for a small company applying the Small Companies Regulations (and for Irish companies, the Companies Act 2014, as amended). A note on the FRC website explains that there are some slight differences between the disclosure requirements of Section 1A and those in the Small LLP Regulations; LLPs should apply the equivalent requirements of the Small LLP Regulations rather than Section 1A. However, additional disclosures may be needed in order for the financial statements to give a true and fair view. Appendix E of Section 1A includes a list of disclosures that are specifically encouraged (and which may nevertheless be necessary for the financial statements to give a true and fair view). Small entities are also encouraged to consider and provide other disclosures from full FRS 102 that are relevant to material transactions, other events or conditions of the small entity in order for the financial statements to give a true and fair view. Specific disclosures are not required if the information is not material, except where required by the CA 2006 regardless of materiality. *[FRS 102.1A.16-20]*. See 7.2 and 11 below.

While 8.1 to 10 below refer to the formats applicable to LLPs, detailed guidance on LLPs is outside the scope of this chapter.

8.1   Formats

A small entity must present a statement of financial position and an income statement (showing its profit or loss for the period) in accordance with the requirements for a balance sheet and profit and loss account set out in Part 1 of Schedule 1 to the Small Companies Regulations (or Part 1 of Schedule 1 to the Small LLP Regulations). Irish small entities instead refer to Part II of Schedule 3A to the Companies Act 2014. *[FRS 102.1A.4, 12, 14]*.

Small entities that do not report under the CA 2006 (or for Irish small entities, the Companies Act 2014) also comply with these requirements, except to the extent that these requirements are not permitted by any statutory framework under which such entities report. *[FRS 102.1A.4]*. Therefore, such entities may have a more restricted choice (or need to make certain modifications to the formats adopted).

A UK company subject to the small companies regime must follow one of the formats included in Part 1 of Schedule 1 to the Small Companies Regulations. An LLP subject to the small LLPs regime must follow one of the formats included in Part 1 of Schedule 1 to the Small LLP Regulations.

Part 1 of Schedule 1 to the Small Companies Regulations (and Part 1 of Schedule 1 to the Small LLP Regulations) allow a choice of:

- statutory formats (see 8.1.1, 9.1 and 10.1 below);
- abridged formats (see 8.1.2, 9.2 and 10.2 below); and
- adapted formats (see 8.1.3, 9.3 and 10.3 below)

for the statement of financial position (referred to as 'the balance sheet' in company and LLP law) and income statement (referred to as 'the profit and loss account' in company and LLP law).

The statutory formats for a small entity in the UK are set out in Section B of Part 1 of Schedule 1 to the Small Companies Regulations (and Section B of Part 1 of Schedule 1 to the Small LLP Regulations). The abridged formats and adapted formats allow certain abridgements and adaptations to be made to the statutory formats.

Further discussion relevant to formats can be found in the following sections:

- 8.1.4 below addresses the modifications to the formats required in consolidated financial statements (where prepared – see 6.2 above). Abridged formats are not available for use in consolidated financial statements;
- 8.1.5 below addresses changes in formats;
- 8.2 below addresses the General Rules to the formats; and
- 9 and 10 below cover the content of the statement of financial position and income statement respectively, depending on the format adopted.

8.1.1   Statutory formats

UK companies and LLPs have a choice of two balance sheet and two profit and loss account statutory formats, with the line items required set out in Section B of Part 1 of Schedule 1 to the Small Companies Regulations (and Section B of Part 1 of Schedule 1 to the Small LLP Regulations). *[1 Sch 1 (SC), 1 Sch 1 (LLP SC)]*. See 9.1 and 10.1 below.

The General Rules to the formats (see 8.2 below) apply to the statutory formats.

Statutory formats, as modified by Schedule 6 to the Small Companies Regulations (or Schedule 4 to the Small LLP Regulations), can also be used in group accounts (see 8.1.4 below). *[6 Sch 1(1A) (SC), 4 Sch 1(1A) (LLP SC)]*.

Irish small entities instead refer to Part II of Schedule 3A to the Companies Act 2014.

8.1.2   Abridged formats

Abridged formats, where appropriate to the circumstances of the company's (or the LLP's) business, can be used in individual financial statements. Abridged formats are not available in group accounts, *[6 Sch 1(1A) (SC), 4 Sch 1(1A) (LLP SC)]*, and are not permitted under Irish law (and so cannot be used by Irish small entities). *[FRS 102.1AA.1(b), 1AB.1(b)]*.

FRS 102 does not provide guidance on in what circumstances it may be appropriate to use abridged formats (which would show less information in the profit and loss account and balance sheet).

The abridged formats derive from the statutory formats but show fewer headings (i.e. those denoted by roman numerals or letters) in the balance sheet and combine line items (by presenting a single line item for 'gross profit or loss') in the profit and loss account. *[1 Sch 1A(1)-(2) (SC), 1 Sch 1A(1)-(2) (LLP SC)]*. See 9.2 and 10.2 below.

Abridged formats cannot be applied by a company that was a charity at any time within that year. There is no similar statutory exclusion for an LLP (although it would be unlikely that an LLP would be a charity). *[1 Sch 1A(4) (SC), 1 Sch 1A (LLP SC)]*. However, Appendix III to FRS 102 extends this restriction beyond charitable companies and states that abridged formats are not available to small entities that are charities. *[FRS 102 Appendix III.11E]*.

To use abridged formats, all of the members of the company (or the LLP) must have consented to the drawing up of the abridged balance sheet and / or abridged profit and loss account. Consent may only be given as regards the preparation of, as appropriate, the balance sheet or profit and loss account in respect of the preceding financial year. *[1 Sch 1A(1)-(3) (SC), 1 Sch 1A(1)-(3) (LLP SC)]*. The implication is that consent is required to be obtained each year in respect of the preceding financial year, before the date of approval of the financial statements for the preceding financial year. The Small Companies Regulations and Small LLP Regulations provide no further requirements on how such consent is obtained.

Appendix III to FRS 102 explains that when a small entity that is not a company chooses to prepare abridged financial statements, it should ensure that: *[FRS 102 Appendix III.11E]*

- similar consent is obtained from the members of its governing body, taking into account its legal form; and
- abridged financial statements would not be prohibited by relevant laws or regulation.

Where the balance sheet or profit and loss account is abridged pursuant to paragraph 1A of Schedule 1 to the Small Companies Regulations (or paragraph 1A of Schedule 1 to the Small LLP Regulations), the directors of the company (or designated members of the LLP) must deliver to the Registrar a statement by the company (or by the LLP) that all the members of the company (or of the LLP) have consented to the abridgement. *[s444(2A), s444(2A) (LLP)]*. While there is no specific requirement to do so, we consider it would also be helpful for annual accounts that include abridged formats to include a statement that all the members of the company (or of the LLP) have consented to the abridgement in the statements made below the balance sheet (and above the directors' signature).

So far as is practicable, the provisions of paragraphs 2 to 9A of the General Rules to the formats (see 8.2 below) apply to the balance sheet or profit or loss account of a company (or an LLP), notwithstanding any such abridgment pursuant to paragraph 1A. *[1 Sch 1C (SC), 1 Sch 1C (LLP SC)]*.

8.1.3   Adapted formats

Paragraph 1B of Schedule 1 to the Small Companies Regulations (and paragraph 1B of Schedule 1 to the Small LLP Regulations) set out the adaptations to the statutory formats permitted for the balance sheet and profit and loss account. These provide limited guidance on the content of the adapted formats, leaving the detail to UK accounting standards. Irish small entities applying adapted formats refer to paragraph 2(2) and paragraph 2(3) of Schedule 3A to the Companies Act 2014. *[FRS 102.1AA.4, 1AB.3]*.

A company's directors (or the members of an LLP) may adapt one of the balance sheet formats in Section B of Part 1 of Schedule 1 to the Small Companies Regulations (or Section B of Part 1 of Schedule 1 to the Small LLP Regulations), so to distinguish between current and non-current items in a different way, provided that: *[1 Sch 1B(1) (SC), 1 Sch 1B(1) (LLP SC)]*

(a)   the information given is at least equivalent to that which would have been required by the use of such format had it not been thus adapted; and

(b)   the presentation of those items is in accordance with generally accepted accounting principles or practice.

Chapter 5

Similarly, a company's directors (or the members of an LLP) may adapt, otherwise than pursuant to paragraph 1A(2), one of the profit and loss account formats in Section B of Part 1 of Schedule 1 to the Small Companies Regulations (or Section B of Part 1 of Schedule 1 to the Small LLP Regulations), provided that: *[1 Sch 1B(2) (SC), 1 Sch 1B(2) (LLP SC)]*

(a)   the information given is at least equivalent to that which would have been required by the use of such format had it not been thus adapted; and

(b)   the presentation is in accordance with generally accepted accounting principles or practice.

The reference to 'otherwise than pursuant to paragraph 1A(2)' means that an entity making an adaptation to combine specified line items as a single line item for 'gross profit' must apply the abridged format requirements in paragraph 1A (including obtaining the consent of all the members each year and filing the required statement of consent with the Registrar). See 8.1.2 above.

So far as is practicable, the provisions of paragraphs 2 to 9A of the General Rules to the formats (see 8.2 below) apply to the balance sheet or profit or loss account of a company (or an LLP), notwithstanding any such adaptation pursuant to paragraph 1B. *[1 Sch 1C(SC), 1 Sch 1C (LLP SC)]*.

Small entities applying adapted formats for the balance sheet and profit and loss account follow the requirements for adapted formats in Section 1A which allow a presentation of the balance sheet and profit and loss account which is much closer to IAS 1. Section 1A specifies that, at a minimum, certain line items are presented on the face of the statement of financial position and income statement, with further sub-classifications of items in the statement of financial position in the notes to the financial statements (see 9.3 and 10.3 below). In general, few difficulties should arise over classification of line items where adapted formats are applied since the required line items are aligned with the categories of assets and liabilities discussed in FRS 102. Some areas to watch on classification are, however, discussed at Chapter 6 at 5.1 and 6.5.

In our view, small entities applying Section 1A could also choose to follow the adapted formats set out in Sections 4 and 5 as these simply require more detailed analysis. See Chapter 6 at 4 to 6.

In addition, Schedule 1 to the Small Companies Regulations (and Schedule 1 to the Small LLP Regulations) require supplementary information in respect of certain line items in the balance sheet and profit and loss account to be given in the notes to the accounts. See 11.1 below. One complexity is that this information is in respect of line items found in the statutory formats, which may not align completely with the line items used where the adapted formats are applied. See discussion at 9.3 below.

Adapted formats, as modified by Schedule 6 to the Small Companies Regulations (or Schedule 4 to the Small LLP Regulations), can also be used in group accounts (see 8.1.4 below).

8.1.4   *Consolidated financial statements*

Section 1A does not require an entity to prepare group accounts. *[FRS 102.1A.21]*. A small entity may be required by other regulations (or may choose) to prepare group accounts. For accounting periods beginning on or after 1 January 2017, there are circumstances where a company subject to the small companies regime (or an LLP subject to the small LLPs regime) may be required to prepare group accounts under the CA 2006 (or SI 2008/1911). See 6.2 above.

Part 1 of Schedule 6 to the Small Companies Regulations (and Part 1 of Schedule 4 to the Small LLP Regulations) address the balance sheet and profit and loss account formats applicable to group accounts of UK companies (or of LLPs), modifying the formats applicable for individual accounts, as set out in Part 1 of Schedule 1 to the Small Companies Regulations (or Part 1 of Schedule 1 to the Small LLP Regulations).

The group accounts must comply so far as practicable with the provisions of Schedule 1 to the Small Companies Regulations (or Schedule 1 to the Small LLP Regulations), as if the undertakings included in the consolidation (the group) were a single company (or LLP). The group accounts are treated as so complying with any provision of the schedules listed above if they comply instead with the corresponding provision of Schedule 6 to the Regulations (or Schedule 3 to the LLP Regulations). *[Regulations (SC) 8, 6 Sch 1(1) (SC), LLP SC Regulations 6, 4 Sch 1(1) (LLP SC)].*

Irish small entities refer to Schedule 4A to the Companies Act 2014. *[FRS 102.1A.22].* The discussion below relates to the formats applicable to small entities in the UK.

8.1.4.A   Modifications to formats for purposes of consolidated financial statements

The formats required in group accounts (relevant to both adapted formats and statutory formats) must identify non-controlling interests (see 8.1.4.B below).

In addition, certain modifications (which are the same for UK companies and LLPs) are made to the statutory formats for the group balance sheet and profit and loss account.

In the group balance sheet statutory formats, the line items in B.III 'Investments in participating interests' (or the line items in A.III for an LLP) presented in the individual balance sheet statutory formats are replaced with the line items in Figure 5.1 below. *[6 Sch 1(2) (SC), 4 Sch 1(2) (LLP SC)].* Shares and loans to group undertakings will only be relevant in consolidated financial statements for those subsidiary undertakings excluded from consolidation (see Chapter 8 at 3.4). Group undertakings, associated undertakings and participating interests are defined in Chapter 6 at 5.3.4.C to 5.3.4.E.

Figure 5.1   Analysis of investments

B	Fixed assets	
III	Investments	
	1	Shares in group undertakings
	2	Interests in associated undertakings
	3	Other participating interests
	4	Loans to group undertakings and undertakings in which a participating interest is held
	5	Other investments other than loans
	6	Others

In the group profit and loss account statutory formats, the line item 'income from participating interests' presented in the individual profit and loss account statutory formats is replaced by two items: 'Income from interests in associated undertakings' and 'Income from other participating interests'. *[6 Sch 1(3) (SC), 4 Sch 1(3) (LLP SC)].*

Chapter 5

8.1.4.B   Non-controlling interest

Under FRS 102, non-controlling interest is defined as 'the equity in a subsidiary not attributable, directly or indirectly, to a parent'. *[FRS 102 Appendix I]*. See Chapter 8 at 3.7.

The requirements for non-controlling interest in Section 9 (or indeed Section 22 – *Liabilities and Equity*) also apply to a small entity. *[FRS 102.1A.1, 22(a)]*. An entity shall present non-controlling interest in the consolidated statement of financial position within equity, separately from the equity of the owners of the parent *[FRS 102.9.20]* and shall disclose non-controlling interest in the profit or loss of the group separately in the statement of comprehensive income (or income statement, if presented). *[FRS 102.9.21]*.

Schedule 6 to the Small Companies Regulations (and Schedule 4 to the Small LLP Regulations) modify the balance sheet and profit and loss account formats to reflect non-controlling interest as follows: *[6 Sch 17 (SC), 4 Sch 17 (SC LLP)]*

'(1)   The formats set out in Section B of Part 1 of Schedule 1 to these Regulations have effect in relation to group accounts with the following additions.

(2)   In the Balance Sheet Formats there must be shown, as a separate item and under the heading "non-controlling interests", the amount of capital and reserves attributable to shares in subsidiary undertakings included in the consolidation held by or on behalf of persons other than the parent company [LLP] and its subsidiary undertakings.

(3)   In the Profit and Loss Account Formats there must be shown, as a separate item and under the heading "non-controlling interests", the amount of any profit or loss attributable to shares in subsidiary undertakings included in the consolidation held by or on behalf of persons other than the parent company [LLP] and its subsidiary undertakings.'

The heading used in the balance sheet is treated as one which has a letter assigned, meaning that it must be included on the face of the balance sheet. However, the heading used in the profit and loss account is treated as one which has an Arabic number assigned (allowing the adaptations permitted by the General Rules to the formats, as described at 8.2 below). *[6 Sch 17(4) (SC), 4 Sch 17(4) (LLP SC)]*.

The statutory requirements for presentation of non-controlling interests would permit a presentation consistent with the requirements of FRS 102. In most cases, the amounts shown as non-controlling interest under FRS 102 and the amounts required by the Small Companies Regulations or Small LLP Regulations will be the same. There is a theoretical possibility that the amounts required by FRS 102 and the Small Companies Regulations or Small LLP Regulations may differ (see Chapter 6 at 4.5 and Chapter 8 at 3.7). In such a case, two totals are strictly required to be presented to meet the requirements of both FRS 102 and the statutory requirements.

The above paragraph refers to modifications to the statutory formats (in Section B of Part 1 of Schedule 1 to the Small Companies Regulations and Section B of Part 1 of Schedule 1 to the Small LLP Regulations) (see 8.1.1 above). In our view, the same requirements for presentation of non-controlling interest apply to adapted formats (see 8.1.3 above) because the General Rules to the formats require that any adaptations made need to be 'at least equivalent' to the information required in the statutory formats. *[1 Sch 1B (SC), 6 Sch 1 (SC), 1 Sch 1B (LLP SC), 4 Sch 1 (LLP SC)]*.

In our view, these requirements also apply to a small entity (other than a UK company or LLP), to the extent permitted by its statutory framework. While Section 1A does not explicitly refer to the formats required for consolidated financial statements (which are not *required* to be prepared by a small entity), it does require that a small entity that prepares consolidated financial statements shall comply so far as practicable with the requirements of Section 1A as if it were a single entity (Schedule 6 of the Small Companies Regulations, paragraph 1(1)), subject to any restrictions or exemptions set out in legislation. *[FRS 102.1A.22(c)]*.

Figure 5.2 below illustrates the presentation of non-controlling interest in the statement of financial position for a company subject to the small companies regime. Figure 5.3 below illustrates the allocation of profit or loss to owners of the parent and to non-controlling interest where a separate income statement is presented by a company subject to the small companies regime. The terminology 'non-controlling interests' in the Small Companies Regulations (rather than 'non-controlling interest' in FRS 102) is used.

Figure 5.2   *Presentation of non-controlling interest in statement of financial position – small UK company*

	£'000
Capital and reserves	
Called up share capital	12,075
Share premium account:	493
Capital redemption reserve	500
Merger reserve	6,250
Profit and loss account	27,882
Equity attributable to owners of the parent	47,200
Non-controlling interests	360
	47,560

Figure 5.3   *Presentation of non-controlling interest in income statement (where presented separately) – small UK company*

	£'000
Profit before taxation	7,786
Tax on profit:	(3,339)
Profit after taxation and profit for the financial year	4,447
Profit for the financial year attributable to:	
Owners of the parent	4,209
Non-controlling interests	238

A small entity is not required to prepare a statement of changes in equity or a statement of comprehensive income (although this is encouraged where there are transactions with equity holders or items of other comprehensive income – see discussion at 8 above). *[FRS 102.1A.9, 5.1A, 6.1A]*. See Chapter 6 at 4.5 for guidance on the presentation of non-controlling interest in such statements, if presented.

Chapter 5

8.1.5   Changes in formats

The General Rules to the formats (see 8.2 below) require that once a company's (or an LLP's) balance sheet or profit and loss account has been prepared for any financial year using one of the formats (in Section B of Part 1 of Schedule 1 to the Small Companies Regulations or Section B of Part 1 of Schedule 1 to the Small LLP Regulations), the company's directors (or members of the LLP) must use the same format in preparing Companies Act accounts (non-IAS accounts, for an LLP) for subsequent financial years, unless in their opinion there are special reasons for a change. Particulars of any such change must be given in a note to the accounts in which the new format is first used, and the reasons for the change must be explained. *[1 Sch 2 (SC), 6 Sch 1(1) (SC), 1 Sch 2 (LLP SC), 4 Sch 1(1) (LLP SC)].*

While this paragraph refers to the statutory formats (see 8.1.1 above), the General Rules apply so far as is practicable to abridged formats (which are derived from the statutory formats) (see 8.1.2 above) and adapted formats (see 8.1.3 above). Therefore, in our view, the same requirements apply to changes in the statutory format used and also changes between abridged, adapted and statutory formats. *[1 Sch 1C (SC), 1 Sch 2 (SC), 6 Sch 1(1) (SC), 1 Sch 1C (LLP SC), 1 Sch 2 (LLP SC), 4 Sch 1(1) (LLP SC)].*

A change in the format applied would be regarded as a change in accounting policy for the purposes of FRS 102 and, therefore, would be retrospectively effected. See Chapter 9 at 3.4 for the requirements on changes in accounting policy.

8.2   General Rules to the formats

The following discussion relates to the General Rules to the formats (see definition in 3 above) which apply to balance sheet and profit and loss account formats included in Schedule 1 to the Small Companies Regulations (and Schedule 1 to the Small LLP Regulations).

The General Rules to the formats also cover changes in formats (see 8.1.5 above).

8.2.1   General Rules governing the form of the statutory formats

Subject to the following provisions of the Schedule:

- every balance sheet of a company (or an LLP) must show the items listed in either of the balance sheet formats; and

- every profit and loss account of a company (or LLP) must show the items listed in either of the profit and loss account formats

in Section B of Part 1 of Schedule 1 to the Small Companies Regulations (or Section B of Part 1 of Schedule 1 to the Small LLP Regulations), i.e. the statutory formats. References in the Schedule to the items listed must be read together with any of the notes following the formats in Section B which apply to those items, which may also permit alternative positions for any particular items.

Subject to paragraph 1A, the items in the balance sheet and profit and loss account statutory formats must be shown in the order and under the headings and sub-headings given in the particular format used, but the letters or numbers assigned to that item in the format do not need to be given (and are not in practice). *[1 Sch 1 (SC), 1 Sch 1 (LLP SC)].*

While the Small Companies Regulations and Small LLP Regulations refer to 'Subject to paragraph 1A' (which provides for abridged formats), it seems likely that this is a drafting error and should read 'Subject to paragraphs 1A and 1B' to cover both the abridged formats and the adapted formats (see 8.2.2 below). This would be consistent with the Regulations and LLP Regulations, where the equivalent paragraph reads 'Subject to paragraph 1A' (which refers to the adapted formats, since the abridged formats are not available under the Regulations or LLP Regulations). *[1 Sch 1(3), 1 Sch 1(3) (LLP)].*

While there are two statutory formats – format 1 and format 2 – available for the balance sheet, only format 1 is commonly used. Both format 1 and format 2 profit and loss accounts are commonly used. There are some differences in detail in the line items required in the LLP statutory formats compared to the company statutory formats.

See Figures 5.4 and 5.5 at 9.1 and 9.1.2 below for the format 1 balance sheet and Figures 5.10 to 5.13 at 10.1 below for the format 1 and 2 profit and loss accounts applicable for the individual accounts of a UK company and an LLP. Each of the headings and sub-headings denoted with a capital letter or Roman numeral must be presented on the face of the balance sheet.

The individual line items in the statutory balance sheet and profit and loss account formats (and their related notes), which are similar to those in the Regulations and LLP Regulations, are discussed in Chapter 6 at 5.3 and 6.6.

8.2.2   Abridged formats and adapted formats

Paragraph 1A sets out the requirements for abridged formats (see 8.1.2 above and 9.2 and 10.2 below) and paragraph 1B sets out the requirements for adapted formats (see 8.1.3 above and 9.3 and 10.3 below).

8.2.3   General Rules applying to statutory, abridged and adapted formats

The following provisions in the General Rules to the formats apply to the statutory formats (in Section B of Part 1 of Schedule 1 to the Small Companies Regulations and Section B of Part 1 of Schedule 1 to Small LLP Regulations). *[1 Sch 1 (SC), 1 Sch 1 (LLP SC)].* These provisions also apply so far as is practicable, to the abridged formats and adapted formats. *[1 Sch 1C (SC), 1 Sch 1C (LLP SC)].*

Chapter 5

The Small Companies Regulations and Small LLP Regulations do not provide further guidance on how 'so far as is practicable' is to be interpreted, but in our view, this phrase is needed because the General Rules to the formats have been written from the perspective of the statutory formats, e.g. they refer to items given an Arabic number which may not have a direct counterpart in the abridged formats or adapted formats. In other cases, such as in relation to corresponding amounts (meaning comparatives), there are no difficulties in applying the requirements. We do not consider that 'so far as is practicable' allows small companies or small LLPs flexibility to regard the General Rules to the formats as optional, where abridged formats or adapted formats are used.

The Small Companies Regulations and Small LLP Regulations require that every profit and loss account must show 'profit or loss before taxation' as a line item on the face of the profit and loss account. *[1 Sch 6 (SC), 1 Sch 6 (LLP SC)]*. This line item is not required for a qualifying partnership preparing statutory accounts.[8]

The General Rules to the formats allow any item to be shown in a company's (or an LLP's) balance sheet or profit and loss account in greater detail than required by the particular format used. The balance sheet or profit and loss account may include an item representing or covering the amount of any asset or liability, income or expenditure not otherwise covered by any of the items listed in the format used. However, preliminary expenses; the expenses of, and commission on, any issue of shares (relevant for a company only); the expenses of, and commission on, any issue of debentures; and the costs of research may not be treated as assets in the balance sheet. *[1 Sch 3 (SC), 1 Sch 3 (LLP SC)]*. A qualifying partnership preparing statutory accounts is not subject to the above rules on which types of costs may not be treated as assets in the balance sheet.[9]

Where the special nature of the company's (or the LLP's) business requires it, the company's directors (or the members of the LLP) *must* adapt the arrangement, headings and sub-headings otherwise required in respect of items given an Arabic number in the balance sheet or profit and loss account format used. The directors (or the members of the LLP) *may* combine items to which Arabic numbers are given in the formats if their individual amounts are not material to assessing the state of affairs or profit or loss of the company (or the LLP) for the financial year in question; or the combination facilitates that assessment. In the latter case, the individual amounts of any items combined must be disclosed in a note to the accounts. *[1 Sch 4 (SC), 1 Sch 4 (LLP SC)]*.

Where adapted formats are used, any amendments made would need to comply 'so far as is practicable' with the General Rules to the formats. An entity may amend the descriptions used in the line items required in the statement of financial position (or the sub-classifications of those line items required), the ordering of items or aggregation of similar items in the statement of financial position, according to the nature of the small entity and its transactions to provide information that is relevant to an understanding of the small entity's financial position, providing that the information given is at least equivalent to that required by the balance sheet format had it not been adapted. *[FRS 102.1AA.5]*. Similarly, a small entity may include additional line items in the income statement, amend the descriptions used, and the ordering of items, when this is necessary to explain the elements of financial performance, providing the information given is at least equivalent to that required by the profit and loss account format had it not been adapted. *[FRS 102.1AB.4].*

FRS 102's requirements on materiality and aggregation are discussed at 7.6 above.

A corresponding amount (i.e. comparative) for the immediately preceding financial year must be shown for every item shown in the balance sheet or profit and loss account. Where that corresponding amount is not comparable with the amount shown in the current financial year, the corresponding amount may be adjusted. Particulars of the non-comparability and of any adjustment must be disclosed in a note to the accounts. *[1 Sch 7 (SC), 1 Sch 7 (LLP SC)].* This statutory requirement would permit FRS 102's requirements on restatement of comparatives to be followed. Where amounts are not restated, e.g. due to transitional provisions in accounting policies or where it is impracticable to determine the effects of a change in accounting policies on earlier periods, *[FRS 102.10.11-12]*, a note to the accounts will need to disclose the non-comparability. FRS 102's requirements on comparatives are discussed at 7.5 above.

The heading or sub-heading required for a particular item in the balance sheet or profit and loss account format must be presented where there is an amount for that item in either the current or immediately preceding financial year; otherwise, the heading or sub-heading must be omitted. *[1 Sch 5 (SC), 1 Sch 5 (LLP SC)].*

Amounts in respect of items representing assets or income may not be set off against amounts in respect of items representing liabilities or expenditure (as the case may be), or *vice versa*. *[1 Sch 8 (SC), 1 Sch 8 (LLP SC)].* FRS 102's requirements on offset are discussed in Chapter 6 at 9.1.1.C.

The company's directors (or the members of an LLP) must, in determining how amounts are presented within items in the profit and loss account and balance sheet, have regard to the substance of the reported transaction or arrangement, in accordance with generally accepted accounting principles or practice. *[1 Sch 9 (SC), 1 Sch 9 (LLP SC)].*

Where an asset or liability relates to more than one item in the balance sheet, the relationship of such asset or liability to the relevant items must be disclosed either under those items or in the notes to the accounts. *[1 Sch 9A (SC), 1 Sch 9A (LLP SC)].*

Examples of situations where this may be relevant include:

- items which are partly reported in debtors: amounts falling due within one year and debtors: amounts falling due after more than one year, where reported separately on the balance sheet (in the statutory or abridged formats);
- items which are partly reported in creditors: amounts falling due within one year and creditors: amounts falling due after more than one year (in the statutory or abridged formats); and
- items which are partly reported as current and non-current assets or liabilities (in the adapted formats).

This disclosure requirement does not appear to extend to reporting the relationship between assets and liabilities that derive from a single transaction (e.g. an asset acquired on a finance lease has an impact both on tangible fixed assets and lease creditors) nor, say, to identifying the associated deferred tax consequences of an asset or liability. Where a *single* asset or liability is required to be reported as more than one line item in the statement of financial position, e.g. split accounting for a convertible loan between equity and liability elements, or a loan at off-market rates made by a parent to its subsidiary is split between investment and loan asset, it would seem appropriate, in our view, to disclose the relationship between these line items.

9   STATEMENT OF FINANCIAL POSITION

A small entity must present a statement of financial position in accordance with the requirements for a balance sheet set out in either Part 1 *General Rules and Formats* of Schedule 1 to the Small Companies Regulations or Part 1 *General Rules and Formats* of Schedule 1 to the Small LLP Regulations. Irish small entities instead refer to Part II of Schedule 3A to the Companies Act 2014.

Small entities that do not report under the CA 2006 (or for Irish small entities, the Companies Act 2014) must also comply with the above requirement, except to the extent not permitted by any statutory framework under which such entities report. *[FRS 102.1A.4, 12]*.

As noted at 8.1 above, a small entity applying Schedule 1 to the Small Companies Regulations (or Schedule 1 to the Small LLP Regulations) has the following three alternatives: *[FRS 102.1AA.1]*

- apply the required statutory balance sheet formats (subject to any permitted flexibility – see the General Rules to the formats at 8.2 above) – see 9.1 below;
- draw up an abridged balance sheet – see 9.2 below; or
- adapt one of the balance sheet formats – see 9.3 below.

Irish law does not provide for the preparation of abridged statutory financial statements. Consequently, the option to prepare an abridged balance sheet is not available to small entities in the Republic of Ireland. This is not the same as abridgement for filing purposes. *[FRS 102.1AA.2]*.

The financial statements of a small entity choosing to apply Section 1A shall contain on the statement of financial position in a prominent position above the signature(s) of the director(s) (or designated member(s) of the LLP), a statement that the financial statements are prepared in accordance with the provisions applicable to companies subject to the small companies regime (or for LLPs, that the financial statements are prepared in accordance with the provisions applicable to LLPs subject to the small LLPs regime). For Irish small entities, this is required by section 324(4A) of the Companies Act 2014. Other entities may refer to the small entities regime. *[FRS 102.1A.6A, s414(3), s414(3) (LLP)]*. This statement will be required if Section 1A is applied and also if any of the statutory exemptions available to the small companies regime (in the UK or Republic of Ireland) or small LLPs regime are taken.

The financial statements of an Irish small entity must also include a statement as to whether the financial statements have been prepared in accordance with Section 1A of FRS 102. The effect of any material departure from Section 1A and the reasons for it must be noted in the financial statements (section 291(7) of the Companies Act 2014). *[FRS 102.1AD.3]*. A small entity in the UK is encouraged (but is not required) to give a statement of compliance with Section 1A. *[FRS 102.1AE.1]*.

Example 5.2 provides an example of the statutory statement which combines it with the statement of compliance with FRS 102. While the statement that the financial statements have been prepared in accordance with the provisions applicable to companies subject to the small companies regime (or to LLPs subject to the small LLPs regime, or to the small entities regime) is to be made on the face of the balance sheet, the statement of compliance with Section 1A could instead be made in the notes to the financial statements.

Example 5.2:   *Use of small companies regime (or small LLPs regime) and statement of compliance with FRS 102*

These financial statements have been prepared in accordance with the provisions applicable to companies subject to the small companies regime / [LLPs subject to the small LLPs regime] and in accordance with Financial Reporting Standard 102 'The Financial Reporting Standard applicable in the UK and Republic of Ireland', applying Section 1A – Small Entities.

9.1   Statutory balance sheet (format 1)

Schedule 1 to the Small Companies Regulations (and Schedule 1 to the Small LLP Regulations) provide a choice of two statutory formats for the balance sheet. Format 1 is a vertical format and is adopted by virtually all UK companies and LLPs. Format 2 presents assets separately from liabilities (including capital and reserves) and is rarely used.

This chapter only discusses the format 1 balance sheet. Irish small entities instead refer to Part II of Schedule 3A to the Companies Act 2014. *[FRS 102.1A.12]*.

Figure 5.4 below sets out the format 1 individual balance sheet for a small UK company. This needs to be read together with the notes to the formats discussed at 9.1.1 below.

In particular, amounts falling due after more than one year must be shown separately for each item included under debtors (items C.II.1-3). Section 4 of FRS 102 requires that where the amount of debtors due after more than one year is so material in the context of the total net current assets that in the absence of disclosure of the debtors due after more than one year on the face of the statement of financial position readers may misinterpret the financial statements, the amount should be disclosed on the face of the statement of financial position within current assets. In most cases, it will be satisfactory to disclose the amount due after more than one year in the notes to the financial statements. *[FRS 102.4.4A]*. While this paragraph does not directly apply to small entities applying Section 1A, we would generally expect this practice to continue to be followed by a small entity applying Section 1A and using the statutory formats.

Figure 5.4   Format 1 individual balance sheet – small UK company

A			Called up share capital not paid*
B			Fixed assets
	I		Intangible assets
		1	Goodwill
		2	Other intangible assets
	II		Tangible assets
		1	Land and buildings
		2	Plant and machinery etc.
	III		Investments**
		1	Shares in group undertakings and participating interests
		2	Loans to group undertakings and undertakings in which the company has a participating interest
		3	Other investments other than loans
		4	Other investments
C			Current assets
	I		Stocks
		1	Stocks
		2	Payments on account
	II		Debtors
		1	Trade debtors
		2	Amounts owed by group undertakings and undertakings in which the company has a participating interest
		3	Other debtors*
	III		Investments
		1	Shares in group undertakings
		2	Other investments
	IV		Cash at bank and in hand
D			Prepayments and accrued income*
E			Creditors: amounts falling due within one year
		1	Bank loans and overdrafts
		2	Trade creditors
		3	Amounts owed to group undertakings and undertakings in which the company has a participating interest
		4	Other creditors*
F			Net current assets (liabilities)
G			Total assets less current liabilities
H			Creditors: amounts falling due after more than one year
		1	Bank loans and overdrafts
		2	Trade creditors
		3	Amounts owed to group undertakings and undertakings in which the company has a participating interest
		4	Other creditors*
I			Provisions for liabilities
J			Accruals and deferred income*
K			Capital and reserves**
	I		Called up share capital
	II		Share premium account
	III		Revaluation reserve
	IV		Other reserves~
	V		Profit and loss account

> *   The notes to format 1 provide alternative positions for prepayments and accrued income, and accruals and deferred income. Prepayments and accrued income may be shown within sub-heading C.II.3 and accruals and deferred income may be shown within E.4, H.4 or both (as the case may require). Called up share capital not paid may also be shown within C.II.3.
>
> **   Modifications are required in group accounts (see discussion below and 8.1.4 above).
>
> ~   There is no breakdown of 'Other reserves' in the formats in the Small Companies Regulations (unlike the Regulations).

The main modifications required for the group balance sheet format are the identification of non-controlling interests and changes to item B.III in Figure 5.4 above. See 8.1.4 above.

The balance sheet statutory formats set out in the Small Companies Regulations (and Small LLP Regulations) distinguish between fixed assets and current assets. 'Fixed assets' are assets of a company (or an LLP) which are intended for use on a continuing basis in the company's (or the LLP's) activities, and 'current assets' are assets not intended for such use. FRS 102 broadens the definitions to refer to 'an entity'. *[8 Sch 3 (SC), 5 Sch 3 (LLP SC), FRS 102 Appendix I].* See Chapter 6 at 5.2.2.

In addition, the balance sheet statutory formats distinguish between creditors: amounts falling due within one year; and creditors: amounts falling due after more than one year. In distinguishing amounts between the two categories of creditor, the deciding factor is the earliest date of payment. Section 4 provides further guidance, which while not directly scoped into Section 1A is relevant as the same distinction would be made for the statutory formats under the Regulations. A creditor is classified as due within one year when the entity does not have an unconditional right, at the end of the reporting period, to defer settlement of the creditor for at least 12 months after the reporting date. *[FRS 102.4.7].* This is consistent with the statutory requirements that a loan is treated as falling due for repayment, and an instalment of a loan is treated as falling due for payment, on the earliest date on which the lender could require repayment or (as the case may be) payment, if the lender exercised all options and rights available to him. *[8 Sch 6 (SC), 5 Sch 6 (LLP SC), FRS 102.4.7].* See Chapter 6 at 5.2.3.

The headings for the format 1 balance sheet in the Small Companies Regulations (and Small LLP Regulations) are slightly more simplified than the headings for the format 1 balance sheet in Schedule 1 to the Regulations (and LLP Regulations) but the guidance on the headings included in the latter at Chapter 6 at 5.3 remains relevant. However, the disclosures in the notes to the accounts required by the Small Companies Regulations (and Small LLP Regulations) are fewer than those required by the Regulations (and LLP Regulations).

Each of the headings and sub-headings denoted with a capital letter or Roman numeral, as set out in Figure 5.4 above, must be presented on the face of the format 1 balance sheet for the individual accounts of a company in the order and under the headings and sub-headings given. The format 1 balance sheet includes sub-headings, denoted with an Arabic number. The General Rules to the formats (see 8.2 above), which must be complied with, explain further the presentation of line items with an Arabic number.

Where an asset or liability relates to more than one item in the balance sheet, the relationship of such asset or liability to the relevant items must be disclosed either under those items or in the notes to the accounts. *[1 Sch 9A (SC), 1 Sch 9A (LLP SC)].* See discussion of this requirement at 8.2 above.

FRS 102 has accounting requirements for various items that do not have separate line items in format 1, but which would be presented separately on the face of the statement of financial position under IAS 1. Such items include investment property, financial assets, biological assets, cash and cash equivalents and deferred tax. FRS 102's requirement (in Section 4) to present additional line items on the face of the statement of financial position where relevant to an understanding of the entity's financial position does not apply to small entities applying Section 1A, *[FRS 102.1A.7, 4.3]*, but the General Rules to the formats provide flexibility to present line items in additional detail (see 8.2 above). So, for example, a property company may distinguish its investment property from other tangible fixed assets. The presentation of additional line items might require use of boxes and subtotals in order to comply with the balance sheet formats.

9.1.1   Notes to the formats

Certain alternative positions for line items are indicated in Figure 5.4 above. In addition, the notes on the balance sheet formats clarify that:

- amounts representing goodwill (item B.I.1) must only be included to the extent that the goodwill was acquired for valuable consideration. This is consistent with the requirements of FRS 102 that internally generated goodwill is not recognised; *[FRS 102.18.8C(f)]*

- amounts in respect of concessions, patents, licences, trademarks and similar rights and assets must only be included at item B.I.2 if either the assets were acquired for valuable consideration and are not required to be shown under goodwill or the assets in question were created by the company itself. FRS 102 has more restrictive requirements over recognition of internally developed intangible assets (where a policy of capitalisation is adopted, instead of a policy of expensing internally developed intangible assets). See Chapter 16 at 3.3.3;

- amounts falling due after more than one year must be shown separately for each item included under debtors (items C.II.1-3);

- within other creditors (items E4, H4 and J), there must be shown separately:

  (a)   the amount of any convertible loans; and

  (b)   the amount for creditors in respect of taxation and social security.

Payments received on account of orders must be included in so far as they are not shown as deductions from stocks. In our view, the offset rules in FRS 102 would not permit payments received on account to be shown as deductions from stocks;

- in determining the amount shown as net current assets (liabilities) (item F), any prepayments and accrued income must be taken into account, wherever shown; and

- the amount of allotted share capital and amount of called up share capital which has been paid up must be shown separately (item K.1).

The notes to the formats also require that where other investments (at item B.III.4 or C.III.2) include own shares, the nominal value of such shares must be shown separately. This accounting treatment is not permitted by FRS 102, which requires own shares to be accounted as a deduction against equity. *[FRS 102.22.16]*.

9.1.2   Modifications of the format 1 balance sheet for small LLPs

The format 1 balance sheet in the Small LLP Regulations differs in the following respects:

- A – Called up share capital is omitted so the headings above are A – Fixed Assets to I – Accruals and deferred income;

- A.III.2 (B.III.2 in company formats) is loans to group undertakings and undertakings in which the LLP has a participating interest;

- B.II.2 (C.II.2 in company formats) is amounts owed by group undertakings and undertakings in which the LLP has a participating interest;

- D.3 and G.3 (E.3 and H.3 in company formats) are amounts owed to group undertakings and undertakings in which the LLP has a participating interest;

- there is an additional item, J – Loans and other debts due to members. Note (7) to the LLP balance sheet formats requires that the following amounts must be shown separately under this item – the aggregate amount of money advanced to the LLP by the members by way of loan; the aggregate amount of money owed to members by the LLP in respect of profits; and any other amounts; and

- K – Capital and reserves is replaced with K – Members' other interests (with sub-headings: K.I – Members' capital, K.II – Revaluation reserve and K.III – Other reserves).

The notes to the LLP format 1 balance sheet are the same as detailed at 9.1.1 above for companies except for the additional requirement in note (7) to analyse loans and other debts due to members discussed above and the omission of items relating to shares. In particular, the amount falling due after more than one year must be shown separately for each item included under debtors (items B.II.1 to B.II.3).[10] See the further discussion of the presentation of debtors: amounts falling due after more than one year at 9.1 above.

Figure 5.5 below sets out the format 1 individual balance sheet for a small LLP. This needs to be read together with the notes to the formats.

Figure 5.5   Format 1 individual balance sheet – small LLP

A	Fixed assets	
I	**Intangible assets**	
	1	Goodwill
	2	Other intangible assets
II	**Tangible assets**	
	1	Land and buildings
	2	Plant and machinery etc.
III	**Investments****	
	1	Shares in group undertakings and participating interests
	2	Loans to group undertakings and undertakings in which the LLP has a participating interest
	3	Other investments other than loans
	4	Other investments
B	Current assets	
I	**Stocks**	
	1	Stocks
	2	Payments on account
II	**Debtors**	
	1	Trade debtors
	2	Amounts owed by group undertakings and undertakings in which the LLP has a participating interest
	3	Other debtors*
III	**Investments****	
	1	Shares in group undertakings
	2	Other investments
IV	**Cash at bank and in hand**	
C	Prepayments and accrued income*	
D	Creditors: amounts falling due within one year	
	1	Bank loans and overdrafts
	2	Trade creditors
	3	Amounts owed to group undertakings and undertakings in which the LLP has a participating interest
	4	Other creditors*
E	Net current assets (liabilities)	
F	Total assets less current liabilities	

G	Creditors: amounts falling due after more than one year	
	1	Bank loans and overdrafts
	2	Trade creditors
	3	Amounts owed to group undertakings and undertakings in which the LLP has a participating interest
	4	Other creditors*
H	Provisions for liabilities	
I	Accruals and deferred income*	
SORP	*Net assets attributable to members*	
	Represented by:#	
J	Loans and other debts due to members	
K	Members' other interests	
	I	Members' capital
	II	Revaluation reserve
	III	Other reserves~

*   The notes to format 1 provide alternative positions for prepayments and accrued income, and accruals and deferred income. Prepayments and accrued income may be shown within sub-heading B.II.3 and accruals and deferred income may be shown within D.4, G.4 or both (as the case may require).

**   Modifications required in group accounts (see discussion below and 8.1.4 above).

~   There is no breakdown of 'Other reserves' in the formats in the Small LLP Regulations (unlike the LLP Regulations).

\#   The LLP SORP requires a total for net assets attributable to members, and total members' interests (as a memorandum item) to be disclosed on the face of the balance sheet. See the discussion below this figure (and Figure 5.6 below).

The main modifications required for the group balance sheet format are the identification of non-controlling interests and changes to item A.III in Figure 5.5 above (see 8.1.4 above).

The LLP SORP provides further guidance on members' interests and the application of the statutory formats for LLPs. The SORP requires the face of the balance sheet to show a total for 'net assets attributable to members' (i.e. a balance sheet total before 'loans and other debts due to members' (item J) and 'members' other interests' (item K)). In addition, 'total members' interests' (i.e. 'loans and other debts due to members' (item J) and 'members' other interests' (item K) less any amounts due from members included in debtors) should be disclosed as a memorandum item on the balance sheet. The SORP also provides illustrations of LLP balance sheets for different situations (depending on whether the partnership interests are classified as equity or a liability or part equity / part liability). *[LLP SORP.58, Appendix 1, Appendix 2]*. As explained at 11.5 below, small LLPs are not subject to all the disclosure requirements in the LLP SORP. However, in our view, it would be helpful for a small LLP to present these subtotals on the face of the balance sheet, where statutory formats are used.

Chapter 5

This format is illustrated in Figure 5.6 below (the capital letters for the line items are not required to be shown but are presented for convenience).

LLPs with no equity, e.g. because of the classification of the partnership interests in the LLP, will not have items to report for 'Members' other interests' in the balance sheet.

Figure 5.6   Presentation of small LLP balance sheet (following LLP SORP)

		£'000
	....	
	Net assets attributable to members	x
	Represented by:	£'000
J	**Loans and other debts due to members within one year**	
	Members' capital classified as liability	x
	Other amounts	x
		x
K	**Members' other interests**	
	Members' capital classified as equity	x
	Members' other interests – other reserves classified as equity	x
		x
		x
	Total members' interests	
	Amounts due from members	(x)
	Loans and other debts due to members	x
	Members' other interests	x
		x

Based on the example in Exhibit B of Appendix 1 of the LLP SORP for an LLP (with some equity). See discussion above this figure.

Detailed guidance on issues specific to LLPs is outside the scope of this chapter.

9.2   Abridged balance sheet (format 1)

Where appropriate to the circumstances of a company's (or an LLP's) business, the company's directors (or members of the LLP) may, with reference to one of the formats in Section B of Part 1 to Schedule 1 to the Small Companies Regulations (or Section B of Part 1 to Schedule 1 to the Small LLP Regulations), draw up an abridged balance sheet showing only those items in that format preceded by letters and Roman numerals provided that: *[1 Sch 1A(1) (SC), 1 Sch 1A(1) (LLP SC)]*

(a)   in the case of format 1, note (5) (for companies) and note (3) (for LLPs) of the notes to the formats is complied with;

(b)   in the case of format 2, notes (5) and (10) (for companies) and notes (3) and (8) (for LLPs) of those notes are complied with (not discussed in this chapter); and

(c)   all of the members of the company (or LLP) have consented to the drawing up of the abridged balance sheet.

See 8.1.2 above for discussion of when abridged formats, which are only available in individual accounts of a small entity in the UK, are permitted to be used.

Note (5) (for companies) and note (3) (for LLPs) require separate disclosure of the amount falling due after more than one year for each item included under debtors in Figure 5.7 below (i.e. items C.II.1 to C.II.3 for companies and items B.II.1 to B.II.3 for LLPs).

Therefore, the abridged balance sheet must include the headings denoted by letters and Roman numerals in the statutory balance sheet format (see 9.1 above), with separate disclosure required of the amounts falling due after more than one year for each item included under debtors. As discussed at 9.1 above, Section 4 provides guidance on when it may be appropriate to present this information on the face of the balance sheet. While this paragraph does not directly apply to small entities applying Section 1A, we would expect this practice to continue to be followed by a small entity applying Section 1A and using the abridged formats.

So far as is practicable, the provisions of paragraphs 2 to 9A of the General Rules to the formats (see 8.2 above) apply to the balance sheet or profit or loss account of a company (or an LLP), notwithstanding any such abridgement pursuant to paragraph 1A of Schedule 1 to the Small Companies Regulations (or paragraph 1A of Schedule 1 to the Small LLP Regulations). *[1 Sch 1C (SC), 1 Sch 1C (LLP SC)].*

Where an asset or liability relates to more than one item in the balance sheet, the relationship of such asset or liability to the relevant items must be disclosed either under those items or in the notes to the accounts. *[1 Sch 9A (SC), 1 Sch 9A (LLP SC)].* See 8.2 above.

Figure 5.7 below sets out an abridged format 1 balance sheet for a small UK company taking full advantage of the permitted abridgements. We only discuss the format 1 balance sheet in this publication as format 2 is rarely used.

Figure 5.7   Format 1 abridged balance sheet – small UK company

A		Called up share capital not paid*
B		Fixed assets
	I	Intangible assets
	II	Tangible assets
	III	Investments
C		Current assets
	I	Stocks
	II	Debtors* **
	III	Investments
	IV	Cash at bank and in hand
D		Prepayments and accrued income*
E		Creditors: amounts falling due within one year*
F		Net current assets (liabilities)
G		Total assets less current liabilities
H		Creditors: amounts falling due after more than one year*
I		Provisions for liabilities
J		Accruals and deferred income*
K		Capital and reserves
	I	Called up share capital
	II	Share premium account
	III	Revaluation reserve
	IV	Other reserves~
	V	Profit and loss account

*   The notes to format 1 provide alternative positions for prepayments and accrued income, and accruals and deferred income. Prepayments and accrued income may be shown within sub-heading C.II and accruals and deferred income may be shown within E or H or both (as the case may require). Called up share capital not paid may also be shown within C.II.

**   Amounts falling due after more than one year for each item included under debtors (item C.II) must be shown separately (Note (5) to the balance sheet format).

~   There is no breakdown of 'Other reserves' in the formats in the Small Companies Regulations (unlike the Regulations).

Figure 5.8 below sets out an abridged format 1 balance sheet for an LLP taking full advantage of the permitted abridgements. As explained at 9.1.2 above, the LLP SORP requires a total for 'net assets attributable to members', and 'total members' interests' (as a memorandum item) to be disclosed on the face of the balance sheet. *[LLP SORP.58, Appendix 1, Appendix 2]*. As explained at 11.5 below, small LLPs are not subject to all the disclosure requirements in the LLP SORP. However, in our view, it would be helpful for a small LLP to present these subtotals on the face of the balance sheet, where abridged formats are used.

Figure 5.8   *Format 1 abridged balance sheet – small LLP*

A	Fixed assets	
	I	Intangible assets
	II	Tangible assets
	III	Investments
B	Current assets	
	I	Stocks
	II	Debtors* **
	III	Investments
	IV	Cash at bank and in hand
C	Prepayments and accrued income*	
D	Creditors: amounts falling due within one year*	
E	Net current assets (liabilities)	
F	Total assets less current liabilities	
G	Creditors: amounts falling due after more than one year*	
H	Provisions for liabilities	
I	Accruals and deferred income*	
SORP	*Net assets attributable to members*	
	Represented by#	
J	Loans and other debts due to members	
K	Members' other reserves	
	I	Members' capital
	II	Revaluation reserve
	III	Other reserves~

*   The notes to format 1 provide alternative positions for prepayments and accrued income, and accruals and deferred income. Prepayments and accrued income may be shown within sub-heading B.II and accruals and deferred income may be shown within D or G or both (as the case may require).

**   Amounts falling due after more than one year for each item included under debtors (item B.II) must be shown separately (Note (3) to the balance sheet format).

~   There is no breakdown of 'Other reserves' in the formats in the Small LLP Regulations (unlike the LLP Regulations).

\#   The LLP SORP requires a total for net assets attributable to members, and total members' interests (as a memorandum item) to be disclosed on the face of the balance sheet (see the discussion above this figure and Figure 5.6 at 9.1.2 above).

As all the headings set out in Figures 5.7 and 5.8 above are preceded with a capital letter or Roman numeral, they must be presented on the face of the format 1 balance sheet for the individual accounts in the order and under the headings and sub-headings given.

The only difference to the statutory formats is the abridgement. The disclosures required by the Small Companies Regulations and Small LLP Regulations are still required. Therefore, the guidance on statutory formats at 9.1 above remains relevant where abridged formats are used.

Chapter 5

A small entity choosing to apply paragraph 1A(1) of Schedule 1 to the Small Companies Regulations (or paragraph 1A(1) of Schedule 1 to the Small LLP Regulations) and draw up an abridged balance sheet must still meet the requirement for the financial statements to give a true and fair view. A small entity must therefore also consider the requirements of paragraph 1A.16 (see 7.2 and 8 above, and 11 below) and provide any additional disclosure that is necessary in the notes to the financial statements, for example in relation to disaggregating the information in the balance sheet. *[FRS 102.1A.16, 1AA.2]*. In considering what level of disaggregation may be appropriate in order for the financial statements to give a true and fair view, in our view, entities should have regard to FRS 102's requirements on materiality and aggregation (see 7.6 above).

9.3   Adapted balance sheet

Adapted formats may be used to distinguish between current and non-current items in a different way (to the statutory formats), provided that the information given is at least equivalent to that which would have been required by the use of the statutory format had it not been thus adapted and the presentation of those items is in accordance with generally accepted accounting principles or practice. *[1 Sch 1B(1) (SC), 1 Sch 1B(1) (LLP SC)]*. The detail, however, is left to accounting standards, namely Section 1A.

An entity choosing to apply paragraph 1B(1) of Schedule 1 to the Small Companies Regulations (or paragraph 1B(1) of Schedule 1 to the Small LLP Regulations) and adapt one of the balance sheet formats shall, as a minimum, include in its statement of financial position the line items presented in Figure 5.9 below, distinguishing between those items that are current and those that are non-current (see 9.3.1 and 9.3.2 below). Irish small entities instead refer to paragraph 2(2) of Schedule 3A to the Companies Act 2014. *[FRS 102.1AA.3]*. To comply with this requirement, an entity must present as separate classifications: current assets and non-current assets, and current liabilities and non-current liabilities. *[FRS 102.1AA.6]*.

Where adapted formats are used, there is no requirement to disclose debtors: amounts falling due after more than one year or to classify creditors: amounts falling due within or after more than one year. *[FRS 102.4.4A, 4.7]*. Section 4 clarifies this in respect of adapted formats under full FRS 102. While Section 1A is silent on this matter, this will also be the case where adapted formats are used in accordance with Section 1A.

Figure 5.9   Balance sheet – line items included in adapted formats

(a)	Property, plant and equipment
(b)	Investment property carried at fair value through profit or loss
(c)	Intangible assets
(d)	Financial assets (excluding amounts shown under (e), (f), (j) and (k))
(e)	Investments in associates
(f)	Investments in jointly controlled entities
(g)	Biological assets carried at cost less accumulated depreciation and impairment
(h)	Biological assets carried at fair value through profit or loss
(i)	Inventories
(j)	Trade and other receivables
(k)	Cash and cash equivalents
(l)	Trade and other payables
(m)	Provisions
(n)	Financial liabilities (excluding amounts shown under (l) and (m))
(o)	Liabilities and assets for current tax
(p)	Deferred tax liabilities and deferred tax assets (classified as non-current)
(q)	Non-controlling interest, presented within equity separately from the equity attributable to the owners of the parent#
(r)	Equity attributable to the owners of the parent~

~ For LLPs, additional line items are required on the face of the balance sheet – see the discussion below this figure and Figure 5.6 at 9.1.2 above.
\# Not required in individual financial statements.

Chapter 5

The LLP SORP states that, in order for the adapted formats to show the equivalent information to the statutory formats, 'loans and other debts due to members' (item J in the statutory formats) and 'members' other interests' (item K in the statutory formats) must be separately disclosed on the face of the balance sheet. Balance sheet item K includes 'Members' capital', 'Revaluation reserve' and 'Other reserves' insofar as they are classified as equity, which are also required to be disclosed separately on the face of the balance sheet. *[LLP SORP.26C, 55]*. In our view, these requirements also apply to small LLPs as they are required to present equivalent information to the statutory formats.

The face of the balance sheet should also show the 'net assets attributable to members of the LLP (i.e. a balance sheet total before 'loans and other debts due to members' (item J) and 'members' other interests' (item K)). In addition, 'total members' interests' (being the total of 'loans and other debts due to members' (item J) and 'members' other interests' (item K) less any amounts due from members in debtors) should be disclosed as a memorandum item on the face of the balance sheet. *[LLP SORP.26C, 58]*. These are the same additional disclosures required by the LLP SORP where statutory formats are used – see 9.1.2 above. As explained at 11.5 below, small LLPs are not subject to all the disclosure requirements in the LLP SORP. However, in our view, it would be helpful for a small LLP to present these subtotals on the face of the balance sheet, where adapted formats are used.

Detailed guidance on issues specific to LLPs is outside the scope of this chapter.

The line items for the balance sheet, where adapted formats are used under Section 1A, are the same as those required where the full standard FRS 102 is applied. *[FRS 102.1AA.3, 4.2A]*.

See Chapter 6 at 5.1 for application issues on the above line items. In addition, an illustrative statement of financial position (using adapted formats) relevant to both Section 1A and Section 4 is included in Example 6.3 in Chapter 6 at 5.1.14.

While line items (o) and (p) appear to combine liabilities and assets for current tax and deferred tax respectively, the assets will need to be shown separately from the liabilities. Deferred tax is always classified as non-current.

The line item (q) for non-controlling interest (see 8.1.4.B above) is relevant only where consolidated financial statements are prepared.

So far as is practicable, the provisions of paragraphs 2 to 9A of the General Rules to the formats (see 8.2 above) apply to the adapted formats. *[1 Sch 1C (SC), 1 Sch 1C (LLP SC)].* Where an asset or liability relates to more than one item in the balance sheet, the relationship of such asset or liability to the relevant items must be disclosed either under those items or in the notes to the accounts. *[1 Sch 9A (SC), 1 Sch 9A (LLP SC)].*

In addition, the following sub-classifications of the line items presented must be disclosed either in the statement of financial position or in the notes: *[FRS 102.1AA.4]*

- property, plant and equipment in classifications appropriate to the entity;
- goodwill and other intangible assets;
- investments, showing separately shares and loans;
- trade and other receivables showing separately amounts due from related parties, and amounts due from other parties;
- trade and other payables, showing separately amounts payable to trade suppliers, and amounts payable to related parties; and
- classes of equity, such as called up share capital, share premium, retained earnings, revaluation reserve, fair value reserve and other reserves.

The sub-classifications of line items required in the notes to the financial statements are less extensive than those required under Section 4.

The descriptions of the line items in the statement of financial position set out in paragraph 1AA.3 (and of the sub-classifications of those line items set out in paragraph 1AA.4) and the ordering of items or aggregation of similar line items, may be amended according to the nature of the small entity and its transactions, to provide information that is relevant to an understanding of the entity's financial position, providing the information given is at least equivalent to that required by the balance sheet format had it not been adapted. *[FRS 102.1AA.5].*

While the adapted formats are closely based on IAS 1, Section 1A does not require IAS 1's disclosure of the amount expected to be recovered or settled after more than twelve months for each asset and liability line that combines amounts expected to be recovered or settled: *[IAS 1.61]*

(a)   no more than twelve months after the reporting period; and

(b)   more than twelve months after the reporting period.

The Small Companies Regulations (and Small LLP Regulations) set out supplementary information to be given in the notes to the accounts which apply where statutory formats, abridged formats or the adapted formats are used. One complexity is that the information required sometimes refers to items found in the statutory formats (which may differ to the line items identified where the adapted formats are used). For example, the adapted formats do not refer to fixed assets, creditors: amounts falling due within one year, creditors: amounts falling due after more than one year, investments, land or buildings, or turnover. A UK company (or an LLP) using adapted formats in Companies Act accounts (non-IAS accounts, for an LLP) will, therefore, need to identify which of its assets, liabilities or revenue streams must be included in the required disclosures. While the classification of non-current assets and current assets used in adapted formats differs to the fixed assets and current assets classification required in statutory formats, the statutory definition of 'fixed assets' is relevant for the purposes of disclosures in respect of fixed assets in the Small Companies Regulations (and Small LLP Regulations). See Chapter 6 at 5.2.2.

In addition, the Small Companies Regulations (and Small LLP Regulations) frequently require analyses and reconciliations to be given for Arabic-numbered sub-headings found in the statutory balance sheet formats. Section 1A includes nearly all the statutory disclosures in the Small Companies Regulations (which are similar to those in the Small LLP Regulations) but restates these disclosures in a way that can be applied even if statutory formats are not used (see 11 below).

Where Section 1A refers to, say, 'In respect of each item which is shown under the general item fixed assets', in our view, it may be appropriate to give the information required for each of the sub-classifications of fixed assets required to be presented by paragraph 1AA.4 (as listed above). This is because these sub-classifications in effect stand in place of the Arabic-numbered headings identified in the statutory formats.

9.3.1   Current and non-current assets

The definitions of current and non-current assets discussed below apply only where an entity chooses to use adapted formats in accordance with paragraph 1B(1) of Schedule 1 to the Small Companies Regulations (or paragraph 1B(1) of Schedule 1 to the Small LLP Regulations). Irish small entities instead refer to paragraph 2(2) of Schedule 3A to the Companies Act 2014.

FRS 102 defines non-current assets as assets of the entity which: *[FRS 102 Appendix I]*

(a)   it does not expect to realise, or intend to sell or consume, in its normal operating cycle (see Chapter 6 at 5.1.1.A);

(b)   it does not hold primarily for the purpose of trading (see Chapter 6 at 5.1.1.B);

(c)   it does not expect to realise within 12 months after the reporting period; or

(d)   are cash or cash equivalents restricted from being exchanged or used to settle a liability for at least 12 months after the reporting period.

The adapted formats also require that deferred tax assets are always classified as non-current. *[FRS 102.1AA.3]*.

'Cash or cash equivalents' are also defined in the FRS 102 Glossary, and should be interpreted in a manner consistent with Section 7 (see Chapter 7 at 3.3).

FRS 102 defines current assets as 'assets of an entity which are not non-current assets'. *[FRS 102 Appendix I]*. This differs to IAS 1, which defines current assets, with non-current assets as the residual. IAS 1 requires an entity to classify an asset as current if the asset meets any of the conditions in (a) to (d) of paragraph 66 of IAS 1. The conditions in (a) to (d) above of FRS 102's definition of 'non-current assets' are broadly the converse of the conditions (a) to (d) in IAS 1's definition of a current asset. In our view, the FRC intended that the classification of assets as non-current and current should be consistent with the requirements of paragraph 66 of IAS 1. However by choosing to define non-current assets, rather than current as in IAS 1, there are potential ambiguities in the wording of the definition, which we consider are unintended. For example, if meeting *any* of (a) to (d) below would qualify an asset as a non-current asset under FRS 102, this would not in fact be aligned with IAS 1. For instance, an asset may not be held primarily for the purpose of trading (so meets (b) in the definition) but if it is expected to be realised within twelve months after the reporting period (so does not meet (c) in the definition), IAS 1 would require this asset to be classified as current. *[IAS 1.66].*

FRS 102 provides no additional guidance beyond the definition above. However, since the intention is to provide a format more aligned with IAS 1, management may consider, as permitted by the hierarchy in Section 10 – *Accounting Policies, Estimates and Errors*, the requirements of IAS 1 for further guidance. See Chapter 6 at 5.1.1 for further discussion of the classification of current and non-current assets.

9.3.2   Current and non-current liabilities

The definitions of current liabilities and non-current liabilities discussed below apply only where an entity chooses to use adapted formats in accordance with paragraph 1B(1) of Schedule 1 to the Small Companies Regulations (or paragraph 1B(1) of Schedule 1 to the Small LLP Regulations). Irish small entities instead refer to paragraph 2(2) of Schedule 3A to the Companies Act 2014.

FRS 102 defines current liabilities as liabilities of the entity which: *[FRS 102 Appendix I]*

(a)   it expects to settle in its normal operating cycle (see Chapter 6 at 5.1.2.A);

(b)   it holds primarily for the purpose of trading (see Chapter 6 at 5.1.2.B);

(c)   are due to be settled within 12 months after the reporting period (see Chapter 6 at 5.1.2.C); or

(d)   it does not have an unconditional right to defer settlement for at least 12 months after the reporting period. (See Chapter 6 at 5.1.2.D).

Meeting any one of (a) to (d) leads to the liability being required to be classified as current.

The FRS 102 Glossary defines non-current liabilities as liabilities of the entity which are not current liabilities (i.e. the residual). *[FRS 102 Appendix I].* This approach is consistent with IAS 1. *[IAS 1.69].* The adapted formats also require that deferred tax liabilities are always classified as non-current. *[FRS 102.1AA.3].*

10   INCOME STATEMENT (OR PROFIT AND LOSS ACCOUNT)

A small entity must present its profit or loss for a period in an income statement in accordance with the requirements for a profit and loss account set out in either Part 1 *General Rules and Formats* of Schedule 1 to the Small Companies Regulations or Part 1 *General Rules and Formats* of Schedule 1 to the Small LLP Regulations. Irish small entities instead refer to Part II of Schedule 3A to the Companies Act 2014. *[FRS 102.1A.14].*

Small entities that do not report under the CA 2006 (or for Irish entities, the Companies Act 2014) must also comply with the above requirement except to the extent that these requirements are not permitted by any statutory framework under which such entities report. *[FRS 102.1A.4. 14].*

As noted at 8.1 above, a small entity applying Schedule 1 to the Small Companies Regulations (or Schedule 1 to the Small LLP Regulations) has the following three alternatives: *[FRS 102.1AB.1]*

- apply the required statutory profit and loss formats (subject to any permitted flexibility – see the General Rules to the formats at 8.2 above) – see 10.1 below;
- draw up an abridged profit and loss account – see 10.2 below; or
- adapt one of the profit and loss account formats – see 10.3 below.

Irish law does not provide for the preparation of abridged statutory financial statements. Consequently, the option to prepare an abridged profit and loss account is not available to small entities in the Republic of Ireland. This is not the same as abridgement for filing purposes. *[FRS 102.1AB.2].*

An income statement presents all items of income and expense recognised in a reporting period, excluding the items of other comprehensive income. This is referred to as the profit and loss account in the CA 2006. *[FRS 102 Appendix I].* Consequently, the income statement must include line items that add down to the profit or loss for the year. This is the case, even if the detailed analysis of certain line items is presented in the notes to the accounts, where this is permitted by the General Rules to the formats (where statutory or abridged formats are used) (see 8.2 above) or the line items are not required on the face of the income statement (where adapted formats are used).

A small company (or small LLP) is not required to present a separate line item (and columnar analysis) for discontinued operations on the face of the separate income statement (or profit or loss section of a single statement of comprehensive income, if any). This is required where adapted formats or statutory formats are used in full FRS 102 (see Chapter 6 at 6.8). *[FRS 102.1A.7, 5.7E-F].*

FRS 102 includes additional requirements on presentation of the profit and loss account that are relevant whatever format is used. For instance:

- guidance on operating profit, where this is presented (see Chapter 6 at 6.7.3); *[FRS 102.5.9B]*
- incoming dividends and similar income receivable are recognised at an amount that includes any withholding tax but excludes other taxes, such as attributable tax credits. Any withholding tax suffered is shown as part of the tax charge (see Chapter 26 at 3.3 and 8.1.2); *[FRS 102.29.19]*
- Section 28 – *Employee Benefits* – does not specify how the cost of a defined benefit plan should be presented in the income statement. Therefore, entities may present the cost as a single item or disaggregate the cost into components presented separately; and
- Section 23 – *Revenue* – includes guidance on measurement of revenue, including principal versus agent considerations. See Chapter 20 at 3.2.

Where Sections 8 to 35 require further analyses of items included in the income statement to be disclosed, these requirements do not apply to financial statements prepared in accordance with Section 1A. *[FRS 102.1A.7]*.

There is no requirement for a small entity to present a full statement of comprehensive income (although, as explained at 8 above, this is encouraged, where gains or losses are recognised in other comprehensive income). *[FRS 102.1A.9]*.

10.1   Statutory profit and loss account

Schedule 1 to the Small Companies Regulations (and Schedule 1 to the Small LLP Regulations) provide a choice of two statutory formats for the profit and loss account. Irish small entities instead refer to Part II of Schedule 3A to the Companies Act 2014. *[FRS 102.1A.14]*.

Format 1 analyses expenses by function and is illustrated at Figure 5.10 below (for a small UK company) and at Figure 5.11 below (for a small LLP). Format 2 analyses expenses by nature and is illustrated at Figure 5.12 below (for a small UK company) and at Figure 5.13 below (for a small LLP).

The main modifications required for group profit and loss account formats are the identification of non-controlling interests and replacing 'income from participating interests' with 'income from interests in associated undertakings' and 'income from other participating interests' (see 8.1.4 above). *[6 Sch 1(3), 6 Sch 17 (SC), 4 Sch 1(3) (LLP SC), 4 Sch 17 (LLP SC)]*.

Figure 5.10 below sets out the profit and loss account, analysing expenses by function (format 1) for a small UK company.

Figure 5.10   *Format 1 individual profit and loss account – small UK company*

1	Turnover
2	Cost of sales
3	Gross profit or loss
4	Distribution costs
5	Administrative expenses
6	Other operating income
7	Income from shares in group undertakings
8	Income from participating interests†
9	Income from other fixed asset investments
10	Other interest receivable and similar income
11	Amounts written off investments
12	Interest payable and similar expenses
	Profit or loss before taxation*
13	Tax on profit or loss
14	Profit or loss after taxation
19	Other taxes not shown under the above items
20	Profit or loss for the financial year†

*   While not in format 1, every profit and loss account must show the amount of a company's profit or loss before taxation (1 Sch 6, Small Companies Regulations).

†   See discussion above (and 8.1.4 above) for modifications in group accounts.

Figure 5.11 below sets out the profit and loss account, analysing expenses by function (format 1) for a small LLP.

The LLP SORP provides further guidance on application of the statutory and formats for LLPs. The SORP requires that the 'profit or loss for the financial year before members' remuneration and profit shares' (the final line item in the statutory formats), 'members' remuneration charged as an expense' (including related employment costs) and the 'profit or loss for the financial year available for discretionary division among members' are separately presented on the face of the profit and loss account (or statement of comprehensive income). The basis on which each element of remuneration (as defined) has been treated in the financial statements should be disclosed and explained by way of note. The SORP provides guidance and illustrations of LLP profit or loss accounts for different situations, including where the partnership interest is classified as equity, liability or part equity / part liability. *[LLP SORP.20, 21, 51-54, Appendix 1, Appendix 2].*

In our view, small LLPs should also present these additional line items on the face of the profit and loss account (or statement of comprehensive income, if any).

Figure 5.11   *Format 1 individual profit and loss account – small LLP*

1	Turnover	
2	Cost of sales	
3	Gross profit or loss	
4	Distribution costs	
5	Administrative expenses	
6	Other operating income	
7	Income from shares in group undertakings	
8	Income from participating interests†	
9	Income from other fixed asset investments	
10	Other interest receivable and similar income	
11	Amounts written off investments	
12	Interest payable and similar expenses	
	Profit or loss before taxation*	
13	Tax on profit or loss	
14	Profit or loss after taxation	
19	Other taxes not shown under the above items	
20	Profit or loss for the financial year before members' remuneration and profit shares	
SORP	*Members' remuneration charged as an expense~*	
SORP	*Profit or loss for the financial year available for discretionary division among members~*	

* While not in format 1, every profit and loss account must show the amount of an LLP's profit or loss before taxation (1 Sch 6, Small LLP Regulations).

† See discussion above (and 8.1.4 above) for modifications in group accounts.

~ Supplementary presentation requirements in the LLP SORP. See discussion above this figure.

Figure 5.12 below sets out the profit and loss account, analysing expenses by nature (format 2) for a small UK company.

Figure 5.12   Format 2 individual profit and loss account – small UK company

1		Turnover	
2		Change in stocks of finished goods and in work in progress	
3		Own work capitalised	
4		Other operating income	
5	(a)	Raw materials and consumables	
	(b)	Other external charges	
6		Staff costs	
	(a)	wages and salaries	
	(b)	social security costs	
	(c)	other pension costs	
7	(a)	depreciation and other amounts written off tangible and intangible fixed assets	
	(b)	amounts written off current assets, to the extent that they exceed write-offs which are normal in the undertaking concerned	
8		Other operating expenses	
9		Income from shares in group undertakings	
10		Income from participating interests†	
11		Income from other fixed asset investments	
12		Other interest receivable and similar income	
13		Amounts written off investments	
14		Interest payable and similar expenses	
		Profit or loss before taxation*	
15		Tax on profit or loss	
16		Profit or loss after taxation	
21		Other taxes not shown under the above items	
22		Profit or loss for the financial year†	

*   While not in format 2, every profit and loss account must show the amount of a company's profit or loss before taxation (1 Sch 6, Small Companies Regulations).

†   See discussion above (and 8.1.4 above) for modifications in group accounts.

Figure 5.13 below sets out the profit and loss account, analysing expenses by nature (format 2) for a small LLP. See comments on the requirements of the LLP SORP discussed immediately above Figure 5.11.

Figure 5.13   *Format 2 individual profit and loss account – small LLP*

1	Turnover
2	Change in stocks of finished goods and in work in progress
3	Own work capitalised
4	Other operating income
5	(a) Raw materials and consumables
	(b) Other external charges
6	Staff costs
	(a) wages and salaries
	(b) social security costs
	(c) other pension costs
7	(a) depreciation and other amounts written off tangible and intangible fixed assets
	(b) amounts written off current assets, to the extent that they exceed write-offs which are normal in the undertaking concerned
8	Other operating expenses
9	Income from shares in group undertakings
10	Income from participating interests†
11	Income from other fixed asset investments
12	Other interest receivable and similar income
13	Amounts written off investments
14	Interest payable and similar expenses
	Profit or loss before taxation*
15	Tax on profit or loss
16	Profit or loss after taxation
21	Other taxes not shown under the above items
22	Profit or loss for the financial year before members' remuneration and profit shares
SORP	*Members' remuneration charged as an expense~*
SORP	*Profit or loss for the financial year available for discretionary division among members~*

*   While not in format 2, every profit and loss account must show the amount of an LLP's profit or loss before taxation (1 Sch 6, Small LLP Regulations).

†   See discussion above (and 8.1.4 above) for modifications in group accounts.

~   Supplementary presentation requirements in the LLP SORP. See discussion above Figure 5.11.

The line items in the formats need to be read together with the notes to the formats. *[1 Sch 1(2) (SC), 1 Sch 1(2) (LLP SC)]*. These require that:

- cost of sales, distribution costs and administrative expenses (format 1, items 2, 4 and 5) are stated after taking into account any necessary provisions for depreciation or diminution in value of assets;

- in income from other fixed asset investments and other interest receivable and similar income (format 1, items 9 and 10, format 2, items 11 and 12), income and interest derived from group undertakings must be shown separately from income and interest derived from other sources. In addition, for LLPs, interest receivable from members must not be included under this item; and

- in interest payable and similar expenses (format 1, item 12 and format 2, item 14), the amount payable to group undertakings must be shown separately. In addition, for LLPs, interest payable to members must not be included under this item.

The individual line items in the profit and loss account formats in the Small Companies Regulations (and Small LLP Regulations) are the same as in the Regulations (and LLP Regulations) and are discussed in Chapter 6 at 6.6 (although disclosures in other sections of FRS 102, as referred to in that discussion, are generally not mandated for small entities applying Section 1A). *[FRS 102.1A.7]*.

The General Rules to the formats (see 8.2 above) apply. As all of the line items are denoted with Arabic numbers, these allow a degree of flexibility in the profit and loss account formats.

10.2   Abridged profit and loss account

Where appropriate to the circumstances of a company's (or an LLP's) business, the company's directors (or members of the LLP's) may, with reference to one of the formats in Section B of Part 1 to Schedule 1 to the Small Companies Regulations (or Section B of Part 1 to Schedule 1 to the Small LLP Regulations), draw up an abridged profit and loss account, combining under one item called 'Gross profit or loss':

(a)   items 1, 2, 3 and 6 in the case of format 1; and

(b)   items 1 to 5 in the case of format 2

provided that, in either case, all of the members of the company (or of the LLP) have consented to the drawing up of the abridged profit and loss account. *[1 Sch 1A(2) (SC), 1 Sch 1A(2) (LLP SC)]*.

See 8.1.2 above for discussion of when abridged formats, which are only available in individual accounts, are permitted to be used.

So far as is practicable, the provisions of paragraphs 2 to 9A of the General Rules to the formats (see 8.2 above) apply to the profit or loss account, notwithstanding any such abridgement pursuant to paragraph 1A of Schedule 1 to the Small Companies Regulations (or paragraph 1A of Schedule 1 to the Small LLP Regulations). *[1 Sch 1C (SC), 1 Sch 1C (LLP SC)]*.

Figure 5.14 below sets out an abridged format 1 profit and loss account for a small UK company taking full advantage of the permitted abridgements.

Figure 5.14   *Abridged format 1 profit and loss account – small UK company*

1, 2, 3, 6*	Gross profit or loss (combines: turnover, cost of sales, gross profit or loss, other operating income)
4	Distribution costs
5	Administrative expenses
7	Income from shares in group undertakings
8	Income from participating interests
9	Income from other fixed asset investments
10	Other interest receivable and similar income
11	Amounts written off investments
12	Interest payable and similar expenses
	Profit or loss before taxation**
13	Tax on profit or loss
14	Profit or loss after taxation
19	Other taxes not shown under the above items
20	Profit or loss for the financial year

*   Disaggregation of gross profit or loss and disclosing turnover may be necessary in the notes to the financial statements in order to give a true and fair view (see FRS 102.1AB.2).

**   While not in format 1, every profit and loss account must show the amount of a company's profit or loss before taxation (1 Sch 6, Small Companies Regulations).

Figure 5.15 below sets out an abridged format 2 profit and loss account for a small UK company taking full advantage of the permitted abridgements.

Figure 5.15   *Abridged format 2 profit and loss account – small UK company*

1-5*	Gross profit (combines items 1 to 5 in format 2)
6	Staff costs
	(a) wages and salaries
	(b) social security costs
	(c) other pension costs
7	(a) depreciation and other amounts written off tangible and intangible fixed assets
	(b) amounts written off current assets, to the extent that they exceed write-offs which are normal in the undertaking concerned
8	Other operating expenses
9	Income from shares in group undertakings
10	Income from participating interests
11	Income from other fixed asset investments
12	Other interest receivable and similar income
13	Amounts written off investments
14	Interest payable and similar expenses
	Profit or loss before taxation**
15	Tax on profit or loss
16	Profit or loss after taxation
21	Other taxes not shown under the above items
22	Profit or loss for the financial year

*   Disaggregation of gross profit or loss and disclosing turnover may be necessary in the notes to the financial statements in order to give a true and fair view (see FRS 102.1AB.2).

**   While not in format 2, every profit and loss account must show the amount of a company's profit or loss before taxation (1 Sch 6, Small Companies Regulations).

Chapter 5

The abridged formats for LLPs are exactly the same as for UK companies, except that the final line is 'profit or loss for the financial year before members' remuneration and profit shares'. Since abridged formats are the same as statutory formats (with certain line items combined), the discussion in connection with the statutory formats of an LLP, immediately above Figure 5.11 at 10.1 above, is also relevant to abridged formats. In our view, small LLPs should also present the additional line items for 'members' remuneration charged as an expense' and 'profit or loss for the financial year available for discretionary division among members' on the face of the abridged profit and loss account (or statement of comprehensive income, if any).

Figure 5.16 below sets out an abridged format 1 profit and loss account for a small LLP taking full advantage of the permitted abridgements and illustrating the supplementary presentation requirements in the LLP SORP.

Figure 5.16   *Abridged format 1 profit and loss account – small LLP*

1, 2, 3, 6*	Gross profit or loss (combines: turnover, cost of sales, gross profit or loss, other operating income)
4	Distribution costs
5	Administrative expenses
6	Other operating income
7	Income from shares in group undertakings
8	Income from participating interests
9	Income from other fixed asset investments
10	Other interest receivable and similar income
11	Amounts written off investments
12	Interest payable and similar expenses
	Profit or loss before taxation**
13	Tax on profit or loss
14	Profit or loss after taxation
19	Other taxes not shown under the above items
20	Profit or loss for the financial year before members' remuneration and profit shares
SORP	*Members' remuneration charged as an expense~*
SORP	*Profit or loss for the financial year available for discretionary division among members~*

*	Disaggregation of gross profit or loss and disclosing turnover may be necessary in the notes to the financial statements in order to give a true and fair view (see FRS 102.1AB.2).
**	While not in format 1, every profit and loss account must show the amount of an LLP's profit or loss before taxation (1 Sch 6, Small LLP Regulations).
~	Supplementary presentation requirements in the LLP SORP. See discussion above this figure.

Figure 5.17 below sets out an abridged format 2 profit and loss account for a small LLP taking full advantage of the permitted abridgements and illustrating the supplementary presentation requirements in the LLP SORP.

Figure 5.17   *Abridged format 2 profit and loss account – small LLP*

1-5*	Gross profit (combines items 1 to 5 in format 2)
6	Staff costs
(a)	wages and salaries
(b)	social security costs
(c)	other pension costs
7 (a)	depreciation and other amounts written off tangible and intangible fixed assets
(b)	amounts written off current assets, to the extent that they exceed write-offs which are normal in the undertaking concerned
8	Other operating expenses
9	Income from shares in group undertakings
10	Income from participating interests
11	Income from other fixed asset investments
12	Other interest receivable and similar income
13	Amounts written off investments
14	Interest payable and similar expenses
	Profit or loss before taxation**
15	Tax on profit or loss
16	Profit or loss after taxation
21	Other taxes not shown under the above items
22	Profit or loss for the financial year before members' remuneration and profit shares
SORP	*Members' remuneration charged as an expense~*
SORP	*Profit or loss for the financial year available for discretionary division among members~*

*   Disaggregation of gross profit or loss and disclosing turnover may be necessary in the notes to the financial statements in order to give a true and fair view (see FRS 102.1AB.2).

**   While not in format 2, every profit and loss account must show the amount of an LLP's profit or loss before taxation (1 Sch 6, Small LLP Regulations).

~   Supplementary presentation requirements in the LLP SORP. See discussion above Figure 5.16.

The only difference to the statutory formats is the abridgement. The disclosures required by the Small Companies Regulations (for a UK company) and by the Small LLP Regulations (for an LLP) are still required. Therefore, the guidance on statutory formats at 10.1 above remains relevant where abridged formats are used.

Chapter 5

A small entity choosing to apply paragraph 1A(2) of Schedule 1 to the Small Companies Regulations (or paragraph 1A(2) of Schedule 1 to the Small LLP Regulations) and draw up an abridged profit and loss account must still meet the requirement for the financial statements to give a true and fair view. A small entity must therefore also consider the requirements of paragraph 1A.16 (see 7.2 and 8 above, and 11 below) and provide any additional disclosure that is necessary in the notes to the financial statements, for example in relation to disaggregating gross profit or loss and disclosing turnover. *[FRS 102.1A.16, 1AB.2]*. In considering what level of disaggregation may be appropriate in order for the financial statements to give a true and fair view, in our view, entities should have regard to FRS 102's requirements on materiality and aggregation (see 7.6 above).

10.3   Adapted profit and loss account

Adapted formats may be used provided that the information given is at least equivalent to that which would have been required by the use of the statutory format had it not been thus adapted and the presentation is in accordance with generally accepted accounting principles or practice. *[1 Sch 1B(2) (SC), 1 Sch 1B(2) (LLP SC)]*. The detail, however, is left to accounting standards, namely Section 1A.

A small entity choosing to apply paragraph 1B(2) of Schedule 1 to the Small Companies Regulations (or paragraph 1B(2) of Schedule 1 to the Small LLP Regulations) and adapt one of the profit and loss account formats shall, as a minimum, include in its income statement line items that present amounts (a) to (f) for the period (as set out in Figure 5.18 below). Irish small entities instead refer to paragraph 2(3) of Schedule 3A to the Companies Act 2014. *[FRS 102.1AB.3]*.

The main modification required for group profit and loss account formats is the identification of non-controlling interests (see 8.1.4.B above).

Figure 5.18   Profit and loss account – line items included in adapted formats

(a)	Revenue	
(b)	Finance costs	
(c)	Share of the profit or loss of investments in associates and jointly controlled entities accounted for using the equity method	
(d)	Profit or loss before taxation	
(e)	Tax expense (excluding tax allocated to other comprehensive income or equity)	
(f)	Profit or loss~	
~	The LLP SORP requires further line items for LLPs. See discussion below this figure.	

The LLP SORP provides guidance on adapted formats which we would expect to apply to all LLPs (including small LLPs) as the adaptations are intended to provide equivalent information to the statutory formats. Therefore, adapted formats show a line item for 'profit or loss for the financial year before members' remuneration and profit shares'. 'Members' remuneration charged as an expense' (which would include related employment costs) must then be deducted as an additional expense, *[LLP SORP.26C, 51-54, Appendix 1]*, presumably coming to the final line item of 'profit or loss for the financial year available for discretionary division among members' (which would correspond to item (f) in Figure 5.18 above). This would be the same presentation on the face of the profit or loss account (or statement of comprehensive income) as discussed for statutory formats at 10.1 above.

So far as is practicable, the provisions of paragraphs 2 to 9A of Section A of the General Rules to the formats (see 8.2 above) apply to the profit or loss account, notwithstanding any such adaptation pursuant to paragraph 1B of Schedule 1 to the Small Companies Regulations (or paragraph 1B of Schedule 1 to the Small LLP Regulations). *[1 Sch 1C (SC), 1 Sch 1C (LLP SC)].*

A small entity may include additional line items in the income statement and should amend the descriptions used in the line items set out in (a) to (f) in Figure 5.18 above, and the ordering of items, when this is necessary to explain the elements of financial performance, providing the information given is at least equivalent to that required by the profit and loss account format had it not been adapted. *[FRS 102.1AB.4].*

Example 6.4 in Chapter 6 at 6.5.2 illustrates a statement of comprehensive income for an entity using adapted formats in the full standard which provides an analysis of expenses. A small entity presenting only an income statement would omit the lines after 'profit for the year' in Example 6.4.

An analysis of expenses is not explicitly required by Section 1A (since Section 5 does not apply), *[FRS 102.1A.7, 5.5B],* but a small entity may consider additional analysis necessary to explaining elements of financial performance. In this regard, it is notable that, where abridged formats are used, Section 1A requires a small entity to provide any additional disclosure that is necessary for a true and fair view in the notes to the financial statements, for example, in relation to disaggregating gross profit or loss (see 10.2 above). *[FRS 102.1AB.2].*

The Small Companies Regulations and Small LLP Regulations set out disclosures to be given in the notes to the financial statements which apply where statutory formats, abridged formats or the adapted formats are used. One complexity is that the information required sometimes refers to items found in the statutory formats (which may differ to the line items identified where the adapted formats are used). See discussion at 9.3 above.

11   INFORMATION TO BE PRESENTED IN THE NOTES TO THE FINANCIAL STATEMENTS

A small entity must present sufficient information in the notes to the financial statements to meet the requirement for the financial statements to give a true and fair view of the assets, liabilities, financial position and profit or loss of the small entity for the reporting period. *[FRS 102.1A.16].*

A small entity is not required to comply with the disclosure requirements of Section 3 (to the extent set out in paragraph 1A.7 – see 7.1 above) and Sections 8 to 35. However, because those disclosures are usually considered relevant to giving a true and fair view, a small entity is encouraged to consider and provide any of those disclosures that are relevant to material transactions, other events or conditions of the small entity in order to meet the requirement (for the financial statements to give a true and fair view) set out in paragraphs 1A.5 (see 7.2 above) and 1A.16. *[FRS 102.1A.17].*

Appendix C of Section 1A sets out certain minimum requirements, based on the statutory requirements for UK companies subject to the small companies regime (see 11.1 below). *[FRS 102.1A.18].*

Chapter 5

The list is not quite exhaustive and some additional statutory disclosures are noted at 11.2 below. Section 1A also specifically encourages a small entity to give certain FRS 102 disclosures listed in Appendix E of Section 1A which may nevertheless be necessary to give a true and fair view (see 11.3 below). *[FRS 102.1A.20].* Statutory disclosures relevant to consolidated financial statements are noted at 11.4 below.

In accordance with paragraph 3.16B, a small entity need not provide a specific disclosure (including those set out in paragraph 1A.18 and Appendix C or Appendix D to Section 1A, as relevant) if the information resulting from that disclosure is not material, except when required by the CA 2006 (for Irish entities, the Companies Act 2014) regardless of materiality. *[FRS 102.1A.17A].*

Entities subject to a SORP may find that the SORP recommends additional disclosures.

11.1 Minimum requirements – Appendix C

A small entity in the UK must provide, at a minimum, when relevant to its transactions, other events and conditions, the disclosures in Appendix C. Disclosures that are immaterial need not be given, except when required by the CA 2006 regardless of materiality (see 7.6 above for examples of such disclosures). *[FRS 102.1A.17A, 1A.18, 1AC.1].*

Appendix C, which is an integral part of Section 1A, sets out the disclosure requirements for small entities based on the requirements of UK company law, i.e. the statutory requirements in the Small Companies Regulations. The disclosure requirements are shown below in italicised font, consistent with Appendix C. Other than substituting company law terminology with the equivalent terminology used in FRS 102 (as set out in Appendix II – *Table of equivalence for company law terminology* – of FRS 102), the FRC states that the drafting is as close as possible to that set out in company law.

A note on the FRC website explains that there are some slight differences between the disclosure requirements of Section 1A and those in the Small LLP Regulations; LLPs should apply the equivalent requirements of the Small LLP Regulations rather than Section 1A. See 11.5 below.

Appendix C highlights disclosures in Sections 8 to 35 of FRS 102 that are similar to its requirements, noting that in many cases compliance with the similar requirement of FRS 102 will result in compliance with the requirements in Appendix C. However, a small entity in the UK must ensure it complies with all the disclosure requirements of Appendix C. Paragraphs in FRS 102 that have been cross referenced in Appendix C are also highlighted in the other sections of the standard with an asterisk. Appendix D takes a similar approach (note that the asterisk by paragraph 6.3(c) of FRS 102 relates to a legal requirement in the Republic of Ireland only). *[FRS 102.1A.19, 1AC.1].*

11.1.1 Structure of notes

- *The notes must be presented in the order in which, where relevant, the items to which they relate are presented in the statement of financial position and in the income statement. [1 Sch 42(2) (SC), 1 Sch 42(2) (LLP SC)].*

  Paragraphs 8.3 and 8.4 address similar requirements (see Chapter 6 at 8.1). *[FRS 102.1AC.2].*

11.1.2 Accounting policies

- *The accounting policies adopted by the small entity in determining the amounts to be included in respect of items shown in the statement of financial position and in determining the profit or loss of the small entity must be stated (including such policies with respect to the depreciation and impairment of assets). [1 Sch 44 (SC), 1 Sch 44 (LLP SC)].*

Paragraph 8.5 addresses similar requirements for disclosing significant accounting policies. Including information about the judgements made in applying the small entity's accounting policies, as set out in paragraph 8.6, may be useful to users of the small entity's financial statements (see Chapter 6 at 8.2 and 8.3). *[FRS 102.1AC.3].*

- *If any amount is included in a small entity's statement of financial position in respect of development costs, the note on accounting policies must include the following information:*

    (a) *the period over which the amount of those costs originally capitalised is being or is to be written off; and*

    (b) *the reasons for capitalising the development costs in question. [1 Sch 21(2) (SC), 1 Sch 21(2) (LLP SC)].*

Paragraph 18.27(a) addresses similar requirements to paragraph 1AC.4(a) (see Chapter 16 at 3.5.2). *[FRS 102.1AC.4].*

- *Where development costs are shown or included as an asset in the small entity's financial statements and the amount is not treated as a realised loss because there are special circumstances justifying this, a note to the financial statements must state the reasons for showing development costs as an asset and that it is not a realised loss. [s844, FRS 102.1AC.5].*

See Chapter 6 at 10.1.3 for discussion of this disclosure requirement. This disclosure does not apply to a small LLP.

- *Where in exceptional cases, the useful life of intangible assets cannot be reliably estimated, there must be disclosed in a note to the financial statements the period over which those intangible assets are being written off and the reasons for choosing that period. [1 Sch 22(4) (SC), 1 Sch 22(4) (LLP SC)].*

Intangible assets include goodwill. Paragraphs 18.27(a) (see Chapter 16 at 3.5.2) and 19.25(g) (see Chapter 17 at 4.1) address similar disclosure requirements. *[FRS 102.1AC.6].*

11.1.3 Changes in presentation and accounting policies and corrections of prior period errors

- *Where there is a change in the presentation of a small entity's statement of financial position or income statement, particulars of any such change must be given in a note to the financial statements in which the new presentation is first used, and the reasons for the change must be explained. [1 Sch 2(2) (SC), 1 Sch 2(2) (LLP SC)].*

Paragraphs 3.12 and 3.13 address similar requirements (see 7.5.2 above), *[FRS 102.1AC.7],* but the statutory reference given is strictly for changes in formats (see 8.1.5 above).

- *Where the corresponding amount for the immediately preceding reporting period is not comparable with the amount to be shown for the item in question in respect of the reporting period, and the corresponding amount is adjusted, the particulars of the non-comparability and of any adjustment must be disclosed in a note to the financial statements. [1 Sch 7(2) (SC), 1 Sch 7(2) (LLP SC)].*

This is likely to be relevant where there has either been a change in accounting policy or the correction of a material prior period error. Paragraphs 10.13, 10.14 and 10.23 address similar requirements (see 7.5.2 and 8.2.3 above, and Chapter 9 at 3.7.1 and 3.7.3). *[FRS 102.1AC.8]*.

The statutory disclosures require particulars of the non-comparability, whether or not any adjustment is made. However, in most cases, a change in accounting policy, a correction of a prior period error or a reclassification would be retrospectively effected.

- *Where any amount relating to a preceding reporting period is included in any item in the income statement, the effect must be stated. [1 Sch 61(1) (SC), 1 Sch 59(1) (LLP SC), FRS 102.1AC.9].*

11.1.4   True and fair override

- *If it appears to the small entity that there are special reasons for departing from any of the principles set out in company law in preparing the small entity's financial statements in respect of any reporting period, it may do so, in which case particulars of the departure, the reasons for it, and its effects must be given in the notes to the financial statements. [1 Sch 10(2) (SC), 1 Sch 10(2) (LLP SC)].*

This is only expected to occur in special circumstances. Paragraphs 3.4 and 3.5 address similar requirements. *[FRS 102.1AC.10]*.

See 7.2 above and Chapter 6 at 9.2. The general principles – the going concern presumption, consistency (in applying accounting policies and measurement bases), use of prudence, use of the accruals basis, separate determination of individual assets and liabilities (no offsetting); and the requirement that the opening balance sheet for a financial year corresponds to the closing balance sheet for the previous financial year– in the Small Companies Regulations and Small LLP Regulations are the same as those set out in the Regulations and LLP Regulations, as discussed in Chapter 6 at 9.1. *[1 Sch 11-15A (SC), 1 Sch 11-15A (LLP SC)].*

There is an additional related statutory requirement for companies and LLPs not separately identified in Appendix C to Section 1A. *[s396(5), s404(5), s396(5) (LLP), s404(5) (LLP)].* However, this appears to be because it is required by paragraphs 3.5 and 3.6, which are not scoped out for a small entity applying Section 1A. Therefore, the following disclosures of paragraphs 3.5 and 3.6 apply to all entities applying Section 1A making use of the 'true and fair override'. See 7.2.1 above.

- *When an entity departs from a requirement of FRS 102 (in special circumstances, in order to give a true and fair view – see paragraph 3.4) or from a requirement of applicable legislation, it shall disclose:*

(a) *that management has concluded that the financial statements give a true and fair view of the entity's financial position, financial performance and, when required to be presented, cash flows;*

(b) *that it has complied with FRS 102 or applicable legislation, except that it has departed from a particular requirement of the standard or applicable legislation to the extent necessary to give a true and fair view; and*

(c) *the nature and effect of the departure, including the treatment that FRS 102 or applicable legislation would require, the reason why that treatment would be so misleading in the circumstances that it would conflict with the objective of financial statements set out in Section 2 and the treatment adopted.* [FRS 102.3.5].

- *When an entity has departed from a requirement of FRS 102 or applicable legislation in a prior period and that departure affects the amounts recognised in the financial statements for the current period, it shall make the disclosures set out in (c) above.* [FRS 102.3.6].

11.1.5   Notes supporting the statement of financial position

11.1.5.A   An asset or liability relating to more than one item in the statement of financial position

- *Where an asset or liability relates to more than one item in the statement of financial position, the relationship of such asset or liability to the relevant items must be disclosed either under those items or in the notes to the financial statements.* [1 Sch 9A (SC), 1 Sch 9A (LLP SC), FRS 102.1AC.11].

See discussion at 8.2 above concerning situations where this disclosure requirement may apply.

11.1.5.B   Fixed assets (general)

- *In respect of each item which is shown under the general item 'fixed assets' in the small entity's statement of financial position, the following information must be given:* [FRS 102.1AC.12]

(a) *the aggregate amounts (on the basis of cost or revaluation) in respect of that item as at the date of the beginning of the reporting period and as at the reporting date respectively;*

(b) *the effect on any amount shown in the statement of financial position in respect of that item of:*

(i) *any revision of the amount in respect of any assets included under that item made during the reporting period as a result of revaluation;*

(ii) *acquisitions during the reporting period of any assets;*

(iii) *disposals during the reporting period of any assets; and*

(iv) *any transfers of assets of the small entity to and from that item during the reporting period.* [1 Sch 48(1)-(2) (SC), 1 Sch 47(1)-(2) (LLP SC)].

- *In respect of each item within paragraph 1AC.12 above, there must also be stated:* [FRS 102.1AC.13]

  (a) the cumulative amount of provisions for depreciation and impairment of assets included under that item as at the date of the beginning of the reporting period and as at the reporting date respectively;

  (b) the amount of any such provisions made in respect of the reporting period;

  (c) the amount of any adjustments made in respect of any such provisions during the reporting period in consequence of the disposal of any such assets; and

  (d) the amount of any other adjustments made in respect of any such provisions during the reporting period. [1 Sch 48(3) (SC), 1 Sch 47(3) (LLP SC)].

These two paragraphs apply to all fixed assets, including investment property, plant and equipment, intangible assets (including goodwill), fixed asset investments, biological assets and heritage assets recognised in the statement of financial position.

Each item refers to a class of fixed assets shown separately either in the statement of financial position or in the notes to the financial statements. These reconciliations need not be presented for prior periods.

FRS 102 addresses similar requirements for investment property (paragraph 16.10(e)), property, plant and equipment (paragraphs 17.31(d) and (e)), intangible assets other than goodwill (paragraphs 18.27(c) and (e)), goodwill (paragraph 19.26), biological assets (paragraphs 34.7(c) and 34.10(e)) and heritage assets (paragraphs 34.55(e) and (f)), recognised in the statement of financial position. [FRS 102.1AC.13]. These are discussed in Chapter 14 at 3.6.1, Chapter 15 at 3.9.1, Chapter 16 at 3.5.2, Chapter 17 at 4.2, Chapter 31 at 2.6.3 and 2.7.2, and Chapter 31 at 5.2.4 respectively. [FRS 102.1AC.13].

'Fixed assets' means assets of an entity which are intended for use on a continuing basis in the entity's activities, and 'current assets' means assets not intended for such use. [8 Sch 3 (SC), 5 Sch 3 (LLP SC), FRS 102 Appendix I]. (See 9.1 above and Chapter 6 at 5.2.2). However, the above disclosures are still required even if adapted formats with a non-current and current analysis of assets and liabilities are applied (see 9.3 above).

11.1.5.C   Fixed assets (measured at revalued amounts)

Section 1A clarifies that the following disclosure requirements in paragraphs 1AC.14 to 1AC.18 apply where:

- investments in subsidiaries, associates and joint ventures are measured at fair value with changes in fair value recognised in other comprehensive income;

- property, plant and equipment are revalued using the revaluation model set out in paragraphs 17.15B to 17.15F; and

- intangible assets other than goodwill are revalued using the revaluation model set out in paragraphs 18.18B to 18.18H.

These requirements do not apply to investment property and biological assets measured at fair value through profit or loss. [FRS 102.1AC.14-18]. This is because such accounting for investment property and biological assets is in accordance with the fair value accounting rules (see Chapter 6 at 10.4) rather than being a revaluation under the alternative accounting rules (see Chapter 6 at 10.2), which is what the disclosures in paragraphs 1AC.14 to 1AC.18 below concern.

The disclosures in respect of fixed assets (measured at revalued amounts using the alternative accounting rules) are as follows:

- *Where fixed assets are measured at revalued amounts the items affected and the basis of valuation adopted in determining the amounts of the assets in question in the case of each such item must be disclosed in the note on accounting policies.* *[1 Sch 34(2) (SC), 1 Sch 34(2) (LLP SC), FRS 102.1AC.14].*

Paragraphs 9.27(b), 17.31(a) and 18.29A(c) address similar disclosure requirements (see Chapter 8 at 4.6.1, Chapter 15 at 3.9.1 and Chapter 16 at 3.5.4).

- *Where any fixed assets of the small entity (other than listed investments) are included under any item shown in the small entity's statement of financial position at a revalued amount, the following information must be given:*

  (a) *the years (so far as they are known to the directors) in which the assets were severally valued and the several values;*

  (b) *in the case of assets that have been valued during the reporting period, the names of the persons who valued them or particulars of their qualifications for doing so (and whichever is stated), the bases of valuation used by them.* *[1 Sch 49 (SC), 1 Sch 48 (LLP SC)].*

Paragraphs 17.32A(a) and (c), 18.29A(a) and (c), and 34.55(e)(ii) address similar requirements (see Chapter 15 at 3.9.1, Chapter 16 at 3.5.4 and Chapter 31 at 5.2.4). These paragraphs do not require the names or qualifications of the persons who valued the fixed assets to be disclosed. *[FRS 102.1AC.15].*

A 'listed investment' means an investment as respects which there has been granted a listing on (a) a recognised investment exchange other than an overseas investment exchange (both as defined in Part 18 of the Financial Services and Markets Act 2000) or (b) a stock exchange of repute outside the UK. *[8 Sch 5 (SC), 5 Sch 5(LLP SC)].* A list of recognised investment exchanges (and recognised overseas investment exchanges) is available on the Financial Conduct Authority website. AIM is not a recognised investment exchange.

- *In the case of each item in the statement of financial position measured at a revalued amount, the comparable amounts determined according to the historical cost accounting rules must be shown in a note to the financial statements.* *[1 Sch 34(3) (SC), 1 Sch 34(3) (LLP SC)].*

The comparable amounts refers to the aggregate amount of cost and the aggregate of accumulated depreciation and accumulated impairment losses that would have been required according to the historical cost accounting rules (see Chapter 6 at 10.1). *[1 Sch 34(4) (SC), 1 Sch 34(4) (LLP SC)].*

Paragraphs 17.32A(d) and 18.29A(d) address similar requirements (see Chapter 15 at 3.9.1 and Chapter 16 at 3.5.4). *[FRS 102.1AC.16].*

- *Where fixed assets are measured at revalued amounts, the following information must be given in tabular form:*

  (a) *movements in the revaluation reserve in the reporting period, with an explanation of the tax treatment of items therein; and*

  (b) *the carrying amount in the statement of financial position that would have been recognised had the fixed assets not been revalued.* [1 Sch 54(2) (SC), 1 Sch 53(2) (LLP SC)].

  Paragraphs 6.3A (see Chapter 6 at 7.1), 17.32A(d), 18.29A(d), and 29.27(a) (see Chapter 15 at 3.9.1, Chapter 16 at 3.5.4 and Chapter 26 at 11.2) address similar requirements. *[FRS 102.1AC.17].*

- *The treatment for taxation purposes of amounts credited or debited to the revaluation reserve must be disclosed in a note to the financial statements.* [1 Sch 35(6) (SC), 1 Sch 35(3) (LLP SC)].

  Paragraph 29.27(a) (see Chapter 26 at 11.2) addresses similar requirements. *[FRS 102.1AC.18].*

11.1.5.D   Capitalisation of borrowing costs

- *Where a small entity adopts a policy of capitalising borrowing costs, the inclusion of interest in determining the cost of the asset and the amount of the interest so included is disclosed in a note to the financial statements.* [1 Sch 27(3) (SC), 1 Sch 27(3) (LLP SC)].

  Paragraph 25.3A(a) addresses a similar requirement to the second part of this (see Chapter 22 at 3.7.1). *[FRS 102.1AC.19].*

11.1.5.E   Impairment of assets

- *Provisions for impairment of fixed assets (including fixed asset investments) must be disclosed separately in a note to the financial statements if not shown separately in the income statement.* [1 Sch 19(3) (SC), 1 Sch 19(3) (LLP SC)].

  Paragraph 27.32(a) (see Chapter 24 at 8) addresses similar requirements. *[FRS 102.1AC.20].*

- *Any provisions for impairment of fixed assets that are reversed because the reasons for which they were made have ceased to apply must be disclosed (either separately or in aggregate) in a note to the financial statements if not shown separately in the income statement.* [1 Sch 20(2) (SC), 1 Sch 20(2) (LLP SC)].

  Paragraph 27.32(b) (see Chapter 24 at 8) addresses similar requirements. *[FRS 102.1AC.21].* The statutory disclosure requirement states that any amounts written back must be recognised in the profit and loss account and disclosed separately in a note to the accounts if not shown separately in the profit and loss account. *[1 Sch 20(2) (SC), 1 Sch 20(2) (LLP SC)].* It is not clear why Section 1A refers to 'either separately or in aggregate' for the disclosure of impairment reversals (it does not do so for the disclosure of impairment provisions).

11.1.5.F   Fair value measurement

- *Where financial instruments or other assets have been measured in accordance with the fair value accounting rules there must be stated:*

  (a) *the significant assumptions underlying the valuation models and techniques used to determine the fair values;*

(b)   *for each category of financial instrument or other asset, the fair value of assets in that category and the change in value:*

     (i)   *included directly in the income statement; or*

     (ii)   *credited to or (as the case may be) debited from the fair value reserve, in respect of those assets. [1 Sch 51(2)(a)-(b) (SC), 1 Sch 50(2)(a)-(b) (LLP SC)].*

This does not apply where financial instruments or other assets are measured at fair value only on initial recognition. This applies where financial instruments, certain inventories, investment property, and biological assets are subsequently measured at fair value through profit or loss, which is permitted or required by paragraphs 9.26(c), 11.14(b), 11.14(d)(iii), 11.14(d)(iv), 12.8, 13.4A, 14.4(d), 15.9(d), 16.7 and 34.4.

Paragraphs 11.41, 11.43, 11.48(a)(i), 11.48(a)(ii), 12.28, 12.29(c) and 12.29(e) address similar disclosure requirements for financial instruments. See Chapter 10 at 11.2.

Paragraphs 16.10(a) and 16.10(e)(ii) address similar disclosure requirements for investment property. See Chapter 14 at 3.6.1.

Paragraphs 34.7(b) and 34.7(c)(i) address similar disclosure requirements for biological assets. See Chapter 31 at 2.6.3. *[FRS 102.1AC.22].*

The requirement in paragraph 51(2)(b) of Schedule 1 to the Small Companies Regulations, and paragraph 50(2)(b) of Schedule 1 to the Small LLP Regulations and Section 1A refers to 'change in value ... in respect of those *assets*' [emphasis added]. This looks like a drafting error, when compared to both Directive 2013/34/EU (the Accounting Directive) and the previous disclosure requirement for financial instruments. In our view, the disclosure is intended to be 'in respect of those financial instruments or other assets'.

- *Where financial instruments or other assets have been measured in accordance with the fair value accounting rules there must be stated for each class of derivatives, the extent and nature of the instruments, including significant terms and conditions that may affect the amount, timing and certainty of future cash flows. [1 Sch 51(2)(c) (SC), 1 Sch 50(2)(c) (LLP SC), FRS 102.1AC.23].*

- *Where any amount is transferred to or from the fair value reserve during the reporting period, there must be stated in tabular form:*

     (a)   *the amount of the reserve as at the beginning of the reporting period and as at the reporting date respectively; and*

     (b)   *the amount transferred to or from the reserve during that year. [1 Sch 51(3) (SC), 1 Sch 50(3) (LLP SC)].*

Paragraphs 6.3A (see Chapter 6 at 7.1), 12.29(c) and 12.29(d) (see Chapter 10 at 11.2) address similar requirements. *[FRS 102.1AC.24].* See Chapter 6 at 10.3 for use of the fair value reserve, where certain financial instruments are held at fair value.

11.1.5.G   Financial instruments measured at fair value

- *Financial instruments which under international accounting standards may be included in accounts at fair value, may be so included, provided that the disclosures required by such accounting standards are made. [1 Sch 36(4) (SC), 1 Sch 36(4) (LLP SC)].*

This only applies in certain circumstances, for example, it does not apply to derivatives. It applies where investments in subsidiaries, associates and joint ventures are measured at fair value through profit or loss. When it applies, the disclosures required by Section 11 – *Basic Financial Instruments* – that relate to financial assets and financial liabilities measured at fair value, including paragraph 11.48A, shall be given. *[FRS 102.1AC.26]*.

The explanatory guidance above is consistent with our view that this disclosure applies only to financial instruments that are held at fair value subject to the requirements of paragraph 36(4) to Schedule 1 to the Small Companies Regulations (or paragraph 36(4) to Schedule 1 to the Small LLP Regulations). Therefore, the disclosures would not apply to all financial instruments held at fair value but would apply to those financial instruments held at fair value that are listed in paragraphs 36(2) and (3) of those Schedules but are permitted to be held at fair value in accordance with EU-adopted IFRS. *[s474(1), s474(1) (LLP)]*.

See Chapter 6 at 10.3.1 and Chapter 10 at 6.4 for further explanation of this disclosure requirement.

We consider that this disclosure applies to all small entities applying Section 1A with such financial instruments, whether or not subject to the statutory disclosure requirements of paragraph 36(4). *[FRS 102.1A.4]*.

11.1.5.H   *Indebtedness, guarantees and financial commitments*

- *For the aggregate of all items shown under 'creditors' in the small entity's statement of financial position there must be stated the aggregate of the following amounts:* *[FRS 102.1AC.27]*

  (a) *the amount of any debts included under 'creditors' which are payable or repayable otherwise than by instalments and fall due for payment or repayment after the end of the period of five years beginning with the day next following the reporting date; and*

  (b) *in the case of any debts so included which are payable or repayable by instalments, the amount of any instalments which fall due for payment after the end of that period.* *[1 Sch 55(1) (SC), 1 Sch 54(1) (LLP SC)]*.

- *In respect of each item shown under 'creditors' in the small entity's statement of financial position there must be stated the aggregate amount of any debts included under that item in respect of which any security has been given by the small entity with an indication of the nature and form of any such security.* *[1 Sch 55(2) (SC), 1 Sch 54(2) (LLP SC)]*.

  Paragraphs 11.46, 13.22(e), 16.10(c), 17.32(a) and 18.28(c) address similar requirements. *[FRS 102.1AC.28]*. See Chapter 10 at 11.2, Chapter 11 at 3.6.2, Chapter 15 at 3.9.1 and Chapter 16 at 3.5.2.

- *The total amount of any financial commitments, guarantees and contingencies that are not included in the balance sheet must be stated.* *[1 Sch 57(1) (SC), 1 Sch 55(1) (LLP SC)]*.

  The total amount of any commitments concerning pensions must be separately disclosed. *[1 Sch 57(3) (SC), 1 Sch 55(3) (LLP SC)]*.

The total amount of any commitments which are undertaken on behalf of or for the benefit of:

(a) any parent, fellow subsidiary or any subsidiary of the small entity (see definition in Chapter 3 at 3.1.2); or

(b) any undertaking in which the small entity has a participating interest (see definition in Chapter 6 at 5.3.4.D);

must be separately stated and those within (a) must also be stated separately from those within (b). [1 Sch 57(4) (SC), 1 Sch 55(4) (LLP SC)].

Such commitments can arise in a variety of situations including in relation to group entities, investments, property, plant and equipment, leases and pension obligations. Paragraphs 15.19(d), 16.10(d), 17.32(b), 18.28(d), 20.16, 21.15, 28.40A(a), 28.40A(b), 28.41A(d), 33.9(b)(ii) and 34.62 address similar requirements. *[FRS 102.1AC.29].* See Chapter 13 at 3.11, Chapter 14 at 3.6.1, Chapter 15 at 3.9.1, Chapter 16 at 3.5.2, Chapter 18 at 3.11.1.B, Chapter 19 at 3.10.3 and 3.10.7, Chapter 25 at 3.12.3 and 3.12.4.B, and Chapter 30 at 3.2.3.A.

- *An indication of the nature and form of any valuable security given by the small entity in respect of commitments, guarantees and contingencies within paragraph 1AC.29 must be given. [1 Sch 57(2) (SC), 1 Sch 55(2) (LLP SC)].*

  Paragraphs 11.46, 13.22(e), 16.10(c), 17.32(a) and 18.28(c) address similar requirements. *[FRS 102.1AC.30].* See Chapter 10 at 11.2.2, Chapter 11 at 3.6.2, Chapter 15 at 3.9.1 and Chapter 16 at 3.5.2.

- *If in any reporting period a small entity is or has been party to arrangements that are not reflected in its statement of financial position and at the reporting date the risks or benefits arising from those arrangements are material, the nature and business purpose of the arrangements must be given in the notes to the financial statements to the extent necessary for enabling the financial position of the small entity to be assessed. [s410A, s410A (LLP)].*

  Examples of off-balance sheet arrangements include risk and benefit-sharing arrangements or obligations arising from a contract such as debt factoring, combined sale and repurchase arrangements, consignment stock arrangements, take or pay arrangements, securitisation arranged through separate entities, pledged assets, operating lease arrangements, outsourcing and the like. In many cases, the disclosures about financial commitments and contingencies required by paragraphs 1AC.29 and 1AC.30 will also address such arrangements. *[FRS 102.1AC.31].*

  See Chapter 6 at 8.7 for discussion of off-balance sheet arrangements, and 11.4.2.D below (in respect of any consolidated financial statements).

11.1.6 Notes supporting the income statement

- *The amount and nature of any individual items of income or expenses of exceptional size or incidence must be stated. [1 Sch 61(2) (SC), 1 Sch 59(2) (LLP SC)].*

  Paragraph 5.9A addresses a similar requirement in relation to material items. *[FRS 102.1AC.32].* See Chapter 6 at 6.7.5.

Chapter 5

11.1.7   Information about employee numbers

- *The notes to a small entity's financial statements must disclose the average number of persons employed by the small entity in the reporting period. [s411(1), s411(1) (LLP), FRS 102.1AC.33].*

The average number is ascertained by determining the number of persons employed under contracts of service by the company for each month in the financial year (whether throughout the month or not – so including both part- and full-time employees), adding together all the monthly numbers and dividing by the numbers of months in the financial year. *[s411(3)-(4), s411(3)-(4) (LLP)].* See Chapter 6 at 8.6 and 11.4.2.B below (in respect of any consolidated financial statements).

11.1.8   Related party disclosures

- *Where the small entity is a subsidiary, the following information must be given in respect of the parent of the smallest group for which consolidated financial statements are drawn up of which the small entity is a member:*
  - *(a)   the name of the parent which draws up the consolidated financial statements;*
  - *(b)   the address of the parent's registered office (whether in or outside the UK); or*
  - *(c)   if it is unincorporated, the address of its principal place of business. [1 Sch 65 (SC), 1 Sch 63 (LLP SC)].*

Paragraph 33.5 addresses a similar requirement to paragraph (a). *[FRS 102.1AC.34].* See Chapter 30 at 3.2.1. In the Small LLP Regulations (c) reads 'if it is incorporated, the address of its principal place of business'. This differs to the Small Companies Regulations and appears to be a drafting error.

11.1.8.A   Related party transactions

- *Particulars must be given of material transactions the small entity has entered into that have not been concluded under normal market conditions with:*
  - *(a)   owners holding a participating interest (see definition in Chapter 6 at 5.3.4.D) in the small entity;*
  - *(b)   companies in which the small entity itself has a participating interest; and*
  - *(c)   the small entity's directors [or members of its governing body].*

  Particulars must include:
  - *(a)   the amount of such transactions;*
  - *(b)   the nature of the related party relationship; and*
  - *(c)   other information about the transactions necessary for an understanding of the financial position of the small entity.*

  Information about individual transactions may be aggregated according to their nature, except where separate information is necessary for an understanding of the effects of the related party transactions on the financial position of the small entity.

  Particulars need not be given of transactions entered into between two or more members of a group provided that any subsidiary which is a party to the transaction is wholly-owned by such a member. [1 Sch 66 (SC), 1 Sch 64 (LLP SC)].

Although disclosure is only required of material transactions with the specified related parties that have not been concluded under normal market conditions, small entities disclosing all transactions with such related parties would still be compliant with company law.

Transactions with directors, or members of an entity's governing body, include directors' remuneration (see 11.1.8.B below) and dividends paid to directors.

Paragraphs 33.9 and 33.14 address similar requirements for all related parties. *[FRS 102.1AC.35].* See Chapter 30 at 3.2.3. However, the categories of related party that information must be reported for and details required under full FRS 102 differ slightly to the requirements of paragraph 1AC.35.

LLP law specifies that particulars must be given of material transactions the small LLP has entered into that have not been concluded under normal market conditions with: (a) members of the LLP that are related parties; and (b) undertakings in which the LLP itself has a participating interest. A note on the FRC website clarifies that where the statutory disclosure requirements in the Small LLP Regulations differ, the statutory requirements for small LLPs (rather than the disclosures in Section 1A) should be followed. Not all members of LLPs may qualify as related parties. The LLP SORP provides further guidance on identifying related parties. *[LLP SORP.128-131].*

See Chapter 30 at 1.1.2 for discussion on the meaning of the exemption from disclosing transactions involving wholly owned subsidiaries. The formats themselves require certain information containing transactions and balances with group undertakings and participating interests.

While the disclosure in Section 1A is only required for transactions 'not concluded under normal market conditions', the FRC has clarified that disclosure of all transactions with the related parties concerned would meet the requirements. *[FRS 102.1AC.35].* This would avoid the difficulties in assessing whether a transaction, say with a director, is 'concluded under normal market conditions'.

11.1.8.B   Directors' remuneration disclosures

There are no statutory directors' remuneration disclosures required by the Small Companies Regulations. However, paragraph 1AC.35 (see 11.1.8.A above) confirms that directors' remuneration (or where the entity is not a company, the remuneration of the entity's governing body) still requires disclosure as a related party transaction. Section 1A contains no further detail as to the basis on which this remuneration should be disclosed. However, it is clear that the disclosures may be given for the small entity's directors (or members of its governing body) in aggregate.

Small entities applying Section 1A are not required to provide disclosure of key management personnel compensation in total. Key management personnel may include persons other than directors of the reporting entity. In addition, key management personnel compensation may include amounts paid on behalf of the reporting entity or its parent (and therefore include transactions not entered into, or where the cost is not borne, by the small entity). *[FRS 102.33.6-7A].* In our view, one approach to disclosing directors' remuneration might be to disclose the element of key management compensation in total that relates to the directors, separately disclosing compensation that is not provided by the reporting entity. Where necessary for an understanding of the financial position of the reporting entity, other information about the transactions might be required. This might sometimes be the case, for example, where long-term incentive plan or share-based payment awards have been made to a director and the amount of the transaction disclosed (say, the expense recognised) does not fully provide an understanding of the effect on the financial position of the reporting entity (which could include commitments). See Chapter 30 at 3.1.1.B and 3.2.2 for a discussion of key management personnel compensation. Since the Small Companies Regulations are not specific, other approaches may be acceptable.

11.1.8.C   Advances, credits and guarantees

• *Details of advances and credits granted by the small entity to its directors and guarantees of any kind entered into by the small entity on behalf of its directors must be shown in the notes to the financial statements.*

  The details required of an advance or credit are:

  (a) *its amount;*

  (b) *an indication of the interest rate;*

  (c) *its main conditions;*

  (d) *any amounts repaid;*

  (e) *any amounts written off; and*

  (f) *any amounts waived.*

  There must also be stated in the notes to the financial statements the totals of amounts stated under (a), (d), (e) and (f).

  The details required of a guarantee are:

  (a) *its main terms;*

  (b) *the amount of the maximum liability that may be incurred by the small entity; and*

  (c) *any amount paid and any liability incurred by the small entity for the purpose of fulfilling the guarantee (including any loss incurred by reason of enforcement of the guarantee).*

  There must also be stated in the notes to the financial statements the totals of amounts stated under (b) and (c). [s413].

Paragraph 33.9 addresses similar requirements for all related parties. See Chapter 30 at 3.2.3.

A small entity that is not a company shall provide this disclosure in relation to members of its governing body. *[FRS 102.1AC.36].* For this reason, we believe that a small LLP should give this disclosure (although there is no equivalent statutory requirement).

See Chapter 6 at 8.8 for discussion of the scope and content of this disclosure and 11.4.2.C below (in respect of any consolidated financial statements).

11.1.9   Other requirements

- *The financial statements must state:*

  (a)   *the part of the UK in which the small entity is registered;*

  (b)   *the small entity's registered number;*

  (c)   *whether the small entity is a public or a private company and whether the small entity is limited by shares or by guarantee;*

  (d)   *the address of the small entity's registered office; and*

  (e)   *where appropriate, the fact that the entity is being wound up.* *[s396, s396 (LLP)].*

  Paragraph 3.24(a) (which is actually scoped in by Section 1A – see 7 above) has similar disclosure requirements, i.e. the legal form of the entity, its country of incorporation, and the address of its registered office (or principal place of business, if different). *[FRS 102.1AC.37].*

  Paragraph 1AC.37(c) above is not required for a small LLP.

  This disclosure is discussed further in Chapter 6 at 8.5.

  See also 7.7 above which addresses the general requirements of FRS 102 on identification of the financial statements.

- *Where items to which Arabic numbers are given in the formats have been combined, unless they are not material, the individual amounts of any items which have been combined must be disclosed in a note to the financial statements.* *[1 Sch 4(3) (SC), 1 Sch 4(3) (LLP SC), FRS 102.1AC.38].*

  See the discussion on the General Rules to the formats at 8.2 above.

- *The nature and financial effect of material events arising after the reporting date which are not reflected in the income statement or statement of financial position must be stated.* *[1 Sch 64 (SC), 1 Sch 62 (LLP SC)].*

  Paragraphs 32.10 and 32.11 address similar requirements. See Chapter 29 at 3.2.2 and 3.5.2. *[FRS 102.1AC.39].*

11.2   Statutory disclosures not noted in Section 1A

Financial statements of a small entity will also need to comply with any statutory requirements arising from the CA 2006 and applicable regulations, or other legal framework that applies to the small entity.

Section 1A does not contain a complete list of all statutory requirements for a small company (or LLP) applying the small companies regime (or small LLPs regime). Some additional disclosures are noted below. The statutory disclosures in group accounts (where voluntarily prepared) are set out at 11.4 below.

11.2.1   Audited financial statements only

A company subject to the small companies regime and an LLP subject to the small LLPs regime is not required to disclose remuneration receivable by the company's auditor. *[s494, s494 (LLP)].*[11]

A small company which has entered into a liability limitation agreement (that purports to limit the liability owed to a company by its auditor in respect of any negligence, default, breach of duty or breach of trust, occurring in the course of the audit of the accounts, of which the auditor may be guilty in relation to the company *[s534]*) must disclose its principal terms, the date of the resolution approving the agreement or the agreement's principal terms or, in the case of a private company, the date of the resolution waiving the need for such approval. This disclosure is required in a note to the annual accounts for the financial year to which the agreement relates, unless the agreement was entered into too late for it to be reasonably practicable for the disclosure to be made in those accounts (in which case, the disclosure is made in a note to the company's next following accounts).[12] This disclosure does not apply to a small LLP.

11.2.2   Audit exemption statement

If a small company takes advantage of an exemption from audit of its annual accounts, its balance sheet will need to contain a statement by the directors to the effect that:

(a)   the company is exempt from audit under section 477 (small companies), section 479A (subsidiary companies) or section 480 (dormant companies) or under section 482 (non-profit-making companies subject to public sector audit) of the CA 2006, stating the relevant exemption;

(b)   the members have not required the company to obtain an audit of its accounts for the year in question in accordance with section 476 of the CA 2006; and

(c)   the directors acknowledge their responsibilities for complying with the requirements of the CA 2006 with respect to accounting records and the preparation of accounts.

The statement must appear above the signature of the director required by section 414 of the CA 2006 (see 11.2.5 below). *[s475, s414]*.

LLPs have a similar but not identical audit exemption statement.

If a small LLP takes advantage of an exemption from audit of its annual accounts, its balance sheet will need to contain a statement by the members of the LLP to the effect that:

(a)   the LLP is exempt from audit under section 477 (small LLPs), section 479A (subsidiary LLPs) or section 480 (dormant LLPs) of the CA 2006 (as applied to LLPs), stating the relevant exemption; and

(b)   the members acknowledge their responsibilities for complying with the requirements of the CA 2006 (as applied to LLPs) with respect to accounting records and the preparation of accounts.

The statement must appear above the signature of the designated member of the LLP required by section 414 of the CA 2006, as applied to LLPs (see 11.2.5 below). *[s475 (LLP), s414(LLP)]*.

Companies House guidance *Company accounts guidance* and *LLP accounts,* available on the Companies House website includes suitable wordings of the audit exemption statements.

11.2.3   Group accounts not prepared by a parent company

A parent company applying the small companies regime (or a parent LLP applying the small LLPs regime) need not disclose use of the exemption from preparing group accounts. *[s399(2A)-(2B), s399(2A)-(2B) (LLP)]*.

Since a company subject to the small companies regime (or an LLP subject to the small LLPs regime) are exempt from preparing group accounts, the disclosures required where the exemptions from preparing group accounts in sections 400 and 401 of the CA 2006 are taken are not noted here.

11.2.4   Other disclosures

Where fixed asset investments (falling under item B.III in the statutory balance sheet format for companies and item A.III for LLPs – see 9.1 above) are included at a value determined on any basis which appears to the directors to be appropriate in the circumstances of the company, particulars of the method of valuation adopted and of the reasons for adopting it must be disclosed in a note to the accounts. *[1 Sch 32(3) (SC), 1 Sch 32(3) (LLP SC)]*.

This disclosure only applies where the valuation is in accordance with the alternative accounting rules. FRS 102 only permits use of the alternative accounting rules for fixed asset investments that are investments in subsidiaries, associates or jointly controlled entities carried at fair value with changes in value recognised in other comprehensive income (except where required to be recognised in profit or loss). This is an accounting policy choice, to be applied consistently to all investments in a single class. See Chapter 8 at 3.4.1, 4.1 and 4.2. Following the Triennial review 2017, an entity may also adopt this accounting policy choice for measuring investments in another group entity in scope of Section 11 (thus the investments are not subsidiaries, associates or jointly controlled entities to the reporting entity). *[FRS 102.11.7, 14(d)]*. See Chapter 10 at 8.3.2. However, as such fixed asset investments are carried at fair value, this disclosure would not apply.

However, the alternative accounting rules may also be used where investments in subsidiaries, associates or jointly controlled entities are carried using a deemed cost in individual or separate financial statements on transition. *[FRS 102.35.10(f)]*. See Chapter 32 at 5.9. In such circumstances, the above disclosure will be required.

11.2.5   Approval of annual accounts

The annual accounts of a company must be approved by the board of directors and the company's balance sheet signed on behalf of the board by a director of the company. *[s414(1)-(2)]*. The annual accounts of an LLP must be approved by the members and the balance sheet is signed on behalf of all the members by a designated member. *[s414(1)-(2) (LLP)]*.

Where this is the case, the balance sheet must contain, in a prominent position above the signature(s) of the director(s) (or designated member(s) of the LLP), a statement that the financial statements have been prepared in accordance with the provisions applicable to companies subject to the small companies regime (or for LLPs, that the financial statements are prepared in accordance with the provisions applicable to LLPs subject to the small LLPs regime). *[s414(3), s414(3) (LLP)]*. See 12 below. Following the Technical Review 2017, this statutory requirement has been included in Section 1A and adapted for other small entities. *[FRS 102.1A.6A]*. See 7.1.1 and 9 above, which also discuss the related statement of compliance.

Chapter 5

11.3   Specifically encouraged disclosures – Appendix E

A small entity is also encouraged to make the disclosures set out in Appendix E to Section 1A, which may nevertheless be necessary to give a true and fair view and meet the requirements of paragraph 1A.5. *[FRS 102.1A.20]*. While the FRC cannot mandate disclosures not included in the Accounting Directive (as implemented into UK and Irish law), this statement implies that the disclosures below should generally be given, where relevant, since they may be necessary to give a true and fair view.

When relevant to its transactions, other events and conditions, a small entity in the UK is encouraged to provide the following disclosures: *[FRS 102.1AE.1]*

(a)   a statement of compliance with FRS 102 as set out in paragraph 3.3, adapted to refer to Section 1A (see 7.1.1 and 9 above);

(b)   a statement that it is a public benefit entity as set out in paragraph PBE 3.3A (see 7.1.1 above);

(c)   the disclosures relating to material uncertainties related to events or conditions that cast significant doubt upon the small entity's ability to continue as a going concern as set out in paragraph 3.9 (see 7.3 above and Chapter 6 at 9.3);

(d)   dividends declared and paid or payable during the period (for example, as set out in paragraph 6.5(b)); and

(e)   on first-time adoption of FRS 102, an explanation of how the transition has affected its financial position and financial performance as set out in paragraph 35.13 (see Chapter 32 at 6.2 and 6.3).

Paragraph 6.5(b) requires the information on dividends to be presented in the statement of income and retained earnings (which may not be presented by a small entity applying Section 1A). In our view, this disclosure could be presented in the notes to the financial statements. Paragraph 1AC.35 may require dividends to certain categories of related parties (such as directors) to be disclosed separately. *[FRS 102.1AC.35]*.

Where relevant to its transactions, other events and conditions, a small entity in the Republic of Ireland is encouraged to give the disclosures in items (b), (c) and (e) above. *[FRS 102.1AE.2]*. Appendix D (which is based on the statutory disclosure requirements for small entities in the Republic of Ireland) already requires disclosures similar to items (a) and (d) above. *[FRS 102.1AD.3, 1AD.35]*.

11.4   Disclosures in consolidated financial statements

FRS 102 does not require a small entity that is a parent entity to prepare consolidated financial statements. *[FRS 102.1A.21]*. However, some small entities may choose to (or may be required, for example, by their statutory framework) to prepare consolidated financial statements.

Section 1A addresses the preparation of consolidated financial statements, including the disclosures required (see 6.2.1 above). A small entity: *[FRS 102.1A.22(b)-(d)]*

- is encouraged to provide the disclosures set out in paragraph 9.23 (see 11.4.1 below) (small entities in the Republic of Ireland are required to provide certain of these disclosures);
- must comply with the disclosure requirements specified in Section 1A as if the group were a single entity (as required by Schedule 6 of the Small Companies Regulations, paragraph 1(1), or for small entities in the Republic of Ireland, by Schedule 4A to the Companies Act 2014, paragraph 2(1)), subject to any restrictions or exemptions set out in legislation (see 11.1 and 11.3 above, and 11.4.2 below); and
- must provide any disclosures in Schedule 6 to the Small Companies Regulations (see 11.4.3 and 11.4.4 below). Small entities in the Republic of Ireland refer instead to Schedule 4A to, and sections 294, 296, 307 to 309, 317, 320, 321 and 323 of, the Companies Act 2014.

A UK company subject to the small companies regime must comply with the statutory disclosure requirements of the CA 2006 and Schedule 6 to the Small Companies Regulations.

Similarly, an LLP subject to the small LLPs regime must comply with the statutory disclosure requirements in the CA 2006 as applied to LLPs (set out in SI 2008/1911) and Schedule 4 to the Small LLP Regulations. These largely overlap with the disclosures required by Section 1A alone (although some additional disclosures are noted at 11.2 above and 11.4.2 below).

The modifications made to the formats for group accounts in the Small Companies Regulations and Small LLP Regulations are addressed at 8.1.4 above.

11.4.1   FRS 102 disclosures encouraged

Section 1A encourages a small entity to provide the following disclosures in consolidated financial statements: *[FRS 102.1A.22(b), FRS 102.9.23]*

- the fact that the financial statements are consolidated financial statements;
- the basis for concluding that control exists when the parent does not own, directly or indirectly through subsidiaries, more than half of the voting power;
- any difference in the reporting date of the financial statements of the parent and its subsidiaries used in the preparation of the consolidated financial statements;
- the nature and extent of any significant restrictions (e.g. resulting from borrowing arrangements or regulatory requirements) on the ability of subsidiaries to transfer funds to the parent in the form of cash dividends or to repay loans;
- the name of any subsidiary excluded from consolidation and the reason for exclusion; and
- the nature and extent of its interests in unconsolidated special purpose entities, and the risks associated with those interests (this was added by the Triennial review 2017).

Chapter 5

11.4.2   *Statutory disclosures – Part 15 of CA 2006*

11.4.2.A   *General disclosures*

Companies Act group accounts (for an LLP, non-IAS group accounts) must state, in respect of the parent company (or parent LLP): *[s404(A1), s404(A1) (LLP)]*

- the part of the UK in which the company (or LLP) is registered;
- the company's (or LLP's) registered number;
- whether the company is a public or a private company and whether it is limited by shares or by guarantee (no equivalent disclosure for an LLP);
- the address of the company's (or LLP's) registered office, and
- where appropriate, the fact that the company (or LLP) is being wound up.

These are the same as the disclosures required by a company (or an LLP) preparing Companies Act individual accounts (for an LLP, non-IAS individual accounts). Those disclosures are included in paragraph 1AC.37 (see 11.1.9 above). *[FRS 102.1A.22, 1AC.37]*. See Chapter 6 at 8.5 for further discussion.

11.4.2.B   *Section 408 exemption from presenting the individual profit and loss account*

Parent companies (or parent LLPs) preparing group accounts in accordance with the CA 2006 (for LLPs, the CA 2006 as applied to LLPs) can take advantage of the section 408 exemption not to present the individual profit and loss account (providing the conditions for use of the exemption are met).

References in Part 15 to the profit and loss account include notes to the accounts giving information required by any provision of the CA 2006 and that is required or allowed by any such provision to be given in a note to the company's accounts. *[s472, s472 (LLP)]*.

The company's (or LLP's) individual balance sheet must show the profit or loss for the financial year. While section 408, as amended, now refers to showing the 'profit *and* loss' [emphasis added] for the financial year on the balance sheet, we believe this is intended to mean 'profit *or* loss', as before.

The disclosures of certain information supplementing the profit and loss account in paragraphs 1AC.9 and 1AC.32 – see 11.1.3 and 11.1.6 above – must be given in the individual accounts as well as for the group. *[1 Sch 61, 1 Sch 59 (LLP), FRS 102.1A.22, 1AC.9, 1AC.32]*.

In addition, the notes to the accounts of a company subject to the small companies regime (or an LLP subject to the small LLPs regime) must disclose the average number of persons employed: *[s411, s411(LLP), FRS 102.1A.22, 1AC.33]*

(a) by the company (or LLP) (in the individual accounts – see paragraph 1AC.33 at 11.1.7); and

(b) by the company (or LLP) and its consolidated subsidiary undertakings (in the group accounts).

This disclosure is discussed further in Chapter 6 at 8.6.

The section 408 exemption would not extend to individual financial statements prepared under other statutory frameworks, unless explicitly permitted by these frameworks. See Chapter 1 at 6.3.2.

11.4.2.C   Advances, credits and guarantees granted to directors

In the case of a parent company preparing group accounts, the notes to the group accounts must include details of:

- advances and credits granted to the directors of the parent company, by that company or by any of its subsidiary undertakings (as defined in section 1162 of the CA 2006); and
- guarantees of any kind entered into on behalf of the directors of the parent company, by that company or by any of its subsidiary undertakings.

The details required in respect of advances, credits and guarantees are those set out in sections 413(3) to 413(5). The information required is the same as that discussed at 11.1.8.C above which sets out the equivalent statutory disclosure required in individual accounts (where group accounts are not prepared). Where group accounts are prepared, only the disclosure required in the group accounts is given. *[s413, FRS 102.1A.22, 1AC.36]*.

While paragraph 1AC.36 incorporates the disclosure required in individual accounts into Section 1A, in our view, the reference in paragraph 1A.22(c) to 'subject to any restrictions or exemptions set out in legislation' allows a small entity applying Section 1A to only give the information required by section 413 in the group accounts. This is particularly because the FRC does not intend to mandate disclosures for companies subject to the small companies regime beyond those required by law.

While this statutory disclosure requirement does not apply to LLPs, the same disclosures are required in respect of the members of an LLP's governing body by virtue of paragraph 1AC.36 and paragraph 1A.22(c) (see (c) at 6.2.1 above). In our view, parent LLPs preparing group accounts need only give the equivalent information to that required in group accounts of a parent company.

This disclosure is discussed further in Chapter 6 at 8.8.

11.4.2.D   Off-balance sheet arrangements

In group accounts, the disclosures required by section 410A for off balance sheet arrangements (paragraph 1AC.31) (see 11.1.5.H above) apply as if the undertakings included in the consolidation were a single company. Therefore, the disclosures are required for both the consolidated group and the company. *[s410A, s410A (LLP), FRS 102.1A.22, 1AC.31]*. This disclosure is discussed further in Chapter 6 at 8.7.

11.4.2.E   Audited financial statements

A company subject to the small companies regime and an LLP subject to the small LLPs regime is not required to disclose remuneration receivable by the company's auditor for auditing the annual accounts for financial years beginning on or after 1 January 2016. *[s494, s494 (LLP)]*.[13]

See 11.2.1 above for disclosures of limited liability limitation agreements in individual accounts. *[s538]*. Only the disclosures required in individual accounts are required where group accounts are also prepared.

11.4.2.F   Audit exemption statement

See 11.2.2 above for the disclosures required in respect of the audit exemption. *[s475, s475 (LLP)]*. Only the disclosures required in individual accounts are required where group accounts are also prepared.

Chapter 5

11.4.3   *Statutory disclosures (CA 2006) – Small Companies Regulations and Small LLP Regulations*

The group accounts of a UK company (or an LLP) must comply so far as practicable with the requirements of Schedule 1 to the Small Companies Regulations (or Schedule 1 to the Small LLP Regulations) as if the undertakings included in the consolidation were a single company (or LLP). *[FRS 102.1A.22(c)]*. There are certain modifications to the formats (see 8.1.4 above).

Therefore, where group accounts are prepared, the Schedule 1 disclosures (see 11.1 and 11.2.4 above) are given for both the individual company (or LLP) and for the consolidated group (i.e. the parent and the undertakings included in the consolidation, as a single unit).

Part 1 of Schedule 6 to the Small Companies Regulations (and Part 1 of Schedule 4 to the Small LLP Regulations) require certain disclosures specific to group accounts (unless not material). *[6 Sch 5(SC), 4 Sch 5 (LLP SC)]*. The disclosures are as follows:

- Where assets and liabilities to be included in the group accounts have been valued or otherwise determined by undertakings according to accounting rules differing from those used for the group accounts, the values or amounts must be adjusted so as to accord with the rules used for the group accounts (unless not material for the purposes of giving a true and fair view). If it appears to the directors of the parent company (or parent LLP) that there are special reasons for departing from this requirement, particulars of any such departure, the reasons for it and its effect must be given in a note to the accounts. *[6 Sch 3 (SC), 4 Sch 3 (LLP SC)]*.

  Since Section 9 requires consolidation adjustments to be made to align with the group accounts, disclosure of departures would not be expected in practice. *[FRS 102.9.17]*.

- Any differences of accounting rules as between a parent company's (or parent LLP's) individual accounts for a financial year and its group accounts must be disclosed in a note to the group accounts and the reasons for the difference given. *[6 Sch 4 (SC), 4 Sch 4 (LLP SC)]*.

- Unless the exemption in paragraph 16 of Schedule 6 to the Small Companies Regulations (paragraph 16 of Schedule 4 to the Small LLP Regulations) applies (see below), the following information with respect to acquisitions taking place in the financial year must be stated in a note to the accounts: *[6 Sch 13 (SC), 4 Sch 13 (LLP SC)]*

  (a) the name of the undertaking acquired or, where a group was acquired, the name of the parent undertaking of that group;

  (b) whether the acquisition has been accounted for by the acquisition or the merger method of accounting; and

  (c) in relation to an acquisition which significantly affects the figures shown in the group accounts:

      (i) the composition and fair value of the consideration for the acquisition given by the parent company (or parent LLP) and its subsidiary undertakings; and

    (ii) where the acquisition method of accounting has been adopted, the book values immediately prior to the acquisition and the fair values at the date of the acquisition, of each class of assets and liabilities of the undertaking or group acquired (in tabular form), including the amount of any goodwill or negative consolidation difference arising on the acquisition together with an explanation of any significant adjustments made.

        In respect of an acquired group, the above amounts are disclosed after any set-offs and other adjustments required by Schedule 6 to the Small Companies Regulations (or Schedule 4 to the Small LLP Regulations) in respect of group accounts.

- Unless the exemption in paragraph 16 of Schedule 6 to the Small Companies Regulations (paragraph 16 of Schedule 4 to the Small LLP Regulations) applies, a note to the accounts must state the cumulative amount of goodwill (net of any goodwill attributed to subsidiary undertakings or businesses disposed of prior to the balance sheet date) resulting from acquisitions in that and earlier financial years which has been written off otherwise than in the consolidated profit and loss account for that or any earlier financial year. *[6 Sch 14 (SC), 4 Sch 14 (LLP SC)].*

In our view, this would apply to any cumulative goodwill taken to reserves prior to application of FRS 10 – *Goodwill and intangible assets*, even though the goodwill, in effect, ceases to exist for accounting purposes on transition to FRS 102.

- Unless the exemption in paragraph 16 of Schedule 6 to the Small Companies Regulations (paragraph 16 of Schedule 4 to the Small LLP Regulations) applies, where during the financial year there has been a disposal of an undertaking or group which significantly affects the figure shown in the group accounts, a note to the accounts must state: *[6 Sch 15 (SC), 4 Sch 15 (LLP SC)]*

    (a) the name of that undertaking or, as the case may be, of the parent undertaking of that group, and

    (b) the extent to which the profit or loss shown in the group accounts is attributable to profit or loss of that undertaking or group.

The information required by paragraphs 13 to 15 of Schedule 6 to the Small Companies Regulations (paragraphs 13 to 15 of Schedule 4 to the Small LLP Regulations) need not be disclosed with respect to an undertaking which: (a) is established under the law of a country outside the UK, or (b) carries on business outside the UK, if in the opinion of the directors of the parent company (or the members of the parent LLP), the disclosure would be seriously prejudicial to the business of that undertaking or to the business of the parent company (or the parent LLP) or any of its subsidiary undertakings; and the Secretary of State agrees that the information should not be disclosed. *[6 Sch 16 (SC), 4 Sch 16 (LLP SC)].*

Chapter 5

A parent company and parent LLP have slightly different disclosures where the merger method of accounting is applied, reflecting the different requirements for use of the merger method in the Small Companies Regulations and Small LLP Regulations.

- Where an acquisition has taken place in the financial year and the merger method of accounting has been adopted, the notes to a company's accounts must also disclose: *[6 Sch 16A (SC)]*

  (a)   the address of the registered office of the undertaking acquired (whether in or outside the UK);

  (b)   the name of the party referred to in paragraph 10(a) of Schedule 6 to the Small Companies Regulations, i.e. the ultimate controlling party;

  (c)   the address of the registered office of that party in (b) (whether in or outside the UK); and

  (d)   the information required by paragraph 11(6) of Schedule 6 to the Small Companies Regulations, i.e. the adjustment to consolidated reserves made in applying the merger accounting method. This adjustment (explained further in Chapter 17 at 5.3.3) is the difference between:

  (i)   the aggregate of (1) the fair value of consideration (except in respect of shares covered by (2)) for the acquisition of shares in the undertaking acquired, determined at the date of acquisition of those shares and (2) the 'appropriate amount' for shares issued by the parent company or its subsidiary undertakings in consideration for the acquisition of shares in the undertaking acquired (where merger relief or group reconstruction relief is taken).

  The 'appropriate amount' used in (2) is nominal value (in relation to shares where merger relief is taken) and nominal value together with any minimum premium value (in relation to shares where group reconstruction relief is taken); and

  (ii)   the nominal value of the issued share capital of the undertaking acquired held by the parent company and its subsidiary undertakings. *[6 Sch 11(5)-(7) (SC)]*.

  Where a group is acquired, references to 'shares of the undertaking acquired' are construed as references to 'shares of the parent undertaking of the group'. *[6 Sch 12 (SC)]*.

- Where an acquisition has taken place in the financial year and the merger method of accounting has been adopted, the notes to the accounts of an LLP must also disclose the names and the addresses of the registered offices of the undertakings concerned (whether in or outside the UK). *[4 Sch 16A (LLP SC)]*.

The requirements of paragraphs 17 to 20 and 22 of Schedule 1 to the Small Companies Regulations (paragraphs 17 to 20 and 22 of Schedule 1 to the Small LLP Regulations) apply to any goodwill relating to an interest in an associated undertaking shown by the equity method of accounting. *[6 Sch 20(1) (SC), 4 Sch 20(1) (LLP SC)].* In our view, this would include the disclosures of the amortisation period used and the reasons (where the useful life of the goodwill cannot be reliably estimated); and of any provision for diminution or write-back of provision for diminution of goodwill relating to an interest in an associated undertaking (see commentary at 11.4.4.C below on meaning of associated undertaking). *[FRS 102.1AC.6, 20-21].* See 11.1.2 and 11.1.5.E above for details of the disclosures.

The statutory disclosures on related party transactions (see 11.1.8.A above) apply in group accounts to transactions which the parent company or other undertakings included in the consolidation have entered into with certain categories of related parties, unless they are intra-group transactions. *[1 Sch 66 (SC), 6 Sch 20B (SC), 1 Sch 64 (LLP SC), 4 Sch 20B (LLP SC), FRS 102.1AC.35].* This clarification appears to simply be an application of the general requirement to present disclosures required by Schedule 1 in individual accounts for the consolidated group.

11.4.4 Statutory disclosures (CA 2006) – information about related undertakings

Disclosures in respect of related undertakings are still required in group accounts and are set out in Part 2 of Schedule 6 to the Small Companies Regulations and Part 2 of Schedule 4 to the Small LLP Regulations. The previous requirements for individual accounts set out in Schedule 2 to the Small Companies Regulations and Schedule 2 to the Small LLP Regulations were removed for financial years beginning on or after 1 January 2016.

Information need not be disclosed in relation to an undertaking that is established under the law of a country outside the UK or carries on business outside the UK if the conditions in section 409(4) of the CA 2006 are met, i.e. disclosure would be seriously prejudicial (to the business of: that undertaking, the parent company (or the parent LLP), any of its subsidiary undertakings, or other consolidated undertakings), in the opinion of the directors or the members of the LLP; and the Secretary of State agrees that the information need not be disclosed. Where this is the case, disclosure is required in the notes to the accounts of the fact that this exemption is taken. *[Regulations (SC) 10, LLP SC Regulations 7, s409(4)-(5), s409(4)-(5) (LLP)].*

In respect of the discussion below, references to 'group' means the parent company (or parent LLP) and its subsidiary undertakings. *[6 Sch 21 (SC), 4 Sch 21 (LLP SC)].* A 'group' therefore includes subsidiary undertakings excluded from consolidation.

Chapter 5

References in the disclosure requirements below to shares held by the parent company or the group are to be construed as follows:

- for the purposes of paragraphs 23, 27(4), 27(5), 28 to 30 of Schedule 6 to the Small Companies Regulations (information about holdings in subsidiary and other undertakings) (paragraphs 23, 26(4), 26(5), 27 to 29 of Schedule 4 to the Small LLP Regulations), there must be attributed to the parent company (or parent LLP) shares held on its behalf by any person. Shares held on behalf of a person other than the company (or LLP) must be treated as not held by the parent company (or parent LLP);

- references to shares held by the group are to any shares held by or on behalf of the parent company (or parent LLP) or any of its subsidiary undertakings. Any shares held on behalf of a person other than the parent company (or parent LLP) or any of its subsidiary undertakings are not to be treated as held by the group; and

- shares held by way of security must be treated as held by the person providing the security: *[6 Sch 37 (SC), 4 Sch 35 (LLP SC)]*

  (a) where apart from the right to exercise them for the purpose of preserving the value of the security, or of realising it, the rights attached to the shares are exercisable only in accordance with his instructions, and

  (b) where the shares are held in connection with the granting of loans as part of normal business activities and apart from the right to exercise them for the purpose of preserving the value of the security, or of realising it, the rights attached to the shares are exercisable only in his interests.

Part 2 of Schedule 6 to the Small Companies Regulations (Part 2 of Schedule 4 to the Small LLP Regulations) requires the following disclosures (at 11.4.4.A to 11.4.4.G below) to be given. These disclosures must be presented in full in the financial statements.

11.4.4.A   *Subsidiary undertakings*

The following information must be stated with respect to the undertakings that are subsidiary undertakings of the parent company at the end of the financial year:

- the name of each undertaking;
- the address of the undertaking's registered office (whether in or outside the UK);
- if the undertaking is unincorporated, the address of its principal place of business;
- whether the subsidiary undertaking is included in the consolidation (i.e. consolidated), *[s474(1), s474(1) (LLP)]*, and, if it is not, the reasons for excluding it from consolidation; and
- for each subsidiary undertaking, by virtue of which of the conditions specified in section 1162(2) or (4) of the CA 2006 it is a subsidiary undertaking of its immediate parent undertaking. This is not required to be given where the relevant condition is section 1162(2)(a) (holding a majority of voting rights) and the immediate parent undertaking holds the same proportion of shares in the undertaking as it holds voting rights. *[6 Sch 22 (SC), 4 Sch 22 (LLP SC)]*.

The following information must be given with respect to the shares of a subsidiary undertaking held (a) by the parent company (or parent LLP) and (b) by the group (separately, if the information for (a) and (b) is different):

- the identity of each class of shares held; and
- the proportion of the nominal value of the shares of that class represented by those shares. *[6 Sch 23 (SC), 4 Sch 23 (LLP SC)]*.

There must be shown with respect to each subsidiary undertaking not included in the consolidation, unless not material:

- the aggregate amount of capital and reserves as at the end of its relevant financial year; and
- its profit or loss for that year.

The relevant financial year is the subsidiary's financial year (where this ends on the same date as the company's (or LLP's) financial year); otherwise, it is the subsidiary's financial year that ends last before the end of the company's (or LLP's) financial year.

This information need not be given if:

- the group's investment in the undertaking is included in the accounts by way of the equity method of valuation; or
- the undertaking is not required by any provision of the CA 2006 to deliver a copy of its balance sheet for its relevant financial year and does not otherwise publish that balance sheet in the UK or elsewhere and the holding in the group is less than 50% of the nominal value of the shares in the undertaking. *[6 Sch 24 (SC), 4 Sch 24 (LLP SC)]*.

11.4.4.B   *Shares of company held by subsidiary undertakings*

The number, description and amount of the shares in the company held by or on behalf of its subsidiary undertakings must be disclosed.

However, this disclosure does not apply in relation to shares where the subsidiary undertaking is concerned as:

- personal representative; or
- trustee (unless the company or any of its subsidiary undertakings is beneficially interested under the trust, otherwise than by way of security only for the purposes of a transaction entered into by it in the ordinary course of business which includes the lending of money). Part 2 of Schedule 2 to the Small Companies Regulations provides interpretation on a beneficial interest under a trust (although this schedule now appears to have been removed). *[6 Sch 25 (SC)]*.

This disclosure does not apply to an LLP.

11.4.4.C   *Associated undertakings*

Where an undertaking included in the consolidation has an associated undertaking, the following information must be stated:

- the name of the associated undertaking;
- the address of the undertaking's registered office (whether in or outside the UK);
- if the undertaking is unincorporated, the address of its principal place of business;
- with respect to the shares of the undertaking held (a) by the parent company (or parent LLP) and, separately, (b) by the group:
  (i)   the identity of each class of shares held; and

(ii)   the proportion of the nominal value of the shares of that class represented by those shares.

This information is required even if paragraph 20(3) applied to the group accounts (which allows that the equity method need not be applied if the amounts are not material). *[6 Sch 27 (SC), 4 Sch 26 (LLP SC)].*

An 'associated undertaking' is defined in paragraph 19 of Schedule 6 to the Small Companies Regulations (paragraph 19 of Schedule 4 to the Small LLP Regulations) (see Chapter 6 at 5.3.4.E). This will generally include a jointly controlled entity and an associate under FRS 102. However, the definition includes a requirement for a 'participating interest' (not a feature of the definitions of a jointly controlled entity or an associate in FRS 102).

There are additional disclosures in relation to joint ventures (as defined in paragraph 18 of Schedule 6 to the Small Companies Regulations (paragraph 18 of Schedule 4 to the Small LLP Regulations)) that are included in the group accounts by the method of proportional consolidation. *[6 Sch 26 (SC), 4 Sch 25 (LLP SC)].* These are not discussed in this chapter because jointly controlled entities are equity accounted under FRS 102 and accordingly the disclosures are unlikely to apply.

11.4.4.D   *Other significant holdings of parent company or group*

A holding is significant for the purpose of the disclosures in paragraphs 29, 30, 32 and 33 of Schedule 6 to the Small Companies Regulations if:

- it amounts to 20% or more of the nominal value of any class of shares in the undertaking; or

- for the disclosures for (a) the parent company / LLP, the amount of the holding (as stated or included in the company's / LLP's individual accounts) exceeds 20% of the amount of the company's / LLP's assets (as so stated); or

- for the disclosures for (b) the group, the amount of the holding (as stated or included in the group accounts) exceeds 20% of the amount of the group's assets (as so stated). *[6 Sch 28, 31 (SC), 4 Sch 27, 30 (LLP SC)].*

Separate disclosures are required for where (a) the parent company / LLP has a significant holding and (b) the group has a significant holding in an undertaking.

Where at the end of the financial year, (a) the parent company / parent LLP or (b) the group has a significant holding in an undertaking which is not one of its subsidiary undertakings and does not fall within paragraph 26 (joint ventures) or paragraph 27 (associated undertakings) of Schedule 6 to the Small Companies Regulations (paragraphs 24 and 26 of Schedule 4 to the Small LLP Regulations) (see 11.4.4.A and 11.4.4.C above), the following information must be stated: *[6 Sch 28-33 (SC), 4 Sch 27-32 (LLP SC)]*

- the name of the undertaking;

- the address of the undertaking's registered office (whether in or outside the UK);

- if the undertaking is unincorporated, the address of its principal place of business;

- with respect to the shares of the undertaking held by the parent company / LLP (for the disclosures for (a) the parent) and, separately with respect to the shares of the undertaking held by the group (for the disclosures for (b) the group):

  (i)   the identity of each class of shares held;

(ii)   the proportion of the nominal value of the shares of that class represented by those shares; and

(iii) if material, the aggregate amount of the capital and reserves of the undertaking as at the end of its relevant financial year and its profit or loss for that year.

The relevant financial year is the undertaking's financial year (where this ends on the same date as the company's / LLP's financial year); otherwise, it is the undertaking's financial year that ends last before the end of the company's / LLP's financial year.

This information need not be given in respect of an undertaking if the undertaking is not required by any provision of the CA 2006 to deliver a copy of its balance sheet for its relevant financial year and does not otherwise publish that balance sheet in the UK or elsewhere and the company's / LLP's holding (in respect of the disclosures for (a) the parent) or group's holding (in respect of the disclosures for (b) the group) is less than 50% of the nominal value of the shares in the undertaking.

11.4.4.E   *Parent company's or group's membership of qualifying undertakings*

The following information must be stated where, at the end of the financial year, the parent company or group is a member of a qualifying undertaking: *[6 Sch 34 (SC)]*

- the name and legal form of the undertaking (if the information is material);
- the address of the undertaking's registered office (whether in or outside the UK) or if it does not have such an office, its head office (whether in or outside the UK) (if the information is material); and
- where the undertaking is a qualifying partnership, either:

(a)   that a copy of the latest accounts of the undertaking has been or is to be appended to a copy of the company's accounts sent to the registrar under section 444 of the CA 2006; or

(b)   the name of at least one body corporate (which may be the company) in whose group accounts the undertaking has been or is to be dealt with on a consolidated basis (this means full consolidation, proportional consolidation or the equity method of accounting). This information need not be given if the notes to the company's accounts disclose that advantage has been taken of the exemption conferred by regulation 7 of the Partnerships (Accounts) Regulations 2008.

A qualifying undertaking is a qualifying partnership or an unlimited company meeting the criteria in paragraph 34(7) of Schedule 6 to the Small Companies Regulations. A qualifying partnership (and a member thereof) are as defined in the *Partnerships (Accounts) Regulations 2008*. Full details of these definitions are not provided here.

This disclosure does not apply to an LLP.

Chapter 5

11.4.4.F   Parent undertaking drawing up accounts for a larger group

Where the parent company / parent LLP is itself a subsidiary undertaking, with respect to that parent undertaking of the company which heads:

(a)   the largest group of undertakings for which group accounts are drawn up and of which that company is a member, and

(b)   the smallest such group of undertakings,

the following information must be stated:

* the name of the parent undertaking;
* if the undertaking is incorporated outside the UK, the country in which it is incorporated;
* if it is unincorporated, the address of its principal place of business; and
* if copies of the group accounts referred to above are available to the public, the addresses from which copies of those group accounts can be obtained. *[6 Sch 35 (SC), 4 Sch 33 (LLP SC)]*.

This is similar to but not the same as the disclosure required in individual accounts by paragraph 1AC.34 (see 11.1.8 above).

11.4.4.G   Identification of ultimate parent

Where the parent company / parent LLP is itself a subsidiary undertaking, the following information must be stated: *[6 Sch 36 (SC), 4 Sch 34 (LLP SC)]*

* the name of the company or body corporate (if any) regarded by the directors as being the company's / LLP's ultimate parent company (for an LLP, ultimate parent); and
* its country of incorporation, if outside the UK (if known to the directors or to the members of the LLP).

11.5   Limited liability partnerships – considerations

A note on the FRC website explains that there are some slight differences between the disclosure requirements of Section 1A and those in the Small LLP Regulations. LLPs should apply the equivalent requirements of the Small LLP Regulations rather than Section 1A. Where differences for an LLP have been identified in the disclosures included in Appendix C, these are noted in the detailed disclosures at 11.1 above.

An LLP subject to the small LLPs regime remains in scope of the LLP SORP which addresses recognition and measurement, presentation and disclosure considerations specific to LLPs. See Chapter 1 at 4.7 and Chapter 3 at 2.3 on application of SORPs.

Small LLPs applying Section 1A are required to comply with the disclosure requirements of Section 1A rather than those of the SORP except that small LLPs must give the disclosures about how loans and other debts due to members rank in relation to unsecured creditors, as required by paragraphs 63 and 64 (information on members' interests) of the SORP. With this exception, the SORP should not be interpreted as removing or not permitting exemptions for certain smaller entities in legislation or accounting standards (which take precedence over the SORP in the event of conflicting requirements), including those from the need to prepare group accounts or cash flow statements.

The SORP also encourages small LLPs applying Section 1A to present a reconciliation of the movement in 'members' other interests' (statement of changes in equity).

The financial statements of small LLPs must give a true and fair view. Judgement will therefore be required in determining whether further disclosures beyond those included in Section 1A of FRS 102 are needed to ensure that the financial statements give a true and fair view. Depending on the individual facts and circumstances, some or all of the disclosures in the SORP and the rest of FRS 102 may be needed in order for the LLP's financial statements to give a true and fair view. *[LLP SORP.27-28, 59, 63-64]*.

Detailed guidance on LLPS is outside the scope of this chapter.

11.6   Small entities in the Republic of Ireland – considerations

A small entity in the Republic of Ireland must provide, at a minimum, when relevant to its transactions, other events and conditions, the disclosures in Appendix D (unless not material, except when required by the Companies Act 2014 regardless of materiality). *[FRS 102.1A.17A, 18, 1AD.1]*.

Appendix D, which is an integral part of Section 1A, sets out the disclosure requirements for small entities based on the requirements of the Companies Act 2014 (as amended by the Companies (Accounting) Act 2017. Other than substituting company law terminology with the equivalent terminology used in FRS 102 (as set out in Appendix II – *Table of equivalence for company law terminology*– of FRS 102), the FRC states that the drafting is as close as possible to that set out in company law. References in Appendix D to sections of the Companies Act 2014 are to the sections of that Act, as amended by the Companies (Accounting) Act 2017 and references to Schedule 3A are to Schedule 3A of the Companies Act 2014.

Appendix D highlights disclosures in Sections 8 to 35 of FRS 102 that are similar to its requirements, noting that in many cases compliance with the similar requirement of FRS 102 will result in compliance with the requirements in Appendix D. However, a small entity in the Republic of Ireland must ensure it complies with all the disclosure requirements of Appendix D. Paragraphs in FRS 102 that have been cross referenced in Appendix D are also highlighted in the other sections of the standard with an asterisk. *[FRS 102.1A.19, 1AD.1]*.

In general, the disclosures in Appendix D are similar to those in Appendix C, although the detailed wording may differ as the drafting has been kept as close as possible to that set out in Irish law. Therefore, a small entity in the Republic of Ireland should refer directly to Appendix D in order to identify the disclosures required.

A small entity in the Republic of Ireland that is subject to Irish law must also ensure that it complies with any statutory requirements, including disclosures. A detailed discussion of Irish law is outside the scope of this publication.

12   SMALL COMPANIES AND LLPS – STATUTORY EXEMPTIONS

There are two sets of exemptions available for small companies (and small LLPs):

- the small companies regime (and small LLPs regime) – which applies to the preparation and / or filing of the financial statements; and

- the small companies exemption – which applies to the preparation and / or filing of the strategic report and directors' report. There is no equivalent for small LLPs (as LLPs are not generally required to prepare a strategic report or directors' report).

A traded LLP or a banking LLP is required to prepare a strategic report. *[s414A(1), s414A(1) ((LLP)].*[14] As discussed at 4.4.2. above, such an LLP would not qualify for the small LLPs regime. *[s384(1) (LLP)].*

These exemptions are available in both Companies Act accounts and IAS accounts. The discussion in this section sets out the requirements in the CA 2006 and Small Companies Regulations and small LLPs regime. This section is not intended to cover companies or LLPs applying the micro-entity provisions. See Chapter 1 at 6.4.

A company subject to the small companies regime (or an LLP subject to the small LLPs regime) must meet certain small size criteria and not be excluded from the small companies regime (or small LLPs regime), i.e. it must not be one of the types of ineligible company (or LLP) nor a member of an ineligible group. See 4 above.

A company entitled to the small companies exemption must meet the same small size criteria as for the small companies regime and must not be an ineligible company (although it may be a member of an ineligible group). The criteria to be subject to the small companies regime are, therefore, more onerous than for the small companies exemption; companies subject to the small companies regime will also qualify for the small companies exemption. See 12.2 below.

These exemptions operate independently from each other – a company entitled to both the small companies regime and the small companies exemption may choose to apply both, neither, the small companies regime only or the small companies exemption only.

A company that is subject to the small companies regime is entitled to apply the Small Companies Regulations, which require fewer disclosures in the financial statements and the directors' report than the Regulations. Similarly, an LLP that is subject to the small LLPs regime is entitled to apply the Small LLP Regulations, which require fewer disclosures in the financial statements than the LLP Regulations. See 12.1 below.

The exemptions from preparing group accounts available for small companies and LLPs are discussed at 6.2 above.

A company that takes advantage of the small companies exemption is not required to prepare a strategic report and is entitled to certain disclosure exemptions in the directors' report. *[s414A(2), s414B, s415A].* See 12.2 below.

Companies subject to the small companies regime or taking advantage of the small companies exemption are also entitled to certain (but different) filing exemptions. *[s444, s444A].* LLPs subject to the small LLPs regime have the same filing exemptions as companies subject to the small companies regime. *[s444 (LLP)].* See 13 below.

If a company's accounts are prepared in accordance with the small companies regime, the company's balance sheet must contain, in a prominent position above the signature(s) of the director(s), a statement to the effect that the accounts have been prepared in accordance with the provisions applicable to companies subject to the small companies regime. A similar statement on the balance sheet is required above the signature(s) of the designated member(s) of the LLP, where the accounts of an LLP are prepared in accordance with the small LLPs regime. This statement does not apply where the company or LLP applies the micro-entity provisions (see Chapter 1 at 6.4). *[s414(3)(b), s414(3)(b) (LLP)]*. This requirement has been included in Section 1A (and adapted for other small entities). See 7.1.1 and 9 above.

Where a company has taken advantage of the small companies exemption in preparing the directors' report, a statement to this effect is required in the directors' report, in a prominent place above the signature of the director (or secretary) signing on behalf of the board. *[s419(2)]*. The statement made in the directors' report refers to the small companies exemption *even if* the company is also subject to the small companies regime.

12.1　Use of the small companies and small LLPs regimes

Companies subject to the small companies regime (see 4.3 above), whether preparing Companies Act accounts or IAS accounts, must provide the disclosures required by the CA 2006, the Small Companies Regulations and other applicable regulations, but are exempt from certain disclosures required by companies not subject to the small companies regime.

Similarly, LLPs subject to the small LLPs regime (see 4.4 above), whether preparing Companies Act accounts or IAS accounts, must provide the disclosures required by the CA 2006 (as applied to LLPs by SI 2008/1911), the Small LLP Regulations and other applicable regulations, but are exempt from certain disclosures required by LLPs not subject to the small LLPs regime.

The disclosures of the relevant accounting standard followed should also be given.

12.1.1　*Small Companies Regulations and Small LLP Regulations*

The Small Companies Regulations (and Small LLP Regulations) contain significantly fewer disclosures than the Regulations (and LLP Regulations).

The statutory disclosures required for a company applying Section 1A are set out at 11 above (and where group accounts are prepared, at 11.4 above). The disclosures for LLPs are generally the same as those for companies, although there are a few differences and LLPs preparing FRS 102 financial statements are also subject to the LLP SORP. Special considerations for LLPs are highlighted at 11.5 above.

SI 2015/980 and SI 2016/575 removed a number of schedules from the Small Companies Regulations and Small LLP Regulations, significantly reducing the disclosures required. Figure 5.19 below sets out the schedules that continue to apply.

Chapter 5

Figure 5.19   *Schedules that apply in the Small Companies Regulations and Small LLP Regulations (as amended)*

Small Companies Regulations
Schedule 1 (Companies Act individual accounts)
Schedule 5 (Matters to be dealt with in directors' report)*
Schedule 6 (Group accounts)
  – Part 1
  – Part 2*
Schedule 7 (Definition of 'provision')
Schedule 8 (General interpretation)*

* Applies to both Companies Act accounts and IAS accounts

Small LLP Regulations
Schedule 1 (Non-IAS individual accounts)

Schedule 4 (Group Accounts)
  – Part 1
  – Part 2*

Schedule 5 (General interpretation)*
Note this includes the definition of a provision.
* Applies to both non-IAS accounts and IAS accounts

The following schedules in the Small Companies Regulations have been removed:

- Schedule 2 (Information about related undertakings where company not preparing group accounts (Companies Act or IAS individual accounts)) – but disclosures of related undertakings are still required in group accounts and are included in Part 2 of Schedule 6 (see 11.4.4 above);

- Schedule 3 (Information about directors' benefits: remuneration (Companies Act or IAS accounts)) – but disclosures may still be required as related party transactions under company law or accounting standards (see 11.1.8.A and 11.1.8.B above for the requirements under Section 1A); and

- Schedule 4 (Companies Act abbreviated accounts for delivery to Registrar of Companies).

The following schedules in the Small LLP Regulations have been removed:

- Schedule 2 (Information about related undertakings where LLP not preparing group accounts (non-IAS or IAS individual accounts)) – but disclosures of related undertakings are still required in group accounts and are included in Part 2 of Schedule 4 to the Small LLP Regulations (see 11.4.4 above); and

- Schedule 3 (Non-IAS abbreviated accounts for delivery to Registrar of Companies).

A company subject to the small companies regime preparing Companies Act accounts must comply with all applicable requirements of the Small Companies Regulations. Similarly, an LLP subject to the small LLPs regime preparing non-IAS accounts must comply with all applicable requirements of the Small LLP Regulations.

A company subject to the small companies regime preparing IAS accounts need not comply with Schedule 1 nor, where group accounts are prepared, Part 1 of Schedule 6 to the Small Companies Regulations. These schedules set out the formats for the profit and loss account and balance sheet, recognition and measurement principles, and disclosure requirements in Companies Act accounts. Similarly, an LLP subject to the small LLPs regime preparing IAS accounts need not comply with Schedule 1 nor Part 1 of Schedule 4 to the Small LLP Regulations.

However, both Companies Act group accounts (non-IAS group accounts for an LLP) and IAS group accounts must give the information on related undertakings in Part 2 of Schedule 6 to the Small Companies Regulations (Part 2 of Schedule 4 to the Small LLP Regulations).

For Companies Act accounts (non-IAS accounts for an LLP), the schedules in the Small Companies Regulations (and Small LLP Regulations) provide simpler formats and reduced disclosures compared to the corresponding schedules in the Regulations (and LLP Regulations). However, companies are treated as complying with Schedule 1 and, in respect of group accounts, Part 1 of Schedule 6 to the Small Companies Regulations if they comply with the corresponding provision of Schedule 1 and / or Part 1 of Schedule 6 to the Regulations. *[Regulations (SC) 3(3), 8(2)].* Similarly, LLPs are treated as complying with Schedule 1 and, in respect of group accounts, Part 1 of Schedule 4 to the Small LLP Regulations if they comply with the corresponding provision of Schedule 1 and / or Schedule 3 to the LLP Regulations. *[LLP SC Regulations 3(3), 6(2)].*

FRS 101 and full FRS 102 (where Section 1A is not applied) require use of the formats included in the Regulations (or LLP Regulations). Our view is that companies subject to the small companies regime (and LLPs subject to the small LLPs regime) can still apply FRS 101 or full FRS 102 but must use the formats in Schedule 1 to the Regulations or Schedule 1 to the LLP Regulations (rather than the formats in Schedule 1 to the Small Companies Regulations or Schedule 1 to the Small LLP Regulations). However, this does not preclude the small company or small LLP taking advantage of *other* exemptions applicable to companies subject to the small companies regime (or LLPs subject to the small LLPs regime).

Companies subject to the small companies regime (and LLPs subject to the small LLPs regime) are entitled to apply Section 1A (see 4 above). Companies subject to the small companies regime that choose to apply Section 1A should follow the formats in Schedule 1 to the Small Companies Regulations or Small LLP Regulations.

12.1.2 Disclosure exemptions for small companies and small LLPs regime in IAS accounts and Companies Act accounts

UK companies subject to the small companies regime (and LLPs subject to the small LLPs regime) benefit from the following disclosure exemptions:

- the financial impact of off-balance sheet arrangements on the company / LLP (and where group accounts are prepared, on the consolidated group) is not required. However, the nature and business purpose of the arrangements, to the extent necessary for enabling the financial position of the company / LLP (and where group accounts are prepared, of the consolidated group) to be assessed, must be disclosed. *[s410A, s410A (LLP)].* See 11.1.5.H and 11.4.2.D above and Chapter 6 at 8.7);

- information analysing employee numbers by category and staff costs is not required, although the total average number of persons employed by the company / LLP (and where group accounts are prepared, the consolidated group) must be disclosed (see 11.1.7 and 11.4.2.B above and Chapter 6 at 8.6); *[s411, s411 (LLP)]* and

- remuneration receivable by the company's (or LLP's) auditor. The disclosure is removed entirely for financial years beginning on or after 1 January 2016.[15] *[s494, s494 (LLP)].* See 11.2.1 and 11.4.2.E above.

The above exemptions from certain disclosures included in Part 15 of the CA 2006 apply both to Companies Act accounts (non-IAS accounts, for an LLP) and IAS accounts.

In addition, the disclosures in Schedule 1 to the Small Companies Regulations and Schedule 1 to the Small LLP Regulations are significantly fewer than those required for companies applying the Regulations, and are largely set out in Appendix C of Section 1A (see 11.1 above). These disclosures only apply to Companies Act accounts (for a company) and non-IAS accounts (for an LLP).

The disclosures at 11.2 above (except for 11.2.4), and in respect of group accounts, at 11.4.2 and 11.4.4 above, apply both to IAS accounts and Companies Act accounts (or non-IAS accounts for an LLP). A company preparing IAS individual and / or group accounts gives the same disclosure as that set out at 11.1.9 and 11.4.2.A above but must also state that the individual accounts (and any group accounts) are prepared in accordance with international accounting standards, i.e. EU-adopted IFRS. *[s397(1), s406(1), s474, s397 (LLP), s406 (LLP), s474 (LLP)].*

A company (or LLP) is not required to comply with Schedule 2 to the Small Companies Regulations, although disclosures for related undertakings (set out in Part 2 of Schedule 6 to the Small Companies Regulations and Part 2 of Schedule 4 to the Small LLP Regulations) are required in any group accounts (see 11.4.4 above). These disclosure exemptions apply to both Companies Act accounts (non-IAS accounts for an LLP) and IAS accounts.

As Schedule 3 (directors' remuneration) has been removed, the previous statutory directors' remuneration disclosures are not required for a small company. There was no equivalent of the disclosure required by Schedule 3 in the Small LLP Regulations; particulars of members and members' remuneration are required for large and medium-sized LLPs only.

However, Section 1A (and the related statutory disclosure requirement in the Small Companies Regulations) require separate disclosure of related party transactions, where not concluded under normal market conditions, for the small entity's directors (or members of the entity's governing body) and certain other categories of related parties. Paragraph 1AC.35 of Section 1A clarifies that such transactions include directors' remuneration and dividends paid to directors (see 11.1.8.A above).

An entity applying full FRS 102, FRS 101 or IFRS would need to comply with related party disclosures in those accounting standards. However, certain disclosure exemptions are available under the reduced disclosure framework in individual financial statements under FRS 101, *[FRS 101.7, 8(j), 8(k)]*, and FRS 102. *[FRS 102.1.8, 1.9, 1.12(e)].* See Chapter 2 at 6.1 and 6.1.10, Chapter 3 at 3.3.4 and 3.5. Intra-group transactions involving wholly owned subsidiaries of a group are exempt from disclosure in both FRS 102 individual and consolidated financial statements. *[FRS 102.1AC.35, 33.1A].* Use of this exemption – unlike the same exemption in FRS 101 – does not use the reduced disclosure framework and need not be disclosed. See Chapter 30 at 1.1.2. There are no disclosure exemptions under IAS 24 – *Related Party Disclosures*.

12.1.3   Disclosure exemptions for small companies – directors' report and strategic report

Where a company is subject to the small companies regime, it will also qualify for the small companies exemption. Therefore, the company is not required to prepare a strategic report and is entitled to disclosure exemptions set out in the CA 2006 in relation to the directors' report. See 12.2.1 and 12.2.2 below.

In addition, a company subject to the small companies regime would prepare a directors' report in accordance with Schedule 5 to the Small Companies Regulations. *[5 Sch (SC)]*. Schedule 5 requires disclosure in respect of political donations and expenditure and the employment of disabled persons. As discussed below, Schedule 5 excludes many of the directors' report disclosures required by Schedule 7 to the Regulations (which applies to companies not applying the small companies regime).

Where any of the above exemptions are taken, the required statement in the directors' report that the company has taken advantage of the small companies exemption in preparing the directors' report must be made. See 12 above.

Companies subject to the small companies regime are not required to give the following disclosures in the directors' report (that would be required where a company instead applies Schedule 7 to the Regulations):

- use of financial instruments – financial risk management objectives, policies and risk exposures;
- details of important post balance sheet events;
- an indication of likely future developments;
- an indication of research and development activities;
- an indication of branches outside the UK;
- information about employee involvement;
- engagement with employees;*
- engagement with suppliers, customers and others in a business relationship with the company;* and
- a statement of corporate governance arrangements.*

* These requirements (which are subject to certain exemptions, including size criteria) have been introduced into Schedule 7 to the Regulations for financial years beginning on or after 1 January 2019. There are no equivalent directors' report requirements in Schedule 5 to the Small Companies Regulations.[16]

The above list excludes those disclosures in Schedule 7 to the Regulations that are applicable to quoted companies, companies with securities admitted to trading on a regulated market or public companies acquiring their own shares. This is because such companies are likely to be public companies and therefore not to qualify for the small companies regime.

12.2   Criteria for use of the small companies exemption

A company is entitled to the small companies exemption in relation to the directors' report (see 12.2.1 below) and the strategic report (see 12.2.2 below) for a financial year if it is entitled to prepare financial statements for the year in accordance with the small companies regime (see 4.3 above) or would be so entitled but for being or having been a member of an ineligible group. *[s415A(1), s414B]*.

The company must, therefore, meet the same small size criteria as for the small companies regime (and if the company is a parent company, it must head a small group). The company must also not have been an ineligible company itself at any time during the financial year to which the accounts relate (but may still use the small companies exemption if it was a member of an ineligible group at any time during that financial year).

The small companies exemption is available both to companies preparing Companies Act accounts and companies preparing IAS accounts (i.e. prepared using EU-adopted IFRS).

12.2.1   Disclosure exemptions for the small companies exemption – directors' report

There are relatively few disclosure exemptions remaining for companies entitled to the small companies exemption contained in the CA 2006 itself.

Companies entitled to the small companies exemption are exempt from including the amount recommended by the directors to be paid by way of dividend (required by section 416(3)). *[s415A(2)].*

If a company is entitled to the small companies exemption, the directors' report must still include:

- the names of persons who were, at any time during the financial year, directors of the company; *[s416(1)(a)]* and
- the statement as to disclosure of relevant information to auditors (unless the company has taken advantage of an audit exemption). *[s418].*

Where the company is entitled to the small companies exemption (but not subject to the small companies regime), the company must comply with the more extensive content requirements for the directors' report in Schedule 7 to the Regulations. *[Regulations 10, 7 Sch].* Where the company is entitled to the small companies regime, it may comply with Schedule 5 to the Small Companies Regulations which has fewer disclosures for the directors' report, as explained at 12.1.3 above.

Where any of the above exemptions are taken, the required statement in the directors' report that the company has taken advantage of the small companies exemption in preparing the directors' report must be made. See 12 above.

12.2.2   Small companies exemption from preparing strategic report

A company entitled to the small companies exemption is not required to prepare a strategic report. *[s414A(2)].*

While there is no statutory requirement to do so, we would recommend that, where a company entitled to the small companies exemption takes advantage of the exemption not to prepare a strategic report, a statement is included in the directors' report, above the signature of the director or secretary to explain that it has done so.

12.3   Potential impact of Brexit on UK small companies regime

At the time of writing this chapter, the company law requirements have not been altered as a result of Brexit. However, the government has published draft legislative proposals – *The Accounts and Reports (Amendment) (EU Exit) Regulations 2018*. Based on the content of these draft proposals, the principal changes are as follows:

- The definition of an ineligible group in section 384 for the purposes of the small companies regime (see 4.3.3 and 4.4.2 above) will refer to a body corporate (other than a company) whose shares are admitted to trading on a UK regulated market (rather than, as now, a regulated market in an EEA State). In addition, a 'traded company' is to be redefined as a company any of whose transferable securities are admitted to trading on a UK regulated market. There are also changes to the definition of a MIFID investment firm.

- There are changes to the list of undertakings in section 399(2B) excluded from using the small group accounts exemption (see 6.2 above). These undertakings must be established under the law of any part of the UK (rather than, as now, an EEA State), and must have to prepare accounts in accordance with Part 15 of the CA 2006 (rather than, as now, the Accounting Directive). The list of undertakings now includes an undertaking whose transferable securities are admitted to trading on a UK regulated market, a credit institution (as defined in the draft legislation) or insurance undertaking (as defined in the draft legislation).

The draft legislation proposes that these changes come into effect for financial years beginning on or after exit day. The draft legislation is subject to Parliamentary approval and may be impacted by any transitional arrangements negotiated with the EU.

13   FILING REQUIREMENTS – SMALL COMPANIES AND SMALL LLPS

13.1   Small companies and small LLPs regimes

Companies subject to the small companies regime have two choices:

- to deliver a copy of the full accounts and reports sent to members and a copy of the auditor's report (unless the company has taken advantage of an audit exemption) to the Registrar; or
- to deliver a copy of the balance sheet but choose to omit a copy of the profit or loss account and / or the directors' report.

This exemption not to deliver a copy of the directors' report or profit and loss account is available to both IAS accounts and Companies Act accounts. *[s444(1), s444(3)].*

In addition, Companies Act group accounts delivered to the Registrar need not give the information required by paragraph 25 of Schedule 6 to the Small Companies Regulations, i.e. shares of the company held by subsidiary undertakings (see 11.4.4.B above). *[Regulations (SC) 11(b), 6 Sch 25 (SC)].*

The requirements for LLPs subject to the small LLPs regime are similar, although as there is no equivalent of the directors' report in LLP law, there are no related filing exemptions. LLPs subject to the small LLPs regime have two choices:

- to deliver a copy of the full accounts sent to members and a copy of the auditor's report (unless the LLP has taken advantage of an audit exemption) to the Registrar; or
- to deliver a copy of the balance sheet but choose to omit a copy of the profit or loss account.

This exemption not to deliver a copy of the profit and loss account is available to both IAS accounts and non-IAS accounts. *[s444(1) (LLP), s444(3) (LLP)].*

Chapter 5

Where the balance sheet or profit and loss account is abridged pursuant to paragraph 1A of Schedule 1 to the Small Companies Regulations (or paragraph 1A of Schedule 1 to the Small LLP Regulations), the directors of the company (or members of the LLP) must deliver to the Registrar a statement by the company (or the LLP) that all the members of the company (or all the members of the LLP) have consented to the abridgement. *[s444(2A), s444(2A) (LLP)]*. See 8.1.2, 9.2 and 10.2 above. While there is no specific requirement to do so, we consider it would also be helpful for annual accounts that include abridged formats to include a statement that all the members of the company (or of the LLP) have consented to the abridgement in the statements made below the balance sheet (and above the directors' signature).

References to the 'profit or loss account' above include its related notes. References in Part 15 to the profit and loss account include notes to the accounts giving information which is required by any provision of the CA 2006 or EU-adopted IFRS, and required or allowed by any such provision to be given in a note to the company's accounts. *[s472, s 472 (LLP)]*.

13.2   Statements required in accounts delivered to Registrar

Where the directors of a company deliver to the Registrar a copy of the company's profit or loss account under section 444(1)(b)(i) of the CA 2006, the directors of the company must also deliver a copy of the auditor's report on the accounts (and any directors' report) delivered, unless the company is exempt from audit and the directors have taken advantage of the audit exemption. *[s444(2)]*.

Similarly, where the designated members of an LLP deliver to the Registrar a copy of the LLP's profit or loss account under section 444(1)(b) of the CA 2006, the members of the LLP must also deliver a copy of the auditor's report on the accounts delivered, unless the LLP is exempt from audit and the members have taken advantage of the audit exemption. *[s444(2) (LLP)]*.

Where the directors of a company (or designated members of an LLP) do not deliver a copy of the company's (or LLP's) profit or loss account, the copy of the company's (or LLP's) balance sheet delivered to the Registrar must disclose that fact and the notes to the balance sheet must:

- state whether the auditor's report was qualified or unqualified;
- where that report was qualified, disclose the basis of the qualification (reproducing any statement under section 498(2)(a) or (b) or section 498(3), if applicable);
- where that report was unqualified, include a reference to any matters to which the auditor drew attention by way of emphasis; and
- state:
  - the name of the auditor and (where the auditor is a firm) the name of the person who signed the auditor's report as senior statutory auditor (where more than one person is appointed auditor, the reference to 'name of the auditor' refers to the 'names of all the auditors'); or
  - if the conditions in section 506 (circumstances in which names may be omitted) are met, that a resolution has been passed (LLPs instead state that a determination has been made) and notified to the Secretary of State in accordance with that section.

The above disclosures do not apply if the company (or LLP) is exempt from audit and the directors of the company (or members of the LLP) have taken advantage of the audit exemption, or if the company (or LLP) qualifies as a micro-entity and the accounts are prepared in accordance with any of the micro-entity provisions. *[s444(5A)-(5C), s444(5A)-(5C) (LLP)]*.

Where the directors of a company do not deliver a copy of the company's profit or loss account or a copy of the directors' report, the copy of the company's balance sheet delivered to the Registrar must contain in a prominent position that the company's annual accounts [and reports] have been delivered in accordance with the provisions applicable to the small companies regime. *[s444(5)]*. Similarly, where the designated members of an LLP do not deliver a copy of the company's profit or loss account, the copy of the LLP's balance sheet delivered to the Registrar must contain in a prominent position that the LLP's annual accounts have been delivered in accordance with the provisions applicable to the small LLPs regime. *[s444(5) (LLP)]*.

This statement should be included above the directors' signature and printed name of the director signing on behalf of the board (or for an LLP, the signature of the designated member of the LLP signing on behalf of the members). See Example 5.3 below for a company subject to the small companies regime, where a copy of the company's profit and loss account has not been delivered to the Registrar (and therefore, a copy of the auditor's report is not delivered to the Registrar). In this example, the auditor's report was unqualified and did not contain an emphasis of matter reference. While the statement is not required to state that there was no emphasis of matter reference, it may be helpful to do so. Had the auditor's report contained a qualification or emphasis of mater, disclosure of the basis of qualification and the emphasis of matter reference would be required (as explained above).

Example 5.3:   *Disclosures where a copy of the profit and loss account is not delivered to the Registrar by a company subject to the small companies regime*

Statement (below balance sheet but above directors' signature)
These accounts [and reports] have been delivered in accordance with the provisions applicable to companies subject to the small companies regime.
The directors have not delivered a copy of the company's profit and loss account to the Registrar, as permitted by section 444(1) and in accordance with section 444(5A) of the Companies Act 2006.
[…]

Note 1 to the balance sheet (extract)
[…]
The auditor's report on the accounts and reports for the financial year ended x/x/x, which was audited by [name of audit firm] and signed on behalf of the auditor by [name of senior statutory auditor] as Senior Statutory Auditor, was unqualified and did not contain any matters to which the auditor drew attention by way of emphasis.

This statement (and if applicable, the note to the balance sheet concerning the auditor's report) are required in the copy of the accounts and reports delivered to the Registrar (but not in the accounts and reports prepared for members).

This statement is *in addition* to any statements required in the accounts and reports prepared for members (and consequently also included in the copy of the accounts and reports delivered to the Registrar), where the accounts for members are prepared in

Chapter 5

accordance with the small companies regime (or small LLPs regime) (see 7.1.1, 11.2.5 and 12 above – example wording is at 9 above) or where the company has taken advantage of the small companies exemption in preparing the directors' report (see 12.2.1 above).

While there is no specific requirement to do so, we consider it would also be helpful for annual accounts that include abridged formats to include a statement that all the members of the company (or of the LLP) have consented to the abridgement in the statements made below the balance sheet (and above the directors' signature). See 13.1 above.

In all cases, the copies of the balance sheet and, for a company, any directors' report delivered to the Registrar must be signed by and state the name of the person who signed it on behalf of the board (or the members, in the case of an LLP). *[s444(6), s444A(3), s444(6) (LLP)]*.

13.3   Small companies exemption

A company entitled to the small companies exemption only (see 12.2 above) is not required to deliver a copy of the directors' report but must deliver a copy of the annual accounts and a copy of the auditor's report on the accounts (and any directors' report that it delivers), unless the company has taken advantage of an audit exemption. *[s444A(1)-(2)]*. While there is no statutory requirement to make a statement, it may be helpful to explain that the company is taking advantage of the small companies exemption in not delivering the directors' report.

The copies of the balance sheet and, for a company, any directors' report delivered to the Registrar must be signed by and state the name of the person who signed it on behalf of the board (or the members, in the case of an LLP). *[s444A(3)]*.

References

1 *Charities SORP (FRS 102): Accounting and Reporting by Charities: Statement of Recommended Practice applicable to charities preparing their accounts in accordance with the Financial Reporting Standard applicable in the UK and Republic of Ireland (FRS 102)*, Charity Commission and Office of the Scottish Charity Regulator, 2014.
2 *The Companies, Partnerships and Groups (Accounts and Reports) Regulations 2015* (SI 2015/980), para. 2(4).
3 *The Unregistered Companies Regulations 2009* (SI 2009/2436).
4 https://registers.esma.europa.eu/publication/searchRegister?core=esma_registers_upreg
5 *The Limited Liability Partnerships, Partnerships and Groups (Accounts and Audit) Regulations* 2016 (SI 2016/575), para. 63.

6 *Guidance on the Going Concern Basis of Accounting and Reporting on Solvency and Liquidity Risks – Guidance for directors of companies that do not apply The UK Corporate Governance Code*, FRC, April 2016, para. 3.5.
7 *The Statutory Auditors Regulations 2017* (SI 2017/1164), para. 2(5)(a), Schedule 3 para. 4.
8 *Partnerships (Accounts) Regulations 2008* (SI 2008/569), para. 4 and Schedule, para. 2(1)(a).
9 *Partnerships (Accounts) Regulations 2008* (SI 2008/569), para. 4 and Schedule, para. 2(1)(a).
10 Note 3 to the balance sheet formats in Section B of Part 1 of Schedule 1 to SI 2008/1913.
11 *The Statutory Auditors and Third Country Auditors Regulations 2016* (SI 2016/649), paras. 1(4)(a), 18(2)(a).

12 *Companies (Disclosure of Auditor Remuneration and Liability Limitation Agreements) Regulations 2008* (SI 2008/489), para. 8.

13 *The Statutory Auditors and Third Country Auditors Regulations 2016* (SI 2016/649), paras. 1(4)(a), 18(2)(a).

14 The Statutory Auditors Regulations 2017 (SI 2017/1164), para. 2(5)(a), Schedule 3 para. 4.

15 *The Statutory Auditors and Third Country Auditors Regulations 2016* (SI 2016/649), paras. 1(4)(a), 18(2)(a).

16 *The Companies (Miscellaneous Reporting) Regulations 2018* (SI 2018/860), paras. 1(4), 13-14.

Chapter 6

Presentation of financial statements

Chapter 6

Chapter 6

Chapter 6

Chapter 6

List of examples

Chapter 6

Chapter 6

Presentation of financial statements

1 INTRODUCTION

The following sections of FRS 102 – *The Financial Reporting Standard applicable in the UK and Republic of Ireland* – address the presentation, i.e. the form, content and structure, of financial statements:

- Section 3 – *Financial Statement Presentation*;
- Section 4 – *Statement of Financial Position*;
- Section 5 – *Statement of Comprehensive Income and Income Statement*;
- Section 6 – *Statement of Changes in Equity and Statement of Income and Retained Earnings*;
- Section 7 – *Statement of Cash Flows*; and
- Section 8 – *Notes to the Financial Statements*.

The above sections cover the content of a complete set of FRS 102 financial statements of an entity applying the full version of FRS 102, as issued in March 2018, including the primary statements and notes required, the concept of a true and fair view, and general principles underlying preparation of financial statements.

This chapter deals only with Sections 3 to 6 (see 3 to 7 below) and Section 8 (see 8 below). Section 7 is addressed in Chapter 7. FRS 102's requirements on presentation overlap with Section 1 – *Scope* (which covers the reduced disclosure framework – see Chapter 3), Section 2 – *Concepts and Pervasive Principles* (see Chapter 4) and Section 10 – *Accounting Policies, Estimates and Errors* (see Chapter 9). These sections are referred to in places in this chapter.

Small entities applying the small entities regime in FRS 102 apply the simpler presentation and disclosure requirements in Section 1A – *Small Entities*. These are based on the statutory requirements for companies subject to the small companies regime. See Chapter 5.

Chapter 6

Statutory accounts prepared in accordance with FRS 102 by UK companies are Companies Act accounts and must also comply with statutory requirements included in:

- the Companies Act 2006 ('CA 2006'); and

- *The Large and Medium-sized Companies and Groups (Accounts and Reports) Regulations 2008* (SI 2008/410), as amended ('the Regulations') or *The Small Companies and Groups (Accounts and Directors' Report) Regulations 2008* (SI 2008/409), as amended ('the Small Companies Regulations').

In particular, Companies Act accounts are required to give a true and fair view, and to comply with the applicable regulations governing the form and content of the balance sheet and profit and loss account and additional notes. *[s396, s404].*

Similarly, LLPs preparing statutory accounts and reports in accordance with FRS 102 prepare non-IAS accounts and must comply with the requirements of:

- *The Limited Liability Partnerships (Accounts and Audit) (Application of Companies Act 2006) Regulations 2008* (SI 2008/1911), as amended; and

- *The Small Limited Partnerships (Accounts) Regulations 2008* ('Small LLP Regulations') (SI 2008/1912) and *The Large and Medium-sized Limited Liability Partnerships (Accounts) Regulations 2008* ('the LLP Regulations') (SI 2008/1913), as amended.

Non-IAS accounts are required to give a true and fair view and comply with the applicable regulations governing the form and content of the balance sheet and profit and loss account and additional notes. *[s396 (LLP), s404 (LLP)].*

Chapter 1 at 6 provides information on the CA 2006 requirements for statutory accounts and reports for UK companies. The requirements for the accounts of LLPs are similar to those for UK companies. LLPs are not required to prepare statutory reports such as a strategic or directors' report.

FRS 102 mandates that UK companies and LLPs comply with the requirements for a balance sheet and profit and loss account in the applicable schedules to the Regulations or the LLP Regulations. *[FRS 102.4.2, 5.5].* Sections 4 and 5 extend this requirement to other entities except to the extent that this conflicts with the statutory frameworks that apply to their financial statements. *[FRS 102.4.1, 5.1].*

The Regulations, LLP Regulations and FRS 102 share basic principles underlying the preparation of financial statements such as going concern, prudence, accruals, materiality, aggregation, and consistency, although the Regulations and LLP Regulations restrict further when profits may be reported in the profit and loss account (see 9 below). The Regulations and LLP Regulations also set out certain requirements for recognition and measurement of assets and liabilities (see 10 below), namely the historical cost accounting rules, the alternative accounting rules and the fair value accounting rules.

1.1   Applicability to UK companies, LLPs, and other entities

Except where otherwise stated, the rest of this chapter covers the presentation requirements for UK companies and for LLPs and highlights the main changes to the presentation requirements made by *Amendments to FRS 102 – The Financial Reporting Standard Applicable in the UK and Republic of Ireland – Triennial review 2017: Incremental improvements and clarifications* (Triennial review 2017).

UK GAAP (prior to implementation of FRS 100 – *Application of Financial Reporting Requirements*, FRS 101 – *Reduced Disclosure Framework – Disclosure exemptions from EU-adopted IFRS for qualifying entities* – and FRS 102) is referred to as 'previous UK GAAP'.

While this chapter (see 4 below) addresses which profit and loss account and balance sheet formats are applied by a UK banking company (applying Schedule 2 to the Regulations – see definition at 4.2.2 below), a UK insurance company (applying Schedule 3 to the Regulations – see definition at 4.2.3 below) or, in group accounts, by the holding company of a banking or insurance group, it does not address the content of such formats in detail.

LLPs, qualifying partnerships (unless exempt under regulation 7 of *The Partnerships (Accounts) Regulations 2008*) and certain other entities preparing annual accounts in accordance with Part 15 of the CA 2006 (see 4.2.4 and 4.2.5 below) are subject to similar requirements to those for UK companies preparing Companies Act accounts, modified as necessary by the regulations that govern the content of their annual accounts. The formats for qualifying partnerships are based on those required for UK companies with the modifications discussed at 4.2.4. The formats applicable to LLPs are addressed throughout this chapter, but the main focus of the chapter is on UK companies. The *Statement of Recommended Practice – Accounting by Limited Liability Partnerships* (January 2017) ('LLP SORP') issued by Consultative Committee of Accounting Bodies (CCAB) provides additional guidance on the requirements of both FRS 102 and the LLP Regulations. The LLP SORP applies to accounting periods beginning on or after 1 January 2016. The LLP SORP is referred to, where relevant, but its requirements are not covered in detail in this publication.

The presentation requirements in Sections 4 and 5 apply to all entities, whether or not they report under the CA 2006. Entities that do not report under the CA 2006 shall comply with these requirements and with the Regulations (or, where applicable, the LLP Regulations), where referred to, except to the extent that these requirements are not permitted by any statutory framework under which such entities report. *[FRS 102.4.1, 5.1]*.

1.2 Irish companies

In 2017, the Republic of Ireland transposed the Accounting Directive into Irish law. The Companies (Accounting) Act 2017 amended the Companies Act 2014 to introduce the small companies regime and a micro-companies regime (similar to but not identical to the UK small companies regime and micro-entities regime) into Irish law. These changes were effective for financial years beginning on or after 1 January 2017 (but could be early applied for financial years beginning on or after 1 January 2015, provided the financial statements had not yet been approved). The Triennial review 2017 amended Section 1A to reflect these changes. See Chapter 5 at 4.5.

1.3 Other entities

Other entities that apply FRS 102 may include entities required by their governing legislation, or other regulation or requirement to prepare financial statements that present a true and fair view. Entities that are not UK companies need to satisfy themselves that FRS 102 does not conflict with any relevant legal obligations. *[FRS 102 Appendix III.41]*.

The FRC sets out summary information concerning the statutory frameworks for certain entities whose financial statements are required to present a true and fair view, including: building societies; UK, Scottish and Northern Ireland charities (accruals accounts), friendly societies; industrial and provident societies; occupational pension schemes. The FRC also comment on how application of FRS 102 relates to the required statutory framework. *[FRS 102 Appendix III.42]*. However, in some cases, these statutory frameworks, particularly for charities, may have changed so entities should make sure that the current legal requirements are referred to.

2　SUMMARY OF FRS 102'S PRESENTATION REQUIREMENTS

The statutory accounts of a UK company prepared in accordance with FRS 102 are Companies Act accounts. The statutory accounts of an LLP prepared in accordance with FRS 102 are non-IAS accounts. The requirements applying to LLP annual accounts are very similar to the requirements for company annual accounts. Certain other entities, including qualifying partnerships (unless exempt under regulation 7 of *The Partnerships (Accounts) Regulations 2008*) are also required to prepare statutory accounts in accordance with Part 15 of the CA 2006 (see 4.2.4 and 4.2.5 below).

The discussion below relates to the presentation requirements of full FRS 102. Section 1A can be applied by an entity subject to the small entities regime. Section 1A has simpler presentation and disclosures and is discussed further in Chapter 5. However, small entities are not required to apply Section 1A and could instead apply full FRS 102 or provide additional disclosures or present additional primary statements to those required by Section 1A.

In December 2017, FRS 102 was updated as part of the Triennial review 2017. Changes impacting presentation are discussed in the relevant sections below. These changes are effective for accounting periods beginning on or after 1 January 2019. Early application is permitted subject to all amendments being early adopted (with some exceptions to this) and disclosure of early adoption being made. See Chapter 3 at 1.3.

A complete set of FRS 102 financial statements contains: a statement of financial position, a statement of comprehensive income (either as a single statement or as a separate income statement and statement of comprehensive income), a statement of cash flows (unless exempt, see 3.5 below), a statement of changes in equity, and accompanying notes to the financial statements (together with comparatives). In certain circumstances, a statement of income and retained earnings can be presented instead of the statement of comprehensive income and statement of changes in equity. Other titles for the primary statements – such as a balance sheet or profit and loss account – can be used as long as they are not misleading.

FRS 102 specifies the content of the primary financial statements and notes. The profit and loss account section of the statement of comprehensive income and the statement of financial position must follow the profit and loss account and balance sheet formats respectively set out in the Regulations or LLP Regulations, as applicable. The Regulations and LLP Regulations allow UK companies (other than banking and insurance companies) and LLPs to make use of adapted formats as an alternative to the statutory formats. Where adapted formats are used, Sections 4 and 5 set out the line items required on the face of the statement of financial position (which must also present separate classifications for current assets, non-current assets, current liabilities, and non-current liabilities) and statement of comprehensive income. The adapted formats in FRS 102 are close to, but not exactly the same as, IAS 1 – *Presentation of Financial Statements* – formats. FRS 102 also requires supplementary analyses of certain line items to be presented in the statement of financial position or in the notes. An entity that does not report under the CA 2006 must also follow the same formats so long as these do not conflict with the statutory framework under which it reports. FRS 102 includes supplementary requirements on presentation of discontinued operations, which apply both to statutory and adapted formats. The requirements for the other primary financial statements are based on (but are simpler than) the requirements in IAS 1. See 4 to 8 below.

Financial statements must give a true and fair view of the financial position, financial performance and cash flows (when required to be presented) of the entity. This usually requires compliance with FRS 102, with additional disclosure where needed. However, FRS 102 provides for a 'true and fair override', consistent with the 'true and fair override' provided for in the CA 2006. See 9.2 below.

Like IAS 1 and the Regulations, FRS 102 sets out basic principles underlying the preparation of financial statements such as going concern, accruals, materiality and aggregation, consistency and offset. See 9 below.

A statement of compliance with FRS 102 (and, where applicable, with FRS 103 – *Insurance Contracts*) is required. FRS 102 contains certain requirements (marked 'PBE') to be applied only by public benefit entities. An entity that is a public benefit entity that applies these paragraphs must make an explicit and unreserved statement that it is a public benefit entity. See 3.8 below.

The notes to the financial statements should include: the basis of preparation; accounting policies (including judgements made and key sources of estimation uncertainty); disclosures required by FRS 102 not presented elsewhere in the financial statements; and information relevant to understanding the financial statements not presented elsewhere in the financial statements. Entities applying FRS 102 may also be subject to other disclosure requirements deriving from statutory or other regulatory frameworks, e.g. a UK company's statutory accounts must be prepared in accordance with Part 15 of the CA 2006 and the Regulations. See 9 below.

FRS 102 provides for a reduced disclosure framework in the individual financial statements of qualifying entities, i.e. members of a group included in publicly available consolidated financial statements intended to give a true and fair view. In particular, a qualifying entity need not present an individual cash flow statement. See Chapter 3 at 3.

IFRS 8 – *Operating Segments* – is scoped in for publicly traded companies. If an entity discloses disaggregated information not complying with IFRS 8, this shall not be described as segment information. *[FRS 102.1.5]*. See 3.3.2 below.

A comparison of the presentational requirements in FRS 102 and IFRS is presented at 11 below.

3   COMPOSITION OF FINANCIAL STATEMENTS

Financial statements are a structured representation of the financial position, financial performance and cash flows of an entity. *[FRS 102 Appendix I]*. Section 2 (see Chapter 4) explains the objective of financial statements and the concepts and pervasive principles underlying financial statements.

Section 3 explains the requirement that financial statements give a 'true and fair view', what compliance with the standard requires and what a complete set of financial statements contains. *[FRS 102.3.1]*. Sections 4 to 8 set out the requirements in relation to the different components of financial statements. Each component of a complete set of financial statements is discussed in more detail at 5 to 8 below, with the exception of the Statement of Cash Flows (which is discussed in Chapter 7).

UK companies preparing Companies Act accounts must also comply with the CA 2006 and the Regulations or the Small Companies Regulations (and other applicable regulations), which set out further recognition, measurement and disclosure requirements. Similarly, LLPs preparing non-IAS accounts must also comply with SI 2008/1911 (which applies the accounts and audit provisions of CA 2006 to LLPs), the LLP Regulations or the Small LLP Regulations (and other applicable regulations), which set out further recognition, measurement and disclosure requirements.

The statutory requirements in the Regulations and LLP Regulations are addressed, where appropriate, in the relevant sections below.

The general principles in the Regulations, LLP Regulations and FRS 102 (which are similar) are discussed at 9 below. See 10 below for a discussion of the three accounting models in the Regulations and LLP Regulations for the recognition and measurement of assets and liabilities:

*   historical cost accounting rules;

*   alternative accounting rules (which provide an alternative measurement basis to the historical cost rules, usually at a valuation); and

*   fair value accounting rules (which may be applied to living animals and plants, financial instruments, investment properties, and certain categories of stocks).

FRS 102's requirements are generally consistent with but are often more restrictive than those in the Regulations and LLP Regulations. Certain areas where FRS 102's requirements are in conflict with the Regulations (and consequently, also with the LLP Regulations) are highlighted in Appendix III to FRS 102. The Small Companies Regulations and Small LLP Regulations, where applied, have the same general principles and accounting models (albeit with fewer related disclosures). See Chapter 5 at 7.2.

3.1   Key definitions

The following definitions, included in the Glossary to FRS 102, are relevant to presentation: *[FRS 102 Appendix I]*

Term	Definition
Current assets*	Assets of the entity which: (a) for an entity choosing to apply paragraph 1A(1) of Schedule 1 to the Regulations are not non-current assets*; (b) for all other entities, are not fixed assets.
Current liabilities for the purposes of an entity applying paragraph 1A(1) of Schedule 1 to the Regulations*	Liabilities of the entity which: (a) it expects to settle in its normal operating cycle; (b) it holds primarily for the purpose of trading; (c) are due to be settled within 12 months after the reporting period; or (d) it does not have an unconditional right to defer settlement for at least 12 months after the reporting period.
Equity	The residual interest in the assets of the entity after deducting all its liabilities.
Expenses	Decreases in economic benefits during the reporting period in the form of outflows or depletions of assets or incurrences of liabilities that result in decreases in equity, other than those relating to distributions to equity investors.
Fair value	The amount for which an asset could be exchanged, a liability settled, or an equity instrument granted could be exchanged, between knowledgeable, willing parties in an arm's length transaction. In the absence of any specific guidance provided in the relevant section of the FRS, the guidance in Appendix 2 to Section 2 shall be used in determining fair value.
Performance	The relationship of the income and expenses of an entity, as reported in the statement of comprehensive income.
Financial position	The relationship of the assets, liabilities, and equity of an entity as reported in the statement of financial position.
Financial statements	Structured representation of the financial position, financial performance and cash flows of an entity. [General purpose financial statements (generally referred to simply as financial statements) are financial statements directed to the general financial information needs of a wide range of users who are not in a position to demand reports tailored to meet their particular information needs.]
Fixed assets	Assets of an entity which are intended for use on a continuing basis in the entity's activities.
Income	Increases in economic benefits during the reporting period in the form of inflows or enhancements of assets or decreases of liabilities that result in increases in equity, other than those relating to contributions from equity investors.

Chapter 6

Term	Definition
Income statement	Financial statement that presents all items of income and expense recognised in a reporting period, excluding the items of other comprehensive income (referred to as the profit and loss account in the Act).
LLP Regulations	The Large and Medium-sized Limited Liability Partnerships (Accounts) Regulations 2008 (SI 2008/1913).
Material	Omissions or misstatements of items are material if they could, individually or collectively, influence the economic decisions of users taken on the basis of the financial statements. Materiality depends on the size and nature of the omission or misstatement judged in the surrounding circumstances. The size or nature of the item, or a combination of both, could be the determining factor.
Non-current assets*	Assets of the entity which: (a) it does not expect to realise, or intend to sell or consume, in its normal operating cycle; (b) it does not hold primarily for the purpose of trading; (c) it does not expect to realise within 12 months after the reporting period; or (d) are cash or cash equivalents restricted from being exchanged or used to settle a liability for at least 12 months after the reporting period.
Non-current liabilities*	Liabilities of the entity which are not current liabilities.
Other comprehensive income	Items of income and expense (including reclassification adjustments) that are not recognised in profit or loss as required or permitted by this FRS or by law.
Profit or loss (or income and expenditure)	The total of income less expenses, excluding the components of other comprehensive income. NB In the not for profit sector, this may be known as income and expenditure (and the profit and loss account, as an income and expenditure account). *[s474(2)]*.
Reporting period	The period covered by financial statements or by an interim financial report.
Regulations	The Large and Medium-sized Companies and Groups (Accounts and Reports) Regulations 2008 (SI 2008/410).
Small Companies Regulations	The Small Companies and Groups (Accounts and Directors' Report) Regulations 2008 (SI 2008/409).
Small entity	A small entity is: (a) a company meeting the definition of a small company as set out in section 382 or 383 of the CA 2006 and not excluded from the small companies regime by section 384; (b) an LLP qualifying as small and not excluded from the small LLPs regime, as set out in LLP Regulations; or (c) any other entity that would have met the criteria in (a) had it been a company incorporated under company law.

Small LLP Regulations	*The Small Limited Liability Partnerships (Accounts) Regulations 2008 (SI 2008/1912).*
Statement of Recommended Practice (SORP)	An extant Statement of Recommended Practice developed in accordance with Policy on Developing Statements of Recommended Practice (SORPs). SORPs recommend accounting practices for specialised industries or sectors. They supplement accounting standards and other legal and regulatory requirements in the light of the special factors prevailing or transactions undertaken in a particular industry or sector.
Statement of comprehensive income	A financial statement that presents all items of income and expense recognised in a period, including those items recognised in determining profit or loss (which is a subtotal in the statement of comprehensive income) and items of other comprehensive income. If an entity chooses to present both an income statement and a statement of comprehensive income, the statement of comprehensive income begins with profit or loss and then displays the items of other comprehensive income.
Total comprehensive income	The change in equity during a period resulting from transactions and other events, other than those changes resulting from transactions from equity participants (equal to the sum of profit or loss and other comprehensive income).
Turnover	The amounts derived from the provision of goods and services, after deduction of: (a) trade discounts; (b) value added tax; and (c) any other taxes based on the amounts so derived.

*   The definitions of non-current assets and non-current liabilities are relevant where an entity applies paragraph 1A(1) of Schedule 1 to the Regulations or paragraph 1A(1) of Schedule 1 to the LLP Regulations (i.e. uses adapted formats).

This chapter also makes many references to certain concepts in the Regulations and LLP Regulations. Unless otherwise indicated, these references should be interpreted as follows:

- 'General Rules to the formats' means the General Rules included in Section A of Part 1 of Schedule 1 to the Regulations and Section A of Part 1 of Schedule 1 to the LLP Regulations;
- 'Statutory formats' means the formats in Section B of Part 1 of Schedule 1 to the Regulations and Section B of Part 1 of Schedule 1 to the LLP Regulations; and
- 'Adapted formats' means the formats permitted by paragraph 1A of Schedule 1 to the Regulations and paragraph 1A of Schedule 1 to the LLP Regulations (as an alternative to the 'statutory formats').

3.2   Objectives of sections in FRS 102 addressing presentation of financial statements

The objective of financial statements is to provide information about the financial position, performance and, when required to be presented, cash flows of an entity that is useful for economic decision-making by a broad range of users who are not in a position to demand reports tailored to meet their particular information needs.

Chapter 6

Financial statements also show the results of the stewardship of management – the accountability of management for the resources entrusted to it. *[FRS 102.2.2-3]*.

Sections 3 to 8, which address presentation of financial statements, include the following objectives:

- to set out the requirement that the financial statements of an entity shall give a true and fair view, what compliance with FRS 102 requires and what is a complete set of financial statements; *[FRS 102.3.1]*

- to set out the information that shall be presented in a statement of financial position (referred to as the 'balance sheet' under the CA 2006) and how to present it; *[FRS 102.4.1]*

- to require an entity to present total comprehensive income for a period, being its financial performance for the period – in one or two statements – and to set out the information that shall be presented in those statements and how to present it; *[FRS 102.5.1]*

- to set out requirements for presenting the changes in an entity's equity for a period either in a statement of changes in equity, or if specified conditions are met and an entity chooses, in a statement of income and retained earnings; *[FRS 102.6.1]*

- to set out the information required in a statement of cash flows and how to present it. See Chapter 7 for further details; *[FRS 102.7.1]* and

- to set out the principles underlying information to be presented in the notes to the financial statements and how to present it. In addition, nearly every section of FRS 102 requires disclosures that are normally presented in the notes. *[FRS 102.8.1]*.

3.3   Interim financial reports and segmental reporting

3.3.1   *Interim financial reporting*

FRS 102 does not address the presentation of interim financial reports. Entities preparing such reports must describe the basis for preparing and presenting such information. FRS 104 – *Interim Financial Reporting* – sets out a basis for the preparation and presentation of interim financial reports that an entity may apply. *[FRS 102.3.25]*. See Chapter 34 for discussion of the requirements of FRS 104.

3.3.2   *Segmental reporting*

IFRS 8 applies to an entity whose debt or equity instruments are publicly traded, or that files, or is in the process of filing, its financial statements with a securities commission or other regulatory organisation for the purpose of issuing any class of instruments in a public market, or an entity that chooses to provide information described as segment information.

If an entity discloses disaggregated information, but that information does not comply with IFRS 8's requirements, the information shall not be described as segment information. *[FRS 102.1.5]*.

The determination of whether a group falls into the scope of IFRS 8 relates solely to the parent entity, rather than to subsidiaries within the group. *[IFRS 8.BC23]*. Therefore, IFRS 8 does not apply to a group headed by a parent that has no listed financial instruments, even if the group contains a subsidiary that has any of its equity or debt instruments traded in a public market. Of course, a subsidiary with publicly traded debt or equity instruments preparing FRS 102 financial statements would be required to provide segment information in accordance with IFRS 8 in its financial statements.

IFRS 8 describes a 'public market' as including a domestic or foreign stock exchange or an over-the-counter market, including local and regional markets, *[IFRS 8.2]*, but does not define what would make some markets 'public' and others not. In our view, a market is 'public' when buyers and sellers (market participants) can transact with one another (directly; through agents; or in a secondary market) at a price determined in that market. A public market does not exist when the buyers and sellers can transact only with the entity itself (or an agent acting on its behalf). The requirement for an entity to list its securities on a stock exchange is not the sole factor in determining whether the entity is in scope of IFRS 8. Its securities must be traded in a public market meeting the criteria above.

See Chapter 32 of EY International GAAP 2019 for a discussion of the scope of IFRS 8 and its requirements for segmental reporting.

3.3.2.A   Segmental disclosures of turnover

A UK company preparing Companies Act accounts (or an LLP preparing non-IAS accounts) must give the following disclosures in the notes to the accounts:

- where the company (or LLP) has carried on business of two or more classes during the financial year that, in the opinion of the directors (or of the members of the LLP), differ substantially from each other, the amount of the turnover attributable to each class of business together with the description of the class; and

- where the company (or LLP) has supplied geographical markets during the financial year that, in the opinion of the directors (or of the members of the LLP), differ substantially from each other, the amount of the turnover attributable to each such market.

The directors (or the members of the LLP) should have regard to the manner in which the company's (or LLP's) activities are organised in making the above analysis. Classes of business (or markets) which, in the opinion of the directors (or of the members of the LLP), do not differ substantially from each other must be treated as one class (or market). Amounts attributable to a class of business (or market) that are not material may be included in the amount stated in respect of another class of business (or market).

Where disclosure of any of the information required would, in the opinion of the directors (or of the members of the LLP), be seriously prejudicial to the interests of the company (or the LLP), that information need not be disclosed, but the fact that any such information has not been disclosed must be stated. *[1 Sch 68, 1 Sch 65 (LLP)]*.

For group accounts, the disclosures are given for the company (or LLP) and undertakings included in the consolidation (i.e. consolidated undertakings). *[6 Sch 1(1), 3 Sch 1 (LLP)]*.

The above requirements do not apply for a company subject to the small companies regime or an LLP subject to the small LLPs regime.

3.4   Frequency of reporting and period covered

An entity must present a complete set of financial statements (including comparative information) at least annually.

When the end of an entity's reporting period changes and annual financial statements are presented for a period longer or shorter than one year, the entity shall disclose that fact, the reason for using a longer or shorter period, and the fact that comparative amounts presented in the financial statements (including the related notes) are not entirely comparable. *[FRS 102.3.10]*.

Normally, financial statements are consistently prepared covering a one year period, which, for a UK company or LLP, will generally end with the last day of the accounting reference period (based on the accounting reference date notified to the Registrar).

Some entities, particularly in the retail sector, present financial statements for a 52-week period. This practice is permitted by the CA 2006 – companies (and LLPs) may prepare financial statements to a financial year end, not more than 7 days before or after the end of the accounting reference period, as the directors (or members of the LLP) may determine. *[s390(2)(b), s391, s390(2)(b) (LLP), s391 (LLP)]*. While FRS 102 does not explicitly address this issue, we consider that financial statements prepared in accordance with FRS 102 can be made up to a financial year end, not more than 7 days from the end of the accounting reference period.

3.5   Components of a complete set of financial statements

A complete set of financial statements under FRS 102 (for an entity not applying Section 1A) includes all of the following, each of which should be presented with equal prominence: *[FRS 102.3.17, 3.21]*

- a statement of financial position as at the reporting date (see 4 and 5 below);
- a statement of comprehensive income for the reporting period (see 4 and 6 below) to be presented either as:
  - a single statement of comprehensive income, displaying all items of income and expense recognised during the period including those items recognised in determining profit or loss (which is a subtotal in the statement of comprehensive income) and items of other comprehensive income; or
  - a separate income statement and a separate statement of comprehensive income. In this case, the statement of comprehensive income begins with profit or loss and then displays the items of other comprehensive income;
- a statement of changes in equity for the reporting period (see 7 below);
- a statement of cash flows (unless exempt) for the reporting period (see Chapter 7); and
- notes, comprising significant accounting policies and other explanatory information (see 8 below).

In addition to information about the reporting period, FRS 102 also requires comparative information in respect of the preceding period for all amounts presented in the current period's financial statements. Therefore, a complete set of financial statements includes, at a minimum, two of each of the required financial statements and related notes. *[FRS 102.3.14, 3.20]*. Comparative information, including the statutory requirements of the Regulations and LLP Regulations, is discussed at 3.6 below.

Chapter 7 at 3.1 sets out exemptions from preparing a cash flow statement. Qualifying entities (see Chapter 3 at 3.1 and 3.3.2) using the reduced disclosure framework in individual financial statements are also exempt. FRS 102 further exempts a small entity (as defined in Chapter 5 at 4) from preparing a cash flow statement. This cash flow exemption is available both to small entities applying Section 1A and to small entities applying the full version of FRS 102, unless it is required to prepare one by an applicable SORP or law or other relevant regulation. *[FRS 102.3.1B]*.

Sections 4 and 5 require that the balance sheet and profit and loss account formats in Part 1 of the applicable schedule of the Regulations or LLP Regulations are followed in presenting the statement of financial position and the 'profit and loss' section of the statement of comprehensive income. These formats include both the statutory formats and the adapted formats available as an alternative to statutory formats under Schedule 1 to the Regulations and Schedule 1 to the LLP Regulations. *[FRS 102.4.2, FRS 102.5.5, 7]*. See 4 below for further discussion of the formats.

Other titles for the financial statements can be used, as long as they are not misleading. *[FRS 102.3.22]*. For instance, an entity may wish to refer to a balance sheet (for the statement of financial position) or the profit and loss account (instead of an income statement, where total comprehensive income is presented in two statements).

If an entity has no items of other comprehensive income in any of the periods presented, it may present only an income statement (or a statement of comprehensive income in which the 'bottom line' is labelled profit or loss). *[FRS 102.3.19]*.

If the only changes to equity during the periods presented in the financial statements arise from profit or loss, payments of dividends, corrections of prior period errors and changes in accounting policy, the entity may present a single statement of income and retained earnings in place of the statement of comprehensive income and statement of changes in equity. *[FRS 102.3.18]*.

FRS 102 explains that notes contain information in addition to that presented in the primary statements above, and provide narrative descriptions or disaggregations of items presented in those statements and information about items that do not qualify for recognition in those statements. *[FRS 102.8.1]*.

3.6 Comparative information

Except when FRS 102 permits or requires otherwise, an entity presents comparative information in respect of the preceding period for all amounts presented in the current period's financial statements. *[FRS 102.3.14]*. This means that the requirement to present comparative information applies both to mandatory and voluntary information presented for the current period.

The Regulations and LLP Regulations also require only one comparative period to be presented for the balance sheet and profit and loss account formats. *[1 Sch 7, 1 Sch 7 (LLP)]*. The Regulations and LLP Regulations do not specifically require comparative note disclosures but, as noted above, these are required by FRS 102 (unless specifically exempted). Other statutory or regulatory frameworks may require further periods to be presented.

Chapter 6

In certain cases, FRS 102 provides specific exemptions from presenting comparatives. For example, there is no requirement to present comparatives for the reconciliations of movements in the number of shares outstanding, or of the movements in the carrying amounts of investment property, property, plant and equipment, intangible assets, goodwill, negative goodwill, provisions or biological assets. *[FRS 102.4.12(a)(iv), 16.10(e), 17.31(e), 18.27(e), 19.26-19.26A, 21.14, 34.7(c), 34.10(e)].* These exemptions are addressed in the relevant chapters of this publication. The Triennial review 2017 clarified that an entity providing reconciliations of items of fixed assets in accordance with paragraph 51 of Schedule 1 to the Regulations, need not present these reconciliations for prior periods. *[FRS 102.3.14A].*

The General Rules to the formats (see 4.4 below) require that for each item presented in the balance sheet and profit and loss account, the corresponding amount for the immediately preceding financial year (i.e. the comparative) must also be shown. *[1 Sch 7(1), 1 Sch 7(1) (LLP)].*

The heading or sub-heading required for a particular item in the balance sheet or profit and loss account format must be presented where there is an amount for that item in either the current or immediately preceding financial year; otherwise, the heading or sub-heading must be omitted. *[1 Sch 5 (SC), 1 Sch 5 (LLP SC)].*

3.6.1   Comparative information for narrative and descriptive information

An entity shall include comparative information for narrative and descriptive information when it is relevant to an understanding of the current period's financial statements. *[FRS 102.3.14].*

3.6.2   Consistency of, and reclassifications of comparative information

The objective of comparative information is comparability of an entity's financial statements through time to identify trends in its financial position and performance, and to enable users to compare the financial statements of different entities to evaluate their relative financial position, performance and cash flows. *[FRS 102.2.11].*

Consequently, an entity must retain the presentation and classification of items in the financial statements from one period to the next unless: *[FRS 102.3.11]*

- it is apparent, following a significant change in the nature of the entity's operations or a review of its financial statements, that another presentation or classification would be more appropriate having regard to the criteria for selection and application of accounting policies in Section 10 (see Chapter 9); or

- FRS 102 (or another applicable FRS) requires a change in presentation.

When entities change the presentation or classification of items in the financial statements, the comparatives must be reclassified, unless this is impracticable (in which case the reason should be disclosed). When comparative amounts are reclassified, the nature of the reclassification, the amount of each item (or class of items) reclassified and the reasons for the reclassification must be disclosed. Applying a requirement is impracticable when the entity cannot apply it after making every reasonable effort to do so. *[FRS 102.3.12-13, FRS 102 Appendix I].*

This situation should be distinguished from a reclassification due to a change in use of an asset. An example would be a reclassification out of investment property because it ceases to meet the definition of investment property in the current period. This would be treated as a transfer arising in the current period and not lead to a reclassification of comparatives. *[FRS 102.16.9]*.

In addition, the initial application of a policy to revalue property, plant and equipment (or intangible assets, where the strict criteria are met) is treated as a revaluation in accordance with Section 17 – *Property, Plant and Equipment* – and Section 18 – *Intangible Assets other than Goodwill* – respectively. *[FRS 102.10.10A]*. This means that it is reflected as an adjustment in the period of application of the revaluation policy rather than retrospectively.

Restatements of comparatives may also arise from:

- changes in accounting policy (see Chapter 9 at 3.4);
- correction of prior period errors (see Chapter 9 at 3.6);
- presentation of discontinued operations (see 6.8 below); and
- hindsight adjustments in respect of provisional fair values of identifiable assets, liabilities and contingent liabilities arising on business combinations (see Chapter 17 at 3.7.4).

FRS 102 (unlike IAS 1) does not require presentation of a third balance sheet at the beginning of the preceding period when there is a retrospective restatement due to an accounting policy change, reclassification or correction of a material error. *[IAS 1.10(f), 40A-D]*. See Chapter 9 at 2.2.

Where the comparative shown in the balance sheet and profit and loss account formats is not comparable with the amount shown in the current period, the General Rules to the formats (see 4.4 below) permit the comparative to be adjusted. Particulars of the non-comparability and of any adjustment must be disclosed in a note to the accounts. *[1 Sch 7(2), 1 Sch 7(2) (LLP)]*. This statutory requirement would permit FRS 102's requirements on restatement of comparatives to be followed. Where amounts are not restated, e.g. due to transitional provisions in accounting policies or where it is impracticable to determine the effects of a change in accounting policies on earlier periods, *[FRS 102.10.11-12]*, a note to the financial statements will need to disclose the non-comparability.

3.7   Identification of the financial statements

It is commonly the case that financial statements will form only part of a larger annual report, regulatory filing or other document, but FRS 102 only applies to the financial statements (including the notes). Chapter 1 at 6 addresses the content of the statutory annual report and accounts for a UK company (and Chapter 5 addresses this for a UK company applying the small companies regime). An LLP is not required to prepare a members' report, but the LLP SORP requires certain information to be disclosed which may be included in a separate members' report. *[LLP SORP.30-31]*. A traded LLP or a banking LLP is also required to prepare a strategic report. *[s414A(1), s414A(1) (LLP)]*. This requirement post-dates the publication of the LLP SORP.[1]

Accordingly, FRS 102 requires that an entity clearly identifies the financial statements and the notes, and distinguishes them from other information in the same document.

In addition, the entity must display the following information prominently, and repeat it when necessary, for an understanding of the information presented: *[FRS 102.3.23]*

- the name of the reporting entity and any change in its name from the end of the preceding reporting period;
- whether the financial statements cover the individual entity or a group of entities;
- the date of the end of the reporting period and the period covered by the financial statements;
- the presentation currency, as defined in Section 30 – *Foreign Currency Translation* (discussed in Chapter 27 at 3.1 and 3.7); and
- the level of rounding, if any, used in presenting amounts in the financial statements.

In practice, these requirements can be met through the use of appropriate headings for pages, statements, notes and columns etc., for example: the inclusion of a basis of preparation note within the accounting policies; the use of appropriate titles for the primary financial statements, distinguishing group and company; and the use of appropriate headings in the columns in the primary financial statements (and notes to the financial statements). Entities will need to consider how best to present the required information where financial statements are made available electronically.

Financial statements are usually presented to an appropriate level of rounding, such as thousands or millions of currency units. An appropriate level of rounding can avoid obscuring useful information (and hence 'cut clutter' – see 9.4.1 below) but entities need to ensure that material information is not omitted. The level of rounding used must be clearly disclosed in the primary statements and notes to the financial statements. Entities are not precluded from using lower levels of rounding in certain notes to the financial statements. For example, where the financial statements are presented in millions of units of the presentation currency, it may be appropriate to include information on directors' remuneration at a lower level of rounding. In all cases, it is important that the units used are clearly stated.

FRS 102 requires disclosures in the notes to the financial statements concerning the legal form of the entity, its country of incorporation and the address of its registered office (or principal place of business, if different from the registered office). *[FRS 102.3.24(a)]*. See 8.5 below.

The statutory accounts of a UK company or LLP must also include certain disclosures concerning its legal form and registration. *[s396(A1), s404(A1), s396(A1) (LLP), s404(A1) (LLP)]*. See 8.5 below.

3.8   Statement of compliance

A set of financial statements prepared in accordance with FRS 102 must contain an explicit and unreserved statement of compliance with FRS 102 in the notes to the financial statements. Financial statements must not be described as complying with FRS 102 unless they comply with *all* the requirements of the standard. *[FRS 102.3.3, FRS 100.9]*. This is similar to the requirement in IAS 1 for an entity preparing its financial statements to give an explicit and unreserved statement of compliance with IFRSs. *[IAS 1.16]*.

FRS 102 additionally requires a public benefit entity (see Chapter 31 at 6 for the definition of a public benefit entity) that applies the 'PBE' prefixed paragraphs to make an explicit and unreserved statement that it is a public benefit entity. *[FRS 102.PBE3.3A].* This is because FRS 102 has specific requirements reserved for public benefit entities (prefixed with 'PBE'), which must not be applied directly, or by analogy by entities that are not public benefit entities (other than, where specifically directed, entities within a public benefit entity group). *[FRS 102.1.2].* See Chapter 3 at 2.5.2.

FRS 103 requires that an entity whose financial statements comply with FRS 103 shall, in addition to the statement of compliance made in accordance with FRS 102, make an explicit and unreserved statement of compliance with FRS 103 in the notes to the financial statements. *[FRS 103.1.12].*

An example (for an entity not applying Section 1A) is presented at Example 6.1 below. See Chapter 5 at 11.2.5 and 11.3 for an example where an entity applies Section 1A.

Example 6.1: Statement of Compliance – illustrative wording

These financial statements were prepared in accordance with Financial Reporting Standard 102 'The Financial Reporting Standard applicable in the UK and Republic of Ireland' [and Financial Reporting Standard 103 'Insurance Contracts']*. [The [company / entity] is a public benefit entity as defined in Financial Reporting Standard 102 'The Financial Reporting Standard applicable in the UK and Republic of Ireland']*.

*delete as applicable.

In special circumstances when management concludes that compliance with any requirement of FRS 102 or applicable legislation (only where it allows for a true and fair override) is inconsistent with the requirement to give a true and fair view, the entity shall depart from that requirement to the extent necessary to give a true and fair view, giving the required disclosures set out in paragraph 3.5 of FRS 102. *[FRS 102.3.4-5].* See 9.2 below for further discussion of the 'true and fair override' under FRS 102 (and where applicable, the CA 2006) together with the implications for the statement of compliance.

3.8.1 Statement that financial statements have been prepared in accordance with applicable accounting standards

The Regulations (and LLP Regulations) require a large UK company preparing Companies Act accounts (or a large LLP preparing non-IAS accounts) to state in the notes to the accounts whether the accounts have been prepared in accordance with applicable accounting standards, giving particulars of any material departure from those standards and the reasons for it (see Chapter 1 at 4.6.1). *[1 Sch 45, 1 Sch 45 (LLP)].*

This statement is also required in the group accounts of a medium-sized company or LLP (see Chapter 1 at 6.6.2.A) but not in its individual accounts. *[Regulations 4(2A), 1 Sch 45, LLP Regulations 4(2A), 1 Sch 45 (LLP)].*

Where a 'true and fair override' in accordance with paragraph 3.5 of the standard (see 9.2 below) is applied in the financial statements, the above statement will need to include or refer to the disclosures of the override.

Financial statements prepared in accordance with FRS 102 are prepared in accordance with applicable accounting standards (which are defined in section 464 of CA 2006). *[s464, s464 (LLP)].*

Chapter 6

3.8.2   Statements of Recommended Practice (SORPs)

FRS 100 requires certain disclosures where a SORP applies to an entity, including in respect of departures from the accounting treatment or disclosure requirements of a SORP. *[FRS 100.6-8]*. See Chapter 1 at 4.7 for the disclosures required and a list of the extant SORPs.

In addition, Chapter 3 at 1.3.4 and 2.3 includes guidance on application of SORPs and lists recent updates to the SORPs.

4   COMPANY LAW FORMATS

Sections 4 and 5 cover the requirements for the statement of financial position and statement of comprehensive income (and income statement, where the statement of comprehensive income is presented as two statements) respectively. These sections require that an entity presents: *[FRS 102.4.2, FRS 102.5.5, 7]*

- its statement of financial position (known as the balance sheet under the CA 2006), and
- the items in the statement of comprehensive income (whether as a single statement or in two statement form) required to be included in a profit and loss account

in accordance with the requirements in Part 1 of the applicable schedule to the Regulations or Part 1 of Schedule 1 to the LLP Regulations.

UK companies (applying Schedule 1 to the Regulations) or LLPs must therefore present a balance sheet and profit and loss account using either the statutory or adapted formats.

Only statutory formats are available for banking companies and insurance companies or where the parent of a banking or insurance group prepares consolidated financial statements.

The formats required by different types of entity (and in consolidated financial statements) are discussed in more detail at 4.1 below. This discussion does not address the formats applicable to an entity qualifying for the small entities regime that chooses to apply Section 1A (see Chapter 5 at 8).

Sections 4 and 5 apply to *all* FRS 102 reporters (apart from small entities applying Section 1A), whether or not they report under the CA 2006. Entities that do not report under the CA 2006 are required to comply with the requirements set out in Sections 4 and 5 and with the Regulations (or, where applicable, the LLP Regulations) where referred to in Sections 4 and 5, except to the extent that these requirements are not permitted by any statutory framework under which such entities report. *[FRS 102.1A.7, 4.1-1A, 5.1-1A]*.

4.1   Required formats – balance sheet and profit and loss account

4.1.1   Individual financial statements

An entity must present its statement of financial position; and, in the statement of comprehensive income (or in the separate income statement), the items to be included in a profit and loss account in accordance with one of the following requirements for individual financial statements: *[FRS 102.4.2, FRS 102.5.5, 7]*

- Part 1 *General Rules and Formats* of Schedule 1 to the Regulations – applies to companies other than banking companies (defined in section 1164) and insurance companies (defined in section 1165). *[Regulations 3]*.

- Part 1 *General Rules and Formats* of Schedule 2 to the Regulations – applies to banking companies. *[Regulations 5]*.

- Part 1 *General Rules and Formats* of Schedule 3 to the Regulations – applies to insurance companies. *[Regulations 6]*.

- Part 1 *General Rules and Formats* of Schedule 1 to the LLP Regulations – applies to limited liability partnerships (LLPs). *[LLP Regulations 3]*.

Schedule 1 to the Regulations and Schedule 1 to the LLP Regulations provide a choice of:

- statutory formats (as set out in Section B of Part 1 of those schedules) – see 5.2, 5.3 and 6.6 below; or

- adapted formats (as permitted by paragraph 1A of Schedule 1 to the Regulations and paragraph 1A of Schedule 1 to the LLP Regulations) – see 4.1.3, 5.1 and 6.5 below.

Schedule 2 and Schedule 3 to the Regulations provide only for statutory formats.

The Regulations require that the individual accounts of a banking or insurance company contain a statement that they are prepared in accordance with the provisions of the Regulations relating to banking or insurance companies, as the case may be. *[Regulations 5(3), 6(3)]*. The definitions of a banking company and an insurance company are given at 4.2.2 and 4.2.3 below.

While not directly relevant to formats, it is worth noting that disclosures from paragraph 42 of Schedule 1 to the Regulations (and paragraph 42 of Schedule 1 to the LLP Regulations) onwards are required to be given in the notes to the accounts and certain Schedule 1 disclosures are required to be given in the note on the accounting policies rather than in the notes to the accounts.

In addition, these notes must be presented in the order in which, where relevant, the items to which they relate are presented in the balance sheet and in the profit and loss account. *[1 Sch 42, 1 Sch 42 (LLP)]*.

4.1.2   Consolidated financial statements

The consolidated statement of financial position and consolidated statement of comprehensive income (or consolidated income statement, where the two-statement approach is used) of a group must be presented in accordance with the requirements for a consolidated balance sheet and consolidated profit and loss account of Schedule 6 to the Regulations or Schedule 3 to the LLP Regulations. *[FRS 102.4.2, FRS 102.5.5, 7]*.

Schedule 6 to the Regulations addresses the balance sheet and profit and loss account formats applicable to group accounts of companies, modifying the formats included in the earlier schedules. The group accounts must comply, so far as practicable with the provisions of Schedule 1 to the Regulations (including the formats) as if the undertakings included in the consolidation were a single company. *[Regulations 9, 6 Sch 1(1)]*.

The parent company of a group (other than a banking or insurance group) applies Part 1 of Schedule 6 to the Regulations. The parent company of a banking group (defined in section 1164(4)-(5)) applies Part 1 (as modified by Part 2) of Schedule 6 to the Regulations. The parent company of an insurance group (defined in section 1165(5)-(6)) applies Part 1 (as modified by Part 3) of Schedule 6 to the Regulations. *[Regulations 9]*.

Chapter 6

This means that the parent company of a group (other than a banking or insurance group) follows the formats in Schedule 1 to the Regulations in its group accounts. The parent of a banking group follows the formats in Schedule 2 to the Regulations in its group accounts. The parent of an insurance group follows the formats in Schedule 3 to the Regulations. In each case, Schedule 6 to the Regulations sets out the modifications required to the respective formats used in the individual accounts.

The Regulations require that the group accounts prepared by a parent of a banking or insurance group must make a statement that they are prepared in accordance with the provisions of the Regulations relating to banking groups or insurance groups, as the case may be. *[Regulations 9(4)].*

It is possible for the parent company of a banking and insurance group to be required to follow the formats in Schedule 1 to the Regulations in its individual accounts (i.e. where it is not a banking or insurance company itself).

Schedule 3 to the LLP Regulations similarly addresses the balance sheet and profit and loss formats applicable to group accounts of LLPs. *[LLP Regulations 6, 3 Sch 1 (LLP), FRS 102.4.2, FRS 102.5.5, 7].* The parent LLP follows the formats in Schedule 1 to the LLP Regulations, with certain modifications to the formats used in the individual accounts.

The modifications for group accounts for companies (other than banking and insurance companies) and LLPs are addressed at 4.5 (presentation of non-controlling interest), and in the introductory sections at 5.1 and 6.5 (adapted formats) and 5.2 and 6.6 (statutory formats) below. Where adapted formats (see 4.1.3 below) are used, the only modification is in relation to non-controlling interests.

4.1.3   Adapted formats

Adapted formats can be used by UK companies (applying Schedule 1 to the Regulations) and LLPs respectively.

Paragraph 1A of Schedule 1 to the Regulations (and paragraph 1A of Schedule 1 to the LLP Regulations) set out the adaptations to the statutory formats permitted for the balance sheet and profit and loss account. Paragraph 1A (set out in full below) refers to the formats in Section B of Part 1 of Schedule 1 to the Regulations (and Section B of Part 1 of Schedule 1 to the LLP Regulations); these are the statutory formats for a UK company (other than a banking or insurance company) and LLP that is not applying the micro-entity provisions.

A company's directors (or the members of an LLP) may adapt one of the balance sheet formats in Section B of Part 1 of Schedule 1 to the Regulations (or Section B of Part 1 of Schedule 1 to the LLP Regulations) so to distinguish between current and non-current items in a different way, provided that: *[1 Sch 1A(1), 1 Sch 1A(1) (LLP)]*

(a)   the information given is at least equivalent to that which would have been required by the use of such format had it not been thus adapted; and

(b)   the presentation of those items is in accordance with generally accepted accounting principles or practice.

Similarly, a company's directors (or the members of an LLP) may adapt one of the profit and loss account formats in Section B of Part 1 of Schedule 1 to the Regulations (or Section B of Part 1 of Schedule 1 to the LLP Regulations), provided that: *[1 Sch 1A(2), 1 Sch 1A(2) (LLP)]*

(a) the information given is at least equivalent to that which would have been required by the use of such format had it not been thus adapted; and

(b) the presentation of those items is in accordance with generally accepted accounting principles or practice.

So far as is practicable, the provisions of paragraphs 2 to 9A of Section A of Part 1 of Schedule 1 to the Regulations (or the same paragraphs in the LLP Regulations) (i.e. the General Rules to the formats – see 4.4 below) apply to a company's (or an LLP's) balance sheet or profit or loss account, notwithstanding any such adaptation pursuant to paragraph 1A. *[1 Sch 1A(3), 1 Sch 1A(3) (LLP)]*.

Adapted formats, as modified by Schedule 6 to the Regulations (or Schedule 3 to the LLP Regulations) (see 4.1.2 above) may also be used in group accounts of a parent company of a group (other than a banking group or insurance group) and in the group accounts of a parent LLP. *[6 Sch 1(1), 3 Sch 1 (LLP)]*. Adapted formats are not permitted to be used in the group accounts of banking groups or insurance groups because their group accounts are drawn up in accordance with Schedule 2 and Schedule 3 to the Regulations (with modifications), which do not allow for adapted formats.

Paragraph 1A provides limited guidance on the content of the adapted formats, leaving the detail to UK accounting standards. Indeed, Appendix III to FRS 102 states that 'for entities within its scope, FRS 102 sets out a framework for the information to be presented by those entities choosing to adapt the formats'. *[FRS 102 Appendix III.38]*.

Entities applying adapted formats for the balance sheet and profit and loss account must, therefore, follow the requirements for adapted formats in Sections 4 and 5, which allow a presentation on the balance sheet and profit and loss account which is much closer to IAS 1. These formats may be attractive to certain entities, e.g. where the formats assist comparability with competitors or where IFRS is used for group reporting but FRS 102 has been adopted in the individual accounts of group undertakings.

Sections 4 and 5 specify that, at a minimum, certain line items are presented on the face of the statement of financial position and statement of comprehensive income (or income statement, where the two statement approach is used), with further sub-classifications of certain line items presented in the statement of financial position in the notes to the financial statements. In addition, FRS 102 sets out when additional line items must be presented and how adapted formats can be modified (see 4.4.3, 5.1 and 6.5 below). *[FRS 102.4.2C, 4.3, 5.5C, 5.9]*. In general, few difficulties should arise over classification of line items where adapted formats are applied since the required line items are aligned with the categories of assets and liabilities discussed in FRS 102. Some areas to watch on classification are, however, discussed at 5.1 and 6.5 below.

In addition, Schedule 1 to the Regulations (and Schedule 1 to the LLP Regulations) require supplementary information in respect of certain line items in the balance sheet and profit and loss account to be given in the notes to the accounts. One complexity is that this information is in respect of line items found in the statutory formats, which may not align completely with the line items used where the adapted formats are applied.

See 5.1 and 6.5 below for further discussion of adapted formats.

Chapter 6

4.2   Which formats should be applied?

4.2.1   UK companies and LLPs applying FRS 102 (but not Section 1A)

4.1.1 and 4.1.2 above explain which formats are applied by UK companies and LLPs applying the full version of FRS 102, rather than the small entities regime in Section 1A. The requirements of FRS 102 are consistent with the requirements of company and LLP law.

The definitions of banking company, banking group, insurance company, and insurance group are relevant to determining which formats are required. See 4.2.2 and 4.2.3 below.

Unregistered companies (that are in scope of *The Unregistered Companies Regulations 2009* (SI 2009/2436)), and not applying Section 1A, would apply Schedule 1 to the Regulations.[2] Unregistered companies are generally outside the scope of this publication.

4.2.2   Definition of banking company and banking group

A 'banking company' means a person who has permission under Part 4A of the Financial Services and Markets Act 2000 to accept deposits, other than:

- a person who is not a company; and
- a person who has such permission only for the purpose of carrying on another regulated activity in accordance with permission under that Part.

This definition is to be read with section 22 of the Financial Services and Markets Act 2000, any relevant order under that section and Schedule 2 to the Financial Services and Markets Act 2000. *[s1164(2)-(3)]*.

A 'banking group' means a group (i.e. a parent undertaking and its subsidiary undertakings) where the parent company is a banking company or where: *[s1164(4), s1173(1)]*

- the parent company's principal subsidiary undertakings are wholly or mainly credit institutions; and
- the parent company does not itself carry on any material business apart from the acquisition, management and disposal of interests in subsidiary undertakings.

For the purposes of the definition of 'banking group', the 'principal subsidiary undertakings' are the subsidiary undertakings of the company whose results or financial position would principally affect the figures shown in the group accounts and the 'management of interests in subsidiary undertakings' includes the provision of services to such undertakings. *[s1164(5)]*.

A credit institution is defined as a credit institution within the meaning of Article 4(1)(1) of Regulation (EU) No. 575/2013 of the European Parliament and of the Council, i.e. as 'an undertaking the business of which is to take deposits or other repayable funds from the public and to grant credits for its own account.' *[s1173(1)]*.

4.2.3   Definition of insurance company and insurance group

An 'insurance company' means:

- an authorised insurance company (i.e. a person (whether incorporated or not) who has permission under Part 4A of the Financial Services and Markets Act 2000 to effect or carry out contracts of insurance); or
- any other person (whether incorporated or not) who:

- carries on insurance market activity (as defined in section 316(3) of the Financial Services and Markets Act 2000); or
- may effect or carry out contracts of insurance under which the benefits provided by that person are exclusively or primarily benefits in kind in the event of accident to or breakdown of a vehicle.

Neither expression includes a friendly society within the meaning of the Friendly Societies Act 1992. *[s1165(2)-(4)].*

References to 'contracts of insurance' and 'to the effecting or carrying out of such contracts' must be read with section 22 of the Financial Services and Markets Act 2000, any relevant order under that section and Schedule 2 to the Financial Services and Markets Act 2000. *[s1165(8)].*

An 'insurance group' means a group (i.e. parent undertaking and its subsidiary undertakings) where the parent company is an insurance company or where: *[s1165(5)]*

- the parent company's principal subsidiary undertakings are wholly or mainly insurance companies; and
- the parent company does not itself carry on any material business apart from the acquisition, management and disposal of interests in subsidiary undertakings.

For the purposes of the definition of 'insurance group', the 'principal subsidiary undertakings' are the subsidiary undertakings of the company whose results or financial position would principally affect the figures shown in the group accounts and the 'management of interests in subsidiary undertakings' includes the provision of services to such undertakings. *[s1165(6)].*

4.2.4   Qualifying partnerships (not applying Section 1A)

A qualifying partnership (as defined in the *Partnerships (Accounts) Regulations 2008*) (SI 2008/569), unless exempt under regulation 7 of SI 2008/569, is required to prepare the like annual accounts and reports as would be required, if the partnership were a company under Part 15 of the CA 2006 and under the Small Companies Regulations or the Regulations, as the case may be.

Part 1 of the Schedule to these regulations sets out certain modifications and adaptations to be made to the Regulations and Small Companies Regulations for these purposes. In addition, modifications may be necessary to take account of the fact that partnerships are unincorporated. For the purposes of the formats, there is no requirement for the profit and loss account to show profit or loss before taxation.[3]

Consequently, the requirements for qualifying partnerships preparing statutory accounts are the same (subject to the modifications and adaptations noted above) as for UK companies (see 4.2.1 above).

4.2.5   Other entities required to prepare statutory accounts in accordance with Part 15 of the CA 2006

Certain other entities are required by regulations to prepare annual accounts as if the entity is a company subject to Part 15 of the CA 2006 and these regulations specify the formats to be applied for the balance sheet and profit and loss account. Some examples are given below.

Chapter 6

The Bank Accounts Directive (Miscellaneous Banks) Regulations 2008 (SI 2008/567) requires a 'qualifying bank' (as defined in those regulations) to prepare such annual accounts and directors' report as if it were a banking company (or the parent company of a banking group) in accordance with Schedule 2 to the Regulations (with certain adaptations or modifications set out in the Schedule to SI 2008/567).

Similarly, an insurance undertaking (as defined in *The Insurance Accounts Directive (Miscellaneous Insurance Undertakings) Regulations 2008* (SI 2008/565)) must prepare the like annual accounts and directors' report as if it were an insurance company (or the parent company of an insurance group) in accordance with Schedule 3 to the Regulations (with certain adaptations or modifications).

Sometimes, other law may apply. For example, the preparation of the accounts of a European public limited-liability company (SE) is governed directly by Articles 61 and 62 of Council Regulation (EC) 2157/2001. The rules applicable to the preparation of accounts of public limited-liability companies under the law of the Member State in which the SE's registered office is situated are followed (there are modifications for an SE which is a credit or financial institution or an insurance undertaking).

The entities described above would not be eligible to apply Section 1A. Such entities discussed above are generally outside the scope of this publication. However, it is important that all entities determine the statutory framework, if any, that applies to the preparation of their financial statements.

4.2.6   Other entities (not applying Section 1A)

Other entities (not applying Section 1A) must apply the formats included in one of Schedules 1 to 3 to the Regulations or in the LLP Regulations, except to the extent that these requirements are not permitted by any statutory framework under which such entities report. *[FRS 102.4.1, 4.1A, 4.2, 5.1, 5.5, 5.7]*. The Basis for Conclusions to FRS 102 states that 'it was concluded that all entities applying FRS 102 would be required to follow company law formats as this would promote consistency between reporting entities regardless of the legal framework under which they operate'. *[FRS 102.BC.A15]*.

As FRS 102 does not specify which format should be used, management of such entities must apply judgement in determining the most appropriate format to apply for the circumstances of the entity concerned, where the statutory framework is not prescriptive.

4.3   Changes in formats

The General Rules to the formats (see 4.4 below) require that once a company's (or an LLP's) balance sheet or profit and loss account has been prepared for any financial year using one of the formats (in Section B of Part 1 of Schedule 1 to the Regulations or Section B of Part 1 of Schedule 1 to the LLP Regulations), the company's directors (or the members of an LLP) must use the same format in preparing Companies Act accounts (non-IAS accounts, for an LLP) for subsequent financial years, unless in their opinion there are special reasons for a change. Particulars of any such change must be given in a note to the accounts in which the new format is first used, and the reasons for the change must be explained. *[1 Sch 2, 6 Sch 1, 1 Sch 2 (LLP), 3 Sch 1 (LLP)]*.

There are similar rules for changes in statutory profit and loss account formats for banking companies in Schedule 2 to the Regulations. *[2 Sch 3, 6 Sch 1]*. There is no choice of statutory balance sheet formats in Schedule 2 to the Regulations. There is no choice of statutory formats in Schedule 3 to the Regulations.

While this paragraph refers to the statutory formats, the General Rules apply so far as is practicable to adapted formats. *[1 Sch 1A(3), 1 Sch 1A(3) (LLP)]*. Therefore, in our view, the same requirements apply to changes in the statutory format used and a change between statutory formats and adapted formats.

A change in the format applied would also be regarded as a change in accounting policy for the purposes of FRS 102 and, therefore, would be retrospectively effected. Accounting policies are defined as 'the specific principles, bases, conventions, rules and practices applied by an entity in preparing and presenting financial statements'. *[FRS 102 Appendix I, FRS 102.10.2]*. See Chapter 9 at 3.4 for the requirements on changes in accounting policy.

4.4   General Rules to the formats

The following discussion relates to the General Rules to the formats which apply to balance sheet and profit and loss account formats included in Schedule 1 to the Regulations (and Schedule 1 to the LLP Regulations). The General Rules to the formats applicable to Schedule 2 (banking companies) and Schedule 3 (insurance companies) to the Regulations, not addressed here, are more restrictive.

The General Rules to the formats also cover changes in formats (see 4.3 above).

4.4.1   *General Rules governing the form of the statutory formats*

Subject to paragraph 1A (which provides for adapted formats – see 4.1.3 above) and the following provisions of the Schedule,

- every balance sheet of a company (or an LLP) must show the items listed in either of the balance sheet formats;
- every profit and loss account of a company (or an LLP) must show the items listed in either of the profit and loss account formats

in Section B of Part 1 of Schedule 1 to the Regulations (or Section B of Part 1 of Schedule 1 to the LLP Regulations), i.e. the statutory formats.

The items in the balance sheet and profit and loss account statutory formats must be shown in the order and under the headings and sub-headings given in the particular format used, but the letters or numbers assigned to that item in the format do not need to be given (and are not in practice). References in the Schedule to items listed must be read together with any of the notes following the formats in Section B which apply to those items, which may also permit alternative positions for any particular items. *[1 Sch 1, 1 Sch 1 (LLP)]*. The individual line items in the statutory balance sheet and profit and loss account formats are discussed respectively at 5.3 and 6.6 below.

While there are two statutory formats, format 1 and format 2, available for the balance sheet, only format 1 is commonly used. Both format 1 and format 2 profit and loss accounts are commonly used. There are some differences in detail in the line items required in the LLP statutory formats compared to the company statutory formats.

See Figure 6.4 at 5.2 below for the format 1 balance sheet and Figures 6.16 to 6.19 at 6.6 below for the format 1 and format 2 profit and loss accounts for the individual accounts of a UK company and an LLP. Each of the headings and sub-headings denoted with a capital letter or Roman numeral must be presented on the face of the balance sheet.

4.4.2   Adapted formats (Companies applying Schedule 1 to the Regulations and LLPs only)

Paragraph 1A of Schedule 1 to the Regulations and paragraph 1A of Schedule 1 to the LLP Regulations permit the use of adapted formats. See 4.1.3 above and 4.4.3, 5.1 and 6.5 below.

4.4.3   General Rules applying to statutory formats and adapted formats

The following provisions in the General Rules to the formats apply to the statutory formats and, so far as is practicable, to the adapted formats. *[1 Sch 1A(3)]*.

The Regulations (and LLP Regulations) do not provide further guidance on how 'so far as is practicable' is to be interpreted, but in our view, this phrase is needed because the General Rules have been written from the perspective of the statutory formats, e.g. they refer to items given an Arabic number which may not have a direct counterpart in the adapted formats. In other cases, such as in relation to corresponding amounts (i.e. comparatives), there are no difficulties in applying the requirements. We do not consider that 'so far as is practicable' allows companies or LLPs flexibility to regard the General Rules to the formats as optional.

Schedule 1 to the Regulations and the LLP Regulations require that every profit and loss account must show 'profit or loss before taxation' as a line item on the face of the profit and loss account. Previously, the line item required was 'profit or loss on ordinary activities before taxation'. *[1 Sch 6, 1 Sch 6 (LLP)]*. This change was not in fact made to the formats in Schedule 2 and Schedule 3 to the Regulations. The line item 'profit or loss before taxation' is not required for a qualifying partnership preparing statutory accounts (see 4.2.4 above).[4]

The General Rules to the formats allow any item to be shown in a company's (or an LLP's) balance sheet or profit and loss account in greater detail than required by the particular format used. The balance sheet or profit and loss account may include an item representing or covering the amount of any asset or liability, income or expenditure not otherwise covered by any of the items listed in the format used. However, preliminary expenses; the expenses of, and commission on, any issue of shares or debentures (relevant for a company only); and the costs of research may not be treated as assets in the balance sheet. *[1 Sch 3, 1 Sch 3 (LLP)]*. A qualifying partnership preparing statutory accounts is not subject to the above rules on which types of costs may not be treated as assets in the balance sheet.[5]

Where the special nature of the company's (or the LLP's) business requires it, the company's directors (or the members of the LLP) *must* adapt the arrangement, headings and sub-headings otherwise required in respect of items given an Arabic number in the balance sheet or profit and loss account format used. The directors (or the members of the LLP) *may* combine items to which Arabic numbers are given in the formats if their individual amounts are not material to assessing the state of affairs or profit or loss of the company (or the LLP) for the financial year in question; or the combination facilitates that assessment. In the latter case, the individual amounts of any items combined must be disclosed in a note to the accounts. *[1 Sch 4, 1 Sch 4 (LLP)]*.

FRS 102's requirements on materiality and aggregation are discussed at 9.4 below.

FRS 102 contains additional requirements that are consistent with the General Rules. Additional line items, headings and subtotals are required to be added where relevant to an understanding of the entity's financial position or financial performance (this applies both to statutory and adapted formats – see 5.1, 5.2 and 6.7 below). *[FRS 102.4.3, 5.9]*. Where additional detail is provided on the face of the balance sheet or profit and loss account, it is usual to provide a subtotal for the heading.

There was no need for FRS 102 to explain how the statutory formats could be amended, as this is covered in the General Rules to the formats. However, amendments to the adapted formats, which do not include Arabic-numbered items, would need to comply so far as is practicable with the General Rules to the formats. Sections 4 and 5 therefore explain what amendments may be made to the line items required for adapted formats. An entity may amend the descriptions used, the ordering of items and the aggregation of similar items in the statement of financial position (including the sub-classifications of certain line items in the statement of financial position required to be presented in the statement of financial position or the notes to the financial statements), according to the nature of the entity and its transactions, to provide information relevant to an understanding of the entity's financial position, providing the information given is at least equivalent to that required by the balance sheet format had it not been adapted. *[FRS 102.4.2C]*. Similarly, an entity may include additional line items in the income statement, amend the descriptions used, and the ordering of items when this is necessary to explain the elements of financial performance, providing the information given is at least equivalent to that required by the profit and loss account format had it not been adopted. *[FRS 102.5.5C]*.

The heading or sub-heading required for a particular item in the balance sheet or profit and loss account format must be presented where there is an amount for that item in either the current or immediately preceding financial year; otherwise, the heading or sub-heading must be omitted. *[1 Sch 5 (SC), 1 Sch 5 (LLP SC)]*.

A corresponding amount (i.e. comparative) for the immediately preceding financial year must be shown for every item shown in the balance sheet or profit and loss account. Where that corresponding amount is not comparable with the amount shown in the current financial year, the corresponding amount may be adjusted. Particulars of the non-comparability and of any adjustment must be disclosed in a note to the accounts. *[1 Sch 7, 1 Sch 7 (LLP)]*. This statutory requirement would permit FRS 102's requirements on restatement of comparatives to be followed. Where amounts are not restated, e.g. due to transitional provisions in accounting policies or where it is impracticable to determine the effects of a change in accounting policies on earlier periods, *[FRS 102.10.11-12]*, a note to the accounts will need to disclose the non-comparability. FRS 102's requirements on comparatives are discussed at 3.6 above.

Amounts in respect of items representing assets or income may not be set off against amounts in respect of items representing liabilities or expenditure (as the case may be), or *vice versa*. *[1 Sch 8, 1 Sch 8 (LLP)]*. FRS 102's requirements on offset are discussed at 9.1.1.C below.

The company's directors (or the members of an LLP) must, in determining how amounts are presented within items in the profit and loss account and balance sheet, have regard to the substance of the reported transaction or arrangement, in accordance with generally accepted accounting principles or practice. *[1 Sch 9, 1 Sch 9 (LLP)]*.

Finally, where an asset or liability relates to more than one item in the balance sheet, the relationship of such asset or liability to the relevant items must be disclosed either under those items or in the notes to the accounts. *[1 Sch 9A, 1 Sch 9A (LLP)]*.

Examples of situations where this may be relevant include:

- items which are partly reported in debtors: amounts falling due within one year and debtors: amounts falling due after more than one year, where reported separately on the balance sheet, (in the statutory formats);
- items which are partly reported in creditors: amounts falling due within one year and creditors: amounts falling due after more than one year (in the statutory formats); and
- items which are partly reported as current and non-current assets or liabilities (in the adapted formats).

This disclosure requirement does not appear to extend to reporting the relationship between assets and liabilities that derive from a single transaction (e.g. an asset acquired on a finance lease has an impact both on tangible fixed assets and lease creditors) nor, say, to identifying the associated deferred tax consequences of an asset or liability. Where a *single* asset or liability is required to be reported as more than one line item in the statement of financial position, e.g. split accounting for a convertible loan between equity and liability elements, or a loan at off-market rates made by a parent to its subsidiary is split between investment and loan asset, it would seem appropriate, in our view, to disclose the relationship between these line items.

4.5   Non-controlling interests in consolidated financial statements

FRS 102, the Regulations and LLP Regulations address the presentation of non-controlling interest. These requirements are relevant to consolidated financial statements, prepared using statutory or adapted formats.

Under FRS 102, a non-controlling interest is defined as 'the equity in a subsidiary not attributable, directly or indirectly, to a parent'. Equity is 'the residual interest in the assets of the entity after deducting all its liabilities'. Owners (as referred to below) are 'holders of instruments classified as equity'. *[FRS 102 Appendix I]*.

FRS 102 requires that non-controlling interest is presented in the consolidated statement of financial position within equity, separately from the equity of the owners of the parent. *[FRS 102.9.20]*.

The statement of changes in equity (see 7.1 below) presents: *[FRS 102.6.3]*

- total comprehensive income, showing separately the total amounts attributable to owners of the parent and non-controlling interests; and
- since non-controlling interest is a component of equity, a reconciliation of the changes in the carrying amount of non-controlling interest.

In addition, the statement of comprehensive income (or separate income statement, where presented) shows as allocations of profit or loss and total comprehensive income: *[FRS 102.5.6, 5.7A-C, 9.21]*

- the profit or loss for the period attributable to the owners of the parent separately from the profit or loss for the period attributable to non-controlling interest; and
- the total comprehensive income attributable to the owners of the parent separately from the total comprehensive income attributable to non-controlling interest.

The statutory requirements for presentation of non-controlling interests (see 4.5.1 below) would permit a presentation consistent with the requirements of FRS 102. In most cases, the amounts shown as non-controlling interest under FRS 102 (see Chapter 8 at 3.7) and the amounts required by the Regulations (or LLP Regulations) (see 4.5.1 below) will be the same. There is a theoretical possibility that the amounts required by FRS 102 (which has a wider definition) and the Regulations (or LLP Regulations) may differ. In such a case, two totals are strictly required to be presented to meet both the requirements of FRS 102 and the Regulations (or LLP Regulations).

4.5.1 Presentation requirements of non-controlling interests in the Regulations and LLP Regulations

Schedule 6 to the Regulations (and Schedule 3 to the LLP Regulations) modify the balance sheet and profit and loss account formats used in the group accounts of a parent company (of a group that is not a banking or an insurance group) or of a parent LLP as follows: *[6 Sch 17, 3 Sch 17 (LLP)]*

'(1) The formats set out in Section B of Part 1 of Schedule 1 to these Regulations have effect in relation to group accounts with the following additions.

(2) In the balance sheet formats there must be shown, as a separate item and under the heading "non-controlling interests", the amount of capital and reserves attributable to shares in subsidiary undertakings included in the consolidation held by or on behalf of persons other than the parent company [LLP] and its subsidiary undertakings.

(3) In the profit and loss account formats there must be shown, as a separate item and under the heading "non-controlling interests", the amount of any profit or loss attributable to shares in subsidiary undertakings included in the consolidation held by or on behalf of persons other than the parent company [LLP] and its subsidiary undertakings.'

The heading for 'non-controlling interests' used in the balance sheet is treated as if it has a letter assigned, meaning that it must be included on the face of the balance sheet. However, the heading used in the profit and loss account is treated as if it has an Arabic number assigned (allowing the adaptations permitted by the General Rules to the formats, as described at 4.4 above). *[6 Sch 17(4), 3 Sch 17(4) (LLP)]*.

The above paragraph refers to modifications to the statutory formats (in Section B of Part 1 of Schedule 1 to the Regulations and Section B of Part 1 of Schedule 1 to the LLP Regulations). In our view, the same requirements for presentation of non-controlling interest apply to adapted formats (see 4.1.3 above) because the General Rules to the formats require that any adaptations made need to be 'at least equivalent' to the information required in the statutory formats. *[1 Sch 1A, 6 Sch 1, 1 Sch 1A (LLP), 3 Sch 1 (LLP)].*

Modifications are made to paragraph 17(4) for the group accounts of parent companies of banking and insurance groups, as follows: *[6 Sch 25, 36]*

- paragraph 17(1) refers to Schedule 2 to the Regulations (for banking groups) and Schedule 3 to the Regulations (for insurance groups);
- paragraph 17(3) requires that the profit and loss account format must show, under the heading "non-controlling interests", separate items for:
  - the amount of any profit or loss on ordinary activities; and
  - the amount of any profit or loss on extraordinary activities,

  attributable to shares in subsidiary undertakings included in the consolidation held by or on behalf of persons other than the parent company and its subsidiary undertakings;
- paragraph 17(4) has more restrictive presentation requirements (which effectively would require the non-controlling interest to be presented as a separate line item on the face of the balance sheet or profit and loss account).

Extraordinary activities are not expected in practice (see 6.7.6 below) so the main effect is that the amount of profit or loss *on ordinary activities* (this heading is still used in the Schedule 2 and Schedule 3 formats) will need to be attributed to non-controlling interests. FRS 102 requires, in any case, that non-controlling interest is presented on the face of the statement of financial position and as an allocation of profit (and total comprehensive income) on the face of the statement of comprehensive income (and separate income statement, if any).

4.5.2   *Illustrative examples of presentation of non-controlling interests*

Figure 6.1 below illustrates the presentation of non-controlling interests in the statement of financial position for a UK company under FRS 102 (and is consistent with the Regulations). The terminology 'non-controlling interests' in the Regulations (rather than 'non-controlling interest' in FRS 102) is used.

Figure 6.1   *Presentation of non-controlling interests in statement of financial position*

	£'000
Capital and reserves	
Called up share capital	12,075
Share premium account	493
Capital redemption reserve	500
Merger reserve	6,250
Profit and loss account	27,882
Equity attributable to owners of the parent company	47,200
Non-controlling interests	360
	47,560

See also Figure 6.3 at 5.1 below and Example 6.3 at 5.1.14 below for the presentation of non-controlling interest in the statement of financial position in adapted formats.

Example 6.7 at 7.1.2 below illustrates the presentation of non-controlling interest in the statement of changes in equity.

FRS 102 allows the statement of comprehensive income to be shown as a single statement or using the two-statement approach (with a separate income statement). *[FRS 102.5.2]*.

Figure 6.2 below illustrates the allocation of profit or loss to owners of the parent and to non-controlling interest where a separate income statement is presented. Where a separate income statement is presented, an allocation of total comprehensive income between owners of the parent and the non-controlling interest would also be presented at the end of the statement of total comprehensive income. *[FRS 102.5.6, 5.7B, 5.7C]*.

See also Example 6.5 at 6.5.2 below which illustrates the presentation for the statement of comprehensive income (with a separate income statement) using adapted formats.

Figure 6.2   *Presentation of non-controlling interests in separate income statement*

	£'000
Profit before taxation	7,786
Tax on profit	(3,339)
Profit after taxation and profit for the financial year	4,447
Profit for the financial year attributable to:	
Owners of the parent company	4,209
Non-controlling interests	238

Where a single statement of comprehensive income is presented (see 6.3 below), these allocations of profit or loss and of total comprehensive income would both be presented as two lines below the total comprehensive income for the period. *[FRS 102.5.7A-C]*. See Example 6.4 at 6.5.2 below which illustrates this for a single statement of comprehensive income using adapted formats.

5   STATEMENT OF FINANCIAL POSITION

The requirements in FRS 102 for entities not applying Section 1A, are set out below and at 5.1 to 5.5.

Section 4 applies to all entities, whether or not they report under the CA 2006. Entities that do not report under the CA 2006 should comply with the requirements of Section 4 and with the Regulations (or where applicable, the LLP Regulations) where referred to in Section 4, except to the extent that these requirements are not permitted by any statutory framework under which such entities report. A small entity applying Section 1A is not required to comply with Section 4. *[FRS 102.4.1, 4.1A]*.

The statement of financial position (referred to as the balance sheet in CA 2006) presents an entity's assets, liabilities and equity at the end of the reporting period. *[FRS 102.4.1]*.

An entity presents its statement of financial position in accordance with the requirements in Part 1 of the applicable schedule to the Regulations or Part 1 of Schedule 1 to the LLP Regulations. *[FRS 102.4.2]*. The formats required by different types of entity (and in consolidated financial statements) are discussed in more detail in 4.1 and 4.2 above.

Part 1 of Schedule 1 to the Regulations and Part 1 of Schedule 1 to the LLP Regulations, provide a choice of:

- one of two balance sheet statutory formats (as set out in Section B of the relevant Part); or
- adapted formats.

Schedule 2 (banking companies) and Schedule 3 (insurance companies) to the Regulations require use of the statutory formats and do not allow use of adapted formats. This chapter does not set out the statutory formats for banking and insurance companies.

The consolidated statement of financial position of a group must be presented in accordance with the requirements for a consolidated balance sheet in Schedule 6 to the Regulations (or, where applicable, Schedule 3 to the LLP Regulations). *[FRS 102.4.2]*. How adapted formats and statutory formats are applied in consolidated financial statements is further explained in 4.1.2 above and 5.1 and 5.2 below.

This part of the chapter is set out as follows:

- 5.1 – Adapted formats (including implementation issues)
- 5.2 – Statutory formats – format 1 balance sheet
- 5.3 – Implementation issues for statutory formats – format 1 balance sheet
- 5.4 – Additional disclosures in respect of share capital (or equivalent) (adapted formats and statutory formats); and
- 5.5 – Information on disposal groups to be presented in the notes (adapted formats and statutory formats)

Certain classification issues are highlighted in the commentary on the statutory and adapted formats. In particular, the line items in the statutory formats are not always aligned with the accounting requirements in FRS 102 (e.g. 'tangible fixed assets' in the statutory formats would include property, plant and equipment, investment properties and other items).

Some additional analyses of line items and disclosures required by the Regulations (and LLP Regulations) in the notes to the accounts are highlighted at 5.3 below. Disclosures in the Regulations and LLP Regulations (unless they derive directly from the notes to the statutory formats so only apply to the statutory format) are also required where adapted formats are used. These disclosures are not separately noted in the discussion in 5.1 below on adapted formats.

Disclosures relating to the statement of financial position specifically required by FRS 102 are set out at 5.4 and 5.5 below. Therefore, these apply where adapted formats or statutory formats are used. These sections also discuss similar disclosures found in the Regulations or LLP Regulations.

5.1   Adapted formats (including application issues)

An entity choosing to apply paragraph 1A(1) of Schedule 1 to the Regulations and adapt one of the balance sheet formats (see 4.1.3 above) shall, as a minimum, include in its statement of financial position the line items presented in Figure 6.3 below, distinguishing between those items that are current and those that are non-current (see 5.1.1 and 5.1.2 below). *[FRS 102.4.2A]*. To comply with this requirement, an entity must present as separate classifications: current and non-current assets, and current and non-current liabilities. *[FRS 102.4.2D]*.

FRS 102 refers only to the Regulations, because at the time that this paragraph was added in to FRS 102, the LLP Regulations did not permit the use of adapted formats. Since paragraph 1A(1) of Schedule 1 to the LLP Regulations now allows the use of adapted formats, this paragraph should be read as extending to LLPs.

FRS 102's presentation requirements for adapted formats are similar to but not identical to IAS 1.

Figure 6.3   Adapted formats – balance sheet

(a)	Property, plant and equipment
(b)	Investment property carried at fair value through profit and loss
(c)	Intangible assets
(d)	Financial assets (excluding amounts shown under (e), (f), (j) and (k))
(e)	Investments in associates
(f)	Investments in jointly controlled entities
(g)	Biological assets carried at cost less accumulated depreciation and impairment
(h)	Biological assets carried at fair value through profit and loss
(i)	Inventories
(j)	Trade and other receivables
(k)	Cash and cash equivalents
(l)	Trade and other payables
(m)	Provisions
(n)	Financial liabilities (excluding amounts shown under (l) and (m))
(o)	Liabilities and assets for current tax
(p)	Deferred tax liabilities and deferred tax assets (classified as non-current)
(q)	Non-controlling interest, presented within equity separately from the equity attributable to the owners of the parent#
(r)	Equity attributable to the owners of the parent~

~   The LLP SORP requires a total for net assets attributable to members, and total members' interests (as a memorandum item) to be disclosed on the face of the statement of financial position. These disclosures are retained where adapted formats are used and 'loans and other debts due to members' and 'members' other interests' (items J and K in the statutory formats for LLPs) are shown as line items on the face of the statement of financial position. See Figure 6.6 at 5.2.1 below and the discussion below.

\#   Not required in individual financial statements.

FRS 102 simply provides a list of items which must, as a minimum, be presented in the statement of financial position. An illustrative example statement of financial position is included in Example 6.3 at 5.1.14 below.

The LLP SORP requires that, in order for the adapted formats to show the equivalent information to the statutory formats, 'loans and other debts due to members' (item J in the statutory formats) and 'members' other interests' (item K in the statutory formats) must be separately disclosed on the face of the balance sheet. The face of the balance sheet should show the total for net assets attributable to members (i.e. the total of 'loans and other debts due to members' and 'members' other interests') and disclose total members' interests (being the total of 'loans and other debts due to members' and 'members' other interests', less any 'amounts due from members' in debtors) as a memorandum item. *[LLP SORP.26C, 58]*. Detailed guidance on issues specific to LLPs is outside the scope of this chapter.

In general, few difficulties should arise over classification of line items since the required line items are aligned with the categories of assets and liabilities discussed in FRS 102. The line items required in adapted formats (and some implementation issues on classification) are discussed at 5.1.3 to 5.1.13 below.

While line items (o) and (p) appear to combine liabilities and assets for current tax and deferred tax respectively, the assets will need to be shown separately from the liabilities. Deferred tax is always classified as non-current.

Line item (q) for non-controlling interest (see 4.5 above) is only relevant where consolidated financial statements are prepared.

So far as is practicable, paragraphs 2 to 9A of the General Rules to the formats apply to the adapted formats. *[1 Sch 1A(3), 1 Sch 1A(3) (LLP)]*.

Section 4 requires that the following sub-classifications of the line items presented must be disclosed either in the statement of financial position or in the notes: *[FRS 102.4.2B]*

- property, plant and equipment in classifications appropriate to the entity;
- intangible assets and goodwill in classifications appropriate to the entity;
- investments, showing separately shares and loans;
- trade and other receivables showing separately amounts due from related parties, amounts due from other parties, prepayments and receivables arising from accrued income not yet billed;
- inventories, showing separately, amounts of inventories:
  - held for sale in the ordinary course of business;
  - in the process of production for such sale; and
  - in the form of materials or supplies to be consumed in the production process or in the rendering of services;
- trade and other payables, showing separately amounts payable to trade suppliers, payable to related parties, deferred income and accruals; and
- classes of equity, such as share capital, share premium, retained earnings, revaluation reserve, fair value reserve and other reserves.

An entity must present additional line items, headings and subtotals in the statement of financial position when such presentation is relevant to an understanding of the entity's financial position. *[FRS 102.4.3]*. This requirement also applies to statutory formats.

The descriptions of the line items in the statement of financial position used in paragraph 4.2A (listed in Figure 6.3 above) and of the sub-classifications of line items set out in paragraph 4.2B (see immediately above); and the ordering of items or aggregation of similar line items, may be amended according to the nature of the entity and its transactions, to provide information that is relevant to an understanding of the entity's financial position, providing the information given is at least equivalent to that required by the balance sheet format had it not been adapted. *[FRS 102.4.2C]*.

Paragraph 4.3 explains when additional line items are required and paragraph 4.2C clarifies the flexibility in the presentation requirements where adapted formats are used (for statutory formats, the General Rules to the formats set out the flexibility for Arabic numbered items, but Arabic numbered items are not used in the adapted formats). Paragraphs 4.3 and 4.2C are similar to requirements in IAS 1. *[IAS 1.55, 57]*. See 4.4 above.

Judgement is needed in determining whether to present additional line items (which might include further disaggregation of the line items required in the statement of financial position, as set out in Figure 6.3), where material and relevant. IAS 1, which has a similar requirement, states that line items are included when the size, nature or function of an item or aggregation of similar items is such that separate presentation is relevant to an understanding of the entity's financial position. The judgement about whether to present additional items separately is based on an assessment of the nature and liquidity of assets, the function of assets within the entity, and the amounts, nature and timing of liabilities. *[IAS 1.57-58]*. IAS 1 further notes that use of different measurement bases (such as cost or revaluation) for different classes of assets suggests that their nature or function differs. *[IAS 1.59]*. The statement of financial position in the adapted formats already shows line items for investment property and biological assets by measurement basis. An FRS 102 reporter may find IAS 1's guidance helpful but is not required to follow this; the principle is to focus on whether additional analysis is relevant to an understanding of the entity's financial position. Any amendments would need to comply with, so far as is practicable, the requirements of the General Rules to the formats governing modifications of the formats (see 4.4 above).

Where adapted formats are used, there is no requirement to disclose debtors: amounts falling due after more than one year or to classify creditors between creditors: amounts falling due within one year and creditors: amounts falling due after more than one year. *[FRS 102.4.4A, 4.7]*. Adapted formats distinguish instead between current assets, current liabilities, non-current assets and non-current liabilities. *[FRS 102.4.2A]*.

FRS 102 does not contain IAS 1's requirement to disclose the amount expected to be recovered or settled after more than twelve months, for each asset and liability line item that combines amounts expected to be recovered or settled no more than twelve months after the reporting period, and more than twelve months after the reporting period. *[IAS 1.61]*.

Other analyses of line items are specified by other sections of FRS 102 (refer to the relevant chapters of this publication) or by the Regulations (or LLP Regulations). These disclosures are not set out at 5.1 and 6.5 below (as they are covered in the relevant chapters of this publication), although some of the latter are highlighted at 5.2, 5.3 and 6.6 below in respect of the statutory formats. The additional disclosures required by other sections of the standard will generally be more straightforward than where the statutory formats are applied, since the line items in the adapted formats are aligned with FRS 102.

The Regulations (and LLP Regulations) require supplementary information to be given in the notes to the accounts which apply where statutory formats or the adapted formats are used. One complexity is that the information required sometimes refers to items found in the statutory formats (which may differ to the line items identified where the adapted formats are used). For example, the adapted formats do not refer to fixed assets, creditors: amounts falling due within one year, creditors: amounts falling due after more than one year, investments, land or buildings, or turnover. A UK company (or an LLP) using adapted formats in Companies Act accounts (non-IAS accounts, for an LLP) will, therefore, need to identify which of its assets, liabilities, revenue streams needs to be included in the required disclosures. While the classification of non-current assets and current assets used in adapted formats differs to the fixed assets and current assets classification required in statutory formats, the statutory definition of 'fixed assets' (see 5.2.2 below) is relevant for the purposes of disclosures in respect of fixed assets in the Regulations (and the LLP Regulations).

In addition, the Regulations (and the LLP Regulations) frequently require analyses and reconciliations to be given for Arabic-numbered sub-headings in the statutory balance sheet formats. As noted above, adapted formats require various sub-classifications to be presented in the statement of financial position or notes to the financial statements. The statutory disclosures are often required 'in respect of each item which is or would but for paragraph 4(2)(b) be shown' under a particular heading (meaning the items are combined on the face of the balance sheet or profit or loss account in order to facilitate assessment of the state of affairs or profit or loss). An example is the reconciliation of movements in fixed assets, or the reconciliation of movements in reserves (discussed at 7.1.1 below). In our view, it may be appropriate to give the information for each of the relevant sub-classifications identified. This is because these sub-classifications in effect stand in place of the Arabic-numbered headings identified in the statutory formats. There is overlap here with the reconciliations of the carrying amounts of certain assets required by FRS 102 but the Regulations (and the LLP Regulations) require separate fixed asset reconciliations for cost and cumulative provision for depreciation and diminution. See 5.2.2 below.

5.1.1   *Definitions of current and non-current assets (adapted formats only)*

The definitions of current and non-current assets discussed below apply only where an entity chooses to use adapted formats in accordance with paragraph 1A(1) of Schedule 1 to the Regulations (or paragraph 1A(1) of Schedule 1 to the LLP Regulations).

FRS 102 defines non-current assets. Current assets are the assets of the entity which are not non-current assets (i.e. the residual). *[FRS 102 Appendix I]*. This differs to IAS 1 which defines current assets and non-current assets are the residual. *[IAS 1.66]*.

We have set out below the definition of 'non-current assets', as included in the FRS 102 Glossary.

Non-current assets are defined as: 'Assets of the entity which: *[FRS 102 Appendix I]*

(a)   it does not expect to realise, or intend to sell or consume, in its normal operating cycle (see 5.1.1.A below);

(b)   it does not hold primarily for the purpose of trading (see 5.1.1.B below);

(c)   it does not expect to realise within 12 months after the reporting period; or

(d)   are cash or cash equivalents restricted from being exchanged or used to settle a liability for at least 12 months after the reporting period'.

The adapted formats also require that deferred tax assets are always classified as non-current. *[FRS 102.4.2A(p)]*.

'Cash or cash equivalents' are defined in the FRS 102 Glossary and should be interpreted in a manner consistent with Section 7 (see Chapter 7 at 3.3).

IAS 1 requires an entity to classify an asset as current if it meets any of the conditions in (a) to (d) of paragraph 66 of IAS 1. The conditions in (a) to (d) above of FRS 102's definition of 'non-current assets' are broadly the converse of the conditions in (a) to (d) in IAS 1's definition of a current asset.

In our view, the FRC intended that the classification of assets as non-current and current should be consistent with the requirements of paragraph 66 of IAS 1, however by choosing to define non-current assets, rather than current as in IAS 1, there are potential ambiguities in the wording of the definition, which we consider are unintended. For example, if meeting *any* of (a) to (d) above would qualify an asset as a non-current asset under FRS 102, this would not in fact be aligned with IAS 1. For instance, an asset may not be held primarily for the purpose of trading (so meets (b) in the definition) but if it is expected to be realised within twelve months after the reporting period (so does not meet (c) in the definition), IAS 1 would require this asset to be classified as current. *[IAS 1.66(c)]*.

FRS 102 provides no additional guidance beyond the definition above. However, since the intention is to provide a format more aligned with IAS 1, management may consider, as permitted by the hierarchy in Section 10, the requirements of IAS 1 for further guidance. The guidance presented at 5.1.1.A to E below refers to IAS 1's requirements, where appropriate.

The current portion of non-current financial assets would be classified as current, consistent with IFRS. *[IAS 1.68]*.

5.1.1.A   Operating cycle

Item (a) of the definition of non-current assets above distinguishes between current and non-current based on the length of the normal operating cycle. The concept of 'operating cycle' is not further explained in FRS 102 but IAS 1 states that 'the operating cycle of an entity is the time between the acquisition of assets for processing and their realisation in cash or cash equivalents. When the entity's normal operating cycle is not clearly identifiable, it is assumed to be twelve months.' *[IAS 1.68]*. IAS 1 does not provide any further guidance on how to determine if an entity's operating cycle is 'clearly identifiable'. In some businesses, the time involved in producing goods or providing services varies significantly from one customer project to another. In such cases, it may be difficult to determine what the normal operating cycle is. Management must consider all facts and circumstances and judgement to determine whether it is appropriate to consider that the operating cycle is clearly identifiable, or whether the twelve months default is to be used.

Chapter 6

IAS 1 further explains that when an entity supplies goods or services within a clearly identifiable operating cycle, separate classification of current and non-current assets and liabilities on the face of the statement of financial position provides useful information by distinguishing the net assets that are continuously circulating as working capital from those used in long-term operations. It also highlights assets that are expected to be realised within the current operating cycle, and liabilities that are due for settlement within the same period. *[IAS 1.62]*.

Current assets, therefore, include assets (such as inventories and trade receivables) that are sold, consumed or realised as part of the normal operating cycle even when they are not expected to be realised within twelve months after the reporting period. *[IAS 1.68]*.

5.1.1.B   Held for the purpose of trading

Current assets include assets held primarily for the purpose of trading, for example, some financial assets classified as trading in accordance with IFRS 9 – *Financial Instruments* – or IAS 39 – *Financial Instruments: Recognition and Measurement*, where these standards are applied to the recognition and measurement of financial instruments.

However, consistent with IFRS practice, a classification as 'held for trading' (e.g. as required for a derivative, that is not hedge accounted) does not necessarily mean the financial asset is 'held for the purpose of trading' for the purposes of current / non-current classification.

5.1.1.C   Assets previously classified as non-current but subsequently held for sale

FRS 102 does not include the concept in IFRS of non-current assets and disposal groups held for sale, and the adapted formats, therefore, do not require separate presentation for such items.

FRS 102 does not address whether items such as property, plant and equipment should be reclassified as current if expected to be realised within twelve months after the reporting period. In our view, an entity should generally continue to classify property, plant and equipment intended to be disposed of as non-current unless it is expected to be realised within 12 months after the reporting period (in which case it must be classified as current).

However, an entity that, in the course of its ordinary activities, routinely sells items of property, plant and equipment that it has held for rental to others, should transfer such assets to inventory when they cease to be rented and become held for sale, consistent with IFRS requirements. *[IAS 16.68A]*. See Chapter 15 at 3.7.1. The inventory should then be classified as current or non-current in accordance with the definitions at 5.1.1, with particular reference to item (a) of the definition of non-current asset.

5.1.1.D   Post-employment benefits

The question arises as to whether the current / non-current analysis needs to be made for defined benefit plan balances. IAS 19 – *Employee Benefits* – does not specify whether such a split should be made, on the grounds that it may sometimes be arbitrary. *[IAS 19.133, BC200]*. In practice, few if any IFRS reporters make this split.

No similar statement is included in FRS 102, but where the same concern over the arbitrary nature of a split arises, in our view, FRS 102 reporters are able to follow the practice of some IFRS reporters and report such balances as non-current.

5.1.2 Definitions of current liabilities and non-current liabilities (adapted formats only)

FRS 102 defines current liabilities, with non-current liabilities being 'liabilities of the entity which are not current liabilities' (i.e. the residual). *[FRS 102 Appendix I].*

Current liabilities are defined as liabilities of the entity which:

(a) it expects to settle in its normal operating cycle (see 5.1.2.A below);

(b) it holds primarily for the purpose of trading (see 5.1.2.B below);

(c) are due to be settled within 12 months after the reporting period (see 5.1.2.C below); or

(d) it does not have an unconditional right to defer settlement for at least 12 months after the reporting period (see 5.1.2.D below).

Meeting any one of (a) to (d) leads to the liability being required to be classified as current.

The adapted formats also require that deferred tax liabilities are always classified as non-current. *[FRS 102.4.2A(p)].*

5.1.2.A Operating cycle

The concept of 'operating cycle' is explained at 5.1.1.A above.

IAS 1 explains that some current liabilities, such as trade payables and some accruals for employee and other operating costs, are part of the working capital used in the normal operating cycle, and are classified as current liabilities even if they are due to be settled more than twelve months after the reporting period. The same normal operating cycle applies to the classification of an entity's assets and liabilities and when not clearly identifiable, is assumed to be twelve months. *[IAS 1.70].*

5.1.2.B Held for the purpose of trading

Current liabilities include assets held primarily for the purpose of trading, for example, some financial liabilities classified as trading in accordance with IAS 39 or IFRS 9.

However, consistent with IFRS practice, a classification as 'held for trading' (e.g. as required for a derivative, that is not hedge accounted) does not necessarily mean the financial liability is 'held for the purpose of trading' for the purposes of current / non-current classification.

5.1.2.C Due for settlement within 12 months

Some current liabilities are not settled as part of the normal operating cycle but are due for settlement within twelve months after the end of the reporting period. Examples given by IAS 1 include bank overdrafts, the current portion of non-current financial liabilities, dividends payable, income taxes and other non-trade payables.

Financial liabilities that provide financing on a long-term basis (i.e. are not part of the working capital used in the entity's normal operating cycle) and are not due for settlement within twelve months after the end of the reporting period are

Chapter 6

non-current liabilities. *[IAS 1.71]*. As explained at 5.1.2.D below, there must be an unconditional right, as at the end of the reporting period, to defer settlement for at least twelve months thereafter, in order for a liability to be reported as non-current.

5.1.2.D   No unconditional right to defer settlement

The assessment of a liability as current or non-current is applied strictly. IAS 1 provides further guidance on this part of the current liability definition.

The key point is that for a liability to be classified as non-current requires that the entity has, *at the end of the reporting period*, an unconditional right to defer its settlement for at least twelve months thereafter. Consequently, a liability is classified as current when:

- it is due to be settled within twelve months after the reporting period even if the original term was for a period longer than twelve months and an agreement to refinance or reschedule payments, on a long-term basis is completed after the reporting period and before the financial statements are authorised for issue; *[IAS 1.72, 76]*

- an entity breaches a provision of a long-term loan arrangement on or before the end of the reporting period, with the effect that the liability becomes payable on demand (even if the lender agreed, after the reporting period and before the authorisation of the financial statements for issue, not to demand payment as a consequence of the breach). *[IAS 1.74, 76]*.

However, the liability would be classified as non-current if the lender agreed by the end of the reporting period to provide a period of grace ending at least twelve months after the reporting period, within which the entity can rectify the breach and during which the lender cannot demand immediate repayment. *[IAS 1.75]*.

Accordingly, as explained in IAS 1, liabilities would be non-current if an entity expects, and has the discretion, to refinance or roll over an obligation for at least twelve months after the reporting period under an existing loan facility, even if it would otherwise be due within a shorter period. However, when refinancing or rolling over the obligation is not at the discretion of the entity, the obligation is classified as current. *[IAS 1.73]*.

Section 11 – *Basic Financial Instruments* – requires specific disclosures where there is a breach of terms or other default in respect of a loan payable recognised at the end of the reporting period (see Chapter 10 at 11.2.3). A qualifying entity that is not a financial institution preparing individual financial statements is exempt from this disclosure (under the reduced disclosure framework), providing that the equivalent disclosures required by the standard are given in the publicly available consolidated financial statements of the group in which the qualifying entity is consolidated. *[FRS 102.1.8, 1.12(c), 11.47]*.

Conditions of breach or default at the end of the reporting period may, however, be material for disclosure in the financial statements (even if no specific disclosure applies), whether adapted formats or statutory formats are applied. A breach or default arising (or its rectification) after the end of the reporting period, while not one of the examples specifically listed in Section 32 – *Events after the End of the Reporting Period*, may be a material post-balance sheet event requiring disclosure (see Chapter 29 at 3.5.2) *[FRS 102.32.10-11]*, and may also be relevant to the going concern assessment and related disclosures (see 9.3 below).

Example 6.2 below illustrates the operation of the above requirements.

Example 6.2: **Determining whether liabilities should be presented as current or non-current**

Scenario 1

An entity has a long-term loan arrangement containing a debt covenant. The specific requirements in the debt covenant have to be met as at 31 December every year. The loan is due in more than 12 months. The entity breaches the debt covenant at or before the period end. As a result, the loan becomes payable on demand.

Scenario 2

Same as scenario 1, but the loan arrangement stipulates that the entity has a grace period of 3 months to rectify the breach and during which the lender cannot demand immediate repayment.

Scenario 3

Same as scenario 1, but the lender agreed not to demand repayment as a consequence of the breach. The entity obtains this waiver:

(a) at or before the period end and the waiver is for a period of more than 12 months after the period end;

(b) at or before the period end and the waiver is for a period of less than 12 months after the period end;

(c) after the period end but before the financial statements are authorised for issue.

Scenario 4

An entity has a long-term loan arrangement containing a debt covenant. The loan is due in more than 12 months. At the period end, the debt covenants are met. However, circumstances change unexpectedly and the entity breaches the debt covenant after the period end but before the financial statements are authorised for issue.

As discussed at Chapter 10 at 11.2.3, Section 11 (subject to any exemption taken under the reduced disclosure framework in individual accounts of a qualifying entity) requires the following disclosures for any loans payable recognised at the reporting date, for which there is a breach of terms or default of principal, interest, sinking fund, or redemption terms that has not been remedied by the reporting date:

• details of that breach or default;

• the carrying amount of the related loans payable at the reporting date; and

• whether the breach or default was remedied, or the terms of the loans payable were renegotiated, before the financial statements were authorised for issue. *[FRS 102.1.8, 1.12(c), 11.47].*

The table below sets out whether debt is to be presented as current or non-current and whether the above disclosures are required.

	Scenario 1	Scenario 2	Scenario 3(a)	Scenario 3(b)	Scenario 3(c)	Scenario 4
At the period end, does the entity have an unconditional right to defer the settlement of the liability for at least 12 months?	no	no	yes	no	no	yes
Classification of the liability	current	current	non-current	current	current	non-current
Are the above Section 11 disclosures required?	yes	yes	no	yes	yes	no

5.1.2.E   Post-employment benefits

Refer to the discussion at 5.1.1.D above. In our view, where the same concern over the arbitrary nature of a split arises, FRS 102 reporters are able to follow the practice of some IFRS reporters and report such balances as non-current.

5.1.3   *Property, plant and equipment*

FRS 102 defines 'property, plant and equipment' as tangible assets that:

- are held for use in the production or supply of goods or services, for rental to others, or for administrative purposes; and

- are expected to be used during more than one period. *[FRS 102 Appendix I].*

See Chapter 15 at 3.2 and 3.3. Investment property is a separate classification from property, plant and equipment but sometimes an investment property may have mixed use, e.g. partly used for rental and partly for owner occupation. A component for property, plant and equipment may be required to be separated (see 5.1.4 below).

Specific types of assets that may be recorded as property, plant and equipment in certain circumstances are discussed below. Chapter 15 at 3.3.1.B, 3.3.1.E and 3.3.1.F also addresses other less common classification issues including: environmental and safety equipment; the classification of items as inventory or property, plant and equipment where minimum levels are maintained; and the production stripping costs of mines.

Where adapted formats are used, FRS 102 requires that sub-classifications of property, plant and equipment that are appropriate to the entity are presented, either on the face of the statement of financial position or in the notes. *[FRS 102.4.2B(a)].*

5.1.3.A   *Heritage assets*

FRS 102 sets out separate requirements for heritage assets, being tangible and intangible assets with historic, artistic, scientific, technological, geophysical or environmental qualities that are held and maintained principally for their contribution to knowledge and culture (see Chapter 31 at 5). *[FRS 102 Appendix I].* Therefore, heritage assets can in principle be tangible or intangible assets.

5.1.3.B   *Exploration and evaluation of mineral resources*

IFRS 6 – *Exploration for and Evaluation of Mineral Resources*, which is applied by FRS 102 reporters operating in the exploration for and / or evaluation of mineral resources, *[FRS 102.34.11],* requires entities within its scope to classify exploration and evaluation assets as either intangible or tangible assets according to the nature of the assets acquired and apply the classification consistently. *[IFRS 6.15].*

For example, drilling rights should be presented as intangible assets, whereas vehicles and drilling rigs are tangible assets. A tangible asset that is used in developing an intangible asset should still be presented as a tangible asset. However, 'to the extent that a tangible asset is consumed in developing an intangible asset, the amount reflecting that consumption is part of the cost of the intangible asset'. For example, the depreciation of a portable drilling rig would be capitalised as part of the intangible exploration and evaluation asset that represents the costs incurred on active exploration projects. *[IFRS 6.16, BC33].* See Chapter 31 at 3.

5.1.3.C   *Service concession arrangements*

FRS 102 distinguishes two principal categories of service concession arrangements: a financial asset model and an intangible asset model. Sometimes, a service concession arrangement may contain both types *[FRS 102.34.13-15]* (see Chapter 31 at 4).

However, Section 35 – *Transition to this FRS* – permits first-time adopters (that are operators of service concession arrangements) to continue to account for service concession arrangements entered into before the date of transition using the same accounting policies as applied at the date of transition (see Chapter 32 at 5.10). *[FRS 102.35.10(i)]*. FRS 5 Application Note F – *Private Finance Initiative and Similar Contracts* – distinguished between arrangements where the property was the asset of the operator (and a tangible fixed asset was recognised) and where the property was the asset of the grantor / purchaser (and a financial asset / debtor was recognised by the operator). Where the transition exemption is taken, the previous UK GAAP classification would continue to be used.

5.1.3.D   Software development costs

The definition of an intangible asset within Section 18 requires that it is an identifiable non-monetary asset without physical substance. *[FRS 102.18.2, FRS 102 Appendix I]*. However, intangible assets can be contained in or on a physical medium such as a compact disc (in the case of computer software), legal documentation (in the case of a licence or patent) or film, requiring an entity to exercise judgement in determining whether to apply Section 17 or Section 18. FRS 102 provides no further guidance on this issue. Management may consider, as permitted by the hierarchy in Section 10, the guidance in IAS 38 – *Intangible Assets*, which has the same definition of an intangible asset. See Chapter 15 at 3.3.1.D and Chapter 16 at 3.2.2 and 4.1 for discussion of the classification of such costs. Some entities may have reclassified such costs compared to previous UK GAAP on transition to FRS 102.

5.1.3.E   Spare parts and similar equipment

Spare parts, stand-by equipment and servicing equipment are recognised in accordance with Section 17 when they meet the definition of property, plant and equipment. Otherwise, such items are classified as inventory. *[FRS 102.17.5]*. See Chapter 15 at 3.3.1.A for further discussion of this requirement.

5.1.4   Investment property

The definition of investment property is explained in Chapter 14 at 3.1. As this definition differs from that in previous UK GAAP, some entities may have reclassified items on transition to FRS 102. Sometimes, also, property may have mixed use (e.g. partly owner-occupied and partly held for rental) which may be required to be split into components for investment property and property, plant and equipment. See Chapter 14 at 3.1.7 and Chapter 15 at 3.3.4.

Only investment property at fair value through profit and loss is required to be presented as a separate line item on the face of the statement of financial position in adapted formats (see Figure 6.3 at 5.1 above). *[FRS 102.4.2A(b)]*. It is not clear whether the standard intends that investment property accounted for using the cost model (in Section 17) is subsumed within the line item for property, plant and equipment or not. However, since investment property accounted for using the cost model does not strictly fall within FRS 102's definition of property, plant and equipment and has a different function, in our view, it may be appropriate, where material, to include additional line items or headings in the statement of financial position to distinguish investment property accounted for at cost. *[FRS 102.4.3]*.

5.1.5   Intangible assets

FRS 102's definition of an intangible asset is discussed in detail in Chapter 16 at 3.2. Specific types of assets that may sometimes fall to be classified as intangible assets and sometimes as property, plant and equipment are discussed at 5.1.3.A to 5.1.3.D above.

Where adapted formats are used, FRS 102 requires that sub-classifications of intangible assets and goodwill appropriate to the entity are presented, either on the face of the statement of financial position or in the notes. *[FRS 102.4.2B(b)]*.

5.1.5.A   Goodwill and negative goodwill

FRS 102 does not specify that positive goodwill is shown as a separate line item on the face of the statement of financial position in adapted formats but requires that sub-classifications of intangible assets and goodwill appropriate to the entity are presented, either on the face of the statement of financial position or in the notes. *[FRS 102.4.2A, 4.2B(b)]*.

Goodwill does not strictly fall within the definition of an intangible asset since it is not identifiable; therefore, we would expect that entities disclose positive goodwill, if material, separately on the face of the statement of financial position. *[FRS 102.4.3]*. Indeed, presentation of goodwill on the face of the statement of financial position does appear to be implied by the requirements in Section 19 – *Business Combinations and Goodwill* – for presentation of negative goodwill, as described below.

Where the acquirer's interest in the net amount of the identifiable assets, liabilities and provisions for contingent liabilities recognised exceeds the cost of the business combination, FRS 102 requires that the resulting excess (i.e. 'negative goodwill') is separately disclosed on the face of the statement of financial position, immediately below positive goodwill, and followed by a subtotal of the net amount of the positive goodwill and the excess. *[FRS 102.19.24(b)]*. See Chapter 17 at 3.8.3.

5.1.6   Financial assets and financial liabilities

FRS 102 requires the following line items to be presented on the face of the statement of financial position (see Figure 6.3 at 5.1 above): *[FRS 102.4.2A]*

(d)   financial assets (excluding items shown under (e), (f), (j) and (k)) (see Chapter 10);

(e)   investments in associates (see Chapter 12);

(f)   investments in jointly controlled entities (see Chapter 13);

(j)   trade and other receivables;

(k)   cash and cash equivalents (see Chapter 7);

(l)   trade and other payables; and

(n)   financial liabilities (excluding items shown under (l) and (m)) (see Chapter 10).

'Cash or cash equivalents' are defined in the FRS 102 Glossary and should be interpreted in a manner consistent with Section 7 (see Chapter 7).

FRS 102 requires that investments in associates and investments in jointly controlled entities are presented as separate line items in adapted formats for both individual and consolidated financial statements. Unlike IAS 1, 'investments in associates and jointly controlled entities accounted using the equity method' (which is only permitted in FRS 102 consolidated financial statements) are not required to be separately presented. However, the 'share of the profit or loss of investments in associates and jointly controlled entities accounted for using the equity method' is a separate line item in the adapted formats for the statement of comprehensive income (or separate income statement, where the two-statement form is used) (see 6.5 below). *[FRS 102.5.5B(c), 5.7A]*.

FRS 102 requires additional line items, headings and sub-headings (where material) to be presented in the statement of financial position, where relevant to an understanding of the financial position. *[FRS 102.4.3]*. This might be the case, for example, where investments in associates and investments in jointly controlled entities are required to be held as part of an investment portfolio at fair value through profit or loss in consolidated financial statements. *[FRS 102.14.4A-B, 15.9A-B]*. See Chapter 12 at 3.3.1.B and Chapter 13 at 3.6.3.B.

Where adapted formats are used, FRS 102 requires that further sub-classifications are presented, either on the face of the statement of financial position or in the notes, for: *[FRS 102.4.2B(c), (d), (f)]*

(a) investments, showing separately shares and loans;

(b) trade and other receivables, showing separately amounts due from related parties (same definition as for Section 33 – *Related Party Disclosures* – as discussed in Chapter 30 at 3.1), amounts due from other parties, prepayments and receivables arising from accrued income not billed; and

(c) trade and other payables, showing separately amounts payable to trade suppliers, payable to related parties, deferred income and accruals.

FRS 102 does not define 'investment'. Nevertheless, (a) above requires the reporting entity to disclose financial assets constituting investments, distinguishing between shares and loans. Where loans are involved, this is likely to require judgement as to whether the loan is in the nature of an investment or is an 'other receivable' (see 5.3.4.A below).

The sub-classifications at (b) and (c) are similar to but not the same as the line items required where the statutory formats are applied. See 5.1.13.B below for discussion of the classification of contract assets and liabilities. FRS 102 further requires the carrying amounts at the reporting date of financial assets and financial liabilities measured at fair value through profit or loss to be disclosed either in the statement of financial position or in the notes. The disclosure may be made separately by category of financial instrument. Financial liabilities that are not held as part of a trading portfolio and are not derivatives shall be shown separately. *[FRS 102.11.41]*.

This analysis only applies to financial assets and liabilities that are in scope of Sections 11 or 12, or IFRS 9, or IAS 39 whichever standard is applied to the recognition and measurement of financial instruments. *[FRS 102.11.2, 11.7, 12.2, 12.3-5]*. See Chapter 10 at 11.2.3. The above disclosures (with the exception of those relating to measurement at fair value through profit and loss) are not required in individual financial statements of a qualifying entity that is not a financial institution using the reduced disclosure framework, providing that the equivalent disclosures required by the standard are given in the publicly available consolidated financial statements of the group in which the qualifying entity is consolidated. *[FRS 102.1.8, 1.12(c)]*.

Chapter 6

5.1.7   *Biological assets*

FRS 102 defines a biological asset as 'a living animal or plant'. *[FRS 102 Appendix I]*. Section 34 – *Specialised Activities* – provides an accounting policy choice, for each class of biological asset (and its related agricultural produce), to apply the fair value model or cost model (see Chapter 31 at 2).

Where adapted formats are applied, an entity must present separately on the face of the statement of financial position: *[FRS 102.4.2A(g)-(h)]*

- biological assets carried at cost less accumulated depreciation and impairment; and
- biological assets carried at fair value through profit and loss.

5.1.8   *Inventories*

Where adapted formats are used, FRS 102 requires that inventories are shown on the face of the statement of financial position. *[FRS 102.4.2A(i)]*.

An analysis of inventories, sub-classified between (a) to (c) below, is presented either on the face of the statement of financial position or in the notes. *[FRS 102.4.2B(e)]*.

FRS 102 defines inventories as assets: *[FRS 102 Appendix I, FRS 102.13.1]*

(a)   held for sale in the ordinary course of business; or

(b)   in the process of production for such sale; or

(c)   in the form of materials or supplies to be consumed in the production process or in the rendering of services.

See Chapter 11 at 3.2 which addresses scope issues relevant to classification of inventories such as:

- classification of core inventories as property, plant and equipment or inventories;
- classification of broadcast rights as intangible assets or inventory;
- spare parts and servicing equipment (see below); and
- real estate inventory held for short term sale.

Inventories also include 'inventories held for distribution at no or nominal consideration', which could include items distributed to beneficiaries by public benefit entities (such as charities) and some advertising and promotional material (such as brochures not despatched). *[FRS 102.13.4A, 18.8C(d), Appendix III.36]*. See Chapter 11 at 3.3.11.

Inventories also include agricultural produce harvested from biological assets (e.g. grapes, milk or felled trees – see Chapter 11 at 3.3.12 and Chapter 31 at 2.3) and work in progress arising under construction contracts, including directly related service contracts (see 5.1.13.B below). *[FRS 102.13.2]*. Service providers may also have inventories, effectively their work in progress (see Chapter 11 at 3.3.10).

Spare parts and servicing equipment are carried as inventory and recognised in profit or loss as consumed unless they meet the definition of property, plant and equipment. *[FRS 102.17.5]*.

Sometimes, assets not categorised as inventories are later transferred to inventories. An example is a property previously held as an investment property, which is transferred to inventory because it is reclassified as property under development with a view to sale. While FRS 102 is not as explicit as IFRSs, properties under development with a view to sale would fall within its definition of inventories. *[FRS 102.16.9, 16.10(e)(iv), IAS 40.57(b)].* Another example is where a car rental company acquires vehicles with the intention of holding them as rental cars for a limited period and then selling them. Chapter 15 at 3.7.1 addresses the accounting for such transfer, based on the requirements of IFRS, i.e. they are transferred to inventories at their carrying amount when they cease to be rented and become held for sale. The subsequent sale of such assets is presented gross (i.e. revenue and cost of sales). *[IAS 16.68A].*

5.1.9   Provisions

A provision is defined as a liability of uncertain timing or amount. *[FRS 102 Appendix I].* See Chapter 19 at 3.

Provisions that are current and non-current will need to be reported as separate classifications in adapted formats (unlike for balance sheet statutory formats, where there is a single line item for provisions for liabilities).

5.1.10   Current tax

Current tax assets and current tax liabilities must be shown as separate line items on the face of the statement of financial position, classified as appropriate as current and / or non-current.

FRS 102 includes rules on offset of current tax assets and liabilities (see Chapter 26 at 10.1.1). *[FRS 102.29.24].*

FRS 102 defines current tax as the amount of income tax payable (refundable) in respect of the taxable profit (tax loss) for the current period or past reporting periods. *[FRS 102.29.2, FRS 102 Appendix I].* See Chapter 26 at 3 for discussion of what is 'income tax' under FRS 102, which is relevant to classification.

5.1.11   Deferred tax

Deferred tax assets and liabilities must be shown as separate line items on the face of the statement of financial position, but classified as non-current. *[FRS 102.4.2A].*

FRS 102 includes rules on offset of deferred tax assets and liabilities (see Chapter 26 at 10.1.1). *[FRS 102.29.24A].*

Section 29 – *Income Tax* – requires deferred tax liabilities to be presented within provisions for liabilities and deferred tax assets to be presented within debtors unless an entity has chosen to adopt the adapted formats in which case they are required to be disclosed separately and classified as non-current. *[FRS 102.29.23].*

Chapter 6

Certain of the statutory disclosures in the Regulations (and LLP Regulations) may cause particular complexity because under the statutory formats, deferred tax is included as a line item within provisions. In particular, UK companies preparing Companies Act accounts must state the provision for deferred tax separately from any other tax provisions and reconcile movements in deferred tax (as it is a line item under provisions). *[1 Sch 59-60, 1 Sch 57-58 (LLP)]*. See 5.3.11 and 5.3.13.B below. In our view, this disclosure is also likely required where adapted formats are used, even though deferred tax is not shown as a provision in the balance sheet.

5.1.12   Equity

Equity attributable to the owners of the parent, and to non-controlling interest (see 4.5 above) must be presented as separate line items within equity.

Where adapted formats are used, separate sub-classifications for classes of equity such as: share capital, share premium, retained earnings, revaluation reserve, fair value reserve and other reserves are required, either on the face of the statement of financial position or in the notes. *[FRS 102.4.2B(g)]*. This list mirrors the classes of equity that are required to be shown on the face of the balance sheet (or in respect of the fair value reserve, may be presented in the notes) where the statutory formats are applied. See 5.3.12 below for further explanation of these reserves.

The amount of the revaluation reserve must be shown in the balance sheet under a separate sub-heading in the position given for the item 'revaluation reserve' under 'Capital and reserves' of the statutory balance sheet formats. *[1 Sch 35(2)]*. The adapted formats do not include the same headings as set out in the format 1 or format 2 balance sheets in the statutory formats (see 5.2 below). However, in our view, this requirement means that the revaluation reserve should be presented on the face of the statement of financial position (in order to give equivalent information to the statutory formats). Indeed, for the same reason, we would encourage entities to present on the face of the statement of financial position the classes of equity that would be so required, if statutory formats were used.

FRS 102's requirement to present a statement of changes in equity and the disclosures in the Regulations and LLP Regulations relating to reserves are discussed at 7 below.

5.1.13   Other application issues

5.1.13.A   Lease premiums

Under IAS 17 – *Leases*, premiums relating to an operating lease over land and / or buildings are classified as a prepayment (albeit there may be a non-current element). Such payments would not be classified as property, plant and equipment under IFRSs. The definitions of property, plant and equipment in FRS 102 (and IFRSs) are similar and, consequently, in our view, it would be appropriate to report an upfront operating lease premium as a prepayment under FRS 102, classified as appropriate as current or non-current.

5.1.13.B   Construction contracts

The percentage of completion method is applied to construction contracts and revenue from rendering services. *[FRS 102.23.21]*. See Chapter 20 at 3.11 for further discussion of construction contracts.

FRS 102 requires that, for construction contracts, an entity shall present the gross amount due from customers for contract work as an asset, and the gross amount due to customers for contract work as a liability. *[FRS 102.23.32]*. The Triennial review 2017 added additional guidance on how these two amounts are determined. *[FRS 102.23.33-34]*. See Chapter 20 at 3.11.

While FRS 102 implies that a single contract asset (being the aggregate of contracts in an asset position) and / or a single contract liability (being the aggregate of contracts in a liability position) should be presented (rather than disaggregated across several lines), there is no requirement to present these on the face of the statement of financial position. This is left to the judgement of the reporting entity, but FRS 102 requires additional line items, headings and subtotals when relevant to an understanding of the entity's financial position. *[FRS 102.4.3]*.

Where adapted formats are used, certain sub-classifications of trade and other receivables and trade and other payables must be presented, either on the face of the statement of financial position or in the notes (see 5.1.6 above). This requirement would also apply to contract assets and contract liabilities presented within these line items on the face of the statement of financial position. Contract assets and liabilities are akin to accrued income not billed and deferred income, but should be presented separately. *[FRS 102.23.32]*. Where material prepayments, inventory or advance payment creditors have been included in the contract balances (see discussion below), we consider that it may be appropriate to distinguish these amounts. In addition, it would be appropriate to show separately contract balances with related parties and others.

Where it is probable that the total contract costs will exceed total contract revenue, FRS 102 requires immediate recognition of the expected loss and a corresponding provision for an onerous contract (and cross refers to Section 21 – *Provisions and Contingencies*). *[FRS 102.23.26]*. Whilst this could imply that the provision element of the overall contract liability is to be presented within provisions, we consider it more likely that the standard is intending a single contract asset and liability to be presented (as was required previously by IAS 11 – *Construction Contracts*, the IFRS on which this part of Section 23 is derived). However, we would expect that full disclosures for provisions in accordance with Section 21 (and the statutory requirements for a UK company (or LLP) included in the Regulations (or LLP Regulations)) are provided, regardless of the presentation adopted.

Chapter 6

Where the stage of completion is determined by reference to contract costs incurred for work performed to date as a proportion of estimated total costs, costs relating to future activity, such as for materials or prepayments, are excluded. *[FRS 102.23.22(a)]*. Such costs are, however, recognised as an asset, where it is probable that the costs will be recovered. *[FRS 102.23.23]*. FRS 102 does not address the classification of such assets, e.g. whether part of the contract asset or liability, or as separate inventory or prepayments (but IAS 11, from which this part of Section 23 is derived, comments that such costs are often classified as contract work in progress). *[IAS 11.27]*.

FRS 102 requires that the contract asset or liability is determined after deducting progress billings. *[FRS 102.23.33, 23.34]*. FRS 102 does not address the presentation of advances but in the Illustrative Examples to IAS 11, from which this part of Section 23 is derived, advances are not included in the determination of the contract asset or liability but are shown separately.

Progress billings not yet received (including any contract retentions) would be included in trade receivables.

5.1.13.C   Assets and disposal groups held for sale

FRS 102 does not include a concept of assets and disposal groups held for sale, comparable to that in IFRS 5 – *Non-current Assets Held for Sale and Discontinued Operations.*

FRS 102, therefore, does not require an entity to present a non-current asset classified as held for sale or the assets of a disposal group held for sale separately from other assets in the statement of financial position, nor the liabilities of a disposal group held for sale separately from other liabilities in the statement of financial position. *[IFRS 5.38, IAS 1.54]*.

This does not preclude entities presenting additional analysis in the notes to the financial statements but it would be odd to show a classification that simply does not exist in FRS 102. See also the disclosures at 5.5 below.

5.1.13.D   Post-employment benefit assets and liabilities

FRS 102, like IFRSs does not specify where in the statement of financial position a net asset or net liability in respect of a defined benefit plan should be presented, nor whether such balances should be shown separately on the face of the statement of financial position or only in the notes. This is left to the judgement of the reporting entity, but FRS 102 requires additional line items, headings and subtotals when relevant to an understanding of the entity's financial position. *[FRS 102.4.3]*. Classification of post-employment benefit assets and liabilities as current or non-current is discussed at 5.1.1.D and 5.1.2.E above.

Employers with more than one plan may find that some are in surplus while others are in deficit. The general rules in FRS 102 prohibit offsetting of such balances. *[FRS 102.2.52]*. Deferred tax is presented separately from defined benefit pensions balances.

See 5.3.13.D below for discussion of disclosures also relevant to a UK company preparing Companies Act accounts (or an LLP preparing non-IAS accounts).

5.1.13.E   Compound instruments

FRS 102 requires that an entity issuing a convertible or compound instrument must allocate the proceeds between the liability component and the equity component. *[FRS 102.22.13]*. This classification is permitted by the Regulations (and LLP Regulations) which require that, in determining how amounts are presented within items in the balance sheet, the directors of the company (or the members of the LLP) must have regard to the substance of the reported transaction or arrangement, in accordance with generally accepted accounting principles or practice (see 4.4 above). *[1 Sch 9, 1 Sch 9 (LLP)]*.

Appendix 2 of Technical Release 02/17BL: *Guidance on Realised and Distributable Profits under the Companies Act 2006* ('TECH 02/17BL') includes numerical illustrations of the treatment of compound instruments.

5.1.13.F   Government grants

FRS 102 sets out two models for recognising government grants – the accrual model and the performance model (see Chapter 21).

Where the performance model is used, FRS 102 states that grants received before the revenue recognition criteria are satisfied are recognised as a liability. *[FRS 102.24.5B(c)]*.

Where the accrual model is used, FRS 102 requires that government grants related to assets are recognised in income on a systematic basis over the expected useful life of the asset. Where part of a grant relating to an asset is deferred, it is recognised as deferred income and not deducted from the carrying amount of the asset. *[FRS 102.24.5F-G]*. FRS 102 does not address the presentation where a grant has been received but does not meet the recognition criteria (in paragraph 24.3A), but it would be logical to present this as a liability rather than deferred income (consistent with the requirement for the performance model).

While FRS 102 does not require government grants to be presented separately on the face of the statement of financial position, the standard specifically requires disclosure of the nature and amounts of grants recognised in the financial statements. *[FRS 102.24.6(b)]*.

5.1.14   Illustrative statement of financial position (adapted formats)

Example 6.3 illustrates a statement of financial position using the adapted formats. This includes some additional line items to those listed in Figure 6.3 at 5.1 above. Situations when additional line items may be or are required to be presented are explained at 5.1 above.

Chapter 6

Example 6.3:   Illustrative statement of financial position (adapted formats)

XYZ GROUP – STATEMENT OF FINANCIAL POSITION AS AT
31 DECEMBER 201Y

	£'000 201Y	£'000 201X
ASSETS		
Non-current assets		
Property, plant and equipment	85,050	69,423
Investment property carried at fair value through profit or loss	20,080	19,560
Goodwill	78,003	91,200
Other intangible assets	65,270	78,000
Investments in associates	34,000	28,800
Investments in jointly controlled assets	38,050	28,800
Biological assets carried at cost	44,000	56,000
Deferred tax	10,563	9,765
	375,016	352,748
Current assets		
Inventories	45,080	28,333
Trade and other receivables	38,789	45,634
Cash and cash equivalents	31,200	56,445
	115,069	130,412
Total assets	490,085	483,160
Trade and other payables	63,566	44,289
Current portion of long-term borrowings	50,000	50,000
Financial liabilities – derivatives	10,200	5,436
Provisions	14,350	—
Total current liabilities	138,116	99,725
Non-current liabilities		
Deferred tax	39,679	46,555
Long-term borrowings	150,000	200,000
Financial liabilities – derivatives	20,789	18,423
Provisions	27,600	—
Defined benefit pension plan	66,341	81,977
Total non-current liabilities	304,409	346,955
Total liabilities	442,525	446,680
Net assets	47,560	36,480
EQUITY		
Share capital	12,075	10,000
Share premium	500	500
Revaluation reserve	3,300	3,100
Other reserves	5,976	(774)
Fair value reserve – cash flow hedges	1,859	2,524
Retained earnings	23,521	21,008
Equity attributable to owners of the parent	47,231	36,358
Non-controlling interests	329	122
Total equity	47,560	36,480

5.2 Statutory formats – format 1 Balance Sheet

Section B of Part 1 of Schedule 1 to the Regulations (and Section B of Part 1 of Schedule 1 to the LLP Regulations) provide a choice of two statutory formats for the balance sheet. Format 1 is a vertical format and is adopted by virtually all UK companies and LLPs. Format 2 presents assets separately from capital, reserves and liabilities and is rarely used.

This chapter discusses only the format 1 balance sheets applicable to companies (other than banking or insurance companies) and LLPs. The formats in Schedule 3 applicable to insurance companies and groups are discussed in Chapter 33 at 8. This publication does not discuss the formats in Schedule 2 applicable to banking companies and groups. See 4.1 and 4.2 above for discussion as to which formats apply to which types of entity.

Each of the headings and sub-headings denoted with a capital letter or Roman numeral, as set out in Figure 6.4 below, must be presented on the face of the format 1 balance sheet for the individual accounts in the order and under the headings and sub-headings given. The format 1 balance sheet includes sub-headings, denoted with an Arabic number, which though shown in Figure 6.4, can be (and often are in practice) presented in the notes to the accounts. The General Rules to the formats (see 4.4 above) explain further the presentation of line items with an Arabic number. The individual line items in the format 1 balance sheet are discussed respectively at 5.3 below.

The line items in the formats need to be read together with the notes to the formats in Part 1 of Section B of Schedule 1 to the Regulations and Part 1 of Section B of Schedule 1 to the LLP Regulations. *[1 Sch 1, 1 Sch 1 (LLP)].*

The modifications required to format 1 in a UK company's group accounts are:

- the identification of non-controlling interests (see 4.5 above); and
- the sub-heading 'Participating interests' (item B III.3 in format 1) is replaced by 'Interests in associated undertakings' and 'Other participating interests' (see 5.3.4.D and 5.3.4.E below). *[6 Sch 17, 6 Sch 20].*

The General Rules to the formats (see 4.4 above) must be complied with.

Chapter 6

Figure 6.4   *Format 1 individual balance sheet (UK company other than a banking company or insurance company)*

A	Called up share capital not paid*		
B	Fixed assets		
	I		Intangible assets
		1	Development costs
		2	Concessions, patents, licences, trade marks and similar rights and assets
		3	Goodwill
		4	Payments on account
	II		Tangible assets
		1	Land and buildings
		2	Plant and machinery
		3	Fixtures, fittings, tools and equipment
		4	Payments on account and assets in course of construction
	III		Investments
		1	Shares in group undertakings
		2	Loans to group undertakings
		3	Participating interests**
		4	Loans to undertakings in which the company has a participating interest
		5	Other investments other than loans
		6	Other loans
		7	Own shares#
C	Current assets		
	I		Stocks
		1	Raw materials and consumables
		2	Work in progress
		3	Finished goods and goods for resale
		4	Payments on account
	II		Debtors
		1	Trade debtors
		2	Amounts owed by group undertakings
		3	Amounts owed by undertakings in which the company has a participating interest
		4	Other debtors
		5	Called up share capital not paid*
		6	Prepayments and accrued income*
	III		Investments
		1	Shares in group undertakings
		2	Own shares
		3	Other investments
	IV		Cash at bank and in hand
D	Prepayments and accrued income*		
E	Creditors: amounts falling due within one year		
		1	Debenture loans
		2	Bank loans and overdrafts
		3	Payments received on account
		4	Trade creditors
		5	Bills of exchange payable
		6	Amounts owed by group undertakings
		7	Amounts owed to undertakings in which the company has a participating interest
		8	Other creditors including taxation and social security
		9	Accruals and deferred income*

F	Net current assets (liabilities)		
G	Total assets less current liabilities		
H	Creditors: amounts falling due after more than one year		
		1	Debenture loans
		2	Bank loans and overdrafts
		3	Payments received on account
		4	Trade creditors
		5	Bills of exchange payable
		6	Amounts owed by group undertakings
		7	Amounts owed to undertakings in which the company has a participating interest
		8	Other creditors including taxation and social security
		9	Accruals and deferred income*
I	Provisions for liabilities		
		1	Pensions and similar obligations
		2	Taxation, including deferred taxation
		3	Other provisions
J	Accruals and deferred income*		
K	Capital and reserves**		
	I		Called up share capital
	II		Share premium account
	III		Revaluation reserve
	IV		Other reserves
		1	Capital redemption reserve
		2	Reserve for own shares
		3	Reserves provided for by the articles of association
		4	Other reserves, including the fair value reserve
	V		Profit and loss account

*   The notes to format 1 provide alternative positions for prepayments and accrued income, and accruals and deferred income, as sub-headings at C-II.6 (for prepayments and accrued income) and at E.9 and H.9 (for accruals and deferred income). Called up share capital not paid may also be shown at C-II.5.

** Modifications required in group accounts (see discussion above Figure 6.4)

\#   This presentation would not be consistent with FRS 102 which would show own shares as a deduction from equity. [FRS 102.22.16]

See 5.2.1 below for modification of the format 1 balance sheet for LLPs.

An entity is required to present additional line items, headings and subtotals in the statement of financial position when such presentation is relevant to an understanding of the entity's financial position. *[FRS 102.4.3]*. Judgement is needed in determining whether additional items should be presented, where material and relevant (see discussion, including relevant IAS 1 guidance at 5.1 above). Any amendments would need to comply with the General Rules to the formats (see 4.4 above).

FRS 102, like IFRSs, has accounting requirements for various items that do not have separate line items in format 1, but which would be presented separately on the face of the statement of financial position under IAS 1. Such items include investment property, financial assets, biological assets, cash and cash equivalents and deferred tax. FRS 102 generally requires separate disclosures of the amounts of these items in the notes to the financial statements (and sometimes requires reconciliations of the movements in the balances of such items). As noted above, FRS 102 requires additional line items to be presented on the face of the statement of financial position where relevant to an understanding of the entity's financial position. So, for example, a property company may distinguish its investment property from other tangible fixed assets. The presentation of additional line items might require use of boxes and subtotals in order to comply with the balance sheet statutory formats.

5.2.1   Modifications of format 1 balance sheet for LLPs

The main headings in the format 1 balance sheet in the LLP Regulations differ to those in Figure 6.4 at 5.2 above in the following respects:

- A – Called up share capital is omitted so the main headings are A – Fixed Assets to I – Accruals and deferred income.

- There is an additional item J – Loans and other debts due to members. The following amounts must be shown separately under this item – the aggregate amount of money advanced to the LLP by the members by way of loan, the aggregate amount of money owed to members by the LLP in respect of profits, and any other amounts.

- In addition, K – Capital and reserves is replaced with K – Members' other interests (with sub-headings K.I – Members' capital, K.II – Revaluation reserve and K.III – Other reserves, including the fair value reserve).

The subheadings in format 1 for LLPs are generally similar to format 1 for companies (apart from referring to LLPs and differences related to above).

As explained at 5.2 above, the format 1 balance sheet includes sub-headings denoted with an Arabic number, which though shown in Figure 6.5, can be (and often are in practice) presented in the notes to the accounts.

Figure 6.5   *Format 1 individual balance sheet (for an LLP)*

A			Fixed assets
	I		Intangible assets
		1	Development costs
		2	Concessions, patents, licences, trade marks and similar rights and assets
		3	Goodwill
		4	Payments on account
	II		Tangible assets
		1	Land and buildings
		2	Plant and machinery
		3	Fixtures, fittings, tools and equipment
		4	Payments on account and assets in course of construction
	III		Investments
		1	Shares in group undertakings
		2	Loans to group undertakings
		3	Participating interests**
		4	Loans to undertakings in which the LLP has a participating interest
		5	Other investments other than loans
		6	Other loans
B			Current assets
	I		Stocks
		1	Raw materials and consumables
		2	Work in progress
		3	Finished goods and goods for resale
		4	Payments on account

	II		Debtors
		1	Trade debtors
		2	Amounts owed by group undertakings
		3	Amounts owed by undertakings in which the LLP has a participating interest
		4	Other debtors
		5	Prepayments and accrued income*
	III		Investments
		1	Shares in group undertakings
		2	Other investments
	IV		Cash at bank and in hand
C			**Prepayments and accrued income***
D			**Creditors: amounts falling due within one year**
		1	Debenture loans
		2	Bank loans and overdrafts
		3	Payments received on account
		4	Trade creditors
		5	Bills of exchange payable
		6	Amounts owed by group undertakings
		7	Amounts owed to undertakings in which the LLP has a participating interest
		8	Other creditors including taxation and social security
		9	Accruals and deferred income*
E			**Net current assets (liabilities)**
F			**Total assets less current liabilities**
G			**Creditors: amounts falling due after more than one year**
		1	Debenture loans
		2	Bank loans and overdrafts
		3	Payments received on account
		4	Trade creditors
		5	Bills of exchange payable
		6	Amounts owed by group undertakings
		7	Amounts owed to undertakings in which the LLP has a participating interest
		8	Other creditors including taxation and social security
		9	Accruals and deferred income*
H			**Provisions for liabilities**
		1	Pensions and similar obligations
		2	Taxation, including deferred taxation
		3	Other provisions
I			**Accruals and deferred income***
SORP			*Net assets attributable to members:*
			Represented by:#
J			**Loans and other debts to members**
K			**Members' other interests****
	I		Members' capital
	II		Revaluation reserve
	III		Other reserves, including the fair value reserve

*   The notes to format 1 provide alternative positions for prepayments and accrued income, and accruals and deferred income, as sub-headings at B-II.5 (for prepayments and accrued income) and at D.9 and G.9 (for accruals and deferred income).

**   Modifications required in group accounts (see discussion below).

\#   The LLP SORP requires a total for net assets attributable to members, and total members' interests (as a memorandum item) to be disclosed on the face of the statement of financial position. See Figure 6.6 below.

Chapter 6

The modifications required to format 1 in group accounts are:

- the identification of non-controlling interests (see 4.5 above);and
- the sub-heading 'Participating interests' (item A.III.3 in format 1) is replaced by 'Interests in associated undertakings' and 'Other participating interests' (see 5.3.4.D and 5.3.4.E below). *[3 Sch 17 (LLP), 3 Sch 20 (LLP)].*

The LLP SORP provides further guidance on members' interests and application of the statutory formats for LLPs. The LLP SORP requires that the face of the statement of financial position shows a total for net assets attributable to members. In addition, total members' interests (being the total of 'loans and other debts due to members' and 'members' other interests', i.e. the amounts in items J and K in the statutory formats, less any 'amounts due from members' in debtors) should be disclosed as a memorandum item on the face of the statement of financial position. *[LLP SORP.58].*

The SORP provides illustrative examples of LLP balance sheets (using statutory formats) for different situations (depending on whether the partnership interests are classified as equity or a liability or part equity / part liability). *[LLP SORP.58, Appendix 1, Appendix 2].* In these illustrative examples, a subtotal labelled 'Net assets attributable to members' is drawn in the formats before items J and K and items J and K are then presented below this subtotal, as shown in Figure 6.6 below (the capital letters for the line items are not required to be shown but are presented for convenience below). As discussed at 5.1 above, we expect that this presentation will also be required where adapted formats are used.

LLPs with no equity, e.g. because of the classification of the partnership interests in the LLP, will not have items to report for 'members' other interests' in the balance sheet.

Detailed guidance on issues specific to LLPs is outside the scope of this chapter.

Figure 6.6   Presentation of LLP balance sheet (following SORP)

		£'000
	....	
	Net assets attributable to members	x
	Represented by:	£'000
J	Loans and other debts due to members within one year	
	Members' capital classified as liability	x
	Other amounts	x
		x
K	Members' other interests	
	Members' capital classified as equity	x
	Members' other interests – other reserves classified as equity	x
		x
		x
	Total members' interests	
	Amounts due from members	(x)
	Loans and other debts due to members	x
	Members' other interests	x
		x

Based on the example in Exhibit B of Appendix 1 of the LLP SORP for an LLP (with some equity)

5.2.2   Fixed assets and current assets

The balance sheet statutory formats set out in the Regulations and LLP Regulations distinguish between fixed assets and current assets, defining 'fixed assets' with 'current assets' as the residual.

'Fixed assets' are assets of a company (or an LLP) which are intended for use on a continuing basis in the company's (or the LLP's) activities, and 'current assets' are assets not intended for such use. FRS 102 broadens the definitions to refer to 'an entity'. *[10 Sch 4, 4 Sch 3 (LLP), FRS 102 Appendix I].*

Current assets include debtors, even if due after more than one year. In instances where the amount of debtors due after more than one year is so material in the context of the total net current assets that in the absence of disclosure of the debtors due after more than one year on the face of the statement of financial position readers may misinterpret the financial statements, the amount should be disclosed on the face of the statement of financial position within current assets. In most cases, it will be satisfactory to disclose the amount due after more than one year in the notes to the financial statements. *[FRS 102.4.4A].* This requirement does not apply where an entity uses the adapted formats. Since LLP law now permits the use of adapted formats, this dispensation extends to LLPs.

Note (5) on the balance sheet formats in Section B of Part 1 of Schedule 1 to the Regulations (and the equivalent requirement for LLPs)[6] state that the amount falling due after more than one year must be shown separately for each item included under debtors.

A UK company preparing Companies Act accounts (or an LLP preparing non-IAS accounts) must disclose the following in the notes to the accounts, for *each* category of fixed assets shown in the balance sheet (or would be so shown, if Arabic-numbered line items were not combined as permitted by paragraph 4(2)(b) of the General Rules to the formats – see 4.4 above): *[1 Sch 51, 1 Sch 49 (LLP)]*

- the gross cost (based on the historical cost – see 10.1 below) or valuation (using the alternative accounting rules – see 10.2 below) at the beginning and end of the financial year;
- the effects on the amounts shown for gross cost / valuation of:
  - any revaluations of any assets made during the financial year;
  - acquisitions of any assets during the financial year;
  - disposals of any assets during the financial year; and
  - any transfers of assets (to and from that category) during the financial year;
- the cumulative amount of provisions for depreciation or diminution in value at the beginning and end of the financial year;
- the amount of any provisions for depreciation and diminution made in respect of the financial year;
- the amount of any adjustments to such provisions arising from the disposal of any assets; and
- the amount of any other adjustments in respect of such provisions for depreciation and diminution.

Chapter 6

Where the Regulations (or LLP Regulations) require disclosures in respect of fixed assets or current assets, in our view, these disclosures need to be given where statutory formats or adapted formats are used. See 5.1 above for discussion on applying these requirements where adapted formats are used.

The above statutory requirements overlap with FRS 102's requirements to provide reconciliations of changes in the carrying amounts for each class of property, plant and equipment *[FRS 102.17.31(e)]* (see Chapter 15 at 3.9.1); each class of intangible asset *[FRS 102.18.27(e)]* (see Chapter 16 at 3.5.2); goodwill and negative goodwill (separately) *[FRS 102.19.26, 26A]* (see Chapter 17 at 4.2); investment property at fair value through profit or loss *[FRS 102.16.10(e)]* (see Chapter 14 at 3.6); and biological assets (separately for each class carried under the cost model and each class carried under the fair value model) *[FRS 102.34.7(c), 34.10(e)]* (see Chapter 31 at 2.6.3 and 2.7.2).

The Regulations (and LLP Regulations) require separate fixed asset reconciliations for cost and cumulative provision for depreciation and diminution whereas FRS 102 only requires reconciliation of the carrying amounts.

Comparatives are not required for the reconciliations required by FRS 102, the Regulations (and LLP Regulations). This is because comparatives are specifically exempted under the equivalent reconciliation requirement in FRS 102 (and the Regulations and LLP Regulations do not specify whether comparatives are required for notes disclosures). See 3.6 above.

A UK company preparing Companies Act accounts (or an LLP preparing non-IAS accounts) must also give additional disclosures in the notes to the accounts where the alternative accounting rules are applied. See 10.2.4 below.

5.2.3   Creditors: amounts falling due within one year and creditors: amounts falling due after more than one year

The Regulations (and LLP Regulations) distinguish between:

- Creditors: amounts falling due within one year; and
- Creditors: amounts falling due after more than one year.

These two line items are shown on the face of the balance sheet in the format 1 balance sheet. In distinguishing amounts between the two categories of creditor, the deciding factor is the earliest date of payment.

FRS 102 states that an entity shall classify a creditor as due within one year when the entity does not have an unconditional right, at the end of the reporting period, to defer settlement of the creditor for at least twelve months after the reporting date. For example, this would be the case if the earliest date on which the lender, exercising all available options and rights, could require repayment or (as the case may be) payment was within twelve months after the reporting date. *[FRS 102.4.7]*. This requirement does not apply where an entity uses the adapted formats. Since LLP law now permits the use of adapted formats, this dispensation extends to LLPs.

FRS 102's requirements are intended to be consistent with the requirements in the Regulations (and LLP Regulations) which state that a loan or advance (including a liability comprising a loan or advance) is treated as falling due for repayment, and an instalment of a loan or advance is treated as falling due for payment, on the earliest date on which the lender could require repayment or (as the case may be) payment, if he exercised all options and rights available to him. *[10 Sch 9, 4 Sch 6 (LLP)].* However, without the full statutory definition, the final sentence of paragraph 4.7 of FRS 102 might appear confusing because it is not clear why a distinction between repayment and payment is being made. This sentence is intended to illustrate when an entity does not have an unconditional right to defer settlement of the creditor (which must be assessed as at the end of the reporting period). A loan is not classified as a creditor: amounts falling due within one year merely because it happens to have been repaid within twelve months of the reporting date.

IAS 1 also includes detailed guidance on the impact of refinancing liabilities that management may consider, as permitted by the hierarchy in Section 10. While IAS 1 requires classification between current and non-current liabilities (which is a different determination), one part of IAS 1's definition of a current liability is that a liability is current if the entity 'does not have an unconditional right to defer settlement of the liability for at least twelve months after the reporting period'. This is consistent with the definition of a creditor due within one year in FRS 102, the Regulations (and the LLP Regulations). *[IAS 1.69(d)].* See 5.1.2.D above.

5.3 Application issues for statutory formats – format 1 balance sheet

In most cases, it will be straightforward to identify in which line items to present assets and liabilities in the format 1 balance sheet. The discussion in this section provides a commentary on each heading and subheading included in the format 1 balance sheet and on the related notes on the balance sheet formats (as included in Section B of Part 1 of Schedule 1 to the Regulations or Section B of Part 1 of Schedule 1 to the LLP Regulations). The extracts shown relate to the statutory formats (and the related notes on the balance sheet formats) included in Section B of Part 1 of Schedule 1 to the Regulations. However, except where indicated, the line items required are the same for LLPs (although often these will have different capital letter-Roman numeral-Arabic number references – see 5.2 above).

In our view, the notes on the balance sheet formats in Section B form part of the statutory formats for the balance sheet. Therefore, entities following the statutory formats in Schedule 1 to the Regulations (or Schedule 1 to the LLP Regulations) must comply with the balance sheet format adopted (including the related notes on that format in Section B). This is the case even if the entity is not a UK company or LLP subject to those statutory requirements.

Where disclosures in the Regulations (or LLP Regulations) are discussed in this section, these are not intended to be comprehensive but to highlight additional disclosures *directly* related to a specific line item. The disclosures required for the line items in the notes to the accounts highlighted here are also required in the notes to the accounts where adapted formats are used (unless they relate to the notes on the balance sheet formats in Section B, as referred above). The disclosures highlighted do not cover all the related disclosures in the Regulations or LLP Regulations.

5.3.1 Called up share capital not paid

This line item can be presented in the position of Called up share capital not paid (item A) on the face of the balance sheet. Alternatively, this line item can be presented either on the face of the balance sheet or in the notes to the accounts as item 5 within Current assets – Debtors (C.II) (see 5.3.6.E below).[7]

Called up share capital and paid up share capital are explained at 5.3.12.A below. Called up share capital not paid can arise, for example, because calls made on the shares have not been paid, or where the share capital is 'paid up' because the amounts are payable on a specified future date under the articles or terms of allotment or other arrangement for payment of those shares (and therefore is called up share capital), but has not yet been settled. *[s547]*.

5.3.2   Intangible assets

Figure 6.7 shows the analysis required in respect of intangible assets (on the face of the balance sheet or in the notes to the accounts – see 4.4 above) under format 1.

Figure 6.7   Analysis of intangible assets

B	Fixed assets	
I	Intangible assets	
	1	Development costs
	2	Concessions, patents, licences, trade marks and similar rights and assets
	3	Goodwill
	4	Payments on account

Intangible assets are not defined in the Regulations (or LLP Regulations), but include the line items listed in Figure 6.7 above. Note (2) on the balance sheet formats (and the equivalent requirement for LLPs)[8] state that amounts are only included in the balance sheet as concessions, patents, licences, trade marks and similar rights and assets if either the assets were acquired for valuable consideration and are not required to be shown under goodwill, or the assets in question were created by the company (or the LLP) itself.

FRS 102 financial statements must apply the more restrictive requirements of the standard (see 5.1.5 above and Chapter 16). Specific types of assets that may sometimes fall to be classified as intangible assets and sometimes as property, plant and equipment are discussed at 5.1.3.A to 5.1.3.D above. The format 1 balance sheet includes a line item for payments on account, i.e. advance payments made for intangible fixed assets.

Note (3) on the balance sheet formats (and the equivalent requirement for LLPs)[9] state that amounts representing goodwill are only included to the extent that the goodwill was acquired for valuable consideration. Therefore, consistent with FRS 102, internally generated goodwill cannot be capitalised. *[FRS 102.18.8C(f)]*.

The Regulations and LLP Regulations do not address the presentation of negative goodwill, but FRS 102's requirements on presentation of negative goodwill, which also apply to statutory formats, are addressed at 5.1.5.A above.

FRS 102, the Regulations (and the LLP Regulations) require reconciliations of movements in intangible assets (comparatives are not required). FRS 102 requires reconciliations of changes in the carrying amounts to be given for each class of intangible asset, for goodwill, and for negative goodwill. *[FRS 102.18.27(e), 19.26, 19.26A]*. See Chapter 16 at 3.5.2 and Chapter 17 at 4.2. See 5.2.2 above for the requirements for reconciliations of movements in fixed assets in the Regulations (and the LLP Regulations) for UK companies preparing Companies Act accounts (and LLP accounts preparing non-IAS accounts). These disclosures apply where statutory formats or adapted formats are used.

5.3.3 Tangible fixed assets

Figure 6.8 shows the analysis required (on the face of the balance sheet or in the notes to the accounts – see 4.4 above) in respect of tangible fixed assets under format 1.

Figure 6.8 *Analysis of tangible fixed assets*

B	Fixed assets	
II	Tangible assets	
	1	Land and buildings
	2	Plant and machinery
	3	Fixtures, fittings, tools and equipment
	4	Payments on account and assets in course of construction

The Regulations (and LLP Regulations) define fixed assets (see 5.2.2 above) but not tangible fixed assets. While FRS 102 does not define the term 'tangible assets', these differ from intangible assets in that they are assets 'with physical substance'.

The distinction between fixed assets and current assets is usually clear and the statutory definition is not normally interpreted to mean that individual assets are transferred to current assets when a decision to dispose of them has been made. See 5.3.13.C below.

The format 1 balance sheet includes a line item for payments on account, i.e. advance payments made for tangible fixed assets.

Tangible fixed assets would include property, plant and equipment, as defined in FRS 102. The definition of property, plant and equipment and some classification issues are discussed at 5.1.3 above and Chapter 15 at 3.2 and 3.3. Investment property would also be classified within tangible fixed assets in the statutory formats (see 5.3.3.A below). However, in our view, it would be appropriate to report an upfront operating lease premium as a prepayment under FRS 102 (see 5.1.13.A above), classified as appropriate between debtors: amounts falling due within one year and debtors: amounts falling due after more than one year.

In practice, most UK companies relegate the sub-headings within tangible assets denoted by an Arabic number to the notes to the accounts, showing only the net book value of tangible assets on the face of the balance sheet.

A UK company preparing Companies Act accounts (or an LLP preparing non-IAS accounts) must also disclose, in the notes to the accounts, 'land and buildings' analysed between freehold land and leasehold land, with leasehold land analysed between land held on a long lease (meaning the unexpired term at the end of the financial year is not less than 50 years) and leasehold land held on a short lease (i.e. a lease that is not a long lease). *[1 Sch 53, 10 Sch 7, 1 Sch 51 (LLP)]*. This disclosure applies where adapted formats or statutory formats are used.

FRS 102, the Regulations (and the LLP Regulations) require reconciliations of movements in tangible fixed assets (comparatives are not required). FRS 102 requires reconciliations of changes in the carrying amounts to be given for each class of property, plant and equipment *[FRS 102.17.31(e)]* (see Chapter 15 at 3.9.1); investment property at fair value through profit or loss *[FRS 102.16.10(e)]* (see Chapter 14 at 3.6); and biological assets (separately for each class carried under the cost model and each class carried under the fair value model) *[FRS 102.34.7(c), 34.10(e)]* (see Chapter 31 at 2.6.3 and 2.7.2). See 5.2.2 above for the requirements for reconciliations of movements in fixed assets in the Regulations (and the LLP Regulations) for UK companies preparing Companies Act accounts (and LLP accounts preparing non-IAS accounts). These disclosures apply where statutory formats or adapted formats are used.

5.3.3.A   Investment property

As noted at 5.3.3 above, investment property would be included within tangible fixed assets in the statutory formats. The Regulations (and LLP Regulations) do not require presentation of investment property on the face of the balance sheet but do permit items to be shown in greater detail. FRS 102 requires additional line items, headings and subtotals when relevant to an understanding of the entity's financial position (see 4.4 above). Therefore, some entities may consider it appropriate to present investment property as a separate line item on the face of the balance sheet.

Chapter 14 at 3.1 explains the definition of investment property. Some property may have mixed use (e.g. partly owner-occupied and partly held for rental) which may be required to be split into components for investment property and property, plant and equipment. See Chapter 14 at 3.1.7 and Chapter 15 at 3.3.4. In the statutory formats, both components would qualify to be presented as tangible fixed assets. Nevertheless, such a split would be relevant for measurement and for the purposes of FRS 102's disclosures.

5.3.4   Investments

Figure 6.9 shows the analysis required in respect of investments (on the face of the balance sheet or in the notes to the accounts – see 4.4 above) under format 1.

Figure 6.9   Analysis of investments

B	Fixed assets	
III	Investments	
	1	Shares in group undertakings
	2	Loans to group undertakings
	3	Participating interests†
	4	Loans to undertakings in which the company has a participating interest
	5	Other investments other than loans
	6	Other loans
	7	Own shares*

† In group accounts, this line item is replaced by two items: 'Interests in associated undertakings' and 'Other participating interests'
* Line item B.III.7 is not included in format 1 in the LLP Regulations. In addition, the equivalent line item to B.III.4 refers to an LLP rather than a company.

C	Current assets	
III	Investments	
	1	Shares in group undertakings
	2	Own shares*
	3	Other investments

* Line item CIII.2 is not included in format 1 in the LLP Regulations

5.3.4.A   Current assets or fixed asset investments?

The format 1 balance sheet distinguishes between fixed asset and current asset investments. It is necessary to apply the general rule that a fixed asset is one which is 'intended for use on a continuing basis in the entity's activities' and a current asset is one not intended for such use (see 5.2.2 above). However, this is an unhelpful distinction for investments which, by their nature, are not intended for use in an entity's activities at all, whether on a continuing basis or not.

Current asset investments may include cash equivalents, meaning: short-term, highly liquid investments that are readily convertible to cash (i.e. cash on hand and demand deposits) and that are subject to an insignificant risk of changes in value. *[FRS 102 Appendix I]*. Examples of current asset investments that may qualify as cash equivalents, but do not fall within the statutory heading 'cash at bank and in hand', include investments in money market funds. Current asset investments may also include investments that do not qualify as cash equivalents but are still of a short-term nature, and investments held for trading purposes.

Investments in shares in subsidiaries or associates or trade investments will generally be fixed asset investments. Indeed, FRS 102 states that, unless otherwise required under the Regulations, investments in associates should be classified as fixed assets. *[FRS 102.14.11]*. However, entities frequently make loans to subsidiaries or associates, which are often repayable on demand. Management will need to exercise judgement in determining whether such loans are debtors or are a fixed asset investment in nature. For example, loan financing provided for the long-term, with no intention of repayment in the foreseeable future, may be more of a fixed asset investment in nature, even where the balance is strictly repayable on demand.

Discussion of the different sub-headings required to be shown for investments is included below. Care must be taken not to offset amounts owed by group undertakings with amounts owed to the same group undertaking or other group undertakings where the offset criteria are not met. The same principle applies to balances with undertakings in which the entity has a participating interest. Offset is required when, and only when, the entity has both a currently legally enforceable right to set off the balances and an intention either to settle on a net basis, or to realise the asset and settle the liability simultaneously. *[FRS 102.11.38A, 12.25B]*.

A UK company preparing Companies Act accounts (or an LLP preparing non-IAS accounts) must disclose the following in the notes to the accounts:

- the amount of listed investments included in each line item under current asset or fixed asset investments shown in the balance sheet (or would be so shown, if Arabic-numbered line items were not combined as permitted by paragraph 4(2)(b) of the General Rules to the formats – see 4.4 above);
- the aggregate market value of the listed investments, where this differs from their carrying amount in the financial statements; and
- both the market value and the stock exchange value of any investments (where the market value is higher than the stock exchange value).

A listed investment is an investment which has been granted a listing on a recognised investment exchange other than an overseas investment exchange (both as defined in

Part 18 of the Financial Services and Markets Act 2000) or a stock exchange of repute outside the UK. *[1 Sch 54, 10 Sch 8, 1 Sch 52 (LLP), 4 Sch 5 (LLP)].* A list of recognised investment exchanges (and recognised overseas investment exchanges) is available on the Financial Conduct Authority website. AIM is not a recognised investment exchange. This disclosure applies where adapted formats or statutory formats are used.

See 5.2.2 above for the requirements for reconciliations of movements in fixed assets in the Regulations (and the LLP Regulations) for UK companies preparing Companies Act accounts (and LLP accounts preparing non-IAS accounts). In this case, the general rules on comparatives in FRS 102 would appear to apply (see 3.6 above), and comparatives are required for the reconciliation. This is because FRS 102 has no comparable disclosure requirement to reconcile movements in investments (and, therefore, does not provide an exemption from comparatives as in the case of other reconciliations included in FRS 102). These disclosures apply where statutory formats or adapted formats are used.

5.3.4.B   Group undertakings, participating interests and associated undertakings

FRS 102 does not require investments in associates and jointly controlled entities to be presented on the face of the statement of financial position in either the individual or consolidated financial statements, where the statutory formats are used.

Disclosure of the carrying amount of investments in associates is required and, separately, the carrying amount of investments in jointly controlled entities. *[FRS 102.14.12(b), 15.19(b)].* This could be presented in the notes to the financial statements, although the standard requires additional line items, headings and subtotals when relevant to an understanding of the entity's financial position. *[FRS 102.4.3].*

The line items in format 1 in the Regulations (and LLP Regulations) refer to group undertakings, participating interests and associated undertakings. These terms are explained at 5.3.4.C to 5.3.4.E below.

All UK companies (and LLPs) must also comply with the extensive requirements of regulation 7 and Schedule 4 to the Regulations (and the equivalent requirements for LLPs)[10] in relation to information about related undertakings. This information must be presented in full in the company's (or the LLP's) accounts. These requirements apply both to Companies Act accounts (non-IAS accounts, for an LLP) and IAS accounts.

5.3.4.C   Group undertakings

A 'group undertaking' means a parent undertaking or subsidiary undertaking of the reporting entity, or a subsidiary undertaking of any parent undertaking (i.e. a fellow subsidiary undertaking) of the reporting entity. *[s1161(5), s1161(5) (LLP)].* Parent and subsidiary undertakings are defined in section 1162 of the CA 2006. *[s1162, s1162 (LLP)].* See Chapter 3 at 3.1.2 and Chapter 8 at 3.2.

FRS 102 defines a subsidiary as an entity that is controlled by the parent. Control is the power to govern the financial and operating policies of an entity so as to obtain benefits from its activities. The standard goes on to explain in what circumstances control exists or can exist. *[FRS 102.9.4-6A].* These circumstances are similar but not identical to those included in the definition of a subsidiary undertaking under section 1162.

Although there are slight differences in wording emphasis between the definition of a subsidiary undertaking in section 1162 and the requirements of Section 9 – *Consolidated and Separate Financial Statements*, we would expect to see few conflicts arising in practice between Section 9 and the CA 2006 (see Chapter 8 at 3.2).

5.3.4.D   Participating interest

A 'participating interest' means an interest held by, or on behalf of, an undertaking (or in group accounts, by, or on behalf of, the parent and its consolidated subsidiary undertakings) in the shares of another undertaking which it holds on a long-term basis for the purpose of securing a contribution to its activities (or in group accounts, the consolidated group's activities) by the exercise of control or influence arising from or related to that interest.

A holding of 20% or more of the shares of the undertaking is presumed to be a participating interest unless the contrary is shown. An interest in shares of another undertaking includes an interest which is convertible into an interest in shares and an option to acquire shares or any such interest, even if the shares are unissued until the conversion or exercise of the option.

In the context of the statutory formats, 'participating interest' does not include an interest in a group undertaking (see 5.3.4.C above). *[10 Sch 11, 4 Sch 8 (LLP)].*

5.3.4.E   Associated undertaking

An 'associated undertaking' is an undertaking in which an undertaking included in the consolidation:

- has a participating interest (as defined at 5.3.4.D above) and over whose operating and financial policy it exercises a significant influence; and
- which is not a subsidiary undertaking of the parent company or a joint venture dealt with in accordance with paragraph 18 of Schedule 6 to the Regulations (or the equivalent requirement for LLPs).[11] The proportional consolidation permitted by this paragraph is not consistent with the requirements of FRS 102. *[FRS 102.15.9A-B].*

An undertaking holding 20% or more of the voting rights in another undertaking is presumed to exercise a significant influence over it unless the contrary is shown. Voting rights mean the rights conferred on shareholders in respect of their shares (or where the undertaking does not have a share capital, on members) to vote at general meetings of the undertaking on all, or substantially all matters. Paragraphs 5 to 11 of Schedule 7 to the CA 2006 apply in determining whether 20% or more of the voting rights are held. *[6 Sch 19, 3 Sch 19 (LLP)].*

The term 'associated undertaking' in the Regulations (and LLP Regulations) will generally include both an associate (see Chapter 12 at 3.2 and 5.1) and a jointly controlled entity (see Chapter 13 at 3.3 and 4.1), as defined under FRS 102. *[FRS 102.14.2-3, 15.8, Appendix I].* However, FRS 102's definition of an associate does not require the existence of a participating interest so it is theoretically possible that an associate under the standard may not be an associated undertaking under the Regulations (or LLP Regulations).

5.3.4.F   Own shares

While 'own shares' have a sub-heading under investments in the balance sheet formats, FRS 102 requires investments in own shares to be treated as treasury shares and deducted from equity. *[FRS 102.22.16]*. Consequently, this line item will not be used under FRS 102. The format 1 balance sheet has an alternative position 'reserve for own shares' within the capital and reserves section which will be used under FRS 102 (see 5.3.12.G below).

5.3.5   Stocks

Figure 6.10 shows the analysis required in respect of stocks (on the face of the balance sheet or in the notes to the accounts – see 4.4 above) under format 1.

Figure 6.10   Analysis of stocks

C	Current assets	
I	Stocks	
	1	Raw materials and consumables
	2	Work in progress
	3	Finished goods and goods for resale
	4	Payments on account

The items reported under stocks in the balance sheet formats will generally correspond with inventories under FRS 102, which are assets: *[FRS 102.13.1, FRS 102 Appendix I]*

- held for sale in the ordinary course of business; or
- in the process of production for such sale; or
- in the form of materials or supplies to be consumed in the production process or in the rendering of services.

See also 5.1.8 above and Chapter 11 at 3.2, which discuss certain classification issues in respect of inventories (including transfers to inventories from other categories of assets), which are also relevant to classification under format 1.

Note (8) on the balance sheet formats (and the equivalent requirement for LLPs)[12] state that payments on account of orders must be shown within creditors in so far as they are not shown as deductions from stocks. We would not expect payments on account to be deducted from stock (or inventory) as this would not meet the offset requirements of FRS 102, and therefore all payments on account must be shown within creditors.

The presentation of construction contracts (which is not specifically addressed in the Regulations (or LLP Regulations)) is discussed at 5.3.13.A below.

5.3.6 *Debtors (including prepayments and accrued income)*

Figure 6.11 shows the analysis required in respect of debtors (on the face of the balance sheet or in the notes to the accounts – see 4.4 above) under format 1.

Figure 6.11 *Analysis of debtors*

C	**Current assets**	
II	Debtors	
	1	Trade debtors
	2	Amounts owed by group undertakings
	3	Amounts owed by undertakings in which the company has a participating interest**
	4	Other debtors
	5	Called up share capital not paid*
	6	Prepayments and accrued income*

> *   Format 1 provides alternative positions for called up share capital not paid at heading A and prepayments and accrued income at heading D. In format 1 in the LLP Regulations, called up share capital is omitted and the alternative position for prepayments and accrued income is at heading C (i.e. the same as heading D in the company balance sheet formats).
>
> ** In format 1 in the LLP Regulations, amounts owed by undertakings in which the LLP has a participating interest.

While all debtors are reported within current assets, debtors include amounts falling due within and amounts falling due after more than one year.

As discussed at 5.2.2 above, where the amount of debtors due after more than one year is so material in the context of total net current assets that in the absence of disclosure of the debtors due after more than one year on the face of the statement of financial position the financial statements may be misinterpreted, the amount should be disclosed on the face of the statement of financial position within current assets. In most cases, it will be satisfactory to disclose the amount due after more than one year in the notes to the financial statements. *[FRS 102.4.4A]*.

Note (5) on the balance sheet formats (and the equivalent requirement for LLPs)[13] state that the amount falling due after more than one year must be shown separately for each item included under debtors.

5.3.6.A *Trade debtors*

Trade debtors are generally amounts receivable from customers, e.g. relating to amounts invoiced to customers, as well as debit balances owed by suppliers. The amounts in trade debtors are stated net of any bad debt provisions or write offs, and the effects of credit notes and other rebates.

Care must be taken not to offset any debit balances in trade debtors with trade creditors (and *vice versa*) where the offset criteria are not met.

The separate line items for 'amounts owed by group undertakings' and 'amounts owed by undertakings in which the company / LLP has a participating interest' will include trade debtors due from group undertakings and participating interests respectively (see 5.3.6.C below).

5.3.6.B   *Construction contracts*

The Regulations (and LLP Regulations) do not specifically address the presentation of construction contracts. Contract assets may include amounts receivable under contracts that have not yet been invoiced (and, therefore, are not recorded in trade debtors). See 5.3.13.A below.

5.3.6.C   *Amounts owed by group undertakings, and by undertakings in which the company has a participating interest*

The line items 'amounts owed by group undertakings' and 'amounts owed by undertakings in which the company has a participating interest' include all amounts owed by such undertakings e.g. loans regarded as current assets, dividends and interest receivable, trading items such as current accounts and balances with group treasury companies. The meanings of 'group undertaking' and 'participating interest' are discussed at 5.3.4.C and 5.3.4.D above.

As noted at 5.3.4.A above, management must exercise judgement in determining whether amounts owed by group undertakings or undertakings in which the entity has a participating interest are debtors or fixed asset investments. Again, care must be taken not to offset debtors and creditors where the offset criteria in FRS 102 are not met.

5.3.6.D   *Other debtors*

This will cover debtors other than those identified in other line items, e.g. amounts receivable from a sale of property, plant and equipment.

5.3.6.E   *Called up share capital not paid*

The format 1 balance sheet permits called up share capital not paid to alternatively be shown in the position of line item A, i.e. on the face of the balance sheet (see 5.3.1 above).

5.3.6.F   *Prepayments and accrued income*

Prepayments and accrued income can alternatively be shown on the face of the balance sheet (line item D).[14]

Prepayments and accrued income are not defined in FRS 102 or the Regulations (or LLP Regulations. Prepayments arise where payments are made in advance of receiving goods or services and must meet the definition and recognition criteria of an asset, including recoverability, in FRS 102 (see Chapter 4 at 3.3.1).

FRS 102 prohibits the recognition as an intangible asset of expenditure such as: internally developed brands, logos, publishing titles, customer lists and items similar in substance; start-up activities; training activities; advertising and promotional activities (except for inventories held for distribution at no or nominal consideration – see Chapter 11 at 3.3.11); relocation and reorganisation costs; and internally generated goodwill. However, the standard does not preclude recognition of a prepayment where payment for goods or services is made in advance of the delivery of the goods or rendering of the services. *[FRS 102.18.8C-D].*

As noted at 5.3.3 above, in our view, it would be appropriate to report an upfront operating lease premium as a prepayment under FRS 102, classified as appropriate between debtors: amounts falling due within one year and debtors: amounts falling due after more than one year.

While the format 1 balance sheet combines prepayments and accrued income into one line item, these two items can have separate characteristics. The Conduct Committee has challenged the aggregation of prepayments and accrued income as the assets differ in nature and liquidity, noting that this is particularly relevant to companies with long-term contracts where revenue recognition is a critical judgement. See the *Technical Findings of the Conduct Committee's Financial Reporting Review Panel 2015-2016*, available on the FRC website. As noted at 4.4 above, the balance sheet formats allow any item to be shown in greater detail and FRS 102 requires additional line items, headings and subtotals when relevant to an understanding of the entity's financial position.

5.3.7 Cash at bank and in hand

The Regulations (and LLP Regulations) do not define cash at bank and in hand. This line item would include bank deposits with notice or maturity periods. Such bank deposits may or may not meet FRS 102's definition of 'cash' (i.e. cash on hand and demand deposits) or 'cash equivalents' (i.e. short-term, highly liquid investments that are readily convertible to known amounts of cash and that are subject to an insignificant risk of changes in value). *[FRS 102.7.2, Appendix I].* See Chapter 7 at 3.2 and 3.3 for the definitions of cash and cash equivalents.

Care is needed with applying the requirements on offset of financial assets and financial liabilities, particularly in group arrangements with a bank (such as cash pooling arrangements) where there are rights of offset. The contractual terms and conditions, and how these operate in practice can vary widely. A right of offset alone is insufficient to meet the requirements on offset of financial assets and financial liabilities. Offset of a financial asset and liability is required when, and only when, an entity currently has a legally enforceable right to set off the recognised amounts and intends either to settle on a net basis, or to realise the asset and settle the liability simultaneously. *[FRS 102.11.38A, 12.25B].* See Chapter 10 at 11.1.

Chapter 6

5.3.8   *Creditors: amounts falling due within one year. Creditors: amounts falling due after more than one year*

Figure 6.12 shows the analysis required in respect of creditors (on the face of the balance sheet or in the notes to the accounts – see 4.4 above) under format 1.

Figure 6.12   *Analysis of creditors: amounts falling due within one year*

E		Creditors: amounts falling due within one year
	1	Debenture loans
	2	Bank loans and overdrafts
	3	Payments received on account
	4	Trade creditors
	5	Bills of exchange payable
	6	Amounts owed to group undertakings
	7	Amounts owed to undertakings in which the company has a participating interest**
	8	Other creditors including taxation and social security
	9	Accruals and deferred income*
H		Creditors: amounts falling due within one year
	1	Debenture loans
	2	Bank loans and overdrafts
	3	Payments received on account
	4	Trade creditors
	5	Bills of exchange payable
	6	Amounts owed to group undertakings
	7	Amounts owed to undertakings in which the company has a participating interest**
	8	Other creditors including taxation and social security
	9	Accruals and deferred income*

*   Format 1 provides an alternative position for accruals and deferred income, at heading J. In format 1 in the LLP Regulations, the alternative position for accruals and deferred income is at heading I (i.e. the same as heading J in the company balance sheet formats).

**   In format 1 in the LLP Regulations, amounts owed to undertakings in which the LLP has a participating interest.

The same line items are required for creditors: amounts falling due within one year, and creditors: amounts falling due after more than one year. See 5.2.3 above for discussion of these two categories of creditors.

In addition, the General Rules to the formats (see 4.4 above) require that, in determining how amounts are presented within items in the balance sheet, the directors of the company (or the members of the LLP) must have regard to the substance of the reported transaction or arrangement, in accordance with generally accepted accounting principles or practice. *[1 Sch 9, 1 Sch 9 (LLP)]*. This provision facilitates the presentation of shares (such as certain preference shares), which are required to be classified as liabilities under accounting standards, to be shown as creditors rather than as called up share capital under the balance sheet statutory format. See Chapter 10 at 5. Note, however, that disclosures required by the Regulations in the notes to the accounts in relation to share capital (see, for example, the disclosures listed in 5.4.2 below) still apply, even if the shares are classified as a liability.

The General Rules to the formats allow or, where the special nature of the company's business requires this, require certain adaptations to the balance sheet formats, as well as allowing line items to be shown in greater detail. The analysis of creditors is another area where entities may need to be mindful that FRS 102 requires additional line items, headings and subtotals when relevant to an understanding of the entity's financial position. For example, it may be appropriate to present preference shares classed as a liability, finance lease creditors and other items separately from other creditors.

UK companies preparing Companies Act accounts (and LLPs preparing non-IAS accounts) must state in the notes to the accounts, for the aggregate of all items shown under 'creditors' in the balance sheet, the aggregate of:

(a) the amount of any debts included under 'creditors' which are payable or repayable otherwise than by instalments and fall due for payment or repayment after the end of the period of five years beginning with the day next following the end of the financial year; and

(b) for debts included under 'creditors' which are payable or repayable by instalments, the amount of any instalments which fall due for payment after the end of that period.

In relation to each debt which is taken into account in (a) or (b) above, the terms of payment or repayment and rate of any interest payable on the debt must be stated. If the number of debts is such that, in the opinion of the directors (or the members of the LLP), the statement required would be of excessive length, a general indication of the terms of payment or repayment and the rates of any interest payable on the debts can be given.

For each item shown under 'creditors' in the balance sheet, the aggregate amount of any debts included under that item in respect of which any security has been given by the company (or by the LLP), and an indication of the nature and the form of the securities given must also be stated. *[1 Sch 61, 1 Sch 59 (LLP)].* This disclosure applies where adapted formats or statutory formats are used.

Where any outstanding loans made under the authority of section 682(2)(b), (c) or (d) of the CA 2006 (various cases of financial assistance by a company for the purchase of its own shares) are included under any item shown in the company's balance sheet, the aggregate amount of those items must be disclosed for each item in question. *[1 Sch 64(2)].* This disclosure applies where adapted formats or statutory formats are used.

5.3.8.A   Debenture loans

The format 1 balance sheet has separate line items for debenture loans and bank loans and overdrafts. Therefore, bank loans and overdrafts need to be shown separately, even if they might also qualify as a debenture loan.

Note (7) on the balance sheet formats (and the equivalent requirement for LLPs)[15] state that the amount of any convertible loans (within debenture loans) must be shown separately.

A 'debenture' is not defined in the CA 2006, except that it is stated to include 'debenture stock, bonds and other securities of a company [LLP], whether or not constituting a charge on the assets of the company.' *[s738, s738 (LLP)].* In general use, a 'debenture' is a term applying to any document evidencing a loan. For the purposes of the statutory formats, this would generally mean a debt instrument issued by the company (or the LLP) with a written loan agreement, and usually giving some form of security or charge over its assets (although this is not an essential feature).

UK companies preparing Companies Act accounts (and LLPs preparing non-IAS accounts) must make the following disclosures in the notes to the accounts: *[1 Sch 50, 1 Sch 48 (LLP)]*

- if the company (or the LLP) has issued any debentures during the financial year, the classes of debentures issued during the financial year, and for each class of debentures, the amount issued and consideration received by the company (or the LLP) for the issue; and

- where any of the company's (or the LLP's) debentures are held by a nominee of or trustee for the company (or the LLP), the nominal amount of the debentures and the amount at which they are stated in the company's (or the LLP's) accounting records.

This disclosure applies where adapted formats or statutory formats are used.

5.3.8.B   Bank loans and overdrafts

In relation to bank loans and overdrafts, care is needed with applying the requirements on offset of financial assets and financial liabilities, particularly in group arrangements with a bank (such as cash pooling arrangements) where there are rights of offset. See 5.3.7 above for discussion of offset in respect of group cash pooling arrangements.

5.3.8.C   Payments on account

As noted at 5.3.5 above we would not expect payments on account to be deducted from stock (or inventory) as this would not meet the offset requirements of FRS 102. Also see 5.3.13.A below for a discussion of how construction contract balances might be reflected in the balance sheet formats.

5.3.8.D   Trade creditors

Trade creditors are generally amounts payable to suppliers of goods and services, e.g. relating to amounts invoiced by suppliers (and could include credit balances due to trade debtors).

Care must be taken not to offset any debit balances in trade debtors with trade creditors (and *vice versa*) where the offset criteria are not met. The separate line items for 'amounts owed to group undertakings' and 'amounts owed to undertakings in which the entity has a participating interest' will include trade creditors due to group undertakings and participating interests respectively (see 5.3.8.F below).

5.3.8.E   Bills of exchange

A bill of exchange is a written instrument used mainly in international trade, where one party agrees to pay an amount to another party on demand or on a specified date. The bill can often be transferred by the holder of the bill to a bank or finance house at a discount.

5.3.8.F   Amounts owed to group undertakings, and to undertakings in which the company has a participating interest

The line items 'amounts owed to group undertakings' and 'amounts owed to undertakings in which the company has a participating interest' include all amounts owed by such undertakings which could include loans, dividends and interest payable, trading items such as current accounts and balances with group treasury companies.

The meanings of 'group undertaking' and 'participating interest' are discussed at 5.3.4.C and 5.3.4.D above. Care must be taken not to offset debtors and creditors where the offset criteria are not met.

5.3.8.G   Other creditors, including taxation and social security

Other creditors are creditors that do not belong in other line items.

Note (9) on the balance formats (and the equivalent requirement for LLPs)[16] state that the amount for creditors in respect of taxation and social security must be shown separately from the amount for other creditors. Taxation and social security creditors would include corporation tax, VAT, PAYE and National Insurance, and other taxes, including overseas taxation. This analysis can be given in the notes to the accounts.

In fact, FRS 102 does not explicitly require separate disclosure of the current tax creditor, although it requires disclosure of information that would enable users of the financial statements to evaluate the nature and financial effect of the current and deferred tax consequences of recognised transactions and other events. *[FRS 102.29.25]*.

Deferred tax liabilities are not included in this heading but in 'Provisions for liabilities' (see 5.3.11 below).

5.3.8.H   Accruals and deferred income

Accruals and deferred income can alternatively be shown on the face of the balance sheet (line item J).[17] FRS 102 does not define accruals but under previous UK GAAP, the distinction presented below was drawn between accruals and provisions.

Accruals are liabilities to pay for goods or services that have been received or supplied but have not been paid, invoiced or formally agreed with the supplier including amounts due to employees (for example, amounts relating to accrued holiday pay). Although it is sometimes necessary to estimate the amount or timing of accruals, the uncertainty is generally much less than for provisions. *[FRS 12.11(b)]*.

Deferred income may arise where cash is received in advance of meeting the conditions for recognising the related revenue, e.g. rental income received in advance or where cash is received for goods not yet delivered or services not yet rendered. In addition, deferred income may arise in relation to government grants related to assets (which are recognised in income on a systematic basis over the expected useful life of the asset). *[FRS 102.24.5F-G]*. See 5.3.13.H below.

While the format 1 balance sheet combines accruals and deferred income into one line item, these two items can have separate characteristics. The Conduct Committee has challenged the aggregation of accruals and deferred income as these liabilities differ in nature and liquidity, noting that this is particularly relevant to companies with long-term contracts where revenue recognition is a critical judgement. See the *Technical Findings of the Conduct Committee's Financial Reporting Review Panel 2015-2016*, available on the FRC website. As noted at 4.4 above, the balance sheet formats allow any item to be shown in greater detail and FRS 102 requires additional line items, headings and subtotals when relevant to an understanding of the entity's financial position.

Chapter 6

5.3.9   Net current assets / (liabilities)

The format 1 balance sheet requires a subtotal to be shown for net current assets / (liabilities) on the face of the balance sheet.

Note (11) on the balance sheet formats (and the equivalent requirement for LLPs)[18] state that any amounts shown under 'prepayments and accrued income' must be taken into account in determining net current assets / (liabilities), wherever shown (see 5.3.6.F above). Therefore, net current assets / (liabilities) for a company will represent the amounts reported at item C in format 1 plus prepayments and accrued income (at item D, if shown separately) less creditors: amounts falling due within one year (at item E). For LLPs, net current assets / (liabilities) is the sum of the amounts reported at item B in format 1 plus prepayments and accrued income (at item C, if shown separately) less creditors: amounts falling due within one year (at item D). See Figure 6.4 at 5.2 and Figure 6.5 at 5.2.1 above.

5.3.10   Total assets less current liabilities

The format 1 balance sheet requires a subtotal to be shown for total assets less current liabilities on the face of the balance sheet. This subtotal would be the sum of fixed assets and net current assets / (liabilities) (see 5.3.9 above).

While the format 1 balance sheet does not require a net assets subtotal (with a balancing subtotal for capital and reserves), most companies give this. Sometimes companies have presented a balancing subtotal for 'capital and reserves' together with 'creditors: amounts falling due within one year', a practice not precluded by the Regulations (or LLP Regulations).

5.3.11   Provisions for liabilities

Figure 6.13 shows the analysis required (on the face of the balance sheet or in the notes to the accounts – see 4.4 above) in respect of provisions for liabilities under format 1.

Figure 6.13   Analysis of provisions for liabilities

I	Provisions for liabilities
1	Pensions and similar obligations
2	Taxation, including deferred taxation
3	Other provisions

References to 'provisions for liabilities' in the Regulations (and LLP Regulations) are 'to any amount retained as reasonably necessary for the purpose of providing for any liability the nature of which is clearly defined and which is either likely to be incurred, or certain to be incurred but uncertain as to amount or as to the date on which it will arise'. *[9 Sch 2, 4 Sch 10 (LLP)].* FRS 102 defines a provision more succinctly as 'a liability of uncertain timing or amount.' *[FRS 102 Appendix I].*

The General Rules to the formats (see 4.4 above) allow or, where the special nature of the company's business requires this, require certain adaptations to the balance sheet formats, as well as allowing line items to be shown in greater detail. The analysis of provisions is an area where entities may need to be mindful that FRS 102 requires additional line items, headings and subtotals when relevant to an understanding of the entity's financial position.

FRS 102 requires an entity to present a reconciliation of each class of provision (comparatives are not required) and requires further narrative disclosures for each class of provision. *[FRS 102.21.14, 21.17, 21.17A]*. See Chapter 19 at 3.10.2.

UK companies preparing Companies Act accounts (and LLPs preparing non-IAS accounts) must give:

- particulars of each material provision included in the line item 'Other provisions' in the notes to the accounts; *[1 Sch 59(3), 1 Sch 57(3) (LLP)]*

- particulars of any pension commitments included in the balance sheet, giving separate particulars of any commitment relating wholly or partly to pensions payable to past directors of the company (or past members of the LLP); *[1 Sch 63(5)-(6), 1 Sch 60(4) (LLP)]*

- where there have been transfers to provisions, or from any provisions (otherwise than for the purpose for which the provision was established) relating to any of the provisions required to be shown as separate line items in the balance sheet (or would be so shown, if Arabic-numbered line items were not combined as permitted by paragraph 4(2)(b) of the General Rules to the formats – see 4.4 above), the company (or the LLP) must disclose the following in tabular form, in the notes to the accounts, in respect of the aggregate of provisions included in the same item:

  - the amount of the provisions as at the beginning and end of the financial year;

  - any amounts transferred to or from the provisions during that year; and

  - the source and application respectively of any amounts transferred.

  Comparatives are not required (since these are specifically exempted under the equivalent reconciliation requirement in FRS 102). *[1 Sch 59(1)-(2), 1 Sch 57(1) (LLP)-(2)]*.

The above reconciliation required by the Regulations (and LLP Regulations) is similar to that required by FRS 102. However, the statutory requirement would also apply to movements in deferred tax provisions (see 5.3.13.B below) and pension provisions, as these are line items under 'provisions for liabilities'. In respect of pension provisions, FRS 102 already requires reconciliations of defined benefit obligations and plan assets, which provide similar information, albeit not for the net balance. *[FRS 102.28.41(e)-(f)]*. See Chapter 25 at 3.12.4.

The above disclosures apply where adapted formats or statutory formats are used.

5.3.12 Capital and reserves

Figure 6.14 shows the analysis required in respect of capital and reserves under format 1 for a UK company.

For an LLP, K – Capital and reserves is replaced with K – Members' other interests (with sub-headings K.I – Members' capital, K.II – Revaluation reserve and K.III – Other reserves, including the fair value reserve). The items shown in K – Members' other interests are equity for an LLP. However, members' interests classified as a liability would be shown in J – Loans and other debts due to members (see 5.2.1 above), which does not have an equivalent in the format 1 balance sheet for a UK company.

Figure 6.14   Analysis of capital and reserves – UK company

K	Capital and reserves	
I	Called up share capital	
II	Share premium account	
III	Revaluation reserve	
IV	Other reserves	
	1	Capital redemption reserve
	2	Reserve for own shares
	3	Reserves provided for by the articles of association
	4	Other reserves, including the fair value reserve
V	Profit and loss account	
	See discussion above for the line items required for K – Members' other interests in the LLP Regulations.	

The capital and reserves section of the balance sheet includes a number of line items denoted by a Roman numeral which must be presented on the face of the balance sheet, with no adaptation of the order of the headings or description used permitted. The analysis of other reserves may be presented in the notes to the accounts, where permitted by the General Rules to the formats (see 4.4 above).

FRS 102's requirement to present a statement of changes in equity; the disclosures in the Regulations and LLP Regulations relating to capital and reserves, the disclosures in the LLP Regulations relating to loans and other debts due to members; and the LLP SORP's related requirement to show a reconciliation of members' interests, are discussed at 5.4 and 7 below.

5.3.12.A   Called up share capital

Called up share capital, in relation to a company, means so much of its share capital as equals the aggregate amounts of the calls made on its shares (whether or not those calls have been paid) together with:

- any share capital paid up without being called; and
- any share capital to be paid on a specified future date under the articles, the terms of allotment of the relevant shares or any other arrangements for payment of those shares.

Uncalled share capital is to be construed accordingly. *[s547]*.

The concept of called up share capital is not relevant to an LLP.

Shares allotted by a company, and any premium on them, may be paid up in money or money's worth (including goodwill and know-how). This does not prevent a company allotting bonus shares to its members, or from paying up, with sums available for the purpose, any amounts for the time being unpaid on any of its shares (whether on account of the nominal value of the shares or by way of premium). There are additional restrictions in Chapter 5 of Part 17 of the CA 2006 for payment of shares for public companies. *[s582]*.

The CA 2006 does not require that the shares issued are fully paid although a public company must not allot a share except where at least one quarter of the nominal value of the share and all of any premium on it is paid up (with an exception for shares allotted in pursuance of an employees' share scheme). *[s586]*.

A share in a company is deemed 'paid up' (as to its nominal value or any premium on it) in cash, or allotted for cash, if the consideration received for the allotment or payment up in cash is:

- cash received by the company;
- a cheque received by the company in good faith that the directors have no reason for suspecting will not be paid;
- a release of a liability of the company for a liquidated sum;
- an undertaking to pay cash to the company at a future date; or
- payment by any other means giving rise to a present or future entitlement (of the company or a person acting on the company's behalf) to a payment, or credit equivalent to payment, in cash. This can include a settlement bank's obligation to make payment under the settlement system operated by Euroclear UK & Ireland (also known as the CREST system).

Cash includes foreign currency. The payment of cash to a person other than the company or an undertaking to pay cash to a person other than the company is consideration other than cash. *[s583]*.

Called up share capital not paid is explained at 5.3.1 above.

FRS 102's requirements on recording issuances of equity instruments are consistent with the presentation of called up share capital in the Regulations (see Chapter 10 at 5.5).

Parts 17 and 18 of the CA 2006 address a company's share capital and the acquisition by a limited company of its own shares respectively. There are a number of ways in which share capital can be altered, not all of which are noted below.

In particular, share capital of a limited company may be reduced, either by special resolution supported by a solvency statement (available for private companies limited by shares only) or by special resolution confirmed by the court. *[s641-s651]*.

In addition, Part 18 of the CA 2006 sets out provisions for redemption and purchases of share capital by a limited company (and for private companies limited by shares to make payments out of capital). There are a number of restrictions governing when these procedures can be used which are not covered in this chapter. These procedures may also affect other reserves and some of the ways in which that can happen are referred to at 5.3.12.B, 5.3.12.C and 5.3.12.F below.

There are more statutory restrictions over how the share capital of a limited company may be altered than for an unlimited company. *[s617]*. However, its articles and other agreements may set out how the share capital of an unlimited company may be altered.

There are detailed rules in the CA 2006 which this chapter does not set out in full. Other regulatory requirements may also be relevant to transactions involving shares and it is important that companies take appropriate legal and professional advice in this area.

5.3.12.B   Share premium account

Share premium account is a statutory reserve that arises on the issue of share capital. It is beyond the scope of this chapter to explain the rules governing share premium in detail, but the summary below explains how share premium arises and can be applied or reduced. The concept of a share premium account is not relevant to an LLP.

Chapter 6

If a company issues shares at a premium, whether for cash or otherwise, a sum equal to the aggregate amount or value of the premiums on those shares must be transferred to an account called the share premium account, except to the extent that merger relief (as set out in sections 612 and 613) and group reconstruction relief (as set out in section 611) apply. Chapter 8 at 4.2.1 discusses how these reliefs operate. *[s610(1), (5), (6)]*.

Where on issuing shares, a company has transferred a sum to the share premium account, that sum can be used to write off the expenses of the issue of those shares and any commission paid on the issue of those shares. Share premium may be used to pay up new shares to be allotted to members as fully-paid bonus shares. *[s610(2)-(3)]*.

Share premium also arises when treasury shares are sold for proceeds that exceed the purchase price paid by the company. The excess must be transferred to the share premium account. *[s731(3)]*. This would include sales of the treasury shares by the company to an ESOP.

The share premium account of a limited company having a share capital may be reduced either by special resolution supported by a solvency statement (available for private companies limited by shares only) or by special resolution confirmed by the court. *[s610(4), s641-s651]*.

Where a limited company purchases (or redeems) shares, normally the purchase (or redemption) must be made out of distributable profits of the company or out of the proceeds of a fresh issue of shares made for the purposes of financing the purchase (or for the purposes of the redemption). However, any premium payable on the purchase (or redemption) of the shares must be paid out of distributable profits, unless the shares were originally issued at a premium and the purchase (or redemption) is made in whole or in part out of proceeds of a fresh issue. In the latter case, the share premium account (rather than distributable profits) may be reduced up to an amount equal to the lower of (a) the aggregate of the premiums received by the company on issue of the shares purchased (or redeemed) and (b) the current amount of the company's share premium account (including any premiums transferred to share premium account in respect of the new shares). *[s687, s692]*.

There are exceptions to the above requirements where:

- a private limited company purchases or redeems its own shares out of capital under Chapter 5 of Part 18 of the CA 2006; *[s687(1), s692(1)]* or
- a private limited company (if authorised to do so by the articles) purchases its own shares out of capital otherwise than in accordance with Chapter 5 up to an aggregate purchase price in a financial year of the lower of: *[s692(1ZA)]*
  - £15,000; or
  - the nominal value of 5% of its fully paid share capital as at the beginning of the financial year.

This means that where section 692(1ZA) applies, Chapter 5 of Part 18 of the CA 2006 does not apply. Chapter 5 of Part 18 allows a private limited company, subject to any restrictions or prohibitions in its articles, to make a payment in respect of the redemption or purchase of its own shares otherwise than out of distributable profits or the proceeds of a fresh issue. The permissible capital payment is the amount of the price of redemption or purchase of the shares after deducting any available profits of the company and the proceeds of any fresh issue of shares made for the purposes of the redemption or purchase. *[s709-s723]*.

Share premium account may also be reduced when a private limited company makes a payment out of capital (under Chapter 5 of Part 18 of the CA 2006) or a payment under section 692(1ZA)) Where the permissible capital payment (together with any proceeds of a fresh issue applied in making the redemption or purchase of the company's own shares) is greater than the nominal amount of the shares redeemed or purchased, the amount of fully paid share capital, share premium account, capital redemption reserve or revaluation reserve (if in credit) may be reduced by the amount of the excess. *[s734]*.

5.3.12.C   Revaluation reserve

The revaluation reserve arises where an asset is carried at valuation using the alternative accounting rules in the Regulations (or LLP Regulations). *[1 Sch 35, 1 Sch 35 (LLP)]*. See 10.2 below.

The amount of the revaluation reserve is presented in the position given for the item 'revaluation reserve' under capital and reserves in the balance sheet formats. The name 'revaluation reserve' must be used (previously there was flexibility on what the reserve was called in the formats). *[1 Sch 35(2), 1 Sch 35(2) (LLP)]*.

The uses of the revaluation reserve (and associated disclosures) are explained further at 10.2.3 and 10.2.4 below.

5.3.12.D   Reserves provided for by the Articles of Association

Where the articles specifically provide for reserves to be established, this line item is used. This is not relevant to LLPs.

5.3.12.E   Other reserves

The General Rules to the formats (see 4.4 above) allow or, where the special nature of the company's business requires this, require certain adaptations to the balance sheet formats, as well as allowing line items to be shown in greater detail.

The analysis of other reserves is an area where entities may need to be mindful that FRS 102 requires additional line items, headings and subtotals when relevant to an understanding of the entity's financial position. *[FRS 102.4.3]*.

The sub-headings within the 'Other reserves' category are discussed at 5.3.12.F to 5.3.12.H below.

5.3.12.F   Capital redemption reserve

The capital redemption reserve is a statutory reserve which is established when: *[s733, s734]*

- the shares of a limited company are redeemed or purchased wholly out of the company's profits – the amount by which the company's issued share capital is diminished on cancellation of the redeemed or purchased shares (i.e. the nominal value of the shares redeemed or purchased) is transferred to capital redemption reserve;
- the shares of a limited company are redeemed or purchased wholly or partly out of the proceeds of a fresh issue and the aggregate amount of the proceeds is less than the aggregate nominal value of the shares redeemed or purchased – the shortfall is

transferred to capital redemption reserve. This does not apply to a private company if, in addition to the proceeds of the fresh issue, the company applies a payment out of capital under Chapter 5 of Part 18 of the CA 2006 or under section 692(1ZA) in making the redemption or purchase;

- a private company makes a redemption or purchase of own shares out of capital (under Chapter 5 of Part 18 of the CA 2006) or a payment under section 692(1ZA), and the permissible capital payment (as defined in section 734 for these purposes, which would include any proceeds of a fresh issue used for the redemption or purchase) is less than the nominal amount of the shares redeemed or purchased – the shortfall is transferred to capital redemption reserve; and

- where treasury shares are cancelled – the share capital is reduced by the nominal amount of the shares cancelled and that amount transferred to capital redemption reserve.

The concept of a capital redemption reserve is not relevant to an LLP.

As with the share premium account, the capital redemption reserve may:

- be used to pay up new shares to be allotted to members as fully-paid bonus shares; *[s733(5)]*

- be reduced by a limited company having a share capital either by special resolution supported by a solvency statement (available for a private company limited by shares only) or by special resolution confirmed by the court; *[s733(6), s641-s651]* and

- be reduced, to the extent permitted by section 734 of the CA 2006, when a private limited company makes a payment out of capital (under Chapter 5 of Part 18 of the CA 2006) or a payment under section 692(1ZA). Where the permissible capital payment (together with any proceeds of a fresh issue applied in making the redemption or purchase of the company's own shares) is greater than the nominal amount of the shares redeemed or purchased, the amount of fully paid share capital, share premium account, capital redemption reserve or revaluation reserve (if in credit) may be reduced by the amount of the excess. *[s709-723, s734]*.

It is beyond the scope of this chapter to explain the detailed rules and procedures and accounting governing redemptions / purchases of shares, treasury shares and the capital redemption reserve (but the summary above highlights the main ways the capital redemption reserve may arise, be utilised or reduced).

5.3.12.G   Reserve for own shares

The reserve for own shares is used where:

- a company issues shares to or purchases its own shares to be held by an ESOP (see Chapter 23 at 13.3).

   This applies in individual and consolidated financial statements (where the company is the sponsoring entity of the ESOP – as FRS 102 requires that the ESOP is treated for accounting purposes as an extension of the company), and in consolidated financial statements that consolidate the ESOP (where the company is not the sponsoring entity of the ESOP); or

- where shares are held as treasury shares (see Chapter 10 at 5.6.3). *[FRS 102.22.16]*.

Note (4) on the balance sheet formats states that the nominal value of the own shares held must be shown separately in the notes to the accounts. This note strictly refers to own shares presented as an asset (which is not permitted under FRS 102) but entities commonly disclose this information even where own shares are presented in equity. Where treasury shares are held, there are further statutory disclosures (see 5.4.2 below).

This line item is not relevant for LLPs.

5.3.12.H   Other reserves, including fair value reserve (item K.IV.4)

Other reserves reported at item K.IV.4 would include a reserve arising where merger relief (under sections 612 and 613) or group reconstruction relief (under section 611) is taken, but the company chooses to record a reserve equivalent to the share premium that would have been recorded but for the relief (as permitted by section 615).

Where a UK company prepares Companies Act accounts (or an LLP prepares non-IAS accounts), the fair value accounting rules in the Regulations (or LLP Regulations) (see 10.3 below) have the effect that the changes in fair value: *[1 Sch 40, 1 Sch 40 (LLP)]*

- of the hedging instrument in respect of cash-flow hedges and hedges of net investment in foreign operations (to the extent effective);
- relating to exchange differences on monetary items forming part of the company's net investment in a foreign entity (see below); and
- of available-for-sale financial assets

must or, in the case of available-for-sale financial assets, may be recognised in a separate statutory reserve (the fair value reserve). This would be an 'Other reserve (including fair value reserve)' in the statutory formats. Available-for-sale financial assets may arise where a company chooses to apply the recognition and measurement provisions of IAS 39.

FRS 102 requires that exchange differences arising on translation of a foreign operation in the financial statements that include that foreign operation (including a monetary item that forms part of the net investment in that foreign operation) are recognised in other comprehensive income and accumulated in equity. However, there is no requirement to accumulate these in a separate reserve. *[FRS 102.30.13, 30.22]*. See Chapter 27 at 3.7. Entities are not, however, precluded from doing so, and the fair value accounting rules in the Regulations (and LLP Regulations) imply that exchange differences on monetary items forming part of the company's or LLP's net investment in a foreign entity may be, at least in some circumstance, accumulated within the fair value reserve. However, the fair value accounting rules apply to a financial instrument measured at fair value (or to assets and liabilities qualifying as hedged items under a fair value hedge accounting system). It is not clear that this requirement to accumulate the exchange differences in the statutory fair value reserve would apply to a monetary item such as a loan to a foreign entity (which would usually be recorded at amortised cost). See 10.3.2 below.

5.3.12.I   Profit and loss account

The profit and loss account reserve (or retained earnings) arises from the accumulation of the results for the year, and other items taken to other comprehensive income or to equity, but not classified in another reserve.

Chapter 6

Where profits are unrealised, companies may prefer to report these in a reserve other than retained earnings, so as to distinguish these from other profits that are realised.

There is no separate line item for the profit and loss account in the LLP formats.

5.3.13   *Other application issues*

5.3.13.A   *Construction contracts*

FRS 102's requirements on presentation of construction contracts are discussed at 5.1.13.B above. This discussion is equally applicable to the statutory formats, subject to the following observations.

In our view, it would be appropriate to include the contract asset as a line item within debtors (see 5.3.6 above) and the contract liability within creditors (see 5.3.8 above). Progress billings not yet received (including any contract retentions) would be included in trade debtors (rather than trade receivables as in the adapted formats). Advances, where reported separately, would be disclosed as 'payments received on account' within 'creditors: amounts falling due within one year' and 'creditors: amounts falling due after more than one year', as appropriate. The sub-classifications required by paragraph 4.2B of FRS 102 where adapted formats are used are not required where statutory formats are used.

5.3.13.B   *Deferred tax*

FRS 102 requires deferred tax liabilities to be presented within 'provisions for liabilities' (see 5.3.11 above) and deferred tax assets to be presented within debtors. *[FRS 102.29.23]*. There is no requirement to present deferred tax separately on the face of the statement of financial position. FRS 102 includes rules on offset of deferred tax assets and liabilities (see Chapter 26 at 10.1.1). *[FRS 102.29.24A]*.

This presentation is consistent with the statutory formats in the Regulations (and LLP Regulations) but differs from the presentation of deferred tax under the adapted formats in FRS 102 (see 5.1 above) or in IFRSs as a non-current asset and / or non-current liability shown on the face of the statement of financial position. *[IAS 1.54, 56]*.

Deferred tax assets may include amounts due after more than one year. See 5.2.2 above for the disclosure requirements for 'debtors: amounts falling due after more than one year' in FRS 102 and the Regulations (and LLP Regulations), where statutory formats are used.

FRS 102 requires that the amount of deferred tax liabilities and deferred tax assets at the end of the reporting period for each type of timing difference and the amount of unused tax losses and tax credits is disclosed separately. *[FRS 102.29.27(e)]*. So while deferred tax is not required to be shown on the face of the statutory balance sheet, this disclosure would be required in the notes. FRS 102's full disclosures for deferred tax are set out in Chapter 26 at 11.

A UK company preparing Companies Act accounts (or an LLP preparing non-IAS accounts) must state the provision for deferred tax separately from any other tax provisions. *[1 Sch 60, 1 Sch 58 (LLP)]*. This should not lead to additional disclosure since deferred tax will of course be shown already on the face of the statement of financial position for adapted formats and, as noted above, FRS 102 required disclosure of deferred tax balances in the notes.

Where there have been transfers to and from deferred tax, the amount of the provision at the beginning and end of the year, and the movements in that provision must also be disclosed in the notes to the accounts (see 5.3.11 above). *[1 Sch 59, 1 Sch 57 (LLP)].* This disclosure is required where statutory formats are used and, in our view, is also likely required where adapted formats are used, even though deferred tax is not shown as a provision in the balance sheet (in order to give equivalent information).

5.3.13.C   Assets and disposal groups held for sale

FRS 102 does not include a concept of assets and disposal groups held for sale, comparable to that in IFRS 5. Therefore, an entity is not required to present a non-current asset classified as held for sale and the assets of a disposal group held for sale separately from other assets in the statement of financial position and the liabilities of a disposal group held for sale separately from other liabilities in the statement of financial position. *[IFRS 5.38, IAS 1.54].*

In addition, FRS 102 does not permit such presentation of disposal groups in the statement of financial position because the General Rules to the formats (see 4.4 above) do not allow the aggregation of different line items into two lines, being assets and liabilities of the disposal group, in this way. This does not preclude entities presenting additional analysis in the notes to the financial statements. See also the disclosures at 5.5 below.

As noted at 5.3.3 above, the statutory definition of a fixed asset is not normally interpreted to mean that individual assets are transferred to current assets when a decision to dispose of them has been made (but see 5.1.8 above which sets out some situations where we would expect a change in use of the asset to lead to reclassification as inventory). Nevertheless, some companies do make such transfers.

5.3.13.D   Post-employment benefit assets and liabilities

FRS 102 does not explicitly address the presentation of post-employment benefit assets and liabilities.

The format 1 balance sheet includes a line item 'pensions and similar liabilities' within provisions for liabilities (see 5.3.11 above). There is no specific line item for pension surpluses but in our view, a pension asset could be presented as a separate line item within debtors. Defined benefit assets may include amounts due after more than one year. See 5.2.2 above for the disclosure requirements in FRS 102 and in the Regulations (and LLP Regulations) for 'debtors: amounts due after more than one year'.

However, under previous UK GAAP, FRS 17 – *Retirement benefits* – required presentation of the pension asset or liability (net of deferred tax) separately on the face of the balance sheet following other net assets and before capital and reserves. Where an employer had more than one scheme, the total of any defined benefit assets and the total of any defined benefit liabilities were shown separately on the balance sheet. *[FRS 17.47, 49].* Appendix II to FRS 17 stated that 'The Board has received legal advice that these requirements do not contravene the Companies Act 1985'. *[FRS 17 Appendix II.6].*

As a result, there is likely to be divergence in practice in the presentation of defined benefit pension surpluses and deficits under FRS 102 (although the related deferred tax asset or liability should be shown separately, as offsetting is not permitted). Disclosure requirements for defined benefit plans are discussed in Chapter 25 at 3.12.4.

Chapter 6

The Regulations (and LLP Regulations) require certain disclosures in Companies Act accounts (non-IAS accounts, for an LLP) for pension commitments included in the balance sheet (see 5.3.11 above) and, for pension commitments not included in the balance sheet (see 8.7.1 below).

Where there have been transfers to and from provisions for liabilities (which as noted above, may include pension provisions), the amount of the provision at the beginning and end of the year, and the movements in that provision must also be disclosed in the notes to the accounts (see 5.3.11 above). *[1 Sch 59, 1 Sch 57 (LLP)].* As noted at 5.3.11 above, FRS 102 also requires a reconciliation of movements in plan assets and plan liabilities. *[FRS 102.28.41(e)-(f)].*

These disclosures are relevant to adapted formats and statutory formats.

5.3.13.E   *Biological assets*

The format 1 balance sheet does not include a line item for biological assets, which should be reported within either tangible fixed assets (e.g. an apple orchard) or stock (e.g. farmed salmon), as appropriate.

FRS 102 requires reconciliations of changes in the carrying amounts to be given for biological assets (separately for each class carried under the cost model and each class carried under the fair value model) (see Chapter 31 at 2.6.3 and 2.7.2). *[FRS 102.34.7(c), 34.10(e)].*

See 5.2.2 above for the requirements for reconciliations of movements in fixed assets in the Regulations (and the LLP Regulations) for UK companies preparing Companies Act accounts (and LLP accounts preparing non-IAS accounts). These disclosures apply where statutory formats or adapted formats are used.

Comparatives are not required for the reconciliations required by FRS 102 or the Regulations (and LLP Regulations).

5.3.13.F   *Financial assets and financial liabilities*

The format 1 balance sheet does not include specific line items for financial assets and financial liabilities. Financial assets will generally be reported, as appropriate, within 'cash at bank and in hand', 'debtors', 'current asset investments' or 'fixed asset investments'. Financial liabilities will generally be reported, as appropriate, within 'creditors: amounts falling due within one year' and 'creditors: amounts falling due after more than one year' or 'provisions for liabilities' (e.g. contingent consideration on a business combination).

FRS 102 requires further analyses of specified categories of financial assets and financial liabilities to be disclosed either in the statement of financial position or in the notes to the financial statements (see 5.1.6 above for details). The Regulations and LLP Regulations also include various disclosures, some of which have been highlighted in the relevant sections above and also in respect of financial instruments held at fair value (see 10.3.1 and 10.3.4 below).

5.3.13.G   Compound instruments

See 5.1.13.E above. The discussion is equally applicable to statutory formats.

5.3.13.H   Government grants

FRS 102 sets out two models for recognising government grants – the accrual model and the performance model (see Chapter 21). There is no specific line for government grants in the balance sheet statutory formats.

The discussion at 5.1.13.F above on presentation and disclosure of government grants under the two models is equally applicable to statutory formats.

5.4   Additional disclosures in respect of share capital (or equivalent) (adapted formats and statutory formats)

FRS 102 (see 5.4.1 below) and the Regulations (see 5.4.2 below) require similar disclosures in respect of share capital.

5.4.1   FRS 102 disclosures in respect of share capital (or equivalent)

FRS 102 requires an entity with share capital to disclose the following information, either in the statement of financial position or in the notes: *[FRS 102.4.12]*

(a)   for each class of share capital:

  (i)   the number of shares issued and fully paid, and issued but not fully paid;

  (ii)   par value per share, or that the shares have no par value;

  (iii)   the rights, preferences and restrictions attaching to that class including restrictions on the distribution of dividends and the repayment of capital;

  (iv)   shares in the entity held by the entity or by its subsidiaries, associates or joint ventures;

  (v)   shares reserved for issue under options and contracts for the sale of shares, including the terms and amounts; and

(b)   a description of each reserve within equity.

The Triennial review 2017 removed the requirement to present a reconciliation of the number of shares outstanding at the beginning and at the end of the period, for each class of share capital. Therefore, this reconciliation is only required for accounting periods beginning before 1 January 2019 and where the Triennial review 2017 amendments have not been early adopted.

An entity without share capital, such as a partnership or trust, must disclose information equivalent to that required by (a) above, showing changes during the period in each category of equity, and the rights, preferences and restrictions attaching to each category of equity. *[FRS 102.4.13].*

5.4.2   Information required by the Regulations in respect of share capital

Some of the FRS 102 disclosure requirements overlap with the disclosure requirements in relation to share capital included in the Regulations for UK companies preparing Companies Act accounts.

The Regulations require the following disclosures in the notes to the accounts:

- the amount of allotted share capital and, separately, the amount of called up share capital which has been paid up (this may be given on the face of the statement of financial position or in the notes);[19]
- where shares of more than one class have been allotted, the number and aggregate nominal value of shares of each class allotted; *[1 Sch 47(1)(a)]*
- where shares are held as treasury shares, the number and aggregate nominal value of the treasury shares and, where shares of more than one class have been allotted, the number and aggregate nominal value of the shares of each class held as treasury shares; *[1 Sch 47(1)(b)]*
- where any part of the allotted share capital consists of redeemable shares: *[1 Sch 47(2)]*
  - the earliest and latest dates on which the company has power to redeem those shares;
  - whether those shares must be redeemed in any event or are liable to be redeemed at the option of the company or of the shareholder; and
  - whether any (and if so, what) premium is payable on redemption.
- if the company has allotted any shares during the financial year: *[1 Sch 48]*
  - the classes of shares allotted; and
  - for each class of shares, the number allotted, their aggregate nominal value, and the consideration received by the company for the allotment.
- with respect to any contingent right to the allotment of shares in the company (i.e. any option to subscribe for shares and any other right to require the allotment of shares to any person whether arising on the conversion into shares of securities of any other description or otherwise), particulars of: *[1 Sch 49]*
  - the number, description and amount of the shares in relation to which the right is exercisable;
  - the period during which it is exercisable; and
  - the price to be paid for the shares allotted;
- if any fixed cumulative dividends on the company's shares are in arrear: *[1 Sch 62]*
  - the amount of the arrears; and
  - the period for which the dividends or, if there is more than one class, each class of them are in arrear; and
- the number, description and amount of the shares in the company held by, or on behalf of, its subsidiary undertakings (except where the subsidiary undertaking is concerned as personal representative, or, subject to certain exceptions, as trustee). *[4 Sch 3]*.

The LLP Regulations do not include the above disclosures (as not relevant) although the following information is required in the notes to the accounts in respect of loans and other debts due to members: *[1 Sch 47 (LLP)]*

- the aggregate amount of loans and other debts due to members as at the date of the financial year;
- the aggregate amounts contributed by members during the financial year;
- the aggregate amounts transferred to or from the profit and loss account during that year;
- the aggregate amounts withdrawn by members or applied on behalf of members during that year;
- the aggregate amount of loans and other debts due to members as at the balance sheet date; and
- the aggregate amount of loans and other debts due to members that fall due after more than one year.

The LLP SORP provides further guidance on this disclosure, adding further related disclosures, and requires a reconciliation of the movement in members' interests analysed between 'members' other interests' and 'loans and other debts due to members' (which would meet the requirements of paragraph 4.13 of FRS 102 (see 5.4.1 above) and the statutory requirements in paragraph 47 of Schedule 1 to the LLP Regulations). *[LLP SORP.60]*.

Detailed guidance on issues specific to LLPs is outside the scope of this chapter.

The LLP SORP made changes to the disclosures required for small LLPs (see Chapter 5 at 11.5).

5.5 Information on disposal groups to be presented in the notes (adapted formats and statutory formats)

FRS 102 requires only limited disclosures where there is, at the end of the reporting period, a disposal group. As discussed at 5.1.13.C and 5.3.13.C above, FRS 102 does not include a concept of assets and disposal groups held for sale, comparable to that in IFRS 5.

If, at the reporting date, an entity has a binding sale agreement for a major disposal of assets, or a disposal group, the entity must disclose in the notes to the financial statements: *[FRS 102.4.14]*

- a description of the asset(s) or the disposal group;
- a description of the facts and circumstances of the sale; and
- the carrying amount of the assets or, for a disposal group, the carrying amounts of the underlying assets and liabilities.

FRS 102 defines a disposal group as 'a group of assets to be disposed of, by sale or otherwise, together as a group in a single transaction, and liabilities directly associated with those assets that will be transferred in the transaction. The group includes goodwill acquired in a business combination if the group is a cash-generating unit to which goodwill has been allocated in accordance with the requirements of paragraphs 27.24 to 27.27 of this FRS'. *[FRS 102 Appendix I]*.

Chapter 6

6   STATEMENT OF COMPREHENSIVE INCOME

This part of the chapter sets out the requirements in FRS 102 for entities not applying Section 1A.

FRS 102 requires an entity to present its total comprehensive income for a period, i.e. its financial performance for period, in one or two statements. Financial performance is the relationship of the income and expenses of an entity as reported in the statement of comprehensive income. *[FRS 102 Appendix I]*.

Definitions of terms applicable to the statement of comprehensive income are at 3.1 above.

This part of the chapter is set out as follows:

- 6.1 – Format of the statement of comprehensive income (adapted formats and statutory formats);
- 6.2 – Items reported in other comprehensive income (adapted formats and statutory formats);
- 6.3 – Single statement approach (adapted formats and statutory formats);
- 6.4 – Two-statement approach (adapted formats and statutory formats);
- 6.5 – Adapted formats;
- 6.6 – Statutory formats – format 1 and 2 profit and loss accounts;
- 6.7 – Requirements applicable to both approaches (adapted formats and statutory formats);
- 6.8 – Presentation of discontinued operations (adapted formats and statutory formats); and
- 6.9 – Earnings per share (adapted formats and statutory formats).

6.1   Format of the statement of comprehensive income (adapted formats and statutory formats)

Part 1 of Schedule 1 to the Regulations (and Part 1 of Schedule 1 to the LLP Regulations) provide a choice of:

- one of two profit and loss account statutory formats (as set out in Section B of the relevant Part); or
- use of adapted formats.

Schedule 2 (banking companies) and Schedule 3 (insurance companies) to the Regulations require use of the statutory formats and do not allow use of adapted formats. The statutory formats for insurance companies are discussed in Chapter 33 at 8. This publication does not set out or discuss the statutory formats for banking companies.

The consolidated statement of comprehensive income or income statement (depending on the option taken) of a group must be presented in accordance with the requirements for a consolidated profit and loss account of Schedule 6 to the Regulations (or, where applicable, Schedule 3 to the LLP Regulations). *[FRS 102.5.5, 5.7]*. How adapted formats and statutory formats are applied in consolidated financial statements is further explained in 4.1.2 above and 6.5 and 6.6 below.

Section 5's requirements to present a statement of comprehensive income in either single statement form or in two-statement form are discussed below. The single statement form is discussed at 6.3 below and the two-statement form at 6.4 below. Items presented in other comprehensive income under both forms are discussed at 6.2 below. Adapted formats (see 6.5 below) and statutory formats (see 6.6 below) can be used under both the single statement and two statement forms of the statement of comprehensive income. Supplementary requirements in FRS 102 relevant to the statement of comprehensive income are discussed at 6.7 to 6.9 below. The discussion at 6.1 to 6.4 and 6.7 to 6.9 below is relevant to both adapted formats and statutory formats.

An entity must present its total comprehensive income for a period either: *[FRS 102.5.2, FRS 102 Appendix I]*

- in a single statement of comprehensive income which presents all items of income and expense recognised in the period (and includes a subtotal for profit or loss); or

- in two statements – an income statement (referred to as the profit and loss account in the CA 2006) and a statement of comprehensive income, in which case the income statement presents all items of income and expense recognised in the period except those that are recognised in total comprehensive income outside of profit or loss as permitted or required by FRS 102.

A change from the single-statement approach to the two-statement approach, or *vice versa*, is a retrospective change in accounting policy to which Section 10 applies. *[FRS 102.5.3]*. See Chapter 9 at 3.4.

These requirements apply both to consolidated and individual financial statements.

6.1.1 *Section 408 exemption in group accounts*

Where a UK company (or an LLP) prepares group accounts in accordance with the CA 2006, the company (or the LLP) can take advantage of the exemption in section 408 of the CA 2006 not to present the individual profit and loss account and certain related notes (providing the conditions for use of the exemption are met). See Chapter 1 at 6.3.2.

References in Part 15 to the profit and loss account include notes to the accounts giving information required by any provision of the CA 2006 and that is required or allowed by any such provision to be given in a note to the company's accounts. *[s472]*.

The section 408 exemption, where used, provides that:

- the company's (or the LLP's) individual profit and loss account need not contain the information specified in paragraphs 65 to 69 of Schedule 1 to the Regulations (or paragraphs 62 to 67 of Schedule 1 to the LLP Regulations); *[Regulations 3(2), 1 Sch 65-69, LLP Regulations 3(2), 1 Sch 62-67 (LLP)]* and

- the company's (or the LLP's) individual profit and loss account must be approved by the directors (or the members of the LLP) in accordance with section 414(1) of the CA 2006, but may be omitted from the company's (or the LLP's) annual accounts. *[s414(1), s414(1) (LLP)]*.

The exemption is conditional on the company's (or the LLP's) individual balance sheet showing the company's (or LLP's) profit or loss for the financial year (determined in accordance with the CA 2006) and disclosing use of the section 408 exemption in the annual accounts.

6.2   Items reported in other comprehensive income (adapted formats and statutory formats)

Other comprehensive income means items of income and expense (including reclassification adjustments), that are not recognised in profit or loss as required or permitted by FRS 102. *[FRS 102 Appendix I]*. Therefore, profit and loss is the default category; all comprehensive income is part of profit and loss unless FRS 102 permits or requires otherwise. See definitions at 3.1 above.

Tax expense / (income) is recognised in other comprehensive income where the transaction or other event that resulted in the tax is recognised in other comprehensive income. *[FRS 102.29.22]*. See Chapter 26 at 8.

FRS 102 requires the following items to be included in other comprehensive income:

(a)   changes in revaluation surplus relating to property, plant and equipment *[FRS 102.17.15E-F]* (see Chapter 15 at 3.6.3), and changes in revaluation surplus relating to intangible assets *[FRS 102.18.18G-H]* (see Chapter 16 at 3.4.2.C);

(b)   remeasurements of the net defined benefit liability of defined benefit plans. These remeasurements comprise actuarial gains and losses, the return on plan assets excluding amounts included in net interest on the net defined benefit liability and any change in the amount of a defined benefit plan surplus that is not recoverable excluding amounts included in net interest on the net defined benefit liability *[FRS 102.28.23(d), 28.25, 28.25A]* (see Chapter 25 at 3.6.10.B);

(c)   exchange gains and losses arising from translating the financial statements of a foreign operation (including in consolidated financial statements, exchange differences on a monetary item that forms part of the net investment in the foreign operation). However, under FRS 102 (unlike IAS 21 – *The Effects of Changes in Foreign Exchange Rates*), cumulative exchange differences accumulated in equity are not reclassified to profit or loss on disposal of a net investment in a foreign operation *[FRS 102.9.18A, 30.13]* (see Chapter 27 at 3.7 and 3.8);

(d)   the effective portion of fair value gains and losses on hedging instruments in a cash flow hedge or a hedge of the foreign exchange risk in a net investment in a foreign operation. The amounts taken to equity in respect of the hedge of the foreign exchange risk in a net investment in a foreign operation are not reclassified to profit or loss on disposal or partial disposal of the foreign operation *[FRS 102.12.23, 12.24, 12.25A]* (see Chapter 10 at 10.8 and 10.9);

(e)   fair value gains and losses through other comprehensive income, where an investor that is not a parent measures its interests in jointly controlled entities, *[FRS 102.15.9(c), 15.14-15.15A]*, and investments in associates in its individual financial statements using the fair value model *[FRS 102.14.4(c), 14.9-10A]* (see Chapter 12 at 3.3.4 and Chapter 13 at 3.6.2);

(f)   fair value gains and losses through other comprehensive income for investments in subsidiaries, associates and jointly controlled entities in a parent's separate financial statements and in consolidated financial statements for certain excluded subsidiaries *[FRS 102.9.9, 9.9A, 9.9B(b), 9.26(b), 9.26A]* (see Chapter 8 at 3.4 and 4.2.2); and

(g) any unrealised gain arising on an exchange of business or non-monetary assets for an interest in a subsidiary, jointly controlled entity or associate, *[FRS 102.9.31(c)]*, (see Chapter 8 at 3.8).

Of the above items, only the amounts taken to other comprehensive income in relation to cash flow hedges (at (d) above) may be reclassified to profit or loss in a subsequent period under FRS 102.

Where the entity applies the recognition and measurement requirements of IAS 39 or IFRS 9 to financial instruments, further items are reported in other comprehensive income (see 6.2.1 below).

The Regulations and LLP Regulations restrict when unrealised profits can be reported in the profit and loss account. Consequently, certain unrealised profits may be required to be reported in other comprehensive income (see 6.2.2 below).

6.2.1   Items reported in other comprehensive income where an entity chooses to apply the recognition and measurement provisions of IAS 39 or IFRS 9

Where the recognition and measurement requirements of IAS 39 or IFRS 9 are applied to financial instruments, as permitted by FRS 102, the following items would also be reported in other comprehensive income in accordance with the requirements of the applicable accounting standard:

(a) gains and losses on remeasuring available-for-sale financial assets (if the entity chooses to apply IAS 39); *[IAS 39.55(b)]*

(b) gains and losses on remeasuring investments in equity instruments designated as measured at fair value through other comprehensive income (if the entity chooses to apply IFRS 9 – see 10.2 below); *[IFRS 9.4.1.4, 5.7.1(b), 5.7.5-6]*

(c) the effective portion of gains and losses on hedging instruments in a cash flow hedge or hedge of a net investment in a foreign operation (if the entity chooses to apply IAS 39 or IFRS 9); *[IAS 39.95-102, IFRS 9.6.5.11-14]*

(d) for liabilities designated as at fair value through profit or loss, fair value changes attributable to changes in the liability's credit risk, unless this would create or enlarge an accounting mismatch in profit and loss (if the entity chooses to apply IFRS 9). *[IFRS 9.4.2.2, 5.7.1(c), 5.7.7-9, FRS 102 Appendix III.12C]*.

This accounting treatment will usually require use of a 'true and fair override' for a UK company or LLP since it breaches the requirements of the Regulations, Small Companies Regulations, LLP Regulations or Small LLP Regulations – see 10.3 below); and

(e) gains and losses on financial assets that are debt instruments (meeting the specified criteria) that are carried at fair value through other comprehensive income (if the entity chooses to apply IFRS 9 – see 10.3 below). *[IFRS 9.4.1.2A, 5.7.1(d), 5.7.10-11]*.

Only items (a), (e) and the effective portion of gains and losses on hedging instruments in a cash flow hedge at (c) above may be reclassified to profit or loss in a subsequent period. The amounts taken to equity in respect of the hedge of the foreign exchange risk in a net investment in a foreign operation are not reclassified to profit or loss on disposal or partial disposal of the foreign operation. *[FRS 102.9.18A, 30.13]*.

The requirements of IAS 39 and IFRS 9 are discussed in Chapters 42 to 54 of EY International GAAP 2019. However, EY International GAAP 2019 reflects the reduced applicability of IAS 39 by covering its requirements only at a high level. IAS 39 is covered in more detail in EY International GAAP 2018.

6.2.2   *Impact of realised and unrealised profits on items reported in other comprehensive income*

UK companies preparing Companies Act accounts (and LLPs preparing non-IAS accounts) need to be mindful of the statutory requirement that 'only profits realised at the balance sheet are to be included in the profit and loss account' (see 9.1.1 below). *[1 Sch 13(a), 1 Sch 13(a) (LLP)]*.

Notwithstanding this restriction, changes in the value of a financial instrument or in the value of an investment property or a living animal or plant measured using the fair value accounting rules (in paragraphs 36, 38 and 39 of Schedule 1 to the Regulations and the same paragraphs in the LLP Regulations) must be reflected in the profit and loss account. This is subject to the requirements of paragraphs 40(3) and (4) of Schedule 1 to the Regulations (and the same paragraphs in the LLP Regulations) for available-for-sale financial assets, hedge accounting and for exchange differences on monetary items forming part of the net investment in a foreign entity, which permit or require certain movements on financial instruments to be reflected in a statutory 'fair value reserve'. *[1 Sch 40(2)-40(4), 1 Sch 40(2) (LLP)-40(4) (LLP)]*. See 10.3.2 and 10.4.1 below.

While UK companies and LLPs may now measure stocks at fair value using the fair value accounting rules (see 10.4 below), paragraph 40 above does not specify where fair value changes arising on stock are presented. FRS 102 allows stock to be measured at fair value less costs to sell in restrictive circumstances; in such circumstances, the fair value changes are recognised in profit or loss. *[FRS 102.13.3]*. See 10.3 and 10.4 below for a fuller discussion of the fair value accounting rules.

FRS 101 requires that 'an entity shall recognise all items of income and expense arising in a period in profit or loss unless an IFRS requires or permits otherwise *or unless prohibited by the Act'* [emphasis added]. *[FRS 101.AG1(k)]*. The Triennial review 2017 added this same requirement into FRS 102. *[FRS 102.5.8]*. Whilst FRS 102 prior to the Triennial review 2017, did not include the words above, there are reasons to believe that the same treatment was intended. For example, FRS 102's requirements for exchanges of businesses and non-monetary assets for an interest in a subsidiary, jointly controlled entity or an associate state that 'any unrealised gain arising on the exchange shall be recognised in other comprehensive income'. *[FRS 102.9.31(c)]*.

Where the standard is explicit that it requires that a particular gain must be reported in profit or loss but this would conflict with the Regulations or LLP Regulations, the entity should consider whether a 'true and fair override' of the requirements of the CA 2006 is appropriate (see 9.2 below). Where the standard is not explicit, notwithstanding that profit and loss is the default location for gains and losses, in our view, entities should look to Appendix III, which highlights the company law requirements on realised profits. However, such considerations are only relevant to entities subject to the Regulations or LLP Regulations (or corresponding requirements in another statutory or regulatory framework that applies to the entity).

Whether profits are available for distribution must be determined in accordance with applicable law. TECH 02/17BL provides guidance on the determination of the profits available for distribution (under the CA 2006). *[FRS 102 Appendix III.29].* See Chapter 1 at 6.8.

6.3   Single-statement approach (adapted formats and statutory formats)

In the single-statement approach, an entity must present the items to be included in a profit and loss account in accordance in accordance with the requirements in Part 1 of the applicable schedule to the Regulations or Part 1 of Schedule 1 to the LLP Regulations.

The consolidated statement of comprehensive income of a group must be presented in accordance with the requirements of Schedule 6 to the Regulations (or, where applicable, Schedule 3 to the LLP Regulations). *[FRS 102.5.5].*

The formats required by different types of entity (and in consolidated financial statements) are discussed in more detail in 4.1, 4.2 and 6.1 above.

A subtotal for profit or loss is included in the statement of comprehensive income. *[FRS 102 Appendix I].*

In addition, the statement of comprehensive income must include line items that present: *[FRS 102.5.5A]*

(a)   each component of other comprehensive income recognised as part of total comprehensive income outside profit or loss as permitted or required by FRS 102 classified by nature (excluding amounts in (b)). These components must be shown either net of related tax, or gross of related tax (with a single amount shown for the aggregate amount of income tax relating to those components);

(b)   the share of the other comprehensive income of associates and jointly controlled entities accounted for by the equity method; and

(c)   total comprehensive income.

Chapter 6

The statement of comprehensive income must also show the allocation of profit or loss for the period and of total comprehensive income for the period attributable to non-controlling interest and owners of the parent. *[FRS 102.5.6]*. See 4.5 above for a discussion of how this allocation should be presented under the formats for the group profit and loss account.

See Example 6.4 at 6.5.2 below for an example of a single statement of comprehensive income, in this case using adapted formats.

6.4   Two-statement approach (adapted formats and statutory formats)

Under the two-statement approach, an entity must present in an income statement, the items to be included in a profit and loss account in accordance with the requirements in Part 1 of the applicable schedule to the Regulations or Part 1 of Schedule 1 to the LLP Regulations.

The consolidated statement of comprehensive income of a group must be presented in accordance with the requirements of Schedule 6 to the Regulations (or, where applicable, Schedule 3 to the LLP Regulations). *[FRS 102.5.7]*.

The formats required by different types of entity (and in consolidated financial statements) are discussed in more detail in 4.1, 4.2 and 6.1 above.

The income statement must show the allocation of profit or loss for the period attributable to non-controlling interest and owners of the parent. *[FRS 102.5.7B]*.

The statement of comprehensive income (whether adapted formats or statutory formats are used) begins with profit or loss as its first line and then includes, as a minimum, line items that present:

(a)   each component of other comprehensive income recognised as part of total comprehensive income outside profit or loss as permitted or required by the standard classified by nature (excluding amounts in (b)). These components must be shown either net of related tax, or gross of related tax (with a single amount shown for the aggregate amount of income tax relating to those components);

(b)   the share of the other comprehensive income of associates and jointly controlled entities accounted for by the equity method; and

(c)   total comprehensive income.

The statement of comprehensive income must also show the allocation of total comprehensive income for the period attributed to non-controlling interest and owners of the parent. *[FRS 102.5.7A-C]*.

See 4.5 above for a discussion of how the allocations of profit or loss and total comprehensive income should be presented under the formats for the group profit and loss account.

See Example 6.5 at 6.5.2 for an example statement of comprehensive income (where a two-statement form is applied).

6.5   Adapted formats

An entity choosing to apply paragraph 1A(2) of Schedule 1 to the Regulations and adapt one of the profit and loss account formats (see 4.1 above for discussion as to which formats apply to which types of entity) shall, as a minimum:

- include in its statement of comprehensive income (under the single statement form) line items that present amounts (a) to (j) for the period (as set out in Figure 6.15 below); *[FRS 102.5.5B]* and

- include in its income statement (under the two-statement form) line items that present amounts (a) to (g) for the period (as set out in Figure 6.15 below), with profit or loss as the last line. The statement of comprehensive income shall begin with profit or loss as its first line and shall display as a minimum line items (h) to (j), with total comprehensive income as its last line. *[FRS 102.5.7A]*.

The main modification required for group profit and loss account using adapted formats is the identification of non-controlling interests (see 4.5, 6.3 and 6.4 above). *[FRS 102.5.6, 5.7A-C]*.

Figure 6.15   *Profit and loss account – UK company (other than a banking company or insurance company) and LLP – adapted formats*

(a)	Revenue
(b)	Finance costs
(c)	Share of the profit or loss of investments in associates and jointly controlled entities accounted for using the equity method
(d)	Profit or loss before taxation
(e)	Tax expense (excluding tax allocated to items (h) and (i) below or to equity)
(f)	A single amount comprising the total of:*
	(i) the post-tax profit or loss of a discontinued operation, and
	(ii) the post-tax gain or loss attributable to the impairment or on the disposal of the assets or disposal group(s) constituting discontinued operations
(g)	Profit or loss~
(h)	Each item of other comprehensive income classified by nature (excluding amounts in (i))
(i)	Share of other comprehensive income of associates and jointly controlled entities accounted for using the equity method
(j)	Total comprehensive income

*   As set out in paragraph 5.7E (including a column for discontinued operations – see 6.8 below)

–   The LLP SORP(2017) requires that LLPs using adapted formats show a line item for 'members' remuneration charged as an expense' as an additional expense.

While FRS 102 refers to the Regulations, the same requirements apply to LLPs since paragraph 1A(2) of Schedule 1 to the LLP Regulations also allows the use of adapted formats.

The LLP SORP requires that adapted formats show a line item for 'profit or loss for the financial year before members' remuneration and profit shares' (in order to give equivalent information to the statutory formats). 'Members' remuneration charged as an expense' (which would include related employment costs) must then be deducted as an additional expense, coming to the final line item of 'profit or loss for the financial year available for discretionary division among members' (which would correspond to item (g) in Figure 6.15 above). This would be the same presentation on the face of the profit or loss account (or statement of comprehensive income) as discussed for statutory formats at 6.6 below.

So far as is practicable, paragraphs 2 to 9A of the General Rules to the formats – see 4.4 above) apply to the income statement (or profit and loss account section of the single statement of comprehensive income), notwithstanding any such adaptation pursuant to paragraph 1A. *[1 Sch 1A(3), 1 Sch 1A(3) (LLP)]*.

An entity may include additional line items in the income statement and amend the descriptions used in the line items set out in (a) to (j) and the ordering of items, when this is necessary to explain the elements of financial performance, providing the information given is at least equivalent to that required by the profit and loss account format had it not been adapted. *[FRS 102.5.5C]*. The effect of paragraph 5.5C is to clarify that there is flexibility in the presentation requirements where adapted formats are used (for statutory formats, the General Rules to the formats clearly set out the flexibility for Arabic numbered items, but Arabic numbered items are not used in the adapted formats). While this requirement is included under the single statement approach, in our view, this is also intended to apply to the two statement approach.

The requirement (see 6.7.2 below) that an entity shall present additional line items, headings and subtotals in the statement of comprehensive income (and in the income statement, where presented) when such presentation is relevant to an understanding of the entity's financial performance also applies to adapted formats. *[FRS 102.5.9]*. Factors to be considered in determining whether to present additional line items, which are highlighted by IAS 1 (which has a similar requirement), include materiality and the nature and function of the items of income and expense. *[IAS 1.86]*.

6.5.1   Other implementation issues (adapted formats)

Schedule 1 to the Regulations (and Schedule 1 to the LLP Regulations) state that adapted formats may be used provided that the information given is at least equivalent to that which would have been required by the use of the statutory format had it not been thus adapted and the presentation is in accordance with generally accepted accounting principles or practice. *[1 Sch 1A(2), 1 Sch 1A(2) (LLP)]*.

The detail of adapted formats is left to accounting standards. The minimum items that FRS 102 requires to be presented in the statement of comprehensive income (in one or two statements), the ability to adapt the headings, and the requirement to present additional line items where relevant to an understanding of financial performance are discussed at 6.5 above.

Section 5 includes additional requirements relevant to the statement of comprehensive income (see 6.7 below) that apply to adapted formats and statutory formats. These include the presentation of turnover, guidance on operating profit (if presented), presentation of an analysis of expenses (see 6.5.2 and 6.7.4 below) and disclosure of the nature and amount of material items included in total comprehensive income (often called 'exceptional items', although that term is not used in the standard). FRS 102's requirements for presentation of discontinued operations are discussed at 6.8 below, and for earnings per share (for those entities required to or choosing to present this) at 6.9 below.

These requirements are generally self-explanatory. However, adapted formats must present revenue on the face of the income statement (or single statement of comprehensive income) (see 6.5 above). *[FRS 102.5.5B]*. FRS 102's requirement to present turnover on the face of the income statement (or statement of comprehensive income, if presented) *[FRS 102.5.7D]* (see 6.7.1 below) implies that an additional analysis of revenue between turnover and other components of revenue (if any) is required on the face of the income statement (or single statement of comprehensive income). FRS 102 also requires a detailed sub-analysis of revenue, which can be presented in the notes. *[FRS 102.23.30(b)]*. See Chapter 20 at 3.12.

Other sections of FRS 102 require supplementary analyses of certain line items presented on the face of the income statement (or profit or loss section of the statement of comprehensive income), which may be included in the notes to the financial statements. See relevant chapters of this publication.

FRS 102 also includes further guidance relevant to presentation in the statement of comprehensive income. For instance:

- incoming dividends and similar income receivable are recognised at an amount that includes any withholding tax but excludes other taxes, such as attributable tax credits. Any withholding tax suffered is shown as part of the tax charge. See further discussion at Chapter 26 at 3.3 and 8.1.2; *[FRS 102.29.19]* and

- Section 28 – *Employee Benefits* – does not specify how the cost of a defined benefit plan should be presented in the profit and loss account. Therefore, entities may present the cost as a single item or disaggregate the cost into components presented separately;

- Section 23 – *Revenue* – includes guidance on measurement of revenue, including principal versus agent considerations. See Chapter 20 at 3.2. *[FRS 102.23.4]*.

The Regulations (and LLP Regulations) require UK companies preparing Companies Act accounts (and LLPs preparing non-IAS accounts) to give further supplementary information in respect of certain line items in the notes to the accounts. These disclosures are relevant where adapted formats or statutory formats are used. One complexity is that the information required by the Regulations (or LLP Regulations) is generally framed in respect of line items required in the statutory formats (e.g. turnover), whereas the headings used in the statutory formats may differ to those included where the adapted formats are used. Further information on certain of these statutory disclosures is given in 6.6 below.

FRS 102, the Regulations and LLP Regulations require numerous further disclosures (which may be given in the notes) concerning items recognised in profit or loss. Refer to the disclosure sections of the relevant chapters in this publication.

6.5.2 Illustrative statement of comprehensive income (adapted formats)

Example 6.4 below illustrates a single statement of comprehensive income, where the adapted formats are used. This is based on an illustrative example in IAS 1's Implementation Guidance, modified to illustrate the requirements of FRS 102. In particular,

- FRS 102 does not require separate presentation in other comprehensive income between items that will not be reclassified to profit or loss and items that may be reclassified subsequently to profit or loss;

- earnings per share information has not been illustrated (see 6.9 below for entities required to present earnings per share information); *[FRS 102.1.4]*

- where there are discontinued operations, FRS 102 requires a line-by-line analysis with columns for continuing, discontinued and total operations (see 6.8 below). Example 6.4 shows only the 'total column' required; *[FRS 102.5.5B, 5.7E]* and

- an analysis of expenses should be presented, either in the income statement or in the notes to the financial statements, which is equivalent to what would have been presented if statutory formats had been used (see 6.6 below). *[FRS 102.5.5B]*.

Chapter 6

The Triennial review 2017 added the requirement in the final bullet point above into FRS 102, where adapted formats are being used. We do not expect this change to significantly affect the amounts presented in the financial statements as, prior to the Triennial review 2017, FRS 102 already required an analysis of expenses by nature or by function. This requirement, which was in paragraph 5.11 of the previous version of FRS 102, has now been removed (see 6.7.4 below).

Example 6.4:   *Presentation of comprehensive income in a single statement*

XYZ Group – Statement of profit or loss and other comprehensive income for the year ended 31 December 201Y

	201Y £'000 Total	201X £'000 Total
Revenue	390,000	355,000
Cost of sales	(245,000)	(230,000)
Gross profit	145,000	125,000
Other income	20,667	11,300
Distribution costs	(9,000)	(8,700)
Administrative expenses	(20,000)	(21,000)
Other expenses	(2,100)	(1,200)
Finance costs	(8,000)	(7,500)
Share of profit of associates[1]	35,100	30,100
Profit before taxation	161,667	128,000
Income tax expense	(40,417)	(32,000)
Profit for the year from continuing operations	121,250	96,000
Loss for the year from discontinued operations	–	(30,500)
PROFIT FOR THE YEAR	121,250	65,500
Other comprehensive income:		
Gains on property revaluation	933	3,367
Remeasurements of defined benefit pension plans	(667)	1,333
Available-for-sale financial assets[4][5]	(24,000)	26,667
Exchange differences on translating foreign operations[4]	5,334	10,667
Cash flow hedges[4]	(667)	(4,000)
Share of gain (loss) on property revaluation of associates[2]	400	(700)
Income tax[3]	4,667	(9,334)
Other comprehensive income for the year, net of tax	(14,000)	28,000
TOTAL COMPREHENSIVE INCOME FOR THE YEAR	107,250	93,500
Profit attributable to:		
Owners of the parent	97,000	52,400
Non-controlling interests	24,250	13,100
	121,250	65,500
Total comprehensive income attributable to:		
Owners of the parent	85,800	74,800
Non-controlling interests	21,450	18,700
	107,250	93,500

Alternatively, items of other comprehensive income could be presented in the statement of comprehensive income net of tax, as follows.

Statement of comprehensive income section (alternative presentation)

	201Y £'000	201X £'000
Other comprehensive income for the year, after tax:		
Gains on property revaluation	600	2,700
Remeasurements of defined benefit pension plans	(500)	1,000
Available-for-sale financial assets[(4)(5)]	(18,000)	20,000
Exchange differences on translating foreign operations[(4)]	4,000	8,000
Cash flow hedges[(4)]	(500)	(3,000)
Share of gain (loss) on property revaluation of associates[(2)]	400	(700)
Other comprehensive income for the year, net of tax[(3)]	(14,000)	28,000

(1) This means the share of associates' profit attributable to owners of the associates, i.e. it is after tax and non-controlling interests in the associates.

(2) This means the share of associates' gain (loss) on property revaluation attributable to owners of the associates, i.e. it is after tax and non-controlling interests in the associates.

(3) Unlike IAS 1, there is no requirement for the notes to disclose income tax relating to each item of other comprehensive income, although the aggregate current and deferred tax relating to items that recognised as items of other comprehensive income or equity is required in the notes. *[FRS 102.29.27(a)]*.

(4) Unlike IAS 1, items in other comprehensive income are not analysed between items that will be reclassified to profit and loss and items that may be reclassified subsequently to profit and loss. Exchange differences on translating foreign operations are not subsequently reclassified under FRS 102. The change in fair value of the hedging item recognised in other comprehensive income in respect of cash flow hedges and hedges of a net investment in a foreign operation and the amounts reclassified to profit or loss in respect of cash flow hedges in the period are required to be disclosed in the notes. *[FRS 102.12.29(c)-(d), 12.29A]*.

FRS 102 requires an analysis of other comprehensive income by item in the statement of changes in equity or in the notes to the accounts. *[FRS 102.6.3A]*.

(5) An FRS 102 reporter will only have available-for-sale financial assets if it adopts IAS 39 for recognition and measurement of financial instruments.

Example 6.5 below shows the statement of comprehensive income using the two-statement form. This is relevant for both adapted formats and statutory formats because the requirements for the statement of comprehensive income derive from Section 5 (rather than the formats in the Regulations (or LLP Regulations)). As in Example 6.4, the items in other comprehensive income may alternatively be presented net of tax.

The separate income statement (not presented in Example 6.5) would follow the requirements for adapted formats (see 6.5 above) (where permitted for use) or statutory formats (see 6.6 below) and would show the allocation of profit between owners of the parent and non-controlling interest.

Example 6.5 is adapted from an illustrative example in IAS 1, but modified to illustrate the requirements of FRS 102. Example 6.5 looks the same as the latter part of the single statement of comprehensive income presented in Example 6.4 above but only shows the allocation of total comprehensive income between owners of the parent and non-controlling interest. The footnotes included in Example 6.5 relate to the same footnotes as in Example 6.4.

Chapter 6

Example 6.5:   Statement of comprehensive income illustrating the presentation of comprehensive income in two statements

XYZ Group – Statement of profit or loss and other comprehensive income for the year ended 31 December 201Y

	201Y £'000	201X £'000
Profit for the year	121,250	65,500
Other comprehensive income:		
Gains on property revaluation	933	3,367
Remeasurements of defined benefit pension plans	(667)	1,333
Available-for-sale financial assets[(4)(5)]	(24,000)	26,667
Exchange differences on translating foreign operations[(4)]	5,334	10,667
Cash flow hedges[(4)]	(667)	(4,000)
Share of gain (loss) on property revaluation of associates[(2)]	400	(700)
Income tax [(3)]	4,667	(9,334)
Other comprehensive income for the year, net of tax	(14,000)	28,000
TOTAL COMPREHENSIVE INCOME FOR THE YEAR	107,250	93,500
Total comprehensive income attributable to:		
Owners of the parent	85,800	74,800
Non-controlling interests	21,450	18,700
	107,250	93,500

6.6   Statutory formats – format 1 and format 2 profit and loss accounts

An entity must present in the statement of comprehensive income, or in the separate income statement, the items to be presented in a profit and loss account in accordance with one of the profit and loss account statutory formats in Part 1 of the applicable schedule to the Regulations or Part 1 of Schedule 1 to the LLP Regulations. *[FRS 102.5.5, FRS 102.5.7].* See 4.1, 4.2 and 6.1 above for discussion as to which formats apply to which types of entity.

The following discussion relates only to the profit and loss account statutory formats for companies applying Schedule 1 to the Regulations and for LLPs. The formats in Schedule 3 to the Regulations applicable to insurance companies and groups are discussed in Chapter 33 at 8. It is beyond the scope of this publication to discuss the formats in Schedule 2 to the Regulations applicable to banking companies and groups. See 4.2.2 and 4.2.3 above for the definitions of banking and insurance companies and groups. However, there is less flexibility to adapt the formats in Schedule 2 and Schedule 3 to the Regulations. These formats still refer to 'profit or loss on ordinary activities before taxation', 'taxation on profit or loss on ordinary activities', 'profit (or loss) on ordinary activities after taxation' and the headings relating to extraordinary items (albeit the latter are not used in practice).

Section B of Part 1 of Schedule 1 to the Regulations (and Section B of Part 1 of Schedule 1 to the LLP Regulations) provide a choice of format 1 and format 2 for the profit and loss account.

The format 1 profit and loss account, which analyses expenses by function, for a UK company (other than a banking company or insurance company) is presented at Figure 6.16 below.

Figure 6.16   *Format 1 profit and loss account (UK company other than a banking company or insurance company)*

1	Turnover
2	Cost of sales
3	Gross profit or loss
4	Distribution costs
5	Administrative expenses
6	Other operating income
7	Income from shares in group undertakings
8	Income from participating interests†
9	Income from other fixed asset investments
10	Other interest receivable and similar income
11	Amounts written off investments
12	Interest payable and similar expenses
	Profit or loss before taxation*
13	Tax on profit or loss
14	Profit or loss after taxation
19	Other taxes not shown under the above items
20	Profit or loss for the financial year

*   While not in format 1, every profit and loss account must show the amount of a company's profit or loss before taxation (1 Sch 6, Regulations).

†   See discussion below for modifications in group accounts.

The format 1 profit and loss account for an LLP is presented at Figure 6.17 below.

Figure 6.17   *Format 1 profit and loss account (LLP)*

1	Turnover
2	Cost of sales
3	Gross profit or loss
4	Distribution costs
5	Administrative expenses
6	Other operating income
7	Income from shares in group undertakings
8	Income from participating interests†
9	Income from other fixed asset investments
10	Other interest receivable and similar income
11	Amounts written off investments
12	Interest payable and similar expenses
	Profit or loss before taxation*
13	Tax on profit or loss
14	Profit or loss after taxation
19	Other taxes not shown under the above items
20	Profit or loss for the financial year before members' remuneration and profit shares
SORP	*Members' remuneration charged as an expense*
SORP	*Profit or loss for the financial year available for discretionary division among members*

*   While not in format 1, every profit and loss account must show the amount of an LLP's profit or loss before taxation (1 Sch 6, LLP Regulations).

†   See discussion below for modifications in group accounts.

SORP   Requirements for formats included in the LLP SORP rather than the LLP Regulations.

Chapter 6

The final line in the format 1 and format 2 profit and loss accounts in the LLP Regulations is 'profit or loss for the financial year before members' remuneration and profit shares'. The LLP SORP provides further guidance on application of the statutory formats for LLPs, and requires that 'profit or loss for the financial year before members' remuneration and profit shares', 'members' remuneration charged as an expense' and 'profit or loss for the financial year available for discretionary division among members' is presented. The basis on which each element of remuneration has been treated in the accounts should be disclosed and explained by way of note. *[LLP SORP.51-54]*. The SORP provides guidance and illustrations of LLP profit or loss account for different situations. Detailed guidance on issues specific to LLPs is outside the scope of this publication. The format 2 profit and loss account, which analyses expenses by nature, for a UK company is presented at Figure 6.18 below.

Figure 6.18   *Format 2 for the profit and loss account (UK company other than a banking company or insurance company)*

1	Turnover	
2	Change in stocks of finished goods and in work in progress	
3	Own work capitalised	
4	Other operating income	
5	(a)	Raw materials and consumables
	(b)	Other external expenses
6	Staff costs	
	(a)	wages and salaries
	(b)	social security costs
	(c)	other pension costs
7	(a)	Depreciation and other amounts written off tangible and intangible fixed assets
	(b)	Amounts written off current assets, to the extent that they exceed write-offs which are normal in the undertaking concerned~
8	Other operating expenses	
9	Income from shares in group undertakings	
10	Income from participating interests†	
11	Income from other fixed asset investments	
12	Other interest receivable and similar income	
13	Amounts written off investments	
14	Interest payable and similar expenses	
	Profit or loss before taxation*	
15	Tax on profit or loss	
16	Profit or loss after taxation	
21	Other taxes not shown under the above items	
22	Profit or loss for the financial year	

*   While not in format 2, every profit and loss account must show the amount of a company's profit or loss before taxation (1 Sch 6, Regulations).

†   See discussion below for modifications in group accounts.

The format 2 profit and loss account for an LLP is presented at Figure 6.19 below. Additional line items are required by the SORP, as discussed above.

Figure 6.19   Format 2 for the profit and loss account (LLP)

1		Turnover
2		Change in stocks of finished goods and in work in progress
3		Own work capitalised
4		Other operating income
5	(a)	Raw materials and consumables
	(b)	Other external expenses
6		Staff costs
	(a)	wages and salaries
	(b)	social security costs
	(c)	other pension costs
7	(a)	Depreciation and other amounts written off tangible and intangible fixed assets
	(b)	Amounts written off current assets, to the extent that they exceed write-offs which are normal in the undertaking concerned~
8		Other operating expenses
9		Income from shares in group undertakings
10		Income from participating interests†
11		Income from other fixed asset investments
12		Other interest receivable and similar income
13		Amounts written off investments
14		Interest payable and similar expenses
		Profit or loss before taxation*
15		Tax on profit or loss
16		Profit or loss after taxation
21		Other taxes not shown under the above items
22		Profit or loss for the financial year before members' remuneration and profit shares
SORP		*Members' remuneration charged as an expense*
SORP		*Profit or loss for the financial year available for discretionary division among members*

*	While not in format 2, every profit and loss account must show the amount of an LLP's profit or loss before taxation (1 Sch 6, LLP Regulations).
†	See discussion below for modifications in group accounts.
SORP	Requirements for formats included in the LLP SORP (2017) rather than the LLP Regulations.

The main modification required for group profit and loss account statutory formats is the identification of non-controlling interests (see 4.5, 6.3 and 6.4 above) and replacing 'income from participating interests' with 'income from associated undertakings' and 'income from other participating interests' (see 6.6.5 below).

The line items in the formats need to be read together with the notes to the formats in Part 1 of Section B of Schedule 1 to the Regulations (and Part 1 of Section B of Schedule 1 to the LLP Regulations). *[1 Sch 1, 1 Sch 1 (LLP)]*. The individual line items in the profit and loss account formats (together with the relevant notes to the statutory formats) are discussed at 6.6.1 to 6.6.14 below.

The General Rules to the formats (see 4.4 above) apply. As all of the line items are denoted with Arabic numbers, these allow a degree of flexibility in the profit and loss account formats. FRS 102 further requires that an entity shall present additional line items, headings and subtotals in the statement of comprehensive income (and in the separate income statement, where presented) when such presentation is relevant to an understanding of the entity's financial performance. *[FRS 102.5.9]*. See 6.7.2 below.

Section 5 includes additional requirements relevant to the statement of comprehensive income (see 6.7 below). FRS 102's requirements for presentation of discontinued operations are discussed at 6.8 below, and for earnings per share (for those entities required to or choosing to present this) at 6.9 below.

Other sections of FRS 102 also require supplementary analysis of certain line items presented on the face of the income statement (or profit or loss section of the statement of comprehensive income), which may be included in the notes to the financial statements. The Regulations (and LLP Regulations) require UK companies preparing Companies Act accounts (and LLPs preparing non-IAS accounts) to give further supplementary information in respect of certain line items in the notes to the accounts. These disclosures are relevant where adapted formats or statutory formats are used. Some of these disclosures are highlighted in the discussion of line items at 6.6.1 to 6.6.14 below.

FRS 102, the Regulations and LLP Regulations require numerous further disclosures (which may be given in the notes to the financial statements) concerning items recognised in profit or loss. The LLP Regulations generally include similar disclosures to the Regulations. Refer to the disclosure sections of other chapters of this publication.

6.6.1   Turnover (format 1 and format 2)

Turnover, in relation to a company (or LLP), is defined as 'the amounts derived from the provision of goods and services, after deduction of:

(a)   trade discounts,

(b)   value added tax, and

(c)   any other taxes based on the amounts so derived.' *[s474(1), s474(1) (LLP), FRS 102 Appendix I]*.

FRS 102 has the same definition as in section 474(1).

FRS 102 further requires that turnover is presented on the face of the income statement (or statement of comprehensive income, if presented). *[FRS 102.5.7D]*. See 6.7.1 below.

Not all income reported in the profit and loss account is turnover, nor is the concept of turnover synonymous with revenue. For example, a company may receive rental or interest income – while these would be types of revenue under FRS 102, these may or may not fall to be reported as turnover. Similarly, an entity whose business includes renting out properties to tenants would include rental income within turnover, but this may be 'other operating income' for another entity. An entity whose business is as a lessor and receives finance lease income would report that interest income in the position of the turnover line (although it may well be described as finance lease income), but an entity that merely receives interest income on its bank deposits or other investments would report that interest income as 'other interest receivable and similar income'. Where significant judgement is applied in determining which sources of revenue qualify as turnover, it may be appropriate to include an accounting policy for turnover and explain these judgements.

See 3.3.2.A above for the segmental disclosures of turnover required in Companies Act accounts (or non-IAS accounts, for an LLP).

6.6.2 Cost of sales. Distribution costs. Administrative expenses (format 1)

The format 1 profit and loss account requires a functional classification of expenses – between cost of sales, distribution costs and administrative expenses. These categories of cost are not defined in the Regulations (or LLP Regulations). The allocation of costs will depend on the particular circumstances of an entity's business, and should be applied consistently. Judgement may be required in allocating costs to certain functions and, where this is the case, it may be appropriate to include an accounting policy for the allocation of expenses explaining significant judgements taken (see 8.3 below). The following discussion provides guidance for the types of items that often fall within these headings.

Cost of sales for a manufacturer would generally include production costs (including direct material, payroll and other costs and direct and indirect overheads attributable to the production function) and adjustments for opening and closing inventory. For a service provider, these would include the costs of providing the service.

Distribution costs would generally include transport and warehousing costs for the distribution of finished goods. Selling and marketing costs (such as advertising, payroll costs of the selling, marketing and distribution functions, sales commission and overheads attributable to the selling, marketing and distribution functions) are often included in this heading.

Administrative expenses would generally include payroll costs of general management and administrative staff, general overheads, property costs not classified within cost of sales or distribution costs, bad debts, professional fees and often goodwill amortisation and impairment.

Note (14) on the profit and loss account formats (format 1) (and the equivalent requirement for LLPs)[20] require that cost of sales, distribution costs and administrative expenses are stated after taking into account any necessary provisions for depreciation or diminution in value of assets.

UK companies and LLPs sometimes show other line items (e.g. research and development costs) or amend or combine other line items, taking advantage of the flexibility available in the Regulations. FRS 102 requires additional line items, headings and subtotals when relevant to an understanding of the entity's financial performance (see 6.7.2 below). *[FRS 102.5.9]*.

6.6.3 Gross profit (format 1)

The format 1 profit and loss account requires gross profit or loss, i.e. turnover less cost of sales, to be shown as a separate line item.

6.6.4 Other operating income (format 1 and format 2)

Other operating income is not defined in the Regulations (or LLP Regulations). In practice, this line item would often include government grant income, operating lease income, other rental income or negative goodwill amortisation.

This line item may include exchange gains arising from trading transactions, following previous UK GAAP practice. While this has not been included in FRS 102, the Legal Appendix to SSAP 20 – *Foreign currency translation* – stated that 'Gains or losses arising from trading transactions should normally be included under "Other operating income or expense" while those arising from arrangements which may be considered as financing should be disclosed separately as part of "Other interest receivable / payable and similar income / expense". ...'. *[SSAP 20.68]*.

6.6.5   Income from shares in group undertakings. Income from participating interests (format 1 and format 2)

The formats for the individual profit and loss account include 'income from shares in group undertakings', and 'income from participating interests'. Dividend income from shares in group undertakings and from participating interests would be included within these line items.

For the group profit and loss account statutory formats, 'income from participating interests' is replaced with 'income from associated undertakings' and 'income from other participating interests'. Income from associated undertakings would usually include the share of the profit or loss of associates and jointly controlled entities. Income from shares in group undertakings will not arise in consolidated financial statements unless there are unconsolidated subsidiaries.

The meanings of group undertakings, participating interests and associated undertakings are explained at 5.3.4.C to 5.3.4.E above.

Incoming dividends and similar income receivable are recognised at an amount that includes any withholding tax but excludes other taxes, such as attributable tax credits. Any withholding tax suffered is shown as part of the tax charge. *[FRS 102.29.19]*. See 6.6.9 below.

FRS 102 requires separate disclosure of the entity's share of the profit or loss of associates accounted for using the equity method and the entity's share of any discontinued operations of such associates. *[FRS 102.14.14]*. The same information is required for jointly controlled entities. *[FRS 102.15.20]*. There is no requirement to present this information on the face of the statement of comprehensive income (or separate income statement). However, entities may consider adapting the heading 'income from associated undertakings' to show the share of the profit or loss of investments in associates and jointly controlled entities (even if the analysis of this between investments in associates and jointly controlled entities is relegated to the notes).

FRS 102 does not address where fair value movements are presented in the profit and loss account formats when investments in subsidiaries, associates and jointly controlled entities are carried at fair value through profit and loss in consolidated and / or individual financial statements. *[FRS 102.9.9-9B, 9.26, 9.26A, 14.4-4B, 15.9-9B]*. Chapter 8 at 3.4 and 4, Chapter 12 at 3.3.1, and Chapter 13 at 3.6.2 and 3.6.3 discuss the situations where this accounting is required or permitted. In our view, entities may present fair value gains and fair value losses on such investments, where material, adjacent to income from shares in group undertakings and income from participating interests (but disclosed separately). FRS 102 would require additional line items on the face of the statement of comprehensive income (or separate income statement), where relevant to an understanding of the entity's financial performance (see 6.7.2 below). Where this accounting is used, all the disclosures in Section 11 in respect of such investments will be required, as explained at 10.3.1 below. *[FRS 102.9.27B]*.

6.6.6   *Income from other fixed asset investments. Other interest receivable and similar income (format 1 and format 2)*

The formats have two line items – 'income from other fixed asset investments', and 'other interest receivable and similar income'. Note (15) on the profit and loss account formats (format 1 and format 2) (and the equivalent requirement for LLPs)[21] state that income and interest derived from group undertakings must be shown separately from income and interest derived from other sources. For LLPs, interest receivable from members must also not be included under these line items.

Incoming dividends and similar income receivable are recognised at an amount that includes any withholding tax but excludes other taxes, such as attributable tax credits. Any withholding tax suffered is shown as part of the tax charge. *[FRS 102.29.19]*. See 6.6.9 below.

In our view, entities may present fair value gains and fair value losses on other fixed asset investments, where material, adjacent to income from other fixed asset investments, but disclosed separately.

Section 28 does not specify how the net interest on the net defined benefit liability should be presented in the profit and loss account (see Chapter 25 at 3.6.10.A). The net interest could be either a positive or negative figure. In our view, net interest could be presented in either 'other finance income', 'interest payable' or another component of profit or loss provided the basis of allocation is explained.

'Other interest receivable and similar income' may include exchange gains arising from financing arrangements, e.g. loans, following previous UK GAAP practice. See 6.6.4 above.

The presentation of gains on settlement of financial liabilities is not addressed by FRS 102. In our view, entities may show the gains on settlement within 'other interest receivable and similar income', or where material, present the gains adjacent to interest receivable and similar income but disclosed separately.

FRS 102 requires, *inter alia*, further analyses of income, expense and net gains or net losses (including fair value changes) by specified category of financial instrument. Interest expense and interest income (calculated using the effective interest method) for financial assets and financial liabilities not at fair value, and impairment losses for each class of financial asset must also be disclosed. There are also extensive disclosures for financial instruments at fair value through profit or loss (that are not financial liabilities held as part of a trading portfolio nor derivatives). These can be disclosed in the notes to the financial statements. *[FRS 102.11.48-48A, 12.26]*. Certain of these disclosures are not required where the reduced disclosure framework is applied in individual financial statements of a qualifying entity that is not a financial institution. *[FRS 102.1.8, 1.12(c)]*. See Chapter 10 at 11.

6.6.7   *Amounts written off investments (format 1 and format 2)*

The line item 'amounts written off investments' would be used for impairments of fixed asset investments (including investments in subsidiaries, associates and jointly controlled entities) carried at cost less impairment in the individual financial statements. It would be usual to present a write-back of a previous provision under the same heading as where the provision was originally recognised (in the same way as an adjustment to reverse a bad debt provision would also be shown within administrative expenses).

The positioning of this line item between 'other interest income receivable and similar income' and 'interest payable and similar charge' is below where many entities would position operating profit, where presented (see 6.7.3 below). FRS 102 is silent on where impairments of investments should be presented. Nevertheless, some entities may find it appropriate, based on the nature of their business, to report 'amounts written off investments' within operating profit.

FRS 102 requires disclosure of impairment losses for each class of financial asset, i.e. a grouping that is appropriate to the nature of the information disclosed and that takes into account the characteristics of the financial assets. *[FRS 102.11.48(c)]*. In addition, disclosure of impairment losses and reversals of impairment losses (and the line items in which those impairment losses are included) is required separately for investments in associates and investments in jointly controlled entities. *[FRS 102.27.33(e)-(f)]*.

In addition, a UK company preparing Companies Act accounts (or an LLP preparing non-IAS accounts) must disclose separately in a note to the accounts (if not shown separately in the profit and loss account): *[1 Sch 19(3), 1 Sch 20(2), 1 Sch 19(3) (LLP), 1 Sch 20(2) (LLP)]*

- provisions for diminution in value; and
- any amounts written back in respect of such provisions.

These disclosures apply where the fixed asset investment is accounted for using the historical cost rules (see 10.1 below). The application of the historical cost depreciation and diminution rules (including these disclosures) to fixed assets accounted for using the alternative accounting rules (i.e. at revaluation) is explained at 10.2.2 below. The disclosures do not apply to fixed asset investments held at fair value using the fair value accounting rules (see 10.3 below).

6.6.8   Interest payable and similar expenses (format 1 and format 2)

'Interest payable and similar expenses' would include finance costs on financial liabilities (including shares classified as a financial liability or where a component of the share is classified as a financial liability).

Note (16) on the profit and loss account formats (format 1 and format 2) (and the equivalent requirement for LLPs)[22] states that interest payable to group undertakings must be shown separately from income and interest derived from other sources. For LLPs, interest payable to members must also not be included under these line items. The LLP SORP explains how interest payable to members is treated (and when it falls to be treated as part of members' remuneration as an expense). *[LLP SORP.21, 54]*.

The presentation of losses on settlement of financial liabilities is not addressed by FRS 102. In our view, entities may show the losses on settlement within other interest payable and similar expenses, or, where material, present the losses adjacent to other interest payable and similar expenses but disclosed separately.

Section 28 does not specify how the net interest on the net defined benefit liability should be presented in the profit and loss account (see Chapter 25 at 3.6.10.A). The net interest could be either a positive or negative figure. In our view, net interest could be presented in either 'other finance income', 'interest payable' or another component of profit or loss provided the basis of allocation is explained.

This line item may also include exchange losses arising from financing arrangements, such as loans, following previous UK GAAP practice. See 6.6.4 above.

FRS 102 does not address the presentation of unwind of discounts on provisions. However, FRS 12 – *Provisions, contingent liabilities and contingent assets* – required this to be disclosed as other finance costs adjacent to interest. *[FRS 12.48]*. In our view, entities can continue to follow this previous UK GAAP presentation of unwind of discounts under FRS 102.

FRS 102 requires, *inter alia*, further analyses of income, expense and net gains or net losses (including fair value changes) by specified category of financial instrument. Interest expense and interest income (calculated using the effective interest method) for financial assets and financial liabilities not at fair value, and impairment losses for each class of financial asset must also be disclosed. There are also extensive disclosures for financial instruments at fair value through profit or loss (that are not financial liabilities held as part of a trading portfolio nor derivatives). These can be disclosed in the notes to the financial statements. *[FRS 102.11.48-48A, 12.26]*. Certain of these disclosures are not required where the reduced disclosure framework is applied in individual financial statements of a qualifying entity that is not a financial institution. *[FRS 102.1.8, 1.12(c)]*. See Chapter 10 at 11.

In addition, a UK company preparing Companies Act accounts (or an LLP preparing non-IAS accounts) must state in the notes to the accounts: the amount of interest on or any similar charges in respect of: (1) bank loans and overdrafts, and (2) loans of any other kind made to the company (or the LLP). This analysis is not required in relation to interest or charges on loans to the company (or the LLP) from group undertakings but applies to all other loans, whether made on security of debentures or not. *[1 Sch 66, 1 Sch 63 (LLP)]*.

6.6.9 Tax on profit (or loss) (format 1 and format 2)

Tax includes current and deferred tax. FRS 102 states that income tax includes all domestic and foreign taxes that are based on taxable profit. Income taxes also include taxes, such as withholding tax on distributions payable by a subsidiary, associate or joint venture to the reporting entity. *[FRS 102.29.1]*. In some situations, entities may need to apply judgement in determining whether a particular tax or tax credit is an income tax and whether to classify interest and penalties as tax. See Chapter 26 at 3.2. FRS 102 requires disclosures of judgements in applying accounting policies with the most significant effect on the financial statements – see 8.3 below.

Incoming dividends and similar income receivable are recognised at an amount that includes any withholding tax but excludes other taxes, such as attributable tax credits. Any withholding tax suffered is shown as part of the tax charge. *[FRS 102.29.19]*.

A UK company preparing Companies Act accounts (or an LLP preparing non-IAS accounts) must give further disclosures in respect of tax on profit or loss in the notes to the accounts. *[1 Sch 67, 1 Sch 64 (LLP)]*. FRS 102's disclosures in respect of current and deferred tax are discussed in Chapter 26 at 11.

6.6.10   Own work capitalised (format 2)

The format 2 profit and loss account includes a line item for 'own work capitalised'.

Own work capitalised may arise, for example, where an entity capitalises the directly attributable costs of constructing its own property, plant and equipment. *[FRS 102.17.10]*. The costs are reported in the relevant line items and a credit item is shown in own work capitalised.

6.6.11   Staff costs (format 2)

The format 2 profit and loss account has a line item for 'staff costs', to be analysed between wages and salaries, social security costs and pension costs (see 8.6 below for the definitions). The format 1 profit and loss account does not have a line item for staff costs.

UK companies and LLPs, whether preparing Companies Act accounts (non-IAS accounts, for an LLP) or IAS accounts, must disclose information on staff numbers and on staff costs in the notes to the accounts (insofar as not stated elsewhere in the accounts). *[s411, s411(LLP)]*. See 8.6 below. There are certain disclosure exemptions for UK companies subject to the small companies regime and LLPs subject to the small LLPs regime.

6.6.12   Depreciation and other amounts written off tangible and intangible fixed assets and amounts written off current assets to the extent that they exceed write-offs which are normal in the undertaking concerned (format 2)

The format 2 profit and loss account has separate line items for 'depreciation and other amounts written off tangible and intangible fixed assets' and 'amounts written off current assets to the extent that they exceed write offs which are normal in the undertaking concerned'.

Entities may also show provisions against current assets under different headings, e.g. changes in stocks / raw materials and consumables (for inventory – see 6.6.13 below) or 'other operating expenses' (e.g. this heading might be used for bad debts – see 6.6.14 below). Judgement is needed as to whether such provisions exceed write offs that are normal and fall to be presented as amounts written off current assets to the extent that they exceed write offs which are normal in the undertaking concerned.

6.6.13   Changes in stocks of finished goods and work in progress and raw materials and consumables (format 2)

The format 2 profit and loss account includes separate line items for the 'change in stocks of finished goods and work in progress' and for 'raw materials and consumables'.

'Raw materials and consumables' would include purchases of raw materials and consumables, adjusted for changes in stocks of raw materials and consumables.

6.6.14   *Other external expenses and other operating expenses (format 2)*

The format 2 profit and loss account includes separate line items for: 'other external expenses' and for 'other operating expenses'. The Regulations and LLP Regulations do not define these terms. There is therefore likely to be diversity in practice in the allocation of costs between these headings, but a consistent policy should be followed.

'Other operating expenses' may include exchange losses arising from trading transactions, following previous GAAP practice. See 6.6.4 above.

6.7   Requirements applicable to both approaches (adapted formats and statutory formats)

FRS 102 includes supplementary requirements relating to the statement of comprehensive income (beyond the requirements to follow the formats permitted by the Regulations or LLP Regulations).

6.7.1   *Disclosure of turnover on the face of the statement of comprehensive income (or separate income statement)*

Turnover must be disclosed on the face of the income statement (or statement of comprehensive income, if presented). *[FRS 102.5.7D]*.

However, not all income reported in the profit and loss account is turnover, nor is the concept of turnover synonymous with revenue. See 6.6.1 above.

FRS 102 also requires a detailed analysis of revenue (which may be included in the notes to the financial statements) showing at a minimum: revenue arising from the sale of goods, the rendering of services, interest, royalties, dividends, commissions, grants and any other significant type of revenue. Contract revenue recognised as revenue must also be disclosed. *[FRS 102.23.30(b), 23.31]*.

6.7.2   *Additional line items, headings and subtotals*

An entity shall present additional line items, headings and subtotals in the statement of comprehensive income (and in the income statement, if presented) when such presentation is relevant to an understanding of the entity's financial performance. *[FRS 102.5.9]*. Judgement is needed in determining whether additional items should be presented, where material and relevant. Factors to be considered, highlighted by IAS 1 (which has a similar requirement), include materiality and the nature and function of the items of income and expense. *[IAS 1.86]*.

While any amendments to the income statement (or profit and loss section of the statement of comprehensive income) would need to comply with the General Rules to the formats (see 4.4 above), the statutory formats provide flexibility since the profit and loss account line items are denoted with Arabic numbers.

Where adapted formats are used, any amendments made would need to comply so far as is practicable with the General Rules to the formats. FRS 102 explains that an entity may include additional line items in the income statement and amend the descriptions used in paragraph 5.5B (i.e. for the line items (a) to (j)) (see Figure 6.15 at 6.5 above) and the ordering of items, when this is necessary to explain the elements of financial performance, providing the information given is at least equivalent to that required by the profit and loss account format had it not been adapted. *[FRS 102.5.5C]*. The effect of this is to clarify the extent of flexibility available in the presentation requirements where adapted formats are used (for statutory formats, the General Rules to the formats clearly set out the flexibility for Arabic numbered items, but Arabic numbers do not appear in the adapted formats). While this requirement is included under the single statement approach, in our view, this is intended to also apply where the two statement approach is applied.

6.7.2.A   *Presentation of alternative performance measures*

A press release on additional and exceptional items issued by the FRC in 2013 includes guidance relevant to the presentation of additional subtotals, particularly alternative performance measures, by FRS 102 reporters. See 6.7.5.B below. The FRC also completed a thematic review in November 2017 on the use of alternative performance measures, the findings of which can be used to assess and enhance disclosures in this area.[23]

The presentation of alternative performance measures has been considered by the IASB. While these requirements have not been included in FRS 102 and so are not mandatory, the recent amendments to IAS 1 are discussed below.

Amendments to IAS 1 – *Disclosure Initiative* – explains that when an entity presents subtotals in accordance with paragraph 85 of IAS 1 (which is similar to the requirements of paragraphs 5.5C and 5.9 of FRS 102, discussed at 6.7.2 above), those subtotals must:

- be comprised of line items made of amounts recognised and measured in accordance with IFRS;

- be presented and labelled in a manner that makes the line items that constitute the subtotal clear and understandable;

- be consistent from period to period; and

- not be displayed with more prominence than the subtotals and totals required in IFRS for the statement(s) presenting profit or loss and other comprehensive income. *[IAS 1.85A]*.

An entity shall present the line items in the statement(s) presenting profit or loss and other comprehensive income that reconcile any such 'additional subtotals' presented, with the subtotals or totals required in IFRS for such statements. *[IAS 1.85B]*.

In addition, in June 2015, ESMA published its final guidance on presentation of Alternative Performance Measures. This applies to regulated information and prospectuses published by issuers of securities admitted to trading on a regulated market from July 2016. The guidelines do not apply to the financial statements but would apply to the management report (e.g. the strategic report) of entities in scope. ESMA have also published a series of 'question and answer' documents, the latest being published in October 2017, to support this guidance. All of the guidance is available on the ESMA website.[24] It is likely that most entities in scope of the ESMA guidance will be applying EU-adopted IFRS. The FRC's thematic review noted above, refers to the ESMA guidance and considered whether alternative performance measures disclosed in the strategic reports it reviewed, were consistent with these guidelines.

6.7.3 Disclosure of operating profit

FRS 102 does not require disclosure of 'operating profit'. If an entity elects to disclose operating profit, the entity should ensure that the amount disclosed is representative of activities that would normally be regarded as 'operating', e.g. it would be inappropriate to exclude items clearly related to operations (such as inventory write-downs and restructuring and relocation expenses) because they occur irregularly or infrequently or are unusual in amount. The Triennial review 2017 further adds that it would be inappropriate to exclude profits or losses on the sale of property, plant and equipment, investment property and intangible assets. Similarly, it would be inappropriate to exclude items on the grounds that they do not involve cash flows, such as depreciation and amortisation expenses. However, the Triennial review 2017 added that profits or losses on the disposal of a discontinued operation should be excluded from operating profit. *[FRS 102.5.9B]*. The illustrative example of a statement of comprehensive income presented in the Appendix to Section 5, has been amended accordingly.

The income statement (or profit and loss section of the statement of comprehensive income) identifies separate line items for the share of the profit or loss of investments in associates and jointly controlled entities accounted for using the equity method in adapted formats (see 6.5 above). For entities presenting a measure of operating profit using the adapted formats, in our view, it is acceptable for an entity to determine which investments form part of its operating activities and include their results in that measure, with the results of non-operating investments excluded from it. Another acceptable alternative would be to exclude the results of all associates and jointly controlled entities from operating profit.

6.7.4 Analysis of expenses by nature or function

The statutory formats in Schedule 1 to the Regulations (and Schedule 1 to the LLP Regulations) (see 6.6 above) require an analysis of expenses by nature (where the format 2 profit and loss account is adopted) or by function (where the format 1 profit and loss account is adopted), and where the adapted formats available in those schedules are used (see 6.5 above), FRS 102 requires an analysis of expenses to be presented either in the income statement or in the notes to the financial statements, which is equivalent to what would have been presented if the statutory formats had been adopted. *[FRS 102.5.5B]*. The Triennial review 2017 removed from FRS 102 the previous requirement to, unless otherwise required under the Regulations, present an analysis of expenses using a classification based on either the nature of expenses or the function of expenses within the entity, whichever provides information that is reliable and more relevant. However, this change in the Triennial review 2017 was made to reduce duplication of what is already a requirement of the Regulations. *[FRS 102.BC.B5.5]*. Therefore, we do not expect this change to affect the amounts presented in financial statements,

Where an entity applies FRS 102 but is not required to prepare its accounts in accordance with the CA 2006, we consider that the entity must comply with the formats (and disclosures in the notes to the statutory formats, where the statutory formats are applied) but is not required to give the other statutory disclosures.

Schedule 1 to the Regulations (and the LLP Regulations) require certain information about the nature of expenses to be provided as line items in format 2 and in the notes to the accounts where format 1 is applied:

- the format 2 profit and loss account includes line items for staff costs (see 6.6.11 above) and 'depreciation and other amounts written off tangible and intangible fixed assets' (see 6.6.12 above);

- all UK companies (and LLPs), except companies subject to the small companies regime (and LLPs subject to the small LLPs regime) must present the analysis of staff costs in the notes to the accounts, insofar as not stated elsewhere in the accounts (see 8.6 below). This requirement applies both to Companies Act accounts (non-IAS accounts, for an LLP) and IAS accounts; and

- note (17) on the profit and loss account formats (and the equivalent requirement for LLPs)[25] state that the amount of depreciation and other amounts written off tangible and intangible fixed assets must be disclosed in a note to the accounts where the format 1 profit and loss account is used.

In addition, a UK company preparing Companies Act accounts (or an LLP preparing non-IAS accounts) must disclose separately in a note to the accounts (if not shown separately in the profit and loss account): *[1 Sch 19(3), 1 Sch 20(2), 1 Sch 19(3) (LLP), 1 Sch 20(2) (LLP)]*

- provisions for diminution in value of fixed assets; and

- any amounts written back in respect of such provisions.

These disclosures must be given where statutory or adapted formats are used. These disclosures apply where the fixed assets in question are accounted for using the historical cost rules (see 10.1 below). The application of the historical cost depreciation and diminution rules (including these disclosures) to fixed assets accounted for using the alternative accounting rules (i.e. at revaluation) is explained at 10.2.2 below. The disclosures do not apply to fixed asset investments held at fair value using the fair value accounting rules (see 10.3 below).

The statutory disclosures overlap with disclosures in FRS 102 of depreciation, amortisation and impairment charges (see Chapter 15 at 3.9, Chapter 16 at 3.5.2, Chapter 17 at 4.2, Chapter 24 at 8 and Chapter 31 at 2.7.2), *[FRS 102.17.31(e), 18.27(e), 19.26-26A, 27.32-33, 34.10]*, defined contribution expense, *[FRS 102.28.40]*, and the cost of defined benefit plans (see Chapter 25 at 3.12). *[FRS 102.28.41(g)]*.

6.7.5   Presentation of 'exceptional items'

FRS 102 does not use the phrase 'exceptional items' nor does the standard contain prescriptive presentation requirements for exceptional items. When items included in total comprehensive income are material, their nature and amount must be disclosed separately in the statement of comprehensive income (and in the income statement, if presented) or in the notes. *[FRS 102.5.9A]*. The level of prominence given to such items is left to the judgement of the entity concerned. Materiality is discussed at 9.4 below.

A UK company preparing Companies Act accounts (or an LLP preparing non-IAS accounts) must state the amount, nature and effect of any individual items of income and expenditure which are of exceptional size or incidence in the notes to the accounts. *[1 Sch 69(2), 1 Sch 67(2) (LLP)]*.

Many UK companies preparing financial statements using EU-adopted IFRS (to which the statutory disclosure above does not apply) continue to refer to 'exceptional items' and this is likely to be the case under FRS 102 as well. Since FRS 102 does not use the term 'exceptional items', it is important that entities clearly define what items are considered to be an 'exceptional item' (or other similar term used) and state this in the accounting policies included in the financial statements. The FRC published a press release on exceptional items in December 2013 (see 6.7.5.B below).

FRS 102 does not give examples of such items, but IAS 1 states that circumstances that would give rise to the separate disclosure of items of income and expense include:
[IAS 1.98]

(a) write-downs of inventories to net realisable value or of property, plant and equipment to recoverable amount, as well as reversals of such write-downs;

(b) restructurings of the activities of an entity and reversals of any provisions for the costs of restructuring;

(c) disposals of items of property, plant and equipment;

(d) disposals of investments;

(e) discontinued operations;

(f) litigation settlements; and

(g) other reversals of provisions.

See 6.8 below for FRS 102's requirements on presentation of discontinued operations.

6.7.5.A   *Presentation in the statement of comprehensive income*

As entities reporting under FRS 102 must follow the formats for the profit and loss account in the Regulations (or LLP Regulations), exceptional items will need to be included within the appropriate statutory format headings, where the statutory formats are used. In most cases, attributing exceptional items to the relevant format heading will be straightforward.

The General Rules to the formats (see 4.4 above) allow the profit and loss account to include income or expenditure not otherwise covered by any of the items listed in the statutory format, and permit or require certain adaptations to the line items given an Arabic number.

There is potentially more flexibility over presentation of exceptional items where adapted formats (see 6.5 above) are used, although (subject to any amendments permitted by paragraph 5.5C of FRS 102) the minimum items required must be presented on the face of the statement of comprehensive income.

FRS 102 does not specify categories of exceptional items that must be reported below operating profit. However, it does include guidance on items that it would be inappropriate to exclude from operating profit. See 6.7.3 above.

6.7.5.B   *FRC Press release on exceptional items*

In December 2013, the FRC issued Press Release PN 108 on the need to improve reporting of additional and exceptional items by companies and ensure consistency in their presentation. It noted that the Financial Reporting Review Panel had identified a significant number of companies that report exceptional items on the face of the income statement and include subtotals to show the profit before such items (sometimes referred to as 'underlying profit'). While the FRC stated that many companies present additional line items in the income statement to provide clear and useful information on the trends in the components of their profit in the income statement, as required by IAS 1, the FRC has identified a number where the disclosure fell short of the consistency and clarity required, with a consequential effect on the profit reported before such items.

The FRC set out the following factors that companies should have regard to, in judging what to include in additional items and underlying profit:

- the approach taken in identifying additional items that qualify for separate presentation should be even handed between gains and losses, clearly disclosed and applied consistently from one year to the next. It should also be distinguished from alternative performance measures used by the company that are not intended to be consistent with IFRS principles;

- gains and losses should not be netted off in arriving at the amount disclosed unless otherwise permitted;

- where the same category of material items recurs each year and in similar amounts (for example, restructuring costs), companies should consider whether such amounts should be included as part of underlying profit;

- where significant items of expense are unlikely to be finalised for a number of years or may subsequently be reversed, the income statement effect of such changes should be similarly identified as additional items in subsequent periods and readers should be able to track movements in respect of these items between periods;

- the tax effect of additional items should be explained;

- material cash amounts related to additional items should be presented clearly in the cash flow statement;

- where underlying profit is used in determining executive remuneration or in the definition of loan covenants, companies should take care to disclose clearly the measures used; and

- management commentary on results should be clear on which measures of profit are being commented on and should discuss all significant items which make up the profit determined according to IFRSs.

While the press release refers to IFRSs, the same factors would apply to FRS 102 financial statements.

6.7.6   Presentation of extraordinary items

An entity applying the adapted formats or statutory formats in Schedule 1 to the Regulations shall not present or describe any items of income or expense as extraordinary items in the statement of comprehensive income (or in the income statement, if presented) or in the notes. *[FRS 102.5.10]*. This requirement also applies to LLPs. The concept of extraordinary items also does not appear in Schedule 1 to the Regulations and Schedule 1 to the LLP Regulations.

However, Schedules 2 and 3 to the Regulations do refer to extraordinary items, so theoretically the concept of an extraordinary items still exists in those schedules. FRS 102 states that 'extraordinary items are material items possessing a high degree of abnormality which arise from events or transactions that fall outside the ordinary activities of the reporting entity and which are not expected to recur.' The additional line items required to be disclosed by paragraph 5.9 (see 6.7.2 above) and material items required to be disclosed by paragraph 5.9A (see 6.7.5 above) are not extraordinary items when they arise from the entity's ordinary activities. In addition, extraordinary items do not include prior period items merely because they relate to a prior period. *[FRS 102.5.10B]*.

Ordinary activities are defined as 'any activities which are undertaken by a reporting entity as part of its business and such related activities in which the reporting entity engages in furtherance of, incidental to, or arising from, these activities. Ordinary activities include any effects on the reporting entity of any event in the various environments in which it operates, including the political, regulatory, economic and geographical environments, irrespective of the frequency or unusual nature of the events'. *[FRS 102.5.10A]*.

While this guidance has not been included in FRS 102, Appendix II to FRS 101 (which has similar requirements to FRS 102 in respect of extraordinary items) states that 'entities should note that extraordinary items are extremely rare as they relate to highly abnormal events or transactions'. *[FRS 101 Appendix II.11]*. Consequently, we do not anticipate that banking and insurance companies still permitted to disclose extraordinary items will do so in practice under FRS 102.

6.8 Presentation of discontinued operations (adapted formats and statutory formats)

FRS 102 requires an entity to disclose on the face of the income statement (or statement of comprehensive income) an amount comprising the total of:

(a) the post-tax profit or loss of discontinued operations (see definition at 6.8.1 below); and

(b) the post-tax gain or loss attributable to the impairment or on the disposal of the assets or disposal group(s) constituting discontinued operations (see 5.5 above for the definition of disposal group).

A line-by-line analysis must be presented in the income statement (or statement of comprehensive income), with columns presented for continuing operations, discontinued operations and for total operations. This requirement applies both to adapted formats (this is line item (f) – see Figure 6.15 at 6.5 above) and statutory formats. *[FRS 102.5.5B, 5.7E]*. This means more detailed disclosure than is commonly seen under IFRS 5, but the line-by-line analysis is to enable compliance with the profit and loss account formats in the Regulations (or the LLP Regulations).

There is no requirement to analyse other comprehensive income between continuing and discontinued operations.

The disclosures for discontinued operations must relate to operations discontinued by the end of the reporting period for the latest period presented, with re-presentation of prior periods where applicable. *[FRS 102.5.7F]*.

An entity must also disclose its share of the profit or loss of associates accounted for using the equity method and its share of any discontinued operations of such associates, *[FRS 102.14.14]*, and the same information for jointly controlled entities. *[FRS 102.15.20]*.

6.8.1   Definition of discontinued operation

FRS 102 defines a discontinued operation as a component of an entity (i.e. operations and cash flows that can be clearly distinguished, operationally and for financial reporting purposes from the rest of the entity) that has been disposed of and: *[FRS 102 Appendix I]*

(a)   represented a separate major line of business or geographical area of operations;

(b)   was part of a single co-ordinated plan to dispose of a separate major line of business or geographical area of operations; or

(c)   was a subsidiary acquired exclusively with a view to resale.

The definition of discontinued operations in FRS 102 differs to that included in IFRS 5 in that it refers to 'a component of an entity *that has been disposed of'* whereas IFRS 5 refers to a 'component of an entity that *either has been disposed of or is classified as held for sale'* [emphasis added]. As noted at 6.8 above, the presentation of discontinued operations relates to operations disposed of at the reporting date.

IFRS 5, which has the same definition of a component as in FRS 102, clarifies that 'a component of an entity will have been a cash-generating unit or a group of cash-generating units while being held for use'. *[IFRS 5.31]*. Under both IFRSs and FRS 102, a cash generating unit is 'the smallest identifiable group of assets that generates cash inflows that are largely independent of the cash inflows from other assets or groups of assets'. *[IFRS 5 Appendix A, FRS 102.27.8, FRS 102 Appendix I]*. See Chapter 24 at 4.2. Management may consider IFRS 5's guidance on a component, as permitted by the hierarchy in Section 10. *[FRS 102.10.4-6]*.

FRS 102 does not clarify the phrase 'has been disposed of'. In our view, the phrase 'has been disposed of' may be interpreted more widely than a sale. An entity's management must use judgement in developing and applying an accounting policy and may consider the requirements and guidance in IFRS 5. IFRS 5's requirements would be consistent with a view that a component meeting any of the criteria (a) to (c) is discontinued if, at the end of the reporting period, the component is an abandoned operation, or the entity has partially disposed of (but lost control of) the operation or has distributed the operation. However, since the phrase 'has been disposed of' has not been explained further in FRS 102, different interpretations of what this means may be sustained.

6.8.2   Adjustments to amounts previously presented in discontinued operations in prior periods

FRS 102 does not address adjustments to amounts previously presented in discontinued operations. Given the absence of specific requirements in FRS 102, management may consider the requirements and guidance of IFRSs in this area.

IFRS 5 requires that adjustments in the current period to amounts previously presented in discontinued operations that are directly related to the disposal of a discontinued operation in a prior period are classified separately in discontinued operations. The nature and amount of such adjustments must be disclosed. Examples given of circumstances in which these adjustments may arise include the following: *[IFRS 5.35]*

- the resolution of uncertainties that arise from the terms of the disposal transaction, such as the resolution of purchase price adjustments and indemnification issues with the purchaser;

- the resolution of uncertainties that arise from and are directly related to the operations of the component before its disposal, such as environmental and product warranty obligations retained by the seller; and

- the settlement of employee benefit plan obligations, provided that the settlement is directly related to the disposal transaction.

6.8.3   Trading between continuing and discontinued operations

Discontinued operations remain consolidated in group financial statements and therefore, any transactions between discontinued and continuing operations are eliminated as usual in the consolidation. As a consequence, the amounts ascribed to the continuing and discontinued operations will be income and expense only from transactions with counterparties external to the group. Importantly, this means the results presented on the face of the income statement will not necessarily represent the activities of the operations as individual entities, particularly when there has been significant trading between the continuing and discontinued operations. Some might consider the results for the continuing and discontinued operations on this basis to be of little use to readers of accounts. An argument could be made that allocating external transactions to or from the discontinued operations would yield more meaningful information.

One approach would be to fully eliminate transactions for the purpose of presenting the income statement then provide supplementary information.

6.8.4   First-time adoption

There is no longer an exception for discontinued operations on first time adoption. The first-time adoption exception for discontinued operations was removed by the Triennial review 2017. However, this exception remains applicable for accounting periods beginning before 1 January 2019 (or before adoption of the Triennial review 2017 amendments, if earlier) The exception stated that, on first-time adoption of FRS 102, an entity shall not retrospectively change the accounting that it followed under its previous financial reporting framework for discontinued operations. See Chapter 32 at 4.3 of EY UK GAAP 2017 for discussion of the (eliminated) transition exception.

6.8.5   Example of presentation of discontinued operations

Example 6.6:   Presentation of discontinued operations

Statement of comprehensive income

For the year ended 31 December 201Y

	201Y Continuing operations	201Y Discontinued operations	201Y Total	201X Continuing operation (as restated)	201X Discontinued operations (as restated)	201X Total
	CU	CU	CU	CU	CU	CU
Turnover	4,200	1,232	5,432	3,201	1,500	4,701
Cost of sales	(2,591)	(1,104)	(3,695)	(2,281)	(1,430)	(3,711)
Gross profit	1,609	128	1,737	920	70	990
Administrative expenses	(452)	(110)	(562)	(418)	(120)	(538)
Other operating income	212	–	212	198	–	198
Operating profit	1,369	18	1,387	700	(50)	650
Profit on disposal of operations*	–	301	301	–	–	–
Interest receivable and similar income	14	–	14	16	–	16
Interest payable and similar expenses	(208)	–	(208)	(208)	–	(208)
Profit before taxation	1,175	319	1,494	508	(50)	458
Taxation	(390)	(4)	(394)	(261)	3	(258)
Profit after taxation and profit for the financial year	785	315	1,100	247	(47)	200
Other comprehensive income						
Actuarial losses on defined benefit pension plans			(108)			(68)
Deferred tax movement relating to actuarial losses			28			18
Total comprehensive income for the year			1,020			150

*   This line was moved from above Operating profit to below Operating Profit as part of the Triennial review 2017. See 6.7.3 above.

The above example is taken from the Appendix to Section 5 (which accompanies but is not part of that section, and provides guidance on application of paragraph 5.7E for presenting discontinued operations). In our view, it would also be good practice to include 'as restated' in the total column in the comparatives.

6.9   Earnings per share (adapted formats and statutory formats)

IAS 33 – *Earnings per Share* – must be followed by an entity whose ordinary shares or potential ordinary shares are publicly traded or that files, or is in the process of filing its financial statements with a securities commission or other regulatory organisation for the purpose of issuing ordinary shares in a public market. IAS 33 also applies to an entity that chooses to disclose voluntarily earnings per share (EPS). *[FRS 102.1.4]*.

IAS 33 requires an entity to present the basic and diluted EPS for profit or loss from continuing operations attributable to ordinary equity holders of the parent entity, and for total profit or loss attributable to ordinary equity holders of the parent entity. This must be given for each class of ordinary share that has a different right to share in profit for the period. *[IAS 33.9, 33.66]*. Basic and diluted EPS must be presented with equal prominence in the statement of comprehensive income (or on the face of the income statement, if presented) for every period for which a statement of comprehensive income is presented. *[IAS 33.66-67A]*.

An entity may disclose basic and diluted EPS for discontinued operations *either* in the statement of comprehensive income (or on the face of the income statement, if presented) *or* in the notes. *[IAS 33.68-68A].*

Basic and diluted EPS is presented even if the amounts are negative, i.e. a loss per share. *[IAS 33.69].* If basic and diluted EPS are equal, dual presentation can be achieved in one line in the statement of comprehensive income. *[IAS 33.67].*

IAS 33 provides further requirements on the calculation of basic and diluted EPS and on the accompanying disclosures. See Chapter 33 of EY International GAAP 2019 for further details.

7 STATEMENT OF CHANGES IN EQUITY

An entity must present a statement of changes in equity, or if certain conditions are met and an entity chooses to, a statement of income and retained earnings (see 7.2 below). *[FRS 102.6.1].*

Equity is the residual interest in the assets of the entity after deducting all its liabilities. It may be sub-classified in the statement of financial position. For example, sub-classifications may include funds contributed by shareholders, retained earnings, and gains or losses recognised directly in equity. *[FRS 102.2.22, FRS 102 Appendix I].*

Section 22 – *Liabilities and Equity* – requires certain financial instruments – that would otherwise meet the definition of a liability – to be classified as equity because they represent the residual interest in the net assets of the entity. Puttable financial instruments, and instruments (or components of instruments) that contain obligations only on liquidation are, therefore, classified as equity providing the criteria for equity classification are met. *[FRS 102.22.4-5].*

See Chapter 10 at 5 for the classification of financial instruments as debt or equity.

FRS 102's requirements for the statement of changes in equity are similar to those included in IFRSs.

The Regulations and LLP Regulations do not require a statement of changes in equity to be presented but do require an analysis of movements on reserves and certain disclosures relating to dividends and appropriations. In practice, the analysis of movements in reserves could be combined with the statement of changes in equity. See 7.1 below.

7.1 Information to be presented in the statement of changes in equity

The statement of changes in equity presents an entity's profit or loss for a reporting period, other comprehensive income for the period, the effects of changes in accounting policies and corrections of material errors recognised in the period and the amounts of investments by, and dividends and other distributions to, equity investors during the period. *[FRS 102.6.2].*

The effects of corrections of material errors and changes in accounting policies are presented as retrospective adjustments of prior periods rather than as part of profit or loss in the period in which they arise. *[FRS 102.5.8].* This is why such errors and changes in accounting policies are reported as separate line items in the statement of changes in equity (or, if presented, the statement of income and retained earnings). *[FRS 102.6.3(b), 6.5(c), (d)].* The retrospective adjustments for material errors and changes in accounting policy are consistent with the requirements of IFRSs.

The statement of changes in equity shows: *[FRS 102.6.3-3A, FRS 102 Appendix I]*

(a)   total comprehensive income for the period (the sum of profit and loss and other comprehensive income – see 6 above) showing separately the total amounts attributable to owners of the parent and to non-controlling interests (see 4.5 above);

(b)   for each component of equity, the effects of retrospective application (of accounting policies) or retrospective restatement recognised in accordance with Section 10; and

(c)   for each component of equity, a reconciliation between the carrying amount at the beginning and the end of the period, separately disclosing changes resulting from:

(i)   profit or loss;

(ii)   other comprehensive income (which must be analysed by item, either in the statement of changes in equity or in the notes); and

(iii)   the amounts of investments by, and dividends and other distributions to, owners, showing separately issues of shares, purchase of own share transactions, dividends and other distributions to owners, and changes in ownership interests in subsidiaries that do not result in a loss of control.

It can be seen that (a) above is effectively a sub-total of the sum of the items required by (c)(i) and (c)(ii). Items required to be recognised in other comprehensive income are listed at 6.2 above.

FRS 102 does not define a 'component of equity'. However, IAS 1, which has a similar requirement to (c) above, states that 'components of equity' include, for example, each class of contributed equity, the accumulated balance of each class of other comprehensive income and retained earnings. *[IAS 1.108]*.

In our view, the components presented should (as a minimum) include the components of capital and reserves relating to the headings and subheadings set out in the statutory formats (see 5.3.12 above), bearing in mind that an analysis of movements in these reserves is already required by the Regulations (or LLP Regulations) (see below) However, other components of equity might include, for example, the cash flow hedge reserve or fair value movements accumulated in equity on available-for-sale financial assets (where IAS 39 is applied). For UK companies and LLPs, these reserves would be included within the statutory fair value reserve required by the fair value accounting rules (see 10.3 below).

Where adapted formats are used, FRS 102 requires separate sub-classifications for classes of equity (such as share capital, share premium, retained earnings, revaluation reserve and fair value reserve) to be shown either on the face of the statement of financial position or in the notes to the financial statements (see 5.1.12 above). *[FRS 102.4.2B(g)]*. These sub-classifications are likely to represent, at a minimum, components of equity for the purposes of the statement of changes in equity.

7.1.1   Related disclosures in the Regulations and LLP Regulations

Where there have been transfers to or from any reserves (and the reserves are shown as separate line items in the balance sheet, or would be so shown, if Arabic-numbered line items were not combined as permitted by paragraph 4(2)(b) of the General Rules to the formats – see 4.4 above), a UK company preparing Companies Act accounts (or an

LLP preparing non-IAS accounts) must disclose, in the notes to the accounts, in respect of the aggregate of reserves included in the same item:

- the amount of the reserves at the beginning and end of the financial year;
- any amounts transferred to or from the reserve during that year; and
- the source and application respectively of any amounts transferred.

This information must be presented in tabular form. *[1 Sch 59(1)-(2), 1 Sch 57(1) (LLP)-(2)].* Comparatives are required under the general requirements of FRS 102 (as there is not a specific exemption). *[FRS 102.3.14].*

This disclosure requirement is relevant to both statutory formats and adapted formats. For statutory formats, the movements in reserves will include the headings and sub-headings listed in the statutory formats (see 5.3.12 above). For adapted formats, in our view, it would be appropriate to present the movements in reserves for the classes of equity identified on the face of the statement of financial position or in the notes to the financial statements (see 5.1.12 above), which would normally be the same components of equity identified when presenting the statement of changes in equity. *[FRS 102.4.2B(g)].*

UK companies preparing Companies Act accounts (relevant to adapted formats and statutory formats) are required to state in the notes to the accounts: *[1 Sch 43]*

- any amount set aside to (or proposed to be set aside to), or withdrawn from (or proposed to be withdrawn from) reserves;
- the aggregate amount of dividends paid in the financial year (other than those for which a liability existed at the immediately preceding balance sheet date);
- the aggregate amount of dividends that the company is liable to pay at the balance sheet date; and
- the aggregate amount of dividends that are proposed before the date of approval of the accounts, and not otherwise disclosed above.

The LLP Regulations only require LLPs preparing non-IAS accounts to state in the notes to the accounts any amount set aside to (or proposed to be set aside to), or withdrawn from (or proposed to be withdrawn from) reserves. *[1 Sch 43 (LLP)].*

Particulars must be given of the proposed appropriation of profit or treatment of loss or, where applicable, particulars of the actual appropriation of profits or treatment of the losses. *[1 Sch 72B, 1 Sch 70B (LLP)].*

Where an entity declares dividends to holders of its equity instruments after the end of the reporting period, those dividends are not recognised as a liability because no obligation exists at that time, but FRS 102 permits an entity to show the dividend as a segregated component of retained earnings at the end of the reporting period. *[FRS 102.32.8].* However, the Triennial review 2017 has introduction an exception to this requirement to allow the tax effects of dividends which qualify as gift aid payments by subsidiaries to their charitable parents to be taken into account at the reporting date when it is probable that the gift aid payment will be made in the following nine months; *[FRS 102.29.14A].* See Chapter 26 at 7.6.1.

FRS 102 requires an entity to *disclose* the fair value of non-cash assets distributed to its owners in the reporting period (except when the non-cash assets are ultimately controlled by the same parties before and after the distribution). *[FRS 102.22.18]*.

7.1.2   Example of statement of changes in equity

FRS 102 does not include an illustrative statement of changes in equity. Example 6.7 illustrates the requirements below.

An analysis is required of other comprehensive income by item in the statement of changes in equity or in the notes to the accounts. *[FRS 102.6.3A]*. The detail in which this analysis must be presented is not specified.

Example 6.7:   Combined statement of changes in equity

XYZ Group – Statement of changes in equity for the year ended 31 December 201Y
(£'000)

	Called up share capital	Share premium account	Re-valuation reserve	Capital redemp-tion reserve	Own shares	Merger reserve	Fair value reserve	Profit and loss account	Equity owners of parent	Non-controll-ing interest	Total equity
Balance at 1 January 201X	10,000	500	3,000	–	(774)	–	3,098	16,849	32,673	85	32,758
Changes in accounting policy	–	–	–	–	–	–	–	600	600	–	600
Restated balance	10,000	500	3,000	–	(774)	–	3,098	17,449	33,273	85	33,358
Profit for the year	–	–	–	–	–	–	–	4,872	4,872	35	4,907
Other comprehensive income	–	–	100	–	–	–	(574)	(541)	(1,015)	2	(1,013)
Total comprehensive income for the year [a]	–	–	100	–	–	–	(574)	4,331	3,857	37	3,894
Dividends paid	–	–	–	–	–	–	–	(1,170)	(1,170)	–	(1,170)
Share based payment expense	–	–	–	–	–	–	–	398	398	–	398
Balance at 31 December 201X	10,000	500	3,100	–	(774)	–	2,524	21,008	36,358	122	36,480

Profit for the year	–	–	–	–	–	–	–	4,674	4,674	235	4,909
Other comprehensive income	–	–	200	–	–	–	(665)	732	267	3	270
Total comprehensive income for the year (b)	–	–	200	–	–	–	(665)	5,406	4,941	238	5,179
Dividends paid	–	–	–	–	–	–	–	(1,400)	(1,400)	(31)	(1,431)
New shares issued	2,575	100	–	–	–	6,250	–	–	8,925	–	8,925
Share issue costs	–	(100)	–	–	–	–	–	–	(100)	–	(100)
Share buy back	(500)	–	–	500	–	–	–	(1,800)	(1,800)	–	(1,800)
Share based payment expense	–	–	–	–	–	–	–	307	307	–	307
Balance at 31 December 201Y	12,075	500	3,300	500	(774)	6,250	1,859	23,521	47,231	329	47,560

(a) The amount included in retained earnings for 201X of £4,331,000 represents profit attributable to owners of the parent of £4,872,000 less remeasurement losses (net of tax) on defined benefit pension plans of £541,000 (gross £676,000 less tax £135,000).

The amount included in the cash flow hedge reserve for 201X comprises a loss on cash flow hedges of £574,000 (£717,000 less tax £143,000) which represented losses (net of tax) transferred to cash flow hedge of £774,000 less reclassification of losses (net of tax) to profit and loss of £200,000. The amount included in non-controlling interest of £2,000 for 2015 relates to exchange translation gains (no attributable tax).

The amount included in the revaluation surplus of £100,000 for 201X represents the share of other comprehensive income of associates of £100,000 (gross £120,000 less tax £20,000). Other comprehensive income of associates relates solely to gains or losses on property revaluation.

(b) The amount included in retained earnings for 201Y of £5,406,000 represents profit attributable to owners of the parent of £4,674,000 plus remeasurement gains on defined benefit pension plans of £732,000 (£915,000 less tax £183,000).

The amount included in the cash flow hedge reserve for 201Y comprises a loss on cash flow hedges of £665,000 (£831,000 less tax £166,000) which represented losses (net of tax) transferred to cash flow hedge of £900,000 less reclassification of losses (net of tax) to profit and loss of £235,000. The amount included in non-controlling interest of £3,000 for 201Y relates to exchange translation gains (no attributable tax).

The amount included in the revaluation surplus of £200,000 for 201Y represents the share of other comprehensive income of associates of £200,000 (gross £240,000 less tax £40,000). Other comprehensive income of associates relates solely to gains or losses on property revaluation.

The LLP SORP provides detailed guidance on the statement of changes in equity (and on the SORP's requirement for an LLP to present, either as a primary statement or in the notes, a reconciliation of members' interests). The SORP defines members' interests as comprising both 'other members' interests' and 'loans and other debts due to members' less any amounts due from members in debtors and specifies the format for the reconciliation of members' interests. Comparatives, i.e. the full table reconciling movements in the comparative year, are required, where this reconciliation is presented as a primary statement. *[LLP SORP.59-60A]*.

Not all LLPs have equity (e.g. if the LLP's partnership interests are classified entirely as liabilities). The LLP SORP clarifies that no statement of changes in equity is required in such circumstances (unless a reconciliation of members' interests is presented as a primary statement) but requires that a statement should be made on the face of one of the primary statements or in the notes to the accounts that the LLP has no equity and consequently a statement of changes in equity is not given. *[LLP SORP.59A]*.

7.2   Statement of income and retained earnings

The purpose of a statement of income and retained earnings is to present an entity's profit or loss and changes in retained earnings for a reporting period.

An entity is permitted (but is not required) to present a statement of income and retained earnings in place of a statement of comprehensive income and a statement of changes in equity if the only changes to its equity in the periods for which financial statements are presented arise from: *[FRS 102.6.4]*

* profit or loss;
* payment of dividends;
* corrections of prior period errors; and
* changes in accounting policy.

In essence, this means that the statement of income and retained earnings may be presented where the entity does not have items of other comprehensive income, investments by equity investors or non-dividend distributions to equity investors in the current or comparative periods presented.

The statement of income and retained earnings shows the following items in addition to the information required in the statement of comprehensive income by Section 5: *[FRS 102.6.5]*

* retained earnings at the beginning of the reporting period;
* dividends declared and paid or payable during the period;
* restatements of retained earnings for corrections of prior period material errors;
* restatements of retained earnings for changes in accounting policy; and
* retained earnings at the end of the reporting period.

See Example 6.8 which illustrates a statement of income and retained earnings.

The LLP SORP does not recommend that LLPs present a statement of income and retained earnings, on the grounds that it will be of little benefit to users of LLP financial statements in most cases. *[LLP SORP.26A]*.

Example 6.8:   *Statement of income and retained earnings (extract)*

	201Y	201X Restated
	£'000	£'000
Profit before taxation	1,494	458
Taxation	(394)	(258)
Profit after taxation and profit for the financial year	1,100	200
Retained earnings brought forward at 1 January 1Y		
(1 January 1X) – as originally reported	12,285	13,500
Prior period adjustment – changes in accounting policy	(1,820)	(2,235)
Prior period adjustment – correction of error	(1,900)	(1,900)
Retained earnings brought forward at 1 January 1Y		
(1 January 1X)– as restated	8,565	9,365
Dividends paid [or payable]	(1,500)	(1,000)
Retained earnings carried forward at 31 December 1Y		
(31 December 1X)	8,165	8,565

8   NOTES TO THE FINANCIAL STATEMENTS

FRS 102 sets out the principles underlying the information to be presented in the notes and how to present it. Notes contain information in addition to that presented in the primary statements. Notes provide narrative descriptions or disaggregations of items presented in those statements and information about items that do not qualify for recognition in those statements. Most sections of FRS 102 require disclosures that are normally presented in the notes. *[FRS 102.8.1]*.

UK companies preparing Companies Act accounts are required by the CA 2006 (principally Part 15), the Regulations and other applicable regulations to disclose certain information in the notes to the accounts. See, for example, the disclosures identified in Chapter 1 at 6.7. Similarly, LLPs preparing non-IAS accounts are required by the CA 2006 (as applied to LLPs by SI 2008/1911), the LLP Regulations and other applicable regulations to disclose certain information in the notes to the accounts. Certain of these statutory disclosures have been commented on in the discussion of the statutory formats at 5.3 and 6.6 above (because they represent additional analyses for line items required in the balance sheet or profit and loss account) but the disclosures generally apply where adapted formats are used as well.

This section looks at, in particular, the statutory disclosures on staff costs; off-balance sheet arrangements; guarantees, contingencies and commitments; and directors' advances, credits and guarantees.

Chapter 6

Statutory disclosures relevant to specific accounting topics are addressed in other chapters of this publication. This publication is not intended to include a comprehensive discussion of all such disclosures. In particular, this publication does not cover the statutory disclosures required in the notes to Companies Act accounts and IAS accounts relating to directors' remuneration (in accordance with Schedule 5 to the Regulations), or of the profit (including members' remuneration) attributable to the member of an LLP with the largest entitlement to profit (including members' remuneration). *[1 Sch 66 (LLP)].* The LLP SORP provides further guidance on disclosure of members' remuneration for LLPs. *[LLP SORP.20, 51-54, 71-73].*

This publication also does not address the disclosure of auditor remuneration for auditing of the annual accounts and other services, required by section 494 of the CA 2006 and *The Companies (Disclosure of Auditor Remuneration and Liability Limitation Agreements) Regulations 2008* (SI 2008/489, as amended by SI 2011/2198 and SI 2016/649). *[s494, s494 (LLP)].*

TECH 14/13 FRF – *Disclosure of Auditor Remuneration*, issued by the ICAEW in December 2013, provides guidance on disclosure of auditor remuneration. TECH 14/13 FRF does not reflect the amendments that were made by SI 2016/649:[26]

- to remove the requirement for companies subject to the small companies regime to disclose, in a note to the annual accounts, the amount of any remuneration receivable by the auditor for the auditing of those accounts.

    This disclosure remains for medium-sized companies; and

- to restrict the conditions for exemption for a subsidiary company, from disclosing remuneration for services other than the auditing of the company's accounts in the subsidiary's individual accounts, to situations where the statutory auditor of the subsidiary company is the same as the statutory auditor of the parent that is required to prepare and does prepare group accounts in accordance with the CA 2006 (which consolidate the subsidiary).

    The other conditions for use of this exemption by a subsidiary company were unchanged. There was also no change to the conditions for the same exemption for the individual accounts of a parent company.

The changes made by SI 2016/649 also affect LLPs *[s494 (LLP)]* and entities such as qualifying partnerships (unless exempt under regulation 7 of *The Partnerships (Accounts) Regulations 2008)* that are required to comply with these disclosures (see 4.2.4 and 4.2.5 above).[27]

8.1   Structure of the notes

FRS 102 requires the presentation of notes to the financial statements that: *[FRS 102.8.2]*

(a)   present information about the basis of preparation of the financial statements and the specific accounting policies used;

(b)   disclose the information required by FRS 102 that is not presented on the face of the primary statements; and

(c)   provide information that is not presented elsewhere in the financial statements, but is relevant to an understanding of any of them.

The notes should, as far as practicable, be presented in a systematic manner. Each item in the financial statements should be cross-referenced to any related information in the notes. *[FRS 102.8.3]*.

The notes are normally presented in the following order: *[FRS 102.8.4]*

(a)   a statement that the financial statements have been prepared in compliance with FRS 102 (see 3.8 above);

(b)   a summary of significant accounting policies applied (see 8.2 below);

(c)   supporting information for items presented in the financial statements, in the sequence in which each statement and each line item is presented; and

(d)   any other disclosures.

The Triennial review 2017 removed most references to 'a summary of' where the requirements relating to significant accounting policies are referred to in Section 8. We do not consider this to be a substantive change and the level of detail required in relation to accounting policies is the same as was required in the previous version of FRS 102. See 8.2 below. The reference to 'a summary of' was not removed from paragraph 8.4(b) of FRS 102 however we do not consider this to be intentional or have substantive implications.

These requirements of FRS 102 are consistent with the traditional order of financial statements. The Regulations require that the notes to the accounts of a company give the information set out in Part 3 of Schedule 1, 2 or 3 to the Regulations, as applicable, in the order in which, where relevant, the items to which they relate are presented in the balance sheet and in the profit and loss account. *[1 Sch 42(2)]*. The LLP Regulations similarly require that the notes to an LLP's accounts give the information set out in Part 3 of Schedule 1 to the LLP Regulations in this same order. *[1 Sch 42(2) (LLP)]*. The same applies in group accounts of UK parent companies and parent LLPs. *[6 Sch 1(1), 3 Sch 1 (LLP)]*. This requirement is emphasised by way of a footnote to paragraph 8.4 in FRS 102 which states: 'Company law requires the notes to be presented in the order in which, where relevant, the items to which they relate are presented in the statement of financial position and in the income statement'. In our view, this restriction only applies to those entities subject to such statutory restrictions. Beside UK companies and LLPs, these restrictions also impact other entities such as qualifying partnerships (unless exempt under regulation 7 of *The Partnerships (Accounts) Regulations 2008*) that are required to prepare their annual accounts in accordance with the CA 2006 (see 4.2.4 and 4.2.5 below).

In recent years, a number of entities have adopted a different placement of information with the aim of ensuring that the financial statements are understandable and avoid immaterial clutter that can obscure useful information. For example, some entities have grouped the notes to the financial statements so that these deal with related accounting topics and / or integrated the accounting policies for particular items within the relevant notes. Some entities have distinguished between the most significant accounting policies and other accounting policies, which may be relegated to an appendix to the financial statements. As FRS 102 refers to 'normally presented in the following order', this allows some flexibility subject to meeting, where relevant, the statutory requirements.

The IASB has an ongoing Disclosure Initiative looking at materiality, principles for disclosure in the notes to the financial statements and other presentation and disclosure matters which may be of interest to FRS 102 reporters. As part of this initiative, in

December 2014, the IASB published Amendments to IAS 1 – *Disclosure Initiative*. The amendments clarify, *inter alia*, that entities have flexibility over the order of the notes (i.e. these do not need to be presented in the traditional order highlighted above), provided that the notes are presented in a systematic manner.

IAS 1 requires that an entity must, as far as practicable, present notes in a systematic manner (and in determining this, must consider understandability and comparability of its financial statements). Each item in the primary statements should be cross referenced to related information in the notes. *[IAS 1.113]*. Examples of a systematic ordering or grouping of notes given by IAS 1 include: *[IAS 1.114]*

- giving prominence to the areas of its activities that the entity considers to be most relevant to an understanding of its financial performance and position, such as grouping together information about particular operating activities;

- grouping together information about items measured similarly such as assets measured at fair value; or

- a presentation similar to that discussed in paragraph 8.4 of FRS 102.

In July 2014, the FRC Lab published a report – *Accounting policies and integration of related financial information*, following a project involving 16 companies and 19 institutional investors, analysts and representative organisations (supplemented by an online survey) which looked at:

- accounting policies: which policies are disclosed, the content of what is disclosed and their placement;

- the notes to the financial statements: the ordering, grouping and combining notes; and

- the financial review: its integration with the primary statements.

The FRC Lab report found that most investors viewed the combining of tax expense and tax balance sheet notes as logical but there was little support for combining other notes. The case for significant change in note order has not been made with some investors preferring the traditional order, some preferring company-specific ordering and some expressing no preference. Investors valued consistency of note order across companies and time; a table of contents was considered helpful, especially where notes are ordered differently. Most investors preferred the traditional approach of placing management commentary and financial statement information in separate sections of the annual report, while some saw merit in increased analysis of financial statement line items that an integrated commentary can provide.

UK companies, LLPs and entities required to prepare their accounts in accordance with the CA 2006 that experiment with alternative methods of structuring the notes will need to ensure that they comply with the statutory requirements on note structure referred to above.

8.2 Significant accounting policies

The disclosure of significant accounting policies should include the measurement basis (or bases) used in preparing the financial statements and the other accounting policies used that are relevant to an understanding of the financial statements. *[FRS 102.8.5]*. FRS 102 explains that measurement is the process of determining the monetary amounts at which assets, liabilities, income and expenses are measured in the financial statements and involves the selection of a basis of measurement. Section 2 specifies which measurement basis an entity must use for many types of assets, liabilities, income and expenses. Examples of common measurement bases are historical cost and fair value. *[FRS 102.2.33-34]*.

Judgement is clearly required when deciding which are the significant accounting policies and the level of detail required in the disclosure of accounting policies. In recent years, the FRC has continued to comment on the quality of disclosure of accounting policies, including particularly revenue recognition policies. The FRC's Corporate Reporting Review function has challenged companies where the information is not company-specific or is generic (including boilerplate text from accounting standards); and where accounting policies that might have been expected given the business model described were not present (e.g. if the business model includes distinct and significant revenue streams described in the business review; accounting policies relevant to each stream would be expected). Accounting policies should be given for material transactions, particularly if unusual or non-recurring but the FRC does not expect immaterial or irrelevant policies to be disclosed. Industry-specific accounting policies should be clearly disclosed, avoiding industry specific jargon.[28]

The FRC Lab Report – *Accounting policies and integration of related financial information*, which is available on the FRC website, highlights the views of investors (including consensus views on the attributes of significant policies and qualities for the content of policy disclosures) and sets out 'dos and don'ts' from the FRC's Corporate Reporting Review team. Subsequently, the FRC Lab published a report that looked at approaches taken to the presentation of significant accounting policies and other accounting policies by one listed company.[29]

Disclosure of particular accounting policies is especially useful to users when those policies are selected from alternatives allowed in FRS 102 (e.g. the accrual or performance model for government grants). Indeed, as indicated below, FRS 102 often explicitly requires accounting policies, where material, to be disclosed in such situations. In addition, disclosure is useful where it relates to significant accounting policies not specifically required to be disclosed but which have been selected by management in accordance with the hierarchy in Section 10.

Chapter 6

FRS 102 specifically requires disclosure (where material) of certain accounting policies, including:

- the accounting policies adopted for the recognition of revenue (including the methods adopted to determine the stage of completion of transactions involving the rendering of services and the methods used to determine construction contract revenue recognised in the period and the stage of completion of construction contracts in progress); *[FRS 102.23.30(a), 23.31(b), (c)]*

- the measurement basis (or bases) used for financial instruments and the other accounting policies used for financial instruments that are relevant to an understanding of the financial statements; *[FRS 102.11.40, 12.26]*

- the accounting policies adopted in measuring inventories, including the cost formula used; *[FRS 102.13.22(a)]*

- for each class of property, plant and equipment, the measurement bases used for determining the gross carrying amount; *[FRS 102.17.31(a)]*

- a description of the methods used to account for the investments in subsidiaries, jointly controlled entities and associates in the separate financial statements of a parent; *[FRS 102.9.27(b)]*

- the accounting policy for investments in associates and for investments in jointly controlled entities in individual and consolidated financial statements; *[FRS 102.14.12(a), 15.19(a)]*

- the accounting policy adopted for grants; *[FRS 102.24.6(a)]*

- the accounting policy adopted for each category of termination benefits that an entity provides to its employees; *[FRS 102.28.43]*

- the accounting policies adopted for heritage assets, including details of the measurement bases used; *[FRS 102.34.55(c)]* and

- the measurement basis used for public benefit entity concessionary loans and any other accounting policies which are relevant to the understanding of these transactions within the financial statements. *[FRS 102.PBE.34.95]*.

FRS 102 also specifically requires disclosure (where material) of methods used in applying accounting policies, including:

- for all financial assets and financial liabilities measured at fair value, the basis for determining fair value e.g. quoted market price in an active market or a valuation technique (and when a valuation technique is used, the assumptions applied in determining fair value for each class of financial assets and financial liabilities); *[FRS 102.11.43, 12.26]*

- the methods used to establish the amount of fair value change attributable to changes in own credit risk for financial instruments measured at fair value through profit or loss (not required for financial liabilities held as part of a trading portfolio nor derivatives). (If the change cannot be measured reliably or is not material, that fact must be stated); *[FRS 102.11.48A(b), 12.26]*

- the methods and significant assumptions applied in: *[FRS 102.16.10(a), 17.32A, 18.29A, 34.7(b), 34.7B, 34.10A]*

  - determining the fair value of investment property;

- estimating the fair values of items of property, plant and equipment stated at revalued amounts;
- estimating the fair values of intangible assets accounted for at revalued amounts;
- determining the fair value of each class of biological asset (where the fair value model is applied); and
- determining the fair value at the point of harvest of each class of agricultural produce (under the fair value model, and for any agricultural produce measured at fair value less costs to sell at the point of harvest under the cost model).

- for each class of intangible assets, the useful lives or the amortisation rates used and the reasons for choosing those periods, and the amortisation methods used; *[FRS 102.18.27(a)-(b)]*
- for each business combination (excluding any group reconstructions) effected during the period, the useful life of goodwill, and if this cannot be reliably estimated, supporting reasons for the period chosen; *[FRS 102.19.25(g)]*
- for each class of property, plant and equipment, the useful lives or the depreciation rates used, and the depreciation methods used; *[FRS 102.17.31(b)-(c)]* and
- for each class of biological asset measured using the cost model, the useful lives or depreciation rates used, and the depreciation methods used. *[FRS 102.34.10(c)-(d)]*.

A UK company preparing Companies Act accounts (or an LLP preparing non-IAS accounts) is also required to disclose the accounting policies used in determining the amounts to be included in respect of items shown in the balance sheet and in determining the profit or loss of the company (or the LLP), in the notes to the accounts. *[1 Sch 44, 1 Sch 44 (LLP)]*.

The Regulations (and LLP Regulations) specifically require the note on accounting policies to include:

- accounting policies with respect to depreciation and diminution in value of assets; *[1 Sch 44, 1 Sch 44 (LLP)]*
- the items affected and the basis of valuation adopted for each item measured using the alternative accounting rules, e.g. where property, plant and equipment is revalued (see 10.2 below); *[1 Sch 34(2), 1 Sch 34(2) (LLP)]* and
- the amortisation period for capitalised development costs, together with the reasons for capitalising the development costs (see 10.1.3 below). *[1 Sch 21, 1 Sch 21 (LLP)]*.

The notes to the accounts must also include the following:

- where in exceptional cases the useful life of intangible assets (including goodwill) cannot be reliably estimated, the amortisation period (which must not exceed ten years) chosen by the directors (or the members of the LLP), together with the reasons for choosing that period; and *[1 Sch 22, 1 Sch 22 (LLP)]*
- the basis of translating sums denominated in foreign currencies into sterling (or the currency in which the accounts are drawn up). *[1 Sch 70, 1 Sch 68 (LLP)]*.

While not required by the Regulations (or LLP Regulations), it would be usual to make these disclosures in the note on accounting policies.

It is common for financial statements to disclose the accounting convention used in their preparation. An example is given below, although the nature of the departures from the historical cost convention will depend on an entity's accounting policies.

Chapter 6

Example 6.9:   Accounting convention

The financial statements are prepared in accordance with the historical cost convention, except for the revaluation of property, plant and equipment at market value under the alternative accounting rules and application of the fair value accounting rules to derivative financial assets and liabilities and hedging relationships.

8.3   Judgements in applying accounting policies

Significant accounting policies or other notes must disclose the judgements, apart from those involving estimations, that management has made in the process of applying the entity's accounting policies and that have the most significant effect on the amounts recognised in the financial statements. *[FRS 102.8.6]*.

Examples of judgements in applying accounting policies include: whether a lease is classified as an operating or finance lease; whether a transaction is a business combination or an asset transaction; and whether the entity is acting as principal or agent in a revenue transaction.

FRS 102 specifically requires disclosure of certain judgements (although in general, there are fewer such disclosures required than under IFRSs), for example:

- the basis for concluding that control exists when the parent does not own (directly or indirectly through subsidiaries) more than half the voting power of an investee; *[FRS 102.9.23]*

- the name of any subsidiary excluded from consolidation and the reason for exclusion; *[FRS 102.9.23]*

- the reasons for a change in functional currency of either the reporting entity or a significant foreign operation; *[FRS 102.30.27]*

- material uncertainties related to events or conditions that cast significant doubt upon the entity's ability to continue as a going concern; and *[FRS 102.3.8-9]*

- the basis of preparation and the reasons, when adopting the non-going concern basis. *[FRS 102.3.8-9]*.

8.4   Information about key sources of estimation uncertainty

The notes to the financial statements should also disclose information about the key assumptions concerning the future, and other key sources of estimation uncertainty at the reporting date, that have a significant risk of causing a material adjustment to the carrying amounts of assets and liabilities within the next financial year. In respect of those assets and liabilities, the notes shall include details of their nature and their carrying amount as at the end of the reporting period. *[FRS 102.8.7]*.

FRS 102 specifically requires disclosure of certain key assumptions, e.g. the principal actuarial assumptions used (including discount rates, expected rates of salary increases, medical cost trend rates and any other material actuarial assumptions used). *[FRS 102.28.41(k)]*. See also some of the disclosures of methods and assumptions noted at 8.3 above.

In addition, the Regulations (and LLP Regulations) require that the notes to the accounts include the significant assumptions underlying the valuation models and techniques used to determine financial instruments, investment property, living animals and plants and stocks measured at fair value (under the fair value accounting rules) (see 10.3.4 and 10.4.3 below). *[1 Sch 55(2)(a), 1 Sch 53(2)(a) (LLP)]*.

IAS 1 includes the same requirement as FRS 102 on disclosure of key sources of estimation uncertainty. *[IAS 1.125]*, but contains considerably more explanatory guidance that management may consider, as permitted by the hierarchy in Section 10, in determining how to make the above disclosure. See Chapter 3 at 5.2 of EY International GAAP 2019.

8.5   Other notes disclosures in the presentation sections of FRS 102

An entity shall disclose in the notes to the financial statements: *[FRS 102.3.24]*

- the legal form of the entity, its country of incorporation and the address of its registered office (or principal place of business, if different from the registered office); and

- a description of the nature of the entity's operations and its principal activities unless this is disclosed in the business review (or similar statement) accompanying the financial statements.

An entity's principal activities will often be explained in the strategic report as part of the business review.

The date the financial statements were authorised for issue and who gave that authorisation must be disclosed. If the entity's owners or others have the power to amend the financial statements after issue, the entity shall disclose that fact. *[FRS 102.32.9]*. See Chapter 29 at 3.5.1.

The above requirement overlaps with the requirements in the CA 2006 for the company's directors to approve the annual accounts and for a director, on behalf of the board, to sign the company balance sheet (with the printed name of the director signing on behalf of the board stated in published and filed copies).[30] *[s414, s433, s444-447]*. For LLPs, the same requirements apply but the annual accounts are approved by the members of the LLP and are signed, on behalf of the members, by a designated member. *[s414 (LLP), s433 (LLP), s444 (LLP)-s447 (LLP)]*. However, the disclosures on authorisation of the financial statements required by FRS 102 are also often included as a separate note to the financial statements.

In addition, individual and group accounts of a company (or an LLP) must state:

- the part of the UK in which the company (or the LLP) is registered;

- the company's (or the LLP's) registered number;

- whether the company is a public or private company and whether it is limited by shares or by guarantee (no equivalent disclosure for LLPs);

- the address of the company's (or the LLP's) registered office; and

- where appropriate, the fact that the company (or the LLP) is being wound up.

This disclosure requirement applies to both Companies Act accounts (non-IAS accounts, for an LLP) and IAS accounts. *[s396(A1), s397(1), s404(A1), s406(1), s396(A1) (LLP), s397(1) (LLP), s404(A1) (LLP), s406(1) (LLP)]*.

Chapter 6

8.6 Staff numbers and costs (and number of members of an LLP)

A UK company (or an LLP) must disclose in the notes to the annual accounts: *[s411(1), s411(2), s411 (5), s411(1) (LLP), s411(2) (LLP), s411(5) (LLP)]*

(a) the average number of persons employed by the company (or the LLP) in the financial year:

(b) the average number of persons within each category of persons so employed.

> This means an analysis of (a) by category selected by the company's directors (or the members of the LLP), having regard to the manner in which the company's (or the LLP's) activities are organised;

(c) in respect of all persons employed by the company (or the LLP) during the financial year under contracts of service, the aggregate amounts of:

> (i)   wages and salaries paid or payable in respect of the year to those persons;
>
> (ii) social security costs incurred by the company (or the LLP) on their behalf; and
>
> (iii) other pension costs so incurred

unless stated elsewhere in the company's (or the LLP's) accounts.

This disclosure applies both to Companies Act accounts (non-IAS accounts, for an LLP) and IAS accounts. The information in (c) may already be stated elsewhere in the company's (or the LLP's) accounts where the format 2 profit and loss account is used.

UK companies subject to the small companies regime (and LLPs subject to the small LLPs regime) are only required to disclose the information in (a) above (see Chapter 5 at 11.1.6 and 11.4.2.C).

Where group accounts are prepared, the information in (a) to (c) above is required both for the consolidated group (i.e. the company (or the LLP) and its consolidated subsidiary undertakings) *[s411(7), s411(7) (LLP)]* and for the company (or the LLP).

The average number of persons employed is determined by dividing the 'relevant annual number' by the number of months in the financial year. The relevant annual number is determined by ascertaining the number of persons employed under contracts of service by the company (or the LLP) for each month in the financial year (whether throughout the month or not – so including both part-time and full-time employees) and then adding together all the monthly numbers. The number of persons so employed in each category is determined in a similar way. *[s411(3)-(4), s411(3) (LLP)-(4) (LLP)]*.

Wages and salaries, and social security costs are determined by reference to payments made or costs incurred in respect of all persons employed by the company (or the LLP) during the financial year under contracts of service. *[s411(5), s411(5) (LLP), 4 Sch 12 (LLP), 10 Sch 14]*.

Social security costs mean any contributions by the company (or the LLP) to any state social security or pension scheme, fund or arrangement. *[s411(6), s411(5) (LLP), 4 Sch 12 (LLP), 10 Sch 14]*.

Pension costs include any costs incurred by the company (or the LLP) in respect of any pension scheme established for the purpose of providing pensions for current or former employees; any sums set aside for the future payment of pensions directly by the company (or the LLP) to current or former employees; and any pensions paid directly to such persons without having first been set aside. *[s411(6), s411(6) (LLP), 4 Sch 12 (LLP), 10 Sch 14]*.

Pension costs exclude contributions to a state pension scheme – these are disclosed as social security costs.

The disclosures relate to persons employed on 'contracts of service' with the company (or the LLP) (meaning an employment contract) and, therefore, exclude self-employed people such as contractors or consultants. Executive directors generally have a contract of service, but non-executive directors may have contracts for services (rather than a contract of service). Where this is the case, the non-executive directors would be excluded from the above disclosure. All directors fall within the scope of statutory directors' remuneration disclosures (as noted at 8 above, these are beyond the scope of this publication).

In groups, employees with contracts of service with one entity (such as the parent or a corporate services entity) may be seconded to another group entity or paid by another entity, sometimes with costs recharged. In such cases, we would recommend that entities supplement the statutory disclosures for persons with contracts of service with additional information on staff costs and staff numbers, explaining the particular situation, including the impact on the profit and loss account.

LLPs preparing non-IAS accounts must also disclose the average number of members of the LLP in the financial year. This is computed by dividing the relevant annual number (i.e. determining the number of members of the LLP for all or part of each month in the financial year, and then adding together all the monthly numbers) by the number of months in the financial year. *[1 Sch 66(1)-(2) (LLP)].*

FRS 102 also includes disclosures in respect of share-based payment and employee benefits (see Chapter 23 at 14 and Chapter 25 at 3.12).

8.7 Off balance sheet arrangements

A UK company (or an LLP) must disclose the following information in the notes to the accounts if, in any financial year, the company (or the LLP) is or has been party to arrangements that are not reflected in its balance sheet and, at the balance sheet date, the risks or benefits arising from those arrangements are material:

(a) the nature and business purpose of the arrangements; and

(b) the financial impact of the arrangements on the company (or the LLP).

The information need only be given to the extent necessary for enabling the financial position to be assessed.

This disclosure applies both to Companies Act accounts (non-IAS accounts, for an LLP) and IAS accounts.

UK companies subject to the small companies regime (and LLPs subject to the small LLPs regime) are only required to give the disclosure in (a) above – see Chapter 5 at 11.1.5.H and 11.4.2.E).

In group accounts, the disclosures relate to the company and the undertakings included in the consolidation. *[s410A, s410A (LLP)].* Where group accounts are prepared, the information in (a) and (b) is given for both the consolidated group and the company (or the LLP).

Chapter 6

Section 410A implements the requirement for disclosure of 'off-balance sheet arrangements' included in Directive 2006/46/EC. Recital 9 to the EU Directive states:

'Such off-balance sheet arrangements could be any transactions or agreements which companies may have with entities, even unincorporated ones that are not included in the balance sheet. Such off-balance sheet arrangements may be associated with the creation or use of one or more Special Purpose Entities (SPEs) and offshore activities designed to address, *inter alia*, economic, legal, tax or accounting objectives. Examples of such off-balance sheet arrangements include risk and benefit-sharing arrangements or obligations arising from a contract such as debt factoring, combined sale and repurchase agreements, consignment stock arrangements, take or pay arrangements, securitisation arranged through separate companies and unincorporated entities, pledged assets, operating leasing arrangements, outsourcing and the like. Appropriate disclosure of the material risks and benefits of such arrangements that are not included in the balance sheet should be set out in the notes to the accounts or the consolidated accounts.'

The examples listed in Recital 9 are not to be taken as exhaustive. FRS 102 and / or the Regulations (and LLP Regulations) already require disclosures about certain off-balance sheet arrangements. The Regulations (and LLP Regulations) also, *inter alia*, require certain disclosures including in relation to the nature and form of security given for debts (see 5.3.8 above) and in respect of guarantees, contingencies and other financial commitments (see 8.7.1 below). As discussed at 8.3 above, FRS 102 also requires significant judgements in applying accounting policies to be disclosed.

UK companies and LLPs will, however, still need to consider whether the disclosures given are sufficient to meet the requirements of section 410A and whether the entity is party to material off-balance sheet arrangements not required to be disclosed by FRS 102 that should be disclosed in accordance with section 410A.

8.7.1   *Guarantees, contingencies and commitments*

A UK company preparing Companies Act accounts (or an LLP preparing non-IAS accounts) must give the following information in a note to the accounts: *[1 Sch 63, 1 Sch 60 (LLP)]*

(a)   particulars must be given of any charge on the assets of the company (or the LLP) to secure the liabilities of any other person, including the amount secured;

(b)   particulars and the total amount of any financial commitments, guarantees and contingencies that are not included in the balance sheet must be disclosed, together with an indication of the nature and form of any valuable security given by the company (or the LLP) in respect of such commitments, guarantees and contingencies;

(c)   the total amount of any pension commitments (within (b) above) that are not included in the balance sheet must be separately disclosed;

(d)   separate particulars of any pension commitment (within (c) above) relating wholly or partly to pensions payable to past directors of the company (or to past members of the LLP) must be given;

(e)   the total amount of any commitments, guarantees and contingencies (within (b) above) that are not included in the balance sheet undertaken on behalf or for the benefit of:

(i)   any parent undertaking or fellow subsidiary undertaking of the company (or LLP);

(ii)   any subsidiary undertaking of the company (or LLP); or

(iii) any undertaking in which the company (or LLP) has a participating interest

must be separately stated and those within each of paragraphs (i), (ii) and (iii) must also be stated separately from those within any other of those paragraphs; and

(f)   particulars must also be given of any pension commitments which are included on balance sheet, with separate particulars given for any pension commitment relating wholly or partly to pensions payable to past directors of the company.

Part (e) above appears to require the totals for (i), (ii), (iii) (and the sum of the totals for (i) to (iii)) to be separately stated.

See 5.3.4.C and 5.3.4.D above and Chapter 3 at 3.1.2 for guidance on the relevant definitions.

Where group accounts are prepared, the disclosures are given for both the consolidated group (i.e. the company (or LLP) and its consolidated subsidiary undertakings) and the individual company (or LLP). *[6 Sch 1(1), 3 Sch 1(1) (LLP)].*

8.8   Directors' advances, credits and guarantees

A UK company preparing Companies Act accounts or IAS accounts must disclose the information concerning directors' advances, credits and guarantees required by section 413 of the CA 2006. There is no equivalent disclosure for LLPs.

A company that does not prepare group accounts must disclose in the notes to its individual accounts: *[s413(1)]*

- advances and credits granted by the company to its directors; and
- guarantees of any kind entered into by the company on behalf of its directors.

A parent company that prepares group accounts must disclose in the notes to the group accounts: *[s413(2)]*

- advances and credits granted to the directors of the parent company, by that company or by any of its subsidiary undertakings; and
- guarantees of any kind entered into on behalf of the directors of the parent company, by that company or by any of its subsidiary undertakings.

The details required for an advance or credit are: *[s413(3), (5)]*

- its amount – for each advance or credit and totals in aggregate;
- an indication of the interest rate;
- its main conditions;
- any amounts repaid – for each advance or credit and totals in aggregate;
- any amounts written off – for each advance or credit and totals in aggregate; and
- any amounts waived – for each advance or credit and totals in aggregate.

Chapter 6

The details required for a guarantee are: *[s413(4), (5)]*

- its main terms;
- the amount of the maximum liability that may be incurred by the company (or its subsidiary) – for each guarantee and totals in aggregate; and
- any amount paid and any liability incurred by the company (or its subsidiary) for the purpose of fulfilling the guarantee (including any loss incurred by reason of enforcement of the guarantee) – for each guarantee and also totals in aggregate.

Disclosure is required: *[s413(6)-(7)]*

- in respect of persons who were directors of the company at any time in the financial year to which the financial statements relate; and
- for every advance, credit or guarantee that subsisted at any time in the financial year:
  - whenever it was entered into;
  - whether or not the person concerned was a director of the company at the time it was entered into; and
  - in relation to an advance, credit or guarantee involving a subsidiary undertaking of the company, whether or not that undertaking was a subsidiary undertaking at the time the advance, credit or guarantee was entered into.

There are certain exemptions for banking companies (and the holding companies of credit institutions (see definitions at 4.2.2 above), as explained at 8.8.1 below.

The terms advances, credits, and guarantees are not defined in the CA 2006 itself. The rules governing the lawfulness of transactions in Part 10 of the CA 2006 refer to loans, quasi-loans (including related guarantees or provision of security) and credit transactions. While these terms do not align with the terms used in section 413, loans and quasi-loans and credit transactions would generally be considered as advances and credits; and guarantees or provision of security would be disclosed as guarantees (of any kind).

The requirements appear to require disclosure of each advance or credit, or guarantee made. This could be arduous in some contexts, as the definition of advances and credits could include directors' current accounts or personal purchases made using a company credit card (as well as loans and outstanding credit card balances provided by banks or finance subsidiaries of certain retailers).

8.8.1   *Banking companies and holding companies of credit institutions*

A banking company or the holding company of a credit institution is only required to disclose: *[s413(8)]*

- the total amounts of advances and credits granted by the company (or in group accounts, by the company and its subsidiary undertakings); *[s413(5)(a)]* and

- the total amounts of the maximum liability that may be incurred by the company (or its subsidiary) in respect of guarantees entered into by the company (or in group accounts, by the company and its subsidiary undertakings). *[s413(5)(c)]*.

9 GENERAL PRINCIPLES FOR PREPARATION OF FINANCIAL STATEMENTS

The objective of financial statements is to provide information about the financial position, performance and cash flows of an entity that is useful for economic decision-making by a broad range of users who are not in a position to demand reports tailored to meet their particular information needs. Financial statements also show the results of the stewardship of management – the accountability of management for the resources entrusted to it. *[FRS 102.2.2-3]*. As noted at 3.5 above, not all entities are required to prepare a cash flow statement.

FRS 102's general principles for preparation of financial statements are covered in Section 2 (see Chapter 4), Section 3 (covered in this chapter) and Section 10 (see Chapter 9).

The selection of accounting policies is also critical in the preparation of financial statements. The requirements on selection of accounting policies and on accounting estimates are in Section 10. Disclosures of accounting policies, judgements and estimates are covered at 8.2 to 8.4 above.

This section concentrates on FRS 102's requirement for financial statements to give a true and fair view, the adoption of the going concern basis, and materiality and aggregation, i.e. the issues which are addressed in Section 3. There are similar requirements in the Regulations (and LLP Regulations), as highlighted at 9.1 below.

9.1 Requirements of the Regulations (and LLP Regulations)

The Regulations (and LLP Regulations) include:

- the requirement for accounts to give a true and fair view, and the concept of a 'true and fair override' (see 9.2 below);

- general principles for the preparation of financial statements, similar to those included in FRS 102 (see 9.1.1 below);

- recognition and measurement principles, where assets and liabilities are measured under the historical cost convention, alternative accounting rules and fair value accounting rules (see 10 to 10.4 below);

- presentation requirements for the balance sheet and profit and loss formats (see 4 to 6 above); and

- disclosure requirements, principally in the notes to the accounts (see Chapter 1 at 6.7, and the relevant chapters of this publication).

Chapter 6

9.1.1   *General principles for preparation of financial statements*

The general principles set out in the Regulations and the LLP Regulations for the preparation of financial statements are: *[1 Sch 10-15A, 1 Sch 10-15A (LLP), 1 Sch 40(2), 1 Sch 40(2) (LLP)]*

- the company (or the LLP) is presumed to be carrying on business as a going concern (see 9.3 below);

- accounting policies (and measurement bases) must be applied consistently within the same accounts and from one financial year to the next (see 3.6.2 above);

- the amount of any item must be determined on a prudent basis, and in particular:

  - only profits realised at the balance sheet date are to be included in the profit and loss account (except where fair value changes of financial instruments, investment property or living animals or plants are required to be included in the profit and loss account by the fair value accounting rules – see 10.3 and 10.4 below);

  - all liabilities which have arisen in respect of the financial year to which the accounts relate or a previous financial year must be taken into account, including those which only became apparent between the balance sheet date and the date on which it is signed on behalf of the Board (or the members of the LLP) in accordance with section 414 of the CA 2006; and

  - all provisions for diminution of value must be recognised, whether the result of the financial year is a profit or loss;

- all income and charges relating to the financial year to which the accounts relate must be taken into account without regard to the date of receipt or payment (i.e. accruals basis);

- in determining the aggregate amount of any item, the amount of each individual asset or liability that falls to be taken into account must be determined separately (i.e. no offsetting); and

- the opening balance sheet for each financial year must correspond to the closing balance sheet for the preceding financial year.

In addition, at the balance sheet date, any provision made must represent the best estimate of the expenses likely to be incurred or, in the case of a liability, of the amount required to meet that liability; and provisions must not be used to adjust the values of assets. *[9 Sch 2A-2B, 1 Sch 13(d) (LLP)-(e) (LLP)]*. This requirement has been included within the general principles in the LLP Regulations but in Schedule 9 to the Regulations (see 10.1.5 below).

The above principles apply in both individual and group accounts. *[6 Sch 1(1), 3 Sch 1(1) (LLP)]*.

Schedules 2 and 3 to the Regulations (and the Small Companies Regulations, which are addressed in Chapter 5) have the same requirements. However, the prohibition on presenting unrealised profits in the profit and loss account (unless permitted by the fair value accounting rules) in Schedule 3 to the Regulations is also subject to note (9) to the profit and loss account formats in that schedule concerning the presentation of unrealised gains and losses on investments. Only the references in Schedule 1 to the Regulations and Schedule 1 to the LLP Regulations are noted below.

9.1.1.A   Substance over form

FRS 102 does not have a separate section on 'substance over form' but requires that 'transactions and other events and conditions should be accounted for and presented in accordance with their substance and not merely their legal form. This enhances the reliability of financial statements.' *[FRS 102.2.8]*. See Chapter 4 at 3.2.5.

In addition, where an FRS does not specifically address a transaction, management must use its judgement in developing and applying an accounting policy that results in relevant and reliable information. *[FRS 102.10.4]*. One of the characteristics of reliable information is that the financial statements 'reflect the economic substance of transactions, other events and conditions, and not merely the legal form'. *[FRS 102.10.4(b)(ii)]*. In June 2014, the FRC issued updated guidance – *True and Fair* – which refers to the above requirement and makes the point that 'if material transactions are not accounted for in accordance with their substance it is doubtful whether the accounts present a true and fair view'.

The General Rules to the formats (see 4.4 above) require that items in the balance sheet and profit and loss account formats are presented, having regard to the substance of the reported transaction or arrangement, in accordance with generally accepted accounting principles or practice. *[1 Sch 9, 1 Sch 9 (LLP)]*. This requirement facilitates the presentation of certain shares as liabilities in accordance with FRS 102.

9.1.1.B   Prudence

FRS 102 identifies prudence as 'the inclusion of a degree of caution in the exercise of the judgements needed in making the estimates required under conditions of uncertainty, such that assets or income are not overstated and liabilities or expenses are not understated. However, the exercise of prudence does not allow the deliberate understatement of assets or income, or the deliberate overstatement of liabilities or expenses. In short, prudence does not permit bias'. *[FRS 102.2.9]*. See Chapter 4 at 3.2.6.

However, FRS 102 does not specifically refer to realised profits. A UK company preparing Companies Act accounts (or an LLP preparing non-IAS accounts) is required to prepare the profit and loss account section of the statement of comprehensive income (or separate income statement) in accordance with the Regulations (or the LLP Regulations). As discussed in Appendix III to FRS 102, the issue of realised profits is pertinent to whether a gain is reported in profit or loss in Companies Act accounts. *[FRS 102 Appendix III.25-27]*. Consequently, UK companies preparing Companies Act accounts (and LLPs preparing non-IAS accounts) must present certain gains in other comprehensive income instead. Profit or loss and other comprehensive income, including the concept of realised profits, are discussed further at 6.2 above.

FRS 102 involves more use of fair values than previous UK GAAP. In particular, UK companies should be mindful that not all gains (even if recognised in profit or loss) may be distributable. Appendix III to FRS 102 states that entities measuring financial instruments, investment properties, and living animals and plants at fair value should note that they may transfer such amounts to a separate non-distributable reserve, instead of a transfer to retained earnings, but are not required to do so. Presenting fair value movements that are not distributable profits in the separate reserve may assist with identification of profits available for that purpose. *[FRS 102 Appendix III.28]*. Appendix III further notes that the determination of profits available for distribution is a complex area where accounting and company law interface and that companies may refer to TECH 02/17BL, or any successor document, to determine profits available for distribution. *[FRS 102 Appendix III.29].*

9.1.1.C   Offset

FRS 102 prohibits offset of assets and liabilities, or income and expenses, unless required or permitted by an FRS (meaning, at present, FRS 102 itself or FRS 103, where applied). *[FRS 102.2.52].* See Chapter 4 at 3.12. This is similar to the requirement in the General Rules to the formats (see 4.4 above) that amounts in respect of items representing assets or income may not be set off against amounts in respect of items representing liabilities or expenditure (as the case may be), or *vice versa. [1 Sch 8, 1 Sch 8 (LLP)].*

FRS 102 sets out when financial assets and liabilities *[FRS 102.11.38A, 12.25B]* (see Chapter 10 at 11.1), employee benefits *[FRS 102.28.3(a), 28.14, 28.30]* (see Chapter 25 at 3.6.9 and 3.8.2), current tax, and deferred tax *[FRS 102.29.24-24A],* (see Chapter 26 at 10.1.1) must be offset. Where the offset criteria are met, FRS 102 is effectively saying that there is a single asset or liability.

In respect of the profit and loss account, if an entity's normal operating activities do not include buying and selling fixed assets (including investments and operating assets), gains and losses on disposal of fixed assets (net of related selling expenses) are reported. *[FRS 102.2.52(b)].* Expenses for a provision are permitted to be shown net of the amount recognised for reimbursement of the provision. *[FRS 102.21.9].*

FRS 102 also permits cash flows from operating, investing and financing activities to be presented on a net basis where specified criteria are met. *[FRS 102.7.10A-10D].*

Appendix III to FRS 102 explains how the requirements on government grants (no offsetting), reimbursement of provisions (offsetting permitted in profit and loss account only) and financial assets (offsetting required when, and only when the criteria are met) are consistent with the Regulations. *[FRS 102 Appendix III.22-23].*

9.2   True and fair view and compliance with FRS 102

The FRC's *Foreword to Accounting Standards* (March 2018) explains that accounting standards are applicable to the financial statements of a reporting entity that are required to give a true and fair view of its financial position at the reporting date and of its profit or loss (or income and expenditure) for the reporting period. The whole essence of accounting standards is to provide for recognition, measurement, presentation and disclosure for specific aspects of financial reporting in a way that reflects economic reality and hence provides a true and fair view. The *Foreword to Accounting Standards* refers to information about 'true and fair' on the FRC's website (e.g. the guidance *True and Fair* issued in June 2014). *[Foreward.4-6].*

True and Fair notes, *inter alia*, that accounting standards are developed after full due process and 'these processes should result in accounting standards that, in the vast majority of cases, are complied with when presenting a true and fair view'. Where the accounting standards clearly address an issue, but the requirements are insufficient to fully explain the issue, the solution is normally additional disclosure. However, a company must depart from a particular accounting standard where required in order to meet the requirement for the accounts to give a true and fair view. The guidance notes that these circumstances are more likely to arise when the precise circumstances were not contemplated during the development of the relevant standard.

The FRC expects preparers, those charged with governance and auditors to stand back and ensure that the financial statements as a whole give a true and fair view, provide additional disclosures where compliance with an accounting standard is insufficient to give a true and fair view, to use the true and fair override where compliance with the standards does not result in the presentation of a true and fair view and to ensure that the consideration they give to these matters is evident in their deliberations and documentation.[31]

9.2.1 True and fair view – requirements of FRS 102 and the Regulations

FRS 102 requires that financial statements shall give a true and fair view of the assets, liabilities, financial position, financial performance and, when required to be presented, cash flows of an entity. *[FRS 102.3.2, FRS 102 Appendix I]*.

Section 393 of the CA 2006 also requires that the directors of a UK company (or the members of an LLP) must not approve the annual accounts unless they are satisfied that they give: *[s393, s393 (LLP)]*

- in the case of the individual accounts, a true and fair view of the assets, liabilities, financial position and profit or loss of the company (or of the LLP);

- in the case of the group accounts (if any), a true and fair view of the assets, liabilities, financial position and profit or loss of the undertakings included in the consolidation as a whole, so far as concerns members of the company (or of the LLP).

The 'undertakings included in the consolidation' means the parent company (or the parent LLP) and its consolidated subsidiary undertakings and is referred to as 'the group' below.

Companies Act accounts (or non-IAS accounts, for an LLP) must include:

- a balance sheet that gives a true and fair view of the company's (or of the LLP's) state of affairs (and, where applicable, the group's state of affairs, so far as concerns members of the company (or of the LLP)) as at the end of the financial year;

- a profit and loss account that gives a true and fair view of the company's (or of the LLP's) profit or loss (and, where applicable, the group's profit or loss, so far as concerns members of the company (or of the LLP)) for the financial year.

The accounts must comply with regulations made by the Secretary of State as to the form and content of the individual (and where applicable, the consolidated) balance sheet and profit and loss account, and additional information to be provided by way of notes to the accounts. *[s396(1)-(3), s404(1)-(3), s396(1) (LLP)-s396(3) (LLP), s404(1) (LLP)-s404(3) (LLP)]*.

Application of FRS 102, with additional disclosure when necessary, is presumed to result in financial statements that give a true and fair view of the financial position, financial performance and, when required to be presented, cash flows of entities within the scope of the standard. *[FRS 102.3.2(a)]*.

An important point here is that all paragraphs of FRS 102 have equal authority. Some sections include appendices containing implementation guidance or examples, some of which are an integral part of the standard and others provide application guidance

Chapter 6

(each specifies its status). We would generally expect that entities follow such guidance unless there is a valid reason. The presumption that application of FRS 102 (with any necessary additional disclosure) results in a true and fair view is subject to the override set out in paragraph 3.4 (and for entities preparing financial statements subject to the CA 2006, the true and fair override). *[FRS 102.3.4]*. See 9.2.2 below.

The additional disclosures referred to in paragraph 3.2(a) are necessary when compliance with the specific requirements in the standard is insufficient to enable users to understand the effect of particular transactions, other events and conditions on the entity's financial position and financial performance. *[FRS 102.3.2]*.

This is consistent with the statutory requirement that if compliance with the regulations, and any other provisions made by or under the CA 2006, as to matters to be included in a company's (or on an LLP's) individual accounts (and, where applicable, group accounts) or in notes to those accounts would not be sufficient to give a true and fair view, the necessary additional information must be given in the accounts or in a note to them. *[s396(4), s404(4), s396(4) (LLP), s404(4) (LLP)]*.

9.2.2   The 'true and fair override' – requirements of FRS 102 and the Regulations

In special circumstances when management concludes that compliance with any requirement of FRS 102 or applicable legislation (only when it allows for a true and fair override) is inconsistent with the requirement to give a true and fair view, the entity shall depart from that requirement in the manner set out in paragraph 3.5. *[FRS 102.3.4]*.

When an entity departs from a requirement of FRS 102, or from a requirement of applicable legislation, it shall disclose:

(a)   that management has concluded that the financial statements give a true and fair view of the entity's financial position, financial performance and, when required to be presented, cash flows;

(b)   that it has complied with FRS 102 or applicable legislation, except that it has departed from a particular requirement of the standard or applicable legislation to the extent necessary to give a true and fair view; and

(c)   the nature and effect of the departure including the treatment that FRS 102 or applicable legislation would require, the reason why that treatment would be so misleading in the circumstances that it would conflict with the objective of financial statements set out in Section 2 (see 9 above), and the treatment adopted. *[FRS 102.3.5]*.

When an entity has departed from a requirement of FRS 102 or applicable legislation in a prior period and that departure affects the amounts recognised in the financial statements for the current period, it shall make the disclosures set out in (c) above. *[FRS 102.3.6]*.

These disclosures are consistent with the statutory disclosures that: if in special circumstances, compliance with any of those provisions is inconsistent with the requirement to give a true and fair view, the directors must depart from that provision to the extent necessary to give a true and fair view. Particulars of any such departure, the reasons for it and its effect must be given in a note to the accounts. *[s396(5), s404(5), s396(5) (LLP), s404(5) (LLP)]*.

FRS 102 does not explain what is required by the 'effect' of the departure, but in our view, consistent with previous UK GAAP, this means 'financial effect'. In the absence of guidance in FRS 102, management may consider the requirements of IFRSs. Where there is a departure from IFRSs in the current period (or a departure was made in a previous period which impacts the amounts recognised in the financial statements in the current period), IAS 1 requires disclosure, for each period presented, of the financial impact of the departure on each item in the financial statements that would have been reported in complying with the requirement. *[IAS 1.20(d), 21]*.

In addition, where it appears to the directors of the company (or members of the LLP) that there are special reasons for departing from any of the general principles (see 9.1.1 above) in preparing the company's (or the LLP's) accounts for the financial year, the particulars of the departure, the reasons for it and its effect should be disclosed in a note to the accounts. *[1 Sch 10(2), 1 Sch 10(2) (LLP)]*. Appendix III to FRS 102 highlights certain instances where the requirements of FRS 102 result in a departure from the requirements of the Regulations in order to give a 'true and fair view'. These examples, which are not exhaustive, are relevant to UK companies preparing Companies Act accounts. They are also relevant to LLPs preparing non-IAS accounts– except that the conditions for merger accounting differ for UK companies and LLPs.

Large and medium-sized companies (and LLPs) must state in the notes to the accounts (see 3.8.1 above) whether the accounts have been prepared in accordance with applicable accounting standards, giving particulars of any material departures from those standards and the reasons. *[1 Sch 45, 1 Sch 45 (LLP)]*. Medium-sized companies (and LLPs) are exempt from making this statement in individual accounts. *[Regulations 4(2A), LLP Regulations 4(2A)]*. Consistent with previous UK GAAP, in our view, it would be appropriate for this statement to either include or cross refer any disclosures of the true and fair override. *[FRS 18.62]*.

9.3   Going concern

FRS 102 requires management, when preparing financial statements, to make an assessment of an entity's ability to continue as a going concern. An entity is a going concern unless management either intends to liquidate the entity or to cease trading, or has no realistic alternative but to do so. In assessing whether the going concern assumption is appropriate, management takes into account all available information about the future, which is at least, but is not limited to, twelve months from the date when the financial statements are authorised for issue. *[FRS 102.3.8, FRS 102 Appendix I]*.

When management is aware, in making its assessment, of material uncertainties related to events or conditions that cast significant doubt upon the entity's ability to continue as a going concern, those uncertainties must be disclosed in the financial statements. *[FRS 102.3.9]*.

When financial statements are not prepared on a going concern basis, that fact must be disclosed, together with the basis on which the financial statements are prepared and the reason why the entity is not regarded as a going concern. *[FRS 102.3.9]*.

FRS 102 states that an entity shall not prepare its financial statements on a going concern basis if management determines after the reporting period either that it intends to liquidate the entity or to cease trading or that it has no realistic alternative but to do so.

Chapter 6

Deterioration in operating results and financial position after the reporting period may indicate a need to consider whether the going concern assumption is no longer appropriate. If the going concern assumption is no longer appropriate, the effect is so pervasive that a fundamental change in the basis of accounting rather than an adjustment to the amounts recognised within the original basis of accounting is required, and therefore the disclosure requirements in paragraph 3.9, as described above, apply. *[FRS 102.32.7A-B].*

FRS 102 provides no further guidance concerning what impact there should be on the financial statements if it is determined that the going concern basis is not appropriate. Accordingly, entities will need to consider carefully their individual circumstances to arrive at an appropriate basis.

FRS 102's requirements are supplemented by the FRC's April 2016 *Guidance on the Going Concern Basis of Accounting and Reporting on Solvency and Liquidity Risks – Guidance for directors of companies that do not apply The UK Corporate Governance Code* ('2016 FRC Guidance'). See 9.3.1 below.

9.3.1   2016 FRC Guidance on Going Concern

The 2016 FRC Guidance is non-mandatory best practice guidance which aims to provide a proportionate and practical guide for directors of companies not applying the *UK Corporate Governance Code* (the Code).[32]

While the 2016 FRC Guidance refers to directors and companies for simplicity, the guidance notes that it is also likely to be relevant to other entities. Small and micro-companies must still assess whether the going concern basis of accounting is appropriate, but are excluded from the scope of the 2016 FRC Guidance Nevertheless, aspects of the guidance may still be helpful to such entities – as explained in Chapter 5 at 7.3.1.

Companies applying the Code are also excluded from the guidance. This is because such companies are subject to more onerous requirements under the Code, and under the Listing Rules (for premium listed companies), and are covered by separate FRC guidance (see 9.3.2 below). More complex and other publicly traded entities that are not required to apply the Code may also wish to refer to that other guidance as an alternative.

The FRC decided to issue separate, simplified guidance for directors of companies not applying the Code. In particular, there is no requirement for such companies to prepare a 'viability statement'. The term 'going concern' refers to the going concern basis of preparation in the financial statements.[33] However, the ideas about integrating the assessment of the going concern basis of preparation with the assessment of principal risks (and that the disclosures fall out from this process) which are key parts of the FRC guidance for companies applying the Code (see 9.3.2 below) are retained.

The 2016 FRC Guidance considers the related requirements in:

- accounting standards – which require disclosure in the financial statements on the going concern basis of accounting and material uncertainties; and

- company law – which requires disclosure in the strategic report of principal risks and uncertainties, which may include risks that might impact solvency and liquidity.[34]

9.3.1.A Overview of approach

A company faces many risks. In making their assessment of principal risks, directors are encouraged to consider a broad range of business risks, including both financial and non-financial (for example, operational, competitive, market or regulatory factors may ultimately impact on solvency or liquidity).

The principal risks and uncertainties, i.e. those matters that could significantly affect the development, performance, position and future prospects of the company, are required to be disclosed in the strategic report. These will generally be the matters that the directors regularly monitor and discuss because of their likelihood, the magnitude of their potential effect or a combination of the two.

Some of the principal risks may have the potential to threaten the company's ability to continue in operation because of their impact on solvency, i.e. the risk that a company will be unable to meet its liabilities in full, and liquidity, i.e. the risk that a company will be unable to meet its liabilities as they fall due. Insolvency is likely to be preceded by a lack of liquidity. An example of a principal risk that could have an impact on solvency or liquidity might be if a company is dependent on a single customer. If the customer ceased purchasing the company's products or services, or became unable to pay its debts to the company, the company may be unable to meet its liabilities as they fall due and in an extreme case, loss of the customer might have the potential to render the company insolvent.[35]

Some solvency and liquidity risks may be so significant that they highlight material uncertainties that may cast significant doubt on a company's ability to adopt the going concern basis of accounting in the future. These material uncertainties must be disclosed in accordance with the requirements of accounting standards. In extreme circumstances, such risks may crystallise, thus making liquidation of the company inevitable and the going concern basis of accounting inappropriate.[36]

The guidance summarises the process for determining which disclosures are necessary as follows:

- identification of risks and uncertainties, including those relating to solvency and liquidity and other potential threats to continue in operation;
- determining which of the identified risks and uncertainties are principal risks, requiring disclosure in the strategic report; *[s414C(2)(b)]*
- considering whether there are material uncertainties requiring disclosure in accordance with accounting standards; *[FRS 102.3.8, 3.9]*
- in extreme circumstances, considering whether it is appropriate to adopt the going concern basis of accounting; *[FRS 102.3.9]* and
- considering whether disclosures additional to those explicitly required by law, regulation or accounting standards are necessary to provide a true and fair view. *[s393]*.[37]

The guidance covers factors for directors to consider when determining whether the going concern basis of accounting is appropriate (and whether material uncertainties should be identified); making an assessment of the solvency and liquidity risks that might constitute principal risks for a company requiring disclosure in the strategic report; guidance on the assessment periods for the going concern basis of accounting and those risks; guidance on

Chapter 6

the assessment process; and summaries of the related reporting requirements (including auditor reporting). It also addresses the application of the guidance to half-yearly financial reports and preliminary announcements.[38]

It is beyond the scope of this publication to set out the guidance in full but some of its considerations are set out below. Auditor reporting is not covered here.

9.3.1.B   The assessment process – principal risks and going concern basis of accounting

Section 5 of the 2016 FRC Guidance provides further factors to consider and techniques that may be applied in:

- identifying principal risks and uncertainties (which may include solvency and liquidity risks); and

- assessing whether the going concern basis of preparation is appropriate and whether there are material uncertainties.

The factors discussed include: forecasts and budgets; the timing of cash flows; sensitivity analysis; products; services and markets; financial and operational risk management; borrowing facilities; contingent liabilities; subsidiary companies; and companies owned by, or dependent on the government.

The directors should assess which factors are likely to be relevant to their company, which will vary according to the size, complexity and particular circumstances of the company, its industry and the general economic environment. Some factors will be more relevant for the assessment of the principal risks disclosures in the strategic report and others more relevant for the assessment of the going concern basis of accounting. The level of detail and the time horizon of the assessment may also differ for these purposes as longer-term assessments, such as for the strategic report disclosures, are likely to be performed at a higher, more aggregated level.[39]

The assessment of solvency and liquidity risks should consider the likelihood and possible effects of those risks materialising. The period of assessment for solvency and liquidity risks, in the context of the requirement to disclose principal risks will be a matter of judgement for the directors based on the particular circumstances of the company (but this will usually be longer than twelve months, and will depend on the nature of the business, its stage of development, investment and planning horizons and other factors). Similarly, the extent of the assessment process, will be a matter of judgement for the directors based on the size, complexity and particular circumstances of the company. Given the forward-looking nature of the assessment, the level of detail and accuracy of the information available relating to the future will vary.[40]

The going concern assessment period, as required by FRS 102, must cover a period of at least twelve months from the date of approval of the financial statements. In making their assessment, the directors should consider all available information about the future at the date they approve the financial statements, such as the information from budgets and forecasts. The guidance recommends best practice that the assessment should be proportionate to the size, complexity and the particular circumstances of the company and documented in sufficient detail to explain the directors' conclusion with respect to the going concern basis of accounting at the date of approval of the financial statements.[41]

The going concern assessment may result in three possible outcomes:

- the going concern basis of accounting is appropriate and there are no material uncertainties;
- the going concern basis is appropriate but there are material uncertainties related to events or conditions that may cast significant doubt upon the company's ability to continue to adopt the going concern basis of accounting in the future; or
- the going concern basis of accounting is not appropriate.

In the first two cases, the going concern basis of accounting is adopted.[42]

The guidance explains that the threshold for departing from the going concern basis of accounting is very high as there are often realistic alternatives to liquidation, even if they depend on uncertain events.[43]

However, events or conditions might result in the going concern basis of accounting becoming inappropriate in future accounting periods. The directors, in performing their assessment, should consider all available information about the future, the realistically possible outcomes of events and changes in conditions and the realistically possible responses to such events and conditions that would be available to the directors. Uncertainties relating to such events or conditions are considered material if their disclosure could reasonably be expected to affect the economic decisions of shareholders and other users of the financial statements, which is a matter of judgement. In making this judgement, the directors should consider the uncertainties arising from their assessment, both individually and in combination with others. The guidance highlights that key focus areas to consider include the magnitude of the potential impacts of the uncertain future events or changes in conditions on the company and the likelihood of their occurrence, the realistic availability and likelihood of mitigating actions and whether these uncertain future events or changes in conditions are unusual, rather than occurring with sufficient regularity to allow the directors to make predictions about them with a high degree of confidence. The guidance states that uncertainties should not usually be considered material if the likelihood that the company will not be able to continue to use the going concern basis of accounting is assessed to be remote, however significant the assessed potential impact.[44]

9.3.1.C   Going concern disclosures

There are no specific disclosure requirements where the going concern basis of accounting is adopted and there are no material uncertainties identified. The disclosures set out in paragraph 3.9 of FRS 102 (see 9.3 above) must be given where the going concern basis of accounting is appropriate but material uncertainties have been identified, and where the going concern basis of accounting is not appropriate.

The 2016 FRC Guidance recommends as best practice that: where material uncertainties are identified, the financial statements should disclose clearly the existence and nature of the material uncertainty, including a description of the principal events or conditions that may cast significant doubt on the entity's ability to continue as a going concern and the directors' plans to deal with these events or conditions. Directors may also wish to bear in mind the obligation of the auditor to report if an appropriate level of clarity in the disclosure of material uncertainties has not been achieved.[45]

Chapter 6

However, in all cases, additional disclosures may be required to give a true and fair view. The guidance gives some example scenarios of where disclosures may be appropriate even where it has been concluded that there are no material uncertainties.[46] These are only illustrative examples, and the conclusions reached and appropriateness of disclosures required will clearly depend on facts and circumstances.

In addition, accounting standards may require relevant disclosures. The main FRS 102 disclosure requirements highlighted in the guidance include: risks arising from financial instruments, defaults and covenant breaches, significant judgements, key estimation uncertainty, and contingent liabilities. *[FRS 102.8.6, 8.7, 11.47, 11.48A(f), 21.15, 34.23-30].*[47] The Regulations also require disclosures in the directors' report providing an indication of the company's financial risk management objectives and policies (including the policy for hedging each major type of forecasted transaction for which hedge accounting is used) and the exposure of the company to price risk, credit risk, liquidity risk and cash flow risk, where material. *[7 Sch 6].*[48]

The guidance recommends as best practice that the principal risks and uncertainties are described in a clear, concise and understandable way but that there is no need to specifically label risks as solvency and liquidity risks when other descriptions can more easily set out their nature and potential impacts.[49] The guidance includes a reminder that the principal risks identified must only include those risks that are material to an understanding of the business. Immaterial information obscures key messages and detracts from the understandability of the information provided in the annual report.[50]

Where relevant, the description of the principal risks and uncertainties (together with their potential impact on the business, management and mitigation) should also highlight any linkage with the disclosures relating to the going concern basis of accounting, material uncertainties and risks in the financial statements.[51]

The directors may also consider placement of the disclosures to facilitate effective communication. For example, it may be helpful to group disclosures in one place. However, where law or regulation sets out the location, and the information is presented outside the specified component of the annual report (such as the strategic report, or the financial statements), the information will need to be included as an integral part of the specified component by way of cross referencing identifying the nature and location of the required information. A component is not complete without the information that is cross referenced and the cross referenced information must be included in the annual report. This differs from 'signposting' which helps users locate complementary information within or outside the annual report. A component must meet its legal and regulatory requirements without reference to signposted information.[52]

9.3.2   *Companies that are applying the Code*

As noted at 9.3.1 above, companies applying the Code are subject to more onerous requirements under the Code and for premium listed companies, under the Listing Rules. While most companies applying the Code are likely to be IFRS reporters, some entities applying FRS 102 (that are not required to prepare group accounts) are premium-listed companies and others may choose voluntarily to apply the Code. Therefore, some brief remarks on the Code and the requirements in the

Listing Rules are included below, although entities should refer to the Guidance noted below for further detail.

In September 2014, the FRC issued *Guidance on Risk Management, Internal Control: and Related Financial and Business Reporting* ('2014 FRC Guidance'). This guidance is aimed primarily at entities subject to the Code. At the time of writing, this guidance has not been updated to reflect changes made in the 2018 version of the Code which is effective for accounting periods beginning on or after 1 January 2019. However, the Code states that this guidance is still relevant. In addition, in July 2018 the FRC also issued *Guidance on Board Effectiveness* to also support application of the Code's principles.

The Listing Rules require a premium listed company to state how it has applied the main principles of the Code and to:

- make a statement of compliance; or
- explain the code provisions, if any, which it has not complied with; the period, if any, for which it did not comply (where those code provisions are of a continuing nature); and the reasons for non-compliance.[53]

In addition, the Listing Rules require the directors to make the statements in the annual financial report on:

- the appropriateness of adopting the going concern basis of preparation (containing the information set out in Code provision C1.3), and
- their assessment of the prospects of the company (containing the information set out in Code provision C2.2),

prepared in accordance with the 2014 FRC Guidance.[54] At the time of writing this publication, the Listing Rules have not been updated to reflect the amended references within the 2018 version of the Code and still refer to the 2016 version. The two requirements above are set out in provisions 30 and 31 of the 2018 version of the Code.

The 2018 version of the Code' itself contains a main principle that the Board should determine the nature and extent of the principal risks the company is willing to take in order to achieve its long-term strategic objectives. The Board should establish procedures to manage risk and oversee the internal control framework.

This main principle is supported by a number of interrelated Code provisions. The 2014 FRC Guidance states that directors should perform a robust assessment of the principal risks (including solvency and liquidity risks) and determine how these will be managed and mitigated. This then informs the Board's assessment of the longer-term viability of the company as well as the Board's assessment of whether the going concern basis of preparation remains appropriate, identifying any material uncertainties. The Board is also responsible for monitoring and reviewing (on an ongoing basis) the effectiveness of the risk management and internal control systems. The aim is that the above processes will be integrated with the Board's ongoing business planning and risk management processes and the disclosures required in the annual report and financial statements will be informed by these processes.

Chapter 6

The key, related provisions in the 2018 version of the Code are as follows:

- The directors should confirm in the annual report that they have carried out a robust assessment of the emerging and principal risks facing the company, including those that would threaten its business model, future performance, solvency liquidity and reputation. The directors should describe those risks and explain how they are being managed or mitigated (Code provision 28).

- The Board should monitor the company's risk management and internal control systems and, at least annually, carry out a review of their effectiveness, and report on that review in the annual report. The monitoring and review should cover all material controls, including financial, operational and compliance controls (Code provision 29).

- In annual and half-yearly financial statements, the directors should state whether they considered it appropriate to adopt the going concern basis of accounting in preparing them, and identify any material uncertainties to the company's ability to continue to do so over a period of at least twelve months from the date of approval of the financial statements (Code provision 30).

- Taking account of the company's current position and principal risks, the directors should explain in the annual report how they have assessed the prospects of the company, over what period they have done so and why they consider that period to be appropriate. The directors should state whether they have a reasonable expectation that the company will be able to continue in operation and meet its liabilities as they fall due over the period of their assessment, drawing attention to any qualifications or assumptions as necessary (Code provision 31).

Companies required to apply DTR 7.2 must include in the corporate governance statement a description of the main features of the company's internal control and risk management systems in relation to the financial reporting process. In group accounts, this covers the undertakings included in the consolidation, taken as a whole.[55]

The 2014 FRC Guidance summarises the Board's responsibilities for risk management and internal control; the establishment of, monitoring and review of risk management and internal control systems; and the Board's related business and financial reporting responsibilities. It is beyond the scope of this publication to cover the guidance in detail.

Section 6, Appendix A and Appendix D of the 2014 FRC Guidance include relevant guidance on adoption of the going concern basis of accounting (including disclosures on material uncertainties) in the financial statements, as well as reporting on principal risks and uncertainties (in the strategic report).

9.4   Materiality and aggregation

Financial statements result from processing large numbers of transactions or other events that are aggregated into classes according to their nature or function. The final stage in the process of aggregation and classification is the presentation of condensed and classified data, which form line items in the financial statements. *[FRS 102.3.16]*.

FRS 102 reporters must comply with the balance sheet and profit and loss account formats set out in the Regulations (or LLP Regulations) (see 4.1 and 4.2 above for which formats apply to which entity). FRS 102 requires an entity to present additional line items, headings and subtotals where relevant to an understanding of the financial position or financial performance. *[FRS 102.4.3, 5.5C, 5.9]*.

The extent of aggregation versus detailed analysis is clearly a judgemental one, with either extreme eroding the usefulness of the information. FRS 102 resolves this issue with the concept of materiality (see Chapter 4 at 3.2.3). 'Material' is defined as follows: 'Omissions or misstatements of items are material if they could, individually or collectively, influence the economic decisions of users taken on the basis of the financial statements. Materiality depends on the size and nature of the omission or misstatement judged in the surrounding circumstances. The size or nature of the item, or a combination of both, could be the determining factor.' However, it is inappropriate to make, or leave uncorrected, immaterial departures from the standard to achieve a particular presentation of an entity's financial position, financial performance or cash flows. *[FRS 102.2.6, FRS 102 Appendix I]*.

FRS 102 requires each material class of similar items to be presented separately and items of a dissimilar nature or function to be presented separately unless they are immaterial. *[FRS 102.3.15]*. If a line item is not individually material, it is aggregated with other items either in those statements or in the notes. An item that may not warrant separate presentation in those financial statements may warrant separate presentation in the notes. The Triennial review 2017 added additional guidance into FRS 102 on materiality and states that an entity should decide, taking into consideration all relevant facts and circumstances, how it aggregates information in the financial statements, which includes the notes. An entity should not reduce the understandability of its financial statements by obscuring material information with immaterial information or by aggregating material items that have different natures or functions. *[FRS 102.3.16, 16A]*.

The General Rules to the formats (see 4.4 above) allow the directors of a company (or members of an LLP) to combine items denoted with Arabic numbers in the statutory balance sheet and profit and loss account formats if their individual amounts are not material to assessing the state of affairs or profit or loss of the company (or of the LLP) for the financial year in question, or where the combination facilitates that assessment (in which case, the individual amounts of the line items combined must be disclosed in the notes). *[1 Sch 4(2), 1 Sch 4(2) (LLP)]*.

FRS 102 states that an entity need not provide a specific disclosure required by the standard if the information resulting from that disclosure is not material, and this is the case even if FRS 102 contains a list of specific requirements or describes them as minimum requirements. *[FRS 102.3.16B]*. UK companies preparing Companies Act accounts must also comply with the disclosure requirements of the Regulations. The Regulations permit that 'amounts which in the particular context of any provision of Schedules 1, 2 or 3 to these Regulations are not material may be disregarded for the purposes of that provision.' *[10 Sch 10]*. However, certain disclosures required by the Act must be given regardless of materiality, such as information on subsidiary undertakings. *[FRS 102.3.16B]*. The LLP Regulations have the same requirements in respect of Schedule 1 to the LLP Regulations. *[4 Sch 7 (LLP)]*.

9.4.1   *'Cutting Clutter'*

In recent years, there has been increased recognition that the length and complexity of annual reports and financial statements can obscure key messages and make them less understandable. This has led to a regulatory focus on 'cutting clutter' with the aim of making financial statements more concise and relevant. The FRC have published a number of papers including *Louder than Words: Principles and actions for making corporate reports less complex and more relevant* (June 2009), *Cutting Clutter: Combating clutter in annual reports* (April 2011), and *Thinking about Disclosures in a broader context: A road map for a disclosure framework* (October 2012). 'Cutting clutter' has been a recurrent message in the annual Corporate Reporting Review and a focus of the FRC Lab, for instance, Lab Insight Report – *Towards Clear and Concise Reporting* (August 2014) which contains many useful observations.

Amendments to IAS 1 – *Disclosure Initiative* – clarifies the concept of materiality and aggregation which, while not directly applicable, may be helpful for FRS 102 reporters to consider. See 8.1 above.

While much of the regulatory focus has been on IFRS financial statements (and IFRS has more extensive disclosure requirements compared to FRS 102), the general messages above are also relevant for FRS 102 financial statements.

10   RECOGNITION AND MEASUREMENT, PRESENTATION AND DISCLOSURE – COMPANIES ACT ACCOUNTS

FRS 102 financial statements prepared by a UK company are Companies Act accounts and, therefore, must comply with the recognition and measurement rules included in the applicable schedule of the Regulations (or the Small Companies Regulations). Similarly, FRS 102 financial statements prepared by an LLP are non-IAS accounts that must comply with the recognition and measurement rules included in the LLP Regulations (or Small LLP Regulations).

Appendix III to FRS 102 provides an overview of how FRS 102's requirements address UK company law requirements (written from the perspective of a company to which the CA 2006 applies) and highlights certain areas where following FRS 102's requirements may necessitate use of the 'true and fair override' (see 9.2.2 above). Appendix III is not comprehensive and, therefore, it is useful to have an understanding of the key recognition and measurement principles included in the Regulations and LLP Regulations. The recognition and measurement principles in the Small Companies Regulations and Small LLP Regulations are the same (although these have simpler disclosures). See Chapter 5 at 7.2.

Schedules 1 to 3 to the Regulations (and Schedule 1 to the LLP Regulations) set out fundamental accounting principles such as: going concern, use of consistent accounting policies, prudence, no offsetting of assets and liabilities (or income and expense), and that the opening balance sheet for each financial year corresponds to the closing balance sheet for the preceding financial year. See 9.1.1 above.

The Regulations (and LLP Regulations) also set out the following three models for the recognition and measurement of assets and liabilities:

- historical cost accounting rules (see 10.1 below);
- alternative accounting rules (see 10.2 below); and
- fair value accounting rules (see 10.3 and 10.4 below).

The main requirements of the three models are set out below. However, entities preparing FRS 102 financial statements also need to comply with the requirements of FRS 102, which are sometimes more restrictive than the statutory requirements.

References given below are to Schedule 1 to the Regulations and Schedule 1 to the LLP Regulations only, but there are equivalent paragraphs in Schedule 2 or Schedule 3 to the Regulations (albeit sometimes with modifications to those in Schedule 1).

10.1   Historical cost accounting rules

FRS 102 makes use of the historical cost accounting rules for the following assets:

- basic financial instruments, except for: *[FRS 102.11.8, 11.14]*
    - investments in non-derivative financial instruments that are equity of the issuer that are publicly traded or whose fair value can otherwise be measured reliably; or
    - investments in another group entity when the holder chooses an accounting policy that is not cost less impairment; or
    - debt instruments and commitments to receive a loan and to make a loan to another entity (meeting specified conditions) that are designated at fair value through profit or loss on initial recognition;
- investments in equity instruments that are not publicly traded and whose fair value cannot otherwise be measured reliably and contracts linked to such instruments that, if exercised, will result in delivery of such instruments; *[FRS 102.12.8(a)]*
- financial instruments that are not permitted by the Regulations, Small Companies Regulations, LLP Regulations or the Small LLP Regulations to be measured at fair value through profit or loss (see 10.3.1 below); *[FRS 102.12.8(c)]*
- inventories – except for inventories measured at fair value less costs to sell through profit or loss (in active markets only) and inventories held for distribution at no or nominal consideration; *[FRS 102.13.3-4A, FRS 102 Appendix III.37]*
- property, plant and equipment – where the cost model is applied; *[FRS 102.17.15-15A]*
- investment property rented to another group company and transferred to property, plant and equipment; *[FRS 102.16.1A]*
- intangible assets – where the cost model is applied; *[FRS 102.18.18-18A]*
- goodwill; *[FRS 102.19.22-23]*
- biological assets – where the cost model is applied; *[FRS 102.34.3A, 34.8-9]*
- investments in subsidiaries, associates and joint ventures in separate or individual financial statements – where the cost model is applied; *[FRS 102.9.26(a), 9.26A, 14.4(a), 14.5-6, 15.9(a), 15.10-11]* and
- investments in excluded subsidiaries in consolidated financial statements – where the cost model is applied. *[FRS 102.9.9, 9.9A, 9.9B(b)]*.

Chapter 6

Under the historical cost accounting rules,

- fixed assets are included at cost (i.e. purchase price or production cost) subject to any provisions for depreciation or diminution in value; *[1 Sch 17, 1 Sch 17 (LLP)]* and

- current assets are included at the lower of cost (i.e. purchase price or production cost) and net realisable value. Where the reasons for which any provision was made have ceased to apply to any extent, the provision must be written back to the extent that it is no longer necessary. *[1 Sch 23-24, 1 Sch 23-24 (LLP)]*.

Fixed assets are assets which are intended for use on a continuing basis in the company's (or the LLP's) activities, and current assets are assets not intended for such use. *[10 Sch 4, 4 Sch 3 (LLP)]*. These recognition and measurement requirements apply whether statutory formats or adapted formats (which distinguish between non-current assets and current assets) are used.

The definition of purchase price and production cost used in the historical cost accounting rules is addressed at 10.1.1 below. The requirements for depreciation or diminution in the historical cost accounting rules are addressed at 10.1.2 below. Some other areas relevant to certain assets or liabilities only are addressed at 10.1.3 to 10.1.5 below.

10.1.1   Definition of purchase price and production cost

The 'purchase price' is the sum of the actual price paid (including cash and non-cash consideration) for the asset and any expenses incidental to its acquisition (and then subtracting any incidental reductions in the cost of acquisition). *[1 Sch 27(1), 10 Sch 12, 1 Sch 27(1) (LLP), 4 Sch 11 (LLP)]*.

The 'production cost' is the sum of the purchase price of the raw materials and consumables used and directly attributable production costs. *[1 Sch 27(2), 1 Sch 27(2) (LLP)]*.

The Regulations (and LLP Regulations) also permit the inclusion of: *[1 Sch 27(3), 1 Sch 27(3) (LLP)]*

- a reasonable proportion of costs incurred by the company (or the LLP) which are only indirectly attributable to the production of the asset (but only to the extent that they relate to the period of production); and

- interest on capital borrowed to finance the production of that asset (to the extent it accrues in respect of the period of production), provided that a note to the accounts discloses that interest is capitalised in the cost of that asset, and gives the amount of interest so capitalised.

Distribution costs may not be included in the production cost of a current asset. *[1 Sch 27(4), 1 Sch 27(4) (LLP)]*.

The purchase price or production cost of stocks and any fungible assets (including investments) may be determined by one of the following methods:

- last in, first out (LIFO) – this method is not permitted by FRS 102;
- first in, first out (FIFO);
- weighted average price; and
- any other method reflecting generally accepted best practice

provided that the method chosen appears to the directors (or the members of the LLP) to be appropriate in the circumstances of the company (or the LLP). *[1 Sch 28(1)-(2), 1 Sch 28(1) (LLP)-(2) (LLP)]*. Fungible assets are assets which are substantially indistinguishable one from another. *[10 Sch 5, 1 Sch 28(6) (LLP)]*.

Where an item shown in the balance sheet includes assets whose purchase price or production cost has been determined using any of the above methods, the notes to the accounts must disclose the amount of the difference, if material, between: *[1 Sch 28(3)-(5), 1 Sch 28(3) (LLP)-(5) (LLP)]*

- the carrying amount of that item; and
- the amount that would have been shown in respect of that item, if assets of any class included under that item at an amount determined using any of the above methods had instead been included at their replacement cost as at the balance sheet date.

  The most recent actual purchase price or production cost before the balance sheet date may be used instead of replacement cost as at that date, but only if the former appears to the directors (or the members of the LLP) to constitute the more appropriate standard of comparison in the case of assets of that class.

Where there is no record of the purchase price or production cost (or of any price, expenses or cost relevant for determining the purchase price or production cost) or any such record cannot be obtained without unreasonable expense or delay, the purchase price or production cost of the asset must be taken to be the value ascribed in the earliest available record of its value made on or after its acquisition or production by the company (or the LLP). *[1 Sch 29, 1 Sch 29 (LLP)]*.

The Regulations (and LLP Regulations) also permit tangible fixed assets and raw materials and consumables (within current assets) to be included at a fixed quantity and value, but only where the assets are constantly being replaced, their overall value is not material to assessing the company's (or the LLP's) state of affairs, and their quantity, value and composition are not subject to material variation. *[1 Sch 26, 1 Sch 26 (LLP)]*. Some companies capitalise minor items (such as tools, cutlery, small containers, sheets and towels) at a fixed amount when they are originally provided as a form of capital 'base stock' where the continual loss and replacement of stock does result in a base amount that does not materially vary. This treatment is not in principle compliant with FRS 102 and would only be acceptable where the items in question are immaterial.

Where the amount repayable on any debt owed by a company (or by an LLP) exceeds the value of the consideration received in the transaction giving rise to the debt, the Regulations (and the LLP Regulations) allow the difference to be treated as an asset, which must then be written off by reasonable amounts each year (and must be completely written off before repayment of the debt). The current amount should be disclosed in a note to the accounts, if it is not shown as a separate item in the company's (or the LLP's) balance sheet. *[1 Sch 25, 1 Sch 25 (LLP)]*. However, this treatment would not comply with FRS 102's requirements on initial measurement of financial liabilities *[FRS 102.11.13]* (see Chapter 10 at 7).

Chapter 6

10.1.1.A   FRS 102's requirements

FRS 102's requirements for measuring cost are consistent with but more prescriptive than the Regulations (and LLP Regulations). For example,

- Property, plant and equipment and intangible assets – Only costs directly attributable to bringing the asset to the location and condition necessary for it to be capable of operating in the manner intended by management are permitted to be included in the cost of property, plant and equipment. *[FRS 102.17.10(b)]*. Section 17 includes detailed requirements on which types of costs are capitalised and clarifies the accounting for income and related expenses of incidental operations during construction or development. *[FRS 102.17.10-12]*. Section 17 also provides more detailed guidance on what costs are included in purchase price and on the cost of property, plant and equipment exchanged for other assets. *[FRS 102.17.10, 17.14]*. See Chapter 15 at 3.4.

- Intangible assets – Where an intangible asset is separately acquired, any directly attributable cost of preparing the asset for its intended use forms part of cost. *[FRS 102.18.10]*. Where a policy of capitalising internally generated intangible assets is adopted, the cost comprises all directly attributable costs necessary to create, produce and prepare the asset to be capable of operating in the manner intended by management. *[FRS 102.18.8K, 18.10-10A]*. Section 18 also provides more detailed guidance on what costs are included in purchase price and addresses the cost of intangible assets exchanged for other assets. *[FRS 102.18.10, 18.13]*. See Chapter 16 at 3.3.

- Borrowing costs – An entity is permitted by Section 25 – *Borrowing Costs* – to either expense borrowing costs or to adopt a policy of capitalising borrowing costs directly attributable to the acquisition, construction or production of a qualifying asset (which must be applied consistently to a class of qualifying assets). Section 25's requirements are more detailed than the Regulations (and LLP Regulations) and specify the period for which borrowing costs can be capitalised, and how to determine the amounts capitalised. *[FRS 102.25.1-2D]*. See Chapter 22 at 3.

- Inventories – The cost of inventories includes all costs of purchase, costs of conversion (direct production costs and allocated variable and fixed production overheads) and other costs incurred in bringing the inventories to their present location and condition. *[FRS 102.13.5-15]*. As noted above, the Regulations (and LLP Regulations) prohibit capitalisation of 'distribution costs'. FRS 102's requirements on cost (including the meaning of 'distribution costs' in this context) and the methods that can be used to determine cost *[FRS 102.13.16-18]* are discussed further at Chapter 11 at 3.3.

10.1.2   Depreciation and diminution of fixed assets

Where a fixed asset has a limited useful economic life, its purchase price or production cost less its estimated residual value (if any) must be reduced by provisions for depreciation calculated to write off that amount systematically over the period of the asset's useful economic life. *[1 Sch 18, 1 Sch 18 (LLP)]*.

Intangible assets must be written off over the useful economic life of the intangible asset. Where in exceptional cases the useful life of intangible assets cannot be reliably estimated, such assets must be written off over a period chosen by the directors of the company (or members of the LLP) that must not exceed ten years. A note to the accounts must disclose that period, together with the reasons for choosing it. *[1 Sch 22, 1 Sch 22 (LLP)].*

Where a fixed asset investment (falling to be included under item B.III in the company balance sheet statutory formats or item A.III in the LLP balance sheet statutory formats – see 5.3.4 above) has diminished in value, provisions for diminution in value *may* [emphasis added] be made in respect of it and its carrying amount reduced accordingly. *[1 Sch 19(1), 1 Sch 19(1) (LLP)].*

Provisions for diminution in value *must* [emphasis added] be made in respect of any fixed asset which has diminished in value, if the reduction in value is expected to be permanent (whether the fixed asset has a limited useful economic life or not). *[1 Sch 19(2), 1 Sch 19(2) (LLP)].*

Notwithstanding the distinction made in company and LLP law between permanent and temporary diminutions, FRS 102's requirements on impairment (on financial assets in Sections 11 and 12 *[FRS 102.11.21-32, 12.13]*, or in Section 27 – *Impairment of Assets*) should be applied. See Chapter 10 at 8.5 and Chapter 24.

Where the reasons for which any provision for diminution was made have ceased to apply to any extent, the provision must be written back to the extent that it is no longer necessary. Provisions made in respect of goodwill must not be written back to any extent. *[1 Sch 20(1), 1 Sch 20(1) (LLP)].*

The Regulations (and LLP Regulations) contain a general principle that 'all provisions for diminution of value must be recognised, whether the result of the financial year is a profit or loss'. *[1 Sch 13(c), 1 Sch 13(c) (LLP)].* FRS 102's requirements for impairment of financial assets (at cost or amortised cost) in Section 11 and impairment of other assets in Section 27 are consistent with this principle (see Chapter 10 at 8.5 and Chapter 24 respectively).

Provisions for diminution must be charged to the profit and loss account. Similarly, any amounts written back must be recognised in the profit and loss account. The provisions made and any write-backs must be disclosed separately in a note to the accounts, if not shown separately in the profit and loss account. *[1 Sch 19(3), 1 Sch 20(2), 1 Sch 19(3) (LLP), 1 Sch 20(2)(LLP)].*

The requirements above also apply to any goodwill relating to an interest in an associated undertaking (e.g. an associate or jointly controlled entity), shown by the equity method of accounting. *[6 Sch 21(1), 3 Sch 21(1) (LLP)].*

10.1.2.A   FRS 102's requirements

The requirements for measuring depreciation, amortisation and impairment in FRS 102 are consistent with the Regulations (and LLP Regulations) but more prescriptive. For example, Section 17 contains detailed requirements on depreciation of property, plant and equipment *[FRS 102.17.16-23]*. See Chapter 15 at 3.5.

FRS 102 generally reflects the requirements of the Regulations and LLP Regulations on goodwill and intangible amortisation. See Chapter 16 at 3.4.3 and Chapter 17 at 3.8.2.

Appendix III to FRS 102 notes that the requirement in paragraph 22 of Schedule 1 to the Regulations which requires intangible assets to be written off over their useful lives is broadly consistent with FRS 102, except that FRS 102 allows for the possibility that an intangible asset will have a residual value, in which case it is the depreciable amount of the intangible asset that is amortised. In practice, it will be uncommon for an intangible asset to have a residual value (an entity should assume that the residual value is zero other than in specific circumstances). *[FRS 102.18.21, 18.23]*. In those cases where an intangible asset has a residual value that is not zero, the amortisation of the depreciable amount of an intangible asset over its useful economic life is a departure from the requirements of paragraph 22 of Schedule 1 to the Regulations for the overriding purpose of giving a true and fair view, requiring the disclosures in the notes to the financial statements of the 'particulars of the departure, the reasons for it and its effect' (paragraph 10(2) of Schedule 1 to the Regulations) (see 9.2.2 above). *[FRS 102 Appendix III.37A]*. See also Chapter 16 at 3.4.3.

FRS 102 requires amortisation of goodwill on a systematic basis over its finite useful life, so there is no residual value, consistent with the Regulations. *[FRS 102.19.23(a)]*.

FRS 102 does not distinguish between temporary and permanent diminutions in value. Section 27 (see Chapter 24) requires provisions for impairment of property, plant and equipment; investment property measured using the cost model; biological assets measured using the cost model; intangible assets; and goodwill to be recognised when the recoverable amount of the asset is less than its carrying amount. *[FRS 102.27.1, 27.5]*. Similarly, Sections 11 and 12 contain specific requirements for recognition of impairment of financial assets measured at cost or amortised cost, where there is objective evidence of impairment (see Chapter 10 at 8.5). *[FRS 102.11.21-26, 12.13]*.

FRS 102 prohibits the reversal of goodwill impairment. *[FRS 102.27.28, 27.31(b)]*.

10.1.3   Development costs

Development costs may be included in 'Other intangible assets' under fixed assets in the balance sheet statutory formats set out in Section B of Part 1 to the Regulations (or Section B of Part 1 to the LLP Regulations) where this is in accordance with generally accepted accounting principles or practice. If any amount is included in a company's (or an LLP's) balance sheet in respect of development costs, the note on accounting policies must include the period over which the amount of those costs originally capitalised is being or is to be written off and the reasons for capitalising the development costs in question. *[1 Sch 21, 1 Sch 21 (LLP)]*. These disclosures are similar to those required by FRS 102. *[FRS 102.18.27(a)]*. The reference to the statutory formats should not preclude the ability to capitalise development costs, where adapted formats are used.

Development costs shown as an asset are treated as a realised loss for the purposes of section 830 (distributions to be made out of profits available for the purpose), except where: *[s844]*

- there are 'special circumstances' in the company's case justifying the directors' decision not to treat these as a realised loss; and
- in Companies Act accounts, the note to the accounts referred to in paragraph 21 of Schedule 1 to the Regulations (and for IAS accounts, in any note to the accounts) states that the amount of the development costs shown as an asset is not to be treated as a realised loss, together with the circumstances relied upon to justify the directors' decision to that effect.

TECH 02/17BL clarifies that this would be the case where the costs are carried forward in accordance with applicable accounting standards. *[s844, TECH 02/17BL.2.38]*.

The reference to 'special circumstances' in section 844 of the CA 2006 has not changed notwithstanding that the Regulations no longer refer to 'special circumstances'.

The requirement to treat development costs as a realised loss does not apply to any part of that amount representing an unrealised profit made on revaluation of those costs. *[s844(2)]*.

Where the company is an investment company (as defined in section 833 of CA 2006), there are similar requirements except that the references to 'realised loss' above instead refer to 'realised revenue loss' for the purposes of section 832 (distributions by investment companies out of accumulated revenue profits). *[s844(1)]*.

Section 844 is not relevant to LLPs.

10.1.4   Equity method in respect of participating interests

The Regulations (and LLP Regulations) allow the use of the equity method to account for participating interests (see definition in 5.3.4.D above). The Basis for Conclusions accompanying FRS 102 explains that FRS 102 already includes a number of options for accounting for such investments, and therefore this option was not introduced. *[FRS 102.BC.A28 (a)]*. Consequently, use of the equity method for accounting for such investments in separate or individual financial statements is not permitted by FRS 102 and therefore this is not discussed further.

10.1.5   Provisions for liabilities

The Regulations (and LLP Regulations) define provisions for liabilities as 'any amount retained as reasonably necessary for the purpose of providing for any liability the nature of which is clearly defined and which is either likely to be incurred, or certain to be incurred but uncertain as to amount or as to the date on which it will arise'. *[9 Sch 2, 4 Sch 10 (LLP)]*.

The Regulations (and LLP Regulations) also add that 'at the balance sheet date, a provision must represent the best estimate of the expenses likely to be incurred or, in the case of a liability, of the amount required to meet that liability' and 'provisions must not be used to adjust the value of assets'. *[9 Sch 2A-2B, 1 Sch 13(d)-(e) (LLP)]*.

FRS 102 defines a provision more succinctly as 'a liability of uncertain timing or amount' and also requires measurement at the best estimate of the amount required to settle the obligation at the balance sheet date. This is the amount an entity would rationally pay to settle the obligation at the end of the reporting period or to transfer it to a third party at that time. *[FRS 102.21.1, 21.7, FRS 102 Appendix I]*. The requirements in FRS 102 are, therefore, consistent with, but more detailed than, the Regulations (and LLP Regulations). See Chapter 19 at 3.

10.2   Alternative accounting rules

Under the alternative accounting rules, an asset is carried at a revalued amount (on one of the permitted bases – see 10.2.1 below). *[1 Sch 32, 1 Sch 32 (LLP)]*. The most familiar use of the alternative accounting rules is for revaluation of property, plant and equipment, but all of the other revaluations listed below follow a similar model. There is no reclassification to profit or loss (for the period) of amounts previously accumulated in equity where the alternative accounting rules are applied.

FRS 102's requirements for revaluations of the following assets make use of the alternative accounting rules:

- Property, plant and equipment (including investment property rented to another group company and transferred to property, plant and equipment) carried at a revalued amount, being the fair value at the date of revaluation less any subsequent accumulated depreciation and subsequent accumulated impairment losses. The revaluation model must be applied to all items of property, plant and equipment in the same class (i.e. having a similar nature, function or use in the business). *[FRS 102.17.15, 17.15B-F]*. See Chapter 15 at 3.6;

- Intangible fixed assets carried at a revalued amount, being the fair value at the date of revaluation less any subsequent accumulated amortisation and subsequent accumulated impairment losses. The revaluation model must be applied to all intangible assets in the same class, and revaluations are only permitted provided that the fair value can be determined by reference to an active market. *[FRS 102.18.18, FRS 102.18.18B-H]*. In practice, it is rare to meet the criteria for revaluation of an intangible fixed asset. See Chapter 16 at 3.4.2;

- Investments in subsidiaries, associates and jointly controlled entities, where a policy of fair value through other comprehensive income is applied in individual or separate financial statements. *[FRS 102.9.26(b), 9.26A, 14.4(c), 15.9(c)]*. See Chapter 8 at 4.2, Chapter 12 at 3.3.1 and 3.3.4, and Chapter 13 at 3.6.2 and 3.6.3.A.

- Investments in subsidiaries excluded from consolidation carried at fair value through other comprehensive income in consolidated financial statements. *[FRS 102.9.9, 9.9A, 9.9B(b)]*. See Chapter 8 at 3.4.

- When IFRS 9 is applied, investments in equity instruments that are designated as measured at fair value through other comprehensive income. *[IFRS 9.4.1.4, 5.7.1(b), 5.7.5-6]*.

  This accounting differs significantly from the accounting for available-for-sale financial assets under IAS 39 (which is explicitly covered by the fair value accounting rules) and for debt securities under IFRS 9. In particular, there is no reclassification to profit or loss of previous amounts accumulated in equity or on disposal of the financial asset. There is also no separate accounting for impairments. With the exception of dividends received, all fair value changes are recognised in other comprehensive income. Therefore, in our view, this accounting is not permitted by the fair value accounting rules but is permitted under the alternative accounting rules for fixed asset investments.

Financial assets carried at fair value in accordance with Sections 11 and 12 or IAS 39 are generally measured using the fair value accounting rules rather than the alternative accounting rules (see 10.3 below). In our view, where financial assets are carried at fair value in accordance with IFRS 9, this also makes use of the fair value accounting rules (except for the situation discussed above).

10.2.1 Assets that may be revalued under the alternative accounting rules in the Regulations

Under the alternative accounting rules in the Regulations (and the LLP Regulations):
[1 Sch 32, 1 Sch 32(LLP)]

- tangible fixed assets may be included at market value determined as at the date of their last valuation or at their current cost;
- fixed asset investments (falling to be included under item B.III in the company balance sheet statutory formats and item A.III in the LLP balance sheet statutory formats – see 5.3.4 above) may be included either:
  - at a market value determined as at the date of their last valuation; or
  - at a value determined on a basis which appears to the directors (or the members of the LLP) to be appropriate in the company's (or the LLP's) circumstances (but in this latter case, particulars of the method of valuation adopted and of the reasons for adopting it must be disclosed in a note to the accounts); and
- intangible fixed assets (other than goodwill) may be included at current cost.

The Regulations and the LLP Regulations no longer permit use of the alternative accounting rules for current asset investments and stocks.

10.2.1.A FRS 102's requirements

FRS 102's requirements for the revaluation of property, plant and equipment and intangible assets at fair value are consistent with but more prescriptive than the alternative accounting rules. See Chapter 15 at 3.6 and Chapter 16 at 3.4.2.

Where investments in subsidiaries, associates and joint ventures are measured at fair value through other comprehensive income in separate or individual financial statements (or investments in subsidiaries that are excluded from consolidation are measured at fair value through other comprehensive income in consolidated financial statements), a directors' valuation (that does not equate to fair value) is not permitted.

As noted at 10.2 above, where other fixed asset or current asset investments are included at fair value under FRS 102, this generally makes use of the fair value accounting rules.

When investments in subsidiaries, associates and joint ventures are carried using the cost model in separate or individual financial statements under FRS 102, the previous GAAP carrying amount at the date of transition may be used as a deemed cost as at the date of transition. *[FRS 102.35.10(f)]*. Where a deemed cost contains a past revaluation subject to the alternative accounting rules (e.g. for investment property transferred to property, plant and equipment at a deemed cost), the requirements of the alternative accounting rules continue to apply. See Chapter 32 at 3.5.3, 5.5 and 5.9.

10.2.2   *Application of the depreciation and diminution rules under the alternative accounting rules*

Where the carrying amount of an asset is determined under the alternative accounting rules, *[1 Sch 32, 1 Sch 32 (LLP)]*, as discussed at 10.2.1 above, the latest revalued amount on that basis is the starting point – instead of its purchase price or production cost or any previous revalued amount – for determining the amount to be included for the asset in the accounts. Therefore, the rules on depreciation or provisions for diminution (or impairment) of the asset apply with the latest revalued amount (on the above basis) substituted instead of references to the asset's purchase price or production cost. *[1 Sch 33(1), 1 Sch 33(1) (LLP)]*.

With this modification, the rules in paragraphs 17 to 21, 23 to 25 of Schedule 1 to the Regulations (and the same paragraphs in Schedule 1 to the LLP Regulations) continue to apply. *[1 Sch 30, 33, 1 Sch 30, 33 (LLP)]*. These rules, which are the same that apply under the historical cost accounting rules, include the disclosure requirements for provisions for diminution and write-backs of such provisions highlighted at 10.1.2 above. *[1 Sch 19(3), 1 Sch 20(2), 1 Sch 19(3), 1 Sch 20(2) (LLP)]*.

The Regulations (and LLP Regulations) refer to the provision for depreciation or diminution calculated using the latest revalued amount (on the above basis) as the 'adjusted amount' and the provision for depreciation or diminution calculated using the historical cost accounting rules as the 'historical cost amount'. *[1 Sch 33(2), 1 Sch 33(2) (LLP)]*.

The Regulations (and LLP Regulations) allow a company (or an LLP) to include under the relevant profit and loss account heading the amount of provision for depreciation for a revalued fixed asset based on historical cost, provided that the difference between the historical cost amount and the adjusted amount is shown separately in the profit and loss account or in a note to the accounts. *[1 Sch 33(3), 1 Sch 33(3) (LLP)]*. This paragraph appears to be intended to allow presentation of the depreciation charge relating to the historical cost amount in a different line item in the profit and loss account rather than allowing the total depreciation charge shown in the profit and loss account to be based on the historical cost amount. However, FRS 102 requires that depreciation (based on the revalued amount) is charged to profit or loss (unless another section requires the depreciation to be recognised as part of the cost of an asset). *[FRS 102.17.18, 18.21]*. We would therefore not expect depreciation on the historical cost component to be separately presented in the profit and loss account formats.

The treatment of revaluations under the Regulations (and LLP Regulations) is discussed at 10.2.3 and 10.2.4 below.

10.2.3   *Revaluation reserve*

Under the alternative accounting rules, the initial recognition of the asset is at its purchase price or production cost (as defined at 10.1.1 above). Purchase price includes any expenses incidental to its acquisition (and subtracts any incidental reductions in its cost of acquisition). *[FRS 102 Appendix III.34, 1 Sch 27, 35(1), 1 Sch 27 (LLP), 35(1) (LLP)]*.

When an asset is subsequently revalued under the alternative accounting rules, the amount of any profit or loss arising from that determination (after allowing, where appropriate, for any provisions for depreciation or diminution in value made otherwise than by reference to the value so determined and any adjustments of any such provisions made in light of that determination) must be credited or (as the case may be) debited to a separate revaluation reserve. *[1 Sch 35(1), 1 Sch 35(1) (LLP)]*. In effect, this means that the revaluation establishes a new 'cost' for the asset and the revaluation gain or loss is based on the difference between the revalued amount and the previous carrying amount of the asset.

The amount of the revaluation reserve must be shown in the balance sheet under a separate sub-heading in the position given for the item 'revaluation reserve' (using that heading) under 'capital and reserves' (for an LLP, under 'members' other interests') in the statutory balance sheet formats. *[1 Sch 35(2), 1 Sch 35(2) (LLP)]*.

FRS 102 requires that a revaluation increase is recognised in other comprehensive income and accumulated in equity, except that a revaluation increase is recognised in profit or loss to the extent it reverses a revaluation decrease of the same asset previously recognised in profit or loss. A revaluation decrease is recognised in other comprehensive income to the extent of any previously recognised revaluation increase accumulated in equity in respect of that asset, with any excess recognised in profit or loss. *[FRS 102.17.15E-F, 18.18G-H]*. FRS 102's requirements, in effect, regard a downward revaluation that reverses previously recognised revaluation increases accumulated in equity as a 'revaluation adjustment' but where a downward revaluation exceeds the previously recognised revaluation increases accumulated in equity, the excess is recognised in profit or loss (as if a diminution in value).

The Regulations specify that UK companies may apply the statutory revaluation reserve as follows:

(a) an amount may be transferred from the revaluation reserve to the profit and loss account, if the amount was previously charged to the profit and loss account or represents a realised profit; *[1 Sch 35(3)(a)]*

(b) an amount may be transferred from the revaluation reserve on capitalisation. *[1 Sch 35(3)(b)]*. Capitalisation means applying an amount to the credit of the revaluation reserve in wholly or partly paying up unissued shares in the company to be allotted to the members of the company as fully or partly paid shares, i.e. a bonus issue of shares; and *[1 Sch 35(4)]*

(c) an amount may be transferred to or from the revaluation reserve in respect of the taxation relating to any profit or loss credited or debited to the reserve. The treatment for taxation purposes of amounts credited or debited to the revaluation reserve must be disclosed in a note to the accounts. *[1 Sch 35(3)(c), 1 Sch 35(6)]*.

The use of the revaluation reserve described in (a) is consistent with:

- FRS 102's accounting for a revaluation increase that reverses a revaluation decrease of the same asset previously recognised in profit and loss;

- where depreciation or an impairment has been charged based on a revalued amount (exceeding historical cost), the excess depreciation (i.e. the depreciation based on the revalued amount less that which would have been charged based on historical cost) may be transferred from the revaluation reserve to the profit and loss account reserve (as a reserves transfer in equity); and

- on sale of a revalued fixed asset, the amount in the revaluation reserve, where realised on the sale, could be transferred to the profit and loss account reserve (as a reserves transfer in equity).

Chapter 6

The revaluation reserve must be reduced to the extent that the amounts transferred to it are no longer necessary for the purposes of the valuation method used and the revaluation reserve must not be reduced except as noted above. *[1 Sch 35(3), 35(5)].* Although the word 'reduced' is ambiguous in the context of a reserve that may contain (in law) either debit or credit balances, the intention is to prevent companies from charging costs, e.g. valuation fees, directly to the reserve or from releasing credits to the profit and loss account, except in ways permitted by the Regulations. These provisions would also permit a company changing policy from revaluation to cost to write back the reduction in carrying value against any credit balance in the revaluation reserve.

The revaluation reserve may also be reduced, to the extent permitted by section 734 of the CA 2006, when a private limited company makes a payment out of capital (under Chapter 5 of Part 18 of the CA 2006) or a payment under section 692(1ZA). Where the permissible capital payment (together with any proceeds of a fresh issue applied in making the redemption or purchase of the company's own shares) is greater than the nominal amount of the shares redeemed or purchased, the amount of fully paid share capital, share premium account, capital redemption reserve or revaluation reserve (if in credit) may be reduced by the amount of the excess. *[s734].*

There are no equivalent rules for LLPs. Appendix 5 – *Legal Opinion* – to the LLP SORP advises on certain matters relating to profits of an LLP, and comments on the revaluation reserve of an LLP.

Care needs to be taken on transition to identify whether a statutory revaluation reserve must be created or maintained. Where an asset is carried at a deemed cost (based on a previous GAAP revaluation which would include historic revaluations or fair value at the date of transition), this makes use of the alternative accounting rules. This is discussed in Chapter 32 at 3.5.3, 5.5 and 5.9.

10.2.4   Disclosures

Where the alternative accounting rules are used for any items shown in the accounts, the items affected and the basis of valuation adopted must be disclosed in the note on accounting policies. *[1 Sch 34(2), 1 Sch 34(2) (LLP)].*

For each balance sheet item affected, the comparable amounts determined according to the historical cost accounting rules must be shown in a note to the accounts. The comparable amounts required to be disclosed are: *[1 Sch 34(4), 1 Sch 34(3) (LLP)]*

- the aggregate amount (i.e. aggregate cost) which would be required to be shown for that balance sheet item if the amounts to be included in respect of all the assets covered by that item were determined according to the historical cost accounting rules; and

- the aggregate amount of the cumulative provisions for depreciation or diminution in value which would be permitted or required in determining those amounts according to the historical cost accounting rules.

Where any fixed assets (other than listed investments – see 5.3.4.A above) are included at a valuation under the alternative accounting rules, the following information is required to be disclosed in a note to the accounts: *[1 Sch 52, 1 Sch 50 (LLP)]*

- the years (so far as they are known to the directors (or the members of the LLP)) in which the assets were severally valued and the several values; and

- where the assets have been valued during the financial year:
  - the names of the persons who valued them or particulars of their qualifications for doing so; and
  - the bases of valuations used by them.

This requirement applies to fixed assets, i.e. assets of a company / LLP which are intended for use on a continuing basis in the company's / LLP's activities *[10 Sch 4, 4 Sch 3 (LLP), FRS 102 Appendix I]* (see 5.2.2 above) where adapted formats or statutory formats are used.

10.3   Fair value accounting rules – financial instruments

Under FRS 102, where an entity carries financial assets or financial liabilities at fair value, or where a financial instrument is used in hedge accounting, this generally makes use of the fair value accounting rules. This is the case whatever policy choice (i.e. Section 11 and Section 12, IFRS 9 or IAS 39) the entity applies to the recognition and measurement of financial instruments. Situations that are covered by the alternative accounting rules instead are listed at 10.2 above.

The fair value accounting rules are based on those in the Accounting Directive which are intended to be consistent with application of IAS 39. Therefore they allow for financial instruments to be accounted at fair value through profit or loss, or as available-for-sale financial assets.

Where financial assets or financial liabilities are measured at fair value under Sections 11 and 12, the accounting is always fair value through profit or loss (and falls within the fair value accounting rules).

Where IFRS 9 is applied, whether fair value changes are recognised in profit or loss or in other comprehensive income depends on the type of financial instrument held at fair value. Our view is that accounting for investments in equity instruments at fair value through other comprehensive income under IFRS 9 makes use of the alternative accounting rules instead of the fair value accounting rules (see 10.2 above).

However, the following situations for accounting for financial instruments at fair value under IFRS 9 do not fall neatly within the fair value accounting rules:

(a) designation of a financial liability at fair value through profit and loss; and *[IFRS 9.4.2.2, 5.7.1(c), 5.7.7-9]*

(b) investments in debt instruments classified as measured at fair value through other comprehensive income which are held within a business model whose objective is achieved by both collecting contractual cash flows and selling financial assets and the contractual terms of the financial assets give rise on specified dates to cash flows that are solely payments of principal and interest on the principal amount outstanding. *[IFRS 9.4.1.2A, 5.7.1(d), 5.7.10-11]*.

In situation (a) above, fair value changes attributable to changes in the credit risk of the liability (often referred to as 'own credit risk') are presented in other comprehensive income, unless that treatment would create or enlarge an accounting mismatch in profit or loss. *[IFRS 9.4.2.2, 5.7.1(c), 5.7.7-9]*. Appendix III to FRS 102 explains that, where entities applying IFRS 9 record fair value gains and losses attributable to changes in credit risk in other comprehensive income, this will usually be a departure from the requirements of paragraph 40 of Schedule 1 to the Regulations (which requires fair value gains and losses on financial instruments measured at fair value to be recorded in profit or loss, except when the financial instrument is a hedging instrument or an available-for-sale security), for the overriding purpose of giving a true and fair view. *[FRS 102 Appendix III.12C]*. See 9.2.2 above.

Appendix III does not discuss situation (b) above. Where investments in certain debt instruments are measured at fair value through other comprehensive income under IFRS 9, the model used for accounting for changes in the fair value of a debt instrument through other comprehensive income is similar to that for an available-for-sale financial asset under IAS 39 (although it is not described as 'available-for-sale'). In our view, it can be inferred from the silence on the matter in Appendix III to FRS 102 that this model is included within the fair value accounting rules and does not therefore require the use of a true and fair override to apply.

In addition, particular care needs to be taken where Sections 11 and 12 or IAS 39 is used, as in some situations the fair value accounting rules in the Regulations (or the LLP Regulations) do not permit use of fair value. This conflict does not exist where IFRS 9 is applied (as IFRS 9 is the extant IFRS). Where accounting for the financial instrument at fair value would conflict with the Regulations (or the LLP Regulations) where Sections 11 and 12 or IAS 39 are applied, the financial instrument (for Sections 11 and 12) or financial asset (for IFRS 9) is required to be carried at amortised cost. *[FRS 102.12.8(c)]*. See 10.3.1 below.

The fair value accounting rules also apply to certain commodity-based contracts (which are generally required to be accounted for as financial instruments under accounting standards). References to 'derivatives' in the fair value accounting rules include commodity-based contracts that give either contracting party the right to settle in cash or in some other financial instrument, except where such contracts:
[10 Sch 2, 4 Sch 1 (LLP)]

- were entered into for the purpose of, and continue to meet the company's (or the LLP's) expected purchase, sale or usage requirements;
- were designated for such purpose at their inception; and
- are expected to be settled by delivery of the commodity.

Where Schedule 2 to the Regulations is applied, the definition of a derivative and commodity contract is in that schedule.

10.3.1   Which financial instruments may be included at fair value under the Regulations and LLP Regulations?

10.3.1.A   Overview

As noted at 10.3 above, FRS 102 allows a choice of policy for the recognition and measurement of financial instruments and the situations in which financial instruments are carried at fair value differ depending on the choice applied.

However, certain types of financial instruments are prohibited from being carried at fair value by company (or LLP) law. As noted at 10.3 above, FRS 102 requires such instruments to be carried at amortised cost (where Sections 11 and 12, or IFRS 9 are applied). *[FRS 102.11.2A, 12.2A, 12.8(c)]*. Chapter 10 at 6.4 discusses types of financial instruments where the accounting in Sections 11 and 12 may conflict with the Regulations and LLP Regulations – meaning that amortised cost treatment is required under FRS 102.

Paragraph 36 of Schedule 1 to the Regulations permits financial instruments, whose fair values can be reliably measured (see 10.3.1.B below), to be included at fair value. However, certain types of financial instruments are prohibited from being included at fair value by paragraphs 36(2) and 36(3) of Schedule 1 to the Regulations, unless the financial instrument falls within paragraph 36(4) of Schedule 1 to the Regulations. *[1 Sch 36(4)]*. The items listed in paragraphs 36(2) and 36(3) may, therefore, still be held at fair value, subject to meeting the requirements in paragraph 36(4) of Schedule 1 to the Regulations, i.e. the accounting is permitted by EU-adopted IFRSs and the disclosures required by such accounting standards are given. See 10.3.1.C and 10.3.1.D below. The accounting would also need to comply with the accounting standard, FRS 101 or FRS 102, adopted.

The same requirements (as paragraph 36) are included in paragraph 44 of Schedule 2 (for banking companies) and paragraph 30 of Schedule 3 (for insurance companies) to the Regulations, *[2 Sch 44, 3 Sch 30]*, and paragraph 36 of Schedule 1 to the LLP Regulations. *[1 Sch 36 (LLP)]*. References below to paragraph 36 are to paragraph 36 of Schedule 1 to the Regulations and paragraph 36 of Schedule 1 to the LLP Regulations but also apply to the same requirements for banking companies and insurance companies (and to small companies and small LLPs).

It is, therefore, important to ensure that the use of fair value accounting is indeed permitted by EU-adopted IFRS.

For application of paragraph 36(4) under FRS 101, see Chapter 2 at 6.3.

10.3.1.B   Determination of reliable fair values

Where the fair value accounting rules are applied, financial instruments (including derivatives) may be included at fair value, only where this can be determined reliably in accordance with paragraph 37 of Schedule 1 to the Regulations (or paragraph 37 of Schedule 1 to the LLP Regulations). *[1 Sch 36(1), (5), 1 Sch 36(1) (LLP), (5) (LLP)]*.

The fair value of a financial instrument is determined as follows: *[1 Sch 37, 1 Sch 37 (LLP)]*

(a)   if a reliable market can readily be identified for the financial instrument, by reference to its market value;

(b)   if a reliable market cannot readily be identified for the financial instrument but can be identified for its components or for a similar instrument, by reference to the market value of its components or of the similar instrument; or

(c)   if neither (a) nor (b) apply, a value resulting from generally accepted valuation models and techniques that must ensure a reasonable approximation of the market value.

See Chapter 10 at 8.6 for FRS 102's requirements on determining fair values of financial instruments, which set out a similar (but not identically worded) fair value hierarchy. *[FRS 102.11.27-32, 12.10-12]*.

Chapter 6

10.3.1.C   *Financial instruments held at fair value subject to paragraph 36(4) of Schedule 1 to the Regulations (and equivalent requirements)*

Paragraphs 36(2)(c) and 36(3) of the Regulations (and its equivalents) list certain types of financial instruments which are not allowed to be held at fair value – unless this is permitted by the requirements of paragraph 36(4) (and its equivalents) – as follows:

- financial liabilities, unless they are held as part of a trading portfolio or are derivatives;
- financial instruments (other than derivatives) held to maturity;
- loans and receivables originated by the company (or the LLP) and not held for trading purposes;
- interests in subsidiary undertakings, associated undertakings and joint ventures;
- equity instruments issued by the company (or the LLP);
- contracts for contingent consideration in a business combination; or
- other financial instruments with such special characteristics that the instruments, according to generally accepted accounting principles or practice, should be accounted for differently from other financial instruments. *[1 Sch 36(2)-36(3), 1 Sch 36(2) (LLP)-(3) (LLP)].*

FRS 102 allows a choice of applying either IAS 39, IFRS 9, or Sections 11 and 12 for the recognition and measurement of financial instruments. The situations in which financial instruments are carried at fair value under FRS 102 will differ depending on the choice taken. Following the adoption by the EU of IFRS 9, this standard is now the principal point of reference for which financial instruments may be included in the accounts at fair value when referring to paragraph 36(4) of Schedule I to the Regulations.

Furthermore, the Regulations (and its equivalents) were written with the application of the previously extant IAS 39 in mind. Terms such as 'loans and receivables', 'held to maturity' and 'held for trading' are not defined in FRS 102. The Regulations indicate that these terms are defined in the Accounting Directive (Directive 2013/34/EU) and Directive 91/674/EEC (for insurance undertakings) and in paragraph 96 of Schedule 2 to the Regulations (for banking companies). *[10 Sch 3(1), 4 Sch 2(1) (LLP)].* Some of these terms are no longer used in IFRS 9 and therefore it would be necessary to refer back to definitions under the version of IAS 39 extant immediately before the introduction of IFRS 9.

Interests in subsidiary undertakings are as defined in section 1162 of the CA 2006; interests in associated undertakings are as defined in paragraph 19 of Schedule 6 to the Regulations (and paragraph 19 of Schedule 3 to the LLP Regulations) and interests in joint ventures are as defined in paragraph 18 of Schedule 6 to the Regulations (and paragraph 18 of Schedule 3 to the LLP Regulations). *[1 Sch 36(6), 1 Sch 36(6) (LLP)].* See 5.3.4.C to 5.3.4.E above and Chapter 3 at 3.1.2 for guidance on the definitions.

Paragraph 36(4) states that 'financial instruments which under international accounting standards may be included in accounts at fair value, may be so included, provided that the disclosures required by such accounting standards are made.' *[1 Sch 36(4), 1 Sch 36(4) (LLP)].* International accounting standards means EU-adopted IFRS in accordance with the IAS Regulation. *[s474].* This is also the meaning of 'international accounting standards' included in Article 8.6 of the Accounting Directive. Accordingly, reference is made to IFRS 9, in determining whether certain financial instruments may be held at fair value and the required disclosures.

Not all the types of financial instruments listed in paragraphs 36(2) and 36(3) may be held at fair value under FRS 101 and FRS 102 (even if they meet the conditions in paragraph 36(4)). The situations where financial instruments would appear to be held at fair value in accordance with paragraph 36(4) for an FRS 102 reporter are set out in Chapter 3 at 3.4.1, and for an FRS 101 reporter in Chapter 2 at 6.3.

FRS 102 permits or requires investments in subsidiaries, associates and joint ventures to be measured at fair value in consolidated and / or individual financial statements. However, such items are still held at fair value subject to the requirements of paragraph 36(4) (and its equivalents). Investments in subsidiaries held at fair value through profit or loss in consolidated financial statements would meet the requirements of paragraph 36(4) in situations where this accounting would be permitted under EU-adopted IFRS (such as IFRS 10 – *Consolidated Financial Statements*). Where accounting at fair value through profit or loss is not permitted by EU-adopted IFRS, this would generally be a departure from the requirements of paragraph 36(4) and require the use of the true and fair override. Note also that in consolidated financial statements, carrying investments in associates or joint ventures at fair value through profit or loss may conflict with the requirement to apply the equity method in Schedule 6 to the Regulations (or Schedule 3 to the LLP Regulations), also requiring use of the true and fair override. *[6 Sch 21, 3 Sch 21 (LLP)]*. See 9.2.2 above for discussion of the true and fair override.

10.3.1.D   Disclosures where paragraph 36(4) of Schedule 1 to the Regulations applies

Appendix III to FRS 102 comments that an entity applying FRS 102 and holding financial instruments measured at fair value may be required to provide the disclosures required by paragraph 36(4). *[FRS 102 Appendix III.13]*.

As noted at 10.3.1.C above, the disclosures required by paragraph 36(4) (and its equivalents) are those in extant EU-adopted IFRS, as confirmed by *Appendix II – Note on Legal requirements* to FRS 101 which addresses the same paragraph. *[FRS 101 Appendix II.2.7]*. The most logical interpretation of this is that an entity should make all material disclosures required by IFRS 7 – *Financial Instruments: Disclosures* – and IFRS 13 – *Fair Value Measurement* – in respect of such financial instruments.

However, Appendix III to FRS 102 states that the disclosures required by paragraph 36(4) have been incorporated into Section 11. Some of the disclosure requirements of Section 11 apply to all financial instruments measured at fair value, whilst others (such as paragraph 11.48A) apply only to certain financial instruments (this does not include financial instruments held as part of a trading portfolio nor derivatives). The disclosure requirements of paragraph 11.48A will predominantly apply to certain financial liabilities, however, there may be instances where paragraph 36(3) requires that the disclosures must also be provided in relation to financial assets, e.g. investments in subsidiaries, associates or jointly controlled entities measured at fair value (see paragraph 9.27B of FRS 102). *[FRS 102 Appendix III.13]*.

While this guidance implies that FRS 102 reporters complying in full with the disclosures included in Sections 11 and 12 will be meeting the disclosure requirements of paragraph 36(4) (and its equivalents), we consider that particular care needs to be taken with both the scope of the disclosures and which disclosures are required. In any event,

FRS 102 reminds entities that they must ensure that they comply with any relevant legal requirements applicable to them and that the standard does not necessarily contain all legal disclosure requirements. *[FRS 102.1.2A]*.

The disclosure requirements of Sections 11 and 12 apply to financial instruments within the scope of whichever accounting standard is applied for recognition and measurement of financial instruments. *[FRS 102.11.1, 11.2, 11.7, 12.1, 12.2, 12.3, 12.26]*. A qualifying entity (that is not a financial institution) applying the reduced disclosure framework in its individual financial statements (see Chapter 3 at 3) may benefit from certain disclosure exemptions from Sections 11 and 12 but must still give the disclosures required by Section 11 for any financial instruments held at fair value subject to the requirements of paragraph 36(4) (and its equivalents). *[FRS 102.1.8, 1.12(c)]*.

However, paragraph 11.48A, which is excluded from the disclosure exemptions in the reduced disclosure framework, has a more restricted scope than other paragraphs in Section 11. It states that: 'An entity, *including an entity that is not a company*, shall provide the following disclosures only for financial instruments measured at *fair value through profit or loss in accordance with paragraph 36(4) of Schedule 1 to the Regulations* (and the equivalent requirements of the Small Companies Regulations, the LLP Regulations, and the Small LLP Regulations) ....' [emphasis added]. Paragraph 11.48A clarifies that its requirements do not apply to financial liabilities held as part of a trading portfolio nor derivatives. *[FRS 102.11.48A]*. However, the reference to an 'entity, including an entity that is not a company' appears to suggest that these disclosures should be given by entities that are not subject to the statutory requirements in paragraph 36(4) (or its equivalents) if they hold financial instruments that would fall within that paragraph, if the entity had been a UK company.

FRS 102 also requires a parent adopting a policy of accounting for its investments in subsidiaries, associates or jointly controlled entities at fair value through profit or loss in its separate financial statements to comply with the requirements of paragraph 36(4) by applying the disclosure requirements of Section 11 to those investments. *[FRS 102.9.27B]*. This means that all applicable disclosures in Section 11 must be given in respect of those investments. In our view, the same requirement would also apply where investments in subsidiaries, associates or jointly controlled entities are held at fair value through profit or loss in consolidated financial statements or in the individual financial statements of an investor or venturer (that is not a parent).

Particular care should also be taken where IAS 39 or IFRS 9 is applied to the recognition and measurement of financial instruments, as financial instruments held at fair value (but not through profit or loss) may in principle be held at fair value subject to paragraph 36(4) (or its equivalents). Examples might include an available-for-sale financial asset or debt instrument at fair value through other comprehensive income that falls within the financial instruments listed in paragraph 36(3). Section 11 and Section 12's disclosure requirements for financial instruments at fair value, including paragraph 11.48A, are generally framed in respect of financial instruments at fair value through profit or loss.

10.3.2 Accounting for changes in fair value of financial instruments

The following requirements apply where a financial instrument is valued in accordance with: *[1 Sch 40(1), 1 Sch 40(1) (LLP)]*

- paragraph 36 of Schedule 1 to the Regulations (or paragraph 36 of Schedule 1 to the LLP Regulations) – i.e. the financial instrument is measured at fair value; or

- paragraph 38 of Schedule 1 to the Regulations (or paragraph 38 of Schedule 1 to the LLP Regulations) – i.e. it is a hedged asset or liability (or identified portion of such an asset or liability) qualifying as a hedged item under a fair value hedge accounting system and included at the amount required under that system (see 10.3.3.A below).

Notwithstanding the general requirement that only realised profits are included in the profit and loss account, *[1 Sch 13, 1 Sch 13 (LLP)]*, a change in the value of the financial instrument must be included in the profit and loss account. *[1 Sch 40(2), 1 Sch 40(2) (LLP)]*.

However, there are exceptions to this general rule, as follows: *[1 Sch 40(3)-40(4), 1 Sch 40(3) (LLP)-(4) (LLP)]*

(a) the financial instrument accounted for is a hedging instrument under a hedge accounting system that allows some or all of the change in value not to be shown in the profit and loss account (see 10.3.3 below); or

(b) the change in value relates to an exchange difference arising on a monetary item that forms part of a company's (or an LLP's) net investment in a foreign entity (see below); or

(c) the financial instrument is an available-for-sale financial asset (and is not a derivative).

This treatment is permitted where IAS 39 is applied to the recognition and measurement of financial instruments by a FRS 102 reporter. See also the discussion at 10.3 above in respect of accounting for certain debt instruments classified as measured at fair value through other comprehensive income under IFRS 9.

In respect of (a) and (b) above, the amount of the change in value must be credited to (or as the case may be) debited from a separate reserve (the fair value reserve). In respect of (c) above, the amount of the change in value may be credited to (or as the case may be) debited from a separate reserve (the fair value reserve). *[1 Sch 40(3)-(4), 1 Sch 40(3) (LLP)-(4) (LLP)]*. The fair value reserve must be adjusted to the extent that the amounts shown in it are no longer necessary for the purposes of paragraphs 40(3) and 40(4). The treatment for taxation purposes of amounts credited to or debited to the fair value reserve must be disclosed in a note to the accounts. *[1 Sch 41, 1 Sch 41 (LLP)]*.

FRS 102 requires that exchange differences arising on a monetary item that in substance forms part of a company's net investment in a foreign operation (which may include long-term receivables or loans, but not trade receivables or payables) are recognised in other comprehensive income (and accumulated in equity) in the financial statements that include the foreign operation and the reporting entity (e.g. consolidated financial statements). Such items are recognised in profit or loss in the separate financial statements of the reporting entity or the individual financial statements of the foreign operation, as appropriate. *[FRS 102.30.12-13]*. See Chapter 27 at 3.7. While not explicitly stated by the Regulations (and LLP Regulations), it seems that (b) is intended to address accounts that include the foreign operation and the reporting entity. Moreover, given the scope of paragraph 40 (see above), it is not clear that (b) would apply to a monetary item such as a loan to a foreign entity measured at amortised cost.

10.3.3   Hedge accounting

10.3.3.A   Fair value hedge accounting

A company (or an LLP) may include any assets and liabilities, or identified portions of such assets or liabilities, that qualify as hedged items under a fair value hedge accounting system at the amount required under that system. *[1 Sch 38, 1 Sch 38 (LLP)].*

The fair value accounting rules, therefore, permit the adjustments made to hedged items under fair value hedge accounting under IAS 39, IFRS 9 and Section 12. See Chapter 10 at 10 and Chapter 49 of EY International GAAP 2019.

10.3.3.B   Cash flow hedge and net investment hedge accounting

Where the financial instrument accounted for is a hedging instrument under a hedge accounting system that allows some or all of the change in value not to be shown in the profit and loss account, the amount of the change in value must be credited to (or as the case may be) debited from a separate reserve ('the fair value reserve'). *[1 Sch 40(3), 1 Sch 40(3) (LLP)].*

The fair value reserve must be adjusted to the extent that the amounts shown in it are no longer necessary for the purposes of paragraph 40(3) of Schedule 1 to the Regulations (or paragraph 40(3) in Schedule 1 to the LLP Regulations). The treatment for taxation purposes of amounts credited to or debited to the fair value reserve must be disclosed in a note to the accounts. *[1 Sch 41, 1 Sch 41 (LLP)].*

The fair value accounting rules, therefore, support hedge accounting of a net investment of a foreign operation and cash flow hedge accounting under IAS 39, IFRS 9 and Section 12. Under these forms of hedge accounting, the entity recognises in other comprehensive income only the effective portion of the hedge and amounts accumulated in equity are reclassified in profit or loss, where required by Section 12, IAS 39 or IFRS 9 for cash flow hedge accounting. FRS 102 does not permit reclassification of exchange differences accumulated in equity arising from hedges of a net investment of a foreign operation. See Chapter 10 at 10 and Chapter 49 of EY International GAAP 2019.

10.3.4   Disclosures required by the Regulations and LLP Regulations

Where financial instruments have been valued in accordance with paragraph 36 (i.e. at fair value) (see 10.3.1 above) or paragraph 38 (see 10.3.3.A above) of Schedule 1 to the Regulations (or paragraphs 36 or 38 of Schedule 1 to the LLP Regulations), the notes to the accounts must include: *[1 Sch 55, 1 Sch 53 (LLP)]*

- the significant assumptions underlying the valuation models and techniques used to determine the fair value of the instruments (this is situation (c) at 10.3.1.B above);
- in the case of financial instruments, their purchase price, the items affected and the basis of valuation (Schedule 3 to the Regulations only); *[3 Sch 73(2)(b)]*

- for each category of financial instrument, the fair value of the assets in that category and the changes in value:
  - included directly in the profit and loss account, or
  - credited to or (as the case may be) debited from the fair value reserve

  in respect of those assets.

  Despite referring to 'assets', in our view, having regard to the underlying Accounting Directive requirement, this disclosure is likely intended to apply to both financial assets and financial liabilities;

- for each class of derivatives, the extent and nature of the instruments, including significant terms and conditions that may affect the amount, timing and certainty of future cash flows; and

- where any amount is transferred to or from the fair value reserve during the financial year, there must be stated in tabular form:
  - the amount of the reserve as at the date of the beginning of the financial year and as at the balance sheet date respectively;
  - the amount transferred to or from the reserve during that year; and
  - the source and application respectively of the amounts so transferred.

Appendix III to FRS 102 notes that most of these disclosures will be satisfied by equivalent requirements of the standard but entities will need to take care to ensure appropriate disclosure of derivatives is provided. *[FRS 102 Appendix III.12D]*.

Where the company (or LLP) has derivatives that it has *not* included at fair value, there must also be stated for each class of derivatives, the fair value of the derivatives in that class (if such a value can be determined in accordance with the requirements set out in 10.3.1.B above) and the extent and nature of the derivatives. *[1 Sch 56, 1 Sch 54 (LLP)]*. This situation should rarely arise under FRS 102 since derivatives are required to be measured at fair value.

Further disclosures are required where:

- the company (or LLP) has financial fixed assets that could be included at fair value under paragraph 36 of Schedule 1 to the Regulations (or paragraph 36 of Schedule 1 to the LLP Regulations) (see 10.3.1 above);
- the amount at which those items are included under any item in the company's (or the LLP's) accounts is in excess of their fair value; and
- the company (or the LLP) has not made provision for diminution in value of those assets in accordance with paragraph 19(1) of Schedule 1 to the Regulations (or paragraph 19(1) of Schedule 1 to the LLP Regulations) (see 10.1.2 above).

In such circumstances, there must also be stated:

- the amount at which either the individual assets or appropriate groupings of those individual assets are included in the company's (or LLP's) accounts;
- the fair value of those assets or groupings; and
- the reasons for not making a provision for diminution in value of those assets, including the nature of the evidence that provides the basis for the belief that the amount at which they are stated in the accounts will be recovered. *[1 Sch 57, 1 Sch 55 (LLP)]*.

Chapter 6

10.4   Investment properties, living animals and plants, and stocks

10.4.1   *Fair value accounting rules under the Regulations and LLP Regulations*

The fair value accounting rules allow:

- investment property;
- living animals and plants; and
- stocks

to be included at fair value, provided that, as the case may be, all such investment property, living animals and plants, and stocks are so included where their fair value can reliably be determined. Fair value, for these purposes, is 'fair value determined in accordance with generally accepted accounting principles or practice'. *[1 Sch 39, 1 Sch 39 (LLP), FRS 102 Appendix III.26].*

Notwithstanding the general requirement that only realised profits are included in the profit and loss account, *[1 Sch 13, 1 Sch 13 (LLP)],* a change in the value of the investment property or living animal or plant must be included in the profit and loss account. *[1 Sch 40(1)-40(2), 1 Sch 40(1) (LLP)-(2) (LLP)].*

The Regulations (and LLP Regulations) do not specify how changes in the fair value of stock are recognised under the fair value accounting rules. However, FRS 102 requires that fair value gains are only recognised in profit or loss on inventories measured at fair value less costs to sell. This accounting is only permitted where the entity operates in an active market, where sale can be achieved at published prices, and inventory is a store of readily realisable value. *[FRS 102.13.3].*

10.4.2   *FRS 102's requirements for fair value accounting*

FRS 102's requirements for investment property (see Chapter 14 at 3.2 and 3.3) and biological assets (see Chapter 31 at 2) make use of the fair value accounting rules described at 10.4 above.

FRS 102 requires that investment property (including property held by a lessee under an operating lease, that would otherwise meet the definition of investment property, that an entity elects (on a property-by-property basis) to treat as investment property) is measured at fair value at each reporting date with changes in fair value recognised in profit or loss. The Triennial review 2017 removed the undue cost or effort exemption from the previous version of FRS 102 that enabled some investment property to be accounted for as property, plant and equipment using the cost model in Section 17. Therefore, this exemption is only available for accounting periods beginning before 1 January 2019 and where the Triennial review 2017 amendments are not being early adopted. However, the Triennial review 2017 did introduce an accounting policy choice between a cost or fair value model, where investment property is rented to another group entity, see Chapter 14 at 3.2 and 3.3. *[FRS 102.16.1, 16.1A, 16.7].*

FRS 102 permits an entity engaged in agricultural activity a policy choice for each class of biological asset (and its related agricultural produce) to use either the fair value model or cost model. *[FRS 102.34.3A-B].*

Like the Regulations (and LLP Regulations), FRS 102 only permits use of fair value for biological assets where fair value can be measured reliably. *[FRS 102.34.6A]*. However, FRS 102's requirements for biological assets permit a policy choice of the fair value or cost models to be applied to a class of assets whereas the Regulations (and LLP Regulations) would require the fair value model, if adopted, to be applied to all such biological assets, where the fair value can reliably be determined.

Under FRS 102, inventories held for distribution are measured at the lower of cost adjusted, when applicable, for any loss of service potential and replacement cost. *[FRS 102.13.4A]*. Appendix III to FRS 102 explains this is an application of fair value accounting and notes that for inventories, including those held for distribution at no or nominal value (particularly items distributed to beneficiaries by public benefit entities), there is unlikely to be a significant difference between replacement cost and fair value. *[FRS 102 Appendix III.37]*.

While not noted in Appendix III, where inventories are measured at fair value less costs to sell, *[FRS 102.13.3]*, this presumably also applies the fair value accounting rules (assuming there is unlikely to be a significant difference between fair value and fair value less costs to sell).

10.4.3 Disclosures required by the Regulations and LLP Regulations

Where the amounts included in the accounts in respect of stocks, investment property, or living animals and plants have been determined using the fair value accounting rules, the balance sheet items affected and the basis of valuation adopted in the case of each such item must be disclosed in a note to the accounts. *[1 Sch 58(1), (2), 1 Sch 56(1) (LLP), (2) (LLP)]*.

In respect of investment property accounted for using the fair value accounting rules, for each balance sheet item affected, the comparable amounts determined according to the historical cost accounting rules or the differences between those comparable amounts and the amounts actually shown in the balance sheet in respect of that item must be disclosed in a note to the accounts. *[1 Sch 58(3)-(4), 1 Sch 56(3) (LLP)-(4) (LLP)]*. This is a similar disclosure to that required where an item is valued subject to the alternative accounting rules and is explained further at 10.2.4 above.

Where stocks, investment property, or living animals and plants have been fair valued in accordance with paragraph 39 of Schedule 1 to the Regulations (or paragraph 39 of Schedule 1 to the LLP Regulations) (see 10.4.1 above), the notes to the accounts must include: *[1 Sch 55, 1 Sch 53 (LLP)]*

- the significant assumptions underlying the valuation models and techniques used to determine the fair value of the assets; and
- for each category of asset, the fair value of the assets in that category and the changes in value included directly in the profit and loss account in respect of those assets.

These disclosures are similar to those required by the same paragraph for financial instruments held at fair value (see 10.3.4 above). However, disclosures in respect of the fair value reserve are only relevant for financial instruments held at fair value.

Chapter 6

11   SUMMARY OF DIFFERENCES BETWEEN FRS 102 AND IFRS

This Appendix refers to the Regulations and LLP Regulations in the context of the columns addressing FRS 102 (not applying the small entities regime in Section 1A). The Regulations and LLP Regulations apply to statutory accounts prepared by UK companies and LLPs not applying the small companies regime, small LLPs regime or micro-entity provisions. For simplicity, the comparison is for a UK company preparing its financial statements in accordance with Schedule 1 to the Regulations or an LLP. Other UK companies and certain other entities are subject to similar statutory requirements (but there may be some differences, particularly in relation to the formats applied).

All relevant schedules in the Regulations (or LLP Regulations) apply to the statutory accounts of a UK company (or an LLP) prepared in accordance with FRS 102 – which are Companies Act accounts (or non-IAS accounts, for an LLP). Only certain schedules in the Regulations (or LLP Regulations) apply to statutory accounts prepared by UK companies (or LLPs) in accordance with EU-adopted IFRS, which are IAS accounts. Therefore, many of the requirements in the Regulations referred to in the FRS 102 columns do not apply to IAS accounts (although they do apply to FRS 101 financial statements).

FRS 102 requires all entities to follow the applicable formats for the profit and loss account and balance sheet set out in the Regulations (or LLP Regulations), except to the extent that these conflict with the entity's statutory framework. While UK companies applying Schedule 1 to the Regulations and LLPs are able to follow adapted or statutory formats, banking and insurance companies (and groups) must follow the applicable statutory formats in Schedules 2 and 3 to the Regulations (which differ). The other disclosure requirements of the Regulations (or LLP Regulations) only apply to entities subject to these statutory requirements.

	FRS 102	*IFRS*
Complete set of financial statements	A complete set of financial statements (see 3.5 above) includes a: • statement of financial position; • statement of comprehensive income (either as a single statement or as a separate income statement and statement of comprehensive income); • statement of cash flows (unless exempt); • statement of changes in equity; and • related notes. In certain circumstances, a statement of income and retained earnings can be presented as an alternative to a statement of changes in equity and a statement of comprehensive income. Comparatives must be presented. FRS 102 includes guidance on comparatives for narrative as well as numerical information. FRS 102 permits the use of other titles – such as balance sheet or profit and loss account for the primary statements – as long as they are not misleading.	IFRS has the same components for a complete set of financial statements as FRS 102. There is more extensive guidance on comparatives. However, there are no exemptions from presenting a cash flow statement, and a statement of income and retained earnings is not available as an alternative primary statement.

Application of company law formats for profit and loss account and balance sheet	The income statement (or profit and loss section of statement of comprehensive income) and statement of financial position of all entities must comply with the applicable profit and loss account and balance sheet formats set out in the Regulations or the LLP Regulations, except to the extent that these requirements are not permitted by any statutory framework under which such entities report. FRS 102 permits use of adapted formats (which are similar to IAS 1 formats) as an alternative to statutory formats where Schedule 1 to the Regulations or the LLP Regulations are applied. See 4 to 6 above. Additional line items, headings and subtotals must be presented when relevant to an understanding of the financial position or financial performance (see 6.7.2 above). The General Rules to the formats (and FRS 102) explain the flexibility available to amend line items (see 4.4 above). The LLP SORP also has additional requirements relevant to the presentation of FRS 102 financial statements of LLPs.	The statement of financial position and statement of comprehensive income follow the requirements of IAS 1 which sets out minimum line items to be presented on the face of these primary statements. The formats in the Regulations and the LLP Regulations do not apply. IAS 1 also requires additional line items, headings and subtotals to be presented when relevant to an understanding of the financial position or financial performance. IAS 1 generally provides more flexibility to amend its formats compared to FRS 102. However, IAS 1 includes more guidance on the use of additional line items, including reconciliation of additional subtotals presented with the subtotals and totals required by IFRS.
Definition of discontinued operations	Discontinued operations (see 6.8 above) are defined as a component of an entity that has been disposed of and: • represented a separate major line of business or geographical area of operations, or • was part of a single coordinated plan to dispose of a separate major line of business or geographical area of operations; or • was a subsidiary acquired exclusively with a view to resale. FRS 102 requires that the operations have been disposed of by the reporting date. There is no further guidance on the definition of discontinued operations.	IFRS 5 has the same definition of discontinued operation as FRS 102, except that the definition refers to a component of an entity that either has been disposed of or is classified as held for sale. IFRS 5 includes extensive guidance on the definition. It is explicit that discontinued operations include sales of operations leading to loss of control, operations held for distribution (or distributed) and abandoned operations (in the period of abandonment).
Presentation of discontinued operations	FRS 102 requires a columnar line-by-line analysis of continuing, discontinued and total operations to be presented on the face of the statement of comprehensive income (or separate income statement) down to an amount that comprises the total of post-tax profit or loss of discontinued operations and the post-tax gain or loss attributed to the impairment or on the disposal of the assets or disposal group(s) constituting discontinued operations. See 6.8 above.	IFRS permits a one line presentation of discontinued operations comprising the total of post-tax profit or loss of discontinued operations and the post-tax gain or loss recognised on the measurement to fair value less costs to sell or on the disposal of the assets or disposal group(s) constituting the discontinued operation. No columnar analysis of each line item is required. Additional analysis of this subtotal and other disclosures regarding discontinued operations are required in the notes.
Operating profit subtotal	An operating profit subtotal is not required but FRS 102 includes guidance, where operating profit is presented. See 6.7.3 above.	Like FRS 102, IAS 1 does not require an operating profit subtotal to be presented. Its basis of conclusions includes similar guidance to FRS 102 on operating profit, where this is presented.

Chapter 6

	FRS 102	IFRS
Exceptional items	FRS 102 requires separate disclosure (in the notes or in the statement of comprehensive income / income statement) of the nature and amount of material items included in total comprehensive income. FRS 102 does not use the term 'exceptional items' (although the term is used in the Regulations and LLP Regulations). Like other profit and loss account items, exceptional items should be included in the applicable heading. The adapted formats are less prescriptive as to the headings required than statutory formats. FRS 102 does not specify 'exceptional items' to be presented below operating profit. See 6.7.5 above.	IAS 1 has the same requirements as FRS 102 (although the requirements of the Regulations or LLP Regulations do not apply).
Extraordinary items	Extraordinary items are not permitted where Schedule 1 to the Regulations or the LLP Regulations are applied. See 6.7.6 above.	IAS 1 does not have a concept of an extraordinary item.
Current and fixed assets (balance sheet statutory formats)	*Statutory formats* The statutory formats in Schedule 1 to the Regulations and the LLP Regulations distinguish between current and fixed assets. Fixed assets are defined as assets of a company which are intended for use on a continuing basis in the company's activities, and current assets are assets not intended for such use. Current assets include debtors, even if these include items expected to be realised after more than one year. The definition of current and fixed assets differs to that for current and non-current assets in IAS 1. FRS 102 requires disclosure of the amounts of debtors due after more than one year on the face of the statement of financial position where the amounts are so material in the context of net current assets, that the financial statements may otherwise be misinterpreted. The analysis of amounts due within and after more than one year must be presented for each line item in debtors in the notes (if not on the face of the balance sheet). See 5.2.2 above.	IAS 1 distinguishes between current assets (defined) and non-current assets (the residual), which are separate classifications on the statement of financial position. A presentation based on liquidity can be used where it provides reliable and more relevant information. Line items containing amounts falling due within and after more than one year must be separately analysed in the notes.

Creditors: amounts falling due within and after more than one year (balance sheet statutory formats)	*Statutory formats* The statutory formats in Schedule 1 to the Regulations and the LLP Regulations distinguish between Creditors: amounts falling due within one year and Creditors: amounts falling due after more than one year. These differ from the definitions of current and non-current liabilities in IAS 1. For example, under IAS 1, an item which is not due for settlement within 12 months is reported as a current liability if the entity expects to settle it in its operating cycle. See 5.2.3 above.	IAS 1 distinguishes between current liabilities and non-current liabilities, which are separate classifications on the statement of financial position. IAS 1 has detailed guidance on when a financial liability should be classified as current or non-current. A presentation based on liquidity can be used instead of a current-non-current analysis where it provides reliable and more relevant information. Line items containing amounts falling due within and after more than one year must be separately analysed in the notes.
Adapted balance sheet formats in Schedule 1 to the Regulations	*Adapted formats* Where adapted formats in Schedule 1 to the Regulations or the LLP Regulations are applied, the statement of financial position must show the headings specified in Section 4 (similar to IAS 1), with separate classifications for current assets, non-current assets, current liabilities and non-current liabilities (see 5.1 above). FRS 102 specifies a supplementary analysis of certain headings to be given in the statement of financial position or in the notes.	IAS 1 distinguishes between current assets, non-current assets, current liabilities and non-current liabilities which are separate classifications on the statement of financial position. A presentation based on liquidity can be used instead of a current-non-current analysis where it provides reliable and more relevant information. Line items containing amounts falling due within and after more than one year must be separately analysed in the notes (this is not required under FRS 102, where adapted formats are applied).
Provisions	*Statutory formats* There is a single heading 'provisions for liabilities' in the balance sheet formats in Schedule 1 to the Regulations and the LLP Regulations. See 5.3.11 above. *Adapted formats* Where adapted formats in Schedule 1 to the Regulations or the LLP Regulations are applied, the presentation of provisions is consistent with IAS 1. See 5.1.9 above.	IAS 1 requires current and non-current provisions to be shown as separate line items on the face of the statement of financial position.
Deferred tax	*Statutory formats* Deferred tax is shown as a debtor or within provisions for liabilities under the balance sheet formats in Schedule 1 to the Regulations and the LLP Regulations. See 5.3.13.B above. *Adapted formats* Where adapted formats in Schedule 1 to the Regulations or the LLP Regulations are applied, the presentation of deferred tax is consistent with IAS 1. See 5.1.11 above.	IAS 1 requires deferred tax to be shown as a separate line item on the face of the statement of financial position, classified as a non-current asset or non-current liability.

Chapter 6

	FRS 102	*IFRS*
Retirement benefits	*Statutory formats* The presentation of assets and liabilities under defined benefit schemes is not addressed by FRS 102. An asset would generally be presented as a debtor and a liability as a provision, under Schedule 1 to the Regulations or LLP Regulations. An alternative is to apply the presentation previously used in FRS 17 (but not net of deferred tax). See 5.3.13.D above. *Adapted formats* Where adapted formats in Schedule 1 to the Regulations or the LLP Regulations are applied, there is no specified line item for defined benefit scheme assets or liabilities. Presentation is likely to be similar to IFRS practice (although FRS 102 is silent on the analysis between current and non-current). See 5.1.13.D above.	IFRS does not require assets and liabilities under defined benefit schemes to be analysed between current and non-current. Many IFRS reporters show such assets and liabilities as non-current in practice.
Assets and disposal groups held for sale	*Statutory and adapted formats* FRS 102 does not require separate presentation of assets and disposal groups held for sale. See 5.1.13.C and 5.3.13.C above. FRS 102 requires disclosures where, at the reporting date, an entity has a binding sale agreement for a major disposal of assets or a disposal group (see 5.5 above).	IAS 1 requires separate presentation in the statement of financial position of: • the total of assets classified as held for sale and assets included in disposal groups classified as held for sale in accordance with IFRS 5; and • liabilities included in disposal groups classified as held for sale in accordance with IFRS 5. Additional information is required in the notes.
Presentation of non-controlling interest in consolidated financial statements	*Statutory and adapted formats* FRS 102 requires presentation of non-controlling interest as a separate component of equity in the consolidated statement of financial position. The profit or loss and total comprehensive income for the period attributable to non-controlling interest must be shown in the statement of comprehensive income. Schedule 6 to the Regulations and Schedule 3 to the LLP Regulations require presentation of non-controlling interest, meaning the amount of capital and reserves (and profit or loss) attributable to shares in subsidiary undertakings held by or on behalf of persons other than the parent and its subsidiary undertakings. This amount will usually be the same as non-controlling interest under FRS 102, although in theory differences may arise. See 4.5 above.	IAS 1 has the same presentational requirement for non-controlling interest as FRS 102. The requirements of Schedule 6 to the Regulations and Schedule 3 to the LLP Regulations do not apply.

Statement of changes in equity (SOCIE) and Statement of Income and Retained Earnings	The SOCIE is a primary statement. Where the only movements in equity arise from profit or loss, dividends, corrections of errors or changes in accounting policy, a statement of income and retained earnings can be presented instead of the SOCIE and a statement of comprehensive income. The SOCIE can be combined with the analysis of movements in reserves required by Schedule 1 to the Regulations or the LLP Regulations. See 7 above.	IAS 1 has the same requirements as FRS 102 except that there is no alternative to present a statement of income and retained earnings. While the analysis of the reserves required by Schedule 1 to the Regulations or the LLP Regulations is not required under IFRSs, similar information is presented in the SOCIE.
Items to be reported in other comprehensive income	Items reported in other comprehensive income include *inter alia*: • revaluations of property, plant and equipment; • revaluations of investments in subsidiaries, associates and jointly controlled entities (at fair value through other comprehensive income); • remeasurement gains and losses on defined benefit schemes; • exchange gains and losses on retranslation of foreign operations; and • cash flow hedges and net investment hedges. Further categories of other comprehensive income arise where IAS 39 or IFRS 9 is applied. Exchange gains and losses on retranslation of foreign operations are not subsequently reclassified to profit or loss on 'disposal' / loss of control. Schedule 1 to the Regulations and the LLP Regulations require that only realised profits are included in profit or loss (except for fair value movements in profit or loss, where the fair value accounting rules are applied). See 6.2 above.	Items reported in other comprehensive income may differ to FRS 102 (where Sections 11 and 12 are applied) principally because of different accounting requirements for financial instruments under IFRSs. Unlike FRS 102, the items must be grouped on the statement of comprehensive income between: • items that may be reclassified to profit and loss in a subsequent period; and • items that may be reclassified subsequently to profit and loss (which, unlike FRS 102, include exchange gains and losses on retranslation of foreign operations). The statutory requirements on only including realised profits (with certain exceptions) in profit or loss do not apply.
Prior year adjustments	Prior year adjustments are required for retrospective correction for material errors, changes in accounting policies and reclassifications of items. The adjustment is shown as an item in the statement of changes in equity (or where presented, statement of income and retained earnings). See 3.6.2 and 7 above.	IAS 1's requirements are the same as FRS 102 (except there is no statement of income and retained earnings). IAS 1 additionally requires presentation of a third balance sheet at the beginning of the comparative period, where there is a restatement of comparatives.

Chapter 6

	FRS 102	*IFRS*
Presentation of associates and jointly controlled entities	*Statutory formats* Schedules 1 and 6 to the Regulations and the LLP Regulations only require fixed asset investments to be presented as a main heading on the face of the balance sheet. In group accounts, income from associated undertakings – which would generally include both associates and jointly controlled entities accounted by the equity method – is a line item in the profit and loss account formats. See 5.3.4.B and 6.6.5 above. *Adapted formats* Where adapted formats in Schedule 1 to the Regulations or the LLP Regulations are applied, • investments in associates and investments in jointly controlled entities are separate line items on the face of the statement of financial position (the line items do not distinguish whether the investments are accounted for by the equity method); and • a single line for the share of profits or losses of investments in jointly controlled entities and associates accounted for by the equity method is shown on the face of the statement of comprehensive income. See 5.1 and 6.5 above. *FRS 102 supplementary requirements (applicable to both statutory and adapted formats)* • The share of other comprehensive income of associates and jointly controlled entities accounted for by the equity method (combined) is a line item on the face of the statement of comprehensive income. • The carrying amounts of investments in associates and the carrying amounts of investments in jointly controlled entities are disclosed (this can be in the notes). • The share of profits or losses of investments (and the share of any discontinued operations) of jointly controlled entities accounted for by the equity method; and of associates accounted for by the equity method are disclosed (this can be in the notes). • There are other disclosures, but generally less extensive than IFRS.	IAS 1's presentational requirements for investments in associates and joint ventures on the face of the primary statements are similar to those for investments in associates and jointly controlled entities where adapted formats are applied in FRS 102. However, the statement of financial position only has a single line item for investments accounted for using the equity method. IFRS generally has more extensive disclosures for associates and joint arrangements (including joint ventures), including financial information on individually material investments in joint ventures and associates (unless an exemption applies).

Reduced disclosure framework (and other disclosure exemptions)	*Reduced disclosure framework* The reduced disclosure framework is available in individual financial statements of qualifying entities only, where the conditions for its use are met. The reduced disclosure framework allows for exemption from preparing a cash flow statement, certain financial instruments disclosures (for non-financial institutions), certain share-based payment disclosures and disclosure of key management personnel compensation. The share-based payment and financial instruments disclosure exemptions require 'equivalent disclosures' to be included in the publicly available consolidated financial statements in which the qualifying entity is consolidated. *Related party transactions – all entities* FRS 102 does not require disclosure of intra-group related party transactions (providing that any subsidiary that is party to the transaction is wholly owned by a member of the group). *Cash flow exemptions* FRS 102 does not require the following entities to prepare a cash flow statement: • mutual life assurance companies; • retirement benefit plans; • investment funds that meet certain conditions (i.e. that substantially all of the entity's investments are highly liquid and are carried at fair value and a statement of changes in net assets is provided); • a small entity (applying Section 1A or the full version of FRS 102)). SORPs may restrict use of this exemption, e.g. the Charities SORP (FRS 102), Update Bulletin 1 only allows small charities below a lower size threshold to omit a cash flow statement.	There are no reduced disclosures for subsidiaries and parents, cash flow exemptions or exemptions for small entities available under IFRSs.
Notes: judgements and estimation uncertainty	FRS 102 requires disclosure of: • judgements, apart from those involving estimations, in applying accounting policies; and • key assumptions and sources of estimation uncertainty at the reporting date that have a significant risk of causing a material adjustment to the carrying amounts of assets and liabilities within the next financial year. See 8.3 and 8.4 above.	Same requirement as FRS 102 but IAS 1 provides more guidance on disclosure of judgements and key assumptions and sources of estimation uncertainty.

Chapter 6

	FRS 102	*IFRS*
Notes: sources of disclosure requirements	FRS 102 and the CA 2006, the Regulations or LLP Regulations (and other applicable regulations) include disclosure requirements for the notes. The LLP SORP also has additional disclosure requirements relevant to FRS 102 financial statements of LLPs.	IFRS's disclosures are more extensive than those required by FRS 102. The disclosures required by Schedules 1 to 3, and 6 to the Regulations or Schedules 1 and 3 to the LLP Regulations do not apply to IAS accounts. However, IAS accounts must comply with disclosures in the CA 2006, and other applicable schedules of the Regulations or LLP Regulations (and other applicable regulations).
Statement of compliance	A statement of compliance that the financial statements are prepared in accordance with FRS 102 (and where applicable, FRS 103) is required. Where an entity is a public benefit entity, a statement to this effect must also be included. The Regulations (and the LLP Regulations) require large and medium-sized companies (and LLPs) to state that the accounts have been prepared in accordance with applicable accounting standards, giving particulars of any departures. Medium-sized companies (and LLPs) do not need to give this statement in their individual accounts. See 3.8 above.	A statement of compliance that the financial statements are prepared in accordance with IFRSs (or EU-adopted IFRSs, where applicable) is required. The requirements in the Regulations (and the LLP Regulations) to state that the accounts have been prepared in accordance with applicable accounting standards do not apply.

References

1 The Statutory Auditors Regulations 2017 (SI 2017/1164), para. 2(5)(a), Schedule 3 para. 4.
2 *Unregistered Companies Regulations 2009* (SI 2009/2436, para. 10 (amended by SI 2013/1972, para. 2).
3 *Partnerships (Accounts) Regulations 2008* (SI 2008/569), para. 4 and Schedule.
4 *Partnerships (Accounts) Regulations 2008* (SI 2008/569), para. 4 and Schedule.
5 *Partnerships (Accounts) Regulations 2008* (SI 2008/569), para. 4 and Schedule.
6 LLPs – Note 3 on the balance sheet formats in Section B of Part 1 of Schedule 1 to LLP Regulations (SI 2008/1913).
7 Note 1 on the balance sheet formats in Section B of Part 1 of Schedule 1 to SI 2008/410.
8 LLPs – Note 1 on the balance sheet formats in Section B of Part 1 of Schedule 1 to SI 2008/1913.
9 LLPs – Note 2 on the balance sheet formats in Section B of Part 1 of Schedule 1 to SI 2008/1913.
10 LLPs – Regulation 5 and Schedule 2 to SI 2008/1913.
11 LLPs – para. 18 of Schedule 3 to SI 2008/1913.
12 LLPs – Note 6 on the balance sheet formats in Section B of Part 1 of Schedule 1 to SI 2008/1913.
13 LLPs – Note 3 on the balance sheet formats in Section B of Part 1 of Schedule 1 to SI 2008/1913.
14 Note 6 on the balance sheet formats in Section B of Part 1 of Schedule 1 to SI 2008/410. For LLPs, the alternative position is line item C (note 4 to the balance sheet formats in Section B of Part 1 of Schedule 1 to SI 2008/1913).

15 LLPs – Note 5 on the balance sheet formats in Section B of Part 1 of Schedule 1 to SI 2008/1913.

16 LLPs – Note 7 on the balance sheet formats in Section B of Part 1 of Schedule 1 to SI 2008/1913.

17 Note 10 on the balance sheet formats in Section B of Part 1 of Schedule 1 to SI 2008/410. For LLPs, the alternative position is line item I (note 8 on the balance sheet formats in Section B of Part 1 of Schedule 1 to SI 2008/1913).

18 LLPs – Note 9 on the balance sheet formats in Section B of Part 1 of Schedule 1 to LLP Regulations (SI 2008/1913).

19 Note 12 on the balance sheet formats in Section B of Part 1 of Schedule 1 to SI 2008/410.

20 LLPs – Note 12 on the profit and loss accounts (format 1) in Section B of Part 1 of Schedule 1 to SI 2008/1913.

21 LLPs – Note 13 on the profit and loss account formats (format 1) in Section B of Part 1 of Schedule 1 to SI 2008/1913.

22 LLPs – Note 14 on the profit and loss account formats (format 1) in Section B of Part 1 of Schedule 1 to SI 2008/1913.

23 Corporate Reporting Thematic Review-Alternative Performance Measures (APMs), November 2017.

24 www.esma.europa.eu/

25 LLPs – Note 15 on the profit and loss accounts (format 1) in Section B of Part 1 of Schedule 1 to SI 2008/1913.

26 *The Statutory Auditors and Third Country Auditors Regulations 2016* (SI 2016/649), paras. 1(4), 18.

27 *Partnership (Accounts) Regulations*, para. 4(2)

28 See, for example, the FRC's Corporate Reporting Review: Annual Report 2015 (October 2015), section 5.2.

29 Lab case study report – William Hill: accounting policies, FRC Lab, February 2015.

30 The Registrars' Rules require that the filed copy of the annual accounts is also signed by a director.

31 *True and Fair*, FRC, June 2014.

32 *Going Concern and Liquidity Risks: Lessons for Companies and Auditors – Final Report and Recommendations of the Panel of Inquiry*, The Sharman Inquiry, June 2012.

33 *Guidance on the Going Concern Basis of Accounting and Reporting on Solvency and Liquidity Risk – Guidance for directors of companies that do not apply The UK Corporate Governance Code*, April 2016, FRC, Summary and paras. 1.1-1.4.

34 *Guidance on the Going Concern Basis of Accounting and Reporting on Solvency and Liquidity Risk – Guidance for directors of companies that do not apply The UK Corporate Governance Code*, April 2016, FRC, para. 2.1.

35 *Guidance on the Going Concern Basis of Accounting and Reporting on Solvency and Liquidity Risk – Guidance for directors of companies that do not apply The UK Corporate Governance Code*, April 2016, FRC, paras. 2.3, 4.1-4.3.

36 *Guidance on the Going Concern Basis of Accounting and Reporting on Solvency and Liquidity Risk – Guidance for directors of companies that do not apply The UK Corporate Governance Code*, April 2016, FRC, para. 2.2.

37 *Guidance on the Going Concern Basis of Accounting and Reporting on Solvency and Liquidity Risk – Guidance for directors of companies that do not apply The UK Corporate Governance Code*, April 2016, FRC, para. 2.4.

38 *Guidance on the Going Concern Basis of Accounting and Reporting on Solvency and Liquidity Risk – Guidance for directors of companies that do not apply The UK Corporate Governance Code*, April 2016, FRC, Summary.

39 *Guidance on the Going Concern Basis of Accounting and Reporting on Solvency and Liquidity Risk – Guidance for directors of companies that do not apply The UK Corporate Governance Code*, April 2016, FRC, paras. 5.1-5.19.

40 *Guidance on the Going Concern Basis of Accounting and Reporting on Solvency and Liquidity Risk – Guidance for directors of companies that do not apply The UK Corporate Governance Code*, April 2016, FRC, paras. 4.4-4.7.

41 *Guidance on the Going Concern Basis of Accounting and Reporting on Solvency and Liquidity Risk – Guidance for directors of companies that do not apply The UK Corporate Governance Code*, April 2016, FRC, paras. 3.5-3.6.

42 *Guidance on the Going Concern Basis of Accounting and Reporting on Solvency and Liquidity Risk – Guidance for directors of companies that do not apply The UK Corporate Governance Code*, April 2016, FRC, para. 3.8.

43 *Guidance on the Going Concern Basis of Accounting and Reporting on Solvency and Liquidity Risk – Guidance for directors of companies that do not apply The UK Corporate Governance Code*, April 2016, FRC, para. 3.1.

Chapter 6

44 *Guidance on the Going Concern Basis of Accounting and Reporting on Solvency and Liquidity Risk – Guidance for directors of companies that do not apply The UK Corporate Governance Code*, April 2016, FRC, paras. 3.2-3.4.

45 *Guidance on the Going Concern Basis of Accounting and Reporting on Solvency and Liquidity Risk – Guidance for directors of companies that do not apply The UK Corporate Governance Code*, April 2016, FRC, para. 3.8.

46 *Guidance on the Going Concern Basis of Accounting and Reporting on Solvency and Liquidity Risk – Guidance for directors of companies that do not apply The UK Corporate Governance Code*, April 2016, FRC, paras. 3.9-3.10.

47 *Guidance on the Going Concern Basis of Accounting and Reporting on Solvency and Liquidity Risk – Guidance for directors of companies that do not apply The UK Corporate Governance Code*, April 2016, FRC, para. 4.10.

48 *Guidance on the Going Concern Basis of Accounting and Reporting on Solvency and Liquidity Risk – Guidance for directors of companies that do not apply The UK Corporate Governance Code*, April 2016, FRC, para. 4.11.

49 *Guidance on the Going Concern Basis of Accounting and Reporting on Solvency and Liquidity Risk – Guidance for directors of companies that do not apply The UK Corporate Governance Code*, April 2016, FRC, para. 4.3.

50 *Guidance on the Going Concern Basis of Accounting and Reporting on Solvency and Liquidity Risk – Guidance for directors of companies that do not apply The UK Corporate Governance Code*, April 2016, FRC, paras. 6.1-6.2.

51 *Guidance on the Going Concern Basis of Accounting and Reporting on Solvency and Liquidity Risk – Guidance for directors of companies that do not apply The UK Corporate Governance Code*, April 2016, FRC, para. 4.9.

52 *Guidance on the Going Concern Basis of Accounting and Reporting on Solvency and Liquidity Risk – Guidance for directors of companies that do not apply The UK Corporate Governance Code*, April 2016, FRC, paras. 6.3-6.7.

53 *Listing Rules*, FCA, LR 9.8.6(5)-(6).

54 *Listing Rules*, FCA, LR 9.8.6(3).

55 *Disclosure and Transparency Rules*, FCA, DTR 7.2.5 and DTR 7.2.10.

Chapter 7   Statement of cash flows

Chapter 7   Statement of cash flows

1   INTRODUCTION

A statement of cash flows provides useful information about an entity's activities in generating cash to repay debt, distribute dividends or reinvest to maintain or expand operating capacity; about its financing activities, both debt and equity; and about its investing and spending of cash. This information, when combined with information in the rest of the financial statements, is useful in assessing factors that may affect the entity's liquidity, financial flexibility, profitability and risk.

Section 7 – *Statement of Cash Flows* – is based on the equivalent IFRS standard IAS 7 – *Statement of Cash Flows*. However a number of the explanatory paragraphs within IAS 7 have not been incorporated into Section 7 of FRS 102.

The statement of cash flows required provides information about the changes in cash and cash equivalents for a reporting period, classifying these between operating activities, investing activities and financing activities. *[FRS 102.7.1].*

2   COMPARISON BETWEEN SECTION 7 AND IFRS

Apart from the scope exemptions discussed at 2.1 below, Section 7 of FRS 102 is essentially the same as IAS 7. However, a number of the explanatory paragraphs from IAS 7 have been excluded. The paragraphs that have been excluded generally provide further detail, although applying Section 2 – *Concepts and Pervasive Principles* – could well lead a preparer of the financial statements to the same answer under FRS 102 in most situations. The principal differences are discussed at 2.1 to 2.3 below.

2.1   Entities exempt from preparing a statement of cash flows

There are no exemptions from preparing a statement of cash flows in IAS 7.

In contrast, FRS 102 allows the following entities an exemption from preparing a statement of cash flows:

- qualifying entities (see Chapter 3);
- mutual life assurance companies;
- retirement benefit plans; and
- investment funds meeting certain conditions. *[FRS 102.1.12(b), FRS 102.7.1A].*

Additionally, a financial institution that undertakes the business of effecting or carrying out insurance contracts should include the cash flows of their long-term business only to the extent of cash transferred and available to meet the obligations of the company or group as a whole. *[FRS 102.7.10E]*.

A small entity is not required to comply with Section 7 even if it does not apply Section 1A – *Small Entities*. *[FRS 102.7.1B]*. However, a small entity may be required to prepare a statement of cash flows by an applicable Statement of Recommended Practice (SORP), for example small charities with gross income exceeding £500,000 are required by the *Charities SORP (FRS 102)* to prepare a cash flow statement (see Chapter 5 at 7.1). *[FRS 102.3.1B]*.

2.2   Presentation using the indirect method

IAS 7 allows an alternative presentation for the indirect method whereby the net cash flow from operating activities may be presented by showing the revenues and expenses disclosed in the statement of comprehensive income and the changes during the period in inventories and operating receivables and payables. *[IAS 7.20]*.

This alternative presentation option is not available under Section 7.

2.3   Cash flows of discontinued operations

IFRS 5 – *Non-current Assets Held for Sale and Discontinued Operations* – requires an entity to disclose the net cash flows attributable to the operating, investing and financing activities of discontinued operations. These disclosures can be presented either on the face of the statement of cash flows or in the notes. Disclosure is not required for disposal groups that are newly acquired subsidiaries which are classified as held for sale on acquisition in accordance with IFRS 5. *[IFRS 5.33(c)]*.

FRS 102 does not contain any requirements to make disclosures in respect of cash flows from discontinued operations. However, aggregate cash flows arising from obtaining or losing control of subsidiaries or other businesses are shown separately within investing activities. *[FRS 102.7.10]*.

3   THE REQUIREMENTS OF SECTION 7 FOR A STATEMENT OF CASH FLOWS

Section 7 specifies how entities report information about the historical changes in cash and cash equivalents and has a relatively flexible approach, which allows them to be applied to all entities including financial institutions. This flexibility can be seen, for example, in the way entities can determine their own policy for the classification of interest and dividend cash flows, provided that they are separately disclosed and this is applied consistently from period to period. Additional disclosure is encouraged where this provides information on an entity's specific circumstances.

3.1   Scope

Section 7 is not mandatory for entities that are 'qualifying entities' (see Chapter 3). In substance, this means that most subsidiaries, regardless of the percentage of voting rights controlled within a group, and parents that also prepare publicly available consolidated financial statements, will not need to prepare a statement of cash flows in their individual financial statements. However, a qualifying entity that prepares consolidated financial statements will have to prepare a statement of cash flows in those consolidated financial statements.

The following entities are also not required to produce a statement of cash flows:

- mutual life assurance companies;
- retirement benefit plans; or
- investment funds that meet all of the following conditions:
  - substantially all of the entity's investments are highly liquid;
  - substantially all of the entity's investments are carried at market value; and
  - the entity provides a statement of changes in net assets. *[FRS 102.7.1A]*.

A financial institution that undertakes the business of effecting or carrying out insurance contracts (other than mutual life assurance companies scoped out above) should include the cash flows of their long-term business only to the extent of cash transferred and available to meet obligations of the company or group as a whole. *[FRS 102.7.10E]*.

A small entity is not required to prepare a cash flow statement. *[FRS 102.7.1B, FRS 102.1A.7]*. This exemption applies even if the small entity does not use the small entities accounting regime in Section 1A. However, a small entity may be required to prepare a statement of cash flows by an applicable SORP, for example, small charities with gross income exceeding £500,000 are required by the *Charities SORP (FRS 102)* to prepare a cash flow statement (see Chapter 5 at 7.1). *[FRS 102.3.1B]*.

3.2   Terms used by Section 7

The following terms are used in Section 7 with the meanings specified: *[FRS 102 Appendix I]*

Term	Definition
Cash	Cash on hand and demand deposits.
Cash equivalents	Short term, highly liquid investments that are readily convertible to known amounts of cash and that are subject to an insignificant risk of changes in value.
Cash flows	Inflows and outflows of cash and cash equivalents.
Financing activities	Activities that result in changes in the size and composition of contributed equity and borrowings of the entity.
Investing activities	The acquisition and disposal of long-term assets and other investments not included in cash equivalents.
Operating activities	The principal revenue-producing activities of the entity and other activities that are not investing or financing activities.
Statement of cash flows	Financial statement that provides information about the changes in cash and cash equivalents of an entity for a period, showing separately changes during the period from operating, investing and financing activities.

Chapter 7

3.3   Cash and cash equivalents

Since the purpose of the statement of cash flows is to provide information about changes in cash and cash equivalents, the definitions of cash and cash equivalents given in the Glossary of FRS 102 (see 3.2 above) are essential to its presentation. It is important to understand the reporting entity's cash management policies, especially when considering whether balances should be classified as cash equivalents. Section 7 states that cash equivalents (which may include some short-term investments) are:

- short-term;
- highly liquid;
- readily convertible into known amounts of cash; and
- subject to an insignificant risk of changes in value. *[FRS 102.7.2]*.

Further guidance is provided on the components of cash equivalents by stating that an investment normally qualifies as a cash equivalent only when it has a short maturity of three months or less from the date of acquisition. Bank overdrafts are normally considered financing activities unless they are repayable on demand and form an integral part of an entity's cash management, in which case they are a component of cash and cash equivalents. *[FRS 102.7.2]*.

In practice, however, determining the components of cash equivalents can be difficult. This is discussed further at 3.3.1 to 3.3.3 below.

An entity must disclose the components of cash and cash equivalents and present a reconciliation of the amounts in the cash flow statement to the equivalent amounts in the balance sheet. *[FRS 102.7.20]*. This reconciliation is needed because the Large and Medium-sized Companies and Groups (Accounts and Reports) Regulations 2008 (SI 2008/410) (the Regulations) require the separate presentation of cash at bank and in hand on the face of the balance sheet. Banking Entities that apply Schedule 2 formats must include as cash only balances at central banks and loans and advances to banks repayable on demand within cash on the balance sheet. *[FRS 102.7.20A]*.

FRS 102 states that a complete set of financial statements should include in the notes a summary of significant accounting policies, which would include a policy on how the entity determines cash equivalents. *[FRS 102.3.17(e)]*. These cash equivalents would need to meet the four conditions shown above to qualify as a cash equivalent, namely that they are short term, highly liquid investments that are readily convertible to known amounts of cash and that are subject to an insignificant risk of changes in value.

The effect of any changes in the policy for determining components of cash and cash equivalents, for example, a change in the classification of financial instruments previously considered to be part of an entity's investment portfolio, should be reported under Section 10 – *Accounting Policies, Estimates and Errors. [FRS 102.10.11(d)]*. This would require comparatives to be restated and additional disclosures given, including the reasons for the change in policy.

On the contrary, if an entity changes the purpose for which it holds certain investments, for example a deposit which was previously held for short term cash management is now held in order to generate an investment return, this would be considered a change in facts and circumstances, which would be accounted for prospectively. In these circumstances, the reclassification out of cash and cash equivalents would appear as a reconciling item in the cash flow statement, rather than as an investing cash outflow.

3.3.1   Short-term investments

As discussed at 3.3 above, for an investment to qualify as a cash equivalent it must be readily convertible to a known amount of cash and be subject to an insignificant risk of changes in value. Normally only an investment with a short maturity of, say, three months or less from the date of acquisition qualifies as a cash equivalent. Whilst Section 7 does not address the matter, it would seem logical that equity instruments will not normally meet the definition of cash equivalents as they have no maturity date and are usually exposed to a not insignificant risk of changes in value. One exception to this is where an equity instrument is a cash equivalent in substance, such as redeemable preference shares acquired within a short period to their maturity date.

When the standard refers to a 'known amount of cash' it means that the amount should be known or determinable at the date on which the investment is acquired. Accordingly, traded commodities, such as gold bullion, would not normally be expected to be cash equivalents because the proceeds to be realised from such commodities is determined at the date of disposal rather than being known or determinable when the investment is made.

3.3.2   Money market funds

Entities commonly invest in money market-type funds (MMF) such as an open-ended mutual fund that invests in money market instruments like certificates of deposit, commercial paper, treasury bills, bankers' acceptances and repurchase agreements. Although there are different types of money market funds, they generally aim to provide investors with a low-risk, low-return investment while preserving the value of the assets and maintaining a high level of liquidity. The question then arises as to whether investments in such funds can be classified as cash equivalents.

As noted below, entities may consider the underlying investments of the fund when assessing the significance of the risk of changes in value, however when determining whether classification as a cash equivalent is appropriate, the unit of account is the investment in the money market fund itself.

In order to meet the definition of a cash equivalent, an investment must be short term; highly liquid; readily convertible to a known amount of cash; and subject to insignificant risk of changes in value. Section 7 considers a maturity date of three months or less from the date of acquisition to be short-term in the context of maturity, however money market funds generally do not have a legal maturity date. However, if the investments are puttable and can be sold back to the fund at any time, they may meet the short term criterion.

Typically, investments in money market funds are redeemed directly with the fund, therefore in assessing liquidity of the investment, focus should be on the liquidity of the fund itself. In making this assessment, entities should consider the nature of any redemption restrictions in place as these may prevent the redemption of the investment in the short term. Alternatively, if a money market fund investment is quoted in an active market, it might be regarded as highly liquid on that basis.

The short-term and highly liquid investment must also be readily convertible into known amounts of cash which are subject to an insignificant risk of changes in value. *[FRS 102.7.2].*

To determine that the potential change in value of an investment in a money market fund is insignificant, an entity has to be able to conclude that the range of possible returns is very small. This evaluation is first made at the time of acquiring the investment and reassessment is required if the facts and circumstances change. The evaluation will involve consideration of factors such as the maturity of the underlying investments of the fund; the credit rating of the fund; the nature of the investments held by the fund (i.e. their fair values are not subject to volatility); the extent of diversification in the portfolio (which would normally need to be very high); the investment policy of the fund; and any mechanisms by the fund to guarantee returns (for example by reference to short-term money market interest rates).

Investments are often held for purposes other than to act as an integral part of an entity's cash management. It is therefore important, even where the criteria above are met, to understand why the entity has invested in a particular money market fund. Where an investment otherwise satisfies the criteria in paragraph 2 of section 7, but does not form an integral part of an entity's cash management, it should not be classified as a cash equivalent.

Substantial judgement may be required in assessing whether an investment in money market funds can be classified as a cash equivalent. As noted at 3.3 above, entities are required to disclose the policies adopted in determining the composition of cash equivalents and, where relevant, this should include the policy applied and judgements made in classifying investments in money market funds.

3.3.3   Investments with maturities greater than three months

An investment qualifies as a cash equivalent only when it has a short maturity of, say, three months or less from the date of acquisition. *[FRS 102.7.2]*. Therefore, an investment with a term on acquisition of, say, nine months is not reclassified as a cash equivalent from the date on which there is less than three months remaining to its maturity. If such reclassifications were permitted, the statement of cash flows would have to reflect movements between investments and cash equivalents. This would be misleading because no actual cash flows would have occurred.

An entity might justify including in cash equivalents a fixed deposit with an original term longer than three months if it effectively functions like a demand deposit. Typically, a fixed deposit will carry a penalty charge for withdrawal prior to maturity. A penalty will usually indicate that the investment is held for investment purposes rather than for the purpose of meeting short-term cash needs. However, some fixed deposits carry a penalty whereby the entity will forego the higher interest that it would have received if held to maturity, but would still receive interest at a prevailing demand deposit rate. In this case, it may be arguable that there is effectively no significant penalty for early withdrawal, as the entity receives at least the same return that it otherwise would have in a demand deposit arrangement. Where an entity classifies such an investment as a cash equivalent, on the basis that it is held for meeting short-term cash needs, then interest should be accrued on a consistent basis. In this example, the entity should consider accruing interest receivable at the demand deposit rate, thus reflecting their expectation that the deposit will be withdrawn before its maturity date.

3.3.4   Restrictions on the use of cash and cash equivalents

As discussed at 3.13 below, an entity must disclose, together with a commentary by management, the amount of significant cash and cash equivalent balances held by the entity that are not available for use by the entity. *[FRS 102.7.21]*. The nature of the restriction must be assessed to determine if the balance is ineligible for inclusion in cash equivalents because the restriction results in the investment ceasing to be highly liquid or readily convertible. For example, when an entity covenants to maintain a minimum level of cash or deposits as security for certain short term obligations, and provided that no amounts are required to be designated for that specific purpose, such balances could still be regarded as cash equivalents, albeit subject to restrictions, as part of a policy of managing resources to meet short-term commitments.

However, an entity may be required formally to set aside cash, for example by way of a deposit into an escrow account, as part of a specific project or transaction, such as the acquisition or construction of a property. In such circumstances, it is necessary to consider the terms and conditions relating to the account and the conditions relating to both the entity's and counterparty's access to the funds within it to determine whether it is appropriate for the deposit to be classified as cash equivalents.

3.4   Information to be presented in the statement of cash flows

The statement of cash flows reports inflows and outflows of cash and cash equivalents during the period classified under:

- operating activities (see 3.5 below);
- investing activities (see 3.6 below); and
- financing activities (see 3.7 below). *[FRS 102.7.3]*.

This classification is intended to allow users to assess the impact of these three types of activities on the financial position of the entity and the amount of its cash and cash equivalents. Although the presentation is not required to follow this layout, we would expect it to be followed in practice. Comparative figures are required for all items in the statement of cash flows and the related notes. *[FRS 102.3.14]*.

Section 7 provides no guidance on how to report different types of cash flows arising from a single transaction. However, there is no prohibition on split presentation so, for example, when the cash repayment of a loan includes both interest and capital, the interest element may be classified as an operating activity and the capital element classified as a financing activity.

3.5   Reporting cash flows from operating activities

Operating activities are the principal revenue-producing activities of the entity and other activities that are not investing or financing activities. *[FRS 102.7.4, Appendix I]*. This means that operating is the 'default' category, with all cash flows that do not fall within either the investing or financing classifications being automatically deemed to be operating.

Chapter 7

Cash flows from operating activities generally result from transactions and other events that enter into the determination of profit or loss. Examples include:

- cash receipts from the sale of goods and the rendering of services;
- cash receipts from royalties, fees, commissions and other revenue;
- cash payments to suppliers for goods and services;
- cash payments to and on behalf of employees;
- cash payments or refunds of income tax, unless they are can be specifically identified with financing and investing activities;
- cash receipts and payments from investments, loans and other contracts held for dealing or trading purposes, which are similar to inventory acquired specifically for resale; and
- cash advances and loans made by financial institutions. *[FRS 102.7.4].*

An example of an item that enters into the determination of profit or loss that is not usually an operating cash flow is the proceeds from the sale of property, plant and equipment, which are usually included in cash flows from investing activities. *[FRS 102.7.4].*

Cash flows from operating activities may be presented using either:

- the indirect method; or
- the direct method. *[FRS 102.7.7].*

FRS 102 does not express a preference for the method to be used.

3.5.1   Indirect method

Under the indirect method, an entity presents a reconciliation determining the net cash flow from operating activities by adjusting a measure of profit or loss disclosed in the statement of comprehensive income (or separate income statement if presented) for the effects of:

- changes during the period in inventories and operating receivables and payables;
- non-cash items such as depreciation, provisions, deferred tax, accrued income/(expenses) not yet received/(paid) in cash, unrealised foreign currency gains and losses, undistributed profits of associates, and non-controlling interests; and
- all other items for which the cash effects relate to investing or financing activities. *[FRS 102.7.8].*

Prior to the *Amendments to FRS 102 Triennial review 2017 – Incremental improvements and clarifications (Triennial review 2017)*, cash flow statements prepared using the indirect method should have used profit after tax as a starting point.[1] While we expect some companies will continue to follow this approach, other measures of profit which appear as subtotals on the income statement, such as operating profit or profit before tax, may be used.

The reconciliation of net cash flows from operating activities may be presented either on the face of the cash flow statement or in a note.[2]

3.5.2   Direct method

The direct method arrives at the same value for net cash flow from operating activities, but does so by disclosing major classes of gross cash receipts and gross cash payments. Such information may be obtained either:

- from the accounting records of the entity (essentially based on an analysis of the cash book); or
- by adjusting sales, cost of sales and other items in the statement of comprehensive income (or income statement if presented) for:
    - changes during the period in inventories and operating receivables and payables;
    - other non-cash items; and
    - other items for which the cash effects are investing or financing cash flows. *[FRS 102.7.9]*.

3.6   Reporting cash flows from investing activities

Unless a net presentation is permitted under FRS 102 (see 3.8 below), an entity should present separately major classes of gross cash receipts and gross cash payments arising from investing and financing activities. *[FRS 102.7.10]*.

Investing activities are defined as the acquisition and disposal of long-term assets and other investments not included in cash equivalents. *[FRS 102.7.5]*. This separate category of cash flows allows users of the financial statements to understand the extent to which expenditures have been made for resources intended to generate future income and cash flows. Cash flows arising from investing activities include:

- payments to acquire, and receipts from the sale of, property, plant and equipment, intangibles and other long-term assets (including payments relating to capitalised development costs and self-constructed property, plant and equipment);
- payments to acquire, and receipts from the sale of, equity or debt instruments of other entities and interests in joint ventures, including the net cash flows arising from obtaining or losing control of subsidiaries or other businesses (other than payments and receipts for those instruments considered to be cash equivalents or those held for dealing or trading purposes);
- advances and loans made to, and repaid by, other parties (other than advances and loans made by a financial institution); and
- payments for, and receipts from, futures contracts, forward contracts, option contracts and swap contracts, except when the contracts are held for dealing or trading purposes, or the cash flows are classified as financing activities.

When a contract is accounted for as a hedge, an entity should classify the cash flows of the contract in the same manner as the item being hedged. *[FRS 102.7.5]*.

Chapter 7

3.7   Reporting cash flows from financing activities

Financing activities are defined as those activities that result in changes in the size and composition of the contributed equity and borrowings of the entity. *[FRS 102.7.6]*.

Cash flows arising from financing activities include:

- proceeds from issuing shares or other equity instruments;
- payments to owners to acquire or redeem the entity's shares;
- proceeds from issuing, and outflows to repay, debentures, loans, notes, bonds, mortgages and other short or long-term borrowings; and
- payments by a lessee for the reduction of the outstanding liability relating to a finance lease. *[FRS 102.7.6]*.

Major classes of gross receipts and gross payments arising from financing activities should be reported separately, except for those items that are permitted to be reported on a net basis, as discussed at 3.8 below. *[FRS 102.7.10]*.

3.8   Reporting cash flows on a net basis

In general, major classes of gross receipts and gross payments should be reported separately, except to the extent that net presentation is specifically permitted. *[FRS 102.7.10]*. Operating, investing or financing cash flows may be reported on a net basis if they arise from:

- cash flows that reflect the activities of customers rather than those of the entity and are thereby made on behalf of customers; or
- cash flows that relate to items in which the turnover is quick, the amounts are large, and the maturities are short. *[FRS 102.7.10A]*.

Examples of cash receipts and payments that reflect the activities of customers rather than those of the entity include:

- the acceptance and repayment of demand deposits by a bank;
- funds held for customers by an investment entity; and
- rents collected on behalf of, and paid over to, the owners of properties. *[FRS 102.7.10B]*.

Other transactions where the entity is acting as an agent or collector for another party would be included in the category of cash receipts and payments that reflect the activities of the customers rather than those of the entities, such as the treatment of cash receipts and payments relating to concession sales.

Examples of cash receipts and payments in which turnover is quick, the amounts are large and the maturities are short include advances made for and the repayment of:

- principal amounts relating to credit card customers;
- the purchase and sale of investments; and
- other short-term borrowings, such as those with a maturity on draw down of three months or less. *[FRS 102.7.10C]*.

Financial institutions may report certain cash flows on a net basis. *[FRS 102.7.10D]*. These cash flows are:

- cash receipts and payments for the acceptance and repayment of deposits with a fixed maturity date;

- the placement of deposits with and withdrawal of deposits from other financial institutions; and

- cash advances and loans made to customers and the repayment of those advances and loans. *[FRS 102.34.33]*.

3.9   Foreign currency cash flows

Cash flows arising from transactions in a foreign currency should be reported in the entity's functional currency in the statement of cash flows by applying the exchange rate between the functional currency and the foreign currency at the date of the cash flow or an exchange rate that approximates the actual rate (for example, a weighted average exchange rate for the period). *[FRS 102.7.11]*. Similarly, the cash flows of a foreign subsidiary should be translated using the exchange rate between the group's presentation currency and the foreign currency of the subsidiary at the date of the cash flow or at an exchange rate that approximates the actual rate. *[FRS 102.7.12]*.

Unrealised gains and losses arising from changes in foreign currency exchange rates are not cash flows. However, to reconcile cash and cash equivalents at the beginning and the end of the period, the effect of exchange rate changes on cash and cash equivalents held or due in a foreign currency must be presented in the statement of cash flows. Therefore, an entity should remeasure cash and cash equivalents held during the reporting period (such as amounts of foreign currency held and foreign currency bank accounts) at period-end exchange rates. The entity should present the resulting unrealised gain or loss separately from cash flows from operating, investing and financing activities. *[FRS 102.7.13]*. This is illustrated in the example at 3.17 below.

3.10   Interest and dividends

An entity is required to disclose separately cash flows from interest and dividends received and paid, and their classification as either operating, investing or financing activities should be applied in a consistent manner from period to period. *[FRS 102.7.14]*.

Interest paid can either be classified as an operating cash flow (because it is included in profit and loss) or as a financing cash flow because it is a cost of obtaining financial resources.

Interest and dividends received can either be classified as operating cash flows, as they are included in profit and loss, or they may be classified as investing cash flows because they represent returns on investments. *[FRS 102.7.15]*.

Dividends paid can either be classified as a financing cash flow (because they are a cost of obtaining financial resources) or as a component of cash flows from operating activities because they are paid out of operating cash flows. *[FRS 102.7.16]*.

The flexibility in the above paragraphs of Section 7 means that all of these treatments are equally acceptable. Nevertheless, it could be argued that entities which do not include interest or dividends received within revenue should not include interest or dividends in operating cash flows because cash flows from operating activities are primarily derived from the principal revenue-producing activities of the entity. *[FRS 102.7.4]*. On this basis, interest paid would be a financing cash flow and interest and dividends received classified as investing cash flows. *[FRS 102.7.15]*. Such entities would also treat dividends paid as a financing cash flow, because they are a cost of obtaining financial resources. *[FRS 102.7.16]*.

3.11   Income tax

Cash flows arising from taxes on income should be separately disclosed within operating cash flows unless they can be specifically identified with investing or financing activities. Where tax cash flows are allocated over more than one class of activity, FRS 102 requires that the total amount of taxes paid be disclosed. *[FRS 102.7.17]*. It is possible to match elements of tax expense to transactions for which cash flows are classified under investing or financing activities. However, taxes paid are usually classified as cash flows from operating activities because it is often impracticable to match tax cash flows with specific elements of tax expense and because those tax cash flows may arise in a different period from the underlying transaction.

3.12   Non cash transactions

Non-cash transactions only ever appear in a statement of cash flows as adjustments to profit or loss for the period when using the indirect method of presenting cash flows from operating activities (as discussed at 3.5.1 above). Investing and financing transactions that do not involve cash or cash equivalents are always excluded from the statement of cash flows. Disclosure is required elsewhere in the financial statements in order to provide all relevant information about these investing and financing activities. *[FRS 102.7.18]*. Examples of such non-cash transactions include:

- acquiring assets by assuming directly related liabilities or by means of a finance lease;
- issuing equity as consideration for the acquisition of another entity; and
- the conversion of debt to equity. *[FRS 102.7.19]*.

Asset exchange transactions and the issue of bonus shares out of retained earnings are other examples of investing and financing transactions that do not involve cash or cash equivalents but require disclosure.

3.13 Disclosure of cash and cash equivalents not available for use

The amount of significant cash and cash equivalent balances held by the entity that are not available for use by the entity should be disclosed, together with a commentary by management. *[FRS 102.7.21]*. These restrictions may be due to foreign exchange controls or legal restrictions.

3.14 Direct cash flows arising from insurance contracts

FRS 103 – *Insurance Contracts* – requires that, when an insurance entity presents its operating cash flows using the direct method, it should separately disclose cash flows arising from insurance contracts. *[FRS 103.4.5(a)]*.

3.15 Cash flows arising from the exploration of mineral resources

As discussed in Chapter 31 at 3.1, an entity applying FRS 102 which is engaged in the exploration for and/or evaluation of mineral resources must apply IFRS 6 – *Exploration for and Evaluation of Mineral Resources*. IFRS 6 requires that an entity discloses the amounts of operating and investing cash flows arising from the exploration for and evaluation of mineral resources. *[IFRS 6.24(b)]*.

3.16 Analysis of changes in net debt

The Triennial review 2017 introduced a requirement for entities to disclose an analysis of changes in net debt in the period.

Net debt consists of the borrowings of an entity, together with any related derivatives and obligations under finance leases, less any cash and cash equivalents. *[FRS 102 Appendix I]*.

The analysis should show changes in net debt from the beginning to the end of the reporting period, separately showing those movements resulting from:

- the cash flows of the entity;
- the acquisition and disposal of subsidiaries;
- new finance leases entered into;
- other non-cash changes; and
- the recognition of changes in market value and exchange rate movements.

No comparative analysis need be provided for prior periods.

When several balances (or parts thereof) from the statement of financial position have been combined to form the components of opening and closing net debt, sufficient detail should be given to enable users to identify these balances. *[FRS 102.7.22]*.

Chapter 7

The example at 3.17 below demonstrates one way in which the analysis of changes in net debt could be provided.

3.17   Example statement of cash flows using the indirect method

The following is an example of a statement of cash flows and related notes prepared using the indirect method.

Group statement of cash flows

	20X1 £000	20X0 £000
Net cash (outflow)/inflow from operating activities	(859)	3,964
Investing activities		
Dividends from joint venture	700	545
Dividends from associates	135	105
Interest received	993	345
Dividends received	200	160
Payments to acquire intangible fixed assets	(575)	(1,010)
Payments to acquire tangible fixed assets	(11,423)	(3,110)
Receipts from sales of tangible fixed assets	8,625	2,765
Payments to acquire investments	(465)	(230)
Receipts from sales of investments	125	–
Proceeds from sale of subsidiary undertaking (net of cash & cash equivalents disposed of)	2,172	–
Purchase of subsidiary undertaking (net of cash & cash equivalents acquired)	(270)	–
Net cash flow from investing activities	217	(430)
Financing activities		
Dividends paid to non-controlling interests	(30)	(30)
Dividends paid to preference shareholders	(175)	(175)
Interest paid	(973)	(1,075)
Interest element of finance lease rental payments	(40)	(50)
Issue costs on new long-term loans	(50)	(56)
Issue of ordinary share capital	175	–
Share issue costs	(100)	–
Purchase of own shares	(1,700)	–
Share purchase costs	(100)	–
New long-term loans	4,660	4,500
Repayment of long-term loans	(500)	–
Repayments of capital element of finance leases and hire purchase contracts	(370)	(243)
Equity dividends paid	(1,431)	(1,170)
Net cash flow from financing activities	(634)	1,701
(Decrease)/Increase in cash and cash equivalents	(1,276)	5,235
Effect of exchange rates on cash and cash equivalents	(120)	(78)
Cash and cash equivalents at 1 January	7,560	2,403
Cash and cash equivalents at 31 December	6,164	7,560

Notes to the statement of cash flows
Reconciliation of profit to net cash (outflow)/inflow from
operating activities

	20X1	20X0
	£000	£000
Group profit for the year before taxation	8,694	7,547
Adjustments to reconcile profit for the year to net cash flow from operating activities		
Loss on revaluation of investment properties	350	474
Depreciation and impairment of tangible fixed assets	5,590	2,610
Amortisation of development expenditure	125	40
Amortisation of patents	50	10
Amortisation of goodwill	160	25
Share-based payment	412	492
Difference between pension charge and cash contributions	(46)	(196)
Increase in provision for maintenance warranties	200	50
Increase in provision for National Insurance contributions on share options	4	4
Provision for maintenance warranties utilised	(219)	(25)
Deferred government grants released	(1,012)	(530)
Share of income from associates and joint ventures	(2,910)	(1,262)
(Profit)/loss on disposal of tangible fixed assets	(1,250)	850
Loss on disposal of fixed asset investments	350	–
Loss on sale of discontinued operations	2,037	–
Net finance costs	167	820
Working capital movements		
Increase in debtors	(4,475)	(2,694)
Increase in stocks	(4,332)	(2,529)
Decrease in creditors	(1,917)	(389)
Taxation		
Corporation tax paid (including advance corporation tax)	(2,379)	(1,218)
Overseas tax paid	(458)	(115)
	(9,553)	(3,583)
Net cash (outflow)/inflow from operating activities	(859)	3,964

Cash and cash equivalents
Cash and cash equivalents comprise the following;

	Group	Group
	At	*At*
	31 December	*31 December*
	20X1	20X0
	£000	£000
Cash at bank and in hand	5,441	69,291
Short-term deposits	1,483	2,039
	6,924	11,330
Bank overdrafts	(760)	(3,770)
Cash and cash equivalents	6,164	7,560

Chapter 7

Analysis of changes in net debt

	Cash and cash equivalents £000	Bank borrowings £000	Derivatives £000	Net debt £000
As at 1 January 20X1	7,560	(2,753)	(180)	4,627
Cash flows	(1,276)	(4,160)	224	(5,212)
Interest		(406)	(34)	(440)
Fair value changes and exchange rate movements	(120)	357	419	656
As at 31 December 20X1	6,164	(6,962)	429	(369)

4   PRACTICAL ISSUES

4.1   VAT and other taxes

The presentation of VAT and other (non-income) taxes is not addressed in FRS 102 (or IAS 7).

In our view, consistent with the guidance that existed under previous UK GAAP, cash flows should be shown net of VAT and other sales taxes unless the tax is irrecoverable by the reporting entity. The net movement on the amount payable, or receivable from, the taxing authority should be allocated to cash flows from operating activities unless a different treatment is more appropriate to the particular circumstances concerned. Where restrictions apply to the recoverability of such taxes, the irrecoverable amount should be allocated to the expenditures affected by the restrictions. If this is impracticable, the irrecoverable tax should be included under the most appropriate standard heading. *[FRS 1.39]*.

4.2   Cash flows from factoring of trade receivables

Section 7 does not address the classification of cash receipts arising from the factoring of trade receivables. In these circumstances, an entity uses a factoring structure to produce cash flows from trade receivables more quickly than would arise from normal collection from customers, generally by transferring rights over those receivables to a financial institution. In our view, the classification of the cash receipt from the financial institution depends on whether the transfer gives rise to the de-recognition of the trade receivable, or to the continued recognition of the trade receivable and the recognition of a financial liability for the funding received from the debt factor.

Only to the extent that the factoring arrangement results in the de-recognition of the original trade receivable would it be appropriate to regard the cash receipt from factoring in the same way as any other receipt from the sale of goods and rendering of services and classify it in operating activities. *[FRS 102.7.4(a)]*. In cases where the trade receivable is not derecognised and a liability is recorded, the nature of the arrangement is a borrowing secured against trade receivables and accordingly we believe that the cash receipt from factoring should be treated in the same way as any short-term borrowing and included in financing activities. *[FRS 102.7.6(c)]*. The later cash inflow from the customer for settlement of the trade receivable would be included in operating cash flows and the reduction in the liability to the financial institution would be a financing outflow. Following the same principle in

Section 11 – *Basic Financial Instruments* – for the disclosure of income and expenditure relating to a transferred asset that continues to be recognised, *[FRS 102.11.34]*, these two amounts would not be netted off in the statement of cash flows. However, it would be acceptable for the entity to disclose the net borrowing receipts from, or repayments to, the financial institution, if it was determined that these relate to advances made for and the repayment of short-term borrowings such as those which have a maturity period of three months or less.(see 3.8 above). *[FRS 102.7.10C]*.

In some cases, the factoring agreement requires customers to remit cash directly to the financial institution. When the transfer does not give rise to de-recognition of the trade receivable, we believe that the later satisfaction of the debt by the customer can be depicted either;

- as a non-cash transaction. No cash flows would be reported at the time of the ultimate de-recognition of the trade receivable and the related factoring liability; or
- as a transaction in which the debt factor collects the receivable as agent of the entity and then draws down amounts received in settlement of the entity's liability to the financial institution. In this case the entity would report an operating cash inflow from the customer and a financing cash outflow to the financial institution.

4.3 Acquisition of property, plant and equipment on deferred terms

The purchase of assets on deferred terms can be a complicated area because it may not be clear whether the associated cash flows should be classified under investing activities, as capital expenditure, or within financing activities, as the repayment of borrowings. FRS 102 includes the following requirements:

- when an entity acquires an asset under a finance lease, the acquisition of the asset is a non-cash transaction; *[FRS 102.7.19]* and
- the payments to reduce the outstanding liability relating to a finance lease are financing cash flows. *[FRS 102.7.6]*.

In our view, this distinction should be applied in all cases where financing is provided by the seller of the asset, with the acquisition and financing being treated as a non-cash transaction and disclosed accordingly. Subsequent payments to the seller are then included in financing cash flows. Nevertheless, if the period between acquisition and payment is not significant, the existence of credit terms should not be interpreted as changing the nature of the cash payment from investing to financing. The period between acquisition and payment would be regarded as significant if it gave rise to the seller recognising imputed interest under Section 23 – *Revenue*. *[FRS 102.23.5]*. Therefore, the settlement of a short-term payable for the purchase of an asset is an investing cash flow, whereas payments to reduce the liability relating to a finance lease or other financing transactions with the seller for the purchase of an asset should be included in financing cash flows.

Chapter 7

4.4   Additional considerations for groups

Section 7 does not distinguish between single entities and groups, and there is no specific guidance as to how an entity should prepare a consolidated statement of cash flows. In the absence of specific requirements, cash inflows and outflows would be treated in the same way as income and expenses under Section 9 – *Consolidated and Separate Financial Statements*. Applying these principles, the statement of cash flows presented in the consolidated financial statements should reflect only the flows of cash and cash equivalents into and out of the group, i.e. consolidated cash flows are presented as those of a single economic entity. *[FRS 102 Appendix I]*. As intragroup balances and transactions are eliminated on consolidation, intragroup cash flows (such as payments and receipts for intra-group sales, management charges, dividends, interest and financing arrangements) should also be eliminated. *[FRS 102.9.15]*. However, dividends paid to non-controlling shareholders in subsidiaries represent an outflow of cash from the perspective of the shareholders in the parent entity. They should, accordingly, be included under cash flows from financing activities or operating activities, in accordance with the entity's determined policy for classification of dividend cash flows (see 3.10 above).

4.4.1   Acquisitions and disposals resulting in an entity obtaining or losing control

The aggregate cash flows arising from obtaining or losing control of subsidiaries or other businesses are shown separately within investing activities. *[FRS 102.7.10]*.

Such amounts should be shown net of cash acquired on acquisition of the subsidiary or disposed of with the subsidiary. *[FRS 102.7.5(c)-(d)]*. FRS 102 does not explicitly require the disclosure of the cash or overdrafts acquired as part of an acquisition. However, if the cash or overdraft acquired was material it may be regarded as a major class of gross cash receipts or payments and separate presentation would be required.[3]

4.4.2   Settlement of amounts owed by the acquired entity

A question that sometimes arises is how to treat a payment made by the acquirer to settle amounts owed by a new subsidiary, either to take over a loan that is owed to the vendor by that subsidiary or to extinguish an external borrowing.

Payments made to acquire debt instruments of other entities are normally included under investing activities. *[FRS 102.7.5]*. Therefore, the payment to the vendor is classified under the same cash flow heading irrespective of whether it is regarded as being part of the purchase consideration or the acquisition of a debt. This presentation can be contrasted with the repayment of debt owed to a third party, such as a bank, by the new subsidiary after the acquisition, using funds provided by the parent, which is a cash outflow from financing activities. *[FRS 102.7.6]*.

4.5 Cash flows in subsidiaries, associates and joint ventures

4.5.1 Dividends from associates and joint ventures

Cash dividends received from equity accounted associates and joint ventures should be classified as operating or investing activities in accordance with the entity's determined policy for other dividends received (see 3.10 above). Where the net cash inflow from operating activities is determined using the indirect method, and the measure of profit used includes the group's share of profits or losses from equity accounted investments, those amounts will appear as a non-cash reconciling item in the reconciliation of cash flows from operating activities (see 3.5.1 above).

4.5.2 Dividend payments to non-controlling interests

Dividends paid to non-controlling interest holders in subsidiaries are included under cash flows from financing activities or operating activities, in accordance with the entity's determined policy for dividends paid (see 3.10 above).

4.5.3 Group treasury arrangements

Some groups adopt treasury arrangements by which cash resources are held centrally, either by the parent entity or by a designated subsidiary. Any excess cash is transferred to the designated group entity. In some cases a subsidiary might not even have its own bank account, with all receipts and payments being made directly from centrally controlled funds. Subsidiaries record an intercompany receivable when otherwise they would have held cash and bank deposits at each period end. A question that arises is whether or not a statement of cash flows should be presented when preparing the separate financial statements of such a subsidiary given that there is no cash or cash equivalents balance held at each period end. In our view, the preparation of the statement of cash flows should be based upon the entity's actual cash flows during the period regardless of cash and cash equivalents balance held at each period end. The cash and cash equivalents may fluctuate from being positive to overdrawn or nil as the subsidiary needs cash to conduct its operations, to pay its obligations and to provide returns to its investors, or sweeps up excess cash to the designated group entity. This approach is consistent with the requirements in Section 3 – *Financial Statement Presentation* – that all entities should prepare a statement of cash flows which forms an integral part of the financial statements. [FRS 102.3.17].

Where the subsidiary makes net deposits of funds to, or net withdrawals of funds from the designated group entity during the reporting period, a further question arises as to how movements should be presented in the subsidiary's statement of cash flows. Normally these transactions give rise to intercompany balances. Therefore, the net deposits or net withdrawals should be shown as investing activities or financing activities, respectively.

Chapter 7

In extremely rare cases the intercompany balances may meet the definition of cash equivalents and be regarded as short-term highly liquid investments that are readily convertible into known amounts of cash and are subject to insignificant risk of changes in value. *[FRS 102.7.2]*. However, in most cases such funds are transferred to the designated group entity for an indeterminate term and the fact that both the subsidiary and designated group entity are controlled by the parent company makes it difficult to conclude that the subsidiary could demand repayment of amounts deposited independently of the wishes of the parent company.

5   SUMMARY OF GAAP DIFFERENCES

The following table shows the differences between FRS 102 and IFRS.

	FRS 102	*IFRS*
Entities exempt from preparing a cash flow statement	• Qualifying entities; • mutual life assurance companies; • retirement benefit plans; and • investment funds that meet certain conditions. In addition, financial institutions that undertake insurance contracts should include cash flows in respect of their long-term business only to the extent of cash transferred and available to meet the obligations of the company or group as a whole. Small entities are not required to comply with the requirements of Section 7.	No exemptions available.
Alternative presentation of indirect method	Not permitted.	Net cash flows from operating activities may be presented by showing revenues and expenses disclosed in the statement of comprehensive income and changes in inventories and operating receivables and payables.
Presentation of cash flows from discontinued operations	No specific disclosure requirements.	Net cash flows attributable to operating, investing and financing cash flows of discontinued operations should be disclosed.

References

1 *Staff Education Note 1 Cash flow statements (SEN 1)*, FRC, December 2013, footnote 5.

2 *SEN 1*, FRC, December 2013, footnote 4.
3 *SEN 1*, FRC, December 2013, p.8.

Chapter 8

Consolidated and separate financial statements

Chapter 8

Chapter 8

List of examples

Chapter 8

Chapter 8

Consolidated and separate financial statements

1 INTRODUCTION

Section 9 – *Consolidated and Separate Financial Statements* – addresses the preparation and accounting for consolidated financial statements as well as accounting for investments in subsidiaries, associates and jointly controlled entities in individual and separate financial statements. It also contains guidance on consolidation of special purpose entities and the accounting for intermediate payment arrangements.

Although Section 9 is based on the IFRS for SMEs, it has been amended to comply with the requirements of UK Company Law, as well as being expanded to reflect guidance contained in several sources of previous UK GAAP and UK Company Law including FRS 2 – *Accounting for subsidiary undertakings*, FRS 5 – *Reporting the substance of transactions*, UITF 31 – *Exchanges of businesses or other non-monetary assets for an interest in a subsidiary, joint venture or associate*, UITF 32 – *Employee benefit trusts and other intermediate payment arrangements* – and UITF 38 – *Accounting for ESOP trusts*. By using the IFRS for SMEs as its basis, Section 9 therefore incorporates some requirements and guidance of IFRS that existed prior to the issuance of IFRS 10 – *Consolidated Financial Statements* – being IAS 27 – *Consolidated and Separate Financial Statements* (IAS 27 (2012)) and SIC 12 – *Consolidation – Special Purpose entities*.

As part of the *Amendments to FRS 102 Triennial review 2017 – Incremental improvements and clarifications* (Triennial review 2017), issued in December 2017, the FRC considered making amendments to update FRS 102 for the control model in IFRS 10. However, following feedback, the FRC concluded that no changes should be made other than an additional disclosure requirement regarding unconsolidated structured entities (see 3.9.1 below). *[FRS 102.BC.B9.2-4]*.

Therefore, in contrast to most sections of FRS 102, the requirements of Section 9 are not based on current IFRS.

2   COMPARISON BETWEEN SECTION 9 AND IFRS

As explained above, Section 9 is an amalgamation of requirements that existed in previous UK GAAP and IFRS extant before the issuance of IFRS 10. This means that there are a number of significant differences compared with IFRS. These are discussed below.

2.1   Requirement to prepare consolidated financial statements

Section 9 contains various exemptions from the basic requirement that a parent prepare consolidated financial statements. These exemptions are aligned with UK Company Law (see 3.1.1 below). In addition, a parent is required to prepare consolidated financial statements only if it is a parent at the end of the financial year. *[FRS 102.9.2]*.

IFRS 10 has different exemptions from consolidation compared to those exemptions permitted by Section 9. *[IFRS 10.4]*. In particular, the financial statements in which an intermediate parent is consolidated must be prepared under IFRS (although, in certain circumstances, financial statements prepared under a national GAAP that is identical with IFRS in all respects could be considered to be under IFRS) rather than an equivalent GAAP for that intermediate parent to be exempt from preparing consolidated financial statements. IFRS also has no exemption from consolidation for small groups. In addition, consolidated financial statements must be prepared if an entity is a parent at any time during its financial year (unless otherwise exempt).

This means that more parents are likely to be exempt from preparing consolidated financial statements under FRS 102 than under IFRS.

2.2   Investment entities

Section 9 states that a subsidiary held as part of an investment portfolio is not consolidated but, instead, recognised at fair value through profit or loss (see 3.4.2 below). *[FRS 102.9.9C(a)]*.

IFRS 10 states that a parent must determine whether it is an investment entity. *[IFRS 10.27]*. An investment entity should measure all subsidiaries (other than those subsidiaries that are not investment entities whose main purpose and activities are providing services that relate to the investment entity's investment activities) at fair value through profit or loss. *[IFRS 10.31-32]*. IFRS 10 also has more detailed conditions for the use of the exception to consolidation than Section 9. *[IFRS 10 Appendix B.85A-J]*.

This means that there could be accounting differences between FRS 102 and IFRS in respect of investment entities since the Section 9 exception applies to a subsidiary whereas the IFRS exception applies to a parent. IFRS 10 also has more detailed conditions for the use of the exception than Section 9.

2.3   Definition of control

Section 9 defines control as the power to govern the financial and operating policies of an entity so as to obtain benefits from its activities. *[FRS 102.9.4]*.

IFRS 10 states that an investor controls an investee when it is exposed, or has rights, to variable returns from its involvement with the investee and has the ability to affect those returns though its power over the investee. *[IFRS 10.16].*

The difference in the definition of control (and the related application guidance) means that there will be circumstances when an entity is controlled by a parent under FRS 102 and not controlled under IFRS 10 (and *vice versa*). Likely areas of difference include potential voting rights, where control is exercised through an agent, control of special purpose entities (see 2.4 below), interests held as trustee or fiduciary and *de facto* control.

2.4 Special purpose entities and structured entities

Section 9 provides guidance on circumstances that indicate that an entity may control a special purpose entity which is defined as an entity created to establish a narrow objective (see 3.3 below). A risks and rewards model applies for special purpose entities which is different from the single control model in IFRS 10. No additional disclosures are required for special purpose entities.

IFRS 12 – *Disclosure of Interests in Other Entities* – defines a structured entity as an entity designed so that voting or similar rights are not the dominant factor in deciding who controls the entity. *[IFRS 12 Appendix A].* No specific guidance is given on circumstances that indicate when an entity may control a structured entity because reporting entities are expected to apply the single control model in IFRS 10 in determining the entities they control. In addition, separate disclosures are required in respect of structured entities in which a reporting entity has an interest.

This means that a special purpose entity under FRS 102 will not always be a structured entity under IFRS and *vice versa* and that the entity may be consolidated under FRS 102 but not consolidated under IFRS 10 (and *vice versa*).

2.5 Subsidiaries excluded from consolidation

Section 9 states that subsidiaries are excluded from consolidation if they operate under severe long term restrictions or are held exclusively with a view to subsequent resale (see 3.4 below). *[FRS 102.9.9].* These exceptions are aligned with UK Company Law.

IFRS 10 does not have similar exceptions. However, a subsidiary which operates under severe long term restrictions may fail to meet the definition of a subsidiary in IFRS 10 (due to lack of control) and therefore the effect may be the same. Differences between IFRS 10 and Section 9 in respect of investment entities (subsidiaries held as part of an investment portfolio are included in Section 9's definition of subsidiaries held exclusively with a view to resale) are discussed at 2.2 above.

2.6 Accounting for a retained interest in a disposal where control is lost in consolidated financial statements

Section 9 states that when a parent loses control of a subsidiary but the former parent continues to hold an investment in that entity then the carrying amount of the net assets (and goodwill) attributable to the investment at the date that control

Chapter 8

is lost is regarded as the cost on initial measurement of the retained investment (see 3.6.3 below). *[FRS 102.9.19]*.

IFRS 10 states that when a parent loses control of a subsidiary any retained interest in the former subsidiary must be recognised at fair value on the date that control is lost. *[IFRS 10.25(b)]*.

2.7   Accounting for exchange differences on the disposal of a foreign operation in consolidated financial statements

Section 9 states that the cumulative amount of any exchange differences that relate to a foreign subsidiary recognised in equity are not recycled to profit or loss on disposal (i.e. loss of control) of the subsidiary (see 3.6.3 below). *[FRS 102.9.18A]*.

IAS 21 – *The Effects of Changes in Foreign Exchange Rates* – states that exchange differences that relate to a foreign subsidiary recognised in equity are reclassified to profit or loss on disposal (i.e. loss of control). *[IAS 21.48]*.

2.8   Initial measurement of non-controlling interest in consolidated financial statements

Section 9 states that non-controlling interest is initially recognised and measured as the non-controlling interest's share in the identifiable net assets as recognised and measured in accordance with the requirements for a business combination (see 3.7.1 below). *[FRS 102.9.13(d), 19.14A]*.

IFRS 3 – *Business Combinations* – allows an accounting policy choice (for each business combination) for the acquirer to initially recognise non-controlling interests (that are present ownership interests and entitle their holders to a proportionate share of the entity's net assets in the event of liquidation) at either the net amount of the identifiable assets or at fair value. All other components of non-controlling interests are initially measured at their acquisition-date fair values unless another measurement basis is required by IFRSs. *[IFRS 3.19]*.

There is no policy choice under FRS 102 to measure non-controlling interest at fair value. FRS 102 also does not distinguish between different categories of non-controlling interest and therefore implies that all non-controlling interests are measured the same way based on present ownership interest (see 3.7 below).

2.9   Accounting for exchanges of business or other non-monetary assets for an interest in a subsidiary in consolidated financial statements

Section 9 addresses the accounting where a reporting entity exchanges a business, or other non-monetary assets, for an interest in another entity that thereby becomes a subsidiary of the reporting entity. See Chapter 12 at 2.5 and Chapter 13 at 2.6 where the interest in another entity thereby becomes an associate or joint venture.

To the extent that the reporting entity retains an indirect or direct ownership interest in the business, or other non-monetary assets, exchanged, that retained interest should be treated as having been owned by the reporting entity throughout the transaction and included at its pre-transaction carrying amount.

To the extent that the fair value of the consideration received exceeds the carrying value of the part of the business, or other non-monetary assets exchanged and no longer owned by the reporting entity, together with any related goodwill and cash given up, a gain is recognised. Any unrealised gains arising are reported in other comprehensive income.

To the extent that the fair value of the consideration received is less than the carrying value of the part of the business, or other non-monetary assets exchanged no longer owned by the reporting entity, together with any related goodwill and cash given up, a loss is recognised (see 3.8 below). *[FRS 102.9.31].*

IFRS 10 does not distinguish between realised and unrealised gains for equivalent transactions and requires the gain or loss, realised or unrealised, to be recognised in profit or loss. *[IFRS 10 Appendix B.98].* Additionally, when the transferred assets remain controlled by the acquirer after the business combination the assets must be measured at their carrying amount immediately before the transfer and no gain or loss is recognised. *[IFRS 3.38].*

2.10   Cost of investment in a subsidiary in separate financial statements

When an investment in subsidiary is measured using the cost model and merger relief or group reconstruction relief is available, in respect of shares issued as consideration, then these reliefs allow the initial carrying amount of the investment to be equal to either the previous carrying amount of the investment in the transferor's books (if group reconstruction relief is available) or the nominal value of the shares issued (if merger relief is available). *[FRS 102 Appendix III.24].* See 4.2.1 below.

IAS 27 requires the cost of an investment in a subsidiary to be measured at the carrying amount of its share of the equity items shown in the separate financial statements of the original parent (or original entity) for certain types of group reorganisation when a new parent is established. *[IAS 27.13-14].* Otherwise, 'cost' is normally as defined by the Glossary to IFRS (i.e. the amount of cash equivalents paid or the fair value of the consideration given). There is no option to use the nominal value of the shares issued, nor generally the previous carrying amount of the investment in the transferor's books, as cost. However, one situation where we believe it would be acceptable to measure cost based on the carrying amount of the investment in the transferor's books under IFRS is in a common control transaction where an investment in a subsidiary constituting a business is acquired in a share-for-share exchange.

This means that, in circumstances when an entity which uses the cost model for measuring investments in subsidiaries is entitled to use group reconstruction relief or merger relief, the 'cost' is likely to be different under FRS 102 and IFRS.

Chapter 8

2.11   Use of the equity method for accounting for investments in subsidiaries, associates and jointly controlled entities in separate or individual financial statements

FRS 102 does not permit the use of the equity method for accounting for investments in subsidiaries, associates and jointly controlled entities in separate financial statements. *[FRS 102.BC.A28(a)].*

IAS 27 permits the use of the equity method for accounting for investments in subsidiaries, associates and joint ventures in separate financial statements. *[IAS 27.10].* See 2.12 below.

2.12   Accounting for investments in separate financial statements

FRS 102 requires an entity to apply the same accounting policy (i.e. cost less impairment, fair value through other comprehensive income or fair value through profit or loss) for all investments in a single class. Examples of classes of investments are investments in subsidiaries held as part of an investment portfolio, investments in subsidiaries not held as part of an investment portfolio, associates and jointly controlled entities. *[FRS 102.9.26].*

IAS 27 requires an entity to apply the same accounting (i.e. cost, in accordance with IFRS 9 – *Financial Instruments* – or using the equity method) for each category of investments. *[IAS 27.10].* 'Category' is not defined but we take this to mean that it would be permissible for a parent that is not an investment entity to account for all subsidiaries at cost and all associates under IFRS 9.

2.13   Intermediate payment arrangements in separate financial statements

Section 9 defines an intermediate payment arrangement and states that when an entity has *de facto* control of such an arrangement the entity shall account for it as an extension of its own business in its separate financial statements (see 4.5 below). *[FRS 102.9.35].*

IFRS has no guidance on accounting for intermediate payment arrangements. In our view, as explained in Chapter 30 of EY International GAAP 2019, an intermediate payment arrangement under IFRS can be accounted for in the separate financial statements of the entity that has *de facto* control either as an extension of the entity or as an investment in a subsidiary.

2.14   Disclosure differences

Disclosure differences between FRS 102 and IFRS are discussed at 5 below.

3   CONSOLIDATED FINANCIAL STATEMENTS

Consolidated financial statements are designed to extend the reporting entity to embrace other entities which are subject to its control. They involve treating the net assets and activities of subsidiaries held by the parent entity as if they were part of the parent entity's own net assets and activities; the overall aim is to present the results and state of affairs of the group as if they were those of a single entity.

The following key terms in Section 9 are defined in the Glossary: *[FRS 102 Appendix I]*

Term	Definition
Consolidated financial statements	The financial statements of a parent and its subsidiaries presented as those of a single economic entity.
Control (of an entity)	The power to govern the financial and operating policies of an entity so as to obtain benefits from its activities.
Held exclusively with a view to subsequent resale	An interest: • for which a purchaser has been identified or is being sought, and which is reasonably expected to be disposed of within approximately one year of its date of acquisition; or • that was acquired as a result of the enforcement of a security, unless the interest has become part of the continuing activities of the group or the holder acts as if it intends the interest to become so; or • which is held as part of an investment portfolio.
Held as part of an investment portfolio	An interest is held as part of an investment portfolio if its value to the investor is through fair value as part of a directly or indirectly held basket of investments rather than as media through which the investor carries out business. A basket of investments is indirectly held if an investment fund holds a single investment in a second investment fund which, in turn, holds a basket of investments. In some circumstances, it may be appropriate for a single investment to be considered an investment portfolio, for example when an investment fund is first being established and is expected to acquire additional investments.
Non-controlling interest	The equity in a subsidiary not attributable, directly or indirectly, to a parent.
Parent	An entity that has one or more subsidiaries.
Subsidiary	An entity, including an unincorporated entity such as a partnership, that is controlled by another entity (known as the parent).

3.1   Requirement to present consolidated financial statements

The basic legal framework for consolidated financial statements in the UK is found in the Companies Act 2006 (CA 2006). This requires that a company which is a parent company at the end of a financial year must prepare group accounts for that year unless it is exempt from the requirement. *[s399(2)]*. The group accounts must be consolidated and must give a true and fair view of the state of affairs as at the end of the financial year, and the profit or loss for the financial year of the undertakings included in the consolidation as a whole, so far as concerns members of the company. *[s404(1)-(2)]*.

Section 9 replicates the requirements of the CA 2006 by requiring that, unless exempt, an entity which is a parent at its year end shall present consolidated financial statements in which it consolidates all its investments in subsidiaries in accordance with FRS 102. *[FRS 102.9.2]*. An entity that was a parent at the beginning of a year but sold all of its

Chapter 8

subsidiaries during the year is not required to present consolidated financial statements for that year. Such an entity would therefore prepare individual financial statements for that year and the comparatives will be the separate financial statements prepared for the previous year, not the consolidated financial statements for the previous year.

Parents that do not report under the CA 2006 (e.g. overseas entities) are required to comply with the requirements of Section 9, and of the Companies Act when referred to in Section 9, unless these requirements are not permitted by any statutory framework under which such entities report. *[FRS 102.9.1]*.

Consolidated financial statements are the financial statements of a parent and its subsidiaries presented as those of a single economic entity. A subsidiary is defined in terms of control as an entity that is controlled by the parent. Control is the power to govern the financial and operating activities of an entity so as to gain benefit from its activities. *[FRS 102.9.4]*.

The CA 2006 defines a subsidiary slightly differently to Section 9 although the clear intent of the FRC is that it is expected that the 'answer' will be the same except in very exceptional circumstances. This is discussed at 3.2 below.

When an entity is not controlled by an investor but that investor has an interest in the entity, the investment in that entity will be accounted for as follows:

- where the investing entity does not have significant influence or joint control the investment will be accounted for as a financial instrument using one of the accounting policy choices permitted under Section 11 – *Basic Financial Instruments* – or Section 12 – *Other Financial Instruments Issues*;

- where the investing entity has significant influence but not joint control the investment will be accounted for as an associate under Section 14 – *Investments in Associates*; and

- where the investing entity has joint control the investment will be accounted for under Section 15 – *Investments in Joint Ventures*.

Potential future changes to company law requirements arising from Brexit are discussed at 3.1.1.G below.

3.1.1   Exemptions from preparing consolidated financial statements

As well as various rules on exclusion of particular subsidiaries from consolidation (see 3.4 below), there are a number of provisions which exempt parent companies from having to prepare consolidated financial statements at all. Most of these exemptions replicate those permitted under the CA 2006 and specific reference is made by Section 9 to the legislation.

A parent is exempt from the requirement to prepare consolidated financial statements on any one of the following grounds: *[FRS 102.9.3]*

- When its immediate parent is established under the law of a European Economic Area (EEA) (see 3.1.1.A below):

  - The parent is a wholly-owned subsidiary. Exemption is conditional on compliance with certain further conditions set out in section 400(2) of the CA 2006.

- The immediate parent holds 90% or more of the allotted shares in the entity and the remaining shareholders have approved the exemption. Exemption is conditional on compliance with certain further conditions set out in section 400(2) of the CA 2006.

- The immediate parent holds more than 50% (but less than 90%) of the allotted shares of the entity, and notice requesting the preparation of consolidated financial statements has not been served on the entity by shareholders holding in aggregate at least 5% of the allotted shares in the entity (such notice must be served at least six months before the end of the financial year to which it relates). *[s400(1)(c)]*. Exemption is conditional on compliance with certain further conditions set out in section 400(2) of the CA 2006.

- When its parent is not established under the law of an EEA State (see 3.1.1.B and 3.1.1.C below):

  - The parent is a wholly-owned subsidiary. Exemption is conditional on compliance with certain further conditions set out in section 401(2) of the CA 2006.

  - The parent holds 90% or more of the allotted shares in the entity and the remaining shareholders have approved the exemption. Exemption is conditional on compliance with certain further conditions set out in section 401(2) of the CA 2006.

  - The parent holds more than 50% (but less than 90%) of the allotted shares of the entity, and notice requesting the preparation of consolidated financial statements has not been served on the entity by shareholders holding in aggregate at least 5% of the allotted shares in the entity (such notice must be served at least six months before the end of the financial year to which it relates). *[s401(1)(c)]*. Exemption is conditional on compliance with certain further conditions set out in section 401(2) of the CA 2006.

- The parent, and the group headed by it, qualify as small as set out in section 383 of the CA 2006 and are considered eligible for the exemption as determined by reference to sections 384 and 399(2A)-(2B) of the CA 2006 (see 3.1.1.D below).

- All of the parent's subsidiaries are required to be excluded from consolidation by section 402 of the CA 2006 (see 3.1.1.E below).

- For a parent not reporting under the CA 2006, if its statutory framework does not require the preparation of consolidated financial statements (see 3.1.1.F below).

When an immediate parent (section 400) or parent (section 401) holds more than 90% but less than 100% of the allotted shares the wording above implies that *all* the other shareholders *must* approve the exemption from preparing consolidated financial statements otherwise the exemption cannot be applied. Neither section 400 nor section 401 explain the form of the approval required.

For this purpose, shares held by a wholly-owned subsidiary of the parent or held on behalf of the parent undertaking or a wholly-owned subsidiary, should be attributed to the parent undertaking. *[s400(3), s401(3)]*. Shares held by directors of a company for the purpose of complying with any share qualification requirement should be disregarded for determining for the purposes of this section whether the company is a wholly-owned subsidiary. *[s400(5), s401(5)]*.

The term 'allotted shares' is not restricted and includes all classes of shares and not just ordinary shares or voting shares, including shares that are classified as a liability under FRS 102 (see Chapter 10 at 5.2). The term 'allotted shares' rather than 'allotted share capital' suggests that it is the number of shares rather than their monetary amount which should be considered although this is not clear.

The exemptions in respect of sections 400 and 401 of CA 2006 referred to above do not apply if any of the parent's transferable securities are admitted to trading on a regulated market of any EEA State within the meaning of EC Directive 2014/65/EC (i.e. a 'traded company' as defined by section 474(1) of CA 2006). *[FRS 102.9.3]*. This requirement repeats a restriction already contained within both sections 400 and 401 although not within sections 400(2) and 401(2) referred to above. *[s400(4), s401(4)]*.

3.1.1.A   *Parent that is a subsidiary of an immediate EEA parent*

The exemption from preparing consolidated financial statements for intermediate parents that are wholly or majority owned subsidiaries of an immediate EEA parent is conditional on compliance with certain further conditions as set out below: *[s400(2)]*

(a)   the company must be included in consolidated accounts for a larger group drawn up to the same date, or to an earlier date in the same financial year, by a parent undertaking established under the law of an EEA State;

(b)   those accounts must be drawn up and audited, and that parent undertaking's annual report must be drawn up according to that law:

   (i)   in accordance with the provisions of Directive 2013/34/EU of the European Parliament and of the Council (the Accounting Directive) on the annual financial statements, consolidated financial statements and related reports of certain types of undertakings; or

   (ii)   in accordance with international accounting standards (see 3.1.1.C) ;

(c)   the company must disclose in the notes to its individual accounts that it is exempt from the obligation to prepare and deliver group accounts;

(d)   the company must state in its individual accounts the name of the parent undertaking that draws up the group accounts referred to above and:

   (i)   the address of the undertaking's registered office (whether in or outside the United Kingdom); or

   (ii)   if it is unincorporated, the address of its principal place of business;

(e)   the company must deliver to the registrar, within the period for filing its accounts and reports for the financial year in question, copies of,

   (i)   those group accounts; and

   (ii)   the parent undertaking's annual report,

   together with the auditor's report on them;

(f)   there must be a certified translation of any document delivered to the registrar under (e) above if they are not in English.

The EEA states are the 28 member states of the European Union (EU) plus Iceland, Lichtenstein and Norway. The national GAAPs of the 28 member states of the EU should be compliant with the Accounting Directive (as EU States were required to implement the Directive by 20 July 2015). In order for the exemption to be taken if the parent is established in the other three countries, it will need to be established whether that country GAAP is in accordance with the Accounting Directive or in accordance with international accounting standards.

UK company law states that 'included in the consolidation', in relation to group accounts, or 'included in consolidated group accounts' means that the undertaking is included in the accounts by the method of full (and not proportional) consolidation, and references to an undertaking excluded from consolidation shall be construed accordingly. *[s474(1)]*. Therefore, if a parent is included at fair value through profit or loss in the financial statements of an investment entity parent it would not be entitled to the exemption.

One situation where the exemption may not be available is in the accounting period when a parent company becomes a subsidiary of another EEA company. Under the legislation, the exemption is not available if the company has not been included in a set of consolidated accounts of the new parent made up to a date which is coterminous or earlier than its own reporting date. It should be noted that the requirement is not that the particular accounts of the company will be included in a set of consolidated accounts of the parent, but that the company is included in such accounts made up to a date which is coterminous or earlier than its own reporting date. This is illustrated in Example 8.1 below.

Example 8.1:   *Accounting period in which parent entity becomes a subsidiary*

Entity A (a parent) is acquired by Entity B (a parent undertaking established in an EEA state) in October 2019. Entity A has an accounting period ending 31 December 2019. Entity B has an accounting period ending 31 March 2020.

Entity A is unable to use the section 400 exemption from preparing consolidated financial statements for its accounting period ending 31 December 2019 because it has not been included in consolidated accounts drawn up to 31 December 2019 or earlier in that financial year.

Even where the year ends of the intermediate parent company and the parent company are the same, problems can arise. The directors of the intermediate parent company have to state in the company's individual financial statements that they are exempt from the obligation to prepare consolidated financial statements. However, some of the conditions which have to be met may not have taken place by the time the directors approve the financial statements of the intermediate parent. For example, the consolidated accounts in which the intermediate parent is to be included, may not have been prepared and audited; this will be the case if the intermediate parent company has a timetable which requires audited accounts to be submitted prior to the audit report on the consolidated accounts being signed.

Potential future changes to company law requirements arising from Brexit are discussed at 3.1.1.G below.

Chapter 8

3.1.1.B   Intermediate parents that are subsidiaries of non EEA parents

The exemption from preparing consolidated financial statements for intermediate parents that are wholly or majority owned subsidiaries of non EEA parents is conditional on compliance with certain further conditions as set out below: *[s401(2)]*

(a)   the company and all of its subsidiary undertakings must be included in consolidated accounts for a larger group drawn up to the same date, or to an earlier date in the same financial year, by a parent undertaking;

(b)   those accounts and, where appropriate, the group's annual report, must be drawn up:

  (i)   in accordance with the provisions of the Accounting Directive on the annual financial statements, consolidated financial statements and related reports of certain types of undertakings;

  (ii)   in a manner equivalent to consolidated accounts and consolidated annual reports so drawn up;

  (iii)   in accordance with international accounting standards adopted pursuant to the IAS Regulation; or

  (iv)   in accordance with accounting standards which are equivalent to such international accounting standards, as determined pursuant to Commission Regulation (EC) No. 1569/2007 of 21 December 2007 (the 2007 Commission Regulation) establishing a mechanism for the determination of equivalence of accounting standards applied by third country issuers of securities pursuant to Directives 2003/71/EC and 2004/109/EC of the European Parliament and of the Council;

(c)   the group accounts must be audited by one or more persons authorised to audit accounts under the law under which the parent undertaking which draws them up is established;

(d)   the company must disclose in its individual accounts that it is exempt from the obligation to prepare and deliver group accounts;

(e)   the company must state in its individual accounts the name of the parent undertaking that draws up the group accounts referred to above and:

  (i)   the address of the undertaking's registered office (whether in or outside the United Kingdom); or

  (ii)   if it is unincorporated, the address of its principal place of business;

(f)   the company must deliver to the registrar, within the period for filing its accounts and reports for the financial year in question, copies of:

  (i)   the group accounts; and

  (ii)   where appropriate the consolidated annual report,

  together with the auditor's report on them;

(g)   there must be a certified translation of any document delivered to the registrar under (f) above if they are not in English.

The condition described at (a) above is different to the equivalent condition for intermediate parents that are subsidiaries of an immediate EEA parent (see 3.1.1.A above) as it also requires all subsidiaries of the intermediate parent to be included in the larger consolidation. As discussed at 3.1.1.A above, UK company law states that 'included in the consolidation' means included by way of full consolidation.

The comments at 3.1.1.A above, including Example 8.1, apply here also.

The concept of equivalence for the purposes of (b)(ii) and (b)(iv) above is discussed at 3.1.1.C below.

Potential future changes to company law requirements arising from Brexit are discussed at 3.1.1.G below.

3.1.1.C   Equivalence for the purposes of the section 401 exemption for intermediate parents that are subsidiaries of non EEA parents

The exemption from preparing consolidated financial statements for intermediate parents that are subsidiaries of non EEA parents is conditional on the higher parent's consolidated financial statements being drawn up:

- either in accordance with the provisions of the Accounting Directive, or *in a manner equivalent* to consolidated accounts and consolidated annual reports so drawn up; or

- in accordance with international standards adopted pursuant to the IAS Regulation (i.e. EU-adopted IFRS), or in accordance with accounting standards which are *equivalent* to EU-adopted IFRS as determined pursuant to the 2007 Commission Regulation.

The Application Guidance to FRS 100 states that whether a particular set of consolidated financial statements are drawn up in a manner equivalent to consolidated financial statements that are in accordance with the Accounting Directive requires an analysis of the facts. The Application Guidance exists to prevent companies and their auditors from adopting an overly cautious approach in response to uncertainty about whether exemptions can be used. *[FRS 100.AG4]*.

The Application Guidance to FRS 100 also states that it is generally accepted that the reference to equivalence in section 401(2)(b)(ii) of the CA 2006 does not mean compliance with every detail of the Accounting Directive. When assessing whether consolidated financial statements of a higher non-EEA parent are drawn up in a manner equivalent to consolidated financial statements drawn up in accordance with the Accounting Directive, it is necessary to consider whether they meet the basic requirements of the Accounting Directive; in particular, the requirement to give a true and fair view, without implying strict conformity with each and every provision. A qualitative approach is more in keeping with the deregulatory nature of the exemption than a requirement to consider the detailed requirements on a checklist basis. *[FRS 100.AG5]*.

Consolidated financial statements of the higher parent will meet the exemption or the test of equivalence in the Accounting Directive if they are intended to give a true and fair view and: *[FRS 100.AG6]*

- are prepared in accordance with FRS 102;

- are prepared in accordance with EU-adopted IFRS;

- are prepared in accordance with IFRS, subject to the consideration of the reasons for any failure by the European Commission to adopt a standard or interpretation; or

- are prepared using other GAAPs which are closely related to IFRS, subject to the consideration of the effect of any differences from EU-adopted IFRS.

Chapter 8

Consolidated financial statements of the higher parent prepared using other GAAPs or the IFRS for SMEs should be assessed for equivalence with the Accounting Directive based on the particular facts, including the similarities to and differences from the Accounting Directive.

In accordance with Commission Regulation (EC) No. 1569/2007 of 21 December 2007 (see (b)(iv) at 3.1.1.B above), the European Commission has identified the following GAAPs as equivalent to international accounting standards. *[FRS 100.AG7]*. This means that these GAAPs are equivalent to international accounting standards as a matter of law:

Equivalent GAAP	*Applicable from*
GAAP of Japan	1 January 2009
GAAP of the United States of America	1 January 2009
GAAP of the People's Republic of China	1 January 2012
GAAP of Canada	1 January 2012
GAAP of the Republic of Korea	1 January 2012

In addition, third country issuers were permitted to prepare their annual consolidated financial statements and half-yearly consolidated financial statements in accordance with the Generally Accepted Accounting Principles of the Republic of India for financial years starting before 1 April 2016. For reporting periods beginning on or after 1 April 2016, in relation to GAAP of the Republic of India, equivalence should be assessed on the basis of the particular facts. *[FRS 100.AG7]*.

3.1.1.D   Exemption from preparing consolidated financial statements for small groups

A company is exempt from the requirement to prepare group accounts if, at the end of its financial year the company: *[s399(2A)(a)]*

- is subject to the small companies regime; or
- would be subject to the small companies regime but for being a public company.

This exemption is further conditional on the company not being a member of a group which, at any time during the financial year, includes an undertaking falling within section 399(2B) as a member (see Chapter 5 at 6.2 for a list of these ineligible undertakings). *[s399(2A)-(2B)]*.

Consequently, a parent is exempt from preparing consolidated financial statements if both the parent and the group headed by it qualify as small as set out in section 383 and the parent and the group are considered eligible for the exemption as determined by reference to sections 384 and 399(2A)-(2B). *[FRS 102.9.3(e)]*. This means that some companies subject to the small companies regime will not be able to take advantage of the exemption.

The detailed criteria for a small company and a small group are discussed in Chapter 5 at 4.

3.1.1.E   *Exemption due to all subsidiaries excluded from consolidation*

This exemption is similar to the exemption in the CA 2006 which states that a parent is exempt from the requirement to produce group accounts if, under section 405, all of its subsidiary undertakings could be excluded from consolidation in Companies Act group accounts. *[s402]*.

The circumstances in which subsidiaries can be excluded from consolidation, including differences between the CA 2006 and FRS 102, are discussed at 3.4 below.

3.1.1.F   *Exemption under statutory framework*

This exemption applies to those entities not required to report under the CA 2006. It applies only if preparation of consolidated financial statements is not required by the applicable statutory framework.

3.1.1.G   *Potential impact of Brexit on exemptions from preparing consolidated financial statements*

At the time of writing this chapter, the company law requirements discussed at 3.1.1 to 3.1.1.E have not been altered as a result of Brexit. However, the government has published draft legislative proposals – *The Accounts and Reports (Amendment) (EU Exit) Regulations 2018*. Based on the content of these draft proposals:

- The section 400 exemption (see 3.1.1.A above) will apply to an intermediate parent that is a subsidiary of an immediate UK parent rather than to a subsidiary of an immediate EEA parent. The intermediate parent must instead be included in consolidated accounts of a UK parent. Those consolidated accounts and the parent's annual report must be drawn up in accordance with Part 15 of the CA 2006 (or if the UK parent is not a company, the applicable legal requirements) or in accordance with EU-adopted IFRS.

- The section 401 exemption (see 3.1.1.B above) will similarly apply to an intermediate parent that is a subsidiary of a non-UK parent rather than a subsidiary of a non-EEA parent. The parent's consolidated accounts (and where appropriate, the group's annual report) – in which the intermediate parent and all its subsidiaries are included – must be drawn up in accordance with Part 15 of the CA 2006 (or in a manner equivalent) or in accordance with EU-adopted IFRS (or equivalent accounting standards).

For the majority of UK parents that are subsidiaries of an immediate EEA parent, this change is unlikely to have any practical impact as it is expected that those parents that previously used the section 400 exemption from consolidation will be able to take advantage of the amended section 401 exemption from preparing consolidated financial statements. However, as discussed at 3.1.1.B above, there are some subtle wording differences between section 400 and section 401 which may mean that some entities are no longer exempt from the requirement to prepare consolidated financial statements.

The draft proposals also contain changes to the companies excluded from the small companies regime and to the eligibility conditions for use of the small group accounts exemption. *[s384, s399(2B)]*.

Chapter 8

The draft legislation proposes that these changes come into effect for financial years beginning on or after exit day. The draft legislation is subject to Parliamentary approval and may be impacted by any transitional arrangements negotiated with the EU.

3.2   The definition of a subsidiary

The question of the definition of a subsidiary is fundamental to any discussion of consolidated financial statements. The question is also related to the subject of off-balance sheet financing, because frequently this hinges on whether the group balance sheet should embrace the financial statements of an entity which holds certain assets and liabilities that management may not wish to include in the consolidated financial statements.

A subsidiary is defined in terms of control as an entity that is controlled by the parent. *[FRS 102.9.4]*.

Control (of an entity) is the power to govern the financial and operating policies of an entity so as to obtain benefits from its activities. *[FRS 102.9.4]*.

The definition requires two criteria for control:

- power over the financial and operating policies; and
- benefits from the entity's activities to be obtained from that power.

Although FRS 102 does not define what financial and operating policies are, these are generally understood to include such areas as budgeting, capital expenditures, treasury management, dividend policy, production, marketing, sales and human resources.

Although no guidance is given as to what benefits means, we believe that these are not restricted to gains resulting from the entity's activities such as dividends or increases in the value of the investment in the entity but could also include benefits such as cross-selling received by the investor as a result of its power over the entity.

There is no requirement to actually exercise control. The requirement is to have the power to do so. Hence, a passive investor that has the necessary power still controls a subsidiary.

There is a rebuttable presumption that control exists when the parent owns, directly or indirectly, more than half of the voting power of an entity. That presumption may be overcome in exceptional circumstances if it can be clearly demonstrated that such ownership does not constitute control. *[FRS 102.9.5]*. No examples of such exceptional circumstances are provided and it would seem that there is a high hurdle to overcome this presumption.

Control also exists when the parent owns half or less of the voting power but it has: *[FRS 102.9.5]*

- power over more than half of the voting rights by virtue of an agreement with other investors;
- power to govern the financial and operating policies of the entity under a statute or an agreement;
- power to appoint or remove the majority of the members of the board of directors or equivalent governing body and control of the entity is by that board or body; or
- power to cast the majority of votes at meetings of the board of directors or equivalent governing body and control of the entity is by that board or body.

These points above extend the control concept from control of a company in a general meeting to control of the board, or control of an entity by other means.

Control can also be achieved by having options or convertible instruments that are currently exercisable. *[FRS 102.9.6]*. See 3.2.1 below.

Control can also be exercised by having an agent with the ability to direct the activities for the benefit of the controlling entity. *[FRS 102.9.6]*. See 3.2.2 below.

Control can also exist when the parent has the power to exercise, or actually exercises, dominant influence or control over the undertaking, or it and the undertaking are managed on a unified basis. *[FRS 102.9.6A]*. No further guidance is provided by FRS 102 in respect of dominant influence. However, the CA 2006 states that an undertaking shall not be regarded as having the right to exercise dominant influence over another undertaking unless it has a right to give directions with respect to the operating and financial policies of that other undertaking which its directors are obliged to comply with whether or not they are for the benefit of that other undertaking. *[7 Sch 4(1)]*.

Entities that are not controlled by voting or similar rights or those that are created with legal arrangements that impose strict requirements over their operations pose special problems. As a result, Section 9 provides guidance on determining who controls these types of entity, described as 'special purpose entities'. See 3.3 below.

For UK companies, the CA 2006 defines an entity as a parent undertaking in relation to another undertaking, a subsidiary undertaking, if: *[s1162(2)]*

- it holds a majority of the voting rights in the undertaking; or
- it is a member of the undertaking and has the right to appoint or remove a majority of its board of directors; or
- it has the right to exercise dominant influence over the undertaking:
  - by virtue of provisions contained in the undertaking's articles; or
  - by virtue of a control contract; or
- it is a member of the undertaking and controls alone, pursuant to an agreement with other shareholders or members, a majority of the voting rights in the undertaking.

For this purpose, an entity is treated as a member of another undertaking if any of its subsidiary undertakings is a member of that undertaking or if any shares in that other undertaking are held by a person acting on behalf of the undertaking or any of its subsidiary undertakings. *[s1162(3)]*.

An undertaking is also a parent undertaking in relation to a subsidiary undertaking if: *[s1162(4)]*

- it has the power to exercise, or actually exercises, dominant influence or control over it; or
- it and the subsidiary undertaking are managed on a unified basis.

A parent undertaking shall be treated as the parent undertaking of undertakings in relation to which any of its subsidiary undertakings are, or are to be treated as, parent undertakings; and references to its subsidiary undertakings shall be construed accordingly. *[s1162(5)]*.

Chapter 8

Schedule 7 to CA 2006 provides supplementary guidance supporting the definition of a subsidiary.

Although there are slight differences in wording emphasis between this definition and the requirements in FRS 102, in our view, we would expect to see few conflicts arising in practice between FRS 102 and the CA 2006 that would require the use of a true and fair override.

3.2.1   *Potential voting rights*

Control can be achieved by having options or convertible instruments that are currently exercisable. *[FRS 102.9.6]*. These instruments may be shares, warrants, share call options, debt or equity instruments that are convertible into instruments that have the potential, if exercised or converted, to give the entity power or reduce another party's voting power over the financial and operating policies of another entity.

The existence and effect of potential voting rights must be considered when assessing whether an entity has the power to govern the financial and operating policies of another entity so as to obtain benefits from its activities. When an option to acquire a controlling interest in an entity has not yet been exercised, but can be freely exercised by its holder (that is, it could be exercised and, if exercised, would give the holder control) the holder in effect has the power of veto and has the power to govern the entity's financial and operating policies.

Potential voting rights are not currently exercisable or convertible when they cannot be exercised or converted until a future date or until the occurrence of a future event. Example 8.2 illustrates the meaning of currently exercisable.

Example 8.2:   *Potential voting rights – meaning of currently exercisable*

An entity (A) holds 40% of another entity (B). It also holds loan notes in B convertible, at A's option, into further shares in B, which if issued would give A a 60% interest in B. A can require conversion of its loan notes into shares at any time on or after the fifth anniversary of their issue.

Until that fifth anniversary occurs, A cannot exercise its conversion rights. Therefore, they are not currently exercisable and B is not (absent other circumstances) controlled by A and therefore not a subsidiary of A. Once the fifth anniversary has occurred, A's option to convert the loan into shares of B is currently exercisable. Therefore, at that date, A has control over the majority of the voting rights of B, such that B therefore becomes a subsidiary of A at that date.

An entity must exercise judgement when determining whether potential voting rights are currently exercisable. A literal reading might suggest that unless the potential voting right is exercisable immediately, the entity ignores the potential voting right when assessing control. In practice, however, many potential voting rights are not exercisable immediately but rather only exercisable after giving notice (e.g. options over the shares of unlisted entities often include a notice period of several days or a week). In practice, a short notice period is usually ignored when assessing whether the rights are currently exercisable.

FRS 102 provides no guidance on whether the intention of management or the financial ability to exercise or convert a potential voting right are factors that must be considered in assessing whether those rights give control. In the absence of guidance, under the hierarchy in Section 10 – *Accounting Policies, Estimates and Errors* – an entity could look to the requirements and guidance in EU-adopted IFRS relating to similar issues. In this case, there are two possible sources of reference, IFRS 10 (the extant standard) and

IAS 27 (2012) (the standard on which much of Section 9's control model is based). Both IFRS 10 and IAS 27 (2012) are clear that the intention of management should be ignored in assessing whether potential voting rights give control. *[IFRS 10 Appendix B.22, IAS 27.15 (2012)].* In respect of the financial ability to exercise or convert a potential voting right, IFRS 10 states that the financial ability of an investor to pay the exercise price should be considered when evaluating whether an option is substantive. *[IFRS 10 Appendix B.23(a)].* In contrast, IAS 27 (2012) stated that the financial ability to exercise or convert a potential voting right is not considered in assessing control. *[IAS 27.15 (2012)].*

3.2.2   Control exercised through an agent

Control can be achieved by having an agent with the ability to direct the activities for the benefit of the controlling entity. *[FRS 102.9.6].*

The overall relationship between the investor and the agent must be assessed to determine whether the 'agent' is acting as an agent for the controlling entity or as a principal in its own right.

3.2.3   Interests held as trustee or fiduciary, or as security

A reporting entity may hold, as a trustee or fiduciary on behalf of others, an interest in another entity that either on its own or when combined with any interest held on its own account, gives the reporting entity control of the majority of the voting rights in, or the ability to appoint or remove a majority of the members of the board of the other entity. This raises the question of whether that other entity is controlled by the reporting entity.

In our view, interests held in another entity on behalf of others generally do not give a reporting entity control over that other entity. Control is 'the power to govern the financial and operating policies of an entity *so as to obtain benefits from its activities*' (emphasis added). *[FRS 102.9.4].* A trustee or other fiduciary exercises any decision-making powers relating to assets under its management so as to obtain benefits not for itself, but for those on whose behalf it exercises the powers. The CA 2006 states that rights held by a person in a fiduciary capacity shall be treated as not held by that person. Similarly, rights held by a person as nominee for another (if such rights are exercisable only on that other person's instructions or with that other person's consent or concurrence), are regarded as held by the other. *[7 Sch 6-7, 9(2)-(3)].*

Rights attached to shares by way of a security are normally treated as held by the person providing the security if, apart from the ability to exercise them for the purpose of preserving the value of the security, rights are only exercisable upon that person's instructions. The same applies when shares are held in connection with the granting of loans as part of normal business activities. *[7 Sch 8, 9(2)-(3)].*

Rights are treated as held by a parent undertaking if they are held by any of its subsidiary undertakings. *[7 Sch 9(1)].*

As illustrated in Example 8.3, consolidation is still required if an entity legally owns and controls an investment, even if the risks and rewards have been passed on to a third party. Determining whether an entity controls an investment or merely holds an interest in a fiduciary capacity requires a careful assessment of the facts and circumstances.

Chapter 8

Example 8.3:   Control over investment vehicle by an insurance entity

An insurance entity makes certain investments on behalf of unit-linked contract holders. One of those investments is an interest of more than 50% in an investment fund. The unit-linked contract holders are not the legal owner of the investment in the fund. In addition, the insurance entity is under no obligation to return the shares in the underlying investment to the unit-linked contract holders upon termination of the contract. The insurance entity is the legal owner and the unit-linked contract holders have no direct relationship with (and decision-making powers over) the investment fund.

The unit-linked contracts do not diminish the insurance entity's ability to control the investment fund. Therefore, the presumption is that the insurance entity consolidates the investment fund unless it can be demonstrated that it does not have control. While the insurance entity holds a matched position of units in the investment fund and unit-linked contracts, it is under no obligation to hold an investment in the units of the investment fund. Conversely, the unit-linked contract holders have no direct legal rights that entitle them to the units in the investment fund that are owned by the insurance entity. In other words, the insurance entity does not hold the units in the investment fund in a fiduciary capacity.

3.2.4   De facto control

De facto control over an entity by a minority shareholder (e.g. a shareholder holding less than a majority of the voting rights) may arise in a number of ways. A common example is when other shareholders are widely dispersed, and when a sufficient number of other shareholders regularly fail to exercise their rights as shareholders (e.g. to vote at general meetings), such that the minority shareholder wields the majority of votes actually cast.

De facto control is not specifically addressed by FRS 102. In our view, FRS 102 does not necessarily require consolidation of entities subject only to *de facto* control since the definition of control refers to the power to govern the financial and operating policies of an entity and power is explained as representing the ability to do or effect something, whether actively or passively (see 3.2 above). It follows from the definition that control involves the ability:

- to make decisions without the support or consent of other shareholders; and
- to give directions with respect to the operating and financial policies of the entity concerned, with which directions the entity's directors are obliged to comply.

Accordingly, control does not exist where an investor must obtain the consent of one or more other shareholders in order to govern the operating and financial policies of the investee.

To have the ability to govern the financial and operating policies of an entity, an investor must be able to hold the management of the entity accountable. It is therefore unlikely that *de facto* control over an entity can exist unless the investor has the power to appoint and remove a majority of its governing body (i.e. normally the board of directors in the case of a company). This power is normally exercisable by holders of the voting shares in general meeting.

In practice, *de facto* control is most likely to be evidenced where an investor with less than a 50% voting interest is able to have its chosen candidates (re)nominated for election to an entity's board of directors and its votes exceed 50% of the votes typically cast in the entity's election of directors. For example, if typically only 70% of the eligible votes are cast on resolutions for the appointment of directors, a minority holding of 40% might give *de facto* control if the remaining shares are widely held (for example, no party has an interest of sufficient size either of itself or with a small number of others, to block decisions).

The question also arises as to whether *de facto* control can exist where a minority voting interest represents less than 50% of votes typically cast in elections of directors, for example, a voting interest of 30% where, typically, 70% of the eligible votes are cast in elections. It is highly unlikely that *de facto* control exists in this case. As control is unilateral, when assessing whether *de facto* control exists, the entity does not consider the possibility that other shareholders will cast their votes in the same way as the entity.

The determination of whether *de facto* control exists is based on facts and circumstances. It is unlikely to be sufficiently certain that *de facto* control exists until actions taken provide evidence of control – i.e. control must be actively exercised. In general, the more that the legal or contractually-based powers that are held in relation to an entity fall short of 50% of the total powers, the greater is the need for evidence of actively exercised *de facto* control.

3.3   Special purpose entities (SPEs)

An SPE is described as an entity created to accomplish a narrow objective (e.g. to effect a lease, undertake research and development activities, securitise financial assets or facilitate employee shareholdings under remuneration schemes, such as Employee Share Ownership Plans (ESOPs)). An SPE may take the form of a corporation, trust, partnership or unincorporated entity. SPEs are often created with legal arrangements that impose strict requirements over the operations of the SPE. *[FRS 102.9.10]*.

The requirements for SPEs do not apply to a post-employment benefit plan or other long-term employee benefit plans to which Section 28 – *Employee Benefits* – applies. *[FRS 102.9.12]*.

Intermediate payment arrangements that are special purpose entities which are controlled by an entity are accounted for in the separate financial statements of that entity using the parent extension method. See 4.5 below.

In our view, the description of an SPE is broader than a separate legal entity. For example, a parcel of 'ring fenced' assets and liabilities within a larger legal entity, such as a cell in a protected cell entity, might be an SPE. A portfolio of securitised assets and the related borrowings might also be an SPE.

The sponsor (or entity on whose behalf the SPE was created) frequently transfers assets to the SPE, obtains the right to use assets held by the SPE or performs services for the SPE, while other parties ('capital providers') may provide funding to the SPE. An entity that engages in transactions with an SPE (frequently the creator or sponsor) may in substance control the SPE. For example, an entity might have a beneficial interest in an SPE, which may take the form of a debt instrument, an equity instrument, a participation right, a residual interest or a lease. Some beneficial interests provide the holder with a fixed or stated rate of return, while others give the holder rights or access to other future economic benefits of the SPE's activities. In most cases, the creator or sponsor (or the entity on whose behalf the SPE was created) retains a significant beneficial interest in the SPE's activities, even though it may own little or none of the SPE's equity.

Unless a parent is not required to prepare consolidated financial statements – see 3.1 above – a parent entity shall prepare consolidated financial statements that include the entity and any SPEs that are controlled by that entity. In addition to the circumstances

Chapter 8

described at 3.2 above, the following circumstances may indicate that an entity controls an SPE (this is not an exhaustive list): *[FRS 102.9.11]*

- the activities of the SPE are being conducted on behalf of the entity according to its specific business needs;
- the entity has ultimate decision-making powers over the activities of the SPE even if the day-to-day decisions have been have been delegated;
- the entity has rights to obtain the majority of the benefits of the SPE and therefore may be exposed to risks incidental to the activities of the SPE; and
- the entity retains the majority of the residual or ownership risks related to the SPE or its assets.

Activities are likely to be conducted on behalf of the entity according to its specific business needs where the reporting entity created the SPE, directly or indirectly. Examples of decision-making powers over the activities of the SPE even where those decisions have been delegated, by for example setting up an auto pilot mechanism, would include the power to unilaterally dissolve the SPE or the power to change, or veto proposed changes to, the SPE's charter or byelaws. Rights to obtain benefits and exposure to risks incidental to the activities of the SPE may arise through statute, contract, agreement, trust deed or any other scheme, arrangement or device. Such rights to benefits in an SPE may be indicators of control when they are specified in favour of an entity that is engaged in transactions with an SPE and that entity stands to gain those benefits from the financial performance of the SPE. Residual or ownership risks may arise through the guarantee of a return or credit protection directly or indirectly through the SPE to outside investors who provide substantially all of the capital to the SPE. As a result of the guarantee, the entity could retain residual or ownership risks and the investors are, in substance, only lenders because their exposure to gains and losses is limited.

No relative weight is given to the various indicators when determining whether an SPE should be consolidated. However, control of an entity comprises the ability to govern the entity's financial and operating policies so as to obtain benefits from the activities of the entity. *[FRS 102.9.4]*. The ability to control decision-making alone is not sufficient to establish control, but must be accompanied by the objective of obtaining benefits from the entity's activities. This reminder counters arguments of those seeking to establish an off-balance sheet SPE, who tend to argue that a third party (such as a charitable trust) owns all the voting rights. However, if the trust does not obtain any real benefit from the SPE, (which is typically the case) this indicates that the trust does not control the SPE.

3.3.1   Benefits need not necessarily be financial

As discussed at 3.3 above, the first of the indicators of whether an entity is an SPE is that its activities are being conducted on behalf of the reporting entity according to its specific business needs.

In our view, this indicator does not necessarily require that the reporting entity has any direct financial benefit. The 'benefit' might be the avoidance of negative outcomes, or operational benefits.

3.3.2 Majority of the benefits and risks

In our view, the reference to the majority of benefits and risks in the third and fourth indicators at 3.3 above refer to the majority of benefits and risks that are likely to arise in practice, rather than to the majority of all theoretically possible benefits and risks as illustrated by Example 8.4.

Example 8.4: Assessment of majority of benefits and risks of an SPE

An SPE is established to undertake a securitisation of financial assets. The SPE has only nominal equity, but issues £1,000 of debt – £100 subordinated debt to the reporting entity and £900 senior debt to a financial institution. The SPE buys £1,000 of receivables from the reporting entity.

The terms of the two classes of debt have the effect that the reporting entity bears the first £100 of any credit losses and the financial institution the remainder. This could suggest that the financial institution is bearing the majority of the risks, since it has £900 of the possible £1,000 bad debt risk. However, if (as is likely to be the case) bad debt risk is in the range of 5% to 7%, all the losses that are likely to occur will be borne by the reporting entity as the holder of the subordinated debt. Therefore, the reporting entity should consolidate the SPE because it retains the majority of residual or ownership risks of the SPE.

3.3.3 Subsequent reassessment of control of an SPE

FRS 102 is silent on whether an entity must reassess who controls an SPE after inception. In our view, the basic principles of consolidation must be considered. Consolidation is required when there is control. Ordinarily, for an SPE, one would not expect changes in control after inception. However, in our view, reassessing whether a reporting entity continues to control an SPE is required when:

(a)   there is a change in the contractual arrangements between the parties to the SPE; or

(b)   any of the parties take steps to strengthen its position and, in doing so, acquires a greater level of control.

Reassessment of which party controls an SPE is a difficult issue; each situation must be assessed based on the facts and circumstances.

An example of the situation in (b) is that if in a period of financial difficulty, commercial paper cannot be reissued for longer than a certain period, the agreement governing the structure may require the assets to be liquidated. The liquidity provider, knowing that a sale of the assets in that difficult environment is likely to result in losses, might decide to extend the life of the structure by buying the new issue of commercial paper. This was not an action that was anticipated in the original agreement and may mean that the liquidity provider has changed the relative contractual positions of the parties to the SPE and taken effective control.

So long as the initial control assessment is not called into question (e.g. because it was based on incomplete or inaccurate information), subsequent changes in the relationship due to changes in the risk profile, or market events, do not necessarily mean that there has been any transfer of control between the parties. For example, the impairment of the assets owned by an SPE would not necessarily trigger reassessment. Similarly, if the losses incurred by an SPE exceed the capital provided to it, such that the residual risk now lies with another party, (for example the SPE sponsor), this event alone would not necessarily trigger reassessment. However, when events such as these occur, the party bearing the residual risk often takes steps to protect its position, which in turn might trigger a reassessment of whether that party controls the SPE and therefore consolidates the SPE.

3.3.4   Securitisation transactions

SPEs are most commonly found in, but are not unique to, the financial services sector, where they are used as vehicles for securitisation of financial assets such as mortgages or credit card receivables. The effect of these requirements combined with the derecognition provisions of Section 11 – *Basic Financial Instruments* – may be that:

- a securitisation transaction qualifies as a sale of the financial asset concerned (which is thus, in principle, derecognised, or removed from the financial statements); but

- the 'buyer' is an SPE, so that the asset is immediately re-recognised through consolidation of the SPE.

3.4   Subsidiaries excluded from consolidation

In general, a parent should consolidate all subsidiaries in its consolidated financial statements. However, there are various circumstances under which it is considered appropriate not to consolidate particular subsidiaries but instead either deal with them in some other manner or to exclude them from the consolidated financial statements altogether.

The CA 2006 *permits* subsidiaries to be excluded from consolidation on certain grounds. *[s405]*. Within the constraints of the CA 2006, FRS 102 *requires* exclusion from consolidation on certain grounds and interprets how the CA 2006 is to be applied.

A subsidiary is required to be excluded from consolidation when: *[FRS 102.9.9]*

- severe long-term restrictions substantially hinder the exercise of the rights of the parent over the assets or management of the subsidiary (see 3.4.1 below); or

- the interest in the subsidiary is held exclusively with a view to subsequent resale and the subsidiary has not previously been consolidated in the consolidated financial statements prepared in accordance with FRS 102 (see 3.4.2 below).

A subsidiary may be excluded from consolidation if its inclusion is not material for the purpose of giving a true and fair view (but two or more undertakings may be excluded only if they are not material taken together). *[FRS 102.9.9A]*. This exclusion option was added by the Triennial review 2017 in order to align FRS 102 with the identical exclusion permitted by section 405(2) of the CA 2006. *[s405(2)]*. FRS 102 did not mention this specific exemption previously but the amendments made by the Triennial review 2017 should not cause any change in practice.

The CA 2006 permits subsidiaries to be excluded from consolidation in extremely rare circumstances when the information necessary for the preparation of group accounts cannot be obtained without disproportionate expense or undue delay. *[s405(3)(b)]*. However, FRS 102 does not permit a subsidiary to be excluded from consolidation on the grounds that the financial statements cannot be obtained without disproportionate expense or undue delay unless its inclusion is not material (individually or collectively for more than one subsidiary) for the purpose of giving a true and fair view in the context of the group. *[FRS 102.9.8A]*.

It is stated explicitly by FRS 102 that a subsidiary is not excluded from consolidation because its business activities are dissimilar to those of other entities within the consolidation. In the opinion of the FRC, relevant information is provided by consolidating such subsidiaries and disclosing additional information in the consolidated financial statements about the different business activities of subsidiaries. *[FRS 102.9.8]*.

3.4.1 Subsidiaries excluded from consolidation due to severe long term restrictions

A subsidiary excluded from consolidation because severe long-term restrictions substantially hinder the exercise of the rights of the parent over the assets or management of the subsidiary is accounted for in the consolidated financial statements as if it is an investment in a subsidiary in separate financial statements using an accounting policy choice selected by the parent (i.e. either at cost less impairment, at fair value with changes in fair value recognised through other comprehensive income (or profit or loss to the extent that it reverses revaluation movements in profit or loss or where the revaluation reserve would otherwise be negative), or at fair value with changes in fair value recognised in profit and loss – see 4.2 below). *[FRS 102.9.26]*. However, if the parent still exercises a significant influence over the subsidiary it should be treated as an associate using the equity method in the consolidated financial statements. *[FRS 102.9.9B]*. In our view, consistent with the requirements for disposal where control is lost (see 3.6.3 below), the initial cost of the investment in the subsidiary in these circumstances should be the carrying amount of the net assets (and goodwill) attributable to the investment on the date that the severe long term restrictions affected the parent's exercise of its rights over the subsidiary. *[FRS 102.9.19]*.

A true and fair override may be required for subsidiaries excluded from consolidation that are held at fair value through profit or loss as this accounting is not permitted by the CA 2006 in circumstances where this would not be permitted by IFRS 10. *[FRS 102 Appendix III.17, 1 Sch 36]*.

FRS 102 does not provide any examples of situations in which a subsidiary might be subject to severe long term restrictions that hinder the exercise of the parent's rights over the assets or management of the subsidiary. However, examples might include:

- insolvency or administration of the subsidiary; or
- veto powers held by a third party (e.g. powers held by a lender due to covenant breaches); or
- the existence of severe restrictions over remittance of funds (e.g. dividends) if they prevent the parent from obtaining benefits of the subsidiary.

FRS 102 provides no guidance as to the accounting if the severe long-term restrictions cease and the parent's rights are restored. In our view, consistent with the guidance contained in previous UK GAAP, when the severe long-term restrictions cease and the parent's rights are restored, the amount of the unrecognised profit or loss that accrued during the period of restriction for that subsidiary should be separately disclosed in the consolidated profit and loss account of the period in which control is resumed. Similarly, any amount previously charged for impairment that needs to be written back as a result of restrictions ceasing in profit or loss in the period in which control is resumed should be separately disclosed. *[FRS 2.28]*. This is different from the accounting for a subsidiary in which control has been lost whereby the regaining of control would be treated as a business combination achieved in stages (a step acquisition) under Section 19 – *Business Combinations and Goodwill* (see Chapter 17 at 3.11).

3.4.2   *Subsidiaries held exclusively with a view to subsequent resale*

A subsidiary held exclusively with a view to subsequent resale is an interest: *[FRS 102 Appendix I]*

- for which a purchaser has been identified or is being sought, and which is reasonably expected to be disposed of within approximately one year of its date of acquisition; or

- that was acquired as a result of the enforcement of a security, unless the interest has become part of the continuing activities of the group or the holder acts as if it intends the interest to become so; or

- which is held as part of an investment portfolio (see 3.4.2.A below).

For a subsidiary to be classified as held exclusively with a view to subsequent resale it must not have been consolidated previously in consolidated financial statements prepared under FRS 102. *[FRS 102.9.9(b)]*.

A subsidiary excluded from consolidation on the grounds that is held exclusively for resale is accounted for in the consolidated financial statements as follows: *[FRS 102.9.9C]*

- a subsidiary held as part of an investment portfolio is measured at fair value with changes in fair value recognised in profit or loss; and

- a subsidiary not held as part of an investment portfolio is accounted for as if it was an investment in a subsidiary in separate financial statements (i.e. either at cost less impairment, at fair value with changes in fair value recognised in other comprehensive income (or profit or loss to the extent that it reverses revaluation movements in profit or loss or where the revaluation reserve would otherwise be negative) or at fair value with changes in fair value recognised in profit or loss – see 4.2 below).

A true and fair override may be required for subsidiaries excluded from consolidation that are held at fair value through profit or loss (whether or not these are subsidiaries held as part of an investment portfolio) as this accounting is not permitted by the CA 2006 in circumstances where this would not be permitted by IFRS 10. *[FRS 102 Appendix III.17, 1 Sch 36]*.

FRS 102 provides no guidance as to the accounting if a subsidiary is no longer considered to be held exclusively with a view to subsequent resale. In our view, the subsidiary should be consolidated from the date of the change in circumstances using the fair values of the identifiable assets and liabilities of the subsidiary at the date of the original acquisition with a catch-up adjustment to reflect subsequent movements to the date that the subsidiary is no longer held exclusively with a view to subsequent resale. This is because the subsidiary has always been controlled by the parent from the date of the original acquisition. This is also consistent with the requirement in the Regulations that identifiable assets and liabilities acquired must be included in the consolidated balance sheet at their fair values at the date of the acquisition. *[6 Sch 9]*.

3.4.2.A   *Subsidiary held as part of an investment portfolio*

A subsidiary is held as part of an investment portfolio if its value to the investor is through fair value as part of a directly or indirectly held basket of investments rather than as media through which the investor carries out business. A basket of investments is indirectly held if an investment fund holds a single investment fund in a second investment fund which, in turn, holds a basket of investments. In some circumstances, it may be appropriate for a single investment to be considered an investment portfolio, for example when an investment fund is first being established and is expected to acquire additional investments. *[FRS 102 Appendix I].*

The concept that an interest held as part of an investment portfolio meets the definition of an interest held exclusively with a view to subsequent resale is an interpretation of company law. The Basis for Conclusions which accompanies FRS 102 notes that this was developed in order to provide a solution for investment entities to avoid those entities having to elect to prepare EU-adopted IFRS in order to be exempt from consolidating their investments. *[FRS 102.BC.B9.6-9].*

The entities most likely to be affected by this exception are:

- subsidiaries of private equity or venture capital funds; and

- investment fund subsidiaries of banks, insurers, asset managers and property managers.

The investment portfolio exception from consolidation is considerably different from that granted by the investment entity exception to IFRS 10. It applies to an individual subsidiary rather than to a parent, contains no requirement for the parent to have an exit strategy for its investment portfolio and the definition explicitly refers to indirectly held investments. It is therefore anticipated that this will have a wider application than the investment entity exception in IFRS 10 and that there may be considerable diversity in practice, especially in the financial services industry, as to what is considered to be an interest in an investment portfolio.

The last sentence of the definition of 'a subsidiary held as part of an investment portfolio' clarifies that, in some circumstances (e.g. when an investment fund is first established), it may be appropriate for a single investment to be considered an investment portfolio. This clarification, which was added by the Triennial review 2017, is consistent with IFRS 10 which does not preclude an entity from meeting the definition of an investment entity simply because it has only one investment. *[IFRS 10 Appendix B.85P].*

Many investment group structures have intermediate holding companies which are established for tax optimisation purposes or which provide investment-related services and activities. There is no explicit guidance as to whether such intermediate holding companies are treated as interests held as part of an investment portfolio (and therefore measured at fair value through profit or loss) or whether they are not considered as such (and therefore consolidated). For a subsidiary to be held as part of an investment portfolio, FRS 102 requires the value of the interest to the investor to be through fair value, rather than as a media through which the investor carries out business. Therefore, if an entity is holding an investment in a subsidiary as a means of carrying on business, it would not appear to be holding it with a view to resale. Similarly, if an intermediate holding company is performing substantial investment-related services and activities it would not appear to be held as part of an investment portfolio. When an intermediate holding company is considered to be a media through which the parent carries on business it would be consolidated by the parent but the parent would look through the intermediate holding company and account for the underlying investments in the subsidiaries of the intermediate holding company as indirectly held portfolio investments.

3.4.3   Limited partnerships

A limited partnership is made up of one or more 'general partners' and one or more 'limited partners'. Limited partnerships which are 'Qualifying Partnerships' are required to prepare statutory financial statements in accordance with the CA 2006. FRS 102 has no specific consolidation guidance for limited partnerships. Under the Limited Partnership Act 1907, a limited partner is prevented from taking an active role in the affairs of the entity. Therefore, where a company is the sole general partner of a limited partnership, the limited partnership may meet the definition of a subsidiary (see 3.2 above). However, the general partner's investment in a limited partnership is often only nominal in amount and the funding is often provided by the limited partners.

Therefore, determining whether the general partner should consolidate a limited partnership requires judgement and consideration of the facts and circumstances. One situation which might indicate that the limited partnership should be consolidated is where there are guarantees given by the limited partnership which might, if called, fall due to the general partner because the general partner will potentially be subject to majority of risks of the partnership. One situation where the definition of a subsidiary may not be met is where the general partner can be dismissed without cause by the limited partner.

3.5   Consolidation procedures

Consolidated financial statements present financial information about a group as a single economic entity. Therefore, in preparing consolidated financial statements an entity should: *[FRS 102.9.13]*

- combine the financial statements of the parent and its subsidiaries line by line by adding together like items of assets, liabilities, equity, income and expenses;

- eliminate the carrying amount of the parent's investment in each subsidiary and the parent's portion of equity of each subsidiary;

- measure and present non-controlling interest in the profit or loss of consolidated subsidiaries for the reporting period separately from the interest of the owners of the parent; and

- measure and present non-controlling interest in the net assets of consolidated subsidiaries separately from the parent shareholders' equity in them. Non-controlling interest in the net assets consists of:

  - the amount of the non-controlling interest's share in the identifiable net assets (consisting of the identifiable assets, liabilities and contingent liabilities as recognised and measured in accordance with Section 19, if any) at the date of the original combination; and

  - the non-controlling interest's share of changes in equity since the date of the combination or other acquisition.

The proportions of profit or loss and changes in equity allocated to owners of the parent and to the non-controlling interests are determined on the basis of existing ownership interests and do not reflect the possible exercise or conversion of options or convertible instruments. *[FRS 102.9.14]*. This means that, for example, although a parent may have control of an entity through the ability to exercise a currently exercisable option (see 3.2.1 above) the parent's and non-controlling interest's allocation of profit and loss and equity are not generally affected until the option is actually exercised. Example 8.5 illustrates this principle.

Example 8.5: Potential voting rights

Entities A and B hold 40% and 60%, respectively, of the equity of Entity C. A also holds a currently exercisable option over one third of B's shareholding in C, which, if exercised, would give A a 60% interest in C. This would, absent exceptional circumstances, lead to the conclusion that C is a subsidiary of A. However, in preparing its consolidated financial statements, A attributes 60% of the results and net assets of C to non-controlling interests.

The following is discussed in more detail below:

- intragroup balances and transactions – see 3.5.1;
- uniform reporting dates and reporting period – see 3.5.2;
- uniform accounting policies – see 3.5.3; and
- consolidating foreign operations – see 3.5.4.

The accounting for non-controlling interest is discussed further at 3.7 below.

3.5.1 Intragroup balances and transactions

Intragroup balances and transactions, including income, expenses and dividends must be eliminated in full. Profits and losses resulting from intragroup transactions that are recognised in assets, such as inventory and property, plant and equipment, must also be eliminated in full. *[FRS 102.9.15]*. Example 8.6 below illustrates this.

Example 8.6: Eliminating intragroup transactions

Entity A holds a 75% interest in Entity B. A sold inventory with a cost of £100 to B for £200 (i.e. a profit of £100). B still held the inventory at the end of the reporting period.

As well as the intragroup sale between A and B, the unrealised profit of £100 is eliminated from the group's point of view in consolidation (the consolidation adjustment is DR turnover in A £200, CR inventory in B £100, CR cost of sales in A £100). The profit from the sale of inventory of £100 is reversed against the group profit and loss. As the parent made the sale, no amount of the eliminated profit is attributed to the non-controlling interest.

If the fact pattern were reversed such that B sold inventory to A, and A still held the inventory at the end of the reporting period, the same consolidation journal entries above would still be reversed in the consolidated financial statements. However, in this instance, as the subsidiary made the sale, £25 of the eliminated profit (i.e. the non-controlling interest's 25% share of the £100 profit) would be allocated to the non-controlling interest.

If the inventory held by B had been sold to a third party for £300 before the end of the reporting period (resulting in a profit in A of £100 for the sale to B at £200 and a profit in B of £100 for the sale to a third party at £300) no intragroup elimination of profit is required. The group has sold an asset with a cost of £100 for £300 creating a profit to the group of £200. In this case, the intra-group elimination is limited to the sale between A and B (DR turnover in A £200, CR cost of sales in B £200).

Even though losses on intragroup transactions are eliminated in full, they may still indicate an impairment, under Section 27 – *Impairment of Assets*, that requires recognition in the consolidated financial statements. *[FRS 102.9.15]*. For example, if a parent sells a property to a subsidiary at fair value and this is lower than the carrying amount of the asset, the transfer may indicate that the property (or the cash-generating unit to which that property belongs) is impaired in the consolidated financial statements. This will not always be the case as the asset's value-in-use may be sufficient to support the higher carrying value. See Chapter 24 at 4.1.

Intragroup transactions give rise to a tax expense or benefit in the consolidated financial statements under Section 29 – *Income Tax* – which applies to timing differences that arise from the elimination of profits and losses arising from intragroup transactions. *[FRS 102.9.15]*. See Chapter 26 at 6.1.

3.5.2   *Uniform reporting dates and reporting period*

The directors of a parent company have an obligation under the CA 2006 to secure that, except where in their opinion there are good reasons against it, the financial year of each of its subsidiary undertakings coincides with the company's own financial year. *[s390(5)]*.

Similarly, FRS 102 states that the financial statements of the parent and its subsidiaries used in the preparation of consolidated financial statements shall be prepared as of the same reporting date, and for the same reporting period, unless it is impracticable to do so. *[FRS 102.9.16]*. Impracticability is discussed in Chapter 9 at 3.1.

When the reporting date and reporting period of a subsidiary are not the same as the parent's reporting date and reporting period, the consolidated financial statements must be made up: *[FRS 102.9.16]*

- from the financial statements of the subsidiary as of its last reporting date before the parent's reporting date, adjusted for the effects of significant transactions or events that occur between the date of those financial statements and the date of the consolidated financial statements, provided that the reporting date is no more than three months before that of the parent; or

- from interim financial statements prepared by the subsidiary as at the parent's reporting date.

This is consistent with the requirements of the Regulations. *[6 Sch 2(2)]*.

3.5.3   *Uniform accounting policies*

Consolidated financial statements must be prepared using uniform accounting policies for like transactions and other events and conditions in similar circumstances. Therefore, if a member of the group uses accounting policies other than those adopted in the consolidated financial statements for like transactions and events in similar circumstances, appropriate adjustments are to be made to its financial statements in preparing the consolidated financial statements. *[FRS 102.9.17]*.

However, as an exception to this rule, using non-uniform accounting policies for insurance contracts (and related deferred acquisition costs and related intangible assets, if any) is permitted if this is a continuation of an accounting policy used under previous GAAP. *[FRS 103.2.6(c)]*.

Other than for insurance contracts, non-uniform accounting policies are not permitted (unless the directors invoke a true and fair override) by FRS 102. The Regulations are more lenient and allow non-uniform accounting policies if it appears to the directors that there are special reasons for it and these reasons and their effect are disclosed – but an entity must comply with both FRS 102 and the Regulations. *[6 Sch 3(2)]*.

3.5.4   Consolidating foreign operations

Section 9 does not specifically address how to consolidate subsidiaries that are foreign operations. Section 30 – *Foreign Currency Translation* – states that when a group contains individual entities with different functional currencies, the items of income and expense and financial position of each entity are expressed in a common currency so that consolidated financial statements may be presented. *[FRS 102.30.17]*. No preference is stated as to whether the financial statements of a foreign operation are translated directly into the presentation currency of the group (known as the direct method) or translated into the functional currency of any intermediate parent and then translated into the presentation currency of the group (known as the step-by-step method). In our view, either method is acceptable provided it is applied consistently.

In incorporating the assets, liabilities, income and expenses of a foreign operation with those of the reporting entity, normal consolidation procedures are followed, such as the elimination of intragroup balances and intragroup transactions. However, an intragroup monetary asset, whether short-term or long-term, cannot be eliminated against the corresponding intragroup liability (or asset) without showing the results of the currency fluctuations in the consolidated financial statements which must be reflected in either profit or loss or other comprehensive income as appropriate. *[FRS 102.30.22]*.

3.6   Acquisitions and disposals of subsidiaries

In consolidated financial statements, except where a business combination is accounted for by using the merger accounting method (see Chapter 17 at 5.3) or, for certain public benefit entity combinations accounted for under Section 34 – *Specialised Activities*, the income and expenses of a subsidiary are included from the acquisition date until the date on which the parent ceases to control the subsidiary. *[FRS 102.9.18]*.

FRS 102 observes that a parent may cease to control a subsidiary with or without a change in absolute or relative ownership levels, for example, when a subsidiary becomes subject to the control of a government, court, administrator or regulator. *[FRS 102.9.18]*. Deemed disposals that may result in loss of control could also arise for other reasons including:

- a group does not take up its full allocation in a rights issue by a subsidiary in the group;
- a subsidiary declares scrip dividends that are not taken up by its parent, so that the parent's proportional interest is diminished;
- another party exercises its options or warrants issued by a subsidiary;
- a subsidiary issues shares to a third party; or
- a contractual arrangement by which a group obtained control over a subsidiary is terminated or changed.

Example 8.9 at 3.6.3 below illustrates a deemed disposal.

The Basis for Conclusions states that the requirements of FRS 102 dealing with acquisitions and disposals of subsidiaries in consolidated financial statements are based on the 2004 version of IFRS 3 and are considered to provide a coherent model for increases and decreases in stakes held in another entity that is consistent with UK company law. *[FRS 102.BC.B9.11]*.

Chapter 8

3.6.1   Accounting for an acquisition where control is achieved in stages

When a parent acquires control of a subsidiary in stages, Section 9 refers to the requirements of paragraphs 11A and 14 of Section 19, applied at the date control is achieved. *[FRS 102.9.19B]*. This means that when control is achieved in stages, the cost of the business combination is the aggregate of the fair values of the assets given, liabilities assumed and the equity instruments issued by the acquirer at the date of each transaction in the series. *[FRS 102.19.11A]*. See Chapter 17 at 3.11.

3.6.2   Accounting for an increase in a controlling interest in a subsidiary

When a parent increases its controlling interest in a subsidiary, the identifiable assets and liabilities and a provision for contingent liabilities of the subsidiary are not revalued to fair value and no additional goodwill is recognised at the date the controlling interest is increased. *[FRS 102.9.19C]*.

The transaction is accounted for as a transaction between equity holders and accordingly the non-controlling interest shall be adjusted to reflect the change in the parent's interest in the subsidiary's net assets and any difference between the amount by which the non-controlling interest is so adjusted and the fair value of the consideration paid is recognised directly in equity and attributed to equity holders of the parent. No gain or loss is recognised on these changes in equity. *[FRS 102.9.19D, 22.19]*. Example 8.7 illustrates the accounting for increasing a controlling interest in a subsidiary.

Example 8.7:   Increase in controlling interest in subsidiary

A parent with a 70% controlling interest in a subsidiary purchases an additional 20% interest in that subsidiary for cash proceeds of £250. Following the purchase, the parent has a 90% controlling interest in the subsidiary. The carrying value of the subsidiary's net assets excluding goodwill is £450 and there is £50 of goodwill remaining from the subsidiary's acquisition.

The parent accounts for the acquisition of the additional 20% interest as follows:

	Dr	Cr
Cash		£250
Non-controlling interest (20% of £450)	£90	
Equity	£160	

The guidance on reattribution of items of other comprehensive income and accounting for transaction costs discussed at 3.6.4 below apply here also.

3.6.3   Accounting for a disposal of a subsidiary when control is lost

When a parent ceases to control a subsidiary, a gain or loss is recognised in the consolidated statement of comprehensive income (or in the income statement if presented) calculated as the difference between: *[FRS 102.9.18A]*

- the proceeds from the disposal (or the event that resulted in the loss of control); and
- the proportion of the carrying amount of the subsidiary's net assets, including any related goodwill, disposed of (or lost) as at the date of disposal (or date control is lost).

The gain or loss calculated above shall also include those amounts that have been recognised in other comprehensive income in relation to that subsidiary, where those amounts are required to be reclassified to profit or loss upon disposal in accordance with other sections of FRS 102. Amounts that are not required to be reclassified to profit or loss upon disposal of the related assets or liabilities in accordance with other sections of FRS 102 are transferred directly to retained earnings. *[FRS 102.9.18B]*.

The cumulative amount of any exchange differences that relate to a foreign subsidiary recognised in equity in accordance with Section 30 is not recognised in profit or loss as part of the gain or loss on disposal of the subsidiary and is transferred directly to retained earnings. *[FRS 102.9.18A]*.

FRS 102 permits only the following unrealised gains and losses recognised in other comprehensive income to be recycled through profit or loss upon disposal of a subsidiary:

- unrealised gains and losses on available-for-sale (AFS) investments (if the entity has elected to use IAS 39 – *Financial Instruments: Recognition and Measurement* – for recognition and measurement of financial instruments); *[FRS 102.11.2(b), 12.2(b)]*

- unrealised gains and losses on debt instruments at fair value through other comprehensive income (if the entity has elected to use IFRS 9 for recognition and measurement of financial instruments); *[FRS 102.11.2(c), 12.2(c)]*

- unrealised gains and losses on cash flow hedges (except for the portion attributable to a hedge of a net investment in a foreign operation); *[FRS 102.12.23-24]* and

- unrealised gains and losses arising from the application of shadow accounting for insurance contracts. *[FRS 103.2.11]*.

No other unrealised gains and losses that have been recognised in other comprehensive income are recycled upon disposal of a subsidiary.

If an entity ceases to be a subsidiary but the former parent continues to hold:

- an investment that is not an associate or a jointly controlled entity, that investment shall be accounted for as a financial asset in accordance with Section 11 or Section 12 (see Chapter 10) from the date the entity ceases to be the subsidiary;

- an associate, that associate shall be accounted for in accordance with Section 14 (see Chapter 12); or

- a jointly controlled entity, that jointly controlled entity shall be accounted for in accordance with Section 15 (see Chapter 13).

The carrying amount of the net assets (and goodwill) attributable to the investment at the date that the entity ceases to be a subsidiary shall be regarded as cost on initial measurement of the financial asset, investment in associate or jointly controlled entity, as appropriate. In applying the equity method to investments in associate or jointly controlled entities as required above, the requirements in respect of the recognition of implicit goodwill and fair value adjustments (see Chapter 12 at 3.3.2.D), shall not be applied. *[FRS 102.9.19]*.

Example 8.8 below illustrates the accounting for a disposal of a subsidiary:

Example 8.8:   Disposal of a subsidiary

A parent sells an 85% interest in a wholly owned subsidiary as follows:

- after the sale the parent accounts for its remaining 15% interest at fair value as an other financial instrument under Section 12;
- the subsidiary did not recognise any amounts in other comprehensive income;
- net assets of the subsidiary before the disposal including goodwill are £500; and
- cash proceeds from the sale of the 85% interest are £750.

The parent accounts for the disposal of the 85% interest as follows:

	Dr	Cr
Other financial instrument (15% of the net assets before disposal of £500)	£75	
Cash	£750	
Net assets of the subsidiary derecognised (summarised)		£500
Gain on loss of control of subsidiary		£325

The gain recognised on the loss of control of the subsidiary is calculated as follows:

Cash proceeds on disposal of 85% interest	£750
Carrying amount of 85% interest (85% × £500)	£(425)
	£325

In this example, the cost on initial measurement of the financial instrument is not its fair value. Therefore, when that financial instrument is subsequently measured at fair value, there will be a 'Day 2' gain or loss as the cost of the investment is adjusted to fair value.

A deemed disposal that results in loss of control of a subsidiary is accounted for as a regular disposal. This is illustrated in Example 8.9 below.

Example 8.9:   Deemed disposal through share issue by subsidiary

A parent entity P owns 600,000 of the 1,000,000 shares issued by its subsidiary S, giving it a 60% interest. The carrying value of S's net identifiable assets in the consolidated financial statements of P is £120 million. The non-controlling interest is £48 million (40% of £120 million). In addition, goodwill with a carrying value of £15 million remains from the acquisition.

Subsequently, S issues 500,000 shares to a new investor for £80 million. As a result, P's 600,000 shares now represent 40% of the 1,500,000 shares issued by S in total and S becomes an associate of P.

This results in a gain of £3 million on disposal, calculated as follows:

	Dr	Cr
Interest in S (40% of increased net assets of £200 million plus 40/60 of goodwill of £15 million)	£90m	
Non-controlling interest	£48m	
Gain on disposal		£3m
Net assets of S (previously consolidated)		£120m
Goodwill (previously shown separately)		£15m

As this is a deemed disposal resulting from the share issue of a subsidiary, P needs to consider whether the profit resulting is realised or unrealised. If unrealised, the profit would be taken to other comprehensive income and not to profit or loss.

3.6.4 Accounting for a part disposal of a subsidiary when control is retained

Where a parent reduces its holding in a subsidiary and control is retained, it shall be accounted for as a transaction between equity holders and the carrying amount of the non-controlling interest shall be adjusted to reflect the change in the parent's interest in the subsidiary's net assets. Any difference between the amount by which the non-controlling interest is so adjusted and the fair value of the consideration paid or received, if any, shall be recognised directly in equity and attributed to equity holders of the parent. No gain or loss shall be recognised at the date of disposal and the entity shall not recognise any change in the carrying amount of assets (including goodwill) or liabilities as a result of the transaction. *[FRS 102.9.19A, 22.19]*.

FRS 102 is not clear whether a portion of goodwill should be regarded as now being attributable to the non-controlling interest in computing the difference to be taken to equity in these circumstances. However, we believe the most logical treatment is that the parent should reallocate a proportion of the goodwill between controlling and non-controlling interest when there is a decrease in the parent's ownership interest without loss of control. Otherwise, any gain or loss recognised upon a subsequent loss of control or goodwill impairment would not reflect the ownership interest applicable to that non-controlling interest.

Example 8.10 below illustrates the accounting for a disposal where control is retained.

Example 8.10: Disposal of a subsidiary where control is retained

A parent sells a 20% interest in a wholly owned subsidiary for cash proceeds of £250. Parent still retains an 80% controlling interest in the subsidiary. The carrying value of the subsidiary's net assets excluding goodwill is £450 and there is £50 of goodwill remaining from the subsidiary's acquisition.

In the consolidated financial statements, we believe the parent should account for this transaction as follows, reallocating goodwill to the non-controlling interest:

	Dr	Cr
Cash	£250	
Non-controlling interest (20% of £500, i.e. including goodwill)		£100
Equity		£150

FRS 102 is silent as to whether amounts recognised in other comprehensive income and equity should be reattributed when a change in ownership in a subsidiary occurs that does not result in the loss of control. In our view, it is logical that such a reattribution should occur and this is consistent with Section 30 which requires that the accumulated exchange differences arising from translation which relate to a foreign operation that is consolidated but not wholly-owned that are attributable to the non-controlling interest are allocated to, and recognised as part of, non-controlling interest. *[FRS 102.30.20]*.

Although FRS 102 is clear that changes in a parent's ownership interest in a subsidiary that do not result in loss of control of the subsidiary are equity transactions, it does not specifically address how to account for related transaction costs. In our view, any directly attributable costs incurred to sell a non-controlling interest in a subsidiary without loss of control are deducted from equity. Whether the costs are attributable to the parent or to the non-controlling interest depends on whether the costs have been incurred by the parent (in which case the costs are attributable to parent equity) or the subsidiary with the non-controlling interest (in which case the cost would be allocated between parent equity and non-controlling interest based on their respective shares).

3.7　Non-controlling interest in subsidiaries

A non-controlling interest is the equity in a subsidiary not attributable, directly or indirectly, to a parent. *[FRS 102 Appendix I]*. The reference to 'equity' in the definition of non-controlling interest refers to those 'equity instruments' of a subsidiary that are not held, directly or indirectly, by its parent. This also means that financial instruments that are legally equity but classified as a liability in accordance with Section 22 – *Liabilities and Equity* – are not included within the definition of non-controlling interest.

The principle underlying accounting for non-controlling interest is that all residual economic interest holders of any part of the consolidated entity have an equity interest in that consolidated entity. This principle applies regardless of the decision-making ability of that interest holder and where in the group that interest is held. Therefore, any equity instruments issued by a subsidiary that are not owned by the parent (apart from those that are required to be classified as financial liabilities) are non-controlling interests, including:

- ordinary shares;
- convertible debt and other compound financial instruments;
- preference shares (including both those with, and without, an entitlement to a *pro rata* share of net assets on liquidation);
- warrants;
- options over own shares; and
- options under share-based payment transactions.

Options and warrants are non-controlling interests, regardless of whether they are vested and of the exercise price (e.g. whether they are 'in-the-money').

The definition of non-controlling interest in FRS 102 is wider than the definition in the Regulations which states that non-controlling interests in the statement of financial position must show the amount of capital and reserves attributable to shares in subsidiary undertakings (i.e. the definition in the CA 2006 is restricted to shares). *[6 Sch 17(2)]*. When differences arise between the definitions used in FRS 102 and the Regulations, it may be necessary to disclose both FRS 102 and CA 2006 amounts for non-controlling interest. See Chapter 6 at 4.5.

3.7.1　*Accounting and presentation of non-controlling interest*

A non-controlling interest in the net assets of a subsidiary is initially measured at the non-controlling interest's share of the identifiable net assets (consisting of the identifiable assets, liabilities and contingent liabilities as recognised and measured in accordance with the requirements for a business combination, if any – see Chapter 17 at 3.8 and Example 17.14) at the date of the original combination. *[FRS 102.9.13(d), 19.14A]*. There is no option under FRS 102 to measure non-controlling interest at fair value.

FRS 102 does not distinguish between non-controlling interest that is a present ownership interest and entitles holders of that interest to a proportionate share of the entity's net assets in the event of liquidation and other components of non-controlling interest (e.g. perpetual debt classified as equity under Section 22). The implication is that all non-controlling interest is measured the same way based on present ownership interest. This means that any non-controlling interest, such as options, are valued at nil if they are not entitled to a present ownership interest. See Chapter 17 at 3.7.

Non-controlling interest shall be presented within equity, separately from equity of the owners of the parent, in the consolidated financial statement of financial position. *[FRS 102.9.20]*.

Non-controlling interest in the profit or loss of the group is required to be disclosed separately in the statement of comprehensive income (or income statement, if presented). *[FRS 102.9.21]*.

Profit or loss and each component of other comprehensive income should be attributed to the owners of the parent and to non-controlling interest. Total comprehensive income should be attributed to the owners of the parent and to non-controlling interest even if this results in non-controlling interest having a deficit balance. *[FRS 102.9.22]*. This approach is consistent with the fact that the controlling and non-controlling interest participate proportionately in the risks and rewards of an investment in the subsidiary. When the non-controlling interest in a subsidiary is in deficit, there is no requirement to make a provision in the group financial statements for any legal or commercial obligation (whether formal or implied) to provide for finance that may not be recoverable in respect of the accumulated losses attributable to the non-controlling interest.

A proportion of profit or loss, other comprehensive income and changes in equity is only attributed to those ownership instruments included within non-controlling interest if they give rise to an existing (or present) ownership interest. Non-controlling interests that include potential voting rights that require exercise or conversion (such as options, warrants, or share-based payment transactions) generally do not receive an allocation of profit or loss (see 3.2.1 above). *[FRS 102.9.14, 22]*.

Where a subsidiary has granted options over its own shares under an equity-settled share-based payment transaction, the share-based payment expense recognised in profit or loss will be attributable to the parent and any other non-controlling interest that has a present legal ownership in the subsidiary.

FRS 102 is silent on the accounting for shares of profit or loss on undeclared dividends in respect of outstanding cumulative preference shares classified as equity that are held by a non-controlling interest. In our view, an entity has an accounting policy choice whether to allocate to the non-controlling interest a portion of the profit or loss after adjusting for such dividends (whether or not declared), or only after adjusting for the declared dividends. The first choice (i.e. profit or loss is after adjusting for dividends on outstanding cumulative preference shares whether or not declared) is the one required by IFRS 10. *[IFRS 10 Appendix B.95]*.

Chapter 8

3.7.1.A   *Measurement of non-controlling interest where an associate holds an interest in a subsidiary*

FRS 102 does not explain how to account for non-controlling interest when the group owns an associate which has a holding in a subsidiary. It is therefore unclear whether non-controlling interest should be computed based on the ownership interests held by the group (i.e. by the parent and any consolidated subsidiary), or whether it should also take into account the indirect ownership of the subsidiary held by the associate. The reciprocal interests can also give rise to a measure of double-counting of profits and net assets between the investor and its associate.

We believe that there are two possible approaches to determine the amount of non-controlling interest in the subsidiary:

(a)   the non-controlling interest is determined after considering the associate's ownership of the subsidiary ('look through approach'); or

(b)   the non-controlling interest is determined based on the holdings of the group in the subsidiary ('black box approach').

An entity should apply the chosen approach consistently.

In applying the 'look through approach', the parent must not recognise the share of the subsidiary's results recognised by the associate applying the equity method, in order to avoid double-counting. The 'black box approach' will often lead to reporting higher consolidated net assets and results than when using the 'look through approach' as this adjustment is not made, although the amounts attributed to owners of the parent should be the same under both approaches. The two approaches are illustrated in Example 8.11 below.

Example 8.11:   *Measurement of non-controlling interest where an associate accounted using the equity method holds an interest in a subsidiary*

Parent P owns directly 60% of subsidiary S. P also directly owns 40% of associate A that in turn holds a 30% interest in S. S has earned profits of £1,000,000 in the period and has net assets of £3,000,000 (which are consolidated in both P's consolidated financial statements and equity accounted by A) at the reporting date. A has net assets of £1,100,000 (excluding its share of the net assets of S). There are no transactions between A and S (which was not acquired in a business combination).

Approach 1 ('look through approach')

This approach involves determining the ownership attributable to the non-controlling interest (NCI) after considering A's ownership of S. This approach views the equity method as primarily a method of consolidation (albeit on a single line), as further discussed in Chapter 14 at 3.3.2.

Therefore, under the 'look through' approach, P's total ownership interest in S is 72% (and the NCI's interest is 28%). P's effective ownership interest of 72% in S represents 60% held directly and an additional effective interest of 12% (40% × 30%) via A.

Therefore, P consolidates the profits of S of £1,000,000, with:

Profits of S attributable to owners of P	£720,000 (£1,000,000 × 72%)
Profits of S attributable to the non-controlling interests	£280,000 (£1,000,000 × 28%)

However, when equity accounting for A, P does not recognise its share of S's results recognised by the associate A of £120,000 (£1,000,000 × (40% × 30%)). This is to avoid double counting as S's results have already been consolidated and P's effective ownership of 12% of S that is indirectly held via A has been attributed to owners of the parent.

The assets and liabilities of S are consolidated, with:

Net assets of S attributable to owners of P	£2,160,000 (72% × £3,000,000)
Net assets of S attributable to the non-controlling interests	£840,000 (28% × £3,000,000)
Investment in A	£440,000 (Note 1)

Note 1 – when equity accounting for A, P does not recognise its share of S's net assets recognised by A of £360,000 (£3,000,000 × (40% × 30%)) to avoid double-counting as the net assets of S owned by A have already been included in the amounts attributable to the owners of P. Therefore, the investment in A is reported at P's 40% share of A's net assets (excluding A's share of S), i.e. 40% × £1,100,000.

Approach 2 ('black box approach')

Under this approach (the 'black box approach'), when determining NCI, P considers the ownership interests in S not held by the group (i.e. by P and its subsidiaries). This approach views the equity method as primarily a method of valuing an investment, as further discussed in Chapter 11 at 7.2.

Accordingly, P's ownership interest is 60% and the NCI's ownership interest is 40%.

Therefore, P consolidates the profits of S of £1,000,000, with:

Profits of S attributable to owners of P	£600,000 (60% × £1,000,000)
Profits of S attributable to the non-controlling interests	£400,000 (40% × £1,000,000)

The assets and liabilities of S are consolidated, with:

Net assets of S attributable to owners of P	£1,800,000 (60% × £3,000,000)
Net assets of S attributable to the non-controlling interests	£1,200,000 (40% × £3,000,000)
Investment in A	£800,000 (Note 2)

Note 2 – when equity accounting for A, P does not eliminate its share of S's results of £120,000 and net assets of £360,000. Therefore, the investment in A is reported at P's 40% share of A's net assets (including the associate's share of S), i.e. 40% × (£1,100,000 + (30% × £3,000,000)).

The results and net assets in respect of S that are attributed to owners of P are the same as in Approach 1. However, the total consolidated results and net assets exceed those reported in Approach 1 by £120,000 and £360,000 respectively (being P's effective ownership interest of 12% in S's profits and net assets that are equity accounted in Approach 2). While this approach has the merit that the attribution of S's profits and net assets to NCI reflects the 40% ownership interests in S not held by the group, a downside is the double counting of 12% of S's profits that are equity accounted by A.

3.7.2   Call and put options over non-controlling interest

Some business combinations involve options over some or all of the outstanding shares. For example, the acquirer might have a call option, i.e. the right to acquire the outstanding shares at a future date for a particular price. Alternatively, the acquirer might have granted a put option to other shareholders whereby they have the right to sell their shares to the acquirer at a future date for a particular price. In some cases, there may be a combination of put and call options, the terms of which may be equivalent or different.

FRS 102 gives no guidance on how to account for such options in a business combination. There is also no guidance when such contracts are entered into following a business combination. Therefore, when determining the appropriate accounting in such situations, Sections 9, 11, 12 and 22 must be considered.

Chapter 8

3.7.2.A   Call options only

Call options are considered when determining whether an entity has obtained control as discussed at 3.2.1 above. Once it is determined whether an entity has control over another entity, the proportions of profit or loss and change in equity allocated to the parent and non-controlling interests are based on the existing (or present) ownership interests and generally do not reflect the possible exercise or conversion of potential voting rights under call options. *[FRS 102.9.14].*

A call option is likely to give the acquiring entity present access to returns associated with the ownership interest in limited circumstances:

- when the option price is fixed with a low exercise price and it is agreed between the parties that either no dividends will be paid to the other shareholders or the dividend payments lead to an adjustment of the option exercise price; or

- the terms are set such that the other shareholders effectively receive only a lender's return.

The acquiring entity has present access to the returns associated with ownership interest in these circumstances because any accretion in the fair value of the underlying ownership interest under the option (for example, due to improved financial performance of the acquiree subsequent to the granting of the call option) is likely to be realised by the acquirer.

If a call option gives the acquiring entity present access to returns over all of the shares held by non-controlling shareholders, then there will be no non-controlling interest presented in equity. The acquirer accounts for the business combination as though it acquired a 100% interest. The acquirer also recognises a financial liability to the non-controlling shareholders under the call option. Changes in the carrying amount of the financial liability are recognised in profit or loss. If the call option expires unexercised, then the acquirer has effectively disposed of a partial interest in its subsidiary in return for the amount recognised as the 'liability' at the date of expiry and accounts for the transaction as a change in ownership interest without a loss of control, as discussed at 3.6.4 above.

A call option may not give present access to the returns associated with that ownership interest where the option's terms contain one or more of the following features:

- the option price has not yet been determined or will be the fair value of the shares at the date of exercise (or a surrogate for such a value);

- the option price is based on expected future results or net assets of the subsidiary at the date of exercise; or

- it has been agreed between the parties that, prior to the exercise of the option, all retained profits may be freely distributed to the existing shareholders according to their current shareholdings.

If a call option does not give present access to the returns associated with the ownership interest, the instruments containing the potential voting rights are accounted for as a derivative financial asset by the holder in accordance with Sections 11 and 12 unless the derivative meets the definition of an equity instrument of the entity in Section 22.

3.7.2.B   *Put options only*

In the context of the consolidated financial statements, a put option held by a non-controlling interest is a form of puttable instrument in that it gives the holder the right to sell the shares in the subsidiary (presented as equity of the group) back to the group. Although it is clear that a put option is usually recognised as a liability, there are a number of decisions that must be made in order to account for the arrangements, including:

- the measurement of the liability under the non-controlling interest put;
- whether the terms of the non-controlling interest put mean that it gives the parent a present ownership interest in the underlying securities; and
- whether or not a non-controlling interest continues to be recognised if the liability is measured based on its redemption amount, i.e. whether the parent recognises both the non-controlling interest and the financial liability for the non-controlling interest put.

In the latter case, there are a number of additional decisions that must be made, in particular the basis on which the non-controlling interest is recognised.

When the put option is a liability, Section 22 offers no guidance as to how that liability should be measured. Section 22 does not contain the requirement in IAS 32 – *Financial Instruments: Presentation* – that an obligation for an entity to purchase its own equity instruments for cash or another financial asset gives rise to a financial liability for the present value of the redemption amount (for example, the present value of the forward purchase price, option price or other redemption amount). *[IAS 32.23]*. In our view, as no guidance is contained in Section 22, unless the parent elects to consider the requirements and guidance in IAS 32 as permitted by paragraph 10.6 of FRS 102 (see Chapter 9), the financial liability for the put option is a derivative which should be measured at fair value according to Sections 11 and 12.

In our view, in the same way as for call options, an entity has to consider whether the terms of the transaction give it present access to the returns associated with the shares subject to the put option.

If it is concluded that the acquirer has a present ownership interest in the shares concerned, it is accounted for as an acquisition of those underlying shares, and no non-controlling interest is recognised. Thus, if the acquirer has granted a put option over all of the remaining shares, the business combination is accounted for as if the acquirer has obtained a 100% interest in the acquiree. No non-controlling interest is recognised when the acquirer completes the purchase price allocation and determines the amount of goodwill to recognise. In this situation, in our view, the acquirer would recognise a liability for the present value of the amount required to be paid under the put option to obtain the interest (i.e. the redemption amount), rather than measuring it as a derivative. Changes in the carrying amount of the financial liability are recognised in profit or loss. If the put option is exercised, the financial liability is extinguished by the payment of the exercise price. If the put option is not exercised, then the entity has effectively disposed of a partial interest in its subsidiary, without loss of control, in return for the amount recognised as the financial liability at the date of expiry. The entity accounts for the transaction as discussed at 3.6.4 above, and measures the non-controlling interest as of the date that the put option expires.

Chapter 8

When the terms of the transaction do not provide a present ownership interest in the shares subject to the put option, the entity will initially recognise both the non-controlling interest based on present ownership interest and the financial liability under the put at fair value as a derivative. If the put option is exercisable at fair value then the fair value of the derivative liability is zero. All subsequent changes in the liability are recognised in profit or loss. Given the absence of guidance in Section 22 as to how a put option should be measured, an entity could, alternatively, under the FRS 102 hierarchy, look to IAS 32 for guidance. As stated above, IAS 32 states that an obligation for an entity to purchase its own equity instruments for cash or another financial asset gives rise to a financial liability for the present value of the redemption amount. If an entity chooses to do this (i.e. apply IAS 32) then different accounting policy choices are available which are discussed in Chapter 7 of EY International GAAP 2019.

3.7.2.C   *Combination of put and call options*

In some business combinations, there might be a combination of call and put options, the terms of which may be equivalent or may be different.

The appropriate accounting for such options is determined based on the discussions in 3.7.2.A and 3.7.2.B above. However, where there is a call and put option with equivalent terms, particularly at a fixed price, the combination of the options is more likely to mean that they give the acquirer a present ownership interest.

In such cases, where the options are over all of the shares not held by the parent, the acquirer has effectively acquired a 100% interest in the subsidiary at the date of the business combination. The entity may be in a similar position as if it had acquired a 100% interest in the subsidiary with either deferred consideration (where the exercise price is fixed) or contingent consideration (where the settlement amount is not fixed, but is dependent upon a future event).

3.7.2.D   *Call and put options entered into in relation to existing non-controlling interest*

The discussion at 3.7.2.A and 3.7.2.B above focused on call and put options entered into at the same time as control is gained of the subsidiary. However, an entity may enter into the options with non-controlling shareholders after gaining control. The appropriate accounting policy will still be based on the discussions at 3.7.2.A and 3.7.2.B above.

Where the entity already has a controlling interest and as a result of the options now has a present ownership interest in the remaining shares concerned the non-controlling interest is no longer recognised within equity. The transaction is accounted for as an acquisition of the non-controlling interest, i.e. it is accounted for as an equity transaction (see 3.6.2 above), because such acquisitions are not business combinations under Section 19.

3.8   Exchanges of businesses or other non-monetary assets for an interest in a subsidiary, jointly controlled entity or associate

A reporting entity may exchange a business, or other monetary asset, for an interest in another entity, and that other entity becomes a subsidiary, jointly controlled entity or associate of the reporting entity. The accounting issues that arise from these transactions are whether they should be accounted for at fair value or at previous book values and how the gain on the transaction should be reported.

The principles behind the requirements for these transactions (derived from previous UK GAAP) are that the only exception to the use of fair values should be in rare circumstances where the transaction is artificial and has no substance and that any unrealised gains should not be reported in profit or loss.

Accordingly, the following accounting treatment applies in the consolidated financial statements of the reporting entity: *[FRS 102.9.31]*

- to the extent that the reporting entity retains an ownership interest in the business, or other non-monetary assets, exchanged, even if that interest is then held through another entity, that retained interest, including any related goodwill, is treated as having been owned by the reporting entity throughout the transaction and should be included at its pre-transaction carrying amount;

- goodwill is recognised as the difference between:

  - the fair value of the consideration given; and

  - the fair value of the reporting entity's share of the pre-transaction identifiable net assets of the other entity.

  The consideration given for the interest acquired in the other entity will include that part of the business, or other non-monetary assets, exchanged and no longer owned by the reporting entity. The consideration may also include cash or monetary assets to achieve equalisation of values. Where it is difficult to value the consideration given, the best estimate of its value may be given by valuing what is acquired;

- to the extent that the fair value of the consideration received by the reporting entity exceeds the carrying value of the part of the business, or other non-monetary assets exchanged and no longer owned by the reporting entity, and any related goodwill together with any cash given up, the reporting entity should recognise a gain. Any unrealised gain arising on the exchange is recognised in other comprehensive income; and

- to the extent that the fair value of the consideration received by the reporting entity is less than the carrying value of the part of the business, or other non-monetary assets no longer owned by the reporting entity, and any related goodwill, together with any cash given up, the reporting entity should recognise a loss. The loss should be recognised as an impairment in accordance with Section 27 or, for any loss remaining after an impairment review of the relevant assets, in profit or loss.

The accounting treatment can be illustrated in Examples 8.12 and 8.13 below:

Example 8.12: Creation of subsidiary by contribution of existing business (1)

A and B are two major pharmaceutical companies, which agree to form a new company (Newco) in respect of a particular part of each of their businesses. B will own 60% of Newco, and A 40%. The parties agree that the total value of the new business is £250m.

B's contribution to the venture is one of its businesses, the net assets of which are included in B's consolidated balance sheet at £85m (including remaining unamortised goodwill of £15m). The fair value of the separable net assets of the business contributed by B is considered to be £120m which consists of £140m of gross assets less a £20m bank loan. The implicit fair value of the business contributed is £150m (60% of total fair value £250m).

The separable net assets of the business to be contributed by A have a carrying amount of £50m, but their fair value is considered to be £80m. A also has unamortised goodwill remaining of £10m. The implicit fair value of the business contributed is £100m (40% of total fair value £250m).

The book and fair values of the businesses contributed by A and B can therefore be summarised as follows:

(in £m)	A Book value	A Fair value	B Book value	B Fair value
Separable net assets	50	80	70	120
Goodwill	10	20	15	30
Total	60	100	85	150

How should B account for this transaction in its consolidated financial statements?

B accounts for the transaction on the basis that it has retained 60% of its existing business and has exchanged a 40% interest in that business for a 60% interest in the business contributed by A. It therefore continues to record the 60% retained at book value and recognise a gain or loss on disposal of the 40% calculated as the difference between the book value of the net assets and the consideration received (being the fair value of the 60% interest in A's business). The difference between the fair value of the 40% interest in the business given up and the new net assets acquired (i.e. the 60% of A's former assets) represents goodwill.

This gives rise to the following accounting entries.

	Dr	Cr
Net assets of Newco[1]	£150m	
Non-controlling interest in Newco[2]		£60m
Goodwill[3]	£21m	
Net assets contributed to Newco[4]		£85m
Other comprehensive income (gain on disposal)[5]		£26m

1   Book value of B's separable net assets + fair value of A's separable net assets (£70m+£80m) = £150m. In reality there would be a number of entries to consolidate these on a line-by-line basis.

2   40% of (book value of B's separable net assets + fair value of A's separable net assets) i.e. 40% × (£70m+£80m) = £60m.

3   Fair value of business given up by B less fair value of separable net assets of A's business acquired, i.e. 40% of £150m less 60% of £80m = £12m, plus 60% of B's goodwill of £15m retained (£9m) = £21m.

4   Previous carrying amount of net assets contributed by B (including goodwill), now deconsolidated (although now reconsolidated in accounting for Newco). In reality there would be a number of entries to deconsolidate these on a line-by-line basis.

5   Fair value of business received, less book value of assets disposed of, 60% of £100m – 40% of £85m = £26m.

The gain on the transaction in Example 8.12 is unrealised because qualifying consideration has not been received. Therefore, the gain is accounted for in other comprehensive income as only realised profits can be recognised in profit or loss. Where part or all of the gain is realised then that portion can be taken to profit and loss. This is illustrated in Example 8.13 below:

Example 8.13:   Creation of subsidiary by contribution of existing business (2)

Assume the same fact pattern as in Example 8.12 above, except that B was to receive a stake of only 50% in Newco (but still have control) and that A paid £25m direct to B in compensation for the reduction in the stake from 60% to 50%. As in Example 8.12 above, the separable net assets of B (book value of £120m) includes a bank loan of £20m which is equal to its fair value.

How should B account for this transaction in its consolidated financial statements?

B accounts for the transaction on the basis that it has retained 50% of its existing business and has exchanged a 50% interest in that business for a 50% interest in the business contributed by A plus cash of £25m. It therefore continues to record the 50% retained at book value and recognise a gain or loss on disposal of the 50% calculated as the difference between the book value of the net assets and the consideration received (being the fair value of the 50% interest in A's business plus cash of £25m). The difference between the fair value of the 50% interest in A's business given up and the new net assets acquired (i.e. the 50% of A's former assets) represents goodwill.

This gives rise to the following accounting entries.

	Dr	Cr
Net assets of Newco[1]	£150.0m	
Non-controlling interest in Newco[2]		£75.0m
Cash	£25.0m	
Goodwill[3]	£17.5m	
Net assets contributed to Newco[4]		£85.0m
Profit and loss (gain on disposal)[5]		£5.0m
Other comprehensive income (gain on disposal)[5]		£27.5m

1   Book value of B's separable net assets + fair value of A's separable net assets (£70m+£80m) = £150m. In reality there would be a number of entries to consolidate these on a line-by-line basis.

2   50% of (book value of B's separable net assets + fair value of A's separable net assets) i.e. 50% × (£70m+£80m) = £75m.

3   Fair value of business given up by B (net of amount of cash of £25m received from A to achieve equalisation of values) less fair value of separable net assets of A's business acquired, i.e. 50% of £150m less £25m, less 50% of £80m = £10m, plus 50% of B's goodwill of £15m retained (£7.5m) = £17.5m.

4   Previous carrying amount of net assets (including goodwill) contributed by B, now deconsolidated (although now consolidated in accounting for Newco). In reality there would be a number of entries to deconsolidate these on a line-by-line basis.

5   Fair value of business received (50% of £100m) plus cash received of £25m less book value of assets disposed of i.e. (50% of £85m), The gain on disposal of £32.5m has been split based on an allocation between 'realised' and 'unrealised' as explained below.

FRS 102 does not explain how a realised gain can be distinguished from an unrealised gain. In Example 8.13 above, we have used a 'top slicing' approach whereby as much as the total gain as is backed by net cash is treated as realised (i.e. £5m). 'Top slicing' is the recommended approach to determining realised profits for exchanges of assets in paragraph 3.18 of the ICAEW/ICAS Technical Release 02/17BL – *Guidance on Realised and Distributable Profits under the Companies Act 2006* (TECH 02/17BL). Paragraph 3.18A of TECH 02/17BL states that when the consideration received comprises a combination of assets and liabilities, the profit will be realised only to the extent of any net balance (i.e. cash less liabilities) of qualifying consideration received. In Example 8.13 above, the realised profit of £5m consists of the cash received of £25m less the bank loan assumed of £20m.

No gain or loss is recognised in those rare cases where the artificiality or lack of substance of the transaction is such that a gain or loss on the exchange could not be justified. When a gain or loss on the exchange is not taken into account because the transaction is artificial or has no substance, the circumstances should be explained. *[FRS 102.9.32]*. There is no elaboration as to the circumstances where this might be applicable.

Chapter 8

3.9   Disclosures in consolidated financial statements

3.9.1   Disclosures in consolidated financial statements required by Section 9 of FRS 102

A limited amount of disclosures in respect of consolidated financial statements are required by FRS 102. This is because certain disclosures are already required by the Regulations.

The following disclosures are required by Section 9 of FRS 102: *[FRS 102.9.23]*

- the fact that the statements are consolidated financial statements;
- the basis for concluding that control exists when the parent does not own, directly or indirectly through subsidiaries, more than half of the voting power;
- any difference in the reporting date of the financial statements of the parent and its subsidiaries used in the preparation of the consolidated financial statements;
- the nature and extent of any significant restrictions (e.g. resulting from borrowing arrangements or regulatory requirements) on the ability of subsidiaries to transfer funds to the parent in the form of cash dividends or to repay loans; and
- the name of any subsidiary excluded from consolidation and the reasons for its exclusion; and
- the nature and extent of its interests in unconsolidated special purpose entities, and the risks associated with such entities.

In addition, where a gain or loss on an exchange of a business or other non-monetary asset for an investment in a subsidiary, associate or jointly controlled entity has not been recognised because of the artificiality or lack of substance of the transaction, these circumstances should be explained (see 3.8 above).

The disclosure in the last bullet point above regarding unconsolidated special purpose entities was introduced by the Triennial review 2017 to improve information available to users about such entities. It is a principle-based disclosure derived from IFRS 12. *[FRS 102.BC.B9.4]*. The equivalent requirement in paragraph 24 of IFRS 12 refers to disclosure of information that enables users of the financial statements to understand the nature and extent of interests in unconsolidated structured entities and to evaluate the nature of, and changes in, risks associated with those interests. The principle-based requirement in paragraph 24 is followed by detailed disclosure requirements in paragraphs 25-31 of IFRS 12. Considering the different wording in FRS 102, which omits a requirement to disclose 'changes in risk' and the reference in the Basis for Conclusions to a 'principle-based disclosure' we do not believe that the FRC intends this disclosure to be as detailed as that required for unconsolidated structured entities under IFRS 12. However, management may consider the requirements and guidance in IFRS 12 useful in determining what type of detail to provide. Unlike IFRS, FRS 102 does not require any specific disclosures in respect of consolidated structured entities. This disclosure is also not required in separate or individual financial statements.

3.9.2   Disclosures in consolidated financial statements in respect of subsidiary undertakings required by the Regulations

The following disclosures are required by the Regulations in consolidated financial statements in respect of subsidiaries except for business combinations which are provided in Chapter 17:

- the name of each subsidiary undertaking and the address of the undertaking's registered office (whether in or outside the United Kingdom) and, if unincorporated, the address of its principal place of business. There is no relief available to limit this disclosure to those of the principal subsidiaries if it is of excessive length; *[4 Sch 1]*

- for each subsidiary, there must be stated the identity of each class of shares held and the proportion of the nominal value of that class of shares held, with separate information on the interest held by the parent and by the group, if different; *[4 Sch 17]*

- for entities that are subsidiaries other than because the immediate parent holds a majority of the voting rights which are in the same proportion of the shares held, the reasons why the subsidiary has been consolidated; *[4 Sch 16(3)]*

- for each subsidiary not included in the consolidation the reasons for excluding the subsidiary from the consolidation; *[4 Sch 16(2)]*

- for each subsidiary not included in the consolidated accounts: *[4 Sch 2]*
    - the aggregated amount of its capital and reserves as at the end of its relevant financial year; and
    - its profit or loss for that year.

  This information is not required if the subsidiary is included in the consolidated accounts under the equity method of accounting or if the subsidiary is not required by the CA 2006 to deliver a copy of its balance sheet for its relevant financial year and does not otherwise publish its balance sheet anywhere in the world and the company's holding is less than 50% of the nominal value of the shares (or if the information is not material);

- when during the financial year, there has been a disposal of an undertaking or group which significantly affects the figures in the group accounts: *[6 Sch 15]*
    - the name of the undertaking or of the parent undertaking of the disposed group; and
    - the extent to which the profit or loss shown in the group accounts is attributable to profit of loss of that undertaking or group.

  This disclosure need not be given for an undertaking which is either established outside the United Kingdom or carries on business outside the United Kingdom if the disclosure is seriously prejudicial to the business of that undertaking or of the parent company or any of its subsidiary undertakings and the Secretary of State agrees; *[6 Sch 16]*

- any differences of accounting rules as between a parent's individual accounts for a financial year and its group accounts, and the reason for the differences; *[6 Sch 4]*

- the number, description and amount of shares in the parent company held by or on behalf of subsidiary undertakings. *[4 Sch 3]*.

See Chapter 12 at 5.4.1 and Chapter 13 at 4.3.1 for disclosures required by the Regulations in consolidated financial statements for investments in associates and jointly controlled entities.

Chapter 8

4   INDIVIDUAL AND SEPARATE FINANCIAL STATEMENTS

The CA 2006 requires accounts to be prepared for each financial year. These are referred to as the company's individual accounts. *[s394]*. Other statutory frameworks will apply for those entities that are not required to produce Companies Act individual accounts. *[FRS 102.9.23A]*.

The following key terms are defined in the FRS 102 Glossary: *[FRS 102 Appendix I]*

Term	*Definition*
Individual financial statements	The accounts that are required to be prepared by an entity in accordance with the CA 2006 or relevant legislation, for example: • 'individual accounts', as set out in section 394 of the CA 2006; • 'statement of accounts', as set out in section 132 of the Charities Act 2011; or • 'individual accounts', as set out in section 72A of the Building Societies Act 1986. Separate financial statements are included in the meaning of this term.
Separate financial statements	Those presented by a parent in which the investments in subsidiaries, associates or jointly controlled entities are accounted for either at cost or fair value rather than on the basis of the reported results and net assets of the investees. Separate financial statements are included within the meaning of individual financial statements.

Both individual and separate financial statements as defined by FRS 102 are Companies Act individual accounts).

An entity that is not a parent (i.e. an entity that does not have subsidiaries) prepares individual financial statements and not separate financial statements. *[FRS 102.9.24]*.

4.1   Accounting for associates and jointly controlled entities in individual financial statements of an entity that is not a parent

An entity that is not a parent accounts for investments in associates and jointly controlled entities using either:

- a cost model, i.e. at cost less impairment;
- a fair value model, i.e. at fair value with changes in fair value recognised in other comprehensive income (or profit or loss to the extent that it reverses revaluation movements in profit or loss or where the revaluation reserve would otherwise be negative); or
- at fair value with changes in fair value recognised in profit or loss. *[FRS 102.9.25, FRS 102.14.4, FRS 102.15.9]*.

There is no option to use equity accounting in individual financial statements prepared under FRS 102 (although this option exists under IFRS and Schedule 1 to the Regulations). *[FRS 102.BC.A28(a)]*. However, the individual financial statements of an investor that is not a parent shall disclose summarised financial information about investments in associates and jointly controlled entities, along with the effect of including those investments as if they had been accounted for using the equity method. Investing entities that are exempt from preparing consolidated financial statements, or would be exempt if they had subsidiaries, are exempt from this requirement. *[FRS 102.14.15A, 15.21A].*

In its individual financial statements, an entity that is not a parent need not measure associates using the same accounting model as jointly controlled entities. However, Sections 14 and 15 do not explicitly address whether all associates or all jointly controlled entities must all be accounted for using the same model. There is an explicit requirement in Section 9 for an entity that is a parent to apply the same accounting policy to all investments in a single class. As discussed at 4.2 below, in our view, associates or jointly controlled entities held as part of an investment portfolio could be considered as a separate class from other associates or jointly controlled entities in the separate financial statements of a parent. While Sections 14 and 15 do not specifically refer to different classes of associates and jointly controlled entities, we believe that an entity that is not a parent may similarly adopt a different accounting policy in accounting for associates and jointly controlled entities held as part of an investment portfolio to that applied to other associates and jointly controlled entities in its individual financial statements.

The cost and fair value measurements for associates and jointly controlled entities are further discussed in Chapters 12 and 13.

4.2 Accounting for subsidiaries, associates and jointly controlled entities in separate financial statements of an entity that is a parent

Separate financial statements are defined as those financial statements presented by a parent in which the investments in subsidiaries, associates or jointly controlled entities are accounted for at either cost, or fair value rather than on the basis of the reported results and net assets of the investees. Separate financial statements are included within the meaning of individual financial statements. *[FRS 102.9.24].*

A parent preparing separate financial statements must select and adopt a policy of accounting for investments in subsidiaries, associates and jointly controlled entities either: *[FRS 102.9.26]*

- at cost less impairment;
- at fair value with changes in fair value recognised in other comprehensive income (or profit or loss) in accordance with paragraphs 15E and 15F of Section 17 – *Property, Plant and Equipment*; or
- at fair value with changes in fair value recognised in profit or loss. Guidance on fair value is provided in Section 2 – *Concepts and Pervasive Principles* (see Chapter 4 at 3.13).

A policy of measuring subsidiaries, associates and jointly controlled entities at fair value through profit or loss is permitted by paragraph 36(4) of Schedule 1 to Regulations (and its equivalents in Schedules 2 and 3) without the use of a true and fair override. However, additional disclosures are required – see 4.6.1 below.

There is no option to use equity accounting in separate financial statements prepared under FRS 102 (although this option exists under IFRS and Schedule 1 to the Regulations). *[FRS 102.BC.A28(a)].*

A parent that is exempt from the requirement to prepare consolidated financial statements (see 3.1.1 above) and therefore presents separate financial statements as its only financial statements must also account for its investments in subsidiaries, associates and jointly controlled entities as above. *[FRS 102.9.26A]*.

A parent must apply the same accounting policy for all investments in a single class (for example subsidiaries that are held as part of an investment portfolio, those subsidiaries not held as part of an investment portfolio, associates or jointly controlled entities) but it can elect different policies for different classes. *[FRS 102.9.26]*. Although not mentioned as an example of a class of investments, it appears that associates and jointly controlled entities which are held as part of an investment portfolio (and therefore required to be measured at fair value through profit or loss) could also be a separate class from associates and jointly controlled entities which are not held as part of an investment portfolio. Otherwise, an investor with, say, an associate held as part of an investment portfolio – that wished to maintain the same accounting in the consolidated and separate financial statements – would be required to measure all associates at fair value through profit or loss.

This restriction means that a parent cannot use a different accounting policy for a class of investments even where individual investments within that class have different characteristics. The Triennial review 2017 amended paragraph 26 of Section 9 to clarify that a subsidiary excluded from consolidation which is held as part of an investment portfolio is a separate class of investment. Subsidiaries that are excluded from consolidation because they are held as part of an investment portfolio are required to be measured at fair value through profit or loss. *[FRS 102.9.9C(a)]*. While the term 'class' has not been referenced to Appendix 1: Glossary to FRS 102, generally a class is taken to mean a grouping of assets of a similar nature and use in an entity's operations. Although the examples given for separate classes of investments differentiate between subsidiaries held as part of an investment portfolio and those that are not so hold, in our view, this does not preclude the election of a different accounting policy for different classes of subsidiaries. For example, an entity may consider it appropriate to account for investments in subsidiaries held exclusively with a view to resale (including those not held as part of an investment portfolio) at fair value, while applying the cost model to other investments in subsidiaries.

If an entity has elected to measure subsidiaries at fair value but the fair value of one or more subsidiaries is not reliably measurable its carrying amount at the last date the asset was reliably measureable becomes its new cost. The entity should measure the asset at this cost less impairment, if any, until a reliable measure of fair value becomes available. *[FRS 102.2A.6]*.

There is no option under FRS 102 to use a directors' valuation (typically, net assets), an out-of-date market value (except when a reliable measure of fair value is no longer available for an asset measured at fair value) or current cost to value an investment in a subsidiary, associate or jointly controlled entity in individual or separate financial statements where such measurements are not the equivalent of fair value at the reporting date.

FRS 102 does not distinguish between different types of entity (e.g. banking entities, insurance entities and other entities). The cost model is not permitted by Schedule 3 to the Regulations for individual or separate financial statements so an insurer is able only to use fair value measurement for investments in subsidiaries.

4.2.1   *Cost of investment in a subsidiary, associate or jointly controlled entity*

Section 9 does not define 'cost' of investment. However, Section 2 – *Concepts and Pervasive Principles* – states that for assets, 'historical cost' is the amount of cash or cash equivalents paid or the fair value of the consideration given to acquire the asset at the time of its acquisition. *[FRS 102.2.34(a)]*. The Regulations state that the purchase price of an asset is determined by adding to the actual price paid any expenses incidental to its acquisition (and then subtracting any incidental reductions in the cost of acquisition). *[1 Sch 27(1)]*. This definition in the Regulations is consistent with Section 17 and the requirements for exchanges of businesses or other non-monetary assets for an interest in a subsidiary, jointly controlled entity or associate (see 3.8 above), which state that cost is normally either the purchase price paid (including directly attributable costs) or the fair value of non-monetary assets exchanged. *[FRS 102.9.31, 17.10]*. The purchase price would generally represent the fair value of the consideration given to purchase the investment consistent with the guidance in respect of exchanges of businesses or other non-monetary assets (see 3.8 above) and the requirements in respect of measuring the cost of a business combination (see Chapter 17 at 3.6).

When shares have been issued as consideration for the investment, the Appendix on Legal Requirements which accompanies FRS 102 states that where the cost model is adopted, sections 611 to 615 of the CA 2006 set out the treatment where 'merger relief' or 'group reconstruction relief' is available. These reliefs reduce the amount required to be included in share premium and also allow the initial carrying amount of the investment to be adjusted downwards so it is equal to either the previous carrying amount of the investment in the transferor's books (in most circumstances) or the nominal value of the shares issued, depending on which relief applies. The Note on Legal Requirements goes on to state that this relief is not available where the fair value model is used, so the investment's carrying amount may not be reduced, although the provisions in the CA 2006 in respect of amounts required to be recorded in share premium remain relevant. *[FRS 102 Appendix III.24]*. In our view, the decision whether or not to use this relief to measure cost is an accounting policy choice that must be applied consistently for all transactions of this type.

In addition, section 615 permits the relief to be reflected in determining the amount at which the shares or other consideration provided for the shares issued are recognised. Therefore, when applying the cost method, any other consideration transferred may also be measured at an amount which reflects the relief available. *[FRS 102 Appendix III.24A]*.

Group reconstruction relief applies when the company issuing shares is:

- a wholly owned subsidiary of another company (the holding company); and
- allots shares:
  - to the holding company; or
  - to another wholly-owned subsidiary of the holding company;

  in consideration for the transfer of non-cash assets of a company (the transferor company) that is a member of the group of companies that comprises the holding company and all its wholly-owned subsidiaries.

When the shares in the issuing company allotted in consideration are issued at a premium, the issuing company (i.e. the subsidiary) is not required to transfer any amount in excess of the minimum premium value (i.e. the amount, if any, by which the base value of the consideration exceeds the aggregate nominal value of the shares) to the share premium account. The base value of the consideration for the shares allotted is the amount by which the base value of the assets transferred (i.e. the cost of the assets to the transferor company or, if less, the amount at which those assets are stated in the transferor company's accounting records immediately before the transfer) exceeds the base value of any liabilities (i.e. the amount at which they are stated in the transferor company's accounting records immediately before the transfer) of the transferor company as part of the consideration for the assets transferred. *[s611]*.

Merger relief applies when a company that issues shares (the issuing company) has secured at least a 90% equity holding in another company in pursuance of an arrangement providing for the allotment of equity shares in the issuing company on terms that the consideration for the share allotted is to be provided: *[s612]*

- by the issue or transfer to the issuing company of equity shares in the other company; or
- by the cancellation of any such shares not held by the issuing company.

If the equity shares (i.e. shares in a company's equity share capital *[s548]*) in the issuing company allotted pursuant to this arrangement are issued at a premium the requirements of the CA 2006 relating to the establishment of a share premium account do not apply to the premiums on those shares.

In addition, where the arrangement also provides for the allotment of any shares in the issuing company on terms that the consideration for those shares is to be provided:

- by the issue or transfer to the issuing company of non-equity shares in the other company; or
- by the cancellation of any such shares in that company not held by the issuing company,

the relief relating to the establishment of the share premium account extends to any shares in the issuing company on those terms in pursuant of the arrangement.

Merger relief cannot be used in a transaction falling within the scope of group reconstruction relief.

For the purpose of determining the 90% equity holding for the purposes of merger relief: *[s613]*

- it does not matter whether any of the shares acquired in the other company were in pursuance of the arrangement;
- shares in the other company held as treasury shares are excluded in determining the nominal amount of that other company's share capital;
- where there is more than one class of shares, a 90% or more equity holding must be met in relation to each class; and
- shares in the other company held by the issuing company's holding company, subsidiary, or a subsidiary of the issuing company's holding company or by its nominees are treated as being held by the issuing company.

The amount of the premium which is not included in the share premium account by virtue of either group reconstruction relief or merger relief may also be disregarded in determining the amount at which any shares or other consideration provided for the shares issued is to be included in the company's balance sheet. *[s615]*.

Examples 8.14 and 8.15 illustrate the application of group reconstruction relief and merger relief on the cost of an investment in a subsidiary.

Example 8.14: *Group reconstruction relief and cost of investment*

Company B (a wholly owned subsidiary of Company A) issues 100 £1 ordinary shares to its holding company, A, in return for an investment in Company C held by A. The investment in C was previously carried by A as its original cost of £400. The fair value of C (and the shares issued by A) at the date of the transaction is £1,000.

How should B account for this transaction in its separate financial statements?

The decision depends on B's accounting policy for its investments in subsidiaries. If B's accounting policy is to carry its investments in subsidiaries at cost less impairment then we believe that B has an accounting policy choice to determine cost as either the previous carrying value of the investment in the transferor's books (by taking group reconstruction relief) or at fair value as follows:

	Dr	Cr
Investment in subsidiary	£400	
Share capital		£100
Share premium		£300

OR

	Dr	Cr
Investment in subsidiary	£1,000	
Share capital		£100
Share premium		£300
Merger reserve		£700

If B's accounting policy is to carry its investments at fair value (whether or not gains and losses on remeasurement are taken through profit and loss or through other comprehensive gains) then the investment in subsidiary must be measured at fair value.

As discussed above, regardless of the accounting policy election, section 611 permits the investor to restrict the amount transferred to share premium to the minimum premium value (i.e. the amount by which the base cost of assets transferred exceeds the base value of any liabilities transferred). In this example, B has elected to restrict the amount transferred to share premium in this way.

Example 8.15: *Merger relief and cost of investment*

Company A issues 100 £1 ordinary shares to a third party for 100% of the ordinary shares of Company B, and pays cash of £200. The fair value of Company B (and the total consideration paid by Company A) is £1,000.

How should A account for this transaction in its separate financial statements?

The decision depends on A's accounting policy for its investments in subsidiaries. If A's accounting policy is to carry its investments in subsidiaries at cost less impairment then we believe that A has an accounting policy choice as follows:

	Dr	Cr
Investment in subsidiary	£300	
Share capital		£100
Cash		£200

OR

	Dr	Cr
Investment in subsidiary	£1,000	
Share capital		£100
Merger reserve		£700
Cash		£200

Chapter 8

As discussed above, Appendix III of FRS 102 states that where the cost model is applied section 615 allows the initial carrying amount to be adjusted downwards so that it reflects the nominal value of the shares issued (and any minimum share premium required by group reconstruction relief) depending on the relief applied. Alternatively, an entity could ignore this option to reduce the carrying amount and use the fair value of B as its cost.

If B's accounting policy is to carry its investments at fair value (whether or not gains and losses on remeasurement are taken through profit and loss or through other comprehensive gains) then the investment in subsidiary must be measured at fair value.

In the 'fair value' example above, the excess of the consideration is described as a 'merger reserve'. Neither the CA 2006 nor FRS 102 specify the title of this reserve. However, given that the share premium requirements of the CA 2006 do not apply when merger relief is used, we believe that it is not appropriate to establish a reserve as 'share premium'.

Section 9 provides no guidance on accounting for contingent consideration on the acquisition of a subsidiary, associate or jointly controlled entity in individual or separate financial statements. However, we believe the guidance on contingent consideration (and adjustments to the cost of the combination) in a business combination discussed in Chapter 17 at 3.6.2 should be applied to the cost of investment in subsidiary in the parent's separate financial statements. This means that the cost at the acquisition date should include the estimated amount of the contingent consideration if it is probable and can be measured reliably. If contingent consideration is not recognised at the acquisition date but subsequently becomes probable and can be measured reliably, the additional consideration is treated as an adjustment to the cost of the investment. If future events that at the acquisition date were expected to occur do not occur, or the estimate needs to be revised, the cost of the investment should be adjusted accordingly. *[FRS 102.19.12-13A]*.

4.2.1.A   *Cost of investment in a subsidiary, associate or jointly controlled entity acquired in stages*

It may be that an investment in a subsidiary, associate or jointly controlled entity was acquired in stages so that, up to the date on which control, significant influence or joint control was first achieved the initial investment was accounted for as a financial asset at fair value under one of the accounting policy choices for recognition and measurement of financial instruments (i.e. Sections 11 and 12, IFRS 9 or IAS 39 – see Chapter 10 at 4). *[FRS 102.11.2, 12.2]*. This raises the question of what the carrying amount should be in the separate financial statements when the cost method is applied. In our view, the cost of the investment is the sum of the consideration given for each tranche. This is because 'historical cost' is the amount of cash or cash equivalents paid or the fair value of the consideration given to acquire the asset at the time of its acquisition. *[FRS 102.2.34(a)]*.

Any difference between the sum of the consideration given and the fair value of the investment should be reversed and reflected in other comprehensive income resulting in an adjustment to the component of equity containing the cumulative valuation gains and losses, i.e. retained earnings if the investment had been treated as at fair value through profit or loss or the 'available-for-sale reserve' where the investment has been treated as available-for-sale by an entity using the recognition and measurement provisions of IAS 39 or the revaluation reserve where the investment has been measured at fair value through other comprehensive income using the recognition and measurement provisions of IFRS 9 (see Chapter 10 at 4).

If changes to the carrying amount of the investment had resulted from an impairment charge, this charge may not necessarily be reversed. This is because the investment must still be considered for impairment in the separate financial statements of the investor. Therefore, additional consideration must be given as to whether Section 11 or Section 27 permit reversals of impairment and whether there are indicators that the impairment can be reversed, based on the classification of the investment.

4.2.2 Fair value of investment

Fair value is the amount for which an asset could be exchanged, a liability settled, or an equity instrument granted could be exchanged, between knowledgeable willing parties in an arm's length transaction. In the absence of any specific guidance provided in the relevant section of FRS 102, the guidance in the Appendix to Section 2 (see Chapter 4 at 3.13) is used in determining fair value. *[FRS 102 Appendix I].*

4.3 Group reorganisations

Group reorganisations involve the restructuring of the relationships between companies in a group by, for example, setting up a new holding company, changing the direct ownership of a subsidiary with a group or transferring businesses from one company to another. FRS 102 provides no explicit guidance on how to account for group reorganisations in separate financial statements. However, when the group reorganisation involves investments in subsidiaries, the requirements of Section 9 to account for investment in subsidiaries at either cost or fair value (see 4.2 above) will apply. When the cost model is applied, the discussion at 4.2.1 above should also be considered.

Example 8.16 below illustrates three scenarios for the accounting in the separate financial statements of a parent which measures investments in subsidiaries at cost less impairment and transfers one subsidiary to another subsidiary.

Example 8.16: *Cost of investment in subsidiary following transfer of subsidiary to another subsidiary*

Parent A has two wholly owned subsidiaries and measures those subsidiaries at cost less impairment. Both Subsidiary B and Subsidiary C have a carrying amount of £30 prior to the transaction.

Parent A transfers Subsidiary B to Subsidiary C.

In these scenarios, it is assumed that Subsidiary B has a recoverable amount of not less than £30 prior to the transaction, and that the increased investment in Subsidiary C is also recoverable.

Scenario 1 – transfer for nil consideration

The total cost of Parent A's investment in its subsidiaries does not change. Parent A's investment in Subsidiary B is not impaired as Parent A still owns and controls Subsidiary B (indirectly) via Subsidiary C.

Therefore, the accounting entries for Parent A are:

	Dr	Cr
Investment in Subsidiary C	£30	
Investment in Subsidiary B		£30

Parent A's total cost of investment in Subsidiary C is now £60 which reflects the commercial substance of the transaction.

Chapter 8

Scenario 2 – transfer for fair value, £40 consideration (intragroup receivable)

Parent A has received a financial asset as consideration for the sale of Subsidiary B to Subsidiary C. In accordance with Section 11 of FRS 102, Parent A recognises the financial asset at transaction price (also its initial fair value) of £40, derecognises the investment in Subsidiary B and recognises a gain of £10 in profit or loss if the receivable is considered to be qualifying consideration (if not, the gain is recognised in other comprehensive income).

Therefore, the accounting entries for Parent A are:

	Dr	Cr
Receivable from Subsidiary C	£40	
Investment in Subsidiary B		£30
Profit or loss		£10

Scenario 3 – transfer for an amount less than fair value, £20 consideration (intragroup receivable)

Parent A has received a financial asset as consideration for the sale of Subsidiary B to Subsidiary C. In accordance with Section 11 of FRS 102, Parent A recognises the financial asset at transaction price (also its initial fair value) of £20, derecognises the investment in Subsidiary B of £30 and recognises an increase in its investment in Subsidiary C of £10. No loss is recognised by Parent A because Parent A still owns and controls Subsidiary B (indirectly).

Therefore, the accounting entries for Parent A are:

	Dr	Cr
Receivable from Subsidiary C	£20	
Investment in Subsidiary B		£30
Investment in Subsidiary C	£10	

Accounting for a group reorganisation that is the acquisition of a business which is not an entity should, in individual financial statements, follow the requirements applicable to group reorganisations dealing with the application of merger accounting in individual financial statements as discussed in Chapter 17 at 5.4.

4.4   Common control transactions in individual and separate financial statements

Transactions often taken place between a parent entity and its subsidiaries or between subsidiaries within a group that may or may not be carried out at fair value. FRS 102 provides no accounting guidance on such transactions.

The CA 2006 states that where a company makes a distribution consisting of, or including, or treated as arising in consequence of the sale, transfer or other disposition of a non-cash asset such a distribution can be made at an undervalue only if the company has positive distributable reserves at the time of the distribution. *[s845]*. When a company makes a distribution of a non-cash asset, any part of that asset which represents an unrealised profit, can be treated as a realised profit for the purpose of determining the lawfulness of the distribution. *[s846]*.

In addition, group reconstruction relief can be applied when a subsidiary issues shares in exchange for a non-cash asset (see 4.2.1 above).

The following sections deal with common transactions between entities under common control. See also Chapter 17 at 5.4 for accounting for group reconstructions in individual financial statements.

4.4.1 Capital contributions

One form of transaction which is sometimes made within a group is a 'capital contribution', where one company injects funds in another (usually its subsidiary) in the form of a non-returnable gift. Whenever capital contributions are made, complex tax considerations can arise and should be addressed.

Capital contributions have no legal status in the UK – the term is not used anywhere in the CA 2006 or in FRS 102. This has led to uncertainty over the appropriate accounting treatment in the financial statements of both the giver and the receiver of the capital contribution.

4.4.1.A Treatment in the financial statements of the paying company

In the most common situation, where the contribution is made by a parent to one of its subsidiaries, the treatment is relatively straightforward; the amount of the contribution should be added to the cost of the investment in the subsidiary. As with any fixed asset, it will be necessary to write down the investment whenever it is determined that its value has been impaired; this should be considered when subsequent dividends are received from the subsidiary which could be regarded as having been met out of the capital contribution and hence representing a return of it.

When the contribution is made to a fellow-subsidiary, it can be usually presumed that the contribution was made on the direction of the entities' parent. However, facts and circumstances may indicate otherwise. If the contribution was made on the direction of the parent, consistent with the guidance issued by the FRC in *Staff Education Note 16 – Financing transactions* (SEN 16) – in respect of financing transactions (see Chapter 10 at 7.2.2 and 7.2.3), we believe the paying subsidiary should account for the transaction in equity as if it were a distribution to the parent. If the contribution was made for a reason other than that the entities are controlled by the same owner then the contribution should be accounted for as an expense through profit or loss. It is not possible to regard the contribution as an asset of any kind; it is neither an investment in the other company, nor can it be treated as a monetary receivable, since by definition there is no obligation on the part of the recipient to return it.

There may be circumstances in which the nature of the transaction gives rise to a funding commitment and therefore the recognition of a liability. Funding commitments are discussed in Chapter 19 at 3.9.

4.4.1.B Treatment in the financial statements of the receiving company

A subsidiary shall include a capital contribution received from its parent within equity and it should be reported in the statement of changes in equity. In terms of where it should be shown within equity, the most common treatment historically has been to credit the amount received to a separate reserve with a suitable title, such as 'capital contribution', or 'capital reserve'.

Notwithstanding this, the contribution may in some circumstances be regarded for distribution purposes as a realised profit, and accordingly be available to be paid out by way of dividend. However, where the contribution received is in the form of a non-monetary asset it is doubtful whether this should be the case. This is the position taken in TECH 02/17BL which regards the contribution of assets from owners in their capacity as such as giving rise to a 'profit', but whether it is a realised profit will depend on the assets contributed meeting the definition of qualifying consideration. Where a contribution is regarded for distribution purposes as a realised profit, it may be appropriate to reclassify the reserve to which the contribution was originally taken as part of the profit and loss account balance (i.e. to retained earnings).

Where the contribution is received from a fellow-subsidiary, as per 4.4.1.A above, it can be usually presumed that the contribution was made on the direction of the entities' parent. However, facts and circumstances may indicate otherwise. If the contribution was made on the direction of the parent, consistent with the guidance issued by the FRC in SEN 16, we believe the receiving subsidiary should account for the transaction in equity as if it were a capital contribution from the parent. If the contribution was made for a reason other than that the entities are controlled by the same owner then the contribution should be accounted for as income through profit or loss (if the contribution is a realised profit for distribution purposes) or other comprehensive income (if the contribution is not a realised profit).

4.4.1.C   *Contribution and distribution of non-monetary assets*

These transactions involve transfers of inventory, property, plant and equipment, intangible assets, investment property and investments in subsidiaries, associates and joint ventures from one entity to another for no consideration. These arrangements are not contractual but are equity transactions: either in specie capital contributions (an asset is gifted by a parent to a subsidiary) or non-cash distributions (an asset is given by a subsidiary to its parent).

The relevant sections of FRS 102 (Sections 13, 16, 17 and 18) refer to assets being recognised at cost. Similarly, investments in subsidiaries, associates and jointly controlled entities may be recognised at cost as discussed at 4.1 and 4.2 above.

In our view, a choice exists as to how the cost is determined. The choice is:

- recognise the transaction at the consideration agreed between the parties (i.e. recognise it at zero); or
- recognise the transaction at fair value, regardless of the agreed consideration of zero, with the difference between that amount and fair value recognised as an equity transaction (capital contribution).

It is in practice more common for an entity that has received an asset in what is purely an equity transaction to recognise it at fair value.

Where the assets are being transferred as part of a group reconstruction (involving the transfer of a business from one group entity to another), *[FRS 102 Appendix I]*, and merger accounting is applied, they can also be recognised at the book values in the financial statements of the transferor (see Chapter 17 at 5.4.2 which also discusses whether the book values should be those shown in the individual financial statements or consolidated financial statements).

When fair value is used to determine cost, part of the difference between fair value and zero may reflect additional goods and services but, once they have been accounted for, any remaining difference will be a contribution or distribution of equity for a subsidiary or an increase in the investment held or distribution received by the parent.

The entity that gives away the asset must reflect the transaction. A parent that makes an in specie capital contribution to its subsidiary will recognise an increase in investment in that subsidiary provided the increase does not result in impairment of the investment. One view is that the transaction lacks substance for the parent since it has simply swapped a direct investment in a non-monetary asset for an indirect investment in the same asset via its subsidiary. If the transaction lacks substance, the parent recognises the additional cost of investment in the subsidiary at the carrying amount of the non-monetary asset given up. This accounting would usually be appropriate if the subsidiary was a newly incorporated company or when the subsidiary is wholly owned. If the transaction is considered to have substance to the parent, it could choose to recognise its additional investment in the subsidiary at the fair value of the consideration given, i.e. the fair value of the non-monetary asset given up. Any gain recognised as a result of this accounting would be unrealised and recognised in other comprehensive income, since the additional investment received in the subsidiary, an unquoted subsidiary, would not be regarded as qualifying consideration (see also Chapter 17 at 5.4.4.A).

A subsidiary that makes a distribution in specie to its parent shall account for the transaction by derecognising the distributed asset at its carrying value against retained earnings. The Basis for Conclusions explains that a distribution to a shareholder does not generate a profit and therefore FRS 102 does not include a requirement to recognise a liability to pay a dividend at fair value (as opposed to carrying value). *[FRS 102.BC.B22.1]*. However, disclosure of the fair value of dividends is required (except when the non-cash assets are ultimately controlled by the same parties both before and after the distribution – as would generally be the case for a dividend from a subsidiary to a parent). *[FRS 102.22.18]*. As the distribution received by the parent is a non-monetary asset, this is unlikely to represent 'qualifying consideration' under TECH 02/17BL and therefore is an unrealised profit and should not be reflected in the parent's income statement, but in other comprehensive income.

Consistent with the treatment of capital contributions discussed at 4.4.1.A and 4.4.1.B above, contributions and distributions of non-monetary assets between fellow subsidiaries can be generally presumed to have been made on the direction of the entities' parent and should therefore also be accounted for as equity transactions.

4.4.1.D   *Incurring expenses and settling liabilities without recharges*

Entities frequently incur costs that provide a benefit to fellow group entities, e.g. audit, management or advertising fees, and do not recharge the costs. The beneficiary is not party to the transaction and does not directly incur an obligation to settle a liability. It may elect to recognise the cost, in which case it will charge profit or loss and credit retained earnings with equivalent amounts; there will be no change to its net assets. If the expense is incurred by the parent, the parent could elect to increase the investment in the subsidiary rather than expensing the amount. This could lead to a carrying value that might be impaired. However, if the expense relates to a share-based payment there is no policy choice as expenses incurred for a subsidiary must be added to the carrying amount of the parent and recognised by the subsidiary (see Chapter 23 at 13). Consistent with the treatment of capital contributions and contributions and distributions of non-monetary assets discussed at 4.4.1.A to 4.4.1.C above, incurring expenses without recharges on behalf of fellow subsidiaries can be generally presumed to have been made on the direction of the entities' parent and, if recognised, should therefore also be accounted for as equity transactions.

Many groups recharge expenses indirectly, by making management charges, or recoup the funds through intra-group dividends, and in these circumstances it would be inappropriate to recognise the transaction in any entity other than the one that makes the payment.

A parent or other group entity may settle a liability on behalf of a subsidiary. If this is not recharged, the liability will have been extinguished in the entity's accounts. This raises the question of whether the gain should be taken to profit or loss or to equity. FRS 102 defines revenue as the gross inflow of economic benefits during the period arising in the course of ordinary activities of the entity when those inflows result in increases in equity, other than increases relating to contributions from equity participants. *[FRS 102 Appendix I]*. Except in unusual circumstances, the forgiveness of debt will usually be a contribution from owners and therefore ought to be taken to equity. It will usually be appropriate for a parent to add the payment to the investment in the subsidiary as a capital contribution, subject always to any impairment of the investment.

If one subsidiary settles a liability of its fellow subsidiary then, consistent with 4.4.1.A above, it can be generally presumed that the contribution was made on the direction of the entities' parent and we believe the settling subsidiary should account for the transaction in equity as a distribution to the parent. If the contribution was made for a reason other than that the entities are controlled by the same owner then the settlement should be accounted for as an expense through profit or loss.

4.4.2   *Transactions involving non-monetary assets*

4.4.2.A   *The parent exchanges property, plant and equipment for a non-monetary asset of the subsidiary*

The exchange of an asset for another non-monetary asset is accounted for by recognising the received asset at fair value unless the transaction lacks commercial substance or the fair value of neither the asset received nor the asset given up is reliably measurable. *[FRS 102.17.14]*.

If the exchange is of assets with dissimilar values this indicates that, unless the difference means that other goods and services are being provided (e.g. a management fee) that the transaction includes an equity contribution. This means that the entity has the following accounting choice:

- recognise the transaction as an exchange of assets at fair value with an equity transaction. Any difference between the fair value of the asset received and the fair value of the asset given up is an equity transaction (or capital contribution) while the difference between the carrying value of the asset given up and its fair value is recognised in other comprehensive income as it is not a realised profit; or

- recognise the transaction as an exchange of assets at fair value of the asset received. Any difference between the fair value of the asset received and the carrying value of the asset given up is recognised in other comprehensive income as it is not a realised profit.

When the first alternative is used, the difference will be accounted by the subsidiary as a contribution or distribution of equity; and by the parent as an increase in the investment held in the subsidiary or a distribution received. As discussed at 4.4.1.C, a distribution received by the parent will be recognised in other comprehensive income as it is not a realised profit. Consistent with the treatment of capital contributions discussed at 4.4.1.A and 4.4.1.B above, contributions and distributions of non-monetary assets between fellow subsidiaries can be generally presumed to have been made on the direction of the entities' parent and should therefore also be accounted for as equity transactions.

4.4.2.B   Acquisition and sale of assets for shares

These transactions include the transfer of inventory, property, plant and equipment, intangible assets, investment property and investments in subsidiaries, jointly controlled entities and associates by one entity in return for the shares of the other entity. These transactions are usually between a parent and subsidiary where the subsidiary is the transferee that issues shares to the parent in exchange for the assets received.

For the subsidiary, transactions that involve the transfer of inventory, property, plant and equipment, intangible assets and investment property in exchange for shares are within the scope of Section 26 – *Share-based Payment*. Accordingly, the assets should be recognised at fair value unless that fair value cannot be estimated reliably. If the entity cannot estimate reliably the fair value of the goods or services received, the entity should measure their value, and the corresponding increase in equity, by reference to the fair value of the equity instruments granted. *[FRS 102.26.7]*.

However, some subsidiaries that are wholly owned are entitled to group reconstruction relief on share issues (see 4.2.1 above) and therefore the question arises as to whether the asset received can be recorded at a cost net of group reconstruction relief (usually the previous carrying amount of the transferor) rather than fair value (the usual approach for share-based payments). The Appendix on Legal Requirements to FRS 102 refers to using group reconstruction relief only in terms of the 'cost' of investments in subsidiaries. *[FRS 102 Appendix III.24]*. It is therefore not clear whether the FRC intended that the application of group reconstruction relief could be extended to asset purchases.

For the parent, based on 4.2.1 above, the cost of the new investment should be recorded at the fair value of the consideration given (i.e. the fair value of the asset sold). However, where it is considered that the transaction lacks substance for the parent, it recognises the additional cost of investment in the subsidiary at the carrying amount of the non-monetary asset given up. This accounting would generally be appropriate if the subsidiary was a newly incorporated company or when the subsidiary is wholly owned. If the transaction is considered to have substance to the parent, it could choose to recognise its additional investment in the subsidiary at the fair value of the consideration given, i.e. the fair value of the non-monetary asset given up. Any gain recognised as a result of this accounting would be unrealised and recognised in other comprehensive income, since the additional investment received in the subsidiary, an unquoted subsidiary, would not be regarded as qualifying consideration.

Chapter 8

4.4.2.C   Acquisition and sale of assets for cash (or equivalent)

These transactions include the transfer of inventory, property, plant and equipment, intangible assets, investment property and investments in subsidiaries, jointly controlled entities and associates by one entity in return for cash or an equivalent consideration such as an inter-company loan. The transactions can be between a parent and a subsidiary or between fellow subsidiaries. Often in these transactions the consideration received is not fair value but the carrying value of the transferred asset in the transferee entity.

Consistent with the guidance at 4.4.1.C above, we believe that a choice exists as to how the entity acquiring the asset determines cost. The choice is:

- recognise the asset at the consideration agreed between the parties; or
- recognise the asset at fair value, regardless of the agreed consideration, with the difference between the consideration and fair value recognised as an equity transaction (or capital contribution).

When fair value is used to determine cost, the difference will be a contribution or distribution of equity for the subsidiary or an increase in the investment held in the subsidiary or a distribution received by the parent. As discussed at 4.4.1.C, a distribution received by the parent will be recognised in other comprehensive income as it is not a realised profit. Consistent with the treatment of capital contributions discussed at 4.4.1.A and 4.4.1.B above, contributions and distributions of non-monetary assets between fellow subsidiaries can be generally presumed to have been made on the direction of the entities' parent and should therefore also be accounted for as equity transactions.

The entity that sells the asset (and the entity that purchases the asset) must recognise the consideration received (or paid) in accordance with its accounting policy choice under Sections 11 or 12 if the consideration is a financial asset (or financial liability) – see 4.4.3 below.

4.4.3   Financial instruments within the scope of Sections 11 and 12

Section 11 requires the initial recognition of financial assets and financial liabilities to be transaction price unless the arrangement constitutes a financing arrangement when it should be measured at the present value of future payments discounted at a market interest rate. *[FRS 102.11.13]*.

A loan provided or received at zero (or a below market) rate of interest constitutes a financing transaction. For loans other than those repayable on demand or where the concessions available not to account initially at present value for certain loans (such as public benefit entity concessionary loans and loans made to small entities by a director or his group of close family members (where that group contains a shareholder) are not taken, a difference arises between the amount of the cash received or advanced and the present value of the loan. This difference reflects the fact that the lender has made a loan at a lower than market rate of interest and thereby has provided an additional benefit to the borrower. When a loan is made at a non-market rate of interest and the lender and the borrower are related parties because one owns the other or the lender and the borrower are owned by the same person, the difference arising on initial recognition of the loan would generally be accounted for in equity as a distribution or capital contribution for a subsidiary (or fellow subsidiary) or an increase in the investment held in the subsidiary or a distribution received by the parent. The accounting for these transactions is discussed in Chapter 10 at 7.2.2 and 7.2.3.

When an entity has elected to apply IAS 39 and/or IFRS 9 to recognise and measure financial instruments (as permitted by Sections 11 and 12) the initial recognition is fair value. Any difference between the fair value and the terms of the agreement are recognised as an equity transaction (i.e. either as a distribution or a capital contribution) for a subsidiary (or fellow subsidiary) or an increase in the investment held or a distribution received by a parent. See Chapter 10 at 7.2.3.

4.4.4 Financial guarantee contracts – parent guarantee issued on behalf of subsidiary

When an entity has elected to apply IAS 39 and/or IFRS 9 to its financial instruments financial guarantees must be initially recognised at fair value. Otherwise, they are recognised under Section 21 – *Provisions and Contingencies* – which means that a liability does not need to be recognised if it is not probable.

When a financial guarantee is initially recognised at fair value, it is normally appropriate for a parent that gives a guarantee to treat the debit that arises on recognising the guarantee at fair value as an additional investment in its subsidiary. The situation is different for the subsidiary or fellow subsidiary that is the beneficiary of the guarantee. There will be no separate recognition of the financial guarantee unless it is provided to the lender separate and apart from the original borrowing, does not form part of the overall terms of the loan and would not transfer with the loan if it were to be assigned by the lender to a third party. This means that few guarantees will be reflected separately in the financial statements of the entities that benefit from the guarantees. In any event the amounts are unlikely to be significant.

4.5 Intermediate payment arrangements

The requirements in respect of intermediate payment arrangements are, in substance, designed to 'consolidate' an employee benefit trust (EBT) or employee share option trust (ESOP) in individual or separate financial statements. It is explained in the Basis for Conclusions that these requirements (derived from previous UK GAAP) have been added to Section 9 to avoid an entity that has no entities that it controls other than an intermediate payment arrangement from having to prepare consolidated financial statements. *[FRS 102.BC.B9.5]*.

FRS 102 does not define intermediate payment arrangements. However, Section 9 states that intermediate payment arrangements may take a variety of forms and that: *[FRS 102.9.33]*

- the intermediary is usually established by a sponsoring entity and constituted as a trust, although other arrangements are possible;
- the relationship between the sponsoring entity and the intermediary may take different forms. For example, when the intermediary is constituted as a trust, the sponsoring entity will not have a right to direct the intermediary's activities.

However, in these and other cases the sponsoring entity may give advice to the intermediary or may be relied upon by the intermediary to provide the information it needs to carry on its activities. Sometimes, the way the intermediary has been set up gives it little discretion in the broad nature of its activities;

- the arrangements are most commonly used to pay employees, although they are sometimes used to compensate supplies of goods and services other than employee services. Sometimes, the sponsoring entity's employees and other suppliers are not the only beneficiaries of the arrangement. Other beneficiaries may include past employees and their dependants, and the intermediary may be entitled to make charitable donations;

- the precise identity of the persons or entities that will receive payments from the intermediary, and the amounts that they will receive, are not usually agreed at the outset;

- the sponsoring entity often has the right to appoint or veto the appointment of the intermediary's trustees (or its directors or the equivalent); and

- the payments made to the intermediary and the payments made by the intermediary are often cash payments but may involve other transfers of value.

Examples of intermediate payment arrangements are ESOPs and EBTs that are used to facilitate employee shareholders under remuneration schemes. Section 9 states that in a typical employee trust arrangement for share-based payments, an entity makes payments to a trust or guarantees borrowing by the trust and the trust uses its funds to accumulate assets to pay the entity's employees for services the employees have rendered to the entity.

Section 9 considers that although the trustees of an intermediary must act at all times in accordance with the interests of the beneficiaries of the intermediary, most intermediaries (particularly those established as a means of remunerating employees) are specifically designed so as to serve the purposes of the sponsoring entity, and to ensure that there will be minimal risk of any conflict arising between the duties of the trustees of the intermediary and the interest of the sponsoring entity, such that there is nothing to encumber implementation of the wishes of the sponsoring entity in practice. Where this is the case, the sponsoring entity has *de facto* control. *[FRS 102.9.33].*

An amendment made by the Triennial review 2017 clarifies that it is possible for an entity to be owned by a trust established for the benefit of employees without the entity controlling the trust. The example provided is one where the entity is a co-operative, owned by its employees, and all of the shares are held in trust for the individual employees but the shares never vest in individual employees, with dividends from the company being distributed to employees solely in accordance with the provisions of the trust deed. *[FRS 102.9.33A].*

4.5.1 Accounting for intermediate payment arrangements

When a sponsoring entity makes payments (or transfers assets) to an intermediary, there is a rebuttable presumption that the entity has exchanged one asset for another and that the payment itself does not represent an immediate expense. To rebut this presumption at the time the payment is made to the intermediary, the entity must demonstrate: *[FRS 102.9.34]*

- it will not obtain future economic benefit from the amounts transferred; or
- it does not have control of the right or other access to future economic benefit it is expected to receive.

When a payment to an intermediary is an exchange by the sponsoring entity of one asset for another, any asset the intermediary acquires in a subsequent exchange transaction will also be under the control of the entity. Accordingly, assets and liabilities of the intermediary will be accounted for by the sponsoring entity as an extension of its own business and recognised in its own individual financial statements. An asset will cease to be recognised as an asset of the sponsoring entity when, for example, the asset of the intermediary vests unconditionally with identified beneficiaries. *[FRS 102.9.35]*.

A sponsoring entity may distribute its own equity instruments, or other equity instruments to an intermediary in order to facilitate employee shareholdings under a remuneration scheme. When this is the case and the sponsoring entity has control, or *de facto* control, of the assets and liabilities of the intermediary, the commercial effect is that the sponsoring entity is, for all practical purposes, in the same position as if it had purchased the shares directly. *[FRS 102.9.36]*.

When an intermediary entity holds the sponsoring entity's equity instruments, the sponsoring entity shall account for the equity instruments as if it had purchased them directly. The sponsoring entity shall account for the assets and liabilities of the intermediary in its individual (or separate) financial statements as follows: *[FRS 102.9.37]*

- the consideration paid for the equity instruments of the sponsoring entity shall be deducted from equity until such time that the equity instruments vest unconditionally with employees;
- consideration paid or received for the purchase or sale of the sponsoring entity's own equity instruments shall be shown as separate amounts in the statement of changes in equity;
- other assets and liabilities of the intermediary shall be recognised as assets and liabilities of the sponsoring entity;
- no gain or loss shall be recognised in profit or loss or other comprehensive income on the purchase, sale, issue or cancellation of the entity's own equity instruments;
- finance costs and any administration expenses shall be recognised on an accruals basis rather than ad funding payments are made to the intermediary; and
- any dividend income arising on the sponsored entity's own equity instruments shall be excluded from profit or loss and deducted from the aggregate of dividends paid.

Chapter 8

Example 8.17 below illustrates the application of these requirements.

Example 8.17:   EBTs in individual or separate financial statements of sponsoring entity

A sponsoring entity lends its EBT £1,000,000 which the EBT uses to make a market purchase of 200,000 shares in the entity. Employees of the entity are beneficiaries of the trust and, a short while after purchase, the shares vest unconditionally with the identified beneficiaries in exchange for a payment of £200,000. During the period the EBT pays £100,000 of administration costs.

In the separate or individual financial statements of the entity, on the basis that the sponsoring entity accounts for the EBT as an extension of its own business the following accounting entries result:

	£'000	£'000
Equity	1,000	
Cash (market purchase of shares)		1,000
Equity		200
Cash (Shares vest to employees)	200	
Profit or loss	100	
Cash (administration expenses)		100

No entries are made for the 'loan' between the sponsoring entity and the EBT as this is considered to be a transaction by the sponsoring entity with itself.

Any share-based payment charges incurred by the sponsoring employee in respect of the shares granted to the employees are accounted for separately under Section 26.

4.6   Disclosures in individual and separate financial statements

4.6.1   *Disclosures required by Section 9 in separate financial statements*

The following disclosures are required where a parent prepares separate financial statements:

- that the statements are separate financial statements;
- a description of the methods used to account for investments in subsidiaries, associates and jointly controlled entities; *[FRS 102.9.27]*
- a parent that uses one of the exemptions from presenting consolidated financial statements (described in 3.1 above) shall disclose the grounds on which the parent is exempt; *[FRS 102.9.27A]* and
- when a parent adopts a policy of accounting for its subsidiaries, associates or jointly controlled entities at fair value with changes in fair value recognised in profit or loss, it must make the disclosures required by Section 11 (see Chapter 10 at 11.2.2) in order to comply with the requirements of paragraph 36(4) of Schedule 1 to the Regulations (and the equivalent paragraphs in Schedules 2 and 3). *[FRS 102.9.27B]*. These disclosures must be made even if the parent is a qualifying entity (see Chapter 1) since they are required by the Regulations.

4.6.2 Disclosures required by Section 9 in individual and separate financial statements in respect of intermediate payment arrangements

When a sponsoring entity recognises the assets and liabilities held by an intermediary, it should disclose sufficient information in the notes to its financial statements to enable users to understand the significance of the intermediary and the arrangement in the context of the sponsoring entity's financial statements. This should include: *[FRS 102.9.38]*

- a description of the main features of the intermediary including the arrangements for making payments and for distributing equity instruments;

- any restrictions relating to the assets and liabilities of the intermediary;

- the amount and nature of the assets and liabilities held by the intermediary which have not yet vested unconditionally with the beneficiaries of the arrangement;

- the amount that has been deducted from equity and the number of equity instruments held by the intermediary, which have not yet vested unconditionally with the beneficiaries of the arrangement;

- for entities that have their equity instruments listed or publicly traded on a stock exchange or market, the market value of the equity instruments held by the intermediary which have not yet vested unconditionally with employees;

- the extent to which the equity instruments are under options to employees, or have been conditionally gifted to them; and

- the amount that has been deducted from the aggregate dividends paid by the sponsoring entity.

4.6.3 Additional disclosures in respect of investments in subsidiaries in separate financial statements required by the CA 2006 and the Regulations

The following disclosures are required by the CA 2006 and the Regulations in respect of subsidiaries, in separate financial statements:

- the name of each subsidiary undertaking and the address of the undertaking's registered office (whether in or outside the United Kingdom) and, if unincorporated, the address of its principal place of business. There is no relief available to limit this disclosure to those of the principal subsidiaries if it is of excessive length; *[4 Sch 1]*

- for each subsidiary not included in the consolidated accounts:*[4 Sch 2]*

    - the aggregated amount of its capital and reserves as at the end of its relevant financial year; and

    - its profit or loss for that year.

    This information is not required if the subsidiary is included in the consolidated accounts under the equity method of accounting or if the subsidiary is not required by the CA 2006 to deliver a copy of its balance sheet for its relevant financial year and does not otherwise publish its balance sheet anywhere in the world and the company's holding is less than 50% of the nominal value of the shares (or if the information is not material);

- the number, description and amount of shares in the parent company held by or on behalf of subsidiary undertakings must be disclosed; *[4 Sch 3]*

Chapter 8

If the company is not required to prepare group financial statements:

- the reasons why that is the case; *[4 Sch 10(1)]*

- if the reason is that all the subsidiaries fall within the exclusions provided in section 405 (see 3.1.1.E and 3.4 above), with respect to each subsidiary which exclusion applies; *[4 Sch 10(2)]*

- for each subsidiary, the identity of each class of shares held and the proportion of the nominal value of that class of shares held, with shares held directly by the company itself distinguished from those attributed to the company held by subsidiaries; *[4 Sch 11]*

- when a subsidiary undertaking's financial year does not end with that of the company the date on which the last financial year ended (last before the end of the company's financial year); *[4 Sch 12]*

- if exempt by virtue of section 400 (see 3.1.1 and 3.1.1.A above), the fact that it is so exempt from the obligation to prepare and deliver group accounts and, in respect of the undertaking in whose consolidated financial statements it is included, the name, the address of the undertaking's registered office (whether in or outside the UK) and, if unincorporated, address of its principal place of business; *[s400(2)(c)-(d)]*

- if exempt by virtue of section 401 (see 3.1.1 and 3.1.1.B above), the fact that it is so exempt from the obligation to prepare and deliver group accounts and, in respect of the undertaking in whose consolidated financial statements it is included, the name, the address of the undertaking's registered office (whether in or outside the UK) and, if unincorporated, address of its principal place of business. *[s401(2)(d)-(e)]*.

Disclosures in respect of investments in associates and jointly controlled entities in separate financial statements are discussed in Chapters 12 at 5.4.2 and Chapter 13 at 4.3.2 respectively.

5   SUMMARY OF GAAP DIFFERENCES

The key differences between FRS 102 and IFRS are set out below.

	FRS 102	*IFRS*
Requirement to prepare consolidated financial statements	Required only if an entity is a parent at the reporting date.	Required if an entity was a parent at any time during the reporting period.
Exemptions from consolidation for parents	Companies subject to the small companies regime are exempt provided they are not a member of a group which, at any time during the financial year, has an ineligible member. Intermediate parents are exempt (subject to conditions) if included in consolidated financial statements of a parent prepared under the EU Accounting Directive, IFRS or an 'equivalent' GAAP (to either).	No exemption for small companies. Intermediate parents are exempt (subject to conditions) but only if included in consolidated financial statements of parent prepared under IFRS (although in certain circumstances financial statements prepared under a national GAAP that is identical with IFRS in all respects could be considered to be under IFRS).
Definition of control	Investor has the power to govern the financial and operating policies of an entity so as to obtain benefits from its activities. Limited application guidance.	Investor is exposed, or has rights to variable returns from involvement with the investee and has the ability to affect those returns through its power over the investee. More detailed application guidance.
Subsidiaries excluded from consolidation	Subsidiaries are excluded from consolidation if they operate under severe long term restrictions or are held exclusively with a view to subsequent resale.	No similar concepts. However, a subsidiary which operates under severe long-term restrictions may fail to meet the IFRS definition of a subsidiary due to lack of control.
Investment entities	Subsidiary held as part of an investment portfolio is not consolidated, but recognised at fair value through profit or loss.	A parent that is an investment entity must measure all subsidiaries (other than those providing investment management services that are not investment entities) at fair value through profit or loss.
Special purpose entity/Structured entity	A special purpose entity is an entity created to establish a narrow objective. Control of a special purpose entity is a risks/reward model.	A structured entity is an entity designed so that voting or similar rights are not the dominant factor in deciding who controls it. Same control criteria as for other entities.
Initial measurement of non-controlling interests in a business combination	Measured at the non-controlling interest's share of the net amount of the identifiable assets, liabilities and contingent liabilities recognised.	Accounting policy choice for acquirer to recognise non-controlling interests (that are present ownership interests and entitle the holder to a proportionate share of net assets in the event of a liquidation) at either their share of net amount of identifiable assets or at fair value. Other non-controlling interests must be recognised at fair value.

Chapter 8

	FRS 102	*IFRS*
Accounting for retained interest on loss of control of a subsidiary	Carrying amount of net assets (and goodwill) is cost on initial measurement of retained investment.	Retained investment must be recognised at fair value on date that control is lost.
Cumulative exchange differences on disposal of a foreign operation when control of a subsidiary is lost	Not recycled to profit or loss.	Recycled to profit or loss.
Cumulative exchange differences on partial disposal of a foreign operation without loss of control	Not recycled to profit or loss.	Recycled to non-controlling interest on a proportionate basis.
Exchanges of business or other non-monetary assets for an interest in a subsidiary in consolidated financial statements	Gains that are not realised are reported in other comprehensive income.	No distinction between realised and unrealised gains and all gains/losses reported in profit or loss.
Investments in subsidiaries, associates and jointly controlled entities in individual and separate financial statements	Accounting policy choice for each class (subsidiaries which are held as part of an investment portfolio, subsidiaries that are not held as part of an investment portfolio, associates and jointly controlled entities) to measure at either cost, fair value through other comprehensive income or fair value through profit or loss. The equity method of accounting is not permitted.	Accounting policy choice for each category to measure at either cost, fair value through other comprehensive income, fair value through profit or loss or under the equity method of accounting.
Cost of investment in a subsidiary in separate financial statements	Merger relief and group reconstruction relief is available, in certain circumstances, that permits cost to be equal to the nominal value of shares issued (merger relief) or cost to the transferor (or if lower, the previous carrying amount of the investment) in the transferor's books (group reconstruction relief).	No option to use nominal value of the shares issued or generally the previous carrying amount of the investment in the transferor's books. A new parent must measure cost at the carrying amount of its share of the equity items of the original parent for certain group reconstructions.
Intermediate payment arrangements	Accounted for as an extension of the parent's own business in its separate financial statements.	No guidance. In practice, an entity could use either the parent extension method or treat as an investment in subsidiary.
Disclosures in consolidated financial statements (key differences)		
Non-controlling interests that are material to the reporting entity	Summarised financial information is not required.	Summarised financial information is required for each subsidiary with material non-controlling interests.

Interests in consolidated special purpose or structured entities	No specific disclosures required for consolidated special purpose entities (would be included within the general disclosure requirements for subsidiaries).	Disclosures required in respect of contractual arrangements, obligations and intentions to provide financial support to consolidated structured entities.
Investments in unconsolidated special purpose/structured entities	Disclosure of the nature and extent of interests and the risks associated with those entities. Basis for Conclusions refers to disclosure as 'principle based'. No additional guidance.	Disclosure of nature and extent of interests and nature of and changes in the risks associated with those entities. Extensive additional guidance and mandated disclosures (in addition to disclosures required by other IFRSs).
Significant restrictions and financial support provided to subsidiaries	Disclosure of significant restrictions on ability to transfer funds to parent.	As well as disclosure of significant restrictions, disclosures required of guarantees, provisions of financial support (contractual and non-contractual) and current intentions to provide financial support.
Changes in ownership interest of a subsidiary that do not result in loss of control	No separate schedule required.	Separate schedule required showing the effects on equity attributable to owners of the parent of any changes.
Unconsolidated subsidiaries	The Regulations require disclosure of the capital and reserves and profit and loss for each material subsidiary not included in the consolidated financial statements.	Separate disclosure required of significant restrictions and financial support. No requirement to disclose the capital and reserves and profit and loss for each material subsidiary not included in the consolidated financial statements.
Differences of accounting rules as between a parent's group and individual accounts	Disclosure required by the Regulations.	No disclosure requirement.

Disclosures in individual and separate financial statements
(key differences)

Investments in unconsolidated special purpose/structured entities	No specific disclosures required (in addition to those required by other sections of FRS 102).	Extensive disclosures required (in addition to disclosures required by other IFRSs).
Intermediate payment arrangements	Various disclosures required.	No specific disclosures required for intermediate payment arrangements (although these may be structured entities – see above).

Chapter 9   Accounting policies, estimates and errors

Chapter 9

588   *Chapter 9*

List of examples

Chapter 9   Accounting policies, estimates and errors

1   INTRODUCTION

Section 10 – *Accounting Policies, Estimates and Errors* – sets out the requirements for:
(a) selecting and applying the accounting policies used in preparing financial statements:
(b) accounting for changes in accounting estimates; and (c) accounting for corrections of
errors in prior period financial statements. *[FRS 102.10.1]*.

Overall, Section 10 is similar to IAS 8 – *Accounting Policies, Changes in Accounting
Estimates and Errors*.

2   COMPARISON BETWEEN SECTION 10 AND IFRS

The principal differences between Section 10 and IFRS are in respect of:

- the hierarchy established where the accounting for a transaction is not specifically
  addressed within the standard (see 2.1 below); and

- presentation and disclosures (see 2.2 below).

The disclosure requirements of Section 10 are less onerous to a reporting entity than
those of IAS 8.

2.1   Hierarchy for selecting accounting policies

Where a section or standard does not specifically address a transaction, other event or
condition, Section 10 permits but does not require an entity's management to refer to
EU-adopted IFRS in the hierarchy established to determine how judgement is used in
developing and applying an accounting policy. *[FRS 102.10.6]*. IAS 8's equivalent wording
refers to any other standard setting body that uses a similar conceptual framework (to
IFRS). *[IAS 8.12]*. This may result in different accounting policies being applied under
FRS 102 for a particular transaction, event or condition compared to IFRS.

2.2   Key presentation and disclosure differences

IAS 8 requires disclosure of the impact of a new IFRS that is issued but not effective.
[IAS 8.30]. Section 10 does not require disclosure of the impact on the financial statements

of future periods of changes to FRS 102 that have been issued but are not yet effective. This would apply both to changes to individual sections of FRS 102 and changes to IFRSs which are being applied by a reporting entity under paragraphs 1.4, 1.5 and 1.7 or 11.2(b) and 11.2(c) of FRS 102 (for example IAS 33 – *Earnings per Share*).

IAS 1 – *Presentation of Financial Statements* – requires a third statement of financial position in such circumstances. *[IAS 1.40A]*. FRS 102 does not require a third statement of financial position as at the beginning of the preceding period to be presented whenever an accounting policy is applied retrospectively or a retrospective restatement or reclassification is made in the financial statements.

3   REQUIREMENTS OF SECTION 10 FOR ACCOUNTING POLICIES, ESTIMATES AND ERRORS

Section 10 sets out the requirements for selecting and applying accounting policies, as well as accounting for changes in accounting estimates and corrections of errors in prior period financial statements. *[FRS 102.10.1.]*

3.1   Terms used in Section 10

The following definitions are introduced: *[FRS 102 Appendix I]*

Accounting policies are the specific principles, bases, conventions, rules and practices applied by an entity in preparing and presenting financial statements.

A *change in accounting estimate* is an adjustment of the carrying amount of an asset or a liability, or the amount of the periodic consumption of an asset, that results from the assessment of the present status of, and expected future benefits and obligations associated with, assets and liabilities. Changes in accounting estimates result from new information or new developments and, accordingly, are not corrections of errors.

Errors are omissions from, and misstatements in, the entity's financial statements for one or more prior periods arising from a failure to use, or misuse of, reliable information that: (a) was available when financial statements for those periods were authorised for issue; and (b) could reasonably be expected to have been obtained and taken into account in the preparation and presentation of those financial statements.

Applying a requirement is *impracticable* when the entity cannot apply it after making every reasonable effort to do so.

3.2   Selection and application of accounting policies

The whole purpose of accounting standards is to specify the accounting policies and presentation and disclosure requirements that should be applied by an entity. Entities applying FRS 102 do not therefore have a free hand in selecting accounting policies. However, a reporting entity should select accounting policies to account for transactions, other events or conditions when financial reporting standards provide multiple choices or do not address accounting for such transactions, other events or conditions.

Accounting policies are defined as the specific principles, bases, conventions, rules and practices applied by an entity in preparing and presenting financial statements. *[FRS 102 Appendix I, 10.2]*. This means that an accounting policy is not just a question of how to measure a transaction but also how items are classified and presented in the financial statements. For example, an entity makes an accounting policy choice as to whether to adopt a single statement of comprehensive income or adopt a two statement presentation. Similarly, an entity makes an accounting policy choice as to whether to present operating cash flows under the direct or indirect method.

The starting point of Section 10 is that if an FRS specifically addresses a transaction, other event or condition, an entity shall apply that FRS. However, the requirement need not be followed if the effect of doing so would not be material. *[FRS 102.10.3]*. See Chapter 4 at 3.2.3 for further details on materiality.

There will be circumstances where a particular event, transaction or other condition is not specifically addressed by an FRS. When this is the case, Section 10 sets out a hierarchy of guidance to use. The primary requirement of the hierarchy is that management should use its judgement in developing and applying an accounting policy that results in information that is: *[FRS 102.10.4]*

- relevant to the economic decision-making needs of users; and
- reliable in that the financial statements:
  - represent faithfully the financial position, financial performance and cash flows of the entity;
  - reflect the economic substance of transactions, other events and conditions, and not merely the legal form;
  - are neutral, i.e. free from bias;
  - are prudent; and
  - are complete in all material respects.

In support of the primary requirement that management should apply judgement in developing and applying appropriate accounting policies, Section 10 gives guidance on how management should apply this judgement. This guidance comes in two 'strengths' – certain things which management is required to consider and others which it may consider, as follows.

Management is *required* to refer to and consider the applicability of the following sources in descending order of authority:

- the requirements and guidance in an FRS dealing with similar and related issues;
- where an entity's financial statements are within the scope of a Statement of Recommended Practice (SORP), the requirements and guidance in that SORP dealing with similar and related issues; and
- the definitions, recognition criteria and measurement concepts for assets, liabilities, income and expenses and the pervasive principles in Section 2 – *Concepts and Pervasive Principles*. *[FRS 102.10.5]*.

Management *may* also consider the requirements and guidance in EU-adopted IFRS dealing with similar and related issues. However, entities should exercise caution in considering the guidance in EU-adopted IFRS dealing with similar issues as not all of the sections in FRS 102 are based on EU-adopted IFRS. In addition, Section 1 – *Scope* – requires certain entities to apply IAS 33 (as adopted in the EU), IFRS 8 – *Operating Segments* (as adopted in the EU) – or IFRS 6 – *Exploration for and Evaluation of Mineral Resources* (as adopted in the EU) – and therefore, where applicable, the accounting policies required by those standards should be followed. *[FRS 102.10.6]*.

Section 10 does not state that an entity may refer to any GAAP other than EU-adopted IFRS. However, in our opinion, an entity would not be prevented from continuing with an accounting policy for a transaction that was applied under previously extant UK GAAP, where FRS 102 does not specifically address the matter, provided the policy was consistent with the guidance, definitions, criteria and concepts contained in the sources referred to by the hierarchy above.

The hierarchy implies that it is not possible to apply an accounting policy for a transaction using the criteria in Section 2 where the accounting for that transaction is specifically addressed by FRS 102 (since Section 2 can only be consulted in the absence of specific guidance). However, Section 3 – *Financial Statement Presentation* – states that there may be special circumstances where management concludes that compliance with FRS 102 would be so misleading that it would conflict with the objective of financial statements of entities as set out with Section 2. In such circumstances, an entity can depart from the specific requirements of FRS 102 by use of a true and fair override. *[FRS 102.3.4]*. See Chapter 6 at 9.2.2 for discussion of the use of the true and fair override.

The hierarchy in Section 10 does not refer to UK Company Law. The implication from Section 10 is that, where choice is available, an accounting policy should be selected on its merits based on the criteria in FRS 102 (relevance and reliability) rather than to comply with the law (e.g. *The Large and Medium-sized Companies and Groups (Accounts and Reports) Regulations 2008 (SI 2008/410)* (the Regulations). Some accounting policy choices permitted or required by FRS 102, for example measuring certain financial liabilities at fair value through profit or loss, are not allowed by the Regulations. However, Section 3 requires an entity to make disclosures when it has departed from a requirement of applicable legislation. *[FRS 102.3.5-6]*.

3.3   Consistency of accounting policies

An entity shall select and apply its accounting policies consistently for similar transactions, other events or obligations unless an FRS specifically requires or permits categorisation of items for which different policies may be appropriate. If an FRS requires or permits such categorisation, an appropriate accounting policy shall be selected and applied consistently to each category. *[FRS 102.10.7]*.

There is no requirement in FRS 102 for each entity within a group to have consistent accounting policies in their separate or individual financial statements. Indeed, FRS 102 anticipates that this will not be the case by requiring consolidated financial statements to be adjusted where a member of the group uses accounting policies other than those adopted in the consolidated financial statements for like transactions and events. *[FRS 102.9.17]*. The Regulations also do not require each entity within a group to have consistent accounting policies. However, Section 10 requires an entity to select accounting policies that are both relevant to the economic decision-making needs of its users and reliable. *[FRS 102.10.4]*. Therefore, factors that one group entity would take into account in setting its accounting policies should normally also apply to other group entities.

3.4   Changes in accounting policies

An entity shall change an accounting policy only if the change: *[FRS 102.10.8]*

- is required by an FRS; or
- results in the financial statements providing reliable and more relevant information about the effects of transactions, other events or conditions on the entity's financial position, financial performance or cash flows.

This means that a change in accounting policy cannot be made on an arbitrary basis.

Reliability is defined as the quality of information that makes it free from material error and bias and represents faithfully that which it either purports to represent or could reasonably be expected to represent. *[FRS 102.2.7]*. Relevance is defined as the quality of information that allows it to influence the economic decisions of users by helping them evaluate past, present or future events or confirming, or correcting, their past evaluations. *[FRS 102.2.5]*.

If an FRS allows a choice of accounting treatment (including the measurement basis) for a specified transaction or other event or condition and an entity changes its previous choice, then that is a change in accounting policy. *[FRS 102.10.10]*.

As noted at 3.2 above, an accounting policy is not restricted to measurement of a transaction but also includes how items are classified and presented in the financial statements. Therefore, changes in presentation, such as a decision to adopt a change from a single statement of comprehensive income approach to a two statement approach is a change in accounting policy. *[FRS 102.5.3]*.

The following are stated specifically not to be changes in accounting policies: *[FRS 102.10.9]*

- the application of an accounting policy for transactions, other events and conditions that differ in substance from those previously occurring;
- the application of a new accounting policy for transactions, other events or conditions that did not occur previously or were not material; and
- a change to the cost model when a reliable measure of fair value is no longer available (or *vice versa*) for an asset that an FRS would otherwise require or permit to be measured at fair value.

Chapter 9

3.4.1   Applying changes in accounting policies

An entity shall account for changes in accounting policies as follows: *[FRS 102.10.11]*

- a change in an accounting policy resulting from a change in the requirements of an FRS are accounted for in accordance with the transitional provisions, if any, specified in that amendment;

- where an entity has elected under paragraph 2 of Section 11 – *Basic Financial Instruments* – to follow IAS 39 – *Financial Instruments: Recognition and Measurement* – and/or IFRS 9 – *Financial Instruments* – and the requirements of IAS 39 and/or IFRS 9 change, then the entity should account for that change in accounting policy in accordance with the transition provisions, if any, specified in the revised IAS 39 and/or IFRS 9;

- where, under paragraphs 1.4, 1.5 or 34.11 of FRS 102, an entity is required or has elected to apply IAS 33, IFRS 8 or IFRS 6 and the requirements of those standards change, the entity shall account for the change in accordance with the transitional provisions, if any, specified in those standards as amended; and

- all other changes in accounting policy are accounted for retrospectively (see 3.4.2 below).

As an exception to the above, the initial application of a policy to revalue assets in accordance with Section 17 – *Property, Plant and Equipment* – or Section 18 – *Intangible Assets other than Goodwill* – is a change in accounting policy to be dealt with as a revaluation in accordance with those sections. *[FRS 102.10.10A]*. This means that the revaluation is accounted for prospectively using the fair value at the date of the revaluation. *[FRS 102.17.15B, 18.18B]*.

When an entity is applying an accounting policy based on an IFRS, other than the specific IFRSs referred to above (IFRS 6, IFRS 8, IFRS 9, IAS 33 and IAS 39), and that IFRS changes, an issue arising is whether the entity is obliged to also change its accounting policy to align to the amended IFRS. We believe that such a change is at the discretion of the entity. In our view, such a change is permitted only if it satisfies the relevance and reliability criteria and is not otherwise inconsistent with the FRS 102 hierarchy (see 3.2 above). All such accounting policy changes should be accounted for retrospectively regardless of the specific transitional rules that may apply in the IFRS (because the change does not meet any of the exceptions from retrospective application listed above).

3.4.2   Retrospective application of accounting policy changes

When a change in accounting policy is applied retrospectively in accordance with 3.4.1 above, the entity applies the new accounting policy to comparative information for prior periods to the earliest date for which it is practicable, as if the new accounting policy had always been applied. *[FRS 102.10.12]*.

The following example illustrates how to apply retrospective accounting.

Example 9.1:   Retrospective application of change in accounting policy (ignoring tax)

Entity A makes a voluntary change in its accounting policy for measuring its investment in an associate in its separate financial statements to change the measurement basis from cost less impairment to fair value through profit or loss. Fair value through profit and loss is considered by Entity A to be more relevant than cost less impairment. The change is made in Entity A's annual reporting period ending 31 December 2019. The fair value of the investment was £9,500 at 31 December 2019, £10,000 at 31 December 2018 and £9,000 at 31 December 2017, respectively. The cost less impairment of the investment in associate was £5,000 at 31 December 2019, 31 December 2018 and 31 December 2017, respectively.

In its statement of changes in equity, Entity A restates its equity at 1 January 2018 by £4,000 to account for the difference between fair value and cost less impairment of the investment in associate at that date. This difference is credited to retained earnings. If the unrealised fair value gain is not a distributable profit, Entity A may wish, instead of crediting retained earnings, to create a separate non-distributable reserve within equity.

Entity A restates its profit and loss account for the year-ended 31 December 2018 to recognise the fair value gain of £1,000 on the investment in associate during the year. If the unrealised fair value gain is not a distributable profit, Entity A may wish to make a transfer of the unrealised gain in the statement of changes in equity from retained earnings to a separate non-distributable reserve within equity.

Entity A records a fair value loss of £500 in profit or loss for the year-ended 31 December 2019.

As discussed above, applying a new accounting policy retrospectively means applying it as if that policy had always been applied. This implies that hindsight should not be used when applying a new accounting policy, either in making assumptions about what management's intentions would have been in a prior period or estimating the amounts recognised, measured or disclosed in a prior period. Hence, retrospectively applying a new accounting policy requires distinguishing information that provides evidence of circumstances that existed on the prior period date(s) from that information which would have been available when the financial statements for that prior period(s) were authorised for issue.

In certain circumstances, it might be impracticable to restate the financial statements of prior years for a change in accounting policy. Applying a requirement is impracticable when the entity cannot apply it after making every reasonable effort to do so. *[FRS 102 Appendix I].* Impracticability could arise when the relevant information for the prior years, for example fair value that is not based on an observable price or input, is not available and the entity is unable to calculate the amount after making every reasonable effort.

IAS 8 contains additional guidance on impracticability which is not included in Section 10 but which might be helpful to users and which could be applied via the hierarchy (see 3.2 above). This guidance states that it is impracticable to apply a change in accounting policy retrospectively or to correct an error retrospectively (see 3.6 below) if: *[IAS 8.5]*

- the effects of the retrospective application or retrospective restatement are not determinable;
- the retrospective application or retrospective restatement requires assumptions about what management's intent would have been in that period; or
- the retrospective application or retrospective restatement requires significant estimates of amounts and that it is impossible to distinguish objectively information about those estimates that:
  - provides evidence of circumstances that existed on the date(s) as at which those amounts are to be recognised, measured or disclosed; and
  - would have been available when the financial statements for that prior period were authorised for issue, from other information.

When it is impracticable to determine the individual-period effects of a change in accounting policy on comparative information for one or more prior periods presented, the entity applies the new accounting policy to the carrying amounts of assets and liabilities as at the beginning of the earliest period for which retrospective application is practicable, which may be the current period, and shall make a corresponding adjustment to the opening balance of each affected component of equity for that period. *[FRS 102.10.12]*.

3.5   Changes in accounting estimates

Estimates are a fundamental feature of financial reporting, reflecting the uncertainties inherent in business activities. The use of reasonable estimates is an essential part of the preparation of financial statements and does not undermine their reliability. *[FRS 102.2.30]*. FRS 102 does not define estimation techniques or accounting estimates. However, examples of estimates within FRS 102 include bad debt provisions, inventory obsolescence provisions, fair values of financial assets or liabilities and useful lives of depreciable assets.

Estimates will need revision as changes occur in the circumstances on which they are based or as a result of new information or more experience. Hence, a change in accounting estimate is an adjustment to the carrying amount of an asset or a liability, or the amount of the periodic consumption of an asset, that results from the present status of, and expected future benefits and obligations associated with, assets and liabilities. Changes in accounting estimates result from new information or new developments and, accordingly, are not corrections of errors. *[FRS 102.10.15]*. Errors do not result from changes in circumstances or the availability of new information. See 3.6 below.

The distinction between an accounting policy and an accounting estimate is particularly important because a very different accounting treatment is applied when there are changes in accounting policies or accounting estimates. When it is difficult to distinguish a change in an accounting policy from a change in an accounting estimate, the change is treated as a change in an accounting estimate. *[FRS 102.10.15]*.

By its nature, a change in an accounting estimate is not caused by a prior period event. Consequently, the effect of a change in accounting estimate is required to be recognised prospectively in profit or loss by including it in: *[FRS 102.10.16]*

- the period of the change, if the change affects that period only; or
- the period of the change and future periods, if the change affects both.

An example of a change in estimate which would affect the current period only is a change in an estimate of bad debts relating to receivables recognised in the previous period. An example of a change which would affect both current and future periods is a change in the estimated useful life of a depreciable asset.

Some changes in accounting estimates will give rise to changes in assets and liabilities, or relate to an item of equity. In those circumstances, the reporting entity adjusts the carrying amount of the related asset, liability or equity item in the period of the change. *[FRS 102.10.17]*.

3.6   Corrections of prior period errors

Errors can arise in respect of the recognition, measurement, presentation or disclosure of elements of financial statements. Such errors include the effects of mathematical mistakes, mistakes in applying accounting policies, oversights or misinterpretations of facts, and fraud. *[FRS 102.10.20]*.

FRS 102 states that information provided in financial statements should be reliable and in order to be reliable it should be free from material error. *[FRS 102.2.7]*.

Prior period errors are omissions from, and misstatements in, an entity's financial statements for one or more prior periods arising from a failure to use, or misuse of, reliable information that: *[FRS 102.10.19]*

- was available when financial statements for those periods were authorised for issue; and
- could reasonably be expected to have been obtained and taken into account in the preparation and presentation of those financial statements.

When it is discovered that material prior period errors have occurred, Section 10 requires that they be corrected in the first set of financial statements prepared after the discovery. The correction should be excluded from the statement of comprehensive income for the period in which the error is discovered. Rather, it is corrected retrospectively by adjusting prior periods. This is done by: *[FRS 102.10.21]*

- restating the comparative amounts for the prior period(s) presented in which the error occurred; or
- if the error occurred before the earliest period presented, restating the opening balances of assets, liabilities and equity for the earliest prior period presented.

This process corrects the recognition, measurement and disclosure of amounts of elements of financial statements as if a prior year error had never occurred.

The same caution on the use of hindsight in applying a new accounting policy (see 3.4.2 above) applies to correction of prior period errors. As is the case for the retrospective application of a change in accounting policy, retrospective restatement for the correction of prior period material errors is not required to the extent that it is impracticable to determine the period-specific effects on comparative information for one or more periods presented. In that case, the entity restates the opening balances of assets, liabilities and equity for the earliest period for which retrospective statement is practicable (which may be the current period). *[FRS 102.10.22]*. As discussed at 3.4.2 above, IAS 8 contains additional guidance on impracticability.

3.7   Disclosure of a change in accounting policy, a change in accounting estimate and prior period errors

3.7.1   Disclosure of a change in accounting policy

The disclosure requirements distinguish between a change in accounting policy that is mandatory (i.e. caused by a change to an FRS) and a change that is voluntarily.

For changes in an accounting policy caused by an amendment to an FRS that have an effect on the current period, any prior period or which might have an effect on future periods, an entity must disclose: *[FRS 102.10.13]*

- the nature of the change in accounting policy;
- for the current period and each prior period presented, to the extent practicable, the amount of the adjustment for each financial statement line item presented;
- the amount of the adjustment relating to periods before those presented, to the extent practicable; and
- an explanation if it is impracticable to determine the amounts to be disclosed above.

Therefore the nature of an accounting policy change that has been made and is expected to impact future periods should be disclosed but the financial impact of such a change need not be quantified.

Financial statements of subsequent periods need not repeat these disclosures.

When a voluntary change in accounting policy has an effect on the current period or any prior period, an entity shall disclose the following: *[FRS 102.10.14]*

- the nature of the change in accounting policy;
- the reasons why applying the new accounting policy provides reliable and more relevant information;
- to the extent practicable, the amount of the adjustment for each financial statement line item affected, showing separately the amounts:
  - for the current period;
  - for each prior period presented; and
  - in the aggregate for periods before those presented; and
- an explanation if it is impracticable to determine the amounts to be disclosed for each financial statement line item above.

Financial statements of subsequent periods need not repeat these disclosures.

3.7.2   *Disclosure of a change in accounting estimate*

Disclosure is required of the nature of any change in an accounting estimate and the effect of the change on assets, liabilities, income and expense for the current period and, if practicable, the effect of the change on one or more future periods. *[FRS 102.10.18]*.

This means that where a change in accounting estimate affects future periods, such as a change in the estimated useful life of a depreciable asset, the reporting entity should provide users of the accounts information regarding the future impact of that change, if practicable. IAS 8 also requires this disclosure. *[IAS 8.39-40]*.

In contrast to a change in accounting policy, there is no requirement to disclose the impact of a change in accounting estimate on each financial statement line item.

3.7.3   Disclosure of prior period errors

The following is required to be disclosed in respect of material prior period errors:
[FRS 102.10.23]

- the nature of the prior period error;
- for each prior period presented, to the extent practicable, the amount of the correction for each financial statement line item affected;
- to the extent practicable, the amount of the correction at the beginning of the earliest prior period presented; and
- an explanation if it is impracticable to determine the amounts to be disclosed above.

Financial statements of subsequent periods need not repeat these disclosures.

These disclosures are similar to those required for a change in accounting policy.

There is no exemption from disclosure of a prior period error on the grounds that such information might prejudice seriously the position of the reporting entity.

The following example illustrates the disclosures required for a retrospective restatement of a prior period error.

Example 9.2:   Retrospective restatement of prior period error

During 2019, Beta Co discovered that some products that had been sold during 2018 were incorrectly included in inventory at 31 December 2018 at £6,500.

Beta's accounting records for 2019 show sales of £104,000, cost of goods sold of £86,500 (including £6,500 for the error in opening inventory), and income taxes of £5,250.

In 2018, Beta reported:

	£
Sales	73,500
Cost of goods sold	(53,500)
Profit before income taxes	20,000
Income taxes	(6,000)
Profit	14,000

The 2018 opening retained earnings were £20,000 and closing retained earnings were £34,000.

Beta's income tax rate was 30 per cent for 2019 and 2018. It had no other income or expenses.

Beta had £5,000 of share capital throughout, and no other components of equity except for retained earnings. Its shares are not publicly traded and it does not disclose earnings per share.

Beta Co
Extract from the statement of comprehensive income

	2019 £	(restated) 2018 £
Sales	104,000	73,500
Cost of goods sold	(80,000)	(60,000)
Profit before income taxes	24,000	13,500
Income taxes	(7,200)	(4,050)
Profit	16,800	9,450

Chapter 9

Beta Co
Statement of Changes in Equity

	Share capital £	Retained earnings £	Total £
Balance at 1 January 2018	5,000	20,000	25,000
Profit for the year ended 31 December 2018 as restated	–	9,450	9,450
Balance at 31 December 2018	5,000	29,450	34,450
Profit for the year ended 31 December 2019	–	16,800	16,800
Balance at 31 December 2019	5,000	46,250	51,250

Extracts from the Notes

1. Some products that had been sold in 2018 were incorrectly included in inventory at 31 December 2018 at £6,500. The financial statements of 2018 have been restated to correct this error. The effect of the restatement on each financial statement line item affected is shown below.

	Effect on 2018 £
Increase in cost of goods sold	(6,500)
Decrease in income tax expense	1,950
Decrease in profit	(4,550)
Decrease in inventory	(6,500)
Decrease in income tax payable	1,950
Decrease in equity	(4,550)

3.8   Amendments to Section 10 from the Triennial review 2017

The amendments to FRS 102 from the Triennial review 2017 are effective for periods beginning on or after 1 January 2019. Very few amendments were made to this section, the most substantive being to describe it as setting out 'requirements' rather than 'guidance',

4   COMPANY LAW MATTERS

4.1   Corrections of prior period errors and defective accounts

If a company's previous annual report and accounts did not comply with the Companies Act 2006 (for example due to an error), s454 of the Act allows the directors to revise any such reports and accounts (often referred to as the Defective Accounts regime). If an entity corrects errors by way of a prior year adjustment in its latest financial statements, the directors should always consider carefully whether to revise the earlier financial statements, although it is common practice not to do so.

5　　SUMMARY OF GAAP DIFFERENCES

The following table shows the differences between FRS 102 and IFRS.

	FRS 102	*IFRS*
Hierarchy reference to other standard setters	May refer to EU-adopted IFRS.	May refer to other standard setting bodies with similar conceptual framework.
Impracticability	Relief for prior year restatements if impracticable.	Relief for prior year restatements if impracticable (more guidance compared to FRS 102).
Disclosures	Disclose nature of accounting policy change arising from an amendment to an FRS that might affect future periods. Third balance sheet not required for prior period restatements.	Disclose both nature and impact of IFRSs issued but not effective Third balance sheet required for prior period restatements.

Chapter 10   Financial instruments

List of examples

Chapter 10   Financial instruments

1   INTRODUCTION

Section 22 – *Liabilities and Equity,* Section 11 – *Basic Financial Instruments* – and Section 12 – *Other Financial Instruments Issues* – contain the accounting and disclosure requirements for financial instruments. Section 34 – *Specialised Activities* – contains additional disclosure requirements for financial instruments that apply to financial institutions.

Section 22's requirements for classifying issued instruments as either liabilities or equity are closely modelled on those in IAS 32 – *Financial Instruments: Presentation*, but without the detailed guidance.

Section 11 deals with what are termed 'basic' financial instruments, which are certain non-complex debt instruments and equity securities. It sets out the criteria for basic financial instruments and how they are measured, along with the impairment requirements. It also includes the derecognition requirements for financial instruments, and various disclosure provisions for all financial instruments. Section 11 has been structured to provide all the financial instrument accounting requirements for many entities, who do not enter into more complex transactions.

Section 12 applies to all other financial instruments, which need to be measured at fair value through profit or loss, and addresses the hedge accounting requirements. It also contains associated disclosure provisions.

However, instead of applying the recognition and measurement requirements of Section 11 and 12, FRS 102 reporters have the choice of applying the recognition and measurement provisions of IAS 39 – *Financial Instruments: Recognition and Measurement* (as adopted in the EU) – or IFRS 9 – *Financial Instruments* (as adopted in the EU). This accounting policy choice applies to all financial instruments – entities cannot decide to elect to use IAS 39 or IFRS 9 only for certain items. Consistent with any change in accounting policy, a subsequent change in this accounting policy choice is allowed only when the change will lead to more reliable and relevant information. *[FRS 102.10.8(b)].*

The classification and measurement requirements in Sections 11 and 12 are simpler and less stringent compared to IAS 39 and IFRS 9: instruments are classified as either basic or other, and measurement is at amortised cost, cost or fair value.

The impairment requirements in Section 11 have been drawn from IAS 39's incurred loss model. The FRC has delayed amending FRS 102 to adopt an expected loss impairment approach similar to that of IFRS 9; should any changes be incorporated to FRS 102, their effective date is not expected to be earlier than 1 January 2022.

The FRS 102 hedge accounting requirements are similar to those in IFRS 9, but with some simplifications and without the detailed guidance of IFRS 9. Accordingly, FRS 102 incorporates a more principles-based approach to hedge accounting compared to IAS 39.

The FRC issued an updated version of FRS 102 in March 2018, following the issue of the Amendments to FRS 102 – *The Financial Reporting Standard application in the UK and Republic of Ireland – Triennial review 2017 – Incremental improvements and clarifications* – issued in December 2017 ('the Triennial review 2017'). The Triennial review 2017 includes amendments to Sections 11, 12 and 22 to FRS 102 as issued in September 2015. These amendments are effective for accounting periods beginning on or after 1 January 2019.

The main amendments are as follows:

(i)   Accounting policy choices: Even though IFRS 9 has superseded IAS 39 for those entities applying IFRS, the FRC decided to maintain the option of continuing to apply IAS 39 (in the form applicable immediately prior to the effective date of IFRS 9) until the FRS 102 requirements for impairment of financial assets have been amended to reflect IFRS 9 or it is otherwise decided not to amend FRS 102 further in relation to IFRS 9. *[FRS 102.BC.B11.5]*. For further details see 4 below.

(ii)   Initial measurement of equity instruments and use of merger relief or group reconstruction relief: The requirements for initial measurement of equity instruments in Section 22 were updated to include explicit reference to the impact of the use of merger relief or group reconstruction relief. For further details see 5.5.2.A below.

(iii)   Debt for equity swaps: Prior to the Triennial review 2017 amendments, Section 22 was silent on the accounting for debt for equity swaps. Although it required equity instruments to be initially recognised at fair value, resulting in equivalent accounting to that required by IFRIC 19 – *Extinguishing Financial Liabilities with Equity Instruments*, it contained no scope exemptions for transactions that would not be within the scope of IFRIC 19 (such as common control transactions) or the conversion of convertible debt. *[FRS 102.BC.B22.2]*. Section 22 now incorporates guidance on the accounting treatment of these types of transactions, prohibiting the recognition of profit or loss on extinguishment of the financial liability. For further details see 5.5.2.B below.

(iv)   Derivatives: The Triennial review 2017 incorporated a more direct reference to 'derivatives' in certain paragraphs of Sections 11 and 12. Previously, these paragraphs avoided the use of the word 'derivative' creating ambiguity for stakeholders. Given that 'derivative' is already defined in FRS 102, this change improved the drafting. One consequence of this is a change to the definition of a financial liability, but this is not expected to have any practical effects. *[FRS 102.BC.B11.7]*. See 3 below.

(v)   Investment in equity instruments: Prior to the Triennial review 2017, basic equity instruments were defined as investments in non-convertible preference shares and non-puttable ordinary shares or preference shares. This definition in Section 11 created an anomaly whereby certain preference shares had a different classification in the books of the issuer and the holder. The reference to such investments in shares was amended to 'non-derivative financial instruments that are equity of the issuer' resolving the anomaly previously observed. *[FRS 102.BC.B11.30-31]*. For further details see 6.1.1 below.

(vi) Basic financial instruments: Prior to the Triennial review 2017, the conditions required for debt instruments to be classified as 'basic' were prescriptive. This prescription caused significant problems in applying FRS 102 as it led to a number of judgement areas and implementation difficulties. The current text in FRS 102 now includes a principle-based approach for classification of debt instruments as a 'basic' financial instrument. The description requires a 'basic' debt instrument to give rise to cash flows on specified dates that constitute reasonable compensation for the time value of money, credit risk and other basic lending risks and costs. *[FRS 102.BC.B11.11-13]*. For further details see 6.1.2 below.

(vii) Loans with two-way compensation clauses: In addition to the incorporation of the principle-based approach for classification of debt instruments discussed at (vi) above, the conditions for classification of a debt instrument as basic were amended to make specific reference to reasonable compensation from either the holder or the issuer for the early termination. This amendment was incorporated mainly in response to issues observed in accounting for social housing loans where these clauses are more prevalent. *[FRS 102.BC.B11.16-18]*. For further details see 6.1.2.E below.

(viii) Classification subsequent to initial recognition: FRS 102 as issued in September 2015 was silent on the need to reassess classification subsequent to initial recognition. The Triennial review 2017 amendments clarified that once classification of a financial instrument is determined at initial recognition, no re-assessment is required at subsequent dates unless there is a modification of contractual terms. *[FRS 102.BC.B11.20]*. For further details see 6.3 below.

(ix) Directors' loans: Prior to the Triennial review 2017, all financing transactions (except for public benefit entity concessionary loans) were required to be initially measured at the present value of the discounted cash flows. Feedback from stakeholders raised concerns about the implications for loans from directors to a small company in which the director was also a shareholder. The Triennial review 2017 introduced a simplified accounting for small entities in relation to loans from a group of close family members of a director where the group includes at least one shareholder of the entity or, in the case of limited liability partnerships, a member of the entity. This relief allows the resulting basic financial liability of a small entity to be carried at transaction price (with no subsequent recognition of interest expense). *[FRS 102.BC.B11.32-39]*. For further details see 7.2.3 below.

(x) Investments in other group entities: The Triennial review 2017 incorporated an accounting policy choice for investments in non-derivative instruments that are equity of the issuer and the issuer is a member of the same group as the holder: (a) cost less impairment; (b) fair value with changes recognised in other comprehensive income; or (c) fair value with changes in fair value recognised in profit or loss. Once chosen, the accounting policy must be consistently applied to all investments in a single class. See 8.1 below.

(xi) Fair value measurement guidance: Prior to the Triennial review 2017 amendments, Section 11 contained guidance on fair value measurement. These paragraphs were cross-referenced from a number of sections of FRS 102 when fair value measurement was permitted or required. As these paragraphs are of general application, rather than relevant only to financial instruments, and illustrate a measurement basis described in Section 2 – *Concepts and Pervasive Principles*, they were moved to a new appendix to Section 2. This did not change the scope and application of the guidance, although some improvements were made to the guidance.

(xii) Disclosures: When IFRS 9 was finalised, amendments were also made to IFRS 7 – *Financial Instruments: Disclosures* – to reflect the new requirements of IFRS 9. In particular, many changes were made to IFRS 7 in relation to the new expected credit loss approach to impairment of financial assets. As a result, some of the disclosure requirements of FRS 102 would have been inconsistent with the application of the recognition and measurement requirements of IFRS 9. The Triennial review 2017 introduced a number of changes to the disclosure requirements to ensure that entities applying the recognition and measurement requirements of IFRS 9 through the accounting policy choice discussed at 4 below, are providing relevant information about the impairment of financial assets. *[FRS 102.BC.B11.50-51]*. For further details see 11.2 below.

When an entity first applies the Triennial review 2017 amendments above, retrospective application is required. *[FRS 102.1.19]*.

2   COMPARISON BETWEEN SECTIONS 11, 12, 22 AND IFRS

The comparable extant IFRSs are IAS 32, IFRS 9 and IFRS 7. The main differences between FRS 102 and IFRS are discussed below. The discussion also includes a comparison to IAS 39 which is relevant for those entities that choose the option to apply IAS 39 for the purposes of recognition and measurement (see 4 below).

2.1   Differences between Section 22 and IAS 32

A contractual obligation or even a potential obligation for an entity to purchase its own equity instruments for cash or another financial asset may be treated as a derivative within the scope of Section 12 and measured at fair value through profit or loss. In contrast, IAS 32 requires measurement at the present value of the financial liability's (gross) redemption amount. This is further illustrated at 5.3.1 below.

Another potential difference arises in relation to the classification of contracts that will or may be settled by the exchange of a fixed amount of cash or another financial asset for a fixed number of the entity's own equity instruments. The IFRS Interpretations Committee concluded that any obligation denominated in a foreign currency represents a variable amount of cash and, consequently, a contract settled by an entity delivering a fixed number of its own equity instruments in exchange for a fixed amount of foreign currency should be classified as a liability. There is no similar explicit interpretation under FRS 102, and therefore, a judgement may be made on whether a fixed amount of foreign currency represents a fixed amount of cash or not, which in turn will affect the conclusion on the classification of such instrument. See 5.3.2 below.

The Triennial review 2017 incorporated explicit accounting requirements for the initial measurement of equity instruments issued to settle a financial liability in particular circumstances. The circumstances covered by this amendment coincide with the scope exclusions in IFRIC 19 leading to the potential for divergence in the accounting. See 5.3.3 below.

2.2 Comparison between Sections 11, 12 and IFRS

2.2.1 Classification and measurement

FRS 102 has a two tiered measurement model: amortised cost/cost or fair value through profit or loss. That is, debt instruments may be measured at amortised cost if they meet the criteria or, if they do not, at fair value through profit or loss, while equities (and certain derivatives on equities) have to be measured at fair value through profit or loss and only at cost in limited circumstances. Hence, entities which prefer to recognise debt or equity securities at fair value through other comprehensive income may choose to opt to apply IAS 39 or IFRS 9.

For basic debt securities, the criteria to recognise them at amortised cost under FRS 102 are less stringent than under IFRS 9, as explained at 8.1.1.A. Unlike under IFRS, there is no concept in FRS 102 of 'held for trading'. Basic debt instruments that are held for trading purposes are not automatically required to be recorded at fair value, and entities will need to elect to use the 'fair value option' if they wish to record these instruments at fair value rather than at amortised cost.

In the case of investments in equity instruments, FRS 102 requires measurement at fair value through profit or loss (unless fair value cannot be measured reliably, in which case they must be measured at cost less impairment). Unless such investments are held for trading, IFRS provides the option to designate these investment as: a) at fair value through other comprehensive income under IFRS 9, in which case changes in fair value are recognised in other comprehensive income with no impact on profit or loss; or b) available for sale under IAS 39, in which case changes in fair value are recognised in other comprehensive income, with recycling to profit or loss in case of impairment or de-recognition.

The complex embedded derivative separation rules in IAS 39 and IFRS 9 do not exist in FRS 102 and many financial instruments containing embedded derivatives, including financial liabilities, will need to be measured at fair value through profit or loss under FRS 102.

2.2.2 Impairment

Section 11 uses the same principles and criteria as the incurred loss model under IAS 39 with one major difference: under FRS 102, assets which have been individually assessed for impairment and found not to be impaired do not subsequently need to be included in a collective assessment of impairment.

By contrast, the IFRS 9 expected credit loss model is complex. Entities are required to recognise either 12-month or lifetime expected credit losses, depending on whether there has been a significant increase in credit risk since initial recognition or not. The measurement of expected credit losses must reflect a probability-weighted outcome, the time value of money and be based on reasonable and supportable information.

2.2.3   Hedge accounting

The requirements for assessing hedge effectiveness for hedge accounting are based on a simplified version of the IFRS 9 requirements and are significantly different compared to IAS 39. Entities are not required to perform an onerous quantitative effectiveness assessment to demonstrate that the hedge relationship in any period was highly effective, using the 80%-125% bright line. Instead, the FRS 102 effectiveness test uses a different approach based on IFRS 9 that focuses on the existence of an economic relationship between the hedged item and hedging instrument. IFRS 9 has additional effectiveness requirements that are not replicated within FRS 102. However, there is a need to measure any actual hedge ineffectiveness and record it in the same way as under IFRS 9 and IAS 39.

A significant difference to IAS 39 is that, consistent with IFRS 9, under the FRS 102 hedge accounting rules it is possible to designate risk components of non-financial items where these are separately identifiable and reliably measurable.

2.2.4   Presentation and disclosures

The disclosure requirements in FRS 102 for financial instruments are less onerous than those of IFRS 7 and IFRS 13 – *Fair Value Measurement.*

3   SCOPE OF SECTIONS 11, 12 AND 22

This section covers the scope of Sections 11, 12, 22 and the key definitions used. *[FRS 102 Appendix I].*

3.1   Definitions

Term	Definition
Active market	A market in which all the following conditions exist: (a) the items traded in the market are homogeneous; (b) willing buyers and sellers can normally be found at any time; and (c) prices are available to the public.
Amortised cost (of a financial asset or financial liability)	The amount at which the financial asset or financial liability is measured at initial recognition minus principal repayments, plus or minus the cumulative amortisation using the effective interest method of any difference between that initial amount and the maturity amount, and minus any reduction (directly or through the use of an allowance account) for impairment or uncollectability.
Compound financial instrument	A financial instrument that, from the issuer's perspective, contains both a liability and an equity element.
Derecognition	The removal of a previously recognised asset or liability from an entity's statement of financial position.

Derivative	A financial instrument or other contract with all three of the following characteristics:
	(a) its value changes in response to the change in a specified interest rate, financial instrument price, commodity price, foreign exchange rate, index of prices or rates, credit rating or credit index, or other variable (sometimes called the 'underlying'), provided in the case of a non-financial variable that the variable is not specific to a party to the contract;
	(b) it requires no initial net investment or an initial net investment that is smaller than would be required for other types of contracts that would be expected to have a similar response to changes in market factors; and
	(c) it is settled at a future date.
Effective interest method	A method of calculating the amortised cost of a financial asset or a financial liability (or a group of financial assets or financial liabilities) and of allocating the interest income or interest expense over the relevant period.
Effective interest rate	The rate that exactly discounts estimated future cash payments or receipts through the expected life of the financial instrument or, when appropriate, a shorter period to the carrying amount of the financial asset or financial liability.
Equity	The residual interest in the assets of the entity after deducting all its liabilities.
Fair value	The amount for which an asset could be exchanged, a liability settled, or an equity instrument granted could be exchanged, between knowledgeable, willing parties in an arm's length transaction. In the absence of any specific guidance provided in the relevant section of FRS 102, the guidance in Appendix to Section 2 – *Concepts and Pervasive Principles* – must be used in determining fair value.
Financial asset	Any asset that is:
	(a) cash;
	(b) an equity instrument of another entity;
	(c) a contractual right:
	(i) to receive cash or another financial asset from another entity, or
	(ii) to exchange financial assets or financial liabilities with another entity under conditions that are potentially favourable to the entity; or
	(d) a contract that will or may be settled in the entity's own equity instruments and is:
	(i) a non-derivative for which the entity is or may be obliged to receive a variable number of the entity's own equity instruments; or
	(ii) a derivative that will or may be settled other than by the exchange of a fixed amount of cash or another financial asset for a fixed number of the entity's own equity instruments. For this purpose the entity's own equity instruments do not include instruments that are themselves contracts for the future receipt or delivery of the entity's own equity instruments.

Term	*Definition*
Financial instrument	A contract that gives rise to a financial asset of one entity and a financial liability or equity instrument of another entity.

Financial liability	Any liability that is:
	(a) a contractual obligation:
	   (i) to deliver cash or another financial asset to another entity; or
	   (ii) to exchange financial assets or financial liabilities with another entity under conditions that are potentially unfavourable to the entity, or
	(b) a contract that will or may be settled in the entity's own equity instruments and is:
	   (i) a non-derivative for which the entity is or may be obliged to deliver a variable number of the entity's own equity instruments; or
	   (ii) a derivative that will or may be settled other than by the exchange of a fixed amount of cash or another financial asset for a fixed number of the entity's own equity instruments. For this purpose the entity's own equity instruments do not include instruments that are themselves contracts for the future receipt or delivery of the entity's own equity instruments.

Firm commitment	Binding agreement for the exchange of a specified quantity of resources at a specified price on a specified future date or dates.
Forecast transaction	Uncommitted but anticipated future transaction.
Hedging gain or loss	Change in fair value of a hedged item that is attributable to the hedged risk.
Highly probable	Significantly more likely than probable.
Liquidity risk	The risk that an entity will encounter difficulty in meeting obligations associated with financial liabilities that are settled by delivering cash or another financial asset.
Market risk	The risk that the fair value or future cash flows of a financial instrument will fluctuate because of changes in market prices. Market risk comprises three types of risk: currency risk, interest rate risk and other price risk. Interest rate risk – the risk that the fair value or future cash flows of a financial instrument will fluctuate because of changes in market interest rates. Currency risk – the risk that the fair value or future cash flows of a financial instrument will fluctuate because of changes in foreign exchange rates. Other price risk – the risk that the fair value or future cash flows of a financial instrument will fluctuate because of changes in market prices (other than those arising from interest rate risk or currency risk), whether those changes are caused by factors specific to the financial instrument or its issuer, or factors affecting all similar financial instruments traded in the market.
Non-controlling interest	The equity in a subsidiary not attributable, directly or indirectly, to a parent.
Probable	More likely than not.

Publicly traded (debt or equity instruments)	Traded, or in process of being issued for trading, in a public market (a domestic or foreign stock exchange or an over-the-counter market, including local and regional markets).
Transaction costs (financial instruments)	Incremental costs that are directly attributable to the acquisition, issue or disposal of a financial asset or financial liability, or the issue or reacquisition of an entity's own equity instrument. An incremental cost is one that would not have been incurred if the entity had not acquired, issued or disposed of the financial asset or financial liability, or had not issued or reacquired its own equity instrument.
Treasury shares	An entity's own equity instruments, held by that entity or other members of the consolidated group.

3.2 Scope

Sections 11, 12 and 22 contain scope exceptions which are largely consistent with those in IFRS 9, IAS 39 and IAS 32. The guidance in Sections 11, 12 and 22 should be applied to all financial instruments except for the following:

(i) Investments in subsidiaries, associates and joint ventures, (see Section 9 – *Consolidated and Separate Financial Statements*, Section 14 – *Investments in Associates* – and Section 15 – *Investments in Joint Ventures* – respectively.

(ii) Employers' rights and obligations under employee benefit plans, to which Section 28 – *Employee Benefits* – applies, except for the determination of the fair value of plan assets.

(iii) Insurance contracts (including reinsurance contracts) that the entity issues and reinsurance contracts that the entity holds, which are subject to FRS 103 – *Insurance Contracts.*

(iv) Leases (see Section 20 – *Leases*), except for certain aspects such as derecognition of related receivables and payables and impairment of finance lease receivables, or if the lease could, as a result of non-typical contractual terms, result in a loss to the lessor or the lessee (see Chapter 18 at 3.1.3).

(v) Contracts for contingent consideration in a business combination to which Section 19 – *Business Combinations and Goodwill* – applies. This exemption applies only to the acquirer.

(vi) Any forward contract between an acquirer and a selling shareholder to buy or sell an acquiree that will result in a business combination at a future acquisition date. The terms of the forward contract should not exceed a reasonable period normally necessary to obtain the required approval and to complete the transaction.

(vii) Financial instruments, contracts and obligations to which Section 26 – *Share-based Payment* – applies, except that the classification requirements discussed at 5 below should be applied to treasury shares issued, purchased, sold, transferred or cancelled in connection with share-based payment arrangements.

(viii) Financial instruments issued by an entity with a discretionary participation feature (see FRS 103).

(ix) Reimbursement assets (see Section 21 – *Provisions and Contingencies*).

(x)   Financial guarantee contracts to which Section 21 applies; *[FRS 102.11.7, 12.3, 22.2]*

(xi)   Contracts to buy or sell non-financial items such as commodities, inventory or property, plant and equipment are excluded from the scope of Section 12 (as they are not financial instruments), unless:

(a)   the contract imposes risks on the buyer/seller that are not typical of such contracts. For example, Section 12 may apply when the buyer/seller is required to absorb losses unrelated to price movements of the underlying non-financial items, to default by one of the counterparties or to fluctuations in foreign exchange rates; *[FRS 102.12.4]* or

(b)   the contract can be settled net in cash or another financial instrument and it does not meet the 'own use' exception. That is, Section 12 does apply to contracts for non-financial instruments that can be net settled and that were not entered into for, and continue to be held without, the purpose of the receipt or delivery of a non-financial item in accordance with an entity's expected purchase, sale or usage requirements. *[FRS 102.12.5]*.

The differences in the scope of FRS 102 compared to that of IFRS are:

(i)   Certain loan commitments are scoped out of IFRS 9 and IAS 39 and scoped into IAS 37 – *Provisions, Contingent Liabilities and Contingent Assets* – while, under FRS 102, all loan commitments are within the scope of either Section 11 or 12. When applying IFRS 9, loan commitments that are otherwise out of scope are still subject to the impairment requirements of IFRS 9. We do not expect this scope difference to have a significant impact in practice.

(ii)   Financial guarantee contracts are scoped out of Sections 11 and 12 and are accounted for under Section 21. Under IFRS, financial guarantee contracts are accounted for in accordance with IFRS 9 or IAS 39 and are generally measured at fair value on initial recognition (subject to certain exemptions), regardless of whether or not it is considered probable that the guarantee will be called, unless the entity has elected under IFRS 4 – *Insurance Contracts* – or IFRS 17 – *Insurance Contracts* – to continue the application of insurance contract accounting.

4   RECOGNITION AND MEASUREMENT: ACCOUNTING POLICY CHOICE

As discussed at 1 above, entities can choose for recognition and measurement to apply either:

(i)   Sections 11 and 12.

or

(ii)   IAS 39 (as adopted in the EU) as the standard applies prior to the application of IFRS 9.

An entity should apply the version of IAS 39 that applied immediately prior to IFRS 9 superseding IAS 39. A copy of that version will be retained for reference on the FRC website.

Entities should apply the so-called 'EU carve-out of IAS 39', which amended paragraph 81A and related Application Guidance in IAS 39, with respect to the fair value hedge of interest rate exposures of a portfolio of financial assets and liabilities.

or

(iii) IFRS 9 (as adopted in the EU), and IAS 39 (as amended following the publication of IFRS 9) as far as it remains applicable when IFRS 9 is applied. *[FRS 102.11.2, 12.2]*.

On application of IFRS 9 entities are permitted to continue to apply the IAS 39 hedge accounting requirements with respect to the fair value hedge of interest rate exposures of a portfolio of financial assets and liabilities. Hence, following the publication of IFRS 9, IAS 39 was amended to include only the guidance necessary to continue to apply such a hedge relationship. *[IFRS 9.6.1.3]*.

The above choice of guidance represents an *accounting policy choice* that *only* applies *for recognition and measurement* of financial instruments. *[FRS 102.11.2, 12.2]*. The disclosure requirements of Sections 11 and 12 (discussed at 11.2 below) and the presentation requirements of Sections 11 and 12 for offsetting on the statement of financial position (discussed at 11.1 below) are still applicable regardless of the accounting policy choice above. In addition, the disclosure requirements of Section 34 are also applicable for financial institutions and when the risks arising from financial instruments are particularly significant to the business (see 11.2.4 below).

There is no accounting policy choice to use IAS 32 in relation to the classification by the issuer of instruments as equity or liability, and therefore, Section 22 must be applied.

4.1 Impact of the accounting policy choice

In applying this accounting policy choice, preparers of financial statements should bear in mind the consequences implied in choosing the application of IAS 39 or IFRS 9. Below there is a list of the most significant ones:

a. *Applicability*: The choice must be made for all financial instruments *[FRS 102.11.2, 12.2]* and be applied for classification and measurement, impairment and hedge accounting. Entities cannot decide to elect to use IAS 39 or IFRS 9 with IAS 39 to the extent it remains applicable only for certain items.

b. *Scope*: When an entity chooses to apply IAS 39 or IFRS 9, it applies the scope of the relevant standard to its financial statements. *[FRS 102.11.2, 12.2]*. Therefore there could be situations where instruments that are out of the scope of Sections 11 and 12 could be within the scope of IAS 39 or IFRS 9; examples of this are embedded derivatives in non-financial contracts (which are discussed at 6.1.4 below) and financial guarantees (which are discussed in Chapter 19 at 2.2). Furthermore, entities should bear in mind that IAS 39 and IFRS 9 have their own exclusions from the scope; in such cases, the references to other IFRSs should be interpreted as to the relevant sections of FRS 102.

c. *Definitions*: IAS 39 and IFRS 9 have their own definitions which in some cases differ from those in FRS 102, including the definition of fair value (see 8.6 below).

d. *Disclosure requirements*: As mentioned at 4 above, the disclosure requirements of Sections 11 and 12 are applicable regardless of the accounting policy choice for recognition and measurement. However, such disclosure requirements were written based on the definitions and scope of FRS 102. Entities applying IAS 39 and IFRS 9 should interpret these requirements to make reference to the equivalent definitions in IFRS.

Disclosure requirements under FRS 102 are less onerous than those in IFRS 7. Entities applying IAS 39 and IFRS 9 are not required to comply with the additional disclosures of IFRS 7 although they should consider whether any additional disclosures should be made to enable users of the financial statements to evaluate the significance of financial instruments for their financial position and performance. *[FRS 102.11.42]*.

The recognition and measurement requirements of IAS 39 are discussed in EY International GAAP 2018. The recognition and measurement requirements of IFRS 9 are discussed in EY International GAAP 2019.

The recognition and measurement requirements of Sections 11 and 12 are discussed in the rest of this Chapter.

4.2   Changes in accounting policy choice for recognition and measurement of financial instruments

Section 10 – *Accounting Policies, Estimates and Errors* – contains the requirements for determining when a change in accounting policy is appropriate, how such a change should be accounted for and what information should be disclosed. Chapter 9 discusses in detail the requirements of Section 10. Below we discuss the relevant aspects resulting from the application of the accounting policy choice described at 4 above. *[FRS 102.11.2, 12.2]*.

4.2.1   *Mandatory changes in accounting policy*

When an entity has elected to apply the recognition and measurement provisions of IFRS 9 and the requirements of IFRS 9 change, the entity should account for that change in accounting policy in accordance with the transitional provisions, if any, specified in the revised IFRS 9. *[FRS 102.10.11(b)]*.

The accounting policy choice described at 4 above allows the use of IAS 39 (as adopted in the EU). Even though IFRS 9 has superseded IAS 39, the FRC decided to maintain the option of continuing to apply IAS 39 (in the form applicable immediately prior to the effective date of IFRS 9) until the FRS 102 requirements for impairment of financial assets have been amended to reflect IFRS 9 or it is otherwise decided not to amend FRS 102 further in relation to IFRS 9. *[FRS 102.BC.B11.5]*. Hence there is no requirement for entities to mandatorily apply IFRS 9, rather than IAS 39 for classification and measurement of financial instruments.

4.2.2   *Voluntary changes*

An entity can voluntarily change its accounting policy only if the change results in the financial statements providing reliable and more relevant information about the effects of transactions, other events or conditions on the entity's financial position, financial performance or cash flows. *[FRS 102.10.8(b)]*.

In the case of a change from IAS 39 to IFRS 9, it would appear logical to apply the transition provisions of IFRS 9. A change from IAS 39 or IFRS 9 to Sections 11 and 12 is not discussed in FRS 102, hence as there are no specific transitional provisions any change must be applied retrospectively. *[FRS 102.10.11(d)].* The transition rules of Section 35 will not apply in these circumstances as they apply only upon first-time adoption of FRS 102.

5 FINANCIAL LIABILITIES AND EQUITY

5.1 Introduction

The classification of issued instruments as either debt or equity is within the scope of Section 22 which contains the principles for classifying an instrument, or its components, as a liability or equity by the issuer. Unlike Sections 11 and 12, there is no accounting policy choice available to apply IAS 32. Section 22 must be applied regardless of the choice in relation to recognition and measurement of financial instruments.

The overriding principle in Section 22 is that those instruments, or components of an instrument, with terms such that the issuer does not have an unconditional right to avoid delivering cash or another financial asset to settle a contractual obligation represent a financial liability. Classification between liability and equity is a complex matter and requires identifying and assessing the components of the instrument and their terms.

In addition, Section 22 discusses the initial recognition and subsequent measurement requirements for an entity's own equity instruments. The initial recognition and subsequent measurement from the point of view of the holder of the instrument is covered by Sections 11 and 12 and are further discussed at 7 and 8 below.

5.2 Scope and definitions

Equity is defined as the residual interest in the assets of an entity after deducting all its liabilities. This is identical to the definition in IAS 32, but Section 22 elaborates on it by stating that equity includes investments by the owners of an entity plus retained profits, or minus losses and distributions to owners. *[FRS 102.22.3].*

A financial liability is:

(a) a contractual obligation:

  (i) to deliver cash or another financial asset to another entity; or

  (ii) to exchange financial assets or financial liabilities with another entity under conditions that are potentially unfavourable to the entity; or

(b) a contract that will or may be settled in the entity's own equity instruments and is:

  (i) a non-derivative for which the entity is or may be obliged to deliver a variable number of the entity's own equity instruments; or

  (ii) a derivative that will or may be settled other than by the exchange of a fixed amount of cash or another financial asset for a fixed number of the entity's own equity instruments. For this purpose, the entity's own equity instruments do not include instruments that are themselves contracts for the future receipt or delivery of the entity's own equity instruments. *[FRS 102.22.3].*

The basic premise of FRS 102 is similar to IAS 32 in the sense that an instrument can only be classified as equity under FRS 102 if the issuer has an unconditional right to avoid delivering cash or another financial instrument, or, if it is settled through own equity instruments, it is an exchange of a fixed amount of cash for a fixed number of the entity's own equity instruments. In all other cases, it would be classified as a financial liability.

FRS 102 provides some examples of instruments that are classified as financial liabilities as there is a contractual obligation to make the payments and the issuer has no discretion to avoid them:

(a)   instruments that oblige the issuer to make payments to the holder before liquidation (e.g. a mandatory dividend); *[FRS 102.22.5(c)]* and

(b)   preference shares that provide for mandatory redemption by the issuer for a fixed or determinable amount at a fixed or determinable future date, or the holder has the right to require the issuer to redeem the instrument at or after a particular date for a fixed or determinable amount. *[FRS 102.22.5(e)]*.

Although in many cases the classification of an instrument as equity or liability will be straightforward, certain instruments may contain terms that can be more problematic. We further discuss these issues at 5.3 to 5.6 below

5.3   Key differences between Section 22 and IAS 32

5.3.1   *Obligation to repurchase own equity*

Under IAS 32, contracts that contain an obligation or even a potential obligation for an entity to pay cash or another financial asset to purchase its own equity instruments will give rise to a liability for the present value of the redemption amount (e.g. the present value of the forward repurchase price or option exercise price). *[IAS 32.23]*. Section 22 does not contain this requirement and in such cases, the obligation/potential obligation would presumably meet the definition of a derivative (see 3.1 above) that must be measured at fair value through profit or loss. This could result in a potentially significant measurement difference.

For example, if a listed entity grants a written put option to a counterparty to sell the entity's own shares back to it for a fixed price at some point in the future, under IAS 32, the listed entity will need to measure that potential obligation at the present value of that fixed price. There would be a corresponding reduction in recorded equity. This is regardless of whether that option is likely to be exercised by the counterparty. In contrast, under FRS 102, the option would be treated as a derivative, measured at fair value through profit or loss, with no reduction in recorded equity.

5.3.2   *Derivatives contracts to acquire a fixed number of own equity instruments*

Other potential differences arise in relation to the classification of contracts that will or may be settled by the exchange of a fixed amount of cash or another financial asset for a fixed number of the entity's own equity instruments. The potential differences are as follows:

(a) In April 2005, the IFRS Interpretations Committee considered whether the reference to 'fixed amount of cash' included a fixed amount of foreign currency. The Interpretations Committee noted that although this matter was not directly addressed in IAS 32, it was clear that, when the question is considered in conjunction with guidance in other international standards, particularly IAS 39, any obligation denominated in a foreign currency represents a variable amount of cash. Consequently, the Interpretations Committee concluded that a contract settled by an entity delivering a fixed number of its own equity instruments in exchange for a fixed amount of foreign currency should be classified as a liability. Even though this conclusion was reached based on the guidance in IAS 39, we believe the same answer applies when considering IFRS 9. There is no similar explicit interpretation under FRS 102, and therefore, a judgement could be made on whether a fixed amount of foreign currency represents a fixed amount of cash or not, which in turn will affect the conclusion on the classification of such instrument. In our view, this judgement should be treated as an accounting policy choice which should be applied consistently in the assessment of instruments with this feature.

(b) IAS 32 further clarifies that rights, options or warrants to acquire a fixed number of the entity's own equity instruments for a fixed amount of *any currency* are equity instruments if the entity offers those instruments *pro rata* to all of its existing owners of the same class of its own non-derivative equity instruments. *[IAS 32.11]*. This clarification is only relevant when a fixed amount of foreign currency is not considered to be a fixed amount of cash, as such contracts should otherwise be classified as a liability. FRS 102 does not explicitly address this point due to the fact that it is also silent on the treatment of contracts involving a fixed amount of foreign currency as discussed in (a) above; hence an FRS 102 reporting entity could reach the same result by interpreting that a fixed amount of foreign currency represents a fixed amount of cash.

5.3.3 Settlement of a financial liability with equity instruments

The Triennial review 2017 incorporated into Section 22 explicit accounting requirements for the initial measurement of equity instruments issued to settle a financial liability in particular circumstances. The circumstances covered by this amendment coincide with the scope exclusions in IFRIC 19. This leads to a situation where FRS 102 mandates a specific accounting outcome for circumstances where under IFRS there is no equivalent guidance and therefore there is an accounting policy choice. This could lead to a potential GAAP difference on the initial measurement of the equity issued. We further discuss this issue at 5.5.2.B below.

5.4 Contingent settlement provisions

Some financial instruments contain contingent settlement provisions whereby settlement is dependent on the occurrence or non-occurrence of uncertain future events beyond the control of both the issuer and the holder, and the issuer does not have the unconditional right to avoid settling in cash or by delivery of another financial asset when such an event happens. This could be the case where settlement is dependent on events such as amendments to tax legislation, regulatory requirements or changes in interest rates or price indices, or even changes in the credit rating of the issuer. These are events which the issuer and the holder cannot prevent from happening; consequently, such instruments should be classified as financial liabilities unless they are included in the following exclusions: *[FRS 102.22.3A, 4]*

(i)   the part of the contingent settlement provision that could require settlement in cash or another financial asset is not *genuine*; or

(ii)   the issuer can be required to settle the obligation in cash or another financial asset only in the event of liquidation of the issuer; or

(iii) the instrument can be put by the holder back to the issuer and meets the criteria described at 5.4.3 below; or

(iv)   the instrument contains obligations arising only on liquidation and meets the criteria described at 5.4.2 below.

5.4.1   Contingencies that are 'not genuine'

FRS 102 does not contain any guidance as to what constitutes a contingent settlement provision that is 'not genuine'. The guidance within IAS 32 states that 'not genuine' refers to the occurrence of an event that is extremely rare, highly abnormal or very unlikely to occur. *[IAS 32.AG28]*. Terms that are contained within a contract are normally intended to have a commercial effect, thus, a high hurdle should apply to demonstrate that a specific term is not genuine. Nevertheless, individual facts and circumstances would need to be evaluated on a case by case basis.

5.4.2   Instruments that contain obligations only on liquidation

In respect of (ii) above, a contingent settlement provision that is only effective on liquidation of the issuer may be ignored and the instrument would be treated as an equity instrument, as different rights and obligations apply in the event of liquidation. However, if the instrument provides for settlement on the occurrence of events that could lead to liquidation such as insolvency, the exclusion does not apply and the instrument would be a financial liability.

The exclusion noted in (iv) above, is only applicable to financial instruments, or components of instruments, that are subordinate to all other classes of instruments; when such instruments impose on the entity an obligation to deliver to another party a *pro rata* share of the net assets of the entity, only on liquidation, they are classified as equity. *[FRS 102.22.4(b)]*. It could be interpreted that these instruments are equity based purely on the exclusion in (ii) discussed in the preceding paragraph. Hence, at first sight, the additional exclusion in (iv) for these instruments appears irrelevant.

IAS 32 includes guidance that clarifies that the equivalent exclusion in (ii) does not apply to circumstances where the obligation arises because liquidation is either certain to occur and beyond the control of the entity (e.g. a limited life entity), or is not certain to occur but the holder of the instrument has the option to enforce liquidation. *[IAS 32.16C, 16D]*. Although not explicitly included within the guidance in FRS 102, we believe that the FRC wrote exclusions (ii) and (iv) with that IAS 32 guidance in mind. We therefore consider that in the circumstances described (i.e. when liquidation is either certain to occur and beyond the control of the entity, or is not certain to occur but the holder of the instrument has the option to enforce liquidation), the financial instruments, or its components, would be classified as a liability unless they meet the criteria of being the most subordinate class of instrument and the obligation is to deliver a *pro rata* share of the net assets in accordance with the exclusion in (iv). This assertion is supported by the example of preference shares that provide for mandatory redemption at 5.2 above.

Another example of the application of the requirements of the exclusion in (iv) is given in FRS 102: If on liquidation the holders of an instrument receive a *pro rata* share of the net assets, but this amount is subject to a maximum amount (a ceiling) and the excess net assets are distributed to a charity organisation, the instrument would be classified as a financial liability. *[FRS 102.22.5(a)]*. This is because such terms have the effect of fixing or restricting the residual return, which is not in line with the definition of equity. This example highlights the importance of meeting the exact criteria given in the standard.

5.4.3   Puttable instruments

'Puttable instruments' are defined as financial instruments that give the holder the right to sell that instrument back to the issuer for cash or another financial asset, or are automatically redeemed or repurchased by the issuer on the occurrence of an uncertain future event or the death or retirement of the instrument holder. *[FRS 102.22.4(a)]*. In most cases, puttable instruments would meet the definition of a financial liability, such as a corporate bond that provides the holder with the option to require the issuer to redeem the instrument for cash or another financial asset at a future date. The option held by the holder means that the issuer does not have an unconditional right to avoid delivering cash, thus, the puttable instrument meets the definition of a financial liability. However, if a puttable instrument meets *all* the five criteria stated below, it will, as an exception, be classified as an equity instrument:

(i)   The instrument entitles the holder to a *pro rata* share of an entity's net assets on liquidation.

(ii)   The instrument is in the class of instruments that is most subordinate to all other classes of instruments (i.e. it is the most junior class of instrument in the hierarchy to be applied if the entity were to be liquidated).

(iii)   All puttable instruments in the most subordinate class have identical features.

(iv)   Apart from the put feature, the instrument does not contain any other liability features and is not a contract that will or may be settled in the entity's own equity instruments, as set out at 5.2 above.

(v)   The total expected cash flows attributable to the instrument over the instrument's life are based substantially on the profit or loss, the change in the recognised net assets or the change in the fair value of the recognised and unrecognised net assets of the entity over the instrument's life (excluding any effects of the instrument). *[FRS 102.22.4(a)]*.

If all the criteria mentioned above are met, a puttable instrument will be classified by exception as an equity instrument. These criteria are intended to prevent an inappropriate classification of such instruments in the financial statements of entities such as some open-ended mutual funds, unit trusts, limited life entities, partnerships and co-operative entities. FRS 102 provides the following examples of application of this classification requirement:

(a)   A puttable instrument is classified as equity if, when the put option is exercised, the holder receives a *pro rata* share of the net assets of the entity, determined by dividing the entity's net assets on liquidation into units of equal amounts and multiplying the resulting amount by the number of the units held by the financial instrument holder. However, if the holder is entitled to an amount measured on some other basis the instrument is classified as a liability. *[FRS 102.22.5(b)]*.

(b)   A puttable instrument classified as equity in a subsidiary's financial statements is classified as a liability in the consolidated financial statements of its parent, as they will not be the most subordinate instrument issued by the consolidated group. *[FRS 102.22.5(d)]*.

(c)   Members' shares in co-operative entities are classified as equity if the entity has an unconditional right to refuse redemption of the members' shares or the redemption is unconditionally prohibited by local law, regulation or the entity's governing charter. *[FRS 102.22.6]*.

We would not expect many FRS 102 adopters to have issued puttable instruments. Thus, we do not elaborate upon them any further in this book, but further information can be found in EY International GAAP 2019.

5.5   Recognition and measurement of issued equity instruments

FRS 102 contains accounting recognition criteria for equity instruments, including options and warrants over equity instruments, unlike IAS 32 which only addresses the treatment of transaction costs. At 5.5.1 to 5.5.3 below we address the recognition requirements for equity instruments issued by the reporting entity. The initial recognition and measurement requirements for the holder of investments in equity instruments and for financial liabilities are discussed at 7 below.

5.5.1   Initial recognition

Section 22 states that an entity should recognise the issue of shares or other equity instruments as equity when it issues those instruments and another party is obliged to provide cash or other resources to the entity in exchange for those instruments:

(i)   If the entity receives cash before the equity instruments are issued and it cannot be required to repay the cash, the entity should recognise an increase in equity for the consideration received.

(ii)   If the equity instruments are subscribed for, but have not been issued or called up, and the entity has not yet received the cash or other resources, the entity cannot recognise an increase in equity. *[FRS 102.22.7]*.

5.5.2   Initial measurement

The general rule is that equity instruments must initially be measured at the fair value of the cash or other resources received or receivable, net of transaction costs (see definition at 3.1 above). Any income tax related to those transactions costs should be accounted for in accordance with Section 29 – *Income Tax* (see Chapter 26). If payment is deferred and the time value of money is material, the initial measurement should be on a present value basis. *[FRS 102.22.8-9]*. No guidance is provided in this context as to the appropriate discount rate, although the guidance on financing transactions set out at 7.2.2 below would be appropriate. This would require the use of a market rate of interest for the amount receivable.

The Triennial review 2017 introduced two exceptions to this general rule. These are discussed below at 5.5.2.A and 5.5.2.B.

5.5.2.A Merger relief or group reconstructions relief under the Companies Act

The general rule at 5.5.2 does not apply when merger relief or group reconstruction relief under the Companies Act 2006 are applied. *[FRS 102.22.8]*. Merger relief and group reconstruction relief have an impact on the accounting considerations for capital and reserves of the issuer for certain group reconstructions. The requirements for these reliefs and the considerations for the related accounting are further discussed in Chapter 17 at 5.4 for consolidated financial statements and in Chapter 8 at 4.2.1 for separate financial statements.

As the use of these reliefs affect the accounting for capital and reserves of the issuer, they have an impact on the overall initial measurement of the equity instruments issued. The Companies Act indicates that when the reliefs are applied, the amount that is not required to be included in share premium can be disregarded in determining the value of the assets received as consideration provided for the shares issued. *[s615]*. Therefore, depending on whether acquisition accounting or merger accounting is applied, the point of reference to determine the value of the consideration received will vary, and so will the measurement of the equity instruments issued.

5.5.2.B Settlement of financial liability with equity instrument

The general rule at 5.5.2 above should not be applied to transactions in which a financial liability is extinguished (partially or in full) by the issue of equity instruments in any of the following circumstances:

(a) the creditor is also a direct or indirect shareholder and is acting in its capacity as a direct or indirect existing shareholder;

(b) the creditor and the entity are controlled by the same party or parties before and after the transaction and the substance of the transaction includes an equity distribution by, or contribution to, the entity; or

(c) the extinguishment is in accordance with the original terms of the financial liability. *[FRS 102.22.8A]*.

In these circumstances there is no gain or loss recognised in profit or loss as the result of such a transaction. *[FRS 102.22.8A]*.

This exception is consistent with the scope exclusions in IFRIC 19. However, FRS 102 addresses the accounting for those circumstances excluded from the scope of IFRIC 19, but no equivalent IFRS guidance exists. This could lead to a potential GAAP difference on the initial measurement of the equity issued. Our view is that due to the scope exclusion from IFRIC 19 and the lack of other specific accounting guidance, IFRS would allow for the transactions subject to this exception to be accounted for either: a) recognising no profit or loss (consistent with FRS 102); or b) recognising the difference between the fair value of the equity instruments issued and the carrying amount of the liability settled in profit or loss (as for items within the scope of IFRIC 19).

5.5.3   Presentation

Exactly how the increase in equity arising on the issue of shares or other equity instruments is presented is determined by applicable laws. For instance, the nominal value of the shares may need to be presented separately from any premium received. *[FRS 102.22.10]*.

5.6   Other topics

Section 22 also includes provisions that deal with the accounting for certain instruments and transactions involving equity instruments issued by the reporting entity. These are described at 5.6.1 to 5.6.6 below. The FRS 102 accounting requirements in respect of compound instruments, treasury shares and distributions to owners are based on the explicit guidance included in IAS 32. The other topics are not explicitly addressed by IAS 32, but are consistent with practice under IFRS.

5.6.1   Exercise of options, right and warrants

Equity issued by means of exercise of options, rights, warrants and similar equity instruments must be accounted for according to the principles discussed at 5.5 above. *[FRS 102.22.11]*.

5.6.2   Bonus issues and share splits

Capitalisation or bonus issues of shares (sometimes referred to as stock dividend) entail the issue of new shares to shareholders in proportion to their existing holdings. For example, an entity might give its shareholders one bonus share for every four shares held.

Another common transaction is a share or stock split, which involves dividing an entity's existing shares into multiple shares. For example, in a share split, shareholders may receive five additional shares for each share held and, in certain cases, the previously outstanding shares may be cancelled and replaced by the new shares.

Bonus issues and stock splits do not change total equity; however an entity should reclassify amounts within equity as required by applicable laws. *[FRS 102.22.12]*. These transactions must be permitted by an entity's articles of association as well as comply with provisions of the applicable laws. For instance, for a bonus issue the entity may utilise one of its existing reserves such as the share premium account, retained earnings or capital redemption reserve to issue the bonus shares. The relevant reserve is debited with the nominal value of the shares issued while issued share capital is credited with an equivalent amount, if the bonus shares meet the criteria to be accounted for as equity.

5.6.3   Compound instruments

Some issued financial instruments cannot be classified in their entirety as either an equity instrument or a financial liability. These instruments subject to a single contract that contain both a liability and equity component are known as compound instruments.

A typical example is a convertible bond, whereby the issuer is obligated to pay principal and interest, but the holder also has an option to convert their holding into a fixed number of equity shares of the issuer. Consequently, from the issuer's perspective, the bond contains two components, a financial liability represented by the obligation to deliver cash payments and an equity element, represented by the obligation to deliver a fixed number of equity shares (see discussion at 5.2 above).

However, not all convertible debt instruments are considered to be compound financial instruments. For example, a convertible bond that allows for conversion into a variable number of shares: since the obligation on conversion is to deliver a variable number of shares, there is no equity element. Thus the entire liability would be recorded at fair value through profit or loss, as it would not be a basic debt instrument (see 6.1 below).

5.6.3.A   *Initial recognition and measurement*

The proceeds from issuing a compound instrument must be allocated between the two components. To perform that allocation, the issuer must:

(i)   First calculate the liability component by computing the fair value of a similar bond that does not have the conversion option. In essence, the entity would need to work out the fair value of the bond assuming it had issued it without the option to convert to its own equity. See 8.6 below for further information on how to calculate fair value.

(ii) Calculate the equity element as the residual amount (i.e. the difference between the proceeds received and the fair value of the liability).

(iii) Transaction costs arising from the instrument's issue are allocated to the liability and equity components on the basis of their relative fair values.

This allocation should not be revised subsequently. *[FRS 102.22.13-14].*

5.6.3.B   *Subsequent measurement*

The subsequent measurement of the liability component of a compound instrument will depend on whether it meets the criteria to be accounted for as a basic financial instrument (i.e. at amortised cost). If not, it has to be subsequently measured at fair value through profit or loss. *[FRS 102.22.15].* Subsequent measurement of financial liabilities is further discussed at 8 below.

After initial recognition, the equity component is not re-measured.

5.6.4   *Treasury shares*

Treasury shares are equity instruments of an entity that have been issued and subsequently reacquired by the entity. When acquiring treasury shares, the entity must deduct from equity the fair value of the consideration given. No gain or loss should be recognised in profit or loss arising from the purchase, sale, transfer or cancellation of treasury shares. *[FRS 102.22.16].*

5.6.5   *Distributions to owners*

Distributions to owners (i.e. holders of an entity's equity instruments) are accounted for as a reduction in equity. *[FRS 102.22.17].*

An entity should disclose the fair value of any non-cash assets that have been distributed to its owners during the reporting period, except when the non-cash assets are ultimately controlled by the same parties both before and after the distributions. *[FRS 102.22.18].*

5.6.6   *Non-controlling interest and transactions in shares of a consolidated subsidiary*

Chapter 17 deals with business combinations and goodwill while Chapter 8 addresses the measurement and presentation of non-controlling interests. In the parent's consolidated accounts, a non-controlling interest is measured as the share of the subsidiary's net assets at fair value at the date of acquisition, adjusted for any changes in the subsidiary's net assets subsequent to acquisition, which are attributable to the non-controlling interest. It is presented within equity.

Where there is a change in the equity interests of the respective parties (i.e. parent and non-controlling interest) in the subsidiary without the parent losing control, for example, the parent's equity interest in the subsidiary increases from 60% to 65%, the non-controlling interest balance is re-measured to the parent's revised attributable share of the subsidiary's net assets. If a difference arises between the re-measurement of the non-controlling interest and the fair value of the consideration paid by the parent, any difference is recognised in equity and attributed to equity holders of the parent, with no gain or loss recognised in profit or loss. There is no re-measurement of the subsidiary's carrying amounts of assets (including goodwill) or liabilities as result of this transaction. *[FRS 102.22.19]*.

6   CLASSIFICATION

Section 11 provides a definition of a financial instrument as follows: a financial instrument is a contract that gives rise to a financial asset of one entity and a financial liability or equity instrument of another entity. *[FRS 102.11.3]*. This is identical to the definition in IAS 32.

FRS 102 introduces two categories of financial instruments:

1.   Basic financial instruments; and

2.   Other financial instruments.

All financial instruments within the scope of Sections 11 and 12 (see 3.2 above) must be categorised as either a 'basic' or 'other' financial instrument. This categorisation will drive whether the accounting guidance in Section 11 or 12, respectively, should be applied.

The category of basic financial instruments is not defined. Instead, a list of conditions that basic instruments would ordinarily satisfy, and examples of instrument types that normally satisfy those conditions is provided. 'Other' or non-basic financial instruments are defined as a default category of all financial instruments that fail to meet the conditions to be a basic financial instrument.

Prior to the Triennial review 2017, the conditions required for debt instruments to be classified as 'basic' were prescriptive. This prescription caused significant problems in applying FRS 102 as it led to a number of areas of judgement and implementation difficulties. *[FRS 102.BC.B11.11]*. The current text in FRS 102 now includes a principle-based approach for classification of debt instruments as a 'basic' financial instrument. *[FRS 102.11.8(bA)]*. This amendment addressed most of the implementation issues identified. We further discuss this at 6.1.2 below.

6.1 'Basic' financial instruments

Section 11 deals with the classification and accounting for basic financial instruments. It introduces the term 'basic financial instrument' by providing a list of financial instruments that shall be accounted for as basic financial instruments:

- Cash (cash on hand and demand deposits).

- Investments in non-derivative financial instruments that are equity of the issuer (e.g. most ordinary shares and certain preference shares) (hereinafter referred to as 'basic equity instruments'). See 6.1.1 below.

- Debt instruments that meet the principle-based description of 'basic' (hereinafter referred to as 'basic debt instruments'). See 6.1.2 below.

- Loan commitments that meet certain conditions (hereinafter referred to as 'basic loan commitments'). See 6.1.3 below. *[FRS 102.11.8]*.

6.1.1 Basic equity instruments

Section 11 includes as 'basic', investments in non-derivative financial instruments that are equity of the issuer. *[FRS 102.11.8(d)]*. Defining basic equity instruments in this fashion ensures consistency in the treatment from the point of view of the issuer and the holder.

Investments in subsidiaries, associates and joint ventures that are accounted for in accordance with Section 9, Section 14 or Section 15 are outside the scope of Sections 11 and 12, and therefore are not considered basic equity instruments.

Prior to the Triennial review 2017, basic equity instruments were defined as investments in non-convertible preference shares and non-puttable ordinary shares or preference shares. This definition in Section 11 created an anomaly whereby certain preference shares had a different classification in the books of the issuer and the holder. The issuer of the preference shares was required by Section 22 to assess whether such instruments were classified as equity or liability based on their substance (see 5 above); some non-puttable preference shares could then have been classified as basic debt instruments and carried at amortised cost by the issuer (see 6.1.2 below). However, in contrast, the holder was required to classify the same non-puttable preference shares as basic equity instruments based on their legal form and carry these instruments at fair value. This anomaly has been resolved by the Triennial review 2017.

6.1.2 Basic debt instruments

The term 'debt instrument' is not defined in FRS 102. But examples of debt instruments are given as an account, note or loan receivable or payable. *[FRS 102.11.8(b)]*. A debt instrument can be a financial asset or a financial liability, depending on whether the entity is the debtor or creditor in the instrument. However, the assessment must first be made as to whether the issued instrument is a liability or equity from the point of view of the issuer (see 5 above).

Prior to the Triennial review 2017, FRS 102 set out six conditions a debt instrument had to satisfy in order to be classified as 'basic. *All* six conditions needed to be satisfied. The conditions were in many respects similar to the IFRS 9 'contractual characteristics test', to determine whether a financial asset qualifies to be measured at amortised cost and, although not exactly the same, would often give the same outcome. However, there is no equivalent of the IFRS 9 'business model test' in FRS 102.

The six conditions have been retained in the current text of FRS 102 and any debt instrument that meets all six conditions continues to be considered 'basic'. But in addition FRS 102 now indicates that a debt instrument should be classified as 'basic' if it is consistent with the principle-based description of a 'basic' financial instrument. The description requires a 'basic' debt instrument to give rise to cash flows on specified dates that constitute reasonable compensation for the time value of money, credit risk and other basic lending risks and costs (e.g. liquidity risk, administrative costs associated with holding the instrument and lender's profit margin). Such reasonable compensation is dependent on the prevailing economic conditions and monetary policies in operation. *[FRS 102.11.9A, BC.B11.11-12].*

Most 'plain vanilla' debt instruments will satisfy either the six conditions or the principle-based description of a 'basic' debt instrument and can therefore be accounted for at amortised cost. These include, *inter alia*:

(a) trade accounts and notes receivable/payable, and loans from banks or third parties;
  [FRS 102.11.10(a)]

(b) accounts payable in a foreign currency (however, any change in the amount payable because of a change in the exchange rate is recognised in profit or loss);
  [FRS 102.11.10(b)]

(c) loans to or from subsidiaries or associates that are due on demand; *[FRS 102.11.10(c)]*

(d) a debt instrument that would become immediately receivable if the issuer defaults on an interest or principal payment; *[FRS 102.11.10(d)]*

(e) commercial paper and commercial bills; *[FRS 102.11.5(c)]* and

(f) bonds and similar instruments. *[FRS 102.11.5(e)].*

Contractual terms that introduce exposure to unrelated risks or volatility (e.g. changes in equity prices or commodity prices) are inconsistent with the principle-based description of a 'basic' debt instrument. *[FRS 102.11.9A],* and therefore debt instruments with such terms would be within the scope of Section 12. These instruments include, *inter alia*, derivatives (such as options, rights, warrants, future contracts, forward contracts and interest rate swaps that can be settled in cash or by exchanging another financial instrument) and investments in convertible debt. *[FRS 102.11.6(b), 11].*

We further discuss how the six conditions and the description of a basic financial instrument interact in assessing classification of financial instruments at 6.1.2.A to 6.1.2.F below.

6.1.2.A   Condition 1 – Contractual return to the holder

In order for a debt instrument to be classified as 'basic', the contractual return to the holder, assessed in the currency in which the debt instrument is denominated, must be:

(i) a fixed amount;

(ii) a positive fixed rate or a positive variable rate; or

(iii) a combination of a positive or a negative fixed rate and a positive variable rate (e.g. LIBOR plus 200 basis points or LIBOR less 50 basis points, but not 500 basis points less LIBOR). *[FRS 102.11.9(a)].*

A variable rate is defined for this purpose as a rate which varies over time and is linked to a single observable interest rate, or to a single relevant observable index of general price inflation of the currency in which the instrument is denominated – see Condition 2 below – provided such links are not leveraged. *[FRS 102.11.9 fn 35]*.

FRS 102 does not provide a definition of leverage. However, FRS 102 gives the example of interest on a loan that is referenced to 2 times the bank's standard variable rate. In the example, even though the return is linked to an observable interest rate, the link is leveraged and therefore fails to meet the condition. A leveraged link to an observable interest rate is also inconsistent with the principle-based description of a 'basic' debt instrument because it increases the variability of cash flows so that they do not represent reasonable compensation for the time value of money, credit risk or other basic lending risks and costs. *[FRS 102.11.9.E5]*.

The contractual return must be assessed in the currency in which the debt instrument is denominated. *[FRS 102.11.9 fn 35]*. We believe this clarification is included to avoid concluding that a return would not be determinable (as required by Condition 3 below) when subject to foreign currency fluctuations. When a debt instrument is denominated in a currency other than the functional currency, the impact of the changes in the exchange rate are accounted for as required by Section 30 – *Foreign Currency Translation* – (see Chapter 27).

The following contractual returns meet Condition 1:

(a) A fixed amount: FRS 102 provides the example of a zero-coupon loan. *[FRS 102.11.9.E1]*. For a zero-coupon loan, the holder's return is the difference between the nominal value of the loan and the issue price. The holder (lender) receives a fixed amount when the loan matures and the issuer (borrower) repays the loan.

(b) A positive fixed rate or a positive variable rate: This is the case when a single interest rate is specified in the debt instrument. In our view, examples of variable rates would be a bank's standard variable rate ('SVR'), LIBOR, SONIA, Euribor and the Bank of England base rate, but this is not an exhaustive list.

One of the examples in FRS 102 clarifies that, even though Condition 1 is not explicit about it, a negative variable rate would be consistent with the principle-based description of a basic debt instrument when that variable rate reflects prevailing economic conditions and monetary policies. This is because in such a case, the negative interest rate represents reasonable compensation for basic lending risks. *[FRS 102.11.9.E3A]*. In our view, even though the example refers to a negative variable rate, the same considerations and conclusion would apply to a fixed negative rate that reflects the prevailing conditions in the market.

(c) A combination of a positive or a negative fixed rate and a positive variable rate (e.g. LIBOR plus 200bp or LIBOR less 50bp). That is, a combination of rates meet the condition provided they do not contain a deduction of variable interest (e.g. interest on a loan charged at 10 per cent less 6-month LIBOR over the life of the loan). The effect of deducting a variable rate from a positive fixed rate is that the interest on the loan increases as and when the variable rate decreases and *vice versa* (so called inverse floating interest). Therefore the resulting rate cannot be considered to be reasonable compensation for the time value of money, credit risk or other basic lending risks and costs and the instrument cannot be classified as 'basic'. *[FRS 102.11.9.E6]*.

FRS 102 provides the example of a loan with interest payable at the bank's SVR plus 1 per cent throughout the life of the loan. A bank's SVR is a permitted variable rate in accordance with the definition of variable rate. The combination of a positive fixed rate (i.e. plus 1 per cent) and a positive variable rate is a permitted return by this condition. The combination of a bank's SVR plus a fixed interest rate of 1 per cent therefore meets Condition 1. *[FRS 102.11.9.E3]*.

6.1.2.B   Condition 2 – Link to inflation

The contract may provide for repayments of the principal or the return to the holder (but not both) to be linked to a single relevant observable index of general price inflation of the currency in which the debt instrument is denominated, provided such links are not leveraged. *[FRS 102.11.9(aA)]*.

The three main aspects of this condition are:

(i)   The link to inflation can be for either the repayment of principal or the return of the holder, but should not be such that the inflation adjusted interest rate is applied to the inflation adjusted principal, as this would imply leverage.

(ii)   The inflation index must be a single relevant observable index of general price inflation and must be denominated in the currency of the debt instrument. Common examples would be the Retail Price Index (RPI) and the Consumer Price Index (CPI) in the UK. Other indexes that do not measure general price inflation of goods and services would not be acceptable.

FRS 102 provides the example of interest on a Sterling denominated mortgage that is linked to the UK Land Registry House Price Index (HPI) plus 3 per cent; even though the index may appear to be relevant for a mortgage (as it measures inflation for residential properties in the UK), it does not measure general price inflation, and therefore it fails to meet Condition 2. The link to HPI is also inconsistent with the principle-based description of a basic debt instrument as it introduces exposure to risk that is not consistent with a basic lending arrangement. *[FRS 102.11.9.E7]*.

(iii)   The link to inflation must not be leveraged. Similar to the condition discussed at 6.1.2.A above, a term that amplifies the inflation impact on the return is likely to make the instrument fail the 'basic' definition.

6.1.2.C   Condition 3 – Variation of the return

The contract may provide for a determinable variation of the return to the holder during the life of the instrument, provided that:

(i)   the new rate satisfies Condition 1 and the variation is not contingent on future events other than:

(a)   a change of a contractual variable rate;

(b)   to protect the holder against credit deterioration of the issuer;

(c) changes in levies applied by a central bank or arising from changes in relevant taxation or law; or

(ii) the new rate is a market rate of interest and satisfies Condition 1. *[FRS 102.11.9(aB)].*

The crux of Condition 3 is that variations in the rate after initial recognition are permitted provided that:

- The variations are not contingent on future events, except in the limited scenarios mentioned above. These limited scenarios are designed to allow variations in the return driven by changes in the credit risk of the borrower and costs of lending, both of which are considered to be inherent to the determination of interest rates. Increasing the interest rate due to a decline in the borrower's credit worthiness would be acceptable. For example, if a borrower breaches a debt covenant that was stipulated in the loan agreement, the bank would be entitled to increase the interest rate to ensure that its return from the loan mitigates its increased credit risk. Finally, if a rate change is required due to changes in levies or legislation or regulations, this would be permitted.

- Variations in the rate other than those discussed above are only allowed when the new rate is a market rate of interest.

Contractual terms that give the lender the unilateral option to change the terms of the contract are not 'determinable' for this purpose. *[FRS 102.11.9(aB)].* When the lender has the unilateral option to change the terms of the contract without stipulating which rate it can change to, it would fail to meet the conditions of a basic instrument. In this respect, we do not believe that the unilateral right of a bank to change its SVR represents a change in the terms of the contract. Also, if the option to change the terms was restricted to a market rate of interest, then the terms would pass this condition.

Some examples of the application of this condition are provided below:

- A fixed interest rate loan with an initial tie-in period which reverts to the bank's SVR after the tie-in period. *[FRS 102.11.9.E2].*

  The initial fixed rate is a return that meets Condition 1 (see 6.1.2.A above). A bank's SVR is an observable interest rate and, in accordance with the definition of a variable rate, since the link to such single observable interest rate is not leveraged, it is a permissible link that meets Condition 1. Furthermore, the variation of the interest rate after the tie-in period is non-contingent, hence Condition 3(i) is also met.

- A loan with interest payable at the bank's SVR less 1 per cent throughout the life of the loan, with the condition that the interest rate can never fall below 2 per cent. *[FRS 102.11.9.E4].*

  Condition 3(i)(a) permits variation of a return to a holder (lender) that is contingent on a change of a contractual variable rate, when that rate satisfies Condition 1. In this example the contractual variable rate is the bank's SVR. The variation of the return to the holder is between the bank's SVR less 1 per cent and 2 per cent, depending on the bank's SVR. For example, if the bank's SVR is less than 3 per cent, the return to the holder is fixed at 2 per cent; if the bank's SVR is higher than 3 per cent, the return to the holder is the bank's SVR less 1 per cent. The combination of a variable rate less a fixed rate satisfies Condition 1. Therefore the interest rate on the loan provides a determinable contractual variation of the return that meets the condition of Condition 3(i)(a).

- A loan with a condition that the interest rate is reset to a higher rate if a set number of payments is missed. *[FRS 102.11.9.E4A]*.

  In this case, the missed payments are an indicator of credit deterioration of the issuer. The interest rate reset condition therefore meets Condition 3(i)(b) above, provided the new rate meets Condition 1.

- An instrument with a variable interest rate that changes based on variations in the credit rating of the issuer; i.e. if the credit rating deteriorates, the rate increases, and if it improves, the rate decreases.

  The change in interest rate is contingent on a future event. Condition (3)(i)(b) allows changes contingent on future events to protect against credit deterioration of the issuer, but it does not mention changes based on credit improvement. We believe the fact that the rate could decrease when the credit rating improves does not contradict the principle that variations in the return caused by contingent future events should only occur to protect against the deterioration of credit risk. This is because variations in the return driven by credit risk are considered to be consistent with a basic lending arrangement and therefore with the principle-based description of a 'basic' debt instrument (See 6.1.2 above). Therefore, provided that the variable interest rate satisfies Condition 1, we believe this arrangement also satisfies Condition 3(i)(b) above.

6.1.2.D   Condition 4 – Loss of principal or interest

The main focus of this condition is the possibility of losing principal or interest for the holder as a result of a contractual provision. Subordination of the debt instrument to other debt instruments does not affect the contractual right of the holder to the principal repayment. *[FRS 102.11.9(b)]*. Furthermore, the possibility of the issuer not repaying the amounts because of financial difficulties is not a contractual provision of the instrument, and therefore should not be considered in assessing this condition.

FRS 102 provides an example of applying this condition in practice. In example 2 at 6.1.2.C, it is determined that the existence of the floor protects the holder against the risk of losing the principal amount of loan in circumstances where the negative fixed spread exceeds the positive variable rate. Without the floor, Condition 4 may not be met. *[FRS 102.11.9.E4]*. This could be interpreted as an indication that any negative market interest rate would fail this condition. However, as discussed at 6.1.2.A, a negative rate would be consistent with the principle-based description of a basic debt instrument, when that variable rate reflects prevailing economic conditions and monetary policies, and would therefore not prevent the instrument from being classified as 'basic'. *[FRS 102.11.9.E3A]*.

In assessing Condition 4, it is important to differentiate between debt instruments with terms linked to the performance of an underlying asset or basket of assets, (e.g. a securitisation or a non-recourse loan) and debt instruments where the assets of the borrower are concentrated in one asset or a limited group of assets.

In the first case, the cash flows are contractually limited to the cash flows generated by an underlying asset or basket of assets and their realisation value in the case of a shortfall. Since there is a contractual linkage to the performance of the underlying asset or basket of assets, the risk of loss of principal derives from a contractual term; therefore the instrument would fail Condition 4 and should be classified as non-basic. In these types of arrangement, the assessment gets more complicated when there are several tranches linked to the performance of the underlying asset or basket of assets through a 'waterfall'. Depending on their subordination in the waterfall, the resulting contractual risk of losing principal or interest will affect the assessment of Condition 4; more senior tranches are more likely to meet the condition while more junior tranches would fail the condition as they will absorb losses first.

In the case of the concentration of assets of the borrower, there may be a similar economic effect without the contractual linkage; i.e. there is credit risk associated with whether the concentrated assets will be able to generate enough cash flows to service the debt instrument payments. For example, if an entity issues two loans, one more senior than the other and has no assets and liabilities other than a property, the question arises whether both or either of the loans fail Condition 4. In our view, the most senior loan does not fail the condition as long as it is unlikely for it to suffer losses when the lower ranking loan is sufficient to absorb the losses first. On the other hand, even though the subordinated loan is not contractually linked and according to Section 11 subordination should be ignored for classification purposes, *[FRS 102.11.9(b)]*, it is in substance constructed to absorb the first losses on the underlying assets in a similar manner to a contractually linked loan, in which case it would fail Condition 4. Therefore, the terms of some lending arrangements where the borrower has a concentration of assets may not be consistent with a basic lending arrangement and judgement will be required to conclude on their classification.

6.1.2.E   Condition 5 – Prepayment options

Contractual provisions that permit the borrower to prepay a debt instrument, or permit the holder to put it back to the issuer before maturity, must not be contingent on future events, other than to protect:

(i)   the holder against the credit deterioration of the issuer (for instance, as a consequence of defaults, credit downgrades or loan covenant breaches), or a change in control of the issuer; or

(ii)   to protect the holder or the issuer against changes in levies applied by a central bank or arising from changes in relevant taxation or law.

The inclusion of contractual terms that as a result of the early termination require reasonable compensation from either the holder or the issuer for the early termination does not constitute, in itself, a breach of Condition 5. *[FRS 102.11.9(c)]*.

Even though FRS 102 refers to contractual provisions that permit prepayment, we believe automatic prepayment provisions (i.e. those provisions that require, rather than permit, prepayment) should also be assessed on the same basis. Therefore, automatic prepayment provisions that would trigger prepayment in circumstances other than those listed above would cause the debt instrument to fail to meet this condition.

The following paragraphs discuss the key terms necessary to understand this Condition.

Contingent event considerations

Determining what is considered to be a contingent future event and whether the event meets the conditions above, particularly in relation to events under the control of the parties to the contract, requires further discussion.

If the lender has the right to require prepayment upon an event under the control of the borrower, such a provision would not be considered to be contingent on future events, as it represents a choice of the borrower, and hence would not contravene condition 5. This is consistent with the approach for contingent settlement provisions applied to the classification of equities and liabilities (see 5.4 above).

In this regard, FRS 102 provides the following example:

Example 10.1:   Early repayment on subordinated debt contingent on repayment of senior debt

Bank A lends £10 million to Entity S. Entity S has an option to repay this loan at any time. Entity S's parent, Entity P, also lends it £10 million. The loans have the same maturity date but the loan from Bank A is senior to the loan from Entity P. Entity S has the right to repay the loan to Entity P at par plus accrued interest at any time after the loan from Bank A has been repaid. *[FRS 102.11.9.E9]*.

Early repayment terms that are within the control of the issuer are not contingent on future events. Therefore if early repayment of both loans is within Entity S's control, the prepayment option in the loan from Entity P is not considered to be contingent, and does not breach Condition 5.

If early repayment of the loan from Bank A was not within the control of Entity S, then the prepayment option in the loan from Entity P would be contingent on a future event other than those permitted by Condition 5.

In such a case, the entities would need to assess whether the terms are consistent with the principle-based description of a 'basic' debt instrument. The nature of the contingent event may be an indicator when assessing the terms, but is not in itself a determinative factor. The restriction on the prepayment feature in the loan from Entity P would be consistent with the principle-based description because it exists simply to enforce its subordination relative to another debt instrument (see discussion on subordination at 6.1.2.D above). The restriction on Entity S's ability to exercise the prepayment option in the loan from Entity P would not therefore cause the loan from Entity P to fail classification as 'basic'. *[FRS 102.11.9.E9]*.

Reasonable compensation

Compensation in the event of prepayment may be payable by either party that chooses to exercise the early termination option, however, no guidance is provided as to what would be considered a reasonable amount of compensation. In this regard, we believe that entities will have a fair degree of discretion and that judgement will need to be exercised.

In our view, if the amount of the prepayment compensation to the lender substantially represents the fair value of the instrument at that point, the compensation would normally be considered reasonable. That is, the prepayment amount represents the present value of the remaining contractual interest and principal payments at the point of prepayment, discounted by the current market interest rate for the remaining tenure. For example, if a six year bond is prepaid at the end of the third year, the prepayment amount will be approximately the sum of the contractual interest and principal amounts due over the remaining three years, discounted using the current market interest rate for a bond with similar characteristics.

A penalty on prepayment that is contractually pre-determined would not automatically fail to meet this condition but should be assessed in order to conclude whether such compensation in essence represents a reasonable amount of compensation or not. An example would be a mortgage loan with a prepayment penalty clause where the amount is intended to represent present value of lost interest, even if calculated in a different manner.

Examples of payments that would not be considered reasonable compensation for early termination could include penalty payments that are something other than lost interest; e.g. when it is linked to an index other than a general inflation index.

Compensating party

In June 2016, the FRC identified that many otherwise straight-forward fixed rate loan agreements, particularly in the social housing sector, include different types of prepayment compensation provisions. These provisions require the borrower to pay the lender or the lender to pay the borrower, depending on whether current market interest rates are below or above the agreed fixed rate. Prior to the Triennial review 2017, the guidance in FRS 102 focused on compensation to the holder and did not explicitly address compensation that was paid to the borrower. This had led to diversity in practice largely driven by differing views on the application of Condition 4, specifically whether such a payment to the borrower represents a loss of principal and/or interest to the lender or not. The amendments introduced by the Triennial review 2017 addressed this issue and Condition 5 now explicitly indicates that compensation could be paid by either the holder or the issuer. *[FRS 102.BC.B11.16-18]*. This solution in consistent with the conclusion reached by the IASB in *Prepayment Features with Negative Compensation – Amendments to IFRS 9*.

6.1.2.F   Condition 6 – Extension options

Contractual provisions may permit the extension of the term of the debt instrument, provided that the return to the holder and any other contractual provisions applicable during the extended term satisfy conditions 1 to 5. *[FRS 102.11.9(e)]*.

In assessing compliance with this condition, entities must consider the fact that the extension option is a contingent event and its exercise will most likely cause a variation of return. In such a case, Condition 3(ii) would be applicable since the contingent event does not correspond to the three circumstances allowed under Condition 3(i); therefore in order for the instrument to be considered as 'basic', the rate of interest for the extended period would need to be a prevailing market rate of interest at the time of exercising the option. However, in our view, extension options for which the rate applicable to the extended period are based on an agreed fixed rate or fixed amount would be consistent with the principle-based description of a 'basic' debt instrument, and hence the instrument could be classified as 'basic'. *[FRS 102.11.9A]*.

6.1.3   Basic loan commitments

Loan commitments are not defined in FRS 102 but they are essentially firm commitments to provide credit under pre-specified terms and conditions, as defined in IFRS 9 and IAS 39. *[IFRS 9.BCZ2.2, IAS 39.BC15]*. Accordingly loan commitments are financial instruments and therefore within the scope of Chapters 11 and 12 (see 3.1 above). *[FRS 102.11.7, 12.3]*. Examples would include a mortgage offer to an individual or a committed borrowing facility granted to a company. Within the terms of the loan commitment, the borrower could have the option or the obligation to borrow from the lender.

For a loan commitment to qualify as basic debt instrument, the following two conditions must be met:

(i)   the commitment cannot be settled net in cash; and

(ii)   the loan to be received/paid when the commitment is executed, is expected to be a basic financial instrument under Section 11 (see discussion at 6.1.2 above). *[FRS 102.11.8(c)]*.

6.1.4   Embedded derivatives

It is important to note that, unlike IAS 39 and IFRS 9, Sections 11 and 12 do not contain the concept of separating embedded derivatives. An embedded derivative is a component of a hybrid (combined instrument) that also includes a non-derivative host contract with the effect that some of the cash flows of the combined instrument vary in a way similar to a standalone derivative. *[IAS 39.10, IFRS 9.4.3.1]*. As the rules for separating embedded derivatives have not been included in Sections 11 and 12, it is likely that many financial instruments that contain embedded derivatives that are not closely related to the host instrument will not meet the conditions for basic financial instruments. Hence the whole instrument will be considered as an 'other' financial instrument, in the scope of Section 12. This is different from IFRS which requires an embedded derivative that is not closely related to the host instrument to be separated and measured at fair value through profit or loss, while the host instrument can be measured at amortised cost:

(i)   only by the issuer in the case of IFRS 9, or

(ii)   by both the issuer and the holder in the case of IAS 39.

6.2   Other financial instruments

All financial instruments that are not 'basic' are dealt with in Section 12. Examples of financial instruments that do not normally meet the conditions for classification as basic, and are therefore within the scope of Section 12, include:

(a)   asset-backed securities, such as collateralised mortgage obligations, repurchase agreements and securitised packages of receivables;

(b)   derivatives (e.g. options, rights, warrants, futures contracts, forward contracts and interest rate swaps);

(c)   financial instruments that qualify and are designated as hedging instruments in accordance with the requirements in Section 12; and

(d)   commitments to make a loan to another entity and commitments to receive a loan, if the commitment can be settled net in cash. *[FRS 102.11.6]*.

Even though FRS 102 mentions repurchase agreements as an example of financial instruments that would usually fail the conditions to be classified as basic, in practice most such contracts would fail to meet the de-recognition criteria and would be accounted for as basic collateralised loans.

Other financial instruments are mostly required to be measured at fair value through profit or loss. We further discuss their accounting treatment at 7.2 and 8.1 below.

6.3 Reclassifications

Prior to the Triennial review 2017, FRS 102 was silent on reclassification between basic instruments and other instruments. Following the amendments, FRS 102 now includes guidance that the initial classification assessment of a financial instrument should take into account the relevant contractual terms dealing with the returns and any subsequent contractual variations relating to returns, prepayments and extensions of terms etc. Once the classification of a financial instrument is determined at initial recognition, re-assessment is only required at subsequent dates if there is a modification of the contractual terms that is relevant to an assessment of the classification. *[FRS 102.11.6A].*

However, the amended wording in FRS 102 still does not address circumstances where the features that caused an instrument to fail the basic instrument criteria expire. The wording only requires reassessment when there is a modification of contractual terms but, in our view, it does not prohibit or mandate reassessment in other circumstances. Considering that it would be onerous and unhelpful to users to require an instrument to continue to be classified as non-basic once all the non-basic features have expired, we believe entities ought to be able to revert to accounting for such instruments as basic, within the scope of Section 11, when the terms that caused the instrument.

6.4 Financial instruments not permitted to be measured at fair value through profit or loss by UK Company Law

6.4.1 Legal requirements

Notwithstanding whether they are basic or non-basic, financial instruments must be measured at amortised cost if they are not permitted by law to be measured at fair value through profit or loss. *[FRS 102.12.8(c), 1 Sch 36 (SC), 1 Sch 36, 2 Sch 44, 3 Sch 30, 1 Sch 36 (LLP SC), 1 Sch 36 (LLP)].*

The financial instruments in the list below may be included in the financial statements at fair value through profit or loss only if fair value is permitted in accordance with EU-adopted IFRS:

(i) financial liabilities, unless they are held as part of a trading portfolio or are derivatives (see definition of derivatives at 3.1 above);

(ii) financial instruments to be held to maturity, other than derivatives;

(iii) loans and receivables originated by the company unless they are held for trading;[2]

(iv) interests in subsidiary undertakings, associated undertakings and joint ventures;

(v) equity instruments issued by the company (outside the scope of Sections 11 and 12);

(vi) contracts for contingent consideration in a business combination (outside the scope of Sections 11 and 12); and

(vii) other financial instruments with such special characteristics that the instruments, according to generally accounting principles or practice should be accounted for differently from other financial instruments. *[FRS 102 Appendix III.12].*

In addition, the law stipulates that a financial instrument can only be held at fair value when its fair value can be reliably measured. *[1 Sch 36(5) (SC), 1 Sch 36(5), 2 Sch 44(5), 3 Sch 30(5), 1 Sch 36(5) (LLP SC), 1 Sch 36(5) (LLP)].*

The law requires that all fair value gains on financial instruments measured at fair value be recognised in the profit and loss account except when the financial instrument is a hedging instrument or an available-for-sale security. *[1 Sch 40 (SC), 1 Sch 40, 2 Sch 48, 3 Sch 34, 1 Sch 40 (LLP SC), 1 Sch 40 (LLP)].*

The Small Companies Regulations, the Regulations, the LLP (SC) and the LLP Regulations were written with the application of IAS 39 in mind and terms such as 'loans and receivables', 'held to maturity', 'held for trading' and 'available for sale' are not defined in FRS 102, although it would be logical to apply the same definitions as set out in IAS 39.

6.4.2   *Impact of the legal restrictions*

IFRS 9 became effective for accounting periods beginning on or after 1 January 2018 and replaced IAS 39 at that point. Therefore IFRS 9 is now the point of reference for determining which financial instruments may be accounted for at fair value through profit or loss under EU-adopted IFRS.

The following financial instruments are either required or allowed to be carried at fair value through profit or loss according to IFRS 9:

1. *Financial assets that fail the business model or contractual cash flows assessment:* IFRS 9 requires financial instruments to be recognised at fair value through profit and loss unless they pass both the following 'tests':

   (a) the contractual terms of the financial asset give rise on specified dates to cash flows that are solely payments of principal and interest on the principal amount outstanding; and

   (b) the financial asset is not held within a business model whose objective is either to hold financial assets in order to collect contractual cash flows, or to collect contractual cash flows and sell the financial assets. *[IFRS 9.4.1.4].*

   These usually include investments in equity instruments, derivatives and debts instruments held for trading.

2. *Financial liabilities held for trading*

3. *Hybrid contracts:* when an embedded derivative that is required by IFRS 9 to be separated from its host contract cannot be measured separately either at acquisition or at the end of the reporting period, IFRS 9 requires that the hybrid contract is designated at profit and loss. *[IFRS 9.4.3.6].*

4. *Fair value option:* IFRS 9 also permits designation at fair value through profit or loss (the fair value option) on initial recognition of a financial liability in any of the following circumstances:

   (a) where doing so eliminates or reduces a measurement or recognition inconsistency, i.e. 'an accounting mismatch';

   (b) a group of financial instruments is managed and their performance evaluated on a fair value basis; or

Chapter 10

(c) for a hybrid financial instrument which contains an embedded derivative, unless the embedded derivative does not significantly modify the cash flows or it is clear, with little or no analysis, that separation of that derivative would be prohibited. *[IFRS 9.4.2.2, 4.3.5, FRS 102 Appendix III.12A]*. In this case, the main point is that the fair value option is available for a hybrid instrument but only as long as the embedded derivative could be recognised separately.

IFRS 9 also permits designation of the fair value option on initial recognition of a financial asset in circumstance a) above.

Given that the comparison is to IFRS 9, entities that choose to apply IFRS 9 for recognition and measurement as an accounting policy choice under FRS 102 will not be subject to any legal restrictions (see 4.1 above). However, the legal restrictions could have an impact on entities that instead choose Sections 11 and 12 or IAS 39 for recognition and measurement of financial instruments. We discuss the potential impact in more detail at 6.4.2.A and 6.4.2.B below. We also discuss the restriction on recognition of gains and losses through other comprehensive income for entities choosing to apply IFRS 9 at 6.4.2.C

6.4.2.A   Impact on entities that choose to apply Sections 11 and 12 of FRS 102

Due to the legal restrictions, as set out above, a debt financial instrument that fails to be classified as 'basic' under FRS 102 can only be recorded at fair value though profit or loss if fair value is permitted in accordance with EU-adopted IFRS – which for periods starting on or after 1 January 2018 is IFRS 9.

We expect in most cases those financial instruments which would fail to be classified as 'basic' under FRS 102 would be required or permitted to be recorded at fair value through profit or loss under IFRS 9, therefore the impact of the restrictions is expected to be limited.

The basis for conclusions to FRS 102 highlights as one of those limited areas of impact from the restrictions the example of financial instruments for which the cash flows are linked to non-financial variables specific to one party to the contract. The examples below arise from analysing hybrid contracts with a host that contains one or more embedded instruments linked to non-financial variables.

Hybrid contracts – Financial assets

The holders of debt instruments that are linked to non-financial variables specific to one party to the contract would usually fail the assessment of contractual cash flows characteristics under IFRS 9 and therefore would be required to be carried at fair value through profit or loss. FRS 102 would require financial assets that are similarly linked to non-financial variables specific to one party to the contract to be classified as 'other' and measured at fair value through profit or loss. Therefore there would be no divergence, so the issue has limited impact on financial assets.

The basis for conclusions to FRS 102 clarifies that when the hybrid instrument could only be measured at fair value under IFRS by using the available-for-sale classification, such instrument could not be carried at fair value through profit or loss under Sections 11 and 12 since fair value changes were required to be recorded through other comprehensive income under IFRS. *[FRS 102.BC.B11.24]*. This clarification was written in the context of IAS 39. However, following the effective date of IFRS 9, we would expect most financial assets linked to non-financial variables would fail to pass the required contractual characteristics test and would be required to be carried at fair value through profit or loss. Thus only in rare occasions would the legal restrictions prevent the type of debt instruments previously classified as available-for-sale under IAS 39 from being carried at fair value through profit or loss under Sections 11 and 12.

Hybrid contracts – financial liabilities

A financial liability arising from a hybrid contract is not problematic when:

(a)   the hybrid contract is held for trading; or

(b)   the fair value option is applied on the basis that 1) fair value is used to address an accounting mismatch, or that 2) the instruments are managed on a fair value basis. This is because the fair value option in FRS 102 (see 8.4. below) is consistent with these two routes under the fair value option in IFRS 9.

But the analysis of the legal restrictions applicable to a financial liability arising from a hybrid contract under different circumstances requires additional considerations. The only other route available under the fair value option in IFRS 9 (see 4.(c) at 6.4.2 above) requires the embedded instrument in the hybrid contract to meet, amongst others, the following two conditions:

i)   a separate instrument with the same terms as the embedded feature would meet the definition of a derivative, and for that purpose; and

ii)   the underlying to that embedded instrument should not be a non-financial variable specific to one of the parties to the contract.

The FRC has acknowledged the existence of divergent views on what constitutes a non-financial variable. Examples of where differing views arise include measures of performance such as turnover, profits or EBITDA. The FRC was unable to resolve this divergence as to do so would involve interpreting EU-adopted IFRS on an issue on which the IFRS Interpretations Committee had so far not reached a definitive conclusion. *[FRS 102.BC.B11.23]*. Hence the assessment of whether the underlying in the embedded instrument is a non-financial variable specific to one of the parties to the contract may have an impact on the ability of the entity to use the fair value option for that hybrid instrument under IFRS 9, and hence may prohibit a fair value through profit or loss classification under FRS 102.

Given the wording in the law and the lack of clarity as to what constitutes a non-financial variable specific to one of the parties to the contract, there is diversity in practice in the assessment of when non-basic debt instruments are required by law, and hence by FRS 102, to be recorded at amortised cost. Practice under IFRS has been to interpret 'non-financial variable specific to one of the parties to the contract' quite broadly, such that no separation of an embedded derivative is permitted under IFRS 9. Hence it is likely that situations may arise such that entities conclude that financial liabilities classified as non-basic debt instruments under FRS 102, contain an embedded derivative for which the underlying is a 'non-financial variable' specific to one of the parties to the contract, which must therefore be recorded at amortised cost, unless held for trading or one of other two routes for the fair value option (to address an accounting mismatch or when managed on a fair value basis) is applicable.

The below is an example of the analysis required to apply the legal restrictions discussed above.

Example 10.2: A loan with interest equal to a percentage of the profits of the issuer

Bank A has given Entity X a loan for which the interest payable equals a percentage of the profits of Entity X. The contractual return is neither a fixed rate or amount, nor a variable rate linked to a single observable interest rate or index of general price inflation. Therefore, the return breaches Condition 1.

In addition, the loan is inconsistent with the principle-based description of a 'basic' debt instrument because the linkage to the profits of Entity X introduces exposure to a risk that is not consistent with a basic lending arrangement.

The instrument would therefore be classified as 'other' financial instrument and would be measured at fair value by the holder (Bank A). However, Entity X will need to consider whether measurement at fair value is permitted by the Regulations. The Regulations prohibit the measurement of financial liabilities at fair value, except for those held as part of a trading portfolio, those that are derivatives and when permitted by EU-adopted IFRS.

If the loan has an embedded derivative that requires separation, Entity X would be permitted under IFRS 9 to apply the fair value option and accounting for the debt at fair value through profit or loss. However, if the terms of the debt include 'a non-financial variable specific to a party to a contract', then separation of the associated embedded derivative is prohibited, and the fair value option is similarly not available for that reason.

Therefore, if the issuer concludes that the issuer's profits are 'a non-financial variable specific to a party to a contract' and that the instrument could not otherwise be measured at fair value under EU–adopted IFRS, then it must measure the instrument at amortised cost, rather than at fair value. *[FRS 102.11.9.E10]*.

Non-hybrid contracts

The basis for conclusion also acknowledges that though there may be other non-basic financial instruments that EU-adopted IFRS would not permit to be measured at fair value through profit or loss, it is expected such instruments would be rare in practice. *[FRS 102.BC.B11.25]*.

6.4.2.B Impact on entities that choose to apply IAS 39

IFRS 9 became effective for accounting periods beginning on or after 1 January 2018. Entities choosing to continue to apply IAS 39 for periods starting on or after 1 January 2018 may need to assess whether there are any restrictions to the use of fair value when compared to IFRS 9. However, we expect that only in rare circumstances would IFRS 9 not allow an instrument to be carried at fair value through profit or loss when IAS 39 allows it.

6.4.3.C Impact on entities that choose to apply IFRS 9

The endorsement of IFRS 9 eliminated any legal restrictions discussed at 6.4.1 above on the inclusion in the financial statements of financial instruments at fair value through profit or loss for entities choosing to apply IFRS 9 as an accounting policy choice under FRS 102. *[FRS 102.12.8(c), 1 Sch 36 (SC), 1 Sch 36, 2 Sch 44, 3 Sch 30, 1 Sch 36 (LLP SC), 1 Sch 36 (LLP)]*.

However, under the current wording of the law, the use of fair value accounting through other comprehensive income is still only allowed for a financial instrument that is a hedging instrument or an available-for-sale security. *[FRS 102 Appendix III.12C, 1 Sch 40 (SC), 1 Sch 40, 2 Sch 48, 3 Sch 34, 1 Sch 40 (LLP SC), 1 Sch 40 (LLP)]*.

IFRS 9 has the following circumstances in which fair value gains or losses are recorded in other comprehensive income:

(i)   when fair value changes in respect of financial liabilities attributable to changes in own credit risk are recorded in other comprehensive income unless that treatment would create or enlarge an accounting mismatch in profit or loss; *[IFRS 9.5.7.7-9]*

(ii)   if, on initial recognition, an entity makes an irrevocable election to present in other comprehensive income subsequent changes in the fair value of an equity instrument that is neither held for trading nor contingent consideration; *[IFRS 9.5.7.5-6]* and

(iii) investment in debt instruments measured at fair value through other comprehensive income which are held within a business model whose objective is achieved by both collecting contractual cash flows and selling financial assets and the contractual terms of the financial assets give rise on specified dates to cash flows that are solely payments of principal and interest on the principal amount outstanding. *[IFRS 9.4.1.2A]*.

The Note on Legal Requirements to FRS 102 states that accounting for fair value gains and losses on financial liabilities attributable to changes in credit risk in other comprehensive income in accordance with IFRS 9 will usually be a departure from the requirement of the Regulations and will therefore require the use of a true and fair override if such accounting is applied in the financial statements. *[FRS 102 Appendix III.12C]*.

The Note on Legal Requirements is silent about the other two circumstances in IFRS 9, described above, in which fair value gains and losses are recorded in other comprehensive income. In our view:

(a)   accounting for changes in the fair value of an equity instrument through other comprehensive income (without recycling of fair value changes to profit and loss) makes use of the alternative accounting rules in the Small Company Regulations, the Regulations, the LLP (SC) and LLP Regulations and does not therefore require the use of a true and fair override (see Chapter 6 at 10.3); and

(b)   the model used for accounting for changes in the fair value of a debt instrument through other comprehensive income is similar, but not identical, to the available-for-sale asset model under IAS 39. In our view, it is inferred from the Accounting Council's silence on the matter that this model is included within the fair value accounting rules in the Small Company Regulations, the Regulations, the LLP (SC) and the LLP Regulations (see Chapter 6 at 10.3) and does not therefore require the use of a true and fair override to apply.

7   INITIAL RECOGNITION AND MEASUREMENT

7.1   Initial recognition

An entity should recognise a financial asset or a financial liability only when the entity becomes a party to the contractual provisions of the instrument. *[FRS 102.11.12, 12.6]*.

Planned future transactions (forecast transactions), no matter how likely, should not be recognised as financial assets or liabilities since the entity has not become a party to a contract.

7.2 Initial measurement

7.2.1 General rule

Basic financial instruments within the scope of Section 11 will be initially measured at the transaction price, adjusted for transaction costs, unless they are subsequently measured at fair value though profit or loss (see exception in 7.2.2 below).

For basic financial instruments designated as at fair value through profit or loss and other financial instruments within the scope of Section 12, initial measurement will be at fair value, which is normally the transaction price. *[FRS 102.11.13, 12.7]*.

In essence, the main difference in the initial measurement is in the treatment of transaction costs. Transaction costs are capitalised as part of the initial carrying value for those financial instruments subsequently measured at amortised cost or cost, and expensed to the profit or loss account for those instruments that are subsequently measured at fair value through profit or loss.

7.2.2 Exception: financing transactions

There is one exception to the general rule of initially measuring a financial instrument measured at amortised cost at its transaction price, in the case of 'financing transactions'. In October 2015, the FRC issued Staff Education Note 16 – *Financing Transactions* – ('SEN 16'), which provides guidance on the measurement requirements applicable to financing transactions.

A financing transaction is an arrangement for which payment is deferred beyond normal business terms or is financed at a rate of interest that is not a market rate. FRS 102 provides the example of a seller providing interest-free credit to a buyer for the sale of goods or an interest-free or below market interest rate loan made to an employee. *[FRS 102.11.13, 12.7]*.

Sections 11 and 12 require financing transactions to be initially measured at the present value of the future payments, discounted at a market rate of interest for a similar debt instrument as determined at initial recognition and adjusted for transaction costs. *[FRS 102.11.13, 12.7]*. By requiring the instrument to be recorded initially at its net present value, the future yield will be approximately the market rate. When there is no initial payment at the time of the transaction, the difference between the net present value and the transaction price is effectively interest income or expense and is accounted for in the subsequent measurement of the receivable/payable by applying the effective interest method under the amortised cost model.

In applying this requirement to the sale of goods or services on deferred payment terms, an entity may use the current cash price of the goods or services on an arm's length basis as an estimate for the present value of the future payments. However, if there is no cash sale alternative or the cash selling price is the same as the price when buying on credit, the entity must calculate the present value of the future cash flows.

It should be noted that the present value of a financial asset or financial liability that is repayable on demand is equal to the undiscounted cash amount payable reflecting the lender's right to demand immediate payment. This would not constitute a financing transaction.

Consider the following examples:

Example 10.3:   *The sale of goods on deferred payment terms*

SEN 16 provides the example of a manufacturer that sells a piece of machinery to a customer on credit for £1,000 on 1 January 2019, agreeing with the customer that full payment is due in two years' time on 31 December 2021. Under normal business terms the piece of machinery is sold for cash and the current cash selling price is £900. Sales taxes are ignored in this example.

On 1 January 2019 the manufacturer recognises the revenue from the sale at the cash selling price of the piece of machinery of £900. The trade receivable is also measured at the cash selling price of £900 as an estimate of the present value of the future receipts. The manufacturer records the following accounting entries when the piece of machinery is sold:

Dr Trade receivable	£900	
Cr Revenue		£900

Each subsequent year, the manufacturer recognises the interest earned based on the annual effective interest rate of 5.4%* in the period with the following accounting entries.

For the year ended 31 December 2019, interest income is calculated applying the effective interest rate (5.4%) on the opening balance (£900):

Dr Trade receivable	£49	
Cr Interest income		£49

For the year ended 31 December 2020, interest income is calculated applying the effective interest rate (5.4%) on the opening balance of the year (£949):

Dr Trade receivable	£51	
Cr Interest income		£51

On 1 January 2019 the purchase of the piece of machinery is recorded by the customer at the cash selling price of £900. The customer also records a trade payable measured at the cash selling price of £900 as an estimate of the present value of the future payments. The customer records the following accounting entries when the piece of machinery is purchased:

Dr Property, plant and equipment	£900	
Cr Trade payable		£900

Each subsequent year, the customer recognises the finance cost for the period with the following accounting entries based on the calculations described above for the seller.

For the year ended 31 December 2019:

Dr Interest expense	£49	
Cr Trade payable		£49

For the year ended 31 December 2020:

Dr Interest expense	£51	
Cr Trade payable		£51

---

*   The effective interest rate was calculated as the annual compound rate that discounts the transaction price of £1,000 payable in 2 years to the £900 cash price.

In Example 10.3 above, after initial recognition both the manufacturer and the customer account for this basic debt instrument at amortised cost using the effective interest method; the difference of £100 between the present value of £900 and the transaction price of £1,000 is therefore recorded as interest income (for the manufacturer) or interest expense (for the customer) over the two years until payment is due from the customer, at which time the amortised cost will match the transaction price of £1,000 as illustrated in the example above.

Chapter 10

Example 10.4: *Parent company provides a loan to its subsidiary at an off market interest rate*

A parent lends £100,000 to its subsidiary at 4% per annum for three years. Interest is payable annually in arrears, while the principal repayment is due at maturity. If the subsidiary were to borrow the same amount from a bank, it would be charged 5%. Hence, 5% would represent the market interest rate and this would constitute a financing transaction as the parent has lent to the subsidiary at an off market rate. The calculation of the present value would take into account the sum of the annual interest payments of £4,000 and the principal repayment at the end of three years, discounted by 5% as follows:

Present value = £4,000 / 1.05 + £4,000 / 1.05^2 + (£4,000 + £100,000) / 1.05^3 = £97,277

In this example, the parent would record a loan receivable from its subsidiary of £97,277 in its separate financial statements.

The accounting for financing transactions raises the question of how to account for the difference between the initial measurement and the transaction price. When the transaction is a fixed term loan with no interest or with a below market rate of interest, the cash exchanged upon initial recognition will differ from present value calculated in accordance with the initial measurement rules for financing transactions discussed above (as shown in Example 10.4 above). This difference reflects that the lender has made a loan at a lower than market rate of interest and thereby has provided an additional benefit to the borrower. FRS 102 does not set out specific accounting requirements for that difference on initial recognition of the financing transaction. Where FRS 102 does not specifically address the accounting for a transaction, an entity applies judgement to select an accounting policy that results in relevant and reliable information. FRS 102 sets out the hierarchy of the sources an entity should consider for that analysis (see Chapter 9 at 3.2).

To determine the accounting treatment for the difference, an entity should assess the particular facts and circumstances of each arrangement. In that regard it is particularly important to establish the reasons a lender decided to make a loan at a non-market rate of interest.

In most cases, these types of loans take place between related parties. When that is the case, SEN 16 states that the accounting for the difference will be determined by the nature of the related party relationship:

a. Fixed term loans between a parent and a subsidiary: Loans between parents and their subsidiaries are often made on interest-free terms. It can be presumed that a loan is made on these terms because the parent owns and controls its subsidiary. The difference between the amount initially paid or received and the present value of a fixed-term loan at a market rate of interest represents in essence a capital contribution from the parent to the subsidiary (when the parent is the lender) or a distribution from the subsidiary to the parent (when the subsidiary is the lender).

b. Fixed term loans between fellow subsidiaries: In a situation where fellow subsidiaries enter into a loan which constitutes a financing transaction, it can generally be presumed that the loan was made on the direction of their parent. However, sometimes the facts and circumstances may indicate otherwise, for example when a fixed term interest-free loan is made in return for receiving goods or services at a discounted price, in which case the recognition of the financing component may have an impact on the accounting for the related goods or services acquired.

If an interest-free loan is made on the direction of the parent, the subsidiaries account for the transaction as if it had been conducted through the parent. The lending subsidiary accounts for the measurement difference as a distribution to its parent (i.e. as if it had made a loan to its parent) and the borrowing subsidiary accounts for the loan as a contribution from its parent (i.e. as if it had received a loan from its parent). The transaction is not required to be reflected in the parent's own financial statements because the parent is not directly involved.

c.   Fixed term loans between entities owned by the same person: In some instances a fixed term interest-free loan is made between entities that are not members of the same group, but the entities are related parties because they are owned and controlled by the same person. Unless the facts and circumstances indicate that the loan is made on these terms for a reason other than that the entities are controlled by the same owner, the accounting for the loan will be the same as shown above for a fixed term interest-free loan between fellow subsidiaries.

d.   Fixed-term loans between entities and their directors: A fixed term interest-free loan may be made between an entity and its director(s). The accounting for the measurement difference arising on the initial recognition of the loan will depend on whether the loan was made in the director's capacity as a shareholder or for another reason. For example, in a situation where a director is the majority shareholder it can be presumed that the loan was made in the director's capacity as a shareholder. This presumption can be rebutted, if, for example, loans between the entity and other third parties without an ownership interest in the entity (e.g. employees) are made on the same or similar terms.

If a fixed term interest-free loan is made between the entity and a director in its capacity as a shareholder, the accounting for the loan is similar to the accounting for a fixed term interest-free loan between a parent and its subsidiary shown above.

If an interest-free loan is made between an entity and a director who has no direct ownership interest in the entity, the terms of the loan and the reasons for making it should be assessed carefully as this is relevant for determining the appropriate accounting under FRS 102. For example, an entity may offer interest-free loans to all employees, including its directors, as an additional employee benefit. Often these loans are made for a specific purpose, for example to purchase a travel season ticket. In this situation the entity accounts for the measurement difference as an employee benefit cost in accordance with Section 28 – *Employee Benefits*.

When a director without ownership interest makes a loan to the entity, the director's motives have to be identified, as the director would not normally directly benefit from making a loan on these terms. The appropriate accounting for the measurement difference will be dependent on the individual circumstances of each transaction.

If the reporting entity is a small entity, there is some relief in the accounting of these types of loans. We further discuss this situation at 7.2.3 below.

In all of the scenarios of fixed term loans between related parties described above, the debits and credits for the cash exchanged and the resulting basic debt instrument are the same. Taking the information in Example 10.4 above:

For the lender:

Dr Loan receivable	£97,277	
Cr Cash		£100,000

For the borrower:

Dr Cash	£100,000	
Cr Loan payable		£97,277

The table below shows how the difference of £2,723 would be accounted for in each of the scenarios discussed above:

	Lender	Borrower	Lender books (Dr)	Borrower books (Cr)
a)	Parent	Subsidiary	Investment in subsidiary [*1]	Capital contribution (equity)
a)	Subsidiary	Parent	Distribution to parent (equity) [*2]	Distribution received from subsidiary [*3]
b)	Subsidiary	Subsidiary	Distribution to parent (equity) [*2]	Capital contribution from parent (equity)
c)	Entities owned by the same person		Distribution (equity) [*2]	Capital contribution (equity)
d)	Director (as Shareholder)	Entity		Capital contribution (equity)
d)	Entity	Director (as shareholder)	Distribution to owner (equity) [*2]	
d)	Entity	Director (as Director)	Employee benefits (P&L)	

*1 Investments in subsidiaries are subject to impairment under Section 27 – *Impairment of Assets*. An entity should apply the relevant accounting requirements in FRS 102 to determine whether an investment is impaired.

*2 A distribution is recorded as a reduction of equity. A distribution recorded in the financial statements in accordance with FRS 102 may not be a distribution as a matter of law. The legal requirements on distributable profits are not addressed here. For limited companies subject to CA 2006, the ICAEW/ICAS Technical Release TECH 02/17BL – *Guidance on Realised and Distributable Profits under the Companies Act 2006* ('TECH 02/17BL') considers issues concerning the determination of distributable profits and entities may refer to this or any successor document for more guidance.

*3 For limited companies subject to the CA 2006, only profits realised at the reporting date are included in profit or loss. Therefore, depending on whether the distribution corresponds to realised gains and losses or not, the distribution received from the subsidiary could be reflected in the income statement or as OCI respectively. The legal requirements on realised profits are not addressed here. TECH 02/17BL considers issues concerning the determination of realised profits and entities may refer to this or any successor document for more guidance.

After initial recognition both the lender and the borrower will account for this basic debt instrument at amortised cost using the effective interest method over the term of the loan, at the end of which the amortised cost will match the transaction price. The effective interest rate used for this purpose will reflect a market rate of interest. *[FRS 102.11.14(a)(iii)]*.

7.2.3   Financing transactions with simplified accounting

Prior to the Triennial review 2017, all financing transactions (except for public benefit entity concessionary loans – see Chapter 31 at 6.2) were required to be measured according to the exception discussed at 7.2.2 above. Feedback from stakeholders raised concerns about the implications for loans from directors to a company in which the director was also a shareholder. As this type of loans is often made by directors, especially to small companies, because funding is unavailable, it is difficult to determine an appropriate market rate for a similar debt instrument.

The FRC continues to believe that the accounting for financing transactions as discussed at 7.2.2 above is generally appropriate accounting as it reflects the fact that such transactions contain both an interest-bearing loan and the transfer of value representing the benefit compared to market rates of interest. However, it recognises that occasional specific exemptions may be granted in order to meet the principle of providing proportionate and practical solutions. For that reason the Triennial review 2017 included an amendment to provide simplified accounting for certain loans from directors for small entities (we further discuss the definition of small entity in Chapter 5 at 4.1).

The simplified accounting is intended to provide relief to small owner-managed businesses. As discussed at 7.2.2 above, transactions between entities within a group are subject to other considerations, including the nature of transactions between the entities and whether a distribution or investment has occurred. Therefore the simplified accounting was not extended to transactions between group entities.

In determining the scope of the simplified accounting, the FRC took into consideration that some small businesses are operated and financed by a group of family members who may have varying interests in the business. It also considered that similar relief should be provided when the small entity is a limited liability partnership instead of a company. *[FRS 102.BC.B11.32-39]*.

The resulting relief allows a basic financial liability of a small entity to be carried at transaction price (with no subsequent recognition of interest expense) if it is a loan from a person who is within a director's group of close family members, when that group contains at least one shareholder (for a company) or member (for a limited liability partnership) in the entity. This covers situations where the director is a shareholder (including those where the person is the sole director-shareholder of the entity), but also situations where the director is not a shareholder but a close family member is. *[FRS 102.11.13A]*. On the other hand, a loan from a director who is not a shareholder and has no close family members that are shareholders will not qualify for this relief. *[FRS 102.BC.B11.38]*.

For purposes of the relief, close family members of the family of a person is defined as those family members who may be expected to influence, or be influenced by, that person in their dealings with the entity including:

(a) that person's children and spouse or domestic partner;

(b) children of that person's spouse or domestic partner; and

(c) dependants of that person or that person's spouse or domestic partner. *[FRS 102 Appendix I].*

It could occur that after initial recognition, the entity ceases to be a small entity. In such a case, it will no longer be able to take advantage of this simplified accounting and will be required to remeasure the financial liability at its present value. However the entity is only required to apply the accounting for financing transactions prospectively from the first reporting date after it ceases to be a small entity. FRS 102 allows the present value to be determined on the basis of the facts and circumstances existing at that time or at the date the financing arrangement was entered into. *[FRS 102.11.13B].*

On the other hand, if after initial recognition an entity qualifies as a small entity, it is allowed to take advantage of the simplified accounting, but if it chooses to do so, it must apply this accounting retrospectively. *[FRS 102.11.13C].*

7.2.4 Difference between fair value and transaction price

As noted at 7.2.1 above, even though financial instruments within the scope of Section 12 are required to be initially measured at fair value, Section 12 acknowledges that the initial fair value is 'normally' the transaction price. *[FRS 102.12.7].* A difference will only arise in rare circumstances where fair value does not equate to the transaction price.

One such example is the wholesale markets for dealers in financial instruments, where such dealers are able to recognise a profit, being the margin that has been 'locked in' as a result of the differential between the price charged to a customer and the prices available to the dealer in wholesale markets.

In addition, in some markets, dealers charge minimal or no explicit transaction costs but instead quote differential prices for purchases and sales. Such prices are often referred to as 'bid' and 'asking' (or 'offer') prices. The term bid-ask spread is normally interpreted as the difference between the quoted bid and offer prices. The following example illustrates this point:

Example 10.5: *Application of a bid-ask spread in the initial measurement of a financial instrument to be measured at fair value through profit or loss*

A company acquires a quoted bond in an active market, where no explicit transaction costs are charged but separate bid and offer prices are quoted. On acquisition, the bond has an asking price of £102,000, which is the amount the purchaser is required to pay, and a bid price of £97,000, which is what the seller would receive were it to sell the bond. The fair value of a quoted asset is deemed to be its bid price (see 8.6 below for further fair value discussion) and this suggests that the entity should initially measure the bond at £97,000. This would result in an immediate loss of £5,000, the difference between the initial fair value and the cash paid. Section 11 does not address the accounting for the £5,000 loss; however, in our view, this should be treated as a transaction cost (in which case it would be included in the initial measurement if the bond is not carried at fair value through profit or loss) rather than a dealing loss, which would be consistent with the accounting under IFRS.

8   SUBSEQUENT MEASUREMENT

8.1   Introduction

The subsequent measurement of financial instruments depends on the type of instrument:

- Basic debt instruments are measured at amortised cost using the effective interest method with the following exceptions:

    (i)   The amortised cost for non-interest bearing basic debt instruments payable or receivable within one year on normal business terms (i.e. that do not constitute a financing transaction) is calculated as the undiscounted amount expected to be paid or received instead of using the effective interest method. See 8.2.1 below.

    (ii)   Basic debt instruments that are financing transactions (see 7.2.2 above) but qualify for either of the two exceptions below are carried at transaction price:

    (a)   a basic financial liability of a small entity that is a loan from a person who is within a director's group of close family members, when that group contains at least one shareholder or member in the entity (see 7.2.3 above); or

    (b)   a public benefit entity concessionary loan (see Chapter 31 at 6.2). *[FRS 102.11.13A, 14]*.

- Basic commitments to receive or make a loan are measured at cost less impairment. *[FRS 102.11.14(c)]*.

- All basic debt instruments and basic commitments to receive or make a loan may be designated as at fair value through profit or loss upon initial recognition when certain criteria are met. *[FRS 102.11.14(b)]*. We further discuss this 'fair value option' at 8.4 below.

- Investments in non-derivative instruments that are equity of the issuer and the issuer is not a member of the same group as the holder and derivatives linked to such instruments that, if exercised, will result in the delivery of such instruments, must be measured at fair value through profit or loss; however if fair value cannot be measured reliably, they must be measured at cost less impairment. *[FRS 102.11.14(d), 12.8(a)]*.

- Investments in non-derivative instruments that are equity of the issuer and the issuer is a member of the same group as the holder must be accounted for in line with an accounting policy choice which is required to be applied to all investments in a single class:

    (i)   cost less impairment;

    (ii)   fair value with changes recognised in other comprehensive income, except for the following changes that are required to be recognised in profit or loss:

    (a)   decreases that exceed cumulative fair value gains accumulated in other comprehensive income in respect of that instruments, and

    (b)   increases that reverse decreases previously recognised in profit or loss in accordance with (a) in respect of the same instrument;

    (iii)   fair value with changes in fair value recognised in profit or loss. *[FRS 102.11.14(d), 17.15E-15F]*.

- All other instruments within the scope of Section 12 are measured at fair value through profit or loss, with the exception of:

    (a) Financial instruments that are not permitted to be measured at fair value through profit or loss by the Small Company Regulations, the Regulations, the Small LLP Regulations or the LLP Regulations; such instruments will be measured at amortised cost. *[FRS 102.12.8(c)]*. We discuss further these legal restrictions at 6.4 above.

    (b) Hedging instruments in a designated hedging relationship accounted for in accordance with the cash flow hedge rules (see 10.8 below). *[FRS 102.12.8(b)]*.

8.1.1   Comparison to IFRS

8.1.1.A   IFRS 9

The classification of financial assets and liabilities under FRS 102 is generally symmetrical, that is instruments classified as basic financial assets by the holder are usually classified as basic financial liabilities by the issuer.

By contrast, IFRS 9 requires two different approaches for the classification of financial assets and financial liabilities. Under IFRS 9, the classification of financial assets is based on two tests: a) the contractual characteristics test, and b) the business model test. Only those debt instruments that both pass the contractual characteristics test and are held within a business model with the objective to collect contractual cash flows can be carried at amortised cost. Under FRS 102, debt instruments that qualify as basic are expected to pass the IFRS 9 contractual characteristics test; however, FRS 102 has no business model test and therefore, regardless of whether they are held for trading or for purposes other than collecting cash flows, they are not prevented from being carried at amortised cost.

In addition, under IFRS 9 there are two categories of financial assets carried at fair value through other comprehensive income, for which there are no equivalent categories available under FRS 102:

(a) debt instruments that pass the contractual characteristics test and are held within a business model for which the purpose is collecting contractual cash flows and selling, in which case, gains or losses recognised in other comprehensive income are recycled into profit or loss upon impairment or derecognition; and

(a) equity instruments that are not held for trading can be designated at fair value through other comprehensive income, in which case gains or losses recognised in other comprehensive income are never recycled into profit or loss.

Under IFRS 9, the classification of financial liabilities generally allows for the use of amortised cost, unless the fair value option is applied. On the other hand, under FRS 102 the classification of financial liabilities follows the same criteria as for financial assets, and any instrument for which the terms are not consistent with the principle-based description of a basic debt instrument would be classified as other and carried at fair value through profit or loss.

Furthermore, in the case of financial liabilities with embedded derivatives, under IFRS 9 there is a requirement to separate certain embedded derivatives and carry the host financial liability at amortised cost, while under FRS 102 such an instrument must be treated as a single other financial liability and carried at fair value through profit or loss.

There are two main differences for the fair value option under FRS 102 and IFRS 9:

i.   Under IFRS 9, a financial liability that contains an embedded derivative which could be separated in the way discussed in the preceding paragraph can be designated at fair value through profit or loss. When this designation occurs, the accounting will be consistent with FRS 102.

ii.   Under FRS 102, financial assets can be designated at fair value if they are managed and their performance is evaluated on a fair value basis. Under IFRS 9 there is no equivalent option as such financial assets are required to be carried at fair value through profit or loss.

Under IFRS 9, when financial liabilities are designated at fair value through profit or loss, the effect of changes in own credit risk on its fair value must be recognised in other comprehensive income.

8.1.1.B   IAS 39

Compared to IAS 39, Section 11 contains less stringent conditions for a debt instrument to be measured at amortised cost. Under IAS 39, only financial assets that are classified as loans and receivables or held to maturity can be subsequently measured at amortised cost. For the former category, the financial asset must not be quoted in an active market and must contain fixed or determinable payments while for the latter category, in addition to the financial asset having fixed or determinable payments, the entity must have the positive intention and ability to hold it to maturity. *[IAS 39.9]*. This means that, for example, most quoted debt securities, which could not be classified as a loan and receivable under IAS 39, will probably qualify for measurement at amortised cost under Section 11. Furthermore, under Section 11 entities need not worry about the requirement to hold debt securities to maturity and the consequential 'tainting rules' for held-to-maturity securities if they fail to do so.

Another difference is that FRS 102 does not have the concept of the 'trading book' contained in IAS 39, so all basic debt instruments will be recorded at amortised cost, irrespective of the reason they were acquired or the purpose for which they are held, unless the entity makes use of the 'fair value option' (see 8.4 below).

8.2   Amortised cost and the effective interest method

The *amortised cost* of a financial instrument is defined as the amount at which it was measured at initial recognition minus principal repayments, plus or minus the cumulative amortisation using the 'effective interest method' of any difference between that initial amount and the maturity amount, and minus any reduction (directly or through the use of an allowance account) for impairment or uncollectability. *[FRS 102.11.15]*.

The *effective interest method* is a method of calculating the amortised cost of a financial instrument (or group of instruments) and of allocating the interest income or expense over the relevant period. *[FRS 102 Appendix I]*.

The *effective interest rate* is the rate that exactly discounts *estimated future cash* payments or receipts through the *expected life* of the financial instrument or, when appropriate, a shorter period, to the carrying amount of the financial asset or financial liability. *[FRS 102 Appendix I]*. The effective interest rate is determined on the basis of the carrying amount of the financial asset or liability at initial recognition. Under the effective interest method:

(a) the amortised cost of a financial asset (liability) is the present value of future cash receipts (payments) discounted at the effective interest rate; and

(b) in the absence of capital repayments, the interest expense (income) in a period equals the carrying amount of the financial liability (asset) at the beginning of a period multiplied by the effective interest rate for the period. *[FRS 102.11.16]*.

Estimated cash flows

It is important to note that the effective interest rate is normally based on estimated, not contractual cash flows and there is a presumption that the cash flows and the expected life of a group of similar financial instruments can be estimated reliably. When calculating the effective interest rate at initial recognition, an entity must estimate cash flows considering all contractual terms of the financial instrument (e.g. prepayment, call and similar options) and known credit losses that have already been incurred. For variable rate financial assets and variable rate financial liabilities (see 6.2.1.A above) the current market rate of interest or index of general price inflation may be used when estimating the contractual cash flows. These cash flows must also include any related fees, finance charges paid or received, transaction costs and other premiums or discounts. It must not include possible future credit losses not yet incurred. *[FRS 102.11.17-18]*.

Future credit losses will be accounted for in line with the impairment model of FRS 102 that is based on incurred credit losses (see 8.5 below). The requirement to consider incurred credit losses on initial recognition in the calculation of the effective interest rate may be particularly important for financial assets acquired at a deep discount, as such a discount will likely reflect incurred credit losses. FRS 102 requires such incurred credit losses to be included in the estimated cash flows when computing the effective interest rate on initial recognition. The estimated cash flows should reflect the impact of the incurred credit losses in the form of expected repayments lower than the contractual cash flows and additional costs required for settlement (e.g. foreclosure costs for a collateralised loan).

Expected life

The effective interest rate should be calculated over the expected life of the instrument, consistent with the estimated cash flows approach. *[FRS 102.11.16]*.

Prepayment, call and similar options that allow the debt instrument to be settled prior to its contractual maturity can have a significant impact in estimating the expected life. The assessment of the impact of these options on the expected life should be considered at initial recognition and at the subsequent measurement dates. *[FRS 102.11.17, 20]*.

Whilst payments, receipts, discounts and premiums included in the effective interest method calculation are normally amortised over the expected life of the instrument, there may be situations when they are amortised over a shorter period. This will be the case when the variable to which they relate reprices to market rates before the expected maturity of the instrument. In such cases, the appropriate amortisation period is the period to the next re-pricing date. *[FRS 102.11.18]*.

Changes in cash flows

For variable rate financial assets and liabilities, periodic re-estimation of cash flows to reflect changes in market rates of interest or an index of general price inflation alters the effective interest rate. If such instruments are recognised initially at an amount equal to the principal receivable or payable at maturity, re-estimating the future interest payments normally has no significant effect on the carrying amount of the asset or liability. *[FRS 102.11.19]*. This is typically interpreted to mean that entities should simply account for periodic floating rate payments on an accruals basis in the period to which they relate. However, there is a view that entities should forecast all future cash flows and so estimate the floating rate payments over the instrument life, with an adjustment to this rate whenever expectations change, treated in accordance with the approach described in the next paragraph. We would not expect most FRS 102 reporters to take the latter view.

In contrast to the treatment of variable rates, in cases where estimates of payments or receipts (e.g. expectations of prepayments) are revised, an adjustment is required to the carrying amount of the financial asset or financial liability (or group of financial instruments) to reflect actual and revised estimated cash flows. The revised carrying amount is recalculated by computing the present value of the revised estimated future cash flows at the financial instrument's original effective interest rate (assuming it is a fixed rate instrument) or at the most recent effective interest rate if it is a variable rate instrument. The adjustment is recognised as income or expense in profit or loss at the date of the revision. *[FRS 102.11.20]*.

These requirements are identical to those in paragraphs B5.4.5 and B5.4.6 of IFRS 9 (and AG7 and AG8 of IAS 39). The point to note is that changing cash flow assumptions such as, for instance, estimates of prepayments, has potentially a significant impact on profit or loss, as this involves booking 'catch up' adjustments to the recorded value of the financial instrument through profit or loss.

Examples

A simple example for determining the amortised cost for a five year bond is shown below. This example is based on the example included in Section 11. *[FRS 102.11.20]*.

Example 10.6:   *Determining the effective interest rate and its application to the measurement of amortised cost*

A bond is acquired for £95,000 on 1 January 2019 and transaction costs amount to £1,000. The interest rate on the bond is 4%, paid annually in arrears, and the redemption value at maturity, which is in five years, is £100,000. The expected cash flows are the annual interest payments of £4,000 (i.e. 4% multiplied by the redemption value of £100,000) and a final bullet repayment of £100,000. The initial carrying amount is the acquisition price of £95,000 and £1,000 of transaction costs, equating to £96,000. The effective interest rate of 4.922% is the rate that discounts the expected cash flows to the initial carrying amount.

The formula is as follows:

£4,000 / (1 + 4.922%) + £4,000 / (1 + 4.922%)² + £4,000 / (1 + 4.922%)³ + £4,000 / (1 + 4.922%)⁴ + (£100,000 + £4,000) / (1 + 4.922%)⁵ = £96,000

Year	Carrying amount at the beginning of the period (£)	Interest income @ 4.922% (£)*	Cash inflow (£)	Carrying amount at the end of the period (£)
2019	96,000	4,725	(4,000)	96,725
2020	96,725	4,761	(4,000)	97,486
2021	97,486	4,798	(4,000)	98,284
2022	98,284	4,838	(4,000)	99,122
2023	99,122	4,878	(104,000)	–

*   Interest income for each period has been calculated by applying the effective interest rate of 4.922% on the carrying amount at the beginning of the period.

The accounting for amortised cost in the case of financing transactions (see 7.2.2 above) is usually straightforward once the effective interest rate is determined and follows a pattern similar to that presented in Example 10.6 above. However, certain circumstances or terms could require more consideration. Example 10.7 below discusses the instance of certain more problematic terms observed in intra-group loans.

Example 10.7:   Rolling intra-group loans

A subsidiary has received an interest free inter-company loan from its parent which has a rolling 367-day notice period. There are no other characteristics that would affect its classification as a basic debt instrument. If the loan is not called before the reporting date, the loan will remain in place for more than a year.

As the instrument is not repayable within one year, FRS 102 does not allow it to be measured at the undiscounted cash flow and requires the use of amortised cost. Since at each reporting date it would be at least 367 days until the payment is due, the entities should continue to measure the loan at an amount that takes account of the 367-day discount. Until notice is given, in order to determine the amortised cost at each reporting date the subsidiary will estimate the cash flows (which would be the bullet payment of the full amount of the loan) and will discount the cash flows using the effective interest rate. In practice, this means that at each reporting date the carrying value of the loan will remain the same. However, between each reporting date, interest would be charged on the loan on an ongoing basis. How should the resulting interest be accounted for?

Following the logic at 7.2.2 above for financing transactions, the interest resulting from applying amortised cost to a contractually interest-free loan between a parent and a subsidiary would result in a capital contribution. Until notice is given, the resulting interest would continually be added to the carrying amount of the investment of the parent in the subsidiary:

On initial recognition:

In the subsidiary's books:

Dr. Cash	100	
Cr. Loan payable		90
Cr. Equity		10

In the parent's books:

Dr. Loan receivable	90	
Dr. Investment in subsidiary	10	
Cr. Cash		100

Between reporting periods:

Dr. Interest expense	10	
Cr. Loan payable		10

Dr. Loan receivable	10	
Cr. Interest income		10

However, at each reporting date, the carrying amount (which would reflect the initial measurement plus any accrued interest from the last reporting date) would need to be adjusted to reflect the amortised cost at that date taking into consideration the treatment of changes in cash flows. As discussed at 8.2 above, the resulting adjustment should be recognised in profit or loss.

In the subsidiary's books:		In the parent's books:	
Dr. Loan payable	10	Dr. Interest income	10
Cr. Interest expense	10	Cr. Loan receivable	10

This adjustment would offset the interest charged during the period. The net effect is that no interest is charged until notice is given. This is consistent with the accounting for a loan that is repayable on demand, where no interest is charged regardless of the ultimate duration. Once notice is given, the resulting interest is included in the amortised cost which at the maturity date will match the maturity amount.

Use of contractual terms

FRS 102 is silent on the rare cases when it is not possible to estimate reliably the cash flows or the expected life of a financial instrument (or group of instruments). We believe that, as suggested by IFRS, in such situations the contractual cash flows over the full contractual term of the financial instrument (or group of instruments) may be used as a reasonable estimate. *[IFRS 9 Appendix I, IAS 39.9].*

8.2.1   Debt instruments due within 1 year

Basic non-interest bearing debt instruments that are payable or receivable within one year must be measured at their undiscounted amount expected to be paid or received, unless the arrangement is a financing transaction as explained at 7.2.2. *[FRS 102.11.14(a)(ii)].* FRS 102 refers to this method as amortised cost but clarifies that in calculating the amortised cost for these instruments, the amortisation using the effective interest method does not apply. *[FRS 102.11.15].* The underlying objective of the one year rule was to simplify the measurement basis for trade receivables, which are by their nature, normally short-term and interest free.

On the other hand, basic interest-bearing debt instruments due within one year are not excluded from the general rules on amortised cost, hence amortisation using the effective interest method is required. Prior to the Triennial review 2017, FRS 102 did not differentiate between the treatment of basic interest bearing and non-interest bearing instruments that were due within one year. This could have been interpreted to mean that on initial recognition the instrument would be recognised at the total of principal plus interest, with immediate recognition of the interest in profit or loss. The updated language in FRS 102 has resolved this inadvertent omission.

Chapter 10

8.3   Measurement at cost

Loan commitments within the scope of Section 11 and equity instruments for which a fair value cannot be reliably measured are measured at cost less impairment. *[FRS 102.11.14(c)-(d), 12.8(a)]*. At 8.3.1 and 8.3.2 below we discuss certain considerations in determining cost for financial instruments carried at cost less impairment. The calculation of impairment is discussed at 8.5 below.

8.3.1   Loan commitments

Basic commitments to receive a loan and to make a loan that are within the scope of Section 11 (see 6.1.3 above) must be measured at cost (which may sometimes be nil) less impairment. *[FRS 102.11.14(c)]*. The reference to cost is presumably in respect of any fees or premiums that have been paid by the borrower (representing a financial asset) and received by the lender (representing a financial liability).

FRS 102 is silent on how such costs should be accounted for once the loan is effectively withdrawn or if it is never utilised. Therefore, the entity will have to use judgement in developing and applying an accounting policy that results in reliable and relevant information. In our view, it would be acceptable to follow the guidance in IFRS 9, although other judgements could also be acceptable. The guidance in IFRS 9 in relation to *commitment fees received by the entity to originate a loan* is as follows:

(a)   If it is probable that the entity will enter into a specific lending arrangement, the commitment fee received is regarded as compensation for an ongoing involvement with the acquisition of a financial instrument. Together with the related transaction costs, the commitment fee is deferred and recognised as an adjustment to the effective interest rate when the loan is drawn. If the commitment expires without the entity making the loan, the fee is recognised as revenue on expiry.

(b)   On the other hand, if it is unlikely that a specific lending arrangement will be entered into, the commitment fee is recognised as revenue on a time-proportionate basis over the commitment period. *[IFRS 9 Appendix B.5.4.2]*.

We expect the treatment by the issuer would be symmetrical; in the case described at (b), the resulting charge would represent compensation for the service provided by the lender, i.e. availability of cash during the commitment period.

8.3.2   Investments in equity instruments

As long as a reliable measure of fair value is available, investments in equity instruments should be measured at fair value through profit or loss. *[FRS 102.11.14(d)(iv), 12.8]*. But when a reliable measure of fair value is not available, investments in equity instruments are carried at cost less impairment. *[FRS 102.11.14(d)(v), 12.8(a)]*.

As discussed at 6.4.1 above, the requirement to use cost less impairment for those equity investments that cannot be reliably measured is similar to that in IAS 39 (but not IFRS 9). The hurdle to overcome before concluding on the unreliability of the fair value measurement in a market that is not active is high, since FRS 102 assumes that normally it is possible to estimate the fair value of equity instruments that an entity has acquired from an outside party (see 8.6.5 below).

8.4   The fair value option

Basic debt financial instruments and basic commitments to receive or make a loan may, upon initial recognition, be designated as at fair value through profit or loss, provided that doing so results in more relevant information. This will be because either:

(i)   use of fair value eliminates or significantly reduces a measurement or recognition inconsistency (sometimes referred to as 'an accounting mismatch') that would otherwise arise; or

(ii)   a group of debt instruments or debt instruments and other financial assets is managed and its performance is evaluated on a fair value basis, in accordance with a documented risk management or investment strategy, and information is provided on that basis to the entity's key management personnel (as defined in Section 33 – *Related Party Disclosures*), for example, members of the entity's board of directors and its chief executive officer. *[FRS 102.11.14(b)]*.

This is similar to the fair value option under IAS 39 (for financial assets and liabilities) and under IFRS 9 (for financial liabilities), where designation is only possible at initial recognition of a financial instrument and not thereafter. However, unlike IAS 39 and IFRS 9, FRS 102 does not contain the further provision that the designation at initial recognition is irrevocable. *[IAS 39.50(b), IFRS 9.4.4.2]*. Having said that, we do not believe that it was the FRC's intention for the designation to be revocable.

The fair value option has a greater relevance under FRS 102 than under IAS 39 or IFRS 9, as there is no concept in the measurement rules of 'held for trading'. Basic debt instruments that are held for trading purposes are not automatically measured at fair value through profit or loss. To do so requires the use of the fair value option, on the grounds that such instruments are managed and their performance is evaluated on a fair value basis. This means that entities have a choice of whether to apply amortised cost or fair value for such instruments.

One of the reasons for including the fair value option in FRS 102 was to mitigate some of the anomalies that would result from a mixed measurement model. It eliminates problems arising where financial assets are measured at fair value and related financial liabilities are measured at amortised cost, or *vice versa*. Its use can eliminate the burden of designating hedges, tracking and analysing hedge effectiveness, which is discussed at 10 below.

An example is the issuance of debt to fund the acquisition of trading assets such as bonds or equities. As the trading assets are bought and sold frequently to maximise/minimise their profits/losses, it may make sense to measure the assets, together with their funding at fair value through profit or loss. This would avoid an accounting mismatch that would otherwise arise by measuring the assets at fair value through profit or loss and the liabilities at amortised cost.

In respect of the second situation in which the fair value option may be applied, the requirement is that the group of instruments must be managed and its performance evaluated on a fair value basis and information is provided on that basis to key management personnel. As a result, the accounting would be consistent with the underlying business objective for the portfolio as that is how its performance is assessed. We would not expect an entity to prepare any incremental documentation to satisfy this requirement, provided that existing documentation in relation to the entity's risk management or investment strategy, as authorised by key management personnel, is consistent with the use of the fair value option. The key requirement is that performance is actually managed and evaluated on a fair value basis. It is unlikely that outside the financial services or commodity trading sectors, there will be many entities that use the fair value option in this situation. Further information on the fair value option can be found in EY International GAAP 2019.

The wording of the second situation, 'a group of debt instruments or debt instruments and other financial assets' is a little odd, as it is unlikely that debt instruments would be managed together with other financial assets, such as equities. We believe this situation was intended to include the managing of debt instruments together with derivatives (which could result in a financial liability or financial asset). It is also unclear why other financial liabilities cannot form part of the portfolio. However, it is likely that most entities will not be troubled by this phrasing.

8.5   Impairment of financial assets measured at cost or amortised cost

8.5.1   Introduction

The concept of impairment is relevant to financial assets that are measured at cost or amortised cost. FRS 102 uses the same principles and criteria as the incurred loss model under IAS 39, but with one major difference. Unlike IAS 39, under FRS 102 there is no requirement for assets that have been individually assessed for impairment and found not to be impaired to be subsequently included in a collective assessment of impairment. *[IAS 39.64]*. The FRS 102 requirements are set out at 8.5.2 below.

The FRC had originally suggested that the impairment requirements of FRS 102 would be updated to reflect the IFRS 9 'expected loss' impairment model, once it was finalised. However, although IFRS 9 was completed in July 2014, the FRC has not incorporated changes to its impairment model. The IFRS 9 expected credit loss model is complex and practical experience of its application is still at an early stage, so it is no surprise that the FRC would not wish to introduce this model soon. Any amendments to FRS 102 to reflect such a major change will require consideration of the appropriate timing. The FRC agrees with respondents that, in most cases, it will be preferable to learn from IFRS implementation experience in determining whether, and if so how and when, FRS 102 should be amended. *[FRS 102.BC.A.45]*. However, if entities desire to use the expected credit loss model, they are able to choose to apply IFRS 9 for recognition and measurement purposes as discussed at 4 above.

The effect of moving from the current incurred loss model of FRS 102 and IAS 39 to the IFRS 9 expected loss approach is that entities recognise impairment losses earlier. Under IFRS 9 entities are required to recognise either 12-month or lifetime expected credit losses, depending on whether there has been a significant increase in credit risk since initial recognition or not. The measurement of expected credit losses must reflect a probability-weighted outcome, the time value of money and be based on reasonable and supportable information. Further information regarding impairment under IFRS 9 can be found in EY International GAAP 2019.

In the sections below, comparisons and references to IFRS are mostly made to IAS 39 as its principles and criteria are also based on incurred credit losses. We do not further discuss differences with the expected credit loss approach in IFRS 9 as it is substantially different.

8.5.2   *Recognition of impairment*

Under FRS 102, an assessment should be made at the end of each reporting period as to whether there is any objective evidence of impairment of financial assets that are measured at cost or amortised cost. *[FRS 102.11.21, 12.13]*. Financial assets carried at fair value through profit or loss are not subject to an impairment assessment, since decreases in value are reflected in the fair value and related profit or loss.

8.5.2.A   *Individual and group assessment*

All equity instruments recorded at cost, regardless of their size, and other financial assets that are individually significant must be assessed individually for impairment. *[FRS 102.11.24(a)]*. There is no guidance in FRS 102 as to how 'individually significant' should be interpreted, and it will therefore require judgement.

All other financial assets that are not individually significant should be assessed either individually, or grouped on the basis of similar credit risk characteristics. *[FRS 102.11.24]*. As previously mentioned, assets that have been individually assessed for impairment and found not to be impaired do not subsequently need to be included in a collective assessment of impairment. Even though this appears to be a difference with IAS 39, in practice the same conclusion may be reached.

Grouping financial assets based on similar credit risk characteristics will be a matter of judgement for individual reporters. For example, a bank might split its loans to customers into several categories such as unsecured retail loans, secured retail loans, corporate loans and mortgages. Further stratification of these groupings may be appropriate; for example, mortgages might be split based on their loan-to-value ratios, or the location of the properties, while smaller corporate loans might be split based on the industry in which the borrower operates. A non-financial institution, might stratify their trade receivables based on their country of operation, lines of business or even brand names.

8.5.2.B   *Objective evidence of impairment*

Objective evidence that a financial asset or group of assets is impaired includes observable data about loss events. Examples of loss events include:

(i)   significant financial difficulty of the issuer or obligor;

(ii)   a breach of contract such as a default or delinquency in interest or principal payments;

(iii) the creditor, for economic or legal reasons relating to the debtor's financial difficulty, granting to the debtor a concession that the creditor would not otherwise consider;

(iv)   it is probable that the debtor will enter bankruptcy or other financial reorganisation; or

(v)   for a group of financial assets, observable data indicating that there has been a measurable decrease in the estimated future cash flows from the group since the initial recognition of those assets, even though the decrease cannot yet be identified with the individual financial assets in the group, such as adverse national or local economic conditions or adverse changes in industry conditions. *[FRS 102.11.22]*.

The above is not an exhaustive list and other factors may also be evidence of impairment, including significant changes with an adverse effect that have taken place in the technological, market, economic or legal environment in which the issuer operates. *[FRS 102.11.23]*.

If such evidence exists, an impairment loss should be recognised in profit or loss immediately. *[FRS 102.11.21]*.

8.5.3 Measurement of impairment

8.5.3.A Financial assets carried at amortised cost

For financial assets carried at amortised cost for which there is objective evidence of impairment, the impairment loss is measured as the difference between the asset's carrying amount and the present value of estimated cash flows, discounted at the asset's original effective interest rate. If it is a variable rate asset, the discount rate for measuring the impairment loss is the current effective interest rate. *[FRS 102.11.25(a)]*. Subsequently, the amortised cost of an impaired financial asset is calculated by applying the effective interest rate on the carrying amount net of impairment. *[FRS 102.11.15(d)]*.

The following example builds on Example 10.6 to illustrate the measurement of impairment.

Example 10.8: Calculating the impairment loss for amortised cost debt instruments

For a bond measured at amortised cost, at the end of 2020, due to continuing deterioration in the borrower's financial performance, the lender assesses that 25% of all future cash flows (in 2021 to 2023) will not be recoverable. The future cash flows that were due were the 4% coupon per annum (i.e. £100,000 × 4%) and the principal repayment of £100,000 at the end of 2023, which works out to £4,000 in 2021 and 2022 respectively and £104,000 in 2023. If the 25% default rate were to be applied to these cash flows, the revised cash inflows would be £3,000 in 2021 and 2022 and £78,000 in 2023. As mentioned above, the impairment loss will be the difference between the present value of the revised future cash flows less the carrying amount before the impairment, which was £97,486. The present value of the revised future cash flows is £73,114 after discounting by the original effective interest rate of 4.922%. This is worked out as:

£3,000 / (1 + 4.922%) + £3,000 / (1 + 4.922%)^2 + £78,000 / (1 + 4.922%)^3 = £73,114. Hence, the impairment loss is £24,372, being the difference between £97,486 and £73,114.

Year	Carrying amount at the beginning of the period (£)	Interest income @ 4.922% * (£)	Cash inflow (£)	Impairment loss (£)	Carrying amount at the end of the period (£)
2019	96,000	4,725	(4,000)	–	96,725
2020 (pre-impairment)	96,725	4,761	(4,000)	–	97,486
2020 (post-impairment)	97,486	–	–	(24,372)	73,114
2021	73,114	3,599	(3,000)	–	73,713
2022	73,713	3,628	(3,000)	–	74,341
2023	74,341	3,659	(78,000)	–	–

* Interest income for each period has been calculated by applying the effective interest rate of 4.922% on the carrying amount at the beginning of the period, which includes any impairment provision.

8.5.3.B   *Financial assets carried at cost*

For investments in equity instruments and basic loan commitments to receive a loan measured at cost, the impairment loss will be the difference between the instrument's carrying amount and a best estimate of the amount that the entity would receive if it were sold at the reporting date. The best estimate will inevitably be an approximation and may be zero. *[FRS 102.11.25(b)]*.

In the case of investments in equity instruments carried at cost denominated in a foreign currency, the assessment for impairment should be carried out in the functional currency of the reporting entity, as the cost of such investments is not remeasured after initial recognition. Therefore, a change in exchange rates could have an impact on their impairment.

8.5.3.C   *Commitments to make a loan*

Section 11 requires that basic commitments either to receive a loan or to make a loan to another party should be measured at cost less impairment. *[FRS 102.11.14(c)]*. As discussed at 8.3.1, in the case of a basic commitment to make a loan, we would expect cost to refer to any fees or premiums received from the borrower, in which case the cost will represent a financial liability to the lender. Given that the impairment rules in Section 11 for loan commitments state that the impairment loss is the difference between the asset's carrying amount and the best estimate (which will necessarily be an approximation) of the amount (which might be zero) that the entity would receive for the asset if it were to be sold at the reporting date, *[FRS 102.11.25(b)]*, this is problematic. First, as already mentioned, the loan commitment will be a liability and not an asset and second, the entity will need to pay to be relieved of the commitment. We assume that entities are expected to substitute the references to 'asset' and 'receive' with 'liability' and 'pay'.

We note that this will give a similar result to applying Section 21, even though loan commitments are explicitly excluded from its scope. *[FRS 102.21.1B]*. Financial institutions that applied IAS 39 were required to measure impairment on commitments to make a loan in accordance with IAS 37, which is also similar in its requirements to Section 21. However, in practice, such institutions often calculated the amount using a similar approach to that used for measuring loss allowances on the loans themselves under IAS 39. This differs from the treatment under IFRS 9, where loan commitments are subject to the assessment of expected credit losses.

8.5.4   Reversal of impairment

If, in a subsequent period, the amount of the impairment loss decreases and the decrease can be objectively related to an event occurring after the impairment was recognised (such as an improvement in the debtor's credit rating), the previously recognised impairment loss should be reversed and recognised in profit or loss, either directly or by adjusting an allowance account. However, the reversal should not result in a carrying amount of the asset that exceeds what its amortised cost would have been had the impairment not been recognised. *[FRS 102.11.26]*.

FRS 102 does not specifically prohibit the reversal of impairment in the case of investments in equity instruments. This constitutes a difference compared to IAS 39, since the IASB could not find an acceptable way to distinguish reversals of impairment losses from other increases in fair value of available-for-sale equity instruments. Therefore, it decided to preclude such reversals for equity instruments. *[IAS 39.BC129-130]*. This also differs from IFRS 9, where equities, even those carried at fair value through other comprehensive income, are not subject to impairment.

8.6   Fair value

FRS 102 defines fair value as the amount for which an asset could be exchanged, a liability settled, or an equity instrument granted could be exchanged, between knowledgeable, willing parties in an arm's length transaction. FRS 102 goes on to say that, in the absence of any specific guidance provided in the relevant section of this FRS, the guidance in relation to the fair value in the Appendix to Section 2 should be used. *[FRS 102 Appendix I]*.

This definition of fair value is similar to that found in the version of IAS 39 prior to issuance of IFRS 13 and appears to be focused on the notion of an 'exit price'. This differs from IFRS 13 which defines fair value as 'the price that would be received to sell an asset or paid to transfer a liability in an orderly transaction between market participants at the measurement date'. *[IFRS 13.9]*.

The difference in definitions could lead to different measurements of fair values, in particular for financial liabilities as the amount to settle a liability required by FRS 102 to determine fair value may differ from the amount paid to transfer the same liability, which is the definition of fair value under IFRS 13 (see 8.6.4.A below).

During the Triennial review 2017 process, the FRC considered amending key definitions relating to fair value included in Appendix to Section 2 for greater consistency with IFRS 13. However, respondents to the Triennial review 2017 consultation highlighted those amendments could have led to unintended consequences, particularly for certain entities that had only recently applied the fair value requirements in FRS 102. In addition, Appendix to Section 2 only provides a methodology for approaching fair value measurement. As a result, the definition of fair value was not amended, and only minor changes were made to Appendix to Section 2, for example to emphasise that it is a methodology and give further practical guidance. *[FRS 102.BC.B11.43-46]*.

8.6.1   Hierarchy used to estimate fair value

As mentioned above, the key guidance on how to calculate fair values is contained in the Appendix to Section 2. The guidance sets out a hierarchy to estimate fair value for which the best evidence of fair value is a quoted price in an active market. *[FRS 102.2A.1]*. Figure 10.1 below shows the fair value hierarchy to be used.

Figure 10.1: Hierarchy

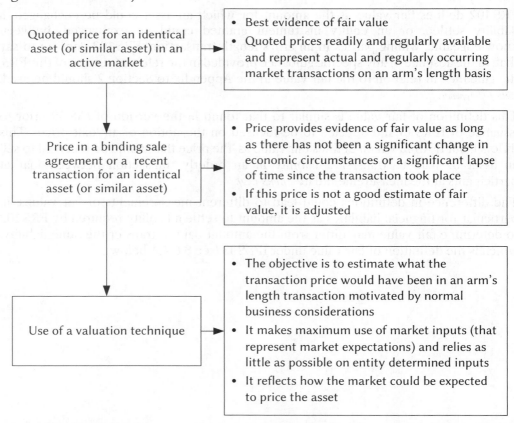

Reporting entities should measure fair value using the highest available level within the hierarchy. FRS 102 is explicit that the best evidence of fair value is a quoted price for an identical or similar instrument in an active market and only when such quoted prices are unavailable, does an entity use the price of a recent transaction for an identical instrument and failing that, a valuation technique. *[FRS 102.2A.1-3]*. However, the above guidance is somewhat theoretical and no examples are provided to illustrate its application.

8.6.2   Quoted price in an active market

'Active market' is defined as 'a market in which all the following conditions exist:

(a)   the items traded in the market are homogeneous;

(b)   willing buyers and sellers can normally be found at any time; and

(c)   prices are available to the public.' *[FRS 102 Appendix I]*.

Based on the above definition, most equities and bonds that are listed on an exchange for which there is a liquid secondary market in terms of regular trading will be considered to be traded in an active market. In addition, instruments that are frequently traded in over-the-counter markets (i.e. instruments that are not listed on an exchange), such as interest rate swaps and options, foreign exchange derivatives and credit default swaps, and for which there are available quotes may also be captured if closing prices are published.

The requirement that the best evidence of fair value is a quoted price for an identical asset in an active market is similar to that in IFRS 13. However, FRS 102 does not reproduce the additional guidance contained in IFRS 13 that the fair value of a portfolio of financial instruments is the product of the number of units of the instrument and its quoted market price, known as 'p times q'. *[IFRS 13.80]*. This guidance means that an entity which has a very large holding of an actively traded financial instrument is unable to adjust the quoted price to reflect any discount or premium that might arise if the holding were to be unloaded onto the market. Given that this guidance is not contained in FRS 102, some might read it as not to require the use of p times q in these circumstances.

8.6.3   Price of a recent transaction

The use of the price of a recent transaction for an identical instrument is a simple valuation technique. However, what requires some judgement is determining whether that price is representative of fair value or not. An adjustment is required if the last transaction is not a good estimate of fair value. This could be the situation if there has been a significant change in economic circumstances, a significant lapse in time or the price of the transaction reflects an amount that an entity was forced to pay or receive in a forced transaction, involuntary liquidation or distressed sale. *[FRS 102.2A.1(b)]*.

8.6.4   Other valuation techniques

In addition to the use of the price of a recent transaction for an identical instrument, other valuation techniques could include reference to the current fair value of another instrument that is substantially the same as the instrument being measured, discounted cash flow analysis and option pricing models. If there is a valuation technique commonly used by market participants to price the asset and that technique has been demonstrated to provide reliable estimates of prices obtained in actual market transactions, the entity uses that technique. *[FRS 102.2A.1(c), 2A.2]*.

The objective of using a valuation technique is to establish what the transaction price would have been on the measurement date in an arm's length exchange, motivated by normal business considerations. Fair value is estimated on the basis of the results of a valuation technique that makes maximum use of market inputs, and relies as little as possible on entity-determined inputs. A valuation technique would be expected to arrive at a reliable estimate of the fair value if:

a)   it reasonably reflects how the market could be expected to price the asset; and

b)   the inputs to the valuation technique reasonably represent market expectations and measures of the risk return factors inherent in the asset. *[FRS 102.2A.3]*.

Many entities applying FRS 102 will not enter into instruments that are required to be recorded at fair value through profit or loss and for which a quoted price in active markets is not available. However if they do invest in, or issue complex instruments that must be fair valued but do not have quoted prices in active markets, they may have to draw upon the larger body of guidance within IFRS 13 in making judgements regarding how to measure fair value, especially regarding the use of valuation techniques. Further information regarding IFRS 13 can be found in EY International GAAP 2019.

8.6.4.A   Consideration of own credit risk

Although guidance in IFRS 13 on valuation techniques may be helpful in some circumstances, caution should be taken in applying the guidance. For instance, IFRS 13 is clear that entities must include in the fair value of financial liabilities such as derivatives any changes in fair value attributable to their own credit risk. *[IFRS 13.42]*. This has the unintuitive consequence that such entities will record profits on revaluation when their credit risk increases. FRS 102 has no specific equivalent requirement, although entities are required to disclose the effect of own credit risk on liabilities recorded at fair value through profit or loss (see 11.2.2 below) for those financial liabilities that do not form part of a trading book and are not derivatives. This could be interpreted to imply that fair value for such liabilities should include the effects of changes in own credit risk; however, since FRS 102 determines that fair value of a liability should be measured on a settlement basis rather than at the amount paid to transfer it (see 8.6 above), the consideration of own credit risk would be an accounting policy choice.

8.6.5   Fair value not reliably measurable

For instruments that do not have a quoted market price in an active market, fair value is considered reliably measurable when the range of reasonable fair value estimates is not significant or the probabilities of the various estimates within the range can be reasonably assessed and used in estimating fair value. There are many situations in which the variability in the range of reasonable fair value estimates of assets that do not have a quoted market price is likely not to be significant. Normally it is possible to estimate the fair value of an asset that an entity has acquired from an outside party. However, if the range of reasonable fair value estimates is significant, and the probabilities of the various estimates cannot be reasonably assessed, an entity is precluded from measuring the asset at fair value. *[FRS 102.2A.4-5]*.

No further guidance is provided to assess significance or probabilities in this context, hence, entities will need to exercise judgement. However, we believe that the bar for determining that a fair value measurement is not reliably measurable is relatively high and is limited to investments such as equity holdings in private companies, for which the investee has no comparable peers.

If, initially, fair value can be reliably measured, but such measurement ceases to be reliable at a subsequent date, a financial instrument's carrying amount at the last date it was reliably measurable becomes its new cost. Going forward, the instrument should be measured at its new cost less impairment until a reliable measure of fair value becomes available again. *[FRS 102.2A.6, 12.9]*.

8.6.6 Financial liabilities due on demand

The fair value of a financial liability that is due on demand is deemed to be not less than the amount payable on demand, discounted from the first date that the amount could be required to be paid. *[FRS 102.12.11]*. The logic is that a rational lender would demand repayment if the fair value were ever less than the net present value of the amount repayable, even though in practice many people do not withdraw their demand deposits in such circumstances. No guidance is provided in this context as to the appropriate discount rate, although the guidance on financing transactions set out at 7.2.2 above would be appropriate. This requirement is identical to that in IFRS 13.47, hence, further information can be found in EY International GAAP 2019.

9 DERECOGNITION

9.1 Introduction

The FRS 102 derecognition requirements are located in Section 11, paragraphs 33 to 38, however, they are also applicable to:

(a) financial assets and financial liabilities within the scope of Section 12; *[FRS 102.12.14]* and

(b) receivables recognised by a lessor and payables recognised by a lessee. *[FRS 102.11.7(c)]*.

9.2 Derecognition of financial assets

The FRS 102 derecognition principles for financial assets are similar to those in IFRS 9 and IAS 39 but they have been simplified and do not contain the full body of guidance that can be found in IFRS 9 and IAS 39. While it would be possible to draw on the additional guidance in IFRS 9 (and IAS 39, which is essentially the same as IFRS 9) to interpret the requirements of FRS 102, we believe that the FRC deliberately intended the FRS 102 derecognition test to be simpler. Consequently, a wider range of transactions will perhaps qualify for derecognition under IFRS than under FRS 102, but most adopters of FRS 102 are unlikely to enter into such transactions.

Under FRS 102, a financial asset is derecognised only when:

(a) the contractual rights to the cash flows from the financial asset expire or are settled; or

(b) the entity transfers to another party substantially all of the risks and rewards of ownership of the financial asset; or

(c) the entity, despite having retained some, but not substantially all, risks and rewards of ownership, has transferred control of the asset to another party and the other party has the practical ability to sell the asset in its entirety to an unrelated third party and is able to exercise that ability unilaterally and without needing to impose additional restrictions on the transfer. *[FRS 102.11.33]*.

The above requirements were clarified as part of the Triennial review 2017, although it always was, and still is our belief that the guidance should be viewed as broadly equivalent to the model set out in IFRS 9 and IAS 39, with the exception of pass-through arrangements (see 9.2.4.A below). That is, there are three situations:

(i)   where the transferor has transferred substantially all the risks and rewards, as set out in (b) above, in which case it should derecognise the asset; or

(ii) where the transferor has neither transferred nor retained substantially all the risks and rewards, in which case the accounting treatment depends on whether control has been transferred, as set out in (c) above; or

(iii) where the transferor has retained substantially all the risks and rewards, in which case the asset should not be derecognised.

This third situation will include transactions such as repurchase obligations (i.e. repos), stock lending agreements and factoring arrangements when the transferee has recourse to the transferor and hence has retained substantially all the risks and rewards. This is consistent with the following example from FRS 102:

Example 10.9:   The sale of trade receivables with retention of risks

A company sells a group of its accounts receivable to a bank at less than their face amount. The company continues to handle collections from the debtors on behalf of the bank, including sending monthly statements, and the bank pays the entity a market rate fee for servicing the receivables. The company is obliged to remit promptly to the bank any and all amounts collected. The company has also agreed to buy back from the bank any receivables for which the debtor is in arrears as to principal or interest for more than 120 days. *[FRS 102.11.35]*.

As the entity has retained the risk of slow payment or non-payment, it should not derecognise the assets but must treat the proceeds from the bank as a loan secured by the receivables.

Where financial assets are transferred, the derecognition assessment first needs to consider the extent to which the entity is still exposed to the risk and rewards associated with the asset following the transfer. If the entity has retained some of the risks and rewards it will also need to consider whether it still has control over the asset. In essence, the substance of the transaction needs to be evaluated in assessing derecognition; the mere transfer of legal ownership is not sufficient.

In most cases, we would expect the application of these requirements by FRS 102 reporters to be straightforward. That is, in the case of a financial asset such as a loan which is settled on its scheduled maturity date or is redeemed before maturity by the borrower in accordance with the stipulated terms of the loan, the loan would be derecognised on settlement. Another simple example would be the unconditional sale of a financial asset for a fixed price. It is only when an entity embarks on more complex transactions, such as factoring or securitisations, that the application of the requirements become more challenging.

9.2.1   Transfer of risks and rewards of ownership of the asset

FRS 102 does not provide any guidance as to what constitutes the transfer to another party of substantially all the risks and rewards of ownership. *[FRS 102.11.33(b)]*. The analysis needs to take into account all facts and circumstances and the most common risks to be evaluated will usually include credit risk, foreign exchange risk, late payment risk and price risk.

In the case of trade receivables, which are usually short-term in nature, the main risks are normally late payment risk (e.g. the debtor does not settle within the stipulated credit period such as 30 days or 90 days, but does eventually make payment in full for the amount due) or credit risk (i.e. the debtor is unable to make full payment for the amount owing and it results in a bad debt for the creditor). In most cases, we would expect the issue of whether substantially all risks and rewards have been transferred to be uncontroversial.

9.2.1.A   *Sale with option to buy back or sell back at some point in the future*

The analysis is more challenging when the asset is sold but either party or both have an option to buy/sell back the asset at some point in the future. In order to analyse the implications of the option on the risk and rewards assessment, the exercise price of the option relative to the current fair value of the asset would need to be considered, together with the term of the option.

In the case of a call option that is deeply in the money (i.e. the exercise price of the option is favourable when compared to the current market price of the asset and is expected to remain so), it is highly likely that the option will be exercised by the transferor before expiry. Consequently, derecognition would not be appropriate based on 9.2(iii) above, as the transferor has retained substantially all the risks and rewards. However, if the circumstances were reversed, that is, the option is deeply out of the money and is highly unlikely to go into the money before maturity, derecognition would be appropriate as the transferor has transferred substantially all risks and rewards. In these situations, it is almost impossible to set bright lines as to when an option is considered deeply in or out of the money, hence, judgement is required by evaluating all relevant facts and circumstances on a case by case basis.

9.2.1.B   *Sale of trade receivables*

The same assessment will need to be made in respect of the sale of trade receivables, by analysing the extent to which the seller has retained any risks and rewards following the sale. If the seller has not retained substantially any of the risks and rewards, derecognition would be appropriate. However, if the seller agrees to reimburse the buyer for all likely bad debts and late payments that will occur, the seller has retained substantially all risks and rewards, thus, derecognition would not be appropriate. Take the following example:

Example 10.10:   The sale of trade receivables with no retention of risks

Consider the same fact pattern discussed in Example 10.9, except that the company has no obligation to the bank for slow payment or non-payment by the debtors. In this case, the company has transferred to the bank substantially all of the risks and rewards of ownership of the receivables.

Accordingly, the company removes the receivables from its statement of financial position (i.e. derecognises them), and it shows no liability in respect of the proceeds received from the bank. The company recognises a loss calculated as the difference between the carrying amount of the receivables at the time of sale and the proceeds received from the bank. The company recognises a liability to the extent that it has collected funds from the debtors but has not yet remitted them to the bank. *[FRS 102.11.35]*.

Determination of whether the seller has transferred or retained substantially all the risks and rewards will be more difficult in situations where the seller retains, for example, the risk associated to the first £10m of future credit losses. The answer will depend on an assessment of the quality of the receivables that were sold. If it is likely that the first £10m of future losses represent a substantial portion of the total losses that are expected to occur, derecognition would not be appropriate as the seller has retained substantially all the risks and rewards. On the other hand, if the first £10m represents an immaterial portion of the total expected future losses, derecognition may be appropriate, as it is clear that the seller has transferred substantially all the risks and rewards.

9.2.2   *Transfer of control of the financial asset*

In between the two extremes of transferring or retaining substantially all the risks and rewards, the transferor may have retained some risks and rewards. The derecognition assessment is then dependent on whether the transferor has retained control of the asset or not. This will depend on whether the transferee has the practical ability to sell the asset in its entirety to an unrelated third party and whether the transferee is able to exercise that ability unilaterally and without needing to impose additional restrictions on the transfer. *[FRS 102.11.33(c)]*.

This is where the second challenge arises, as no further guidance is given in FRS 102 on what is meant by 'practical ability'. IFRS 9 and IAS 39 contain the following guidance:

'An entity has not retained control of a transferred asset if the transferee has the practical ability to sell the transferred asset. An entity has retained control of a transferred asset if the transferee does not have the practical ability to sell the transferred asset. A transferee has the practical ability to sell the transferred asset if it is traded in an active market because the transferee could repurchase the transferred asset in the market if it needs to return the asset to the entity. For example, a transferee may have the practical ability to sell a transferred asset if the transferred asset is subject to an option that allows the entity to repurchase it, but the transferee can readily obtain the transferred asset in the market if the option is exercised. A transferee does not have the practical ability to sell the transferred asset if the entity retains such an option and the transferee cannot readily obtain the transferred asset in the market if the entity exercises its option'. *[IFRS 9 Appendix B.3.2.7, IAS 39.AG42]*.

In our view, most FRS 102 reporters will use this guidance when assessing the practical ability test. Consider the following example, which helps illustrate these requirements:

Example 10.11:   *The sale of quoted bonds subject to a call option to buy them back*

Company Y holds 8,000 corporate bonds issued by a listed company, Company X. Similar to Company X's equity shares, the corporate bonds are listed on an exchange and are subject to regular trading in the market. The market price of the bonds at 31 December 2019 is at par £100, thus, the investment's fair value is £800,000. The bonds meet the criteria to be classified as basic financial instruments and are thus measured at amortised cost. However, there is currently no material difference between the amortised cost and the fair value of the bonds. On the same day, Company Y sells the bonds to a hedge fund for £750,000 but simultaneously obtains a call option to buy back the bonds on 31 December 2020 for £850,000. The sale agreement does not prevent the hedge fund from selling, exchanging or pledging the bonds to another party.

In these circumstances, due to the existence of the option, it is assessed that Company Y has retained some, but not substantially all risk and rewards of ownership of the bonds. This is because it will be able to benefit from fair value movements above the call option exercise price of £850,000 by exercising the option, however, it is not exposed to fair value movements below the call option exercise price.

In addition, because the bonds are listed and traded on an active market, (see 3.1 above for the definition of an active market), it is considered that the hedge fund has the practical ability to sell the bonds. Even if the hedge fund sells the bonds and Company Y decides to exercise its call option, the hedge fund can repurchase the bonds in the market in order to sell them back to Company Y. Therefore, Company Y has transferred control of the bonds to the hedge fund. Consequently, Company Y derecognises the bonds and recognises an option asset, which is a new right that has arisen following the transfer. At 31 December 2019, the call option is 'out of the money' because the exercise price of £850,000 is greater than the fair value of £800,000. The premium paid on the option is £50,000, being the difference between the fair value of the bonds of £800,000 and the sale consideration of £750,000. The following accounting entries would be made by Company Y:

Dr. Cash received from sale	£750,000	
Dr. Fair value of call option	£ 50,000	
Cr. Bond holding in Company X		£800,000

The call option is a derivative, which falls within the scope of Section 12 and thus would need to be measured at fair value through profit or loss until it expires (see 8.1 above). In this example, the practical ability test has been satisfied as the bonds are listed on an exchange and they are regularly traded; however, being exchange-listed is not necessarily itself a requirement, it is sufficient for there to be an active market.

In the example above, if the corporate bonds were not traded in an active market, with all other things being equal, the transaction would have failed the practical ability test and the corporate bonds would not have been derecognised. See further discussion on the accounting in this situation at 9.2.3.B and 9.2.4.B below.

9.2.3   Accounting for derecognition of financial assets

9.2.3.A   Transfers that qualify for derecognition

When it is concluded that the transfer qualifies for derecognition, the asset should be derecognised and any rights and obligations retained or created should be recognised separately. The carrying amount of the transferred asset must be allocated between the rights or obligations retained and those transferred on the basis of their relative fair values at the *transfer date*. Newly created rights and obligations must be measured at their fair values at that date. Any difference between the consideration received and the amounts recognised and derecognised is recognised in profit or loss. *[FRS 102.11.33]*.

These accounting requirements are explained by Example 10.10 at 9.2.1.B above.

9.2.3.B   Transfers that do not qualify for derecognition

If a transfer does not result in derecognition because the entity has retained substantially all risks and rewards of ownership of the transferred asset, the entity should continue to recognise the transferred asset in its entirety and should recognise a financial liability for the consideration received. The asset and liability should not be offset. In subsequent periods, the entity should recognise any income on the transferred asset and any expense incurred on the financial liability. *[FRS 102.11.34]*. This describes the gross presentation of assets and liabilities in the statement of financial position and their related income and expenses in the income statement to represent the substance of a collateralised borrowing transaction.

FRS 102 only refers to transactions where the entity has retained substantially all risks and rewards. For transactions where the transferor has retained some, but not substantially all the risks and rewards, but has retained control of the financial assets (see 9.2.2 above), we would also expect a financial liability to be recognised. These are transactions where there is a continuing involvement with the assets. We further discuss these transactions at 9.2.4.B below.

9.2.4   Comparison with IFRS

9.2.4.A   What is a transfer?

As discussed at **9.2.1** above, Section 11 provides no guidance on what is meant by a 'transfer of risks and rewards'. In fact, unlike IFRS, FRS 102 does not even define the meaning of 'transfer'. Under IFRS, an entity transfers all or a part of a financial asset (the transferred financial asset) if, and only if, it either: *[IFRS 9.3.2.4]*

(a)   transfers the contractual rights to receive the cash flows of that financial asset; or

(b)   retains the contractual rights to receive the cash flows of that financial asset, but assumes a contractual obligation to pay the cash flows to one or more recipients in an arrangement (pass through arrangements).

IFRS 9 and IAS 39 address in some detail many complex arrangements that do not qualify for derecognition because they do not meet their transfer criteria. In particular, IFRS 9 and IAS 39 have additional guidance on the treatment of pass-through arrangements. *[IAS 39.19, IFRS 9.3.2.5]*. For instance, under this guidance a securitisation of short-term receivables, in which amounts collected are invested in further receivables would not pass the transfer criteria under IFRS. In contrast, under Section 11, the reinvestment on its own would not automatically be a reason to prevent derecognition. However, judgement would need to be applied to assess the extent of risks and rewards that have been transferred (see **9.2.1** above). Further guidance on the treatment under IFRS is provided on this topic in EY International GAAP 2019.

9.2.4.B   Continuing involvement

Situations in which the transferor has retained some, but not substantially all, risks and rewards of ownership as described at **9.2** above, give rise to another difference from the IFRS derecognition requirements. This is the measurement of the transferor's ongoing involvement with the transferred asset. For example, if the bonds in Example 10.11 were not traded in an active market, the hedge fund would not have the practical ability to sell them because it must be able to reacquire them if Company Y exercises the call option. In these circumstances, as Company Y has not transferred control and has retained some risks and rewards, according to FRS 102, derecognition would not be appropriate. *[FRS 102.11.33(c)]*.

Under IFRS the bonds would only be recognised to the extent of the transferor's 'continuing involvement', that is, the extent to which Company Y is exposed to changes in the value of the transferred asset. *[IFRS 9.3.2.16, IAS 39.30]*. IFRS provides more detailed guidance on the application of continuing involvement accounting to transferred assets measured at fair value when such transferred assets are subject to a transferor's call option or to a transferee's put option. This guidance ensures that the net carrying amount of the asset and the associated liability is the fair value of the call or put option. Further guidance on the treatment on this topic under IFRS is provided in EY International GAAP 2019.

FRS 102 is silent on the accounting for these types of transactions, particularly on what happens at the point that an option is either exercised or expires. Considering the example of the call option in the first paragraph, there will be a difference between the consideration received of £750,000 (see Example 10.11 above) and the settlement of the financial liability at a later date, which either will be either:

(a) £850,000 – the amount paid when the call option is exercised; or

(b) £800,000 – the carrying value of the financial asset derecognised if the call option expires without being exercised.

Entities will be required to apply judgement in order to determine how to best account for fact patterns as the one discussed above. However, we expect most entities applying Sections 11 and 12 for recognition and measurement will not enter these types of transactions.

9.3   Accounting for collateral

FRS 102 also deals with the accounting consequences of transactions where a transferor provides non-cash collateral to the transferee. The accounting for non-cash collateral by the transferor and the transferee depends on:

(a) whether the transferee has the right to sell or repledge the collateral; and

(b) whether the transferor has defaulted.

If the transferee has the right by contract to sell or re-pledge the collateral, the transferor should reclassify that asset in its statement of financial position separately from other assets. For example, it could be disclosed as a loaned asset or pledged asset.

If the transferee sells collateral pledged to it, it should recognise the proceeds from the sale and a liability measured at fair value for its obligation to return the collateral.

If the transferor defaults under the terms of the contract and is no longer entitled to redeem the collateral, it should derecognise the collateral, and the transferee should recognise the collateral as its asset, initially measured at fair value or, if it has already sold the collateral, derecognise its obligation to return the collateral.

In all circumstances, the transferor must continue to recognise the collateral as its asset, unless the transferor has defaulted and is no longer entitled to redeem the collateral. *[FRS 102.11.35]*.

9.4   Derecognition of financial liabilities

9.4.1   General rule: extinguishment

The derecognition requirements for financial liabilities are identical to those in IFRS 9 and IAS 39; i.e. an entity should derecognise a financial liability or part of a financial liability only when it is extinguished. In essence, a financial liability or a part of it is only extinguished when the obligations specified in the contract are discharged, are cancelled or expire. *[FRS 102.11.36]*.

9.4.2   Exchange and modification

If an existing borrower and lender exchange financial instruments with substantially different terms or substantially modify the terms of an existing financial liability, the transaction should be accounted for as an extinguishment of the original financial liability and the recognition of a new one. *[FRS 102.11.37]*.

FRS 102 does not contain the additional guidance in IFRS 9 and IAS 39 on what constitutes 'substantially different'. While that guidance may be used by an entity reporting under FRS 102, it is, itself, not without issues of interpretation and we do not believe that it must be applied under FRS 102; hence we do not discuss it further here. Further details can be found in EY International GAAP 2019.

The subsequent accounting for exchanges or modifications that fail derecognition is discussed at 9.5 below.

9.4.3   Gains and losses on derecognition

Any difference that may arise between the carrying amount of the financial liability that has been extinguished or transferred to another party and the consideration paid, including any non-cash assets transferred or liabilities assumed, is recognised in profit or loss. *[FRS 102.11.38]*.

9.5   Exchange or modification that does not qualify for derecognition

FRS 102 does not provide specific guidance on the subsequent accounting where it is determined that an exchange of financial instruments with different terms is not a substantial modification of the terms of the existing financial asset or liability. We believe that entities have an accounting policy choice to either:

(a)   account for the changes in cash flows prospectively through a revised effective interest rate; or

(b)   adjust the carrying amount of the financial liability to reflect the modified cash flows, discounted at the original effective interest rate of the existing financial liability (see 8.2 above). This is consistent with practice under IAS 39 but represents a difference with IFRS 9 since, in July 2017, the IASB confirmed that when a financial liability measured at amortised cost is modified without resulting in derecognition, a gain or loss should be recognised in profit or loss.

10   HEDGE ACCOUNTING

10.1   Introduction

The hedge accounting model in FRS 102 is designed to allow entities to reflect their hedging activities in the financial statements in a manner that is consistent with the entity's risk management objectives. The hedge accounting approach in FRS 102 is based on a simplified version of that in IFRS 9. Hedge accounting is optional and an entity can choose not to designate exposures it is economically hedging. In that case the normal measurement rules in Sections 11 and 12 will apply.

Of course, if the entity has chosen to apply IAS 39 or IFRS 9 to its financial instruments, then it will apply the hedge accounting requirements of those standards (see 4 above).

The two main elements of a hedging relationship are the hedging instrument and the hedged item. Provided the qualifying conditions in Section 12 are met, hedge accounting can be applied prospectively from the date all of the conditions are met and documented. This section focuses on the definitions and criteria for hedge accounting under FRS 102.

10.1.1   What is hedge accounting?

Every entity is exposed to business risks from its daily operations. Many of those risks have an impact on the cash flows or the value of assets and liabilities, and therefore, ultimately affect profit or loss. In order to manage these risk exposures, companies often enter into derivative contracts (or, less commonly, other financial instruments) to hedge them. 'Hedging' can therefore be seen as a risk management activity in order to change an entity's risk profile.

Applying FRS 102 to those risk management activities can result in accounting mismatches when the gains or losses on a hedging instrument are not recognised in the same period(s) and/or in the same place in the financial statements as gains or losses on the hedged exposure. The idea of hedge accounting is to reduce this mismatch by changing either the measurement or (in the case of certain firm commitments) recognition of the hedged exposure, or alternatively, the accounting for the hedging instrument.

Under FRS 102, all derivatives are recorded on the balance sheet at fair value with subsequent fair value changes recorded in the profit and loss account. *[FRS 102.11.6(b), 12.8].* The impact on profit or loss from derivatives may be reduced if the hedge accounting criteria are met. FRS 102 describes three types of hedging relationships:

(i)   fair value hedges (see 10.7 below);

(ii)   cash flow hedges (see 10.8 below); and

(iii)   hedges of net investments in foreign operations (see 10.9 below). *[FRS 102.12.19].*

The resultant hedge accounting entries depend on the type of hedge accounting relationship.

For example, an entity with sterling functional currency may expect highly probable future revenue of US$200 in 3 months' time. As £/US$ foreign currency exchange rates change, the revenue recognised by the entity in profit or loss will also change, as the entity's cash flows are exposed to foreign exchange risk. In order to reduce this potential profit or loss volatility, the entity may enter into a forward currency contract to pay US$200 and receive a fixed sterling equivalent. Under FRS 102, the forward currency contract will be recorded at fair value through profit or loss, and the forecast revenue will not be recognised until it occurs, resulting in a measurement and timing mismatch in profit or loss. If FRS 102 hedge accounting is applied, the forward currency contract would be accounted for differently, in order to reduce the mismatch. This is an example of a cash flow hedge, as the hedging instrument is reducing variability in the cash flows of the hedged item. The associated hedge accounting is to remove the effective portion of the change in fair value of the hedging derivative from profit or loss, and recognise it initially in other comprehensive income (OCI), thereby reducing volatility in profit or loss. The amounts recorded in OCI are then recycled to be reflected in profit or loss at the same time as the forecast revenue is recognised, so that the revenue is recorded as the hedged rate (see 10.8.3 below).

Figure 10.2: Cash flow hedge accounting model

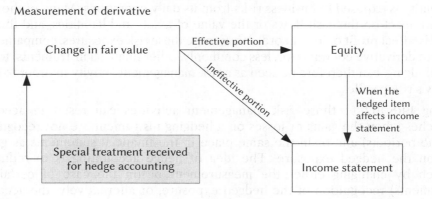

The special treatment for hedge accounting of a net investment in a foreign operation is consistent with that described above for a cash flow hedge (see 10.9 below).

An entity may also transact a derivative that converts a fixed exposure into a variable one. This is described as a fair value hedge. An example of a fair value hedge would be an entity that has issued fixed rate debt and enters into an interest rate swap in which it receives a fixed rate and pays a variable rate of interest on an underlying notional value. The entity might view this as converting the fixed interest flow into a variable interest flow, but this activity is described in the standard as eliminating variability in fair value with respect to interest rate risk. On application of FRS 102 (without hedge accounting) the interest rate swap would be accounted for at fair value through profit or loss whilst the debt would be held at amortised cost, resulting in an accounting mismatch. If FRS 102 hedge accounting is applied to this fact pattern, an adjustment would be made to the carrying amount of the debt and to profit or loss, to reflect the revaluation of the debt with respect to interest rate risk. This hedge accounting adjustment would mitigate some of the volatility in profit or loss from fair value changes in the derivative (see 10.7.3 below).

Figure 10.3: Fair value hedge accounting model

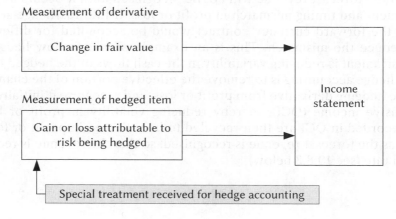

10.1.2 Hedge accounting overview

An entity may choose to designate a hedging relationship between a hedging instrument and a hedged item in order to achieve hedge accounting. *[FRS 102.12.18].* Prior to hedge accounting being applied, all of the following steps must have been completed:

- identification of eligible hedged item(s) and hedging instrument(s) (see 10.2 and 10.3 below);
- ensuring that the hedge relationship meets the definition of one of the permitted types (a fair value, cash flow or net investment hedge) (see 10.7, 10.8 and 10.9 below);
- ensuring that the hedge relationship is consistent with the entity's risk management objective for undertaking the hedges (see 10.4.2 below);
- assessing that there is an economic relationship between the hedged item(s) and hedging instrument(s) (see 10.4.3 below);
- formal designation of the hedge relationship, including identification of the hedged risk (see 10.4.4 below); and
- the sources of hedge ineffectiveness are determined and documented (see 10.5 below).

Once these requirements are met, hedge accounting can be applied prospectively, but the ongoing qualifying criteria and assessments must continue to be met, otherwise hedge accounting will cease (see 10.10 below).

The table below summarises the application of hedge accounting for the three types of hedge relationships:

Figure 10.4: Accounting for hedge relationships

Hedge type	Fair value	Cash flow	Net investment
Hedged item	Carrying amount adjusted for changes in fair value with respect to the hedged risk. Adjusted through profit or loss.	N/A	N/A
Hedging instrument	N/A	No change to carrying amount, but effective portion of change in fair value is recorded in OCI.	No change to carrying amount, but effective portion of change in fair value is recorded in OCI.
Resultant profit or loss	Ineffective portion	Ineffective portion	Ineffective portion

As it can be seen from the above, for a fair value hedge, an adjustment is made to the carrying value of the hedged item to reflect the change in value of the hedged risk, with an offset to profit or loss for the change in value of the hedging instrument. Where the offset is not complete, this will result in ineffectiveness to be recorded in profit or loss (see 10.5 below).

However, for both a cash flow and net investment hedge, the carrying amount of the hedged item, which for a cash flow hedge may not even yet be recognised, is unchanged. The effect of cash flow and net investment hedge accounting is to defer the effective portion of the change in value of the hedging instrument in OCI. Any ineffective portion will remain in profit or loss as ineffectiveness.

10.2   Hedged items

10.2.1   Introduction

A hedged item can be a recognised asset or liability, an unrecognised firm commitment, a highly probable forecast transaction, a net investment in a foreign operation, or a component of any such item, provided the item is reliably measurable. *[FRS 102.12.16]*.

Recognised assets and liabilities can include financial items and non-financial items such as inventory.

Only assets, liabilities, firm commitments and forecast transactions with a party external to the reporting entity can qualify as hedged items. This means that hedge accounting can only be applied to transactions between entities in the same group in the individual financial statements of those entities, and not in the consolidated financial statements. Three exceptions to this rule are given: *[FRS 102.12.16A]*

(i)   transactions with subsidiaries, where the subsidiaries are not consolidated in the consolidated financial statements;

(ii)   a hedge of the foreign currency risk of an intragroup monetary item if that foreign currency risk affects consolidated profit or loss; and

(iii) foreign currency risk of a highly probable forecast intragroup transaction denominated in a currency other than the functional currency of the entity entering into the transactions, if the foreign currency risk affects consolidated profit or loss.

By way of example, foreign currency risk from intra group monetary items will usually affect consolidated profit or loss when the intra group monetary item is transacted between two group entities that have different functional currencies, as it will not be eliminated on consolidation.

10.2.2   Components

FRS 102 permits components of an item to be hedged (including combinations of components). For example, an item may be hedged with respect to the risks associated with only a portion of its cash flow variability or fair value change, as long as the risk component is separately identifiable and reliably measurable. *[FRS 102.12.16C]*. For example, if an entity issued debt paying a coupon of LIBOR + 2%, it would be possible to only include the LIBOR component of the total interest rate exposure within the hedge accounting relationship. Similarly, for fixed rate debt, it would also be possible to identify, say, a 5% coupon component of debt paying a 6% fixed rate coupon.

If a risk component is contractually specified, as in the above LIBOR debt issued example, it would usually be considered separately identifiable. In this circumstance, the contractually specified risk component would usually be referenced to observable data, such as a published price index. Therefore, the risk component would usually also be considered reliably measurable.

Ordinary purchase or sales agreements sometimes contain clauses that determine the contract price via a specified formula linked into a benchmark commodity price. Accordingly these contracts may also contain components that are separately identifiable and reliably measurable. Examples of contractually specified risk components in purchase and sale contracts are as follows:

(a) the price of wires contractually linked in part to a copper benchmark price and in part to a variable tolling charge reflecting energy costs; and

(b) the price of coffee contractually linked in part to a benchmark price of Arabica coffee and in part to transportation charges that include a diesel price indexation.

While it is certainly easier to determine that a risk component is separately identifiable and reliably measurable if it is specified in the contract, it is not a requirement that a component must be contractually specified in order for it to be eligible as a hedged item. We believe that in order to determine that the risk component is separately identifiable and reliably measurable and qualify for hedging, it must have a distinguishable effect on changes in the value or the cash flows that an entity is exposed to.

The fact that a commodity is a major physical input in a production process does not automatically translate into a separately identifiable effect on the price of the item as a whole, but it might. For example, although crude oil price changes might influence the long term price of plastic toys to some degree, they are unlikely to have a distinguishable effect on the retail price in the short term. Similarly, the price for pasta at food retailers in the medium to long term also responds to changes in the price for wheat, but there is no distinguishable direct effect of wheat price changes on the retail price for pasta, which remains unchanged for longer periods even though the wheat price changes. If retail prices are periodically adjusted in a way that also directionally reflects the effect of wheat price changes, that is not sufficient to constitute a separately identifiable risk component. The evaluation would always have to be based on relevant facts and circumstances.

An example of a risk component that has a distinguishable effect on changes in the cash flows an entity is exposed to is provided in the application guidance to IFRS 9.

Example 10.11: Hedge of a non-contractually specified risk component

An entity purchases a particular quality of coffee of a particular origin from its supplier under a contract that sets out a variable price linked to the benchmark price for coffee. The price is represented by the coffee futures price plus a fixed spread, reflecting the different quality of the coffee purchased compared to the benchmark plus a variable logistics services charge reflecting that the delivery is at a specific manufacturing site of the entity. The fixed spread is set for the current harvest period. For the deliveries that fall into the next harvest period this type of supply contract is not available.

The entity analyses the market structure for its coffee supplies, taking into account how the eventual deliveries of coffee that it receives are priced. The entity can enter into similar supply contracts for each harvest period once the crop relevant for its particular purchases is known and the spread can be set. In that sense, the knowledge about the pricing under the supply contracts also informs the entity's analysis of the market structure more widely, including forecast purchases which are not yet contractually specified. This allows the entity to conclude that its exposure to variability of cash flows resulting from changes in the benchmark coffee price is a risk component that is separately identifiable and reliably measurable for coffee purchases under the variable price supply contract for the current harvest period as well as for forecast purchases that fall into the next harvest period. *[IFRS 9 Appendix B.6.3.10(b)].*

Other components that can be hedged include selected contractual cash flows and a specified part of the nominal amount of an item and combinations of these items. *[FRS 102.12.16].* FRS 102 does not provide detail on what is meant by a 'specified part of the nominal amount of an item'. The hedge accounting rules in FRS 102 are based on IFRS 9 which states that such a component of a nominal amount could be a proportion of an entire item (such as, 60% of a fixed rate loan of £10 million) or a layer component (for example, the first £6 million of sales). *[IFRS 9 Appendix B.6.3.16].*

IFRS 9 contains some restrictions when hedging a layer component that includes a prepayment option. In particular, a layer component that includes a prepayment option does not qualify as a hedged item in a fair value hedge if the fair value of the prepayment option is affected by changes in the hedged risk (unless the changes in fair value of the prepayment option as a result of changes in the hedged risk are included when measuring the change in fair value of the hedged item). However, this restriction is not included in FRS 102 and there is no requirement to analogise to the requirements of IFRS 9 or to assume that IFRS 9 applies where FRS 102 is silent. Hence, an entity applying FRS 102 does not encounter this issue and can designate a layer component in a fair value hedge, although the effect of the related prepayment option on the layer's fair value with respect to the hedged risk will still need to be included.

In FRS 102, risk components may also include a designation of changes in the cash flows or the fair value of a hedged item above or below a specified price or other variable (i.e. a one-sided risk). *[FRS 102.12.16C]*. For example, an entity could hedge the cash flow losses resulting from an increase in the price of a forecast commodity purchase above a specified level. This would be useful when economically hedging with options, which only provide protection above or below a specified price level.

An issue that entities have faced under IAS 39 and IFRS 9 is the prohibition on hedge accounting for changes in LIBOR when the hedged item attracts a 'sub-LIBOR' interest rate, e.g. LIBOR–0.25%. Application of hedge accounting to the LIBOR component is not permitted under IFRS because the hedged component cannot be more than the total cash flows of the hedged item. Part of the rationale for this prohibition is that if LIBOR fell to 0.25% in this example, any changes in LIBOR below 0.25% would not ordinarily cause any further variability in cash flows on the hedged item, as there is usually an inherent floor. Whilst this restriction is not explicit in FRS 102, the logic would appear to be equally valid. However, an entity could still achieve hedge accounting by designating the cash flows of the hedged item in their entirety (e.g. LIBOR–0.25%) with, for example, a LIBOR swap as the hedging instrument, although some ineffectiveness may arise and need to be recorded in profit or loss.

10.2.3   Groups of items as hedged items

Hedging relationships typically include a single hedging instrument (e.g. an interest rate swap) hedging a single item (e.g. a loan). However, for operational reasons entities often economically hedge several items together on a group basis (e.g. a number of purchases in a foreign currency could be hedged with a single forward contract).

FRS 102 explains that a hedged item can either be a single item or a group of items, including components of items, provided that all of the following conditions for groups of items are met:

(i)   the group consists of items that are individually eligible hedged items;

(ii)   the items in the group share the same risk;

(iii) the items in the group are managed together on a group basis for risk management purposes; and

(iv)   the group does not include items with offsetting risk positions. *[FRS 102.12.16B]*.

Whether the items in the group are managed together on a group basis is a matter of fact, i.e. it depends on an entity's behaviour and cannot be achieved by mere documentation. Examples of groups of items that could be eligible for hedging if all of the conditions are met are a portfolio of customer loans that pay interest based on LIBOR, or a portfolio of shares of Swiss companies that replicates the Swiss Market Index (SMI).

Hedge accounting for a net position (e.g. a group of assets and liabilities or income and expenses) is not permitted, as this would include offsetting risk positions. However, where an entity undertakes economic hedge accounting of a net position, the entity could still achieve hedge accounting under FRS 102 by designating a specified component of the gross hedged items. For example, consider an entity with sterling functional currency that has forecast foreign currency sales of €100 and purchases of €80, both in 6 months. It hedges the net exposure using a single forward contract to sell €20 in 6 months. Hedge accounting could be achieved by designating the forward contract as hedging €20 of the €100 forecast sales.

10.3 Hedging instruments

10.3.1 Introduction

FRS 102 defines a hedging instrument as a financial instrument measured at fair value through profit or loss that is a contract with a party external to the reporting entity and is not a written option unless:

(i) the written option is an offset to a purchased option in the hedged item and the combination is not a net written option; or

(ii) the written option is combined with a purchased option and the combination is not a net written option. *[FRS 102.12.17, 17C]*.

Entities are therefore permitted to designate derivatives as hedging instruments, but also non-derivative financial assets or non-derivative financial liabilities that are accounted for at fair value through profit or loss are eligible hedging instruments. This can be helpful if an entity does not have access to derivatives markets or does not want to be subject to margining requirements and could also be operationally simpler than transacting derivatives.

If a derivative is not measured at fair value (for example, if the fair value cannot be reliably measured), then the derivative cannot be designated as a hedging instrument. *[FRS 102.11.32]*. With the exception of certain written options, the circumstances in which a derivative recorded at fair value through profit or loss may be designated as a hedging instrument are not restricted, provided the relevant conditions for hedge accounting are met. The reason written options cannot be designated as hedging instruments is because net options written by an entity do not reduce risk exposure or the potential effect on profit or loss. In practice many so-called 'zero cost collars' (i.e. a combination of a put and call option, one of which is purchased and the other sold, priced so that the premiums offset to zero) are transacted as legally separate written and purchased options. However, the standard includes an example of a zero cost interest rate collar to illustrate circumstances under which a written option is combined with a purchased option such that the combination is not a net written option, and hence is eligible as a hedging instrument (as per exception (ii) above). *[FRS 102.12.17C]*.

FRS 102 also permits the foreign currency risk component of a non-derivative financial instrument (for example, a basic foreign currency loan carried at amortised cost) to be designated as a hedging instrument in the hedge of foreign currency risk. *[FRS 102.12.17B]*. This is illustrated in the following example.

Example 10.12:   Hedging using a foreign currency component of a non-derivative instrument

Company J has GBP functional currency. J issued fixed rate debt with principal of JPY 5 million due on maturity in two years. J had also entered into a fixed price sales commitment, accounted for as an executory contract, for JPY 5 million that will be paid in two years.

J could designate the foreign currency component of the fixed rate debt as a hedging instrument for the foreign currency exposure associated with the future receipt of JPY 5m on the fixed price sales commitment.

Similarly as for hedged items, a hedging instrument must be a contract with a party external to the reporting entity and there are no exceptions to this. *[FRS 102.12.17(b)]*.

10.3.2   Combinations of hedging instruments

A combination of instruments that individually meet the criteria to be treated as hedging instruments to be designated in a hedge relationship are permitted to be jointly designated in the hedging relationship. Hence a purchased bond measured at fair value through profit or loss and an interest rate swap could be jointly designated as 'the hedging instrument'. *[FRS 102.12.17A]*.

10.3.3   Proportions and components of instruments

FRS 102 specifies that a hedging instrument can only be designated:

- in its entirety;
- a proportion (e.g. 50% of the nominal amount of the instrument): or
- by separating the spot risk element of a foreign currency contract and excluding the forward element, or by separating the intrinsic value of an option and excluding the time value. *[FRS 102.12.17A]*.

The requirement to designate an instrument in its entirety is consistent with IFRS 9 and IAS 39. The reason given for that original guidance in IAS 39 is because there is normally a single fair value measure for a hedging instrument in its entirety and the factors that cause changes in its fair value are co-dependent. *[IAS 39.74]*.

Similar to IFRS 9 and IAS 39, this means that the entity cannot designate a 'partial-term' component of a financial instrument as the hedging instrument. For example, in the case of a five year interest rate swap hedging a four year exposure, the swap payments and receipts over the next four years (i.e. ignoring those in year five) could not be designated as the hedging instrument. Instead, the whole derivative (i.e. including payments and receipts in year five) must be designated as the hedging instrument, although the hedging relationship may itself last for only four years. Likewise, components of particular cash flows in the hedging instrument cannot be designated in hedge relationships.

It is possible to designate a proportion of the entire hedging instrument, such as 50% of the notional amount, in a hedging relationship. The proportion that is not designated is available for designation within other hedge relationships, such that a maximum of 100% of the notional is designated as a hedging instrument. Any proportions of an instrument not designated within hedge relationships are accounted under the usual FRS 102 classification and measurement guidance.

The ability to separate the spot risk in a forward foreign currency contract or the intrinsic value in an option contract, and exclude the forward element and time value respectively from the hedge relationship was introduced as part of the Triennial review 2017. The option to apply this treatment is consistent with IAS 39. *[IAS 39.74]*. The excluded elements of the hedging instrument (i.e. the forward element of a foreign exchange contract, or the time value of an option contract) are accounted under the usual FRS 102 classification and measurement guidance, which will be at fair value through profit or loss for derivatives. Hence the application of this amendment has minimal effect on the accounting for hedging instruments in a fair value hedge (see 10.7.3 below); fair value changes in the forward element of forward contracts and time value of option contracts would previously form part of hedge ineffectiveness, whereas on application of the amendment, such fair value changes are deemed to be outside the hedge relationship but will still be recognised in the profit or loss, albeit possibly in a different line. Application of the amendment could have more of an impact on accounting for cash flow and net investment hedges, as not all ineffectiveness is always recognised in profit and loss due to the 'lower of' accounting (see 10.8.3 and 10.9.2 below).

There could be some hedge relationships for which it will be easier to determine that an economic relationship exists between the hedged item and the hedging instrument if the forward element of forward contracts or time value of option contracts are excluded from the hedge relationship. For example, if based on the current market situation, the majority of fair value movements of a purchased option (designated as a hedging instrument) are expected to arise from changes in the time value, no offset will arise for changes in the time value unless the time value also exists in the hedged item (see 10.4.3 below).

Although the amendment brings FRS 102 into line with IAS 39 on this particular issue, IFRS 9 has additional guidance that has not been included in FRS 102. IFRS 9 includes guidance on the ability to exclude cross currency basis from a hedging instrument, and to achieve a 'cost of hedging' treatment for the excluded portions of a hedging derivative. Given FRS 102 is silent on these issues, even after the Triennial review 2017, we do not believe it is possible to apply the IFRS 9 guidance on excluding cross currency basis from a hedging instrument, or costs of hedging.

The exclusion of the forward element of a foreign currency contract or the time value of an option from an existing hedge relationship would be a change to the documented hedged item and risk management objective. Such a change can only be accommodated by discontinuing an existing hedge relationship and starting a new one (see 10.4.2 below). Although the Triennial review 2017 amendments are generally applied retrospectively, we believe that the need to start a new hedge relationship in order to separate the spot risk element of a foreign currency contract and exclude the forward element, or to separate the intrinsic value of an option and exclude the time value, means the amendment can only be applied prospectively, once all the criteria for hedge accounting are met for such a strategy (see 10.4.1 below).

As noted at 10.3.1 above, for a hedge of foreign currency risk, the foreign currency risk component of a non-derivative financial instrument can be designated as a hedging instrument.

10.4   Criteria for hedge accounting

10.4.1   Introduction

In order to qualify for hedge accounting a hedging relationship has to consist of eligible hedging instruments and eligible hedged items as described at 10.2 and 10.3 above. In addition:

(i)   the hedging relationship must be consistent with the entity's risk management objectives for undertaking hedges;

(ii)   there must be an economic relationship between the hedged item and hedging instrument;

(iii)   the entity must document the hedging relationship; and

(iv)   the entity must determine and document causes of hedge ineffectiveness. *[FRS 102.12.18].*

Each of these criteria is discussed below.

An entity is required to discontinue hedge accounting if the conditions for hedge accounting are no longer met. *[FRS 102.12.25(b)].* This means that there is an ongoing requirement to assess whether the criteria are met. We would expect entities to undertake the assessment, at a minimum, at each reporting date. If it is determined that the criteria are no longer met, then the standard says that hedge accounting should be discontinued prospectively. No further guidance is provided in FRS 102 as to what is meant by 'discontinued prospectively'. IAS 39 states that hedge accounting ceases from the date the hedge relationship last met the effectiveness requirements. *[IAS 39.AG113],* whereas IFRS 9 states that discontinuation applies prospectively from the date on which the qualifying criteria are no longer met. *[IFRS 9 Appendix B.6.5.22].* Given the lack of guidance, in FRS 102 and the fact that IAS 39 and IFRS 9 have different requirements, we believe an accounting policy choice can be made as to the date as of which hedge accounting is discontinued.

10.4.2   Risk management objectives

Hedge accounting must reflect the entity's risk management objectives for undertaking a hedge. The risk management objective is set at the level of an individual hedging relationship and defines how a particular hedging instrument is designated to hedge a particular hedged item. For example, a risk management objective for an entity with sterling functional currency might be to designate a foreign exchange forward contract in a hedge of the foreign exchange risk of the first €1m of sales in March 2019 or to designate a particular interest rate swap in a fair value hedge of £10m fixed rate debt. If this objective for the hedge relationship changed, then hedge accounting should cease (see 10.10 below). Accordingly, the risk management objective should be written in such a way that it can be determined if it has changed, and therefore whether discontinuation is required or not. *[FRS102.12.25(b)].*

10.4.3   Economic relationship

FRS 102 states that 'an economic relationship between a hedged item and hedging instrument exists when the entity expects that the values of the hedged item and hedging instrument will typically move in opposite directions in response to movements in the same risk, which is the hedged risk'. *[FRS102.12.18A].*

Chapter 10

This relationship should be based on an economic rationale rather than just by chance, as could be the case if the relationship is based only on a statistical correlation. However, although a statistical correlation on its own is not sufficient to determine the existence of an economic relationship, it may provide corroboration of an economic rationale.

Where statistical correlation or other quantitative methods are applied to demonstrate the existence of an economic relationship, the standard does not provide any bright lines or other success criteria, hence judgement will be required.

This requirement will quite obviously be fulfilled for many hedging relationships, for example if the underlying of the hedging instrument matches, or is closely aligned with the hedged risk in the hedged item. For example, an economic relationship clearly exists when hedging the 3 month LIBOR variable interest rate payable on a £100,000 loan with a 3 month LIBOR (pay fixed, receive floating) interest rate swap with a notional of £100,000. This is because the present value of the changes in the cash flows of the loan and the swap would move systematically in opposite directions in response to changes in the underlying interest rate. However, an economic relationship is unlikely to exist when an entity hedges a currency exposure using a different currency where the two currencies are not pegged or otherwise formally linked.

Even when there are differences between the hedged item and the hedging instrument, the economic relationship will often be capable of being demonstrated using a qualitative assessment. However, when the critical terms of the hedging instrument and hedged item are not closely aligned, it may be necessary to undertake a quantitative assessment.

IFRS 9 includes additional effectiveness criteria such as that credit risk must not dominate the hedge relationship and an appropriate hedge ratio must be used. *[IFRS 9.6.4.1(c)]*. There is no expectation that these criteria must be applied for hedge accounting under FRS 102.

10.4.4 Documentation

The FRS 102 documentation requirements are intended to be relatively informal and undemanding (compared to those of IAS 39 or IFRS 9) and should not pose a significant administrative burden on entities. However, appropriate documentation remains an important element of hedge accounting under FRS 102, and hedge accounting cannot be applied until the documentation criteria are met. *[FRS102.12.18(d)-(e)]*. The documentation supporting the hedge relationship should include the identification of:

(i)   the hedging instrument;

(ii) the hedged item;

(iii) the economic relationship between the hedging instrument and hedged item;

(iv) the nature of the risk being hedged;

(v)   how the hedge fits in with the entity's risk management objectives for undertaking hedges; and

(vi) the possible causes of hedge ineffectiveness within the hedge relationship.

Designation of a hedge relationship takes effect prospectively from the date all of the criteria for hedging are met. In particular, hedge accounting can be applied only from the date all of the necessary documentation is completed (although there are different rules for transition to FRS 102 – see Chapter 32 at 5.16). Hedge relationships cannot be designated retrospectively. *[FRS102.12.18]*.

Hedge designation need not take place at the time a hedging instrument is entered into. For example, a derivative contract may be designated and formally documented as a hedging instrument any time after entering into the derivative contract. However, hedge accounting will only apply prospectively from the date of documentation of the hedge designation, provided all the other conditions are met.

10.5   Hedge ineffectiveness

Hedge ineffectiveness is the difference between the fair value change of a hedging instrument and the fair value change of the hedged item attributable to the hedged risk. It is required to be recorded in profit or loss. Hedge ineffectiveness can arise due to several reasons and the possible causes of hedge ineffectiveness in hedge relationships must be documented by an entity at the outset. *[FRS 102.12.18(e)]*.

When considering possible causes of ineffectiveness in a hedge relationship, mismatches between the designated hedged item and the hedging instrument should be considered. For example, mismatches in the following terms are likely to be causes of ineffectiveness:

(i)   maturity;

(ii)   volume or nominal amount;

(iii)   cash flow dates;

(iv)   interest rate or other market index basis, or quality and location basis differences;

(v)   day count methods;

(vi)   credit risk, including the effect of collateral; and

(vii)   the extent that the hedging instrument is already 'in', or 'out of the money' when first designated.

For example, if the interest rates on the hedging instrument and hedged item differ (e.g. 3 month LIBOR versus 6 month LIBOR), ineffectiveness will arise. Similarly, if an entity hedges a forecast commodity purchase using a forward contract, unless the forward contract is for the purchase of the same quantity of the same commodity at the same time and location as the hedged forecast purchase, there will be some ineffectiveness. Furthermore, changes in the counterparty's credit risk and the value of collateral held, will be reflected in the fair value of the hedging instrument but not necessarily in the hedged item, resulting in ineffectiveness.

Unlike under IFRS 9 and IAS 39, there is no explicit requirement to include changes in the entity's own credit risk in the valuation of derivatives (see 8.6.4.A above), therefore, it is possible that these will not form part of hedge ineffectiveness. This is supported by the Illustrative Examples that frequently say that, for simplicity, they have ignored counterparty credit risk but do not mention own credit risk.

As mentioned at 10.4.4 above, it is possible to designate a hedging instrument in a hedging relationship subsequent to its inception. For non-option derivatives, such as forwards or interest rate swaps, any fair value at inception of the hedge is likely to create 'noise' that may not be fully offset by changes in the hedged item, especially in the case of a cash flow hedge. This is because the derivative contains a 'financing' element (the initial fair value), gains and losses on the remeasurement of which will not be replicated in the hedged item and therefore the hedge contains an inherent source of ineffectiveness.

Another cause of ineffectiveness could be derivative valuation inputs that are not replicated when revaluing the hedged item (in addition to credit risk mentioned above). The hedged item is fair valued for the hedged risk only, whilst the hedging instrument is fair valued in its entirety. This means that ineffectiveness will arise as the hedging instrument will be fair valued for more than just the hedged risk. For example, the hedged item might be fair valued for interest rate risk only, whilst the hedging instrument's fair value may additionally change due to factors such as liquidity.

Ineffectiveness can also arise between interest rate reset dates when using hedging instruments such as interest rate swaps in fair value hedges. This is often referred to as the 'most recently fixed-floating leg' issue. The payments on the floating leg of an interest rate swap are typically 'fixed' at the beginning of a reset period and paid at the end of that period. Between these two dates the swap is no longer a pure pay-fixed receive-variable (or *vice versa*) instrument because not only is the next payment fixed, but the next receipt is also fixed. So although fair value changes in the fixed rate hedged item should provide some offset to fair value changes in the pay fixed leg of the swap, there is no offset from the hedged item for the fair value of the most recently fixed floating leg.

10.6 Hedging relationships

There are three types of hedging relationships in FRS 102, defined as follows: *[FRS 102.12.19]*

A *fair value hedge*: a hedge of the exposure to changes in the fair value of a recognised asset or liability or an unrecognised firm commitment, or a component of any such item that are attributable to a particular risk and could affect profit or loss.

A *cash flow hedge*: a hedge of the exposure to variability in cash flows that is attributable to a particular risk associated with all, or a component of, a recognised asset or liability (such as all or some future interest payments on variable rate debt) or a highly probable forecast transaction, and could affect profit or loss.

A *net investment hedge*: a hedge of a net investment in a foreign operation.

These relationships are considered further in the remainder of this section.

10.7 Fair value hedges

10.7.1 Introduction

Typically a fair value hedge is undertaken where an entity wishes to convert a fixed rate exposure into a variable one. The fair value of an exposure that contractually pays a fixed or 'locked in' market index, such as an interest rate or a commodity price, is sensitive to changes in that market index. By converting the fixed index into a variable one, that fair value sensitivity is reduced. In many circumstances an entity may actually be more focused on creating variable rate cash flows, rather than eliminating fair value sensitivity. However the two economic perspectives are not dissimilar and both would fall within the FRS 102 description of a fair value hedge for accounting purposes.

An example of a fair value hedge is a hedge of the exposure to changes in the fair value of a fixed rate debt instrument (not measured at fair value through profit or loss) as a result of changes in interest rates – if interest rates increase, the fair value of the debt decreases and *vice versa*. If the debt instrument were to be sold before maturity, the fair value changes would affect profit or loss. Such a hedge could be entered into either by the issuer or by the holder.

Another example of a fair value hedge is where an entity wishes to eliminate the ongoing price risk from inventory. If an entity holds 100 tonnes of commodity A as inventory, for which they paid a price of 1 per tonne, the entity may wish to protect the value of that inventory against future changes in the market price that would affect profit or loss when the inventory is sold. In this case the entity would transact a derivative to sell that inventory forward at a locked in price.

10.7.2   Hedges of firm commitments

A hedge of a fixed price firm commitment (for instance, a hedge of the change in fuel price relating to an unrecognised contractual commitment by an electricity utility to purchase fuel at a fixed price) is considered a hedge of an exposure to a change in fair value. Accordingly, such a hedge is a fair value hedge.

However, a hedge of the foreign currency risk of a firm commitment may be accounted for as a fair value hedge or as a cash flow hedge. *[FRS 102.12.19A]*. This is because foreign currency risk affects both fair values and cash flows. This would mean that a foreign currency cash flow hedge of a forecast transaction need not be re-designated as a fair value hedge when the forecast transaction becomes a firm commitment.

10.7.3   Accounting for fair value hedges

From the date the conditions for hedge accounting are met, a fair value hedge should be accounted for as follows:

(i)   the gain or loss on the hedging instrument shall be recognised in profit or loss; and

(ii)   the hedging gain or loss on the hedged item shall adjust the carrying amount of the hedged item (if applicable). *[FRS 102.12.20]*.

The gain or loss on the hedging instrument will be the change in its fair value (subject to any excluded elements, see 10.3.3 above). Accordingly, the application of FRS 102 hedge accounting does not change the usual measurement requirements for the hedging instrument. The hedging gain or loss on the hedged item is the change in its value attributable to the hedged risk, and this must be added to, or subtracted from, the carrying value of the hedged item. This has the effect that the carrying amount of the hedged item is a hybrid value. For example, in the case of hedged debt, the carrying amount is a combination of amortised cost plus the change in the valuation due to changes in interest rates since hedge designation.

To the extent these amounts differ, a net amount will be recognised in profit or loss, commonly referred to as hedge 'ineffectiveness' (see 10.5 above). For fair value hedges all ineffectiveness is recognised in profit or loss.

The following example illustrates the basic mechanics of fair value hedge accounting.

Example 10.13: Fair value hedge mechanics

On 1 January 2019 an investor purchases a fixed rate debt security for £100 and classified it as a basic financial instrument recorded at amortised cost (see 6.1.2 above). To protect the value of the investment, the investor entered into a hedge by transacting a derivative (e.g. an interest rate swap) with a nil fair value. The interest rate swap pays fixed rate and receives variable rate interest. During 2019 interest rates fall such that by the end of the year, the change in value of the fixed rate debt attributable to the hedged risk (interest rate) since designation is £10. Other factors that might influence the full fair value of the debt are not included within the hedging gain or loss, as the hedged risk is solely interest rate risk. Meanwhile, the derivative fair value has fallen by £9, resulting in a liability of that amount.

The investor would record the following accounting entries:

	£	£
1 January 2019		
Dr Debt security	100	
Cr Cash		100
To reflect the acquisition of the security.		
Dr Derivative	nil	
Cr Cash		nil
To record the acquisition of the derivative at its fair value of nil.		
31 December 2019		
Dr Profit or loss	9	
Cr Derivative		9
To recognise the decrease in the derivative's fair value.		
Dr Debt security	10	
Cr Profit or loss		10
To recognise the change (increase) in value of the fixed rate debt attributable to the hedged risk		

In this example, it can be seen that ineffectiveness of £1 has been recognised as a credit to profit or loss, reflecting some mismatches between the hedged debt security and the hedging derivative.

Where the hedged item is a financial instrument for which the effective interest method of accounting is used, the adjustment to the hedged item referred to above, should be amortised to profit or loss. Amortisation may begin as soon as the adjustment exists and should begin no later than when the hedged item ceases to be adjusted for hedging gains and losses. The amortisation should be based on a recalculated effective interest rate at the date amortisation begins. *[FRS 102.12.22]*. For the fair value hedge of an exposure that is issued at par and redeems at par, any fair value adjustments to the hedged exposure during its life will automatically reverse through the natural unwind or pull to par of the revaluation adjustment, and hence amortisation is not necessary.

When the hedged item is an unrecognised firm commitment (see 10.7.2 above), the cumulative hedging gain or loss on the hedged item attributable to the hedged risk is recognised as an asset or liability with a corresponding gain or loss recognised in profit or loss. The initial carrying amount of the asset or liability that results from the entity meeting the firm commitment is adjusted to include the cumulative hedging gain or loss on the hedged item that was recognised in the statement of financial position. *[FRS 102.12.20-21]*.

The following example, based on Example 1 in the Appendix to Section 12, provides a more detailed illustration of the mechanics of a simple fair value hedge and in particular, a fair value hedge of a firm commitment.

Example 10.14:   Fair value hedge accounting – hedge of forward foreign currency risk of an unrecognised firm commitment

A hedge of the foreign currency risk of an unrecognised firm commitment may be accounted for as a cash flow or fair value hedge. This example illustrates fair value hedge accounting.

On 9 June 2019 an entity with US$ functional currency, enters into a purchase agreement with a third party to buy a piece of machinery in CHF, a foreign currency for CHF515,000. On the same day, the entity enters into a forward currency contract to buy CHF500,000 for US$1,000,000. Under the purchase agreement, the machinery will be delivered and paid for on 30 March 2020, the same day the forward currency contract is required to be settled.

In this example the hedged item is the total of the commitment of CHF515,000 and the hedging instrument is the forward contract to buy CHF500,000. Since the nominal amounts of the two contracts do not match, hedge ineffectiveness arises. It should be noted that in practice an entity could avoid ineffectiveness arising for this reason by identifying an amount of CHF500,000 of the total commitment as the hedged item (see 10.2.2).

For simplification, this example disregards other sources of ineffectiveness, e.g. counterparty credit risk associated with the forward currency contract. Also it is assumed that the effect of discounting is immaterial.

The entity's financial year ends on 31 December.

This example assumes that the qualifying conditions for hedge accounting are met from 9 June 2019.

The table below sets out the applicable forward exchange rates, the fair value of the forward currency contract (the hedging instrument) and the hedging gains/losses on the purchase commitment (the hedged item) on the relevant dates. This example ignores the effects of discounting.

	9 June 2019	*31 Dec 2019*	*30 March 2020*
Forward exchange rate (US$:CHF)	2:1	2.2:1	2.16:1
Forward currency contract (hedging instrument)			
Fair value	Nil	CHF500,000 × US$0.2:FC = US$100,000	CHF500,000 × SDU0.16:FC = US$80,000 [1]
Fair value change	Nil	US$100,000 – 0 = US$100,000	US$80,000 – US$100,000 = (US$20,000)
Purchase commitment (hedged item)			
Cumulative hedging (loss) [2]	nil	(CHF515,000) × US$0.2:CHF = (US$103,000)	(CHF515,000) × US$0.16:CHF = (US$82,400)
Hedging (loss)/gain	Nil	(US$103,000) – 0 = (US$103,000)	(US$82,400) – (US$103,000) = US$20,600

1   This is the fair value of the contract prior to settlement.
2   The commitment is fair valued only for the hedged risk, which in this example is the forward exchange rate risk.

9 June 2019

Note that there are no hedge accounting entries on 9 June 2019.

31 December 2019

Accounting entries:

	Dr	Cr
Forward currency contract	US$100,000	
Profit or loss		US$100,000

To recognise the fair value gain of US$100,000 on the forward currency contract in profit or loss.

Profit or loss	US$103,000	
Hedged item (commitment)		US$103,000

To record the cumulative hedging loss of US$103,000 on the commitment as a liability with a corresponding loss recognised in profit or loss.

30 March 2020

Accounting entries:

	Dr	Cr
Profit or loss	US$20,000	
Forward currency contract		US$20,000

To recognise the fair value loss of US$20,000 on the forward currency contract in profit or loss.

Hedged item (commitment)	US$20,600	
Profit or loss		US$20,600

To recognise the hedging gain on the commitment of US$20,600 in profit or loss with a corresponding adjustment to the recognised liability from US$103,000 to US$82,400.

Hedged item (commitment)	US$82,400	
Property, plant and equipment (PP&E)		US$82,400

To adjust the machinery's carrying amount to include the cumulative hedging loss on the hedged item of US$82,400.

Cash	US$80,000	
Forward currency contract		US$80,000

To reflect the settlement of the forward currency contract in cash for US$80,000 is shown above.

Property, plant and equipment (PP&E)	US$1,112,400	
Cash		US$1,112,400

To reflect the purchase of the machinery at the applicable spot rate of US$2.16:CHF1 for US$1,112,400 (settled in cash) is shown above.

10.8   Cash flow hedges

10.8.1   Introduction

Typically a cash flow hedge is undertaken where an entity wishes to convert a variable rate exposure into a fixed one. An example of a cash flow hedge is the use of an interest rate swap to change floating rate debt to fixed rate debt. The cash flows being hedged are the future interest payments.

An entity with GBP functional currency may have highly probable monthly forecast sales in a foreign currency over the next year. In order to eliminate variability from changes in foreign currency risk in the highly probable forecast revenue, the entity may transact a series of foreign currency forward contracts to lock in the GBP equivalent for that revenue. This scenario is an example of a cash flow hedge of foreign exchange risk.

10.8.2   Highly probable forecast transactions

FRS 102 permits a cash flow hedge of a forecast transaction only where it is considered highly probable. *[FRS102.12.16A]*. The glossary to FRS 102 defines 'highly probable' and 'forecast transaction' (see 3.1 above). To meet the 'highly probable' criteria, entities are not required to predict and document the exact date a forecast transaction is expected to occur but should be able to identify and document the forecast transaction within a reasonably specific and generally narrow range of time from a most probable date, as a basis for determining fair values and assessing hedge effectiveness.

The high probability of a transaction should be supported by observable facts and attendant circumstances and should not be based solely on management intent, because intentions are not verifiable. In making this assessment, entities may find it helpful to consider the following (although this is not an exhaustive list):

(i)   the frequency of similar past transactions;

(ii)   the financial and operational ability to carry out the transaction;

(iii)   whether there has already been a substantial commitments of resources to a particular activity, e.g. a manufacturing facility that can be used in the short run only to process a particular type of commodity;

(iv)   the extent of loss or disruption of operations that could result if the transaction does not occur;

(v)   the likelihood that transactions with substantially different characteristics might be used to achieve the same business purpose, e.g. there may be several ways of raising cash ranging from a short-term bank loan to a public share offering; and

(vi)   the entity's business plan.

The length of time until a forecast transaction is projected to occur is also a consideration in determining probability. Other factors being equal, the more distant a forecast transaction is, the less likely it is to be considered highly probable and the stronger the evidence that would be needed to support an assertion that it is highly probable. For example, a transaction forecast to occur in five years may be less likely to occur than a transaction forecast to occur in only one year. However, forecast interest payments for the next 20 years on variable-rate debt would typically be highly probable if supported by an existing contractual obligation.

In addition, the greater the physical quantity or future value of a forecast transaction in proportion to transactions of the same nature, the less likely it is that the transaction would be considered highly probable and the stronger the evidence that would be required to support such an assertion. For example, less evidence would generally be needed to support forecast sales of 500,000 units in the next month than 950,000 units when recent sales have averaged 950,000 units for each of the past three months.

A history of having designated hedges of forecast transactions and then determining that the forecast transactions are no longer expected to occur, would call into question both the ability to accurately predict forecast transactions and the propriety of using hedge accounting in the future for similar forecast transactions. However there are no prescriptive 'tainting' provisions in this area and entities are not automatically prohibited from using cash flow hedge accounting if a forecast transaction fails to occur. Instead, whenever such a situation arises, the particular facts, circumstances and evidence would normally need to be assessed to determine whether doubt has, in fact, been cast on an entity's ongoing hedging strategies.

If a hedged forecast transaction is no longer considered to be highly probable, the hedge must be discontinued prospectively (see 10.4.1 above and 10.10 below).

10.8.3   Accounting for cash flow hedges

From the date the conditions for hedge accounting are met, a cash flow hedge should be accounted for as follows:

(a) the separate component of equity associated with the hedged item (cash flow hedge reserve) is adjusted to the lower of the following (in absolute amounts):

   (i)   the cumulative gain or loss on the hedging instrument from the date the conditions for hedging are met; and

   (ii) the cumulative change in fair value on the hedged item (i.e. the present value of the cumulative change of expected future cash flows) from the date the conditions for hedging are met;

(b) the portion of the gain or loss on the hedging instrument that is determined to be an effective hedge (i.e. the portion that is offset by the change in the cash flow hedge reserve calculated in accordance with (a)) is recognised in OCI;

(c) any remaining gain or loss on the hedging instrument (or any gain or loss required to balance the change in the cash flow hedge reserve calculated in accordance with (a)), is hedge ineffectiveness that is recognised in profit or loss. The reference to 'balance' here refers to the difference between the effective part of a hedge recorded in OCI and the fair value change on the derivative;

(d) the amount that has been accumulated in the cash flow hedge reserve in accordance with (a) above is accounted for as follows:

   (i)   if a hedged forecast transaction subsequently results in the recognition of a non-financial asset or non-financial liability, or a hedged forecast transaction for a non-financial asset or non-financial liability becomes a firm commitment for which fair value hedge accounting is applied, the entity shall remove that amount from the cash flow hedge reserve and include it directly in the initial cost or other carrying amount of the asset or liability (commonly referred to as a 'basis adjustment');

(ii) for cash flow hedges other than those covered by (i), that amount shall be reclassified from the cash flow hedge reserve to profit or loss in the same period or periods during which the hedged expected future cash flows affect profit or loss (for example, in the periods that interest income or interest expense is recognised or when a forecast sale occurs);

(iii) if the amount accumulated in the cash flow hedge reserve is a loss, and all or part of that loss is not expected to be recovered, the amount of the loss not expected to be recovered shall be reclassified to profit or loss immediately. *[FRS102.12.23]*.

The cash flow hedge mechanics described in (a) to (c) above are often referred to as the 'lower of' calculation. This can be explained more easily by way of an example.

Example 10.15: Cash flow hedge mechanics – 'lower of' calculation

	Scenario A	Scenario B
Change in value of the hedged item (i.e. the present value of the cumulative change of expected future cash flows)	110	100
Change in the fair value of the hedging instrument	(100)	(110)
'Lower of' exposure	Hedging instrument	Hedged item
Accounting entries:		
Other comprehensive income	Dr 100	Dr 100
Profit or loss	Nil	Dr 10
Derivative	Cr 100	Cr 110
Ineffectiveness recognised	Nil	(10)

It can be seen from the above example that, for cash flow hedges, ineffectiveness is only recognised in profit or loss to the extent that the absolute change in fair value of the hedging instrument exceeds the absolute change in fair value of the hedged item. This comparison of value changes should be undertaken on a cumulative basis, i.e. the change in value over the life of the designated hedge relationship since inception.

If the hedging instrument's cumulative fair value changes are less than the cumulative fair value changes of the hedged item, no ineffectiveness is recorded in profit or loss (i.e. the full fair value change of the derivative would be recorded in OCI). If the hedging instrument's cumulative fair value changes are more than the cumulative fair value changes of the hedged item, the excess is recorded as ineffectiveness in profit or loss.

In practice entities often use what is called the 'hypothetical derivative' method to measure ineffectiveness in a cash flow hedge. As its name suggests, the hypothetical derivative method involves establishing a notional derivative that would be the ideal hedging instrument for the hedged exposure (normally an interest rate swap or forward contract with no unusual terms and a zero fair value at inception of the hedge relationship). The fair value of the hypothetical derivative is then used as a proxy for the net present value of the change in hedged future cash flows (requirement (a)(ii) above) against which changes in value of the actual hedging instrument are compared to measure ineffectiveness. The Appendix to Section 12 illustrates the use of the hypothetical derivative method to measure ineffectiveness (see Example 10.17 below).

In order to meet the requirements of (d) above, consideration must be given to the nature of the hedged item. The following are some examples of how amounts recorded in OCI are subsequently recycled.

Example 10.16: Cash flow hedge mechanics – recycling

	Hedge of purchase of fixed asset in foreign currency	Monthly forecast sale of gas	Floating rate debt
Hedged risk	Foreign currency.	Gas price.	Interest rates.
Timing of recognition of hedged item	Purchase date.	Throughout each month.	Debt is already recognised, but interest is accrued over the remaining life of the debt.
Timing of recycling of effective portion from OCI to profit or loss	Full amount recycled and included in cost of the fixed asset when purchased (a 'basis' adjustment), subsequently recognised in profit and loss through depreciation, impairment or sale of hedged fixed asset.	The relevant component of the effective portion for each month of gas sales is recycled each month.	The relevant component of the effective portion for each hedged interest accrual is to be recycled. This is often achieved by recycling, each period, the net interest accrual on the derivative from OCI into profit or loss.

The purpose of the recycling is so that the impact of the cash flow hedge is reflected in profit or loss to match the timing of recognition of the hedged item. We believe the reclassification from accumulated other comprehensive income to profit or loss should be recognised in the same line item in profit or loss as the hedged transaction to reflect the offsetting effect of hedge accounting (see 10.11 below).

The following example, based on Example 2 in the Appendix to Section 12, illustrates in more detail how to account for a cash flow hedge.

Example 10.17: Cash flow hedge accounting – hedge of variability in cash flows in a floating rate loan due to interest rate risk

This example illustrates the accounting for a cash flow hedge of interest rate risk associated with a floating rate loan. An entity, with sterling functional currency, borrows money at a floating rate and enters into an interest rate swap with the effect of paying a fixed rate overall.

On 1 January 2019, an entity borrows £10,000,000 from a bank at a floating rate of 3-month LIBOR plus 2.5%. The interest is payable annually in arrears on 31 December. The loan is repayable on 31 December 2021.

On 1 January 2019 the entity also enters into an interest rate swap with a third party, under which it receives 6-month LIBOR and pays a fixed rate of interest of 4.5%. The notional amount of the swap is £10,000,000. The swap is settled annually in arrears on 31 December and expires on 31 December 2021.

The LIBOR rates on the loan and the interest rate swap are reset and fixed annually in advance on 31 December based on the expected LIBOR rates applicable at that time. Note that in practice the loan and swap interest rates would be reset and paid more frequently than assumed for the purpose of simplification in this example, in keeping with the 3-month and 6-month LIBOR fixings.

The entity hedges the variability of the interest rate payments on the bank loan based on 3-month LIBOR. It should be noted that because the entity receives interest based on 6-month LIBOR under the interest rate swap, ineffectiveness will arise because the expected cash flows of the hedged item and the hedging instrument differ. The fair value of the interest rate swap may be affected by other factors that cause ineffectiveness, for example counterparty credit risk, but these have been disregarded in this example. This example also ignores the effect of discounting.

There are no transaction costs.

The entity's financial year ends on 31 December.

This example assumes that the qualifying conditions for hedge accounting are met from 1 January 2019.

The table below sets out the applicable LIBOR rates, interest payments and swap settlements. The fair values of the interest rate swap and the hedged item shown in the table are shown for illustrative purposes only.

Note that in practice, when forecast variable interest rate payments are the hedged item, the fair value of a hypothetical swap, that would be expected to perfectly offset the hedged cash flows, is used as a proxy of the fair value of the hedged item. The hypothetical derivative in this scenario is a fixed to floating interest rate swap with terms that match those of the loan and a fixed rate of 4.3%, which for the purpose of this example, is the interest rate where the fair value of the hypothetical swap is nil at the inception of the hedging relationship.

	1 Jan 2019	*31 Dec 2019*	*31 Dec 2020*	*31 Dec 2021*
Actual 3-month LIBOR	4.3%	5%	3%	n/a
Actual 6-month LIBOR	4.5%	4.9%	3.2%	n/a
Interest payments based on 3-month LIBOR	n/a	£10 × (4.3% + 2.5%) = £680,000	£10 × (5% + 2.5%) = £750,000	£10 × (3% + 2.5%) = £550,000
Interest rate swap (hedging instrument)				
Fair value[4]	nil	£78,000	(£89,000)[1]	(£130,000)[2]
Fair value change	nil	£78,000 – 0 = £78,000	(£89,000) – £78,000 = (£167,000)	(£130,000) – (£40,000)[3] – (£89,000) = (£1,000)
Swap settlement receipts/(payments) based on 6-month LIBOR	n/a	£10m × (4.5% – 4.5%) = nil	£10m × (4.9% – 4.5%) = £40,000	£10m × (3.2% – 4.5%) = (£130,000)
Hedged item				
Fair value[4]	nil	(£137,000)	£59,000	£130,000

Key to table:

1:   This valuation is determined before the receipt of the cash settlement of £40,000 due on 31 December 2020.
2:   This valuation is determined before the payment of the cash settlement of £130,000 due on 31 December 2021.
3:   £40,000 is the settlement of the interest rate swap as at 31 December 2020 which affects the fair value of the swap, but is not included in the fair value of the swap at 31 December 2020 of £89,000.
4:   The fair values of the interest rate swap and the hedged item shown in the table are those given in Example 2 in the standard, but may not reflect the market data given.

31 December 2019

Accounting entries:

Note that the accounting entries shown are only those relevant to demonstrate the effects of hedge accounting. In practice other accounting entries would be required, e.g. an entry to recognise the loan liability.

	Periodic		Cumulative	
	Dr	Cr	Dr	Cr
Interest rate swap	£78,000		£78,000	
OCI		£78,000		£78,000

The cash flow hedge reserve is adjusted to the lower of (in absolute amounts) the cumulative gain on the hedging instrument (i.e. the interest rate swap), which equals its fair value, of £78,000 and the cumulative change in fair value of the hedged item, which equals its fair value of (£137,000).

The gain of £78,000 on the interest rate swap is recognised in OCI.

The fixed interest element on the hypothetical swap is £430,000, the same amount as the variable rate component. The variability of 3-month LIBOR did therefore not affect profit or loss during the period. The reclassification adjustment is nil. (Note that no accounting entry is shown here).

Profit or loss (interest)	£680,000		£680,000
Cash		£680,000	£680,000

In respect of the interest payments on the loan. Note that in practice the accrual and payment of interest may be recorded in separate accounting entries.

31 December 2020

Accounting entries:

	Periodic		Cumulative	
	Dr	Cr	Dr	Cr
OCI	£137,000		£59,000	
Profit or loss (ineffectiveness)	£30,000		£30,000	
Interest rate swap		£167,000		£89,000

The cash flow hedge reserve is adjusted to the lower of (in absolute amounts) the cumulative loss on the hedging instrument (i.e. the interest rate swap) which equals its fair value of (£89,000) and the cumulative change in fair value of the hedged item, which equals its fair value of £59,000. The cash flow hedge reserve moves from £78,000 to (£59,000), a change of (£137,000).

A loss of £137,000 on the interest rate swap is recognised in OCI, as this part of the loss is fully off-set by the change in the cash flow hedge reserve. The remainder of the loss on the interest rate swap of £30,000 is recognised in profit or loss.

	Dr	Cr	Dr	Cr
OCI	£70,000		£129,000	
Profit or loss (interest)		£70,000	£610,000	

The fixed interest element on the hypothetical swap is £430,000, whilst the variable rate component is £500,000. The variability of 3-month LIBOR affects profit or loss during the period by £70,000. Accordingly, the reclassification adjustment is £70,000.

Profit or loss (interest)	£750,000		£1,360,000
Cash		£750,000	£1,430,000

In respect of the interest payments on the loan. Note that in practice the accrual and payment of interest may be recorded in separate accounting entries.

Cash	£40,000		£1,390,000
Interest rate swap		£40,000	£129,000

In respect of the settlement of the swap.

31 December 2021

Accounting entries:

Description	Periodic		Cumulative	
	Dr	Cr	Dr	Cr
OCI	£1,000		£130,000	
Interest rate swap		£1,000		£130,000

The cash flow hedge reserve is adjusted to the lower of (in absolute amounts) the cumulative loss on the hedging instrument (i.e. the interest rate swap) which equals the fair value of (£130,000) and the cumulative change in fair value of the hedged item, which equals its fair value of £130,000.

The cash flow hedge reserve moves from (£129,000) to (£130,000), a change of (£1,000). The loss of £1,000 on the interest rate swap is recognised in OCI.

Description	Dr	Cr	Dr	Cr
Profit or loss (interest)	£130,000		£1,490,000	
OCI		£130,000		nil

The fixed interest element on the hypothetical swap is £430,000, whilst the variable rate component is £300,000. The variability of 3-month LIBOR affects profit or loss during the period by (£130,000). Accordingly, the reclassification adjustment is (£130,000).

Description	Dr	Cr	Dr	Cr
Profit or loss (interest)	£550,000		£2,040,000	
Cash		£550,000		£1,940,000

In respect of the interest payments on the loan. Note that in practice the accrual and payment of interest may be recorded in separate accounting entries.

Description	Dr	Cr	Dr	Cr
Interest rate swap	£130,000		nil	
Cash		£130,000		£2,070,000

For illustrative purposes the accounting entry for the settlement of the swap is shown above.

The table below summarises the effects of the accounting entries shown above on the interest rate swap, profit or loss and other comprehensive income.

Description	Interest rate Swap	Other comprehensive income	Profit or loss
	£	£	£
31 December 2019			
Opening balance	nil	nil	–
Interest on the loan			680,000
Interest rate swap fair value movement	78,000	(78,000)	–
Closing balance	78,000	(78,000) [1]	680,000

31 December 2020			
Opening balance	78,000	(78,000)	680,000
Interest on the loan			750,000
Interest rate swap fair value movement	(167,000)	137,000	30,000
Settlement receipt interest rate swap	(40,000)	–	
Reclassification from cash flow hedge reserve	–	70,000	(70,000)
Closing balance	(129,000)	129,000 [1]	1,390,000
31 December 2021			
Opening balance	(129,000)	129,000[1]	1,390,000
Interest on the loan			550,000
Interest rate swap movement	(1,000)	1,000	
Settlement receipt interest rate swap	130,000	–	
Reclassification from cash flow hedge reserve	–	(130,000)	130,000
Closing balance	nil	nil[1]	2,070,000

1   This is the balance of the cash flow hedge reserve.

10.9 Hedges of net investments in foreign operations

10.9.1 *Introduction*

Many reporting entities have investments in foreign operations which may be subsidiaries, associates, joint ventures or branches. Section 30 requires an entity to determine the functional currency of each of its foreign operations as the currency of the primary economic environment of that operation. When translating the results and financial position of its foreign operation into a presentation currency, on consolidation foreign exchange differences should be recognised in other comprehensive income (with no reclassification to profit or loss in future periods).

From the perspective of an investor (e.g. a parent) it is clear that an investment in a foreign operation is likely to give rise to a degree of foreign currency exchange rate risk and an entity with many foreign operations may be exposed to a number of foreign currency risks.

FRS 102 defines a net investment in a foreign operation as 'the amount of the reporting entity's interest in the net assets of that operation'. *[FRS 102 Appendix I]*. A hedge of a net investment in a foreign operation is a hedge of the foreign currency exposure, not a hedge of the change in the value of the investment. The net investment hedge accounting rules can also be applied to a monetary item that is accounted for as part of the net investment (see Chapter 27 at 3.7.4). For example, if a parent grants a foreign currency loan to an overseas subsidiary and settlement is neither planned nor likely in the foreseeable future, the loan can be hedged as part of the net investment in the foreign subsidiary.

Net investment hedge accounting can be applied only when the net assets of the foreign operation (and not fair value or cost less impairment) are included in the financial statements. This will be the case for consolidated financial statements, financial statements in which investments such as associates or joint ventures are accounted for using the equity method or those that include a branch or a joint operation. Investments in foreign operations may be held directly by a parent entity or indirectly by its subsidiary or subsidiaries. Accordingly it is also possible to achieve net investment hedge accounting of a foreign branch in an entity's standalone financial statements under FRS 102, if the other requirements for hedge accounting are met, as confirmed in April 2015 when the FRC issued *FRS 102 – Editorial amendments and clarification statements.*

10.9.2   Accounting for net investment hedges

Hedges of a net investment in a foreign operation, including a hedge of a monetary item that is accounted for as part of the net investment, are accounted for similarly to cash flow hedges from the date the conditions for hedging are met:

(i)   the portion of the gain or loss on the hedging instrument that is determined to be an effective hedge is recognised in other comprehensive income; and

(ii)   the ineffective portion is recognised in profit or loss.

The effective portion is determined by applying the same cash flow hedge 'lower of' accounting, as explained at 10.8.3 above. However, the cumulative gain or loss on the hedging instrument relating to the effective portion of the hedge that has been accumulated in equity is not reclassified from equity to profit or loss in subsequent periods. *[FRS102.12.24]*. This ensures consistency with Section 30 which requires that foreign exchange gains and losses relating to the consolidation of a subsidiary are not recycled on disposal of the subsidiary. *[FRS 102.30.13]*.

The following example, based on the Appendix to Section 12, illustrates how to account for a simple net investment hedge.

Example 10.18:   Hedge accounting: net investment in a foreign operation

On 1 April 2019 an entity with sterling functional currency acquires an investment in an overseas subsidiary (with functional currency NZ$) at a cost of NZ$1,200,000. On the same day the entity takes out a loan with a third party of NZ$1,200,000 to finance the investment. This example disregards the effects of interest or other transaction costs associated with the loan.

This example assumes that the foreign operation makes losses of NZ$200,000 in 2019 and profits of NZ$100,000 in 2020. The reduction in value below NZ$1,200,000 causes ineffectiveness.

The entity's financial year ends on 31 December.

This example assumes that the qualifying conditions for hedge accounting are met from 1 April 2019.

The table below sets out the applicable exchange rates, the carrying amount of the loan and the foreign exchange gains and losses on the loan, as well as the retranslation differences on the foreign investment recognised in OCI in accordance with Section 30– *Foreign Currency Translation* (see Chapter 27).

	1 April 2019	*31 December 2019*	*31 December 2020*
Spot exchange rate £:NZ$	0.35:1	0.3:1	0.45:1
Loan (hedging instrument)			
	£	£	£
Carrying amount	420,000	360,000	540,000
	(= NZ$1,200,000 × 0.35)	(= NZ$1,200,000 × 0.3)	(=NZ$1,200,000 × 0.45)
Cumulative gain/(loss)	nil	60,000	(120,000)
		(= 420,000 – 360,000)	(= 420,000 – 540,000)
Periodic gain/(loss)	nil	60,000	(180,000)
		(= 420,000 – 360,000)	(= 360,000 – 540,000)

Investment in foreign operation (hedged item)

Translation effect of profit or loss in the period at the date of the transactions and assets and liabilities at the closing rate	nil	5,000 [1]	7,500 [2]
Translation of the opening net assets at the closing rate	nil	(60,000)	150,000 [3]
Total retranslation gain/(loss)	nil	(55,000)	157,500
Cumulative retranslation gain/(loss)	nil	(55,000) (= (55,000) + nil)	102,500 (=(55,000) + 157,500)

1   The calculation is based on the translation of the NZ$200,000 loss at the average rate of 0.325 £:NZ$. *[FRS 102.30.13(a)].*
2   The calculation is based on the translation of the NZ$100,000 profit at the average rate of 0.375 £:NZ$. *[FRS 102.30.13(a)].*
3   The calculation is based on the opening net assets of NZ$1,000,000, after the losses of NZ$200,000 during 2019. *[FRS 102.30.13(b)].*

31 December 2019

A component of equity is adjusted to the lower of (in absolute amounts) the cumulative exchange gain on the loan of £60,000 and the cumulative retranslation difference on the net investment of (£55,000).

A gain of £55,000 is recognised in OCI, with the remainder of the gain on the loan of £5,000 is recognised in profit or loss.

Accounting entries:

Note that only the accounting entry in relation to net investment hedge accounting are shown. Other accounting entries in relation to the loan and the investment in the foreign operation would be required in practice.

	Dr £	Cr £
Loan	60,000	
OCI		55,000
Profit or loss		5,000

31 December 2020

A component of equity is adjusted to the lower of (in absolute amounts) the cumulative exchange loss on the loan of £120,000 and the cumulative exchange difference on the net investment of £102,500.

The amount recorded in equity changes from £55,000 to (£102,500), a change of (£157,500). A loss of £157,500 is recognised in OCI, and the remainder of the loss on the loan of £22,500 is recorded in profit or loss.

Accounting entries:

	Dr £	Cr £
OCI	157,500	
Profit or loss	22,500	
Loan		180,000

10.10   Discontinuing hedge accounting

Hedge accounting should be discontinued prospectively if any of the following occurs:

(i)   the hedging instrument expires, is sold or terminated;

(ii)   the conditions for hedge accounting are no longer met (see 10.4 above); or

(iii)   the entity elects to discontinue the hedge. *[FRS102.12.25].*

If the entity elects to voluntarily discontinue a hedge, it must document its decision and the discontinuation would be effective prospectively from that date.

The conditions for hedge accounting include a requirement that the hedge relationship is consistent with the entity's risk management objective for undertaking hedges. Should that objective change, then the condition is no longer met and the hedge relationship must be discontinued. Similarly if the documented hedged risk, hedged item or hedging instrument no longer exists, or have been replaced with an alternate, then hedge accounting for that hedge relationship must cease prospectively. A new hedge relationship may be designated in order to achieve hedge accounting prospectively, once all the conditions are met.

Following discontinuation in a fair value hedge, any adjustment to the hedged item arising as a result of fair value hedging, is amortised as discussed at 10.7.3 above, or written off to profit or loss if the hedged item no longer exists.

In a cash flow hedge, if the hedged future cash flows are no longer expected to occur, the amount that has been accumulated in the cash flow hedge reserve is reclassified from the cash flow hedge reserve to profit or loss immediately.

If cash flow hedge accounting is discontinued and the hedged future cash flows are still expected to occur (for example a future cash flow that is no longer highly probable may still be expected to occur), the cumulative gain or loss in the cash flow hedge reserve should either:

(i)   remain in equity and be recycled to profit or loss in line with 10.8.3(d) above or

(ii)   be recorded in profit or loss immediately if the amount is a loss and is not expected to be recovered. *[FRS 102.12.23(d), 25A].*

In a net investment hedge, the amount that has been accumulated in equity is not reclassified to profit or loss.

10.10.1   Rollover strategies

IAS 39 and IFRS 9 sometimes permit a hedging relationship to continue where a hedging instrument is 'rolled-over', replacing an expired or terminated hedging instrument. For example, both standards state that an entity shall discontinue hedge accounting if the hedging instrument 'expires or is sold, terminated or exercised...the replacement or rollover of a hedging instrument is not an expiration or termination if such replacement or rollover is part of the entity's documented hedging strategy'. *[IFRS 9.6.5.6, IAS 39.101(a)].*

Similarly, FRS 102 states that an entity shall discontinue hedge accounting if the hedging instrument has 'expired, is sold, terminated or exercised'. However, FRS 102 is silent on the issue of rollover strategies. The absence of guidance in FRS 102 does not mean that the guidance in IFRS automatically applies and in this situation, it would appear the difference in the two standards is deliberate. FRS 102 is a simplification of IFRS and it was not intended that every rule in IFRS would apply to entities applying FRS 102. Hence, under FRS 102, a hedge relationship is discontinued when the hedging instrument expires regardless of whether the instrument is rolled over.

10.10.2   Novation of derivatives

IAS 39 and IFRS 9 both contain guidance on dealing with novation of derivatives that are part of a hedging relationship – the guidance was added following an Interpretations Committee discussion on the topic of mandated novation of derivatives to a central clearing party. A novation in this context is the act of replacing an existing counterparty to a derivative with a new party, such that all the obligations to the derivative contract must now be performed by the new party. The Interpretations Committee confirmed that a change in the counterparty of a derivative results in derecognition of the derivative. As noted at 10.10.1 above, it follows therefore that a hedge relationship would be discontinued if the derivative is novated, unless the change in counterparty is part of a documented replacement strategy or roll over strategy. IAS 39 was amended to include an additional exception such that a novation of a derivative in a hedge relationship would not result in discontinuation of the hedge relationship if the novation was as a consequence of laws or regulation requiring a change to a central clearing counterparty. The same guidance also appears in IFRS 9.

The basis for conclusions for IAS 39 explain the principle why a derivative is derecognised when it is novated to another counterparty: financial assets are derecognised when the contractual rights to the cash flows expire; whilst financial liabilities are extinguished when the debtor is legally released from primary responsibility for the liability. In a novation, both of these conditions are met. These conditions are also set out in FRS 102 implying that a derivative that is novated under FRS 102 would also need to be derecognised and the existing hedge would need to be terminated. *[FRS 102.11.33, 36]*. However, unlike IAS 39, FRS 102 does not contain the 'exception' for novations that are part of a documented hedging strategy or with a central clearing counterparty. Therefore, in our view, novations result in termination of the hedging relationship under FRS 102.

Due to various regulatory changes and political events such as the probable end of IBOR benchmark interest rates, the departure of the UK from the European Union ('Brexit') and the 'ring fencing' of certain activities of banks, how these might all affect cash flow hedge accounting has been the subject of discussion. Entities could find that the counterparty to some of their existing hedging derivatives may change to a different legal entity within an existing banking group, as banks make their preparations for Brexit or compliance with ring fencing regulations. In these circumstances, the entity will need to conclude whether such a change in counterparty would require discontinuation of the existing hedge relationship and its replacement with a new one.

10.10.3   The replacement of IBOR benchmark interest rates

As a result of the reforms mandated by the Financial Stability Board following the Financial Crisis, regulators are pushing for IBOR to be replaced by new 'official' benchmark rates, known as Risk Free Rates (RFRs). For instance, in the UK, the new official benchmark will be the reformed Sterling Overnight Interest Average (SONIA) and banks will no longer be required to quote LIBOR beyond the end of 2021. Such a change will necessarily affect future cash flows in both contractual floating rate financial instruments currently referenced to IBOR, and highly probably forecast transactions for which IBOR is designated as the hedged risk. This raises a number of accounting questions, many of which relate to hedge accounting.

This raises a number of accounting questions, many of which relate to hedge accounting. Two key questions are whether:

(i)   there continues to be an IBOR component of future variable cash flows if it is known that IBOR will not exist in its current form beyond the end of 2021 (or the equivalent date for other jurisdictions) (see 10.8.2 above); and

(ii)   a change of designated hedged risk from IBOR to the new RFR should result in a de-designation and re-designation of existing hedge relationships for interest rate risk.

Issue (i) above is the most urgent, as it is possible that IBOR will cease to be a component of future variable cash flows well in advance of 2021. We believe that, as at the date of writing, it is possible to consider that IBOR is still a component of variable interest rates in the context of the market structure and that IBOR and RFR interest rates are equivalent for the purposes of cash flow hedge accounting. Hence, at present, it is still possible to designate IBOR as a risk component in a cash flow hedge. However, this conclusion may become invalid once RFRs take over from IBOR as the main interest rate market benchmarks.

10.11   Presentation

FRS 102 does not address how hedges should be presented in profit or loss in the financial statements. IFRS reporters normally try to reflect the effect of the hedged item and hedging instrument in the financial statements so that they offset.

For derivatives designated in effective hedge relationships, the profit or loss related to the effective portion of the hedging instrument would normally be presented in the same line that the profit or loss arising on the hedged item is recorded. However, this is not mandated. It would also be acceptable to present the profit or loss from hedging derivatives similarly to non-hedging derivatives, if an entity so chooses as its accounting policy.

If a hedge does not qualify for hedge accounting, the profit or loss arising on the derivative would not necessarily be presented in the same income or expenditure line as the item that it was intended to hedge. The default is for the gain or loss to be recorded in trading income. However, gains or losses on interest rate derivatives are sometimes presented in interest income or expense. Also, gains and losses on currency derivatives may be presented in the foreign currency revaluation income or expense line. Presentation may be appropriate in cost of goods sold if the entity does not enter into derivatives for trading purposes and, hence, does not have a line item for trading instruments.

Presentation policies should be applied consistently to all similar instruments and should be clearly described in the accounting policies.

11   PRESENTATION AND DISCLOSURES

11.1   Offsetting of financial instruments

11.1.1   Requirements

The rules regarding the offsetting, sometimes called 'netting', of a financial asset and a financial liability are contained in both Sections 11 and 12. However, the guidance is identical, that is, a financial asset and a financial liability should be offset and the net amount presented in the statement of financial position when and only when, an entity:

(a)   currently has a legally enforceable right to set off the recognised amounts; and

(b)   intends either to settle on a net basis, or to realise the asset and settle the liability simultaneously. *[FRS 102.11.38A, 12.25B].*

The offsetting principle set out above is identical to that in IAS 32 but without the additional guidance contained in IAS 32. The IASB decided to incorporate additional guidance into IAS 32 to deal with historical ambiguities as well as emerging practical application issues arising from the growth in the clearing of financial instruments. The additional guidance has helped to clarify aspects such as current legal enforceability and simultaneous settlement. We would expect FRS 102 reporters to default to the guidance within IAS 32 where helpful, but this would not itself be a requirement. Further information on offsetting under IAS 32 can be found in EY International GAAP 2019.

The effect of the offsetting rules described above is that, when the requirements are met, in effect the entity presents a single financial asset or liability which represents the net cash flow intended to be received or paid. When the requirements are not met, the financial asset and the financial liability need to be presented separately.

11.1.2   Interaction with derecognition rules

It is worth clarifying that offsetting and derecognition are different. Offsetting does not result in derecognition of the financial asset or liability from the statement of financial position, but in their net presentation in the statement of financial position as either a net financial asset or a net financial liability. Offsetting does not have an impact on the income statement as there is no gain or loss arising from the net presentation.

When a transfer of financial assets does not qualify for derecognition, the entity has to recognise an associated liability as discussed at 9.2.3.B above. In such cases, the financial asset retained in the statement of financial position and the resulting financial liability cannot be offset. *[FRS 102.11.34].*

11.2   Disclosures

11.2.1   Introduction

The disclosures contained in Section 11 are also applicable to financial instruments within the scope of Section 12, where relevant. *[FRS 102.12.26].* The disclosure requirements of Sections 11 and 12 apply to all entities regardless of their accounting policy choice for recognition and measurement of financial instruments (see 4 above).

However, a qualifying entity which is not a financial institution (i.e. most subsidiaries and parents in their separate financial statements) is not required to make all of the disclosures required by Sections 11 and 12, providing the equivalent disclosures are included in the consolidated financial statements of the group in which the entity is consolidated. *[FRS 102.1.8, 9, 12(c)]*. The August 2014 version of FRS 102 exempted qualifying entities that were not financial institutions from *all* disclosures required by Sections 11 and 12. Nevertheless, all entities (including qualifying entities) preparing Companies Act accounts were required to make certain disclosures in respect of financial instruments. To remove this inconsistency, the July 2015 amendments to FRS 102 removed some of the disclosure exemptions for qualifying entities that are not financial institutions. These disclosures apply to all entities, even those that do not prepare financial statements in accordance with UK company law. Therefore, for a qualifying entity that is not a financial institution that is not required to prepare Companies Act accounts, certain disclosures are now required that were not previously. *[FRS 102.1.12(c)]*.

When IFRS 9 was finalised, amendments were also made to IFRS 7 to reflect the new requirements of IFRS 9. In particular, many changes were made to IFRS 7 in relation to the new expected credit loss approach to impairment of financial assets. As a result, some of the disclosure requirements of FRS 102 would have been inconsistent with the application of the recognition and measurement requirements of IFRS 9. Consequently the Triennial review 2017 introduced a number of changes to the disclosure requirements to ensure that entities applying the recognition and measurement requirements of IFRS 9 through the accounting policy choice discussed at 4 above are providing relevant information about the impairment of financial assets. *[FRS 102.BC.B11.50-51]*.

In addition, the Triennial review 2017 updated the disclosure requirements in relation to the statement of financial position to: (a) remove the requirement to disclose the carrying amounts of categories of financial assets and financial liabilities other than those carried at fair value though profit or loss; and (b) clarify that when the risks arising from financial instruments are particularly significant to the business of the entity, additional disclosure may be required. See 11.2.3 below.

As a result of the interaction of requirements described above, 11.2.2 to 11.2.5 below summarise the disclosure requirements on a cumulative basis, starting with the minimum FRS 102 disclosure requirements applicable to all reporting entities, followed by:

- the additional disclosures applicable to entities that do not take the qualifying entity exemptions;

- the additional disclosures applicable to financial institutions according to Section 34; and

- the additional disclosures applicable to entities reporting under UK company law.

11.2.2   *Disclosures applicable to all entities, including qualifying entities*

The disclosure requirements for all entities, including qualifying entities, are listed below:

Accounting policies

(i)   In its significant accounting policies, the measurement basis (or bases) used for financial instruments and the other accounting policies used for financial instruments that are relevant to an understanding of the financial statements. *[FRS 102.11.40]*. Even though

FRS 102 does not explicitly stipulate it, we expect the accounting policy to include disclosure of which standard was chosen and applied by the entity for recognition and measurement of financial instruments, as this constitutes an accounting policy choice.

Statement of financial position – categories

(ii) Separate disclosure of the carrying amounts at the reporting date of:

(a) financial assets measured at fair value through profit or loss;

(b) financial liabilities measured at fair value through profit or loss. Those that are not held as part of a trading portfolio and are not derivatives should be shown separately; *[FRS 102.11.41]*

This disclosure may be made separately by category of financial instrument.

(iii) For all financial assets and financial liabilities measured at fair value, the basis for determining fair value, (e.g. quoted market price in an active market or a valuation technique). When a valuation technique is used, the assumptions applied in determining fair value for each class of financial assets or financial liabilities. For example, if applicable, information about the assumptions relating to prepayment rates, rates of estimated credit losses, and interest rates or discount rates. *[FRS 102.11.43]*.

Collateral

(iv) When an entity has pledged financial assets as collateral for liabilities or contingent liabilities, the carrying amount of the financial assets pledged as collateral and the terms and conditions relating to its pledge. *[FRS 102.11.46]*.

Items of income, expense, gains or losses

(v) An entity should disclose income, expense, net gains or net losses, including changes in fair value, recognised on financial assets measured at fair value through profit or loss, financial liabilities measured at fair value through profit or loss (with separate disclosure of movements on those which are not held as part of a trading portfolio and are not derivatives). *[FRS 102.11.48(a)(i)-(ii)]*.

Financial instruments at fair value through profit or loss

(vi) An entity should provide the disclosures below only for financial instruments that are measured at fair value in accordance with paragraph 36(4) of Schedule 1 to the Regulations (see 6.4.1 above):

(a) financial liabilities, unless they are held as part of a trading portfolio or are derivatives;

(b) financial instruments to be held to maturity, other than derivatives;

(c) loans and receivables originated by the company unless they are held for trading;

(d) interests in subsidiary undertakings, associated undertakings and joint ventures;

(e) equity instruments issued by the company;

(f) contracts for contingent consideration in a business combination; and

(g) other financial instruments with such special characteristics that the instruments, according to generally accounting principles or practice should be accounted for differently from other financial instruments.

The disclosure requirements are as follows: *[FRS 102.11.48A]*

- For a financial liability designated at fair value through profit or loss, the amount of change, during the period and cumulatively, in the fair value of the financial instrument that is attributable to changes in the credit risk of that instrument, determined either:
    - as the amount of change in its fair value that is not attributable to changes in market conditions that give rise to market risk; or
    - using an alternative method the entity believes more faithfully represents the amount of change in its fair value that is attributable to changes in the credit risk of the instrument.
- The method used to establish the amount of change attributable to changes in own credit risk, or, if the change cannot be measured reliably or is not material, that fact.
- The difference between the financial liability's carrying amount and the amount the entity would be contractually required to pay at maturity to the holder of the obligation.
- If an instrument contains both a liability and an equity feature, and the instrument has multiple features that substantially modify the cash flows and the values of those features are interdependent (such as a callable convertible debt instrument), the existence of those features.
- If there is a difference between the fair value of a financial instrument at initial recognition and the amount determined at that date using a valuation technique, the aggregate difference yet to be recognised in profit or loss at the beginning and end of the period and a reconciliation of the changes in the balance of this difference.
- Information that enables users of the entity's financial statements to evaluate the nature and extent of relevant risks arising from financial instruments to which the entity is exposed at the end of the reporting period. These risks typically include, but are not limited to, credit risk, liquidity risk and market risk. The disclosure should include both the entity's exposure to each type of risk and how it manages those risks.

The purpose of these disclosures above is compliance with the disclosures in EU-adopted IFRS when using fair value accounting according to paragraph 36(4) of Schedule 1 to the Regulations. These disclosure requirements will predominantly apply to certain financial liabilities. However, there may be instances where the Regulations requires that the disclosures must also be provided in relation to financial assets, for example investments in subsidiaries, associates or jointly controlled entities measured at fair value. *[FRS 102. 9.27B, Appendix III.13,].*

Hedging

(vii) For fair value hedges, the following disclosures must be provided:
  (a) the amount of the change in fair value of the hedging instrument recognised in profit or loss for the period; and
  (b) the amount of the change in fair value of the hedged item recognised in profit or loss for the period. *[FRS 102.12.28].*

(viii) For cash flow hedges, entities are required to disclose:

    (a)   the amount of the change in fair value of the hedging instrument that was recognised in other comprehensive income during the period; *[FRS 102.12.29(c)]*

    (b)   the amount, if any, that was reclassified from equity to profit or loss for the period; *[FRS 102.12.29(d)]* and

    (c)   the amount, if any, of any hedge ineffectiveness recognised in profit or loss for the period (i.e. any ineffectiveness). *[FRS 102.12.29(e)]*.

11.2.3 Additional disclosures for entities not taking the qualifying entity exemptions

Entities that are not qualifying entities (or do not avail themselves of the disclosure exemptions available to qualifying entities) and qualifying entities that are financial institutions, should include the following disclosures in their financial statements in addition to those discussed at 11.2.2 above:

Statement of financial position – categories

(i)   Information that enables users of an entity's financial statements to evaluate the significance of financial instruments for its financial position and performance. For example, for long-term debt, such information would normally include the terms and conditions of the debt instrument (such as interest rate, maturity, repayment schedule, and restrictions that the debt instrument imposes on the entity). When the risks arising from financial instruments are particularly significant to the business (for example because they are principal risks for the entity), additional disclosure may be required. The disclosure requirements for financial institutions at 11.2.4 below, include examples of disclosure requirements for risks arising from financial instruments that may be relevant in such cases. *[FRS 102.11.42, 34.19]*.

    In order to comply with the above, an entity that has taken the accounting policy choice to apply the recognition and measurement provisions of IAS 39 or IFRS 9 may need to consider additional disclosure based on IFRS 7, as it relates to the recognition and measurement policies applied. *[FRS 102.BC.B11.50]*.

(ii)   The fact that a reliable measure of fair value is no longer available for any financial instrument that would otherwise be required to be measured at fair value through profit or loss, if that is the case, and the carrying amount of those financial instruments. *[FRS 102.11.44]*.

Derecognition

(iii) If an entity has transferred financial assets to another party in a transaction that does not qualify for derecognition, for each class of such financial assets:

    (a)   the nature of the assets;

    (b)   the nature of the risks and rewards of ownership to which the entity remains exposed; and

    (c)   the carrying amounts of the assets and of any associated liabilities that the entity continues to recognise. *[FRS 102.11.45]*.

Defaults and breaches on loans payable

(iv)   For loans payable recognised at the reporting date for which there is a breach of terms or default of principal, interest, sinking fund, or redemption terms that has not been remedied by the reporting date:

   (a)   details of that breach or default;

   (b)   the carrying amount of the related loans payable at the reporting date; and

   (c)   whether the breach or default was remedied, or the terms of the loans payable were renegotiated, before the financial statements were authorised for issue. *[FRS 102.11.47]*.

Items of income, expense, gains or losses

(v)   An entity should disclose the following items of income, expense, gains or losses:

   (a)   income, expense, net gains or net losses, including changes in fair value, recognised on:

      (1)   financial assets measured at amortised cost;

      (2)   financial liabilities measured at amortised cost; and

      (3)   when an entity has made the accounting policy choice to apply the recognition and measurement provisions of IFRS 9 (see 4 above), financial instruments measured at fair value through other comprehensive income;

   (b)   total interest income and total interest expense (calculated using the effective interest method) for financial assets or financial liabilities that are not measured at fair value through profit or loss; and

   (c)   the amount of any impairment loss for each class of financial asset. A class of financial asset is a grouping that is appropriate to the nature of the information disclosed and that takes into account the characteristics of the financial assets. When an entity has made the accounting policy choice to apply the recognition and measurement provisions of IFRS 9 (see 4 above), the groupings shall be based on whether the amount is equal to 12-month expected credit risk losses, equal to the lifetime expected credit losses or financial assets that are purchased or originated credit-impaired. *[FRS 102.11.48]*.

Hedging

(vi)   When hedge accounting is applied, entities are required to disclose the following, separately for each type of hedging relationships:

   (a)   a description of the hedge relationship;

   (b)   a description of the financial instruments designated as hedging instruments and their fair values at the reporting date;

   (c)   a description of the hedged item; and

   (d)   the nature of the risks being hedged. *[FRS 102.12.27]*.

(vii)   For cash flow hedges, entities are required to disclose:

   (a)   the periods when the cash flows are expected to occur and when they are expected to affect profit or loss;

   (b)   a description of any forecast transaction for which hedge accounting had previously been used, but which is no longer expected to occur. *[FRS 102.12.29]*.

(viii) For a hedge of net investment in a foreign operation entities must disclose separately:

   (a)   the amounts recognised in other comprehensive income (i.e. fair value changes in the hedging instrument that were effective hedges); and

   (b)   the amounts recognised in profit or loss (as ineffectiveness). *[FRS 102.12.29A]*.

11.2.4   Additional disclosures required for financial institutions

For financial institutions (as defined in Chapter 3 at 2.5.1.A) additional disclosures are required to be provided in:

(a)   the individual financial statements of the financial institution; and

(b)   the consolidated financial statements of a group containing a financial institution when the financial instruments held by the financial institution are material to the group. Where this is the case, the disclosures apply regardless of whether the principal activity of the group is being a financial institution or not. However, the disclosures only need to be given in respect of financial instruments held by entities within the group that are financial institutions. *[FRS 102.11.48B, 34.17]*.

The required disclosures are as follows:

Significance of financial instruments for financial position and performance

(i)   A disaggregation of the statement of financial position line item by class of financial instrument. A class is a grouping of financial instruments that is appropriate to the nature of the information disclosed and that takes into account the characteristics of those financial instruments. *[FRS 102.34.20]*.

Impairment

(ii)   Unless a financial institution has made the accounting policy choice at 4 above to apply recognition and measurement provision of IFRS 9, where a separate allowance account is used to record impairments, a reconciliation of changes in that account during the period for each class of financial asset. *[FRS 102.34.21]*.

(iii)   When a financial institution has made the accounting policy choice at 4 above to apply the recognition and measurement provisions of IFRS 9, it must disclose information that enables users of its financial statements to understand the effect of credit risk on the amount, timing and uncertainty of future cash flows. This shall include:

   (a)   an explanation of the financial institution's credit risk management practices and how they relate to the recognition and measurement of expected credit losses;

   (b)   a reconciliation from the opening balance to the closing balance of the loss allowance, in a table, showing separately the changes during the period for:

      (1)   the loss allowance measured at an amount equal to 12-month expected credit losses;

      (2)   the loss allowance measured at an amount equal to lifetime expected credit losses (showing separately the amount relating to financial instruments for which credit risk has increased significantly since initial recognition); and

      (3)   financial assets that are purchased or originated credit-impaired.

(c)   by credit risk rating grade, the gross carrying amount of financial assets and the exposure to credit risk on loan commitments and financial guarantee contracts (showing separately information for financial instruments for which the loss allowance is measured at an amount equal to 12-month expected credit losses, for which the loss allowance is measured at an amount equal to lifetime expected credit losses, and that are purchased or originated credit-impaired financial assets).

Fair value

(iv) For financial instruments held at fair value in the statement of financial position, for each class of financial instrument, an analysis of the level in the fair value hierarchy into which the fair value measurements are categorised. *[FRS 102.34.22]*.

In order to simplify the preparation of disclosures about financial instruments for the entities affected, whilst increasing the consistency with disclosures required by EU-adopted IFRS, the three levels in the fair value hierarchy required for disclosures are aligned with those in IFRS 13:

(a)   Level 1: The unadjusted quoted price in an active market for identical assets or liabilities that the entity can access at the measurement date.

(b)   Level 2: Inputs other than quoted prices included within Level 1 that are observable (i.e. developed using market data) for the asset or liability, either directly or indirectly.

(c)   Level 3: Inputs are unobservable (i.e. for which market data is unavailable) for the asset or liability.

Even though they are based on similar considerations, the hierarchy to estimate fair value discussed at 8.6.1 is not aligned with the disclosure requirements.

Nature and extent of risks arising from financial instruments

(v)   Information that enables users of the financial institution's financial statements to evaluate the nature and extent of credit risk, liquidity risk and market risk arising from financial instruments to which the institution is exposed at the end of the reporting period. *[FRS 102.34.23]*.

(vi) For each type of risk arising from financial instruments:

(a)   the exposures to risk and how they arise;

(b)   the institution's objectives, policies and processes for managing the risk and the methods used to measure the risk; and

(c)   any changes from the previous period. *[FRS 102.34.24]*.

Credit risk

(vii) By class of financial instrument that is not subject to the impairment requirements of IFRS 9 as a consequence of the accounting policy choice at 4 above:

(a)   the amount that best represents the institution's maximum exposure to credit risk at the end of the reporting period. This disclosure is not required for financial instruments whose carrying amount best represents the maximum exposure to credit risk;

(b)   a description of collateral held as security and of other credit enhancements, and the extent to which these mitigate credit risk;

(c)   the amount by which any related credit derivatives or similar instruments mitigate that maximum exposure to credit risk. *[FRS 102.34.25(a)-(c)].*

(viii) Unless a financial institution has made the accounting policy choice at 4 above to apply the recognition and measurement requirements of IFRS 9, an analysis by class of financial asset of:

(a)   information about the credit quality of financial assets that are neither past due nor impaired. *[FRS 102.34.25(d)].*

(b)   the age of financial assets that are past due as at the end of the reporting period but not impaired; and

(c)   the financial assets that are individually determined to be impaired as at the end of the reporting period, including the factors the financial institution considered in determining that they are impaired. *[FRS 102.34.26].*

(ix) When financial or non-financial assets are obtained by taking possession of collateral held as security or calling on other credit enhancements (e.g. guarantees), and such assets meet the recognition criteria in other sections of FRS 102, a financial institution should disclose:

(a)   the nature and carrying amount of the assets obtained; and

(b)   when the assets are not readily convertible into cash, its policies for disposing of such assets or for using them in its operations. *[FRS 102.34.27].*

Liquidity risk

(x)   A maturity analysis for financial liabilities that shows the remaining contractual maturities at undiscounted amounts separated between derivative and non-derivative financial liabilities. *[FRS 102.34.28].*

Market risk

(xi) A sensitivity analysis for each type of market risk (e.g. interest rate risk, currency risk, other price risk) the financial institution is exposed to, showing the impact on profit or loss and equity. Details of the methods and assumptions used should be provided. If a sensitivity analysis, such as value-at-risk is prepared, that reflects interdependencies between risk variables (e.g. interest rates and exchange rates) and the financial institution uses such analysis to manage financial risks, it may use that sensitivity analysis instead. *[FRS 102.34.29-30].*

Capital

(xii) Information that enables users of the financial institution's financial statements to evaluate its objectives, policies and processes for managing capital.

(a)   qualitative information about its objectives, policies and processes for managing capital, including:

(1)   a description of what it manages as capital;

(2)   when the institution is subject to externally imposed capital requirements, the nature of those requirements and how those requirements are incorporated into the management of capital; and

(3)   how it is meeting its objectives for managing capital.

(b) summary quantitative data about what the financial institution manages as capital. Some regard some financial liabilities (e.g. some forms of subordinated debt) as part of capital. Others regard capital as excluding some components of equity (e.g. components arising from cash flow hedges);

(c) any changes in the above from the previous period;

(d) whether during the period the financial institution complied with any externally imposed capital requirements to which it is subject;

(e) when the financial institution has not complied with such externally imposed capital requirements, the consequences of such non-compliance.

A financial institution must base all these disclosures on the information provided internally to key management personnel. *[FRS 102.34.31].*

A financial institution may manage capital in a number of ways and be subject to a number of different capital requirements. For example, a conglomerate may include entities that undertake insurance activities and banking activities and those entities may operate in several jurisdictions. When an aggregate disclosure of capital requirements and how capital is managed would not provide useful information or would distort a financial statement user's understanding of the financial institution's capital resources, the financial institution should disclose separate information for each capital requirement to which the entity is subject. *[FRS 102.34.32].*

Reporting cash flows on a net basis

(xiii) Where a statement of cash flows is presented, cash flows arising from each of the following activities may be reported on a net basis:

(a) cash receipts and payments for the acceptance and repayment of deposits with a fixed maturity date;

(b) the placement of deposits with and withdrawal of deposits from other financial institutions; and

(c) cash advances and loans made to customers and the repayment of those advances and loans. *[FRS 102.34.33].*

11.2.5   Disclosures applicable to all entities reporting under UK company law

The Small Companies Regulations, the Regulations, the LLP (SC) and LLP Regulations require various disclosures in respect of financial instruments. Entities reporting under such regulations, including qualifying entities, will be required to disclose the following in addition to those discussed at 11.2.2 to 11.2.4 above:

(i) the amount of fixed asset or current asset investments ascribable to listed investments; *[1 Sch 54(1), 3 Sch 72]*

(ii) the aggregate amount of listed investments where this is different from the amount recorded in the financial statements (and both market value and stock exchange value if market value is higher); *[1 Sch 54(2)]*

The following must be disclosed where financial instruments are recorded at fair value:

(iii) significant assumptions underlying any valuation models and techniques used where the fair value has been determined using generally accepted valuation techniques and models; *[1 Sch 55(2)(a), 2 Sch 66(2)(a), 3 Sch 73(2)(a)]* (iv)　the purchase price, the items affected and the basis of valuation (insurers only); *[3 Sch 73(2)(b)]*

(v)　the fair value of each category of financial instrument and the changes in value reported in profit and loss or credited/debited to the fair value reserve; *[1 Sch 55(2)(b), 2 Sch 66(2)(b), 3 Sch 73(2)(c)]*

(vi)　for each class of derivatives, the extent and nature of the instruments including significant terms and conditions that may affect the amount, timing and uncertainty of future cash flows; *[1 Sch 55(2)(c), 2 Sch 66(2)(c), 3 Sch 73(2)(d)]*

(vii)　where any amount is transferred to or from the fair value reserve, there must be stated in tabular form, the amount of the reserve at the beginning and end of the reporting period, the amount transferred to/from the reserve in the year and the source and application of the amounts so transferred. *[1 Sch 55(3), 2 Sch 66(3), 3 Sch 72(3)]*.

We believe the disclosure requirements included in (iii) and (v) above will in most cases be satisfied by disclosure requirements in FRS 102 discussed at 11.2.2(ii), 11.2.2(iii) and 11.2.2(v) above.

In addition, entities should disclose:

(viii)　the fair values of any derivatives not included at fair value together with the extent and nature of the derivatives. *[1 Sch 56, 2 Sch 67, 3 Sch 74]*. This disclosure requirement would apply, for example, in the case of a derivative where the underlying investment is an equity instrument for which fair value cannot be reliably measured;

(ix)　the fair value of instruments that could be measured at fair value but are measured at a higher amount (i.e. amortised cost) and reasons for not making a provision for diminution in value, together with the evidence that provides a basis for recoverability of the amount in the financial statements; *[1 Sch 57, 2 Sch 68, 3 Sch 75]*

(x)　for each item within fixed assets, the balance at the beginning and end of the year, the effect of any revision of the amount in respect of any assets made during that year on any basis, acquisitions and disposals during that year, any transfers of fixed assets in and out of that item of the balance sheet; *[1 Sch 51, 2 Sch 62, 3 Sch 69]*

(xi)　for the aggregate of all items shown under 'creditors' in the company's balance sheet, the aggregate of the following amounts:

(a)　the amount of any debts which fall due after five years from the date of the balance sheet which are payable other than by instalments; and

(b)　the amount of any debts which are payable in instalments, the amount of any instalments which fall due for payment after the end of five years;

(c)　for each debt falling to be taken into account in (a) and (b) above, the terms of payment or repayment and the rate of any interest payable on the debt. If the number of debts is such that, in the opinion of the directors, compliance with this requirement would result in excessive length, it is sufficient to provide a general indication of the terms of payment or repayment and the rates of any interest payable on those debts. *[1 Sch 61, 3 Sch 79]*.

(xii)　if any debentures were issued during the year, the following information must be given:

(a)　the classes of debentures issued; and

(b)　the amount issued and the consideration received in respect of each class of debenture. *[1 Sch 50, 2 Sch 61, 3 Sch 68]*.

12   SUMMARY OF GAAP DIFFERENCES

The following table shows the differences between FRS 102 and IFRS.

	FRS 102	*IFRS 9/IAS 32/IAS 39*
Definitions	Fair value is defined as the amount for which an asset could be exchanged, *a liability settled*, or an equity instrument granted could be exchanged, between knowledgeable, willing parties in an arm's length transaction.	Fair value is defined as the price that would be received to sell an asset *or paid to transfer a liability* in an orderly transaction between market participants at the measurement date.
Liabilities and equity	Similar principle to IFRS but less guidance. A contractual obligation to purchase own equity instruments for cash or another financial asset is considered to be a derivative. Contracts to exchange a fixed amount of equity instrument for a fixed amount of foreign currency could be classified as a liability or equity depending on interpretation.	IAS 32 requires a contractual obligation to purchase own equity instruments for cash or another financial asset to be measured at the present value of the gross redemption amount. Contracts to exchange a fixed amount of equity instrument for a fixed amount of foreign currency are classified as a liability.
Accounting policy choice	• Option to apply the recognition and measurement requirements of Sections 11 and 12, IAS 39 or IFRS 9. No matter the option chosen, entities must apply disclosure requirements of Sections 11 and 12	• Option to apply hedge accounting requirements of IAS 39 in full
Classification and Measurement	• Instruments are classified as basic or other. • All basic instruments other than investments in equity instruments are carried at amortised cost or cost less impairment. • Investments in equity instruments and all other instruments must be carried at fair value, except when not reliably measured or prohibited by law. • No concept of held for trading, thus, such instruments could theoretically be measured at amortised cost unless the fair value option is elected. • No concept of fair value through other comprehensive income.	• Under IFRS 9, classification of financial assets is based on a contractual characteristics test and business model test leading to the following classifications: 1. Amortised cost 2. Fair value through OCI (with or without recycling) 3. Fair value through profit or loss • Financial liabilities can be carried at amortised cost, although the fair value option is available under certain circumstances (and for financial assets but in more restricted circumstances). • Changes in fair value due to own credit risk of financial liabilities designated at fair value are recognised through OCI.

Derivatives	No concept of embedded derivatives. Derivatives recognised and measured at fair value through profit or loss.	Derivatives and certain embedded derivatives in financial liabilities or non-financial items are recognised and measured at fair value through profit or loss.
Impairment	Incurred loss model with assessment of objective evidence of impairment. Credit losses for impaired assets calculated based on present value of discounted cash flows.	IFRS 9 is an expected loss model. Recognition of 12-month expected credit loss until there is a significant increase in credit risk at which point life time expected losses are recognised.
Derecognition	Similar principles to IFRS but less guidance. No concept of 'continuing involvement' or 'pass through' unlike IFRS 9.	Complex rules.
Disclosures	Disclosures as set out in Sections 11 and 12 and additional disclosures if considered a financial institution (Section 34).	Extensive disclosures (IFRS 7 and IFRS 13).
Hedge accounting	Similar principles to IFRS 9 but simpler. Does not include rebalancing, aggregated exposures or costs of hedging.	IAS 39: Rules based standard IFRS 9: Uses IAS 39 as the basis for the mechanics of hedge accounting, but more principled approach with additional features such as rebalancing, aggregated exposures and costs of hedging.
Hedged items – risk components	Risk components permitted for financial and non-financial instruments.	IAS 39: Only for financial items. IFRS 9: Similar to FRS 102.
Hedging instruments – non derivatives	Based on simplified version of IFRS 9. Non-derivative financial assets or liabilities at FVTPL are eligible as hedging instruments.	IAS 39: Non-derivatives may be hedging instruments only for FX risks. IFRS 9: Similar to FRS 102.
Hedge effectiveness assessment	Prospective only, a simpler version of IFRS 9 approach, could be qualitative in many instances	IAS 39: A quantitative retrospective and prospective test is required (80%-125%). IFRS 9: Prospective assessment only, likely to be qualitative in many instances.

Chapter 11 — Inventories

List of examples

Chapter 11   Inventories

1   INTRODUCTION

Section 13 of FRS 102 – *Inventories* – addresses the measurement and disclosure requirements for inventories.

There were no changes to the recognition or measurement requirements of Section 13 as a result of *Amendments to FRS 102 Triennial review 2017 – Incremental improvements and clarifications (Triennial review 2017)*. There was, however, a change to the disclosure requirement. See 3.6.2 below.

The principles of Section 13 are broadly consistent with IFRS.

2   COMPARISON BETWEEN SECTION 13 AND IFRS

The accounting for inventories under IFRS is addressed by IAS 2 – *Inventories*. Section 13 and IAS 2 both use the principle that the primary basis of accounting for inventories is cost unless the amount that the inventories are expected to realise is lower than cost. Where this is the case, the inventories are written down to that amount.

Generally under Section 13 and IAS 2, the cost of inventories comprises all costs of purchase and costs of conversion based on normal levels of activity and other costs incurred in bringing inventories to their present location and condition.

Both accounting frameworks allow the use of costing methods, such as standard costing, provided they approximate to cost.

There are, however, some areas of potential difference between the frameworks in accounting for inventories. These differences mainly arise where more specific requirements are contained within IAS 2 than are provided under Section 13. These areas are summarised at 4 below.

3   REQUIREMENTS OF SECTION 13 FOR INVENTORIES

3.1   Terms used in Section 13

The following terms are used in Section 13 with the meanings specified. *[FRS 102 Appendix I].*

Term	Definition
Asset	A resource controlled by the entity as a result of past events and from which future economic benefits are expected to flow to the entity.
Fair value	The amount for which an asset could be exchanged, a liability settled, or an equity instrument granted could be exchanged, between knowledgeable, willing parties in an arm's length transaction. In the absence of any guidance provided in the relevant section of FRS 102, the guidance in the Appendix to Section 2 – *Concepts and Pervasive Principles* – shall be used.
Fair value less costs to sell	The amount obtainable from the sale of an asset or cash-generating unit in an arm's length transaction between knowledgeable, willing parties, less the costs of disposal.
Inventories	Assets: (a) held for sale in the ordinary course of business; (b) in the process of production for such sale; or (c) in the form of materials or supplies to be consumed in the production process or in the rendering of services.
Inventories held for distribution at no or nominal consideration	Assets that are: (a) held for distribution at no or nominal consideration in the ordinary course of operations; (b) in the process of production for distribution at no or nominal consideration in the ordinary course of operations; or (c) in the form of material or supplies to be consumed in the production process or in the rendering of services at no or nominal consideration.
Non-exchange transaction	A transaction whereby an entity receives value from another entity without directly giving approximately equal value in exchange, or gives value to another entity without directly receiving approximately equal value in exchange.
Public benefit entity	An entity whose primary objective is to provide goods or services for the general public, community or social benefit and where any equity is provided with a view to supporting the entity's primary objectives rather than with a view to providing a financial return to equity providers, shareholders or members.
Public benefit entity group	A public benefit entity parent and all of its wholly-owned subsidiaries.
Qualifying asset	An asset that necessarily takes a substantial period of time to get ready for its intended use or sale.
Service potential	The capacity to provide services that contribute to achieving an entity's objectives. Service potential enables an entity to achieve its objectives without necessarily generating net cash inflows.

3.2 Scope

Inventories are assets: *[FRS 102 Appendix I]*

(a)   held for sale in the ordinary course of business;

(b)   in the process of production or sale; or

(c)   in the form of materials or supplies to be consumed in the production process or in the rendering of services.

Inventories can include all types of goods purchased and held for resale including, for example, merchandise purchased by a retailer. The term also encompasses finished goods produced, or work in progress being produced by the entity, and includes materials and supplies awaiting use in the production process. If the entity is a service provider, its inventories may be intangible (e.g. the costs of the service for which the entity has not yet recognised the related revenue).

Section 13 applies to all inventories, except: *[FRS 102.13.2]*

(a)   work in progress arising under construction contracts, including directly related service contracts (addressed in Section 23 – *Revenue* – see Chapter 20);

(b)   financial instruments (addressed in Section 11 – *Basic Financial Instruments* – and Section 12 – *Other Financial Instruments Issues* – see Chapter 10); and

(c)   biological assets related to agricultural activity and agricultural produce at the point of harvest (addressed in Section 34 – *Specialised Activities* – see Chapter 31).

In addition, the measurement provisions of Section 13 do not apply to inventories measured at fair value less costs to sell through profit and loss at each reporting date. *[FRS 102.13.3]*. Although these inventories are scoped out of the measurement requirements of Section 13, the disclosure requirements of Section 13 continue to apply.

Section 13 states that inventories should not be measured at fair value less costs to sell unless it is a more relevant measure of the entity's performance (i.e. more relevant than cost and estimated selling price less costs to complete and sell) because the entity operates in an active market where sale can be achieved at published prices, and inventory is a store of readily realisable value. *[FRS 102.13.3]*. 'Relevance' will be judged by the criteria in Section 2 and is discussed in Chapter 4 at 3.2.2. Measuring inventories at fair value less costs to sell is permitted by company law. *[1 Sch 39, 1 Sch 39 (LLP)]*. However, the Regulations (and LLP Regulations) do not specify how changes in the fair value of stocks are recognised under the fair value accounting rules. Section 13 requires that fair value movements are recognised in profit or loss on inventories measured at fair value less costs to sell. Although the Regulations require that that only profits realised at the balance sheet date are to be included in the profit and loss account, *[1 Sch 13, 1 Sch 13 (LLP)]*, the measurement of inventory at fair value less costs to sell through profit or loss is permitted only where the entity operates in an active market, where sale can be achieved at published prices, and inventory is a store of readily realisable value, *[FRS 102.13.3]*, and therefore would not require the use of a true and fair override.

The criteria for the use of measurement at fair value less costs in Section 2 of FRS 102 described above is different from that contained in IAS 2 which is limited to certain types of inventories (e.g. agricultural produce and inventories held by commodity broker-traders). *[IAS 2.3]*. In addition, IAS 2 does not contain a requirement that an entity operates in an active market or that inventory is a store of readily realisable value for fair value measurement to be applied.

3.2.1   Scope and recognition issues

For entities operating in some industries, it may not always be clear whether certain assets fall in scope of Section 13 or are covered by another section of FRS 102. Scope issues that entities may encounter include:

- classification of core inventories as property, plant and equipment or inventory. Core inventories arise in industries where certain processes or storage arrangements require a core of inventory to be present in the system at all times. For example, in order for a crude oil refining process to take place, the plant must contain a certain minimum quantity of oil which can only be taken out once the plant is abandoned;

- classification of broadcast rights as intangible assets or inventory;

- classification of emission rights as intangible assets or inventory; and

- classification of crypto-currencies.

These scope issues are discussed at Chapter 22 of EY International GAAP 2019.

3.2.1.A   Spare parts

Many entities carry spare parts for items of property, plant and equipment. Section 17 – *Property, Plant and Equipment* – requires that spare parts, stand-by equipment and servicing equipment are recognised as property, plant and equipment if they meet the definition of property, plant and equipment; *[FRS 102.17.5]* that is, they are tangible assets that:

(a)   are held for use in the production or supply of goods or services, for rental to others, or for administrative purposes; and

(b)   are expected to be used during more than one period. *[FRS 102 Appendix I]*.

Otherwise, such items are classified as inventory. *[FRS 102.17.5]*.

There are, of course, practical considerations when determining whether major spare parts should be classified as inventory or property, plant and equipment and these considerations are discussed further at 3.3.1.A of Chapter 15.

3.2.1.B   Real estate inventory held for short term sale

Many real estate businesses develop and construct residential properties for sale, often consisting of several units. The strategy is to make a profit from the development and construction of the property rather than to make a profit in the long term from general price increases in the property market. The intention is to sell the property units as soon as possible following their construction, and is therefore in the ordinary course of the entity's business. When construction is complete it is not uncommon for individual property units to be leased at market rates to earn revenues to partly cover expenses such as interest, management fees and real estate taxes. Large-scale buyers of property, such as insurance companies, are often reluctant to buy unless tenants are *in situ*, as this assures immediate cash flows from the investment.

It is our view that if it is in the entity's ordinary course of business (supported by its strategy) to hold property for short-term sale rather than for long-term capital appreciation or rental income, the entire property (including the leased units) should be accounted for and presented as inventory. This will continue to be the case as long as it remains the intention to sell the property in the short term. Rent received should be included in other income as it does not represent a reduction in the cost of inventory.

Investment property, which is accounted for under Section 16 – *Investment Property* – is defined as 'property (land or a building, or part of a building, or both) held by the owner or by the lessee under a finance lease to earn rentals or for capital appreciation or both, rather than for: (a) use in the production or supply of goods or services or for administrative purposes; or (b) for sale in the ordinary course of business'. *[FRS 102 Appendix I]*. Therefore in the case outlined above, the property does not meet the definition of investment property. Properties intended for sale in the ordinary course of business – no matter whether leased out or not – are outside the scope of Section 16.

The accounting for real estate inventory is discussed in Chapter 22 of EY International GAAP 2019.

3.2.1.C   Consignment stock

A seller may enter into an arrangement with a distributor where the distributor sells inventory on behalf of the seller. Such consignment arrangements are common in certain industries, such as the automotive industry. Under Section 23 – *Revenue* – the seller would recognise revenue only when the goods are sold by the distributor to a third party. *[FRS 102.23A.6]*.

Similarly, entities may enter into sale and repurchase agreements with a customer where the seller agrees to repurchase inventory under particular circumstances. For example, a seller may agree to repurchase any inventory that the customer has not sold to a third party after six months.

Section 13 provides no specific guidance on the recognition or derecognition of inventory subject to consignment or similar arrangements. Entities should therefore use judgement in developing an appropriate and consistent accounting policy for recognising and derecognising consignment inventory that reflects the commercial substance of these transactions. *[FRS 102.10.4-6]*.

3.3   Measurement

Inventories in scope of the measurement provisions of Section 13 should be measured at the lower of cost and estimated selling price less costs to complete and sell. *[FRS 102.13.4]*.

3.3.1   What is included in the cost of inventories?

The cost of inventories should include all costs of purchase, costs of conversion and other costs incurred in bringing inventories to their present location and condition. *[FRS 102.13.5]*.

Other costs should be included in the cost of inventories only to the extent that they are incurred in bringing them into their present location and condition. *[FRS 102.13.11]*. For example, design costs for a special order for a particular customer may be included in inventory.

3.3.2   Costs of purchase of inventories

The cost of purchase of inventories comprises the purchase price, transport, handling and other costs directly attributable to the acquisition of finished goods, materials and services. It also includes import duties and other unrecoverable taxes. Trade discounts, rebates and other similar items should be deducted in arriving at the cost of purchase. *[FRS 102.13.6]*.

Entities sometimes purchase inventories on deferred settlement terms. In some cases, the arrangement contains an unstated financing element, for example, a difference between the purchase price for normal credit terms and the deferred settlement amount. In these cases, the difference is usually recognised as an interest expense over the period of the financing. It is not added to the cost of inventories unless the inventory is a qualifying asset under Section 25 – *Borrowing Costs* – and the entity adopts a policy of capitalising finance costs. *[FRS 102.13.7]*. Inventories manufactured over a short period of time are not qualifying assets. Only inventories produced in small quantities over a long time period of time are likely to be qualifying assets under Section 25. Qualifying assets are discussed further in Chapter 22.

3.3.3   Costs of conversion

The cost of conversion of inventories includes costs directly related to the units of production, such as direct labour. It also includes a systematic allocation of the fixed and variable production overheads that are incurred in converting materials into finished goods. Fixed production overheads are those indirect costs of production that remain relatively constant regardless of the volume of production, such as depreciation and maintenance of factory buildings and equipment, and the cost of factory management and administration. Variable production overheads are those indirect costs of production that vary directly, or nearly directly, with the volume of production, such as indirect materials and indirect labour. *[FRS 102.13.8]*. It must be remembered that the inclusion of overheads is not optional.

The allocation of fixed production overheads should be based on the normal capacity of the production facilities. Normal capacity is defined as 'the production expected to be achieved on average over a number of periods or seasons under normal circumstances, taking into account the loss of capacity resulting from planned maintenance.' While actual capacity may be used if it approximates to normal capacity, increased overheads may not be allocated to production as a result of low production or idle plant. Unallocated overheads must be recognised as an expense in the period in which they are incurred. In periods of abnormally high production, the amount of fixed overhead allocated to each unit of production is decreased, as otherwise inventories would be recorded at an amount in excess of cost. *[FRS 102.13.9]*.

The allocation of variable production overheads should be based on the actual use of the production facilities in the period. *[FRS 102.13.9]*.

Some entities may have an obligation to dismantle, remove and restore a production site at some future date. For example, mining companies may have obligations to decommission mines and rehabilitate the impacted area on closure of the mine. Although provisions for such obligations are not specifically addressed by Section 21 – *Provisions and Contingencies*, the recognition criteria within Section 21 may require entities to record a provision for these obligations. If the obligation arises as a result of production of inventory during the period, costs in respect of the obligation incurred during the period (measured in accordance with Section 21) should be included within production overheads to be allocated to the cost of inventories. *[FRS 102.13.8A]*. The estimated costs to dismantle, remove and restore a site which arise either when an item of property, plant or equipment is acquired or as a consequence of having used the property, plant or equipment for purposes other than to produce inventories during the period should be recognised as part of the cost of that item of property, plant and equipment. *[FRS 102.17.10]*.

Example 11.1:   Inclusion of costs for obligations within production overheads

An entity operates an offshore oilfield where its licensing agreement requires it to remove the oil rig at the end of production and restore the seabed. Ninety per cent of the eventual costs relate to the removal of the oil rig and restoration of damage caused by building it. Ten per cent of the eventual costs arise from the extraction of oil. The ten per cent of costs that arise through the extraction of oil are recognised as a liability when the oil is extracted. The amount of the additional provision recognised each year as a result of the extraction of oil should be part of the production overheads to be allocated to the cost of inventory. The ninety percent of costs that relate to the removal of the oil rig and restoration of damage caused by building it would be recognised as part of the cost of the oil rig.

3.3.4   Costs excluded from inventories

The following are examples of costs that should not be included in the cost of inventories: *[FRS 102.13.13]*

(a)   abnormal amounts of wasted materials, labour or other production costs;

(b)   storage costs, unless those costs are necessary during the production process before a further production stage;

(c)   administrative overheads that do not contribute to bringing inventories to their present location and condition; and

(d)   selling costs.

These costs should be recognised as expenses in the period in which they are incurred.

3.3.5   Storage and distribution costs

Storage costs are not permitted to be included in the cost of inventories unless they are necessary in the production process. This appears to prohibit including the costs of the warehouse and the overheads of a retail outlet as part of inventory, as neither of these is a prelude to a further production stage.

When it is necessary to store raw materials or work in progress prior to a further processing or manufacturing stage, the cost of such storage should be included in production overheads. For example, it would appear reasonable to allow the costs of storing maturing stocks, such as cheese, wine or whisky, in the cost of production.

Although distribution costs in the general sense are obviously a cost of bringing an item to its present location, company law prohibits them from being added to the cost of stock. However, the Regulations do not define distribution costs. *[1 Sch 27(4)]*. The question therefore arises as to whether costs of transporting inventory from one location to another are eligible.

Costs of distribution to the customer are not allowed; they are selling costs and FRS 102 prohibits their inclusion in the carrying value of inventory. *[FRS 102.13.13(d)]*. It therefore seems probable that distribution costs of inventory whose production process is complete should not normally be included in its carrying value.

If the inventory is transferred from one of the entity's storage facilities to another and the condition of the inventory is not changed at either location, none of the warehousing costs should be included in inventory costs. The same argument appears to preclude transportation costs between the two storage facilities being included in inventory costs.

For large retailers, such as supermarkets, transport and logistics are essential to their ability to move goods from central distribution centres to initial points of sale at a particular location in an appropriate condition. It therefore seems reasonable to conclude that such costs are an essential part of the production process and can be included in the cost of inventory.

3.3.6   General and administrative overheads

FRS 102 specifically prohibits administrative overheads that do not contribute to bringing inventories to their present location and condition from being included in the cost of inventories. *[FRS 102.13.13(c)]*. Costs and overheads that do contribute should be included in costs of conversion. There is a judgement to be made about such matters, as on a very wide interpretation, any department in an entity could be considered to make a contribution to inventories. For example, the accounts department will normally support the following functions:

- production – by paying direct and indirect production wages and salaries, by controlling purchases and related payments, and by preparing periodic financial statements for the production units;
- marketing and distribution – by analysing sales and by controlling the sales ledger; and
- general administration – by preparing management accounts and annual financial statements and budgets, by controlling cash resources and by planning investments.

Only those costs of the accounts department that can be reasonably allocated to the production function can be included in the cost of conversion. Part of the management and overhead costs of a large retailer's logistical department may be included in cost if it relates to bringing the inventory to its present location and condition. These types of cost are unlikely to be material in the context of the inventory total held by organisations. In our view, an entity wishing to include a material amount of overhead of a borderline nature must ensure it can sensibly justify its inclusion under the provisions of FRS 102 by presenting an analysis of the function and its contribution to the production process similar to the bulleted section above.

3.3.7   Borrowing costs

In limited circumstances, borrowing costs may be included in the cost of inventories. Section 25 allows entities to adopt an accounting policy of capitalising borrowing costs that are directly attributable to the acquisition, construction or production of a qualifying asset as part of the cost of that asset. *[FRS 102.25.2]*. Qualifying assets are assets that necessarily take a substantial period of time to get ready for their intended use or sale, and may include inventories. *[FRS 102 Appendix I]*. Inventories that are manufactured in large quantities on a repetitive basis are unlikely to meet the definition of qualifying assets. However, any manufacturer that produces small quantities of inventories over a long period of time will have an accounting policy choice as to whether to include borrowing costs in the cost of these inventories. This is discussed further in Chapter 22.

3.3.8   *Inventories acquired through a non-exchange transaction*

Entities may sometimes enter into non-exchange transactions whereby the entity gives value to or receives value from another entity without directly receiving or giving approximately equal value in exchange. *[FRS 102 Appendix I]*.

Where inventories are acquired through a non-exchange transaction, their cost should be measured at their fair value as at the date of acquisition. *[FRS 102.13.5A]*. For entities other than public benefit entities, the fair value of inventories acquired through a non-exchange transaction should be determined by reference to the guidance in the Appendix to Section 2, which is discussed in Chapter 4.

For public benefit entities and entities within a public benefit entity group, Section 34 and the related Appendix B provide additional guidance on non-exchange transactions. As part of their normal business operations, public benefit entities may receive donations of cash, goods and services, and legacies which would meet the definition of non-exchange transactions. Public benefit entities and entities within a public benefit entity group should recognise inventories acquired through a non-exchange transaction at fair value only when required by Section 34. *[FRS 102.13.5A]*. Accounting for non-exchange transactions by public benefit entities and entities within a public benefit entity group is discussed further in Chapter 31 at 6.

3.3.9   *Joint products and by-products*

A production process may result in more than one product being produced simultaneously, for example when joint products are produced or where there is a main product and a by-product. If the costs of raw materials or converting each product are not separately identifiable, they should be allocated between the products on a rational and consistent basis. This may be, for example, based on the relative sales value of each of the products, either at the stage in the production process when the products become separately identifiable, or once production is complete. If the value of the by-product is immaterial, as is often the case, it should be measured at selling price less costs to complete and sell, with this amount then deducted from the cost of the main product. *[FRS 102.13.10]*.

3.3.10   *Service providers*

FRS 102 deals specifically with the inventories of service providers – effectively their work in progress. For this type of business, FRS 102 requires the labour and other costs of personnel directly engaged in providing the service, including supervisory personnel and attributable overheads, to be included in the costs of inventories. However, labour and other costs relating to sales and general administrative personnel must be expensed as incurred. Inventories should not include profit margins or non-attributable overheads. *[FRS 102.13.14]*.

As discussed at 3.3.3 above, FRS 102 requires attributable overheads to be allocated to the cost of inventories based on normal levels of capacity. Determining a normal level of activity may be difficult in the context of service industries where the 'inventory' is intangible and based on work performed for customers that has not yet been recognised as income. Entities must take care to establish an appropriate benchmark to avoid the distortions that could occur if overheads were attributed on the basis of actual 'output'.

Chapter 11

3.3.11   Inventories held for distribution at no or nominal consideration

Inventories held for distribution at no or nominal consideration includes items such as advertising and promotional material, and also items that may be distributed to beneficiaries by public benefit entities. *[FRS 102 Appendix III.36].*

FRS 102 requires inventories held for distribution at no or nominal consideration to be measured at the lower of cost adjusted, when applicable, for any loss of service potential and replacement cost. *[FRS 102.13.4A].*

IFRS requires advertising and promotional activities to be expensed as incurred, unless the entity has paid in advance for advertising goods or services that have not yet been made available to the entity, in which case a prepayment asset is recognised. *[IAS 38.69-70].* In contrast, FRS 102 requires advertising and promotional material (being inventory held for distribution at no or nominal value) to be carried at the lower of cost (adjusted for any loss of service potential) and replacement cost. *[FRS 102.13.4A].* FRS 102 provides no further guidance on how, or at what unit of account, service potential should be measured. It does not specify whether this should be at the individual asset level (e.g. the extent to which an individual catalogue is expected to generate future revenue for the entity) or based on a class of promotional material (e.g. the extent to which all catalogues printed for a particular year / season are expected to generate future revenue for the entity). In our view, an entity wishing to recognise a material inventory balance for advertising and promotional expenditure must ensure that it can sensibly justify how the entity will derive future benefit from the use of the materials.

The measurement basis described above (i.e. lower of cost adjusted for loss of service potential and replacement cost) is an application of fair value accounting as permitted by Schedule 1 to the Regulations, however for inventories held for distribution at no or nominal value (particularly items distributed to beneficiaries by public benefit entities) there is unlikely to be a significant difference between replacement cost and fair value. *[FRS 102 Appendix III.37].*

The carrying amount of inventories held for distribution at no or nominal consideration should be recognised as an expense when the inventories are distributed. *[FRS 102.13.20A].*

3.3.12   Agricultural produce harvested from biological assets

Inventories comprising agricultural produce that an entity has harvested from its biological assets should be measured on initial recognition, at the point of harvest, at either: *[FRS 102.13.15]*

- their fair value less estimated costs to sell; or
- the lower of cost and estimated selling price less costs to complete and sell.

For the purposes of applying Section 13, this amount becomes the cost of the inventories at that date.

3.3.13   Cost measurement methods

FRS 102 allows the use of standard costing methods, the retail method or most recent purchase price for measuring the cost of inventories if the result approximates cost. *[FRS 102.13.16]*.

Standard costs should take into account normal levels of materials and supplies, labour, efficiency and capital utilisation. They must be reviewed regularly and revised where necessary. *[FRS 102.13.16]*.

The retail method measures cost by reducing the sales value of the inventory by the appropriate percentage gross margin. This method is typically used in businesses with high volumes of various line items of inventory, where similar marks-ups are applied to ranges of inventory items or groups of items. It may be unnecessarily time-consuming to determine the cost of the period-end inventory on a conventional basis. Consequently, the most practical method of determining period-end inventory may be to record inventory on hand at selling prices, and then convert it to cost by removing the normal mark-up.

A judgemental area in applying the retail method is in determining the margin to be removed from the selling price of inventory in order to convert it back to cost. The percentage has to take account of circumstances in which inventories have been marked down to below original selling price. Adjustments have to be made to eliminate the effect of these markdowns so as to prevent any item of inventory being valued at less than both its cost and its net realisable value. In practice, however, entities that use the retail method apply a gross profit margin computed on an average basis appropriate for departments and/or ranges, rather than applying specific mark-up percentages.

As noted above, FRS 102 also allows the use of the most recent purchase price as a cost measurement method. This method arrives at the cost of stock by applying the latest purchase price to the total number of units in stock. IAS 2 is silent on the use of this methodology. In practice, the use of the most recent purchase price is not a common method of measuring the cost of inventory. Where it is used, care should be taken to ensure that the result does approximate to the actual cost of inventories.

Items of inventory that are not interchangeable (i.e. where one item of inventory cannot easily be replaced with another item of inventory held by the entity) and goods or services produced and segregated for specific projects should have their costs specifically identified. *[FRS 102.13.17]*. These costs should be matched with the goods or services physically sold. Due to the clerical effort required, this is likely to be feasible only where there are relatively few high value items being bought or produced. Consequently, it would normally be used where inventory comprised items such as antiques, jewellery and vehicles in the hands of dealers.

Chapter 11

When inventory comprises a large number of ordinarily interchangeable items, FRS 102 requires inventory to be measured using either a first-in, first-out (FIFO) or a weighted average cost formula. *[FRS 102.13.18]*. The FIFO method assumes that when inventories are sold or used in a production process, the oldest are sold or used first. Consequently, the balance of inventory on hand at any point represents the most recent purchases or production. The weighted average method involves the computation of an average unit cost by dividing the total cost of units by the total number of units. The average unit cost then has to be revised with every receipt of inventory, or at the end of predetermined periods. In practice, where it is not possible to value inventory on an actual costs basis, the FIFO method is generally used. However, the weighted average method is widely used in computerised inventory systems. In times of low inflation, or where inventory turnover is relatively quick, the FIFO and weighted average methods give similar results.

The last-in, first-out (LIFO) method of measuring the cost of inventory is not permitted by FRS 102. *[FRS 102.13.18]*. The LIFO method assumes that when inventories are sold or used in a production process, the most recent purchases are sold or used first. This method is an attempt to match current costs with current revenues so that the profit and loss account excludes the effects of holding gains. However, this results in inventories being stated on balance sheet at amounts which may bear little or no relationship to recent cost levels.

FRS 102 makes it clear that the same cost formula should be used for all inventories having a similar nature and use to the entity. However, different cost formulas may be justified for inventories with a different nature or use. *[FRS 102.13.18]*.

3.3.14   Additional company law considerations

As an alternative to the historical cost accounting rules set out above, the Regulations allow that where materials and consumables inventories are of a kind that are constantly being replaced they may be recorded at a fixed quantity and value if: *[1 Sch 26, 1 Sch 26 (LLP)]*

- their overall value is not material to the company; and
- their quality, value and composition are not subject to material variation.

This treatment is not generally permitted by Section 13 and would be appropriate only if the result approximated the cost of inventories as determined by applying the measurement requirements of Section 13.

3.4   Impairment of inventories

In accordance with the requirements of Section 27 – *Impairment of Assets*, entities should assess inventories for impairment at the end of each reporting period. Inventories are impaired if their carrying value exceeds their selling price less costs to complete and sell. Inventories may become impaired due to damage, obsolescence or declining selling prices. Where inventories are impaired, the carrying amount should be written down to selling price less costs to complete and sell. *[FRS 102.13.19]*. The reduction in carrying value is an impairment loss and should be recognised immediately in profit or loss. *[FRS 102.27.2]*.

Assessing inventories for impairment should normally be done on an item-by-item basis. However, in many circumstances it will be impracticable to determine the selling price less costs to complete and sell on this basis. Where this is the case, items of inventory may be grouped. This may be the case for items of inventory relating to the same product line that have similar purposes or end uses and are produced and marketed in the same geographical area. *[FRS 102.27.3]*.

3.4.1   *Selling price less costs to complete and sell*

Section 32 – *Events after the End of the Reporting Period* – states that 'the sale of inventories after the end of a reporting period may give evidence about their selling price at the end of the reporting period for the purpose of assessing impairment at that date.' *[FRS 102.32.5(b)(ii)]*. Events that have impacted selling prices after the end of the reporting period, such as damage to inventories as a result of a warehouse fire post year end, would not be relevant to the assessment of impairment at end of the reporting period. Other than this, FRS 102 gives no guidance on how to determine selling price or what costs should be included when assessing costs to complete and sell.

The requirement to measure inventories at the lower of cost and selling price less costs to complete and sell under FRS 102 is similar to the requirement under IFRS to carry inventories at the lower of cost and net realisable value. Entities may therefore choose to look to IFRS for further guidance in this area.

IFRS defines net realisable value as 'the estimated selling price in the ordinary course of business less the estimated costs of completion and the estimated costs necessary to make the sale.' *[IAS 2.6]*.

IFRS is explicit that materials and other supplies held for use in the production of inventories are not written down below cost if the final product in which they are to be used is expected to be sold at or above cost. *[IAS 2.32]*. Whilst this is not explicit in FRS 102, we consider that this is consistent with the measurement principle of FRS 102. As such, we would not expect a whisky distiller, for example, to write down an inventory of grain because of a fall in the grain price, so long as it expected to sell the whisky at a price sufficient to recover cost. Conversely, if a provision is required in respect of finished goods, then work in progress and raw materials should also be reviewed to see if any further provision is required.

In estimating net realisable value, IFRS requires that entities should take into consideration the purpose for which inventory is held. For example, the net realisable value of inventory held to satisfy firm sales contracts is based on that contract price. *[IAS 2.31]*. This reflects the fact that net realisable value, unlike fair value, is an entity specific value. In our view, selling price less costs to complete and sell is also an entity specific measure intended to reflect the amount that the entity actually expects to make from selling particular inventories.

In our view, costs to complete and sell should comprise only direct and incremental costs to complete and sell the inventory and should not include any profit margin on these activities. They should also not include overheads or the costs of the distribution channel, such as shops, since these costs will be incurred regardless of whether or not any sale of this inventory actually takes place. The only situation in which the cost of a shop might be considered to be included in these selling costs might be when one shop is entirely dedicated to selling impaired goods.

Chapter 11

3.4.2   *Reversal of impairment of inventory*

As noted at 3.4 above, FRS 102 requires entities to assess inventories for impairment at the end of each reporting period. When the circumstances that previously caused inventories to be written down no longer exist, or when there is clear evidence of an increase in selling price less costs to complete and sell because of changed economic circumstances, the amount of the write down is reversed. The amount of the reversal cannot be greater than the amount of the original write down. This means that the new carrying amount of inventories following the reversal of an impairment will be the lower of its cost and the revised selling price less costs to complete and sell. *[FRS 102.27.4]*.

3.5   Recognition of inventory in profit or loss

When inventories are sold, the carrying amount of those inventories should be recognised as an expense in the period in which the related revenue is recognised. *[FRS 102.13.20]*.

However, some inventories go into the creation of another asset, such as self-constructed property, plant or equipment. In this case, the inventories form part of the cost of the other asset and are accounted for subsequently in accordance with the section of FRS 102 relevant to that asset type. *[FRS 102.13.21]*.

Any impairment loss on inventory should be recognised immediately as an expense in profit or loss. *[FRS 102.27.2]*.

The carrying amount of inventories held for distribution at no or nominal consideration (as discussed at 3.3.11 above) is recognised as an expense when the inventories are distributed. *[FRS 102.13.20A]*.

3.6   Presentation and disclosure

3.6.1   *Presentation of inventories*

As discussed in Chapter 6 at 5, UK companies and qualifying partnerships applying Schedule 1 to the Regulations are permitted to use 'adapted formats' as an alternative to the statutory formats as set out in section B of Part 1 of Schedule 1. FRS 102's presentation requirements for adapted formats are similar but not identical to formats included in IAS 1 – *Presentation of Financial Statements*. The two alternatives are set out below.

Where entities apply the statutory balance sheet formats, they are required by Schedule 1 to the Regulations to present inventories on the face of the balance sheet. Inventories should be further analysed, either on the face of the balance sheet or within the notes to the accounts, into:

- raw materials and consumables;
- work in progress;
- finished goods and goods for resale; and
- payments on account.

The classifications used in the disaggregation may be adapted dependent upon the nature of the company's business. *[1 Sch 4(1)]*. In practice, most companies present the disaggregation as a note to the financial statements.

Where 'adapted formats' are used, FRS 102 requires that inventories are shown on the face of the balance sheet. *[FRS 102.4.2A]*. Inventories should be further analysed, either in the statement of financial position or the notes, between amounts of inventories: *[FRS 102.4.2B]*

- held for sale in the ordinary course of business;
- in the process of production for such sale; and
- in the form of materials or supplies to be consumed in the production process or in the rendering of services.

3.6.2   Disclosure of inventories

FRS 102 requires an entity to disclose the following: *[FRS 102.13.22]*

- the accounting policies adopted in measuring inventories, including the cost formula used;
- the total carrying amount of inventories and the carrying amount in classifications appropriate to the entity;
- impairment losses recognised or reversed in profit or loss in accordance with Section 27 (see Chapter 24); and
- the total carrying amount of inventories pledged as security for liabilities.

The Triennial review 2017 removed the requirement to disclose the amount of inventories recognise as an expense in the period.

The disclosure requirements of FRS 102 are similar to those required by IFRS, although IAS 2 also contains additional disclosure requirements not replicated in Section 13.

Where an entity has included borrowing costs in cost of inventories (see 3.3.7 above), the disclosure requirements of Section 25 will also be relevant. See Chapter 22 at 3.7.

3.6.2.A   Additional company law disclosures

The Regulations includes the following additional disclosure requirements with respect to inventories:

- if finance costs are included in the cost of inventory, this fact, along with the amount included; *[1 Sch 27(3)]*
- for large and medium companies where a costing method (such as FIFO, weighted average price or similar) has been applied, the difference between carrying value and replacement cost of inventories where this is material. *[1 Sch 28(3)]*. This may be determined by reference to the most recent purchase or production cost before the balance sheet date if this is considered by the directors of the company to give a more appropriate comparison; *[1 Sch 28(5)]* and
- where there has been a departure from the historical cost convention, the fact that this is the case, the balances affected and the basis of valuation adopted. *[1 Sch 34]*.

4   SUMMARY OF GAAP DIFFERENCES

The following table shows the differences between FRS 102 and IFRS.

	FRS 102	*IFRS*
Scope	Section 13 applies to inventories other than work in progress under construction contracts, financial instruments and biological assets related to agricultural activity and agricultural produce at the point of harvest. The measurement rules of Section 13 also exclude inventories measured at fair value less costs to sell through profit or loss. See 3.2 above.	IAS 2 is similar to FRS 102 although there is a specific exclusion for commodity broker-dealers who measure inventories at fair value through profit or loss rather than a general exclusion for inventories measured in this way. In addition, IAS 2 does not explicitly exclude from its scope work in progress arising under construction contracts. Such contracts would be accounted for under IFRS 15 – *Revenue from Contracts with Customers.*
Measurement of inventory	Inventories are measured at the lower of cost and estimated selling price less costs to complete and sell. Section 13 provides prescriptive guidance on what may be and what should not be included in the cost of inventory. For inventories that meet the definition of qualifying assets, entities may choose to adopt an accounting policy of capitalising borrowing costs. See 3.3 above.	The measurement of inventory is similar to FRS 102, although borrowing costs must be capitalised if inventories meet the definition of qualifying assets.
Costs of inventories of a service provider	Section 13 provides specific guidance on the cost of inventories of a service provider. Inventories of a service provider are measured at the cost of their production. Costs consist primarily of the labour and other costs of personnel directly involved in providing the service, including supervisory personnel, and attributable overheads. See 3.3.10 above.	IAS 2 contains no guidance on cost of inventories of a service provider. IFRS 15 provides guidance on the accounting for costs to fulfil a contract. Costs to fulfil a contract, as defined in IFRS 15, are divided into two categories: (a) costs that give rise to an asset; and (b) costs that are expensed as incurred. IFRS 15 does not specifically deal with the classification and presentation of contract costs.
Impairment of inventory	FRS 102 provides limited guidance on assessing estimated selling price less costs to complete and sell. See 3.4 above.	IAS 2 refers to 'net realisable value' rather than 'estimated selling price less costs to complete and sell' and provides substantial guidance on the identification of net realisable value. However, it is unlikely that a GAAP difference would arise in practice.
Inventory purchased on deferred payment terms	If the inventory is a qualifying asset and the entity adopts a policy of capitalising borrowing costs, the interest expense should be added to the cost of inventory. See 3.3.2 above.	If the inventory is a qualifying asset, the interest expense must be added to the cost of inventory.

Inventories held for distribution at no or nominal consideration	These inventories should be measured at cost adjusted, where applicable, for any loss of service potential. The carrying amount of those inventories should be recognised as an expense when they are distributed. See 3.3.11 above.	No guidance on inventories held for distribution at no or nominal consideration.
Advertising and promotional expenditure	This expenditure may meet the definition of 'inventories held for distribution at no or nominal consideration' and could therefore be recognised as inventory. See 3.3.11 above.	IAS 38 – *Intangible Assets* – requires the cost of advertising and promotional material, such as mail order catalogues, to be recognised as an expense once the entity gains access to those materials. A GAAP difference may therefore arise.
Inventories acquired through non exchange transactions	Where an entity receives inventories without giving approximately equal value in exchange, the cost of the inventories should be measured as their fair value at the date of acquisition. See 3.3.8 above.	IFRS provides no specific guidance on inventories that are acquired through a non-exchange transaction.
Disclosures	FRS 102 requires fewer disclosures that IAS 2, although Company Law disclosures are also required. See 3.6.2 above.	IAS 2 requires some additional disclosures beyond those required by FRS 102. Company law disclosures are not required by entities reporting under IFRS.

Chapter 12

Investments in associates

List of examples

Chapter 12

Chapter 12

Investments in associates

1   INTRODUCTION

Section 14 – *Investments in Associates* – applies to investments in associates in consolidated financial statements and in the individual financial statements of an investor that is not a parent.

2   COMPARISON BETWEEN SECTION 14 AND IFRS

There are a number of differences between the accounting and disclosure requirements in Section 14 compared to IFRS (IAS 28 – *Investments in Associates and Joint Ventures*). The key differences are discussed in the section below and summarised at 6 below.

2.1   Measurement – individual and separate entity financial statements

Section 14 permits entities that are not parents to account for their investment in associates at cost less impairment, at fair value with changes in fair value recognised through other comprehensive income (unless reversing a revaluation decrease of the same investment previously recognised in profit or loss, in which case the revaluation increase is recognised in profit or loss, or where a revaluation decrease exceeds increases previously recognised in respect of the same investment, in which case the excess is recognised in profit or loss) or at fair value with changes in fair value recognised through profit or loss (see 3.3.1.A below). *[FRS 102.14.4]*. The same accounting policy choice is available for an investor preparing separate financial statements in accordance with Section 9 – *Consolidated and Separate Financial Statements. [FRS 102.9.26]*.

Under IFRS, an entity that is not a parent must prepare financial statements whereby its investments in associates are accounted for under the equity method accounting unless it meets the criteria for exemption. *[IAS 28.16, 17]*. An election is available for investments in associates held by, or indirectly through, a venture capital organisation, mutual fund, unit trust or similar entities including investment-linked insurance funds, to measure their investment in an associate at fair value through profit or loss in accordance with IFRS 9 – *Financial Instruments. [IAS 28.18]*. This election extends to portions of an investment held indirectly through a venture capital organisation, mutual fund, unit trust or similar entities including investment-linked insurance funds, whereby the investor may elect to measure the portion of the investment so held at fair value through profit and loss in accordance with IFRS 9, regardless of whether the vehicle the investment is held through has significant influence over that portion of the investment. If this election is made, the equity method must be applied to the remaining portion of the investment in an associate that is not held through such a vehicle. *[IAS 28.19]*. This election also applies in the investor's individual financial statements, but in any case, an investor preparing separate financial statements under IFRS, has an accounting policy choice of measuring investments in associates at cost, fair value in accordance with IFRS 9 or the equity method of accounting. *[IAS 27.10]*.

2.2   Investment portfolios / funds

Under Section 14, an investor that is a parent and has investments in associates that are held as part of an investment portfolio is required to measure those investments at fair value with changes in fair value recognised in profit or loss in the consolidated financial statements. *[FRS 102.14.4B]*. However, under IAS 28, the measurement of investments in associates at fair value through profit or loss in consolidated financial statements is an option that is only available for an entity which is a venture capital organisation, or a mutual fund, unit trust and similar entities including investment-linked insurance funds or one which holds its investments indirectly through such an entity. *[IAS 28.18]*.

2.3   Accounting for the acquisition of an associate

Section 14 requires the use of Section 19 – *Business Combinations and Goodwill* – to determine the implicit goodwill on the acquisition of an associate. This goodwill is then amortised over its useful life. *[FRS 102.14.8(c), 19.23]*.

Under IAS 28, the implicit goodwill is not amortised.

2.4   Loss of significant influence

Section 14 requires that where loss of significant influence is as a result of a partial disposal, a gain or loss is recognised based on the disposal proceeds and the carrying amount relating to the proportion disposed of. The carrying value of the equity interest retained at the date significant influence is lost becomes the cost of the retained investment and there is no re-measurement of the retained interest at fair value. *[FRS 102.14.8(i)(i)]*.

If the loss of significant influence is for reasons other than a partial disposal, for example a change in circumstances such as the associate issuing shares to third parties, no gain or loss is recognised and the carrying value of the equity-accounted investment at the date significant influence is lost becomes the cost of the retained investment. *[FRS 102.14.8(i)(ii)]*.

Under IFRS, where loss of significant influence is as a result of a partial disposal, a gain or loss is recognised based on any difference between the disposal proceeds together with the fair value of any retained interest and the carrying amount of the total interest in the associate.

Similarly under IFRS if the loss of significant influence is for reasons other than a partial disposal, for example a change in circumstances such as the associate issuing shares to third parties, a gain or loss is recognised based on the fair value of the retained interest and the carrying amount of the interest in the associate at that date. *[IAS 28.22]*.

2.5   Transactions to create an associate

Section 9 – *Consolidated and Separate Financial Statements* – sets out the requirements in respect of transactions where an investor may exchange a business, or other non-monetary asset, for an interest in another entity, and that other entity becomes an associate of the investor. To the extent that the fair value of the consideration received by the investor exceeds the carrying value of the part of the business, or other non-monetary assets exchanged and no longer owned by the investor, and any related goodwill together with any cash given up, the investor should recognise a gain. Any unrealised gain arising on the exchange is recognised in other comprehensive income. To the extent that the fair value of the consideration received is less than the carrying value of what has been exchanged, together with any related goodwill and cash given up, a loss is recognised (see 3.3.2.K below). *[FRS 102.9.31].*

IFRS does not distinguish between realised and unrealised gains for equivalent transactions and requires that gain or loss, realised or unrealised, to be recognised in profit or loss. *[IFRS 10 Appendix B.98].*

2.6   Long term interests in associates

FRS 102 does not address the concept of long term interests in associates or the accounting for such interests, although it is widely accepted practice that long term loans which are not intended to be repaid in the near future can be regarded as forming part of the investor's net investment in the associate. As there are no explicit accounting requirements for long term interest in associates in FRS 102, an entity must make an accounting policy choice as to how such interests are accounted for and presented.

An amendment to IAS 28 with an effective date of 1 January 2019 has clarified that long term interests in an associate, for which equity accounting is not applied, are within the scope of IFRS 9, for example long term loans from the investor to the associate. The amendment clarifies that the impairment requirements of IFRS 9 should be applied before the impairment requirements of IAS 28 when recognising impairment losses in relation to such long term interests.

3   REQUIREMENTS OF SECTION 14 FOR INVESTMENTS IN ASSOCIATES

3.1   Introduction

3.1.1   Scope

Section 14 applies to investments in:

- associates in consolidated financial statements; and
- investments in associates in the individual financial statements of an investor that is not a parent (see 3.3.1.A below).

An entity that is a parent accounts for investments in associates in its separate financial statements in accordance with paragraphs 9.26 and 9.26A of FRS 102, as appropriate (see Chapter 8 at 4.2). *[FRS 102.14.1].*

3.1.2   Terms used in Section 14

The following key terms are used in Section 14 with the meanings specified:
[FRS 102 Appendix I]

Term	Definition
Associate	An entity, including an unincorporated entity such as a partnership, over which the investor has significant influence and that is neither a subsidiary nor an interest in a joint venture.
Consolidated financial statements	The financial statements of a parent and its subsidiaries presented as those of a single economic entity.
Held as part of an investment portfolio	An interest is held as part of an investment portfolio if its value to the investor is through fair value as part of a directly or indirectly held basket of investments rather than as a media through which the investor carries out business. A basket of investments is indirectly held if an investment fund holds a single investment in a second investment fund which, in turn, holds a basket of investments. In some circumstances, it may be appropriate for a single investment to be considered an investment portfolio, for example when an investment fund is first being established and is expected to acquire additional investments.
Individual financial statements	The accounts that are required to be prepared by an entity in accordance with the Act or relevant legislation, for example: (a) 'individual accounts', as set out in section 394 of the Act; (b) 'statement of accounts', as set out in section 132 of the Charities Act 2011; or (c) 'individual accounts', as set out in section 72A of the Building Societies Act 1986. Separate financial statements are included in the meaning of this term.
Impracticable	Applying a requirement is impracticable when the entity cannot apply it after making every reasonable effort to do so.
Parent	An entity that has one or more subsidiaries.
Separate financial statements	Those presented by a parent in which the investments in subsidiaries, associates or jointly controlled entities are accounted for either at cost or fair value rather than on the basis of the reported results and net assets of the investees. Separate financial statements are included within the meaning of individual financial statements.
Significant influence	Significant influence is the power to participate in the financial and operating policy decisions of the associate but is not control or joint control over those policies.
Subsidiary	An entity, including an unincorporated entity such as a partnership, which is controlled by another entity (known as the parent).

3.2 Definitions of an associate, and related terms

3.2.1 Associate

Section 14 defines an associate as an entity, including an unincorporated entity such as a partnership, over which an investor has significant influence and that is neither a subsidiary nor an interest in a joint venture. *[FRS 102.14.2]*.

A similar definition is contain in UK Company law which defines an *'associated undertaking'* as an undertaking in which an undertaking included in the consolidation has a participating interest and over whose operating and financial policy it exercises a significant influence, and which is not:

- a subsidiary undertaking of the parent company; or
- a joint venture dealt with in accordance with the paragraph on joint ventures. *[6 Sch 19(1)]*.

A *'participating interest'* is an interest held by an undertaking in the shares of another undertaking which it holds on a long-term basis for the purpose of securing a contribution to its activities by the exercise of control or influence arising from or related to that interest. The interest in shares includes interests which are convertible into shares or options to acquire shares, regardless whether or not they are currently exercisable. Additionally, interests held on behalf of an undertaking are to be treated as held by it. *[10 Sch 11(1), (3)-(4)]*.

3.2.2 Significant influence

Fundamental to the definition of an associate is the concept of significant influence. This is defined as 'the power to participate in the financial and operating policy decisions of the associate but is not control or joint control over those policies'. *[FRS 102.14.3]*.

Under Section 14, a holding of 20% or more of the voting power of the investee (held directly or indirectly, through subsidiaries) is presumed to give rise to significant influence, unless it can be clearly demonstrated that this is not the case. Conversely, a holding of less than 20% of the voting power is presumed not to give rise to significant influence, unless it can be clearly demonstrated that significant influence does exist. The existence of a substantial or majority interest of another investor does not necessarily preclude the investor from having significant influence. *[FRS 102.14.3]*. UK company law also contains a rebuttable presumption of significant influence when an undertaking holds 20% or more of the voting rights of another undertaking unless the contrary is shown. *[6 Sch 19(2)]*.

An entity should consider both ordinary shares and other categories of shares in determining its voting rights.

Other factors need to be considered to determine whether significant influence exists or not and to potentially rebut any presumptions above regarding voting power. There is no further guidance in Section 14 on how significant influence is demonstrated. Under the FRS 102 hierarchy set out in Section 10 – *Accounting Policies, Estimates and Errors* – we can look to the guidance in IAS 28 which notes that significant influence can be evidenced in one or more of the following ways:

(a)   representation on the board of directors or equivalent governing body of the investee;

(b)   participation in policy-making processes, including participation in decisions about dividends and other distributions;

(c)   material transactions between the entity and the investee;

(d)   interchange of managerial personnel; or

(e)   provision of essential technical information. *[IAS 28.6].*

Significant influence may also exist over another entity through potential voting rights (see 3.2.2.D below).

An entity loses significant influence over an investee when it loses the power to participate in the financial and operating policy decisions of that investee. The loss of significant influence can occur with or without a change in absolute or relative ownership levels. It could occur, for example, as a result of a contractual agreement or when an associate becomes subject to the control of a government, court, administrator or regulator.

An entity with an interest in an associate will need to evaluate the facts and circumstances, whenever a change to those facts and circumstances is identified, to assess whether it is still able to exercise significant influence over the financial and operating policies of the investee.

The accounting for loss of significant influence over an associate is discussed at 3.3.2.J below.

3.2.2.A   Lack of significant influence

The presumption of significant influence due to the existence of 20% or more of the voting power can sometimes be rebutted, for example when (see section 4.1 of Chapter 11 of EY International GAAP 2019):

• the investor has failed to obtain representation on the investee's board of directors;

• the investee or other shareholders are opposing the investor's attempts to exercise significant influence;

• the investor is unable to obtain timely financial information or cannot obtain more information – required to apply the equity method – than shareholders that do not have significant influence; or

• a group of shareholders that holds the majority ownership of the investee operates without regard to the views of the investor.

Determining whether the presumption of significant influence has been rebutted requires considerable judgement and sufficient evidence to justify rebutting the presumption.

3.2.2.B   Holdings of less than 20% of the voting power

Although there is a presumption that an investor that holds less than 20% of the voting power in an investee cannot exercise significant influence, *[FRS 102.14.3(b)]*, where investments give rise to only slightly less than 20% of the voting power careful judgement is needed to assess whether significant influence may exist.

For example, an investor may be able to exercise significant influence in the following circumstances:

- the investor's voting power is much larger than that of any other shareholder of the investee;
- the corporate governance arrangements may be such that the investor is able to appoint members to the board, supervisory board or significant committees of the investee. The investor will need to apply judgement to determine whether representation in the respective boards or committees is enough to provide significant influence; or
- the investor has the power to veto significant financial and operating decisions.

3.2.2.C   Voting rights in UK company law

The provisions of paragraphs 5 to 11 of Schedule 7 to the 2006 Act (parent and subsidiary undertakings: rights to be taken into account and attribution of rights) apply in determining whether an undertaking holds 20% or more of the voting rights in another undertaking. *[6 Sch 19(4)]*.

The '*voting rights*' in an undertaking are the rights conferred on shareholders in respect of their shares or, in the case of an undertaking not having a share capital, on members, to vote at general meetings of the undertaking on all, or substantially all, matters. *[6 Sch 19(3)]*.

Voting rights on shares held as security remain the rights of the provider of the security, and are not taken into account if the rights are only exercisable in accordance with instructions from the provider of the security or in his interest. *[7 Sch 8 (CA)]*. Similarly, voting rights that are held in a fiduciary capacity by the entity are treated as not held by the entity. *[7 Sch 6 (CA)]*. Voting rights held by a nominee on behalf of the entity should be treated as held by the entity. Rights are regarded as held as nominee for another if the rights are only exercisable on the other's instruction or with the other's consent. *[7 Sch 7 (CA)]*.

The voting rights referred to above should be reduced by any rights held by the undertaking itself. *[7 Sch 10 (CA)]*.

3.2.2.D   Potential voting rights

An entity may own share warrants, share call options, debt or equity instruments that are convertible into ordinary shares, or other similar instruments that have the potential, if exercised or converted, to give the entity voting power or reduce another party's voting power over the financial and operating policies of another entity (potential voting rights).

Section 14 requires that an entity should consider the existence and effect of potential voting rights in deciding whether significant influence exists. *[FRS 102.14.8(b)]*. Whilst not explicitly stated in Section 14, by using the GAAP hierarchy in Section 10, and applying the guidance in Section 9 Paragraph 6, such potential voting rights should only be considered if they are currently exercisable or convertible.

Potential voting rights are not currently exercisable or convertible when they cannot be exercised or converted until a future date or until the occurrence of a future event. The meaning of currently exercisable or convertible is discussed further in Chapter 8 at 3.2.1.

Consistent with that discussion, IAS 28 (on which the requirements of Section 14 are based) states that in assessing whether potential voting rights contribute to significant influence, an entity must examine all facts and circumstances (including the terms of exercise of the potential voting rights (both of the reporting entity and of other parties) and any other contractual arrangements whether considered individually or in combination) that affect potential voting rights, except the intention of management and the financial ability to exercise or convert those potential voting rights. *[IAS 28.8]*.

3.2.2.E   *Voting rights held in a fiduciary capacity*

Voting rights on shares held as security by an entity remain the rights of the provider of the security, and are generally not taken into account if the rights are only exercisable in accordance with instructions from the provider of the security or in his interest. Similarly, voting rights that are held in a fiduciary capacity may not be those of the entity itself. However, if voting rights are held by a nominee on behalf of the entity, they should be taken into account. *[7 Sch 6-7 (CA)]*.

3.3   Measurement

3.3.1   *Accounting policy options*

3.3.1.A   *Investor not a parent*

An entity that is not a parent shall account for its investments in associates in its individual financial statements using either:

- the cost model (see 3.3.3 below);
- fair value with changes in other comprehensive income (unless reversing a revaluation decrease of the same investment previously recognised in profit or loss, in which case the revaluation increase is recognised in profit or loss, or where a revaluation decrease exceeds increases previously recognised in respect of the same investment, in which case the excess is recognised in profit or loss) (see 3.3.4 or below); or
- fair value with changes in fair value recognised in profit or loss (see 3.3.4 below and Chapter 4). *[FRS 102.14.4]*.

The measurement options are an accounting policy choice. Section 14 does not contain the additional guidance in Section 9 that requires a parent to apply the same accounting policy for all investments in a single class. *[FRS 102.9.26]*. A class is a grouping of assets of a similar nature and use in an entity's operations. However, applying the FRS 102 GAAP hierarchy discussed in Chapter 9 at 3.2, it would seem logical for the same accounting policy to be applied to the same class of associates. A discussion of the meaning of class of investment in this context is in Chapter 8 at 4.2 and, in our view, associates held as part of an investment portfolio, which are required to be measured at fair value through profit or loss, are a separate class of investment.

There is no option in Section 14 to use the equity method of accounting in individual financial statements even though permitted by Regulations. However, the individual financial statements of an investor that is not a parent must disclose summarised financial information about its investments in associates, along with the effect of including those investments as if they had been accounted for using the equity method. Investing entities that are exempt from preparing consolidated financial statements, or would be exempt if they had subsidiaries, are exempt from this requirement. *[FRS 102.14.15A].*

Schedule 1 to the Regulations permits the equity method of accounting to be applied in respect of participating interests in the individual entity accounts of an investor. *[1 Sch 29A].* However, this option cannot be applied by an investor in preparing their individual entity accounts in accordance with FRS 102 as it is not available in paragraph 14.4 of Section 14. *[FRS 102.BC.A.28].*

3.3.1.B   *Investor that is a parent*

An investor that is a parent should, in its consolidated financial statements, account for all of its investments in associates using the equity method of accounting (see 3.3.2 below). *[FRS 102.14.4A].*

The exception to this is when the investment in an associate is held as part of an investment portfolio. These investments shall be measured at fair value with changes in fair value recognised in profit or loss in the consolidated financial statements. *[FRS 102.14.4B].*

An investment is held as part of an investment portfolio if its value to the investor is through fair value as part of a directly or indirectly held basket of investments rather than as a media through which the investor carries out business. A basket of investments is indirectly held if an investment fund holds a single investment in a second investment fund which, in turn, holds a basket of investments. In some circumstances, it may be appropriate for a single investment to be considered an investment portfolio, for example when an investment fund is first being established and is expected to acquire additional investments. (see Chapter 8 at 3.4.2.A). *[FRS 102 Appendix I].*

An entity that is a parent should account for its investments in associates in its separate financial statements in accordance with paragraphs 9.26 and 9.26A of Section 9 (see Chapter 8 at 4.2). *[FRS 102.14.1].*

3.3.2   *Equity method*

Section 14 defines the equity method as a method of accounting whereby the investment is initially recognised at transaction price (including transaction costs) and is subsequently adjusted to reflect the investor's share of:

- profit or loss;
- other comprehensive income; and
- equity of the associate. *[FRS 102.14.8].*

The investor's share of the investee's profit or loss is recognised in the investor's profit or loss. *[FRS 102.5.5, 6 Sch 20(3)].* The investor's share of the investee's other comprehensive income is recognised in the investor's statement of comprehensive income. *[FRS 102.5.5A].*

Transaction costs are defined in FRS 102 in the context of financial instruments as incremental costs that are directly attributable to the acquisition, issue or disposal of a financial asset or liability. An incremental cost is one that would not have been incurred if the entity had not acquired, issued or disposed of the financial asset or liability. *[FRS 102 Appendix I].*

In the context of Section 14, transaction costs will comprise any costs directly attributable to the acquisition of the interest in the associate.

The application of the equity method is illustrated in Example 12.1 below and the key features of the method are explained in the paragraphs that follow.

Example 12.1:   Application of the equity method

On 1 January 2019 entity A acquires a 35% interest in entity B, over which it is able to exercise significant influence. Entity A paid £475,000 for its interest in B. At that date the book value of B's net assets was £900,000, and their fair value £1,100,000, the difference of £200,000 relates to an item of property, plant and equipment with a remaining useful life of 10 years. During the year to 31 December 2019, B made a profit of £80,000 and paid a dividend of £120,000 on 31 December 2019. Entity B also had a gain in other comprehensive income of £20,000 during the year. Goodwill is assumed to have a 10 year useful life. For the purposes of the example, any deferred tax implications have been ignored.

Entity A accounts for its investment in B under the equity method as follows:

	£	£
Acquisition of investment in B		
Share in book value of B's net assets: 35% of £900,000	315,000	
Share in fair valuation of B's net assets: 35% of (£1,100,000 – £900,000) *	70,000	
Goodwill on investment in B: £475,000 – £315,000 – £70,000 *	90,000	
Cost of investment		475,000
Profit during the year		
Share in the profit reported by B: 35% of £80,000	28,000	
Adjustment to reflect additional depreciation on fair value adjustment*	(7,000)	
35% of ((£1,100,000 – £900,000) ÷ 10 years)		
Goodwill amortisation *(£90,000 ÷ 10 years)	(9,000)	
Share of profit in B recognised in income by A		12,000
Share of other comprehensive income recognised by A: 35% of £20,000		7,000
Dividend received by A during the year		
35% of £120,000		(42,000)
At 31 December 2019		
Share in book value of B's net assets:		
£315,000 + 35% (£80,000 – £120,000 + £20,000)	308,000	
Share in fair valuation of B's net assets: £70,000 – £7,000 *	63,000	
Goodwill on investment in B: £90,000 – £9,000*	81,000	
Closing balance of A's investment in B		452,000

*   These line items are normally not presented separately, but are combined with the ones immediately above.

Through its significant influence over the associate the investor has an interest in the associate's performance and, as a result, a return on its investment. The investor accounts for this interest by extending the scope of its financial statements so as to include its share of profits or losses of the associate. As a result the application of the equity method provides more informative reporting of the net assets and profit or loss of the associate, rather than simply recognising income on the basis of distributions received, which may bear little relation to the performance of the associate.

3.3.2.A   Date of commencement of equity accounting

An investor begins equity accounting for an associate from the date on which it gains significant influence over the associate (and is not otherwise exempt from equity accounting for it). In most situations, this will be when the investor purchases the investment in the associate. However, it may be that the investor only obtains significant influence over the investee at some date after having purchased its ownership interest. FRS 102 does not explicitly deal with this situation, but the investor should account for the associate by applying its selected accounting policy for such piecemeal acquisitions as discussed at 4.1.2 below.

3.3.2.B   Distributions and other adjustments to carrying amount

Distributions received from an associate will reduce the carrying amount of the investment. Adjustments to the carrying amount may also be necessary due to changes in the associate's equity from items of its other comprehensive income. *[FRS 102.14.8(a)]*.

Such changes could include those arising from the revaluation of property, plant and equipment and from foreign exchange translation differences. The investor's share of the investee's other comprehensive income is recognised in the investor's statement of comprehensive income. *[FRS 102.5.5A]*. Distributions received in excess of the carrying amount of the associate are dealt with at 4.2 below.

3.3.2.C   Potential voting rights and share of the investee

In applying the equity method, the proportionate share of the associate to be accounted for, in many cases, will be based on the investor's ownership interest in the ordinary shares of the investee.

Although potential voting rights need to be considered in determining whether significant influence exists (see 3.2.2.D above) an investor should measure its share of profit or loss and other comprehensive income of the associate as well as its share of changes in the associate's equity based on present ownership interests. Those measurements should not reflect the possible exercise or conversion of potential voting rights. *[FRS 102.14.8(b)]*.

If an associate has outstanding cumulative preference shares that are held by parties other than the investor and that are classified as equity, the investor should compute its share of profits or losses after adjusting for the dividends on such shares, whether or not the dividends have been declared.

Example 12.2:   Cumulative preference shares issued by an associate

An entity holds an investment of 30% in the ordinary shares of an associate that has net assets of £200,000 and net profit for the year of £24,500. The associate has issued 5,000 cumulative preference shares with a nominal value of £10 which entitle its holders to a 9% cumulative preference dividend. The cumulative preference shares are classified by the associate as equity in accordance with the requirements of Section 22 – *Liabilities and Equity*. The associate has not declared dividends on the cumulative preference shares in the past two years.

The investor calculates its share of the associate's net assets and net profit as follows:

	£
Net assets	200,000
9% Cumulative preference shares	(50,000)
Undeclared dividend on cumulative preference shares	
2 years × 9% × £50,000 =	(9,000)
Net assets value attributable to ordinary shareholders	141,000
Investor's 30% share of the net assets	42,300
Net profit for the year	24,500
Share of profit of holders of cumulative preference shares	
9% of £50,000 =	(4,500)
Net profit attributable to ordinary shareholders	20,000
Investor's 30% share of the net profit	6,000

If the investor also owned all of the cumulative preference shares then its share in the net assets of the associate would be £42,300 + £50,000 + £9,000 = £101,300. Its share in the net profit would be £6,000 + £4,500 = £10,500.

When an associate has a complicated equity structure with several classes of equity shares that have varying entitlements to net profits and equity, the investor needs to assess carefully the rights attaching to each class of equity share in determining the appropriate percentage of ownership interest.

Example 12.3:   Preference shares with a liquidation preference

Entity A has issued 10,000 preference shares with a nominal value of £0.10. The preference shareholders are entitled to a cumulative dividend equal to 25% of the net profits, 35% of the equity upon liquidation and have a liquidation preference in respect of the nominal value of the shares. Entity A has also issued ordinary shares that are entitled to the remainder of the net profits and equity upon liquidation.

An investor that holds 40% of the ordinary shares of Entity A will need to assess carefully what its appropriate share in the profits and equity of Entity A is. The investor would take the liquidation preference into account in calculating its interest in the associate or joint venture to the extent that there is economic substance to that right.

Section 14 does not address the situation where in a group, shares in the associate are held by the parent and its subsidiaries. However, based on the requirements of IAS 28, it is clear that a group's share in an associate is the aggregate of the holdings in that associate by the parent and its subsidiaries. Holdings in the associate by the group's other associates or joint ventures are ignored for this purpose. *[IAS 28.27]*.

Example 12.4:   *Share in an associate*

Parent A holds a 100% investment in subsidiary B, which in turn holds a 25% investment in associate Z. In addition, parent A also holds a 30% investment in associate C and a 50% investment in joint venture D, each of which holds a 10% investment in associate Z.

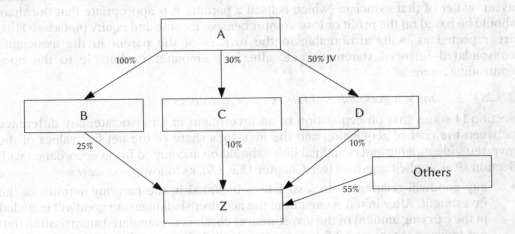

In its consolidated financial statements parent A accounts for a 25% investment in associate Z under the equity method because:

- the investments in associate Z held by associate C and joint venture D should not be taken into account; and

- parent A fully consolidates the assets of subsidiary B, which include a 25% investment in associate Z.

Section 14 does not address the situation where an associate itself has subsidiaries, associates or jointly controlled entities. However, based on the Companies Act 2006 (CA 2006) and the requirements of IAS 28, it is clear that profits or losses, other comprehensive income and net assets taken into account when the investor applies the equity method should be those recognised in the associate's consolidated financial statements, but after any adjustments necessary to give effect to uniform accounting policies (see 3.3.2.H below).

It may be that the associate does not own all the shares in some of its subsidiaries, in which case its consolidated financial statements will include non-controlling interests. Under the CA 2006, any non-controlling interests are presented in the consolidated statement of financial position within equity, separately from the equity of the owners of the parent. Profit or loss and each component of other comprehensive income are attributed to the owners of the parent and to the non-controlling interests. *[FRS 102.6.3(a)].*

The profit or loss and other comprehensive income reported in the associate's consolidated financial statements will include 100% of the amounts relating to the subsidiaries, but the overall profit or loss and total comprehensive income will be split between the amounts attributable to the owners of the parent (i.e. the associate) and those attributable to the non-controlling interests. The net assets in the associate's consolidated statement of financial position will also include 100% of the amounts relating to the subsidiaries, with any non-controlling interests in the net assets presented in the consolidated statement of financial position within equity, separately from the equity of the owners of the parent.

Section 14 does not address whether the investor's share, for equity accounting purposes, of the associate's profits, other comprehensive income and net assets should be based on the amounts before or after any non-controlling interests in the associate's consolidated financial statements. However, as the investor's interest in the associate is as an owner of that associate (which is itself a parent), it is appropriate that the share should be based on the profit or loss, comprehensive income and equity (net assets) that are reported as being attributable to the owners of the parent in the associate's consolidated financial statements, i.e. after any amounts attributable to the non-controlling interests.

3.3.2.D   *Implicit goodwill and fair value adjustments*

Section 14 states that on acquisition of an investment in an associate, any difference between the cost of acquisition and the investor's share of the net fair values of the investee's identifiable assets and liabilities should be accounted for in accordance with Section 19 as implicit goodwill (see Chapter 17 at 3.9), as follows: *[FRS 102.14.8(c)]*

- any goodwill relating to an associate is included in the carrying amount of the investment. After initial recognition, the acquirer shall measure goodwill included in the carrying amount of the investment at cost less accumulated amortisation (but not impairment, see 3.3.2.E below). Goodwill shall be considered to have a finite useful life and shall be amortised on a systematic basis over its life. If, in exceptional cases, an entity is unable to make a reliable estimate of the useful life of goodwill, the life shall not exceed 10 years. Any amortisation shall be recognised against the investor's share of the associate's profit or loss; *[FRS 102.19.23]*

- if the acquirer's interest in the net amount of the associate's identifiable assets, liabilities and provisions for contingent liabilities exceeds the cost of the investment (also referred to as negative goodwill), the acquirer must (after reassessing the identification and measurement of the acquiree's assets and liabilities and the measurement of the cost of the combination) recognise the excess up to the fair value of the non-monetary assets acquired in the associate's profit or loss in the periods in which the non-monetary assets are recovered. Any excess exceeding the fair value of the non-monetary assets acquired shall be recognised in profit or loss in the periods expected to be benefited (see Chapter 17 at 3.9.3). *[FRS 102.19.24]*.

Section 14 also states that an investor should adjust its share of the associate's profits or losses after acquisition in order to account, for example, for additional depreciation or amortisation of the depreciable assets or amortisable assets (including goodwill) on the basis of the excess of their fair values over their carrying amounts at the time the investment was acquired. *[FRS 102.14.8(c)]*.

3.3.2.E   *Impairment*

An entity will have to test the carrying value of its investment in an associate for impairment only if an event has occurred that indicates that it will not recover the carrying value. *[FRS 102.27.7]*.

The most common of these events, trading losses in the associate, will automatically have been taken into account in determining the carrying value of the investment, leaving only the remaining net carrying amount (i.e. after deducting the share of trading losses) to be assessed for impairment.

Determining whether an investment in an associate is impaired may be more complicated than is apparent at first sight, as it involves carrying out several separate impairment assessments:

- *Underlying assets of the associate*

  It is generally not appropriate for the investor simply to multiply the amount of the impairment charge recognised in the investee's own books by the investor's percentage of ownership, because the investor should measure its interest in an associate's identifiable net assets at fair value at the date of acquisition of an associate (see 3.3.2.D above). Therefore, if the value that the investor attributes to the associate's net assets differs from the carrying amount of those net assets in the associate's own books, the investor should restate any impairment losses recognised by the associate and also needs to consider whether it needs to recognise any impairments that the associate itself did not recognise in its own books.

  Any goodwill recognised by an associate needs to be separated into two elements. Goodwill that existed at the date the investor acquired its interest in the associate is not an identifiable asset of the associate from the perspective of the investor. That goodwill should be combined with the investor's goodwill on the acquisition of its interest in the associate and any impairment losses of that goodwill recognised in the financial statements of the associate should be reversed when the investor applies the equity method. However, goodwill that arises on subsequent acquisitions by the associate should be accounted for as such in the books of the associate and tested for impairment in accordance with Section 27 – *Impairment of Assets* – by the associate. The investor should not make any adjustments to the associate's accounting for that goodwill.

- *Investment in the associate*

  As well as reflecting any impairment in the underlying assets of the associate using the equity method as discussed above, Section 14 requires an investor to test the overall investment in the associate for impairment as a single asset in accordance with Section 27. Any goodwill included as part of the carrying amount of the investment in the associate is not tested separately for impairment but is tested as part of the overall investment as a whole. *[FRS 102.14.8(d)].*

- *Other interests that are not part of the equity interest in the associate*

  The investor must also apply Section 11 – *Basic Financial Instruments* – in order to determine whether it is necessary to recognise any additional impairment loss with respect to that part of the investor's interest in the associate that does not comprise its net investment in the associate. This could include, for example, trade receivables and payables, and collateralised long-term receivables, but might also include preference shares or loans (see 3.3.2.I below). In this case, however, the impairment is calculated in accordance with Section 11, and not Section 27.

Chapter 12

Where the carrying amount of an investment in an associate is tested for impairment in accordance with Section 27, an impairment loss is recognised against the entire investment and is not allocated to any individual asset, including goodwill, which forms part of the carrying amount of the associate. In addition, any reversal of that impairment loss is recognised to the extent that the recoverable amount of the investment exceeds the carrying amount, subject to the reversal not exceeding the carrying amount that would have been determined had no impairment loss been recognised in previous years. *[FRS 102.27.30].*

Example 12.5:   *Impairment losses recognised by an associate*

Entity A has a 40% interest in Entity B. Entity A has significant influence over Entity B and accounts for its investment under the equity method.

At 31 December 2019, Entity B, which prepares its financial statements under FRS 102, has carried out impairment tests under Section 27 and recognised an impairment loss of £140,000 calculated as follows:

	Carrying amount £'000	Recoverable amount £'000	Impairment loss £'000
CGU A	210	300	n/a
CGU B	250	450	n/a
CGU C	540	400	140
Total	1,000	1,150	140

In accounting for its associate, Entity B, in its consolidated financial statements for the year ended 31 December 2019, should Entity A reflect its 40% share of this impairment loss of £140,000?

As indicated above, it is generally not appropriate for the investor simply to multiply the amount of the impairment recognised in the investee's own books by the investor's percentage of ownership, because the investor should initially measure its interest in an associate's identifiable net assets at fair value at the date of acquisition of an associate. Accordingly, appropriate adjustments based on those fair values are made for impairment losses recognised by the associate (see 3.3.2.D above).

Prior to the recognition of the impairment loss by Entity B, the carrying amount of Entity A's 40% interest in the net assets of Entity B, after reflecting fair value adjustments made by Entity A at the date of acquisition, together with the goodwill arising on the acquisition is as follows:

	Carrying amount reflecting fair value adjustments made by Entity A £'000
CGU A	140
CGU B	100
CGU C	320
Net assets	560
Goodwill	40
Investment in associate	600

In applying the equity method, Entity A should compare its 40% share of the cash flows attributable to each of Entity B's CGUs to determine the impairment loss it should recognise in respect of Entity B. Accordingly, in equity accounting for its share of Entity B's profit or loss, Entity A should recognise an impairment loss of £180,000 calculated as follows:

	Carrying amount reflecting fair value adjustments made by Entity A £'000	Recoverable amount (40%) £'000	Impairment loss £'000
CGU A	140	120	20
CGU B	100	180	n/a
CGU C	320	160	160
Net assets	560	460	180

In addition, after applying the equity method, Entity A should calculate whether any further impairment loss is necessary in respect of its investment in its associate.

The carrying amount of Entity A's investment in Entity B under the equity method after reflecting the impairment loss of £180,000 would be as follows:

	Carrying amount after impairment loss £'000
CGU A	120
CGU B	100
CGU C	160
Net assets	380
Goodwill	40
Investment in associate	420

Based on Entity A's 40% interest in the total recoverable amount of Entity B of £460,000, Entity A would not recognise any further impairment loss in respect of its investment in the associate.

It should be noted that the impairment loss recognised by Entity A of £180,000 is not the same as if it had calculated an impairment loss on its associate as a whole i.e. by comparing its 40% share of the total recoverable amount of Entity B of £460,000 to its investment in the associate of £600,000 (prior to reflecting any impairment loss on its share of Entity B's net assets). Such an approach would only be appropriate if Entity B did not have more than one CGU.

3.3.2.F   Investor's transactions with associates

Section 14 requires unrealised profits and losses resulting from what it refers to as 'upstream' (associate to investor) and 'downstream' (investor to associate) transactions between an investor (including its consolidated subsidiaries) and an associate to be eliminated from the investor's financial statements to the extent of investor's interest in the associate. Unrealised losses on such transactions may provide evidence of an impairment of the asset transferred. *[FRS 102.14.8(e)].*

'Upstream' transactions are, for example, sales of assets from an associate to the investor. 'Downstream' transactions are, for example, sales or contributions of assets from the investor to its associate.

Section 14 provides no further guidance as to how this broadly expressed requirement translates into accounting entries, but we suggest that the following would be appropriate:

- in the income statement, the adjustment should be taken against either the investor's profit or the share of the associate's profit, according to whether the investor or the associate recorded the profit on the transaction, respectively; and

- in the statement of financial position:

  - if the asset subject to the transaction is held by the associate, the adjustment should be made against the carrying amount for the associate (illustrated at Example 12.6 below); or

  - if the asset subject to the transaction is held by the investor, entities have an accounting policy choice as to where the adjustment is made. It would be acceptable to make the adjustment either against the carrying amount for the associate or against the asset which was the subject of the transaction. This latter approach is illustrated in Example 12.7 below.

Examples 12.6 and 12.7 below illustrate the adjustment against the asset which is the subject of the transaction. Both examples deal with the reporting entity H and its 40% associate A. The journal entries are based on the premise that H's financial statements are initially prepared as a simple aggregation of H and the relevant share of its associate. The entries below would then be applied to the numbers at that stage of the process.

Example 12.6:   Elimination of profit on sale by investor to associate ('downstream transaction')

On 1 December 2019 H sells inventory costing £750,000 to A for £1 million. On 10 January 2020, A sells the inventory to a third party for £1.2 million. What adjustments are made in the group financial statements of H at 31 December 2019 and 31 December 2020?

In the year ended 31 December 2019, H has recorded revenue of £1 million and cost of sales of £750,000. However since, at the reporting date, the inventory is still held by A, only 60% of this transaction is regarded by FRS 102 as having taken place (in effect with the other shareholders of A). This is reflected by the consolidation entry:

	£	£
Dr. Revenue	400,000	
Cr. Cost of sales		300,000
Cr. Investment in A		100,000

This effectively defers recognition of 40% of the sale and offsets the deferred profit against the carrying amount of H's investment in A.

During 2019, when the inventory is sold on by A, this deferred profit can be released to group profit or loss, reflected by the following accounting entry.

	£	£
Dr. Opening reserves	100,000	
Dr. Cost of sales	300,000	
Cr. Revenue		400,000

Opening reserves are adjusted because the financial statement working papers (if prepared as assumed above) will not include the consolidation adjustments and will already include this profit in opening reserves, since it forms part of H's opening reserves.

An alternative approach would be to eliminate the profit on 40% of the sale against the cost of sales, as follows:

	£	£
Dr. Cost of sales	100,000	
Cr. Investment in A		100,000

An argument in favour of this approach is that the revenue figures should not be adjusted because the sales to associates need to be disclosed as related party transactions. However, this may be outweighed by the drawback of the approach, namely that it causes volatility in H's reported gross margin as revenue and the related net margin are not necessarily recognised in the same accounting period.

Example 12.7: Elimination of profit on sale by associate to reporting entity ('upstream transaction')

This is the mirror image of the transaction in Example 12.6 above. On 1 December 2019 A sells inventory costing £750,000 to H for £1,000,000. On 10 January 2020, H sells the inventory to a third party for £1.2 million. What adjustments are made in the group financial statements of H at 31 December 2019 and 31 December 2020?

H's share of the profit of A as included on the financial statement working papers at 31 December 2019 will include a profit of £250,000 (£1,000,000 – £750,000), 40% of which (£100,000) is regarded under FRS 102 as unrealised by H, and is therefore deferred and offset against closing inventory:

	£	£
Dr. Share of A's result (income statement)	100,000	
Cr. Inventory		100,000

In the following period when the inventory is sold H's separate financial statements will record a profit of £200,000 and A's individual financial statements will record no profit. On consolidation, the total profit must be increased by the £100,000 deferred from the previous period. The entry is:

	£	£
Dr. Opening reserves	100,000	
Dr. Share of A's result (income statement)		100,000

Again, opening reserves are adjusted because the financial statement working papers (if prepared as assumed above) will already include this profit in opening reserves, this time, however, as part of H's share of the opening reserves of A.

A slightly counter-intuitive consequence of this treatment is that at the end of 2019 the investment in A in H's consolidated statement of financial position will have increased by £100,000 more than the share of profit of associates as reported in group profit or loss and in 2020 by £100,000 less (this would be avoided if the adjustment were to be made against the carrying amount of the associate). This is because the statement of financial position adjustment at the end of 2019 is made against inventory rather than the carrying value of the investment in A, which could be seen as reflecting the fact that A has, indeed, made a profit. It might therefore be necessary to indicate in the notes to the financial statements that part of the profit made by A is regarded as unrealised by the group in 2019 and has therefore been deferred until 2020 by offsetting it against inventory.

Note that unrealised losses on upstream and downstream transactions may provide evidence of an impairment in the asset transferred. *[FRS 102.14.8(e)]*.

The effect of these requirements is illustrated in Examples 12.8 and 12.9 below.

Example 12.8: Sale of asset from an investor to associate at a loss

Entity A holds 40% of entity B, giving it significant influence. B acquires a property from A for £8 million cash and the property was recorded in the financial statements of A at £10 million. £8 million is agreed to be the fair market value of the property. How should A account for these transactions?

The required accounting entry by A is as follows:

	£m	£m
Dr. Cash (1)	8	
Dr. Loss on sale (2)	2	
Cr. Property (3)		10

(1)   £8 million received from B.

(2)   Loss on sale of property £2 million (£8 million received from B less £10 million carrying value = £2 million) not adjusted since the transaction indicated an impairment of the property. In effect, it is the result that would have been obtained if A had recognised an impairment charge immediately prior to the sale and then recognised no gain or loss on the sale.

(3)   Derecognition of A's original property.

Example 12.9:   *Sale of asset from associate to an investor at a loss*

Entity A holds 40% of entity B giving it significant influence. B acquires a property for £8 million from an independent third party C. The property is then sold to A for £7 million, which is agreed to be its market value. How should A account for these transactions?

The required accounting entry by A is as follows:

	£m	£m
Dr. Property (1)	7.0	
Dr. Share of loss of B (2)	0.4	
Cr. Investment in B		0.4
Cr. Cash (3)		7.0

(1)   £7 million paid to B not adjusted since the transaction indicated an impairment of B's asset.

(2)   Loss in B's books is £1 million (£8 million cost of property less £7 million proceeds of sale). A recognises its 40% share because the transaction indicates an impairment of the asset. In effect, it is the result that would have been obtained if B had recognised an impairment charge immediately prior to the sale and then recognised no gain or loss on the sale.

(3)   £7 million consideration for the property.

Elimination of 'downstream' unrealised profits in excess of the investment

Occasionally an investor's share of the unrealised profit on the sale of an asset to an associate exceeds the carrying value of the investment held. In that case, to what extent is any profit in excess of the carrying value of the investment eliminated?

Section 14 provides no guidance on the elimination of 'downstream' unrealised gains in excess of the investment. Consequently, an investor needs to determine an appropriate policy for dealing with such a situation. We believe that the investor could either recognise the excess as 'deferred income' or restrict the elimination to the amount required to reduce the investment to zero.

Loans and borrowings between the reporting entity and its associates

The requirement in section 14 to eliminate partially unrealised profits or losses on transactions with associates is expressed in terms of transactions. In our view, the requirement for partial elimination of profits does not apply to items such as interest paid on loans and borrowings between the reporting entity and its associates, since such loans and borrowings do not involve the transfer of assets giving rise to gains or losses. Moreover, they are not normally regarded as part of the investor's share of the net assets of the associate, but as separate transactions, except in the case of loss-making associates, where interests in long-term loans and borrowings may be required to be accounted for as if they were part of the reporting entity's equity investment in determining the carrying value of the associate against which losses may be offset (see 3.3.2.I below). Likewise, loans and borrowings, and indeed other payables and receivables, between the reporting entity and its associates should not be eliminated in the reporting entity's consolidated accounts because associates are not part of the group.

However, if the associate has capitalised the borrowing costs then the investor would need to eliminate a relevant share of the profit, in the same way it would eliminate a share of the capitalised management or advisory fees charged to an associate.

Cash flow statement

FRS 102 is silent on how cash flows relating to transactions with an associate should be presented in the consolidated cash flow statement. It is generally accepted that no adjustment should be made in respect of these cash flows, as the associate is not a member of the group and hence is not subject to the requirements on elimination of intragroup transactions as set out in paragraph 15 of Section 9. This contrasts with the requirement, in any consolidated statement of cash flows, to eliminate the cash flows between members of the group in the same way that intragroup transactions are eliminated in the profit and loss account and statement of financial position.

3.3.2.G Date of associate's financial statements

In applying the equity method, the investor should use the financial statements of the associate as of the same date as the financial statements of the investor unless it is impracticable to do so. *[FRS 102.14.8(f)].*

Applying a requirement is impracticable when the entity cannot apply it after making every reasonable effort to do so. *[FRS 102 Appendix I].*

Otherwise an investor should use the most recent available financial statements of the associate. Adjustments must then be made for the effects of significant transactions or events, for example a sale of a significant asset or a major loss on a contract, that occurred between that date and the date of the investor's financial statements. *[FRS 102.14.8(f)].* There are no exemptions from this requirement despite the fact that it may be quite onerous in practice, for example, because the associate might need to produce non statutory or interim financial statements so that the investor can comply with this requirement.

3.3.2.H Associate's accounting policies

If an associate uses accounting policies different from those of the investor for like transactions and events in similar circumstances, adjustments must be made to conform the associate's accounting policies to those of the investor when the associate's financial statements are used by the investor in applying the equity method unless it is impracticable to do so. *[FRS 102.14.8(g)].*

In practice, this may be difficult, since an investor's influence over an associate, although significant, may still not be sufficient to ensure access to the relevant underlying information in sufficient detail to make such adjustments with certainty. Restating the financial statements of an overseas associate to FRS 102 may require extensive detailed information that may simply not be required under the associate's local GAAP (for example, in respect of business combinations, share-based payments, financial instruments and revenue recognition).

3.3.2.1   Losses in excess of investment

An investor in an associate should recognise its share of the losses of the associate until its share of losses equals or exceeds the carrying amount of its investment in the associate, at which point the investor discontinues recognising its share of further losses. *[FRS 102.14.8(h)].*

Once the investor's interest is reduced to zero, additional losses are provided for, and a liability is recognised in accordance with Section 21 – *Provisions and Contingencies* (see Chapter 19), but only to the extent that the investor has incurred legal or constructive obligations or made payments on behalf of the associate. If the associate subsequently reports profits, the investor resumes recognising its share of those profits only after its share of the profits equals the share of losses not recognised. The practical effect of this is that an entity needs to track the off balance sheet losses of its associates in order to calculate subsequent income to be recognised from that associate. *[FRS 102.14.8(h)].*

In addition to the recognition of losses arising from application of the equity method, an investor in an associate must consider the requirements of Section 27 in respect of impairment losses. An investor also needs to consider Section 11 in order to determine whether it is necessary to recognise any additional impairment loss with respect to that part of the investor's interest in the associate that does not comprise its net investment in the associate (see 3.3.2.E above).

Section 14 does not address any long-term interests that, in substance, form part of the investor's net investment in the associate. For example, an item for which settlement is neither planned nor likely to occur in the foreseeable future might be regarded as being, in substance, an extension of the entity's investment in that associate. An investor would need to consider whether these interests are recoverable in accordance with Section 27. IAS 28, on which Section 14 is based, considers that such items include: *[IAS 28.38]*

- preference shares; or
- long-term receivables or loans (unless supported by adequate collateral), but do *not* include:
  - trade receivables;
  - trade payables; or
  - any long-term receivables for which adequate collateral exists, such as secured loans.

Example 12.10: Accounting for a loss-making associate

At the beginning of the year entity H invests £5 million to acquire a 30% equity interest in an associate, entity A. In addition, H lends £9 million to the associate, but does not provide any guarantees or commit itself to provide further funding. How should H account for the £20 million loss that the associate made during the year?

H's share in A's loss is £20 million × 30% = £6 million. If H's loan to A is considered part of the net investment in the associate then the carrying amount of the associate is reduced by £6 million, from £14 million (= £5 million + £9 million) to £8 million. This would generally be done by reducing the equity interest to nil and reducing the loan to £8 million. However, if the loan is not part of the net investment in the associate then H accounts for the loss as follows:

- the equity interest in the associate is reduced from £5 million to zero;

- a loss of £1 million remains unrecognised because H did not provide any guarantees and has no commitments to provide further funding. If in the second year, however, A were to make a profit of £10 million then H would only recognise a profit of £2 million (= £10 million × 30% – £1 million). However, if in the second year H were to provide a £1.5 million guarantee to A and A's net profit were nil, then H would need to recognise an immediate loss of £1 million (i.e. the lower of the unrecognised loss of £1 million and the guarantee of £1.5 million) because it now has a legal obligation in respect of A's debts; and

- as there are a number of indicators of impairment, the loan from H to A should be tested for impairment in accordance with FRS 102 Section 11.

3.3.2.J   Discontinuing the equity method

An investor discontinues the use of the equity method from the date that significant influence ceases. The subsequent accounting depends upon the nature of the retained investment.

If the associate becomes a subsidiary (because control is obtained), it will be accounted for in accordance with Section 19 (i.e. a step-acquisition, see Chapter 17 at 2.10).

If an investment in an associate becomes an investment in a joint venture it will account for its investment in accordance with Section 15 – *Investments in Joint Ventures* (i.e. it will continue to be accounted for under the equity method, see Chapter 13).

Otherwise the retained investment should be accounted for as a financial asset in accordance with Section 11 or Section 12 – *Other Financial Instruments Issues* – as discussed below. *[FRS 102.14.8(i)]*.

If an investor disposes of some or all of its investment, such that it no longer has significant influence over the investee, it will discontinue the use of the equity method. In such situations, the entity derecognises the associate and recognises in profit or loss any difference between the:

(a)   the proceeds from the disposal; and

(b)   the carrying amount of the investment in the associate relating to the proportion disposed of or lost at the date significant influence is lost. *[FRS 102.14.8(i)(i)]*.

The investor accounts for any retained interest as a financial asset in accordance with Section 11 or Section 12 as appropriate. The carrying amount of the proportion retained in the investment at the date that it ceases to be an associate shall be regarded as its cost on initial measurement as a financial asset.

Where an investor ceases to have significant influence due to a change in circumstances other than by partial disposal, for example, as a result of changes to the board of directors or equivalent governing body of the associate that results in a loss of significant influence, the investor will discontinue the use of the equity method. In that case, the investor does not recognise a profit or loss, but regards the carrying amount of the investment at that date as the new cost basis in accordance with Sections 11 or 12. *[FRS 102.14.8(i)(ii)]*.

If an investor loses significant influence as a result of a disposal the gain or loss arising on that disposal shall also include amounts recognised in other comprehensive income in relation to that associate where those amounts are required to be reclassified to profit or loss on disposal. *[FRS 102.14.8(i)]*. Under FRS 102 this includes cash flow hedges which have not yet been reclassified to profit or loss. Amounts that are not required to be reclassified to profit or loss upon disposal shall be transferred directly to retained earnings. *[FRS 102.14.8(i)]*.

A deemed disposal, for example, where the associate has issued shares to a new investor, would be accounted for as a regular disposal and hence a profit or loss would be recognised as set out above. The original investor would need to consider whether any profit resulting from the transaction is realised or unrealised. If unrealised, it would be taken to other comprehensive income and not to profit or loss.

3.3.2.K   *Transactions to create an associate*

An investor may exchange a business, or other non-monetary asset, for an interest in another entity, and that other entity becomes an associate of the investor. The accounting issues that arise from these transactions are whether they should be accounted for at fair value or at previous book values and how the gain on the transaction should be reported.

The requirements in respect of such transactions are set out in Section 9 (see Chapter 8 at 3.8). The principles are that the only exception to the use of fair values should be in rare circumstances where the transaction is artificial and has no substance and that any unrealised gains should not be reported in profit or loss.

Accordingly, the following accounting treatment should be applied in the consolidated financial statements of the reporting entity:

- to the extent that the reporting entity retains an ownership interest in the business, or other non-monetary assets, exchanged, even if that interest is then held through the associate, that retained interest, including any related goodwill, is treated as having been owned by the reporting entity throughout the transaction and should be included at its pre-transaction carrying amount;

- goodwill is recognised as the difference between:

  - the fair value of the consideration given; and

  - the fair value of the reporting entity's share of the pre-transaction identifiable net assets of the other entity.

  The consideration given for the interest acquired in the associate will include that part of the business, or other non-monetary assets, exchanged and no longer owned by the reporting entity. The consideration may also include cash or monetary assets to achieve equalisation of values. Where it is difficult to value the consideration given, the best estimate of its value may be given by valuing what is acquired;

- to the extent that the fair value of the consideration received by the reporting entity exceeds the carrying value of the part of the business, or other non-monetary assets exchanged and no longer owned by the reporting entity, and any related goodwill together with any cash given up, the reporting entity should recognise a gain. Any unrealised gain arising on the exchange is recognised in other comprehensive income; and

- to the extent that the fair value of the consideration received by the reporting entity is less than the carrying value of the part of the business, or other non-monetary assets no longer owned by the reporting entity, and any related goodwill, together with any cash given up, the reporting entity should recognise a loss. The loss should be recognised as an impairment in accordance with Section 27 or, for any loss remaining after an impairment review of the relevant assets, in profit or loss. *[FRS 102.9.31].*

The most common situation for these transactions in practice is the contribution of a business for equity in an associate (or joint venture).

Examples 13.7 and 13.8 in Chapter 13 illustrate the required accounting for such transactions.

Section 9 does not explain how a realised gain can be distinguished from an unrealised gain. In Example 13.8 in Chapter 13, we have used a 'top slicing' approach whereby as much of the total gain as is backed by cash is treated as realised (i.e. £10m). 'Top slicing' is the recommended approach in determining realised profits for exchanges of assets in paragraph 3.18 of the ICAEW/ICAS TECH 02/17BL – *Guidance on Realised and Distributable Profits under the Companies Act 2006.* Paragraph 3.18A of the guidance states that when the consideration received comprise a combination of assets and liabilities, the profit will be realised only to the extent of any net balance (i.e. cash less liabilities) of qualifying consideration received.

No gain or loss is recognised in those rare cases where the artificiality or lack of substance of the transaction is such that a gain or loss on the exchange could not be justified. When a gain or loss on the exchange is not taken into account because the transaction is artificial or has no substance, the circumstances should be explained. *[FRS 102.9.32].* There is no elaboration in the standard as to the circumstances where this might be applicable.

3.3.3 Cost model

An investor that is not a parent, and that chooses to adopt the cost model, should measure its investments in associates at cost less any accumulated impairment losses. Section 27 will apply to the recognition and measurement of impairment losses. *[FRS 102.14.5].*

Section 14 does not define 'cost' of investment. However, Section 2 – *Concepts and Pervasive Principles* – defines 'historical cost' as the amount of cash or cash equivalents paid or the fair value of the consideration given to acquire the asset at the time of its acquisition. *[FRS 102.2.34(a)].* The Regulations state that the purchase price of an asset is determined by adding to the actual price paid any expenses incidental to its acquisition and then subtracting any incidental reductions in the cost of the acquisition. *[1 Sch 27(1)].* Consistent with this, Section 17 – *Property, Plant and Equipment*, states that cost is normally either the purchase price paid (including directly attributable costs) or the fair value of non-monetary assets exchanged. *[FRS 102.17.10, 14].* The purchase price would generally represent the fair value of the consideration given to purchase the investment consistent with the guidance in respect of exchanges of businesses or other non-monetary items assets (see Chapter 8 at 3.8) and the requirements in respect of measuring the cost of a business combination (see Chapter 17 at 3.6).

An investor will recognise distributions received from its investments in associates as income irrespective of whether the distributions are from accumulated profits of the associate arising before or after the date of acquisition. *[FRS 102.14.6].*

3.3.4 Fair value model

An investor that is not a parent, and that chooses to adopt the policy of accounting for its associate at fair value through other comprehensive income, should initially recognise its investment at the transaction price. *[FRS 102.14.9].* 'Transaction price' is not defined, but it is presumably the same as its cost.

At each subsequent reporting date, the investor should measure its investments in associates at fair value using the fair value guidance in the Appendix to Section 2 of FRS 102. *[FRS.102.14.10]*.

Where the fair value through other comprehensive income model is used, increases in the carrying amount of the investment as a result of a revaluation to fair value are recognised in other comprehensive income and accumulated in equity i.e. a revaluation reserve. If a revaluation increase reverses a revaluation decrease of the same investment that was previously recognised as an expense, it must be recognised in profit or loss. *[FRS 102.17.15E]*. Decreases as a result of revaluation are recognised in other comprehensive income to the extent of any previously recognised revaluation increase accumulated in revaluation reserve in respect of the same investment. If a revaluation decrease exceeds the revaluation gains accumulated in revaluation reserve in respect of that investment, the excess is recognised in profit or loss. *[FRS 102.17.15F]*. This means that it is not permissible to carry a negative revaluation reserve in respect of each investment in associates at fair value.

Where the fair value through profit or loss model is used, increases and decreases in the carrying amount of the investment as a result of a revaluation to fair value are recognised in profit or loss.

An investor will recognise distributions received from its investments in associates accounted for at fair value through other comprehensive income as income irrespective of whether the distributions are from accumulated profits of the associate arising before or after the date of acquisition. *[FRS 102.14.10A]*.

3.4   Presentation and disclosures

3.4.1   Presentation

Under the Companies Act formats, investments in participating interests are classified under fixed asset investments in the balance sheet (see Chapter 6 at 5.3.4). When 'adapted formats' (see Chapter 6 at 5.1) are used, investments in associates must be shown as a separate balance sheet item and distinguished between current and non-current items. *[FRS 102.4.2A]*.

Goodwill relating to an associate is included in the carrying amount of the investment. *[FRS 102.14.8(c)]*.

As set out at 2.6 above, there is no guidance in FRS 102 as to how long term interests (such as long term loans for which no payment is intended in the foreseeable future) in associates should be presented and therefore an entity must make an accounting policy choice as to the presentation of such interests. Entities frequently make loans to associates, the terms of which are repayable on demand, but there is no intention of repayment in the foreseeable future. In these circumstances, for entities applying the Companies Act formats, management will need to exercise judgement in determining whether such a loan is a debtor or a fixed asset investment in nature (see Chapter 6 at 5.3.4). For entities applying the adapted formats, such loans will need to be classified as appropriate between current or non-current assets (see Chapter 6 at 5.1.1).

In the profit and loss account, for entities applying the Companies Act formats, income from interests in associates should be shown as one line item in the profit and loss account. *[6 Sch 20]*. For entities applying the adapted formats, the share of the profit or loss of associates and jointly controlled entities accounted for using the equity method must be included as one line item in the profit and loss account. *[FRS 102.5.5B]*.

3.4.2   Disclosures

The disclosures required under Section 14 in respect of investments in associates are set out below. Additional disclosures required by the CA 2006 are discussed at 3.4.2.E below.

3.4.2.A   General requirements

In both consolidated and individual financial statements where an entity holds an investment in an associate the following should be disclosed:

- the accounting policy for investments in associates;
- the carrying amount of investments in associates; and
- the fair value of investments in associates accounted for using the equity method for which there are published price quotations. *[FRS 102.14.12]*.

3.4.2.B   Consolidated financial statements

An investor shall disclose separately:

- its share of the profit or loss of associates accounted for in accordance with the equity method; and
- its share of any discontinued operations of such associates. *[FRS 102.14.14]*.

3.4.2.C   Individual financial statements of investors that are not parents

An investor should disclose:

- summarised financial information about the investments in associates ; and
- the effect of including those investments as if they had been accounted for using the equity method. *[FRS 102.14.15A]*.

Summarised financial information is not defined in FRS 102, but using the GAAP hierarchy to refer to IFRS 12 – *Disclosure of Interests in Other Entities*, it would seem appropriate to include: current assets, non-current assets, current liabilities, non-current liabilities, revenue, profit or loss from continuing operations, post-tax profit or loss from discontinued operations, other comprehensive income, total comprehensive income. This list is not exhaustive and other items may need to be considered if deemed material. *[IFRS 12 Appendix B.12]*.

For investments accounted for in accordance with the cost model, an investor is required to disclose the amount of dividends and any other distributions recognised as income. *[FRS 102.14.13]*.

For investments in associates accounted for in accordance with fair value through other comprehensive income, an investor shall make the disclosures required by Section 11 paragraphs 11.43 and 11.44 (this is notwithstanding the fact that paragraph 11.43 refers to fair value through profit or loss, but the intention is clearly to make these disclosures for fair value through other comprehensive income): *[FRS 102.14.15]*

- the basis for determining fair value (e.g. quoted market price in an active market or a valuation technique. If the latter is used, the assumptions applied in determining fair value for each class of financial assets or liabilities must be disclosed); and

- if a reliable measure of fair value is no longer available for financial instruments that would otherwise be required to be measured at fair value through profit or loss this fact shall be disclosed and the carrying amount of those financial instruments.

For investments in associates accounted for at fair value through profit or loss, the above disclosures will also apply (see Chapter 6 at 10.3.1.D.

Investors in associates that are exempt from preparing consolidated financial statements, or would be exempt if they had any subsidiaries, are exempt from these requirements. *[FRS 102.14.15A]*. This would apply to an entity which failed the small company criteria and which had no subsidiaries, but only associates and joint ventures.

3.4.2.D   *Additional company law disclosures – consolidated financial statements*

The Regulations also require that the following information must be given where an undertaking included in the consolidation has an interest in an associated undertaking:

- the name of the associate;
- the country in which the associate is incorporated for those incorporated outside the United Kingdom;
- the address of the registered office of the associate;
- The identity and proportion of the nominal value of each class of share held disclosing separately those held by the:
  - parent company; and
  - group. *[4 Sch 19]*.

3.4.2.E   *Additional company law disclosures – individual financial statements*

In individual financial statements the Regulations require additional disclosures in respect of significant holdings in undertakings, other than subsidiary entities. A holding is deemed significant if:

- it amounts to 20% or more of the nominal value of any class of shares in the undertaking; or
- the amount of the holding as stated in the company's individual accounts exceeds 20% of the stated net assets of the company. *[4 Sch 4]*.

In practice, this definition will capture most investments in associates. The resulting disclosures in individual financial statements are:

- the name of each associate;
- the address of the registered office of each associate;
- the address of each associate's principal place of business if unincorporated;
- the identity and proportion of the nominal value of each class of share held. *[4 Sch 5]*.

For each associate detailed above there must also be disclosed the aggregate amount of the capital and reserves as at the end of its relevant financial year of each entity and its profit or loss for that year (unless the associate is not required to publish its balance sheet anywhere in the world and the holding is less than 50% of the nominal value of the shares, or the information is not material). *[4 Sch 6]*.

A parent that is exempt under sections 400 or 401 of the Act from the requirement to prepare group accounts is not required to give the additional disclosures listed above in its separate financial statements if it discloses, in the notes to its accounts, the aggregate investment in all significant holdings in undertakings (including its associates) determined by way of the equity method of valuation. *[4 Sch 13]*.

A parent that prepares consolidated financial statements and discloses the information described at 3.4.2.D above in respect of its associates is not required to give the disclosures otherwise required by paragraphs 5 and 6 of Schedule 4 of the Regulations in its individual financial statements. *[4 Sch 4]*.

4 PRACTICAL ISSUES

4.1 Changes in ownership interest

4.1.1 *Initial carrying amount of an associate following loss of control of an entity*

Under Section 9, if a parent entity loses control of an entity, then at the date that the entity ceases to be a subsidiary the retained interest is measured at the carrying amount of the net assets (and goodwill) attributable to the investment and shall be regarded as the cost on initial measurement of the financial asset or investment in the associate, as appropriate. In applying the equity method to a retained investment in an associate as required in Section 9, paragraph 9.19 states that the requirements of Section 14, paragraph 14.8(c) shall not be applied. *[FRS 102.9.19]*.

This means that in the case of a retained interest in an associate, there is no need to re-determine the implicit goodwill and fair values of the associate's assets and liabilities at the date it becomes an associate.

Example 12.11: Accounting for retained interest in an associate following loss of control of an entity

Entity A owns 100% of the shares of Entity B. The interest was originally purchased for £500,000 and £40,000 of directly attributable costs relating to the acquisition were incurred. On 30 June 2019, Entity A sells 60% of the shares to Entity C for £1,300,000. As a result of the sale, Entity C obtains control over Entity B, but by retaining a 40% interest, Entity A determines that it still has significant influence over Entity B.

At the date of disposal, the carrying amount of the net assets of Entity B in Entity A's consolidated financial statements is £1,200,000 and there is also goodwill of £200,000 relating to the acquisition of Entity B. The fair value of the identifiable assets and liabilities of Entity B is £1,600,000. The fair value of Entity A's retained interest of 40% of the shares of Entity B is £800,000.

Upon Entity A's sale of 60% of the shares of Entity B, it deconsolidates Entity B and accounts for its investment in Entity B as an associate using the equity method of accounting.

Entity A's initial carrying amount of the associate must be based on the carrying value of the net assets (and goodwill) of the retained interest, i.e. £560,000 or 40% of the carrying amount of the net assets and goodwill totalling £1,400,000.

4.1.2   *Piecemeal acquisition of an associate*

There is no guidance in FRS 102 on how to account for the piecemeal acquisition of an associate and so different approaches could be applied in practice.

4.1.2.A   *Existing investment becoming an associate*

An entity may gain significant influence over an existing investment upon acquisition of a further interest or due to a change in circumstances. Section 14 gives no guidance on how an investor should account for an existing investment that subsequently becomes an associate.

It is clear under Section 19 that in a business combination where control over an acquiree is achieved in stages following a series of transactions, the cost of the business combination is the aggregate of the fair values of the assets given, liabilities assumed and equity instruments issued by the acquirer at the date of each transaction in the series. *[FRS 102.19.11A]*. It might be argued that a similar approach should be adopted when an associate is acquired in stages.

4.1.3   *Step increase in an existing associate*

An entity may acquire an additional interest in an existing associate that continues to be an associate accounted for under the equity method. FRS 102 does not explicitly deal with such transactions.

In these situations, we believe that the purchase price paid for the additional interest is added to the existing carrying amount of the associate and the existing interest in the associate is not remeasured.

This increase in the investment must still be notionally split between goodwill and the additional interest in the fair value of the net assets of the associate. This split is based on the fair value of the net assets at the date of the increase in the associate. However, no remeasurement is made for previously unrecognised changes in the fair values of identifiable net assets.

Paragraph 14.8(c) of FRS 102 establishes the requirement that the cost of an investment in an associate is allocated between the purchase of a share of the fair value of net assets and the goodwill. This requirement is not limited to the initial application of equity accounting, but applies to each acquisition of an investment. However, this does not result in any revaluation of the existing share of net assets.

Rather, the existing ownership interests are accounted for under paragraph 14.8 of FRS 102, whereby the carrying value is adjusted only for the investor's share of the associate's profits or losses and other recognised equity transactions. No entry is recognised to reflect changes in the fair value of assets and liabilities that are not recognised under the accounting policies applied for the associate.

Example 12.12 below illustrates an increase in ownership of an associate that continues to be an associate.

Example 12.12: Accounting for an increase in the ownership of an associate

Entity A obtains significant influence over Entity B by acquiring an investment of 25% at a cost of £3,000 in January 2017. At the date of the acquisition of the investment, the fair value of the associate's net identifiable assets is £10,000. The investment is accounted for under the equity method in the consolidated financial statements of Entity A.

In January 2019, Entity A acquires an additional investment of 20% in Entity B at a cost of £4,000, increasing its total investment in Entity B to 45%. The investment is, however, still an associate and still accounted for using the equity method of accounting.

For the purposes of the example, directly attributable costs have been ignored and it is assumed that no profit or loss arose during the period since the acquisition of the first 25%. The implicit goodwill on the initial acquisition of the associate of £500 is assumed to have a 10 year useful life, therefore goodwill amortisation of £100 has been recognised over the two year period between the initial investment of 25% and the purchase of the additional interest of 20%. Therefore, the carrying amount of the investment immediately prior to the additional investment is £2,900 (£3,000 – £100). However, an asset held by the associate has increased in value by £5,000 so that the fair value of the associate's net identifiable assets is now £15,000.

To summarise, amounts are as follows:

	£
Fair value of net assets of Entity B in 2017	10,000
Increase in fair value	5,000
Fair value of net assets of Entity B in 2019	15,000

As a result of the additional investment, the equity-accounted amount for the associate increases by £4,000. The notional goodwill applicable to the second tranche of the acquisition is £1,000 [£4,000 – (20% × £15,000)].

The impact of the additional investment on Entity A's equity-accounted amount for Entity B is summarised as follows:

	% held	Carrying amount	Share of net assets	Goodwill included in investment
		£	£	£
Existing investment	25	2,900	2,500	400
Additional investment	20	4,000	3,000	1,000
Total investment	45	6,900	5,500	1,400

The accounting described above applies when the additional interest in an existing associate continues to be accounted for as an associate under the equity method. The accounting for an increase in an associate that becomes a subsidiary is discussed in Chapter 17.

4.1.4 Step increase in an existing associate that becomes a joint venture

In the situation discussed at 4.1.3 above, the acquisition of the additional interest did not result in a change in status of the investee; i.e. the associate remained an associate. However, an entity may acquire an additional interest in an existing associate that becomes a joint venture. In this situation, although FRS 102 does refer to an associate that becomes a joint venture, it does not actually contain any specific guidance as to what should be done. *[FRS 102.14.8(i)]*. However, as a joint venture is also accounted under the equity method, the accounting described in Example 12.12 above would seem to apply.

4.2　Distributions received in excess of the carrying amount

When an associate makes dividend distributions to the investor in excess of the investor's carrying amount it is not immediately clear how the excess should be accounted for. A liability under Section 21 should only be recognised if the investor is obliged to refund the dividend, or has incurred a legal or constructive obligation or made payments on behalf of the associate. In the absence of such obligations, it would seem appropriate that the investor recognises the excess in net profit for the period. When the associate subsequently makes profits, the investor should only start recognising profits when they exceed the excess cash distributions recognised in net profit plus any previously unrecognised losses (see 3.3.2.I above).

4.3　Equity transactions in an associate's financial statements

The financial statements of an associate that are used for the purposes of equity accounting by the investor may include items within its statement of changes in equity that are not reflected in the profit or loss or components of other comprehensive income, for example, dividends or other forms of distributions, issues of equity instruments and equity-settled share-based payment transactions. Where the associate has subsidiaries and consolidated financial statements are prepared, those financial statements may include the effects of changes in the parent's (i.e. the associate's) ownership interest and non-controlling interest in a subsidiary that did not arise from a transaction that resulted in loss of control of that subsidiary.

Although the description of the equity method in Section 14 (together with the requirements in Section 5 – *Statement of Comprehensive Income and Income Statement* - requires that the investor's share of the profit or loss of the associate is recognised in the investor's profit or loss, and the investor's share of changes in items of other comprehensive income of the associate is recognised in other comprehensive income of the investor, *[FRS 102.14.8]*, no explicit reference is made to other items that the associate may have in its statement of changes in equity.

Investors will therefore need to determine an appropriate accounting treatment for these different types of transactions that may be accounted for by the associate in its statement of changes in equity.

5   SUMMARY OF GAAP DIFFERENCES

The key differences between FRS 102 and IFRS in accounting for associates are set out below.

	FRS 102	*IFRS*
Individual and separate entity financial statements	An entity that is not a parent (i.e. has no subsidiaries) or is a parent that prepares separate financial statements, has the option to account for its investments in associates using either the cost model, at fair value through other comprehensive income or at fair value through profit or loss.	An entity that is not a parent (i.e. has no subsidiaries) must account for its investments in associates under the equity accounting method unless it meets criteria for exemption. An entity that is a parent but prepares separate financial statements also has the option of using the equity method of accounting.
Investment portfolios / funds	Investments in associates held as part of an investment portfolio should be measured at fair value through profit or loss in the consolidated financial statements of an investor that is a parent.	Venture capital organisations and similar entities can choose to measure investments in associates at fair value through profit or loss. Investment entities would elect to choose this option.
Implicit goodwill and fair value adjustments on acquisition of an associate	Follows the requirements of Section 19. Goodwill should be amortised over its finite useful life, but if, in exceptional cases, an entity is unable to makes a reliable estimate of the useful life of goodwill, the life shall not exceed 10 years.	Follows the IFRS requirements regarding business combinations. Implicit goodwill is not amortised.
Loss of significant influence of an equity-accounted associate that does not become a subsidiary or an jointly controlled entity	If loss of significant influence is as a result of a partial disposal, a gain or loss is recognised based on the disposal proceeds and the carrying amount relating to the proportion disposed of. The carrying value of the equity interest retained at the date significant influence was lost becomes the cost of the retained investment. If the loss of significant influence is for reasons other than a partial disposal, no gain or loss is recognised and the carrying value of the equity-accounted investment at the date significant influence is lost becomes the cost of the retained investment.	If loss of significant influence is as a result of a partial disposal, a gain or loss is recognised based on the disposal proceeds together with the fair value of any retained interest and the carrying amount of the total interest in the associate. If loss of significant influence is for reasons other than a partial disposal, a gain or loss is recognised based on the fair value of the retained interest and the carrying amount of the interest in the associate at that date.
Exchange of business or other non-monetary assets for an interest in an associate in the consolidated financial statement.	Gains that are not realised are reported in other comprehensive income.	No distinction between realised and unrealised gains and all gains/losses are reported in profit or loss.

Chapter 12

Chapter 13

Investments in joint ventures

List of examples

Chapter 13   Investments in joint ventures

1   INTRODUCTION

Section 15 – *Investments in Joint Ventures* – sets out the accounting and disclosure requirements for joint ventures in consolidated financial statements, separate financial statements of a venturer that is a parent and individual financial statements of a venturer that is not a parent. *[FRS 102.15.1]*.

The accounting requirements in Section 15 are based on the IASB's IFRS for SMEs, which in turn were derived from those in the then IAS on the topic, IAS 31 – *Interests in Joint Ventures*. It therefore does not reflect the requirements of IFRS 11 – *Joint Arrangements* – which is now the effective IFRS relevant to this topic. Although based on the IFRS for SMEs, Section 15 has also been amended, principally in relation to certain aspects of the accounting and disclosures for investments in a jointly controlled entity in the individual financial statements of a venturer that is not a parent.

A 'joint venture' is a contractual arrangement whereby two or more parties undertake an economic activity that is subject to joint control. The exact form of the strategic investment can vary and Section 15 addresses that variation by classifying joint ventures into three categories: jointly controlled assets, jointly controlled operations and jointly controlled entities.

Joint ventures are commonplace in many industry sectors, often as a means of pooling resources or expertise, risk sharing or new product development. The term is sometimes used loosely to describe any commercial partnership type arrangement but it is important to emphasise that only those where contractually-based joint control exists will fall within the scope of Section 15.

2   COMPARISON BETWEEN SECTION 15 AND IFRS

There are differences between the accounting and disclosure requirements in Section 15 compared with IFRS 11. The key differences are discussed below and summarised at 5 below.

2.1   Scope and classification

As noted above, Section 15 classifies joint ventures as either jointly controlled operations, jointly controlled assets or jointly controlled entities.

IFRS 11 addresses joint arrangements and only makes the distinction between joint operations and joint ventures. This distinction is based on the rights and obligations under the arrangement, rather than focussing on the legal form of the entity. *[IFRS 11.14]*. Where the parties with joint control have an interest in the net assets of the arrangement then the arrangement will be a joint venture, *[IFRS 11.16]*, which is the equivalent of a jointly controlled entity under Section 15. Otherwise, where the parties with joint control have rights to underlying assets and obligations for liabilities the arrangement will be a joint operation. *[IFRS 11.15]*. Determining the appropriate classification under IFRS 11 involves an assessment of a venturer's rights and obligations under the arrangement, based on the detailed guidance within the standard.

Generally, arrangements that are jointly controlled operations or jointly controlled assets under Section 15 would be joint operations under IFRS 11. Although many arrangements that are jointly controlled entities under Section 15 would be classified as joint ventures under IFRS 11 some would have to be classified as joint operations due to the requirement to assess rights and obligations rather than focussing on the legal form of the entity.

2.2   Measurement – individual and separate entity financial statements

Section 15 permits entities that are not parents to account for their investment in jointly controlled entities using either cost less impairment, at fair value with changes in fair value recognised through other comprehensive income (unless reversing a revaluation decrease of the same investment previously recognised in profit or loss, in which case the revaluation increase is recognised in profit or loss, or where a revaluation decrease exceeds increases previously recognised in respect of the same investment, in which case the excess is recognised in profit or loss) or at fair value with changes in fair value recognised through profit or loss (see **3.6.2** below). *[FRS 102.15.9]*. The same accounting policy choice is available for a venturer accounting for their investment in jointly controlled entities that is preparing separate financial statements in accordance with Section 9 – *Consolidated and Separate Financial Statements*. *[FRS 102.9.26]*.

Under IFRS, an entity that is not a parent must prepare individual financial statements in which its investments in jointly controlled entities are accounted for under the equity accounting method unless it meets the criteria for exemption. *[IAS 28.16-17]*. An entity preparing separate financial statements under IFRS has an accounting policy choice of measuring investments in jointly controlled entities at cost, in accordance with IFRS 9 – *Financial Instruments*, or using the equity method of accounting. *[IAS 27.10]*.

2.3   Investment portfolios / funds

Under Section 15, a venturer that is a parent and has investments in jointly controlled entities that are held as part of an investment portfolio is required to measure those investments at fair value through profit or loss with changes in fair value recognised in profit or loss in the consolidated financial statements (see **3.6.3.B** below). *[FRS 102.15.9B]*. However, under IFRS, the measurement of investments in joint ventures at fair value through profit or loss is an option that is only available for an entity which is a venture capital organisation or a mutual fund, unit trust and similar entities including investment-linked insurance funds or one which holds its investments indirectly through such an entity. *[IAS 28.18]*.

2.4   Accounting for the acquisition of a jointly controlled entity

Section 15 (via Section 14 – *Investments in Associates*) requires the use of Section 19 – *Business Combinations and Goodwill* – to determine the implicit goodwill on the acquisition of a jointly controlled entity. The implicit goodwill is then amortised over its useful life. *[FRS 102.14.8(c), 19.23]*. Under IFRS, implicit goodwill is not amortised.

2.5   Loss of joint control where the jointly controlled entity does not become a subsidiary or associate

Section 15 (via Section 14) requires that where loss of joint control is as a result of a partial disposal, a gain or loss is recognised based on the disposal proceeds and the carrying amount relating to the proportion disposed of. The carrying value of the equity interest retained at the date joint control is lost becomes the cost of the retained investment and there is no measurement of the retained interest at fair value.

If the loss of joint control is for reasons other than a partial disposal, for example a change in circumstances such as the joint venture issuing shares to third parties, no gain or loss is recognised and the carrying value of the equity-accounted investment as at the date at which joint control is lost becomes the cost of the retained investment. *[FRS 102.14.8(i)]*.

Under IFRS, where loss of joint control is as a result of a partial disposal, a gain or loss is recognised based on any difference between the disposal proceeds together with the fair value of any retained interest and the carrying amount of the total interest in the joint venture.

If the loss of joint control is for reasons other than a partial disposal, a gain or loss is recognised based on the fair value of the retained interest and the carrying amount of the interest in the joint venture at that date. *[IAS 28.22]*.

2.6   Transactions to create a jointly controlled entity

Section 9 sets out the requirements in respect of transactions where a venturer may exchange a business, or other non-monetary asset, for an interest in another entity, and that other entity becomes a jointly controlled entity of the venturer. To the extent that the fair value of the consideration received by the venturer exceeds the carrying value of the part of the business, or other non-monetary assets exchanged and no longer owned by the venturer, and any related goodwill together with any cash given up, the venturer should recognise a gain. Any unrealised gain arising on the exchange is recognised in other comprehensive income. To the extent that the fair value of the consideration received is less than the carrying value of what has been exchanged, together with any related goodwill and cash given up, a loss is recognised (see 3.9 below).

IFRS, does not distinguish between realised and unrealised gains for equivalent transactions and requires that gain or loss, realised or unrealised, to be recognised in profit or loss. *[IFRS 10 Appendix B.98]*.

3   REQUIREMENTS OF SECTION 15 FOR INVESTMENTS IN JOINT VENTURES

3.1   Scope

Section 15 applies to investments in:

- joint ventures in consolidated financial statements;
- joint ventures in the individual financial statements of a venturer that is not a parent (see 3.6.2 below); and
- jointly controlled operations and jointly controlled assets in the separate financial statements of a venturer that is a parent (see 3.6.3 below).

A venturer that is a parent accounts for interests in jointly controlled entities in its separate financial statements in accordance with paragraphs 9.26 and 9.26A of FRS 102, as appropriate (see Chapter 8 at 4.2). *[FRS 102.15.1]*.

3.2   Terms used in Section 15

Terms defined within Section 15 are explained in this chapter. Those and other relevant terms used within Section 15 but defined elsewhere within FRS 102 have the meanings specified in the Glossary as shown in the following table: *[FRS 102 Appendix I]*

Term	Definition
Consolidated financial statements	The financial statements of a parent and its subsidiaries presented as those of a single economic entity.
Control (of an entity)	The power to govern the financial and operating policies of an entity so as to obtain benefits from its activities.
Held as part of an investment portfolio	An interest is held as part of an investment portfolio if its value to the investor is through fair value as part of a directly or indirectly held basket of investments rather than as a media through which the investor carries out business. A basket of investments is indirectly held if an investment fund holds a single investment in a second investment fund which, in turn, holds a basket of investments. In some circumstances, it may be appropriate for a single investment to be considered an investment portfolio, for example when an investment fund is first being established and is expected to acquire additional investments.
Individual financial statements	The accounts that are required to be prepared by an entity in accordance with the Act or relevant legislation, for example: (a) 'individual accounts', as set out in section 394 of the Act; (b) 'statement of accounts', as set out in section 132 of the Charities Act 2011; or (c) 'individual accounts', as set out in section 72A of the Building Societies Act 1986. Separate financial statements are included in the meaning of this term.

Joint control	The contractually agreed sharing of control over an economic activity. It exists only when the strategic financial and operating decisions relating to the activity require the unanimous consent of the parties sharing control (the venturers).
Jointly controlled entity	A joint venture that involves the establishment of a corporation, partnership or other entity in which each venturer has an interest. The entity operates in the same way as other entities, except that a contractual arrangement between the venturers establishes joint control over the economic activity of the entity.
Joint venture	A contractual arrangement whereby two or more parties undertake an economic activity that is subject to joint control. Joint ventures can take the form of jointly controlled operations, jointly controlled assets or jointly controlled entities.
Parent	An entity that has one or more subsidiaries.
Separate financial statements	Those presented by a parent in which the investments in subsidiaries, associates or jointly controlled entities are accounted for either at cost or fair value rather than on the basis of the reported results and net assets of the investees. Separate financial statements are included within the meaning of individual financial statements.
Subsidiary	An entity, including an unincorporated entity such as a partnership, which is controlled by another entity (known as the parent).
Venturer	A party to a joint venture that has joint control over that joint venture.

Chapter 13

3.3 Definition of a joint venture and related terms

Section 15 defines a joint venture as 'a contractual arrangement whereby two or more parties undertake an economic activity that is subject to joint control'. *[FRS 102.15.3]*.

An economic activity is not defined in FRS 102 but is intended to be broadly based given that joint ventures can take many forms (see 3.3.5 below).

Joint control is defined as 'the contractually agreed sharing of control over an economic activity, and exists only when the strategic financial and operating decisions relating to the activity require the unanimous consent of the parties sharing control (the venturers)'. *[FRS 102.15.2]*.

Although FRS 102 does not define what strategic, financial and operating decisions would cover, these are generally understood to include areas such as budgeting, capital expenditure, treasury management, dividend policy, production, marketing, sales and human resources.

FRS 102 defines control (of an entity) as 'the power to govern the financial and operating policies of an entity so as to obtain benefits from its activities'. *[FRS 102 Appendix I]*. The concept of control is discussed further in Chapter 8.

A venturer is defined as 'a party to a joint venture that has joint control over that joint venture'. *[FRS 102 Appendix I]*.

Section 15 offers no further guidance on the following: parties to a joint venture that are not venturers and the nature of the contractual arrangements or joint control (in particular the concept of unanimous consent) which are key to an understanding of a joint venture. These aspects are discussed in the following sections making reference to additional guidance in IFRS 11 when relevant. As Section 10 – *Accounting Policies, Estimates and Errors,* requires management to use its judgement in developing and applying an accounting policy when a transaction is not specifically addressed by the standard, management may consider the requirements and guidance in IFRS dealing with similar and related issues. *[FRS 102.10.5-6].*

3.3.1   'Venturer' versus 'investor'

In addition to 'venturers', there may well be other investors in the joint venture. In the absence of a definition of an 'investor' in FRS 102, it is clear from the definition of a 'venturer' that an investor in a joint venture must be 'a party to a joint venture that does not have joint control over the joint venture'. This is illustrated by Example 13.1.

Example 13.1:   'Venturer' versus 'investor'

A, B and C establish a fourth entity D, of which A owns 40%, B 11% and C 49%. A and B enter into a contractual arrangement whereby any financial and operating decisions taken by A and B relating to the activity of D require the unanimous consent of A and B. A simple majority of D's shareholders only is required for all major decisions. An analysis based on the relevant definitions would regard A and B as being 'venturers', and C as an 'investor', in D.

The interest of an 'investor' in a jointly controlled entity should be treated as either:

- an associate within the scope of Section 14 if the investor has significant influence over the entity (see Chapter 12); or

- otherwise as a financial asset within the scope of Section 11 – *Basic Financial Instruments* – or Section 12 – *Other Financial Instruments Issues* (see Chapter 10).
   [FRS 102.15.18].

3.3.2   Contractual arrangement

Contractual arrangements can be evidenced in several ways. An enforceable contractual arrangement is often, but not always, in writing (although we expect unwritten agreements to be rare in practice). Statutory mechanisms can create enforceable arrangements, either on their own or in conjunction with contracts between the parties. A contractual arrangement may be incorporated into the articles or other formation documents of the entity.

The contractual arrangement sets out the terms upon which the parties agree to share control over the activity that is the subject of the arrangement. IFRS 11 provides some relevant guidance on the aspects generally specified in the contractual arrangement for a joint arrangement which could equally be applied to a joint venture under FRS 102:

(a)   the purpose, activity and duration of the joint arrangement;

(b)   how the members of the board of directors, or equivalent governing body, of the joint arrangement, are appointed;

(c)   the decision-making process: the matters requiring decisions from the parties, the voting rights of the parties and the required level of support for those matters. The decision-making process reflected in the contractual arrangement establishes joint control of the arrangement;

(d)   the capital or other contributions required of the parties; and

(e)   how the parties share assets, liabilities, revenues, expenses or profit or loss relating to the joint arrangement. *[IFRS 11 Appendix B.4].*

3.3.3   Joint control and unanimous consent

In order to establish whether joint control of an arrangement exists, it is necessary to establish whether the contractual arrangement gives all the parties to that arrangement (or a group of the parties) control of the arrangement in the collective sense. That means the parties (or a group thereof) must need to act together to direct the strategic, financial and operating policies of the arrangement. It follows that there must be at least two parties for there to be joint control.

Section 15 includes the specific requirement for 'unanimous consent' in the definition of joint control. Unanimous consent essentially means that any party to the arrangement can prevent any of the other parties, or group of the other parties, from making decisions of a strategic, financial or operating nature without its consent. This ensures that no single party can control the arrangement. This means, for example, that none of the parties to the contractual arrangement should have a casting vote that enables it to resolve a deadlock, as that would constitute a form of unilateral control. *[FRS 102.15.2]*.

Care is required in situations where a contractual arrangement may identify one venturer as the operator or manager of the joint venture. The operator does not control the joint venture if it acts within the financial and operating policies agreed by the venturers in accordance with the contractual arrangement and delegated to the operator. If, however, the operator does have the power to govern (i.e. not merely to execute) the financial and operating policies of the economic activity, the operator controls the venture and the venture is a subsidiary of the operator and not a joint venture.

3.3.4   Potential voting rights

An entity may own share warrants, share call options, debt or equity instruments that are convertible into ordinary shares, or other similar instruments that have the potential, if exercised or converted, to give the entity voting power or reduce another party's voting power over the financial and operating policies of another entity (potential voting rights).

Potential voting rights are not directly addressed in Section 15. Nevertheless, the existence of potential voting rights may be relevant to an assessment of joint control, as explained in Section 9, since control can be achieved by having options or convertible instruments that are currently exercisable. *[FRS 102.9.6]*. However, the contractual arrangement giving rise to joint control will tend to override relative ownership interests (voting and potential voting rights). This is an issue that will need to be addressed in the light of individual facts and circumstances.

3.3.5   Types of joint venture

Section 15 explains that joint ventures can take one of three forms, all sharing the common characteristics of an underlying contractual arrangement and joint control. The three forms are:

- jointly controlled operations (see 3.4 below);
- jointly controlled assets (see 3.5 below); and
- jointly controlled entities (see 3.6 below).

Chapter 13

3.4   Jointly controlled operations

3.4.1   Definition

Jointly controlled operations arise when a joint venture is established that does not involve the formation of a separate corporation, partnership or other entity or financial structure that exists separately from the venturers. Instead the joint venture uses assets and other resources of the venturers. In such a case each venturer will use its own property, plant and equipment and carries its own inventories. It also incurs its own expenses and liabilities and raises its own finance, which represent its own obligations. The joint venture activities may be carried out by the venturer's employees alongside the venturer's similar activities. The joint venture agreement usually provides a means by which the revenue from the sale of the joint product and any expenses incurred in common are shared among the venturers. *[FRS 102.15.4].*

An example of a jointly controlled operation might be where two or more venturers combine their operations, resources and expertise in order to jointly manufacture, market and distribute a particular product. Each venturer undertakes a different part of the manufacturing process and bears its own costs. Revenue from the sale of the product is then shared on the basis of the contractual arrangement. There is no separate entity conducting the business of manufacturing and selling the product. It is merely an extension of the venturers' existing businesses.

3.4.2   Accounting requirements for jointly controlled operations

In respect of its interests in jointly controlled operations, a venturer recognises in its financial statements:

- the assets that it controls and the liabilities that it incurs; and
- the expenses that it incurs and its share of the income that is earns from the sale of goods or services by the joint venture. *[FRS 102.15.5].*

As the assets, liabilities, income and expenses will already be reflected in the individual financial statements of the venturer (including the separate financial statements of a venturer that is a parent) then no adjustments or other consolidation procedures are required in respect of these items if the venturer presents consolidated financial statements.

When venturers are funding the operations of a jointly controlled operation they may need to account for a receivable or payable from other venturers, as illustrated in Example 13.2 below.

Example 13.2:   Loans to jointly controlled operations

Two entities – A and B – each own half of a jointly controlled operation. In the joint venture agreement, revenue from the sale of the joint product and expenses incurred in common are shared equally between the A and B. Entity A has lent £400 to the jointly controlled operation, while entity B has lent £300. How should entity A account for its loan?

The jointly controlled operation has total borrowings of £400 + £300 = £700. A's share in the borrowings of £350 (=50% of £700) should be offset against its receivable of £400. Entity A should, therefore, account for a net receivable from its joint venture partner of £50 (=£400 – £350).

The jointly controlled operation is not a separate legal entity and under the joint venture agreement A has a business relationship only with B. Gross presentation of a receivable of £200 (=£400 – 50% of £400) and a liability of £150 (=50% of £300) would therefore not be appropriate.

3.5   Jointly controlled assets

3.5.1   *Definition*

Jointly controlled assets arise in circumstances where one or more assets are contributed to or acquired for the purpose of the joint venture and those assets are jointly controlled and often jointly owned. *[FRS 102.15.6]*.

The assets are used to obtain benefits for the venturers, who may each take a share of the output from the assets and bear an agreed share of the expenses incurred. Such ventures do not involve the establishment of an entity or financial structure separate from the venturers themselves, so that each venturer has control over its share of future economic benefits through its share in the jointly controlled assets.

Joint ventures of this type are particularly common in extractive industries. For example, a number of oil companies may jointly control and operate an oil pipeline. Each venturer uses the pipeline to transport its own product in return for which it bears an agreed proportion of the operating expenses of the pipeline. Another example of a jointly controlled asset could be that two entities jointly control a commercial property, each taking a share of the rents received and bearing a share of the expenses.

3.5.2   *Accounting requirements for jointly controlled assets*

In respect of its interest in a jointly controlled asset, a venturer recognises in its financial statements:

- its share of the jointly controlled assets, classified according to their nature (i.e. a share in a jointly controlled pipeline should be shown within property, plant and equipment rather than as an investment);
- any liabilities that it has incurred (e.g. those it has incurred in financing its share of the assets);
- its share of any liabilities incurred jointly with the other venturers in relation to the joint venture;
- any income from the sale or use of its share of the output of the joint venture, together with its share of any expenses incurred by the joint venture; and
- any expenses that it has incurred in respect of its interest in the joint venture (e.g. those relating to financing the venturer's interest in the assets and selling its share of the output). *[FRS 102.15.7]*.

As with jointly controlled operations, the assets, liabilities, income and expenses will already be reflected in the individual financial statements of the venturer (including the separate financial statements of a venturer that is a parent), therefore no adjustments or other consolidation procedures are required in respect of these items if the venturer presents consolidated financial statements. Separate accounting records may be limited to a record of the expenses incurred in common, and ultimately borne by the venturers according to their agreed shares. Similarly, financial statements may not be prepared for the joint venture itself, although the venturers may prepare management accounts in order to assess the performance of the joint venture.

Chapter 13

3.6   Jointly controlled entities

3.6.1   Definition

Section 15 defines a jointly controlled entity as 'a joint venture that involves the establishment of a corporation, partnership or other entity in which each venturer has an interest'. The entity would operate in the same way as other entities except that the venturers would have joint control over the entity and its economic activities by virtue of the existence of a contractual arrangement between them. *[FRS 102.15.8]*.

A jointly controlled entity controls the assets of the joint venture, incurs liabilities and expenses and earns income. It manages the joint venture and may enter into contracts in its own name and raise finance for the purposes of the joint venture activity. Each venturer is entitled to a share of the results of the jointly controlled entity based on the requirements in the joint venture agreement.

There are a number of different considerations for the accounting for interests in jointly controlled entities depending on whether the venturer is a parent or not, and if a parent, the financial statements being prepared. These are discussed in the sections that follow.

3.6.2   Venturer that is not a parent

Where a venturer is an entity that is not a parent and hence only prepares individual financial statements, in those financial statements it has a choice of how to account for all of its interests in jointly controlled entities. It can apply either:

(a)   the cost model (see 3.6.2.A below);

(b)   fair value with changes in fair value recognised in other comprehensive income (unless reversing a revaluation decrease of the same investment previously recognised in profit or loss, in which case the revaluation increase is recognised in profit or loss, or where a revaluation decrease exceeds increases previously recognised in respect of the same investment, in which case the excess is recognised in profit or loss) (see 3.6.2.B below); or

(c)   fair value with changes in fair value recognised in profit or loss. *[FRS 102.15.9]*.

In terms of the option to carry interests in jointly controlled entities at fair value through profit or loss or fair value through other comprehensive income, fair value in that context should be determined by reference to the guidance in Appendix 2 to Section 2 – *Concepts and Pervasive Principles*, (see Chapter 4 at 3.13). *[FRS 102.15.9(d)]*.

There is no option in Section 15 to use the equity method of accounting in individual financial statements (this option exists under IFRS) even though permitted by the Regulations (see 4.2 below). However, the individual financial statements of a venturer that is not a parent must disclose summarised financial information about its investments in jointly controlled entities, along with the effect of including those investments as if they had been accounted for using the equity method. Investing entities that are exempt from preparing consolidated financial statements, or would be exempt if they had subsidiaries, are exempt from this requirement. *[FRS 102.15.21A]*.

3.6.2.A   Cost model

A venturer that is not a parent, and that chooses to adopt the cost model, should measure its investments in jointly controlled entities at cost less any accumulated impairment losses. Section 27 – *Impairment of Assets* – will apply to the recognition and measurement of impairment losses. *[FRS 102.15.10]*.

Section 15 does not define 'cost' of investment. However, Section 2 defines 'historical cost' as the amount of cash or cash equivalents paid or the fair value of the consideration given to acquire the asset at the time of its acquisition. *[FRS 102.2.34(a)]*. The Regulations state that the purchase price of an asset is determined by adding to the actual price paid any expenses incidental to its acquisition and then subtracting any incidental reductions in the cost of the acquisition. *[1 Sch.27(1)]*. Consistent with this, Section 17 – *Property, Plant and Equipment* – states that cost is normally either the purchase price paid (including directly attributable costs) or the fair value of non-monetary assets exchanged. *[FRS 102.17.10, 14]*. The purchase price would generally represent the fair value of the consideration given to purchase the investment consistent with the guidance in respect of exchanges of businesses or other non-monetary assets (see Chapter 8 at 3.8) and the requirements in respect of measuring the cost of a business combination (see Chapter 17 at 3.6).

A venturer will recognise distributions received from its investments in jointly controlled entities as income irrespective of whether the distributions are from accumulated profits of the jointly controlled entity arising before or after the date of acquisition. *[FRS 102.15.11]*.

Chapter 13

3.6.2.B   Fair value model

A venturer that is not a parent, and that chooses to adopt the policy of accounting for its jointly controlled entity at fair value through other comprehensive income or fair value through profit or loss, should initially recognise its investment at the transaction price. *[FRS 102.15.14]*. 'Transaction price' is not defined, but it is presumably the same as its cost (see 3.6.2.A above).

At each subsequent reporting date, the venturer should measure its investments in jointly controlled entities at fair value using the fair value guidance in the Appendix to Section 2 of FRS 102. *[FRS 102.15.15]*.

Where the fair value through other comprehensive income model is used, increases in the carrying amount of the investment as a result of a revaluation to fair value are recognised in other comprehensive income and accumulated in equity i.e. revaluation reserve. If a revaluation increase reverses a revaluation decrease of the same investment that was previously recognised as an expense, it must be recognised in profit or loss. *[FRS 102.17.15E]*. Decreases as a result of revaluation are recognised in OCI to the extent of any previously recognised revaluation increase accumulated in revaluation reserve in respect of the same investment. If a revaluation decrease exceeds the revaluation gains accumulated in revaluation reserve in respect of that investment, the excess is recognised in profit or loss. *[FRS 102.17.15F]*. This means that it is not permissible to carry a negative revaluation reserve in respect of each investment in jointly controlled entities at fair value (see Chapter 15 at 3.6.3).

Where the fair value through profit or loss model is used, increases and decreases in the carrying amount of the investment as a result of a revaluation to fair value are recognised in profit or loss.

A venturer will recognise distributions received from its investments in jointly controlled entities as income irrespective of whether the distributions are from accumulated profits of the jointly controlled entity arising before or after the date of acquisition. *[FRS 102.15.15A]*.

3.6.3   Venturer that is a parent

3.6.3.A   Separate financial statements

A venturer that is a parent accounts for interests in jointly controlled entities in its separate financial statements in accordance with the requirements of Section 9 (see also Chapter 8 at 4.2). *[FRS 102.15.1]*.

The parent is required to apply a policy of accounting for its investments in jointly controlled entities either :

- at cost less impairment (i.e. a cost model);
- at fair value with changes in fair value recognised in other comprehensive income (unless reversing a revaluation decrease of the same investment previously recognised in profit or loss, in which case the revaluation increase is recognised in profit or loss, or where a revaluation decrease exceeds increases previously recognised in respect of the same investment, in which case the excess is recognised in profit or loss) ; or

- at fair value with changes in fair value recognised in profit or loss (guidance on fair value is provided in Section 2). *[FRS 102.9.26]*.

The discussion at 3.6.2.A and 3.6.2.B above with respect to the cost model and the fair value model will be relevant for a parent applying either of these models.

The same choices apply to a parent that is exempt in accordance with Section 9 paragraph 9.3 from the requirement to present consolidated financial statements and therefore presents separate financial statements as its only financial statements. *[FRS 102.9.26A]*.

Section 9 states that a parent must apply the same accounting policy for all investments in a single class (for example investments in subsidiaries that are held as part of an investment portfolio, those that are not so held, associates or jointly controlled entities) but it can elect different policies for different classes. *[FRS 102.9.26]*.

Although Section 15 does not state so explicitly, it appears that, although associates and jointly controlled entities do not need to be measured the same way, all investments in a single class must be measured the same way. There is an explicit requirement in Section 9 for an entity that is a parent to apply the same accounting policy for all investments in a single class, the implications of which are discussed in Chapter 8 at 4.2. In our view, this implies that jointly controlled entities held as part of an investment portfolio are separate classes of investments. Section 15 requires investments in jointly controlled entities that are held as part of an investment portfolio to be measured at fair value through profit or loss in the parent's consolidated financial statements, rather than under the equity method (see 3.6.3.B below). *[FRS 102.15.9A-B]*.

3.6.3.B   Consolidated financial statements

In its consolidated financial statements, a venturer that is a parent accounts for all of its investments in jointly controlled entities using the equity method, except where its investments in jointly controlled entities are held as part of an investment portfolio. In this case such investments in jointly controlled entities are required to be measured at fair value in its consolidated financial statements with the changes in fair value recognised in profit or loss. *[FRS 102.15.9A-B]*.

Investments in jointly controlled entities are held as part of an investment portfolio if their value to the venturer is through fair value changes in a directly or indirectly held basket of investments rather than as a means through which the venturer carries out business. A basket of investments is held indirectly if a venturer holds a single investment in a second investment fund which, in turn, holds a basket of investments. In some circumstances, it may be appropriate for a single investment to be considered an investment portfolio, for example when an investment fund is first being established and is expected to acquire additional investments (see Chapter 8 at 3.4.2.A). *[FRS 102 Appendix I]*.

3.7   Equity method

3.7.1   *Overview*

The equity method is explained in Section 14. It is described as a method of accounting whereby the investment is initially recognised at transaction price (including transaction costs) and is subsequently adjusted to reflect the investor's share of:

- profit or loss;
- other comprehensive income; and
- equity of the associate. *[FRS 102.14.8]*.

The investor's share of the investee's profit or loss is recognised in the investor's profit or loss. *[FRS 102.5.5, 6 Sch 20(3)]*. The investor's share of the investee's other comprehensive income is recognised in the investor's statement of comprehensive income. *[FRS 102.5.5A, 6 Sch 20(3)]*.

The requirements of the equity method described above should be applied to jointly controlled entities, substituting 'joint control' for 'significant influence' and 'jointly controlled entity' for 'associate'. *[FRS 102.15.13]*.

3.7.2   *Summary of the equity method*

The equity method is discussed in detail in Chapter 12. The key aspects of the equity method as applicable to an investment in a jointly controlled entity are therefore as follows: *[FRS 102.14.8]*

- a venturer should commence equity accounting for a jointly controlled entity from the date it begins to have joint control over the entity (see Chapter 12 at 3.3.2.A);

- distributions received from the jointly controlled entity reduce the carrying amount of the investment. Adjustments to the carrying amount may also be required as a consequence of changes in the jointly controlled entity's equity arising from items of other comprehensive income (see Chapter 12 at 3.3.2.B);

- in applying the equity method, the proportionate share of the jointly controlled entity to be accounted for, in many cases, will be based on the venturer's ownership interest in the ordinary shares of the entity. A venturer should measure its share of profit or loss and other comprehensive income of the jointly controlled entity as well as its share of changes in the jointly controlled entities' equity based on present ownership interests. Those measurements should not reflect the possible exercise or conversion of potential voting rights (see Chapter 12 at 3.3.2.C);

- on acquisition of the investment in a jointly controlled entity a venturer accounts for any difference (whether positive or negative) between the cost of acquisition and its share of the fair values of the net identifiable assets of the jointly controlled entity in accordance with Section 19, as implicit goodwill (see Chapter 17 at 3.9). A venturer adjusts its share of the jointly controlled entity's profits or losses after acquisition to account for additional depreciation or amortisation of the jointly controlled entity's depreciable or amortisable assets (including goodwill) on the basis of the excess of their fair values over their carrying amounts at the time the investment was acquired (see Chapter 12 at 3.3.2.D). If negative goodwill arises (the acquirer's interest in the net amount of the associate's identifiable assets, liabilities and provisions for contingent liabilities exceeds the cost of the investment), the acquirer must (after reassessing the identification and measurement of the acquiree's assets and liabilities and the measurement of the cost of the combination) recognise the excess up to the fair value of the non-monetary assets acquired in the jointly controlled entity's profit or loss in the periods in which the non-monetary assets are recovered. Any excess exceeding the fair value of the non-monetary assets acquired shall be recognised in profit or loss in the periods expected to be benefited. *[FRS 102.19.24]*. If the interest in the jointly controlled entity is acquired on a piecemeal basis then the approach to such acquisitions is discussed, in the context of equity accounting, in Chapter 12 at 4.1.2 to 4.1.4;

- if there is an indication that an investment in a jointly controlled entity may be impaired a venturer shall test the entire carrying amount of the investment for impairment in accordance with Section 27 (see Chapter 24) as a single asset. Any goodwill included as part of the carrying amount of the investment in the jointly controlled entity is not tested separately for impairment but, rather, as part of the test for impairment of the investment as a whole (see Chapter 12 at 3.3.2.E);

- the venturer eliminates unrealised profits and losses resulting from upstream (jointly controlled entity to investor) and downstream (investor to jointly controlled entity) transactions to the extent of the venturer's interest in the jointly controlled entity. Unrealised losses on such transactions may provide evidence of an impairment of the asset transferred (see Chapter 12 at 3.3.2.F);

- in applying the equity method, the investor uses the financial statements of the jointly controlled entity as of the same date as the financial statements of the investor unless it is impracticable to do so. If it is impracticable, the investor uses the most recent available financial statements of the jointly controlled entity, with adjustments made for the effects of any significant transactions or events occurring between the accounting period ends (see Chapter 12 at 3.3.2.G);

- if the jointly controlled entity uses accounting policies that differ from those of the investor, the investor adjusts the jointly controlled entity's financial statements to reflect the investor's accounting policies for the purpose of applying the equity method unless it is impracticable to do so (see Chapter 12 at 3.3.2.H);

- if a venturer's share of losses of a jointly controlled entity equals or exceeds the carrying amount of its investment in the jointly controlled entity, the venturer discontinues recognising its share of further losses. After the venturer's interest is reduced to zero, the venturer recognises a provision for additional losses (see Section 21 – *Provisions and Contingencies*) only to the extent that the venturer has incurred legal or constructive obligations or has made payments on behalf of the jointly controlled entity. If the jointly controlled entity subsequently reports profits, the venturer resumes recognising its share of those profits only after its share of the profits equals the share of losses not recognised (see Chapter 12 at 3.3.2.I); and

- a venturer discontinues the use of the equity method from the date that joint control ceases. The subsequent accounting depends on the nature of any retained investment. If the investment becomes a subsidiary (because control is obtained),

Chapter 13

it will be accounted for in accordance with Section 19 (i.e. a step-acquisition, see Chapter 17 at 3.11). If the investment becomes an associate, it will be accounted for in accordance with Section 14 (i.e. it will continue to be accounted for under the equity method, see Chapter 12). Otherwise, on a full or partial disposal, a profit or loss will be recognised based on the difference between the disposal proceeds and the carrying amount relating to the proportion of the jointly controlled entity disposed of. Any retained investment should be accounted for as a financial asset in accordance with Section 11 or Section 12 (see Chapter 12 at 3.3.2.J for further discussion).

3.8   Transactions between a venturer and joint venture

3.8.1   Background

It is common for venturers to transact with the joint venture, in particular on the formation of the venture. Typical transactions include:

- the venturers contribute cash to the venture in proportion to their agreed relative shares. The venture then uses some or all of the cash to acquire assets from the venturers for use in the venture;

- the venturers contribute other assets (or a mixture of cash and other assets) to the joint venture with fair values in proportion to the venturers' agreed relative shares in the venture; and

- the venturers contribute other assets to the joint venture with fair values not in proportion to the venturers' agreed relative shares. Cash 'equalisation' payments are then made between the venturers so that the overall financial position of the venturers corresponds to their agreed relative shares in the venture.

3.8.2   Requirements

When a venturer contributes or sells assets to a joint venture, Section 15 requires that the recognition of any portion of a gain or loss from the transaction should reflect the substance of the transaction. While the assets are retained by the joint venture, and provided the venturer has transferred the significant risks and rewards of ownership, the venturer should only recognise that portion of the gain or loss that is attributable to the interests of the other venturers in its consolidated financial statements. However, the venturer should recognise the full amount of any loss when the contribution or sale provides evidence of an impairment loss. *[FRS 102.15.16].*

These requirements are illustrated in the following examples:

Example 13.3:   Sale of asset from venturer to joint venture at a profit

Two entities A and B establish a joint venture involving the creation of a jointly controlled entity C in which A and B each hold 50%. A and B each contribute £5 million in cash to the joint venture in exchange for equity shares. C then uses £8 million of its £10 million cash to acquire from A a property recorded in the financial statements of A at £6 million. It is agreed that £8 million is the fair value of the property. How should A account for these transactions?

The accounting entry for A is as follows:

	£m	£m
Dr. Cash (1)	3	
Dr. Investment in joint venture C(2)	4	
Cr. Property (3)		6
Cr. Gain on sale (4)		1

(1)   £8 million received from C less £5 million contributed to C.

(2)   £5 million initial investment in C, less £1 million (share of profit eliminated – see (4) below. In effect, this treatment represents that A still holds 50% of the property at its original carrying value to A (50% of £6 million = £3 million) plus 50% of the cash held by the joint venture (50% of £2 million = £1m)

(3)   Derecognition of A's original property.

(4)   Gain on sale of property £2 million (£8 million received from C less £6 million carrying value = £2 million), less 50% eliminated (so as to reflect only profit attributable to interest of other venturer B) = £1 million.

In Example 13.3 above, the elimination of A's share of the profit has been made against the asset that was the subject of the transaction and now held by A. This is based on our suggested approach for the elimination of unrealised profits and losses resulting from downstream transactions (investor to jointly controlled entity) under Section 14, discussed in Chapter 12 at 3.3.2.F. It is also consistent with the treatment where a venture exchanges a non-monetary asset for an interest in another entity that becomes a jointly controlled entity of a venture (see 3.9 below).

Example 13.4:   Sale of asset from venturer to joint venture at a loss

Two entities A and B establish a joint venture involving the creation of a jointly controlled entity C in which A and B each hold 50%. A and B each contribute £5 million in cash to the joint venture in exchange for equity shares. C then uses £8 million of its £10 million cash to acquire from A a property recorded in the financial statements of A at £10 million. £8 million is agreed to be the fair market value of the property. How should A account for these transactions?

The accounting entry for A is as follows:

	£m	£m
Dr. Cash (1)	3	
Dr. Investment in joint venture C (2)	5	
Dr. Loss on sale (3)	2	
Cr. Property (4)		10

(1)   £8 million received from C less £5 million contributed to C.

(2)   £5 million initial investment in C. In effect, this treatment represents that A still holds 50% of the property at the current fair value (50% of £8 million = £4 million) plus 50% of the cash held by the joint venture (50% of £2 million = £1m).

(3)   Loss on sale of property £2 million (£8 million received from C less £10 million carrying value = £2 million) not adjusted since the transaction indicated an impairment of the property. In effect, it is the result that would have been obtained if A had recognised an impairment charge immediately prior to the sale and then recognised no gain or loss on the sale.

(4)   Derecognition of A's original property.

When a venturer purchases an asset from a joint venture, the venturer should not recognise its share of the profits of the joint venture from the transaction until it resells the assets to an independent party or otherwise realises its carrying amount. For example on an item of property, plant and equipment, this will occur as the asset is depreciated or written down for impairment; therefore the appropriate proportion of the previously unrecognised profit can be recognised as the asset's carrying value is reduced. A venturer should recognise its share of the losses resulting from these transactions in the same way as profits except that losses shall be recognised immediately when they represent an impairment loss. *[FRS 102.15.17]*.

These requirements are illustrated in the following examples:

Example 13.5:   Sale of asset from joint venture to venturer at a profit

Two entities A and B establish a joint venture involving the creation of a jointly controlled entity C in which A and B each hold 50%. A and B each contribute £5 million in cash to the joint venture in exchange for equity shares. C then uses £8 million of its £10 million cash to acquire a property from an independent third party D. The property is later sold to A for £12 million, which is agreed to be its market value. How should A account for these transactions?

The required accounting entry for A is:

	£m	£m
Dr. Property (1)	10	
Dr. Investment in joint venture C (2)	7	
Cr. Cash (3)		17

(1)   £12 million paid to C less elimination of A's share of the profit made by C £2 million (50% of [£12 million sales proceeds less £8 million cost to C]).

(2)   £5 million initial investment in C plus profit on sale of property by C that is attributable to B). In effect, this treatment represents A's 50% interest in the cash held by the joint venture (50% of £14 million).

(3)   £5 million cash contributed to C plus £12 million consideration paid for property.

In Example 13.5 above, the elimination of A's share of the profit made by C has been made against the asset that was the subject of the transaction and now held by A. This is based on our suggested approach for the elimination of unrealised profits and losses resulting from upstream transactions (jointly controlled entity to investor) under Section 14, discussed in Chapter 12 at 3.3.2.F.

Example 13.6:   Sale of asset from joint venture to venturer at a loss

Two entities A and B establish a joint venture involving the creation of a jointly controlled entity C in which A and B each hold 50%. A and B each contribute £5 million in cash to the joint venture in exchange for equity shares. C then uses £8 million of its £10 million cash to acquire a property from an independent third party D. The property is then sold to A for £7 million, which is agreed to be its market value. How should A account for these transactions?

The accounting entry for A is:

	£m	£m
Dr. Property (1)	7.0	
Dr. Investment in joint venture C (2)	4.5	
Dr. Share of loss of C (3)	0.5	
Cr. Cash (4)		12.0

(1)   £7 million paid to C not adjusted since the transaction indicated an impairment of C's asset.

(2)   £5 million initial investment in C less A's 50% share of loss in C's books of £1 million (£8 million cost of property less £7 million proceeds of sale). In effect, it is the result that would have been obtained if C had recognised an impairment charge immediately prior to the sale and then recognised no gain or loss on the sale.

(3)   Loss in C's books is £1 million (£8 million cost of property less £7 million proceeds of sale). A recognises its 50% share because the transaction indicates an impairment of the asset. In effect, it is the result that would have been obtained if C had recognised an impairment charge immediately prior to the sale and then recognised no gain or loss on the sale.

(4)   €5 million cash contributed to C plus €7 million consideration for property.

It may be that transactions occur between a venturer and a joint venture in assets, such as inventories, which are destined for onward sale in the normal course of business by the buying party. The accounting adjustments required are the same as for similar transactions between an investor and its associate – see Examples 12.6 and 12.7 in Chapter 12 at 3.3.2.F.

3.8.3   *Loans and borrowings between the venturer and joint ventures*

Section 15's requirement to eliminate partially unrealised profits or losses on transactions with joint ventures is expressed in terms of transactions involving the transfer of assets. This raises the question of whether this requirement is generally intended to apply to items such as interest paid on loans between joint ventures and the reporting entity.

In our view, the requirement for partial elimination of profits or losses does not apply to items such as interest paid on loans and borrowings between the reporting entity and its joint ventures, since such loans do not involve the transfer of assets giving rise to gains or losses. Moreover, the loans are not normally regarded as part of the venturer's share of the net assets of the joint venture, but as separate transactions, except in the case of loss-making joint ventures, where interests in long-term loans may be accounted for as if they were part of the reporting entity's equity investment in determining the carrying value of the joint venture against which losses may be offset.

However, if the joint venture has capitalised the borrowing costs then the investor would need to eliminate a relevant share of the profit, in the same way it would eliminate a share of the capitalised management or advisory fees charged to a joint venture.

3.9   Transactions to create a jointly controlled entity

A venturer may exchange a business, or other non-monetary asset, for an interest in another entity, and that other entity becomes a jointly controlled entity of the venturer. The accounting issues that arise from these transactions are whether they should be accounted for at fair value or at previous book values and how the gain on the transaction should be reported.

The requirements in respect of such transactions are set out in Section 9 (see also Chapter 8 at 3.8) and the principles behind the requirements are derived from previous UK GAAP. The principles are that the only exception to the use of fair values should be in rare circumstances where the transaction is artificial and has no substance and that any unrealised gains should not be reported in profit or loss.

Chapter 13

Accordingly, the following accounting treatment applies in the consolidated financial statements of the reporting entity:

- to the extent that the reporting entity retains an ownership interest in the business, or other non-monetary assets, exchanged, even if that interest is then held through the jointly controlled entity, that retained interest, including any related goodwill, is treated as having been owned by the reporting entity throughout the transaction and should be included at its pre-transaction carrying amount;

- goodwill is recognised as the difference between:
  - the fair value of the consideration given; and
  - the fair value of the reporting entity's share of the pre-transaction identifiable net assets of the other entity.

  The consideration given for the interest acquired in the jointly controlled entity will include that part of the business, or other non-monetary assets, exchanged and no longer owned by the reporting entity. The consideration may also include cash or monetary assets to achieve equalisation of values. Where it is difficult to value the consideration given, the best estimate of its value may be given by valuing what is acquired;

- to the extent that the fair value of the consideration received by the reporting entity exceeds the carrying value of the part of the business, or other non-monetary assets exchanged and no longer owned by the reporting entity, and any related goodwill together with any cash given up, the reporting entity should recognise a gain. Any unrealised gain arising on the exchange is recognised in other comprehensive income; and

- to the extent that the fair value of the consideration received by the reporting entity is less than the carrying value of the part of the business, or other non-monetary assets no longer owned by the reporting entity, and any related goodwill, together with any cash given up, the reporting entity should recognise a loss. The loss should be recognised as an impairment in accordance with Section 27 or, for any loss remaining after an impairment review of the relevant assets, in profit or loss. *[FRS 102.9.31]*.

The most common situation for these transactions in practice is the contribution of a business for equity in a joint venture (or associate), and such a transaction forms the basis of illustrating the above accounting requirements in Example 13.7 below.

Example 13.7:   *Creation of a jointly controlled entity by the transfer of non –*
monetary assets (1)

A and B are two companies which agree to form a jointly controlled entity (JV Co) in respect of a particular part of each of their businesses. A will own 40% of the JV Co, and B 60%. The parties agree that the total value of the new business is £250m.

A's contribution to the venture is one of its subsidiaries, the net assets of which are included in A's consolidated balance sheet at £60m (including remaining unamortised goodwill of £10m). The fair value of the separable net assets of the subsidiary contributed by A is considered to be £80m. The implicit fair value of the business contributed is £100m (40% of total fair value £250m).

B also contributes a subsidiary, the net assets of which have a carrying amount of £85m (including remaining unamortised goodwill of £15m). The fair value of the separable net assets is considered to be £120m. The implicit fair value of the business contributed is £150m (60% of total fair value £250m).

The book and fair values of the businesses contributed by A and B are summarised as follows:

(in £m)	A Book value	A Fair value	B Book value	B Fair value
Separable net assets	50	80	70	120
Goodwill	10	20	15	30
Total	60	100	85	150

How should A account for the set-up of the jointly controlled entity?

The required entries in A would be:

	£m	£m
Dr. Share of net assets of JV Co (1)	68	
Dr. Goodwill (2)	16	
Cr. Net assets contributed to JV Co (3)		60
Cr. Other comprehensive income (gain on disposal) (4)		24

(1) 40% of (book value of A's separable net assets + fair value of B's separable net assets), i.e. 40% × (£50m+£120m) = £68m.

(2) Fair value of consideration given by A less fair value of separable net assets of B's business acquired, i.e. 60% of £100m less 40% of £120m = £12m (which can also be 'proved' as being 40% of B's inherent goodwill of £30m), plus 40% of A's original goodwill of £10m retained (£4m) = £16m. This goodwill will be included in the total carrying value of JV Co.

(3) Previous carrying amount of net assets contributed by A, now deconsolidated. In reality there would be a number of entries to deconsolidate these on a line-by-line basis.

(4) Fair value of consideration received, less book value of assets disposed of, i.e. 40% of £150m – 60% of £60m = £24m (which can also be 'proved' as being 60% of the £40m difference between the book value and fair value of A's business).

The gain on the transaction in Example 13.7 is unrealised because qualifying consideration has not been received. Therefore, the gain is accounted for in other comprehensive income as only realised profits can be recognised in profit or loss. *[FRS 102.9.31(c)]*. Where part or all of the gain is realised then that portion can be taken to profit or loss. This is illustrated in Example 13.8 below:

Example 13.8:   Creation of a jointly controlled entity by the transfer of non –
monetary assets (2)

Assume the same fact pattern as in Example 13.7 above, except that A was to receive a stake of only 36% in JV Co. In that case it would be expected that A, having contributed assets worth 40% of the combined entity, would receive a cash payment of £10m (4% of £250m) directly from B in compensation for the reduction in the stake from 40% to 36%.

How should A account for the set-up of the jointly controlled entity?

The required entries in A would be:

	£m	£m
Dr. Share of net assets of JV Co (1)	61.2	
Dr. Cash	10.0	
Dr. Goodwill (2)	14.4	
Cr. Net assets contributed to JV Co (3)		60.0
Cr. Profit and loss (gain on disposal)		10.0
Cr. Other comprehensive income (gain on disposal (4)		15.6

(1)   36% of (book value of A's separable net assets + fair value of B's separable net assets), i.e. 36% × (£50m+£120m) = £61.2m.

(2)   Fair value of consideration given by A (net of £10m cash received from B) less fair value of separable net assets of B's business acquired, i.e. 64% of £100m (£64m) less £10m = £54m, less 36% of £120m = £10.8m (which can also be 'proved' as being 36% of B's goodwill of £30m), plus 36% of A's goodwill of £10m retained (£3.6m) = £14.4m. This goodwill will be included in the total carrying value of JV Co.

(3)   Previous carrying amount of net assets contributed by A, now deconsolidated. In reality there would be a number of entries to deconsolidate these on a line-by-line basis.

(4)   Fair value of consideration received (including £10m cash received from B), less book value of assets disposed of, i.e. 36% of £150m = £54m plus £10m cash = £64m – 64% of £60m = £25.6m (which can also be 'proved' as being 64% of the £40m difference between the book value and fair value of A's business). The gain on disposal of £25.6m has been split based on an allocation between 'realised' and 'unrealised' profit. It has been assumed that no liabilities were transferred to A as part of the consideration, and therefore all the profit backed by cash is treated as realised. This approach is further explained below.

Section 9 does not explain how a realised gain can be distinguished from an unrealised gain. In Example 13.7 above, we have used a 'top slicing' approach whereby as much of the total gain as is backed by cash is treated as realised (i.e. £10m). 'Top slicing' is the recommended approach to determining realised profits for exchanges of assets in paragraph 3.18 of the ICAEW/ICAS TECH 02/17BL – *Guidance on Realised and Distributable Profits under the Companies Act 2006*. Paragraph 3.18A of the guidance states that when the consideration received comprise a combination of assets and liabilities, the profit will be realised only to the extent of any net balance (i.e. cash less liabilities) of qualifying consideration received.

No gain or loss is recognised in those rare cases where the artificiality or lack of substance of the transaction is such that a gain or loss on the exchange could not be justified. When a gain or loss on the exchange is not taken into account because the transaction is artificial or has no substance, the circumstances should be explained. *[FRS 102.9.32]*. There is no elaboration as to the circumstances where this might be applicable.

3.10   Variable profit share

Venturers may not always be entitled to a fixed proportion of the profit of a jointly controlled entity. Venturers that each have a 50% interest in a joint venture may, for example, agree that;

- in the initial three years of operation one of the venturers will be entitled to 75% of the profits in order to recover its investment quicker;

- the venturers are entitled to a fixed proportion of cash flows 'as defined in the joint venture agreement'; or

- the profit of the joint venture will be distributed based on an alternative measure of profitability such as earnings before interest, tax, depreciation and amortisation (EBITDA).

It may not be appropriate in those cases for the venturers to account for 50% of the profit of the joint venture. Instead, they would need to take into account the substance of the profit sharing arrangements that apply in each reporting period, in determining their share of the profits and net assets of the joint venture. A venturer's profit share may therefore differ from its share in the net assets of the joint venture. This situation is not unlike the situation that arises in the case of an investment in an associate that has different classes of equity (see Chapter 12 at 3.3.2.C).

3.11   Disclosures

Section 15 requires the following disclosures in individual and consolidated financial statements:

(a)   the accounting policy for recognising investments in jointly controlled entities;

(b)   the carrying amount of investments in jointly controlled entities;

(c)   the fair value of investments in jointly controlled entities accounted for using the equity method for which there are published price quotations; and

(d)   the aggregate amount of commitments relating to joint ventures, including the venturers share in the capital commitments that have been incurred jointly with other venturers, as well as the share of the capital commitments of the joint ventures themselves. *[FRS 102.15.19]*.

For jointly controlled entities accounted for in accordance with the equity method, a venturer should disclose separately its share of the profit or loss of such investments and its share of any discontinued operations of such jointly controlled entities. *[FRS 102.15.20]*.

For jointly controlled entities accounted for at fair value through other comprehensive income, a venturer should make the disclosures required by paragraphs 11.43 and 11.44 (this is notwithstanding the fact that paragraph 11.44 refers to fair value through profit or loss, but the intention is clearly to make these disclosures for fair value through other comprehensive income): *[FRS 102.15.21]*

- the basis for determining fair value (e.g. quoted market price in an active market or a valuation technique. If the latter is used, the assumptions applied in determining fair value for each class of financial assets or liabilities must be disclosed); and

- if a reliable measure of fair value is no longer available for financial instruments that would otherwise be required to be measured at fair value through profit or loss this fact shall be disclosed and the carrying amount of those financial instruments.

For investments in associates accounted for at fair value through profit or loss, the above disclosures will also apply (see Chapter 6 at 10.3.1.C).

The individual financial statements of a venturer that is not a parent should disclose summarised financial information about its investments in the jointly controlled entities, along with the effect of including those investments as if they had been accounted for using the equity method. Summarised financial information is not defined in FRS 102, but using the GAAP hierarchy to refer to IFRS 12 – *Disclosure of Interests in Other Entities*, it would seem appropriate to include: current assets, non-current assets, current liabilities, non-current liabilities, revenue, profit or loss from continuing operations, post-tax profit or loss from discontinued operations, other comprehensive income, total comprehensive income. This list is not exhaustive and other items may need to be considered if deemed material. *[IFRS 12 Appendix B.12]*. Investing entities that are exempt from preparing consolidated financial statements, or would be exempt if they had subsidiaries, are exempt from this requirement. *[FRS 102.15.21A]*.

4   COMPANY LAW MATTERS

4.1   Jointly controlled entities

The Companies Act does not define a 'joint venture', but paragraph 18 of Schedule 6 of the Regulations refers to a 'joint venture' as an undertaking that is managed 'jointly with one or more undertakings not included in the consolidation' in its description of non-corporate joint ventures that are permitted to be dealt with in consolidated financial statements by way of proportional consolidation. *[6 Sch 18]*. The disclosure requirements for 'joint ventures' are framed in the context of such joint ventures that are proportionally consolidated, *[4 Sch 18]*, and hence under FRS 102, these requirements will not be relevant.

However, jointly controlled entities that are equity accounted will be captured by the accounting and disclosure requirements in paragraph 19 of Schedule 6 of the Regulations which refer to 'associated undertakings'.

An '*associated undertaking*' is defined in the Regulations as an undertaking in which an undertaking included in the consolidation has a participating interest and over whose operating and financial policy it exercises a significant influence, and which is not:

- a subsidiary undertaking of the parent company; or

- a joint venture accounted for by proportional consolidation. *[6 Sch 19(1)]*.

A '*participating interest*' is defined as an interest held by an undertaking in the shares of another undertaking which it holds on a long-term basis for the purpose of securing a contribution to its activities by the exercise of control or influence arising from or related to that interest. The interest in shares includes interests which are convertible into shares or options to acquire shares, regardless of whether or not they are currently exercisable. Additionally, interests held on behalf of an undertaking are to be treated as held by it. *[10 Sch 11(1), 11(3)-(4)]*.

Hence an equity interest in a jointly controlled entity, given the nature of the joint control, will meet the definition of an associated undertaking for the purposes of the Regulations.

4.2 Measurement in individual entity accounts

Schedule 1 to the Regulations permits the equity method of accounting to be applied in respect of participating interests in the individual entity accounts of a venturer. *[1 Sch 29A]*. However, since FRS 102 already included a number of options for accounting for such investments, this option was not introduced to FRS 102. Consequently, this option cannot be applied by a venturer in preparing their individual entity accounts in accordance with FRS 102 (see 3.6.2 above). *[FRS 102.BC.A.28]*.

4.3 Presentation and disclosure

4.3.1 Consolidated financial statements

The Regulations require that equity accounted investments in jointly controlled entities are presented as fixed asset investments in the balance sheet. *[6 Sch 20]*. When 'adapted formats' (see Chapter 6 at 5.1) are used, investments in jointly controlled entities must be shown as a separate balance sheet item and distinguished between current and non-current items. *[FRS 102.4.2A]*.

Goodwill relating to a jointly controlled entity is included in the carrying amount of the investment. *[FRS 102.15.13]*.

There is no guidance in FRS 102 as to how long term interests (such as long term loans for which no payment is intended in the foreseeable future) in jointly controlled entities should be presented and therefore an entity must make an accounting policy choice as to how such interests are presented. Entities frequently make loans to jointly controlled entities, the terms of which are repayable on demand, but there is no intention of repayment in the foreseeable future. In these circumstances, for entities applying Schedule 1 to the Regulations, management will need to exercise judgement in determining whether such a loan is a debtor or a fixed asset investment in nature (see Chapter 6 at 5.3.4). For entities applying the adapted formats, such loans will need to be classified as appropriate between current or non-current assets (see Chapter 6 at 5.1.1).

In the profit and loss account, for entities applying the formats of Schedule 1 to the Regulations, income from interests in joint controlled entities should be shown as one line item in the profit and loss account. *[6 Sch 20]*. For entities applying the adapted formats, the share of the profit or loss of associates and jointly controlled entities accounted for using the equity method must be included as a single line item in the profit and loss account. *[FRS 102.5.5B]*. The format of the profit and loss account and balance sheet under FRS 102 are discussed further in Chapter 6.

Chapter 13

The Regulations also require that the following information must be given where an undertaking included in the consolidation has an interest in an 'associated undertaking' (which, as discussed at 4.1 above, will also be relevant for equity accounted jointly controlled entities):

- the name of the jointly controlled entity;
- the country in which the jointly controlled entity is incorporated for those incorporated outside the United Kingdom;
- the address of the registered office of the jointly controlled entity;
- the identity and proportion of the nominal value of each class of share held, disclosing separately those held by the:
  - parent company; and
  - group. *[4 Sch 19]*.

4.3.2   *Individual financial statements*

In individual financial statements the Regulations require additional disclosures in respect of significant holdings in undertakings, other than subsidiary entities. A holding is deemed significant if:

- it amounts to 20% or more of the nominal value of any class of shares in the undertaking; or
- the amount of the holding as stated in the company's individual accounts exceeds 20% of the stated net assets of the company. *[4 Sch 4]*.

In practice, this definition will capture most investments in jointly controlled entities. The resulting disclosures in individual accounts are:

- the name of each jointly controlled entity;
- the address of the registered office of each jointly controlled entity;
- the address of each jointly controlled entity's principal place of business if unincorporated; and
- the identity and proportion of the nominal value of each class of share held. *[4 Sch 5]*.

Additional disclosure would also be required in respect of each jointly controlled entity detailed above of:

- the aggregate amount of the capital and reserves of each entity; and
- the profit or loss for the year of each entity. *[4 Sch 6]*.

The additional disclosures just mentioned are not required when the jointly controlled entity is not required to publish its balance sheet anywhere in the world and the holding is less than 50% of the nominal value of the shares (or the information is not material). *[4 Sch 6]*.

A parent is not required to provide the additional disclosures of paragraph 6 of Schedule 4 in the Regulations in its individual financial statements if it is exempt under sections 400 or 401 of the Act from the requirement to prepare group accounts and the company discloses, in the notes to its accounts, the aggregate investment in the relevant jointly controlled entities determined by way of the equity method of valuation. *[4 Sch 13]*.

A parent that prepares consolidated financial statements and discloses the information described at 4.3.1 above in respect of its jointly controlled entities is not required to give the above disclosures in its individual financial statements. *[4 Sch 4].*

5   SUMMARY OF GAAP DIFFERENCES

The key differences between FRS 102 and IFRS in accounting for joint ventures are set out below.

	FRS 102	*IFRS*
Classification	Classifies joint ventures as either jointly controlled operations, jointly controlled assets or jointly controlled entities with different accounting considerations for each. Classification as jointly controlled entity requires existence of a separate legal entity.	Defines joint arrangements and classifies them between joint operations and joint ventures. Classification as a joint venture depends on assessment of the venturer's rights and obligations over the arrangement.
Accounting for jointly controlled operations	A venturer recognises in its financial statements: • the assets that it controls and the liabilities that it incurs; and • the expenses that it incurs and its share of the income that it earns from the sale of goods or services by the joint venture.	A joint operator recognises: • assets, including any share of assets held jointly; • liabilities, including its share of any liabilities incurred jointly; • revenue from the sale of its share of the output by the joint operation; • share of the revenue from the sale of the output by the joint operation; and • expenses, including its share of any expenses incurred jointly. The accounting and measurement for each of these items is in accordance with the applicable IFRS.
Accounting for jointly controlled assets	A venturer recognises in its financial statements: • its share of the jointly controlled assets, classified according to their nature; • any liabilities that it has incurred; • its share of any liabilities incurred jointly with the other venturers in relation to the joint venture; • any income from the sale or use of its share of the output of the joint venture together with its share of any expenses incurred by the joint venture; and • any expenses that it has incurred in respect of its interest in the joint venture.	Although IFRS does not have a concept of jointly controlled assets, such assets would normally qualify as joint operations as defined by IFRS 11. The accounting for joint operations is, in substance, the same as the accounting for jointly controlled assets under FRS 102.

Chapter 13

	FRS 102	IFRS
Individual and separate entity financial statements	An entity that is not a parent or is a parent that prepares separate financial statements, has the option to account for its investments in jointly controlled entities using either the cost model, fair value through other comprehensive income or at fair value through profit or loss.	An entity that is not a parent must prepare financial statements whereby its investments in jointly controlled entities are accounted for under the equity accounting method unless it meets criteria for exemption. An entity that is a parent but prepares separate financial statements has the option to account for its investment in jointly controlled entities at cost, in accordance with IFRS 9 or the equity method of accounting.
Investment portfolios / funds	Investments in jointly controlled entities held as part of an investment portfolio should be measured at fair value through profit or loss in the consolidated financial statements of a venturer that is a parent.	Venture capital organisations and similar entities can choose to measure investments in joint ventures at fair value through profit or loss.
Accounting for jointly controlled entities	Apart from those held as above, jointly controlled entities are equity accounted in the consolidated financial statements of a venturer.	Apart from those held as above or are to be classified as held for sale under IFRS 5, joint ventures are equity accounted in the consolidated financial statements of a venturer.
Implicit goodwill and fair value adjustments on acquisition of an equity-accounted jointly controlled entity	Follows the requirements of Section 19 of FRS 102. Goodwill should be amortised over its finite useful life, but if, in exceptional cases, an entity is unable to makes a reliable estimate of the useful life of goodwill, the life shall not exceed 10 years.	Follows the IFRS requirements regarding business combinations. Implicit goodwill is not amortised.
Loss of joint control of an equity-accounted jointly controlled entity that does not become a subsidiary or an associate	• If loss of joint control is as a result of a partial disposal, a gain or loss is recognised based on the disposal proceeds and the carrying amount relating to the proportion disposed of. The carrying value of the equity interest retained at the date joint control is lost becomes the cost of the retained investment. • If the loss of joint control is for reasons other than a partial disposal, no gain or loss is recognised and the carrying value of the equity-accounted investment at the date joint control is lost becomes the cost of the retained investment.	• If loss of joint control is as a result of a partial disposal, a gain or loss is recognised based on the disposal proceeds together with the fair value of any retained interest and the carrying amount of the total interest in the joint venture. • If loss of joint control is for reasons other than a partial disposal, a gain or loss is recognised based on the fair value of the retained interest and the carrying amount of the interest in the joint venture at that date.
Exchange of business or other non-monetary assets for an interest in a joint venture in consolidated financial statement.	• Gains that are not realised are reported in other comprehensive income.	• No distinction between realised and unrealised gains and all gains/losses are reported in profit or loss.

Chapter 14   Investment property

Chapter 14   Investment property

1   INTRODUCTION

What primarily distinguishes investment property from other types of property interest is that its cash flows (from rental or sale) are largely independent of those from other assets held by the entity. By contrast, property used by an entity for administrative purposes or for the production or supply of goods or services do not generate cash flows themselves but do so only in conjunction with other assets. Therefore, FRS 102 proposes a different model for investment properties than for property plant and equipment ('PP&E') under Section 17 – *Property, Plant and Equipment*. For investment properties rented to another group entities, an entity has an accounting policy choice (see 3.1.2 below).

Section 16 – *Investment Property* – applies to accounting for investments in land or buildings that meet the definition of investment property (see 3.1 below) and some property interests held by a lessee under an operating lease that are classified as investment property (see 3.1.5 below). This chapter discusses the version of Section 16 contained in the March 2018 version of FRS 102, which incorporates the *Amendments to FRS 102 The Financial Reporting Standard applicable in the UK and Republic of Ireland – Triennial review 2017 – Incremental improvements and clarifications* (Triennial review 2017) issued by the FRC in December 2017.

The principal Triennial review 2017 amendments which affect Section 16 are:

- the removal of 'undue cost or effort' exemptions (see 3.3.2 below);

- classification of investment property whose fair value can no longer be measured reliably; and

- introduction of an accounting policy choice for entities that rent investment property to another group entity, whereby entities can choose to measure the investment property either at cost (less depreciation and impairment) or at fair value (see 3.1.2 below).

Other Triennial review 2017 amendments are editorial in nature and/or intended to merely clarify rather than change the accounting treatment. For example, additional guidance is added when accounting for properties with mixed use (see 3.1.7 below) and accounting for transfers of assets to or from investment property (see 3.4 below).

The principal effective date for these amendments is accounting periods beginning on or after 1 January 2019, with early application permitted provided all amendments are applied at the same time (see Chapter 3 at 1.3). The amendments are applied retrospectively (see Chapter 9 at 3.4.2) with limited transitional provision available (see 3.1.2 below).

2   COMPARISON BETWEEN SECTION 16 AND IFRS

There are some key differences between accounting for investment properties under Section 16 compared to IFRS (IAS 40 – *Investment Property*). These are discussed at 2.1 to 2.6 below. The summary at 4 below contains the major GAAP differences.

2.1   Measurement basis after initial recognition

Section 16 requires all property meeting the definition of investment property (whose fair value can be measured reliably on an on-going basis) and property interests held by a lessee under an operating lease that are classified as investment property, to be measured at fair value (see 3.3 below). *[FRS 102.16.1]*. For investment properties rented to another group entities, an entity has an accounting policy choice (see 3.1.2 below). Property interests held under operating leases may be accounted for as investment property on a property-by-property basis provided that the property would otherwise meet the definition of an investment property and the fair value of the property interest can be measured on an on-going basis (see 3.1.5 below). *[FRS 102.16.3]*.

IAS 40 permits entities an accounting policy choice to use either cost or fair value for investment properties. Once an entity chooses a measurement basis, it must apply that basis to all of its investment properties. However, there are some exceptions for insurers and similar entities. *[IAS 40.30-32C]*. IAS 40 does not identify a preferred alternative although the fair value model seems to be the more widely adopted model amongst entities in real estate sector.

Under IFRS, insurance companies and other entities that hold specified assets, including investment properties, whose fair value or return is directly linked to the return paid on specific liabilities (i.e. liabilities that are secured by such investment properties), can choose either the fair value or cost model for all such properties without it affecting the choice available for all the other investment properties that they may hold. However, for an insurer or other entity that operates an internal property fund that issues notional units, with some units held by investors in linked contracts and others held by the entity, all properties within such a fund must be held on the same basis because IAS 40 does not permit the entity to measure the property held by such a fund partly at cost and partly at fair value. *[IAS 40.32A-32B]*.

If an entity reporting under IFRS has a leased property that meets the definition of investment property and it elects to apply the fair value model in IAS 40 to its investment properties, the entity must also apply that fair value model to its right-of-use assets. *[IFRS 16.34]*. Conversely, for an entity that chooses to apply the cost model to its investment property, the entity must apply the cost model in IFRS 16 – *Leases* – to right-of-use assets that meet the definition of investment property.

2.2 Valuation method

The definition of fair value in FRS 102 is identical to the IAS 39 – *Financial Instruments: Recognition and Measurement* – definition of fair value prior to the adoption of IFRS 13 – *Fair Value Measurement*. Fair value as defined by FRS 102 is 'the amount for which an asset could be exchanged... between knowledgeable willing parties in an arm's length transaction'. *[FRS 102 Appendix I]*. Hence the FRS 102 definition is a transaction (entry) price.

The IFRS 13 definition of fair value is 'the price that would be received to sell an asset...in an orderly transaction between market participants at the measurement date'. *[IFRS 13.9]*. The IFRS measurement is an exit price from the perspective of a market participant that holds the asset rather than a transaction (entry) price and is a market based measurement rather than an entity specific measurement.

Therefore, differences may arise between FRS 102 and IAS 40 in respect of how fair value measurement is determined.

2.3 Mixed use property

Section 16 states that a property that has mixed use should be separated between investment property and PP&E if the resulting portions could be sold separately or leased out separately under a finance lease. Section 16 further requires consideration of whether the separate investment property component can be fair valued. That is, if the fair value of the investment property component cannot be reliably measured, the entire property is accounted for as PP&E in accordance with Section 17 (see 3.1.7 below). *[FRS 102.16.4]*.

Similar to above, IAS 40 requires that a property that has mixed use should be separated between the owner-occupied element and the investment property element only if the two elements could be sold (or leased under a finance lease) separately. However, the entire property is accounted for as PP&E only in the event that no separation is possible and if a significant proportion is used for non-investment property purposes. If no separation is possible and if an insignificant proportion is used for non-investment property purposes, the entire property is an investment property. *[IAS 40.10]*.

IAS 40 emphasises that it is only in exceptional cases and only on initial recognition (either by acquisition or change in use) that the entity will be able to conclude that it will not be able to reliably measure the investment property's fair value on a continuing basis. *[IAS 40.53]*. Accordingly, if separation is possible but on initial recognition the fair value of the investment property element cannot be reliably measured on a continuing basis, the property is still classified as investment property but is measured using the cost model in IAS 16 – *Property, Plant and Equipment* – for owned investment property or cost model in accordance with IFRS 16 for investment property held by a lessee as a right-of-use asset, until its disposal. The investment property element is assumed to have a nil residual value (see also 2.4 below). *[IAS 40.53]*.

2.4 Inability to reliably measure fair value

Section 16 requires investment property to be measured at fair value at each reporting date. The Appendix to Section 2 – *Concepts and Pervasive Principles* – provides guidance on determining fair value (see 3.3.1 below). *[FRS 102.16.7]*. If a reliable measure of fair value is no longer available for an asset measured at fair value, its carrying amount at the last date the asset was reliably measurable becomes its new cost. The entity should measure the asset at this cost amount less impairment, if any, until a reliable measure of fair value becomes available (see 3.3.4 below). *[FRS 102.2A.6]*.

Although there is a choice under IAS 40 whether to apply either the fair value or cost model, where an entity adopts the fair value model, 'there is a rebuttable presumption that an entity can reliably measure the fair value of an investment property on a continuing basis' and only in exceptional circumstances and only on initial recognition (either by acquisition or change in use) of an investment property may that presumption be rebutted. *[IAS 40.53]*. In such exceptional cases, the property should be measured using the cost model in IAS 16 for owned investment property, or the cost model in accordance with IFRS 16 for investment property held by a lessee as a right-of-use asset, until its disposal. The property is assumed to have a nil residual value. *[IAS 40.53]*. Once a property is initially recognised at its fair value, it must always be so recognised until disposed of or reclassified for owner-occupation or development for subsequent sale in the ordinary course of the business, even if comparable market transactions become less frequent or market prices become less easily available. *[IAS 40.55]*.

2.5   Investment property rented to another group entity

Section 16 states that if investment property (or part of such property) is rented to another group entity, that property (or the part of that property that is rented to another group entity) should be accounted for either at fair value in accordance with Section 16 or by transferring the property to PP&E and applying the cost model in accordance with Section 17 (see 3.1.2 below). *[FRS 102.16.4A-4B]*. Accordingly, the treatment of such property in the individual accounts and in the group accounts would be the same if an entity chooses to account for such property in its individual accounts as PP&E.

Under IFRS, if an entity owns property that is leased to, and occupied by, its parent or another subsidiary, that property meets the definition of an investment property from the perspective of the entity that owns it. There is no option to treat the property as PP&E in the individual financial statements. In the consolidated financial statements the property does not qualify as investment property because the property is owner-occupied from the perspective of the group. Therefore, the lessor treats the property as investment property in its individual financial statements but the same property would be treated differently, i.e. as PP&E, in the consolidated financial statements. *[IAS 40.15]*.

2.6   Disclosures

The disclosure requirements of Section 16 are less extensive than those of IFRS and are discussed at 3.6 below.

3 REQUIREMENTS OF SECTION 16 FOR INVESTMENT PROPERTY

3.1 Definition, scope and initial recognition of investment property

Section 16 applies to investment property. *[FRS 102.16.1]*. Investment property is defined as property (land or a building, or part of a building, or both) held by the owner or by the lessee under a finance lease to earn rentals or capital appreciation or both. *[FRS 102 Appendix I]*.

This means that any entity, whatever the underlying nature of its business, can hold investment property assets if its intention on initial recognition (either by acquisition or by transfer – see 3.4 below) is to hold them for rent or for capital appreciation or both. Subsequent to initial recognition, reclassifications of assets into and from investment property are discussed at 3.4 below. An investment property can also be held under an operating lease (see 3.1.5 below).

In contrast, property held (by the owner or by the lessee under a finance lease) for use in the production or supply of goods or services or for administrative purposes (commonly referred to as 'owner-occupied'), or property held or under construction for sale in the ordinary course of business is not investment property. *[FRS 102 Appendix I]*. However, a property which has mixed use should be separated between PP&E and investment property (see 3.1.7 below).

Section 16 applies to the measurement in a lessee's financial statements of investment property interests held under a finance lease and of lessee's property interests under an operating lease that are classified as investment property and to the measurement in a lessor's financial statements of investment property provided to a lessee under an operating lease (see 3.1.5 and 3.1.8 below). However, it does not deal with other accounting matters that are dealt with in Section 20 – *Leases* (see Chapter 18).

Prior to the Triennial review 2017 amendments, only investment property whose fair value could be measured reliably without 'undue cost or effort' on an on-going basis could be accounted for at fair value through profit or loss. Otherwise, the investment property was accounted for as PP&E using the cost model in Section 17 until a reliable measure of fair value becomes available and it is expected that fair value will be reliably measurable on an on-going basis. See 3.3.2 and 3.3.4 below for discussion of the Triennial review 2017 amendments on 'undue cost or effort' and on classification of investment property whose fair value can no longer be measured reliably, respectively.

The Triennial review 2017 amendments also added a paragraph 1A to Section 16 to clarify that Section 16 does not apply to investment property rented to another group entity and transferred to PP&E (see 3.1.2 below).

3.1.1   Investment property under construction

Section 16 does not explicitly address investment property under construction. However, it states that an entity should determine the cost of a self-constructed investment property in accordance with paragraphs 10 to 14 of Section 17. *[FRS 102.16.5]*. This implies that investment property under construction is within the scope of Section 16 and that classification as an investment property is determined at initial recognition, instead of when construction is completed. In summary, these paragraphs require cost to comprise of purchase price, costs directly attributable to bringing the asset to the location and condition necessary for it to be capable of operating in the manner intended by management, the initial estimate of costs of dismantling and removing the item and restoring the site and any capitalised borrowing costs in accordance with Section 25 – *Borrowing Costs*.

This reference to Section 17 implies that the FRC believes that an investment property under construction should normally be recognised and measured initially at cost under Section 17 on the grounds that the fair value cannot be reliably measurable until completion. However, if the fair value can be reliably measured during construction then FRS 102 would require that investment property under construction is held at fair value. See 3.2 below for measurement of investment property at initial recognition.

3.1.2   Investment property leased to other group entities

A property leased to other group entities is within the scope of Section 16 as it meets the definition of an investment property. *[FRS 102.16.1, 16.4A-4B]*. This classification in the lessor's individual financial statements will apply even if the rental is not at arm's length and the individual entity is not in a position to benefit from capital appreciation, provided the definition of an investment property is met.

In consolidated financial statements transactions between group entities, including income and expenses in respect of inter-group leased property should be eliminated in accordance with Section 9 – *Consolidated and Separate Financial Statements* (see Chapter 8 at 3.5.1). Property owned by one group company but leased to another will be classified as PP&E (being owner-occupied) from the perspective of the group as a whole.

During the drafting of the Triennial review 2017 amendments, a significant amount of feedback from stakeholders suggested that the cost of obtaining a fair value for an investment property that is rented to another group entity far outweighs the benefit, as the information is of little use when the investment property would be treated as PP&E in the consolidated financial statements. *[FRS 102.BC.B16.2]*. As a result, the Triennial review 2017 amendments introduced an accounting policy choice. *[FRS 102.BC.B16.3]*. The amended Section 16 states that an entity that rents investment property to another group entity should account for those properties either:

(a)   at fair value with changes in fair value recognised in profit or loss in accordance with Section 16; or

(b)   by transferring them to PP&E and applying the cost model in accordance with Section 17.

The Appendix to Section 2 provides guidance on determining fair value (see 3.3.1 below). An entity choosing to apply (b) above should provide all the disclosures required by Section 17, other than those related to fair value measurement. *[FRS 102.16.4A]*.

When only part of a property is rented to another group entity and the remainder is used for other purposes (such as being rented to an external third party or owner-occupied), the accounting policy choice described above only applies to the component of that property that is rented to another group entity. *[FRS 102.16.4B]*.

Section 16 is not explicit whether the accounting policy choice described above can be applied on a property-by-property basis. As currently written, it appears that an entity's accounting policy choice must be applied to all of its investment properties (or part of such property) rented to another group entities.

If an entity subsequently changes its previous choice of accounting policy, this represents a change in accounting policy and should be accounted for retrospectively (see Chapter 9 at 3.4). *[FRS 102.10.10, 10.12]*.

As discussed at 1 above, the Triennial review 2017 amendments are applied retrospectively with limited transitional provision available. In particular, when an entity first applies the Triennial review 2017 amendments, as an exception to retrospective application, an entity may elect to measure an investment property rented to another group entity, that is measured on an ongoing basis at cost less accumulated depreciation and accumulated impairment losses, at its fair value and use that fair value as its deemed cost at the date of transition for the Triennial review 2017 amendments. *[FRS 102.1.19(a)]*.

This transitional provision allows the use of fair value at the date of transition for applying the Triennial review 2017 amendments as 'deemed cost', instead of restating to historical cost, for investment property rented out to other group entities which is accounted for as PP&E. The transitional provision may be applied on a property-by-property basis. This option is similar to paragraph 35.10(c) of FRS 102 which permits first-time adopters to use a fair value at the transition date as the 'deemed cost' of an item of PP&E, an investment property or an intangible asset (which is available on an item-by-item basis – see Chapter 32 at 5.5.1). *[FRS 102 Appendix III.40B]*.

If an entity elects to take this transitional exemption, this asset is measured under the alternative accounting rules rather than under the historical cost accounting rules. Therefore, any upwards revaluation compared to the historical cost amounts that would have been recorded at the date of transition must be recognised in a revaluation reserve as required by the Regulations. *[1 Sch 35(1)]*. The additional disclosures required by paragraph 34 of Schedule 1 to the Regulations must be given. *[FRS 102 Appendix III.40C]*. These disclosures are discussed in Chapter 6 at 10.2.4.

Subsequently, there may be transfers of reserves to the extent the entity is realising the revaluation reserve. The alternative accounting rules allow that an amount may be transferred from the revaluation reserve to the profit and loss account, if the amount was previously charged to the profit and loss account or represents a realised profit. *[1 Sch 35(3)]*. Therefore, where depreciation or an impairment has been charged based on the deemed cost which exceeds the historical cost, the excess depreciation or impairment (over that which would have been charged based on historical cost) may be transferred from the revaluation reserve to retained earnings (as a reserves transfer). Similarly, on sale of the asset, the amount in the revaluation reserve, where realised on sale, could be transferred to retained earnings (as a reserves transfer in equity). See Chapter 15 at 3.6.3.A and more generally on the use of the revaluation reserve, see also Chapter 6 at 10.2.3.

Associates and joint ventures are not part of a group. Therefore, a property owned by a group but leased to an associate or a joint venture would be accounted for as investment property in the consolidated financial statements of the group (provided, of course, it meets the definition of an investment property).

3.1.3   *Property with the provision of ancillary services*

Section 16 provides no guidance on the impact (if any) of ancillary services on the classification of a property as an investment property where such services are provided by the owner to the user of the investment property.

However, the definition of an investment property requires that the property should be held for capital appreciation and/or rentals rather than for use in the production or supply of goods and services. Therefore, if an owner provides ancillary services to the user of the investment property, exercise of judgement will be required to determine whether or not the property is being held for capital appreciation/rentals or for the income generated by the supply of those ancillary goods and services.

It would be reasonable to consider the related guidance in IFRS. IAS 40 states that if the owner supplies ancillary services to the user of the investment property, the property will not qualify as an investment property unless these services are an insignificant component of the arrangement as a whole. For example, security and maintenance services are described as being insignificant. *[IAS 40.11]*.

The crucial issue is the extent to which the owner retains significant exposure to the risks of running a business. IAS 40 uses the example of a hotel. An owner-managed hotel, for example, would be precluded from being an investment property as the services provided to guests are a significant component of the commercial arrangements. *[IAS 40.12-13]*.

However, the nature of the asset in question is not the key factor; rather it is the nature of the owner's interest in the asset. If the owner's position is, in substance, that of a passive investor, any property may be treated as investment property. If, in contrast, the owner has outsourced day-to-day functions while retaining significant exposure to variation in the cash flows generated by the operations that are being executed in the building, a property should rather be treated as owner-occupied property. *[IAS 40.13]*.

IAS 40 refers to owner-managed hotels as being precluded from being investment property. Hotel properties that are leased on arm's length terms to hotel operators may, however, fall to be accounted for as investment property. This is more likely to be the case when:

- the payments under the lease are not significantly determined by the results of the hotel operator (see 3.1.10 below), rather they reflect the general market for such properties; and
- the nature of the owner's rights in the arrangements with the operator is not divergent from those usually expected under a property lease.

IAS 40 acknowledges that this question of significance can require judgements to be made. It specifies that an entity should develop consistent criteria for use in such instances that reflect the provisions described above. *[IAS 40.14]*. If significant, disclosure of this judgement would be required by Section 8 – *Notes to the Financial Statements. [FRS 102.8.6]*.

3.1.4 Land

The definition of an investment property refers to land as well as buildings. Therefore, land is investment property if it is held to earn rentals or for capital appreciation or both. This is in contrast to land that is held for sale in the ordinary course of business (typically in the shorter term) or held for the production or supply of goods and services or for administrative purposes.

A situation may arise where an entity has land but has not yet decided what this land will be used for. Section 16 is silent on this matter but IAS 40 provides guidance that if, on initial recognition, land is held for a currently undetermined future use, i.e. if an entity has not determined whether it will use the land as owner-occupied property or for sale in the ordinary course of business, it is deemed to be held for capital appreciation and must be classified as investment property. *[IAS 40.8]*.

3.1.5 Property interests held under operating leases

Section 16 applies to property interests held by a lessee under an operating lease that are classified as investment property. *[FRS 102.16.1]*. A lessee in an operating lease is permitted to classify and account for its interest in the property as an investment property using Section 16 if, and only if:

- the property would otherwise meet the definition of an investment property; and
- the lessee can measure the fair value of the property interest on an on-going basis (or prior to the Triennial review 2017 amendments, the lessee can measure the fair value of the property interest without undue cost or effort on an on-going basis – see 3.3.2 below). *[FRS 102.16.3]*.

The Appendix to Section 2 provides guidance on determining fair value (see 3.3.1 below). This classification alternative is available on a property-by-property basis so that a lessee may decide to classify some property interests held under an operating lease as investment property and leave the others off the balance sheet. *[FRS 102.16.3]*.

The accounting for investment properties held on operating leases is discussed at 3.2.4 below.

3.1.6 Social benefit entities

Section 16 specifically excludes properties whose main purpose is to provide social benefits, from being accounted for as investment properties. For example, social housing held by a public benefit entity (i.e. an entity whose primary objective is to provide goods or services for the general public, community or social benefit and where any equity is provided with a view to supporting the entity's primary objectives rather than with a view to providing a financial return to equity providers, shareholders or members). Such properties held primarily for the provision of social benefits are properties held to supply services, which do not meet the definition of an investment property, and therefore, are accounted for as PP&E in accordance with Section 17. *[FRS 102.16.3A]*.

3.1.7   Properties with mixed use

A property may have mixed use and could be partly owner-occupied and partly held for rental. For example, an entity may own a building and occupy some floors for its own use but also sub-lease other floors to tenants.

As a result of the Triennial review 2017 amendments, the guidance on separating components of a mixed use property has been expanded and the use of 'undue cost or effort' exemption when determining fair value has been removed (see 3.3.2 below).

Section 16 now requires that mixed use property should be separated between investment property and PP&E if the resulting portions could be sold separately or leased out separately under a finance lease. *[FRS 102.16.4].* In cases where the components of a mixed use property can be physically and legally separated but the fair value of the investment property component cannot be measured reliably, the entire property should be accounted for as PP&E in accordance with Section 17. The Appendix to Section 2 provides guidance on determining fair value (see 3.3.1 below). *[FRS 102.16.4].*

Section 16 does not provide further guidance if the components of a mixed use property cannot be physically and legally separated but the fair value of the entire property can be measured reliably. It would be reasonable to consider the related guidance in IFRS. Under IAS 40, in the event that no separation is possible, the property is an investment property only if an insignificant proportion is used for non-investment property purposes. *[IAS 40.10].* The setting of a threshold to evaluate whether or not something is significant or insignificant depends on judgement and circumstances.

Criteria used in the assessments described above should be applied consistently and if significant, disclosure of these judgements would be required by Section 8. *[FRS 102.8.6].*

Prior to the Triennial review 2017 amendments, Section 16 required mixed use property to be separated and accounted for as investment property or PP&E, as applicable for the relevant components. However, if the entity could not reliably measure the fair value of the investment property components without undue cost or effort, then the entity would have accounted for the entire property as PP&E in accordance with Section 17. Accordingly, Section 16 required consideration only of whether the separate investment property element could be fair valued. It did not require that the property could actually be physically and legally separated between investment property and PP&E.

3.1.8   Property leased to others

Properties leased to third parties under one or more operating lease are generally investment properties, whether they are owned freehold by the reporting entity or held under a leasehold interest. Under IFRS, this will also apply if the property is currently vacant while tenants are being sought. *[IAS 40.8].*

However, in our view, an exception should be made in those cases where, despite being leased out, properties have been held for sale in the ordinary course of business since their initial recognition (either by acquisition or transfer – see 3.4.2 below). Leasing of property prior to sale is a common practice in the real estate industry in order to minimise cash outflows whilst the entity seeks a buyer and because prospective buyers may view the existence of such lease contracts positively, especially those that wish to acquire property for investment purposes.

In those circumstances – and notwithstanding that they are leased to tenants under operating leases – they should be accounted for as inventory under Section 13 – *Inventories* – as long as it remains the intention to hold such properties for short-term sale in the ordinary course of business. The rent received would be recorded in profit or loss and would not be treated as a reduction in the cost of inventory.

Property that is leased to a third party under a finance lease is not an investment property but is accounted for under Section 20 (see Chapter 18).

3.1.9   Property held or under construction for sale in the ordinary course of business

Property held, or being constructed, with the intention of sale in the ordinary course of business is not an investment property. This includes property acquired exclusively for sale in the near future or for development and resale (such property is accounted for as inventory under Section 13 (see Chapter 11)) and property being built or developed under construction contract for third parties (covered by Section 23 – *Revenue* (see Chapter 20).

In practice, the classification between investment property and property intended for sale in the ordinary course of business is often a difficult judgement. There is only a fine line between:

- a property held for capital appreciation, and therefore classified as investment property; and

- a property intended for sale in the ordinary course of business, which would be classified as inventory. This might be the case where, for example, the owner will undertake activities to increase the property's value prior to sale or where there is uncertainty in obtaining permits required from relevant authorities prior to commencing construction activities. In the latter case, the property, e.g. land, may continue to appreciate in value during the period where there are no development activities – see 3.2.5 below.

As set out at 3.1.8 above, the receipt of rental income from a property would not necessarily be the deciding factor. Certainly, other than for land (see 3.1.4 above), there is no deemed 'default' classification when the future use of a property has not yet been determined.

However, this judgement is important because whilst Section 16 allows property held as inventory to be reclassified as investment property when the property first meets the definition of investment property, it is more difficult to reclassify investment property as inventory (see 3.4.1 below). Accordingly, an entity should develop criteria so that it can exercise that judgement consistently in accordance with the definition of investment property and with the related guidance in Section 16. If significant, disclosure of this judgement would be required by Section 8. *[FRS 102.8.6]*.

3.1.10   Property where rentals are determined by reference to the operations in the property

It may also be inappropriate to consider a property as investment property if the owner is significantly exposed to the operation of the business in the property through a linkage between the rentals charged and the performance of the business.

Chapter 14

A common example is the incidence of turnover or profit-related rents in retail leases. If the turnover or profit-related element is a very significant proportion of total rental then consideration should be given to whether the landlord is so exposed to the performance of the underlying retail business as to make classification of the property as investment property inappropriate. This will be a matter of judgement, including the consideration of any other facts and circumstances (for example, the length of the lease to the tenant). If significant, disclosure of this judgement would be required by Section 8. *[FRS 102.8.6]*.

3.2   Measurement at initial recognition

An entity should recognise an asset in the statement of financial position when it is probable that the future economic benefits will flow to the entity and the asset has a cost or value that can be measured reliably. *[FRS 102.2.37]*. These recognition criteria apply for any costs incurred, whether initially or subsequently.

Section 16 requires an investment property to be measured at its cost at initial recognition. The cost of purchased investment property comprises its purchase price and any directly attributable costs such as legal fees, brokerage fees, property transfer taxes and other transaction costs. *[FRS 102.16.5]*.

Although specific reference to Section 17 is made only when determining the cost of a self-constructed investment property (see 3.2.3 below), we consider that the principles in Section 17 must still be applied to the recognition of costs of acquired investment property. These principles, together with the discussions of other practical issues, are set out in detail in Chapter 15 at 3.4.

3.2.1   *Deferred payments*

In considering the purchase price, if payment for the property is deferred beyond normal credit terms, the present value of all future payments is calculated in order to arrive at the cost. *[FRS 102.16.5]*.

3.2.2   *Exchange for monetary and/or non-monetary assets*

Section 16 is silent on how to measure the cost of an investment property acquired in part or in whole in exchange for a non-monetary asset.

However, guidance is contained in Section 17 in respect of how to measure the cost of an item of PP&E in exchange for a non-monetary asset or combination of monetary and non-monetary assets. This states that the cost of acquired asset is measured at fair value unless:

- the exchange transaction lacks commercial substance; or
- the fair value of neither the asset received nor the asset given up is reliably measurable. In that case, the asset's cost is measured at the carrying amount of the asset given up. *[FRS 102.17.14]*.

This is further discussed in Chapter 15 at 3.4.4.

3.2.3   *Self-constructed property*

To determine the cost of a self-constructed investment property, Section 16 refers to the guidance in paragraphs 10 to 14 of Section 17 (see Chapter 15). *[FRS 102.16.5]*. This means that only those costs that are allowed by Section 17 can be capitalised and that capitalisation ceases when the asset has reached the condition necessary for it to be capable of operating in the manner intended by management. Therefore, start-up costs and operating losses incurred before the investment property achieves the planned occupancy level are not to be capitalised because at the date of physical completion, the asset would be capable of operating in the manner intended by management.

In addition to the purchase price and directly attributable costs, the cost of a self-constructed investment property also comprises the initial estimate of costs (if any) of dismantling and removing the property and restoring the site on which it is located and any borrowing costs capitalised in accordance with Section 25 (see Chapter 22). *[FRS 102.17.10]*. Paragraphs 11 to 14 of Section 17 referred to above also provide guidance in determining which costs are not capitalisable, treatment of income and expenses of incidental operations during construction of a property, accounting for deferred payments and accounting for exchanges of assets when acquiring a property.

These are further discussed in Chapter 15 at 3.4.1 to 3.4.4.

3.2.4 Property interests held under a finance or operating lease

The initial cost of a property interest held under a lease and classified as an investment property should be as prescribed for a finance lease by paragraphs 9 and 10 of Section 20. This applies even if the property interest would otherwise be classified as an operating lease if it was within the scope of Section 20 (see 3.1.5 above).

This means that initial cost of the asset is the lower of the fair value of the property and the present value of the minimum lease payments. An equivalent amount is recognised as a liability. Any premium paid for a lease would be included in the minimum lease payments for this purpose thus forming part of the cost of the asset but are clearly excluded from the liability as it has already been paid. *[FRS 102.16.6]*.

3.2.5 Expenditure prior to planning permissions/zoning consents

In UK, as well as in many jurisdictions, permissions from relevant authorities are required prior to development of new or existing property, and the ability to start physical construction of the development depends on these permissions.

Application for such permissions supports the entity's intention as to the use of the property and may be considered as a factor in classifying the asset. However, unless an entity is considering a number of possible uses of the asset at its initial recognition, the uncertainty in obtaining relevant permission would usually not affect the classification of the property which, as described at 3.1 above, is mainly based on the entity's intention when the property is first acquired. Subsequent to initial recognition, assets might be reclassified into and from investment property (see 3.4.2 below).

The likelihood of obtaining such permissions, however, is relevant in recognition and measurement of any additional costs to the property. Developers typically incur significant costs prior to such permissions being granted and such permissions are rarely guaranteed. Therefore, in assessing whether such pre-permission expenditure can be capitalised – assuming it otherwise meets the criteria – a judgement must be made, at the date the expenditure is incurred, of whether there is sufficient probability that the relevant permissions will be granted. Conversely, if during the application and approval process it is no longer expected that necessary permits will be granted, capitalisation of pre-permission

Chapter 14

expenditure should cease and any related amounts that were previously capitalised should be written off. Under the fair value model, it would not affect the measurement of the investment property in the statement of financial position; it would only affect presentation of write-off of expenses and fair value gains and losses in the income statement. If, however, the cost model is used due to the fact that the fair value of investment property can no longer be measured reliably (see 3.3.4 below), the carrying amount of any related property subject to development or redevelopment (or, if appropriate, the cash generating unit where such an asset belongs) should be tested for impairment, where applicable, in accordance with Section 27 – *Impairment of Assets* (see Chapter 24).

3.2.6   Income from tenanted property during development

An issue that can arise is whether rental and similar income generated by existing tenants in a property development may be capitalised and offset against the cost of developing that property.

Section 17 requires that the income and related expenses of incidental operations are recognised in profit or loss and included in their respective classifications of income and expense (see Chapter 15 at 3.4.2). *[FRS 102.17.12]*. In our view there should not be a measurement difference between the cost of a property development dealt with under Section 16 and the cost of development dealt with under Section 17. We consider that rental and similar income from existing tenants are incidental operations to the development and therefore should not be capitalised against the costs of the development. Rather such rental and similar income should be recognised in profit or loss in accordance with the requirements of Section 20 (see Chapter 18), together with related expenses. For these purposes it is irrelevant whether the investment property is held at fair value, or in certain cases, at cost (see 3.3 below).

3.2.7   Payments by the vendors to the purchaser

In some instances, a transaction for the purchase of an investment property may include an additional element where the vendor repays an amount to the purchaser – perhaps described as representing a rental equivalent for a period of time.

The question then arises whether, in the accounts of the purchaser, this payment should be recorded as income (albeit perhaps recognised over a period of time) or as a deduction from the acquisition cost of the investment property on initial recognition.

In our view such amounts are an integral part of the acquisition transaction and should invariably be treated as a deduction from the acquisition cost of the investment property because the payment is an element of a transaction between a vendor and purchaser of the property, rather than a landlord and tenant. In the event that the repayments by the vendor are spread over time, the present value of those payments should be deducted from the cost of the investment property and an equivalent receivable recognised against which those payments are amortised.

3.2.8   Acquisition of investment property or business combination

The judgement required to determine whether the acquisition of investment property is an acquisition of an asset or a group of assets – or a business combination within the scope of Section 19 – *Business Combinations and Goodwill* – should be made with reference to Section 19 (see Chapter 17 at 3.2). This judgement will rest upon the facts and circumstances of each acquisition. If significant, disclosure of this judgement would be required by Section 8. *[FRS 102.8.6]*.

The definition of a business is applied regardless of whether the entity purchases a property directly or, in the case of consolidated financial statements, via the shares in another entity.

3.3 Measurement after initial recognition

Once recognised, an investment property should be measured at fair value at each reporting date (except in the cases described in 3.1.2 and 3.1.7 above and in 3.3.4 below) with changes in fair value recognised in profit or loss. If a property interest held under a lease is classified as an investment property, the item accounted for at fair value is that interest only and not the underlying property. *[FRS 102.16.7]*. See 3.3.1 below for discussion on determining the fair value of an investment property.

The FRC's appendix on the legal requirements of FRS 102 clarifies that fair value movements on investment properties can be included in the profit and loss account under paragraph 40 of Schedule 1 of the Regulations despite the fact that unrealised gains on investment properties are not usually realised profits as defined by the Companies Act. *[FRS 102 Appendix III.27]*.

Although the default reserve within equity for fair value movements on investment property is retained earnings, the FRC observes that entities measuring investment properties at fair value may transfer such amounts to a separate non-distributable reserve, instead of a transfer to retained earnings, but are not required to do so. Presenting fair value movements that are not distributable profits in a separate reserve may assist with the identification of profits available for that purpose. *[FRS 102 Appendix III.28]*. Any such transfer from retained earnings to a non-distributable reserve should be made in the statement of changes in equity.

Unless carried under the cost model in certain cases as discussed at 3.1.2 and 3.1.7 above, no depreciation is required on investment properties as the Regulations do not require depreciation of investment properties measured under the fair value accounting rules.

Section 16 permits an entity to subdivide investment property into classes such that some classes may be measured at cost, and others at fair value (for example, investment property rented to another group entity – see 3.1.2 above). The FRC's appendix on the legal requirements of FRS 102 takes the view that such requirement that allows certain class of investment property to be held at fair value and other class of such items at cost is 'consistent with the most reasonable and common sense interpretation' of paragraph 39 of Schedule 1 of the Regulations which permits investment property to be included at fair value provided that the fair value can reliably be determined. *[FRS 102 Appendix III.37D]*.

Prior to the Triennial review 2017 amendments, only an investment property whose fair value could be measured reliably without undue cost or effort on an on-going basis was measured at fair value through profit or loss. Accordingly, all other investment property (i.e. investment property whose fair value could not be reliably measured without undue cost or effort) was measured using the cost model in Section 17. See also 3.3.2 below for discussion on the concept of 'undue cost or effort'.

3.3.1   Determining fair value

Fair value is 'the amount for which an asset could be exchanged... between knowledgeable, willing parties in an arm's length transaction'. *[FRS 102 Appendix I]*.

Section 16 emphasises that if a property interest held under a lease is classified as investment property, the fair value to be determined is the leasehold interest and not the underlying property. *[FRS 102.16.7]*.

Section 16 refers to the guidance on determining fair value in the Appendix to Section 2. *[FRS 102.16.7]*. This provides a methodology in approaching fair value measurement whenever fair value measurement is permitted or required. See Chapter 4 at 3.13 for the detailed discussion of such guidance.

In practice, the fair value estimate arrived at under FRS 102 may be similar to that estimated for 'market value' as defined by the Royal Institution of Chartered Surveyors ('RICS') and the International Valuation Standards Council ('IVSC'). Their definition of 'market value' being 'the estimated amount for which an asset or liability should exchange on the valuation date between a willing buyer and a willing seller in an arm's length transaction, after proper marketing and where the parties had each acted knowledgeably, prudently and without compulsion.'[1]

Many entities use an external valuer to estimate fair value based on the RICS and/or IVSC Valuation Standards. In practice, the use of an independent valuer with a recognised and relevant professional qualification and with recent experience in the location and category of the investment property being valued is generally preferred by many entities over valuations prepared in-house, albeit there is no requirement for an entity to use an independent valuer in determining the fair value of investment property. However, if there has been no such independent valuation, this must be disclosed (see 3.6.1 below). *[FRS 102.16.10(b)]*.

3.3.2   Undue cost or effort

Prior to the Triennial review 2017 amendments, Section 16 required only investment property that could be measured at fair value without undue cost or effort to be measured at fair value; any that could not were accounted for as PP&E using the cost model in Section 17. *[FRS 102.BC.B16.1]*. However, FRS 102 did not define 'undue cost or effort'.

The FRC observed implementation issues when applying the concept of 'undue cost or effort'. It was noted that entities needed to apply judgement in determining whether an exemption was available in their circumstances, which led to the exemptions being applied inconsistently in similar circumstances and therefore different costs being incurred in the preparation of financial statements. It was noted that not all entities were applying sufficient rigour in assessing the availability of the undue cost or effort exemptions; it is not an accounting policy choice. In response to these issues, the undue cost or effort exemptions that existed in FRS 102 were removed. *[FRS 102.BC.A47-48]*.

The FRC particularly noted that in the UK, entities should generally be able to obtain a fair value for an investment property, without undue cost or effort, which would provide useful, decision-relevant information to users of the financial statements. Therefore as part of the Triennial review 2017, and in line with the response to implementation issues described above, the undue cost or effort exemption in relation to investment property was removed. *[FRS 102.BC.B16.1].*

3.3.3   Double-counting of assets and liabilities

Section 16 does not address the potential for double-counting assets and liabilities that are recorded separately in the balance sheet, but also included within a valuation of an investment property. Common examples include air-conditioning, lifts and fixtures and fittings, all of which may be recorded separately on the balance sheet as tangible fixed assets and also included within a valuation obtained for a furnished investment property.

An entity would need to consider the specific inputs included in the investment property valuation to assess whether it includes assets and liabilities which are also recognised separately on the balance sheet. If so, an adjustment is required to avoid double-counting these assets or liabilities.

When an entity separately recognises prepaid or accrued operating lease income and lease incentives in the balance sheet, the investment property valuation may also include such items. If so, an adjustment is required to avoid double-counting the asset or liability.

If a property valuation of investment property held under a lease is obtained net of the valuer's estimate of the present value of the future lease obligations, (which is usually the case), an amount should be added back by adjusting for the finance lease obligation recognised in the financial statements, to arrive at the fair value of the investment property for the purposes of the financial statements, since the lease obligation is already recognised in the balance sheet.

In our view, an adjustment will always be required to avoid double-counting assets or liabilities.

3.3.4   Inability to determine fair value of investment property

Prior to the Triennial review 2017, paragraph 8 of Section 16 stated that if a reliable measure of fair value was no longer available without undue cost or effort for an item of investment property measured using the fair value model, the entity should have thereafter accounted for that item as PP&E in accordance with Section 17 until a reliable measure of fair value became available. The carrying amount of the investment property on that date became its cost under Section 17. The related amount of this change was required to be disclosed as part of the reconciliation between the carrying amounts of investment property at the beginning and end of the period. It was considered a change of circumstances and not a change in accounting policy.

Paragraph 9 of Section 16 also stated that other than the requirement described above, an entity would transfer a property to, or from, investment property only when the property first meets, or ceases to meet, the definition of investment property.

The Triennial review 2017 amendments resulted in deletion of paragraph 8 of Section 16 as described above and paragraph 9 of Section 16 was clarified that unless otherwise required by FRS 102, an entity would transfer a property to, or from, investment property only when the property first meets, or ceases to meet, the definition of investment property (see 3.4 below).

Consequently, an investment property whose fair value can no longer be measured reliably should still be classified as investment property, instead of transferring and accounting for it as PP&E. However, following the guidance on determining fair value in the Appendix to Section 2, if a reliable measure of fair value is no longer available for an investment property measured at fair value, its carrying amount at the last date the investment property was reliably measurable becomes its new 'cost'. The entity should measure the investment property at this 'cost' less impairment (if any), until a reliable measure of fair value becomes available (see Chapter 4 at 3.13.5). *[FRS 102.2A.6, BC.B16.4]*.

The FRC particularly noted that in the UK, entities should generally be able to obtain a fair value for an investment property, which would provide useful, decision-relevant information to users of the financial statements. *[FRS 102.BC.B16.1]*. Further, the FRC noted that prior to the introduction of FRS 102, investment properties were required to be measured at open market value. *[FRS 102.BC.B16.4]*. Therefore, it appears reasonable to expect that in practice, the inability to determine fair value of investment property would occur only in exceptional cases.

The accounting consequences when the fair value cannot be measured reliably for investment property under construction and mixed use property are discussed at 3.1.1 and 3.1.7 above, respectively.

3.4   Transfers of assets to or from investment property

The instances where Section 16 explicitly requires transfers of investment property to PP&E are the following:

- when an entity chooses to account for investment property (or part of such property) that is rented to another group entity by transferring the property to PP&E and applying the cost model in accordance with Section 17 (see 3.1.2 above); and

- when the entire mixed use property is accounted for as PP&E because the fair value of the investment property component cannot be measured reliably (see 3.1.7 above).

As discussed at 3.3.4 above, the Triennial review 2017 amendments clarified that unless otherwise required by FRS 102, an entity would transfer a property to, or from, investment property only when the property first meets, or ceases to meet, the definition of investment property. *[FRS 102.16.9]*. This means that, unless specifically required by FRS 102 (such as items described above), there should be evidence that a change in use has occurred to support a transfer of property. Accordingly, a change in management's intentions, in isolation, would not be enough to support a transfer of property. This is because management's intentions, alone, do not provide evidence of a change in use. Observable actions toward effecting a change in use must have been taken by the entity during the reporting period to provide evidence that such a change has occurred.

The assessment of whether a change in use has occurred is based on an assessment of all the facts and circumstances and judgement is needed to determine whether a property qualifies as investment property.

3.4.1   Transfers from investment property to inventory

Transfers to inventory are more difficult to deal with by way of the application of a general principle since it is a common practice in the real estate industry to hold investment properties as assets 'available' for sale. This is especially the case when an entity believes it is economical to sell the assets before they reach their peak of capital growth, or when recycling of equity (selling owned property to buy new property) presents more opportunities for capital appreciation, or in situations where an entity urgently needing cash for operations wants to release money tied up in real estate properties. FRS 102 does not provide further guidance on this therefore, it would be reasonable to consider the related guidance in IFRS.

Under IFRS, unless there is development with a view to sale, it may not be possible to reclassify investment property as inventory even if the entity holding that property changes its intentions and is no longer holding that property for rental or capital appreciation. Accordingly, when an entity decides to dispose of an investment property without development, it should continue to classify the property as an investment property until it is derecognised (see 3.5 below) and should not reclassify it as inventory. Similarly, if an entity begins to redevelop an existing investment property for continued future use as investment property, the property remains an investment property and is not reclassified as owner-occupied property during the redevelopment. *[IAS 40.58]*.

3.4.2   Accounting treatment of transfers

The Triennial review 2017 amendments added further guidance in accounting for transfers of investment property.

3.4.2.A   Transfer from investment property to owner-occupied property

When a property ceases to meet the definition of an investment property, for example it becomes owner-occupied, the deemed cost for subsequent accounting as PP&E (in accordance with Section 17 – see Chapter 15) should be its fair value at the date of change in use. *[FRS 102.16.9A]*.

The carrying amount of the investment property at the date of transfer becomes its 'cost'. There is no ability to restate the asset back to cost less depreciation and impairment, and reverse out previous fair value gains.

Where the 'cost' of such property described above is not the historical cost amount, under UK law the property is being carried at a revalued amount under the alternative accounting rules. Consequently, any upwards revaluation compared to the historical cost amounts should be transferred to the statutory revaluation reserve (as a reserves transfer) and the statutory disclosures for revalued assets would apply. *[1 Sch 34-35]*. Subsequently, there may be transfers of reserves to the extent the entity is realising the revaluation reserve. The alternative accounting rules allow that an amount may be transferred from the revaluation reserve to the profit and loss account, if the amount was previously charged to the profit and loss account or represents a realised profit. *[1 Sch 35(3)]*. Therefore, where depreciation or an impairment has been charged based on the deemed cost which exceeds the historical cost, the excess depreciation or impairment (over that which would have been charged based on historical cost) may be transferred from the revaluation reserve to retained earnings (as a reserves transfer). Similarly, on sale of the asset, the amount in the revaluation reserve, where realised on sale, could be transferred to retained earnings (as a reserves transfer in equity). See Chapter 15 at 3.6.3.A and more generally on the use of the revaluation reserve, see also Chapter 6 at 10.2.3.

Investment property transferred to PP&E where the fair value of that property can still be measured reliably, for example a transfer to PP&E because the property is no longer held to earn rentals and/or capital appreciation, can be measured subsequently under either the cost or revaluation models of Section 17 (provided that where the revaluation model is selected, this should be applied to all items of PP&E in the same class) – see Chapter 15.

3.4.2.B   *Transfer from investment property to inventories*

When a property ceases to meet the definition of an investment property and it becomes inventory, the deemed cost for subsequent accounting as an inventory (in accordance with Section 13 – see Chapter 11) should be its fair value at the date of change in use. *[FRS 102.16.9A]*.

The carrying amount of the investment property at the date of transfer becomes its 'cost'. There is no ability to restate the asset back to cost less depreciation and impairment, and reverse out previous fair value gains. However, using such cost as 'deemed cost' of any investment property transferred to inventory – which is usually then carried using the cost model at the lower of cost and net realisable value – may represent a departure from Company Law where this 'cost' is not the same as the historical cost amount. Inventories are no longer permitted to be stated at their current cost under the alternative accounting rules nor does this 'deemed cost' apply the fair value accounting rules. Therefore, in some situations, use of 'deemed cost' would require necessary disclosures relating to the true and fair override of Company Law. *[1 Sch 10(2)]*.

Please also see other practical considerations discussed at 3.1.9 and 3.4.1 above.

3.4.2.C   *Transfer from owner-occupied property to investment property*

If an owner-occupied property becomes an investment property, an entity should apply Section 17 up to the date of change in use. The entity should treat any difference at that date between the carrying amount of the property in accordance with Section 17 and its fair value in the same way as a revaluation in accordance with Section 17. *[FRS 102.16.9B]*.

If the owner-occupied property had not previously been revalued, the transfer to investment property does not imply that the entity has now chosen a policy of revaluation for other property accounted for under Section 17 in the same class. The treatment depends on whether it is a decrease or increase in value and whether the asset had previously been revalued or impaired in value (see Chapter 15 at 3.6.4).

While not explicitly addressed in Section 16 or Section 17, if an item of PP&E had not previously been revalued, the revaluation arising on transfer to investment property that is recognised in other comprehensive income may, but is not required to, be accumulated in retained earnings because the asset is measured under fair value accounting rules going forward.

When an item of PP&E that has previously been revalued (e.g. a revaluation reserve was created or retained on measuring the PP&E at deemed cost on transition to FRS 102) or that had been previously measured under the revaluation model in Section 17 is transferred to investment property, in our view, any amounts in the revaluation reserve may likewise, but are not required to, be transferred to retained earnings via the statement of changes in equity (as this is no longer a revaluation under the alternative accounting rules).

However, as discussed at 3.3 above, an entity is not precluded from transferring the revaluation reserve to a separate non-distributable reserve, instead of to retained earnings, because this may assist with the identification of distributable profits. *[FRS 102 Appendix III.28]*. Any such transfer from retained earnings to a non-distributable reserve is a reserves transfer that should be shown in the statement of changes in equity.

Subsequently, when an item of PP&E is derecognised (see 3.5 below), any amount accumulated in the revaluation reserve (or in a separate non-distributable reserve) relating to that item, where realised on derecognition, could be transferred to retained earnings. Again, any transfer is made directly from such reserves to retained earnings, and not through profit or loss. *[1 Sch 35(3)]*.

See Chapter 6 at 10.2.3 for further discussion on the use of the revaluation reserve.

3.4.2.D   Transfer from inventories to investment property

For a transfer from inventories to investment property that will be carried at fair value, any difference between the fair value of the property at that date and its previous carrying amount should be recognised in profit or loss. *[FRS 102.16.9C]*. This treatment appears consistent with the treatment of sales of inventories.

3.5   Derecognition

Accounting for disposals of investment property is not addressed specifically within Section 16. However Section 17 has requirements and guidance in respect of derecognition of PP&E, including replacement of parts, which can be applied to investment properties. See Chapter 15 at 3.7 for further guidance.

3.6   Presentation and disclosures

The main disclosure requirements of Section 16 and other sections of FRS 102 relating to investment property are set out at 3.6.1 below. Other disclosures required by the Companies Act in respect of investment property are set out at 3.6.2 below.

See Chapter 6 for the detailed discussion of the requirements for financial statement presentation relevant to investment property.

Chapter 14

3.6.1   *Disclosures required by Section 16*

The following disclosures are required:

- the methods and significant assumptions applied in determining the fair value;

- the extent to which the fair value (as measured or disclosed in the financial statements) is based on a valuation by an independent valuer who holds a recognised and relevant professional qualification and has recent experience in the location and class of the investment property being valued. If there has been no such valuation, that fact should be disclosed (e.g. a statement that the fair value of investment property is based on internal appraisals rather than on a valuation by an independent valuer as described above);

- the existence and amounts of any restrictions on the realisability of investment property or the remittance of income and proceeds of disposal;

- contractual obligations to purchase, construct or develop investment property or for repairs, maintenance or enhancements; and

- a reconciliation between the carrying amounts of investment property at the beginning and end of the period; showing separately:

  - additions, disclosing separately additions resulting from acquisitions through business combinations;

  - net gains and losses arising from fair value adjustments;

  - transfers to and from PP&E – see 3.4 above (or prior to the Triennial review 2017 amendments, transfers to PP&E when fair value can no longer be measured reliably without undue cost or effort – see 3.3.2 above);

  - transfers to and from inventories – see 3.4 above (or prior to the Triennial review 2017 amendments, transfers to and from inventories and owner-occupied property); and

  - other changes (e.g. disposals).

The reconciliation need not be presented for prior periods. *[FRS 102.16.10]*.

All relevant disclosures required for leases which a reporting entity has entered into must be disclosed in accordance with Section 20 (see Chapter 18). *[FRS 102.16.11]*.

Prior to the Triennial review 2017 amendments, all of the above disclosures were required explicitly only for all investment property accounted for at fair value through profit or loss.

As a consequence of the Triennial review 2017, such explicit reference to 'all investment property accounted for at fair value through profit or loss' was deleted. This may mean that the above disclosures are also applicable to investment properties whose fair value can no longer be measured reliably. Such properties are still classified as investment property but are measured at cost amount less impairment, if any, until a reliable measure of fair value becomes available (see 3.3.4 above). *[FRS 102.2A.6]*. However, it is reasonable to expect that only those disclosures that are considered relevant to such properties would be provided. For example, the first two bullet points above might not be relevant.

Entities might also need to consider providing further information about such properties whose fair value can no longer be measured reliably and may consider the disclosures required by IAS 40 such as:

- the reconciliation described above could disclose the amounts for such investment property held at cost separately from amounts relating to other investment property held at fair value;
- a description of such investment property;
- an explanation of why fair value cannot be measured reliably;
- if possible, the range of estimates within which fair value is highly likely to lie; and
- on disposal of investment property not carried at fair value:
  - the fact that the entity has disposed of investment property not carried at fair value;
  - the carrying amount of that investment property at the time of sale; and
  - the amount of gain or loss recognised. *[IAS 40.78].*

The reconciliation described above may also need to show impairment losses and reversals of impairment losses, together with corresponding accumulated opening and ending balances.

Section 27 requires disclosure of impairment losses and reversals of impairment losses including the line item(s) in the statement of comprehensive income (or the income statement, if presented) in which those impairment losses are included or reversed. It also requires an entity to disclose a description of the events and circumstances that led to the recognition or reversal of the impairment loss (see Chapter 24 at 8).

The disclosure requirements for investment properties carried at cost (e.g. investment property rented to another group entity measured under the cost model and mixed use property but the fair value of the investment property component cannot be measured reliably – see 3.1.2 and 3.1.7 above, respectively) are set out in Section 17 (see Chapter 15 at 3.9).

3.6.2   Additional disclosures required by the Regulations

The following disclosures are required by the Regulations for investment properties measured at fair value through profit or loss in addition to those required by Section 16:

- the fair value and the changes in value included in the profit and loss account; *[1 Sch 55, 2 Sch 66, 3 Sch 73]*
- the balance sheet items affected and the basis of valuation adopted in determining the amounts of the assets; *[1 Sch 58, 2 Sch 69, 3 Sch 76]*
- the comparable amounts determined under the historical accounting rules (aggregate cost and cumulative depreciation) or the differences between the fair value and historical cost, had the asset always been recorded at historical cost; *[1 Sch 58, 2 Sch 69, 3 Sch 76]* and
- an analysis of land and buildings between freehold tenure and leasehold tenure splitting the land held on leasehold tenure between land held on long lease (50 years or more) and short lease. *[1 Sch 53, 2 Sch 64, 3 Sch 71, 10 Sch 7].*

Chapter 14

4   SUMMARY OF GAAP DIFFERENCES

The key differences between FRS 102 and IFRS in accounting for investment properties (IP) are set out below.

	FRS 102	*IFRS*
Measurement and recognition		
Measurement basis at initial recognition	The initial cost of a property interest held under a lease and classified as an IP is the lower of the fair value (FV) of the property and the present value of the minimum lease payments. Any premiums paid would be included in the minimum lease payments thus forming part of the asset (see 3.2.4 above).	An IP held by a lessee as a right-of-use asset should be recognised and measured initially at cost in accordance with IFRS 16.
	If payment for the asset is deferred beyond normal credit terms, the cost is the present value of all future payments (see 3.2.1 above). Although expected to be materially similar, it is not the cash price equivalent at the recognition date like in IAS 40.	If payment for the asset is deferred beyond normal credit terms, interest is recognised over the period of credit i.e. the measurement of cost of IP is the cash price equivalent at the recognition date.
	No explicit requirements on exchanges of assets. It is expected to follow guidance in Section 17 (see 3.2.2 above) which is similar to IFRS except that any resulting gain or loss is likely to be an unrealised profit or loss and would be reported in OCI.	Subject to conditions (e.g. transaction has economic substance and fair value is reliably measurable), IAS 40 requires all acquisitions of IP in exchange for non-monetary assets, or a combination of monetary and non-monetary assets, to be measured at fair value. Any resulting gain or loss is reported in the income statement.
Measurement basis after initial recognition	IP is measured at FV, except for IP (or part of such property) rented to another group entity which can be accounted for in an entity's individual accounts either at FV in accordance with Section 16 or by transferring the property to PP&E and applying the cost model in accordance with Section 17 (see 3.3 and 3.1.5 above).	An entity has a choice between FV or cost model in measuring IP, with certain exceptions for insurers and similar entities. While there is a choice between FV or cost model in measuring IP, there is no option to classify a property rented to another group entity as PP&E in an entity's individual financial statements (see 2.1 above).
	Property interest held under operating lease may be accounted for as investment property on a property-by-property basis provided that the property would otherwise meet the definition of an IP and the FV of the property interest can be measured on an on-going basis (see 3.1.5 above).	If FV model in IAS 40 is applied to IP, a right-of-use asset is measured using such model if the leased property meets the definition of IP. Conversely, if IP is measured using the cost model, a right-of-use asset that meets the definition of IP is measured using the cost model in IFRS 16 (see 2.1 above).

Valuation method	FV is the amount for which an asset could be exchanged between knowledgeable willing parties in an arm's length transaction. The definition is a transaction (entry) price (see 3.3.1 above).	FV is the price that would be received to sell an asset in an orderly transaction between market participants at the measurement date. The IFRS measurement is an exit price from the perspective of a market participant that holds the asset rather than a transaction (entry) price and is a market based measurement rather than an entity specific measurement. Further, FV for non-financial assets is the value attributable to the 'highest and best use' of that asset by a market participant even if the entity intends a different use.
Inability to reliably measure FV	If a reliable measure of fair value is no longer available for an asset measured at fair value, its carrying amount at the last date the asset was reliably measurable becomes its new cost. The entity should measure the asset at this cost amount less impairment, if any, until a reliable measure of fair value becomes available (see 3.3.4 above). See also similar issue below which is specific to 'Mixed use properties'.	Only in exceptional cases and only on initial recognition (either by acquisition or change in use) that an entity will be able to conclude that it will not be able to reliably measure the IP's FV on a continuing basis. If this exceptional situation occurs, that property is then accounted for using the cost model in IAS 16 (for owned IP) or in IFRS 16 (for IP held as a right-of-use asset) until disposal date and the property is assumed to have a nil residual value.
Mixed use properties	Separated if the IP and PP&E components can be sold separately or leased out under a finance lease separately but if FV for the IP component cannot be measured reliably, the entire property is accounted for as PP&E, There is no explicit guidance when a reliable measure of FV of the IP component becomes available subsequently (see 3.1.7 above).	Separated if the IP and PP&E components can be sold or leased (under a finance lease) separately. It is only in exceptional cases and only on initial recognition (either by acquisition or change in use) that the entity will be able to conclude that it will not be able to reliably measure the IP's fair value on a continuing basis. In the event that no separation is possible, the entire property is accounted for as PP&E only if significant proportion is used for non-IP purposes (see 2.3 above).
Ancillary services	No guidance (see 3.1.3 above)	Where ancillary services are significant, a property should be accounted for as owner-occupied (i.e. PP&E) rather than as investment property
Transfers of IP	Section 16 is silent on transfers of a revaluation surplus to retained earnings. However, the Regulations permit such transfers of amounts if the amount represents realised profit (see 3.4.2 above).	IAS 40 provides more detailed guidance on accounting of transfers of IP, including revaluation surplus to retained earnings i.e. when the related asset is derecognised.
Property held for provision of social benefits	Not classified as IP but accounted for as PP&E (see 3.1.6 above)	No specific guidance

Chapter 14

	FRS 102	IFRS
Disclosures – FV model		
FV hierarchy disclosures	No requirement	Required to be disclosed
Classification of IP	No specific disclosure requirement although Section 8 would require disclosure of significant judgements made when applying accounting policies	Criteria used to distinguish IP from other assets, where classification is difficult is required to be disclosed by IAS 40
Reconciliation between carrying amounts at beginning and end of the period	The reconciliation need not be presented for prior periods (see 3.6.1 above)	Reconciliation of the relevant comparative period(s) should be disclosed
Inability to reliably measure FV	For mixed use properties (see above), no other disclosures required other than the amounts of transfers to PP&E which are included in the reconciliation of carrying amounts of IP at beginning and end of the period. Entities, however, may consider providing similar disclosures required by IFRS for IP measured using cost, less any impairment, during the period that fair value cannot measured reliably (see 3.6.1 above).	In addition to disclosing the reconciliation of carrying amounts at beginning and end of the period for such investment property separately from amounts relating to other investment property, extra disclosures are required such as a description of the IP and reasons for why FV cannot be reliably measured, possible range of estimates within which FV is highly likely to lie, and specific details on subsequent disposal of such IP (i.e. the fact that the entity has disposed of IP not carried at FV; the carrying amount of that IP at the time of sale and the amount of gain or loss recognised).
Amounts recognised in profit or loss	There are no specific items recognised in profit or loss that are required to be disclosed in the notes to the financial statements.	Amounts recognised in relation to direct operating expenses are required to be disclosed separately for let and vacant IP, and the cumulative change in FV recognised in P&L on a sale of IP from a pool of assets under the cost model into a pool of assets under the FV model

References

1 *The IVS Framework*, International Valuation Standards 2013, IVSC, June 2013, para. 29.

Chapter 15   Property, plant and equipment

List of examples

Chapter 15

Chapter 15   Property, plant and equipment

1   INTRODUCTION

This chapter covers the accounting for property, plant and equipment and for investment property that is rented to another group entity when the reporting entity chooses to use the cost model as permitted by paragraph 4A of Section 16 – *Investment Property* (see Chapter 14).

Overall, FRS 102 (Section 17 – *Property, Plant and Equipment*) is largely similar to IFRS (IAS 16 – *Property, Plant and Equipment*). Both Section 17 and IAS 16 have similar definitions of property, plant and equipment ('PP&E') and both require that such assets are initially recorded at cost and subsequently carried using either a cost model or a revaluation model. Revaluation gains and losses are recognised in the statement of other comprehensive income except for losses below cost (which are recognised in profit and loss) and for gains to the extent that they reverse previously recognised losses in profit and loss.

2   COMPARISON BETWEEN SECTION 17 AND IFRS

As discussed at 1 above, Section 17 is largely similar to IFRS. However, there are also certain key differences which are discussed at 2.1 to 2.6 below. The table at 4 below contains a summary of the major GAAP differences.

2.1   Accounting for non-current assets held for sale

FRS 102 does not have a 'held-for-sale' category for non-current assets. A plan to dispose of an asset before the previously expected date is an indicator of impairment that triggers the calculation of the asset's recoverable amount for the purpose of determining whether the asset is impaired. *[FRS 102.17.26]*. Therefore, there is no reclassification of assets or suspension of depreciation – see 3.5.7.B below. However, in our view, if 'adapted formats' of presentation of the financial statements are used, an entity should generally continue to classify PP&E intended to be disposed of as non-current unless it is expected to be realised within 12 months after the reporting period, in which case it must be classified as current (see Chapter 6 at 5.1.1.C).

IFRS 5 – *Non-current Assets Held for Sale and Discontinued Operations* – requires that an item of PP&E should be classified as held for sale if its carrying amount will be recovered principally through a sale transaction rather than continuing use, though continuing use is not in itself precluded for assets classified as held for sale. *[IFRS 5.6]*. Once this classification has been made, depreciation ceases, even if the asset is still being used, but the assets must be carried at the lower of their previous carrying amount and fair value less costs to sell. *[IFRS 5.15]*.

2.2   Revenue-based depreciation method

The use of 'revenue expected to be generated' as the basis to depreciate PP&E is not explicitly prohibited under FRS 102 (see 3.5.6 below).

In contrast, IAS 16 states that a depreciation method that is based on revenue which is generated by an activity that includes the use of an asset is not appropriate. *[IAS 16.62A]*.

2.3   Intra-group investment property

Under FRS 102 an entity can choose to bring investment properties rented to another group entity within the scope of Section 17 if it applies the cost model to their subsequent measurement (see 3.2 below).

This option is not available under IAS 40 – *Investment Property* – although IAS 40 permits cost less impairment as a measurement option. Under IAS 40 property rented to other group entities is classified as an investment property if it meets the definition of investment property.

2.4   Bearer plants

Section 34 – *Specialised Activities* – does not make a distinction between biological assets and bearer plants. Therefore, bearer plants are treated as biological assets and accounted for in accordance with Section 34.

In contrast, IAS 41 – *Agriculture* – does distinguish between biological assets and bearer plants. IAS 41 defines a bearer plant as a living plant which is used in the production or supply of agricultural produce, is expected to bear produce for more than one period and has a remote chance of being sold as agricultural produce, except for incidental scrap sales. *[IAS 41.5]*. Bearer plants are scoped out of IAS 41 and instead fall in the scope of IAS 16. *[IAS 41.1]*.

2.5   Disposal of PP&E

Under FRS 102 the date of disposal is determined in accordance with the criteria in Section 23 – *Revenue* – for the recognition of revenue from the sale of goods. *[FRS 102.17.29]*. Section 23 is based on IAS 18 – *Revenue* – which has been superseded by IFRS 15 – *Revenue from Contracts with Customers*. IFRS 15 made several consequential amendments to IAS 16. Under IAS 16 the date of disposal of an item of PP&E is the date that the recipient obtains control of that item in accordance with the requirements for determining when a performance obligation is satisfied in IFRS 15. *[IAS 16.69]*. Therefore there may be differences in the date that PP&E disposed is derecognised under FRS 102 compared to IAS 16.

Under FRS 102 gains and losses on disposal are calculated as the difference between any net disposal proceeds and the carrying value of the item of PP&E. *[FRS 102.17.30]*. Section 17 does not provide further guidance on how the disposal proceeds should be determined. However, IAS 16 requires that the amount of consideration on disposal to be included in the gain or loss on derecognition of PP&E should be determined in accordance with the requirements for determining the transaction price in IFRS 15. In addition subsequent changes to the estimated amount of consideration included in the gain or loss should be accounted for in accordance with the requirements for changes in transaction price in IFRS 15. *[IAS 16.72].* As a result of this difference the gain or loss on disposal calculated under FRS 102 may be different to that calculated under IAS 16. See 3.7 below for further details of the requirements in relation to derecognition of PP&E under FRS 102.

2.6   Disclosures

The disclosure requirements of Section 17 (see 3.9 below) are less extensive than those of IAS 16. In addition, unlike IAS 16, Section 17 does not require comparative information to be presented in the reconciliation of the carrying amount from the beginning to the end of the reporting period.

3   REQUIREMENTS OF SECTION 17 FOR PROPERTY, PLANT AND EQUIPMENT

3.1   Terms used in Section 17

The main terms used throughout Section 17 are as follows: *[FRS 102 Appendix I]*

Term	Definition
Borrowing costs	Interest and other costs incurred by an entity in connection with the borrowing of funds.
Depreciable amount	The cost of an asset, or other amount substituted for cost (in the financial statements), less its residual value.
Depreciated replacement cost	The most economic cost required for the entity to replace the service potential of an asset (including the amount that the entity will receive from its disposal at the end of its useful life) at the reporting date.
Depreciation	The systematic allocation of the depreciable amount of an asset over its useful life.
Property, plant and equipment	Tangible assets that: (a) are held for use in the production or supply of goods or services, for rental to others, or for administrative purposes; and (b) are expected to be used during more than one period.
Recoverable amount	The higher of an asset's (or cash-generating unit's) fair value less costs to sell and its value in use.
Residual value	The estimated amount that an entity would currently obtain from disposal of the asset, after deducting the estimated costs of disposal, if the asset were already of the age and in the condition expected at the end of its useful life.
Useful life	The period over which an asset is expected to be available for use by an entity, or the number of production or similar units expected to be obtained from the asset by an entity.

3.2   Scope of Section 17

Section 17 applies to the accounting for:

(a)   PP&E; and

(b)   investment property that is rented to another group entity when the reporting entity chooses to use the cost model as permitted by paragraph 4A of Section 16 (see Chapter 14). *[FRS 102.17.1].*

Section 17 does not apply to:

- PP&E classified as investment property (see Chapter 14), except where the investment property is rented to another group company and the reporting entity chooses to apply the cost model;

- biological assets related to agricultural activity (see Chapter 31);

- heritage assets (see Chapter 31); and

- mineral rights and mineral reserves such as oil, gas, and similar 'non-regenerative' resources (see Chapter 31). *[FRS 102.17.3].*

The scope of Section 17 has been amended following the *Amendments to FRS 102 Triennial review 2017 – Incremental improvements and clarifications* (Triennial review 2017). Prior to this amendment, investment properties whose fair value could not be measured reliably without undue cost or effort were within the scope of Section 17. The FRC consider that, in the UK, entities should generally be able to obtain a fair value for an investment property without undue cost or effort and therefore this exemption was removed. *[FRS 102.BC.B16.1].*

In place of the undue cost or effort exemption, the Triennial review 2017 amendments now bring investment properties rented to another group entity within the scope of Section 17 if the entity chooses to apply the cost model to their subsequent measurement. This scope amendment was in response to a significant amount of feedback received by the FRC that suggested the cost of obtaining a fair value for an investment property that is rented to another group entity far outweighs the benefit, as the information is of little use when the investment property would be treated as PP&E in the consolidated financial statements. *[FRS 102.BC.B16.2].*

This amendment is effective for periods beginning on or after 1 January 2019, with early adoption permitted provided that all the Triennial review 2017 amendments are applied at the same time. *[FRS 102.1.18].* The amendment can either be applied retrospectively or the investment property may be recorded at a deemed cost equal to its fair value at the date of transition to the Triennial review 2017 amendments. *[FRS 102.1.19].* The 'date of transition' is not defined but our view is that this means the beginning of the earliest period presented when first applying the December 2017 amendments). As the use of deemed cost applies the alternative accounting rules, a revaluation reserve would be recorded on any fair value uplift above the historical cost amount at this point (and the company law disclosures relating to use of the alternative accounting rules would be required).

Although Section 17 scopes out biological assets and mineral resources, any PP&E used in developing or maintaining such resources would be within scope. Section 17 is silent as to whether a biological asset meeting the definition of a 'bearer plant' (e.g. fruit tree) is within its scope. However, Section 34 does not make a distinction between biological assets and bearer plants. Therefore, bearer plants are treated as biological assets and accounted for in accordance with Section 34 (see Chapter 31 at 2.2.2).

Other sections of FRS 102 may require an item of PP&E to be recognised on a basis different from that required by Section 17. For example Section 20 – *Leases* – has its own rules regarding recognition and measurement. See Chapter 18 for a description of how an item of PP&E held under a finance lease is recognised and initially measured. However, once an item of PP&E has been recognised as a finance lease under Section 20, its treatment thereafter is in accordance with Section 17.

3.3   Recognition

An item of PP&E should be recognised (i.e. its cost included as an asset in the statement of financial position), only if it is probable that future economic benefits associated with the item will flow to the entity and if its cost can be measured reliably. *[FRS 102.17.4]*.

3.3.1   *Aspects of recognition*

3.3.1.A   *Spare parts and minor items*

Spare parts, stand-by equipment and servicing equipment are recognised in accordance with Section 17 when they meet the definition of PP&E. Otherwise, such items are classified as inventory. *[FRS 102.17.5]*.

The wording above reflects an amendment made as part of the Triennial review 2017 and is now consistent with the wording used in paragraph 8 of IAS 16. Prior to the amendment Section 17 contained a requirement that spare parts and servicing equipment that can only be used in connection with an item of PP&E must be classified as PP&E. The Triennial review 2017 amendments to FRS 102 are effective for periods beginning on or after 1 January 2019, with early adoption permitted provided that all the Triennial review 2017 amendments are applied at the same time. *[FRS 102.1.18]*. The amendment should be applied retrospectively.

Some types of business may have a very large number of minor items of PP&E such as spare parts, tools, pallets and returnable containers, which nevertheless are used in more than one accounting period. There are practical problems in recording them on an asset-by-asset basis in an asset register; they are difficult to control and frequently lost. The main consequence is that it becomes very difficult to depreciate them. Generally, entities write off such immaterial assets as expenses in the period of addition. Section 17 does not prescribe what actually constitutes a single item of PP&E. Therefore, in our view, entities have to apply judgement in defining PP&E in their individual circumstances. It may be appropriate to aggregate some parts (such as tools, moulds and dies) and to apply the requirements of Section 17 to the aggregate amount (presumably without having to identify the individual assets).

Materiality judgements are considered when deciding how an item of PP&E should be accounted for. Major spare parts, for example, qualify as PP&E, while smaller spares would be carried as inventory and as a practical matter many companies have a minimum value for capitalising assets.

Chapter 15

3.3.1.B   *Environmental and safety equipment*

There may be expenditures forced upon an entity by legislation that requires it to buy 'assets' that do not meet the recognition criteria because the expenditure does not directly increase the expected future benefits expected to flow from the asset. Examples would be safety or environmental protection equipment. While Section 17 has no specific guidance, it would be reasonable to consider the related guidance in IFRS.

IAS 16 explains that these expenditures qualify for recognition as they allow future benefits in excess of those that would flow if the expenditure had not been made; for example, a plant might have to be closed down if these environmental testing expenditures were not made. *[IAS 16.11].*

An entity may voluntarily invest in environmental equipment even though it is not required by law to do so. The entity can capitalise those investments in environmental and safety equipment in the absence of a legal requirement as long as:

• the expenditure meets the definition of an asset; or

• there is a constructive obligation to invest in the equipment.

If the entity can demonstrate that the equipment is likely to increase the economic life of the related asset, the expenditure meets the definition of an asset. Otherwise, the expenditure can be capitalised when the entity can demonstrate all of the following:

• the entity can prove that a constructive obligation exists to invest in environmental and safety equipment (e.g. it is standard practice in the industry, environmental groups are likely to raise issues or employees demand certain equipment to be present);

• the expenditure is directly related to improvement of the asset's environmental and safety standards; and

• the expenditure is not related to repairs and maintenance or forms part of period costs or operational costs.

Consistent with IAS 16, whenever safety and environmental assets are capitalised, the resulting carrying amount of the asset, and any related asset, are required to be reviewed for impairment in accordance with Section 27 – *Impairment of Assets* (see 3.5.7 below).

3.3.1.C   *Property economic benefits and property developments*

Section 17 requires that PP&E is recognised only when it is probable that future economic benefits associated with the item will flow to the entity.

For example, in relation to property development, many jurisdictions require permissions prior to development whilst developers, including entities developing property for their own use, typically incur significant costs prior to such permissions being granted.

In assessing whether such pre-permission expenditures can be capitalised – assuming they otherwise meet the criteria – a judgement must be made at the date the expenditure is incurred of whether it is sufficiently probable that the relevant permission will be granted. Such expenditure does not become part of the cost of the land; to the extent that it can be recognised it will be as part of the cost of a separate building. Furthermore, if the granting of necessary permits is no longer expected during the application and approval process, capitalisation of pre-permission expenditures should cease and any related amounts that were previously capitalised should be written off in accordance with Section 27.

3.3.1.D   *Classification as PP&E or intangible assets*

The restrictions in Section 18 – *Intangible Assets other than Goodwill* – in respect of capitalising certain internally-generated intangible assets focus attention on the treatment of many internal costs. In practice, items such as computer software purchased by entities are frequently capitalised as part of a tangible asset, for example as part of an accounting or communications infrastructure. Equally, internally written software may be capitalised as part of a tangible production facility, and so on. Judgement must be exercised in deciding whether such items are to be accounted for under Section 17 or Section 18, and this distinction becomes increasingly important if the two sections prescribe differing treatments in any particular case.

Both Section 17 and Section 18 do not refer to this type of asset, however, it is reasonable to consider guidance provided in IFRS. IAS 38 – *Intangible Assets* – states that an entity needs to exercise judgement in determining whether an asset that incorporates both intangible and tangible elements should be treated as PP&E or as an intangible asset, for example:

- computer software that is embedded in computer-controlled equipment that cannot operate without that specific software is an integral part of the related hardware and is treated as PP&E;
- application software that is being used on a computer is generally easily replaced and is not an integral part of the related hardware, whereas the operating system normally is integral to the computer and is included in PP&E; and
- a database that is stored on a compact disc is considered to be an intangible asset because the value of the physical medium is wholly insignificant compared to that of the data collection. *[IAS 38.4]*.

It is worthwhile noting that as the 'parts approach' in Section 17 (see 3.3.2 below) requires an entity to account for significant parts of an asset separately, this raises 'boundary' problems between Section 17 and Section 18 when software and similar expenditure are involved. We believe that where Section 17 requires an entity to identify significant parts of an asset and account for them separately, the entity needs to evaluate whether any software-type intangible part is actually integral to the larger asset or whether it is really a separate asset in its own right. The intangible part is more likely to be an asset in its own right if it was developed separately or if it can be used independently of the item of PP&E.

3.3.1.E   *Classification of items as inventory or PP&E when minimum levels are maintained*

Entities may acquire items of inventory on a continuing basis, either for sale in the ordinary course of business or to be consumed in a production process or when rendering services. This means there will always be a core stock of that item (i.e. a minimum level of inventory is maintained). This does not in itself turn inventory into an item of PP&E, since each individual item will be consumed in a single

Chapter 15

operating cycle. However, there may be cases where it is difficult to judge whether an item is part of inventory or is an item of PP&E. This may have implications on measurement because, for example, PP&E has a revaluation option (see 3.6 below) that is not available for inventory.

In our view, an item of inventory is accounted for as an item of PP&E if it:

- is not held for sale or consumed in a production process or during the process of rendering services;

- is necessary to operate or benefit from an asset during more than one operating cycle; and

- cannot be recouped through sale (or is significantly impaired after it has been used to operate the asset or benefit from that asset).

This applies even if the part of inventory that is an item of PP&E cannot be physically separated from the rest of inventories.

Consider the following examples:

- An entity acquires the right to use an underground cave for gas storage purposes for a period of 50 years. The cave is filled with gas, but a substantial part of that gas will only be used to keep the cave under pressure in order to be able to get gas out of the cave. It is not possible to distinguish the gas that will be used to keep the cave under pressure and the rest of the gas.

- An entity operates an oil refining plant. In order for the refining process to take place, the plant must contain a certain minimum quantity of oil. This can only be taken out once the plant is abandoned and would then be polluted to such an extent that the oil's value is significantly reduced.

- An entity sells gas and has at any one time a certain quantity of gas in its gas distribution network.

In the first example, therefore, the total volume of gas must be virtually split into (i) gas held for sale and (ii) gas held to keep the cave under pressure. The former must be accounted for under Section 13 – *Inventories*. The latter must be accounted for as PP&E and depreciated over the period the cave is expected to be used.

In the second example the part of the crude that is necessary to operate (in technical terms) the plant and cannot be recouped (or can be recouped but would then be significantly impaired), even when the plant is abandoned, should be considered as an item of PP&E and amortised over the life of the plant.

In the third example the gas in the pipeline is not necessary to operate the pipeline. It is held for sale or to be consumed in the production process or process of rendering services. Therefore this gas is accounted for as inventory.

3.3.1.F   *Production stripping costs of surface mines*

Under FRS 102, there is no specific guidance on production stripping costs of surface mines. However, the approach in Section 17 in relation to accounting for parts (see 3.3.2 below) seems to be consistent with the specific guidance provided in IFRS.

IFRIC 20 – *Stripping Costs in the Production Phase of a Surface Mine* – states that costs associated with a 'stripping activity asset' (i.e. the costs associated with gaining access to a specific section of the ore body) are accounted for as an additional component of an existing asset. Other routine stripping costs are accounted for as current costs of production (i.e. inventory).

The Interpretations Committee's intention was to maintain the principle of IAS 16 by requiring identification of the *component* of the ore body for which access had been improved, as part of the criteria for recognising stripping costs as an asset. An entity will have to allocate the stripping costs between the amount capitalised (as it reflects the future access benefit) and the amount that relates to the current-period production of inventory. This allocation should be based on a relevant production measure.

This component approach follows the principle of separating out parts of an asset that have costs that are significant in relation to the entire asset and when the useful lives of those parts are different. *[IAS 16.45]*.

3.3.2   Accounting for parts ('components') of assets

Section 17 has a single set of recognition criteria, which means that subsequent expenditure must also meet these criteria before it is recognised.

Parts of an asset are to be identified so that the cost of replacing a part may be recognised (i.e. capitalised as part of the asset) and the previous part derecognised. These parts are often referred to as 'components'. 'Parts' are distinguished from day-to-day servicing but they are not otherwise identified and defined; moreover, the unit of measurement to which Section 17 applies (i.e. what comprises an item of PP&E) is not itself defined.

Section 17 requires the initial cost of an item of PP&E to be allocated to its 'major components' and each component should be depreciated separately where there are different patterns of consumption of economic benefits. *[FRS 102.17.6, 16]*. 'Major components' is not defined and this will therefore require the exercise of judgement after considering the specific facts and circumstances. However, parts that have a cost that is significant in relation to the total cost of the asset will usually be a 'major component'.

An entity will have to identify the major components of the asset on initial recognition in order for it to depreciate the asset properly. There is no requirement to identify all components. Section 17 requires entities to derecognise an existing part or component when it is replaced, regardless of whether it has been depreciated separately. If it is impracticable for an entity to identify the carrying amount of the replaced part, it may be estimated using the current cost of the replacement part as a proxy for the original cost of the replaced part and adjusting it for depreciation and impairment. *[FRS 102.17.6]*. This is consistent with the treatment for 'major inspections' discussed at 3.3.3.A below.

Given there is no requirement to identify all components, an entity may not actually identify the parts or components of an asset until it incurs the replacement expenditure, as in the following example.

Chapter 15

Example 15.1:   Recognition and derecognition of parts

An entity buys a piece of machinery with an estimated useful life of ten years for £10 million. The asset contains two identical pumps, which are assumed to have the same useful life as the machine of which they are a part. After seven years one of the pumps fails and is replaced at a cost of £200,000. The entity had not identified the pumps as separate parts and does not know the original cost. It uses the cost of the replacement part to estimate the carrying value of the original pump. With the help of the supplier, it estimates that the cost would have been approximately £170,000 and that this would have a remaining carrying value after seven year's depreciation of £51,000. Accordingly it derecognises £51,000 and capitalises the cost of the replacement.

3.3.2.A   Land and buildings

Section 17 requires that the land and the building elements of property are treated as separate assets and accounted for separately, even when they are acquired together. *[FRS 102.17.8]*.

3.3.3   Initial and subsequent expenditure

Section 17 makes no distinction in principle between the initial costs of acquiring an asset and any subsequent expenditure upon it. In both cases any and all expenditure has to meet the recognition rules, and be expensed in profit or loss if it does not.

A distinction is drawn between servicing and more major expenditures. Day-to-day servicing (e.g. repairs and maintenance of PP&E, which largely comprises labour costs and minor parts) should be recognised in profit or loss as incurred. *[FRS 102.17.15]*. However, if the cost involves replacing a part of the asset, this replacement part should be recognised, i.e. capitalised as part of the PP&E, if the recognition criteria are met. The carrying amount of the part that has been replaced should be derecognised. *[FRS 102.17.6]*. Identification of replaced parts to be derecognised is discussed at 3.3.2 above.

Examples of parts which may require replacement at regular intervals during the life of the asset include the roofs of buildings, relining a furnace after a specified number of hours of use, or replacing the interiors of an aircraft several times during the life of the airframe. There could also be parts which may involve less frequently recurring replacements, such as replacing the interior walls of a building.

Section 17 does not state that these replacement expenditures necessarily qualify for recognition. For example, aircraft interiors are clearly best treated as separate components as they have a useful life different from that of the asset of which they are part. With the other examples, such as interior walls, it is less clear why they meet the recognition criteria. However, replacing internal walls or similar expenditures may extend the useful life of a building while upgrading machinery may increase its capacity, improve the quality of its output or reduce operating costs. Hence, this type of expenditure may give rise to future economic benefits.

3.3.3.A   Cost of major inspections

A condition of continuing to operate an item of PP&E (e.g. a bus) may include a requirement to perform regular major inspections for faults regardless of whether parts of the item are replaced. Section 17 requires the cost of each major inspection performed to be recognised in the carrying amount of the item of PP&E as a replacement (and considered a separate part) if the recognition criteria are satisfied (see 3.3 above). Any remaining carrying amount of the cost of the previous major inspection (as distinct from physical parts) is derecognised. This is done regardless of whether the cost of the previous major inspection was identified in the transaction in which the item was acquired or constructed. If necessary, the estimated cost of a future similar inspection may be used as an indication of what the cost of the existing inspection component was when the item was acquired or constructed. *[FRS 102.17.7]*. Accordingly, if the element relating to the inspection had previously been identified, it would have been depreciated between that time and the current overhaul. However, if it had not previously been identified, the recognition and derecognition rules still apply, but Section 17 appears to allow the entity to reconstruct the carrying amount of the previous inspection (i.e. to estimate the net depreciated carrying value of the previous inspection that will be derecognised using the estimated cost of a future similar inspection as an indication of the cost of the existing inspection component that must be derecognised).

3.3.4 Properties with mixed use

There may be instances where a property has mixed use, for example, it could be partly owner-occupied and partly held for rental. Section 16 – *Investment Property* – provides guidance relating to the allocation of mixed use property between investment property and PP&E (see Chapter 14 at 3.1.7).

3.4 Measurement at initial recognition

Section 17 draws a distinction between measurement at initial recognition (i.e. the initial treatment of an item of PP&E on acquisition) and measurement after initial recognition (i.e. the subsequent treatment of the item). Measurement after initial recognition is discussed at 3.5 and 3.6 below.

Section 17 states that 'an entity shall measure an item of property, plant and equipment at initial recognition at its cost'. *[FRS 102.17.9]*. What may be included in the cost of an item is discussed below.

3.4.1 Elements of cost and cost measurement

The cost of an item of PP&E comprise all of the following:

(a) its purchase price, including import duties and non-refundable purchase taxes, after deducting trade discounts and rebates;

(b) any costs directly attributable to bringing the asset to the location and condition necessary for it to be capable of operating in the manner intended by management. These can include the costs of site preparation, initial delivery and handling, installation and assembly, and testing of functionality;

(c) the initial estimate of the costs, recognised and measured in accordance with Section 21 – *Provisions and Contingencies* – of dismantling and removing the item and restoring the site on which it is located, the obligation for which an entity incurs either when the item is acquired or as a consequence of having used the item during a particular period for purposes other than to produce inventories during that period; and

(d) any borrowing costs capitalised in accordance with paragraph 25.2 of Section 25 – *Borrowing Costs*. *[FRS 102.17.10]*.

The purchase price of an individual item of PP&E may be an allocation of the price paid for a group of assets. While FRS 102 does not provide specific guidance when an entity acquires a group of assets that do not comprise a business, it is reasonable that the principles in Section 19 – *Business Combinations and Goodwill* – are applied to allocate the entire cost to individual items (see Chapter 17), except for the fact that such allocation does not give rise to goodwill. Accordingly, the entity would identify and recognise the individual identifiable assets acquired (including those assets that meet the definition of, and recognition criteria for intangible assets in Section 18) and liabilities assumed. The cost of the group of assets would be allocated to the individual identifiable assets and liabilities on the basis of their relative fair values at the date of purchase.

When there is no record of the purchase price or production cost of any asset of a company or of any price, expenses or costs relevant for determining its purchase price or production cost, or any such record cannot be obtained without unreasonable expense or delay, The Large and Medium-sized Companies and Groups (Accounts and Reports) Regulations 2008 (the Regulations or SI 2008/410), as amended, allow the purchase price or production cost of the asset to be the value ascribed to it in the earliest available record of its value made on or after its acquisition or production by the company. *[1 Sch 29].*

If an asset is used to produce inventories, the costs of obligations to dismantle, remove or restore the site on which it has been located are dealt with in accordance with Section 13 (discussed in Chapter 11).

Note that all site restoration costs and other environmental restoration and similar costs must be estimated and capitalised at initial recognition, in order that such costs can be recovered over the life of the item of PP&E, even if the expenditure will only be incurred at the end of the item's life. The obligations are calculated in accordance with Section 21.

A common instance of (c) above is dilapidation obligations in lease agreements, under which a lessee is obliged to return premises to the landlord in an agreed condition. Arguably, a provision is required whenever the 'damage' is incurred. Therefore, if a retailer rents two adjoining premises and knocks down the dividing wall to convert the premises into one and has an obligation to make good at the end of the lease term, the tenant should immediately provide for the costs of so doing. The 'other side' of the provision entry is an asset that will be amortised over the lease term, notwithstanding the fact that some of the costs of modifying the premises may also have been capitalised as leasehold improvement assets. This is discussed in more detail in Chapter 19.

3.4.1.A   'Directly attributable' costs

This is the key issue in the measurement of cost. Section 17 gives examples of types of expenditure that are, and are not, considered to be directly attributable. The following are examples of those types of expenditure that are considered to be directly attributable and hence may be included in cost at initial recognition: *[FRS 102.17.10(b)]*

- costs of site preparation;
- initial delivery and handling costs;
- installation and assembly costs; and
- cost of testing of functionality.

While FRS 102 has no further guidance relating to costs of testing whether the asset is functioning properly, it is reasonable and common practice to recognise costs after deducting the net proceeds from selling any items produced while bringing the asset to its location and condition (such as samples produced when testing equipment). Income received during the period of construction of PP&E is considered further at 3.4.2 below.

In our view, amounts charged under operating leases during the construction period of an asset may also be a directly attributable cost that may be included as part of the cost of the PP&E if those lease costs are 'directly attributable to bringing the asset to the location and condition necessary for it to be capable of operating in the manner intended by management'. *[FRS 102.17.10(b)]*. This may be the case, for example, where a building is constructed on land that is leased under an operating lease. This approach must be applied consistently.

Other types of costs expected to be considered to be directly attributable costs are the following:

- costs of employee benefits (as defined in Section 28 – *Employee Benefits*) arising directly from the construction or acquisition of the item of property, plant and equipment. This means that the labour costs of an entity's own employees (e.g. site workers, in-house architects and surveyors) arising directly from the construction, or acquisition, of the specific item of PP&E may be recognised; and

- professional fees.

3.4.1.B　Borrowing costs

Entities are not required to capitalise borrowing costs. However, in line with item (d) at 3.4.1 above and Section 25, such costs may be capitalised in respect of certain qualifying assets to the extent that entities choose to capitalise borrowing costs in respect of such assets. The treatment of borrowing costs is discussed separately in Chapter 22.

3.4.1.C　Costs that are not PP&E costs

The following costs are not costs of PP&E and must be recognised as an expense when they are incurred: *[FRS 102.17.11]*

- costs related to opening a new facility;
- costs of introducing a new product or service (including costs of advertising and promotional activities);
- costs of conducting business in a new territory or with a new class of customer (including costs of staff training); and
- administration and other general overhead costs.

These costs should be accounted for (in general, expensed as incurred) in the same way as similar costs incurred as part of the entity's on-going activities.

Administration and other general overhead costs are not costs of an item of PP&E. This means that employee costs not related to a specific asset, such as site selection activities and general management time, do not qualify for capitalisation.

Chapter 15

3.4.1.D   Cessation of capitalisation

Only those costs directly attributable to bringing the asset to the location and condition for it to be capable of being operated in a manner intended by management can be capitalised. *[FRS 102.17.10(b)]*. Once that has occurred capitalisation should cease. This will usually be the date of practical completion of the physical asset. An entity is not precluded from continuing to capitalise costs during an initial commissioning period that is necessary for installation or assembly or testing equipment.

3.4.1.E   Self-built assets

Section 17 is silent on construction costs of an item of self-built PP&E. If an asset is self-built by the entity, the same general principles apply as for an acquired asset i.e. only those costs directly attributable to bringing the asset to the location and condition for it to be capable of being operated in a manner intended by management can be capitalised. This includes assembly costs. *[FRS 102.17.10(b)]*. Consistent with IAS 16 and common practice, abnormal amounts of wasted resources, whether labour, materials or other resources, should not be included in the cost of self-built assets. *[IAS 16.22]*. Section 25, discussed in Chapter 22, contains criteria relating to the recognition of any interest as a component of a self-built item of PP&E

If the same type of asset is made for resale by the business, it should be recognised at cost of production, but including attributable overheads in accordance with Section 13 (see Chapter 11 at 3.3.3). *[FRS 102.13.8-9]*.

3.4.1.F   Deferred payment

The cost of an item of PP&E is its cash price equivalent at the recognition date. This means that if payment is made in some other manner, the cost to be capitalised is the normal cash price. If the payment terms are extended beyond 'normal' credit terms, the cost to be recognised must be the present value of all future payments. *[FRS 102.17.13]*. Accordingly, any difference between the present value and the total payments must be treated as an interest expense over the period of credit. Assets held under finance leases are discussed in Chapter 18.

3.4.1.G   Land and buildings to be redeveloped

It is common for property developers to acquire land with an existing building where the planned redevelopment necessitates the demolition of that building and its replacement with a new building that is to be held to earn rentals or will be owner occupied. Whilst Section 17 requires that the building and land be classified as two separate items, *[FRS 102.17.8]*, in our view it is appropriate, if the existing building is unusable or likely to be demolished by any party acquiring it, that the entire, or a large part of, the purchase price be allocated to land. Similarly, subsequent demolition costs should be treated as being attributable to the cost of the land.

Owner-occupiers may also replace existing buildings with new facilities for their own use or to rent to others. Here the consequences are different and the carrying amount of the existing building cannot be rolled into the costs of the new development. The existing building must be depreciated over its remaining useful life to reduce the carrying amount of the asset to its residual value (presumably nil) at the point at which it is demolished. Consideration will have to be given as to whether the asset is impaired in accordance with Section 27. Many properties do not directly generate independent cash inflows (i.e. they are part of a cash-generating unit) and reducing the useful life will not necessarily lead to an impairment of the cash-generating unit, although by the time the asset has been designated for demolition it may no longer be part of a cash-generating unit (see Chapter 24).

Developers or owner-occupiers replacing an existing building with a building to be sold in the ordinary course of their business will deal with the land and buildings under Section 13 (see Chapter 11 at 3.2.1.B).

3.4.1.H   Transfers of assets from customers

Section 17 has no specific guidance on transfers of assets from customers other than for circumstances when the transfer involves an exchange of assets – see 3.4.4 below. Transfers that are government grants are within the scope of Section 24 – *Government Grants* (discussed in Chapter 21). Assets used in a service concession or resources from non-exchange transactions are within the scope of Section 34 (see Chapter 31). Accordingly, an entity applying FRS 102 may use the principles set out in these sections of FRS 102 and at 3.4.4 below – i.e. recognition of the asset transferred at fair value. *[FRS 102.17.14, 24.5, 34.14].*

3.4.1.I   Variable consideration

The final purchase price of an item of PP&E is not always known when the terms include a variable or contingent amount that is linked to future events that cannot be determined at the date of acquisition. The total consideration could vary based on the performance of an asset – for example, the revenue or EBITDA generated, for a specified future period, by the asset or a business in which the asset is used. Generally, we would believe that a financial liability relating to variable consideration arises on the purchase of an item of PP&E and any measurement changes to that liability would be recorded in the statement of profit or loss as required by Section 12 – *Other Financial Instruments Issues*. However, in some instances contracts are more complex and it can be argued that the subsequent changes to the initial estimate of the purchase price should be are capitalised as part of the asset, similar to any changes in a decommissioning liability (see 3.4.3 below). Further, many consider that these are executory payments that are not recognised until incurred.

In the absence of specific guidance, an entity should develop an accounting policy for variable consideration relating to the purchase of PP&E in accordance with the hierarchy in Section 10 – *Accounting Policies, Estimates and Errors. [FRS 102.10.4-6].* In practice, there are different approaches for treating the estimated future variable payments. Some entities do not capitalise these amounts upon initial recognition of the asset and then either expense or capitalise any payments as they are incurred. Other entities include an estimate of future amounts payable on initial recognition with a corresponding liability being recorded. Under this approach subsequent changes in the liability are either capitalised or expensed. An entity should exercise judgement in developing and consistently applying an accounting policy that results in information that is relevant and reliable in its particular circumstances. *[FRS 102.10.4].* For more discussion see Chapter 16 at 4.3.

3.4.2   *Incidental and non-incidental income*

The cost of an item of PP&E includes any costs directly attributable to bringing the asset to the location and condition necessary for it to be capable of operating in the manner intended by management. *[FRS 102.17.10(b)]*. However, during the construction of an asset, an entity may enter into incidental operations that are not, in themselves, necessary to meet this objective.

Using a building site as a car park prior to starting construction is an example of an incidental operation. Income and expenses related to incidental operations are recognised in profit or loss because incidental operations during construction or development of PP&E are not necessary to bring an item to the location and operating condition intended by management. *[FRS 102.17.12]*. These income and expenses would be included in their respective classifications of income and expense in profit and loss and not included in determining the cost of the asset.

However, if some income is generated wholly and necessarily as a result of the process of bringing the asset into the location and condition for its intended use, for example from the sale of samples produced when testing the equipment concerned to determine whether the asset is functioning properly, then the income should be credited to the cost of the asset. It appears reasonable that the cost of such testing is reduced by the net proceeds from selling any items produced while bringing the asset to that location and condition. It will be a matter of judgement as to when the asset is in the location and condition intended by management, but capitalisation (including the recording of income as a credit to the cost of the asset) ceases when the asset is fully operational, regardless of whether or not it is yet achieving its targeted levels of production or profitability.

If the asset is *already in* the location and condition necessary for it to be capable of being used in the manner intended by management then capitalisation should cease and depreciation should start. In these circumstances all income earned from using the asset must be recognised as revenue in profit or loss and the related costs should include an element of depreciation of the asset.

3.4.2.A   *Income received during the construction of property*

One issue that commonly arises is whether rental and similar income generated by existing tenants in a property development may be capitalised and offset against the cost of developing that property.

The relevant question is whether the leasing arrangements with the existing tenants are a necessary activity to bring the development property to the location and condition necessary for it to be capable of operating in the manner intended by management. Whilst the existence of the tenant may be a fact, it is not a necessary condition for the building to be developed to the condition intended by management; the building could have been developed in the absence of any existing tenants.

Therefore, rental and similar income from existing tenants are incidental to the development and should not be capitalised. Rather rental and similar income should be recognised in profit or loss in accordance with the requirements of Section 20 together with related expenses.

3.4.2.B   Liquidated damages during construction

Income may arise in other ways, for example, liquidated damages received as a result of delays by a contractor constructing an asset. Normally such damages received should be set off against the asset cost – the purchase price of the asset is reduced to compensate for delays in delivery.

3.4.3   Accounting for changes in decommissioning and restoration costs

Section 17 requires the initial estimate of the costs of dismantling and removing an item of PP&E and restoring the site on which it is located to be included as part of the item's cost. This applies whether the obligation is incurred either when the item is acquired or as a consequence of having used the item during a particular period for purposes other than to produce inventories during that period (see 3.4.1 above). *[FRS 102.17.10(c)].* However, Section 17 does not address the extent to which an item's carrying amount should be affected by changes in the estimated amount of dismantling and site restoration costs that occur *after* the estimate made upon initial measurement. Accordingly, an entity may consider the approach applied by IFRIC 1 – *Changes in Existing Decommissioning, Restoration and Similar Liabilities* (see Chapter 19 at 4.1).

IFRIC 1 applies to any decommissioning, restoration or similar liability that has been both included as part of the cost of an asset measured in accordance with IAS 16 (or Section 17) and recognised as a liability in accordance with IAS 37 – *Provisions, Contingent Liabilities and Contingent Assets* (or Section 21). *[IFRIC 1.2].* It deals with the impact of events that change the measurement of an existing decommissioning, restoration or similar liability. Events include a change in the estimated cash flows, a change in the discount rate and the unwinding of the discount. *[IFRIC 1.3].*

Detailed discussion and requirements of IFRIC 1 can be found in Chapter 27 at 6.3.1 of EY International GAAP 2019.

3.4.4   Exchanges of assets

An entity might swap an asset it does not require in a particular area, for one it does from another area – the opposite being the case for the counterparty. Such exchanges are common in the telecommunications, media and leisure businesses, particularly after an acquisition. Governmental competition rules sometimes require such exchanges. The question arises whether such transactions give rise to a gain in circumstances where the carrying value of the outgoing facility is less than the fair value of the incoming one. This can occur when carrying values are less than market values, although it is possible that a transaction with no real commercial substance could be arranged solely to boost apparent profits.

Section 17 requires all acquisitions of PP&E in exchange for non-monetary assets, or a combination of monetary and non-monetary assets, to be measured at fair value, unless:

(a)   the exchange transaction lacks commercial substance; or

(b)   the fair value of neither the asset received nor the asset given up is reliably measurable.

In that case, the asset's cost is measured at the carrying amount of the asset given up. *[FRS 102.17.14].*

Chapter 15

The recognition of income from an exchange of assets does not depend on whether the assets exchanged are dissimilar. If fair value cannot be reliably measured for either asset, then the exchange is measured at the carrying value of the asset the entity no longer owns. For example, if the new asset's fair value is higher than the carrying amount of the old asset, a gain may be recognised.

This requirement is qualified by a 'commercial substance' test (see 3.4.4.A below). If it is not possible to demonstrate that the transaction has commercial substance, assets received in exchange transactions will be recorded at the carrying value of the asset given up. Accordingly, there is no gain on such a transaction.

If the transaction passes the 'commercial substance' test, then the exchanged asset is to be recorded at its fair value. As discussed in 3.7 below, Section 17 requires gains or losses on items that have been derecognised to be included in profit or loss in the period of derecognition but does not allow gains on derecognition to be classified as revenue (except for certain assets previously held for rental – see 3.7.1 below). *[FRS 102.17.28]*. However, under current UK law, this gain is likely to be an unrealised profit and therefore should be included in other comprehensive income (OCI) i.e. only profits realised at the balance sheet date are to be included in the profit and loss account. *[1 Sch 13(a)]*. For consolidated financial statements, the gain is also recognised in OCI if the new asset acquired is an interest in another entity (see Chapter 8). *[FRS 102.9.31(c)]*.

3.4.4.A   *Commercial substance*

Section 17 does not provide further guidance on 'commercial substance' and therefore the application of this term will involve judgement and careful consideration of facts and circumstances. In addition, an entity may also consider the guidance provided under IFRS – the commercial substance test was put in place as an anti-abuse provision to prevent gains in income being recognised when the transaction had no discernible effect on the entity's economics. *[IAS 16.BC21]*. The commercial substance of an exchange is to be determined by forecasting and comparing the future cash flows budgeted to be generated by the incoming and outgoing assets. For there to be commercial substance, there must be a significant difference between the two forecasts. IAS 16 sets out this requirement as follows:

'An entity determines whether an exchange transaction has commercial substance by considering the extent to which its future cash flows are expected to change as a result of the transaction. An exchange transaction has commercial substance if:

(a)   the configuration (risk, timing and amount) of the cash flows of the asset received differs from the configuration of the cash flows of the asset transferred; or

(b)   the entity-specific value of the portion of the entity's operations affected by the transaction changes as a result of the exchange; and

(c)   the difference in (a) or (b) is significant relative to the fair value of the assets exchanged.' *[IAS 16.25]*.

As set out in the definitions of IAS 16, entity-specific value is the net present value of the future predicted cash flows from continuing use and disposal of the asset. Post-tax cash flows should be used for this calculation. IAS 16 contains no guidance on the discount rate to be used for this exercise, nor on any of the other parameters involved, but it does suggest that the result of these analyses might be clear without having to perform detailed calculations. *[IAS 16.25]*. Care will have to be taken to ensure that the transaction has commercial substance as defined in IAS 16 if an entity receives a similar item of PP&E in exchange for a similar asset of its own. Commercial substance may be difficult to demonstrate if the entity is exchanging an asset for a similar one in a similar location. However, in the latter case, the risk, timing and amount of cash flows could differ if one asset were available for sale and the entity intended to sell it whereas the previous asset could not be realised by sale or only sold over a much longer timescale. It is feasible that such a transaction could meet the conditions (a) and (c) above. However, it would be unusual if the entity-specific values of similar assets differed enough in any arm's length exchange transaction to meet condition (c).

Other types of exchange are more likely to pass the 'commercial substance' test, for example exchanging an interest in an investment property for one that the entity uses for its own purposes. The entity has exchanged a rental stream and instead has an asset that contributes to the cash flows of the cash-generating unit of which it is a part. In this case it is probable that the risk, timing and amount of the cash flows of the asset received would differ from the configuration of the cash flows of the asset transferred.

3.4.5   Assets held under finance leases

The cost at initial recognition of assets held under finance leases is determined in accordance with Section 20, *[FRS 102.20.9-10]*, as described in Chapter 18.

3.5   Measurement after initial recognition: cost model

Section 17 allows one of two alternatives to be chosen as the accounting policy for measurement of PP&E after initial recognition. The choice made must be applied to an entire class of PP&E, which means that not all classes are required to have the same policy. *[FRS 102.17.15]*.

The first alternative is the cost model whereby the item is carried at cost less any accumulated depreciation and less any accumulated impairment losses. *[FRS 102.17.15A]*. The other alternative, the revaluation model, is discussed at 3.6 below.

Whichever model is used after initial recognition, the provisions discussed in 3.5.1 to 3.5.7 below are applicable:

3.5.1   Depreciation by component of an item of PP&E

Section 17 links its recognition concept of a component of an asset, discussed at 3.3.2 above, with the analysis of assets for the purpose of depreciation. Each major component of an item of PP&E with significantly different patterns of consumption of economic benefits must be depreciated separately over its useful life, which means that the initial cost must be allocated between the major components by the entity. Other assets are depreciated over their useful lives as a single asset. *[FRS 102.17.16]*. Components are identified by their patterns of consumption of economic benefits and they may have the same useful lives and depreciation method. Practically, they could be grouped for the purposes of calculating depreciation charge.

Section 17 does not provide guidance for depreciating the remainder of an asset that has not separately been identified into components. These may consist of other components that are individually not significant. An entity may consider the approach in IAS 16 and thus, the entity may use estimation techniques to calculate an appropriate depreciation method for all of these parts. *[IAS 16.46]*. An entity may also depreciate separately components that are not significant in relation to the whole.

The depreciation charge for each period is recognised in profit or loss unless it forms part of the cost of another asset, for example, the depreciation of manufacturing PP&E is included in the costs of inventories (see Chapter 11). *[FRS 102.17.17]*. Similarly, depreciation of PP&E used for development activities may be included in the cost of an intangible asset recognised in accordance with Section 18 (see Chapter 16 at 3.3.3).

3.5.2   Depreciable amount and residual values

The *depreciable amount* of an item of PP&E is its cost or valuation less its estimated residual value. The *residual value* of an asset is the estimated amount that an entity would currently obtain from disposal of the asset, after deducting the estimated costs of disposal, if the asset were already of the age and in the condition expected at the end of its useful life. *[FRS 102 Appendix I]*.

Factors such as a change in how an asset is used, significant unexpected wear and tear, technological advancement, and changes in market prices may indicate that the residual value or useful life of an asset has changed since the most recent annual reporting date. Entities should assess if such indicators exist. If such indicators are present, an entity should review its previous estimates and, if current expectations differ, amend the residual value, depreciation method or useful life. The entity should account for the change in residual value, depreciation method or useful life as a change in an accounting estimate in accordance with paragraphs 15 to 18 of Section 10 (see Chapter 9). *[FRS 102.17.19]*. This requirement applies to all items of PP&E, and therefore is applicable to all components of them.

The residual value of an item of PP&E today is the estimated amount that an entity would currently obtain from disposal of the asset, after deducting the estimated costs of disposal, if the asset were already of the age and assuming that it was already in the condition it will be in at the end of its useful life. This would mean that price changes (e.g. due to inflation) would be taken into account only up to the reporting date and expectations as to future increases or decreases of asset's disposal value after the reporting date are not taken into account. Accordingly, Section 17 contains an element of continuous updating of an asset's carrying value because it is the current amount of a future value.

As any change in the residual value directly affects the depreciable amount, it may also affect the depreciation charge. This is because the depreciable amount (i.e. the amount actually charged to profit or loss over the life of the asset) is calculated by deducting the residual value from the cost or valuation of the asset, although for these purposes the residual value would be capped at the asset's carrying amount (see 3.1 above). In periods of rising prices, the residual value for assets will typically appreciate in value (e.g. buildings). Accordingly, where residual value rises over time the depreciation charge on an asset is likely to decline and may cease altogether when the residual value exceeds the asset's carrying value.

Many items of PP&E have a negligible residual value because they are kept for significantly all of their useful lives. Residual values are of no relevance if the entity intends to keep the asset for significantly all of its useful life. If an entity uses residual values based on prices fetched in the market for a type of asset that it holds, it must also demonstrate an intention to dispose of that asset before the end of its economic life.

The requirement concerning the residual values of assets highlights how important it is that residual values are considered and reviewed in conjunction with the review of useful lives. The useful life is the period over which the entity expects to use the asset, not the asset's economic life.

3.5.3   Depreciation charge

Section 17 requires the depreciable amount of an asset to be allocated on a systematic basis over its useful life. *[FRS 102.17.18]*.

As described above, depreciation must be charged on all items of PP&E. This requirement applies even to PP&E measured under the revaluation model, even if the fair value of the asset at the year-end is higher than the carrying amount, as long as the residual value of the item is lower than the carrying amount. If the residual value exceeds the carrying amount, no depreciation is charged until the residual value once again decreases to less than the carrying amount. Repair and maintenance of an asset would not of itself negate the need to depreciate it.

3.5.4   Useful lives

One of the critical assumptions on which the depreciation charge depends is the useful life of the asset. Useful life is defined as either:

• the period over which an asset is expected to be available for use by an entity; or
• the number of production or similar units expected to be obtained from the asset by an entity. *[FRS 102 Appendix I]*.

As discussed at 3.5.2 above, the asset's useful life should be estimated on a realistic basis and reviewed at the end of each reporting period for indicators that would suggest it has changed. The effects of changes in useful life are recognised prospectively, over the remaining useful life of the asset. *[FRS 102.17.19]*.

The useful life is the period over which the present owner will benefit and not the total potential life of the asset; the two will often not be the same.

It is quite possible for an asset's useful life to be shorter than its economic life. Many entities have a policy of disposing of assets when they still have a residual value, which means that another user can benefit from the asset. This is particularly common with property and motor vehicles, where there are effective second-hand markets, but less usual for plant and machinery. For example, an entity may have a policy of replacing all of its motor vehicles after three years, so this will be their estimated useful life for depreciation purposes. The entity will depreciate them over this period down to the estimated residual value. The residual values of motor vehicles are often easy to obtain and the entity will be able to reassess these residuals in line with the requirements of the standard.

Judgement is necessary in determining the useful life of an asset. Section 17 provides the following guidance about the factors to be considered when determining the useful life of an asset:

(a)   The expected usage of the asset. Usage is assessed by reference to the asset's expected capacity or physical output.

(b)   Expected physical wear and tear, which depends on operational factors such as the number of shifts for which the asset is to be used and the repair and maintenance programme, and the care and maintenance of the asset while idle (see 3.5.4.A below).

(c)   Technical or commercial obsolescence arising from changes or improvements in production, or from a change in the market demand for the product or service output of the asset (see 3.5.4.C below).

(d)   Legal or similar limits on the use of the asset, such as the expiry dates of related leases. *[FRS 102.17.21]*.

Factor (d) above states that the 'expiry dates of related leases' is considered when determining the asset's useful life. Generally, the useful life of the leasehold improvement is the same or less than the lease term, as defined by Section 20 (see Chapter 18). However, a lessee may be able to depreciate an asset whose useful life exceeds the lease term over a longer period if the lease includes an option to extend that the lessee expects to exercise, even if the option is not considered 'reasonably certain' at inception (a higher threshold than the estimate of useful life in Section 17). In such a case, the asset may be depreciated either over the lease term or over the shorter of the asset's useful life and the period for which the entity expects to extend the lease.

3.5.4.A   Repairs and maintenance

The initial assessment of the useful life of the asset will take into account the expected routine spending on repairs and expenditure necessary for it to achieve that life. Although Section 17 implies that this refers to an item of plant and machinery, care and maintenance programmes are relevant to assessing the useful lives of many other types of asset. For example, an entity may assess the useful life of a railway engine at thirty-five years on the assumption that it has a major overhaul every seven years. Without this expenditure, the life of the engine would be much less certain and could be much shorter. Maintenance necessary to support the fabric of a building and its service potential is also taken into account in assessing its useful life. Eventually, it will always become uneconomic for the entity to continue to maintain the asset so, while the expenditure may lengthen the useful life, it is unlikely to make it indefinite.

Note that this applies whether the expenditure is capitalised because it meets the definition of a 'major inspection' (see 3.3.3.A above) or if it is repairs and maintenance that is expensed as incurred.

3.5.4.B   Land

As discussed in 3.3.2.A above, land and buildings are separable assets and must be accounted for separately, even when they are acquired together. *[FRS 102.17.8]*. Land, which generally has an unlimited life, is not usually depreciated. *[FRS 102.17.16]*. A building is a depreciable asset and its useful life is not affected by an increase in the value of the land on which it stands.

Although land generally has an unlimited useful life, there may be circumstances in which depreciation could be applied to land. In those instances in which land has a finite life it will be either used for extractive purposes (a quarry or mine) or for some purpose such as landfill; it will be depreciated in an appropriate manner but it is highly unlikely that there will be any issue regarding separating the interest in land from any building element. However, the cost of such land may include an element for site dismantlement or restoration (see 3.4.3 above), in which case this element will have to be separated from the land element and depreciated over an appropriate period (i.e. the period of benefits obtained by incurring these costs) which will often be the estimated useful life of the site for its purpose and function. An entity engaged in landfill on a new site may make a provision for restoring it as soon as it starts preparation by removing the overburden. It will separate the land from the 'restoration asset' and depreciate the restoration asset over the landfill site's estimated useful life. If the land has an infinite useful life, an appropriate depreciation basis will have to be chosen that reflects the period of benefits obtained from the restoration asset.

While FRS 102 provides no specific guidance related to revision of estimated costs, an entity may consider the approach applied by IFRIC 1 (see 3.4.3 above and Chapter 19 at 4.1). Accordingly, if the estimated costs are revised, in accordance with IFRIC 1, the adjusted depreciable amount of the asset is depreciated over its useful life. Therefore, once the related asset has reached the end of its useful life, all subsequent changes in the liability will be recognised in profit or loss as they occur, irrespective of whether the entity applies the cost or revaluation model. *[IFRIC 1.7]*.

3.5.4.C   Technological change

A current or expected future reduction in the market demand for the product or service output of an asset may be evidence of technical or commercial obsolescence. Expected future reductions in the selling price of an item that was produced using an asset could also indicate the expectation of technical or commercial obsolescence of the asset, which, in turn, might reflect a reduction of the future economic benefits embodied in the asset. If an entity anticipates technical or commercial obsolescence, it should reassess the residual value of an asset, its useful life or the pattern of consumption of future economic benefits. *[FRS 102.17.19]*. In such cases, it might be more appropriate to use a diminishing balance method of depreciation to reflect the pattern of consumption (see 3.5.6.B below).

The effects of technological change are often underestimated. It affects many assets, not only high technology plant and equipment such as computer systems. For example, many offices that have been purpose-built can become obsolete long before their fabric has physically deteriorated, for reasons such as the difficulty of introducing computer network infrastructures or air conditioning, poor environmental performance or an inability to meet new legislative requirements such as access for people with disabilities. Therefore, the estimation of an asset's useful life is a matter of judgement and the possibility of technological change must be taken into account.

3.5.5   When depreciation starts and ceases

Section 17 is clear on when depreciation should start and finish, and sets out the requirements as follows:

- Depreciation of an asset begins when it is available for use, which is defined further as occurring when the asset is in the location and condition necessary for it to be capable of operating in the manner intended by management. This is the point at which capitalisation of costs relating to the asset cease.

- Depreciation of an asset ceases when the asset is derecognised. *[FRS 102.17.20]*.

Therefore, an entity does not stop depreciating an asset merely because it has become idle or has been retired from active use, unless the asset is fully depreciated. However, if the entity is using a usage method of depreciation (e.g. the units of production method) the depreciation charge can be zero while there is no production. *[FRS 102.17.20]*. Of course, a prolonged period in which there is no production may raise questions as to whether the asset is impaired: an asset becoming idle is a specific example of an indication of impairment in Section 27 (see Chapter 24). *[FRS 102.27.9(f)]*.

3.5.6   Depreciation methods

Section 17 does not prescribe a particular method of depreciation. It simply states that 'an entity shall select the depreciation method that reflects the pattern in which it expects to consume the asset's future economic benefits', mentioning straight-line, diminishing balance and units of production methods as possibilities. *[FRS 102.17.22]*. The overriding requirement is that the depreciation charge reflects the pattern of consumption of the benefits the asset brings over its useful life, and is applied consistently from period to period unless there is a change in the expected pattern of consumption of those future economic benefits. *[FRS 102.17.22-23]*.

Section 17 contains an explicit requirement that the depreciation method be reviewed to determine if there is an indication that there has been a significant change since the last annual reporting date in the pattern by which an entity expects to consume an asset's future economic benefits. This could mean, for example, concluding that the straight-line method was no longer appropriate and changing to a diminishing balance method. If there has been such a change, the depreciation method should be changed to reflect it. However, under paragraphs 15 to 18 of Section 10 (see Chapter 9), this change is a change in accounting estimate and not a change in accounting policy. *[FRS 102.17.23]*. This means that the consequent depreciation adjustment should be made prospectively, i.e. the asset's depreciable amount should be written off over current and future periods. *[FRS 102.10.16]*.

Some industries use revenue as a practical basis to depreciate PP&E. These industries argue that there is a linear relationship between revenue and the units of production method (discussed below at 3.5.6.C). Unlike IFRS, FRS 102 does not explicitly prohibit the use of revenue as the basis to depreciate assets.

3.5.6.A   Straight-line method

The straight-line method of depreciation is well known and understood. Its simplicity makes it the most commonly used method in practice. The method is time-based and involves the use of a fixed percentage of the original cost of the asset in spreading the depreciable amount evenly over the useful life of the asset resulting in a constant depreciation charge over such period. It is considered the most appropriate method to use when the pattern of consumption of future economic benefits of an asset is expected to be constant year-on-year or when such pattern cannot be readily determined.

3.5.6.B   Diminishing balance method

The diminishing balance method involves determining a percentage depreciation that will write off the asset's depreciable amount over its useful life. This involves calculating a rate that will reduce the asset's carrying amount to its residual value at the end of the useful life.

Example 15.2:   Diminishing balance depreciation

An asset costs £6,000 and has a life of four years and a residual value of £1,500. It calculates that the appropriate depreciation rate on the declining balance is 29% and that the depreciation charge in years 1-4 will be as follows:

		£
Year 1	Cost	6,000
	Depreciation at 29% of £6,000	1,757
	Carrying amount	4,243
Year 2	Depreciation at 29% of £4,243	1,243
	Carrying amount	3,000
Year 3	Depreciation at 29% of £3,000	879
	Carrying amount	2,121
Year 4	Depreciation at 29% of £2,121	621
	Carrying amount	1,500

The sum of digits method is another form of the diminishing balance method, but one that is based on the estimated life of the asset and which can easily be applied if the asset has a residual value. If an asset has an estimated useful life of four years then the digits 1, 2, 3, and 4 are added together, giving a total of 10. Depreciation of four-tenths, three-tenths and so on, of the cost of the asset, less any residual value, will be charged in the respective years. The method is sometimes called the 'rule of 78', 78 being the sum of the digits 1 to 12.

Example 15.3:   Sum of the digits depreciation

An asset costs £10,000 and is expected to be sold for £2,000 after four years. The depreciable amount is £8,000 (£10,000 – £2,000). Depreciation is to be provided over four years using the sum of the digits method.

		£
Year 1	Cost	10,000
	Depreciation at 4/10 of £8,000	3,200
	Carrying amount	6,800
Year 2	Depreciation at 3/10 of £8,000	2,400
	Carrying amount	4,400
Year 3	Depreciation at 2/10 of £8,000	1,600
	Carrying amount	2,800
Year 4	Depreciation at 1/10 of £8,000	800
	Carrying amount	2,000

Chapter 15

3.5.6.C   *Units of production method*

Under this method, the asset is written off in line with its estimated total output. By relating depreciation to the proportion of productive capacity utilised to date, it reflects the fact that the useful economic life of certain assets, principally machinery, is more closely linked to its usage and output than to time. This method is normally used in extractive industries, for example, to amortise the costs of development of productive oil and gas facilities.

The essence of choosing a fair depreciation method is to reflect the consumption of economic benefits provided by the asset concerned. In most cases the straight-line basis will give perfectly acceptable results, and the vast majority of entities use this method. Where there are instances, such as the extraction of a known proportion of a mineral resource, or the use of a certain amount of the total available number of working hours of a machine, it may be that units of production method will give fairer results.

3.5.7   *Impairment*

All items of PP&E accounted for under Section 17 are subject to the impairment requirements of Section 27 – *Impairment of Assets*. That section explains when and how an entity reviews the carrying amount of its assets, how it determines the recoverable amount of an asset, and when it recognises or reverses an impairment loss. *[FRS 102.17.24]*. Impairment is discussed in Chapter 24.

There is no requirement in Section 17 for an automatic impairment review if no depreciation is charged.

3.5.7.A   *Compensation for impairment*

The question has arisen about the treatment of any compensation an entity may be due to receive as a result of an asset being impaired. For example an asset that is insured might be destroyed in a fire, so repayment from an insurance company might be expected. These two events – the impairment and any compensation – are separate economic events and should be accounted for separately as follows:

- impairments of PP&E are recognised in accordance with Section 27 (see Chapter 24);

- derecognition of items retired or disposed of should be recognised in accordance with Section 17 (derecognition is discussed at 3.7 below); and

- compensation from third parties for PP&E that is impaired, lost or given up is included in profit and loss only when the compensation is virtually certain. *[FRS 102.17.25]*.

3.5.7.B   *PP&E held for sale*

An entity's plan to dispose of an asset before the previously expected date is an indicator of impairment that triggers the calculation of the asset's recoverable amount for the purpose of determining whether the asset is impaired. *[FRS 102.17.26, 27.9(f)]*. If the asset is impaired, then the carrying amount of the asset should be written down to its recoverable amount.

Although the entity plans to dispose of the asset, depreciation should continue until the asset is disposed. In addition, the plan to dispose an asset might indicate that the residual value or the remaining life of the asset needs adjustment even if there is no impairment.

3.6   Measurement after initial recognition: revaluation model

If the revaluation model is adopted, PP&E is initially recognised at cost and subsequently measured at fair value less subsequent accumulated depreciation and impairment losses. *[FRS 102.17.15B]*. In practice, 'fair value' will usually be the market value of the asset. There is no requirement for a professional external valuation or even for a professionally qualified valuer to perform the appraisal, although in practice professional advice is often sought.

Section 17 does not prescribe the frequency of revaluations and simply states that revaluations are to be made with sufficient regularity to ensure that the carrying amount does not differ materially from the fair value at the end of the reporting period. *[FRS 102.17.15B]*. When the fair value of a revalued asset differs materially from its carrying amount, a further revaluation is necessary. As some items of PP&E have frequent and volatile changes in fair value, these would need to be revalued more frequently (e.g. annually).

If the revaluation model is adopted, all items within a class of assets are to be revalued simultaneously. This prevents selective revaluations particularly choosing to revalue only those assets that have significantly increased in value. A class of PP&E is a grouping of assets of a similar nature, function or use in an entity's business. *[FRS 102.17.15]*. This is not a precise definition. The following could be examples of separate classes of asset:

- land;
- land and buildings;
- machinery;
- ships;
- aircraft;
- motor vehicles;
- furniture and fixtures; and
- office equipment.

These are very broad categories of asset and it is possible for them to be classified further into groupings of assets of a similar nature and use. Office buildings and factories or hotels and fitness centres, could be separate classes of asset. If the entity used the same type of asset in two different geographical locations, e.g. clothing manufacturing facilities for similar products or products with similar markets, say in the United Kingdom and the Republic of Ireland, it is likely that these would be seen as part of the same class of asset. However, if the entity manufactured pharmaceuticals and clothing, both in European facilities, then few would argue that these could be assets with a sufficiently different nature and use to be a separate class. Ultimately, it must be a matter of judgement in the context of the specific operations of individual entities.

A rolling valuation of a class of assets could be made provided that the class is revalued over a short period of time and that the valuations are kept up to date. In practice, a rolling valuation is usually performed if the value of the assets changes very insignificantly (in which case the valuations may only be performed less frequently) because if a significant change is revealed, then presumably a new revaluation for the entire class is required to keep the valuation up to date.

3.6.1   The meaning of fair value

Fair value is defined as the amount for which an asset could be exchanged, a liability settled, or an equity instrument granted could be exchanged, between knowledgeable, willing parties in an arm's length transaction. In the absence of any specific guidance provided in the relevant section of FRS 102, the guidance in the Appendix to Section 2 – *Concepts and Pervasive Principles* – should be used in determining fair value (see Chapter 4). *[FRS 102 Appendix I].*

Section 17 describes the process of determining fair value for assets within its scope. For land and buildings, fair value is usually determined from market-based evidence by appraisal that is normally undertaken by professionally qualified valuers (although income or depreciated replacement cost approaches are permitted if no such evidence is available because of the specialised nature of the item of PP&E – see 3.6.2 below). For other items of PP&E, the fair value is usually their market value determined by appraisal. *[FRS 102.17.15C-D].* Section 17 does not imply that fair value and market value are synonymous, although it states that the fair value of items of PP&E is usually their market value determined by appraisal. *[FRS 102.17.15C].*

3.6.2   Fair value in the absence of market-based evidence

If there is no market-based evidence of fair value because of the specialised nature of the item of PP&E and the item is rarely sold except as part of a continuing business an entity may need to estimate fair value using an income or a depreciated replacement cost (DRC) approach (see 3.6.2.A and 3.6.2.B below). *[FRS 102.17.15D].*

The basis underlying the income or DRC approach is that the asset is so specialised that there is no market value for it. There are three main subsets of such assets: (a) those that are only ever sold as part of a business; (b) assets primarily used to provide services to the public (whether on a paying or non-paying basis); and (c) assets that are so specialised by nature of their size or location or similar features that there is no market for them.

Examples of specialised properties include:

- oil refineries and chemical works where, usually, the buildings are no more than housings or cladding for highly specialised plant;
- power stations and dock installations where the building and site engineering works are related directly to the business of the owner, it being highly unlikely that they would have a value to anyone other than a company acquiring the undertaking;
- schools, colleges, universities and research establishments where there is no competing market demand from other organisations using these types of property in the locality;
- hospitals, other specialised health care premises and leisure centres where there is no competing market demand from other organisations wishing to use these types of property in the locality; and
- museums, libraries, and other similar premises provided by the public sector.

In addition, there may be no market-based evidence for properties of such specialised construction, arrangement, size or specification that it is unlikely that there would be a single purchaser. The same may be the case even for standard properties in geographical areas remote from main business centres, perhaps originally located there for operational or business reasons that no longer exist. This could occur if the buildings were of such an abnormal size for the district that no market for them would exist.

3.6.2.A   Income approach to fair value

Section 17 does not define what it means by an income approach. However, a definition is provided in IFRS 13 – *Fair Value Measurement* – which states that the *income approach* converts future amounts (e.g. cash flows or income and expenses) to a single discounted amount. The fair value reflects current market expectations about those future amounts. In the case of PP&E, this will usually mean using a discounted cash flow technique. *[IFRS 13.B10, B11].*

Further discussion of this valuation technique can be found in Chapter 14 of EY International GAAP 2019.

3.6.2.B   Depreciated replacement cost

Depreciated replacement cost is defined as the most economic cost required for the entity to replace the service potential of an asset (including the amount that the entity will receive from its disposal at the end of its useful life) at the reporting date. *[FRS 102 Appendix I].* The objective of DRC is to make a realistic estimate of the current cost of constructing an asset that has the same service potential as the existing asset.

As a DRC valuation is based on replacement cost, it is likely to give a higher valuation than one using market-based evidence that reflects the actual current condition of the asset. For this reason, it is necessary to ensure that the asset really is so specialised that such evidence cannot be obtained. It is also necessary to be satisfied that the potential profitability of the business is adequate to support the value derived on a DRC basis.

DRC approaches are often applied to the valuation of plant and machinery, as distinct from property assets, where there is rarely a market from which to derive a fair value.

3.6.3   Accounting for revaluation surpluses and deficits

With respect to any determination of the value of an asset of a company on any basis of the alternative accounting rules, the amount of any profit or loss arising from that determination must be credited or (as the case may be) debited to a separate reserve ('the revaluation reserve') as required by the Companies Act. *[1 Sch 35(1)].*

Accordingly, increases as a result of revaluation are recognised in OCI and accumulated in equity i.e. revaluation reserve. If a revaluation increase reverses a revaluation decrease of the same asset that was previously recognised as an expense, it may be recognised in profit or loss. *[FRS 102.17.15E].* Decreases as a result of revaluation are recognised in OCI to the extent of any previously recognised revaluation increase accumulated in revaluation reserve in respect of the same asset. If a revaluation decrease exceeds the revaluation gains accumulated in revaluation reserve in respect of that asset, the excess is recognised in profit or loss. *[FRS 102.17.15F].* This means that it is not permissible under Section 17 to carry a negative revaluation reserve in respect of any item of PP&E.

The same rules apply to impairment losses. Any impairment loss of a revalued asset should be treated as a revaluation decrease in accordance with Section 17. *[FRS 102.27.6]*.

3.6.3.A   *Depreciation of revalued assets*

The fundamental objective of depreciation is to reflect in operating profit the cost of use of an item of PP&E (i.e. the amount of economic benefits consumed) in the period. This requires a charge to operating profit even if the asset has changed in value or has been revalued.

Section 17 is not specific as to the base amount of an item of PP&E to be used when computing the depreciation charge for the period. It might be best to use the average carrying value during the year, or else, the opening or closing balance may be used provided that it is used consistently in each period. In practice, the depreciation charge is generally based on the opening value and the written down asset is revalued as at the end of accounting period. The depreciation charge should be recognised as an expense, unless it qualifies to be capitalised as part of another asset (see discussion at 3.5.1 above).

While not explicitly addressed in Section 17, the revaluation surplus included in OCI may be transferred directly to retained earnings as the surplus is realised. *[1 Sch 35(3)]*. Accordingly, the difference between depreciation based on the revalued carrying amount of the asset and depreciation based on its original cost may be transferred from the revaluation reserve to retained earnings as the asset is used by the entity. Any depreciation of the revalued part of an asset's carrying value is considered realised by being charged to profit or loss. Thus a transfer may be made of an equivalent amount from the revaluation surplus to retained earnings. However any transfer is made directly from revaluation surplus to retained earnings and not through profit or loss. This is illustrated in Example 15.4 below. Any remaining balance may be transferred from revaluation reserve to retained earnings when the asset is derecognised (see 3.7 below). Revaluation gains or losses arising from the disposal of PP&E are not recycled to profit or loss.

Example 15.4:   *Effect of depreciation on the revaluation reserve*

On 1 January 2016 an entity acquired an asset for £1,000. The asset has an economic life of ten years and is depreciated on a straight-line basis. The residual value is assumed to be £nil. At 31 December 2019 (when the cost net of accumulated depreciation is £600) the asset is valued at £900. The entity accounts for the revaluation by debiting the carrying value of the asset (using either of the methods discussed below) £300 and crediting £300 to the revaluation reserve. At 31 December 2019 the useful life of the asset is considered to be the remainder of its original life (i.e. six years) and its residual value is still considered to be £nil. In the year ended 31 December 2020 and in later years, the depreciation charged to profit or loss is £150 (£900/6 years remaining).

Accordingly, the treatment thereafter for each of the remaining 6 years of the asset's life, is to transfer £50 (£300/6 years) each year from the revaluation reserve to retained earnings (not through profit or loss). This avoids the revaluation reserve being maintained indefinitely even after the asset ceases to exist, which does not seem sensible. This treatment is also permitted by Companies Act which allows amounts to be transferred to the profit and loss account reserve if the amount has previously been charged in that account or is a realised profit. A transfer is possible because the amount of £50 is a realised profit in terms of the Companies Act. *[s841(5), 1 Sch 35(3)]*.

The effect on taxation, both current and deferred, of a policy of revaluing assets is recognised and disclosed in accordance with Section 29 – *Income Tax*. This is dealt with in Chapter 26.

FRS 102 does not provide specific guidance on accounting for accumulated depreciation when an item of PP&E is revalued. There are two usual methods of adjusting the carrying amount when an item of PP&E is revalued. At the date of revaluation, the asset is treated in one of the following ways:

- The accumulated depreciation is eliminated against gross carrying amount of the asset and the carrying amount is then restated to the revalued amount of the asset.

- The gross carrying amount is adjusted in a manner that is consistent with the revaluation of the carrying amount of the asset. For example, the gross carrying amount may be restated by reference to observable market data or it may be restated proportionately to the change in the carrying amount of the asset. The accumulated depreciation at the date of the revaluation is adjusted to equal the difference between the gross carrying amount and the carrying amount of the asset after taking into account accumulated impairment losses.

The first method available eliminates the amount of accumulated depreciation to the extent of the difference between the revalued amount and the carrying amount of the asset immediately before revaluation. This is illustrated in Example 15.5.

Example 15.5:   *Revaluation by eliminating accumulated depreciation*

On 31 December, a building has a carrying amount of £40,000, being the original cost of £70,000 less accumulated depreciation of £30,000. A revaluation is performed and the fair value of the asset is £50,000. The entity would record the following journal entries:

	Dr £	Cr £
Accumulated depreciation	30,000	
Building		20,000
Asset revaluation reserve		10,000

	Before £	After £
Building at cost	70,000	
Building at valuation		50,000
Accumulated depreciation	30,000	–
Carrying amount	40,000	50,000

Under the observable market data approach, the gross carrying amount will be restated and its difference compared to the revalued amount of the asset will be absorbed by the accumulated depreciation. Using the example above, assume the gross carrying amount is restated to £75,000 by reference to the observable market data and the accumulated depreciation will be adjusted to £25,000 (i.e. the gross carrying amount of £75,000 less the carrying amount adjusted to its revalued amount of £50,000).

Alternatively, the gross carrying amount is restated proportionately to the change in carrying amount (i.e. a 25% uplift) resulting in the same revaluation movement as the methods above but the cost and accumulated depreciation carried forward reflect a gross cost of the asset of £87,500 and accumulated depreciation of £37,500. This method may be used if an asset is revalued using an index to determine its depreciated replacement cost (DRC) (see 3.6.2.B above).

3.6.4   Reversals of downward valuations

Section 17 requires that, if an asset's carrying amount is increased as a result of a revaluation, the increase should be credited directly to OCI and accumulated in equity. However, the increase should be recognised in profit or loss to the extent that it reverses a revaluation decrease of the same asset previously recognised in profit or loss. *[FRS 102.17.15E].*

If the revalued asset is being depreciated, the full amount of any reversal is not taken to profit or loss. Rather, the reversal should take account of the depreciation that would have been charged on the previously higher book value. The text of Section 17 does not specify this treatment but such treatment is consistent with Section 27, which states:

> 'The reversal of an impairment loss shall not exceed the carrying amount of the asset above the carrying amount that would have been determined (net of amortisation or depreciation) had no impairment loss been recognised for the asset in prior years'. *[FRS 102.27.30(c)].*

The following example demonstrates a way in which this could be applied:

Example 15.6:   Reversal of a downward valuation

An asset has a cost of £1,000,000, a life of 10 years and a residual value of £nil. At the end of year 3, when the asset's depreciated cost is £700,000, it is revalued to £350,000. This write down below cost of £350,000 is taken through profit or loss.

The entity then depreciates the asset by £50,000 per annum, so as to depreciate the revalued carrying amount of £350,000 over the remaining 7 years.

At the end of year 6, the asset's carrying amount is £200,000 but it is now revalued to £500,000. The effect on the entity's asset is as follows:

	£000
Valuation	
At the beginning of year 6	350
Surplus on revaluation	150
At the end of the year	500
Accumulated depreciation	
At beginning of year 6 *	100
Charge for the year	50
Accumulated depreciation written back on revaluation	(150)
At the end of the year	–
Carrying amount at the end of year 6	500
Carrying amount at the beginning of year 6	250

* Two years' depreciation (years 4 and 5) at £50,000 per annum.

Upon the revaluation in year 6 the total uplift in the asset's carrying amount is £300,000 (i.e. £500,000 less £200,000). However, only £200,000 is taken through profit or loss. £100,000 represents depreciation that would otherwise have been charged to profit or loss in years 4 and 5. This is taken directly to the revaluation surplus in OCI.

From the beginning of year 7 the £500,000 asset value will be written off over the remaining four years at £125,000 per annum.

In Example 15.6 above, the amount of the revaluation that is credited to the revaluation surplus in OCI represents the difference between the carrying amount that would have resulted had the asset always been held on a cost basis since initial recognition (£400,000) and the carrying amount on a revalued basis (£500,000).

This might be considered as an extreme example. Most assets that are subject to a policy of revaluation would not show such marked changes in value and it would be expected that there would be valuation movements in the intervening years rather than dramatic losses and gains in years 3 and 6. However, we consider that in principle this is the way in which downward valuations should be recognised.

There may be major practical difficulties for any entity that finds itself in the position of reversing revaluation deficits on depreciating assets, although whether in practice this eventuality often occurs is open to doubt. If there is any chance that it is likely to occur, the business would need to continue to maintain asset registers on the original, pre-write down, basis.

3.6.5 Adopting a policy of revaluation

Although the adoption of a policy of revaluation by an entity that has previously used the cost model is a change in accounting policy, it is not dealt with as a prior year adjustment in accordance with Section 10. Instead, the change is treated as a revaluation during the year. *[FRS 102.10.10A]*. This means that the entity is not required to obtain valuation information about comparative periods.

3.6.6 Assets held under finance leases

Once assets held under finance leases have been capitalised as items of PP&E, their subsequent accounting is the same as for any other asset so they do not constitute a separate class of assets. Therefore such assets may also be revalued using the revaluation model but, if the revaluation model is used, then the entire class of assets (both owned and those held under finance lease) must be revalued. *[FRS 102.17.15]*.

Whilst it is not explicit in Section 17, in our view, to obtain the fair value of an asset held under a finance lease for financial reporting purposes, the assessed value must be adjusted to take account of any recognised finance lease liability. Accordingly, if the entity obtains an asset valuation net of the valuer's estimate of the present value of future lease obligations, which is usual practice, to the extent that the lease obligations have already been accounted for in the balance sheet as a lease obligation, an amount must be added back to arrive at the fair value of the asset for the purposes of the financial statements. Such a valuation adjustment is achieved by adjusting for the finance lease obligation recognised in the financial statements. This is consistent with the mechanism discussed at 3.3.3 of Chapter 14.

For disclosure purposes PP&E acquired under a finance lease should be considered to be the same class of asset as those with a similar nature that are owned. Consequently, there is no need to provide separate reconciliations of movements in owned assets from assets held under finance leases (see 3.9 below).

3.7 Derecognition

Derecognition i.e. removal of the carrying amount of the item from the financial statements of the entity, occurs when an item of PP&E is either disposed of, or when no further economic benefits are expected to flow from its use or disposal. *[FRS 102.17.27]*. The disposal of an item of PP&E may occur in a variety of ways (e.g. by sale, by entering into a finance lease or by donation). The actual date of disposal is determined in accordance with the criteria in Section 23 for the recognition of revenue from the sale of goods. Section 20 applies to disposal by way of a sale and leaseback. *[FRS 102.17.29]*. Revenue recognition under Section 23 is discussed in Chapter 20. All gains and losses on derecognition must be included in profit and loss for the period (although, except as discussed in 3.7.1 below, gains should not be classified as revenue) when the item is derecognised, unless another standard applies, e.g. under Section 20, a sale and leaseback transaction might not give rise to a gain. *[FRS 102.17.28]*. See Chapter 18 at 3.10 for more detail.

Gains and losses are to be calculated as the difference between any net disposal proceeds and the carrying value of the item of PP&E. *[FRS 102.17.30]*. This means that any revaluation surplus relating to the asset disposed of is transferred directly to retained earnings when the asset is derecognised and not reflected in profit or loss.

Replacement of 'parts' of an asset requires derecognition of the carrying value of the original part, even if that part was not being depreciated separately. In these circumstances, it might be acceptable to estimate using the cost of a replacement part to be a guide to the original cost of the replaced part, if that cannot be determined. See discussion at 3.3.2 above.

Any consideration received on the disposal of an item should be recognised at its fair value. If deferred credit terms are given, the consideration for the sale is the cash price equivalent, and any surplus is treated as interest revenue using the effective yield method as required by Section 23 (see Chapter 20).

There could be a few fully depreciated assets still in use. For those fully depreciated assets that are no longer in use, it may be practical to derecognise them, rather than continue to carry them at their gross cost and accumulated depreciation.

3.7.1   Sale of assets held for rental

If an entity, in the course of its ordinary activities, routinely sells PP&E that it has held for rental to others, it should transfer such assets to inventories at their carrying amount when they cease to be rented and are then held for sale. Accordingly, the proceeds from the sale of such assets should be recognised as revenue. While this is not specified in Section 17, this treatment appears reasonable and is consistent with the specific provisions in IAS 16 paragraph 68A. In contrast, the sale of investment property is generally not recognised as revenue.

A number of entities sell assets that have previously been held for rental, for example, car rental companies that may acquire vehicles with the intention of holding them as rental cars for a limited period and then selling them. One issue is whether the sale of such assets, which arguably have a dual purpose of being rented out and then sold, should be presented gross (revenue and cost of sales) or net (gain or loss) in profit or loss.

It would be reasonable to consider the IFRS conclusion in this scenario. The IASB concluded that the presentation of gross revenue, rather than a net gain or loss, would better reflect the ordinary activities of some such entities. Accordingly, when preparing statement of cash flows, both (i) the cash payments to manufacture or acquire assets held for rental and subsequently held for sale; and (ii) the cash receipts from rentals and sales of such assets would be presented as from operating activities. *[IAS 7.14]*. This is intended to avoid initial expenditure on purchases of assets being classified as investing activities while inflows from sales are recorded within operating activities.

3.7.2 Partial disposals and undivided interests

Section 17 requires an entity to derecognise 'an item' of PP&E on disposal or when it expects no future economic benefits from its use or disposal. *[FRS 102.17.27]*.

Items of PP&E are recognised when their costs can be measured reliably and it is probable that future benefits associated with the asset will flow to the entity. *[FRS 102.17.4]*. Section 17 does not prescribe the unit of measurement for recognition, i.e. what constitutes an item of PP&E.

However, items that are derecognised were not necessarily items on initial recognition. The item that is being disposed of may be part of a larger 'item' bought in a single transaction that can be subdivided into parts (i.e. separate items) for separate disposal; an obvious example is land or many types of property. The principle is the same as for the replacement of parts, which may only be identified and derecognised so that the cost of the replacement part may be recognised (see 3.3.2 above). The entity needs to identify the cost of the part disposed of by allocating the carrying value on a systematic and appropriate basis.

Section 17 assumes that disposal will be of a physical part (except in the specific case of major inspections and overhauls – see 3.3.3.A above). However, some entities enter into arrangements in which they dispose of part of the benefits that will be derived from the assets.

Although Section 17 defines an asset by reference to the future economic benefits that will be controlled by the entity as a result of the acquisition, it does not address disposals of a proportion of these benefits. An entity may dispose of an undivided interest in the whole asset (sometimes called an ownership 'in common' of the asset). This means that all owners have a proportionate share of the entire asset (e.g. the purchaser of a 25% undivided interest in 100 acres of land owns 25% of the whole 100 acres). These arrangements are common in, but are not restricted to, the extractive and property sectors. Vendors have to determine how to account for the consideration they have received from the purchaser. This will depend on the details of the arrangement and, in particular, whether the entity continues to control the asset or if there is joint control.

3.7.2.A Joint control

In some cases there may be joint control over the asset (e.g. sale of an asset to a joint venture), in which case the arrangement will be within scope of Section 15 – *Investments in Joint Ventures* – which will determine how to account for the disposal and the subsequent accounting. Joint control is discussed in Chapter 13.

The retained interest will be analysed as a jointly controlled operation (JCO), a jointly controlled assets (JCA) or a jointly controlled entity (JCE). Undivided interests cannot be accounted for as joint ventures in the absence of joint control.

3.7.2.B Vendor retains control

If the asset is not jointly controlled in the subsequent arrangement, the vendor might retain control over the asset. The vendor will recognise revenue or it will be a financing arrangement. If it is the former, then the issue is the period and pattern over which revenue is recognised.

If the vendor retains control then it will not meet the criteria in Section 23 for treating the transaction as a sale, i.e. recognising revenue on entering into the arrangement. As discussed in Chapter 20, the entity must retain neither continuing managerial involvement to the degree usually associated with ownership nor effective control over the goods sold in order to recognise revenue from the sale of goods. *[FRS 102.23.10]*.

The arrangement could be akin to a lease, especially if the disposal is for a period of time. However, arrangements are only within the scope of Section 20 if they relate to a specified asset. Generally, a portion of a larger asset that is not physically distinct is not considered to be a specified asset. See Chapter 18.

If it is not a lease and the vendor continues to control the asset, the arrangement might be best characterised as akin to a performance obligation for services to be spread over the term of the arrangement. That is, the initial receipt would be a liability and recognised in profit and loss over time.

Alternatively, it could be a financing-type arrangement, in which case the proceeds would be classified as a financial liability. In effect, the vendor is trading a share of any revenue to which it is entitled in exchange for funding by the purchaser of one or more activities relating to the asset. The purchaser receives a return that is comparable to a lender's rate of return out of the proceeds of production. This could be by receiving a disproportionate share of output until it has recovered its costs (the financing it has provided) as well as the agreed rate of return for the funding. These arrangements are found in the extractive sector, e.g. carried interests and farm-outs (Chapter 31). In the development stage of a project, the asset in question will be classified as PP&E or as an intangible asset under Section 18. Under a carried interest arrangement the carried party transfers a *portion* of the risks and rewards of a property, in exchange for a funding commitment from the carrying party.

3.7.2.C   Partial sale of a single-asset entity

Certain assets, particularly properties, may be bought and sold by transferring ownership of a separate legal entity formed to hold the asset (a 'single-asset' entity) rather than the asset itself. The asset could be realised through either an outright sale or partial disposal. If the asset is sold in its entirety the gain or loss on disposal is the difference between the net disposal proceeds and the carrying amount of the asset (which, in this example, is assumed to be equal to the carrying amount of the investment in a single-asset entity). *[FRS 102.17.30]*. This scenario may be straight-forward but in instances where there is a partial disposal of an investment in a single-asset entity (including a partial disposal of an asset) that results in a loss of control, the type of investment that is retained should be considered in determining the gain or loss on disposal.

If the retained interest is not a joint venture within the scope of Section 15, the structure should be assessed to determine whether the retained interest represents an undivided interest in the asset or an investment in an entity. This assessment is important if the structure would result in a different amount of gain or loss on disposal. Therefore, if the retained interest represents an undivided interest in the asset, the accounting result is the same as that for an investment in a jointly controlled asset i.e. a gain or loss is recognised only to the extent of the portion sold, because the sale of a portion of the shares in the entity that holds the asset is regarded as a partial sale of the asset. However, if the retained interest represents an investment in an entity, a gain or loss is recognised as if 100% of the investment in the single-asset entity had been sold because control has been lost. This is consistent with principles when an entity lost control of a subsidiary or lost joint control of a jointly controlled entity – see Chapter 8 and Chapter 13, respectively. A financial asset or an interest in an associate is recognised, as appropriate, for the ownership interest retained. *[FRS 102.9.19, 15.18]*.

3.8 Presentation of PP&E

A entity reporting under Schedule 1 using the 'statutory formats' (see Chapter 6 at 5.2) is required to present PP&E on the face of statement of financial position. The main heading should be 'Tangible assets'. The following required subheadings may be shown either on the face of the statement of financial position or in the notes:

- land and buildings;
- plant and machinery;
- fixtures, fittings, tools and equipment; and
- payments on account and assets in course of construction.

Subheadings may not be limited to those above.

A Schedule 1 entity using the 'adapted formats' (see Chapter 6 at 5.1) is required to present property, plant and equipment as a separate line item on the statement of financial position. FRS 102 also requires that sub-classifications of property, plant and equipment that are appropriate to the entity are presented, either on the face of the statement of financial position or in the notes. *[FRS 102.4.2B(a)]*. As discussed at 2.1 above, if 'adapted formats' of presentation of the financial statements are used, an entity should generally continue to classify PP&E intended to be disposed of as non-current unless it is expected to be realised within 12 months after the reporting period, in which case it must be classified as current.

3.9 Disclosures

The main disclosure requirements of Section 17 are set out at 3.9.1 below. Other disclosures required by other sections of FRS 102 and Companies Act in respect of PP&E are included in 3.9.2 and 3.9.3 below, respectively.

3.9.1 Disclosures required by Section 17

For each class of PP&E the following should be disclosed in the financial statements:

- the measurement bases used for determining the gross carrying amount (e.g. cost or revaluation);
- the depreciation methods used;
- the useful lives or the depreciation rates used;
- the gross carrying amount and the accumulated depreciation (aggregated with accumulated impairment losses) at the beginning and end of the reporting period;

Chapter 15

- a reconciliation of the carrying amount at the beginning and end of the reporting period, which need not be presented for prior periods, showing separately the following:
  - additions;
  - disposals;
  - acquisitions through business combinations;
  - revaluations;
  - transfers to or from investment property (see Chapter 14 at 3.4);
  - impairment losses recognised or reversed in profit or loss during the period under Section 27;
  - depreciation for the period; and
  - other changes. *[FRS 102.17.31]*.

Where an entity has chosen to account for investment properties rented to other group entities using the cost model it should disclose their carrying amount at the end of the reporting period. *[FRS 102.17.31A]*.

An entity should also disclose the following:

- the existence and carrying amounts of PP&E to which the entity has restricted title or that is pledged as security for liabilities; and
- the amount of contractual commitments for the acquisition of PP&E. *[FRS 102.17.32]*.

In addition to above disclosures, if items of PP&E are stated at revalued amounts, the following should be disclosed:

- the effective date of the revaluation;
- whether an independent valuer was involved;
- the methods and significant assumptions applied in estimating the items' fair values; and
- for each revalued class of PP&E, the carrying amount that would have been recognised had the assets been carried under the cost model. *[FRS 102.17.32A]*.

The requirement under the last bullet point above can be quite onerous for entities, as it involves maintaining asset register information in some detail in order to meet it.

When both the cost model and the revaluation model have been used, the gross carrying amount for that basis in each category will have to be disclosed (however the standard requires that if revaluation is adopted the entire class of PP&E must be revalued – see 3.6 above). The selection of the depreciation method, useful lives or depreciation rates used is a matter of judgement and the disclosure should provide information to allow users to review the policies selected by management and to compare them with other entities.

All of the disclosures above (other than those related to fair value measurement) are also relevant to an entity that chooses to measure investment properties rented to another group entity under the cost model. *[FRS 102.17.30A]*.

3.9.2 Disclosures required by other sections of FRS 102 in respect of PP&E

In addition to the above disclosures, other sections of FRS 102 require disclosures of specific information relating to PP&E:

- If, at the reporting date, an entity has a binding sale agreement for a major disposal of assets (i.e. PP&E held for sale), a description of the facts and circumstances of the planned sale, and the carrying amount of the assets, is required to be disclosed. *[FRS 102.4.14]*. See Chapter 6 for further details.

- In accordance with Section 10, the nature and effect of any changes in accounting estimate (e.g. depreciation methods, useful lives, residual values, estimated cost of dismantling, removing or restoring items of PP&E) that have a material effect on the current or future periods must be disclosed. *[FRS 102.10.18]*. See Chapter 9 for further details.

- Disclosures required for a lessee under finance lease agreement or a lessor under operating lease agreement (i.e. the party that recognises the PP&E in its statement of financial position) are covered by Section 20. See Chapter 18 for details.

- In the case of PP&E that is impaired, disclosures are required by Section 27. See Chapter 24 for further details.

- Disclosures in relation to borrowing costs that are capitalised as part of the cost of an item of PP&E are required by Section 25. See Chapter 22 for details.

3.9.3 Additional disclosures required by the Companies Act and the Regulations

The following disclosures are required by the Companies Act and the Regulations in respect of PP&E in addition to those disclosures required by FRS 102:

- An analysis of freehold, long leasehold and short leasehold in respect of disclosures of land and buildings. *[1 Sch 53]*. For this purpose, a 'lease' is defined to include an agreement for a lease and a 'long lease' as a lease which has 50 years or more to run at the end of the financial year in question, otherwise, it would be a 'short lease'. *[10 Sch 7]*.

- In addition to the disclosures described at 3.9.1 above, the following information should be given for any PP&E that are measured using the revaluation model (i.e. alternative accounting rules) and that have been valued during the financial year:
    - the year of valuation and the amounts of the revaluation;
    - in the year of valuation, the names of the persons who valued them or particulars of their qualifications for doing so; and
    - the bases of valuation used by them. *[1 Sch 52]*.

- The treatment for taxation purposes of amounts credited or debited to the revaluation reserve must be disclosed in a note to the accounts. *[1 Sch 35(6)]*.

- Where an entity has determined the purchase price or production cost of any asset for the first time using the value ascribed to it in the earliest available record of its value made on or after its acquisition or production by the company, this fact should be disclosed in the notes to its financial statements (see 3.4.1 above). *[1 Sch 64(1)]*.

Chapter 15

4   SUMMARY OF GAAP DIFFERENCES

The key differences between FRS 102 and IFRS in accounting for PP&E are set out below.

	FRS 102	*IFRS*
Scope	Applies to all items of PP&E except for biological assets related to agricultural activity, heritage assets, mineral rights and reserves and PP&E classified as held for sale. For periods beginning on or after 1 January 2019 (or where the December 2017 Amendments to FRS 102 are early adopted), investment properties rented to another group entity where (as permitted by paragraph 4A of Section 16) the reporting entity chooses to apply the cost model (see 3.5 above) are within the scope of Section 17. For periods beginning prior to 1 January 2019 (and where the December 2017 Amendments to FRS 102 are not early adopted), investment properties (including investment properties under construction) whose fair value cannot be measured reliably without undue cost or effort are within the scope of Section 17. A plan to dispose of an asset (i.e. held-for-sale asset) before the previously expected date is an indicator of impairment (i.e. no reclassification or suspension of depreciation – although see 2.1 above). Section 34 does not make a distinction between biological assets and bearer plants. Therefore, bearer plants are treated as biological assets and accounted for in accordance with Section 34.	Applies to all items of PP&E except PP&E classified as held for sale, biological assets related to agricultural activity, mineral rights and reserves and investment properties held at fair value. Recognition and measurement of exploration and evaluation assets are also excluded from its scope. Entities using the cost model for investment properties (including investment properties under construction) use the cost method as prescribed in IAS 16. PP&E classified as held for sale is accounted for under IFRS 5. Biological assets meeting the definition of 'bearer plants' are within the scope of IAS 16.
Classification of computer software	No specific guidance on classification of computer software. We expect entities will follow the guidance under IFRS (see 3.3.1.D above).	Most computer software is an intangible asset whereas computer software which is integral to a tangible asset remains in tangible assets.
Cost	If payment for the asset is deferred beyond normal credit terms, the cost is the present value of all future payments (although expected to be materially similar, it is not the cash price equivalent at the recognition date like in IAS 16). Capitalisation of directly attributable borrowing costs in respect of a qualifying asset is permitted but not required. Subject to conditions (e.g. transaction has economic substance and fair value is reliably measurable), FRS 102 requires all acquisitions of PP&E in exchange for non-monetary assets, or a combination of monetary and non-monetary assets, to be measured at fair value. Any resulting gain or loss is likely to be an unrealised profit or loss and would be reported in OCI.	If payment for the asset is deferred beyond normal credit terms, interest is recognised over the period of credit (unless capitalised per IAS 23 – *Borrowing Costs*) i.e. the measurement of cost of a PP&E is the cash price equivalent at the recognition date. Borrowing costs related to a qualifying asset must be capitalised. Subject to conditions (e.g. transaction has economic substance and fair value is reliably measurable), IAS 16 requires all acquisitions of PP&E in exchange for non-monetary assets, or a combination of monetary and non-monetary assets, to be measured at fair value. Any resulting gain or loss is reported in the income statement.

Revaluation model	Assets are revalued to 'fair value', determined from market-based evidence by appraisal for land and buildings or 'market value' determined by appraisal for other items of PP&E. Where there is no market-based evidence, due to the specialised nature of the asset and it is rarely sold, an estimation using an income or depreciated replacement cost approach may be used.	Assets are revalued to 'fair value', which is defined by IFRS for non-financial assets as being the value attributable to the 'highest and best use' of that asset by a market participant even if the entity intends a different use.
	Section 17 does not have detailed guidance on accumulated depreciation when assets are revalued. However, we expect that FRS 102 adopters will follow the approach similar to IFRS (see 3.6.3.A above).	IAS 16 provides detailed guidance on accumulated depreciation when assets are revalued.
	Section 17 is silent on transfers of a revaluation surplus to retained earnings. However, the Regulations permit such transfers of amounts if the amount represents realised profit (see 3.6.3.A above).	IAS 16 provides detailed guidance on transfers of revaluation surplus to retained earnings – i.e. as the asset is used by an entity or when the related asset is derecognised.
Depreciation of assets / impairment	Depreciation ceases at the end of the useful life or on disposal of the asset.	Depreciation of an asset ceases when the asset is either classified as held for sale or derecognised.
	No equivalent guidance in respect of non-depreciation if an asset's residual value is equal to or exceeds its carrying amount. However, we expect that FRS 102 adopters will follow an approach similar to IFRS (see 3.5.2 above).	If an asset's residual value is equal to or exceeds its carrying amount the asset is not depreciated until its residual value subsequently decreases to an amount below the assets' carrying amount.
	There is no explicit prohibition of the use of 'revenue expected to be generated' as the basis to depreciate PP&E.	The use of revenue-based depreciation is inappropriate and thus, prohibited
	Reassessment of depreciation methods and residual values are only required if there is an indication that it has changed since the most recent annual reporting date. There is no specific requirement to perform a mandatory annual impairment review for assets with no depreciation (as immaterial) or for assets where the remaining useful life exceeds 50 years.	Depreciation methods and residual value should be reassessed at least annually. Depreciation methods are changed if there is a significant change in the expected pattern of consumption. There is no specific requirement to perform a mandatory annual impairment review for assets with no depreciation (as immaterial) or for assets where the remaining useful life exceeds 50 years.

Chapter 15

	FRS 102	IFRS
Disposal of PP&E	Under FRS 102 the date of disposal is determined in accordance with the criteria in Section 23 – *Revenue* – for the recognition of revenue from the sale of goods. *[FRS 102.17.29]*. Section 23 is based on IAS 18 which has been superseded by IFRS 15.	Under IAS 16 the date of disposal of an item of PP&E is the date that the recipient obtains control of that item in accordance with the requirements for determining when a performance obligation is satisfied in IFRS 15. *[IAS 16.69]*.
	Under FRS 102 gains and losses on disposal are to be calculated as the difference between any net disposal proceeds and the carrying value of the item of PP&E. *[FRS 102.17.30]*. Section 17 does not provide further guidance on how the disposal proceeds should be determined.	IAS 16 requires that the amount of consideration on disposal to be included in the gain or loss on derecognition of PP&E should be determined in accordance with the requirements for determining the transaction price in IFRS 15. In addition subsequent changes to the estimated amount of consideration included in the gain or loss should be accounted for in accordance with the requirements for changes in transaction price in IFRS 15. *[IAS 16.72]*
Disclosures	Reconciliation disclosure (i.e. opening balances to ending balances) required only for the current period.	Reconciliation disclosure (i.e. opening balances to ending balances) required for both current and comparative period.
	Where an entity has chosen to account for investment properties rented to other group entities using the cost model it should disclose their carrying amount at the end of the reporting period (see 3.9.1 above).	

Chapter 16 Intangible assets other than goodwill

Chapter 16

Chapter 16   Intangible assets other than goodwill

1   INTRODUCTION

Intangible assets represent a significant class of assets for a wide range of entities. The existence of a corporate identity or brand; intellectual property rights protecting an entity's knowledge, products and processes; or contractual and other rights to exploit both physical and intellectual resources can be as important to an entity's success as its physical asset base and infrastructure. The cost and uncertainty of outcomes associated with developing these types of assets from scratch contribute in part to the premiums paid by acquirers of businesses that already have these attributes. Accordingly, there has for some time been a strong link between accounting for intangible assets and accounting for business combinations.

Section 18 – *Intangible Assets other than Goodwill* – addresses the nature, recognition and measurement of intangible assets other than goodwill. It also sets out the disclosure requirements. The accounting for goodwill is addressed in Section 19 – *Business Combinations and Goodwill* (See Chapter 17). Section 18 does not address the impairment of intangible assets, which is dealt with in Section 27 – *Impairment of Assets* (see Chapter 24).

The FRC changed the criteria for recognising intangible assets acquired in a business combination following the Triennial review 2017. As a result, entities will be required to recognise fewer intangible assets acquired in a business combination separately from goodwill. The FRC believes this will reduce the costs of compliance, whilst still providing users with useful information about the business combination. Entities may adopt a policy to separately recognise additional intangible assets acquired in a business combination if this provides useful information to the entity and the users of its financial statements. When an entity chooses to recognise such intangible assets separately from goodwill, it shall apply that policy consistently to the relevant class of intangible assets. These requirements are set out at 3.3.2.A. below.

There are some differences between the accounting for intangible assets under Section 18 compared to IFRS. The key differences are discussed at 2 below.

2   COMPARISON BETWEEN SECTION 18 AND IFRS

2.1   Intangible assets acquired in a business combination

Entities applying FRS 102 are required to recognise fewer intangible assets acquired in a business combination separately from goodwill than under IFRS, although they may voluntarily adopt an accounting policy to separately recognise additional intangible assets in business combinations, provided that this policy is applied consistently to the relevant class of intangible assets.

In business combinations under FRS 102, entities must recognise intangible assets separately from goodwill when all of the following three conditions are satisfied:

(a)   the recognition criteria in paragraph 4 of Section 18 are met (see 3.3 below);

(b)   the intangible asset arises from contractual or other legal rights; and

(c)   the intangible asset is separable. *[FRS 102.18.8]*.

This requirement is more restrictive than IAS 38 – *Intangible Assets* – which requires intangible assets to be recognised separately from goodwill where it is either separable or arises from contractual or other legal rights. *[IAS 38.33]*. However, entities applying FRS 102 can choose to adopt an accounting policy to recognise intangible assets separately from goodwill where the recognition criteria in paragraph 4 of Section 18 are met and only one of conditions (b) or (c) above is met, *[FRS 102.18.8]*, resulting in an approach closer to that required by IAS 38. The requirements of FRS 102 in respect of intangible assets acquired in a business combination are discussed at 3.3.2.A below.

2.2   Indefinite lived intangible assets

Under FRS 102 all intangible assets are considered to have a finite life. *[FRS 102.18.19]*. If an entity cannot make a reliable estimate of the useful life of an intangible asset, the life should not exceed ten years. Section 18 explicitly states that an entity is only expected to be unable to make a reliable estimate of the useful life of an intangible asset 'in exceptional cases'. *[FRS 102.18.20]*.

IAS 38 requires an intangible asset to be regarded as having an indefinite life when there is no foreseeable limit to the period over which the asset is expected to generate net cash inflows for the entity. *[IAS 38.88]*. Intangible assets with indefinite useful lives are not amortised. *[IAS 38.107]*.

2.3   Development costs

Section 18 allows an entity to capitalise expenditure incurred in developing an intangible asset, provided certain criteria are met. *[FRS 102.18.8H]*. Alternatively, an entity may choose to expense development expenditure as incurred. The policy adopted must be applied consistently to all development projects. *[FRS 102.18.8K]*.

IAS 38 does not allow an accounting policy choice as to whether development costs can be capitalised or expensed. An intangible asset arising from the development phase of a project must be capitalised if certain criteria (the same as those in Section 18) are met. *[IAS 38.57]*.

2.4 Advertising and promotional activities

Under FRS 102, promotional stocks, such as catalogues and other promotional material may be recognised as an asset if they meet the definition of inventories held for distribution at no or nominal consideration *[FRS 102.18.8C]* (see Chapter 11 at 3.3.11).

IAS 38 does not allow entities to capitalise expenditure on advertising and promotional activities, including mail order catalogues. *[IAS 38.69(c)]*.

2.5 Intangible assets acquired by way of government grant

Section 18 requires intangible assets acquired by way of a grant to be recorded at fair value at the date the grant is received or receivable. *[FRS 102.18.12]*.

IAS 38, in contrast, permits an accounting policy choice between recognising the intangible asset at fair value or at a nominal amount. *[IAS 38.44, IAS 20.23]*.

2.6 Disclosures

There are some differences between the disclosure requirements of Section 18 and IFRS. These are discussed at 5 below.

3 REQUIREMENTS OF SECTION 18 FOR INTANGIBLE ASSETS OTHER THAN GOODWILL

3.1 Terms used in Section 18

The following terms are used in Section 18 with the meanings specified: *[FRS 102 Appendix I]*

Term	Definition
Active market	A market in which all the following conditions exist: (a) the items traded in the market are homogeneous; (b) willing buyers and sellers can normally be found at any time; and (c) prices are available to the public.
Amortisation	The systematic allocation of the depreciable amount of an asset over its useful life.
Asset	A resource controlled by an entity as a result of past events and from which future economic benefits are expected to flow to the entity.
Class of assets	A grouping of assets of a similar nature and use in an entity's operations.
Depreciable amount	The cost of an asset, or other amount substituted for cost (in the financial statements), less its residual value.
Development	The application of research findings or other knowledge to a plan or design for the production of new or substantially improved materials, devices, products, processes, systems or services before the start of commercial production or use.

Term	*Definition*
Fair value	The amount for which an asset could be exchanged, a liability settled, or an equity instrument granted could be exchanged, between knowledgeable, willing parties in an arm's length transaction. In the absence of any specific guidance provided in the relevant section of FRS 102, the guidance in the Appendix to Section 2 – *Concepts and Pervasive Principles* – shall be used in determining fair value.
Identifiable	An asset is identifiable when: (a) it is separable, i.e. capable of being separated or divided from the entity and sold, transferred, licensed, rented or exchanged, either individually or together with a related contract, asset or liability; or (b) it arises from contractual or other legal rights, regardless of whether those rights are transferable or separable from the entity or from other rights and obligations.
Impairment loss	For assets other than inventories, the amount by which the carrying amount of an asset exceeds its recoverable amount.
Intangible asset	An identifiable non-monetary asset without physical substance.
Inventories held for distribution at no or nominal consideration	Assets that are: (a) held for distribution at no or nominal consideration in the ordinary course of operations; (b) in the process of production for distribution at no or nominal consideration in the ordinary course of operations; or (c) in the form of material or supplies to be consumed in the production process or in the rendering of services at no or nominal consideration.
Monetary items	Units of currency held and assets and liabilities to be received or paid in a fixed or determinable number of units of currency.
Non-exchange transaction	A transaction whereby an entity receives value from another entity without directly giving approximately equal value in exchange, or gives value to another entity without directly receiving approximately equal value in exchange.
Public benefit entity	An entity whose primary objective is to provide goods or services for the general public, community or social benefit and where equity is provided with a view to supporting the entity's primary objectives rather than with a view to providing a financial return to equity providers, shareholders or members.
Research	Original and planned investigation undertaken with the prospect of gaining new scientific or technical knowledge and understanding.
Residual value	The estimated amount that an entity would currently obtain from disposal of an asset, after deducting the estimated costs of disposal, if the asset were already of the age and in the condition expected at the end of its useful life.
Useful life	The period over which an asset is expected to be available for use by an entity or the number of production or similar units expected to be obtained from the asset by an entity.

3.2   Scope and definition

Section 18 applies to all intangible assets, other than the following:

- goodwill (dealt with by Section 19). *[FRS 102.18.1]*. See Chapter 17;
- intangible assets held for sale in the ordinary course of business (dealt with by Section 13 – *Inventories* – and Section 23 – *Revenue*). *[FRS 102.18.1]*. See Chapter 11 and Chapter 20;
- financial assets (dealt with by Section 11 – *Basic Financial Instruments* – and Section 12 – *Other Financial Instruments Issues*). *[FRS 102.18.3(a)]*. See Chapter 10;
- heritage assets (dealt with by Section 34 – *Specialised Activities*). *[FRS 102.18.3(b)]*. See Chapter 31;
- exploration for and evaluation of mineral resources, such as oil, natural gas and similar non-regenerative resources (dealt with by Section 34) and expenditure on the development and extraction of such resources. *[FRS 102.18.3(c)]*. See Chapter 31; and
- deferred acquisition costs and intangible assets arising from contracts in the scope of FRS 103 – *Insurance Contracts*. However, the disclosure requirements of Section 18 apply to intangible assets arising from contracts in the scope of FRS 103. *[FRS 102.18.3(d)]*. See Chapter 34.

FRS 102 defines an intangible asset as 'an identifiable non-monetary asset without physical substance'. *[FRS 102 Appendix I]*. The essential characteristics of intangible assets are therefore that they:

- are identifiable (see 3.2.1 below);
- lack physical substance (see 3.2.2 below);
- are controlled by the entity (see 3.2.3 below); and
- will give rise to future economic benefits for the entity (see 3.2.4 below).

However, in order to determine whether an intangible asset that meets all of these criteria should be recognised, an entity must also consider whether it satisfies the applicable recognition criteria set out within Section 18. The principles for the recognition of intangible assets are discussed at 3.3 below.

3.2.1   Identifiability

An asset is identifiable when it:

(a)   is separable, i.e. capable of being separated or divided from the entity and sold, transferred, licensed, rented or exchanged, either individually or together with a related contract, asset or liability; or

(b)   arises from contractual or other legal rights, regardless of whether those rights are transferable or separable from the entity or from other rights and obligations.
[FRS 102 Appendix I].

Applying this definition means that assets arising from contractual rights alone may meet the definition of an intangible asset under FRS 102. One example of such an asset is a licence that, legally, is not transferable except by sale of the entity as a whole. However, preparers should not restrict their search for intangible assets to those embodied in contractual or other legal rights. Non-contractual rights may also meet the definition of an intangible asset if the right could be sold, transferred, licensed, rented or exchanged.

Chapter 16

3.2.2   Lack of physical substance

The definition of an intangible asset requires that it lacks physical substance. However, intangible assets can be contained in or on a physical medium such as a digital storage device (in the case of computer software), legal documentation (in the case of a licence or patent) or film, requiring an entity to exercise judgement in determining whether to apply Section 18 or Section 17 – *Property, Plant and Equipment.* FRS 102 provides no further guidance on this issue. Where there is no specific guidance within FRS 102, Section 10 – *Accounting Policies, Estimates and Errors* – allows entities to consider the requirements in IFRS in developing an accounting policy. *[FRS 102.10.4-6]*. Entities may therefore choose to look to IFRS for further guidance. IAS 38 provides the following relevant examples: *[IAS 38.4-5]*

- software that is embedded in computer-controlled equipment that cannot operate without it is an integral part of the related hardware and is treated as property, plant and equipment;
- the operating system of a computer is normally integral to the computer and is included in property, plant and equipment;
- software which is not an integral part of the related hardware is treated as an intangible asset; and
- research and development expenditure may result in an asset with physical substance (e.g. a prototype), but as the physical element is secondary to its intangible component, the related knowledge, it is treated as an intangible asset.

It is worthwhile noting that the 'parts approach' in Section 17 requires an entity to account for significant components of an asset separately if they have significantly different patterns of consumption of economic benefits. *[FRS 102.17.6]*. This raises 'boundary' problems between Section 17 and Section 18 when software and similar expenditure is involved. We believe that where Section 17 requires an entity to identify parts of an asset and account for them separately, the entity needs to evaluate whether any intangible-type part is actually integral to the larger asset or whether it is really a separate asset in its own right. The intangible part is more likely to be an asset in its own right if it was developed separately or if it can be used independently of the item of property, plant and equipment of which it apparently forms part.

3.2.3   Control

In the context of intangible assets, control normally results from legal rights, in the way that copyright, a restraint of trade agreement or a legal duty on employees to maintain confidentiality would protect the economic benefits arising from market and technical knowledge. While it will be more difficult to demonstrate control in the absence of legal rights, legal enforceability of a right is not a necessary condition for control. An entity may be able to control the future economic benefits in some other way, for example, through custody. However, determining that this is the case in the absence of observable contractual or other legal rights requires the exercise of judgement based on an understanding of the specific facts and circumstances involved.

For example, an entity usually has insufficient control over the future economic benefits arising from an assembled workforce (i.e. a team of skilled workers, or specific management or technical talent) or from training for these items to meet the definition of an intangible asset. There would have to be other legal rights before control could be demonstrated.

Similarly, an entity would not usually be able to recognise an asset for an assembled portfolio of customers or a market share. In the absence of legal rights to protect or other ways to control the relationships with customers or the loyalty of its customers, the entity usually has insufficient control over the expected economic benefits from these items to meet the definition of an intangible asset.

3.2.4   Future economic benefits

The future economic benefit of an asset is its potential to contribute, directly or indirectly, to the flow of cash and cash equivalents to the entity. Those cash flows may come from using the asset or from disposing of it. *[FRS 102.2.17]*.

Future economic benefits include not only future revenues from the sale of products or services but also cost savings or other benefits resulting from the use of the asset by the entity. For example, the use of intellectual property in a production process may create future economic benefits by reducing future production costs rather than increasing future revenues.

3.3   Recognition and initial measurement of an intangible asset

An item that meets the definition of an intangible asset (see 3.2 above) should be recognised if and only if, at the time of initial recognition of the expenditure: *[FRS 102.18.4]*

(a)   it is probable that the expected future economic benefits that are attributable to the asset will flow to the entity; and

(b)   the cost or value of the asset can be measured reliably.

'Probable' is defined as 'more likely than not'. *[FRS 102 Appendix I]*. In assessing whether expected future economic benefits are probable, the entity should use reasonable and supportable assumptions representing management's best estimate of the set of economic conditions that will exist over the useful life of the asset. *[FRS 102.18.5]*. In making the judgement over the degree of certainty attached to the flow of future economic benefits attributable to the use of the asset, the entity considers the evidence available at the time of initial recognition, giving greater weight to external evidence. *[FRS 102.18.6]*.

The test that the item meets both the definition of an intangible asset and the criteria for recognition is performed at the time of initial recognition of the expenditure. On initial recognition, any intangible asset meeting these criteria should be measured at cost. *[FRS 102.18.9]*. If these criteria are not met at the time the expenditure is incurred, an expense is recognised and it is never reinstated as an asset. *[FRS 102.18.17]*.

The guidance in Section 18 on the recognition and initial measurement of intangible assets takes account of the way in which an entity obtained the asset. Separate rules for recognition and initial measurement apply for intangible assets depending on whether they were:

- acquired separately (see 3.3.1 below);
- acquired as part of a business combination (see 3.3.2 below);
- generated internally (see 3.3.3 below);
- acquired by way of government grant (see 3.3.4 below); or
- obtained in an exchange of assets (see 3.3.5 below).

3.3.1   Separately acquired intangible assets

3.3.1.A   Recognition of separately acquired intangible assets

Separately acquired intangible rights will normally be recognised as assets, provided that they meet the definition of an intangible asset in Section 18.

The criteria for recognising an intangible asset are set out at 3.3 above. The probability recognition criterion in (a) at 3.3 above is always considered satisfied for intangible assets that are separately acquired. *[FRS 102.18.7]*. It is assumed that the price paid to acquire an intangible asset separately usually reflects expectations about the probability that the future economic benefits embodied in it will flow to the entity. In other words, the entity always expects there to be a flow of economic benefits, even if it is uncertain about the timing or amount. In addition, the cost of a separately acquired intangible asset can usually be measured reliably, as required in recognition criterion (b) at 3.3 above, especially in the case of a monetary purchase consideration.

However, not all external costs incurred to secure intangible rights automatically qualify for capitalisation as separately acquired assets, because they do not meet the definition of an intangible asset in the first place. An entity that subcontracts the development of intangible assets (e.g. development-and-supply contracts or R&D contracts) to other parties (its suppliers) must exercise judgement in determining whether it is acquiring an intangible asset or whether it is obtaining goods and services that are being used in the development of an intangible asset by the entity itself. For example, if the entity pays a supplier upfront or by milestone payments during the course of a project, it will not necessarily recognise an intangible asset on the basis of those payments. Only those costs that are incurred after it becomes probable that economic benefits are expected to flow to the entity will be part of the cost of an intangible asset. If a supplier is working on an internal project for the entity, costs can only be capitalised after the criteria have been met for recognising an internally developed intangible asset (see 3.3.3 below).

In determining whether a supplier is providing services to develop an internally generated intangible asset, it can be useful to consider the terms of the supply agreement, in particular whether the supplier is bearing a significant proportion of the risks associated with a failure of the project. For example, if the supplier is always compensated under a development-and-supply contract for development services and tool costs irrespective of the project's outcome, the entity on whose behalf the development is undertaken should account for those activities as its own.

3.3.1.B   Initial measurement of separately acquired intangible assets

The cost of a separately acquired intangible asset comprises:

(a)   its purchase price, including import duties and non-refundable purchase taxes, after deducting trade discounts and rebates; and

(b)   any directly attributable cost of preparing the asset for its intended use. *[FRS 102.18.10]*.

Section 18 does not elaborate on what costs may be directly attributable to preparing a separately acquired intangible asset for its intended use. Examples may include:

- costs of employee benefits arising directly from bringing the asset to its working condition;
- professional fees arising directly from bringing the asset to its working condition; and
- costs of testing whether the asset is functioning properly.

Capitalisation of expenditure should cease when the asset is in the condition necessary for it to be capable of operating in the manner intended by management. This may well be before the date on which it is brought into use.

3.3.2   Intangible assets acquired as part of a business combination

3.3.2.A   Recognition of intangible assets acquired as part of a business combination

The FRC modified the criteria for recognising intangible assets acquired in a business combination following the Triennial review 2017. These changes are mandatory for accounting periods beginning on or after 1 January 2019, with early adoption allowed provided that all of the amendments to FRS 102 are applied at the same time (with exceptions for certain amendments relating to financial instruments and income tax) and that this fact is disclosed. *[FRS 102.1.18]*. These changes are applied prospectively, i.e. without restating comparative information, and therefore an entity should not subsume intangible assets that previously have been separately recognised within goodwill. *[FRS 102.1.19]*.

Intangible assets that are acquired in a business combination must be recognised separately from goodwill when all of the following three conditions are met:

(a)   the recognition criteria in paragraph 4 of Section 18 are met (see 3.3 above);

(b)   the intangible asset arises from contractual or other legal rights; and

(c)   the intangible asset is separable (i.e. capable of being separated or divided from the entity and sold, transferred, licenced, rented or exchanged either individually or together with a related contract, asset or liability). *[FRS 102.18.8]*.

In addition, an entity can choose to recognise intangible assets separately from goodwill for which the recognition criteria in paragraph 4 of Section 18 are satisfied and only one of condition (b) or (c) above is met. *[FRS 102.18.8]*.

Where an entity chooses to recognise such additional intangible assets, this policy must be applied to all intangible assets in the same class (i.e. having a similar nature, function or use in the business), and must be applied consistently to all business combinations. Section 18 adds that licences are an example of a category of intangible asset that may be treated as a separate class, however, further subdivision may be appropriate, for example, where different types of licences have different functions within the business. *[FRS 102.18.8]*. When this accounting policy choice is adopted, the acquirer is required to disclose the nature of those additional intangible assets and to explain why they have been separated from goodwill. *[FRS 102.18.28A]*.

The previous version of Section 18 defined intangible assets as separable *or* arising from contractual or other legal rights, with the only restriction being to prohibit the recognition of intangible assets that are acquired in a business combination and arise from legal or other contractual rights where there is no history or evidence of exchange transactions for the same or similar assets, and otherwise estimating fair value would be dependent on

Chapter 16

immeasurable variables. By requiring the recognition in a business combination of intangible assets that meet the general recognition criteria and are *both* separable *and* arising from contractual or other legal rights, the amended version of the Standard requires fewer intangible assets to be recognised separately from goodwill. However, as noted above, these new requirements must be applied prospectively (i.e. an entity should not restate comparative information), and therefore an entity should not subsume intangible assets that previously have been separately recognised within goodwill. *[FRS 102.1.19]*.

It follows that where an entity chooses to adopt a policy of recognising additional intangible assets separately from goodwill (where the recognition criteria in paragraph 4 of Section 18 are satisfied and only one of conditions (b) or (c) above is met *[FRS 102.18.8]*), comparatives are not restated to separate from goodwill those intangible assets arising from legal or other contractual rights that had not been recognised due to the restriction in the previous version of the Standard. *[FRS 102.1.19]*.

If an intangible asset is acquired in a business combination, the cost of that intangible asset is its fair value at the acquisition date. *[FRS 102.18.11]*. As the fair value of an intangible asset should reflect expectations about the probability that the future economic benefits embodied in it will flow to the entity, the probability criterion is always assumed to be satisfied for intangible assets acquired as part of a business combination. In other words, the existence of a fair value means that an inflow of economic benefits is considered to be probable, in spite of any uncertainties about timing or amount.

In making its amendments to Section 18, the FRC considered requests for further guidance on which intangible assets are expected to meet the criteria for separate recognition in a business combination. The analysis of technical issues in Part B of the Basis for Conclusions provides examples of intangible assets that would normally satisfy all three criteria for recognition noted above. These include licences, copyrights, trademarks, internet domain names, patented technology and legally protected trade secrets. Examples of intangible assets that would not normally satisfy all three criteria include customer lists, customer relationships and unprotected trade secrets (such as recipes or formulae), as no contractual or legal right exists that would give rise to expected future economic benefits. *[FRS 102.BC.B18.10]*.

The separability criterion of Section 18 requires an acquired intangible asset to be *capable* of being separated or divided from the acquiree. *[FRS 102.18.8(c)]*. This is regardless of the intentions of the acquirer. An intangible asset that is not individually separable from the acquiree or combined entity can still be recognised separately from goodwill if it could be separable in combination with a related contract, identifiable asset or liability. *[FRS 102.18.8(c)]*. For example an acquiree owns a registered trademark and documented but unpatented technical expertise used to manufacture the trademarked product. The entity could not transfer ownership of the trademark without everything else necessary for the new owner to produce an identical product or service. Because the unpatented technical expertise must be transferred if the related trademark is sold, it is separable. In this example, the asset is separable but not contractual, such that the unpatented technical expertise would only be recognised separately from goodwill under FRS 102 where the acquirer applies a policy of recognising intangible assets separately from goodwill for which the recognition criteria in paragraph 4 of Section 18 are satisfied and only one of the conditions (b) or (c) above are met.

The process of identifying intangible assets in a business combination might involve, for example:

- determining whether the entity has chosen to recognise additional intangible assets, or to restrict recognition only to those that meet all three recognition criteria noted above;

- reviewing the list of items that the FRC believes would usually meet the recognition criteria for an intangible asset referred to above;

- examining documents such as those related to the acquisition, other internal documents produced by the entity, public filings, press releases, analysts' reports, and other externally available documents; and

- comparing the acquired business to similar businesses and their intangible assets.

Intangible assets differ considerably between industries and between individual entities. Therefore, considerable expertise and careful judgement is required in determining whether there are intangible assets that need to be recognised and valued separately.

3.3.2.B   *Initial measurement of intangible assets acquired as part of a business combination*

The cost of an intangible asset acquired in a business combination is its fair value at the acquisition date. *[FRS 102.18.11]*. Section 18 provides no specific guidance on how to determine the fair value of intangible assets acquired in a business combination. Therefore the guidance in the Appendix to Section 2 – *Concepts and Pervasive Principles* – should be used. *[FRS 102 Appendix I]*. The Appendix to Section 2 requires fair value to be determined using the following methodology:

(a)   the best evidence of fair value is a quoted price for an identical asset (or similar asset) in an active market. This is usually the current bid price.

(b)   when quoted prices are unavailable, the price in a binding sale agreement or a recent transaction for an identical asset (or similar asset) in an arm's length transaction between knowledgeable, willing parties provides evidence of fair value. However, this price may not be a good estimate of fair value if there has been a significant change in economic circumstances or a significant period of time between the date of the binding sale agreement or the transaction, and the measurement date. If the entity can demonstrate that the last transaction price is not a good estimate of fair value (e.g. because it reflects the amount than an entity would receive or pay in a forced transaction, involuntary liquidation or distress sale), that price is adjusted.

(c)   if the market for the asset is not active and any binding sale agreements or recent transactions for an identical asset (or similar asset) on their own are not a good estimate of fair value, an entity estimates the fair value by using another valuation technique. The objective of using another valuation technique is to estimate what the transaction price would have been on the measurement date in an arm's length exchange motivated by normal business considerations. *[FRS 102.2A.1]*.

Some intangible assets may be traded in an active market, for example certain licenses, such as taxi licenses. However, the unique nature of many intangible assets means that they are unlikely to have a quoted market price. Similarly, there are unlikely to be recent transactions in identical assets. Therefore fair value will most frequently be determined using valuation techniques. The objective of using a valuation technique is to estimate what the transaction price would have been on the measurement date in an arm's length exchange motivated by normal business considerations. The valuation technique used should make maximum use of market inputs and rely as little as possible on entity-determined inputs. *[FRS 102.2A.3]*. If there is a valuation technique commonly used by market participants to price the asset and that has been demonstrated to provide reliable estimates of prices obtained in actual market transactions, the entity should use that technique. *[FRS 102.2A.2]*.

In practice there are three broad approaches to valuing intangible assets:

(a)   the market approach, which determines fair value based on observable market prices and comparable market transactions;

(b)   the cost approach, the premise of which is that an investor would pay no more for an intangible asset than the cost to recreate it; and

(c)   the income approach, which involves identifying the expected cash flows or economic benefits to be derived from the ownership of the particular intangible asset.

The recognition and initial measurement requirements for intangible assets acquired in a business combination are discussed further in Chapter 17 at 6.3.

3.3.3   Internally generated intangible assets

It may be difficult to decide whether an internally generated intangible asset qualifies for recognition because of problems in:

(a)   confirming whether and when there is an identifiable asset that will generate expected future economic benefits; and

(b)   determining the cost of the asset reliably, especially in cases where the cost of generating an intangible asset internally cannot be distinguished from the cost of maintaining or enhancing the entity's internally generated goodwill or of running day-to-day operations.

To avoid the inappropriate recognition of an asset, Section 18 requires that internally generated intangible assets are not only tested against the general requirements for recognition and initial measurement (discussed at 3.2 above), but also meet criteria which confirm that the related activity or project is at a sufficiently advanced stage of development, is both technically and commercially viable and includes only directly attributable costs. Those criteria comprise guidance on accounting for intangible assets in the research phase (see 3.3.3.A below), the development phase (see 3.3.3.B below) and on measurement of an internally generated intangible asset (see 3.3.3.C below).

To assess whether an internally generated asset meets the criteria for recognition, an entity classifies the generation of the asset into a research phase and a development phase. *[FRS 102.18.8A]*. If an entity cannot distinguish the research phase from the development phase, then all expenditure is treated as research and is recognised as an expense when it is incurred. *[FRS 102.18.8B, 18.8E]*.

3.3.3.A   Research

Section 18 gives the following examples of research activities: *[FRS 102.18.8G]*

(a)   activities aimed at obtaining new knowledge;

(b)   the search for, evaluation and final selection of, applications of research findings and other knowledge;

(c)   the search for alternatives for materials, devices, products, processes, systems or services; and

(d)   the formulation, design, evaluation and final selection of possible alternatives for new or improved material, devices, projects, processes, systems or services.

An entity cannot recognise an intangible asset arising from research or from the research phase of an internal project. Instead, any expenditure on research or the research phase of an internal project should be expensed as incurred. *[FRS 102.18.8E]*. In the research phase of an internal project the entity cannot demonstrate that there is an intangible asset that will generate probable future economic benefits. *[FRS 102.18.8F]*.

If an entity cannot distinguish the research phase from the development phase, it should treat the expenditure on that project as if it were incurred in the research phase only and recognise an expense accordingly. *[FRS 102.18.8B]*.

3.3.3.B   Development

Section 18 gives the following examples of development activities: *[FRS 102.18.8J]*

(a)   the design, construction and testing of pre-production or pre-use prototypes and models;

(b)   the design of tools, jigs, moulds and dies involving new technology;

(c)   the design, construction and operation of a pilot plant that is not of a scale economically feasible for commercial production; and

(d)   the design, construction and testing of a chosen alternative for new or improved materials, devices, products, processes, systems or services.

In the development phase of an internal project, an entity can, in some instances, identify an intangible asset and demonstrate that the asset will generate probable future economic benefits. This is because the development phase of a project is further advanced than the research phase. *[FRS 102.18.8I]*.

Entities have an accounting policy choice whether or not to capitalise qualifying development expenditure. Entities may either recognise an internally generated intangible asset arising from the development phase of a project (provided that specific recognition criteria are met, see below) or recognise the expenditure in profit or loss as incurred. Where an entity adopts a policy of capitalising expenditure in the development phase, the policy should be applied consistently to all expenditure that meets the recognition criteria set out in Section 18. Expenditure that does not meet the conditions for capitalisation must be expensed as incurred. *[FRS 102.18.8K]*.

Chapter 16

An intangible asset arising from development may be recognised if, and only if, the entity can demonstrate all of the following: *[FRS 102.18.8H]*

(a)   the technical feasibility of completing the intangible asset so that it will be available for use or sale;

(b)   its intention to complete the intangible asset and use or sell it;

(c)   its ability to use or sell the intangible asset;

(d)   how the intangible asset will generate probable future economic benefits. Among other things, the entity can demonstrate the existence of a market for the output of the intangible asset or the intangible asset itself or, if it is to be used internally, the usefulness of the intangible asset;

(e)   the availability of adequate technical, financial and other resources to complete the development and to use or sell the intangible asset; and

(f)   its ability to measure reliably the expenditure attributable to the intangible asset during its development.

It may be challenging to demonstrate each of the above conditions because:

- condition (b) relies on management intent; and

- conditions (c), (e) and (f) are entity-specific, i.e. whether development expenditure meets any of these conditions depends both on the nature of the development activity itself and the financial position of the entity.

Evidence may be available in the form of:

- a business plan showing the technical, financial and other resources needed and the entity's ability to secure those resources;

- a lender's indication of its willingness to fund the plan confirming the availability of external finance; and

- detailed project information demonstrating that an entity's costing systems can measure reliably the cost of generating an intangible asset internally, such as salary and other expenditure incurred in securing copyrights or licences or developing computer software.

In any case, an entity should maintain books and records in sufficient detail that allow it to prove whether it meets the conditions set out in (a) to (f) above. Certain types of product (e.g. pharmaceuticals, aircraft and electrical equipment) require regulatory approval before they can be sold. Regulatory approval is not one of the criteria for recognition and therefore entities are not prohibited from capitalising development costs in advance of approval. However, in some industries regulatory approval is vital to commercial success and its absence indicates significant uncertainty around the possible future economic benefits. This is the case in the pharmaceuticals industry, where it is rarely possible to determine whether a new drug will secure regulatory approval until it is actually granted. Accordingly it is common practice in this industry for costs to be expensed until such approval is obtained.

3.3.3.C   Measurement of internally generated intangible assets

The cost of an internally generated intangible asset is the sum of the expenditure incurred from the date when the intangible asset first meets the recognition criteria in Section 18 set out at 3.3 above and the conditions for capitalising development costs set out at 3.3.3.B above. *[FRS 102.18.10A]*.

Costs incurred before these criteria are met are expensed and cannot be reinstated retrospectively. *[FRS 102.18.17]*.

The cost of an internally generated intangible asset comprises all directly attributable costs necessary to create, produce, and prepare the asset to be capable of operating in the manner intended by management. Examples of directly attributable costs are: *[FRS 102.18.10B]*

(a)   costs of materials and services used or consumed in generating the intangible asset;

(b)   costs of employee benefits arising from the generation of the intangible asset;

(c)   fees to register a legal right; and

(d)   amortisation of patents and licences that are used to generate the intangible asset.

Borrowing costs eligible for capitalisation under Section 25 – *Borrowing Costs* – may be recognised as an element of the cost of an internally generated intangible asset, provided the entity adopts an accounting policy of capitalising eligible borrowing costs. See Chapter 22.

Indirect costs and general overheads, even if they can be allocated on a reasonable and consistent basis to the development project, should not be recognised as part of the cost of any intangible asset.

3.3.3.D   Expenditure that does not qualify for recognition as an internally generated intangible asset

Expenditure on the following items must be recognised as an expense and should not be recognised as intangible assets: *[FRS 102.18.8C]*

(a)   internally generated brands, logos, publishing titles, customer lists and items similar in substance;

(b)   start-up activities (i.e. start-up costs), which include establishment costs such as legal and secretarial costs incurred in establishing a legal entity, expenditure to open a new facility or business (i.e. pre-opening costs) and expenditure for starting new operations or launching new products or processes (i.e. pre-operating costs);

(c)   training activities;

(d)   advertising and promotional activities (unless it meets the definition of inventories held for distribution at no or nominal consideration. See 3.3.3.E below);

(e)   relocating or reorganising part or all of an entity; and

(f)   internally generated goodwill.

For these purposes no distinction is made between costs that are incurred directly by the entity and those that relate to services provided by third parties. However, Section 18 does not prevent an entity from recording a prepayment as an asset if it pays for the delivery of goods before obtaining a right to access those goods. Similarly, a prepayment can be recognised when payment is made before services are received. *[FRS 102.18.8D]*.

3.3.3.E   *Advertising and promotional expenditure*

As set out at 3.3.3.D above, FRS 102 generally requires expenditure on advertising and promotional activities to be recognised as an expense as incurred. However, Section 18 gives an exception for advertising and promotional activities that meet the definition of inventories held for distribution at no or nominal consideration. *[FRS 102.18.8C(d)].*

Items covered by this definition may include stocks of brochures and other marketing material. Advertising and promotional expenditure that meets the definition of inventories held for distribution at no or nominal consideration should be included within inventories. This is discussed further in Chapter 11 at 3.3.11.

3.3.4   *Intangible assets acquired by way of a grant*

An intangible asset may sometimes be acquired free of charge, or for nominal consideration, by way of a government grant. Governments frequently allocate airport-landing rights, licences to operate radio or television stations, emission rights, import licences or quotas, or rights to access other restricted resources.

Section 18 does not set out any separate recognition criteria for intangible assets acquired by way of a grant. The recognition criteria for government grants are set out in Section 24 – *Government Grants* (see Chapter 21).

The cost of an intangible asset acquired by way of a grant is its fair value at the date the grant is received or receivable in accordance with Section 24 in respect of government grants or, for public benefit entities, Section 34 (see Chapter 32) in respect of incoming resources from non-exchange transactions. *[FRS 102.18.12].* Some permits allocated by government, such as milk quotas, are freely traded and therefore have a readily ascertainable fair value. However, it may be difficult to reliably measure the fair value of every kind of permit allocated by governments because they may have been allocated for nil consideration, may not be transferable and may only be bought and sold as part of a business. Despite this, FRS 102 does not permit entities to recognise intangible assets acquired by way of government grant at a nominal value.

3.3.5   *Exchanges of assets*

An entity might swap certain intangible assets that it does not require or is no longer allowed to use for those of a counterparty that has other surplus assets. For example, it is not uncommon for airlines and media groups to exchange landing slots and newspaper titles, respectively, to meet demands of competition authorities.

Section 18 requires intangible assets acquired in exchange for non-monetary assets, or a combination of monetary and non-monetary assets, to be measured at fair value unless: *[FRS 102.18.13]*

(a)   the exchange transaction lacks commercial substance; or

(b)   the fair value of neither the asset received nor the asset given up is reliably measurable.

If the fair value of neither the asset received, nor the asset given up, can be measured reliably the acquired intangible asset is measured at the carrying amount of the asset given up. *[FRS 102.18.13(b)].*

The acquired intangible asset should also be measured at the carrying amount of the asset given up if the exchange transaction lacks commercial substance. This is because it would not be appropriate to recognise a gain or loss on a transaction that lacks commercial substance. FRS 102 provides no guidance to assist entities in assessing whether a transaction has commercial substance. Under IFRS, IAS 38 requires that an entity determines whether an exchange transaction has commercial substance by considering the extent to which its future cash flows are expected to change as a result of the transaction. *[IAS 38.46]*. A similar assessment may need to be made under Section 18. In some cases, the assessment may be clear without an entity having to perform detailed calculations.

3.4   Subsequent measurement

Section 18 permits an entity to choose between two alternative treatments for the subsequent measurement of intangible assets: *[FRS 102.18.18]*

- the cost model; or
- the revaluation model.

When the revaluation model is selected, it must be applied to all intangible assets in the same class of asset. If an intangible asset in a class of revalued intangible assets cannot be revalued because there is no active market for this asset, the asset is carried at its cost less any accumulated amortisation and impairment losses. *[FRS 102.18.18]*. A class of assets is a grouping of assets of a similar nature and use in an entity's operations. *[FRS 102 Appendix I]*. Examples of separate classes of intangible asset may include:

(a)   brand names;

(b)   mastheads and publishing titles;

(c)   computer software;

(d)   licences and franchises;

(e)   copyrights, patents and other industrial property rights, service and operating rights;

(f)   recipes, formulae, models, designs and prototypes; and

(g)   intangible assets under development.

3.4.1   Cost model for measurement of intangible assets

Under the cost model, an entity should measure its intangible assets at cost less accumulated amortisation and any accumulated impairment losses. *[FRS 102.18.18A]*. The rules on amortisation of intangible assets are discussed at 3.4.3 below and impairment is discussed at 3.4.5 below.

3.4.2   Revaluation model for measurement of intangible assets

The revaluation model is only available if there is an active market for the intangible asset. *[FRS 102.18.18B]*. This will only rarely be the case (see 3.4.2.A below). Accordingly, Section 18 does not allow fair value to be determined indirectly, for example by using the same valuation techniques applied to estimate the fair value of intangible assets acquired in a business combination.

After initial recognition an intangible asset should be carried at a revalued amount, which is its fair value at the date of the revaluation less any subsequent accumulated amortisation and subsequent accumulated impairment losses. *[FRS 102.18.18B]*. To prevent an entity from circumventing the recognition rules of Section 18, the revaluation model does not allow: *[FRS 102.18.18C]*

- the revaluation of intangible assets that have not previously been recognised as assets; or
- the initial recognition of intangible assets at amounts other than cost.

These rules are designed to prevent an entity from recognising at a 'revalued' amount an intangible asset that was never recorded because its costs were expensed as they did not, at the time, meet the recognition criteria. Section 18 does not permit recognition of past expenses as an intangible asset at a later date. *[FRS 102.18.17]*.

However, an entity is permitted to apply the revaluation model to the whole of an intangible asset even if only part of its cost was originally recognised as an asset because it did not meet the criteria for recognition until part of the way through the development process. *[FRS 102.18.18F]*.

Where the revaluation model is applied, assets in the same class should be revalued at the same time. To do otherwise would allow selective revaluation of assets and the reporting of a mixture of costs and values as at different dates within the same asset class.

3.4.2.A   Revaluation is allowed only if there is an active market

An entity can only elect to apply the revaluation model if the fair value can be determined by reference to an active market for the intangible asset. *[FRS 102.18.18B]*. An active market is a market in which all the following conditions exist: *[FRS 102 Appendix I]*

(a)   the items traded in the market are homogeneous;

(b)   willing buyers and sellers can normally be found at any time; and

(c)   prices are available to the public.

Few intangible assets will be eligible for revaluation as such an active market would be uncommon. By their very nature most intangible assets are unique or entity-specific. Intangible assets such as brands, newspaper mastheads, music and film publishing rights, patents or trademarks are ineligible for revaluation because each such asset is unique. The existence of a previous sale and purchase transaction is not sufficient evidence for the market to be regarded as active because of the requirement in the definition for a sufficient frequency and volume of transactions to allow the provision of ongoing pricing information. In addition, if prices are not available to the public, this is evidence that an active market does not exist.

If an intangible asset in a class of revalued intangible assets cannot be revalued because there is no active market for that particular asset, the asset should be carried at its cost less any accumulated amortisation and impairment losses. *[FRS 102.18.18]*.

If the fair value of a previously revalued intangible asset can no longer be determined by reference to an active market, the valuation is 'frozen' at the date of the last revaluation by reference to the active market. The carrying amount of the asset is reduced thereafter by subsequent accumulated amortisation and any subsequent accumulated impairment losses. *[FRS 102.18.18E]*.

3.4.2.B   *Frequency of revaluations*

If there is an active market, Section 18 requires revaluation to be performed 'with sufficient regularity to ensure that the carrying amount does not differ materially from that which would be determined using fair value at the end of the reporting period'. *[FRS 102.18.18D]*. Section 18 lets entities judge for themselves the frequency of revaluations depending on the volatility of the fair values of the underlying intangible assets. Significant and volatile movements in quoted prices may necessitate annual revaluation, whereas a less frequent update would be required for intangibles whose price is subject only to insignificant movements. Nevertheless, since an entity can only revalue assets for which a price is quoted in an active market, there should be no impediment to updating that valuation at each reporting date. As noted at 3.4.2 above, where the revaluation model is applied, assets in the same class should be revalued at the same time.

3.4.2.C   *Accounting for gains and losses on revaluations*

Increases in an intangible asset's carrying amount as a result of a revaluation should be recognised in other comprehensive income and accumulated in equity, except to the extent that the revaluation reverses previous revaluation decreases of the same asset that were recognised in profit or loss. In this case, the increases should be recognised in profit or loss. *[FRS 102.18.18G]*. Conversely, decreases in an intangible asset's carrying amount as a result of a revaluation should be recognised in other comprehensive income to the extent of any previous revaluation increases of the same asset that are accumulated in equity. Any excess revaluation loss should be recognised in profit or loss. *[FRS 102.18.18H]*.

For UK entities, the Regulations require that revaluation surpluses, net of provisions for amortisation or impairment, must be shown in the balance sheet within a separate reserve (the revaluation reserve) and not within retained earnings. *[1 Sch 35]*.

3.4.3   *Amortisation of intangible assets*

After initial recognition, Section 18 requires an entity to allocate the depreciable amount of an intangible asset on a systematic basis over its useful life. *[FRS 102.18.21]*. Depreciable amount is the cost, or other amount substituted for cost, of the intangible asset, less its residual value. *[FRS 102 Appendix I]*. The amortisation charge for each period depends on the useful life of the intangible asset, the amortisation method applied and the residual value of the intangible asset. These factors are discussed at 3.4.3.A, B and C below.

The amortisation charge for each period should be recognised in profit or loss, unless another section of FRS 102 requires the cost to be recognised as part of the cost of an asset. For example, the amortisation of an intangible asset may be included in the costs of inventories or property, plant and equipment. *[FRS 102.18.21]*.

Amortisation must be charged on all intangible assets. This requirement applies even to intangible assets measured under the revaluation model. For guidance on depreciation of revalued assets see Chapter 15 at 3.6.3.A.

3.4.3.A   Assessing the useful life of an intangible asset

The useful life of an intangible asset is: *[FRS 102 Appendix I]*

(a)   the period over which an asset is expected to be available for use by an entity; or

(b)   the number of production or similar units expected to be obtained from the asset by an entity.

Thus, if appropriate, the useful life of an intangible asset should be expressed as a number of production or similar units rather than a period of time.

For the purposes of FRS 102, all intangible assets including those under the revaluation model, should be considered to have a finite useful life. *[FRS 102.18.19]*.

Where an intangible asset arises from contractual or other legal rights, its useful life is the shorter of:

•   the period of the contractual or other legal rights; and

•   the period over which the entity expects to use the asset. *[FRS 102.18.19]*.

If the contractual or other legal rights can be renewed, the useful life of the intangible asset should include the renewal period only if there is evidence to support renewal by the entity without significant cost. *[FRS 102.18.19]*. An entity needs to exercise judgement in assessing what it regards as a significant cost. The following factors may indicate that an entity is able to renew the contractual or other legal rights without significant cost:

(a)   there is evidence, possibly based on experience, that the contractual or other legal rights will be renewed. If renewal is contingent upon the consent of a third party, this includes evidence that the third party will give its consent;

(b)   there is evidence that any conditions necessary to obtain renewal will be satisfied; and

(c)   the cost to the entity of renewal is not significant when compared with the future economic benefits expected to flow to the entity from renewal.

If there is no evidence to support renewal of the contractual or legal rights by the entity without significant cost, then the useful life of the intangible asset must not include the renewal period. In this case, the original asset's useful life ends at the contractual renewal date. If the rights are then renewed at the renewal date, we would expect the renewal cost to be treated as the cost to acquire a new intangible asset.

In our view, a number of factors may be considered in estimating the useful life of an intangible asset, including:

(a)   the expected usage of the asset by the entity and whether the asset could be managed efficiently by another management team;

(b)   typical product life cycles for the asset and public information on estimates of useful lives of similar assets that are used in a similar way;

(c)   technical, technological, commercial or other types of obsolescence;

(d)   the stability of the industry in which the asset operates and changes in the market demand for the products or services output from the asset;

(e)   expected actions by competitors or potential competitors;

(f)   the level of maintenance expenditure required to obtain the expected future economic benefits from the asset and the entity's ability and intention to reach such a level;

(g)   the period of control over the asset and legal or similar limits on the use of the asset, such as the expiry dates of related leases; and

(h)   whether the useful life of the asset is dependent on the useful life of other assets of the entity.

If an entity is unable to make a reliable estimate of the useful life of an intangible asset, the life should not exceed ten years. *[FRS 102.18.20]*. However, this should not be considered an automatic default. Entities should not underestimate the useful life of an intangible asset on the basis of this requirement. Similarly, it should not be used to justify a useful life of ten years for an intangible asset for which a shorter useful life may be appropriate. Section 18 explicitly states that an entity is only expected to be unable to make a reliable estimate of the useful life of an intangible asset 'in exceptional cases'. *[FRS 102.18.20]*.

3.4.3.B   Amortisation method

An entity should choose an amortisation method that reflects the pattern in which it expects to consume the asset's future economic benefits. If the entity cannot determine that pattern reliably, it should use the straight-line method. *[FRS 102.18.22]*. A variety of amortisation methods may be used to depreciate an intangible asset on a systematic basis over its useful life. The straight-line method is most commonly seen in practice. The unit of production method or reducing balance method are also sometimes seen. Whilst an amortisation method based on estimated total output (a unit of production method) may be appropriate, an amortisation method based on the pattern of expected revenues is not. This is because a revenue-based method reflects a pattern of generation of economic benefits from operating the business (of which the asset is a part), rather than the consumption of the economic benefits embodied in the asset itself. The difference is more obvious when unit prices are expected to increase over time.

Amortisation should begin when the intangible asset is available for use, i.e. when it is in the location and condition necessary for it to be usable in the manner intended by management. Therefore, even if an entity is not using the asset, it should still be amortised if it is available for use. Amortisation should cease when the asset is derecognised. (See 3.4.6 below). *[FRS 102.18.22]*.

3.4.3.C   Residual value

Section 18 requires entities to assume a residual value of zero for an intangible asset, unless there is a commitment by a third party to purchase the asset at the end of its useful life or there is an active market for the asset from which to determine its residual value and it is probable that such a market will exist at the end of the asset's useful life. *[FRS 102.18.23]*.

Given the definition of 'active market' (see 3.4.2.A above) it seems highly unlikely that – in the absence of a commitment by a third party to buy the asset – an entity will ever be able to prove that the residual value of an intangible asset is other than zero.

3.4.3.D   *Amortisation of intangible assets with a residual value*

The Note on Legal Requirements to FRS 102 provides guidance on the amortisation of intangible assets which have a residual value. When an intangible asset has a residual value, it is the depreciable amount that is amortised. *[FRS 102 Appendix III.37A].* See 3.4.3 above. As noted at 3.4.3.C above, the FRC believes that it is uncommon for an intangible asset to have a residual value and FRS 102 requires an entity to assume that the residual value is zero unless there is a commitment by a third party to purchase the asset at the end of its useful life or there is an active market for the asset from which to determine its residual value and it is probable that such a market will exist at the end of the asset's useful life. *[FRS 102.18.23].*

However, in those cases where an intangible asset does have a residual value that is not zero, the amortisation of the depreciable amount of the asset over its useful economic life is a departure from the requirements of paragraph 22 of Schedule 1 to the Regulations (and its equivalents in Schedules 2 and 3 to the Regulations and to the LLP Regulations respectively) since the regulations require intangible assets to be written off over their useful economic lives. In those circumstances, the FRC states that entities must invoke a true and fair override and make the disclosures required by paragraph 10(2) of Schedule 1 to the Regulations for the use of a true and fair override. *[FRS 102 Appendix III.37A].*

3.4.3.E   *Review of amortisation period and amortisation method*

Factors such as a change in how an intangible asset is used, technological advancement, or changes in market prices may indicate that the residual value or useful life of an intangible asset has changed since the most recent annual reporting date. If such indicators are present, management should review previous estimates and, if current expectations differ, amend the residual value, amortisation method or useful life to reflect current expectations. *[FRS 102.18.24].*

Changes in residual value, amortisation method or useful life should be accounted for prospectively as a change in accounting estimate in accordance with Section 10 of FRS 102. *[FRS 102.18.24].*

If the residual value of an intangible asset increases to an amount greater than the asset's carrying amount, the asset's amortisation charge would be zero until its residual value decreases to an amount below the asset's carrying amount.

3.4.4   *Subsequent expenditure*

Entities may sometimes incur expenditure on an acquired intangible asset after its initial recognition or on an internally generated intangible asset after its completion.

Section 18 provides no separate rules on the recognition of subsequent expenditure on intangible assets. Instead, subsequent expenditure that meets the general recognition criteria for intangible assets, discussed at 3.3 above, may be recognised as an addition to an intangible asset. In practice, it is expected that most subsequent expenditure on intangible assets will maintain the expected future economic benefits embodied in the existing intangible asset and will not satisfy the recognition criteria in Section 18. Therefore only rarely would we expect subsequent expenditure to be recognised in the carrying amount of an asset.

3.4.5   Impairment losses

Entities should refer to the requirements of Section 27 to determine whether an intangible asset is impaired. *[FRS 102.18.25]*. See Chapter 24.

Section 27 requires entities to assess at each reporting date whether these is any indication that an intangible asset may be impaired. If there are indicators of impairment, the entity must estimate the recoverable amount of the intangible asset. *[FRS 102.27.7]*. Section 27 explains how the entity should do this and when it should recognise or reverse an impairment loss. *[FRS 102.18.25]*.

If there are indicators that an intangible asset is impaired, this could indicate that the entity should review the remaining useful life, amortisation method or residual value of the intangible asset, even if no impairment loss is recognised for the asset. *[FRS 102.27.10]*.

3.4.6   Retirements and disposals

An intangible asset should be derecognised on disposal or when no future economic benefits are expected from its use or disposal. *[FRS 102.18.26]*.

The gain or loss on derecognition, being the difference between the net disposal proceeds and the carrying amount of the asset, *[FRS 102.2.52(b)]*, should be accounted for in profit or loss. *[FRS 102.18.26]*. This means that any revaluation surplus relating to the asset disposed of is transferred directly to retained earnings and not reflected in profit or loss.

3.5   Presentation and disclosure

The main requirements of Section 18 are set out below, but it may be necessary to refer also to the disclosure requirements of Section 27 in the event of an impairment of an intangible asset (see Chapter 24).

3.5.1   Presentation of intangible assets

Entities are required by Schedule 1 of the Regulations to present a separate heading for intangible assets on the face of the balance sheet. Intangible assets should be analysed into the following sub-headings, either on the face of the balance sheet, or within the notes to the accounts:

- development costs;
- concessions, patents, licenses, trade-marks and similar rights and assets;
- goodwill; and
- payments on account.

However, company law permits all entities to adapt the subheadings set out above to suit the nature of the entity's business. *[1 Sch 4(1)]*.

3.5.2   General disclosures

Section 18 requires certain disclosures to be presented by class of intangible assets.

The following must be disclosed for each class of intangible assets: *[FRS 102.18.27]*

(a) the useful lives or the amortisation rates used and the reasons for choosing those periods;

(b) the amortisation methods used;

Chapter 16

(c)   the gross carrying amount and any accumulated amortisation (aggregated with accumulated impairment losses) at the beginning and end of the period;

(d)   the line item(s) of the statement of comprehensive income (or the income statement, if presented) in which any amortisation of intangible assets is included; and

(e)   a reconciliation of the carrying amount at the beginning and end of the reporting period showing separately:

   (i)   additions, indicating separately those from internal development and those acquired separately;

   (ii)   disposals;

   (iii)   acquisitions through business combinations;

   (iv)   revaluations;

   (v)   amortisation;

   (vi)   impairment losses; and

   (vii) other changes.

The reconciliation in (e) above does not need to be presented for prior periods.

In addition to the disclosures required above, any impairment of intangible assets is to be disclosed in accordance with Section 27. *[FRS 102.27.33(d)]*. The nature and effect of any change in useful life, amortisation method or residual value estimates should be disclosed. *[FRS 102.10.18]*.

Entities are also required to provide the following information, to the extent that they apply: *[FRS 102.18.28]*

(a)   a description, the carrying amount and remaining amortisation period of any individual intangible asset that is material to the entity's financial statements;

(b)   for intangible assets acquired by way of a grant and initially recognised at fair value:

   (i)   the fair value initially recognised for these assets; and

   (ii)   their carrying amounts.

(c)   the existence and carrying amounts of intangible assets to which the entity has restricted title or that are pledged as security for liabilities; and

(d)   the amount of contractual commitments for the acquisition of intangible assets.

3.5.3   *Disclosure of research and development expenditure*

Entities should disclose the aggregate amount of research and development expenditure recognised as an expense during the period (i.e. the amount of expenditure incurred internally on research and development that has not been capitalised as an intangible asset or as part of the cost of another asset that meets the recognition criteria of FRS 102). *[FRS 102.18.29]*.

Where an entity has elected to capitalise development costs, company law requires disclosure of: *[1 Sch 21(2)]*

(a) the period over which the amount of the costs that were originally capitalised is being written off; and

(b) the reasons for capitalising the development costs.

Unamortised development costs included as an asset in a company's accounts should be treated as a realised loss for the purpose of calculating a company's distributable profits. However, in special circumstances directors may be able to justify a decision that unamortised development costs included as an asset in a company's accounts should not be treated as a realised loss. In such cases, the circumstances relied upon by the directors in reaching this justification must be disclosed. *[s844]*.

The Regulations also require that the directors' report of large and medium-sized companies and groups should contain an indication of the activities of the company (and its subsidiary undertakings) in the field of research and development. *[7 Sch 7(c)]*.

3.5.4 Additional disclosures when the revaluation model is applied

If intangible assets are accounted for at revalued amounts, an entity should disclose the following: *[FRS 102.18.29A]*

(a) the effective date of the revaluation;

(b) whether an independent valuer was involved;

(c) the methods and significant assumptions applied in estimating the assets' fair values; and

(d) for each revalued class of intangible assets, the carrying amount that would have been recognised had the assets been carried under the cost model.

UK Company law requires the following additional disclosures:

(a) the years in which the intangible assets were separately valued (so far as known to the directors) and the separate values;

(b) for intangible assets that have been revalued in the financial year, the names of the persons who valued them or particulars of their qualifications for doing so, and the basis of valuation used by them. *[1 Sch 52]*. However, as FRS 102 allows the use of the revaluation model only where fair value can be determined by reference to an active market, this company law requirement is likely to be of limited relevance to FRS 102 reporters; and

(c) Separate disclosure of the revaluation reserve on the company balance sheet. *[1 Sch 35(2)]*.

3.5.5 Disclosures for additional intangible assets recognised as part of a business combination

When, as part of a business combination, an acquirer elects to recognise intangible assets separately from goodwill for which the recognition criteria in paragraph 4 of Section 18 are satisfied and only one of condition (b) or (c) above is met (see 3.3.2.A above), the nature of those additional intangible assets and the reason why they have been separated from goodwill must be disclosed. *[FRS 102.18.28A]*.

Chapter 16

4   PRACTICAL ISSUES

4.1   Website costs

There is no specific guidance on the accounting for website development costs under FRS 102. Given their lack of physical substance, it is likely that these costs would be classified as intangible assets under FRS 102 (see 3.2.2 above). However, certain elements related to developing a website, such as web servers, do have physical substance. Entities may therefore have to exercise judgement in determining whether to apply Section 18 or Section 17 to the elements of a website with physical substance.

Website costs classified as intangible assets would be subject to the specific recognition requirements for internally generated intangible assets within Section 18.

4.2   Measurement of intangible assets: income from incidental operations while an asset is being developed

When an entity generates income while it is developing or constructing an asset, the question arises as to whether this income should reduce the initial carrying value of the asset being developed or be recognised in profit or loss. Section 18 is silent on this issue. For IFRS reporters, IAS 38 requires the entity to consider whether the activity giving rise to income is necessary to bring the asset to the condition necessary for it to be capable of operating in the manner intended by management, or not. Entities reporting under FRS 102 may consider applying a similar assessment. IAS 38 requires the income and related expenses of incidental operations (being those not necessary to develop the asset for its intended use) to be recognised immediately in profit or loss and included in their respective classifications of income and expense. *[IAS 38.31].*

Whilst IAS 38 is not explicit on the matter, it follows that when the activity is determined to be necessary to bring the intangible asset into its intended use, any income should be deducted from the cost of the asset. An example would be where income is generated from the sale of samples produced during the testing of a new process or from the sale of a production prototype. However, care must be taken to confirm whether the incidence of income indicates that the intangible asset is ready for its intended use, in which case capitalisation of costs would cease, revenue would be recognised in profit or loss and the related costs of the activity would include a measure of amortisation of the asset.

4.3   Measurement of intangible assets: intangible assets acquired for contingent consideration

The consideration payable on acquisition of an intangible asset may sometimes be contingent upon a specified future event or condition. For example, an entity may acquire an intangible asset for consideration comprising a combination of up-front payment, guaranteed instalments for a number of years and additional amounts that vary according to future activity (revenue, profit or number of units output).

Transactions involving contingent consideration are often very complex and payment can be dependent on a number of factors. In the absence of specific guidance in Section 18, entities will be required to determine an appropriate accounting treatment based on the commercial circumstances of the transaction. In practice there are two general approaches. One approach includes the fair value of all contingent payments in the initial measurement of the asset. The other approach considers that these arrangements contain executory contracts that are only accounted for when one of the contracting parties perform. Under both approaches, contingent payments are either capitalised when incurred if they meet the definition of an asset, or expensed as incurred.

4.4 Industry specific practical issues

Entities in certain industries may encounter issues in accounting for intangible assets that are common across the industry. Industry specific issues are not explicitly addressed by Section 18. Entities encountering the following industry specific issues may wish to consider guidance in Chapter 17 of EY International GAAP 2019 in formulating appropriate accounting policies under FRS 102:

- research and development in the pharmaceutical industry;
- rate-regulated activities;
- emission trading schemes;
- accounting for green certificates or renewable energy certificates;
- accounting for REACH costs;
- television and telecommunications programme and broadcast rights; and
- crypto-assets.

5 SUMMARY OF GAAP DIFFERENCES

The following table shows the differences between FRS 102 and IFRS.

	FRS 102	IFRS
Software development costs	No specific guidance. We would expect entities to look to the guidance in IFRS. See 3.2.2 above.	Required to use judgement to assess which element is more significant when an asset incorporates both tangible and intangible elements. Software that is not integral to related hardware is treated as an intangible asset.
Cost of separately acquired intangible assets	Comprises purchase price, import duties and non-refundable taxes, trade discounts and rebates; and directly attributable costs of preparing the asset for its intended use. See 3.3.1.B above	Similar to FRS 102, with additional guidance provided.

	FRS 102	IFRS
Intangible assets acquired in a business combination *(accounting periods beginning on or after 1 January 2019 or where the Triennial review 2017 amendments to FRS 102 have been early adopted)*	Required only to recognise separately from goodwill those intangible assets that satisfy the general recognition criteria (see 3.3 above), and both of the following conditions are met: (a) the intangible asset arises from contractual or other legal rights; and (b) the intangible asset is separable. Entities can voluntarily adopt an accounting policy to recognise additional intangible assets of a particular class separately from goodwill where only one of conditions (a) or (b) are met. See 3.3.2.A above.	Must recognise separately from goodwill where the intangible asset meets the general recognition criteria in IAS 38 and either: (a) the intangible asset arises from contractual or other legal rights, or; (b) the intangible asset is separable (i.e. capable of being separated or divided from the entity and sold, transferred, licenced, rented or exchanged either individually or together with a related contract, asset or liability).
Intangible assets acquired in a business combination *(accounting periods beginning prior to 1 January 2019 and where the Triennial review 2017 amendments to FRS 102 have not been early adopted)*	The previous version of Section 18 defined intangible assets as separable *or* arising from contractual or other legal rights, with the only restriction being to prohibit the recognition of intangible assets that are acquired in a business combination and arise from legal or other contractual rights where there is no history or evidence of exchange transactions for the same or similar assets, and otherwise estimating fair value would be dependent on immeasurable variables. See 3.3.2.A above.	Must recognise separately from goodwill where the intangible asset meets the general recognition criteria in IAS 38 and either: (a) the intangible asset arises from contractual or other legal rights, or; (b) the intangible asset is separable (i.e. capable of being separated or divided from the entity and sold, transferred, licenced, rented or exchanged either individually or together with a related contract, asset or liability). Presumes that intangible assets acquired in a business combination can always be measured reliably.
Intangible assets acquired by government grant	Cost of the asset is its fair value at the date the grant is received or receivable. See 3.3.4 above.	Accounting policy choice – measure at fair value or a nominal amount.
Advertising and promotional expenditure	Certain advertising and promotional expenditure should be carried as an asset within inventories. See 3.3.3.E above.	Expenditure on advertising and promotional activities is recognised as an expense when it is incurred.
Development expenditure	Accounting policy choice – an entity may recognise an intangible asset arising from development or from the development phase of an internal project if certain criteria are met. See 2.3 above.	An entity must recognise an intangible asset arising from development or from the development phase of an internal project if certain criteria (which are consistent with FRS 102) are met.

Amortisation	Intangible assets are amortised over a finite useful life. If an entity is unable to make a reliable estimate, the useful life should not exceed ten years.	Intangible assets with finite useful lives are amortised over their useful lives. An intangible asset with an indefinite useful life is not amortised.
	Renewal periods are included in the useful life of intangible assets that arise from contractual or legal right conveyed for a finite term only if there is evidence to support renewal by the entity without significant cost.	Consistent with FRS 102. Additionally, IAS 38 provides examples of indicators that an entity could renew the contractual or legal rights without significant cost.
	Review the amortisation method, useful life and residual value of intangible assets if there are indicators that any of these have changed. See 3.4.3 above.	Review the amortisation method, useful life and residual value of intangible assets at least at each financial year end.
Impairment reviews	Required if there are indicators of impairment. See 3.4.5 above.	Consistent with FRS 102 except impairment reviews required annually and whenever indicators of impairment for indefinite lived intangibles.
Intangible assets acquired in exchange for non-monetary assets	Measured at fair value unless the exchange transaction lacks commercial substance; or the fair value of neither the asset received nor the asset given up is reliably measurable. In that case, the asset's cost is measured at the carrying amount of the asset given up. See 3.3.5 above.	Similar to FRS 102. IAS 38 additionally provides guidance on determining whether a transaction has commercial substance.
Disclosures	The disclosures required by FRS 102 are set out at 3.5 above. The reconciliation table (i.e. opening balances to ending balances) is required only for current period.	Similar to FRS 102. IFRS requires a reconciliation of the carrying amount of intangible assets at the beginning and end of the reporting period for both the current and comparative period. In addition, there are some differences in the items to be included in the reconciliation table

Chapter 16

Chapter 17   Business combinations and goodwill

Chapter 17

Chapter 17

List of examples

Chapter 17

Chapter 17   Business combinations and goodwill

1   INTRODUCTION

Section 9 – *Consolidated and Separate Financial Statements* – which is dealt with in Chapter 8 of this publication, *inter alia*, addresses the preparation of consolidated financial statements by parents. Its focus is on matters such as when consolidated financial statements should be prepared, what entities should be considered to be part of the group for the purposes of inclusion therein, and the mechanics of how such entities should be dealt with in the consolidated financial statements. It also deals with the accounting for disposals of, and increased interests in, existing subsidiaries of the group.

Section 19 – *Business Combinations and Goodwill* – applies to the accounting for business combinations. A business combination is defined as 'the bringing together of separate entities or businesses into one reporting entity'. *[FRS 102.19.3, Appendix I]*. While this chapter is written primarily in the context of an entity becoming a subsidiary of another, the guidance also applies to individual financial statements in situations where an entity purchases (or combines with) an unincorporated business, for example, through the acquisition of the trade and net assets, including goodwill, of another entity.

Section 19 requires all business combinations (with limited exceptions) to be accounted for by applying the purchase method. The exceptions are for group reconstructions meeting specified criteria (see 5 below), and for public benefit entity combinations that are in substance a gift or that are a merger (dealt with by Section 34 – *Specialised Activities* – see Chapter 31 at 6).

Section 19 provides guidance on the most common issues facing preparers in relation to the accounting for business combinations – namely, defining a business combination, identifying the acquirer, determining the acquisition date, measuring the cost of the business combination, and then allocating that cost to the acquirer's interest in the identifiable assets and liabilities of the acquiree. It also addresses the initial and subsequent accounting treatment of goodwill or any excess over cost of the acquirer's interest in the identifiable assets and liabilities of the acquiree (negative goodwill).

Section 19 also addresses the accounting for group reorganisations. It permits the use of the merger method of accounting for group reorganisations meeting specified criteria. Group reorganisations generally involve the restructuring of the relationships between companies in a group by, for example, setting up a new holding company, changing the direct ownership of a subsidiary within a group, or transferring businesses from one company to another. Most of these changes should have no impact on the consolidated financial statements of the ultimate parent (provided there are no non-controlling interests affected), because they are purely internal and cannot affect the group when it is being portrayed as a single entity. However, such transactions may impact the consolidated financial statements (if prepared) of a parent (at a lower level in the group) that did not previously control the subsidiaries or businesses transferred. Such transactions can also have a significant impact on the financial statements of the individual companies in the group. However, this chapter addresses only the accounting in individual financial statements for the transfer of a business from another group company. The accounting in individual financial statements for the transfer of an investment in subsidiary is addressed in Chapter 8 at 4.2 to 4.4.

1.1   Background

There were traditionally two distinctly different forms of reporting the effects of a business combination; acquisition accounting (or the purchase method) and merger accounting (or the pooling of interests method). These two methods look at business combinations from quite different perspectives. An acquisition is seen as the absorption by the acquirer of the target; there is continuity only of the acquirer, with only the post-acquisition results of the target reported in earnings of the acquirer, and the comparatives remaining those of the acquirer. In contrast, a merger is seen as the uniting of the interests of two formerly distinct shareholder groups, and in order to present continuity of both entities there is retrospective restatement to show the enlarged entity as if the two entities had always been together, by combining the results of both entities pre- and post-combination and restating the comparatives. Over the years, the accounting landscape has changed in attempts to distinguish between the circumstances when each of these methods is appropriate.

Another area of historical debate when it comes to accounting for business combinations using the purchase method has been how to treat any difference between the cost of the acquisition and the cost of the identifiable assets and liabilities of the acquiree. Where the amounts allocated to the assets and liabilities are less than the overall cost, the difference is accounted for as goodwill. Over the years, there have been different views on how goodwill should be accounted for, but the general method has been to deal with it as an asset. The question has been: should goodwill be amortised over its economic life or should it not be amortised at all, but subjected to some form of impairment test? Where the cost has been less than the value allocated to the identifiable assets and liabilities, then this has traditionally been treated as negative goodwill. The issue has then been how such a credit should be released to the income statement.

1.2   The FRS 102 approach to business combinations and goodwill

The business combinations section of FRS 102 is broadly based on the equivalent section of the IFRS for SMEs. Consequently, Section 19 is – subject to some amendments made by the Financial Reporting Council – ultimately derived from the version of IFRS 3 – *Business Combinations* – prior to the amendments made by the IASB in 2008 (IFRS 3 (2004)).

As it relates to the two matters discussed at 1.1 above:

- FRS 102 prohibits merger accounting in all but two instances:

  - Group reconstructions: Merger accounting permitted by FRS 6 – *Acquisitions and mergers* ('FRS 6') – for group reconstructions has been carried forward into FRS 102. The Basis for Conclusions that accompanies FRS 102, asserts that the accounting provided by FRS 6 is well understood and provides useful requirements. In practice, the introduction of FRS 102 was not expected to change the accounting for group reconstructions. *[FRS 102.BC.B19.1].*

  - Public benefit entities: A type of merger accounting is required, in certain circumstances, for combinations between public benefit entities. The Basis for Conclusions notes concern as to whether acquisition accounting appropriately caters for such combinations, particularly if there is a gift of one entity to another in a combination at nil or nominal consideration, or where two or more organisations genuinely merge to form a new entity. *[FRS 102.BC.B34J.1].* See Chapter 31 at 6.4.

- In the treatment of goodwill, FRS 102 is largely consistent with the principles of previous UK GAAP – positive goodwill is to be recognised as an asset and amortised over its useful life. There is no longer provision for a determination of indefinite lived goodwill. Where, 'in those exceptional cases' an entity is otherwise unable to make a reliable estimate of the useful life, the presumed maximum life for goodwill is restricted to 10 years to be consistent with company law. *[FRS 102.BC.B18.1].* Negative goodwill is recognised and separately disclosed on the face of the statement of financial position, and subsequently amortised. See 3.9 below.

2 KEY DIFFERENCES BETWEEN SECTION 19 AND IFRS

As Section 19 is not based on the current version of IFRS 3, but has been derived from IFRS 3 (2004), this means that there are a number of significant differences to the requirements of IFRS 3.

2.1 Method of accounting

IFRS 3 requires all business combinations within its scope to be accounted for using the purchase method – one difference to FRS 102 being that IFRS 3 excludes business combinations under common control from its scope, whereas FRS 102 specifically caters for group reconstructions (allowing group reconstructions meeting specified criteria to be accounted for using the merger method of accounting). What constitutes a 'business combination under common control' under IFRS 3 however is wider than what meets the definition of a 'group reconstruction' under FRS 102 (see 5.1 below). Additionally, IFRS 3 makes no special provisions for business combinations involving public benefit entities.

Another difference is that the 'purchase method' required by FRS 102 is conceptually different from that in IFRS 3. FRS 102 is a 'cost-based' approach, whereby the cost of the business combination is allocated to the assets and liabilities acquired. In contrast, IFRS 3 adopts an approach whereby the various components of a business combination

Chapter 17

are measured at their acquisition-date fair values (albeit with a number of exceptions). This results in a number of the differences, which are identified below.

2.2   Definition of a business combination

The definition of a business combination in FRS 102 is 'the bringing together of separate entities or businesses into one reporting entity'. *[FRS 102.19.3, Appendix I]*.

IFRS 3 defines a business combination as 'a transaction or other event in which an acquirer obtains control of one or more businesses'. *[IFRS 3 Appendix A]*. It is notable that the Basis of Conclusions accompanying IFRS 3 identifies that the definition is intended to include all transactions and events initially included in the scope of IFRS 3 (2004). *[IFRS 3.BC11]*.

FRS 102's definition is identical to that in IFRS 3 (2004), so it follows that there are not likely to be differences in practice as a result of the differing definitions of a 'business combination'. However, differences could arise as a result of the definition of a 'business'.

2.3   Definition of a business

Like FRS 102, IFRS 3 includes an explicit definition of what constitutes a business. However, by inclusion of the additional italicised words in the definition of a business – 'An integrated set of activities and assets *that is capable of being* conducted and managed ...' [emphasis added] *[IFRS 3 Appendix A]* – IFRS 3's definition of a business is wider than that in FRS 102. Additionally, FRS 102 indicates that a business generally consists of three different elements – (1) inputs, (2) processes applied to those inputs, and (3) resulting outputs which together are, or will be, used to generate revenues. *[FRS 102 Appendix I]*. IFRS 3 further defines these elements, and clarifies that a business would be required to have only the first two of these three elements (i.e. inputs and processes), which together have the ability to create outputs. *[IFRS 3 Appendix B.7-8]*. As such, although businesses usually have outputs, under IFRS 3 they would not need to be present for an integrated set of activities and assets to be a business. Consequently, it is possible certain acquisitions that would constitute a business under IFRS 3 would not do so under FRS 102. In addition, IFRS 3 contains application guidance on the definition of a business, which FRS 102 does not. *[IFRS 3 Appendix B.7-12]*.

In October 2018, the IASB issued an amendment to the definition of a business in IFRS 3 and related application guidance. This amendment clarifies how an entity determines whether it has acquired a business or a group of assets and applies to business combinations for which the acquisition date is, or asset acquisitions that occur, on or after the beginning of the first annual reporting period beginning on or after 1 January 2020 (with earlier application permitted).

The new definition of a business is 'an integrated set of activities and assets that is capable of being conducted and managed for the purpose of providing goods and services to customers, generating investment income (such as dividends or interest) or generating other income from ordinary activities'. *[IFRS 3 Appendix A]*.

The amendment includes an optional 'concentration test' designed to simplify the evaluation of whether an integrated set of activities and assets constitutes a business. Under the amendment, an integrated set of activities and assets is not a business if substantially all of the fair value of the gross assets acquired (excluding cash and cash equivalents, deferred tax assets and goodwill resulting from the effects of deferred tax liabilities) is concentrated in a single identifiable asset or group of similar identifiable assets. If this concentration test, which is optional on a transaction-by-transaction basis, is applied and the set of activities and assets is determined not to be a business, no further assessment is needed.

In addition, the IASB decided that in order to be considered a business, an acquisition must include, at a minimum, an input and a substantive process that together significantly contribute to the ability to create outputs. Additional guidance is provided to help evaluate whether a substantive process is acquired. Not all the vendor's inputs and processes have to be acquired for the integrated set of activities and assets to qualify as a business.

The amendment also:

- removes the statement that a set of activities and assets is a business if market participants can replace the missing elements and continue to produce outputs;

- revises the definition of outputs to focus on goods and services provided to customers, investment income or other income from ordinary activities (i.e. consistent with the new definition of a business); and

- removes the presumption that if goodwill is present, the integrated set of activities and assets is a business (also a feature of the definition in FRS 102).

The application of this approach under IFRS could lead to additional scenarios in which the definition of a business differs between IFRS 3 and FRS 102.

2.4   Identifying an acquirer

FRS 102 includes as an explicit step in applying the purchase method 'identifying an acquirer', *[FRS 102.19.7(a)]*, and identifies that the acquirer is the combining entity that obtains control of the other combining entities or businesses. *[FRS 102.19.8]*.

FRS 102 further includes three indicators in assisting the identification of the acquirer: *[FRS 102.19.10]*

- If the fair value of one of the combining entities is significantly greater than that of the other combining entity, the entity with the greater fair value is likely to be the acquirer.

- If the business combination is effected through an exchange of voting ordinary equity instruments for cash or other assets, the entity giving up cash or other assets is likely to be the acquirer.

- If the business combination results in the management of one of the combining entities being able to dominate the selection of the management team of the resulting combined entity, the entity whose management is able so to dominate is likely to be the acquirer.

IFRS 3 likewise explicitly requires that, for each business combination, one of the combining entities be identified as the acquirer, i.e. the entity that obtains control of another entity, the acquiree. *[IFRS 3.6]*. As for guidance on identifying that acquirer, IFRS 3 in the first instance refers to the guidance in IFRS 10 – *Consolidated Financial Statements* ('IFRS 10'); and failing a clear indication from IFRS 10, sets out specific indicators. *[IFRS 3.6-7, Appendix B.14-18]*.

Chapter 17

There is some level of consistency between the indicators contained in FRS 102 and IFRS 3. For example, IFRS 3's consideration of the first indicator noted above (relative fair value of the combining entities) is similar, although not identical as follows, 'The acquirer is usually the combining entity whose relative size (measured in, for example, assets, revenues or profit) is significantly greater than that of the other combining entity or entities'. *[IFRS 3 Appendix B.16]*. However the guidance included in IFRS 3 is more extensive than that in FRS 102.

While FRS 102 gives rise to the possibility of a reverse acquisition by requiring identification of the acquirer, the accounting treatment for reverse acquisitions is not explicitly mentioned in FRS 102. In contrast, IFRS 3 defines a reverse acquisition, as well as containing specific requirements about reverse acquisition accounting and providing an example illustrating the accounting for a reverse acquisition. *[IFRS 3 Appendix B.19-27, IE1-15]*.

2.5   Cost of a business combination

2.5.1   *Acquisition expenses*

The inclusion of directly attributable costs within the cost of a business combination (effectively reflecting them within goodwill) under FRS 102 differs significantly from IFRS 3, which requires that acquisition-related transaction costs are expensed.

2.5.2   *Contingent consideration*

FRS 102 requires recognition of any contingent consideration to be made at the acquisition date if the adjustment is 'probable and can be measured reliably'. *[FRS 102.19.12]*. If the potential adjustment is not recognised at the acquisition date, but subsequently becomes probable and can be measured reliably, the additional consideration is treated as an adjustment to the cost of the combination. *[FRS 102.19.13]*. Similarly, if the future events that, at the acquisition date, were expected to occur do not occur, or the estimate needs to be revised, the cost of the business combination is adjusted accordingly. *[FRS 102.19.13A]*.

Some clarifications to FRS 102's requirements for contingent consideration were made as part of the *Amendments to FRS 102 Triennial review 2017 – Incremental improvements and clarifications (Triennial review 2017)*. See discussion at 3.6.2 below.

In contrast, under IFRS 3, the acquisition-date fair value of any contingent consideration is recognised as part of the consideration transferred in acquiring the business – regardless of whether payment is probable or can be measured reliably. The obligation for the contingent consideration is classified as equity or a financial liability based on the definition of an equity instrument and a financial liability in IAS 32 – *Financial Instruments: Presentation*. Contingent consideration that is classified as equity is not remeasured. *[IFRS 3.58]*. This contrasts with FRS 102, under which, we believe that contingent consideration classified as equity would be adjusted for the number of equity instruments issued, but not changes to their fair value (see 3.6.5 below).

Under IFRS, subsequent changes in the fair value of the contingent consideration classified as a financial liability are not accounted for as adjustments to the consideration transferred, but are reflected in profit or loss – they therefore do not result in changes to goodwill as they would under FRS 102. *[IFRS 3.58]*.

2.5.3   *Contingent payments to employees or selling shareholders*

FRS 102 provides no guidance on the accounting to be applied where further contingent amounts may be payable to vendors who become, or continue to be, key employees of the acquiree subsequent to the acquisition.

In contrast, IFRS 3 specifically identifies a transaction that remunerates employees or former owners of the acquiree for future services as not part of the cost of the business combination, *[IFRS 3.52(b)]*, and contains specific guidance to assist in the determination of whether arrangements for contingent payments to employees or selling shareholders are contingent consideration in the business combination or are separate transactions. *[IFRS 3 Appendix B.54-55]*. That guidance specifically states that 'a contingent consideration arrangement in which the payments are automatically forfeited if employment terminates is remuneration for post-combination services'. *[IFRS 3 Appendix B.55(a)]*.

Under FRS 102, we believe that an acquirer must make this same distinction and therefore identify contingent consideration that is, in substance, compensation for future services, and account for this separately from the cost of the combination. This is because Section 2 – *Concepts and Pervasive Principles* – includes as one of the qualitative characteristics of information in financial statements 'substance over form', requiring that 'transactions and other events and conditions should be accounted for and presented in accordance with their substance and not merely their legal form'. *[FRS 102.2.8]*. Therefore, where a vendor is also a continuing employee, it is necessary to determine whether payments are made to them in their capacity as vendor or as employee.

2.6   Measurement period

Under FRS 102, provisional amounts in the first post-acquisition financial statements are to be finalised within twelve months after the acquisition date. If amendments are required to those provisional amounts, they are made retrospectively by restating comparatives, i.e. by accounting for them as if they were made at the acquisition date. Beyond twelve months after the acquisition date, adjustments to the initial accounting are recognised only to correct a material error in accordance with Section 10 – *Accounting Policies, Estimates and Errors. [FRS 102.19.19]*.

These FRS 102 provisions are broadly consistent with IFRS 3; one nuance being the measurement period afforded by IFRS 3 ends at the sooner of: (i) one year from the acquisition date; and (ii) when the acquirer receives the information it was seeking about the facts and circumstances that existed as of the acquisition date or learns that it cannot obtain more information. *[IFRS 3.45]*. This distinction may have little practical difference.

2.7   Initial measurement of acquiree's assets, liabilities and contingent liabilities

FRS 102 requires the acquiree's identifiable assets and liabilities and a provision for those contingent liabilities (that satisfy the recognition criteria in paragraph 19.20) to be measured at their fair values at the acquisition date (except for deferred tax, employee

Chapter 17

benefit arrangements and share-based payments, which are to be recognised and measured in accordance with the respective section of FRS 102). *[FRS 102.19.14]*.

Section 19 offers no guidance on how to derive this acquisition date fair value. Section 2 states that 'fair value is the amount for which an asset could be exchanged, a liability settled, or an equity instrument granted could be exchanged, between knowledgeable, willing parties in an arm's length transaction. In the absence of any specific guidance provided in the relevant section of this FRS, when fair value measurement is permitted or required the guidance in the appendix to this section shall be applied'. *[FRS 102.2.34(b)]*.

IFRS 3 includes a similar requirement to measure the identifiable assets acquired and liabilities assumed at their acquisition-date fair values. *[IFRS 3.18]*. Consistent with FRS 102, there is specific recognition and measurement guidance for deferred tax, employee benefits and share-based payments. However, unlike FRS 102, IFRS 3 includes specific guidance on the recognition and measurement of indemnification assets, *[IFRS 3.27-28]*, re-acquired rights, *[IFRS 3.29]*, assets held for sale, *[IFRS 3.31]*, operating leases and intangible assets. *[IFRS 3.14, Appendix B.28-40]*. For the purpose of IFRS 3, the definition of 'fair value' is that in IFRS 13 – *Fair Value Measurement*, being 'the price that would be received to sell an asset or paid to transfer a liability in an orderly transaction between market participants at the measurement date.' *[IFRS 13.9]*. It is explicitly an exit price. Where IFRS 3 requires assets and liabilities to be measured at fair value, the guidance in IFRS 13 would be applied.

2.8   Recognising intangible assets separately from goodwill

As noted below, the requirements in FRS 102 in respect of intangible assets recognised separately from goodwill have changed as a result of the Triennial review 2017, effective for periods beginning on or after 1 January 2019. See also discussion at 3.7.1.A below.

Under FRS 102, an intangible asset acquired in a business combination is separately recognised if it:

(a)   meets the recognition criteria (i.e. it is probable that the expected future economic benefits attributable to the asset will flow, and that the fair value of the intangible asset can be measured reliably);

(b)   arises from contractual or legal rights; and

(c)   is separable (i.e. capable of being separated or divided from the entity and sold, transferred, licensed, rented or exchanged either individually or together with a related contract, asset or liability).

In addition, an entity may choose to recognise additional intangible assets acquired in a business combination separately from goodwill for which (a) is satisfied and only one of (b) or (c) is met. However, where an entity chooses to recognise such additional intangible assets, this policy must be applied to all intangible assets in the same class (i.e. having a similar nature, function and use in the business) and consistently to all business combinations. *[FRS 102.18.8]*. See 3.7.1.A below.

IFRS 3, in contrast, requires identifiable assets, i.e. those meeting either the separable or contractual-legal criterion (so either (b) or (c) above) to be recognised separately from goodwill. *[IFRS 3.14, Appendix B.31-34]*. In addition, the probability and the reliable measurement criterion is always considered to be satisfied for intangible assets in a business combination. *[IAS 38.33]*. Consequently, FRS 102 does not require intangible assets to be recognised separately in as many situations as IFRS, although entities applying FRS 102 do have a policy choice as to whether to recognise more intangible assets.

The Illustrative Examples accompanying IFRS 3 provide a large number of examples of identifiable intangible assets acquired in a business combination. *[IFRS 3.IE16-44]*.

As part of the Triennial review 2017, the FRC provided examples of intangible assets that would normally meet all three criteria (a) to (c) above, and those that would not. Customer relationships are given as an example of an intangible asset that would not normally satisfy all three criteria 'as no contractual or legal right exists that would give rise to expected future economic benefits.' *[FRS 102.BC.B18.10]*. This is a potential area of difference from IFRS 3, which contains examples of customer relationships that are considered to meet the contractual-legal criterion. *[IFRS 3.IE23-30]*. However, the option under FRS 102 to recognise additional intangible assets satisfying (a) and either (b) or (c) of the criteria above could be used to mitigate any potential difference with IFRS 3 in this regard.

2.9   Deferred tax

FRS 102 provides that when the amount that can be deducted for tax for an asset (other than goodwill) that is recognised in a business combination is less (more) than the value at which it is recognised, a deferred tax liability (asset) shall be recognised for the additional tax that will be paid (avoided) in respect of that difference. Similarly, a deferred tax asset (liability) shall be recognised for the additional tax that will be avoided (paid) because of a difference between the value at which a liability is recognised and the amount that will be assessed for tax. The amount attributed to goodwill shall be adjusted by the amount of deferred tax recognised. *[FRS 102.29.11]*.

The treatment under FRS 102 will be largely consistent with the requirements of IFRS.

2.10   Step acquisitions

Where a parent acquires control of a subsidiary following a series of transactions, the cost of the business combination is the aggregate of the fair values of the assets given, liabilities assumed, and equity instruments issued by the acquirer at the date of each transaction in the series, *[FRS 102.19.11A]*, whereas the 'normal' rules on allocating the cost of the business combination to the acquisition-date fair value of the identifiable assets, liabilities and contingent liabilities apply. *[FRS 102.19.14]*.

This approach differs to the requirements under IFRS 3, whereby the acquirer remeasures any previously held equity investment in the acquiree immediately before obtaining control at its acquisition-date fair value and recognises any resulting gain or loss in profit or loss or other comprehensive income, as appropriate. In addition, any changes in the value of the acquirer's equity interest in the acquiree recognised in other comprehensive income is reclassified on the same basis that would be required if the acquirer had directly disposed of the previously held equity investment. *[IFRS 3.42]*. The acquisition-date fair value of the previously held equity interest is included in the computation of goodwill or gain on bargain purchase recognised under IFRS 3. *[IFRS 3.32, 34]*.

Chapter 17

2.11   Non-controlling interests in a business combination

FRS 102 requires that, at the acquisition date, any non-controlling interest in the acquiree is stated at the non-controlling interest's share in the net amount of the identifiable assets, liabilities and contingent liabilities recognised and measured in accordance with Section 19. *[FRS 102.9.13(d), 19.14A]*.

This differs from IFRS 3 where, for those non-controlling interests that are present ownership interests and entitle their holders to a proportionate share of the entity's net assets in the event of liquidation, there is a choice of two methods in measuring non-controlling interests arising in a business combination:

- Option 1, to measure the non-controlling interest at its acquisition date fair value; or
- Option 2, to measure the non-controlling interest at the proportionate share of the present ownership instruments' value of net identifiable assets acquired.

All other non-controlling interests (for example, preference shares not entitled to a *pro rata* share of net assets upon liquidation, equity component of convertible debt and other compound financial instruments, share warrants, etc.) are measured at their acquisition-date fair value (unless another measurement basis is required by IFRS). *[IFRS 3.19]*. FRS 102 is silent on the measurement of such components of non-controlling interests, the implication being they are valued at nil if they are not entitled to a present ownership interest.

2.12   Subsequent accounting for goodwill

FRS 102 requires goodwill acquired in a business combination to be recognised as an asset and amortised on a systematic basis over its useful life. FRS 102 mandates that goodwill shall have a finite useful life, and further, if in exceptional circumstances the entity is unable to make a reliable estimate of the useful life of goodwill, the life shall not exceed 10 years. *[FRS 102.19.23]*.

This contrasts with IFRS 3, under which goodwill is not amortised, but instead subjected to (at least) annual impairment tests under IAS 36 – *Impairment of Assets*. *[IFRS 3 Appendix B.63(a)]*. FRS 102 requires, instead, a review for impairment indicators at each reporting date, with impairment tests performed only where indications of such impairment exist. *[FRS 102.19.23, 27.7]*.

Where negative goodwill arises, FRS 102 requires the acquirer to reassess the identification and measurement of the acquiree's identifiable assets, liabilities and contingent liabilities and the measurement of the cost of the combination. Having undertaken that reassessment, any excess remaining after that reassessment is required to be recognised and separately disclosed on the face of the statement of financial position on the acquisition date, immediately below goodwill, and followed by a subtotal of the net amount of goodwill and the negative goodwill. Subsequently, negative goodwill up to the fair value of non-monetary assets is recognised in profit or loss in the periods in which the non-monetary assets are recovered. Any negative goodwill in excess of the fair value of non-monetary assets is recognised in profit or loss in periods expected to benefit. *[FRS 102.19.24]*.

This treatment differs to IFRS 3 whereby any excess of the acquirer's interest in the net fair value of the acquiree's identifiable assets, liabilities and contingent liabilities over cost (i.e. negative goodwill) is recognised by the acquirer immediately in profit or loss. *[IFRS 3.34]*.

2.13 Disclosures

The FRS 102 disclosure requirements are considerably less extensive than those under IFRS 3; for example, IFRS 3 requires specific disclosures in respect of the following areas that are not included in FRS 102: *[IFRS 3 Appendix B.64]*

- the primary reasons for the business combination and a description of how the acquirer obtained control of the acquiree;
- a qualitative description of the factors that make up the goodwill recognised;
- contingent consideration and indemnification assets;
- acquired receivables;
- the total amount of goodwill that is expected to be deductible for tax purposes;
- transactions recognised separately from the business combination;
- acquisition-related costs;
- bargain purchases;
- non-controlling interests;
- business combinations achieved in stages;
- revenue and profit of the combined entity as though the acquisition date of all business combinations had been at the beginning of the year;
- provisional amounts and measurement period adjustments;
- adjustments to contingent consideration in subsequent periods; and
- an explanation of significant gains or losses relating to the identifiable assets acquired and liabilities assumed in a business combination in the current or previous reporting period. *[IFRS 3 Appendix B.67]*.

The Triennial review 2017 added a requirement to FRS 102, to provide a qualitative description of the nature of intangible assets included in goodwill. *[FRS 102.19.25(fA)]*. This is similar in nature to the requirement in IFRS 3 above, which requires a qualitative description of the factors that make up goodwill. However, the FRS 102 requirement is more specific in actually referring to intangible assets included in goodwill.

3 REQUIREMENTS OF SECTION 19 FOR BUSINESS COMBINATIONS AND GOODWILL

A business combination is defined by FRS 102 as 'the bringing together of separate entities or businesses into one reporting entity'. *[FRS 102.19.3, Appendix I]*. This applies not only when an entity becomes a subsidiary of another, but also when an entity purchases (or combines with) an unincorporated business, for example, through the acquisition of the trade and net assets, including any goodwill, of another entity.

3.1 Scope of Section 19

Section 19 deals with all business combinations except: *[FRS 102.19.2]*

- the formation of a joint venture; and
- the acquisition of a group of assets that does not constitute a business.

In addition to Section 19, public benefit entities must consider the requirements of Section 34 in accounting for specific types of business combination. *[FRS 102.PBE19.2A. PBE34.75-86]*.

The first exception above scopes out the requirements of Section 19 for the accounting for the formation of a joint venture. In such circumstances, in the financial statements of the newly formed joint venture, that entity would need to determine an appropriate accounting policy to account for the transaction.

While worded similarly to an original exception in IFRS 3, *[IFRS 3.2(a)]*, that exception under IFRS was clarified as part of the *Annual Improvements to IFRSs 2011-2013 Cycle* to make it clear that the exception applies only to the accounting for the formation of a joint arrangement in the financial statements of the joint arrangement itself. FRS 102 contains no such clarification, but we consider the exception similarly does not apply to the accounting for the formation of the joint venture in the consolidated financial statements of the venturers. That said, Section 19 does not apply directly because the venturers have not obtained control of the joint venture. However, to the extent that the joint venture includes a business not previously held by the venturer, many of the requirements would apply indirectly.

If the formation of the joint venture has arisen as a result of the venturer exchanging a business, or other non-monetary asset, for an interest in another entity that becomes a jointly-controlled entity of the venturer, the requirements of Section 9 apply to consolidated financial statements prepared by the venturer. As discussed in Chapter 13 at 3.9, these include, *inter alia*, the requirement to recognise goodwill as the difference between the fair value of the consideration given and the fair value of the reporting entity's share of the pre-transaction identifiable net assets of the other entity. *[FRS 102.9.31(b)]*. If the formation of the joint venture has not arisen as a result of the venturer exchanging a business, or other non-monetary asset, but the venturer has acquired an investment in a jointly-controlled entity, as discussed in Chapter 13 at 3.7.2, the initial recognition requirements of the equity method apply in terms of accounting for any difference between the cost of acquisition and the investor's share of the fair values of the net identifiable assets of the jointly-controlled entity. *[FRS 102.14.8(c)]*.

The second exception is a truism in that Section 19 applies only to business combinations – so if the group of assets is not a business, Section 19 does not apply, nor does it specify how to account for a group of assets. The initial recognition and measurement of the assets acquired will depend on the nature of the particular assets and the requirements of FRS 102 for such assets. Many assets, such as property, plant and equipment, intangible assets or inventories, are required to be measured initially at cost. Therefore it will be necessary to make some apportionment of the overall cost of the group of assets to the individual assets.

One possible approach to making such an allocation would be to apply the guidance in IFRS 3 for the acquisition of a group of assets that is not a business, which is to allocate the cost to the individual identifiable assets and liabilities on the basis of their relative fair values at the date of purchase, *[IFRS 3.2(b)]*, but other approaches may be appropriate. Whatever approach is used to allocate the overall cost to the individual assets or liabilities, no goodwill arises since goodwill is recognised only in a business combination.

It may be difficult to determine whether or not an acquired group of assets constitutes a business (see 3.2.1 below for the definition of a business and a business combination), and this decision can have a considerable impact on an entity's reported results and the presentation of its financial statements. Accounting for a business combination differs considerably from accounting for an asset acquisition in a number of important respects:

- goodwill (positive or negative) arises only on business combinations;
- assets acquired and liabilities assumed are generally accounted for at fair value in a business combination, while they are assigned a carrying amount based on an allocation of the overall cost in an asset acquisition;
- deferred tax assets and liabilities are recognised if the transaction is a business combination, but not recognised if it is an asset acquisition; and
- disclosures are more onerous for business combinations than for asset acquisitions.

3.1.1   Application of the purchase method

FRS 102 requires all business combinations to be accounted for by applying the purchase method, except for: *[FRS 102.19.6]*

- group reconstructions which may be accounted for by using the merger accounting method; and
- public benefit entity combinations that are in substance a gift or that are a merger which shall be accounted for in accordance with Section 34.

The accounting for group reconstructions under FRS 102 is discussed at 5 below.

Public benefit entity combinations are discussed in Chapter 31 at 6.4.

3.2   Identifying a business combination

3.2.1   Business combination defined

FRS 102 defines a business combination as 'the bringing together of separate entities or businesses into one reporting entity'. *[FRS 102.19.3]*. It then goes on to say that 'the result of nearly all business combinations is that one entity, the acquirer, obtains control of one or more other businesses, the acquiree'. *[FRS 102.19.3]*.

For this purpose, FRS 102 defines a 'business' as 'an integrated set of activities and assets conducted and managed for the purpose of providing:

(a)   a return to investors; or

(b)   lower costs or other economic benefits directly and proportionately to policyholders or participants'.

'A business generally consists of inputs, processes applied to those inputs, and resulting outputs that are, or will be, used to generate revenues. If goodwill is present in a transferred set of activities and assets, the transferred set shall be presumed to be a business.' *[FRS 102 Appendix I]*.

Chapter 17

3.2.2   *Inputs, processes and outputs*

FRS 102 does not discuss further the meaning or interaction of inputs, processes or outputs. However, the application guidance to IFRS 3 expands upon them as follows:

[IFRS 3 Appendix B.7]

- Input: Any economic resource that creates, or has the ability to create, outputs when one or more processes are applied to it. Examples include non-current assets (including intangible assets or rights to use non-current assets), intellectual property, the ability to obtain access to necessary materials or rights and employees.

- Process: Any system, standard, protocol, convention or rule is a process if, when applied to an input or inputs, it either creates or has the ability to create outputs. Examples include strategic management processes, operational processes and resource management processes. These processes typically are documented, but an organised workforce having the necessary skills and experience following rules and conventions may provide the necessary processes that are capable of being applied to inputs to create outputs. Accounting, billing, payroll and other administrative systems typically are not processes used to create outputs so their presence or exclusion generally will not affect whether an acquired set of activities and assets is considered a business.

- Output: The result of inputs and processes applied to those inputs that provide or have the ability to provide a return in the form of dividends, lower costs or other economic benefits directly to investors or other owners, members or participants.

As noted at 2.3 above, the IASB has issued an amendment to the definition of a business and related application guidance in IFRS 3, which will apply to business combinations for which the acquisition date is, or asset acquisitions occurring, on or after the beginning of the first annual reporting period beginning on or after 1 January 2020 (with earlier application permitted). The changes to the application guidance may lead to different determinations of what constitutes a business under IFRS 3 compared to FRS 102 (which has no application guidance). The amendment also makes some clarifications to the descriptions above of inputs and processes and narrows the definition of outputs by focusing on goods and services provided to customers and by removing the reference to an ability to reduce costs, in order to better distinguish between a business combination and an asset acquisition.

As discussed at 3.1 above, the acquisition of a group of assets – notwithstanding that they may be held within a separate entity or entities – which do not constitute a business is excluded from the scope of Section 19. In some situations, there may be difficulties in determining whether or not an acquisition of a group of assets constitutes a business, and judgement will need to be exercised based on the particular circumstances.

The following are examples from extractive and real estate industries that illustrate the issues.

Example 17.1: Extractive industries – definition of a business (1)

E&P Co A (an oil and gas exploration and production company) acquires a mineral interest from E&P Co B, on which it intends to perform exploration activities to determine if reserves exist. The mineral interest is an unproven property and there have been no exploration activities performed on the property.

Inputs – mineral interest

Processes – none

Output – none

Conclusion

In this scenario, we do not believe E&P Co A acquired a business. While E&P Co A acquired an input (mineral interest), it did not acquire any processes and there were no outputs.

Example 17.2: Extractive industries – definition of a business (2)

E&P Co A acquires a property similar to that in Example 17.1 above, except that oil and gas production activities are in place. The target's employees are not part of the transferred set. E&P Co A will take over the operations by using its own employees.

Inputs – oil and gas reserves

Processes – operational processes associated with oil and gas production

Output – revenues from oil and gas production

Conclusion

In this scenario, we generally consider that E&P Co A acquired a business. The acquired set has all three components of a business (inputs, processes and outputs) and is providing a return to its owners. Although the employees are not being transferred to the acquirer, E&P Co A is able to produce outputs by:

- supplying the employees necessary to continue production; and
- integrating the business with its own operations while continuing to produce outputs.

Example 17.3: Real estate – definition of a business (1)

Company A acquires land and a vacant building from Company B. No processes, other assets or employees (for example, leases and other contracts, personnel, or a leasing office) are acquired in the transaction.

Inputs – land and vacant building

Processes – none

Output – none

Conclusion

In this scenario, we do not believe Company A acquired a business. While Company A acquired inputs (land and a vacant building), it did not acquire any processes and there were no outputs.

Example 17.4: Real estate – definition of a business (2)

Company A acquires an operating hotel, the hotel's employees, the franchise agreement, inventory, reservations system and all 'back office' operations.

Inputs – non-current assets, franchise agreement and employees

Processes – operational and resource management processes associated with operating the hotel

Output – revenues from operating the hotel

Conclusion

In this scenario, we generally believe Company A acquired a business. The acquired set has all three components of a business (inputs, processes and outputs) and is providing a return to its owners.

Chapter 17

There is a rebuttable presumption that if goodwill arises on the acquisition, the acquisition is a business. *[FRS 102 Appendix I]*. If, for example, the total fair value of an acquired set of activities and assets is £15 million and the fair value of the net identifiable assets is only £10 million, the existence of value in excess of the fair value of identifiable assets (i.e. goodwill) creates a presumption that the acquired set is a business. However, care should be exercised to ensure that all of the identifiable net assets have been identified and measured appropriately. While the absence of goodwill may be an indicator that the acquired activities and assets do not represent a business, it is not presumptive.

3.2.3   Differing combination structures

FRS 102 indicates that a business combination may be structured in a variety of ways for legal, taxation or other reasons. It may involve: *[FRS 102.19.4]*

- the purchase by an entity of the equity of another entity;
- the purchase of all the net assets of another entity;
- the assumption of the liabilities of another entity; or
- the purchase of some of the net assets of another entity that together form one or more businesses.

It may be effected by the issue of equity instruments, the transfer of cash, cash equivalents or other assets, or a mixture of these. The transaction may be between the shareholders of the combining entities or between one entity and the shareholders of another entity. It may involve the establishment of a new entity to control the combining entities or net assets transferred, or the restructuring of one or more of the combining entities. *[FRS 102.19.5]*. Whatever the legal structure, if it is a 'business combination' then the requirements of Section 19 apply (unless it is specifically excluded).

As indicated above, a business combination may involve the purchase of the net assets, including any goodwill, of another entity rather than the purchase of the equity of the other entity. Such a combination does not result in a parent-subsidiary relationship. Nevertheless, the acquirer (even if it is a single entity), will account for such a business combination in its individual or separate financial statements and consequently in any consolidated financial statements.

3.3   The purchase method (acquisition accounting)

All business combinations (apart from those excluded from the scope of Section 19, group reconstructions which may be accounted for by using the merger accounting method and certain public benefit entity combinations) are accounted for by applying the purchase method. *[FRS 102.19.6]*. The purchase method is commonly referred to as acquisition accounting.

As discussed at 1.1 above, the purchase method views a business combination from the perspective of the combining entity that is identified as the acquirer. The acquirer recognises the assets acquired and liabilities and contingent liabilities assumed, including those not previously recognised by the acquiree.

Applying the purchase method involves the following steps: *[FRS 102.19.7]*

- identifying an acquirer (3.4 below);
- determining the acquisition date (3.5 below)
- measuring the cost of the business combination (3.6 below); and

- allocating, at the acquisition date, the cost of the business combination to the assets acquired and liabilities and provisions for contingent liabilities assumed (3.7 below).

3.3.1   Company law issues

The purchase method as outlined in Section 19 corresponds with the description of the acquisition method in UK company law: *[6 Sch 9]*

- the identifiable assets and liabilities of the undertaking acquired must be included in the consolidated balance sheet at their fair values as at the date of acquisition;

- the income and expenditure of the undertaking acquired must be brought into the group accounts only as from the date of the acquisition;

- there must be set off against the acquisition cost of the interest in the shares of the undertaking held by the parent company and its subsidiary undertakings the interest of the parent company and its subsidiary undertakings in the adjusted capital and reserves of the undertaking acquired;

- the resulting amount if positive must be treated as goodwill, and if negative as a negative consolidation difference; and

- negative goodwill may be transferred to the consolidated profit and loss account where such a treatment is in accordance with the principles and rules of Part 2 of Schedule 1 to these Regulations.

The accounting for goodwill (positive or negative) under Section 19 is discussed at 3.9 below.

3.4   Identifying an acquirer

Section 19 requires that an acquirer shall be identified for all business combinations accounted for by applying the purchase method. The acquirer is the combining entity that obtains control of the other combining entities or businesses. *[FRS 102.19.8]*.

Control is defined as 'the power to govern the financial and operating policies of an entity or business so as to obtain benefits from its activities'. *[FRS 102.19.9]*. Section 19 cross-references to Section 9 for a description of control of one entity by another in the context of identifying subsidiaries for the purposes of consolidation:

'Control is presumed to exist when the parent owns, directly or indirectly through subsidiaries, more than half of the voting power of an entity. That presumption may be overcome in exceptional circumstances if it can be clearly demonstrated that such ownership does not constitute control. Control also exists when the parent owns half or less of the voting power of an entity but it has: *[FRS 102.9.5]*

(a)   power over more than half of the voting rights by virtue of an agreement with other investors;

(b)   power to govern the financial and operating policies of the entity under a statute or an agreement;

(c)   power to appoint or remove the majority of the members of the board of directors or equivalent governing body and control of the entity is by that board or body; or

(d)   power to cast the majority of votes at meetings of the board of directors or equivalent governing body and control of the entity is by that board or body.'

Chapter 17

'Control can also be achieved by having options or convertible instruments that are currently exercisable or by having an agent with the ability to direct the activities for the benefit of the controlling entity', *[FRS 102.9.6]*, and 'can also exist when the parent has the power to exercise, or actually exercises, dominant influence or control over the undertaking or it and the undertaking are managed on a unified basis.' *[FRS 102.9.6A]*.

The requirements of Section 9 relating to 'control' are discussed in Chapter 8 at 3.2.

Section 19 notes that although it may sometimes be difficult to identify an acquirer, there are usually indicators that one exists. For example: *[FRS 102.19.10]*

- If the fair value of one of the combining entities is significantly greater than that of the other combining entity, the entity with the greater fair value is likely to be the acquirer.

- If the business combination is effected through an exchange of voting ordinary equity instruments for cash or other assets, the entity giving up cash or other assets is likely to be the acquirer.

- If the business combination results in the management of one of the combining entities being able to dominate the selection of the management team of the resulting combined entity, the entity whose management is able so to dominate is likely to be the acquirer.

Determination of the acquirer may require significant judgement and consideration of the pertinent facts and circumstances must be considered.

3.4.1   Reverse acquisitions

While not explicitly mentioned in FRS 102, it is implicitly recognised that in some business combinations, commonly referred to as reverse acquisitions, the acquirer is the entity whose equity interests have been acquired and the issuing entity is the acquiree. This might be the case when, for example, a private entity arranges to have itself 'acquired' by a small public entity as a means of obtaining a stock exchange listing and, as part of the agreement, the directors of the public entity resign and are replaced with directors appointed by the private entity and its former owners. Although legally the issuing public entity is regarded as the parent and the private entity is regarded as the subsidiary, the legal subsidiary is the acquirer if it has the power to govern the financial and operating policies of the legal parent so as to obtain benefits from its activities. See 3.10 below for further discussion on reverse acquisitions.

3.4.2   Newly incorporated entities formed to effect a business combination

Occasionally, a new entity is formed to issue equity instruments to effect a business combination between, for example, two other entities. FRS 102 does not explicitly deal with this situation, but it is dealt with in IFRS 3 and was dealt with under previous UK GAAP in FRS 6. IFRS 3 requires that one of the combining entities that existed before the combination be identified as the acquirer. *[IFRS 3 Appendix B.18]*. Similarly, FRS 6 required that where the combination of the entities other than the new parent would have been an acquisition, one of the combining entities would be identified as having the role of the acquirer. This acquirer and the new parent company would be first combined by using merger accounting, and the other entities would be treated as having been acquired by this combined company. *[FRS 6.14]*.

FRS 102 contains no such explicit guidance that a new entity would not generally be identified as the acquirer. However, we believe that the same approach should be adopted when a new entity effects a business combination. The substance of the transaction is that one of the two other entities has acquired the other, but they have been brought together legally under the new entity rather than one of these entities acquiring the other. The new entity, itself, has little substance other than as a vehicle to hold the shares in the combining entities, and may have been structured in this way for legal, taxation or other reasons. Therefore, in such a transaction, the combination between the new entity and the identified acquirer is effectively the same as if a new entity had been inserted above an existing entity. Such a 'group reconstruction' would be accounted for under merger accounting (see 5.3 below). Reverse acquisition accounting (see 3.4.1 above) is unlikely to be appropriate in this situation because the definition of a business combination (see 3.2.1 above) generally involves an acquirer obtaining control of a business, *[FRS 102.19.3]*, and a newly formed entity would not meet the definition of a business.

However, that is not to say that a new entity that is established to effect a business combination cannot ever be identified as the acquirer. For example, there may be situations where a new entity is established and used on behalf of a group of investors or another entity to acquire a controlling interest in a 'target entity' in an arm's length transaction and the consideration is cash or other assets.

Example 17.5:   Business combination effected by a Newco for cash consideration

Entity A intends to acquire the voting shares (and therefore obtain control) of Target Entity. Entity A incorporates Newco and uses this entity to effect the business combination. Entity A provides a loan at commercial interest rates to Newco. The loan funds are used by Newco to acquire 100% of the voting shares of Target Entity in an arm's length transaction. The group structure post-transaction is as follows:

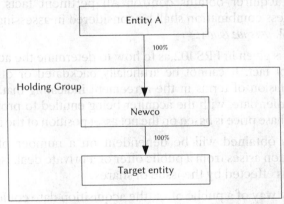

Newco is required to prepare consolidated financial statements for the Holding Group (the reporting entity). (In most situations like this, Newco would be exempt from preparing consolidated financial statements – see Chapter 8 at 3.1).

The acquirer is the entity that obtains control of the acquiree. Whenever a new entity is formed to effect a business combination other than through the issue of shares, it is appropriate to consider whether Newco is an extension of one of the transacting parties. If it is an extension of the transacting party (or parties) that ultimately gain control of the other combining entities, Newco is the acquirer.

In this situation, Entity A has obtained control of Target Entity in an arm's length transaction, using Newco to effect the acquisition. The transaction has resulted in a change in control of Target Entity and Newco is in effect an extension of Entity A acting at its direction to obtain control for Entity A. Accordingly, Newco would be identified as the acquirer at the Holding Group level.

If, rather than Entity A establishing Newco, a group of investors had established it as the acquiring vehicle through which they obtained control of Target Entity then, we believe, Newco would be regarded as the acquirer since it is an extension of the group of investors.

3.5   Determining the acquisition date

The determination of the acquisition date is critical to accounting for a business combination, as it is both the date from which the results of the acquiree are incorporated into the financial statements of the acquirer, and the date on which the cost of the business combination is allocated to the fair values of the assets acquired and liabilities and provisions for contingent liabilities assumed. The acquisition date is the date on which the acquirer obtains control of the acquiree. *[FRS 102.19.3]*.

The acquirer's statement of comprehensive income incorporates the acquiree's profits or losses after the acquisition date by including the acquiree's income and expenses based on the cost of the business combination to the acquirer. For example, depreciation expense included after the acquisition date in the acquirer's statement of comprehensive income that relates to the acquiree's depreciable assets shall be based on the fair values of those depreciable assets at the acquisition date, i.e. their cost to the acquirer. *[FRS 102.19.16]*.

Application of the purchase method starts from the acquisition date, which is the date on which the acquirer obtains control of the acquiree. Because control is the power to govern the financial and operating policies of an entity or business so as to obtain benefits from its activities, it is not necessary for a transaction to be closed or finalised at law before the acquirer obtains control. All pertinent facts and circumstances surrounding a business combination shall be considered in assessing when the acquirer has obtained control. *[FRS 102.19.10A]*.

No further guidance is given in FRS 102 as to how to determine the acquisition date, but it is clearly a matter of fact. It cannot be artificially backdated or otherwise altered, for example, by the inclusion of terms in the agreement indicating that acquisition is to be effective as of an earlier date, with the acquirer being entitled to profits arising after that date, even if the purchase price is based on the net asset position of the acquiree at that date.

The date control is obtained will be dependent on a number of factors, including whether the acquisition arises from a public offer or a private deal, is subject to approval by other parties, or is effected by the issue of shares.

For an acquisition by way of a public offer, the acquisition date could be when the offer has become unconditional as a result of a sufficient number of acceptances being received or at the date that the offer closes. In a private deal, the date would generally be when an unconditional offer has been accepted by the vendors.

It can be seen from the above that one of the key factors is that the offer is 'unconditional'. Thus, where an offer is conditional on the approval of the acquiring entity's shareholders then until that approval has been received, it is unlikely that control will have been obtained. Where the offer is conditional upon receiving some form of regulatory approval, then it will depend on the nature of that approval. Where it is a substantive hurdle, such as obtaining the approval of a competition authority, it is unlikely that control could have been obtained prior to that approval. However, where the approval is merely a formality, or 'rubber-stamping' exercise, then this would not preclude control having been obtained at an earlier date.

Where the acquisition is effected by the issue of shares, then the date of control will generally be when the exchange of shares takes place.

However, as indicated above, whether control has been obtained by a certain date is a matter of fact, and all pertinent facts and circumstances surrounding a business combination need to be considered in assessing when the acquirer has obtained control.

3.6 Measuring the cost of the business combination

Having identified the acquirer, the next step is for the acquirer to measure the cost of the business combination. Section 19 requires this to be the aggregate of: *[FRS 102.19.11]*

- the fair values, at the acquisition date, of assets given, liabilities incurred or assumed, and equity instruments issued by the acquirer, in exchange for control of the acquiree (see 3.7.3 below); plus
- any costs directly attributable to the business combination.

In a step acquisition, i.e. where control is achieved in a series of transactions, the cost of the business combination is the aggregate of the fair values of the assets given, liabilities assumed, and equity instruments issued by the acquirer at the date of each transaction in the series. *[FRS 102.19.11A]*. The accounting treatment for step acquisitions is discussed further at 3.11 below.

Where equity instruments issued by the acquirer are given as consideration to the vendor, the fair value of those equity instruments is determined based on the guidance in Section 2. *[FRS 102.2A1-2A6]*. It should be noted that while 'merger relief' and 'group reconstruction relief' under the CA 2006 include relief from recognising share premium where certain conditions are met, this affects the accounting considerations for capital and reserves of the issuing entity only, and is not relevant for the purposes of measuring the cost of the combination in connection with application of the purchase method – see 5.5 below for discussion of merger relief and group reconstruction relief.

3.6.1 Costs directly attributable to the combination

The cost of a business combination includes any costs directly attributable to the combination. FRS 102 does not indicate what types of costs these might be, but we consider that they would include costs such as professional fees paid to accountants, legal advisers, valuers and other consultants to effect the combination. General administrative costs, including the costs of maintaining an acquisitions department, and other costs that cannot be directly attributed to the particular combination being accounted for are not included in the cost of the combination: They are recognised as an expense when incurred. Only incremental internal costs should be included.

It may be that an entity engages another party to investigate or assist in identifying a potential target. Whether any fee payable to such party can be included as part of the cost of the business combination will depend on whether the work performed can be regarded as directly attributable to that particular business combination. Where the fee is payable only if the combination takes place then it should be included as part of the cost.

Transaction costs (for financial instruments) are incremental costs that are directly attributable to the acquisition, issue or disposal of a financial asset or liability, or the issue of an entity's own equity instrument. *[FRS 102 Appendix I]*. These costs are not included as costs of the business combination, but are accounted for as costs of issuing those instruments. *[FRS 102.11.13, 22.9]*. They therefore do not affect the measurement of goodwill in the business combination.

Where professional advisors provide advice on all aspects of the business combination, including the arranging and issuing of financial liabilities and / or issuing equity instruments, it will be necessary for some allocation of the fees payable to be made, possibly by obtaining a breakdown from the relevant advisor.

It may be that an entity, at its balance sheet date, is in the process of acquiring another business and has incurred costs that are considered to be directly attributable to that expected business combination. At the balance sheet date, the entity has not yet obtained control over the business. In this situation how should the costs be accounted for? One view is that the costs must be expensed since at the balance sheet date there has been no business combination. However, we believe that since directly attributable costs are to be included in the cost of a business combination, then the costs should be carried forward as an asset from the date that is considered probable that the business combination will be completed. Any costs incurred prior to the date that it is considered probable that the business combination will be completed should be expensed, and remain written off regardless of whether the acquisition takes place; they cannot be reinstated and capitalised at a later date. In the subsequent period, when the business combination is completed, the costs carried forward will be reclassified as part of the cost of the business combination (and therefore into goodwill). If in the subsequent period it is no longer considered probable that the business combination will be completed, then the costs initially recognised as an asset will be expensed to the income statement.

3.6.2 Adjustments to the cost of a business combination contingent on future events ('Contingent consideration')

FRS 102 recognises that the terms of a business combination agreement may provide for an adjustment to the cost of the combination contingent on future events, and requires that, in such cases, the acquirer includes an estimate of that adjustment (reflecting the time value of money, if material) in the cost of the combination at the acquisition date if the adjustment is probable (i.e. more likely than not) and can be measured reliably. *[FRS 102.19.12]*.

Such future events might relate to a specified level of profit being maintained or achieved in future periods. A provision for an adjustment is more likely to be made in those situations where the contingent consideration is based on the acquiree maintaining a level of profits which it is currently earning (either for a particular period or as an average over a set period) or achieving profits which it is currently budgeting.

If the potential adjustment is not recognised at the acquisition date but subsequently becomes probable and can be measured reliably, the additional consideration shall be treated as an adjustment (reflecting the time value of money, if material) to the cost of the combination. *[FRS 102.19.13]*. If the future events that, at the acquisition date, were expected to occur do not occur, or the estimate needs to be revised, the cost of the business combination is adjusted accordingly. *[FRS 102.19.13A]*. Any subsequent adjustments in respect of contingent consideration will consequently be reflected in the carrying amount of goodwill. However, if an impairment loss has already been recognised in respect of the goodwill (see Chapter 24), this may require a further impairment loss to be recognised.

FRS 102 does not address whether these adjustments should be reflected retrospectively or prospectively. In our view, changes in the probability of an event occurring (or not) reflect conditions arising after the acquisition date and so represent a change in estimate. Changes in accounting estimates are accounted for prospectively (see Chapter 9 at 3.5).

If contingent consideration is adjusted for the time value of money, the unwinding of any discounting is recognised as a finance cost in profit or loss, in the period it arises. *[FRS 102.19.13B]*.

The Triennial review 2017 clarified that the time value of money should be taken into account when determining contingent consideration (if material) and that subsequent adjustments to contingent consideration should be recognised in the cost of the combination. It is not expected that these clarifications will lead to significant changes in practice.

FRS 102 does not provide guidance on determining the discount rate to be used in respect of contingent consideration. In our view, an entity can determine an accounting policy, to be applied consistently, either by analogy to financial liabilities at amortised cost or to provisions. This is further explained in Example 17.6 below.

The following example illustrates how changes to discount rates could be considered.

Example 17.6:   Discount rate in contingent consideration subsequently adjusted

Entity A acquired Entity B on 31 December 2018 and the consideration includes £8 million that is contingent on meeting a profit target by 31 December 2021.

At the date of acquisition it was considered probable that the acquiree would meet the profit target, when the appropriate discount rate was 8%. Accordingly, £6,350,658 (see table below) was recognised as part of the cost of the business combination in the financial statements for 31 December 2018.

At 31 December 2019, Entity A's assessment remains that payment of £8 million at 31 December 2021 is probable, so its estimate of cash flows is the same as the prior period end. However, changes in circumstances at 31 December 2019 mean that the discount rate would be 7%. Should Entity A adjust its contingent consideration liability for the update in discount rate?

The relevant present values are as follows:

	PV at 8% £	PV at 7% £
31 December 2018	6,350,658	6,530,383
Interest for 2019	508,053	457,127
31 December 2019	6,858,711	6,987,510
Interest for 2020	548,696	489,126
31 December 2020	7,407,407	7,476,636
Interest for 2021	592,593	523,364
31 December 2021	8,000,000	8,000,000

Whether the discount rate is updated at 31 December 2019 is not clear from FRS 102. A contingent consideration liability could be considered similar to a financial liability (which would not qualify as a basic instrument under Section 11 – *Basic Financial Instruments*) or a provision. However, the accounting by the acquirer for contingent consideration in a business combination is out of scope of both Section 12 – *Other Financial Instrument Issues* – and Section 21 – *Provisions and Contingencies*. *[FRS 102.12.3(g), 21.1]*. In our view, an entity applies the hierarchy in paragraph 5(a) of Section 10 to refer to other relevant guidance within FRS 102 regarding discounted liabilities. Therefore, Entity A analogises to the discounting of either a financial liability at amortised cost or a provision. Under an amortised cost model, the discount rate would not be updated. *[FRS 102.11.16, 20]*. Analogising to a provisions model the discount rate would be updated at each reporting date. *[FRS 102.21.11]*.

Therefore, depending on the entity's chosen policy, the liability is discounted at the rate determined at 31 December 2018 (following an amortised cost model) or 31 December 2019 (following a provisions model). Following an amortised cost model, the liability accretes at the original discount rate of 8%, interest of £508,053 is recognised in the income statement for 2019 and no adjustment is made to goodwill. Following a provisions model, the same interest would be recognised in the income statement and an adjustment of £128,799 is made to the cost of the combination (and therefore goodwill) to record the liability at £6,987,510 at 31 December 2019. This adjustment to goodwill arises from a change in the present value of the estimated cash flows. As a change in estimate, the adjustment is made at the date of change rather than calculated retrospectively. The resulting liability is reassessed at each reporting date thereafter for changes in estimated cash flows (and changes in discount rate when following a provisions model), and any necessary adjustment made to the cost of the combination (and therefore goodwill).

3.6.3   Distinguishing 'contingent consideration' from other arrangements

Other than noting that the cost of a business combination is the aggregate of 'the fair values, at the acquisition date, of assets given, liabilities incurred or assumed, and equity instruments issued by the acquirer, *in exchange for control of the acquiree'*[emphasis added], *[FRS 102.19.11]*, FRS 102 provides no further guidance in distinguishing between consideration given in exchange for control of the acquiree and payments pertaining to other arrangements.

It is important to be able to identify those arrangements that represent contingent consideration and those that do not because contingent consideration generally results in some form of adjustment to the accounting for a business combination (including goodwill). Notwithstanding the structuring of a purchase agreement, which may be for legal, tax, or other reasons, transactions and other events and conditions should be accounted for and presented in accordance with their substance and not merely their legal form. *[FRS 102.2.8]*.

In our view, an arrangement that provides for additional payments to be made to the vendors of an acquiree should be accounted for as contingent consideration if the payment:

(a)   is made as consideration for the acquisition of a controlling interest in the acquiree (based on the substance of the arrangement); *and*

(b)   is contingent on future events that relate to the value of the acquiree (for example, an acquirer makes an additional cash payment if the acquiree achieves a profit target).

It is necessary to consider the substance of the arrangement to determine whether additional payments are made as consideration for the acquisition of a controlling interest in the acquiree (criterion (a) above). Where a vendor has a continuing relationship with the acquirer (for example, an on-going customer or supplier relationship) it is necessary to determine in what capacity payments are made to the vendor. As there is no specific guidance, the following factors may be considered in evaluating the substance of the arrangement:

- whether the additional payments are linked to the on-going relationship;
- what are the reasons for the additional payments; and
- the nature of the formula for determining the additional payments.

Criterion (b) above involves a consideration of whether the contingency relates to the value of the acquiree. If it is not clear what the contingency relates to, it will be necessary to consider its nature carefully in order to determine whether it should be accounted for as contingent consideration or separately from the business combination.

3.6.3.A   Examples of 'contingent consideration' relating to the value of the acquiree

Arrangements that provide for additional payments to be made to the vendors of an acquiree that are contingent on future events relating to the value of the acquiree, and thus will result in adjustments to the cost of the business combination, can take a number of forms. Examples include:

- an additional payment of £X million if the acquiree's profit in the year after acquisition exceeds £Y million;
- an additional payment of £X million if a drug currently under development receives regulatory approval at a later date; and
- an additional payment of Z% of actual EBITDA of the acquiree in the year after acquisition.

The first example of an 'earn-out' clause – whereby the acquirer agrees to pay additional amounts if the future earnings of the acquiree exceed specified amounts – is a typical example of contingent consideration relating to the value of the acquiree. The second example is where the contingency relates to a key business-related milestone that will have an impact on the value of the acquiree.

In both of these examples, there is uncertainty linked to a specific event as to whether an additional payment will be made (profit exceeding X or drug approval). In the third case, which also relates to the value of the acquiree, there will be an additional payment (on the assumption that a negative EBITDA is highly unlikely for that business) but there is uncertainty as to how much the payment will be.

In our view, FRS 102 requires an adjustment to the cost of the business combination in all of these situations. 'Future events' should include events that affect the amount of the payment and not just those that affect whether a specified payment is required or not. Thus, any consideration for a business combination where the amount or the timing is unknown with certainty is contingent consideration.

3.6.3.B   Example of an arrangement that is not 'contingent consideration'

The following example illustrates an arrangement where the additional payments that may be made to the vendors under the business combination agreement should not be accounted for as 'contingent consideration' under FRS 102.

Example 17.7:   Vendor retains a customer relationship with acquiree and is entitled to volume rebates on purchases it makes

Target is a subsidiary of Vendor Entity. Target provides goods and services to Vendor Entity that represent a significant portion of Target's business. Acquirer acquires 100% of the issued shares of Target. The purchase price is considered to represent the fair value of Target.

As part of the business combination agreement, Acquirer agrees to pay Vendor Entity a volume rebate for the next 5 years if Vendor Entity's purchases from Target exceed a specified amount in each of those years. The volume rebate offered is consistent with terms offered to other customers.

The volume rebate agreement with the vendor should not be accounted for as contingent consideration because it is not consideration for the acquisition of control in Target. The purchase price paid for the issued shares of Target is considered to represent fair value of Target; and Acquirer will be required to pay the volume rebates only in the event that Vendor Entity's purchases exceed a specified amount. The volume rebate arrangement is merely a means of securing Vendor Entity's custom for the next five years. Therefore, whilst the volume rebate arrangement arises by virtue of Acquirer having acquired Target, it does not

Chapter 17

represent additional consideration for the acquisition of a controlling interest in Target. Additionally, the contingency does not relate to the value of the business acquired because payment is contingent on Vendor Entity's future purchases exceeding a specified amount.

3.6.4   Contingent consideration relating to future services

A particular example of a situation where vendors may have a continuing relationship with the acquirer is where they become, or continue to be, key employees of the acquiree subsequent to the acquisition.

While IFRS 3 specifically identifies a transaction that remunerates employees or former owners of the acquiree for future services as not part of the cost of the business combination, *[IFRS 3.52(b)]*, FRS 102 does not distinguish between contingent consideration that, in substance, is additional purchase price and contingent consideration that, in substance, represents compensation for future services. However, consistent with the discussion at 3.6.3 above, we believe that an acquirer must make such a distinction and therefore identify contingent consideration that is, in substance, compensation for future services, and account for this separately from the cost of the combination. This is because Section 2 includes as one of the qualitative characteristics of information in financial statements 'substance over form', requiring that 'transactions and other events and conditions should be accounted for and presented in accordance with their substance and not merely their legal form'. *[FRS 102.2.8]*. Therefore, where a vendor is also a continuing employee it is necessary to determine whether payments are made to them in their capacity as vendor or as employee.

If, for example, the consideration takes the form of share-based payments, it is necessary to determine how much of the share-based payment relates to the acquisition of control (which forms part of the cost of combination, accounted for under Section 19) and how much relates to the provision of future services (which is a post-combination operating expense accounted for under Section 26 – *Share-based Payment*). This would be the case if, for example, the vendor of an acquired entity receives a share-based payment for transferring control of the entity and for remaining in continuing employment.

In the absence of specific guidance, entities will need to apply judgement for evaluating the substance of the contingent consideration or determining an appropriate split. In making such a judgement, entities may consider the requirements and guidance in EU-adopted IFRS dealing with similar or related issues. *[FRS 102.10.6]*. IFRS 3 contains specific guidance for determining whether arrangements for contingent payments to employees or selling shareholders are contingent consideration in the business combination or are separate transactions. This includes consideration of a number of indicators relating to continuing employment, duration of continuing employment, level of remuneration, incremental payments to employees, number of shares owned, linkage to valuation, formula for determining consideration, and other agreements and issues. *[IFRS 3 Appendix B.54-55]*.

In making such an evaluation, all terms of the agreement have a critical role in this assessment, and the reasons for structuring the terms of the transaction in a particular way, and the identity of the initiator, should be understood. Nevertheless, when the agreement includes employment conditions such that the payments are forfeited upon termination of employment, all or a portion of, the additional payments will generally be classified as employment compensation.

3.6.5 Contingent consideration to be settled by equity instruments

In some business combination agreements involving contingent consideration, it may be that additional consideration will not be settled by cash, but by shares.

Section 19 makes no explicit reference to such a situation. Section 11 scopes out from its provisions 'Financial instruments that meet the definition of an entity's own equity', *[FRS 102.11.7(b)]*, while Section 12 and Section 22 – *Liabilities and Equity* – both scope out from their respective requirements 'Contracts for contingent consideration in a business combination' (this exemption applies only to the acquirer). *[FRS 102.12.3(g), 22.2(c)]*.

Section 26 applies to 'share-based payment transactions'. *[FRS 102.26.1]*. Section 26 does not explicitly scope out transactions in which an entity acquires goods as part of the net assets acquired in a business combination to which Section 19 applies nor equity instruments issued in a business combination in exchange for control of an acquiree. On this matter, IFRS 2 – *Share-based Payment* – explicitly scopes these out from its requirements. *[IFRS 2.5]*.

In our view, while not explicitly excluded, as the nature of a business combination is fundamentally different from a transaction to acquire goods or services, we do not consider that the provisions of Section 26 should extend to equity instruments issued in a business combination.

In practice, there is a wide variety of share-settled contingent consideration arrangements, but they are generally based on one of two models:

- arrangements whereby shares are issued to a particular value based on certain conditions being met, e.g. if profits are £A then additional consideration of £M will be given, to be satisfied by shares based on the share price at date of issue; or

- arrangements whereby a particular number of shares are issued if certain conditions are met, e.g. if profits are £A then X shares will be issued, but if profits are £B then Y shares will be issued.

The issues that need to be considered in accounting for such arrangements are:

- If the consideration is recognised, should it be classified as a liability or as equity?

- How should the consideration be valued, both on initial recognition and if reassessed at a later date?

Example 17.8: Share-settled contingent consideration (1)

Entity P acquires a 100% interest in Entity S on 31 December 2019. As part of the consideration arrangements, additional consideration will be payable on 1 January 2023, based on Entity S meeting certain profit targets over the three years ended 31 December 2022, as follows:

Profit target (average profits over 3 year period)	Additional consideration
£1m but less than £1.25m	£5m
£1.25m but less than £1.5m	£6m
£1.5m+	£7.5m

Any additional consideration will be satisfied by issuing the appropriate number of shares with a value equivalent to the additional consideration payable based on Entity P's share price at 1 January 2023.

At the date of acquisition, Entity P considers that it is probable that Entity S will meet the first profit target, but not the others.

How should Entity P classify the additional consideration in its financial statements for the year ended 31 December 2019, and what amount should be recognised in respect of it?

As discussed above, contracts for contingent consideration are specifically scoped out of Section 22, and we consider the provisions of Section 26 should not apply. In our view the principles of Section 22 are relevant to determining the appropriate classification of such arrangements. On that basis, the contingent consideration in this situation is 'a contract that will or may be settled in the entity's own equity instruments and is a non-derivative for which the entity is or may be obliged to deliver a variable number of the entity's own equity instruments', *[FRS 102.22.3(b)]*, and therefore classification as a liability seems appropriate.

On the basis that the consideration is reflected as a liability then, as with contingent consideration payable in cash, the amount to be recognised at 31 December 2019 should be the present value of the £5m consideration expected to be payable on 1 January 2023.

If at 31 December 2020, Entity P considers that is it is probable that Entity S will now meet the second target, it should remeasure the liability at that date to the present value of the £6m that is now expected to be payable on 1 January 2023 with a corresponding adjustment to goodwill, having reflected the unwinding of the discount on the original £5m in the income statement. In determining the present value as at 31 December 2020, whether the discount rate is updated at that date or remains the original discount rate calculated at initial recognition depends on the accounting policy adopted by Entity P. This is further explained in Example 17.6 above.

In the above example, the arrangement was of the type where the shares issued to settle the consideration were equivalent to a particular value. However, what if the arrangement was of the type where a particular number of shares are to be issued to satisfy the consideration?

Example 17.9:   *Share-settled contingent consideration (2)*

Entity P acquires a 100% interest in Entity S on 31 December 2019. As part of the consideration arrangements, additional consideration will be payable on 1 January 2023, based on Entity S meeting certain profit targets over the three years ended 31 December 2022, as follows:

Profit target	*Additional consideration*
Year ended 31 December 2020 – £1m+	100,000 shares
Year ended 31 December 2021 – £1.25m+	150,000 shares
Year ended 31 December 2022 – £1.5m+	200,000 shares

Each target is non-cumulative. If the target for a particular year is met, the additional consideration will be payable, irrespective of whether the targets for the other years are met or not. If a target for a particular year is not met, no shares will be issued in respect of that year. At the date of acquisition, Entity P considers that it is probable that Entity S will meet the first profit target, but not the others.

How should Entity P classify the additional consideration in its financial statements for the year ended 31 December 2019, and what amount should be recognised in respect of it?

Although Section 22 does not strictly apply, we consider that its principles are relevant to determining whether this type of arrangement is classified as a financial liability or equity.

Section 22 does not consider a contract to be equity where it is 'a contract that will or may be settled in the entity's own equity instruments and is a non-derivative for which the entity is or may be obliged to deliver a variable number of the entity's own equity instruments'. *[FRS 102.22.3(b)]*.

In this scenario, as each of the targets are independent of one another, this arrangement can be regarded as being three distinct contingent consideration arrangements that are assessed separately. As either zero or the requisite number of shares will be issued if each target is met, the obligation in respect of each arrangement is classified as equity.

If the targets were dependent on each other, for example, if they were based on an average for the three year period, a specified percentage increase on the previous year's profits, or the later targets were forfeited if the earlier targets were not met, the classification would be assessed on the overall arrangement. As this would mean that a variable number of shares may be delivered, the obligation under such an arrangement would have to be classified as a financial liability.

On the basis that the consideration is reflected as equity, we believe that the amount recognised for the consideration should be based on the requirements of Section 19 in respect of equity instruments issued as consideration, i.e. at the fair value at the date of exchange (31 December 2019). However, in this situation the fair value of the 'equity instrument' at the date of exchange would need to take into account, for example, an allowance for any estimated dividends on the shares that will not be payable during the period until they are issued on 1 January 2023.

One other issue that arises in this situation is whether adjustments should be made to the consideration, and thus goodwill, to reflect subsequent changes in the fair value of the shares such that the consideration is ultimately measured at Entity P's share price at the date the shares are finally issued. Although the requirements for contingent consideration would generally require subsequent changes in the estimate of the consideration that will ultimately be given to be recognised, we do not believe that this should reflect such changes in fair value. Under FRS 102, equity instruments are measured based on the fair value of cash or other resources received or receivable at the date of initial recognition. *[FRS 102.22.7-8]*. Once an equity instrument has been recognised, changes in the fair value of the equity instrument are not recognised in the financial statements.

Since, at 31 December 2019, Entity P considers that is it is not probable that Entity S will meet the second profit target (i.e. as at 31 December 2021), no amount is reflected in equity for that second profit target. If, at 31 December 2020, the second profit target becomes probable, then the financial statements at that date need to reflect that Entity P now expects to issue an additional 150,000 shares. As discussed above, we do not believe that any change should be made to reflect changes in the value of Entity P's shares since the date of exchange (31 December 2019), and so the additional consideration of 150,000 shares should be valued using the same value per share as the original estimated consideration of 100,000 shares, with a consequent adjustment to goodwill.

3.7 Allocating the cost of the business combination to the assets acquired and liabilities and contingent liabilities assumed

Having determined the cost of the business combination, the next stage is to allocate that cost to the assets acquired and liabilities and contingent liabilities assumed.

FRS 102 requires that the acquirer shall, at the acquisition date, allocate the cost of a business combination by recognising the acquiree's identifiable assets, liabilities and a provision for those contingent liabilities that satisfy the recognition criteria (see below) at their fair values at that date. There is an exception for deferred tax assets and liabilities, employee benefit assets and liabilities and share-based payment arrangements – which are subject to separate requirements, discussed at 3.7.2 below. Any difference between the cost of the business combination and the acquirer's interest in the net amount of the identifiable assets, liabilities and provisions for contingent liabilities so recognised is accounted for as goodwill or negative goodwill (see 3.9 below). *[FRS 102.19.14]*.

The acquirer recognises separately the acquiree's identifiable assets, liabilities and contingent liabilities (except for deferred tax assets and liabilities, employee benefit assets and liabilities and share-based payment arrangements) at the acquisition date only if they satisfy the following criteria at that date: *[FRS 102.19.15]*

- In the case of an asset, it is probable that any associated future economic benefits will flow to the acquirer, and its fair value can be measured reliably.

- In the case of a liability other than a contingent liability, it is probable that an outflow of resources will be required to settle the obligation, and its fair value can be measured reliably.

- In the case of a contingent liability, its fair value can be measured reliably.

The identifiable assets acquired and liabilities assumed must meet the definition of assets (i.e. resources controlled by the entity as a result of past events and from which future economic benefits are expected to flow to the entity) and liabilities (i.e. present obligations of the entity arising from past events, the settlement of which is expected to result in an outflow from the entity of resources embodying economic benefits). *[FRS 102 Appendix I]*.

The recognition criteria for contingent liabilities are different from those of other assets and liabilities. FRS 102 reflects IFRS 3 in that, whilst not meeting the recognition criteria under the standard in the financial statements of the acquiree, the contingent liability has a fair value, which reflects market expectations about any uncertainty surrounding the possibility that an outflow of resources will be required to settle the possible or present obligation. *[IFRS 3.23]*. Accordingly, under FRS 102, the allocation of the cost of the business combination includes the separate recognition of the acquiree's contingent liabilities, if their fair value can be reliably measured. *[FRS 102.19.20]*.

Since the recognition of this liability is not what would be required by Section 21, Section 19 includes requirements for the subsequent measurement of such liabilities. Accordingly, after their initial recognition, the acquirer measures contingent liabilities that are recognised separately in accordance with paragraph 19.15(c) at the higher of: *[FRS 102.19.21]*

(a)   the amount that would be recognised in accordance with Section 21; and

(b)   the amount initially recognised less amounts previously recognised as revenue in accordance with Section 23 – *Revenue*.

The implications of part (a) of this requirement are clear. Part (b) implies that if the provision turns out to be lower than the amount initially recognised on acquisition, it is not reduced until the contingency no longer exists; the reference to Section 23 presumably applies where the contingent liability related to a revenue-earning activity.

If the fair value of a contingent liability cannot be measured reliably, the acquirer discloses the information about that contingent liability as required by Section 21 (see Chapter 19 at 3.10.3). *[FRS 102.19.20]*.

The recognition criteria make no reference to contingent assets of the acquiree. However, an asset is recognised in a business combination only if it meets the recognition criteria; i.e. it is probable that any associated future economic benefits will flow to the acquirer, and its fair value can be measured reliably. *[FRS 102.19.15]*. When the flow of future economic benefits from a contingent asset is virtually certain, then the related asset is not a contingent asset, and its recognition is appropriate. *[FRS 102.2.38]*.

3.7.1   Acquiree's identifiable assets and liabilities

3.7.1.A   Acquiree's intangible assets

The allocation of the cost of the business combination includes the separate recognition of the acquiree's intangible assets. This is irrespective of whether the asset had been recognised by the acquiree before the business combination.

An intangible asset is defined as an identifiable non-monetary asset without physical substance. Such an asset is identifiable when: *[FRS 102 Appendix I]*

- it is separable, i.e. capable of being separated or divided from the entity and sold, transferred, licensed, rented or exchanged, either individually or together with a related contract, asset or liability; or

- it arises from contractual or other legal rights, regardless of whether those rights are transferable or separable from the entity or from other rights and obligations.

An intangible asset acquired in a business combination is separately recognised if it:

(a)   meets the recognition criteria (i.e. (i) it is probable that the expected future economic benefits attributable to the asset will flow; and (ii) that the fair value of the intangible asset can be measured reliably);

(b)   arises from contractual or legal rights; and

(c)   is separable (i.e. capable of being separated or divided from the entity and sold, transferred, licensed, rented or exchanged either individually or together with a related contract, asset or liability).

In addition, an entity may choose to recognise additional intangible assets acquired in a business combination separately from goodwill for which (a) is satisfied and only one of (b) or (c) applies. The decision to recognise such additional intangible assets is a policy choice, to be applied consistently to a class of intangible assets (having a similar nature, function or use in the business). Licences are an example of a category of intangible asset that may be treated as a separate class, however, further subdivision may be appropriate, for example, where different types of licences have different functions within the business. *[FRS 102.18.8]*.

Where additional intangibles are recognised, the nature of the intangible assets and the reason why they have been separated from goodwill must be disclosed. *[FRS 102.18.28A]*.

Under the previous version of FRS 102, applicable to periods beginning prior to 1 January 2019, an intangible asset acquired in a business combination is separately recognised so long as: (i) its fair value can be measured reliably; and (ii) either one of (b) or (c) applies.

Additionally, prior to the Triennial review 2017 amendments, an intangible asset acquired in a business combination arising from legal or contractual rights was not recognised where there was no history of exchange transactions for the same or similar assets and otherwise estimating fair value would be dependent on immeasurable variables. This guidance has now been removed in response to feedback that it was not clear.

Chapter 17

The FRC considers that the revised requirements are 'a proportionate solution that permits the separate recognition of a larger number of intangible assets when this information provides useful information to the reporting entity and the users of its financial statements.' *[FRS 102.BC.B18.8]*. Although this may lead to greater inconsistency between entities, the FRC felt that it enables more information to be provided in some circumstances and that the additional disclosure of the nature of the additional intangible assets separated from goodwill, *[FRS 102.19.25(fA)]*, would assist in drawing comparisons. *[FRS 102.BC.B18.9]*.

The FRC considers that examples of intangible assets that would normally satisfy all three criteria (a) to (c) include: licences, copyrights, trademarks, internet domain names, patented technology and legally protected trade secrets. Examples of intangible assets that would not normally satisfy all three criteria include customer lists, customer relationships and unprotected trade secrets (such as secret recipes or formulas) as no contractual or legal right exists that would give rise to expected future economic benefits. *[FRS 102.BC.B18.10]*.

The guidance in the Illustrative Examples of IFRS 3 might also be relevant to the identification of specific items although some differences to FRS 102 may arise as explained below the following table. *[IFRS 3.IE16-IE44]*. The table below summarises the items included in the Illustrative Examples that the IASB regards as meeting the definition of an intangible asset. It is clear that the IASB envisages a wide range of items meeting the definition of an intangible asset, and therefore potentially being recognised separately from goodwill. Reference should be made to the Illustrative Examples for any further explanation about some of these items.

Intangible assets arising from contractual or other legal rights (regardless of being separable)	Other intangible assets that are separable
Marketing-related • Trademarks, trade names, service marks, collective marks and certification marks • Internet domain names • Trade dress (unique colour, shape or package design) • Newspaper mastheads • Non-competition agreements	
Customer-related • Order or production backlogs • Customer contracts and the related customer relationships	• Customer lists • Non-contractual customer relationships
Artistic-related • Plays, operas and ballets • Books, magazines, newspapers and other literary works	

• Musical works such as compositions, song lyrics and advertising jingles • Pictures and photographs • Video and audio-visual material, including films, music videos and television programmes	
Contract-based • Licensing, royalty and standstill agreements • Advertising, construction, management, service or supply contracts • Lease agreements • Construction permits • Franchise agreements • Operating and broadcasting rights • Servicing contracts such as mortgage servicing contracts • Employment contracts • Use rights such as drilling, water, air, timber-cutting and route authorities	
Technology-based • Patented technology • Computer software and mask works • Trade secrets such as secret formulas, processes or recipes	• Unpatented technology • Databases, including title plants

It can be seen from the table that customer relationships can potentially fall under either category. In the IASB's view, 'Customer relationships meet the contractual-legal criterion if an entity has a practice of establishing contracts with its customers, regardless of whether a contract exists at the acquisition date.' *[IFRS 3.IE28]*. In such cases, it does not matter whether the relationship is separable. It would only be if the relationship did not arise from a contract that recognition depends on the separability criterion.

As noted at 2.8 above, the IASB's view of the contractual nature of customer relationships appears to differ from the FRC's view expressed in the Basis of Conclusions as discussed above. Therefore, IFRS 3's guidance on customer relationships may not be relevant to an entity preparing financial statements under FRS 102.

3.7.1.B Reorganisation provisions and future operating losses

FRS 102 makes it clear that the acquirer recognises separately only the identifiable assets, liabilities and contingent liabilities of the acquiree that existed at the acquisition date and satisfy the recognition criteria (see 3.7 above). *[FRS 102.19.14, 15-15C, 18]*.

Therefore, the acquirer must recognise liabilities for terminating or reducing the activities of the acquiree as part of allocating the cost of the combination only to the extent that the acquiree has, at the acquisition date, an existing liability for restructuring recognised in accordance with Section 21. *[FRS 102.19.18(a)]*.

Chapter 17

Similarly, the acquirer, when allocating the cost of the combination, must not recognise liabilities for future losses or other costs expected to be incurred as a result of the business combination. *[FRS 102.19.18(b)]*.

3.7.2   Exceptions to the general recognition and measurement rules

Section 19 makes three exceptions from the general requirements of recognising and measuring the acquiree's assets and liabilities at their acquisition-date fair values.

3.7.2.A   Deferred tax assets and liabilities

The acquirer must recognise and measure a deferred tax asset or liability arising from the assets acquired and liabilities assumed in accordance with Section 29 – *Income Tax*. *[FRS 102.19.15A]*. To require the normal fair value treatment on acquisition would have resulted in immediate gains or losses being recognised when the deferred tax assets and liabilities were subsequently measured in accordance with Section 29, for example where fair values reflected the effects of discounting, but measurement under Section 29 would be on an undiscounted basis.

Under Section 29, when the amount that can be deducted for tax for an asset (other than goodwill) that is recognised in a business combination is less (more) than the value at which it is recognised, a deferred tax liability (asset) is recognised for the additional tax that will be paid (avoided) in respect of that difference. Similarly, a deferred tax asset (liability) is recognised for the additional tax that will be avoided (paid) because of a difference between the value at which a liability is recognised and the amount that will be assessed for tax. The amount attributed to goodwill (or negative goodwill) is adjusted by the amount of deferred tax recognised. *[FRS 102.29.11]*.

In determining the amount that can be deducted for tax an entity considers the manner in which the entity expects, at the end of the reporting period, to recover or settle the carrying amount of the asset or liability. *[FRS 102.29.11A]*.

The requirement to recognise deferred tax in a business combination, which is discussed further in Chapter 26 at 6.6, is an exception to the general 'timing differences' approach in Section 29.

3.7.2.B   Employee benefit assets and liabilities

The acquirer recognises and measures a liability (or asset, if any) related to the acquiree's employee benefit arrangements in accordance with Section 28 – *Employee Benefits*. *[FRS 102.19.15B]*. See Chapter 25.

3.7.2.C   Share-based payment transactions

The acquirer recognises and measures a share-based payment in accordance with Section 26 – *Share-based Payment*. *[FRS 102.19.15C]*. See Chapter 23.

Equity instruments granted to the employees of the acquiree in their capacity as employees (e.g. in return for continued service following the business combination) do not form part of the consideration for the business combination and are therefore within the scope of Section 26 as a share-based payment transaction, as are the cancellation, replacement or modification of a share-based payment transaction as the result of a business combination or other equity restructuring.

If a vendor of an acquired business remains as an employee of that business following the business combination and receives a share-based payment for transferring control of the entity and for remaining in continuing employment, it is necessary to determine how much of the share-based payment relates to the acquisition of control (and therefore forms part of the consideration for the business combination) and how much relates to the provision of future services (which is a post-combination operating expense, see 3.6.4 above).

3.7.3   Determining the acquisition-date fair values

There is no specific guidance in Section 19 on the determination of the fair value of particular assets and liabilities. However, in Appendix I to FRS 102, fair value is defined as 'the amount for which an asset could be exchanged, a liability settled... between knowledgeable, willing parties in an arm's length transaction. In the absence of any specific guidance provided in the relevant section of this FRS, the guidance in the Appendix to Section 2 – *Concepts and Pervasive Principles* – shall be used in determining fair value'. *[FRS 102 Appendix I]*. See Chapter 10 at 8.6 for discussion of this guidance.

Other guidance that might be relevant to the determination of the fair values of specific items includes that in other sections of FRS 102 (see 3.7.3.A to 3.7.3.H below) and also guidance included in IFRS 3 and IFRS 13.

3.7.3.A   Property, plant and equipment

In approaching the recognition and measurement of, for example, property, plant and equipment of the acquiree, the acquirer might look to the revaluation guidance included within Section 17 – *Property, Plant and Equipment. [FRS 102.17.15C-D]*. This refers to the guidance in the Appendix to Section 2 and notes that:

'The fair value of land and buildings is usually determined from market-based evidence by appraisal that is normally undertaken by professionally qualified valuers. The fair value of items of plant and equipment is usually their market value determined by appraisal. If there is no market-based evidence of fair value because of the specialised nature of the item of property, plant and equipment and the item is rarely sold, except as part of a continuing business, an entity may need to estimate fair value using an income or a depreciated replacement cost approach.' *[FRS 102.17.15C-D]*.

Since assets are recognised at their acquisition-date fair values, it follows that the acquirer does not recognise a separate provision or valuation allowance for assets – such as accumulated depreciation.

3.7.3.B   Intangible assets

Section 18 – *Intangible Assets other than Goodwill*, provides no guidance on the determination of fair value and so the general guidance in the Appendix to Section 2 is used.

Under IFRS, there are three broad approaches to valuing intangible assets that correspond to the valuation approaches referred to in IFRS 13. *[IFRS 13.62]*. These are the market, income and cost approaches. The diagram below shows these valuation

Chapter 17

approaches, together with some of the primary methods used to measure the fair value of intangible assets that fall under each approach, shown in the boxes on the right.

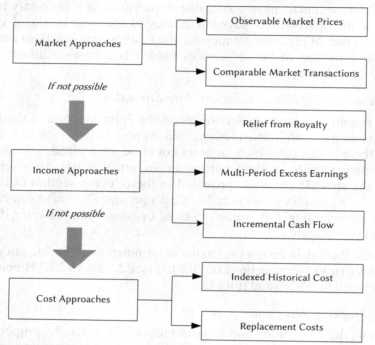

Income-based approaches are the most commonly used of the three in respect of intangible assets. These involve identifying the expected cash flows or economic benefits to be derived from the ownership of the particular intangible asset, and calculating the fair value of an intangible asset at the present value of those cash flows.

Two income-based methods that are commonly used to value intangible assets are:

- the Multi Period Excess Earnings Method ('MEEM'); and
- the Relief from Royalty method.

The MEEM is a residual cash flow methodology that is often used in valuing the primary intangible asset acquired.

The Relief from Royalty method is often used to calculate the value of a trademark or trade name. This approach is based on the concept that if an entity owns a trademark, it does not have to pay for the use of it and therefore is relieved from paying a royalty. The amount of that theoretical payment is used as a surrogate for income attributable to the trademark. The valuation is arrived at by computing the present value of the after-tax royalty savings, calculated by applying an appropriate royalty rate to the projected revenue, using an appropriate discount rate.

3.7.3.C   Inventories

Section 13 – *Inventories*, provides no guidance on determination of fair value.

One way of approaching inventory valuation on a business combination is as follows:

- finished goods are valued using selling prices less the costs of disposal and a reasonable profit allowance for the selling effort of the acquirer based on profit for similar finished goods;
- work in progress is valued using selling prices of finished goods less the sum of the costs to complete, the costs of disposal and a reasonable profit allowance for the completing and selling effort based on profit for similar finished goods; and
- raw materials are valued using current replacement costs.

Example 17.10:   Fair value of work in progress

Entity A acquires Entity B on 30 June 2019. Entity B operates a dairy business and included in its inventory at the date of acquisition was work in progress being inventory of cheddar cheese in cellars of the dairy left to mature for a year. The carrying amount of this inventory, being the costs incurred to the date of acquisition, is £400,000.

The intention is to sell the cheese once it has matured. The sales price of fully-matured cheese of the same quality at 30 June 2019 is £900,000. Future storage, marketing and selling expenses required to complete the process and market the product to retailers are estimated at £185,000.

How should the fair value of the work in progress be determined?

Based on the guidance above, the work in progress would be valued using selling prices of finished goods less the sum of the costs to complete, the costs of disposal and a reasonable profit allowance for the completing and selling effort based on profit for similar finished goods. Judgement is required by entities in calculating a reasonable profit allowance relating to the completing and selling efforts.

One approach would be to use the cost structure of Entity B to determine the reasonable profit allowance for subsequent costs to be incurred. Accordingly, it may be that if Entity B had not been acquired by Entity A, it would have incurred total costs of £585,000. Based on the estimated selling price of £900,000, this would result in an overall profit of £315,000. Consequently, the profit allowance to be made for the completing and selling effort would be £100,000 (being £315,000 × £185,000 ÷ £585,000). On this basis, the fair value of the work in progress would be £615,000 (being £900,000 − £185,000 − £100,000).

3.7.3.D   Financial instruments

Financial instruments traded in an active market should be valued at their quoted price, which is usually the current bid price. When quoted prices are unavailable, the price in a binding sale agreement or a recent transaction for an identical asset (or similar asset) in an arm's length transaction between knowledgeable, willing parties provides evidence of fair value. However, this price may not be a good estimate of fair value if there has been a significant change in economic circumstances or a significant period of time between the date of the binding sale agreement or the transaction, and the measurement date. If the market for the asset is not active and any binding sale agreements or recent transactions for an identical asset (or similar asset) on their own are not a good estimate of fair value, an entity estimates the fair value by using another valuation technique. *[FRS 102.2A.1]*. Further guidance on these concepts is provided in Chapter 4 at 3.3, which addresses the Appendix to Section 2.

Under the above guidance, receivables would likely be valued based on the present values of the amounts to be received, determined at appropriate current interest rates, less allowances for uncollectibility and collection costs, if necessary. As receivables are recognised and measured at fair value at the acquisition date, any uncertainty about collections and future cash flows are included in the fair value measure – and therefore, the acquirer should not recognise a separate provision or valuation allowance. In other words,

Chapter 17

an acquirer cannot 'carry over' any provision or valuation allowance already recognised by the acquiree. Generally, discounting is not required for short-term receivables, beneficial contracts and other identifiable assets when the difference between the nominal and discounted amounts is not material.

Similarly, accounts and notes payable, long-term debt, liabilities, accruals and other claims payable should be valued using the present values of amounts to be disbursed in settling the liabilities determined at appropriate current interest rates. Again, discounting is not generally required for short-term liabilities when the difference between the nominal and discounted amounts is not material.

3.7.3.E   *Investments in an associate or jointly controlled entity*

Where one of the identified assets is an investment in an associate or a jointly controlled entity, the fair value should be determined in accordance with the above guidance for financial instruments, rather than calculating a fair value based on the appropriate share of the fair values of the identifiable assets, liabilities and contingent liabilities of the associate or jointly controlled entity. By doing so, any goodwill relating to the associate or jointly controlled entity is subsumed within the carrying amount of the associate or jointly controlled entity rather than within the goodwill arising on the overall business combination. Nevertheless, although this fair value is effectively the 'cost' to the group to which equity accounting is applied, the underlying fair values of the identifiable assets, liabilities and contingent liabilities also need to be determined to apply equity accounting (see Chapter 12 at 3.3.2).

If the fair value exercise results in an excess of assets over the fair value of the consideration (commonly referred to as 'negative goodwill'), in accordance with the requirements discussed at 3.9.3 below, the acquirer should challenge the fair value placed on the associate or jointly controlled entity as it re-challenges the values placed on all of the assets, liabilities and contingent liabilities of the acquiree to ensure that the value has not been overstated. *[FRS 102.14.8(c), 19.24(a)].*

3.7.3.F   *Onerous contracts and operating leases*

A provision for an onerous contract that would be recognised under Section 21 by the acquiree at the acquisition date, should be recognised and measured at its fair value on allocation of the cost of the business combination.

An onerous contract is one in which the 'unavoidable costs of meeting the obligations under the contract exceed the economic benefits expected to be received under it. The unavoidable costs under a contract reflect the least net cost of exiting from the contract, which is the lower of the cost of fulfilling it and any compensation or penalties arising from failure to fulfil it. For example, an entity may be contractually required under an operating lease to make payments to lease an asset for which it no longer has any use.' *[FRS 102.21A.2].* Therefore, an onerous contract is a contract that is directly loss-making, not simply uneconomic by reference to current prices. However, in allocating the cost of a business combination, the acquirer should go further than considering just onerous contracts that are directly loss-making. We believe that contracts that are 'onerous' by reference to market conditions at the date of acquisition should be recognised as liabilities. This is consistent with the requirements for intangible assets.

In addition to contracts which are onerous, in allocating the cost of a business combination to the assets acquired, liabilities and contingent liabilities assumed, we consider that favourable contracts should be recognised as intangible assets and unfavourable contracts recognised as liabilities.

3.7.3.G   Contingent liabilities

No specific guidance is included in FRS 102 in determining the fair value of a contingent liability. Its fair value would be based on the amount that a third party would charge to assume those contingent liabilities. This amount would reflect all expectations about possible cash flows and not the single most likely or the expected maximum or minimum cash flow. Many contingent liabilities are so defined because it is not probable that an outflow of resources embodying economic benefits will be required to settle the obligation – even though the minimum cash flow may be zero, a third party would still charge a sum to assume the contingent liability.

3.7.3.H   Deferred revenue

An acquiree may have recorded deferred revenue at the date of acquisition for a number of reasons. For example, it might represent upfront payments for services or products that have yet to be delivered, or payments for delivered goods or services sold as a part of a multiple-element arrangement that could not be accounted for separately from undelivered items included in the same arrangement.

In accounting for a business combination, an acquirer should recognise a liability for deferred revenue of the acquiree only if it relates to an outstanding performance obligation assumed by the acquirer. Such performance obligations would include obligations to provide goods or services or the right to use an asset.

The measurement of the deferred revenue liability should be based on the fair value of the obligation at the date of acquisition, which will not necessarily be the same as the amount of deferred revenue recognised by the acquiree. In general, the fair value would be less than the amount recognised by the acquiree, as the amount of revenue that another party would expect to receive for meeting that obligation would not include any profit element relating to the selling or other efforts already completed by the acquiree.

Example 17.11: Deferred revenue of an acquiree

Target is an electronics company that sells contracts to service all types of electronics equipment for an upfront annual fee of £120,000. Acquirer purchases Target in a business combination. At the acquisition date, Target has one service contract outstanding with six months remaining and for which £60,000 of deferred revenue is recorded in Target's pre-acquisition financial statements.

To fulfill the contract over its remaining 6-month term, Acquirer estimates that another party would expect to receive £54,000 for fulfilling that obligation. It has estimated that the other party would incur direct and incremental costs of £45,000, and expect a profit margin for that fulfillment effort of 20%, i.e. £9,000, and would, thus, expect to receive £54,000.

Accordingly, Acquirer should recognise a liability of £54,000 in respect of the deferred revenue obligation.

However, if the acquiree's deferred revenue does not relate to an outstanding performance obligation but to goods or services that have already been delivered, no liability should be recognised by the acquirer.

Chapter 17

3.7.4   Subsequent adjustments to fair values

If the initial accounting for a business combination is incomplete by the end of the reporting period in which the combination occurs, the acquirer recognises provisional amounts for the items for which the accounting is incomplete. Within twelve months of the acquisition date, the acquirer retrospectively adjusts the provisional amounts recognised as assets and liabilities at the acquisition date to reflect new information obtained, i.e. the adjustments are accounted for as if they were made at the acquisition date. *[FRS 102.19.19]*.

Therefore, FRS 102 requires the allocation of the cost of the business combination to be completed within twelve months of the acquisition date. Where, as a result of completing the initial accounting, adjustments to the provisional values are identified, FRS 102 requires them to be recognised from the acquisition date. Although not explicitly stated in FRS 102, this means that:

(a)   the carrying amount of the identifiable asset, liability or contingent liability that is recognised or adjusted as a result of completing the initial accounting is calculated as if its fair value at the acquisition date had been recognised from that date;

(b)   goodwill is adjusted from the acquisition date by an amount equal to the adjustment to the fair value at the acquisition date of the identifiable asset, liability or contingent liability being recognised or adjusted; and

(c)   comparative information presented for the periods before the initial accounting for the combination is complete is presented as if the initial accounting had been completed from the acquisition date. This includes any additional depreciation, amortisation or other profit or loss effect recognised as a result of completing the initial accounting.

These requirements are illustrated in the following example; the deferred tax implications have been ignored.

Example 17.12:   Finalisation of provisional values upon completion of initial accounting

Entity A prepares financial statements for annual periods ending on 31 December. Entity A acquired Entity B on 30 September 2018, in relation to which it sought an independent appraisal for an item of property, plant and equipment acquired in the combination. However, the appraisal was not finalised by the time Entity A completed its 2018 annual financial statements in which it recognised a provisional fair value for the asset of £30,000, and a provisional value for acquired goodwill of £100,000. The item of property, plant and equipment had a remaining useful life at the acquisition date of five years. Goodwill is amortised over its useful life of 10 years.

Six months after the acquisition date, Entity A received the independent appraisal, which estimated the asset's fair value at the acquisition date at £40,000.

In preparing its 2019 financial statements, Entity A is required to recognise any adjustments to provisional values as a result of completing the initial accounting from the acquisition date.

Part (a) at 3.7.4 above means that an adjustment is made to the carrying amount of the item of property, plant and equipment. That adjustment is measured as the fair value adjustment at the acquisition date of £10,000, less the additional depreciation that would have been recognised had the asset's fair value at the acquisition date been recognised from that date (£500 for three months' depreciation to 31 December 2018), i.e. an increase of £9,500.

Part (b) means that the carrying amount of goodwill is adjusted to reflect the increase in value of the asset at the acquisition date of £10,000. The decrease in goodwill will be net of £250 being the reduced amortisation charge for the three months to 31 December 2018, i.e. a decrease of £9,750.

Part (c) means the 2018 comparative information is to be restated to reflect these adjustments. Accordingly, the 2018 balance sheet is restated by increasing the carrying amount of property, plant and equipment by £9,500, reducing goodwill by £9,750 and reducing retained earnings by £250. The 2018 income statement is restated to include additional depreciation of £500 and a reduction in amortisation of goodwill of £250.

While FRS 102 does not mandate disclosures on these matters, we consider it appropriate that Entity A would disclose in its 2018 financial statements that the initial accounting for the business combination has been determined only provisionally, and explain why this is the case. In its 2019 financial statements it would disclose the amounts and explanations of the adjustments to the provisional values recognised during the current reporting period. Therefore, Entity A would disclose that:

- the fair value of the item of property, plant and equipment at the acquisition date has been increased by £10,000 with a corresponding decrease in goodwill; and

- the 2018 comparative information is restated to reflect this adjustment, including additional depreciation of £500 and reduced amortisation of goodwill of £250 relating to the year ended 31 December 2018.

The above example illustrates a situation where a provisional value of an asset was finalised at a different amount as part of the completion of the initial accounting. By contrast, the following example illustrates the identification of a new asset as a result of finalising the business combination accounting.

Example 17.13: Identification of an asset upon completion of initial accounting

Entity C prepares financial statements for annual periods ending on 31 December. Entity C acquired Entity D on 30 November 2018. Entity C engaged an independent appraiser to assist with the identification and determination of fair values to be assigned to the acquiree's assets, liabilities and contingent liabilities and the cost of the business combination. However, the appraisal was not finalised by the time Entity C completed its 2018 annual financial statements, and therefore the amounts recognised in its 2018 annual financial statements were on a provisional basis.

As part of the work carried out in finalising the initial accounting, it was identified by the independent appraiser that Entity D had an intangible asset (meeting all of Section 18's recognition and identification criteria) with a fair value at the date of acquisition of £20,000. However, this had not been identified at the time when Entity C was preparing its 2018 annual financial statements. Thus, no value had been included for this intangible asset.

In preparing its 2019 financial statements, Entity C is required to recognise any adjustments to provisional values as a result of completing the initial accounting from the acquisition date. In this case, no value had been recognised, and indeed, the intangible asset had not even been identified at the time of preparing its 2018 financial statements. So, can an adjustment be made under the provisions of paragraph 19.19?

In our view, an adjustment is appropriate. The requirements are not limited to measurement adjustments. Adjustments to recognise subsequently identified assets or liabilities are permitted as a result of completing the initial accounting. The initial accounting involves the identification as well as the measurement of the acquiree's assets, liabilities and contingent liabilities.

It is important that any adjustments to the provisional allocation reflect conditions as they existed at the date of the acquisition, rather than being affected by subsequent events; the objective is to determine the fair values of the items at the date of acquisition. There is a parallel to be drawn here with the accounting treatment of events subsequent to the balance sheet date. Only those events which provide further evidence of conditions as they existed at the acquisition date should be taken into account.

Beyond twelve months after the acquisition date, adjustments to the initial accounting for a business combination are to be recognised only to correct a material error in accordance

Chapter 17

with Section 10. *[FRS 102.19.19]*. This would probably be the case only if the original allocation were based on a complete misinterpretation of the facts that were available at the time; it would not apply simply because new information had come to light which changed the acquiring management's view of the value of the item in question.

Adjustments to the initial accounting for a business combination after it is complete are not made for the effect of changes in estimates. In accordance with Section 10, the effect of a change in estimate is recognised in the current and future periods (see Chapter 9 at 3.5). *[FRS 102.10.15-17]*.

Section 10 requires, to the extent practicable, an entity to correct a material error retrospectively, and to restate the comparative information for the prior period(s) in which the error occurred. *[FRS 102.10.21]*. The accounting is similar to that outlined above for adjustments upon completion of initial accounting. The only difference being that there is no time limit as to when such adjustments may be required. Section 10 also has specific disclosure requirements in respect of material prior period errors (see Chapter 9 at 3.7.3). *[FRS 102.10.23]*.

3.8   Non-controlling interests

A non-controlling interest is the equity in a subsidiary not attributable, directly or indirectly, to a parent. *[FRS 102 Appendix I]*.

Both Sections 9 and 19 address the initial recognition and measurement of any non-controlling interests arising on a business combination, being the non-controlling interest's share of the net amount of the identifiable assets, liabilities and contingent liabilities recognised and measured in accordance with Section 19 at the acquisition date. *[FRS 102.9.13(d), 19.14A]*.

Consequently, where the acquirer obtains less than a 100% interest in the acquiree, a non-controlling interest in the acquiree is recognised reflecting the non-controlling interest's proportion of the net identifiable assets, liabilities and contingent liabilities of the acquiree at their attributed fair values at the date of acquisition; no amount is included for any goodwill relating to the non-controlling interests. There is no option under FRS 102 to measure non-controlling interests at fair value.

FRS 102 does not distinguish between non-controlling interests that are present ownership interests and entitle their holders to a proportionate share of the entity's net assets in the event of liquidation and other components of non-controlling interests (e.g. perpetual debt classified as equity under Section 22). The implication is that all non-controlling interests are measured the same way based on present ownership interest. This means that any non-controlling interests, such as options, are valued at nil if they are not entitled to a present ownership interest.

The measurement of non-controlling interests in a business combination is illustrated in Example 17.14 below.

Example 17.14: Initial measurement of non-controlling interest in a business combination

Parent acquires 80% of the ordinary shares of Target for £950 in cash. The fair value of Target's identifiable net assets is £850. The impact of the business combination, and the measurement of non-controlling interest, is as follows:

	Dr	Cr
Fair value of identifiable net assets	£850	
Goodwill (£950 – (80% × £850))	£270	
Cash		£950
Non-controlling interest (20% × £850)		£170

The ordinary shares are present ownership interests and entitle their holders to a proportionate share of the Target's net assets in the event of liquidation. They are measured at the non-controlling interest's proportionate share of the identifiable net assets of Target.

3.9   Goodwill

FRS 102 defines 'goodwill' in terms of its nature, rather than in terms of its measurement. It is defined as 'future economic benefits arising from assets that are not capable of being individually identified and separately recognised'. *[FRS 102 Appendix I].*

Section 19 addresses accounting for goodwill both at the time of a business combination and subsequently. *[FRS 102.19.14].*

3.9.1   Initial recognition

Section 19 requires that an acquirer, at the acquisition date, recognises goodwill acquired in a business combination as an asset. However, rather than attributing a fair value to the goodwill directly, the initial measurement of goodwill is required to be its cost, being the excess of the cost of the business combination over the acquirer's interest in the net amount of the identifiable assets, liabilities and contingent liabilities recognised and measured in accordance with FRS 102. *[FRS 102.19.14, 22].* Thus, as discussed at 3.8 above, no amount is included for any goodwill relating to the non-controlling interests.

FRS 102 considers goodwill acquired in a business combination to represent a payment made by the acquirer in anticipation of future economic benefits from assets that are not capable of being individually identified and separately recognised.

Since goodwill is measured as the residual cost of the business combination after recognising the acquiree's identifiable assets, liabilities and contingent liabilities, then, to the extent that the acquiree's identifiable assets, liabilities and contingent liabilities do not satisfy the criteria for separate recognition at the acquisition date, there is a resulting effect on the amount recognised as goodwill. Section 19 makes an explicit statement that this will be the case if the fair value of a contingent liability cannot be measured reliably. *[FRS 102.19.20(a)].*

3.9.2   Subsequent measurement

After initial recognition, an acquirer measures goodwill acquired in a business combination at cost less accumulated amortisation and accumulated impairment losses. *[FRS 102.19.23].* Section 19 defers to Section 18 and Section 27 – *Impairment of Assets* – for the detailed requirements in relation to amortisation and impairment, respectively. Section 19 requires that goodwill is to be amortised on a systematic basis over a finite useful life following the principles of paragraphs 19 to 24 of Section 18, and that Section 27 is to be followed for recognising and measuring any impairment of goodwill. *[FRS 102.19.23].*

Chapter 17

However, Section 19 states that 'if, in exceptional cases, an entity is unable to make a reliable estimate of the useful life of goodwill, the life shall not exceed 10 years'. *[FRS 102.19.23(a)]*. This is consistent with UK company law. *[1 Sch 22]*.

If the useful life of goodwill cannot be reliably estimated, disclosure must be made of the reasons supporting the period chosen (which cannot exceed 10 years). *[FRS 102.19.25(g)]*.

See Chapter 16 at 3.4.3.A and Chapter 24 for further discussion of the requirements of Sections 18 and 27 regarding estimating the useful life, and impairment, respectively.

3.9.3   *Excess over cost of acquirer's interest in the net fair value of acquiree's identifiable assets, liabilities and contingent liabilities (negative goodwill)*

In some business combinations, the acquirer's interest in the net fair value of the acquiree's identifiable assets, liabilities and contingent liabilities exceeds the cost of the combination. That excess is commonly referred to as 'negative goodwill'.

Where such an excess arises, Section 19 requires the acquirer to reassess the identification and measurement of the acquiree's identifiable assets, liabilities and contingent liabilities and the measurement of the cost of the combination. *[FRS 102.19.24(a)]*.

Having undertaken that reassessment, any excess remaining after that reassessment is then required to be recognised and separately disclosed on the face of the statement of financial position, immediately below goodwill, and followed by a subtotal of the net amount of goodwill and the excess (i.e. negative goodwill). *[FRS 102.19.24(b)]*.

Following initial recognition on the statement of financial position, negative goodwill up to the fair value of the non-monetary assets acquired is recognised in profit or loss in the periods in which the non-monetary assets are recovered. *[FRS 102.19.24(c)]*. The reference to 'non-monetary assets', which includes items such as inventories, may not actually postpone recognition of negative goodwill for very long. FRS 102 does not specify whether, for example, to allocate negative goodwill to non-monetary assets on a *pro rata* basis or to specific assets. This determination will lead to different profiles of amortisation. For example, since inventories are usually turned over relatively quickly, any negative goodwill up to the fair value of the inventories (or allocated on the basis of the fair value of the inventories) may be released to the profit and loss account over a short period following the acquisition.

The secondary basis on which negative goodwill should be released to profit or loss involves that element, if any, of negative goodwill in excess of the fair values of non-monetary assets acquired. This element should be released in the periods expected to benefit. *[FRS 102.19.24(c)]*. The exact meaning of this wording is not completely clear, but any reasonable interpretation is likely to be acceptable. It is unusual for negative goodwill to exceed the non-monetary assets acquired.

3.10   Reverse acquisitions

In some business combinations, commonly referred to as reverse acquisitions, the acquirer is the entity whose equity interests have been acquired and the issuing entity is the acquiree (see 3.4.1 above). This might be the case when, for example, a private entity arranges to have itself 'acquired' by a small public entity as a means of obtaining a stock exchange listing and, as part of the agreement, the directors of the public entity resign and are replaced with directors appointed by the private entity and its former owners. Although legally the issuing public entity is regarded as the parent and the private entity is regarded as the subsidiary, the legal subsidiary is the acquirer if it has the power to govern the financial and operating policies of the legal parent so as to obtain benefits from its activities.

A reverse acquisition generally occurs when the owners of a company being 'acquired' (Company B) receive as consideration sufficient voting shares of the 'acquiring company' (Company A) so as to obtain control over the new combined entity. The acquisition is 'reverse' because, from an economic point of view, the acquirer (Company A) is being taken over by the acquiree (Company B).

Since the CA 2006 regards Company A as being the parent undertaking of Company B, it requires Company A to prepare consolidated accounts. In preparing those accounts, Company A is required by the CA 2006 to acquisition account for the acquisition of its subsidiary undertaking, Company B. *[6 Sch 9]*.

In these circumstances, as Company B obtains control (power to govern the financial and operating policies of an entity so as to obtain benefits from its activities, *[FRS 102 Appendix I]*) of Company A, and is therefore the acquirer under FRS 102, Company A should be deemed to have been acquired by Company B and reverse acquisition accounting should be applied.

To adopt reverse acquisition accounting represents a departure from company law which does not envisage such occurrence. Such departure is required where it is necessary to give a true and fair view. In such circumstances, there should be disclosure of a true and fair view override departure from the CA 2006, and disclosure of the particulars, reasons and effect. *[s404(5)]*.

In the absence of guidance within FRS 102, the discussion that follows is based on the guidance in IFRS 3. *[IFRS 3 Appendix B.19-27]*.

3.10.1 Measuring the cost of the business combination

In a reverse acquisition, the accounting acquirer usually issues no consideration for the accounting acquiree; equity shares are issued to the owners of the accounting acquirer (i.e. the legal subsidiary) by the accounting acquirer (i.e. the legal parent). In a reverse acquisition, the cost of the business combination is deemed to have been incurred by the legal subsidiary in the form of equity instruments issued to the owners of the legal parent. The cost of the combination is based on the number of equity instruments the legal subsidiary would have had to issue to provide the same percentage ownership interest of the combined entity to the owners of the legal parent as they have in the combined entity as a result of the reverse acquisition. The fair value of the number of equity instruments so calculated is used as the cost of the combination.

If the fair value of the equity instruments of the legal parent is used as the basis for determining the cost of the combination, it is the total fair value of all the issued equity instruments of the legal parent before the business combination that is used. This might be the case, for example, where the fair value of the legal subsidiary's shares is not clearly evident.

Chapter 17

Example 17.15:   Reverse acquisition – calculating the cost of the business combination using the fair value of the equity shares of the legal subsidiary

Entity A, the entity issuing equity instruments and therefore the legal parent, is acquired in a reverse acquisition by Entity B, the legal subsidiary, on 30 September 2019.

Balance sheets of Entity A and Entity B immediately before the business combination are:

	Entity A £	Entity B £
Tangible fixed assets	1,300	3,000
Debtors	500	700
	1,800	3,700
Creditors: amounts falling due within one year	300	600
Creditors: amounts falling due after more than one year	400	1,100
	700	1,700
Net assets	1,100	2,000
Capital and reserves		
Called up share capital		
100 £1 ordinary shares	100	
60 £1 ordinary shares		60
Share premium account	200	540
Profit and loss account	800	1,400
	1,100	2,000

On 30 September 2019, Entity A issues 2.5 shares in exchange for each ordinary share of Entity B. All of Entity B's shareholders exchange their shares in Entity B. Therefore, Entity A issues 150 ordinary shares in exchange for all 60 ordinary shares of Entity B, and so has 250 issued shares in total.

The fair value of each ordinary share of Entity B at 30 September 2019 is £40. The quoted market price of Entity A's ordinary shares at that date is £16.

The fair values of Entity A's identifiable assets and liabilities at 30 September 2019 are the same as their carrying amounts, with the exception of tangible fixed assets. The fair value of Entity A's tangible fixed assets at 30 September 2019 is £1,500. (For the purposes of illustration, deferred tax implications have been ignored.) Therefore, the fair value of Entity A's net assets is £1,300 (£1,100 plus £200).

As a result of the issue of 150 ordinary shares by Entity A, Entity B's shareholders own 60 per cent of the issued shares of the combined entity (i.e. 150 shares out of 250 issued shares). The remaining 40 per cent is owned by Entity A's shareholders. If the business combination had taken place in the form of Entity B issuing additional ordinary shares to Entity A's shareholders in exchange for their ordinary shares in Entity A, Entity B would have had to issue 40 shares for the ratio of ownership interest in the combined entity to be the same. Entity B's shareholders would then own 60 out of the 100 issued shares of Entity B and therefore 60 per cent of the combined entity.

As a result, the cost of the business combination is £1,600 (i.e. 40 shares each with a fair value of £40). In this example, this is the same as calculated using the fair value of the equity issued by Entity A (100 shares with a fair value per share of £16, i.e. £1,600).

3.10.2   Preparation and presentation of consolidated financial statements

Since the legal parent is the acquiree for accounting purposes, the consolidated financial statements prepared following a reverse acquisition reflect the fair values of the assets, liabilities and contingent liabilities of the legal parent, not those of the legal subsidiary.

Therefore, the cost of the business combination is allocated by measuring the identifiable assets, liabilities and contingent liabilities of the legal parent that satisfy the recognition criteria at their fair values at the acquisition date. Any excess of the cost of the combination over the acquirer's interest in the net fair value of those items is then accounted for as goodwill.

In Example 17.15 above, goodwill of £300 would be calculated as the difference between the cost of the combination of £1,600 and the fair value of the assets acquired of £1,300.

Although the accounting for a reverse acquisition reflects the legal subsidiary as being the acquirer, the consolidated financial statements prepared following a reverse acquisition are issued under the name of the legal parent (accounting acquiree). Consequently, we believe that they should be described in the notes as a continuation of the financial statements of the legal subsidiary (accounting acquirer), with one adjustment, which is to adjust retrospectively the accounting acquirer's legal capital to reflect the legal capital of the accounting acquiree. Comparative information presented in those consolidated financial statements is therefore that of the legal subsidiary (accounting acquirer) – not that originally presented in the financial statements of the legal parent (accounting acquiree) – but is adjusted to reflect the legal capital of the legal parent (accounting acquiree).

Because the consolidated financial statements represent the continuation of the financial statements of the legal subsidiary except for its capital structure, the consolidated financial statements reflect:

- the assets and liabilities of the legal subsidiary (accounting acquirer) recognised and measured at their pre-combination carrying amounts, i.e. not at their acquisition-date fair values;

- the assets and liabilities of the legal parent (accounting acquiree) recognised and measured in accordance with Section 19, i.e. generally at their acquisition-date fair values;

- the retained earnings and other equity balances of the legal subsidiary (accounting acquirer) *before* the business combination, i.e. not those of the legal parent (accounting acquiree);

- the amount recognised as issued equity interests in the consolidated financial statements determined by adding the issued equity interest of the legal subsidiary (accounting acquirer) outstanding immediately before the business combination to the fair value of the legal parent (accounting acquiree). However, the equity structure (i.e. the number and type of equity interests issued) reflects the equity structure of the legal parent (accounting acquiree), including the equity interests the legal parent issued to effect the combination. Accordingly, the equity structure of the legal subsidiary (accounting acquirer) is restated using the exchange ratio established in the acquisition agreement to reflect the number of shares of the legal parent (accounting acquiree) issued in the reverse acquisition;

- any non-controlling interest's proportionate share of the legal subsidiary's (accounting acquirer's) pre-combination carrying amounts of retained earnings and other equity interests (as discussed at 3.10.3 below); and

Chapter 17

- the income statement for the current period reflects that of the legal subsidiary (accounting acquirer) for the full period together with the post-acquisition results of the legal parent (accounting acquiree) based on the attributed fair values.

Example 17.16: Reverse acquisition – consolidated balance sheet at date of the business combination

If we consider the transaction in Example 17.15 above with the cost of consideration of £1,600, the consolidation at the date of the business combination would be as follows, using the guidance in IFRS 3. As discussed below and shown in Example 17.17, additional adjustments would be required to equity for a UK company.

	Entity A	Entity B	Consolidation adjustments	Consolidated
	£	£	£	£
Tangible fixed assets	1,300	3,000	200 [1]	4,500
Goodwill			300 [2]	300
Debtors	500	700		1,200
	1,800	3,700		6,000
Creditors: amounts falling due within one year	300	600		900
Creditors: amounts falling due after one year	400	1,100		1,500
	700	1,700		2,400
Net assets	1,100	2,000		3,600
Capital and reserves				
Called up share capital				
100 £1 ordinary shares	100		(100) [3]	–
60 £1 ordinary shares		60	1,600 [3]	1,660
Share premium account	200	540	(200) [3]	540
Profit and loss account	800	1,400	(800) [3]	1,400
	1,100	2,000		3,600

[1] To recognise Entity A's tangible fixed assets at their fair value at the acquisition date.

[2] To recognise goodwill on consolidation, representing the difference between the cost of the combination, £1,600, and the fair value of Entity A's net assets acquired, £1,300.

[3] To recognise the cost of the acquisition and to eliminate Entity A's share capital and reserves as at the date of the acquisition.

The equity as shown above would require further adjustment in a UK company. As stated above, the amount of share capital in the consolidated balance sheet does not equal the nominal value of either Entity B's share capital (£60) or that of Entity A following the acquisition (£250). Although the total share capital and share premium (issued equity) in the consolidated balance sheet of £2,200 is equivalent to the total as it would have been if Entity B had been the legal acquirer, the equity structure (i.e. the number and type of equity instruments issued) should reflect that of the legal parent and in a UK GAAP context, the amounts for share capital and related reserves, such as share premium, in the consolidated financial statements should also reflect the legal position. On this basis, a reserve, often called a 'reverse acquisition reserve' would be reflected as illustrated below.

Example 17.17:   Reverse acquisition – recognition of a reverse acquisition reserve

	Entity A	Entity B	Consolidation adjustments	Consolidated
	£	£	£	£
Tangible fixed assets	1,300	3,000	200 [1]	4,500
Goodwill			300 [2]	300
Debtors	500	700		1,200
	1,800	3,700		6,000
Creditors: amounts falling due within one year	300	600		900
Creditors: amounts falling due after one year	400	1,100		1,500
	700	1,700		2,400
Net assets	1,100	2,000		3,600
Capital and reserves				
Called up share capital				
100 £1 ordinary shares	100		150 [3]	250
60 £1 ordinary shares		60	(60) [4]	
Share premium account	200	540	(540) [4]	200
Reverse acquisition reserve			1,750	1,750
Profit and loss account	800	1,400	(800) [5]	1,400
	1,100	2,000		3,600

[1] To recognise Entity A's tangible fixed assets at their fair value at the acquisition date.

[2] To recognise goodwill on consolidation, representing the difference between the cost of the combination, £1,600, and the fair value of Entity A's net assets acquired, £1,300.

[3] To recognise the nominal value of the shares issued by Entity A on the acquisition. Merger relief applies and so no share premium has been recognised on the transaction.

[4] To eliminate the share capital and share premium of Entity B (as the capital reserves on this basis reflect those of the legal acquirer).

[5] To eliminate the profit and loss reserves of Entity A.

3.10.3   Non-controlling interests

In some reverse acquisitions, it may be that some of the owners of the legal subsidiary (accounting acquirer) might not exchange their equity interests for equity interests of the legal parent (accounting acquiree), but retain their interest in the equity instruments of the legal subsidiary. Those owners are treated as a non-controlling interest in the consolidated financial statements after the reverse acquisition. That is because the owners of the legal subsidiary that do not exchange their equity interests for equity interests of the legal acquirer have an interest in only the results and net assets of the legal subsidiary – not in the results and net assets of the combined entity. Conversely, even though the legal parent is the acquiree for accounting purposes, the owners of the legal parent have an interest in the results and net assets of the combined entity.

The assets and liabilities of the legal subsidiary are measured and recognised in the consolidated financial statements at their pre-combination carrying amounts. Therefore, in a reverse acquisition, the non-controlling interest reflects the

Chapter 17

non-controlling shareholders' proportionate interest in the pre-combination carrying amounts of the legal subsidiary's net assets. These requirements are illustrated in the following example.

Example 17.18: *Reverse acquisition – non-controlling interests*

This example uses the same facts in Example 17.15 above, except that in this case only 56 of Entity B's ordinary shares are tendered for exchange rather than all 60. Because Entity A issues 2.5 shares in exchange for each ordinary share of Entity B, Entity A issues only 140 (rather than 150) shares. As a result, Entity B's shareholders own 58.3 per cent of the issued shares of the combined entity (i.e. 140 shares out of 240 issued shares).

As in Example 17.15 above, the cost of the business combination is calculated by assuming that the combination had taken place in the form of Entity B issuing additional ordinary shares to the shareholders of Entity A in exchange for their ordinary shares in Entity A. In calculating the number of shares that would have to be issued by Entity B, the non-controlling interest is ignored. The majority shareholders own 56 shares of Entity B. For this to represent a 58.3 per cent ownership interest, Entity B would have had to issue an additional 40 shares. The majority shareholders would then own 56 out of the 96 issued shares of Entity B and therefore 58.3 per cent of the combined entity.

As a result, the cost of the business combination is £1,600 (i.e. 40 shares each with a fair value of £40). This is the same amount as when all 60 of Entity B's ordinary shares are tendered for exchange (see Example 17.15 above). The cost of the combination does not change simply because some of Entity B's shareholders do not participate in the exchange.

The non-controlling interest is represented by the four shares of the total 60 shares of Entity B that are not exchanged for shares of Entity A. Therefore, the non-controlling interest is 6.7 per cent. The non-controlling interest reflects the non-controlling shareholders' proportionate interest in the pre-combination carrying amounts of the net assets of the legal subsidiary. Therefore, the consolidated balance sheet is adjusted to show a non-controlling interest of 6.7 per cent of the pre-combination carrying amounts of Entity B's net assets (i.e. £134 or 6.7 per cent of £2,000).

The consolidated balance sheet at 30 September 2019 (the date of the business combination) reflecting the non-controlling interest is as follows (the intermediate columns for Entity B, non-controlling interest (NCI), Entity A and UK legal capital adjustments are included to show the workings):

	Entity B	NCI[1]	Entity A	UK legal capital adjustments[2]	Consolidated
	Book values		Fair values		
	£	£	£	£	£
Tangible fixed assets	3,000		1,500		4,500
Debtors	700		500		1,200
Goodwill			300		300
	3,700		2,300		6,000
Creditors: amounts falling due within one year	600		300		900
Creditors: amounts falling due after one year	1,100		400		1,500
	1,700		700		2,400
Net assets	2,000		1,500		3,600

Capital and reserves					
Called up share capital					
240 £1 ordinary shares (Entity A)	60	(4)	1,600	(1,416)	240
Share premium account	540	(36)		(304)	200
Profit and loss account	1,400	(94)	–		1,306
Non-controlling interest	–	134	–		134
Reverse acquisition reserve	–		–	1,720	1,720
	2,000		1,600		3,600

[1] The non-controlling interest of £134 has two components. The first component is the reclassification of the non-controlling interest's share of the accounting acquirer's retained earnings immediately before the acquisition (£1,400 × 6.7 per cent or £93.80). The second component represents the reclassification of the non-controlling interest's share of the accounting acquirer's issued equity (£600 × 6.7 per cent or £40.20).

[2] A UK company makes adjustments to present the share capital structure of the legal parent, Entity A, with an equivalent entry to reverse acquisition reserve.

3.11   Business combinations achieved in stages (step acquisitions)

So far, this chapter has discussed business combinations which result from a single purchase transaction. However, in practice, some subsidiaries are acquired in a series of steps which take place over an extended period, during which the underlying value of the subsidiary is likely to change, both because of the trading profits (or losses) which it retains and because of other movements in the fair value of its assets and liabilities. This raises questions regarding how to determine the cost of the business combination, allocating that cost to the assets acquired and liabilities and provisions for contingent liabilities assumed, and the resulting goodwill.

Where a parent acquires control of a subsidiary in stages, FRS 102 requires the transaction to be accounted for in accordance with paragraphs 19.11A and 19.14, applied at the date control is achieved. *[FRS 102.9.19B]*. Accordingly:

- the cost of the business combination is the aggregate of the fair values of the assets given, liabilities incurred or assumed, and equity instruments issued by the acquirer at the date of each transaction in the series; *[FRS 102.19.11A]* and

- the normal rules on allocation of the cost of the business combination under the purchase method apply whereby 'the acquirer shall, *at the acquisition date* [emphasis added], allocate the cost of a business combination by recognising the acquiree's identifiable assets, liabilities and contingent liabilities ... *at their fair values at that date* [emphasis added]'. *[FRS 102.19.14]*.

This approach is consistent with the requirements of the CA 2006, whereby goodwill must be recognised as the difference between the fair value at the acquisition date of the identifiable assets and liabilities of the undertaking acquired and the acquisition cost of the interest in the shares of the undertaking. *[6 Sch 9]*.

The following example illustrates the application of these principles.

Example 17.19:   Business combination achieved in stages (step acquisition) (1)

Company A acquires a 10% ownership interest in Company B on 1 January 2015 for £5 million cash. Company A acquired a further 20% ownership interest in Company B for £10 million cash on 1 January 2017 and obtained significant influence. At 1 January 2019, Company A's equity-accounted interest in Company B

Chapter 17

was £18 million. Company A acquired a further 30% of Company B for £30 million cash on 1 January 2019, and obtained control. The fair value of Company B's identifiable net assets at 1 January 2019 was £60 million.

In accordance with paragraph 19.11A, the cost of the business combination is £45 million, being the aggregate of the cash paid at each stage in exchange for control. Company A's share of the identifiable net assets of Company B is £36 million (being 60% of £60 million), resulting in goodwill of £9 million.

Company A will record the following entries in its consolidated financial statements at the date of the business combination:

	Dr £m	Cr £m
Identifiable net assets of Company B	60	
Goodwill (£45m – (60% of £60m))	9	
Non-controlling interest (40% of £60m)		24
Cash		30
Equity investment in Company B		18
Other comprehensive income[1]	3	

[1] This 'dangling entry' represents the difference between previous cash paid (£15m) and the share of the net assets at date control is obtained (£18m). As this is not a profit or loss it should be taken to other comprehensive income.

FRS 102's approach to step acquisitions is a practical means of applying the purchase method because it does not require retrospective assessments of the fair value of the identifiable assets and liabilities of the subsidiary. However, the FRC notes that in certain circumstances not using the fair values at the dates of earlier purchases may result in accounting that is inconsistent with the way the investment has been treated previously and, for that reason, may fail to give a true and fair view. *[FRS 102 Appendix III.19].*

For example, when an associate becomes a subsidiary, using the method required by the Regulations and paragraph 9.19B of FRS 102 to calculate goodwill has the effect that the group's share of profits or losses and reserve movements of its associate becomes reclassified as goodwill (usually negative goodwill). *[FRS 102 Appendix III.20].*

A similar problem may arise where an entity has substantially restated its investment in an undertaking that subsequently becomes its subsidiary. For example, where such an investment has been impaired, the application of the purchase method as set out in the Regulations would increase reserves and create an asset (goodwill). *[FRS 102 Appendix III.20].*

Consequently, the FRC acknowledges that, in the rare cases where the method for calculating goodwill set out in company law and paragraph 9.19B (as discussed above) would be misleading, the goodwill should be calculated as the sum of the goodwill arising from each purchase of an interest in the relevant undertaking, adjusted as necessary for any subsequent impairment. In such circumstances, goodwill arising on each purchase is calculated as the difference between the cost of that purchase and the fair value at the date of that purchase of the identifiable assets and liabilities attributable to the interest purchased. The difference between the goodwill calculated using this method and that calculated using the method provided by company law and FRS 102 is shown in reserves. Section 404(5) of the CA 2006 sets out the disclosures required in cases where the statutory requirement is not applied. Paragraph 3.5 sets out the disclosures when an entity departs from a requirement of FRS 102 or from a requirement of applicable legislation (see Chapter 6 at 9.2.2). *[FRS 102 Appendix III.21].* This is illustrated in Example 17.20 below.

Example 17.20: Business combination achieved in stages (step acquisition) (2)

Company A acquires a 100% holding in Company B as a result of two separate transactions, several years apart, as set out in the table below.

Transaction number	Holding acquired	Fair value of net assets	Total value of investee	Price paid	Cumulative price paid
1	49%	£8m	£10m	£4.9m	£4.9m
2	51%	£30m	£40m	£20.4m	£25.3m

At the time of the first investment, Company A determined that it had significant influence of Company B and that it was neither a subsidiary nor an interest in a jointly controlled entity. In its consolidated financial statements, Company A accordingly accounted for its investment in Company B using the equity method, in accordance with Section 14 – *Investments in Associates,* with the investment initially recognised at £4.9 million.

Company A subsequently obtained control of Company B through a transaction with Company B's other shareholder, paying £20.4 million in return for acquiring its 51% interest in Company B. At that date, the carrying value of Company A's 49% investment in Company B, accounted for under the equity method, was £10.8 million, having reflected £5.9 million for its share of profits of £12 million.

Applying the purchase method as stipulated by FRS 102 would result in Company A determining the cost of the business combination at £25.3 million, and recognising identifiable net assets of Company B at the acquisition date of £30 million – resulting in the recognition of negative goodwill of £4.7 million. This is despite the fact that Company A had paid more than its proportionate share of the fair value of the net assets at each transaction. There would also be a debit of £5.9 million taken to other comprehensive income, being the difference between the original price paid (£4.9 million) and the investment under the equity method (£10.8 million). This is effectively the reversal of the previously recognised equity-accounted share of profits. As discussed at 3.9.3 above, Company A would recognise this negative goodwill in profit or loss in the periods in which the non-monetary assets are recovered.

However, assuming that this accounting for goodwill is considered misleading, goodwill would be calculated as £6.1 million, being £1.0 million for the first transaction (£4.9 million – £3.9 million (49% × £8.0 million)) and £5.1 million for the second transaction (£20.4 million – £15.3 million (51% × £30.0 million)). The difference between this goodwill of £6.1 million and the negative goodwill of £4.7 million (calculated using the method provided by company law and FRS 102), i.e. £10.8 million, is to be taken to reserves (presumably through other comprehensive income). This difference of £10.8 million, together with the previously calculated debit to other comprehensive income of £5.9 million, means that a credit of £4.9 million is taken to other comprehensive income. This effectively represents 49% of the fair value increase of £10 million in the assets of Company B at the date of the business combination (i.e. £30 million – £20 million, being £8 million plus £12 million (Company B profits recognised between transaction 1 and 2)).

4 DISCLOSURES RELATING TO BUSINESS COMBINATIONS AND GOODWILL

The disclosure requirements of FRS 102 in relation to business combinations and goodwill are discussed at 4.1 to 4.3 below. The CA 2006 contains a number of detailed disclosure requirements. Some of these duplicate those contained in FRS 102 but there are a few additional matters in the legislation, and these are considered at 4.3.3 below.

Chapter 17

4.1   Business combinations during the reporting period

For each business combination, excluding any group reconstruction (see 5.6 below for disclosure requirements in respect of group reconstructions), that was effected during the period, the acquirer shall disclose the following: *[FRS 102.19.25]*

- the names and descriptions of the combining entities or businesses;
- the acquisition date;
- the percentage of voting equity instruments acquired;
- the cost of the combination and a description of the components of that cost (such as cash, equity instruments and debt instruments);
- the amounts recognised at the acquisition date for each class of the acquiree's assets, liabilities and contingent liabilities, including goodwill;
- a qualitative description of the nature of intangible assets included in goodwill (see 3.7.3.B above);
- the useful life of goodwill, and if this cannot be reliably estimated, supporting reasons for the period chosen (see 3.9.2 above); and
- the periods in which any negative goodwill (see 3.9.3 above) will be recognised in profit or loss.

Disclosure is required of the amounts of revenue and profit or loss of the acquiree since the acquisition date included in the consolidated statement of comprehensive income. Such disclosure should be provided for individual business combinations that are material or in aggregate for business combinations that are not individually material. *[FRS 102.19.25A]*.

As discussed at 3.7.4 above, the accounting for a business combination may be based on provisional amounts which are later retrospectively adjusted to reflect their finalisation within twelve months after the acquisition date. FRS 102 is silent as to whether any disclosures are required about the use of provisional amounts and their subsequent finalisation. Nonetheless, we believe good practice would be to disclose where provisional fair values have been used, and explain why that is the case. As any subsequent adjustments will be accounted for retrospectively by restating comparatives, we would expect disclosure that such adjustments have been made, and the reasons.

4.2   Goodwill reconciliations

In addition to disclosures for business combinations effected during the period, an acquirer should disclose a reconciliation of the carrying amount of goodwill at the beginning and end of the reporting period, showing separately: *[FRS 102.19.26]*

- changes arising from new business combinations;
- amortisation;
- impairment losses;
- disposals of previously acquired businesses; and
- other changes.

A similar reconciliation is also required in respect of any negative goodwill – albeit with no impairment, and with 'amortisation' replaced by 'amounts recognised in profit or loss in accordance with paragraph 19.24(c)'. *[FRS 102.19.26A]*.

Reconciliations need not be presented for prior periods. *[FRS 102.19.26-26A]*.

Section 27 requires further disclosures be made in respect of the amount of the impairment losses and reversals on goodwill (including the line items in which included), together with a description of the events and circumstances leading to the recognition or reversal of the impairment loss (see Chapter 24 at 8). *[FRS 102.27.32-33A]*.

4.3 Other disclosures

4.3.1 Contingent liabilities

Where contingent liabilities of the acquiree cannot be reliably measured, the acquirer discloses the information about that contingent liability as required by Section 21 (see Chapter 19 at 3.10.3). *[FRS 102.19.20(b)]*.

4.3.2 Step acquisitions

As discussed at 3.11 above, in rare cases where the method for calculating goodwill set out in company law and paragraph 9.19B would be misleading, the goodwill should be calculated as the sum of goodwill arising from each purchase of an interest in the relevant undertaking adjusted as necessary for any subsequent impairment. Where the FRS 102 or statutory requirement is not applied, paragraph 3.5 sets out the necessary disclosures when applying a 'true and fair override' (see Chapter 6 at 9.2.2).

4.3.3 Company law disclosures

The CA 2006 contains a number of detailed disclosure requirements that are relevant for business combinations to be shown in the notes to the financial statements. *[6 Sch 13]*. Some of these duplicate those contained in FRS 102 but there are a few additional matters in the legislation that need to be considered.

The CA 2006 requires disclosure of the names of subsidiaries acquired, and whether they have been accounted for by the acquisition or the merger method of accounting, even if they do not significantly affect the figures shown in the consolidated financial statements. *[6 Sch 13(2)]*.

In relation to an acquisition which significantly affects the figures shown in the consolidated financial statements, the CA 2006 requires disclosures of: *[6 Sch 13(3)-(4)]*

- the composition and the fair value of the consideration for the acquisition given by the parent company and its subsidiary undertakings;
- where the acquisition method of accounting has been adopted:
  - the book values immediately prior to the acquisition of each class of assets and liabilities of the undertaking or group acquired (to be stated in tabular form);
  - the fair values at the date of acquisition, of each class of assets and liabilities of the undertaking or group acquired (to be stated in tabular form);
  - a statement of the amount of any goodwill or negative consolidation difference arising on the acquisition;
  - an explanation of any significant adjustments made.

There must also be stated the cumulative amount of goodwill resulting from acquisitions in that and earlier years which has been written off otherwise than in the consolidated profit and loss account. That figure must be shown net of any goodwill attributable to subsidiary undertakings or businesses disposed of prior to the balance sheet date. *[6 Sch 14]*. This disclosure requirement would apply in limited circumstances only, for example when the entity has legacy amounts of goodwill written off directly to reserves, which was a policy permitted under previous UK GAAP prior to the introduction of FRS 10 – *Goodwill and intangible assets*. Under FRS 102, such amounts are never recycled to profit or loss.

UK company law provides an exemption from disclosing the above information in certain circumstances. It need not be disclosed with respect to an undertaking which:

- is established under the law of a country outside the United Kingdom, or
- carries on business outside the United Kingdom,

if in the opinion of the directors of the parent company the disclosure would be seriously prejudicial to the business of that undertaking or to the business of the parent company or any of its subsidiary undertakings and the Secretary of State agrees that the information should not be disclosed. *[6 Sch 16]*.

5   GROUP RECONSTRUCTIONS

Section 19 requires that all business combinations (except certain public entity combinations) should be accounted for by applying the purchase method except for group reconstructions which *may* be accounted for using the merger accounting method [emphasis added]. *[FRS 102.19.6]*.

The Basis for Conclusions explains that FRS 102 retains the accounting permitted by FRS 6 for group reconstructions. It was noted that whilst EU-adopted IFRS does not provide accounting requirements for business combinations under common control, the accounting required by FRS 6 is well understood and provides useful information. Therefore these requirements were carried forward into FRS 102. In practice, the introduction of FRS 102 was not expected to change the accounting for group reconstructions. *[FRS 102.BC.B19.1]*.

Under FRS 102, the use of the merger accounting method for group reconstructions is optional. In most cases where the criteria to apply the merger accounting method are met, the acquirer will wish to use the merger accounting method, thereby avoiding the need to determine fair values of the identifiable assets, liabilities and contingent liabilities of the acquiree as well as the fair value of the consideration given.

Where the option of using the merger accounting method is not taken, it would seem that the purchase method (acquisition accounting) needs to be used. Historically, FRS 6 stated 'acquisition accounting would require the restatement at fair value of the assets and liabilities of the company transferred, and the recognising of goodwill, which is likely to be inappropriate in the case of a transaction that does not alter the relative rights of the ultimate shareholders', *[FRS 6.78]*, and this sentence in FRS 6 was used as support for the argument that application of acquisition accounting was unlikely to give a true and fair view. While FRS 102 contains no such health warning, the position is likely to remain the same that, in certain circumstances, notwithstanding that it is permitted (or required, where the strict criteria for use of the merger accounting method are not met) by company law and FRS 102, the application of the purchase method and all that it entails would not be appropriate, and that a 'true and fair override' to apply the merger accounting method may be necessary.

In addition, as discussed at 3.4 above, when applying the purchase method, it is necessary to identify the accounting acquirer. In certain group reconstructions, particularly those effected using a newly incorporated entity, the accounting acquirer is not necessarily the legal acquirer and it may be that use of the merger accounting method is more appropriate than use of the purchase method in these scenarios. Further factors to consider when determining the most appropriate method in the context of individual financial statements are given at 5.4.1.A below.

5.1   Scope and applicability to various structures

FRS 102 defines a group reconstruction as any one of the following arrangements: *[FRS 102 Appendix I]*

- the transfer of an equity holding in a subsidiary from one group entity to another;
- the addition of a new parent entity to a group;
- the transfer of equity holdings in one or more subsidiaries of a group to a new entity that is not a group entity but whose equity holders are the same as those of the group's parent;
- the combination into a group of two or more entities that before the combination had the same equity holders;
- the transfer of the business of one group entity to another; or
- the transfer of the business of one group entity to a new entity that is not a group entity but whose equity holders are the same as those of the group's parent.

The final two bullets in the list above were added by the Triennial review 2017 to incorporate in certain circumstances, the transfer of a business, in addition to the transfer of equity holdings. *[FRS 102.BC.B19.2]*. This, however, codified generally accepted practice, which regarded such transfers as group reconstructions.

Additionally, FRS 102 identifies that while the wording explaining the merger accounting method (see 5.3 below) is drafted in terms of an acquirer or issuing entity issuing shares as consideration for the transfer to it of shares in the other parties to the combination, the provisions also apply to other arrangements that achieve similar results. *[FRS 102.19.28]*.

5.2   Qualifying conditions

Under FRS 102, group reconstructions may be accounted for by using the merger accounting method provided: *[FRS 102.19.27]*

- the use of the merger accounting method is not prohibited by company law or other relevant legislation (see 5.2.1);
- the ultimate equity holders remain the same, and the rights of each equity holding, relative to the others, are unchanged; and
- no non-controlling interest in the net assets of the group is altered by the transfer.

Chapter 17

The third condition must be considered, for example, when the group reconstruction involves transfers in or out of a sub-group with a non-controlling interest. In such a case, the non-controlling interest is likely to be affected by the transfer and the transaction might not qualify for merger accounting as a result.

The following example illustrates one issue that could arise when analysing the second condition.

Example 17.21: Insertion of a new parent company onto a group

Company A owns 100% of each of Companies B and C. Company A is owned by two individuals, X owns 85% and is the controlling party, while Y owns 15%.

Y wishes to exit the business. To facilitate this, Newco is incorporated to become the new parent company of the group. Newco issues shares to X in exchange for all X's shares in Company A. Y sells their shares to Newco in return for loan notes of £2m. These are settled immediately following the transaction by Company A declaring and paying a dividend of £2m to Newco, and Newco using the resulting cash to settle the liability.

In the consolidated financial statements of Newco, can it apply the merger accounting method?

The definition of a group reconstruction in FRS 102 includes the addition of a new parent entity to a group (see 5.1 above). However, viewed as a whole, the transaction results in X and Y having different ownership interests in the group after the transaction, since Y exits. This contravenes the requirements in paragraph 19.27 of FRS 102 that the relative rights of the equity holders remain unchanged (see 5.2 above). However, in our view, the substance of the transaction has two separate elements: the insertion of Newco (a group reconstruction) and the exit of Y. Therefore, in our view, merger accounting may be applied in Newco's consolidated financial statements and a true and fair override is required in respect of the requirements in paragraph 19.27 of FRS 102 that the relative rights of the equity holders remain unchanged.

5.2.1   Company law considerations

UK company law sets out requirements that have to be met in consolidated financial statements before merger accounting can be applied. The conditions laid down in the Regulations for accounting for an acquisition of a subsidiary undertaking as a merger are that: *[6 Sch 10]*

(a)   the undertaking whose shares are acquired is ultimately controlled by the same party both before and after the acquisition (see 5.2.1.A);

(b)   the control referred to above is not intended to be transitory (see 5.2.1.B); and

(c)   the adoption of the merger method of accounting accords with generally accepted accounting principles or practice (see 5.2.1.C).

The conditions set out in the Regulations apply only to consolidated financial statements and where an undertaking becomes a subsidiary undertaking of the parent company. *[6 Sch 7(1)]*. They do not apply to group reconstructions involving a business which is not a subsidiary undertaking.

There are no longer restrictions over the extent of the consideration not in the form of equity shares or over the percentage shareholding in the acquiree obtained, which were conditions of merger accounting under now superseded company law.

5.2.1.A   The same controlling party before and after the acquisition

The undertaking must be controlled by the same party both before and after the transaction. Accordingly, for example, the transfer of a 75% subsidiary from one group entity to another would qualify for the merger accounting method (assuming the other conditions under the Regulations and FRS 102 are met).

A transaction in which a new parent is inserted above an existing group might not meet the requirements for use of the merger accounting method. This is because the undertaking whose shares are acquired (e.g. the previous ultimate parent of a group) will have the same equity holders as before, and it may be that there is no single controlling party either before or after the transaction. The Basis of Conclusions to FRS 102 observes that paragraph 10 of Schedule 6 to the Regulations is generally consistent with paragraph 19.27 (reproduced at 5.2 above). However, if an entity considers that, for the overriding purpose of giving a true and fair view, merger accounting should be applied in circumstances other than those set out in paragraph 10 of Schedule 6 to the Regulations, it may do so providing the relevant disclosures are made in the notes to the financial statements. *[FRS 102.BC.A3.30]*. This situation is an example of when a true and fair override might be appropriate in order to use the merger accounting method in the consolidated financial statements of the new parent. See Chapter 6 at 9.2.2 for a discussion of the true and fair override and the disclosures required.

Other arrangements meeting the definition of a group reconstruction under FRS 102 involving equity holders that are the same, but with no single controlling party, may also need to invoke 'a true and fair override' in order to apply the merger method of accounting.

In some cases, a newly incorporated company might be involved in a transaction and in certain circumstances it might be identified as an acquirer, meaning that the purchase method is appropriate (see 5.2.1.B below).

5.2.1.B   Control is not intended to be transitory

The note on legal requirements in Appendix III to FRS 102 provides no additional guidance on this criterion. IFRS 3 contains a similar requirement within its scope exemption for business combinations under common control. *[IFRS 3 Appendix B.1]*. This criterion addresses concerns that business combinations between parties acting at arm's length – that would otherwise be accounted using the purchase method – could be structured through the use of 'grooming' transactions so that, for a brief period immediately before and after the combination, the combining entities or businesses are under common control.

Judgement will be required when assessing whether control is transitory in certain scenarios; for example, when a transaction that qualifies as a group reconstruction under FRS 102 is completed at the same time as other transactions that result in a change of control.

Often a reorganisation involves the formation of a new entity (Newco) to facilitate the sale of part of an organisation. In our view, an intention to sell the businesses or go to an Initial Public Offering (IPO) shortly after the reorganisation does not, by itself, prevent the use of the common control exemption. Whether or not control is 'transitory' should be assessed by looking at the duration of control of the businesses in the period both before and after the reorganisation – it is not limited to an assessment of the duration of control only after the reorganisation.

Chapter 17

Example 17.22: Formation of Newco to facilitate disposal of businesses

Entity A currently has two businesses operated through Entity X and Entity Y. The group structure (ignoring other entities within the group) is as follows:

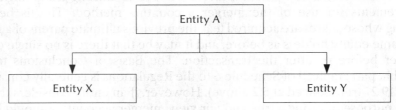

Entity A proposes to combine the two businesses (currently housed in two separate entities, Entity X and Entity Y) into the one entity and then spin-off the combined entity as part of an IPO. Both of the businesses have been owned by Entity A for several years. The internal reconstruction will be structured such that Entity A will establish a new entity (Newco) and transfer its interests in Entity X and Entity Y to Newco, resulting in the following group structure:

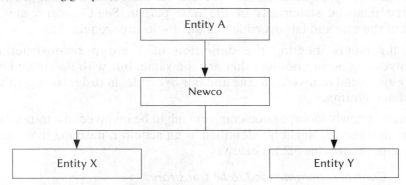

After the IPO, Newco will no longer be under the control of Entity A.

In the consolidated financial statements of Newco, is it entitled to use the merger accounting method?

The question of whether the entities or businesses are under common control applies to the combining entities that existed before the combination, excluding Newco, i.e. Entity X and Entity Y. These entities have clearly been under the common control of Entity A, and remain so after the transfer.

If Newco were preparing consolidated financial statements without there being an intended IPO, it would be entitled to use the merger accounting method (assuming that all other conditions for merger accounting in the CA 2006 and paragraph 19.27 of FRS 102 are met). However, as the purpose of the transaction was to facilitate the disposal of the businesses by way of the IPO, such that Entity A no longer has control over Entity X and Entity Y, does this mean that common control is 'transitory' and the merger accounting method cannot be applied?

In our view, the answer is 'no'. Common control is not considered to be transitory and therefore the reorganisation does not breach the transitory control condition for use of merger accounting in the CA 2006. This is consistent with the ordinary meaning of 'transitory', something which is fleeting, brief or temporary. The common control of Entity X and Entity Y was not fleeting in the fact pattern as both entities had been controlled by Entity A for several years. Assuming all other legal conditions and those in paragraph 19.27 of FRS 102 are met, Newco may apply the merger accounting method in its consolidated financial statements.

Although this example involves a new entity, the same considerations apply regardless of the manner in which the internal reconstruction may have been structured. For example, Entity X may have acquired Entity Y or the trade and assets of Entity Y, with Entity X then being the subject of an IPO. In such a situation, Entity X would be entitled to use the merger accounting method with respect to the group reconstruction (assuming all other legal conditions and those in paragraph 19.27 of FRS 102 had been met). By contrast, if Entity Y had only recently come into the group, this could indicate that control is transitory.

However, if such a restructuring was an integral part of another transaction such as a sale or disposal via an IPO, the circumstances may be such that Newco could be regarded as the acquirer if it is considered to be effectively an extension of the new owners. There may be scenarios that appear similar to Example 17.22 above, but in which Newco might be identified as the acquirer and therefore use of the purchase method might be appropriate – for example, where a parent uses a Newco to facilitate a public flotation of shares in a group of subsidiary companies (i.e. as in Example 17.22 above), but in this case the acquisition of the subsidiaries is conditional on an IPO of Newco. A Newco incorporated by the existing parent of the subsidiaries concerned would not generally be identified as the acquirer, but in this particular situation the critical distinguishing factor is that the acquisition of the subsidiaries is conditional on an IPO of Newco. This means that there has been a substantial change in ownership of the subsidiaries by virtue of the IPO.

Example 17.23: *Business combination effected by a Newco for cash consideration (spin-off transaction)*

Entity A proposes to spin off two of its existing businesses (currently housed in two separate entities, Sub 1 and Sub 2) as part of an IPO. The existing group structure is as follows:

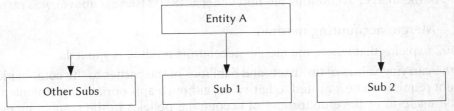

To facilitate the spin off, Entity A incorporates a new company (Newco) with nominal equity and appoints independent directors to the Board of Newco.

Newco signs an agreement to acquire Sub 1 and Sub 2 from Entity A conditional on the IPO proceeding. Newco issues a prospectus offering to issue shares for cash to provide Newco with funds to acquire Sub 1 and Sub 2. The IPO proceeds and Newco acquires Sub 1 and Sub 2 for cash. Entity A's nominal equity leaves virtually 100% ownership in Newco with the new investors.

Following the IPO, the respective group structures of Entity A and Newco appear as follows:

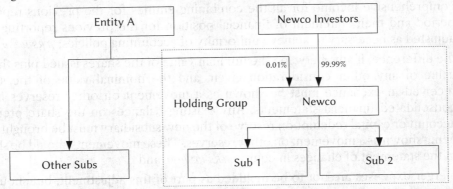

In this case, we believe it might be appropriate to identify Newco as the acquirer. The Newco investors have obtained control and virtually 100% ownership of Sub 1 and Sub 2 in an arm's length transaction, using Newco to effect the acquisition. The transaction has resulted in a change in control of Sub 1 and Sub 2 (i.e. Entity A losing control and Newco investors, via Newco, obtaining control). Newco could in effect be considered as an extension of the Newco investors since:

- the acquisition of Sub 1 and Sub 2 was conditional on the IPO proceeding so that the IPO is an integral part of the transaction as a whole, evidencing that Entity A did not have control of the transaction / entities; and

- there is a substantial change in the ownership of Sub 1 and Sub 2 by virtue of the IPO (i.e. Entity A only retains a negligible ownership interest in Newco).

Accordingly, Newco might be identified as the acquirer at the Holding Group level and use of the purchase method might be appropriate.

Whether a Newco formed to facilitate an IPO is capable of being identified as an acquirer depends on the facts and circumstances and ultimately requires judgement. If, for example, Entity A incorporates Newco and arranges for it to acquire Sub 1 and Sub 2 prior to the IPO proceeding, Newco might be viewed as an extension of Entity A or possibly an extension of Sub 1 or Sub 2. This is because the IPO and the reorganisation may be seen not as part of one integral transaction, but as two separate transactions. In that situation, Newco would not be the acquirer. This situation is discussed in Example 17.22 above.

5.2.1.C   Adoption of the merger accounting method accords with GAAP

This criterion is met for group reconstructions meeting the criteria set out in Section 19 for use of the merger accounting method under FRS 102 (see 5.2 above). *[FRS 102.19.27]*.

5.3   Merger accounting method

FRS 102 explains that where the merger accounting method is applied:

(a)   the carrying values of the assets and liabilities of the parties to the combination are not required to be adjusted to fair value, although appropriate adjustments should be made to achieve uniformity of accounting policies in the combining entities; *[FRS 102.19.29]*

(b)   the results and cash flows of all the combining entities should be brought into the financial statements of the combined entity from the beginning of the financial year in which the combination occurred, adjusted so as to achieve uniformity of accounting policies;

(c)   the comparative information should be restated by including the total comprehensive income for all the combining entities for the previous reporting period and their statement of financial position for the previous reporting date, adjusted as necessary to achieve uniformity of accounting policies; *[FRS 102.19.30]*

(d)   the difference, if any, between the nominal value of the shares issued plus the fair value of any other consideration given, and the nominal value of the shares received in exchange must be shown as a movement on other reserves in the consolidated financial statements. Any existing balances on the share premium account or capital redemption reserve of the new subsidiary must be brought in by being shown as a movement on other reserves. These movements should be shown in the statement of changes in equity; *[FRS 102.19.31]* and

(e)   merger expenses are not to be included as part of this adjustment, but should be charged to the statement of comprehensive income as part of profit or loss of the combined entity at the effective date of the group reconstruction. *[FRS 102.19.32]*.

These requirements in FRS 102 are similar to those contained in the Regulations when accounting for the acquisition of a subsidiary under the merger method of accounting in Companies Act group accounts. *[6 Sch 11]*.

The above wording explaining the merger accounting method is drafted in terms of an acquirer or issuing entity issuing shares as consideration for the transfer of shares in the other parties to the combination, *[FRS 102.19.28]*, and refers to consolidated financial statements. The application of the above requirements in the context of consolidated financial statements are discussed further at 5.3.1 to 5.3.5 below.

However, FRS 102 indicates that the provisions also apply to other arrangements that achieve similar results. *[FRS 102.19.28]*. In particular, the definition of a group reconstruction also includes arrangements such as the acquisition by an individual entity of the trade and net assets of another entity within the same group. Particular issues relating to the application of the above requirements in the context of individual financial statements are discussed at 5.4 below and Examples 17.27 to 17.33 demonstrate the application of the merger accounting method in the individual financial statements.

5.3.1   Carrying values of assets and liabilities

For group reconstructions involving the transfer of an equity holding in a subsidiary from one group entity to another, no adjustments would be expected to be required to conform accounting policies. This is because in the preparation of the consolidated financial statements of the ultimate parent entity, uniform accounting policies would have been expected to be adopted by all members of the group. However, it may be necessary to make adjustments where the combining entities have used different accounting policies when preparing their own financial statements. This is more likely to be the case for a group reconstruction involving the combination into a group of two or more entities that before the combination had the same equity holders.

The main issue relating to the use of carrying values is whether the amounts for the transferred entity (or entities) should be based on the carrying values reported at the level of:

(a)   financial statements of the transferred entity; or

(b)   the consolidated financial statements of the parent.

The carrying amounts with respect to the reporting entity are the same as those in its existing financial statements prior to the transfer of the other entity.

In our view, either basis would be acceptable. Using the carrying values reported in the financial statements of the transferred entity is more straightforward. Rather than the assets and liabilities being reported in two previous sets of financial statements, they are now reported in a single set of financial statements. Indeed, the Regulations state that 'the assets and liabilities of the undertaking acquired must be brought into the group accounts at the figures at which they stand in the undertaking's accounts, subject to any adjustment authorised or required by this Schedule'. *[6 Sch 11(2)]*. However, where the transferred entity had been previously acquired by the parent, using the carrying values (including any fair value adjustments and goodwill arising on that acquisition) reported in the consolidated financial statements of the parent may be more appropriate. This results in the assets and liabilities being reported on the same basis as if the transferred

Chapter 17

entity had been acquired by the reporting entity at the time the transferred entity was acquired by the parent, and could be considered to provide information that may be more relevant to the parent.

5.3.2   *Restatement of financial information prior to the date of the combination*

The description of the merger accounting method explicitly requires the results (and cash flows) of all combining entities to be included from the beginning of the financial year and for comparatives to be restated. *[FRS 102.19.30]*. This will be appropriate where the entity applying the merger accounting method in its consolidated financial statements and the entity (or entities) transferred to it under the group reconstruction have been under the control of the ultimate parent or common controlling party for at least that period of time. Indeed, this is consistent with the equivalent requirements in the Regulations which are as follows:

- the income and expenditure of the undertaking acquired must be included in the group accounts for the entire financial year, including the period before the acquisition; and

- the group accounts must show corresponding amounts relating to the financial year as if the undertaking acquired had been included in the consolidation throughout that year. *[6 Sch 11(3), (4)]*.

Effectively, the use of the merger accounting method results in the consolidated financial statements reflecting information as if the new sub-group had existed for the entire duration of the period covered by the financial statements. However, where the entities have come under the common control of the ultimate parent or common controlling party at a date after the beginning of the comparative period, this will not have been the case. In that situation, we believe that the results (and cash flows) of the transferred entity (or entities) should be included only from the date that it, and the entity applying the merger method of accounting, came under the control of the parent or the controlling party. This is the earliest date that the sub-group could have been created, and the results (and cash flows) should reflect that position.

5.3.3   *Equity eliminations*

As well as combining the assets and liabilities of the companies concerned, it will be necessary to eliminate the share capital of the new subsidiary against the cost of the investment as stated in the balance sheet of the new holding company. This is in principle a straightforward exercise, but when the two amounts do not equate to each other, the question arises of what to do with the difference, positive or negative.

The description of the merger accounting method at 5.3 above appears to presume that the cost of the investment will normally be carried at the nominal value of the shares of the new holding company which have been issued to effect the combination, together with the fair value of any other consideration given. (The ability to record these shares at nominal rather than fair value on issue depends on qualifying for merger relief under section 612 of the CA 2006, which is discussed at 5.5.1 below.) This will not be the case in a group reconstruction falling within the ambit of group reconstruction relief under section 611 of the CA 2006 (see 5.5.2 below) where, as a result of recognising a minimum premium value in share premium, the cost of investment reflects an amount in excess of the nominal value of the shares issued. However, we believe that this cost should be used in determining the difference to be accounted for under FRS 102, consistent with the requirements of the CA 2006 (see 5.5.2 below). *[6 Sch 11(5), (7)]*.

FRS 102 requires the difference to be shown as a movement on other reserves in the consolidated financial statements and also to be shown in the statement of changes in equity. *[FRS 102.19.31]*. The CA 2006 also requires such difference to be shown as a movement in consolidated reserves. *[6 Sch 11(6)]*. However, neither FRS 102 nor the legislation specifies any particular reserve.

Where the cost of the investment is less than the nominal value of the share capital of the subsidiary, the elimination of these two amounts will leave a residual credit in shareholders' funds in the consolidated balance sheet; this is generally classified as some form of capital reserve (or merger reserve).

Where the reverse situation applies, the net debit has to be eliminated against consolidated reserves. There are no particular rules on the matter, but common practice is to eliminate against a merger or similar reserve, or retained earnings, although some companies create a separate debit reserve. To the extent that the subsidiary has reserves that may be reclassified to profit or loss in the future under FRS 102, e.g. a cash flow hedge reserve, a fair value available-for-sale reserve (where IAS 39 – *Financial Instruments: Recognition and Measurement* – is applied) or a reserve arising from debt assets at fair value through other comprehensive income under IFRS 9 – *Financial Instruments*, it would not be appropriate to eliminate any debit adjustment against such reserves.

Apart from the effects of dealing with any imbalance as discussed above, there is no other elimination of the reserves of the subsidiary, which are combined with those of the holding company, in contrast to the treatment under the purchase method. However, some of the subsidiary's other reserves may need to be reclassified in order to make sense in the context of the group financial statements.

FRS 102 requires that any existing balance on the share premium account or capital redemption reserve of the new subsidiary undertaking should be brought in by being shown as a movement on other reserves. *[FRS 102.19.31]*. This is because these statutory reserves do not relate to the share capital of the reporting entity. Again, this difference should be shown in the statement of changes in equity. *[FRS 102.19.31]*. Such a difference should probably be taken to the same reserve as that on the elimination of the share capital of the subsidiary, because in reality the distinction between share capital and share premium can be considered arbitrary in this context.

Although the discussion above deals with the equity eliminations required, the application of the merger method of accounting also requires comparative information in the consolidated financial statements to be restated (see 5.3.2 above). Assuming the new subsidiary is being included from the beginning of the comparative period, this will generally mean that where share capital has been issued by the reporting entity to effect the group reconstruction, in applying the merger method of accounting, it should also be treated as if it had been in issue at the beginning of that period. However, if the subsidiary had issued any share capital between that date and the date of the group reconstruction, the equivalent amount of shares issued by the reporting entity to acquire those shares should be treated as if the shares had been issued on the same date as the subsidiary, not at the beginning of the comparative period. Where the reporting entity has given any other form of consideration to effect the group reconstruction, e.g. cash or incurred an inter-company financial liability, arguably this should also be accounted for as if the liability for such consideration arose at the beginning of the comparative period, but this then raises an issue as to whether the liability should be discounted to its present value at that date, with any unwinding of the discount reflected in the consolidated profit or loss. However, we believe it would be acceptable to account for the liability for such consideration at the date of the reorganisation, with the corresponding debit being reflected in the consolidated statement of equity at that time.

5.3.4   Expenses of the merger

One other question which sometimes arises in this context is how to account for the expenses of the merger. FRS 102 requires that all merger expenses should be charged to the statement of comprehensive income as part of profit or loss of the combined entity at the effective date of the group reconstruction. *[FRS 102.19.32]*.

However, some of these costs may be regarded as share issue expenses and therefore qualify to be written off against any share premium account recognised by the holding company in respect of the shares issued to effect the group reconstruction. FRS 102 does not prohibit the subsequent charging of such costs to the share premium account by means of a transfer between reserves.

5.3.5   Non-coterminous accounting periods

Particular practical problems in applying the merger method of accounting can arise when the accounting periods of the combining companies do not match each other. For many group reconstructions involving existing companies within a group, this should not be an issue as the ultimate controlling parent may have taken steps to ensure that its subsidiaries had coterminous accounting periods (or prepared interim financial statements as at the ultimate controlling parent's reporting date). However, for some forms of group reconstructions that may not be the case and the requirement (in applying merger accounting) to restate the consolidated financial statements retrospectively can cause difficulties.

Company law dictates that directors of a company, as well as preparing individual accounts for a company's financial year (based on its accounting reference period), must also prepare group accounts for the same year. *[s399(2)]*. The Companies Act group accounts so prepared must give a true and fair view in respect of the accounting period of the parent company, *[s404(2)]*, so this will require the period used by the subsidiary to be made to conform to that of its parent rather than the other way round. Naturally, the parent could change its own accounting reference date, but this can be amended only for the future, not retrospectively. It will therefore be necessary to try to draw up financial statements for the subsidiary at each of the relevant balance sheet dates of its new parent company.

Another treatment which may be appropriate is to use non-coterminous years for the comparative figures, with the result that there will be the need to deal with the effects of either a 'gap' or an overlapping period as an adjustment to reserves. However, the use of such non-coterminous financial statements would be appropriate only if the consolidated financial statements present materially the same picture as if coterminous years had been used. As indicated in Chapter 8 at 3.5.2, the Regulations and Section 9 require that, in preparing consolidated financial statements, a subsidiary's reporting date can be used only if it is no more than three months before that of the parent, and that adjustments are made for the effects of significant transactions or events that occur between the subsidiary's reporting date and those of the consolidated financial statements.

A particular problem can arise when a company is incorporated for the purpose of acting as the new parent company in a group reconstruction. The accounting reference period of the group must by law be that of the parent company, so this may result in the inadvertent creation of an accounting period which is not the one the group would have preferred. Moreover, unless the company has been in existence for two years, arguably its statutory accounts should not be able to deal with the results of the group for the current and comparative periods, because strictly they should go back only as far as the date of incorporation of the parent company.

However, in practice, particularly in situations where a new top holding company is set up as part of a group reconstruction, many companies simply produce consolidated financial statements for the more relevant period(s), as if the company had always been in existence. Only the individual financial statements of the new top holding company are prepared for the period from the date of incorporation. The justification for this approach is based on the more specific provisions of the Regulations relating to group accounts:

- the consolidated balance sheet and profit and loss account must incorporate in full the information contained in the individual accounts of the undertakings included in the consolidation; *[6 Sch 2(1)]* and

- the principles of the merger accounting method require information for the undertaking acquired to be included for an entire year, with comparatives for the previous year. *[6 Sch 11(3)-(4)]*.

Consider the following example:

Example 17.24: Merger accounting by a newly incorporated parent company

Company A is incorporated on 1 April 2019 to effect a group reorganisation on 1 July 2019 whereby it will become the new parent entity of an existing group, headed by Company B. Company B has a financial year ending on 31 December and has prepared consolidated financial statements for the year ended 31 December 2018. Company A gives notice to have an accounting reference date of 31 December and will prepare consolidated financial statements made up to 31 December 2019. In doing so, Company A has determined that it is appropriate to account for the acquisition of the existing group under the merger method (invoking a true and fair override, if necessary – see 5.2.1.A above).

As indicated above, arguably the statutory consolidated financial statements should include the existing Company B group for only the 9 month period from the date of incorporation of Company A. Nevertheless, this does not really provide relevant information to the shareholders of the group who have continued to have an interest in the Company B group. Common practice would be for Company A to present the year ended 31 December 2019 (with comparatives for the year ended 31 December 2018). The notes to the financial statements will need to explain the basis on which the consolidated financial statements have been drawn up.

If Company A had instead been incorporated on 1 October 2018, a similar problem arises, but again, a pragmatic approach is to prepare accounts for the same two year period. However, this may be appropriate only because Company A is a Newco and therefore is assumed to have no trade in the period from 1 October to 31 December 2018.

Chapter 17

5.4   Application of merger accounting in individual financial statements

5.4.1   *Hive transactions*

A common transaction in the individual financial statements of entities within a group is the transfer of trade and assets from one entity to another. These result in different accounting issues, which are discussed at 5.4.1.A to 5.4.4 below. This guidance focuses on three variations of a transfer of trade and assets from:

- a subsidiary to a parent, ('hive up');
- one subsidiary to a fellow subsidiary, ('hive across'); and
- a parent to a subsidiary, ('hive down').

In all of the following discussion and examples in 5.4.1.A to 5.4.4 below, it is assumed that the conditions for the use of merger accounting in FRS 102 are met (see 5.2 above), i.e.:

- the ultimate equity holders remain the same, and the rights of each equity holder, relative to the others, are unchanged; and
- no non-controlling interest in the net assets of the group is altered by the transfer.

The other condition is that the use of the merger accounting method is not prohibited by company law or other relevant legislation. *[FRS 102.19.27]*. All of the following examples relate to individual accounts. Therefore, the conditions for use of the merger accounting method included in the Regulations and LLP Regulations do not apply; these conditions apply only in group accounts. *[6 Sch 10, 6 Sch 10 (LLP)]*.

In addition, it is assumed that the trade and assets transferred meet the definition of a business in the Glossary to FRS 102, *[FRS 102 Appendix I]*, (see 3.2.1 above).

5.4.1.A   *Use of the merger accounting method or the purchase method for hive transactions?*

Group reconstructions meeting the specified conditions *may* be accounted for by using the merger accounting method [emphasis added]. *[FRS 102.19.27]*. This suggests that use of the purchase method is also available for such group reconstructions.

As required by Section 10, an entity must select and apply consistent accounting policies for similar transactions (see Chapter 9 at 3.2 to 3.3). *[FRS 102.10.7]*.

There may be circumstances in which the purchase method is not appropriate for a group reconstruction. In our view, where the purchase method is selected, the transaction must have substance from the perspective of the reporting entity. This is because the purchase method results in the reassessment of the value of the net assets of one or more of the entities involved and / or the recognition of goodwill. As discussed at 5 above, FRS 6 noted these as reasons why the purchase method may be inappropriate for some group reconstructions. Careful consideration is required of all of the facts and circumstances from the perspective of each entity, before it is concluded that a transaction has substance. If there is no substance to the group reconstruction, the merger accounting method should be applied.

In our view, when evaluating whether the hive transaction has substance and in determining an appropriate accounting policy, the following factors should be taken into account:

- The purpose of the transaction

  It is important to understand the economics and objectives of a transaction in relation to all of the parties to it. These will often inform management's judgements as to the appropriate accounting.

- Whether or not the transaction is a business combination

  See 3.2.1 above for a full discussion of the definition of a business and of a business combination. Importantly, Section 19 states that 'the result of nearly all business combinations is that one entity, the acquirer, obtains control of one or more other businesses, the acquiree.' *[FRS 102.19.3]*. Therefore, if the transaction is not a business combination, use of the purchase method is generally not appropriate.

  One example where this is relevant is in the case of a hive up (see 5.4.2 below). It may be difficult to categorise a hive up transaction as a business combination because there is no acquirer that obtains control of a business; the parent already controlled the business that has been transferred to it.

  In assessing whether the transaction is a business combination, it is relevant to consider the existing activities of the entities involved in the transaction and whether the transaction is bringing businesses together into a 'reporting entity' that did not exist before. Some transfers of businesses may be more in the nature of a continuation of an existing business (or part of a business) than a business combination.

- Whether or not the transaction involves a newly incorporated entity (Newco)

  As discussed at 3.4.2 above, it is difficult to identify Newco as the acquirer in a business combination and so merger accounting is likely to be more appropriate where a business has been transferred to a Newco. However, in some cases, a group reconstruction involving a Newco may be undertaken in connection with an IPO or spin off or other change in control and significant change in ownership and in some circumstances, it may be possible to identify the Newco as the acquirer (see the discussion at 5.2.1.B above). The accounting will depend on a careful analysis of the facts and circumstances and ultimately requires judgement.

- Whether or not the transaction is conducted at fair value

  If the transaction is equivalent to an arm's length transaction between third parties then it may be appropriate to apply the purchase method. An example of this is a business combination for which the consideration paid is cash or loan (with formally documented interest and / or repayment terms), of an amount commensurate to the fair value of the trade and assets acquired (i.e. of the business, including goodwill).

  It may often be difficult to obtain a reliable estimate of the fair value of shares issued by an entity as consideration for the transfer of the trade and assets in a group reconstruction. It would be difficult to apply the purchase method in such circumstances.

  In addition, the economic substance of the transaction may be the same irrespective of the number of shares issued; for example, in a hive down to a wholly owned subsidiary. Therefore, in our view, the merger accounting method is often more appropriate for transactions involving share consideration.

If an entity concludes that use of the purchase method is appropriate for a particular transaction, then Section 19's requirements regarding the application of the purchase method apply. *[FRS 102.19.6-6A]*. In particular, it is important to determine which party is the accounting acquirer (see 3.4 above).

5.4.1.B   *Transactions at undervalue and section 845 of the CA 2006*

When an entity sells an asset (or a group of assets and liabilities, for example, a business) for an amount that is less than its fair value (including for nil consideration), the entity is making a transfer at undervalue because it is not receiving an arm's length consideration. Therefore, the entity must consider whether it is making a distribution under Part 23 of the CA 2006 and whether it has sufficient distributable reserves to do so. In the context of hive transactions, this is particularly relevant when the transaction involves a transfer of value from a group entity to its direct or indirect parent / owner or to a fellow subsidiary. An example of a transfer of value by the transferor (the selling entity) is a hive up or hive across in which the consideration received by the entity is less than the fair value of the trade and assets sold. An example of a transfer of value by the transferee (the purchasing entity) is a hive down or hive across in which the consideration paid by the entity exceeds the fair value of the trade and assets purchased.

It is not the intention of this publication to discuss all the requirements relating to the lawfulness of undervalue transactions, which is an area where an entity may need to obtain appropriate legal advice on the specific transaction. However, sections 845 and 846 of the CA 2006 are often relevant to such transactions and are briefly discussed below.

Section 845 of the CA 2006 applies to a company in determining the 'amount of a distribution' in relation to the sale, transfer or other disposition of a non-cash asset, providing that:

- the company has 'profits available for distribution' at the time of the distribution; and,
- if the amount of the distribution were to be determined in accordance with section 845, the company could make the distribution without contravening Part 23 of the CA 2006.

For the purposes of section 845, the profits available for distribution are treated as increased by the amount (if any) by which the amount or value of the consideration for the disposition exceeds the book value of the asset. The book value of the asset is the amount at which the asset is stated in the relevant accounts of the transferor used to support the distribution (or if not stated in those accounts, nil). *[s845]*. Where any part of the amount at which the asset is stated in the relevant accounts represents an unrealised profit (for example, where an item of property, plant and equipment has been revalued), that profit is treated as a realised profit for the purpose of determining the lawfulness of the distribution. *[s846]*.

If section 845 applies, the amount of the distribution is the amount by which the book value of the asset exceeds any consideration received. If the consideration exceeds the book value, the amount of the distribution is nil.

Example 17.25:   Application of section 845

Entity A has a property, measured at cost less impairment, with a book value of £750,000. Entity A has distributable reserves of £600,000. Entity A sells the property to its parent, Entity P.

In the following scenarios, what is the amount of any distribution in law?

Entity A receives cash of the following amounts, from Entity P, in consideration for the property:

- £750,000: Distribution is measured as (£750,000 – £750,000 = £nil).
- £150,000: Distribution is measured as (£750,000 – £150,000 = £600,000).
- £nil: Distribution would be measured as (£750,000 – £nil = £750,000). Entity A does not have sufficient distributable reserves for this transaction, so it cannot be conducted as planned (see discussion following Example 17.26 below).

Example 17.26: Application of sections 845 and 846

Entity B has a property, measured at revaluation under Section 17, with a carrying value of £900,000. Entity B purchased the property for £600,000 and the related revaluation reserve is £300,000. Entity B has distributable reserves of £150,000. Entity B sells the property to its parent, Entity P for £475,000.

The carrying value of the property exceeds the consideration received by £425,000 (£900,000 less £475,000), which is the amount at which the distribution is measured under section 845. Entity B has only £150,000 of reserves available for distribution. However, by virtue of section 846, the revaluation reserve of £300,000 is considered realised for the purpose of distributing the property to which the revaluation reserve relates. Therefore, total profits available for distribution are £450,000 which are sufficient to cover the amount of the distribution.

Detailed worked examples demonstrating the application of sections 845 and 846 are provided in the ICAEW/ICAS Technical Release TECH 02/17BL – *Guidance on Realised and Distributable Profits under the Companies Act 2006. [TECH 02/17BL Appendix 1].*

It is important that the transferor company has positive profits available for distribution (as defined) sufficient to cover the amount of the distribution (as defined). In a transaction to sell an asset at book value, the amount of the distribution is nil but if the transferor has nil or negative profits available for distribution, it would not be able to enter into the transaction as planned. However, alternative structures for the transaction could be considered. For example, the buyer could pay an amount equal to fair value (in the case of a sale of trade and assets, the fair value of the business) for the transaction. The asset could also be sold at book value plus an amount exceeding the deficit on distributable reserves. (This is because, for the purposes of section 845, the profits available for distribution are treated as increased by the amount of any excess of the consideration for the transfer over the book value of the asset. While the amount of the distribution is nil, in order to effect the transaction, there must be a positive (not a nil) balance on profits available for distribution after such adjustment for that excess.) Another possibility is that the seller might be in a position to effect a capital reduction in order to create positive profits available for distribution prior to the transaction. An entity may often need to obtain legal advice in order to structure the transaction appropriately.

Undervalue transactions in group reconstructions are often undertaken in such a way that intermediate holding companies are affected. For example, one subsidiary sells its trade and assets to another, and there is an intermediate holding company between the selling subsidiary and the common parent of both the selling and buying subsidiaries. That intermediate holding company must also consider the adequacy of its distributable reserves (including the effects of any impairment in its investment in the subsidiary) when its subsidiary conducts a transaction at undervalue. See 5.4.3.B below.

5.4.1.C   *Balances arising from merger accounting and realised profits*

As discussed at 5.4.6 below, application of merger accounting often results in balances within equity, which may be a debit or a credit. TECH 02/17BL contains guidance on debits within equity arising on group reconstructions. Paragraph 9.41 of TECH 02/17BL notes that although the guidance is written in the context of IFRS 3 it is equally applicable to a group reconstruction accounted for under FRS 102. The following is guidance within TECH 02/17BL:

- Where the accounting is to recognise the net assets acquired at the transferor's book amounts (rather than at their fair values), the consideration paid, say, measured at the nominal value of the shares issued plus the value of the cash element, may exceed the book amount of the net assets acquired. This will leave a debit difference to be recognised. It is not goodwill. The debit is sometimes referred to as a 'merger difference' and is recorded in equity. *[TECH 02/17BL.9.36]*.

- A business combination involving members of the same group is completed under the direction of the controlling party, the common parent. Consequently, any excess paid by the acquirer over the book amount of the vendor's net assets is accounted for in a similar manner to a distribution or return of capital to the common parent. Distributions and returns of capital are dealt with through equity, and therefore it is logical also to recognise the debit in equity. *[TECH 02/17BL.9.37]*.

- Such a debit directly to equity is not necessarily, however, a distribution as a matter of law. This is because the debit described above is determined on a book basis, whereas the question as to whether there would be an actual distribution is determined by whether the company gives consideration other than an issue of its shares, to its parent or a fellow subsidiary, with a fair value in excess of the fair value of the net assets and business acquired. Accordingly the debit may form part of an actual distribution or may not. *[TECH 02/17BL.9.38]*.

- In a case where the debit in equity does not form part of an actual distribution, then at the date of acquisition the debit does not represent a loss; the acquiring company has purchased net assets worth at least the book value of the consideration given but, under the appropriate accounting, has recognised these at a lower amount. The difference between the two is the amount of the debit. As the debit is not a loss at all, it is neither realised nor unrealised. However, it can subsequently become a realised loss. *[TECH 02/17BL.9.39]*.

- To the extent that the assets, if they had been recognised at the higher amount, together with any goodwill that would have been recognised, would have been written down, say, by depreciation or impairment, an equivalent amount of the debit becomes a realised loss. It is a realised, rather than unrealised, loss because, had the debit been carried as an asset, any write down for depreciation or impairment would be required, by section 841 and the principles of realisation, to be regarded as realised. *[TECH 02/17BL.9.40]*.

A debit adjustment to reserves in a public company would result in a restriction to the reserves available for distribution via the 'net assets test' in section 831 of the CA 2006. *[s831]*.

The guidance in TECH 02/17BL discussed above deals with the situation where there is a net debit to be taken to equity as a result of merger accounting. However, for some group reconstructions, the net amount to be recognised is a credit (see 5.4.6 below). In determining whether this credit represents realised profits or not, reference should be made to the guidance in TECH 02/17BL. Paragraph 3.18 recommends a 'top slicing' approach in determining realised profits for exchanges of assets where the consideration received is partly 'qualifying' consideration and partly other consideration. This means that where an asset is sold partly for qualifying consideration and partly for other consideration (for example, a mixed consideration of cash and a freehold property), any profit arising is a realised profit to the extent that the fair value of the consideration received is in the form of qualifying consideration. *[TECH 02/17BL.3.18].* Paragraph 3.18A expands on the application of 'top slicing' when the consideration received comprises a combination of assets and liabilities. For example, this will often be the case on a transfer of trade and assets for no consideration. The guidance states that any liabilities are first deducted from the amount of qualifying consideration received, therefore the profit will be realised only to the extent of any net balance (i.e. cash less liabilities) of qualifying consideration received. *[TECH 02/17BL.3.18-18A].*

5.4.2 Hive up transactions

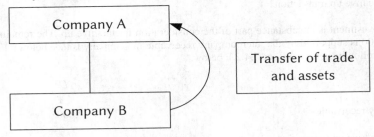

5.4.2.A Hive up immediately after acquisition

Example 17.27: Hive up immediately after acquisition

- Company A acquires Company B on 31 December 2018 in a business combination for £5,000 cash. Company B has net assets with a book value in its individual financial statements of £2,800 and a fair value of £3,500 (including deferred tax adjustments arising on the business combination). Goodwill of £1,500 arises in the consolidated financial statements of Company A, also prepared under FRS 102.

- On 1 January 2019, Company B sells its trade and assets to Company A in consideration for an intercompany receivable of £2,800 equal to the book value of net assets in Company B's individual financial statements.

- Company B has positive distributable reserves (see 5.4.1.B above).

- Company A prepares consolidated and individual financial statements under FRS 102. Company A and Company B use consistent accounting policies.

Company A uses the merger accounting method for the hive up (see 5.4.1.A above). However, in this particular case of a hive up immediately after acquisition, using the merger accounting method achieves the same result as applying the purchase method.

In using the merger accounting method, Company A must determine which are the appropriate book values of net assets of Company B to use, those from its consolidated financial statements or from Company B's individual financial statements. In our view, it is appropriate for Company A to use the consolidated book values of net assets (including goodwill) relating to Company B's trade and assets. This reflects the substance of the transaction, which is equivalent to Company A purchasing the trade and assets directly from the third party, combined with the acquisition of a cash shell Company B. Using the consolidated book values has the effect that the same assets (including goodwill) and liabilities are presented in relation to the trade and assets acquired in both the consolidated and individual financial statements of Company A.

Company B is selling its trade and assets for a consideration equal to the book value of the net assets in its individual financial statements, which is less than fair value of the trade and assets (i.e. the business). Since it has positive distributable reserves, section 845 applies (see 5.4.1.B above) and, in this case, because

Company B receives an intercompany receivable equal to the book value of its net assets, the amount of the distribution is measured at nil.

The hive up results in the following entries in Company A's separate financial statements and Company B's individual financial statements:

Company A	Dr	Cr
	£	£
Investment in Company B	5,000	
Cash		5,000
To record the initial purchase of Company B		
Goodwill	1,500	
Net assets (at acquisition date fair value)	3,500	
Intercompany payable		2,800
Investment in Company B		2,200
To record the hive up transaction		

The credit to investment is in substance part of the consideration for the hive up. The remaining investment balance of £2,800 is supported by the intercompany receivable in Company B (see below). For a discussion of impairment following a hive up, see 5.4.2.F below.

Company B	Dr	Cr
	£	£
Intercompany receivable	2,800	
Net assets		2,800
To record the hive up transaction		

5.4.2.B   *Other forms of consideration*

Share consideration: It is unlikely that a hive up would be effected by shares since this would result in the subsidiary holding shares in its parent, which is generally prohibited by section 136 of the CA 2006. *[s136]*.

Nil consideration: If Company B gifted its business to its parent Company A, it would need sufficient profits available for distribution to cover the book value of the net assets distributed. In this example, this would have the effect that, instead of the intercompany receivable recorded above, a distribution in equity would be recorded for the same amount. An entity would never have quite sufficient reserves to distribute the entirety of its net assets because some of those net assets will be represented by share capital and premium. An entity may need to obtain legal advice in order to structure the transaction appropriately. For example, Company B might conduct a capital reduction in advance of the hive up (although one share, that is not a redeemable share, must always be left outstanding) and a nominal consideration could be paid for any share capital remaining. *[s641]*.

Company A would record the same goodwill and net assets for the hive up of Company B's trade and assets as shown in the example above, together with a credit to the carrying amount of its investment in Company B of £5,000 (less any amount supported by nominal consideration paid to Company B).

5.4.2.C Hive up sometime after acquisition

Example 17.28: Hive up sometime after acquisition

- Assume the facts are the same as Example 17.27, at 5.4.2.A above, but Company B was acquired on 31 December 2015 by Company A. Since acquisition, Company B has recorded profits of £600 per year in its individual financial statements. Goodwill is amortised over 10 years and the property is depreciated over 30 years from the acquisition date.

- On original acquisition, in Company A's consolidated financial statements, property that was recorded in Company B's individual financial statements at historical cost of £125 was ascribed a fair value of £1,000. A deferred tax liability of £175 (at a substantively enacted tax rate of 20%) arose on the fair value adjustment (20% × (£1000 – £125)), giving a net of tax adjustment to the fair values of the identifiable net assets acquired of £700.

- On 1 January 2019, Company B sells its trade and assets to Company A, in consideration for an intercompany receivable of £4,600 (£2,800 plus £1,800 cumulative profits for three years) equal to the book value of net assets in Company B's individual financial statements.

- Company B has positive distributable reserves (see 5.4.1.B above).

- Company A prepares consolidated and individual financial statements under FRS 102. Company A and Company B use consistent accounting policies.

Company A uses the merger accounting method to account for the transaction in its individual financial statements. As in Example 17.27 at 5.4.2.A above, Company A must determine which are the appropriate book values of net assets of Company B to use, those from its consolidated financial statements or from Company B's individual financial statements. In our view, it would generally be most appropriate to use the consolidated book values of the net assets (including goodwill) relating to Company B's trade and assets.

If, as seems likely, the fair value of the trade and assets transferred exceeds the consideration received (based on the book value of the related net assets in its individual financial statements), Company B would be making an undervalue transfer (see 5.4.1.B above). However, since Company B has positive distributable reserves and is paid book value for its net assets, the amount of the distribution is zero in accordance with section 845 and there is also no accounting effect of the distribution to reflect in Company B's equity.

The hive up results in the following entries in Company A's separate financial statements and Company B's individual financial statements:

Company A	Dr £	Cr £
Goodwill[1]	1,050	
Net assets[2]	5,230	
Intercompany payable		4,600
Investment[3]		400
Merger reserve[4]		1,280
To record the hive up transaction		

[1]Goodwill of £1,500 arising on original acquisition has been amortised for three years at £150 per year. Note that goodwill is not remeasured at the date of hive up.

[2]Net assets of Company B in Company A's consolidated financial statements are £3,500 at the date of acquisition and Company B has made £1,800 cumulative profits in the three years post-acquisition. There was a fair value adjustment on property of £700 (net of deferred tax), depreciated for three years of its 30 year useful economic life, giving accumulated depreciation net of unwind of deferred tax of £70. Therefore, the net assets of Company B in A's consolidated financial statements at the date of hive up are £5,230 (£3,500 plus £1,800 less £70).

Chapter 17

[3]Company A's investment has been written down to the amount that can be supported by the intercompany receivable in Company B of £4,600: i.e. £5,000 (from original acquisition) less £4,600. For a discussion of impairment following a hive up, see 5.4.2.F below.

[4]An adjustment in equity, sometimes to a separate reserve (in this example, the merger reserve), is recorded for the merger accounting difference arising. *[FRS 102.19.31]*. The merger reserve represents the cumulative profits made by Company B as shown in Company A's consolidated financial statements, i.e. cumulative profit of £1,800 less £70 net depreciation / deferred tax unwind on the property fair value adjustment less goodwill amortisation of £450. The reserve would be assessed to determine whether any amount of it represents a realised profit using the guidance in TECH 02/17BL (see 5.4.1.C above).

Company B	Dr £	Cr £
Intercompany receivable	4,600	
Net assets		4,600
To record the hive up transaction		

5.4.2.D   Other forms of consideration

There are similar considerations to those discussed in Example 17.27 at 5.4.2.A above.

5.4.2.E   Hive up of a business not previously acquired

Example 17.29:   Hive up of a business not previously acquired

- Company B has been owned by Company A since incorporation. Company A has an investment in Company B of £1,000.
- On 1 January 2019, Company B sells a business (trade and assets) to Company A, in consideration for an intercompany receivable equal to the book value of net assets (relating to that business) of £4,600 in Company B's individual financial statements.
- Company B has positive distributable reserves before and after the transaction (see 5.4.1.B above).
- Company A prepares consolidated and individual financial statements. Company A and Company B use consistent accounting policies.

As in Examples 17.27 (at 5.4.2.A above) and 17.28 (at 5.4.2.C above), Company A uses the merger accounting method for the hive up in its individual financial statements. This may be an undervalue transfer if the fair value of the trade and assets exceeds the book value of the related net assets in Company B's individual financial statements. Since Company B has positive distributable reserves and is paid book value for the net assets, the amount of the distribution is nil in accordance with section 845 and there is also no accounting effect of the distribution to reflect in Company B's equity.

In this case, the book values of the net assets of the business hived up are the same in the individual financial statements of Company B and the consolidated financial statements of Company A, and therefore are the only book values that can be used to account for the hive up in Company A's individual financial statements. More generally, the book values of net assets from a selling subsidiary's individual financial statements may be subject to accounting policy alignment. Therefore, the accounting in both companies is straightforward, since both companies recognise / derecognise net assets at the book value of £4,600 and an equivalent intercompany balance. In this example, the carrying amount of the investment in Company B remains supported by the intercompany receivable of £4,600 held by Company B. In situations where the investment carrying amount would not be supported as a consequence of the hive up, a credit to the investment would be recorded with an adjustment to equity for any difference between the net assets recorded in Company A's books and the credit to the cost of investment.

For a discussion of impairment following a hive up, see 5.4.2.F below.

5.4.2.F   Assessing the parent's carrying value of investment for impairment

After a hive up, the parent company may need to assess whether the carrying value of its investment in the subsidiary transferring its trade and assets remains recoverable.

In Example 17.29 at 5.4.2.E above, it is clear that there is no impairment since the intercompany receivable of £4,600 held by Company B following the hive up is in excess of the investment of £1,000. However, in other cases, there might be an apparent 'impairment' in value, if the carrying value of the parent's investment exceeds the consideration given for the hive up.

Example 17.30: Debit merger difference ('impairment') arises on hive up

- Company A acquired Company B on 31 December 2014, for a fair value of £10,000, when Company B's net assets were stated in its individual financial statements at £6,000.

- On 1 January 2019, Company B sells its trade and assets to Company A in consideration for an intercompany receivable of £7,500 equal to the book value of net assets in Company B's individual financial statements.

- On 1 January 2019, the carrying value of Company B's net assets (including goodwill) from Company A's consolidated financial statements is £11,500.

- Company B has positive distributable reserves.

- The value in use / fair value of Company B supported the carrying value of Company A's cost of investment of £10,000 prior to the hive up. There is no remaining trade in Company B after the hive up.

- Company A applies merger accounting, and recognises the net assets of Company B at their book values from Company B's individual financial statements, i.e. £7,500, and an intercompany payable for the same amount.

Subsequent to the hive up, Company A assesses its investment in Company B and identifies that the intercompany receivable of £7,500 held by Company B does not support the investment carrying value of £10,000. There is an apparent 'impairment' of £2,500. However, Company A has suffered no loss and so it would not be appropriate for it to recognise an impairment loss in profit or loss as a result of the hive up. This is because there is no change to the net assets that it controls; they have simply moved between the legal entities. Company A must recognise the reduction in the cost of investment, which is in substance part of the consideration paid by Company A for the hive up. Therefore, it is appropriate to consider the debit of £2,500 as a merger accounting difference to be recognised in equity in Company A. It is not goodwill, since the application of the merger accounting method does not result in the recognition of new goodwill. *[FRS 102.19.29-32]*. See 5.4.1.C above for a discussion of whether such merger accounting differences result in realised profits and losses.

In this scenario, accounting for the hive up using the book values of the net assets (including goodwill) of the subsidiary in the consolidated financial statements generally avoids or mitigates an overall debit arising on the transaction. This is because the investment is essentially exchanged for the net assets (including goodwill) relating to the hive up as included in the consolidated financial statements. If this were the appropriate accounting in Company A, the amounts it would record are:

Company A	Dr £	Cr £
Net assets	11,500	
Intercompany payable		7,500
Investment[1]		2,500
Merger reserve[2]		1,500
To record the hive up transaction		

[1]To write down the investment to the amount receivable in Company B.

[2]An adjustment in equity, sometimes to a separate reserve (in this example, the merger reserve), is recorded for the merger accounting difference arising. *[FRS 102.19.31]*. The reserve would be assessed to determine whether any amount of it represents a realised profit using the guidance in TECH 02/17BL (see 5.4.1.C above).

Although the investment is written down to the same amount (£7,500) using the book values of Company B from either Company B's individual financial statements or Company A's consolidated financial statements, when the latter amounts are used to account for the hive up, no overall debit arises on the transaction. Instead, a credit balance arises of £1,500, essentially representing the increase in the consolidated net assets (including goodwill) of Company B since its original acquisition, which is reflected in the net assets recorded on the hive up, but not in the consideration that was agreed between the two parties.

Care should be taken that any genuine impairment in the parent's investment in its subsidiary, i.e. one resulting from factors other than the hive up, is identified and recognised appropriately in the parent's profit or loss. This is because otherwise a debit merger accounting difference recorded in equity may inappropriately include a true impairment loss.

5.4.3   Hive across transactions

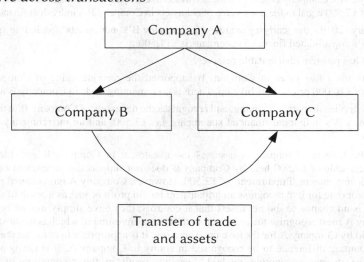

Similar issues arise when considering a hive across transaction, as when considering a hive up (see 5.4.2 above): the seller must consider whether it is making a sale at undervalue (see 5.4.1.B above), and the buyer must consider the appropriate basis on which to recognise the net assets acquired in its individual financial statements (see 5.4.1.A above).

5.4.3.A   Hive across for intercompany consideration

Example 17.31:   Hive across for intercompany consideration

- On 1 January 2019, Company B transfers its trade and assets to Company C, for an intercompany receivable of £6,000 equal to the book value of Company B's net assets in its individual financial statements.
- The fair value of Company B's trade and assets (i.e. the business) is £12,500 at the date of transfer.
- Company B has positive distributable reserves (see 5.4.1.B above).
- Company A prepares consolidated and individual financial statements under FRS 102. Company A, Company B and Company C use consistent accounting policies.
- Company A has a cost of investment in Company B of £7,000 and in Company C of £1,000.
- Company A's consolidated financial statements at 31 December 2018 show amortised goodwill of £1,500 and net assets of £8,500 in respect of Company B's trade and assets, as Company A had acquired Company B in a previous transaction.

As discussed at 5.4.1.A above, Company C must determine whether to apply the merger accounting method or the purchase method to the hive across.

Company C applies the merger accounting method to the hive across. It must consider which book values of net assets to use, those from Company B's individual financial statements or from Company A's consolidated financial statements. Which is most appropriate will depend on specific facts and circumstances. Since Company B has been previously acquired, using the book values of net assets (including goodwill) from the consolidated financial statements may be more appropriate. There may be other circumstances in which the book values from Company B's individual financial statements would be considered most appropriate, for example, if the substance of the transaction were a continuation of the trade and assets hived across, as would be the case if Company C were newly incorporated for the purpose of the transaction.

If Company C uses the consolidated book values of net assets (including goodwill), the accounting is similar to that shown in Example 17.28 at 5.4.2.C above, except that a credit to equity (for example, to a separate merger reserve) will arise for all of the difference between the book values recognised and the consideration given of £6,000, and there is no investment to be credited.

If, in different circumstances, Company C were to use the individual book values of net assets, the accounting is similar to that shown in Example 17.29 at 5.4.2.E above, with net assets and an intercompany payable recognised of £6,000.

Company C uses the consolidated book values of net assets (including goodwill), so the accounting in each of Companies B and C is as follows:

Company C	Dr £	Cr £
Goodwill	1,500	
Net assets	8,500	
Intercompany payable		6,000
Merger reserve[1]		4,000
To record the hive up transaction		

[1] See 5.4.1.C above for a discussion of whether such merger accounting differences result in realised profits and losses.

Company B	Dr £	Cr £
Intercompany receivable	6,000	
Net assets		6,000
To record the hive up transaction		

The common parent, Company A, must also consider the effect of the hive across on its financial statements. In the consolidated financial statements, the transaction has no effect. In Company A's individual financial statements, there is a cost of investment in Company B of £7,000 but Company B contains only a receivable of £6,000. On the face of it, there is an apparent 'impairment' in the cost of investment in Company B, but Company A has suffered no loss because it has simply transferred assets from one subsidiary to another. Therefore, it would be inappropriate to recognise an impairment loss in Company A's profit or loss. In our view, it is appropriate for Company A to reallocate an appropriate amount of its investment in Company B to its investment in Company C. Company A's total investment in its subsidiaries B and C remains the same.

5.4.3.B Intermediate parent companies in a hive across transaction

When there is an intermediate parent above the seller in a hive across (for example, between Companies A and B in Example 17.31 at 5.4.3.A above), there are further legal and accounting considerations for the intermediate parent.

This situation is addressed by TECH 02/17BL which highlights that such transactions have potential to be unlawful, even if the intermediate parent suffers no accounting impairment loss. TECH 02/17BL states that when the seller transacts at an undervalue (see 5.4.1.B above) the actual value of the intermediate parent's investment in its subsidiary is diminished by the transfer, and so it is possible that knowledge of the proposed transaction and passive acquiescence in it may result in its being, in law, a distribution by the intermediate parent. If so, and if the intermediate parent has insufficient profits available for distribution, then it will be unlawful. *[TECH 02/17BL.9.71].*

Another issue for intermediate parents to consider is whether an impairment of the cost of investment in the selling subsidiary (or in any intermediate parent companies in the group structure above the selling subsidiary) arises as a result of the hive across transaction. If the business remaining in the selling subsidiary after a hive across does not support the carrying value of the investment in the selling subsidiary, its immediate parent company may need to recognise an impairment loss. This may also affect subsequent intermediate parent companies up the chain in the group structure. This does not affect the common parent company of the buying and selling subsidiaries, but may affect intermediate parents above the selling subsidiary as far as the common parent. See Example 17.31 at 5.4.3.A above for considerations of the common parent in a hive across.

5.4.3.C   Other forms of consideration

Share consideration: Similarly to a hive up transaction, it is unlikely that a hive across would be effected by shares since this would result in cross-holdings within the group, which may add complexity to a group structure.

Nil consideration: If Company B gifted its business to Company C, the considerations and accounting for Company B would be similar to those described in Example 17.27 at 5.4.2.A above.

Company C would record a credit to equity, representing the capital contribution of a gifted business. Capital contributions are assessed to determine whether any portion represents a realised profit in accordance with section 3 of TECH 02/17BL.

As discussed in Example 17.31 at 5.4.3.A above, Company A must consider whether the carrying amount of its investment in Company B remains recoverable, and may need to reallocate an appropriate amount of its investment in Company B to its investment in Company C.

5.4.4   Hive down transactions

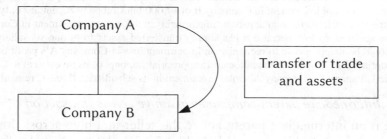

5.4.4.A   Hive down for share consideration

Example 17.32: Hive down for share consideration

- On 1 January 2019, Company A transfers its trade and assets to Company B, its wholly owned subsidiary, in exchange for the issue of shares from Company B, with nominal value of £300.

- The book value of net assets in Company A's financial statements immediately before transfer is £2,500 and comprise property of £1,100, inventory of £1,200, trade receivables of £700 and payables of £1,000 and £500 of cash.

- Company A is not part of a wider group. Therefore, the book values of its net assets are the same in the individual and consolidated financial statements that contain Company A.

- Company A has a policy of revaluation of property, which is stated in its financial statements at 31 December 2018 at £1,100. Its original cost was £700.

- Company A and Company B prepare financial statements. Company A and Company B use consistent accounting policies.

As discussed at 5.4.1.A above, Company B must determine whether to apply the merger accounting method or the purchase method to the hive down.

Company B applies the merger accounting method to the hive down and so recognises the net assets of £2,500. Group reconstruction relief is relevant to this transaction since Company B, a wholly owned subsidiary, is issuing shares to its parent Company A for consideration that is (at least in part) non-cash assets. *[s611].* While group reconstruction relief is optional (see Chapter 8 at 4.2.1), Company B chooses to make use of this relief.

Group reconstruction relief establishes the minimum premium value to be recognised in share premium account. For further discussion and examples of the operation of group reconstruction relief, see 5.5.2 below and Chapter 8 at 4.2.1. In this example, Company B is required to recognise a 'minimum premium value', which is 'the amount (if any) by which the base value of the consideration for the shares allotted (being the base value of the assets transferred less the base value of any liabilities of the transferor company assumed by the issuing company) exceeds the aggregate nominal value of the shares.' *[s611].*

The base value of the assets transferred is taken as:

- the cost of those assets to the transferor company, or
- if less, the amount at which those assets are stated in the transferor company's accounting records immediately before the transfer.

The base value of the liabilities assumed is taken as the amount at which they are stated in the transferor company's accounting records immediately before the transfer. *[s611].*

Broadly speaking, base value is often equal to the book value of the assets and liabilities in the transferring entity's records immediately before transfer, although this would not be true of assets carried at fair value or valuation, if the resulting carrying amount is higher than the original cost to the transferor.

In this example, the base value of the property is its original cost of £700. The base value of the remaining assets and liabilities is the book value of £1,400.

Therefore, Company B recognises the following accounting entries:

Company B	Dr £	Cr £
Net assets	2,500	
Share capital[1]		300
Share premium (minimum premium value)[2]		1,800
Merger reserve[3]		400
To record the hive up transaction		

[1] Recognised at the nominal value of shares issued.

[2] Base value of net assets is £2,100 (£700 property plus £1,400 other net assets), minimum premium value is the base value less the nominal value of shares issued of £300.

[3] The difference above of £400, between the book value of net assets recognised and the required entries to share capital and premium, arises as a result of the revaluation of property of £400. This difference can be credited to an unrealised reserve where group reconstruction relief is taken.

Company A must derecognise its net assets and recognise the investment in Company B arising from the issue of shares. One view is that the transaction lacks substance for Company A, since it has simply swapped a direct investment in trade and assets for an indirect investment in the same trade and assets, via Company B. If the transaction lacks substance, Company A recognises the additional cost of investment in Company B at the carrying amount of the net assets given up. This accounting would usually be appropriate if Company B were a newly incorporated company or when Company B is wholly owned.

If a hive down transaction is considered to have substance to Company A (for example, this might be the case if Company B is not a wholly owned subsidiary), it could choose to recognise its additional investment in Company B at the fair value of the consideration given, i.e. the fair value of the trade and assets given up. Any gain recognised as a result of this accounting would be unrealised and recognised in other comprehensive income, since the additional investment received in Company B, an unquoted subsidiary, would not be regarded as qualifying consideration.

5.4.4.B   Other forms of consideration

Cash or other monetary assets: If the consideration paid is cash or other monetary assets such as a receivable, under merger accounting, any difference between the book values of net assets recognised and the consideration paid would be recognised in equity.

If Company B overpays for the trade and assets of its parent (including goodwill), in comparison to their fair value, this could be a distribution of value to its parent. See 5.4.1.B above.

In Company A, any excess of consideration received over the carrying amount of the net assets sold would be recognised as a gain. If realised, the gain will be recognised in profit or loss; if unrealised, the gain will be recognised in other comprehensive income. The gain will be realised only if the consideration represents qualifying consideration (see section 3 of TECH 02/17BL). Care should be taken in determining whether an intercompany receivable represents qualifying consideration.

If the consideration is less than the net assets sold or is gifted for no consideration, Company A is making a capital contribution to its wholly owned subsidiary. The difference would be debited to its investment in Company B, which is then assessed for impairment. In Company B, the gift of Company A's business would result in a credit to equity, for example, to a merger or capital contribution reserve. Whether this reserve is realised or not is assessed using the guidance in TECH 02/17BL, discussed at 5.4.1.C above.

5.4.5   Financial information prior to the date of the combination

The description of the merger accounting method explicitly requires the results (and cash flows) of all combining entities to be included from the beginning of the financial year and for comparatives to be restated. *[FRS 102.19.30]*. While these paragraphs are framed in the context of a parent combining with a new subsidiary, and will apply to consolidated financial statements prepared by the parent, the definition of a group reconstruction includes, for example, the hive transactions discussed at 5.4.1 to 5.4.4, above.

Application of the requirement to restate comparative information to such transactions, *[FRS 102.19.30]*, would mean that the entity accounting for the acquired business under the merger method of accounting would include the results of that business from the beginning of the financial year and in the comparative year in its individual financial statements. However, in the context of individual financial statements, consideration needs to be given to paragraph 13(a) of Schedule 1 to the Regulations which requires that only profits realised at the reporting date are included in profit or loss. *[FRS 102 Appendix III.25]*.

This results in two possible approaches, of which the former is most common practice (note that legal mergers can create complexities and are not addressed in this guidance):

- Since the pre-transaction profits of the acquired business are not profits (and consequently cannot be realised profits) of the acquiring entity, they should not be included in the acquiring entity's profit and loss account. For UK companies, the Regulations require that only realised profits (with limited exceptions relating to the fair value accounting rules) are included in the profit and loss account. *[1 Sch 13, 40]*. The acquiring entity 'merger accounts' in its individual financial statements on a prospective basis only from the date of transfer, rather than reflecting it from the beginning of the financial year and for comparative periods.

- If the profits of the acquired business represented realised profits of that business, the acquiring entity could reflect the transfer from the beginning of the financial year and comparatives could be restated. The fact that the cumulative pre-transaction profits of the acquired business are not realised profits of the acquiring entity could be dealt with by disclosure or by transferring those profits to a 'non-distributable' reserve.

FRS 102 does not explicitly deal with this issue. However, in our view, the first approach should be applied in statutory accounts of a UK company. This does not preclude presentation of the pre-transaction and comparative profits using the second approach on a pro forma basis. Such information may be particularly relevant where a group reconstruction represents the continuation of an existing business – for example, where a business is transferred to a newly incorporated group entity. In our view, however, such pro forma figures are not required to be given. In this context, it is notable that the Statement of Recommended Practice *Accounting by Limited Liability Partnerships* ('LLP SORP') issued by CCAB effective for LLPs adopting FRS 102 recommends use of the first approach in relation to the application of merger accounting on initial transition of an existing entity to a single-entity LLP for the same reasons as explained above. However, the LLP SORP also considers that the second approach gives relevant information and recommends presentation of pro forma numbers on that basis. *[LLP SORP Appendix 4]*.

Where the company applying the merger method of accounting is a newly-incorporated company, the company law requirements relating to a company's first accounting period will also need to be considered (see 5.4.7 below). This will further restrict the capability of including the pre-transaction results of the acquired business, and is another reason for using a prospective approach.

5.4.6 Equity eliminations

As discussed at 5.3.3 above, the merger method of accounting under FRS 102 involves an equity elimination relating to the difference between the share capital of the new subsidiary (and any share premium or capital redemption reserve) and the cost of the investment as stated in the balance sheet of the new holding company.

However, in the context of applying the merger method in a hive transaction, there is no share capital (or share premium or capital redemption reserve) of the business transferred requiring elimination. Therefore, the difference to be shown as a movement on other reserves relates to the nominal value of any shares issued plus any share

Chapter 17

premium recognised plus the fair value of any other consideration given by the acquiring entity. This difference will always be a debit to reserves (i.e. debit reserves, credit consideration transferred).

As indicated at 5.3.3 above, there are no particular requirements governing where to eliminate any debit adjustments in reserves arising on the application of the merger method of accounting in consolidated financial statements. The same is true for any debit adjustment for individual financial statements.

For some group reconstructions, the nominal value of the shares issued plus any share premium recognised plus the fair value of any other consideration given will be less than the book amount of the net assets acquired in the group reconstruction. In that situation, there will be a net credit to be taken to equity equivalent to the reserves being recognised in applying the merger accounting method in respect of the trade and assets acquired, less the debit adjustment relating to the nominal value of the shares issued plus the fair value of any other consideration given.

We recommend that the net credit is taken to a separate merger reserve.

Whether any net debit or credit arising from applying the merger accounting method represents a realised loss or profit is discussed at 5.4.1.C above.

5.4.7   Newly incorporated companies

It may be that in certain hive transactions involving the acquisition of the trade and net assets within the same group, the company acquiring the business is a newly incorporated company.

As discussed at 5.3.5 above, when a company is incorporated for the purpose of acting as the new parent company in a group reconstruction (Newco), it might not have been in existence for the entirety of the current and comparative period that would have been presented in respect of the transferred business if no reorganisation had occurred. In contrast to common practice in consolidated financial statements, individual financial statements cannot be prepared for a period prior to incorporation. In addition, as discussed at 5.4.5, hive transactions in individual financial statements of UK companies are accounted for prospectively from the date of the reorganisation. Therefore, Newco must present financial statements for its actual period since incorporation, recognising the hive transaction from the date that it takes place. However, if considered relevant, the pre-reorganisation period(s) could be given as supplementary pro forma information, as explained in Example 17.33 below.

Example 17.33:   Merger accounting in individual financial statements by a newly incorporated company

Parent A sets up a newly incorporated subsidiary, Subsidiary B, on 1 April 2019 to effect a group reorganisation on 1 July 2019 whereby Subsidiary B will acquire the trade and assets of an existing subsidiary of Parent A, Subsidiary C. All companies within Parent A's group have financial years ending on 31 December. Subsidiary C has prepared individual financial statements for the year ended 31 December 2018. Subsidiary B gives notice to have an accounting reference date of 31 December and will prepare its first individual financial statements made up to 31 December 2019. In doing so, Subsidiary B will account for the acquisition of the former business of Subsidiary C under the merger method of accounting.

Company law dictates that directors of a company prepare individual accounts for each financial year, *[s394]*, and that a company's first financial year is required to begin with the date of its incorporation and ending with its accounting reference date. *[s391(5)]*. In addition, Companies Act individual accounts must, in the case of the profit and loss account, give a true and fair view of the profit or loss of the company for the financial year. *[s396(2)(b)]*. Accordingly, the statutory individual financial statements of Subsidiary B can only be for the 9 month period from the date of its incorporation. Also, Subsidiary B includes the results of the business acquired from 1 July 2019 in its individual financial statements. However, if it wished to present information about its underlying business for what it might consider to be for a more relevant period, i.e. for the year ended 31 December 2019 (with comparatives for the year ended 31 December 2018), it could do so in supplementary pro-forma form.

This approach is recommended in the LLP SORP in relation to the application of merger accounting on initial transition of an existing entity to a single-entity LLP for the same reasons as explained at 5.4.5 above. *[LLP SORP Appendix 4]*.

5.5 Implications on the share premium account

Under the CA 2006, a company issuing shares at a premium must transfer a sum equal to the aggregate amount or value of premiums on those shares to an account called 'the share premium account'. *[s610(1)]*.

UK company law includes certain relief – 'merger relief' and 'group reconstruction relief' – from recognising share premium at all, or in full, where certain conditions are met. These reliefs, which are discussed further below, impact the accounting considerations for capital and reserves of the issuing entity only, but are not relevant for the purposes of measuring the cost of the combination in connection with application of the purchase method.

The implications of these reliefs in measuring the cost of investments in subsidiaries in separate financial statements are discussed further in Chapter 8 at 4.2.1.

5.5.1 Merger relief

The rules on merger relief and those on merger accounting are frequently confused with each other. However, not only are they based on the satisfaction of different criteria, they in fact have quite distinct purposes. As discussed at 5.3 above, merger accounting is a form of financial reporting which applies to a group reconstruction meeting certain qualifying conditions, but although the merger relief provisions were originally brought in to facilitate merger accounting, merger relief is purely a legal matter to do with the maintenance of capital for the protection of creditors and has very little to do with accounting *per se*. Moreover, merger relief may be available under transactions which are accounted for as acquisitions, rather than mergers, and the two are not interdependent in that sense.

Section 612 of the CA 2006 broadly relieves companies from the basic requirement of section 610 to set up a share premium account in respect of equity shares issued in exchange for shares in another company in the course of a transaction which results in the issuing company securing at least a 90% holding in the equity shares of the other company. The precise wording of section 612 (and related sections) should be considered carefully in order to ensure that any particular transaction falls within its terms. 'Equity shares' mean shares in a company's equity share capital. *[s548]*. See Chapter 8 at 4.2.1.

Over the years there have been some differences of legal opinion as to whether merger relief is in fact *compulsory* when the conditions of section 612 are met, or whether it is optional.

Chapter 17

The CA 2006 says that where the conditions are met, then section 610 'does not apply to the premiums on those shares' issued. Therefore some people argue that the effect of this relief is simply to make section 610 optional rather than mandatory, but the more prevalent view is it makes it illegal to set up a share premium account. Therefore, if a company wishes to set up a share premium account where merger relief is available, we recommend that the directors take legal advice.

Where merger relief is taken, and the purchase method is applied, as the cost of the business combination is based on the fair value, any amount that would have been taken to share premium account needs to be reflected in another reserve, generally a 'merger reserve' in the consolidated financial statements. Where merger accounting is applied, such an amount is not reflected in any 'merger reserve' as the mechanics of merger accounting uses the nominal value of shares issued. Whether such a reserve arises in the separate financial statements is discussed in Chapter 8 at 4.2.1.

It should be noted, however, that merger relief is not applicable in a case falling within the ambit of 'group reconstruction relief' (see 5.5.2 below). *[s612(4)]*.

5.5.2 Group reconstruction relief

Section 611 of the CA 2006 provides a partial relief from the basic requirement to Section 610 as regards transfers to the share premium account where the issuing company is a wholly-owned subsidiary of another company (the holding company) and allots shares to that other company or another wholly-owned subsidiary of the holding company in consideration for the transfer to the issuing company of non-cash assets of a company (the transferor company) that is a member of the group of companies that comprises the holding company and all its wholly-owned subsidiaries. *[s611(1)]*.

Application of the relief in this instance means that just a 'minimum premium value' is required to be transferred to the share premium account – that amount being the amount (if any) by which the base value (see Chapter 8 at 4.2.1) of the consideration for the shares allotted exceeds the aggregate nominal value of the shares. *[s611(2)-(5)]*.

Where group reconstruction relief is taken, and the purchase method is applied, as the cost of the business combination is based on the fair value, any amount that would otherwise have been taken to share premium account needs to be reflected in another reserve, generally a 'merger reserve' in the consolidated financial statements. Where merger accounting is applied, such an amount is not reflected in any 'merger reserve' as the mechanics of merger accounting uses the nominal value of shares issued (or the base value of the consideration).

Chapter 8 at 4.2.1 provides further detail and examples of the application of merger relief and group reconstruction relief in separate financial statements and Example 17.32 above demonstrates an application of group reconstruction relief to a hive down.

5.6 Disclosure requirements

As discussed at 4 above, group reconstructions are scoped out of the 'normal' business combination disclosures required by FRS 102. Instead, FRS 102 provides that, for each group reconstruction that was effected during the period, the combined entity shall disclose: *[FRS 102.19.33, 6 Sch 13(1)-(2)]*

- the names of the combining entities (other than the reporting entity);
- whether the combination has been accounted for as an acquisition or a merger; and
- the date of combination.

Additional disclosures required by the CA 2006 for a group reconstruction accounted for as a merger are:

- if the transaction significantly affects the figures shown in the group accounts, the composition and fair value of the consideration given by the parent company and its subsidiary undertakings (subject to the exemption in paragraph 16 of Schedule 6, as noted below); *[6 Sch 13(3)]*
- any adjustment to consolidated reserves as a result of setting off the following amounts:
    - the aggregate of:
        (i) the appropriate amount in respect of qualifying shares issued by the parent or its subsidiary undertakings (i.e. the nominal value of any shares subject to either merger or group reconstruction relief, together with the minimum premium value for shares subject to group reconstruction relief) in consideration for the acquisition of shares in the undertaking acquired; and
        (ii) the fair value of any other consideration given, determined as at the date of the acquisition,
      against
    - the nominal value of the issued share capital of the undertaking acquired held by the parent company and its subsidiary undertakings; *[6 Sch 11(6)]*
- the address of the registered office of the undertaking acquired (whether in or outside the United Kingdom); *[6 Sch 16A(a)-(b)]* and
- the name of the ultimate controlling party that controls the undertaking whose shares are acquired and its registered office (whether in or outside the United Kingdom). *[6 Sch 16A(c)-(d)]*.

Additional disclosures required by the CA 2006 for a group reconstruction accounted for as an acquisition are discussed at 4.3.3 above.

The requirement above regarding the fair value and composition of consideration need not be given with respect to an undertaking which:

- is established under the law of a country outside the United Kingdom; or
- carries on business outside the United Kingdom,

if in the opinion of the directors of the parent company the disclosure would be seriously prejudicial to the business of that undertaking or to the business of the parent company or any of its subsidiary undertakings and the Secretary of State agrees that the information should not be disclosed. *[6 Sch 16]*.

Chapter 17

6   SUMMARY OF GAAP DIFFERENCES

The key differences between FRS 102 and IFRS in accounting for business combinations are set out below.

	FRS 102	IFRS
Method of accounting for business combinations	Purchase method used for all business combinations except certain group reconstructions and public benefit entity combinations.	Purchase method used for all business combinations (apart from common control transactions that may be accounted for by pooling of interests or merger accounting if applying the GAAP hierarchy).
Common control transactions	Merger accounting permitted for certain group reconstructions (and certain public benefit entity combinations). Merger method of accounting explained.	Out of scope.
Definition of a business	Integrated set of activities and assets conducted and managed for providing a return to investors or lower costs or other economic benefits to policyholders or participants. A business contains inputs, processes and outputs.	Integrated set of activities and assets capable of being conducted and managed for providing return in form of dividends, or lower costs or other economic benefits to investors or other owners, members or participants. A business is required to have only inputs and processes, which together are or will be used to create outputs. Additional Application Guidance. The definition of a business and related Application Guidance has recently been amended from above (see 2.3 and 3.2 above).
Identifying the acquirer	There must be an acquirer for all business combinations using purchase method.	There must be an acquirer for all business combinations within scope of IFRS 3.
Acquisition expenses	Capitalise as part of cost of combination / goodwill.	Expense.
Contingent consideration	Recognise if probable and can be reliably measured. Subsequent adjustments to goodwill. No specific guidance relating to contingent consideration that may be classified as equity.	Fair value. Subsequent adjustments to profit or loss for contingent consideration classified as a financial liability. No subsequent adjustment for contingent consideration classified as equity.
Contingent payments to employees or selling shareholders	No specific guidance, but consideration of 'substance over form' required.	Contingent consideration forfeited if employment terminates is post employment remuneration. Additional Application Guidance.

Initial measurement of acquiree's assets, liabilities and contingent liabilities	Fair value (except deferred tax, employee benefits, share-based payments).	Fair values (except deferred tax, employee benefits, share-based payments, assets held for sale, reacquired rights, indemnification assets).
Recognition of intangible assets separate from goodwill	Recognise at fair value if (a) meet recognition criteria (i.e. probable cash flows and fair value can be measured reliably), (b) are separable and (c) arise from contractual or legal rights. Option to recognise if meet (a) and only one of (b) or (c). This policy choice must be applied consistently to a class of intangible assets and to all business combinations.	Recognise at fair value if meets either separability or contractual – legal criterion (regardless of being separable). Probability and reliable measurement criteria always considered to be satisfied for intangible assets acquired in a business combination.
Step acquisitions	Cost of business combination is aggregate of fair values of assets given, liabilities assumed and equity instruments issued at each stage of transaction plus any directly attributable costs. True and fair override may be used in certain circumstances to compute goodwill as the sum of the goodwill arising on each step.	Existing interest held immediately before control is achieved is remeasured at fair value with gain or loss recognised in profit or loss. Fair value of the existing equity interest is used in computing the cost of the combination / goodwill. Changes in value in other comprehensive income reclassified to profit or loss.
Non-controlling interests	Measure at proportionate share of net assets. No specific guidance for any non-controlling interests that are not entitled to a present ownership interest, the implication being they are valued at nil.	Policy choice for each business combination to use fair value or share of net assets for interests entitled to proportionate net assets share. Otherwise, fair value.
Positive goodwill	Amortise on systematic basis over its finite useful life (cannot be indefinite). If, in exceptional circumstances, no reliable estimate of useful life can be made, the maximum life is 10 years. Test for impairment if impairment indicators.	Not amortised. Measured at cost less impairment. Mandatory annual impairment test.
Negative goodwill	Amount up to fair value of non-monetary assets recognised in periods in which non-monetary assets are recovered. Excess amortised over periods expected to benefit.	Immediate gain in profit or loss.
Disclosures	Less onerous disclosure requirements.	Extensive disclosure requirements.

Chapter 17

Chapter 18   Leases

List of examples

Chapter 18

Chapter 18   Leases

1   INTRODUCTION

Section 20 – *Leases* – follows the precedent of earlier UK and international accounting standards such as SSAP 21 – *Leases and Hire Purchase Contracts* – and IAS 17 – *Leases*. However, for annual periods beginning on or after 1 January 2019, IAS 17 is replaced by IFRS 16 – *Leases* – which introduces significant changes to lease accounting under IFRS. There are significant differences between Section 20 and IFRS 16 in respect of lessee accounting. This, and other key differences, are discussed at 2 below. Lessor accounting under IFRS 16 is substantially unchanged from that required under IAS 17.

Although a lease is an agreement whereby the lessor conveys to the lessee the right to use an asset for an agreed period of time in return for a payment or series of payments, companies are required in certain circumstances to capitalise these assets in their statements of financial position, together with the corresponding obligations, irrespective of the fact that legal title to those assets is vested in another party.

A finance lease is essentially regarded as an entitlement to receive, and an obligation to make, a stream of payments that are substantially the same as blended payments of principal and interest under a loan agreement. Consequently, the lessee accounts for an asset and the obligation to pay the amount due under the lease contract; the lessor accounts for its investment in the amount receivable under the lease contract rather than for the leased asset itself. An operating lease, on the other hand, is regarded primarily as an uncompleted contract committing the lessor to provide the use of an asset in future periods in exchange for consideration similar to a fee for a service payable by the lessee. The lessor continues to account for the leased asset itself rather than any amount receivable in the future under the contract.

The term 'lease' also applies to arrangements that do not take the form of leases. Instead, they may combine rights to use assets and the provision of services or outputs, for agreed periods of time in return for a payment or series of payments, e.g. outsourcing arrangements that include the provision of assets and services. Entities have to consider the substance of these arrangements to see if they are, or contain, leases. If so, then the elements identified as a lease will be subject to the requirements of Section 20.

There were no substantial changes made to Section 20 as a result of *Amendments to FRS 102 Triennial review 2017 – Incremental improvements and clarifications (Triennial review 2017)*.

2   COMPARISON BETWEEN SECTION 20 AND IFRS (IFRS 16)

Section 20 closely resembles IAS 17. However, for annual periods beginning on or after 1 January 2019, IAS 17 is replaced by IFRS 16 which introduces significant changes to lease accounting under IFRS. There are significant differences between Section 20 and IFRS 16, particularly in respect of lessee accounting. Lessor accounting under IFRS 16 is substantially unchanged from that required under IAS 17.

As part of the Triennial review 2017, the FRC considered whether to amend FRS 102 to incorporate the requirements of IFRS 16, effective from 1 January 2022.[1] However, it was concluded that further evidence-gathering and analysis needs to be undertaken before a decision is made on the most appropriate timetable and approach for reflecting the principles of IFRS 16 in FRS 102, if at all.[2]

2.1   Lessee accounting

Under Section 20, lessee accounting for a lease is driven by whether the lease is classified as an operating lease or a finance lease. For an operating lease, the lessee generally recognises lease payments as an expense on a straight-line basis over the lease term (see 3.8.1 below). Lessees recognise finance leases as assets and liabilities in their statement of financial position at the commencement date of the lease at amounts equal to the fair value of the leased item, or, if lower, at the present value of the minimum lease payments. Subsequent to initial recognition and measurement of finance leases, lessees accrete the lease liability to reflect interest and reduce the liability to reflect lease payments. The related asset is depreciated in accordance with the depreciation requirements of Section 17 – *Property, Plant and Equipment* – or Section 18 – *Intangible Assets other than Goodwill*. (See 3.7.1 below).

IFRS 16 does not distinguish between finance and operating leases for lessees. Under IFRS 16, a lessee recognises a lease liability and a right-of-use asset on balance sheet for most leases. Lessees are permitted to make an accounting policy election, by class of underlying asset to which the right of use relates, to apply a method like Section 20's operating lease accounting and not recognise right-of-use assets and lease liabilities for leases with a lease term of 12 months or less. *[IFRS 16.5(a), Appendix A]*. Lessees are also permitted to make an election, on a lease-by-lease basis, to apply a method similar to Section 20's operating lease accounting to leases for which the underlying asset is of low value. *[IFRS 16.5(b)]*.

For all other leases, under IFRS 16, the lessee's lease liability is initially measured at the present value of lease payments to be made over the lease term. *[IFRS 16.26]*. The right-of-use asset is initially measured at the amount of the lease liability, adjusted for lease prepayments, lease incentives received, the lessee's initial direct costs associated with the lease, and an estimate of restoration, removal and dismantling costs. *[IFRS 16.24]*.

Subsequent to initial recognition and measurement, lessees accrete the lease liability to reflect interest and reduce the liability to reflect lease payments. *[IFRS 16.36]*. The related right-of-use asset is accounted for either by applying a cost model and is depreciated in accordance with the depreciation requirements of IAS 16 – *Property, Plant and Equipment*, *[IFRS 16.29-31]*, or by applying a remeasurement model. *[IFRS 16.29, 34-35]*.

2.2 Lessor accounting – Leases of land and buildings

When a lease includes both land and building elements, IFRS 16 requires that a lessor assess the classification of each element as a finance lease or an operating lease separately. The lease payments (including any lump-sum upfront payments) are allocated between land and buildings in proportion to the relative fair values of the interests in each element, i.e. the leasehold interest in the land and buildings at the inception of the lease. *[IFRS 16 Appendix B.55-57].*

FRS 102 is silent about separating the land and buildings elements of leases. Generally, in the context of the UK property market, the minimum lease payments are attributed to a single leased asset and land and buildings are not separately accounted for. Only those leases of land and buildings that are of such length that they allow the lessee to redevelop the site are likely to include a significant value for the land element. In such cases, it may be necessary for the lessor to account separately for the building and the land.

2.3 Lessor accounting – Straight-line basis for lease payments

IFRS 16 requires all operating lease payments to be recognised as income on a straight-line basis, unless another systematic basis is more representative of the pattern in which benefit from use of the underlying asset is diminished. *[IFRS 16.81].*

FRS 102 contains this same requirement with one exception: if lease payments increase annually by fixed increments intended to compensate for expected annual inflation over the lease period, the fixed minimum increment that reflects expected general inflation will be recognised as an income as incurred. *[FRS 102.20.25(b)].* See the discussion at 3.8.2 below.

2.4 Lease modifications

Section 20 provides no specific guidance on accounting for lease modifications. Entities therefore have to use their judgement in developing an appropriate accounting policy. *[FRS 102.10.4].* Accounting for lease modifications is discussed at 3.9 below.

Under IFRS 16, a lessor accounts for a modification to an operating lease as a new lease from the effective date of the modification, considering any prepaid or accrued lease payments relating to the original lease as part of the lease payments for the new lease. *[IFRS 16.87].* For other lease modifications (i.e. finance leases for lessors and leases other than shot-term for lessees), the accounting by both lessee and lessor depends upon whether the modification is considered to give rise to a separate lease or a change in the accounting for the existing lease. A modification results in a separate lease when the modification increases the scope of the lease by adding the right to use one or more underlying assets, and the consideration for the lease increases commensurate with the stand-alone selling price for the increase in scope and any adjustments to that stand-alone selling price reflect the circumstances of the particular contract. *[IFRS 16.44, 79].* If the modification results in a separate lease, the lease is accounted for in the same manner as other new leases. IFRS 16 contains specific guidance on the accounting for a modification that does not result in a separate lease. The accounting for lease modifications under IFRS 16 is discussed in Chapter 24 of EY International GAAP 2019.

Chapter 18

2.5   Sale and leasebacks

Under Section 20, the accounting for a sale and leaseback transaction by a seller-lessee depends upon whether the leaseback is classified as a finance lease or an operating lease. If the leaseback is classified as an operating leaseback, the accounting further depends upon whether the transaction is established at fair value.

Under IFRS 16, both the seller-lessee and buyer-lessor use the definition of a sale in IFRS 15 – *Revenue from Contracts with Customers* – to determine whether a sale has occurred in a sale and leaseback transaction. *[IFRS 16.99]*. If the transfer of the underlying asset satisfies the requirements of IFRS 15 to be accounted for as a sale, the transaction will be accounted for as a sale and leaseback by both the seller-lessee and buyer-lessor. *[IFRS 16.100]*. If not, then the transaction will be accounted for as a financing transaction by both parties. *[IFRS 16.103]*.

2.6   Subleases – Accounting by the intermediate lessor

Section 20 provides no specific guidance in respect of subleases. The accounting by an intermediate lessor therefore depends upon whether the sublease is classified as an operating lease or a finance lease, based on the extent to which risks and rewards incidental to ownership of the leased asset are passed to the sub-lessee.

IFRS 16 also requires the intermediate lessor to classify the sublease as an operating or finance lease by reference to the right-of-use asset that arises under the head lease, rather than by reference to the underlying leased asset (for example, the item of property, plant or equipment that is subject to the lease), However, where the head lease is a short-term lease that the sub-lessor, as lessee, has elected to account for applying a method like Section 20's operating lease accounting (i.e. by recognising lease payments as an expense on a straight-line basis over the lease term rather than recognising a right-of-use asset and a lease liability) – see 2.1 above – the sublease should be classified as an operating sublease by the intermediate lessor. *[IFRS 16 Appendix B.58]*.

3   REQUIREMENTS OF SECTION 20 FOR LEASES

3.1   Scope

Section 20 applies to leases, except for: *[FRS 102.20.1]*

- leases to explore for or use minerals, oil, natural gas and similar non-regenerative resources;
- licensing agreements for such items as motion picture films, video recordings, plays, manuscripts, patents and copyrights (see 3.1.1 below);
- measurement of property held by lessees that is accounted for as investment property and measurement of investment property provided by lessors under operating leases. Investment properties are accounted for in accordance with Section 16 – *Investment Property* (see Chapter 14);

- measurement of biological assets held by lessees under finance leases and biological assets provided by lessors under operating leases. Biological assets are addressed in Section 34 – *Specialised Activities* (see Chapter 31); and

- leases that could lead to a loss to the lessor or the lessee as a result of non-typical contractual terms (see 3.1.3 below).

3.1.1   Licensing agreements

FRS 102 does not define a licensing agreement so the distinction between 'leases' and 'licensing agreements' is not clear.

A conventional licence over an intangible asset such as a film or video commonly gives a non-exclusive 'right of access' to show or view the video simultaneously with many others but not a 'right of use' of the original film or video itself because the licensee does not control that asset. Arguably, this puts such a conventional licence outside the scope of Section 20. The relationship between rights of access to and rights of use over the underlying asset is explored further at 3.2 below.

Intangible assets themselves may be the subject of leases, as discussed below.

3.1.2   Arrangements over intangible assets

Section 20 applies to leases over intangible assets although there are additional issues when the right is not tangible.

First, the 'right' in question must be an asset that meets the definition of an intangible asset in Section 18 – *Intangible Assets other than Goodwill* – (see Chapter 16). Second, because many of these rights are either acquired for an up-front sum or for a series of periodic payments and by definition the period covered by the payments equals the life of the right, there is divergence in practice in how to account for them, i.e. whether they are leases (and if so, whether finance or operating leases) or whether they are acquisitions of assets on deferred payment terms.

Many intangible assets are capable of being subdivided with the part subject to the lease itself meeting the definition of an intangible asset. If the rights are exclusive, the part will meet the definition of an intangible asset because it is embodied in legal rights that allow the acquirer to control the benefits arising from the asset. For example, an entity might sell to another entity rights to distribute its product in a particular geographical market. If the right is not on an exclusive basis then it may not be within scope of Section 20, e.g. it may be a licensing agreement as discussed at 3.1.1 above. Other arrangements may, on analysis, prove to be for services and not for a right of use of an intangible asset. See 3.1.4 below.

It is irrelevant to the analysis whether the original right is recognised in the financial statements of the lessor prior to the inception of the arrangement.

Rights that do meet the definition of an intangible asset often have a finite life, e.g. a radio station may acquire a licence that gives it a right to broadcast over specified frequencies for a period of seven years. Yet the underlying asset on which the right depends exists both before and after the 'right' has been purchased and may have an indefinite life, as is the case with the broadcast spectrum. Many intangible rights can be purchased for an upfront sum, which will be accounted for as the acquisition of an intangible asset that is capitalised at cost. As an alternative to up-front purchase, an entity may pay for the same right in a series of instalments over a period of time. Does it become an operating lease because it is only a short period out of the life of the underlying asset? Usually the answer is no: these rights will not be accounted for as operating leases by comparison to the total life of the underlying asset as the arrangement is over the *right* in question.

If the arrangement is considered to be a lease, then it will be accounted for in accordance with Section 20, whatever the pattern of payment. If it is a finance lease then the asset will be measured using the methodology prescribed by FRS 102 described at 3.7 below.

If, rather than as a lease, the arrangement is seen as the acquisition of an asset on deferred payment terms, the effective interest rate method is mandated. The effective interest rate is the rate that exactly discounts estimated future cash payments or receipts through the expected life of the financial instrument or, when appropriate, a shorter period, to the carrying amount of the financial asset or financial liability. The effective interest rate is determined on the basis of the carrying amount of the financial asset or liability at initial recognition. *[FRS 102.11.16]*. This will take account of estimated future cash payments or receipts through the expected life of the financial instrument that may include some of the 'contingent' payments that are excluded from the measurement of finance leases (see 3.4.5 below).

Therefore, there are arguments as to whether there are assets and liabilities to be recognised and, even if recognition is accepted, measurement depends on the view that is taken of the applicable Section. In the absence of a clear principle, there is likely to be diversity in practice.

3.1.3 Leases with non-typical contractual terms classified as financial instruments

Certain leases are not accounted for as leases in accordance with Section 20 but instead classified as financial instruments within scope of Section 12 – *Other Financial Instruments Issues* – if the lease could, as a result of non-typical contractual terms, result in a loss to the lessor or the lessee. The Basis for Conclusions to FRS 102 states that this could include contractual terms that are unrelated to changes in the price of the leased asset, changes in foreign exchange rates, or a default by one of the counterparties. *[FRS 102.BC.B20.1]*. The Basis for Conclusions also notes that 'the reference to "changes in the price of the leased asset" is framed widely and in practice it does not expect many leases to fall within the scope of Section 12.' Section 12 is addressed in Chapter 10. *[FRS 102.BC.B20.2]*.

Although it is not clear precisely what contractual terms are referred to, it is likely that this does *not* refer to rents that vary according to:

- non-financial variables specific to the parties to the contract, e.g. rents that vary with future sales or amount of future use; or
- future price indices and future market rates of interest that are relevant to the parties to the contract.

Accounting for these contingent rents is addressed by Section 20 (see 3.4.5 below). Briefly, they are excluded from the minimum lease payments so do not affect the measurement of assets and liabilities in finance leases; instead, whatever the classification of the lease, they are treated as income or an expense as incurred.

3.1.4 Arrangements that include services

Agreements that transfer the right to use assets contain leases even if the lessor is obliged to provide substantial services in connection with the operation or maintenance of the assets. *[FRS 102.20.2]*. Costs for services are excluded from the minimum lease payments in assessing or measuring leases; see the definition in 3.3 below and the discussion at 3.8.1.B and 3.8.2 below.

A contract for services that does not transfer the right to use assets from one contracting party to the other will not be accounted for under Section 20. *[FRS 102.20.2]*. Instead, the provider of services will recognise revenue by applying the principles in Section 23 – *Revenue* – while the purchaser will recognise costs as incurred (see Chapter 20). However, these contracts have to be examined carefully to see if they do, in fact, contain an embedded lease arrangement. See 3.2 below.

Service concession arrangements also contain services as well as the provision of assets. There are separate accounting requirements for these arrangements, which are characterised by control of the asset and services by the 'grantor', a public sector body, a public benefit entity or other entity operating to fulfil a public service obligation. The contractual terms of certain contracts or arrangements may meet both the scope requirements of Section 20 and those of Section 34 that pertain to service concessions. Where this is the case, the arrangement must be accounted for as a service concession in accordance with the requirements of Section 34 (see Chapter 31). *[FRS 102.34.12C]*.

3.2 Determining whether an arrangement contains a lease

Some arrangements do not take the legal form of leases. Instead, they may combine rights to use assets and the provision of services or outputs, for agreed periods of time in return for a payment or series of payments. Examples include outsourcing arrangements, telecommunication contracts that provide rights to capacity and take-or-pay contracts. *[FRS 102.20.3]*. Entities have to consider the substance of these arrangements to see if they are, or contain, leases.

This will depend on whether: *[FRS 102.20.3A]*

(a) a specific asset or assets must be used in order to fulfil the arrangement (see 3.2.1 below); and

(b) the arrangement conveys a right to use the asset. This will be the case where the arrangement conveys to the purchaser the right to control the use of the underlying asset (see 3.2.2 below).

3.2.1 A specified asset

Section 20 does not include much additional explanation. It notes that an asset may be explicitly or implicitly identified; in neither case does this automatically mean that the arrangement contains a lease. Although a specific asset may be explicitly identified in an arrangement, it is not the subject of a lease if fulfilment of the arrangement is not dependent on the use of the specified asset. An asset is implicitly specified if, for example, the supplier owns or leases only one asset with which to fulfil the obligation and it is not economically feasible or practicable for the supplier to perform its obligation through the use of alternative assets. *[FRS 102.20.3A].*

For example, an arrangement in which an entity (the purchaser) outsources its product delivery department to another organisation (the supplier) will not contain a lease if the supplier is obliged to make available a certain number of delivery vehicles of a certain standard specification and the supplier is a delivery organisation with many suitable vehicles available.

The arrangement is more likely to contain a lease if the supplier identifies specific vehicles out of its fleet and those vehicles must be used to provide the service. If the supplier has to supply and maintain a specified number of specialist vehicles in the purchaser's branding, then this arrangement is likely to contain a lease. These arrangements may be commercially more akin to outsourcing the purchaser's acquisitions of delivery vehicles rather than its delivery functions.

Similar issues would have to be taken into account if data processing functions are outsourced as these may require substantial investment by the supplier in computer hardware dedicated to the use of a single customer.

Some arrangements may allow the supplier to replace the specified asset with a similar asset if the original asset is unavailable (e.g. because one of the delivery vehicles has broken down). As this is in effect a warranty obligation it does not preclude lease treatment.

The supplier may have a substantive right to substitute other vehicles at will for the vehicles it has identified. This is common in transport arrangements where a contract may identify the original asset (e.g. a particular truck, aircraft or ship) used for the service but the supplier is not obliged to use the asset identified by the contract. Fulfilment of the arrangement would not then be dependent on the use of the specified asset and the identification of the asset does not indicate that the arrangement contains a lease.

Where arrangements are likely to contain leases (e.g. delivery vehicles in branding, dedicated hardware), the purchaser cannot be unaware that there are specific assets underlying the service. There would have been negotiations between supplier and purchaser that would probably be reflected in the contract documentation. By contrast, if the purchaser does not know what assets are used to provide the service (beyond the fact that they are trucks and computers, of course), and in the circumstances it is reasonable not to know, it is plausible that there is no underlying lease in the arrangement. This remains true even if the supplier has dedicated specific assets to the service being provided and expects their cost to be recouped during the course of the contractual relationship.

3.2.1.A   Parts of assets and the unit of account

Some issues relating to units of account in relation to intangible rights are discussed at 3.1.2 above; this section deals more directly with parts (or 'components') of physical assets.

Some arrangements transfer the right to use an asset that is a part of a larger asset which raises the issue of whether and when such rights should be accounted for as leases.

Generally, a portion of a larger asset that is not physically distinct is not considered to be a specified asset. Therefore an arrangement that allows an entity to use a quarter of the capacity of a whole pipeline will not usually be considered to contain a lease.

However, some arrangements refer to physical 'parts' of larger assets. For example, a plant may contain more than one production unit or line that might be regarded as a single 'part' (because each makes the same product) or alternatively each of its units or lines might be regarded as separate 'parts'. Depending on other aspects of the arrangement, a particular production line may be the asset that is the subject of a lease, if the supplier cannot transfer production to a different line to supply the goods.

Similar examples from the telecommunications industry include fibre optical cable, satellite and wireless tower arrangements. Fibre agreements vary from those that allow use of the whole cable, through those that specify the wavelength or spectrum within a fibre to the most common arrangements which are essentially for transmission capacity within the vendor's fibre cable or network. As a result, arrangements have to be examined carefully to determine if they do specify an asset.

3.2.2   A right to use the asset

The arrangement will not contain a lease unless it conveys a right to use the asset. This will be the case where the arrangement conveys to the purchaser the right to control the use of the underlying asset. *[FRS 102.20.3A]*. Section 20 does not give any further explanation.

IFRS also requires entities to assess whether an arrangement conveys a right to control the use of an identified asset in order to determine whether that arrangement contains a lease, but provides more guidance on making this assessment. *[IFRS 16 Appendix B9-31]*. Applying the hierarchy in Section 10 – *Accounting Policies, Estimates and Errors* – entities may choose to look to the requirements of IFRS 16 in developing an accounting policy in this area. Identification of a lease under IFRS 16 is discussed in Chapter 24 of EY International GAAP 2019.

3.3   Terms used in Section 20

The following terms in Section 20 are defined in the Glossary to FRS 102:

[FRS 102 Appendix I]

Term	*Definition*
Asset	A resource controlled by the entity as a result of past events and from which future economic benefits are expected to flow to the entity.
Commencement of lease term	The date from which the lessee is entitled to exercise its right to use the leased asset. It is the date of initial recognition of the lease (i.e. the recognition of the assets, liabilities, income or expenses resulting from the lease, as appropriate).
Contingent rent	That portion of the lease payments that is not fixed in amount but is based on the future amount of a factor that changes other than with the passage of time (e.g. percentage of future sales, amount of future use, future price indices, and future market rates of interest).
Fair value	The amount for which an asset could be exchanged, a liability settled, or an equity instrument granted could be exchanged, between knowledgeable, willing parties in an arm's length transaction. In the absence of any specific guidance provided in the relevant section of FRS 102, the guidance in the Appendix to Section 2 *Concepts and Pervasive Principles* shall be used in determining fair value.
Finance lease	A lease that transfers substantially all the risks and rewards incidental to ownership of an asset. Title may or may not eventually be transferred. A lease that is not a finance lease is an operating lease.
Fixed assets	Assets of an entity which are intended for use on a continuing basis in the entity's activities.
Gross investment in a lease	The aggregate of: (a) the minimum lease payments receivable by the lessor under a finance lease; and (b) any unguaranteed residual value accruing to the lessor.
Inception of the lease	The earlier of the date of the lease agreement and the date of commitment by the parties to the principal provisions of the lease.

Interest rate implicit in the lease	The discount rate that, at the inception of the lease, causes the aggregate present value of:
	(a) the minimum lease payments; and
	(b) the unguaranteed residual value to be equal to the sum of:
	    (i) the fair value of the leased asset; and
	    (ii) any initial direct costs of the lessor.

Lease	An agreement whereby the lessor conveys to the lessee in return for a payment or series of payments the right to use an asset for an agreed period of time.

Lease incentives	Incentives provided by the lessor to the lessee to enter into a new or renew an operating lease. Examples of such incentives include up-front cash payments to the lessee, the reimbursement or assumption by the lessor of costs of the lessee (such as relocation costs, leasehold improvements and costs associated with pre-existing lease commitments of the lessee), or initial periods of the lease provided by the lessor rent-free or at a reduced rent.
Lease term	The non-cancellable period for which the lessee has contracted to lease the asset together with any further terms for which the lessee has the option to continue to lease the asset, with or without further payment, when at the inception of the lease it is reasonably certain that the lessee will exercise the option.
Lessee's incremental borrowing rate (of interest)	The rate of interest the lessee would have to pay on a similar lease or, if that is not determinable, the rate that, at the inception of the lease, the lessee would incur to borrow over a similar term, and with a similar security, the funds necessary to purchase the asset.

Minimum lease payments	The payments over the lease term that the lessee is or can be required to make, excluding contingent rent, costs for services and taxes to be paid by and reimbursed to the lessor, together with:
	
	(a) for a lessee, any amounts guaranteed by the lessee or by a party related to the lessee; or
	
	(b) for a lessor, any residual value guaranteed to the lessor by:
	
	  (i) the lessee;
	  (ii) a party related to the lessee; or
	  (iii) a third party unrelated to the lessor that is financially capable of discharging the obligations under the guarantee.
	
	However, if the lessee has an option to purchase the asset at a price that is expected to be sufficiently lower than fair value at the date the option becomes exercisable for it to be reasonably certain, at the inception of the lease, that the option will be exercised, the minimum lease payments comprise the minimum payments payable over the lease term to the expected date of exercise of this purchase option and the payment required to exercise it.

Net investment in a lease	The gross investment in a lease discounted at the interest rate implicit in the lease.
Onerous contract	A contract in which the unavoidable costs of meeting the obligations under the contract exceed the economic benefits expected to be received under it.
Operating lease	A lease that does not transfer substantially all the risks and rewards incidental to ownership. A lease that is not an operating lease is a finance lease.

3.4   Lease classification

A lease is classified as a finance lease if it transfers substantially all the risks and rewards incidental to ownership. A lease is classified as an operating lease if it does not transfer substantially all the risks and rewards incidental to ownership. *[FRS 102.20.4]*.

Chapter 18

The individual circumstances of a lessor and lessee may differ in respect of a single lease contract. As a result, the application of the definitions to the circumstances of the lessor and lessee may result in the same lease being classified differently by them. For example, a lease may be classified as an operating lease by the lessee and as a finance lease receivable by the lessor if it includes a residual value guarantee provided by a third party. Residual value guarantors are discussed further at 3.4.6.A below.

Lease classification is made at the inception of the lease, *[FRS 102.20.8]*, which is the earlier of the date of the lease agreement or of a commitment by the parties to the principal provisions of the lease. *[FRS 102 Appendix I]*. Classification is not changed during the term of the lease unless the lessee and the lessor agree to change the provisions of the lease (other than simply by renewing the lease), in which case the lease classification must be re-evaluated (see 3.4.3 below). *[FRS 102.20.8]*.

3.4.1 Classification as finance or operating leases

The classification of leases is based on the extent to which the risks and rewards incidental to ownership of a leased asset lie with the lessor or the lessee. Risks include the possibilities of losses from idle capacity or technological obsolescence and of variations in return due to changing economic conditions. Rewards may be represented by the expectation of profitable operation over the asset's economic life and of gain from appreciation in value or realisation of a residual value.

Some national standards, including SSAP 21 under previous UK GAAP, include the rebuttable presumption that the transfer of substantially all of the risks and rewards occurs if, at the inception of the lease, the present value of the minimum lease payments amounts to substantially all (normally 90% or more) of the fair value of the leased asset.[3] Section 20 provides no numerical guidelines to be applied in classifying a lease as either finance or operating. Lease classification should not be reduced to a single pass or fail test.

Instead, Section 20 takes a more principles-based substance over form approach. It makes the statement that the classification of a lease depends on the substance of the transaction rather than the form of the contract, and lists a number of examples of situations that individually or in combination would normally lead to a lease being classified as a finance lease: *[FRS 102.20.5]*

(a) the lease transfers ownership of the asset to the lessee by the end of the lease term;

(b) the lessee has the option to purchase the asset at a price which is expected to be sufficiently lower than the fair value at the date the option becomes exercisable such that, at the inception of the lease, it is reasonably certain that the option will be exercised (frequently called a 'bargain purchase' option);

(c) the lease term is for the major part of the economic life of the asset even if title is not transferred;

(d) at the inception of the lease the present value of the minimum lease payments amounts to at least substantially all of the fair value of the leased asset; and

(e) the leased assets are of a specialised nature such that only the lessee can use them without major modifications being made.

All of these are indicators that the lessor will only look to the lessee to obtain a return from the leasing transaction, so it can be presumed that the lessee will, in fact, pay for the asset.

Title does not have to be transferred to the lessee for a lease to be classified as a finance lease. The point is that the lease will almost certainly be classified as a finance lease if title does transfer.

Options such as those referred to under (b) are common in lease agreements. The bargain purchase option is designed to give the lessor its expected lender's return (comprising interest on its investment perhaps together with a relatively small fee), but no more, over the life of the agreement.

Lease term (criterion(c)) must be measured by reference to economic life, which is the period for which the asset is expected to be usable by one or more users, not the physical life. The economic life will usually be shorter than the physical life if the asset is subject to technological obsolescence. A computer may be capable of use for six or seven years but would rarely be used beyond three years. It is not so well appreciated that buildings suffer from technological obsolescence which means that an office building with a fabric life of sixty years may have an economic life of half of that. It becomes increasingly hard to adapt buildings to rapidly-changing IT or energy efficiency requirements. The residual value of these assets at the end of the economic life is minimal.

The economic life would therefore include additional lease terms with the same or different lessees. It is not the same as the useful life which is specific to the lessee and is the estimated remaining period, from the commencement of the lease term but without the limitation of the lease term, over which the entity expects to consume the economic benefits embodied in the asset (see 3.7.1.D below).

Criteria (c) and (d) above also include the unquantified expressions 'major part of' and 'substantially all', which means that judgement must be used in determining their effect on the risks and rewards of ownership. By contrast, in US GAAP the equivalent to (c) above in Accounting Standards Codification [ASC] 840 – *Leases*[4] – does quantify when a lease will be a capital lease (the equivalent of a finance lease). In ASC 840, if the lease term is equal to 75% or more of the estimated economic life of the leased asset, the lease will normally be a capital lease (there is an exception if the beginning of the lease term falls within the last 25% of the total estimated economic life of the leased asset, including earlier years of use, where this criterion is not used for purposes of classifying the lease).[5] In practice, if the lease is for the major part of the economic life of the asset, it is unlikely that the lessor will rely on any party other than the lessee to obtain its return from the lease. This would still not be conclusive evidence that the lease should be classified as a finance lease. There could be other terms that indicate that the significant risks and rewards of ownership rest with the lessor, e.g. lease payments might be reset periodically to market rates or there might be significant technological, obsolescence or damage risks borne by the lessor.

Similarly, whilst (d) above refers to the present value of the minimum lease payments being at least 'substantially all of the fair value of the asset', it does so without putting a percentage to it; FRS 102, unlike previous UK GAAP, has no '90% test'. However, we see no harm in practice in at least applying the '90% test' as a rule of thumb benchmark as part of the overall process in reaching a judgement as to the classification of a lease. Clearly, though, it cannot be applied as a hard and fast rule.

For an example of the 90% test, see Example 18.4 at 3.5 below. In that example, the present value of the minimum lease payments is calculated to be 92.74% of the asset's fair value; as this exceeds 90%, this would normally indicate that the lease is a finance lease. Nevertheless, the other criteria discussed above would need to be considered as well.

Consequently, we would stress that the 90% test is not an explicit requirement and should not be applied as a rule or in isolation, but it may be a useful tool to use in practice in attempting to determine the economic substance of a lease arrangement.

Section 20 provides the following indicators of situations that, individually or in combination, could also lead to a lease being classified as a finance lease: *[FRS 102.20.6]*

(a) if the lessee can cancel the lease, the lessor's losses associated with the cancellation are borne by the lessee;

(b) gains or losses from the fluctuation in the residual value of the leased asset accrue to the lessee (for example, in the form of a rent rebate equalling most of the sales proceeds at the end of the lease); and

(c) the lessee has the ability to continue the lease for a secondary period at a rent which is substantially lower than market rent.

Section 10 notes that these examples are only indicators and are not always conclusive. If it is clear from other features that the lease does not transfer substantially all risks and rewards incidental to ownership, the lease is classified as an operating lease. For example, this may be the case if ownership of the asset is transferred to the lessee at the end of the lease for a variable payment equal to the asset's then fair value, or if there are contingent rents, as a result of which the lessee does not have substantially all risks and rewards incidental to ownership. *[FRS 102.20.7]*.

Other considerations that could be made in determining the economic substance of the lease arrangement include the following:

• Are the lease rentals based on a market rate for use of the asset (which would indicate an operating lease) or a financing rate for use of the funds, which would be indicative of a finance lease? and

• Is the existence of put and call options a feature of the lease? If so, are they exercisable at a predetermined price or formula (indicating a finance lease) or are they exercisable at the market price at the time the option is exercised (indicating an operating lease)?

These two considerations mean that an arrangement for the whole of an asset's useful life may be an operating lease, as may an agreement in which the lessee has a right to obtain title to the asset at market value.

3.4.1.A   *Residual values guaranteed by the lessee*

One of the indicators listed in Section 20 that may lead to a lease being classified as a finance lease is where gains or losses from fluctuation in the fair value of the residual accrue to the lessee. *[FRS 102.20.6]*. However, this does not mean that a lease where the residual is guaranteed by the lessee will necessarily be classified as a finance lease. The lease itself may be structured so that the most likely outcome of events relating to the residual value indicates that no significant risk will attach to the lessee.

Example 18.1: A lease structured such that the most likely outcome is that the lessee has no significant residual risk

Brief details of a motor vehicle lease are:

Fair value   –   £10,000
Rentals   –   20 monthly payments of £300, followed by a final rental of £2,000

At the end of the lease, the lessee sells the vehicle as agent for the lessor and if it is sold for:

(i)   more than £3,000, the sales proceeds are paid to the lessor and 99% of the excess is repaid to the lessee; or

(ii) less than £3,000, the sales proceeds are paid to the lessor and lessee pays the deficit to the lessor up to a maximum of 4 pence per mile above 25,000 miles p.a. on average that the leased vehicle has done.

The net present value of the minimum lease payments excluding the guarantee amounts to £7,365.

This lease involves a guarantee by the lessee of the residual value of the leased vehicle of £3,000, as a result of (ii) above. However, the guarantee will only be called on if both:

(a)   the vehicle's actual residual value is less than £3,000; and

(b)   the vehicle has travelled more than 25,000 miles per year on average over the lease term.

Further, the lessee is only liable to pay a certain level of the residual; namely, £100 for each 2,500 miles above 25,000 miles that the vehicle has done (if the lessee chooses the drive such an amount).

Classification depends on the substance of the arrangement as described above. In assessing the risks and rewards of ownership, the entity will take account of the residual guarantee, which may be zero if the lessee chooses not to drive the vehicle over 25,000 miles.

The risks and rewards of ownership are determined in a lease classification by the substance of the arrangement, including the substance of any residual guarantee arrangements.

Therefore the guarantee would be considered in evaluating the substance of the arrangement on a qualitative basis, to the extent that experience or expectations of the sales price and/or mileage that vehicles have driven (and the inter-relationship between these) indicate that a residual payment by the lessee will be made.

If a lease is determined to be a finance lease, Section 20 requires initial recognition of the asset at fair value or at the net present value of the minimum lease payments. The residual value guarantee could then affect the asset's residual value as explained in Example 18.10 at 3.7.4.A below.

3.4.1.B   Rental rebates

FRS 102 suggests that it is an indicator that the lease is a finance lease if the gains or losses from the fluctuation in the fair value of the residual accrue to the lessee, e.g. in the form of a rent rebate equalling most of the sales proceeds at the end of the lease. *[FRS 102.20.6]*. This is because a lessee that obtains most of the sales proceeds has received most of the risks and rewards of the residual value in the asset. This would indicate that the lessor has already been compensated for the transaction and hence that it is a finance lease.

Other leases require the asset to be sold at the end of the lease but the lessor receives the first tranche of proceeds and only those proceeds above a certain level are remitted to the lessee. These arrangements may have a different significance as the lessor may be taking the proceeds to meet its unguaranteed residual value. Lessors are prepared to take risks on residual values of such assets if there is an established and reliable market in which to sell them. This could mean that the gains or losses from the fluctuation in the fair value of the residual do not fall predominantly to the lessee and, in the absence of other factors, could indicate that it is an operating lease.

Example 18.2: *Rental rebates*

The lease arrangements are as in Example 18.1 except that at the end of the lease, the lessee sells the vehicle as an agent for the lessor, and if it is sold for

(i) up to £3,000, all of the sales proceeds are paid to the lessor; or

(ii) more than £3,000, the sales are paid to the lessor and 99% of excess is repaid to the lessee. The lessee does not have to make good any deficit, should one arise.

In this example, it appears that the lessor is using the sale proceeds to meet its unguaranteed residual value but it is also taking the first loss provision. Only thereafter does the lessee gain or lose from the fluctuations in the fair value. The lessee's minimum lease payments have a net present value of £7,365, it has not guaranteed the residual value at all and is not exposed to any risk of any fall in value, although it may benefit from increases in the fair value in excess of £3,000. On balance this indicates that the arrangement is an operating lease.

3.4.2   Inception and commencement of the lease

It is important to distinguish between the inception of the lease (when leases are classified) and the commencement of the lease term (when recognition takes place).

The *inception* of the lease is the earlier of the date of the lease agreement and the date of commitment of the parties to the principal terms of the lease. *[FRS 102 Appendix I]*. This is the date on which a lease is classified as a finance or operating lease.

The *commencement* of the lease term is the date on which the lessee is entitled to exercise its right to use the leased asset and is the date of initial recognition of the assets, liabilities, income and expenses of the lease in the financial statements. *[FRS 102 Appendix I]*.

This means that the entity makes an initial calculation of the assets and liabilities under a finance lease at inception of the lease but does not recognise these in the financial statements until the commencement date, if this is later. The amounts in the initial calculation may in some circumstances be revised. It is not uncommon for the two dates to be different, especially if the asset is under construction. Section 20 requires the lessee under a finance lease to recognise the asset at its fair value or, if lower, at the present value of the minimum lease payments, determined at the inception of the lease. *[FRS 102.20.9]*. This means that, if the final cost of the asset, and hence its fair value, is not known until after the date of inception, hindsight should be used to establish that fair value.

Sometimes lease payments may be adjusted for changes in the lessor's costs during the period between inception and commencement. The lease may allow for changes in respect of costs of construction, acquisition costs, changes in the lessor's financing costs and any other factor, such as changes in general price levels, during the construction period. Such changes are also relevant in establishing the fair value and minimum lease payments for the purposes of Section 20. In our view, changes to the lease payments as a result of such events should be deemed to take place at inception of the lease and be taken into account in establishing whether it is a finance or operating lease at inception and, if it is a finance lease, the amount at which the asset and liability should be recorded (see 3.7 below). A contract might estimate the cost of construction to be £1 million but allow for additional specific increased costs of up to 5% to be reflected in increased payments made by the lessee. If those increased costs are incurred, then the fair value and minimum lease payments at inception will take account of the increased cost of the asset (£1.05 million) and the increased lease payments.

The fair value may be known at inception but payment delayed until commencement, which may happen with large but routinely constructed assets such as aircraft or railway locomotives. The lease liability will increase between the date of inception and the date of commencement, taking account of payments made and the interest rate implicit in the lease. Again, this is not addressed by Section 20 but, in our view, the lessee ought to add the increase in the liability until the commencement date to the asset. It is not a finance cost on the liability (no liability is recognised prior to commencement) and nor need it be an expense. It is not appropriate to recognise at commencement the liability that was calculated at inception as that would change the interest rate implicit in the lease.

Circumstances in which lease classification might be changed are discussed at 3.4.3 below.

3.4.3   Changes to the classification of leases

Classification is not changed during the term of the lease unless the lessee and the lessor agree to change the provisions of the lease (other than simply by renewing the lease), in which case the lease classification must be re-evaluated. *[FRS 102.20.8]*.

Changes in estimates (for example, changes in estimates of the economic life or of the residual value of the leased item) or changes in circumstances (for example, default by the lessee) do not result in the lease being reclassified for accounting purposes.

The distinction between changes to the provisions of the lease and changes in estimate is that the former, unlike the latter, are always the result of agreements between the lessee and lessor.

Section 20 does not address the measurement of these changes. References to the relevant parts of this chapter in which the changes are dealt with are given below.

(a)   Changes to the provisions or terms of an existing lease ('modifications')

Changes to the provisions or terms of an existing lease (referred to here as 'modifications') are changes to the contractual terms and conditions that are not part of the original lease. Modifications that affect a lease's classification are those that affect the risks and rewards incidental to ownership of the asset by changing the terms and cash flows of the existing lease. Examples of modifications that could affect classification include those that change the duration of the lease and the number, amount and timing of lease payments or the inclusion or an option to acquire not previously part of the lease terms.

The revised agreement resulting from the modification is considered as if it were a new agreement which should be accounted for appropriately, as a finance or operating lease, prospectively over the remaining term of the lease.

FRS 102 does not give any specific guidance on how to assess whether modified lease terms give rise to a new classification so the general classification rules described in 3.4.1 above must be applied. Nor does it explain how to measure modifications of leases if

Chapter 18

changes affect the value of the assets and liabilities for both lessor and lessee. These issues are discussed at 3.9 below. See 3.9.1 below for discussion on how to assess whether the classification has changed, based on the revised cash flows, and see 3.9.2 below for how to account for the reclassification.

If lease terms are modified but the classification does not change, the entity will still have to account for the modified cash flows. How to account for the changes if a finance lease remains a finance lease is discussed at 3.9.3.A below. Accounting for changes to the terms of operating leases, where those changes do not result in reclassification, is considered at 3.9.3.B below.

Some changes to lease terms will not affect the cash flows at all, e.g. those that change terms such as the names of the contracting parties. Other changes could affect only the lessor, e.g. a transfer from one lessor to another that requires no consent or other action by the lessee and where there is no change to the lease cash flows.

(b)   the lessor and lessee renew the lease

If the lessee and lessor renew the lease, this could mean one of the following:

- Exercising an option to extend the lease or purchase the underlying asset, when these options were included in the original lease but exercise of the options was not considered probable at its inception. Changes in circumstances or intentions do not give rise to a new classification of the original lease, unless they indicate that the initial classification was made in error because it was not based on the substance of the arrangement at the time it was entered into. This means that the intention to exercise a renewal option in a lease originally classified as an operating lease will not change that classification.

- Entering into a new lease with the lessor. For example, an entity may have a right to 'renew' a lease of business premises for a further term after expiry of the initial term at the market rent at the date the new agreement is entered into. This is not a change to the terms of the original lease. It may be under the terms of a statutory right to extend commercial leases found in many jurisdictions, whose purpose is to ensure that businesses are not forced to relocate. This is similar in effect to an option to extend at market value so under a risks and rewards model the secondary term would not pass the significant risks and rewards to the lessee.

   The lessor and lessee could revoke the original lease and enter into a new one in its place, which would also be considered a renewal. It is necessary to ensure that the new lease terms are at fair value at the time it is entered into so it does not reflect, for example, underpayments made by the lessee under the terms of the original lease.

- Extending the existing lease without changing any other term, e.g. with the consent of the lessor, continuing to use the asset for a period of time after the original expiry at the original rental. This has to be distinguished on the facts from a negotiation between the lessee and lessor that changes the terms of the original lease before its expiry, although this will probably also include other changes such as a different rental.

A new, renewed or extended lease will be classified on its own terms without any consideration of the terms and provisions of the original lease.

Example 18.3:   Lease classification

Consider the following scenarios:

(a) Entity A leases a motor vehicle from Entity B for a non-cancellable three-year period. At the inception of the lease, the lease was assessed as an operating lease. The lease did not contain any explicit option in the lease contract to extend the term of the lease. A short period of time before the end of the lease term, Entity A applies to Entity B to extend the lease for a further two years. This extension is granted by the leasing company at fair value.

Entity A's negotiations result in a renewed (i.e. new) lease, not a change in the provisions of the original lease, which will be accounted for on its own terms. This does not affect the classification of the original lease.

(b) Entity C leases a machine tool from Entity D for 5 years, expecting to purchase a new asset after the lease expires. After 3 years, Entity C concludes that it is more economically viable for it to lease the asset from Entity D for a total of 8 years. The lessor agrees to revised lease terms and the lease is extended by 3 years, giving a total term of 8 years. At the same time the lease payments for years 4 and 5 are revised so that Entity C will pay a new rental for each of the years 4 to 8.

This is a lease modification as it has resulted in a change to the terms of the original lease. The entity will have to assess whether the revised lease is an operating or finance lease.

(c) Entity E leases an asset from Entity F for 10 years. The lease includes a purchase option under which Entity E may purchase the asset from Entity F at the end of the lease. The exercise price is fair value. Entity E is required to give notice of its intention to purchase no later than the end of the eighth year of the lease (since this arrangement allows Entity F time to market the leased asset for sale). On inception, Entity E classifies the lease as an operating lease, believing it was not reasonably certain that it would exercise the option. Near the end of the eighth year of the lease, Entity E serves notice that it will purchase the asset, thereby creating a binding purchase commitment.

Entity E exercises an option that was not considered reasonably certain at inception; this is a change in estimate and does not affect lease classification. Many entities would consider the arrangement to be executory at the time that the notice is given even though there is a legal obligation to make the option payment and therefore would account for the purchase option only when it is exercised.

3.4.4   Lease term

The lease term is the non-cancellable period for which the lessee has contracted to lease the asset together with any further terms for which the lessee has the option to continue to lease the asset, with or without further payment, when at the inception of the lease it is reasonably certain that the lessee will exercise the option. *[FRS 102 Appendix I].*

A lease may contain terms that effectively force the lessee to continue to use the asset for the period of the agreement. Arguably, the substance of the transaction should be taken into account. Therefore, a lease may be non-cancellable if it can be cancelled only:

(a) on the occurrence of a remote contingency;

(b) with the permission of the lessor;

(c) if the lessee enters into a new lease with the same lessor for the same or an equivalent asset; or

(d) if the lessee is required to pay additional amounts that make it reasonably certain at inception that the lessee will continue the lease.

An example of (d) is a requirement that the lessee pays a termination payment equivalent to the present value of the remaining lease payments.

3.4.5   Contingent rent and minimum lease payments

Contingent rent is that portion of the lease payments that is not fixed in amount but is based on the future amount of a factor that changes other than with the passage of time (e.g. percentage of future sales, amount of future use, future price indices, and future market rates of interest). *[FRS 102 Appendix I].*

In the case of finance leases, contingent rents are excluded from minimum lease payments. Lessees charge contingent rents as expenses in the periods in which they are incurred. *[FRS 102.20.11].*

Contingent payments will be taken into account in assessing whether substantially all of the risks and rewards of ownership have been transferred; for example, property rentals that are periodically reset to market rates would tend to indicate that risks and rewards rest with the lessor – see the discussion at 3.4.1 above. This still leaves open to debate whether a particular 'contingency' is in fact contingent or is so certain that it ought to be reflected in the minimum lease payments for the purposes of classifying the lease. In practice this will always be based on an assessment of the individual circumstances.

For operating leases, FRS 102 is not explicit on the treatment of contingent rent. Current practice is to exclude an estimate of such amounts from the total operating lease payments or lease income to be recognised on a straight-line basis over the lease term. Accordingly, contingent lease payments or receipts under operating leases are generally recognised in the period in which they are incurred. Views are divided on whether minimum lease payments determined at the inception of the lease are revised on the occurrence of the contingency, e.g. whether minimum lease payments change when there are rent revisions that are stipulated in the original lease agreement, either for straight-line recognition or disclosure purposes. In the case of contingencies based on an index, such as a retail price index, it is our view that disclosure should reflect all contingencies that have occurred in future minimum lease disclosures. This is on the basis that the contingency has occurred and Section 20 specifies disclosure of future minimum lease payments. *[FRS 102.20.16, 30].* If the initial payment before any indexation changes was 100 per year and at the end of year 1, the index was 102.5, the minimum lease payments for disclosure purposes at the end of year 1 would be 102.5 for each remaining year of the lease term.

Section 20 excludes from its scope 'leases that could lead to a loss to the lessor or the lessee as a result of non-typical contractual terms'. *[FRS 102.20.1(e)].* These contractual terms would be unrelated to changes in the price of the leased asset, changes in foreign exchange rates, or a default by one of the counterparties. *[FRS 102.BC.B20.1].* Generally we would expect this to exclude contingent rents relating to the factors described above as they are not included in the measurement of assets and liabilities. Leases excluded from scope on this basis are discussed at 3.1.3 above and 3.6 below.

3.4.6   *Residual values*

The guaranteed residual value is:

(a)   for a lessee, the part of the residual value that is guaranteed by itself or by one of its related parties. The amount of the guarantee is the maximum amount that could, in any event, become payable; and

(b)   for a lessor, the part of the residual value that is guaranteed by the lessee, a party related to the lessee, or by a third party unrelated to the lessor who is financially capable of discharging the obligations under the guarantee. *[FRS 102 Appendix I].*

This means that the lessor's unguaranteed residual value is any part of the residual value of the leased asset, whose realisation is not assured or is guaranteed solely by a related party of the lessor. If the net present value of the residual value of an asset is significant and is not guaranteed by the lessee or a party related to it, then the lease is likely to be classified as an operating lease by the lessee. The lessee will not bear the risks of recovering the significant residual value; consequently it is unlikely that 'substantially all' of the risks and rewards of ownership will have passed to the lessee. However, as can be seen from Example 18.1 at 3.4.1.A above, the provision of a residual value guarantee by a lessee does not necessarily mean that the lease will not be classified as an operating lease by the lessee.

There are frequently problems of interpretation regarding the significance of residual values in lease classification. Lessees may find it difficult to obtain information in order to calculate the unguaranteed residual values.

If lessees guarantee all or part of the residual value of the asset, this has to be taken into account in the lease classification.

If a related party, e.g. a member of the same group as the lessee, guarantees the residual, this can result in recognition of a finance lease in the consolidated financial statements and an operating lease in the individual entity. This assumes that there are no intra-group arrangements that transfer the guarantee back to the lessee.

3.4.6.A   *Residual value guarantors*

A lessee and lessor may legitimately classify the same lease differently if the lessor has received a residual value guarantee provided by a third party. Residual value guarantors undertake to acquire the assets from the lessor at an agreed amount at the end of the lease term because they can dispose of the assets in a ready and reliable market. As a result, such a lease is an operating lease for the lessee and a finance lease for the lessor. Residual value guarantors may be prepared to take the residual risk with many types of assets as long as there is a second-hand market. This is particularly common with vehicle leases where there is an efficient second-hand market, including price guides, many car dealers and car auctions.

Chapter 18

3.5   Calculating the net present value of the minimum lease payments

An entity will frequently have to calculate the net present value of the minimum lease payments in order to classify a lease as a finance or operating lease as well as in accounting for finance leases. In order to do so, it must consider the residual value of the asset and whether there are any residual value guarantors. Once it has this information then it can calculate the implicit interest rate and present value of minimum lease payments, as in the following example:

Example 18.4:   Calculation of the implicit interest rate and present value of minimum lease payments

Details of a non-cancellable lease are as follows:

(i)   Fair value = £10,000

(ii)   Five annual rentals payable in advance of £2,100

(iii)   Lessor's unguaranteed estimated residual value at end of five years = £1,000

The implicit interest rate in the lease is that which gives a present value of £10,000 for the five rentals plus the total estimated residual value at the end of year 5. This rate can be calculated as 6.62%, as follows:

Year	Capital sum at start of period £	Rental paid £	Capital sum during period £	Finance charge (6.62% per annum) £	Capital sum at end of period £
1	10,000	2,100	7,900	523	8,423
2	8,423	2,100	6,323	419	6,742
3	6,742	2,100	4,642	307	4,949
4	4,949	2,100	2,849	189	3,038
5	3,038	2,100	938	62	1,000
		10,500		1,500	

In other words, 6.62% is the implicit interest rate that, at the inception of the lease, causes the aggregate present value of the minimum lease payments (£10,500) and the unguaranteed residual value (£1,000) to be equal to the fair value of the leased asset. Lessor's initial direct costs have been excluded for simplicity.

This implicit interest rate is then used to calculate the present value of the minimum lease payments, i.e. £10,500 discounted at 6.62%. This can be calculated at £9,274, which is 92.74% of the asset's fair value, indicating that the present value of the minimum lease payments is substantially all of the fair value of the leased asset and a finance lease is therefore indicated.

It would be appropriate for the lessee to record the asset at £9,274 as the present value of the minimum lease payments is lower than the fair value and this would take account of the lessor's residual interest in the asset.

The lessor will know all of the information in the above example, as it will have been used in the pricing decision for the lease. However, the lessee may not know either the fair value or the unguaranteed residual value and, therefore, not know the implicit interest rate. In such circumstances the lessee will substitute its incremental borrowing rate. *[FRS 102.20.10]*. The lessee is also unlikely to know the lessor's initial direct costs even if the other information is known, but this is unlikely to have more than a marginal effect on the implicit interest rate.

3.5.1   Fair value

Fair value is defined as the amount for which an asset could be exchanged, a liability settled, or an equity instrument granted could be exchanged, between knowledgeable, willing parties in an arm's length transaction. *[FRS 102 Appendix I]*. Additional guidance is given in the appendix to Section 2 (see Chapter 4). Although the additional guidance does not refer to Section 20, it is used as guidance in establishing the fair value of property, plant and equipment and will therefore be relevant in establishing the fair value of assets held under leases. *[FRS 102.17.15C]*.

In practice, the transaction price, i.e. the purchase price of the asset that is the subject of the lease, will be its fair value, unless there is evidence to the contrary.

3.6 Leases as financial instruments

Leases 'that could lead to a loss to the lessor or the lessee as a result of non-typical contractual terms' are out of scope of Section 20. *[FRS 102.20.1(e)]*. This could include contractual terms that are unrelated to any of the following:

- changes in the price of the leased asset;
- changes in foreign exchange rates; or
- a default by one of the counterparties. *[FRS 102.BC.B20.1]*.

These leases with non-typical contractual terms are, in effect, financial instruments that are carried at fair value in accordance with Section 12 (see Chapter 10).

In general the lease rights and obligations that come about as a result of FRS 102 are recognised and measured in accordance with the rules in Section 20 and are not included within the scope of Section 11 or Section 12. The exceptions are:

- derecognition and impairment of receivables recognised by a lessor; and
- derecognition of payables recognised by a lessee arising under a finance lease.

In these cases the derecognition requirements (in paragraphs 11.33 to 11.35 and paragraphs 11.36 to 11.38, addressing respectively derecognition of financial assets and financial liabilities) and impairment accounting requirements (in paragraphs 11.21 to 11.26) apply. These are discussed at 3.7.4.B below.

Finance lease assets and liabilities are not necessarily stated at the same amount as they would be if they were measured as financial instruments. The most obvious differences are those between the interest rate implicit in the lease (IIR) and the effective interest rate, both of which are defined in the Glossary. *[FRS 102 Appendix I]*. The IIR (as described at 3.5 above) is the discount rate that, at the inception of the lease, causes the aggregate present value of the minimum lease payments (receivable during the non-cancellable lease term and any option periods that it is reasonably certain at inception the lessee will exercise) and the unguaranteed residual value to be equal to the sum of the fair value of the leased asset and any initial direct costs of the lessor. The effective interest rate, by contrast, is the rate that exactly discounts estimated future cash payments or receipts through the expected life of the financial instrument. The latter may include payments that would be considered contingent rentals, and hence excluded from the calculation of the IIR, and may take account of cash flows over a different period.

3.7 Accounting for finance leases

Lessees recognise finance leases as assets and liabilities in their statements of financial position at the commencement of the lease term at amounts equal at the inception of the lease to the fair value of the leased item or, if lower, at the present value of the minimum lease payments. In calculating the present value of the minimum lease payments the discount factor is the interest rate implicit in the lease, if this is practicable to determine; if not, the lessee's incremental borrowing rate should be used. Any initial direct costs of the lessee are added to the asset. 'Fair value' and 'minimum lease payments' are defined at 3.5.1 and 3.4.5 above.

The fair value and the present value of the minimum lease payments are both determined as at the inception of the lease. *[FRS 102.20.9]*. At commencement, the asset and liability for the future lease payments are recognised in the statement of financial position at the same amount (except for any incremental costs that are directly attributable to negotiating and arranging a lease, that are added to the recognised asset). As discussed at 3.4.2 above, the initial calculation of the asset and liability at inception of the lease may differ from the amount determined at lease commencement. The terms and calculations of initial recognition by lessees are discussed further at 3.7.1 below.

Lease payments made by the lessee are apportioned between the finance charge and the reduction of the outstanding liability. The finance charge should be allocated to periods during the lease term using the effective interest method so as to produce a constant periodic rate of interest on the remaining balance of the liability for each period. This is covered at 3.7.1.B below.

Lessors recognise assets held under a finance lease as receivables in their statements of financial position and present them as a receivable at an amount equal to the net investment in the lease. Lessors who are not manufacturers or dealers include costs that they have incurred in connection with arranging and negotiating a lease as part of the initial measurement of the finance lease receivable. Initial recognition by lessors, which is in many respects a mirror image of lessee recognition, follows at 3.7.2 below. The recognition of finance income and other issues in connection with subsequent measurement of the lessor's assets arising from finance leases is dealt with at 3.7.2.A below.

Residual values, to which finance leases are very sensitive, are discussed at 3.7.3 below.

The consequences of terminating a finance lease are described at 3.7.4 below. Subleases and back-to-back leases are discussed at 3.7.4.C below, as the principal accounting issue is the whether or not the conditions for derecognition are met by the intermediate party.

Manufacturer or dealer lessors have specific issues with regard to recognition of selling profit and finance income. These are dealt with at 3.7.5 below.

3.7.1   Accounting by lessees

3.7.1.A   Initial recognition

At commencement of the lease, the right of use and obligations for the future lease payments are recorded in the statement of financial position at the same amount. This is equal to the fair value of the leased asset or, if lower, the present value of the minimum lease payments, determined at the inception of the lease. *[FRS 102.20.9]*. The present value of the minimum lease payments is calculated using the interest rate implicit in the lease or, if this cannot be determined, at the lessee's incremental borrowing rate. *[FRS 102.20.10]*. An example of the calculation is given in Example 18.4 at 3.5 above.

Initial direct costs of the lessee, which are incremental costs directly attributable to negotiating and arranging the lease, are added to the asset. *[FRS 102.20.9]*.

3.7.1.B Allocation of finance costs

Lease payments must be apportioned between the finance charge and the reduction of the outstanding liability using the effective interest method. The finance charge is allocated to periods during the lease term so as to produce a constant periodic rate of interest on the remaining balance of the liability. *[FRS 102.11.16, 20.11]*.

A lessee must charge contingent rents as expenses in the periods in which they are incurred. *[FRS 102.20.11]*.

Example 18.5: Allocation of finance costs

In Example 18.4 above, the present value of the lessee's minimum lease payments was calculated at £9,274 by using the implicit interest rate of 6.62%. The total finance charges of £1,226 (total rentals paid of £10,500 less their present value of £9,274) are allocated over the lease term as follows:

Year	Liability at start of period £	Rental paid £	Liability during period £	Finance charge (6.62% per annum) £	Liability at end of period £
1	9,274	2,100	7,174	475	7,649
2	7,649	2,100	5,549	368	5,917
3	5,917	2,100	3,817	253	4,070
4	4,070	2,100	1,970	130	2,100
5	2,100	2,100	–	–	–
		10,500		1,226	

In practice, when allocating the finance charge to periods during the lease term, entities may sometimes use some form of approximation to simplify the calculation. Two methods that are used as approximations are the sum of digits method, which is based on allocating the finance charge based on the cumulative number of payments still outstanding, or the straight-line method. While Section 20 makes no mention of simplified methods, there is of course no prohibition on using an approximation if differences between that method and that mandated by Section 20 are not material.

3.7.1.C Recording the liability

The carrying amount of the liability will always be calculated in the same way, by adding the finance charge to the outstanding balance and deducting cash paid. The liability in each of the years, as apportioned between the current and non-current liability, is as follows:

Example 18.6: Lessee's liabilities and interest expense

The entity entering into the lease in Example 18.4 will record the following liabilities and interest expense in its statement of financial position:

Year	Liability at end of period £	Current liability at end of period £	Non-current liability at end of period £	Interest expense (at 6.62%) for the period £
1	7,649	2,100	5,549	475
2	5,917	2,100	3,817	368
3	4,070	2,100	1,970	253
4	2,100	2,100	–	130
5	–	–		
				1,226

Chapter 18

3.7.1.D   Accounting for the leased asset

At commencement of the lease, the asset and liability for the future lease payments are recorded in the statement of financial position at the same amount, with initial direct costs of the lessee then being added to the asset. *[FRS 102.20.9]*. These are costs that are directly attributable to the lease in question and are added to the carrying value in an analogous way to the treatment of the acquisition costs of property, plant and equipment.

Accounting for the leased asset follows the general rules for accounting for property, plant and equipment or intangible assets. A finance lease gives rise to a depreciation expense for depreciable assets as well as a finance expense for each accounting period. The depreciation policy for depreciable leased assets should be consistent with that for depreciable assets that are owned, and the depreciation recognised should be calculated in accordance with Section 17 (see Chapter 15) or Section 18 (see Chapter 16). If there is no reasonable certainty that the lessee will obtain ownership by the end of the lease term, the asset should be depreciated over the shorter of the lease term and its useful life. *[FRS 102.20.12]*.

Section 20 does not address the situation in which an entity expects to extend a lease but it is not reasonably certain at inception that it will do so. In our view, the entity is not precluded from depreciating assets either over the lease term or over the shorter of the asset's useful life and the period for which the entity expects to extend the lease.

Because the interest expense and depreciation must be calculated separately and are unlikely to be the same it is not appropriate simply to treat the lease payments as an expense for the period. This is demonstrated in the following example.

Example 18.7:   Lessee's depreciation and interest expense

The entity that has entered into the lease agreement described in Example 18.4 will depreciate the asset (whose initial carrying value, disregarding initial direct costs, is £9,274) on a straight-line basis over five years in accordance with its depreciation policy for owned assets, i.e. an amount of £1,855 per annum. The balances for asset and liability in the financial statements in each of the years 1-5 will be as follows:

Year	Carrying value of asset at end of period £	Total liability at end of period £	Total charged to income statement* £	Lease payments £
1	7,419	7,649	2,330	2,100
2	5,564	5,917	2,222	2,100
3	3,709	4,070	2,108	2,100
4	1,855	2,100	1,985	2,100
5	–	–	1,855	2,100
			10,500	10,500

*   The total charge combines the annual depreciation of £1,855 and the interest calculated according to the IIR method in Example 18.4, which is in aggregate the initial carrying value of the asset of £9,274 and the total finance charge of £1,226, i.e. the total rent paid of £10,500. Note that this example assumes that the asset is being depreciated to a residual value of zero over the lease term, which is shorter than its useful life.

A lessee must also assess at each reporting date whether an asset leased under a finance lease is impaired. *[FRS 102.20.12]*.

Assets held under finance leases may also be revalued using the revaluation model but the entire class of assets (both owned and those held under finance lease) must be revalued. *[FRS 102.17.15]*.

Whilst it is not explicit in Section 20, in our view, to obtain the fair value of an asset held under a finance lease for financial reporting purposes, the assessed value should be adjusted to avoid double counting of any recognised finance lease liability.

3.7.2   Accounting by lessors

Under a finance lease, a lessor retains legal title to an asset but passes substantially all the risks and rewards of ownership to the lessee in return for a stream of rentals. In substance, therefore, the lessor provides finance and expects a return thereon.

Lessors are required to recognise assets held under a finance lease in their statement of financial position as a receivable at an amount equal to the net investment in the lease. The net investment in a lease is the lessor's gross investment discounted at the interest rate implicit in the lease. The gross investment in the lease is the aggregate of:

(a)   the minimum lease payments receivable by the lessor under a finance lease; and

(b)   any unguaranteed residual value accruing to the lessor. *[FRS 102.20.17]*.

Initial direct costs (costs that are incremental and directly attributable to negotiating and arranging a lease) may include commissions, legal fees and internal costs. They are included in the measurement of the net investment in the lease at inception, except in the case of finance leases involving manufacturer or dealer lessors. *[FRS 102.20.18]*.

As they are included in the initial measurement of the finance lease receivable, they reduce the amount of income recognised over the lease term.

At any point in time the net investment comprises the gross investment after deducting gross earnings allocated to future periods. The lessor's gross investment is, therefore, the same as the aggregate figures used to calculate the implicit interest rate and the net investment is the present value of those same figures – see Example 18.4 above. Therefore, at inception, the lessor's net investment in the lease is the cost of the asset as increased by its initial direct costs. The difference between the net and gross investments is the gross finance income to be allocated over the lease term. Example 18.8 below illustrates this point.

3.7.2.A   Allocation of finance income

The lease payments received from the lessee, excluding costs for services, are treated as repayments of principal and finance income; in other words, they reduce both the principal and the unearned finance income. Finance income should be recognised at a constant periodic rate of return on the lessor's net investment in the finance lease. *[FRS 102.20.19]*.

If there is an indication that the estimated unguaranteed residual value used in computing the gross investment in the lease has changed significantly, the income allocation over the lease term should be revised. Any reduction in amounts accrued is recognised immediately in profit or loss (see 3.7.3.A below). *[FRS 102.20.19]*.

In Example 18.8 below, we examine the same fact pattern used in Example 18.4 at 3.5 above, but from the lessor's perspective:

Chapter 18

Example 18.8:   The lessor's gross and net investment in the lease

The lease has the same facts as described in Example 18.4, i.e. the asset has a fair value of £10,000, the lessee is making five annual rentals payable in advance of £2,100 and the total unguaranteed estimated residual value at the end of five years is estimated to be £1,000. The lessor's direct costs have been excluded for simplicity.

The lessor's gross investment in the lease is the total rents receivable of £10,500 and the unguaranteed residual value of £1,000. The gross earnings are therefore £1,500. The initial carrying value of the receivable is its fair value of £10,000, which is also the present value of the gross investment discounted at the interest rate implicit in the lease of 6.62%.

Year	Receivable at start of period £	Rental received £	Finance income (6.62% per annum) £	Gross investment at end of period £	Gross earnings allocated to future periods £	Receivable at end of period £
1	10,000	2,100	523	9,400	977	8,423
2	8,423	2,100	419	7,300	558	6,742
3	6,742	2,100	307	5,200	251	4,949
4	4,949	2,100	189	3,100	62	3,038
5	3,038	2,100	62	1,000	–	1,000
		10,500	1,500			

The gross investment in the lease at any point in time comprises the aggregate of the rentals receivable in future periods and the unguaranteed residual value, e.g. at the end of year 2, the gross investment of £7,300 is three years' rental of £2,100 plus the unguaranteed residual of £1,000. The net investment, which is the amount at which the debtor will be recorded in the statement of financial position, is £7,300 less the earnings allocated to future periods of £558 = £6,742.

If the lessor's initial direct costs of £500 are included, then it is likely that these will be recouped by the lessor through higher rental charges, as in the following example.

Year	Receivable at start of period £	Rental received £	Finance income (6.62% per annum) £	Gross investment at end of period £	Gross earnings allocated to future periods £	Receivable at end of period £
1	10,500	2,213	549	8,835	1,017	7,818
2	8,835	2,213	438	7,061	558	6,503
3	7,061	2,213	321	5,169	251	4,918
4	5,169	2,213	196	3,151	62	3,089
5	3,151	2,213	62	1,000	–	1,000
		11,066	1,566			

The lessor has recovered an additional 566 from the lessee (11,066 – 10,500); this is the additional debtor of 500 for the initial direct costs, together with interest at 6.62%.

3.7.3   Residual values

Residual values have to be taken into account in assessing whether a lease is a finance or operating lease as well as affecting the calculation of the IIR and finance income.

- Unguaranteed residual values have to be estimated in order to calculate the IIR and finance income receivable under a finance lease. If there is an indication that the estimated unguaranteed residual value has changed significantly, the income allocation over the lease term is revised, and any reduction in respect of amounts accrued is recognised immediately in profit or loss. Any impairment in the residual must be taken into account. *[FRS 102.20.19]*. This is illustrated at 3.7.3.A below.

- Residual values can be guaranteed by the lessee or by a third party. The effects of third party guarantees on risks and rewards are described at 3.4.6.A above.

- The terms of a lease guarantee can affect the assessment of the risks and rewards in the arrangement as in Example 18.1 at 3.4.1.A above.

- A common form of lease requires the asset to be sold at the end of the lease term. The disposition of the proceeds has to be taken into account in assessing who bears residual risk, as described at 3.4.1.B above.

3.7.3.A   Unguaranteed residual values

Income recognition by lessors can be extremely sensitive to the amount recognised as the asset's residual value. This is because the amount of the residual directly affects the computation of the amount of finance income earned over the lease term – this is illustrated in Example 18.9 below. If there has been a reduction in the estimated value, the income allocation over the lease term is revised and any reduction in respect of amounts accrued is recognised immediately. *[FRS 102.20.19]*. Section 20 provides no guidance regarding the estimation of unguaranteed residual values.

Example 18.9:   Reduction in residual value

Taking the same facts as used in Example 18.4 above, the lessor concludes at the end of year 2 that the residual value of the asset is only £500 and revises the income allocation over the lease term accordingly. It continues to apply the same implicit interest rate, 6.62%, as before.

Year	Receivable at start of period £	Rental received £	Finance income (6.62% per annum) £	Gross investment at end of period* £	Gross earnings allocated to future periods £	Receivable at end of period £
2	8,423	2,100	419	6,800	471	6,329
3	6,329	2,100	280	4,700	191	4,509
4	4,509	2,100	160	2,600	31	2,569
5	2,569	2,100	31	500	–	500

*   The gross investment in the lease now takes account of the revised unguaranteed residual of £500, rather than the original £1,000.

The lessor will have to write off £413, being the difference between the carrying amount of the receivable as previously calculated in Example 18.8 and the revised balance above (£6,742 – £6,329). This is the present value as at the end of year 2 of £500 and represents the part of the unguaranteed residual written off.

This is the same method as is used for impairment of lease receivables, which is within the scope of Section 11. *[FRS 102.11.7(c)]*. Impairment of leases is described at 3.7.4.B below.

3.7.4   Termination of finance leases

The expectations of lessors and lessees regarding the timing of termination of a lease may affect the classification of a lease as either operating or finance. This is because it will affect the expected lease term, level of payments under the lease and expected residual value of the lease assets.

Termination during the primary lease term will generally not be anticipated at the lease inception because the lessee can be assumed to be using the asset for at least that period. In addition, early termination is made less likely because most leases are non-cancellable. A termination payment is usually required which will give the lessor an amount equivalent to most or all of the rental receipts which would have been received if no termination had taken place, which means that it is reasonably certain at inception that the lease will continue to expiry.

However, there are consequences if the lease is terminated. The issues for finance lessees and lessors are discussed in the following sections.

3.7.4.A   Termination of finance leases by lessees

Finance lease payables recognised by a lessee are subject to the derecognition provisions of Section 11. *[FRS 102.11.7(c)]*.

Section 11 requires an entity to derecognise (i.e. remove from its statement of financial position) a financial liability (or a part of a financial liability) when, and only when, it is 'extinguished', that is, when the obligation specified in the contract is discharged, cancelled, or expires. *[FRS 102.11.36]*. This is discussed in Chapter 10.

The difference between the carrying amount of all or part of a financial liability extinguished or transferred to another party and the consideration paid, including any non-cash assets transferred or liabilities assumed, is to be recognised in profit or loss. *[FRS 102.11.38]*.

In order to identify the part of a liability derecognised, an entity allocates the previous carrying amount of the financial liability between the part that continues to be recognised and the part that is derecognised based on the relative fair values of those parts on the date of the partial derecognition.

Unless it is part of a renegotiation or business combination or similar larger arrangement, the lessee will derecognise the capitalised asset on early termination of a finance lease, with any remaining balance of the capitalised asset being written off as a loss on disposal. Any payment made by the lessee will reduce the lease obligation that is being carried in the statement of financial position. If either a part of this obligation is not eliminated or the termination payment exceeds the previously existing obligation, then the remainder or excess will be included as a gain or loss respectively on derecognition of a financial liability.

A similar accounting treatment is required where the lease terminates at the expected date and there is a residual at least partly guaranteed by the lessee. For the lessee, a payment made under such a guarantee will reduce the obligation to the lessor as the guaranteed residual would obviously be included in the lessee's finance lease obligation. If any part of the guaranteed residual is not called on, then the lessee would treat this as a profit on derecognition of a financial liability.

The effect on the derecognition of the capitalised asset will depend on the extent to which the lessee expected to make the residual payment as this will have affected the level to which the capitalised asset has been depreciated. For example, if the total guaranteed residual was not expected to become payable by the lessee, then the depreciation charge may have been calculated to give a net book value at the end of the lease term equal to the residual element not expected to become payable. If this estimate was correct then the remaining obligation will equal the net book value of the relevant asset, so that the gain on derecognition of the liability will be equal to the loss on derecognition of the asset.

Example 18.10: Early termination of finance leases by lessees

In Example 18.1 at 3.4.1.A. above there is effectively a guarantee of a residual of £3,000 dependent on the mileage done by the leased vehicle. Assuming that the lease is capitalised as a finance lease, if the lessee considers at the lease inception that the guarantee will not be called on, then the lessee will depreciate the vehicle to an estimated residual value of £3,000 over the lease term. In the event the lessee's estimate is found to be correct, then the loss on disposal of the asset at its written down value will be equal and opposite to the gain on derecognition of the lease obligation of £3,000. However, if, for example, £1,000 of the guarantee was called on, whereas the lessee had estimated that it would not be, then the net book value of £3,000 (which assumes that the lessee had not previously adjusted the residual value of the leased asset for depreciation purposes, nor impaired the leased asset) and the unused guarantee of £2,000 will both be derecognised. As a result, a loss of £1,000 will be shown on disposal of the vehicle.

3.7.4.B   Termination and impairment of finance leases by lessors

Although lease receivables are not financial instruments, the carrying amounts recognised by a lessor are subject to the derecognition and impairment provisions of Section 11 (see Chapter 10). Generally, a financial asset is derecognised when the contractual rights to the cash flows from that asset have expired. *[FRS 102.11.33(a)]*. This will apply to most leases at the end of the term when the lessor has no more right to cash flows from the lessee.

If the cash flows from the financial asset have not expired, it is derecognised when, and only when, the entity 'transfers' the asset within the specified meaning of the term in FRS 102, and the transfer has the effect that the entity has either: *[FRS 102.11.33(b)-(c)]*

- transferred substantially all the risks and rewards of the asset; or
- the entity retains some significant risks and rewards of ownership but has transferred control of the asset to another party. The other party has the practical ability to sell the asset in its entirety to an unrelated third party and is able to exercise that ability unilaterally and without needing to impose additional restrictions on the transfer. In this case, the entity must:

  (i)   derecognise the asset; and

  (ii)   recognise separately any rights and obligations retained or created in the transfer.

These requirements are relevant to lease situations such as sub-leases and back-to-back leases.

If a lease receivable is impaired, for example, because the lessee is in default of lease payments, the amount of the impairment is measured as the difference between the carrying value of the receivable and the present value of the estimated future cash flows, discounted at the implicit interest rate used on initial recognition. Therefore, if the lessor makes an arrangement with the lessee and reschedules and/or reduces amounts due under the lease, the loss is by reference to the new carrying amount of the receivable, calculated by discounting the estimated future cash flows at the original implicit interest rate. *[FRS 102.11.25]*. This is the same methodology that was used in Example 18.9 at 3.7.3.A above to reflect a reduction in the estimated residual value.

Chapter 18

Any termination payment received by a lessor on an early termination will reduce the lessor's net investment in the lease shown as a receivable. The recognition of a gain or loss on early termination will depend upon the amount of termination payment received and the value of the leased asset returned to the lessor on termination of the lease. If the sum of the termination payment and value of the asset returned is greater than the carrying amount of the net investment, the lessor will account for a gain on derecognition of the lease; conversely, if the sum of the termination payment and value of the leased asset returned is smaller than the net investment, a loss will be shown. If the leased asset is retained by the lessee on early termination of the lease, the gain or loss recognised by the lessor will depend upon whether the termination payments is greater or smaller than the net investment in the lease.

Losses on termination in the ordinary course of business are less likely to arise because a finance lease usually has termination terms so that the lessor is compensated fully for early termination and the lessor has legal title to the asset. The lessor can continue to include the asset in current assets as a receivable to the extent that sales proceeds or new finance lease receivables are expected to arise. If the asset is then re-leased under an operating lease, the asset may be transferred to property, plant and equipment and depreciated over its remaining useful life. There is no guidance about the amount at which the asset is recognised in PP&E. Although the net investment (i.e. the lease receivable recognised by the lessor) is not a financial instrument (see 3.6 above) and there is no specific guidance, the most straightforward method is for entities to use the carrying amount of the net investment as the cost of the reacquired item of PP&E.

3.7.4.C   Sub-leases and back-to-back leases

It is common for entities whose business is the leasing of assets to third parties to finance these assets themselves through leasing arrangements. There are also arrangements in which a party on-leases assets as an intermediary between a lessor and a lessee while taking a variable degree of risk in the transaction. The appropriate accounting treatment by the intermediate party depends on the substance of the series of transactions. Either the intermediate party will act as lessee to the original lessor and lessor to the ultimate lessee or, if in substance it has transferred the risks and rewards of ownership, it may be able to derecognise the assets and liabilities under its two lease arrangements and recognise only its own commission or fee income. Therefore, in practice, this only creates accounting issues if the lease between the original lessor and the intermediate party is a finance lease.

These are known as sub-leases or back-to-back leases. The difference between the two arrangements is that, for a back-to-back lease, the terms of the two lease agreements match to a greater extent than would be the case for a sub-lease arrangement. This difference is really only one of degree.

The accounting treatment adopted by the lessor and ultimate lessee will not be affected by the existence of sub-leases or back-to-back leases. The original lessor has an agreement with the intermediate party, which is not affected by any further leasing of the assets by the intermediate party unless the original lease agreement is thereby replaced.

Similarly, the ultimate lessee has a lease agreement with the intermediate party. The lessee will have use of the asset under that agreement and must make a decision, in the usual way, as to whether the lease is of a finance or operating type under the requirements of Section 20.

The important decision to be made concerns whether the intermediate party is acting as both lessee and lessor in two related but independent transactions or whether the nature of the interest is such that it need not recognise the rights and obligations under the leases in its financial statements.

In order to analyse the issues that may arise, the various combinations of leases between lessor/intermediate and intermediate/lessee are summarised in the following table:

| | Lessor | Intermediate party | | Lessee |
	Lease to Intermediate	Lease from Lessor	Lease to Lessee	Lease from Intermediate
(1)	Operating lease	Operating lease	Operating lease	Operating lease
(2)	Finance lease	Finance lease	Operating lease	Operating lease
(3)	Finance lease	Finance lease	Finance lease	Finance lease

Only in unusual circumstances could there be an operating lease from the lessor to the intermediate and a finance lease from the intermediate to the lessee. The intermediate would have to acquire an additional interest in the asset from a party other than the lessor in order to be in a position to transfer substantially all of the risks and rewards incidental to ownership of that asset to the lessee.

There are no significant accounting difficulties for the intermediate party regarding (1), an operating lease from the lessor to the intermediate and from the intermediate to the lessee. The intermediate may be liable to the lessor if the lessee defaults, e.g. in some forms of property lease assignment, in which case it would have to make an appropriate provision, but otherwise both contracts are executory and will be accounted for in the usual way.

In situation (2), the intermediate will record at commencement of the lease term an asset acquired under a finance lease and an obligation to the lessor of an equal and opposite amount. As it has granted an operating lease to the lessee, its risks and rewards incidental to ownership of the asset exceed those assumed by the lessee under the lease. It is appropriate for the intermediate party to record an item of PP&E, which it will have to depreciate.

However, under scenario (3), the intermediate is the lessee under a finance lease with the lessor and lessor under a finance lease with the lessee. Its statement of financial position, *prima facie*, records a finance lease receivable from the lessee and a finance lease obligation to the lessor. Both of these are treated as if they are financial instruments for derecognition purposes (see 3.6 above).

The intermediate may be in a position to derecognise its financial asset and liability if it 'transfers' the asset within the specified meaning of the term in FRS 102. 'Transfer' can mean one of two things.

- The entity has transferred substantially all the risks and rewards of the asset to another party. *[FRS 102.11.33(b)]*.
- The entity has transferred control of the asset to another party while retaining some significant risks and rewards of ownership. The other party must have the practical ability to sell the asset in its entirety to an unrelated third party and must be able to exercise that ability unilaterally and without needing to impose additional restrictions on the transfer. In this case, the entity must derecognise the asset, and recognise separately any rights and obligations retained or created in the transfer. *[FRS 102.11.33(c)]*.

Chapter 18

Agents do not retain significant risks and rewards of ownership. An intermediate party that is acting as an agent for the original lessor must be able to demonstrate that it has transferred substantially all the risks and rewards of the asset to another party. If so, then it can derecognise its interest in the two leases. It should not include any asset or obligation relating to the leased asset in its statement of financial position. The income received by the intermediary should be taken to profit or loss on a systematic and rational basis.

If, on the other hand, the intermediate party is taken to be acting as both lessee and lessor in two independent although related transactions, the assets and obligations under finance leases should be recognised in the normal way.

It should not be inferred that all situations encountered can be relatively easily analysed. In practice this is unlikely to be the case, as the risks and rewards will probably be spread between the parties involved.

3.7.5 *Manufacturer or dealer lessors*

Manufacturers or dealers often offer customers the choice of either buying or leasing an asset. While there is no selling profit on entering into an operating lease because it is not the equivalent of a sale, a finance lease of an asset by a manufacturer or dealer lessor gives rise to two types of income:

(a) the profit or loss equivalent to the profit or loss resulting from an outright sale of the asset being leased, at normal selling prices, reflecting any applicable volume or trade discounts; and

(b) the finance income over the lease term. *[FRS 102.20.20]*.

If the customer is offered the choice of paying the cash price for the asset immediately or paying for it on deferred credit terms then, as long as the credit terms are the manufacturer or dealer's normal terms, the cash price (after taking account of applicable volume or trade discounts) can be used to determine the selling profit. However, in many cases such an approach should not be followed as the manufacturer or dealer's marketing considerations often influence the terms of the lease. For example, a car dealer may offer 0% finance deals instead of reducing the normal selling price of his cars. It would be wrong in this instance for the dealer to record a profit on the sale of the car and no finance income under the lease.

Sales revenue is therefore to be based on the fair value of the asset (i.e. usually the cash price) or, if lower, the present value of the minimum lease payments computed at a market rate of interest. As a result, selling profit is restricted to that which would apply if a commercial rate of interest were charged. The cost of sale is reduced to the extent that the lessor retains an unguaranteed residual interest in the asset. Selling profit is recognised in accordance with the entity's policy for outright sales. *[FRS 102.20.21]*. This also means that the entity will ignore artificially low rates of interest quoted by the lessor; profit will be restricted by substituting a market rate of interest. *[FRS 102.20.22]*.

Initial direct costs should be recognised as an expense in the income statement at the inception of the lease when the selling profit is recognised. *[FRS 102.20.22]*. This is not the same as the treatment when a lessor arranges a finance lease where the costs are added to the finance lease receivable; this is because the costs are related mainly to earning the selling profit.

If the manufacturer or dealer is in the relatively unlikely position of incurring an overall loss because the total rentals receivable under the finance lease are less than the cost to it of the asset then this loss should be taken to the income statement at the inception of the lease. This emphasises the importance of calculating an appropriate market interest rate.

If the manufacturer or dealer does not conduct other leasing business, an estimate will have to be made of the implicit rate for the leasing activity.

Example 18.11: Manufacturer or dealer lessors

A company manufactures specialised machinery. The company offers customers the choice of either buying or leasing the machinery. A customer chooses to lease the machinery. Details of the arrangement are as follows:

(i)   The lease commences on 1 January 20X1 and lasts for three years.

(ii) The lessee makes three annual rentals payable in arrears of £57,500.

(iii) The leased machinery is returned to the lessor at the end of the lease.

(iv) Fair value of the machinery is £150,000, which is equivalent to the selling price of the machinery.

(v)   The machinery cost £100,000 to manufacture. The lessor incurred costs of £2,500 to negotiate and arrange the lease.

(vi) The expected useful life of the machinery is 3 years. The machinery has an expected residual value of £10,000 at the end of year three. The estimated residual value does not change over the term of the lease.

(vii) The interest rate implicit in the lease is 10.19%.

The lessor classifies the lease as a finance lease.

The cost to the lessor of providing the machinery for lease consists of the book cost of the machinery (£100,000), plus the initial direct costs associated with entering into the lease (£2,500), less the future income expected from disposing of the machinery at the end of the lease (the present value of the unguaranteed residual value of £10,000, being £7,475). This gives a cost of sale of £95,025.

The lessor records the following entries at the commencement of the lease:

	Debit £	Credit £
Lease receivable	150,000	
Cost of sales	95,025	
Inventory		100,000
Revenue		142,525
Creditors / cash (initial direct costs)		2,500

The sales profit recognised by the lessor at the commencement of the lease is therefore £47,500 (£142,525 − £95,025). This is equal to the fair value of the machinery of £150,000, less the book value of the machinery (£100,000) and the initial direct costs of entering into the lease (£2,500). Revenue is equal to the lease receivable (£150,000), less the present value of the unguaranteed residual value (£7,475).

Lease payments received from the lessee will then be allocated over the lease term as follows:

Year	Lease receivable at the start of the year (£)	Lease payments (£)	Interest income (10.19% per annum) (£)	Decrease in lease receivable (£)	Lease receivable at the end of the year (£)
	(a)	(b)	(c)	(d)=(b)–(c)	(e)=(a)–(d)
1	150,000	57,500	15,280	42,220	107,780
2	107,780	57,500	10,979	46,521	61,260
3	61,260	57,500	6,240	51,260	10,000

The lessor will record the following entries:

		Debit £	Credit £
Year 1	Cash	57,500	
	Lease receivable		42,220
	Interest income		15,280
Year 2	Cash	57,500	
	Lease receivable		46,521
	Interest income		10,979
Year 3	Cash	57,500	
	Lease receivable		51,260
	Interest income		6,240

At the end of the three year lease term, the leased machinery will be returned to the lessor, who will record the following entries:

	Debit £	Credit £
Inventory	10,000	
Lease receivable		10,000

3.8   Accounting for operating leases

3.8.1   *Operating leases in the financial statements of lessees*

Lease payments under an operating lease, excluding costs for services such as insurance and maintenance, are to be recognised as an expense on a straight-line basis over the lease term unless:

(a)   another systematic basis is representative of the time pattern of the user's benefit, even if the payments are not on that basis; or

(b)   the payments to the lessor are structured to increase in line with expected general inflation (based on published indexes or statistics) to compensate for the lessor's expected inflationary cost increases. *[FRS 102.20.15]*.

Payments that vary because of factors other than general inflation will not meet condition (b). *[FRS 102.20.15(b)]*.

Generally, the only bases that are considered acceptable under (a) apart from the straight-line basis are those where rentals are based on a unit of use or unit of production.

Section 20 requires straight-line recognition of the lease expenses that do not fall within (b) even when amounts are not payable on this basis. This does not require the entity to anticipate contingent rental increases, such as those that will result from a periodic re-pricing to market rates or those that are based on some other index. Although FRS 102 is not explicit on this point, we expect that entities will expense these contingent rents as incurred.

However, lease payments may vary over time for other reasons that will have to be taken into account in calculating the annual charge. Described in more detail below are some examples: leases that are inclusive of services and leases with increments intended to substitute for inflation.

Lease incentives are another feature that may affect the cash flows under a lease; they are dealt with in more detail at 3.8.1.C (for lessees) and 3.8.2.A (for lessors).

3.8.1.A   *Lease payments intended to compensate for inflation*

There are some lease payments that increase annually by fixed increments intended to compensate for expected annual inflation over the lease period. Others allow for an annual increase in line with an index but with a fixed minimum increment. As long as the fixed minimum increment reflects expected general inflation, this element of the rental payment will be recognised as an expense as incurred. *[FRS 102.20.15]*. The amount in excess of the fixed minimum increment is a contingent rent and, as discussed above, contingent rents are usually excluded from the lease payments and expensed as incurred.

Escalating payments may be structured to compensate for factors other than expected inflation, e.g. a lessee may arrange a lease that increases in line with expected sales or utilisation of the asset. These annual rent expenses will be recognised on a straight-line basis.

Example 18.12: *Lease payments containing fixed increments*

(a) Entity A operates in a country in which the consensus forecast by local banks is that the general price level index, as published by the government, will increase by an average of 10% annually over the next five years. Entity A leases some office space for five years under an operating lease. The lease payments are structured to reflect the expected 10% annual general inflation (cost and prices index (CPI)) over the five-year term of the lease as follows:

Year	Annual rental £
1	100,000
2	110,000
3	121,000
4	133,000
5	146,000

Entity A recognises annual rent expense equal to the amounts owed to the lessor as shown above.

(b) Entity B has negotiated a lease under which the payments increase by 10% per annum, in order to correspond to the expected growth in its retail activity. The lease payments are the same as above. The increases in rental are not compensation for expected annual inflation. Entity B will recognise an annual rent expense on a straight-line basis of £122,000 each year (the sum of the amounts payable under the lease divided by five years).

(c) Entity C leases a property at an initial rent of £1,000,000 per annum. The lease has a non-cancellable term of 20 years and rent increases annually in line with the CPI of the country in which the property is situated but with a minimum increase of 2% and a maximum of 5% per annum. The estimated long-term rate of inflation in the country in question is 2.5%.

The rental payment charged by the lessor, which will include a minimum increase of 2% per annum whatever the actual rate of inflation, will be recognised as an expense as incurred. The entity will not be obliged to make a straight-line adjustment for the 2% minimum increase. The fixed minimum increment is considered to be a proxy for expected general inflation. It is reasonable to have a range rather than a single figure.

This analysis would be the same if the estimated long-term rate of inflation were some other figure within the range, e.g. 2% or 3%, as long as both the long-term rate and minimum and maximum increases were reasonable estimates in the circumstances of the country in question.

3.8.1.B   *Leases that include payments for services*

There is a wide range of services that can be subsumed into a single 'lease' payment. For a vehicle, the payment may include maintenance and servicing. Property leases could include cleaning, security, reception services, gardening, utilities and local and property taxes. Single payments for operating facilities may include lease payments for the plant and the costs of operating them. The costs of services should be excluded to arrive at the lease payments. This is straightforward enough if the payments are made by the lessor and quantified in the payments made by the lessee. It will be somewhat less so if, for example, the lessor makes all maintenance payments but does not specify the amounts; instead, payments are increased periodically to take account of changes in such costs. In such a case the lessee will have to estimate the amount paid for services and deduct them from the total. The remaining payments, which relate solely to the right to use the asset, will then be spread on a straight-line basis over the non-cancellable term of the lease.

3.8.1.C   *Lease incentives – accounting by lessees*

Incentives that may be given by a lessor to a lessee as an incentive to enter into a new or renewed operating lease agreement include an up-front cash payment to the lessee or the reimbursement or assumption by the lessor of costs of the lessee, such as relocation costs, leasehold improvements and costs associated with a pre-existing lease commitment of the lessee. Alternatively, the lessor may grant the lessee rent-free or reduced rent initial lease periods.

The lessee should recognise the aggregate benefit of incentives as a reduction of rental expense over the lease term, on a straight-line basis unless another systematic basis is representative of the time pattern of the lessee's benefit from the use of the leased asset. *[FRS 102.20.15A]*.

Costs incurred by the lessee, including costs in connection with a pre-existing lease (for example, costs for termination, relocation or leasehold improvements), are to be accounted for by the lessee in accordance with the relevant section of FRS 102. *[FRS 102.20.15A]*.

The following two examples illustrate how to apply the requirements:

Example 18.13:   Accounting for lease incentives

Example 1

An entity agrees to enter into a new lease arrangement with a new lessor. As an incentive for entering into the new lease, the lessor agrees to pay the lessee's relocation costs. The lessee's moving costs are £1,000. The new lease has a term of 10 years, at a fixed rate of £2,000 per year.

The lessee recognises relocation costs of £1,000 as an expense in Year 1. Both the lessor and lessee would recognise the net rental consideration of £19,000 (£2,000 for each of the 10 years in the lease term, less the £1,000 incentive) over the 10 year lease term using a single amortisation method.

Example 2

An entity agrees to enter into a new lease arrangement with a new lessor. The lessor agrees to a rent-free period for the first three years. The new lease has a term of 20 years, at a fixed rate of £5,000 per annum for years 4 to 20.

Net consideration of £85,000 consists of £5,000 for each of 17 years in the lease term. Both the lessor and lessee would recognise the net consideration of £85,000 over the 20-year lease term using a single amortisation method.

Incentives must be spread over the lease term. Incentives are seen in the context of the total cash flows under the lease and, except where the benefit of the lease is not directly related to the time during which the entity has the right to use the asset, cash flows are taken on a straight-line basis.

There is a similar argument when lessees contend that they should not be obliged to spread rentals over a void period as they are not actually benefiting from the property during this time – it is a fit-out period or a start-up so activities are yet to increase to anticipated levels. However, the argument against this is really no different to the above: the lessee's period of benefit from the use of the asset is the lease term, so the rentals should be spread over the lease term, including the initial period.

Section 35 – *Transition to this FRS* – includes a transition exemption that allows first-time adopters of FRS 102 to choose to continue their previous accounting treatment for lease incentives provided the lease term commenced before the date of transition. *[FRS 102.35.10(p)]*. Transition to FRS 102 is discussed in Chapter 33.

3.8.1.D   Onerous contracts

If an operating lease becomes onerous, the entity must also apply Section 21 – *Provisions and Contingencies* (see Chapter 19). *[FRS 102.20.15B]*.

An onerous contract as defined is one in which the unavoidable costs of meeting the obligations under the contract exceed the economic benefits expected to be received under it (see 3.3 above).

The appendix to Section 21 expands on onerous contracts. 'The unavoidable costs under a contract reflect the least net cost of exiting from the contract, which is the lower of the cost of fulfilling it and any compensation or penalties arising from failure to fulfil it. For example, an entity may be contractually required under an operating lease to make payments to lease an asset for which it no longer has any use.' *[FRS 102.21A.2]*.

In an onerous lease, there is a present obligation as a result of a past obligating event. The obligating event is the signing of the lease contract, which gives rise to a legal obligation and the entity is contractually required to pay out resources for which it will not receive commensurate benefits. The entity has to recognise the present obligation under the contract as a provision. *[FRS 102.21A.2]*. This is measured at the best estimate of the amount required to settle the obligation at the reporting date.

Care must be taken to ensure that the lease itself is onerous. If an entity has a number of retail outlets and one of these is loss-making, this is not sufficient to make the lease onerous. However, if the entity vacates the premises and could reasonably sub-let them only at an amount less than the rent it is paying, then the lease becomes onerous and the entity should provide for its best estimate of the unavoidable costs of the lease. The unavoidable costs of the lease will be the remaining lease commitment reduced by the estimated sub-lease rentals that the entity could reasonably obtain, regardless of whether or not the entity intends to enter into a sublease.

Accounting for onerous contracts is discussed in more detail in Chapter 19.

3.8.2 Operating leases in the financial statements of lessors

Lessors should present assets subject to operating leases in their statements of financial position according to the nature of the asset, i.e. usually as PP&E or as an intangible asset. *[FRS 102.20.24]*.

Lease income from operating leases should be recognised in income on a straight-line basis over the lease term, unless another systematic basis is representative of the time pattern of the lessee's benefit from the leased asset. *[FRS 102.20.25]*. Generally, the only other basis that is encountered is based on unit-of-production or service.

In the same way as for lessees, payments to the lessor that are structured to increase in line with expected general inflation (based on published indexes or statistics) to compensate for the lessor's expected inflationary cost increases are exempt from the requirement to be accounted for on a straight-line basis. This is the mirror image of accounting by lessees, so the guidance described in detail at 3.8.1.A above is also relevant for lessors. *[FRS 102.20.25]*.

Lease income excludes receipts for services provided such as insurance and maintenance. Section 23 provides guidance on how to recognise service revenue (see Chapter 20). Costs, including depreciation, incurred in earning the lease income are recognised as an expense. *[FRS 102.20.26]*. Initial direct costs incurred specifically to earn revenues from an operating lease are added to the carrying amount of the leased asset and allocated to profit or loss as an expense over the lease term on the same basis as the lease income. *[FRS 102.20.27]*. This means that the costs will be depreciated on a straight-line basis if this is the method of recognising the lease income, regardless of the depreciation basis of the asset.

As there are no specific requirements about depreciation in Section 20, the entity will depreciate leased assets in a manner that is consistent with the entity's policy for similar assets under Section 17 (see Chapter 15). This also means that the lessor is obliged to consider the residual value, useful life and depreciation method of the assets if there is any indication that these have changed since the last financial statements were prepared. *[FRS 102.17.19, 23]*. There are similar requirements in the case of intangible assets in Section 18 (see Chapter 16) although they rarely have a residual value because of the conditions that must apply before recognition. *[FRS 102.18.23-24]*. These assets are also tested for impairment in a manner consistent with other tangible and intangible fixed assets applying the requirements of Section 27 – *Impairment of Assets* (see Chapter 24). *[FRS 102.20.28]*.

Manufacturer or dealer lessors do not recognise any selling profits on entering into operating leases because they are not the equivalent of a sale. *[FRS 102.20.29]*.

3.8.2.A   Lease incentives – accounting by lessors

In negotiating a new or renewed operating lease, a lessor may provide incentives for the lessee to enter into the arrangement. In the case of a property lease, the tenant may be given a rent-free period but other types of incentive may include up-front cash payments to the lessee or the reimbursement or assumption by the lessor of lessee costs such as relocation costs, leasehold improvements and costs associated with a pre-existing lease commitment of the lessee. FRS 102 requires the lessor to recognise the aggregate cost of incentives as a reduction of rental income over the lease term, on a straight-line basis unless another systematic basis is representative of the time pattern over which the benefit of the leased asset is diminished. *[FRS 102.20.25A]*. Lessor accounting is, therefore, the mirror image of lessee accounting for the incentives, as described at 3.8.1.C above.

Section 35 includes a transition exemption that allows first-time adopters of FRS 102 to choose to continue their previous accounting treatment for lease incentives provided the lease term commenced before the date of transition. *[FRS 102.35.10(p)]*. Transition to FRS 102 is discussed in Chapter 32.

3.8.3   Payments made in connection with the termination of operating leases

Payments for terminating operating leases are extremely common. FRS 102 states that any such costs incurred by the lessee, such as costs for termination of a pre-existing lease, relocation or leasehold improvements are to be accounted for in accordance with the applicable section of the FRS. *[FRS 102.20.15A]*. Example 18.14 below addresses a situation for a variety of payments that might arise in connection with terminating an operating lease over a property and suggests ways in which they might be accounted for.

Example 18.14:   Payments made in connection with terminating an operating lease

Treatment in the financial statements of

Transaction	Lessor	Old tenant	New tenant
Lessor pays			
Old tenant – lessor intends to renovate the building	Expense immediately, or Capitalise as part of the carrying amount of the leased asset if the payment meets the definition of construction costs in Section 17 (note 1)	Recognise income immediately (note 1)	
Old tenant – new lease with higher quality tenant	Expense immediately (note 1)	Recognise income immediately (note 1)	
New tenant – an incentive to occupy	Deferred lease incentive amortised over the lease term on a straight-line basis (see 3.8.2.A above)		Deferred lease incentive amortised over the lease term on a straight-line basis (see 3.8.1.C above)
Building alterations specific to the tenant with no further value to the lessor after completion of the lease period	Deferred lease incentive amortised over the lease term on a straight-line basis (see 3.8.2.A above)		Leasehold improvements capitalised and depreciated. Deferred lease incentive amortised over the lease term on a straight-line basis (see 3.8.1.C above)
Old tenant pays			
Lessor, to vacate the leased premises early	Recognised as income immediately to the extent not already recognised (note 2)	Recognised as expense immediately to the extent not already recognised (note 2)	
New tenant to take over the lease		Recognise as an expense immediately (note 3)	Recognise as income immediately, unless compensation for above market rentals, in which case amortise over expected lease term (note 3)

New tenant pays

Lessor to secure the right to obtain a lease agreement	Recognise as deferred revenue and amortise over the lease term on a straight-line basis (see 3.8.2.A above)	Recognise as a prepayment and amortise over the lease term on a straight-line basis (see 3.8.1.C above)
Old tenant to buy out the lease agreement	Recognise as a gain immediately (note 4)	Recognise as an intangible asset with a finite economic life (note 4)

Note 1   A payment by a lessor to a lessee to terminate the lease is not dealt with under Section 20. If the lessor's payment meets the definition of a cost of an item of PP&E, which might be the case if the lessor intends to renovate, it must be capitalised. *[FRS 102.17.4]*. If not, the payment will be expensed, as it does not meet the definition of an intangible asset in Section 18 (see Chapter 16). *[FRS 102 Appendix I]*. A payment by a lessor to a lessee to terminate the lease in order to re-let it to another tenant does not meet the definition of initial direct costs for arranging a new lease. *[FRS 102.20.9]*. This is because the cost is incurred in relation to the lease with the old tenant, and is not directly related to the new lease, even if the new lease has been entered into. As the lessee has no further performance obligation the receipt should be income.

Note 2   A payment made by the lessee to the lessor to get out of a lease agreement does not meet the appropriate definitions of an asset in Section 17 (see Chapter 15) or Section 18 (as above) and does not fall within Section 20 as there is no longer a lease – the payments are not for the use of the asset. Therefore it should be expensed. Similarly, from the lessor's perspective, income should be recorded. However, if the payment to the lessor to vacate the premises was already stipulated in the original lease contract and the payment was assessed as probable during the life of the contract, both the lessee and lessor would have accrued this over the lease term in accordance with the principles of Section 20.

Note 3   A payment made by an existing tenant to a new tenant to take over the lease would also not meet the definition of an asset under Section 17 or Section 18 (see notes above) and falls outside Section 20 as the lease no longer exists. The old tenant must expense the cost. The new tenant will recognise the payment as income except to the extent that it is compensation for an above-market rental (similar in nature to an incentive to enter into a lease), in which case the receipt is deferred and amortised over the lease term (see 3.8.1.C above).

Note 4   The new tenant has made a payment to an old tenant, and while it is in connection with the lease arrangements, it is not directly related to the actual lease as it was made to a party outside the lease contract. Therefore it cannot be accounted for under Section 20. The old tenant will treat the receipt as a gain immediately. Any remaining balances of the lease will be removed and a net gain (or loss) recorded. The payment by the lessee will generally meet the definition of an intangible asset and therefore will be amortised over the useful life, being the term of the lease. However, if other conditions and circumstances in the arrangement mean that this definition is not met, the payment will be expensed in the period in which it is incurred.

3.8.3.A   *Compensation for loss of profits*

Compensation amounts paid by lessors to lessees are sometimes described as 'compensation for loss of profits' or some similar term. This is a method of calculating the amount to be paid and the receipt is not a substitute for the revenue or profits that the lessee would otherwise have earned. The description will not affect the treatment described above.

3.9 Accounting for modifications to leases

Lessees may renegotiate lease terms for a variety of reasons. They may wish to extend the term over which they have a right to use the asset or to alter the number of assets that they have a right to use. They may consider that the lease is too expensive by comparison with current market terms. The renegotiations may deal with several such issues simultaneously.

Lessors may also renegotiate leases, for example one lessor may sell the lease to another that offers to provide the lease service more cheaply to the lessee, usually because the new lessor's transactions have different tax consequences.

Lease contracts may allow for changes in payments if specified contingencies occur, for example a change in taxation or interest rates.

As described at 3.4.3 above, classification is not changed during the term of the lease, i.e. after its inception, unless the lessee and the lessor agree to change the provisions of the lease (other than simply by renewing the lease), in which case the lease classification must be re-evaluated. *[FRS 102.20.8]*. This means that an agreement that is reclassified (e.g. an operating lease is reassessed as a finance lease or *vice versa*) will be accounted for prospectively in accordance with the revised terms. However, FRS 102 provides no practical guidance on what to take into account to determine whether there would have been a different classification. It does not explain how to account for the consequences of modifications, whether or not they would lead to a different classification. These matters are described below.

Other changes to lease terms that do not lead to reclassification but that nevertheless need to be accounted for, for example variations due to changes in rates of taxation or interest rates, are discussed at 3.9.3 below.

Changes in estimates, for example changes in estimates of the economic life or of the residual value of the leased item, or changes in circumstances, for example default by the lessee, do not result in a different classification. Changes in estimates also include the renewal of a lease or the execution of a purchase option, if these were not considered probable at the inception of the lease (see 3.4.3 above).

3.9.1 Determining whether there is a different classification

This section addresses ways of assessing whether the lease classification has changed. Accounting for reclassified leases is addressed at 3.9.2 below while changes that do not result in reclassification but that must nevertheless be addressed are considered at 3.9.3 below.

While the focus of the section is on ways of quantifying differences between the original and modified lease, all features of any arrangement must be considered as part of an assessment of whether or not the modified lease transfers substantially all of the risks and rewards of ownership. However, in order for a change to the provisions of a lease to result in a change of classification, it must be one that affects the risks and rewards incidental to ownership of the asset by changing the terms and cash flows of the existing lease. An example of such a change is a renegotiation that changes the lease's duration and/or the payments due under the lease.

One of the indicators used in practice is an assessment of the net present value of the minimum lease payments and whether or not these amount to substantially all of the fair value of the leased asset. An entity might use this test to help assess whether the revised lease is a finance or operating lease, in conjunction with a reassessment of the other factors described at 3.4.1 above. Therefore, the entity might use one of the following methods to calculate the net present value:

(a) recalculate, as per the original date of inception of the lease, the net present value of the minimum lease payments based on the revised lease term and cash flows (and revised residual value, if relevant), which will result in a different implicit interest rate to that used in the original calculation;

(b) take into consideration the changes in the agreement but calculate the present value of the asset and liability using the interest rate implicit in the original lease. This approach is consistent with the remeasurement of the carrying value of financial instruments applying the effective interest rate method. This will result in a 'catch up' adjustment as at the date of the reassessment; or

(c) consider the revised agreement to be a new lease and assess the classification based on the terms of the new agreement and the fair value and useful life of the asset at the date of the revision. The inference of this method, unlike (a) and (b), is that the entity already considers that there is likely to be a new classification to the lease, based on an assessment of other factors.

The methodology is straightforward in the case of (a) and (c) above as it involves using updated cash flows, either from inception (method (a)) or from the date of the revised agreement (method(c)) to calculate the net present value, using the methodology described at 3.5 above and illustrated in Example 18.15 below. A lessee under a lease originally classified as an operating lease will be able to apply both of these methods but method (b) will not be available to it unless it has sufficient information to be able to calculate the IIR at the inception of the original lease. Lessees that are party to more complex leases or sale and leaseback arrangements are more likely to have the necessary information available to them.

Each of these three approaches is likely to lead to a different net present value for the minimum lease payments.

Example 18.15: *Modifying the terms of leases*

Details of a non-cancellable lease taken out on the first day of the year are as follows:

(i)   Fair value = £25,000.

(ii) Estimated useful life of asset = 8 years.

(iii) Five annual rentals payable in advance of £4,200.

(iv) At the end of year 5, the asset must be sold and all proceeds up to £8,292 taken by the lessor. If any amount in excess of £8,292 is received, 99% of the excess is repaid to the lessee.

The lease does not contain any renewal options.

The lessee assesses this as an operating lease because the terms suggest that substantially all of the risks and rewards of ownership have not been transferred to it – the lease term is only 62.5% of the useful life of the asset and there is clearly significant residual value.

At the end of year 2, the parties renegotiate the lease, with the changes coming into effect on the first day of year 3. The lease term is to be extended for a further two years, making the term seven years in total. Payments for the four years 3-6 have been reduced to £4,000 and £1,850 is payable for year 7. At the time of the renegotiation the estimated fair value of the asset is £17,500 and its residual value at the end of year 7 is £1,850.

Chapter 18

The implicit interest rate in the original lease can be calculated because the maximum amount receivable by the lessor on the sale of the asset at the end of the lease term is the residual value (on the assumption that the lessor disregards any potential upside in its contingent 1%); the IIR is 5.92%, as follows:

Year	Capital sum at start of period £	Rental paid £	Capital sum during period £	Finance charge (5.92% per annum) £	Capital sum at end of period £
1	25,000	4,200	20,800	1,231	22,031
2	22,031	4,200	17,831	1,056	18,887
3	18,887	4,200	14,687	869	15,556
4	15,556	4,200	11,356	672	12,028
5	12,028	4,200	7,828	464	8,292
		21,000		4,292	

This supports the lessee's assessment that this is an operating lease as the present value of the minimum lease payments (the rentals to be paid over the term discounted at the IIR of 5.92%) is £18,780, which is 75% of the fair value of the asset at the commencement of the lease.

If these revised terms had been in existence at inception then the implicit interest rate and NPV calculation would have been as follows. This corresponds to (a) above.

Year	Capital sum at start of period £	Rental paid £	Capital sum during period £	Finance charge (4.10% per annum) £	Capital sum at end of period £
1	25,000	4,200	20,800	853	21,653
2	21,653	4,200	17,453	715	18,168
3	18,168	4,000	14,168	581	14,749
4	14,749	4,000	10,749	441	11,190
5	11,190	4,000	7,190	294	7,484
6	7,484	4,000	3,484	143	3,627
7	3,627	1,850	1,777	73	1,850
		26,250		3,100	

The NPV of the lessee's minimum lease payments (per the rentals paid above) is £23,603 which is 94% of the fair value of the asset at the commencement of the lease. The lease would be classified as a finance lease.

Method (b) results in the following calculation:

Year	Capital sum at start of period £	Rental paid £	Capital sum during period £	Finance charge (5.92% per annum) £	Capital sum at end of period £
1	25,000	4,200	20,800	1,231	22,031
2	22,031	4,200	17,831	1,056	18,887
3	**17,566**	4,000	13,566	803	14,369
4	14,369	4,000	10,369	613	10,982
5	10,982	4,000	6,982	414	7,396
6	7,396	4,000	3,396	201	3,597
7	3,597	1,850	1,747	103	1,850
		26,250		4,421	

The present value of the total payments over the revised lease term at the original discount rate of 5.92% is £22,585, which is 90.3% of the fair value of the asset at commencement of the lease. In addition, the residual value of £1,850 would have had a present value of only £1,237; it is a feature of the methodology that the present value of the lease payments and the present value of the residual do not add up to the fair value of the asset at inception. In order to make the computation, an adjustment is made to the capital amount as at the date that the lease is renegotiated. The outstanding amount is recomputed from £18,887 (the balance at the end of year 2 calculated using the original assumptions) to £17,566, the amount that corresponds to the new assumptions. Note that it is not relevant that the method results in a change to the 'capital sum' of only 7% ((18,887 − 17,566) ÷ 18,887). The assessment is based on the net present value of the minimum lease payments over the lease term and other features of the revised agreement.

If method (c) is applied, the modified lease is considered as if it were a new five year lease. The IIR calculated prospectively over the remaining term is now 6.13%:

Year	Capital sum at start of period £	Rental paid £	Capital sum during period £	Finance charge (6.13% per annum) £	Capital sum at end of period £
3	17,500	4,000	13,500	827	14,327
4	14,327	4,000	10,327	633	10,960
5	10,960	4,000	6,960	426	7,386
6	7,386	4,000	3,386	207	3,593
7	3,593	1,850	1,743	107	1,850
		17,850		2,200	

The present value of the remaining payments discounted at the IIR of 6.13% is £16,126, which is 92.15% of the fair value of the asset (£17,500) at the date of entering into the new lease.

In this example, all three methods result in a present value of the minimum lease payments that exceeds 90% but this would not, of course, always be the case.

3.9.2 Accounting for reclassified leases

If the original lease was a finance lease and the revised lease is an operating lease, then the balances relating to the finance lease must be derecognised. For the lessee, this involves derecognising both the asset (which will have been depreciated up to the point of derecognition over the shorter of the useful life or the lease term) and the finance lease liability. Finance lease derecognition is discussed further at 3.7.4 above.

If the original lease was an operating lease and the revised lease is a finance lease, then any balances resulting from recognising the lease cost on a straight-line basis will be expensed and the balances relating to the finance lease must be recognised for the first time.

The most obvious way in which to account for the revised finance lease is as a new lease as from the date on which the terms were changed, either based on an implicit interest rate modified to reflect the revised lease term and revised cash flows (method (a) in 3.9.1 above) or the revised lease term, cash flows, and fair value of the assets as at the date of revision (method (c) in 3.9.1 above). In the facts as in Example 18.15 above, the assets and liabilities under the finance lease would be recognised initially as:

- £16,655, being the present value of the revised remaining lease payments applying method (a) from 3.9.1 above; or
- £16,126, being the present value of the revised remaining lease payments applying method (c) from 3.9.1 above.

However, it is also acceptable to recognise the new lease using method (b) above, by taking into consideration the changes in the agreement but calculating the present value of the asset and liability by using the interest rate implicit in the original lease. This uses an accepted methodology and is consistent with the fact that there has, in fact, only been a change to the original terms and not a completely new lease; it also has the advantage that the revised fair value of the asset does not have to be known. In the facts as in Example 18.15 above, this means that the asset and liability would be recorded at £16,178.

If the original lease agreement and the revised lease agreement are both finance leases, then the modification will have accounting consequences that are discussed in the following section.

3.9.3   Changes to leases terms that do not result in reclassification

3.9.3.A   Accounting for changes to the terms of finance leases

If the rights under a finance lease have changed without a change in the classification, these changes to lease term and cash flows must be accounted for.

The two most obvious methods of calculating the impact of the changes are as follows:

(a)   Even though the classification has not changed, the revised agreement is accounted for as if it were a new lease. The calculation will be based on the fair value and useful life of the asset at the date of the revision.

(b)   Use the original IIR to discount the revised minimum lease payments and (for a lessee) adjust any change in lease liability to the carrying amount of the asset. Lessors will adjust the carrying value of the asset, taking gains or losses to income.

These are described at 3.9.1 above (method (c) and method (b)). For lessees, both of these methods will affect the carrying value of the asset and hence its future amortisation.

Another method that might be considered is to reflect changes prospectively over the remaining term of the lease; this is only likely to be appropriate if the cash flows are modified but all other rights remain unchanged, e.g. the effects of a tax or interest variation clause.

3.9.3.B   Accounting for changes to the terms of operating leases

Lessees may renegotiate terms with lessors, e.g. in circumstances in which the lessee has financial difficulties or where there is evidence that the lease terms are at higher than market rates.

Operating leases may include explicit or implicit options to extend the lease and the extension may have different payment terms. If there is a formal option, the lessee might be required to give notice to the lessor of its intention to extend at a set date before the lease expires. There may be similar arrangements with purchase options.

The revised terms should be taken into account prospectively from the date of the agreement. Both previously recognised amounts and aggregate future minimum lease payments should be recognised on a straight-line basis prospectively over the remaining revised lease term, whether or not the original lease contract contained a renewal option. A catch-up adjustment as if the new terms had always existed is not consistent with the fact that the modification is a change in estimate and these are normally accounted for prospectively.

If the lessee renews a lease or exercises a purchase option, it does not have to re-assess the classification of a lease if the renewal and exercise were not considered probable at the inception of the lease (see 3.4.3 above). There may still be accounting consequences in connection with spreading the lease costs because of FRS 102's requirement to expense lease costs on a straight-line basis over the lease term, save in unusual circumstances (see 3.8.1 and 3.8.1.A above).

3.10 Sale and leaseback transactions

These transactions involve the original owner of an asset selling it and immediately leasing it back. The lease payment and the sale price are usually interdependent because they are negotiated as a package. The accounting treatment of a sale and leaseback transaction depends on the type of lease. *[FRS 102.20.32].*

Sometimes, instead of selling the asset outright, the original owner will lease the asset to the other party under a finance lease and then lease it back. Such a transaction is known as a 'lease and leaseback' and has similar effects so for these purposes is included within the term 'sale and leaseback'.

Sale and leaseback transactions are a fairly common feature in sectors that own many properties, such as the retail and hotel industries. Many parties are involved as buyer/lessors, not only finance houses and banks but also pension funds and property groups. From a commercial point of view, the important point of difference lies between an entity that decides that it is cheaper to rent than to own – and is willing to pass on the property risk to the landlord – and an entity which decides to use the property as a means of raising finance – and will therefore retain the property risk. However from the accounting point of view, a major consideration is whether a profit can be reported on such transactions.

These parties will be termed the seller/lessee and buyer/lessor respectively.

The buyer/lessor will treat the lease in the same way as it would any other lease that was not part of a sale and leaseback transaction. The accounting treatment of the transaction by the seller/lessee depends on the type of lease involved, i.e. whether the leaseback is under a finance or an operating lease.

3.10.1 Sale and finance leaseback

In order to assess whether the leaseback is under a finance lease, the seller/lessee will apply the qualitative tests that are described at 3.4.1 above. If a sale and leaseback transaction results in a finance lease, any excess of sales proceeds over the carrying amount should not be recognised immediately as income by a seller/lessee. Instead, the excess is deferred and amortised over the lease term. *[FRS 102.20.33].*

It is inappropriate to show a profit on disposal of an asset which has then, in substance, been reacquired by the entity under a finance lease as the lessor is providing finance to the lessee with the asset as security.

The implication of Section 20 is that the previous carrying value is left unchanged, with the sales proceeds being shown as a liability, usually accounted for under Section 11 (see Chapter 10). The creditor balance represents the finance lease liability under the leaseback. This treatment is consistent with Section 23 (see Chapter 20) as the seller/lessee has by definition not transferred to the buyer the significant risks and rewards of ownership of the goods. *[FRS 102.23.10(a)]*. Therefore it would not be recorded as a sale.

However, another way of accounting for the transaction is for the asset to be restated to its fair value (or the present value of the minimum lease payments, if lower) in exactly the same way as any other asset acquired under a finance lease.

Both treatments have the same net effect on the income statement.

Example 18.16:   Sale and finance leaseback – accounting for the excess sale
proceeds

An asset that has a carrying value of £700 and a remaining useful life of 7 years is sold for £1,200 and leased back on a finance lease. If this is accounted for as a financing transaction with the property used as security for a loan, the asset will remain at £700 and will be amortised over the remaining 7 years at £100 per year.

If it is accounted for as a disposal of the original asset and the acquisition of an asset under a finance lease for £1,200, the excess of sales proceeds of £500 over the original carrying value should be deferred and amortised (i.e. credited to profit or loss) over the lease term.

The net impact on income of the charge for depreciation based on the carrying value of the asset held under the finance lease of £171 and the amortisation of the deferred income of £71 is the same as the annual depreciation of £100 based on the original carrying amount.

If the sales value is less than the carrying amount, the apparent 'loss' does not need to be taken to profit or loss unless there has been an impairment under Section 27. There may be an obvious reason why the sales proceeds are less than the carrying value; for example, the fair value of a second-hand vehicle or item of plant and machinery is frequently lower than its carrying amount, especially soon after the asset has been acquired by the entity. This fall in fair value after sale has no effect on the asset's value-in-use. What this means is that in the absence of impairment, a deficit (sales proceeds lower than carrying value) may be deferred in the same manner as a profit and spread over the lease term.

3.10.2   Sale and operating leaseback

If a sale and leaseback transaction results in an operating lease, and it is clear that the transaction is established at fair value, any profit or loss should be recognised immediately by the seller/lessee. If the sale price is below fair value, any profit or loss should be recognised immediately unless the loss is compensated for by future lease payments at below market price, in which case it should be deferred and amortised in proportion to the lease payments over the period for which the asset is expected to be used. If the sale price is above fair value, the excess over fair value should be deferred and amortised over the period for which the asset is expected to be used. *[FRS 102.20.34]*.

The rationale behind these treatments is that if the sales value is not based on fair values then it is likely that the normal market rents will have been adjusted to compensate. For example, a sale at above fair value followed by above-market rentals is similar to a loan of the excess proceeds by the lessor that is being repaid out of the rentals. Accordingly, the transaction should be recorded as if it had been based on fair value.

Where the sales value is less than fair value there may be legitimate reasons for this to be so, for example where the seller has had to raise cash quickly. In such situations, as the rentals under the lease have not been reduced to compensate, the profit or loss should be based on the sales value.

The following table is intended to assist in interpreting the various permutations of facts and circumstances.

Sale price established at fair value	Carrying amount equal to fair value	Carrying amount less than fair value
Profit	no profit	recognise profit immediately
Loss	no loss	not applicable
Sale price below fair value		
Profit	no profit	recognise profit immediately
Loss *not* compensated for by future lease payments at below market price	recognise loss immediately	recognise loss immediately
Loss compensated for by future lease payments at below market price	defer and amortise loss	defer and amortise loss
Sale price above fair value		
Profit	defer and amortise profit	defer and amortise excess profit
Loss	no loss	no loss

3.10.3 Sale and leaseback arrangements with put and call options

Sale and leaseback arrangements may also include features such as repurchase options. These are not directly addressed by FRS 102 but affect the disposition of risks and rewards in the overall arrangement.

If a lease arrangement includes an option that can only be exercised by the seller/lessee at the then fair value of the asset in question, the risks and rewards inherent in the residual value of the asset have passed to the buyer/lessor. The option amounts to a right of first refusal to the seller/lessee.

Where there is both a put and a call option in force on equivalent terms at a determinable amount other than the fair value, it is clear that the asset will revert to the seller/lessee. It must be in the interests of one or other of the parties to exercise the option so as to secure a profit or avoid a loss, and therefore the likelihood of the asset remaining the property of the buyer/lessor rather than reverting to the seller must be remote. In such a case, this is a bargain purchase option and the seller/lessee has entered into a finance leaseback.

However, the position is less clear where there is only a put option or only a call option in force, rather than a combination of the two. The overall commercial effect will have to be evaluated and one-sided options may be an indication that the arrangement contains non-typical contractual terms which will put it out of scope of lease accounting altogether (see 3.1.3 above).

These arrangements are not common in practice and further discussion is beyond the scope of this publication.

3.11   Disclosures

The disclosure requirements of Section 20 are set out below.

3.11.1   *Disclosures by lessees*

In addition to the specific disclosure requirements for finance and operating leases set out below, Section 3 – *Financial Statement Presentation* – contains the requirement to disclose accounting policies (see Chapter 6).

3.11.1.A   *Disclosure of finance leases*

Lessees must make the following disclosures for finance leases: *[FRS 102.20.13]*

(a)   the net carrying amount at the end of the reporting period by class of asset;

(b)   the total of future minimum lease payments at the end of the reporting period, for each of the following periods:

    (i)   not later than one year;

    (ii)   later than one year and not later than five years; and

    (iii)   later than five years; and

(c)   a general description of the lessee's significant leasing arrangements including, for example, information about contingent rent, renewal or purchase options and escalation clauses, subleases, and restrictions imposed by lease arrangements.

In addition, the requirements for disclosure about assets in accordance with Sections 17, 18 and 27 apply to lessees for assets leased under finance leases (see Chapters 15, 16 and 24). *[FRS 102.20.14]*.

There is no requirement to disclose separately depreciation, amortisation or impairment of assets held under finance leases from owned assets or to disclose separately lease obligations in the statement of financial position.

3.11.1.B   *Disclosure of operating leases*

A lessee must make the following disclosures for operating leases: *[FRS 102.20.16]*

(a)   the total of future minimum lease payments under non-cancellable operating leases for each of the following periods:

    (i)   not later than one year;

    (ii)   later than one year and not later than five years; and

    (iii)   later than five years; and

(b)   lease payments recognised as an expense.

As discussed at 3.4.5 above, in the case of contingencies based on an index, it is our view that disclosure should reflect all contingencies that have occurred in future minimum lease disclosures. This is on the basis that the contingency has occurred and Section 20 specifies disclosure of future minimum lease payments. *[FRS 102.20.16]*.

3.11.2 Disclosures by lessors

3.11.2.A Disclosure of finance leases

A lessor must make the following disclosures for finance leases: *[FRS 102.20.23]*

(a) a reconciliation between the gross investment in the lease at the end of the reporting period, and the present value of minimum lease payments receivable at the end of the reporting period.

In addition, a lessor must disclose the gross investment in the lease and the present value of minimum lease payments receivable at the end of the reporting period, for each of the following periods:

(i) not later than one year;

(ii) later than one year and not later than five years; and

(iii) later than five years;

(b) unearned finance income;

(c) the unguaranteed residual values accruing to the benefit of the lessor;

(d) the accumulated allowance for uncollectible minimum lease payments receivable;

(e) contingent rents recognised as income in the period; and

(f) a general description of the lessor's significant leasing arrangements, including, for example, information about contingent rent, renewal or purchase options and escalation clauses, subleases, and restrictions imposed by lease arrangements.

3.11.2.B Disclosure of operating leases

Lessors must disclose the following for operating leases: *[FRS 102.20.30]*

(a) the future minimum lease payments under non-cancellable operating leases for each of the following periods:

(i) not later than one year;

(ii) later than one year and not later than five years; and

(iii) later than five years;

(b) total contingent rents recognised as income; and

(c) a general description of the lessor's significant leasing arrangements, including, for example, information about contingent rent, renewal or purchase options and escalation clauses, and restrictions imposed by lease arrangements.

As discussed at 3.4.5 above, in the case of contingencies based on an index, it is our view that disclosure should reflect all contingencies that have occurred in future minimum lease disclosures. This is on the basis that the contingency has occurred and Section 20 specifies disclosure of future minimum lease payments. *[FRS 102.20.30]*.

The requirements for disclosure about assets in accordance with Sections 17, 18 and 27 apply to lessors for assets provided under operating leases (see Chapters 15, 16 and 24). *[FRS 102.20.31]*.

Chapter 18

3.11.3   *Disclosures of sale and leaseback transactions*

Disclosure requirements for lessees and lessors apply equally to sale and leaseback transactions. The required description of significant leasing arrangements includes description of unique or unusual provisions of the agreement or terms of the sale and leaseback transactions. *[FRS 102.20.35].*

4   SUMMARY OF GAAP DIFFERENCES

The differences between FRS 102 and IFRS in accounting for leases are set out below.

	FRS 102	*IFRS*
Lessee accounting model	Lessee accounting is driven by whether the lease is classified as an operating lease or a finance lease.	IFRS 16 does not distinguish between finance and operating leases for lessees. Under IFRS 16, a lessee recognises a lease liability and a right-of-use asset on balance sheet for most leases.
Lessor accounting – Leases of land and buildings	FRS 102 is silent about separating the land and buildings elements of leases.	Leases of land are to be assessed separately from building leases and the leases over land classified as finance or operating leases in accordance with the general rules.
Lessor accounting – Straight-line basis for lease payments	Operating lease rentals should be recognised in the income statement on a straight-line basis with one exception: if lease payments increase annually by fixed increments intended to compensate for expected annual inflation over the lease period, the fixed minimum increment that reflects expected general inflation will be recognised as income as incurred.	All operating lease receipts are recognised as income on a straight-line basis, unless another systematic basis is more appropriate.
Lease modifications	Section 20 provides no specific guidance in respect of lease modifications.	A lessor accounts for modifications to an operating lease as a new lease from the effective date of the modification. For other lease modifications, the accounting for both lessee and lessor depends upon whether the modification is considered to give rise to a separate lease or a change in the accounting for the existing lease.

Sale and leaseback accounting	The accounting for a sale and leaseback transaction by a seller-lessee depends upon whether the leaseback is classified as a finance lease or an operating lease. If the leaseback is classified as an operating leaseback, the accounting further depends upon whether the transaction is established at fair value	Both the seller-lessee and buyer-lessor use the definition of a sale in IFRS 15 to determine whether a sale has occurred in a sale and leaseback transaction. If the transfer of the underlying asset satisfies the requirements of IFRS 15 to be accounted for as a sale, the transaction will be accounted for as a sale and leaseback by both the seller-lessee and buyer-lessor. If not, then the transaction will be accounted for as a financing transaction by both parties.
Subleases – accounting by intermediate lessor	Section 20 provides no specific guidance in respect of subleases. The accounting by an intermediate lessor therefore depends upon whether the sublease is classified as an operating lease or a finance lease, based on the extent to which risks and rewards incidental to ownership of the leased asset are passed to the sub-lessee.	Where the head lease is a short-term lease that the entity, as lessee, has elected to account for applying a method like Section 20's operating lease accounting, the intermediate lessor classifies the sublease as an operating lease. Otherwise, the intermediate lessor classifies the sublease as a finance lease or an operating lease by reference to the right-of-use asset that arises under the head lease, rather than by reference to underlying leased asset

References

1 *Consultation Document Triennial review of UK and Ireland accounting standards – Approach to Changes in IFRS*, FRC, September 2016.
2 *Feedback Statement – Consultation Document Triennial review of UK and Ireland accounting standards – Approach to Changes in IFRS*, FRC, June 2017.
3 SSAP 21.15.

4 ASC 840 is superseded by ASC 842, with the effective date depending on the type of entity. Although ASC 842 does not require the use of bright-lines for lease classification in the same way as ASC 840, the implementation guidance in ASC 842-10-55 states that a reasonable approach to applying the lease classification criteria would be to conclude that seventy-five percent or more of the remaining economic life of the underlying asset is a major part of the remaining economic life of that underlying asset.

Chapter 18

Chapter 19

Provisions and contingencies

List of examples

Chapter 19

Provisions and contingencies

1 INTRODUCTION

Section 21 – *Provisions and Contingencies* – addresses the recognition, measurement and disclosure of provisions and the disclosure of contingent liabilities and contingent assets.

The principle of Section 21 for the recognition and measurement of provisions is consistent with that applied by IAS 37 – *Provisions, Contingent Liabilities and Contingent Assets*. A provision should be recognised by an entity if the entity has a present obligation (legal or constructive) as a result of a past event, payment is probable and the amount expected to settle the obligation can be measured reliably. *[FRS 102.21.4]*.

The approach to contingent liabilities and contingent assets under Section 21 is also consistent with that taken by IAS 37. These items should not be recognised on balance sheet but may require disclosure. *[FRS 102.21.12]*. The only exception to this is for contingent liabilities of an acquiree in a business combination, which should be recognised on the balance sheet of the acquirer. *[FRS 102.19.14]*.

However, IAS 37 provides more guidance than Section 21 in certain areas. In addition, there are some minor differences between Section 21 and the equivalent guidance under IFRS. These are addressed at 2 below.

There were no substantial changes made to Section 21 by the FRC as a result of *Amendments to FRS 102 Triennial review 2017 – Incremental improvements and clarifications (Triennial review 2017)*.

2 COMPARISON BETWEEN SECTION 21 AND IFRS

As stated at 1 above, Section 21 and IAS 37 apply the same principle to the recognition and measurement of provisions. The approach to the disclosure of provisions, contingent liabilities and contingent assets is also consistent between Section 21 and IAS 37. The key differences between Section 21 and IFRS are set out at 2.1 to 2.3 below.

2.1 Scope – provisions, contingent liabilities and contingent assets covered by another section

Section 21 does not apply to provisions, contingent liabilities and contingent assets covered by another section of FRS 102. However, where those other sections contain no specific requirements to deal with contracts that have become onerous, Section 21 applies to those contracts. *[FRS 102.21.1]*. This will include, for example, onerous leases and loss-making revenue contracts other than construction contracts. The recognition of provisions for loss making construction contracts is addressed by Section 23. *[FRS 102.23.26]*.

Under IAS 37, where a provision, contingent liability or contingent asset is covered by another IFRS and that IFRS contains no specific requirements to deal with onerous contracts, there is no general requirement that IAS 37 be applied to those contracts. However, IAS 37 states that it does apply to:

- any lease that becomes onerous before the commencement date of the lease;

- short-term leases and leases of low-value assets which are recognised as an expense in accordance with paragraph 6 of IFRS 16 – *Leases* – and have become onerous; and

- contracts with customers that are, or have become, onerous. *[IAS 37.5]*.

2.2 Scope – financial guarantee contracts

Financial guarantee contracts are included in the scope of Section 21 when an entity has chosen to apply the requirements of Sections 11 – *Basic Financial Instruments* – and 12 – *Other Financial Instruments Issues*, for the recognition and measurement of financial instruments. Section 21 does not apply to financial guarantee contracts where:

(a) an entity has chosen to apply IAS 39 – *Financial Instruments: Recognition and Measurement* – and / or IFRS 9 – *Financial Instruments* – to its financial instruments; or

(b) an entity has elected under FRS 103 – *Insurance Contracts* – to continue the application of insurance contract accounting. *[FRS 102.21.1A]*. See 3.2.1.B below.

Under IFRS, financial guarantee contracts are generally accounted for by the issuer in accordance with IAS 32 – *Financial Instruments: Presentation*, IAS 39, IFRS 9 and IFRS 7 – *Financial Instruments: Disclosures*. Financial guarantee contracts issued are generally measured at fair value on initial recognition (subject to certain exemptions), regardless of whether or not it is considered probable that the guarantee will be called, unless the entity has elected under IFRS 4 – *Insurance Contracts* – or IFRS 17 – *Insurance Contracts* – to continue the application of insurance contract accounting. Financial guarantee contracts held are not within the scope of IAS 39 or IFRS 9, nor IFRS 4. As no IFRS applies specifically to the holder of financial guarantee contracts, the holder of financial guarantee contracts may look to the requirements of IAS 37 addressing contingent assets or reimbursement assets in developing an appropriate accounting policy.

2.3   Disclosures

The disclosures required by Section 21 are discussed at 3.10 below.

Section 21 does not refer specifically to the following two specific disclosures required by IAS 37. These are:

- the disclosure of major assumptions concerning future events that may affect the amount required to settle an obligation where this is necessary to provide adequate information; *[IAS 37.85(b)]* and

- a separate line item in the reconciliation of opening and closing provision balances showing the increase during the period in the discounted amount arising from the passage of time and the effect of any change in discount rate. *[IAS 37.84(e)]*. Section 21 allows the line showing additions to provisions in the period to include adjustments that arise from changes in measuring the discounted amount. *[FRS 102.21.14(a)(ii)]*.

Section 21 requires an entity to disclose the expected amount and timing of any payments resulting from an obligation. *[FRS 102.21.14(b)]*. IAS 37 requires disclosure only of the expected timing of payments resulting from an obligation. *[IAS 37.85(a)]*.

Like IAS 37, Section 21 offers an exemption from certain disclosures that would otherwise be required in those extremely rare cases where disclosure of some or all of the information required can be expected to prejudice seriously the position of the entity in a dispute with other parties. *[FRS 102.21.17]*. Under the seriously prejudicial exemption in IAS 37, entities must disclose the general nature of the dispute, together with the fact that, and the reason, the information otherwise required by the standard has not been disclosed. *[IAS 37.92]*. Section 21 includes much more fulsome disclosure requirements in the case where information is considered seriously prejudicial. These requirements are set out at 3.10.5 below and significantly reduce the usefulness of the seriously prejudicial exemption under Section 21.

Section 21 requires an entity to disclose the nature and business purpose of any financial guarantee contracts it has issued, regardless of whether a provision is required or contingent liability disclosed. *[FRS 102.21.17A]*. This is not specifically required under IFRS. In addition, to the extent a provision is recognised, or contingent liability disclosed, for financial guarantee contracts, the general provisions or contingent liabilities disclosures set out at 3.10 below are also required. This is not required under IFRS as financial guarantee contracts are excluded from the scope of IAS 37.

3   REQUIREMENTS OF SECTION 21 FOR PROVISIONS AND CONTINGENCIES

3.1   Terms used in Section 21

The following terms are used in Section 21 with the meanings specified. *[FRS 102 Appendix I]*.

Term	*Definition*
Provision	A liability of uncertain timing or amount.
Liability	A present obligation of the entity arising from past events, the settlement of which is expected to result in an outflow from the entity of resources embodying economic benefits.
Contingent liability	(a) a possible obligation that arises from past events and whose existence will be confirmed only by the occurrence or non-occurrence of one or more uncertain future events not wholly within the control of the entity; or (b) a present obligation that arises from past events but is not recognised because: (i) it is not probable that an outflow of resources embodying economic benefits will be required to settle the obligation; or (ii) the amount of the obligation cannot be measured with sufficient reliability.
Contingent asset	A possible asset that arises from past events and whose existence will be confirmed only by the occurrence or non-occurrence of one or more uncertain future events not wholly within the control of the entity.
Onerous contract	A contract in which the unavoidable costs of meeting the obligations under the contract exceed the economic benefits expected to be received under it.
Probable	More likely than not.
Constructive obligation	An obligation that derives from an entity's actions where: (a) by an established pattern of past practice, published policies or a sufficiently specific current statement, the entity has indicated to other parties that it will accept certain responsibilities; and (b) as a result, the entity has created a valid expectation on the part of those other parties that it will discharge those responsibilities.

Financial guarantee contract	A contract that requires the issuer to make specified payments to reimburse the holder for a loss it incurs because a specified debtor fails to make payments when due in accordance with the original or modified terms of a debt instrument.
Executory contract	A contract under which neither party has performed any obligations or both parties have partially performed their obligations to an equal extent. *[FRS 102.21.1B(c)]*.
Present value	A current estimate of the present discounted value of the future net cash flows in the normal course of business.
Restructuring	A programme that is planned and controlled by management and materially changes either: (a) the scope of the business undertaken by the entity; or (b) the manner in which that business is conducted.
Impracticable	Applying a requirement is impracticable when the entity cannot apply it after making every reasonable effort to do so.

3.2   Scope

Section 21 applies to all provisions, contingent liabilities and contingent assets other than those covered by other sections of FRS 102. Where those other sections contain no specific requirements to deal with contracts that become onerous, Section 21 applies to those contracts. *[FRS 102.21.1]*.

Financial guarantee contracts are included in the scope of Section 21 when an entity has chosen to apply the requirements of Sections 11 and 12 for the recognition and measurement of financial instruments. Section 21 does not apply to financial guarantee contracts where:

- the entity has chosen to apply IAS 39 and / or IFRS 9 to its financial instruments (see Chapter 10); or

- the entity has elected under FRS 103 to continue the application of insurance contract accounting. *[FRS 102.21.1A]*.

Where an entity has chosen to apply IAS 39 and / or IFRS 9 to its financial instruments, the issuer of financial guarantee contracts will account for those contracts as financial instruments under those standards. However, financial guarantee contracts held are not within scope of IAS 39, IFRS 9, or FRS 103 and therefore would fall in scope of Section 21 regardless of whether the elections set out in paragraph 1A of Section 21 are applied.

The requirements of Section 21 relating to financial guarantee contracts are discussed at 3.3.5.F below.

The following table lists the specific types of transaction or circumstances referred to in Section 21 that might give rise to a provision, contingent liability or contingent asset. In some cases, the transaction is identified in Section 21 only to prohibit recognition of any liability, such as for future operating losses (see 3.3.4.A below). This chapter does not address those items identified below as falling outside the scope of Section 21.

Types of transactions or circumstances referred to	In scope	Out of scope	Another section
Restructuring costs	●		
Product warranties / refunds	●		
Legal claims	●		
Reimbursement rights	●		
Future operating costs (e.g. training)	●		
Future operating losses	●		
Onerous contracts	●		
Financial guarantee contracts	●		
Provisions for depreciation, impairment or doubtful debts		●	Section 17 / Section 27 / Section 11 / Section 12
Executory contracts (unless onerous)		●	
Financial Instruments in the scope of Section 11		●	Section 11
Financial Instruments in the scope of Section 12		●	Section 12
Contingent liabilities acquired in a business combination		●	Section 19
Leases (unless onerous operating leases)		●	Section 20
Construction contracts		●	Section 23
Employee benefits		●	Section 28
Income taxes		●	Section 29
Insurance contracts		●	FRS 103

3.2.1   Items outside the scope of Section 21

3.2.1.A   Executory contracts, except where the contract is onerous

Section 21 does not apply to executory contracts unless they are onerous. Executory contracts are contracts under which neither party to the contract has performed any of their obligations or where both parties have performed their obligations to an equal extent. *[FRS 102.21.1B(c)]*. This means that contracts such as supplier purchase contracts and capital commitments, which would otherwise fall within the scope of Section 21, are exempt unless the contract becomes onerous. Onerous contracts are addressed at 3.3.5.A below.

3.2.1.B   Financial instruments

Section 21 does not apply to financial instruments (including loan commitments) that are within the scope of Section 11 – *Basic Financial Instruments* – or Section 12 – *Other Financial Instruments Issues*. *[FRS 102.21.1B(a)]*.

As noted at 3.2 above, an entity must apply Section 21 to financial guarantee contracts unless it has chosen to apply IAS 39 or IFRS 9 to its financial instruments or FRS 103 to continue to account for these guarantees as insurance contracts. *[FRS 102.21.1A]*.

3.2.1.C   Insurance contracts

Insurance contracts (including reinsurance contracts) that an entity issues and reinsurance contracts that the entity holds fall within the scope of FRS 103 and not FRS 102. *[FRS 102.21.1B]*. An insurance contract is defined as 'a contract under which one party (the insurer) accepts significant insurance risk from another party (the policyholder) by agreeing to compensate the policyholder if a specified uncertain future event (the insured event) adversely affects the policyholder'. *[FRS 102 Appendix I]*. A reinsurance contract is 'an insurance contract issued by one insurer (the reinsurer) to compensate another insurer (the cedant) for losses on one or more contracts issued by the cedant'. *[FRS 102 Appendix I]*.

Section 21 also excludes from its scope financial instruments issued by an entity with a discretionary participation feature that are within the scope of FRS 103. *[FRS 102.21.1B]*. These features are most commonly found in life insurance policies and are essentially contractual rights of the holder to receive, as a supplement to guaranteed benefits, significant additional benefits whose amount or timing are contractually at the discretion of the issuer and based on the performance of the insurer, a fund or a specified pool of investments. *[FRS 102 Appendix I]*.

3.2.1.D   Areas covered by other sections of FRS 102

Section 21 does not apply to those provisions covered by other sections of FRS 102. *[FRS 102.21.1]*. However, other than financial instruments and insurance contracts which are explicitly excluded from its scope, Section 21 does not provide any more examples of what transactions or circumstances this exclusion is intended to cover. Examples of other transactions and circumstances which are covered elsewhere and that we would therefore expect to fall outside the scope of Section 21 are included in the table at 3.2 above. However, where those other sections of the FRS do not contain specific requirements on accounting for onerous contracts, Section 21 should be applied. *[FRS 102.21.1]*.

Section 21 notes that the word 'provision' is sometimes used in the context of items such as depreciation, impairment of assets and doubtful debts. Such provisions are not covered by Section 21 because they are adjustments to the carrying amount of assets rather than recognition of liabilities. *[FRS 102.21.3]*.

3.2.1.E   *Provisions compared to other liabilities*

The feature distinguishing provisions from other liabilities, such as trade creditors and accruals, is the existence of uncertainty about the timing or amount of the future expenditure required in settlement. This distinction is not explicitly made in FRS 102 but is explained in IAS 37, which compares provisions to:

(a)   trade payables – liabilities to pay for goods or services that have been received or supplied and have been invoiced or formally agreed with the supplier; and

(b)   accruals – liabilities to pay for goods or services that have been received or supplied but have not been paid, invoiced or formally agreed with the supplier, including amounts due to employees (for example, amounts relating to accrued vacation pay). Although it is sometimes necessary to estimate the amount or timing of accruals, the uncertainty is generally much less than for provisions. *[IAS 37.11]*.

For trade creditors and their associated accruals, there is little uncertainty regarding either the amount of the obligation (which would be determined by the contracted price for the goods and services being provided) or of the timing of settlement (which would normally occur within an agreed period following transfer of the goods and services in question and the issue of an invoice). In practice, however, contracts can be more complex and give rise to a wide range of possible outcomes in terms of the amount or timing of payment. In these circumstances, the difference between provisions and other liabilities is less obvious and judgement may be required to determine where the requirement to make an estimate of an obligation indicates a level of uncertainty about timing or amount that is more indicative of a provision. Such judgements, if significant to the amounts recognised in the financial statements, would merit disclosure (see Chapter 6 at 8.3). *[FRS 102.8.6]*.

One reason why this distinction matters is that provisions are subject to narrative disclosure requirements regarding the nature of the obligation and the uncertainties over timing and amount; and to quantitative disclosures of movements arising from their use, remeasurement or release that do not apply to other payables (see 3.10 below). In fact, although questions of recognition and measurement are important, transparency of disclosure is also a very significant matter in relation to accounting for provisions and ensuring that their effect is properly understood by users of the financial statements.

3.3   Determining when a provision should be recognised

Section 21 requires that a provision should be recognised only when:

(a)   an entity has an obligation at the reporting date as a result as a result of a past event;

(b)   it is probable (i.e. more likely than not) that the entity will be required to transfer economic benefits in settlement; and

(c)   the amount of the obligation can be measured reliably. *[FRS 102.21.4]*.

No provision should be recognised unless all of these conditions are met. Each of these conditions is discussed separately below.

Where all of these three conditions are met, a provision should be recognised as a liability in the statement of financial position. In most cases, the recognition of a provision results in an immediate expense in profit or loss. However, in some cases, it may be appropriate to recognise the amount of the provision as part of the cost of an asset such as inventories or property plant and equipment. *[FRS 102.21.5]*. A common case when a provision is recognised as part of the cost of an asset is in relation to decommissioning costs (see 4.1 below).

3.3.1 The entity has an obligation at the reporting date as a result of a past event

An obligation at the reporting date can be either a legal obligation that can be enforced by law, or a constructive obligation. A constructive obligation arises when an entity has created a valid expectation in other parties that it will discharge the obligation. *[FRS 102.21.6]*. This may be as a result of past practice, published policies or a sufficiently specific current statement. *[FRS 102 Appendix I]*. The entity must have no realistic alternative to settling the obligation, whether legal or constructive, in order to meet condition (a) of the recognition criteria for provisions set out at 3.3 above. *[FRS 102.21.6]*.

The following example from Section 21 illustrates how a constructive obligation may be created. *[FRS 102.21A.5]*.

Example 19.1: Recognising a provision because of a constructive obligation

Refunds policy

A retail store has a policy of refunding purchases by dissatisfied customers, even though it is under no legal obligation to do so. Its policy of making refunds is generally known.

In this scenario, the sale of the product gives rise to a constructive obligation because the store, through its policy and past conduct, has created a valid expectation on the part of its customers that a refund will be given if they are dissatisfied with their purchase.

The assessment of whether an entity has a constructive obligation may not always be straightforward, but in our opinion will have to be accompanied by evidence of communication between the entity and the affected parties in order to be able to conclude that they have a valid expectation that the entity will honour its obligations. In this context, an internal memo or board decision is not sufficient. It is not necessary for the entity to know the identity of the other party. In Example 19.1 above, the other party comprises all the retail store customers and they were aware of the entity's returns policy. Restructuring provisions give rise to another case where judgment is needed to determine whether a valid expectation exists, as discussed at 3.3.5.B below.

In addition to an entity having an obligation at the reporting date, the obligation must arise as a result of a past event. Obligations that will arise from an entity's future actions do not satisfy condition (a) of the recognition criteria set out at 3.3 above, regardless of how likely the future actions are to occur, and even if they are contractual. *[FRS 102.21.6]*. This is illustrated in the following scenarios. *[FRS 102.21.6, 21A.8]*.

Example 19.2: No provision without a past obligating event

Scenario 1: Requirement to fit smoke filters

An entity may intend or need to carry out expenditure to fit smoke filters in a particular type of factory in the future, as a result of either legal requirements or commercial pressures.

In this scenario, the entity can avoid the expenditure required to fit smoke filters by its future actions, for example by changing its method of operation or selling the factory. It therefore has no obligation at the reporting date arising as a result of a past event and no provision is recognised.

Scenario 2: Staff retraining as a result of changes to the income tax system

The government introduces changes to the income tax system. As a result of those changes, an entity in the financial services sector will need to retrain a large proportion of its administrative and sales workforce in order to ensure continued compliance with tax regulations. At the end of the reporting period, no retraining of staff has taken place.

In this scenario, no obligating event for recognising a provision (the retraining itself) has taken place at the reporting date to create a present obligation.

Sometimes it is not always clear whether a present obligation exists as a result of a past event, in which case judgement is required. A common example is a lawsuit, in which the responsibility of the defendant has not yet been established. IAS 37, which shares consistent principles with Section 21 regarding the recognition of provisions, suggests that entities would recognise an obligation if, taking account of all available evidence it is 'more likely than not' that a present obligation exists at the end of the reporting period. *[IAS 37.15]*. In this context, 'all available evidence' would include the opinion of experts together with any additional evidence provided by events after the reporting period. *[IAS 37.16]*. Indeed, Section 32 – *Events after the End of the Reporting Period* – cites the settlement of a court case as such an example of facts that might indicate the existence of an obligation at the reporting date. *[FRS 102.32.5(a)]*.

3.3.2 A transfer of economic benefits is probable

A transfer of economic benefits is considered probable if it is more likely than not to occur. *[FRS 102.21.4]*. In practice this is taken as meaning a probability of greater than 50%.

Where an entity has a number of similar obligations, the probability that a transfer of economic benefits will occur should be based on the class of obligations as a whole. Whilst this is not explicitly stated in Section 21, it is implied in an example in the Appendix, where a manufacturer recognises a provision for warranties given at the time of sale to purchasers of its product. The obligating event is the sale of a product with a warranty and an outflow of resources in settlement is determined to be probable for the warranties as a whole (i.e. it is more likely than not that the entity will have to honour some warranties claims). *[FRS 102.21A.4]*. Warranty provisions are discussed further at 3.3.5.C below.

3.3.3 The amount of the obligation can be measured reliably

Section 21 provides no guidance on how this condition should be applied. The general concept of reliability in Section 2 – *Concepts and Pervasive Principles* – (see Chapter 4) requires only that information is free from material error and bias and faithfully represents that which it either purports to represent or could reasonably be expected to represent. Financial statements are not free from bias (i.e. not neutral) if, by the selection or presentation of information, they are intended to influence the making of a decision or judgement in order to achieve a predetermined result or outcome. *[FRS 102.2.7]*. In addition, to be reliable, the information in financial statements must be complete within bounds of materiality and cost. *[FRS 102.2.10]*. Combined with the requirement that a provision is measured at the 'best estimate' of the amount required to settled the obligation at the reporting date, *[FRS 102.21.7]*, it could be argued that only in rare cases would a lack of a reliable measure prohibit recognition of an obligation. Under the hierarchy set out in Section 10 – *Accounting Policies, Estimates and Errors* – entities may consider the requirements of IAS 37 which takes the view that a sufficiently reliable estimate can almost always be made for a provision where an entity can determine a range of possible outcomes. Hence IAS 37 contends that it will only be in extremely rare cases that a range of outcomes cannot be determined. *[IAS 37.25]*. Whether such a situation is as rare as IAS 37 asserts may be open to question, especially for entities trying to determine estimates relating to potential obligations that arise from litigation and other legal claims. However, given the consistent principles applied by Section 21 and IAS 37 to the recognition of provisions, we would expect entities applying FRS 102 to apply a similarly thorough approach in assessing whether a reliable estimate can be made of the amount of an obligation.

In the event that a present obligation cannot be measured reliably, it is regarded as a contingent liability, *[FRS 102 Appendix I]*, (see 3.4 below).

3.3.4 Cases where recognition of a provision is prohibited

3.3.4.A Future operating losses

Section 21 prohibits the recognition of provisions for future operating losses. *[FRS 102.21.11B]*. This is illustrated by Example 1 in the Appendix to Section 21, which is reproduced below. *[FRS 102.21A.1]*.

Example 19.3: Future operating losses

An entity determines that it is probable that a segment of its operations will incur future operating losses for several years.

In this situation, no provision is recognised. There is no past event that obliges the entity to pay out and expected future losses do not meet the definition of a liability. However, the expectation of future losses may be an indicator that one or more assets are impaired.

As alluded to in Example 19.3, it would be wrong to assume that the prohibition of provisions for future operating losses in Section 21 has effectively prevented the effect of future operating losses from being anticipated. They may sometimes be recognised as a result of requirements in another section of FRS 102. For example:

- under Section 27 – *Impairment of Assets* – the carrying amount of an asset is compared with its recoverable amount when there is an indicator of impairment. If the recoverable amount is lower than the carrying amount then the asset must be impaired to its recoverable amount. The calculation of the recoverable amount should include the effect of any future operating losses (or sub-standard operating profits) on the value of the asset. See Chapter 24;

- under Section 27, inventories are written down to selling price less costs to complete and sell to the extent that they will not be recovered from future revenues, rather than leaving the difference between carrying amount and selling prices less costs to complete and sell to show up as a future operating loss. See Chapter 11 at 3.4; and

- under Section 23 – *Revenue* – provision is made for losses expected on construction contracts when it is probable that contract costs will exceed contract revenue. See Chapter 20 at 3.9.9.

This is therefore a rather more complex issue than Section 21 acknowledges. Indeed, Section 21 itself has to navigate closely the dividing line between the general prohibition of the recognition of future losses and the recognition of contractual or constructive obligations that are expected to give rise to losses in future periods.

3.3.4.B   Staff training costs

Example 19.2 at 3.3.1 above reproduces an example from Section 21 where the government introduces changes to the income tax system. An entity needs to retrain a large proportion of its administrative and sales workforce in order to ensure continued compliance with tax regulations. Section 21 argues that there is no present obligation until the actual training has taken place and so no provision should be recognised. In many cases the need to incur training costs could also be avoided by the entity by its future actions. For example, the cost could be avoided by hiring new staff who were already appropriately trained.

3.3.5   Examples of provisions in Section 21

3.3.5.A   Onerous contracts

Although future operating losses in general cannot be provided for, Section 21 requires that 'if an entity has an onerous contract, the present obligation under the contract shall be recognised and measured as a provision'. *[FRS 102.21.11A]*.

FRS 102 defines an onerous contract as a 'contract in which the unavoidable costs of meeting the obligations under the contract exceed the economic benefits expected to be received under it.' *[FRS 102 Appendix I]*. This seems to require that the contract is onerous to the point of being directly loss-making, not simply uneconomic by reference to current prices.

The unavoidable costs under a contract reflect the least net cost of exiting from the contract. This is the lower of the cost of fulfilling it and any compensation or penalties arising from failure to fulfil it. *[FRS 102.21A.2]*. This evaluation does not require an intention by the entity to fulfil or to exit the contract. It does not even require there to be specific terms in the contract that apply in the event of its termination or breach. Its purpose is to recognise only the unavoidable costs to the entity. In the absence of specific clauses in the contract relating to termination or breach the unavoidable cost could include an estimation of the cost of walking away from the contract and having the other party go to court for compensation for the resultant breach.

There is a subtle yet important distinction between making a provision in respect of the unavoidable costs under a contract (reflecting the least net cost of what the entity has to do) compared to making an estimate of the cost of what the entity *intends* to do. The first is an obligation, which merits the recognition as a provision. The second is a choice of the entity, which fails the recognition criteria because it does not exist independently of the entity's future actions, *[FRS 102.21.6]*, and is therefore akin to a future operating loss.

Example 19.4:   Onerous supply contract

Entity P negotiated a contract in 2016 for the supply of components when availability in the market was scarce. It agreed to purchase 100,000 units per annum for 5 years commencing 1 January 2017 at a price of £20 per unit. Since then, new suppliers have entered the market and the typical price of a component is now £5 per unit. Whilst its activities are still profitable (Entity P makes a margin of £6 per unit of finished product sold) changes to the entity's own business means that it will not use all of the components it is contracted to purchase. As at 31 December 2019, Entity P expects to use 150,000 units in future and has

55,000 units in inventory. The contract requires 200,000 units to be purchased before the agreement expires in 2021. If the entity terminates the contract before 2021, compensation of £1 million per year is payable to the supplier. Each finished product contains one unit of the component.

Therefore, the entity expects to achieve a margin of £900,000 (150,000 × £6) on the units it will produce and sell; but will make a loss of £15 (£20 – £5) per unit on each of the 105,000 components (55,000 + 200,000 – 150,000) it is left with at the end of 2021 and now expects to sell in the components market.

In considering the extent to which the contract is onerous, Entity P in the example above must compare the net cost of the excess units purchased of £1,575,000 (105,000 × £15) with the related benefits, which includes the profits earned as a result of having a secure source of supply. Therefore the supply contract is onerous (directly loss making) only to the extent of the costs not covered by related revenues, justifying a provision of £675,000 (£1,575,000 – £900,000).

Section 21 gives the example of a contractual requirement to make payments under an operating lease for an asset which is no longer used by a business as an example of an onerous contract. However, it provides no specific guidance on the recognition or measurement of provisions for onerous leases. The most common examples of onerous contracts in practice relate to leasehold property. The recognition and measurement of provisions for vacant leasehold property is discussed at 4.10 below. The recognition and measurement of provisions for occupied leasehold property is discussed in detail in Chapter 27 at 6.2.1 of EY International GAAP 2019.

3.3.5.B   Restructuring provisions

An entity should recognise a provision for restructuring costs only when it has a legal or constructive obligation at the reporting date to carry out the restructuring. *[FRS 102.21.11D]*.

The specific requirements within Section 21 for the recognition of a restructuring provision seek to define the circumstances that give rise to a constructive obligation to restructure. Section 21 restricts the recognition of a restructuring provision to cases when an entity:

- has a detailed formal plan for the restructuring identifying at least:
  - the business or part of a business concerned;
  - the principal locations affected;
  - the location, function, and approximate number of employees who will be compensated for terminating their services;
  - the expenditures that will be undertaken; and
  - when the plan will be implemented; and
- has raised a valid expectation in those affected that it will carry out the restructuring by starting to implement that plan or announcing the main features to those affected by it. *[FRS 102.21.11C]*.

A restructuring is defined as 'a programme that is planned and controlled by management, and materially changes either:

- the scope of a business undertaken by an entity; or
- the manner in which that business is conducted'. *[FRS 102 Appendix I]*.

In practice a restructuring may include changes such as the sale or termination of a line of business, the closure of business locations in a country or region, changes in management structure or fundamental reorganisations that have a material effect on the nature and focus of the entity's operations. Whilst the definition of a restructuring may be widely interpreted, there must be a material change to either the scope of the business or the way in which it is conducted, which goes beyond normal changes arising as a result of operating in a dynamic business environment. This may be a subjective judgement. However, it is important in order to prevent entities from classifying all kinds of operating costs as restructuring costs, thereby inviting the user of the accounts to perceive them differently from the 'normal' costs of operating in a dynamic business environment.

The following examples taken from the Appendix to Section 21 illustrate how a constructive obligation for a restructuring may or may not be created. *[FRS 102.21A.6-7]*.

Example 19.5:   *The effect of timing of the creation of a constructive obligation on the recognition of a restructuring provision*

Scenario 1: Closure of a division – no implementation before the end of the reporting period

On 12 December 2019 the board of an entity decided to close down a division. Before the end of the reporting period (31 December 2019) the decision was not communicated to any of those affected and no other steps had been taken to implement the decision.

In these circumstances, no provision is recognised at 31 December 2019 because the actions of management prior to this date are insufficient to create a constructive obligation.

Scenario 2: Closure of a division – Communication and implementation before the end of the reporting period

On 12 December 2019, the board of an entity decided to close a division making a particular product. On 20 December 2019 a detailed plan for closing the division was agreed by the board, letters were sent to customers warning them to seek an alternative source of supply, and redundancy notices were sent to the staff of the division.

The communication of management's decision to customers and employees on 20 December 2019 creates a valid expectation that the division will be closed, thereby giving rise to a constructive obligation from that date. Accordingly a provision is recognised at 31 December 2019 for the best estimate of the costs of closing the division.

In practice it can be very difficult to determine whether it is appropriate to recognise a provision for the future costs of a restructuring programme. The determination of whether an organisational change is a material change or just part of a process of continuous improvement is a subjective judgement. Once it has been established that the activities in question constitute a restructuring rather than an ongoing operating cost, it can be difficult to determine whether management's actions before the reporting date have been sufficient to have 'raised a valid expectation in those affected'. *[FRS 102.21.11C(b)]*. Even if a trigger point is easily identifiable, such as the date of an appropriately detailed public announcement, it might not necessarily commit management to the whole restructuring, but only to specific items of expenditure such as redundancy costs. When the announcement is less clear, referring for example to consultations, negotiations or voluntary arrangements, particularly with employees, judgement is required. Furthermore, taken on its own, the 'valid expectation' test is at least as open to manipulation as one based on the timing of a board decision. Entities anxious to accelerate or postpone recognition of a liability could do so by advancing or deferring an event that signals such a commitment, such as a public announcement, without any change to the substance of their position.

In these situations it is important to consider all the related facts and circumstances and not to focus on a single recognition criterion. The objective of the analysis is to determine whether there is a past obligating event at the reporting date. The guidance in Section 21 about restructuring, referring as it does to constructive obligations and valid expectations is ultimately aimed at properly applying the principle in Section 21 that only those obligations arising from past events and existing independently of an entity's future actions are recognised as provisions. *[FRS 102.21.6]*. In essence, a restructuring provision qualifies for recognition if, as at the reporting date, it relates to a detailed plan of action from which management cannot realistically withdraw.

Section 21 does not address which costs may or may not be included within a restructuring provision. IAS 37, which contains consistent principles to Section 21 on the measurement of provisions, imposes criteria to restrict the types of cost that can be provided for. They specify that a restructuring provision should include only the direct expenditures arising from the restructuring, which are those that are both:

- necessarily entailed by the restructuring; and
- not associated with the ongoing activities of the entity. *[IAS 37.80]*.

IAS 37 gives specific examples of costs that may not be included within the provision, because they relate to the future conduct of the business. Such costs include:

- retraining or relocating continuing staff;
- marketing; and
- investing in new systems and distribution networks. *[IAS 37.81]*.

Given the consistent principles of Section 21 with IAS 37 in respect of the recognition of provisions, including restructuring provisions, entities may consider it appropriate under the hierarchy in Section 10 to apply the criteria above in quantifying a restructuring provision under Section 21. The application of these criteria would ensure that entities do not contravene the general prohibition in Section 21 against provisions for operating losses. *[FRS 102.21.11B]*.

Costs that should and should not be included in a restructuring provision under IAS 37 are discussed further in Chapter 27 at 6.1.4 of EY International GAAP 2019.

3.3.5.C Warranty provisions

Warranty provisions are specifically addressed by Example 4 in the Appendix to Section 21, which is reproduced in Examples 19.7 and 19.8 at 3.7.1 and 3.7.2 below.

In Examples 19.7 and 19.8 the assessment of the probability of an outflow of economic resources is made across the population of warranties as a whole, and not using each potential claim as the unit of account. This makes it more likely that a provision will be recognised, because the probability criterion is considered in terms of whether at least one item in the population will give rise to a payment. Recognition then becomes a matter of reliable measurement and entities calculate an expected value of the estimated warranty costs.

3.3.5.D Refunds policy

Example 5 from the Appendix of Section 21 (reproduced in Example 19.1 above) addresses a retail store that has a policy of refunding goods returned by dissatisfied customers. There is no legal obligation to do so, but the company's policy of making refunds is generally known. The example argues that the conduct of the store has created a valid expectation on the part of its customers that it will refund purchases. The obligating event is the original sale of the item, and the probability of some economic outflow is greater than 50%, as there will nearly always be some customers demanding refunds. Hence, a provision should be made for the best estimate of the amount required to settle the refunds. *[FRS 102.21A.5]*.

The assessment of whether a provision is required may be straightforward when the store has a very specific and highly publicised policy on refunds. However, some stores' policies on refunds might not be so clear cut. A store may offer refunds under certain conditions, but not widely publicise its policy. In these circumstances, there might be doubt as to whether the store has created a valid expectation on the part of its customers that it will honour all requests for a refund.

3.3.5.E   Litigation and other legal costs

The Appendix to Section 21 includes an example of a court case to illustrate how the principles of Section 21 distinguish between a contingent liability and a provision in such situations. This example is reproduced in Example 19.6 at 3.4 below. However, the assessment of the particular case in the example is clear-cut. In most situations, assessing the need to provide for legal claims is one of the most difficult tasks in the field of provisioning. This is due mainly to the inherent uncertainty in the judicial process itself, which may be very long and drawn out. Furthermore, this is an area where either provision or disclosure might risk prejudicing the outcome of the case, because they give an insight into the entity's own view on the strength of its defence that can assist the claimant. Similar considerations apply in other related areas, such as tax disputes.

Whether an entity should make provision for the costs of settling a case or to meet any award given by a court will depend on a reasoned assessment of the particular circumstances, based on appropriate legal advice. The evidence to be considered should also include any additional evidence occurring after the end of the reporting period that confirms whether the entity had a present obligation at the reporting date. This is relevant if, for example, the court case is settled in the period between the reporting date and the date on which the financial statements are authorised for issue. *[FRS 102.32.5(a)]*.

3.3.5.F   Financial guarantee contracts

A financial guarantee contract is a 'contract that requires the issuer to make specified payments to reimburse the holder for a loss it incurs because a specified debtor fails to make payments when due in accordance with the original or modified terms of a debt instrument'. *[FRS 102 Appendix I]*.

As discussed at 3.2 above, in some cases, financial guarantee contracts may be excluded from the scope of Section 21. For financial guarantee contracts in the scope of Section 21, a provision should be recognised if the general recognition criteria for provisions are met. This would include it being probable that the issuer would be required to make a payment under the guarantee.

3.4 Contingent liabilities

A contingent liability is defined as:

- a possible obligation that arises from past events and whose existence will be confirmed only by the occurrence or non-occurrence of one or more uncertain future events not wholly within the control of the entity; or

- a present obligation that arises from past events but is not recognised because:

  - it is not probable that an outflow of resources embodying economic benefits will be required to settle the obligation; or

  - the amount of the obligation cannot be measured with sufficient reliability.

  [FRS 102 Appendix I].

The term 'possible' is not defined in FRS 102. Literally, it could mean any probability greater than 0% and less than 100%. However, since 'probable' is defined as 'more likely than not', *[FRS 102 Appendix I]*, it would be reasonable to use the term 'possible' in the context of contingent liabilities as meaning a probability of 50% or less. Accordingly, the above definition restricts contingent liabilities to those where either the existence of an obligation or an outflow of economic resources is less than 50% probable, or in those rare cases when a probable obligation cannot be measured with sufficient reliability.

Section 21 requires that contingent liabilities should not be recognised as liabilities on the balance sheet. The only exception to this is contingent liabilities of an acquiree in a business combination. *[FRS 102.21.12]*. Such contingent liabilities are covered by the requirements of Section 19 – *Business Combinations and Goodwill* (see Chapter 17).

Information about contingent liabilities should be disclosed unless the probability of an outflow of resources is remote (see 3.10 below). *[FRS 102.21.12]*. When an entity is jointly and severally liable for an obligation (see 3.7.6 below), the part of the obligation that is expected to be met by other parties is treated as a contingent liability and disclosed. *[FRS 102.21.12]*.

Although it is not explicitly required by Section 21, we would expect contingent liabilities to be assessed continually to determine whether an outflow of resources embodying economic benefits has become probable. Where this becomes the case, then the provision should be recognised in the period in which the change in probability occurs, except in the circumstances where no reliable estimate can be made. This is illustrated by Example 9 to Section 21, which is reproduced below. *[FRS 102.21A.9]*.

Example 19.6: *When the likelihood of an outflow of economic benefits becomes probable*

A customer has sued Entity X, seeking damages for injury the customer allegedly sustained from using a product sold by Entity X. Entity X disputes liability on grounds that the customer did not follow directions in using the product. Up to the date the board authorised the financial statements for the year to 31 December 2018 for issue, the entity's lawyers advise that it is probable that the entity will not be found liable. However, when the entity prepares the financial statements for the year to 31 December 2019, its lawyers advise that, owing to developments in the case, it is now probable that the entity will be found liable.

At 31 December 2018, no provision is recognised and the matter is disclosed as a contingent liability unless the probability of any outflow is regarded as remote. On the basis of evidence available when the financial statements were approved, there is no obligation as a result of a past event.

At 31 December 2019, a provision is recognised for the best estimate of the amount required to settle the obligation as at that date. The fact that an outflow of economic benefits is now believed to be probable means that there is a present obligation. The expense is recognised in profit or loss. It is not a correction of an error in 2018 because, on the basis of the evidence available when the 2018 financial statements were approved, a provision should not have been recognised at that time.

3.5   Contingent assets

A contingent asset is defined as 'a possible asset that arises from past events and whose existence will be confirmed only by the occurrence or non-occurrence of one or more uncertain future events not wholly within the control of the entity'. *[FRS 102 Appendix I]*. In contrast to the case of contingent liabilities (see 3.4 above), the word 'possible' in the context of contingent assets is not confined to a probability level of 50% or less because Section 21 states that a contingent asset should never be recognised. *[FRS 102.21.13]*.

Only when the flow of economic benefits to the entity is virtually certain is the related asset not contingent and capable of recognition. *[FRS 102.21.13]*. 'Virtually certain' is not defined in FRS 102. However, in addressing the same requirements in IAS 37, this has been interpreted as being as close to 100% as to make the remaining uncertainty insignificant. We would expect a similar interpretation under FRS 102.

Contingent assets should be disclosed when an inflow of economic benefits is probable, *[FRS 102.21.13]*, with 'probable' meaning 'more likely than not'. *[FRS 102 Appendix I]*. The disclosure requirements for contingent assets are discussed at 3.10.4 below.

As with contingent liabilities, we would expect contingent assets to be assessed continually to ensure that developments are appropriately reflected in the financial statements. If it has become virtually certain that an inflow of economic benefits will arise, the asset and the related income should be recognised in the period in which the change occurs.

3.6   How probability determines whether to recognise or disclose

The following matrix summarises the treatment of contingencies under Section 21:

Likelihood of outcome	*Accounting treatment: contingent liability*	*Accounting treatment: contingent asset*
Virtually certain	Recognise	Recognise
Probable	Recognise	Disclose
Possible, but not probable	Disclose	No disclosure permitted
Remote	No disclosure required	No disclosure permitted

FRS 102 does not put a numerical measure of probability on either 'virtually certain' or 'remote'. In our view, the use of such measures would downgrade a process requiring the exercise of judgement into a mechanical exercise. It is difficult to imagine circumstances when an entity could reliably determine an obligation to be, for example, 92%, 95% or 99% likely, let alone be able to compare those probabilities objectively. Accordingly, we think it is reasonable to regard 'virtually certain' as describing a likelihood that is as close to 100% as to make any remaining uncertainty insignificant; to see 'remote' as meaning a likelihood of an outflow of resources that is not significant; and for significance to be a matter for judgement and determined according to the merits of each case.

3.7 Initial measurement

3.7.1 Best estimate of provision

Section 21 requires the amount recognised as a provision to be the best estimate of the amount required to settle the obligation at the reporting date. This is the amount an entity would rationally pay to settle the obligation at the end of the reporting period or to transfer it to a third party at that time. *[FRS 102.21.7]*.

It is implicit in the definition of a provision that there are often uncertainties around the amount of the outflow required by an entity. Section 21 sets out different approaches to dealing with these uncertainties in arriving at an estimate of the provision, depending upon whether it arises from a single obligation or from a large population of items.

Where a provision arises from a single obligation, the individual most likely outcome may be the best estimate of the amount required to settle the obligation. However, even in such a case, the other possible outcomes should be considered. When the other possible outcomes are mostly higher than the most likely outcome, the best estimate will be higher than the individual most likely amount. Conversely, when other possible outcomes are mostly lower, the best estimate will be lower than the individual most likely amount. *[FRS 102.21.7(b)]*. In effect, this adjustment builds into the measure of the provision an allowance to reflect the risk that the actual outcome is an amount other than the individual most likely outcome.

When the provision involves a large population of items, the best estimate of the amount required to settle the obligation should reflect the weighting of all possible outcomes by their associated probabilities, i.e. a probability-weighted expected value calculation should be performed. *[FRS 102.21.7(a)]*. This method is illustrated by Example 4 in the Appendix to Section 21, which considers the estimation of a provision for product warranties, as set out below. *[FRS 102.21A.4]*.

Example 19.7: Calculation of expected value: warranties

A manufacturer gives warranties at the time of sale to purchasers of its product. Under the terms of the contract for sale, the manufacturer undertakes to make good, by repair or replacement, manufacturing defects that become apparent within three years from the date of sale. On the basis of experience, it is probable that there will be some claims under the warranties. Accordingly it is determined that the obligating event is the sale of a product with a warranty and an outflow of resources in settlement is probable for the warranties as a whole (i.e. it is more likely than not that the manufacturer will have to settle some warranties given on past sales). The entity therefore recognises a provision for the best estimate of the costs of making good under the warranty products sold before the reporting date.

In 2019, goods are sold for £1,000,000. Experience indicates that 90 per cent of products sold require no warranty repairs; 6 per cent of products require minor repairs costing 30 per cent of the sale price; and 4 per cent of products require major repairs or replacement costing 70 per cent of sale price. Therefore, estimated warranty costs are:

Possible outcome	Probability weighted cost	Expected value (£)
No repair required	£1,000,000 × 90% × 0	0
Minor repairs	£1,000,000 × 6% × 30%	18,000
Major repairs	£1,000,000 × 4% × 70%	28,000
Expected value		46,000

Where the provision involves a large population of items and there is a continuous range of possible outcomes, and each point in that range is as likely as any other, the mid-point of the range is used as the best estimate of the amount required to settle the obligation. *[FRS 102.21.7(a)].*

3.7.2   Discounting the estimated cash flows to a present value

When the effect of the time value of money is material, the amount of a provision should be the present value of the amount expected to be required to settle the obligation. The discount rate (or rates) should be a pre-tax rate (or rates) that reflect(s) current market assessments of the time value of money and the risks specific to the liability. The risks specific to the liability should be reflected either in the discount rate or in the estimation of the amounts required to settle the obligation, but not both. *[FRS 102.21.7].*

This requirement is illustrated in the following example taken from the Appendix to Section 21. *[FRS 102.21A.4].*

Example 19.8:   Discounting the estimated cash flows to a present value

The fact pattern is the same as Example 19.7 above, with the probability-weighted estimate of total warranty costs for goods sold in 2019 expected to be £46,000. In this case, the expenditures for warranty repairs and replacements are expected to be made 60 per cent in 2020, 30 per cent in 2021 and 10 per cent in 2022, in each case at the end of the period. Because the estimated cash flows already reflect the probabilities of the cash outflows, and assuming there are no other risks or uncertainties that must be reflected, to determine the present value of those cash flows the entity uses a 'risk free' discount rate based on government bonds with the same term as the expected cash outflows (6 per cent for one-year bonds and 7 per-cent for two-year and three-year bonds). Calculation of the present value, at the end of 2019, of the estimated cash flows related to the warranties for products sold in 2019 is as follows:

Year		Expected cash payments (£)	Discount rate	Discount factor	Present value (£)
1	60% × £46,000	27,600	6%	0.9434 (at 6% for 1 year)	26,038
2	30% × £46,000	13,800	7%	0.8734 (at 7% for 2 years)	12,053
3	10% × £46,000	4,600	7%	0.8163 (at 7% for 3 years)	3,755
Present value					41,846

The entity will recognise a warranty obligation of £41,846 at the end of 2019 for products sold in 2019.

FRS 102 gives no further guidance on how an entity should determine the appropriate discount rate to use. However, the example above refers to a government bond rate with a similar term as the related obligation. This is consistent with the application of similar requirements in IAS 37.

The main types of provision where the impact of discounting will be significant are those relating to decommissioning and other environmental restoration liabilities, which are discussed at 4.1 and 4.2 below.

3.7.2.A   Real or nominal rate

Section 21 does not indicate whether the discount rate should be a real discount rate or a nominal discount rate. The discount rate to be used depends on whether:

- the future cash flows are expressed in current prices, in which case a real discount rate (which excludes the effects of general inflation) should be used; or

- the future cash flows are expressed in expected future prices, in which case a nominal discount rate (which includes a return to cover expected inflation) should be used.

Either alternative is acceptable, and these methods may produce the same amount for the initial present value of the provision. However, the effect of the unwinding of the discount will be different in each case (see 3.8.1 below).

3.7.2.B   Adjusting for risk and using a government bond rate

Section 21 requires that risk is taken into account in the calculation of a provision, but gives little guidance as to how this should be done. It merely states that the risks specific to the liability should be reflected in either the discount rate or in the estimate of the amounts required to settle the obligation, but not in both. *[FRS 102.21.7]*. One may use a discount rate that reflects the risk associated with the liability (a risk-adjusted rate). The following example, taken from the Accounting Standard Board's (ASB's) Working Paper *Discounting in Financial Reporting*[1] shows how an entity might calculate such a risk adjusted rate.

Example 19.9:   Calculation of a risk-adjusted rate

A company has a provision for which the expected value of the cash outflow in three years' time is £150, and the risk-free rate (i.e. the nominal rate unadjusted for risk) is 5%. However, the possible outcomes from which the expected value has been determined lie within a range between £100 and £200. The company is risk averse and would settle instead for a certain payment of, say, £160 in three years' time rather than be exposed to the risk of the actual outcome being as high as £200. The effect of risk in calculating the present value can be expressed as either:

(a)   discounting the risk-adjusted cash flow of £160 at the risk-free (unadjusted) rate of 5%, giving a present value of £138; or

(b)   discounting the expected cash flow (which is unadjusted for risk) of £150 at a risk-adjusted rate that will give the present value of £138, i.e. a rate of 2.8%.

As can be seen from this example, the risk-adjusted discount rate is a *lower* rate than the unadjusted (risk-free) discount rate. This may seem counter-intuitive initially, because the experience of most borrowers is that banks and other lenders will charge a higher rate of interest on loans that are assessed to be higher risk to the lender. However, in the case of a provision a risk premium is being suffered to eliminate the possibility of the actual cost being higher (thereby capping a liability), whereas in the case of a loan receivable a premium is required to compensate the lender for taking on the risk of not recovering its full value (setting a floor for the value of the lender's financial asset). In both cases the actual cash flows incurred by the paying entity are higher to reflect a premium for risk. In other words, the discount rate for an asset is increased to reflect the risk of recovering less and the discount rate for a liability is reduced to reflect the risk of paying more.

A problem with changing the discount rate to account for risk is that this adjusted rate is a theoretical rate, as it is unlikely that there would be a market assessment of the risks specific to the liability alone. *[FRS 102.21.7]*. However the lower discount rate in the above example is consistent with the premise that a risk-adjusted liability should be higher than a liability without accounting for the risk that the actual settlement amount is different to the estimate. It is also difficult to see how a risk-adjusted rate could be obtained in practice. In the above example, it was obtained only by reverse-engineering; it was already known that the net present value of a risk-adjusted liability was £138, so the risk-adjusted rate was just the discount rate applied to unadjusted cash flow of £150 to give that result.

The alternative approach, to adjust the cash flows instead of using a risk-adjusted discount rate, *[FRS 102.21.7]*, is conceptually more straightforward, but still presents the problem of how to adjust the cash flows for risk. It could be inferred from Example 19.7 at 3.7.1 above that estimated cash flows which reflect the probabilities of cash outflows represent risk adjusted cash flows. However, whilst a best estimate based solely on the expected value approach or the mid-point of a range addresses the uncertainties relating to there being a variety of possible outcomes, it does not fully reflect risk, because the actual outcome could still be higher or lower than the estimate. Nevertheless, adjusting estimated cash flows to reflect risk may be easier than attempting to risk-adjust the discount rate.

Where the risks specific to the liability are reflected in the estimated cash flows, they should not also be included in the discount rate. *[FRS 102.21.7]*. The discount rate to be applied in this case should therefore be a risk free rate. As suggested in Example 19.8 at 3.7.2 above, it would be appropriate to apply a government bond rate with a similar currency and remaining term as the provision. It follows that because a risk-adjusted rate is always lower than the risk-free rate, an entity cannot justify the discounting of a provision at a rate higher than a government bond rate with a similar currency and term as the provision.

In recent years, government bond rates have been more volatile as markets have changed rates to reflect (among other factors) heightened perceptions of sovereign debt risk. The question has therefore arisen whether government bond rates, at least in certain jurisdictions, should continue to be regarded as the default measure of a risk-free discount rate. Whilst the current volatility in rates has highlighted the fact that no debt (even government debt) is totally risk free, the challenge is to find a more reliable measure as an alternative. Any adjustment to the government bond rate to 'remove' the estimate of sovereign debt risk is conceptually flawed, as it not possible to isolate one component of risk from all the other variables that influence the setting of an interest rate. Another approach might be to apply some form of average bond rate over a period of 3, 6 or 12 months to mitigate the volatility inherent in applying the spot rate at the period end. However, this is clearly inappropriate given the requirements in Section 21 to determine the best estimate of an obligation by reference to the expenditure required to settle it 'at the reporting date' *[FRS 102.21.7]* and to determine the discount rate on the basis of 'current market assessments' of the time value of money. *[FRS 102.21.7]*.

With 'risk' being a measure of potential variability in returns, it remains the case that in most countries a government bond will be subject to the lowest level of variability in that jurisdiction. As such, it normally remains the most suitable of all the observable measures of the time value of money in a particular country. When government bond rates are negative or, more likely, result in a negative discount rate once adjusted for risk, we believe that it is not appropriate to apply a floor of zero to the discount rate as this would result in an understatement of the liability. As discussed above, and at 3.7.2.A, there are various approaches to determining an appropriate discount rate. It may sometimes be the case that one or more of the acceptable approaches result in a negative discount rate whereas the application of an alternative permitted approach would not. In order to avoid some of the presentational difficulties associated with a negative discount rate, entities faced with a negative real discount rate before risk adjustment may wish to consider the alternative approach of discounting expected future cash flows expressed in future prices, at a nominal discount rate (see 3.7.2.A above), if the nominal rate is not negative. Similarly, entities that are faced with a negative risk-adjusted discount rate only because of risk adjustment (i.e. where risk free rates themselves are not negative) may wish to adopt the alternative approach of adjusting the estimated future cash flows to reflect the risks associated with the liability, rather than risk-adjusting the discount rate.

3.7.2.C   Own credit risk is not taken into account

In adjusting either the estimated cash flows or discount rate for risk, an entity should not adjust for its own credit risk (i.e. the risk that the entity could be unable to settle the amount finally determined to be payable). This is because Section 21 requires either the discount rate or estimated cash flows to reflect 'the risks specific to the liability'. *[FRS 102.21.7]*. Credit risk is a risk of the entity rather than a risk specific to the liability.

3.7.3   Anticipating future events that may affect the estimate of cash flows

The amount that an entity expects will be required to settle an obligation in future may depend upon expectations and assumptions concerning future events, such as changes in legislation or technological advances. Section 21 does not address the extent to which such expectations should be built into an entity's best estimate of the amount required to settle the obligation. IAS 37 provides guidance in this area. Given the consistent principles of Section 21 and IAS 37 regarding the measurement of provisions, entities may therefore look to IAS 37 for further guidance. IAS 37 states that 'future events that may affect the amount required to settle an obligation shall be reflected in the amount of a provision where there is sufficient objective evidence that they will occur'. *[IAS 37.48]*.

The requirement for objective evidence means that it is not appropriate to reduce the best estimate of future cash flows simply by assuming that a completely new technology will be developed before the liability is required to be settled. There will need to be sufficient objective evidence that such future developments are likely. For example, an entity may believe that the cost of cleaning up a site at the end of its life will be reduced by future changes in technology. The amount recognised has to reflect a reasonable expectation of technically qualified, objective observers, taking account of all available evidence as to the technology that will be available at the time of the clean-up. It would be appropriate to include, for example, expected cost reductions associated with increased experience in applying existing technology. *[IAS 37.49]*.

Similarly, if new legislation is to be anticipated, IAS 37 requires that there needs to be evidence both of what the legislation will demand and whether it is virtually certain to be enacted and implemented. In many cases sufficient objective evidence will not exist until the new legislation is enacted. *[IAS 37.50]*.

3.7.4   Provisions should exclude gains on expected disposal of assets

An entity should exclude gains from the expected disposal of assets from the measurement of a provision. *[FRS 102.21.8]*. We would instead expect such gains to be recognised at the time specified by the relevant section of FRS 102 dealing with the assets concerned. This is likely to be of particular relevance in relation to restructuring provisions which are discussed at 3.3.5.B above.

3.7.5   Reimbursement of amounts required to settle a provision

An entity may sometimes be reimbursed all or part of an amount required to settle a provision, for example through an insurance claim. The reimbursement should be recognised only when it is virtually certain that the entity will receive the reimbursement on settlement of the obligation. *[FRS 102.21.9]*. It should be recognised as an asset in the statement of financial position and should not be offset against the provision. *[FRS 102.21.9]*. However, the expense relating to a provision can be presented net of reimbursement in the income statement. *[FRS 102.21.9]*. The amount recognised for the reimbursement should not exceed the amount of the provision. *[FRS 102.21.9]*.

Except when an obligation is determined to be joint and several (see 3.7.6 below), any form of net presentation in the balance sheet is prohibited. This is because the entity would remain liable for the whole cost if the third party failed to pay for any reason, for example as a result of the third party's insolvency.

3.7.6   Joint and several liability

When an entity is jointly and severally liable for an obligation, it recognises only its own share of the obligation, based on the amount that it is probable that the entity will pay. The remainder that is expected to be met by other parties is treated as a contingent liability. *[FRS 102.21.12]*.

Arguably, the economic position in the case of joint and several liability is no different than if the entity was liable for the whole obligation but expected to be reimbursed part of the amount required to settle the provision under the terms of an insurance contract.

In both cases, the entity is exposed to further loss in the event that the other parties are unable or unwilling to pay. However, in the case of joint and several liability, the entity and the parties with whom it shares liability each have a direct (albeit shared) obligation for the past event. This contrasts with the case where the entity expects to be reimbursed part of the amount required to settle a provision. In this case, the insurance company from whom the reimbursement is expected has a contractual relationship only with the entity and has no direct obligation for the past event itself. Accordingly, any disclosed liability should not be reduced on the basis that the entity holds valid insurance against the obligation.

3.8   Subsequent measurement of provisions

After initial recognition, provisions should be reviewed at each reporting date and adjusted to reflect the current best estimate of the amount required to settle the obligation. *[FRS 102.21.11]*. Any adjustments to the amounts previously recognised should be recognised in profit or loss unless the provision was originally recognised as part of the cost of an asset. *[FRS 102.21.11]*.

An entity should charge against a provision only those expenditures for which the provision was originally recognised. *[FRS 102.21.10]*. Therefore, if a provision is no longer required, the amount of the provision should be reversed. Provisions may not be redesignated or used for expenses for which the provision was not originally recognised.

When a provision is measured at the present value of the amount required to settle the obligation, the unwinding of the discount should be recognised as a finance cost in profit or loss in the period it arises. *[FRS 102.21.11]*. However, the amount of finance cost recognised as an unwinding of the discount depends upon whether the provision has been discounted at a real or a nominal rate, and also whether the entity has used a risk free or risk adjusted discount rate. This is not addressed by Section 21 but is discussed at 3.8.1 and 3.8.2 below. In addition, Section 21 provides no guidance on the effect of changes in interest rates on the discount rates applied. This is discussed at 3.8.3 below.

3.8.1   *Unwinding of the discount: impact of using real or nominal discount rates*

As discussed at 3.7.2.A above, Section 21 provides no guidance on whether a real or nominal discount rate should be used to discount a provision. Whilst both methods may produce the same figure for the initial present value of the provision, the effect of the unwinding of the discount will be different in each case. This is best illustrated by way of an example.

Example 19.10:   Effect on future profits of choosing a real or nominal discount rate

A provision is required to be set up for an expected cash outflow of £100,000 (estimated at current prices), payable in three years' time. The appropriate nominal discount rate is 7.5%, and inflation is estimated at 5%.

If the provision is discounted using the nominal rate, the expected cash outflow has to reflect future prices. Accordingly, if prices increase at the rate of inflation, the cash outflow will be £115,762 (£100,000 × 1.05^3). The net present value of £115,762, discounted at 7.5%, is £93,184 (£115,762 × 1 ÷ $(1.075)^3$).

If all assumptions remain valid throughout the three-year period, the movement in the provision would be as follows:

	Undiscounted cash flows	Provision
	£	£
Year 0	115,762	93,184
Unwinding of discount (£93,184 × 0.075)		6,989
Revision to estimate		–
Year 1	115,762	100,173
Unwinding of discount (£100,173 × 0.075)		7,513
Revision to estimate		–
Year 2	115,762	107,686
Unwinding of discount (£107,686 × 0.075)		8,076
Revision to estimate		–
Year 3	115,762	115,762

If the provision is calculated based on the expected cash outflow of £100,000 (estimated at current prices), then it needs to be discounted using a real discount rate. This may be thought to be 2.5%, being the difference between the nominal rate of 7.5% and the inflation rate of 5%. However, it is more accurately calculated using the Fisher relation (an equation used to estimate the relationship between real and nominal interest rates under inflation) or formula as 2.381%, being $(1.075 \div 1.05) - 1$. Accordingly, the net present value of £100,000, discounted at 2.381%, is £93,184 ($£100,000 \times 1 \div (1.02381)^3$), the same as the calculation using future prices discounted at the nominal rate.

If all assumptions remain valid throughout the three-year period, the movement in the provision would be as follows:

	Undiscounted cash flows	Provision
	£	£
Year 0	100,000	93,184
Unwinding of discount (£93,184 × 0.02381)		2,219
Revision to estimate (£100,000 × 0.05)	5,000	4,770
Year 1	105,000	100,173
Unwinding of discount (£100,173 × 0.02381)		2,385
Revision to estimate (£105,000 × 0.05)	5,250	5,128
Year 2	110,250	107,686
Unwinding of discount (£107,686 × 0.02381)		2,564
Revision to estimate (£110,250 × 0.05)	5,512	5,512
Year 3	115,762	115,762

Although the total expense in each year is the same under either method, what will be different is the allocation of the change in provision between operating costs (assuming the original provision was treated as an operating expense) and finance charges. It can be seen from the second table in the above example that using the real discount rate will give rise to a much lower finance charge each year. However, this does not lead to a lower provision in the balance sheet at the end of each year. Provisions have to be revised annually to reflect the current best estimate of the amount required to settle the obligation. *[FRS 102.21.11]*. Thus, the provision in the above example at the end of each year needs to be adjusted to reflect current prices at that time (and any other adjustments that arise from changes in the estimate of the provision), as well as being adjusted for the unwinding of the discount. For example, the revised provision at the end of Year 1 is £100,173, being £105,000 discounted for two years at 2.381%. After allowing for the unwinding of the discount, this required an additional provision of £4,770.

3.8.2 Unwinding of the discount: impact of using risk-free or risk-adjusted discount rates

The decision made by an entity to use a risk free or risk adjusted discount rate impacts on the unwinding of the discount and the amount recognised in finance costs in respect of the unwind. This is illustrated in the following example:

Example 19.11: Effect on future profits of choosing a risk-free or risk-adjusted discount rate

A company is required to make a provision for which the expected value of the cash outflow in three years' time is £150, when the risk-free rate (i.e. the rate unadjusted for risk) is 5%. However, the possible outcomes from which the expected value has been determined lie within a range between £100 and £200. The reporting entity is risk averse and would settle instead for a certain payment of, say, £160 in three years' time rather than be exposed to the risk of the actual outcome being as high as £200. The measurement options to account for risk can be expressed as either:

(a) discounting the risk-adjusted cash flow of £160 at the risk free (unadjusted) rate of 5%, giving a present value of £138; or

(b) discounting the expected cash flow (which is unadjusted for risk) of £150 at a risk-adjusted rate that will give the present value of £138, i.e. a rate of 2.8%

Assuming that there are no changes in estimate required to be made to the provision during the three-year period, alternative (a) will unwind to give an overall finance charge of £22 and a final provision of £160. Alternative (b) will unwind to give an overall finance charge of £12 and a final provision of £150.

In Example 19.11 above, the unwinding of different discount rates gives rise to different provisions. The difference of £10 (£22 – £12) relates to the risk adjustment that has been made to the provision. As the actual date of settlement comes closer, the estimates of the range of possible outcomes (and accordingly the expected value of the outflow) and the premium the entity would accept for certainty will converge. As such, the effect of any initial difference related to the decision to apply a risk-free or risk-adjusted rate will be lost in the other estimation adjustments that would be made over time.

3.8.3 The effect of changes in interest rates on the discount rate applied

Section 21 requires the discount rate to reflect current market assessments of the time value of money. *[FRS 102.21.7]*. It follows that where interest rates change, the provision should be recalculated on the basis of revised interest rates. This will give rise to an adjustment to the carrying value of the provision, but Section 21 does not address how this should be classified in the income statement. We believe that the adjustment to the provision is a change in accounting estimate, as defined in Section 10. Accordingly, it should be reflected in the line item of the income statement in which the expense establishing the provision was originally recorded. Where the original provision was recorded as part of the cost of an asset such as inventory or property, plant and equipment, the effect of any subsequent adjustment to discount rates should be added to or deducted from the cost of the asset to which the provision relates.

Calculating this adjustment is not straightforward either, because Section 21 gives no guidance on how it should be done. For example, should the new discount rate be applied during the year or just at the year-end and should the rate be applied to the new estimate of the provision or the old estimate? Because Section 21 requires the value of a provision to reflect the best estimate of the expenditure required to settle the obligation to be assessed as at the end of the reporting period, *[FRS 102.21.7]*, it would appear that the effect of a change in the estimated discount rate is accounted for prospectively from the end of the reporting period. This is illustrated in the following example:

Example 19.12:   Accounting for the effect of changes in the discount rate

A provision is required to be set up for an expected cash outflow of £100,000 (estimated at current prices), payable in three years' time. The appropriate nominal discount rate is 7.5%, and inflation is estimated at 5%. At future prices the cash outflow will be £115,762 (£100,000 × 1.05³). The net present value of £115,762, discounted at 7.5%, is £93,184 (£115,762 × 1 ÷ (1.075)³).

At the end of Year 2, all assumptions remain valid, except it is determined that a current market assessment of the time value of money and the risks specific to the liability would require a decrease in the discount rate to 6.5%. Accordingly, at the end of Year 2, the revised net present value of £115,762, discounted at 6.5%, is £108,697 (£115,762 ÷ 1.065).

The movement in the provision would be reflected as follows:

	Undiscounted cash flows	Provision
	£	£
Year 0	115,762	93,184
Unwinding of discount (£93,184 × 0.075)		6,989
Revision to estimate		–
Year 1	115,762	100,173
Unwinding of discount (£100,173 × 0.075)		7,513
	115,762	107,686
Revision to estimate (£108,697 – £107,686)		1,011
Year 2	115,762	108,697
Unwinding of discount (£108,697 × 0.065)		7,065
Revision to estimate		–
Year 3	115,762	115,762

In Year 2, the finance charge is based on the previous estimate of the discount rate and the revision to the estimate of the provision would be charged to the same line item in the income statement that was used to establish the provision of £93,184 at the start of Year 1.

3.9   Funding commitments (other than loan commitments)

The requirements of FRS 102 regarding funding commitments, other than commitments to make a loan, are set out in Section 34 – *Specialised Activities*, rather than in Section 21. Nevertheless, an entity is required to consider the requirements of both Section 21 and Section 2 when accounting for funding commitments. *[FRS 102.34.58]*. Loan commitments fall within the scope of Section 11 and Section 12. *[FRS 102.34.57]*. In our opinion, it would also be appropriate to regard other commitments to provide resources that will result in the recognition of a financial instrument as being within the scope of Sections 11 and 12 (see Chapter 10).

3.9.1   Recognition of a funding commitment as a liability

Section 34 requires that an entity recognises a liability and, usually, a corresponding expense, when it has made a commitment that it will provide resources to another party, if, and only if:

(a)   the definition and recognition criteria for a liability have been satisfied (see 3.3 above);

(b)   the obligation (which may be a constructive obligation) is such that the entity cannot realistically withdraw from it; and

(c)   the entitlement of the other party to the resources does not depend on the satisfaction of performance-related conditions. *[FRS 102.34.59]*.

The definition of a liability requires that there be a present obligation, and not merely an expectation of a future outflow. *[FRS 102.34A.1]*. A general statement that the entity intends to provide resources to certain classes of potential beneficiaries in accordance with its objectives does not in itself give rise to a liability, as the entity may amend or withdraw its policy, and potential beneficiaries do not have the ability to insist on their fulfilment. Similarly, a promise to provide cash conditional on the receipt of future income in itself may not give rise to a liability where the entity cannot be required to fulfil it if the future income is not received and it is probable that the economic benefits will not be transferred. *[FRS 102.34A.2]*.

A liability is recognised only for a commitment that gives the recipient a valid expectation that payment will be made and from which the grantor cannot realistically withdraw. One of the implications of this is that a liability only exists where the commitment has been communicated to the recipient. *[FRS 102.34A.3]*.

Commitments that are performance-related will be recognised when those performance-related conditions are met. *[FRS 102.34.60]*. Performance-related conditions are defined in FRS 102 as conditions that require the performance of a particular level of service or units of output to be delivered, with payment of, or entitlement to, the resources conditional on that performance. *[FRS 102 Appendix I]*. Commitments are not recognised if they are subject to performance-related conditions. In such a case, the entity is required to fulfil its commitment only when the performance-related conditions are met and no liability exists until that time. *[FRS 102.34A.4]*.

A commitment may contain conditions that are not performance-related conditions. For example, a requirement to provide an annual financial report to the grantor may serve mainly as an administrative tool because failure to comply would not release the grantor from its commitment. This may be distinguished from a requirement to submit a detailed report for review and consideration by the grantor of how funds will be utilised in order to secure payment. A mere restriction on the specific purpose for which the funds are to be used does not in itself constitute a performance-related condition. *[FRS 102.34A.5]*.

Whether an arrangement gives rise to a funding commitment and when such commitments are recognised is a matter of judgement based on the facts and circumstances of the case, as illustrated in Example 19.13 below.

Example 19.13: Accounting for donations to non-profit organisations

An entity decides to enter into an arrangement to 'donate' £1m in cash to a university. A number of different options are available for the arrangement and the entity's management want to determine whether the terms of these options make any difference to the timing, measurement or presentation of the £1m expenditure, as follows:

Option 1:
The entity enters into an unenforceable contract to contribute £1m for general purposes. The benefits to the entity are deemed only to relate to its reputation as a 'good corporate citizen'; the entity does not receive any consideration or significant benefit from the university in return for the donation.

Option 2:
As per Option 1 except the entity publishes a press release in relation to the donation and announcing that payment is to be made in equal instalments of £200,000 over 5 years.

Option 3:
As per Option 2, except that the contract is legally enforceable in the event that the entity does not pay all the instalments under the contract.

Option 4:
As per Option 2, except that the entity is only required to make the donation if the university raises £4m from other sources.

Option 5:
As per Option 2, except that the contract is legally enforceable and the funds will be used for research and development activities specified by the entity. The entity will retain proprietary rights over the results of the research.

Applying the requirements in respect of funding commitments discussed above:

- In Option 1, the contract is unenforceable, there is no announcement or conditions preceding payment and there is no exchange of benefits. Accordingly, an expense would be recognised only when the entity transfers cash to the university.

- For Option 2, it may be appropriate for the entity to conclude that the entity's announcement of the donation to be paid by instalments indicates that there is a constructive obligation because the entity has created a valid expectation that it will make all of the payments promised. Alternatively, it could determine that once the first instalment is paid, the entity has created a valid expectation that it will make the remaining payments. This is a matter of judgement. In this case the entity would recognise an expense and a liability, measured at the net present value of the 5 instalments of £200,000, at the point when it is determined that a constructive obligation exists.

- Option 3 involves an enforceable contract with no exchange of benefits. Therefore a liability and an expense are recognised on signing the enforceable contract, measured at the present value of the 5 instalments of £200,000.

- Under Option 4, the contract is unenforceable and the donation is subject to a performance condition. In these circumstances, no liability exists until the performance condition is met (i.e. when the additional funds have been raised). *[FRS 102.34.60]*. Only then would a liability and expense be recognised, measured at the net present value of the £1m promised.

- Option 5 involves an enforceable contract. Therefore a liability is recognised when the contract is signed. In addition, there is an exchange of benefits relating to the research and development activities performed on behalf of the entity. Whether these benefits have a value close to the present value of the 5 instalments of £200,000 is a matter of judgement. If it is determined that this is an exchange transaction, the entity would apply the criteria in Section 18 – *Intangible Assets other than Goodwill* – to determine whether an asset or expense could be recognised for the related research and development costs (see Chapter 16).

Where the arrangement gives rise to an exchange transaction rather than a donation, the expenditure incurred by the donor is recorded in accordance with the relevant section of FRS 102. An exchange transaction is a reciprocal transfer in which each party receives and sacrifices approximately equal value. Assets and liabilities are not recognised until each party performs their obligations under the arrangement.

3.10 Presentation and disclosure

3.10.1 Presentation of provisions

For UK companies and LLPs preparing financial statements using statutory formats rather than 'adapted formats', provisions within the scope of Section 21 would fall within the statutory caption 'Other provisions' within the heading 'Provisions for liabilities'. 'Other provisions' can be shown either on the face of the balance sheet or in the notes to the accounts. See Chapter 6 at 5.3.11.

Companies and LLPs using 'adapted formats' must present current and non-current provisions separately on the face of the balance sheet. *[FRS 102.4.2A]*. See Chapter 6 at 5.1.9.

3.10.2 Disclosures about provisions

For each class of provision an entity should provide a reconciliation showing:

(a) the carrying amount at the beginning and end of each period;

(b) additions during the period, including adjustments that result from changes in measuring the discounted amount;

(c) amounts charged against the provision during the period; and

(d) unused amounts reversed during the period. *[FRS 102.21.14]*.

Disclosure (b) requires additions in the period and adjustments that result from changes in measuring the discounted amount to be disclosed as one line item in the reconciliation. This differs from the disclosure requirements of IAS 37, which requires the disclosure of additions during the period and the increase in the discounted amount of the provision arising from the passage of time and the effect of any changes in discount rates as separate line items within the reconciliation. *[IAS 37.84]*.

In addition, for each class of provision, an entity should disclose:

(a) a brief description of the nature of the obligation and the expected amount and timing of any resulting payments;

(b) an indication of the uncertainties about the amount or timing of those outflows; and

(c) the amount of any expected reimbursements, stating the amount of any asset that has been recognised for the expected reimbursement. *[FRS 102.21.14]*.

Disclosure (a) requires disclosure of the expected amount and timing of any resulting payments. This differs from IAS 37 which requires disclosure only of the expected timing of outflows. *[IAS 37.85(a)]*. In many cases, the expected amount of the payments will be the same as the carrying amount of the provision at the end of the period. However, where a provision has been discounted to its present value it is unclear from Section 21 whether the disclosure of the expected amount of payments should be expressed based on current prices or expected future prices.

Comparative information is not required for any of the disclosures about provisions. *[FRS 102.21.14]*.

Where a transfer has been made to any provision for liabilities, or from any provision for liabilities other than for the purpose for which the provision was established, UK Company Law (i.e. the Regulations) and the LLP Regulations require disclosure, in tabular form, of:

• the amount of provisions at the beginning and the end of the year and as at the balance sheet date;

• any amounts transferred to or from provisions during the year; and

• the source and application of any amounts so transferred.

Particulars must be given of each provision included within the statutory heading 'other provisions' in any case where the amount of that provision is material. *[1 Sch 59, 2 Sch 70, 3 Sch 77, 1 Sch 57 (LLP)]*.

3.10.3   Disclosures about contingent liabilities

Unless the possibility of any outflow of resources in settlement is remote, an entity should disclose, for each class of contingent liability at the reporting date, a brief description of the nature of the contingent liability and, when practicable:

• an estimate of its financial effect, measured in accordance with paragraphs 7 to 11 of Section 21 (see 3.7 above);

• an indication of the uncertainties relating to the amount or timing of any outflow; and

• the possibility of any reimbursement. *[FRS 102.21.15]*.

If it is impracticable to make one or more of these disclosures, that fact should be stated. *[FRS 102.21.15]*. Applying a requirement is impracticable when the entity cannot apply it after making every reasonable effort to do so. *[FRS 102 Appendix I]*.

Section 21 does not define or put a numerical measure of probability on the term 'remote'. In our view, it is reasonable to interpret 'remote' as meaning a likelihood of an outflow of resources that is not significant (see 3.6 above).

The Regulations and LLP Regulations require disclosure of the particulars and the total amount of any financial commitments, guarantees and contingencies that are not included in the balance sheet. *[1 Sch 63(2), 2 Sch 77(1), 3 Sch 81(2), 1 Sch 60(2) (LLP)]*. An indication of the nature and form of any valuable security given by the entity in respect of those commitments, guarantees and contingencies must be given. *[1 Sch 63(3), 2 Sch 77(2), 3 Sch 81(3), 1 Sch 60(3) (LLP)]*. The total amount of those commitments concerning pensions must be separately disclosed. *[1 Sch 63(4), 2 Sch 77(3), 3 Sch 81(4), 1 Sch 60(4)]*. The entity must also state separately the total amount of those commitments, guarantees and contingencies which are undertaken on behalf of, or for the benefit of:

(a)   any parent undertaking or fellow subsidiary undertaking of the entity,

(b)   any subsidiary undertaking of the entity, or

(c)   any undertaking in which the entity has a participating interest. *[1 Sch 63(7), 2 Sch 77(6), 3 Sch 81(7), 1 Sch 60(7) (LLP)]*.

3.10.4 Disclosures about contingent assets

If an inflow of economic benefits is probable (more likely than not) but not virtually certain, an entity should disclose:

- a description of the nature of the contingent assets at the end of the reporting period; and

- when practicable, an estimate of their financial effect, measured using the principles set out in paragraphs 7 to 11 of Section 21 (see 3.7 above).

If it is impracticable to make one or more of these disclosures, that fact should be stated. *[FRS 102.21.16]*. Applying a requirement is impracticable when the entity cannot apply it after making every reasonable effort to do so. *[FRS 102 Appendix I]*.

3.10.5 Disclosure when information is seriously prejudicial

In extremely rare cases, disclosure of some or all of the information required (by the disclosure requirements at 3.10.2 to 3.10.4 above) can be expected to prejudice seriously the position of the entity in a dispute with other parties on the subject matter of the provision, contingent liability or contingent asset. In such circumstances, an entity need not disclose all of the information required (by 3.10.2 to 3.10.4 above) insofar as it relates to the dispute, but should disclose at least the following: *[FRS 102.21.17]*

- in relation to provisions:
  - (a) a table showing the reconciliation required by 3.10.2 above in aggregate, including the source and application of any amounts transferred to or from provisions during the reporting period;
  - (b) particulars of each provision in any case where the amount of the provision is material; and
  - (c) the fact that, and reason why, the information required by 3.10.2 above has not been disclosed.
- in relation to contingent liabilities:
  - (a) particulars and the total amount of contingent liabilities (excluding those which arise out of insurance contracts) that are not included in the statement of financial position;
  - (b) the total amount of contingent liabilities which are undertaken on behalf of or for the benefit of:
    - (i) any parent or fellow subsidiary of the entity;
    - (ii) any subsidiary of the entity;
    - (iii) any entity in which the reporting entity has a participating interest,

    shall each be stated separately; and
  - (c) the fact that, and reason why, the information required by 3.10.3 above has not been disclosed.

In relation to contingent assets, the entity should disclose the general nature of the dispute, together with the fact that, and reason why, the information required by 3.10.4 above has not been disclosed. *[FRS 102.21.17]*.

3.10.6 *Disclosures about financial guarantee contracts*

An entity should disclose the nature and business purpose of any financial guarantee contracts it has issued. *[FRS 102.21.17A]*. This appears to be required regardless of whether the financial guarantee contract meets the recognition criteria for provisions or the disclosure criteria for contingent liabilities discussed at 3.3 and 3.4 above. In addition, if applicable, the disclosures required for provisions (see 3.10.2 above) or contingent liabilities (see 3.10.3 above) should also be provided. *[FRS 102.21.17A]*.

The Regulations and LLP Regulations also require disclosure of the particulars of any financial commitments that have not been provided for and are relevant to assessing the entity's state of affairs. *[1 Sch 63(2), 2 Sch 77(1), 3 Sch 81(2), 1 Sch 60(2) (LLP)]*.

3.10.7 *Disclosures about funding commitments (other than loan commitments)*

An entity that has made a funding commitment (see 3.9 above) is required to disclose the following:

(a)   the commitment made;

(b)   the time-frame of that commitment;

(c)   any performance-related conditions attached to that commitment; and

(d)   details of how that commitment will be funded. *[FRS 102.34.62]*.

Separate disclosure is required for recognised and unrecognised commitments. Within each category, disclosure can be aggregated provided that such aggregation does not obscure significant information. *[FRS 102.34.63]*. Accordingly, material commitments should be disclosed separately.

For funding commitments that are not recognised, it is important that full and informative disclosures are made of their existence and of the sources of funding for these unrecognised commitments. *[FRS 102.34A.6]*.

4   OTHER EXAMPLES OF PROVISIONS

Section 21 provides specific guidance in respect of a limited number of situations, which are discussed at 3.3.4 and 3.3.5 above. This section considers other common provisions not addressed specifically by Section 21. As there is no specific guidance on accounting for these provisions within FRS 102, entities may, under the hierarchy set out in Section 10, refer to the requirements and guidance of IFRS in formulating an appropriate accounting policy for these obligations. Accordingly, it would be appropriate to refer to Chapter 27 of EY International GAAP 2019.

4.1   Decommissioning provisions

Decommissioning costs arise when an entity is required to dismantle or remove an asset at the end of its useful life and to restore the site on which it has been located, for example, when an oil rig or nuclear power station reaches the end of its economic life.

Section 17 – *Property, Plant and Equipment* – observes that the cost of an item of property, plant and equipment includes the initial estimate of the costs, recognised and measured in accordance with Section 21, of dismantling and removing the item and restoring the site on which it is located, the obligation for which an entity incurs either when the item is acquired or as a consequence of having used the item during a particular period for purposes other than to produce inventories during that period. *[FRS 102.17.10(c)]*. See Chapter 15 at 3.4.1. However, Section 21 provides no specific guidance on decommissioning provisions.

Examples in the appendices to IAS 37 illustrate that the decommissioning liability is recognised as soon as the obligation arises, rather than being built up as the asset is used over its useful life. This is because the construction of the asset (and the environmental damage caused by it) creates the past obliging event requiring restoration in the future.

Given that Section 21 and IAS 37 apply the same principles to the recognition and measurement of provisions, we believe that this approach is also appropriate for entities reporting under FRS 102. The accounting for decommissioning provisions under IFRS is discussed in detail in Chapter 27 at 6.3 of EY International GAAP 2019. Chapter 27 also discusses:

- IFRIC 1 – *Changes in Existing Decommissioning, Restoration and Similar Liabilities* – which provides guidance on how to account for the effect of changes in measurement of existing provisions for obligations to dismantle, remove or restore items of property, plant and equipment; and

- IFRIC 5 – *Rights to Interests arising from Decommissioning, Restoration and Environmental Rehabilitation Funds* – which addresses the accounting by an entity when it participates in a 'decommissioning fund', with the purpose of segregating assets to fund some or all of the costs of decommissioning or environmental liabilities for which it has to recognise a provision under IAS 37.

Section 21 provides no specific guidance on the matters addressed within IFRIC 1 and IFRIC 5. However, the approach applied by IFRIC 1 is consistent with the approach commonly applied in practice by entities within and outside of the oil and gas industry.

4.2 Environmental provisions

IAS 37 sets out two examples of circumstances where environmental provisions would be required, both in relation to contaminated land. The examples illustrate that an entity can have an obligation to clean up contaminated land either as a result of legislation or as a result of a widely publicised environmental policy. The accounting applied in these examples is consistent with the principles of Section 21. These examples and the recognition and measurement of environmental provisions are discussed in Chapter 27 at 6.4 of EY International GAAP 2019.

4.3 Liabilities associated with emissions trading schemes

A number of countries around the world either have, or are developing, schemes to encourage reduced emissions of pollutants, in particular of greenhouse gases. These schemes comprise tradable emissions allowances or permits, an example of which is a 'cap and trade' model whereby participants are allocated emission rights or allowances equal to a cap (i.e. a maximum level of allowable emissions) and are permitted to trade those allowances.

Whilst there is currently no guidance under IFRS on accounting for cap and trade emission rights schemes, a discussion of the methods applied in practice can be found in Chapter 27 at 6.5 of EY International GAAP 2019.

4.4   EU Directive on Waste Electrical and Electronic Equipment

This Directive, which came into force in the UK on 2 January 2007, regulates the collection, treatment, recovery and environmentally sound disposal of waste electrical or electronic equipment (WE&EE). It applies to entities involved in the manufacture and resale of electrical or electronic equipment, including entities (both European and Non-European) that import such equipment into the EU.

The Directive states that the cost of waste management for historical household equipment should be borne by producers of that type of equipment that are in the market during a period to be specified in the applicable legislation of each Member State (the measurement period). The Directive states that each Member State should establish a mechanism to have producers contribute to costs proportionately e.g. in proportion to their respective share of the market by type of equipment.

IFRIC 6 – *Liabilities arising from Participating in a Specific Market – Waste Electrical and Electronic Equipment* –clarifies that the obligation under the Directive is linked to participation in the market during the measurement period, with their being no obligation unless and until a market share exists during the measurement period. The obligation is not linked to the production or sale of the items to be disposed of. The application of IFRIC 6 is discussed in Chapter 27 at 6.7 of EY International GAAP 2019.

4.5   Levies charged on entities operating in a specific market

When governments or other public authorities impose levies on entities in relation to their activities, it is not always clear when the liability to pay a levy arises and when a provision should be recognised. In May 2013, the IFRS Interpretations Committee issued IFRIC 21 – *Levies* – to address this question. It requires that, for levies within its scope, an entity should recognise a liability only when the activity that triggers payment, as identified by the relevant legislation, occurs. *[IFRIC 21.8]*. Given that Section 21 and IAS 37 apply the same principles to the recognition and measurement of provisions, entities may wish to apply the guidance in IFRIC 21 to the recognition of liabilities for levies under FRS 102. IFRIC 21 is discussed further in Chapter 27 at 6.8 of EY International GAAP 2019.

4.5.1   UK Apprenticeship levy

Since 6 April 2017, UK employers with an annual pay bill in excess of £3 million are required to pay a levy of 0.5% of that bill. Payments are made via the PAYE system, along with payroll taxes. Amounts paid by the employer are recorded in the employer's account on the government controlled 'Digital Apprenticeship System' (DAS). Payments made under the levy are credited to the employer's DAS account and are immediately available to fund certain approved apprenticeship training for, or assessment of, new hires or existing employees. Payments to the training provider are made directly by the government, with a corresponding reduction is made to the employer's DAS balance. The employer cannot recover cash directly from the DAS account, and amounts paid into the DAS expire after 24 months, i.e. they cannot be applied against training costs incurred after that time.

Government also contribute to apprenticeship costs, through a 'top-up' of £1 for every £10 paid in through the levy system, and through, in some cases, co-investment funding.

As discussed above, IFRIC 21 provides specific guidance on accounting for levies under IFRS. Whilst there is no equivalent guidance in Section 21, entities may wish to apply it to the recognition of liabilities for levies under FRS 102, since Section 21 is consistent with the principles of IAS 37. However, whilst IFRIC 21 addresses the recognition of liabilities to pay levies, entities are required to apply other Standards to decide whether recognition of a liability to pay a levy gives rise to an asset or expense. *[IFRIC 21.3]*. In our view, for employers that expect to enter into apprenticeships that meet the requirements for utilisation of funds in their DAS account within the 24 month life of those funds, the payment under the levy represents a prepayment for approved training services expected to be received and should be recognised an asset until the approved training occurs. An expense will be recognised when the training is delivered. Employers that do not expect to incur qualifying training costs before their entitlement to the funds expire should recognise the payment of the levy as an expense.

Both the government 'top-up' element of funding, and any benefit received under co-investment funding would meet the definition of government grants within FRS 102, and should therefore be accounted for in accordance with Section 24. See Chapter 21.

4.6 Repairs and maintenance of owned assets

IAS 37 includes an example within the appendices illustrating how the principles for the recognition of a provision are applied strictly in the case of an obligation to incur repairs and maintenance costs in the future on owned assets. This is the case even when this expenditure is substantial, distinct from what may be regarded as routine maintenance and essential to the continuing operations of the entity, such as major refit or refurbishment of the asset. This is discussed in Chapter 27 at 5.2 of EY International GAAP 2019.

Repairs and maintenance provisions for owned assets are generally prohibited under IAS 37. Given that Section 21 and IAS 37 apply the same principles to the recognition and measurement of provisions, we would also not generally expect provisions for repairs and maintenance of owned assets to be recognised under FRS 102.

4.7 Dilapidations and other provisions relating to leased assets

Whilst it is not generally appropriate to recognise provisions that relate to repairs and maintenance of owned assets (including assets held under finance leases) the position can be different in the case of obligations relating to assets held under operating leases.

Operating leases often contain clauses which specify that the lessee should incur periodic charges for maintenance, make good dilapidations or other damage occurring during the rental period or return the asset to the configuration that existed as at inception of the lease. These contractual provisions may restrict the entity's ability to change its future conduct to avoid the expenditure. The contractual obligations in a lease could therefore create an environment in which a present obligation could exist as at the reporting date from which the entity cannot realistically withdraw.

The recognition of provisions relating to leased assets is discussed in Chapter 27 at 6.9 of EY International GAAP 2019.

4.8 Self-insurance

Another situation where entities sometimes make provisions is self-insurance which arises when an entity decides not to take out external insurance in respect of a certain category of risk because it would be uneconomic to do so. The same position may arise when a group insures its risks with a captive insurance subsidiary, the effects of which have to be eliminated on consolidation. In fact, the term 'self-insurance' is potentially misleading, since it really means that the entity is not insured at all and will settle claims from third parties from its own resources in the event that it is found to be liable. Accordingly, the recognition criteria in Section 21 should be applied, with a provision being justified only if there is a present obligation as a result of a past event; if it is probable that an outflow of resources will occur; and a reliable estimate can be determined. *[FRS 102.21.4]*. FRS 103 – *Insurance Contracts* – also clarifies that self-insurance is not insurance as there is no insurance contract because there is no agreement with another party. *[FRS 103 Appendix II.19(c)]*.

Therefore, losses are recognised based on their actual incidence and any provisions that appear in the balance sheet should reflect only the amounts expected to be paid in respect of those incidents that have occurred by the end of the reporting period.

In certain circumstances, a provision will often be needed not simply for known incidents, but also for those which insurance companies call IBNR – Incurred But Not Reported – representing an estimate of claims that have occurred at the end of the reporting period but which have not yet been notified to the reporting entity. We believe that it is appropriate that provision for such expected claims is made.

4.9 Parent company guarantees given in connection with audit exemption

The Companies Act 2006 exempts some subsidiary companies from the requirement to be audited, subject to a number of conditions. One of the conditions requires that the parent company files with the registrar a statutory guarantee of all of the outstanding financial liabilities of the subsidiary at the end of the financial year for which the subsidiary seeks an exemption from audit. *[s394A, s479A]*. In our view, the statutory guarantee is not a contract. It therefore does not meet the definition of a financial guarantee contract within FRS 102 and should be accounted for under Section 21. If it is only a remote possibility that the guarantee will be called upon by the subsidiary's creditors, the parent does not recognise a provision nor disclose the guarantee in their separate financial statement. If it is possible (but not probable) that the guarantee will be called upon, the parent should disclose a contingent liability in their separate financial statements. If it is probable that the guarantee will be called upon, the parent must recognise a provision for the best estimate of the amount required to settle the obligation under the guarantee at the reporting date.

4.10 Recognition of provisions for vacant leasehold property

The most common example of an onerous contract in practice relates to leasehold property. From time to time entities may hold vacant leasehold property which they have substantially ceased to use for the purpose of their business and where sub-letting is either unlikely, or would be at a significantly reduced rental from that being paid by the entity. In these circumstances, the obligating event is the signing of the lease contract (a legal obligation) and when the lease becomes onerous, an outflow of resources embodying economic benefits is probable. Accordingly, a provision is recognised for the best estimate of the unavoidable lease payments.

Entities have to make systematic provision when such properties become vacant, and on a discounted basis where the effect is sufficiently material. Indeed, it is not just when the properties become vacant that provision would be required, but that provision should be made at the time the expected economic benefits of using the property fall short of the unavoidable costs under the lease. This may occur prior to an entity physically vacating a property. The recognition of onerous lease provisions for occupied leasehold property when the entity has no current intention of vacating the property is addressed in Chapter 27 at 6.2.1.B of EY International GAAP 2019. For vacant, or soon to be vacated, leasehold property consideration will need to be given to the point in time at which the lease becomes onerous and whether this may occur prior to the property being physically vacated. In our view, it may be appropriate to recognise an onerous lease provision prior to physically vacating a property if an entity has made a commitment to vacate from which it cannot realistically withdraw or if the unavoidable costs of meeting the obligations under the lease exceed the economic benefits expected to be received under that lease.

Nevertheless, where a provision is to be recognised a number of difficulties remain. The first is how the provision should be calculated. It is unlikely that the provision will simply be the net present value of the future rental obligation, because if a substantial period of the lease remains, the entity will probably be able either to agree a negotiated sum with the landlord to terminate the lease early, or to sub-lease the building at some point in the future. Hence, the entity will have to make a best estimate of its future cash flows taking all these factors into account.

Another issue that arises from this is whether the provision in the statement of financial position should be shown net of any cash flows that may arise from sub-leasing the property, or whether the provision must be shown gross, with a corresponding asset set up for expected cash flows from sub-leasing only if they meet the recognition criteria of being 'virtually certain' to be received. Whilst the expense relating to a provision can be shown in the income statement net of reimbursement, *[FRS 102.21.9]*, the strict offset criteria (see 3.7.5 above) would suggest the latter to be required, as the entity would normally retain liability for the full lease payments if the sub-lessee defaulted. However, neither FRS 102 nor IAS 37 make explicit reference to this issue. It is common for entities to apply a net approach for such onerous contracts. Indeed, it could be argued that because an onerous contract provision relates to the excess of the unavoidable costs over the expected economic benefits, *[FRS 102.21A.2]*, there is no corresponding asset to be recognised. In its 2005 exposure draft of proposed amendments to IAS 37, the IASB confirmed that if an onerous contract is an operating lease, the unavoidable cost of the contract is the remaining lease commitment reduced by the estimated rentals that the entity could reasonably obtain, regardless of whether or not the entity intends to enter into a sublease.[2] Given the consistent principles of Section 21 and IAS 37 regarding the measurement of provisions, we would also expect this to be the case for entities reporting under FRS 102.

In the past, some entities may have maintained that no provision is required for vacant properties, because if the property leases are looked at on a portfolio basis, the overall economic benefits from properties exceed the overall costs. However, this argument is not sustainable under FRS 102, as the definition of an onerous contract refers specifically to costs and economic benefits *under the contract.* *[FRS 102 Appendix I].*

It is more difficult to apply the definition of onerous contracts to the lease on a head office which is not generating revenue specifically. If the definition were applied too literally, one might end up concluding that all head office leases should be provided against because no specific economic benefits are expected under them. It would be more sensible to conclude that the entity as a whole obtains economic benefits from its head office, which is consistent with the way in which corporate assets are allocated to other cash generating units for the purposes of impairment testing (see Chapter 24 at 4.6.7). However, this does not alter the fact that if circumstances change and the head office becomes vacant, or the unavoidable costs of meeting the obligations under the head office lease come to exceed the economic benefits expected to be received, a provision should then be made in respect of the lease.

IAS 37 requires that any impairment loss that has occurred in respect of assets dedicated to an onerous contract is recognised before establishing a provision for the onerous contract. *[IAS 37.69].* For example, any leasehold improvements that have been capitalised should be written off before provision is made for excess future rental costs.

5 SUMMARY OF GAAP DIFFERENCES

	FRS 102	*IFRS*
Scope – Provisions, contingent liabilities and contingent assets covered by another Section / Standard	Section 21 does not apply to provisions, contingent liabilities and contingent assets covered by another section of FRS 102. However, where those other sections contain no specific requirements to deal with contracts that have become onerous, Section 21 applies to those contracts. This will include, for example, onerous leases, and loss making revenue contracts other than construction contracts. The recognition of provisions for loss making construction contracts is addressed by Section 23.	In contrast to FRS 102, where a provision, contingent liability or contingent asset is covered by another Standard and that Standard contained no specific requirements to deal with onerous contracts, there is no general requirement that IAS 37 be applied to those contracts. However, IAS 37 applies specifically to certain onerous leases and to contracts with customers that are, or have become, onerous.
Scope – Financial guarantee contracts	Financial guarantee contracts are in scope of Section 21 unless: • the entity has chosen to apply IAS 39 or IFRS 9 to its financial instruments; or • the entity has elected under FRS 103 to continue the application of insurance contract accounting.	Financial guarantee contracts are out of scope of IAS 37. They are accounted for as financial instruments unless the entity has elected under IFRS 4 or IFRS 17 to continue the application of insurance contract accounting.

Disclosure –Provisions	Included within the disclosure requirements for provisions is a requirement to disclose the expected amount of payments resulting from an obligation. There is no requirement to disclose: Major assumptions concerning future events that may affect the amount required to settle an obligation; or a separate line item in the reconciliation of opening and closing provision balances showing the increase during the period in the discounted amount arising from the passage of time and the effect of any change in discount rate.	Included within the disclosure requirements for provisions are requirements to disclose: Major assumptions concerning future events that may affect the amount required to settle an obligation where this is necessary to provide adequate information; and a separate line item in the reconciliation of opening and closing provision balances showing the increase during the period in the discounted amount arising from the passage of time and the effect of any change in discount rate. There is no requirement to disclose the expected amount of payments resulting from an obligation.
Disclosure when information is seriously prejudicial	Section 21 includes much more fulsome disclosure requirements in the case where information is considered seriously prejudicial than is required under IFRS. The disclosure requirements are set out in 3.10.5 above and significantly reduce the usefulness of the seriously prejudicial exemption under Section 21 compared to IFRS.	Under the seriously prejudicial exemption in IAS 37, entities must disclose the general nature of the dispute, together with the fact that, and the reason why, the information otherwise required by the standard has not been disclosed.
Disclosure – Financial guarantee contracts	An entity must disclose the nature and business purpose of any financial guarantee contracts in scope of Section 21, regardless of whether a provision is required. In addition, to the extent a provision is recognised for financial guarantee contracts, or a contingent liability disclosed, the general provision / contingent liability disclosures within Section 21 are also required.	There is no specific requirement for entities to disclose the nature and business purpose of any financial guarantee contracts it has issued. Financial guarantee contracts are in scope of the disclosure requirement of IFRS 7(if the issuer has elected to apply IFRS 9 or IAS 39 to the contracts), or IFRS 4 / IFRS 17, not IAS 37.

References

1 *Discounting in Financial Reporting*, ASB, April 1997.
2 *Exposure Draft of Proposed Amendments to IAS 37 Provisions, Contingent Liabilities and Contingent Assets* (IAS 37 ED) and *IAS 19 – Employee Benefits* (IAS 19 ED), IASB, June 2005, para. 58.

Chapter 20 Revenue

List of examples

Chapter 20

Chapter 20   Revenue

1   INTRODUCTION

1.1   Scope

Section 23 – *Revenue* – applies to revenue arising from: *[FRS 102.23.1]*

- the sale of goods (whether produced by the entity for the purpose of sale or purchased for resale);
- the rendering of services;
- construction contracts in which the entity is the contractor; and
- the use by others of entity assets yielding interest, royalties or dividends.

Section 23 does not apply to revenue or other income arising from: *[FRS 102.23.2]*

- lease agreements (Section 20 – *Leases*);
- dividends and other income arising from investments that are accounted for using the equity method (Section 14 – *Investments in Associates* – and Section 15 – *Investments in Joint Ventures*);
- changes in the fair value of financial assets and liabilities or their disposal (Section 11 – *Basic Financial Instruments* – and Section 12 – *Other Financial Instruments Issues*);
- changes in the fair value of investment property (Section 16 – *Investment Property*);
- initial recognition and changes in the fair value of biological assets related to agricultural activity, the initial recognition of agricultural produce and incoming resources from non-exchange transactions for public benefit entities (Section 34 – *Specialised Activities*); and
- transactions and events dealt with in FRS 103 – *Insurance Contracts*.

2   COMPARISON BETWEEN SECTION 23 AND IFRS

Section 23 is based on the requirements in IFRSs extant before the issuance of IFRS 15 – *Revenue from Contracts with Customers*. This means that there are number of significant differences compared with IFRS. This section compares Section 23 with IFRS 15 that was issued in May 2014 and replaces IAS 11 – *Construction Contracts*,

IAS 18 – *Revenue*, IFRIC 13 – *Customer Loyalty Programmes*, IFRIC 15 – *Agreements for the Construction of Real Estate*, IFRIC 18 – *Transfers of Assets from Customers* – and SIC Interpretation 31 – *Revenue – Barter transactions involving advertising services*. IFRS 15 is effective for periods beginning on or after 1 January 2018. IFRS 15 is discussed in Chapter 28 of EY International GAAP 2019.

In September 2016, the FRC issued a Consultation Document *Triennial review of UK and Ireland accounting standards: Approach to changes in IFRS*. The consultation document proposed that, in the longer term, the revenue requirements of FRS 102 should be aligned with IFRS 15, however, no significant changes were expected before 2022. In feedback on this consultation issued in 2017, the FRC agreed that further analysis was needed on the timetable and approach for reflecting IFRS 15 in FRS 102.

Amendments to FRS 102 – *The Financial Reporting Standard applicable in the UK and Republic of Ireland – Triennial Review 2017 – Incremental Improvements and Clarifications* (December 2017) (Triennial review 2017) has made only limited amendments to Section 23 but did not seek to incorporate any aspects of IFRS 15. The FRC confirm that any amendments to FRS 102 to reflect major changes to IFRS, such as IFRS 15, will be considered on a case by case basis including the appropriate timing, noting that it will be preferable to learn from IFRS implementation experience before considering changes to FRS 102. *[FRS 102.BC.A44]*.

The principles and guidance in Section 23 were based on the superseded IAS 11, IAS 18, IFRIC 13, IFRIC 15, IFRIC 18 and SIC 31 (the superseded IFRSs) and therefore, were very similar. Whilst there were differences in the written content of the standards, differences in accounting between Section 23 and the superseded IFRSs were not necessarily expected to arise in practice. Areas of potential difference between Section 23, based on the superseded IFRSs, and IFRS 15 are discussed at 2.1 below.

2.1   Differences to IFRS 15

Section 23 is based on the principle of risk and rewards whereas the core principal in IFRS 15 is transfer of control. Under IFRS 15 an entity recognises revenue at an amount that reflects the consideration to which the entity expects to be entitled in exchange for transferring goods or services to a customer. The principles in IFRS 15 are applied using the following five steps:

1.   Identify the contract(s) with a customer.
2.   Identify the performance obligations in the contract.
3.   Determine the transaction price.
4.   Allocate the transaction price to the performance obligations in the contract.
5.   Recognise revenue when (or as) the entity satisfies a performance obligation.

IFRS 15 includes more requirements and/or provides more guidance than Section 23 or the superseded IFRSs related to revenue recognition on a number of topics including, but not limited to, the following:

2.1.1 Combining contracts

IFRS 15 provides more stringent requirements on when to combine contracts than the requirements in the superseded IFRSs. IAS 11 (superseded) allowed an entity to combine contracts with several customers, provided the relevant criteria for combination were met. In contrast, the contract combination requirements in IFRS 15 only apply to contracts with the same customer or related parties of the customer. Unlike IFRS 15, IAS 11 (superseded) did not require that contracts be entered into at or near the same time.

Overall, the criteria are generally consistent with the underlying principles in the superseded IFRSs on combining contracts. However, IFRS 15 explicitly requires an entity to combine contracts if one or more of the criteria in IFRS 15 are met.

2.1.2 Contract modification

The requirement in IFRS 15 to determine whether to treat a change in contractual terms as a separate contract or a modification to an existing contract is similar to the requirements in IAS 11 (superseded) for construction contracts. In contrast, IAS 18 (superseded) did not provide detailed application guidance on how to determine whether a change in contractual terms should be treated as a separate contract or a modification to an existing contract. Despite there being some similarities to superseded IFRSs, the requirements in IFRS 15 for contract modifications are much more detailed.

2.1.3 Customer options

Section 23 or the superseded IFRSs did not provide application guidance on how to distinguish between an option and a marketing offer (i.e. as an expense). Nor did they address how to account for options that provide a material right. IFRS 15 requires on the amount of the transaction price to be allocated to the customer option. IFRS 15 includes a requirement to identify and allocate contract consideration to an option (that has been determined to be a performance obligation) on a relative stand-alone selling price basis.

2.1.4 Sale with a right of return

IFRS 15 is not expected to materially change the net impact of arrangements involving sale of products with a right of return. However, there may be some differences as Section 23 or IAS 18 (superseded) did not specify the presentation of a refund liability or the corresponding debit. IFRS 15 requires that a return asset be recognised in relation to the inventory that may be returned. In addition, the refund liability is required to be presented separately from the corresponding asset (i.e. on a gross basis, rather than a net basis).

2.1.5   Variable consideration

Under Section 23 and superseded IFRSs, preparers often deferred measurement of variable consideration until revenue was reliably measurable, which could be when the uncertainty is removed or when payment is received. Furthermore, superseded IFRSs permitted recognition of contingent consideration, but only if it was probable that the economic benefits associated with the transaction would flow to the entity and the amount of revenue could be reliably measured. Some entities, therefore, deferred recognition until the contingency was resolved. In contrast, the constraint on variable consideration in IFRS 15 is an entirely new way of evaluating variable consideration and is applicable to all types of variable consideration in all transactions.

2.1.6   Revenue recognised over time

Under IFRS 15, for each performance obligation identified in the contract, an entity is required to consider at contract inception whether it satisfies the performance obligation over time (i.e. whether it meets one of the three criteria for over-time recognition) or at a point in time. This evaluation requires entities to perform analyses that might differ from Section 23 or superseded IFRSs. For example, entities that enter into contracts to construct real estate for a customer no longer need to determine whether the contract either meets the definition of a construction contract (in order to apply Section 23 or superseded IAS 11) or is for the provision of services (under superseded IAS 18) so as to recognise revenue over time. Instead, under IFRS 15, an entity needs to determine whether its performance obligation is satisfied over time by evaluating the three criteria for over-time recognition. If an entity does not satisfy a performance obligation over time, the performance obligation is satisfied at a point in time.

2.1.7   Licences of intellectual properties

IFRS 15 provides more detailed application guidance than the superseded IFRSs for recognising revenue from licences of intellectual property that differs in some respects from the requirements for other promised goods or services.

Revenue recognition under IFRS 15 depends on the classification of licences. According to IFRS 15, a licence provides either (i) A right to access the entity's intellectual property throughout the licence period, which results in revenue that is recognised over time or (ii) A right to use the entity's intellectual property as it exists at the point in time in which the licence is granted, which results in revenue that is recognised at a point in time.

2.1.8 Warranties

IFRS 15 provides more detailed guidance on accounting for warranties than Section 23 or IAS 18 (superseded). Under IFRS 15, warranties are classified either as assurance-type warranties or as service-type warranty. The requirements for assurance-type warranties are essentially the same as the in practice IAS 18 (superseded). The requirements for service-type warranties may differ, particularly in relation to the amount of transaction price that is allocated to the warranty performance obligation. Under Section 23 and IAS 18 (superseded), entities that provided separate extended warranties often defer an amount equal to the stated price of the warranty and recorded that amount as revenue evenly over the warranty period. IFRS 15 requires an entity to defer an allocated amount, based on a relative stand-alone selling price allocation.

2.1.9 Contract costs

IFRS 15 represents a significant change in practice for entities that previously expensed the costs of obtaining a contract and are required to capitalise them under IFRS 15. Entities need to evaluate all sales commissions paid to employees and capitalise any costs that are incremental, regardless of how directly involved the employee was in the sales process or the level or title of the employee.

In addition, this may be a change for entities that previously capitalised costs to obtain a contract, particularly if the amounts capitalised were not incremental and, therefore, would not be eligible for capitalisation under IFRS 15, unless explicitly chargeable to the customer regardless of whether the contract is obtained.

2.1.10 Presentation and disclosures

IFRS 15 provides explicit presentation and disclosure requirements that are more detailed than under Section 23 or superseded IFRSs. Key areas that could be impacted with presentation and disclosure requirements in IFRS 15 include, but are not limited to, the following:

- disaggregation of revenue;
- contract balances;
- performance obligations;
- significant judgement;
- assets recognised from the costs to obtain or fulfil a contract; and
- accounting policy disclosures.

Chapter 20

3 REQUIREMENTS OF SECTION 23 FOR REVENUE

3.1 Terms used by Section 23

The following are the key terms in Section 23: *[FRS 102 Appendix I]*

Term	Definition
Agent	An entity is acting as an agent when it does not have exposure to the significant risks and rewards associated with the sale of goods or the rendering of services. One feature indicating that an entity is acting as an agent is that the amount the entity earns is predetermined, being either a fixed fee per transaction or a stated percentage of the amount billed to the customer.
Asset	A resource controlled by the entity as a result of past events and from which future economic benefits are expected to flow to the entity.
Construction contract	A contract specifically negotiated for the construction of an asset or a combination of assets that are closely interrelated or independent in terms of their design, technology and function or their ultimate purpose or use.
Imputed rate of interest	The more clearly determinable of either: (a) the prevailing rate for a similar instrument of an issuer with a similar credit rating; or (b) a rate of interest that discounts the nominal amount of the instrument to the current cash sales price of the goods or services.
Onerous contract	A contract in which the unavoidable costs of meeting the obligations under the contract exceed the economic benefit expected to be received under it.
Principal	An entity is acting as a principal when it has exposure to the significant risks and rewards associated with the sale of goods or the rendering of services. Features that indicate that an entity is acting as a principal include: (a) the entity has the primary responsibility for providing the goods or services to the customer or for fulfilling the order, for example by being responsible for the acceptability of the products or services ordered or purchased by the customer; (b) the entity has inventory risk before or after the customer order, during shipping or on return; (c) the entity has latitude in establishing prices, either directly or indirectly, for example by providing additional goods or services; and (d) the entity bears the customer's credit risk for the amount receivable from the customer.
Revenue	The gross inflow of economic benefits during the period arising in the course of the ordinary activities of an entity when those inflows result in increases in equity, other than increases relating to contributions from equity participants.

This section focuses on the requirements of Section 23 and also refers to the Appendix to Section 23 which provides guidance for applying the requirements in recognising revenue. The Appendix, however, does not form part of Section 23.

3.2 Measurement of revenue

Revenue within the scope of Section 23 shall only be recognised if it meets, at a minimum, the following two criteria: *[FRS 102.23.10(c)-(d), 14(a)-(b), 28]*

- revenue can be measured reliably; and
- it is *probable* that the economic benefits associated with the transaction will flow to the entity.

'Probable' is defined as 'more likely than not'. *[FRS 102 Appendix I]*. The consideration receivable may not be regarded to be probable until the actual consideration is received or when a condition is met that removes any uncertainty.

In addition to the above criteria, there are other conditions that need to be met for the recognition of revenue from the sale of goods and the rendering of services. *[FRS 102.23.10, 14]*. These are further discussed below at 3.4 and 3.5 respectively.

Revenue shall be measured at the fair value of the consideration received or receivable taking into account trade discounts, prompt settlement discounts and volume rebates allowed by the entity. *[FRS 102.23.3]*. Section 23 also requires an entity to exclude from revenue amounts collected on behalf of third parties such as sales taxes and value added taxes (VAT). *[FRS 102.23.4]*.

3.2.1 Discounts, rebates and sales incentives

Where an entity provides sales incentives to a customer when entering into a contract, these are usually treated as rebates and will be included in the measurement of (i.e. deducted from) revenue when the goods are delivered or services provided.

Where the incentive is in the form of cash, revenue will be recognised at a reduced amount taking into account the rebate factor from the cash incentive.

Prompt settlement discounts (for example, customers are offered a reduction of 5% of the selling price for paying an invoice within 7 days instead of the usual 60 days) should be estimated at the time of sale and deducted from revenues.

Non-cash incentives take a variety of forms. Where the seller provides 'free postage' this would impose an additional cost on the entity but would not impact revenue. However, where the seller provides free delivery and *undertakes this service itself,* this would either be a separate component of a multiple element transaction to which some of the transaction price should be allocated (see 3.3.1 below), or more commonly, where risks and rewards of the goods are not transferred to the customer until delivery, the total revenue will not be recognised until that point.

Non-cash incentives may comprise products or services from third parties. If these are provided as part of a sales transaction they will represent separate components of a multiple element transaction to which revenue must be attributed. The seller will need to determine whether they are acting as an agent or principal for that element of the transaction. If the seller is acting as agent and has no further obligations in respect of that component, then it will immediately recognise the margin on that element as its own revenue. If acting as principal, it will recognise the full transaction price as revenue but it will need to defer any element that relates to the provision of the good or service by the third party if that party still needs to provide that good or service (for example where the incentive is in the form of a voucher that is redeemable by the third party at a later date). Principal versus agent and multiple element arrangements are discussed in further detail below at 3.2.2 and 3.3 respectively.

Some of these non-cash incentives e.g. money off vouchers, air miles or loyalty cards, may fall under the scope of loyalty awards which is discussed at 3.3.2 below.

3.2.2   *Principal versus agent*

An entity shall include in revenue only the gross inflows of economic benefits received and receivable by the entity on its own account and not the revenue collected on behalf of any third parties. If the entity is an agent, it shall include in revenue only the amount of its commission as any amounts collected on behalf of the principal are not revenue of the entity. *[FRS 102.23.4].*

FRS 102 provides the following definitions for identifying whether an entity is acting as principal or agent.

'An entity is acting as a principal when it has exposure to the significant risks and rewards associated with the sale of goods or the rendering of services. Features that indicate that an entity is acting as a principal include:

- the entity has the primary responsibility for providing the goods or services to the customer or for fulfilling the order, for example by being responsible for the acceptability of the products or services ordered or purchased by the customer;

- the entity has inventory risk before or after the customer order, during shipping or on return;

- the entity has latitude in establishing prices, either directly or indirectly, for example by providing additional goods or services; and

- the entity bears the customer's credit risk for the amount receivable from the customer.' *[FRS 102.23A.38, Appendix I].*

'An entity is acting as an agent when it does not have exposure to the significant risks and rewards associated with the sale of goods or the rendering of services. One feature indicating that an entity is acting as an agent is that the amount the entity earns is predetermined, being either a fixed fee per transaction or a stated percentage of the amount billed to the customer.' *[FRS 102.23A.39, Appendix I].*

Further guidance, added by the Triennial review 2017, is provided in the Appendix to Section 23 which notes that determining whether an entity is acting as a principal or as an agent requires judgement and consideration of all relevant facts and circumstance. *[FRS 102.23A.37].*

When an entity has entered into a contract as an undisclosed agent, it is normally acting as principal. *[FRS 102.23A.40].*

Amounts collected by an agent on behalf of a principal are not revenue for the agent. Instead, revenue for the agent is the amount of commission. *[FRS 102.23A.41].*

3.2.3　Deferred payments

If the consideration receivable from the sale of goods or services is deferred, and the arrangement is in effect a financing transaction, the fair value of the consideration is the present value of all the future receipts calculated using an imputed rate of interest. Examples of a financing transaction are when an entity provides interest-free credit to the buyer or the entity accepts a note receivable bearing a below-market interest rate from the buyer as consideration.

Section 23 sets out two methods to arrive at the appropriate rate of interest. The imputed rate of interest is, depending on which is the more clearly determinable, either:

- the prevailing rate for a similar instrument of an issuer with a similar credit rating; or
- a rate of interest that discounts the nominal amount of the instrument to the current cash sales price of the goods or services. *[FRS 102.23.5]*.

The difference between the nominal amount of the consideration and the present value of all future receipts is recognised as interest revenue using the effective interest method. *[FRS 102.23A.13]*.

3.2.4　Exchanges of goods and services

Entities may enter into transactions which involve exchanging or the swapping of goods or services, also known as barter transactions. An example is the exchange of commodities such as oil or milk where suppliers exchange inventories in different locations to fulfil demand. Other examples include exchanges of capacity in the telecommunications sector and barter of advertising services.

An entity shall not recognise revenue if: *[FRS 102.23.6]*

- the entity exchanges goods or services for goods and services that are of a similar nature and value; or
- the transaction lacks commercial substance even if the goods or services are dissimilar.

Hence an entity shall recognise revenue from the exchange of goods or services for dissimilar goods or services as long as the transaction has commercial substance. The entity shall then measure the transaction at: *[FRS 102.23.7]*

- the fair value of the goods or services received adjusted by the amount of any cash or cash equivalents transferred; or
- if the above cannot be measured reliably, at the fair value of the goods or services given up adjusted by the amount of any cash or cash equivalents transferred; or
- if the fair value of neither the goods or services received nor the goods or services given up can be measured reliably, then revenue is recognised at the carrying amount of the goods or services given up adjusted by the amount of any cash or cash equivalents transferred.

3.3　Identification of the revenue transaction

3.3.1　Separately identifiable components

The revenue recognition criteria in Section 23 are usually applied separately to each transaction. However, if there are 'separately identifiable components' of a single transaction, the revenue recognition criteria will be applied to each component to reflect the substance of the transaction. Entities should analyse the transactions in accordance with their economic substance to determine whether there are separately identifiable components and whether they should be combined or separated for revenue recognition purposes. In assessing whether there are separately identifiable components, an entity should consider whether it has in the past sold the individual components separately or plans to do so in the future. However, absent such evidence, the components may still be deemed to be separately identifiable if the individual components are sold separately by others in the market.

For example, if the sale of a product included an identifiable amount for subsequent servicing, the entity would apply the recognition criteria to the separately identifiable components i.e. the sale of the product and the sale of the servicing element. *[FRS 102.23.8]*. The Appendix to Section 23 includes an example which sets out that the seller defers the identifiable amount for subsequent servicing and recognises it as revenue over the period the service is performed. The amount that is deferred will cover the expected costs of the services together with a reasonable profit on those services. *[FRS 102.23A.19]*. Section 23 does not explain what constitutes a 'reasonable profit'.

If two or more transactions are linked in such a way that the commercial effect cannot be understood without reference to the series of transactions as whole, then the recognition criteria would be applied to the linked transactions together. For example, if an entity sells goods and at the same time enters into a separate agreement to repurchase the goods at a later date, the entity would apply the recognition criteria to the two transactions together. *[FRS 102.23.8]*.

The basic principle for measurement of revenue under FRS 102 requires that revenue is measured at its fair value. Therefore, the separately identifiable components should be recorded at their fair value. However a contract with multiple elements may have a contract fair value that is lower than the aggregate of the fair values of the separately identifiable components. The difference between these two fair values should be allocated to the separable identifiable components, using an appropriate allocation method.

Example 20.1:   Accounting for differences in the contract fair value and the fair values of the separately identifiable components

An entity sells a software product for £10,000 and also provides support and maintenance services for £2,000 per annum. The entity sells these two products and services together to a customer for a contract value of £11,000. In other words, a total discount of £1,000 has been given.

Using the relative fair value approach, the discount allocated to the software product is £833 (£1,000 × (£10,000 / £12,000)) and the discount allocated to the support and maintenance services is £167 (£1,000 × (£2,000 / £12,000)).

FRS 102 does not provide additional guidance in identifying the separate components of a transaction and how revenue should be allocated to these components. An allocation of revenue based on relative fair values would be considered an appropriate basis but this is not an explicit requirement of FRS 102 and other bases may be appropriate. As such, an entity must use its judgement to select the most appropriate methodology, taking into consideration all relevant facts and circumstances.

See 3.5 below for discussion on accounting for revenue from rendering of services. Some of the practical implementation issues in accounting for revenue on the separation (unbundling) and linking (bundling) of contractual arrangements, including accounting for contracts that include the receipt of initial fees are discussed at 4 below.

3.3.2 Loyalty awards

An entity may grant its customers a loyalty award, as part of a sales transaction, that the customer may redeem in the future for free or discounted goods or services. For example, money-off vouchers, air miles offered by airlines and retail stores that provide loyalty cards used to earn points as purchases are made, which can be used against future purchases. The award credit shall be accounted for as a separately identifiable component of the initial sales transaction, as discussed at 3.3.1 above. The fair value of the consideration received, or receivable, shall be allocated between the award credits and the other components of the sale. The consideration allocated to the award credits shall be their fair value which is the amount for which the award credits could be sold separately. *[FRS 102.23.9]*.

The appendix to Section 23 provides an example that illustrates how Section 23 may be applied in practice. *[FRS 102.23A.16-17]*.

Example 20.2: Sale with a customer loyalty award

An entity sells product A for £100. Purchasers of product A get an award credit enabling them to buy product B for £10. The normal selling price of product B is £18. The entity estimates that 40 per cent of the purchasers of product A will use their award to buy product B at £10. The normal selling price of product A, after taking into account discounts that are usually offered but that are not available during this promotion, is £95.

The fair value of the award credit is 40 per cent × [£18 − £10] = £3.20. The entity allocates the total revenue of £100 between product A and the award credit by reference to their relative fair values of £95 and £3.20 respectively. Therefore:

(a) Revenue for product A is £100 × [£95 ÷ (£95 + £3.20)] = £96.74

(b) Revenue for product B is £100 × [£3.20 ÷ (£95 + £3.20)] = £3.26

The example illustrates that a number of factors should be taken into account including:

- the percentage of awards expected to be redeemed;
- the normal selling price of the initial sales of goods or service when the loyalty award is not available; and
- the normal selling price for the goods or service for which the voucher is being offered against.

The entity would then allocate the total consideration received or receivable, between the initial sales goods or service and the award credit according to their relative fair values.

If the sales incentive is in the form of a voucher that is issued independently of a sales transaction (e.g. one that entitles the customer to money off if they choose to make a purchase) there will be no impact on revenue at this time. They also do not give rise to a liability unless the products or services would be sold at a loss, in which case a provision for an onerous contract may be required in accordance with Section 21 – *Provisions and Contingencies*.

3.4   Sale of goods

Revenue from the sale of goods is recognised when all of the following conditions are satisfied: *[FRS 102.23.10]*

- the significant risks and rewards of ownership of the goods has been transferred to the buyer;

- the entity no longer has any continuing managerial involvement usually associated with ownership nor effective control over the goods sold;

- the amount of revenue can be measured reliably;

- it is probable that the economic benefits associated with the transaction will flow to the entity; and

- the costs incurred (or to be incurred) in respect of the transaction can be measured reliably.

Assessing when an entity has transferred the significant risks and rewards of ownership to the buyer requires the specific circumstances of the transaction to be assessed. The transfer of risks and rewards usually coincides with the transfer of the legal title or when possession of the goods is passed to the buyer, as is the case for most retail sales. However the transfer of risks and rewards can occur at a different time to the transfer of legal title or taking possession of the goods. *[FRS 102.23.11]*.

If an entity retains the significant risks of ownership, it does not, therefore, recognise the revenue. Examples of when an entity may retain the significant risks and rewards of ownership are: *[FRS 102.23.12]*

- when an entity retains an obligation for unsatisfactory performance not covered by normal warranties;

- when the receipt of revenue from a sale is contingent on the buyer selling the goods;

- when the goods are shipped but are subject to installation and the installation is a significant part of the contract and is incomplete; and

- when the buyer has the right to rescind the purchase for a reason specified in the sale contract or at the buyer's sole discretion without any reason and the entity is uncertain about the probability of return.

An entity recognises the revenue on a sale if the entity retains only an insignificant risk of ownership. For example, the seller would recognise the sale if the entity retains the legal title to the goods solely to protect the collectability of the amount due. *[FRS 102.23.13]*.

3.4.1   *Goods with a right of return*

Where an entity sells goods with a right of return, as commonly seen for clothing or on-line retailers, the entity recognises the revenue in full, if the entity can estimate the returns reliably. A provision for the returns would then be recognised against revenue, in accordance with Section 21. *[FRS 102.23.13]*.

If the entity cannot estimate the returns reliably, the revenue is recognised when the shipment has been formally accepted by the buyer or the goods have been delivered and the time period for rejection has elapsed (see 3.4.3(b) below).

3.4.2 'Bill and hold' sales

The term 'bill and hold' sale is used to describe a transaction where delivery is delayed at the buyer's request, but the buyer takes title and accepts billing.

Under the guidance provided in the Appendix to Section 23, revenue is recognised when the buyer takes title, provided: *[FRS 102.23A.3]*

(a) it is probable that delivery will be made;

(b) the item is on hand, identified and ready for delivery to the buyer at the time the sale is recognised;

(c) the buyer specifically acknowledges the deferred delivery instructions; and

(d) the usual payment terms apply.

Revenue is not recognised when there is simply an intention to acquire or manufacture the goods in time for delivery.

3.4.3 Goods shipped subject to conditions

The Appendix to Section 23 identifies scenarios where goods are shipped subject to various conditions: *[FRS 102.23A.4-7]*

(a) Installation and inspection

Revenue is normally recognised when the buyer accepts delivery, and installation and inspection are complete. Revenue is recognised immediately upon the buyer's acceptance of delivery when:

(i) the installation process is simple in nature, e.g. the installation of a factory-tested television receiver which only requires unpacking and connection of power and antennae; or

(ii) the inspection is performed only for purposes of final determination of contract prices, for example, shipments of iron ore, sugar or soya beans.

(b) On approval when the buyer has negotiated a limited right of return

If there is uncertainty about the possibility of return, revenue is recognised when the shipment has been formally accepted by the buyer or the goods have been delivered and the time period for rejection has elapsed.

(c) Consignment sales under which the recipient (buyer) undertakes to sell the goods on behalf of the shipper (seller)

Revenue is recognised by the shipper when the goods are sold by the recipient to a third party.

(d) Cash on delivery sales

Revenue is recognised when delivery is made and cash is received by the seller or its agent.

3.4.4 Layaway sales (goods delivered when final payment made)

The term 'layaway sales' applies to transactions where the goods are delivered only when the buyer makes the final payment in a series of instalments. Revenue from such sales is recognised when the goods are delivered. However, when experience indicates that most sales are ultimately completed, revenue may be recognised when a significant deposit is received, provided the goods are on hand, identified and ready for delivery to the buyer. *[FRS 102.23A.8]*.

3.4.5   Payments in advance

In certain sectors, for example, furniture and kitchen retail, payment or partial payment is received from the customer when an order is placed for the goods. This is often well in advance of delivery for goods which are not presently held in inventory, if, for example, the goods are still to be manufactured or will be delivered directly to the customer by a third party. In such cases, revenue is recognised when the goods are delivered to the customer. *[FRS 102.23A.9]*.

In other sectors, for example, utilities, companies receive advance payments from customers for services to be provided in the future. In some cases, these advance payments are long term in nature. The issue that arises is whether or not interest should be accrued on these advances and if so, how revenue should be measured in these circumstances.

Section 23 requires entities to measure revenue 'at the fair value of the consideration received or receivable'. *[FRS 102.23.3]*. It also refers to the situations in which an entity either provides interest-free credit to the buyer or accepts a note receivable bearing a below-market interest rate from the buyer as consideration for the sale of goods. If the arrangement effectively constitutes a financing transaction, Section 23 requires that the entity determines the fair value of the consideration by discounting all future receipts using an imputed rate of interest. *[FRS 102.23.5]*. However, Section 23 does not address the reverse situation of the receipt of interest-free advances from customers. A similar rationale may be applied to justify the accruing of interest, i.e. there is a financing element to the transaction and this must be taken into account, if revenue is to be measured at the fair value of the consideration at the time the good or service is provided.

Given this lack of clarity we believe it is a policy choice under FRS 102 of whether to accrue interest on advance payments received from customers. If interest is accrued it will be calculated based upon the incremental borrowing rate of the entity and revenue will ultimately be recognised based upon the nominal value of the advance payments received from customers plus this accrued interest. Whichever accounting policy is adopted, it should be applied consistently. Alternatively, an entity could apply the guidance in IFRS 15 following the hierarchy in Section 10. IFRS 15 states that an entity should adjust the promised amount of consideration for the effects of the time value of money if the timing of payments agreed to by the parties to the contract (either explicitly or implicitly) provides the customer or the entity with a significant benefit of financing the transfer of goods or services to the customer. *[IFRS 15.60]*. Accordingly, IFRS 15 clarifies the accounting for significant financing benefit is consistent for both the benefit obtained by the customer and the entity.

3.4.6   Sale and repurchase agreements

Sale and repurchase agreements take many forms: the seller concurrently agrees to repurchase the same goods at a later date, or the seller has a call option to repurchase, or the buyer has a put option to require the repurchase, by the seller, of the goods.

In a sale and repurchase agreement for an asset other than a financial asset, the terms of the agreement need to be analysed to determine whether, in substance, the seller has transferred the risks and rewards of ownership to the buyer hence revenue is recognised. When the seller has retained the risks and rewards of ownership, even though legal title has been transferred, the transaction is a financing arrangement and does not give rise to revenue. *[FRS 102.23A.10].* Sale and leaseback arrangements, repurchase agreements and options are discussed in Chapter 18. For a sale and repurchase agreement on a financial asset, the derecognition provisions of Section 11 apply (see Chapter 10 at 9).

3.4.7 Subscriptions to publications

Publication subscriptions are generally paid in advance and are non-refundable. As the publications will still have to be produced and delivered to the subscriber, the subscription revenue cannot be regarded as having been earned until production and full delivery takes place. This is the approach adopted by Section 23, which requires that revenue is recognised on a straight-line basis over the period in which the items are despatched when the items involved are of similar value in each time period. When the items vary in value from period to period, revenue is recognised on the basis of the sales value of the item despatched in relation to the total estimated sales value of all items included in the subscription. *[FRS 102.23A.12].*

3.4.8 Consignment sales

The Appendix to Section 23 provides examples for consignment sales and sales to intermediate parties. When goods are shipped subject to conditions e.g. consignment sales under which the buyer agrees to sell the goods on behalf of the seller, the seller recognises the revenue only when the goods are sold by the buyer to a third party. *[FRS 102.23A.6].* Another example is when sales are made to intermediate parties such as distributors, dealers or others for resale. The seller generally recognises revenue from such sales when the risks and rewards of ownership have been transferred. However, if the buyer is acting, in substance, as an agent, the sale is treated as a consignment sale. *[FRS 102.23A.11].*

3.5 Rendering of services

Section 23 requires that for transactions involving the rendering of services that are incomplete at the end of the reporting period, revenue shall be recognised based on the stage of completion if the outcome can be estimated reliably. The outcome of a transaction can be estimated reliably when all of the following are satisfied: *[FRS 102.23.14]*

- the amount of revenue can be measured reliably;
- it is probable that the economic benefits associated with the transaction will flow to the entity;
- the stage of completion at the end of the reporting period can be measured reliably; and
- the costs incurred for the transaction and the costs to complete can be measured reliably.

When the outcome of a transaction cannot be estimated reliably, revenue can be recognised only to the extent of the expenses recognised that is probable will be recovered. *[FRS 102.23.16].*

See 3.6 below for further guidance for applying the percentage of completion method and related examples on the application of Section 23 to the rendering of services.

When the services are performed by an 'indeterminate number of acts over a specified period of time' an entity shall recognise the revenue on a straight-line basis over the specified period or another method if that method better reflects the stage of completion. *[FRS 102.23.15]*.

3.5.1   Contingent fee arrangements

When a specific act is much more significant than any other act, the entity shall postpone the recognition of revenue until that significant act is executed. *[FRS 102.23.15]*. For example, when fees are contingent on the performance of a significant act.

3.6   Percentage of completion method

Section 23 also provides guidance on the possible methods that are available to entities to determine the stage of completion. The percentage of completion method is used to recognise revenue from rendering services and also from construction contracts which is discussed at 3.9.6 below.

An entity shall use the most reliable method for measuring the work performed to arrive at the stage of completion. Possible methods include: *[FRS 102.23.22]*

- the proportion of costs incurred for work performed to date (excluding costs related to future activity such as materials and prepayments) compared to the estimated total costs;
- surveys of work performed; and
- completion of a physical proportion of the contract work or completion of a proportion of the service contract.

Payments received in advance including progress payments do not always reflect the work performed. An entity shall also, when necessary, review and revise the estimates of revenue and costs as the work or service progresses. *[FRS 102.23.21-22]*.

If costs are incurred in relation to future activity, such as material or prepayments, and the costs will be recovered, the entity shall recognise those costs as an asset. *[FRS 102.23.23]*. If recovery of the costs is not probable, the entity shall expense those costs immediately. *[FRS 102.23.24]*.

If an amount is recognised as revenue, and at a later date, the collectability of that amount is not probable, the entity shall recognise the uncollectable amount as an expense and not an adjustment to the revenue. *[FRS 102.23.27]*.

The Appendix to Section 23 also provides a number of examples to provide guidance on the application of Section 23 to the rendering of services which are explained at 3.6.1 to 3.6.7 below.

3.6.1   Installation fees

Installation fees are recognised as revenue by reference to the stage of completion of the installation, unless they are incidental to the sale of a product in which case they are recognised when the goods are sold. *[FRS 102.23A.18]*. However, in certain circumstances where the installation fees are linked to a contract for future services (for example, in the telecommunications industry: see 4.3 below) it may be more appropriate to defer such fees over either the contract period or the average expected life of the customer relationship, depending on the circumstances.

3.6.2 Advertising commissions

Performance of the service is considered as the critical event for the recognition of revenue derived from the rendering of advertising services. Consequently, media commissions are recognised when the related advertisement or commercial appears before the public. Production commissions are recognised by reference to the stage of completion of the project. *[FRS 102.23A.20]*. Barter transactions involving advertising services are addressed at 3.2.4 above.

3.6.3 Insurance agency commissions

The critical event for the recognition of insurance agency commissions is the commencement or renewal date of the policy. Hence, insurance agency commissions received or receivable which do not require the agent to render further service are recognised as revenue on the effective commencement or renewal dates of the related policies. However, when it is probable that the agent will be required to render further services during the life of the policy, the commission, or part of it, is deferred and recognised as revenue over the period of the policy. *[FRS 102.23A.21]*.

3.6.4 Financial services fees

The recognition of revenue for financial service fees depends on the purpose of the fees and the basis of accounting for any associated financial instrument. The description of the fee may not be indicative of the nature and substance of the services provided therefore entities will need to distinguish the fees that are an integral part of the effective interest rate, fees that are earned over the period the services are provided and fees that are earned on the occurrence of a significant act. *[FRS 102.23A.21A]*.

3.6.5 Admission fees

Admission fees to 'artistic performances, banquets and other special events' are recognised when the event takes place. If there is a subscription to a number of events, fees may be allocated on a basis that reflects the extent to which services are performed at each event. *[FRS 102.23A.22]*.

3.6.6 Tuition fees

Tuition fee revenue is recognised over the period of instruction. *[FRS 102.23A.23]*.

3.6.7 Initiation, entrance and membership fees

Revenue recognition depends on the nature of the services provided. If the fee permits membership only, and all other services or products are paid for separately, or if there is a separate annual subscription, the fee is recognised as revenue immediately as long as no significant uncertainty as to its collectability exists. If the fee entitles the member to services or publications to be provided during the membership period, or to purchase goods or services at prices lower than those charged to non-members, it is recognised on a basis that reflects the timing, nature and value of the benefits provided. *[FRS 102.23A.24]*.

3.7   Franchise fees

Franchise agreements between franchisors and franchisees can vary widely both in complexity and in the extent to which various rights, duties and obligations are explicitly addressed. There is no standard franchise agreement which would dictate standard accounting practice for the recognition of all franchise fee revenue. Therefore, only a full understanding of the franchise agreement will reveal the substance of a particular arrangement so that the most appropriate accounting treatment can be determined. The following are the more common areas which are likely to be addressed in any franchise agreement and which will be relevant to the reporting of franchise fee revenue:

(a)   *rights transferred by the franchisor:* the agreement gives the franchisee the right to use the trade name, processes, know-how of the franchisor for a specified period of time or in perpetuity;

(b)   *the amount and terms of payment of initial fees:* payment of initial fees (where applicable) may be fully or partially due in cash, and may be payable immediately, over a specified period or on the fulfilment of certain obligations by the franchisor;

(c)   *amount and terms of payment of continuing franchise fees:* the franchisee will normally be required to pay a continuing fee to the franchisor – usually on the basis of a percentage of gross revenues; and

(d)   *services to be provided by the franchisor, both initially and on a continuing basis:* the franchisor will usually agree to provide a variety of services and advice to the franchisee, such as:

- site selection;
- the procurement of fixed assets and equipment – these may be either purchased by the franchisee, leased from the franchisor or leased from a third party (possibly with the franchisor guaranteeing the lease payments);
- advertising;
- training of franchisee's personnel;
- inspecting, testing and other quality control programmes; and
- book-keeping services.

The Appendix to Section 23 includes a broad discussion of the receipt of franchise fees, stating that they are recognised as revenue on a basis that reflects the purpose for which the fees were charged. *[FRS 102.23A.25]*. The following methods of franchise fee recognition are appropriate:

- *Supplies of equipment and other tangible assets:* the fair value of the assets sold are recognised as revenue when the items are delivered or title passes; *[FRS 102.23A.26]*

- *Supplies of initial and subsequent services:*

  - fees for continuing services, whether part of the initial fee or a separate fee, are recognised as revenue as the services are performed. When the separate fee does not cover the cost of the continuing services together with a reasonable profit, part of the initial fee, to cover the costs of continuing services and to provide a reasonable profit on those services is deferred and recognised as revenue as the services are performed; *[FRS 102.23A.27]*

- the franchise agreement may provide for the franchisor to supply tangible assets, such as equipment or inventories, at a price lower than that charged to others or at a price that does not provide a reasonable profit on those sales. In which case, part of the initial fee to cover estimated costs in excess of that price and to provide a reasonable profit on those sales, is deferred and recognised over the period the goods are likely to be sold to the franchisee. The remaining initial fee is recognised as revenue when performance of all the initial services and other obligations (such as assistance with site selection, staff training, financing and advertising) has been substantially performed by the franchisor; *[FRS 102.23A.28]*

- the initial services and other obligations under an area franchise agreement may depend on the number of individual outlets established in the area. In which case, the fees attributable to the initial services are recognised as revenue in proportion to the number of outlets for which the initial services have been substantially completed; *[FRS 102.23A.29]*

- if the initial fee is collectible over an extended period and there is significant uncertainty that it will be collected in full, the fee is recognised as the cash is received; *[FRS 102.23A.30]*

- *Continuing Franchise Fees*: fees charged for the use of continuing rights granted by the agreement, or for other services provided during the period of the agreement, are recognised as the services are provided or the rights used; *[FRS 102.23A.31]* and

- *Agency Transactions*: transactions under the franchise agreement may, in substance, involve the franchisor acting as agent for the franchisee. For example, the franchisor may order supplies and arrange for their delivery to the franchisee at no profit. Such transactions do not give rise to revenue. *[FRS 102.23A.32]*.

In summary, it is necessary to break down the initial fee into its various components, e.g. the fee for franchise rights, fee for initial services to be performed by the franchisor, fair value of tangible assets sold etc. The initial fee for individual components may be recognised as revenue at different stages. The portion that relates to the franchise rights may be recognised in full immediately unless part of it has to be deferred because the continuing fee does not cover the cost of continuing services to be provided by the franchisor plus a reasonable profit. In this case a portion of the initial fee should be deferred and recognised as services are provided. The fees for initial services should only be recognised when the services have been 'substantially performed' (it is unlikely that substantial performance will have been completed before the franchisee opens for business).

3.8 Interest, royalties and dividends

If an entity's assets are used by others, yielding interest, royalties or dividends, an entity shall recognise that revenue when it is probable that the entity will receive the economic benefits associated with the transaction and the amount of the revenue can be measured reliably. *[FRS 102.23.28]*.

The following bases shall be used to recognise revenue: *[FRS 102.23.29]*

- interest shall be recognised using the effective interest method – see Chapter 10 at 8.2. When calculating the effective interest rate, any related fees, finance charges paid or received, transaction costs and other premiums or discounts shall be included;

- royalties shall be recognised on an accruals basis in accordance with the substance of the relevant agreement; and

- dividends shall be recognised when the shareholder's right to receive payment is established.

3.8.1   *Licence fees and royalties*

Fees and royalties paid for the use of an entity's assets (such as trademarks, patents, software, music copyright, record masters and motion picture films) are normally recognised in accordance with the substance of the agreement. As a practical matter, this may be on a straight-line basis over the life of the agreement, for example, when a licensee has the right to use certain technology for a specified period of time. *[FRS 102.23A.34]*.

Therefore, under normal circumstances, the accounting treatment of advance royalties or licence receipts is straightforward; under the accruals concept the advance should be treated as deferred income when received, and released to the profit and loss account when earned under the terms of the licence or royalty agreement.

Companies in the media sector often enter into arrangements in which one party receives upfront sums of a similar nature, e.g. a music company may receive fees from another party for content that will be accessed via the internet, e.g. digital downloading or streaming of music. If so, the same considerations apply and revenue will be recognised when earned under the terms of the licence or royalty agreement. Often the terms of such arrangements call for the music company to make its current product (past recordings) available and may also require that the future product be made available to the other party in exchange for an upfront payment (often called a 'minimum guarantee') that is recouped against future amounts owed to the music company by the other party. This revenue will generally be recognised over the term of the arrangement. However, in cases where there is no expectation or obligation to provide future content (arrangement is for past recordings only), revenue would generally be recognised by the music company once its product has been made available to the other party. In the latter instance, the arrangement would likely be viewed as an in-substance sale, as discussed below.

Advance receipts may comprise a number of components that may require revenue to be recognised on different bases. Advance royalty or licence receipts have to be distinguished from assignments of rights that are, in substance, sales. The Appendix to Section 23 explains the following:

'An assignment of rights for a fixed fee or non-refundable guarantee under a non-cancellable contract which permits the licensee to exploit those rights freely and the licensor has no remaining obligations to perform is, in substance, a sale. An example is a licensing agreement for the use of software when the licensor has no obligations subsequent to delivery. Another example is the granting of rights to exhibit a motion picture film in markets where the licensor has no control over the distributor and expects to receive no further revenues from the box office receipts. In such cases, revenue is recognised at the time of sale.' *[FRS 102.23A.35]*.

Software revenue recognition and the granting of rights to exhibit motion pictures are discussed at 4.2 and 4.5 below respectively, but in-substance sales are not restricted to these sectors. Some arrangements in the pharmaceutical sector can also be accounted for as in-substance sales.

Licence fees or royalties may be receivable only on the occurrence of a future event, in which case revenue will be recognised only when it is probable that the fee or royalty will be received. This is normally when the event has occurred. *[FRS 102.23A.36]*.

3.8.2 Dividends

Dividends are recognised when the shareholder's right to receive payment is established. *[FRS 102.23.29(c)]*.

3.9 Construction contracts

Section 23 also brings into its scope construction contracts.

3.9.1 Differences to IAS 11 (superseded) for construction contracts

Although the construction contracts section of Section 23 is based on IAS 11 (superseded), there are a number of paragraphs of IAS 11 (superseded) which have been omitted from FRS 102. In general these provided further guidance on specific areas.

3.9.1.A Construction of a separate asset

IAS 11 (superseded) provided guidance on accounting where either the contract provides for the construction of an additional asset at the option of the customer, or may be amended to include the construction of an additional asset. The standard had concluded that this should be treated as a new contract if:

- the asset differs significantly in design, technology or function from the asset or assets covered by the original contract; or
- the price of the asset is negotiated without regard to the original contract price.

This guidance has been omitted from FRS 102. Preparers could refer this guidance given the similarities between FRS 102 and IAS 11 (superseded). This is discussed further at 4.6 below.

3.9.1.B Contract revenue

IAS 11 (superseded) also provided guidance on the composition of contract revenue. This has not been included in FRS 102. See 3.9.4 below for further discussion on this.

3.9.1.C Contract costs

IAS 11 (superseded) provided further guidance on the composition of contract costs, which has not been included in FRS 102. See 3.9.5 below for further discussion on this.

3.9.1.D Recognition of contract revenue and expenses

Although FRS 102 states that the percentage of completion method must be used when the outcome of the contract can be reliably estimated, and that an entity shall recognise as an expense immediately any costs whose recovery is not probable, it provides no further guidance on the recognition of contract revenue and expenses. Further discussion on this is given at 4.7 below.

3.9.2   *Whether an arrangement is a construction contract*

Determining whether an arrangement is a construction contract is critical as this determines whether revenue is recognised using the percentage of completion method under Section 23. Otherwise revenue is not recognised until the risks and rewards of ownership and control have passed. The definition of a construction contract is at 3.1 above.

The underlying principle of Section 23 is that, once the outcome of a construction contract can be estimated reliably, revenue (and costs) associated with the construction contract should be recognised by reference to the stage of completion of the contract activity at the end of the reporting period. *[FRS 102.23.17]*.

3.9.3   *Combination and segmentation of contracts*

The requirements in Section 23 should usually be applied separately to each construction contract. However, in order to reflect the substance of the transaction it may be necessary for a contract to be sub-divided and apply Section 23 individually to each component, or to a group of contracts to be treated as one. *[FRS 102.23.18]*. FRS 102 provides guidance on two separate cases. The first case is where a single contract covers the construction of a number of separate assets, each of which is in substance a separate asset. This would be treated as a separate contract for each asset provided that the following criteria are met: *[FRS 102.23.19]*

- separate proposals have been submitted for each asset;
- each asset has been subject to separate negotiation, and the contractor and customer are able to accept or reject that part of the contract relating to each asset; and
- the costs and revenues of each asset can be identified.

The second case is effectively the reverse of the first and deals with situations where in substance there is only a single contract with a customer, or a group of customers. A group of contracts should be treated as a single contract where: *[FRS 102.23.20]*

- the group of contracts is negotiated as a single package;
- the contracts are so closely interrelated that they are, in effect, part of a single project with an overall profit margin; and
- the contracts are performed concurrently or in a continuous sequence.

3.9.4   *Contract revenue*

FRS 102 does not define what should be included in contract revenue, therefore preparers could refer to the guidance in IAS 11 (superseded). Alternatively, preparers could follow IFRS 15 – see Chapter 28 of EY International GAAP 2019 – for further guidance using the hierarchy in Section 10. Under IAS 11 (superseded) contract revenue comprises the amount of revenue initially agreed by the parties together with any variations, claims and incentive payments as long as it is probable that they will result in revenue and can be measured reliably. It is also worth noting that the overriding principles of Section 23 are that revenue must be able to be reliably measured and that a flow of economic benefits to the entity is probable, and that these are the same principles as noted above in IAS 11 (superseded). Section 23 states that such revenue is to be measured at the fair value of the consideration received and receivable. *[FRS 102.23.3]*. In this context, measurement of fair value includes the process whereby the consideration is to be revised as events occur and uncertainties are resolved. These may include contractual matters such as increases in revenue in a fixed price contract as a result of cost escalation clauses or, when a contract involves a fixed price per unit of output, contract revenue may increase as the number of units is increased. Penalties for delays may reduce revenue. In addition variations and claims must be taken into account. Variations are instructions by the customer to change the scope of the work to be performed under the contract, including changes to the specification or design of the asset or to the duration of the contract. Variations may only be included in contract revenue when it is probable that the customer will approve the variation and the amount to be charged for it, and the amount can be reliably measured.

Given the extended periods over which contracts are carried out and changes in circumstances prevailing whilst the work is in progress, it is quite normal for a contractor to submit claims for additional sums to a customer. Claims may be made for costs not included in the original contract or arising as an indirect consequence of approved variations, such as customer caused delays, errors in specification or design or disputed variations. Because their settlement is by negotiation (which can in practice be very protracted), they are subject to a high level of uncertainty; consequently, no credit should be taken for these items unless negotiations have reached an advanced stage such that:

- it is probable that the customer will accept the claim; and
- the amount that it is probable will be accepted by the customer can be measured reliably.

This means that, as a minimum, the claims must have been agreed in principle and, in the absence of an agreed sum, the amount to be accrued must have been carefully assessed.

Contracts may provide for incentive payments, for example, for an early completion or superior performance. They may only be included in contract revenue when the contract is at such a stage that it is probable the required performance will be achieved and the amount can be measured reliably.

3.9.5 Contract costs

The Triennial review 2017 clarified that costs that relate directly to a contract and are incurred in securing the contract are also included as part of the contract costs if they can be separately identified and measured reliably and it is probable that the contract will be obtained. When costs incurred in securing a contract are recognised as an expense in the period in which they are incurred, they are not included in contract costs if the contract is obtained in a subsequent period. *[FRS 102.23.17A]*.

Section 23 only covers revenue from construction contracts, and does not cover the amounts that should be included in contract costs in the percentage of completion method calculation.

Although Section 13 – *Inventories* – excludes from its scope work in progress arising under construction contracts, this can be used to determine the costs to be included in the percentage of completion method. This is due to the hierarchy in Section 10 that requires users to consider the requirements of other Sections in FRS 102 in developing and applying an accounting policy for an event or transaction. *[FRS 102.10.5]*. Under Section 13 costs of inventories include all costs of purchase, costs of conversion and other costs incurred in bringing the inventories to their present location and condition. *[FRS 102.13.5]*. Costs of conversion include costs directly related to the units of production, such as direct labour. They also include a systematic allocation of fixed and variable production overheads that are incurred in converting materials into finished goods. *[FRS 102.13.8]*. Although not dealing directly with construction contracts the above guidance can be applied in broad terms to construction contracts.

Again, preparers could refer to IAS 11 (superseded) for further guidance in this area as that standard deal specifically with construction contract costs. Alternatively, preparers could follow IFRS 15 – see Chapter 28 of EY International GAAP 2019 for further guidance using the hierarchy in Section 10. The following details the relevant guidance in IAS 11 (superseded) which have been omitted from FRS 102.

Directly related costs would normally include:

- site labour costs, including site supervision;
- costs of materials used in construction;
- depreciation of plant and equipment used on the contract;
- costs of moving plant, equipment and materials to and from the contract site;
- costs of hiring plant and equipment;
- costs of design and technical assistance that is directly related to the contract;
- the estimated costs of rectification and guarantee work, including expected warranty costs; and
- claims from third parties.

If the contractor generates incidental income from any directly related cost, e.g. by selling surplus materials and disposing of equipment at the end of the contract, this is treated as a reduction of contract costs.

The second category of costs comprises those attributable to contract activity in general that can be allocated to a particular contract. These include design and technical assistance not directly related to an individual contract, insurance, and construction overheads such as the costs or preparing and processing the payroll for the personnel working on the contract. These must be allocated using a systematic and rational method, consistently applied to all costs having similar characteristics. Allocation must be based on the normal level of construction activity.

There are various costs that, in most circumstances, were specifically precluded by IAS 11 (superseded) from being attributed to contract activity or allocated to a contract. These are general administration costs, selling costs, research and development costs and the depreciation of idle plant and equipment that is not used on a particular contract. However, the entity is allowed to classify general administration costs and research and development as contract costs if they are specifically reimbursable under the terms of the contract.

Costs may be attributed to a contract from the date on which it is secured until its final completion. Additionally, the costs relating directly to the contract, which have been incurred in gaining the business, may be included in contract costs if they have been incurred once it is probable the contract will be obtained. These costs must be separately identified and measured reliably. Costs that have been written off cannot be reinstated if the contract is obtained in a subsequent period.

3.9.5.A Borrowing costs

Borrowing costs may be specific to individual contracts or attributable to contract activity in general. Section 25 – *Borrowing Costs*, requires capitalisation of borrowing costs that are directly attributable to the acquisition, construction or production of qualifying assets. *[FRS 102.25.2]*. We would expect users to apply this by analogy to construction contracts and to include borrowing costs which are directly attributable to the asset being constructed.

3.9.5.B Inefficiencies

Section 13 specifically excludes from the cost of inventories 'abnormal amounts of wasted materials, labour or other production costs'. *[FRS 102.13.13(a)]*. There is no such requirement in Section 23 and this is reflected in a degree of uncertainty about how to account for inefficiencies and 'abnormal costs' incurred during the course of a construction contract. If these costs are simply added to the total contract costs, this may affect the stage of completion if contract activity is estimated based on the total costs that have been incurred.

Referring to the principles of IAS 11 (superseded), it is clear that abnormal costs and inefficiencies that relate solely to a particular period ought to be expensed in that period as they are not 'costs that relate directly to a specific contract'. The issue is often a practical one on how to distinguish such costs from revisions of estimates that can be more reasonably treated as contract costs.

Usually, inefficiencies that result from an observable event can be identified and expensed. For example, if a major supplier collapses and the materials from another supplier are more expensive, the additional costs ought to be identifiable without undue difficulty and represent an inefficiency that ought to be expensed. By contrast, an unexpected increase in costs of materials unrelated to such an event may simply be a revision to the estimate of costs. Other situations may be less clear. It is relatively easy to distinguish cases at either extreme but much less so when issues are marginal, where judgement will have to be exercised.

3.9.6 Percentage of completion method

FRS 102 requires the percentage of completion method to be used in order to recognise revenue from construction contracts. Estimates of revenue and costs should be reviewed and, when necessary, revised as the construction contract progresses. *[FRS 102.23.21]*. This will include any contract inefficiencies which do not relate to a specific period (see 3.9.5.B above).

The percentage of completion method is applied on a cumulative basis in each accounting period to the current estimates of revenue and costs. FRS 102 does not specify how to use these revised estimates, however IAS 11 (superseded) clarified that revised estimates must be used in determining the amount of revenue and expenses recognised in profit or loss in the period in which the change is made, and in subsequent periods. Alternatively, preparers could follow IFRS 15 – see Chapter 28 of EY International GAAP 2019 for further guidance using the hierarchy in Section 10. Refer to section 2.1.6 above that highlights over time recognition of revenue under IFRS 15.

Section 23 allows the stage of completion of a transaction or contract to be determined in a number of ways, including: *[FRS 102.23.22]*

- the proportion that costs incurred for work performed to date bear to the estimated total costs. Costs incurred for work performed to date do not include costs relating to future activity, such as for materials or prepayments;

- surveys of work performed; and

- completion of a physical proportion of the contract work or completion of a proportion of the service contract.

These could, of course, give different answers regarding the stage of completion of the contract as demonstrated in the following example:

Example 20.3:   Determination of revenue

A company is engaged in a construction contract with an expected sales value of £10,000. It is the end of the accounting period during which the company commenced work on this contract and it needs to compute the amount of revenue to be reflected in the profit and loss account for this contract.

Scenario (i)	Stage of completion is measured by the proportion that contract costs incurred for work performed to date bear to the estimated total contract costs

The company has incurred and applied costs of £4,000. £3,000 is the best estimate of costs to complete. The company should therefore recognise revenue of £5,714, being the appropriate proportion of total contract value, and computed thus:

$$\frac{4,000}{7,000} \times 10,000 = 5,714$$

Scenario (ii)	Stage of completion is measured by surveys of work performed

An independent surveyor has certified that at the period-end the contract is 55% complete and that the company is entitled to apply for cumulative progress payments of £5,225 (after a 5% retention). In this case the company would record revenue of £5,500 being the sales value of the work done. (If it is anticipated that rectification work will have to be carried out to secure the release of the retention money then this should be taken into account in computing the stage of completion – but the fact that there is retention of an amount does not, in itself, directly impact the amount of revenue to be recorded.)

Scenario (iii)	Stage of completion is measured by completion of a physical proportion of the contract work

The company's best estimate of the physical proportion of the work it has completed is that it is 60% complete. The value of the work done and, therefore, the revenue to be recognised is £6,000.

In each of the above scenarios the computation of the amount of revenue is quite independent of the question of how much profit (if any) should be taken. This is as it should be, because even if a contract is loss making the sales price will be earned and this should be reflected by recording revenue as the contract progresses. In the final analysis, any loss arises because costs are greater than revenue, and costs should be reflected through cost of sales. Different methods of determining revenue will, as disclosed above, produce different results, which highlights the importance of disclosing the method adopted by the entity.

Where an entity uses a method of determining the stage of completion other than by measuring the proportion of costs incurred to date compared to the total estimated contract costs, an entity may find that the profit margin recognised is not in line with expectations due to the timing of the recognition of costs. For example, a survey of work performed may indicate that the work is 70% complete, but significantly more costs have been incurred, resulting in a lower than expected profit margin and costs that cannot be expensed under this method recorded as an asset. It is not clear in FRS 102 how such costs could be treated as work in progress. Likewise, if costs incurred are lower than expected, it would normally be inappropriate for entities to accrue for costs not yet incurred. In this circumstance, entities may need to reassess whether the method selected for determining the stage of completion is the most appropriate. The method chosen should accurately reflect the progress in the contract and should be applied consistently.

There are of course other ways of measuring work done, e.g. labour hours, which depending upon the exact circumstances might lead to a more appropriate basis for computing revenue.

If the stage of completion is determined by reference to the contract costs incurred to date, it is fundamental that this figure includes only those contract costs that reflect work actually performed so far. Any contract costs that relate to future activity on the contract must be excluded from the calculation.

3.9.7   The determination of contract revenue and expenses

FRS 102 provides no illustrative examples on the determination of contract revenue and expenses. Preparers could refer to the Illustrative Examples in IAS 11 (superseded) for further guidance. The following example is based on an illustrative example from IAS 11 (superseded).

Example 20.4:   *Cumulative example – the determination of contract revenue and expenses*

The following example illustrates the determination of the stage of completion of a contract and the timing of the recognition of contract revenue and expenses, measured by the proportion that contract costs incurred for work performed to date bear to the estimated total contract costs.

A construction contractor has a fixed price contract to build a bridge. The initial amount of revenue agreed in the contract is £9,000. The contractor's initial estimate of contract costs is £8,000. It will take 3 years to build the bridge.

By the end of year 1, the contractor's estimate of contract costs has increased to £8,050.

In year 2, the customer approves a variation resulting in an increase in contract revenue of £200 and estimated additional contract costs of £150. At the end of year 2, costs incurred include £100 for standard materials stored at the site to be used in year 3 to complete the project.

The contractor determines the stage of completion of the contract by calculating the proportion that contract costs incurred for work performed to date bear to the latest estimated total contract costs. A summary of the financial data during the construction period is as follows:

	Year 1 £	Year 2 £	Year 3 £
Initial amount of revenue agreed in contract	9,000	9,000	9,000
Variation	–	200	200
Total contract revenue	9,000	9,200	9,200
Contract costs incurred to date	2,093	6,168	8,200
Contract costs to complete	5,957	2,023	–
Total estimated contract costs	8,050	8,200	8,200
Estimated profit	950	1,000	1,000
Stage of completion	26%	74%	100%

The constructor uses the percentages calculated as above to calculate the revenue, contract costs and profits over the term of the contract. The stage of completion for year 2 (74%) is determined by excluding from contract costs incurred for work performed to date the £100 of standard materials stored at the site for use in year 3 ((£6,138 – £100) / £8,200 = 74%).

The amounts of revenue, expenses and profit recognised in profit or loss in the three years are as follows:

	To date £	Recognised in prior years £	Recognised in current years £
Year 1			
Revenue (9,000 × 26%)	2,340	–	2,340
Expenses	2,093	–	2,093
Profit	247	–	247
Year 2			
Revenue (9,200 × 74%)	6,808	2,340	4,468
Expenses			
(6,168 incurred less 100 of materials in storage)	6,068	2,093	3,975
Profit	740	247	493
Year 3			
Revenue (9,200 × 100%)	9,200	6,808	2,392
Expenses	8,200	6,068	2,132
Profit	1,000	740	260

This does not mean that contract activity is necessarily based on the total costs that have been incurred by the entity. Contract costs that relate to future activity, such as for inventories or prepayments, should be deferred and recognised as an asset if it is probable that the costs will be recovered. *[FRS 102.23.23]*.

FRS 102 requires that where it is not probable that costs will be recovered, these costs should be expensed immediately. *[FRS 102.23.24]*. FRS 102 again does not provide any examples of situations in which this may occur, however IAS 11 (superseded) provided further guidance in this area. There may be deficiencies in the contract, which means that it is not fully enforceable. Other problems may be caused by the operation of law, such as the outcome of pending litigation or legislation or the expropriation of property. The customer or the contractor may be unable for some reason to complete the contract.

3.9.8 Inability to estimate the outcome of a contract reliably

When the outcome of a construction contract cannot be estimated reliably, an entity will first have to determine whether it has incurred costs that it is probable will be recovered under the contract. It can then recognise revenue to the extent of these costs. Contract costs should be recognised as an expense in the period in which they are incurred, *[FRS 102.23.25]*, unless, of course, they relate to future contract activity, such as materials purchased for future use on the contract as explained above.

It is often difficult to estimate the outcome of a contract reliably during its early stages. This means that it is not possible to recognise contract profit. However, the entity may be satisfied that at least some of the contract costs it has incurred will be recovered and it will be able to recognise revenue to this extent.

3.9.9 Loss making contracts and uncollectible revenue

As soon as the entity considers that it is probable that the contract costs will exceed contract revenue it must immediately recognise the expected loss as an expense, with a corresponding provision for an onerous contract. *[FRS 102.23.26]*.

Where the collectability of an amount already recognised as contract revenue is no longer probable, the entity shall recognise the uncollectible amount as an expense rather than as an adjustment of the amount of contract revenue. *[FRS 102.23.27]*.

3.9.10 Examples of construction contract revenue recognition under the principles of Section 23

The Appendix to Section 23 provides two examples in relation to the construction of real estate to help determine when the percentage of completion method should be used.

An entity that undertakes the construction of real estate, directly or through subcontractors, and enters into an agreement with one or more buyers before construction is complete, shall account for the agreement using the percentage of completion method, only if: *[FRS 102.23A.14]*

- the buyer is able to specify the major structural elements of the design of the real estate before construction begins and/or specify major structural changes once construction is in progress (whether it exercises that ability or not); or

- the buyer acquires and supplies construction materials and the entity provides only construction services.

If the entity is required to provide services together with construction materials in order to perform its contractual obligation to deliver real estate to the buyer, the agreement shall be accounted for as the sale of goods. In this case, the buyer does not obtain control or the significant risks and rewards of ownership of the work in progress in its current state as construction progresses. Rather the transfer occurs only on delivery of the completed real estate to the buyer. *[FRS 102.23A.15]*.

3.11   Disclosures

The following disclosures are required for revenue: *[FRS 102.23.30]*

- the accounting policies adopted for revenue recognition including the methods to determine the stage of completion involving rendering of services;
- the amount of revenue recognised during the period, showing separately, at a minimum, the amount of each category arising from:
  - i.   the sale of goods;
  - ii.   the rendering of services;
  - iii. interest;
  - iv.   royalties;
  - v.   dividends;
  - vi.   commissions;
  - vii. grants; and
  - viii. any other significant types of revenue.

FRS 102 also requires the following disclosures in relation to construction contracts: *[FRS 102.23.31]*

- the amount of contract revenue recognised as revenue in the period;
- the methods used to determine the contract revenue recognised in the period; and
- the methods used to determine the stage of completion of contracts in progress.

In addition, an entity should present: *[FRS 102.23.32]*

- the gross amount due from customers for contract work, as an asset; and
- the gross amount due to customers for contract work, as a liability.

The Triennial review 2017 clarified that for all contracts in progress for which contract expenses plus recognised profits (less recognised losses) exceed progress billings, the gross amount due from customers for contract work is the net amount of: *[FRS 102.23.33]*

- costs recognised as contract expenses plus recognised profits; less
- the sum of recognised losses and progress billings.

The Triennial review 2017 clarified that for all contracts in progress for which progress billings exceed contract expenses plus recognised profits (less recognised losses), the gross amount due to customers for contract work is the net amount of: *[FRS 102.23.34]*

- costs recognised as contract expenses plus recognised profits; less
- the sum of recognised losses and progress billings.

The Triennial review 2017 also clarified that costs incurred less costs recognised as contract expenses shall be presented as contract work in progress within inventories, unless an entity has chosen to adapt its statement of financial position in accordance with paragraph 2A of Section 4. *[FRS 102.23.35]*.

4   PRACTICAL ISSUES

Although Section 23 lays down general principles of revenue recognition, there is a lack of specific guidance in relation to matters such as multiple-element revenue arrangements and industry specific issues. Section 10 provides additional guidance if an FRS does not specifically address a transaction, event or condition, and requires that management shall use its judgement in developing and applying an accounting policy that results in information that is relevant and reliable. *[FRS 102.10.4]*. In making the judgement, management may also consider the requirements and guidance in EU-adopted IFRS dealing with similar and related issues. *[FRS 102.10.6]*. Management may therefore need to consider the requirements and guidance in IFRS 15 in dealing with the practical implementation issues discussed below.

4.1   Receipt of initial fees

It is common practice in certain industries to charge an initial fee at the inception of a service (or signing of a contract) followed by subsequent service fees. These can present revenue allocation problems. As it is not always clear what the initial fee represents, it is necessary to determine what proportion, if any, of the initial fee has been earned on receipt, and how much relates to the provision of future services. For example, if an initial fee is paid on signing a contract, before this receipt is recognised as revenue, the entity needs to consider a number of factors including what the customer is receiving in return for the initial fee, whether the entity has delivered a service for which the initial consideration is a fair consideration, and whether a service is yet to be delivered following receipt of the fee.

The fact the initial fee is non-refundable does not, of itself, support revenue recognition on receipt. In some cases, large initial fees are paid for the provision of a service, whilst continuing fees are relatively small in relation to future services to be provided. If it is probable that the continuing fees will not cover the cost of the continuing services to be provided plus a reasonable profit, then a portion of the initial fee should be deferred over the period of the service contract such that a reasonable profit is earned throughout the service period. Accounting for initial fees requires judgement and, as such, practice does vary. Entities must assess the terms and conditions for each individual contract in order to conclude on the appropriate revenue recognition treatment for initial fees.

4.2   Software revenue recognition

The software services industry face a number of issues such as when to recognise revenue from contracts to develop software, software licensing fees, customer support services and data services. However, these issues have not been addressed in Section 23. Instead, Section 23 provides only one sentence of guidance: 'fees from the development of customised software are recognised as revenue by reference to the stage of completion of the development, including completion of services provided for post-delivery service support.' *[FRS 102.23A.33]*. IAS 18 (superseded) did not address these issues either, therefore, preparers could follow IFRS 15 – see Chapter 28 of EY International GAAP 2019 for further guidance using the hierarchy in Section 10.

Software arrangements range from those that simply provide a licence for a single software product, to those that require significant production, modification or customisation of the software. Arrangements may also include multiple products or services.

Because of the nature of the products and services involved, applying the general revenue recognition principles to software transactions can sometimes be difficult. As a result, software companies have used a variety of methods to recognise revenue, often producing significantly different financial results from similar transactions.

4.2.1   Accounting for a software licence

If the arrangement is for a simple provision of a licence for a single software product, then the guidance for accounting for licences, as discussed at 3.8.1 above, should be applied.

4.2.2   Accounting for software arrangements with multiple elements

Software arrangements may provide licences for many products or services such as additional software products, upgrades/enhancements, rights to exchange or return software or post-contract customer support (PCS).

As noted at 3.3 above, in certain circumstances it is necessary to apply the recognition criteria to the separately identifiable components of a single transaction in order to reflect the substance of the transaction. *[FRS 102.23.8]*. However, as discussed at 3.5 above, when services are performed by an indeterminate number of acts over a specified period of time, an entity shall recognise revenue on a straight-line basis over that period, unless another method better reflects the stage of completion. *[FRS 102.23.15]*.

It is likely that many software contracts will fall somewhere between these two extremes and so entities must use their judgement in order to select the most appropriate methodology, taking into consideration all relevant facts and circumstances.

4.2.3   Accounting for arrangements which require significant production, modification or customisation of software

Where companies are running well-established computer installations with systems and configurations that they do not wish to change, off-the-shelf software packages are generally not suitable for their purposes. For this reason, some software companies will enter into a customer contract whereby they agree to customise a generalised software product to meet the customer's specific requirements. A simple form of customisation is to modify the system's output reports so that they integrate with the customer's existing management reporting system. However, customisation will often entail more involved obligations, e.g. having to translate the software so that it is able to run on the customer's specific hardware configuration, data conversion, system integration, installation and testing.

The question that arises, therefore, is what is the appropriate basis on which a software company recognises revenue when it enters into a contract that involves significant obligations? Section 23 includes guidance on accounting for construction contracts and it is our view that this guidance, including the percentage of completion method, may also be applied to other contracts with separately identifiable components. *[FRS 102.23.18]*. The percentage of completion method is discussed at 3.6 and 3.9.6 above.

Consequently, where an entity is able to make reliable estimates as to the extent of progress towards completion of a contract, the related revenues and the related costs, and where the outcome of the contract can be assessed with reasonable certainty, the percentage of completion method of profit recognition should be applied.

4.3   Revenue recognition issues in the telecommunications sector

There are significant revenue recognition complexities that affect the telecommunications sector, and about which FRS 102 and the superseded IFRSs are effectively silent. However, preparers could follow IFRS 15 – see Chapter 28 of EY International GAAP 2019 – for further guidance using the hierarchy in Section 10. The complexities differ depending upon the type of telecommunications services being considered. Recognition issues may differ between fixed line (principally voice and data) services and wireless (principally mobile voice and data) services. In addition customers may purchase elements of both as part of a bundled package.

A number of general factors underlie the accounting issues. For example, local regulatory laws may dictate the way business is done by the operators, there may be restrictions on the discounting of handsets, handsets may be branded in some countries but not in others, both branded and unbranded handsets may co-exist in the same country and there may be varying degrees of price protection.

4.3.1   *Recording revenue for multiple service elements ('bundled offers')*

Section 23 states that when necessary to reflect the substance of the transaction, revenue shall be recognised for the separately identifiable components of a single transaction and refers specifically to situations where the selling price of a product includes an identifiable amount for subsequent servicing, in which case that amount is deferred and recognised as revenue over the period during which the service is performed. *[FRS 102.23A.19]*. This is directly relevant to some aspects of multiple deliverable arrangements offerings, where customers are offered a 'bundle' of assets and services.

When a consumer enters into a mobile phone contract with a provider, the contract may be a package that includes a handset and various combinations of talktime, text messages and data allowances (internet access). The bundle may also include fixed line products, such as voice, video and broadband services.

Consumers may pay for their bundle of assets and services in a number of different ways: a payment for the handset (which may be discounted); connection charges related to activation of the handset; monthly fixed or usage-based payments; and prepayments by credit card or voucher. None of these payments may relate directly to the cost of the services being provided by the operator, and operators also may offer loyalty programs that entail the provision of future services at substantially reduced prices.

As there is no specific guidance within FRS 102 (nor the superseded IFRSs) on the subject of multiple deliverable arrangements beyond the brief references as noted above, companies will need to apply judgement in applying the requirements of Section 23 relevant to the facts and circumstances of each transaction.

Chapter 20

4.3.1.A   *Accounting for handsets and monthly service arrangements*

Many of the mobile operators that provide handsets to customers who subscribe to service contracts do so at heavily discounted prices or even free of charge. Most telecommunications operators have an accounting policy under which handsets and airtime are separately identifiable components but they apply a form of 'residual method' to the amount of revenue taken for the sale of the handset, recognising no more than the amount contractually receivable for it.

However, although FRS 102 requires revenue to be measured at its fair value, it is not definitive on the method of allocation. Usually, an allocation of revenue based on relative fair values would be considered an appropriate basis but this is not an explicit requirement. This is discussed at 3.3 above.

4.3.1.B   *'Free' services*

'Free' services are often included in the monthly service arrangement for contract subscribers as an additional incentive to encourage subscribers to sign up for a fixed contract period, typically one or two years.

'Free' services can either be provided up-front as inclusive services for a fixed monthly fee, or as an incentive after a specific threshold has been exceeded, intended to encourage subscribers to spend more than their specified amount.

As a result, one of the challenges for mobile operators is the accounting treatment for the 'free' service period. In our opinion, the total amount that is contractually required to be paid by the customer is recognised as revenue rateably over the entire service period, including the period in which the 'free' services are provided.

The following example illustrates the accounting for free minutes granted at subscription date by a mobile operator to a subscriber:

Example 20.5:   *Accounting for free minutes*

An operator enters into a service contract with a customer for a period of 12 months. Under the contract specifications, for the first two months the customer is offered 60 free minutes talktime per month and for the remaining 10 months of the contract the customer will pay a fixed fee of £30 per month for 60 minutes of communication per month. The operator considers the recoverability of the amounts due under the contract from the customer to be probable.

In our view, since the free minutes offer is linked to the non-cancellable contract, the fee receivable for the non-cancellable contract is spread over the entire contract term.

Consequently, the fixed fee of £300 (£30 × 10 months) to be received from the subscriber would be recognised on a straight-line basis over the 12 month contract period, being the stage of completion of the contract. The operator therefore would recognise £25 each month over the twelve month period (£30 × 10 / 12 = £25).

4.3.1.C   *Connection and up-front fees*

Connection fees can be a feature of both the wireless (mobile) and the fixed line activities. Accordingly, connection and up-front fees are an issue for both fixed line and mobile operators.

When the mobile telecoms industry was in its infancy, upfront costs such as connection fees, contract handling fees, registration fees, fees for changing plans etc., were commonly charged by operators. Such charges have been phased out over the years and are no longer a common feature in the UK.

Nevertheless, there are still occasions in which a telecommunications operator charges its subscribers a one-time non-refundable fee for connection to its network. The contract for telecommunications services between the operator and the subscriber has either a finite or an indefinite life and includes the provision of the network connection and on-going telecommunications services. The direct/incremental costs incurred by the operator in providing the connection service are primarily the technician's salary and related benefits; this technician provides both connection and physical installation services at the same time.

In such cases, the connection service and the telecommunications services have to be analysed in accordance with their economic substance in order to determine whether they should be combined or segmented for revenue recognition purposes. When the connection transaction is bundled with the service arrangement in such a way that the commercial effect cannot be understood without reference to the two transactions as a whole, the connection fee revenue should be recognised over the expected term of the customer relationship under the arrangement which generated the connection. In our view, the expected term of the customer relationship may not necessarily be the contract period, but may be the estimated average life of the customer relationship, provided that this can be estimated reliably.

Charging fees for connection to a fixed telephone line remains relatively common. Although connection fees are commonly recognised over the contract period, upfront recognition of the non-refundable fee may be possible if there is a clearly demonstrable separate service and it is provided at the inception of the contract.

4.3.2 'Gross versus net' issues

The difficulty of deciding whether to record revenue gross or net is pervasive in the telecommunications sector. The problem occurs because of the difficulty in deciding whether the parties involved in any particular agreement are acting as principal or agent. Section 23 sets out that in an agency relationship, the amounts collected on behalf of the principal are not revenue and instead, revenue is the amount of commission. *[FRS 102.23.4]*.

The principal versus agent assessment is further discussed at 3.2.2 above but does not necessarily help decide the matter in many telecoms scenarios. A frequent arrangement is where there is data content provided by third parties that is subject to a separate provider agreement.

Content, such as music, navigation and other downloads such as 'apps' can either be included in the monthly price plan, or purchased separately on an *ad hoc* basis. Operators can either develop the content in-house, or use third party providers to offer a range of items to their subscribers, with charges based either on duration (news, traffic updates etc.) or on quantity (number of ringtones, games etc.).

The issue is whether the operator should report the content revenue based on the gross amount billed to the subscriber because it has earned revenue from the sale of the services, or the net amount retained (that is, the amount billed to the subscriber less the amount paid to a supplier) because it has only earned a commission or fee. Is the substance of the transaction with the supplier one of buying and on-selling goods or selling goods on consignment (i.e. an agency relationship)? The two most important considerations for most of these arrangements are:

- whether the operator has the primary responsibility for providing the services to the customer or for fulfilling the order, for example by being responsible for the acceptability of the services ordered or purchased by the customer; and

- whether it has latitude in establishing prices, either directly or indirectly, for example by providing additional goods or services.

Inventory risk is unlikely to be relevant for a service provision and credit risk may be only a weak indicator as the amounts are individually small and may be paid to access the download.

Therefore, if the content is an own-brand product or service, then the revenue receivable from subscribers should be recorded as revenue by the operator, and the amounts payable to the third party content providers should be recorded as costs.

By contrast, if the content is a non-branded product/service that is merely using the mobile operator's network as a medium to access its subscriber base, then the amounts receivable from subscribers should not be recorded as revenue. The operator's revenue will comprise only the commissions receivable from the content providers for the use of the operator's network.

4.3.3   Accounting for roll-over minutes

Where an operator offers a subscriber a finite number of call minutes for a fixed amount per period with the option of rolling over any unused minutes, the question arises as to how the operator should account for the unused minutes that the subscriber holds. The operator is not obliged to reimburse the subscriber for unused minutes, but is obliged (normally subject to a ceiling) to provide the accumulated unused call minutes to the subscriber until the end of the contract, after which they expire.

In such cases, revenue is recognised at the time the minutes are used. Any minutes unused at the end of each month should be recognised as deferred revenue.

However, in some instances, the operator has relevant and reliable evidence that shows that a portion of those unused minutes will not be used before the expiration of the validity period. In that case, the operator could consider an alternative revenue recognition policy that would take account of the probability of unused minutes at the end of the validity period in the computation of the revenue per minute used by the subscriber. This would result in allocating a higher amount of revenue per minute used.

When the validity period expires, any remaining balance of unused minutes would be recognised as revenue immediately, since the obligation of the operator to provide the contractual call minutes is extinguished.

4.3.4   Accounting for the sale of prepaid calling cards

Prepaid cards are normally sold by an operator either through its own sales outlet or through distributors. The credit sold with the cards may have an expiry date that varies from one operator to another, although, in certain limited jurisdictions (not the UK), there is no expiry date. For example, prepaid cards may be sold with an initial credit of £10 covering 60 minutes of communication and the credit has a validity period of 90 days from the date of activation. If not used within this period, the credit is lost.

When the cards are sold through distributors, the distributor is usually obliged to sell the cards to the customers at the face value of the card. On sale of the card, the distributor pays the operator the face value less a commission. The distributor has a right to return unsold cards to the operator. Once the distributor has sold the cards, it has no further obligation to the operator.

In our view, when an operator sells calling cards directly, revenue is recognised at the time the minutes are used. Any minutes unused at the end of each month should be recognised as deferred revenue. However, if the operator has relevant and reliable evidence that shows that a portion of those unused minutes will not be used before the expiration of the validity period then it could consider an alternative revenue recognition policy. This would take account of the probability of unused minutes at the end of the validity period in the computation of the revenue per minute recognised as the minutes are used by the customer.

When an operator sells calling cards through a distributor, the revenue is required to be recognised based on the substance of the arrangement with the distributor.

It is usually the case that the distributor is in substance acting as an agent for the operator. The revenue associated with the sale of the calling card is recognised when the subscriber uses the minutes. The difference between the card's usage value, which is charged to the subscriber, and the amount paid to the operator is the distributor's commission.

In our view, unless the distributor is also an operator or the calling card could be used on any operator's network (which is rare), it would be difficult to conclude that the distributor is the principal in the arrangement with the subscriber, because the distributor would not have the capacity to act as the principal under the terms of the service provided by the calling card to the subscriber (see 3.2.2 and 4.3.2 above).

4.4 Excise taxes and goods and services taxes: recognition of gross versus net revenues

Many jurisdictions around the world raise taxes that are based on components of sales or production. These include excise taxes and goods and services or value added taxes. In some cases, these taxes are, in effect, collected by the entity from customers on behalf of the taxing authority. In other cases, the taxpayer's role is more in the nature of principal than agent. The regulations (for example, excise taxes in the tobacco and drinks industries) differ significantly from one country to another. The practical accounting issue that arises concerns the interpretation of whether excise taxes and goods and services taxes be deducted from revenue (net presentation) or included in the cost of sales and, therefore, revenue (gross presentation). *[FRS 102.23.4].*

The appropriate accounting treatment will depend on the particular circumstances. In determining whether gross or net presentation is appropriate, the entity needs to consider whether it is acting in a manner similar to that of an agent or principal.

4.5 Film exhibition and television broadcast rights

Revenue received from the licensing of films for exhibition at cinemas and on television should be recognised in accordance with the general recognition principles discussed in this chapter.

Contracts for the television broadcast rights of films normally allow for multiple showings within a specific period; these contracts usually expire either on the date of the last authorised telecast, or on a specified date, whichever occurs first. Rights for the exhibition of films at cinemas are generally sold either on the basis of a percentage of the box office receipts or for a flat fee.

The Appendix to Section 23 states that 'an assignment of rights for a fixed fee or non-refundable guarantee under a non-cancellable contract that permits the licensee to exploit those rights freely and the licensor has no remaining obligations to perform is, in substance, a sale'. When a licensor grants rights to exhibit a motion picture film in markets where it has no control over the distributor and expects to receive no further revenues from the box office receipts, revenue is recognised at the time of sale. *[FRS 102.23A.35]*.

Therefore, it is our view that the revenue from the sale of broadcast, film or exhibition rights may be recognised in full upon commencement of the licence period provided the following conditions are met:

(a)   a contract has been entered into;

(b)   the film is complete and available for delivery;

(c)   there are no outstanding performance obligations, other than having to make a copy of the film and deliver it to the licensee; and

(d)   collectability is reasonably assured.

This applies even if the rights allow for multiple showings within a specific period for a non-refundable flat fee and the contract expires either on the date of the last authorised telecast, or on a specified date, whichever occurs first. The sale can be recognised even though the rights have not yet been used by the purchaser. We do not believe it is appropriate to recognise revenue prior to the date of commencement of the licence period since it is only from this date that the licensee is able to freely exploit the rights of the licence and hence has the rewards of ownership. *[FRS 102.23.10(a)]*.

When the licensor is obliged to perform any significant acts or provide any significant services subsequent to delivery of the film to the licensee – for example to promote the film – it would be appropriate to recognise revenue as the acts or services are performed (or, as a practical matter, on a straight-line basis over the period of the licence). *[FRS 102.23.15]*.

Rights for the exhibition of a film at cinemas may be granted on the basis of a percentage of the box office receipts, in which case revenue should be recognised as the entitlement to revenue arises based on box office receipts.

If the fees only become payable when the box office receipts have exceeded a minimum level, revenue should not be recognised until the minimum level has been achieved. The Appendix to Section 23 sets out that revenue that is contingent on the occurrence of a future event is recognised only when it is probable that the fee or royalty will be received, which is normally when the event has occurred. *[FRS 102.23A.36]*.

4.6   Construction of a separate asset

An area where it is necessary to consider whether contracts should be combined is in contract options and additions. Combining of contracts is important because of its potential impact on the recognition of revenue and profits on transactions. If any optional asset is treated as part of the original contract, contract revenue will be recognised using the percentage of completion method over the combined contract.

FRS 102 does not specifically consider the option of an additional asset, only whether a contract covering a number of assets should be treated as a separate construction contract for each asset. This is discussed further at 3.9.3 above.

IAS 11 (superseded) considered the circumstances in which a contract that gives a customer an option for an additional asset (or is amended in this manner) and concluded that this should be treated as a new contract if:

- the asset differs significantly in design, technology of function from the asset or assets covered by the original contract; or
- the price of the asset is negotiated without regard to the original contract price.

This means, for example, that the contract for an additional, identical asset would be treated as a separate contract if its price was negotiated separately from the original contract price. Costs often decline with additional production, not only because of the effects of initial costs but also because of the 'learning curve' (the time taken by the workforce to perform activities decreases with practice and repetition). This could result in a much higher profit margin on the additional contract. If, for example, a government department takes up its option with a defence contractor for five more aircraft, in addition to the original twenty five that had been contracted for, but the option was unpriced and the new contract is priced afresh, then it cannot be combined with the original contract regardless of the difference in profit margins. The combining of contracts may also have unexpected results. If, for example, an entity has a contract with a government to build two satellites and a priced option to build a third, it may be obliged to combine the contracts at the point at which the option is exercised. This could well be in a different accounting period to the commencement of the contract and there will be a cumulative catch up of revenue and probably profits. In subsequent periods results will be based on the combined contracts.

4.7 The recognition of contract revenue and expenses

IAS 11 (superseded) identifies two types of construction contract, fixed price and cost plus contracts. This differentiation is not made in FRS 102. Preparers could refer IAS 11 (superseded) for further guidance. Alternatively, preparers could follow IFRS 15 – see Chapter 28 of EY International GAAP 2019 for further guidance using the hierarchy in Section 10.

In the case of a fixed price contract, IAS 11 (superseded) states that the outcome of a construction contract can be estimated reliably when all the conditions discussed below are satisfied:

- First, it must be probable that the economic benefits associated with the contract will flow to the entity, which must be able to measure total contract revenue reliably. As discussed further below, these conditions will usually be satisfied when there are adequate contractual arrangements between parties.

- Second, both the contract costs to complete the contract and the stage of contract completion at the end of the reporting period must be able to be measured reliably.

- Third, the entity must be able to identify and measure reliably the contract costs attributable to the contract so that actual contract costs incurred can be compared with prior estimates. This means that it must have adequate resources and budgeting systems.

Cost plus contracts are not subject to all of the same uncertainties as fixed price contracts. As with any transaction, it must be probable that the economic benefits associated with the contract will flow to the entity in order to recognise income at all. In most contracts this will be evidenced by the contract documentation. The fundamental criterion for a cost plus contract is the proper measurement of contract costs. Therefore, the contract costs attributable to the contract, whether or not specifically reimbursable, must be clearly identified and measured reliably.

There are certain general principles that apply whether the contract is classified as a fixed cost or as a cost plus. Recognition of revenue is by reference to the 'stage of completion method', and contact revenue and costs are recognised as revenue and expenses in profit or loss in the period in which the work is performed.

This does not mean that contract activity is necessarily based on the total costs that have been incurred by the entity. As noted at 3.9.7 above contract costs that relate to future contract activity (i.e. that activity for which revenue has not yet been recognised) may be deferred and recognised as an asset as long as it is probable that they will be recovered. These costs are usually called contract work in progress. Otherwise, contract costs are recognised in the profit or loss as they are incurred.

Importantly, neither does it mean that an entity can determine what it considers to be an appropriate profit margin for the whole contract and spread costs over the contract so as to achieve this margin, thereby classifying deferred costs as work in progress.

5   SUMMARY OF GAAP DIFFERENCES

Key differences between FRS 102 and IFRS 15 in accounting for revenue are set out below.

	FRS 102	*IFRS 15*
Revenue recognition	Based on the principles in superseded IAS 18 and IAS 11 that was essentially based on the principle of risks and rewards	Based on transfer of control which is the core principle and includes more detailed guidance than in legacy standards
Disclosures – Amount of revenue recognised during the period	Amount of revenue for each category from the sale of goods, rendering of services interest, royalties, dividends, commissions, grants and 'other significant types' of revenue	Quantitative and qualitative information by providing disaggregated revenue from contracts with customers into categories that depict how the nature, amount, timing and uncertainty of revenue and cash flows are affected by economic factors
Segmental disclosures	Entities with publically traded debt or equity instruments shall disclose segmental information in line with IFRS 8 – *Operating Segments* – revenues from external customers, intra-segment revenues, revenue that is 10% or more of the combined revenue of all operating segments and a reconciliation of the reportable segments' revenues to the total entity revenue	Entities within the scope of IFRS 8 shall also disclose sufficient information to enable users of financial statements to understand the relationship between the disclosure of disaggregated revenue and revenue information that is disclosed for each reportable segment, if the entity applies IFRS 8

Chapter 20

Chapter 21   Government grants

List of examples

Chapter 21   Government grants

1   INTRODUCTION

Government grants typically involve a transfer of resources by a government body to an entity to support specified activities or projects. The transfer of funds is usually dependent on past or future compliance with certain conditions relating to the entity's operating activities. The exact nature of the support varies over time as governments and their priorities change.

The main accounting issue that arises from government grants is how to deal with the benefit that the grant represents in the profit and loss account. Section 24 – *Government Grants* – gives an accounting policy choice over one of two models for recognising the benefit; the performance model and the accrual model. *[FRS 102.24.4]*. These methods are discussed at 3.4 and 3.5 below.

Section 24 also recognises that an entity may receive other forms of government assistance, such as free technical or marketing advice and the provision of guarantees, including assistance which cannot reasonably have a value placed upon them. Rather than prescribe how these should be accounted for, it requires disclosure about such assistance. *[FRS 102.24.6(d), 7]*.

The FRC made only a minor change to Section 24 as a result of the *Amendments to FRS 102 Triennial review 2017 – Incremental improvements and clarifications* (Triennial review 2017), issued in December 2017, The change clarified that the accounting for incoming resources from non-exchange transactions other than government grants is addressed in Section 34 – *Specialised Activities*. See 3.2 below and Chapter 31 at 6.3. *[FRS 102.PBE24.1A]*.

2   COMPARISON BETWEEN SECTION 24 AND IFRS

There are some differences between the accounting and disclosure requirements in Section 24 compared to IFRS (IAS 20 – *Accounting for Government Grants and Disclosure of Government Assistance*). The key differences are discussed at 2.1 to 2.3 below and are summarised at 4 below.

2.1   Recognition

Section 24 provides an accounting policy choice for recognising grants as income using either a performance model or an accrual model. *[FRS 102.24.4]*. The performance model means the grant is recognised as income as the performance related conditions are met. *[FRS 102.24.5B]*. The accrual model means that the grant is recognised as income when the related expenses are recognised. *[FRS 102.24.5D]*.

IAS 20 follows an accruals-based approach requiring grants to be recognised in profit or loss on a systematic basis as the entity recognises the related expense. *[IAS 20.12]*. IAS 20 does not permit a performance model approach.

2.2   Measurement

Section 24 requires that all government grants are measured on initial recognition at the fair value of the asset received or receivable. *[FRS 102.24.5]*.

IAS 20 allows non-monetary government grants to be recorded initially at fair value, or alternatively at a nominal amount. *[IAS 20.23]*.

2.3   Presentation

Section 24 prohibits the deferred element of a grant that relates to an asset being deducted from the carrying amount of the asset. *[FRS 102.24.5G]*.

IAS 20 allows two options, presenting the deferred element either as deferred income or as a deduction against the asset. *[IAS 20.24]*.

3   REQUIREMENTS OF SECTION 24 FOR GOVERNMENT GRANTS

3.1   Terms used in Section 24

The following terms are used in Section 24 with the meanings specified:

Term	Definition
Class of assets	A grouping of assets of a similar nature and use in an entity's operations. *[FRS 102 Appendix I]*.
Fair value	The amount for which an asset could be exchanged, a liability settled, or an equity instrument granted could be exchanged, between knowledgeable, willing parties in an arm's length transaction. In the absence of any specific guidance provided in the relevant Section of FRS 102, the guidance in the Appendix to Section 2 – Concepts *and* Pervasive Principles – shall be used in determining fair value. *[FRS 102 Appendix I]*.
Government	Government, government agencies and similar bodies whether local, national or international. *[FRS 102 Appendix I]*.
Government assistance	Action by government designed to provide an economic benefit specific to an entity or range of entities qualifying under specified criteria. *[FRS 102.24.7]*.
Government grant	Assistance by government in the form of a transfer of resources to an entity in return for past or future compliance with specified conditions relating to the operating activities of the entity. *[FRS 102 Appendix I]*.

Liability	A present obligation of the entity arising from past events, the settlement of which is expected to result in an outflow from the entity of resources embodying economic benefits. *[FRS 102 Appendix I]*.
Operating activities	The principal revenue-producing activities of the entity and other activities that are not investing or financing activities. *[FRS 102 Appendix I]*.
Performance-related condition	A condition that requires the performance of a particular level of service or units of output to be delivered, with payment of, or entitlement to, the resources conditional on that performance. *[FRS 102 Appendix I]*.

3.2 Scope

The accounting requirements in Section 24 apply to all government grants, defined as assistance by government in the form of a transfer of resources to an entity in return for past or future compliance with specified conditions relating to the operating activities of the entity. *[FRS 102 Appendix I]*. In this context, the term 'government' includes government agencies and similar bodies whether local, national or international. *[FRS 102 Appendix I]*.

The Triennial review 2017 added clarification that the accounting for incoming resources from non-exchange transactions other than government grants is addressed in Section 34 – *Specialised Activities*. See Chapter 31 at 6.3. *[FRS 102.PBE24.1A]*.

A government grant is distinguished from 'government assistance', defined as action by government designed to provide an economic benefit specific to an entity or range of entities qualifying under specified criteria. Examples of government assistance include free technical or marketing advice and the provision of guarantees. *[FRS 102.24.7]*.

The recognition and measurement provisions of Section 24 do not apply to government assistance that does not meet the definition of a grant and to grants in the form of government assistance that:

- cannot reasonably have a value placed on them; *[FRS 102.24.2]*
- comprise transactions with government that cannot be distinguished from the normal trading transactions of the entity; *[FRS 102.24.2]* or
- are provided in the form of benefits that are available in determining taxable profit or loss or are determined or limited on the basis of income tax liability such as income tax holidays, investment tax credits, accelerated depreciation allowances and reduced income tax rates. *[FRS 102.24.3]*.

FRS 102 does not provide examples of assistance that might be incapable of reasonable measurement or examples of transactions that are indistinguishable from the normal trading transactions of the entity. Such examples might include cases when financial guarantees are provided by government in the absence of any commercial alternative source or where the entity is being favoured by a government's procurement policy. The treatment of investment tax credits is discussed further at 3.2.1 below and in Chapter 26 at 3.4.

Whilst the recognition and measurement provisions of Section 24 do not apply to the forms of government assistance noted above, certain disclosures are required, as discussed at 3.8 below.

3.2.1 Investment tax credits

As discussed at 3.2 above, investment tax credits are cited as an example of government assistance excluded from the scope of Section 24. Taxes based on income are required to be accounted under Section 29 – *Income Tax*. *[FRS 102.24.3]*. This implies that those investment tax credits that are excluded from the scope of Section 24 would be accounted for under Section 29 (see Chapter 26). However, if government assistance is described as an investment tax credit, but it is neither determined nor limited by the entity's income tax liability nor provided in the form of an income tax deduction, such assistance should be accounted for as a government grant under Section 24.

Investment tax credits are not defined in FRS 102 and can take different forms and be subject to different terms. Sometimes a tax credit is given as a deductible expense in computing the entity's tax liability, and sometimes as a deduction from the tax liability, rather than as a deductible expense. In some cases, the assistance is chargeable to corporation tax and in others it is not. Entitlement to assistance can be determined in a variety of ways. Investment tax credits may relate to direct investment in property, plant and equipment, research and development or other specific activities. Some credits may be realisable only through a reduction in current or future corporation tax payable, while others may be settled directly in cash if the entity is loss-making or otherwise does not have sufficient corporation tax payable to offset the credit within a certain period. Access to the credit may be limited according to the total of all taxes paid to the government providing the assistance, including employment taxes (such as PAYE and NIC) and VAT, in addition to corporation tax. There may be other conditions associated with receiving the investment tax credit, for example with respect to the conduct and continuing activities of the entity, and the credit may become repayable if ongoing conditions are not met.

This raises the question as to how an entity should assess whether a particular investment tax credit gives rise to assistance in the form of benefits that are available in determining taxable profit or loss or are determined or limited on the basis of income tax liability *[FRS 102.24.3]* and, therefore, whether Section 24 or Section 29 should be applied. In our view, such a judgment would be informed by reference to the following factors, as applied to the specific facts and circumstances relating to the incentive:

Feature of credit	Indicator of Section 24 treatment	Indicator of Section 29 treatment
Method of realisation	Directly settled in cash where there are insufficient taxable profits to allow credit to be fully offset, or available for set off against payroll taxes, VAT or amounts owed to government other than income taxes payable.	Only available as a reduction in income taxes payable (i.e. benefit is forfeit if there are insufficient income taxes payable). However, the longer the period allowed for carrying forward unused credits, the less relevant this indicator becomes.
Number of conditions not related to tax position (e.g. minimum employment, ongoing use of purchased assets)	Many.	None or few.

Restrictions as to nature of expenditure required to receive the grant	Highly specific.	Broad criteria encompassing many different types of qualifying expenditure.
Tax status of grant income	Taxable.	Not taxable.

In group accounts in which entities from a number of different jurisdictions may be consolidated, it may be desirable that all investment tax credits should be consistently accounted for, either as a government grant or as an element of income tax. However, the fact that judgement is required in making this determination may mean that predominant practice by FRS 102 reporters relating to a specific type of tax credit has evolved differently from predominant practice by FRS 102 reporters in accounting for a substantially similar credit in another tax jurisdiction. We believe that, in determining whether the arrangement is of a type that falls within the scope of Section 24 or Section 29, an entity should consider the following factors in the order listed below:

- the predominant local determination by FRS 102 reporters as to whether a specific credit in the relevant tax jurisdiction falls within the scope of Section 24 or Section 29;

- if there is no predominant local consensus, the group wide approach to determining whether Section 24 or Section 29 applies to such a credit; and

- in the absence of a predominant local consensus or a group wide approach to making the determination, the indicators listed in the table above should provide guidance.

This may mean that an entity operating in a number of territories adopts different accounting treatments for apparently similar arrangements in different countries. However, this approach at least ensures a measure of comparability between different FRS 102 reporters operating in the same tax jurisdiction.

The treatment of investment tax credits accounted under Section 29 is discussed in Chapter 26 at 3.4.

Example 21.1:   UK research and development expenditure credit (RDEC)

Eligible entities in the UK are entitled to an investment tax credit known as the RDEC (sometimes referred to colloquially as the 'above-the-line' tax credit). Features of the tax credit relevant to an accounting analysis are:

- entities are generally entitled to a gross credit of 11% of qualifying R&D expenditure (with some entities entitled to a higher rate);

- the gross credit is treated as taxable income;

- the available credit is first set against the entity's corporation tax liability for the current period;

- the amount of any remaining credit (net of corporation tax) is 'capped' by reference to employment expenditure (measured by reference to the entity's PAYE and NIC liabilities);

- any remaining credit (net of corporation tax and the employment costs cap) can be carried back or carried forward to reduce the entity's corporation tax liability for certain earlier and later periods, or ceded by way of group relief;

- any unrecovered excess can be offset against the entity's other outstanding tax liabilities (e.g. PAYE and NIC); and

- any amount not recovered in any of the ways listed above is recoverable in cash from the tax authority (HMRC).

Should the RDEC credit be treated as a government grant or an element of income tax?

Analysis of these features by reference to the criteria suggested above leads us to the view that the RDEC credit is more appropriately regarded as a government grant, and therefore reflected in profit before tax. In particular, the benefits of the tax credit are capable of being realised in cash where there is insufficient corporation tax capacity; the tax credit relates to specific qualifying expenditure; and the grant income is determined on a pre-tax basis and is itself taxable.

Such an analysis requires a thorough understanding of the rules applying to the particular relief. Other seemingly similar reliefs should be treated as income taxes under Section 29 if, for example, the relief is not itself taxable; the relief could only be recovered by offset against other liabilities to corporation tax; or, where there is a cash payment alternative, the expected cash inflow approximates more closely to the value of the tax benefit rather than to the value of the expenditure incurred.

As noted above, an RDEC credit is treated as taxable income and so will affect the current tax liability in two ways as illustrated in the following example.

Example 21.2: *Illustration of RDEC credit consequences on current tax liability*

A company engages in research and development activity and has incurred qualifying research and development expenditure of £1,000,000 which results in a gross RDEC credit of £110,000. The company has a current tax liability of £150,000 and its tax rate is 20%.

Subject to meeting the recognition criteria (see 3.3.1 below) the gross RDEC of £110,000 will be initially recognised by the following entries:

	£	£
Current tax receivable (1)	110,000	
Deferred income(2)		110,000

(1) The receivable is ultimately 'current tax receivable' as the amount is recoverable from HMRC to reduce payments of corporation tax. However, it may be considered appropriate to reflect it initially as an 'other receivable' until a right of set off has been established against the current tax liability.

(2) The timing of the release of the deferred income to profit or loss will be governed by the requirements of Section 24 (see 3.3.3 below).

The £110,000 receivable will then be applied to reduce the current tax liability of £150,000.

However, the gross RDEC credit is taxable so there would be a current tax charge arising from the £110,000 RDEC receivable of £22,000 (at a 20% rate):

	£	£
Current tax charge (profit and loss)	22,000	
Current tax liability		22,000

So the consequence of a gross RDEC credit on the current tax liability is a net reduction of £88,000 (receivable of £110,000 offset against an additional liability of £22,000).

Additionally, there may be deferred tax arising on the transaction to the extent that the £110,000 is recognised in profit or loss on a different basis to immediate recognition (e.g. deferred under Section 24). However for simplicity, deferred tax is not considered in this example, nor is the need to utilise the RDEC credit against anything other than the current tax liability.

3.3 Recognition and measurement

3.3.1 *General conditions for recognition*

Section 24 requires that government grants should be recognised only when there is reasonable assurance that:

(a) the entity will comply with the conditions attaching to them; and

(b) the grants will be received. *[FRS 102.24.3A].*

The standard does not define 'reasonable assurance'. However, we would not expect an entity to recognise government grants before it was at least probable (or 'more likely than not') *[FRS 102 Appendix I]* that the entity would comply with the conditions attached to the grants (even though these conditions may relate to future performance and other future events) and that the grants would be received.

3.3.2 *Measurement*

All government grants are measured on initial recognition at the fair value of the asset received or receivable. *[FRS 102.24.5].* The asset will normally be cash but could be a non-monetary asset such as land or other resources.

In this context, fair value is the amount for which an asset could be exchanged, between knowledgeable, willing parties in an arm's length transaction. Where guidance on determining the fair value of a specific asset is not available in the relevant section of FRS 102, the guidance in the Appendix to Section 2 – *Concepts and Pervasive Principles* – should be used (see Chapter 4). *[FRS 102 Appendix I].*

3.3.3 *Basis of recognition in income*

Section 24 provides entities with an accounting policy choice over the method of recognition of government grants in the income statement:

*   the performance model (see 3.4 below); or

*   the accrual model (see 3.5 below).

The policy choice must be applied on a class-by-class basis. *[FRS 102.24.4].*

A class of assets is defined in FRS 102 as a grouping of assets of a similar nature and use in an entity's operations. *[FRS 102 Appendix I].* A class of financial assets is a grouping that is appropriate to the nature of the information disclosed and that takes into account the characteristics of the financial assets. *[FRS 102.11.48(c)].* Therefore, it would appear that government grants of a similar nature and subject to similar conditions should be recognised in income in a similar way.

Any accounting policy choice should be made according to the requirements of Section 10 – *Accounting Policies, Estimates and Errors*. This requires that the chosen accounting policy results in information that is relevant to the decision-making needs of users of the financial statements and reflects the economic substance of transactions, other events and conditions, and not merely their legal form. *[FRS 102.10.4].* In that regard, an understanding of the purpose for which the grant was awarded is a relevant consideration.

3.4   The performance model

Under this model, grant income is recognised by reference to the achievement of performance-related conditions, as follows:

- If there are no imposed, specified future performance-related conditions on the entity, then the grant is recognised in income when the grant proceeds are received or receivable.

- If there are imposed, specified future performance-related conditions on the entity, then the grant is recognised in income only when the performance-related conditions are met.

- Any grant received in advance of being able to be recognised as income under either of the above circumstances is recognised as a liability. *[FRS 102.24.5B]*.

FRS 102 defines a performance-related condition as a condition that requires the performance of a particular level of service or units of output to be delivered, with payment of, or entitlement to, the resources conditional on that performance. *[FRS 102 Appendix I]*.

When the performance model is applied, a grant with no performance-related conditions will be recognised in income in full when received or receivable (i.e. when the general recognition requirements at 3.3.1 above are met), irrespective of the nature or timing of the expenditure to which it is contributing.

If a performance-related condition operates over time, the question arises as to how the grant is recognised. In the Financial Reporting Council's *Staff Education Note 8 – Government Grants* – (SEN 8) an example is illustrated where a grant contributed to the build cost of a factory but with a performance-related condition of usage and employment (see Example 21.3 below). SEN 8 states that 'the mechanism for recognising the grant during the specified period would depend on the detailed terms and conditions, but it would not generally be based on the expected useful life of the building'.[1]

One of the most relevant terms and conditions to consider in determining how income should be recognised in profit or loss will be how any potential obligation to repay the grant varies as the performance period elapses. There are two most likely scenarios:

(a) If the potential obligation to repay the grant remains equal to the full amount of the grant throughout the performance period and that obligation is only discharged in full at the end of the performance period then, in our view, the full grant should be recognised in profit or loss at the end of the performance period.

(b) If the potential obligation to repay the grant reduces as the performance period elapses then it may be appropriate to recognise the release of the grant to income over the performance period in line with the corresponding reduction in the amount potentially repayable.

Example 21.3:   *Grant towards a fixed asset – the performance model*

A manufacturing company secures a UK government grant of £200,000 as an incentive to open a factory in a region of high unemployment. There are no further conditions associated with the grant, other than that it is used to pay for the construction of this factory. A second grant is secured from the European Union of £130,000 in relation to the construction of the same factory. An additional condition relating to this grant is that the company continues to operate the factory for a period of five years, subject to repayment of the grant on a time-apportioned basis. The company constructs the factory for a total cost of £600,000 and begins to use it. In the same year in which the factory begins operating the company receives both grants. The company has a policy of depreciating buildings over a useful life of 50 years.

How should the company recognise the grants in the income statement?

Under the performance model, the whole of the UK government grant is recognised in income when the factory is opened, because this is the only condition imposed under the grant. However, the grant from the European Union is subject to an additional condition requiring use of the asset for at least five years. This grant would be recognised in income evenly over that five year period.

3.5   The accrual model

Under this model, the entity is required to classify a grant as relating to either revenue or assets. *[FRS 102.24.5C]*.

3.5.1   *Grants relating to revenue*

Grants relating to revenue should be recognised in the income statement on a systematic basis that matches them with the related costs that they are intended to compensate. *[FRS 102.24.5D]*.

Grants that become receivable as compensation for costs or losses already incurred or to give immediate financial support to the entity with no future related costs should be recognised in income when they become receivable. *[FRS 102.24.5E]*.

Most problems accounting for grants relate to implementing the requirement to match the grant against the costs that it is intended to compensate. This apparently simple principle can be difficult to apply in practice. This is because it is sometimes unclear what the essence of the grant was and, therefore, what costs are being subsidised. Moreover, grants are sometimes given for a particular kind of expenditure that forms part of a larger project, making the allocation a more subjective matter. For example, government assistance that is in the form of a training grant could be recognised in income in any of the following ways:

(a)   matched against direct training costs;

(b)   recognised over a period of time against the salary costs of the employees being trained, for example over the estimated duration of the project;

(c)   recognised over the estimated period for which the company or the employees are expected to benefit from the training;

(d)   matched against total project costs together with other project grants receivable;

(e)   recognised in income systematically over the life of the project, for example, the total grant receivable may be allocated to revenue on a straight-line basis;

(f)   allocated against project costs or income over the period over which the grant is paid (instead of over the project life); or

(g)   recognised in income when received in cash.

Chapter 21

Depending on the circumstances, any of these approaches might produce an acceptable result. However, our observations on these alternative methods are as follows:

- method (a) could lead to recognition of the grant as income in advance of its receipt, since the major part of the direct training costs will often be incurred at the beginning of a project and payment of the grant is usually made retrospectively to the related expenditure. As the total grant receivable may be subject to adjustment, this may not be prudent or may lead to a mismatch of costs and revenues;

- methods (b) to (e) all rely on different interpretations of the expenditure to which the grant is expected to contribute, and could all represent an appropriate form of matching;

- method (f) might not appear to relate to the actual expenditure profile, but, in the absence of better evidence, the period of payment of the grant might in fact give an indication of the duration of the project for which the expenditure is to be subsidised; and

- method (g) is unlikely to be an appropriate method *per se*, as the cash receipt profile may be influenced by factors other than the expenditure profile. However, it may approximate to one of the other methods, or may, in the absence of any conclusive indication as to the expenditure intended to be subsidised by the grant, be the only practicable method that can be adopted.

In the face of the problems described above of attributing a grant to related costs, it is difficult to offer definitive guidance. Entities will have to exercise judgement in determining how the matching principle should be applied. The only overriding considerations are that the method should be systematically and consistently applied, and that, for material grants, the policy adopted should be adequately disclosed.

3.5.2   Grants relating to assets

Grants relating to assets should be recognised in the income statement on a systematic basis over the expected useful life of the asset. *[FRS 102.24.5F]*.

For grants relating to depreciable assets, this means they are usually recognised as income over the periods, and in the proportions, in which depreciation on those assets is charged. Grants relating to non-depreciable assets may also require the fulfilment of certain obligations, in which case they would be recognised as income over the periods in which the costs of meeting the obligations are incurred. For example, a grant of land may be conditional upon the erection of a building on the site and it may be appropriate to recognise it as income over the life of the building.

The Regulations prohibit the offset of items that represent assets against items that represent liabilities. *[1 Sch 8]*. FRS 102 does not therefore permit grants relating to an asset to be deducted from the carrying amount of the asset. The grant should instead be recognised as deferred income. *[FRS 102.24.5G]*.

3.6   Repayment of government grants

A government grant that becomes repayable should be recognised as a liability when the repayment meets the definition of a liability. *[FRS 102.24.5A]*.

3.7 Presentation

Where part of a grant is deferred to be released over the expected useful life of a related asset it should be recognised as deferred income. *[FRS 102.24.5G]*.

FRS 102 does not state where grant income should be presented in the income statement. The most appropriate caption will usually be as part of other operating income, possibly separately identified if significant. Wherever presented, the approach taken should be consistently applied from year to year.

3.8 Disclosure requirements

An entity is required to disclose the following in respect of government grants:

(a) the accounting policy adopted for government grants in particular whether the performance or accrual model has been adopted;

(b) the nature and amount of grants recognised in the financial statements;

(c) unfulfilled conditions and other contingencies attaching to grants that have been recognised in income; and

(d) an indication of any other forms of government assistance from which the entity has directly benefitted. *[FRS 102.24.6]*.

Through (d), Section 24 requires certain disclosures for all forms of government assistance even though it only includes government grants, as defined, in scope of its accounting requirements. For the purposes of item (d) above, other forms of government assistance is defined as action by government designed to provide an economic benefit specific to an entity or a range of entities qualifying under specified criteria, such as free technical or marketing advice and the provision of guarantees. *[FRS 102.24.7]*.

4 SUMMARY OF GAAP DIFFERENCES

The key differences between FRS 102 and IFRS in accounting for government grants are set out below.

	FRS 102	*IFRS*
Recognition	Accounting policy choice using either a performance model (grant is recognised as income as the performance related conditions are met) or an accrual model (grant is recognised as income when the related expenses are recognised).	Only allows accrual model.
Measurement	All government grants are measured on initial recognition at the fair value of the asset received or receivable.	Allows non-monetary government grants to be recorded at a nominal amount as an alternative to fair value.
Presentation	Prohibits the deferred element of a grant that relates to an asset being deducted from the carrying amount of the asset.	Allows two options, deferred income or deduction against the asset.

Chapter 21

References

1 Accounting and Reporting Policy: FRS 102 –
Staff Education Note 8 Government Grants,
Financial Reporting Council, para. 16.

Chapter 22   Borrowing costs

List of examples

Chapter 22   Borrowing costs

1   INTRODUCTION

A common question when determining the initial measurement of an asset is whether or not borrowing (or finance) costs incurred on its acquisition or during the period of its construction should be capitalised as part of the cost of the asset or expensed through profit or loss. Section 25 – *Borrowing Costs* – specifies the accounting for borrowing costs.

2   COMPARISON BETWEEN SECTION 25 AND IFRS

Overall, Section 25 is consistent with UK company law which allows an entity to have accounting policy choice as to whether to capitalise borrowing costs when certain criteria are satisfied. This is different to IFRS since IAS 23 – *Borrowing Costs* – requires capitalisation of borrowing costs when the criteria are satisfied.

The key differences between Section 25 and IFRS are also discussed below. See 4 below for the summary of such GAAP differences.

2.1   Capitalisation of borrowing costs

Under FRS 102, capitalisation of borrowing costs directly attributable to the acquisition, construction or production of a qualifying asset is an accounting policy choice applied separately to each class of qualifying assets (see 3.3 below).

Under IFRS, capitalisation of borrowing costs is mandatory for most qualifying assets (i.e. there is no accounting policy choice). However, capitalisation is an accounting policy choice for a qualifying asset measured at fair value or inventories that are manufactured, or otherwise produced, in large quantities on a repetitive basis. *[IAS 23.4]*.

2.2   General borrowings

Under FRS 102, the general borrowings on which the capitalisation rate is based, exclude the borrowings specifically for the purpose of obtaining either qualifying or non-qualifying assets. Therefore, only the general borrowings are included in the computation of the capitalisation rate (see 3.5.3.B below).

IFRS explicitly excludes only the borrowings that are specifically for the purpose of obtaining qualifying assets, thus together with all the general borrowings, specific borrowings to obtain non-qualifying assets are also included in computing the capitalisation rate.

2.3   Expenditure on qualifying assets

Under FRS 102, for the purpose of applying the capitalisation rate to the expenditure on the qualifying asset, the expenditure on the asset is the average carrying amount of the asset during the period, including borrowing costs previously capitalised. *[FRS 102.25.2C]*.

Under IFRS, the average carrying amount of the asset during a period, including borrowing costs previously capitalised, is regarded as a reasonable approximation of the expenditures to which the capitalisation rate is applied in that period. Expenditures on a qualifying asset are explicitly limited to those expenditures that have resulted in payments of cash, transfers of other assets or the assumption of interest-bearing liabilities and reduced by any progress payments received and grants received in connection with the asset. *[IAS 23.18]*.

2.4   Disclosure differences

Disclosure differences between FRS 102 and IFRS are discussed at 4 below.

3   THE REQUIREMENTS OF SECTION 25 FOR BORROWING COSTS

3.1   Terms used in Section 25

The main terms used throughout Section 25 are as follows: *[FRS 102 Appendix I]*

Term	Definition
Borrowing costs	Interest and other costs incurred by an entity in connection with the borrowing of funds.
Effective interest method	A method of calculating the amortised cost of a financial asset or a financial liability (or a group of financial assets or financial liabilities) and of allocating the interest income or interest expense over the relevant period.
Qualifying asset	An asset that necessarily takes a substantial period of time to get ready for its intended use or sale. Depending on the circumstances any of the following may be qualifying assets: • inventories; • manufacturing plants; • power generation facilities; • intangible assets; and • investment properties. Financial assets and inventories that are produced over a short period of time, are not qualifying assets. Assets that are ready for their intended use or sale when acquired are not qualifying assets.

These definitions are discussed in the relevant sections below.

3.2 Scope of Section 25

Section 25 applies to borrowing costs. Borrowing costs are interest and other costs incurred by an entity in connection with the borrowing of funds. Borrowing costs include:

- interest expense calculated using the effective interest method as set out in Section 11 – *Basic Financial Instruments* (see Chapter 10);
- finance charges in respect of finance leases as set out in Section 20 – *Leases* (see Chapter 18); and
- exchange differences arising from foreign currency borrowings to the extent that they are regarded as an adjustment to interest costs (see 3.5.4 below). *[FRS 102.25.1].*

Section 25 does not deal with the actual or imputed costs of equity used to fund the acquisition or construction of an asset. This would mean that any distributions or other payments made in respect of equity instruments, as defined by Section 22 – *Liabilities and Equity*, are not within the scope of Section 25. Conversely, interest and dividends payable on instruments that are legally equity but classified as financial liabilities under FRS 102 appear to be within the scope of Section 25 (see 3.5.5.D below).

When an entity adopts a policy of capitalising borrowing costs (see 3.3 below), Section 25 addresses whether or not to capitalise borrowing costs as part of the cost of the asset. The identification and measurement of finance costs are not directly dealt with in Section 25 and it does not address many of the ways in which an entity may finance its operations or other finance costs that it may incur. Examples of these other finance costs and their eligibility for capitalisation under Section 25 are discussed at 3.5.5 below.

Section 25 does not preclude the classification of costs, other than those it identifies, as borrowing costs. However, they must meet the basic criterion in Section 25, i.e. that they are 'costs that are directly attributable to the acquisition, construction or production of a qualifying asset', which would, therefore, preclude treating the unwinding of discounts on provisions as borrowing costs. Many unwinding discounts are treated as finance costs in profit or loss. These include discounts relating to various provisions such as those for onerous leases and decommissioning costs. These finance costs will not be borrowing costs under Section 25 because they do not arise in respect of funds borrowed by the entity that can be attributed to a qualifying asset. Therefore, they cannot be capitalised. *[FRS 102.25.1, 2].* In addition, as in the case of exchange differences, capitalisation of such costs should be permitted only 'to the extent that they are regarded as an adjustment to interest costs' (see 3.5.4 below). *[FRS 102.25.1].*

3.3 Accounting for borrowing costs

For borrowing costs directly attributable to the acquisition, construction or production of a qualifying asset, Section 25 provides an accounting policy choice to either:

- capitalise those borrowing costs; or
- recognise all borrowing costs as an expense in profit or loss in the period in which they are incurred. *[FRS 102.25.2].*

Accordingly, all borrowing costs should be recognised as an expense in profit or loss in the period in which they are incurred unless a policy of capitalising borrowing costs is adopted.

Chapter 22

In addition, borrowing costs that are not directly attributable to a qualifying asset must be expensed as incurred.

Where an entity adopts a policy of capitalisation of borrowing costs for qualifying assets, it should be applied consistently to a class of qualifying assets. *[FRS 102.25.2].* The definition of class is discussed at 3.5.1 below.

Since an entity has a policy choice, a change in accounting policy (i.e. capitalisation versus expense) would require retrospective restatements in accordance with Section 10 – *Accounting Policies, Estimates and Errors. [FRS 102.10.11(d), 12].*

3.4   Definition of a qualifying asset

Section 25 defines a qualifying asset as 'an asset that necessarily takes a substantial period of time to get ready for its intended use or sale. Depending on the circumstances any of the following may be qualifying assets:

- inventories;
- manufacturing plants;
- power generation facilities;
- intangible assets; and
- investment properties.' *[FRS 102 Appendix I].*

Financial assets (which we consider include equity instruments of another entity) and inventories that are produced over a short period of time, are not qualifying assets. Assets that are ready for their intended use or sale when acquired are also not qualifying assets. *[FRS 102 Appendix I].*

Section 25 is silent as to whether other types of assets not mentioned in the definition (e.g. owner occupied property, biological assets including bearer plants) can be qualifying assets. In our view, there is nothing to prohibit other assets meeting the definition of a qualifying asset.

Section 25 does not define 'substantial period of time' and this will therefore require the exercise of judgement after considering the specific facts and circumstances. In practice, an asset that normally takes twelve months or more to be ready for its intended use will usually be a qualifying asset.

3.5   Borrowing costs eligible for capitalisation

Borrowing costs are eligible for capitalisation as part of the cost of a qualifying asset if they are directly attributable to the acquisition, construction or production of that qualifying asset (whether or not the funds have been borrowed specifically). *[FRS 102.25.2].*

Section 25 starts from the premise that borrowing costs that are directly attributable to the acquisition, construction or production of a qualifying asset are those borrowing costs that would have been avoided if the expenditure on the qualifying asset had not been made. *[FRS 102.25.2A].* Recognising that it may not always be easy to identify a direct relationship between particular borrowings and a qualifying asset and to determine the borrowings that could otherwise have been avoided, Section 25 includes separate requirements for specific borrowings and general borrowings (see 3.5.2 and 3.5.3 below).

3.5.1   Class of qualifying assets

Where an entity adopts a policy of capitalisation of borrowing costs, it should be applied consistently to a class of qualifying assets. *[FRS 102.25.2]*. There is no specific definition of a 'class of qualifying assets'. However, a 'class of assets' is defined as 'a grouping of assets of a similar nature and use in an entity's operations.' *[FRS 102 Appendix I]*. Therefore, it may be possible to have a capitalisation policy only in relation to plant under construction but not to machinery under construction or inventories that are qualifying assets.

3.5.2   Specific borrowings

To the extent that an entity borrows funds specifically for the purpose of obtaining a qualifying asset, the borrowing costs that are directly related to that qualifying asset can be readily identified. The borrowing costs eligible for capitalisation are the actual borrowing costs incurred on those specific borrowings during the period less any investment income on the temporary investment of those borrowings. *[FRS 102.25.2B]*.

Entities frequently borrow funds in advance of expenditure on qualifying assets and may temporarily invest the borrowings. Section 25 makes it clear that any investment income earned on the temporary investment of those borrowings needs to be deducted from the borrowing costs incurred and only the net amount capitalised (see Example 22.2 below).

There is no restriction in Section 25 on the type of investments in which the funds can be invested but, in our view, to maintain the conclusion that the funds are specific borrowings, the investment must be of a nature that does not expose the principal amount to the risk of not being recovered. The more risky the investment, the greater is the likelihood that the borrowing is not specific to the qualifying asset. If the investment returns a loss rather than income, such losses are not added to the borrowing costs to be capitalised.

3.5.3   General borrowings

To the extent that funds applied to obtain a qualifying asset form part of the entity's general borrowings, Section 25 requires the application of a capitalisation rate to the expenditure on that asset in determining the amount of borrowing costs eligible for capitalisation. However, the amount of borrowing costs an entity capitalises during a period should not exceed the amount of borrowing costs it incurred during that period. *[FRS 102.25.2C]*.

The capitalisation rate used in an accounting period should be the weighted average of rates applicable to the general borrowings of the entity that are outstanding during the period. This excludes borrowings made specifically for the purpose of obtaining other qualifying assets (see 3.5.3.B). The capitalisation rate is then applied to the expenditure on the qualifying asset. For this purpose, the expenditure on the asset is the average carrying amount of the asset during the period, including borrowing costs previously capitalised. *[FRS 102.25.2C]*.

Section 25 does not provide specific guidance regarding interest income earned from temporarily investing excess general funds. However, any interest income earned is unlikely to be directly attributable to the acquisition or construction of a qualifying asset. In addition, the capitalisation rate required by Section 25 focuses on the

Chapter 22

borrowings of the entity outstanding during the period of construction or acquisition and does not include temporary investments. As such, borrowing costs capitalised should not be reduced by interest income earned from the investment of general borrowings nor should such income be included in determining the appropriate capitalisation rate.

In some circumstances, it may be appropriate for all borrowings made by the group (i.e. borrowings of the parent and its subsidiaries) to be taken into account in determining the weighted average of the borrowing costs. In other circumstances, it may be appropriate for each subsidiary to use a weighted average of the borrowing costs applicable to its own borrowings. It is likely that this will largely be determined by the extent to which borrowings are made centrally (and, perhaps, interest expenses met in the same way) and passed through to individual group companies via intercompany accounts and intra-group loans. The capitalisation rate is discussed further at 3.5.3.E below.

There may be practical difficulties in identifying a direct relationship between particular borrowings and a qualifying asset and in determining the borrowings that could otherwise have been avoided. This could be the case if the financing activity of an entity is co-ordinated centrally, for example, if an entity borrows to meet its funding requirements as a whole and the construction of the qualifying asset is financed out of general borrowings. Other circumstances that may cause difficulties (and which are identified by IAS 23) include the following: *[IAS 23.11]*

• a group which has a treasury function and uses a range of debt instruments to borrow funds at varying rates of interest and lends those funds on various bases to other entities in the group; or

• a group which has loans denominated in or linked to foreign currencies and the group operates in highly inflationary economies or there are fluctuations in exchange rates.

In these circumstances, determining the amount of borrowing costs that are directly attributable to the acquisition of a qualifying asset may be difficult and require the exercise of judgement.

3.5.3.A   *Borrowing costs on borrowings related to completed qualifying assets*

As noted at 3.5.3 above, determining general borrowings will not always be straightforward and, as a result, the determination of the amount of borrowing costs that are directly attributable to the acquisition of a qualifying asset is difficult and the exercise of judgement is required.

A question that arises is whether a specific borrowing undertaken to obtain a qualifying asset ever changes its nature into a general borrowing. Differing views exist as to whether or not borrowings change their nature throughout the period they are outstanding. Some consider that once the asset for which the borrowing was incurred has been completed, and the entity chooses to use its funds on constructing other assets rather than repaying the loan, this changes the nature of the loan into a general borrowing. However, to the extent that the contract links the repayment of the loan to specific proceeds generated by the entity, its nature as a specific borrowing would be preserved. Others take the view that once the borrowing has been classified as specific, its nature does not change while it remains outstanding.

Entities may wish to consider using the related guidance in IFRS as permitted by Section 10 (see Chapter 9 at 3.2). In December 2017, the IASB issued the *Annual Improvements to IFRSs 2015-2017 Cycle* which amended paragraph 14 of IAS 23. The amendments clarified that when a qualifying asset is ready for its intended use or sale, an entity treats any outstanding borrowings made specifically to obtain that qualifying asset as part of general borrowings. *[IAS 23.BC14D]*. These amendments apply to accounting periods beginning on or after 1 January 2019.

Refer also to further discussion in 3.6.3 below to determine when all the activities necessary to prepare the qualifying asset for its intended use or sale are 'substantially' complete.

3.5.3.B   *General borrowings related to specific non-qualifying assets*

Another question that arises is regarding the treatment of general borrowings used to purchase a specific asset other than a qualifying asset for the purpose of capitalising borrowing costs.

Section 25 explicitly states that the capitalisation rate to be used should be the weighted average of rates applicable to the entity's 'general borrowings that are outstanding during the period'. *[FRS 102.25.2C]*. This means that any specific borrowings related to obtaining either qualifying assets or non-qualifying assets would be excluded. Therefore, only the general borrowings are included in the computation of capitalisation rate.

3.5.3.C   *Expenditure on the asset*

Section 25 explicitly states that for purposes of applying the capitalisation rate to the expenditure on the qualifying asset, 'the expenditure on the asset is the average carrying amount of the asset during the period, including borrowing costs previously capitalised'. *[FRS 102.25.2C]*.

Accordingly, unlike in IFRS (see 2.3 above), expenditure is not restricted to that resulting in the payment of cash, the transfer of other assets or the assumption of interest-bearing liabilities. Therefore, in principle, costs of a qualifying asset that have only been accrued but have not yet been paid in cash would also be included although, by definition, no interest can have been incurred on an accrued payment. The same principle can be applied to non-interest bearing liabilities e.g. non-interest-bearing trade payables or retention money that is not payable until the asset is completed.

A related issue that can arise in practice is about whether an entity includes expenditures on a qualifying asset incurred before obtaining general borrowings in determining the amount of borrowing costs eligible for capitalisation. Consider the fact pattern below:

- an entity constructs a qualifying asset;
- the entity has no borrowings at the start of the construction of the qualifying asset;
- partway through construction, it borrows funds generally and uses them to finance the construction of the qualifying asset; and
- the entity incurs expenditures on the qualifying asset both before and after it incurs borrowing costs on the general borrowings.

An entity applies paragraph 25.2D(a) of FRS 102 to determine the commencement date for capitalising borrowing costs. This paragraph requires an entity to begin capitalising borrowing costs when it meets all of the following conditions:

- it incurs expenditures on the asset;
- it incurs borrowing costs; and
- it undertakes activities necessary to prepare the asset for its intended use or sale (see also 3.6.1 below). *[FRS 102.25.2D(a)].*

Applying paragraph 25.2D(a) of FRS 102 to the fact pattern described above, the entity would not begin capitalising borrowing costs until it incurs borrowing costs.

Once the entity incurs borrowing costs and therefore satisfies all the three conditions described above, it then applies paragraph 25.2C of FRS 102 to determine the expenditures on a qualifying asset to which it applies the capitalisation rate. In doing so, we believe, the entity does not disregard expenditures on the qualifying asset incurred before the entity obtains the general borrowings. For this purpose, the expenditure on the asset is the average carrying amount of the asset during the period, including borrowing costs previously capitalised.

The above issue was also discussed by the International Financial Reporting Interpretations Committee (the 'Interpretations Committee') in its June 2018[1] and September 2018[2] meetings and a similar conclusion was reached.

3.5.3.D   *Assets carried below cost in the statement of financial position*

An asset may be recognised in the financial statements during the period of production on a basis other than cost, i.e. it may have been written down below cost as a result of being impaired. An asset may be impaired when its carrying amount or expected ultimate cost, including costs to complete and the estimated capitalised interest thereon, exceeds its estimated recoverable amount or net realisable value (see 3.6.2.A below).

The question then arises as to whether the calculation of interest to be capitalised should be based on the cost or carrying amount of the impaired asset. It could be argued that in this case, cost should be used, as this is the amount that the entity or group has had to finance. However, Section 25 explicitly states that the expenditure on the asset is the average carrying amount (not the cost) of the asset during the period. Nevertheless, in the case of an impaired asset, the continued capitalisation based on cost (instead of average carrying value) of the asset may well necessitate a further impairment. Accordingly, although the amount capitalised will be different, this should not affect net profit or loss as this is simply an allocation of costs between finance costs and impairment expense.

3.5.3.E   *Calculation of capitalisation rate*

As noted at 3.5.3 above, determining general borrowings will not always be straightforward, it will be necessary to exercise judgement to meet the main objective – a reasonable measure of the directly attributable finance costs.

The following example illustrates the practical application of the method of calculating the amount of finance costs to be capitalised:

Example 22.1: Calculation of capitalisation rate (no investment income)

On 1 April 20X2 a company engages in the development of a property, which is expected to take five years to complete, at a cost of £6,000,000. The statements of financial position at 31 December 20X1 and 31 December 20X2, prior to capitalisation of interest, are as follows:

	31 December 20X1 £	31 December 20X2 £
Development property	–	1,200,000
Other assets	6,000,000	6,000,000
	6,000,000	7,200,000
Loans		
5.5% debenture stock	2,500,000	2,500,000
Bank loan at 6% p.a.	–	1,200,000
Bank loan at 7% p.a.	1,000,000	1,000,000
	3,500,000	4,700,000
Shareholders' equity	2,500,000	2,500,000

The bank loan with an effective interest rate of 6% was drawn down to match the development expenditure on 1 April 20X2, 1 July 20X2 and 1 October 20X2.

Expenditure was incurred on the development as follows:

	£
1 April 20X2	600,000
1 July 20X2	400,000
1 October 20X2	200,000
	1,200,000

If the bank loan at 6% p.a. is a new borrowing specifically to finance the development then the amount of interest to be capitalised for the year ended 31 December 20X2 would be the amount of interest charged by the bank of £42,000 ((£600,000 × 6% × 9/12) + (£400,000 × 6% × 6/12) + (£200,000 × 6% × 3/12)).

However, if all the borrowings were general (i.e. the bank loan at 6% was not specific to the development) and would have been avoided but for the development, then the amount of interest to be capitalised would be:

$$\frac{\text{Total interest expense for period}}{\text{Weighted average total borrowings}} \times \text{Development expenditure}$$

Total interest expense for the period

	£
£2,500,000 × 5.5%	137,500
£1,200,000 (as above)	42,000
£1,000,000 × 7%	70,000
	249,500

Therefore the capitalisation rate would be calculated as:

$$\frac{249,500}{3,500,000 + 700,000^*} = 5.94\%$$

* Weighted average total borrowings is computed as the sum of £3,500,000 (or £3,500,000 × 12/12) and £700,000 (or (£600,000 × 9/12) + (£400,000 × 6/12) + (£200,000 × 3/12)).

The capitalisation rate would then be applied to the expenditure on the qualifying asset, resulting in an amount to be capitalised of £41,580 as follows:

	£
£600,000 × 5.94% × 9/12	26,730
£400,000 × 5.94% × 6/12	11,880
£200,000 × 5.94% × 3/12	2,970
	41,580

In this example, all borrowings are at fixed rates of interest and the period of construction extends at least until the end of the period, simplifying the calculation. The same principle is applied if borrowings are at floating rates i.e. only the interest costs incurred during that period, and the weighted average borrowings for that period, will be taken into account.

Note that the company's shareholders' equity (i.e. equity instruments – see further discussion at 3.5.5.D below) cannot be taken into account. Also, at least part of the outstanding general borrowings is presumed to finance the acquisition or construction of qualifying assets. Regardless of whether they are financing qualifying or non-qualifying assets, all of the outstanding borrowings are presumed to be general borrowings – unless they are specific borrowings (see discussions at 3.5.3.A and 3.5.3.B above).

The above example also assumes that loans are drawn down to match expenditure on the qualifying asset. If, however, a loan is drawn down immediately and investment income is received on the unapplied funds, then the calculation differs from that in Example 22.1 above. This is illustrated in Example 22.2 below.

Example 22.2:   Calculation of amount to be capitalised – specific borrowings with investment income

Same fact pattern as in Example 22.1 above except that in this example, a bank loan of £6,000,000 with an effective interest rate of 6% was taken out on 31 March 20X2 and fully drawn. The total interest charge for the year ended 31 December 20X2 was consequently £270,000.

However, investment income was also earned at 3% on the unapplied funds during the period as follows:

	£
£5,400,000 × 3% × 3/12	40,500
£5,000,000 × 3% × 3/12	37,500
£4,800,000 × 3% × 3/12	36,000
	114,000

Consequently, the amount of interest to be capitalised for the year ended 31 December 20X2 is:

	£
Total interest charge	270,000
Less: investment income	(114,000)
	156,000

3.5.4 Exchange differences as a borrowing cost

An entity may borrow funds in a currency that is not its functional currency e.g. a Euro loan financing a development in a company which has Sterling as its functional currency. This may have been done on the basis that, over the period of the development, the borrowing costs, even after allowing for exchange differences, were expected to be less than the interest cost of an equivalent Sterling loan.

Section 25 defines borrowing costs as including exchange differences arising from foreign currency borrowings to the extent that they are regarded as an adjustment to interest costs. *[FRS 102.25.1(c)]*. Section 25 does not expand on this point. Therefore, judgement will be required in its application and appropriate disclosure of accounting policies and judgements would provide users with the information they need to understand the financial statements (see 3.7.2 below).

In our view, as exchange rate movements are partly a function of differential interest rates, in many circumstances the foreign exchange differences on directly attributable borrowings will be an adjustment to interest costs that can meet the definition of borrowing costs. However, care is needed if there are fluctuations in exchange rates that cannot be attributed to interest rate differentials. In such cases, we believe that a practical approach is to limit exchange losses taken as borrowing costs such that the total borrowing costs capitalised do not exceed the amount of borrowing costs that would be incurred on functional currency equivalent borrowings, taking into consideration the corresponding market interest rates and other conditions that existed at inception of the borrowings.

If this approach is used and the construction of the qualifying asset takes more than one accounting period, there could be situations where in one period only a portion of foreign exchange differences could be capitalised. However, in subsequent years, if the borrowings are assessed on a cumulative basis, foreign exchange losses previously expensed may now meet the recognition criteria. The two methods of dealing with this are illustrated in Example 22.3 below.

In our view, whether foreign exchange gains and losses are assessed on a discrete period basis or cumulatively over the construction period is a matter of accounting policy, which must be consistently applied. As alluded to above, Section 8 requires clear disclosure of significant accounting policies and judgements that are relevant to an understanding of the financial statements (see 3.7.2 below).

Example 22.3: Foreign exchange differences in more than one period

Method A – The discrete period approach

The amount of foreign exchange differences eligible for capitalisation is determined for each period separately. Foreign exchange losses that did not meet the criteria for capitalisation in previous years are not capitalised in subsequent years.

Method B – The cumulative approach

The borrowing costs to be capitalised are assessed on a cumulative basis based on the cumulative amount of interest expense that would have been incurred had the entity borrowed in its functional currency. The amount of foreign exchange differences capitalised cannot exceed the amount of foreign exchange losses incurred on a cumulative basis at the end of the reporting period. The cumulative approach looks at the construction project as a whole as the unit of account ignoring the occurrence of reporting dates. Consequently, the amount of the foreign exchange differences eligible for capitalisation as an adjustment to the borrowing cost in the period is an estimate, which can change as the exchange rates vary over the construction period.

An illustrative calculation of the amount of foreign exchange differences that may be capitalised under Method A and Method B is set out below.

	Year 1 £	Year 2 £	Total £
Interest expense in foreign currency (A)	25,000	25,000	50,000
Hypothetical interest expense in functional currency (B)	30,000	30,000	60,000
Foreign exchange loss (C)	6,000	3,000	9,000
Method A – Discrete Approach			
Foreign exchange loss capitalised – lower of C and (B minus A)	5,000	3,000	8,000
Foreign exchange loss expensed	1,000	–	1,000
Method B – Cumulative Approach			
Foreign exchange loss capitalised	5,000*	4,000**	9,000
Foreign exchange loss expensed	1,000	(1,000)	–

*   Lower of C and (B minus A) in Year 1.

**   Lower of C and (B minus A) in total across the two years. In this example this represents the sum of the foreign exchange loss of £3,000 capitalised using the discrete approach plus the £1,000 not capitalised in year 1.

3.5.5   Other finance costs as a borrowing cost

An entity may incur other finance costs. Section 25 does not specifically address these. Below are examples of other finance costs including discussion on their eligibility for capitalisation under Section 25.

3.5.5.A   Derivative financial instruments

Many derivative financial instruments such as interest rate swaps, floors, caps and collars are commonly used to manage interest rate risk on borrowings. The most straightforward and commonly encountered derivative financial instrument used to manage interest rate risk is a floating to fixed interest rate swap, as in the following example.

Example 22.4:   Floating to fixed interest rate swaps

Entity A has borrowed £4 million for five years at a floating interest rate to fund the construction of a building. In order to hedge the cash flow interest rate risk arising from these borrowings, A has entered into a matching pay-fixed receive-floating interest rate swap, based on the same underlying nominal sum and duration as the original borrowing, that effectively converts the interest on the borrowings to fixed rate. The net effect of the periodic cash settlements resulting from the hedged and hedging instruments is as if A had borrowed £4 million at a fixed rate of interest.

Section 25 is silent on the use of hedging instruments in determining directly attributable borrowing costs. Section 12 – *Other Financial Instruments Issues* – sets out the basis on which derivatives are recognised and measured. Accounting for hedges is discussed in Chapter 10 at 10.

An entity may consider that a specific derivative financial instrument, such as an interest rate swap, is directly attributable to the acquisition, construction or production of a qualifying asset. If the instrument does not meet the conditions for hedge accounting then the effects on income will be different from those if it does, and they will also be dissimilar from year to year. What is the impact of the derivative on borrowing costs eligible for capitalisation? In particular, does the accounting treatment of the derivative financial instrument affect the amount available for capitalisation? If hedge accounting is not adopted, does this affect the amount available for capitalisation?

The following examples illustrate the potential differences.

Example 22.5: Cash flow hedge of variable-rate debt using an interest rate swap

Entity A is constructing a building and expects it to take 18 months to complete. To finance the construction, on 1 January 20X1, the entity issues an eighteen month, £20,000,000 variable-rate note payable, due on 30 June 20X2 at a floating rate of interest plus a margin of 1%. At that date the market rate of interest is 8%. Interest payment dates and interest rate reset dates occur on 1 January and 1 July until maturity. The principal is due at maturity. On 1 January 20X1, the entity also enters into an eighteen month interest rate swap with a notional amount of £10,000,000 from which it will receive periodic payments at the floating rate and make periodic payments at a fixed rate of 9%, with settlement and rate reset dates every 30 June and 31 December. The fair value of the swap is zero at inception.

On 1 January 20X1, the debt is recorded at £20,000,000. No entry is required for the swap on that date because its fair value was zero at inception.

During the eighteen month period, floating interest rates change as follows:

	Floating rate	Rate paid by Entity A on note payable
Period to 30 June 20X1	8%	9%
Period to 31 Dec 20X1	8.5%	9.5%
Period to 30 June 20X2	9.75%	10.75%

Under the interest rate swap, Entity A receives interest at the market floating rate as above and pays at 9% on the nominal amount of £10,000,000 throughout the period.

At 31 December 20X1, the swap has a fair value of £37,500, reflecting the fact that it is now in the money as Entity A is expected to receive a net cash inflow of this amount in the period until the instrument is terminated. There are no further changes in interest rates prior to the maturity of the swap and the fair value of the swap declines to zero at 30 June 20X2. Note that this example excludes the effect of issue costs and discounting. In addition, it is assumed that, if Entity A is entitled to, and applies, hedge accounting, there will be no ineffectiveness.

The cash flows incurred by the entity on its borrowing and interest rate swap are as follows:

	Cash payments Interest on principal £	Interest rate swap (net) £	Total £
30 June 20X1	900,000	50,000	950,000
31 Dec 20X1	950,000	25,000	975,000
30 June 20X2	1,075,000	(37,500)	1,037,500
Total	2,925,000	37,500	2,962,500

There are a number of different ways in which Entity A could calculate the borrowing costs eligible for capitalisation, including the following.

(i)   The interest rate swap meets the conditions for, and entity A applies, hedge accounting. The finance costs eligible for capitalisation as borrowing costs will be £1,925,000 in the year to 31 December 20X1 and £1,037,500 in the period ended 30 June 20X2.

(ii) Entity A does not apply hedge accounting. Therefore, it will reflect the fair value of the swap in income in the year ended 31 December 20X1, reducing the net finance costs by £37,500 to £1,887,500 and increasing the finance costs by an equivalent amount in 20X2 to £1,075,000. However, if it considers that it is inappropriate to reflect the fair value of the swap in borrowing costs eligible for capitalisation, it capitalises costs based on the net cash cost on an accruals accounting basis. In this case this will give the same result as in (i) above.

(iii) Entity A does not apply hedge accounting and considers only the costs incurred on the borrowing, not the interest rate swap, as eligible for capitalisation. The borrowing costs eligible for capitalisation would be £1,850,000 in 20X1 and £1,075,000 in 20X2.

In our view, all these methods are valid interpretations of Section 25; however, the preparer will need to consider the most appropriate method in the particular circumstances after taking into consideration the discussion below.

In particular, if using method (ii), it is necessary to demonstrate that the gains or losses on the derivative financial instrument are directly attributable to the construction of a qualifying asset. In making this assessment it is necessary to consider the term of the derivative and this method may not be appropriate if the derivative has a different term to the underlying directly attributable borrowing.

Based on the facts in this example, and assuming that entering into the derivative financial instrument is considered to be related to the borrowing activities of the entity, method (iii) may not be an appropriate method to use because it appears to be inconsistent with the underlying principle of Section 25 – that the costs eligible for capitalisation are those costs that would have been avoided if the expenditure on the qualifying asset had not been made. *[FRS 102.25.2A]*. However, method (iii) may be an appropriate method to use in certain circumstances where it is not possible to demonstrate that the gains or losses on a specific derivative financial instrument are directly attributable to a particular qualifying asset, rather than being used by the entity to manage its interest rate exposure on a more general basis.

Note that method (i) appears to be permitted under US GAAP for fair value hedges. IAS 23 makes reference in its basis of conclusion that under US GAAP, derivative gains and losses (arising from the effective portion of a derivative instrument that qualifies as a fair value hedge) are considered to be part of the capitalised interest cost. IAS 23 does not address such derivative gains and losses. *[IAS 23.BC21]*.

Whichever policy is chosen by an entity, it needs to be consistently applied in similar situations.

3.5.5.B   *Gains and losses on derecognition of borrowings*

If an entity repays borrowings early, in whole or in part, then it may recognise a gain or loss on the early settlement. Such gains or losses include amounts attributable to expected future interest rates; in other words, the settlement includes an estimated prepayment of the future cash flows under the instrument. The gain or loss is a function of relative interest rates and how the interest rate of the instrument differs from current and anticipated future interest rates. There may be circumstances in which a loan is repaid while the qualifying asset is still under construction. Section 25 does not address this issue.

Section 11 requires that gains and losses on extinguishment of debt should be recognised in profit or loss (see Chapter 10 at 9.4.3). Accordingly, in our view, gains and losses on derecognition of borrowings are not eligible for capitalisation. Decisions to repay borrowings early are not usually directly attributable to the qualifying asset but to other circumstances of the entity.

The same approach would be applied to gains and losses arising from a refinancing when there is a substantial modification of the terms of borrowings as this is accounted for as an extinguishment of the original financial liability and the recognition of a new financial liability (see Chapter 10 at 9.4.2 to 9.4.3).

3.5.5.C   Gains or losses on termination of derivative financial instruments

If an entity terminates a derivative financial instrument, for example, an interest rate swap, before the end of the term of the instrument, it will usually have to either make a payment or receive a payment, depending on the fair value of the instrument at that time. The fair value is typically based on expected future interest rates; in other words it is an estimated prepayment of the future cash flows under the instrument.

The treatment of the gain or loss for the purposes of capitalisation will depend on the following:

- the basis on which the entity capitalises the gains and losses associated with derivative financial instruments attributable to qualifying assets (see 3.5.5.A above); and
- whether the derivative is associated with a borrowing that has also been terminated.

Entities must adopt a treatment that is consistent with their policy for capitalising the gains and losses from derivative financial instruments that are attributable to qualifying investments (see 3.5.5.A above).

The accounting under Section 12 will differ depending on whether the instrument has been designated as a hedge or not. Assuming the instrument has been designated as a cash flow hedge and that the borrowing has not also been repaid, the entity will usually maintain the cumulative gain or loss on the hedging instrument, subject to reclassification to profit or loss during the same period that the hedged cash flows affect profit or loss. In such a case, the amounts that are reclassified from other comprehensive income will be eligible for capitalisation for the remainder of the period of construction.

Similarly, assuming the instrument has been designated as a fair value hedge and that the borrowing has not also been repaid, entities would continue to recognise the cumulative gain or loss on the hedging instrument in the carrying amount of the hedged item and would form part of the ongoing determination of amortised cost of the financial liability using the effective interest rate method. Interest expense calculated using the effective interest method is eligible for capitalisation for the remainder of the period of construction (see 3.2 above).

If the entity is not hedge accounting for the derivative financial instrument, but considers it to be directly attributable to the construction of the qualifying asset then it will have to consider whether part of the gain or loss relates to a period after construction is complete.

Chapter 22

If the underlying borrowing is also terminated then the gain or loss will not be capitalised and the treatment will mirror that applied on derecognition of the borrowing, as described at 3.5.5.B above.

3.5.5.D   *Dividends payable on shares classified as financial liabilities*

An entity might finance its operations in whole or in part by the issue of preference shares and in some circumstances these will be classified as financial liabilities (see Chapter 10). In some circumstances the dividends payable on these instruments would meet the definition of borrowing costs. For example, an entity might have funded the development of a qualifying asset by issuing redeemable preference shares that are redeemable at the option of the holder and so are classified as financial liabilities under Section 22. In this case, the 'dividends' would be treated as interest and meet the definition of borrowing costs and so could be capitalised following the principles on specific borrowings discussed at 3.5.2 above.

Companies with outstanding preference shares which are treated as liabilities under Section 22 might subsequently obtain a qualifying asset. In such cases, these preference share liabilities would be considered to be part of the company's general borrowings. The related 'dividends' would meet the definition of borrowing costs and could be capitalised following the principles on general borrowings discussed at 3.5.3 above – i.e. that they are directly attributable to a qualifying asset.

If these shares were both irredeemable, but still treated as liabilities under Section 22 (see Chapter 10), and the only general borrowings, it would generally be difficult to demonstrate that such borrowings would have been avoided if the expenditure on the qualifying asset had not been made. In such a case capitalisation of related 'dividends' would not be appropriate, unless the qualifying asset is demonstrably funded (at least partly) by such borrowings. In cases where such instruments were just a part of a general borrowing 'pool', it would be appropriate to include applicable 'dividends' in determining the borrowing costs eligible for capitalisation (see 3.5.3 above), notwithstanding the fact that these instruments are irredeemable, provided that:

- at least part of any of the general borrowings in the pool was applied to obtain the qualifying asset; or
- it can be demonstrated that at least part of the fund specifically allocated for repaying any of the redeemable part of the pool was used to obtain the qualifying asset.

Capitalisation of dividends or other payments made in respect of any instruments that are classified as equity in accordance with Section 22 is not appropriate as these instruments would not meet the definition of financial liabilities. In addition, as discussed at 3.2 above, Section 25 does not deal with the actual or imputed cost of equity, including preferred capital not classified as a liability.

3.5.6   *Capitalisation of borrowing costs in hyperinflationary economies*

While Section 31 – *Hyperinflation* – provides guidance in situations where an entity's functional currency is the currency of a hyperinflationary economy, it does not provide specific guidance on the impact of inflation to accounting for borrowing costs. Thus, under the GAAP hierarchy in Section 10 (see Chapter 9 at 3.2) entities may wish to consider the specific guidance in IFRS. Under IFRS, in situations where IAS 29 – *Financial Reporting in Hyperinflationary Economies* – applies, an entity needs to distinguish between borrowing costs that compensate for inflation and those incurred in order to acquire or construct a qualifying asset.

IAS 29 states that '[t]he impact of inflation is usually recognised in borrowing costs. It is not appropriate both to restate the capital expenditure financed by borrowing and to capitalise that part of the borrowing costs that compensates for the inflation during the same period. This part of the borrowing costs is recognised as an expense in the period in which the costs are incurred.' *[IAS 29.21]*.

Accordingly, IAS 23 specifies that when an entity applies IAS 29, the borrowing costs that can be capitalised should be restricted and the entity must expense the part of borrowing costs that compensates for inflation during the same period in accordance with paragraph 21 of IAS 29 (as described above). *[IAS 23.9]*.

Detailed discussion and requirements of IAS 29 can be found in Chapter 16 of EY International GAAP 2019.

3.5.7 Group considerations

3.5.7.A Borrowings in one company and development in another

A question that can arise in practice is whether it is appropriate to capitalise interest in the group financial statements on borrowings that appear in the financial statements of a different group entity from that carrying out the development. Based on the underlying principle of Section 25, capitalisation in such circumstances would only be appropriate if the amount capitalised fairly reflected the interest cost of the group on borrowings from third parties that could have been avoided if the expenditure on the qualifying asset were not made.

Although it may be appropriate to capitalise interest in the group financial statements, the entity carrying out the development should not capitalise any interest in its own financial statements as it has no borrowings. If, however, the entity has intra-group borrowings then interest on such borrowings may be capitalised in its own financial statements.

3.5.7.B Qualifying assets held by joint ventures

A number of sectors carry out developments through the medium of joint ventures (see Chapter 13) – this is particularly common with property developments. In such cases, the joint venture may be financed principally by equity and the joint venturers may have financed their participation in this equity through borrowings.

In situations where the joint venture is classified as a jointly controlled entity (JCE) in accordance with Section 15 – *Investments in Joint Ventures*, it is not appropriate to capitalise interest in the JCE on the borrowings of the venturers as the interest charge is not a cost of the JCE. Neither would it be appropriate to capitalise interest in the financial statements of the venturers, whether in separate or consolidated financial statements, because the qualifying asset does not belong to them. The investing entities have an investment in a financial asset (i.e. an equity instrument of another entity) which is excluded by Section 25 from being a qualifying asset (see 3.4 above).

In situations where the joint venture is classified as a jointly controlled operation (JCO) or jointly controlled assets (JCA) in accordance with Section 15 and the venturers are accounting for their own and their share of the assets, liabilities, revenue and expenses of the JCO or JCA, then the venturers could capitalise borrowing costs incurred that relate to their own qualifying asset or their share of any qualifying asset. Borrowing costs eligible for capitalisation would be based on the venturer's obligation for the loans of such JCO or JCA together with any direct borrowings of the venturer itself if the venturer funds part of the acquisition of such joint venture's qualifying asset.

3.6   Commencement, suspension and cessation of capitalisation

3.6.1   *Commencement of capitalisation*

Section 25 requires that an entity capitalise borrowing costs as part of the cost of a qualifying asset from the point when the entity first meet all of the following conditions:

- it incurs expenditure on the asset;
- it incurs borrowing costs; and
- it undertakes activities necessary to prepare the asset for its intended use or sale.
  [FRS 102.25.2D(a)].

Section 25 has no further guidance on 'activities necessary to prepare an asset for its intended use or sale'. However, some guidance is provided by IAS 23 which states that the activities necessary to prepare an asset for its intended use or sale can include more than the physical construction of the asset. Necessary activities can start before the commencement of physical construction and include, for example, technical and administrative work such as the activities associated with obtaining permits prior to the commencement of the physical construction. *[IAS 23.19].* However, the general principle in capitalisation and recognition of an asset apply, therefore, borrowing costs are only capitalised as part of the cost of the asset when it is probable that they will result in future economic benefits to the entity and the costs can be measured reliably. *[FRS 102.2.27].* Borrowing costs cannot be capitalised if the permits that are necessary for the construction are not expected to be obtained. Accordingly, a judgement must be made, at the date the expenditure is incurred, as to whether it is sufficiently probable that the relevant permits will be granted. Consequently, if during the application and approval process of such permits it is no longer expected that the necessary permits will be granted, capitalisation of borrowing costs should cease, any related borrowing costs that were previously capitalised should be written off in accordance with Section 27 – *Impairment of Assets* – and accordingly, the carrying amount of any related qualifying asset subject to development or redevelopment (or, if appropriate, the cash generating unit where such an asset belongs) should be tested for impairment, where applicable (see 3.6.2.A below).

Borrowing costs may not be capitalised during a period in which there are no activities that change the condition of the asset. For example a house-builder or property developer may not capitalise borrowing costs on its 'land bank' i.e. that land which is held for future development. Borrowing costs incurred while land is under development are capitalised during the period in which activities related to the development are being undertaken. However, borrowing costs incurred while land acquired for building purposes is held without any associated development activity represent a holding cost of the land. Such costs do not qualify for capitalisation and hence would be considered a period cost (i.e. expensed as incurred). *[IAS 23.19]*.

An entity may make a payment to a third party contractor before that contractor commences construction activities. It is unlikely to be appropriate to capitalise borrowing costs in such a situation until the contractor commences activities that are necessary to prepare the asset for its intended use or sale. However, that would not preclude the payment being classified as a prepayment until such time as construction activities commence.

3.6.2   Suspension of capitalisation

An entity may incur borrowing costs during an extended period in which it suspends the activities necessary to prepare an asset for its intended use or sale. In such a case, Section 25 states that capitalisation of borrowing costs should be suspended during extended periods in which active development of the asset has paused. *[FRS 102.25.2D(b)]*. Such costs are costs of holding partially completed assets and do not qualify for capitalisation. However, no further guidance is provided. For example, Section 25 does not distinguish between extended periods of interruption (when capitalisation would be suspended) and periods of temporary delay that are a necessary part of preparing the asset for its intended purpose (when capitalisation is not normally suspended).

Applying guidance provided by IAS 23, an entity does not normally suspend capitalising borrowing costs during a period when it carries out substantial technical and administrative work. Also, capitalising borrowing costs would not be suspended when a temporary delay is a necessary part of the process of getting an asset ready for its intended use or sale. For example, capitalisation would continue during the extended period in a situation where construction of a bridge is delayed by temporary adverse weather conditions or high water levels, if such conditions are common during the construction period in the geographical region involved. *[IAS 23.21]*. Similarly, capitalisation continues during periods when inventory is undergoing slow transformation – for example, inventories taking an extended time to mature such as Scotch whisky or Cognac.

Borrowing costs incurred during extended periods of interruption caused, for example, by a lack of funding or a strategic decision to hold back project developments during a period of economic downturn are not considered a necessary part of preparing the asset for its intended purpose and should not be capitalised.

3.6.2.A   Impairment considerations

When it is determined that capitalisation is appropriate, an entity continues to capitalise borrowing costs that are directly attributable to the acquisition, construction or production of a qualifying asset as part of the cost of the asset even if the capitalisation causes the expected ultimate cost of the asset to exceed its net realisable value (for inventories that are qualifying assets) or recoverable amount (for all other qualifying assets).

When the carrying amount of the qualifying asset exceeds its recoverable amount or net realisable value (depending on the type of asset), the carrying amount of the asset must be written down or written off in accordance with the Section 27 (see Chapter 24). In certain circumstances, the amount of the write-down or write-off is written back in accordance with Section 27. Section 25 does not have specific guidance in instances where an asset is incomplete thus, an entity may wish to consider the related guidance in IFRS. Under IAS 23, if the asset is incomplete, the impairment assessment is performed by considering the expected ultimate cost of the asset. *[IAS 23.16]*. The expected ultimate cost, which will be compared to recoverable amount or net realisable value, must include costs to complete and the estimated capitalised interest thereon.

3.6.3 Cessation of capitalisation

Section 25 requires capitalisation of borrowing costs to cease when substantially all the activities necessary to prepare the qualifying asset for its intended use or sale are complete. *[FRS 102.25.2D(c)]*.

IAS 23 provides additional guidance that may be useful in assisting preparers of financial statements as to when a qualifying asset is considered as complete, including when such assets are completed in parts. IAS 23 states that an asset is normally ready for its intended use or sale when the physical construction of the asset is complete, even though routine administrative work might still continue. If minor modifications, such as the decoration of a property to the purchaser's or user's specification, are all that are outstanding, this indicates that substantially all the activities are complete. *[IAS 23.23]*. In some cases there may be a requirement for inspection (e.g. to ensure that the asset meets safety requirements) before the asset can be used. Usually 'substantially all the activities' would have been completed before this point in order to be ready for inspection. In such a situation, capitalisation would cease prior to the inspection.

When the construction of a qualifying asset is completed in parts and each part is capable of being used while construction continues on other parts, capitalisation should cease for the borrowing costs on the portion of borrowings attributable to that part when substantially all the activities necessary to prepare that part for its intended use or sale are completed. *[IAS 23.24]*. An example of this might be a business park comprising several buildings, each of which is capable of being fully utilised individually while construction continues on other parts. *[IAS 23.25]*. This principle also applies to single buildings where one part is capable of being fully utilised even if the building as a whole is incomplete (for example, individual floors of a high-rise office building).

For a qualifying asset that needs to be complete in its entirety before any part can be used as intended, it would be appropriate to capitalise related borrowing costs until all the activities necessary to prepare the entire asset for its intended use or sale are substantially complete. An example of this is an industrial plant, such as a steel mill, involving several processes which are carried out in sequence at different parts of the plant within the same site. *[IAS 23.25]*.

However, other circumstances may not be as straightforward. As neither IAS 23 nor IAS 16 – *Property, Plant and Equipment* – provide guidance on what constitutes a 'part', it will therefore depend on particular facts and circumstances and may require the exercise of judgement as to what constitutes a 'part'. Disclosure of this judgement is required if it is significant to the understanding of the financial statements (see 3.7.2 below).

3.6.3.A *Borrowing costs on 'land expenditures'*

An issue may arise about when an entity ceases capitalising borrowing costs on land, for example, consider the fact pattern below:

- an entity acquires and develops land and thereafter constructs a building on that land – the land represents the area on which the building will be constructed;
- both the land and the building meet the definition of a qualifying asset; and
- the entity uses general borrowings to fund the expenditures on the land and construction of the building.

The issue is whether the entity ceases capitalising borrowing costs incurred in respect of expenditures on the land ('land expenditures') once it starts constructing the building or whether it continues to capitalise borrowing costs incurred in respect of land expenditures while it constructs the building.

In our view, in applying Section 25 to determine when to cease capitalising borrowing costs incurred on land expenditures, an entity considers:

- the intended use of the land; and
- in applying paragraph 25.2D(c) of FRS 102, whether the land is capable of being used for its intended purpose while the construction continues on the building.

Land and buildings are used for owner-occupation (and therefore recognised as property, plant and equipment applying Section 17); rent or capital appreciation (and therefore recognised as investment property applying Section 16 – *Investment Property*); or for sale (and therefore recognised as inventory applying Section 13). The intended use of the land is not simply for the construction of a building on the land, but rather to use it for one of these three purposes.

If the land is not capable of being used for its intended purpose while construction continues on the building, the entity considers the land and the building together to assess when to cease capitalising borrowing costs on the land expenditures. In this situation, the land would not be ready for its intended use or sale until substantially all the activities necessary to prepare both the land and building for that intended use or sale are complete (see 3.6.3 above).

The above issue was also discussed by the Interpretations Committee in its June 2018[3] and September 2018[4] meetings and a similar conclusion was reached.

3.7 Disclosures

The disclosure requirements of Section 25 are set out at 3.7.1 below. Disclosures in respect of borrowing costs required by other sections of FRS 102 and The Large and Medium-sized Companies and Groups (Accounts and Reports) Regulations 2008 ('The Regulations') in respect of borrowing costs are set out at 3.7.2 and 3.7.3 below.

3.7.1 Disclosures required by Section 25

When a policy of capitalising borrowing costs is not adopted, Section 25 does not require any additional disclosure. *[FRS 102.25.3]*. However, other sections of FRS 102 require certain disclosures in respect of borrowing costs (see 3.7.2 below).

Where a policy of capitalisation is adopted, an entity should disclose:

- the amount of borrowing costs capitalised in the period; and
- the capitalisation rate used. *[FRS 102.25.3A]*.

3.7.2 Disclosures required by other sections of FRS 102 in respect of borrowing costs

In addition to the disclosure requirements in Section 25, an entity may need to disclose additional information in relation to its borrowing costs in order to comply with requirements in other sections of FRS 102. These include:

- presentation requirements for items of profit or loss including interest payable, are addressed by Section 5 – *Statement of Comprehensive Income and Income Statement* (see Chapter 6); *[FRS 102.5.5, 5.5B]*
- disclosure of total interest expense (using effective interest method for financial liabilities that are not at fair value through profit or loss) is required by Section 11 (see Chapter 10); *[FRS 102.11.48(b)]* and
- Section 8 (see Chapter 6) requires disclosure of the following:
  - the measurement bases used in preparing the financial statements and other accounting policies used that are relevant to an understanding of the financial statements (e.g. clear policy to adopt capitalisation of borrowing costs); *[FRS 102.8.5]* and
  - the significant judgements made in the process of applying an entity's accounting policies that have the most significant effect on the recognised amounts (e.g. criteria in determining a qualifying asset or a 'part' of a qualifying asset, including definition of 'substantial period of time'; determination of capitalisation rate; and treatment of foreign exchange gains and losses as part of borrowing costs, including any derivatives used to hedge such foreign exchange exposures). *[FRS 102.8.6]*.

3.7.3 Additional disclosures required by The Regulations

Where a policy of capitalisation is adopted, The Regulations require an entity to disclose in the notes: *[1 Sch 27(3), 2 Sch 35(3), 3 Sch 45(3)]*

- the fact that interest is included in determining the production cost of the qualifying asset (usually achieved by a clear accounting policy – see 3.7.2 above); and
- the aggregate amount of interest so included in the cost of qualifying assets.

4   SUMMARY OF GAAP DIFFERENCES

The key differences between FRS 102 and IFRS in accounting for borrowing costs are set out below.

	FRS 102	*IFRS*
Scope	Section 25 applies to all 'qualifying assets' which is defined in the same way as IAS 23 but has no reference to 'bearer plants'. However, we expect entities will follow the guidance under IFRS.	IAS 23 applies to all qualifying assets and has same definition of qualifying asset as FRS 102 except that it includes biological assets that meet the definition of bearer plants.
	Borrowing costs include finance charges in respect of finance leases as set out in Section 20.	Borrowing costs include interest in respect of liabilities recognised in accordance with IFRS 16 – *Leases*.
Capitalisation of borrowing costs	Capitalisation of eligible borrowing costs in respect of qualifying assets is a policy choice (i.e. optional).	Capitalisation of eligible borrowing costs is mandatory. However, IAS 23 need not be applied to a qualifying asset measured at fair value or inventories that are manufactured or otherwise produced, in large quantities on a repetitive basis.
	Where an entity adopts a policy of capitalisation of borrowing costs, it should be applied consistently to a class of qualifying assets.	An accounting policy choice exists only for a qualifying asset measured at fair value or inventories that are manufactured or otherwise produced, in large quantities on a repetitive basis. Capitalisation of eligible borrowing costs is mandatory for all other qualifying assets.
	There is no guidance concerning the impact of inflation to the treatment of borrowing costs when an entity's functional currency is the currency of a hyperinflationary economy.	When an entity applies IAS 29, it recognises as an expense the part of borrowing costs that compensates for inflation during the same period.
Capitalisation rate	The capitalisation rate is the weighted average of rates applicable to general borrowings outstanding in the period. This excludes borrowings made specifically for the purpose of obtaining other qualifying assets and non-qualifying assets.	The capitalisation rate is the weighted average of the borrowing costs applicable to borrowings outstanding in the period other than borrowings made specifically for the purpose of obtaining a qualifying asset. This means that specific borrowings to acquire non-qualifying assets would be included in the computation.
	For purposes of applying the capitalisation rate to the expenditure on the qualifying asset, the expenditure on asset is the average carrying amount of the asset during the period, including borrowing costs previously capitalised.	Expenditures on a qualifying asset are explicitly limited to those expenditures that have resulted in payments of cash, transfers of other assets or the assumption of interest-bearing liabilities and reduced by any progress payments received and grants received in connection with the asset. However, IAS 23 accepts that, when funds are borrowed generally, the average carrying amount of the asset during a period, including borrowing costs previously capitalised, is normally a reasonable approximation of the expenditure to which the capitalisation rate is applied in that period.

Chapter 22

	FRS 102	*IFRS*
Commencement, suspension and cessation of capitalisation	No further guidance on 'activities that are necessary to prepare the asset for its intended use or sale'. However, we expect entities will follow the guidance under IFRS.	Additional guidance is provided e.g. borrowing costs incurred are expensed if the asset is held without any associated development activities i.e. activities that change the physical condition of the asset.
	No further guidance about treatment of borrowing costs in periods of temporary delay. However, we expect entities will follow the guidance under IFRS.	Capitalisation is not normally suspended when substantial technical and administrative work are being carried out or when a temporary delay is a necessary part of the process of getting an asset ready for its intended use or sale.
	No further guidance about cessation of capitalisation of borrowing costs for qualifying assets being constructed in parts. However, we expect entities will follow the guidance under IFRS.	Explicit guidance is provided for construction of a qualifying asset in parts and each part is capable of being used or sold while construction continues on other parts.
Disclosures	If the company adopts a policy of capitalising borrowing costs, disclosure is required of the amount of borrowing costs capitalised during the period and the capitalisation rate used. It also needs to disclose the aggregate amount of interest so included in the cost of qualifying assets.	An entity should disclose the amount of borrowing costs capitalised during the period and the capitalisation rate used.

References

1 *IFRIC Update*, June 2018.
2 *IFRIC Update*, September 2018.
3 *IFRIC Update*, June 2018.
4 *IFRIC Update*, September 2018.

Chapter 23   Share-based payment

Chapter 23

Chapter 23

Chapter 23

List of examples

Chapter 23

Chapter 23   Share-based payment

1   INTRODUCTION

1.1   Background

Most share-based payment transactions undertaken by entities are awards of shares and options as remuneration to employees, in particular senior management and directors. One advantage of shares and options as remuneration is that they need not entail any cash cost to the entity. If an executive is entitled under a bonus scheme to a free share, the entity can satisfy this award simply by printing another share certificate, which the executive can sell, so that the cash cost of the award is effectively borne by shareholders rather than by the entity itself. However, this very advantage was the source of controversy surrounding share-based remuneration.

Investors became increasingly concerned that share-based remuneration was resulting in a significant cost to them, through dilution of their existing shareholdings. As a result, there emerged an increasing consensus among investors that awards of shares and share options should be recognised as a cost in the financial statements.

Accounting for share-based payment transactions is addressed in Section 26 – *Share-based Payment*. However, many of the requirements of Section 26 are virtually impossible to interpret without recourse to IFRS 2 – *Share-based Payment* – from which many of the requirements and definitions of Section 26 were ultimately derived.

The IASB published IFRS 2 in February 2004. There have been three subsequent sets of amendments to IFRS 2 as well as a number of clarifications through the IASB's Annual Improvements process. The most recent amendments to IFRS 2 were published in June 2016 and were mandatory for accounting periods beginning on or after 1 January 2018 for entities applying IFRS. These June 2016 amendments have not been incorporated into FRS 102 but are referred to, where relevant, in the discussions of IFRS 2 in this chapter.

1.2   Scope of Chapter 23 and referencing convention

This chapter generally discusses the requirements of Section 26 for entities applying FRS 102 in accounting periods beginning on or after 1 January 2019. It is based on the March 2018 version of FRS 102 which includes the amendments in 2017. Section 26 has had incremental improvements and clarifications made to it as a result of the

Amendments to FRS 102 Triennial review 2017 – Incremental improvements and clarifications (Triennial review 2017), with retrospective effect. The March 2018 version of FRS 102 is referred to as 'FRS 102' throughout this chapter.

As noted at 1.1 above, the requirements of Section 26 are virtually impossible to interpret without recourse to IFRS 2, which contains extensive application and implementation guidance. Without this guidance, the practical application of the requirements of Section 26 is difficult and we therefore draw on the guidance in IFRS 2 as part of the explanation in this chapter, applying the hierarchy on selecting accounting policies as set out in Section 10 – *Accounting Policies, Estimates and Errors* (see Chapter 9 at 3.2).

The application of Section 26 – and IFRS 2 – to a variety of practical situations is unclear. Whilst this chapter addresses some of the complexities, other areas of discussion are beyond the scope of this publication. EY International GAAP 2019 includes a more detailed analysis in certain areas, as indicated later in this chapter.

1.3   Overview of accounting approach

The overall approach to accounting for share-based payment transactions is complex, in part because it is something of a hybrid. Essentially the total cost (i.e. measurement) of an award is calculated by determining whether the award is a liability or an equity instrument, using criteria somewhat different from those used in accounting for financial instruments but then applying measurement principles based on those generally applicable to financial liabilities or equity instruments. However the periodic allocation (i.e. recognition) of the cost[1] is determined using something closer to a straight-line accruals methodology, which would not generally be used for financial instruments.

This inevitably has the result that, depending on its legal form, a transaction of equal value to the recipient can result in several different potential charges in profit or loss. Moreover, many of the requirements are rules derived from the 'anti-avoidance' approach of IFRS 2. This means that an expense often has to be recorded for transactions that either have no ultimate value to the counterparty or to which, in some cases, the counterparty actually has no entitlement at all.

1.3.1   *Classification differences between share-based payments and financial instruments*

As noted above, not only are there differences between the accounting treatment of liabilities or equity in a share-based payment transaction as compared with that of other transactions involving liabilities or equity instruments (Section 22 – *Liabilities and Equity*), but the classification of a transaction as a liability or equity transaction may differ.

The most important difference is that a share-based payment transaction involving the delivery of equity instruments is always accounted for as an equity transaction, whereas a similar transaction outside the scope of the share-based payment accounting requirements might well be classified as a liability if the number of shares to be delivered varies.

2 COMPARISON BETWEEN SECTION 26 AND IFRS

As a result of the Triennial review 2017 some of the principal differences between Section 26 and IFRS 2 have been eliminated through the incremental improvements and clarifications. This section summarises the remaining principal differences between Section 26 and the requirements of IFRS 2. In some of the areas referred to below, the difference between the standards is explicit but there are others where the lack of guidance or explanation in Section 26 means that it is unclear whether or not a different accounting treatment is intended.

Prior to the Triennial review 2017, Section 26 did not include a definition of 'vesting conditions' or make explicitly clear that service conditions and non-market performance conditions should not be taken into account in determining the fair value of equity-settled share-based payment transaction but in estimating the number of awards expected to vest. The Triennial review 2017 now provides a definition of 'vesting conditions' consistent with that in IFRS 2 and clarifies that service conditions and non-market performance conditions should not be taken into account when estimating the fair value of shares or share options.

All of the areas below, which set out the differences, are addressed in more detail in the remainder of this chapter, as indicated.

2.1 Scope

2.1.1 Definitions and transactions within scope

Unlike IFRS 2, Section 26 does not provide guidance or examples in areas such as:

- the meaning of 'goods' in 'goods and services' when used in the definition of a share-based payment transaction;
- vested transactions;
- transactions with shareholders as a whole;
- business combinations; or
- the interaction with the requirements of FRS 102 relating to financial instruments.

The differences are discussed in more detail at 3.2 and 3.3 below and, in the case of replacement awards in a business combination, at 12 below.

2.2 Recognition

2.2.1 Accounting after vesting date

FRS 102 includes no guidance on accounting for awards after vesting whereas IFRS 2 specifically prohibits a reversal of expense (see 7.1.3 below).

2.3 Measurement of equity-settled share-based payment transactions

2.3.1 Non-vesting conditions

The Triennial review 2017 amended FRS 102 whereby reference to 'non-vesting conditions' has been replaced with 'conditions that are not vesting conditions'. Neither of these terms are defined in FRS 102 or IFRS 2, but IFRS 2 includes examples of such conditions as part of its implementation guidance (see 4 and 7 below).

Section 26 of FRS 102 provides an example of a condition that is not a vesting condition, such as a condition that an employee contributes to a saving plan, which is one of the examples provided in the implementation guidance of IFRS 2 as a non-vesting condition. Therefore we believe that both terms, 'non-vesting conditions' and 'conditions that are not vesting conditions', are similar and we will refer to the terms interchangeably throughout this chapter.

2.3.2   Employees and others providing similar services

Both Section 26 and IFRS 2 distinguish between awards to employees (and others providing similar services) and those to other parties providing goods or services. The recognition and measurement of equity-settled share-based payment transactions differ according to whether the counterparty is treated as an employee.

Section 26 provides no additional guidance on the meaning of 'others providing similar services' whereas IFRS 2 defines/explains this term in Appendix A (see 6.2.1 below).

In dealing with the recognition and measurement of share-based payments, FRS 102 sometimes refers only to employees without specifying the treatment for non-employee awards. In such cases, we assume that a similar accounting treatment is intended for non-employee awards.

2.3.3   Valuation methodology

IFRS 2 requires the use of a market price or an option pricing model for the valuation of equity-settled share-based payment transactions. FRS 102 draws a more explicit distinction than IFRS 2 between the valuation of shares and the valuation of options and appreciation rights. Section 26 specifies the following valuation hierarchy:

- observable market price,
- entity-specific observable market data,
- directors' valuation using a generally accepted methodology

and gives limited examples for both shares and options/appreciation rights of the type of approach that might be taken. *[FRS 102.26.10-11]*. Section 26 does not mandate the use of an option pricing model for the valuation of share options when market prices are unavailable; instead it allows use of a valuation methodology 'such as an option pricing model'.

This approach to valuation was identified by the FRC in earlier versions of FRS 102 as a significant difference between FRS 102 and the IFRS for SMEs (and therefore IFRS 2). In practical terms, it is not entirely clear what alternatives to an option pricing model are likely to provide a reliable indication of the fair value (see 9.2 and 9.3 below).

IFRS 2 includes guidance in Appendix B about the selection and application of option pricing models, none of which is reproduced in FRS 102 (see 9 below).

2.3.4   Awards where fair value cannot be measured reliably

Section 26 assumes as part of its requirements relating to the measurement of equity-settled share-based payment transactions that it will always be possible to derive a fair value for the award (see 9.2 and 9.3 below). IFRS 2 includes an approach based on the intrinsic value of the equity instruments for the 'rare cases' in which an entity is unable to measure reliably the fair value of those instruments. *[IFRS 2.24]*. The intrinsic value approach is not addressed in this chapter.

2.3.5 Cancellation of awards

IFRS 2 makes clear that an award may be cancelled either by the entity or by the counterparty and also that a failure to meet non-vesting conditions should, in certain situations, be considered to amount to the cancellation of an award. Section 26 includes no explicit requirements to mirror those in IFRS 2 (see 7.4.3 and 8.4 below).

2.3.6 Settlement of awards

Section 26 states that a settlement of an unvested equity-settled share-based payment should be treated as an acceleration of vesting. It does not specify the treatment where the fair value of the settlement exceeds the fair value of the award being cancelled. Under IFRS 2, any incremental fair value is expensed at the date of settlement but any settlement value up to the fair value of the cancelled award is debited to equity.

Similarly, Section 26 contains no guidance on the repurchase of vested equity instruments whereas IFRS 2 requires any incremental fair value to be expensed as at the date of repurchase (see 8.4 below).

2.3.7 Replacement awards following a cancellation or settlement

Section 26 includes no guidance on the accounting treatment of equity-settled awards to replace an award cancelled during the vesting period and whether, as under IFRS 2, they may be accounted for on the basis of their incremental fair value rather than being treated as a completely new award (see 8.4.4 below).

2.4 Cash-settled share-based payment transactions

Until the publication of an amendment to IFRS 2 in June 2016, the treatment of service and non-market performance conditions in determining the fair value of a cash-settled share-based payment transaction was unclear. The amendment clarified that the approach should be similar to that for equity-settled share-based payment transactions rather than the probability of such conditions being reflected directly in measuring the fair value of the liability. In the absence of a similar clarification to the wording of paragraph 14 of Section 26, we believe that either interpretation remains valid for cash-settled arrangements under FRS 102 (see 10.3.2.C below).

2.5 Share-based payment transactions with cash alternatives

2.5.1 Entity or counterparty has choice of equity- or cash-settlement

Where the counterparty has a choice of settlement in equity or cash, Section 26 requires the entity to account for the transaction as wholly cash-settled unless the choice of settlement in cash has no commercial substance (in which case the transaction is accounted for as wholly equity-settled). IFRS 2 requires a split accounting approach (between a liability and equity) for such arrangements (see 11.2 below).

There are no significant differences between the requirements of Section 26 and those of IFRS 2 for transactions where the entity has a choice of equity or cash settlement.

Chapter 23

2.5.2 Settlement in cash of award accounted for as equity-settled (or vice versa)

Section 26 contains no guidance on how to account for the settlement in cash of an award accounted for as equity-settled (or *vice versa*). This is specifically addressed in IFRS 2 and discussed at 11.1.1 below.

2.6 Group plans

2.6.1 Accounting by group entity with obligation to settle an award when another group entity receives goods or services

Section 26 makes clear that a group entity receiving goods or services, but with no obligation to settle the transaction with the provider of those goods or services, accounts for a share-based payment transaction as equity-settled. However, prior to the Triennial review 2017 the accounting treatment in the entity settling the transaction was not specified. The accounting has now been clarified to be consistent with IFRS 2 and makes clear that when the entity settles the share-based payment when another group entity receives the goods or services, the entity recognises the transaction as an equity-settled share-based payment transaction only if it is settled in its own equity instruments, otherwise the transaction should be recognised as a cash-settled share-based payment transaction. *[FRS 102.26.2A]*. This is discussed at 3.2.1 and 13.2 below.

2.6.2 Alternative accounting treatment for group plans

Where a share-based payment award is granted by an entity to the employees of one or more members of a group, those members are permitted – as an alternative to the general recognition and measurement requirements of Section 26 – to recognise and measure the share-based payment expense on the basis of a reasonable allocation of the group expense (see 3.2.1 and 13.2.3.A below). There is no corresponding alternative treatment in IFRS 2.

2.7 Government-mandated plans

2.7.1 Unidentifiable goods/services

For certain government-mandated plans where the goods/services received or receivable in exchange for equity instruments are not identifiable, Section 26 requires the award to be valued on the basis of the equity instruments rather than the goods or services. Under IFRS 2, the scope is not restricted to government-mandated plans.

The FRC appeared to address this inconsistency in the Triennial review 2017 by introducing similar wording to that in IFRS 2, where in the absence of specifically identifiable goods or services, other circumstances may indicate that goods or services have been (or will be) received, in which case Section 26 applies. *[FRS 102.26.1]*. However, as noted above, Section 26 appears to restrict the requirements of unidentifiable goods or services only to certain government arrangements, for the fact the requirements are placed within the section heading 'Government-mandated plans' in Section 26. Therefore, it still remains unclear whether entities applying Section 26 should apply the principle more widely (see 3.2.3 below).

2.8 Plans with net settlement for tax withholding obligations

The June 2016 amendment to IFRS 2 introduced an exception for transactions with a net settlement feature for tax withholding obligations. Following application of the amendment, awards meeting the exception criteria will be accounted for in their entirety as equity-settled rather than being separated into an equity-settled element and a cash-settled element. There is no comparable exception for entities applying FRS 102. See 15.3 below.

2.9 Disclosures

The disclosure requirements of Section 26 are generally derived from, but less extensive than, those of IFRS 2. However, Section 26 has three specific requirements that are not found in IFRS 2:

- if a valuation methodology is used to determine the fair value of equity-settled awards, the entity is required to disclose both the method and reason for choosing it;
- for cash-settled share-based payment transactions, an entity is required to disclose how the liability was measured; and
- where the alternative accounting treatment is adopted for group plans, disclosure of this fact is required together with the basis of allocation.

More generally, unlike IFRS, FRS 102 includes exemptions from disclosure for certain entities.

The disclosure requirements are discussed at 14 below.

2.10 First-time adoption

The first-time adoption provisions of FRS 102 are set out in Section 35 – *Transition to this FRS*. The specific requirements relating to share-based payments are discussed at 17 below. Unlike IFRS 1 – *First-time Adoption of International Financial Reporting Standards*, Section 35 does not specify the accounting treatment of an award that was granted prior to transition but subsequently modified.

3 SCOPE OF SECTION 26

This section covers the scope of the share-based payment accounting requirements of Section 26 as follows:

- definitions from Appendix I to FRS 102 that are relevant to determining whether transactions are within the scope of Section 26 (see 3.1 below);
- a discussion of transactions that fall within the scope of Section 26 (see 3.2 below) including group arrangements (see 3.2.1 below), transactions with employee benefit trusts (EBTs) and similar vehicles (see 3.2.2 below) and transactions where the consideration received might not be clearly identifiable (see 3.2.3 below);
- a discussion of transactions that fall outside the scope of Section 26 (see 3.3 below); and
- some examples of situations commonly encountered in practice and a discussion of whether they are within scope of Section 26 (see 3.4 below).

3.1   Definitions

The following definitions from Appendix I: Glossary to FRS 102 are relevant to the scope of Section 26.

Term	Definition
Cash-settled share-based payment transaction	A share-based payment transaction in which the entity acquires goods or services by incurring a liability to transfer cash or other assets to the supplier of those goods or services for amounts that are based on the price (or value) of equity instruments (including shares and share options) of the entity or another group entity.
Equity (equity instrument is not defined)	The residual interest in the assets of the entity after deducting all its liabilities.
Equity-settled share-based payment transaction	A share-based payment transaction in which the entity: (a) receives goods or services as consideration for its own equity instruments (including shares or share options); or (b) receives goods or services but has no obligation to settle the transaction with the supplier.
Group (group entity is not defined)	A parent and all its subsidiaries.
Share-based payment	The equity instruments (including shares and share options), cash or other assets to which a counterparty may become entitled in a share-based payment transaction.
Share-based payment arrangement	An agreement between the entity (or another group entity or any shareholder of any group entity) and another party (including an employee) that entitles the other party to receive: (a) cash or other assets of the entity for amounts that are based on the price (or value) of equity instruments (including shares or share options) of the entity or another group entity; or (b) equity instruments (including shares or share options) of the entity or another group entity, (c) provided the specified vesting conditions, if any, are met.
Share-based payment transaction	A transaction in which the entity: (a) receives goods or services from the supplier of those goods or services (including an employee) in a share-based payment arrangement; or (b) incurs an obligation to settle the transaction with the supplier in a share-based payment arrangement when another group entity receives those goods or services.
Share option	A contract that gives the holder the right, but not the obligation, to subscribe to the entity's shares at a fixed or determinable price for a specific period of time.

The definition of a share-based payment transaction was revised as part of the Triennial review 2017 and is now consistent with IFRS 2.

It will be seen from these definitions that FRS 102 applies not only to awards of shares and share options but also to awards of cash (or other assets) of a value equivalent to the value, or a movement in the value, of a particular number of shares.

3.2 Transactions within the scope of Section 26

Subject to the exceptions noted at 3.3 below, Section 26 must be applied to all share-based payment transactions, including:

(a) equity-settled share-based payment transactions (discussed at 5 to 9 below);

(b) cash-settled share-based payment transactions (discussed at 10 below); and

(c) transactions where either the entity or the supplier of goods or services can choose whether the transaction is to be equity-settled or cash-settled (discussed at 11 below). *[FRS 102.26.1].*

Whilst the boundaries between these types of transaction are reasonably self-explanatory, there may be transactions – as discussed in more detail at 10 and 11 below – that an entity may intuitively regard as equity-settled which are in fact required to be treated as cash-settled.

Although the majority of share-based payment transactions are with employees, the scope of Section 26 is not restricted to employee transactions. For example, if an external supplier of goods or services, including another group entity, is paid in shares or share options, or cash of equivalent value, Section 26 must be applied.

A share-based payment transaction as defined in FRS 102 (see 3.1 above) requires goods or services to be received or acquired, but FRS 102 does not define 'goods' or give any additional guidance as to what might be included within such a term. IFRS 2 includes the following within its scope and it seems appropriate to use this guidance for the purposes of Section 26:

- inventories;
- consumables;
- property, plant and equipment (PP&E);
- intangibles; and
- other non-financial assets. *[IFRS 2.5].*

It will be seen that 'goods' do not include financial assets, which raises some further issues (see 3.3.6 below).

Although not always explicitly stated, the scope of Section 26 extends to:

- certain transactions by other group entities and by shareholders of group entities (see 3.2.1 below);
- transactions with employee benefit trusts ('EBTs') and similar vehicles (see 3.2.2 below);
- certain transactions where the identifiable consideration received appears to be less than the consideration given (see 3.2.3 below); and
- 'all employee' share plans (see 3.2.4 below).

Chapter 23

Section 26 is silent on certain other transactions or arrangements, including vested transactions (see 3.2.5 below), where it is unclear whether the transactions or arrangements fall within the scope of the share-based payment accounting requirements.

In the absence of specific guidance in FRS 102 we suggest that entities follow the requirements of IFRS 2, or general practice that has evolved through the application of IFRS 2, as set out in the sections below.

3.2.1   *Transactions by other group entities and shareholders*

The definition of 'share-based payment transaction' (see 3.1 above) and additional requirements in paragraph 1A of Section 26 have the effect that the scope of Section 26 is not restricted to transactions where the reporting entity acquires goods or services in exchange for providing its own equity instruments (or cash or other assets based on the cost or value of those equity instruments). Within a group of companies it is common for one member of the group (typically the parent) to have the obligation to settle a share-based payment transaction in which services are provided to another member of the group (typically a subsidiary). This transaction is within the scope of Section 26 for the entity receiving the services (even though it is not a direct party to the arrangement between its parent and its employee), the entity settling the transaction and the group as a whole.

Accordingly, Section 26 requires an entity to account for a transaction in which it either:

- receives goods or services when another entity in the same group (or shareholder of any group entity) has the obligation to settle the share-based payment transaction; or
- has an obligation to settle a share-based payment transaction when another entity in the same group receives the goods or services

unless the transaction is clearly for a purpose other than payment for goods or services supplied to the entity receiving them. *[FRS 102.26.1A]*.

Moreover, the definition of 'equity-settled share-based payment transaction' (see 3.1 above) has the effect that the analysis of the transaction as equity-settled or cash-settled (and its accounting treatment) may differ when viewed from the perspective of the entity receiving the goods or services, the entity settling the transaction and the group as a whole depending on whether or not an entity is required to settle the award and whether that settlement is in its own equity instruments.

The Triennial review 2017 clarified that an entity settling a share-based payment transaction is required to account for that transaction as a cash-settled share-based payment transaction when:

- another group entity is receiving the goods and services; and
- the award is not settled with the equity instruments of the settling entity. *[FRS 102.26.2A]*.

3.2.1.A   *Scenarios illustrating scope requirements for group entities*

In this section we consider seven scenarios, all based on the simple structure in Figure 23.1. These scenarios are by no means exhaustive, but cover the situations most commonly seen in practice.

It should be noted that the scenarios below are based on the scope requirements of Section 26 as set out at 3.2.1 above and do not reflect the additional exemption for members of group schemes. This exemption allows the group expense to be allocated between members of the group on a reasonable basis rather than requiring each group entity to recognise and measure its expense in accordance with the general requirements of Section 26. *[FRS 102.26.16]*. The exemption and the accounting treatment of group share schemes generally are discussed in more detail at 13 below.

Figure 23.1:   Scope of IFRS 2

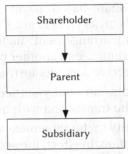

The scenarios assume that:

- the shareholder is not a group entity; and
- the subsidiary is directly owned by the parent company (see also 13.2.1 below in relation to intermediate parent companies).

Scenario	Who grants the award?	Which entity receives the goods or services?	Who settles the award?	On which entity's shares is the award based?	Award settled in shares or cash?
1	Parent	Subsidiary	Parent	Parent	Shares
2	Shareholder	Subsidiary	Shareholder	Parent	Shares
3	Subsidiary	Subsidiary	Subsidiary	Parent	Shares
4	Subsidiary	Subsidiary	Subsidiary	Subsidiary	Shares
5	Parent	Subsidiary	Parent	Subsidiary	Shares
6	Parent	Subsidiary	Parent	Parent	Cash
7	Shareholder	Subsidiary	Shareholder	Parent	Cash

Scenario 1

Parent awards equity shares in Parent to employees of Subsidiary in exchange for services to Subsidiary. Parent settles the award with the employees of Subsidiary.

> *Consolidated financial statements of Parent*
>
> Under the definition of 'share-based payment transaction', 'the entity [i.e. the Parent group] ... receives goods or services ... in a share-based payment arrangement ...'. A share-based payment arrangement includes 'an agreement between the entity ... and another party (including an employee) that entitles the other party to receive ... equity instruments ... of the entity ...'.
>
> The transaction is classified as an equity-settled transaction because it is settled in an equity instrument of the group.

Chapter 23

Separate financial statements of Parent

Parent does not receive the goods or services but it does have the obligation to settle. This is within the scope of paragraph 1A(b) of Section 26 as Parent 'has an obligation to settle a share-based payment transaction when another entity in the same group receives the goods or services'. The transaction is classified as an equity-settled transaction because it is settled in an equity instrument of Parent. *[FRS 102.26.2A]*.

Subsidiary

Under the definition of 'share-based payment transaction', 'the entity [i.e. Subsidiary] ... receives goods or services ... in a share-based payment arrangement ...'. A 'share-based payment arrangement' includes 'an agreement between ... another group entity [i.e. Parent] ... and another party (including an employee) that entitles the other party to receive ... equity instruments of ... another group entity'.

The transaction is classified as an equity-settled transaction because Subsidiary 'has no obligation to settle the transaction with the supplier'.

Even if Subsidiary is not a party to the agreement with its employees, it nevertheless records a cost for this transaction. In effect, the accounting treatment is representing that Subsidiary has received a capital contribution from Parent, which Subsidiary has then 'spent' on employee remuneration. This treatment is often referred to as 'push-down' accounting – the idea being that a transaction undertaken by one group entity (in this case, Parent) for the benefit of another group entity (in this case, Subsidiary) is 'pushed down' into the financial statements of the beneficiary entity.

Scenario 2

Shareholder awards equity shares in Parent to employees of Subsidiary in exchange for services to Subsidiary. Shareholder settles the award with the employees of Subsidiary.

Consolidated financial statements of Parent

Paragraph 1A of Section 26 refers to awards settled by a shareholder of a group entity on behalf of the entity receiving the goods or services.

The transaction is classified as an equity-settled transaction, because the Parent group 'receives goods or services but has no obligation to settle the transaction with [the] supplier'.

Separate financial statements of Parent

Scenario 2 is not within the scope of Section 26 for the separate financial statements of Parent because Parent (as a separate entity) receives no goods or services, nor does it settle the transaction.

Subsidiary

Under the definition of 'share-based payment transaction', 'the entity [i.e. Subsidiary] ... receives goods or services ... in a share-based payment arrangement ...'. A 'share-based payment arrangement' includes 'an agreement between ... another group entity [i.e. Parent] ... and another party (including an employee) that entitles the other party to receive ... equity instruments of ... another group entity'.

The transaction is classified as an equity-settled transaction because Subsidiary 'has no obligation to settle the transaction with the supplier'.

Scenario 3

Subsidiary awards equity shares in Parent to employees of Subsidiary in exchange for services to Subsidiary. Subsidiary settles the award with its employees.

Consolidated financial statements of Parent

Under the definition of 'share-based payment transaction', 'the entity [i.e. the Parent group] ... receives goods or services ... in a share-based payment arrangement ...'. A share-based payment arrangement includes 'an agreement between the entity ... and another party (including an employee) that entitles the other party to receive ... equity instruments ... of the entity ...'

The transaction is classified as an equity-settled transaction because it is settled in an equity instrument of Parent. *[FRS 102.26.2A]*.

Separate financial statements of Parent

Scenario 3 is not within the scope of Section 26 for the separate financial statements of Parent because Parent (as a separate entity) receives no goods or services, nor does it settle the transaction.

Subsidiary

Under the definition of 'share-based payment transaction', 'the entity [i.e. Subsidiary] ... receives goods or services ... in a share-based payment arrangement ...'. A 'share-based payment arrangement' includes 'an agreement between ... another group entity [i.e. Parent] ... and another party (including an employee) that entitles the other party to receive ... equity instruments of ... another group entity'.

The transaction is classified as a cash-settled transaction because Subsidiary has the obligation to settle the award with equity instruments issued by Parent – i.e. a financial asset in Subsidiary's separate financial statements – rather than with Subsidiary's own equity instruments.

However, for the approach in this Scenario to apply, it must be the case that Subsidiary grants the award as a principal rather than acting as agent for Parent. If Subsidiary appears to be granting an award but is really doing so only on the instructions of Parent, as will generally be the case for UK companies, then the approach in Scenario 1 above is more likely to apply. This is discussed in more detail at 13.2.5.B below.

Scenario 4

Subsidiary awards equity shares in Subsidiary to employees of Subsidiary in exchange for services to Subsidiary. Subsidiary settles the award with the employees of Subsidiary.

Consolidated financial statements of Parent

Under the definition of 'share-based payment transaction', 'the entity [i.e. the Parent group] ... receives goods or services ... in a share-based payment arrangement'. A share-based payment arrangement includes 'an agreement between the entity ... and another party (including an employee) that entitles the other party to receive ... equity instruments ... of the entity ...'.

In the consolidated financial statements of Parent, shares of Subsidiary not held by Parent are a non-controlling interest.

Separate financial statements of Parent

Scenario 4 is not within the scope of Section 26 for the separate financial statements of Parent because Parent (as a separate entity) receives no goods or services, nor does it settle the transaction.

Subsidiary

Under the definition of 'share-based payment transaction', 'the entity [i.e. Subsidiary] ... receives goods or services ... in a share-based payment arrangement'. A share-based payment arrangement includes 'an agreement between the entity ... and another party (including an employee) that entitles the other party to receive ... equity instruments ... of the entity ...'.

The transaction is classified as an equity-settled transaction because it is settled in an equity instrument of Subsidiary.

Scenario 5

Parent awards equity shares in Subsidiary to employees of Subsidiary in exchange for services to Subsidiary. Parent settles the award with the employees of Subsidiary.

Consolidated financial statements of Parent

Under the definition of 'share-based payment transaction', 'the entity [i.e. the Parent group] ... receives goods or services ... in a share-based payment arrangement'. A share-based payment arrangement includes 'an agreement between the entity ... and another party (including an employee) that entitles the other party to receive ... equity instruments of the entity ...'.

The transaction is classified as an equity-settled transaction because it is settled in an equity instrument of the group. In the consolidated financial statements of Parent, shares of Subsidiary not held by Parent are a non-controlling interest.

Separate financial statements of Parent

Parent does not receive the goods or services but it does have the obligation to settle. This is within the scope of paragraph 1A(b) of Section 26 as Parent 'has an obligation to settle a share-based payment transaction when another entity in the same group receives the goods or services'. The transaction is classified as a cash-settled transaction as Parent is settling the award not in its own equity instrument but in an equity instrument issued by a subsidiary and held by Parent – i.e. a financial asset in Parent's separate financial statements. *[FRS 102.26.2A]*.

Subsidiary

Under the definition of 'share-based payment transaction', 'the entity [i.e. Subsidiary] ... receives goods or services ... in a share-based payment arrangement'. A 'share-based payment arrangement' includes 'an agreement between ... another group entity [i.e. Parent] ... and another party (including an employee) that entitles the other party to receive equity instruments of the entity...'.

The transaction is classified as an equity-settled transaction, because Subsidiary 'has no obligation to settle the transaction with the supplier'.

Scenario 6

Parent awards cash based on the value of shares in Parent to employees of Subsidiary in exchange for services to Subsidiary. Parent settles the award with the employees of Subsidiary.

Consolidated financial statements of Parent

Under the definition of 'share-based payment transaction', 'the entity [i.e. the Parent group] ... receives goods or services ... in a share-based payment arrangement'. A 'share-based payment arrangement' includes 'an agreement between the entity ... and another party (including an employee) that entitles the other party to receive ... cash ... of the entity ... based on the price (or value) of equity instruments ... of the entity ...'.

The transaction is classified as a cash-settled transaction, because it is settled in cash of the group.

Separate financial statements of Parent

Parent does not receive the goods or services but it does have the obligation to settle. This is within the scope of paragraph 1A(b) of Section 26 as Parent 'has an obligation to settle a share-based payment transaction when another entity in the same group receives the goods or services'. The transaction is classified as a cash-settled transaction, because it is settled not in an equity instrument issued by Parent, but in cash based on the value of shares in Parent.

Subsidiary

When the drafting of the definition of a 'share-based payment transaction' is examined closely, it is not absolutely clear that this arrangement is within the scope of Section 26 for Subsidiary. In order to be a share-based payment *transaction* (and therefore in the scope of Section 26) for the reporting entity, a transaction must also be a share-based payment *arrangement*. A share-based payment arrangement is defined as one in which the counterparty receives (our emphasis added):

- cash or other assets *of the entity; or*
- equity of the entity *or any other group entity*.

As drafted, the definition has the effect that a transaction settled in equity is in the scope of Section 26 for a reporting entity, whether the equity used to settle the transaction is the entity's own equity or that of another group entity. Where a transaction is settled in cash, however, the definition has the effect that a transaction is in the scope of Section 26 for a reporting entity only when that entity's own cash (or other assets) is used in settlement, and not when another group entity settles the transaction.

When read with the general scope requirements in paragraphs 1 and 1A, we believe that the apparent omissions from the definition of 'share-based payment transaction' should be regarded as minor drafting errors and that the transaction should be classified as an equity-settled transaction by Subsidiary, because Subsidiary 'receives goods or services but has no obligation to settle the transaction with the supplier'.

Scenario 7

Shareholder awards cash based on the value of shares in Parent to employees of Subsidiary in exchange for services to Subsidiary. Shareholder settles the award with the employees of Subsidiary.

This transaction is within the scope of paragraph 1A of Section 26 for the consolidated financial statements of Parent and for the separate financial Subsidiary as it is a transaction where the shareholder has an obligation to settle on behalf of the entity receiving the goods or services. However, it does not strictly meet the definitions in Appendix I. As noted at Scenario 6 above, the definitions of 'share-based payment transaction' and 'cash-settled share-based payment transaction' as drafted do not explicitly address any arrangement that is settled in cash by a party other than the reporting entity.

Nevertheless, we believe that the transaction should be treated as being within the scope of Section 26 for the consolidated financial statements of Parent and the separate financial statements of Subsidiary and the transaction accounted for as equity-settled.

3.2.2   Transactions with employee benefit trusts and similar vehicles

It is common for an entity to establish a trust to hold shares in the entity for the purpose of satisfying share-based awards to employees. In such cases, it is often the trust, rather than any entity within the legal group, that actually makes share-based awards to employees. Awards by EBTs and similar vehicles are within the scope of Section 26 and are discussed at 13.3 below.

3.2.3   Transactions where the identifiable consideration received appears to be less than the consideration given

3.2.3.A   Government-mandated plans

A share-based payment transaction as defined (see 3.1 above) involves the receipt of goods or services. Nevertheless, Section 26 also applies to government-mandated plans 'established under law by which equity investors (such as employees) are able to acquire equity without providing goods or services that can be specifically identified (or by providing goods or services that are clearly less than the fair value of the equity instruments granted). This indicates that other consideration has been or will be received (such as past or future employee services) ...'. *[FRS 102.26.17]*.

Such arrangements are treated as equity-settled share-based payment transactions under FRS 102 and the unidentifiable goods or services are measured as the difference between the fair value of the equity instrument and the fair value of any identifiable goods or services received (or to be received) measured at the grant date. *[FRS 102.26.17]*. The determination of the grant date is addressed at 6.3 below.

Section 26 offers no further explanation or guidance as to the type of arrangement that is expected to fall within the scope of this paragraph. The reference to employees and employee services is somewhat puzzling since share-based payment transactions with employees are always measured at the fair value of the share-based payment rather than the fair value of the employee services, identifiable or otherwise.

What is also not made explicitly clear in paragraph 17 is that, in this situation, the fair value of a share-based payment with a non-employee would need to be that of the equity instruments rather than that of the goods or services (as would normally be the case for an award to a non-employee – see 6.1 and 6.4 below).

As Section 26 refers only to 'programmes mandated under law' beneath the heading 'Government-mandated plans', it appears that the standard does not require an entity to apply the requirements of paragraph 17 to other transactions with non-employees in which the value of goods or services received or receivable falls short of the fair value of the equity instruments or cash transferred.

IFRS 2 includes a similar requirement for transactions with non-employees where no specifically identifiable goods or services have been (or will be) received but does not restrict the scope to government-mandated plans. *[IFRS 2.2]*. Section 26 as a result of the Triennial review 2017 clarifications, contains similar wording and requirements in paragraph 26.1 of Section 26 to that of paragraph 2 of IFRS 2, but then goes on to restrict the requirement to government mandated plans.

IFRS 2 asserts that, if the identifiable consideration received (if any) appears to be less than the fair value of consideration given in any share-based payment arrangement, the implication is that, in addition to the identifiable goods and services acquired, the entity must also have received some unidentifiable consideration equal to the difference between the fair value of the share-based payment and the fair value of any identifiable consideration received. Accordingly, the cost of the unidentified consideration must be accounted for in accordance with IFRS 2. *[IFRS 2.13A]*.

For example, if an entity agrees to pay a supplier of services with a clearly identifiable market value of £1,000 by issuing shares with a value of £1,500, IFRS 2 requires the entity to recognise an expense of £1,500. This is notwithstanding the normal requirement of IFRS 2 that an equity-settled share-based payment transaction with a non-employee be recognised at the fair value of the goods or services received (see 6.1 and 6.4 below).

3.2.3.B   Other transactions

In rare circumstances a transaction may occur in which no goods or services are received by the entity. For example, a principal shareholder of an entity, for reasons of estate planning, may transfer shares to a relative. In the absence of indications that the relative has provided, or is expected to provide, goods or services to the entity in exchange for the shares, such a transfer would be outside the scope of Section 26 as a transaction clearly for a purpose other than payment for goods or services supplied to the entity. *[FRS 102.26.1A]*.

Chapter 23

3.2.4 *'All employee' share plans*

Many countries, including the UK, encourage wider share-ownership by allowing companies to award a limited number of free or discounted shares to employees without either the employee or the employer incurring tax liabilities which would apply if other benefits in kind to an equivalent value were given to employees.

There is no exemption from the scope of Section 26 for such plans (unless they are immaterial).

3.2.5 *Vested transactions*

Section 26 does not specifically address the accounting treatment of awards once they have vested. Drawing on the requirements of IFRS 2, a transaction accounted for as a share-based payment does not necessarily cease to be within the scope of Section 26 once it has vested in the counterparty (see 4 below). This is made clear by the numerous provisions of IFRS 2 referring to the accounting treatment of vested awards.

Once equity shares have been unconditionally delivered or beneficially transferred to the counterparty (e.g. as the result of the vesting of an award of ordinary shares, or the exercise of a vested option over ordinary shares), the holder of those shares will often be in exactly the same position as any other holder of ordinary shares and the shares should generally be accounted for under Section 22, rather than under Section 26.

If, however, the holder of a share or vested option enjoys rights not applicable to all holders of that class of share, such as a right to put the share or the option to the entity for cash, or holds a special class of share with rights that do not apply to other classes of equity, the share or option might remain in the scope of Section 26 as long as any such rights continue to apply. The same is true of modifications made after vesting which add such rights to a vested share or option or otherwise alter the life of the share-based payment transaction. The special terms or rights will often be linked to the holder's employment with the entity but could also apply to an arrangement with a non-employee.

The significance of this is that accounting and disclosure requirements could be very different depending on whether or not transactions are considered to be within the scope of Section 26.

3.3 Transactions not within the scope of Section 26

Section 26 simply states that share-based transactions that are clearly for a purpose other than payment to the entity for goods or services are not within its scope. *[FRS 102.26.1A]*. It does not include any more specific examples of transactions that are outside the scope of its requirements. IFRS 2 includes some specific scope exemptions and we imagine that similar exemptions are intended to apply in the application of Section 26. The following transactions are outside the scope of IFRS 2:

- transactions with shareholders as a whole and with shareholders in their capacity as such (see 3.3.1 below);
- transfers of assets in certain group restructuring arrangements (see 3.3.2 below);
- business combinations (see 3.3.3 below);
- combinations of businesses under common control and the contribution of a business to form a joint venture (see 3.3.4 below); and

- transactions in the scope of IAS 32 – *Financial Instruments: Presentation* – and IAS 39 – *Financial Instruments: Recognition and Measurement* – or IFRS 9 – *Financial Instruments* – or Section 22 (see 3.3.5 below). In addition, the scope exemptions in IFRS 2 combined with those in IAS 32 and IAS 39 (or IFRS 9) appear to have the effect that there is no specific guidance in IFRS for accounting for certain types of investments when acquired in return for shares (see 3.3.6 below).

However, as noted at 3.2.4 above, there is no exemption for share schemes aimed mainly at lower- and middle-ranking employees, referred to in different jurisdictions by terms such as 'all-employee share schemes', 'employee share purchase plans' and 'broad-based plans'.

3.3.1 Transactions with shareholders in their capacity as such

IFRS 2 does not apply to transactions with employees (and others) purely in their capacity as shareholders. For example, an employee may already hold shares in the entity as a result of previous share-based payment transactions. If the entity then raises funds through a rights issue, whereby all shareholders (including the employee) can acquire additional shares for less than the current fair value of the shares, such a transaction is not a 'share-based payment transaction' for the purposes of IFRS 2. *[IFRS 2.4].*

3.3.2 Transfer of assets in group restructuring arrangements

In some group restructuring arrangements, one entity will transfer a group of net assets, which does not meet the definition of a business, to another entity in return for shares. Careful consideration of the precise facts and circumstances is needed in order to determine whether, for the separate or individual financial statements of any entity affected by the transfer, such a transfer meets the definition of a share-based payment transaction. If the transfer is considered primarily to be a transfer of goods by their owner in return for payment in shares then, in our view, this should be accounted for as a share-based payment transaction. However, if the transaction is for another purpose and is driven by the group shareholder in its capacity as such, the transaction may be outside the scope of share-based payment accounting (see 3.3.1 above).

Accounting for intra-group asset transfers in return for shares is considered further in Chapter 8 at 4.4.2.B.

3.3.3 Business combinations

IFRS 2 does not apply to share-based payments to acquire goods (such as inventories or property, plant and equipment) in the context of a business combination to which IFRS 3 – *Business Combinations* – applies. We assume that shares issued as consideration for business combinations under Section 19 – *Business Combinations and Goodwill* – are similarly outside the scope of Section 26.

Equity instruments granted to the employees of the acquiree in their capacity as employees (e.g. in return for continued service following the business combination) do not form part of the consideration for the business combination and are therefore within the scope of Section 26 as a share-based payment transaction, as are the cancellation, replacement or modification of a share-based payment transaction as the result of a business combination or other equity restructuring.

If a vendor of an acquired business remains as an employee of that business following the business combination and receives a share-based payment for transferring control of the entity and for remaining in continuing employment, it is necessary to determine how much of the share-based payment relates to the acquisition of control (and therefore forms part of the consideration for the business combination) and how much relates to the provision of future services (which is a post-combination operating expense). There is further discussion on this issue in Chapter 17 at 3.6.4.

3.3.4   Common control transactions and formation of joint arrangements

IFRS 2 also does not apply to a combination of entities or businesses under common control or the contribution of a business on the formation of a joint venture as defined by IFRS 11 – *Joint Arrangements. [IFRS 2.5].*

It should be noted that the contribution of non-financial assets (which do not constitute a business) to a joint venture in return for shares is within the scope of IFRS 2.

IFRS 2 does not directly address other types of transactions involving joint ventures or transactions involving associates, particularly arrangements relating to the employees of associates or joint ventures (see 13 below).

3.3.5   Transactions in the scope of IAS 32, IAS 39 and IFRS 9 or Section 22 (financial instruments)

IFRS 2 does not apply to transactions within the scope of IAS 32, IAS 39 or IFRS 9. Therefore, if an entity enters into a transaction to purchase, in return for shares, a commodity surplus to its production requirements or with a view to short-term profit taking, the contract is treated as a financial instrument under IAS 32 and IAS 39 or IFRS 9 rather than a share-based payment transaction under IFRS 2. *[IFRS 2.6].*

Some practical examples of scope issues involving IFRS 2 and IAS 32 / IAS 39 / IFRS 9 are discussed at 3.4 below.

Whilst Section 26 has no specific corresponding reference to financial assets or liabilities, Section 22 excludes from its scope financial instruments, contracts and obligations under share-based payment transactions (except for the classification requirements that relate to treasury shares) and refers users to Section 26. *[FRS 102.22.2(d)].*

3.3.6   Transactions relating to investments in subsidiaries, associates and joint ventures

As noted at 3.2 above, IFRS 2 applies to share-based payment transactions involving goods or services, with 'goods' defined so as to exclude financial assets. This means that, when (as is commonly the case) an entity acquires an investment in a subsidiary, associate or joint venture for the issue of equity instruments, there is no explicit guidance as to the required accounting in the separate financial statements of the investor when it chooses to apply a policy of 'cost' under paragraph 24 of Section 9 – *Consolidated and Separate Financial Statements* (see Chapter 8 at 4.4.2.B).

3.4 Some practical applications of the scope requirements

This section addresses the application of the scope requirements of Section 26 to a number of situations frequently encountered in practice. The situations are not specifically addressed in Section 26 but the following sections draw on the requirements of Section 26 together with related guidance in IFRS 2 and our experience of the practical application of IFRS 2:

- remuneration in non-equity shares and arrangements with put rights over equity shares (see 3.4.1 below);
- an increase in the counterparty's ownership interest with no change in the number of shares held (see 3.4.2 below);
- awards for which the counterparty has paid 'fair value' (see 3.4.3 below);
- a cash bonus which depends on share price performance (see 3.4.4 below);
- cash-settled awards based on an entity's 'enterprise value' or other formula (see 3.4.5 below); and
- holding own shares to satisfy or 'hedge' awards (see 3.4.6 below).

The following aspects of the scope requirements are covered elsewhere in this chapter:

- employment taxes on share-based payment transactions (see 15 below); and
- instruments such as limited recourse loans that sometimes fall within the scope of the share-based payment, rather than financial instruments, requirements because of the link both to the entity's equity instruments and to goods or services received in exchange (see 16.2 below).

3.4.1 Remuneration in non-equity shares and arrangements with put rights over equity shares

A transaction is within the scope of Section 26 only where it involves the delivery of an equity instrument, or cash or other assets based on the price or value of 'equity instruments (including shares and share options) of the entity or another group entity' (see 3.1 above).

There can sometimes be advantages to giving an employee, in lieu of a cash payment, a share that carries a right to a 'one-off' dividend, or is mandatorily redeemable, at an amount equivalent to the intended cash payment. Such a share would almost certainly be classified as a liability (based on Section 22). Payment in such a share would not fall in the scope of Section 26 since the consideration paid by the entity for services received is a financial liability rather than an equity instrument (see the definitions at 3.1 above).

If, however, the amount of remuneration delivered in this way were equivalent to the value of a particular number of equity instruments issued by the entity, then the transaction would be in scope of Section 26 as a cash-settled share-based payment transaction, since the entity would have incurred a liability (i.e. by issuing the redeemable shares) for an amount based on the price of its equity instruments.

Similarly, if an entity grants an award of equity instruments to an employee together with a put right whereby the employee can require the entity to purchase those shares for an amount based on their fair value, both elements of that transaction are in the scope of Section 26 as a single cash-settled transaction (see 10 below). This is notwithstanding the fact that, in other circumstances, the share and the put right might well be analysed as a single synthetic instrument and classified as a liability with no equity component.

3.4.2   Increase in ownership interest with no change in number of shares held

An increasingly common arrangement, typically found in entities with venture capital investors, is one where an employee (often part of the key management) subscribes initially for, say, 1% of the entity's equity with the venture capitalist holding the other 99%. The employee's equity interest will subsequently increase by a variable amount depending on the extent to which certain targets are met. This is achieved not by issuing new shares but by cancelling some of the venture capitalist's shares. In our view, such an arrangement falls within the scope of Section 26 as the employee is rewarded with an increased equity stake in the entity if certain targets are achieved. The increased equity stake is consistent with the definition of equity as 'a residual interest' notwithstanding the fact that no additional shares are issued.

In such arrangements, it is often asserted that the employee has subscribed for a share of the equity at fair value. However, the subscription price paid must represent a fair value using a Section 26 valuation basis in order for there to be no additional Section 26 expense to recognise (see 3.4.3 below).

3.4.3   Awards for which the counterparty has paid 'fair value'

In certain situations, such as where a special class of share is issued, the counterparty might be asked to subscribe a certain amount for the share which is agreed as being its 'fair value' for taxation or other purposes. This does not mean that such arrangements fall outside the scope of Section 26, either for measurement or disclosure purposes, if the arrangement meets the definition of a share-based payment transaction. In many cases, the agreed 'fair value' will be lower than a fair value measured in accordance with Section 26 because it will reflect the impact of service and non-market performance vesting conditions which are excluded from a Section 26 fair value (see 7 and 9 below). This is addressed in more detail at 16.4.5 below.

3.4.4   Cash bonus dependent on share price performance

An entity might agree to pay its employees a £100 cash bonus if its share price remains at £10 or more over a given period. Intuitively, this does not appear to be in the scope of Section 26, since the employee is not being given cash of equivalent value to a particular number of shares. However, it could be argued that it does fall within the scope of Section 26 on the basis that the entity has incurred a liability, and the amount of that liability is 'based on' the share price (in accordance with the definition of a cash-settled share-based payment transaction) – it is nil if the share price is below £10 and £100 if the share price is £10 or more. In our view, either interpretation is acceptable.

3.4.5   Cash-settled awards based on an entity's 'enterprise value' or other formula

As noted at 3.1 above, Section 26 includes within its scope transactions in which the entity acquires goods or services by incurring a liability 'based on the price (or value) of equity instruments (including shares and share options) of the entity or another group entity'. Employees of an unquoted entity may receive a cash award based on the value of the equity of that entity. Such awards are typically, but not exclusively, made by venture capital investors to the management of entities in which they have invested and which they aim to sell in the medium term. Further discussion of the accounting implications of awards made in connection with an exit event may be found at 16.4 below.

More generally, where employees of an unquoted entity receive a cash award based on the value of the equity, there is no quoted share price and an 'enterprise value' has therefore to be calculated as a surrogate for it. This begs the question of whether such awards are within the scope of Section 26 (because they are based on the value of the entity's equity) or that of Section 28 – *Employee Benefits*.

In order for an award to be within the scope of Section 26, any calculated 'enterprise value' must represent the fair value of the entity's equity. Where the calculation uses techniques recognised by Section 26 as yielding a fair value for equity instruments (as discussed at 9 below), we believe that the award should be regarded as within the scope of Section 26.

An unquoted entity may have calculated the value of its equity based on net assets or earnings (see 9.3 below). In our view, this may be appropriate in some cases.

Where, however, the enterprise value is based on a constant formula, such as a fixed multiple of earnings before interest, tax, depreciation and amortisation (EBITDA), in our view it is unlikely that this will represent a good surrogate for the fair value of the equity on an ongoing basis, even if it did so at the inception of the transaction. It is not difficult to imagine scenarios in which the fair value of the equity of an entity could be affected with no significant change in EBITDA, for example as a result of changes in interest rates and effective tax rates, or a significant impairment of assets. Alternatively, there might be a significant shift in the multiple of EBITDA equivalent to fair value, for example if the entity were to create or acquire a significant item of intellectual property.

The accounting treatment of awards based on the 'market price' of an unquoted entity raises similar issues, as discussed more fully at 7.3.7 below.

3.4.6 Holding own shares to satisfy awards

Entities often seek to 'hedge' the cost of share-based payment transactions by buying their own equity instruments in transactions with existing shareholders. For example, an entity could grant an employee options over 10,000 shares and buy 10,000 of its own shares into treasury, or into its employee benefit trust, at the date that the award is made. If the award is share-settled, the entity will deliver the shares to the counterparty. If it is cash-settled, it may be in a position to sell the shares to raise the cash it is required to deliver to the counterparty. In either case, the cash cost of the award is capped at the amount paid for the shares at the date the award is made, less any amount paid by the employee on exercise. It could of course be argued that such an arrangement only 'hedges' an increase in the price of the shares. If the share price goes down so that the option is never exercised, the entity is left holding 10,000 of its own shares that cost more than they are now worth.

Whilst these strategies may cap the cash cost of share-based payment transactions that are eventually exercised, they will not have any effect on the charge to profit or loss required by Section 26 for such transactions. This is because purchases and sales of own shares are accounted for as movements in equity and are therefore never included in profit or loss, i.e. the recognition of an expense under Section 26 for the share-based payment transaction and accounting for movements in own shares are two completely distinct areas which should be treated separately for accounting purposes (see 5.1 below).

4   GENERAL RECOGNITION PRINCIPLES

The recognition rules in Section 26 are based on a so-called 'service date model'. In other words, an entity is required to recognise the goods or services received or acquired in a share-based payment transaction when it obtains the goods or as the services are received. *[FRS 102.26.3]*. For awards to employees (or others providing similar services), this contrasts with the measurement rules, which normally require a share-based payment transaction to be measured as at the date on which the transaction was entered into, which may be some time before or after the related services are received – see 5 to 8 below.

Where the goods or services received or acquired in exchange for a share-based payment transaction do not qualify for recognition as assets they should be expensed. *[FRS 102.26.4]*. Typically, services will not qualify as assets and should therefore be expensed immediately, whereas goods will generally be initially recognised as assets and expensed later as they are consumed. However, some payments for services may be capitalised (e.g. as part of the cost of PP&E or inventories) and some payments for goods may be expensed immediately (e.g. where they are for items included within development costs written off as incurred).

The corresponding credit entry is, in the case of an equity-settled transaction, an increase in equity and, in the case of a cash-settled transaction, a liability (or decrease in cash or other assets). *[FRS 102.26.3]*.

The primary focus of the discussion in the remainder of this chapter is the application of these rules to transactions with employees, with the accounting treatment of transactions with non-employees addressed at 3.2.3 above and 6.1 and 6.4 below.

4.1   Vesting and vesting conditions

Under Section 26, the point at which a cost is recognised for goods or services depends on the concept of 'vesting'.

A share-based payment to a counterparty is said to vest when it becomes an entitlement of the counterparty. The term is further defined as follows:

'Under a share-based payment arrangement, a counterparty's right to receive cash, other assets or equity instruments of the entity vests when the counterparty's entitlement is no longer conditional on the satisfaction of any vesting conditions.' *[FRS 102 Appendix I]*.

This definition refers only to equity instruments of the entity and omits any reference to equity instruments of other group entities. This appears to be a drafting oversight given that the scope of Section 26 and the definitions of equity- and cash-settled share-based payment transactions in Appendix I to FRS 102 all refer to the equity instruments of the entity and other group entities.

The definition above refers to 'vesting conditions'. Prior to the Triennial review 2017 this term was not defined in FRS 102. However, the standard now defines the term and is consistent with IFRS 2. Vesting conditions are defined as 'conditions that determines whether the entity receives the services that entitle the counterparty to receive cash, other assets or equity instruments of the entity, under a share-based payment arrangement. Vesting conditions are either service conditions or performance conditions.' *[FRS 102 Appendix I]*.

The definition of vesting conditions emphasises the receipt of services by the entity. The recognition principles in FRS 102 using this approach set out the differing accounting treatments, discussed further below, depending on whether the share-based payment transaction includes a service condition. A service condition is, 'a vesting condition that requires the counterparty to complete a specified period of service during which services are provided to the entity. If the counterparty, regardless of the reason, ceases to provide service during the vesting period, it has failed to satisfy the condition. A service condition does not require a performance target to be met.' *[FRS 102 Appendix I]*.

The absence of a service requirement means that an award will vest, or be deemed to vest, immediately as there is no service to be rendered before the counterparty becomes unconditionally entitled to the award. This concept of immediate vesting is reinforced by the fact that FRS 102 requires an entity to presume, in the absence of evidence to the contrary, that services rendered by the counterparty (for example, an employee) as consideration for the share-based payments have already been received. Where there is immediate vesting, the entity is required to recognise the services received, i.e. the cost of the award, in full on the grant date of the award with a corresponding credit to equity or liabilities. *[FRS 102.26.5]*.

If, as will generally be the case for employee awards, the share-based payments do not vest until the counterparty completes a specified period of service, the entity should presume that the services to be rendered by the counterparty as consideration for those share-based payments will be received in the future, during the vesting period, i.e. the period over which the services are being rendered in order for the award to vest. The entity is required to account for those services as they are rendered by the counterparty during the vesting period, with a corresponding increase in equity or liabilities. *[FRS 102.26.6]*. For example, if an employee is granted a share option with a service condition of remaining in employment with an entity for three years, the award vests three years after the date of grant. Accordingly, if the employee is still employed by the entity the cost of the award will be recognised over that three-year period.

As mentioned above, the vesting of awards might also be conditional on performance conditions which require both the counterparty to complete a specified period of service and specified performance targets to be met. Following the amendment to FRS 102 from the Triennial review 2017, the standard includes the following definition of a 'performance condition' consistent with IFRS 2:

Chapter 23

'A vesting condition that requires:

(a)   the counterparty to complete a specified period of service (i.e. a service condition); the service requirement can be explicit or implicit; and

(b)   specified performance target(s) to be met while the counterparty is rendering the service required in (a).

The period of achieving the performance target(s):

(a)   shall not extend beyond the end of the service period; and

(b)   may start before the service period on the condition that the commencement date of the performance target is not substantially before the commencement of the service period;

A performance target is defined by reference to:

(a)   the entity's own operations (or activities) or the operations or activities of another entity in the same group (i.e. a non-market condition); or

(b)   the price (or value) of the entity's equity instruments or the equity instruments of another entity in the same group (including shares and share options) (i.e. a market condition).

A performance target might relate either to the performance of the entity as a whole or to some part of the entity (or part of the group), such as a division or an individual employee.' *[FRS 102 Appendix I].*

Examples of performance conditions are a specified increase in the entity's profit over a specified period of time (a non-market condition – see 7.2 below) or a specified increase in the entity's share price (a market condition – see 7.3 below). *[FRS 102.26.9].* As discussed more fully at 4.2 below, performance conditions refer to performance by an employee (such as a personal sales target) or performance by the entity (or part of the entity), rather than an external performance indicator, such as a general stock market index.

Thus a condition that an award vests if, in three years' time, earnings per share have increased by 10% and the employee is still in employment, is a performance condition. If, however, the award becomes unconditional in three years' time if earnings per share have increased by 10%, irrespective of whether the employee is still in employment, that condition is not a performance condition, but a 'non-vesting' condition because there is no associated service requirement (see 4.2 below).

In addition to the general discussion above and in the remainder this section, specific considerations relating to awards that vest on a flotation or change of control (or similar exit event) are addressed at 16.4 below.

4.2   Non-vesting conditions (conditions that are neither service conditions nor performance conditions)

Some share-based payment transactions are dependent on the satisfaction of conditions that are neither service conditions nor performance conditions. For example, an employee might be given the right to 100 shares in three years' time, subject only to the employee not working in competition with the reporting entity during that time. An undertaking not to work for another entity does not include a requirement for the counterparty to complete a specified period of service with the entity – the employee could sit on a beach for three years and still be entitled to collect the award. Accordingly, such a condition is not regarded as a vesting condition for the purposes of Section 26, but is instead referred to as a 'condition that is not a vesting condition'. *[FRS 102.26.9]*. Alternatively IFRS 2 refers to such a condition as a 'non-vesting condition'. Throughout this chapter we will refer to a 'condition that is not a vesting condition' as a 'non-vesting condition' (see 2.3.1 above).

Section 26 introduces the concept of a non-vesting condition when discussing the measurement of equity-settled awards, providing an example of a condition when an employee contributes to a saving plan as a condition that is not vesting condition, but does not otherwise define the term. *[FRS 102.26.9]*. Given the similarities of approach to recognition and measurement in IFRS 2 and Section 26, we presume that the concept of a non-vesting condition under FRS 102 is intended to be the same as that under IFRS 2 and this is the approach adopted in this chapter. The accounting impact of non-vesting conditions is discussed in detail at 7.4 below.

Although IFRS 2 contains a little more explanation about non-vesting conditions than is found in FRS 102, it does not explicitly define a 'non-vesting condition' but uses the term to describe a condition that is neither a service condition nor a performance condition. However, the concept of the 'non-vesting' condition is not entirely clear and the identification of such conditions is not always straightforward. This has sometimes resulted in differing views on the appropriate classification of certain types of condition depending on whether or not they were considered to be measures of the entity's performance or its activities and hence performance vesting conditions.

As noted at 4.1 above, FRS 102 and IFRS 2 define a vesting condition as a condition that determines whether the entity receives the services that entitle the counterparty to receive payment in equity or cash. Performance conditions are those that require the counterparty to complete a specified period of service and specified performance targets to be met (such as a specified increase in the entity's profit over a specified period of time).

The Basis for Conclusions to IFRS 2 adds that the feature that distinguishes a performance condition from a non-vesting condition is that the former has an explicit or implicit service requirement and the latter does not. *[IFRS 2.BC171A]*.

In issuing its *Annual Improvements to IFRSs 2010-2012 Cycle* in December 2013 the IASB considered whether a definition of 'non-vesting condition' was needed. It decided that 'the creation of a stand-alone definition ... would not be the best alternative for providing clarity on this issue'. *[IFRS 2.BC364]*. Instead, it sought to provide further clarification in the Basis for Conclusions to IFRS 2, as follows:

'...the Board observed that the concept of a non-vesting condition can be inferred from paragraphs BC170-BC184 of IFRS 2, which clarify the definition of vesting conditions. In accordance with this guidance it can be inferred that a non-vesting condition is any condition that does not determine whether the entity receives the services that entitle the counterparty to receive cash, other assets or equity instruments of the entity under a share-based payment arrangement. In other words, a non-vesting condition is any condition that is not a vesting condition.' *[IFRS 2.BC364]*.

Chapter 23

For a condition to be a performance vesting condition, it is not sufficient for the condition to be specific to the performance of the entity. There must also be an explicit or implied service condition that extends to the end of the performance period. For example, a condition that requires the entity's profit before tax or its share price to reach a minimum level, but without any requirement for the employee to remain in employment throughout the performance period, is not a performance condition, but a non-vesting condition.

Specific examples of non-vesting conditions given by IFRS 2 include:

- a requirement to make monthly savings during the vesting period;
- a requirement for a commodity index to reach a minimum level;
- restrictions on the transfer of vested equity instruments; or
- an agreement not to work for a competitor after the award has vested – a 'non-compete' agreement. *[IFRS 2.BC171B, IG24]*.

The IASB has also clarified that a condition related to a share market index target (rather than to the specific performance of the entity's own shares) is a non-vesting condition because a share market index reflects not only the performance of an entity but also that of other entities outside the group. Even where an entity's share price makes up a substantial part of the share market index, the IASB confirmed that this would still be a non-vesting condition because it reflects the performance of other, non-group, entities. *[IFRS 2.BC354-358]*.

Thus, whilst conditions that are not related to the performance of the entity are always, by their nature, non-vesting conditions, conditions that relate to the performance of the entity may or may not be non-vesting conditions depending on whether there is also a requirement for the counterparty to render service.

As noted at 4.1 above, FRS 102 and IFRS 2 define a performance condition. The definition clarifies the extent to which the period of achieving the performance target(s) needs to coincide with the service period and states that this performance period:

(a) shall not extend beyond the end of the service period; and

(b) may start before the service period on the condition that the commencement date of the performance target is not substantially before the commencement of the service period.

There clearly remains an element of judgement in the interpretation of 'substantially' as used in the definition.

There is further discussion of the accounting treatment of non-vesting conditions at 7.4 below.

4.3 Vesting period

As noted at 4.1 above, the vesting period is the period during which all the specified vesting conditions of a share-based payment arrangement are to be satisfied. This is not the same as the exercise period or the life of the option, as illustrated by Example 23.1 below.

Example 23.1:   Meaning of 'vesting period' – award with vesting conditions only

An employee is awarded options that can be exercised at any time between three and ten years from the date of the award, provided the employee remains in service for at least three years from the date of the award. For this award, the vesting period is three years; the exercise period is seven years; and the life of the option is ten years. However, for the purposes of calculating the fair value of the award (see 9 below), the life of the award is taken as the period ending with the date on which the counterparty is most likely actually to exercise the option, which may be some time before the full ten year life expires.

It is also important to distinguish between vesting conditions and other restrictions on the exercise of options and / or trading in shares, as illustrated by Example 23.2 below.

Example 23.2:   Meaning of 'vesting period' – award with vesting conditions and other restrictions

An employee is awarded options that can be exercised at any time between five and ten years from the date of the award, provided the employee remains in service for at least three years from the date of the award. In this case, the vesting period remains three years as in Example 23.1 above, provided that the employee's entitlement to the award becomes absolute at the end of three years – in other words, the employee does not have to provide services to the entity in years 4 and 5. The restriction on exercise of the award in the period after vesting is a non-vesting condition, which would be reflected in the original valuation of the award at the date of grant (see 5, 6 and 9 below).

The accounting implications of vesting conditions, non-vesting conditions and vesting periods for equity-settled transactions are discussed at 5 to 8 below and for cash-settled transactions at 10 below.

5   EQUITY-SETTLED TRANSACTIONS – OVERVIEW

5.1   Summary of accounting treatment

The provisions relating to accounting for equity-settled transactions are complex, even when supplemented by additional guidance as is found in the appendices and implementation guidance to IFRS 2. As noted at 1.2 above, FRS 102 does not replicate this guidance and so we have referred to IFRS 2 to supplement the requirements of FRS 102.

The key points can be summarised as follows.

(a)   All equity-settled transactions are measured at fair value. However, transactions with employees are measured using a 'grant date model' (i.e. the transaction is recorded at the fair value of the equity instrument at the date when it is originally granted), whereas transactions with non-employees are normally measured using a 'service date model' (i.e. the transaction is recorded at the fair value of the goods or services received at the date they are received). As noted at 4 above, all transactions, however *measured*, are *recognised* using a 'service date model' (see 6 below).

(b)   Where an award is made subject to future fulfilment of conditions, a 'market condition' (i.e. one related to the market price (or value) of the entity's equity instruments) or a 'non-vesting condition' (i.e. one that is neither a service condition nor a performance condition) is taken into account in determining the fair value of the award. However, the effect of conditions other than market and non-vesting conditions is ignored in determining the fair value of the award (see 4 above and 7 below).

(c)   Where an award is made subject to future fulfilment of service or performance vesting conditions, its cost is recognised over the period during which the service condition is fulfilled (see 4 above and 7 below). The corresponding credit entry is recorded within equity (see 5.2 below).

(d)   Until an equity instrument has vested (i.e. the entitlement to it is no longer conditional on future service) any amounts recorded are in effect contingent and will be adjusted if more or fewer awards vest than were originally anticipated to do so. However, an equity instrument awarded subject to a market condition or a non-vesting condition is considered to vest irrespective of whether or not that market or non-vesting condition is fulfilled, provided that all other vesting conditions are satisfied (see 7 below).

(e)   No adjustments are made, either before or after vesting, to reflect the fact that an award has no value to the employee or other counterparty e.g. in the case of a share option, because the option exercise price is above the current market price of the share (see 7.1.1 and 7.1.3 below).

(f)   If an equity instrument is cancelled, whether by the entity or the counterparty (see (g) below) before vesting, any amount remaining to be expensed is charged in full at that point (see 8.4 below). If an equity instrument is modified before vesting (e.g. in the case of a share option, by changing the performance conditions or the exercise price), the financial statements must continue to show a cost for at least the fair value of the original instrument, as measured at the original grant date, together with any excess of the fair value of the modified instrument over that of the original instrument, as measured at the date of modification (see 8.3 below).

(g)   Where an award lapses during the vesting period due to a failure by the counterparty to satisfy a non-vesting condition within the counterparty's control, or a failure by the entity to satisfy a non-vesting condition within the entity's control, the lapse of the award is accounted for as if it were a cancellation (see (f) above and 7.4.3 below).

(h)   In determining the cost of an equity-settled transaction, whether the entity satisfies its obligations under the transaction with a fresh issue of shares or by purchasing its own shares in the financial markets or from private company shareholders is completely irrelevant to the charge in profit or loss, although there is clearly a difference in the cash flows. Where own shares are purchased, they are accounted for as treasury shares (see 3.4.6 above).

The requirements summarised in (d) to (g) above can have the effect that an entity is required to record a cost for an award that is deemed to vest for accounting purposes but ultimately has no value to the counterparty because the award either does not vest or vests but is not exercised. These rather counter-intuitive requirements are in part 'anti-abuse' provisions to prevent entities from applying a 'selective' grant date model, whereby awards that increase in value after grant date remain measured at grant date while awards that decrease in value are remeasured. This is discussed further in the detailed analysis at 6 to 8 below.

5.2   The credit entry

As noted at (c) in the summary at 5.1 above, the basic accounting entry for an equity-settled share-based payment transaction is: *[FRS 102.26.3]*

Dr   Profit or loss for the period (employee costs)

    Cr   Equity.

FRS 102 does not prescribe whether the credit should be to a separate reserve or, if the entity chooses to treat it as such, how it should be described. Under the Companies Act 2006, an entity is permitted to credit a separate 'other reserve' rather than the credit being allocated initially to the profit and loss reserve. The 'other reserve' is generally labelled as 'shares to be issued' or 'share-based payment reserve' with the share-based payment credit held within this reserve until the award vests (if an award of free shares), is exercised or lapses (an award of options). When such trigger events occur, it will be appropriate for the entity to make a transfer between reserves.

The FRS 102 credit is not taken to share capital and share premium as these are used to record the legal proceeds of a share issue.

Overall, there will be a net nil impact on equity arising from the FRS 102 accounting as the profit and loss expense is ultimately reflected in the profit and loss reserve and offset by the credit taken directly to equity. The impact on distributable profits of employee share schemes depends on whether or not the reporting entity is a public company. Whilst FRS 102 is not specifically addressed, the effect of the similar accounting requirements of IFRS 2 is discussed in Section 7 of TECH 02/17BL: *Guidance on Realised and Distributable Profits under the Companies Act 2006* (TECH 02/17BL). *[TECH 02/17BL.7]*.

Occasionally there will be a credit to profit or loss (see for instance Example 23.12 at 7.2.4 below) and a corresponding reduction in equity.

6 EQUITY-SETTLED TRANSACTIONS – COST OF AWARDS

6.1 Cost of awards – overview

The general measurement rule in FRS 102 is that an entity must measure the goods or services received, and the corresponding increase in equity, directly, at the fair value of the goods or services received, unless that fair value cannot be estimated reliably. If the fair value of the goods or services received cannot be estimated reliably, the entity must measure their value, and the corresponding increase in equity, indirectly, by reference to the fair value of the equity instruments granted. *[FRS 102.26.7]*.

'Fair value' is defined in Appendix I to FRS 102 as 'the amount for which an asset could be exchanged, a liability settled, or an equity instrument granted could be exchanged, between knowledgeable, willing parties in an arm's length transaction'. The definition goes on to make clear that, in the absence of more specific guidance within individual sections of FRS 102, the Appendix to Section 2 – *Concepts and Pervasive Principles* – should be used in determining fair value. Therefore, where the fair value of a share-based payment is based on the fair value of the goods or services, the Section 2 Appendix guidance should be used. Where the share-based payment is measured on the basis of the fair value of the equity instruments rather than the goods or services, Section 26 has its own specific rules in relation to determining the fair value which differ from the more general fair value measurement requirements of FRS 102 (see 6.5 below).

On their own, the general measurement principles of paragraph 7 of Section 26 might suggest that the reporting entity must determine in each case whether the fair value of the equity instruments granted or that of the goods or services received is more reliably determinable. However, paragraph 7 goes on to clarify that, in the case of transactions with employees and others providing similar services, the fair value of the equity instruments must always be used 'because typically it is not possible to estimate reliably the fair value of the services received' (see 6.2 below). *[FRS 102.26.7]*.

Moreover, transactions with employees and others providing similar services are measured at the date of grant (see 6.2 below), whereas those with non-employees are measured at the date when the entity obtains the goods or the counterparty renders service (see 6.4 below). *[FRS 102.26.8]*.

The overall position can be summarised by the following matrix.

Counterparty	Measurement basis	Measurement date	Recognition date
Employee	Fair value of equity instruments awarded	Grant date	Service date
Non-employee	Fair value of goods or services received or, if goods or services not reliably measurable, fair value of equity instruments awarded	Service date	Service date

One effect of a grant date measurement model is that, applied to a grant of share options that is eventually exercised, it 'freezes' the accounting cost at the (typically) lower fair value at the date of grant. This excludes from the post-grant financial statements the increased cost and volatility that would be associated with a model that constantly remeasured the award to fair value until exercise date.

The price to be paid in accounting terms for the grant date model is that, when an award falls in value after grant date, it continues to be recognised at its higher grant date value. It is therefore quite possible that, during a period of general economic downturn, financial statements will show significant costs for options granted in previous years, but which are currently worthless.

6.2   Transactions with employees and others providing similar services

These will comprise the great majority of transactions accounted for as equity-settled share-based payments under Section 26 and include all remuneration in the form of shares, share options and any other form of reward settled in equity instruments of the entity or a member of its group.

6.2.1   *Who is an 'employee'?*

Given the difference between the accounting treatment of equity-settled transactions with employees and with non-employees, it is obviously important to understand what is meant by 'employees and others providing similar services'. *[FRS 102.26.7]*. FRS 102 does not provide a definition but IFRS 2 defines 'employees and others providing similar services' as individuals who render personal services to the entity and either:

(a)   the individuals are regarded as employees for legal or tax purposes;

(b)   the individuals work for the entity under its direction in the same way as individuals who are regarded as employees for legal or tax purposes; or

(c)   the services rendered are similar to those rendered by employees.

The term encompasses all management personnel, i.e. those persons having authority and responsibility for planning, directing and controlling the activities of the entity, including non-executive directors. *[IFRS 2 Appendix A].*

The implication of (a) and (b) above is that it is not open to an entity to argue that an individual who is not an employee as a matter of law is therefore automatically a non-employee for the purposes of IFRS 2 and FRS 102.

The implication of (b) and (c) above is that, where a third party provides services pursuant to a share-based payment transaction that could be provided by an employee (e.g. where an external IT consultant works alongside an in-house IT team), that third party is treated as an employee rather than a non-employee for the purposes of IFRS 2 and FRS 102.

Conversely, however, where an entity engages a consultant to undertake work for which there is not an existing in-house function, the implication is that such an individual is not regarded as an employee. In other words, in our view, the reference in (c) to 'services ... similar to those rendered by employees' is to services rendered by employees that the entity actually has, rather than to employees that the entity might have if it were to recruit them. Otherwise, the distinction in IFRS 2 and FRS 102 between employees and non-employees would have no effect, since it would always be open to an entity to argue that it could employ someone to undertake any task instead of engaging a contractor.

Exceptionally, there might be cases where the same individual is engaged in both capacities. For example, a director of the entity might also be a partner in a firm of lawyers and be engaged in that latter capacity to advise the entity on a particular issue. It might be more appropriate to regard payment for the legal services as made to a non-employee rather than to an employee.

6.2.2 Basis of measurement

As noted above, equity-settled transactions with employees must be measured by reference to the fair value of the equity instruments granted at 'grant date' (see 6.3 below). *[FRS 102.26.8].* FRS 102 offers no explanation as to why this should be the case, but IFRS 2 asserts that this approach is necessary because shares, share options and other equity instruments are typically only part of a larger remuneration package, such that it would not be practicable to determine the value of the work performed in consideration for the cash element of the total package, the benefit-in-kind element, the share option element and so on. *[IFRS 2.12].*

In essence, this is really an anti-avoidance provision. The underlying concern is that, if an entity were able to value options by reference to the services provided for them, it might assert that the value of those services was zero, on the argument that its personnel are already so handsomely rewarded by the non-equity elements of their remuneration package (such as cash and health benefits), that no additional services are (or indeed could be) obtained by granting options.

Chapter 23

6.3   Grant date

The determination of grant date is critical to the measurement of equity-settled share-based transactions with employees, since grant date is the date at which such transactions must be measured (see 6.2 above). Grant date is defined as:

'The date at which the entity and another party (including an employee) agree to a share-based payment arrangement, being when the entity and the counterparty have a shared understanding of the terms and conditions of the arrangement. At grant date the entity confers on the counterparty the right to cash, other assets or equity instruments of the entity, provided the specified vesting conditions, if any, are met. If that agreement is subject to an approval process (for example, by shareholders), grant date is the date when that approval is obtained.' *[FRS 102 Appendix I].*

In practice, it is not always clear when a shared understanding of the award (and, therefore, grant date) has occurred. Issues of interpretation can arise as to:

- how precise the shared understanding of the terms of the award must be; and
- exactly what level of communication between the reporting entity and the counterparty is sufficient to ensure the appropriate degree of agreement and 'shared understanding'.

As a consequence, the determination of the grant date is often difficult in practice. We discuss the following issues in more detail in the sections below:

- basic determination of grant date (see 6.3.1 below);
- the communication of awards to employees and the rendering of services in advance of grant date (see 6.3.2 below);
- awards where the exercise price or performance target depends on a formula or on a future share price (see 6.3.3 below);
- awards where the exercise price is paid in shares – net settlement of award (see 6.3.4 below);
- an award of equity instruments to a fixed monetary value (see 6.3.5 below);
- awards with multiple service and performance periods (see 6.3.6 below);
- awards subject to modification or discretionary re-assessment by the entity after the original grant date (see 6.3.7 below); and
- mandatory or discretionary awards to 'good leavers' (see 6.3.8 below).

Some arrangements give rise to significant issues of interpretation in relation to the determination of grant date and the appropriate accounting treatment. For example:

- automatic full or *pro rata* entitlement to awards on cessation of employment (see 6.3.8.C below); and
- awards over a fixed pool of shares (including 'last man standing' arrangements) (see 6.3.9 below).

An outline of the nature of these arrangements is given in this chapter but a detailed discussion is beyond the scope of this publication.

6.3.1 Determination of grant date

The definition of 'grant date' in Appendix I to FRS 102 (see 6.3 above) emphasises that a grant occurs only when all the conditions are understood and agreed by the parties to the arrangement and any required approval process has been completed. This is reinforced by the implementation guidance accompanying the same definition in IFRS 2 which, in our view, should also be considered by an entity applying FRS 102.

For example, if an entity makes an award 'in principle' to an employee of options whose terms are subject to review or approval by a remuneration committee or the shareholders, 'grant date' is the later date when the necessary formalities have been completed. *[FRS 102 Appendix I, IFRS 2.IG1-3]*.

The implementation guidance to IFRS 2 emphasises that the word 'agree' is 'used in its usual sense, which means that there must be both an offer and an acceptance of that offer'. Therefore, there cannot be a grant unless an offer by one party has been accepted by the other party. The guidance notes that agreement will be explicit in some cases (e.g. if an agreement has to be signed), but in others it might be implicit, such as when an employee starts to deliver services for the award. *[IFRS 2.IG2]*. Determination of when the counterparty has agreed to an offer will often be an area of judgement that depends on the precise facts and circumstances of a particular situation.

The implementation guidance to IFRS 2 further notes that employees may begin rendering services in consideration for an award before it has been formally ratified. For example, a new employee might join an entity on 1 January and be granted options relating to performance for a period beginning on that date, but subject to formal approval by the remuneration committee at its next quarterly meeting on 15 March. In that case, the entity would typically begin expensing the award from 1 January based on a best estimate of its fair value, but would subsequently adjust that estimate so that the ultimate cost of the award was its actual fair value at 15 March (see 6.3.2 below). *[IFRS 2.IG4]*. This reference to formal approval could be construed as indicating that, in fact, FRS 102 and IFRS 2 require not merely that there is a mutual understanding of the award (which might well have been in existence since 1 January), but also that the entity has completed all processes necessary to make the award a legally binding agreement.

In practice, many situations are much less clear-cut than the examples given in the implementation guidance. Some of the practical interpretation issues are considered further below.

6.3.2 Communication of awards to employees and services in advance of grant date

As discussed at 6.3.1 above, the definition of grant date in FRS 102 together with the implementation guidance to IFRS 2 indicate that, in order for a grant to have been made, there must not merely be a mutual understanding of the terms – including the conditions attached to the award – but there must also be a legally enforceable arrangement. Thus, if an award requires board or shareholder approval for it to be legally binding on the reporting entity, it has not been granted until such approval has been given, even if the terms of the award are fully understood at an earlier date. However, if services are effectively being rendered for an award from a date earlier than the grant date as defined in IFRS 2, the cost of the award should be recognised over a period starting with that earlier date. *[IFRS 2.IG4]*.

In some situations the employee will have a valid expectation of an award, and the entity will have a corresponding obligation, based on an earlier commitment by the entity. However, it might be the case that not all of the precise terms and conditions have been finalised. In our view, provided it is possible to estimate the fair value of the arrangement, an estimated cost for services should be recognised in advance of grant date in such cases as well as in those situations where formal approval does not take place until a later date.

The implications of this approach are illustrated in Example 23.3 below for a situation where formal approval of an award is delayed. It is important, however, to retain a sense of proportion in considering the overall impact on the financial statements. For example, in cases where the share price or value is not particularly volatile, whether the grant date is, say, 1 January or 1 April may not make a great difference to the valuation of the award, particularly when set beside the range of acceptable valuations resulting from the use of estimates in the valuation process.

Example 23.3:   Determination of grant date

Scenario 1

On 1 January an entity advises employees of the terms of a share award designed to reward performance over the following three years. The award is subject to board approval, which is given two month later on 1 March. Grant date is 1 March. However, the cost of the award would be recognised over the three year period beginning 1 January, since the employees would have effectively been rendering service for the award from that date.

Scenario 2

On 1 January an entity's board resolves to implement a share scheme designed to reward performance over the following three years. The award is notified to employees two months later on 1 March. Grant date is again 1 March. *Prima facie*, in this case, the cost of the award would be recognised over the two years and ten months beginning 1 March, since the employees could not be regarded as rendering service in January and February for an award of which they were not aware at that time.

However, if a similar award is made each year, and according to a similar timescale, there might be an argument that, during January and February of each year, the employees are rendering service for an award of which there is high expectation, and that the cost should therefore, as in Scenario 1, be recognised over the full three year period. The broader issue of the accounting treatment for awards of which there is a high expectation is addressed in the discussion of matching share awards at 16.1 below.

Scenario 3

On 1 January an entity advises employees of the terms of a share award designed to reward performance over the following three years. The award is subject to board approval, which is given two months later on 1 March. However, in giving such approval, the board makes some changes to the performance conditions as originally communicated to employees on 1 January. The revised terms of the award are communicated to employees a month later on 1 April. Grant date is 1 April. However, the cost of the award would be recognised over the three year period beginning 1 January, since the employees would have effectively been rendering service for the award from that date.

Examples of situations where an employee might render service in advance of the formal grant date because the precise conditions of an award are outstanding are considered at 6.3.3 to 6.3.6 and at 16.4.1 below.

6.3.3   Exercise price or performance target dependent on a formula or future share price

Some share plans define the exercise price not in absolute terms, but as a factor of the share price. For example, the price might be expressed as:

- a percentage of the share price at exercise date; or
- a percentage of the lower of the share price at grant date and at exercise date.

The effect of this is that, although the actual exercise price is not known until the date of exercise, both the entity and the counterparty already have a shared understanding of how the price will be calculated and it is possible to estimate the outcome on an ongoing basis without the need for additional approval or inputs.

A similar approach might be applied in the setting of performance targets, i.e. they are set by reference to a formula rather than in absolute terms and so do not require further input by the entity or its shareholders.

In order for there to be a shared understanding and a grant date, the formula or method of determining the outcome needs to be sufficiently clear and objective to allow both the entity and the counterparty to make an estimate of the outcome of the award during the vesting period. Accordingly, in our view, grant date is the date on which the terms and conditions (including the formula for calculating the exercise price or performance target) are determined sufficiently clearly and agreed by the entity and the counterparty, subject to the matters discussed at 6.3.2 above.

6.3.4 Exercise price paid in shares (net settlement of award)

Some share awards allow the exercise price to be paid in shares. In practical terms, this means that the number of shares delivered to the counterparty will be the total 'gross' number of shares awarded less as many shares as have, at the date of exercise, a fair value equal to the exercise price.

In our view, this situation is analogous to that described at 6.3.3 above in that, whilst the absolute 'net' number of shares awarded will not be known until the date of exercise, the basis on which that 'net' number will be determined is established in advance. Accordingly, in our view, grant date is the date on which the terms and conditions (including the ability to surrender shares to a fair value equal to the exercise price) are determined and agreed by the entity and the counterparty, subject to the matters discussed at 6.3.2 above.

Such a scheme could be analysed as a share-settled share appreciation right (whereby the employee receives shares to the value of the excess of the value of the shares given over the exercise price), which is accounted for as an equity-settled award.

Awards settled in shares net of a cash amount to meet an employee's tax liability are considered further at 15.3 below.

6.3.5 Award of equity instruments to a fixed monetary value

Some entities may grant awards to employees of shares to a fixed value. For example, an entity might award as many shares as are worth £10,000, with the number of shares being calculated by reference to the share price as at the vesting date. The number of shares ultimately received will not be known until the vesting date. This begs the question of whether such an award can be regarded as having been granted until that date, on the argument that it is only then that the number of shares to be delivered – a key term of the award – is known, and therefore there cannot be a 'shared understanding' of the terms of the award until that later date.

In our view, however, this situation is analogous to those in 6.3.3 and 6.3.4 above in that, whilst the absolute number of shares awarded will not be known until the vesting date, the basis on which that number will be determined is established in advance in a manner sufficiently clear and objective as to allow an ongoing estimate by the entity and by the counterparty of the number of awards expected to vest. Accordingly, in our view, grant date is the date on which the terms and conditions are determined sufficiently clearly and agreed by the entity and the counterparty, subject to the matters discussed at 6.3.2 above.

FRS 102 does not address the valuation of such awards and IFRS 2 does not address it directly. Intuitively, it might seem obvious that an award which promises (subject to vesting conditions) shares to the value of £10,000 must have a grant date fair value of £10,000, adjusted for the time value of money, together with market conditions and non-vesting conditions. However, matters are not so clear-cut, as Example 23.4 illustrates:

Example 23.4:   Award of shares to a fixed monetary value

At the beginning of year 1, the reporting entity grants:

- to Employee A an award of 1,000 shares subject to remaining in employment for three years; and
- to Employee B £10,000 subject to remaining in employment for three years, to be paid in as many shares as are (at the end of year 3) worth £10,000.

Both awards vest, and the share price at the end of year 3 is £10, so that both employees receive 1,000 shares.

The charge for A's award is clearly 1000 × the fair value as at the beginning of year 1 of a share deliverable in three years' time. What is the charge for B's award? A number of potential alternatives exist including:

- the number of shares actually delivered multiplied by the fair value at the grant date (start of year 1)
- An amount based on a grant date estimate of the number of shares (which is not subsequently revisited due to the existence of a market condition);
- £10,000, adjusted for the time value of money.

Whilst there are hints in the Basis for Conclusions to IFRS 2 that the IASB thought that the two awards should be similarly valued, this treatment is not made explicitly clear.

Some argue that an award of shares to a given monetary amount contains a market condition, since the number of shares ultimately delivered (and therefore vesting) depends on the market price of the shares on the date of delivery. This allows the award to be valued at a fixed amount at grant date. We acknowledge that a literal reading of the definition of 'market condition' in FRS 102 and IFRS 2 supports this view, but question whether this can really have been intended. In our view, the essential feature of a share-based payment transaction subject to a market condition must be that the employee's ultimate entitlement to the award depends on the share price rather than the share price simply being used to determine the number of shares.

In our view, the principal question is whether the measurement of the transaction should be based on the overall award or on each share or share equivalent making up the award. In the absence of clear guidance as to the appropriate unit of account, entities may take a number of views on how to value awards of shares to a given value, but should adopt a consistent approach for all such awards.

6.3.6   Awards with multiple service and performance periods

Entities frequently make awards that cover more than one reporting period, but with different performance conditions for each period, rather than a single cumulative target for the whole vesting period. In such cases, the grant date may depend on the precision with which the terms of the award are communicated to employees, as illustrated by Example 23.5 below.

Example 23.5:   Awards with multiple service and performance periods

Scenario 1

At the beginning of year 1, an entity enters into a share-based payment arrangement with an employee. The employee is informed that the maximum potential award is 40,000 shares, 10,000 of which will vest at the end of year 1, and 10,000 more at the end of each of years 2 to 4. Vesting of each of the four tranches of 10,000 shares is conditional on:

(a)   the employee having been in continuous service until the end of each relevant year; and

(b)   revenue targets for each of those four years, as communicated to the employee at the beginning of year 1, having been attained.

In this case, the terms of the award are clearly understood by both parties at the beginning of year 1, and this is therefore the grant date under FRS 102 (subject to issues such as any requirement for later formal approval – see 6.3 above). The cost of the award would be recognised using a 'graded' vesting approach – see 7.2.2 below.

Scenario 2

At the beginning of year 1, an entity enters into a share-based payment arrangement with an employee. The employee is informed that the maximum potential award is 40,000 shares, 10,000 of which will vest at the end of year 1, and 10,000 more at the end of each of years 2 to 4. Vesting of each tranche of 10,000 shares is conditional on:

(a)   the employee having been in continuous service until the end of each relevant year; and

(b)   revenue targets for each of those four years, to be communicated to the employee at the beginning of each relevant year in respect of that year only, having been attained.

In this case, in our view, at the beginning of year 1 there is a clear shared understanding only of the terms of the first tranche of 10,000 shares that will potentially vest at the end of year 1. There is no clear understanding of the terms of the tranches potentially vesting at the end of years 2 to 4 because their vesting depends on revenue targets for those years which have not yet been set.

Accordingly, each of the four tranches of 10,000 shares has a separate grant date (and, therefore, a separate measurement date) – i.e. the beginning of each of years 1, 2, 3 and 4, and a vesting period of one year from the relevant grant date.

In this type of situation, the entity would also need to consider whether, in the absence of a grant date, the employee was nonetheless rendering services in advance of the grant date. However, if targets are unquantified and do not depend on a formula, for example, then it is likely to be difficult to estimate an expense in advance of the grant date (see 6.3.2 above).

A variation on the above two scenarios which is seen quite frequently in practice is an award where the target is quantified for the first year and the targets for subsequent years depend on a formula-based increase in the year 1 target. The formula is set at the same time as the year 1 target. Whether the accounting treatment for scenario 1 above or scenario 2 above is the more appropriate in such a situation is, in our view, a matter of judgement depending on the precise terms of the arrangement (see 6.3.3 above).

6.3.7   Awards subject to modification by entity after original grant date

Some employee share awards are drafted in terms that give the entity discretion to modify the detailed terms of the scheme after grant date. Some have questioned whether this effectively means that the date originally determined as the 'grant date' is not in fact the grant date as defined in FRS 102, on the grounds that the entity's right to modify means that the terms are not in fact understood by both parties in advance.

In our view, this is very often not an appropriate analysis. If it were, it could mean that significant numbers of share-based awards to employees (including most in the UK) would be required to be measured at vesting date, which clearly is not intended under the grant date model in Section 26.

However, the assessment of whether or not an intervention by the entity after grant date constitutes a modification is often difficult. Some situations commonly encountered in practice are considered in the sections below.

6.3.7.A   *Significant equity restructuring or transactions*

Many schemes contain provisions designed to ensure that the value of awards is maintained following a major capital restructuring (such as a share split or share consolidation – see 8.7 below) or a major transaction with shareholders as a whole (such as a major share buyback or the payment of a special dividend). These provisions will either specify the adjustments to be made in a particular situation or, alternatively, may allow the entity to make such discretionary adjustments as it sees fit in order to maintain the value of awards. In some cases the exercise of such discretionary powers may be relatively mechanistic (e.g. the adjustment of the number of shares subject to options following a share split). In other cases, more subjectivity will be involved (e.g. in determining whether a particular dividend is a 'special' dividend for the purposes of the scheme).

In our view, where the scheme rules specify the adjustments to be made or where there is a legal requirement to make adjustments in order to remedy any dilution that would otherwise arise, the implementation of such adjustments would not result in the recognition of any incremental fair value. This assumes that the adjustment would simply operate on an automatic basis to put the holders of awards back to the position that they would have been in had there not been a restructuring and hence there would be no difference in the fair value of the awards before and after the restructuring (or other specified event).

However, where there is no such explicit requirement in the scheme rules or under relevant legislation, we believe that there should be a presumption that the exercise of the entity's discretionary right to modify is a 'modification' as outlined in FRS 102. In such a situation, the fair values before and after the modification may differ and any incremental fair value should be expensed over the remaining vesting period (see 8.3 below).

6.3.7.B   *Interpretation of general terms*

More problematic might be the exercise of any discretion by the entity to interpret the more general terms of a scheme in deciding whether performance targets have been met and therefore whether, and to what extent, an award should vest. In this case, there might be more of an argument that the entity's intervention constitutes a modification.

If such an intervention were not regarded as a modification, then the results might be different depending on the nature of the award and the conditions attached to it. Where an award is subject to a market condition, or to a non-vesting condition, an expense might well have to be recognised in any event, if all the non-market vesting conditions (e.g. service) were satisfied – see 7.3 and 7.4 below.

However, suppose that an award had been based on a non-market performance condition, such as a profit target, which was met, but only due to a gain of an unusual, non-recurring nature. The Board of Directors concludes that this should be ignored, with the effect that the award does not vest. If this is regarded as the exercise of a pre-existing right to ensure that the award vests only if 'normal' profit reaches a given level, then there has been no modification. On this analysis, the award has not vested, and any expense previously recognised would be reversed. If, however, the Board's intervention is regarded as a modification, it would have no impact on the accounting treatment in this case, as the effect would not be beneficial to the employee and so the modification would be ignored under the general requirements of FRS 102 relating to modifications (see 8.3.2 below).

6.3.7.C   Discretion to make further awards

Some schemes may contain terms that give the entity the power to increase an award in circumstances where the recipient is considered to have delivered exceptional performance, or some such similar wording. In our view, unless the criteria for judging such exceptional performance are so clear as to be, in effect, performance conditions, the presumption should be that any award made pursuant to such a clause is granted, and therefore measured, when it is made. There may be circumstances where an award described as 'discretionary' may not truly be so, since the entity has created an expectation amounting to an obligation to make the award. However, we believe that it would be somewhat contradictory to argue that such expectations had been created in the case of an award stated to be for (undefined) exceptional performance only.

6.3.8   'Good leaver' arrangements

It is common for awards to contain a so-called 'good leaver' clause. A 'good leaver' clause is one which makes provision for an employee who leaves before the end of the full vesting period of an award nevertheless to receive some or all of the award on leaving (see 6.3.8.A below).

In other cases, the original terms of an award will either make no reference to 'good leavers' or will not be sufficiently specific to allow the accounting treatment on cessation of employment to be an automatic outcome of the original terms of the scheme. In such cases, and in situations where awards are made to leavers on a fully discretionary basis, the accounting approach differs from that required where the original terms are clear about 'good leaver' classification and entitlement (see 6.3.8.B below).

We refer throughout this section on 'good leavers' to an employee leaving employment, but similar considerations apply when an individual automatically becomes entitled to an award before the end of the original vesting period due to other reasons specified in the terms of the agreement, e.g. attaining a certain age or achieving a specified length of service, even if the individual remains in employment after the relevant date. In these situations, the date of full entitlement is the date on which any services – and therefore expense recognition – cease for the purposes of Section 26.

Chapter 23

Arrangements for a good leaver to receive all, or part, of an award on leaving employment should be distinguished from a situation where an employee leaves with no award and where forfeiture accounting is likely to apply (see 8.4.1.A below).

6.3.8.A   Provision for 'good leavers' made in original terms of award

In some cases the types of person who are 'good leavers' may be explicitly defined in the original terms of the arrangement (common examples being persons who die or reach normal retirement age before the end of the full vesting period, or who work for a business unit that is sold or closed during the vesting period). In other cases, the entity may have the discretion to determine on a case-by-case basis whether a person should be treated as a 'good leaver'.

In addition, some schemes may specify the entitlement of a 'good leaver' on leaving (e.g. that the leaver receive a portion of the award pro-rata to the extent that the performance conditions have been met as at the date of leaving), whereas others leave the determination of the award to the entity at the time that the employee leaves.

Whichever situation applies, any expense relating to an award to a good leaver must be fully recognised by the leaving date (or date of unconditional entitlement, if earlier than the usual vesting date) because, at that point, the good leaver ceases to provide any services to the entity for the award and any remaining conditions attached to the award will be treated as non-vesting rather than vesting conditions (see 4.2 above).

In our view, an award which vests before the end of the original vesting period due to the operation of a 'good leaver' clause is measured at the original grant date only where, under the rules of the scheme as understood by both parties at the original grant date, the award is made:

- to a person clearly identified as a 'good leaver'; and
- in an amount clearly quantified or quantifiable.

Where, as outlined above, the rules of the scheme make clear the categories of 'good leaver' and their entitlement, the entity should assess at grant date how many good leavers there are likely to be and to what extent the service period for these particular individuals is expected to be shorter than the full vesting period. The grant date fair value of the estimated awards to good leavers should be separately determined, where significant, and the expense relating to good leavers recognised over the expected period between grant date and leaving employment (or date of unconditional entitlement). In this situation the entity would re-estimate the number of good leavers and adjust the cumulative expense at each reporting date. This would be a change of estimate rather than a modification of the award as it would all be in accordance with the original terms and would require no discretionary decisions on the part of the entity. We would not generally expect an entity to have significant numbers of good leavers under such an arrangement.

6.3.8.B   Discretionary awards to 'good leavers'

Awards where the arrangements for leavers are clear as at the original grant date of the award are discussed at 6.3.8.A above. However, it is often the case that the entity determines only at, or near, the time that the employee leaves either that the employee is a 'good leaver' or the amount of the award. In such cases, grant date or modification date (see further below) should be taken as the later of the date on which such determination is made, or the date on which the award is notified to the employee.

This is because the employee had no clear understanding at the original grant date of an automatic entitlement to equity instruments other than through full vesting of the award at the end of the full service period.

In our view, an entity should assess the appropriate accounting treatment based on the particular facts and circumstances and the extent to which the discretionary award is linked to the original award. The discretionary award at the time of leaving is considered to be either a modification of an original award in the employee's favour (for example, where vesting conditions are waived to allow an individual to keep an award) or the forfeiture of the original award and the granting of a completely new award on a discretionary basis (see 8.3 and 8.5 below).

In some cases, a good leaver will be allowed, on a discretionary basis, to keep existing awards that remain subject to performance conditions established at the original grant date. In this situation, any conditions that were previously treated as vesting conditions will become non-vesting conditions following the removal of the service requirement (see 4.1 and 4.2 above). This will be the case whether the discretionary arrangement is accounted for as the forfeiture of the old award plus a new grant or as a modification of the original award.

The non-vesting conditions will need to be reflected in the measurement of the fair value of the award as at the date of modification or new grant (although the non-vesting conditions alone will not result in any incremental fair value). Any fair value that is unrecognised as at the date of the good leaver ceasing employment will need to be expensed immediately as there is no further service period over which to recognise the expense.

There is further discussion of modifications at 8.3 below and of replacement and ex gratia awards granted on termination of employment at 8.5 below.

6.3.8.C   Automatic full or pro rata entitlement on cessation of employment

In some cases, entities establish schemes where a significant number of the participants will potentially leave employment before the end of the full vesting period and will be allowed to keep a *pro rata* share of the award.

Such arrangements are encountered relatively infrequently and mostly outside the UK. Accordingly, a detailed discussion of the accounting treatment is beyond the scope of this publication. There is further detail available in EY International GAAP 2019.

6.3.9   Awards over a fixed pool of shares (including 'last man standing' arrangements)

An award over a fixed pool of shares is sometimes granted to a small group of, typically senior, employees. Such awards might involve an initial allocation of shares to each individual but also provide for the redistribution of each employee's shares to the other participants should any individual leave employment before the end of the vesting period. This is often referred to as a 'last man standing' arrangement.

The accounting requirements for such an arrangement are unclear and discussion of the various approaches seen in practice is beyond the scope of this publication. In the absence of specific guidance, several interpretations are possible and these are discussed in EY International GAAP 2019.

Chapter 23

6.4   Transactions with non-employees

In accounting for equity-settled transactions with non-employees, the starting point is that the value of the goods or services received provides the more reliable indication of the fair value of the transaction. The fair value to be used is that at the date on which the goods are obtained or the services rendered. *[FRS 102.26.3, 7-8]*. This implies that, where the goods or services are received on a number of dates over a period, the fair value at each date should be used, although in the case of a relatively short period there may be no great fluctuation in fair value.

If the entity rebuts the presumption that the goods or services provide the more reliable indication of fair value, it may use as a surrogate measure the fair value of the equity instruments granted, but as at the date when the goods or services are received, not the original grant date. However, where the goods or services are received over a relatively short period and the share price does not change significantly, an average share price can be used in calculating the fair value of equity instruments granted.

6.4.1   *Effect of change of status from employee to non-employee (or vice versa)*

Neither FRS 102 nor IFRS 2 gives specific guidance on how to account for an award when the status of the counterparty changes from employee to non-employee (or *vice versa*) but, in all other respects, the award remains unchanged. In our view, the accounting following the change of status will depend on the entity's assessment of whether or not the counterparty is performing the same or similar services before and after the change of status.

If it is concluded that the counterparty is providing the same or similar services before and after the change of status, the measurement approach remains unchanged. However, if the services provided are substantially different, the accounting following the change of status will be determined by the counterparty's new status.

A change of status is rare in practice. A detailed discussion is beyond the scope of this publication but the matter is addressed in EY International GAAP 2019.

6.5   Determining the fair value of equity instruments

As discussed at 6.2 and 6.4 above, FRS 102 requires the following equity-settled transactions to be measured by reference to the fair value of the equity instruments issued rather than that of the goods or services received:

- all transactions with employees; and
- transactions with non-employees where, in rare cases, the entity rebuts the presumption that the fair value of goods or services provided is more reliably measurable.

There will also be situations where the identifiable consideration received (if any) from non-employees appears to be less than the fair value of consideration given. In such cases, an entity will need to determine the fair value of the equity instruments (see 3.2.3 above).

For all transactions measured by reference to the fair value of the equity instruments granted, fair value should be measured at the 'measurement date' – i.e. grant date in the case of transactions with employees and service date in the case of transactions with non-employees. *[FRS 102.26.8]*. Fair value should be based on market prices if available. *[FRS 102.26.10-11]*. In the absence of market prices or other entity-specific market data, a valuation method should be used to estimate what the market price would have been on the measurement date in an arm's length transaction between knowledgeable and willing parties. The technique used should be a generally recognised valuation methodology for valuing equity instruments that is appropriate to the circumstances of the entity and uses market data to the greatest extent possible. *[FRS 102.26.10-11]*.

Paragraphs 10 to 11 of Section 26 contain outline requirements on valuation and are discussed at 9 below, supplemented by guidance from the appendices and implementation guidance to IFRS 2. As noted elsewhere in this chapter, the 'fair value' of equity instruments under Section 26 takes account of some, but not all, conditions attached to an award rather than being a 'true' fair value (see 7.3 and 7.4 below on the treatment of market and non-vesting conditions).

7 EQUITY-SETTLED TRANSACTIONS – ALLOCATION OF EXPENSE

7.1 Overview

Equity-settled transactions, particularly those with employees, raise particular accounting problems since they are often subject to vesting conditions (see 4.1 above) that can be satisfied only over an extended vesting period.

An award of equity instruments that vests immediately is presumed, in the absence of evidence to the contrary, to relate to services that have already been rendered, and is therefore expensed in full at grant date. *[FRS 102.26.5]*. This may lead to the immediate recognition of an expense for an award to which the employee may not be legally entitled for some time, as illustrated in Example 23.6.

Example 23.6: *Award with non-vesting condition only*

An entity grants a director share options, exercisable after three years provided the director does not compete with the reporting entity for a period of at least three years. The 'non-compete' clause is considered to be a non-vesting condition (see 4.2 above and 7.4 below). As this is the only condition to which the award is subject, the award has no vesting conditions and therefore vests immediately. The fair value of the award at the date of grant, including the effect of the 'non-compete' clause, is determined to be £150,000. Accordingly, the entity immediately recognises a cost of £150,000.

This cost can never be reversed, even if the director goes to work for a competitor and loses the award. This is discussed more fully at 7.4 below.

Where equity instruments are granted subject to vesting conditions (as in many cases they will be, particularly where payments to employees are concerned), FRS 102 creates a presumption that they are a payment for services to be received in the future, during the 'vesting period', with the transaction being recognised during that period, as illustrated in Example 23.7. *[FRS 102.26.6, 9]*.

Example 23.7: *Award with service condition only*

An entity grants a director share options on condition that the director remain in employment for three years. The requirement to remain in employment is a service condition, and therefore a vesting condition, which will take three years to fulfil. The fair value of the award at the date of grant, ignoring the effect of the vesting condition, is determined to be £300,000. The entity will record a cost of £100,000 a year in profit or loss for three years, with a corresponding increase in equity.

Chapter 23

In practice, the calculations required by FRS 102 are unlikely to be as simple as that in Example 23.7. In particular:

- the final number of awards that vest cannot be known until the vesting date (because employees may leave before the vesting date, or because relevant performance conditions may not be met); and/or

- the length of the vesting period may not be known in advance (since vesting may depend on satisfaction of a performance condition with no, or a variable, time-limit on its attainment).

In order to deal with such issues, FRS 102 requires a continuous re-estimation process as summarised at 7.1.1 below.

7.1.1   The continuous estimation process of Section 26

The overall objective is that, at the end of the vesting period, the cumulative cost recognised in profit or loss (or, where applicable, included in the carrying amount of an asset), should represent the product of:

- the number of equity instruments that have vested, or would have vested, but for the failure to satisfy a market condition (see 7.3 below) or a non-vesting condition (see 7.4 below); and

- the fair value (excluding the effect of any non-market vesting conditions, but including the effect of any market conditions or non-vesting conditions) of those equity instruments at the date of grant.

It is essential to appreciate that the 'grant date' measurement model in FRS 102 seeks to capture the value of the contingent right to shares promised at grant date, to the extent that the promise becomes (or is deemed to become – see 7.1.2 below) an entitlement of the counterparty, rather than the value of any shares finally delivered. Therefore, if an option vests, but is not exercised because it would not be in the counterparty's economic interest to do so, FRS 102 still recognises a cost for the award.

In order to achieve this outcome, FRS 102 requires the following process to be applied:

(a)   at grant date, the fair value of the award (excluding the effect of any service and non-market performance vesting conditions, but including the effect of any market conditions or non-vesting conditions (conditions that are not vesting conditions)) is determined;

(b)   at each subsequent reporting date until vesting, the entity calculates a best estimate of the cumulative charge to profit or loss at that date, being the product of:

(i)   the grant date fair value of the award determined in (a) above;

(ii)   the current best estimate of the number of awards that will vest (see 7.1.2 below); and

(iii)   the expired portion of the vesting period;

(c)   the charge (or credit) to profit or loss for the period is the cumulative amount calculated in (b) above less the amounts already charged in previous periods. There is a corresponding credit (or debit) to equity; *[FRS 102.26.3-9]*

(d) once the awards have vested, no further accounting adjustments are made to the cost of the award, except in respect of certain modifications to the award – see 8 below; and

(e) if a vested award is not exercised, an entity may (but need not) make a transfer between reserves – see 7.1.3 below.

The overall effect of this process is that a cost is recognised for every award that is granted, except when it is forfeited for failure to meet a vesting condition (see 7.1.2 below). *[FRS 102.26.9].*

It is stated above, service conditions and non-market performance vesting conditions are not taken into account in determining the fair value of an equity-settled share-based payment transaction. This approach was clarified in the Triennial review 2017 in paragraph 9 of Section 26 which requires market conditions and conditions that are not vesting conditions being reflected in the fair value of awards and other vesting conditions being taken into account in estimating the number of awards expected finally to vest.

7.1.2   Vesting and forfeiture

In normal English usage, and in many share scheme documents, an award is described as 'vested' when all the conditions needed to earn it have been met, and as 'forfeited' where it lapses before vesting because one or more of the conditions has not been met.

IFRS 2 uses the term 'forfeiture' in a much more restricted sense to refer to an award that does not vest in IFRS 2 terms. FRS 102 takes a similar approach although it does not specifically refer to 'forfeiture' of an award. Essentially the approach is as follows:

- where an award is subject only to vesting conditions other than market conditions, failure to satisfy any one of the conditions is treated as a forfeiture (and any cumulative expense recognised to date is reversed);

- where an award is subject to both

    - vesting conditions other than market conditions, and

    - market conditions and/or non-vesting conditions,

    failure to satisfy any one of the vesting conditions other than market conditions is treated as a forfeiture. Otherwise (i.e. where all the vesting conditions other than market conditions are satisfied), the award is deemed to vest even if the market conditions and/or non-vesting conditions have not been satisfied; and

- where an award is subject only to non-vesting conditions, it is always deemed to vest.

Where an award has been modified (see 8.3 below) so that different vesting conditions apply to the original and modified elements of an award, forfeiture will not apply to the original award if the service and non-market performance conditions attached to that element have been met. This will be the case even if the service and non-market performance conditions attached to the modified award have not been met and so the modified award is considered to have been forfeited (resulting in the reversal of any incremental expense relating to the modification). Examples 23.24 and 23.25 at 8.3 below illustrate this point.

Chapter 23

As a result of the interaction of the various types of condition, the reference in the summary at 7.1.1 above to the 'best estimate of the number of awards that will vest' really means the best estimate of the number of awards for which it is expected that all non-market vesting conditions will be met.

In practice, however, it is not always clear how that best estimate is to be determined, and in particular what future events may and may not be factored into the estimate. This is discussed further at 7.2 to 7.4 and 8.6 below.

7.1.3 Accounting after vesting

FRS 102 does not address specifically the treatment of share-based payment transactions once they have vested but it seems appropriate to adopt the approach required by IFRS 2.

Once an equity-settled transaction has vested (or, in the case of a transaction subject to one or more market or non-vesting conditions, has been treated as vested – see 7.1.2 above), no further accounting entries are made to reverse the cost already charged, even if the instruments that are the subject of the transaction are subsequently forfeited or, in the case of options, are not exercised. However, the entity may make a transfer between different components of equity. *[IFRS 2.23]*. For example, an entity's accounting policy might be to credit all amounts recorded for share-based transactions to a separate reserve such as 'Shares to be issued'. Where an award lapses after vesting, it would then be appropriate to transfer an amount equivalent to the cumulative cost for the lapsed award from 'Shares to be issued' to another component of equity, usually the profit and loss reserve.

This prohibition against 'truing up' (i.e. reversing the cost of vested awards that lapse) is controversial, since it has the effect that a cost is still recognised for options that are never exercised, typically because they are 'underwater' (i.e. the current share price is lower than the option exercise price), so that it is not in the holder's interest to exercise the option.

7.2 Vesting conditions other than market conditions

7.2.1 Awards with service conditions

Most share-based payment transactions with employees are subject to explicit or implied service conditions. Examples 23.8 and 23.9 below illustrate the application of the allocation principles discussed at 7.1 above to awards subject only to service conditions which are based on the implementation guidance to IFRS 2. *[IFRS 2.IG11]*.

Example 23.8: Award with no change in the estimate of number of awards vesting

An entity grants 100 share options to each of its 500 employees. Vesting is conditional upon the employees working for the entity over the next three years. The entity estimates that the fair value of each share option is £15. The entity's best estimate at each reporting date is that 100 (i.e. 20%) of the original 500 employees will leave during the three year period and therefore forfeit their rights to the share options.

If everything turns out exactly as expected, the entity will recognise the following amounts during the vesting period for services received as consideration for the share options.

Year	Calculation of cumulative expense	Cumulative expense (£)	Expense for period‡ (£)
1	50,000 options × 80%* × £15 × 1/3†	200,000	200,000
2	50,000 options × 80% × £15 × 2/3	400,000	200,000
3	50,000 options × 80% × £15 × 3/3	600,000	200,000

*   The entity expects 100 of its 500 of employees to leave and therefore only 80% of the options to vest.

†   The vesting period is 3 years, and 1 year of it has expired.

‡   In each case the expense for the period is the difference between the calculated cumulative expense at the beginning and end of the period.

Example 23.9:   Award with revised estimate of number of awards vesting due to staff turnover

As in Example 23.8 above, an entity grants 100 share options to each of its 500 employees. Vesting is conditional upon the employee working for the entity over the next three years. The entity estimates that the fair value of each share option is £15.

In this case, however, 20 employees leave during the first year, and the entity's best estimate at the end of year 1 is that a total of 75 (15%) of the original 500 employees will have left before the end of the vesting period. During the second year, a further 22 employees leave, and the entity revises its estimate of total employee departures over the vesting period from 15% to 12% (i.e. 60 of the original 500 employees). During the third year, a further 15 employees leave. Hence, a total of 57 employees (20 + 22 + 15) forfeit their rights to the share options during the three year period, and a total of 44,300 share options (443 employees × 100 options per employee) finally vest.

The entity will recognise the following amounts during the vesting period for services received as consideration for the share options.

Year	Calculation of cumulative expense	Cumulative expense (£)	Expense for period (£)
1	50,000 options × 85% × £15 × 1/3	212,500	212,500
2	50,000 options × 88% × £15 × 2/3	440,000	227,500
3	44,300 options × £15 × 3/3	664,500	224,500

In Example 23.9 above, the number of employees that leave during year 1 and year 2 is not directly relevant to the calculation of cumulative expense in those years, but would naturally be a factor taken into account by the entity in estimating the likely number of awards finally vesting.

7.2.2   Equity instruments vesting in instalments ('graded' vesting)

An entity may make share-based payments that vest in instalments (sometimes referred to as 'graded' vesting). For example, an entity might grant an employee 600 options, 100 of which vest if the employee remains in service for one year, a further 200 after two years and the final 300 after three years. In today's more mobile labour markets, such awards are often favoured over awards which vest only on an 'all or nothing' basis after an extended period.

It is consistent with the overall recognition approach of Section 26 (and with the implementation guidance to IFRS 2) to treat such an award as three separate awards, of 100, 200 and 300 options, on the grounds that the three different vesting periods will mean that the three tranches of the award have different fair values. This may well have the effect that, compared to the expense for an award with a single 'cliff' vesting, the expense for an award vesting in instalments will be for a different amount in total and require accelerated recognition of the expense in earlier periods, as illustrated in Example 23.10 below.

Example 23.10:   Award vesting in instalments ('graded' vesting)

An entity is considering the implementation of a scheme that awards 600 free shares to each of its employees, with no conditions other than continuous service. Two alternatives are being considered:

- All 600 shares vest in full only at the end of three years.

- 100 shares vest after one year, 200 shares after two years and 300 shares after three years. Any shares received at the end of years 1 and 2 would have vested unconditionally.

The fair value of a share delivered in one year's time is £3; in two years' time £2.80; and in three years' time £2.50.

For an employee that remains with the entity for the full three year period, the first alternative would be accounted for as follows:

Year	Calculation of cumulative expense	Cumulative expense (£)	Expense for period (£)
1	600 shares × £2.50 × 1/3	500	500
2	600 shares × £2.50 × 2/3	1,000	500
3	600 shares × £2.50 × 3/3	1,500	500

For the second alternative, the analysis is that the employee has simultaneously received an award of 100 shares vesting over one year, an award of 200 shares vesting over two years and an award of 300 shares vesting over 3 years. This would be accounted for as follows:

Year	Calculation of cumulative expense	Cumulative expense (£)	Expense for period (£)
1	[100 shares × £3.00] + [200 shares × £2.80 × 1/2] + [300 shares × £2.50 × 1/3]	830	830
2	[100 shares × £3.00] + [200 shares × £2.80 × 2/2] + [300 shares × £2.50 × 2/3]	1,360	530
3	[100 shares × £3.00] + [200 shares × £2.80 × 2/2] + [300 shares × £2.50 × 3/3]	1,610	250

At first sight, such an approach seems to be taking account of vesting conditions other than market conditions in determining the fair value of an award, contrary to the basic principle of paragraph 9 of Section 26 (see 7.1.1 above). However, it is not the vesting conditions that are being taken into account *per se*, but the fact that the varying vesting periods will give rise to different lives for the award (which are generally required to be taken into account – see 8.2 and 9 below).

Provided all conditions are clearly understood at the outset, the accounting treatment illustrated in Example 23.10 would apply even if the vesting of shares in each year also depended on a performance condition unique to that year (e.g. that profit in that year must reach a given minimum level), as opposed to a cumulative performance condition (e.g. that profit must have grown by a minimum amount by the end of year 1, 2 or 3). This is because all tranches of the arrangement have the same service commencement date and so for the awards that have a performance condition relating to year 2 or year 3 there is a service condition covering a longer period than the performance condition. In other words, an award that vests at the end of year 3 conditional on profitability in year 3 is also conditional on the employee providing service for three years from the date of grant in order to be eligible to receive the award. This is discussed further at 6.3.6 above.

7.2.3 Transactions with variable vesting periods due to non-market performance vesting conditions

An award may have a vesting period which is subject to variation. For example, the award might be contingent upon the achievement of a particular performance target (such as achieving a given level of cumulative earnings) within a given maximum period, but vesting immediately once the target has been reached. Alternatively, an award might be contingent on levels of earnings growth over a period, but with vesting occurring more quickly if growth is achieved more quickly. Also some plans provide for 're-testing', whereby an original target is set for achievement within a given vesting period, but if that target is not met, a new target and/or a different vesting period are substituted.

FRS 102 has no specific requirements in respect of variable vesting periods – it simply refers to revising the number of awards expected to vest if new information indicates that the number of equity instruments expected to vest differs from previous estimates. *[FRS 102.26.9(a)]*. However, it seems appropriate to follow the requirements of IFRS 2 in this area. Therefore, in such cases, the entity needs to estimate the length of the vesting period at grant date, based on the most likely outcome of the performance condition. Subsequently, it is necessary continuously to re-estimate not only the number of awards that will finally vest, but also the date of vesting, as shown by Example 23.11. *[IFRS 2.15(b), IG12]*. This contrasts with the IFRS 2 treatment of awards with market conditions and variable vesting periods, where the initial estimate of the vesting period may not be revised (see 7.3.4 below).

Example 23.11: Award with non-market vesting condition and variable vesting period

At the beginning of year 1, the entity grants 100 shares each to 500 employees, conditional upon the employees remaining in the entity's employment during the vesting period. The shares will vest:

- at the end of year 1 if the entity's earnings increase by more than 18%;
- at the end of year 2 if the entity's earnings increase by more than an average of 13% per year over the two year period; or
- at the end of year 3 if the entity's earnings increase by more than an average of 10% per year over the three year period.

The award is estimated to have a fair value of £30 per share at grant date. It is expected that no dividends will be paid during the whole three year period.

By the end of the first year, the entity's earnings have increased by 14%, and 30 employees have left. The entity expects that earnings will continue to increase at a similar rate in year 2, and therefore expects that the shares will vest at the end of year 2. The entity expects, on the basis of a weighted average probability, that a further 30 employees will leave during year 2, and therefore expects that an award of 100 shares each will vest for 440 (500 – 30 – 30) employees at the end of year 2.

By the end of the second year, the entity's earnings have increased by only 10% and therefore the shares do not vest at the end of that year. 28 employees have left during the year. The entity expects that a further 25 employees will leave during year 3, and that the entity's earnings will increase by at least 6%, thereby achieving the average growth of 10% per year necessary for an award after 3 years, so that an award of 100 shares each will vest for 417 (500 – 30 – 28 – 25) employees at the end of year 3.

By the end of the third year, a further 23 employees have left and the entity's earnings have increased by 8%, resulting in an average increase of 10.67% per year. Therefore, 419 (500 – 30 – 28 – 23) employees receive 100 shares at the end of year 3.

The entity will recognise the following amounts during the vesting period for services received as consideration for the shares.

Year	Calculation of cumulative expense	Cumulative expense (£)	Expense for period (£)
1	440 employees × 100 shares × £30 × 1/2*	660,000	660,000
2	417 employees × 100 shares × £30 × 2/3*	834,000	174,000
3	419 employees × 100 shares × £30	1,257,000	423,000

* The entity's best estimate at the end of year 1 is that it is one year through a two year vesting period and at the end of year 2 that it is two years through a three year vesting period.

In Example 23.11, which is based on IG Example 2 in the implementation guidance to IFRS 2, it is assumed that the entity will pay no dividends (to any shareholders) throughout the maximum possible three year vesting period. This has the effect that the fair value of the shares to be awarded is equivalent to their market value at the date of grant.

If dividends were expected to be paid during the vesting period, this would no longer be the case. Employees would be better off if they received shares after two years rather than three, since they would have a right to receive dividends from the end of year two.

One solution might be to use the approach in IG Example 4 in the implementation guidance to IFRS 2 (the substance of which is reproduced as Example 23.13 at 7.2.5 below). That Example deals with an award whose exercise price is either £12 or £16, dependent upon various performance conditions. Because vesting conditions other than market conditions are ignored in determining the value of an award, the approach is in effect to treat the award as the simultaneous grant of two awards, whose value, in that case, varies by reference to the different exercise prices.

The same principle could be applied to an award of shares that vests at different times according to the performance conditions, by determining different fair values for the shares (in this case depending on whether they vest after one, two or three years). The cumulative charge during the vesting period would be based on a best estimate of which outcome will occur, and the final cumulative charge would be based on the grant date fair value of the actual outcome (which will require some acceleration of expense is the actual vesting period is shorter than the previously estimated vesting period).

Such an approach appears to be taking account of non-market vesting conditions in determining the fair value of an award, contrary to the basic principle of paragraph 9 of Section 26 (see 7.1.1 above). However, it is not the vesting conditions that are being taken into account *per se*, but the fact that the varying vesting periods will give rise to different lives for the award (which are generally required to be taken into account – see 8.2 and 9 below). That said, the impact of the time value of the different lives on the fair value of the award will, in many cases, be insignificant and it will therefore be a matter of judgement as to how precisely an entity switches from one fair value to another.

Economically speaking, the entity in Example 23.11 has made a single award, the true fair value of which must be a function of the weighted probabilities of the various outcomes occurring. However, under the accounting model for share-settled awards, the probability of achieving non-market performance conditions is not taken into account in valuing an award. If this is required to be ignored, the only approach open is to proceed as in Example 23.11 above and treat the arrangement as if it consisted of the simultaneous grant of three awards.

Some might object that this methodology is not relevant to the award in Example 23.11 above, since it is an award of shares rather than, in the case of Example 23.13 below, an award of options. However, an award of shares is no more than an award of options with an exercise price of zero. Moreover, the treatment in the previous paragraph is broadly consistent with the IFRS 2 treatment of an award vesting in instalments (see 7.2.2 above).

In Example 23.11 above, the vesting period, although not known, is at least one of a finite number of known possibilities. The vesting period for some awards, however, may be more open-ended, such as is frequently the case for an award that vests on a trade sale or flotation of the business. Such awards are discussed further at 16.4 below.

7.2.4 Transactions with variable number of equity instruments awarded depending on non-market performance vesting conditions

More common than awards with a variable vesting period are those where the number of equity instruments awarded varies, typically increasing to reflect the margin by which a particular minimum target is exceeded. In accounting for such awards, the entity must continuously revise its estimate of the number of shares to be awarded in line with the requirement to revise the estimate of the number of equity instruments expected to vest if new information indicates that this number differs from previous estimates. *[FRS 102.26.9(a)].* This is illustrated in Example 23.12 below (which is based on IG Example 3 in the implementation guidance to IFRS 2).

Example 23.12: Award with non-market performance vesting condition and variable number of equity instruments

At the beginning of year 1, an entity grants an option over a variable number of shares (see below), estimated to have a fair value at grant date of £20 per share under option, to each of its 100 employees working in the sales department. The share options will vest at the end of year 3, provided that the employees remain in the entity's employment, and provided that the volume of sales of a particular product increases by at least an average of 5% per year. If the volume of sales of the product increases by an average of between 5% and 10% per year, each employee will be entitled to exercise 100 share options. If the volume of sales increases by an average of between 10% and 15% each year, each employee will be entitled to exercise 200 share options. If the volume of sales increases by an average of 15% or more, each employee will be entitled to exercise 300 share options.

By the end of the first year, seven employees have left and the entity expects that a total of 20 employees will leave by the end of year 3. Product sales have increased by 12% and the entity expects this rate of increase to continue over the next two years, so that 80 employees will be entitled to exercise 200 options each.

By the end of the second year, a further five employees have left. The entity now expects only three more employees to leave during year 3, and therefore expects a total of 15 employees to have left during the three year period. Product sales have increased by 18%, resulting in an average of 15% over the two years to date. The entity now expects that sales will average 15% or more over the three year period, so that 85 employees will be entitled to exercise 300 options each.

By the end of year 3, a further seven employees have left. Hence, 19 employees have left during the three year period, and 81 employees remain. However, due to trading conditions significantly poorer than expected, sales have increased by a 3 year average of only 12%, so that the 81 remaining employees are entitled to exercise only 200 share options.

The entity will recognise the following amounts during the vesting period for services received as consideration for the options.

Year	Calculation of cumulative expense	Cumulative expense (£)	Expense for period (£)
1	80 employees × 200 options × £20 × 1/3	106,667	106,667
2	85 employees × 300 options × £20 × 2/3	340,000	233,333
3	81 employees × 200 options × £20	324,000	(16,000)

This Example reinforces the point that it is quite possible for an equity-settled transaction to give rise to a credit to profit or loss for a particular period during the period to vesting.

7.2.5 Transactions with variable exercise price due to non-market performance vesting conditions

Another mechanism for delivering higher value to the recipient of a share award so as to reflect the margin by which a particular target is exceeded might be to vary the exercise price depending on performance. IFRS 2 requires such an award to be dealt with, in effect, as more than one award and we believe that it is appropriate to adopt a similar approach under FRS 102. The fair value of each award is determined, and the cost during the vesting period based on the best estimate of which award will actually vest, with the final cumulative charge being based on the actual outcome. *[IFRS 2.IG12, IG Example 4].*

This is illustrated in Example 23.13 below.

Example 23.13: Award with non-market performance vesting condition and variable exercise price

An entity grants to a senior executive 10,000 share options, conditional upon the executive remaining in the entity's employment for three years. The exercise price is £40. However, the exercise price drops to £30 if the entity's earnings increase by at least an average of 10% per year over the three year period.

On grant date, the entity estimates that the fair value of the share options, with an exercise price of £30, is £16 per option. If the exercise price is £40, the entity estimates that the share options have a fair value of £12 per option. During year 1, the entity's earnings increased by 12%, and the entity expects that earnings will continue to increase at this rate over the next two years. The entity therefore expects that the earnings target will be achieved, and hence the share options will have an exercise price of £30.

During year 2, the entity's earnings increased by 13%, and the entity continues to expect that the earnings target will be achieved. During year 3, the entity's earnings increased by only 3%, and therefore the earnings target was not achieved. The executive completes three years' service, and therefore satisfies the service condition. Because the earnings target was not achieved, the 10,000 vested share options have an exercise price of £40.

The entity will recognise the following amounts during the vesting period for services received as consideration for the options.

Year	Calculation of cumulative expense	Cumulative expense (£)	Expense for period (£)
1	10,000 options × £16 × 1/3	53,333	53,333
2	10,000 options × £16 × 2/3	106,667	53,334
3	10,000 options × £12	120,000	13,333

At first sight this may seem a rather surprising approach. In reality, is it not the case that the entity in Example 23.13 made a single award, the fair value of which must lie between £12 and £16, as a function of the weighted probabilities of either outcome occurring? Economically speaking, this is indeed the case. However, under the accounting model for equity-settled share-based payments in IFRS 2 and FRS 102, the probability of achieving non-market performance conditions is not taken into account in valuing an award. If this is required to be ignored, the only approach open is to proceed with the 'two award' analysis as above.

7.3 Market conditions

7.3.1 What is a 'market condition'?

The Glossary to FRS 102 defines the term 'market vesting condition', whereas paragraph 9 of Section 26 refers to 'market conditions' and 'market vesting conditions' which sets out the principles of measuring an equity-settled share-based payment. We believe that the terms are synonymous and from here on we will refer to the condition as a market condition. A market condition is defined as 'a condition upon which the exercise price, vesting or exercisability of an equity instrument depends that is related to the market price of the entity's equity instruments, such as attaining a specified share price or a specified amount of intrinsic value of a share option, or achieving a specified target that is based on the market price of the entity's equity instruments relative to an index of market prices of equity instruments of other entities'. *[FRS 102 Appendix I]*. In order for a market condition to be treated as a performance vesting condition rather than as a non-vesting condition, there must also be an implicit or explicit service condition (see 4.2 above).

The 'intrinsic value' of a share option is defined as 'the difference between the fair value of the shares to which the counterparty has the (conditional or unconditional) right to subscribe or which it has the right to receive, and the price (if any) the counterparty is (or will be) required to pay for those shares'. *[FRS 102 Appendix I]*. In other words, an option to acquire for £8 a share with a fair value of £10 has an intrinsic value of £2. A performance condition based on the share price and one based on the intrinsic value of the option are effectively the same, since the values of each will obviously move in parallel.

Section 26 includes a specified increase in the entity's share price as an example of a market condition. *[FRS 102.26.9]*. A market condition often seen in practice, although more common in a listed entity and not specifically mentioned in FRS 102, is a condition based on total shareholder return (TSR). TSR is a measure of the increase or decrease in a given sum invested in an entity over a period on the assumption that all dividends received in the period had been used to purchase further shares in the entity. The market price of the entity's shares is an input to the calculation.

However, a condition linked to a purely internal financial performance measure such as profit or earnings per share is not a market condition. Such measures will affect the share price or value, but are not directly linked to it, and hence are not market conditions.

A condition linked solely to a general market index is not a market condition, but a non-vesting condition (see 4.2 above and 7.4 below), because the reporting entity's own share price is not relevant to the satisfaction of the condition.

However, if the condition were that the entity's own share price had to outperform a general index of shares, that condition would be a market condition because the reporting entity's own share price is then relevant to the satisfaction of the condition.

7.3.2   *Summary of accounting treatment*

The key feature of the accounting treatment of an equity-settled transaction subject to a market condition is that the market condition is taken into account in valuing the award at the date of grant, 'with no subsequent adjustment to the estimated fair value, irrespective of the outcome of the market condition or condition that is not a vesting condition, provided that all other vesting conditions are satisfied'. *[FRS 102.26.9(b)]*. In other words, an award is treated as vesting irrespective of whether the market condition is satisfied, provided that all other service and non-market performance vesting conditions are satisfied. The requirements relating to market conditions can have rather controversial consequences, as illustrated by Example 23.14.

Example 23.14:   Award with market condition

An entity grants an employee an option to buy a share on condition of remaining in employment for three years and the share price at the end of that period being at least £7. At the end of the vesting period, the share price is £6.80. The share price condition is factored into the initial valuation of the option, and the option is considered to vest provided that the employee remains for three years, irrespective of whether the share price does in fact reach £7.

Therefore, an award is sometimes treated as vesting (and a cost is recognised for that award) when it does not actually vest in the natural sense of the word. See also Example 23.16 at 7.3.4 below.

This treatment is clearly significantly different from that for transactions involving a non-market vesting condition, where no cost would be recognised where the conditions were not met. As discussed at 7.2 above, the methodology prescribed for transactions with a vesting condition other than a market condition is to determine the fair value of the option ignoring the condition and then to multiply that fair value by the estimated (and ultimately the actual) number of awards expected to vest based on the likelihood of that non-market vesting condition being met.

In any event, it appears that it may be possible to soften the impact of the rules for market conditions relatively easily by introducing a non-market vesting condition closely correlated to the market condition. For instance, the option in Example 23.14 above could be modified so that exercise was dependent not only upon the £7 target share price and continuous employment, but also on a target growth in earnings per share. Whilst there would not be a perfect correlation between earnings per share and the share price, it would be expected that they would move roughly in parallel, particularly if the entity has historically had a fairly consistent price/earnings ratio. Thus, if the share price target were not met, it would be highly likely that the earnings per share target would not be met either. This would allow the entity to show no cumulative cost for the option, since only one (i.e. not *all*) of the non-market related vesting conditions would have been met.

Similarly, entities in sectors where the share price is closely related to net asset value (e.g. property companies and investment trusts) could incorporate a net asset value target as a non-market performance condition that would be highly likely to be satisfied only if the market condition was satisfied.

The matrices below illustrate the interaction of market conditions and vesting conditions other than market conditions. Matrix 1 summarises the possible outcomes for an award with the following two vesting conditions:

- the employee remaining in service for three years (service condition); and
- the entity's share price increasing by 10% over the vesting period (share price target).

Matrix 1

	Service condition met?	Share price target (market condition) met?	Section 26 expense?
1	Yes	Yes	Yes
2	Yes	No	Yes
3	No	Yes	No
4	No	No	No

It will be seen that, to all intents and purposes, the 'Share price target (market condition) met?' column is redundant, as this is not relevant to whether or not the award is treated as vesting for accounting purposes. The effect of this is that the entity would recognise an expense for outcome 2, even though no awards truly vest.

Matrix 2 summarises the possible outcomes for an award with the same conditions as in Matrix 1, plus a requirement for earnings per share to grow by a general inflation index plus 10% over the period ('EPS target').

Matrix 2

	Service condition met?	Share price target (market condition) met?	EPS target (non-market condition) met?	Section 26 expense?
1	Yes	Yes	Yes	Yes
2	Yes	No	Yes	Yes
3	Yes	Yes	No	No
4	Yes	No	No	No
5	No	Yes	Yes	No
6	No	No	Yes	No
7	No	Yes	No	No
8	No	No	No	No

Again it will be seen that, to all intents and purposes, the 'Share price target (market condition) met?' column is redundant, as this is not relevant to whether or not the award is treated as vesting. The effect of this is that the entity would recognise an expense for outcome 2, even though no awards truly vest. However, no expense would be recognised for outcome 4, which is, except for the introduction of the EPS target, equivalent to outcome 2 in Matrix 1, for which an expense is recognised. This illustrates that the introduction of a non-market vesting condition closely related to a market condition may mitigate the impact of the accounting requirements.

Examples of the application of the accounting treatment for transactions involving market conditions are given at 7.3.3 and 7.3.4 below.

7.3.3   Transactions with market conditions and known vesting periods

Following on from the discussion at 7.3.2 above, the accounting for these transactions is essentially the same as that for transactions without market conditions but with a known vesting period (including 'graded' vesting – see 7.2.2 above), except that adjustments are made to reflect the changing probability of the achievement of the non-market vesting conditions only, as illustrated by Example 23.15 below (based partly on IG Example 5 in the implementation guidance to IFRS 2). *[FRS 102.26.9]*.

Example 23.15:   Award with market condition and fixed vesting period

At the beginning of year 1, an entity grants to 100 employees 1,000 share options each, conditional upon the employees remaining in the entity's employment until the end of year 3. However, the share options cannot be exercised unless the share price has increased from £50 at the beginning of year 1 to more than £65 at the end of year 3.

If the share price is above £65 at the end of year 3, the share options can be exercised at any time during the next seven years, i.e. by the end of year 10. The entity applies an option pricing model which takes into account the possibility that the share price will exceed £65 at the end of year 3 (and hence the share options vest and become exercisable) and the possibility that the share price will not exceed £65 at the end of year 3 (and hence the options will be treated as having vested under Section 26 but will never be exercisable – as explained below). It estimates the fair value of the share options with this market condition to be £24 per option.

FRS 102 requires the entity to recognise the services received from a counterparty who satisfies all other vesting conditions (e.g. services received from an employee who remains in service for the specified service period), irrespective of whether that market condition is satisfied. It makes no difference whether the share price target is achieved, since the possibility that the share price target might not be achieved has already been taken into account when estimating the fair value of the share options at grant date. However, the options are subject to another condition (i.e. continuous employment) and the cost recognised should be adjusted to reflect the ongoing best estimate of employee retention.

By the end of the first year, seven employees have left and the entity expects that a total of 20 employees will leave by the end of year 3, so that 80 employees will have satisfied all conditions other than the market condition (i.e. continuous employment).

By the end of the second year, a further five employees have left. The entity now expects only three more employees will leave during year 3, and therefore expects that a total of 15 employees will have left during the three year period, so that 85 employees will have satisfied all conditions other than the market condition.

By the end of year 3, a further seven employees have left. Hence, 19 employees have left during the three year period, and 81 employees remain. However, the share price is only £60, so that the options cannot be exercised. Nevertheless, as all conditions other than the market condition have been satisfied, a cumulative cost is recorded as if the options had fully vested in 81 employees.

The entity will recognise the following amounts during the vesting period for services received as consideration for the options (which in economic reality do not vest).

Year	Calculation of cumulative expense	Cumulative expense (£)	Expense for period (£)
1	80 employees × 1,000 options × £24 × 1/3	640,000	640,000
2	85 employees × 1,000 options × £24 × 2/3	1,360,000	720,000
3	81 employees × 1,000 options × £24	1,944,000	584,000

7.3.4   Transactions with variable vesting periods due to market conditions

Where a transaction has a variable vesting period due to a market condition, a best estimate of the most likely vesting period will have been used in determining the fair value of the transaction at the date of grant. IFRS 2 requires the expense for that transaction to be recognised over an estimated expected vesting period consistent with the assumptions used in the valuation, without any subsequent revision. *[IFRS 2.15(b), IG14].* FRS 102 does not specify the accounting treatment in this situation but it seems consistent with the general requirement in paragraph 9 of Section 26 that there should be 'no subsequent adjustment to the estimated fair value, irrespective of the outcome of the market condition' to adopt a similar approach to that required by IFRS 2.

This may mean, for example, that if the actual vesting period for an employee share option award turns out to be longer than that anticipated for the purposes of the initial valuation, a cost is nevertheless recorded in respect of all employees who reach the end of the *anticipated* vesting period, even if they do not reach the end of the *actual* vesting period, as shown by Example 23.16 below, which is based on IG Example 6 in the implementation guidance in IFRS 2.

Example 23.16: Award with market condition and variable vesting period

At the beginning of year 1, an entity grants 10,000 share options with a ten year life to each of ten senior executives. The share options will vest and become exercisable immediately if and when the entity's share price increases from £50 to £70, provided that the executive remains in service until the share price target is achieved.

The entity applies an option pricing model which takes into account the possibility that the share price target will be achieved during the ten year life of the options, and the possibility that the target will not be achieved. The entity estimates that the fair value of the share options at grant date is £25 per option. From the option pricing model, the entity determines that the most likely vesting period is five years. The entity also estimates that two executives will have left by the end of year 5, and therefore expects that 80,000 share options (10,000 share options × 8 executives) will vest at the end of year 5.

Throughout years 1 to 4, the entity continues to estimate that a total of two executives will leave by the end of year 5. However, in total three executives leave, one in each of years 3, 4 and 5. The share price target is achieved at the end of year 6. Another executive leaves during year 6, before the share price target is achieved.

IFRS 2 and FRS 102 require the entity to recognise the services received over the expected vesting period, as estimated at grant date, and also require the entity not to revise that estimate. Therefore, the entity recognises the services received from the executives over years 1-5. Hence, the transaction amount is ultimately based on 70,000 share options (10,000 share options × 7 executives who remain in service at the end of year 5). Although another executive left during year 6, no adjustment is made, because the executive had already completed the expected vesting period of 5 years.

The entity will recognise the following amounts during the initial expected five year vesting period for services received as consideration for the options.

Year	Calculation of cumulative expense	Cumulative expense (£)	Expense for period (£)
1	8 employees × 10,000 options × £25 × 1/5	400,000	400,000
2	8 employees × 10,000 options × £25 × 2/5	800,000	400,000
3	8 employees × 10,000 options × £25 × 3/5	1,200,000	400,000
4	8 employees × 10,000 options × £25 × 4/5	1,600,000	400,000
5	7 employees × 10,000 options × £25	1,750,000	150,000

IFRS 2 does not specifically address the converse situation, namely where the award actually vests before the end of the anticipated vesting period. In our view, where this occurs, any expense not yet recognised at the point of vesting should be immediately accelerated. We consider that this treatment is most consistent with the overall requirement of IFRS 2 – and FRS 102 – to recognise an expense for share-based payment transactions 'as the services are received'. *[IFRS 2.7, FRS 102.26.3]*. It is difficult to regard any services being received for an award after it has vested.

Moreover, the prohibition in paragraph 15 of IFRS 2 on adjusting the vesting period as originally determined refers to 'the estimate of the expected vesting period'. In our view, the acceleration of vesting that we propose is not the revision of an estimated period, but the substitution of a known vesting period for an estimate.

Suppose in Example 23.16 above, the award had in fact vested at the end of year 4. We believe that the expense for such an award should be allocated as follows:

Year	Calculation of cumulative expense	Cumulative expense (£)	Expense for period (£)
1	8 employees × 10,000 options × £25 × 1/5	400,000	400,000
2	8 employees × 10,000 options × £25 × 2/5	800,000	400,000
3	8 employees × 10,000 options × £25 × 3/5	1,200,000	400,000
4	8 employees × 10,000 options × £25 × 4/4	2,000,000	800,000

7.3.5 Transactions with multiple outcomes depending on market conditions

In practice, it is very common for an award subject to market conditions to give varying levels of reward that increase depending on the extent to which a 'base line' market performance target has been exceeded. Such an award is illustrated in Example 23.17 below.

Example 23.17: Award with market conditions and multiple outcomes

At the beginning of year 1, the reporting entity grants an employee an award of shares that will vest on the third anniversary of grant if the employee is still in employment. The number of shares depends on the share price achieved at the end of the three-year period. The employee will receive:

* no shares if the share price is below £10.00;
* 100 shares if the share price is in the range £10.00 – £14.99;
* 150 shares if the share price is in the range £15.00 – £19.99; or
* 180 shares if the share price is £20.00 or above.

In effect the entity has made three awards, which need to be valued as follows:

(a) 100 shares if the employee remains in service for three years and the share price is in the range £10.00 – £14.99;

(b) 50 (150 – 100) shares if the employee remains in service for three years and the share price is in the range £15.00 – £19.99; and

(c) 30 (180 – 150) shares if the employee remains in service for three years and the share price is £20.00 or more.

Each award would be valued, ignoring the impact of the three-year service condition but taking account of the share price target. This would result in each tranche of the award being subject to an increasing level of discount to reflect the relative probability of the share price target for each tranche of the award being met. All three awards would then be expensed over the three-year service period, and forfeited only if the awards lapsed as a result of the employee leaving during that period.

It can be seen that the (perhaps somewhat counterintuitive) impact of this is that an equity-settled share-based payment where the number of shares increases in line with increases in the entity's share price may nevertheless have a fixed grant date value irrespective of the number of shares finally awarded.

7.3.6 Transactions with independent market conditions, non-market vesting conditions or non-vesting conditions

7.3.6.A Independent market and non-market vesting conditions

The discussion at 7.3.2 above addressed the accounting treatment of awards with multiple conditions that must all be satisfied, i.e. a market condition *and* a non-market vesting condition. However, entities might also make awards with multiple conditions, only one of which need be satisfied, i.e. the awards vest on satisfaction of either a market condition *or* a non-market vesting condition. Neither FRS 102 nor IFRS 2 provides any explicit guidance on the treatment of such awards and the requirements are far from clear, as illustrated by Example 23.18 below.

Example 23.18: Award with independent market conditions and non-market vesting conditions

An entity grants an employee 100 share options that vest after three years if the employee is still in employment and the entity achieves either:

* an increase in its share price over three years of at least 15%, or
* cumulative profits over three years of at least £200 million.

The fair value of the award, ignoring vesting conditions, is £300,000. The fair value of the award, taking account of the share price condition, but not the other conditions, is £210,000.

In our view, the entity has, in effect, simultaneously issued two awards – call them 'A' and 'B' – which vest as follows:

A   on achievement of three years' service plus minimum share price increase,

B   on achievement of three years' service plus minimum earnings growth.

If the conditions for both awards are simultaneously satisfied, one or other effectively lapses.

It is clear that award A, if issued separately, would require the entity to recognise an expense of £210,000 if the employee were still in service at the end of the three year period. It therefore seems clear that, if the employee does remain in service, there should be a charge of £210,000 irrespective of whether the award actually vests. It would be anomalous for the entity to avoid recording a charge that would have been recognised if the entity had made award A in isolation simply by packaging it with award B.

If in fact the award vested because the earnings condition, but not the market condition, had been satisfied, it would then be appropriate to recognise a total expense of £300,000.

During the vesting period, we believe that the entity should make an assessment at each reporting date of the basis on which the award is expected to vest. It should assess whether, as at that date, the award is expected to vest by virtue of the earnings condition, but not the share price condition, being satisfied. Assume (for example) that the entity assesses at the end of year 1 that the award is likely to vest by virtue of the share price condition, and at the end of year 2 that it is likely to vest by virtue of the earnings condition, and that the award actually does not vest, but the employee remains in service. This would give rise to annual expense as follows:

Year	Calculation of cumulative expense	Cumulative expense (£)	Expense for period (£)
1	210,000 × 1/3	70,000	70,000
2	300,000 × 2/3	200,000	130,000
3	210,000 × 3/3	210,000	10,000

We believe that ongoing reassessment during the vesting period is most consistent with the general accounting approach to awards with a number of possible outcomes.

As for other awards, the accounting treatment would also require an assessment of whether the employee was actually going to remain in service.

Chapter 23

A further question that arises is how the award should be accounted for if both conditions are satisfied. It would clearly be inappropriate to recognise an expense of £510,000 (the sum of the separate fair values of the award) – this would be double-counting, because the employee receives only one package of 100 options. However, should the total expense be taken as £210,000 or £300,000? In our view, it is more appropriate to recognise a cost of £300,000 since the non-market vesting condition has been satisfied.

7.3.6.B   Independent market conditions and non-vesting conditions

Arrangements are also seen where a share-based payment transaction vests on the satisfaction of either a market condition or a non-vesting condition.

In our view, an entity granting an award on the basis of a service condition (and any other non-market vesting conditions) plus either a market condition or a non-vesting condition should measure the fair value of the award at grant date taking into account the probability that either the market condition or the non-vesting condition will be met. The fact that there are two alternative conditions on which the award might vest means that, unless the two conditions are perfectly correlated, the grant date fair value of such an award will be higher than that of an award where there is only one possible basis on which the award might vest. Irrespective of whether the market and/or non-vesting conditions are met, the entity will recognise the grant date fair value provided all other service and non-market vesting conditions are met (i.e. the expense recognition is consistent with that of any award with market and/or non-vesting conditions).

7.3.7   Awards based on the market value of a subsidiary or business unit

Awards with a market condition are frequently based on the market value of the (typically quoted) equity instruments of the parent entity. However, some entities implement share-based remuneration schemes which aim to reward employees by reference to the market value of the equity of the business unit for which they work. The detail of such schemes varies, but the general effect is typically as follows:

- at grant date, the employee is allocated a (real or notional) holding in the equity of the employing subsidiary, the market value of which is measured at grant date; and

- the employee is granted an award of as many shares of the listed parent as have a value, at a specified future date (often at, or shortly after, the end of the vesting period but sometimes at a later date), equal to the increase over the vesting period in the market value of the employee's holding in the equity of the employing subsidiary.

Some take the view that such a scheme contains a market condition, since it depends on the fair value of the subsidiary's shares, with the result that the grant date fair value per share:

- reflects this market condition (see 7.3.2 above); and

- is fixed, irrespective of how many parent company shares are finally issued, since the entity has effectively issued a market-based award with multiple outcomes based on the market value of the equity of a subsidiary (see 7.3.5 above).

In our view, however, the required accounting treatment of such schemes is not as straightforward as suggested by this analysis. A fundamental issue is whether any award dependent on the change in value of the equity of an unquoted entity contains a market condition at all. A market condition is defined (see 7.3.1 above) as one dependent on the 'market price' of the entity's equity. *Prima facie*, if there is no market, there is no market price.

Notwithstanding the absence of a market, some argue that there are generally accepted valuation techniques for unquoted equities which can yield a fair value as a surrogate for market value. The difficulty with that argument, in our view, is that the definition of 'market condition' refers to 'market price' and not to 'fair value'. The latter term is, of course, used extensively elsewhere in Section 26 (and in IFRS 2), which suggests that the two terms were not considered to be interchangeable. This concern is reinforced by that fact that, in the 'valuation hierarchy' for the measurement of share awards in paragraph 10 of Section 26, a quoted market price is given as the preferred (but not the only) method of arriving at fair value (see 9 below).

An entity implementing such an award must therefore make an assessment, in any particular situation, of whether the basis on which the subsidiary equity is valued truly yields a market price (or value) or merely a fair value according to a hypothetical valuation model.

Furthermore, in order for there to be a market condition there needs to be a specified performance target. It is not always clear in such situations that there is such a target if the various outcomes depend on an exchange of shares regardless of the level of market price or value achieved by the subsidiary.

If it is considered that there is no market condition within the arrangement and there is simply an exchange of shares – in effect, using one entity's shares as the currency for the other – then the arrangement might nonetheless be viewed as containing a non-vesting condition (similar to when an arrangement depends on the performance of an index for example (see 4.2 above and 7.4 below)). Like a market condition, a non-vesting condition would be taken into account in determining the fair value of the award and would result in a fixed grant date fair value irrespective of the number of shares finally delivered.

7.3.7.A   Awards with a condition linked to flotation price

The situations discussed above and at 3.4.5 above relate to ongoing conditions linked to the calculated value of an unlisted entity's equity instruments and therefore differ from those where the condition is linked to the market price at which a previously unlisted entity floats. On flotation there is clearly a market and a market price for the entity's equity instruments and the achievement of a specific price on flotation would, in our view, be a market condition when accompanied by a corresponding service requirement (see 16.4 below).

7.4   Non-vesting conditions

Prior to the Triennial review 2017, Section 26 and IFRS 2 referred to 'non-vesting conditions'. Section 26 has been amended whereby the term has now been deleted and replaced with 'conditions that are not vesting conditions', neither terms are defined in FRS 102 or IFRS 2. However, FRS 102 provides an example of a condition that is not a vesting condition, such as a condition that an employee contributes to a saving plan, which is one of the examples provided in the implementation guidance of IFRS 2 as a non-vesting condition. *[FRS 102.26.9(b), IFRS 2.IG24].* Therefore we believe that both terms, 'non-vesting conditions' and 'conditions that are not vesting conditions', are similar and we will refer to the term as a non-vesting condition in this section. FRS 102 does not specify the accounting treatment for non-vesting conditions

Chapter 23

other than to state that '... conditions that are not vesting conditions shall be taken into account when estimating the fair value of the equity instruments granted at the measurement date, with no subsequent adjustment to the estimated fair value, irrespective of the outcome of the ... condition that is not a vesting condition, provided that all other vesting conditions are satisfied'. *[FRS 102.26.9(b)].*

The accounting treatment for awards with non-vesting conditions has some similarities to that for awards with market conditions in that:

- the fair value of the award at grant date is reduced to reflect the impact of the condition; and

- an expense is recognised for the award irrespective of whether the non-vesting condition is met, provided that all vesting conditions (other than market conditions) are met.

However, in some situations under IFRS 2 – and, in the absence of specific guidance, FRS 102 – the accounting for non-vesting conditions differs from that for market conditions as regards the timing of the recognition of expense if the non-vesting condition is not satisfied (see 7.4.3 below).

7.4.1   Awards with no conditions other than non-vesting conditions

Any award that has only non-vesting conditions (e.g. an option award to an employee that may be exercised on a trade sale or IPO of the entity, irrespective of whether the employee is still in employment at that time) must be expensed in full at grant date. This is discussed further at 4.2 above and at 16.4 below, and illustrated in Example 23.6 at 7.1 above.

7.4.2   Awards with non-vesting conditions and variable vesting periods

Neither FRS 102 nor IFRS 2 explicitly addresses the determination of the vesting period for an award with a non-vesting condition but a variable vesting period (e.g. an award which delivers 100 shares when the price of gold reaches a given level, but without limit as to when that level must be achieved, so long as the employee is still in employment when the target is reached). However, given the close similarity between the required treatment for awards with non-vesting conditions and that for awards with market conditions, we believe that entities should follow the guidance for awards with market conditions and variable vesting periods (see 7.3.4 above).

7.4.3   Failure to meet non-vesting conditions

As noted above, the accounting under IFRS 2 – and, in the absence of specific guidance, FRS 102 – for non-vesting conditions sometimes differs from that for market conditions in the timing of the recognition of expense if the non-vesting condition is not satisfied. The treatment depends on the nature of the non-vesting condition, as follows:

- if a non-vesting condition within the control of the counterparty (e.g. making monthly savings in an SAYE scheme) is not satisfied during the vesting period, the failure to satisfy the condition is treated as a cancellation (see 8.4 below), with immediate recognition of any expense for the award not previously recognised; *[IFRS 2.28A, IG24]*

- if a non-vesting condition within the control of the entity (e.g. continuing to operate the scheme) is not satisfied during the vesting period, the failure to satisfy the condition is treated as a cancellation (see 8.4 below), with immediate recognition of any expense for the award not previously recognised; *[IFRS 2.28A, IG24]* but

- if a non-vesting condition within the control of neither the counterparty nor the entity (e.g. a financial market index reaching a minimum level) is not satisfied, there is no change to the accounting and the expense continues to be recognised over the vesting period, unless the award is otherwise treated as forfeited by IFRS 2. *[IFRS 2.BC237A, IG24]*. In our view, the reference to the vesting period would include any deemed vesting period calculated as described in 7.4.2 above.

If an award is forfeited due to a failure to satisfy a non-vesting condition after the end of the vesting period (e.g. a requirement for an employee not to work for a competitor for a two year period after vesting), no adjustment is made to the expense previously recognised, consistent with the general provisions for accounting for awards in the post-vesting period (see 7.1.3 above). This would be the case even if shares previously issued to the employee were required to be returned to the entity.

8 EQUITY-SETTLED TRANSACTIONS – MODIFICATION, CANCELLATION AND SETTLEMENT

8.1 Background

It is quite common for equity instruments to be modified or cancelled before or after vesting. Typically this is done where the conditions for an award have become so onerous as to be virtually unachievable, or (in the case of an option) where the share price has fallen so far below the exercise price of an option that it is unlikely that the option will ever be 'in the money' to the holder during its life. An entity may take the view that such equity awards are so unattainable as to have little or no motivational effect, and accordingly replace them with less onerous alternatives. Conversely, and more rarely, an entity may make the terms of a share award more onerous (possibly because of shareholder concern that targets are insufficiently demanding). In addition an entity may 'settle' an award, i.e. cancel it in return for cash or other consideration.

The provisions in FRS 102 relating to modification, cancellation and settlement are derived from those in IFRS 2 and, where necessary, we have drawn on the guidance in IFRS 2 to supplement and explain the FRS 102 requirements. The provisions in both standards (like the summary of them below) are framed in terms of share-based payment transactions with employees. IFRS 2 and FRS 102 (as a result of the Triennial review 2017) indicates that the provisions are equally applicable to transactions with parties other than employees that are measured by reference to the fair value of the equity instruments granted (see 6.4 above). *[FRS 102.26.12]*. For transactions with parties other than employees, however, all references to 'grant date' should be taken as references to the date on which the third party supplied goods or rendered service.

Chapter 23

In the discussion below, any reference to a 'cancellation' is to any cancellation, whether instigated by the entity or the counterparty. As well as more obvious situations where an award is cancelled by either the entity or the counterparty, cancellations include:

- a failure by the entity to satisfy a non-vesting condition within the control of the entity; and
- a failure by the counterparty to satisfy a non-vesting condition within the control of the counterparty (see 7.4.3 above).

The basic principles of the rules for modification, cancellation and settlement, which are discussed in more detail at 8.3 and 8.4 below, can be summarised as follows:

- As a minimum, the entity must recognise the amount that would have been recognised for the award if it remained in place on its original terms.
- If the value of an award to an employee is reduced (e.g. by reducing the number of equity instruments subject to the award or, in the case of an option, by increasing the exercise price), there is no reduction in the cost recognised in profit or loss.
- However, if the value of an award to an employee is increased (e.g. by increasing the number of equity instruments subject to the award or, in the case of an option, by reducing the exercise price), the incremental fair value must be recognised as a cost. The incremental fair value is the difference between the fair value of the original award and that of the modified award, both measured at the date of modification. *[FRS 102.26.12].*

8.2 Valuation requirements when an award is modified, cancelled or settled

These provisions have the important practical consequence that, when an award is modified, cancelled or settled, the entity must obtain a fair value not only for the modified award, but also for the original award, updated to the date of modification. If the award had not been modified, there would have been no need to obtain a valuation for the original award after the date of grant.

Any modification of a performance condition clearly has an impact on the 'real' value of an award but it may have no direct effect on the value of the award for accounting purposes. As discussed at 7.2 to 7.4 above, this is because market vesting conditions and non-vesting conditions are taken into account in valuing an award whereas non-market vesting conditions are not. Accordingly, by implication, a change to a non-market performance condition will not necessarily affect the expense recognised for the award.

For example, if an award is contingent upon sales of a given number of units and the number of units required to be sold is decreased, the 'real' value of the award is clearly increased. However, as the performance condition is a non-market condition, and therefore not relevant to the original determination of the value of the award, there is no incremental fair value required to be accounted for. However, if the change in the condition results in an increase in the estimated number of awards expected to vest, the change of estimate will however give rise to an accounting charge (see 7.1 to 7.4 above).

If an award is modified by changing the service period, the situation is more complex. A service condition does not of itself change the fair value of the award for the purposes of FRS 102 and IFRS 2, but a change in service period may indirectly change the life of the award, which is relevant to its value (see 9 below). Similar considerations apply where performance conditions are modified in such a way as to alter the anticipated vesting date.

The valuation requirements relating to cancelled and settled awards are considered further at 8.4 below.

8.3 Modification

When an award is modified, the entity must as a minimum recognise the cost of the original award as if it had not been modified (i.e. based on the original grant date fair value, spread over the original vesting period, and subject to the original vesting conditions). *[FRS 102.26.12(b)].*

In addition, a further cost must be recognised for any modifications that increase the fair value of the award. If the modification occurs during the vesting period, this additional cost is spread over the period from the date of modification until the vesting date of the modified award, which might not be the same as that of the original award. *[FRS 102.26.12(a)].* Although not explicitly stated in Section 26, but nevertheless consistent with its requirements, where a modification is made after the original vesting period has expired, and is subject to no further vesting conditions, any incremental fair value should be recognised immediately. *[IFRS 2 Appendix B.43].*

Whether a modification increases or decreases the fair value of an award is determined as at the date of modification, as illustrated by Example 23.19. *[FRS 102.26.12].*

Example 23.19: Does a modification increase or decrease the value of an award?

At the beginning of year 1 an entity granted two executives, A and B, a number of options with a fair value of £100 each.

At the beginning of year 2, A's options are modified such that they have a fair value of £85, their current fair value being £80. This is treated as an increase in fair value of £5 (even though the modified award is worth less than the original award when first granted). Therefore an additional £5 of expense would be recognised in respect of A's options.

At the beginning of year 3, B's options are modified such that they have a fair value of £120, their current fair value being £125. This is treated as a reduction in fair value of £5 (even though the modified award is worth more than the original award when first granted). However, there is no change to the expense recognised for B's options as the entity has to recognise, as a minimum, the original grant date fair value of the options (i.e. £100).

This treatment ensures that movements in the fair value of the original award are not reflected in the entity's profit or loss, consistent with the accounting treatment of other equity instruments.

Appendix B and the implementation guidance to IFRS 2 provide further detailed guidance on these requirements as set out in the following sections.

8.3.1 Modifications that increase the value of an award

8.3.1.A Increase in fair value of equity instruments granted

If the modification increases the fair value of the equity instruments granted, (e.g. by reducing the exercise price or changing the exercise period), the incremental fair value, measured at the date of modification, must be recognised over the period from the date

Chapter 23

of modification to the date of vesting for the modified instruments, as illustrated in Example 23.20 below (which is based on IG Example 7 in the implementation guidance to IFRS 2). *[FRS 102.26.12(a), IFRS 2 Appendix B.43(a)].*

Example 23.20:   *Award modified by repricing*

At the beginning of year 1, an entity grants 100 share options to each of its 500 employees. Each grant is conditional upon the employee remaining in service over the next three years. The entity estimates that the fair value of each option is £15.

By the end of year 1, the entity's share price has dropped, and the entity reprices its share options. The repriced share options vest at the end of year 3. The entity estimates that, at the date of repricing, the fair value of each of the original share options granted (i.e. before taking into account the repricing) is £5 and that the fair value of each repriced share option is £8.

40 employees leave during year 1. The entity estimates that a further 70 employees will leave during years 2 and 3, so that there will be 390 employees at the end of year 3 (500 – 40 – 70).

During year 2, a further 35 employees leave, and the entity estimates that a further 30 employees will leave during year 3, so that there will be 395 employees at the end of year 3 (500 – 40 – 35 – 30).

During year 3, 28 employees leave, and hence a total of 103 employees ceased employment during the original three year vesting period, so that, for the remaining 397 employees, the original share options vest at the end of year 3.

IFRS 2 (and FRS 102) requires the entity to recognise:

- the cost of the original award at grant date (£15 per option) over a three year vesting period beginning at the start of year 1, plus

- the incremental fair value of the repriced options at repricing date (£3 per option, being the £8 fair value of each repriced option less the £5 fair value of the original option) over a two year vesting period beginning at the date of repricing (end of year 1).

This would be calculated as follows.

Year	Calculation of cumulative expense		Cumulative expense (£)	Expense for period (£)
	Original award (a)	Modified award (b)	(a+b)	
1	390 employees × 100 options × £15 × 1/3		195,000	195,000
2	395 employees × 100 options × £15 × 2/3	395 employees × 100 options × £3 × 1/2	454,250	259,250
3	397 employees × 100 options × £15	397 employees × 100 options × £3	714,600	260,350

In effect, the original award and the incremental value of the modified award are treated as if they were two separate awards.

A similar treatment to that in Example 23.20 above is adopted where the fair value of an award subject to a market condition has its value increased by the removal or mitigation of the market condition. *[IFRS 2 Appendix B.43(c)].* Where a vesting condition other than a market condition is changed, the treatment set out at 8.3.1.C below is adopted. The standards do not specifically address the situation where the fair value of an award is increased by the removal or mitigation of a non-vesting condition. It seems appropriate, however, to account for this increase in the same way as for a modification caused by the removal or mitigation of a market condition – i.e. as in Example 23.20 above.

8.3.1.B   *Increase in number of equity instruments granted*

Paragraph 12 of Section 26 on modification of awards begins by referring solely to modifications to the conditions on which equity instruments were granted rather than the number of equity instruments granted. However, in discussing the related accounting treatment, paragraph 12 goes on to refer both to the fair value of an award and to the number of equity instruments granted. If the modification increases the number of equity instruments granted, the fair value of the additional instruments, measured at the date of modification, must be recognised over the period from the date of modification to the date of vesting for the modified instruments. *[FRS 102.26.12(a)].* Although not explicitly stated, it follows that if there is no further vesting period for the modified instruments, the incremental cost should be recognised immediately.

It is often the case, however, that a change in the number of equity instruments granted is combined with other modifications to the award – such situations are considered further at 8.3.2 and 8.3.4 below.

8.3.1.C   *Removal or mitigation of non-market related vesting conditions*

Where a vesting condition, other than a market condition, is modified in a manner that is beneficial to the employee, the modified vesting condition should be taken into account when applying the general requirements of FRS 102 as discussed at 7.1 to 7.4 above – in other words, the entity would continuously estimate the number of awards likely to vest and/or the vesting period. This is consistent with the general principle that vesting conditions, other than market conditions, are not taken into account in the valuation of awards, but are reflected by recognising a cost for those instruments that ultimately vest on achievement of those conditions. See also the discussion at 8.2 above.

The standards do not provide an example that addresses this point specifically, but we assume that the intended approach is as in Example 23.21 below. In this Example, the entity modifies an award in a way that is beneficial to the employee even though the modification does not result in any incremental fair value. The effect of the modification is therefore recognised by basing the expense on the original grant date fair value of the awards and an assessment of the extent to which the modified vesting conditions will be met.

Example 23.21: *Modification of non-market performance condition in employee's favour*

At the beginning of year 1, the entity grants 1,000 share options to each member of its sales team, with exercise conditional upon the employee remaining in the entity's employment for three years, and the team selling more than 50,000 units of a particular product over the three year period. The fair value of the share options is £15 per option at the date of grant.

At the end of year 1, the entity estimates that a total of 48,000 units will be sold, and accordingly records no cost for the award in year one.

During year 2, there is so severe a downturn in trading conditions that the entity believes that the sales target is too demanding to have any motivational effect, and reduces the target to 30,000 units, which it believes is achievable. It also expects 14 members of the sales team to remain in employment throughout the three year performance period. It therefore records an expense in year 2 of £140,000 (£15 × 14 employees × 1,000 options × 2/3). This cost is based on the originally assessed value of the award (i.e. £15) since the performance condition was never factored into the original valuation, such that any change in performance condition likewise has no effect on the valuation and does not result in any incremental fair value.

By the end of year 3, the entity has sold 35,000 units, and the share options vest as the modified performance condition has been met. Twelve members of the sales team have remained in service for the three year period. The entity would therefore recognise a total cost of £180,000 (12 employees × 1,000 options × £15), giving an additional cost in year 3 of £40,000 (total charge £180,000, less £140,000 charged in year 2).

The difference between the accounting consequences for different methods of enhancing an award could cause confusion in some cases. For example, it may sometimes not be clear whether an award has been modified by increasing the number of equity instruments or by lowering the performance targets, as illustrated in Example 23.22.

Example 23.22:   Increase in number of equity instruments or modification of vesting conditions?

An entity grants a performance-related award which provides for different numbers of options to vest after 3 years, depending on different performance targets as follows.

Profit growth	Number of options
5%-10%	100
10%-15%	200
over 15%	300

During the vesting period, the entity concludes that the criteria are too demanding and modifies them as follows.

Profit growth	Number of options
5%-10%	200
over 10%	300

This raises the issue of whether the entity has changed:

(a)   the performance conditions for the vesting of 200 or 300 options; or

(b)   the number of equity instruments awarded for achieving growth of 5%-10% or growth of over 10%.

In our view, the reality is that the change is to the performance conditions for the vesting of 200 or 300 options, and should therefore be dealt with as in 8.3.1.C above rather than 8.3.1.B above. Suppose, however, that the conditions had been modified as follows.

Profit growth	Number of options
5%-10%	200
10%-15%	300
over 15%	400

In that case, there has clearly been an increase in the number of equity instruments subject to an award for a growth increase of over 15%, which would have to be accounted for as such (i.e. under 8.3.1.B above rather than 8.3.1.C above). In such a case, it might seem more appropriate to deal with the changes to the lower bands as changes to the number of shares awarded rather than changes to the performance conditions.

8.3.2   Modifications that decrease the value of an award

This type of modification does not occur very often, as the effect would be somewhat demotivating and, in some cases, contrary to local labour regulations. However, there have been occasional examples of an award being made more onerous – usually in response to criticism by shareholders that the original terms were insufficiently demanding.

The general requirement of FRS 102 and of IFRS 2 (as outlined at 8.3 above) is that, where an award is made more onerous (and therefore less valuable), the financial statements must still recognise the cost of the original award. This rule is in part an anti-avoidance measure since, without it, an entity could reverse the cost of an out-of-the-money award by modifying it so that it was unlikely to vest (for example, by adding unattainable non-market performance conditions) rather than cancelling the award and triggering an acceleration of expense as at 8.4 below.

8.3.2.A   *Decrease in fair value of equity instruments granted*

If the modification decreases the fair value of the equity instruments granted (e.g. by increasing the exercise price or reducing the exercise period), the decrease in value is effectively ignored and the entity continues to recognise a cost for services as if the awards had not been modified. *[FRS 102.26.12(b), IFRS 2 Appendix B.44(a)]*. This approach also applies to reductions in the fair value of an award by the addition of a market condition or by making an existing market condition more onerous. *[IFRS 2 Appendix B.44(c)]*. Although the standards have no specific guidance on this point, we assume that reductions in the fair value resulting from the addition or amendment of a non-vesting condition are similarly ignored, as illustrated in Example 23.23 below.

Example 23.23:   Award modified by replacing a non-market condition with a market condition

At the beginning of year 1, an entity grants 1,000 share options to each of its 10 employees, with exercise conditional upon the employee remaining in the entity's employment for three years, and an earnings per share (EPS) target (non-market condition) being met over the three year period. The fair value of the share options is £15 per option at the date of grant.

At the end of year 1, the entity estimates that all the employees will remain in service until the end of year 3 and that the EPS target will be met. It therefore records a cost of £50,000 for the award in year 1 (£15 × 10 employees × 1,000 options × 1/3).

During year 2, the entity reassesses the arrangement and replaces the EPS target with a share price target (market condition) that must be achieved by the end of year 3. At the date of modification, the fair value of the option with the market condition is £12 and the fair value of the original option is £17. Therefore the fair value of the award has decreased as a result of the modification but, under Section 26, this decrease is not accounted for and the entity must continue to use the original grant date fair value. An expense must be recognised based on this grant date fair value unless the award does not vest due to failure to meet a service or non-market performance condition specified at the original grant date. At the original grant date the conditions were a service condition and a non-market performance condition. With the removal of the non-market performance condition, the only condition that has been in place since grant date is the service condition.

At the end of year 2 the entity estimates that nine employees will fulfil the service condition by the end of year 3. It therefore records a cumulative expense in year 2 of £90,000 (£15 × 9 employees × 1,000 options × 2/3) and an expense for the year of £40,000 (£90,000 – £50,000).

At the end of year 3 the share price target has not been met but eight employees have met the service condition. The entity therefore recognises a cumulative expense of £120,000 (£15 × 8 employees × 1,000 options) and an expense for the year of £30,000 (£120,000 – £90,000).

It can be seen that the only expense reversal relates to those employees who have forfeited their options by failing to fulfil the employment condition. There is no reversal of expense for those employees who met the service condition but whose options did not vest (in real terms) because the market condition was not met. In FRS 102 terms the options of those eight employees vested because all non-market conditions were met and so the entity has to recognise the grant date fair value for those awards. This is the case even though the original grant date fair value did not take account of the effect of the market condition (unlike an award with a market condition specified from grant date). This outcome is the result of the different treatment of market and non-market conditions within Section 26, and the requirement to recognise an expense for an award with a market condition provided all other conditions have been met (see further discussion at 7.3.2 above).

8.3.2.B   *Decrease in number of equity instruments granted*

If the modification reduces the number of equity instruments granted, IFRS 2 requires the reduction to be treated as a cancellation of that portion of the award (see 8.4 below). *[IFRS 2 Appendix B.44(b)]*. Essentially this has the effect that any previously unrecognised cost of the cancelled instruments is immediately recognised in full, whereas the cost of an award whose value is reduced by other means continues to be spread in full over the remaining vesting period.

In situations where a decrease in the number of equity instruments is combined with other modifications so that the total fair value of the award remains the same or increases, it is unclear whether the approach required is one based on the value of the award as a whole or, as in the previous paragraph, one based on each equity instrument as the unit of account. This is considered further at 8.3.4 below.

8.3.2.C   *Additional or more onerous non-market related vesting conditions*

Where a non-market vesting condition is modified in a manner that is not beneficial to the employee, again it is ignored and a cost recognised as if the original award had not been modified, as shown by Example 23.24 (which is based on IG Example 8 in the implementation guidance to IFRS 2). *[IFRS 2 AppendixB.44(c), IG15, IG Example 8]*.

Example 23.24: Award modified by changing non-market performance conditions

At the beginning of year 1, the entity grants 1,000 share options to each member of its sales team, conditional upon the employee remaining in the entity's employment for three years, and the team selling more than 50,000 units of a particular product over the three year period. The fair value of the share options is £15 per option at the date of grant. During year 2, the entity believes that the sales target is insufficiently demanding and increases it to 100,000 units. By the end of year 3, the entity has sold 55,000 units, and the modified share options are forfeited. Twelve members of the sales team have remained in service for the three year period.

On the basis that the original target would have been met, and twelve employees would have been eligible for awards, the entity would recognise a total cost of £180,000 (12 employees × 1,000 options × £15) in accordance with the minimum cost requirements of paragraph 12 of Section 26. The cumulative cost in years 1 and 2 would, as in the Examples above, reflect the entity's best estimate of the *original* 50,000 unit sales target being achieved at the end of year 3. If, conversely, sales of only 49,000 units had been achieved, any cost booked for the award in years 1 and 2 would have been reversed in year 3, since the original target of 50,000 units would not have been met.

It is noted in IG Example 8 that the same accounting result would have occurred if the entity had increased the service requirement rather than modifying the performance target. Because such a modification would make it less likely that the options would vest, which would not be beneficial to the employees, the entity would take no account of the modified service condition when recognising the services received. Instead, it would recognise the services received from the twelve employees who remained in service for the original three year vesting period. Other modifications to vesting periods are discussed below.

8.3.3 Modifications with altered vesting period

Where an award is modified so that its value increases, FRS 102 and IFRS 2 require the entity to continue to recognise an expense for the grant date fair value of the unmodified award over its *original* vesting period, even where the vesting period of the modified award is longer (see 8.3.1 above). This appears to have the effect that an expense may be recognised for awards that do not actually vest, as illustrated by Example 23.25 (which is based on Example 23.20 above).

Example 23.25: Award modified by reducing the exercise price and extending the vesting period

At the beginning of year 1, an entity grants 100 share options to each of its 500 employees, with vesting conditional upon the employee remaining in service over the next three years. The entity estimates that the fair value of each option is £15.

By the end of year 1, the entity's share price has dropped, and the entity reprices its share options. The repriced share options vest at the end of year 4. The entity estimates that, at the date of repricing, the fair value of each of the original share options granted (i.e. before taking into account the repricing) is £5 and that the fair value of each repriced share option is £7.

40 employees leave during year 1. The entity estimates that a further 70 employees will leave during years 2 and 3, and a further 25 employees during year 4, such that there will be 390 employees at the end of year 3 (500 – 40 – 70) and 365 (500 – 40 – 70 – 25) at the end of year 4.

During year 2, a further 35 employees leave, and the entity estimates that a further 30 employees will leave during year 3 and 30 more in year 4, such that there will be 395 employees at the end of year 3 (500 – 40 – 35 – 30) and 365 (500 – 40 – 35 – 30 – 30) at the end of year 4.

During year 3, 28 employees leave, and hence a total of 103 employees ceased employment during the original three year vesting period, so that, for the remaining 397 employees, the original share options would have vested at the end of year 3. The entity now estimates that only a further 20 employees will leave during year 4, leaving 377 at the end of year 4. In fact 25 employees leave, so that 372 satisfy the criteria for the modified options at the end of year 4.

In our view the entity is required to recognise:

- the cost of the original award at grant date (£15 per option) over a three year vesting period beginning at the start of year 1, based on the ongoing best estimate of, and ultimately the actual, number of employees at the end of the *original three year* vesting period;

- the incremental fair value of the repriced options at repricing date (£2 per option, being the £7 fair value of each repriced option less the £5 fair value of the original option) over a three year vesting period beginning at the date of repricing (*end* of year one), but based on the ongoing best estimate of, and ultimately the actual, number of employees at the end of the *modified four year* vesting period.

This would be calculated as follows:

Year	Calculation of cumulative expense		Cumulative expense (£)	Expense for period (£)
	Original award	Modified award		
1	390 employees × 100 options × £15 × 1/3		195,000	195,000
2	395 employees × 100 options × £15 × 2/3	365 employees × 100 options × £2 × 1/3	419,333	224,333
3	397 employees × 100 options × £15	377 employees × 100 options × £2 × 2/3	645,767	226,434
4	397 employees × 100 options × £15	372 employees × 100 options × £2	669,900	24,133

Chapter 23

It may seem strange that a cost is being recognised for the original award in respect of the 25 employees who leave during year 4, who are never entitled to anything. However, in our view, this is consistent with:

- the overall requirement of FRS 102 and IFRS 2 that the minimum cost of a modified award should be the cost that would have been recognised if the award had not been modified; and

- IG Example 8 in IFRS 2 (the substance of which is reproduced in Example 23.24 above) where an expense is clearly required to be recognised to the extent that the original performance conditions would have been met if the award had not been modified.

Moreover, as Examples 23.24 and 23.25 illustrate, the rule in FRS 102 and IFRS 2 requiring recognition of a minimum expense for a modified award (i.e. as if the original award had remained in place) applies irrespective of whether the effect of the modification is that an award becomes less valuable to the employee (as in Example 23.24) or more valuable to the employee (as in Example 23.25).

Where a modified vesting period is shorter than the original vesting period, all of the expense relating to both the original and modified elements of the award should, in our view, be recognised by the end of the modified vesting period as no services will be rendered beyond that date.

8.3.4　Modifications that reduce the number of equity instruments granted but maintain or increase the value of an award ('value for value' exchanges and 'give and take' modifications)

As discussed at 8.3.2.B above, IFRS 2 requires cancellation accounting to be applied to a reduction in the number of equity instruments when a modification reduces both the number of equity instruments granted and the total fair value of the award. *[IFRS 2 Appendix B.44(b)]*. FRS 102 is silent on the accounting treatment of such arrangements and we therefore suggest that entities follow the IFRS 2 requirements. The IFRS 2 approach is consistent with the fact that part of the award has been removed without compensation to the employee. However, a modification of this kind is rarely seen in practice because of the demotivating effect and, in some jurisdictions, a requirement to pay compensation to the counterparty. An entity is more likely to modify an award so that the overall fair value remains the same, or increases, even if the number of equity instruments is reduced. These types of modification, sometimes known as 'value for value' exchanges or 'give and take' modifications, are considered below.

Where an entity reduces the number of equity instruments but also makes other changes so that the total fair value of the modified award remains the same as, or exceeds, that of the original award as at the modification date, it is unclear whether the unit of account for accounting purposes should be an individual equity instrument or the award as a whole. Examples 23.26 and 23.27 below illustrate the two situations and the two approaches.

Example 23.26:　Modification where number of equity instruments is reduced but total fair value is unchanged

At the beginning of year 1, an entity granted an employee 200 share options with a grant date fair value of £9 and a vesting period of three years. During years 1 and 2, the entity recognises a cumulative expense of £1,200 (200 × £9 × 2/3). At the end of year 2 the exercise price of the options is significantly higher than the market price and the options have a fair value of £5 per option. On this date, the entity modifies the award and exchanges the 200 underwater options for 100 'at the money' options with a fair value of £10 each. The total fair value of the new awards of £1,000 (100 × £10) equals the total fair value of the awards exchanged (200 × £5), as measured at the modification date.

View 1 is that the unit of account is an individual option. Taking this approach, the decrease in the number of options from 200 to 100 will be accounted for as a cancellation with an acceleration at the modification date of any unexpensed element of the grant date fair value of 100 options (i.e. recognition of an additional amount of £300 (100 × £9 × 1/3)). The grant date fair value of the remaining 100 options continues to be recognised over the remainder of the vesting period together with their incremental fair value following the modification. Therefore, in year 3, there would be an expense of £300 (for the remaining grant date fair value) plus £500 (100 × (£10 − £5)) for the incremental fair value of 100 options. In total, therefore, an expense of £2,300 is recognised.

View 2 is that the total number of options exchanged is the more appropriate unit of account. In this case, the cancellation of the original options and the grant of replacement options are accounted for as one modification. There would therefore be no acceleration of expense in respect of the reduction in the number of options from 200 to 100 and the grant date fair value of the original award would continue to be recognised over the vesting period. In this case, the total expense recognised would be £1,800 (200 × £9).

Example 23.27: Modification where number of equity instruments is reduced but total fair value is increased

At the beginning of year 1, an entity granted to its employees 1,000 share options with an exercise price equal to the market price of the shares at grant date. There is a two year vesting period and the grant date fair value is £10 per option. The entity's share price has declined significantly so that the share price is currently significantly less than the exercise price. At the end of year 1, the entity decides to reduce the exercise price of the options and, as part of the modification, it also reduces the number of options from 1,000 to 800. At the date of modification, the fair value of the original options is £7 per option and that of the modified options £11 per option.

View 1 is that the unit of account is an individual option. Taking this approach, the decrease in the number of options from 1,000 to 800 will be accounted for as a cancellation of 200 options with an acceleration at the modification date of any remaining grant date fair value relating to those 200 options. The total expense recognised in year 1 is £6,000 ((800 × £10 × ½) + (200 × £10)). The grant date fair value of the remaining 800 options continues to be recognised over the remainder of the vesting period together with the incremental fair value of those awards as measured at the modification date. In total the entity will recognise an expense of £13,200 (original grant date fair value of £10,000 (1,000 × £10) plus incremental fair value of £3,200 (800 × £(11 − 7)).

View 2 is that the unit of account is the total number of options as there are linked modifications forming one package. In this case, the incremental fair value is calculated as the difference between the total fair value before and after the modification. In total the entity will recognise an expense of £11,800 (original grant date fair value of £10,000 (1,000 × £10) plus incremental fair value on modification of £1,800 ((800 × £11) − (1,000 × £7)).

Given the lack of clarity, we believe that an entity may make an accounting policy choice as to whether it considers the unit of account to be an individual equity instrument or an award as a whole. Further detail on the arguments underpinning each of the two approaches is given in EY International GAAP 2019 but is beyond the scope of this publication.

Once made, the accounting policy choice should be applied consistently to all modifications that reduce the number of equity instruments but maintain or increase the overall fair value of an award. Whatever the policy choice, the entity will still need to determine whether or not the amendments to the arrangement are such that it is appropriate to account for the changes as a modification rather than as a completely new award (see 8.4.2 and 8.4.4 below).

Chapter 23

8.3.5 Modification of award from equity-settled to cash-settled (and vice versa)

Occasionally an award that was equity-settled when originally granted is modified so as to become cash-settled, or an originally cash-settled award is modified so as to become equity-settled. FRS 102 provides no explicit guidance on such modifications. IFRS 2 provides no explicit guidance on modifications from equity-settled to cash-settled but the June 2016 amendment clarified IFRS 2 to provide more specific guidance on modifications of awards from cash-settled to equity-settled. In the absence of specific guidance in FRS 102 we believe that it is possible to arrive at a reasonable approach by analogy to the provisions of IFRS 2 in respect of:

- the modification of equity-settled awards during the vesting period (see 8.3 above);
- the addition of a cash-settlement alternative to an equity-settled award after grant date (as illustrated in IG Example 9 in the implementation guidance to IFRS 2);
- the settlement of equity-settled awards in cash (see 8.4 below); and
- the settlement in equity of awards where the entity has a choice of settlement, but which have been accounted for as cash-settled during the vesting period (see 11.1.1.A below).

A detailed discussion of this topic is beyond the scope of this publication but the subject is addressed more fully in EY International GAAP 2019.

8.4 Cancellation and settlement

Paragraph 13 of Section 26 is headed 'cancellations and settlements' but, whilst its treatment of cancellations is consistent with the basic requirement of IFRS 2 (as set out in (a) below), it does not specify the accounting treatment of a settlement (i.e. an award cancelled with some form of compensation). Section 26 also does not address the treatment of replacement awards following a cancellation.

In the absence of specific guidance in FRS 102, we consider it appropriate to follow the full guidance in IFRS 2, as outlined below, for the cancellation, replacement or settlement of an award other than by forfeiture for failure to satisfy the vesting conditions.

When an award accounted for under FRS 102 is settled, it is perhaps debatable whether any incremental amount paid in settlement is required to be expensed, as for IFRS 2 (see (b) below) or whether any difference could be accounted for in equity as would be the case with the repurchase of equity instruments outside a share-based payment transaction. In our view, an approach consistent with that of IFRS 2 is appropriate given the extent to which the requirements of Section 26 generally are derived from those of IFRS 2.

IFRS 2 requires the following approach:

(a) if the cancellation or settlement occurs during the vesting period, it is treated as an acceleration of vesting, and the entity recognises immediately the amount that would otherwise have been recognised for services received over the remainder of the vesting period; *[FRS 102.26.13, IFRS 2.28-29]*

(b) where the entity pays compensation for a cancelled award:

    (i) any compensation paid up to the fair value of the award at cancellation or settlement date (whether before or after vesting) is accounted for as a deduction from equity, as being equivalent to the redemption of an equity instrument;

    (ii) any compensation paid in excess of the fair value of the award at cancellation or settlement date (whether before or after vesting) is accounted for as an expense in profit or loss; and

    (iii) if the share-based payment arrangement includes liability components, the fair value of the liability is remeasured at the date of cancellation or settlement. Any payment made to settle the liability component is accounted for as an extinguishment of the liability; and

(c) if the entity grants new equity instruments during the vesting period and, on the date that they are granted, identifies them as replacing the cancelled or settled instruments, the entity is required to account for the new equity instruments as if they were a modification of the cancelled or settled award. Otherwise it accounts for the new instruments as an entirely new award. *[IFRS 2.28-29]*.

It should be noted that the calculation of any additional expense in (b) above depends on the fair value of the award at the date of cancellation or settlement, not on the cumulative expense already charged. This has the important practical consequence that, when an entity pays compensation on cancellation or settlement of an award, it must obtain a fair value for the original award, updated to the date of cancellation or settlement. If the award had not been cancelled or settled, there would have been no need to obtain a valuation for the original award after the date of grant.

These requirements raise some further detailed issues of interpretation on a number of areas, as follows:

- the distinction between 'cancellation' and 'forfeiture' (see 8.4.1 below);
- the distinction between 'cancellation' and 'modification' (see 8.4.2 below);
- the calculation of the expense on cancellation (see 8.4.3 below); and
- replacement awards (see 8.4.4 and 8.5 below).

8.4.1 Distinction between cancellation and forfeiture

The provisions of IFRS 2 apply when an award of equity instruments is cancelled or settled 'other than a grant cancelled by forfeiture when the vesting conditions are not satisfied'. *[IFRS 2.28]*. The significance of this is that the terms of many share-based awards provide that they are, or can be, 'cancelled', in a legal sense, on forfeiture. IFRS 2 is clarifying that, where an award is forfeited (within the meaning of that term in IFRS 2 – see 7.1.2 above), the entity should apply the accounting treatment for a forfeiture (i.e. reversal of expense previously recognised), even if the award is legally cancelled as a consequence of the forfeiture. FRS 102 does not have such an explicit distinction but we presume that a similar treatment is intended.

8.4.1.A   *Termination of employment by entity*

In some cases, it might not always be immediately clear whether cancellation or forfeiture has occurred, particularly where options lapse as the result of a termination of employment by the entity. For example, an entity might grant options to an employee at the beginning of year 1 on condition of his remaining in employment until the end of year 2. During year 1, however, economic conditions require the entity to make a number of its personnel, including that employee, redundant, as a result of which his options lapse. Is this lapse a forfeiture or a cancellation for accounting purposes?

The uncertainty arises because it could be argued either that the employee will be unable to deliver the services required in order for the options to vest (suggesting a forfeiture) or that the options lapse as a direct result of the employer's actions (suggesting a cancellation).

Any failure to meet a service condition, regardless of the reason, is accounted for under IFRS 2 as a forfeiture rather than as a cancellation. Therefore a situation where the entity terminates the employment contract should be accounted for as a forfeiture and a similar approach should be followed by entities applying FRS 102 as the definition of a service condition is consistent with that in IFRS 2. *[FRS 102 Appendix I]*.

8.4.1.B   *Surrender of award by employee*

It is sometimes the case that an employee, often a member of senior management, will decide – or be encouraged by the entity – to surrender awards during the vesting period. The question arises as to whether this should be treated as a cancellation or forfeiture for accounting purposes. FRS 102 and IFRS 2 allow forfeiture accounting, and the consequent reversal of any cumulative expense, only in situations where vesting conditions are not satisfied. A situation where the counterparty voluntarily surrenders an award and therefore 'fails' to meet the service condition does not, in our view, meet the criteria for treatment as a forfeiture and should be treated as a cancellation of the award by the employee.

8.4.2   *Distinction between cancellation and modification*

One general issue raised by the approach to modification and cancellation in FRS 102 and IFRS 2 is where the boundary lies between 'modification' of an award in the entity's favour and outright cancellation of the award. As a matter of legal form, the difference is obvious. However, if an entity were to modify an award in such a way that there was no realistic chance of it ever vesting (for example, by introducing a requirement that the share price increase 1,000,000 times by vesting date), some might argue that this amounts to a *de facto* cancellation of the award. The significance of the distinction is that, whereas the cost of a 'modified' award continues to be recognised on a periodic basis over the vesting period (see 8.3 above), the remaining cost of a cancelled award is recognised immediately.

Share-based payment 1295

8.4.3   Calculation of the expense on cancellation

The basic accounting treatment for a cancellation and settlement is illustrated in Example 23.28 below.

Example 23.28:   Cancellation and settlement – basic accounting treatment

At the start of year 1 an entity grants an executive 30,000 options on condition that she remain in employment for three years. Each option is determined to have a fair value of £10.

At the end of year 1, the executive is still in employment and the entity charges an expense of £100,000 (30,000 × £10 × 1/3). At the end of year 2, the executive is still in employment. However, the entity's share price has suffered a decline which the entity does not expect to have reversed by the end of year 3, such that the options, while still 'in the money' now have a fair value of only £6.

The entity cancels the options at the end of year 2 and in compensation pays the executive £6.50 per option cancelled, a total payment of £195,000 (30,000 options × £6.50).

FRS 102 and IFRS 2 first require the entity to record a cost as if the options had vested immediately. The total cumulative cost for the award must be £300,000 (30,000 options × £10). £100,000 was recognised in year 1, so that an additional cost of £200,000 is recognised.

As regards the compensation payment, the fair value of the awards cancelled is £180,000 (30,000 options × £6.00). Accordingly, £180,000 of the payment is accounted for as a deduction from equity, with the remaining payment in excess of fair value, £15,000, charged to profit or loss (as required by IFRS 2 – and, in our view, a reasonable approach to apply under FRS 102).

The net effect of this is that an award that ultimately results in a cash payment to the executive of only £195,000 (i.e. £6.50 per option) has resulted in a total charge to profit or loss of £315,000 (i.e. £10.50 per option, representing £10 grant date fair value + £6.50 compensation payment – £6.00 cancellation date fair value).

Example 23.28 illustrates the basic calculation of the required cancellation 'charge'. In more complex situations, however, the amount of the 'charge' may not be so clear-cut, due to an ambiguity in the drafting of paragraph 28(a) of IFRS 2 and paragraph 13 of Section 26, which state that an entity:

> 'shall account for the cancellation or settlement ... as an acceleration of vesting, and therefore shall recognise immediately the amount that otherwise would have been recognised for services received over the remainder of the vesting period.'
>
> *[FRS 102.26.13, IFRS 2.28(a)].*

There is something of a contradiction within this requirement as illustrated by Example 23.29.

Example 23.29:   Cancellation and settlement – best estimate of cancellation expense

At the beginning of year 1, entity A granted 150 employees an award of free shares, with a grant date fair value of £5, conditional upon continuous service and performance targets over a 3-year period from grant date. The number of shares awarded varies according to the extent to which targets (all non-market vesting conditions) have been met, and could result in each employee still in service at the end of year 3 receiving a minimum of 600, and a maximum of 1,000 shares.

Halfway through year 2 (i.e. 18 months after grant date), A is acquired by B, following which A cancels all of its share awards. At the time of the cancellation, 130 of the original 150 employees were still in employment. At that time, it was A's best estimate that, had the award run to its full term, 120 employees would have received 900 shares each. Accordingly, the cumulative expense recognised by A for the award as at the date of takeover would, under the normal estimation processes discussed at 7.1 to 7.4 above, be £270,000 (900 shares × 120 employees × £5 × 18/36).

How should A account for the cancellation of this award?

The opening phrase of paragraph 28(a) of IFRS 2 (echoed in paragraph 13 of Section 26 – 'the entity shall account for the cancellation ...as an acceleration of vesting' – suggests that A should recognise a cost for all 130 employees in service at the date of cancellation. However, the following phrase – '[the entity] shall therefore recognise immediately the amount that would otherwise have been recognised for services received over the remainder of the vesting period' – suggests that the charge should be based on only 120 employees, the best estimate, as at the date of cancellation of the number of employees in whom shares will finally vest. In our view, either reading is possible.

There is then the issue of the number of shares per employee that should be taken into account in the cancellation charge. Should this be 1,000 shares per employee (the maximum amount that could vest) or 900 shares per employee (the amount expected by the entity at the date of cancellation actually to vest)?

In our view, it is unclear whether the intention was that the cancellation charge should be based on the number of shares considered likely, as at the date of cancellation, to vest for each employee (900 shares in this example) or whether it should be based on the maximum number of shares (1,000 shares in this example). Given the lack of clarity, in our view an entity may make an accounting policy choice.

In extreme cases, the entity's best estimate, as at the date of cancellation, might be that no awards are likely to vest. In this situation, no cancellation expense would be recognised. However, there would need to be evidence that this was not just a rather convenient assessment made as at the date of cancellation. Typically, the previous accounting periods would also have reflected a cumulative expense of zero on the assumption that the awards would never vest.

An effect of these requirements is that they create an accounting arbitrage between an award that is 'out of the money' but not cancelled (the cost of which continues to be spread over the remaining period to vesting) and one which is formally cancelled (the cost of which is recognised immediately). Entities might well prefer to opt for cancellation so as to create a 'one-off' charge to earnings rather than continue to show, particularly during difficult trading periods, significant periodic costs for options that no longer have any real value. However, such early cancellation of an award precludes any chance of the cost of the award being reversed through forfeiture during, or at the end of, the vesting period if the original vesting conditions are not met.

8.4.4 Replacement awards

FRS 102 contains no specific requirements or guidance in relation to replacement awards and so we consider it appropriate to draw on those in IFRS 2. The remainder of this section therefore reflects the IFRS 2 requirements. Whilst the requirements relating to accounting for replacement awards are generally clear under IFRS 2, there are nevertheless some issues of interpretation.

As set out at 8.4 above, a new award that meets the criteria in paragraph 28(c) of IFRS 2 to be treated as a replacement of a cancelled or settled award is accounted for as a modification of the original award and any incremental value arising from the granting of the replacement award is recognised over the vesting period of that replacement award.

Where the criteria are not met, the new equity instruments are accounted for as a new grant (in addition to accounting for the cancellation or settlement of the original arrangement). The requirements are discussed in more detail below.

8.4.4.A   Designation of award as replacement award

Whether or not an award is a 'replacement' award (and therefore recognised at only its incremental, rather than its full, fair value) is determined by whether or not the entity designates it as such on the date that it is granted.

Entities need to ensure that designation occurs on grant date as defined by IFRS 2 (and FRS 102) (see 6.3 above). For example, if an entity cancels an award on 15 March and notifies an employee in writing on the same day of its intention to ask the remuneration committee to grant replacement options at its meeting in two months on 15 May, such notification (although formal and in writing) may not strictly meet the requirement for designation on grant date (i.e. 15 May). However, in our view, what is important is that the entity establishes a clear link between the cancellation of the old award and the granting of a replacement award even if there is later formal approval of the replacement award following the communication of its terms to the counterparty at the same time as the cancellation of the old award.

As drafted, IFRS 2 gives entities an apparently free choice to designate any newly granted awards as replacement awards. In our view, however, such designation cannot credibly be made unless there is evidence of some connection between the cancelled and replacement awards. This might be that the cancelled and replacement awards involve the same counterparties, or that the cancellation and replacement are part of the same arrangement.

8.4.4.B   Incremental fair value of replacement award

Where an award is designated as a replacement award, any incremental fair value must be recognised over the vesting period of the replacement award. The incremental fair value is the difference between the fair value of the replacement award and the 'net fair value' of the cancelled or settled award, both measured at the date on which the replacement award is granted. The net fair value of the cancelled or settled award is the fair value of the award, immediately before cancellation, less any compensation payment that is accounted for as a deduction from equity. *[IFRS 2.28(c)].* Thus the 'net fair value' of the original award can never be less than zero (since any compensation payment in excess of the fair value of the cancelled award would be accounted for in profit or loss, not in equity – see Example 23.28 at 8.4.3 above).

There is some confusion within IFRS 2 as to whether a different accounting treatment is intended to result from, on the one hand, modifying an award and, on the other hand, cancelling it and replacing it with a new award on the same terms as the modified award. This is explored in the discussion of Example 23.30 below, which is based on the same fact pattern as Example 23.20 at 8.3.1.A above.

Example 23.30:   Replacement awards – is there an accounting arbitrage between modification and accounting for cancellation and a new grant?

At the beginning of year 1, an entity grants 100 share options to each of its 500 employees. Each grant is conditional upon the employee remaining in service over the next three years. The entity estimates that the fair value of each option is £15.

By the end of year 1, the entity's share price has dropped. The entity cancels the existing options and issues options which it identifies as replacement options, which also vest at the end of year 3. The entity estimates that, at the date of cancellation, the fair value of each of the original share options granted is £5 and that the fair value of each replacement share option is £8.

40 employees leave during year 1. The entity estimates that a further 70 employees will leave during years 2 and 3, so that there will be 390 employees at the end of year 3 (500 – 40 – 70).

During year 2, a further 35 employees leave, and the entity estimates that a further 30 employees will leave during year 3, so that there will be 395 employees at the end of year 3 (500 – 40 – 35 – 30).

During year 3, 28 employees leave, and hence a total of 103 employees ceased employment during the original three year vesting period, so that, for the remaining 397 employees, the replacement share options vest at the end of year 3.

Paragraph BC233 of IFRS 2 suggests that the intention of the IASB was that the arrangement should be accounted for in exactly the same way as the modification in Example 23.20 above.

However, it is not clear that this intention is actually reflected in the drafting of paragraph 28 of IFRS 2 which seems to require the cancellation of the existing award to be treated as an acceleration of vesting – explicitly and without qualification – and any 'new equity instruments' granted to be accounted for in the same way as a modification of the original grant of equity instruments. It does not require this treatment for the cancellation of the *original* instruments, because this has already been addressed as an acceleration of vesting.

The application of, firstly, the main text of IFRS 2 and, secondly, the Basis for Conclusions to IFRS 2 to the entity in Example 23.30 is set out below.

The main text in IFRS 2 appears to require the entity to recognise:

- The entire cost of the original options at the end of year 1 (since cancellation has the effect that they are treated as vesting at that date), based on the 390 employees expected at that date to be in employment at the end of the vesting period. This is not the only possible interpretation of the requirement of paragraph 28(a) – see the broader discussion in Example 23.29 at 8.4.3 above.

- For the options replacing the 390 cancelled awards, the incremental fair value of the replacement options at repricing date (£3 per option, being the £8 fair value of each replacement option less the £5 fair value of each cancelled option) over a two year vesting period beginning at the date of cancellation (end of year 1), based on the (at first estimated and then actual) number of employees at the end of year 3 (i.e. the final number could be less than the estimate of 390).

- For any additional replacement options (i.e. replacement options awarded in excess of the 390 × 100 options that were expected to vest at cancellation date), the full incremental fair value at repricing date (being the £8 fair value of each replacement option) over a two year vesting period beginning at the repricing date (end of year 1). The expense is based on the (at first estimated and then actual) number of employees in excess of 390 at the end of year 3.

This would be calculated as follows:

Year	Calculation of cumulative expense		Cumulative expense (£)	Expense for period (£)
	Original award	Replacement award		
1	390 employees × 100 options × £15	–	585,000	585,000
2	390 employees × 100 options × £15	390 employees × 100 options × £3 × 1/2 5 employees × 100 options × £8 × 1/2	645,500	60,500
3	390 employees × 100 options × £15	390 employees × 100 options × £3 7 employees × 100 options × £8	707,600	62,100

By contrast, the accounting treatment implied by the Basis for Conclusions is as follows (see Example 23.20 above):

Year	Calculation of cumulative expense		Cumulative expense (£)	Expense for period (£)
	Original award (a)	Modified award (b)	(a+b)	
1	390 employees × 100 options × £15 × 1/3	–	195,000	195,000
2	395 employees × 100 options × £15 × 2/3	395 employees × 100 options × £3 × 1/2	454,250	259,250
3	397 employees × 100 options × £15	397 employees × 100 options × £3	714,600	260,350

It can be seen that both the periodic allocation of expense and the total expense differ under each interpretation. This is because, under the first interpretation, the cost of the original award is accelerated at the end of year 1 for all 390 employees expected at that date to be in employment at the end of the vesting period, whereas under the second interpretation a cost is recognised for the 397 employees whose awards finally vest. The difference between the two total charges of £7,000 (£714,600 – £707,600) represents 397 – 390 = 7 employees @ £1,000 (100 options × £10 (£15 + £3 – £8)) each = £7,000.

In practice, the second (modification accounting) approach tends to be seen more frequently. However, we believe that either interpretation is valid, and an entity should adopt one or other consistently as a matter of accounting policy.

In Example 23.30 above, we base the cancellation calculations on 390 employees (the number expected to be employed at the end of the vesting period as estimated at the cancellation date) rather than on 460 employees (the number in employment at the cancellation date). As discussed in Example 23.29 at 8.4.3 above, either approach may be adopted but the selected approach should be applied consistently.

The discussion above relates to situations in which awards are cancelled and replaced for reasons other than expected, or actual, failure by the counterparty to meet a service condition. Changes to awards in contemplation, or as a consequence, of cessation of employment are considered at 6.3.8.B above and at 8.5 and 8.6 below.

8.4.4.C   Replacement of vested awards

The rules for replacement awards summarised in paragraph (c) at 8.4 above apply 'if a grant of equity instruments is cancelled or settled during the vesting period ...'. *[IFRS 2.28]*. FRS 102 does not explicitly state that its requirements relate solely to awards cancelled or settled during the vesting period but this seems to be implied by the references to 'an acceleration of vesting' and 'the remainder of the vesting period'. *[FRS 102.26.13]*. However, if the original award has already vested when a replacement award is granted, there is no question of accelerating the cost of the cancelled award, as it has already been recognised during the vesting period. The issue is rather the treatment of the new award itself. Whilst neither IFRS 2 nor FRS 102 explicitly addresses this point, it appears that such a replacement award should be treated as if it were a completely new award. In other words, its full fair value should be recognised immediately or, if there are any vesting conditions for the replacement award, over its vesting period.

By contrast, the rules in IFRS 2 for modification of awards (discussed in 8.3 above) apply whether the award has vested or not. Paragraphs 26 and 27 of IFRS 2 (modifications) are not restricted to events 'during the vesting period' in contrast to paragraph 28 (cancellation and settlement, including replacement awards), which is restricted to events 'during the vesting period'. *[IFRS 2.26-28]*. In FRS 102, any such distinction is less clear because the paragraph on modifications is written in the context of a modification of vesting conditions and, whilst it refers explicitly to the accounting treatment of modifications during the vesting period, it is silent on the modification of vested awards. *[FRS 102.26.12]*. In the absence of explicit guidance, we believe that it is appropriate to follow the accounting approach of IFRS 2.

The treatment outlined above has the effect that the accounting cost of modifying an already vested award (i.e. the incremental fair value of the modified award) may, at first sight, appear to be lower than the cost of cancelling and replacing it, which requires the full fair value of the new award to be expensed. However, the full fair value of the new replacement award will be reduced by the fair value of the cancelled award that the employee has surrendered as part of the consideration for the new award. This analysis will, in many cases, produce an accounting outcome similar to that of the modification of an unvested award.

8.5 Replacement and ex gratia awards on termination of employment

When an employee's employment is terminated during the vesting period of an award of shares or options, the award will typically lapse in consequence. It is common in such situations, particularly where the employee was part of the senior management, for the entity to make an alternative award, or to allow the employee to retain existing awards, as part of the package of benefits agreed with the employee on termination of employment.

Generally, such an award is an *ex gratia* award – in other words, it is a voluntary award to which the outgoing employee had no legal entitlement under the terms of the original award. However, a number of plan rules set out, in a 'good leaver' clause (see 6.3.8 above), the terms on which any *ex gratia* award may be made, usually by applying a formula to determine, or limit, how much of the original award can be considered to have vested.

In many cases the award will be made on a fully vested basis, i.e. the employee has full entitlement without further conditions needing to be fulfilled. In other cases, however, an employee will be allowed to retain awards that remain subject to the fulfilment of the original conditions (other than future service). Whichever form the award takes, in accounting terms it will be treated as vesting at the date of termination of employment because any remaining conditions will be accounted for as non-vesting conditions in the absence of an explicit or implied service condition (see 4.2 above).

It has not always been clear whether the termination of employment should be accounted for as a forfeiture or as a cancellation. However, as discussed at 8.4.1.A above, if an employee is unable to satisfy a service condition for any reason, this should be accounted for under IFRS 2 as a forfeiture rather than as a cancellation. It appears appropriate for entities accounting under FRS 102 also to apply forfeiture accounting.

IFRS 2 does not specifically address the accounting for any replacement or ex gratia awards granted on termination of employment. It perhaps follows from the treatment of the termination of employment as a forfeiture to:

- reverse any expense relating to the forfeited award; and
- recognise the ex gratia award as a completely new award granted at the date of termination of employment.

However, the guidance is not clear and there might be situations where entities consider it more appropriate to apply modification accounting (recognising the original grant date fair value of the award that would otherwise be forfeited on its original terms (because the service condition would not be met) plus the incremental value of the modified terms). In the absence of clarity, we believe that judgement will be required based on the specific facts and circumstances and the extent to which the changes to the arrangements are considered to be a waiver of existing conditions in connection with the cessation of employment rather than the introduction of a discretionary replacement arrangement on completely new terms.

8.6 Entity's plans for future modification or replacement of award – impact on estimation process at reporting date

As discussed at 7.1.1 and 7.1.2 above, FRS 102 requires an entity to determine a cumulative charge at each reporting date by reference to an estimate of the number of awards that will vest (within the special meaning of that term in FRS 102). The process of estimation at each reporting date should take into account any new information that indicates a change to previous estimates.

In addition to the normal difficulties inherent in any estimation process, it is not entirely clear which anticipated future events should be taken into account in the estimation process and which should not, as illustrated by Example 23.31 below.

Example 23.31: Estimation of number of awards expected to vest – treatment of anticipated future events

At the beginning of year 1, an entity granted an award of 1,000 shares to each of its 600 employees at a particular manufacturing unit. The award vests on completion of three years' service. As at the end of year 1, the entity firmly intends to close the unit, and terminate the employment of employees, as part of a rationalisation programme. This closure would occur part way through year 2. The entity has not, however, announced its intentions or taken any other steps so as to allow provision for the closure.

Under the original terms of the award, the award would lapse on termination of employment. However, the entity intends to compensate employees made redundant by changing the terms of their award so as to allow full vesting on termination of employment.

What is the 'best estimate', as at the end of year 1, of the number of awards expected to vest? Specifically, should the entity:

(a) ignore the intended closure altogether, on the grounds that there is no other recognition of it in the financial statements;

(b) take account of the impact of the intended closure on vesting of the current award, but ignore the intended modification to the terms of the award to allow vesting; or

(c) take account of both the intended closure and the intended modification of the award?

In our view, there is no basis in FRS 102 for accounting for an anticipated future change to the terms of an award. The entity must account for those awards in issue at the reporting date, not those that might be in issue in the future. Accordingly we do not consider approach (c) above to be appropriate if any change to the issued awards was simply an intention.

Equally, we struggle to support approach (a) above. FRS 102 requires the entity to use an estimate of the number of awards expected to vest and its best available estimate as at the end of year 1 must be that the unit will be closed, and the employees' employment terminated, in year 2. This view is supported by the fact that, unlike other areas of accounting such as impairment and provisions, accounting for share-based payment transactions does not explicitly prohibit an entity from taking account of the consequences of reorganisations and similar transactions to which it is not yet committed.

Accordingly, we believe that approach (b) should be followed.

The entity's best estimate, at the end of year 1, must be that none of the awards currently in place will vest (because all the employees will be made redundant and so will not meet the service condition before the end of the vesting period). It therefore applies forfeiture accounting at the end of year 1 and reverses any cost previously recorded for the award.

When the terms of the award are changed at the time of the redundancy in year 2 to allow full vesting, the entity will either recognise the full cost of the new award (as all cost relating to the original award has been reversed) or will treat the revised arrangement as a modification of the original award that is beneficial to the employee. In effect, the modification approach is based on a view that the original award is not now going to lapse because it will be modified before employment ceases and the forfeiture crystallises. In our view, in the absence of clarity in the standard, the entity should assess the more appropriate approach based on the particular facts and circumstances.

Either approach will have what many may see as the less than ideal result that the entity will recognise a credit in profit or loss in year 1 and an expense in year 2, even though there has been no change in management's best estimate of the overall outcome. This follows from the analysis, discussed above, that we do not believe that the entity can account, in year 1, for the award on the basis of what its terms may be in year 2.

The best estimate is made as at each reporting date. A change in estimate made in a later period in response to subsequent events affects the accounting expense from that later period only (i.e. there is no restatement of earlier periods presented).

8.7   Share splits and consolidations

It is relatively common for an entity to divide its existing equity share capital into a larger number of shares (share splits) or to consolidate its existing share capital into a smaller number of shares (share consolidations). The impact of such splits and consolidations is not specifically addressed in either FRS 102 or IFRS 2.

Suppose that an employee has options over 100 shares in the reporting entity, with an exercise price of £1. The entity undertakes a '1 for 2' share consolidation – i.e. the number of shares in issue is halved such that, all other things being equal, the value of one share in the entity after the consolidation is twice that of one share before the consolidation.

IFRS 2 is required to be applied to modifications to an award arising from equity restructurings (FRS 102 is silent on this). *[IFRS 2.BC24]*. In many cases, a share scheme will provide for automatic adjustment so that, following the consolidation, the employee holds options over only 50 shares with an exercise price of £2. As discussed at 6.3.7.A above, all things being equal, it would be expected that the modified award would have the same fair value as the original award and so there would be no incremental expense to be accounted for.

However, it may be that the scheme has no such provision for automatic adjustment, such that the employee still holds options over 100 shares. The clear economic effect is that the award has been modified, since its value has been doubled. It could be argued that, on a literal reading of IFRS 2, no modification has occurred, since the employee holds options over 100 shares at the same exercise price before and after the consolidation. In our view, whilst it seems appropriate to have regard to the substance of the transaction, and treat it as giving rise to a modification, it can be argued that FRS 102 and IFRS 2 as drafted do not require such a treatment.

Sometimes, the terms of an award give the entity discretion to make modifications at a future date in response to more complex changes to the share structure, such as those arising from bonus issues, share buybacks and rights issues where the effect on existing options may not be so clear-cut. These are discussed further at 6.3.7.A above.

9 EQUITY-SETTLED TRANSACTIONS – VALUATION

9.1 Introduction

As noted at 6.1 above, an equity-settled share-based payment transaction is valued either at the fair value of the goods or services received – using the general requirements of FRS 102 for the determination of fair value – or at the fair value of the equity instruments granted – using the specific requirements set out in Section 26. The timing of the fair value measurement, and whether it is based on the goods or services or on the equity instruments, is driven by a number of factors including the relative reliability of measurement and the identity of the counterparty (see 6 above).

In this section we consider the specific requirements in Section 26 for the valuation of shares, share options and equity-settled share appreciation rights. No distinction is drawn between awards to employees and to non-employees and the requirements should therefore be applied to the measurement of employee awards at grant date and non-employee awards at service date.

9.2 Shares

Section 26 requires the fair value of shares (and the related goods or services received) to be determined using the following three-tier measurement hierarchy:

(a) if an observable market price is available for the equity instruments granted, use that price;

(b) if an observable market price is not available, measure the fair value of equity instruments granted using entity-specific observable market data such as:

    (i) a recent transaction in the entity's shares; or

    (ii) a recent independent fair valuation of the entity or its principal assets;

(c) if an observable market price is not available and obtaining a reliable measurement of fair value under (b) is impracticable, indirectly measure the fair value of the shares using a valuation method that uses market data to the greatest extent practicable to estimate what the price of those equity instruments would be on the grant date in an arm's length transaction between knowledgeable, willing parties. The entity's directors should use their judgement to apply a generally accepted valuation methodology for valuing equity instruments that is appropriate to the circumstances of the entity. *[FRS 102.26.10].*

Chapter 23

FRS 102 defines a requirement as 'impracticable' when the entity cannot apply it after making every reasonable effort to do so. *[FRS 102 Appendix I]*.

It seems unlikely that the market price referred to in (a), or the entity-specific observable market data referred to in (b), will be available for the measurement of the vast majority of share-based awards granted by unlisted entities. Most entities will therefore be required to apply the approach required by (c) and use an appropriate valuation methodology.

The selection of an appropriate methodology for valuing the equity of an unlisted entity is beyond the scope of this publication but, in many cases of awards of free shares (which are akin to options with a zero strike price), it is likely that an approach similar to that used for valuing share options will be adopted (see 9.3 below).

FRS 102 states that all market conditions and non-vesting conditions should be taken into account when estimating the fair value of the shares or share options at the measurement date (see further discussion at 7.3 and 7.4 above on market conditions and non-vesting conditions). *[FRS 102.26.9]*. Apart from this, there is no mention of adjusting the market price, or estimated market price, of an entity's shares to take into account the terms and conditions on which they were granted (which would, typically, reduce the value). Many conditions and restrictions attached to awards will be covered by the requirements of paragraph 9. However, this guidance does not specifically address the common situation where the counterparty is not entitled to receive dividends during the vesting period.

Under the requirements of IFRS 2, no adjustment is required to the estimated grant date fair value of shares if the employees are entitled to receive dividends, or dividend equivalents paid in cash, during the vesting period (as they are in no different a position in this respect than if they already held shares). However, where employees are not entitled to receive dividends during the vesting period, IFRS 2 requires the valuation to be reduced by the present value of dividends expected to be paid during the vesting period. *[IFRS 2 Appendix B.31, 33-34]*.

The accounting treatment of awards which give the right to receive dividends during the vesting period is discussed further at 16.3 below.

If an entity is taking approach (c) above in determining a fair value for the equity instruments then it seems appropriate to adjust for all the terms and conditions on which the shares have been awarded (other than those vesting conditions which are not taken into account in the determination of fair value).

Where an entity is using approaches (a) or (b), it might appear that it is required to use an unadjusted market price or other observable price without adjusting for the specific terms and conditions of the share-based payment. However, that seems to be at variance with the requirements of paragraph 9 to take certain conditions into account. In our view, it will generally be more appropriate to adjust the fair value for the terms and conditions on which the right to the equity instrument is granted if the instrument granted is not precisely that for which the market price, or other observable price, is available.

9.3   Share options and equity-settled share appreciation rights

A share option is defined in FRS 102 as 'a contract that gives the holder the right, but not the obligation, to subscribe to the entity's shares at a fixed or determinable price for a specific period of time'. *[FRS 102 Appendix I]*.

A share appreciation right (SAR) is not specifically defined in FRS 102 but is a grant where the counterparty will become entitled either to shares (or, more commonly, to a future cash payment) based on the increase in the entity's share price or value from a specified level over a period of time (see further discussion at 10 below on cash-settled awards).

Section 26 requires the fair value of share options and equity-settled share appreciation rights (and the related goods or services received) to be determined using the following three-tier measurement hierarchy:

(a)   if an observable market price is available for the equity instruments granted, use that price;

(b)   if an observable market price is not available, measure the fair value of share options and share appreciation rights granted using entity-specific observable market data such as for a recent transaction in the share options;

(c)   if an observable market price is not available and obtaining a reliable measurement of fair value under (b) is impracticable, indirectly measure the fair value of share options or share appreciation rights using an alternative valuation methodology such as an option pricing model. The inputs for an option pricing model (such as the weighted average share price, exercise price, expected volatility, option life, expected dividends and the risk-free interest rate) shall use market data to the greatest extent possible. Paragraph 26.10 provides guidance on determining the fair value of the shares used in determining the weighted average share price. The entity shall derive an estimate of expected volatility consistent with the valuation methodology used to determine the fair value of the shares. *[FRS 102.26.11]*.

The fact that Section 26 does not mandate the use of an option pricing model was identified in earlier versions of FRS 102 as a significant difference between FRS 102 and the IFRS for SMEs on which FRS 102 is based (and is also a change from IFRS 2). However, in practice, it is likely that use of a pricing model will often be a practical basis for determining the fair value of share options and appreciation rights.

The treatment of vesting and non-vesting conditions in the determination of the fair value of share options should be considered in the same way as for the fair value of shares (see 9.2 above) as paragraph 9 of Section 26 refers to both shares and share options.

A discussion of valuation methodology is beyond the scope of this publication. Whilst not addressing the subject of valuation in detail, EY International GAAP 2019 draws on the guidance in Appendix B to IFRS 2 relating to the valuation of share-based payments and addresses some aspects of the pricing of options, particularly with respect to employee awards.

10   CASH-SETTLED TRANSACTIONS

Throughout the discussion in this section, 'cash' should be read as including 'other assets' in accordance with the definition of a cash-settled share-based payment transaction (see 3.1 above).

10.1   Scope of requirements

Section 26 notes that cash-settled share-based payment transactions include:

- share appreciation rights (SARs), where employees are entitled to a future cash payment (rather than an equity instrument) based on the increase in an entity's share price from a specified level over a specified period of time; and

- a right to a future cash payment through a grant of shares (including shares to be issued upon the exercise of share options) that are redeemable, either mandatorily (e.g. upon cessation of employment) or at the employee's option. *[FRS 102.26.2]*.

Another type of cash-settled arrangement frequently encountered in practice is a grant of phantom options, where employees are entitled to a cash payment equivalent to the gain that would have been made by exercising options at a notional price over a notional number of shares and then selling the shares at the date of exercise.

As is clear from the inclusion of certain types of redeemable share as a specific example of a cash-settled share-based payment arrangement, FRS 102 looks beyond the simple issue of whether an award entitles an employee to receive instruments that are in form shares or options to the terms of those instruments. The fact that certain redeemable shares would be treated as a cash-settled, not an equity-settled, award is consistent with the fact that a share with these terms would be regarded as a financial liability rather than an equity instrument of the issuer (based on Section 22).

In some cases the boundary between equity-settled and cash-settled schemes may appear somewhat blurred, so that further analysis may be required to determine whether a particular arrangement is equity-settled or cash-settled. Some examples of such arrangements are discussed at 10.2 below.

10.2   What constitutes a cash-settled award?

There are a number of possible circumstances in which, on, or shortly after, settlement of an equity-settled award either:

- the entity incurs a cash outflow equivalent to that which would arise on cash-settlement (e.g. because it purchases its own shares to deliver to counterparties); or

- the counterparty receives cash equivalent to the amount that would arise on cash-settlement (e.g. because the shares are sold for cash on behalf of the counterparty).

Such situations raise the question of whether such schemes are in fact truly equity-settled or cash-settled.

Examples of relatively common mechanisms for delivering the cash-equivalent of an equity-settled award to employees are discussed below. It emerges from the analysis below that, in reality, the accounting for share-based payment transactions is driven by questions of form rather than substance. To put it rather crudely, what matters is often not so much whether the entity has made a cash payment for the fair value of the award, but rather the name of the payee.

The significance of this is that the analysis affects the profit or loss charge for the award, as illustrated by Example 23.32 below.

Example 23.32: Equity-settled award satisfied by purchase of own shares

An entity awards an employee a free share with a fair value at grant date of £5 which has a fair value of £8 at vesting. At vesting the entity acquires one of its own shares from an existing shareholder for £8 for delivery to the employee. If the scheme were treated as cash-settled, there would be a charge to profit or loss of £8 (the fair value at vesting date – see 10.3 below). If it were treated as equity-settled (as required in this case by FRS 102), profit or loss would show a charge of only £5 (the fair value at grant date), with a further net charge of £3 in equity, comprising the £8 paid for the share accounted for as a treasury share or own share less the £5 credit to equity (being the credit entry corresponding to the £5 charge to profit or loss – see 5.2 above).

The analyses below all rely on a precise construction of the definition of a cash-settled share-based payment transaction, i.e. one 'in which the entity acquires goods or services *by incurring a liability to transfer cash or other assets to the supplier of those goods or services* for amounts that are based on the price (or value) of equity instruments (including shares and share options) of the entity or another group entity' (emphasis added). *[FRS 102 Appendix I]*. Thus, if the entity is not actually required – legally or constructively – to pay cash to the counterparty, there is no cash-settled transaction under FRS 102, even though the arrangement may give rise to an external cash flow and, possibly, another form of recognised liability.

Some have raised the question of whether the entity should recognise some form of liability to repurchase own equity in situations where the entity has a stated policy of settling equity-settled transactions using previously purchased treasury or own shares. In our view, the normal provisions of accounting for financial instruments apply and there would be no question of recognising a liability to repurchase own equity on the basis merely of a declared intention. It is only when the entity enters into a forward contract or a call option with a third party that some accounting recognition of a future share purchase may be required.

An entity might sometimes purchase a number of its own shares shortly after issuing a similar number of shares in settlement of an equity-settled transaction. This raises the question of whether such a scheme would be considered as in substance cash-settled. In our view, further enquiry into the detailed circumstances of the purchase is required in order to determine the appropriate analysis.

Broadly speaking, so long as there is no obligation (explicit or implicit) for the entity to settle in cash with the counterparty, such purchase arrangements will not require a scheme to be treated as cash-settled under Section 26. However, in our view, there might be situations in which post-settlement share purchases are indicative of an obligation to the counterparty, such that treatment as a cash-settled scheme would be appropriate.

For example, if the entity were to create an expectation by employees that any shares awarded can always be liquidated immediately, because the entity will ensure that there is a market for the shares, it could well be appropriate to account for such a scheme as cash-settled. This will often be the case with awards granted to the employees of an unlisted company. The treatment of schemes in which the entity has a choice of settlement, but has created an expectation of cash-settlement, provides a relevant analogy (see 11.1.3 below).

Chapter 23

A more extreme example of such a situation would be where the entity has arranged for the shares delivered to the counterparty to be sold on the counterparty's behalf, but has at the same time entered into a contract to purchase those shares. In that situation, in our view, the substance is that:

- the entity has created an expectation by the counterparty of a right to receive cash; and

- the intermediate purchaser or broker is no more than an agent paying that cash to the counterparty on behalf of the entity.

Accordingly, it would be appropriate to account for such an arrangement as a cash-settled award.

Similar issues arise in the application of 'drag along' and 'tag along' rights in the context of an exit event and these are discussed at 16.4.6 below.

10.3 Required accounting for cash-settled share-based payment transactions

10.3.1 Basic accounting treatment

For a cash-settled share-based payment transaction, Section 26 requires an entity to measure the goods or services acquired and the corresponding liability incurred at the fair value of the liability. Until that liability is settled, the entity should remeasure the fair value at each reporting date and at the date of settlement. Any changes in fair value arising from this process of remeasurement should be recognised in profit or loss for the period. *[FRS 102.26.14].*

It is clear that the ultimate cost of a cash-settled transaction must be the actual cash paid to the counterparty, which will be the fair value at settlement date but the liability is recognised and measured as follows:

- at each reporting date between grant and settlement the fair value of the award is determined in accordance with the requirements of Section 26;

- during the vesting period, the liability recognised at each reporting date is the Section 26 fair value of the award at that date multiplied by the expired portion of the vesting period;

- from the end of the vesting period until settlement, the liability recognised is the full fair value of the liability at the reporting date.

Where the cost of services received in a cash-settled transaction is recognised in the carrying amount of an asset (e.g. inventory) in the entity's statement of financial position, the carrying amount of the asset should not be adjusted for changes in the fair value of the liability.

Although paragraph 14 of Section 26 refers to 'fair value' it provides no further guidance about how the fair value of a cash-settled share-based payment liability should be determined. Appendix I to FRS 102 includes a definition of 'fair value' as:

'the amount for which ... a liability [could be] settled ... between knowledgeable, willing parties in an arm's length transaction. In the absence of any specific guidance provided in the relevant section of this FRS, the guidance in the Appendix to Section 2 – *Concepts and Pervasive Principles* – shall be used in determining fair value.'

The reference to 'fair value' in paragraph 14 is not highlighted as a defined term and so it is not clear whether the defined term in Appendix I to FRS 102 is intended to apply to liabilities for cash-settled share-based payments. Section 26 specifies how fair value should be determined for equity-settled share-based payment transactions (see 9.2 and 9.3 above) but contains no specific guidance for cash-settled share-based payment transactions. In our view, an acceptable approach would be to use the guidance in the Appendix to Section 2 but also to draw on IFRS 2 (using the GAAP hierarchy in Section 10) to provide some more practical guidance on the approach to be taken in fair valuing a cash-settled share-based payment transaction.

The Appendix to Section 2 indicates that an appropriate valuation technique should be used and that this might include an option pricing model. The use of a pricing model is consistent with the requirement in IFRS 2 that fair value be determined by applying an option pricing model, taking into account the terms and conditions on which the cash-settled transaction was granted, and the extent to which the employees have rendered service to date.

10.3.2 Application of the accounting treatment

The treatment required by Section 26 for cash-settled transactions is illustrated by Example 23.33 which is based on IG Example 12 in the implementation guidance to IFRS 2.

Example 23.33: Cash-settled transaction with service condition

An entity grants 100 cash-settled share appreciation rights (SARs) to each of its 500 employees, on condition that the employees remain in its employment for the next three years. The SARs can be exercised on the third, fourth and fifth anniversary of the grant date.

During year 1, 35 employees leave. The entity estimates that a further 60 will leave during years 2 and 3 (i.e. the award will vest in 405 employees).

During year 2, 40 employees leave and the entity estimates that a further 25 will leave during year 3 (i.e. the award will vest in 400 employees).

During year 3, 22 employees leave, so that the award vests in 403 employees. At the end of year 3, 150 employees exercise their SARs (leaving 253 employees still to exercise).

Another 140 employees exercise their SARs at the end of year 4, leaving 113 employees still to exercise, who do so at the end of year 5.

The entity estimates the fair value of the SARs at the end of each year in which a liability exists as shown below. The intrinsic values of the SARs at the date of exercise (which equal the cash paid out) at the end of years 3, 4 and 5 are also shown below.

Year	Fair value £	Intrinsic value £
1	14.40	
2	15.50	
3	18.20	15.00
4	21.40	20.00
5		25.00

The entity will recognise the cost of this award as follows:

Year	Calculation of liability	Calculation of cash paid	Liability (£)	Cash paid (£)	Expense for period (£)*
1	405 employees × 100 SARs × £14.40 × 1/3		194,400	–	194,400
2	400 employees × 100 SARs × £15.50 × 2/3		413,333	–	218,933
3	253 employees × 100 SARs × £18.20	150 employees × 100 SARs × £15.00	460,460	225,000	272,127
4	113 employees × 100 SARs × £21.40	140 employees × 100 SARs × £20.00	241,820	280,000	61,360
5	–	113 employees × 100 SARs × £25.00	–	282,500	40,680

*   Liability at end of period + cash paid in period – liability at start of period

The accounting treatment for cash-settled transactions is therefore (despite some similarities in the methodology) significantly different from that for equity-settled transactions. An important practical issue is that, for a cash-settled transaction, the entity must determine the fair value at each reporting date rather than at grant date (and at the date of any subsequent modification or settlement) as would be the case for equity-settled transactions. As Example 23.33 shows, it is not necessary to determine the fair value of a cash-settled transaction at grant date in order to determine the share-based payment expense.

We discuss in more detail below the following aspects of the accounting treatment of cash-settled transactions:

- determining the vesting period (see 10.3.2.A below);
- periodic allocation of cost (see 10.3.2.B below);
- treatment of non-market vesting conditions (see 10.3.2.C below);
- treatment of market conditions and non-vesting conditions (see 10.3.2.D below); and
- treatment of modification, cancellation and settlement (see 10.3.2.E below).

10.3.2.A   Determining the vesting period

The rules for determining vesting periods are the same as those applicable to equity-settled transactions, as discussed at 7.1 to 7.4 above. Where an award vests immediately, there is a presumption that, in the absence of evidence to the contrary, the award is in respect of services that have already been rendered, and should therefore be expensed in full at grant date. *[FRS 102.26.5]*.

Where cash-settled awards are made subject to vesting conditions (as in many cases they will be, particularly where payments to employees are concerned), there is a presumption that the awards are a payment for services to be received in the future, during the 'vesting period', with the transaction being recognised during that period, as illustrated in Example 23.33 above.

10.3.2.B   Periodic allocation of cost

The required treatment for cash-settled transactions is simply to measure the fair value of the liability at each reporting date, *[FRS 102.26.14]*, which might suggest that the full fair value, and not just a time-apportioned part of it, should be recognised at each reporting date – as would be the case for any liability that is a financial instrument measured at fair value.

However, paragraph 14 needs to be read with paragraph 6 which states that if the counterparty is required to complete a specified period of service, the entity 'shall account for those services as they are rendered during the vesting period, with a corresponding increase in ... liabilities'. This indicates that a spreading approach is to be adopted. *[FRS 102.26.6]*.

10.3.2.C   Non-market vesting conditions

FRS 102 does not specifically addresses the impact of vesting conditions (other than service conditions) in the context of cash-settled transactions – the provisions relating to vesting conditions are to be found under headings relating to equity-settled share-based payment transactions.

Where a vesting condition is a minimum service period, the liability should be estimated on the basis of the current best estimate of the number of awards that will vest, this estimate being made exactly as for an equity-settled transaction.

As regards other non-market performance conditions, the treatment is unclear. However, in June 2016, the IASB issued an amendment to IFRS 2 to clarify that entities should not reflect non-market performance conditions in the fair value of a cash-settled share-based payment but should apply a similar approach to that used for equity-settled share-based payments.

In the absence of specific guidance in FRS 102, we believe that entities applying FRS 102 will continue to have an accounting policy choice in determining the fair value of the liability (see 2.4 above). We believe that the fair value of the liability until vesting date may either fully take account of the probability of the vesting conditions being achieved or exclude the conditions. If the latter approach is adopted, the liability recognised by the entity would be adjusted at each reporting date to reflect the entity's current best estimate of the outcome of those conditions. This approach analogises to the treatment of service conditions (and to the equity-settled treatment of service and non-market performance conditions).

10.3.2.D   Market conditions and non-vesting conditions

There is no specific guidance in FRS 102 as to whether a distinction is to be drawn between the treatment of non-vesting conditions and market conditions and that of other non-market vesting conditions, as would be the case for an equity-settled transaction (see 7.2 to 7.4 above).

As discussed at 10.3.2.C above, this is a matter that has been addressed in a recent amendment to IFRS 2. As well as clarifying the treatment of non-market vesting conditions, the amendment confirms the current approach generally applied in practice that market performance conditions and non-vesting conditions should be taken into account in measuring the fair value of the cash-settled share-based payment. There will be no ultimate cost for an award subject to a market condition or non-vesting condition that is not satisfied as any liability would be reversed.

Chapter 23

This differs from the accounting model for equity-settled transactions with market conditions or non-vesting conditions, which can result in a cost being recognised for awards subject to a market or non-vesting condition that is not satisfied (see 7.3 and 7.4 above).

In our view, entities applying FRS 102 should also take market performance conditions and non-vesting conditions into account in measuring the fair value of a cash-settled share-based payment.

10.3.2.E   *Modification, cancellation and settlement*

FRS 102 provides no specific guidance on modification, cancellation and settlement of cash-settled awards. However, as cash-settled awards are accounted for using a full fair value model no such guidance is needed. It is clear that:

- where an award is modified, the liability recognised at and after the point of modification will be based on its new fair value, with the effect of any movement in the liability recognised immediately;

- where an award is cancelled the liability will be derecognised, with a credit immediately recognised in profit or loss; and

- where an award is settled, the liability will be derecognised, and any gain or loss on settlement immediately recognised in profit or loss.

10.4   Modification of award from equity-settled to cash-settled or from cash-settled to equity-settled

As noted at 8.3.5 above, a detailed discussion of this topic is beyond the scope of this publication but is addressed more fully in EY International GAAP 2019.

11   TRANSACTIONS WITH EQUITY AND CASH ALTERNATIVES

Some share-based payment transactions (particularly those with employees) provide either the entity or the counterparty with the choice of settling the transaction either in shares (or other equity instruments) or in cash (or other assets). *[FRS 102.26.15]*.

More detailed guidance is provided as to how that general principle should be applied to transactions:

- where the entity has choice of settlement (see 11.1 below); and
- where the counterparty has choice of settlement (see 11.2 below).

A common type of arrangement seen in practice is the 'matching' award or deferred bonus arrangement where an employee is offered a share award or a cash alternative to 'match' a share award or a cash bonus earned during an initial period. This type of arrangement is discussed further at 16.1 below.

Some share-based payment transactions rather than providing either the entity or the counterparty with a choice between settlement in equity or in cash, offer no choice but instead require an arrangement that will generally be equity-settled to be settled in cash in certain specific and limited circumstances (awards with contingent cash settlement). There will also be situations where there is contingent settlement in equity of an award that is otherwise cash-settled. These types of arrangement are considered in more detail at 11.3 below.

Some awards offer an equity alternative and a cash alternative where the cash alternative is not based on the price or value of the equity instruments. These arrangements are considered at 11.4 below.

11.1 Transactions where the entity has choice of settlement in equity or in cash

Section 26 requires that an entity with a choice of settling a transaction in cash (or other assets) or by transferring equity instruments, should account for the transaction as a wholly equity-settled share-based payment transaction (in accordance with paragraphs 7 to 13 of Section 26) unless:

(a) the choice of settlement in equity instruments has no commercial substance (e.g. because the entity is legally prohibited from issuing shares); or

(b) the entity has a past practice or a stated policy of settling in cash, or generally settles in cash whenever the counterparty asks for cash settlement.

If (a) or (b) applies, the transaction should be accounted for as wholly cash-settled in accordance with paragraph 14 of Section 26. *[FRS 102.26.15A].*

An important practical effect of the above criteria is that some schemes that may appear at first sight to be equity-settled may in fact have to be treated as cash-settled. For example, if an entity has consistently adopted a policy of granting *ex gratia* cash compensation to all those deemed to be 'good' leavers (or all 'good' leavers of certain seniority) in respect of partially vested share options, such a scheme may well be treated as cash-settled for the purposes of FRS 102 to the extent to which there are expected to be such 'good' leavers during the vesting period. 'Good leaver' arrangements are also discussed at 6.3.8 above.

11.1.1 Accounting at date of settlement for awards where there is a choice of equity- or cash-settlement

FRS 102 contains no guidance about how to account as at the date of settlement for an award that has been accounted for as cash-settled but which is settled in equity, or *vice versa*. We suggest the following approach based on the requirements of IFRS 2 or practice that has evolved in the application of that standard.

11.1.1.A Settlement of an award treated as cash-settled during vesting period

IFRS 2 gives no specific guidance as to the accounting treatment on settlement where an entity has accounted for an award as cash-settled but it is settled in equity. However, it is clear from other provisions of IFRS 2, including the general rules on settlement and the provisions relating to settlement of an award where the counterparty has the choice of settlement method, that:

- the liability should be remeasured to fair value through the income statement at settlement date;
- if cash settlement occurs, the cash paid is applied to reduce the liability; and
- if equity settlement occurs, the liability is transferred into equity.

11.1.1.B   Settlement of an award treated as equity-settled during vesting period

When a transaction that has been accounted for as equity-settled is settled, IFRS 2 specifies the following approach:

(a)   subject to (b) below:

   (i)   if the transaction is cash-settled, the cash is accounted for as a deduction from equity; or

   (ii) if the transaction is equity-settled, there is a transfer from one component of equity to another (if necessary); and

(b)   if the entity chooses the settlement alternative with the higher fair value, as at the date of settlement, the entity recognises an additional expense for the excess value given. *[IFRS 2.43]*.

This is illustrated in Examples 23.34 and 23.35 below.

Example 23.34:   Settlement of transaction treated as equity-settled where fair value of cash settlement exceeds fair value of equity settlement

An entity has accounted for a share-based payment transaction where there is a choice of settlement as an equity-settled transaction, and has recognised a cumulative expense of £1,000 based on the fair value at grant date.

At settlement date the fair value of the equity-settlement option is £1,700 and that of the cash-settlement option £2,000. If the entity settles in equity, no further accounting entry is required by IFRS 2. However, there may be a transfer within equity of the £1,000 credited to equity during the vesting period.

If the entity settles in cash, the entity must recognise an additional expense of £300, being the difference between the fair value of the equity-settlement option (£1,700) and that of the cash-settlement option (£2,000). The accounting entry is:

	£	£
Profit or loss (employee costs)	300	
Equity	1,700	
Cash		2,000

Example 23.35:   Settlement of transaction treated as equity-settled where fair value of equity settlement exceeds fair value of cash settlement

As in Example 23.34, an entity has accounted for a share-based payment transaction where there is a choice of settlement as an equity-settled transaction, and has recognised a cumulative expense of £1,000 based on the fair value at grant date.

In this case, however, at settlement date the fair value of the equity-settlement option is £2,000 and that of the cash-settlement option £1,700. If the transaction is settled in equity, the entity must recognise an additional expense of £300, being the difference between fair value of the equity-settlement option (£2,000) and that of the cash-settlement option (£1,700). The accounting entry is:

	£	£
Profit or loss (employee costs)	300	
Equity		300

No further accounting entry is required by IFRS 2. However, there may be a transfer within equity of the £1,300 credited during the vesting period and on settlement.

If the entity settles in cash, no extra expense is recognised, and the accounting entry is:

	£	£
Equity	1,700	
Cash		1,700

It can be seen in this case that, if the transaction is settled in equity, an additional expense is recognised. If, however, the transaction had simply been an equity-settled transaction (i.e. with no cash alternative), there would have been no additional expense on settlement and the cumulative expense would have been only £1,000 based on the fair value at grant date.

As FRS 102 does not specify the accounting for a settlement – either generally (see 8.4 above) or where there is a settlement choice – it is debatable whether the recognition of an additional expense on remeasurement is required, or whether any difference could be accounted for in equity as would be the case with the repurchase of equity instruments outside a share-based payment transaction. However, in our view, it is appropriate to adopt an approach consistent with that of IFRS 2 given the extent to which the requirements of Section 26 generally, including those relating to modification and cancellation, are derived from those of IFRS 2.

11.1.2 Change in classification of award after grant date

Neither FRS 102 nor IFRS 2 specifies whether a transaction where the entity has a choice of settlement in equity or cash should be assessed as equity-settled or cash-settled only at the inception of the transaction or whether this should also be assessed at each reporting date until the transaction is settled.

FRS 102 states that a transaction should be treated as equity-settled unless either criterion (a) or criterion (b) in paragraph 15A of Section 26 applies (see 11.1 above). As it is not specified that this assessment takes place only at inception of the award, in our view FRS 102 requires an ongoing assessment of the relevance of these criteria.

FRS 102 does not specify how to account for a change in classification resulting from a change in the entity's policy or intention. In our view, the most appropriate treatment is to account for such a change as if it were a modification of the manner of settlement of the award (see 10.4 above). Where the entity is able to choose the manner of settlement, the substance of the situation is the same as a decision to modify the manner of settlement of an award which does not already give the entity a choice. These situations are distinct from those where the manner of settlement depends on the outcome of a contingent event outside the entity's control (see 11.3 below).

11.1.3 Economic compulsion for cash settlement (including unlisted entity awards with a presumption of cash settlement)

Some awards may nominally give the reporting entity the choice of settling in cash or equity, while in practice giving rise to an economic compulsion to settle only in cash. In addition to the examples mentioned at 11.1 above, this will often be the case where an entity that is a subsidiary or owned by a small number of individuals, such as members of the same family, grants options to employees. In such cases there will normally be a very strong presumption that the entity will settle in cash in order to avoid diluting the existing owners' interests. Similarly, where the entity is not listed, there is little real benefit for an employee in receiving a share that cannot be realised except when another shareholder wishes to buy it or there is a change in ownership of the business as a whole.

In our view, such schemes are generally most appropriately accounted for as cash-settled schemes from inception. In any event, once the scheme has been operating for a while, it

Chapter 23

is likely that there will be a past practice of cash settlement such that the scheme is required to be treated as a liability under the general provisions of FRS 102 summarised above.

A similar conclusion is often reached even where the terms of the agreement do not appear to offer the entity a choice of settling the award in cash but it has established a constructive obligation or a past practice of so doing (see 10.2 above).

11.2   Transactions where the counterparty has choice of settlement in equity or in cash

Where the counterparty has a choice of settlement in either equity instruments or cash, it will generally be the case that the arrangement will be accounted for as a cash-settled share-based payment transaction (see 10 above).

Section 26 requires an entity to account for a transaction where the counterparty has a choice of settlement in cash (or other assets) or in equity instruments as a wholly cash-settled share-based payment transaction (in accordance with paragraph 14), except for when the conditions set out in paragraph 15C of Section 26 are met. *[FRS 102.26.15B]*. If the choice of settlement in cash (or other assets) has no commercial substance because the cash settlement amount (or value of the other assets) bears no relationship to, and is likely to be lower in value than, the fair value of the equity instruments, the entity should account for the transaction as wholly equity-settled in accordance with paragraphs 7 to 13 of Section 26. *[FRS 102.26.15C]*.

In cases where the fair values of the cash and equity alternatives are similar, the approach required by FRS 102 is broadly consistent with the outcome of the approach required by IFRS 2. IFRS 2 requires a split accounting approach, between liabilities and equity, which mainly has an impact where the fair value of the equity alternative exceeds that of the cash alternative.

FRS 102 has no specific guidance for situations where there is a change of settlement method. The discussions at 11.1.1 and 11.1.2 above may also provide some guidance for transactions where the counterparty has choice of settlement.

11.2.1   *Transactions with settlement alternatives of different value*

In many share-based payment transactions with a choice of settlement, the value of the share and cash alternatives is equal. The counterparty will have the choice between (say) 1,000 shares or the cash value of 1,000 shares. Under FRS 102, this transaction would be accounted for as a cash-settled transaction.

However, it is not uncommon, particularly in transactions with employees, for the equity-settlement alternative to have more value. For example, an employee might be able to choose at vesting between the cash value of 1,000 shares immediately or 2,000 shares (often subject to further conditions such as a minimum holding period, or a further service period). In such a situation, it will need to be decided whether the arrangement falls within paragraph 15C of Section 26 (see 11.2 above) leading to the entire arrangement being accounted for as an equity-settled transaction.

11.2.2   *'Backstop' cash settlement rights*

Some schemes may provide cash settlement rights to the holder so as to cover more or less remote contingencies.

If the terms of the award provide the employee with a general right of cash-settlement, FRS 102 requires the award to be treated as cash-settled. This is the case even if the right of cash settlement is extremely unlikely to be exercised (e.g. because it would give rise to adverse tax consequences for the employee as compared with equity settlement). If, however, the right to cash-settlement is exercisable only in specific circumstances, a more detailed analysis may be required (see 11.3 below).

11.3 Awards requiring cash or equity settlement in specific circumstances (awards with contingent cash or contingent equity settlement)

This section is written with a focus on awards with contingent cash settlement. However, similar considerations will apply in a situation where it is the settlement in equity that depends on the outcome of circumstances outside the control of the entity or both the entity and the counterparty.

Rather than giving either the entity or the counterparty a general right to choose between settlement in equity or in cash, some awards require cash settlement in certain specific and limited circumstances, but otherwise will be equity-settled. These arrangements are sometimes referred to as contingent settlement provisions and are driven by the occurrence or non-occurrence of specific outcomes rather than by choice. Questions arise as to whether such an award should be accounted for as equity-settled or cash-settled and whether this should be re-assessed on an ongoing basis during the vesting period.

Neither FRS 102 nor IFRS 2 has specific guidance on the accounting treatment of such arrangements. In advising on the July 2015 amendments to FRS 102, the Accounting Council noted that respondents to the draft amendments to Section 26 pointed out that this is a subject that has recently been discussed in the context of IFRS 2 although no changes have yet been made, or indeed proposed, to the published guidance. The Accounting Council therefore advised that the need for further amendment for situations where settlement in cash depends on the occurrence of an event outside the control of either party to a transaction should be re-considered as part of the next review of FRS 102.[2] No further amendments were proposed as part of the Triennial review 2017, most likely as a result of no current amendments being proposed to IFRS 2 by the IASB.

In the absence of specific guidance, we consider some possible accounting analyses at 11.3.1 to 11.3.3 below.

11.3.1 Approach 1 – Treat as cash-settled if contingency is outside entity's control

One approach might be to observe that the underlying principle that determines whether an award is accounted for as equity-settled or cash-settled appears to be whether the reporting entity can unilaterally avoid cash-settlement (see 11.1 and 11.2 above). Under this approach, any award where the counterparty has a right to cash-settlement is always treated as a liability, irrespective of the probability of cash-settlement, unless there is no commercial substance. By contrast, an award where the choice of settlement rests with the entity is accounted for as a liability only where the entity's own actions have effectively put it in a position where it has no real choice but to settle in cash.

Applying this approach, it is first of all necessary to consider whether the event that requires cash-settlement is one over which the entity has control. If the event, however unlikely, is outside the entity's control, then under this approach the award should be treated as cash-settled. However, if the event is within the entity's control, the award should be treated as cash-settled only if the entity has a liability by reference to the criteria summarised in 11.1 above.

Whilst, in our view, this is an acceptable accounting approach, it does not seem entirely satisfactory. For example, it is common for an equity-settled share-based payment award to contain a provision to the effect that, if the employee dies in service, the entity will pay to the employee's estate the fair value of the award in cash. The approach above would lead to the conclusion that the award must be classified as cash-settled, on the basis that it is beyond the entity's control whether or not an employee dies in service. This seems a somewhat far-fetched conclusion, and is moreover inconsistent with the accounting treatment that the entity would apply to any other death-in-service benefit.

11.3.2   *Approach 2 – Treat as cash-settled if contingency is outside entity's control and probable*

Under US GAAP,[3] a cash settlement feature that can be exercised only upon the occurrence of a contingent event that is outside the employee's control (such as an initial public offering) does not give rise to a liability until it becomes probable that that event will occur.

In our view, this approach based on the probability of a contingent event that is outside the control of both the counterparty and the entity is also acceptable in the absence of specific guidance in FRS 102 (and IFRS 2) and has frequently been used in practice by entities applying IFRS 2.

The impact of Approach 1 and Approach 2 can be illustrated by reference to an award that requires cash-settlement in the event of a change of control of the entity (see 11.3.3 below).

11.3.3   *Application of Approach 1 and Approach 2 to awards requiring cash settlement on a change of control*

It is not uncommon for the terms of an award to provide for compulsory cash-settlement by the entity if there is a change of control of the reporting entity. Such a provision ensures that there is no need for any separate negotiations to buy out all employee options, so as to avoid non-controlling (minority) interests arising in the acquired entity when equity-settled awards are settled after the change of control.

The determination of whether or not a change of control is within the control of the entity is beyond the scope of this publication.

If the facts and circumstances of a particular case indicate that a change of control is within the entity's control, the conclusion under either Approach 1 or Approach 2 above would be that the award should be treated as cash-settled only if the entity has a liability by reference to the criteria summarised at 11.1 above.

If, however, the change of control is not considered to be within the control of the reporting entity, the conclusion will vary depending on whether Approach 1 or Approach 2 is followed. Under Approach 1, an award requiring settlement in cash on a change of control outside the control of the entity would be treated as cash-settled, however unlikely the change of control may be. Under Approach 2 however, an award requiring settlement in cash on a change of control outside the control of the entity would be treated as cash-settled only if a change of control were probable.

A difficulty with Approach 2 is that it introduces rather bizarre inconsistencies in the accounting treatment for awards when the relative probability of their outcome is considered. As noted at 11.2.2 above, an award that gives the counterparty an absolute right to cash-settlement is accounted for as a liability, however unlikely it is that the counterparty will exercise that right (unless the cash settlement option is considered to have no commercial substance). Thus, under this approach, the entity could find itself in the situation where it treats:

- as a liability: an award with a unrestricted right to cash-settlement for the counterparty, where the probability of the counterparty exercising that right is less than 1%; but
- as equity: an award that requires cash settlement in the event of a change of control which is assessed as having a 49% probability of occurring.

In our view, an entity may adopt either of these accounting treatments, but should do so consistently and state its policy for accounting for such transactions if material.

It should be noted in the selection of an accounting policy that the IASB had discussions – but did not conclude – on whether an approach based on the 'probable' outcome, as set out here, should be applied under IFRS 2 or whether an approach based on the accounting treatment for a compound financial instrument should be used. Any further developments in this area could affect the availability of the alternative treatments in future. The detailed discussions are beyond the scope of this publication but are addressed in EY International GAAP 2019.

There is further discussion at 16.4 below of awards that vest or are exercisable on a flotation or change of control, including the question of whether a cash-settlement obligation rests with the entity itself or with other parties involved in the change of control (see 16.4.6 below).

11.3.4 Accounting for change in manner of settlement where award is contingent on future events outside the control of the entity and the counterparty

When, under Approach 2 above, the manner of settlement of an award changes solely as a consequence of a re-assessment of the probability of a contingent event, there is neither settlement of the award nor modification of its original terms. The terms of the award are such that there have been two potential outcomes, one equity-settled and one cash-settled, running in parallel since grant date. It is as if, in effect, the entity has simultaneously issued two awards, only one of which will vest.

At each reporting date the entity should assess which outcome is more likely and account for the award on an equity- or cash-settled basis accordingly. In our view, any adjustments arising from a switch between the cumulative amount for the cash-settled award and the cumulative amount for the equity-settled award should be taken to profit or loss in the current period. This is similar to the approach for an award with multiple independent vesting conditions (see 7.3.6 above).

When applying an approach where the two outcomes have both been part of the arrangement from grant date, an entity measures the fair value of the equity-settled award only at the original grant date and there is no remeasurement of the equity-settled award on reassessment of the settlement method. As the cash-settled award would be remeasured on an ongoing basis, a switch in the manner of settlement during the period until the shares vest or the award is settled in cash could give rise to significant volatility in the cumulative expense. At the date of vesting or settlement, however, the cumulative expense will equate to either the grant date fair value of the equity-settled approach or the settlement value of the cash-settled approach depending on whether or not the contingent event has happened.

The situation discussed in this section (i.e. an arrangement with two potential outcomes from grant date because the manner of settlement is not within the control of either the entity or the counterparty) is not the same as an award where the manner of settlement is entirely within the entity's control. Where the entity has such control and therefore a choice of settlement, a change in the manner of settlement is treated as a modification with a potential catch-up adjustment through equity (see 10.4 above).

11.4 Cash settlement alternative where the cash sum is not based on share price or value

Some awards may provide a cash-settlement alternative that is not based on the share price. For example, an employee might be offered a choice between 500 shares or £1,000,000 on the vesting of an award. Whilst an award of £1,000,000, if considered in isolation, would obviously not be a share-based payment transaction, in our view it falls within the scope of Section 26 if it is offered as an alternative to a transaction that is within the scope of that Section. FRS 102 has no specific guidance in this area but we draw on the Basis for Conclusions to IFRS 2 which states that the cash alternative may be fixed or variable and, if variable, may be determinable in a manner that is related, or unrelated, to the price of the entity's shares. *[IFRS 2.BC256].*

Under the requirements of paragraphs 15B and 15C of Section 26, the award will be treated as cash-settled unless the option arrangements do not have commercial substance (see 11.2 above).

12 REPLACEMENT SHARE-BASED PAYMENT AWARDS ISSUED IN A BUSINESS COMBINATION

12.1 Background

It is relatively common for an entity (A) to acquire another (B) which, at the time of the business combination, has outstanding employee share options or other share-based awards. If no action were taken by A, employees of B would be entitled, once any vesting conditions had been satisfied, to shares in B. This is not a very satisfactory outcome for either party: A now has non-controlling (minority) shareholders in subsidiary B, which was previously wholly-owned, and the employees of B are the owners of unmarketable shares in an effectively wholly-owned subsidiary.

The obvious solution, adopted in the majority of cases, is for some mechanism to be put in place such that the employees of B end up holding shares in the new parent A. This can be achieved, for example, by:

- A granting options over its own shares to the employees of B in exchange for the surrender of the employees' options over the shares of B; or

- changing the terms of the options so that they are over a special class of shares in B which are mandatorily convertible into shares of A.

FRS 102 contains no guidance about how such a substitution transaction should be accounted for in the consolidated financial statements of A and this area is considered to be beyond the scope of this publication. Under IFRS, the relevant guidance is included in IFRS 3 and the requirements, which are based on accounting for the modification of share-based payments, are addressed in EY International GAAP 2019.

The treatment in the single entity financial statements of B is discussed at 12.2 below.

12.2 Financial statements of the acquired entity

The replacement of an award based on the acquiree's equity with one based on the acquirer's equity appears, from the perspective of the acquired entity, to be a cancellation and replacement. In our view, this should to be accounted for in accordance with the general principles for such transactions (see 8.4 above) but taking into account the specific provisions of Section 26 in respect of group share schemes (see 13 below). Therefore, in addition to considerations about whether this is accounted for as a separate cancellation and new grant or as a modification of the original terms, the acquiree needs to take into account its new status as a subsidiary of the acquirer. If the acquiree's employees are now receiving awards granted by the new parent, the new subsidiary might choose to apply the provisions for groups in paragraph 16 of Section 26 (see 13.2.3.A below) rather than the general approach for an entity receiving goods or services but not obliged to settle the award.

13 GROUP SHARE SCHEMES

In this section we consider various aspects of share-based payment arrangements operated within a group of companies and involving several legal entities. The main areas covered are as follows:

- typical features of a group share scheme (see 13.1 below);

- a summary of the accounting treatment of group share schemes (see 13.2 below);

- EBTs and similar arrangements (see 13.3 below);

- an example of a group share scheme (based on an equity-settled award satisfied by a purchase of shares) illustrating the accounting by the different entities involved (see 13.4 below);

- an example of a group share scheme (based on an equity-settled award satisfied by a fresh issue of shares) illustrating the accounting by the different entities involved (see 13.5 below);

- an example of a group cash-settled transaction where the award is settled by an entity other than the one receiving goods or services (see 13.6 below); and

- the accounting treatment when an employee transfers between group entities (see 13.7 below).

Chapter 23

Associates and joint arrangements do not meet the definition of group entities but there will sometimes be share-based payment arrangements that involve the investor or venturer and the employees of its associate or joint venture. Such arrangements are beyond the scope of this publication but are addressed in EY International GAAP 2019.

13.1   Typical features of a group share scheme

In this section we use the term 'share scheme' to encompass any transaction falling within the scope of Section 26, whether accounted for as equity-settled or cash-settled.

It is common practice for a group to operate a single share scheme covering the employees of the parent and/or several subsidiaries but the precise terms and structures of group share schemes are so varied that it is rare to find two completely identical arrangements. From an accounting perspective, however, group share schemes can generally be reduced to a basic prototype, as described below, which will serve as the basis of the following discussion.

A group scheme typically involves transactions by several legal entities:

- the parent, over whose shares awards are granted and which is often responsible for settling the award (either directly or through a trust);
- the subsidiary employing an employee who has been granted an award ('the employing subsidiary'); and
- in some cases, an employee benefit trust ('EBT') that administers the scheme. The accounting treatment of transactions with EBTs is discussed at 13.3 below.

In practice, it might not always be a simple assessment to determine which entity is receiving an employee's services and which entity is responsible for settling the award. For example, the scheme may be directed by a group employee services entity or an individual might be a director of the parent as well as providing services to other operating entities within the group.

Where an employee services company is involved it will be necessary to evaluate the precise group arrangements in order to decide whether the entity is, in substance, the employer. It will often be the case that the services company is simply administering the arrangements on behalf of the parent entity.

A share-based award is often granted to an employee by the parent, or a group employee services entity, which will in turn have an option exercisable against the EBT for the shares that it may be required to deliver to the employee. Less commonly, the trustees of the EBT make awards to the employees and enter into reciprocal arrangements with the parent.

If the parent takes the view that it will satisfy any awards using existing shares it will often seek to fix the cash cost of the award by arranging for the EBT to purchase, on the day that the award is made, sufficient shares from existing shareholders to satisfy all or part of the award. This will be funded by external borrowings, a loan from the parent, a contribution from the employing subsidiary, or some combination. The cash received from the employee on exercise of the option can be used by the EBT to repay any borrowings.

If the parent takes the view that it will satisfy the options with a fresh issue of shares, these will be issued to the EBT, either:

(a) at the date on which the employee exercises his option (in which case the EBT will subscribe for the new shares using the cash received from the employee together with any non-refundable contribution made by the employing subsidiary – see below). Such arrangements are generally referred to as 'simultaneous funding';

(b) at some earlier date (in which case the EBT will subscribe for the new shares using external borrowings, a loan from the parent or a contribution from the employing subsidiary, or some combination. The cash received from the employee on exercise of the option may then be used by the EBT to repay any borrowings). Such arrangements are generally referred to as 'pre-funding'; or

(c) some shares will be issued before the exercise date as in (b) above, and the balance on the exercise date as in (a) above.

As noted in (a) above, the employing subsidiary often makes a non-refundable contribution to the EBT in connection with the scheme, so as to ensure that employing subsidiaries bear an appropriate share of the overall cost of a group-wide share scheme.

13.2 Accounting treatment of group share schemes – summary

13.2.1 Background

From a financial reporting perspective, it is generally necessary to consider the accounting treatment in:

- the group's consolidated financial statements;
- the parent's separate financial statements; and
- the employing subsidiary's financial statements.

We make the assumption throughout this section on group share schemes that the subsidiary is directly owned by the parent company. In practice, there will often be one or more intermediate holding companies between the ultimate parent and the subsidiary. The intermediate parent company generally will not be the entity granting the award, receiving the goods or services or responsible for settling the award. Therefore, under Section 26, we believe that there is no requirement for the intermediate company to account for the award in its separate financial statements.

The accounting entries to be made in the various financial statements will broadly vary according to:

- whether the award is satisfied using shares already held or a fresh issue of shares;
- whether any charge is made to the employing subsidiary for the cost of awards to its employees;
- whether an EBT is involved. The accounting treatment of transactions undertaken with and by EBTs is discussed in more detail at 13.3 below; and
- the tax consequences of the award. For the purposes of the discussion and illustrative examples below, tax effects are ignored. A more general discussion of the tax effects of share-based payment transactions may be found at 15 below.

The sections below largely discuss the application of the basic requirements of Section 26 to share-based payment transactions within a group of entities. However, in addition to the application of those requirements, Section 26 allows an alternative treatment based on the allocation of a group share-based payment expense to group entities on a reasonable basis (see 13.2.3.A below).

13.2.2   Scope of Section 26 for group share schemes

By virtue of the definition of a 'share-based payment transaction' (see 3.1 and 3.2.1 above), a group share-based payment transaction is in the scope of Section 26 for:

- the consolidated financial statements of the group (the accounting for which follows the general principles set out in 4 to 11 above);

- the separate or individual financial statements of the entity in the group that receives goods or services (see 13.2.3 below); and

- the separate or individual financial statements of the entity in the group (if different from that receiving the goods or services) that settles the transaction with the counterparty. This entity will typically, but not necessarily, be the parent (see 13.2.4 below).

As discussed at 3 above, the scope paragraphs of Section 26, together with the definitions in Appendix I to FRS 102, indicate whether transactions are to be accounted for as equity-settled or as cash-settled in most group situations including:

- transactions settled in the equity of the entity, or in the equity of its parent (see 13.2.5 below); and

- cash-settled transactions settled by a group entity other than the entity receiving the goods or services (see 13.2.6 below).

At 3.2.1.A above, we consider seven scenarios commonly found in practice and outline the approach required by Section 26 in the consolidated and separate or individual financial statements of group entities depending on whether the award is settled in cash or shares and which entity grants the award, has the obligation to settle the award and receives the goods or services. These scenarios do not reflect the alternative treatment for group plans in Section 26 (see 13.2.3.A below).

It is common practice in a group share scheme to require each participating entity in the group to pay a charge, either to the parent or to an EBT, in respect of the cost of awards made under the scheme to employees of that entity. This is generally done either as part of the group's cash-management strategy, or in order to obtain tax relief under applicable local legislation. The amount charged could in principle be at the discretion of the group, but is often based on either the fair value of the award at grant date or the fair value at vesting, in the case of an award of free shares, or exercise, in the case of an award of options.

Neither FRS 102 nor IFRS 2 directly addresses the accounting treatment of such intragroup management charges and other recharge arrangements, which is discussed further at 13.2.7 below. *[IFRS 2 Appendix B.46]*.

Worked examples illustrating how these various principles translate into accounting entries are given at 13.4 to 13.6 below.

13.2.3   Entity receiving goods or services

The entity in a group receiving goods or services in a share-based payment transaction determines whether the transaction should be accounted for as equity-settled or cash settled in its separate or individual financial statements. It does this by assessing the nature of the awards granted and its own rights and obligations.

The entity accounts for the transaction as equity-settled when either the awards granted are the entity's own equity instruments, or the entity has no obligation to settle the share-based payment transaction. Otherwise, the entity accounts for the transaction as cash-settled. Where the transaction is accounted for as equity-settled it is remeasured after grant date only to the extent permitted or required by Section 26 for equity-settled transactions generally, as discussed at 4 to 7 above.

A possible consequence of these requirements is that the amount recognised by the entity may differ from the amount recognised by the consolidated group or by another group entity settling the share-based payment transaction. This is discussed further at 13.6 below.

The cost recognised by the entity receiving goods or services is calculated according to the principles set out above unless the group applies the alternative treatment for group plans in Section 26 (see 13.2.3.A below). The cost under Section 26 is not adjusted for any intragroup recharging arrangements, the accounting for which is discussed at 13.2.7 below.

13.2.3.A   Alternative treatment for group plans

As an alternative to the accounting treatment in paragraphs 3 to 15C of Section 26 (discussed in sections 4 to 11 and 13 of this chapter), in a share-based payment arrangement granted by an entity to the employees of one or more group entities, those group entities are permitted to measure the share-based payment expense on the basis of a reasonable allocation of the group expense. *[FRS 102.26.16]*.

Prior to the Triennial review 2017 it was not clear in Section 26 whether this alternative treatment is intended only to apply in situations where the group expense is calculated on a basis consistent with the requirements of FRS 102. However, the Triennial review 2017 clarified that the alternative treatment is permitted where the group expense is calculated in accordance with FRS 102, IFRS 2 or on an equivalent basis. *[FRS 102.26.16]*.

13.2.4   Entity settling the transaction

As noted at 3.2.1 above, Section 26 was clarified in the Triennial review 2017 by specifying the accounting treatment when the entity settling the transaction does not receive the goods or services. An entity settling a share-based payment transaction when another entity in the group receives the goods or services should recognise the transaction as an equity-settled share-based payment transaction only if it is settled in its own equity instruments, otherwise, the transaction is recognised as a cash-settled share-based payment transaction. *[FRS 102.26.2A]*.

The above requirements relate only to the credit entry – the classification of the transaction as equity- or cash-settled, and its measurement. They do not specify the debit entry, which is therefore subject to the general requirement of IFRS 2 (and Section 26) that a share-based payment transaction should normally be treated as an expense, unless there is the basis for another treatment (see 4 above).

In our view, the settling entity is not always required to treat the transaction as an expense. Instead:

- Where the settling entity is a parent (direct or indirect) of the entity receiving the goods or services and is accounting for the transaction as equity-settled, it will generally account for the settlement of the award as an addition to the cost of its investment in the employing subsidiary (or of that holding company of the employing subsidiary which is the settling entity's directly-held subsidiary). It may then be necessary to review the carrying value of that investment to ensure that it is not impaired.

- Where the settling entity is a parent (direct or indirect) of the entity receiving the goods or services and is accounting for the transaction as cash-settled (whereas the subsidiary will be accounting for the transaction as equity-settled), in our view it has an accounting policy choice for the treatment of the remeasurement of the cash-settled liability. Either:

  - it accounts for the entire award as part of the contribution to the subsidiary and therefore as an addition to the cost of its investment in the employing subsidiary (or of that holding company of the employing subsidiary which is the settling entity's directly-held subsidiary); or

  - after the initial capitalisation of the grant date fair value of the liability, it remeasures the liability through profit or loss.

  Whichever policy is chosen, it may then be necessary to review the carrying value of the investment to ensure that it is not impaired.

- In other cases (i.e. where the settling entity is a subsidiary (direct or indirect) or fellow subsidiary of the entity receiving the goods or services), it should treat the settlement as a distribution, and charge it directly to equity. Whether or not such a settlement is a legal distribution is a matter of law.

We adopt the approach of full capitalisation by the parent entity in the worked examples set out at 13.4 to 13.6 below.

13.2.5   Transactions settled in equity of the entity or its parent

13.2.5.A   Awards settled in equity of subsidiary

Where a subsidiary grants an award to its employees and settles it in its own equity, the subsidiary accounts for the award as equity-settled. *[FRS 102.26.1, FRS 102 Appendix I]*.

The parent accounts for the award as equity-settled in its consolidated financial statements. In its separate financial statements, the parent does not account for the award under FRS 102 because the Parent receives no goods or services, nor does it settle the transaction (see 3.2.1 above). In both cases, the transaction may have implications for other aspects of the financial statements, since its settlement results in the partial disposal of the subsidiary.

Where the parent is responsible for settling the award, it accounts for the transaction as equity-settled in its consolidated financial statements. In its separate financial statements, however, it accounts for the award as cash-settled, since it is settled not in its own equity, but in the equity of the subsidiary (see 3.2.1 and 13.2.4 above). From the perspective of the parent's separate financial statements, the equity of a subsidiary is a financial asset.

13.2.5.B   *Awards settled in equity of the parent*

Where the parent grants an award directly to the employees of a subsidiary and settles it in its own equity, the subsidiary accounts for the award as equity-settled, with a corresponding increase in equity as a contribution from the parent. *[FRS 102.26.1, 1A].*

The parent accounts for the award as equity-settled in both its consolidated and separate financial statements (see 3.2.1 above). *FRS 102.26.2A]*

Where a subsidiary grants an award of equity in its parent to its employees and settles the award itself, it accounts for the award as cash-settled, since it is settled not in its own equity, but in the equity of its parent. From the perspective of the subsidiary's separate or individual financial statements, the equity of the parent is a financial asset. *[FRS 102.26.1].*

This requirement potentially represents something of a compliance burden. For the purposes of the parent's consolidated financial statements the fair value of the award needs to be calculated once, at grant date. For the purposes of the subsidiary's financial statements, however, the basic requirements of Section 26 require the award to be accounted for as cash-settled, with the fair value recalculated at each reporting date. In some cases, the rather unclear wording of paragraph 16 of Section 26 might mean that the arrangements are considered to meet the criteria for the alternative accounting treatment for group schemes. If this were the case, the subsidiary could, in effect, account on an equity-settled basis until the point of settlement (see 13.2.3.A above).

However this approach, which results in equity-settled accounting in the consolidated financial statements and cash-settled accounting in the subsidiary financial statements, applies only when a subsidiary 'grants', and is therefore obliged to settle, such an award. In some jurisdictions, including the UK, it is normal for grants of share awards to be made by the parent, or an employee service company or EBT, rather than by the subsidiary, although the subsidiary may well make recommendations to the grantor of the award as to which of its employees should benefit.

In those cases, the fact that the subsidiary may communicate the award to the employee does not necessarily mean that the subsidiary itself has granted the award. It may simply be notifying the employee of an award granted by another group entity and which the other group company has the obligation to settle. In that case the subsidiary should apply the normal requirement of Section 26 to account for the award as equity-settled.

13.2.6   *Cash-settled transactions not settled by the entity receiving goods or services*

The scope section of Section 26 (see 3 above) considers arrangements in which the parent has an obligation to make cash payments to the employees of a subsidiary linked to the price of either:

- the subsidiary's equity instruments, or
- the parent's equity instruments.

In both cases, the subsidiary has no obligation to settle the transaction. Therefore, unless the alternative accounting rules are applied (see below), the subsidiary accounts for the transaction as equity-settled, recognising a corresponding credit in equity as a contribution from its parent. *[FRS 102.26.1-1A].*

The subsidiary subsequently remeasures the cost of the transaction only for any changes resulting from non-market vesting conditions not being met in accordance with the normal provisions of Section 26 discussed at 4 to 7 above. Section 26 does not specifically make the point – made in IFRS 2 – that this will differ from the measurement of the transaction as cash-settled in the consolidated financial statements of the group. *[IFRS 2 Appendix B.56-57].*

The parent has an obligation to settle the transaction in cash, paragraph 2A of Section 26 requires the parent to account for the transaction as cash-settled in both its consolidated and separate financial statements as the settling entity. *[FRS 102.26.1, 2A].*

The requirement for the subsidiary to measure the transaction as equity-settled is somewhat controversial. The essential rationale for requiring the subsidiary to record the cost of a share-based payment transaction settled by its parent is to reflect that the subsidiary is effectively receiving a capital contribution from its parent.

Using the alternative accounting treatment for group plans set out in Section 26 (see 13.2.3.A above), it appears that the subsidiary in this situation could base its expense either on an equity-settled calculation or on an allocation of the group cash-settled expense.

13.2.7   Intragroup recharges and management charges

As noted at 13.2.2 above, neither FRS 102 nor IFRS 2 deals specifically with the accounting treatment of intragroup recharges and management charges that may be levied on the subsidiary that receives goods or services, the consideration for which is equity or cash of another group entity.

The accounting requirements of FRS 102 for group share schemes derive from requirements in IFRS 2 which evolved, via an Interpretation, from an exposure draft (D17) published in 2005.[4] In the absence of more specific guidance, we suggest that the treatment outlined below is applied to recharge arrangements in place between entities applying FRS 102. For entities applying the Companies Act 2006, the accounting treatment under D17 is also addressed in Section 7 of TECH 02/17BL. *[TECH 02/17BL.7.53-56].*

D17 proposed that any such payment made by a subsidiary should be charged directly to equity, on the basis that it represents a return of the capital contribution recorded as the credit to equity required by IFRS 2 (see 13.2.3 and 13.2.6 above) up to the amount of that contribution, and a distribution thereafter.

In our view, whilst IFRS 2 and FRS 102 as currently drafted clearly do not explicitly require this treatment, this is likely to be the more appropriate analysis for most cases where the amount of the recharge or management charge to a subsidiary is directly related to the value of the share-based payment transaction. Indeed, the only alternative, 'mechanically' speaking, would be to charge the relevant amount to profit or loss. This would result in a double charge (once for the FRS 102 charge, and again for the management charge or recharge) which we consider less appropriate in cases where the amounts are directly related. Accordingly, in the examples at 13.4 to 13.6 below, we apply the treatment originally proposed in D17 to any payments made by the subsidiary for participation in the group scheme.

Many intragroup recharge arrangements are based directly on the value of the underlying share-based payment – typically at grant date, vesting date or exercise date.

In other cases, a more general management charge might be levied that reflects not just share-based payments but also a number of other arrangements or services provided to the subsidiary by the parent. Where there is a more general management charge of this kind, we believe that it is more appropriate for the subsidiary to recognise a double charge to profit or loss rather than debiting the management charge to equity as would be the case for a direct recharge.

IFRS 2 and FRS 102 also do not address how the parent should account for a recharge or management charge received. In our view, to the extent that the receipt represents a return of a capital contribution made to the subsidiary, the parent may choose whether to credit:

- the carrying amount of its investment in the subsidiary; or
- profit or loss (with a corresponding impairment review of the investment).

Even if part of the recharge received is credited to the carrying amount of the investment, any amount received in excess of the capital contribution previously debited to the investment in subsidiary should be accounted for as a distribution from the subsidiary and credited to the income statement of the parent. Where applicable, the illustrative examples at 13.4 to 13.6 below show the entire amount as a credit to the income statement of the parent rather than part of the recharge being treated as a credit to the parent's investment in its subsidiary.

A further issue that arises in practice is the timing of recognition of the recharge by the parties to the arrangement. In the absence of a contractual agreement, the treatment adopted might depend on the precise terms and whether there are contractual arrangements in place, but two approaches generally result in practice:

- to account for the recharge when it is actually levied or paid (which is consistent with accounting for a distribution); or
- to accrue the recharge over the life of the award or the recharge agreement even if, as is commonly the case, the actual recharge is only made at vesting or exercise date.

An entity should choose the more appropriate treatment for its particular circumstances. The first approach is often the more appropriate in a group context where recharge arrangements might be rather informal and therefore not binding until such time as a payment is made. It is also consistent with the overall recognition of the arrangement through equity. The second approach, which is likely to be the more appropriate approach when a liability is considered to exist in advance of the payment date, is closer in some aspects to the accounting treatment of a provision or financial liability but would reflect changes in the liability through equity rather than profit or loss and would build up the liability over the life of the award rather than recognising it in full when a present obligation has been identified.

Whichever accounting treatment is adopted, any adjustments to the amount to be recognised as a recharge, whether arising from a change in the Section 26 expense or other changes, should be recognised in the current period and previous periods should not be restated.

Where applicable, the examples at 13.4 to 13.6 below illustrate the first of the two treatments outlined above and recognise the recharge only when it becomes payable at the date of exercise.

Chapter 23

13.3   Employee benefit trusts ('EBTs') and similar arrangements

13.3.1   *Background*

For some time entities have established trusts and similar arrangements for the benefit of employees. These are known by various names but, for the sake of convenience, in this section we will use the term 'EBT' ('employee benefit trust') to cover all such vehicles by whatever name they are actually known.

The commercial purposes of using such vehicles vary from employer to employer but may include the following:

- An EBT, in order to achieve its purpose, needs to hold shares that have either been issued to it by the entity or been bought by the EBT on the open market.

- In the case of longer-term benefits the use of an EBT may 'ring fence' the assets set aside for the benefit of employees in case of the insolvency of the entity.

- The use of an EBT may be necessary in order to achieve a favourable tax treatment for the entity or the employees, or both.

The detailed features of an EBT will again vary from entity to entity but typical features often include the following:

- The EBT provides a warehouse for the shares of the sponsoring entity, for example by acquiring and holding shares that are to be sold or transferred to employees in the future. The trustees may purchase the shares with finance provided by the sponsoring entity (by way of cash contributions or loans), or by a third-party bank loan, or by a combination of the two. Loans from the entity are usually interest-free. In other cases, the EBT may subscribe directly for shares issued by the sponsoring entity or acquire shares in the market.

- Where the EBT borrows from a third party, the sponsoring entity will usually guarantee the loan, i.e. it will be responsible for any shortfall if the EBT's assets are insufficient to meet its debt repayment obligations. The entity will also generally make regular contributions to the EBT to enable the EBT to meet its interest payments, i.e. to make good any shortfall between the dividend income of the EBT (if any) and the interest payable. As part of this arrangement the trustees may waive their right to dividends on the shares held by the EBT.

- Shares held by the EBT are distributed to employees through an employee share scheme. There are many different arrangements – these may include:
  - the purchase of shares by employees when exercising their share options under a share option scheme;
  - the purchase of shares by the trustees of an approved profit-sharing scheme for allocation to employees under the rules of the scheme; or
  - the transfer of shares to employees under some other incentive scheme.

- The trustees of an EBT may have a legal duty to act at all times in accordance with the interests of the beneficiaries under the EBT. However, most EBTs (particularly those established as a means of remunerating employees) are specifically designed so as to serve the purposes of the sponsoring entity, and to ensure that there will be minimal risk of any conflict arising between the duties of the trustees and the interest of the entity.

13.3.2 Accounting for EBTs

The requirement to treat an EBT as an extension of the entity is included in Section 9 (see Chapter 8 at 4.5). *[FRS 102.9.35-37]*. This treatment has the following broad consequences for the consolidated and separate financial statements of the reporting entity:

- Until such time as the entity's own shares held by the EBT vest unconditionally in employees any consideration paid for the shares should be deducted in arriving at shareholders' equity.

- Other assets and liabilities (including borrowings) of the EBT should be recognised as assets and liabilities in the financial statements of the sponsoring entity.

- No gain or loss should be recognised in profit or loss or other comprehensive income on the purchase, sale, issue or cancellation of the entity's own shares. Consideration paid or received for the purchase or sale of the entity's own shares in an EBT should be shown separately from other purchases and sales of the entity's own shares ('true' treasury shares held by the reporting entity) in the statement of changes in equity.

- Any dividend income arising on own shares should be excluded from profit or loss and deducted from the aggregate of dividends paid. In our view, the deduction should be disclosed if material.

- Finance costs and any administration expenses should be charged as they accrue and not as funding payments are made to the EBT.

The discussion above, and in the remainder of 13 below, focuses on arrangements where the EBT holds unallocated shares of the reporting entity and/or shares that have been allocated to employees in connection with share awards but where the awards have not yet vested. There will also be situations in practice in which an EBT reaches the stage where, or is designed so that, it only holds shares to which employees have full entitlement (i.e. the shares are fully vested). In this situation the shares are beneficially owned and controlled by the individual employees but might remain in trust for tax or other reasons in the period following vesting. Where an EBT does not hold any unvested shares and there are no other assets or liabilities in the EBT over which the entity continues to exercise control, there will be nothing left in the EBT to incorporate into the entity's financial statements by extension.

13.3.3 Illustrative Examples – awards satisfied by shares purchased by, or issued to, an EBT

The following Examples show the interaction of accounting for the EBT with the requirements of Section 26. Example 23.36 illustrates the treatment where an award is satisfied using shares previously purchased by the EBT. Example 23.37 illustrates the treatment where freshly issued shares are used.

Example 23.36: Interaction of accounting for share purchase by EBT and accounting for share-based payment transactions

On 1 January in year 1, the EBT of ABC plc made a market purchase of 100,000 shares of ABC plc at £2.50 per share. These were the only ABC shares held by the EBT at that date.

On 1 May in the same year, ABC granted executives options over between 300,000 and 500,000 shares at £2.70 per share, which will vest at the end of year 1, the number vesting depending on various performance criteria. It is determined that the cost to be recognised in respect of this award under FRS 102 is £0.15 per share.

Four months later, on 1 September, the EBT made a further market purchase of 300,000 shares at £2.65 per share.

At the end of year 1, options vested over 350,000 shares and were exercised immediately.

The accounting entries for the above transactions in the consolidated financial statements of ABC would be as set out below.

	£	£
1 January		
Own shares (equity)	250,000	
Cash		250,000
To record purchase of 100,000 £1 shares at £2.50/share		
1 May – 31 December		
Profit or loss	52,500	
Equity†		52,500
To record cost of vested 350,000 options at £0.15/option		
1 September		
Own shares (equity)	795,000	
Cash		795,000
To record purchase of 300,000 £1 shares at £2.65/share		
31 December		
Cash	945,000	
Equity†1		945,000
Receipt of proceeds on exercise of 350,000 options at £2.70/share		
Equity†	914,375	
Own shares (equity)2		914,375
Release of shares from EBT to employees		

1   This reflects the fact that the entity's resources have increased as a result of a transaction with an owner, which gives rise to no gain or loss and is therefore credited direct to equity.

2   It is necessary to transfer the cost of the shares 'reissued' by the EBT out of own shares, as the deduction for own shares would otherwise be overstated. The total cost of the pool of 400,000 shares immediately before vesting was £1,045,000 (£250,000 purchased on 1 January and £795,000 purchased on 1 September), representing an average cost per share of £2.6125. £2.6125 × 350,000 shares = £914,375.

†   These amounts should all be accounted for in the profit and loss reserve or, until the awards are exercised, a separate reserve for share-based payments.

Example 23.36 illustrates the importance of keeping the accounting for the cost of the shares completely separate from that for the cost of the share-based payment award. In cash terms, ABC has made a 'profit' of £30,625, since it purchased 350,000 shares with a weighted average cost of £914,375 and issued them to the executives for £945,000. However, this 'profit' is accounted for entirely within equity, whereas a calculated expense of £52,500 is recognised in profit or loss.

Example 23.37:   *Interaction of accounting for fresh issue of shares to EBT and accounting for share-based payment transactions*

On 1 January in year 1, the EBT of ABC plc subscribed for 100,000 £1 shares of ABC plc at £2.50 per share, paid for in cash provided by ABC by way of loan to the EBT. In accordance with the Companies Act, these proceeds must be credited to the share capital account up to the par value of the shares issued, with any excess taken to a share premium account. These were the only ABC shares held by the EBT at that date.

On 1 May in the same year, ABC granted executives options over between 300,000 and 500,000 shares at an exercise price of £2.70 per share, which will vest at the end of year 1, the number vesting depending on various performance criteria. It is determined that the fair value to be recognised in respect of this award is £0.15 per share.

Four months later, on 1 September, the EBT subscribed for a further 300,000 shares at £2.65 per share, again paid for in cash provided by ABC by way of loan to the EBT.

At the end of year 1, options vested over 350,000 shares and were exercised immediately.

The accounting entries for the above transactions in the consolidated financial statements of ABC would be as set out below.

	£	£
1 January		
Equity[†1]	250,000	
Share capital		100,000
Share premium		150,000
To record issue of 100,000 £1 shares to EBT at £2.50/share		
1 May – 31 December		
Profit or loss	52,500	
Equity[†]		52,500
To record cost of vested 350,000 options at £0.15/option		
1 September		
Equity[†1]	795,000	
Share capital		300,000
Share premium		495,000
To record issue of 300,000 £1 shares at £2.65/share		
31 December		
Cash	945,000	
Equity[2†]		945,000
Receipt of proceeds on exercise of 350,000 options at £2.70/share		

1   This entry is required to reconcile the legal requirement to record an issue of shares with the fact that, in reality, there has been no increase in the resources of the reporting entity. All that has happened is that one member of the reporting group (the EBT) has transferred cash to another (the parent entity). In our view, this amount should not strictly be accounted for within any 'Own shares reserve' in equity, which should be restricted to shares acquired from third parties, although it is increasingly common in practice to see an entry in 'own shares' to reflect such a holding of shares by an EBT.

2   This reflects the fact that the entity's resources have increased as a result of a transaction with an owner, which gives rise to no gain or loss and is therefore credited direct to equity.

†   These amounts should all be accounted for in the profit and loss reserve (subject to note 1 above) or, until the awards are exercised, a separate reserve for share-based payments.

13.3.4   Financial statements of the EBT

The EBT may be required to prepare financial statements in accordance with requirements imposed by local law or by its own trust deed. The form and content of such financial statements are beyond the scope of this publication.

13.4   Illustrative example of group share scheme – equity-settled award satisfied by purchase of shares

The discussion in 13.4.1 to 13.4.3 below is based on Example 23.38 and addresses the accounting treatment for three distinct aspects of a group share scheme – a share-based payment arrangement involving group entities (see 13.2 above), the use of an EBT (see 13.3 above) and a group recharge arrangement (see 13.2.7 above).

This illustrative example treats the recharge by the parent to the subsidiary as an income statement credit in the individual accounts of the parent and recognises the recharge when it is paid. In some situations, entities might consider it appropriate to apply alternative accounting treatments (see 13.2.7 above).

Example 23.38:   *Group share scheme (purchase of shares)*

On 1 July 20x1 an employee of S Limited, a subsidiary of the H plc group, is awarded options under the H group share scheme over 3,000 shares in H plc at £1.50 each, exercisable between 1 July 20x4 and 1 July 20x7, subject to a service condition and certain performance criteria being met in the three years ending 30 June 20x4.

H plc is the grantor of the award, and has the obligation to settle it. On 1 January 20x2, in connection with the award, the H plc group EBT purchases 3,000 shares from existing shareholders at a price of £2.00 per share, funded by a loan from H plc. On exercise of the option, S Limited is required to pay the differential between the purchase price of the shares and the exercise price of the option (£0.50 per share) to the EBT.

For the purposes of FRS 102, the options are considered to have a fair value at grant date of £1 per option. Throughout the vesting period of the option, H takes the view that the award will vest in full.

The option is exercised on 1 September 20x6, at which point the EBT uses the option proceeds, together with the payment by S Limited, to repay the loan from H plc.

H plc and its subsidiaries have a 31 December year end.

13.4.1   *Consolidated financial statements*

So far as the consolidated financial statements are concerned, the transactions to be accounted for are:

- the purchase of the shares by the EBT and their eventual transfer to the employee; and
- the cost of the award.

Transactions between H plc or S Limited and the EBT are ignored since the EBT is treated as an extension of H plc (see 13.3 above). The accounting entries required are set out below. As in other examples in this chapter, an entry to equity is not allocated to a specific reserve as this will vary between entities (although the most common for an entity complying with the Companies Act 2006 will be the profit and loss reserve or a separate 'other reserve' for share-based payments).

		£	£
y/e 31.12.20x1	Profit or loss (employee costs)*	500	
	Equity		500
1.1.20x2	Own shares (equity)	6,000	
	Cash		6,000
y/e 31.12.20x2	Profit or loss (employee costs)*	1,000	
	Equity		1,000
y/e 31.12.20x3	Profit or loss (employee costs)*	1,000	
	Equity		1,000
y/e 31.12.20x4	Profit or loss (employee costs)*	500	
	Equity		500
1.9.20x6	Cash (option proceeds)†	4,500	
	Equity‡	1,500	
	Own shares (equity)**		6,000

*   Total cost £3,000 (3000 options × £1) spread over 36 months. Charge for period to December 20x1 is 6/36 × £3,000 = £500, and so on. In practice, where options are granted to a group of individuals, or with variable performance criteria, the annual charge will be based on a continually revised cumulative charge (see further discussion at 7.1 to 7.4 above).

†   3,000 options at £1.50 each.

‡   This reflects the fact that the overall effect of the transaction for the group *in cash terms* has been a 'loss' of £1,500 (£6,000 original cost of shares less £4,500 option proceeds received). However, under FRS 102 this is an equity transaction, not an expense.

**   £6,000 cost of own shares purchased on 1 January 20x2 now transferred to the employee. In practice, it is more likely that the appropriate amount to be transferred would be based on the weighted average price of shares held by the EBT at the date of exercise, as in Example 23.36 at 13.3.3 above. In such a case there would be a corresponding adjustment to the debit to equity marked with ‡ above.

13.4.2 Parent

13.4.2.A Accounting by parent where the subsidiary company is the employing company

The parent accounts for the share-based payment transaction under FRS 102 as an equity-settled transaction since the parent settles the award by delivering its own equity instruments to the employees of the subsidiary (see 13.2.4 above). However, as discussed at 13.2.4 above, instead of recording an expense, as in its consolidated financial statements, the parent records an increase in the carrying value of its investment in subsidiary. It might then be necessary to consider whether the ever-increasing investment in subsidiary is supportable or is in fact impaired. As this is a matter to be determined in the light of specific facts and circumstances, it is not considered in this example. Any impairment charge would be recorded in profit or loss.

In addition to accounting for the share-based payment transaction, the parent records the transactions of the EBT and the purchase of shares.

This gives rise to the following entries:

		£	£
y/e 31.12.20x1	Investment in subsidiary*	500	
	Equity		500
1.1.20x2	Own shares (equity)	6,000	
	Cash		6,000
y/e 31.12.20x2	Investment in subsidiary*	1,000	
	Equity		1,000
y/e 31.12.20x3	Investment in subsidiary*	1,000	
	Equity		1,000
y/e 31.12.20x4	Investment in subsidiary*	500	
	Equity		500
1.9.20x6	Cash†	6,000	
	Equity‡	1,500	
	Profit or loss§		1,500
	Own shares** (equity)		6,000

*   Total increase in investment £3,000 (3000 shares × £1 fair value of each option) spread over 36 months. Increase during period to December 20x1 is 6/36 × £3,000 = £500, and so on. In practice, where options were granted to a group of individuals, or with variable performance criteria, the

Chapter 23

annual adjustment would be based on a continually revised cumulative adjustment (see further discussion at 7.1 to 7.4 above).

†　£4,500 option exercise proceeds from employee plus £1,500 contribution from S Limited.

‡　This is essentially a balancing figure representing the fact that the entity is distributing own shares with an original cost of £6,000, but has treated £1,500 of the £6,000 of the cash it has received as income (see § below) rather than as payment for the shares.

§　The £1,500 contribution by the subsidiary to the EBT has been treated as a distribution from the subsidiary (see 13.2.7 above) and recorded in profit or loss. It might then be necessary to consider whether, as a result of this payment, the investment in the subsidiary had become impaired. As this is a matter to be determined in the light of specific facts and circumstances, it is not considered in this example. Any impairment charge would be recorded in profit or loss.

**　£6,000 cost of own shares purchased on 1 January 20x2 now transferred to employee. In practice, it is more likely that the appropriate amount to be transferred would be based on the weighted average price of shares held by the EBT at the date of exercise, as in Example 23.36 at 13.3.3 above.

13.4.2.B　*Parent company as employing company*

If, in Example 23.38, the employing entity were the parent rather than the subsidiary, it would record an expense under FRS 102. It would also normally waive £1,500 of its £6,000 loan to the EBT (i.e. the shortfall between the original loan and the £4,500 option proceeds received from the employee).

As the EBT is treated as an extension of the parent, the accounting entries for the parent would be the same as those for the group, as set out at 13.4.1 above.

13.4.3　*Employing subsidiary*

The employing subsidiary is required to account for the FRS 102 expense and the contribution to the EBT on exercise of the award. This gives rise to the accounting entries set out below. The entries to reflect the expense are required by FRS 102 (see 13.2.3 above). The treatment of the contribution to the EBT as a distribution is discussed at 13.2.7 above.

		£	£
y/e 31.12.20x1	Profit or loss*	500	
	Equity		500
y/e 31.12.20x2	Profit or loss*	1,000	
	Equity		1,000
y/e 31.12.20x3	Profit or loss*	1,000	
	Equity		1,000
y/e 31.12.20x4	Profit or loss*	500	
	Equity		500
1.9.20x6	Equity†	1,500	
	Cash		1,500

* Total cost £3,000 (3000 options × £1) spread over 36 months. Charge for period to December 20x1 is 6/36 × £3,000 = £500, and so on. In practice, where options were granted to a group of individuals, or with variable performance criteria, the annual charge would be based on a continually revised cumulative charge (see further discussion at 7.1 to 7.4 above).

† This should be treated as a reduction of whatever component of equity was credited with the £3,000 quasi-contribution from the parent in the accounting entries above.

13.5 Illustrative example of a group share scheme – equity-settled award satisfied by fresh issue of shares

The discussion in 13.5.1 to 13.5.3 below is based on Example 23.39 and addresses the accounting treatment for three distinct aspects of a group share scheme – a share-based payment arrangement involving group entities (see 13.2 above), the use of an EBT (see 13.3 above) and a group recharge arrangement (see 13.2.7 above). The Example assumes that the share-based payment arrangement is settled by a fresh issue of shares.

This illustrative example treats the recharge by the parent to the subsidiary as an income statement credit in the individual accounts of the parent and recognises the recharge when it is paid. In some situations, entities might consider it appropriate to apply alternative accounting treatments (see 13.2.7 above).

Example 23.39: Group share scheme (fresh issue of shares)

On 1 July 20x1 an employee of S Limited, a subsidiary of the H plc group, is awarded options under the H group share scheme over 3,000 shares in H plc at £1.50 each, exercisable between 1 July 20x4 and 1 July 20x7, subject to a service condition and certain performance criteria being met in the three years ending 30 June 20x4. The fair value of the options on 1 July 20x1 is £1 each.

H plc grants the award and has the obligation to settle it.

When preparing accounts during the vesting period H plc and its subsidiaries assume that the award will vest in full. The options are finally exercised on 1 September 20x6, at which point H plc issues 3,000 new shares to the EBT at the then current market price of £3.50 for £10,500. The EBT funds the purchase using the £4,500 option proceeds received from the employee together with £6,000 contributed by S Limited, effectively representing the fair value of the options at exercise date (3,000 × [£3.50 – £1.50]). H plc and its subsidiaries have a 31 December year end.

13.5.1 *Consolidated financial statements*

The consolidated financial statements need to deal with:

- the charge required by FRS 102 in respect of the award; and
- the issue of shares.

Transactions between H plc or S Limited and the EBT are ignored since the EBT is treated as an extension of H plc (see 13.3 above). The accounting entries required are set out below. As in other examples in this chapter, an entry to equity is not allocated to a specific reserve as this will vary between entities (although the most common for an entity complying with the Companies Act 2006 will be the profit and loss reserve or a separate 'other reserve' for share-based payments).

		£	£
y/e 31.12.20x1	Profit or loss*	500	
	Equity		500
y/e 31.12.20x2	Profit or loss*	1,000	
	Equity		1,000
y/e 31.12.20x3	Profit or loss*	1,000	
	Equity		1,000
y/e 31.12.20x4	Profit or loss*	500	
	Equity		500
1.9.20x6	Cash	4,500	
	Other equity†	6,000	
	Share capital / premium†		10,500

*   Total cost £3,000 (3000 options × £1) spread over 36 months. Charge for period to December 20x1 is 6/36 × £3,000 = £500, and so on. In practice, where options were granted to a group of individuals, or with variable performance criteria, the annual charge would be based on a continually revised cumulative charge (see further discussion at 7.1 to 7.4 above).

†   From the point of view of the consolidated group, the issue of shares results in an increase in net assets of only £4,500 (i.e. the exercise price received from the employee), since the £6,000 contribution from the employing subsidiary to the EBT is an intragroup transaction. However, an entity applying the Companies Act 2006 is required to increase its share capital and share premium accounts by the £10,500 legal consideration for the issue of shares. The £6,000 consideration provided from within the group is effectively treated as a bonus issue.

13.5.2   *Parent*

13.5.2.A   *Accounting by parent where subsidiary is the employing company*

The parent accounts for the share-based payment transaction under FRS 102 as an equity-settled transaction since the parent settles the award by delivering its own equity instruments via its EBT to the employees of the subsidiary (see 13.2.4 above). However, as discussed at 13.2.4 above, instead of recording an expense, as in its consolidated financial statements, the parent records an increase in the carrying value of its investment in subsidiary. It might then be necessary to consider whether the ever-increasing investment in subsidiary is supportable or is in fact impaired. As this is a matter to be determined in the light of specific facts and circumstances, it is not considered in this example. Any impairment charge would be recorded in profit or loss.

In addition to accounting for the share-based payment transaction, the parent records the transactions of the EBT and the issue of shares.

		£	£
y/e 31.12.20x1	Investment in subsidiary*	500	
	Equity		500
y/e 31.12.20x2	Investment in subsidiary*	1,000	
	Equity		1,000
y/e 31.12.20x3	Investment in subsidiary*	1,000	
	Equity		1,000
y/e 31.12.20x4	Investment in subsidiary*	500	
	Equity†		500
1.9.20x6	Cash†	10,500	
	Equity‡	6,000	
	Profit or loss**		6,000
	Share capital/premium‡		10,500

* Total increase in investment £3,000 (3000 shares × £1 fair value of each option) spread over 36 months. Increase during period to December 20x1 is 6/36 × £3,000 = £500, and so on. In practice, where options were granted to a group of individuals, or with variable performance criteria, the annual adjustment would be based on a continually revised cumulative adjustment (see further discussion at 7.1 to 7.4 above).

† £4,500 option exercise proceeds from employee plus £6,000 contribution from the subsidiary.

‡ This assumes that local law requires the entity to record share capital and share premium of £10,500, as in 13.5.1 above. However, FRS 102 *prima facie* requires the £6,000 cash received by the EBT from the subsidiary to be treated as income (see ** below) rather than as part of the proceeds of the issue of shares. In order, in effect, to reconcile these conflicting analyses, £6,000 of the £10,500 required by law to be capitalised as share capital and share premium has been treated as an appropriation out of other equity.

** The £6,000 contribution by the subsidiary to the EBT has been treated as a distribution from the subsidiary (see 13.2.7 above) and recorded in profit or loss. It might then be necessary to consider whether, as a result of this payment, the investment in the subsidiary had become impaired. As this is a matter to be determined in the light of specific facts and circumstances, it is not considered in this Example. Any impairment charge would be recorded in profit or loss.

13.5.2.B   *Parent company as employing company*

If, in Example 23.39, the employing entity were the parent rather than the subsidiary, it would clearly have to record an expense under FRS 102. It would also have to fund the £6,000 shortfall between the option exercise proceeds of £4,500 and the £10,500 issue proceeds of the shares.

As the EBT is treated as an extension of the parent, the accounting entries for the parent would be the same as those for the group, as set out in 13.5.1 above.

13.5.3   Employing subsidiary

The employing subsidiary is required to account for the FRS 102 expense and the contribution to the EBT on exercise of the award. This gives rise to the accounting entries set out below. The entries to reflect the expense are required by FRS 102 (see 13.2.3 above). The treatment of the contribution to the EBT as a distribution is discussed at 13.2.7 above.

		£	£
y/e 31.12.20x1	Profit or loss*	500	
	Equity		500
y/e 31.12.20x2	Profit or loss*	1,000	
	Equity		1,000
y/e 31.12.20x3	Profit or loss*	1,000	
	Equity		1,000
y/e 31.12.20x4	Profit or loss*	500	
	Equity		500
1.9.20x6	Equity†	6,000	
	Cash		6,000

*   Total cost £3,000 (3000 options × £1) spread over 36 months. Charge for period to December 20x1 6/36 × £3,000 = £500, and so on. In practice, where options were granted to a group of individuals, or with variable performance criteria, the annual charge would be based on a continually revised cumulative charge (see further discussion at 7.1 to 7.4 above).

†   £3,000 of this payment should be treated as a reduction of whatever component of equity was credited with the £3,000 quasi-contribution from the parent in the accounting entries above. The remaining £3,000 would be treated as a distribution and deducted from any appropriate component of equity.

13.6   Illustrative example – cash-settled transaction not settled by the entity receiving goods or services

The discussion in 13.6.1 to 13.6.3 below is based on Example 23.40.

Example 23.40:   Cash-settled scheme not settled by receiving entity

On 1 July 20x1 an employee of S Limited, a subsidiary of the H plc group, is awarded a right, exercisable between 1 July 20x4 and 1 July 20x7, to receive cash equivalent to the value of 3,000 shares in H plc at the date on which the right is exercised. Exercise of the right is subject to a service condition and certain performance criteria being met in the three years ending 30 June 20x4. The cash will be paid to the employee not by S, but by H. Throughout the vesting period of the award, H and S take the view that it will vest in full.

The award does in fact vest, and the right is exercised on 1 September 20x6.

The fair value of the award (per share-equivalent) at various relevant dates is as follows:

Date	Fair value £
1.7.20x1	1.50
31.12.20x1	1.80
31.12.20x2	2.70
31.12.20x3	2.40
31.12.20x4	2.90
31.12.20x5	3.30
1.9.20x6	3.50

If the award had been equity-settled (i.e. the employee had instead been granted a right to 3,000 free shares), the grant date fair value of the award would have been £1.50 per share.

H plc and its subsidiaries have a 31 December year end.

13.6.1 Consolidated financial statements

The group has entered into a cash-settled transaction which is accounted for using the methodology discussed at 10.3 above. This gives rise to the following accounting entries:

		£	£
y/e 31.12.20x1	Profit or loss*	900	
	Liability		900
y/e 31.12.20x2	Profit or loss*	3,150	
	Liability		3,150
y/e 31.12.20x3	Profit or loss*	1,950	
	Liability		1,950
y/e 31.12.20x4	Profit or loss*	2,700	
	Liability		2,700
y/e 31.12.20x5	Profit or loss*	1,200	
	Liability		1,200
y/e 31.12.20x6	Profit or loss*	600	
	Liability		600
1.9.20x6	Liability	10,500	
	Cash		10,500

* Charge for period to 31 December 20x1 is 6/36 × 3000 × £1.80 [reporting date fair value] = £900. Charge for year ended 31 December 20x2 is 18/36 × 3000 × £2.70 = £4,050 less £900 charged in 20x1 = £3,150 and so on (refer to Example 23.33 at 10.3.2 above). In practice, where options were granted to a group of individuals, or with variable performance criteria, the annual charge would be based on a continually revised cumulative charge (see further discussion at 10 above).

Chapter 23

13.6.2   *Parent company*

The parent accounts for the share-based payment transaction under FRS 102 as a cash-settled transaction, since the parent settles the award by delivering cash to the employees of the subsidiary (see 13.2.4 above). However, as discussed at 13.2.4 above, instead of recording a cost, as in its consolidated financial statements, the parent records an increase in the carrying value of its investment in subsidiary. It might then be necessary to consider whether the ever-increasing investment in subsidiary is supportable or is in fact impaired. As this is a matter to be determined in the light of specific facts and circumstances, it is not considered in this example. Any impairment charge would be recorded in profit or loss.

This would result in the following accounting entries:

		£	£
y/e 31.12.20x1	Investment in subsidiary*	900	
	Liability		900
y/e 31.12.20x2	Investment in subsidiary*	3,150	
	Liability		3,150
y/e 31.12.20x3	Investment in subsidiary*	1,950	
	Liability		1,950
y/e 31.12.20x4	Investment in subsidiary*	2,700	
	Liability		2,700
y/e 31.12.20x5	Investment in subsidiary*	1,200	
	Liability		1,200
y/e 31.12.20x6	Investment in subsidiary*	600	
	Liability		600
1.9.20x6	Liability	10,500	
	Cash		10,500

* Increase in investment to 31 December 20x1 is 6/36 × 3000 × £1.80 [reporting date fair value] = £900. Increase for year ended 31 December 20x2 is 18/36 × 3000 × £2.70 = £4,050 less £900 charged in 20x1 = £3,150 and so on (refer to Example 23.33 at 10.3.2 above). In practice, where options were granted to a group of individuals, or with variable performance criteria, the annual charge would be based on a continually revised cumulative charge (see further discussion at 10 above).

Where the parent entity was also the employing entity (and therefore receiving goods or services), it would apply the same accounting treatment in its separate financial statements as in its consolidated financial statements (see 13.6.1 above).

13.6.3   *Employing subsidiary*

The employing subsidiary accounts for the transaction as equity-settled, since it receives services, but incurs no obligation to its employees (see 13.2.3 and 13.2.6 above). This gives rise to the following accounting entries:

		£	£
y/e 31.12.20x1	Profit or loss*	750	
	Equity		750
y/e 31.12.20x2	Profit or loss*	1,500	
	Equity		1,500
y/e 31.12.20x3	Profit or loss*	1,500	
	Equity		1,500
y/e 31.12.20x4	Profit or loss*	750	
	Equity		750

*   Charge for period to 31 December 20x1 is $6/36 \times 3000 \times £1.50$ [grant date fair value] = £750, and so on. In practice, where options were granted to a group of individuals, or with variable performance criteria, the annual charge would be based on a continually revised cumulative charge (see further discussion at 7.1 to 7.4 above).

The effect of this treatment is that, while the group ultimately records a cost of £10,500, the subsidiary records a cost of only £4,500.

However, there may be cases where the subsidiary records a higher cost than the group. This would happen if, for example:

- the award vests, but the share price has fallen since grant date, so that the value of the award at vesting (as reflected in the consolidated financial statements) is lower than the value at grant (as reflected in the subsidiary's financial statements); or

- the award does not actually vest because of a failure to meet a market condition and/or a non-vesting condition (so that the cost is nil in the consolidated financial statements) but is treated by FRS 102 as vesting in the subsidiary's financial statements, because it is accounted for as equity-settled (see 7.3 and 7.4 above).

13.7   Employee transferring between group entities

It is not uncommon for an employee to be granted an equity-settled share-based payment award while in the employment of one subsidiary in the group, but to transfer to another subsidiary in the group before the award is vested, with the entitlement to the award remaining unchanged.

Chapter 23

Section 26 does not specifically address the accounting in such cases. For entities applying the special rules for group plans in paragraph 16 of Section 26, that paragraph appears to support an appropriate allocation of the group expense between the employing entities (see 13.2.3.A above). In other cases, we suggest that group entities adopt an approach based on that in IFRS 2. Under IFRS 2, each subsidiary measures the services received from the employee by reference to the fair value of the equity instruments at the date those rights to equity instruments were originally granted, and the proportion of the vesting period served by the employee with each subsidiary. *[IFRS 2 Appendix B.59]*. In other words, for an award with a three-year vesting period granted to an employee of subsidiary A, who transfers to subsidiary B at the end of year 2, subsidiary A will (cumulatively) record an expense of 2/3, and subsidiary B 1/3, of the fair value at grant date. However, any subsidiary required to account for the transaction as cash-settled in accordance with the general principles discussed at 13.2 above accounts for its portion of the grant date fair value and also for any changes in the fair value of the award during the period of employment with that subsidiary. *[IFRS 2 Appendix B.60]*.

After transferring between group entities, an employee may fail to satisfy a vesting condition other than a market condition, for example by leaving the employment of the group. In this situation each subsidiary adjusts the amount previously recognised in respect of the services received from the employee in accordance with the general principles of FRS 102 and IFRS 2 (see 7.1 to 7.4 above). *[IFRS 2 Appendix B.61]*.

14   DISCLOSURES

The disclosure requirements of Section 26 fall into three main categories:

- the nature and extent of share-based payment arrangements (see 14.1 below);
- the measurement of share-based payment arrangements (see 14.2 below); and
- the effect on the financial statements of share-based payment transactions (see 14.3 below).

The requirements apply to all entities applying FRS 102 although a 'qualifying entity', as defined in Section 1 – *Scope* – of FRS 102, may take advantage in its individual financial statements of an exemption from the requirements of paragraphs 18(b), 19 to 21 and 23 of Section 26 provided the following criteria are met:

- if the qualifying entity is a subsidiary, the share-based payment arrangement concerns equity instruments of another group entity;
- if the qualifying entity is an ultimate parent, the share-based payment arrangement concerns its own equity instruments and its separate financial statements are presented alongside the consolidated financial statements of the group;

and, in both cases, provided that the equivalent disclosures required by FRS 102 are included in the consolidated financial statements of the group in which the entity is consolidated. *[FRS 102.1.8-12]*.

14.1 Nature and extent of share-based payment arrangements

IFRS 2 contains a general requirement that an entity should 'disclose information that enables users of the financial statements to understand the nature and extent of share-based payment arrangements that existed during the period' *[IFRS 2.44]* and then lists the minimum disclosures required to meet the overall requirement.

FRS 102 does not include the overall requirement from IFRS 2 but picks up some of the detailed disclosures and requires an entity to 'disclose the following information about the nature and extent of share-based payment arrangements that existed during the period: *[FRS 102.26.18]*

(a) A description of each type of share-based payment arrangement that existed at any time during the period, including the general terms and conditions of each arrangement, such as vesting requirements, the maximum term of options granted, and the method of settlement (e.g. whether in cash or equity). An entity with substantially similar types of share-based payment arrangements may aggregate this information.

(b) The number and weighted average exercise prices of share options for each of the following groups of options:

  (i)   outstanding at the beginning of the period;

  (ii) granted during the period;

  (iii) forfeited during the period;

  (iv) exercised during the period;

  (v)   expired during the period;

  (vi) outstanding at the end of the period; and

  (vii) exercisable at the end of the period.'

The reconciliation in (b) above should, in our view, reflect all changes in the number of equity instruments outstanding. Therefore, in addition to awards with a grant date during the period, the reconciliation should include subsequent additions to earlier grants, e.g. options or shares added to the award in recognition of dividends declared during the period (where this is part of the original terms of the award), and changes to the number of equity instruments as a result of share splits or consolidations and other similar changes.

As drafted, the requirements in (b) above appear to apply only to share options. However, since there is little distinction between the treatment of an option with a zero exercise price and the award of a free share, in our view the disclosures should not be restricted to awards of options.

14.2 Measurement of share-based payment arrangements

IFRS 2 contains a general requirement that an entity should 'disclose information that enables users of the financial statements to understand how the fair value of the goods or services received, or the fair value of the equity instruments granted, during the period was determined' *[IFRS 2.46]* and then lists the minimum disclosures required to meet the overall requirement.

FRS 102 contains its own general disclosure requirements for equity-settled, cash-settled, modified and group share-based payment arrangements but does not mandate the disclosure of specific details other than as set out at 14.2.1 to 14.2.4 below.

14.2.1   Equity-settled arrangements

For equity-settled share-based payment arrangements, FRS 102 requires an entity to 'disclose information about how it measured the fair value of goods or services received or the value of the equity instruments granted. If a valuation methodology was used, the entity shall disclose the method and the reason for choosing it'. *[FRS 102.26.19]*.

Unlike IFRS 2, FRS 102 has no specific requirement to disclose the inputs to an option pricing model and other assumptions made in the determination of fair value.

The requirement in FRS 102 to disclose the reason for choosing the valuation methodology used is not found in IFRS 2 but is consistent with the fact that FRS 102 allows directors to select an appropriate method of valuation rather than requiring the use of an option-pricing model (as is the case in IFRS 2 when market price information is not available).

14.2.2   Cash-settled arrangements

FRS 102 includes a requirement to disclose information about how the liability for a cash-settled arrangement was measured but does not expand on this general requirement. *[FRS 102.26.20]*. There is no direct correlation between this requirement and the disclosure requirements of IFRS 2 as the latter do not specifically address the measurement of cash-settled arrangements. The FRS 102 requirement is therefore potentially more onerous.

14.2.3   Modification of share-based payment arrangements

Where share-based payment arrangements have been modified during the accounting period, FRS 102 requires an explanation of those modifications *[FRS 102.26.21]* although, unlike IFRS 2, there is no specific requirement to disclose the incremental fair value or information about how that incremental value was measured.

14.2.4   Group share-based payment arrangements

If the reporting entity is part of a group share-based payment arrangement and it measures its share-based payment expense on the basis of a reasonable allocation of the expense for the group (in accordance with paragraph 16 of Section 26 – see 13.2.3.A above), then disclosure is required of that fact and of the basis for the allocation. *[FRS 102.26.22]*.

14.3   Effect of share-based payment transactions on financial statements

IFRS 2 contains a general requirement that an entity should 'disclose information that enables users of the financial statements to understand the effect of share-based payment transactions on the entity's profit or loss for the period and on its financial position' *[IFRS 2.50]* and then lists the minimum disclosures required to meet the overall requirement.

FRS 102 does not include such a general requirement but picks up some of the detailed disclosures and requires an entity to 'disclose the following information about the effect of share-based payment transactions on the entity's profit or loss for the period and on its financial position:

(a) the total expense recognised in profit or loss for the period; and

(b) the total carrying amount at the end of the period for liabilities arising from share-based payment transactions'. *[FRS 102.26.23]*.

15 TAXES RELATED TO SHARE-BASED PAYMENT TRANSACTIONS

15.1 Income tax deductions for the entity

The particular issues raised by the accounting treatment for income taxes on share-based payment transactions are discussed in Chapter 26 at 7.7.

15.2 Employment taxes of the employer

An employing entity is required to pay National Insurance on share options and other share-based payment transactions with employees, just as if the employees had received cash remuneration. This raises the question of how such taxes should be accounted for as FRS 102 contains no specific guidance in this area.

The previous version of UK GAAP included UITF Abstract 25: *National Insurance contributions on share option gains* and, in our view, entities should continue to apply the requirements of this interpretation in the absence of more specific guidance. Therefore a provision should be made for National Insurance ('NI') contributions on outstanding share options (and similar awards) that are expected to be exercised. The provision should be:

- calculated at the latest enacted NI rate applied to the difference between the market value of the underlying shares at the reporting date and the option exercise price;

- allocated over the period from grant date to the end of the vesting period, after which it should be updated using the current market value of the shares; and

- expensed through profit or loss unless the options form part of capitalised staff costs.

In some situations the entity may require employees to reimburse the amount of NI paid. This should be treated in accordance with the general rules in Section 21 – *Provisions and Contingencies* – for the reimbursement of the expenditure required to settle a provision.

15.3 Sale or surrender of shares by employee to meet employee's tax liability ('sell to cover' and net settlement)

An award of shares or options to an employee may give rise to a personal tax liability for the employee, often related to the fair value of the award when it vests or, in the case of an option, is exercised. In order to meet this tax liability, employees may wish to sell or surrender as many shares as are needed to raise proceeds equal to the tax liability (sometimes described respectively as 'sell to cover' or 'net settlement').

This *in itself* does not, in our view, require the scheme to be considered as cash-settled, any more than if the employee wished to liquidate the shares in order to buy a car or undertake home improvements. However, if the manner in which the cash is passed to, or realised for, the employee gives rise to a legal or constructive obligation for the employer, then the scheme might well be cash-settled (see 10.2 above), to the extent of any such obligation.

Where employees must pay income tax on share awards, the tax is often initially collected from the employer, but with eventual recourse by the tax authorities to the employee for tax not collected from the employer. Such tax collection arrangements mean that even an equity-settled award results in a cash cost for the employer for the income tax.

In such a situation, the employer may require the employee, as a condition of taking delivery of any shares earned, to indemnify the entity against the tax liability, for example by:

- direct payment to the entity;

- authorising the entity to deduct the relevant amount from the employee's salary; or

- surrendering as many shares to the entity as have a fair value equal to the tax liability.

If the entity requires the employee to surrender the relevant number of shares, in our view the scheme must be treated as cash-settled to the extent of the indemnified amount, as explained in Example 23.41 below.

Example 23.41: Surrendering of vested shares by employee to indemnify liability of entity to pay employee's tax liability (net settlement)

An individual has a personal tax rate of 40% and free shares are taxed at their fair value on vesting. The individual is granted an award of 100 free shares with a grant date fair value of £3 each. The fair value at vesting date is £5, so that the employee's tax liability (required to be discharged in the first instance by the employer via PAYE) is £200 (40% of £500).

If the employee were required to surrender the 40 shares needed to settle the tax liability, in our view the substance of the transaction is that, at grant date, the entity is making an award of only 60 shares (with a grant date fair value of £3 each) and is bearing the cost of the employment tax itself. On this analysis, the entity will have recorded the following entries by the end of the vesting period:

	£	£
Employee costs (based on 60 shares at grant date fair value)	180	
Equity		180
Employee costs (based on 40% of vesting date value)	200	
Employment tax liability		200

The award is then satisfied by the delivery of 60 shares by the entity to the employee.

If, instead of being required to surrender the shares needed to settle the tax liability, the employee has a free choice as to how to indemnify the employer, the employer will have recorded the following entries by the end of the vesting period:

	£	£
Employee costs (based on 100 shares at grant date fair value)	300	
Equity		300
Receivable from employee (based on 40% of vesting date value)	200	
Employment tax liability		200

The award is then satisfied by the delivery of 100 shares to the employee and the employee indicates that he wishes to surrender 40 shares to discharge his obligation to the employer under the indemnity arrangement. The entity therefore receives 40 shares from the employee in settlement of the £200 receivable from him.

In practice, this would almost certainly be effected as a net delivery of 60 shares, but in principle there are two transactions:

- a release of 100 shares to the employee; and
- the re-acquisition of 40 of those shares at £5 each from the employee.

The entity then settles the tax liability:

	£	£
Employment tax liability	200	
Cash		200

Even in this case, however, some might take the view that the substance of the arrangement is that the employee has the right to put 40 shares to the employer, and accordingly 40% of the award should be accounted for as cash-settled, resulting in essentially the same accounting as when the employee is required to surrender 40 shares, as set out above. An entity should therefore make a careful assessment of the appropriate accounting treatment based on the terms of a particular arrangement.

An amendment to IFRS 2, issued in June 2016, introduced an exception to the requirement to split an award into an equity-settled element and a cash-settled element where certain specified criteria relating to an entity's tax withholding obligations are met. The exception means that net-settled arrangements that meet the criteria will be accounted for as entirely equity-settled under IFRS. There is no corresponding exception to the requirements of Section 26 and so the requirement to consider whether an award has an equity-settled portion and a cash-settled portion, and to account accordingly, will continue to apply.

16 OTHER PRACTICAL ISSUES

We consider below the application of Section 26 to the following types of arrangement encountered in practice:

- matching share awards (including deferred bonuses delivered in shares) (see 16.1 below);
- loans to employees to purchase shares (limited recourse and full recourse loans) (see 16.2 below);
- awards entitled to dividends or dividend equivalents during the vesting period (see 16.3 below); and
- awards vesting or exercisable on an exit event or change of control (flotation, trade sale etc.) (see 16.4 below).

16.1 Matching share awards (including deferred bonuses delivered in shares)

As noted in the discussion at 11.2.1 above, in our view the rules in Section 26 for awards where there is a choice of equity- or cash-settlement do not fully address awards where the equity and cash alternatives may have significantly different fair values and vesting periods. A matching share award is an example of the type of scheme giving rise to such issues.

Under a matching share award, the starting point is usually that an employee is awarded a bonus for a one year performance period. At the end of that period, the employee may then be either required or permitted to take all or part of that bonus in shares rather than cash. To the extent that the employee takes shares rather than cash, the employing entity may then be required or permitted to make a 'matching' award of an equal number of shares (or a multiple or fraction of that number). The matching award will typically vest over a longer period.

Whilst such schemes can appear superficially similar, the accounting analysis may vary significantly, according to whether:

- the employee has a choice, or is required, to take some of the 'base' bonus in shares and whether any such shares have to be retained by the employee in order for the matching shares to vest; and/or

- the employer has a choice, or is required, to match any shares taken by the employee.

The detailed accounting for such arrangements is beyond the scope of this publication but is addressed in EY International GAAP 2019. The requirements of FRS 102 and IFRS 2 are not identical for awards where there is a choice of settlement but are closely aligned (see 11 above). However, it is expected that many companies with a matching share scheme will be part of a larger group arrangement and will potentially be able to recognise an expense based on the group expense in accordance with paragraph 16 of Section 26 (see 13.2.3.A above).

16.2 Loans to employees to purchase shares (limited recourse and full recourse loans)

Share awards to employees are sometimes made by means of so-called 'limited recourse loan' schemes. The detailed terms of such schemes vary, but typical features include the following:

- the entity makes an interest-free loan to the employee which is immediately used to acquire shares to the value of the loan on behalf of the employee;

- the shares may be held by the entity, or a trust controlled by it (see 13.3 above), until the loan is repaid;

- the employee is entitled to dividends, except that these are treated as paying off some of the outstanding loan;

- within a given period (say, five years) the employee must either have paid off the outstanding balance of the loan, at which point the shares are delivered to the employee, or surrendered the shares. Surrender of the shares by the employee is treated as discharging any outstanding amount on the loan, irrespective of the value of the shares.

The effect of such an arrangement is equivalent to an option exercisable within five years with an exercise price per share equal to the share price at grant date less total dividends since grant date. There is no real loan at the initial stage. The entity has no right to receive cash or another financial asset, since the loan can be settled by the employee returning the (fixed) amount of equity 'purchased' at grant date.

Indeed, the only true cash flow in the entire transaction is any amount paid at the final stage if the employee chooses to acquire the shares at that point. The fact that the exercise price is a factor of the share price at grant date and dividends paid between grant date and the date of repayment of the 'loan' is simply an issue for the valuation of the option. The fair value of the option will generally need to be based on the employee's implicit right to buy the shares at a future date rather than being the share price at grant date (the face value of the loan).

The loan arrangement might have a defined period during which the employee must remain in service (five years in the example above) and during which there might also be performance conditions to be met. Where this is the case, the FRS 102 expense will be recognised by the entity over this period. However, where, as is frequently the case, such an award is subject to no future service or performance condition, i.e. the 'option' is, in effect, immediately exercisable by the employee should he choose to settle the 'loan', the cost will need to be recognised in full at grant date (see 7.1 above).

Under more complex arrangements, the loan to the employee to acquire the shares is a full recourse loan (i.e. it cannot be discharged simply by surrendering the shares and there can be recourse to other assets of the employee). However, the amount repayable on the loan is reduced not only by dividends paid on the shares, but also by the achievement of performance targets, such as the achievement of a given level of earnings.

The appropriate analysis of such awards is more difficult, as they could be viewed in two ways:

- either the employer has made a loan (which the employee has chosen to use to buy a share), accounted for as a financial asset, and has then entered into a performance-related cash bonus arrangement with the employee, accounted for as an employee benefit; or

- the transaction is a share option where the exercise price varies according to the satisfaction of performance conditions and the amount of dividends on the shares, accounted for under Section 26.

The different analyses give rise to potentially significantly different expenses. This will particularly be the case where one of the conditions for mitigation of the amount repayable on the loan is linked to the price of the employer's equity. As this is a market condition, the effect of accounting for the arrangement under Section 26 may be that an expense is recognised in circumstances where no expense would be recognised if the arrangement were treated as an employee benefit under Section 28.

Such awards need to be carefully analysed, in the light of their particular facts and circumstances, in order to determine the appropriate treatment. Factors that could suggest that Section 26 is the more relevant would, in our view, include:

- the employee can use the loan only to acquire shares;

- the employee cannot trade the shares until the loan is discharged; or

- the entity has a practice of accepting (e.g. from leavers) surrender of the shares as full discharge for the amount outstanding on the loan and does not pursue any shortfall between the fair value of the shares and the amount owed by the employee. This would tend to indicate that, in substance, the loan is not truly full recourse.

Chapter 23

16.3   Awards entitled to dividends or dividend equivalents during the vesting period

Some awards entitle the holder to receive dividends on unvested shares (or dividend equivalents on options) during the vesting period.

For example, an entity might award shares that are regarded as fully vested for the purposes of tax legislation (typically because the employee enjoys the full voting and dividend rights of the shares), but not for accounting purposes (typically because the shares are subject to forfeiture if a certain minimum service period is not achieved). In practice, the shares concerned are often held by an EBT until the potential forfeiture period has expired.

Another variant of such an award that is sometimes seen is where an entity grants an employee an option to acquire shares in the entity which can be exercised immediately. However, if the employee exercises the option but leaves within a certain minimum period from the grant date, he is required to sell back the share to the entity (typically either at the original exercise price, or the lower of that price or the market value of the share at the time of the buy-back).

Such awards do not fully vest for the purposes of Section 26 until the potential forfeiture or buy-back period has expired. The cost of such awards should therefore be recognised over this period.

This raises the question of the accounting treatment of any dividends paid to employees during the vesting period. Conceptually, it could be argued that such dividends cannot be dividends for financial reporting purposes since the equity instruments to which they relate are not yet regarded as issued for financial reporting purposes. This would lead to the conclusion that dividends paid in the vesting period should be charged to profit or loss as an employment cost.

However, the charge to be made for the award under Section 26 will already take account of the fact that the recipient is entitled to receive dividends during the vesting period. Thus, it could be argued that also to charge profit or loss with the dividends paid is a form of double counting. Moreover, whilst the relevant shares may not have been fully issued for financial reporting purposes, the basic Section 26 accounting does build up an amount in equity over the vesting period. It could therefore be argued that – conceptually, if not legally – any dividend paid relates not to an issued share, but rather to the equity instrument represented by the cumulative amount that has been recorded for the award as a credit to equity, and can therefore appropriately be shown as a deduction from equity.

However, this argument is valid only to the extent that the credit to equity represents awards that are expected to vest. It cannot apply to dividends paid to employees whose awards are either known not to have vested or treated as expected not to vest when applying Section 26 (since there is no credit to equity for these awards). Accordingly, we believe that the most appropriate approach is to analyse the dividends paid so that, by the date of vesting, cumulative dividends paid on awards treated by Section 26 as vested are deducted from equity and those paid on awards treated by Section 26 as unvested are charged to profit or loss. The allocation for periods prior to vesting should be based on a best estimate of the final outcome, as illustrated by Example 23.42 below.

Example 23.42: Award with rights to receive (and retain) dividends during vesting period

An entity grants 100 free shares to each of its 500 employees. The shares are treated as fully vested for legal and tax purposes, so that the employees are eligible to receive any dividends paid. However, the shares will be forfeited if the employee leaves within three years of the award being made. Accordingly, for the purposes of Section 26, vesting is conditional upon the employee working for the entity over the next three years. The entity estimates that the fair value of each share (including the right to receive dividends during the Section 26 vesting period) is £15. Employees are entitled to retain any dividend received even if the award does not vest.

20 employees leave during the first year, and the entity's best estimate at the end of year 1 is that 75 employees will have left before the end of the vesting period. During the second year, a further 22 employees leave, and the entity revises its estimate of total employee departures over the vesting period from 75 to 60. During the third year, a further 15 employees leave. Hence, a total of 57 employees (20 + 22 + 15) forfeit their rights to the shares during the three year period, and a total of 44,300 shares (443 employees × 100 shares per employee) finally vest.

The entity pays dividends of £1 per share in year 1, £1.20 per share in year 2, and £1.50 in year 3.

Under FRS 102, the entity will recognise the following amounts during the vesting period for services received as consideration for the shares.

Year	Calculation of cumulative expense	Cumulative expense (£)	Expense for period (£)
1	100 shares × 425 employees × £15 × 1/3	212,500	212,500
2	100 shares × 440 employees × £15 × 2/3	440,000	227,500
3	100 shares × 443 × £15 × 3/3	664,500	224,500

On the assumption that all employees who leave during a period do so on the last day of that period (and thus receive dividends paid in that period), in our view the dividends paid on the shares should be accounted for as follows:

		£	£
Year 1	Dr. Profit or loss (employee costs)[1]	7,500	
	Dr. Equity[1]	42,500	
	Cr. Cash[2]		50,000
Year 2	Dr. Profit or loss (employee costs)[3]	3,300	
	Dr. Equity[3]	54,300	
	Cr. Cash[4]		57,600
Year 3	Dr. Profit or loss (employee costs)[5]	1,590	
	Dr. Equity[5]	67,110	
	Cr. Cash[6]		68,700

1 20 employees have left and a further 55 are anticipated to leave. Dividends paid to those employees (100 shares × 75 employees × £1 = £7,500) are therefore recognised as an expense. Dividends paid to other employees are recognised as a reduction in equity.

2 100 shares × 500 employees × £1.

3 22 further employees have left and a further 18 are anticipated to leave. The cumulative expense for dividends paid to leavers and anticipated leavers should therefore be £10,800 (100 shares × 20 employees × £1 = £2,000 for leavers in year 1 + 100 shares × 40 employees × [£1 + £1.20] for leavers and anticipated leavers in year 2 = £8,800). £7,500 was charged in year 1, so the charge for year 2 should be £10,800 − £7,500 = £3,300. This could also have been calculated as charge for leavers and expected leavers in current year £4,800 (100 shares × 40 [22 + 18] employees × £1.20) less reversal of expense in year 1 for reduction in anticipated final number of leavers £1,500 (100 shares × 15 [75 − 60] employees × £1.00). Dividends paid to other employees are recognised as a reduction in equity.

4 100 shares × 480 employees in employment at start of year × £1.20.

5 15 further employees have left. The cumulative expense for dividends paid to leavers should therefore be £12,390 (£2,000 for leavers in year 1 (see 3 above) + 100 shares × 22 employees × [£1 + £1.20] = £4,840 for

leavers in year 2 + 100 shares × 15 employees × [£1 + £1.20 + £1.50] = £5,550 for leavers in year 3). A cumulative expense of £10,800 (see 3 above) was recognised by the end of year 2, so the charge for year 3 should be £12,390 – £10,800 = £1,590. This could also have been calculated as charge for leavers in current year £2,250 (100 shares × 15 employees × £1.50) less reversal of expense in years 1 and 2 for reduction in final number of leavers as against estimate at end of year 2 £660 (100 shares × 3 [60 – 57] employees × [£1.00 + £1.20]). Dividends paid to other employees are recognised as a reduction in equity.

6   100 shares × 458 employees in employment at start of year × £1.50.

16.4   Awards vesting or exercisable on an exit event or change of control (flotation, trade sale etc.)

Entities frequently issue awards connected to a significant event such as a flotation, trade sale or other change of control of the business. It may be that an award that would otherwise be equity-settled automatically becomes cash-settled if such an event crystallises and the entity has no choice as to the method of settlement (as discussed at 11.3 above).

However, it may also be the case that an award vests only on such an event, which raises various issues of interpretation, as discussed below.

The sections below should be read together with the more general discussions elsewhere in this chapter (as referred to in the narrative below) on topics such as grant date, vesting period, vesting and non-vesting conditions and classification as equity-settled or cash-settled. References to flotation should be read as also including other exit events.

16.4.1   Grant date

Sometimes awards are structured so that they will vest on flotation, or so that they will vest on flotation subject to further approval at that time. For awards in the first category, grant date as defined in FRS 102 will be the date on which the award is first communicated to employees (subject to the normal requirements of Section 26 relating to a shared understanding, offer and acceptance, as discussed at 6.3 above). For awards in the second category, grant date will be at or around the date of flotation, when the required further approval is given.

This means that the cost of awards subject to final approval at flotation will generally be significantly higher than that of awards that do not require such approval. Moreover, as discussed further at 6.3 above, it may well be the case that employees begin rendering service for such awards before grant date (e.g. from the date on which the entity communicates its intention to make the award in principle). In that case, the entity would need to consider making an initial estimate of the value of the award for the purpose of recognising an expense from the date services have been provided, and continually re-assess that value up until the actual grant date. As with any award dependent on a non-market vesting condition, an expense would be recognised only to the extent that the award is considered likely to vest. The classification of a requirement to float as a non-market vesting condition is discussed further at 16.4.3 below.

16.4.2   Vesting period

Many awards that vest on flotation have a time limit – in other words, the award lapses if flotation has not occurred on or before a given future date. In principle, as discussed at 7.2.3 above, when an award has a variable vesting period due to a non-market performance condition, the reporting entity should make a best estimate of the likely vesting period at each reporting date and calculate the Section 26 charge on the basis of that best estimate.

In practice, the likely timing of a future flotation is notoriously difficult to assess months, let alone years, in advance. In such cases, it would generally be acceptable simply to recognise the cost over the full potential vesting period until there is real clarity that a shorter period may be more appropriate. However, in making the assessment of the likelihood of vesting, it is important to take the company's circumstances into account. The likelihood of an exit event in the short- to medium-term is perhaps greater for a company owned by private equity investors seeking a return on their investment than for a long-established family-owned company considering a flotation.

It is worth noting that once an exit event becomes likely, the Section 26 expense will in some cases need to be recognised over a shorter vesting period than was originally envisaged as the probability of the exit event occurring will form the basis at the reporting date of the estimate of the number of awards expected to vest (see also the discussion at 8.6 above).

16.4.3 Is flotation or sale a vesting condition or a non-vesting condition?

There was debate in the past about whether a requirement for a flotation or sale to occur in order for an award to vest was a vesting condition or a non-vesting condition. The argument for it being a non-vesting condition was that flotation or sale may occur irrespective of the performance of the entity. The counter-argument was essentially that the price achieved on flotation or sale, which typically affects the ultimate value of the award (see 16.4.4 below), reflects the performance of the entity and is therefore a non-market performance condition (provided there is an associated service condition).

On the basis of discussions on the interpretation of IFRS 2 by the IASB and the IFRS Interpretations Committee, it appears appropriate to treat a requirement to float or be sold as a performance vesting condition rather than as a non-vesting condition, provided there is also a service condition for the duration of the performance condition (see 4.2 above). If the service period is not at least as long as the duration of the flotation or sale condition, the condition will need to be accounted for as a non-vesting condition.

Even though the condition is deemed to relate to the entity's own operations and therefore generally classified as a performance condition, it will sometimes be concluded that fulfilment of the condition is outside the control of both the entity and the counterparty. The settlement of an award in equity or cash might depend on the outcome of the condition i.e. there might be either cash- or equity-settlement that is entirely contingent on the exit event. Such contingent arrangements are discussed at 11.3 above.

16.4.4 Awards requiring achievement of a minimum price on flotation or sale

Some awards with a condition contingent on flotation (or another similar event) vest only if a minimum price per share is achieved. For example, an entity might grant all its employees share options, the vesting of which is contingent upon a flotation or sale of the shares at a price of at least £5 per share within five years, and the employee still being in employment at the time of the flotation or sale.

Taken alone, the requirement for a flotation or sale to occur is a non-market performance condition (see further below and at 16.4.3 above). However, if a minimum

Chapter 23

market price has to be achieved, the question arises as to whether, in addition to the service requirement, such an award comprises:

- a single market performance condition (i.e. float or sell within five years at a share price of at least £5); or
- two conditions:
  - a market performance condition (share price at time of flotation or sale of at least £5); and
  - a non-market performance condition (flotation or sale achieved within five years).

The significance of this is the issue discussed at 7.3 above, namely that an expense must always be recognised for all awards with a market condition, if *all* the non-market vesting conditions are satisfied, even if the market condition is not. In either case, however, there is a market condition which needs to be factored into the valuation of the award.

If the view is that 'flotation or sale at £5 within five years' is a single market condition, the entity will recognise an expense for the award for all employees still in service at the end of the five year period, since the sole non-market vesting condition (i.e. service) will have been met. Note that this assumes that the full five-year period is considered the most likely vesting period at grant date (see 16.4.2 above).

If, on the other hand, the view is that 'flotation or sale within five years' and 'flotation or sale share price £5' are two separate conditions, and no flotation or sale occurs, no expense will be recognised since the performance element of the non-market vesting condition (i.e. 'flotation or sale within five years') has not been satisfied. However, even on this second analysis, if a sale or flotation is achieved at a price less than £5, an expense must be recognised, even though the award does not truly vest, since the non-market condition (i.e. 'flotation or sale within five years' with its associated service requirement) will have been met.

In our view, the appropriate analysis is to regard 'flotation or sale within five years' and 'flotation or sale share price £5' as two separate conditions.

The example above assumes that there is a service condition equal in duration to the other condition attached to the award and hence the analysis above only considers vesting conditions. If the fact pattern were such that there was no service condition, or a service condition that was of a shorter duration than the other conditions, then those conditions would need to be treated as non-vesting conditions rather than as performance vesting conditions.

16.4.5 Awards 'purchased for fair value'

As noted at 3.4.3 above, entities that are contemplating a flotation or trade sale may invite employees to subscribe for shares (often a special class of share) for a relatively nominal amount. In the event of a flotation or trade sale occurring, these shares may be sold or will be redeemable at a substantial premium. It is often argued that the initial subscription price paid represents the fair value of the share at the time, given the inherent high uncertainty as to whether a flotation or trade sale will in fact occur.

The premium paid on the shares in the event of a flotation or trade sale will typically be calculated in part by reference to the price achieved. The question therefore arises as to whether such awards fall within the scope of Section 26. It might be argued for example that, as the employee paid full fair value for the award at issue, there has been no share-based payment and, accordingly, the award is not within the scope of Section 26.

In our view, in order to determine whether the arrangement falls within the scope of Section 26, it is necessary to consider whether the award has features that would not be expected in 'normal' equity transactions – in particular, a requirement for the holder of the shares to remain in employment until flotation or sale and/or individual buyback arrangements. If this is the case, regardless of the amount subscribed, the terms suggest that the shares are being awarded in connection with, and in return for, employee services and hence that the award is within the scope of Section 26. This may mean that, even if the award has no material fair value once the subscription price has been taken into account (and therefore gives rise to no FRS 102 expense), it may be necessary to make the disclosures required by Section 26.

Moreover, even if the amount paid by the employees can be demonstrated to be fair value for tax or other purposes, that amount would not necessarily meet the valuation requirements of Section 26. Specifically, a 'true' fair value would take into account non-market vesting conditions (such as a requirement for the employee to remain in employment until flotation or a trade sale occurs). However, a valuation for Section 26 purposes would not take such conditions into account (see 6.5 and 7.2.1 above) and would therefore typically be higher than the 'true' fair value.

If the arrangement relates to a special class of share rather than ordinary equity shares, the underlying shares might well be classified under FRS 102 as a liability rather than as equity. However, if the redemption amount is linked to the flotation price of the 'real' equity, the arrangement will be a cash-settled share-based payment transaction under Section 26 (see 3.4.1 above).

It is common in such situations for the cost of satisfying any obligations to the holders of the special shares to be borne by shareholders rather than by the entity itself. This raises a number of further issues, which are discussed at 3.2.1 above and at 16.4.6 below.

16.4.6 'Drag along' and 'tag along' rights

An award might be structured to allow management of an entity to acquire a special class of equity at fair value (as in 16.4.5 above), but (in contrast to 16.4.5 above) with no redemption right on an exit event. However, rights are given:

- to any buyer of the 'normal' equity also to buy the special shares (sometimes called a 'drag along' right);
- to a holder of the special shares to require any buyer of the 'normal' equity also to buy the special shares (sometimes called a 'tag along' right).

Such schemes are particularly found in entities where the 'normal' equity is held by a provider of venture capital, which will generally be looking for an exit in the medium term.

It may well be that, under the scheme, the entity itself is required to facilitate the operation of the drag along or tag along rights, which may involve the entity collecting the proceeds from the buyer and passing them on to the holder of the special shares.

Chapter 23

This raises the issue of whether such an arrangement is equity-settled or cash-settled. The fact that, in certain circumstances, the entity is required to deliver cash to the holder of a share suggests that the arrangement is an award requiring cash settlement in specific circumstances, the treatment of which is discussed at 11.3 above.

However, if the terms of the award are such that the entity is obliged to pass on cash to the holder of the share only if, and to the extent that, proceeds are received from an external buyer, in our view the arrangement may be economically no different to the 'broker settlement' arrangements typically entered into by listed entities.

Under such broker settlement arrangements, the entity may either sell employees' shares in the market on the employees' behalf or, more likely, arrange for a third party broker to do so. A sale of shares on behalf of an employee is undertaken by the entity as agent and does not give rise to an increase in equity and an expense, although a share-based payment expense will be recognised for the award of shares. Such an arrangement does not of itself create a cash-settled award, provided that the entity has not created any obligation to the employees. If, however, the entity has either created an expectation among employees that it will step in to make good any lack of depth in the market, or has indeed itself contracted to repurchase the shares in question, it may well mean that analysis as a cash-settled scheme is more appropriate. However, as the entity may enter into much the same transaction with a broker whether it is selling shares on its own behalf or on behalf of its employees, the challenge is for the entity to be able to demonstrate the true economic nature of the transaction.

Following on from the approach to broker settlement arrangements outlined above, an arrangement where the employees' shares are being sold to an external buyer could be regarded as equity-settled because the entity's only involvement as a principal is in the initial delivery of shares to employees. However, consideration must be given to all the factors that could suggest that the scheme is more appropriately regarded as cash-settled.

In making such an assessment, care needs to be taken to ensure that the precise facts of an arrangement are considered. For example, a transaction where the entity has some discretion over the amount of proceeds attributable to each class of shareholder might indicate that it is inappropriate to treat the entity simply as an agent in the cash payment arrangement. It might also be relevant to consider the extent to which, under relevant local law, the proceeds received can be 'ring fenced' so as not to be available to settle other liabilities of the entity.

It is also the case that arrangements that result in employees obtaining similar amounts of cash can be interpreted very differently under Section 26 depending on how the arrangement is structured and whether, for example:

- the entity is required to pay its employees cash on an exit (having perhaps held shares itself via a trust and those shares having been subject to 'drag along' rights); or

- the employees themselves have held the right to equity shares on a restricted basis with vesting – and 'drag along' rights – taking effect on a change of control and the employees receiving cash for their shares.

The appropriate accounting treatment in such cases requires a significant amount of judgement based on the precise facts and circumstances.

17 FIRST-TIME ADOPTION AND TRANSITIONAL PROVISIONS

17.1 Transitional provisions on first-time adoption of FRS 102

Section 35 sets out the transitional provisions for first-time adoption of FRS 102 and is discussed in Chapter 32. Issues arising from the specific requirements of Section 35 in relation to share-based payment transactions are discussed below.

Subject to the special provisions outlined below, a first-time adopter is not required to apply Section 26:

- to equity instruments (including the equity component of share-based payment transactions previously treated as compound instruments) that were granted before the date of transition to FRS 102; or

- to liabilities arising from share-based payment transactions that were settled before the date of transition to FRS 102. *[FRS 102.35.10(b)]*.

There are special provisions for first-time adopters of FRS 102 that have previously applied IFRS 2, which are discussed further below. The transitional provisions from previous UK GAAP (FRS 20 and the FRSSE) are not covered as entities would have transitioned to FRS 102 some years back.

Where a first-time adopter has previously applied IFRS 2, it should 'apply either IFRS 2 (as applicable) or Section 26 of this FRS at the date of transition' to equity instruments (including the equity component of share-based payment transactions previously treated as compound instruments) granted before the date of transition to FRS 102. Therefore, unlike the full exemption from accounting for pre-transition grants given to those first-time adopters that have not previously accounted for share-based payments, those who have previously applied IFRS 2 are required to continue accounting for ongoing awards either under the previous standard or under Section 26. *[FRS 102.35.10(b)]*. In our view, the intention is simply that an entity may complete the accounting for a pre-transition grant using the original grant date fair value and it is not intended that the application of Section 26 to such grants should necessarily result in a remeasurement. However, there is nothing in paragraph 10(b) of Section 35 to prohibit such a remeasurement (for example, as a result of applying the group allocation arrangements of paragraph 16 of Section 26).

FRS 102 and IFRS 2 are not identical for awards where there is a choice of settlement but are closely aligned (see 11 above), therefore it is less likely that the classification of a share-based payment transaction as equity-settled or cash-settled will differ depending on whether an entity is applying FRS 102 or IFRS 2. If a classification difference does still result from adoption of FRS 102, it appears that an entity could continue with the IFRS 2 classification for existing awards, even if new grants would be classified differently under FRS 102.

There is a lack of clarity in relation to certain other aspects of the requirements for those entities with share-based payments to which IFRS 2 has previously been applied but where the accounting treatment of such arrangements differs, or could differ, under Section 26. For example, it is unclear whether a company which has recognised an expense for a transaction for which no apparent consideration has been received has a choice as to whether it carries on doing so (given that there is no general equivalent of paragraph 13A of IFRS 2 (see 3.2.3 above)).

17.2   Modification of awards following transition

Section 35 does not address the treatment of equity-settled awards granted before the date of transition but modified at a later date. Therefore a first-time adopter (other than one who has previously applied FRS 20 or IFRS 2) could potentially avoid a charge for a new award by modifying (or cancelling or settling) an out of scope old award instead. However, in practice, the potential to do this is likely to be limited to those entities previously applying the FRSSE which, in most cases, are unlikely to have had extensive equity-settled share-based payment arrangements in place prior to transition to FRS 102.

18   SUMMARY OF GAAP DIFFERENCES

The differences between FRS 102 and IFRS are set out below.

	FRS 102	*IFRS 2*
Scope: Definitions and transactions within scope (see 2.1 above)	FRS 102 does not provide guidance or examples in areas such as: 1. the meaning of 'goods' in 'goods and services' when used in the definition of a share-based payment transaction; 2. vested transactions; 3. transactions with shareholders as a whole; 4. business combinations; or 5. interaction with accounting for financial instruments.	IFRS 2 has specific guidance or examples in these areas.
Recognition: Accounting after the vesting date (see 2.2.1 above)	FRS 102 includes no guidance on accounting for awards after vesting.	IFRS 2 specifically prohibits a reversal of the expense once awards have vested.
Measurement of equity-settled transactions: Non-vesting conditions (see 2.3.1 above)	FRS 102 contains no definition of conditions that are not vesting conditions, but the example provided is similar to that provided for non-vesting conditions in IFRS 2.	IFRS 2 does not include a definition of a 'non-vesting condition' but includes examples of such conditions as part of the Implementation Guidance.
Employees and others providing similar services (see 2.3.2 above)	FRS 102 offers no additional guidance on the meaning of 'others providing similar services'.	This term is explained/defined in Appendix A to IFRS 2.
Valuation methodology (see 2.3.3 above)	FRS 102 draws a more explicit distinction than IFRS 2 between the valuation of shares and the valuation of options and appreciation rights. It does not mandate use of an option pricing model in the absence of market price information.	IFRS 2 requires the use of a market price or an option pricing model for the valuation of equity-settled transactions. The standard includes guidance in Appendix B about the selection and application of option pricing models that is not reproduced in FRS 102.
Awards where fair value cannot be measured reliably (see 2.3.4 above)	FRS 102 contains no specific requirements and assumes that it will always be possible to fair value an award.	IFRS 2 includes an approach based on intrinsic value to be used in 'rare cases' where an entity is unable to measure fair value reliably.

Cancellation of awards (see 2.3.5 above)	FRS 102 contains no specific requirements to mirror those in IFRS 2.	IFRS 2 makes clear that an award may be cancelled either by the entity or the counterparty and also that a failure to meet non-vesting conditions should, in certain situations, be considered cancellation of an award.
Settlement of awards (see 2.3.6 above)	FRS 102 states that settlement of an unvested award should be treated as an acceleration of vesting but does not specify the treatment when the settlement value exceeds the fair value of the award being cancelled. Similarly, there is no specific guidance on the repurchase of vested equity instruments.	Under IFRS 2, any incremental fair value is expensed at the date of settlement but any settlement value up to the fair value of the cancelled award is debited to equity. When vested equity instruments are repurchased, IFRS 2 requires any incremental fair value to be expensed at the date of repurchase.
Replacement awards following a cancellation or settlement (see 2.3.7 above)	FRS 102 includes no guidance on the accounting treatment of equity-settled awards to replace a cancelled award.	Under IFRS 2 replacement awards may be accounted for on the basis of their incremental fair value rather than being treated as a completely new award.
Measurement of cash-settled transactions: Treatment of non-market performance conditions in measurement of fair value (see 2.4 above)	FRS 102 does not make it explicitly clear whether service and non-market performance conditions should be incorporated into the determination of fair value or whether they should be taken into account in estimating the number of awards expected to vest.	The June 2016 amendment to IFRS 2 clarifies that non-market performance conditions should be taken into account in estimating the number of awards expected to vest rather than being reflected in the determination of fair value. .
Share-based payment transactions with cash alternatives: Counterparty has choice of settlement in equity or cash (see 2.5.1 above)	FRS 102 requires cash-settled accounting unless there is no commercial substance to the amount of the cash settlement alternative.	IFRS 2 requires a split accounting approach, splitting the arrangement into equity-settled and cash-settled components.
Settlement in cash of award accounted for as equity-settled (or *vice versa*) (see 2.5.2 above)	There is no guidance in FRS 102 on how to account for the settlement in cash of an award accounted for as equity-settled or *vice versa*.	IFRS 2 specifically addresses the accounting for a basis of settlement that differs from the accounting basis.
Group plans: Accounting by group entity with obligation to settle an award when another group entity receives goods or services (see 2.6.1 above)	FRS 102 makes clear that an entity receiving goods or services, but with no obligation to settle the transaction, accounts for the transaction as equity-settled. However, prior to the Triennial review 2017although explicitly within scope, the accounting in the entity settling the transaction was not specified. This is now clarified and consistent with IFRS 2.	IFRS 2 makes clear when the settling entity should treat an award as equity-settled and when as cash-settled.

Chapter 23

	FRS 102	*IFRS 2*
Alternative accounting treatment for group plans (see 2.6.2 above)	Where a share-based payment award is granted by an entity to the employees of one or more group entities, those group entities are permitted – as an alternative to the measurement requirements of FRS 102 – to recognise the share-based payment expense on the basis of a reasonable allocation of the group expense.	IFRS 2 has no corresponding alternative treatment.
Unidentifiable goods or services (see 2.7.1 above)	The Triennial review 2017 clarified the scope of the section, where in the absence of specifically identifiable goods or services, other circumstances may indicate that goods or services have been (or will be) received, which is consistent with IFRS 2. But Section 26 then appears to restrict the requirements for certain government-mandated plans where the goods or services received or receivable are not identifiable, and requires the award to be valued on the basis of the equity instruments rather than the goods or services.	Under IFRS 2, the scope is not restricted to government-mandated plans.
Net settlement of awards for tax withholding obligations (see 2.8 above)	There is no exception comparable to that added to IFRS 2 and entities will need to continue to assess whether a net-settled arrangement has an equity-settled element and a cash-settled element.	The June 2016 amendment to IFRS 2 introduced an exception for arrangements that are net-settled solely to meet an entity's withholding tax obligation in respect of an employee's tax liability. Entities meeting the criteria will account for the net-settled award as equity-settled in its entirety. Where the criteria for the exception are not met, entities will need to continue to assess whether an arrangement has an equity-settled element and a cash-settled element.
Disclosures (see 2.9 above)	The disclosure requirements of FRS 102 are generally derived from, but less extensive than, those of IFRS 2. However, there are certain specific requirements that are not found in IFRS 2. There are disclosure exemptions for certain entities.	There are no exemptions from disclosure under IFRS 2.

References

1 For convenience, throughout this chapter we refer to the recognition of a cost for share-based payments. In some cases, however, a share-based payment transaction may initially give rise to an asset (e.g. where employee costs are capitalised as part of the cost of PP&E or inventories).

2 FRS 102 – *The Financial Reporting Standard applicable in the UK and Republic of Ireland*, September 2015, para Accounting Council Advice (SE).39.

3 FASB Staff Position 123(R)-4, *Classification of Options and Similar Instruments Issued as Employee Compensation That Allow for Cash Settlement upon the Occurrence of a Contingent Event.*

4 D17 – *IFRS 2 – Group and Treasury Share Transactions*, IASB, 2005, para. IE5.

Chapter 23

Chapter 24   Impairment of assets

List of examples

Chapter 24

Chapter 24   Impairment of assets

1   INTRODUCTION

In principle an asset is impaired when an entity will not be able to recover that asset's balance sheet carrying value, either through use or sale. If circumstances arise which indicate assets might be impaired, a review should be undertaken of their cash generating abilities either through use (value in use) or sale (fair value less costs to sell). This review will produce an amount which should be compared with the asset's carrying value. If the carrying value is higher, the difference must be written off as an impairment loss.

These principles are consistent with those under IAS 36 – *Impairment of Assets*, although there are some differences in application as discussed at 2 below. The relevant provisions are set out within Section 27 – *Impairment of Assets* – and are discussed at 3 to 8 below.

2   COMPARISON BETWEEN SECTION 27 AND IFRS

2.1   Scope

The scope of Section 27 includes inventories unlike IAS 36. The requirements for impairment of inventories under IFRS are dealt with in IAS 2 – *Inventories*. Differences between IAS 2 and Section 27 are discussed in Chapter 11.

The scope of Section 27 is discussed at 3.1 below.

2.2   Timing of impairment tests

On an annual basis, entities must consider whether there are indicators of impairment in respect of all assets within the scope of Section 27. Entities need only undertake a full impairment test when such indicators are found. Indicators of impairment are discussed at 4.3 below.

This differs to IAS 36, which requires annual impairment tests for goodwill, indefinite-lived intangibles and intangibles not yet available for use. *[IAS 36.10].*

The timing of impairment tests under Section 27 is discussed at 4.1 below.

2.3   Allocation of goodwill

Under both IAS 36 and Section 27, goodwill acquired in a business combination is allocated to each of the acquirer's CGUs that are expected to benefit from the acquisition, whether or not the acquiree's other assets or liabilities are assigned to those units. *[IAS 36.80, FRS 102.27.25]*.

However, if it is not possible to allocate goodwill to a CGU (or group of CGUs) non-arbitrarily, Section 27 contains provisions that allow entities to test for impairment by determining the recoverable amount of either the acquired entity as a whole (if goodwill relates to a non-integrated acquired entity) or the entire group of entities, excluding non-integrated entities (if goodwill relates to an integrated entity). *[FRS 102.27.27]*. IAS 36 contains no such provision. All goodwill must be allocated to a CGU (or group of CGUs).

The allocation of goodwill under Section 27 is discussed further at 5 below.

2.4   Disclosure differences

Section 27 requires less detailed disclosures than IAS 36. The specific disclosure requirements under Section 27 are discussed at 8 below.

3   REQUIREMENTS OF SECTION 27 FOR IMPAIRMENT

3.1   Objective and scope

Section 27 explains that an impairment loss occurs when the carrying amount of an asset exceeds its recoverable amount, whether that is its value in use or its fair value less costs to sell. If, and only if, the recoverable amount of an asset is less than its carrying amount, the entity should reduce the carrying amount of the asset to its recoverable amount. That reduction is an impairment loss. *[FRS 102.27.5]*. Section 27 has a general application to all assets, but the following are outside its scope: *[FRS 102.27.1]*

- assets arising from construction contracts (see Section 23 – *Revenue*);
- deferred tax assets (see Section 29 – *Income Tax*);
- assets arising from employee benefits (see Section 28 – *Employee Benefits*);
- financial assets within the scope of Section 11 – *Basic Financial Instruments* – or Section 12 – *Other Financial Instruments Issues*;
- investment property measured at fair value (see Section 16 – *Investment Property*);
- biological assets related to agricultural activity measured at fair value less estimated costs to sell (see Section 34 – *Specialised Activities*); and
- deferred acquisition costs and intangible assets arising from contracts within the scope of FRS 103 – *Insurance Contracts*.

A parent, in its separate financial statements, must select and adopt a policy of accounting for the following investments at either cost less impairment; at fair value with changes in fair value recognised in other comprehensive income in accordance with Section 17 – *Property, Plant and Equipment*; or, at fair value with changes in fair value recognised in profit or loss: *[FRS 102.9.26]*

- subsidiaries (as defined in Section 9 – *Consolidated and Separate Financial Statements*);
- associates (as defined in Section 14 – *Investments in Associates*); and
- jointly controlled entities (as defined in Section 15 – *Investments in Joint Ventures*).

When entities make an accounting policy choice to account for these investments at cost less impairment, they fall within scope of Section 27 for impairment purposes. *[FRS 102.9.26]*. Similarly, where an entity that is not a parent makes an accounting policy choice to account for their investments in associates and jointly controlled entities at cost less impairment in their individual financial statements, as permitted by Sections 14 and 15 respectively, those investments also fall within scope of Section 27. *[FRS 102.14.5, 15.10]*. Section 27 also includes within its scope investments in associates and joint ventures accounted for using the equity method in the consolidated accounts of a group. *[FRS 102.14.8(d), 15.13]*. The requirements of Sections 9, 14 and 15 are discussed further in Chapters 8, 12 and 13.

3.2   Terms used in Section 27

The key definitions used in FRS 102 are set out in the Glossary in Appendix I to FRS 102 and are given below. *[FRS 102 Appendix I]*.

Term	*Definition*
Carrying amount	The amount at which an asset or liability is recognised in the statement of financial position.
Cash-generating unit	The smallest identifiable group of assets that generates cash inflows that are largely independent of the cash inflows from other assets or groups of assets.
Depreciated replacement cost	The most economic cost required for the entity to replace the service potential of an asset (including the amount that the entity will receive from its disposal at the end of its useful life) at the reporting date.
Fair value less costs to sell	The amount obtainable from the sale of an asset or cash-generating unit in an arm's length transaction between knowledgeable willing parties, less the costs of disposal.
Impairment loss	The amount by which the carrying amount of an asset exceeds: • in the case of inventories, its selling price less costs to complete and sell; or • in the case of other assets, its recoverable amount.
Recoverable amount	The higher of an asset's (or cash-generating unit's) fair value less costs to sell and its value in use.
Service potential	The economic utility of an asset, based on the total benefit expected to be derived by the entity from use (and/or through sale) of the asset.
Value in use	The present value of the future cash flows expected to be derived from an asset or cash-generating unit.
Value in use (in respect of assets held for their service potential)	The present value to the entity of the asset's remaining service potential if it continues to be used, plus the net amount that the entity will receive from its disposal at the end of its useful life.

Chapter 24

3.3   Impairment of inventories

While Section 27 includes specific requirements relating to the impairment of inventories, readers should refer to Chapter 11 where we have chosen to discuss those requirements together with the other principles on the recognition and measurement of inventories.

4   IMPAIRMENT OF ASSETS OTHER THAN INVENTORIES

4.1   General principles

Section 27 requires entities to assess at each reporting date whether there is any indication that an asset may be impaired. Entities are only required to carry out an impairment test if there is an indication of impairment. An entity is not required to perform an impairment test if there is no indication of impairment. *[FRS 102.27.7]*.

As it might be unduly onerous for all assets in scope to be tested for impairment every year, Section 27 requires assets to be tested only if there is an indication that impairment may have occurred. If there are indications that the carrying amount of an asset may not be fully recoverable, an entity should estimate the recoverable amount. The 'indications' of impairment may relate to either the assets themselves or to the economic environment in which they are operated. Possible indicators of impairment are discussed further at 4.3 below.

The purpose of the impairment test is to ensure that tangible and intangible assets, including goodwill, are not carried at a figure greater than their recoverable amount. This recoverable amount is compared with the carrying value of the asset to determine if the asset is impaired.

Recoverable amount is defined as the higher of fair value less costs to sell (FVLCS) and value in use (VIU); the general principle being that an asset should not be carried at more than the amount it will raise, either from selling it now or from using it. *[FRS 102.27.11]*.

Fair value less costs to sell essentially means what the asset could be sold for, having deducted costs of disposal (incrementally incurred direct selling costs). Value in use is defined in terms of discounted future cash flows, as the present value of the cash flows expected from the future use and eventual sale of the asset at the end of its useful life. As the recoverable amount is to be expressed as a present value, not in nominal terms, discounting is a central feature of the impairment test. Diagrammatically, this comparison between carrying value and recoverable amount, and the definition of recoverable amount, can be shown as follows:

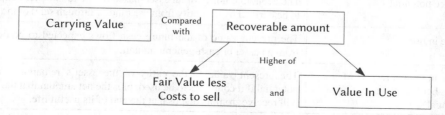

It may not always be necessary to identify both VIU and FVLCS, as if either of VIU or FVLCS is higher than the carrying amount then there is no impairment and no write-down is necessary. Thus, if FVLCS is greater than the carrying amount then no further consideration need be given to VIU, or to the need for an impairment write down. The more complex issues arise when the FVLCS is not greater than the carrying value, and so a VIU calculation is necessary.

If, and only if, the recoverable amount of an asset is less than its carrying amount, the entity should reduce the carrying amount of the asset to its recoverable amount. That reduction is an impairment loss. *[FRS 102.27.5].*

4.2 Testing individual assets or cash generating units

If it is not possible to estimate the recoverable amount of the individual asset, an entity should estimate the recoverable amount of the cash generating unit to which the asset belongs. This may be the case because measuring recoverable amount requires forecasting cash flows, and sometimes individual assets do not generate cash inflows by themselves. An asset's cash generating unit is the smallest identifiable group of assets that includes the asset and generates cash inflows that are largely independent of the cash inflows from other assets or groups of assets. *[FRS 102.27.8].*

The group of assets that is considered together should be as small as is reasonably practicable, i.e. the entity should be divided into as many CGUs as possible – an entity must identify the lowest aggregation of assets that generate largely independent cash inflows. It should be emphasised that the focus is on the asset group's ability to generate cash *inflows*. Cash outflows or any bases for cost allocation have no relevance for the identification of CGUs. The division should not go beyond the level at which each income stream is *capable* of being separately monitored. For example, it may be difficult to identify a level below an individual factory as a CGU but of course an individual factory may or may not be a CGU.

A practical approach to identifying CGUs involves two stages, the first being to work down to the smallest group of assets for which a stream of cash inflows can be identified. These groups of assets will be CGUs unless the performance of their cash inflow-generating assets is dependent on those generated by other assets, or *vice versa* their cash inflows are affected by those of other assets. If the cash inflows generated by the group of assets are not largely independent of those generated by other assets, the second stage is to add other assets to the group to form the smallest collection of assets that generates largely independent cash inflows. The existence of a degree of flexibility over what constitutes a CGU is obvious.

The identification of cash generating units will require judgement and Section 27 itself does not give any further guidance on this area. However, under the hierarchy in Section 10 – *Accounting Policies, Estimates and Errors*, users may wish to refer to the associated guidance in IAS 36.

Under IAS 36, in identifying whether cash inflows from an asset are largely independent of the cash inflows from other assets, entities are advised to consider various factors including:

- how management monitors the entity's operations (such as by product lines, businesses, individual locations, districts or regional areas); or
- how management makes decisions about continuing or disposing of the entity's assets and operations. *[IAS 36.69].*

While monitoring by management may help identify CGUs, it does not override the requirement that the identification of CGUs is based on largely independent cash *inflows*. The following examples illustrate how an entity might identify their CGUs.

Chapter 24

Example 24.1:   Identification of CGUs – Independent cash flows

A bus company provides services under contract with a municipality that requires minimum service on each of five separate routes. Assets devoted to each route and the cash flows from each route can be identified separately. One of the routes operates at a significant loss.

Because the entity does not have the option to curtail any one bus route, the lowest level of identifiable cash inflows that are largely independent of the cash inflows of other assets or groups of assets are the cash inflows generated by the five routes together. The cash generating unit for each route is the bus company as a whole.

Example 24.2:   Identification of CGUs – Management monitoring and decision making

A publisher owns 150 magazine titles of which 70 were purchased and 80 were self-created. The price paid for a purchased magazine title is recognised as an intangible asset. The costs of creating magazine titles and maintaining the existing titles are recognised as an expense when incurred. Cash inflows from direct sales and advertising are identifiable for each magazine title. Titles are managed by customer segments. Management has a policy to abandon old titles before the end of their economic lives and replace them immediately with new titles for the same customer segment.

It is likely that the recoverable amount of an individual magazine title can be assessed. Even though the level of advertising income for a title is influenced, to a certain extent, by the other titles in the customer segment, cash inflows from direct sales and advertising are identifiable for each title. In addition, although titles are managed by customer segments, decisions to abandon titles are made on an individual title basis.

Therefore, it is likely that individual magazine titles generate cash inflows that are largely independent of each other and that each magazine title is a separate cash-generating unit.

In addition to monitoring by management, IAS 36 stresses the significance of an active market for the output of an asset in identifying a CGU. If an active market exists for the output produced by an asset or group of assets, that asset or group of assets should be identified as a cash generating unit, even if some or all of the output is used internally. *[IAS 36.70]*. The existence of an active market means that the assets or CGU could generate cash inflows independently from the rest of the business by selling on the active market. There are active markets for many metals, energy products (various grades of oil product, natural gas) and other commodities that are freely traded.

An active market is defined in FRS 102 as one in which all of the items traded are homogeneous, where willing buyers and sellers can normally be found at any time and which has prices that are available to the public.

Example 24.3:   Identification of CGUs – Active market

Entity M produces a single product and owns plants A, B and C. Each plant is located in a different continent. A produces a component that is assembled in either B or C. The combined capacity of B and C is not fully utilised. M's products are sold worldwide from either B or C. For example, B's production can be sold in C's continent if the products can be delivered faster from B than from C. Utilisation levels of B and C depend on the allocation of sales between the two sites. There is also an active market for A's product.

As there is an active market for its products, it is likely that A is a separate cash-generating unit. Although there is an active market for the products assembled by B and C, cash inflows for B and C depend on the allocation of production across the two sites. It is unlikely that the future cash inflows for B and C can be determined individually. Therefore, it is likely that B and C together are the smallest identifiable group of assets that generates cash inflows that are largely independent.

In determining the value in use of A and B plus C, M adjusts financial budgets/forecasts to reflect its best estimate of future prices that could be achieved in arm's length transactions for A's products.

In practice, different entities will have varying approaches to determining their CGUs. While a CGU as defined in Section 27 is the smallest identifiable group of assets that generates cash inflows that are largely independent, the level of judgement involved means that there is still likely to be a reasonable degree of flexibility in most organisations. In practice, most entities may tend towards larger rather than smaller CGUs to keep the complexity of the process within reasonable bounds, but this leads to the risk that lower level impairments are avoided because poor cash flows from some assets may be offset by better ones from other assets in the CGU.

4.3   Indicators of impairment

An entity should assess at each reporting date whether there is any indication that an asset may be impaired. If any such indication exists, the entity should estimate the recoverable amount of the asset. If there is no indication of impairment, it is not necessary to estimate the recoverable amount. *[FRS 102.27.7]*.

The 'indications' of impairment may relate to either the assets themselves or to the economic environment in which they are operated. Section 27 gives examples of indications of impairment, but makes it clear this is not an exhaustive list. An entity may identify other indications that an asset is impaired that would equally trigger an impairment review.

The indicators given in Section 27 are divided into external and internal indications.

External sources of information:

(a)   During the period, an asset's market value has declined significantly more than would be expected as a result of the passage of time or normal use.

(b)   Significant changes with an adverse effect on the entity have taken place during the period, or will take place in the near future, in the technological, market, economic or legal environment in which the entity operates or in the market to which an asset is dedicated.

(c)   Market interest rates or other market rates of return on investments have increased during the period, and those increases are likely to affect materially the discount rate used in calculating an asset's value in use and decrease the asset's fair value less costs to sell.

(d)   The carrying amount of the net assets of the entity is more than the estimated fair value of the entity as a whole (such an estimate may have been made, for example, in relation to the potential sale of part or all of the entity).

Internal sources of information:

(e)   Evidence is available of obsolescence or physical damage of an asset.

(f)   Significant changes with an adverse effect on the entity have taken place during the period, or are expected to take place in the near future, in the extent to which, or manner in which, an asset is used or is expected to be used. These changes include the asset becoming idle, plans to discontinue or restructure the operation to which an asset belongs, plans to dispose of an asset before the previously expected date, and reassessing the useful life of an asset as finite rather than indefinite.

(g)   Evidence is available from internal reporting that indicates that the economic performance of an asset is, or will be, worse than expected. In this context economic performance includes operating results and cash flows. *[FRS 102.27.9]*.

Chapter 24

While it is not specifically set out in Section 27, the presence of indicators of impairment will not necessarily mean that the entity has to calculate the recoverable amount of the asset. A previous calculation may have shown that an asset's recoverable amount was significantly greater than its carrying amount and it may be clear that subsequent events have been insufficient to eliminate this headroom. Similarly, previous analysis may show that an asset's recoverable amount is not sensitive to one or more of these indicators.

Clearly there is an important judgement to be made in deciding whether an impairment review is needed. As discussed below, once triggered, an impairment review can become a complicated process with serious implications for the financial statements of an entity. Many will therefore wish to avoid performing such a process and thus may wish to argue that there has not been an indication of impairment of significant consequence. Much might turn on the judgement of matters such as whether there has been a *significant* adverse change in the market or just an adverse change.

Section 27 also explains that if there is an indication that an asset may be impaired, this may indicate that the entity should review the remaining useful life, the depreciation (amortisation) method or the residual value for the asset and adjust it in accordance with the applicable section of FRS 102 (e.g. Section 17 – *Property, Plant and Equipment* – and Section 18 – *Intangible Assets other than Goodwill*), even if no impairment loss is recognised for the asset. *[FRS 102.27.10].*

4.3.1 Future performance

The specific wording in (g) above makes clear that FRS 102 requires an impairment review to be undertaken if performance is or will be worse than expected. In particular, there may be indicators of impairment even if the asset is profitable in the current period if budgeted results for the future indicate that there will be losses or net cash outflows when these are aggregated with the current period results.

4.3.2 Individual assets or part of CGU?

Some of the indicators are aimed at individual fixed assets rather than the CGU of which they are a part, for example a decline in the market value of an asset or evidence that it is obsolete or damaged. However, they may also imply that a wider review of the business or CGU is required. For example, if there is a property slump and the market value of the entity's new head office falls below its carrying value this would constitute an indicator of impairment and trigger a review. At the level of the individual asset, as FVLCS is below carrying amount, this might indicate that a write-down is necessary. However, the building's recoverable amount may have to be considered in the context of a CGU of which it is a part. This is an example of a situation where it may not be necessary to re-estimate an asset's recoverable amount because it may be obvious that the CGU has suffered no impairment. In short, it may be irrelevant to the recoverable amount of the CGU that it contains a head office whose market value has fallen.

4.3.3 Interest rates

Including interest rates as indicators of impairment could imply that assets are judged to be impaired if they are no longer expected to earn a market rate of return, even though they may generate the same cash flows as before. However, it may well be that an upward movement in general interest rates will not give rise to a write-down in assets because they may not materially affect the rate of return expected from the asset or CGU itself.

The discount rate used in a VIU calculation should be based on the rate specific for the asset. An entity is not required to make a formal estimate of an asset's recoverable amount if the discount rate used in calculating the asset's VIU is unlikely to be affected by the increase in market rates. For example recoverable amount for an asset that has a long remaining useful life may not be materially affected by increases in short-term rates. Further an entity is not required to make a formal estimate of an asset's recoverable amount if previous sensitivity analyses of the recoverable amount show that it is unlikely that there will be a material decrease in recoverable amount because future cash flows are also likely to increase to compensate for the increase in market rates. Consequently, the potential decrease in recoverable amount may simply be unlikely to result in a material impairment loss.

4.4 Measuring recoverable amount

Section 27 requires the carrying amount to be compared with the recoverable amount when there is an indicator of impairment. The recoverable amount of an asset or a CGU is the higher of its fair value less costs to sell and its value in use. *[FRS 102.27.11]*. If either the FVLCS or the VIU is higher than the carrying amount, the asset is not impaired and it is not necessary to estimate the other amount. *[FRS 102.27.12]*.

Recoverable amount is calculated for an individual asset, unless that asset does not generate cash inflows that are largely independent of those from other assets or groups of assets, in which case the recoverable amount should be estimated for the CGU to which the asset belongs. *[FRS 102.27.8]*.

VIU is defined as the present value of the future cash flows expected to be derived from an asset or CGU. FVLCS is defined as the amount obtainable from the sale of an asset or CGU in an arm's length transaction between knowledgeable, willing parties, less the costs of disposal.

Estimating the VIU of an asset involves estimating the future cash inflows and outflows that will be derived from the continuing use of the asset and from its ultimate disposal, and discounting them at an appropriate rate. *[FRS 102.27.15]*. There can be complex issues involved in determining the relevant cash flows and choosing a discount rate and these are discussed at 4.6 below.

When estimating FVLCS, the best evidence is a price in a binding sale agreement in an arm's length transaction or a market price in an active market. Where such evidence is not available, management should base their estimate of FVLCS on the best information available. *[FRS 102.27.14]*. This can be a complex process as discussed at 4.5 below.

Section 27 mentions circumstances in which it may be appropriate to use an asset or CGU's FVLCS without calculating its VIU, as the measure of its recoverable amount. There may be no reason to believe that an asset's VIU materially exceeds its FVLCS, in which case the asset's FVLCS may be used as its recoverable amount. *[FRS 102.27.13]*. This is the case, for example, if management is intending to dispose of the asset or CGU, as apart from its disposal proceeds there will be few if any cash flows from further use.

It is not uncommon for the FVLCS of an asset to be readily obtainable while the asset itself does not generate largely independent cash inflows, as is the case with many property assets held by entities. If the FVLCS of the asset is lower than its carrying value then the recoverable amount (which means both FVLCS and VIU) will have to be calculated by reference to the CGU of which the asset is a part. However, as explained at 4.3.2 above, it may be obvious that the CGU to which the property belongs has not suffered an impairment. In such a case it would not be necessary to assess the recoverable amount of the CGU.

4.4.1 Consistency and the impairment test

In testing for impairment, entities must ensure that the assets and liabilities included in the carrying amount of the CGU are consistent with the cash flows used to calculate its VIU and FVLCS. There should also be consistency between the cash flows and the discount rate.

A CGU is defined as the smallest identifiable group of assets that generate cash inflows that are largely independent of the cash inflows from other assets or groups of assets. Therefore, we would generally expect that entities would not include liabilities in arriving at the carrying amount of a CGU. However, in order to achieve consistency in the impairment calculation, there are some exceptions. If a buyer would have to assume a liability if it acquired an asset of CGU, then this liability should be deducted from the CGU's carrying amount and recoverable amount, by taking the relevant cash flows into account, in order to perform a meaningful comparison between VIU and FVLCD.

For practical reasons an entity may determine the recoverable amount of a CGU after taking into account assets and liabilities such as receivables or other financial assets, trade payables, pensions and other provisions. In all cases:

- the carrying amount of the CGU must be calculated on the same basis for VIU and FVLCS, i.e. including the same assets and liabilities; and

- it is essential that cash flows are prepared on a consistent basis to the assets and liabilities within CGUs.

4.5 Fair value less costs to sell (FVLCS)

FVLCS is defined as the amount obtainable from the sale of an asset (or CGU) in an arm's length transaction between knowledgeable, willing parties, less the costs of disposal. The best evidence of an asset's FVLCS is a price in a binding sale agreement in an arm's length transaction or a market price in an active market. If there is no binding sale agreement or active market for an asset, FVLCS is based on the best information available to reflect the amount that an entity could obtain, at the reporting date, from the disposal of the asset in an arm's length transaction between knowledgeable, willing parties, after deducting the costs of disposal. In determining this amount, an entity considers the outcome of recent transactions for similar assets within the same industry. *[FRS 102.27.14].*

Section 27 therefore makes clear that if there is a binding sales agreement in an arm's length transaction or an active market then that price *must* be used. In reality, however, there are few active markets for most tangible and intangible assets. An active market is defined as one in which all of the items traded are homogeneous, where willing buyers and sellers can normally be found at any time and which has prices that are available to the public. *[FRS 102 Appendix I].* Consequently, most estimates of fair value will be based on estimates of the market price of the asset in an arm's length transaction. This will involve consideration of the outcome of recent transactions for similar assets in the same industry. The entity will use the best information it has available at the balance sheet date to construct the price payable in an arm's length transaction between knowledgeable, willing parties.

While Section 27 does not mention any other valuation techniques, it may be that the use of such techniques is the only way to obtain the best estimate of fair value. This may be the case where there is no binding sales agreement, where no active market for the asset exists and transactions for similar assets do not happen often enough to provide a reliable measure of fair value. In such cases entities need to rely on other valuation techniques in considering the best information available at the balance sheet date. This is discussed further at 4.5.1 below.

In all cases, FVLCS should take account of estimated disposal costs. These include legal costs, stamp duty and other transaction taxes, costs of moving the asset and other direct incremental costs.

The following simple example illustrates how an entity might determine FVLCS for an asset.

Example 24.4: Estimating FVLCS

An entity owns two ships, one a chemical tanker designed to transport liquids for entities in the chemical industry and the other a container ship supplying the freight industry. The cash inflows for each ship are independent and as such, each ship is considered a CGU.

At the end of 20X0 the chemical tanker has a carrying value of £9,000,000 (original cost (£19,000,000; accumulated depreciation £10,000,000). The original estimate of the life of the tanker was seven years (measured from the date the tanker was first recognised by the entity) and it had an estimated residual value of £5,000,000.

Because of increased port taxes for liquid chemical consignments in the region, the entity has seen a substantial decrease in demand for use of the tanker since the prior year. The market price for the tanker in an active resale market is £6,000,000. Licence and title fees associated with selling the tanker are £200,000.

The reduction in use is an internal indicator that the tanker is impaired.

The price in an active market provides an estimate of fair value. The entity has calculated the VIU of the tanker as £4,500,000 which is lower than the resale value in an active market. Consequently the recoverable amount of the tanker is £5,800,000 (£6,000,000 fair value less £200,000 costs to sell). The entity makes the following entries to record the impairment of the tanker:

Dr. Profit or loss	
(impairment of tanker)	£3,200,000
Cr. Accumulated impairment	
(property, plant and equipment)	£3,200,000

To recognise the impairment loss on property, plant and equipment.

4.5.1 Estimating fair value less costs to sell without an active market

Even where an active market for an asset (or CGU) does not exist, it may be possible to determine fair value provided there is a basis for making a reliable estimate of the amount obtainable from the sale of the asset in an arm's length transaction between knowledgeable and willing parties.

When there is no binding sale agreement or active market for an asset, an entity should consider 'the outcome of recent transactions for similar assets within the same industry'. *[FRS 102.27.14]*. If the entity has only recently acquired the asset or CGU in question then it may be able to demonstrate that its purchase price remains an appropriate measure of FVLCS, although it would have to make adjustments for material costs to sell.

To rely on the outcome of a recent transaction for a similar asset by a third party, the following conditions should be considered:

- the transaction should be in the same industry, unless the asset is generic and its fair value would not be affected by the industry in which the purchaser operates;
- the assets should be shown to be substantially the same as to their nature and condition; and
- the economic environment of the entity should be similar to the environment in which the previous sale occurred (e.g. no material circumstances have arisen since the earlier transaction that affect the value of the asset). This means that previous transactions are particularly unreliable if markets are falling.

It would be unusual to be able to estimate FVLCS reliably from a single market transaction. As discussed below, if reliable market assumptions are known, it is much more likely that a recent market transaction would be one of the factors taken into account in the calculation of FVLCS. For example, if the economic environment is slightly different, or if the asset sold is not exactly the same as the one for which a FVLCS is being estimated, then it may still be possible to use the transaction as a starting point from which adjustments could be made for differing characteristics in the asset or the economic environment. Judgement will be required and consideration will have to be given to all relevant facts and circumstances.

Similarly, if the entity cannot demonstrate that a recent transaction alone provides a reliable estimate of FVLCS, the transaction may be one of the sources of evidence used to validate an estimate of FVLCS using other valuation techniques. This is particularly likely to be the case if the impairment review is of a CGU or CGU group rather than an individual asset, as market transactions for CGUs may be less relevant.

Section 27 itself provides no specific guidance on other valuation techniques, which could be used. However, within the definition of fair value in the Glossary in Appendix I to FRS 102, it is stated that in the absence of any specific guidance provided in the relevant section of this FRS, the guidance in the Appendix to Section 2 *Concepts and Pervasive Principles* should be used in determining fair value.

When quoted prices are unavailable, the price in a binding sale agreement or a recent transaction for an identical asset (or similar asset) in an arm's length transaction between knowledgeable, willing parties provides evidence of fair value. However this price may not be a good estimate of fair value if there has been a significant change in economic circumstances or significant period of time between the date of the binding sale agreement or the transaction, and the measurement date. If the entity can demonstrate that the last transaction price is not a good estimate of fair value (e.g. because it reflects the amount that an entity would receive or pay in a forced transaction, involuntary liquidation or distress sale), that price will have to be adjusted. *[FRS 102.2A.1(b)].*

If the market for the asset is not active and any binding sale agreements or recent transactions for an identical asset (or similar asset) on their own are not a good estimate of fair value, an entity estimates the fair value by using another valuation technique. The objective of using another valuation technique is to estimate what the transaction price would have been on the measurement date in an arm's length exchange motivated by normal business considerations. *[FRS 102.2A.1(c)]*.

Valuation techniques include using the price in a binding sale agreement and recent arm's length market transactions for an identical asset between knowledgeable, willing parties, reference to the current fair value of another asset that is substantially the same as the asset being measured, discounted cash flow analysis and option pricing models. If there is a valuation technique commonly used by market participants to price the asset and that technique has been demonstrated to provide reliable estimates of prices obtained in actual market transactions, the entity uses that technique. *[FRS 102.2A.2]*.

As noted above, the objective of using a valuation technique is to establish what the transaction price would have been on the measurement date in an arm's length exchange motivated by normal business considerations. Fair value is estimated on the basis of the results of a valuation technique that makes maximum use of market inputs, and relies as little as possible on entity-determined inputs. A valuation technique would be expected to arrive at a reliable estimate of the fair value if:

- it reasonably reflects how the market could be expected to price the asset; and
- the inputs to the valuation technique reasonably represent market expectations and measures of the risk return factors inherent in the asset. *[FRS 102.2A.3]*.

It is clear that in calculating FVLCS it may be appropriate to use cash flow valuation techniques such as discounted cash flows or other valuation techniques such as earnings multiples, if it can be demonstrated that they would be used by the relevant 'market participants' i.e. other businesses in the same industry; while the second paragraph emphasises the need to prioritise market inputs i.e. those which are visible to all, over inputs determined by the entity itself.

When selecting and using a valuation technique to estimate FVLCS, an entity would consider all of the following:

- relevance of the available valuation models – this may include consideration of industry practice;
- assumptions used in the model – these should only be those that other market participants would use. They should not be based on management's uncorroborated views or information that would not be known or considered by other market participants; and
- whether there is reliable evidence showing that these assumptions would be taken into account by market participants. For this purpose, it may be necessary for the entity to obtain external advice.

Additionally, when markets are unstable, entities should ensure that multiples remain valid. They should not assume that the basis underlying the multiples remains unchanged.

A discounted cash flow technique may be used if this is commonly used in that industry to estimate fair value. Cash flows used when applying the model may only reflect cash flows that market participants would take into account when assessing fair value. This includes the type of cash flows, for example future capital expenditure, as well as the estimated amount of cash flows. For example, an entity may wish to take into account cash flows relating to future capital expenditure, which would not be permitted for a VIU calculation (see 4.6.3 below). These cash flows can be included if, but only if, other market participants would consider them when evaluating the asset. It is not permissible to include assumptions about cash flows or benefits from the asset that would not be available to or considered by a typical market participant. Obtaining reliable evidence of market assumptions is not straightforward, and may not be available to many entities wishing to apply valuation techniques. However, if the information is available then entities ought to take it into account in calculating FVLCS.

It is also important to ensure that the cash flows included in the discounted cash flow model are consistent with the asset or CGU being tested. For example if working capital balances such as trade debtors and creditors are included in the carrying value of the CGU, the cash inflows and outflows from those assets and liabilities should be included in the related cash flow projections.

4.5.2   Effect of restrictions on fair value

When determining an asset's fair value less costs to sell, consideration should be given to any restrictions imposed on that asset. Costs to sell should also include the cost of obtaining relaxation of a restriction where necessary in order to enable the asset to be sold. If a restriction would also apply to any potential purchaser of an asset, the fair value of the asset may be lower than that of an asset whose use is not restricted. *[FRS 102.27.14A].*

Where a restriction on the sale or use of an asset would apply to any potential purchaser of the asset, the effect of that restriction should be taken into account in pricing the fair value of the asset. Where the restriction is specific to the entity holding the asset and so would not transfer to a potential purchaser, then that restriction would not reduce the fair value of the asset.

The following example illustrates a situation where a certain restriction would apply to any potential purchaser of the asset concerned while a further restriction applies to the specific entity holding the asset, but not to other market participants. Only the first of these restrictions will reduce fair value when compared with an equivalent unrestricted asset.

Example 24.5:   Restrictions on assets

A donor of land specifies that the land must be used by a sporting association as a playground in perpetuity. Upon review of relevant documentation, the association determines that the donor's restriction would not transfer to potential purchasers if the association sold the asset (i.e. the restriction on the use of the land is specific to the association). Furthermore, the association is not restricted from selling the land. Without the restriction on the use of the land, the land could be used as a site for residential development. In addition, the land is subject to an easement (a legal right that enables a utility to run power lines across the land).

Under these circumstances, the effect of the restriction and the easement on the fair value measurement of the land is as follows:

(a) donor restriction on use of land – The donor restriction on the use of the land is specific to the association and thus would not apply to potential purchasers. Therefore, a market participant would not take this restriction into consideration when pricing the land and fair value might therefore be based on a residential development.

(b) easement for utility lines – Because the easement for utility lines would apply to any potential purchaser, the fair value of the land would include the effect of the easement, regardless of whether the land's valuation premise is as a playground or as a site for residential development.

4.6   Value in use (VIU)

Value in use (VIU) is defined as the present value of the future cash flows expected to be derived from an asset or cash-generating unit. *[FRS 102 Appendix I]*.

The calculation of VIU involves the following steps: *[FRS 102.27.15]*

- estimating the future cash inflows and outflows to be derived from continuing use of the asset and from its ultimate disposal; and
- applying the appropriate discount rate to those future cash flows.

The following elements are required to be reflected in the VIU calculation: *[FRS 102.27.16]*

(a) an estimate of the future cash flows the entity expects to derive from the asset;

(b) expectations about possible variations in the amount or timing of those future cash flows;

(c) the time value of money, represented by the current market risk-free rate of interest;

(d) the price for bearing the uncertainty inherent in the asset; and

(e) other factors, such as illiquidity, that market participants would reflect in pricing the future cash flows the entity expects to derive from the asset.

Uncertainty as to the timing of cash flows or the market's assessment of risk in the assets ((d) and (e) above) must be taken into account *either* by adjusting the cash flows or the discount rate. Specifically, the discount rate used to measure an asset's VIU should not reflect risks for which the future cash flow estimates have been adjusted, to avoid double counting. *[FRS 102.27.20]*.

If it is not possible to estimate the recoverable amount of an individual asset, the entity should estimate the recoverable amount of the CGU to which the asset belongs. *[FRS 102.27.8]*. This will frequently be necessary because:

- the single asset may not generate sufficiently independent cash inflows, as is often the case; and
- in the case of the possible impairment of a single asset, FVLCS will frequently be lower than the carrying amount.

Where a CGU is being reviewed for impairment, this will involve calculation of the VIU of the CGU as a whole unless a reliable estimate of the CGU's FVLCS can be made and the resulting FVLCS is above the total of the CGU's net assets.

VIU calculations at the level of the CGU will thus be required when no satisfactory FVLCS is available or FVLCS is below the CGU's carrying amount and:

- goodwill is suspected of being impaired;
- a CGU itself is suspected of being impaired; or

- individual assets are suspected of being impaired and individual future cash flows cannot be identified for them.

In order to calculate VIU there are a series of steps to follow, as set out below. Within each step, we should discuss the practicalities and difficulties in determining the VIU of an asset. The steps in the process are:

1:    Dividing the entity into CGUs (at 4.2 above).

2:    Estimating the future pre-tax cash flows of the CGU under review (at 4.6.1-4.6.4 below).

3:    Identifying an appropriate discount rate and discounting the future cash flows (at 4.6.5 below).

4:    Comparing carrying value with VIU and recognising impairment losses (at 6 below).

Although this process describes the determination of the VIU of a CGU, steps 2 to 4 are the same as those that would be applied to an individual asset if it generated cash inflows independently of other assets.

Example 24.6 illustrates a simple example of how an entity would calculate the VIU of an individual asset following the principles set out at 4.6.1-4.6.5 below.

Example 24.6:   Estimating value in use

Entity A manufactures an electrical component using a specialised machine. During 20X0, one of Entity A's competitors starts producing an alternative component using a less expensive material. The competitor is able to market their product at a lower cost than Entity A and so sales of Entity A's product fall sharply.

Entity A's specialised machine cannot be modified to work with this cheaper material and so at the end of 20X0 they test the machine for impairment. The machine was bought five years ago for £300,000 when its useful life was estimated to be 15 years and the estimated residual value was nil. At 31 December 20X0, after recognising the depreciation change for 20X0, the machine's carrying amount is £200,000 and the remaining useful life is 10 years.

The machine's VIU is calculated using a pre-tax discount rate of 14 per cent per year. Budgets approved by management reflect estimated costs necessary to maintain the level of economic benefit expected to arise from the machine in its current condition.

Assume for simplicity, expected future cash flows occur at the end of the reporting period. An estimation of the VIU of the machine at the end of 20X0 is shown below:

Year	Probability-weighted future cash flow £	Present value factor 14%[1]	Discounted cash flow £
20X1	19,949	0.877193	17,499
20X2	19,305	0.769468	14,855
20X3	18,084	0.674972	12,206
20X4	21,016	0.592080	12,443
20X5	20,767	0.519369	10,786
20X6	19,115	0.455587	8,709
20X7	17,369	0.399637	6,941
20X8	16,596	0.350559	5,818
20X9	14,540	0.307508	4,471
20Y0[2]	12,568	0.269744	3,390
Value in use			97,118

[1] The present value factor is calculated as $k+1/(1+i)^n$ where i is the discount rate and n is the number of periods of discount e.g. for 20Y0 the present value factor is calculated as follows: $1/(1.14)^{10} = 1/3.707221 = 0.269744$.

[2] The expected future cash flow for year 20Y0 includes £2,500 expected to be paid for the disposal of the asset at the end of its useful life. The residual value is nil because it is expected that the machine will be scrapped at the end of 20Y0.

Assuming that the FVLCS is lower than VIU (and thus VIU is the recoverable amount), the calculation of the impairment loss at the end of 20X0 is as follows:

Carrying amount before impairment loss	£200,000
Less recoverable amount	(£97,118)
Impairment loss	£102,882
Carrying amount after impairment loss	£97,118

As a consequence of the impairment loss recognised at 31 December 20X0, the carrying amount of the machine immediately after the impairment recognition is equal to the recoverable amount of the machine i.e. £97,118. In this case, in subsequent periods, assuming all variables remain the same as at the end of 20X0, the depreciable amount will be £97,118, so the depreciation charge will be £9,712 per year.

4.6.1 Estimating the future pre-tax cash flows of the CGU under review

In measuring value in use, estimates of future cash flows should include:

- projections of cash inflows from the continuing use of the asset;
- projections of cash outflows that are necessarily incurred to generate the cash inflows from continuing use of the asset (including cash outflows to prepare the asset for use) and can be directly attributed, or allocated on a reasonable and consistent basis, to the asset; and
- net cash flows, if any, expected to be received (or paid) for the disposal of the asset at the end of its useful life in an arm's length transaction between knowledgeable, willing parties.

An entity may wish to use any recent financial budgets or forecasts to estimate the cash flows, if available. To estimate cash flow projections beyond the period covered by the most recent budgets or forecasts an entity may wish to extrapolate the projections based on the budgets or forecasts using a steady or declining growth rate for subsequent years, unless an increasing rate can be justified. *[FRS 102.27.17]*.

As noted at 4.6 above, uncertainties as to the timing of cash flows or the market's assessment of risk in the assets should be taken into account *either* by adjusting the cash flows or the discount rate. Entities must take care to avoid double counting.

Although not specified in Section 27, our normal expectation would be for entities to apply a similar rule of thumb to that under IAS 36, being the application of a five year maximum, for the period before which a steady or declining growth rate could be assumed. This five year rule is based on general economic theory that postulates above-average growth rates will only be achievable in the short-term, because such above-average growth will lead to competitors entering the market. This increased competition will, over a period of time, lead to a reduction of the growth rate, towards the average for the economy as a whole.

Cash flows can be estimated by taking into account general price changes caused by inflation, or on the basis of stable prices. If inflation is excluded from the cash flow then

Chapter 24

the discount rate selected should also be adjusted to remove the inflationary effect. Generally entities will use whichever method is most convenient to them and that is consistent with the method they use in their budgets and forecasts. It is, of course, fundamental that cash flows and discount rate are both estimated on a consistent basis.

In our view, if the cash inflows generated by an asset or CGU are based on internal transfer pricing, management should use their best estimate of an external arm's length transaction price in estimating the future cash flows to determine the asset's or CGU's VIU.

The cash inflows attributable to an asset or CGU may be generated in a foreign currency. Section 27 does not provide any guidance on this issue, but under the hierarchy in Section 10, companies may wish to consider the guidance in IAS 36. IAS 36 states that foreign currency cash flows should first be estimated in the currency in which they will be generated and then discounted using a discount rate appropriate for that currency. The entity can then translate the present value calculated in the foreign currency using the spot exchange rate at the date of the VIU calculation.

This is to avoid the problems inherent in using forward exchange rates, which would result in double-counting the time value of money, first in the discount rate and then in the forward rate. Arriving at a suitable discount rate could be an extremely difficult exercise as many different factors need to be taken into account including relative inflation rates and relative interest rates as well as appropriate discount rates for the currencies in question. Entities may wish to engage valuers to assist them in this situation.

4.6.2   Financing and taxation

Estimates of future cash flows should not include: *[FRS 102.27.18]*

- cash inflows or outflows from financing activities; or
- income tax receipts or payments.

The first of these exclusions is required because the discount rate applied to the cash flow projections represents the associated financing costs (so to include financing cash flows would be double counting this effect). For consistency, financial liabilities are excluded from the carrying amount of the CGU. Discount rates are discussed further at 4.6.5 below. Similarly, income tax receipts and payments must also be excluded on consistency grounds as Section 27 requires the use of a pre-tax discount rate to be used in the VIU calculation. *[FRS 102.27.20]*.

4.6.3   Restructuring and improvements

While cash flow projections should include costs of day-to-day servicing, future cash flows should be estimated for the asset in its current condition. Estimates of future cash flows should not include estimated future cash inflows or outflows that are expected to arise from: *[FRS 102.27.19]*

- a future restructuring to which an entity is not yet committed; or
- improving or enhancing the asset's performance.

While the restriction on enhanced performance may be understandable, it adds an element of unreality that is hard to reconcile with other assumptions made in the VIU calculation process. For example, the underlying forecast cash flows an entity uses in its VIU calculation are likely to be based on the business as it is actually expected to develop in the future, growth, improvements and all. Producing a special forecast based on unrealistic assumptions, even for this limited purpose, may be difficult.

Nevertheless, Section 27 explicitly states that projected cash flows should not include expenditure to improve or enhance performance of an asset. *[FRS 102.27.19]*. The implication of this requirement is that if an asset is impaired, and even if the entity is going to make the future expenditure to reverse that impairment, the asset will still have to be written down. Subsequently, the asset's impairment can be reversed, to the degree appropriate, after the expenditure has taken place. Reversal of asset impairment is discussed at 7 below.

An assumption of new capital investment is in practice intrinsic to the VIU test. What has to be assessed are the future cash flows of a productive unit such as a factory or hotel. The cash flows, out into the far future, will include the sales of product, cost of sales, administrative expenses, etc. They must necessarily include capital expenditure as well, at least to the extent required to keep the CGU functioning as forecast.

Accordingly, *some* capital expenditure cash flows must be built into the forecast cash flows. Whilst improving capital expenditure may not be recognised, routine or replacement capital expenditure necessary to maintain the function of the asset or assets in the CGU has to be included. Entities must therefore distinguish between maintenance, replacement and enhancement expenditure. This distinction may not be easy to draw in practice, as shown in the following example.

Example 24.7:   *Distinguishing enhancement and maintenance expenditure*

A telecommunications company provides fixed line, telephone, television and internet services. It must develop its basic transmission infrastructure (by overhead wires or cables along streets or railway lines etc.) and in order to service a new customer it will have to connect the customer's home via cable and other equipment. It will extend its network to adjoining areas and perhaps acquire an entity with its own network. It will also reflect changes in technology, e.g. fibre optic cables replacing copper ones.

Obviously, when preparing the budgets which form the basis for testing the network for impairment, it will make assumptions regarding future revenue growth and will include the costs of connecting those customers. However, its infrastructure maintenance spend will inevitably include replacing equipment with the current technology. There is no option of continuing to replace equipment with something that has been technologically superseded. Once this technology exists it will be reflected in the entity's budgets and taken into account in its cash flows when carrying out impairment tests, even though this new equipment will enhance the performance of the transmission infrastructure.

Further examples indicate another problem area – the effects of future expenditure that the entity has identified but which the entity has not yet incurred. An entity may have acquired an asset with the intention of enhancing it in future and may, therefore, have paid for future synergies which will be reflected in the calculation of goodwill. Another entity may have plans for an asset that involve expenditure that will enhance its future performance and without which the asset may be impaired.

Examples could include:

- a TV transmission company that, in acquiring another, would expect to pay for the future right to migrate customers from analogue to digital services; or

- an aircraft manufacturer that expects to be able to use one of the acquired plants for a new model at a future point, a process that will involve replacing much of the current equipment.

Chapter 24

In both cases the long-term plans reflect both the capital spent and the cash flows that will flow from it. There is no obvious alternative to recognising an impairment when calculating the CGU or CGU group's VIU as Section 27 states that the impairment test has to be performed for the asset in its current condition. This means that it is not permitted to include the benefit of improving or enhancing the asset's performance in calculating its VIU.

An entity in this situation may attempt to avoid an impairment write down by calculating the appropriate FVLCS, as this is not constrained by rules regarding future capital expenditure. As discussed above, these cash flows can be included only to the extent that other market participants would consider them when evaluating the asset. It is not permissible to include assumptions about cash flows or benefits from the asset that would not be available to or considered by a typical market participant.

Section 27 contains similar rules with regard to any future restructuring that may affect the VIU of the asset or CGU. The prohibition on including the results of restructuring applies only to those plans to which the entity is not committed. This is because of the general rule that the cash flows must be based on the asset in its current condition so future events that may change that condition should not be taken into account. When an entity becomes committed to a restructuring Section 27 then allows an entity's estimates of future cash inflows and outflows to reflect the cost savings and other benefits from the restructuring, based on the most recent financial budgets/forecasts approved by management.

As is the case for improvement expenditure above, entities will sometimes be required to recognise impairment losses on assets or CGUs that will be reversed once the expenditure has been incurred and the restructuring completed.

4.6.4   Terminal values

In the case of non-current assets, a large component of value attributable to an asset or CGU arises from its terminal value, which is the net present value of all of the forecast free cash flows that are expected to be generated by the asset or CGU after the explicit forecast period.

Where an asset is to be sold at the end of its useful life the disposal proceeds and costs should be based on current prices and costs for similar assets, adjusted if necessary for price level changes if the entity has chosen to include this factor in its forecasts and selection of a discount rate. The entity should ensure that its estimate is based on a proper assessment of the amount that would be received in an arm's length transaction.

However, CGUs usually have indefinite lives, as have some assets, and the terminal value is calculated by having regard to the forecast maintainable cash flows that are expected to be generated by the asset or CGU in the final year of the explicit forecast period ('the terminal year').

It is essential that the terminal year cash flows reflect maintainable cash flows as otherwise any material one-off or abnormal cash flows that are forecast for the terminal year will inappropriately increase or decrease the valuation.

The maintainable cash flow expected to be generated by the asset or CGU is then capitalised by a perpetuity factor based on either:

- the discount rate if cash flows are forecast to remain relatively constant; or
- the discount rate less the long term growth rate if cash flows are forecast to grow.

Care is required in assessing the growth rate to ensure consistency between the long term growth rate used and the assumptions used by the entity generally in its business planning.

4.6.5 Discount rate

After identifying the relevant cash flows for the asset or CGU, the next step is to identify an appropriate discount rate to use in deriving the present value of those cash flows.

The discount rate (rates) used in the present value calculation should be a pre-tax rate (rates) that reflect(s) current market assessments of:

- the time value of money; and
- the risks specific to the asset for which the future cash flow estimates have not been adjusted.

The discount rate (rates) used to measure an asset's value in use should not reflect risks for which the future cash flow estimates have been adjusted, to avoid double-counting. *[FRS 102.27.20]*.

This means the discount rate to be applied should be an estimate of the rate that the market would expect on an equally risky investment. The discount rate specific for the asset or CGU will take account of the period over which the asset or CGU is expected to generate cash inflows and it may not be sensitive to changes in short-term rates.

If at all possible, the rate should be obtained from market transactions or market rates. It should be the rate implicit in current market transactions for similar assets or the weighted average cost of capital (WACC) of a listed entity that has a single asset (or a portfolio of assets) with similar service potential and risks to the asset under review.

In most cases an asset-specific rate will not be available from the market and therefore estimates will be required. Determining the discount rate that investors would require if they were to choose an investment that would generate cash flows of amounts, timing and risk profile equivalent to those that the entity expects to derive from the asset will not be easy.

As a starting point, the entity may take into account the following rates:

- the entity's weighted average cost of capital determined using techniques such as the Capital Asset Pricing Model;
- the entity's incremental borrowing rate; and
- other market borrowing rates.

From that starting point the rate should be adjusted to:

- reflect the specific risks associated with the projected cash flows (such as country, currency, price and cash flow risks);
- exclude risks that are not relevant to the asset or CGU concerned;
- avoid double counting, by ensuring that the discount rate does not reflect risks for which future cash flow estimates have already been adjusted; and
- reflect a pre-tax rate if the basis for the starting rate is post-tax (such as WACC).

Chapter 24

As the rate required is one which is specific to the asset (or CGU) and not to the entity, the discount rate should be independent of the entity's capital structure and the way it financed the purchase of the asset.

In practice many entities will use the WACC as a starting point to estimate the appropriate discount rate. WACC is an accepted methodology based on a well-known formula and widely available information and in addition, many entities already know their own WACC. However, it can only be used as a starting point for determining an appropriate discount rate. Some of the issues that must be taken into account are as follows:

a)   the WACC is a post-tax rate and VIU is required to be calculated using pre-tax cash flows and a pre-tax rate. Converting the former into the latter is not simply a question of grossing up the post-tax rate by the effective tax rate;

b)   other tax factors may need to be considered, whether or not these will result in tax cash flows in the period covered by budgets and cash flows;

c)   an entity's own WACC may not be suitable as a discount rate if there is anything atypical about the entity's capital structure compared with 'typical' market participants;

d)   the WACC must reflect the risks specific to the asset and not the risks relating to the entity as a whole, such as default risk; and

e)   the entity's WACC is an average rate derived from its existing business, yet entities frequently operate in more than one sector. Within a sector, different types of projects may have different levels of risk (e.g. a start-up as against an established product).

The selection of the discount rate is obviously a crucial part of the impairment testing process and in practice it will probably not be possible to obtain a theoretically perfect rate. The objective, therefore, must be to obtain a rate which is sensible and justifiable and in order to do so, specialist advice may be needed. For further discussion on calculation of an appropriate discount rate and on how entities can derive the appropriate pre-tax equivalent rate from a starting point of WACC, readers may wish to refer to Chapter 20 at 7.2 of EY International GAAP 2019. Ultimately the selection of discount rates leaves considerable room for judgement and it is likely that many very different approaches will be applied in practice, even though this may not always be evident from the financial statements. Once the discount rate has been chosen, the future cash flows are discounted in order to produce a present value figure representing the VIU of the CGU or individual asset that is the subject of the impairment test.

4.6.6   Assets held for their service potential

While in a for-profit entity, it is appropriate to determine VIU by measuring the present value of the cash flows derived from an asset or CGU, this may be less relevant in the context of Public Benefit Entities (PBEs). A PBE is defined in FRS 102 as an entity whose primary objective is to provide goods or services for the general public, community or social benefit and where any equity is provided with a view to supporting the entity's primary objectives rather than with a view to providing a financial return to equity providers, shareholders or members.

In a PBE assets may be held not for cash generating purposes but for their service potential i.e. where the benefits are expected to be derived through use of the asset along with proceeds from sale. To acknowledge this, Section 27 includes the following alternative approach for such assets.

For assets held for their service potential a cash flow driven valuation (such as value in use) may not be appropriate. In these circumstances value in use (in respect of assets held for their service potential) is determined by the present value of the asset's remaining service potential plus the net amount the entity will receive from its disposal. In some cases this may be taken to be costs avoided by possession of the asset. Therefore, depreciated replacement cost, may be a suitable measurement model but other approaches may be used where more appropriate. *[FRS 102.27.20A]*.

4.6.7 Corporate assets

An entity may have assets that are inherently incapable of generating cash inflows independently, such as headquarters buildings or central IT facilities that contribute to more than one CGU. The characteristics that distinguish these corporate assets are that they do not generate cash inflows independently of other assets or groups of assets and their carrying amount cannot be fully attributed to one CGU. Section 27 provides no specific guidance on how to deal with such assets, although they would certainly fall within its scope. Under the hierarchy in Section 10, users may consider guidance which is provided under IAS 36.

Corporate assets present a problem in the event of those assets showing indications of impairment. It also raises a question of what those indications might actually be, in the absence of cash inflows directly relating to this type of asset. Some, but not all, of these assets may have relatively easily determinable fair values but while this is usually true of a headquarters building, it could not be for a central IT facility. We have already noted at 4.3.2 above that a decline in value of the asset itself may not trigger a need for an impairment review and it may be obvious that the CGUs of which corporate assets are a part are not showing any indications of impairment – unless, of course, management has decided to dispose of the asset. It is most likely that a corporate asset will show indications of impairment if the CGU or group of CGUs to which it relates are showing indications and this is reflected in the methodology in IAS 36 by which corporate assets are tested.

The corporate asset's carrying value should be tested for impairment along with CGUs. This allocation allows the recoverable amount of all of the assets involved, both CGU and corporate ones, to be considered.

If possible, the corporate assets should be allocated to individual CGUs on a reasonable and consistent basis. If the carrying value of a corporate asset can be allocated on a reasonable and consistent basis between individual CGUs, each CGU should have its impairment test done separately and its carrying value includes its share of the corporate asset.

If the corporate asset's carrying value cannot be allocated to an individual CGU, IAS 36 suggests three steps as noted below. As noted above, indicators of impairment for corporate assets that cannot be allocated to individual CGUs are likely to relate to the CGUs that use the corporate asset as well. First the CGU is tested for impairment and any impairment written off. Then a group of CGUs is identified to which, as a group, all or part of the carrying value of the corporate asset can be allocated. This group should include the CGU that was the subject of the first test. Finally, all CGUs in this group should be tested to determine if the group's carrying value (including the allocation of the corporate asset's carrying value) is in excess of the group's VIU. If it is not in excess the impairment loss should be allocated pro-rata to all assets in the group of CGUs as the allocated portion of the corporate asset.

In the illustrative examples accompanying IAS 36, Example 8 has a fully worked example of the allocation and calculation of a VIU involving corporate assets. Example 24.8 below serves to illustrate the allocation of the corporate asset to CGUs:

Example 24.8:   *Allocation of corporate assets*

An entity comprises three CGUs and a headquarters building. The carrying amount of the headquarters building of 150 is allocated to the carrying amount of each individual cash-generating unit. A weighted allocation basis is used because the estimated remaining useful life of A's cash-generating unit is 10 years, whereas the estimated remaining useful lives of B and C's cash-generating units are 20 years.

Calculation of a weighted allocation of the carrying amount of the headquarters building

End of 20X0	A	B	C	Total
Carrying amount	100	150	200	450
Remaining useful life	10 years	20 years	20 years	
Weighting based on useful life	1	2	2	
Carrying amount after weighting	100	300	400	800
Pro-rata allocation of the building	(100/800)= 12%	(300/800)= 38%	(400/800)= 50%	100%
Allocation of the carrying amount of the building (based on pro-rata above)	18	57	75	150
Carrying amount (after allocation of the building)	118	207	275	600

The allocation need not be made on carrying value or financial measures such as turnover – employee numbers or a time basis might be a valid basis in certain circumstances.

One effect of this pro-rata process is that the amount of the head office allocated to each CGU will change as the useful lives and carrying values change. In the above example, the allocation of the head office to CGU A will be redistributed to CGUs B and C as A's remaining life shortens. The entity will have to ensure that B and C can support an increased head office allocation. Similar effects will be observed if the sizes of any other factor on which the allocation to the CGUs is made change relative to one another.

4.6.8   Overheads and share-based payments

As noted at 4.6.1 above, when measuring VIU, entities should include projections of cash outflows that are:

(i)   necessarily incurred to generate the cash inflows from continuing use of the asset (or CGU); and

(ii)   can be directly attributed, or allocated on a reasonable and consistent basis to the asset (or CGU). *[FRS 102.27.17(b)]*.

Projections of cash outflows should therefore include those for the day-to-day servicing of the asset/CGU as well as future overheads that can be attributed directly, or allocated on a reasonable and consistent basis, to the use of the asset/CGU.

In principle, all overhead costs should be considered and most should be allocated to CGUs when testing for impairment, subject to materiality.

Judgements might however be required to determine how far down to allocate some overhead costs, and what an appropriate allocation basis might be, particularly when it comes to stewardship costs and overhead costs incurred at a far higher level in a group than the CGU/asset being assessed for impairment. Careful consideration of the entity's specific relevant facts and circumstances and cost structure is needed.

Generally, overhead costs that provide identifiable services to a CGU (e.g. IT costs from a centralised function) as well as those that would be incurred by a CGU if it needed to perform the related tasks when operating on a 'stand-alone basis' (e.g. financial reporting function) should be allocated to the CGU being tested for impairment.

Conversely, overhead costs that are incurred with a view to acquire and develop a new business (e.g. costs for corporate development such as M&A activities) would generally not be allocated. These costs are similar in nature to future cash inflows and outflows that are expected to arise from improving or enhancing a CGU's performance which are not considered in the VIU. *[FRS 102.27.19(b)]*.

The selection of a reasonable and consistent allocation basis for overhead costs will require analysis of various factors including the nature of the CGU itself. A reasonable allocation basis for identifiable services may be readily apparent, for example in some cases volume of transaction processing for IT services or headcount for human resource services may be appropriate. However, a reasonable allocation basis for stewardship costs that are determined to be necessarily incurred by the CGU to generate cash inflows may require more analysis. For example, an allocation basis for stewardship costs such as revenue or headcount may not necessarily be reasonable when CGUs have different regulatory environments, (i.e. more regulated CGUs may require more governance time and effort) or maturity stages (i.e. CGUs in mature industries may require less governance effort). The allocation basis may need to differ by type of cost and in some cases may need to reflect an average metric over a period of time rather than a metric for a single period or may need to reflect future expected, rather than historic, metrics.

Overheads not fully pushed down to the lowest level of CGUs might need to be included in an impairment test at a higher group of CGU level if it can be demonstrated that the overhead costs are necessarily incurred and can be attributed directly or allocated on a reasonable and consistent basis at that higher level. After a careful analysis, if this criteria cannot be met, there could be instances when certain overhead costs are excluded from the cash flow projections. *[FRS 102.27.17(b)]*.

Many entities make internal charges, often called management charges, which purport to transfer overhead charges to other group entities. Care must be taken before using these charges as a surrogate for actual overheads as they are often based on what is permitted, (e.g. by the taxation authorities), rather than actual overhead costs. There is also the danger of double counting if a management charge includes an element for the use of corporate assets that have already been allocated to the CGU being tested e.g. an internal rent charge.

In certain situations it may be argued that some stewardship costs are already included in the impairment test through the discount rate used. This would, among other factors, depend on the way the discount rate has been determined, and whether the relevant stewardship cost should be regarded more as a shareholder cost covered in the shareholders' expected return rather than a cost necessarily incurred by the CGU to generate the relevant cash flows. Due to the complexity of such an approach it would need to be applied with appropriate care.

Often employees' remuneration packages include share-based payments. Share-based payments may be cash-settled, equity-settled or give the entity or the counterparty the choice of settlement in equity or in cash. In practice, many share-based payment transactions undertaken by entities are awards of equity settled shares and options. This gives the entity the possibility of rewarding employees without incurring any cash outflows and instead the cash costs are ultimately borne by the shareholders through dilution of their holdings.

When it comes to impairment assessment a question that often faces entities is whether and how to consider share-based payments in the recoverable amount, in particular the VIU calculation? Section 27 itself does not provide any specific guidance in respect of whether or how share-based payments should be considered in determining the recoverable amount.

As Section 27 focuses on cash flows in determining VIU, it seems that expected cash outflows in relation to cash-settled share-based payments would need to be reflected in the VIU calculation. The future expected cash outflow could for example be reflected by the fair value of the award at the balance sheet date, through including the amount of that fair value expected to vest and be paid out in excess of the liability already recognised at that date in the VIU calculation. In such a case the liability already recognised at the date of the VIU determination would not form part of the carrying value of the CGU.

Theoretically this seems to be straight forward, but in practice it can be quite a challenging and judgemental task, particularly when the entity consists of a large number of CGUs. Share-based payments are in general awarded by the parent to employees within the group and any change in the value of share-based payments after the grant date might be disconnected from the performance of the employing CGU. This may be relevant in assessing whether and how such changes in value and the ultimate expected cash flows are allocated to a specific CGU.

What is even less clear is whether an entity should reflect equity-settled share-based payments in the VIU calculation. Such share-based payment transactions will never result in any cash outflows for the entity, and therefore a literal reading of Section 27 may indicate that they can be ignored in determining the recoverable amount. However, some might argue an entity should appropriately reflect all share-based payments in the VIU calculation, whether or not these result in a real cash outflow to the entity. Such share-based payments are part of an employee's remuneration package and therefore costs for services from the employee, which are necessary as part of the overall cash flow generating capacity of the entity. Others may argue that they need to be considered through adjusting the discount rate in order to reflect a higher return to equity holders to counter the dilutive effects of equity settled share based payment awards.

The time span over which the recoverable amount is calculated is often much longer than the time period for which share-based payments have been awarded. Companies and their employees would often expect that further share-based payment awards will be made in the future during the time period used for the recoverable amount calculation. Depending on the respective facts and circumstances an entity would need to consider whether to include the effect of share-based payments over a longer period, considering the discussion above.

5 GOODWILL AND ITS ALLOCATION TO CGUs

Goodwill, by itself, cannot be sold. Nor does it generate cash flows to an entity that are independent of other assets. As a consequence, the fair value of goodwill cannot be measured directly. Therefore, the fair value of goodwill must be derived from measurement of the fair value of the CGU(s) of which the goodwill is a part. *[FRS 102.27.24].*

For the purpose of impairment testing, goodwill acquired in a business combination should, from the acquisition date, be allocated to each of the acquirer's CGUs that are expected to benefit from the synergies of the combination, irrespective of whether other assets or liabilities of the acquiree are assigned to those units. *[FRS 102.27.25].*

Example 24.9: Allocating goodwill to CGUs – a simple example

On 1 January 20X0 Entity A acquired Entity B. As a consequence of the business combination, Entity B became a wholly owned subsidiary of entity A. Entities A and B each have one CGU. Goodwill of £1,000 arose from the business combination, all of which is attributable to synergies of the combination which are expected to arise in Entity B's CGU only.

For the purposes of impairment testing, £1,000 goodwill is allocated to Entity B's CGU. No goodwill is allocated to Entity A's CGU.

Example 24.10: Allocating goodwill to more than one CGU

The facts are the same as Example 24.9. However, in this example, 60 per cent of the goodwill is attributable to synergies of the combination that are expected to occur in Entity A's CGU. The rest of the goodwill is attributable to synergies in Entity B's CGU.

For the purposes of impairment testing, £600 goodwill is allocated to Entity A's CGU and £400 goodwill is allocated to Entity B's CGU.

The examples above are fairly simple, but the allocation of goodwill to individual CGUs or groups of CGUs at the date of acquisition is likely to require significant judgement by management. In some cases management may conclude that it is not possible to allocate goodwill on anything but an arbitrary basis. Section 27 addresses this issue by allowing management to test the associated goodwill for impairment by splitting the entity into two parts.

The requirement is that, if goodwill cannot be allocated to individual CGUs (or groups of CGUs) on a non-arbitrary basis, then for the purposes of testing goodwill the entity should test the impairment of goodwill by determining the recoverable amount of either:

- the acquired entity in its entirety, if the goodwill relates to an acquired entity that has not been integrated. Integrated means the acquired business has been restructured or dissolved into the reporting entity or other subsidiaries; or

- the entire group of entities, excluding any entities that have not been integrated, if the goodwill relates to an entity that has been integrated.

Chapter 24

In applying this requirement, an entity will need to separate goodwill into goodwill relating to entities that have been integrated and goodwill relating to entities that have not been integrated. The entity should also follow the requirements for CGUs in this section when calculating the recoverable amount of, and allocating impairment losses and reversals to assets belonging to, the acquired entity or group of entities. *[FRS102.27.27]*.

It is not clear how often this method will be applied in practice as we would generally expect management to have a reasonable basis of allocating goodwill to individual CGUs or group of CGUs. The application of this is illustrated in the following example.

Example 24.11:   Non-allocated goodwill and integrated/non-integrated subsidiaries

Group A comprises a parent company and several subsidiaries. Management of Group A considers that goodwill cannot be allocated to individual CGUs or groups of CGUs on a non-arbitrary basis.

On 1 January 20X0 Group A acquired 100 per cent of the ordinary share capital of Entity Z for £10,000. Goodwill of £1,000 arose in accounting for that business combination. That goodwill is amortised using the straight line basis over 10 years.

At 31 December 20X0 the total carrying amount of goodwill after amortisation, and any impairment made in prior years, in Group A's consolidated financial statements is £3,900 (note: the £3,900 includes goodwill from a number of business combinations including the acquisition of Entity Z).

On 31 December 20X0, as impairment indicators are present, Group A performs an impairment test on all of its goodwill.

Assume that, at 31 December 20X0, the recoverable amount of Group A (excluding Entity Z) is £34,000, the recoverable amount of Entity Z is £10,500 and the recoverable amount of Group A (including Entity Z) is £44,500.

Scenario 1 – Non-integrated subsidiary – Entity Z is engaged in dissimilar activities from the rest of Group A. Entity Z has therefore not been integrated into Group A.

At 31 December 20X0 the carrying amount of the net assets of Group A and Entity Z were as follows:

	Goodwill	Carrying amount (excluding Goodwill) at 31/12/20X0[1]
	£	£
Group A (excluding Z)	[2]3,000	30,000
Entity Z	[3]900	10,000
Group A	3,900	40,000

[1] After depreciation and amortisation

[2] Goodwill relating to the acquisition of subsidiaries other than Entity Z.

[3] Goodwill relating to the acquisition of Entity Z.

Because Entity Z's activities are not integrated into Group A, in accordance with FRS 102.27.27(a), the goodwill arising on Entity Z is tested separately from the goodwill relating to Group A's other business combinations. The impairment loss is calculated as follows:

Entity Z (non-integrated entity): impairment = £400 (carrying amount £10,900 less recoverable amount £10,500). The impairment loss reduces goodwill by £400.

Group A (excluding Entity Z): no impairment as the recoverable amount of Group A (excluding Entity Z) of £34,000 exceeds the carrying amount of Group A (excluding Entity Z) of £33,000.

Total impairment loss for Group A = £400.

Scenario 2 – Subsidiary is integrated – Entity Z has been integrated into Group A.

At 31 December 20X0 the carrying amount of the net assets of Group A are:

	Goodwill	Carrying amount at 31/12/20X0[1]
	£	£
Group A	[2]3,900	40,000

[1] After depreciation and amortisation

[2] Goodwill relating to the acquisition of subsidiaries including the acquisition of Entity Z.

The goodwill arising on the acquisition of Entity Z is combined with the rest of the goodwill relating to Group A from the date of acquisition of Entity Z. The impairment loss is calculated as follows:

Group A: no impairment because the recoverable amount £44,500 exceeds the carrying amount of £43,900 (£3,900 goodwill plus £40,000 other assets at group carrying amounts).

As can be seen from the example above, an incidental effect of this approach may be to reduce the incidence of write-downs, as the higher the level at which the goodwill is tested for impairment, the more likely that an impairment loss can be avoided. Judgement will be required in order to assess whether an arbitrary allocation of goodwill is genuinely all that is possible.

5.1 Goodwill on non-controlling interests

As required by Section 19 – *Business Combinations and Goodwill*, an acquirer should, at the acquisition date: *[FRS 102.19.22]*

- recognise goodwill acquired in a business combination as an asset; and
- initially measure that goodwill at its cost, being the excess of the cost of the business combination over the acquirer's interest in the net amount of the identifiable assets, liabilities and contingent liabilities recognised and measured in accordance with the various requirements for those assets, liabilities and contingent liabilities.

Non-controlling interests (NCI) are measured at the acquisition date at their proportionate share of the acquiree's identifiable net assets, which excludes goodwill i.e. goodwill attributable to NCI is not recognised in the parent's consolidated financial statements. However the recoverable amount would be calculated for the whole CGU, i.e. part of the recoverable amount of the CGU determined in accordance with Section 27 that is attributable to the non-controlling interest in goodwill.

Therefore, for the purposes of impairment testing of a non-wholly owned CGU with goodwill, the carrying amount of that unit is notionally adjusted, before being compared with its recoverable amount, by grossing up the carrying amount of goodwill allocated to the unit to include the goodwill attributable to the NCI. This notionally adjusted carrying amount is then compared with the recoverable amount of the unit to determine whether the CGU is impaired. *[FRS 102.27.26]*.

There is no specific guidance on how the gross up should be performed, but we expect the default method will be a simple mechanical gross up based on ownership percentages. This is shown in Example 24.12 below. However, in the absence of specific guidance we consider that an entity is not precluded from grossing up goodwill on a basis other than ownership percentages if to do so is reasonable.

Chapter 24

Example 24.12:   Notionally adjusting the carrying amount of goodwill for non-controlling interests

On 30 December 20X0 Entity A acquired 75% of Entity Z. As a consequence of the business combination, Entity Z become a subsidiary of Entity A. Entities A and Z each have one CGU. Goodwill of £750 arose from the business combination, all of which is attributable to synergies of the combination that are expected to occur only in Entity Z's CGU.

In the group's consolidated statement of financial position NCI is measured at their proportionate interest (25%) of the group carrying amount of Entity Z's net assets excluding goodwill.

If Entity Z's CGU was tested for impairment on 31 December 20X0, the £750 goodwill asset allocated to entity Z's CGU would, solely for the purpose of the impairment test at group level, be grossed up by £250 to £1,000 (i.e. it would be notionally increased to include goodwill attributable to the NCI's 25% interest in the CGU).

In the event of an impairment, the entity allocates the impairment loss as usual, first reducing the carrying amount of goodwill allocated to the CGU. However, because only the parent's goodwill is recognised, the impairment loss is apportioned between that attributable to the parent and that attributable to the NCI, with only the former being recognised.

Example 24.15 at 6.4 below shows an impairment calculation where goodwill has been notionally adjusted to take account of NCI.

6   RECOGNISING AND MEASURING IMPAIRMENT LOSSES

An impairment loss occurs when the carrying amount of an asset or CGU exceeds its recoverable amount. The following sections set out how such impairment losses should be recognised.

6.1   Recognising an impairment loss on an individual asset

In the case of individual assets, an entity should recognise an impairment loss immediately in profit or loss, unless the asset is carried at a revalued amount in accordance with another section of FRS 102 (for example in accordance with the revaluation model in Section 17). Any impairment loss of a revalued asset should be treated as a revaluation decrease in accordance with that other section. *[FRS 102.27.6]*.

If there is an impairment loss on an asset that has not been revalued, it is recognised in profit or loss. An impairment loss on a revalued asset is first used to reduce the revaluation surplus for that asset. Only when the impairment loss exceeds the amount in the revaluation surplus for that same asset is any further impairment loss recognised in profit or loss. *[FRS 102.17.15F]*.

An impairment loss will reduce the depreciable amount of an asset and the revised amount will be depreciated or amortised prospectively over the remaining life. However, an entity ought also to review the useful life and residual value of its impaired asset as both of these may need to be revised. The circumstances that give rise to impairments frequently affect these as well. *[FRS 102.27.10]*.

6.2   Recognising an impairment loss on a CGU

An impairment loss should be recognised for a CGU if, and only if, the recoverable amount of the unit is less than the carrying amount of the unit. The impairment loss should be allocated to reduce the carrying amount of the assets of the unit in the following order: *[FRS 102.27.21]*

- first, to reduce the carrying amount of any goodwill allocated to the CGU; and
- then to the other assets of the unit *pro rata* on the basis of the carrying amount of each asset in the CGU.

This principle is illustrated in Example 24.13 below.

Example 24.13: Impairment loss for a CGU with goodwill – a simple example

On 31 December 20X0, Entity T acquires 100% of voting rights in Entity M for £10,000. Entity M has manufacturing plants in three countries, A, B and C, each of which is considered a CGU.

The fair value of identifiable assets in Entity M is £7,000 and goodwill of £3,000 arising on the acquisition has been allocated across the three CGUs A, B and C.

During 20X1, a new government is elected in Country A. It passed legislation that significantly restricts exports of the main product produced by Entity T and its subsidiaries (i.e. Group T). As a result, and for the foreseeable future, Group T's production in Country A will be cut by 40 percent. The significant export restriction and the resulting production decrease require Group T to estimate the recoverable amount of Country A's CGU at the end of 20X1.

Management estimates cash flow forecasts for Country A's operations and determines the CGU's recoverable amount to be £1,360. The carrying amounts of goodwill and identifiable assets of Country A are £800 and £1,833 respectively. The calculation and allocation of the impairment loss for Country A's CGU at the end of 20X1 is as follows:

	Carrying amount	Impairment[1]	Carrying amount after impairment
	£		£
Goodwill	800	(800)	–
Asset A	500	(129)	371
Asset B	457	(118)	339
Asset C	876	(226)	650
Total identifiable assets	1,833	(473)	1,360
Total assets	2,633	(1,273)	1,360

[1] Impairment allocated pro-rata to identifiable assets e.g. for Asset A this is $(500 \div 1,833) \times 473 = 129$.

The impairment loss is recorded first against the carrying amount of goodwill (£800) and next, pro-rata against the carrying amount of Country A's identifiable assets (£473).

However, an entity should not reduce the carrying amount of any asset in the CGU below the highest of: *[FRS 102.27.22]*

- its fair value less costs to sell (if determinable);
- its value in use (if determinable); and
- zero.

Any excess amount of the impairment loss that cannot be allocated to an asset because of the restriction above should be allocated to the other assets of the unit *pro rata* on the basis of the carrying amount of those other assets. *[FRS 102.27.23]*. Example 24.14 below illustrates how this approach would be applied in practice.

Example 24.14: Impairment loss for a CGU with goodwill

An entity's CGU produces a product in a continuous process using three machines i.e. the output of Machine A is the input (raw material) for Machine B, the output of which is the input for Machine C. The output from Machine C is the entity's only marketable product.

After recognising depreciation and amortisation for the year ended 20X0 the carrying amount of the CGU containing Machines A, B and C including Goodwill is £72,220. This can be broken down as £13,000 for Machine A, £29,250 for Machine B, £22,750 for Machine C and £7,220 for goodwill.

As there has been a significant downturn in the market for its products, the entity must conduct an impairment test on the associated CGU. The value in use of the CGU is calculated to be £55,000.

With a carrying value of £72,220 and a value in use of £55,000, this gives rise to an impairment loss of £17,220. The impairment loss is first allocated to the goodwill (£7,220) and then to the other assets of the CGU on a *pro rata* basis reflecting the carrying amount of each asset in the CGU.

Management have been able to determine the FVLCS of Machine A at £12,500. They have not been able to determine the FVLCS or VIU of any other individual asset within the CGU.

Absent the information about the FVLCS of Machine A, the remaining impairment loss of £10,000 (total impairment of £17,220 less £7,220 allocated to goodwill) would be allocated to Machines A, B and C on a pro-rata basis as follows:

	Carrying amount before impairment	Carrying amount in relation to CGU's carrying amount	Notional impairment allocation	Notional carrying amount after impairment
	£	%	£	£
Machine A	13,000	20	2,000	11,000
Machine B	29,250	45	4,500	24,750
Machine C	22,750	35	3,500	19,250
Total	65,000		10,000	55,000

However, this allocation would reduce the carrying amount of Machine A to £11,000, which is lower than its FVLCS of £12,500. Consequently, in accordance with FRS 102.27.22(a), the impairment loss allocated to Machine A is limited to £500 (i.e. £13,000 carrying amount less £12,500 FVLCS). The remaining impairment loss of £1,500 (i.e. £2,000 less £500 allocated to Machine A) is allocated to Machines B and C on the basis of each machine's carrying amount in relation to the total carrying amount of the two machines as follows:

	Carrying amount after first impairment	Carrying amount in relation to CGU's carrying amount	Second impairment allocation
	£	%	£
Machine B	24,750	56.25	844
Machine C	19,250	43.75	656
Total	44,000		1,500

The total impairment loss allocated to each machine is shown below, together with the carrying amounts of Machines A, B and C immediately after recognising the impairment loss.

	Carrying amount before impairment	First impairment allocation	Second impairment allocation	Total impairment	Carrying amount after impairment
	£	£	£	£	£
Machine A	13,000	500	–	500	12,500
Machine B	29,250	4,500	844	5,344	23,906
Machine C	22,750	3,500	656	4,156	18,594
Goodwill	7,220	7,220	–	7,220	–
Total	72,220	15,720	1,500	17,220	55,000

In the above example, the impairment loss is fully allocated across the assets of the CGU. However, as individual assets cannot be written down below the higher of their FVLCS and their VIU, this may not always be the case, thus an element of the impairment charge may not be recognised.

6.3 Recognising an impairment loss on a group of CGUs

It is important when applying the requirements above, that impairment testing is conducted in the right order. If there are indicators of impairment in connection with a CGU with which goodwill is associated, i.e. the CGU is part of a CGU group to which goodwill is allocated, the individual CGU should be tested and any necessary impairment loss taken, before the 'CGU group' goodwill is tested for impairment. These impairment losses and consequent reductions in carrying values are treated in exactly the same way as those for individual assets as explained at 6.1 above.

6.4 Recognising an impairment loss on a CGU with goodwill and non-controlling interests

As noted at 5.1 above, when impairment testing a non-wholly owned CGU with goodwill, the carrying amount of that unit must be notionally adjusted, before being compared with its recoverable amount, by grossing up the carrying amount of goodwill allocated to the unit to include the goodwill attributable to the NCI. *[FRS 102.27.26]*.

If there is an impairment, the entity allocates the impairment loss as usual, first reducing the carrying amount of goodwill allocated to the CGU. However, because only the parent's goodwill is recognised, the impairment loss is apportioned between that attributable to the parent and that attributable to the NCI, with only the former being recognised.

If any impairment loss remains, it is allocated in the usual way to the other assets of the CGU *pro rata* on the basis of the carrying amount of each asset in the CGU.

These requirements are illustrated in the following example.

Example 24.15: A CGU with goodwill and non-controlling interest

Entity X acquires an 80 per cent ownership interest in Entity Y for £1,600 on 1 January 20X0. At that date, Entity Y's identifiable net assets have a fair value of £1,500. Entity X recognises in its consolidated financial statements:

(a) goodwill of £400, being the difference between the cost of the business combination of £1,600 and acquirer's interest in the identifiable net assets of Entity Y of £1,200 (being 80% of £1,500);

(b) Entity Y's identifiable net assets at their fair value of £1,500; and

(c) a non-controlling interest of £300, being the remaining 20% of Entity Y's identifiable net assets.

The group considers Entity Y to be a CGU and the full £400 of goodwill is allocated to that CGU. For simplicity, we should ignore the amortisation of goodwill in this example.

At the end of 20X0, the carrying amount of Entity Y's identifiable assets (excluding goodwill) has reduced to £1,350 and Entity X determines that the recoverable amount of Entity Y is £1,000.

The carrying amount of Entity Y must be notionally adjusted to include goodwill attributable to the non-controlling interest, before being compared with the recoverable amount of £1,000. Goodwill attributable to Entity X's 80% interest in Entity Y at 31 December 20X0 is £400. Therefore, goodwill notionally attributable to the 20% non-controlling interest in Entity Y at the acquisition date is £100, being £400 × 20 ÷ 80. Testing Entity Y for impairment at the end of 20X0 gives rise to an impairment loss of £850 calculated as follows:

	Goodwill £	Identifiable net assets £	Total £
Carrying amount	400	1,350	1,750
Unrecognised non-controlling interest	100	–	100
Notionally adjusted carrying amount	500	1,350	1,850
Recoverable amount			1,000
Impairment loss			850

The impairment loss of £850 is allocated to the assets in the CGU by first reducing the carrying amount of goodwill to zero. Therefore, £500 of the £850 impairment loss for Entity Y is allocated to the goodwill. However, because Entity X only holds a 80% ownership interest in Entity Y, it recognises only 80 per cent of that goodwill impairment loss (i.e. £400). The remaining impairment loss of £350 is recognised by reducing the carrying amounts of Entity Y's identifiable assets, as follows:

	Goodwill £	Identifiable net assets £	Total £
Carrying amount	400	1,350	1,750
Impairment loss	(400)	(350)	(750)
Carrying amount after impairment loss	–	1,000	1,000

Of the impairment loss of £350 relating to Entity Y's identifiable assets, £70 (i.e. 20% thereof) would be attributed to the non-controlling interest.

In this example the same result would have been achieved by just comparing the recoverable amount of £1,000 with the carrying amount of £1,750. However, what if the recoverable amount of the CGU had been greater than the carrying amount of the identifiable net assets prior to recognising the impairment loss?

Assume the same facts as above, except that at the end of 20X0, Entity X determines that the recoverable amount of Entity Y is £1,400. In this case, testing Entity Y for impairment at the end of 20X0 gives rise to an impairment loss of £450 calculated as follows:

	Goodwill £	Identifiable net assets £	Total £
Carrying amount	400	1,350	1,750
Unrecognised non-controlling interest	100	–	100
Notionally adjusted carrying amount	500	1,350	1,850
Recoverable amount			1,400
Impairment loss			450

All of the impairment loss of £450 is allocated to the goodwill. However, Entity X recognises only 80 per cent of that goodwill impairment loss (i.e. £360). This allocation of the impairment loss results in the following carrying amounts for Entity Y in the financial statements of Entity X at the end of 20X0:

	Goodwill £	Identifiable net assets £	Total £
Carrying amount	400	1,350	1,750
Impairment loss	(360)	–	(360)
Carrying amount after impairment loss	40	1,350	1,390

Of the impairment loss of £360, none of it is attributable to the non-controlling interest since it all relates to the majority shareholder's goodwill.

In this case the total carrying amount of the identifiable net assets and the goodwill has not been reduced to the recoverable amount of £1,400, but is actually less than the recoverable amount. This is because the recoverable amount of goodwill relating to the non-controlling interest (20% of [£500 – £450]) is not recognised in the consolidated financial statements.

6.5 Impairment of assets of a subsidiary which is part of a larger CGU

When testing for impairment in consolidated accounts, entities must divide the group into CGUs, being the smallest group of assets that generate largely independent cash inflows. The identification of a group's CGUs may not be consistent with the legal structure of the group, such that the activities of an individual subsidiary may form part of a larger CGU in the group. When this is the case the cash flows attributable to an individual subsidiary may appear not to support the carrying value of that entity's assets, while from a group perspective no impairment is identified as the subsidiary forms part of a larger and profitable CGU.

An example of this would be where plant X manufactures an intermediate product used as an input by plant Y. Plant X is loss making and is owned by subsidiary A, while plant Y is owned by another subsidiary within the group. From a group perspective plants X and Y are one CGU, which is highly profitable. While the cash flows for subsidiary A may not support the carrying value of its assets, from the perspective of the consolidated accounts the CGU is profitable and therefore no impairment is required at that level.

As a result of the different levels at which impairment testing is performed, impairment losses in individual subsidiaries' financial statements may not follow the losses recognised in the consolidated financial statements.

Chapter 24

7   REVERSAL OF AN IMPAIRMENT LOSS

An impairment loss recognised for goodwill should not be reversed in a subsequent period. For all assets other than goodwill, if and only if the reasons for the impairment loss have ceased to apply, an impairment loss should be reversed in a subsequent period. *[FRS 102.27.28-29].*

An entity should assess at each reporting date whether there is any indication that an impairment loss recognised in prior periods may no longer exist or may have decreased. Indications that an impairment loss may have decreased or may no longer exist are generally the opposite of those discussed at 4.3 above. If any such indication exists, the entity should determine whether all or part of the prior impairment loss should be reversed. The procedure for making that determination will depend on whether the prior impairment loss on the asset was based on: *[FRS 102.27.29]*

- the recoverable amount of that individual asset; or

- the recoverable amount of the cash-generating unit to which the asset belongs.

The process to be followed for the reversal of an impairment on an individual asset is discussed at 7.1 below and for a CGU at 7.2 below.

7.1   Reversal where recoverable amount was estimated for an individual impaired asset

When the prior impairment loss was based on the recoverable amount of the individual impaired asset, the following requirements apply: *[FRS 102.27.30]*

(a)   The entity should estimate the recoverable amount of the asset at the current reporting date.

(b)   If the estimated recoverable amount of the asset exceeds its carrying amount, the entity should increase the carrying amount to recoverable amount, subject to the limitation described in (c) below. That increase is a reversal of an impairment loss. The entity should recognise the reversal immediately in profit or loss unless the asset is carried at revalued amount in accordance with another section of FRS 102 (for example, the revaluation model in Section 17). Any reversal of an impairment loss of a revalued asset should be treated as a revaluation increase in accordance with the relevant section of FRS 102.

(c)   The reversal of an impairment loss should not increase the carrying amount of the asset above the carrying amount that would have been determined (net of amortisation or depreciation) had no impairment loss been recognised for the asset in prior years.

(d)   After a reversal of an impairment loss is recognised, the entity should adjust the depreciation (amortisation) charge for the asset in future periods to allocate the asset's revised carrying amount, less its residual value (if any), on a systematic basis over its remaining useful life.

Therefore if there are indications that a previously recognised impairment loss has disappeared or reduced, it is necessary to determine the recoverable amount (i.e. the higher of FVLCS or VIU) so that the reversal can be quantified.

In the event of an individual asset's impairment being reversed, Section 27 makes it clear that the reversal may not raise the carrying value above the figure it would have been (after taking into account the depreciation charge which would have applied) had no impairment originally been recognised. This requirement is illustrated in the example below.

Example 24.16: Impairment reversal for an individually impaired asset

The facts are the same as in Example 24.6. During 20X4, it becomes apparent that the cheaper material used by Entity A's competitor was not fit for purpose and their components need replacement after a year. Sales of Entity A's product start to return to their previous levels. At 31 December 20X4 the machine has a carrying amount of £58,271. Management has reassessed the future cash flows based on changed circumstances since the end of 20X0 and determined VIU at the end of 20X4 to be £122,072. Management believes FVLCS is less than VIU.

At the end of 20X4, the machine's recoverable amount i.e. its VIU (£122,072) is higher than the machine's carrying amount before the recognition of any reversal of the impairment loss recognised in 20X0 (£58,271). It is an indication that the impairment loss recognised in 20X0 no longer exists or may have decreased.

End of 20X4	Machine £
Recoverable amount	122,072
Carrying amount before the reversal of the impairment loss recognised in 20X0	58,271
Difference	63,801

The difference is only an indication of the amount of the reversal because the reversal cannot increase the carrying amount of the asset above the carrying amount that would have been determined had no impairment loss been recognised for the asset in prior years. At 31 December 20X4, the carrying amount that would have been determined, had no impairment loss been recognised for the asset in prior years, is £120,000 (cost £300,000 less accumulated depreciation £180,000). Thus £120,000 is the maximum carrying amount for the asset after the reversal of impairment.

The entity compares the carrying amount at 20X4 if no impairment loss had been recognised, with the carrying amount at 20X4 and determines that the maximum impairment reversal is £61,729.

End of 20X4	Machine £
Cost	300,000
Less notional depreciation since acquisition until 20X4	(180,000)
Notional carrying amount at 31/12/20X4 if no impairment loss had been recognised for the asset in 20X0	120,000
Less carrying amount at the year ended 31/12/20X4, before the reversal of the impairment loss recognised in prior reporting periods	(58,271)
Reversal of prior year's impairment loss	61,729

As a consequence of the reversal of part of the impairment loss recognised at 31 December 20X0, the carrying amount of the machine is £120,000 i.e. equal to the carrying amount that would have been determined had no impairment loss been recognised for the asset in prior years. In subsequent periods, assuming that all variables remain the same as at the end of 20X4, the depreciable amount will be £120,000, so the depreciation charge will be £20,000 (£120,000 depreciable amount depreciated over remaining 6 year remaining useful life).

Chapter 24

7.2   Reversal when recoverable amount was estimated for a cash-generating unit

When the original impairment loss was based on the recoverable amount of the cash-generating unit to which the asset, including goodwill belongs, the following requirements apply: *[FRS 102.27.31]*

(a)   The entity should estimate the recoverable amount of that cash-generating unit at the current reporting date.

(b)   If the estimated recoverable amount of the cash-generating unit exceeds its carrying amount, that excess is a reversal of an impairment loss. The entity should allocate the amount of that reversal to the assets of the unit, except for goodwill, *pro rata* with the carrying amounts of those assets subject to the limitation described in (c) below. Those increases in carrying amounts should be treated as reversals of impairment losses and recognised immediately in profit or loss unless the asset is carried at revalued amount in accordance with another section of this FRS (for example, the revaluation model in Section 17). Any reversal of an impairment loss of a revalued asset should be treated as a revaluation increase in accordance with the relevant section of this FRS.

(c)   In allocating a reversal of an impairment loss for a cash-generating unit, the reversal should not increase the carrying amount of any asset above the lower of:

    (i)   its recoverable amount; and

    (ii)   the carrying amount that would have been determined (net of amortisation or depreciation) had no impairment loss been recognised for the asset in prior periods.

(d)   Any excess amount of the reversal of the impairment loss that cannot be allocated to an asset because of the restriction in (c) above should be allocated *pro rata* to the other assets of the cash-generating unit.

(e)   After a reversal of an impairment loss is recognised, if applicable, the entity should adjust the depreciation (amortisation) charge for each asset in the cash-generating unit in future periods to allocate the asset's revised carrying amount, less its residual value (if any), on a systematic basis over its remaining useful life.

The above requirements are illustrated in the example below.

Example 24.17:   Impairment reversal for a cash generating unit

The facts are the same as those in Example 24.13. In 20X3 the government is still in office in Country A but the business situation is improving. The effects of the export laws on Entity T's production are proving to be less drastic than initially expected by management. As a result, management estimates that production will increase. This favourable change requires Entity T to re-estimate the recoverable amount of the CGU for the net assets of the Country A operations. Management estimates that the recoverable amount of the Country A CGU is now £2,010. Management are unable to estimate the FVLCS or VIU of any individual asset within the CGU. To calculate the reversal of the impairment loss, Entity T compares the recoverable amount and the net carrying amount of Country A's CGU.

	Goodwill	Identifiable assets	Total
	£	£	£
Historical cost	1,000	2,000	3,000
Accumulated amortisation/depreciation[1]	(200)	(167)	(367)
Accumulated impairment loss	(800)	(473)	(1,273)
Carrying amount after impairment loss at 31/12/20X1 20X2 and 20X3	–	1,360	1,360
Depreciation (2 years)[2]	–	(247)	(247)
Carrying amount before impairment reversal	–	1,113	1,113

[1] Goodwill was being amortised over a period of five years (£1000 ÷ 5 years = £200), while the identifiable assets were deemed to have a useful life of 12 years (£2000 ÷ 12 years = £166.70 depreciation per year).
[2] Two years of depreciation based on carrying amount of £1,360 at 1/1/20X4 and remaining useful life of 11 years ((£1,360 ÷ 11 years = £123.6 per year) × 2 years = £247).

Comparing this with the recoverable amount of the CGU:

End of 20X3	CGU A
	£
Recoverable amount	2,010
Carrying amount before the reversal of the impairment loss recognised in 20X1	(1,113)
Difference	897

The difference is only an indication of the amount of the possible reversal because of the restriction in FRS 102.27.31(b)(i), which requires that any impairment reversal can only be applied to assets of the unit other than goodwill (subject to the limitation that the reversal cannot increase the carrying amount of any asset above the lower of its recoverable amount and the carrying amount that would have been determined (net of amortisation or depreciation) had no impairment loss been recognised for the asset in prior periods). As can be seen below, this results in the impairment reversal being restricted to £387.

	Identifiable assets
	£
Carrying amount of identifiable assets before impairment reversal	1,113
Carrying amount assuming no prior period impairment[1]	1,500
Impairment reversal applied to assets	387

[1] Identifiable assets continue to be depreciated over their 12 year useful life @£166.70 per year ((£2000 ÷ 12 years = £166.70 per year) × 3 years) = £500. Gives carrying amount of £2000 less depreciation of £500 = £1,500.

Note: if management were able to estimate the recoverable amount for any of the individual identifiable assets then these amounts (if lower) would be used in restricting the impairment reversal.

8   DISCLOSURES

An entity should disclose the following for each class of assets indicated in the paragraph below: *[FRS 102.27.32]*

- the amount of impairment losses recognised in profit or loss during the period and the line item(s) in the statement of comprehensive income (or in the income statement, if presented) in which those impairment losses are included; and

- the amount of reversals of impairment losses recognised in profit or loss during the period and the line item(s) in the statement of comprehensive income (or in the income statement, if presented) in which those impairment losses are reversed.

The information above is required for each of the following classes of asset: *[FRS 102.27.33]*

- inventories;

- property, plant and equipment (including investment property accounted for by the cost method);

- goodwill;

- intangible assets other than goodwill;

- investments in associates; and

- investments in joint ventures.

An entity should disclose a description of the events and circumstances that led to the recognition or reversal of the impairment loss. *[FRS 102.27.33A]*.

8.1   Companies Act disclosure requirements

Schedule 1 of the *Large and Medium-sized Companies and Groups (Accounts and Reports) Regulations 2008*, (SI 2008/410) (the Regulations), requires provisions for diminution in value to be made in respect of any fixed asset if the reduction in value is expected to be permanent. Where the reasons for the provision have ceased to apply, the provision must be written back to the extent that it is no longer necessary. In either case, amounts not shown in the profit and loss account must be disclosed in the notes to the accounts. *[1 Sch 19-20]*.

As accounts prepared under FRS 102 are Companies Act accounts, entities subject to Schedule 1 to the Regulations have a choice of:

- applying one of the two statutory formats set out in Section B of Part 1 of Schedule 1 to the Regulations; or

- applying paragraph 1A(2) of Schedule 1 to the Regulations and using the 'adapted' formats as set out in Section 5 – *Statement of Comprehensive Income and Income Statement*.

Under Format 2 of Schedule 1 to the Regulations, where expenses are classified by nature, there is a specific line item, 7(a), headed 'Depreciation and other amounts written off tangible and intangible fixed assets' where impairment losses should be shown. Under Format 1, where expenses are classified by function, impairment losses should generally be shown in the same category of expense as depreciation of the relevant asset, with the amount of depreciation and other amounts written off tangible and intangible assets disclosed in a note to the accounts.

Under the adapted format, an entity shall present an analysis of expenses, either in the income statement or the notes, equivalent to what would have been presented had the profit and loss account format not been adapted. *[FRS 102.5.5B]*.

Under both the statutory and adapted formats, FRS 102 requires entities to present additional line items, headings and subtotals in the income statement when such presentation is relevant to an understanding of the entity's financial performance. *[FRS 102.5.9]*. So, in practice, we would not anticipate differences in the level of information given about impairment charges whether entities apply the statutory or adapted formats for the income statement.

The Regulations also require certain information to supplement the balance sheet. In respect of fixed assets, this includes:

- the cumulative amount of provisions for depreciation or diminution in value as at the beginning of the financial year and at the balance sheet date;

- the amount of any such provisions made in respect of the financial year;

- the amount of any adjustments made in respect of any such provisions during that year in consequence of the disposal of any assets; and

- the amount of any other adjustments made in respect of any such provisions during that year. *[1 Sch 51(3)]*.

The statutory disclosures overlap with disclosures in FRS 102 of depreciation, amortisation and impairment charges (see above at 8, Chapter 15 at 3.9 and Chapter 16 at 3.5.2). *[FRS 102.17.31, 18.27(e) 27.32-33]*.

9 SUMMARY OF GAAP DIFFERENCES

The key differences between FRS 102 and IFRS in accounting for impairments are set out below.

	FRS 102	*IFRS*
Timing of impairment tests	Impairment testing required only when indicators of impairment exist.	Mandatory annual testing for goodwill and indefinite lived intangibles.
Assets held for service potential	Possible to use depreciated replacement cost as a measurement model.	Silent.
Guidance on inputs to VIU calculations	No guidance.	Guidance provided on identifying CGUs, allocating goodwill to those CGUs, estimating cash flows and discount rates and treatment of corporate assets.
Allocation of goodwill to CGUs for purposes of impairment testing	Allocated to each of the acquirer's CGUs that are expected to benefit from the acquisition, whether or not the acquiree's other assets or liabilities are allocated to those units. If unable to allocate to CGUs non-arbitrarily, can test based on simplified split between integrated and non-integrated entities.	Allocated to each of the acquirer's CGUs that are expected to benefit from the acquisition, whether or not the acquiree's other assets or liabilities are allocated to those units. Each CGU or group of CGUs to which goodwill is allocated should represent the lowest level at which goodwill is monitored and cannot be larger than an IFRS 8 – *Operating Segments* – operating segment before aggregation.

	FRS 102	*IFRS*
Disclosures	Limited to amount of impairment losses recognised/reversed and circumstances leading to it.	Extensive additional disclosures required in respect of goodwill/indefinite lived intangibles even where no impairment recognised – includes amounts of goodwill/indefinite lived intangibles allocated to particular CGUs, key assumptions, period over which cash flows projected, growth rates and discount rates applied and further detail where a reasonably possible change in a key assumption could give rise to an impairment.

Chapter 25   Employee benefits

Chapter 25

Chapter 25

Chapter 25   Employee benefits

1   INTRODUCTION

Employee benefits typically form a very significant part of any entity's costs, and can take many varied forms. These are covered in two separate sections of FRS 102, Section 28 – *Employee Benefits* – which is dealt with in this chapter, and Section 26 – *Share-based Payment* (which is dealt with in Chapter 23).

Many issues in accounting for employee benefits can be straight forward, such as the allocation of wages paid to an accounting period. In contrast accounting for the costs of retirement benefits in the financial statements of employers presents one of the most difficult challenges within the field of financial reporting. The amounts involved are large, the timescale is long, the estimation process is complex and involves many areas of uncertainty for which assumptions must be made. Section 28 includes limited guidance on the recognition of pension surpluses, which further increases the level of assumptions preparers of financial statements must make in determining appropriate accounting for employee benefits. In March 2018, the FRC published amendments to FRS 102 which resulted in minor changes to this section.

2   COMPARISON BETWEEN SECTIONS 28 AND IFRS

The key differences between Section 28 of FRS 102 and IAS 19 – *Employee Benefits* – are detailed below.

2.1   Past service costs

IAS 19 defines past service costs as the change in the present value of the defined benefit obligation for employee service in prior periods, resulting from a plan amendment (the introduction or withdrawal of, or changes to, a defined benefit plan) or curtailment (a significant reduction by the entity in the number of employees covered by a plan). *[IAS 19.8]*. FRS 102 does not use the term past service costs, but still requires the cost of plan introductions, benefit changes, curtailments and settlements to be recorded in profit or loss. *[FRS 102.28.23(c)]*. As both FRS 102 and IAS 19 require a charge to the profit and loss account the only difference is concerned with disclosure (see 3.12.4 below).

Chapter 25

2.2   Asset ceiling and IFRIC 14 guidance

In practice, defined benefit pension plans tend to be funded on a more prudent basis than would be the case if a surplus or deficit were measured in accordance with FRS 102 or IAS 19. This is usually due to the discount rate being used for funding purposes typically being lower than that specified in FRS 102 and IAS 19. For this reason FRS 102 and IAS 19 valuations may result in a pension surplus, when for funding purposes there is a deficit.

FRS 102 requires that an entity should recognise a plan surplus as a defined benefit asset only to the extent that it is able to recover the surplus either through reduced contributions in the future or through refunds from the plan. *[FRS 102.28.22]*. This is identical to the method used in IAS 19 which refers to the present value of the reduction in future contributions as the asset ceiling. FRS 102 does not elaborate on how this restriction is quantified, however IFRIC 14 – *IAS 19 – The Limit on a Defined Benefit Asset, Minimum Funding Requirements and their Interaction* – provides guidance on this issue.

The lack of guidance provided by FRS 102 will lead to management being required to make a judgement on the amount of a defined benefit pension surplus to be recognised. In making judgements FRS 102 states that management may consider the requirements and guidance in EU-adopted IFRS dealing with similar or related issues, as discussed in Chapter 9 at 3.2. *[FRS 102.10.6]*. The treatment of pension surpluses which was dealt with under previous UK GAAP and EU-adopted IFRS, but with potentially different outcomes as a result of the strict requirements under previous UK GAAP that the amount to be recovered from refunds of the scheme should only reflect those that have been agreed by the pension scheme trustees at the balance sheet date, *[FRS 17.42]*, has led to a diversity in practice under FRS 102.

Due to the problems encountered in practice in applying the asset ceiling test in IAS 19, the issue was considered by the Interpretations Committee, and IFRIC 14 was issued. At present the guidance from IFRIC 14 has not been included within FRS 102. The interpretation set out to address the issues of:

- when refunds or reductions in future contributions should be regarded as available in accordance with the definition of the asset ceiling in IAS 19.8;

- how a minimum funding requirement might affect the availability of reductions in future contributions; and

- when a minimum funding requirement might give rise to a liability.

For entities already recognising assets or liabilities for defined benefit plans in accordance with FRS 102, no additional liabilities should be recognised in respect of an agreement with the defined benefit plan to fund a deficit (such as a schedule of contributions). This is a difference with IFRS which requires a liability to be recognised where deficit funding contributions are not recoverable in the future. This is discussed further at 3.6.7 below.

The requirements of IFRIC 14 are discussed in full in Chapter 31 of EY International GAAP 2019.

2.3 Attributing benefit to years of service

IAS 19 requires benefits to be attributed to the periods in which the obligation to provide post-employment benefits arises. In applying the projected unit credit method, IAS 19 normally requires benefits to be attributed to periods of service under the plan's benefit formula, however if an employee's service in later years will lead to a materially higher level of benefit the benefit should be attributed on a straight line basis from: *[IAS 19.70]*

- the date when service by the employee first leads to benefits under the plan; until
- the date when further service by the employee will lead to no material amount of further benefits under the plan, other than from further salary increases.

FRS 102 also notes that the present value of an entity's obligations under defined benefit plans should include the effects of benefit formulas that give employees greater benefits for later years of service, *[FRS 102.28.16]*, but does not state that this should be attributed on a straight line basis. Given the GAAP hierarchy in Section 10 – *Accounting Policies, Estimates and Errors* – we would expect users to follow the principles in IAS 19, but they are not required to do so.

2.4 Calculation of service cost and net interest following a plan amendment, curtailment or settlement

In February 2018 amendments were issued to IAS 19 which address the accounting when a plan amendment, curtailment or settlement occurs during the reporting period. This guidance has not been replicated in FRS 102. However given that the standard is silent in this area users of FRS 102 may under the GAAP hierarchy turn to IAS 19 for further guidance.

The amendments confirm that an entity should determine the current service cost using actuarial assumptions determined at the start of the annual reporting period. However, if any entity remeasures the net defined benefit liability (asset) on a plan amendment, curtailment or settlement, it should determine the current service cost for the remainder of the annual reporting period after the plan amendment, curtailment or settlement using the actuarial assumptions used to remeasure the net defined benefit liability (asset). *[IAS 19.122A]*.

If an entity remeasures the net defined benefit liability (asset) to determine a past service cost, or a gain or loss on settlement the entity should determine the net interest for the remainder of the annual reporting period after the plan amendment, curtailment or settlement using: *[IAS 19.123A]*

(a) the net defined benefit liability (asset) reflecting the benefits offered after the plan amendment, curtailment or settlement; and

(b) the discount rate used to remeasure the net defined benefit liability (asset)

The entity should also take into account any changes in the net defined benefit liability (asset) during the period resulting from contributions or benefit payments.

When a plan amendment, curtailment or settlement occurs, an entity should recognise and measure any past service cost, or gain or loss on settlement without considering the effect of the asset ceiling. An entity should then determine the effect of the asset ceiling after the plan amendment, curtailment or settlement with any change in that effect, excluding amounts included in net interest, recognised in other comprehensive income. *[IAS 19.101A]*. Accounting for plan amendments, curtailments and settlements is discussed further at 3.6.6 below.

2.5   Presentation

Part 1 of Schedule 1 to the Regulations provides a choice of either two statutory formats or the adapted formats for the balance sheet. This is discussed further in Chapter 6 at 4.

The statutory formats of the *Large and Medium-sized companies and Groups (Accounts and Reports) Regulations 2008* (SI 2008/410) ('The Regulations'), presentation under FRS 102 differ from that required by IAS 1 – *Presentation of Financial Statements*. The Regulations show pension deficits as the first line item within provisions, and pension surpluses are presented in the same place as pension deficits (i.e. after accruals and deferred income) under format 1 of the Regulations, but after prepayments and accrued income under format 2 of the Regulations. FRS 17 – *Retirement benefits* – required defined benefit pension assets or liabilities to be presented after accruals and deferred income, but before capital and reserves. *[FRS 17.47]*. This presentation was based on an interpretation of law. *[FRS 17 Appendix II.6]*. As a result there is likely to be divergence in practice in the presentation of defined benefit pension surpluses and deficits under FRS 102. This is further discussed at 3.12.4 below.

Where the adapted formats are used, neither FRS 102 nor IFRS specify where in the statement of financial position a net asset or a net liability in respect of a defined benefit plan should be presented, nor whether such balances should be shown separately on the face of the balance sheet or only in the notes. This is left to the judgement of the reporting entity, although FRS 102 requires additional line items, headings and subtotals where relevant to an understanding of the entity's financial position. *[FRS 102.4.3]*. Classification of post-employment benefit assets and liabilities as current or non-current is discussed in Chapter 6 at 5.1.1.D.

3   THE REQUIREMENTS OF SECTION 28 FOR EMPLOYEE BENEFITS

3.1   Terms used in Section 28

The following definitions are included within the FRS 102 Glossary. *[FRS 102 Appendix I]*.

Term	Definition
Accumulating compensated absences	Compensated absences that are carried forward and can be used in future periods if the current period's entitlement is not used in full.
Actuarial assumptions	An entity's unbiased and mutually compatible best estimates of the demographic and financial variables that will determine the ultimate cost of providing post-employment benefits.
Actuarial gains and losses	Changes in the present value of the defined benefit obligation resulting from: <ul><li>experience adjustments (the effects of differences between the previous actuarial assumptions and what has actually occurred); and</li><li>the effects of changes in actuarial assumptions.</li></ul>

Assets held by a long term employee benefit fund	An asset (other than non-transferable financial instruments issued by the reporting entity) that:
	
	• is held by an entity (a fund) that is legally separate from the reporting entity and exists solely to pay or fund employee benefits; and
	
	• is available to be used only to pay or fund employee benefits, is not available to the reporting entity's own creditors (even in bankruptcy), and cannot be returned to the reporting entity, unless either:
	
	    • the remaining assets of the fund are sufficient to meet all the related employee benefit obligations of the plan or the reporting entity; or
	
	    • the assets are returned to the reporting entity to reimburse it for employee benefits already paid.

Constructive obligation	An obligation that derives from an entity's actions where: • by an established pattern of past practice, published policies or a sufficiently specific current statement, the entity has indicated to other parties that it will accept certain responsibilities; and • as a result, the entity has created a valid expectation on the part of those other parties that it will discharge those responsibilities.
Defined benefit obligation (present value of)	The present value, without deducting any plan assets, of expected future payments required to settle the obligation resulting from employee service in the current and prior periods.
Defined benefit plans	Post-employment benefit plans other than defined contribution plans.
Defined contribution plans	Post-employment benefit plans under which an entity pays fixed contributions into a separate entity (a fund) and has no legal or constructive obligation to pay further contributions or to make direct benefit payments to employees if the fund does not hold sufficient assets to pay all employee benefits relating to employee service in the current and prior periods.
Employee benefits	All forms of consideration given by an entity in exchange for service rendered by employees.
Funding (of post-employment benefits)	Contributions by an entity, and sometimes its employees, into an entity, or fund, that is legally separate from the reporting entity and from which the employee benefits are paid.
Multi-employer (benefit) plans	Defined contribution plans (other than state plans) or defined benefit plans (other than state plans) that: • pool the assets contributed by various entities that are not under common control; and • use those assets to provide benefits to employees of more than one entity, on the basis that contribution and benefit levels are determined without regard to the identity of the entity that employs the employees concerned.
Net defined benefit liability	The present value of the defined benefit obligation at the reporting date minus the fair value at the reporting date of plan assets (if any) out of which the obligations are to be settled.

Chapter 25

Term	*Definition*
Plan assets (of employee benefit plan)	Plan assets (of an employee benefit plan) are: (a) assets held by a long-term employee benefit fund; and (b) qualifying insurance policies.
Post-employment benefits	Employee benefits (other than termination benefits and short-term employee benefits) that are payable after the completion of employment.
Post-employment benefit plans	Formal or informal arrangements under which an entity provides post-employment benefits for one or more employees.
Projected unit credit method	An actuarial valuation method that sees each period of service as giving rise to an additional unit of benefit entitlement and measures each unit separately to build up the final obligation (sometimes known as the accrued benefit method pro-rated on service or as the benefit/years of service method).

Qualifying insurance policies	An insurance policy issued by an insurer that is not a related party of the reporting entity, if the proceeds of the policy:
	• can be used only to pay or fund employee benefits under a defined benefit plan; and
	• are not available to the reporting entity's own creditors (even in bankruptcy) and cannot be paid to the reporting entity, unless either:
	   • the proceeds represent surplus assets that are not needed for the policy to meet all the related employee benefit obligations; or
	   • the proceeds are returned to the reporting entity to reimburse it for employee benefits already paid.
	A qualifying insurance policy is not necessarily an insurance contract.

Retirement benefit plan	Arrangements whereby an entity provides benefits for employees on or after termination of service (either in the form of an annual income or as a lump sum) when such benefits, or the contributions towards them, can be determined or estimated in advance of retirement from the provisions of a document or from the entity's practice.
State (employee benefit) plan	Employee benefit plans established by legislation to cover all entities (or all entities in a particular category, for example a specific industry) and operated by national or local government or by another body (for example an autonomous agency created specifically for this purpose) which is not subject to control or influence by the reporting entity.
Termination benefits	Employee benefits provided in exchange for the termination of an employee's employment as a result of either: • an entity's decision to terminate an employee's employment before the normal retirement date; or • an employee's decision to accept voluntary redundancy in exchange for those benefits.

3.2 Scope and general recognition principles

Section 28 is not restricted to pensions and other post-retirement benefits, but addresses all forms of consideration (except for share-based payment transactions which are dealt with by Section 26 and discussed in Chapter 23 of this publication) given by an employer in exchange for services rendered by employees or for the termination of employment. *[FRS 102.28.1]*. In particular Section 28 covers:

- Short-term employee benefits, which are employee benefits (other than termination benefits) that are expected to be settled wholly before twelve months after the end of the reporting period in which the employees render the related service. The accounting for these is discussed at 3.3 below.

- Post-employment benefits, which are employee benefits (other than termination benefits and short-term employee benefits) that are payable after the completion of employment. The accounting for these is discussed at 3.4 to 3.6 and 3.10 below.

- Other long-term employee benefits, which are all employee benefits other than short-term employee benefits, post-employment benefits and termination benefits. The accounting for these is discussed at 3.8 below.

- Termination benefits, which are employee benefits provided in exchange for the termination of an employee's employment as a result of either:

  - the entity's decision to terminate an employee's employment before the normal retirement date; or

  - an employee's decision to accept voluntary redundancy in exchange for those benefits. The accounting for these is discussed at 3.9 below.

In Section 28 the term employees includes management and directors. *[FRS 102.28.1]*.

The general recognition principle for all employee benefits is that an entity must recognise the cost of employee benefits to which its employees have become entitled as a result of service rendered to the entity during the period:

- as a liability, after deducting amounts that have been paid either directly to the employees or as a contribution to an employee benefit fund. If the amount paid exceeds the obligation arising from service before the reporting date, an entity should recognise that excess as an asset to the extent that the prepayment will lead to a reduction in future payments or a cash refund; and

- an expense, unless another section of the FRS requires the cost to be recognised as part of the cost of an asset such as inventories or property, plant and equipment. *[FRS 102.28.3]*.

An employee benefit fund may have been set up as an intermediary payment arrangement. Contributions made to the fund need to be accounted for in accordance with paragraphs 9.33 to 9.38 of FRS 102. This means that when the employer is a sponsoring employer of the fund, the assets and liabilities of the fund will be accounted for by the sponsoring employer as an extension of its own business. As a consequence the payments to the employee benefit fund do not extinguish the liability of the employer. *[FRS 102.28.3(a)]*. Accounting for employee benefit funds is discussed in Chapter 23 at 13.3. A pension plan is independent of the employer and is therefore not accounted for as an extension of the employers business.

3.3   Short-term employee benefits

Short-term employee benefits are employee benefits (other than termination benefits) that are expected to be settled wholly before twelve months after the end of the annual reporting period in which the employees render the related service. The following are examples of short-term employee benefits: *[FRS 102.28.4]*

- wages, salaries and social security contributions;
- paid annual leave and paid sick leave;
- profit-sharing and bonuses; and
- non-monetary benefits (such as medical care, housing, cars and free or subsidised goods or services) for current employees.

Accounting for short-term employee benefits is relatively straight forward as no discounting is required due to their short term nature. An entity should recognise the undiscounted amount expected to be paid in respect of short-term benefits attributable to services that have been rendered in the period as an expense or as part of the cost of an asset where required by another section of FRS 102. *[FRS 102.28.5]*. As detailed in the general recognition principles at 3.2 above, any amount of the expense which has not been paid at the reporting date should be recognised as a liability.

Short-term compensated absences occur where the employee does not provide services to the employer but benefits continue to accrue. This may be made for various reasons including absences for annual leave and sick leave. Short-term compensated absences can either be accumulating or non-accumulating absences. Accumulating absences are those that can be carried forward and used in future periods if the entitlement in the current period is not used in full. An entity should recognise the expected cost of accumulating compensated absences when the employees render service that increases their entitlement to future compensated absences. The amount recognised will be the undiscounted additional amount that the entity expects to pay as a result of the unused entitlement that has accumulated at the end of reporting period. This liability should be presented on the balance sheet as falling due within one year at the reporting date. *[FRS 102.28.6]*.

An example of an accumulating compensated absence is holiday not taken in the current year which can be carried forward.

Example 25.1:   Accumulating compensated absences

An entity has 100 employees, who are each entitled to twenty five working days of paid holiday for each year. Unused holiday may be carried forward for one calendar year. Holiday is taken first out of the current year's entitlement and then out of any balance brought forward from the previous year (a LIFO basis). At 31 December 2019, the average unused entitlement is two days per employee. The entity expects, based on past experience which is expected to continue, that 92 employees will take no more than twenty five days of paid holiday in 2020 and that the remaining eight employees will take an average of twenty six and a half days each.

The entity expects that it will pay an additional 12 days of holiday pay as a result of the unused entitlement that has accumulated at 31 December 2019 (one and a half days each, for eight employees). Therefore, the entity recognises a liability equal to 12 days of holiday pay.

Non-accumulating absences are those where there is no entitlement to carry forward unused amounts/days. An entity should record the cost of these absences when they occur at the undiscounted amount of salaries and wages paid or payable for the period of absence. *[FRS 102.28.7]*. Examples of non-accumulating compensating absences include sick leave, maternity leave and jury service.

In applying the general recognition criteria to profit-sharing and bonus payments, an entity should recognise the expected cost of profit-sharing and bonus payments when, and only when: *[FRS 102.28.8]*

- the entity has a present legal or constructive obligation to make such payments as a result of past events (this means that the entity has no realistic alternative but to make the payments); and
- a reliable estimate of the obligation can be made.

A legal obligation may not always be present, however an entity's past practice in paying profit-sharing or bonuses may have established a constructive obligation, requiring the cost to be recognised.

A constructive obligation is defined at 3.1 above.

Cost is not defined in Section 23 and therefore the accounting for such benefits may vary depending on any other standards involved in the recognition of the transaction.

FRS 102 provides no guidance on how to determine whether an estimate may be reliable. In looking for guidance over what is meant by a 'reliable estimate' users may turn to IAS 19. This standard states that a reliable estimate of a constructive or legal obligation under a profit-sharing or bonus plan can usually be made when, and only when: *[IAS 19.22]*

- the formal terms of the plan contain a formula for determining the amount of the benefit;
- the entity determines the amounts to be paid before the financial statements are authorised for issue; or
- past practice gives clear evidence of the amount of the entity's constructive obligation.

Profit-sharing and bonus plans should only be accounted for as short-term benefits when they are expected to be wholly settled within twelve months from the end of the reporting period, plans which are expected to be settled over a longer period should be accounted for as other long-term benefits, which are discussed at 3.8 below.

3.4 Post-employment benefits: distinction between defined contribution plans and defined benefit plans

Post-employment benefits are defined as employee benefits (other than termination benefits and short-term employee benefits) that are payable after the completion of employment. *[FRS 102 Appendix I]*. They include, for example:

- retirement benefits, such as pensions; and
- other post-employment benefits, such as post-employment life insurance and post-employment medical care. *[FRS 102.28.9]*.

Chapter 25

Arrangements whereby an entity provides post-employment benefits are post-employment benefit plans as defined. Section 28 applies to all post-employment benefit plans, whether or not they involve the establishment of a separate legal entity to receive contributions or pay benefits. In some cases, these arrangements are imposed by law rather than by the action of the entity. In some cases these arrangements arise from actions of the entity even in the absence of a formal documented plan. *[FRS 102.28.9]*.

3.4.1   Distinction between defined contribution plans and defined benefit plans

Section 28 draws the natural, but important, distinction between defined contribution plans and defined benefit plans. The determination is made based on the economic substance of the plan as derived from its principal terms and conditions. The approach it takes is to define defined contribution plans, with the defined benefit plans being the default category. These definitions are stated at 3.1 above. Guidance is also provided explaining how to apply the requirements to insured benefits, multi-employer plans (including state plans) and group plans.

Defined contribution plans are post-employment benefit plans under which an entity pays fixed contributions into a separate entity (a fund) and has no legal or constructive obligation to pay further contributions or to make direct benefit payments to employees if the fund does not hold sufficient assets to pay all the employee benefits relating to employee service in the current or prior periods. Thus, the amount of the post-employment benefits received by the employee is determined by the amount of contributions paid by an entity (and perhaps also the employee) to a post-employment benefit plan or to an insurer, together with investment returns arising from the contributions. *[FRS 102.28.10(a)]*.

Defined benefit plans are post-employment benefit plans other than defined contribution plans. Under defined benefit plans, the entity's obligation is to provide the agreed benefits to current and former employees, and actuarial risk (that benefits will cost more or less than expected) and investment risk (that returns on assets set aside to fund the benefits will differ from expectations) are borne, in substance, by the entity. If actuarial or investment experience is worse than expected, the entity's obligation may be increased, and *vice versa* if actuarial or investment experience is better than expected. *[FRS 102.28.10(b)]*.

The most significant difference between defined contribution and defined benefit plans is that, under a defined benefit plan some actuarial risk or investment risk falls on the employer. Consequently because the employer is in substance underwriting the actuarial and investment risks associated with the plan, the expense recognised for a defined benefit plan is not necessarily the amount of the contributions due for the period. In contrast the benefits received by the employee from a defined contribution plan are determined by contributions paid (both by the employer and employee) to the benefit plan or insurance company, together with investment returns, and therefore actuarial and investment risk fall in substance on the employee. Hence the expense of a defined contribution plan is the contributions due for the period from the employer.

Under defined benefit plans the employer's obligation is not limited to the amount that it agrees to contribute to the fund. Rather, the employer is obliged (legally or constructively) to provide the agreed benefits to current and former employees.

An employer's obligation may be increased by a constructive obligation such as the historical practice of discretionary pension increases going beyond the formal terms of the plan or statutory minimum increases.

3.4.2 Multi-employer and state plans

Multi-employer plans, other than state plans, are defined contribution plans or defined benefit plans that: *[FRS 102 Appendix I]*

- pool assets contributed by various entities that are not under common control; and
- use those assets to provide benefits to employees of more than one entity, on the basis that contribution and benefit levels are determined without regard to the identity of the entity that employs the employees.

In the UK these are typically industry wide schemes. They exclude group administration plans, which simply pool the assets of more than one employer under common control, for investment purposes and the reduction of administrative and investment costs, but keep the claims of different employers segregated for the sole benefit of their own employees. The accounting for these plans is dealt with at 3.10 below.

A multi-employer plan should be classified as either a defined contribution plan or a defined benefit plan in accordance with its terms, including any constructive obligation that goes beyond the formal terms of the plan, in the normal way (see 3.4.1 above). However, if sufficient information is not available to use defined benefit accounting for a multi-employer plan that is a defined benefit plan, the entity should account for the plan as if it were a defined contribution plan and make relevant disclosures (see 3.12.3 below). *[FRS 102.28.11]*.

Where an entity participates in a defined benefit plan which is a multi-employer plan, and this plan is accounted for as a defined contribution plan, if the entity has entered into an agreement with the multi-employer plan that determines how the entity will fund a deficit, the entity should recognise a liability for the contributions payable that arise from this agreement (to the extent they are related to the deficit). The resulting expense is recognised in profit or loss. *[FRS 102.28.11A]*.

In the UK the Pensions Act 2004 has required that where a defined benefit plan is underfunded (i.e. it does not have sufficient assets to cover its obligations), the trustees must establish a recovery plan which confirms how the Statutory Funding Objective must be met and the period over which this is to be met. This recovery plan will detail the contributions to be made by each participating employer. From this agreement it may be possible to establish sufficient information to allow defined benefit accounting as the schedule of deficit funding contributions provides information on how the deficit will be funded by each of the participating employers, and hence their share of assets and liabilities.

A state plan is an employee benefit plan established by legislation to cover all entities (or all other entities in a particular category, for example a specific industry) and operated by national or local government or by another body (for example an

Chapter 25

autonomous agency created specifically for this purpose) which is not subject to control or influence by the reporting entity. *[FRS 102 Appendix I]*. A state plan should be accounted for in the same way as a multi-employer plan. *[FRS 102.28.11]*.

Neither FRS 102 nor IAS 19 address the accounting treatment required if sufficient information becomes available for a multi-employer plan which has previously been accounted for as a defined contribution scheme. There are two possible approaches to this:

* record an immediate charge/credit to profit and loss equal to the deficit/surplus; or
* record an actuarial gain or loss in other comprehensive income.

It can be argued that the first approach is correct as starting defined benefit accounting is akin to introducing a new scheme and, as discussed in 3.6.6 below, plan introductions result in the corresponding amount of any increase or decrease in a liability being taken to profit and loss.

On the other hand it could be argued that defined contribution accounting was the best estimate for what the defined benefit accounting should have been given the information available, and the emergence of new information is a change in estimate and therefore recorded as a remeasurement.

Given the lack of guidance in either FRS 102 or IAS 19 we believe that either approach would be acceptable as long as it is applied consistently.

3.4.3   Insured benefits

One factor that can complicate making the distinction between defined benefit and defined contribution plans is the use of external insurers.

Section 28 helps users to make this distinction by stating that where insurance premiums are paid to fund post-employment benefits, the employer should treat the plan as a defined contribution plan unless it has (either directly or indirectly through the plan) a legal or constructive obligation to:

* pay the employee benefits directly when they fall due; or
* pay further amounts if the insurer does not pay all future employee benefits relating to employee service in the current and prior periods.

If a plan involving insurance is determined to be a defined benefit plan, the insurance policies will represent plan assets which are discussed at 3.6.3 below.

If the employer has retained such a legal or constructive obligation it should treat the plan as a defined benefit plan. A constructive obligation could arise indirectly through the plan, through the mechanism for setting future premiums, or through a related party relationship with the insurer. *[FRS 102.28.12]*.

Section 28 provides limited guidance on how to account for the insurance policy, other than requiring that if a plan asset is an insurance policy which exactly matches the timing and amount of some of the benefits payable under the plan, the fair value of the asset is deemed to be the present value of the related obligation (see 3.6.3 below).

Qualifying insurance policies are defined as an insurance policy issued by an insurer that is not a related party of the reporting entity, if the proceeds of the policy: *[FRS 102 Appendix I]*

- can be used only to pay or fund employee benefits under a defined benefit plan; and
- are not available to the reporting entity's own creditors (even in bankruptcy) and cannot be paid to the reporting entity unless either;
  - the proceeds represent surplus assets that are not needed for the policy to meet all the related employee benefit obligations; or
  - the proceeds are returned to the reporting entity to reimburse it for employee benefits already paid.

Qualifying insurance policies are accounted for as plan assets, however Section 28 provides no guidance on accounting for other insurance policies which do not meet the definition of a qualifying insurance policy. Under IAS 19 these are accounted for as reimbursement rights (providing the criteria for recognition as reimbursement rights are met). See 3.6.4 below.

3.5 Defined contribution plans

3.5.1 General

Accounting for defined contribution plans is straightforward under Section 28 as a reporting entity's obligation for each period is determined by the amounts to be contributed for that period. Consequently, no actuarial assumptions are required to be made in order to measure the obligation or the expense and there is no possibility of any actuarial gain or loss to the reporting entity. Moreover, the obligations are measured on an undiscounted basis, except where they are not expected to be settled wholly before twelve months after the end of the period in which the employees render the related service. Where discounting is required, the discount rate should be determined in the same way as for defined benefit plans, which is discussed at 3.6.2.B below. *[FRS 102.28.13A]*. In general, though, it would seem unlikely for a defined contribution scheme to be structured with such a long delay between the employee service and the employer contribution.

Section 28 requires that, when an employee has rendered service during a period, the employer should recognise the contribution payable to a defined contribution plan in exchange for that service: *[FRS 102.28.13]*

- as a liability, after deducting any contribution already paid. If the contribution already paid exceeds the contribution due for service before the end of the reporting period, the excess should be recognised as an asset (prepaid expense) to the extent that the prepayment will lead to, for example, a reduction in future payments or a cash refund; and
- as an expense, unless another section of the FRS requires the cost to be recognised as part of the cost of an asset such as inventories or property, plant and equipment. See Chapters 11 and 15 respectively.

As discussed at 3.4.2 above, Section 28 requires multi-employer defined benefit plans to be accounted for as defined contribution plans in certain circumstances. It is clear that contractual arrangements to make contributions to fund a deficit should be fully provided for (on a discounted basis) even if they are to be paid over an extended period. The unwinding of any discount is recognised as a finance cost in profit or loss. *[FRS 102.18.13A]*.

3.6   Defined benefit plans

Accounting for defined benefit plans is complex because actuarial assumptions are required to measure both the obligation and the expense, and there is a possibility of actuarial gains and losses. Moreover, because the obligations are settled many years after the employees render the related service, the obligations are measured on a discounted basis.

3.6.1   Recognition

In applying the general recognition principle (see 3.2 above) to defined benefit plans, an entity is required to recognise: *[FRS 102.28.14]*

- a liability for its obligations under the defied benefit plans net of plan assets – its 'net defined benefit liability'; and

- the change in that liability during the period as the cost of its defined benefit plans during the period.

Guidance on how to account for these is covered below.

3.6.2   Measurement of plan liabilities

An entity is required to measure the net defined benefit liability for its obligations under defined benefit plans at the net total of the following amounts: *[FRS 102.28.15]*

- the present value of its obligations under defined benefit plans (its defined benefit obligation) at the reporting date; minus

- the fair value at the reporting date of the plan assets (if any) out of which the obligations are to be settled. If the asset is an insurance policy that exactly matches the amount and timing of some or all of the benefits payable under the plan, the fair value of the asset is deemed to be the present value of the related obligation. See 3.6.3 below.

3.6.2.A   Legal and constructive obligations

The present value of an entity's obligations under defined benefit plans at the reporting date should reflect the estimated amount of benefit that employees have earned in return for their service in the current and prior periods, including benefits that are not yet vested (see below) and including the effects of benefit formulas that give employees greater benefits for later years of service. This requires the entity to determine how much benefit is attributable to the current and prior periods on the basis of the plans benefit formula and to make estimates (actuarial assumptions) about demographic variables (such as employee turnover and mortality) and financial variables (such as future increases in salaries and medical costs) that influence the cost of the benefit. The actuarial assumptions should be unbiased (neither imprudent nor excessively conservative), mutually compatible, and selected to lead to the best estimate of the future cash flows that will arise under the plan. *[FRS 102.28.16]*.

Although Section 28 does not use the term 'attribution of benefit to years of service', the fact that it states that defined benefit obligations should reflect the estimated amount of benefit that employees have earned in return for their service, including benefits that are not yet vested, and it requires the effects of benefit formulas that give employees greater benefits for later years of service to be taken into account essentially has the same meaning. In doing this the projected unit credit method is required to be used (see 3.6.2.C below). However, Section 28 does not provide detail on how greater benefits for later years of service should be taken into account. IAS 19 requires that when an employee's service in later years will lead to a materially higher level of benefit, the benefit should be attributed on a straight line basis from: *[IAS 19.70]*

- the date when service by the employee first leads to benefits under the plan; until
- the date when further service by the employee will lead to no material amount of further benefits under the plan, other than from further salary increases.

This requirement is considered necessary because the employee's service throughout the entire period will ultimately lead to benefit at that higher level.

The employee service gives rise to an obligation under a defined benefit plan even if the benefits are conditional on future employment (in other words they have not yet vested). Employee service before the vesting date gives rise to a constructive obligation because, at each successive reporting date, the amount of future service that an employee will have to render before being entitled to the benefit is reduced. When calculating its defined benefit obligation (attributing benefits to years of service) an entity must consider the probability that some employees may not satisfy the vesting requirements (i.e. leave before retirement age). Similarly, although some post-employment benefits (such as post-employment medical benefits) become payable only if a specified event occurs when an employee is no longer employed (such as illness), the obligation is created when the employee renders the service that provides entitlement to the benefit if the specified event occurs. The probability that the specified event will occur affects the measurement of the obligation, but does not determine whether the obligation exists. *[FRS 102.28.26]*.

3.6.2.B   Discount rate

Due to the long timescales involved, post-employment benefit obligations are required to be discounted. The rate used should be determined 'by reference to' the market yield (at the end of the reporting period) on high quality corporate bonds of currency and term consistent with liabilities. In countries where there is no deep market in such bonds, the entity should use the market yields on government bonds instead. *[FRS 102.28.17]*.

FRS 102 does not explain what is meant by 'high quality'. In practice it is considered to mean bonds rated AA or higher by Standard and Poor's, or an equivalent rating from another rating agency.

3.6.2.C   Actuarial methodology

An entity is required to use the projected unit credit method to measure its defined benefit obligation and the related expense. It is defined as an actuarial valuation method that sees each period of service as giving rise to an additional unit of benefit entitlement and measures each unit separately to build up the final obligation. *[FRS 102 Appendix I]*. If defined benefits are based on future salaries, the projected unit method requires an entity to measure its defined benefit obligations on a basis that reflects estimated future salary increases. In addition, the projected unit credit method requires an entity to make various actuarial assumptions in measuring the defined benefit obligation, including discount rates, employee turnover, mortality and (for defined benefit medical plans) medical cost trend rates. *[FRS 102.28.18]*.

As detailed above, this method uses both the vested and non-vested benefits.

IAS 19 provides a simple example of the projected unit credit method: *[IAS 19.68]*

Example 25.2:   The projected unit credit method

A lump sum benefit is payable on termination of service and equal to 1% of final salary for each year of service. The salary in year 1 is 10,000 and is assumed to increase at 7% (compound) each year. The discount rate used is 10% per year. The following table shows how the obligation builds up for an employee who is expected to leave at the end of year 5, assuming that there are no changes in actuarial assumptions. For simplicity, this example ignores the additional adjustment needed to reflect the probability that the employee may leave the entity at an earlier or later date.

Year	1	2	3	4	5
Benefit attributed to:					
– prior years	0	131	262	393	524
– current year (1% of final salary)	131	131	131	131	131
– current and prior years	131	262	393	524	655
Opening Obligation	–	89	196	324	476
Interest at 10%	–	9	20	33	48
Service Cost	89	98	108	119	131
Closing Obligation	89	196	324	476	655

Note:
– The Opening Obligation is the present value of benefit attributed to prior years.
– The Current Service Cost is the present value of benefit attributed to the current year.
– The Closing Obligation is the present value of benefit attributed to current and prior years.

As can be seen in this simple example, the projected unit credit method also produces a figure for service cost and interest cost. These cost components are discussed at **3.6.9** below.

The underlying workings relevant to the above are as follows:

Final salary at year 5 (10,000 compounded at 7%) $10,000 \times (1 + 0.07)^4 = 13,100$

1% of final salary attributed to each year   131

Expected final benefit   5 years $\times$ 1% $\times$ 131,000 = 655

Service cost, being present value of 131 discounted at 10%: e.g.

Year 1 $131 \times (1 + 0.1)^{-4} = 89$

Year 2 $131 \times (1 + 0.1)^{-3} = 98$

Closing obligation, being years served multiplied by present value of 131: e.g.

Year 3   3 years $\times 131 \times (1 + 0.1)^{-2} = 324$

3.6.2.D   Actuarial assumptions

As noted above, the projected unit credit method requires an entity to make various actuarial assumptions in measuring the defined benefit obligation. These are defined as an entity's unbiased and mutually compatible best estimates of the demographic and financial variables that will determine the ultimate cost of providing post-employment benefits. *[FRS 102 Appendix I].*

Demographic assumptions concern the future characteristics of current and former employees (and their dependents) who are eligible for benefits and deal with matters such as:

- mortality, both during and after employment;
- rates of employee turnover, disability and early retirement;
- the proportion of plan members with dependents who will be eligible for benefits; and
- claim rates under medical plans.

Financial assumptions deal with items such as:

- the discount rate (see 3.6.2.B above);
- future salary and benefit levels, excluding the cost of benefits that will be met by the employees;
- in the case of medical benefits, future medical costs, including claim handling costs; and
- price inflation.

The actuarial assumptions must be unbiased (neither imprudent nor excessively conservative), mutually compatible, and selected to lead to the best estimate of the future cash flows that will arise under the plan. *[FRS 102.28.16].*

When the level of defined benefits payable by a scheme are reduced for the amounts that will be paid to employees under government-sponsored benefits, an entity should measure its defined benefit obligations on a basis that reflects the benefits payable under the plans, but only if: *[FRS 102.28.27]*

- those plans were enacted before the reporting date; or
- past history, or other reliable evidence, indicates that those state benefits will change in some predictable manner, for example, in line with future changes in general price levels or general salary levels.

3.6.2.E   Frequency of valuations and use of an independent actuary

An entity must measure its defined benefit obligation and plan assets at the reporting date. *[FRS 102.28.15].* An entity is not required to engage an independent actuary to perform the comprehensive actuarial valuation needed to calculate the defined benefit obligation, nor does it require that a comprehensive valuation to be performed annually. If the principal actuarial assumptions have not changed significantly in periods between the comprehensive actuarial valuations, the defined benefit obligation can be measured by adjusting the prior period measurement for changes in employee demographics such as employee numbers or salary levels. *[FRS 102.28.20].*

In practice we expect that most entities will engage an independent actuary to perform the comprehensive actuarial valuation given its complexity.

3.6.2.F   Equalisation of GMP benefits

On 26 October 2018, the High Court in England and Wales ruled on the equalisation of certain pension benefits payable to men and women.[1] The benefits in question are those accrued in company defined benefit schemes between 1990 and 1997 where the plan was 'contracted out' of the state earnings related pension (SERPS). The pensions concerned must be at least as much as the statutory benefit which they replaced and hence are described as 'guaranteed minimum pensions' or GMP. The court ruled that these pensions should not be different simply due to the sex of the recipient; that is, the benefits must be 'equalised'. Trustees have an obligation to equalise benefits and it is likely that this will require a change to the scheme rules. It is important to note that GMP equalisation is distinct from the equalisation of other elements of pension arrangements which has been dealt with by companies and pension funds in the past.

The court considered different ways in which individual pensions could be equalised; the ruling does not prescribe a single methodology to be applied in all cases. The method to be applied will need to be considered by each scheme based on its own specific circumstances to determine whether and how individual payments will change as a result of equalisation. That assessment of future cash flows will form the basis of the defined benefit obligation in the accounts calculated using the projected unit credit method.

Where a company has not in the past accounted for the higher pension payments resulting from GMP equalisation it should account for any change as a past service cost which occurred on 26th October 2018. Accordingly, the cost should be presented in profit and loss for the period containing that date. *[FRS 102.28.21]*. If material, this will be a disclosable post-balance sheet event for accounts drawn up to a date before 26th October 2018 but would not be accounted for in such periods (see Chapter 29 at 3.5.2). *[FRS 102.32.10]*.

However, if the defined benefit obligation of earlier years reflected the effect of GMP equalisation and it can be evidenced that this was the best estimate of the liability at the time (given the then impending ruling by the High Court, if applicable), then any further adjustment resulting from the ruling would be recognised in OCI as a re-measurement. *[FRS 102.28.23]*. Importantly, such re-estimation would need to be reflected in any accounts prepared after the ruling irrespective of the balance sheet date.

The process of quantifying any effect of equalisation will require directors to perform detailed and 'granular' calculations which may well be a time consuming task. During this process the method to be used and the period of arrears to be taken into account will need to be determined based on the individual circumstances of each scheme.

3.6.3   Measurement of plan assets

Plan assets are required to be measured at fair value at the reporting date, except that if an asset is an insurance policy that exactly matches the amount and timing of some or all of the benefits payable under the plan, the fair value of the asset is deemed to be the present value of the related obligation. The Appendix to Section 2 – *Concepts and Pervasive Principles* – provides guidance on determining the fair value of those plan assets. See Chapter 4 at 3.13. *[FRS 102.28.15(b)]*.

Plan assets are defined as comprising: *[FRS 102 Appendix I]*

- assets held by a long-term employee benefit fund; and
- qualifying insurance policies.

Assets held by a long-term employee benefit fund are an asset (other than non-transferable financial instruments issued by the reporting entity) that: *[FRS 102 Appendix I]*

- is held by an entity (a fund) that is legally separate from the reporting entity and exists solely to pay or fund employee benefits; and

- is available to be used only to pay or fund employee benefits, is not available to the reporting entity's own creditors (even in bankruptcy) and cannot be returned to the reporting entity, unless either:

    - the remaining assets of the fund are sufficient to meet all the related employee benefit obligations of the plan or the reporting entity; or

    - the assets are returned to the reporting entity to reimburse it for employee benefits already paid.

A qualifying insurance policy is defined at 3.4.3 above. A footnote to the definition clarifies that an insurance policy is not necessarily an insurance contract.

3.6.4 Reimbursement rights

Some employers may have in place arrangements to fund defined benefit obligations which do not meet the definition of qualifying insurance policies, but which do provide for another party to reimburse some or all of the expenditure required to settle a defined benefit obligation. In such cases, the expected receipts under the arrangement are not classified as plan assets.

Section 28 states that when an entity is virtually certain that another party will reimburse some or all of the expenditure required to settle a defined benefit obligation, the entity should recognise its right to the reimbursement as a separate asset, which should be treated the same way as other plan assets. The cost of a defined benefit plan recognised in accordance with paragraph 28.23 (i.e. service cost, net interest and the cost of plan introductions, benefit changes, curtailments and settlements) may be presented net of the amounts relating to changes in the carrying amount of the right to reimbursement. *[FRS 102.28.28].*

3.6.5 Longevity swaps

A longevity swap transfers, from a pension scheme to an external party, the risk of members living longer (or shorter) than expected.

Longevity swaps are not specifically dealt with in FRS 102. Therefore, we would expect users to turn to discussions held by the Interpretations Committee on the subject.

The Interpretations Committee was asked in August 2014 to clarify the measurement of longevity swaps held by an entity's defined benefit plan, and in particular discussed whether an entity should:

(a) account for a longevity swap as a single instrument and measure its fair value as part of plan assets (discussed at 3.6.3 above) with changes in fair value being recorded in other comprehensive income; or

(b) split longevity swaps into two components.

The two components in (b) would be a 'fixed leg' and a 'variable leg'. As the variable leg exactly matches some or all of the defined benefit obligation it would represent a

Chapter 25

qualifying insurance policy and be measured at the present value of the related obligation (discussed at 3.4.3 above). The fixed leg comprises a series of fixed payments to be made in return for the receipt of the variable leg receipts. In other words, a longevity swap could be considered to be economically equivalent to the purchase of qualifying insurance (commonly called a 'buy-in') but with the premium paid over a period of time rather than at inception.

The likely effect of disaggregating a longevity swap in this way would be to recognise a loss at inception very similar to that for a buy-in. Conversely, considering the swap as a single instrument measured at fair value would likely have no initial effect as typically its fair value would be zero (that is, a premium neither received nor paid).

If the two legs were to be considered separately, an appropriate accounting policy would need to be applied to the fixed leg. Two possibilities were discussed by the Interpretations Committee as follows. The fixed leg would initially be measured at fair value with subsequent accounting either:

- if treated as part of plan assets, at fair value with interest reported in profit or loss and other changes being included in other comprehensive income (discussed at 3.6.3 above); or

- if a financial liability at amortised cost using the effective interest rate with interest recognised in profit and loss and no other remeasurements.

The Interpretations Committee noted that when such transactions take place, the predominant practice is to account for a longevity swap as a single instrument and measure it at fair value as part of plan assets.

The Interpretations Committee decided not to add this issue to its agenda as it did not expect diversity to develop in the application of IAS 19.[2] Given that the Interpretations Committee decided not to add this to its agenda we believe that either of the subsequent accounting options detailed above would be acceptable.

3.6.6   *Plan introductions, changes, curtailments and settlements*

If a defined benefit plan has been introduced or the benefits have changed in the current period, the entity should increase/(decrease) its net defined benefit liability to reflect the change and recognise the increase/(decrease) as an expense/(income) in profit or loss in the current period. *[FRS 102.28.21]*.

The point in time at which a plan amendment occurs will often be a matter of fact based on the legal entitlements of plan members. Judgement may be required, based on individual facts and circumstances, if the benefits concerned constitute constructive, as opposed to legal, obligations (see 3.6.2.A above).

Sometimes benefit plans are amended in such a way as to allow members a choice, for a limited period, between two or more benefit arrangements. In such cases a plan amendment occurs (and a positive or negative past service cost will be recognised) on the date at which the new arrangement comes into existence (legally or constructively) and not at the later date by which members are required to make their choice. This may mean that the initial accounting for the plan amendment will require estimates to be made of the choices which members will make. However, if it is known, at the time the relevant financial statements are prepared, what choices members have made (for example, because the 'window' for making selections closes before the financial statements are authorised for issue) this definitive data would remove the need for estimation. Any subsequent changes in estimates in the following years resulting from the confirmation process would be a change in estimate and recognised as a remeasurement gain or loss.

Where a defined benefit plan has been curtailed (i.e. the benefits or group of covered employees are reduced) or settled (the relevant part of the employer's obligation is completely discharged) in the current period, the defined benefit obligation should be decreased or eliminated and the resulting gain or loss recognised in profit and loss in the current reporting period. *[FRS 102.28.21A]*. This gain or loss should be disclosed separately as part of the reconciliation of the defined benefit obligation along with the expense/(income) arising from plan introductions and changes. This expense/(income) should be disclosed separately as part of the required reconciliation of the defined benefit obligation. *[FRS 102.28.41(f)(iv)]*. See 3.12.4 below for further details on disclosure requirements.

An employer may acquire an insurance policy to fund all or some of the employee benefits relating to employee service in the current and prior periods. The acquisition of such a policy is not a settlement if the employer retains a legal or constructive obligation to pay further amounts if the insurer does not pay the employee benefits specified in the insurance policy (referred to as a buy-in arrangement – see 3.6.5 above). However, the acquisition of an insurance policy will mean that the entity has an asset which it needs measure at fair value. As discussed at 3.6.3 above, certain insurance policies are valued at an amount equal to the present value of the defined benefit obligation they match. The cost of buying such a policy will typically greatly exceed its subsequent carrying amount as the discount rate used by the insurance company will be lower than that used in an FRS 102 valuation. This raises the question of how to treat the resultant loss. One view might be that because the loss results from exchanging one plan asset for another it is an actuarial loss and therefore should be recognised in other comprehensive income. Another view is that the loss in substance is very similar to a settlement loss and should be recognised in profit or loss. This might be appropriate where the buy-in was entered into to enable the plan to move to a buy-out (or settlement). In our view, either approach is acceptable if applied consistently and, where material, disclosed. The plan assets and plan liabilities would remain to be recorded on the statement of financial position until such time as the settlement had occurred and the entity no longer had any obligations under the plan.

3.6.7 Restriction on plan assets

In practice, defined benefit pension plans tend to be funded on a more prudent basis than would be the case if the surplus or deficit was measured in accordance with FRS 102. This is due to the discount rate used for funding purposes typically being lower than that specified by Section 28. For this reason an FRS 102 valuation may result in a pension asset (surplus), when for funding purposes there is a deficit. FRS 102 states that if the present value of the defined benefit obligation at the reporting date is less than the fair value of plan assets at that date, the plan has a surplus. It goes on to observe that an entity should recognise a plan surplus as a defined benefit asset only to the extent that it is able to recover the surplus either through reduced contributions in the future or through refunds from the plan. *[FRS 102.28.22]*.

No further explanation is given of the meaning of 'reduced contributions in the future or through refunds from the plan'. This lack of guidance will require management to exercise judgement in developing and applying an accounting policy to determine the amount of any defined benefit pension surplus that can be recognised. In making such a judgement, management should refer to and consider the definitions, recognition criteria and measurement concepts for assets, liabilities, income and expenses and the pervasive principles in Section 2 – *Concepts and Pervasive Principles* (see Chapter 9 at 3.2). Section 2 states that recognition is the process of incorporating in the statement of financial position or statement of comprehensive income an item that meets the definition of an asset, liability, equity, income or expense and satisfies the following criteria: *[FRS 102.2.27]*

(a)   it is probable that any future economic benefit associated with the item will flow to or from the entity; and

(b)   the item has a cost or value that can be measured reliably.

One possible way that an entity may interpret the above is that a defined benefit pension surplus is only recognised when it is probable that the entity will receive a refund or reduction in future contributions (i.e. it meets the definition of an asset in the standard).

In exercising judgement when developing and applying an accounting policy when FRS 102 does not specifically address a transaction, other event or condition, management may also consider the requirements and guidance in EU-adopted IFRS dealing with similar or related issues (see Chapter 9 at 3.2).

Due to the problems encountered in practice in applying the asset ceiling test in IAS 19, the Interpretations Committee issued IFRIC 14 in 2007. IFRIC 14 addresses the issues of:

- when refunds or reductions in future contributions should be regarded as available in accordance with the definition of the asset ceiling in IAS 19.8;

- how a minimum funding requirement might affect the availability of reductions in future contributions; and

- when a minimum funding requirement might give rise to a liability.

FRS 102 does not include the requirements of IFRIC 14. However, paragraph 15A of Section 28 states that '[w]here an entity has measured its defined benefit obligation using the projected unit credit method (including the use of appropriate actuarial assumptions), as set out in paragraph 28.18, it should not recognise any additional liabilities to reflect differences from these assumptions and those used for the most recent actuarial valuation of the plan for funding purposes. For the avoidance of doubt, no additional liabilities should be recognised in respect of an agreement with the defined benefit plan to fund a deficit (such as a schedule of contributions).' *[FRS 102.28.15A]*. This means that entities turning to IFRIC 14 under the hierarchy in Section 10 should not recognise a liability for a minimum funding requirement.

3.6.7.A   IFRIC 14 – General requirements concerning the limit on a defined benefit asset

IFRIC 14 clarifies that economic benefits, in the form of refunds or reduced future contributions, are available if they can be realised at some point during the life of the plan or when plan liabilities are settled. In particular, such an economic benefit may be available even if it is not realisable immediately at the end of the reporting period. *[IFRIC 14.8]*. Furthermore, the benefit available does not depend on how the entity intends to use the surplus. The entity should determine the maximum economic benefit available from refunds and reductions in future contributions that are mutually exclusive. *[IFRIC 14.9]*.

3.6.7.B Economic benefit available through a refund

IFRIC 14 observes that an unconditional right to a refund can exist whatever the funding level of a plan at the end of the reporting period. However, if the right to a refund of a surplus depends on the occurrence or non-occurrence of one or more uncertain future events not wholly within an entity's control, the entity does not have an unconditional right and should not recognise the asset. *[IFRIC 14.12]*. Furthermore, the interpretation states that benefits are available as a refund only if the entity has an unconditional right to the refund: *[IFRIC 14.11-12]*

(a) during the life of the plan, without assuming that the plan liabilities must be settled in order to obtain the refund; or

(b) assuming the gradual settlement of the plan liabilities over time until all members have left the plan; or

(c) assuming the full settlement of the plan liabilities in a single event (i.e. as a plan wind up).

The economic benefit available as a refund should be measured as the amount of the surplus at the end of the reporting period (being the fair value of the plan assets less the present value of the defined benefit obligation) that the entity has a right to receive as a refund, less any associated costs. For example if a refund would be subject to a tax other than income tax of the reporting entity it should be measured net of tax. *[IFRIC 14.13]*.

In measuring the amount of a refund available when the plan is wound up (point (c) above), the costs to the plan of settling the plan liabilities and making the refund should be included. For example, a deduction should be made for professional fees if these are paid by the plan rather than the entity, and the costs of any insurance premiums that may be required to secure the liability on wind up. *[IFRIC 14.14]*.

There is currently diversity in practice under IFRS in relation to accounting for costs associated with a pension plan. When a UK pension scheme makes a refund (known in tax law as 'an authorised surplus payment') to an employer, the refund gives rise to a liability for the pension scheme to pay a tax of 35% of the amount refunded (a 'refund tax'). As above, IFRIC 14 requires that taxes other than income taxes should be deducted from the measurement of the refund. *[IFRIC 14.13]*.

Where the refund tax is not considered to be an income tax of the sponsoring employer (based on the fact that it is not charged to the employer and does not appear in the employer's tax calculation) and an entity has a surplus on a scheme (measured under FRS 102 or IAS 19) that is recognised on the basis of a potential refund, IFRIC 14 requires the surplus to be restricted to the net of tax amount (i.e. 65% of the gross surplus is recognised).

Where the refund tax is not deemed to be an income tax (based on the refund tax being economically an income tax of the employer in the sense that it has the effect of claiming back tax relief given to the employer on contributions to the scheme), and this will not be deducted in measuring the refund. Deferred tax should be measured based on management's actual expectation of the manner of recovery of the asset, which may be different to the conclusion reached in respect of the recognition of a pension asset which will be based on the ability to recover the asset. The measurement of deferred tax assets and liabilities is discussed in detail in Chapter 26 at 7.4. If a pension asset is expected to be recovered by way of a refund then the rate of refund tax (currently 35%) should be used to measure the deferred tax asset arising. If however the pension asset is expected to be recovered in another way such as through reductions in future contributions or the 'spending' of the asset (see below) the deferred tax asset will be measured at the substantively enacted rate of tax expected to apply when the asset reverses.

We note that both of the above approaches are seen in practice.

Another relatively common situation in the UK is for pension schemes to have a defined benefit section and a defined contribution section. Trustees may be empowered under the trust deed to use any surplus arising on the defined benefit section in paying up contributions to the defined contribution section. Whilst this is equivalent to obtaining a refund for accounting purposes, it may not be regarded as an 'authorised payment' for tax purposes. Therefore, where an entity is recognising a surplus on a defined benefit section on the basis that it could be refunded through a transfer to a defined contribution section of the same plan, there may be no need to provide for the effect of a refund tax.

It is usually the case that the trustees of a pension fund are independent of the entity. Trustees may have a variety of powers to influence a surplus in a plan. For example:

- setting the investment strategy whereby assets with lower risk and lower return would erode a surplus over time; or the purchase of assets in the form of insurance policies matching all or some of the cash outflows of the plan; or

- full or partial settlement of liabilities; or the improvement of benefits under the plan.

IFRIC 14 makes it clear that for future benefit improvements made by the employer and actuarial gains and losses, the existence of an asset at the end of the reporting period is not affected by possible future changes to the amount of the surplus. If future events occur that change the amount of the surplus, their effects are recognised when they occur. *[IFRIC 14.BC10]*.

IFRIC 14 is also clear that if the right to a refund of a surplus depends on the occurrence or non-occurrence of one or more uncertain future events that are not wholly within an entity's control, the entity does not have an unconditional right and should not recognise a surplus. *[IFRIC 14.11-12]*.

However neither IAS 19 nor IFRIC 14 address the question of whether the entity's right to a refund of a surplus which depends on the occurrence or non-occurrence of uncertain future events means that no surplus should be recognised in any scenario where trustees have the power to 'spend' a surplus.

In June 2015, the IASB issued Exposure Draft *ED/2015/5 – Remeasurement on a Plan Amendment Curtailment or Settlement / Availability of a Refund from a defined Benefit Plan* which proposes amendments to IFRIC 14 to address whether the power of other parties (for example pension trustees) to enhance benefits for plan members or wind up a plan affects the availability of a refund (see 3.6.7.D below). The exposure draft was issued as a response to two requests to the Interpretations Committee, suggesting that there is diversity in practice in this area. In the Basis for Conclusions on the exposure draft the IASB noted that paragraph BC10 of IFRIC 14 had not specifically addressed the circumstances in which trustees have such unconditional powers. The exposure draft proposed that the amount of the surplus that the entity recognises as an asset on the basis of a future refund should not include amounts that other parties can use for other purposes that affect the benefits for plan members, for example by enhancing those benefits without the entity's consent. Until an amendment to IFRIC 14 is issued we expect diversity in practice to continue in this area.

If the amount of a refund is determined as the full amount or a proportion of the surplus, rather than a fixed amount, an entity should make no adjustment for the time value of money, even if the refund is realisable only at a future date. *[IFRIC 14.15]*.

3.6.7.C Economic benefit available through reduced future contributions where there is no minimum funding requirement

IFRIC 14 addresses separately cases where there are minimum funding requirements for contributions relating to future service, and cases where there are no such funding requirements.

This section deals with the situation where there are no such funding requirements. The implications of future service minimum funding requirements are discussed at 3.6.7.D below.

IFRIC 14 requires that the economic benefit available by way of reduced future contributions be determined as the future service cost to the entity for each period over the shorter of the expected life of the plan and the expected life of the entity. The future service cost to the entity excludes amounts that will be borne by employees. *[IFRIC 14.16]*.

Future service costs should be determined using assumptions consistent with those used to determine the defined benefit obligation and with the situation that exists at the end of the reporting period as determined by FRS 102/IAS 19. Accordingly, no future changes to the benefits to be provided by a plan should be assumed until the plan is amended, and a stable workforce in the future should be assumed unless the entity makes a reduction in the number of employees covered by the plan. In the latter case, the assumption about the future workforce should include the reduction. The present value of the future service cost should be determined using the same discount rate as that used in the calculation of the defined benefit obligation (discount rates are discussed at 3.6.2.B above). *[IFRIC 14.17]*.

3.6.7.D Interpretations Committee discussions on IFRIC 14

At 3.6.7.B above we discuss how certain powers of pension fund trustees (to set investment policy, for example) may influence the recognition of a net defined benefit asset by reference to refunds.

The Interpretations Committee received a similar question and, in May 2014, published a description of its initial discussion which is summarised below.

Chapter 25

The Interpretations Committee discussed a question about whether an employer has an unconditional right to a refund of a surplus in the following circumstances:

- the trustee acts on behalf of the plan's members and is independent from the employer; and

- the trustee has discretion in the event of a surplus arising in the plan to make alternative use of that surplus by augmenting the benefits payable to members or by winding up the plan through purchase of annuities, or both.

The question discussed related to a plan that is closed to accrual of future benefits, such that there will be no future service costs, and so no economic benefit is available through a reduction in future contributions. The Interpretations Committee also noted that:

- the fact that an existing surplus at the balance sheet date could be decreased or extinguished by uncertain future events that are beyond the control of the entity is not relevant to the existence of the right to a refund;

- if the trustee can use a surplus by augmenting the benefits in the future, pursuant to the formal terms of a plan (or a constructive obligation that goes beyond those terms), this fact should be considered when the entity measures its defined benefit obligation; and

- the amount of surplus to be recognised could be zero, as a consequence of the measurement of the defined benefit obligation.[3]

In June 2015, the IASB published an exposure draft[4] setting out proposed amendments to IFRIC 14 to require that, when an entity determines the availability of a refund from a defined benefit plan:

- the amount of the surplus that an entity recognises as an asset on the basis of a future refund should not include amounts that other parties (for example, the plan trustees) can use for other purposes without the entity's consent;

- an entity should not assume gradual settlement of the plan as the justification for the recognition of an asset, if other parties can wind up the plan without the entity's consent; and

- other parties' power to buy annuities as plan assets or make other investment decisions without changing the benefits for plan members does not affect the availability of a refund.

The exposure draft also proposed amending IFRIC 14 to confirm that when an entity determines the availability of a refund and a reduction in future contributions, the entity should take into account the statutory requirements that are substantively enacted, as well as the terms and conditions that are contractually agreed and any constructive obligations.

At its April 2017 meeting the Board tentatively decided to finalise the proposed amendments to IFRIC 14, subject to drafting changes.[5] However, some stakeholders subsequently communicated that they believed that the proposed amendments could have a significant effect on some defined benefit plans, particularly those in the United Kingdom. The original proposed amendments to IFRIC 14 included a new paragraph 12A which stated that 'An entity does not have an unconditional right to a refund of a surplus on the basis of assuming the gradual settlement described in paragraph 11(b) if other parties (for example, the plan trustees) can wind up the plan without the entity's consent. Other parties do not have the power to wind up the plan without the entity's consent, if the power is dependent on the occurrence or non-occurrence of one or more uncertain future events not wholly within the other parties' control.' In response to respondents' concerns over the inconsistencies between this new paragraph and paragraphs 11(c) and 14 of IFRIC 14, the Board tentatively decided to replace the reference to other parties' powers to 'wind-up the plan' in this new paragraph with other parties powers to 'settle in full the plan liabilities in a single event (i.e. as a plan wind-up)'. In the United Kingdom although trustees do not generally have the right to legally wind-up a defined benefit plan without the entity's consent, they do generally have the right to settle plan liabilities for individual plan members without an entity's consent if they are 'reasonable'. Although 'reasonable' is not defined in the applicable legislation it is generally understood that this type of partial settlement can be initiated by trustees if plan members would not be worse off as a result of the settlement. It is also understood that trustees do not generally need to obtain consent from plan members to initiate a settlement. Accordingly, trustees could exercise the right to settle liabilities for all plan members in a single event. Entities with defined benefit plans have generally measured the economic benefit available as a refund on a gradual settlement basis applying paragraph 13 of IFRIC 14. Applying the proposed paragraph 12A of IFRIC 14 to United Kingdom defined benefit plans could result in a significantly lower net defined benefit assets in some situations (due to measuring the asset on a wind-up basis in a single event).[6]

In its June 2018 meeting the IASB received an update on the Interpretations Committee's work on how an entity might assess the availability of a refund of a surplus. The Interpretations Committee believe it would be possible to develop a principles-based approach focusing on the distinction between when an entity assumes a gradual settlement of plan liabilities over time and when it assumes full settlement of plan liabilities. The Committee believe that such an approach would however be broader in scope than that of the existing proposed amendments to IFRIC 14 and it is possible that any amendments may need to be exposed for further comments. It was proposed that all possible changes to accounting for employee benefits be considered at the same time and that the IASB would be better placed to consider direction of the IFRIC 14 project when the outcome of the IAS 19 research project (see below) is known. No decisions were reached at the June 2018 Board meeting and the IASB will continue its discussions at a future meeting.

In February 2018, the IASB reviewed its research pipeline and decided to start research on pension benefits that depend on asset returns.[7] Its objective is to assess whether it is feasible to place a cap on asset returns used in estimates of asset-dependent benefits to avoid what is perceived by some to be an anomaly (i.e. benefits being projected based on expected returns that exceed the discount rate, resulting in a liability even though employees will never be paid any amount above the fair value of the reference assets). If the research establishes that this approach would not be feasible the staff expect to recommend no further work on pensions.[8]

Although FRS 102 does not permit minimum funding requirements to be recognised as an additional liability, preparers of FRS 102 financial statements are able to refer to EU IFRS in the absence of specific guidance within FRS 102. As a result, developments in

IAS 19 and IFRIC 14 will be relevant to FRS 102 reporters (as, if under the hierarchy in Section 10, the accounting under these standards is followed any amendments will also need to be followed) and in the case of the discussion above the requirement to recognise a pension surplus.

3.6.8   Tax on defined benefit pension plans

The presentation of income and deferred tax on defined benefit pension schemes along with tax on a pension surplus are discussed in Chapter 26 at 8.4.

3.6.9   Presentation of the net defined benefit liability/asset

FRS 102 requires that an entity present a statement of financial position in accordance with one of the formats prescribed by the Regulations, or using one of the 'adapted formats' (see Chapter 6). The Regulations show pension deficits as the first line item in provisions and pension surpluses either in the same place as a pension deficit under Format 1 of the Regulations, or after prepayments and accrued income under Format 2 of the Regulations. The presentation under FRS 17, which was based on an interpretation of company law, could also be used under FRS 102 as it does not conflict with the Companies Act with the exception that any related deferred tax must not be offset against the pension balance. FRS 17 required defined benefit pension assets or liabilities to be presented, net of deferred tax, after accruals and deferred income, but before capital and reserves (see 2.4 above). As a result there is likely to be divergence in practice in the presentation of defined benefit pension surpluses and deficits under FRS 102.

Where the 'adapted formats' are used, neither FRS 102 nor IFRS specify where in the statement of financial position a net asset or a net liability in respect of a defined benefit plan should be presented, nor whether such balances should be shown separately on the face of the statement of financial position or only in the notes. This is left to the judgement of the reporting entity, but FRS 102 requires additional line items, headings and subtotals where relevant to an understanding of the entity's financial position. *[FRS 102.4.3]*. Classification of post-employment benefit assets and liabilities as current or non-current is discussed in Chapter 6 at 5.1.1.D.

The cost of a defined benefit plan would be included within administration expenses in the income statement, and net interest either within interest receivable and similar income or interest payable and similar charges dependent on whether net interest was an income or expense.

Where an entity has more than one defined benefit pension plan it is possible that it may have a plan with a surplus and another with a deficit. As Section 28 does not deal directly with the presentation of pension plans in the statement of financial position, users are required to look to other sections of FRS 102 which deal with the issue. FRS 102 states that an entity should not offset assets and liabilities unless required or permitted by an FRS. We would therefore expect defined benefit pension surpluses and deficits to be presented separately on the face of the statement of financial position. *[FRS 102.2.52]*.

3.6.10   Treatment of defined benefit plans in profit and loss, and other comprehensive income.

Section 28 requires the cost of a defined benefit plan to be recognised as follows:

- the change in the net defined benefit liability arising from employee service rendered during the reporting period in profit or loss;
- net interest on the defined benefit liability during the reporting period in profit of loss (see 3.6.10.A below);
- the cost of plan introductions, benefit changes, curtailments and settlements in profit or loss (see 3.6.6 above); and
- remeasurement of the net defined benefit liability in other comprehensive income (see 3.6.10.B below).

Where another Section of FRS 102 requires part or all of a cost of employee benefits to be recognised as part of the cost of an asset such as inventories or plant, property and equipment that cost is not recognised in profit or loss. See Chapters 11 and 15 respectively. *[FRS 102.28.3(b)]*.

Some defined benefit plans require employees or third parties to contribute to the cost of the plan. Contributions by employees reduce the cost of benefits to the entity. *[FRS 102.28.23]*.

3.6.10.A   Net interest

The net interest on the net defined benefit liability is determined by multiplying the net defined benefit liability by the discount rate (see 3.6.2.B above), both as determined at the start of the reporting period, taking into account any changes in the net defined liability during the period as a result of contributions and benefit payments. *[FRS 102.28.24]*.

In our view, the requirement to take account of payments to and from the fund implies that an entity should also take account of other significant changes in the net defined benefit liability, for example settlements and curtailments. In February 2018, IAS 19 was amended to clarify that net interest should be determined for the remainder of the period after a plan amendment, curtailment or settlement using:

- the net defined benefit liability (asset) reflecting the benefits offered under the plan and the plan assets after that event; and
- the discount rate used to remeasure that net defined benefit liability (asset).

Although these amendments have not been reproduced in FRS 102 users may turn to IAS 19 for guidance in this regard, and calculate the net interest after significant changes using the net defined benefit liability after the event and possibly the discount rate used to remeasure that net defined benefit liability.

As the net item in the statement of financial position is comprised of two or three separate components (the defined benefit obligation, plan assets and the asset restriction, if any), the net interest is made up of interest unwinding on each of these components in the manner described above. *[FRS 102.28.24A]*. Although, for the purposes of presentation in profit or loss, net interest is a single net amount.

Interest on plan assets calculated as described above will not, other than by coincidence, be the same as the actual return on plan assets. The difference is a remeasurement which is recognised in other comprehensive income. *[FRS 102.28.24B]*.

Chapter 25

3.6.10.B   Remeasurements

Remeasurements of the net defined benefit liability (asset) comprise:

- actuarial gains and losses;
- the return on plan assets, excluding amounts included in net interest on the net defined benefit liability; and
- any change in the amount of a defined benefit plan surplus that is not recoverable (in accordance with paragraph 28.22), excluding amounts included in net interest on the net defined benefit liability. *[FRS 102.28.25]*.

Remeasurements of the net defined benefit liability are recognised in other comprehensive income, and are not reclassified to profit or loss in a subsequent period. *[FRS 102.28.25A]*.

Actuarial gains and losses are changes in the present value of defined benefit obligation resulting from: experience adjustments (the effects of differences between the previous actuarial assumptions and what has actually occurred); and the effects of changes in actuarial assumptions. *[FRS 102 Appendix I]*.

3.7   Costs of administering employee benefit plans

Some employee benefit plans incur costs as part of delivering employee benefits. These costs are generally more significant for post-retirement benefits such as pensions. Examples of costs would include actuarial valuations, audits and the costs of managing any plan assets.

FRS 102 does not include any guidance on accounting for these costs. As noted at 2.2 above entities may refer to IAS 19 using the GAAP hierarchy in Section 10.

IAS 19 deals with some costs, but is silent on others.

The following costs are required to be factored into the measurement of the defined benefit obligation:

- in the case of medical benefits, future medical costs, including claim handling costs (i.e. the costs that will be incurred in processing and resolving claims, including legal and adjuster's fees); and
- taxes payable by the plan on contributions relating to service before the reporting date or on benefits resulting from that service. *[IAS 19.76(b)]*.

The following costs (and no others) are deducted from the return on plan assets:

- the costs of managing the plan assets; and
- any tax payable by the plan itself, other than tax included in the actuarial assumptions used to measure the defined benefit obligation. *[IAS 19.130]*.

As discussed at 3.6.10 above, net interest on the net liability or asset is reported in the profit or loss. This is a wholly computed amount which is uninfluenced by actual asset returns; the difference between actual asset returns and the credit element of the net interest amount forms part of remeasurements reported in other comprehensive income.

So, although not expressed in these terms, costs of administering plan assets and the tax mentioned above are under IAS 19, reported in other comprehensive income.

Both Section 28 and IAS 19 do not address the treatment of any other costs of administering employee benefit plans. However, the Basis for Conclusions of IAS 19 contains the following: 'the Board decided that an entity should recognise administration costs when the administration services are provided. This practical expedient avoids the need to attribute costs between current and past service and future service'. *[IAS 19.BC127]*. The IASB may well have taken that decision, however it did not include such a requirement in the standard.

In our view, such an approach is certainly an acceptable way to account for costs not dealt with in FRS 102; however other approaches could be acceptable, for example, that in relation to closed schemes discussed below. In addition FRS 102 allows only specific items to be presented in other comprehensive income. *[FRS 102.5.5A]*. Costs of administering employee benefit plans are not required or permitted to be recognised in other comprehensive income and therefore should be presented within profit or loss.

One alternative to simple accruals-accounting as costs are incurred could be relevant to closed plans, where employees are no longer exchanging services for defined benefits. In this situation, it is clear that any and all future costs of administering the plan relate to past periods and no attribution is necessary. An entity with such an arrangement may select a policy of full provision of all costs of 'running-off' the plan.

3.8 Other long-term employee benefits

3.8.1 *Meaning of other long-term benefits*

Other long-term employee benefits include items such as the following, if they are not expected to be wholly settled within 12 months after the end of the annual reporting period in which the employees have rendered the related service: *[FRS 102.28.29]*

- long-term paid absences such as long-service or sabbatical leave;
- other long-service benefits;
- long-term disability benefits;
- profit-sharing and bonuses; and
- deferred remuneration.

3.8.2 *Recognition and measurement*

For other long-term benefits a simplified version of the accounting treatment required in respect of defined benefit plans (which is discussed in detail at 3.6 above) is required. The amount recognised as a liability for other long-term employee benefits should be the net total, at the end of the reporting period, of the present value of the defined benefit obligation and the fair value of plan assets (if any) out of which the obligations are to be settled directly. The net change in the liability during the period should be recognised in profit or loss, except to the extent that FRS 102 requires or permits their inclusion in the cost of an asset, such as inventory or property, plant and equipment. *[FRS 102.28.30]*. See Chapters 11 and 15.

In other words, all assets, liabilities, income and expenditure relating to such benefits should be accounted for in the same way as those relating to a defined benefit plan (see 3.6 above), except that remeasurements are recognised in profit or loss (and not in other comprehensive income).

A simple example of a long-term employee benefit would be where an employee receives a bonus of £100,000 in 5 years' time provided he/she continues to stay employed by the entity for this period. This cost will be spread over the 5 year period using the attribution of benefit period method described at 3.6.2.C above.

3.8.3 Long-term benefits contingent on a future event

It may be the case that a long-term benefit becomes payable only on the occurrence of an uncertain future event, for example an initial public offering of an entity's shares (IPO) or an exit event. Such events are binary in nature and would result in payment either to no employees with entitlements under the plan or to all such employees.

As discussed at 3.8.2 above, the projected unit credit method is applied to long-term employee benefits, *[FRS 102.28.30]*, however the key question that arises is whether the accounting should reflect the single best estimate of the outcome; or, the expected value – that is, a weighted average of possible outcomes. Paragraph 26 of Section 28 states that 'the probability that the specified event will occur affects the measurement of the obligation, but does not determine whether the obligation exists'. This sets out the requirement that probability affects measurement. The manner in which probability affects measurement is dealt with in the definition of actuarial assumptions which requires that these are a best estimate of the ultimate cost of providing benefits. *[FRS 102 Appendix A]*. Accordingly, we believe that the best estimate of the outcome of the uncertain event should be used when accounting for long-term employee benefits where the outcome is binary. Therefore if an IPO (or exit event) is not probable the liability should be measured at nil. When the IPO (or exit event) is or becomes probable (that is, more likely than not) the actuarial assumption used in applying the projected unit credit method should reflect the full benefits which would be payable upon the occurrence of the event.

3.9 Termination benefits

Termination benefits occur when an entity is committed, by legislation, by contractual or other agreements with employees or their representatives or by a constructive obligation based on business practice, custom or desire to act equitably, to make payments (or to provide other benefits) to employees when it terminates their employment. *[FRS 102.28.31]*. Rather than being earned through providing services to an entity, termination benefits arise as a result of an event such as a decision to reduce the size of the workforce.

Termination benefits are required to be recognised by an entity as an expense in profit or loss immediately, as they do not provide an entity with future economic benefits. *[FRS 102.28.32]*.

Termination benefits should be recognised as a liability and an expense only when the entity is demonstrably committed either: *[FRS 102.28.34]*

- to terminate the employment of an employee or group of employees before the normal retirement age; or
- to provide termination benefits as a result of an offer made in order to encourage voluntary redundancy.

An entity becomes demonstrably committed to a termination only when it has a detailed formal plan for the termination and is without realistic possibility of withdrawal from the plan. *[FRS 102.28.35]*. Section 21 – *Provisions and Contingencies* – states that a restructuring, which may include termination benefits, gives rise to a constructive obligation only when an entity has a detailed formal plan which identifies at least: *[FRS 102.21.11C]*

- the business or part of a business concerned;
- the principal locations affected;
- the location, function, and approximate number of employees who will be compensated for terminating their services;
- the expenditures that will be undertaken; and
- when the plan will be implemented.

Additionally, the entity must have raised a valid expectation in those affected that it will carry out the restructuring by starting to implement that plan or announcing its main features to those affected by it.

When an entity recognises termination benefits, it may also have to account for a plan amendment or a curtailment of other employee benefits. *[FRS 102.28.33]*.

An entity is required to measure termination benefits at the best estimate of the amount that would be required to settle the obligation at the reporting date. If an offer was made to encourage voluntary redundancy, the measurement of termination benefits should be based on the number of employees expected to accept the offer. *[FRS 102.28.36]*.

Where termination benefits are not due to be settled wholly within 12 months after the end of the reporting period, they should be discounted to their present value using the methodology and discount rate specified as for defined benefit pension schemes (see 3.6.2.B above). *[FRS 102.28.37]*.

Some employers will pay 'stay bonuses' to encourage employees who have been told that they will be made redundant to continue to work for the employer for a further period of time (for example to complete a project). These bonuses are not termination benefits as the individuals are still employed by the entity and the expense does not meet the definition of a termination benefit (see above), and therefore the cost of the stay bonus should be recognised over the period in which the employee is working to earn this bonus.

3.10 Group plans

When an entity participates in a defined benefit plan that shares risks between entities under common control (a group plan), it is required to obtain information about the plan as a whole measured in accordance with FRS 102, on the basis of assumptions that apply to the plan as a whole. If there is a contractual agreement or stated policy for charging the net defined benefit cost of a defined benefit plan as a whole to individual group entities, then the entity is required to recognise the net defined benefit cost based on this allocation in its individual financial statements. *[FRS 102.28.38]*.

If there is no contractual agreement or stated policy for charging the net defined benefit cost to individual group entities, the net defined benefit cost of a defined benefit plan should be recognised in the individual financial statements of the group entity which is the sponsoring employer for the plan. The other group entities should recognise a cost equal to their contribution payable for the period in their individual financial statements. *[FRS 102.28.38].*

As the net defined benefit cost is calculated by reference to both the defined benefit obligation and the fair value of plan assets, recognising a net defined benefit cost requires the recognition of a corresponding net benefit asset or liability in the individual financial statements of any group entity recognising a net defined benefit cost. *[FRS 102.28.38].*

3.11   Death-in service benefits

The provision of death-in service benefits is a common part of employment packages (either as part of a defined benefit plan or on a stand-alone basis). Unfortunately no guidance is provided by FRS 102 or IAS 19 on how to account for such benefits. Guidance had been proposed under E54 – *Employee Benefits October 1996* (the exposure draft preceding earlier versions of IAS 19). We suggest that an appropriate approach could be that:

- death in service benefits provided as part of a defined benefit post-employment plan are factored into the actuarial valuation. In this case any insurance cover should be accounted for in accordance with the normal rules of IAS 19. An important point here is that insurance policies for death in service benefits typically cover only one year, and hence will have a low or negligible value. As a result, it will not be the case that the insurance asset is equal and opposite to the defined benefit obligation;

- other death in service benefits which are externally insured are accounted for by expensing the premiums as they become payable; and

- other death in service benefits which are not externally insured are provided for as deaths in service occur.

An alternative approach could be to view death in service benefits as being similar to disability benefits. The accounting for disability benefits under IAS 19 is as follows:

- Where a long-term disability benefit depends on the length of service of the employee, an obligation arises as the employee renders service, which is to be measured according to the probability that payment will be required and the length of time for which payment is expected to be made.

- If however the level of benefit is the same for all disabled employees regardless of years of service, the expected cost is recognised only when an event causing a disability occurs. *[IAS 19.157].*

Given the lack of any guidance in FRS 102 and IAS 19, we would expect practice to be mixed in accounting for death-in service benefits under FRS 102.

3.12 Disclosures

3.12.1 Disclosures about short-term employee benefits

Section 28 does not require any specific disclosures about short-term employee benefits, *[FRS 102.28.39]*, but preparers of financial statements should also consider the requirements of Section 33 – *Related Party Disclosures* – discussed in Chapter 30 at 3.2.

3.12.2 Disclosures about other long-term benefits

For each category of other long-term benefits that it provides to its employees, an entity should disclose the nature of the benefit, the amount of its obligation and the extent of funding at the reporting date. *[FRS 102.28.42]*.

3.12.3 Disclosures about defined contribution plans

An entity is required to disclose the amount recognised in profit or loss as an expense for defined contribution plans. *[FRS 102.28.40]*.

When a multi-employer plan is treated as a defined contribution plan because sufficient information is not available to use defined benefit accounting (see 3.4.2 above) entities should: *[FRS 102.28.40A]*

- disclose the fact that it is a defined benefit plan and the reason why it is being accounted for as a defined contribution plan, along with any available information about the plan's surplus or deficit and the implications, if any, for the entity;
- include a description of the extent to which the entity can be liable to the plan for other entities' obligations under the terms and conditions of the multi-employer plan; and
- disclose how any liability recognised as a result of the entity entering into an agreement to fund a deficit (see 3.4.2 above) has been determined.

3.12.4 Disclosures about defined benefit plans

As discussed at 3.6.9 above, FRS 102 requires that the statement of financial performance and income statement should be presented in accordance with The Large and Medium sized companies and Groups (Accounts and Reports) Regulations 2008 or the 'adapted formats'.

Chapter 25

3.12.4.A   General disclosures

An entity is required to disclose the following information about defined benefit plans (except for multi-employer defined benefit plans that as treated as defined contribution plans – see 3.4.2 above). If an entity has more than one defined benefit plan, these disclosures may be made in aggregate, separately for each plan, or in such groupings as considered to be the most useful:

- A general description of the type of plan, including funding policy. This includes the amount and timing of the future payments to be made by the entity under any agreement with the defined benefit plan to fund a deficit (such as a schedule of contributions).

- The date of the most recent comprehensive actuarial valuation and, if it was not as of the reporting date, a description of the adjustments that were made to measure the defined benefit obligation at the reporting date.

- A reconciliation of opening and closing balances for each of the following:
  - the net defined benefit obligation;
  - the fair value of the plan assets; and
  - any reimbursement right recognised as an asset.

- Each of the reconciliations above should show each of the following, if applicable:
  - the change in the net defined benefit liability arising from employee service rendered during the period;
  - interest income or expense;
  - remeasurements of the defined benefit liability, showing separately actuarial gains and losses and the return on plan assets less amounts included in interest income/expense above; and
  - plan introductions, changes, curtailments and settlements.

- The cost relating to defined benefit plans for the period, disclosing separately the amounts:
  - recognised in profit or loss as an expense; and
  - included in the cost of an asset.

- For each major class of plan assets, which should include but is not limited to, equity instruments, debt instruments, property, and all other assets, the percentage or amount that each major class constitutes of the fair value of the total plan assets at the reporting date.

- The amounts included in the fair value of plan assets for:
  - each class of the entity's own financial instruments; and
  - any property occupied by, or other assets used by, the entity.

- The return on plan assets.

- The principal actuarial assumptions used, including when applicable:
  - the discount rates;
  - the expected rates of salary increases;
  - medical cost trend rates; and
  - any other material actuarial assumptions used.

The reconciliations above need not be presented for prior periods. *[FRS 102.28.41].*

3.12.4.B   Disclosures for plans which share risks between entities under common control

If an entity participates in a defined benefit plan that shares risks between entities under common control (see 3.10 above) it is required to disclose the following information:

- the contractual agreement or stated policy for charging the cost of a defined benefit plan or the fact that there is no policy;
- the policy for determining the contribution to be paid by the entity; and
- if the entity accounts for an allocation of the net defined benefit cost, all the information required in section 3.12.4.A above.

If the entity accounts for the contributions payable for the period, the following information is also required:

- a general description of the type of plan, including funding policy;
- the date of the most recent comprehensive actuarial valuation and, if it was not as of the reporting date, a description of the adjustments that were made to measure the defined benefit obligation at the reporting date;
- for each major class of plan assets, which should include but is not limited to, equity instruments, debt instruments, property, and all other assets, the percentage or amount that each major class constitutes of the fair value of the total plan assets at the reporting date; and
- the amounts included in the fair value of plan assets for:
  - each class of the entity's own financial instruments; and
  - any property occupied by, or other assets used by, the entity.

This information can be disclosed by cross-reference to disclosures in another group entity's financial statements if: the group entity's financial statements separately identify and disclose the information required about the plan; and that group entity's financial statements are available to users of the financial statements on the same terms as the financial statements of the entity and at the same time as, or earlier than, the financial statements of the entity. *[FRS 102.28.41A].*

3.12.5   Disclosures about termination benefits

For each category of termination benefits provided to employees the following should be disclosed: *[FRS 102.28.43]*

- the nature of the benefit;
- the accounting policy; and
- the amount of its obligation and the extent of funding at the reporting date.

When there is uncertainty about the number of employees who will accept an offer of termination benefits, a contingent liability exists. Section 21 requires the disclosure of contingent liabilities unless the possibility of an outflow in settlement is remote (see Chapter 19 at 3.10). *[FRS 102.28.44].*

4   COMPANIES ACT REQUIREMENTS

4.1   Disclosures

The Companies Act does not require any specific disclosure requirements for employee benefits, however there are numerous disclosure requirements for salaries, pensions and other benefits payable to directors. These requirements are within Schedule 5 to the Large and Medium sized Companies and Groups (Accounts and Reports) Regulations 2008. In addition s411 of the Companies Act requires the disclosure of other pension costs as part of the disclosure of staff costs.

5   SUMMARY OF GAAP DIFFERENCES

The following table shows the key differences between IFRS and FRS 102.

	FRS 102	*IFRS*
Pension surpluses/ asset ceilings	FRS 102 provides little guidance on recognition of plan surpluses, other than it can be recognised to the extent it can be recovered through reductions in future contributions or refunds	IAS 19 allows the recognition of defined benefit surpluses provided that the refund is available, but restricts it to the lower of the refund and the asset ceiling. IFRIC 14 provides guidance on the asset ceiling.
Liability for deficit funding requirements	Under FRS 102, no additional liabilities should be recognised in respect of an agreement with the defined benefit plan to fund a deficit (such as a schedule of contributions).	IFRIC 14 requires a liability to be recorded to the extent that deficit funding contributions payable will not be available after they are paid into the plan.
Presentation	FRS 102 requires primary statements to be presented in accordance with the Regulations, although the presentation under FRS 17 may be applied as it was based on an interpretation of company law (except that deferred tax cannot be offset against the gross pension deficit or surplus). FRS 102 also has fewer disclosure requirements in respect of defined benefit pension schemes (e.g. there is no requirement for sensitivity disclosures) than IAS 19.	Follow the general requirements of IAS 1 for the presentation on the statement of financial position.

References

1 Case number HC-2017-001399, Mr Justice Morgan, final judgement 26.10.18. Colloquially referred to as the Lloyds case, GMP equalisation and similar.
2 *IFRIC Update*, March 2015.
3 *IFRIC Update*, May 2014.
4 *Remeasurement on a Plan Amendment, Curtailment and Settlement/ Availability of a Refund from a Defined Benefit Plan (proposed amendments to IAS 19 and IFRIC 14)*, June 2015.
5 *IASB Update*, April 2017.
6 *IASB Agenda Paper 12C*, July 2017.
7 *IASB Update*, February 2018.
8 *IASB Update*, March 2017.

Chapter 26

Income tax

Chapter 26

List of examples

Chapter 26   Income tax

1   INTRODUCTION

Section 29 – *Income Tax* – not only applies to accounting for income tax, but also to value added tax (VAT) and other similar sales taxes which are not income taxes, *[FRS 102.29.2]*, as discussed at 4 below. Section 29 also covers specific provisions in relation to withholding tax on dividend income (see 3.3 below).

Income tax as described in Section 29 comprises:

- current tax; and
- deferred tax including deferred tax in respect of assets (other than goodwill) and liabilities recognised as a result of a business combination. *[FRS 102.29.2]*.

An entity is required to recognise the current and future tax consequences of transactions and other events that have been recognised in the financial statements. Current tax is the amount of income tax payable (refundable) in respect of the taxable profit (tax loss) for the current period or past reporting periods. Deferred tax represents the income tax payable (recoverable) in respect of the taxable profit (tax loss) for future reporting periods as a result of past transactions or events. *[FRS 102 Appendix I]*.

The requirements applicable to business combinations are discussed at 6.6 below.

The FRC made the following changes to Section 29 as a result of its Triennial review 2017 of FRS 102.

- to allow the tax effects of gift aid payments by subsidiaries to their charitable parents to be taken into account at the reporting date when it is probable that the gift aid payment will be made in the following nine months; *[FRS 102.29.14A]* and
- to require the tax expense (income) effects of distributions to owners to be presented in profit or loss. *[FRS 102.29.22A]*.

These amendments are mandatory for accounting periods beginning on or after 1 January 2019, with early application permitted provided that fact is disclosed. As an exception to the general rule that all amendments should be applied at the same time, the amendments relating to the tax effects of gift aid payments can be applied separately. These requirements are set out at 7.6.1 and 8.1.3 below.

1.1 Allocation of tax income and expense between periods

The most significant accounting question which arises in relation to taxation is how to allocate tax expense (income) between accounting periods. The particular period in which transactions are recognised in the financial statements is determined by FRS 102. However, the timing of the recognition of transactions for the purposes of measuring the taxable profit is governed by tax law, which sometimes prescribes an accounting treatment different from that used in the financial statements. The generally accepted view is that it is necessary for the financial statements to seek some reconciliation between these different treatments.

Broadly speaking, those tax consequences that are legal assets or liabilities at the reporting date are referred to as current tax. The other tax consequences, which are expected to become, or (more strictly) form part of, legal assets or liabilities in a future period, are referred to as deferred tax.

This is illustrated by Example 26.1, and the further discussion at 1.1.1 to 1.1.2 below.

Example 26.1: PP&E attracting tax deductions in advance of accounting depreciation

An item of equipment is purchased on 1 January 2019 for £50,000 and is estimated to have a useful life of five years, at the end of which it will be scrapped. There is no change to the estimated residual amount of zero over the life of the equipment. The depreciation charge will therefore be £10,000 per year for five years.

The applicable corporate tax rate is 30%. No tax deductions are given for depreciation charged in the financial statements. Instead, the cost may be deducted from taxes payable in the year that the asset is purchased. The entity's profit before tax, including the depreciation charge, for each of the five years ended 31 December 2019 to 31 December 2023 is £100,000. All components of pre-tax profit, other than the accounting depreciation, are taxable or tax-deductible.

The entity's tax computations for each year would show the following:[1]

£s	2019	2020	2021	2022	2023
Accounting profit	100,000	100,000	100,000	100,000	100,000
Accounting depreciation	10,000	10,000	10,000	10,000	10,000
Tax depreciation	(50,000)	–	–	–	–
Taxable profit	60,000	110,000	110,000	110,000	110,000
Tax payable @ 30%	18,000	33,000	33,000	33,000	33,000

1.1.1 No provision for deferred tax ('flow through')

If the entity in Example 26.1 above were to account only for the tax legally due in respect of each year ('current tax'), it would report the amounts in the table below in profit or loss. Accounting for current tax only is generally known as the 'flow through' method.

£s	2019	2020	2021	2022	2023	Total
Profit before tax	100,000	100,000	100,000	100,000	100,000	500,000
Current tax (at 1.1 above)	18,000	33,000	33,000	33,000	33,000	150,000
Profit after tax	82,000	67,000	67,000	67,000	67,000	350,000
Effective tax rate (%)	18	33	33	33	33	30

The 'effective tax rate' in the last row of the table above is the ratio, expressed as a percentage, of the profit before tax to the charge for tax in the financial statements, and is regarded a key performance indicator by many preparers and users of financial statements. As can be seen from the table above, over the full five-year life of the asset, the entity pays tax at the statutory rate of 30% on its total profits of £500,000, but with considerable variation in the effective rate in individual accounting periods.

The generally held view is that simply to account for the tax legally payable as above is distortive, and that the tax should therefore be allocated between periods. Under FRS 102 this allocation is achieved by means of deferred taxation (see 1.1.2 below).

1.1.2 Provision for deferred tax (the timing difference approach)

The approach required by Section 29 is known as the 'timing difference' approach, which seeks to measure the impact on future tax payments of the cumulative difference, as at the reporting date, between income or expenditure (in the case of Example 26.1 above, depreciation) in the financial statements and the amounts recognised for the same income or expense in the tax computation. Such differences are known as 'timing differences'. Timing differences are said to 'originate' in those periods in which the cumulative difference between book and tax income (expense) increases and to 'reverse' in those periods in which that cumulative difference decreases. In Example 26.1 above the differences originate and reverse as follows:

£s	2019	2020	2021	2022	2023
Accounting depreciation	10,000	10,000	10,000	10,000	10,000
Tax depreciation	(50,000)	–	–	–	–
(Origination)/reversal	(40,000)	10,000	10,000	10,000	10,000
Cumulative[1]	(40,000)	(30,000)	(20,000)	(10,000)	–

As discussed in more detail at 7 below, Section 29 requires an entity to recognise a liability for deferred tax on the timing difference arising between book and tax depreciation, as follows.

£s	2019	2020	2021	2022	2023
Cumulative difference (per table above)	(40,000)	(30,000)	(20,000)	(10,000)	–
Deferred tax[1]	(12,000)	(9,000)	(6,000)	(3,000)	–
Movement in deferred tax in period	12,000	(3,000)	(3,000)	(3,000)	(3,000)

---

[1] Cumulative timing difference multiplied by the tax rate of 30%. As discussed at 7 below, Section 29 requires deferred tax to be measured by reference to the tax rates and laws expected to apply when the timing differences will reverse.

The deferred tax liability is recognised in the statement of financial position and any movement in the deferred tax liability during the period is recognised as deferred tax income or expense in profit or loss, with the following impact:

£s	2019	2020	2021	2022	2023	Total
Profit before tax	100,000	100,000	100,000	100,000	100,000	500,000
Current tax (at 1.1 above)	18,000	33,000	33,000	33,000	33,000	150,000
Deferred tax	12,000	(3,000)	(3,000)	(3,000)	(3,000)	–
Total tax	30,000	30,000	30,000	30,000	30,000	150,000
Profit after tax	70,000	70,000	70,000	70,000	70,000	350,000
Effective tax rate (%)	30	30	30	30	30	30

It can be seen that the effect of accounting for deferred tax is to present an effective tax rate of 30% in profit or loss for each period.

In the example above, the deferred tax could also have been calculated by comparing the net carrying amount of the asset in the financial statements to its carrying amount for tax purposes (i.e. the amount of future tax deductions available for the asset). For example, at the end of 2019, the carrying amount of the asset would be £40,000 (cost of £50,000 less one year's depreciation of £10,000), and its carrying amount for tax purposes would be nil. The difference between £40,000 and nil is £40,000, the same as the difference between the tax depreciation of £50,000 and the book depreciation of £10,000.

In practice, therefore, deferred tax is often calculated by comparing the carrying amount of an asset and its tax value, since balance sheet carrying amounts are usually easier to 'track' than cumulative income or expenditure. However, such 'short-cut' methods must be applied with great care, since some differences between the book and tax carrying amounts of an asset arise not from timing differences, but from permanent differences (see 1.2 below).

1.2 Permanent differences

Some differences between an entity's taxable profit and accounting profit arise not because the same items are recognised in taxable profit and accounting profit in different periods (i.e. timing differences), but because an item recognised in accounting profit is never recognised in taxable profit and vice-versa. For example:

- An item of PP&E is depreciated but its cost is not deductible for tax purposes other than on sale. An example in the UK would be an industrial building. Any depreciation of such an asset recognised for accounting purposes is a permanent difference.
- In the UK a company may obtain a tax deduction for a share-based payment transaction based on its value at vesting or exercise, which is typically higher than its value at grant, on which the expense in the financial statements is based. Any excess of the tax deduction over the expense recognised in the financial statements is a permanent difference.

As discussed further at 6.5 below, Section 29 requires that deferred tax is not recognised on permanent differences, except for differences arising on first accounting for a business combination accounted for by applying the purchase method. *[FRS 102.29.10]*.

2   KEY DIFFERENCES TO IFRS

2.1   Withholding taxes on dividends and VAT and other sales taxes

The requirements of Section 29 in relation to withholding taxes on dividends (see 3.3 below) are not reflected in IAS 12 – *Income Taxes*, which refers only to withholding taxes payable by a subsidiary, associate or joint arrangement on distributions to the reporting entity. Accordingly, entities moving from IFRS to FRS 102 may find themselves grossing up withholding taxes on dividend income for the first time.[2]

IAS 12 does not include VAT and other similar sales taxes in its scope, whereas Section 29 does (see 4 below). Taxes outside the scope of IAS 12 fall under the general requirements of IAS 37 – *Provisions, Contingent Liabilities and Contingent Assets*. *[IFRIC 21.BC4]*. Specific provisions of other standards, notably in IFRS 15 – *Revenue from Contracts with Customers*, IAS 2 – *Inventories*, IAS 38 – *Intangible Assets*, and IAS 16 – *Property, Plant and Equipment*, result in an accounting treatment for VAT and some other sales taxes that is essentially the same as that required in FRS 102.[3]

2.2   Current tax and deferred tax

The requirements of Section 29 and IAS 12 in respect of the recognition and measurement of current tax are essentially the same.

As regards deferred tax, Section 29 adopts a 'timing difference' approach, except when the entity first recognises assets and liabilities acquired in a business combination accounted for by applying the purchase method (where the treatment is largely the same as IFRS). Timing differences are differences between taxable profits and total comprehensive income as stated in the financial statements that arise from the inclusion of income and expenses in tax assessments in periods different from those in which they are recognised in financial statements. *[FRS 102.29.6]*.

IAS 12 applies a 'temporary difference' approach, whereby deferred tax is recognised on the difference between the carrying amount of an asset or liability and the amount at which that asset or liability is assessed for tax purposes (referred to as its 'tax base'). However, there are some exceptions to this, most notably the initial recognition exception, whereby no deferred tax is recorded on a difference between the carrying amount of an asset or liability and its tax base where that difference arose on the initial recognition of the asset or liability in a transaction which gave rise to no accounting profit or loss and no tax effect and was not a business combination. No such exemption is necessary under a 'timing differences' approach as no timing differences arise on the initial recognition of an asset. *[FRS 102.BC.B29.5]*.

Whilst it had been determined that FRS 102 should be based on a 'timing differences' approach in most circumstances, it was considered important to maintain consistency with IFRS on the recognition of deferred tax arising from a business combination. Accordingly, Section 29 departs from a pure 'timing differences' approach in this respect alone. *[FRS 102.BC.B29.6]*.

Having supplemented the 'timing differences' approach with a requirement to recognise deferred tax on business combinations, the main distinction between Section 29 and IFRS is that IAS 12 requires deferred tax to be recognised on any difference between the carrying amount of an asset or liability and its tax base that arises after the initial recognition of the asset or liability. Section 29 would prohibit the recognition of such differences that are not the result of timing differences. For example, no deferred tax is recognised under Section 29 when: *[FRS 102.BC.B29.7]*

- the tax basis (the tax-deductible amount) of an asset is amended, such as when the legislation changes the amount of future tax relief relating to the asset (see 6.5 below); and

- the tax deduction (or estimated future deduction) for share-based payment exceeds the cumulative amount of the related remuneration expense (see 7.7 below).

3   SCOPE OF SECTION 29

Section 29 applies not only to income tax, but also includes specific provisions in relation to withholding taxes on dividend income (see 3.3 below) and on accounting for Value Added Tax (VAT) and other similar sales taxes that are not income taxes (see 4 below). *[FRS 102.29.2]*.

No transitional reliefs are given for first-time adopters of FRS 102 in respect to the application of Section 29. Accordingly, on transition to FRS 102 entities must apply the requirements of Section 29 on a fully retrospective basis. In particular, deferred tax will arise as a result of the following:

- past revaluations of property, plant and equipment and investment properties (see Chapter 32 at 3.5);

- accounting for business combinations before the date of transition (see Chapter 32 at 5.2); and

- the application of transitional reliefs, such as the use of fair value or a previous revaluation as the deemed cost of certain assets (see Chapter 32 at 5.5.4).

In addition, the transition to FRS 102 can have direct implications for an entity's corporation tax position in the UK. In some cases a current tax liability arises in the year of transition and in others the liability is spread over a period of up to 10 years. Such deferral of the liability to corporation tax can either be automatic or require an election to be made and will require deferred tax to be recognised as at the date of transition to FRS 102 to the extent that this creates a timing difference under Section 29. Entities should refer to relevant guidance issued by HM Revenue & Customs and take professional advice as appropriate.[4]

3.1   Terms used in Section 29

The following terms are used in Section 29 with the meanings specified. *[FRS 102 Appendix I]*.

Term	Definition
Business combination	The bringing together of separate entities or businesses into one reporting entity.
Current tax	The amount of income tax payable (refundable) in respect of the taxable profit (tax loss) for the current period or past reporting periods.

Deferred tax	Income tax payable (recoverable) in respect of the taxable profit (tax loss) for future reporting periods as a result of past transactions or events.
Deferred tax assets	Income tax recoverable in future reporting periods in respect of: (a) future tax consequences of transactions and events recognised in the financial statements of the current and previous periods; (b) the carry forward of unused tax losses; and (c) the carry forward of unused tax credits.
Deferred tax liabilities	Income tax payable in future reporting periods in respect of future tax consequences of transactions and events recognised in the financial statements of the current and previous periods.
Income tax	All domestic and foreign taxes that are based on taxable profits. Income tax also includes taxes, such as withholding taxes, that are payable by a subsidiary, associate or joint venture on distributions to the reporting entity.
Permanent differences	Differences between an entity's taxable profits and its total comprehensive income as stated in the financial statements, other than timing differences.
Probable	More likely than not.
Substantively enacted	Tax rates shall be regarded as substantively enacted when the remaining stages of the enactment process historically have not affected the outcome and are unlikely to do so. A UK tax rate shall be regarded as having been substantively enacted if it is included in either: (a) a Bill that has been passed by the House of Commons and is awaiting only passage through the House of Lords and Royal Assent; or (b) a resolution having statutory effect that has been passed under the Provisional Collection of Taxes Act 1968. (Such a resolution could be used to collect taxes at a new rate before that rate has been enacted. In practice, corporation tax rates are now set a year ahead to avoid having to invoke the Provisional Collection of Taxes Act for the quarterly payment system). A Republic of Ireland tax rate can be regarded as having been substantively enacted if it is included in a Bill that has been passed by the Dáil.
Tax expense	The aggregate amount included in total comprehensive income or equity for the reporting period in respect of current tax and deferred tax.
Taxable profit (tax loss)	The profit (loss) for a reporting period upon which income taxes are payable or recoverable, determined in accordance with the rules established by the taxation authorities. Taxable profit equals taxable income less amounts deductible from taxable income.
Timing differences	Differences between taxable profits and total comprehensive income as stated in the financial statements that arise from the inclusion of income and expenses in tax assessments in periods different from those in which they are recognised in financial statements.

Chapter 26

3.2   What is an 'income tax'?

Section 29 applies to income tax. *[FRS 102.29.2(a)]*. Income tax as defined in FRS 102 Appendix I includes:

- all domestic and foreign taxes that are based on taxable profit; and

- taxes, such as withholding taxes, that are payable by a subsidiary, associate or joint arrangement on distributions to the reporting entity.

This definition is somewhat circular, since 'taxable profit' is, in turn, defined in terms of profits 'upon which income taxes are payable'. *[FRS 102 Appendix I]*.

UK corporation tax is an 'income tax' as defined, since it takes as its starting point the totality of a reporting entity's accounting profits. However, both the UK and overseas jurisdictions raise 'taxes' on sub-components of net profit. These include:

- sales taxes;

- goods and services taxes;

- value added taxes;

- levies on the sale or extraction of minerals and other natural resources;

- taxes on certain goods as they reach a given state of production or are moved from one location to another; or

- taxes on gross production margins.

Taxes that are simply collected by the entity from one third party (generally a customer or employee) on behalf of another third party (generally local or national government) are not 'income taxes' for the purposes of Section 29. This view is supported by the requirement of Section 23 – *Revenue* – that taxes which are collected from customers by the entity on behalf of third parties do not form part of the entity's revenue *[FRS 102.23.4]* (and therefore, by implication, are not an expense of the entity either).

In cases where such taxes are a liability of the entity, they may often have some characteristics both of production or sales taxes (in that they are payable at a particular stage in the production or extraction process and may well be allowed as an expense in arriving at the tax on net profits) and of income taxes (in that they may be determined after deduction of certain allowable expenditure). This can make the classification of such taxes (as income taxes or not) difficult.

Further discussion of factors that are considered in determining whether a particular tax meets the definition of an income tax under IFRS may be found in Chapter 29 at 4.1 of EY International GAAP 2019.

3.2.1   *Levies*

A number of jurisdictions, including the UK, charge levies in relation to certain activities or on certain types of entity, particularly those in the financial services sector. In many cases the levies are expressed as a percentage of a measure of revenue or net assets, or some component(s) of revenue or net assets, at a particular date. Such levies are not income taxes and should be accounted for in accordance with Section 21 – *Provisions and Contingencies* (see Chapter 19).

3.2.2   Tonnage tax

In the UK, entities that operate qualifying vessels that are 'strategically and commercially managed in the UK', can take advantage of the tonnage tax regime. The tonnage tax regime differs from the main corporation tax system in a number of key respects, the most significant from an accounting point of view being that an entity in the tonnage tax regime is not assessed to tax on the basis of its reported profits from qualifying activities. Instead, its corporate tax liability is determined by reference to the qualifying tonnage of qualifying vessels. For this reason, it is not an income tax as defined in Section 29. Another feature of the tonnage tax regime is that a qualifying entity does not receive capital allowances for the cost of its ships.

The accounting implications for vessels taken into the tonnage tax regime are discussed at 6.3.1 below.

3.3   Withholding and similar taxes

As discussed at 3.2 above, Section 29 includes in its scope those taxes, such as withholding taxes, which are payable by a subsidiary, associate or joint arrangement on distributions to the reporting entity. *[FRS 102 Appendix I]*. FRS 102 also sets specific requirements in relation to withholding taxes on income from entities other than a subsidiary, associate or joint venture. This gives rise to further questions of interpretation which are not addressed by the standard.

When an entity pays dividends to its shareholders, it may be required to pay a portion of the dividends to taxation authorities on behalf of shareholders. Outgoing dividends and similar amounts payable shall be recognised at an amount that includes any withholding tax but excludes other taxes, such as attributable tax credits. *[FRS 102.29.18]*.

Incoming dividends and similar income receivable shall be recognised at an amount that includes any withholding tax but excludes other taxes, such as attributable tax credits. Any withholding tax suffered shall be shown as part of the tax charge. *[FRS 102.29.19]*.

The rationale for the treatment as income taxes of taxes payable by a subsidiary, associate or joint arrangement on distributions to the investor is discussed further at 6.4 below. Essentially, however, the reason for considering withholding taxes within the scope of income tax accounting derives from the accounting treatment of the investments themselves. The accounting treatment for such investments – whether by consolidation or the equity method – results in the investor recognising profit that may be taxed twice: once as it is earned by the investee entity concerned, and again as that entity distributes the profit as dividends to the investor. Section 29 ensures that the financial statements reflect both tax consequences.

3.4   Investment tax credits

Investment tax credits are not defined in FRS 102 and can take different forms and be subject to different terms. Sometimes a tax credit is given as a deductible expense in computing the entity's tax liability, and sometimes as a deduction from the tax liability, rather than as a deductible expense. In other cases, the value of the credit is chargeable to corporation tax and in others it is not. Entitlement to investment tax credits can be determined in a variety of ways. Some investment tax credits may relate to direct investment in property, plant and equipment. Other entities may receive investment tax credits relating to research and

Chapter 26

development or other specific activities. Some credits may be realisable only through a reduction in current or future corporation tax payable, while others may be settled directly in cash if the entity is loss-making or otherwise does not have sufficient corporation tax payable to offset the credit within a certain period. Access to the credit may be limited according to total of all taxes paid, including employment taxes (such as PAYE and NIC) and VAT, in addition to corporation tax. There may be other conditions associated with receiving the investment tax credit, for example with respect to the conduct and continuing activities of the entity, and the credit may become repayable if ongoing conditions are not met.

Section 24 of FRS 102 – *Government Grants* – excludes from its scope government assistance that is either provided by way of a reduction in taxable income, or determined or limited according to an entity's income tax liability, citing investment tax credits as an example and then stating that taxes based on income are required to be accounted under Section 29. *[FRS 102.24.3]*. This implies that those investment tax credits that are excluded from the scope of Section 24 should be accounted for as income tax. However, if government assistance is described as an investment tax credit, but it is neither determined or limited by the entity's income tax liability nor provided in the form of an income tax deduction, such assistance should be accounted for as a government grant under Section 24 (see Chapter 21 at 3.2.1).

This raises the question as to how an entity should assess whether a particular investment tax credit gives rise to assistance in the form of benefits that are available in determining taxable profit or loss or are determined or limited on the basis of income tax liability *[FRS 102.24.3]* and, therefore, whether Section 24 or Section 29 should be applied. In our view, such a judgment would be informed by reference to the following factors as applied to the specific facts and circumstances relating to the incentive:

Feature of credit	Indicator of Section 29 treatment (income tax)	Indicator of Section 24 treatment (grant)
Method of realisation	Only available as a reduction in income taxes payable (i.e. benefit is forfeit if there are insufficient income taxes payable). However, the longer the period allowed for carrying forward unused credits, the less relevant this indicator becomes.	Directly settled in cash where there are insufficient taxable profits to allow credit to be fully offset, or available for set off against payroll taxes, VAT or amounts owed to government other than income taxes payable.
Number of conditions not related to tax position (e.g. minimum employment, ongoing use of purchased assets)	None or few.	Many.
Restrictions as to nature of expenditure required to receive the grant.	Broad criteria encompassing many different types of qualifying expenditure.	Highly specific.
Tax status of grant income	Not taxable.	Taxable.

In group accounts, in which entities from different jurisdictions may be consolidated, it may be desirable that all 'investment tax credits' should be consistently accounted for, either as a government grant under Section 24 or as an income tax under Section 29.

However, the judgment as to which section applies is made by reference to the nature of each type of investment tax credit and the conditions attached to it. This may mean that the predominant treatment by FRS 102 reporters for a specific type of tax credit differs from the consensus by FRS 102 reporters in another jurisdiction for what could appear to be a substantially similar credit. We believe that, in determining whether the arrangement is of a type that falls within Section 24 or Section 29, an entity should consider the following factors in the order listed below:

- the predominant local determination by FRS 102 reporters as to whether a specific credit in the relevant tax jurisdiction falls within the scope of Section 24 or Section 29;

- if there is no predominant local consensus, the group-wide approach to determining the section that applies to such a credit should be applied; and

- in the absence of a predominant local treatment or a group-wide approach to making the determination, the indicators listed in the table above should provide guidance.

This may occasionally mean that an entity operating in a number of territories adopts different accounting treatments for apparently similar arrangements in different countries, but it at least ensures a measure of comparability between different FRS 102 reporters operating in the same tax jurisdiction.

Where a tax credit is determined to be in the nature of an income tax, an entity will need to determine whether the related benefit is more appropriately accounted for as a discrete tax asset akin to a tax loss, or as a deduction in respect of a specific asset and therefore akin to accelerated capital allowances. In most cases, we believe that it will generally be more appropriate to treat a tax credit that is accounted for as income tax as a discrete tax asset akin to a tax loss. As a result, the recoverability of any amounts that are unused and available for carry forward to future years would be assessed in accordance with the criteria discussed at 6.2 below.

Example 26.2:   UK research and development expenditure credit (RDEC)

Eligible entities in the UK are entitled to an investment tax credit known as the RDEC (sometimes referred to colloquially as the 'above-the-line' tax credit). Features of the tax credit relevant to an accounting analysis are:

- entities are generally entitled to a gross credit of 10% of qualifying R&D expenditure (with some entities entitled to a higher rate);

- the gross credit is treated as taxable income;

- the available credit is first set against the entity's corporation tax liability for the current period;

- the amount of any remaining credit (net of corporation tax) is 'capped' by reference to employment expenditure (measured by reference to the entity's PAYE and NIC liabilities);

- any remaining credit (net of corporation tax and the employment costs cap) can be carried back or carried forward to reduce the entity's corporation tax liability for certain earlier and later periods, or ceded by way of group relief;

- any unrecovered excess can be offset against the entity's other outstanding tax liabilities (e.g. PAYE and NIC); and

- any amount not recovered in any of the ways listed above is recoverable in cash from the tax authority (HMRC).

Should the RDEC credit be treated as a government grant or an element of income tax?

Analysis of these features by reference to the criteria set out above leads us to conclude that the RDEC credit is more appropriately regarded as a government grant. In particular, the benefits of the tax credit are capable of being realised in cash where there

Chapter 26

is insufficient corporation tax capacity; the tax credit relates to specific qualifying expenditure; and the grant income is determined on a pre-tax basis and is itself taxable.

Such an analysis requires a thorough understanding of the rules applying to the particular relief. Other seemingly similar reliefs should be treated as income taxes under Section 29 if, for example, the relief is not itself taxable; the relief could only be recovered by offset against other liabilities to corporation tax; or, where there is a cash payment alternative, the expected cash inflow approximates more closely to the value of the tax benefit rather than to the value of the expenditure incurred.

3.5   Interest and penalties

UK tax law (and that of other jurisdictions) provide for interest and/or penalties to be paid on late payments of tax. This raises the question of whether or not such penalties fall within the scope of Section 29. The answer can have consequences not only for the presentation of interest and penalties in the income statement; but also for the timing of recognition and on the measurement of amounts recognised. If such penalties and interest fall within the scope of Section 29, they are presented as part of tax expense and measured in accordance with the requirements of that section. Where uncertainty exists as to whether interest and penalties will be applied by the tax authorities, an entity must consider the effect of uncertain tax positions as discussed at 5.2 below. If interest and penalties do not fall within the scope of Section 29, they should be included in profit before tax, with recognition and measurement determined in accordance with other accounting requirements, most likely to be Section 21.

In our view, in the absence of specific guidance in FRS 102 on recognition and measurement of interest and penalties, an entity may apply the hierarchy provided in Section 10 – *Accounting Policies, Estimates and Errors* – and accordingly, consider the guidance in EU-adopted IFRS, *[FRS 102.10.6]*, as described below:

(a)   the determination of whether Section 29 or Section 21 should be applied is not a simple accounting policy choice. Instead, the nature of the particular amount payable or receivable for interest and penalties, how it is calculated and whether this meets the definition of an income tax are relevant to making an appropriate judgement. If Section 29 is determined to apply, then the entity recognises and measures any current tax and deferred tax on that basis. If an entity does not apply Section 29 to interest and penalties, then it applies Section 21 to those amounts;

(b)   paragraph 26 of Section 29 requires an entity to disclose the major components of tax expense (income) and paragraph 14 of Section 21 require a reconciliation of the carrying amount at the beginning and end of the reporting period as well as various other pieces of information. Accordingly, regardless of whether an entity applies Section 29 or Section 21 when accounting for interest and penalties related to income taxes, the entity would disclose information about that interest and those penalties if it is material; and

(c)   paragraph 6 of Section 8 – *Notes to the Financial Statements* – requires disclosure of the judgements that management has made in the process of applying the entity's accounting policies and that have the most significant effect on the amounts recognised in the financial statements.

Factors that are relevant in determining whether an item is accounted as income tax are more fully discussed in Chapter 29 at 4.4 of EY International GAAP 2019.

3.6 State-aid

In the European Union, member states are prohibited from providing 'State Aid', whereby government intervention results in an advantage being conferred on a selective basis to undertakings in a manner that may distort competition. State intervention includes the transfer of resources, for example by grants, guarantees, equity investment or by the provision of tax incentives and tax reliefs. Where the European Commission confirms that State Aid has been provided, it has powers to require the member state to seek recovery of the funds determined to have been transferred.

Where such incentives have been provided under local tax law, the related tax reliefs will have been accounted for under Section 29 on the basis of substantively enacted legislation as at the relevant reporting date. In situations where the European Commission has confirmed the provision of State Aid, recovery may be made either by a revision to local tax legislation or by a direct demand for repayment under EU Regulations, including competition law. The question therefore arises whether the recovery of incentives and reliefs that are now determined to be State Aid should be accounted for as a repayment of income tax under Section 29 or as the payment of a fine or levy in accordance with Section 21.

If recovery of the State Aid is achieved by changes to tax legislation, it follows that Section 29 would apply. However, where recovery does not involve any changes to tax legislation, the answer is not clear. On the one hand the economic substance is that previously claimed tax reliefs are being returned; whereas the legal form of the repayment is a fine or a levy. In our opinion, in these circumstances entities face considerations that are similar to the judgement as to whether interest and penalties should fall in the scope of Section 29 or Section 21 (see 3.5 above).

3.7 Effectively tax-free entities

Certain classes of entity (for example, in the UK, pension funds and certain partnerships) are exempt from income tax, and accordingly are not within the scope of Section 29.

However, a more typical, and more complex, situation is that tax legislation has the effect that certain classes of entities, whilst not formally designated as 'tax-free' in law, are nevertheless exempt from tax provided that they meet certain conditions that, in practice, they are almost certain to meet. Examples in the UK are certain investment vehicles that pay no tax, provided that they distribute all, or a minimum percentage, of their earnings to investors.

Accounting for the tax affairs of such entities raises a number of challenges, as discussed further at 7.6 below.

3.8 Discontinued operations – interaction with Section 5

Section 5 – *Statement of Comprehensive Income and Income Statement* – requires the post-tax results of discontinued operations to be shown separately on the face of the statement of comprehensive income (and any separate income statement presenting the components of profit or loss). This is discussed further in Chapter 6.

Chapter 26

The definitions of income tax, tax expense and taxable profit in Section 29 (see 3.1 above) do not distinguish between the results of continuing and discontinued operations, or the tax on those results. Thus, Section 29 applies not only to the tax income or expense on continuing operations, but also to any tax income or expense relating to the results of discontinued operations.

4. VALUE ADDED TAX ('VAT') AND OTHER SIMILAR SALES TAXES

FRS 102 requires turnover shown in profit or loss to exclude VAT and other similar taxes on taxable outputs, and VAT imputed under the flat rate[5] VAT scheme. Similarly, recoverable VAT and other similar recoverable sales taxes should be excluded from expenses. Irrecoverable VAT that can be allocated to fixed assets and to other items disclosed separately in the financial statements should be included in the cost of those items where it is practical to do so, and the effect is material. *[FRS 102.29.20]*.

5 CURRENT TAX

Current tax is the amount of income taxes payable (refundable) in respect of the taxable profit (tax loss) for the current period or a past reporting period. *[FRS 102 Appendix I]*.

An entity recognises a current tax liability for tax payable on taxable profits for the current and past periods. If the amount already paid for the current and past periods exceeds the tax payable for those periods, the excess should be recognised as a current tax asset. *[FRS 102.29.3]*. An entity should recognise a current tax asset relating to a tax loss that can be carried back to recover tax paid in a previous period. *[FRS 102.29.4]*. Tax losses that can be carried *forward* to future periods are reflected in deferred tax.

Current tax should be measured at the amount expected to be paid to or recovered from the tax authorities by reference to tax rates and laws that have been enacted or substantively enacted by the reporting date, meaning the balance sheet date (see 5.1 below). *[FRS 102.29.5]*. Current tax assets or liabilities should not be discounted. *[FRS 102.29.17]*.

5.1 Enacted or substantively enacted tax legislation

5.1.1 UK

In the UK, legislation is enacted when it receives Royal Assent. For the purposes of FRS 102, tax rates are regarded as substantively enacted when the remaining stages of the enactment process historically have not affected the outcome and are unlikely to do so.

A UK tax rate is regarded as having been substantively enacted if it is included in either:

- a Bill that has been passed by the House of Commons and is awaiting only passage through the House of Lords and Royal Assent; or

- a resolution having statutory effect that has been passed under the Provisional Collection of Taxes Act 1968. Such a resolution is used to collect taxes at a new rate before that rate has been enacted. FRS 102 notes that, in practice, corporation tax rates are now set a year ahead to avoid having to invoke the Provisional Collection of Taxes Act for the quarterly payment system. *[FRS 102 Appendix I]*.

Section 29 refers to 'tax rates *and laws*' [emphasis added] that have been enacted or substantively enacted, *[FRS 102.29.5]*, whereas the definition of 'substantively enacted' in the Glossary in Appendix 1 to FRS 102 refers only to 'tax rates'. In our view, there is no intentional distinction, and the guidance in the glossary should be applied equally to determining whether tax laws or tax rates have been substantively enacted.

5.1.2   Republic of Ireland

FRS 102 provides that a Republic of Ireland tax rate can be regarded as having been substantively enacted if it is included in a Bill that has been passed by the Dáil. *[FRS 102 Appendix I].*

5.1.3   Other jurisdictions

FRS 102 gives no guidance as to how this requirement is to be interpreted in other jurisdictions. For the purposes of IAS 12, however, a consensus has emerged in most jurisdictions as to the meaning of 'substantive enactment' for that jurisdiction. This is discussed more fully in Chapter 29 at 5.1 of EY International GAAP 2019.

5.1.4   Changes to tax rates and laws enacted before the reporting date

Current tax should be measured at the amount expected to be paid to or recovered from the tax authorities by reference to tax rates and laws that have been enacted, or substantively enacted, by the reporting date. *[FRS 102.29.5].* Accordingly, the effects of changes in tax rates and laws on current tax balances are required to be recognised in the period in which the legislation is substantively enacted. There is no relief from this requirement under Section 29, even in circumstances when complex legislation is substantively enacted shortly before the end of an annual or interim reporting period. In cases where the effective date of any rate changes is not the first day of the entity's annual reporting period, current tax would be calculated by applying a blended rate to the taxable profits for the year.

Where complex legislation is enacted shortly before the end of the period, entities might encounter two distinct sources of uncertainty:

- uncertainty about the requirements of the law, which may give rise to uncertain tax treatments as discussed at 5.2; and
- uncertainties arising from incomplete information because entities may not have all the data required to process the effects of the changes in tax laws.

It is not necessary for entities to have a complete understanding of every aspect of the new tax law to arrive at reasonable estimates, and provided that entities make every effort to obtain and take into account all the information they could reasonably be expected to obtain up to the date when the financial statements for the period are authorised for issue, subsequent changes to those estimates would not be regarded as a prior period error under Section 10. *[FRS 102.10.19].* We expect that only in rare circumstances would it not be possible to determine a reasonable estimate. However, these uncertainties may require additional disclosure in the financial statements. Section 8 requires entities to disclose information about key sources of estimation uncertainty at the reporting date that have a significant risk of causing a material adjustment to the carrying amounts of assets and liabilities within the next financial year (see Chapter 6 at 8.4). *[FRS 102.8.7].*

Whilst the effect of changes in tax laws enacted after the end of the reporting period are not taken into account (see 5.1.5 below), information and events that occur between the end of the reporting period and the date when the financial statements are authorised for issue are adjusting events after the reporting period if they provide evidence of conditions that existed as at the reporting date. *[FRS 102.32.2(a), 4]*. Updated tax calculations, collection of additional data, clarifications issued by the tax authorities and gaining more experience with the tax legislation before the authorisation of the financial statements should be treated as adjusting events if they pertain to the position at the balance sheet date. Events that are indicative of conditions that arose after the reporting period should be treated as non-adjusting events. Judgement needs to be applied in determining whether technical corrections and regulatory guidance issued after year-end are to be considered adjusting events.

Where the effect of changes in the applicable tax rates compared to the previous accounting period are material, an explanation of those effects is required to be provided in the notes to the financial statements (see 11.1 below). *[FRS 102.29.27(d)]*.

5.1.5   Changes to tax rates and laws enacted after the reporting date

The requirement for substantive enactment by the end of the reporting period is clear. Section 32 – *Events after the End of the Reporting Period* – identifies the enactment or announcement of a change in tax rates and laws after the end of the reporting period as an example of a non-adjusting event. *[FRS 102.32.11(h)]*. For example, an entity with a reporting period ending on 31 December issuing its financial statements on 20 April the following year would measure its tax assets and liabilities by reference to tax rates and laws enacted or substantively enacted as at 31 December even if these had changed significantly before 20 April and even if those changes had retrospective effect. However, in these circumstances the entity would have to disclose the nature of those changes and provide an estimate of the financial effect of those changes if the impact is expected to be significant (see 11.2 below). *[FRS 102.32.10]*.

5.1.6   Implications of the decision by the UK to withdraw from the EU

On 29 March 2017, the UK Government started the legal process of negotiating a withdrawal by the UK from the European Union (EU). Under the provisions of the relevant laws and treaties, the UK will leave the EU by 29 March 2019, unless either a deal is reached at an earlier date, or the negotiation period is extended by unanimous consent of the European Council. Until that date, the UK remains a member of the EU and all laws and regulations continue to apply on that basis. After that date, the UK will cease to be a member of the EU and will acquire 'third country' status, the terms of which will be defined in a new arrangement that, at the time of writing this Chapter, is still being negotiated.

Tax legislation in EU member states and other countries contains tax exemptions and tax reliefs (e.g. withholding tax and merger relief) that depend on whether or not one or more of the entities involved are EU domiciled. Once the UK leaves the EU, these exemptions and reliefs may no longer apply to transactions between UK entities and entities in those EU member states and other countries. In those cases, additional tax liabilities may crystallise. At the time of writing, it is still uncertain whether any of these exemptions and reliefs will apply to the UK when it ceases to be a member state.

A transitional period to December 2020, during which the status quo is maintained, has been proposed but is itself dependent on an overall agreement being concluded between the EU and the UK. Other scenarios of 'no deal' or a rejection of any proposed agreement by the UK and other national parliaments is still a possibility at this stage.

Accordingly, the withdrawal process by the UK raises significant uncertainty about how the existing tax legislation in the UK and in other countries will apply after the UK ceases to be a member of the EU. It has also raised uncertainty about the future tax status of entities, which may lead to changes in the accounting treatment.

Given the uncertainties on taxation, we believe it is appropriate for entities to continue to apply their current accounting policies, until the position becomes clearer. However, these uncertainties will require additional disclosure in the financial statements of entities reporting in the period leading up to 29 March 2019, to reflect any progress between the parties in defining the terms of the UK's withdrawal and in clarifying the position of the UK as a 'third country' after its withdrawal from the EU becomes effective. Section 8 requires entities to disclose the significant accounting policies used in preparing the financial statements, including the judgements that management has made in applying those accounting policies that have the most significant effect on the amounts recognised in the financial statements. *[FRS 102.8.6]*. Section 8 also requires entities to disclose information about the key assumptions they make about the future, and other key sources of estimation uncertainty at the reporting date, that have a significant risk of causing a material adjustment to the carrying amounts of assets and liabilities within the next financial year. *[FRS 102.8.7]*. Therefore, entities will need to carefully consider the assumptions and estimates made about the future impact of tax positions and consider whether additional disclosure is needed of the uncertainties arising from UK withdrawal from the EU.

As the negotiations for withdrawal come to a conclusion, the uncertainties about tax legislation and the application of Section 29 will be resolved as each jurisdiction confirms the tax status of transactions with UK entities. Therefore, entities will need to consider the current position at each reporting date and may have to revise the accounting treatment and disclosures that have previously been applied. The recognition and measurement of current and deferred taxes will have to reflect the new status of the UK when it becomes effective and have regard to any related legislation when it is substantively enacted (see 5.1.1 above and 7.8.1 below). *[FRS 102.29.5]*. Enactment after the end of the reporting period but before the date of approval of the financial statements is an example of a non-adjusting event, *[FRS 102.32.11(h)]*, requiring entities to disclose the nature of any changes and provide an estimate of their financial effect if the impact is expected to be significant (see 5.1.5 above and 7.8.2 below). *[FRS 102.32.10]*.

5.2 Uncertain tax positions

In recording the amounts of current tax expected to be paid or recovered, *[FRS 102.29.5]*, the entity will sometimes have to deal with uncertainty. For example, tax legislation may allow the deduction of research and development expenditure, but there may be uncertainty as to whether a specific item of expenditure falls within the definition of eligible research and development costs in the legislation. In some cases, it may not be clear how tax law applies to a particular transaction, if at all. In other situations, a tax return might have been submitted to the tax authorities, who are yet to opine on the treatment of certain transactions, or even have indicated that they disagree with the entity's interpretation of tax law.

These situations are commonly referred to as 'uncertain tax positions' or 'uncertain tax treatments' and estimating the outcome of these uncertainties is often one of the most complex and subjective areas in accounting for tax. However, FRS 102 does not specifically address the measurement of uncertain tax positions, beyond the general requirement of the standard to measure current tax at the amount expected to be paid or recovered. *[FRS 102.29.5]*.

When a Standard does not specifically address a transaction other event or condition, FRS 102 requires an entity's management to use its judgment in developing and applying an appropriate accounting policy. *[FRS 102.10.4]*. It would be appropriate to refer to other sections of FRS 102, *[FRS 102.10.5]*, for example to the guidance in Section 21 on the determination of a 'best estimate of the amount required to settle the obligation at the reporting date' *[FRS 102.21.7]* (see Chapter 19 at 3.7.1). An entity may also consider the approaches applied by IFRS reporters dealing with uncertain tax treatments under IFRIC 23 – *Uncertainty over Income Tax Treatments. [FRS 102.10.6]*. These approaches are discussed in Chapter 29 at 9 of EY International GAAP 2019.

One of the judgments required to be made by management is to determine the unit of account. This might be an entire tax computation, individual uncertain positions, or a group of related uncertain positions (e.g. all positions in a particular tax jurisdiction, or all positions of a similar nature or relating to the same interpretation of tax legislation). The estimated outcome could be different depending on whether the probability of outcomes is considered on an item by item basis or across the population of uncertainties as a whole.

Another consideration required in estimating an uncertain tax position is the question of 'detection risk', which refers to the likelihood that the tax authority examines every single amount reported to it by the entity and the extent to which the tax authority has full knowledge of all relevant information. In our view, it is normally not appropriate to assume that the tax authority would not exercise its right to examine amounts reported to it nor to assume that it has less than full knowledge of all relevant information. Accordingly, such 'detection risk' should not feature in the recognition and measurement of uncertain tax positions.

In many jurisdictions, including the UK, the tax law imposes a legal obligation on an entity operating in that jurisdiction to disclose its full liability to tax, or to assess its own liability to tax, and to make all relevant information available to the tax authorities. In such a tax jurisdiction it would be difficult, as a matter of corporate governance, for an entity to record a tax provision calculated on the basis that the tax authority will not become aware of a particular position which the entity has a legal obligation to disclose to that authority.

5.2.1   Classification of uncertain tax positions

Uncertain tax positions generally relate to the estimate of current tax payable or receivable. Any amount recognised for an uncertain current tax position should normally be classified as current tax, and presented (or disclosed) as current or non-current in accordance with the general requirements of Section 4 – *Statement of Financial Position* – and companies' legislation.

However, there are circumstances where an uncertain tax position affects the measurement of timing differences as at the reporting date, or to the tax base of an asset or liability acquired in a business combination and therefore relates to deferred tax. For example, there might be doubt as to the amount of tax depreciation that can be deducted in respect of a particular asset, which in turn would lead to doubt as to the tax base of the asset, or to the cumulative difference between depreciation charged to date and amounts recognised in the tax returns. There may sometimes be an equal and opposite uncertainty relating to current and deferred tax. For example, there might be uncertainty as to whether a particular item of income is taxable, but – if it is – any tax payable will be reduced to zero by a loss carried forward from a prior period. As discussed at 10.1.1.C below, it is not appropriate to offset current and deferred tax items.

5.3 'Prior year adjustments' of previously presented tax balances and expense (income)

The determination of the tax liability for all but the most straightforward entities is a complex process. It may be several years after the end of a reporting period before the tax liability for that period is finally agreed with the tax authorities and settled. Therefore, the tax liability initially recorded at the end of the reporting period to which it relates is no more than a best estimate at that time, which will typically require revision in subsequent periods until the liability is finally settled.

Tax practitioners often refer to such revisions as 'prior year adjustments' and regard them as part of the overall tax charge or credit for the current reporting period whatever their nature. However, for financial reporting purposes, the normal provisions of Section 10 (see Chapter 9) apply to tax balances and the related expense (income). Therefore, the nature of any revision to a previously stated tax balance should be considered to determine whether the revision represents:

- a correction of a material prior period error (in which case it should be accounted for retrospectively, with a restatement of comparative amounts and, where applicable, the opening balance of assets, liabilities and equity at the start of the earliest period presented); *[FRS 102.10.21]* or
- a refinement in the current period of an estimate made in a previous period (in which case it should be accounted for in the current period). *[FRS 102.10.17].*

In some cases the distinction is clear. If, for example, the entity used an incorrect substantively enacted tax rate (see 5.1 above) to calculate the liability in a previous period, the correction of that rate would – subject to materiality – be a prior year adjustment. A more difficult area is the treatment of accounting changes to reflect the resolution of uncertain tax positions (see 5.2 above). These are in practice almost always treated as measurement adjustments in the current period. However, a view could be taken that the eventual denial, or acceptance, by the tax authorities of a position taken by the taxpayer indicates that one or other party (or both of them) were previously taking an erroneous view of the tax law. As with other aspects of accounting for uncertain tax positions, this is an area where considerable judgment may be required.

5.4 Intra-period allocation, presentation and disclosure

The allocation of current tax income and expense to components of total comprehensive income and equity is discussed at 8 below. The presentation and disclosure of current tax income expense and assets and liabilities are discussed at 10 and 11 below.

6 DEFERRED TAX – RECOGNITION

Deferred tax is defined as the amount of income tax payable (recoverable) in respect of the taxable profit (tax loss) for future reporting periods as a result of past transactions or events. *[FRS 102 Appendix I]*. Section 29 requires deferred tax to be recognised in respect of all timing differences at the reporting date (see 6.1 below), subject to further considerations relating to: *[FRS 102.29.6]*

- unrelieved losses and other deferred tax assets (see 6.2 below);
- tax allowances for the cost of a fixed asset when all the conditions for retaining the tax allowances have been met (see 6.3 below); and
- certain timing differences relating to the recognition in the financial statements of income and expenses from a subsidiary, associate, branch or an interest in a joint venture (see 6.4 below).

Deferred tax is usually not recognised in respect of permanent differences (see 6.5 below). *[FRS 102.29.10]*. However, the general 'timing differences approach' of Section 29 does not apply when an entity recognises assets and liabilities in a business combination accounted for by applying the purchase method. In this situation, deferred tax is recognised in respect of the differences between the values recognised in the financial statements for the acquired assets (other than goodwill) and liabilities in the business combination accounted for by applying the purchase method and the respective amounts that can be deducted or otherwise assessed for tax purposes. *[FRS 102.29.11]*. Accounting for deferred tax in a business combination is discussed at 6.6 below.

6.1 Recognition of deferred tax on timing differences

Timing differences are differences between taxable profits and total comprehensive income as stated in the financial statements that arise from the inclusion of income and expenses in tax assessments in periods different from those in which they are recognised in financial statements. *[FRS 102.29.6]*. Timing differences are said to originate in the accounting period in which they first arise or increase and to reverse in subsequent periods when they decrease, eventually to zero.

6.1.1 Examples of timing differences

A deferred tax liability arises when:

- expenditure is recognised for tax purposes before it is recognised in the financial statements; or
- income is recognised in the financial statements before it is recognised for tax purposes.

A deferred tax asset arises when:

- expenditure is recognised for tax purposes after it is recognised in the financial statements; or
- income is recognised in the financial statements after it is recognised for tax purposes.

Examples of timing differences include:

- tax deductions for the cost of property, plant and equipment are recorded before (deferred tax liability) or after (deferred tax asset) the related depreciation is charged to the income statement;
- tax deductions are available in respect of provisions (for example in respect of decommissioning costs) only when payments are made to settle the obligation. In this case, a deferred tax asset will arise when the entity recognises a provision for that obligation in the financial statements;
- expenditure is capitalised in the financial statements, whereas tax deductions are obtained as the expenditure is incurred. Examples include capitalised borrowing costs and capitalised development costs. Another example arises when an entity accounts for tax-deductible loan issue costs (as a reduction in the recorded net proceeds as required by Section 11 – *Basic Financial Instruments* – and Section 12 – *Other Financial Instruments Issues*), whereas tax relief is given when the issue costs are incurred. In these cases a deferred tax liability will be recognised, because the tax deduction is received before the related cost is depreciated or amortised through the income statement;
- pensions liabilities are recognised in the financial statements but are allowed for tax purposes only when contributions are paid at a later date. This will give rise to a deferred tax asset when a pension liability is recorded and a deferred tax liability to the extent that a pension asset is recognised;
- revaluations of property, plant and equipment give rise to a gain or loss recorded through other comprehensive income, but do not attract a tax charge until the asset is sold. In this example, a deferred tax liability would be recognised. A similar situation arises when an asset is sold and the related taxable gain is rolled over into the cost of a replacement asset;
- in consolidated financial statements, the elimination of intra-group profits in inventory will give rise to a timing difference (deferred tax asset) because tax is payable on the inter-company transfer before the sale of the related inventory (by the transferee subsidiary) is recognised in the consolidated income statement;
- where a tax loss or tax credit is not relieved against past or current taxable profits but can be carried forward to reduce future taxable profits, a timing difference arises. Subject to the additional criteria set out at 6.2 below, this may give rise to a deferred tax asset being recognised; and
- where an entity holds an investment in a subsidiary, associate or joint venture and additional tax is payable when dividends are remitted to the investor, a timing difference will arise (deferred tax liability) to the extent that profits are recognised in the consolidated income statement before the related earnings are distributed by the investee. In certain circumstances the related timing difference is not required to be recognised, as explained at 6.4 below.

Chapter 26

6.1.2 Deferred taxable gains

The UK (and some overseas) tax regime mitigates the tax impact of some asset disposals by allowing some or all of the tax liability on such transactions to be deferred, typically subject to conditions, such as a requirement to reinvest the proceeds from the sale of the asset disposed of in a similar 'replacement' asset. The postponement of tax payments achieved in this way may either be for a fixed period (holdover relief) or for an indefinite period until the new asset is disposed of without the sale proceeds being again reinvested in another replacement asset (rollover relief).

The ability to postpone tax payments in this way does not affect the recognition of deferred tax. The original disposal transaction gives rise to a timing difference on which deferred tax must be recognised.

6.2 Restrictions on the recognition of deferred tax assets

Embodied in the definition of an asset in FRS 102 is the expectation of an inflow of future economic benefits. *[FRS 102 Appendix I].* Accordingly, Section 29 restricts the recognition of unrelieved tax losses and other deferred tax assets to the extent that it is probable that they will be recovered against the reversal of deferred tax liabilities or other future taxable profits. Section 29 observes that the very existence of unrelieved tax losses is strong evidence that there may not be other future taxable profits against which the losses will be relieved. *[FRS 102.29.7].*

By contrast to IAS 12, FRS 102 provides no additional guidance on the interpretation of this general requirement. However, in applying the hierarchy set out in Section 10, we believe that the guidance in IAS 12 is relevant in forming a view as to whether to recognise a deferred tax asset under Section 29. Accordingly, in our opinion, the entity needs to consider:

- recovery against the reversal of recognised deferred tax liabilities; and
- the availability of future taxable profits.

6.2.1 Recovery against the reversal of recognised deferred tax liabilities

IAS 12 states that it is 'probable' that there will be sufficient taxable profit if a deferred tax asset can be offset against a deferred tax liability relating to the same tax authority which will reverse in the same period as the asset, or in a period into which a loss arising from the asset may be carried back or forward. *[IAS 12.28].* Any deferred tax liability used as the basis for recognising a deferred tax asset must represent a future tax liability against which the future tax deduction represented by the deferred tax asset can actually be offset. For example, in a tax jurisdiction where revenue and capital items are treated separately for tax purposes, a deferred tax asset representing a capital loss cannot be recognised by reference to a deferred tax liability relating to PP&E against which the capital loss could never be offset in a tax return.

Where there are insufficient deferred tax liabilities relating to the same tax authority to offset a deferred tax asset, the entity should then look to the availability of future taxable profits.

6.2.2   The availability of future taxable profits

A deferred tax asset can be recovered only out of future *taxable* profit. Evidence of future accounting profit is not necessarily evidence of future taxable profit (for example, if significant tax deductions or credits not reflected in the accounting profit are likely to be claimed by the entity in the relevant future periods). Whilst FRS 102 notes that the 'very existence of unrelieved tax losses is strong evidence that there may not be other future taxable profits against which the losses will be relieved', *[FRS 102.29.7]*, we do not believe this represents a prohibition on their recognition in the absence of recognised deferred tax liabilities; just that more convincing evidence of the existence of profits is required.

IAS 12 suggests that a deferred tax asset should be recognised to the extent that:

- it is probable that in future periods there will be sufficient taxable profits:
  - relating to the same tax authority;
  - relating to the same taxable entity; and
  - arising in the same period as the reversal of the difference or in a period into which a loss arising from the deferred tax asset may be carried back or forward; or
- tax planning opportunities are available that will create taxable profit in appropriate periods. *[IAS 12.29]*.

In our view, any deferred tax liability or future taxable profit used as the basis for recognising a deferred tax asset must also represent a future tax liability against which the future tax deduction can actually be realised. For example, where revenue and capital items are treated separately for tax purposes, a deferred tax asset representing a capital loss cannot be recognised by reference to an expected taxable profit from revenue items, against which the capital loss could never be offset in a tax return.

Where a deferred tax asset is recognised on the basis of expected future taxable profits from trading activities, the 'quality' of those profits must be considered. For example, it might be appropriate to give more weight to (say) revenues from existing orders and contracts than to those from merely anticipated future trading. Where an entity expects to recover from a recent loss-making position, greater scepticism as to the speed of a recovery in profits would also be appropriate.

We do not believe that it will generally be appropriate to restrict the assumed availability of future taxable profit to an arbitrary future timeframe (e.g. 3 years, 5 years etc.) unless such a restriction is imposed because losses expire under tax law. For example, it may well be the case that a deferred tax asset recoverable in twenty years from profits from a currently existing long-term supply contract with a creditworthy customer may be more robust than one recoverable in one year from expected future trading by a start-up company. In the UK, it is also relevant that tax losses can normally be carried forward indefinitely.

To the extent that it is not probable that taxable profit will be available against which the unused tax losses, unused tax credits or other timing differences can be utilised, a deferred tax asset is not recognised. *[FRS 102.29.7]*.

6.2.2.A   *Tax planning strategies*

Where an entity recognises a deferred tax asset on the basis that it will be recovered through profits generated as a result of a tax planning strategy, in our view the entity must:

- be able to demonstrate that the strategy is one that it will undertake, not merely one that it could theoretically undertake;

- measure any deferred tax asset recognised on the basis of a tax planning strategy net of any cost of implementing that strategy (measured, where applicable, on an after-tax basis); and

- expect to be in a net taxable profit position at the relevant time. Where the entity is expected to remain tax loss-making (such that the strategy effectively will simply reduce future tax losses), we believe that the strategy does not generally form the basis for recognising a deferred tax asset, except to the extent that it will create *net* future taxable profits.

6.2.2.B   *Future changes to tax rates and laws are ignored*

The assessment as to the probable existence of future taxable profits, including the availability of tax planning strategies, is based on those tax rates and laws that have been enacted or substantively enacted by the reporting date. *[FRS 102.29.12]*. As noted at 5.1 above and at 7 below, the use of enacted rates is applied very strictly. In particular, no account should be taken of changes to tax rates and laws that are announced or enacted after the reporting date, even if they will create a new tax planning opportunity or result in a deductible timing difference ceasing to be recoverable. Section 32 identifies the enactment or announcement of a change in tax rates and laws after the end of the reporting period as an example of a non-adjusting event. *[FRS 102.32.11(h)]*.

6.3   Capital allowances – when all conditions for their retention have been met

Section 29 requires deferred tax to be recognised on timing differences arising when the tax allowances for the cost of a fixed asset are accelerated (i.e. received before the depreciation of the asset is recognised in profit or loss) or decelerated (i.e. received after the depreciation of the asset is recognised in profit or loss). However, any recorded deferred tax should be reversed if and when all conditions for retaining the allowances have been met. *[FRS 102.29.8]*.

A past example of a situation giving rise to such a reversal in the UK related to entities that had previously claimed industrial buildings allowances (IBAs) which ceased to be subject to clawback (or a balancing charge) if the asset had been held for 25 years. However, IBAs were phased out in the UK by 2012.

6.3.1   *Treatment of assets brought into the UK tonnage tax regime*

Companies subject to UK corporation tax, which operate qualifying vessels that are 'strategically and commercially managed in the UK', can take advantage of the tonnage tax regime. The tonnage tax regime differs from the main corporation tax system in a number of key respects, the most significant from an accounting point of view being that an entity in the tonnage tax regime is not assessed to tax on the basis of its reported profits from qualifying activities and does not receive capital allowances for the cost of its ships. Therefore, an entity's operations within the tonnage tax regime are outside the scope of Section 29, because tonnage tax does not meet the definition of an income tax discussed at 3.2 above.

When an entity first enters the tonnage tax regime, not only does it cease to qualify for further capital allowances in relation to the vessels it held at the time of the change, but it is also exempt from any balancing charges on disposals of those vessels made while it is still in the tonnage tax regime. However, if the entity returns to the corporation tax system at a later date, there are rules which may cause this exposure to be reinstated. Membership of the tonnage tax regime is determined for a fixed period, albeit with a renewal option at the entity's discretion; but HMRC also has the power in limited circumstances to withdraw an entity from the tonnage tax regime.

The question therefore arises as to whether an entity entering the tonnage tax regime should derecognise the deferred tax balances related to its vessels on the basis that, 'all conditions for retaining the tax allowances have been met'. *[FRS 102.29.8]*. In our view it is appropriate for entities reporting under FRS 102 to continue the practice applied under previous UK GAAP and IFRS of derecognising the deferred tax balances related to assets brought into the tonnage tax regime unless there is evidence of a real possibility that the entity will become subject to the main corporation tax regime at a later date. Consideration should be given to the need to disclose (as a contingent liability) the financial consequences of a return to the main corporation tax system. An entity should not anticipate the effect of entering the tonnage tax regime before it is evident that the necessary clearances have been granted by the tax authorities.

6.4 Income or expenses from a subsidiary, associate, branch or joint venture

Entities are required to recognise deferred tax on timing differences that arise when income or expenses from a subsidiary, branch, associate or joint venture have been recognised in the financial statements and will be assessed to or allowed for tax in a future period, except where: *[FRS 102.29.9]*

- the reporting entity is able to control the reversal of the timing difference; and
- it is probable that the timing difference will not reverse in the foreseeable future.

Section 29 notes that such timing differences may arise where there are undistributed profits in a subsidiary, branch, associate or joint venture. *[FRS 102.29.9]*. For example, an entity may have recognised in its consolidated financial statements the profits of its subsidiaries or recognised in its consolidated income statement an amount in respect of its share of the earnings of its equity-accounted associates and joint ventures. In cases where the investee is required to deduct withholding tax on any distribution of those profits to its parent, there will be future tax consequences relating to those earnings that have been recognised in the entity's financial statements. Subject to the exception above, deferred tax should be recognised for such timing differences.

6.4.1 'Control' over reversal of timing differences

For this exception to apply, the investor must be able to control the reversal of the timing difference and not expect there to be a reversal in the foreseeable future. *[FRS 102.29.9]*. Section 29 does not discuss what is meant by 'control' in this context.

However, IAS 12, in discussing the similar requirements of IAS 12, takes the following position:

- in respect of a subsidiary or a branch, the parent is able to control when and whether retained earnings are distributed. Therefore, no provision need be made for the tax consequences of distributing profits if the parent has determined that those profits will not be distributed in the foreseeable future; *[IAS 12.40]*

- in the case of a joint venture, no amount is recorded for the tax consequences of distributing the share of profits recognised by the entity in its statement of comprehensive income to the extent that the joint venture agreement requires the consent of the entity before a dividend can be paid and the entity expects that it will not give such consent in the foreseeable future; *[IAS 12.43]* and

- in the case of an associate, however, the investor cannot usually control distribution policy. Therefore provision should be made for the tax consequences of the distribution of the share of profits recognised by the entity from its associate, except to the extent that there is a shareholders' agreement to the effect that those earnings will not be distributed in the foreseeable future. *[IAS 12.42]*.

We believe that an entity should consider these criteria in determining whether it controls the reversal of such timing differences. Of course, if control is deemed to exist, but the entity expects its investee to make a distribution in the foreseeable future, any related tax consequences will have to be recognised at the reporting date.

6.5 Permanent differences

Permanent differences are differences between an entity's taxable profits and its total comprehensive income as stated in the financial statements, other than timing differences. *[FRS 102 Appendix I]*. Permanent differences arise because certain types of income or expenses are non-taxable or disallowable, or because certain tax charges or allowances are greater than or smaller than the corresponding income or expense in the financial statements. *[FRS 102.29.10]*. These latter items are sometimes referred to as 'super-deductible' or 'partially-deductible' assets and liabilities. Under Section 29, deferred tax is not recognised on permanent differences, except when an entity is accounting for assets and liabilities acquired in a business combination accounted for by applying the purchase method (see 6.6 below). *[FRS 102.29.10]*.

A permanent difference generally arises from the tax status of an asset (or liability) at the time of its initial recognition. For example, in the UK certain categories of building attract no tax deduction in respect of their use within the business, but only on a subsequent sale. Conversely, the tax deductions made available may exceed the actual expenditure incurred, such as in the case of certain companies engaged in North Sea exploration activities. Another example of a permanent difference arises where an asset is transferred at book value from one member of a group to another, together with its tax history. In this case, the selling subsidiary derecognises the asset and any related deferred tax; but the buying subsidiary recognises only the asset, despite the fact that the cost may only be partially deductible for tax purposes.

In other cases, a permanent difference can be created as a result of changes in tax law subsequent to the original recognition of the asset, for example when the cost of an asset becomes deductible for tax purposes having previously been disallowed. Such changes can give rise to the recognition of deferred tax assets or liabilities under IFRS, but do not under Section 29, where the effect is recognised prospectively as timing differences arise.

In most cases, the application of this requirement for permanent differences is straightforward – either an item is deductible or assessable for tax, or it is not. However, certain items give rise to accounting income and expenditure of which some is assessable or deductible for tax, and some is not. Accounting for the deferred tax effects of such items can raise some issues of interpretation which particularly affect:

- non-deductible assets subject to revaluation (see 6.5.1 below); and
- partially deductible and super-deductible assets (see 6.5.2.below).

6.5.1 Non-deductible assets subject to revaluation

Where a non-deductible asset is acquired separately (i.e. not as part of a larger business combination), the difference between the original cost of the asset and the amount deductible for tax (i.e. zero) is a permanent difference on which no deferred tax is recognised.

If gains on disposal of such an asset are taxable and the asset is subsequently revalued, however, the revaluation would give rise to a timing difference as it results in the recognition of income which is expected to be taxed at a later date. This is illustrated in Examples 26.3 and 26.4 below.

Example 26.3: Revaluation of non-depreciated, non-deductible asset

On 1 January 2019 an entity paying tax at 20% acquires a non tax-deductible office building for £2,000,000. Application of Section 17 – *Property, Plant and Equipment* – results in no depreciation being charged on the building.

On 1 January 2020 the entity revalues the building to £2,400,000. The revaluation of £400,000 is a timing difference giving rise to a deferred tax expense at 20% of £80,000. This tax expense would be recognised in other comprehensive income with the related revaluation gain (see 8 below).

Example 26.4: Revaluation of depreciated, non-deductible asset

On 1 January 2019 an entity paying tax at 20% acquires a non-tax-deductible office building for £2,000,000. The building is depreciated over 20 years at £100,000 per year to a residual value of zero. The entity's financial year ends on 31 December.

At 31 December 2020, the carrying amount of the building is £1,800,000, and it is revalued upwards by £900,000 to its current market value of £2,700,000. As there is no change to the estimated residual value of zero, or to the expected life of the building, this will be depreciated over the next 18 years at £150,000 per year.

As the building is depreciated in future periods the £900,000 timing difference relating to the revaluation will reverse. However, £1,800,000 of the depreciation charged over a period of 18 years relates to the original cost which is not taxable. Accordingly, in our view, for the purposes of applying Section 29, £900,000 of depreciation charged in future periods should be considered as giving rise to a reversal of the timing difference created by the revaluation, and 18/27 should be considered as giving rise to a permanent difference. For example, in 2021:

Total depreciation £	Permanent difference £	Timing difference £
150,000	100,000	50,000

The revaluation in 2020 gives rise to a timing difference of £900,000 giving rise to a deferred tax charge against OCI at 20% of £180,000 in the year ended 31 December 2020. As the difference reverses in 2021 the entity recognises deferred tax income of £10,000, representing the tax effect at 20% of the £50,000 depreciation relating to the revalued element of the building (see table above).

6.5.2   *Partially deductible and super-deductible assets*

The tax deductions for an asset are generally based on the cost of that asset to the legal entity that owns it. However, in some jurisdictions, certain categories of asset are deductible for tax but for an amount either less than the cost of the asset ('partially deductible') or more than the cost of the asset ('super-deductible').

In such cases the difference between the cost and the tax-deductible amount (whether lower or higher) is a permanent difference as defined in Section 29. Section 29 provides no specific guidance on the treatment of partially deductible and super-deductible assets. The issues raised by such assets are illustrated in Examples 26.5 and 26.6 below.

Example 26.5:   *Partially deductible asset*

An entity acquires an asset with a cost of £100,000, for which tax deductions of only £60,000 are available, in a transaction which is not a business combination. The asset is depreciated to a residual value of zero over 10 years, and qualifies for tax deductions of 20% per year over 5 years. In our view, in applying Section 29, the entity could analyse the annual depreciation of £10,000 per annum into a tax-deductible element of £6,000 and a non-deductible element of £4,000, reflecting the fact that only 60% of the cost of the asset is tax-deductible. Timing differences are then calculated by reference to the interaction of tax deductions claimed with the tax-deductible 'element' of the depreciation as set out below.

Year	Depreciation a	40% non- deductible element b (40% of a)	60% deductible element c (60% of a)	Tax deductions d	Cumulative timing difference c − d
1	10,000	4,000	6,000	12,000	6,000
2	10,000	4,000	6,000	12,000	12,000
3	10,000	4,000	6,000	12,000	18,000
4	10,000	4,000	6,000	12,000	24,000
5	10,000	4,000	6,000	12,000	30,000
6	10,000	4,000	6,000	–	24,000
7	10,000	4,000	6,000	–	18,000
8	10,000	4,000	6,000	–	12,000
9	10,000	4,000	6,000	–	6,000
10	10,000	4,000	6,000	–	–

If the entity pays tax at 30%, the amounts recorded for this transaction during year 1 (assuming that there are sufficient other taxable profits to absorb the tax loss created) would be as follows:

	€
Depreciation of asset	(10,000)
Current tax income[1]	3,600
Deferred tax charge[2]	(1,800)
Net tax credit	1,800
Post tax depreciation	(8,200)

1   £100,000 [cost of asset] × 60% [deductible element] × 20% [tax depreciation rate] × 30% [tax rate]
2   £6,000 [timing difference] × 30% [tax rate] = £1,800 − brought forward deferred tax balance [nil] = £1,800

If this calculation is repeated for all 10 years, the following would be reported in the financial statements.

Year	Depreciation A	Current tax credit b	Deferred tax (charge)/credit c	Total tax credit d (=b+c)	Effective tax rate e (=d/a)
1	(10,000)	3,600	(1,800)	1,800	18%
2	(10,000)	3,600	(1,800)	1,800	18%
3	(10,000)	3,600	(1,800)	1,800	18%
4	(10,000)	3,600	(1,800)	1,800	18%
5	(10,000)	3,600	(1,800)	1,800	18%
6	(10,000)	–	1,800	1,800	18%
7	(10,000)	–	1,800	1,800	18%
8	(10,000)	–	1,800	1,800	18%
9	(10,000)	–	1,800	1,800	18%
10	(10,000)	–	1,800	1,800	18%

This methodology has the result that, throughout the life of the asset, a consistent tax credit is reported in each period. The effective tax rate in each period corresponds to the effective tax rate for the transaction as a whole – i.e. cost of £100,000 attracting total tax deductions of £18,000 (£60,000 at 30%), an overall rate of 18%.

However, this approach cannot be said to be required by Section 29 and other methodologies could well be appropriate, provided that they are applied consistently in similar circumstances.

Example 26.6: Super-deductible asset

The converse situation to that in Example 26.5 arises where tax authorities seek to encourage certain types of investment by giving tax allowances for an amount in excess of the expenditure actually incurred. Suppose that an entity invests £1 million in PP&E, for which tax deductions of £1.2 million are available, in a transaction which is not a business combination. The asset is depreciated to a residual value of zero over 10 years, and qualifies for five annual tax deductions of 20% of its deemed tax cost of £1,200,000.

The methodology we propose in Example 26.5 could be applied 'in reverse' – i.e. with the tax deductions, rather than the depreciation, of the asset being apportioned in the ratio 10:2 into a 'cost' element and a 'super deduction' element, and the timing difference calculated by reference to the 'cost' element as follows.

Year	Depreciation a	Tax deduction b	'Super deduction' element c (=2/12 of b)	Cost element d (=10/12 of b)	Cumulative timing difference a – d
1	100,000	240,000	40,000	200,000	100,000
2	100,000	240,000	40,000	200,000	200,000
3	100,000	240,000	40,000	200,000	300,000
4	100,000	240,000	40,000	200,000	400,000
5	100,000	240,000	40,000	200,000	500,000
6	100,000	–	–	–	400,000
7	100,000	–	–	–	300,000
8	100,000	–	–	–	200,000
9	100,000	–	–	–	100,000
10	100,000	–	–	–	–

Chapter 26

If the entity pays tax at 30%, the amounts recorded for this transaction during year 1 (assuming that there are sufficient other taxable profits to absorb the tax loss created) would be as follows:

	£
Depreciation of asset	(100,000)
Current tax income[1]	72,000
Deferred tax charge[2]	(30,000)
Net tax credit	42,000
Profit after tax	(58,000)

1   £1,200,000 [deemed tax cost of asset] × 20% [tax depreciation rate] × 30% [tax rate]
2   £100,000 [timing difference] × 30% [tax rate] = £30,000 – brought forward balance [nil] = £30,000.

If this calculation is repeated for all 10 years, the following would be reported in the financial statements.

Year	Depreciation a	Current tax credit b	Deferred tax (charge)/credit c	Total tax credit d (=b+c)	Effective tax rate e (=d/a)
1	(100,000)	72,000	(30,000)	42,000	42%
2	(100,000)	72,000	(30,000)	42,000	42%
3	(100,000)	72,000	(30,000)	42,000	42%
4	(100,000)	72,000	(30,000)	42,000	42%
5	(100,000)	72,000	(30,000)	42,000	42%
6	(100,000)	–	30,000	30,000	30%
7	(100,000)	–	30,000	30,000	30%
8	(100,000)	–	30,000	30,000	30%
9	(100,000)	–	30,000	30,000	30%
10	(100,000)	–	30,000	30,000	30%

This results in an effective 42% tax rate for this transaction being reported in years 1 to 5, and a rate of 30% in years 6 to 10, in contrast to the average effective rate of 36% for the transaction as a whole – i.e. cost of £1,000,000 attracting total tax deductions of £360,000 (£1,200,000 at 30%). This is because, in the case of a partially deductible asset as in Example 26.5 above, there is an accounting mechanism (i.e. depreciation) for allocating the non-deductible cost on a straight-line basis. However, in the present case of a super deductible asset there is no basis for spreading the £60,000 tax super-deductions, and these are therefore reflected as current tax income in the years in which they are claimed.

Again, as in Example 26.5 above, no single approach can be said to be required by FRS 102 and other methodologies could well be appropriate, provided that they are applied consistently in similar circumstances.

6.5.3   UK indexation allowance

UK tax legislation provides that when certain types of asset are disposed of the cost of the asset deducted in calculating any taxable gain on disposal may be increased by an 'indexation allowance' that is broadly intended to exclude from taxation any gains arising simply as a result of general price inflation.

On a strict interpretation of the definition of 'permanent difference', an indexation allowance is a permanent difference since it is effectively an item of expenditure that appears in taxable profit, but not in total comprehensive income. However, in our view – supported by long-standing practice under FRS 19 – *Deferred tax* – under which the same issue of interpretation would have arisen – it is more appropriate to deal with indexation allowance in the measurement of the related deferred tax liabilities (see 7.5 below).

6.6 Business combinations

As an exception to the general 'timing differences' approach to the recognition of deferred tax in Section 29, an entity is required to recognise deferred tax on the differences between the values recognised for assets (other than goodwill) and liabilities acquired in a business combination accounted for applying the purchase method and the amounts at which those assets and liabilities will be assessed for tax. *[FRS 102.29.11]*. Any such differences are permanent differences to the acquiring entity as defined in FRS 102, because they arise from:

- gains or losses recognised by (and/or tax charged to or credited by) the acquiree before its acquisition;

- fair value adjustments made by the reporting entity on acquisition (which are effectively recognised in goodwill or negative goodwill, not in total comprehensive income); and

- the effect of permanent differences that were not recognised in the financial statements of the acquired entity.

Accordingly, the amount of deferred tax required to be recognised in a business combination may be greater than just the differences between the fair values of assets and liabilities acquired and their previous carrying amounts in the financial statements of the acquired entity.

This exception to the general 'timing differences' approach of Section 29 requires entities to account for deferred tax arising in a business combination accounted for applying the purchase method using the 'temporary differences' approach of IAS 12. The accounting for deferred taxes in such business combinations is largely consistent with the guidance in IAS 12 except that whilst IAS 12 explicitly prohibits only the recognition of a deferred tax liability relating to the initial recognition of goodwill, *[IAS 12.15(a)]*, Section 29 prohibits the recognition of both a deferred tax liability and a deferred tax asset on goodwill arising in a business combination. *[FRS 102.29.11]*. Accordingly, in the (albeit rare) situation where goodwill is tax deductible and the deductible amount exceeds the value recognised in the financial statements, no asset would be recognised under FRS 102 whereas a deductible temporary difference may qualify for recognition as a deferred tax asset under IAS 12. The recognition and measurement of deferred tax in the context of a business combination is discussed more fully in Chapter 29 at 12 of EY International GAAP 2019.

Chapter 26

Deferred tax recognised in a business combination is reflected in the measurement of goodwill, and not taken to total comprehensive income or equity. *[FRS 102.29.11].* This requirement may lead to the creation of goodwill which, on a literal reading of Section 27 – *Impairment of Assets*, would be required to be immediately impaired, as illustrated by Example 26.7 below.

Example 26.7: *Apparent 'day one' impairment arising from recognition of deferred tax in a business combination*

Entity A, which is taxed at 20%, acquires Entity B for £100m in a transaction that is a business combination. The fair values of the identifiable net assets of Entity B, and the amounts deductible for those net assets for tax purposes are as follows:

	Fair value £m	Tax deduction £m
Brand name	60	–
Other net assets	20	15

This will give rise to the following consolidation journal:

	£m	£m
Goodwill (balance)	33	
Brand name	60	
Other net assets	20	
Deferred tax[1]		13
Cost of investment		100

[1] 20% of (£[60m + 20m] – £15m)

The fair value of the consolidated assets of the subsidiary (excluding deferred tax) and goodwill as presented in the financial statements is now £113m, but the cost of the subsidiary is only £100m. Clearly £13m of the goodwill arises solely from the recognition of deferred tax. However, Section 27, paragraph 18(b), explicitly requires tax to be excluded from the estimate of future cash flows used to calculate any impairment. This raises the question of whether there should not be an immediate impairment write-down of the assets to £100m. In our view, this cannot have been the intention of Section 27, as discussed in Chapter 24.

6.6.1 Determining the manner of recovery of assets and settlement of liabilities

In determining the amount that can be deducted for tax, Section 29 requires an entity to consider the manner in which the entity expects to recover its assets or settle its liabilities recognised in a business combination accounted for by applying the purchase method. *[FRS 102.29.11A].*

The acquirer's assessment of the manner of recovery for the purposes of Section 29 may well differ from that of the acquired entity. For example, the acquired entity might have intended to recover an asset through use, whereas the acquirer intends to sell it. In such a case, in our view, the requirement in Section 19 – *Business Combinations and Goodwill* – to recognise and measure deferred tax arising in a business combination in accordance with Section 29 *[FRS 102.19.15A]* has the effect that the expectations of the acquirer are used to determine the tax base of an item and the measurement of any deferred tax associated with the item. The expected manner of recovery of assets and settlement of liabilities by IFRS reporters is discussed more fully in Chapter 29 at 8.4 of EY International GAAP 2019.

6.6.2 Acquisition of subsidiary not accounted for as a business combination

Occasionally, an entity may acquire a subsidiary which is accounted for as the acquisition of an asset rather than as a business combination. This will most often be the case where the subsidiary concerned is a 'single asset entity' holding a single item of property, plant and equipment which is not considered to comprise a business as defined in FRS 102 (see Chapter 17). Where an asset is acquired in such circumstances, the normal provisions of Section 29 apply. Accordingly, any difference between the cost of the asset and the amount (if any) that will be deductible for tax in respect of that asset is a permanent difference, and deferred tax should not be recognised.

6.6.3 Group reconstructions for which the merger accounting method is used

FRS 102 requires all business combinations to be accounted for using the purchase method, except for:

- group reconstructions, which may be accounted for by using the merger accounting method; and

- public benefit entity combinations that are in substance a gift or that are a merger, which shall be accounted for in accordance with Section 34 – *Specialised Activities. [FRS 102.19.6]*.

With the merger accounting method, the carrying values of the assets and liabilities of the parties to the combination are not required to be adjusted to fair value, although appropriate adjustments are required to be made to achieve uniformity of accounting policies in the combining entities. *[FRS 102.19.29]*.

In our view, this approach applies equally to any deferred tax assets and liabilities of the parties to the combination, such that carrying values would not be adjusted in a transaction accounted for using the merger accounting method.

As discussed in Chapter 17 at 5, the Basis for Conclusions on FRS 102 has noted that FRS 102 should retain the accounting for group reconstructions that was permitted by FRS 6 – *Acquisitions and mergers*. It was noted that whilst EU-adopted IFRS does not provide accounting requirements for the accounting for business combinations under common control, the accounting required by FRS 6 is well understood and provides useful information. Therefore these requirements were carried forward into FRS 102. *[FRS 102.BC.B19.1]*.

In addition, the requirement in Section 19 for an acquirer to 'recognise and measure a deferred tax asset or liability arising from the assets acquired and liabilities assumed' *[FRS 102.19.15A]* is set out in the context of an acquisition to which the purchase method is applied. This requirement, and the statement in Section 29 that 'the amount attributed to goodwill shall be adjusted by the amount of deferred tax recognised', *[FRS 102.29.11]*, seems incongruous with the use of merger accounting, which should not give rise to the recognition of goodwill.

Chapter 26

7   DEFERRED TAX – MEASUREMENT

Like current tax, deferred tax should not be discounted, *[FRS 102.29.17]*, and should be measured by reference to the tax rates and laws that have been enacted or substantively enacted by the reporting date. *[FRS 102.29.12]*. 'Enacted or substantively enacted' for the purposes of deferred tax has the same meaning as for the purposes of calculating current tax, as discussed at 5.1 above.

In measuring deferred tax assets and deferred tax liabilities, an entity is required to apply those enacted rates that are expected to apply to the reversal of the timing difference. *[FRS 102.29.12]*. As noted at 5.1 and 6.2.2.B above, the use of enacted rates is quite clear in the literature. In particular, no account should be taken of changes to tax rates and laws that are announced or enacted after the reporting date, even if they will be applied retrospectively or result in a deductible temporary difference ceasing to be recoverable. Section 32 identifies the enactment or announcement of a change in tax rates and laws after the end of the reporting period as an example of a non-adjusting event. *[FRS 102.32.11(h)]*.

When different tax rates apply to different levels of taxable profit, deferred tax assets and liabilities are measured using the average enacted or substantively enacted rates that are expected to apply to the taxable profit (tax loss) of the periods in which the entity expects the deferred tax asset to be realised or the deferred tax liability to be settled. *[FRS 102.29.13]*.

7.1   Revalued non-depreciable assets and investment property measured at fair value

Section 29 specifies the manner of recovery that should be applied by entities in two situations as follows:

*   deferred tax relating to a non-depreciable asset that is measured using the revaluation model in Section 17 – *Property, Plant and Equipment* – should be measured using the tax rates and allowances that apply to the sale of the asset; *[FRS 102.29.15]* and

*   deferred tax relating to investment property that is measured at fair value in accordance with Section 16 – *Investment Property* – should be measured using the tax rates and allowances that apply to the sale of the asset, except for investment property that has a limited useful life and is held within a business model whose objective is to consume substantially all of the economic benefits embodied in the property over time. *[FRS 102.29.16]*.

These provisions of Section 29 are derived from IAS 12, where they appear as an exception to a more general principle that measurement of deferred tax should have regard to the manner in which an entity expects to recover the asset, or settle the liability, to which the deferred tax relates. *[IAS 12.51, 51B, 51C]*. However, there is no such equivalent general principle expressed in Section 29, although it could be implied from the requirement that deferred tax is measured using the tax rates 'that are expected to apply to the reversal of the timing difference'. *[FRS 102.29.12]*. In measuring deferred tax arising on a business combination accounted for by applying the purchase method, an entity should consider the manner in which it expects, at the end of the reporting period, to recover or settle the carrying amount of its assets and liabilities (see 6.6.1 above). *[FRS 102.29.11A]*. Whilst this requirement applies only to the measurement of deferred tax arising on a business combination accounted for by applying the purchase method, we believe that its underlying principle should be applied more generally. The concept of the 'manner of recovery' is discussed in more detail at 7.4 below.

7.2   Uncertain tax positions

'Uncertain tax positions' are not discussed in FRS 102, but are generally understood to arise when the tax treatment of an item is unclear or is a matter subject to an unresolved dispute between the reporting entity and the relevant tax authority. An uncertain tax position generally occurs where there is an uncertainty as to the meaning of the tax law, or to the applicability of the law to a particular transaction, or both.

As discussed at 5.2 above, uncertain tax positions generally relate to the estimate of current tax payable or receivable. However, in some situations an uncertain tax position affects the measurement of timing differences as at the reporting date, or to the tax base of an asset or liability acquired in a business combination. For example, there might be doubt as to the amount of tax depreciation that can be deducted in respect of a particular asset, which in turn would lead to doubt as to any related deferred tax arising in a business combination, or to the cumulative difference between depreciation charged to date and amounts recognised in the tax returns. In these circumstances the discussion at 5.2 above will also be relevant to the measurement of deferred tax assets and liabilities.

7.3   'Prior year adjustments' of previously presented tax balances and expense (income)

The requirement to revise estimates of amounts recognised as deferred tax assets and liabilities at successive reporting dates is an inevitable consequence of the Standard and, in that respect, the normal requirements of Section 10 apply (see Chapter 9). As discussed in the context of current tax at 5.3 above, the nature of any revision to a previously stated deferred tax balance should be considered to determine whether the revision represents:

- a correction of a material prior period error (in which case it should be accounted for retrospectively, with a restatement of comparative amounts and, where applicable, the opening balance of assets, liabilities and equity at the start of the earliest period presented); *[FRS 102.10.21]* or

- a refinement in the current period of an estimate made in a previous period (in which case it should be accounted for in the current period). *[FRS 102.10.17]*.

7.4   Expected manner of recovery of assets or settlement of liabilities

As noted at 7.1 above, Section 29 requires that in measuring deferred tax arising on a business combination accounted for by applying the purchase method, an entity should consider the manner in which it expects to recover or settle the carrying amount of its assets and liabilities. *[FRS 102.29.11A]*. We believe that this principle should be applied in measuring all deferred tax, in order to meet the requirement of Section 29 to measure deferred tax using the tax rates and laws that are 'expected' to apply to the reversal of the timing difference. *[FRS 102.29.12]*. If a different rate or law would apply to the reversal of the difference depending on the manner of reversal (e.g. depreciation or sale), the expected manner of reversal is an essential input to the assessment of the expected applicable tax rate or law.

Chapter 26

7.4.1   Tax planning strategies to reduce liabilities are not anticipated

As discussed at 6.2.2.A above, we believe that it may be appropriate for an entity to have regard to tax planning strategies in determining whether a deferred tax asset may be recognised.

Some believe that this principle should be extended and have argued that, where an entity has the ability and intention to undertake transactions in the future that will lead to its being taxed at a lower rate, it may take this into account in measuring deferred tax liabilities relating to timing differences that exist at the reporting date and will reverse in future periods when the lower rate is expected to apply.

We believe that this is not appropriate. While tax planning opportunities may be relevant in assessing whether a deferred tax asset should be *recognised*, entities are not permitted to take into account future tax planning opportunities in relation to the measurement of deferred tax liabilities as at the reporting date, nor are entities allowed to anticipate future tax deductions that are expected to become available. Such opportunities do not impact on the *measurement* of deferred tax until the entity has undertaken them, or is at least irrevocably committed to doing so.

7.4.2   Assets and liabilities with more than one manner of recovery (settlement) ('dual-based' assets)

In the UK, and some jurisdictions, the manner in which an entity recovers (settles) the carrying amount of an asset (liability) may affect either or both of:

- the tax rate applicable when the entity recovers (settles) the carrying amount of the asset (or liability); and
- the amount at which the asset or liability is recognised for tax purposes.

For example, in the UK, many types of building are not eligible for capital allowances while they are in use, but are deductible on sale for an amount equal to cost plus indexation allowance. Assets which are treated differently for tax purposes depending on whether their value is recovered through use or sale are commonly referred to as 'dual-based' assets.

In practice, however, many such assets are not realised wholly through use or wholly through sale, but are routinely acquired, used for part of their life and then sold before the end of that life. This is particularly the case with long-lived assets such as property. We set out below the approach which we believe should be adopted in assessing the manner of recovery of:

- depreciable PP&E and intangible assets (see 7.4.2.A below);
- non-depreciable PP&E, investment properties and intangible assets (see 7.4.2.B below); and
- other assets and liabilities (see 7.4.2.C below).

7.4.2.A   Depreciable PP&E and intangible assets

Depreciable PP&E and investment properties are accounted for in accordance with Section 17. Amortised intangibles are accounted for in accordance with Section 18 – *Intangible Assets other than Goodwill.* Sections 17 and 18, which are discussed in detail in Chapters 15 and 16, require the carrying amount of a depreciable asset to be separated into a 'residual value' and a 'depreciable amount'.

'Residual value' is defined as:

'... the estimated amount that an entity would currently obtain from disposal of an asset, after deducting the estimated costs of disposal, if the asset were already of the age and condition expected at the end of its useful life'

and 'depreciable amount' as:

'... the cost of an asset, or other amount substituted for cost ... , less its residual value'. *[FRS 102 Appendix I].*

It is inherent in the definitions of 'residual value' and 'depreciable amount' that, in determining residual value, an entity is effectively asserting that it expects to recover the depreciable amount of an asset through use and its residual value through sale. If the entity does not expect to sell an asset, but to use and scrap it, then the residual value (i.e. the amount that would be obtained from sale) must be nil.

Accordingly, we believe that, in determining the expected manner of recovery of an asset for the purposes of Section 29, an entity should assume that, in the case of an asset accounted for under Section 17 or Section 18, it will recover the residual value of the asset through sale and the depreciable amount through use. Such an analysis is also consistent with the requirement of Section 10 to account for similar transactions consistently (see Chapter 9). This suggests that consistent assumptions should be used in determining both the residual value of an asset for the purposes of Section 17 or Section 18 and the expected manner of its recovery for the purposes of Section 29.

The effect of this treatment is as follows.

Example 26.8: Dual-based asset

As part of a business combination an entity purchases an opencast mine to which there is assigned a fair value of £10 million. The tax system of the jurisdiction where the mine is located provides that, if the site is sold (with or without the minerals *in situ*), £9 million will be allowed as a deduction in calculating the taxable profit on sale. The profit on sale of the land is taxed as a capital item. If the mine is exploited through excavation and sale of the minerals, no tax deduction is available.

The entity intends fully to exploit the mine and then to sell the site for retail development. Given the costs that any developer will need to incur in preparing the excavated site for development, the ultimate sales proceeds are likely to be nominal. Thus, for the purposes of Section 17, the mine is treated as having a depreciable amount of £10 million and a residual value of nil.

On the analysis above:

- as the asset is used, the amount that can be deducted for tax (nil) is £10 million less than the amount at which it is recognised in the financial statements (£10 million); and

- when the asset is finally sold, the amount that can be deducted for tax (£9 million) is £9 million more than the amount at which the residual value is carried (nil).

The entity will therefore provide for a deferred tax liability on the excess of the carrying value of the depreciable amount of the mine over the amount deductible for tax. Whether or not a deferred tax asset can be recognised in respect of the excess of the amount deductible on sale over the carrying amount of the residual value will be determined in accordance with the criteria discussed above. In some tax regimes, capital profits and losses are treated more or less separately from revenue profits and losses to a greater or lesser degree, so that it may be difficult to recognise such an asset due to a lack of suitable taxable profits.

However, we acknowledge that this is not the only possible interpretation of Section 29, and some might persuade themselves that there is a single net deferred tax liability based on the net book-tax difference of £1 million.

7.4.2.B   Non-depreciable PP&E and investment properties at fair value

As noted at 7.1 above, Section 29 requires that where a non-depreciable asset is accounted for using the revaluation model, any deferred tax on the revaluation should be calculated by reference to the tax consequences that would arise on sale of the asset. *[FRS 102.29.15]*. Section 29 also requires any deferred tax asset or liability associated with an investment property that is measured at fair value in accordance with Section 16 is measured by reference to the tax consequences that would arise on sale of the asset, except when the investment property has a limited useful life and the entity's business model is to consume substantially all the economic benefits embodied in the investment property over time. *[FRS 102.29.16]*.

7.4.2.C   Other assets and liabilities

In a number of areas of accounting FRS 102 effectively requires a transaction to be accounted for in accordance with an assumption as to the ultimate settlement of that transaction that may not reflect the entity's expectation of the actual outcome.

For example, if the entity enters into a share-based payment transaction with an employee that gives the employee the right to require settlement in either shares or cash, Section 26 – *Share-based Payment* – requires the transaction to be accounted for on the assumption that it will be settled in cash, however unlikely this may be. Section 28 – *Employee Benefits* – may assert that an entity has a surplus on a defined benefit pension scheme on an accounting basis, when in reality it has a deficit on a funding basis. Similarly, if an entity issues a convertible bond that can also be settled in cash at the holder's option, Section 11 requires the bond to be accounted for on the assumption that it will be repaid, however probable it is that the holders will actually elect for conversion. It may well be that such transactions have different tax consequences depending on the expected manner of settlement, as illustrated in Example 26.9 below.

Example 26.9:   Convertible bond deductible if settled

An entity issues a convertible bond for €1 million. After three years, the holders can elect to receive €1.2 million or 100,000 shares of the entity. If the bond were settled in cash, the entity would receive a tax deduction for the €200,000 difference between its original issue proceeds and the amount payable on redemption. If the bond is converted, no tax deduction is available.

Under Section 11, the premium on redemption of the bond would be accreted as interest over the three year issue period. Since tax relief on the interest is not given until the bond is settled, a deductible timing difference of €200,000 emerges over the issue period. It is assumed that the deferred tax asset relating to this difference would meet the recognition criteria in Section 29 (see 6.2 above).

For various reasons, it is extremely unlikely that the bond will be redeemed in cash.

Example 26.9 raises the issue of whether any deferred tax asset should be recognised in respect of the €200,000 temporary difference.

One view would be that deferred tax should be recognised and measured based on management's actual expectation of the manner of recovery of the asset (or settlement of the liability) to which the deferred tax relates, even where this differs from the expectation inherent in the accounting treatment. The contrary view would be that deferred tax should be recognised and measured based on the expectation inherent in the accounting treatment of the manner of recovery of the asset (or settlement of the liability) to which the deferred tax relates, even where this differs from management's actual expectation.

In our view, the treatment should be based on management's actual expectation. We see a difference between the analysis here and that relating to depreciable PP&E and intangible assets discussed at 7.4.2.A above. In the case of depreciable PP&E and intangibles, Sections 17 and 18 effectively require management to assess whether such assets will be realised through use or sale, and it therefore seems reasonable to use that same assessment for the purpose of measuring deferred tax under Section 29. In the case of the items discussed immediately above, however, FRS 102 may require management to make assumptions that are directly contrary to its expectations, which therefore need not be used for the purposes of Section 29. Therefore, while the entity accretes interest on the bond, it assumes that no tax deduction will be available, because it is unlikely that the liability will be settled in cash.

7.4.3 Timing differences relating to subsidiaries, branches, associates and joint ventures

Such differences, and the special recognition criteria applied to them in Section 29, are discussed in more detail at 6.4 above.

Where deferred tax is recognised on such a timing difference, the question arises as to how it should be measured. Broadly speaking, investors can realise an investment in one of two ways – either indirectly (by remittance of retained earnings or capital) or directly (through sale of the investment). In many jurisdictions, the two means of realisation have very different tax consequences.

In our view, the entity should apply the general principle (discussed above) that, where there is more than one method of recovering an investment, the entity should measure any associated deferred tax asset or liability by reference to the expected manner of recovery of the investment. In other words, to the extent that the investment is expected to be realised through sale, the deferred tax is measured according to the tax rules applicable on sale, but to the extent that the temporary difference is expected to be realised through a distribution of earnings or capital, the deferred tax is measured according to the tax rules applicable on distribution.

Where the expected manner of recovery is through distribution, there may be tax consequences for more than one entity in the group. For example, the paying company may be required to deduct a withholding tax on the dividend paid and the receiving company may suffer income tax on the dividend received. In such cases, provision should be made for the cumulative effect of all tax consequences. A withholding tax on an intragroup dividend is not accounted for in the consolidated financial statements as a withholding tax (i.e. within equity), but as a tax expense in profit or loss, since the group is not making a distribution but transferring assets from a group entity to a parent of that entity.

Chapter 26

7.4.4 *Change in expected manner of recovery of an asset or settlement of a liability*

A change in the expected manner of recovery of an asset or settlement of a liability should be dealt with as an item of deferred tax income or expense for the period in which the change of expectation occurs, and recognised in profit or loss or in other comprehensive income or movements in equity for that period as appropriate (see 8 below).

This may have the effect, in certain situations, that some tax consequences of a disposal transaction are recognised before the transaction itself. For example, an entity might own an item of PP&E which has previously been held for use but which the entity now expects to sell. In our view, any deferred tax relating to that item of PP&E should be measured on a 'sale' rather than a 'use' basis from that point, even though the disposal itself, and any related current tax, may not be accounted for until the disposal occurs.

7.5 UK indexation allowance

A UK company, in computing the taxable gain on the sale of an asset, is allowed to increase the cost of the asset by an indexation allowance, the broad intention of which is to exclude purely inflationary gains from taxation. As noted at 6.5.3 above, on a strict interpretation of the definition of 'permanent difference', an indexation allowance is a permanent difference since it is effectively an item of expenditure that appears in taxable profit, but not in total comprehensive income. However, in our view, supported by long-standing practice under FRS 19 (under which the same issue of interpretation would have arisen), it is more appropriate to take account of the indexation allowance in measuring any deferred tax that would be expected to arise on the sale of an asset.

In our view, deferred tax at the reporting date should be computed based on the indexation that would be available if disposal were to occur at the balance sheet date. Possible increases in the allowance due to future inflation should not be assumed.

The benefit of an indexation allowance can be taken only to the extent that it reduces a tax liability. It cannot be used to create or increase a tax loss. Therefore, a deferred tax asset should not be recognised in respect of an asset whose indexed cost for tax purposes is greater than its carrying amount.

7.6 Effectively tax-free entities

In the UK, and elsewhere, certain types of entity, typically investment vehicles, are exempt from corporate income tax provided that they fulfil certain criteria, which generally include a requirement to distribute all, or a minimum percentage, of their annual income as a dividend to investors. Examples in the UK include investment trusts and real estate investment trusts 'REITs'. This raises the question of how such entities should measure income taxes.

One view would be that such an entity has a liability to tax at the normal rate until the dividend for a year becomes a liability. The liability for a dividend for an accounting period typically arises after the end of that period. Under this analysis, therefore, such an entity would be required, at each period end, to record a liability for current tax at the standard corporate rate. That liability would be released in full when the dividend is recognised as a liability in the following period. This would mean that, on an ongoing basis, the income statement would show a current tax charge or credit comprising:

- a charge for a full liability for the current period; and
- a credit for the reversal of the corresponding liability for the prior period.

In addition, deferred tax would be recognised at the standard tax rate on all timing differences.

A second view would be that the provisions of Section 29 regarding different tax rates for distributed and undistributed tax rates are intended to apply where the only significant factor determining the differential tax rate is the retention or distribution of profit. By contrast, the tax status of an investment fund typically depends on many more factors than whether or not profits are distributed, such as restrictions on its activities, the nature of its investments and other regulatory or listing requirements. On this view, the analysis would be that such an entity can choose to operate within one of two tax regimes (a 'full tax' regime or a 'no tax' regime), rather than that it operates in a single tax regime with a dual tax rate depending on whether profits are retained or distributed.

7.6.1 Subsidiaries of charitable entities

Arrangements whereby tax legislation grants an entity tax-exempt status should be distinguished from those situations where legislation provides allowances and reliefs that allow an entity to effectively extinguish its liability to corporation tax. For example, many charitable entities, including registered providers of social housing and higher education institutions, carry out trading activities through a non-charitable subsidiary. Profits from the subsidiary might be distributed to the parent charity in a tax-efficient manner as a donation which is eligible for corporation tax relief under the gift aid rules, provided it is made during the relevant reporting period or during the following nine months. *[FRS 102.BC.B29.11]*. Such entities that gift-aid 100% of their taxable profits within the required period can therefore achieve an effective tax rate of zero.

However, these are not tax-exempt entities and should therefore account for income taxes, and deferred tax, under Section 29, for the following reasons:

- unlike the entities described at 7.6 above, there are no conditions as to the establishment and conduct of these trading subsidiaries over and above the simple requirement to make a gift-aid payment equal to the otherwise determined taxable profit;
- such gift-aid payments have been determined in law to be distributions of profits, and therefore subject to the same restrictions that apply to the declaration and payment of dividends. An entity would be unable to distribute an amount equal to its taxable profits in any period (as determined under enacted tax laws) if the value of its distributable profits (as determined under accounting standards and the Companies Act) is lower.

For example, a subsidiary that has recognised a significant level of provisions would have to deduct those amounts from its measure of distributable profits, whilst for tax purposes such costs would not be deductible. Any shortfall between the gift-aid payment that it can legally make to its parent and the measure of its taxable profits would result in a corporation tax liability. That is, the subsidiary would have taxable profits and need to recognise a tax expense.

As it performed its triennial review of FRS 102, the FRC was made aware of significant differences in accounting treatment arising in practice in relation to the accounting for payments made, or expected to be made, by a subsidiary to its charitable parent that will qualify for gift aid (expected gift aid payments). *[FRS 102.BC.B29.10]*.

The general rule in Section 29 requires an entity to measure current and deferred taxes at the tax rate applicable to undistributed profits until it recognises a liability to pay a dividend (see 8.1.1 below). When the entity recognises a liability to pay a dividend, it recognises the resulting current or deferred tax liability (asset), and the related tax expense (income). *[FRS 102.29.14]*. The Triennial review 2017 introduced an exception to this requirement when:

(a)   an entity is wholly-owned by one of more charitable entities;

(b)   it is probable that a gift aid payment will be made to a member of the same charitable group, or a charitable venturer, within nine months of the reporting date; and

(c)   that payment will qualify to be set against profits for tax purposes.

If all of these conditions are satisfied, the income tax effects of that gift-aid payment are measured consistently with the tax treatment planned to be used in the entity's income tax filings. Consequently, a deferred tax liability is not recognised in relation to such a gift aid payment. *[FRS 102.29.14A]*. The footnote to paragraph 14A clarifies that in this context, 'charitable' refers to an entity that has been recognised by HMRC as being eligible for certain tax reliefs because of its charitable purposes.

7.7   Share-based payment transactions

The accounting treatment of share-based payment transactions, some knowledge of which is required to understand the discussion below, is dealt with in Chapter 23.

In the UK, and many other jurisdictions, an entity receives a tax deduction in respect of remuneration paid in shares, share options or other equity instruments of the entity. The amount of any tax deduction may differ from the related remuneration expense, and may arise in a later accounting period. For example, in the UK, an entity recognises an expense for employee services in accordance with Section 26 (based on the fair value of the award at the date of grant), but does not receive a tax deduction until the award is exercised (in the case of options) or vests (in the case of free shares). The tax deduction is for the fair value of the award at the date of vesting or exercise (as the case may be), which will be equal to the intrinsic value at that date.

Under Section 29, any tax deduction received in excess of the amount recognised as an expense under Section 26 gives rise to a permanent difference which is recognised as current tax when it is received. However, recognition of the Section 26 expense in advance of the tax deduction being received to the extent of that expense gives rise to timing differences, on which a deferred tax asset should be recognised (subject to the general restrictions discussed at 6.2 above).

Section 29 does not prescribe how these timing differences should be calculated. As the tax relief will ultimately be given for the intrinsic value of the award, this forms a reasonable basis for computing the timing difference, which has generally been followed in practice under UK GAAP. However, practice varies as to whether the timing difference is computed as:

- the lower of (a) the total expected tax deduction based on the intrinsic value at the reporting date and (b) the cumulative share-based payment expense (Approach 1); or
- the lower of (a) the cumulative share-based payment expense and (b) the total expected tax deduction based on the intrinsic value at the reporting date, multiplied by the expired portion of the vesting period at that date (Approach 2).

Where the intrinsic value of the award is equal to, or more than, the grant date fair value used in applying Section 26, the two approaches have the same effect. However, where the intrinsic value falls below the grant date fair value, the two approaches give rise to a different result, as illustrated by Example 26.10 below.

Example 26.10: *Timing differences on share-based payment transactions*

On 1 January 2019, an entity with a reporting date of 31 December makes an award of free shares to an employee with a grant date fair value of £300,000. The vesting period is three years. In applying Section 26, it is assumed throughout the vesting period that the award will vest in full. The award actually vests, and is fully deducted for tax in the year of vesting at its intrinsic value on vesting date.

The expense recognised under Section 26 would therefore be as follows:

Year ending	Expense for period £	Cumulative expense £
31 December 2019	100,000	100,000
31 December 2020	100,000	200,000
31 December 2021	100,000	300,000

The intrinsic value of the award at each reporting date is as follows:

	£
31 December 2019	270,000
31 December 2020	290,400
31 December 2021	320,000

Under Approach 1 above, the timing difference would be calculated as the lower of (a) the total intrinsic value at the reporting date and (b) the cumulative share-based payment expense.

Year ending	Total intrinsic value _a_ £	Cumulative expense _b_ £	Timing difference Lower of _a_ and _b_ £
31 December 2019	270,000	100,000	100,000
31 December 2020	290,400	200,000	200,000
31 December 2021	320,000	300,000	N/A[1]

1   The award vests at this point so that any tax relief is recognised as current tax.

Under Approach 2 above, the timing difference would be calculated as the lower of (a) the cumulative share-based payment expense and (b) the total intrinsic value, multiplied by the expired portion of the vesting period at that date.

Year ending	Total intrinsic value	Pro-rated intrinsic value	Cumulative expense	
	a	b	c	Lower of b and c
	£	£	£	£
31 December 2019	270,000	90,000	100,000	90,000
31 December 2020	290,400	193,600	200,000	193,600
31 December 2021	320,000	320,000	300,000	N/A[1]

1   The award vests at this point so that any tax relief is recognised as current tax.

In our view, either approach is acceptable, but should be adopted consistently.

Under Section 29 all tax on share-based payment transactions is accounted for in profit or loss (in contrast to the allocation between profit or loss and equity required under IFRS).

7.8   Legislation at the end of the reporting period

Deferred tax should be measured by reference to the tax rates and laws, as enacted or substantively enacted by the reporting date, that are expected to apply to the reversal of the timing differences. *[FRS 102.29.12]*.

When different tax rates apply to different levels of taxable profit, deferred tax expense (income) and related deferred tax liabilities (assets) are measured using the average rates that are expected to apply to the taxable profit (tax loss) of the periods in which the deferred tax asset is expected to be realised or the deferred tax liability is expected to be settled. *[FRS 102.29.13]*.

As discussed at 5.1.3 above, FRS 102 does not provide further guidance on actual enactment in other jurisdictions. However, IAS 12 provides some further guidance that is discussed more fully in Chapter 29 at 5.1 of EY International GAAP 2019.

7.8.1   Changes to tax rates and laws enacted before the reporting date

Deferred tax should be measured by reference to the tax rates and laws, as enacted or substantively enacted by the reporting date. *[FRS 102.29.12]*. This requirement for substantive enactment is clear. Changes that have not been enacted by the end of the reporting period are ignored, but changes that are enacted before the reporting date must be applied, even in circumstances when complex legislation is substantively enacted shortly before the end of an annual or interim reporting period.

In cases where the effective date of any enacted changes is after the end of the reporting period, deferred tax should still be calculated by applying the new rates and laws timing differences that are expected to reverse in those later periods. *[FRS 102.29.12]*. When the effective date of any rate changes is not the first day of the entity's annual reporting period, deferred tax would be calculated by applying a blended rate to the taxable profits for each year.

In implementing any amendment to enacted tax rates and laws there will be matters to consider that are specific to the actual changes being made to the tax legislation. However, the following principles from Section 29 and other standards are relevant in all cases where new tax legislation has been enacted before the end of the reporting period.

7.8.1.A   Managing uncertainty in determining the effect of new tax legislation

Where complex legislation is enacted, especially if enactment is shortly before the end of the reporting period, entities might encounter two distinct sources of uncertainty:

- uncertainty about the requirements of the new law, which may give rise to uncertain tax treatments as discussed at 5.2 above; and

- incomplete information because entities may not have all the data required to process the effects of the changes in tax laws.

It is not necessary for entities to have a complete understanding of every aspect of the new tax law to arrive at reasonable estimates, and provided that entities make every effort to obtain and take into account all the information they could reasonably be expected to obtain up to the date when the financial statements for the period are authorised for issue, subsequent changes to those estimates would not be regarded as a prior period error under Section 10. *[FRS 102.10.19]*. Only in rare circumstances would it not be possible to determine a reasonable estimate. However, these uncertainties may require additional disclosure in the financial statements. Section 8 requires entities to disclose information about key sources of estimation uncertainty at the end of the reporting period that have a significant risk of causing a material adjustment to the carrying amounts of assets and liabilities within the next financial year (see Chapter 6 at 8.4). *[FRS 102.8.7]*.

Whilst the effect of changes in tax laws enacted after the end of the reporting period are not taken into account (see 7.8.2 below), information and events that occur between the end of the reporting period and the date when the financial statements are authorised for issue are adjusting events after the reporting period if they provide evidence of conditions that existed as at the reporting date. *[FRS 102.32.2(a), 32.4]*. Updated tax calculations, collection of additional data, clarifications issued by the tax authorities and gaining more experience with the tax legislation before the authorisation of the financial statements should be treated as adjusting events if they pertain to the position at the balance sheet date. Events that are indicative of conditions that arose after the reporting period should be treated as non-adjusting events. Judgement needs to be applied in determining whether technical corrections and regulatory guidance issued after year-end are to be considered adjusting events.

Where the effect of changes in the applicable tax rates compared to the previous accounting period are material, an explanation of those effects is required to be provided in the notes to the financial statements (see 11.1 below). *[FRS 102.29.27]*.

7.8.1.B   Disclosures relating to changes in enacted tax rates and laws

In addition to the disclosures noted at 7.8.1.A above concerning key sources of estimation uncertainty at the end of the reporting period, the following disclosures are required by Section 29 (see 11 below):

- the amount of deferred tax expense (or income) relating to changes in tax rates or the imposition of new taxes; *[FRS 102.29.26(d)]*

- an explanation of changes in the applicable tax rate(s) compared to the previous accounting period. *[FRS 102.29.27(d)]*.

7.8.2   *Changes to tax rates and laws enacted after the reporting date*

The requirement for substantive enactment as at the end of the reporting period is clear. Section 32 identifies the enactment or announcement of a change in tax rates and laws after the end of the reporting period as an example of a non-adjusting event. *[FRS 102.32.11(h)]*. For example, an entity with a reporting period ending on 31 December issuing its financial statements on 20 April the following year would measure its tax assets and liabilities by reference to tax rates and laws enacted or substantively enacted as at 31 December even if these had changed significantly before 20 April and even if those changes have retrospective effect. However, in these circumstances the entity would have to disclose the nature of those changes and provide an estimate of the financial effect of those changes if the impact is expected to be significant (see 11.2 below). *[FRS 102.32.10]*.

8   ALLOCATION OF TAX CHARGE OR CREDIT

Section 29 requires an entity to present changes in current tax and deferred tax as tax income or tax expense, except for those changes that arise on the initial recognition of a business combination accounted for by applying the purchase method, which enter into the determination of goodwill or negative goodwill (see 6.6 above). *[FRS 102.29.21]*.

Section 29 also requires an entity to present tax expense (or tax income) in the same component of comprehensive income (i.e. continuing or discontinued operations, and in profit or loss or in other comprehensive income) or equity as the transaction or other event that resulted in the tax expense (or tax income). *[FRS 102.29.22]*. However, as a result of an amendment made following the Triennial review 2017 of FRS 102, an entity must present the tax income or tax expense effects of distributions to owners in profit or loss. *[FRS 102.29.22A]*. This amendment was made to be consistent with a similar change made to IAS 12. *[FRS 102.BC.B29.19]*.

Except as stated above in relation to distributions to owners, Section 29 does not explicitly require tax that does not directly relate to any particular component of total comprehensive income or equity to be accounted for in profit or loss. In our view, where, under Section 5, total comprehensive income is reported in two statements (an income statement and a statement of comprehensive income), any tax expense or tax income that cannot be directly allocated to a particular component of total comprehensive income or equity should be accounted for in the income statement. This approach is consistent with the requirement of Section 5 that all items are presented in the income statement except those that are permitted or required by FRS 102 to be recognised outside profit or loss *[FRS 102.5.2(b)]* – see Chapter 6.

Section 29 does not address the question of the allocation of income tax expense or income arising from the remeasurement of deferred tax asset or liability subsequent to its initial recognition. In our view such remeasurements should be allocated to the same component of total comprehensive income or equity to which the remeasured item was originally allocated. This approach is consistent with IAS 12. This requirement to have regard to the previous history of a transaction in accounting for its tax effects is commonly referred to as 'backward tracing'.

8.1 Dividends and transaction costs of equity instruments

8.1.1 Dividend subject to differential tax rate

In some jurisdictions, the rate at which tax is paid depends on whether profits are distributed or retained. In other jurisdictions, distribution may lead to an additional liability to tax, or a refund of tax already paid. Section 29 requires current and deferred taxes to be measured using the rate applicable to undistributed profits until a liability to pay a dividend is recognised, at which point the tax consequences of that dividend should also be recognised. *[FRS 102.29.14]*. This is discussed further at 7 above.

Where taxes are remeasured on recognition of a liability to pay a dividend, the difference should normally be recognised in profit or loss rather than directly in equity, even though the dividend itself is recognised directly in equity under FRS 102. Section 29 implicitly takes the view that any additional (or lower) tax liability relates to the original profit now being distributed rather than to the distribution itself. Where, however, the dividend is paid out of profit arising from a transaction that was originally recognised in other comprehensive income or equity, the adjustment to the tax liability should also be recognised in other comprehensive income or equity.

8.1.2 Dividend subject to withholding tax

Where dividends are paid by the reporting entity subject to withholding tax that is required to be paid to the tax authorities on behalf of shareholders, the withholding tax should be included as part of the dividend deducted from equity. Other taxes, such as attributable tax credits, should be excluded from the amount recorded as a dividend. *[FRS 102.29.18]*.

Section 29 requires incoming dividends and similar income to be recognised at an amount that includes any withholding taxes, but excludes other taxes, such as attributable tax credits. Any withholding tax suffered is shown as part of the tax charge. *[FRS 102.29.19]*.

'Attributable tax credits' in this context would include any double tax relief for underlying tax on dividends received by a UK entity.

8.1.2.A Distinction between a withholding tax and a differential rate for distributed profits

These provisions of Section 29 may prove somewhat problematic in practice. There may be little economic difference, from the paying entity's perspective, between a requirement to pay a 5% 'withholding tax' on all dividends and a requirement to pay an additional 5% 'income tax' on distributed profit. Yet, the accounting treatment varies significantly depending on the analysis. If the tax is considered a withholding tax, it is treated as a deduction from equity in all circumstances. If, however, it is considered as an additional income tax, it will generally be treated as a charge to profit or loss (see 8.1.1 above).

8.1.2.B Intragroup dividend subject to withholding tax

Where irrecoverable withholding tax is suffered on intragroup dividends, the withholding tax does not relate to an item recognised in equity in the consolidated financial statements (since the intragroup dividend to which it relates has been eliminated in those financial statements). The tax should therefore be accounted for in profit or loss for the period.

8.1.3   Tax benefits of distributions and transaction costs of equity instruments

It is not entirely clear how FRS 102 requires the tax effects of certain equity transactions to be dealt with, as illustrated by Example 26.11 below.

Example 26.11: Tax deductible distribution on equity instrument

An entity paying tax at 25% has issued €25 million 4% preference shares at par value that are treated as equity instruments for accounting purposes (because coupon payments are subject to an equity dividend blocker and are therefore discretionary). The preference shares are treated as debt for tax purposes (i.e. all coupon payments are deductible in determining taxable profit). The entity makes a payment of €1 million and is able to claim a tax deduction of €250,000. There are no restrictions on the recoverability of that deduction for tax purposes.

In the past, some would have allocated the tax deduction to equity on the basis that it relates to the coupon payment, which was accounted for in equity. Others would have considered the distribution as being sourced from the accumulation of retained earnings originally accounted for in profit or loss and, therefore, have allocated that tax deduction for the dividend payment in profit or loss. However, following the amendment to FRS 102 noted at 8 above, the position is clear. The tax benefits of equity distributions should be recognised in profit or loss. *[FRS 102.29.22A]*.

Whilst some payments in relation to equity instruments, such as the issue costs of equity shares, can clearly be regarded as a transaction cost rather than a distribution of profits to owners, entities will have to exercise judgement in determining the appropriate treatment of other items. In making such a judgement, the legal and regulatory requirements in the entity's jurisdiction would also be relevant, for example if those local requirements stipulate whether a particular payment is, in law, a distribution.

8.2   Gain/loss in profit or loss and loss/gain outside profit or loss offset for tax purposes

It often happens that a gain or loss accounted for in profit or loss can be offset for tax purposes against a gain or loss accounted for in other comprehensive income (or an increase or decrease in equity). This raises the question of how the tax effects of such transactions should be accounted for, as illustrated by Example 26.12 below.

Example 26.12: Loss in other comprehensive income and gain in profit or loss offset for tax purposes

During the year ended 31 December 2019, an entity that pays tax at 20% makes a taxable profit of £50,000 comprising:

- £80,000 trading profit less finance costs accounted for in profit or loss; and
- £30,000 foreign exchange losses accounted for in other comprehensive income ('OCI').

Should the total tax liability of £10,000 (20% of £50,000) be presented as either:

(a) a charge of £10,000 in profit or loss; or

(b) a charge of £16,000 (20% of £80,000) in profit or loss and a credit of £6,000 (20% of £30,000) in other comprehensive income?

In our view, (b) is the appropriate treatment, since the amount accounted for in other comprehensive income represents the difference between the tax that would have been paid absent the exchange loss accounted for in other comprehensive income and the amount actually payable. This indicates that this is the amount of tax that, in the words of paragraph 22 of Section 29, 'resulted' from items that are recognised in equity.

Similar issues may arise where a transaction accounted for outside profit or loss generates a suitable taxable profit that allows recognition of a previously unrecognised tax asset relating to a transaction previously accounted for in profit or loss, as illustrated by Example 26.13 below.

Example 26.13: Recognition of deferred tax asset in profit or loss on the basis of tax liability accounted for outside profit or loss

An entity that pays tax at 20% has brought forward unrecognised deferred tax assets (with an indefinite life) totalling £1 million, relating to trading losses accounted for in profit or loss in prior periods. On 1 January 2019 it invests £100,000 in government bonds, which it holds until they are redeemed for the same amount on maturity on 31 December 2022. For tax purposes, any taxable income arising from revaluation of the bonds can be offset against the brought forward tax losses.

The entity elects to account for the bonds as available-for-sale and therefore carries them at fair value (see Chapter 10). Over the period to maturity the fair value of the bonds at the end of each reporting period (31 December) is as follows:

	£
2019	110,000
2020	115,000
2021	120,000
2022	100,000

Movements in value would be accounted for in other comprehensive income ('OCI'). Taken in isolation, the valuation gains in 2019 to 2022 would give rise to current tax liabilities (at 20%) of £2,000 (2019), £1,000 (2020) and £1,000 (2021). However, these liabilities can be offset against the losses brought forward. This raises the question as to whether there should be either:

(a) no tax charge or credit in either profit or loss or other comprehensive income in any of the periods affected; or

(b) in each period, a current tax charge in other comprehensive income (in respect of the taxable income arising from valuation gains on the bonds) and current tax income in profit or loss (representing the recognition of the previously unrecognised deferred tax asset).

In our view, the treatment in (b) should be followed. Although the previously unrecognised deferred tax asset can only be recovered as the result of the recognition of a current tax liability arising from a transaction accounted for in other comprehensive income, the previously unrecognised asset relates to a trading loss previously recorded in profit or loss. Accordingly, the current tax credit arising from the recognition of the asset is properly accounted for in profit or loss.

8.3 Discontinued operations

As noted above, Section 29 requires tax income and tax expense to be allocated between continuing and discontinued operations. Some of the practical issues raised by this requirement are illustrated by Examples 26.14 to 26.16 below.

Example 26.14: *Profit in continuing operations and loss in discontinued operations offset for tax purposes*

Entity A, which pays tax at 25%, has identified an operation as discontinued for the purposes of Section 5. During the period the discontinued operation incurred a loss of £2 million and the continuing operations made a profit of £10 million. The net £8 million profit is fully taxable in the period, and there is no deferred tax income or expense. In our view, the tax expense should be allocated as follows:

	£m	£m
Dr. Current tax expense (continuing operations)[1]	2.5	
Cr. Current tax income (discontinued operation)[2]		0.5
Cr. Current tax liability[3]		2.0

1. Continuing operations profit £10m @ 25% = £2.5m
2. Discontinued operations loss £2m @ 25% = £0.5m.
3. Net taxable profit £8m @ 25% = £2.0m

The tax allocated to the discontinued operation represents the difference between the tax that would have been paid absent the loss accounted for in discontinued operations and the amount actually payable.

Example 26.15: *Taxable profit on disposal of discontinued operation reduced by previously unrecognised tax losses*

Entity B disposes of a discontinued operation during the current accounting period. The disposal gives rise to a charge to tax of £4 million. However, this is reduced to zero by offset against brought forward tax losses, which relate to the continuing operations of the entity, and for which no deferred tax asset has previously been recognised.

In our view, even though there is no overall tax expense, this should be reflected for financial reporting purposes as follows:

	£m	£m
Dr. Current tax expense (discontinued operation)	4.0	
Cr. Current tax income (continuing operations)		4.0

This allocation reflects that fact that, although the transaction that allows recognition of the brought forward tax losses is accounted for as a discontinued operation, the losses themselves arose from continuing operations. This is essentially the same analysis as is used in Example 26.13 above (where a current tax liability recognised in other comprehensive income gives rise to an equal deferred tax asset recognised in profit or loss).

Example 26.16: *Taxable profit on disposal of discontinued operation reduced by previously recognised tax losses*

Entity B disposes of a discontinued operation during the current accounting period. The disposal gives rise to a charge to tax of £4 million. However, this is reduced to zero by offset against brought forward tax losses, which relate to the entities continuing operations, and for which a deferred tax asset has previously been recognised.

In our view, even though there is no overall tax expense, this should be reflected for financial reporting purposes as follows:

	£m	£m
Dr. Current tax expense (discontinued operation)	4.0	
Dr. Deferred tax expense (continuing operations)	4.0	
Cr. Current tax income (continuing operations)		4.0
Cr. Deferred tax asset (statement of financial position)		4.0

This allocation reflects that fact that, although the transaction that allows recognition of the brought forward tax losses is accounted for as a discontinued operation, the losses themselves arose from continuing operations. This is essentially the same analysis as is used in Example 26.14 above.

8.4 Defined benefit pension plans

Section 28 requires an entity, in accounting for a defined benefit post-employment benefit plan, to recognise actuarial gains and losses relating to the plan in full in other comprehensive income ('OCI'). At the same time, a calculated current (and, where applicable, past) service cost and finance income and expense relating to the plan assets and liabilities are recognised in profit or loss – see Chapter 25.

In the UK, and many other jurisdictions, tax deductions for post-employment benefits are given on the basis of cash contributions paid to the plan fund (or benefits paid when a plan is unfunded).

This significant difference between the way in which defined benefit plans are treated for tax and financial reporting purposes can make the allocation of tax deductions for them between profit or loss and OCI somewhat arbitrary, as illustrated by Example 26.17 below.

Example 26.17: Tax deductions for defined benefit pension plans

At 1 January 2019 an entity that pays tax at 20% has a fully-funded defined benefit pension scheme. During the year ended 31 December 2019 it records a total cost of £1 million, of which £800,000 is allocated to profit or loss and £200,000 to other comprehensive income ('OCI'). In January 2020 it makes a funding payment of £400,000, a tax deduction for which is received through the current tax charge for the year ended 31 December 2019.

Assuming that the entity is able to recognise a deferred tax asset for the entire £1 million charged in 2019, it will record the following entry for income taxes in 2019.

	£	£
Dr. Deferred tax asset [£1,000,000 @ 20%]	200,000	
Cr. Deferred tax income (profit or loss) [£800,000 @ 20%]		160,000
Cr. Deferred tax income (OCI) [£200,000 @ 20%]		40,000

When the funding payment is made in January 2020, the accounting deficit on the fund is reduced by £400,000. This gives rise to a current tax deduction of £80,000 (£400,000 @ 20%), in relation to the contribution paid to the pension scheme, and a deferred tax expense of £80,000 in respect of the reversal of the temporary difference arising as some of the deferred tax asset as at 31 December 2019 is released. The difficulty is how to allocate this movement in the deferred tax asset between profit or loss and OCI, as it is ultimately a matter of arbitrary allocation as to whether the funding payment is regarded as making good (for example):

- £400,000 of the £800,000 deficit previously accounted for in profit or loss;
- the whole of the £200,000 of the deficit previously accounted for in OCI and £200,000 of the £800,000 deficit previously accounted for in profit or loss; or
- a pro-rata share of those parts of the total deficit accounted for in profit or loss and OCI.

In the example above, the split is of relatively minor significance, since the entity was able to recognise 100% of the potential deferred tax asset associated with the pension liability.

Chapter 26

This means that, as the scheme is funded, there will be an equal and opposite amount of current tax income and deferred tax expense. The only real issue is therefore one of presentation, namely whether the gross items comprising this net nil charge are disclosed within the tax charge in profit or loss or in OCI.

In other cases, however, there might be an amount of net tax income or expense that needs to be allocated. Suppose that, as above, the entity recorded a pension cost of £1 million in 2019 but determined that the related deferred tax asset did not meet the criteria for recognition under Section 29. In 2020, the entity determines that an asset of £50,000 can be recognised in view of the funding payments and taxable profits anticipated in 2020 and later years. This results in a total tax credit of £130,000 (£80,000 current tax, £50,000 deferred tax) in 2020, raising the question of whether it should be allocated to profit or loss, to OCI, or allocated on a pro-rata basis. This question might also arise if, as the result of newly enacted tax rates, the existing deferred tax balance were required to be remeasured. In our view, any reasonable method of allocation may be used, provided that it is applied on a consistent basis.

One approach might be to compare the funding payments made to the scheme in the previous few years with the charges made to profit or loss under Section 28 in those periods. If, for example, it is found that the payments were equal to or greater than the charges to profit or loss, it might reasonably be concluded that the funding payments have 'covered' the charge recognised in profit or loss, so that any surplus or deficit on the statement of financial position is broadly represented by items that have been accounted for in OCI.

However, a surplus may also arise from funding the scheme to an amount greater than the liability recognised under Section 28 (for example under a minimum funding requirement imposed by local legislation or agreed with the pension fund trustees). In this case, the asset does not result from previously recognised income but from a reduction in another asset (i.e. cash). The entity should assess the expected manner of recovery of any asset implied by the accounting treatment of the surplus – i.e. whether it has been recognised on the basis that it will be 'consumed' (resulting in an accounting expense) or refunded to the entity in due course.

Where it is concluded that the asset will be 'consumed' (resulting in accounting expense), the entity will need to determine whether such an expense is likely to be recognised in profit or loss or in OCI in a future period.

9 CONSOLIDATED TAX RETURNS AND OFFSET OF TAXABLE PROFITS AND LOSSES WITHIN GROUPS

In some jurisdictions one member of a group of companies may file a single tax return on behalf of all, or some, members of the group. Sometimes this is a mandatory requirement for a parent entity and its eligible subsidiaries operating in the same tax jurisdiction; and sometimes adoption is elective. In other jurisdictions, such as the UK, it is possible for one member of a group to transfer tax losses to one or more other members of the group in order to reduce their tax liabilities. In some groups a company whose tax liability is reduced by such an arrangement may be required, as a matter of group policy, to make a payment to the member of the group that pays tax on its behalf, or transfers losses to it, as the case may be. In other groups no such charge is made.

Such transactions raise the question of the appropriate accounting treatment in the separate financial statements of the group entities involved – in particular, whether the company benefiting from such an arrangement should reflect income (or, more likely, a capital contribution) from another member of the group equal to the tax expense mitigated as a result of the arrangement.

Some argue that the effects of such transactions should be reflected in the separate financial statements of the entities involved. Others argue that, except to the extent that a management charge is actually made (see 9.1 below), there is no need to reflect such transactions in the separate financial statements of the entities involved. This has historically been the normal approach adopted in the UK. Section 29 is silent on the issue and, in our view, no single approach can be said to either be prohibited or required. Accordingly, a properly considered approach may be adopted, provided that it is applied on a consistent basis and the related judgements are disclosed where their impact is believed to be material. In arriving at an appropriate judgement, the discussion at 3.2 and 3.5 above is relevant in considering whether entities should apply Section 29 or another section (such as Section 21). Any judgement should be based on the particular facts and circumstances relating to the legislation giving rise to tax consolidation, the nature of the obligations and rights of entities in the group and local company law. As noted at 3.5 above, where there is a predominant local consensus in evidence or specific guidance issued by regulators in the relevant tax jurisdiction, then we believe that the entity should apply this consensus or guidance.

In the context of payments made by subsidiaries of charitable entities in the UK under the gift aid regime, specific requirements were introduced following the FRC's Triennial review 2017, as discussed at 7.6.1 above.

9.1 Payments for intragroup transfer of tax losses

Where one member of a group transfers tax losses to another member of the group, the entity whose tax liability is reduced may be required, as matter of group policy, to pay an amount of compensation to the member of the group that transfers the losses to it. Such payments are known by different terms in different jurisdictions, but are referred to in the discussion below as 'group relief payments'.

Group relief payments are generally made in an amount equal to the tax saved by the paying company. In some cases, however, payment may be made in an amount equal to the nominal amount of the tax loss, which will be greater than the amount of tax saved. This raises the question of how such payments should be accounted for.

The first issue is whether such payments should be recognised:

- in total comprehensive income; or
- as a distribution (in the case of a payment from a subsidiary to a parent) or a capital contribution (in the case of a payment from a parent to a subsidiary).

Chapter 26

The second issue is, to the extent that the payments are accounted for in total comprehensive income, whether they should be classified as:

- income tax, allocated between profit or loss, other comprehensive income or equity (see 9 above). The argument for this treatment is that the payments made or received are amounts that would otherwise be paid to or received from (or offset against an amount paid to) a tax authority; or

- operating income or expense in profit or loss (on the grounds that, as a matter of fact, the payments are not made to or received from any tax authority).

There is a long-standing practice in the UK that such payments are treated as if they were income taxes. We believe that this practice is appropriate to the extent that the intragroup payment is for an amount up to the amount of tax that would otherwise have been paid by the paying company. Where a tax loss payment is made in excess of this amount, we consider that it is more appropriate to account for the excess not as an income tax but as either:

- a distribution or capital contribution (as applicable); or

- operating income or expense (as applicable).

In considering the applicable treatment, the legal and regulatory requirements in the entity's jurisdiction would also be relevant, for example if those local requirements stipulate whether the excess payment is, in law, a distribution. This is the case in the UK, where payments for group relief in excess of the tax relief are regarded in law as distributions of profit. *[TECH 02/17BL.9.69]*. The chosen treatment should be applied consistently.

10   PRESENTATION

In addition to meeting any requirements specified in FRS 102 discussed below, entities preparing statutory accounts must also comply with relevant legislation in the UK or Ireland, as appropriate.

For entities incorporated in the UK, these regulations are principally The Large and Medium-sized Companies and Groups (Accounts and Reports) Regulations 2008 (Regulations). The Regulations establish prescribed formats for the statutory accounts and include the option to apply 'adapted formats' which are similar but not identical to formats included in IAS 1 – *Presentation of Financial Statements*.

Companies subject to the small companies regime are entitled to apply The Small Companies and Groups (Accounts and Directors' Report) Regulations 2008 (Small Companies Regulations). Micro-entities are entitled to apply The Small Companies (Micro Entities' Accounts) Regulations 2013 (Micro-entity Regulations).

The requirements under the UK Companies Act for statutory accounts and reports are discussed in Chapter 1 at 6. The presentation requirements for financial statements prepared under FRS 102 are explained in Chapter 6, with the application of 'adapted formats' discussed in Chapter 6 at 5.1.

10.1   Statement of financial position

Section 29 requires deferred tax liabilities to be included within provisions for liabilities and deferred tax assets to be included within debtors when an entity applies statutory formats to present its statement of financial position. Where an entity applies the 'adapted formats' permitted under the UK Companies Act (see Chapter 6 at 5.1). *[FRS 102.29.23]*, deferred tax assets and liabilities must be shown as separate line items on the face of the statement of financial position, but classified as non-current. *[FRS 102.4.2A(p)]*.

When the 'statutory formats' are applied, deferred tax assets are included within current assets, even if due after more than one year. However, where the amount of debtors due after more than one year is so material in the context of net current assets that in the absence of disclosure of the debtors due after more than one year on the face of the statement of financial position readers may misinterpret the financial statements, FRS 102 requires the amount to be disclosed on the face of the statement of financial position, but still within current assets. *[FRS 102.4.4A]*.

As noted in Chapter 6 at 5.1.11, certain of the statutory disclosures in the Regulations may cause particular complexity when deferred tax is included as a line item within provisions. In particular, UK companies preparing Companies Act accounts must state the provision for deferred tax separately from any other tax provisions and reconcile movements in deferred tax (as it is a line item under provisions). *[1 Sch 59-60]*. In our view, the reconciliation of movements in deferred tax is also required where 'adapted formats' (as well as statutory formats) are used, even though deferred tax is not shown as a provision in the balance sheet.

Section 29 does not explicitly require separate disclosure of the current tax creditor on the face of the statement of financial position and, as discussed in Chapter 6 at 5.3.8.G, note (9) to the balance sheet statutory formats in Schedule 1 to the Regulations would require current tax to be disclosed within the line item for 'Other creditors, including taxation and social security'. However, where an entity applies the 'adapted formats' permitted under the UK Companies Act, current tax assets and current tax liabilities must be shown as separate line items on the face of the statement of financial position, and classified appropriately as current and/or non-current. *[FRS 102.4.2A(o)]*.

10.1.1 Offset

10.1.1.A Current tax

Current tax assets and liabilities should be offset if, and only if, the entity:

- has a legally enforceable right to set off the amounts; and
- intends either to settle them net or simultaneously. *[FRS 102.29.24]*.

10.1.1.B Deferred tax

Deferred tax assets and liabilities should be offset if, and only if:

- the entity has a legally enforceable right to set off current tax assets and liabilities; and
- the deferred tax assets and liabilities concerned relate to income taxes raised by the same taxation authority on either:
  - the same taxable entity; or
  - different taxable entities which intend to settle their current tax assets and liabilities either on a net basis or simultaneously, in each future period in which significant amounts of deferred tax are expected to be settled or recovered. *[FRS 102.29.24A]*.

The offset criteria for deferred tax are less clear than those for current tax. The position is broadly that, where in a particular jurisdiction current tax assets and liabilities relating to future periods will be offset, deferred tax assets and liabilities relating to that jurisdiction and those periods must be offset (even if the deferred tax balances actually recognised in the statement of financial position would not satisfy the criteria for the offset of current tax).

IAS 12 (from which these requirements are derived) suggests that this slightly more pragmatic approach was adopted in order to avoid the detailed scheduling of the reversal of temporary differences that would be necessary to apply the same criteria as for current tax. However, IAS 12 notes that, in rare circumstances, an entity may have a legally enforceable right of set-off, and an intention to settle net, for some periods but not for others. In such circumstances, detailed scheduling may be required to determine the extent of permitted offset.

10.1.1.C   *Offset of current and deferred tax*

Section 29 contains no provisions allowing or requiring the offset of current tax and deferred tax. Accordingly, in our view, given the general restrictions on offset in Section 2 – *Concepts and Pervasive Principles* (see Chapter 4) current and deferred tax may not be offset against each other and should always be presented gross.

10.2   Statement of comprehensive income

As discussed at 8 above, except for tax relating to distributions to owners that are accounted in profit or loss, the tax expense (or income) should be accounted in the same component of comprehensive income to which it relates.

The results of discontinued operations should be presented on a post-tax basis. *[FRS 102.5.7E].*

The results of equity-accounted entities should be presented on a post-tax basis. *[FRS 102.14.8].*

10.3   Statement of cash flows

Cash flows arising from taxes on income are separately disclosed and classified as cash flows from operating activities, unless they can be specifically identified with financing and investing activities. Where tax cash flows are allocated over more than one class of activity, the total amount of taxes paid should be disclosed. *[FRS 102.7.17].*

11   DISCLOSURE

Section 29 imposes extensive disclosure requirements as summarised below.

11.1   Components of tax expense

The major components of tax expense (or income) should be disclosed separately. These may include: *[FRS 102.29.26]*

(a)   current tax expense (or income);

(b)   any adjustments recognised in the period for current tax of prior periods;

(c)   the amount of deferred tax expense (or income) relating to the origination and reversal of timing differences;

(d) the amount of deferred tax expense (or income) relating to changes in tax rates or the imposition of new taxes;

(e) adjustments to deferred tax expense (or income) arising from a change in the tax status of the entity or its shareholders; and

(f) the amount of tax expense (or income) relating to changes in accounting policies and errors (see Chapter 9 at 3.7).

11.2   Other disclosures required by FRS 102

The following should also be disclosed separately: *[FRS 102.29.27]*

(a) the aggregate current and deferred tax relating to items that are recognised as items of other comprehensive income or equity; and

(b) a reconciliation between the tax expense (income) included in profit or loss and the profit or loss on ordinary activities multiplied by the applicable tax rate;

(c) the amount of the net reversal of deferred tax assets and deferred tax liabilities expected to occur during the year beginning after the reporting period together with a brief explanation for the expected reversal;

(d) an explanation of changes in the applicable tax rate(s) compared with the previous reporting period;

(e) the amount of deferred tax liabilities and deferred tax assets at the end of the reporting period for each type of timing difference;

(f) the amount of unused tax losses and tax credits;

(g) the expiry date, if any, of timing differences, unused tax losses and unused tax credits; and

(h) where different tax rates apply to retained and distributed profits (see 7 above), an explanation of the nature of the potential income tax consequences that would result from the payment of dividends to shareholders.

The requirement at (c) above is noteworthy in that it is not required by IAS 12 nor the IFRS for SMEs. The disclosure should be given on a net basis, which takes account of both the reversal of existing timing differences and the origination of new ones. *[FRS 102.BC.B29.9]*. For example, for timing differences related to property, plant and equipment, an entity needs to compare next year's depreciation charge and next year's tax writing down allowances to see if it reverses or increases the timing difference.

The Basis for Conclusions notes that the net basis provides information that is relevant to the entity's future cash flows, and hence is more relevant than disclosure on a gross basis. The Basis for Conclusions also noted that the additional benefit of disclosure on a net basis outweighed the cost to preparers of forecasting future new timing differences. *[FRS 102.BC.B29.9]*. Given that, unlike the requirement at (e) above, the disclosure does not ask for an analysis for each type of timing difference, it would appear that the disclosure of a single net figure would be sufficient.

In addition, Section 32 requires entities to provide information about the nature of any changes in tax rates or tax laws enacted or announced after the reporting period that have a significant effect on current and deferred tax assets and liabilities. *[FRS 102.32.11(h)]*. An estimate of the financial effect of these changes should also be disclosed, or a statement given that such an estimate cannot be made. *[FRS 102.32.10]*. The requirements of Section 32 are discussed in Chapter 29.

11.3 Disclosures required by entities subject to UK and Irish legislation

Under previous UK and Irish GAAP, accounting standards in many cases included the disclosure requirements for entities established under UK and Irish legislation. This is not the case in FRS 102. Entities should therefore consider any additional requirements arising from legal and regulatory requirements. For example, UK incorporated entities must also comply with the requirements of the Large and Medium-sized Companies and Groups (Accounts and Reports) Regulations 2008, which are discussed further in Chapter 6.

12 SUMMARY OF GAAP DIFFERENCES

The differences between FRS 102 and IFRS are set out below.

	FRS 102	*IFRS*
Deferred tax on unremitted earnings of subsidiaries etc.	Recognise in relation to timing differences only, and subject to a control test.	Control test.
Deferred tax on accelerated capital allowances where conditions for retaining allowances are met.	Derecognise.	Continue to recognise.
Deferred tax relating to effect of changes in tax base (e.g. grant of North Sea Field Allowance).	Not recognised (only changes measurement of previously recognised deferred tax).	Recognised.
Deferred tax on excess tax relief on share-based payments.	Permanent difference, no deferred tax.	Recognise deferred tax in equity.
Discounting of current tax receivable or payable.	Prohibited	Neither prohibited nor required. Entities should consider discounting current tax balances if the amounts involved are material.
Balance sheet classification of current tax assets and liabilities.	Not specified in Section 29. Statutory formats require current tax to be included within 'Other creditors, including taxation and social security'. When an entity applies the 'adapted formats', current tax assets and liabilities are disclosed as separate line items on the face of the balance sheet, classified as current or non-current as appropriate.	Disclosed as separate line items on face of balance sheet, classified as current or non-current as appropriate.

Balance sheet classification of deferred tax assets and liabilities.	Unless the 'adapted formats' are applied, deferred tax assets are shown in the balance sheet as a current asset. Deferred tax liabilities are disclosed within provisions for liabilities. When an entity applies the 'adapted formats', deferred tax assets and liabilities are disclosed as separate line items on the face of the balance sheet, classified as current or non-current as appropriate.	Disclosed as separate line items on face of balance sheet, classified as current or non-current as appropriate.
Disclose split of current tax charge between domestic and foreign tax.	Not specified. Only disclose if UK or Irish law requires it.	Not required.
Disclose effect of double tax relief.	Not specified. Only disclose if UK or Irish law requires it.	Not required.
Disclose effect of previously unrealised losses being utilised.	Not specified. Only disclose if UK or Irish law requires it.	Not required.
Disclose nature of evidence to support recognition of deferred tax assets.	Not required.	Required.
Disclose expected net reversal of timing differences in the following reporting period.	Required.	Not required.

References

1 The tax treatment in this example is purely illustrative, and does not reflect current UK tax law on capital allowances.
2 Practice in this area is diverse under IFRS. In some cases such income is measured gross and in other cases net of withholding taxes. See International GAAP 2019, Chapter 31 at 4.2.
3 *IFRS 15 – Revenue from Contracts with Customers,* para. 8, IAS 2 – *Inventories,* para. 11, and IAS 16 – *Property, Plant and Equipment,* para. 16.

4 *FRS 102 Overview Paper – Tax Implications,* H M Customs & Excise, updated 14 October 2016.
5 The flat rate scheme provides for a simplified calculation of VAT payable by entities with VAT taxable turnover below a certain threshold. Customers are still charged the applicable rate of VAT. Entities do not reclaim input VAT but instead account for output VAT using a fixed percentage according to category of business.

Chapter 26

Chapter 27
Foreign currency translation

List of examples

Chapter 27

Chapter 27   Foreign currency translation

1   INTRODUCTION

1.1   Background

An entity can conduct foreign activities in two ways. It may enter directly into transactions which are denominated in foreign currencies, the results of which need to be translated into the currency in which the company measures its results and financial position. Alternatively, it may conduct foreign operations through a foreign entity, such as a subsidiary, associate, joint venture or branch which keeps its accounting records in terms of its own currency. In this case it will need to translate the financial statements of the foreign entity for the purposes of inclusion in the consolidated financial statements.

This chapter discusses the requirements of Section 30 – *Foreign Currency Translation* – for including foreign currency transactions and foreign operations in the financial statements of an entity and how to translate financial statements into a presentation currency.

Section 30 of FRS 102 is similar to IAS 21 – *The Effects of Changes in Foreign Exchange Rates*, with the differences discussed below. Other differences, not discussed, mainly relate to issues addressed by IAS 21 that are not discussed in FRS 102.

2   COMPARISON BETWEEN SECTION 30 AND IFRS

2.1   Reclassification of foreign exchange differences on disposal of a foreign operation

Under IAS 21 all exchange differences arising on translation of a foreign operation that have been accumulated in equity are reclassified to profit and loss on disposal of the net investment. *[IAS 21.48]*. Section 30 of FRS 102 prohibits such reclassifications on disposal. *[FRS 102.9.18A, 30.13]*.

2.2   Unrealised exchange gains on intercompany balances

Unrealised exchange gains on intercompany balances that are part of the net investment in a foreign operation are recognised in other comprehensive income in the separate financial statements of the reporting entity or the individual financial statements of the foreign operation. Under IAS 21, all such exchange gains are recognised in profit or loss. *[FRS 102.30.13, IAS 21.32]*. The treatment in FRS 102 results from the general restriction in the Companies Act 2006 (CA 2006) from recognising unrealised profits in the profit and loss account (see 3.7.6 and 4 below).

3   REQUIREMENTS OF SECTION 30 FOR FOREIGN CURRENCY TRANSLATION

3.1   Definitions

The definitions of terms used in Section 30 are as follows: *[FRS 102 Appendix I]*

Term	Definition
Closing rate	The spot exchange rate at the end of the reporting period.
Fair value	The amount for which an asset could be exchanged, a liability settled, or an equity instrument granted could be exchanged, between knowledgeable, willing parties in an arm's length transaction. In the absence of any specific guidance provided in the relevant section of FRS 102, the guidance in the Appendix to Section 2 – *Concepts and Pervasive Principles* – should be used in determining fair value.
Financing activities	Activities that result in changes in the size and composition of the contributed equity and borrowings of the entity.
Foreign operation	An entity that is a subsidiary, associate, joint venture or branch of a reporting entity, the activities of which are based or conducted in a country or currency other than those of the reporting entity.
Functional currency	The currency of the primary economic environment in which the entity operates.
Group	A parent and all its subsidiaries.
Monetary items	Units of currency held and assets and liabilities to be received or paid in a fixed or determinable number of units of currency.
Net investment in a foreign operation	The amount of the reporting entity's interest in the net assets of that operation.
Operating activities	The principal revenue-producing activities of the entity and other activities that are not investing or financing activities.
Presentation currency	The currency in which the financial statements are presented.

3.2   Scope

An entity can conduct foreign activities in two ways. It may have transactions in foreign currencies or it may have foreign operations. In addition, an entity may present its financial statements in a foreign currency. Section 30 applies to foreign currency transactions, foreign operations and the translation of financial statements into a presentation currency. *[FRS 102.30.1]*.

Section 30 does not apply to hedge accounting of foreign currency items. This is dealt with in Section 12 – *Other Financial Instruments Issues* (see Chapter 10). *[FRS 102.30.1A]*.

3.3 Summary of the approach required by Section 30

In preparing financial statements, the following approach should be followed:

- Each entity – whether a stand-alone entity, an entity with foreign operations (such as a parent) or a foreign operation (such as a subsidiary or branch) – determines its functional currency. *[FRS 102.30.2]*. This is discussed at 3.4 below.

  In the case of group financial statements, there is not a 'group' functional currency; each entity included within the group financial statements, be it the parent, a subsidiary, associate, joint venture or branch, has its own functional currency.

- Where an entity enters into a transaction denominated in a currency other than its functional currency, it translates the related foreign currency items into its functional currency and reports the effects of the translation in accordance with the requirements of Section 30 discussed at 3.5 below.

- The results and financial position of any individual entity within the reporting entity whose functional currency differs from the presentation currency are translated in accordance with the provisions of Section 30 discussed at 3.7 below.

Many reporting entities comprise a number of individual entities (e.g. a group is made up of a parent and one or more subsidiaries). Entities may also have investments in associates or joint ventures or have branches (see 3.4.2 below). It is necessary for the results and financial position of each individual entity included in the reporting entity to be translated into the currency in which the reporting entity presents its financial statements (if this presentation currency is different from the individual entity's functional currency). *[FRS 102.30.17]*.

3.4 Determination of an entity's functional currency

Functional currency is defined as the currency of 'the primary economic environment in which the entity operates'. This will normally be the currency in which the entity primarily generates and expends cash. *[FRS 102.30.3]*.

Section 30 sets out a number of factors or indicators that an entity should or may need to consider in determining its functional currency. When the factors or indicators are mixed and the functional currency is not obvious, management should use its judgement to determine the functional currency that most faithfully represents the economic effects of the underlying transactions, events and conditions. We believe that as part of this approach, management should give priority to the most important indicators before considering the other indicators, which are designed to provide additional supporting evidence to determine an entity's functional currency.

The following are the most important factors an entity considers in determining its functional currency: *[FRS 102.30.3]*

(a)   the currency:

(i)   that mainly influences sales prices for goods and services. This will often be the currency in which sales prices for its goods and services are denominated and settled; and

(ii)   of the country whose competitive forces and regulations mainly determine the sales prices of its goods and services; and

(b)   the currency that mainly influences labour, material and other costs of providing goods or services. This will often be the currency in which such costs are denominated and settled.

Where the functional currency of the entity is not obvious from the above, the following factors may also provide evidence of an entity's functional currency: *[FRS 102.30.4]*

(a)   the currency in which funds from financing activities (issuing debt and equity instruments) are generated; and

(b)   the currency in which receipts from operating activities are usually retained.

An operation that carries on business as if it were an extension of the parent's operations, will have the same functional currency as the parent. In this context, the term parent is drawn broadly and is the entity that has the foreign operation as its subsidiary, branch, associate or joint venture. Therefore the following additional factors are also considered in determining the functional currency of a foreign operation, particularly whether its functional currency is the same as that of the reporting entity: *[FRS 102.30.5]*

(a)   Whether the activities of the foreign operation are carried out as an extension of the reporting entity, rather than being carried out with a significant degree of autonomy. An example of the former is when the foreign operation only sells goods imported from the reporting entity and remits the proceeds to it. An example of the latter is when the operation accumulates cash and other monetary items, incurs expenses, generates income and arranges borrowings, all substantially in its local currency.

(b)   Whether transactions with the reporting entity are a high or a low proportion of the foreign operation's activities.

(c)   Whether cash flows from the activities of the foreign operation directly affect the cash flows of the reporting entity and are readily available for remittance to it.

(d)   Whether cash flows from the activities of the foreign operation are sufficient to service existing and normally expected debt obligations without funds being made available by the reporting entity.

Since an entity's functional currency reflects the underlying transactions, events and conditions that are relevant to it, once it is determined, Section 30 requires that the functional currency is not changed unless there is a change in those underlying transactions, events and conditions. *[FRS 102.30.15]*. The implication of this is that management of an entity cannot decree what the functional currency is – it is a matter of fact, albeit subjectively determined fact based on management's judgement of all the circumstances.

3.4.1 Intermediate holding companies or finance subsidiaries

For many entities the determination of functional currency will be relatively straightforward. However, for some entities, particularly entities within a group, this may not be the case. One particular difficulty is the determination of the functional currency of an intermediate holding company or finance subsidiary within an international group.

Example 27.1: Functional currency of intermediate holding companies or finance subsidiaries

An international group is headquartered in the UK. The UK parent entity has a functional currency of pound sterling, which is also the group's presentation currency. The group has three international sub-operations, structured as follows:

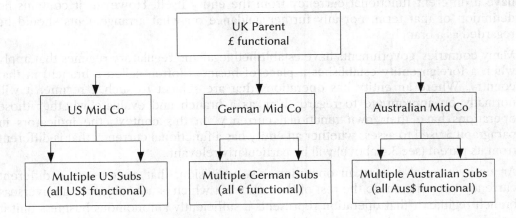

What is the functional currency of the three Mid Cos?

There are a variety of factors to be considered for intermediate holding companies or finance subsidiaries when deciding on the appropriate functional currency. Therefore, there will not be a single analysis applicable to all such entities.

FRS 102 defines a 'foreign operation' as 'an entity that is a subsidiary...the activities of which are based or conducted in a country or currency other than those of the reporting entity' (see 3.1 above). This definition suggests that a foreign operation must have its own 'activities'.

Paragraph 3 of Section 30 states that the functional currency is 'the currency of the primary economic environment in which the entity operates'. However, this is determined by reference to the currency that mainly influences sales prices and the operation's costs (see 3.4 above), and is therefore not directly relevant to intermediate holding companies or finance subsidiaries. Paragraphs 4 and 5 of Section 30 set out a number of factors to consider in determining the functional currency of a foreign operation. The theme running through these factors is the extent to which the activities and cash flows of the foreign operation are independent of those of the reporting entity.

In the case of an intermediate holding company or finance subsidiary, the acid-test question to consider is whether it is an extension of the parent and performing the functions of the parent – i.e. whether its role is simply to hold the investment in, or provide finance to, the foreign operation on behalf of the parent company or whether its functions are essentially an extension of a local operation (e.g. performing selling, payroll or similar activities for that operation) or indeed it is undertaking activities on its own account.

This means that subsidiaries that do nothing but hold investments or borrow money on behalf of the parent will normally have the functional currency of the parent. The borrowings of such companies are frequently guaranteed by the parent, which is itself likely to be a relevant factor. In other words, on whose credit is the lender relying? If the lender is looking to the ultimate parent, then the functional currency is likely to be that of the ultimate parent. However, if the lender is looking to the sub-group, then the functional currency of the companies in the sub-group will be relevant. Accordingly, any analysis that such a company has a functional currency other than that of the parent will require careful consideration of the features of the entity which give rise to that conclusion. Complex situations are likely to require the application of careful management judgement.

As for other entities within a group, the circumstances of each entity should be reviewed against the indicators and factors set out in Section 30. This requires management to use its judgement in determining the functional currency that most faithfully represents the economic effects of the underlying transactions, events and conditions applicable to that entity.

3.4.2   *Branches and divisions*

Section 30 uses the term 'branch' to describe an operation within a legal entity that may have a different functional currency from the entity itself. However, it contains no definition of that term, nor any further guidance on what arrangements should be regarded as a branch.

Many countries' governments have established legal and regulatory regimes that apply when a foreign entity establishes a place of business (often called a branch) in that country. Where an entity has operations that are subject to such a regime, it will normally be appropriate to regard them as a branch and evaluate whether those operations have their own functional currency. In this context, the indicators in paragraph 5 used to assess whether an entity has a functional currency that is different from its parent (see 3.4 above) will be particularly relevant.

An entity may also have an operation, e.g. a division, that operates in a different currency environment to the rest of the entity but which is not subject to an overseas branch regime. If that operation represents a sufficiently autonomous business unit it may be appropriate to view it as a branch and evaluate whether it has a functional currency that is different to the rest of the legal entity. However, in our experience, this situation will not be a common occurrence.

3.5   Reporting foreign currency transactions in the functional currency of an entity

Where an entity enters into a transaction denominated in a currency other than its functional currency then it will have to translate those foreign currency items into its functional currency and report the effects of such translation. The general requirements of Section 30 are discussed at 3.5.1 to 3.5.11 below.

3.5.1   *Initial recognition*

A foreign currency transaction is a transaction that is denominated or requires settlement in a foreign currency, including transactions arising when an entity: *[FRS 102.30.6]*

(a)   buys or sells goods or services whose price is denominated in a foreign currency;

(b)   borrows or lends funds when the amounts payable or receivable are denominated in a foreign currency; or

(c)   otherwise acquires or disposes of assets, or incurs or settles liabilities, denominated in a foreign currency.

On initial recognition, foreign currency transactions should be translated into the functional currency using the spot exchange rate between the foreign currency and the functional currency on the date of the transaction. *[FRS 102.30.7].*

The date of a transaction is the date on which the transaction first qualifies for recognition in accordance with FRS 102. For practical reasons, a rate that approximates the actual rate at the date of the transaction is often used, for example, an average rate for a week or a month might be used for all transactions in each foreign currency occurring during that period. However, if exchange rates fluctuate significantly, the use of the average rate for a period is inappropriate. *[FRS 102.30.8].*

3.5.2   Identifying the date of transaction

The date of a transaction is the date on which it first qualifies for recognition in accordance with FRS 102. Although this sounds relatively straightforward, the following example illustrates the difficulty that can sometimes arise in determining the transaction date:

Example 27.2:   Establishing the transaction date (1)

A UK entity buys an item of inventory from a Canadian supplier. The dates relating to the transaction, and the relevant exchange rates, are as follows:

Date	Event	£1=C$
14 April 2019	Goods are ordered	1.50
5 May 2019	Goods are shipped from Canada and invoice dated that day	1.53
7 May 2019	Invoice is received	1.51
10 May 2019	Goods are received	1.54
14 May 2019	Invoice is recorded	1.56
7 June 2019	Invoice is paid	1.60

Section 13 – *Inventories* – does not make any reference to the date of initial recognition of inventory and Section 11 – *Basic Financial Instruments* – deals with the initial recognition of financial liabilities only in general terms. Generally an entity does not recognise a liability at the time of the commitment but delays recognition until the ordered goods have been shipped or delivered, i.e. the date that the risks and rewards of ownership have passed. Accordingly, it is unlikely that the date the goods are ordered should be used as the date of the transaction.

If the goods are shipped free on board (f.o.b.) then as the risks and rewards of ownership pass on shipment (5 May) then this date should be used.

If, however, the goods are not shipped f.o.b. then the risks and rewards of ownership will often pass on delivery (10 May) and therefore the date the goods are received should be treated as the date of the transaction. In practice, the transaction date will depend on the precise terms of the agreement (which are often based on standardised agreements such as the Incoterms rules).

The dates on which the invoice is received and is recorded are irrelevant to when the risks and rewards of ownership pass and therefore should not, in principle, be considered to be the date of the transaction. In practice, it may be acceptable that as a matter of administrative convenience that the exchange rate at the date the invoice is recorded is used, particularly if there is no undue delay in processing the invoice. If this is done then care should be taken to ensure that the exchange rate used is not significantly different from that ruling on the 'true' date of the transaction.

It is clear from Section 30 that the date the invoice is paid is not the date of the transaction because if it were then no exchange differences would arise on unsettled transactions.

Example 27.2 above illustrated that the date that a transaction is recorded in an entity's books and records is not necessarily the same as the date at which it qualifies for

Chapter 27

recognition under FRS 102. Other situations where this is likely to arise is where an entity is recording a transaction that relates to a period, rather than one being recognised at a single point in time, as illustrated below:

Example 27.3:   Establishing the transaction date (2)

On 30 September 2019 Company A, whose functional currency is the pound sterling, acquires a US dollar bond for US$8,000. The bond carries fixed interest of 5% per annum paid quarterly, i.e. US$100 per quarter. The exchange rate on acquisition is US$1 to £1.50.

On 31 December 2019, the US dollar has appreciated and the exchange rate is US$1 to £2.00. Interest received on the bond on 31 December 2019 is US$100 (= £200).

Although the interest might be recorded only on 31 December 2019, the rate on that date is not the spot rate ruling at the date of the transaction. Since the interest has accrued over the 3 month period, it should be translated at the spot rates applicable to the accrual of interest during the 3 month period. Accordingly, a weighted average rate for the 3 month period should be used. Assuming that the appropriate average rate is US$1 to £1.75 the interest income is £175 (= US$100 × 1.75).

Accordingly, there is also an exchange gain on the interest receivable of £25 (= US$100 × [2.00 – 1.75]) to be reflected in profit or loss. The journal entry for recording the receipt of the interest on 31 December 2019 is therefore as follows:

	£	£
Dr. Cash	200	
Cr. Interest income (profit or loss)		175
Cr. Exchange gain (profit or loss)		25

3.5.3   Using average rates

Rather than using the actual rate ruling at the date of the transaction 'an average rate for a week or month may be used for all foreign currency transactions occurring during that period', if the exchange rate does not fluctuate significantly (see 3.5.1 above). *[FRS 102.30.8]*. For entities which engage in a large number of foreign currency transactions it will be more convenient for them to use an average rate rather than using the exact rate for each transaction.

3.5.4   Dual rates or suspension of rates

One practical difficulty in translating foreign currency amounts is where there is more than one exchange rate for that particular currency depending on the nature of the transaction. In some cases the difference between the exchange rates can be small and therefore it probably does not matter which rate is actually used. However, in other situations the difference can be quite significant. So what rate should be used?

There is no specific guidance on this matter in FRS 102. So in accordance with the hierarchy set out in Section 10 – *Accounting Policies, Estimates and Errors*, an entity could look to the requirements in IFRS for guidance. IAS 21 states that 'when several exchange rates are available, the rate used is that at which the future cash flows represented by the transaction or balance could have been settled if those cash flows had occurred at the measurement date'. *[IAS 21.26]*. Companies would therefore normally look at the nature of the transaction and apply the appropriate exchange rate.

Another practical difficulty which could arise is where, for some reason, exchangeability between two currencies is temporarily lacking at the transaction date or subsequently at the end of the reporting period. Again FRS 102 provides no specific guidance but IAS 21 requires that the rate to be used is 'the first subsequent rate at which exchanges could be made'. *[IAS 21.26]*.

3.5.5 Reporting at the ends of the subsequent reporting periods

At the end of each reporting period, an entity should: *[FRS 102.30.9]*

(a) translate foreign currency monetary items using the closing rate;

(b) translate non-monetary items that are measured in terms of historical cost in a foreign currency using the exchange rate at the date of the transaction; and

(c) translate non-monetary items that are measured at fair value in a foreign currency using the exchange rates at the date when the fair value was determined.

The treatment of exchange differences arising from this is set out at 3.5.6 and 3.5.7 below for monetary and non-monetary items respectively.

3.5.6 Treatment of exchange differences – monetary items

The general rule in Section 30 is that exchange differences on the settlement or retranslation of monetary items should be recognised in profit or loss in the period in which they arise. *[FRS 102.30.10]*.

These requirements can be illustrated in the following examples:

Example 27.4: *Reporting an unsettled foreign currency transaction in the functional currency*

A UK entity purchases plant and equipment on credit from a Canadian supplier for C$328,000 in January 2019 when the exchange rate is £1=C$1.64. The entity records the asset at a cost of £200,000. At the UK entity's year end at 31 March 2019 the account has not yet been settled. The closing rate is £1=C$1.61. The amount payable would be retranslated at £203,727 in the balance sheet and an exchange loss of £3,727 would be reported as part of the profit or loss for the period. The cost of the asset would remain as £200,000.

Example 27.5: *Reporting a settled foreign currency transaction in the functional currency*

A UK entity sells goods to a German entity for €87,000 on 28 February 2019 when the exchange rate is £1=€1.45. It receives payment on 31 March 2019 when the exchange rate is £1=€1.50. On 28 February the UK entity will record a sale and corresponding receivable of £60,000. When payment is received on 31 March the actual amount received is only £58,000. The loss on exchange of £2,000 would be reported as part of the profit or loss for the period.

There are situations where the general rule above will not be applied. The first exception relates to exchange differences arising on a monetary item that, in substance, forms part of an entity's net investment in a foreign operation (see 3.7.4 below). In this situation the exchange differences should be recognised in other comprehensive income and accumulated in equity. However, in general, this treatment applies only in the financial statements that include the foreign operation and the reporting entity (e.g. consolidated financial statements when the foreign operation is a subsidiary). It does not normally apply to the reporting entity's separate financial statements or the financial statements of the foreign operation. This is discussed further at 3.7.6 below.

The next exception relates to hedge accounting for foreign currency items, to which Section 12 applies. The application of hedge accounting requires an entity to account for some exchange differences differently from the treatment required by Section 30. For example, Section 12 requires that exchange differences on monetary items that

Chapter 27

qualify as hedging instruments in a cash flow hedge are recognised initially in other comprehensive income to the extent the hedge is effective. Hedge accounting is discussed in more detail in Chapter 10.

Another situation where exchange differences on monetary items are not recognised in profit or loss in the period they arise would be where an entity capitalises borrowing costs under Section 25 – *Borrowing Costs* – since that section of FRS 102 requires exchange differences arising from foreign currency borrowings to be capitalised to the extent that they are regarded as an adjustment to interest costs (see Chapter 22 at 3.5.4). *[FRS 102.25.1]*.

3.5.7   Treatment of exchange differences – non-monetary items

When non-monetary items are measured at fair value in a foreign currency they should be translated using the exchange rate as at the date when the fair value was determined. *[FRS 102.30.9(c)]*. Therefore, any re-measurement gain or loss will include an element relating to the change in exchange rates. In this situation, the exchange differences are recognised as part of the gain or loss arising on the fair value re-measurement.

When a gain or loss on a non-monetary item is recognised in other comprehensive income, any exchange component of that gain or loss should also be recognised in other comprehensive income. *[FRS 102.30.11]*. For example, Section 17 – *Property, Plant and Equipment* – requires some gains and losses arising on a revaluation of property, plant and equipment to be recognised in other comprehensive income (see Chapter 15 at 3.6.3). When such an asset is measured in a foreign currency, the revalued amount should be translated using the rate at the date the value is determined, resulting in an exchange difference that is also recognised in other comprehensive income.

Conversely, when a gain or loss on a non-monetary item is recognised in profit or loss, e.g. financial instruments that are measured at fair value through profit or loss in accordance with Section 12 (see Chapter 10 at 8.4) or an investment property accounted for using the fair value model (see Chapter 14 at 3.3), any exchange component of that gain or loss should be recognised in profit or loss. *[FRS 102.30.11]*.

The carrying amount of some items is determined by comparing two or more amounts. For example, Section 13 – *Inventories* – requires the carrying amount of inventories to be determined as the lower of cost and estimated selling price less costs to complete and sell. Similarly, in accordance with Section 27 – *Impairment of Assets* – the carrying amount of an asset for which there is an indication of impairment should be the lower of its carrying amount before considering possible impairment losses and its recoverable amount. When such an asset is non-monetary and is measured in a foreign currency, the carrying amount is determined by comparing:

- the cost or carrying amount, as appropriate, translated at the exchange rate at the date when that amount was determined (i.e. the rate at the date of the acquisition for an item measured in terms of historical cost); and

- the estimated selling price less costs to complete or recoverable amount, as appropriate, translated at the exchange rate at the date when that value was determined (e.g. the closing rate at the end of the reporting period).

The effect of this comparison may be that an impairment loss is recognised in the functional currency but would not be recognised in the foreign currency, or *vice versa*.

3.5.8 Determining whether an item is monetary or non-monetary

Section 30 generally requires that monetary items denominated in foreign currencies be retranslated using closing rates at the end of the reporting period and non-monetary items should not be retranslated (see 3.5.6 and 3.5.7 above). Monetary items are defined as 'units of currency held and assets and liabilities to be received or paid in a fixed or determinable number of units of currency'. *[FRS 102 Appendix I]*. Section 30 does not elaborate further on this, however IAS 21 states that 'the essential feature of a monetary item is a right to receive (or an obligation to deliver) a fixed or determinable number of units of currency'. Some examples given by IAS 21 (and which would also apply under FRS 102) are pensions and other employee benefits to be paid in cash; provisions that are to be settled in cash; and cash dividends that are recognised as a liability. More obvious examples are cash and bank balances; trade receivables and payables; and loan receivables and payables.

Conversely, the essential feature of a non-monetary item is the absence of a right to receive (or an obligation to deliver) a fixed or determinable number of units of currency. Examples are amounts prepaid for goods and services (e.g. prepaid rent); goodwill; intangible assets; inventories; property, plant and equipment; and provisions that are to be settled by the delivery of a non-monetary asset. Investments in equity instruments are generally non-monetary items. However there are a number of situations where the distinction may not be altogether clear.

3.5.9 Deposits or progress payments

Entities may be required to pay deposits or progress payments when acquiring certain assets, such as property, plant and equipment or inventories, from foreign suppliers. The question then arises as to whether such payments should be retranslated as monetary items or not.

Example 27.6: Deposits or progress payments

A UK entity contracts to purchase an item of plant and machinery for €10,000 on the following terms:

Payable on signing contract (1 August 2019)	10%
Payable on delivery (19 December 2019)	40%
Payable on installation (7 January 2020)	50%

At 31 December 2019 the entity has paid the first two amounts on the due dates when the respective exchange rates were £1=€1.25 and £1=€1.20. The closing rate at the end of its reporting period, 31 December 2019, is £1=€1.15.

	€	(i) £	(ii) £
First payment	1,000	800	870
Second payment	4,000	3,333	3,478
		4,133	4,348

(i) If the payments made are regarded as prepayments or as progress payments then the amounts should be treated as non-monetary items and included in the balance sheet at £4,133.'

(ii) If the payments made are regarded as deposits, and are refundable, then the amounts could possibly be treated as monetary items and included in the balance sheet at £4,348 and an exchange gain of £215 recognised in profit or loss. A variant of this would be to treat only the first payment as a deposit until the second payment is made, since once delivery is made it is less likely that the asset will be returned and a refund sought from the supplier.

In practice, it will often be necessary to consider the terms of the contract to ascertain the nature of the payments made in order to determine the appropriate accounting treatment.

3.5.10   Investments in preference shares

Entities may invest in preference shares of other entities. Whether such shares are monetary items or not will depend on the rights attaching to the shares. As discussed at 3.5.8 above investments in equity instruments are generally considered to be non-monetary items. Thus, if the terms of the preference shares are such that they are classified by the issuer as equity, rather than as a financial liability, then they are non-monetary items. However, if the terms of the preference shares are such that they are classified by the issuer as a financial liability (e.g. a preference share that provides for mandatory redemption by the issuer for a fixed or determinable amount at a fixed or determinable future date), then it would appear that they should be treated as monetary items.

3.5.11   Assets and liabilities arising from insurance contracts

FRS 103 – *Insurance Contracts* – states that for the purposes of applying the requirements of Section 30 an entity should treat all assets and liabilities arising from an insurance contract as monetary items. *[FRS 103.2.26]*. This means that items such as deferred acquisition costs and unearned premiums that arose in a foreign currency will be retranslated into the entity's functional currency at the closing exchange rate at each reporting date even though they have characteristics that are more akin to a non-monetary item.

3.6   Change in functional currency

Section 30 requires management to use its judgement to determine the entity's functional currency such that it most faithfully represents the economic effects of the underlying transactions, events and conditions that are relevant to the entity (see 3.4 above). Accordingly, once the functional currency is determined, it may be changed only if there is a change to those underlying transactions, events and conditions. For example, a change in the currency that mainly influences the sales prices of goods and services may lead to a change in an entity's functional currency. *[FRS 102.30.15]*.

When there is a change in an entity's functional currency, the entity should apply the translation procedures applicable to the new functional currency prospectively from the date of the change. In other words, an entity translates all items into the new functional currency using the exchange rate at the date of the change. The resulting translated amounts for non-monetary items are treated as their historical cost. *[FRS 102.30.14, 16]*.

Example 27.7:   Change in functional currency

The management of Entity A has considered the functional currency of the entity to be the euro. However, as a result of change in circumstances affecting the operations of the entity, management determines that on 1 January 2019 the functional currency of the entity is now the US dollar. The exchange rate at that date is €1=US$1.20. The balance sheet of Entity A at 1 January 2019 in its old functional currency is as follows:

	€
Property, plant and equipment	200,000
Current assets	
Inventories	10,000
Receivables	20,000
Cash	5,000
	35,000

Current liabilities	
Payables	15,000
Taxation	3,000
	18,000
Net current assets	17,000
	217,000
Long-term loans	120,000
	97,000

Included within the balance sheet at 1 January 2019 are the following items:

- Equipment with a cost of €33,000 and a net book value of €16,500. This equipment was originally purchased for £20,000 in 2013 and has been translated at the rate ruling at the date of purchase of £1=€1.65.

- Inventories with a cost of €6,000. These were purchased for US$6,000 and have been translated at the rate ruling at the date of purchase of €1=US$1.00.

- Payables of €5,000 representing the US$6,000 due in respect of the above inventories, translated at the rate ruling at 1 January 2019.

- Long-term loans of €15,000 representing the outstanding balance of £10,000 on a loan originally taken out to finance the acquisition of the above equipment, translated at £1=€1.50, the rate ruling at 1 January 2019.

Entity A applies the translational procedures applicable to its new functional currency prospectively from the date of change. Accordingly, all items in its balance sheet at 1 January 2019 are translated at the rate of €1=US$1.20 giving rise to the following amounts:

	$
Property, plant and equipment	240,000
Current assets	
Inventories	12,000
Receivables	24,000
Cash	6,000
	42,000
Current liabilities	
Payables	18,000
Taxation	3,600
	21,600
Net current assets	20,400
	260,400
Long-term loans	144,000
	116,400

As far as the equipment that was originally purchased for £20,000 is concerned, the cost and net book value in terms of Entity A's new functional currency are US$39,600 and US$19,800 respectively, being €33,000 and €16,500 translated at €1=US$1.20. Entity A does not go back and translate the £20,000 cost at whatever the £ sterling/US dollar exchange rate was at the date of purchase and calculate a revised net book value on that basis.

Similarly, the inventories purchased in US dollars are included at $7,200, being €6,000 translated at €1=US$1.20. This is despite the fact that Entity A knows that the original cost was $6,000.

As far as the payables in respect of the inventories are concerned, these are included at $6,000, being €5,000 translated at €1=US$1.20. This represents the original amount payable in US dollars. However, this is as it should be since the original payable had been translated into euros at the rate ruling at 1 January 2019 and has just been translated back into US dollars at the same rate. The impact of the change in functional currency is that whereas Entity A had recognised an exchange gain of €1,000 while the functional currency was the euro, no further exchange difference will be recognised in respect of this amount payable. Exchange differences will now arise from 1 January 2019 on those payables denominated in euros, whereas no such differences would have arisen on such items prior to that date.

Similarly, the £10,000 amount outstanding on the loan will be included at $18,000, being €15,000 translated at €1=US$1.20. This is equivalent to the translation of the £10,000 at a rate of £1=US$1.80, being the direct exchange rate between the two currencies at 1 January 2019. In this case, whereas previously exchange gains and losses would have been recognised on movements of the £/€ exchange rate, as from 1 January 2019 the exchange gains and losses will be recognised based on the £/$ exchange rate.

Often an entity's circumstances change gradually over time and it may not be possible to determine a precise date on which the functional currency changes. In these circumstances an entity will need to apply judgement to determine an appropriate date from which to apply the change, which might coincide with the beginning or end of an interim or annual accounting period.

3.7   Use of a presentation currency other than the functional currency

An entity may present its financial statements in any currency (or currencies) (see 3.3 above). If the presentation currency differs from the entity's functional currency, it needs to translate its results and financial position into the presentation currency. For example, when a group contains individual entities with different functional currencies, the results and financial position of each entity are expressed in a common currency so that consolidated financial statements may be presented. *[FRS 102.30.17]*. There is no concept of a 'group' functional currency. Each entity within the group has its own functional currency, and the results and financial position of each entity have to be translated into the presentation currency that is used for the consolidated financial statements.

The requirements of Section 30 in respect of this translation process are discussed below. The procedures to be adopted apply not only to the inclusion of foreign subsidiaries in consolidated financial statements but also to the incorporation of the results of associates and joint ventures. They also apply when the results of a foreign branch are to be incorporated into the financial statements of an individual entity and to a stand-alone entity presenting financial statements in a currency other than its functional currency.

In addition to these procedures, Section 30 has additional provisions that apply when the results and financial position of a foreign operation are translated into a presentation currency so that the foreign operation can be included in the financial statements of the reporting entity by consolidation or the equity method. These additional provisions are covered at 3.7.3 to 3.7.12 below.

3.7.1 Translation to the presentation currency

The method of translation depends on whether the entity's functional currency is that of a hyperinflationary economy or not, and if it is, whether it is being translated into a presentation currency which is that of a hyperinflationary economy or not. A hyperinflationary economy is defined in Section 31 – *Hyperinflation* (see Chapter 28 at 3.2). This chapter covers only the requirements for translating an operation into a presentation currency of a non-hyperinflationary economy. For information on translation to the presentation currency which is that of a hyperinflationary economy refer to Chapter 28.

The results and financial position of an entity whose functional currency is not the currency of a hyperinflationary economy should be translated into a different presentation currency using the following procedures: *[FRS 102.30.18]*

(a) assets and liabilities for each balance sheet presented (i.e. including comparatives) are translated at the closing rate at the date of each respective balance sheet;

(b) income and expenses for each statement of comprehensive income (i.e. including comparatives) are translated at exchange rates at the dates of the transactions; and

(c) all resulting exchange differences are recognised in other comprehensive income.

For practical reasons, the reporting entity may use a rate that approximates the actual exchange rate, e.g. an average rate for the period, to translate income and expense items. However, if exchange rates fluctuate significantly, the use of the average rate for a period is inappropriate. *[FRS 102.30.19]*.

The exchange differences referred to in item (c) above result from: *[FRS 102.30.20]*

- translating income and expenses at the exchange rates at the dates of the transactions and assets and liabilities at the closing rate; and

- translating the opening net assets at a closing rate that differs from the previous closing rate.

This is not completely accurate because, if the entity has had any transactions with equity holders that have resulted in a change in the net assets during the period, there are likely to be further exchange differences that need to be recognised to the extent that the closing rate differs from the rate used to translate the transaction. For example, this would be the case if a parent had subscribed for further equity shares in a subsidiary.

The application of these procedures is illustrated in the following example.

Chapter 27

Example 27.8:   *Translation of a non-hyperinflationary functional currency to a non-hyperinflationary presentation currency*

A UK entity owns 100% of the share capital of a foreign entity which was set up a number of years ago when the exchange rate was £1=FC2. It is consolidating the financial statements of the subsidiary in its consolidated financial statements for the year ended 31 December 2019. The exchange rate at the year-end is £1=FC4 (2018: £1=FC3). For the purposes of illustration, it is assumed that exchange rates have not fluctuated significantly and the appropriate weighted average rate for the year was £1=FC3.5, and that the currency of the foreign entity is not that of a hyperinflationary economy. The income statement of the subsidiary for that year and its balance sheet at the beginning and end of the year in its functional currency and translated into £ are as follows:

Income statement

	FC	£
Sales	35,000	10,000
Cost of sales	(33,190)	(9,483)
Depreciation	(500)	(143)
Interest	(350)	(100)
Profit before taxation	960	274
Taxation	(460)	(131)
Profit after taxation	500	143

Balance sheets	2018 FC	2019 FC	2018 £	2019 £
Property, plant and equipment	6,000	5,500	2,000	1,375
Current assets				
Inventories	2,700	3,000	900	750
Receivables	4,800	4,000	1,600	1,000
Cash	200	600	67	150
	7,700	7,600	2,567	1,900
Current liabilities				
Payables	4,530	3,840	1,510	960
Taxation	870	460	290	115
	5,400	4,300	1,800	1,075
Net current assets	2,300	3,300	767	825
	8,300	8,800	2,767	2,200
Long-term loans	3,600	3,600	1,200	900
	4,700	5,200	1,567	1,300
Share capital	1,000	1,000	500	500
Retained profits*	3,700	4,200	1,500	1,643
Exchange reserve*			(433)	(843)
	4,700	5,200	1,567	1,300

*   The opening balances for 2018 in £ have been assumed and represent cumulative amounts since the foreign entity was set up.

The movement of £(410) in the exchange reserve included as a separate component of equity is made up as follows:

(i)   the exchange loss of £392 on the opening net investment in the subsidiary, calculated as follows:

Opening net assets at opening rate	– FC4,700 at FC3 = A$1 =	£1,567
Opening net assets at closing rate	– FC4,700 at FC4 = A$1 =	£1,175
Exchange loss on net assets		£392

(ii)   the exchange loss of £18, being the difference between the income account translated at an average rate, i.e. £143, and at the closing rate, i.e. £125.

When the exchange differences relate to a foreign operation that is consolidated but not wholly-owned, accumulated exchange differences arising from translation and attributable to non-controlling interests are allocated to, and recognised as part of, non-controlling interests in the consolidated balance sheet. *[FRS 102.30.20].*

3.7.2 Functional currency is that of a hyperinflationary economy

A UK based group preparing consolidated financial statements under FRS 102 might have a subsidiary that operates in, and has a functional currency of, a country subject to hyperinflation. In this case, FRS 102 requires the subsidiary's results and financial position to be adjusted using the procedures specified in Section 31 (see Chapter 28) before translating them into a different presentation currency as follows: All amounts (i.e. assets, liabilities, equity items, income and expenses, including comparatives) are translated at the closing rate at the date of the most recent statement of financial position. However, when amounts are translated into the currency of a non-hyperinflationary economy, comparative amounts should be those that were presented as current year amounts in the relevant prior period financial statements. *[FRS 102.30.21].*

3.7.3 Exchange differences on intragroup balances

The incorporation of the results and financial position of a foreign operation with those of the reporting entity should follow normal consolidation procedures, such as the elimination of intragroup balances and intragroup transactions of a subsidiary. *[FRS 102.30.22].* On this basis, there is a tendency sometimes to assume that exchange differences on intragroup balances should not affect the reported profit or loss for the group in the consolidated financial statements. However, an intragroup monetary asset (or liability), whether short-term or long-term, cannot be eliminated against the corresponding intragroup liability (or asset) without the entity with the currency exposure recognising an exchange difference on the intragroup balance.

This exchange difference will be reflected in that entity's profit or loss for the period (see 3.5.6 above) and, except as indicated at 3.7.4 below, Section 30 requires this exchange difference to continue to be included in profit or loss in the consolidated financial statements. This is because the monetary item represents a commitment to convert one currency into another and exposes the reporting entity to a gain or loss through currency fluctuations. *[FRS 102.30.22].*

3.7.4 Monetary items included as part of the net investment in a foreign operation – general

As an exception to the general rule at 3.7.3 above, where an exchange difference arises on an intragroup balance that, in substance, forms part of an entity's net investment in a foreign operation, the exchange difference is not recognised in profit or loss in the consolidated financial statements, but is recognised in other comprehensive income and accumulated in a separate component of equity. *[FRS 102.30.13, 22].*

The 'net investment in a foreign operation' is defined as being 'the amount of the reporting entity's interest in the net assets of that operation'. *[FRS 102 Appendix I].* This will include a monetary item that is receivable from or payable to a foreign operation for which settlement is neither planned nor likely to occur in the foreseeable future (often referred to as a 'permanent as equity' loan) because it is, in substance, a part of the entity's net investment in that foreign operation. Such monetary items may include long-term receivables or loans. They do not include trade receivables or trade payables. *[FRS 102.30.12]*.

In our view, trade receivables and payables can be included as part of the net investment in the foreign operation, but only if cash settlement is not made or planned to be made in the foreseeable future. However, if a subsidiary makes payment for purchases from its parent, but is continually indebted to the parent as a result of new purchases, then in these circumstances, since individual transactions are settled, no part of the inter-company balance should be regarded as part of the net investment in the subsidiary. Accordingly, exchange differences on such balances should be recognised in profit or loss.

These requirements are illustrated in the following example.

Example 27.9:   *Receivables/payables included as part of net investment in a foreign operation*

A UK entity, A, has a Belgian subsidiary, B. A has a receivable due from B amounting to £1,000,000.

In each of the following scenarios, could the receivable be included as part of A's net investment in B?

Scenario 1

The receivable arises from the sale of goods, together with interest payments and dividend payments which have not been paid in cash but have been accumulated in the inter-company account. A and B agree that A can claim at any time the repayment of this receivable. It is likely that there will be a settlement of the receivable in the foreseeable future.

Although Section 30 states that trade receivables and payables are not included, we do not believe that it necessarily precludes deferred trading balances from being included. In our view, such balances can be included as part of the net investment in the foreign operation, but only if cash settlement is not made or planned to be made in the foreseeable future.

In this scenario, the settlement of A's receivable due from B is not planned; however, it is likely that a settlement will occur in the foreseeable future. Accordingly, the receivable does not qualify to be treated as part of A's net investment in B. The term 'foreseeable future' is not defined and no specific time period is implied. It could be argued that the receivable should only be considered as part of the net investment if it will be repaid only when the reporting entity disinvests from the foreign operation. However, it is recognised that in most circumstances this would be unrealistic and therefore a shorter time span should be considered in determining the foreseeable future.

Scenario 2

The receivable represents a loan made by A to B and it is agreed that the receivable will be repaid in 20 years.

In this scenario, A's receivable due from B has a specified term for repayment. This suggests that settlement is planned. Accordingly, the receivable does not qualify to be treated as part of A's investment in B.

Scenario 3

A and B have previously agreed that the receivable under scenario 2 will be repaid in 20 years but A now decides that it will replace the loan on maturity either with a further inter-company loan or with an injection of equity. This approach is consistent with A's intention to maintain the strategic long-term investment in B.

In this scenario, the words from paragraph 12 of Section 30 '... settlement is neither planned nor likely to occur in the foreseeable future ...' are potentially problematic, since a loan with a fixed maturity must, *prima facie*, have a planned settlement. However, from the date A decides that it will re-finance the inter-company debt upon maturity with a further long-term instrument, or replace it with equity, the substance of the inter-company loan is that it is part of the entity's net investment in the foreign operation, and there is no actual 'intent' to settle the investment without replacement. On this basis, loans with a stated maturity may qualify to be treated in accordance with paragraph 13 of Section 30, with foreign currency gains and losses recognised in other comprehensive income and accumulated in a separate component of equity in the consolidated financial statements. However, in our view, management's intention to refinance the loan must be documented appropriately, for example in the form of a minute of a meeting of the management board or board of directors. In addition, there should not be any established historical pattern of the entity demanding repayment of such inter-company debt without replacement.

Consequently, when the purpose of the loan is to fund a long-term strategic investment then it is the entity's overall intention with regard to the investment and ultimate funding thereof, rather than the specific terms of the inter-company loan funding the investment, that should be considered.

Scenario 4

The receivable arises from the sale of goods, together with interest payments and dividend payments which have not been paid in cash but have been accumulated in the inter-company account. However, in this scenario, A and B agree that A can claim the repayment of this receivable only in the event that the subsidiary is disposed of. A has no plans to dispose of entity B.

In this scenario, the settlement of A's receivable due from B is not planned nor is it likely to occur in the foreseeable future. Although the term 'foreseeable future' is not defined, it will not go beyond a point of time after the disposal of a foreign operation. Accordingly, the receivable does qualify for being treated as part of a net investment in a foreign operation.

The question of whether or not a monetary item is as permanent as equity can, in certain circumstances, require the application of significant judgement.

3.7.5 Monetary items included as part of the net investment in a foreign operation – currency of the monetary item

When a monetary item is considered to form part of a reporting entity's net investment in a foreign operation and is denominated in the functional currency of the reporting entity, an exchange difference will be recognised in the foreign operation's individual financial statements. If the item is denominated in the functional currency of the foreign operation, an exchange difference will be recognised in the reporting entity's separate financial statements, normally in profit or loss, although an unrealised gain is recognised in other comprehensive income (see 3.7.6 below).

In the financial statements that include the foreign operation and the reporting entity (i.e. financial statements in which the foreign operation is consolidated or accounted for using the equity method), such exchange differences are recognised in other comprehensive income and accumulated in a separate component of equity. [FRS 102.30.12-13].

Example 27.10: Monetary item in functional currency of either the reporting entity or the foreign operation

A UK entity has a Belgian subsidiary. On the last day of its financial year, 31 March 2018, the UK entity lends the subsidiary £1,000,000. Settlement of the loan is neither planned nor likely to occur in the foreseeable future, so the UK entity regards the loan as part of its net investment in the Belgian subsidiary. The exchange rate at 31 March 2018 was £1=€1.40. Since the loan was made on the last day of the year there are no exchange differences to recognise for that year. At 31 March 2019, the loan has not been repaid and is still regarded as part of the net investment in the Belgian subsidiary. The relevant exchange rate at that date was £1=€1.50. The average exchange rate for the year ended 31 March 2019 was £1=€1.45.

In the UK entity's separate financial statements no exchange difference is recognised since the loan is denominated in its functional currency of pound sterling. In the Belgian subsidiary's financial statements, the liability to the parent is translated into the subsidiary's functional currency of euros at the closing rate at €1,500,000, giving rise to an exchange loss of €100,000, i.e. €1,500,000 less €1,400,000 (£1,000,000 @ £1=€1.40). This exchange loss is reflected in the Belgian subsidiary's profit or loss for that year. In the UK entity's consolidated financial statements, this exchange loss included in the subsidiary's profit or loss for the year will be translated at the average rate for the year, giving rise to a loss of £68,966 (€100,000@ £1=€1.45). This will be recognised in other comprehensive income and accumulated in the separate component of equity together with an exchange gain of £2,299, being the difference between the amount included in the Belgian subsidiary's income statement translated at average rate, i.e. £68,966, and at the closing rate, i.e. £66,667 (€100,000@ £1=€1.50). The overall exchange loss recognised in other comprehensive income is £66,667. This represents the exchange loss on the increased net investment of €1,400,000 in the subsidiary made at 31 March 2018, i.e. £1,000,000 (€1,400,000 @ £1=€1.40) less £933,333 (€1,400,000 @ £1=€1.50).

If, on the other hand, the loan made to the Belgian subsidiary had been denominated in the equivalent amount of euros at 31 March 2018, i.e. €1,400,000, the treatment would have been as follows:

In the UK entity's separate financial statements, the amount receivable from the Belgian subsidiary would be translated at the closing rate at £933,333 (€1,400,000 @ £1=€1.50), giving rise to an exchange loss of £66,667, i.e. £1,000,000 (€1,400,000 @ £1=€1.40) less £933,333, which is included in its profit or loss for the year. In the Belgian subsidiary's financial statements, no exchange difference is recognised since the loan is denominated in its functional currency of euros. In the UK entity's consolidated financial statements, the exchange loss included in its profit or loss for the year in its separate financial statements will be recognised in other comprehensive income and accumulated in the separate component of equity. As before, this represents the exchange loss on the increased net investment of €1,400,000 in the subsidiary made at 31 March 2018, i.e. £1,000,000 (€1,400,000 @ £1=€1.40) less £933,333 (€1,400,000 @ £1=€1.40).

In most situations, intragroup balances for which settlement is neither planned nor likely to occur in the foreseeable future will be denominated in the functional currency of either the reporting entity or the foreign operation. However, this will not always be the case. If a monetary item is denominated in a currency other than the functional currency of either the reporting entity or the foreign operation, the exchange difference arising in the reporting entity's separate financial statements and in the foreign operation's individual financial statements is also recognised in other comprehensive income, and accumulated in the separate component of equity, in the financial statements that include the foreign operation and the reporting entity (i.e. financial statements in which the foreign operation is consolidated or accounted for using the equity method).

3.7.6   *Monetary items included as part of the net investment in a foreign operation – treatment in individual financial statements*

The exception for exchange differences on monetary items forming part of the net investment in a foreign operation applies only in the consolidated financial statements. It does not normally apply to the reporting entity's separate financial statements or the financial statements of the foreign operation. Rather, the exchange differences will normally be recognised in profit or loss in the period in which they arise in the financial statements of the entity that has the foreign currency exposure. However, as an exception, an unrealised exchange gain is recognised in other comprehensive income. *[FRS 102.30.12-30.13]*. This treatment results from the general restriction in the CA 2006 from recognising unrealised profits in the profit and loss account. The ICAEW/ICAS Technical Release TECH 02/17BL – *Guidance on realised and distributable profits under the Companies Act 2006* (TECH 02/17BL) explains that a receivable for which settlement is neither planned nor likely to occur in the foreseeable future is not qualifying consideration and therefore any cumulative exchange gain on such on an asset is not a realised profit (see 4 below). *[TECH 02/17BL.3.11]*.

3.7.7 Monetary items becoming part of the net investment in a foreign operation

An entity's plans and expectations in respect of an intragroup monetary item may change over time and the status of such items should be assessed each period. For example, a parent may decide that its subsidiary requires refinancing and instead of investing more equity capital in the subsidiary decides that an existing inter-company account, which has previously been regarded as a normal monetary item, should become a long-term deferred trading balance and no repayment of such amount will be requested within the foreseeable future. In our view, such a 'capital injection' should be regarded as having occurred at the time it is decided to redesignate the inter-company account. Consequently, the exchange differences arising on the account up to that date should be recognised in profit or loss and the exchange differences arising thereafter would be recognised in other comprehensive income on consolidation. This is discussed further in the following example.

Example 27.11: Monetary item becoming part of the net investment in a foreign operation

A UK entity has a wholly owned Canadian subsidiary whose net assets at 31 December 2018 were C$2,000,000. These net assets were arrived at after taking account of a liability to the UK parent of £250,000. Using the closing exchange rate of £1=C$2.35 this liability was included in the Canadian company's balance sheet at that date at C$587,500. On 30 June 2019, when the exchange rate was £1=C$2.45, the parent decided that in order to refinance the Canadian subsidiary it would regard the liability of £250,000 as a long-term liability which would not be called for repayment in the foreseeable future. Consequently, the parent thereafter regarded the loan as being part of its net investment in the subsidiary. In the year ended 31 December 2019 the Canadian company made no profit or loss other than any exchange difference to be recognised on its liability to its parent. The relevant exchange rate at that date was £1=C$2.56. The average exchange rate for the year ended 31 December 2019 was £1=C$2.50.

The financial statements of the subsidiary in C$ and translated using the closing rate are as follows:

Balance sheet	31 December 2019		31 December 2018	
	C$	£	C$	£
Assets	2,587,500	1,010,742	2,587,500	1,101,064
Amount due to parent	(640,000)	(250,000)	(587,500)	(250,000)
Net assets	1,947,500	760,742	2,000,000	851,064

Income statement	
Exchange difference	(52,500)

If the amount due to the parent is not part of the parent's net investment in the foreign operation, this exchange loss would be translated at the average rate and included in the consolidated profit and loss account as £21,000. As the net investment was C$2,000,000 then there would have been an exchange loss recognised in other comprehensive income of £69,814, i.e. £851,064 less £781,250 (C$2,000,000 @ £1=C$2.56), together with an exchange gain of £492, being the difference between profit or loss translated at average rate, i.e. £21,000, and at the closing rate, i.e. £20,508.

However, the parent now regards the amount due as being part of the net investment in the subsidiary. The question then arises as to when this should be regarded as having happened and how the exchange difference on it should be calculated. No guidance is given in Section 30.

In our view, the 'capital injection' should be regarded as having occurred at the time it is decided to redesignate the inter-company account. The exchange differences arising on the account up to that date should be recognised in profit or loss. Only the exchange difference arising thereafter would be recognised in other comprehensive income on consolidation. The inter-company account that was converted into a long-term loan becomes part of the entity's (UK parent's) net investment in the foreign operation (Canadian subsidiary) at the moment in time when the entity decides that settlement is neither planned nor likely to occur in the foreseeable future, i.e. 30 June 2019. Accordingly, exchange differences arising on the long-term loan are recognised in other

Chapter 27

comprehensive income and accumulated in a separate component of equity from that date. The same accounting treatment would have been applied if a capital injection had taken place at the date of redesignation.

At 30 June 2019 the subsidiary would have translated the inter-company account as C$612,500 (£250,000 @ £1=C$2.45) and therefore the exchange loss up to that date was C$25,000. Translated at the average rate this amount would be included in consolidated profit or loss as £10,000, with only an exchange gain of £234 recognised in other comprehensive income, being the difference between profit or loss translated at average rate, i.e. £10,000, and at the closing rate, i.e. £9,766. Accordingly, £11,000 (£21,000 less £10,000) offset by a reduction in the exchange gain on the translation of profit or loss of £258 (£492 less £234) would be recognised in other comprehensive income. This amount represents the exchange loss on the 'capital injection' of C$612,500. Translated at the closing rate this amounts to £239,258 which is £10,742 less than the original £250,000.

Some might argue that an approach of regarding the 'capital injection' as having occurred at the beginning of the accounting period would have the merit of treating all of the exchange differences for this year in the same way. However, for the reasons provided above we do not regard such an approach as being acceptable.

Suppose, instead of the inter-company account being £250,000, it was denominated in dollars at C$587,500. In this case the parent would be exposed to the exchange risk; what would be the position?

The subsidiary's net assets at both 31 December 2018 and 2019 would be:

Assets	C$2,587,500
Amount due to parent	(587,500)
Net assets	C$2,000,000

As the inter-company account is expressed in Canadian dollars, there will be no exchange difference thereon in the subsidiary's profit or loss.

There will, however, be an exchange loss in the parent as follows:

C$587,500	@ 2.35 =	£250,000
	@ 2.56 =	£229,492
		£20,508

In the consolidated financial statements some of this amount should be recognised in other comprehensive income as the inter-company account is now regarded as part of the equity investment. For the reasons stated above, in our view it is only the exchange differences that have arisen after the date of redesignation, i.e. 30 June 2019, that should be recognised in other comprehensive income.

On this basis, the exchange loss would be split as follows:

C$587,500	@ 2.35 =	£250,000
	@ 2.45 =	£239,796
		£10,204
	@ 2.45 =	£239,796
	@ 2.56 =	£229,492
		£10,304

The exchange loss up to 30 June 2019 of £10,204 would be recognised in consolidated profit or loss and the exchange loss thereafter of £10,304 would be recognised in other comprehensive income. This is different from when the account was expressed in sterling because the 'capital injection' in this case is C$587,500 whereas before it was effectively C$612,500.

3.7.8 Monetary items ceasing to be part of the net investment in a foreign operation

The situation where a pre-existing monetary item was subsequently considered to form part of the net investment in a foreign operation was discussed at 3.7.7 above.

However, what happens where a monetary item ceases to be considered part of the net investment in a foreign operation, either because the circumstances have changed such that it is now planned or is likely to be settled in the foreseeable future or indeed that the monetary item is in fact settled?

Where the circumstances have changed such that the monetary item is now planned or is likely to be settled in the foreseeable future, then similar issues to those discussed at 3.7.4 above apply; i.e. are the exchange differences on the intragroup balance to be recognised in profit or loss only from the date of change or from the beginning of the financial year? For the same reasons as set out in Example 27.11 above, in our view, the monetary item ceases to form part of the net investment in the foreign operation at the moment in time when the entity decides that settlement is planned or is likely to occur in the foreseeable future. Accordingly, exchange differences arising on the monetary item up to that date are recognised in other comprehensive income and accumulated in a separate component of equity. The exchange differences that arise after that date are recognised in profit or loss.

Consideration also needs to be given as to the treatment of the cumulative exchange differences on the monetary item that have been recognised in other comprehensive income, including those that had been recognised in other comprehensive income in prior years. The treatment of these exchange differences is to recognise them in other comprehensive income and accumulate them in a separate component of equity. *[FRS 102.30.22]*. The principle question is whether the change in circumstances or actual settlement in cash of the intragroup balance represents a disposal or partial disposal of the foreign operation and this is considered in more detail at 3.8 below.

3.7.9   Dividends

If a subsidiary pays a dividend to the parent during the year the parent should record the dividend at the rate ruling when the dividend was declared. An exchange difference will arise in the parent's own financial statements if the exchange rate moves between the declaration date and the date the dividend is actually received. This exchange difference is required to be recognised in profit or loss and will remain there on consolidation.

The same will apply if the subsidiary declares a dividend to its parent on the last day of its financial year and this is recorded at the year-end in both entities' financial statements. There is no problem in that year as both the intragroup balances and the dividends will eliminate on consolidation with no exchange differences arising. However, as the dividend will not be received until the following year an exchange difference will arise in the parent's financial statements in that year if exchange rates have moved in the meantime. Again, this exchange difference should remain in consolidated profit or loss as it is no different from any other exchange difference arising on intragroup balances resulting from other types of intragroup transactions. It should not be recognised in other comprehensive income.

It may seem odd that the consolidated results can be affected by exchange differences on inter-company dividends. However, once the dividend has been declared, the parent now effectively has a functional currency exposure to assets that were previously regarded as part of the net investment. In order to minimise the effect of exchange rate movements entities should, therefore, arrange for inter-company dividends to be paid on the same day the dividend is declared, or as soon after the dividend is declared as possible.

3.7.10   Unrealised profits on intragroup transactions

The other problem area is the elimination of unrealised profits resulting from intragroup transactions when one of the parties to the transaction is a foreign subsidiary.

Example 27.12:   Unrealised profits on intragroup transaction

A UK parent has a wholly owned Swiss subsidiary. On 30 November 2019 the subsidiary sold goods to the parent for CHF1,000. The cost of the goods to the subsidiary was CHF700. The goods were recorded by the parent at £685 based on the exchange rate ruling on 30 November 2019 of £1=CHF1.46. All of the goods are unsold by the year-end, 31 December 2019. The exchange rate at that date was £1=CHF1.52. How should the intragroup profit be eliminated?

Neither Section 30 nor IAS 21 contain specific guidance on this matter. However, US GAAP requires the rate ruling at the date of the transaction to be used.

If the exchange rate ruling at the date of the transaction is used, the profit shown by the subsidiary is CHF300 which translated at £1=CHF1.46 equals £205. Consequently, the goods will be included in the balance sheet at:

Per parent company balance sheet	£685
Less unrealised profit eliminated	£(205)
	£480

It can be seen that the resulting figure for inventory is equivalent to the original CHF cost translated at the rate ruling on the date of the transaction. Whereas if the subsidiary still held the inventory it would be included at £461 (CHF700 @ £1=CHF1.52).

If in the above example the goods had been sold by the UK parent to the Swiss subsidiary then the approach in US GAAP would say the amount to be eliminated is the amount of profit shown in the UK entity's financial statements. Again, this will not necessarily result in the goods being carried in the consolidated financial statements at their original cost to the group.

3.7.11   Non-coterminous period ends

Unlike IAS 21, Section 30 does not deal with situations where a foreign operation is consolidated on the basis of financial statements made up to a different date from that of the reporting entity. However, in accordance with the hierarchy set out in Section 10 an entity could apply the guidance in IAS 21. In such a case, IAS 21 initially states that the assets and liabilities of the foreign operation are translated at the exchange rate at the end of the reporting period of the foreign operation rather than at the date of the consolidated financial statements. However, it then goes on to say that adjustments are made for significant changes in exchange rates up to the end of the reporting period of the reporting entity (i.e. the date of the consolidated financial statements). This approach is consistent with the requirements in paragraph 16(a) of Section 9 – *Consolidated and Separate Financial Statements* – which requires that adjustments be made for the effects of significant transactions that occur between the date of subsidiary financial statements and the date of the consolidated financial statements. The same approach is used in applying the equity method to associates and joint ventures in accordance with IAS 28 – *Investments in Associates and Joint Ventures*.

3.7.12   Goodwill and fair value adjustments

Any goodwill arising on the acquisition of a foreign operation and any fair value adjustments to the carrying amounts of assets and liabilities arising on the acquisition of that foreign operation are treated as assets and liabilities of the foreign operation.

Therefore, they are expressed in the functional currency of the foreign operation and translated at the closing rate in accordance with paragraph 30.18. *[FRS 102.30.23]*.

3.8 Disposal of a foreign operation

Exchange differences resulting from the translation of a foreign operation to a different presentation currency are to be recognised in other comprehensive income and accumulated within a separate component of equity (see 3.7.1 above).

On the disposal of a foreign operation, the exchange differences relating to that foreign operation that have been recognised in other comprehensive income and accumulated in the separate component of equity are not recognised in profit or loss. *[FRS 102.30.13]*. Instead, the cumulative exchange differences relating to the foreign operation that have accumulated in the separate component of equity should be transferred directly to retained earnings on disposal. *[FRS 102.9.18A-18.B]*.

This is a clear difference to IAS 21 which requires reclassification of the exchange differences from equity to profit or loss on disposal of the foreign operation.

Example 27.13: Disposal of a foreign operation

A UK entity has a Swiss subsidiary which was set up on 1 January 2016 with a share capital of CHF200,000 when the exchange rate was £1=CHF1.55. The subsidiary is included in the parent's separate financial statements at its original cost of £129,032. The profits of the subsidiary, all of which it has retained, for each of the three years ended 31 December 2018 were CHF40,000, CHF50,000 and CHF60,000 respectively, so that the net assets at 31 December 2018 are CHF350,000. In the consolidated financial statements the results of the subsidiary have been translated at the respective average rates of £1=CHF1.60, £1=CHF1.68 and £1=CHF1.70 and the net assets at the respective closing rates of £1=CHF1.71, £1=CHF1.65 and £1=CHF1.66. All exchange differences have been recognised in other comprehensive income and accumulated in a separate exchange reserve. The consolidated reserves have therefore included the following amounts in respect of the subsidiary:

	Retained profit £	Exchange reserve £
1 January 2016	–	–
Movement during 2016	25,000	(13,681)
31 December 2016	25,000	(13,681)
Movement during 2017	29,762	5,645
31 December 2017	54,762	(8,036)
Movement during 2018	35,294	(209)
31 December 2018	90,056	(8,245)

The net assets at 31 December 2018 of CHF350,000 are included in the consolidated financial statements at £210,843.

On 1 January 2019 the subsidiary is sold for CHF400,000 (£240,964), thus resulting in a gain on disposal in the parent entity's books of £111,932, i.e. £240,964 less £129,032.

In the consolidated financial statements for 2018, Section 9 and Section 30 requires the cumulative exchange losses of £8,245 to be transferred directly to retained earnings without being recognised in profit or loss. The gain recognised in the consolidated financial statements would be £30,121 (the difference between the proceeds of £240,964 and net asset value of £210,843 at the date of disposal).

Chapter 27

3.9   Tax effects of all exchange differences

Gains and losses on foreign currency transactions and exchange differences arising on translating the results and financial position of an entity (including a foreign operation) into a different currency may have tax effects to which Section 29 – *Income Tax* – applies. The requirements of Section 29 are discussed in Chapter 26. In broad terms the tax effects of exchange differences will follow the reporting of the exchange differences, i.e. they will be recognised in profit or loss except to the extent they relate to exchange differences recognised in other comprehensive income, in which case they will also be recognised in other comprehensive income. *[FRS 102.29.22]*.

3.10   Change of presentation currency

Neither Section 30 nor IAS 21 address how an entity should approach presenting its financial statements if it changes its presentation currency. This is a situation that is commonly faced when the reporting entity determines that its functional currency has changed (see 3.6 above). However, because entities have a free choice of their presentation currency it can occur in other situations too.

Changing presentation currency is, in our view, similar to a change in accounting policy, the requirements for which are set out in Section 10. Therefore, when an entity chooses to change its presentation currency, we consider it appropriate to follow the approach in Section 10 which requires retrospective application except to the extent it is impracticable (see Chapter 9 at 3.4.2). Comparatives should be restated and presented in the new presentation currency. Further, they should be prepared as if this had always been the entity's presentation currency (at least to the extent practicable). The following example illustrates the impact of a change in presentation currency in a relatively simple group.

Example 27.14:   Change of presentation currency

A UK parent, P, was established on 1 January 2017 and issued new shares for £20 million. On the same date it established two wholly owned subsidiaries, S1 and S2 incorporated in the UK and Canada respectively and subscribed £10 million and C$4.5 million for their entire share capital. The functional currency of each group company was determined to be its local currency, i.e. pound sterling for P and S1 and Canadian dollars for S2.

During 2017, S1 made a profit of £800,000, S2 made a profit of C$350,000 and P made a loss of £25,000. On 30 September 2017, P issued new shares for £10 million of which C$4 million was used immediately to subscribe for additional shares in S2.

During 2018, S1 made a profit of £700,000, S2 made a profit of C$750,000 and P made a loss of £30,000 before dividends received from S2. On 30 June 2018, S2 paid dividends (out of profits then made) of C$700,000 to P and on 30 September 2018 P paid dividends of £1,000,000 to its shareholders.

The relevant exchange rates for £1=C$ were as follows:

1 January 2017	2.10
30 September 2017	2.28
31 December 2017	2.35
Average for 2017	2.24
30 June 2018	2.55
30 September 2018	2.63
31 December 2018	2.40
Average for 2018	2.52

Consequently, the statement of changes in equity in P's consolidated financial statements for 2017 and 2018 can be summarised as follows:

	Share capital £	Retained earnings £	Foreign exchange £	Total £
1 January 2017	–	–	–	–
Issue of shares	30,000,000	–	–	30,000,000
Comprehensive income	–	931,250	(287,536)	643,714
31 December 2017	30,000,000	931,250	(287,536)	30,643,714
Comprehensive income	–	967,619	(80,733)	886,886
Dividends	–	(1,000,000)	–	(1,000,000)
31 December 2018	30,000,000	898,869	(368,269)	30,530,600

The comprehensive income reflected within retained earnings represents the profit for each year, calculated as follows:

2017: £800,000 + (C$350,000 ÷ 2.24) – £25,000 = £931,250

2018: £700,000 + (C$750,000 ÷ 2.52) – £30,000 = £967,619

The foreign exchange differences recognised in other comprehensive income can be calculated as follows:

	2017			*2018*		
	C$	Rate	£	C$	Rate	£
Opening net assets*	4,500,000	2.10	2,142,857	8,850,000	2.35	3,765,957
		2.35	1,914,893		2.40	3,687,500
Exchange loss			(227,964)			(78,457)
Additional capital	4,000,000	2.28	1,754,386	–	–	–
		2.35	1,702,128		–	–
Exchange loss			(52,258)			–
Dividend	–	–	–	(700,000)	2.55	(274,510)
					2.40	(291,667)
Exchange loss			–			(17,157)
Profit	350,000	2.24	156,250	750,000	2.52	297,619
		2.35	148,936		2.40	312,500
Exchange (loss)/gain			(7,314)			14,881
	8,850,000		(287,536)	8,900,000		(80,733)

* for 2017, includes the proceeds received for issuing shares on 1 January.

For the year ended 31 December 2019, P decided to change its presentation currency to Canadian dollars. (This may or may not have coincided with a change of P's functional currency.) The remainder of this example illustrates how one might determine the amounts to be included in respect of the comparative period in P's consolidated financial statements for the year ended 31 December 2019.

Chapter 27

The revised statement of changes in equity in P's consolidated financial statements can be summarised as follows and these are the amounts that will be reflected as comparative amounts in P's consolidated financial statements for the year ended 31 December 2019:

	Share capital C$	Retained earnings C$	Foreign exchange C$	Total C$
1 January 2017	–	–	–	–
Issue of shares	64,800,000	–	–	64,800,000
Comprehensive income	–	2,086,000	5,126,729	7,212,729
31 December 2017	64,800,000	2,086,000	5,126,729	72,012,729
Comprehensive income	–	2,438,400	1,452,311	3,890,711
Dividends	–	(2,630,000)	–	(2,630,000)
31 December 2018	64,800,000	1,894,400	6,579,040	73,273,440

FRS 102 does not address the exchange rate to use when recording equity instruments issued such as share capital. In the example P uses the historical exchange rates at the date the equity instruments were issued on the basis that they are non-monetary items (C$64,800,000 = £20,000,000 × 2.10 + £10,000,000 × 2.28). Even if P retranslated those amounts at year end rates any difference arising would simply be recorded in another component of equity and this difference would not affect profit or loss or other comprehensive income in any period.

The calculations showing how these amounts have been determined are shown below.

The comprehensive income reflected within retained earnings represents the profit for each year, calculated as follows:

$$2017: (£800,000 × 2.24) + C\$350,000 – (£25,000 × 2.24) = C\$2,086,000$$

$$2018: (£700,000 × 2.52) + C\$750,000 – (£30,000 × 2.52) = C\$2,438,400$$

In this case, the profit calculated in this way results in the same amount as translating the consolidated profit of £931,250 and £967,619 presented in sterling at the average rate for the period of £1=C$2.24 and £1=C$2.52 respectively. In practice minor differences can arise as a result of imperfections in the average rates used.

Similarly, the net assets presented above are the same as the amounts obtained by translating consolidated net assets of £30,643,714 and £30,530,600 at the closing rates at the end of the relevant period, £1=C$2.35 and £1=C$2.40 respectively. This should always be the case.

However, the foreign exchange reserve is fundamentally different to that in the financial statements presented in sterling. In this case it represents exchange differences arising from the translation of both P's and S1's financial statements into Canadian dollars whereas previously it represented exchange differences arising from the translation of S2's financial statements into sterling.

The foreign exchange differences recognised in other comprehensive income can be calculated as follows:

	£	2017 Rate	C$	£	2018 Rate	C$
Opening net assets*	17,857,143	2.10	37,500,000	26,877,757	2.35	63,162,729
		2.35	41,964,286		2.40	64,506,617
Exchange gain			4,464,286			1,343,888
Additional capital**	8,245,614	2.28	18,800,000	–	–	–
		2.35	19,377,193			
Exchange gain			577,193			–
Dividend received	–	–	–	274,510	2.55	700,000
					2.40	658,824
Exchange loss			–			(41,176)
Dividend paid	–	–	–	(1,000,000)	2.63	(2,630,000)
					2.40	(2,400,000)
Exchange loss			–			230,000
Profit***	775,000	2.24	1,736,000	670,000	2.52	1,688,400
		2.35	1,821,250		2.40	1,608,000
Exchange gain			85,250			(80,400)
	26,877,757		5,126,729	26,822,267		1,452,311

*   for 2017, includes the proceeds received for issuing shares on 1 January (£20,000,000) less amounts invested in S2 (£2,142,857 = C$4,500,000 ÷ 2.10) on the same date.

** reduced by the amounts invested in S2 on the same date (£10,000,000 – (C$4,000,000 ÷ 2.28)).

*** profits of S1 (£800,000 and £700,000 in 2017 and 2018 respectively) less losses of P (£25,000 and £30,000 in 2017 and 2018).

In the example above, it was reasonably straightforward to recreate the consolidated equity balances using the new presentation currency. This is because the group had a very simple structure with operations having only two functional currencies, a short history and few (external and internal) equity transactions. Whilst entities should strive for a theoretically perfect restatement, in practice it is unlikely to be such an easy exercise.

As noted above, where an accounting policy is changed, Section 10 requires retrospective application except to the extent that this is impracticable, in which case an entity should adjust the comparative information to apply the new accounting policy prospectively from the earliest practicable date. A similar approach is, in our view, appropriate when an entity changes its presentation currency.

3.11   Disclosure requirements

Section 30 requires an entity to disclose:

(a)   the amount of exchange differences recognised in profit or loss during the period, except for those arising on financial instruments measured at fair value through profit or loss in accordance with Section 11 and Section 12; *[FRS 102.30.25(a)]*

(b)   the amount of exchange differences recognised in other comprehensive income arising during the period; *[FRS 102.30.25(b)]*

(c)   the currency in which the financial statements are presented. When the presentation currency is different from the functional currency, the entity should state that fact and should disclose the functional currency and the reason for using a different presentation currency. *[FRS 102.30.26]*. For this purpose, in the case of a group, the references to 'functional currency' are to that of the parent; *[FRS 102.30.24]* and

(d)   when there is a change in the functional currency of either the reporting entity (the parent in the case of consolidated financial statements) or a significant foreign operation, that fact and the reason for the change in functional currency. *[FRS 102.30.24, 27]*.

4   UK COMPANY LAW MATTERS

The CA 2006 contains a general prohibition against recognising unrealised profits in profit and loss, although there is an exception to this rule when the fair value provisions of the Act are applied.

TECH 02/17BL provides guidance on realised and distributable profits under the CA 2006. The main aspects of TECH 02/17BL that deal with foreign exchange are:

- Unless there are doubts as to the convertibility or marketability of the currency in question, foreign exchange profits arising on the retranslation of monetary items are realised, irrespective of the maturity date of the monetary item. However, a profit on retranslation of a monetary asset will not be a realised profit where the underlying balance on which the exchange difference arises does not itself meet the definition of 'qualifying consideration' – e.g. some long term intercompany balances. *[TECH 02/17BL.3.21]*. This principle is replicated in FRS 102, see 3.7.6 above.

- Realised profits and losses are measured by reference to the functional currency of the company. *[TECH 02/17BL.11.7]*. Therefore an accounting gain or loss arising from the retranslation of an entity's accounts from its functional currency to a presentation currency is not a profit or loss as a matter of law. It cannot therefore be a realised profit or loss. *[TECH 02/17BL.11.8]*.

- The profit or loss arising on the necessary retranslation of an autonomous branch, from its functional currency into the functional currency of the company, is a realised profit or loss to the extent that the branch net assets were qualifying consideration when the profit or loss arose. *[TECH 02/17BL.11.12]*.

- Where a company's shares, irrespective of whether those shares are classified as equity or debt for accounting purposes, are denominated in a currency other than the company's functional currency, the adjustment arising upon any translation for accounting purposes of the share capital is not a profit or loss at law. Therefore it is not a realised profit or loss. *[TECH 02/17BL.11.18]*.

- Where share capital is denominated in a currency other than the functional currency, it is fixed at that other currency amount. A distribution cannot be made if it would reduce the company's net assets below the level of the company's share capital. *[TECH 02/17BL.11.21]*. This needs to be considered when assessing the distribution that can be made.

5 SUMMARY OF GAAP DIFFERENCES

The key differences between FRS 102 and IFRS in accounting for foreign currency translation are set out below.

	FRS 102	*IFRS*
Disposal of a foreign operation	On disposal of a foreign operation, the exchange differences relating to that foreign operation that have been accumulated in the separate component of equity are not recognised in profit and loss. The cumulative exchange differences are transferred directly to retained earnings on disposal.	Exchange differences arising on translation of a foreign operation that have been accumulated in equity are reclassified to profit and loss on disposal of the net investment.
Exchange gains on intercompany balances forming part of the net investment in a foreign operation	Exchange differences arising on a monetary item that forms part of a reporting entity's net investment in a foreign operation are recognised in profit or loss in the separate financial statements of the reporting entity or the individual financial statements of the foreign operation, as appropriate, except that any unrealised gain is recognised in other comprehensive income.	Exchange differences arising on a monetary item that forms part of a reporting entity's net investment in a foreign operation are recognised in profit or loss in the separate financial statements of the reporting entity or the individual financial statements of the foreign operation, as appropriate.

Chapter 27

Chapter 28   Hyperinflation

Chapter 28   Hyperinflation

1   INTRODUCTION

1.1   The concept of hyperinflation

Accounting standards are applied on the assumption that the value of money (the unit of measurement) is constant over time, which normally is an acceptable practical assumption. However, when the effect of inflation on the value of money is no longer negligible, the usefulness of historical cost based financial reporting is often significantly reduced. High rates of inflation give rise to a number of problems for entities that prepare their financial statements on a historical cost basis, for example:

- historical cost figures expressed in terms of monetary units do not show the 'value to the business' of assets;

- holding gains on non-monetary assets that are reported as operating profits do not represent real economic gains;

- financial information presented for the current period is not comparable with that presented for the prior periods; and

- real capital can be reduced because profits reported do not take account of the higher replacement costs of resources used in the period. Therefore, if calculating a nominal return on capital based on profit, and not distinguishing this properly from a real return of capital, the erosion of capital may go unnoticed in the financial statements. This is the underlying point in the concept of capital maintenance.

For entities used to working in economies with low inflation it is easy to overlook that there are countries where inflation is still a major economic concern. In some of these countries, inflation has reached such levels that (1) the local currency is no longer a useful measure of value in the economy and (2) the general population may prefer not to hold its wealth in the local currency. Instead, they hold their wealth in a stable foreign currency or in non-monetary assets. Such a condition is often referred to as hyperinflation.

1.2   Relevance in the UK

Section 31 – *Hyperinflation* – sets out the accounting requirements for an entity that has a functional currency which is the currency of a hyperinflationary economy. It requires such an entity to prepare financial statements that have been adjusted for the effects of hyperinflation. *[FRS 102.31.1]*. These accounting requirements are set out at 3.4 below.

The UK clearly does not suffer from hyperinflation, but it would be theoretically possible, although extremely unlikely, for a UK company to have the functional currency of a hyperinflationary economy. In that case, the requirements of Section 31 would apply in full to the accounting and disclosures in that company's own financial statements.

A more likely scenario would be that of a UK based group preparing consolidated financial statements under FRS 102 with a subsidiary that operates in, and has a functional currency of, a country subject to hyperinflation. This is discussed at 3.5 below.

2   COMPARISON BETWEEN SECTION 31 AND IFRS

There is little substantive difference between the accounting and disclosure requirements in Section 31 compared to IFRS (IAS 29 – *Financial Reporting in Hyperinflationary Economies*). However, IAS 29 does contain more application guidance.

The Triennial review 2017 amended Section 31 to address situations where non-monetary items, such as property, plant and equipment have been revalued at an earlier date. Under Section 31, the revaluation reserve is not restated when adjustments are made for the effects of hyperinflation, the difference arising being included in retained earnings. This reflects the requirement under company law to maintain a revaluation reserve and is therefore a difference from IAS 29 (see 3.4.1 below).

3   REQUIREMENTS OF SECTION 31 FOR HYPERINFLATION

3.1   Terms used in Section 31

The key terms used within Section 31 have the meanings specified in the following table:
[FRS 102 Appendix I]

Term	Definition
Functional currency	The currency of the primary economic environment in which the entity operates.
Monetary items	Units of currency held and assets and liabilities to be received or paid in a fixed or determinable number of units of currency.
Presentation currency	The currency in which the financial statements are presented.

3.2   A hyperinflationary economy

Section 31 does not establish an absolute level at which an economy is deemed hyperinflationary. An entity should make that judgement by considering all available information including, but not limited to, the following possible indicators of hyperinflation: *[FRS 102.31.2]*

(a)   The general population prefers to keep its wealth in non-monetary assets or in a relatively stable foreign currency. Amounts of local currency held are immediately invested to maintain purchasing power.

(b)   The general population regards monetary amounts not in terms of the local currency but in terms of a relatively stable foreign currency. Prices may be quoted in that currency.

(c)   Sales and purchases on credit take place at prices that compensate for the expected loss of purchasing power during the credit period, even if the period is short.

(d)   Interest rates, wages and prices are linked to a price index.

(e)   The cumulative inflation rate over three years is approaching, or exceeds, 100 per cent.

For reporting under US accounting standards, the International Practices Task Force (IPTF), a task force of the SEC Regulations Committee, monitors the inflation status of different countries. As the IPTF's criteria are similar to those used under IFRS, this provides a useful guide for entities reporting under IFRS, and hence would inform an assessment of whether an economy is hyperinflationary for FRS 102 purposes.

3.3   Measuring unit in the financial statements

Section 31 requires the following approach: *[FRS 102.31.3]*

- amounts in the financial statements of an entity whose functional currency is the currency of a hyperinflationary economy should be stated in terms of the measuring unit current at the end of the reporting period; and

- the comparative information in those financial statements for the previous period required by Section 3 – *Financial Statement Presentation*, paragraph 14, and any information presented in respect of earlier periods, should also be stated in terms of the measuring unit current at the reporting date.

The restatement of financial statements in accordance with Section 31 requires the use of a general price index that reflects changes in general purchasing power. Section 31 says that in most economies there is a recognised general price index, normally produced by the government, which entities will follow. *[FRS 102.31.4]*.

However, as noted below, in more extreme cases of hyperinflation such indices may not be available, especially if the prevailing circumstances that led to hyperinflation significantly impact the operation of governmental and/or social systems.

Section 31 provides no further guidance on what is meant by a general price index. It is generally accepted practice to use a Consumer Price Index (CPI) for this purpose, unless that index is clearly flawed. National statistical offices in most countries issue several price indices that potentially could be used for the purposes of Section 31. Important characteristics of a good general price index include the following:

- a wide range of goods and services has been included in the price index;

- continuity and consistency of measurement techniques and underlying assumptions;

- free from bias;

- frequently updated; and

- available for a long period.

The entity should assess the above characteristics and select the most reliable and most readily available general price index and use that index consistently. It is important that the index selected is representative of the real position of the hyperinflationary currency concerned.

If the general price index is not available for all periods for which the restatement of long-lived assets is required, then FRS 102 offers no guidance. However, using the FRS 102 hierarchy, an entity is permitted to refer to IAS 29 which requires an entity to make an estimate of the price index. The entity could base the estimate, for example, on the movements in the exchange rate between the functional currency and a relatively stable foreign currency. *[IAS 29.17].*

Entities could use a similar approach to estimating a price index when they cannot find a general price index that is sufficiently reliable (e.g. if the national statistical office in the hyperinflationary economy is subject to significant political bias). However, this would only be acceptable if all available general price indices are fatally flawed.

It should be noted that this method of determining the price index is only acceptable if the currency of the hyperinflationary economy is freely exchangeable, i.e. not subject to currency controls and 'official' exchange rates. Entities should be mindful that, especially in the short term, the exchange rate may fluctuate significantly in response to factors other than changes in the domestic price level.

3.4   Procedures for restating historical cost financial statements

3.4.1   *Statement of financial position*

Amounts in the statement of financial position that are not expressed in terms of the measuring unit current at the end of the reporting period are restated by applying a general price index as discussed below. *[FRS 102.31.5].*

Monetary items (money held and items to be received or paid in money) are not restated because they are expressed in terms of the measuring unit current at the end of the reporting period. *[FRS 102.31.6].*

Assets and liabilities linked by agreement to changes in prices, such as index-linked bonds and loans, are adjusted in accordance with the agreement and presented at this adjusted amount in the restated statement of financial position. *[FRS 102.31.7].*

All other assets and liabilities are non-monetary: *[FRS 102.31.8]*

(a)   Some non-monetary items are carried at amounts current at the end of the reporting period, such as net realisable value and fair value, so they are not restated. All other non-monetary assets and liabilities are restated using the approach in (b) to (d) as appropriate.

(b)   Most non-monetary items are carried at cost or cost less depreciation; hence they are expressed at amounts current at their date of acquisition. The restated cost, or cost less depreciation, of each item is determined by applying to its historical cost and accumulated depreciation the change in a general price index from the date of acquisition to the end of the reporting period.

(c)   Some non-monetary items are carried at amounts that were current at dates other than that of acquisition or the reporting date, for example, property, plant and equipment that has been revalued at some earlier date. In these cases, the carrying amounts are restated by applying to the revalued amount the change in a general price index from the date of the revaluation to the end of the reporting period.

(d) The restated amount of a non-monetary item is reduced, in accordance with Section 27 – *Impairment of Assets* (see Chapter 24), when it exceeds its recoverable amount.

At the beginning of the first period of application of Section 31, the components of equity, except retained earnings and any revaluation surplus, are restated by applying a general price index from the dates the components were contributed or otherwise arose. Any revaluation surplus that arose in previous periods is not restated. This is a new requirement brought in by the Triennial review 2017 reflecting the requirement under company law to maintain a revaluation reserve. Restated retained earnings are derived from all the other amounts in the restated statement of financial position, including the effect of not restating the revaluation reserve. Retained earnings is essentially the balancing figure after all other restatements. *[FRS 102.31.9]*.

At the end of the first period in which hyperinflation arises and in subsequent periods, all components of owners' equity are restated by applying a general price index from the beginning of the period or the date of contribution, if later. The changes for the period in owners' equity are disclosed in accordance with Section 6 – *Statement of Changes in Equity and Statement of Income and Retained Earnings* (see Chapter 6). *[FRS 102.31.10]*.

3.4.2 Statement of comprehensive income and income statement

All items in the statement of comprehensive income (and in the income statement, if presented) should be expressed in terms of the measuring unit current at the end of the reporting period. Therefore, all amounts need to be restated by applying the change in the general price index from the dates when the items of income and expenses were initially recognised in the financial statements. If general inflation is approximately even throughout the period, and the items of income and expense arose approximately evenly throughout the period, an average rate of inflation may be appropriate. *[FRS 102.31.11]*.

3.4.3 Statement of cash flows

An entity should express all items in the statement of cash flows in terms of the measuring unit current at the end of the reporting period. *[FRS 102.31.12]*.

3.4.4 Gain or loss on net monetary position

In a period of inflation, an entity holding an excess of monetary assets over monetary liabilities loses purchasing power, and an entity with an excess of monetary liabilities over monetary assets gains purchasing power, to the extent the assets and liabilities are not linked to a price level. An entity should therefore include in profit or loss the gain or loss on the net monetary position, except that any unrealised gain shall be recognised in other comprehensive income. An entity should offset the adjustment to those assets and liabilities linked by agreement to changes in prices (see 3.4.1 above) against the gain or loss on net monetary position. *[FRS 102.31.13]*.

3.4.5   Comparative information

As noted at 3.3 above, comparative information in financial statements should also be stated in terms of the measuring unit current at the end of the reporting period. *[FRS 102.31.3]*. This means the comparative information will require restatement using the relevant general price index.

3.4.6   Economies ceasing to be hyperinflationary

When an economy ceases to be hyperinflationary and an entity discontinues the application of Section 31, it should treat the amounts expressed in the presentation currency at the end of the previous reporting period as the basis for the carrying amounts in its subsequent financial statements. *[FRS 102.31.14]*.

3.5   Accounting for a hyperinflationary subsidiary in consolidated financial statements

As previously mentioned, a more likely scenario relevant to FRS 102 would be that of a UK based group preparing consolidated financial statements under FRS 102 with a subsidiary that operates in, and has a functional currency of, a country subject to hyperinflation. Section 30 – *Foreign Currency Translation* – requires the subsidiary's results and financial position to be adjusted using the procedures specified in Section 31 (see 3.4 above) before translating them into a different presentation currency using the following procedures (added by the Triennial review 2017): *[FRS 102.30.21]*

- all amounts (i.e. assets, liabilities, equity items, income and expenses, including comparatives) shall be translated at the closing rate at the date of the most recent statement of financial position, except that

- when amounts are translated into the currency of a non-hyperinflationary economy, comparative amounts shall be those that were presented as current year amounts in the relevant prior period financial statements.

3.6   Disclosures

An entity which applies Section 31 in its own financial statements should disclose the following: *[FRS 102.31.15]*

(a)   the fact that financial statements and other prior period data have been restated for changes in the general purchasing power of the functional currency;

(b)   the identity and level of the price index at the reporting date and changes during the current reporting period and the previous reporting period; and

(c)   the amount of gain or loss on monetary items.

Chapter 29   Events after the end of the reporting period

List of examples

Chapter 29   Events after the end of the reporting period

1   INTRODUCTION

Section 32 – *Events after the End of the Reporting Period* – defines events after the end of the reporting period and sets out principles for recognising, measuring and disclosing those events that occur between the end of the reporting period and the date when the financial statements are authorised for issue. *[FRS 102.32.1, 2]*. The definition includes all events occurring between those dates irrespective of whether they relate to conditions that existed at the end of the reporting period. The principal issue is determining which events after the end of the reporting period to reflect in the financial statements as adjustments or by providing additional disclosure.

2   COMPARISON BETWEEN SECTION 32 AND IFRS

There are no key differences between Section 32 and the comparable IFRS standard, IAS 10 – *Events after the Reporting Period.*

3   REQUIREMENTS OF SECTION 32 FOR EVENTS AFTER THE END OF THE REPORTING PERIOD

The following key terms in Section 32 are defined in the Glossary: *[FRS 102 Appendix I]*

Reporting date is the end of the latest period covered by financial statements or by an interim financial report.

Reporting period is the period covered by financial statements or by an interim financial report.

The financial statements of an entity present, among other things, its financial position at the end of the reporting period. Therefore, it is appropriate to adjust the financial statements for all events that offer greater clarity concerning the conditions that existed at the end of the reporting period, that occur prior to the date the financial statements are authorised for issue. Section 32 requires entities to adjust the amounts recognised in the financial statements for 'adjusting events' that provide evidence of conditions that existed at the end of the reporting period. *[FRS 102.32.4]*. An entity does not recognise in the financial statements those events that relate to conditions that arose after the reporting period, 'non-adjusting events'. However, if non-adjusting events are material, Section 32 requires certain disclosures about them. *[FRS 102.32.10]*.

Section 32 deals with the accounting for and the disclosure of events after the reporting period, which are defined as 'those events, favourable and unfavourable, that occur between the end of the reporting period and the date when the financial statements are authorised for issue'. *[FRS 102.32.2]*. The definition includes all events that provide evidence of conditions that existed at the end of the reporting period (adjusting events) and those events that are indicative of conditions that arose after the end of the reporting period (non-adjusting events).

Events after the end of the reporting period include all events that occur up to the date the financial statements are authorised for issue, even if those events occur after the public announcement of profit or loss or other financial information. *[FRS 102.32.3]*.

One exception to the general rule of Section 32 for non-adjusting events is when the going concern basis becomes inappropriate after the reporting period. This is treated as an adjusting event (see 3.3 below). *[FRS 102.32.7A]*.

The requirements of Section 32 and practical issues resulting from these requirements are dealt with below.

3.1   Date when financial statements are authorised for issue

Given the definition above, the meaning of 'the date when the financial statements are authorised for issue' is clearly important. Section 32 states that events after the end of the reporting period include all events up to the date that the financial statements are authorised for issue, even if those events occur after the public announcement of profit or loss or other selected financial information. *[FRS 102.32.3]*.

The example below illustrates a situation when an entity releases preliminary information, but not complete financial statements, before the date of the authorisation for issue.

Example 29.1:   Release of financial information before date of authorisation for issue

The management of an entity completes the primary financial statements for the year to 31 December 20X9 on 21 January 20Y0, but has not yet completed the explanatory notes. On 26 January 20Y0, the board of directors reviews the primary financial statements and authorises them for public media release. The entity announces its profit and certain other financial information on 28 January 20Y0. On 1 February 20Y0 an error is discovered in the year-end stock valuation of £1m. On 11 February 20Y0, management issues the financial statements (with full explanatory notes) to the board of directors, which approves the financial statements for filing on 18 February 20Y0. The entity files the financial statements with a regulatory body on 21 February 20Y0.

The financial statements are authorised for issue on 18 February 20Y0 (date the board of directors, approves the financial statements for filing). Therefore, the error discovered in the year-end stock valuation on 1 February 20Y0, before the financial statements have been authorised for issue, is an adjusting event after the end of the reporting period which must be reflected, if material, in the 31 December 20X9 financial statements (see 3.2.1 below).

Example 29.1 illustrates that events after the reporting period include all events up to the date when the financial statements are authorised for issue, even if those events occur after the public announcement of profit or of other selected financial information.

Accordingly, the information in the financial statements might differ from the equivalent information in a preliminary announcement.

3.1.1 Re-issuing financial statements

Section 32 does not address whether and how an entity may amend its financial statements after they have been authorised for issue. Generally, such matters are dealt with in local regulations. There are a number of reasons why financial statements may be re-issued after they have been authorised for issue, such a reason could be that the original financial statements were defective or the entity is re-issuing financial statement for a listing.

If an entity reissues financial statements to correct an error, the UK *Companies (Revision of Defective Accounts and Reports) Regulation 2008 (SI 2008/373)* should be followed in correcting the defective financial statements. The regulations permit the defective financial statements to be either replaced or revised by a supplementary note. If the financial statements are replaced or revised by a supplementary note, they should appropriately reflect all adjusting events, by updating the amounts recognised in the financial statements, and non-adjusting events, to the date when the original financial statements were approved. This means that the financial statements do not reflect events that occurred between the date when the original financial statements were authorised for issue and the date the revised financial statements were authorised for re-issue.

3.2 Recognition and measurement of events occurring after the end of the reporting period

3.2.1 Adjusting events

Adjusting events are 'those that provide evidence of conditions that existed at the end of the reporting period.' *[FRS 102.32.2(a)]*. An entity shall adjust the amounts recognised in its financial statements, including any related disclosures, to reflect adjusting events. *[FRS 102.32.4]*.

The following are examples of adjusting events after the end of the reporting period that require amounts in the financial statements to be adjusted or to recognise items that were not previously recognised: *[FRS 102.32.5(a)-(e)]*

- The settlement after the end of a reporting period of a court case that confirms that the entity had a present obligation at the end of the reporting period. In this situation, an entity adjusts any previously recognised provision related to this court case under Section 21 – *Provisions and Contingencies* – or recognises a new provision. Mere disclosure of a contingent liability is not sufficient because the settlement provides additional evidence of conditions that existed at the end of the reporting period that would give rise to a provision in accordance with Section 21 (see Chapter 19).

- The receipt of information after the end of the reporting period indicating that an asset was impaired at the end of the reporting period, or that the amount of a previously recognised impairment loss for that asset needs to be adjusted. For example:

  - the bankruptcy of a customer that occurs after the end of the reporting period usually confirms that a loss existed at the end of the reporting period on a

> trade receivable and that the entity needs to adjust the carrying amount of the trade receivable (see 4.3 below); and

- • the sale of inventories after the end of the reporting period may give evidence about their selling price at the end of the reporting period for the purpose of assessing impairment at that date (see 4.1 below).

- • The determination after the end of the reporting period of the cost of assets purchased, or the proceeds from assets sold, before the end of the reporting period.

- • The determination after the end of the reporting period of the amount of profit-sharing or bonus payments, if the entity had a legal or constructive obligation at the end of the reporting period to make such payments as a result of events before that date.

- • The discovery of fraud or errors that show that the financial statements are incorrect (see 4.5 below).

In addition, those entities that apply IAS 33 – *Earnings per Share* – as permitted by Section 1 – *Scope* – are required to make adjustments to earnings per share for certain share transactions after the reporting period (such as bonus issues, share splits or share consolidations), even though the transactions themselves are non-adjusting events (see 3.2.2 below).

3.2.2   Non-adjusting events

Non-adjusting events are 'those that are indicative of conditions that arose after the end of the reporting period'. *[FRS 102.32.2(b)]*. An entity shall not adjust the amounts recognised in its financial statements to reflect non-adjusting events. *[FRS 102.32.6]*.

Examples of non-adjusting events are as follows: *[FRS 102.32.7]*

- • A decline in market value of investments between the end of the reporting period and the date when the financial statements are authorised for issue. The decline in market value does not normally relate to the condition of the investments at the end of the reporting period but reflects circumstances that have arisen subsequent to the end of the reporting period.

- • An amount that becomes receivable as a result of a favourable judgement or settlement of a court case after the reporting date but before the financial statements are authorised for issue. This would be a contingent asset at the reporting date (see Section 21 and Chapter 19) and disclosure may be required. However, if an agreement is reached before the financial statements are authorised for issue, on the amount of damages for a judgement that was reached before the reporting date, but that was not previously recognised on the basis it could not be measured reliably, this may constitute an adjusting event. *[FRS 102.32.7(b)]*.

The following are further examples of non-adjusting events after the end of the reporting period that would generally result in disclosure. The disclosures will reflect information that becomes known after the end of the reporting period but before the financial statements are authorised for issue: *[FRS 102.32.11]*

- • a major business combination or disposal of a major subsidiary (Section 19 – *Business Combinations and Goodwill* – does not require any specific disclosures in respect of business combinations occurring after the reporting date);

- announcing a plan to discontinue an operation;
- major purchases of assets, disposal or plans to dispose of assets, or expropriation of major assets by governments;
- the destruction of a major production plant by a fire;
- announcing, or commencing the implementation of a major restructuring;
- the issue or repurchase of an entity's debt or equity instruments;
- abnormally large changes in asset prices or foreign exchange rates;
- changes in tax rates or tax laws enacted or announced that have a significant effect on current and deferred tax assets and liabilities;
- entering into significant commitments or contingent liabilities, for example, by issuing significant guarantees; and
- commencing major litigation arising solely out of events that occurred after the end of the reporting period.

3.3   Going concern

If management determines after the reporting period (but before the financial statements are authorised for issue) either that it intends to liquidate the entity or to cease trading, or that it has no realistic alternative but to do so, the financial statements should not be prepared on the going concern basis. *[FRS 102.32.7A]*.

Deterioration in operating results and financial position after the reporting period may indicate a need to consider whether the going concern assumption is still appropriate. If the going concern assumption is no longer appropriate, Section 32 states that the effect is so pervasive that it results in a fundamental change in the basis of accounting, rather than an adjustment to the amounts recognised within the original basis of accounting. *[FRS 102.32.7B]*.

Section 3 – *Financial Statement Presentation* – contains guidance and specific disclosure requirements when the financial statements are not prepared on a going concern basis or when there are uncertainties that cast significant doubt upon an entity's ability to continue as a going concern – see Chapter 6.

3.4   Dividends

Dividends declared by an entity to holders of its equity instruments after the end of the reporting period are not adjusting events as no obligation exists at the end of the reporting period. However, although dividends declared after the reporting date are not liabilities, entities may present the amount of dividends declared after the end of the reporting period, as a segregated component of retained earnings. *[FRS 102.32.8]*. This allows entities to show the amount of retained earnings that are set aside for future dividends, as at the date the financial statements are authorised for issue.

The accounting for dividends in FRS 102 reflects the legal status of dividends under the Companies Act 2006. ICAEW/ICAS *Technical Release 02/17BL – Guidance on Realised and Distributable Profits under the Companies Act 2006* (TECH 02/17BL) states that a distribution is made when it becomes a legally binding liability of the company, regardless of the date on which it is to be settled. In the case of a final dividend, this is when it is declared by the company in a general meeting or, for private companies, by the members passing a general resolution. In the case of interim dividends authorised under common articles of association, normally no legally binding liability is established prior to payment being made. In such cases, dividends are normally recognised when they are paid although TECH 02/17BL also provides guidance in determining whether an interim dividend is a legally binding liability at a date earlier than when payment is made. *[TECH 02/17BL.2.10]*.

The examples of non-adjusting events discussed at 3.2.2 above do not include declared dividends. However, the Companies Act requires disclosure of any dividends proposed before the date of approval of the financial statements (see 3.5.4 below).

3.5   Disclosures

Section 32 does not require any disclosures in respect of adjusting events as disclosures of such transactions follow the applicable sections in FRS 102 since the financial statements reflect such transactions.

3.5.1   Date when financial statements are authorised for issue

An entity shall disclose the date when the financial statements were authorised for issue and who authorised the financial statements for issue. *[FRS 102.32.9]*.

3.5.2   Non-adjusting events

An entity shall disclose the following for each category of non-adjusting events after the end of the reporting period: *[FRS 102.32.10]*

- the nature of the event; and
- an estimate of its financial effect, or a statement that such an estimate cannot be made.

Examples of non-adjusting events after the end of the reporting period that would generally result in disclosures are provided at 3.2.2 above. It is important to note that the list of examples of non-adjusting events in Section 32, and summarised at 3.2.2 above, is not an exhaustive one; Section 32 requires disclosure of any material non-adjusting event.

3.5.3   Breach of a long-term loan covenant and its subsequent rectification

The rectification of the breach or default of a loan payable, or the renegotiation of the terms of the loan, subsequent to the reporting date is not an adjusting event and therefore does not change the classification of the liability in the statement of financial position from current to non-current.

When a breach or default of a loan payable exists at the reporting date, an entity shall disclose, whether the breach or default was remedied, or the terms of the loan payable was renegotiated, before the financial statements were authorised for issue. *[FRS 102.11.47(c)]*. These disclosures are not required for qualifying entities that are non-financial institutions.

3.5.4 Additional Companies Act 2006 disclosure requirements in respect of reserves and dividends

The following disclosures in respect of reserves and dividends intended to be distributed after the reporting period are required for large and medium sized companies, as defined by The Large and Medium-sized Companies and Groups (Accounts and Reports) Regulations 2008 as amended (the Regulations):

- any amount set aside or proposed to be set aside to, or withdrawn, or proposed to be withdrawn from, reserves; and
- the aggregate amount of dividends that are proposed before the date of approval of the financial statements. *[1 Sch 43, 2 Sch 56, 3 Sch 64]*.

4. PRACTICAL ISSUES

Section 32 alludes to practical issues such as those discussed below. It states that a decline in fair value of investments after the reporting period does not *normally* relate to conditions at the end of the reporting period (see 3.2.2 above). At the same time, Section 32 asserts that the bankruptcy of a customer that occurs after the reporting period *usually* confirms that a loss on a trade receivable existed at the end of the reporting period (see 3.2.1 above). Judgement of the facts and circumstances is required to determine whether an event that occurs after the reporting period provides evidence about a condition that existed at the end of the reporting period, or whether the condition arose subsequent to the reporting period.

4.1 Valuation of inventory

The sale of inventories after the reporting period is normally a good indicator of their selling price at that date. Section 32 states that such sales 'may give evidence about their selling price at the end of the reporting period' *[FRS 102.32.5(b)(ii)]* (see 3.2.1 above). However, in some cases, selling prices decrease because of conditions that did not exist at the end of the reporting period.

Therefore, the problem is determining why selling price decreased. Did it decrease because of circumstances that existed at the end of the reporting period, which subsequently became known, or did it decrease because of circumstances that arose subsequently? A decrease in price is merely a response to changing conditions so it is important to assess the reasons for these changes.

Some examples of changing conditions are as follows:

- Price reductions caused by a sudden increase in cheap imports:

  Whilst it is arguable that the 'dumping' of cheap imports after the reporting period is a condition that arises subsequent to that date, it is more likely that this is a reaction to a condition that already existed such as overproduction in other parts of the world. Thus, it might be more appropriate in such a situation to adjust the value of inventories based on its subsequent selling price.

- Price reductions caused by increased competition:

  The reasons for price reductions and increased competition do not generally arise overnight but normally occur over a period. For example, a competitor may have built up a competitive advantage by investing in machinery that is more efficient. In these circumstances, it is appropriate for an entity to adjust the valuation of its inventories because its own investment in production machinery is inferior to its competitor's and this situation existed at the end of the reporting period.

- Price reductions caused by the introduction of an improved competitive product:

    It is unlikely that a competitor developed and introduced an improved product overnight. Therefore, it is more appropriate to adjust the valuation of inventories to their selling price after that introduction because the entity's failure to maintain its competitive position in relation to product improvements that existed at the end of the reporting period.

Competitive pressures that cause a decrease in selling price after the reporting period are generally additional evidence of conditions that developed over a period and existed at the end of the reporting period. Consequently, their effects normally require adjustment in the financial statements.

However, for certain types of inventory, there is clear evidence of a price at the end of the reporting period and it is inappropriate to adjust the price of that inventory to reflect a subsequent decline. An example is inventories for which there is a price on an appropriate commodities market. In addition, inventory may be physically damaged or destroyed after the reporting period (e.g. by fire, flood, or other disaster). In these cases, the entity does not adjust the financial statements. However, the entity may be required to disclose the subsequent decline in selling price of the inventories if the impact is material (see 3.2.2 above).

4.2   Percentage of completion estimates

Events after the reporting period frequently give evidence about the profitability of construction contracts (or other contracts for which revenue is recognised using a percentage of completion method) that are in progress at the end of the reporting period.

Section 23 – *Revenue* – requires an assessment to be made as of the end of the reporting period, of the outcome of a construction contract to recognise revenue and expenses under the percentage of completion method (see Chapter 20). *[FRS 102.23.17]*. In such an assessment, consideration should be given to events that occur after the reporting period and a determination should be made as to whether they are adjusting or non-adjusting events for which the financial effect is included in the percentage of completion calculation.

4.3   Insolvency of a debtor

The insolvency of a debtor or inability to pay debts usually builds up over a period. Consequently, if a debtor has an amount outstanding at the end of the reporting period and this amount is written off because of information received after the reporting period, the event is normally adjusting. Section 32 states that the 'bankruptcy of a customer that occurs after the end of the reporting period usually confirms that a loss existed at the end of the reporting period' *[FRS 102.32.5(b)(i)]* (see 3.2.1 above). If, however, there is evidence to show that the insolvency of the debtor resulted solely from an event occurring after the reporting period, then the event is a non-adjusting event. If the impact is material, the entity will be required to disclose the impact of the debtor's default.

4.4 Valuation of investment property at fair value and tenant insolvency

The fair value of investment property reflects, among other things, the quality of tenants' covenants and the future rental income from the property. If a tenant ceases to be able to meet its lease obligations due to insolvency after the reporting period, an entity considers how this event is reflected in the valuation at the end of the reporting period.

Professional valuations generally reference the state of the market at the date of valuation without the use of hindsight. Consequently, the insolvency of a tenant is not normally an adjusting event to the fair value of the investment property because the investment property still holds value in the market. However, it would generally be indicative of an adjusting event for any amounts due from the tenant at the end of the reporting period.

Section 32 states that 'a decline in market value of investments between the end of the reporting period and the date when the financial statements are authorised for issue' is a non-adjusting event, as the decline does not normally relate to a condition at the end of the reporting period (see 3.2.2 above). This decline in fair value, however, may be required to be disclosed if material.

4.5 Discovery of fraud after the end of the reporting period

When fraud is discovered after the reporting date the implications on the financial statements should be considered. In particular it should be determined whether the fraud is indicative of a prior period error, and that financial information should be restated, or merely a change of estimate requiring prospective adjustment. Application of the definitions of a prior period error and a change in accounting policy included in Section 10 – *Accounting Policies, Estimates and Errors* – requires judgement in the case of a fraud (see Chapter 9). The facts and circumstances should be evaluated to determine if the discovery of fraud resulted from previous failure to use, or misuse of, reliable information; or from new information. If the fraud meets the definition of a prior period error, the fraud would be an adjusting event as it relates to conditions that existed at the end of the reporting period. However, if the fraud meets the definition of a change in estimate, the application of Section 32 is required to determine whether financial information is required to be adjusted, or whether disclosure is sufficient. The facts and circumstances are evaluated to determine if the fraud provides evidence of circumstances that existed at the end of the reporting period or circumstances that arose after that date. Determining this is a complex task and requires judgement and careful consideration of the specifics to each case.

Chapter 29

Chapter 30

Related party disclosures

List of examples

Chapter 30

Related party disclosures

1 INTRODUCTION

Section 33 – *Related Party Disclosures* – requires an entity to include in its financial statements the disclosures necessary to draw attention to the possibility that its financial position and profit or loss have been affected by the existence of related parties and by transactions and outstanding balances with such entities. *[FRS 102.33.1]*.

Section 33 requires disclosures only. It does not establish any recognition or measurement requirements. Related party transactions are accounted for in accordance with the requirements of the section of FRS 102 applicable to the transaction. The disclosures required by Section 33 are in addition to those required by other sections. For example, a loan to a related party will also be subject to the disclosure requirements of Section 11 – *Basic Financial Instruments*.

1.1 Scope of Section 33

Section 33 applies to all financial statements prepared under FRS 102 including both group and individual financial statements. However, disclosure is not required in consolidated financial statements, of any transactions or balances between group entities that have been eliminated on consolidation (see 1.1.1 below).

In addition to the above, disclosures required by Section 33 need not be given of *transactions* entered into between two members of a group, provided that any subsidiary which is a party to the transaction is wholly owned by such a member (see 1.1.2 below). *[FRS 102.33.1A]*.

1.1.1 Transactions eliminated on consolidation

Although Section 33 does not specifically include a paragraph stating that intra-group transactions eliminated on consolidation are not required to be disclosed in the consolidated financial statements of an entity, this is not so much an exemption as a statement of the obvious since, so far as the group accounts are concerned, such items do not exist. The effect is that no related party disclosures between subsidiary undertakings are required in group accounts. However, disclosure is still required in respect of transactions or balances with associates or joint ventures since these are not 'eliminated' on consolidation, although they may be subject to consolidation adjustments.

1.1.2   Transactions between wholly-owned subsidiaries

The wording of this exemption has been taken directly from UK company law. The exemption may be applied to transactions between entities within a sub-group where the transacting subsidiary is wholly-owned by the intermediate parent of that sub-group, even if that intermediate is not wholly-owned by the ultimate parent. *[FRS 102 Appendix III.40D-E]*.

The Basis for Conclusions clarifies that this exemption applies only to transactions between wholly owned subsidiary undertakings and not to outstanding balances between those entities. This is because the exemption derives from company law and therefore it is not possible to provide an exemption from the disclosure of outstanding balances with group undertakings, though it should be noted that the requirement is for the balances to be disclosed in aggregate. In relation to the format of the balance sheet, company law requires disclosure of outstanding balances in aggregate for group undertakings and, separately, for undertakings in which the company has a participating interest. Compliance with the requirements of Section 4 – *Statement of Financial Position* (see Chapter 6) should satisfy this requirement. *[FRS 102.BC.B33.2]*.

The Note on Legal Requirements clarifies that, in the FRC's view, the exemption may not be applied to transactions between entities in an intermediate parent's sub-group (including the intermediate parent itself) and the entities in the larger group if the intermediate parent is not wholly-owned by the parent of that larger group. Otherwise, related party transactions could be obscured by a partly-owned intermediate parent creating a wholly-owned subsidiary and passing transactions through it. *[FRS 102 Appendix III.40F]*.

Example 30.1 below illustrates the application of the disclosure exemption based on the interpretation above.

Example 30.1:   Application of the exemption from disclosure of transactions between wholly-owned subsidiary undertakings

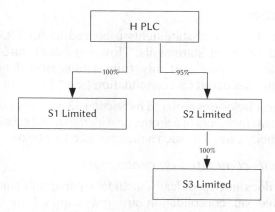

Because H PLC only owns 95% of S2 Limited, the wholly owned subsidiaries exemption cannot be used in (a) the individual company financial statements of H PLC in respect of transactions with S2 Limited and S3 Limited, (b) the individual financial statements of S1 Limited in respect of transactions with S2 Limited and S3 Limited (c) the consolidated and/or individual financial statements of S2 Limited in respect of any transactions with H PLC and S1 Limited or (d) the individual financial statements of S3 Limited in respect of any transactions with H PLC and S1 Limited.

The exemption can be used for any transactions in individual financial statements between H PLC and S1 Limited and between S2 Limited and S3 Limited.

However, if the remaining 5% of S2 Limited (not directly held by H PLC) was held by another wholly owned subsidiary undertaking of H PLC, then S2 Limited would be a wholly owned subsidiary undertaking of H PLC. In those circumstances, the exemption from disclosing transactions with the other entities in the group should be available in the individual financial statements of H PLC, S1 Limited, S2 Limited and S3 Limited and the consolidated financial statements of S2 Limited (as S1 Limited, S2 Limited and S3 Limited would all be wholly owned subsidiary undertakings of the H PLC group).

The exemption has no other conditions: it can be applied, for example, to an entity with an overseas parent, an entity whose parent does not prepare publicly available consolidated financial statements or to an entity whose parent does not prepare consolidated financial statements.

2 COMPARISON BETWEEN SECTION 33 AND IFRS

The principal differences between Section 33 and IAS 24 – *Related Party Disclosures* – are in respect of:

- the scope exemption for wholly-owned subsidiaries (see 2.1 below);
- the state-related exemption (see 2.2 below);
- disclosure of key management compensation (see 2.3 below);
- aggregation of disclosures (see 2.4 below); and
- disclosure of commitments (see 2.5 below).

In summary, the disclosure requirements of Section 33 are less onerous to a reporting entity than those of IAS 24.

2.1 Scope exemption for wholly-owned subsidiaries

Section 33 has an exemption from disclosure of transactions entered into between two members of a group, provided that any subsidiary which is a party to the transaction is wholly-owned by such a member (see 1.1.2 above). IAS 24 does not have such an exemption.

2.2 State-related exemption

Section 33 exempts an entity from disclosing information about related party transactions with a related party that is a state or another entity related because that same state has control, joint control or significant influence over it (see 3.2.3.C below).

IAS 24 has a similar but not identical exemption for government-related entities. However, the IAS 24 exemption is conditional on disclosure of (i) the nature and amount of each individually significant transaction; and (ii) for other transactions that are collectively, but not individually, significant, a qualitative or quantitative indication of their type. *[IAS 24.25-26]*. In addition, under IAS 24, the reporting entity must disclose the name of the government and the nature of its relationship with the reporting entity. In contrast, Section 33 does not require these additional disclosures and the reporting entity is only obliged to disclose the name of the state if the state is the parent of the reporting entity. *[FRS 102.33.11]*. Therefore a state with significant influence over a reporting entity need not be named in FRS 102 financial statements, nor will any transactions and balances with that state be disclosed.

Chapter 30

2.3   Disclosure of key management compensation

Section 33 requires key management compensation to be disclosed only in total. *[FRS 102.33.7]*.

In addition, when an entity is subject to a legal or regulatory requirement to disclose directors' remuneration (or equivalent), it is exempt from the requirement to disclose key management personnel compensation if the key management personnel and directors are the same. *[FRS 102.33.7A]*.

Directors' remuneration is subject to additional company law requirements (see 3.2.4 below).

IAS 24 requires key management compensation to be disclosed in total and also split between short-term employee benefits, post-employment benefits, other long-term benefits, termination benefits and share-based payment. *[IAS 24.17]*.

2.4   Aggregation of disclosures

Section 33 requires related party transaction disclosures to be made in aggregate for the following separate categories (a) entities with control, joint control or significant influence over the reporting entity; (b) entities over which the entity has control, joint control or significant influence (c) key management personnel of the entity or its parent (in the aggregate); and (d) other related parties. *[FRS 102.33.10]*.

IAS 24 has a similar requirement but requires the disclosures to be made separately for seven categories instead of four. *[IAS 24.19]*.

2.5   Disclosure of commitments

Section 33 states that information about 'commitments' should be disclosed if necessary for an understanding of the potential effect of the related party relationship on the financial statements. *[FRS 102.33.9]*.

IAS 24 states explicitly that 'commitments to do something if a particular event occurs or does not occur in the future, including executory contracts (recognised and unrecognised)' are transactions requiring disclosure if they are with a related party. In addition, a commitment is listed as an example of a related party transaction requiring disclosure. *[IAS 24.21(i)]*.

3   REQUIREMENTS OF SECTION 33 FOR RELATED PARTY DISCLOSURES

Section 33 defines a related party and then requires various disclosures of related party transactions, balances and relationships.

3.1   Definition of a related party

A related party is defined as 'a person or entity that is related to the entity that is preparing its financial statements (the reporting entity)'. *[FRS 102.33.2]*.

Preparers should use this definition of 'related party' when applying concepts elsewhere in FRS 102 where this term or similar terms are used and not otherwise defined.

In considering each possible related party relationship, attention is directed to the substance of the relationship and not merely the legal form. *[FRS 102.33.3].*

A related party transaction is defined as 'a transfer of resources, services or obligations between a reporting entity and a related party, regardless of whether a price is charged'. *[FRS 102.33.8].*

The following are considered to be related parties of the reporting entity:

- a person or a close member of that person's family, if that person has either control, joint control, or significant influence over the reporting entity, or is a member of the key management personnel of the reporting entity, or of a parent of the reporting entity (see 3.1.1 below);

- entities that are members of the same group (see 3.1.2 below);

- entities that are associates or joint ventures (see 3.1.3 below);

- entities that are joint ventures of the same third party (see 3.1.4 below);

- entities that are joint ventures and associates of the same third entity (see 3.1.5 below);

- post-employment benefit plans (see 3.1.6 below);

- entities under control or joint control of certain categories of persons or close members of such a person's family (see 3.1.7 below);

- entities under significant influence of certain categories of persons or close members of such a person's family (see 3.1.8 below); and

- entities, or any member of a group of which they are a part, that provide key management personnel services to the reporting entity or its parent (see 3.1.9 below).

3.1.1 Persons or close members of a person's family that are related parties

A person or close member of that person's family is related to a reporting entity if that person: *[FRS 102.33.2(a)]*

(i)   has control or joint control over the reporting entity;

(ii)   has significant influence over the reporting entity; or

(iii) is a member of the key management personnel of the reporting entity or of a parent of the reporting entity.

'Control', 'joint control' and 'significant influence' have the same meanings here as in Section 9 – *Consolidated and Separate Financial Statements*, Section 14 – *Investments in Associates* – and Section 15 – *Investments in Joint Ventures*.

3.1.1.A Close members of a family

Close members of a family of a person are defined as 'those family members who may be expected to influence, or be influenced by, that person in their dealings with the entity' including: *[FRS 102 Appendix I]*

(a)   that person's children and spouse or domestic partner;

(b)   children of that person's spouse or domestic partner; and

(c)   dependants of that person or that person's spouse or domestic partner.

This list of family members is non-exhaustive and does not preclude other family members from being considered as close members of the family of a person. As well as those specific family members described in (a) to (c) above, the definition also applies to any other family members who may be expected to influence or be influenced by that person in their dealings with the reporting entity. For example, this may include parents, siblings or relatives who are even more distant.

The IFRS Interpretations Committee confirmed in May 2015 that the definition of close members of a family of a person under IFRS (which is identical to the definition in FRS 102) appears to provide no scope to argue that there are circumstances in which the specific family members described in (a) to (c) above are not related parties. Dependants are not limited to children and may include other relatives depending on the facts and circumstances.

The Interpretations Committee observed that the definition of close members of the family of a person:

- is expressed in a principle-based manner and involves the use of judgement to determine whether members of the family of a person (including that person's parents) are related parties or not; and

- includes a list of family members that are always considered close members of the family of a person.

The IFRS Interpretations Committee further noted that the list of family members that are always considered 'close members' is non-exhaustive and does not preclude other family members from being considered as close members of the family of a person. Consequently, other family members, including parents or grandparents, could qualify as close members of the family depending on the assessment of specific facts and circumstances.[1]

3.1.1.B   *Key management personnel*

Key management personnel are those persons with authority and responsibility for planning, directing and controlling the activities of an entity, directly or indirectly, including any director (whether executive or otherwise) of that entity. *[FRS 102.33.6].*

A related party includes all key management personnel of a reporting entity and of a parent of the reporting entity. This means that all key management personnel of all parents (i.e. the immediate parent, any intermediate parent and the ultimate parent) of a reporting entity are related parties of the reporting entity.

Some entities may have more than one level of key management. For example, some entities may have a supervisory board, whose members have responsibilities similar to those of non-executive directors, as well as a board of directors that sets the overall operating strategy. All members of either board will be considered to be key management personnel.

The definition of key management personnel is not restricted to directors. It also includes other individuals with authority and responsibility for planning, directing and controlling the activities of an entity. For example, a chief financial officer or a chief operating officer may not be directors but could meet the definition of key management personnel. Other examples of the type of persons who are not directors but may meet the definition of key management personnel include a divisional chief executive or a director of a major trading subsidiary of the entity, but not of the entity itself, who nevertheless participates in the management of the reporting entity. A reference to individuals who are not directors in a reporting entity's strategic review might indicate that those persons are considered to be key management personnel.

Key management personnel are normally employees of the reporting entity (or of another entity in the same group). However, the definition does not restrict itself to employees. Therefore, seconded staff and persons engaged under management or outsourcing contracts may also have a level of authority or responsibility such that they are key management personnel.

A related party of a reporting entity also includes an entity that provides key management personnel services to that reporting entity (see 3.1.9 below). However, it is unclear whether individuals employed by that management entity (e.g. key management personnel of the management entity) can be key management personnel of the reporting entity. IAS 24, which has an identical definition of a related party to FRS 102, does not require a reporting entity to look through a management entity to the compensation paid or payable by the management entity to the management entity's employees or directors on the grounds that it is impracticable to access the detailed information required. *[IAS 24.17A, BC51].* In our view, as FRS 102 provides no specific guidance on this issue, an entity could use the hierarchy in Section 10 – *Accounting Policies, Estimates and Errors* (see Chapter 9) in order to apply the guidance in IAS 24 and not disclose any remuneration paid by a management entity to its employees or directors.

3.1.2 Entities that are members of the same group

'An entity is related to a reporting entity if:

> (i) the entity and the reporting entity are members of the same group (which means that each parent, subsidiary and fellow subsidiary is related to the others).' *[FRS 102.33.2(b)(i)].*

'Parent' and 'subsidiary' have the same meanings as in Section 9. Therefore, all entities that are controlled by the same ultimate parent are related parties. This would include entities where the reporting entity holds less than a majority of the voting rights but which are still considered to be subsidiaries. There are no exceptions to this rule although transactions between wholly-owned subsidiaries are not required to be disclosed (see 1.1.2 above).

3.1.3 Entities that are associates or joint ventures

'An entity is related to a reporting entity if:

...

> (ii) one entity is an associate or joint venture of the other entity (or an associate or joint venture of a member of a group of which the other entity is a member).' *[FRS 102.33.2(b)(ii)].*

'Associate' and 'joint venture' have the same meanings as in Sections 14 and 15 respectively.

In the definition of a related party, an associate includes subsidiaries of the associate and a joint venture includes subsidiaries of the joint venture. Therefore, for example, an associate's subsidiary and the investor that has significant influence over the associate are related to each another. *[FRS 102.33.4A].*

The definition also means that an associate of a reporting entity's parent is also a related party of the reporting entity.

However, the definition does not cause investors in a joint venture to be related to each other (see 3.1.10 below).

3.1.4   *Entities that are joint ventures of the same third party*

'An entity is related to a reporting entity if:

...

> (iii)   both entities are joint ventures of the same third party'. *[FRS 102.33.2(b)(iii)].*

As discussed at 3.1.3 above, a joint venture includes subsidiaries of the joint venture. *[FRS 102.33.4A].*

3.1.5   *Entities that are joint ventures and associates of the same third entity*

'An entity is related to a reporting entity if:

...

> (iv)   one entity is a joint venture of a third entity and the other entity is an associate of the third entity'. *[FRS 102.33.2(b)(iv)].*

This definition treats joint ventures in a similar manner to subsidiaries.

3.1.6   *Post-employment benefit plans*

'An entity is related to a reporting entity if:

...

> (v)   the entity is a post-employment benefit plan for the benefit of employees of either the reporting entity or an entity related to the reporting entity. If the reporting entity is itself such a plan, the sponsoring employers are also related to the reporting entity.' *[FRS 102.33.2(b)(v)].*

The definition is quite wide-ranging and includes post-employment benefit plans of any entity related to the reporting entity. This includes, for example, post-employment benefit plans of an associate or joint venture of the reporting entity or a post-employment benefit plan of an associate of the reporting entity's parent.

Sponsoring employers are also related parties of a post-employment benefit plan.

3.1.7   *Entities under control or joint control of certain persons or close members of their family*

'An entity is related to a reporting entity if:

...

> (vi)   the entity is controlled or jointly controlled by a person or close member of that person's family who has control or joint control over the reporting entity; has significant influence over the reporting entity; or is a member of key management personnel of the reporting entity or of a parent of the reporting entity.' *[FRS 102.33.2(b)(vi)].*

This is intended to cover situations in which an entity is controlled or jointly controlled by a person or close family member of that person and that person or close family member also controls, jointly controls, has significant influence or is a member of key management personnel of the reporting entity.

3.1.8 Entities under significant influence of certain persons or close members of their family

'An entity is related to a reporting entity if:

...

> (vii) a person or a close family member of that person who has control or joint control over the reporting entity has significant influence over the entity or is a member of the key management personnel of the entity (or of a parent of the entity).' *[FRS 102.33.2(b)(vii)]*.

This is the reciprocal of 3.1.7 above and covers situations where a reporting entity is controlled or jointly controlled by a person, or close family member of that person and that person, or close member of that person's family, has significant influence or is a member of key management personnel of the entity (or of a parent of the entity).

Entities that have a director or other member of key management personnel in common are not *de facto* related parties. Similarly, if a member of key management personnel of one entity has significant influence over another entity, this does not make the two entities related parties in the absence of any control or joint control by those persons (see 3.1.10 below).

3.1.9 Entities, or any member of the group of which they are a part, that provide key management personnel services

'An entity is related to a reporting entity if:

...

> (viii) the entity, or any member of a group of which it is a part, provides key management personnel services to the reporting entity or to the parent of the reporting entity.' *[FRS 102.33.2(b)(viii)]*.

This is intended to cover situations in which an entity (described as a 'management entity'), or a member of its group, provides key management personnel services to the reporting entity. As discussed at 3.1.1.B above, in our view, an entity could look to apply the guidance in IAS 24 and not disclose any remuneration paid by a management entity to its employees or directors.

The definition of key management personnel is 'those persons having authority and responsibility for planning, directing and controlling the activities of the entity, directly or indirectly, including any director (whether executive or otherwise)'. *[FRS 102.33.6]*. It therefore follows that to determine whether an entity were providing key management personnel services to another entity, the same attributes would need to be considered.

The effect of the requirement is illustrated in the following example.

*Example 30.2:   Entities that provide key management personnel services to a
reporting entity*

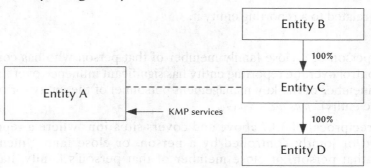

Entity C provides key management personnel (KMP) services to Entity A. For Entity A's financial
statements, Entities B, C and D are all related parties. However, Entity A is not a related party of Entities B,
C and D in their financial statements (i.e. the related party relationship between the management entity and
the reporting entity is not symmetrical).

In addition, an entity is required to disclose separately transactions with entities that
provide key management personnel services. *[FRS 102.33.10(d)]*. The type of transactions
that require disclosure are discussed at 3.2.3 below.

3.1.10   Parties that are not related parties

Having included such a detailed definition of related parties, Section 33 clarifies that the
following are not related parties: *[FRS 102.33.4]*

- two entities simply because they have a director or other member of key
  management personnel in common or because a member of key management
  personnel of one entity has significant influence over the other entity;

- two venturers simply because they share joint control over a joint venture;

- providers of finance, trade unions, public utilities, and departments and agencies of
  a government that do not control, jointly control or significantly influence the
  reporting entity, simply by virtue of their normal dealings with the entity (even
  though they may affect the freedom of action of an entity or participate in its
  decision-making process); and

- a customer, supplier, franchisor, distributor or general agent with whom an entity
  transacts a significant volume of business, simply by virtue of the resulting
  economic dependence.

The reason for these exclusions is that, without them, many entities that are not
normally regarded as related parties could fall within the definition of related party. For
example, a small clothing manufacturer selling 90% of its output to a single customer
could be under the effective economic control of that customer.

These exclusions are effective only where these parties are 'related' to the reporting
entity simply because of the relationship noted above. If there are other reasons why a
party is a related party, the exclusions do not apply.

3.1.11   *Illustrative examples of related party relationships*

The following examples, based on examples in IAS 24 which has the same definition of a related party as Section 33, illustrate the related party relationships discussed at Sections 3.1.1 to 3.1.8 above.

Example 30.3:   Related party relationships between entities

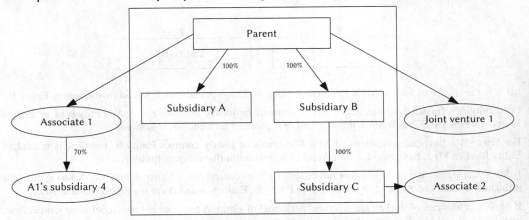

In Parent's consolidated financial statements, Subsidiaries A, B and C, Joint Venture 1, Associates 1 and 2 and Associate 1's subsidiary (referred hereafter as 'Associate 4') are related parties to the group. However, Parent's consolidated financial statements need not disclose transactions entered into with Subsidiaries A, B and C as they would be eliminated on consolidation (see 1.1.1 above).

In Parent's individual financial statements, Subsidiaries A, B and C, Joint Venture 1 and Associates 1, 2 and 4 are related parties. However, Parent need not disclose transactions entered into with Subsidiaries A, B and C as they are 100% owned by Parent (see 1.1.2 above).

For Subsidiary B's consolidated financial statements, Parent, Subsidiary A, Subsidiary C, Joint Venture 1 and Associates 1, 2 and 4 are related parties. However, Subsidiary B need not disclose transactions with Parent or Subsidiaries A and C as both Subsidiary B and Subsidiaries A and C are 100% owned by Parent (see 1.1.2 above).

For Subsidiary A, Subsidiary B and Subsidiary C's individual financial statements, Parent, all fellow subsidiaries, Joint Venture 1 and Associates 1, 2 and 4 are related parties. However, the subsidiaries need not disclose transactions entered into with Parent or the other subsidiaries as all entities party to the any transaction are 100% owned by a member of the group (see 1.1.2 above).

For Joint Venture 1's individual financial statements, Parent, Subsidiaries A, B and C and Associates 1, 2 and 4 are related parties.

For Associate 1's consolidated financial statements, Parent, Subsidiaries A, B and C, Associate 4 and Joint Venture 1 are related parties. However, Associate 1's consolidated financial statements need not disclose transactions entered into with Associate 4 as they would be eliminated on consolidation (see 1.1.1 above). Associate 2 is not a related party.

For Associate 1's individual financial statements, Parent, Subsidiaries A, B and C, Joint Venture 1 and Associate 4 are related parties. Associate 2 is not a related party. Associate 1 must disclose transactions with Associate 4 as Associate 4 is not 100% owned by Associate 1 (see 1.1.2 above).

For Associate 2's individual financial statements, Parent, Subsidiaries A, B and C and Joint Venture 1 are related parties. Associates 1 and Associate 4 are not related to Associate 2.

For Associate 4's individual financial statements, Associate 1, Parent, Subsidiaries A, B and C and Joint Venture 1 are related parties. Associate 2 is not a related party. Subsidiary 4 must disclose transactions with Associate 1 as Subsidiary 4 is not 100% owned by Associate 1 (see 1.1.2 above).

Example 30.4:   Close members of the family holding investments

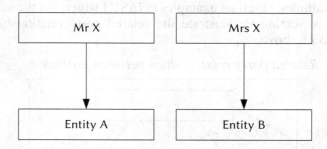

Mr X is the spouse of Mrs X. Mr X has an investment in Entity A and Mrs X has an investment in Entity B.

For Entity A's financial statements, if Mr X controls or jointly controls Entity A, Entity B is related to Entity A when Mrs X has control, joint control or significant influence over Entity B.

For Entity B's financial statements, if Mrs X controls or jointly controls Entity B, Entity A is related to Entity B when Mr X has control, joint control or significant influence over Entity A.

If Mr X has significant influence (but not control or joint control) over Entity A and Mrs X has significant influence (but not control or joint control) over Entity B, Entities A and B are not related to each other.

If Mr X is a member of the key management personnel of Entity A but does not have control or joint control over Entity A and Mrs X is a member of the key management personnel of Entity B, but does not have control or joint control over Entity B then Entities A and B are not related to each other.

3.2   Disclosures of related party transactions, balances and relationships

The following disclosures are required:

- parent–subsidiary relationships (see 3.2.1 below);
- key management personnel compensation (see 3.2.2 below); and
- related party transactions and balances (see 3.2.3 below).

There is no requirement to disclose information about related party transactions in one comprehensive note. However, it may be more useful to users of the financial statements to present information this way.

Section 3 – *Financial Statement Presentation* – requires that, except when FRS 102 permits otherwise (which Section 33 does not), comparative information in respect of the previous period must be disclosed for all amounts reported in the current period's financial statements. *[FRS 102.3.14]*.

3.2.1   Disclosure of parent–subsidiary relationships

An entity shall disclose:

- the name of its parent; and, if different,
- the name of its ultimate controlling party.

If neither the entity's parent nor the ultimate controlling party produces financial statements available for public use, the name of the next most senior parent that does so (if any) shall also be disclosed. *[FRS 102.33.5]*.

The use of the word 'party' means that the disclosure applies to both individuals and to entities. Disclosure must be made even if the parent or ultimate controlling party does not prepare financial statements.

The ultimate controlling party could be a group of individuals or entities acting together. Section 33 is silent on the issue of individuals or entities acting together to exercise joint control as a result of contractual relationships. Two venturers are not related parties simply because they share joint control over a joint venture. *[FRS 102.33.4(b)]*. Section 33 is also silent on whether a group of individuals acting in an informal way could be considered to be the ultimate controlling party of an entity. However, it is likely that such an informal arrangement would at least give such individuals acting collectively significant influence over the reporting entity and as such those individuals collectively would be related parties to the reporting entity.

It is stressed that these relationships between a parent and its subsidiary must be disclosed irrespective of whether there have been related party transactions. *[FRS 102.33.5]*.

3.2.2 Disclosure of key management personnel compensation

An entity is required to disclose key management compensation in total. *[FRS 102.33.7]*.

Compensation includes all employee benefits (as defined in Section 28 – *Employee Benefits*) including those in the form of share-based payments. Employee benefits includes all forms of consideration paid, payable or provided by the entity, or on behalf of the entity (e.g. by its parent or shareholder), in exchange for services rendered to the entity. It also includes such consideration paid on behalf of a parent of the entity in respect of goods and services provided to the entity. *[FRS 102.33.6]*.

A related party includes all key management personnel of a reporting entity and of a parent of the reporting entity. This means that all key management personnel of all parents (i.e. the immediate parent, any intermediate parent and the ultimate parent) of a reporting entity are related parties of the reporting entity. When the reporting entity's financial statements represent a group, key management personnel of subsidiaries might not be key management personnel of the group if those persons do not participate in the management of the group.

Disclosure is required only of key management compensation in total. There is no need to split the amount into its constituent parts. There is also no requirement to disclose individual key management compensation or to name those individuals considered to be key management. In addition, when an entity is subject to a legal or regulatory requirement to disclose directors' remuneration (or equivalent), it is exempt from the requirement to disclose key management personnel compensation if the key management personnel and directors are the same. *[FRS 102.33.7A]*.

One practical difficulty for an entity in a group is that the disclosure of its key management personnel compensation is for the services rendered to the reporting entity. Accordingly, where key management personnel of the reporting entity also provide services to other entities within the group, an apportionment of the compensation is necessary. Likewise, where the reporting entity receives services from key management personnel that are also key management personnel of other entities within the group, the reporting entity may have to impute the compensation received.

Such apportionments and allocations required judgment and an assessment of the time commitment involved.

As discussed at 3.1.1.B above, in our view, an entity could look to apply the guidance in IAS 24 and not disclose any remuneration paid by a management entity to its employees or directors.

Company law requires disclosures in respect of directors' remuneration which are in addition to the requirement to disclose key management personnel compensation (see 3.2.4 below).

3.2.3   Disclosure of related party transactions and balances

3.2.3.A   Definition of and examples of related party transactions

A related party transaction 'is a transfer of resources, services or obligations between a reporting entity and a related party, regardless of whether a price is charged'.

Examples of related party transactions include but are not limited to:

- transactions between an entity and its principal owner(s);
- transactions between an entity and another entity when both entities are under the common control of a single entity or person; and
- transactions in which an entity or person that controls the reporting entity incurs expenses directly that would have been borne by the reporting entity. *[FRS 102.33.8]*.

Section 33 provides the following examples of transactions that shall be disclosed if they are with a related party:

- purchases or sales of goods (finished or unfinished);
- purchases or sales of property and other assets;
- rendering or receiving of services;
- leases;
- transfers of research and development;
- transfers under licence agreements;
- transfers under finance agreements (including loans and equity contributions in cash or in kind);
- provisions of guarantees or collateral;
- settlement of liabilities on behalf of the entity or by the entity on behalf of another party; and
- participation by a parent or a subsidiary in a defined benefit plan that shares risks between group entities. *[FRS 102.33.12]*.

This list is not intended to be exhaustive. Information about commitments should be disclosed if necessary for an understanding of the potential effect of the related party relationship on the financial statements. *[FRS 102.33.9]*.

Items of a similar nature may be disclosed in aggregate except where separate disclosure is necessary for an understanding of the effects of related party transactions on the financial statements of an entity. *[FRS 102.33.14]*.

3.2.3.B   *Disclosures required in respect of related party transactions and outstanding balances*

If an entity has related party transactions of the type described at 3.2.3.A above, it shall disclose the nature of the related party relationship as well as information about the transactions, outstanding balances and commitments necessary for an understanding of the potential effect of the relationship on the financial statements. These disclosure requirements are in addition to the requirements to disclose key management personnel compensation (see 3.2.2 above). However, when, an entity takes advantage of the exemption from disclosing key management personnel compensation (see 3.2.2 above) it is not required to provide additional disclosure about directors' share-based payment arrangements.

At a minimum, disclosures shall include:

- the amount of the transactions;
- the amount of the outstanding balances, and:
    - their terms and conditions, including whether they are secured, and the nature of the consideration to be provided in settlement; and
    - details of any guarantees given or received;
- provisions for uncollectible receivables related to the amount of outstanding balances; and
- the expense recognised during the period in respect of bad or doubtful debts due from related parties. *[FRS 102.33.9].*

The disclosures required above shall be made in aggregate for each of the following separate categories:

- entities with control, joint control or significant influence over the entity;
- entities over which the entity has control, joint control or significant influence;
- key management personnel of the entity or its parent (in the aggregate); and
- other related parties. *[FRS 102.33.10].*

Section 33 stresses that an entity shall not state that related party transactions were made on terms equivalent to those that prevail in arm's length transactions unless such terms can be substantiated. *[FRS 102.33.13].* However, there is no requirement to state that transactions have not been made on an arm's length basis.

There is no exemption from disclosure on the grounds of confidentiality. However, since there is no requirement to disclose the name of a related party (apart from the name of the parent, or if different, the ultimate controlling entity), this lack of exemption is likely to be less of a concern.

In determining whether an entity discloses related party transactions in financial statements, the general concept of materiality is applied. Section 33 does not refer specifically to materiality since this qualitative characteristic is described in Section 2 – *Concepts and Pervasive Principles.* Omissions or misstatements of items are material if they 'individually or collectively, could influence the economic decisions of users taken on the basis of the financial statements. Materiality depends on the size and nature of the omission or misstatement judged in the surrounding circumstances. The size or nature of the item, or a combination of both, could be the determining factor'. *[FRS 102.2.6].*

This may have the effect that any related party transaction whose disclosure is considered sensitive (for tax reasons perhaps) is by definition material because it is expected by the reporting entity to influence a user of the financial statements. Therefore, it may not be possible to avoid disclosing such items on the grounds that they are financially immaterial. In addition, a transaction conducted at advantageous terms to either the related party or the reporting entity is more likely to be material than one conducted at arm's length. Since Section 33 requires disclosure of related party transactions irrespective of whether consideration is received, disclosure cannot be avoided on the argument that, since there is no consideration, the transaction must be immaterial.

3.2.3.C   Disclosure exemption for state-related entities

An entity is exempt from the disclosure requirements discussed at 3.2.3.B above in relation to:

- a state (a national, regional or local government) that has control, joint control or significant influence over the reporting entity; and
- another entity that is a related party because the same state has control, joint control or significant influence over both the reporting entity and the other entity.

This is a generous exemption as there is no requirement to give even an indication of the type of transactions with the state or other state-related entity that is a related party.

However, the entity must still disclose a parent-subsidiary relationship as discussed at 3.2.1 above. *[FRS 102.33.11]*.

3.2.4   Additional UK company law disclosures

UK company law requires disclosures of transactions with directors including disclosure of directors' remuneration and disclosure of directors' advances, credits and guarantees.

These disclosures are in addition to the disclosure of key management personnel compensation discussed at 3.2.2 above.

3.2.4.A   Disclosure of directors' remuneration – all companies

Disclosure of directors' remuneration is required for all entities and disclosures are required for both individual and group financial statements. The requirements are contained in Schedule 5 of *The Large and Medium-sized Companies and Groups (Accounts and Report) Regulations 2008* (SI 2008/410) (The Regulations). It is beyond the scope of this publication to address the requirements at length which differ slightly between AIM listed and unquoted entities that are not AIM listed. The following summarises the major points: *[5 Sch 1-15]*

- Disclosure is required of:
    - the aggregate amount of remuneration paid to or receivable by directors (i.e. all directors including non-executive directors) in respect of qualifying services;
    - gains made by directors on share options in aggregate (as well as the number of directors who exercised share options);
    - the aggregate of the amount of money paid to or receivable by directors and the net value of assets (other than money or share options) received or receivable by directors under long term incentive plans in respect of qualifying services

(as well as the number of directors in respect of whose qualifying services shares were received or receivable under long term incentive schemes);

- the aggregate value of any company contributions paid, or treated as paid, to a pension scheme in respect of directors' qualifying services and contributions by reference to which the rate or amount of any money purchase benefits that may become payable will be calculated; and

- the number of directors to whom retirement benefits are accruing in respect of qualifying services under both money purchase and defined benefit schemes.

- When aggregate remuneration of all directors, share option gains and amounts receivable on long-term incentive plans exceeds £200,000 disclosures are required of the total of those aggregates for the highest paid director of:

  - the amount of remuneration, share option gains and amounts receivable on long-term incentive plans;

  - the amount of any company contributions paid into a money purchase pension scheme;

  - the accrued pension and the amount of the accrued lump sum in respect of any defined benefit pension plan; and

  - whether the director has exercised any share options and whether any shares were received or receivable by that director in respect of qualifying services under a long term incentive scheme.

- Disclosure is required in aggregate of any excess retirement benefits paid or receivable by directors or past directors (compared to their entitlement when the benefits first became payable or as at 31 March 1997, whichever is the later).

- Disclosure is required of the aggregate amount of compensation paid to directors or past directors for loss of office (which includes loss of office as director, loss of any other office in connection with management of the company's affairs and any office as director or otherwise in connection with the management of the affairs of any subsidiary undertaking of the company).

- Disclosure is required of the aggregate amount of any consideration paid to or receivable by third parties (i.e. a person other than the director or a person connected with him or a body corporate controlled by him or the company or any of its subsidiary undertakings) for making available the services of any person as a director of the company or, while a director of the company, as director of any of its subsidiary undertakings or otherwise in connection with the management of the affairs of the company or any of its subsidiary undertakings.

'Qualifying services' are defined as a person's services as director of a company and his services at any time while he is a director of the company as a director of any of its subsidiary undertakings or otherwise in connection with the management of the affairs of the company or any of its subsidiary undertakings.

'Remuneration' means salary, fees, bonuses, sums paid by way of expense allowance (chargeable to UK income tax) and the estimated money value of other benefits received otherwise than in cash. It does not include the value of share options, gains made on exercise of share options, company contributions paid into a pension scheme or amounts paid/receivable under a long term incentive plan.

All amounts disclosed should include sums paid by or receivable from the company, its subsidiary undertakings or any other person. In other words, disclosures are required, regardless of who actually pays the director.

Payments made to persons connected with the director or persons connected with a body corporate 'controlled' by a director (as defined in sections 252-255 of CA 2006) are required to be included in the aggregate remuneration disclosed.

In group financial statements, the directors' remuneration disclosure requirements only extend to directors of the holding company.

In group situations, it is common practice for a holding company, whose directors also act as directors of subsidiary companies, to remunerate the directors in respect of their services to the subsidiary companies. In this situation, remuneration disclosures are still required in the subsidiary company's financial statements and there should be an apportionment of the remuneration received for qualifying services to each subsidiary. It may also be possible that, given the level of services required by each subsidiary company, the remuneration for qualifying services is £nil.

However, in the rare cases that the directors believe that it is not practicable to make such an apportionment, we believe that full disclosure of the total amount received as remuneration would be required, accompanied by a statement that it is not practicable to allocate this amount between services as directors of the company and services as directors of holding and fellow subsidiary companies. The note to the financial statements should explain that the charge disclosed as remuneration has been borne by the holding company or other group company.

It may be the case that a blanket management charge has been charged by a holding company to its subsidiaries in respect of a variety of expenditure incurred on its subsidiaries' behalf, including the remuneration of the subsidiaries' directors. The reporting company should seek to analyse the expenditure between types and thereby arrive at a figure for directors' remuneration.

3.2.4.B   *Directors' remuneration report – quoted companies only*

Quoted companies are required to prepare a directors' remuneration report. A quoted company is a company whose equity share capital is included in the official list of the UK Listing Authority, officially listed in an EEA state or admitted to dealing on either the New York Stock Exchange or NASDAQ. *[s385(2)]*. AIM and OFEX companies are not quoted.

The contents of a directors' remuneration report are specified by Schedule 8 of The Regulations.

3.2.4.C   *Disclosure of directors' advances, credits and guarantees – all companies*

Disclosure of directors' advances, credits and guarantees is required by section 413 of the CA 2006 for all entities. These disclosures are required for each credit, advance or guarantee.

Disclosure is required in respect of all transactions during the reporting period as well as balances outstanding at the reporting date. Disclosure is required of transactions with any person who was a director of the company at any time during the period, irrespective of whether that person was a director at such time that the transaction or arrangement was made. See Chapter 6 at 8.8 for further detail.

3.2.5 Stock exchange requirements

In addition to the requirements of the Companies Act, there are explicit statutory, London Stock Exchange (LSE) and Disclosure and Transparency Rules (DTR) requirements and reliefs regarding disclosure of certain related party transactions and relationships. These disclosure requirements are not addressed in detail in this chapter and reference should be made to the original regulatory requirements. These disclosure requirements go beyond those required by FRS 102.

Both the LSE and AIM have definitions of a related party which differ from the definition in FRS 102. For related party transactions meeting certain thresholds, the Listing Rules require the company to make notification of the related party transaction, and to send a circular containing specified details to shareholders, and to obtain shareholder approval. There are modified rules for smaller related party transactions. AIM Rules 13 and 16 also require notification of related party transactions meeting certain thresholds. Disclosure of certain related party transactions can be required in the financial statements.

4. SUMMARY OF GAAP DIFFERENCES

The following table shows the differences between FRS 102 and IFRS.

	FRS 102	*IFRS*
Transactions between wholly owned subsidiaries	Disclosure exemption available.	No disclosure exemption available.
Disclosure of key management personnel compensation	Disclose in total only. However, no disclosure is required if there is a legal or regulatory requirement to disclose directors' remuneration and the key management personnel and the directors are the same.	Disclose in total and by five categories.
State-related parties	Disclosure exemption available.	Disclosure exemption conditional on certain additional disclosures being made.
Aggregation of disclosures by category	Disclosure by four categories.	Disclosure by seven categories.
Disclosure of commitments	Disclose required if necessary for understanding of relationship.	Explicit statement that the commitment is a type of related party transaction.

References

1 *IFRIC Update*, May 2015, IASB.

Chapter 31   Specialised activities

Chapter 31

List of examples

Chapter 31

Chapter 31   Specialised activities

1   INTRODUCTION

This chapter covers (unless stated otherwise below) the financial reporting requirements for entities applying FRS 102 involved in the following types of specialised activities:

- Agriculture (see 2 below);
- Extractive Activities (see 3 below);
- Service Concession Arrangements (see 4 below);
- Heritage Assets (see 5 below);
- Public Benefit Entities, including incoming resources from non-exchange transactions, public entity business combinations and concessionary loans (see 6 below);
- Financial Institutions (see Chapter 10 at 11.2.4); and
- Funding Commitments (see Chapter 19 at 3.9).

These are all dealt with in Section 34 – *Specialised Activities.* Accounting by retirement benefit plans is outside the scope of this publication.

2   AGRICULTURE

2.1   Introduction

Section 34 sets out the recognition, measurement and disclosure requirements for agricultural activities. While these requirements are based on the IFRS for SMEs, the FRC included in FRS 102 an accounting policy choice to apply either a fair value model or a cost model.

Originally, the proposed requirements for agriculture were largely based on a fair value model in line with IAS 41 – *Agriculture*. It is observed in the Basis for Conclusions that respondents questioned the proposed requirements noting that previous accounting standards did not set out accounting requirements for these transactions and although the proposals included an exemption from applying fair value where there is undue cost or effort, the fair value information is inconsistent with the way most agricultural businesses are managed and would not benefit the users of financial statements. Therefore, an accounting policy choice between a cost model and a fair value model was introduced for biological assets. *[FRS 102.BC.B34A.1-2].*

Respondents in favour of the cost model also expected that the cost model would mean that both biological assets and agricultural produce should be measured at cost although both IFRS and the IFRS for SMEs require agricultural produce to be measured at the point of harvest at fair value less costs to sell. *[FRS 102.BC.B34A.3]*. The Basis for Conclusions further observes that agricultural produce, as opposed to biological assets, should be capable of being measured at fair value without undue cost or effort and should provide more relevant information to users. However, respondents argued that agricultural businesses often manage their business on the basis of cost information and agricultural produce should be permitted to be measured at cost. Therefore, use of the cost model for agricultural produce is limited to those entities that had chosen the cost model for biological assets. Such entities also have the choice of using the fair value model for their agricultural produce. *[FRS 102.BC.B34A.4]*.

2.2 Key differences to IFRS

There are two principal measurement differences between Section 34 and IAS 41: the first relates to the measurement basis for biological assets and related agricultural produce and the second relates to the concept of bearer plants.

2.2.1 Measurement basis

Section 34 permits an accounting policy choice between the fair value model and the cost model. See 2.5 below.

IAS 41 requires the measurement of biological assets at fair value less costs to sell, unless at initial recognition the entity cannot reliably measure the fair value, in which case the entity would measure the biological asset or agricultural produce at historic cost less any accumulated depreciation and any accumulated impairment losses until fair value becomes reliably measurable. *[IAS 41.12]*.

2.2.2 Bearer plants

Section 34 does not make a distinction between biological assets and bearer plants. Therefore, bearer plants are treated as biological assets and accounted for in accordance with Section 34.

IAS 41 does distinguish between biological assets and bearer plants. IAS 41 defines a bearer plant as a living plant which is used in the production or supply of agricultural produce, is expected to bear produce for more than one period and has a remote chance of being sold as agricultural produce, except for incidental scrap sales. *[IAS 41.5]*. Bearer plants are scoped out of IAS 41 and instead fall in the scope of IAS 16 – *Property, Plant and Equipment. [IAS 41.1]*.

2.2.3 Government grants related to biological assets

Government grants related to biological assets are not within the scope of Section 34. Government grants are recognised and measured in accordance with Section 24 – *Government Grants.*

An unconditional government grant related to a biological asset measured at its fair value less costs to sell is within the scope of IAS 41. *[IAS 41.34-35]*.

2.3 Definitions and scope

2.3.1 Definitions

The following terms are used in paragraphs 34.2 to 34.10A of Section 34 with the definitions specified. *[FRS 102 Appendix I]*.

Term	Definition
Agricultural activity	The management by an entity of the biological transformation of biological assets for sale, into agricultural produce or into additional biological assets.
Agricultural produce	The harvested product of the entity's biological assets.
Biological asset	A living animal or plant.

Agricultural activity, as defined in the table above, covers a wide range of activities, such as, raising livestock, forestry, annual or perennial cropping, cultivating orchards and plantations, floriculture, and aquaculture (including fish farming). *[IAS 41.6]*.

These definitions can be illustrated as follows: *[IAS 41.4]*

Biological assets	Agricultural produce	Products that are the result of processing after harvest
Sheep	Wool	Yarn, carpet
Trees in a plantation	Felled trees	Logs, lumber
Plants	Cotton	Thread, clothing
	Harvested cane	Sugar
Dairy cattle	Milk	Cheese
Pigs	Carcass	Sausages, cured hams
Bushes	Leaf	Tea, cured tobacco
Vines	Grapes	Wine
Fruit trees	Picked fruit	Processed fruit

2.3.2 Scope

An entity that is engaged in agricultural activity should determine an accounting policy for each class of biological asset and its related agricultural produce. *[FRS 102.34.2]*. In addition, biological assets held by lessees under finance leases and biological assets provided by lessors under operating leases should be measured in accordance with Section 34. *[FRS 102.20.1(d)]*.

Biological assets may be outside the scope of Section 34 when they are not used in agricultural activity. For example, animals in a zoo (or game park) that does not have an active breeding programme and rarely sells any animals or animal products would be outside the scope of the standard. Another example is activities in the pharmaceutical industry that involve the culture of bacteria. Such activity would not fall within the scope of Section 34. While the bacteria may be considered a biological asset, the development of a culture by a pharmaceutical company would not constitute agricultural activity.

Once harvested, agricultural produce is no longer within the scope of Section 34. At that point, it is measured at its fair value less costs to sell and this measurement becomes the cost at that date when applying Section 13 – *Inventories* – or another applicable section of FRS 102. *[FRS 102.34.5]*.

Section 34 does also not apply to the following:

- land used by the entity for agricultural activity. This falls within the scope of either Section 17 – *Property, Plant and Equipment* (see Chapter 15) or Section 16 – *Investment Property* (see Chapter 14);

- plant and equipment related to agricultural activity. This falls within the scope of Section 17 (see Chapter 15);

- intangible assets related to agricultural activity which fall within the scope of Section 18 – *Intangible Assets other than Goodwill* (see Chapter 16); and

- leased biological assets held by a lessee under an operating lease which fall under Section 20 – *Leases* (see Chapter 18).

2.4   Recognition

An entity should recognise a biological asset or an item of agricultural produce only when:

(a)   the entity controls the asset as a result of past events;

(b)   it is probable that future economic benefits associated with the asset will flow to the entity; and

(c)   the fair value or cost of the asset can be measured reliably. *[FRS 102.34.3]*.

As discussed at 2.3 above, Section 34 only applies to agricultural produce (i.e. harvested crops) at the point of harvest and not prior or subsequent to harvest. Unharvested agricultural produce is considered to be part of the biological asset from which it will be harvested. Therefore, before harvest, agricultural produce should not be recognised separately from the biological asset from which it comes. For example, grapes on the vine are accounted for as part of the vines themselves right up to the point of harvest.

2.5   Measurement

For each class of biological asset and its related agricultural produce, Section 34 provides an entity an accounting policy choice to use either: *[FRS 102.34.3A]*

(a)   the fair value model set out at 2.6 below; or

(b)   the cost model set out at 2.7 below.

However, once an entity has elected to use the fair value model for a class of biological asset and its related agricultural produce, it is not subsequently permitted to change its accounting policy to the cost model. *[FRS 102.34.3B]*.

The Regulations and the LLP Regulations state that if the fair value model is adopted by an entity, it must be adopted for all living animals and plants where their fair value can be reliably be determined. *[1 Sch 39(2), 2 Sch 47(2), 3 Sch 33(2), 1 Sch 39(2)(LLP)]*. However, the Note on legal requirements to FRS 102 states that the ability of an entity to subdivide biological classes such that some classes may be measured cost and others at fair value is consistent with the most reasonable and common sense interpretation of the Regulations. *[FRS 102 Appendix III.37D]*.

2.6 Fair value model

2.6.1 Measurement

If an entity applies the fair value model, it should measure a biological asset on initial recognition and at each reporting date at its fair value less costs to sell. Changes in fair value less costs to sell should be recognised in profit or loss. *[FRS 102.34.4]*. Agricultural produce harvested from an entity's biological assets should be measured at the point of harvest at its fair value less costs to sell. This then becomes the cost at that date when applying Section 13 or another applicable section of FRS 102. *[FRS 102.34.5]*.

Fair value less costs to sell is 'the amount obtainable from the sale of an asset or cash-generating unit in an arm's length transaction between knowledgeable, willing parties, less the costs of disposal.' *[FRS 102 Appendix I]*. The costs of disposal would include costs that are necessary for a sale to occur but that would not otherwise arise, such as commissions to brokers and dealers, levies by regulatory agencies and commodity exchanges, and transfer taxes and duties. *[IAS 41.BC3]*.

2.6.2 Fair value hierarchy

Section 34 provides guidance on determining fair value and establishes a hierarchy that can be summarised as follows:

(a) the price for the asset in an active market (see 2.6.2.A below);

(b) absent an active market, one or more of the following types of market-based data (see 2.6.2.B below):

    (i) the most recent market transaction price;

    (ii) adjusted market prices for similar assets; or

    (iii) sector benchmarks;

(c) the present value of expected net cash flows from the asset (see 2.6.2.C below).

2.6.2.A Active market

When an active market exists for a biological asset or agricultural produce in its present location and condition, the quoted price in that market is the appropriate basis for determining the fair value of that asset. *[FRS 102.34.6(a)]*. Under FRS 102, an active market is one in which all the following conditions exist: *[FRS 102 Appendix I]*

(a) the items traded in the market are homogeneous;

(b) willing buyers and sellers can normally be found at any time; and

(c) prices are available to the public.

If an entity has access to different active markets then it should use the price in the market that it expects to use. *[FRS 102.34.6(a)]*.

2.6.2.B   *Market-based data in the absence of an active market*

If there is no active market then an entity should consider the following types of market-based data in determining fair value: *[FRS 102.34.6(b)]*

(a)   the most recent market transaction price, provided that there has not been a significant change in economic circumstances between the date of that transaction and the end of the reporting period;

(b)   market prices for similar assets with adjustment to reflect differences; and

(c)   sector benchmarks such as the value of an orchard expressed per export tray, bushel, or hectare, and the value of cattle expressed per kilogram of meat.

The above market-based data may suggest different conclusions as to the fair value of a biological asset or an item of agricultural produce. In those cases, an entity considers the reasons for those differences, to arrive at the most reliable estimate of fair value within a relatively narrow range of reasonable estimates. *[FRS 102.34.6(c)]*.

'Relatively narrow range' is not defined further but is presumably included to prevent outlying estimates from being used as a reasonable estimate.

2.6.2.C   *Fair value in the absence of market prices or data*

Fair value may sometimes be readily determinable even though market determined prices or values are not available for a biological asset in its present condition. Therefore, an entity should consider whether the present value of expected net cash flows from the asset discounted at a current market determined rate results in a reliable measure of fair value. *[FRS 102.34.6(d)]*.

The purpose of a calculation of the present value of expected net cash flows is to determine the fair value of a biological asset in its present location and condition. Therefore, in determining the present value of expected net cash flows, an entity includes the net cash flows that market participants would expect the asset to generate in its most relevant market. An entity should ensure that it uses assumptions for determining a discount rate that are consistent with those used in estimating the expected cash flows; this is to avoid double-counting or overlooking risks. In any case, the entity should exclude the cash flows for financing the assets, taxation or re-establishing biological assets after harvest, for example, the cost of replanting trees in a plantation after harvest.

2.6.2.D   *Fair value of a biological asset that is not reliably measurable*

If an entity cannot measure the fair value of a biological asset reliably then it should apply the cost model (see 2.7 below) to that biological asset until such time that the fair value can be reliably measured. *[FRS 102.34.6A]*.

For agricultural produce, the FRC's view is that agricultural produce should be capable of measurement at fair value without undue cost or effort, and should provide more relevant information for users'. *[FRS 102.BC.B34A.4]*. Nonetheless, Section 34 retains the choice of the fair value model or the cost model for agricultural produce, dependent on the treatment of the biological assets to which the agricultural produce is related (see 2.7.1.B below).

2.6.3 Disclosures

An entity should disclose the following information for each class of biological asset that is measured using the fair value model: *[FRS 102.34.7]*

(a)   a description of each class of biological asset;

(b)   the methods and significant assumptions applied in determining the fair value of each class of biological asset; and

(c)   a reconciliation of changes in the carrying amount of each class of biological asset between the beginning and the end of the current period. The reconciliation should include:

    (i)   the gain or loss arising from changes in fair value less costs to sell;

    (ii)   increases resulting from purchases;

    (iii)   decreases attributable to sales;

    (iv)   decreases resulting from harvest;

    (v)   increases resulting from business combinations; and

    (vi)   other changes.

This reconciliation need not be presented for prior periods.

A class of assets is a grouping of assets of a similar nature and use in an entity's operations. *[FRS 102 Appendix I]*. In grouping biological assets into classes in order to make the disclosures above, an entity may consider distinguishing between different types of assets, such as consumable biological assets, bearer biological assets or mature and immature assets. In particular, it should be noted that for the purposes of the reconciliation at (c) above, it would be unhelpful to combine information about annual crops (which are akin to inventory) with that on bearer plant or long-lived biological assets (which are more like property, plant and equipment).

If an entity measures any individual biological assets at cost because fair value cannot be measured reliably (see 2.6.2.D above), it should explain why fair value cannot be reliably measured. If the fair value of such a biological asset becomes reliably measurable during the current period an entity shall explain why fair value has become reliably measurable and the effect of the change. *[FRS 102.34.7A]*.

Finally, an entity should disclose the methods and significant assumptions applied in determining the fair value at the point of harvest of each class of agricultural produce. *[FRS 102.34.7B]*.

2.7   Cost model

2.7.1   Measurement

2.7.1.A   Biological assets

An entity that applies the cost model should measure biological assets at cost less any accumulated depreciation and any accumulated impairment losses. *[FRS 102.34.8]*.

'Historical cost' is the amount of cash or cash equivalents paid or the fair value of the consideration given to acquire the asset at the time of its acquisition. Amortised historical cost is the historical cost of an asset or liability plus or minus that portion of its historical cost previously recognised as an expense or income. *[FRS 102.2.34(a)]*. In determining cost and depreciated cost an entity should consider the guidance in Section 17 (see Chapter 15).

Impairment losses on biological assets measured under the cost model are within the scope of Section 27 – *Impairment of Assets* (see Chapter 24 at 3.1).

2.7.1.B   Agricultural produce

Section 34 requires that in applying the cost model, agricultural produce harvested from an entity's biological assets should be measured at the point of harvest at either: *[FRS 102.34.9]*

(a)   the lower of cost and estimated selling price less costs to complete and sell; or

(b)   its fair value less costs to sell. Any gain or loss arising on initial recognition of agricultural produce at fair value less costs to sell should be included in profit or loss for the period in which it arises.

That amount is then the cost at that date when applying Section 13 or another applicable section of this FRS.

In other words, if an entity elects to measure its biological assets under the cost model, it will still be allowed to measure agricultural produce under the fair value model. However, the converse would not be true, if an entity measures its biological assets under the fair value model then it must measure the resulting agricultural produce under the fair value model as well.

2.7.2   Disclosures

For each class of biological asset measured under the cost model, an entity should disclose the following: *[FRS 102.34.10]*

(a)   a description of each class of biological asset;

(b)   the depreciation method used;

(c)   the useful lives or the depreciation rates used; and

(d)   a reconciliation of changes in the carrying amount of each class of biological asset between the beginning and the end of the current period. The reconciliation shall include:

    (i)   increases resulting from purchases;

    (ii)   decreases attributable to sales;

    (iii)   decreases resulting from harvest;

    (iv)   increases resulting from business combinations;

    (v)   impairment losses recognised or reversed in profit or loss in accordance with Section 27; and

    (vi)   other changes.

    This reconciliation need not be presented for prior periods.

In addition, an entity should disclose, for any agricultural produce measured at fair value less costs to sell, the methods and significant assumptions applied in determining the fair value at the point of harvest of its agricultural produce. *[FRS 102.34.10A]*.

The comments at 2.6.3 above regarding classes of assets apply here also.

2.8 Summary of GAAP differences

The following table shows the differences between FRS 102 and IFRS.

	FRS 102	*IFRS*
Measurement	Accounting policy choice of either the fair value model or the cost model.	Entities must measure biological assets and agricultural produce at fair value less costs to sell unless the fair value cannot be reliably measured at initial recognition. In the latter case, the entity would measure at cost less accumulated depreciation and accumulated impairment losses.
Bearer plants	Definition does not exist in Section 34.	Defined as a living plant used in the production or supply of agricultural produce, expected to bear produce for more than one period and has a remote likelihood of being sold as agricultural produce, except for incidental scrap sales. Such plants are accounted for under IAS 16.
Government grants	Accounting for government grants related to biological assets is not in the scope of Section 34.	Accounting for government grants related to biological assets measured at fair value less costs to sell is set out in IAS 41. Grants related to biological assets measured at cost are in the scope of IAS 20.

3 EXTRACTIVE ACTIVITIES

3.1 Introduction

An entity applying FRS 102 which is engaged in the exploration for and/or evaluation of mineral resources (extractive activities) must apply the requirements of IFRS 6 – *Exploration for and Evaluation of Mineral Resources* (as adopted in the EU). *[FRS 102.34.11].*

IFRS 6 covers the accounting for exploration and evaluation (E&E) expenditures which are 'expenditures incurred by an entity in connection with the exploration for and evaluation of mineral resources before the technical feasibility and commercial viability of extracting a mineral resource are demonstrable'. E&E assets are defined as 'exploration and evaluation expenditures recognised as assets in accordance with the entity's accounting policy'. *[IFRS 6 Appendix A].* IFRS 6 is limited to accounting for E&E expenditures and does not address the other aspects of accounting for entities engaged in these activities. This section will therefore not apply to expenditures incurred before the exploration for, and evaluation of, mineral resources (e.g. expenditures incurred before the entity has obtained legal rights to explore in a specific area) or after the technical feasibility and commercial viability of extracting a mineral resource are demonstrable. *[IFRS 6.5].* Equipment used in the E&E phase, e.g. property, plant and equipment and any other intangibles such as software, are not in the scope of IFRS 6, instead they are in the scope of Sections 17 and 18 respectively.

The scope and objectives of IFRS 6 are covered in further detail in Chapter 39 at 3.1 of EY International GAAP 2019.

Activities outside the E&E phase which are not covered by IFRS 6, may be covered by the following sections of FRS 102:

- Section 13 – *Inventories;*
- Section 17 – *Property, Plant and Equipment;*
- Section 18 – *Intangible Assets other than Goodwill;* or
- Section 20 – *Leases.*

In many of these sections 'minerals and mineral reserves' are excluded from their scope, although the exact wording of the scope exclusions differs between standards.

3.2   Requirements of Section 34 for extractive activities

As noted at 3.1 above, FRS 102 requires an entity engaged in extractive activities to apply the requirements of IFRS 6 to account for E&E expenditures. *[FRS 102.34.11].*

IFRS 6 is not discussed in detail in this publication. Instead, readers are referred to Chapter 39 of EY International GAAP 2019 which covers IFRS 6 in detail.

IFRS 6 contains within it a number of references to other standards. In applying FRS 102, the references within IFRS 6 should be taken to mean the relevant section or paragraph of FRS 102. *[FRS 102.34.11A].* For example, paragraph 6 of IFRS 6 refers to IAS 8 – *Accounting Policies, Changes in Accounting Estimates and Errors.* The relevant section of FRS 102 in this case would be Section 10.

However, when applying paragraph 21 of IFRS 6, which deals with the allocation of E&E assets to cash-generating units or groups of cash-generating units for the purpose of assessing such assets for impairment, Section 34 states that the cash-generating unit or group of cash-generating units should be no larger than an operating segment as defined by FRS 102 and the reference to IFRS 8 – *Operating Segments* – should be ignored. *[FRS 102.34.11B].*

If on first-time adoption, an entity determines that it is impractical to apply any of the requirements related to the assessment of exploration and evaluation assets for impairment to previous comparative amounts, an entity should disclose this fact. *[FRS 102.34.11C].*

On transition to FRS 102, an entity which previously accounted for exploration and development costs for oil and gas properties in the development or production phases under the full cost accounting method may elect to measure these assets on the following basis:

- exploration and evaluation assets at the amount determined under the entity's previous GAAP; and
- assets in the development or production phases at the amount determined for the cost centre under the entity's previous GAAP. The entity shall allocate this amount to the cost centre's underlying assets *pro rata* using reserve volumes or reserve values as of that date.

Both E&E assets and assets in the production and development phases should be tested for impairment, at the date of transition, in accordance with Section 34 (IFRS 6) or Section 27 respectively. *[FRS 102.35.10(j)].*

This transitional provision should eliminate the requirement for a restatement for companies which had previously adopted the full cost method and make the process of allocating E&E assets into cash-generating units required easier under FRS 102.

3.3 Practical implementation issues

Practical issues in the oil and gas industry are covered in Chapter 39 of EY International GAAP 2019.

4 SERVICE CONCESSION ARRANGEMENTS

4.1 Introduction

Service concession arrangements have been developed in many countries as a mechanism for procuring public services using private sector finance and management expertise. Under a service concession arrangement (SCA), private capital is used to provide major economic and social facilities for public use. The concept is that, rather than having bodies in the public sector taking on the entire responsibility and risk of funding and building infrastructure assets such as roads, bridges, railways, hospitals, prisons and schools, some of these should be contracted out to private sector entities from which the public sector bodies would rent the assets and buy services. In the UK, such arrangements are referred to as Public Private Partnerships and formerly as arrangements under the Private Finance Initiative.

Service concession arrangements are of great complexity and are often devised to meet political as well as purely commercial ends. SCAs are contractual arrangements between the public sector body and the private sector operator which set out in great detail the rights of each party, the related performance obligations and measures and the mechanisms for payment. The transactions involved in a typical service concession are wide-ranging and include the construction or refurbishment of infrastructure assets, the delivery of operating and maintenance services, collection of revenues from the public, and the receipt of payments from the public sector body (some of which may have been deferred). As a result, the accounting issues raised by service concessions range across a number of areas, including accounting for construction contracts, property, plant and equipment, leasing, intangible assets, financial instruments, revenue and borrowing costs (as these arrangements are often financed by borrowings of the operator).

The requirements of Section 34 related to service concessions require an entity to determine whether an arrangement meets the definition of a service concession and then directs that entity to the other sections of FRS 102 that should be applied to each component of the transaction. Central to the definition of an SCA is whether the public sector body (or grantor) has control over the infrastructure, by virtue of both its rights under the contract to direct how the assets are used during the concession and thereafter by controlling any significant residual interest in the assets. *[FRS 102.34.12A]*.

An operator first applying FRS 102 can elect to retain the same asset classification (property, plant and equipment or financial asset) as it applied under previous UK GAAP for those service concession arrangements that were entered into before its date of transition and apply Section 34 to SCAs entered into after its date of transition. *[FRS 102.35.10(i)]*. However, no such relief is available to grantors.

Chapter 31

Only minor changes to the Service Concessions part of Section 34 were made by the Triennial review 2017 of FRS 102 (see 4.3.4.A and 4.3.5 below), being:

- to clarify that an entity is not prevented from classifying a financial asset as basic when payment is contingent on the operator meeting specified quality or efficiency conditions; *[FRS 102.34.14]* and

- to require additional disclosures. *[FRS 102.34.16B, 16C]*.

4.2   Key differences to IFRS

Under IFRS, two Interpretations apply to the treatment of service concession arrangements: IFRIC 12 – *Service Concession Arrangements* – and SIC-29 – *Service Concession Arrangements: Disclosures.*

Unlike IFRIC 12, FRS 102 sets out requirements for accounting by the public sector body in an SCA, requiring it to recognise a finance lease liability and related asset, to the extent that it has a contractual obligation to make payments to the operator in respect of the infrastructure assets. *[FRS 102.34.12F]*. IFRIC 12 does not specify the accounting by grantors. *[IFRIC 12.9]*.

For operators in a service concession, Section 34 applies the same control criteria as IFRIC 12 (see 4.3.2 below). However, whilst the resulting accounting principles are very similar to those established in IFRIC 12, what is set out in FRS 102 is very much a simplification of the Interpretation and there is no guidance on how the control criteria might be interpreted in different situations; exactly what is meant by services 'for the benefit of the public'; and how to classify arrangements where only part of the infrastructure is controlled by the grantor (see 4.3.2.A below). In addition, Section 34 does not consider situations where the following features exist in a service concession arrangement:

- assets of the operator are used in the service concession;
- payments are made by the operator to the grantor (for example rentals payable for assets retained by the grantor or for other services provided by the public sector body);
- payments under the service concession contract are variable;
- where both an intangible asset and a financial asset exists; and
- major upgrade, replacement or maintenance works are required at intervals during the concession term.

IFRIC 12 also provides a number of examples, tables and flow charts to assist entities in implementing its requirements. None of these are included in Section 34.

As discussed at 4.3.4.G below, Section 10 implies that entities may also consider the requirements and guidance in IFRIC 12 in these circumstances, *[FRS 102.10.6]*, which are discussed in Chapter 26 of EY International GAAP 2019.

4.3   Requirements of FRS 102 for service concession arrangements

4.3.1   *Definitions used in Section 34 for service concession arrangements*

The following terms are used in paragraphs 34.12 to 34.16C of Section 34 with the definitions specified. *[FRS 102 Appendix I]*.

Term	Definition
Borrowing costs	Interest and other costs incurred by an entity in connection with the borrowing of funds.

Financial asset [extract]	An asset that is:
	(a) cash;
	(c) a contractual right:
	   (i) to receive cash or another financial asset from another entity; or
	   (ii) to exchange financial assets or financial liabilities with another entity under conditions that are potentially favourable to the entity; ...

Infrastructure assets	Infrastructure for public services, such as roads, bridges, tunnels, prisons, hospitals, airports, water distribution facilities, energy supply and telecommunications networks.
Intangible asset	An identifiable non-monetary asset without physical substance. Such an asset is identifiable when: (a) it is separable, i.e. capable of being separated or divided from the entity and sold, transferred, licensed, rented or exchanged, either individually or together with a related contract, asset or liability; or (b) it arises from contractual or other legal rights, regardless of whether those rights are transferable or separable from the entity or from other rights and obligations.
Public benefit entity	An entity whose primary objective is to provide goods or services for the general public, community or social benefit and where any equity is provided with a view to supporting the entity's primary objectives rather than with a view to providing a financial return to equity providers, shareholders or members.
Residual value (of an asset)	The estimated amount that an entity would currently obtain from disposal of an asset, after deducting the estimated costs of disposal, if the asset were already of the age and in the condition expected at the end of its useful life.
Revenue	The gross inflow of economic benefits during the period arising in the course of the ordinary activities of an entity when those inflows result in increases in equity, other than increases relating to contributions from equity participants.
Service concession arrangement (SCA)	An arrangement whereby a public sector body or public benefit entity (the grantor) contracts with a private sector entity (the operator) to construct (or upgrade), operate and maintain infrastructure assets for a specified period of time (the concession period).
Useful life	The period over which an asset is expected to be available for use by an entity or the number of production or similar units expected to be obtained from the asset by an entity.

Chapter 31

4.3.2 Scope

A SCA arises from a contractual agreement between a public sector body or public benefit entity (the grantor) and a private sector entity (the operator) to construct or upgrade, operate and maintain infrastructure assets for a specified period of time (the concession period). The operator is paid for its services over the period of the arrangement. *[FRS 102.34.12]*. Such payments are often referred to as 'unitary charges' because the amounts to be paid under the contract compensate the operator for both services in constructing or upgrading the infrastructure assets and for their maintenance and operation over a longer period.

A common feature of an SCA is the public service nature of the obligation undertaken by the operator, whereby the arrangement contractually obliges the operator to provide services to, or on behalf of, the grantor for the benefit of the public. *[FRS 102.34.12]*. This feature, that the operator is providing services to the public or for public benefit, is often applied to distinguish a service concession from the provision by a private sector entity of outsourcing, leasing or other services to a public sector body or public benefit entity (see 4.3.2.A below).

Specifically an arrangement is an SCA when the following conditions apply: *[FRS 102.34.12A]*

(a) the grantor controls or regulates what services the operator must provide using the infrastructure assets, to whom, and at what price; and

(b) the grantor controls, through ownership, beneficial entitlement or otherwise, any significant residual interest in the assets at the end of the term of the arrangement.

Where the infrastructure assets have no significant residual value at the end of the term of the arrangement (i.e. the concession is for the entire useful life of the related infrastructure), then the arrangement is accounted for as a service concession if the grantor controls or regulates the services provided using the infrastructure as described at (a) above. *[FRS 102.34.12A]*.

For the purpose of condition (b) above, the grantor's control over any significant residual interest should both restrict the operator's practical ability to sell or pledge the infrastructure assets and give the grantor a continuing right of use throughout the concession period. *[FRS 102.34.12A]*. Control over the residual interest does not require that the infrastructure is returned to the grantor at the end of the concession. It is sufficient that the deployment of the infrastructure is controlled by the grantor, as illustrated in the example below.

Example 31.1: Residual arrangements

A gas transmission system is being operated under a concession arrangement with the State Gas Authority. At the end of the term, the grantor will either acquire the infrastructure assets at their net book value, determined on the basis of the contract, or it may decide to grant a new SCA on the basis of a competitive tender, which will exclude the current operator. If the grantor elects to do the latter, the operator will be entitled to the lower of the following two amounts:

(a) the net book value of the infrastructure, determined on the basis of the contract; and

(b) the proceeds of a new competitive bidding process to acquire a new contract.

Although the operator cannot enter the competitive tender, it also has the right to enter into a new concession term but, in order to do so, it must match the best tender offer made. It has to pay to the grantor the excess of the best offer (b) above the amount in (a); should the tender offer be lower than (a), it will receive an equivalent refund.

In this arrangement, the grantor will control the residual. It can choose to take over the activities of the concession itself or it can allow potential operators, including the incumbent, to bid for a second term. The price that might be received by the operator, or paid by the grantor, is not relevant.

FRS 102 states that a concession may contain a group of contracts and sub-arrangements as elements of the SCA as a whole. Such an arrangement is treated as a whole when the group of contracts and sub-arrangements are linked in such a way that the commercial effect cannot be understood without reference to them as a whole. Accordingly, the contractual terms of certain contracts or arrangements may meet both the scope requirements of an SCA under Section 34, as noted above, and a leasing contract under Section 20. Where this is the case, the requirements of Section 34 shall prevail. *[FRS 102.34.12C]*.

4.3.2.A Judgements required in determining whether an arrangement is an SCA

Arrangements within scope will be those that meet the following criteria:

- the arrangement is a contract between a public sector grantor and a private sector operator; *[FRS 102.34.12]*
- the grantor controls or regulates the services; *[FRS 102.34.12A(a)]*
- the grantor controls any significant residual interest; *[FRS 102.34.12A(b)]*
- the infrastructure is constructed or upgraded in order to provide services to, or on behalf of, the public; *[FRS 102.34.12]* and
- the operator has either a contractual right to receive cash from or at the direction of the grantor; or a contractual right to charge users of the service. *[FRS 102.34.13]*.

If an arrangement meets all of these criteria then the concession is in scope of Section 34. The last criterion also determines which accounting model, financial asset or intangible asset, described at 4.3.4 below, should be applied by the operator.

Because of the commercial and contractual complexities of SCAs and seemingly similar arrangements, the determination of whether or to what extent these criteria are met is always likely to be a matter of judgement and there will be different views in practice. Section 34 acknowledges that some arrangements might more appropriately be classified as leases *[FRS 102.34.12C]* and, as noted at 4.3.2 above, where the operator is contracted to provide services to the grantor for its own benefit (rather than providing infrastructure services to the public), depiction of the arrangement as a lease could be more appropriate. For example, where a government department has outsourced its information technology function to a private sector operator, it would be more usual to account for this arrangement as an IT services contract rather than a service concession. However, where the arrangement could be judged to be either a lease or a service concession, it is accounted for using Section 34. *[FRS 102.34.12C]*.

This, and a number of other judgements familiar to IFRS reporters trying to assess whether an arrangement falls within the scope of IFRIC 12, are not addressed in Section 34. These include:

- Determining what constitutes services to the public. Do members of the public have to consume the services being provided (for example by using a road or bridge) or does a wider concept of public benefit apply (for example in the provision of services by private contractors to the Ministry of Defence)?
- Deciding how to classify arrangements where the use of only part of the infrastructure is controlled under the terms of the contract, or for part of the time. For example, a private contractor might be given the contract to build and operate an airport. The services to be provided for passengers, for airport security and to airlines might be regulated under the contract; but the operator might have total freedom over the design, operation and pricing of the parking, retail and other space in the airport complex.

Section 10 of FRS 102 suggests that entities may also consider the requirements and guidance in IFRIC 12 in these circumstances. *[FRS 102.10.6]*. The scope of IFRIC 12 is discussed in Chapter 26 at 2 of EY International GAAP 2019.

Chapter 31

4.3.2.B   Accounting for arrangements determined not to be SCAs under FRS 102

Where an arrangement does not meet both the definition of an SCA and the control criteria noted at 4.3.2 above, Section 34 does not apply and the arrangement should be accounted for in accordance with Section 17, Section 18, Section 20 or Section 23 – *Revenue*, as appropriate, based on the nature of the arrangement. *[FRS 102.34.12D]*.

4.3.3   Accounting by grantors – finance lease liability model

Section 34 requires a grantor to account for its interest in a service concession contract as a finance lease. This is because the grantor in an SCA controls both the use to which the infrastructure is put during the contract term as well as any significant residual interest in the infrastructure at the end of the concession. *[FRS 102.34.12A]*. The contract also requires the grantor to pay the operator for the construction and operation of the assets, or to establish arrangements for the users of the infrastructure to pay the operator themselves.

Therefore, the infrastructure assets are recognised as assets of the grantor together with a liability for its obligation under the concession. *[FRS 102.34.12E]*. The grantor should initially recognise the infrastructure assets and associated liability in accordance with paragraphs 9 and 10 of Section 20. *[FRS 102.34.12F]*. The liability is recognised as a finance lease liability and subsequently accounted for in accordance with paragraph 11 of Section 20. *[FRS 102.34.12G]*. Accounting for finance leases is discussed in Chapter 18.

The infrastructure assets are recognised as property, plant and equipment or as intangible assets, as appropriate, and subsequently accounted for in accordance with Section 17 or Section 18. *[FRS 102.34.12H]*. This includes the determination of useful lives and amortisation methods for the assets; the estimation of residual values, as discussed in Chapters 15 and 16 for property, plant and equipment and for intangible assets respectively. This also includes accounting for impairment as discussed in Chapter 24.

If the grantor is not required to recognise a liability to make payments to the operator, for example, because the operator is expected to charge the users of the infrastructure directly, the grantor shall not recognise the infrastructure assets. *[FRS 102.34.12F]*. In other words, the grantor recognises an asset only to the extent of its obligation to make payments to the operator for the construction of the infrastructure, its upgrade or its residual value at the end of the concession.

4.3.4   Accounting by operators

Accounting by the operator is more complicated, because its involvement in the concession comprises transactions relating to the construction of the infrastructure or its upgrade; the provision of services to the public using the infrastructure; and the collection of payments from either the grantor, users of the service or a combination of both.

Looking first at the infrastructure, because the grantor controls the use of the assets during the concession term and any significant residual interest in them after the contract has ended, *[FRS 102.34.12A]*, an operator in an arrangement determined to be a service concession does not recognise the infrastructure assets as property, plant and equipment. The operator only has a right of access to the assets in order to provide the public service on behalf of the grantor in accordance with the terms specified in the concession. *[FRS 102.34.12I]*.

A service concession contract gives the operator the right to receive payment in return for meeting its obligations to construct, upgrade, operate and maintain the infrastructure assets controlled by the grantor. Accordingly, Section 34 sets out two principal categories of concession:

- in one, the operator receives a financial asset – an unconditional contractual right to receive a specified or determinable amount of cash or another financial asset from, or at the direction of, the grantor in return for constructing (or upgrading) the infrastructure assets and then operating and maintaining the asset for a specified period of time. This category includes guarantees by the grantor to pay for any shortfall between amounts received from users of the public service and specified or determinable amounts; *[FRS 102.34.13(a)]* and

- in the other, the operator receives an intangible asset – a right to charge for the use of the infrastructure assets that it constructs (or upgrades) and then operates and maintains for a specified period of time. A right to charge users is not an unconditional right to receive cash because the amounts are contingent on the extent to which the public uses the service. *[FRS 102.34.13(b)]*.

As noted above, sometimes an SCA may entitle the operator to receive payment from both the grantor and the users of the infrastructure. To the extent that the grantor has given an unconditional guarantee of payment for the construction (or upgrade) of the infrastructure assets, the operator has a financial asset; to the extent that the operator receives a right to charge the public for using the service, the operator has an intangible asset. *[FRS 102.34.13]*.

No guidance is provided in Section 34 on the determination of whether the financial asset model or the intangible asset model is applied. The application of similar requirements under IFRIC 12 is discussed in Chapter 26 at 4.1.2 of EY International GAAP 2019. A comparison between the different models can be illustrated in the following table:

	Arrangement	*Applicable model*
1	Grantor pays – fixed payments	Financial asset
2	Grantor pays – payments vary with demand	Intangible asset
3	Grantor retains demand risk – users pay but grantor guarantees amounts	Financial asset or bifurcated (part financial, part intangible)
4	Grantor retains demand risk – operator collects revenues from users until it achieves specified return	Intangible asset
5	Users pay – no grantor guarantees	Intangible asset

4.3.4.A   Financial asset model

The operator shall recognise a financial asset to the extent it has an unconditional contractual right to receive cash or another financial asset from, or at the direction of, the grantor for the construction (or upgrade) services. The operator shall initially recognise the financial asset at the fair value of the consideration received or receivable, based on the fair value of the construction (or upgrade) services provided. Thereafter, it shall account for the financial asset in accordance with Section 11 – *Basic Financial Instruments* – and Section 12 – *Other Financial Instruments Issues*. *[FRS 102.34.14]*.

Whether the financial asset represents a basic financial instrument within the scope of Section 11 or Section 12 will depend on the terms of the Concession and judgement is required (see Chapter 10). The following example is based on Illustrative Example 1 in IFRIC 12. An amendment to Section 34 following the Triennial review 2017 clarifies that in classifying the financial asset as basic or other, a payment being contingent on the operator ensuring that the infrastructure meets specified quality or efficiency requirements does not prevent its classification as basic. *[FRS 102.34.14]*.

Example 31.2:   Financial asset model – recording the construction asset

Table 1 Concession terms

The terms of the arrangement require an operator to construct a road – completing construction within two years – and maintain and operate the road to a specified standard for eight years (i.e. years 3-10). The terms of the concession also require the operator to resurface the road at the end of year 8. At the end of year 10, the arrangement will end. The operator estimates that the costs it will incur to fulfil its obligations will be:

	Year	£
Construction services (per year)	1-2	500
Operation services (per year)	3-10	10
Road resurfacing	8	100

The terms of the concession require the grantor to pay the operator £200 per year in years 3-10 for making the road available to the public.

For the purpose of this illustration, it is assumed that all cash flows take place at the end of the year.

Table 2 Contract revenue

The operator recognises contract revenue and costs in accordance with Section 23. The costs of each activity – construction, operation, maintenance and resurfacing – are recognised as expenses by reference to the stage of completion of that activity. Contract revenue – the fair value of the amount due from the grantor for the activity undertaken – is recognised at the same time.

The total consideration (£200 in each of years 3-8) reflects the fair values for each of the services, which are:

	Fair value		
Construction	Forecast cost	+	5%
Operation and maintenance	" "	+	20%
Road resurfacing	" "	+	10%
Lending rate to grantor	6.18% per year		

In year 1, for example, construction costs of £500, construction revenue of £525 (cost plus 5 per cent), and hence construction profit of £25 are recognised in the income statement.

Financial asset

The amount due from the grantor meets the definition of a receivable in Section 11. The receivable is measured initially at fair value. It is subsequently measured at amortised cost, i.e. the amount initially recognised plus the cumulative interest on that amount calculated using the effective interest method minus repayments.

Table 3 Measurement of receivable

	£
Amount due for construction in year 1	525
Receivable at end of year 1*	525
Effective interest in year 2 on receivable at the end of year 1 (6.18% × £525)	32
Amount due for construction in year 2	525
Receivable at end of year 2	1,082
Effective interest in year 3 on receivable at the end of year 2 (6.18% × £1,082)	67
Amount due for operation in year 3 (£10 × (1 + 20%))	12
Cash receipts in year 3	(200)
Receivable at end of year 3	961

* No effective interest arises in year 1 because the cash flows are assumed to take place at the end of the year.

4.3.4.B   Intangible asset model

Under this accounting model, the operator recognises an intangible asset to the extent that it receives a right (a licence) to charge users of the public service. The operator shall initially recognise the intangible asset at the fair value of the consideration received or receivable, based on the fair value of the construction (or upgrade) services provided. Thereafter, it shall account for the intangible asset in accordance with Section 18. *[FRS 102.34.15]*. The following example is based on Example 2 in IFRIC 12.

Example 31.3:   Intangible asset model – recording the construction asset

Arrangement terms

The terms of a service arrangement require an operator to construct a road – completing construction within two years – and maintain and operate the road to a specified standard for eight years (i.e. years 3-10). The terms of the arrangement also require the operator to resurface the road when the original surface has deteriorated below a specified condition. The operator estimates that it will have to undertake the resurfacing at the end of the year 8. At the end of year 10, the service arrangement will end. The operator estimates that the costs it will incur to fulfil its obligations will be:

Table 1 Contract costs

	Year	£
Construction services (per year)	1-2	500
Operation services (per year)	3-10	10
Road resurfacing	8	100

The terms of the arrangement allow the operator to collect tolls from drivers using the road. The operator forecasts that vehicle numbers will remain constant over the duration of the contract and that it will receive tolls of £200 in each of years 3-10.

For the purpose of this illustration, it is assumed that all cash flows take place at the end of the year.

Intangible asset

The operator provides construction services to the grantor in exchange for an intangible asset, i.e. a right to collect tolls from road users in years 3-10. In accordance with Section 18, the operator recognises the intangible asset at cost, i.e. the fair value of consideration received or receivable.

Chapter 31

During the construction phase of the arrangement the operator's asset (representing its accumulating right to be paid for providing construction services) is classified as an intangible asset (licence to charge users of the infrastructure). The operator estimates the fair value of its consideration received to be equal to the forecast construction costs plus 5 per cent margin. It is also assumed that the operator adopts the allowed alternative treatment in Section 25 – *Borrowing Costs* – and therefore capitalises the borrowing costs, estimated at 6.7 per cent, during the construction phase:

Table 2 Initial measurement of intangible asset

	£
Construction services in year 1 (£500 × (1 + 5%))	525
Capitalisation of borrowing costs	34
Construction services in year 2 (£500 × (1 + 5%))	525
Intangible asset at end of year 2	1,084

The intangible asset is amortised over the period in which it is expected to be available for use by the operator, i.e. years 3-10. In this case, the directors determine that it is appropriate to amortise using a straight-line method. The annual amortisation charge is therefore £1,084 divided by 8 years, i.e. £135 per year.

Construction costs and revenue

The operator recognises the revenue and costs in accordance with Section 23, i.e. by reference to the stage of completion of the construction. It measures contract revenue at the fair value of the consideration received or receivable. Thus in each of years 1 and 2 it recognises in its income statement construction costs of £500, construction revenue of £525 (cost plus 5 per cent) and, hence, construction profit of £25.

Toll revenue

The road users pay for the public services at the same time as they receive them, i.e. when they use the road. The operator therefore recognises toll revenue when it collects the tolls.

4.3.4.C   Measuring the fair value of construction services

Under both the financial asset model and the intangible asset model, the asset that the operator initially recognises is measured at the fair value of the consideration received or receivable, based on the fair value of the construction (or upgrade) services provided. *[FRS 102.34.14, 15]*. The operator only recognises an asset in respect of the contractual obligations that have been satisfied at this stage, namely the provision of construction or upgrade services. Under Section 34, there is no suggestion that an operator would recognise an asset for the present value of all the contractual payments to be received under the contract (including for operating services).

Section 34 provides no guidance on the calculation of the fair value of the construction (or upgrade) services provided, and no guidance on the allocation of consideration between construction (or upgrade) services and operating services where the operator is paid under a single payment mechanism throughout the term of the concession.

Under IFRIC 12, the value of the construction services is determined in accordance with IFRS 15 – *Revenue from Contracts with Customers*. *[IFRIC 12.14]*. Applying a similar approach under FRS 102 would result in the fair value of the construction (or upgrade) services provided being calculated, and revenue recognised, in accordance with Section 23 (see Chapter 20). This approach has been applied in Examples 31.2 and 31.3 above, where an appropriate profit margin (5%) was added to the construction costs incurred. Under Section 23, revenue would be recognised by reference to the stage of completion of the construction (or upgrade) services.

4.3.4.D   Operating services

Section 34 requires the operator to account for revenue relating to the operating services it performs in accordance with Section 23. *[FRS 102.34.16]*. Accordingly, revenue may be recognised on a straight-line basis over the contract period; or as the infrastructure is used; or as other performance obligations are determined to have been satisfied (see Chapter 20).

4.3.4.E   Borrowing costs incurred during the construction or upgrade phase

Many operators will borrow funds to finance the up-front construction or upgrade costs associated with the SCA. Only under the intangible asset model will an operator have the option to capitalise any borrowing costs. Otherwise, borrowing costs attributable to the concession should be recognised as an expense. Entities should account for their borrowing costs in accordance with Section 25. *[FRS 102.34.16A]*. Accounting for borrowing costs is discussed in Chapter 22.

4.3.4.F   Relief from retrospective application by operators of SCAs

An operator adopting FRS 102 for the first time is not required to apply Section 34 to SCAs that were entered into before the date of transition. Such concessions would continue to be accounted for using the same accounting policies that applied at the date of transition to FRS 102. *[FRS 102.35.10(i)]*. This means that for these contracts, the concession asset would continue to be classified and measured as property, plant and equipment or financial assets in accordance with FRS 5 Application Note F and any financial assets would be accounted for under previous UK GAAP (rather than Section 17 or Sections 11 and 12 of FRS 102). This exemption would continue to apply to those pre-transition date contracts in subsequent financial statements, until such time when the assets and liabilities associated with those transactions, events or arrangements are derecognised. *[FRS 102.35.11A]*.

However, where a concession entered into before the date of transition is renegotiated in a way that significantly modifies the terms of the concession, such that had those terms existed at the outset a different classification would have resulted, then Section 35 requires that the operator should reassess the appropriateness of applying that exemption in the future. *[FRS 102.35.11B]*. This might result in the renegotiated concession being treated as a new arrangement, to which Section 34 would be applied. FRS 102 does not provide guidance on when such classification decisions should be revisited.

Section 34 is applied to all concessions entered into after the date of transition. *[FRS 102.35.10(i)]*.

There are no transitional reliefs available to grantors.

4.3.4.G   Aspects of SCA accounting not addressed in Section 34

As noted at 4.2 above, a number of features often seen in SCAs and familiar to IFRS reporters are not addressed in Section 34. These include accounting for the following features:

- assets of the operator used in the service concession;
- payments made by the operator to the grantor (for example rentals payable for assets retained by the grantor or for other services provided by the public sector body);
- the existence of variable payment terms under the service concession contract;
- where both an intangible asset and a financial asset exists; and
- where a major upgrade, replacement or maintenance works are required at intervals during the concession term.

Chapter 31

Section 10 of FRS 102 suggests that entities may also consider the requirements and guidance in IFRIC 12 in these circumstances. *[FRS 102.10.6]*. These features of service concession arrangements under IFRIC 12 are discussed in Chapter 26 at 4 and 5 of EY International GAAP 2019.

4.3.5 Disclosures relating to service concession arrangements

Section 34 did not originally specify any disclosures. The disclosure requirements introduced by the Triennial review 2017 are set out below.

An operator and a grantor should disclose information that enables users of the entity's financial statements to evaluate the nature and extent of relevant risks arising from service concession arrangements. This information shall typically include, but is not limited to:

(a) a description of the arrangement including any rights, obligations or options arising; and

(b) any significant terms of the arrangement that may affect the amount, timing and certainty of future cash flows. *[FRS 102.34.16B]*.

In addition, an operator should disclose the amount of revenue, profits or losses and other income recognised in the period on exchanging construction services for a financial asset or an intangible asset. *[FRS 102.34.16C]*.

Further detail on what disclosures may be made around the rights, obligations and options of the arrangement are given in SIC-29 for IFRS reporters. These include the rights to use specified assets; obligations to provide or rights to expect provision of services; obligations to acquire or build items of property, plant and equipment; obligations to deliver or rights to receive specified assets at the end of the concession period; renewal and termination options; and other rights and obligations (e.g. major overhauls). However, since this additional guidance is not provided within Section 34 it should be treated as suggested detail rather than a requirement.

Significant terms of the arrangement that may affect the amount, timing and certainty of future cash flows may include the period of the concession, re-pricing dates and the basis upon which re-pricing or re-negotiation is determined.

4.4 Summary of GAAP differences

The following table shows the differences between FRS 102 and IFRS.

	FRS 102	IFRS
Accounting by Grantor	Recognise a finance lease liability and related asset to the extent that there is a contractual obligation to pay for the infrastructure assets.	Not specified in IFRIC 12.

5 HERITAGE ASSETS

Section 34 includes guidance on the accounting for heritage assets, defined as 'Tangible and intangible assets with historic, artistic, scientific, technological, geophysical, or environmental qualities that are held and maintained principally for their contribution to knowledge and culture'. *[FRS 102 Appendix I]*.

In summary, the recognition and measurement accounting requirements for heritage assets are the same as for property, plant and equipment or intangible assets. However, the disclosure requirements are different.

5.1 Key differences to IFRS

Unlike FRS 102, IFRS has no specific requirements for heritage assets. Therefore, heritage assets are accounted for according to their nature under either IAS 16, IAS 38 – *Intangible Assets* – or IAS 40 – *Investment Property*.

5.2 Requirements of FRS 102 for heritage assets

5.2.1 *Terms used in Section 34 on heritage assets*

Heritage assets are 'tangible and intangible assets with historic, artistic, scientific, technological, geophysical, or environmental qualities that are held and maintained principally for their contribution to knowledge and culture'. *[FRS 102 Appendix I]*.

5.2.2 *Scope*

FRS 102 defines heritage assets according to their intended use ('maintained principally for their contribution to knowledge and culture') rather than according to their nature as a tangible or intangible asset. Section 34 states that its paragraphs relating to heritage assets do not apply to investment property, property, plant and equipment or intangible assets that fall within the scope of Section 16, Section 17, and Section 18. *[FRS 102.34.49]*. This is a somewhat circular reference, since the scope of both Sections 17 and 18 (but not Section 16) state that they do not apply to heritage assets. *[FRS 102.17.3, 18.3]*. However, the intent of this wording appears to be clarification that property, plant and equipment and intangible assets with historic, artistic, scientific, technological, geographical or environmental qualities that are not held principally for their contribution to knowledge and culture cannot be heritage assets under Section 34. Investment property is defined as property held to earn rentals or for capital appreciation or both *[FRS 102 Appendix I]* and as such cannot at the same time be held and maintained for its contribution to knowledge and culture.

Section 34 further explains that works of art and similar objects held by commercial companies are not heritage assets as they are not maintained principally for their contribution to knowledge and culture. Instead, such assets should be accounted for in accordance with Section 17. Similarly, heritage assets used by the entity itself, for example historic buildings used for teaching by education establishments, shall also be accounted for under Section 17. The reason for this is that an operational perspective is likely to be most relevant for users of the financial statements. Section 34 goes on to recommend that entities that use historic buildings or similar assets for their own use may consider providing voluntarily the disclosures set out at 5.2.4 below for heritage assets. *[FRS 102.34.50]*. Given that heritage assets are recognised and measured in accordance with Section 17 (see 5.2.3 below), this distinction drawn by the FRC between heritage assets maintained for their contribution to knowledge and culture and heritage assets used for some other purpose affects only disclosure and not recognition and measurement.

5.2.3   Recognition and measurement of heritage assets

The general requirement of Section 34 is that heritage assets should be recognised and measured in accordance with Section 17 or Section 18, as appropriate (i.e. using either the cost model or revaluation model). *[FRS 102.34.51]*. Accounting for property plant and equipment and intangible assets is discussed in Chapters 15 and 16 respectively.

Heritage assets must be recognised in the statement of financial position separately from other assets. *[FRS 102.34.52]*.

It is assumed that when heritage assets have previously been capitalised or are recently purchased that information on the cost or value of the asset will be available. However, when this information is not available, and cannot be obtained at a cost which is commensurate with the benefit to the users of the financial statements, the assets shall not be recognised. *[FRS 102.34.53]*. In those circumstances, additional disclosures are required explaining why the assets are not recognised, the significance and nature of those assets and information helpful in assessing the value of the assets (see 5.2.4 below). *[FRS 102.34.55(d)]*.

At each reporting date, an entity shall apply the requirements of Section 27 to determine whether a heritage asset is impaired and, if so, how to recognise and measure the impairment loss. Section 34 states that physical deterioration, breakage or doubts arising as to an asset's authenticity are examples of impairment indicators for heritage assets. *[FRS 102.34.54]*. The requirements of Section 27 are discussed in Chapter 24.

5.2.4   Disclosures required for heritage assets

An entity should disclose the following for all heritage assets it holds: *[FRS 102.34.55]*

(a)   an indication of the nature and scale of heritage assets held;

(b)   the policy for the acquisition, preservation, management and disposal of heritage assets (including a description of the records maintained by the entity of its collection of heritage assets and information on the extent to which access to the assets is permitted);

(c)   the accounting policies adopted for heritage assets, including details of the measurement bases used;

(d)   for heritage assets that have not been recognised in the statement of financial position (see 5.2.3 above), the notes to the financial statements shall:

    (i)   explain the reasons why;

    (ii)   describe the significance and nature of those assets;

    (iii)   disclose information that is helpful in assessing the value of those heritage assets;

(e)   when heritage assets are recognised in the statement of financial position the following disclosure is required:

    (i)   the carrying amount of heritage assets at the beginning of the reporting period and the reporting date, including an analysis between classes or groups of heritage assets recognised at cost and those recognised at valuation; and

    (ii)   when assets are recognised at valuation, sufficient information to assist in understanding the valuation being recognised (date of valuation, method used, whether carried out by external valuer and if so their qualification and any significant limitations on the valuation);

(f) a summary of transactions relating to heritage assets for the reporting period and each of the previous four reporting periods disclosing;

    (i) the cost of acquisitions of heritage assets;

    (ii) the value of heritage assets acquired by donations;

    (iii) the carrying amount of heritage assets disposed of in the period and proceeds received; and

    (iv) any impairment recognised in the period;

The summary shall show separately those transactions included in the statement of financial position and those that are not;

(g) in exceptional circumstances when it is impracticable to obtain a valuation of heritage assets acquired by donation the reason shall be stated.

Disclosures can be aggregated for groups or classes of heritage assets, provided this does not obscure significant information.

Where it is impracticable to do so, the disclosure of the summary of heritage asset transactions for the reporting period and each of the previous four reporting periods (see above) need not be given for any accounting period earlier than the previous comparable period. If impracticability applies, then a statement shall be made to that effect. *[FRS 102.34.56]*.

There are no additional company law matters particular to heritage assets.

5.3 Summary of GAAP differences

The following table shows the differences between FRS 102 and IFRS.

	FRS 102	*IFRS*
Scope	Applies to heritage assets which do not meet the definition of investment property, property, plant and equipment or intangible assets.	No specific requirements for heritage assets. Accounting will follow the nature of the asset (e.g.: property, plant and equipment, intangible or investment property).
Recognition and measurement	In accordance with Section 17 or Section 18 (which requires depreciated cost or fair value with valuation gains/losses through OCI).	Not applicable.
Disclosures	Separate disclosures are required for heritage assets.	No specific disclosures for heritage assets.

6 PUBLIC BENEFIT ENTITIES

6.1 Introduction

In their advice to the FRC on the issue of the March 2013 version of the standard, the Accounting Council noted that a significant number of public benefit entities apply UK accounting standards, and would be within the scope of FRS 102. Accordingly, the requirements of FRS 102 apply to public benefit entities and other entities, not just to companies. However, FRS 102 includes paragraph numbers prefixed with 'PBE' that must only be applied by public benefit entities, and shall not be applied directly, or by analogy, by entities that are not public benefit entities, other than, where specifically directed, entities within a public benefit entity group. *[FRS 102.1.2]*.

This section deals with the paragraphs in Section 34 preceded with 'PBE' which relate to Public Benefit Entities. Where not discussed elsewhere, the requirements of 'PBE' provisions in other Sections of FRS 102 are listed at 6.6 below.

IFRS does not have a separate section or standard dealing with public benefit entities. Therefore, public benefit entities using IFRS would measure assets and liabilities according to the applicable IFRSs.

6.2   Definitions used in Section 34 on public benefit entities

The following terms are used in Section 34 in relation to public benefit entities with the definitions specified. *[FRS 102 Appendix I]*.

Term	*Definition*
Non-exchange transaction	A transaction whereby an entity receives value from another entity without directly giving approximately equal value in exchange, or gives value to another entity without directly receiving approximately equal value in exchange.
Performance-related condition (in respect of finding commitments)	A condition that requires the performance of a particular level of service or units of output to be delivered, with payment of, or entitlement to, the resources conditional on that performance.
Prevailing market rate	The rate of interest that would apply to the entity in an open market for a similar financial instrument.
Public benefit entity	An entity whose primary objective is to provide goods or services for the general public, community or social benefit and where any equity is provided with a view to supporting the entity's primary objectives rather than with a view to providing a financial return to equity providers, shareholders or members.
Public benefit entity concessionary loan	A loan made or received between a public benefit entity or an entity within a public benefit entity group and another party: (a) at below the prevailing market rate of interest; (b) that is not repayable on demand; and (c) is for the purposes of furthering the objectives of the public benefit entity or public benefit entity parent.
Public benefit entity group	A public benefit entity parent and all of its wholly-owned subsidiaries
Restriction	A requirement that limits or directs the purposes for which a resource may be used that does not meet the definition of a performance-related condition.

Footnote 49 to Appendix I of FRS 102 elaborates that the term 'public benefit entity' does not necessarily imply that the purpose of the entity is for the benefit of the public as a whole. For example, many PBEs exist for the direct benefit of a particular group of people, although it is possible that society as a whole also benefits indirectly. In the FRC's view, the most important factor is what the primary purpose of such an entity is, and that it does not exist primarily to provide economic benefit to investors. Organisations such as mutual insurance companies, other mutual co-operative entities and clubs that provide dividends or other economic benefits directly and proportionately to their owners, members or participants are not PBEs.

The footnote goes on to state that some PBEs undertake certain activities that are intended to make a surplus in order to fund their primary activities and that consideration should be given to the primary purpose of an entity's (or group's) activities in assessing whether it meets the definition of a PBE. PBSs may have received contributions in the form of equity, even though the entity does not have a primary profit motive. However, because of the fundamental nature of public benefit entities, any such contributions are made by the equity holders of the entity primarily to enable the provision of goods and services to beneficiaries rather than with a view to a financial return for themselves. This is different from the position of lenders; loans do not fall into the category of equity. *[FRS 102 Appendix I.fn49].*

6.3 Incoming resources from non-exchange transactions

6.3.1 Introduction

FRS 102 defines a non-exchange transaction as one where an entity receives value from another entity without directly giving approximately equal value in exchange, or gives value to another entity without directly receiving approximately equal value in exchange. *[FRS 102 Appendix I.PBE34.65].*

A non-exchange transaction that meets the definition of a government grant falls under the scope of Section 24, and these are covered in Chapter 21. *[FRS 102.PBE34.64].*

Where public benefit entities, or entities within a public benefit entity group, receive other resources by way of non-exchange transactions then Section 34 (and the additional guidance in its Appendix B) are applied to determine the appropriate accounting. *[FRS 102.PBE34.65].*

In this context, non-exchange transactions can include, but are not limited to, donations (of cash, goods, and services) and legacies (see 6.3.2.C below). *[FRS 102.PBE34.66].*

6.3.2 Recognition

An entity should recognise receipts of resources from non-exchange transactions as follows: *[FRS 102.PBE34.67]*

(a) Transactions that do not impose specified future performance-related conditions on the entity are recognised in income when the resources are received or receivable.

(b) Transactions that do impose specified future performance-related conditions on the entity are recognised in income only when the performance-related conditions are met.

(c) Where resources are received before the revenue recognition criteria are satisfied, the entity recognises a liability.

A 'restriction' is defined as 'a requirement that limits or directs the purposes for which a resource may be used that does not meet the definition of a performance related condition'. *[FRS 102 Appendix I]*. A 'performance condition' is defined as 'a condition that requires the performance of a particular level of service or units of output to be delivered, with payment of, or entitlement to, the resources conditional on that performance'. *[FRS 102 Appendix I]*. The existence of a restriction does not prohibit a resource from being recognised in income when receivable. *[FRS 102.PBE34.68]*. An example of a restriction would be a where a donor requires that a donation must be used to fund a specific activity but the donor does not set any requirements making the donation conditional on achieving specific outputs or service levels from the activity.

The receipt of resources will usually result in an entity recognising an asset and corresponding income for the fair value of resources when those resources become received or receivable. Instances when this may not be the case include where: *[FRS 102.PBE34B.1]*

(a)   an entity received the resources in the form of services (see 6.3.2.A below); or

(b)   there are performance-related conditions attached to the resources, which have yet to be fulfilled (see 6.3.2.B below).

When applying the above recognition requirements, an entity must take into consideration whether the resource being received can be measured reliably and whether the benefits of recognising the resource outweigh the costs. *[FRS 102.PBE34.69]*.

Incoming resources should only be recognised when their fair value can be measured reliably. Hence, where it is impracticable to make a sufficiently reliable estimate of the value of the incoming resource, the related income should be recognised in the financial period when the resource is sold or distributed. A common example would be that of high volume, low value second-hand goods which have been donated for resale. *[FRS 102. PBE34B.2, 4, PBE34.70]*.

Concepts of materiality, and the balance between cost and benefit (see Chapter 4) should be considered when deciding which resources received should be recognised in the financial statements. *[FRS 102.PBE34B.3]*.

An entity should recognise a liability for any resource, previously received and recognised in income, when a subsequent failure to meet restrictions or performance-related conditions attached to it causes repayment to become probable. *[FRS 102.PBE34.71]*.

6.3.2.A   Services

Donations of services that can be reasonably quantified will usually result in the recognition of income and an expense rather than an asset because the service is consumed immediately. An asset will be recognised only when those services are used to produce an asset, in which case the services received will be capitalised as part of the cost of that asset in accordance with the relevant Section of FRS 102. *[FRS 102.PBE34.72]*.

An example would be in the construction of a building where the plumbing and electrical services have been donated. Such donated services would be recognised as a part of the cost of that building provided they meet the recognition criteria in Section 17. *[FRS 102.PBE34B.9]*.

Donated services that can be reasonably quantified should be recognised in the financial statements when they are received. *[FRS 102.PBE34B.8]*. Examples include donated facilities, such as office accommodation, are services that would otherwise have been purchased and services usually provided by an individual or an entity as part of their trade or profession for a fee. *[FRS 102.PBE34B.10]*. Additionally, it is expected that contributions made by volunteers cannot be reasonably quantified and therefore such services should not be recognised. *[FRS 102.PBE34B.11]*.

6.3.2.B   *Performance-related conditions*

Some resources come with performance-related conditions attached requiring the recipient to use the resources to provide a specified level of service to be entitled to retain the resources. An entity should not recognise income from those resources until these performance-related conditions have been met. *[FRS 102.PBE34B.13]*.

However, some requirements are stated so broadly that they do not actually impose a performance-related condition on the recipient. In these cases the recipient should recognise income on receipt of the transfer of resources. *[FRS 102.PBE34B.14]*.

6.3.2.C   *Legacies*

Donations in the form of legacies should be recognised when it is probable that the legacy will be received and its value can be measured reliably. These criteria will normally be met following probate once the executors of the estate have established that there are sufficient assets in the estate, after settling liabilities, to pay the legacy. *[FRS 102.PBE34B.5]*.

Evidence that the executors have determined that a payment can be made may arise on the agreement of the estate's accounts or notification that payment will be made. Where notification is received after the year-end but it is clear that the executors have agreed prior to the year-end that the legacy can be paid, the legacy is accrued in the financial statements. The certainty and measurability of the receipt may be affected by subsequent events such as valuations and disputes. *[FRS 102.PBE34B.6]*.

Entities that are in receipt of numerous immaterial legacies for which individual identification would be burdensome are permitted to take a portfolio approach. *[FRS 102.PBE34B.7]*.

6.3.3   *Measurement*

An entity should measure incoming resources from non-exchange transactions as follows: *[FRS 102.PBE34.73]*

(a)   Donated services and facilities that would otherwise have been purchased should be measured at the value to the entity.

(b)   All other incoming resources from non-exchange transactions should be measured at the fair value of the resources received or receivable.

The value to the entity in (a) above will be the price the entity estimates it would pay in the open market for an equivalent service or facility. *[FRS 102.PBE34B.15]*.

In (b) the fair values are usually the price that the entity would have to pay on the open market for an equivalent resource. *[FRS 102.PBE34B.16]*.

Chapter 31

When there is no direct evidence of an open market value for an equivalent item a value may be derived from sources such as: *[FRS 102.PBE34B.17]*

(a)   the cost of the item to the donor; or

(b)   in the case of goods that are expected to be sold, the estimated resale value (which may reflect the amount actually realised) after deducting the cost to sell the goods.

As noted above, donated services are recognised as income with an equivalent amount recognised as an expense in income and expenditure, unless the expense can be capitalised as part of the cost of an asset. *[FRS 102.PBE34B.18]*.

6.3.4   *Disclosures regarding non-exchange transactions*

An entity should disclose the following relating to non-exchange transactions: *[FRS 102.PBE34.74]*

(a)   the nature and amounts of resources receivable from non-exchange transactions recognised in the financial statements;

(b)   any unfulfilled conditions or other contingencies attaching to resources from non-exchange transactions that have not been recognised in income; and

(c)   an indication of other forms of resources from non-exchange transactions from which the entity has benefited.

The disclosure required by (c) above would include the disclosure of unrecognised volunteer services. *[FRS 102.PBE34B.12]*.

6.4   Public benefit entity combinations

These requirements in Section 34 apply only to public benefit entities entering into the following entity combinations (i.e. business combinations) which involve a whole entity or parts of an entity combining with another entity: *[FRS 102.19.6, PBE34.75]*

•   combinations at nil or nominal consideration which are in substance a gift; and

•   combinations which meet the definition and criteria of a merger.

In all other cases, in particular for combinations which are determined to be acquisitions, public benefit entities should apply the requirements of Section 19 – *Business Combinations and Goodwill* (see Chapter 17). *[FRS 102.19.2A, PBE34.76]*.

6.4.1   *Combinations that are in substance a gift*

The Standard requires that a combination that is in substance a gift should be accounted for in accordance with Section 19 except for following matters: *[FRS 102.PBE34.77]*

(a)   Any excess of the fair value of the assets received over the fair value of the liabilities assumed is recognised as a gain in income and expenditure. This gain represents the gift of the value of one entity to another and should be recognised as income. *[FRS 102.PBE34.78]*.

(b)   Any excess of the fair value of the liabilities assumed over the fair value of the assets received is recognised as a loss in income and expenditure. This loss represents the net obligations assumed, for which the receiving entity has not received a financial reward and should be recognised as an expense. *[FRS 102.PBE34.79]*.

6.4.2   Combinations that are an acquisition

Any entity combination which is: *[FRS 102.PBE34.81]*

*   a combination that is in substance neither a gift nor a merger; or
*   for which merger accounting is not permitted under the statutory framework under which the public benefit entity reports;

should be accounted for as an acquisition in accordance with Section 19.

6.4.3   Combinations that are a merger

Unless it is not permitted by the statutory framework under which a public benefit entity reports, an entity combination that is a merger shall apply merger accounting as prescribed below. If merger accounting is not permitted, an entity combination shall be accounted for as an acquisition in accordance with Section 19. *[FRS 102.PBE34.80]*.

The note on legal requirements to FRS 102 states that, for public benefit entities, the use of merger accounting has not been extended beyond its applicability in company law, or other relevant statutory framework. If a public benefit entity that is a company considers that, for the overriding purpose of giving a true and fair view, merger accounting should be applied in circumstances other than those set out in paragraph 10 of Schedule 6 to the Regulations, it may do so providing the relevant disclosures are made in the notes to the financial statements. *[FRS 102 Appendix III.30A]*.

Under merger accounting the following procedures are applied: *[FRS 102.PBE34.82-85]*

(a)   the carrying value of the assets and liabilities of the parties to the combination are not adjusted to fair value, although adjustments should be made to achieve uniformity of accounting policies across the combining entities;

(b)   the results and cash flows of all the combining entities should be brought into the financial statements of the newly formed entity from the beginning of the financial period in which the merger occurs;

(c)   the comparative amounts (marked as 'combined figures') should be restated by including the results for all the combining entities for the previous accounting period and their statement of financial positions for the previous reporting date; and

(d)   all costs associated with the merger should be charged as an expense in the period incurred.

For each entity combination accounted for as a merger in the reporting period the following disclosures are required in the newly formed entity's financial statements: *[FRS 102.PBE34.86]*

(a)   the names and descriptions of the combining entities or businesses;

(b)   the date of the merger;

(c)   an analysis of the principal components of the current year's total comprehensive income to indicate:

   (i)   the amounts relating to the newly formed merged entity for the period after the date of the merger; and

   (ii)   the amounts relating to each party to the merger up to the date of the merger;

(d)   an analysis of the previous year's total comprehensive income between each party to the merger;

(e)   the aggregate carrying value of the net assets of each party to the merger at the date of the merger; and

(f)   the nature and amount of any significant adjustments required to align accounting policies and an explanation of any further adjustments made to net assets as a result of the merger.

6.4.4   *Relief from applying Section 34 to combinations before transition*

A first-time adopter may elect not to apply the above requirements to public benefit entity combinations that were effected before the date of transition to FRS 102. However, if on first-time adoption a public benefit entity restates any entity combination to comply with this section, it shall restate all later entity combinations. *[FRS 102.35.10(q)]*.

6.5   Public benefit entity concessionary loans

Public benefit entities and other members of a public benefit entity group that make or receive public benefit entity concessionary loans shall refer to the relevant paragraphs of Section 34 for the accounting requirements for such loans. *[FRS 102.PBE11.1A, PBE12.1A]*.

These requirements address the recognition, measurement and disclosure of public benefit entity concessionary loans within the financial statements of public benefit entities or entities within a public benefit entity group. *[FRS 102.PBE34.87]*.

Public benefit entity concessionary loans are defined as loans made or received between a public benefit entity, or an entity within the public benefit entity group, and another party at below the prevailing market rate of interest that are not repayable on demand and are for the purposes of furthering the objectives of the public benefit entity or public benefit entity parent. *[FRS 102.PBE34.88]*.

The prevailing market rate is defined as the rate of interest that would apply to the entity in an open market for a similar financial instrument. *[FRS 102 Appendix I]*.

6.5.1 Accounting policy choice

Entities making or receiving public benefit entity concessionary loans have a policy choice and should use either:

(a) the recognition, measurement and disclosure requirements in Section 11 or Section 12 (see Chapter 10); or

(b) the accounting treatment set out at 6.5.2 below.

A public benefit entity or an entity within a public benefit entity group should apply the same accounting policy to concessionary loans both made and received. *[FRS 102.PBE34.89].*

6.5.2 Accounting requirements

6.5.2.A Initial measurement

A public benefit entity or an entity within a public benefit entity group making or receiving concessionary loans should initially measure these arrangements at the amount received or paid and recognise them in the statement of financial position. *[FRS 102.PBE34.90].*

6.5.2.B Subsequent measurement

In subsequent years, the carrying amount of concessionary loans in the financial statements should be adjusted to reflect any accrued interest payable or receivable. *[FRS 102.PBE34.91].*

To the extent that a loan that has been made is irrecoverable, any impairment loss should be recognised as an expense. *[FRS 102.PBE34.92].*

6.5.2.C Presentation and disclosure

Concessionary loans made and concessionary loans received should be presented by the entity either as separate line items on the face of the statement of financial position or in the notes to the financial statements. *[FRS 102.PBE34.93].*

Concessionary loans should be presented separately between amounts repayable or receivable within one year and amounts repayable or receivable after more than one year. *[FRS 102.PBE34.94].*

The entity should disclose in its significant accounting policies the measurement basis used for concessionary loans and any other accounting policies which are relevant to the understanding of these transactions within the financial statements. *[FRS 102.PBE34.95].*

The entity should also disclose: *[FRS 102.PBE34.96]*

(a) the terms and conditions of concessionary loan arrangements, for example the interest rate, any security provided and the terms of the repayment; and

(b) the value of concessionary loans which have been committed but not taken up at the year end.

Concessionary loans made or received should be disclosed separately. However multiple loans made or received may be disclosed in aggregate, providing that such aggregation does not obscure significant information. *[FRS 102.PBE34.97].*

Chapter 31

6.6 Other disclosures in FRS 102 relating to public benefit entities

The following requirements of FRS 102 are also relevant to public benefit entities:

- A public benefit entity that applies the 'PBE' prefixed paragraphs shall make an explicit and unreserved statement that it is a public benefit entity. *[FRS 102.PBE3.3A]*.

- Property held primarily for the provision of social benefits, e.g. social housing held by a public benefit entity, shall not be classified as investment property and shall be accounted for as property, plant and equipment in accordance with Section 17. *[FRS 102.16.3A]*.

Chapter 32   Transition to FRS 102

Chapter 32

List of examples

Chapter 32

Chapter 32   Transition to FRS 102

1   INTRODUCTION

Section 35 – *Transition to this FRS* – addresses the first-time adoption of FRS 102. The guidance in Section 35 is a simplified version of IFRS 1 – *First-time Adoption of International Financial Reporting Standards* – that contains significant modifications compared to the transition section of the IFRS for SMEs.

The underlying principle in Section 35 is that a first-time adopter should prepare financial statements applying FRS 102 retrospectively. However, there are a number of exemptions that allow and exceptions that require a first-time adopter to deviate from this principle in preparing its opening statement of financial position at the date of transition (i.e. at the beginning of the earliest period presented).

In previous editions of this publication, this chapter has discussed transition from previous UK or Irish GAAP or *The Financial Reporting Standard applicable for Smaller Entities* ('the FRSSE'). Previous UK or Irish GAAP were withdrawn for accounting periods beginning on or after 1 January 2015 and the FRSSE was withdrawn for accounting periods beginning on or after 1 January 2016.

In the future, entities transitioning to FRS 102 are likely to have applied EU-adopted IFRS or FRS 101 – *Reduced Disclosure Framework* (or if previously applying the micro-entities regime, FRS 105 – *The Financial Reporting Standard applicable to the Micro-entities Regime*). This chapter therefore focuses on differences between EU-adopted IFRS (given that FRS 101 follows the same recognition and measurement requirements, with limited exceptions) and FRS 102. Section 35 includes three transition exemptions available for small entities transitioning to FRS 102 for an accounting period beginning before 1 January 2017 that are not addressed in this chapter. These transition exemptions were made available because many entities transitioned from the FRSSE to FRS 102 during their first accounting period beginning on or after 1 January 2016. These transition exemptions are discussed in Chapter 32 at 5.4, 5.19 and 5.20 of EY UK GAAP 2017. However, two of these transition exemptions may have an ongoing effect on recognition and measurement in subsequent financial statements (even if the entity later ceases to be a small entity), as explained in Chapter 5 at 6.3.

Issues to consider in transitioning from FRS 105 are addressed briefly at 7 below.

There may be many reasons why an entity might choose to change its financial reporting framework to FRS 102. These may include:

- the entity ceasing to have its instruments listed on a regulated market;
- a change in ownership of the entity (where a different accounting framework is followed by the new group of which the entity is a member);
- a change in the financial framework followed by the group of which the entity is a member;
- tax and / or distributable profit implications of different financial reporting frameworks;
- a desire to reduce GAAP complexity and disclosure (e.g. arising from IFRS 9, IFRS 15, and IFRS 16); and
- ineligibility to continue applying FRS 105.

1.1   Summary of Section 35

Section 35 applies to the first financial statements prepared in conformity with FRS 102 which include an explicit and unreserved statement of compliance with FRS 102. *[FRS 102.35.3-4]*.

In preparing its opening statement of financial position, an entity must follow the requirements of FRS 102, subject to application of the mandatory exceptions and optional exemptions provided in Section 35. *[FRS 102.35.7]*. Adjustments are recognised directly in retained earnings (or, if appropriate, another category of equity). *[FRS 102.35.8]*. Under the mandatory exceptions, an entity cannot retrospectively change the accounting followed under its previous financial reporting framework for: derecognition of financial assets and liabilities, accounting estimates and measuring non-controlling interests. *[FRS 102.35.9]*. From the date of transition, FRS 102 must be applied in full (except where otherwise provided in Section 35). *[FRS 102.35.7]*.

Section 35 sets out the disclosures required to explain the transition to FRS 102. These include reconciliations from its previous financial reporting framework to FRS 102 of equity at the date of transition and the comparative period end, and of the comparative profit or loss. *[FRS 102.35.12, 13-15]*. There are also certain disclosures where an entity has applied FRS 102 in a previous reporting period but not in its most recent annual financial statements and is re-applying FRS 102. *[FRS 102.35.12A]*.

1.2   Changes made by the Triennial review 2017 to FRS 102

In December 2017, the FRC issued *Amendments to FRS 102 Triennial review 2017 – Incremental improvements and clarifications* (Triennial review 2017). Most changes made to Section 35 by the Triennial review 2017 were editorial amendments.

However, the transition exception for discontinued operations (discussed in Chapter 32 at 4.3 of EY UK GAAP 2017) was removed. In addition, an entity re-applying FRS 102 must disclose the reason it stopped applying FRS 102 previously, the reason for resuming application of FRS 102 and whether it has applied Section 35 or applied FRS 102 retrospectively (see 6.4 below).

This chapter addresses Section 35's requirements as per the March 2018 edition of FRS 102 which incorporates the Triennial review 2017.

1.3 References to IFRS 1

IFRS 1, as referred to throughout this chapter, is the version of IFRS 1 issued as of March 2018. However, as described below, IFRS 1 continues to be amended as changes are made to other IFRSs. Hence, to understand the differences between IFRS 1 and Section 35 on transition, it is important to make reference to the version of IFRS 1 effective for the reporting period.

2 KEY DIFFERENCES BETWEEN SECTION 35 AND IFRS

The transition exceptions and exemptions included in Section 35 are similar to those included in IFRS 1. However, Section 35 omits certain exceptions and exemptions that are included in IFRS 1, but adds certain others and modifies the wording in places. Finally, Section 35 contains significantly less guidance and examples on the application of the transition exceptions and exemptions than IFRS 1. Many transition exemptions in IFRS 1 that do not appear in Section 35 relate to the implementation of IFRSs that do not have a direct counterpart in FRS 102.

IFRS 1 contains specific transition exemptions relating to IFRS 9 – *Financial Instruments* – not included in Section 35. Section 35 does, however, include transition provisions for hedge accounting where IAS 39 – *Financial Instruments: Recognition and Measurement* – or IFRS 9 is to be applied to financial instruments under FRS 102. These are similar to the transition provisions for hedge accounting included in IFRS 1, but include a concession over the timing of completion of the designation and documentation of hedging relationships (see 5.16.3 below). There is also a transition exception for derecognition of financial assets and financial liabilities (see 4.1 below).

In practice, the lack of transition exemptions included in Section 35 relating to IFRS 9 may potentially cause issues if an FRS 101 or IFRS reporter that has applied IAS 39 in its previous financial statements (for an accounting period beginning prior to 1 January 2018) becomes a first-time adopter of FRS 102 and decides to apply IFRS 9 to the recognition and measurement of financial instruments (since transitional provisions of accounting standards generally do not apply on first-time adoption). See discussion at 3.5.5.B below.

This is likely to be an implementation issue of short duration. For accounting periods beginning on or after 1 January 2018, an FRS 101 or IFRS reporter will apply IFRS 9 (and will have applied the transitional provisions set out in that standard in moving to IFRS 9 from IAS 39). However, some entities applying IFRS 9 may have continued to use the hedge accounting provisions of IAS 39, as permitted by the transitional provisions on initial application of IFRS 9. *[IFRS 9.7.2.21].*

Notwithstanding the lack of transition exemptions included in Section 35 relating to IFRS 9, we doubt that the FRC intended that there will be a change to the accounting for financial instruments on later transition to FRS 102, where IFRS 9 continues to be applied. See discussion at 3.5.5.A below.

The main differences between Section 35 and IFRS 1 are listed below:

- Section 35 contains relief where it is impracticable for an entity to restate the opening statement of financial position or make the required disclosures. *[FRS 102.35.11]*.

- The disclosure requirements regarding transition in the annual financial statements are less extensive in Section 35. For example, there are no requirements to:

  - present an opening statement of financial position and related notes; *[FRS 102.35.7]*

  - explain how the transition affects the reported cash flows or to disclose the adjustments made for impairment or reversal of impairment in preparing the opening statement of financial position; *[FRS 102.35.12]*

  - reconcile total comprehensive income determined in accordance with its previous financial reporting framework to FRS 102 (although there is a requirement to reconcile profit or loss); *[FRS 102.35.13(c)]*

  - make certain disclosures relating to designation of financial assets or financial liabilities and to the use of deemed cost; *[IFRS 1.29-31C]* or

  - explain changes to accounting policies or the use of exemptions between the first FRS 102 interim financial report and the first FRS 102 financial statements and update the reconciliations previously included in the interim financial statements. *[IFRS 1.32(c)]*.

- In addition, Section 35 includes the following transition exemptions not in IFRS 1:

  - dormant companies (see 5.13 below); *[FRS 102.35.10(m)]*

  - pre-transition lease incentives (operating leases) (see 5.12 below); *[FRS 102.35.10(p)]*

  - public benefit entity combinations effected pre-transition (see 5.3 below); *[FRS 102.35.10(q)]*

  - deferred development costs as deemed cost (see 5.6 below); *[FRS 102.35.10(n)]* and

  - concessions for small entities, where the entity first adopts FRS 102 for an accounting period beginning before 1 January 2017 (discussed in Chapter 32 at 5.4, 5.19 and 5.20 of EY UK GAAP 2017). *[FRS 102.35.10(b), (u), (v)]*.

Where FRS 102 does not specifically address a transaction, Section 10 – *Accounting Policies, Estimates and Errors* – requires management to use judgement in developing and applying a relevant and reliable accounting policy. In making that judgement, management *must* refer to and consider the sources listed in Section 10, and *may* consider the requirements and guidance in EU-adopted IFRS dealing with similar and related issues. *[FRS 102.10.4-6]*. Consequently, management may refer to the IFRS 1 requirements and guidance relating to the same exception or exemption. However, care should be taken in doing so where the first-time adoption or underlying accounting for the item differs.

3 DEFINITIONS, SCOPE, AND PREPARATION OF THE OPENING FRS 102 STATEMENT OF FINANCIAL POSITION

3.1 Key definitions

The following terms in Section 35 are defined in the Glossary to FRS 102 (or in Section 35, where indicated). Other terms used in Section 35 will be explained in the sections in this chapter addressing the related issue. *[FRS 102 Appendix I]*.

Term	Definition
Carrying amount	The amount at which an asset or liability is recognised in the statement of financial position.
Date of transition	The beginning of the earliest period for which an entity presents full comparative information in a given standard in its first financial statements that comply with that standard.
Deemed cost	An amount used as a surrogate for cost or depreciated cost at a given date. Subsequent depreciation or amortisation assumes that the entity had initially recognised the asset or liability at the given date and that its cost was equal to the deemed cost.
Fair value	The amount for which an asset could be exchanged, a liability settled, or an equity instrument granted could be exchanged, between knowledgeable, willing parties in an arm's length transaction. In the absence of any specific guidance provided in the relevant section of FRS 102, the guidance in the Appendix to Section 2 – *Concepts and Pervasive Principles* – shall be used in determining fair value.
First FRS 102 financial statements	The first financial statements (excluding interim financial statements) in which the entity makes an explicit and unreserved statement of compliance with FRS 102. *[FRS 102.35.4]*.
First-time adopter of FRS 102	An entity that presents its first annual financial statements that conform to FRS 102, regardless of whether its previous financial reporting framework was EU-adopted IFRS or another set of accounting standards.
Opening statement of financial position	The statement of financial position as of its date of transition to FRS 102 (i.e. the beginning of the earliest period presented). *[FRS 102.35.7]*.
Reporting date	The end of the latest period covered by financial statements or by an interim financial report.
Reporting period	The period covered by financial statements or by an interim financial report.

Throughout this chapter, *The Large and Medium-sized Companies and Groups (Accounts and Reports) Regulations 2008* (SI 2008/410), as amended, are referred to as 'the Regulations'. Similarly, *The Large and Medium-sized Limited Liability Partnerships (Accounts) Regulations 2008* (SI 2008/1913), as amended, are referred to as 'the LLP Regulations'.

Chapter 32

3.2 Scope of Section 35

Section 35 applies to a first-time adopter of FRS 102, regardless of whether its previous financial reporting framework was EU-adopted IFRS or another set of generally accepted accounting principles (GAAP) such as its national accounting standards, or another framework such as the local income tax basis. *[FRS 102.35.1]*.

Most FRS 102 reporters will be UK or Irish companies preparing statutory accounts under the Companies Act 2006 ('CA 2006') or the Companies Act 2014 respectively. In such cases, the previous financial reporting framework will be FRS 101, FRS 105, or EU-adopted IFRS.

A first-time adopter (see 3.2.1 below) must apply the requirements of Section 35 in its first financial statements that conform to FRS 102. *[FRS 102.35.3]*. These are the first financial statements (excluding interim financial statements) in which the entity makes an explicit and unreserved statement of compliance with FRS 102. *[FRS 102.35.4]*. These financial statements are referred to as the 'first FRS 102 financial statements' below.

Section 35 also addresses the situation where an entity re-applies FRS 102 after a period of applying a different financial reporting framework (see 3.2.2 below).

3.2.1 Who is a first-time adopter?

Normally, it will be clear whether an entity is a first-time adopter of FRS 102, as defined at 3.1 above. However, Section 35 clarifies that financial statements prepared in accordance with FRS 102 are an entity's first FRS 102 financial statements if, for example, the entity: *[FRS 102.35.4]*

- did not present financial statements for previous periods;

- presented its most recent previous financial statements under previous UK and Republic of Ireland requirements that are not consistent with FRS 102 in all respects; or

- presented its most recent previous financial statements in conformity with EU-adopted IFRS.

The first FRS 102 financial statements must be a complete set of financial statements, as defined in paragraph 3.17 of FRS 102 (see Chapter 6 at 3.5). This means that the financial statements must include a full set of primary statements and notes (together with comparatives). *[FRS 102.35.4-6]*. Small companies are not required to present a cash flow statement and small companies applying Section 1A of FRS 102 are encouraged but not mandated to present a statement of changes in equity or statement of comprehensive income. *[FRS 102.7.1B, 1A.8, 1A.9]*. See Chapter 5 at 8.

The first FRS 102 financial statements of a UK company (or LLP) will usually be the statutory financial statements, but this may not always be the case (e.g. first-time adoption in an offering document). In practice, most companies publishing offering documents are likely to be applying IFRS or EU-adopted IFRS rather than FRS 102.

An entity is not a first-time adopter if it presented financial statements in the previous year that contained an explicit and unreserved statement of compliance with FRS 102 even if its auditors qualified the auditor's report on those financial statements.

3.2.2 Repeat application of FRS 102

An entity that has applied FRS 102 in a previous reporting period, but whose most recent previous annual financial statements did not contain an explicit and unreserved statement of compliance with FRS 102, has a choice *either* to apply Section 35 *or* else to apply FRS 102 retrospectively in accordance with Section 10 as if the entity had never stopped applying FRS 102. *[FRS 102.35.2]*. Such an entity must also disclose the reason it stopped applying FRS 102, the reason it is resuming application of FRS 102 and whether it has applied Section 35 or FRS 102 retrospectively (see 6.4 below).

Repeat application of FRS 102 is unlikely to be an issue faced by many entities for a few years. However, where the entity chooses to re-apply Section 35, it must apply the transition exceptions and exemptions without regard to the elections made when it applied Section 35 previously. The entity will, therefore, apply the transition exceptions and exemptions of Section 35 based on its new date of transition to FRS 102. Where an entity instead chooses to apply FRS 102 retrospectively, it does so as if it had never stopped applying FRS 102. *[FRS 102.35.2]*. Therefore, the entity must retain the transition exceptions and exemptions applied in its first FRS 102 financial statements.

3.3 First-time adoption timeline

An entity's first FRS 102 financial statements must include at least two statements of financial position, two statements of comprehensive income, two separate income statements (if presented), two statements of cash flows (unless exempt) and two statements of changes in equity and related notes. *[FRS 102. 3.17, 3.20, 7.1A-B, 35.5]*. Where permitted by the standard, two statements of income and retained earnings may be included in place of the statements of comprehensive income and statements of changes in equity. *[FRS 102.3.18, 6.4]*. As a small entity is not required to present a statement of comprehensive income or a statement of changes in equity, a small entity's first FRS 102 financial statements need only include at least two statements of financial position, two income statements and related notes. *[FRS 102.1A.8, 10]*.

The beginning of the earliest period for which the entity presents full comparative information in accordance with FRS 102 in its FRS 102 financial statements will be treated as its date of transition. *[FRS 102.35.6, Appendix I]*.

The diagram below shows how the above terms are related for an entity with a December year-end:

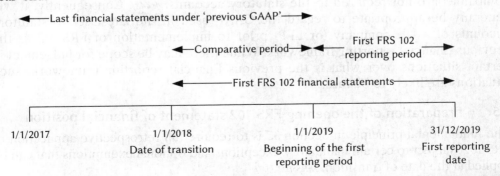

The following example illustrates how an entity should determine its date of transition to FRS 102.

Example 32.1:   Determining the date of transition to FRS 102

(i)   *Entity A's year-end is 31 December and it presents financial statements that include one comparative period. Entity A changes its financial reporting framework to prepare financial statements in conformity with FRS 102 for the first accounting period starting on or after 1 January 2019.*

Entity A's first financial statements in conformity with FRS 102 are for the period ending on 31 December 2019. Its date of transition to FRS 102 is 1 January 2018, which is the beginning of the comparative period included in its first financial statements in conformity with FRS 102.

(ii) *Entity B's year-end is 30 November and it presents financial statements that voluntarily include full information for two comparative periods. Entity B changes its financial reporting framework to prepare financial statements in conformity with FRS 102 for the accounting period ended 30 November 2018.*

Entity B's first financial statements in conformity with FRS 102 are for the accounting period ended 30 November 2018. Its date of transition to FRS 102 is 1 December 2015, which is the beginning of the earliest period for which full comparative information is included in its first financial statements in conformity with FRS 102.

(iii) *Entity C's most recent financial statements under its previous financial reporting framework are for the period from 1 July 2017 to 31 December 2018. Entity C presents its first financial statements (with one comparative period) in conformity with FRS 102 for the period ending 31 December 2019.*

Entity C's date of transition is 1 July 2017. While FRS 102 requires presentation of at least one comparative period, neither FRS 102 (nor the CA 2006, for a UK company) require the comparative period to be a 12-month period. Thus, the entity's date of transition will be the beginning of the earliest comparative period, irrespective of the length of that period. However, the financial statements must disclose that the comparative period is not a 12-month period, the reason why the comparative period is not 12 months and that the periods presented are not entirely comparable. *[FRS 102.3.10, 3.14, 3.17, FRS 102.35.5-6].*

3.4   Determining the previous financial reporting framework

Although FRS 102 does not define 'previous financial reporting framework', it is generally taken to mean the basis of accounting that a first-time adopter used immediately before adopting FRS 102. This is the equivalent term to 'previous GAAP' as used in IFRS 1. *[IFRS 1 Appendix A].*

Most UK companies (and LLPs) are required to prepare and file statutory accounts. *[s394, s441-s447, s394 (LLP), s441-s446 (LLP)].* There are exemptions for certain dormant subsidiary companies (and LLPs) not to prepare and file statutory accounts. *[s394A-s394C, s448A-s448C, s394A-s394C (LLP), s448A-s448C (LLP)].* In addition, certain unlimited companies are not required to file statutory accounts. *[s448].* Consequently, it will generally be appropriate to regard the GAAP used in the latest set of statutory accounts of a UK company (or LLP) prior to implementation of FRS 102 as the previous financial reporting framework. While there may be scope for judgement in certain situations over what is the previous financial reporting framework, such situations are likely to be rare.

3.5   Preparation of the opening FRS 102 statement of financial position

The fundamental principle in Section 35 is to require full retrospective application of FRS 102, subject to certain mandatory exceptions and optional exemptions that can be applied at the date of transition. *[FRS 102.35.7].*

Except as provided in paragraphs 35.9 to 35.11B (which set out certain mandatory exceptions, and optional exemptions to full retrospective application of FRS 102), an entity must, in the opening statement of financial position: *[FRS 102.35.7]*

(a)   recognise all assets and liabilities whose recognition is required by FRS 102;

(b)   not recognise items as assets or liabilities if FRS 102 does not permit such recognition;

(c)   reclassify items that it recognised under its previous financial reporting framework as one type of asset, liability or component of equity, but are a different type of asset, liability or component of equity under FRS 102; and

(d)   apply FRS 102 in measuring all recognised assets and liabilities.

An entity may identify errors under its previous financial reporting framework in transitioning to FRS 102. The standard requires material prior period errors to be adjusted retrospectively, to the extent practicable. *[FRS 102.10.21]*. Such errors should be adjusted at the date of transition. If a first-time adopter becomes aware of errors made under its previous financial reporting framework, the reconciliations required by Section 35 should, to the extent practicable, distinguish the correction of those errors from changes in accounting policies (see 6.3 below). *[FRS 102.35.14]*.

Where the accounting policies applied in the opening statement of financial position under FRS 102 differ from those applied under an entity's previous financial reporting framework, the resulting adjustments arise from transactions, other events or conditions before the date of transition. Therefore, an entity must recognise those adjustments directly in retained earnings (or, if appropriate, another category of equity – see Example 32.2 below) at the date of transition to FRS 102. *[FRS 102.35.8]*.

Example 32.2:   Revaluation of property

On transition to FRS 102, Entity A adopts a policy of revaluation for its freehold property. *[FRS 102.17.15E-F]*. The freehold property, with a net book value of £500,000 under its previous financial reporting framework (where the cost model had been applied), is revalued to £1.1m, being its fair value at the date of transition. A revaluation reserve of £600,000 is recognised at the date of transition.

Under FRS 102, freehold property is revalued through other comprehensive income and consequently deferred tax arises on this timing difference. *[FRS 102.29.6]*. The adjustment to reflect the revaluation (and related deferred tax) is recognised in equity as at the date of transition. *[FRS 102.35.8]*.

If Entity A is a UK company (or LLP) preparing statutory accounts, a statutory revaluation reserve is required to be established by the alternative accounting rules in the Regulations (and LLP Regulations). *[1 Sch 35, 1 Sch 35 (LLP)]*. The related deferred taxation charge arising on the revaluation may be offset against the statutory revaluation reserve in accordance with the alternative accounting rules rather than taken to retained earnings. *[1 Sch 35(3)]*. See 3.5.3 below and Chapter 6 at 10.2, Chapter 15 at 3.6.3 and Chapter 26.

Another example where adjustments (if any) may be reflected in a category of equity other than retained earnings concerns where cash flow hedge accounting is applied under FRS 102. See 5.16 below for further discussion of the hedge accounting transition provisions.

IFRS 1 includes additional requirements and guidance in respect of the transition compared to FRS 102 that can provide further insight into the requirements of Section 35. The application of specific exceptions and exemptions (including any relevant additional guidance in IFRS 1) are addressed at 4 and 5 below, respectively. However, some general issues are discussed below, namely:

- changes of accounting policy made on transition to FRS 102 (see 3.5.1 below);

- impairment testing at the date of transition (see 3.5.2 below);

- use of the historical cost accounting rules, alternative accounting rules, and fair value accounting rules (by UK companies, LLPs and certain other entities) (see 3.5.3 below);

- the impracticability exemption, and subsequent application of transition exemptions (see 3.5.4 below); and

- transition issues where a previous IFRS or FRS 101 reporter applies IFRS 9 to the recognition and measurement of financial instruments under FRS 102 (see 3.5.5 below).

3.5.1   *Changes of accounting policy made on transition to FRS 102*

The fundamental principle in Section 35 is to require full retrospective application of FRS 102. This means that consistent accounting policies should be used in the opening statement of financial position and for all periods presented in an entity's first FRS 102 financial statements. *[FRS 102.10.7, 35.8].*

A first-time adopter is not under a general obligation to ensure that its FRS 102 accounting policies are as similar as possible to its accounting policies under its previous financial reporting framework. Therefore, a first-time adopter could adopt a revaluation model for property, plant and equipment even if it had applied a cost model under its previous financial reporting framework (or *vice versa*).

A first-time adopter would, however, need to take into account the requirements of Section 10 to ensure that its choice of accounting policy results in information that is relevant and reliable. In doing so, in situations where an FRS does not specifically address the issue, management must refer to the hierarchy set out in paragraph 10.5 and may consider the requirements and guidance in EU-adopted IFRS dealing with similar and related issues. *[FRS 102.10.3-6].*

In our view, transitional provisions in other sections of FRS 102, other FRC standards (such as FRS 103 – *Insurance Contracts*), IAS 39 or IFRS 9 (where applied to the recognition and measurement of financial instruments), and other IFRSs that are required to be applied by certain FRS 102 reporters, are ignored when an entity applies Section 35 to the transition. This is the case unless the transitional provisions are stated to apply to a first-time adopter (as is the case for FRS 103), *[FRS 103.6.1-4],* or are provided for as a specific transition exception or exemption in Section 35.

Section 35 contains a number of transition exemptions relating to Section 11 – *Basic Financial Instruments* – and Section 12 – *Other Financial Instruments Issues.* The only transition exemption explicitly referring to the use of IAS 39 or IFRS 9 relates to hedge accounting (see 5.16 below).

TECH 02/17BL – *Guidance on Realised and Distributable Profits under the Companies Act 2006* ('TECH 02/17BL'), issued by the ICAEW and ICAS, provides guidance on how and when transition to a new GAAP affects distributable profits. This guidance is discussed in Chapter 1 at 5.5 and 6.8.

3.5.2 *Impairment testing at the date of transition*

FRS 102 permits first-time adopters to make use of deemed cost for certain assets as the initial carrying amount on transition. Section 35 specifically requires that the carrying amount of exploration and evaluation assets and assets in the development and production phases are tested for impairment when the exemption in paragraph 35.10(j) is taken for oil and gas assets (see 5.7 below). However, while FRS 102 does not specifically call for an impairment test of other assets, a first-time adopter should be mindful that there are no exemptions from full retrospective application of the requirements set out in Section 27 – *Impairment of Assets* (or indeed in relation to the impairment of financial assets under Sections 11 and 12, *[FRS 102.11.21-26, 12.13]*, IAS 39, *[IAS 39.58-70]*, or IFRS 9 *[IFRS 9.5.5.1-5.5.20]*).

Therefore, an entity should consider whether there is an indicator of impairment (or reversal of previous impairment) of assets at the date of transition that might require an impairment test to be performed. In relation to financial assets, an entity should consider whether there is objective evidence that an impairment loss has been incurred (where Sections 11 and 12, or IAS 39 is applied) and should recognise a loss allowance for expected credit losses in accordance with IFRS 9, where that standard is applied.

If an entity uses fair value as deemed cost for assets whose fair value is above cost, an impairment test for other assets may be appropriate as the entity should not ignore indications that the recoverable amount of other assets may have fallen below their carrying amount.

Impairment losses for assets (except goodwill) are reversed under Section 27 if, and only if, the reasons for the impairment loss have ceased to apply. Hence, for assets (other than goodwill), there should be no practical differences between applying Section 27 fully retrospectively or as at the date of transition. *[FRS 102.27.28-29]*. Performing the test at the date of transition should result in recognition of any required impairment as of that date, remeasuring any impairment determined under the entity's previous financial reporting framework to comply with the approach in Section 27, or recognition of any additional impairment or reversing any impairment determined under its previous financial reporting framework that is no longer necessary.

The estimates used to determine whether a first-time adopter recognises an impairment provision at the date of transition to FRS 102 should normally be consistent with estimates made for the same date under its previous financial reporting framework (after adjustments to reflect any difference in accounting policies), unless there is objective evidence that those estimates were in error. If a first-time adopter needs to make estimates for that date that were not necessary under its previous financial reporting framework, such estimates and assumptions should not reflect conditions that arose after the date of transition to FRS 102.

If a first-time adopter's opening FRS 102 statement of financial position reflects impairment losses (e.g. recognised under its previous financial reporting framework or upon transition to FRS 102), any later reversal of those impairment losses (not permitted for goodwill) should be recognised in profit or loss provided that Section 27 does not require such reversal to be treated as a revaluation. *[FRS 102.27.30(b)]*.

Where an entity makes use of deemed cost exemptions at transition, deemed cost is used as a surrogate for cost at the date the deemed cost is established. Therefore, if the carrying

Chapter 32

amount at the date the deemed cost is established reflects previous impairment, these impairment losses cannot be later reversed and also any later impairment losses are reflected in profit or loss. Certain transition exemptions permit use of a deemed cost equal to the carrying amount of the asset as determined under the entity's previous financial reporting framework – an example includes investments in subsidiaries, associates or jointly controlled entities in individual or separate financial statements. *[FRS 102.35.10(f)]*. Where this is the case, we consider that application of Section 27 could lead to a further impairment on transition, but should not lead to a reversal of an impairment determined properly under the entity's previous financial reporting framework (as reflecting a reversal of impairment is not consistent with the deemed cost being equal to the previous financial reporting framework carrying amount). See 5.5 below.

Section 35 does not require specific disclosures regarding any impairment losses recognised or reversed on transition to FRS 102; however, where material, disclosure of such adjustments is likely to be relevant to an explanation of the transition. *[FRS 102.35.12]*. See 6.2 below.

3.5.3   Use of the historical cost accounting rules, alternative accounting rules and fair value accounting rules

A UK company's (or LLP's) statutory accounts prepared in accordance with FRS 102 are Companies Act accounts (non-IAS accounts, for an LLP). Therefore, the company (or LLP), in preparing its FRS 102 opening statement of financial position, should consider whether it makes use of the historical cost accounting rules, alternative accounting rules or fair value accounting rules set out in Part 2 of Schedule 1 to the Regulations (or the equivalent requirements in Schedules 2 and 3 to the Regulations or Schedule 1 to the LLP Regulations).

This is relevant both to whether any adjustments made at the date of transition should be reported in retained earnings or another category of equity, and to subsequent accounting and disclosure requirements. For example, where the revaluation model is applied to property, plant and equipment, a statutory revaluation reserve should be established under the alternative accounting rules. Chapter 6 at 10 explains the historical cost rules, alternative accounting rules and fair value accounting rules in more detail.

3.5.3.A   Deemed cost

A number of the transition exemptions permit an entity to establish a deemed cost that may differ from the historical cost carrying amount under its previous financial reporting framework. The implications of deemed cost are discussed at 5.5 below. For a UK company's (or LLP's) statutory accounts, the deemed cost, in many cases, will need to comply with either the alternative accounting rules or the fair value accounting rules, as applicable. Example 32.2 at 3.5 above illustrates that where a revaluation policy is adopted by a UK company (or LLP), a statutory revaluation reserve is established, where required by the alternative accounting rules. However, even if, for example, a UK company (or LLP) records an item of property, plant and equipment at a deemed cost equal to its fair value at the date of transition or treats a revaluation under its previous financial reporting framework as a deemed cost at the date of the revaluation (see 5.5 below), application of the alternative accounting rules may require the company (or LLP) to establish (or maintain an existing) statutory revaluation reserve.

3.5.3.B   Financial instruments held at fair value

Where financial instruments are measured at fair value under the fair value accounting rules, certain fair value movements are required to be recognised in other comprehensive income and accumulated in the statutory fair value reserve. See Chapter 6 at 10.3. The most common examples relate to fair value movements arising on: cash flow hedges (see Chapter 10 at 10.8), exchange differences in respect of monetary items forming part of a net investment in a foreign operation (and hedges of a net investment in a foreign operation) (see Chapter 10 at 10.9), and, where IAS 39 is applied to the recognition and measurement of financial instruments, available-for-sale financial assets. *[IAS 39.45(d)]*. As discussed in Chapter 6 at 10.3, our view is that the fair value accounting rules also apply to investments in debt instruments accounted at fair value through other comprehensive income in accordance with IFRS 9. *[IFRS 9.4.1.2.A, IFRS 9.5.7.1(d), 5.7.10-11]*. This is because the accounting is similar to that for an available for sale financial asset. Therefore, fair value movements arising on such debt instruments should also be reflected in the statutory fair value reserve. A statutory fair value reserve may sometimes be required for a cash flow hedge on transition, even where hedge accounting is not being used going forward. This will, however, depend on whether IAS 39, or IFRS 9, or Sections 11 and 12 are being used. See 5.16 below for a discussion of the transition provisions for hedge accounting.

By contrast, in our view, accounting for investments in equity instruments at fair value through other comprehensive income in accordance with IFRS 9, *[IFRS 9.4.1.4, 5.7.1(b), IFRS 9.5.7.5-6]*, makes use of the alternative accounting rules and fair value movements should be reflected in the statutory revaluation reserve (see Chapter 6 at 10.2).

Where a financial liability is designated at fair value through profit or loss in accordance with IFRS 9, fair value changes attributable to changes in the credit risk of the liability are accounted in other comprehensive income (unless that treatment would create or enlarge an accounting mismatch). *[IFRS 9.4.2.2, 5.7.1(c), 5.7.7-9]*. Recording such fair value gains and losses attributable to changes in credit risk in other comprehensive income in accordance with IFRS 9 will usually be a departure from the requirement of paragraph 40 of Schedule 1 to the Regulations (which requires fair value gains and losses to be included in the profit and loss account, except where the financial instrument is a hedging instrument or an available for sale security) for the overriding purpose of giving a true and fair view. *[FRS 102.A3.12C]*. This is discussed further at Chapter 6 at 10.3.

Whether or not adjustments are taken to retained earnings or another category of equity, particular care needs to be taken in evaluating whether such adjustments are realised or not for the purposes of determining the distributable profits of a UK company. TECH 02/17BL provides guidance. See also Chapter 1 at 5.5 and 6.8.

3.5.3.C   Investment property – transitional adjustments

Under FRS 102 (as amended by the Triennial review 2017), investment property must be carried at fair value through profit or loss (except for investment property rented to another group entity, where a policy choice is made to transfer the investment property to property, plant and equipment and apply the cost model). *[FRS 102.16.1, 1A, 4A-4B, 7]*. In a UK company's (or LLP's) statutory accounts, this accounting makes use of the fair value accounting rules.

It is possible that a first-time adopter previously accounted for investment property using the cost model as a policy choice under EU-adopted IFRS (or FRS 101). Where the fair value model is applied to the investment property under FRS 102, the adjustment of the carrying amount to fair value at the date of transition should be included in retained earnings (or transferred to a separate non-distributable reserve) as the revaluation applies the fair value accounting rules.

It is also possible that a first-time adopter previously accounted for investment property rented to another group entity at fair value through profit or loss under EU-adopted IFRS (or FRS 101) but, on transition to FRS 102, makes a policy choice to transfer the investment property to property, plant and equipment and to apply the cost model. If this is the case, the investment property will need to be restated to original cost or deemed cost on transition (see 3.5.3.A above and 5.5 below). *[FRS 102.1.19A, Appendix III.40B-40C]*. Where a deemed cost is used on transition for such investment properties to be accounted using the cost model, a statutory revaluation reserve may arise, where the deemed cost exceeds the depreciated historical cost of such properties (see 5.5 below).

On transition, deferred tax should be provided on any revaluation in accordance with Section 29 – *Income Tax*, as this is generally a timing difference recognised on or prior to transition. Deferred tax relating to investment property that is measured at fair value shall be measured using the tax rates and allowances that apply to sale of the asset, except for investment property that has a limited useful life and is held within a business model whose objective is to consume substantially all of the economic benefits embodied in the property over time. *[FRS 102.29.6, 16]*.

3.5.4   Impracticability exemption, and subsequent application of transition exemptions

If it is impracticable for an entity to restate the opening statement of financial position at the date of transition for one or more of the adjustments required by paragraph 35.7(a) to (d) (see 3.5 above), an entity must:

- apply paragraphs 35.7 to 35.10 (i.e. retrospective application of FRS 102, subject to the transition exceptions and exemptions) for such adjustments in the earliest period for which it is practicable to do so; and
- identify which amounts in the financial statements have not been restated.

If it is impracticable for an entity to provide any disclosures required by FRS 102 for any period before the period in which it prepares its first FRS 102 financial statements, the omission shall be disclosed. *[FRS 102.35.11]*.

Applying a requirement is impracticable when an entity cannot apply it, after making every reasonable effort to do so. *[FRS 102 Appendix I]*.

If it is not practical on first-time adoption to apply a particular requirement of paragraph 18 of IFRS 6 – *Exploration for and Evaluation of Mineral Resources* – to previous comparative amounts, an entity shall disclose that fact. *[FRS 102.34.11C]*.

Section 35 states that, where applicable to the transactions, events or arrangements affected by applying the exemptions, an entity may continue to use the exemptions that are applied at the date of transition to FRS 102 when preparing subsequent financial statements, until such time when the assets and liabilities associated with those transactions, events or arrangements are derecognised. *[FRS 102.35.11A]*. This simply confirms that, in preparing FRS 102 financial statements after first-time adoption, the exemptions and exceptions taken at the date of transition continue to be applied as opposed to Section 35 *only* applying to the first FRS 102 financial statements. Once the associated assets and liabilities are derecognised, those transition exemptions cease, in any event, to have any accounting effect.

However, when there is subsequently a significant change in the circumstances or conditions associated with transactions, events or arrangements that existed at the date of transition, to which an exemption has been applied, an entity shall reassess the appropriateness of applying that exemption in preparing subsequent financial statements in order to maintain a true and fair view in accordance with Section 3 – *Financial Statement Presentation*. *[FRS 102.35.11B]*. It is not clear what circumstances are envisaged by this requirement (there is no equivalent text in the IFRS for SMEs), but it appears to permit the possibility of an entity later ceasing to use transition exemptions taken.

Transition exemptions are pragmatic concessions available in the first FRS 102 financial statements that involve a departure from fully retrospectively applying FRS 102. In our view, if an entity did not take a particular transition exemption in its first FRS 102 financial statements, the entity is unable to apply that transition exemption as a 'voluntary change in accounting policy' in later financial statements as this would not meet the requirement that the financial statements provide reliable and more relevant information about the effects of transactions, other events or conditions on the entity's financial position, financial performance or cash flows. *[FRS 102.10.8]*.

3.5.5 Transition issues where a previous IFRS or FRS 101 reporter applies IFRS 9 to the recognition and measurement of financial instruments under FRS 102

For accounting periods beginning on or after 1 January 2018, an FRS 101 or IFRS reporter will apply IFRS 9 (and will have applied the transitional provisions set out in that standard in moving to IFRS 9 from IAS 39). For example, the application of the 'business model' assessment to the classification of financial assets; and any designations of financial assets and / or financial liabilities at fair value through profit or loss or of investments in equity instruments at fair value through other comprehensive income, are based on the facts and circumstances at the date of initial application of IFRS 9. Hedge accounting is (with limited exceptions) applied prospectively from the date of initial application of IFRS 9. The derecognition requirements of IFRS 9 and IAS 39, however, are the same (and there is a transitional provision that IFRS 9 does not apply to financial instruments derecognised prior to the date of initial application of IFRS 9). *[IFRS 9.7.2.1-7.2.26]*. See Chapter 44 at 10.2, Chapter 46 at 5.2, Chapter 47 at 16.2 and Chapter 49 at 13 of EY International GAAP 2019 for further guidance on the above transition requirements.

3.5.5.A Previous IFRS or FRS 101 reporter applying IFRS 9 under its previous financial reporting framework

An entity already applying IFRS 9 under its previous financial reporting framework is likely to continue to apply IFRS 9 to the recognition and measurement of financial instruments if it transitions to FRS 102 in a subsequent accounting period. However, the only transition provisions in Section 35 relating to financial instruments address derecognition of financial assets and financial liabilities (see 4.1 below) and hedge accounting (see 5.16 below). *[FRS 102.35.9(a), 10(t)]*.

As discussed at 3.5.1 above, in our view, the transitional provisions of accounting standards would not apply on first-time adoption of FRS 102 (unless specifically included within Section 35). However, we doubt that the FRC intended that an entity already applying IFRS 9 (or indeed IAS 39, for an accounting period beginning before 1 January 2018) under its previous financial reporting framework should change their accounting treatment when continuing to apply the same accounting policy choice on transition from EU-adopted IFRS or FRS 101 to FRS 102.

As explained at 3.5.1 above, consistent accounting policies should be used in the opening statement of financial position and for all periods presented in an entity's first FRS 102 financial statements. *[FRS 102.10.7, 35.8]*. Therefore, comparatives would need to be presented under IFRS 9. However, this should not generally cause difficulty even if a first-time adopter had used the modified retrospective approach (and not restated comparatives) in the accounting period where IFRS 9 was first applied under its previous financial reporting framework (i.e. IFRS or FRS 101). If the entity transitions to FRS 102 in the following period, the prior year comparative will reflect the amounts presented in the initial period of application of IFRS 9 under its previous financial reporting framework.

The situation is less clear concerning IFRS 9's requirements on hedge accounting as a previous IFRS or FRS 101 reporter was required (with certain exceptions) to apply these prospectively from the date of initial application of IFRS 9. *[IFRS 9.7.2.15, 7.2.17, 7.2.21-26]*. Hedge accounting is also addressed by a specific transition provision in Section 35 (see 5.16.3 below). However, for many entities, the existing hedging relationships under IAS 39 may have continued under IFRS 9 (after consideration of rebalancing), with no accounting adjustments to the hedge accounting required to opening equity on initial application of IFRS 9. Where adjustments on transition to IFRS 9's hedge accounting requirements were reflected in opening equity (for example to reflect IFRS 9's accounting for the 'costs of hedging', where only the hedging option's intrinsic value was designated) or on rebalancing hedges, the question arises as to whether these adjustments should be reflected at the date of transition. Generally, we believe that the adjustments made to opening equity on initial application of IFRS 9 under the previous financial reporting framework would be reflected at the date of transition. In addition, we believe the effects of rebalancing hedges at the date of initial application of IFRS 9 should continue to be reflected in profit or loss in the same way as under IFRS 9. *[IFRS 9.7.2.25(b)]*.

Entities applying IFRS 9 are permitted to choose an accounting policy to continue to apply the hedge accounting provisions of IAS 39 (together with IFRIC 16 – *Hedges of a Net Investment in a Foreign Operation*) on initial application of IFRS 9. *[IFRS 9.7.2.21]*. This concession is located in the section on transition for hedge accounting in IFRS 9 but is more in the nature of an accounting policy choice available within the standard. In addition, while this chapter refers to applying IFRS 9 to the recognition and measurement of financial instruments, FRS 102 strictly refers to 'the recognition and measurement provisions of IFRS 9 – *Financial Instruments* (as adopted by the EU) and

IAS 39 (as amended by IFRS 9).' *[FRS 102.11.2, 12.2]*. Therefore, we believe that an entity already applying IFRS 9 and applying IAS 39 to its hedges can continue to adopt this accounting policy on transition to FRS 102. If the entity changes its policy to apply IFRS 9's hedge accounting requirements on transition to FRS 102, the same issues arise as discussed at 3.5.5.B below.

3.5.5.B   *Previous IFRS or FRS 101 reporter applying IAS 39 under its previous financial reporting framework*

If a first-time adopter had applied IAS 39 under its previous financial framework but changes to IFRS 9 on transition to FRS 102, it will need to apply IFRS 9 retrospectively, subject to the transition provisions on derecognition of financial instruments (see 4.1 below) and on hedge accounting (see 5.16.3 below).

For some entities, application of IFRS 9 may cause implementation difficulties and limit the ability to make designations of financial instruments.

For many entities, the existing hedging relationships under IAS 39 may continue under IFRS 9 (after consideration of rebalancing), with no accounting adjustments to the hedge accounting required to the opening statement of financial position under FRS 102. See Chapter 49 of EY International GAAP 2019 for further discussion of IFRS 9's requirements on hedge accounting.

However, entities will need to consider the following implementation issues in relation to hedge accounting on transition to FRS 102:

- It will be necessary to ensure that all the qualifying criteria for hedge accounting under IFRS 9 are met at the date of transition (except that the entity may complete the designation and documentation of the hedging relationship after the date of transition but before the date of authorisation of the financial statements) in order for hedge accounting for existing hedging relationships to continue from the date of transition. *[IFRS 9.6.4.1, FRS 102.35.10(t)(iv)]*. Otherwise, hedge accounting will need to be discontinued prospectively from the date of transition. *[IFRS 9.6.5.6, 6.5.7, 6.5.10]*.

- If new hedging relationships are identified under IFRS 9 (that were not identified under IAS 39), the opening statement of financial position would not reflect the hedging relationship. However, hedge accounting could be established prospectively from the date all qualifying criteria for hedge accounting under IFRS 9 are met (subject to the concession over the timing of designation and documentation allowed for in the transition provision), which might be prospectively from the date of transition or a later date. *[FRS 102.35.10(t)(iv)]*. See 5.16.3 below.

- Under IAS 39, a hedging relationship that failed the effectiveness tests would have been required to be discontinued. *[IAS 39.88, 91(b), 101(b)]*. Under IFRS 9, the retrospective effectiveness test has been withdrawn, although the qualifying criteria for hedge accounting include ongoing effectiveness requirements such as the existence of an economic relationship between the hedged item and the hedging instrument. *[IFRS 9.6.4.1(c)]*. In these circumstances, the opening statement of financial position of the entity would continue to reflect the discontinuance of the past hedging relationship but, if all the qualifying criteria (subject to the concession over the timing of designation and documentation allowed for in the transition provision) are met at the date of transition, the entity could re-establish hedge accounting prospectively from the date of transition. *[FRS 102.35.10(t)(iv)]*. See 5.16.3 below.

- An entity changing from IAS 39 to IFRS 9 on adoption of FRS 102 may also need to adjust the hedge ratio of the hedging relationship ('rebalancing') in its hedge documentation. It would appear that the effects of any rebalancing would be reflected in profit or loss following the date of transition. This is the same position as would be the case if an ongoing IFRS reporter moved from IAS 39 to IFRS 9. *[IFRS 9.7.2.25(b)]*. IFRS 9's requirements for rebalancing of hedges are discussed in Chapter 49 at 8.2 of EY International GAAP 2019.

- The hedge accounting under IAS 39 differs, or may differ, under IFRS 9 where the intrinsic value of an option (or the spot element of a forward contract) was designated as a hedging instrument. IFRS 9 also permits an entity to exclude the foreign currency basis spread when designating a financial instrument as a hedging instrument (but this was not permitted under IAS 39).

  Under IAS 39, where the time value of an option or the forward element of a foreign currency contract was excluded from the hedging relationship, fair value movements on those elements were recognised in profit or loss. Under IFRS 9, where the time value of an option is excluded from the hedging relationship, the fair value movements on the time value of the option are first recognised in other comprehensive income (and a separate component of equity), with the subsequent treatment depending on the nature of the hedged transaction. A similar treatment may be elected on a hedge-by-hedge basis for the fair value movements attributable to the forward element of foreign currency contracts (and foreign currency basis spread). *[IAS 39.74, IFRS 9.6.5.15-16]*. IFRS 9's accounting for 'costs of hedging' is discussed in Chapter 49 at 7.5 of EY International GAAP 2019.

  In our view, the transitional provisions in IFRS 9 do not apply to a first-time adopter. However, where the time value of an option or the forward element of a foreign currency contract was excluded from the hedging relationship under IAS 39, the above accounting for 'costs of hedging' (where applied for such hedging relationships under IFRS 9) would be applied retrospectively on first-time adoption. This is because there is no change to the hedging relationship, just to the underlying accounting. Consequently, amounts previously reflected in profit or loss (and that are therefore in retained earnings at the date of transition) under the entity's previous financial reporting framework will (for an option) and may (for a foreign currency contract) be reclassified into a separate component of equity on transition (and subsequently be reclassified as a basis adjustment on the later recognition of a non-financial item, or to profit or loss, as appropriate).

  Since IAS 39 did not permit the exclusion of foreign currency basis spread from a hedging relationship, it would appear that the transition provisions may not allow retrospective application of IFRS 9's accounting for 'costs of hedging'. The transition provisions in Section 35 (see 5.16.3 below), *[FRS 102.35.10(t)(iv)]*, do not allow retrospective designation of hedging relationships prior to the date of transition. Therefore, such adjustments would not be reflected in the opening statement of financial position under FRS 102. To separate the foreign currency basis spread would mean a different hedging relationship would be required to be designated under IFRS 9. However, in our view, this hedging relationship could be reflected prospectively from transition, if all the qualifying criteria for hedge accounting (subject to the concession over the timing of designation and documentation allowed for in the transition provision) were met by the date of approval of the financial statements.

For the same reasons as described at 3.5.5.A above, we believe that the entity could continue to apply IAS 39 to its hedges as this is permitted as an accounting policy choice by IFRS 9.

4 MANDATORY EXCEPTIONS TO RETROSPECTIVE APPLICATION

Section 35 prohibits retrospective application of its requirements in some areas, many of which correspond to similar mandatory *exceptions* in IFRS 1. The mandatory exceptions in FRS 102 cover areas where full retrospective application could be costly or onerous, or may involve use of hindsight.

The mandatory exceptions in Section 35 cover the following areas:

- derecognition of financial assets and financial liabilities (see 4.1 below);
- accounting estimates (see 4.2 below); and
- non-controlling interests (see 4.3 below).

Each of the current exceptions is explained further below. The exception for discontinued operations was removed by the Triennial review 2017. However, this exception remains applicable for accounting periods beginning before 1 January 2019 (or before adoption of the Triennial review 2017 amendments, if earlier) and is discussed in Chapter 32 at 4.3 of EY UK GAAP 2017.

However, the exemptions regarding:

- hedge accounting where IFRS 9 or IAS 39 are applied to the recognition and measurement of financial instruments (see 5.16.3 below);
- an entity becoming a first-time adopter in its consolidated financial statements later than its subsidiary, associate or joint venture (see 5.15.2 below); and
- a parent adopting FRS 102 in its separate financial statements earlier or later than in its consolidated financial statements (see 5.15.4 below)

contain certain mandatory requirements.

4.1 Derecognition of financial assets and financial liabilities

Financial assets and liabilities derecognised under an entity's previous financial reporting framework before the date of transition shall not be recognised upon adoption of FRS 102. Conversely, for financial assets and liabilities that would have been derecognised under FRS 102 in a transaction that took place before the date of transition, but that were not derecognised under an entity's previous financial reporting framework, an entity may choose either to derecognise them on adoption of FRS 102, or to continue to recognise them until disposed of or settled. *[FRS 102.35.9(a)]*. Derecognition is defined as the removal of a previously recognised asset or liability from an entity's statement of financial position. *[FRS 102 Appendix I]*.

4.1.1   Implementation issues

There is no further implementation guidance on this transition exception. The main first-time adoption implementation issues are:

- what comprises derecognition of financial assets and financial liabilities under the entity's previous financial reporting framework; and

- whether there are financial assets and financial liabilities that would have been derecognised under FRS 102 in a pre-transition transaction, but were not derecognised under the entity's previous financial reporting framework.

An FRS 102 reporter has an accounting policy choice of applying:

- Section 11 and Section 12 of FRS 102; or

- IAS 39 (as adopted in the European Union); or

- IFRS 9 (as adopted in the European Union) and IAS 39 (as amended following the publication of IFRS 9) (together referred to as IFRS 9 below)

to the recognition and measurement of financial instruments.

FRS 102 defines which version of IAS 39 should be applied for accounting periods beginning on or after 1 January 2018. *[FRS 102.11.2, 12.2]*. See Chapter 10 at 4.

Comparatives need to be restated in accordance with the accounting policy choice applied to the recognition and measurement of financial instruments under FRS 102.

Financial assets and financial liabilities that remain recognised on transition will need to be measured in accordance with the accounting policy choice that the entity applies to the recognition and measurement of financial instruments under FRS 102. Consequently, if the accounting policy adopted differs to that applied under the previous financial framework (generally, FRS 105, IFRS or FRS 101), adjustments may be required on transition to FRS 102.

4.1.2   First-time adopters that previously applied IAS 39 or IFRS 9 and choose to apply IAS 39 or IFRS 9 to the recognition and measurement of financial instruments on adoption of FRS 102

FRS 102 reporters are permitted to apply IAS 39 or IFRS 9 to the recognition and measurement of financial instruments under FRS 102. The derecognition requirements for financial assets and financial liabilities in IAS 39 and IFRS 9 are the same. However, where an exchange or modification of a financial asset or liability is not accounted as an extinguishment (and is therefore not derecognised), the measurement of the financial asset or financial liability may differ under IFRS 9 compared to IAS 39 (depending on the approach taken under IAS 39). *[IAS 39.40, IFRS 9.3.3.2, 5.4.3, BC4.252-253]*.

Under IFRS 9, the modified contractual cash flows of a financial asset or financial liability (that is not accounted as an extinguishment following an exchange or modification), will be discounted at the original effective interest rate, with an adjustment to the carrying amount of the financial liability and profit or loss. *[IFRS 9.3.3.2, 5.4.3, BC4.252-253]*. However, IAS 39 (which only addresses modifications of financial liabilities) does not provide conclusive guidance as to whether an adjustment is made to the carrying amount of the financial liability or financial asset for such changes in contractual cash flows (or whether the effective interest rate must be changed). See Chapter 46 at 3.8 of International GAAP 2019 and Chapter 48 at 3.4.1 and 6.2 of EY International GAAP 2019.

IFRS 1 contains the following transition exception in relation to derecognition of financial assets and financial liabilities. A first-time adopter shall apply the derecognition requirements in IFRS 9:

- prospectively for transactions occurring on or after the date of transition to IFRS; or
- retrospectively from a date of the entity's choosing, provided that the information needed to apply IFRS 9 to financial assets and financial liabilities derecognised as a result of past transactions was obtained at the time of initial accounting.

Prior to implementation of IFRS 9, this exception referred to IAS 39. *[IFRS 1 Appendix B.2-3].*

Moreover, the transitional provisions in IFRS 9 (which are relevant to an ongoing IFRS or FRS 101 reporter) state that the standard does not apply to any items derecognised at the date of initial application. *[IFRS 9.7.2.1].*

Consequently, an entity may have derecognised financial assets or financial liabilities that would not ordinarily qualify for derecognition under IAS 39 or IFRS 9 in transactions occurring prior to the first adoption of IFRS (or FRS 101). Any such financial assets or financial liabilities still in existence at the date of transition remain derecognised on transition to FRS 102 because of the derecognition exception in paragraph 35.9(a). However, the discussion at 4.1.3 below may still be relevant to a previous IFRS or FRS 101 reporter.

4.1.3 Financial assets and financial liabilities previously derecognised

Financial assets and financial liabilities derecognised under the entity's previous financial reporting framework before the date of transition (and consequently not recognised on transition to FRS 102) would be re-recognised if they qualify for recognition as a result of a later transaction or event (i.e. subsequent to the date of transition) using the accounting policy choice that the entity applies to the recognition and measurement of financial instruments under FRS 102, i.e. IAS 39, or IFRS 9, or Sections 11 and 12.

See 4.1.5 below for further discussion of what constitutes derecognition of financial assets and financial liabilities under IAS 39 and IFRS 9, where an entity applies Sections 11 and 12 to the recognition and measurement of financial instruments as an accounting policy choice under FRS 102.

Some arrangements for the transfer of assets, particularly securitisations, may last for some time, with the result that transfers might be made both before and on or after the date of transition under the same arrangement. Where assets were transferred prior to the date of transition and derecognised under the previous financial reporting framework (IFRS or FRS 101), the assets are not re-recognised (unless the transferee is required to be consolidated under FRS 102 – see discussion below). Under FRS 102, transfers on or after the date of transition would be subject to the full requirements of whatever accounting policy choice is applied to the recognition and measurement of financial instruments.

FRS 102's requirements on consolidation of special purpose entities ('SPEs'), *[FRS 102.9.10-12]*, differ from those in IFRS 10 – *Consolidated Financial Statements*. *[FRS 102.BC.B9.2-4]*. Since there are no specific transitional or first-time adoption provisions, FRS 102's requirements must be applied fully retrospectively by first-time adopters. Therefore, financial assets and financial liabilities derecognised on transfer to an SPE that was not consolidated under the entity's previous financial reporting framework (but would be required to be consolidated under FRS 102) will be re-recognised on transition to FRS 102 by way of consolidation of the SPE. This is unless the SPE itself had subsequently achieved derecognition of the items concerned under the entity's previous financial reporting framework before the date of transition, other than by transfer to another entity consolidated by the FRS 102 first-time adopter.

4.1.4   *Financial assets and financial liabilities previously not derecognised*

There may be cases where a financial asset or financial liability would have been derecognised in a pre-transition transaction (under the accounting policy choice applied to the recognition and measurement of financial instruments under FRS 102, i.e. IAS 39, or IFRS 9, or Sections 11 and 12) but was not derecognised under the entity's previous financial reporting framework. As noted at 4.1.2 above, such situations may also arise for a previous IFRS or FRS 101 reporter because of transitional provisions on first-time adoption of IFRS. *[IFRS 1 Appendix B.2-3]*.

On transition to FRS 102, a first-time adopter is permitted to derecognise the financial asset or financial liability in accordance with the derecognition requirements of the accounting policy choice applied to the recognition and measurement of financial instruments under FRS 102. It is unclear whether an entity may apply the choice to continue to recognise or to derecognise financial assets and financial liabilities (which would have been derecognised under FRS 102 in a pre-transition transaction) on a transaction-by-transaction basis or consistently to all such financial assets and financial liabilities. Unless this issue is clarified by the FRC, we believe an entity may apply judgement in interpreting this part of the transition exception.

Where the entity continues to recognise a financial asset or financial liability on transition, it must retrospectively apply the accounting standard that it applies to the recognition and measurement of financial instruments under FRS 102. Consequently, this may lead to a measurement adjustment of the financial asset or financial liability as the recognition and measurement requirements of IAS 39, IFRS 9 and Sections 11 and 12 differ in certain respects. In particular, care should also be taken where an IFRS or FRS 101 reporter had undertaken an exchange or modification of a financial asset or financial liability with the original counterparty prior to the date of transition (but this was not accounted as an extinguishment and therefore not derecognised). *[IAS 39.40, IFRS 9.3.3.2, 5.4.3, BC4.252-253]*.

See 4.1.5.B below and Chapter 10 at 8.2 and 9.4 where Sections 11 and 12 are applied to the recognition and measurement of financial instruments under FRS 102. Where an IFRS or FRS 101 reporter that applied IAS 39 in its last set of IFRS financial statements applies IFRS 9 on adoption of FRS 102, see Chapter 46 at 3.8 and Chapter 48 at 3.4.1 and 6.2 of International GAAP 2019.

4.1.5 Specific implementation issues where a previous IFRS or FRS 101 reporter applies Sections 11 and 12 under FRS 102.

4.1.5.A Financial assets – what is derecognition?

Generally, it will be clear whether a financial asset has been derecognised under IAS 39 or IFRS 9 and therefore must not be re-recognised on transition to FRS 102. However, Section 35 does not specifically address whether derecognition of a part of a financial asset or continued recognition of an asset to the extent of its continuing involvement are regarded as derecognition for the purposes of paragraph 35.9(a).

IAS 39 and IFRS 9 require an entity to determine whether the derecognition requirements are to be applied to a part of a financial asset (or a part of a group of financial assets) or a financial asset (or a group of similar financial assets) in its entirety. *[IAS 39.16, IFRS 9.3.2.2]*. Situations where parts of a financial asset are capable of derecognition under IAS 39 or IFRS 9 include: specifically identified cash flows (e.g. the interest cash flows of a debt instrument, commonly referred to as an interest rate strip), a fully proportionate share of the cash flows (e.g. 90% share of all cash flows of a debt instrument), and a fully proportionate share of specifically identified cash flows (e.g. 90% of the interest cash flows from a financial asset). *[IAS 39.16(a), IFRS 9.3.2.2(a)]*.

Section 11, unlike IAS 39 and IFRS 9, does not refer to derecognition of parts of a financial asset (although it does so in respect of parts of a financial liability). *[FRS 102.11.33, 36, 12.14]*. Nevertheless, in our view, specifically identified cash flows or a fully proportionate share of all or of specifically identified cash flows would meet the definition of a financial asset. Therefore, derecognition of a part of a financial asset in accordance with IAS 39 or IFRS 9 would be regarded as derecognition of a financial asset for the purposes of the transition exception in paragraph 35.9(a). Consequently, the part of the original financial asset derecognised would not be reinstated on transition to FRS 102.

IAS 39 and IFRS 9 state that if the entity neither transfers nor retains substantially all the risks and rewards of ownership of the financial asset but has retained control, it shall continue to recognise the financial asset to the extent of its continuing involvement. IAS 39 and IFRS 9 set out how the continuing involvement in the asset (or part of the asset) and the associated liability should be measured. *[IAS 39.20(c)(ii), 30-35, IFRS 9.3.2.6(c)(ii), 3.2.16-3.2.21]*. See Chapter 48 at 5.3 and 5.4 of EY International GAAP 2019. It would seem unlikely that an entity with assets (or parts of assets) recognised to the extent of the continuing involvement would choose to apply Sections 11 and 12, since these sections do not set out rules for accounting for such arrangements (see Chapter 10 at 9.2.4.B). However, it would not appear that recognising an asset (or part of an asset) to the extent of its continuing involvement could be regarded as derecognition for the purposes of paragraph 35.9(a). Accordingly, if Sections 11 and 12 are applied to the recognition and measurement of financial instruments, in our view, the accounting for the continuing involvement would need to be retrospectively restated.

4.1.5.B Financial liabilities

IAS 39 and IFRS 9 address derecognition of financial liabilities, including when an exchange of debt between an existing borrower and lender, or modification of the terms of existing debt gives rise to derecognition. Hence, it will be clear whether a financial liability has been derecognised under IAS 39 or IFRS 9 prior to the date of transition and therefore must not be re-recognised on transition to FRS 102.

IAS 39, IFRS 9 and Sections 11 and 12 require an entity to derecognise a financial liability (or part of a financial liability) only when it is extinguished (i.e. when the obligation specified in the contract is discharged, is cancelled or expires). *[FRS 102.11.36-38, 12.14, IAS 39.39-42, IFRS 9.3.3.1-4]*. Sections 11 and 12 contain the same basic requirements on accounting for exchanges of a financial liability between an existing borrower and lender and the modification of terms of an existing financial liability as IAS 39 and IFRS 9, but not the related application guidance. *[IAS 39.AG57-63, IFRS 9.B3.3.1-7]*. In particular, the application guidance in IAS 39 and IFRS 9 covers the evaluation of whether an exchange or modification of debt has substantially different terms, and the accounting for an exchange or modification. As discussed in Chapter 10 at 9.4.2, we believe an entity applying Sections 11 and 12 as an accounting policy choice under FRS 102 may, but is not required to, apply this application guidance.

An entity previously applying IAS 39 or IFRS 9 that exchanged or modified debt with the same lender in circumstances where the terms of the exchanged or 'modified' debt are not 'substantially different' would not have accounted for the extinguishment of the original financial liability. *[IFRS 9.3.3.2, IAS 39.40]*. On initial application of FRS 102, there is no exemption from measuring the exchanged or 'modified' debt that continues to be recognised in accordance with the requirements of Sections 11 and 12. The measurement adjustments, if any, required on transition for exchanged or 'modified' debt will depend on the accounting previously adopted under IAS 39 or IFRS 9, as discussed further below, and on the accounting adopted under Sections 11 and 12.

The application guidance in both IAS 39 and IFRS 9 address the treatment of costs or fees associated with the exchange or modification of a financial liability that is not accounted as an extinguishment – requiring that the costs or fees are adjusted against the carrying amount of the liability, and amortised over the remaining term of the modified liability. *[IAS 39.AG62, IFRS 9 Appendix B.3.3.6]*.

Under IFRS 9, the modified contractual cash flows of a financial liability (that is not accounted as an extinguishment following an exchange or modification), will be discounted at the original effective interest rate, with an adjustment to the carrying amount of the financial liability and profit or loss. However, IAS 39 does not provide conclusive guidance as to whether an adjustment is made to the carrying amount of the financial liability for such changes in contractual cash flows (or whether the effective interest rate must be changed). *[IFRS 9.3.3.2, 5.4.3, BC4.252-253]*. See Chapter 48 at 6.2 of EY International GAAP 2019 for further discussion of IFRS 9's requirements on exchange or modification of debt by the original lender.

FRS 102 does not provide any specific guidance on the subsequent accounting where it is determined that an exchange or modification of a financial liability is not an extinguishment of the original financial liability. Even following the clarification of the accounting for such a modification under IFRS 9, the later Triennial review 2017 did not clarify the accounting under FRS 102. In light of this, we believe that entities may apply judgement and adopt an appropriate accounting policy in accounting for changes to the contractual cash flows and for costs or fees for exchange or modification of financial liabilities that are not deemed to be an extinguishment of the original financial liability. For example, under the hierarchy in Section 10, an entity might look to accounting treatments adopted by IFRS reporters applying IAS 39 or IFRS 9. See Chapter 10 at 9.4.2.

4.2   Accounting estimates

4.2.1   *Exception to retrospective application*

On first-time adoption of FRS 102, an entity must not retrospectively change the accounting that it followed under its previous financial reporting framework for accounting estimates. *[FRS 102.35.9(c)]*. However, FRS 102 offers no further guidance in respect of this exception. Since paragraph 35.9(c) does not refer to accounting estimates *at the date of transition*, as other exceptions do, it seems that the exception relates to accounting estimates made under the entity's previous financial reporting framework in *both* the opening statement of financial position at the date of transition and in the comparative period(s) presented. As this is consistent with the corresponding exception in IFRS 1, entities may want to consider the guidance in that standard.

IFRS 1 requires an entity to use estimates under IFRSs that are consistent with the estimates made for the same date under its previous GAAP – after adjusting for any difference in accounting policies – unless there is objective evidence that those estimates were in error. *[IFRS 1.14-17]*. Under IFRS 1, an entity cannot apply hindsight and make 'better' estimates when it prepares its first IFRS financial statements. Therefore, an entity is not allowed to consider subsequent events that provide evidence of conditions that existed at the date of transition (or at the end of the comparative period), but that came to light after the date that the entity's financial statements under its previous financial reporting framework were finalised. If an estimate made under its previous financial reporting framework requires adjustment because of new information after the relevant date, an entity treats this information in the same way as a non-adjusting event after the reporting period. In addition, the exception also ensures that a first-time adopter need not conduct a search for, and change the accounting for, events that might have otherwise qualified as adjusting events, e.g. the resolution of a court case relating to an obligation as at the date of transition or end of the comparative period.

Where FRS 102 requires a first-time adopter to make estimates that were not required under its previous financial reporting framework, the general approach should be to base those estimates on conditions that existed at the date of transition (or, where applicable, the end of the comparative period).

4.2.2   *Post-balance sheet events and correction of errors*

FRS 102 requires changes in accounting estimates to be reflected prospectively. *[FRS 102.10.15-17]*. Adjustments for post-balance sheet events are only made where these provide evidence of conditions existing at the end of the reporting period. *[FRS 102.32.2(a)]*.

So, for example, inventories are accounted at the lower of cost and net realisable value under EU-adopted IFRS, FRS 101 and FRS 102. Assuming the estimate of net realisable value made under the entity's previous financial reporting framework (say, EU-adopted IFRS or FRS 101) was not made in error, any changes in the carrying amount of the inventory due to a reassessment of net realisable value or a sale of the inventory at below its previous financial reporting framework carrying amount in the following period are reflected prospectively.

Section 10 further explains that 'changes in accounting estimates result from new information or new developments and, accordingly, are not corrections of errors. When it is difficult to distinguish a change in an accounting policy from a change in an accounting estimate, the change is treated as a change in an accounting estimate'. *[FRS 102.10.15]*. See Chapter 9 at 3.5.

Material prior period errors identified at transition and in the comparatives must be retrospectively corrected. *[FRS 102.10.21]*.

4.3   Non-controlling interest

The definition and accounting requirements for non-controlling interest in FRS 102 are discussed in Chapter 8 at 3.7. There are some differences in accounting to IFRS 10.

In measuring non-controlling interest, FRS 102's requirements (in Section 9 – *Consolidated and Separate Financial Statements*):

- to allocate profit or loss and total comprehensive income between non-controlling interest and owners of the parent (see Chapter 6 at 4.5 and Chapter 8 at 3.7); *[FRS 102.9.14, 22]*

- for accounting for changes in the parent's ownership interest in a subsidiary that do not result in a loss of control (see Chapter 8 at 3.6.2 and 3.6.4); *[FRS 102.9.19A, C-D, 22.19]* and

- for accounting for a loss of control over a subsidiary (see Chapter 8 at 3.6.3); *[FRS 102.9.18A-19]*

must be applied prospectively from the date of transition to FRS 102 (or from such earlier date as FRS 102 is applied to restate business combinations – see paragraph 35.10(a)). *[FRS 102.35.9(e), 10(a)]*.

The application of the exception is straightforward. It simply states that the accounting in FRS 102 for these matters is applied prospectively from the date of transition (or where pre-transition business combinations are restated in accordance with Section 19 – *Business Combinations and Goodwill*, from the earlier date from which business combinations are restated – see 5.2.1 below). *[FRS 102.35.9(e)]*. Of course, changes to assets and liabilities of a subsidiary with a non-controlling interest made at the date of transition will have a consequential effect on non-controlling interest at that date.

Retrospective changes for previous allocations of profit or loss and total comprehensive income (made prior to the date of transition, or that earlier date from which Section 19 is applied) are prohibited. Consequently, where a provision has been made under the entity's previous financial reporting framework against a non-controlling interest debit balance prior to the date of transition (or that earlier date from which Section 19 is applied), this should not be reversed on transition to FRS 102. In addition, if that subsidiary subsequently earns profits post transition, any past losses absorbed by the parent are not reversed but the profits are attributed to the parent and non-controlling interest based on existing ownership interests. *[FRS 102.9.14, 22]*. This situation may apply to a first-time adopter previously reporting under IFRS, which may be reporting non-controlling interest after taking advantage of the transitional exemptions in IFRS 1 (when it first adopted IFRS) or in IFRS 10 – which are similar to those in paragraph 35.9(e). *[IFRS 10 Appendix C.6, IFRS 1 Appendix B.7]*.

The accounting in FRS 102 for a change in ownership of a subsidiary without loss of control is similar to IFRS 10. *[IFRS 10.23, Appendix B.96]*. However, care should be taken where there are transactions involving changes in non-controlling interest subsequent to the date of transition that do not result in loss of control of a subsidiary. Where the non-controlling interest had been provided against (i.e. losses allocated to the parent) as at the date of transition (or as at the earlier date from which business combinations are restated), the parent should not reallocate any of those losses on re-measuring the non-controlling interest for the change in relative ownership. This means that the non-controlling interest is re-measured at the date of the transaction based upon the 'change in their relative interest' and not by reference to a percentage change of net assets. While FRS 102 is not explicit on what the accounting should be, this approach would be consistent with the approach taken under IFRS.

The accounting for a change in ownership of a subsidiary with loss of control in FRS 102 (see Chapter 8 at 3.6.3) differs to IFRS in a number of respects, notably no reclassification of exchange differences previously recognised in other comprehensive income or remeasurement of any retained interest to fair value (at the date of loss of control). *[IFRS 10.25, Appendix B.97-99A]*. Transactions in the comparative period (or post the date for which business combinations are restated in accordance with Section 19) may, therefore, need to be restated.

The accounting for non-controlling interest under IFRS and FRS 102 may differ also on a business combination (see Chapter 17 at 3.8). *[IFRS 3.32, Appendix B.44-45]*. However, this transition exception does not address such GAAP differences. There is an optional transition exemption that addresses business combinations, discussed at 5.2 below.

The transition exception does not address the presentation requirements for non-controlling interest in the primary financial statements. These are addressed in Chapter 6 at 4.5. The statutory requirements for presentation of non-controlling interests in the Regulations or LLP Regulations are generally aligned with the requirements in FRS 102. However, there is a theoretical possibility that the amounts for non-controlling interest required by FRS 102 (which has a wider definition) and the statutory requirements may differ. In such a case, two totals are strictly required to be presented to meet the requirements of FRS 102 and the Regulations or LLP Regulations.

5 OPTIONAL EXEMPTIONS TO RETROSPECTIVE APPLICATION

5.1 Introduction

Section 35 sets out optional *exemptions* from the general requirement of full retrospective application of the requirements of FRS 102. *[FRS 102.35.10]*. While many of these correspond to exemptions in IFRS 1 (but worded differently), other exemptions are specific to FRS 102.

The optional exemptions in Section 35 cover the following areas:

- Business combinations, including group reconstructions (see 5.2 below).
- Public benefit entity combinations (see 5.3 below).
- Share-based payment transactions (see 5.4 below).
- Fair value as deemed cost (see 5.5 below).
- Previous revaluation as deemed cost (see 5.5 below).
- Deferred development costs as a deemed cost (see 5.6 below).
- Deemed cost for oil and gas assets (see 5.7 below).
- Decommissioning liabilities included in the cost of property, plant and equipment (see 5.8 below).
- Individual and separate financial statements (see 5.9 below).
- Service concession arrangements – accounting by operators (see 5.10 below).
- Arrangements containing a lease (see 5.11 below).
- Lease incentives (operating leases) (see 5.12 below).
- Dormant companies (see 5.13 below).
- Borrowing costs (see 5.14 below).
- Assets and liabilities of subsidiaries, associates and joint ventures (see 5.15 below).
- Hedge accounting (see 5.16 below).
- Designation of previously recognised financial instruments (see 5.17 below).
- Compound financial instruments (see 5.18 below).
- Small entities – fair value measurement of financial instruments (this exemption applied for accounting periods beginning before 1 January 2017 only) and
- Small entities – financing transactions involving related parties (this exemption applied for accounting periods beginning before 1 January 2017 only).

In addition, FRS 103 includes transition exemptions in relation to insurance contracts (see 5.19 below).

The transition exemptions for small entities are discussed in Chapter 32 at 5.4, 5.19 and 5.20 of EY UK GAAP 2017.

Despite being located within the optional transition exemptions, the transition provisions for hedge accounting in paragraph 35.10(t)(iv) are mandatory where IFRS 9 or IAS 39 is applied to the recognition and measurement of financial instruments. *[FRS 102.35.10(t)(iv)]*. In addition, where an entity adopts FRS 102 in its consolidated financial statements later than its subsidiary, associate or joint venture (or a parent adopts FRS 102 in its separate financial statements earlier or later than for its consolidated financial statements), the transition provisions in paragraph 35.10(r) are mandatory. *[FRS 102.35.10(r)]*.

Otherwise, the exemptions are optional, i.e. a first-time adopter can pick and choose the exemption(s) that it wants to apply. There is no hierarchy of exemptions; therefore, when an item is covered by more than one exemption, a first-time adopter has a free choice in determining the order in which it applies the exemptions.

Each of the exemptions is explained further below.

5.2 Business combinations, including group reconstructions

A first-time adopter may elect not to apply Section 19 to business combinations that were effected before the date of transition to FRS 102. However, if a first-time adopter restates any business combination to comply with Section 19, it shall restate all later business combinations.

If a first-time adopter does not apply Section 19 retrospectively, the first-time adopter shall recognise and measure all its assets and liabilities acquired or assumed in a past business combination at the date of transition in accordance with paragraphs 35.7 to 35.9 or if applicable, with paragraphs 35.10(b) to (v) except for: *[FRS 102.35.10(a)]*

- intangible assets other than goodwill – intangible assets subsumed within goodwill shall not be separately recognised; and

- goodwill – no adjustment shall be made to the carrying value of goodwill.

The business combinations exemption permits a first-time adopter not to restate business combinations that occurred prior to its date of transition in accordance with Section 19. Whether or not a first-time adopter elects to restate pre-transition business combinations, it may still need to restate the carrying amounts of the acquired assets and assumed liabilities (see 5.2.3.B and 5.2.3.C below).

The requirements to allocate profit or loss and total comprehensive income between non-controlling interest and owners of the parent; for accounting for changes in the parent's ownership interest in a subsidiary that do not result in a loss of control; and for accounting for a loss of control over a subsidiary must be applied prospectively from the date of transition (or from such earlier date as FRS 102 is applied to restate business combinations). *[FRS 102.35.9(e)].* See 4.3 above.

Paragraphs PBE 34.75 to 34.86 of FRS 102 contain specific requirements on accounting for public benefit entity combinations, which are discussed at 5.3 below.

Unlike IFRS 1, Section 35 provides no guidance beyond the wording of the transition exemption itself. While there may be other approaches, we consider that Appendix C of IFRS 1 can be helpful in interpreting the transition exemption and will refer to that guidance where appropriate. There are some GAAP differences between IFRS 1 and FRS 102 regarding the business combinations exemption; therefore some aspects of the guidance in Appendix C are not relevant. This commentary is organised as follows:

- option to restate business combinations retrospectively (see 5.2.1 below);

- scope of the transition exemption (see 5.2.2 below);

- application of the transition exemption – general (see 5.2.3 below);

- restatement of goodwill (see 5.2.4 below);

- changes in scope of consolidation (see 5.2.5 below); and

- business combinations – transition example (see 5.2.6 below).

5.2.1 Option to restate business combinations retrospectively

A first-time adopter must account for business combinations occurring *after* its date of transition under Section 19. The requirements of Section 19 are discussed in Chapter 17. Therefore, any business combination during the comparative period(s) needs to be restated in accordance with FRS 102.

Chapter 32

An entity may elect to apply Section 19 to business combinations occurring before the date of transition, but must then restate any subsequent business combinations under Section 19. In other words, a first-time adopter can choose any date in the past from which it wants to account for all business combinations under Section 19 without restating business combinations that occurred before that date. Although there is no restriction that prevents retrospective application by a first-time adopter of Section 19 to all past business combinations, in our view, a first-time adopter should not restate business combinations under Section 19 that occurred before the date of transition when this would require undue use of hindsight.

If any pre-transition business combinations are restated, the first-time adopter must also apply FRS 102's requirements on the measurement of non-controlling interests from the date of the earliest business combination that is restated (see 4.3 above).

5.2.1.A Considerations on restatement of business combinations

If the exemption from restating pre-transition business combinations is not applied, the requirements of Section 19 (see Chapter 17) would need to be applied retrospectively. This might be an onerous exercise that might require undue use of hindsight. For example, restatement would require:

- reassessment as to whether the previous financial reporting framework classification of the business combination (as an acquisition by the legal acquirer, reverse acquisition by the legal acquiree, or merger accounting) was appropriate;

- a fair value exercise to be performed, at the date of the business combination, if the purchase method is required. Any adjustments to assets and liabilities may also impact deferred tax and non-controlling interest;

- an adjustment to non-controlling interest arising on a business combination, if this had been initially recognised at fair value under IFRS, as permitted as an accounting policy choice on a transaction-by-transaction basis. *[IFRS 3.19, Appendix B.44-45]*. This treatment is not permitted under Section 19, which would require the non-controlling interest to be initially recognised at the non-controlling interest's share of the net amount of the identifiable assets, liabilities and contingent liabilities recognised and measured in accordance with Section 19 at the acquisition date (see Chapter 17 at 3.8); *[FRS 102.9.13(d), 19.14A]* and

- the amounts recognised in the business combination to be restated under Section 19 and, subsequently, to be accounted for under FRS 102.

The application of the purchase method in Section 19 differs in certain respects from acquisition accounting under IFRS 3 – *Business Combinations*. See Chapter 17 at 3 for details of application of the purchase method under Section 19.

In particular, retrospective application of Section 19 may result in changes to the recognition of intangible assets compared to the entity's previous financial reporting framework. The extent of any differences to IFRS may depend on what policy the entity applies to the recognition of intangible assets, following amendments made to FRS 102 in the Triennial review 2017. *[FRS 102.18.8]*. In addition, FRS 102 requires that the expected future economic benefits attributable to the intangible asset are probable and the fair value of the intangible asset is measured reliably whereas under IFRS, the probability recognition and reliable measurement criteria are always considered to be satisfied. *[IAS 38.33]*. See Chapter 17 at 2.8 and 3.7.1.A.

Section 19 has a general requirement that the acquiree's identifiable assets and liabilities (and contingent liabilities) – providing their fair value can be measured reliably – are measured at their acquisition-date fair values (with recognition and measurement exceptions for deferred tax assets and liabilities, employee benefit assets and liabilities and share-based payment transactions, where the requirements in the relevant section of FRS 102 dealing with these items are followed). *[FRS 102.19.14-21]*. These requirements may differ from those in the entity's previous financial reporting framework. For example, IFRS 3 requires that the identifiable assets and liabilities (and contingent liabilities) are measured at their acquisition-date fair values in accordance with IFRS 13 – *Fair Value Measurement*. However, there are also specific exceptions to the recognition and measurement principles. *[IFRS 3.10, 18-31, IFRS 13.5]*. If a business combination is restated under Section 19, the adjustments to the fair values of the identifiable assets and liabilities (and contingent liabilities) at the date of the business combination (including any changes to deferred tax and non-controlling interest) are reflected as an adjustment to goodwill. Therefore, applying Section 19 to the business combination would mean restatement of goodwill arising on the acquisition, adjusted for any subsequent amortisation and impairment.

Where the exemption not to restate business combinations is taken, any adjustments to the assets and liabilities acquired or assumed (including related deferred tax, which is required on the differences between the values recognised for assets (other than goodwill) and liabilities acquired in a business combination and the amounts at which those assets and liabilities will be assessed for tax *[FRS 102.29.11]* – see Chapter 26 at 6.6) are reflected in retained earnings (or if appropriate, another category of equity). *[FRS 102.35.9]*. See 5.2.3.C below. Where the business combination involves a purchase of trade and assets reflected in the individual financial statements of a UK company, recognising additional deferred tax liabilities on fair value adjustments, but not adjusting goodwill, would have an adverse effect on the company's distributable reserves. This was a particular concern for previous UK GAAP reporters transitioning to FRS 102.

Example 32.3 at 5.2.6 illustrates the impact of applying the transition exemption and retrospectively restating the business combination in accordance with Section 19 of FRS 102 for a previous IFRS reporter.

5.2.2 Scope of the transition exemption

A transaction must be a business combination or a group reconstruction (as defined in FRS 102 – see Chapter 17 at 3.2 and 5.1 respectively) to qualify for the transition exemption; otherwise, it will need to be retrospectively restated subject to the mandatory exceptions and optional exemptions included in Section 35. IFRS does not have a separate accounting concept of a group reconstruction, but certain transactions may fall within the definition of a group reconstruction.

In practice, some such transactions may have qualified as business combinations under common control and either have been accounted as pooling of interests or acquisition accounted (depending on the policy applied by the entity to such transactions under IFRS). Other transactions may not have qualified as business combinations at all under IFRS. So long as the transaction would have met the definition of a group reconstruction, in our view, it will still qualify for the transition exemption.

IFRS 3 has a different and wider definition of a business compared to FRS 102. *[IFRS 3.3, Appendix A, Appendix B.7-12]*. In October 2018, the IASB issued *Definition of a Business – Amendments to IFRS 3* which amend the definition of a business (and related application guidance) in IFRS. This amendment applies to business combinations for which the acquisition date is, and asset acquisitions that occur, on or after the beginning of the first annual reporting period beginning on or after 1 January 2020 (with earlier application permitted). *[IFRS 3 Appendix A]*. See Chapter 17 at 2.3. Some business combinations under IFRS may not be considered business combinations under FRS 102. If this is the case, then the transition exemption would not apply and retrospective adjustment would appear to be required (if the transaction does not fall within the definition of a group reconstruction).

Unlike IFRS 1, Section 35 does not extend the exemption from applying the principles in Section 19 to acquisitions of associates and interests in joint ventures before the date of transition. *[IFRS 1 Appendix C.5]*. These are not business combinations, as defined, and would therefore appear to require retrospective adjustment.

An entity may have consolidated a subsidiary in a business combination prior to the date of transition that is a subsidiary required to be excluded from consolidation under FRS 102. Section 35 does not address this particular circumstance. However, in our view, the subsidiary should be excluded from consolidation in accordance with the general requirements of Section 35 to apply the recognition and measurement requirements of FRS 102. *[FRS 102.35.7(d)]*. Instead, we would expect that the investment in the subsidiary would be accounted in accordance with paragraphs 9.9 to 9.9C of the standard. See 5.2.5.A below and Chapter 8 at 3.4.

5.2.3 Application of the transition exemption – general

Although there are GAAP differences between IFRS 1 Appendix C and Section 35 in respect of the treatment of intangible assets previously subsumed within goodwill (which must not be reinstated as intangible assets under Section 35), the guidance in Appendix C can be helpful in interpreting the transition exemption. The commentary below, therefore, draws on IFRS 1 in suggesting approaches that preparers may want to consider.

5.2.3.A Classification of business combination

If a first-time adopter does not restate a business combination then it would keep the same classification of the business combination (as an acquisition by the legal acquirer, reverse acquisition by the legal acquiree, merger accounting or pooling of interests) as in its financial statements under its previous financial reporting framework. However, if a transaction is restated in accordance with Section 19, the classification of the business combination may change.

5.2.3.B   Recognition and derecognition of assets and liabilities

A first-time adopter that applies the transition exemption should recognise all assets and liabilities at the date of transition that were acquired or assumed in a past business combination, other than:

- financial assets and financial liabilities that fall to be derecognised under the derecognition transition exception in paragraph 35.9(a) (see 4.1 above);

- assets (including goodwill) and liabilities that were not recognised in the acquirer's consolidated statement of financial position in accordance with its previous financial reporting framework that also would not qualify for recognition as an asset or liability under FRS 102 in the separate (or individual) statement of financial position of the acquiree; and

- intangible assets previously subsumed within goodwill.

The entity must exclude items it recognised under its previous financial reporting framework that do not qualify for recognition as an asset or liability under FRS 102 (subject to the derecognition transition exception for financial assets and financial liabilities).

In our view, a first-time adopter may derecognise intangible assets on transition if these do not meet the criteria followed for recognition of intangible assets on a business combination under FRS 102. This is the case even though, for an ongoing FRS 102 reporter, adoption of the new requirements relating to recognition of intangible assets acquired on a business combination is reflected prospectively (see discussion at 3.5.1 above).

No adjustment is made to the carrying amount of goodwill. Any resulting change is recognised by adjusting retained earnings (or another category of equity). *[FRS 102.35.8, 9(a), 10(a)].*

5.2.3.C   Measurement of assets and liabilities

In essence, the approach to recognising and measuring assets and liabilities is to apply FRS 102 retrospectively (subject to the exceptions and exemptions taken at the date of transition), but without revisiting the fair value exercise. This means that where assets and liabilities acquired or assumed in a past business combination were not recognised under the entity's previous financial reporting framework, these should normally be reflected at the amounts that would be recognised in the separate or individual financial statements of the acquiree and no adjustments are made to goodwill. The previous financial reporting framework carrying amounts as at the date of the acquisition are treated as a deemed cost for the purposes of cost-based depreciation and amortisation. This does not preclude the deemed cost exemptions available on transition from being subsequently applied to assets acquired in the business combination that are still held at the date of transition (see 5.5 below).

FRS 102 requires that, where the transition exemption is used, no adjustments are made to the carrying amount of goodwill at the date of transition. *[FRS 102.35.10(a)].* However, 5.2.4 below sets out situations where it may be necessary to adjust the carrying amount of goodwill, notwithstanding this prohibition.

Chapter 32

A first-time adopter should also consider the following implementation issues on measuring assets acquired and liabilities assumed in business combinations:

(a) *Subsequent measurement of assets and liabilities under FRS 102 not based on cost* – Where FRS 102 requires subsequent measurement of some assets and liabilities on a basis that is not based on original cost, such as fair value (e.g. certain financial instruments) or on specific measurement bases (e.g. share-based payment or employee benefits), a first-time adopter must measure these assets and liabilities on that basis in its opening FRS 102 statement of financial position, even if they were acquired or assumed in a past business combination. Any resulting change is recognised by adjusting retained earnings (or another category of equity).

(b) *Previous financial reporting framework carrying amount as deemed cost* – The carrying amounts in accordance with the entity's previous financial reporting framework of assets acquired and liabilities assumed in the business combination, immediately after the business combination, are their deemed cost in accordance with FRS 102 at that date. If FRS 102 requires a cost-based measurement of those assets and liabilities at a later date that deemed cost should be the basis for cost-based depreciation or amortisation from the date of the business combination (i.e. the carrying amounts under the previous financial reporting framework *at the date of the business combination* are 'grandfathered' as at that date).

A first-time adopter would not use the provisionally determined fair values of assets acquired and liabilities assumed (that were later finalised under its previous financial reporting framework) in applying the business combinations exemption. In any case, goodwill is adjusted retrospectively at the date of transition for the changes to the provisional fair values under FRS 101 / EU-adopted IFRS. While neither Section 35 nor IFRS 1 explicitly addresses this issue, this is consistent with how the related transition exemption in Appendix C of IFRS 1 has been applied in practice.

By contrast, under its previous financial reporting framework, the entity may have amortised intangible assets or depreciated property, plant and equipment from the date of the business combination. If this amortisation or depreciation is not in compliance with FRS 102 (or indeed the asset was not amortised or depreciated under the entity's previous financial reporting framework, but this is required under FRS 102 – see the discussion on intangible assets at 5.2.4.F below), this is not 'grandfathered' under the business combination exemption. If the amortisation or depreciation methods and rates are not acceptable and the difference has a material impact on the financial statements, a first-time adopter must adjust the accumulated amortisation or depreciation on transition (see 5.5.2 below).

(c) *Measurement of items not recognised under the entity's previous financial reporting framework*– If an asset acquired or liability assumed in a past business combination was not recognised under the entity's previous financial reporting framework, this does not mean that such items have a deemed cost of zero in the opening FRS 102 statement of financial position. Instead, the acquirer normally recognises and measures those items in its opening statement of financial position on the basis that FRS 102 would require in the statement of financial position of the acquiree. Conversely, if an asset or liability was subsumed in goodwill in accordance with the entity's previous financial reporting framework but would have been recognised separately under Section 19, that asset or liability remains in goodwill unless FRS 102 would require its recognition in the financial statements of the acquiree. However, intangible assets previously subsumed within goodwill under the entity's previous financial reporting framework are not separately recognised. *[FRS 102.35.10(a)]*. Financial assets and financial liabilities that are derecognised in accordance with the derecognition transition exception (see 4.1 above) are not recognised. *[FRS 102.35.9(a)]*.

(d) *Measurement of non-controlling interests and deferred tax* – The measurement of non-controlling interests (see also 4.3 above) and deferred tax follows from the measurement of other assets and liabilities. Consequently, deferred tax and non-controlling interests should be recalculated after all assets acquired and liabilities assumed have been adjusted under Section 35.

The recognition and measurement of deferred tax is addressed in Section 29. Section 29 must be applied retrospectively as no transition exemptions or exceptions apply. In particular, first-time adopters will need to consider what deferred tax would have been recognised at the date of the business combination, as adjusted by subsequent movements in timing differences recognised under Section 29.

Any resulting change in the carrying amount of deferred taxes and non-controlling interest is recognised by adjusting retained earnings or another category of equity.

Some IFRS reporters may have included non-controlling interest at fair value when accounting for the business combination under IFRS 3. *[IFRS 3.19, Appendix B.44-45]*. This may exceed the non-controlling interest based on the proportionate share of the subsidiary's identifiable assets, liabilities (and contingent liabilities) which would be the measurement basis used under FRS 102 at the date of the business combination. *[FRS 102.9.13(d), 19.14A]*. Consequently some of the goodwill recognised under IFRS would relate to the non-controlling interest. Given that goodwill is not restated where the transition exemption in paragraph 35.10(a) is taken, we believe that it is appropriate that non-controlling interest – which represents the equity in a subsidiary not attributable, directly or indirectly, to its parent *[FRS 102 Appendix I]* – continues to include this attributed goodwill.

5.2.4 Restatement of goodwill

Notwithstanding the prohibition in paragraph 35.10(a) from making adjustments to goodwill where past business combinations are not restated, there may be certain situations where an adjustment to goodwill is appropriate. These could include:

- where there is an indicator that the goodwill may be impaired at the date of transition (see 5.2.4.A below);
- the interaction with FRS 102's requirements to restate goodwill for adjustments to contingent consideration (see 5.2.4.B below);
- a potential conflict with FRS 102's requirements to retranslate goodwill and fair value adjustments relating to a foreign operation. (see 5.2.4.C below); and
- changes in the scope of consolidation (see 5.2.5 below).

The transition requirements for negative goodwill (see 5.2.4.D below) and goodwill previously deducted from equity (see 5.2.4.E below) are not explicitly addressed by Section 35, although IFRS 1 Appendix C addresses the latter.

5.2.4.A   Impairment of goodwill

Section 35 does not require an impairment review of goodwill to be performed as at the date of transition. However, there are no exemptions in Section 35 from applying Section 27, which requires that an entity must assess at each reporting date whether there is any indication of impairment. FRS 102 prohibits the reversal of impairment losses relating to goodwill. *[FRS 102.35.7, 27.24, 28].*

For example, an entity may uplift the carrying amount of property, plant and equipment to fair value at the date of transition (by adopting a revaluation policy under FRS 102 or using the deemed cost exemption to state an item of property, plant or equipment at fair value as at the date of transition *[FRS 102.35.10(c)]* – see 5.5 below). As a consequence, the total carrying amount of the acquired net assets including goodwill may exceed the recoverable amount of the relevant cash-generating unit(s) (or groups of cash-generating unit(s)) to which the goodwill is allocated. (Where this allocation cannot be performed on a non-arbitrary basis, Section 27 sets out the approach to be used). Consequently, an impairment of goodwill (and potentially other assets in the cash generating unit(s)) would be recognised. See Chapter 24 at 5.

Section 35 states that no adjustments shall be made to the carrying amount of goodwill at the date of transition (or earlier date from which the first-time adopter restates business combinations under Section 19). *[FRS 102.35.10(a)].* However, it would be inappropriate to recognise an impairment loss on the first day of the comparative period of the FRS 102 financial statements when that impairment already existed at the date of transition itself. Therefore, if there is an indicator of impairment at transition, the goodwill should be reviewed for impairment at the date of transition.

Any impairment losses identified at the date of transition would be reflected in retained earnings in accordance with paragraph 35.8, unless the impairment is allocated to revalued assets (such as property, plant and equipment) where the impairment is accounted as a revaluation decrease in accordance with other sections of FRS 102 and reduces a revaluation surplus on that asset included in the revaluation reserve (see Chapter 6 at 10.2, Chapter 15 at 3.6 and Chapter 24 at 6). *[FRS 102.27.6].*

5.2.4.B   Transition accounting for contingent consideration

Contingent consideration should be remeasured under the general principles in FRS 102 as there are no exemptions under Section 35. FRS 102 requires that the acquirer includes the estimated amount of contingent consideration (reflecting the time value of money, if material) in the cost of the combination at the acquisition date if the adjustment is probable and can be measured reliably. Subsequent changes to the estimate are also reflected as adjustments to the cost of the business combination (with the unwinding of any discount reflected as a finance cost in profit or loss in the period it arises). *[FRS 102.19.12-13B].* See Chapter 17 at 3.6.2.

The requirements of IFRS for accounting for contingent consideration differ significantly from those in FRS 102. In particular, IFRS 3 requires that contingent consideration classified as equity shall not be remeasured and its subsequent settlement shall be accounted for within equity. Other contingent consideration is measured at fair value at each reporting date and changes in fair value are recognised in profit or loss. *[IFRS 3.39-40, 58].* Therefore, it is likely that a previous IFRS or FRS 101 reporter will need to remeasure contingent consideration classified as a liability (or asset) on transition to FRS 102 to reflect the amounts that are probable (and can be measured reliably) rather than the fair value. The situation with contingent consideration classified as equity is more complicated since FRS 102's requirements on contingent consideration arising from a business combination do not distinguish between contingent consideration classified as equity or as a liability. As explained further in Chapter 17 at 3.6.5, in our view, contingent consideration classified as equity is remeasured for changes in the number of equity instruments to be issued (and valued using the fair value at the date of exchange, i.e. the date of acquisition), with adjustments reflected in the cost of combination (and hence goodwill). The estimated amount of contingent consideration classified as equity is not remeasured for subsequent changes in the entity's share price.

Consequently, while paragraph 35.10(a) specifies that no adjustments should be made to goodwill (where the transition exemption is used), Section 19 requires goodwill to be adjusted for changes in the amount of estimated contingent consideration. However, the amount of goodwill recognised by a previous IFRS or FRS 101 reporter would not reflect adjustments to the fair value of contingent consideration made subsequent to the acquisition (unless these qualified as measurement period adjustments). *[IFRS 3.39-40, 45, 58]*. The question therefore arises as to whether a first-time adopter is permitted to adjust goodwill as at the date of transition to reflect the estimated contingent consideration, measured in accordance with Section 19 at that date. Although a conflict between paragraph 35.10(a) and Section 19 arises, in our view, goodwill is not adjusted as at the date of transition, and therefore any resulting change to the estimated contingent consideration is recognised by adjusting retained earnings (or another category of equity) at that date. This view recognises that paragraph 35.10(a) takes precedence. *[FRS 102.35.7, 10(a)]*. This situation differs in certain respects from the situation discussed at 5.2.4.C below with denominating goodwill in a foreign currency as the accounting just changes the *same* goodwill from being viewed as denominated in the functional currency to a foreign currency (rather than remeasuring the goodwill to a different amount, based on estimated contingent consideration).

The interaction between the requirements on contingent consideration and those on financial instruments is rather complicated. Sections 11 and 12 of FRS 102, where applied to the recognition and measurement of financial instruments, scope out the accounting by the acquirer for contracts for contingent consideration in a business combination – and instead refer to Section 19. *[FRS 102.12.3(g)]*. Consequently, goodwill must be adjusted prospectively for re-measurements of contingent consideration that are made subsequent to the date of transition.

An entity that chooses to apply IAS 39 or IFRS 9 to the recognition and measurement of financial instruments, applies the scope of the relevant standard to its financial instruments. *[FRS 102.11.2, 12.2]*. IAS 39 and IFRS 9 specifically address contingent consideration classified as a financial liability that is recognised in a business combination to which IFRS 3 applies. *[IAS 39.9(aa), IFRS 9.4.2.1]*. However, the requirements on accounting for contingent consideration are found primarily in IFRS 3 and so do not apply to entities reporting under FRS 102. *[IFRS 3.39-40, 58, IFRS 9.4.2.1(c)]*. Therefore, such an entity should also normally apply the requirement in paragraph 19.12 that contingent consideration is recognised where the adjustments to consideration are probable and can be measured reliably, with subsequent adjustments to goodwill.

Chapter 32

5.2.4.C   *Goodwill on a pre-transition business combination that is a foreign operation (where not restated under Section 19)*

Section 35 is not explicit on how to treat goodwill relating to an acquisition of a foreign operation in a business combination that is not restated under Section 19.

While paragraph 35.10(a) specifies that no adjustments should be made to goodwill, Section 30 – *Foreign Currency Translation* – requires goodwill arising on the acquisition of a foreign operation to be translated. *[FRS 102.30.23]*. Where a conflict between paragraph 35.10(a) and Section 30 arises, management will need to use judgement to determine an appropriate policy and this may be an area where diversity in practice will emerge. A previous IFRS or FRS 101 reporter will in any event be translating foreign currency goodwill; however, there may be elements of goodwill which were regarded as functional currency goodwill (and not retranslated on an ongoing basis) on transition to IFRS or FRS 101. *[IAS 21.23.47, IFRS 1 Appendix C2-C3]*.

In our view, paragraph 35.10(a) does not preclude management regarding the goodwill as foreign currency goodwill and retranslating the goodwill at the date of transition (and thereafter at each reporting period). An alternative view which could meet the requirements of paragraph 35.10(a) to preserve the carrying amount of goodwill (expressed in the functional currency of the reporting entity) and to comply with Section 30, would be taking the functional currency carrying amount of the goodwill at the date of transition, translating it into the underlying currency of the acquired operations at the transition date exchange rate and thereafter regarding the goodwill as foreign currency goodwill to be retranslated at each reporting period. Another alternative view is that the requirement relates to preserving the carrying amount of the goodwill (i.e. in the reporting entity's functional currency); this view takes a literal reading of the transition exemption in paragraph 35.10(a) and considers that this takes precedence over Section 30's requirements.

5.2.4.D   *Negative goodwill*

FRS 102's accounting requirements for negative goodwill (see Chapter 17 at 3.9.3) differ significantly from those in IFRS 3 where the negative goodwill is recognised immediately in profit or loss. *[FRS 102.19.24, IFRS 3.34]*.

The transition exemption in paragraph 35.10(a) addresses *goodwill*, requiring that no adjustment shall be made to the carrying value of goodwill. Goodwill is defined as 'future economic benefits arising from assets that are not capable of being individually identified and separately recognised' rather than simply as a residual (see Chapter 17 at 3.9). Therefore, goodwill is not the same as the 'excess over cost of acquirer's interest in the net fair value of acquiree's identifiable assets, liabilities and contingent liabilities' (negative goodwill). On the other hand, negative goodwill is not strictly an asset or liability (as defined) and so arguably does not fall within the requirement to restate the opening financial position. *[FRS 102.35.7]*.

In our view, an entity that applies the transition exemption in paragraph 35.10(a) not to restate business combinations is not required to reinstate negative goodwill that was recognised immediately in profit or loss under IFRS. Moreover, for the reasons explained in Chapter 17 at 3.9.3, it may often be the case that negative goodwill would have been fully amortised by the date of transition had FRS 102 been applied.

However, an entity would need to consider carefully whether any accumulated credit in retained earnings represented by negative goodwill is a realised profit in accordance with the guidance in TECH 02/17BL, as this may not always be the case.

5.2.4.E   Goodwill previously deducted from equity

There may be historic circumstances where, under the entity's previous financial framework, some goodwill has been eliminated against reserves. In our view, where the exemption not to restate pre-transition business combinations in accordance with Section 19 is taken, the requirement that no adjustment shall be made to the carrying value of goodwill means that there is no change to the amount of goodwill recognised as an asset (i.e. the goodwill remains eliminated against equity). *[FRS 102.35.10(a)]*. Effectively under FRS 102, such goodwill does not exist for accounting purposes. FRS 102 does not permit or require recycling of goodwill previously deducted from equity to profit or loss when the related operation is disposed of or closed.

5.2.4.F   Goodwill and intangible asset amortisation

FRS 102 requires that goodwill and intangible assets be amortised on a systematic basis over a finite useful life using an amortisation method that reflects the expected pattern of consumption of economic benefits. A straight-line basis is used if the entity cannot determine that pattern reliably. If an entity is unable to make a reliable estimate of the useful life of goodwill or an intangible asset, the useful life shall not exceed ten years. *[FRS 102.18.19-22, 19.23]*. See Chapter 16 at 3.4.3 and Chapter 17 at 3.9.2 for a fuller discussion.

Under IFRS, the acquirer measures goodwill at the amount recognised at the acquisition date less any accumulated impairment losses. *[IFRS 3 Appendix B.63]*. Consequently, goodwill is not amortised.

A first-time adopter may also need to consider the following implementation issues:

(a) *Adjustments to goodwill lives where no restatement of business combinations under Section 19* – Where an entity is not restating the business combination in accordance with Section 19, paragraph 35.10(a) requires that no adjustment is made to the carrying amount of goodwill. Consequently, the requirement in FRS 102 to amortise goodwill over a finite life is accounted for prospectively.

    The Basis for Conclusions to FRS 102 states that 'FRS 102 does not permit goodwill to have an indefinite useful life, unlike current FRS. On transition to FRS 102, entities that previously determined that goodwill had an indefinite useful life will need to reassess goodwill to determine its remaining useful life, and subsequently amortise the goodwill over that period.' *[FRS 102.BC.B35.1]*.

    This does not appear to distinguish between goodwill relating to past business combinations restated in accordance with Section 19 and goodwill that is not restated, but we believe it is intended to apply only where the exemption in paragraph 35.10(a) not to restate business combinations is taken.

    Therefore, an IFRS or FRS 101 reporter is required to reassess the remaining useful life of the goodwill, as at the date of transition and to amortise the goodwill prospectively.

(b) *Restatement of business combinations in accordance with Section 19* – Where a first-time adopter restates a business combination in accordance with Section 19 and has previously ascribed a finite useful life to goodwill, any adjustment to that useful life is accounted for prospectively over the remaining revised useful life determined under FRS 102 as a change in estimate (see 4.2 above).

Where, however, an indefinite useful life was used under the entity's previous financial reporting framework (as required under IFRS), amortisation should be adjusted for retrospectively from the date of the business combination. This is because this is a change in accounting policy (not a change in estimate) and the requirement in paragraph 35.10(a) that no adjustment shall be made to the carrying amount of goodwill does not apply. On transition to FRS 102, however, goodwill and intangible assets *must* be amortised over a finite useful life. Therefore, in our view, a move from an indefinite useful life to a finite useful life for goodwill is required to be retrospectively effected – such that the goodwill at transition represents the carrying amounts after adjusting for amortisation on the basis of the finite useful life determined under FRS 102.

(c)   *Intangible assets* – There are no special transition requirements for intangible assets (other than goodwill) and therefore FRS 102's requirements are applied retrospectively. *[FRS 102.35.7].*

Where an entity amortised an intangible asset over a longer finite useful life than ten years under its previous financial reporting framework, it can continue to use that useful life, where it continues to be a reliable estimate of the useful life. In particular, it would be difficult to argue that the useful life of the intangible asset should simply default to a ten year life. Any changes to the useful life would need to be justified by reference to a change in circumstances (unless the previous life was objectively in error) and be recognised prospectively as a change in estimate (see 4.2 above). However, if an entity ascribed an indefinite useful life to an intangible asset under its previous financial reporting framework, in our view, the intangible asset must be amortised retrospectively over its new finite useful life since this is a change in accounting policy (FRS 102 does not permit use of an indefinite useful life).

The above conclusions apply to all intangible assets, whether acquired separately or in a business combination (and do not depend on whether the business combination is restated in accordance with Section 19 or not).

5.2.5   Changes in scope of consolidation

The scope of consolidation under the entity's previous financial reporting framework may differ from the scope of consolidation under FRS 102. Therefore, a first-time adopter may not have consolidated a subsidiary acquired in a past business combination under its previous financial reporting framework or a subsidiary previously consolidated qualifies to be excluded from consolidation under FRS 102.

Adjustments to the carrying amounts of assets and liabilities of subsidiaries may affect non-controlling interest and deferred tax.

5.2.5.A   *Changes in scope of consolidation compared to the previous financial reporting framework*

Section 9 of FRS 102 states that 'a subsidiary is an entity that is controlled by the parent'. The definition of 'a subsidiary' in Section 9 is generally consistent with (although not identical to) the definition of 'a subsidiary undertaking' included in section 1162 of the CA 2006. However, Section 9 contains additional guidance on 'control' – in relation to currently exercisable options or convertible instruments; where control is exercised through an agent; and Special Purpose Entities – as well as an extended definition of subsidiaries held exclusively for resale (which are excluded from consolidation). *[FRS 102.9.4-9.12, s1162, s1162 (LLP)].*

IFRS 10 has a similar definition that 'a subsidiary is an entity that is controlled by another entity'. *[IFRS 10 Appendix A].* However, IFRS 10 and FRS 102 differ in the wording of the definition of 'control' (and associated guidance) and exclusions from the scope of consolidation. *[FRS 102.9.4-6A].* In many cases, both standards lead to the same determination of whether an entity is or is not a subsidiary. However, a first-time adopter should consider Section 9's requirements on control and the exclusions from the scope of consolidation (discussed in Chapter 8 at 3.3 and 3.4) in order to determine whether any changes are required compared to its previous financial reporting framework. *[FRS 102.9.4-12].*

5.2.5.B   *Previously unconsolidated subsidiaries*

If, under its previous financial reporting framework, an FRS 102 first-time adopter did not consolidate a subsidiary that it is required to consolidate under FRS 102, it must retrospectively apply FRS 102 to the carrying amounts of the assets and liabilities of that subsidiary, subject to the transition exceptions and transition exemptions set out in Section 35. *[FRS 102.35.7].*

FRS 102 does not explain how a first-time adopter should consolidate a subsidiary for the first time (whether because the reporting entity did not consider the entity to be a subsidiary under its previous financial reporting framework or did not prepare consolidated financial statements). However, as set out below, management should apply the requirements of paragraph 35.10(r) (which addresses the accounting for a subsidiary on transition, where a parent becomes a first-time adopter of FRS 102 later than its subsidiary – see 5.15.2 below) and may want to consider paragraphs IG 27 to IG 30 of IFRS 1 (which provide further implementation guidance discussed below) to the extent that these do not conflict with FRS 102.

If an entity becomes a first-time adopter later than its subsidiary, the entity shall in its consolidated financial statements, measure the assets and liabilities of the subsidiary at the same carrying amounts as in the financial statements of the subsidiary, after adjusting for consolidation adjustments and for the effects of the business combination in which the entity acquired the subsidiary. *[FRS 102.35.10(r)].* Where the subsidiary has not previously adopted FRS 102, the reference above to the 'same carrying amounts' is to the amounts FRS 102 would require in the statement of financial position of the subsidiary. *[IFRS 1.IG 27(a)].*

Chapter 32

The amounts of goodwill, assets and liabilities recognised in respect of the subsidiary will depend on whether it was acquired in a business combination or not, and if it was so acquired, whether the business combination is restated in accordance with Section 19 or not. *[FRS 102.35.10(a)].*

(a)   *Subsidiary acquired in a business combination: entity uses the transition exemption in paragraph 35.10(a) not to restate past business combinations –*

Where the business combination is not restated in accordance with Section 19, paragraph 35.10(a) is applied to accounting for the business combination (see 5.2 generally). Section 35 does not explain how to implement paragraph 35.10(a) where the subsidiary has not been previously consolidated (so that no goodwill has been reflected in the consolidated financial statements). In such cases, the entity should adopt an appropriate policy. For example, even if consolidated financial statements were not prepared by the entity under its previous financial reporting framework, the amount of the goodwill, assets and liabilities that would have been recognised had the subsidiary been consolidated under its previous financial reporting framework may be known or determinable (for example, if the amounts were already available for the purposes of group reporting). The CA 2006 also requires the determination of goodwill, as at the date of the acquisition, where a subsidiary undertaking is acquired and accounted for using the acquisition method. *[6 Sch 9, 3 Sch 9 (LLP)].* However, this will not always be the case and, on the basis that no goodwill was reflected in the entity's previous financial reporting framework financial statements, a view could be taken that the transition adjustments to derecognise the cost of investment and recognise the assets and liabilities of the subsidiary may be reflected in retained earnings (or other category of equity), following the general requirements in Section 35. In some cases, the impracticability exemption in paragraph 35.11 may be relevant to the accounting for the business combination (see 3.5.4 above). *[FRS 102.35.11].*

This differs from the requirement in Appendix C4(j) in IFRS 1 to establish a deemed cost of goodwill, being the difference between the carrying amount of the investment and the assets and liabilities of the subsidiary that would be required in the subsidiary's own IFRS financial statements. *[IFRS 1 Appendix C.4(j)].* While pragmatic, this will result in a deemed cost of goodwill which will rarely represent the true goodwill under a previous financial reporting framework, will give a different answer for goodwill depending on the measurement basis used for the investment in the subsidiary in the parent's separate financial statements, and appears to conflict with paragraph 35.10(a)'s requirement that no adjustment is made to the carrying value of goodwill at the date of transition.

Other assets acquired and liabilities assumed *since* the business combination and still held at the acquirer's date of transition are reported at:

- the carrying amounts that FRS 102 would require in the subsidiary's own statement of financial position; or
- where the subsidiary has already adopted FRS 102 before its parent, the amounts included in the subsidiary's statement of financial position in its FRS 102 financial statements,

after adjusting for consolidation procedures. *[FRS 102.35.10(r), IFRS 1.IG 27(a), 30(a)].*

(b) *Subsidiary acquired in a business combination restated under Section 19* – Where the previously unconsolidated subsidiary was acquired in a business combination restated under Section 19, the goodwill and fair values of the identifiable net assets recognised at the date of the business combination would be retrospectively restated. The first-time adopter would need to restate either all pre-transition business combinations or all later business combinations (and apply the requirements of FRS 102 in respect of non-controlling interests from the same date). *[FRS 102.35.9(e), 10(a)].*

Other assets acquired and liabilities assumed *since* the business combination and still held at the acquirer's date of transition are reported at:

- the carrying amounts that FRS 102 would require in the subsidiary's own statement of financial position; or

- where the subsidiary has already adopted FRS 102 before its parent, the amounts included in the subsidiary's statement of financial position in its FRS 102 financial statements,

after adjusting for consolidation procedures. *[FRS 102.35.10(r), IFRS 1.IG 27(a), 30(a)].*

(c) *Subsidiary not acquired in a business combination* – The first-time adopter would adjust the carrying amounts of the subsidiary's assets and liabilities to the amounts that FRS 102 would require in the subsidiary's own statement of financial position (or where the subsidiary has already adopted FRS 102 before its parent, the amounts included in its statement of financial position in its FRS 102 financial statements), after adjusting for consolidation procedures. *[FRS 102.35.10(r), IFRS 1.IG 27(a)].*

Where the subsidiary was not acquired in a business combination, no goodwill is recognised. *[IFRS 1.IG 27(c)].* Instead, any difference between the carrying amounts and the net identifiable assets determined above is treated as an adjustment to retained earnings at the date of transition.

5.2.5.C Previously consolidated entities that are not subsidiaries

A first-time adopter may have consolidated an investment under its previous financial reporting framework that does not meet the definition of a subsidiary under FRS 102. In such a case, the entity should first determine the appropriate classification under FRS 102 (for example, as an associate, jointly controlled entity or financial asset) and then apply Section 35's requirements.

The requirements of FRS 102 should be applied retrospectively subject to any transition exceptions and exemptions available and, where applicable, the use of the impracticability exemption available in paragraph 35.11 (see 3.5.4 above). *[FRS 102.35.7, 11].*

5.2.6 Business combination – transition example

The following example illustrates a number of the considerations relevant to the treatment of business combinations on transition.

Example 32.3:   Business combination example

On 31 December 2017, Entity A purchased Entity B for £1.2m cash consideration (incurring acquisition costs of £10,000) and further contingent cash consideration. The date of transition is 1 January 2018 and Entity A prepares its first FRS 102 financial statements for the accounting period beginning 1 January 2019. Entity A prepared its last annual financial statements in accordance with IFRS.

The assets and liabilities acquired were as follows:

	Book value (and tax base) in B's financial statements £000	Fair value (IFRS) £000	Fair value (Not restating under Section 19) £000	Fair value (Section 19) £000
Intangible asset (brand – 5 year life)	–	200	200	200
Intangible asset (customer contract – 5 year life)	–	300	–	–
Investment property	100	300	300	300
Owner-occupied property (20 year life – nil residual value)	100	500	500	480
Inventory	50	70	70	70
Deferred tax (at 20%)	(40)	(264)	(204)	(200)
Net assets acquired	–	1,106	866	850
Consideration – cash	–	1,200	1,200	1,200
Contingent cash consideration		400	350	350
Transaction costs		10	10	10
Goodwill	–	494	494	710
Adjustment to retained earnings (DR/ (CR))			190	(10)

The entity acquisition accounted for the transaction under IFRS. The fair values for the identifiable assets and liabilities and the goodwill recognised are shown in the second column in the table above. Goodwill, which is not amortised under IFRS, has not been impaired. The fair value of the contingent consideration liability recognised was £400,000 at the date of the business combination and £600,000 as at 31 December 2018. Transaction costs of £10,000 were expensed under IFRS.

The transaction meets the definition of a business combination under FRS 102. An income tax rate of 20% applies in all periods and indexation is ignored. The discount rate used to unwind the contingent consideration is 4%. It is assumed there are no tax effects of fair value movements or of settlement of contingent consideration (so that no deferred tax arose under IFRS and there is no timing difference under FRS 102).

Under FRS 102, Entity A accounts for the owner-occupied property using the cost model (same as IFRS). The investment property is accounted at fair value through profit or loss (under IFRS, the entity had elected the cost model, but any depreciation was immaterial in the first year of ownership). The fair value of the investment property was £350,000 as at 31 December 2018. The present value of the amount of contingent consideration that is estimated as probable to be paid (and can be reliably measured) was £350,000 as at the date of the business combination (and date of transition) and £540,000 as at 31 December 2018.

This example considers the accounting when the business combination is not restated under Section 19 (using the exemption in paragraph 35.10(a)) and when the business combination is restated under Section 19.

Business combination is not restated under Section 19

At the date of transition, Entity A:

- Does not restate the IFRS carrying amount of the owner-occupied property of £500,000, even though its acquisition-date fair value would have differed had Section 19 been applied (this is because Section 19 does not specify application of the highest and best use, as required under IFRS 13). It is assumed that the value in use of the cash generating unit to which the property belongs exceeds the carrying amount of the cash generating unit. The values ascribed under IFRS are treated as deemed cost at the date of the business combination.

- Derecognises the customer contract intangible asset of £300,000 as at the date of transition as Entity A applies a policy of not recognising additional classes of intangible assets that do not meet all three recognition criteria. *[FRS 102.18.8]*.

- Reduces the deferred tax liability by £60,000 relating to the fair value adjustment to derecognise the customer contract intangible asset. *[FRS 102.29.11]*.

- Remeasures the contingent consideration to £350,000, i.e. a reduction of £50,000 in the liability recognised under IFRS. *[FRS 102.19.12]*.

Entity A does not change the carrying amount of goodwill of £494,000 recognised under IFRS at the date of transition, and adjusts retained earnings by £190,000 debit for the reduction in the intangible asset and deferred tax liability and remeasurement of contingent liability above. *[FRS 102.35.10(a)]*. Goodwill is assessed as having a remaining life of 15 years.

In the comparative period, Entity A makes the following adjustments compared to IFRS:

- An increase of £50,000 in the carrying amount of the investment property (to its fair value at 31 December 2018) recognising the fair value gain in profit or loss. This property was carried using the cost model under IFRS (with immaterial depreciation in the comparative period). *[FRS 102.16.7]*.

- The contingent consideration liability is remeasured to £540,000 as at 31 December 2018. There is a consequential increase of £176,000 to the carrying amount of goodwill as at 31 December 2018. leaving £14,000 (i.e. 0.04 × £350,000) unwind of discount in profit or loss. This adjustment to goodwill is made prospectively (rather than restating goodwill at transition). *[FRS 102.19.12-13B]*. Under IFRS, a fair value movement of £200,000 had been recognised in profit or loss, measuring the contingent consideration liability at £600,000. This is reversed. *[IFRS 3.58]*.

- Goodwill amortisation of £32,933 (i.e. £494,000 / 15), based on the goodwill amount as at transition, is recognised as an expense. *[FRS 102.19.23]*. Goodwill is not amortised under IFRS. *[IFRS 3 Appendix B.63]*.

- The reversal of amortisation on the customer contract of £60,000 (i.e. £300,000 / 5) which is recognised as an intangible asset under IFRS but not FRS 102.

- A reduction of £12,000 to deferred tax income (relating to the reversal of deferred tax under IFRS on the customer contract intangible asset amortisation) and an increase in deferred tax expense of £10,000 (relating to the fair value gain on the investment property which was not recognised under IFRS as the cost model was used). *[FRS 102.29.6]*.

Business combination restated under Section 19

Entity A restates the business combination in accordance with Section 19 (as shown in the final column in the table above). Goodwill of £710,000 arising is amortised over 15 years from the date of the business combination. Therefore, the carrying amount of goodwill is increased by £216,000 and the net assets acquired reduced by £216,000 (compared to IFRS) at the date of transition.

In the comparative period, Entity A makes the following adjustments compared to IFRS:

- An increase of £50,000 in the carrying amount of the investment property (to its fair value at 31 December 2018) recognising the fair value gain in profit or loss. This property was carried using the cost model under IFRS (with immaterial depreciation in the comparative period). *[FRS 102.16.7]*.

- The contingent consideration liability is remeasured to £540,000 as at 31 December 2018. There is a consequential increase of £176,000 to the carrying amount of goodwill as at 31 December 2018. leaving £14,000 (i.e. 0.04 × £350,000) unwind of discount in profit or loss. This adjustment to goodwill is made prospectively (rather than restating goodwill at transition). *[FRS 102.19.12-13B]*. Under IFRS, a fair value movement of £200,000 had been recognised in profit or loss, measuring the contingent consideration liability at £600,000. This is reversed. *[IFRS 3.58]*.

- Goodwill amortisation of £47,333 (i.e. £710,000 / 15), based on the goodwill amount as at transition, is recognised as an expense. *[FRS 102.19.23]*. Goodwill is not amortised under IFRS. *[IFRS 3 Appendix B.63]*.

- The reversal of amortisation on the customer contract of £60,000 (i.e. £300,000 / 5) which is recognised as an intangible asset under IFRS but not FRS 102 and £1,000 ((£500,000 − £480,000) / 20) lower depreciation on the owner-occupied property.

- A reduction of £12,200 to deferred tax income (being £12,000 relating to the reversal of deferred tax under IFRS on the customer contract intangible asset amortisation, and £200 relating to the reversal of deferred tax due to lower depreciation on the owner-occupied property), and an increase in deferred tax expense of £10,000 (relating to the fair value gain on the investment property which is not recognised under IFRS as the cost model is used). *[FRS 102.29.6]*.

5.3   Public-benefit entity combinations

A public benefit entity is 'an entity whose primary objective is to provide goods or services for the general public, community or social benefit and where any equity is provided with a view to supporting the entity's primary objectives rather than with a view to providing a financial return to equity providers, shareholders or members.' *[FRS 102 Appendix I]*.

FRS 102 specifies the accounting for different types of public benefit entity combinations (see Chapter 31 at 6). *[FRS 102.PBE34.75-86]*. Entities that are subject to a SORP may find that the relevant SORP contains further guidance specific to transactions in their sector. For example, the *Charities SORP (FRS 102)*, issued by the Charity Commission in England and Wales and the Office of the Scottish Charity Regulator in 2014 (and subsequently updated in 2016 and 2018 by Update Statements 1 and 2), contains guidance on various types of public benefit entity combinations involving charities.[1]

A first-time adopter may elect not to apply paragraphs PBE 34.75 to PBE 34.86 relating to public benefit entity combinations to combinations that were effected before the date of transition to FRS 102. However, if on first-time adoption, a public benefit entity restates any entity combination to comply with this section, it shall restate all later entity combinations. *[FRS 102.35.10(q)]*.

Section 35 does not add further guidance. However, entities may want to interpret paragraph 35.10(q) in the same way as the exemption not to restate pre-transition business combinations (including group reconstructions) in paragraph 35.10(a). See 5.2 above.

5.4   Share-based payment transactions

A first-time adopter is not required to apply Section 26 – *Share-based Payment* – to equity instruments (including the equity component of share-based payment transactions previously treated as compound instruments) that were granted before the date of transition to FRS 102, or to liabilities arising from share-based payment transactions that were settled before the date of transition to FRS 102. In addition, there was a further concession for small entities that first adopted FRS 102 for accounting periods prior to 1 January 2017 not to apply Section 26 to equity instruments granted before the start of the first reporting period that complies with FRS 102.

However, a first-time adopter previously applying IFRS 2 – *Share-based Payment* – shall, in relation to equity instruments (including the equity component of share-based payment transactions previously treated as compound instruments) that were granted before the date of transition to FRS 102, apply IFRS 2 or Section 26 at the date of transition. The same requirement was in effect where first-time adopters previously applied FRS 20 (IFRS 2) – *Share-based payment* (rather than IFRS 2).

Most first-time adopters will now be previous IFRS or FRS 101 reporters. In our view, the intention of the transition exemption is simply that an entity previously applying IFRS 2 may complete the accounting for a pre-transition grant using the original grant date fair value and it is not intended that the application of Section 26 of FRS 102 to such grants should necessarily result in a remeasurement. However, there is nothing in paragraph 10(b) of Section 35 to prohibit such a remeasurement (for example, as a result of applying the group allocation arrangements of paragraph 16 of Section 26).

The classification of a share-based payment transaction as equity-settled or cash-settled will often be the same under FRS 102 and IFRS 2 (although the requirements on classification are not identical). If a classification difference does result from adoption of FRS 102, it appears that an entity could continue with the IFRS 2 classification for existing awards, even if new grants would be classified differently under FRS 102.

The transition exemptions impact the ongoing accounting for the share-based awards to which the exemption was applied. See Chapter 5 at 6.4 (in relation to the concession for small entities) and Chapter 23 at 17.

5.5   Fair value or previous revaluation as deemed cost

A first-time adopter may elect to measure an:

- item of property, plant and equipment,
- an investment property, or
- an intangible asset which meets the recognition criteria and the criteria for revaluation as set out in Section 18 – *Intangible Assets other than Goodwill*,

on the date of transition to FRS 102 at its fair value (see definitions at 3.1 above) and use that fair value as its deemed cost at that date. *[FRS 102.35.10(c)]*. Fair value at the date of transition should reflect the conditions that existed at transition date. FRS 102 requires that, in the absence of specific guidance in the relevant section of the standard dealing with an item, the guidance in the Appendix to Section 2 should be used in determining fair value. *[FRS 102 Appendix I]*.

A first-time adopter may elect to use a revaluation determined under its previous financial reporting framework of an item of property, plant and equipment, an investment property, or an intangible asset (which meets the recognition criteria and the criteria for revaluation as set out in Section 18) at, or before, the date of transition to FRS 102 as its deemed cost at the revaluation date. *[FRS 102.35.10(d)]*.

Establishing the historical cost amounts for an asset may be onerous where the requirements differ from the previous financial reporting framework. A previous IFRS or FRS 101 reporter may have used a deemed cost exemption (similar to those in paragraphs 35.10(c) and (d), discussed above) on first-time adoption of IFRS. *[IFRS 1 Appendix D.5-7]*. Use of a deemed cost exemption would allow a first-time adopter that revalued the property, plant and equipment under its previous financial reporting framework to retain the revalued amount at the date of transition when moving to the cost model on adoption of FRS 102. It would also allow first-time adopters to reflect a one-off revaluation at the date of transition. Section 35 includes further deemed cost exemptions for:

- deferred development costs (see 5.6 below);
- oil and gas properties (see 5.7 below); and
- cost of investments in subsidiaries, associates and joint ventures in separate or individual financial statements (see 5.9 below).

5.5.1   Scope of the deemed cost exemption

The exemptions in paragraphs 35.10(c) and (d) are available on an item-by-item basis (so need not be applied consistently to a class of assets).

In practice, these exemptions are likely to be most useful for items of property, plant and equipment, where there are few restrictions to their application.

Following the Triennial review 2017, investment property is required to be measured at fair value through profit or loss unless it is investment property rented out to another group entity, where the entity has taken the policy choice to transfer it to property, plant and equipment and to account for the investment property using the cost model. *[FRS 102.16.1-1A, 4A-4B, 7]*. See Chapter 14 at 3.1.2.

The deemed cost exemption can only be applied to intangible assets that meet the recognition criteria and criteria for revaluation in Section 18, including the existence of an active market. Therefore, the exemption is of limited practical relevance to intangible assets.

5.5.2   Establishing deemed cost at a date other than transition

If the deemed cost of an asset is determined before the date of transition, then an FRS 102-compliant accounting policy needs to be applied to that deemed cost in the intervening period to determine what the carrying amount of the asset is in the opening FRS 102 statement of financial position. This means that a first-time adopter that uses a revaluation determined under its previous financial reporting framework prior to the date of transition will need to start depreciating the item from the date for which the entity established the revaluation (i.e. deemed cost) not from the date of transition to FRS 102.

This requirement is unlikely to give rise to a GAAP difference where an entity previously adopted IFRS provided the depreciation methods, lives and residual values previously applied remain acceptable under FRS 102. This may be an issue with intangible assets, where an indefinite life may have been determined under IFRS. *[IAS 38.88]*. In our view, the intangible asset must be amortised retrospectively over its new finite useful life since this is a change in accounting policy (FRS 102 does not permit use of an indefinite useful life). See the discussion at 5.2.4.F above. Where it is difficult to apply FRS 102's requirements on depreciation retrospectively, an entity can always use a deemed cost equal to fair value at the date of transition.

5.5.3   Impairment

As deemed cost is a surrogate for cost from the date of the measurement, any later impairment must be recognised in profit or loss. Moreover, any previous impairment recognised prior to the date that the deemed cost is established cannot be reversed. Section 27 does not permit reversal of impairment of an asset above the carrying amount that would have been determined (net of amortisation or depreciation) had no impairment loss been recognised in prior years (i.e. depreciated cost based on the deemed cost at the date of measurement). Goodwill impairment cannot be reversed. *[FRS 102.27.28-31]*.

5.5.4   Deferred tax

Where a deemed cost is established based on a valuation determined under an entity's previous financial reporting framework, or fair value at transition, the past revaluation on or prior to transition generally represents a timing difference for which deferred tax will need to be recognised in accordance with the requirements of Section 29. Under the alternative accounting rules, any deferred tax relating to amounts credited or debited to the revaluation reserve (relating to the same asset) may also be recognised in the revaluation reserve as an alternative to retained earnings. *[1 Sch 35(3)(b), 1 Sch 35(3)(b) (LLP)].*

If, after transition, the deferred tax is remeasured (e.g. because of a change in tax rate) and the asset concerned was revalued outside profit or loss under its previous financial reporting framework, an entity needs to determine whether the resulting deferred tax income or expense should be recognised in, or outside, profit or loss.

FRS 102 requires that an entity shall present tax expense (income) in the same component of total comprehensive income (i.e. continuing or discontinued operations, and profit or loss or other comprehensive income) or equity as the transaction or other event that resulted in the tax expense (income). *[FRS 102.29.22].*

The essence of the argument for where such tax effects should be recognised is whether the reference in paragraph 29.22 to 'other comprehensive income' means items recognised in other comprehensive income under FRS 102 or whether it can extend to the treatment under its previous financial reporting framework. In our view, there are arguments for either approach, i.e. in profit or loss or in other comprehensive income, so long as it is applied consistently.

5.5.5   Revaluation reserve

UK companies (and LLPs) preparing statutory accounts are required by the Regulations (and LLP Regulations) to establish or maintain a statutory revaluation reserve under the alternative accounting rules on transition (see 3.5.3.A above) where property, plant and equipment, investment property (where the cost model is applied – see below) or intangible assets are included at a deemed cost measurement at the date of transition (which exceeds the depreciated historical cost of the item). *[1 Sch 35, 1 Sch 35 (LLP), FRS 102.35.10(d), Appendix III.40B-C].*

While a subsequent impairment of an asset carried at deemed cost should be reflected in profit or loss, this does not preclude a transfer between revaluation reserves and retained earnings in respect of the impairment loss (where it is less than the amount of revaluation reserve related to that asset). Similarly, any excess depreciation (based on revalued amount compared to the historical cost amount) can also be transferred from the revaluation reserve to retained earnings. *[1 Sch 35(3)(a), 1 Sch 35(3)(a) (LLP)].*

FRS 102 requires investment property normally to be carried at fair value through profit or loss. This makes use of the fair value accounting rules under the Regulations (and LLP Regulations). However, following the Triennial review 2017, FRS 102 allows an entity to make a policy choice either to account for investment property rented to another group entity at fair value through profit or loss or to transfer the investment property to property, plant and equipment and apply the cost model. *[FRS 102.16.1, 1A, 4A-4B, 7].* Adjustments on transition (including the treatment of the revaluation reserve) to investment properties are addressed in 3.5.3.C above.

Chapter 6 at 10.2 and 10.4 addresses the alternative accounting rules and fair value accounting rules, including related disclosure requirements, in detail.

5.6 Deferred development costs as a deemed cost

A first-time adopter may elect to measure the carrying amount at the date of transition to FRS 102 for development costs deferred in accordance with SSAP 13 – *Accounting for research and development* – as its deemed cost at that date. *[FRS 102.35.10(n)]*.

This transition exemption is not of relevance to new first-time adopters. The situation for previous UK GAAP reporters is discussed in Chapter 32 at 5.6 of EY UK GAAP 2017. Therefore, new first time adopters must apply Section 18 retrospectively. This provides a choice of policy as to whether to capitalise development costs (meeting the conditions for capitalisation in paragraph 18.8H) or to expense all development costs, to be applied consistently. *[FRS 102.18.8K]*.

Where business combinations are restated in accordance with Section 19, intangible assets (including development costs) should be recognised at their fair values where the recognition criteria in Section 19 (depending on the policy applied – see Chapter 17 at 3.7.1.A) are met, even if a policy of expensing development costs is followed under Section 18.

5.7 Deemed cost for oil and gas assets

A first-time adopter that under its previous financial reporting framework accounted for exploration and development costs for oil and gas properties in the development or production phases, in cost centres that included all properties in a large geographical area may elect to measure oil and gas assets at the date of transition to FRS 102 on the following basis:

(i) exploration and evaluation assets at the amount determined under the entity's previous financial reporting framework;

(ii) assets in the development or production phases at the amount determined for the cost centre under the entity's previous financial reporting framework. The entity shall allocate this amount to the cost centre's underlying assets *pro rata* using reserve volumes or reserve values as of that date.

The entity shall test exploration and evaluation assets and assets in the development and production phases for impairment at the date of transition to FRS 102 in accordance with Section 34 – *Specialised Activities* – or Section 27 respectively and, if necessary, reduce the amount determined in accordance with (i) or (ii) above. For the purposes of this paragraph, oil and gas assets comprise only those assets used in the exploration, evaluation, development or production of oil and gas. *[FRS 102.35.10(j)]*.

Oil and gas entities may account for exploration and development costs for properties in development or production in cost centres that include all properties in a large geographical area, e.g. under the 'full cost accounting method'. However, this method of accounting generally uses a unit of account that is much larger than is acceptable under FRS 102 (or indeed IFRS, which has a similar transition exemption). Applying FRS 102 fully retrospectively would pose significant problems for first-time adopters because – as the IASB noted in paragraph BC47A of IFRS 1 – it would require amortisation 'to be calculated (on a unit of production basis) for each year, using a reserves base that has changed over time because of changes in factors such as geological understanding and prices for oil and gas. In many cases, particularly for older assets, this information may not be available.' Even when such information is available, the effort and cost to determine the opening balances at the date of transition would usually be very high.

To avoid the use of deemed cost resulting in an oil and gas asset being measured at more than its recoverable amount, oil and gas assets are required to be tested for impairment at the date of transition. The deemed cost amounts should be reduced to take account of any impairment charge in accordance with Section 34 (for exploration and evaluation assets) (see Chapter 31 at 3) and Section 27 (for assets in the development and production phases) (see Chapter 24). The requirements of Section 34 are based on those in IFRS 6 (with certain adaptations). Section 34 would, therefore, require an entity to determine an accounting policy for allocating exploration and evaluation assets to cash-generating units for impairment purposes. A cash-generating unit or group of cash-generating units (used for exploration and evaluation assets) shall be no larger than an operating segment (as defined in the Glossary to FRS 102). *[FRS 102.34.11B].*

5.8 Decommissioning liabilities included in the cost of property, plant and equipment

Paragraph 17.10(c) of FRS 102 states that the cost of an item of property, plant and equipment includes the initial estimate of the costs, recognised and measured in accordance with Section 21 – *Provisions and Contingencies*, of dismantling and removing the item and restoring the site on which it is located, the obligation for which an entity incurs either when the item is acquired or as a consequence of having used the item during a particular period for purposes other than to produce inventories during that period. A first-time adopter may elect to measure this component of the cost of an item of property, plant and equipment at the date of transition to FRS 102, rather than on the date(s) when the obligation initially arose. *[FRS 102.35.10(l), 17.10(c)].*

IFRIC 1 – *Changes in Existing Decommissioning, Restoration and Similar Liabilities* – contains more detailed requirements than Section 21. An entity may want to consider IFRIC 1 in accounting for changes in existing decommissioning, restoration and similar liabilities and the guidance on the related first-time adoption exemption in IFRS 1. *[IFRS 1 Appendix D.21].*

The transition exemption, which is based on a comparable exemption in IFRS 1, provides a pragmatic approach to determining the decommissioning component of the carrying amount of an item of property, plant and equipment. Depreciation and impairment losses on the asset can cause differences between the carrying amount of the liability and the amounts included in the carrying amount of the asset. The transition exemption provides an exemption from determining the changes to the carrying amount of the asset that occurred before the date of transition.

Most previous IFRS and FRS 101 reporters should already be following an accounting treatment for decommissioning provisions (and adjustments to the related assets) consistent with FRS 102 and are unlikely to apply the transition exemption. See Chapter 19 at 4.1 for discussion of decommissioning provisions.

Chapter 32

5.9   Individual and separate financial statements

When an entity prepares individual or separate financial statements, paragraphs 9.26, 14.4 and 15.9 require the entity to account for its investments in subsidiaries, associates, and jointly controlled entities either at cost less impairment, or at fair value.

If a first-time adopter measures such an investment at cost, it shall measure that investment at one of the following amounts in its individual or separate opening statement of financial position, as appropriate, prepared in accordance with FRS 102: *[FRS 102.35.10(f)]*

- cost determined in accordance with Section 9, Section 14 – *Investments in Associates* – or Section 15 – *Investments in Joint Ventures at the date of transition*; or

- deemed cost, which shall be the carrying amount at the date of transition as determined under the entity's previous financial reporting framework.

An entity must apply the same accounting policy – i.e. cost, fair value with changes in fair value recognised in comprehensive income (or profit or loss) in accordance with paragraphs 17.15E and 17.15F, or fair value with changes in fair value recognised in profit or loss – to all investments in a single class (for example investments in subsidiaries that are held as part of an investment portfolio, those that are not so held, associates or jointly controlled entities), but can elect different policies for different classes. *[FRS 102.9.26, 26A, 14.1, 4, 15.1, 9]*. See Chapter 8 at 4.1 and 4.2.

Where the cost model is applied, the transition exemption would permit the choice of cost or deemed cost to be applied on an investment-by-investment basis. See 5.9.1 below for specific considerations where cost or deemed cost is used for investments.

The transition exemption allows a first-time adopter to 'grandfather' the carrying amount determined under its previous financial reporting framework at the date of transition as a deemed cost at that date. Unlike the comparable exemption in IFRS 1, *[IFRS 1 Appendix D.14]*, however, Section 35 does not permit use of deemed cost equal to the fair value at the date of transition (unless that happens to be the previous carrying amount).

Investments in subsidiaries, associates and jointly controlled entities in the individual or separate financial statements included at cost or a deemed cost are subject to the impairment requirements of Section 27 (see Chapter 24).

5.9.1   *Use of cost or deemed cost for investments – implementation issues*

Where a UK company acquired an investment accounted for at cost in a share-for-share exchange, FRS 102 permits the initial cost of the investment to be reported either at its fair value at the date of the transaction or at an amount excluding any reliefs that would have been required to be reflected in share premium but for the existence of merger relief or group reconstruction relief. Hence, it is not necessary to establish a 'deemed cost' on transition where the previous carrying amount was net of such reliefs. *[FRS 102 Appendix III.24, 24A, 22.8]*. See Chapter 8 at 4.2.1.

Previous IFRS or FRS 101 reporters that measured investments in subsidiaries, associates and joint ventures at fair value or using the equity method in separate financial statements (but now wish to adopt the cost model on transition to FRS 102) may also wish to use the transition exemption. The equity method is not permitted in individual or separate financial statements under FRS 102. *[FRS 102.9.26, 9.26A, 14.1, 14.4, 15.1, 15.9]*. Previous IFRS or

FRS 101 reporters that used the cost model under IAS 27 – *Separate Financial Statements* – may also wish to use the transition exemption where the carrying amount of the investment under IFRS does not represent cost under FRS 102. Examples of such situations include: where a deemed cost was used on transition to IFRS / FRS 101; where the cost of the investment has been reduced by the amount of pre-acquisition dividends in the past; or where IAS 27 specifies the cost of investment in certain group reorganisations. *[IAS 27.10, 13-14]*. Previous IFRS or FRS 101 reporters may also wish to use the transition exemption where the cost of investment reflects past fair value hedge accounting, which is not being continued under FRS 102 and Sections 11 and 12 are applied.

The deemed cost exemption was also of interest to previous UK GAAP reporters that had revalued investments in the past or retranslated foreign equity investments in the individual accounts (where financed or hedged by foreign borrowings), taking exchange differences on the investment and, where specified conditions were met, exchange differences on the foreign borrowings to reserves. *[SSAP 20.51]*. This situation is discussed further in Chapter 32 at 5.9.1 and 5.16.5 of EY UK GAAP 2017.

Where a UK company (or LLP) preparing statutory accounts uses a deemed cost at the date of transition that reflects a revaluation under its previous financial reporting framework, this would generally mean that the investment is carried at a revalued amount that makes use of the alternative accounting rules. See 3.5.3 and 3.5.3.A above and Chapter 6 at 10.2.

5.10 Service concession arrangements – accounting by operators

A service concession arrangement is defined as 'an arrangement whereby a public sector body, or a public benefit entity (the grantor) contracts with a private sector entity (the operator) to construct (or upgrade), operate and maintain infrastructure assets for a specified period of time (the concession period)'. *[FRS 102.34.12, Appendix I]*. Service concession arrangements can be in place for several years and the accounting can be important to the economics of such arrangements.

A first-time adopter is not required to apply paragraphs 34.12I to 34.16A to service concession arrangements that were entered into before the date of transition to FRS 102. Such service concession arrangements shall continue to be accounted for using the same accounting policies being applied at the date of transition to FRS 102. *[FRS 102.35.10(i), 34.12I, 13-16A]*.

FRS 102 sets out two principal categories of service concession arrangements – a financial asset model and an intangible asset model for accounting for service concession arrangements by operators– based on a simplified version of IFRIC 12 – *Service Concession Arrangements*. See Chapter 31 at 4.3 for discussion of the definition of and accounting requirements for service concession arrangements under FRS 102, as set out in Section 34 of the standard.

Grantors of service concession arrangements are not covered by the transition exemption and are required to follow the finance lease liability model requirements (set out in paragraphs 34.12E to 12H) retrospectively.

See Chapter 31 at 4.2 for a discussion of the key differences between Section 34's requirements and the accounting under IFRIC 12, which generally has more detailed requirements. Previous IFRS or FRS 101 reporters may also have taken advantage of transitional provisions regarding the accounting for service concession arrangements, where it was impracticable to restate retrospectively, on first adoption of IFRS or on first implementation of IFRIC 12. *[IFRS 1 Appendix D.22, IFRIC 12.29-30].* There is further discussion of the implications of the transition exemption for previous UK GAAP reporters in Chapter 32 at 5.10 of EY UK GAAP 2017.

The exemption relates only to the requirements in Section 34 for the accounting by the operator for the service concession arrangement itself, not to all the accounting policies applied by the operator. Therefore, all other assets and liabilities of the operator at the date of transition must be accounted for in accordance with FRS 102 (subject to any other transition exemptions or exceptions in Section 35). The operator must apply Section 34 to all concessions entered into after the date of transition.

However, where a concession entered into before the date of transition is renegotiated in a way that significantly modifies the terms of the concession, such that had those terms existed at the outset a different classification would have resulted, then Section 35 requires that the operator should reassess the appropriateness of applying that exemption in the future. *[FRS 102.35.11B].* This might result in the renegotiated concession being treated as a new arrangement, to which Section 34 would be applied. FRS 102 does not provide guidance on when such classification decisions should be revisited.

Where the transition exemption is not used, operators must account for service concession arrangements retrospectively in accordance with the requirements of paragraphs 34.12I to 16A of FRS 102.

5.11 Arrangements containing a lease

A first-time adopter may elect to determine whether an arrangement existing at the date of transition to FRS 102 contains a lease (see paragraph 20.3A of FRS 102) on the basis of facts and circumstances existing at the date of transition, rather than when the arrangement was entered into. *[FRS 102.20.3A, 35.10(k)].*

Examples of arrangements in which one entity (the supplier) may convey a right to use an asset to another entity (the purchaser), often together with related services, may include outsourcing arrangements, telecommunication contracts that provide rights to capacity and take-or-pay contracts. *[FRS 102.20.3].*

FRS 102 sets out criteria for determining whether an arrangement contains a lease (see Chapter 18 at 3.2). An entity's previous financial reporting framework may not have applied the same criteria in determining whether an arrangement contains a lease. The transition exemption allows an entity to avoid the practical difficulties of going back many years by permitting this assessment to be made at the date of transition.

The transition exemption is similar to the exemption in IFRS 1. IFRS 1 allows a first-time adopter to assess whether a contract existing at the date of transition to IFRS contains a lease by applying paragraphs 9 to 11 of IFRS 16 – *Leases* – to those contracts on the basis of facts and circumstances existing at that date. *[IFRS 1 Appendix D.9].* However, IFRS 1 previously allowed a first-time adopter not to reassess its determination under its previous financial reporting framework of whether the arrangement contains a lease on transition, where the reassessment would give the same outcome as applying IAS 17 – *Leases* – and

IFRIC 4 – *Determining whether an Arrangement contains a Lease* – but was made at a date other than that required by IFRIC 4. *[IFRS 1 Appendix D.9-9A]*. FRS 102 would not permit such assessments made by an entity under its previous financial reporting framework to be 'grandfathered' on transition and requires a first-time adopter to apply Section 20 either fully retrospectively or reassess the determination at the date of transition.

Section 35 does not include any specific exemptions from retrospective application of Section 20 – *Leases* (other than in relation to operating lease incentives, described at 5.12 below). Therefore, a first-time adopter is required to classify leases as operating or finance leases under Section 20, based on the circumstances existing at the inception of the lease or at the date of a subsequent change to the terms of the lease (other than simply by renewing the lease). *[FRS 102.20.8]*.

5.12   Lease incentives (operating leases) – lessees and lessors

A first-time adopter is not required to apply paragraphs 20.15A and 20.25A of FRS 102 to lease incentives provided the term of the lease commenced before the date of transition to FRS 102. The first-time adopter shall continue to recognise any residual benefit or cost associated with these lease incentives on the same basis as that applied at the date of transition to FRS 102. *[FRS 102.35.10(p)]*.

While the wording of the transition exemption is not explicit, in our view, the exemption is available on a lease-by-lease basis.

Where the transition exemption is not taken, the requirements of FRS 102 are applied retrospectively. FRS 102 requires that a lessee in an operating lease recognises the aggregate benefit of lease incentives as a reduction to the lease expense recognised (in accordance with paragraph 20.15) over the lease term, on a straight-line basis unless another systematic basis is representative of the time pattern of the lessee's benefit from the use of the leased asset. Similarly, a lessor in an operating lease recognises the aggregate cost of lease incentives as a reduction to the lease income recognised (in accordance with paragraph 20.25) over the lease term on a straight-line basis, unless another systematic basis is representative of the time pattern over which the lessor's benefit from the leased asset is diminished. *[FRS 102.20.15A, 25A]*.

The requirements of IAS 17 in respect of operating lease incentives are similar to those of FRS 102, so previous IFRS or FRS 101 reporters that applied IAS 17 (as lessees or lessors) – or that are lessors that applied IFRS 16 – are unlikely to take advantage of this transition exemption. The accounting under IFRS 16 for leases by lessees differs significantly to FRS 102, except where the recognition exemptions available for short-term and / or low value leases are taken. *[IFRS 16.5-8, Appendix B.3-8]*. In our view, a lessee could not meaningfully apply this transition exemption to a lease accounted under IFRS 16 as any lease incentives are only one part of accounting for a right-of-use asset.

5.13   Dormant companies

A company within the Companies Act definition of a dormant company (section 1169 of the CA 2006) may elect to retain its accounting policies for reported assets, liabilities and equity at the date of transition to FRS 102 until there is any change to those balances or the company undertakes any new transactions. *[FRS 102.35.10(m)]*. Hence, so long as a company remains dormant, it can retain its accounting policies under its previous financial reporting framework.

Chapter 32

Without this transition exemption, dormant companies would be required to assess whether there are changes to the existing accounting under FRS 102 compared to its previous financial reporting framework. A change in accounting could lead to the company ceasing to be dormant. For UK companies, this could impact on the requirements to prepare and file statutory accounts (as exemptions are available to qualifying subsidiary companies that are dormant companies supported by a statutory guarantee from an EEA parent) and on the availability of audit exemptions. *[s394A-s394C, s448A-s448C, s480-s481]*. The detailed conditions for these exemptions may change as a consequence of exit from the European Union, based on draft legislative proposals – *The Accounts and Reports (Amendment) (EU Exit) Regulations 2018*. The draft legislation proposes that these changes come into effect for financial years beginning on or after exit day. The draft legislation is subject to Parliamentary approval and may be impacted by any transitional arrangements negotiated with the EU.

Dormant companies must, like all FRS 102 reporters, give a complete and unreserved statement of compliance with FRS 102. *[FRS 102.3.3]*. We recommend that dormant companies using the transition exemption should disclose this fact as this is important to explaining the transition *[FRS 102.35.12]* and the accounting policies applied. *[FRS 102.8.5]*.

Where there is potential to become non-dormant in the future, a dormant company may consider whether it is beneficial to take (and accordingly state use of) other exemptions which would not affect its dormant status under the CA 2006. An example of this would be the election to use deemed cost on transition in relation to the cost of investments in subsidiaries, associates and jointly controlled entities – see 5.9 above. *[FRS 102.35.10(f)]*. This is because, if the company becomes non-dormant in the future and can no longer retain its existing accounting policies, it will no longer be a first-time adopter (and so cannot make use of new exemptions at that time). However, in many cases, dormant companies may have simple affairs and other transition exemptions may not be relevant.

While the exemption does not explicitly state this, we consider that the wording of the exemption, in particular its references to accounting policies at the date of transition, more closely supports the view that the exemption is only available to companies that are dormant at the date of transition (until such time as they cease to be dormant) rather than being available to companies that become dormant during the period prior to the first reporting period in which FRS 102 is applied.

In our view, the reference to 'dormant company' is intentional given that the purpose of the exemption was to enable UK dormant companies not to change their status and thereby lose entitlement to various accounting and audit exemptions under the CA 2006. However, the CA 2006 states that 'Any reference in the Companies Acts to a body corporate other than a company being dormant has a corresponding meaning'. *[s1169(4)]*. In our view, this reference could support an extension of the transition exemption to an entity like a dormant LLP that has a comparable status to a dormant company under UK law and benefits from similar exemptions. *[s394-s394C (LLP), s448A-C (LLP), s480-1 (LLP), s1169 (LLP)]*.

5.14   Borrowing costs

An entity electing to adopt an accounting policy of capitalising borrowing costs as part of the cost of a qualifying asset may elect to treat the date of transition to FRS 102 as the date on which capitalisation commences. *[FRS 102.35.10(o)].*

FRS 102 offers a policy choice of expensing borrowing costs as incurred or of capitalising borrowing costs that are directly attributable to the acquisition, construction or production of a qualifying asset as part of the cost of that asset. Where a capitalisation policy is adopted, this must be applied consistently to a class of qualifying assets (see Chapter 22 at 3.2). *[FRS 102.25.2].*

First-time adopters, that want to adopt a capitalisation policy for borrowing costs under Section 25 – *Borrowing Costs*, can use the transition exemption which offers relief by allowing an entity to commence capitalising borrowing costs arising on qualifying assets from the date of transition. That way these entities can avoid difficult restatement issues, such as determining which assets would have qualified for capitalisation of borrowing costs in past periods, which costs met the definition of borrowing costs and determining the amount of borrowing costs that qualified for capitalisation in past periods. However, a previous IFRS reporter would already be capitalising borrowing costs in accordance with IAS 23 – *Borrowing Costs.* There are some differences between IAS 23 and Section 25, for example, under IFRS, capitalisation of borrowing costs is mandatory for most qualifying assets and there are differences in how the capitalisation rate is calculated on general borrowings and expenditure on qualifying assets is determined. See Chapter 22 at 2.

Also, a previous IFRS or FRS 101 reporter may have used the transition exemption under IFRS 1 and therefore may not have fully retrospectively applied IAS 23. This transition exemption allowed a first-time adopter to elect to apply IAS 23 from the date of transition (or from an earlier date as permitted by paragraph 28 of IAS 23). *[IFRS 1 Appendix D.23].* Unlike the comparable IFRS 1 transition exemption, in our view, the FRS 102 transition exemption does not permit grandfathering of the borrowing cost component included in the carrying amounts of a qualifying asset at the date of transition under a previous financial framework.

Therefore, if the amounts capitalised by a previous IFRS or FRS 101 reporter are materially different from a fully retrospective application of Section 25, an adjustment would be needed on transition to FRS 102. In some cases, the impracticability exemption in paragraph 35.11 may be relevant to the accounting for the capitalised borrowing costs (see 3.5.4 above). *[FRS 102.35.11].*

A first-time adopter of IFRS that establishes a deemed cost for an asset (see 5.5 to 5.7 above) cannot capitalise borrowing costs incurred before the measurement date of the deemed cost. *[IFRS 1.IG 23].* While FRS 102 does not include an explicit statement to this effect, it would generally be appropriate to follow the same treatment under FRS 102 where a deemed cost exemption is used. This would avoid an entity that has recognised an asset at a deemed cost equal to its fair value at a particular date increasing its carrying value to recognise interest capitalised before that date. However, the entity could make use of the transition exemption to commence capitalising borrowing costs from the date of transition in accordance with Section 25.

Chapter 32

Where an entity that previously capitalised borrowing costs (which is mandatory for a previous IFRS or FRS 101 reporter) changes its policy on transition to FRS 102 to instead expense borrowing costs for any class of assets, retrospective application of the standard will require derecognition of the carrying amount of the asset relating to capitalised borrowing costs. This is subject to any transition exemptions available, such as establishing a deemed cost, where permitted (see 5.5 to 5.7 above).

5.15 Assets and liabilities of subsidiaries, associates and joint ventures

Within groups, some subsidiaries, associates and joint ventures may have a different date of transition to FRS 102 from the parent, investor or venturer. As this could result in permanent differences between the FRS 102 figures in a subsidiary's own financial statements and those it reports to its parent, FRS 102 includes a special exemption regarding the assets and liabilities of subsidiaries, associates and joint ventures.

Paragraph 35.10(r) contains detailed guidance on the approach to be adopted when a parent adopts FRS 102 before its subsidiary (see 5.15.1 below) and also on when a subsidiary adopts FRS 102 before its parent (see 5.15.2 below).

These provisions also apply when FRS 102 is adopted at different dates by:

- an associate and the entity that has significant influence over it (i.e. the investor in the associate); or

- a joint venture and the entity that has joint control over it (i.e. the venturer in the joint venture).

In the discussion that follows at 5.15.1 to 5.15.3 below, references to a 'parent' should be read as including an investor that has significant influence in an associate or a venturer in a joint venture, and references to a 'subsidiary' should be read as including an associate or a joint venture. References to consolidation adjustments should be read as including similar adjustments made when applying equity accounting.

FRS 102 does not elaborate on exactly what constitutes 'consolidation adjustments' but in our view, these would encompass adjustments required in order to harmonise accounting policies as well as purely 'mechanical' consolidation adjustments such as the elimination of intragroup balances, profits and losses.

Paragraph 35.10(r) also addresses the requirements for a parent that adopts FRS 102 at different dates for the purposes of its consolidated and its separate financial statements (see 5.15.4 below).

5.15.1 *Subsidiary becomes a first-time adopter later than its parent*

If a subsidiary becomes a first-time adopter later than its parent, it shall in its financial statements measure its assets and liabilities at either:

(i) the carrying amounts that would be included in the parent's consolidated financial statements, based on the parent's date of transition to FRS 102, if no adjustments were made for consolidation procedures and for the effects of the business combination in which the parent acquired the subsidiary; or

(ii) the carrying amounts required by the rest of FRS 102, based on the subsidiary's date of transition to FRS 102. These carrying amounts could differ from those described in (i) when:

(a) the exemptions in FRS 102 result in measurements that depend on the date of transition to FRS 102; or

(b) the accounting policies used in the subsidiary's financial statements differ from those in the consolidated financial statements. For example, the subsidiary may use as its accounting policy the cost model in Section 17 – *Property, Plant and Equipment*, whereas the group may use the revaluation model.

A similar election is available to an associate or joint venture that becomes a first-time adopter later than an entity that has significant influence or joint control over it. *[FRS 102.35.10(r)]*.

The following example, which is adapted from an example included in IFRS 1, which has a comparable transition exemption, *[IFRS 1 Appendix D.16]*, illustrates how an entity should apply these requirements. *[IFRS 1.IG Example 8]*.

Example 32.4:   Parent adopts FRS 102 before subsidiary

Background

Entity A presented its first FRS 102 consolidated financial statements in 2017 (having switched from IFRS in its group accounts in advance of moving its subsidiaries from FRS 101 to FRS 102). Subsidiary B, wholly owned by Entity A (its parent) since formation (so not acquired in a business combination), prepares information under FRS 102 for internal consolidation purposes from that date, but Subsidiary B does not present its first FRS 102 financial statements until 2019.

Application of requirements

If Subsidiary B applies option (i) in paragraph 35.10(r), the carrying amounts of its assets and liabilities are the same in both its opening FRS 102 statement of financial position at 1 January 2018 and Entity A's consolidated statement of financial position (except for adjustments for consolidation procedures) and are based on Entity A's date of transition to FRS 102.

Alternatively, Subsidiary B may apply option (ii) in paragraph 35.10(r), and measure all its assets or liabilities based on its own date of transition to FRS 102 (1 January 2018). However, the fact that Subsidiary B becomes a first-time adopter in 2019 does not change the carrying amounts of its assets and liabilities in Entity A's consolidated financial statements.

Under option (ii), a subsidiary would prepare its own FRS 102 financial statements, completely ignoring the FRS 102 elections that its parent used when it adopted FRS 102 for its consolidated financial statements.

Under option (i), the numbers in a subsidiary's FRS 102 financial statements would be as close to those used by its parent as possible. However, differences other than those arising from business combinations (and consolidation adjustments) will still exist in many cases, for example:

- a subsidiary may have hedged an exposure by entering into a transaction with a fellow subsidiary. Such a transaction could qualify for hedge accounting in the subsidiary's own financial statements but not in the parent's consolidated financial statements; or

- a pension plan may have to be classified as a defined contribution plan from the subsidiary's point of view, but is accounted for as a defined benefit plan in the parent's consolidated financial statements.

Chapter 32

The transition exemption will rarely succeed in achieving more than a moderate reduction of the number of reconciling differences between a subsidiary's own reporting and the numbers used by its parent.

More importantly, the choice of option (i) prevents the subsidiary from electing to apply all the other voluntary exemptions offered by Section 35, since the parent had already made the choices for the group at its date of adoption. Therefore, option (i) may not be appropriate for a subsidiary that prefers to use a different exemption, e.g. fair value as deemed cost for property, plant and equipment. Additionally, application of option (i) would be more difficult when a parent and its subsidiary have different financial years. In that case, Section 35 would seem to require the FRS 102 information for the subsidiary to be based on the parent's date of transition, which may not even coincide with an interim reporting date of the subsidiary.

A subsidiary may become a first-time adopter later than its parent, because it previously prepared a reporting package under FRS 102 for consolidation purposes, but did not present a full set of financial statements under FRS 102. Adjustments made centrally to an unpublished reporting package are not considered to be corrections of errors for the purposes of the disclosure requirements in FRS 102. However, a subsidiary is not permitted to ignore misstatements that are immaterial to the consolidated financial statements of its parent but material to its own financial statements. *[IFRS 1.IG31].*

If a subsidiary was acquired after the parent's date of transition to FRS 102, then it cannot apply option (i) because there are no carrying amounts included in the parent's consolidated financial statements, based on the parent's date of transition. Therefore, the subsidiary is unable to use the carrying amounts recognised in the group accounts when it was acquired, since push-down of the group's purchase accounting values is not allowed in the subsidiary's financial statements.

Unlike the comparable IFRS 1 transition exemption, FRS 102 does not explicitly address the situation where a subsidiary that is excluded from consolidation under FRS 102 (and is measured at fair value, either through profit or loss or through other comprehensive income – see Chapter 8 at 3.4) adopts FRS 102 after its parent adopts FRS 102 in its consolidated financial statements. However, in our view, it would make sense for the subsidiary to apply option (ii), i.e. to use the carrying amounts of assets and liabilities based on its own date of transition.

The exemption is also available to associates and joint ventures. This means that in many cases an associate or joint venture that wants to apply option (i) will need to choose which shareholder it considers its investor or venturer for FRS 102 purposes and determine the FRS 102 carrying amount of its assets and liabilities by reference to that investor's or venturer's date of transition to FRS 102.

5.15.2   *Parent becomes a first-time adopter later than its subsidiary*

If an entity becomes a first-time adopter later than its subsidiary (or associate or joint venture) the entity shall, in its consolidated financial statements, measure the assets and liabilities of the subsidiary (or associate or joint venture) at the same carrying amounts as in the financial statements of the subsidiary (or associate or joint venture), after adjusting for consolidation (and equity accounting) adjustments and for the effects of the business combination in which the entity acquired the subsidiary (or transaction in which it acquired the associate or joint venture). *[FRS 102.35.10(r)].*

While located within the transition exemptions, paragraph 35.10(r) does not offer a choice between different accounting alternatives. In fact, while a subsidiary that adopts FRS 102 later than its parent can choose to prepare its first FRS 102 financial statements by reference to its own date of transition to FRS 102 or that of its parent, the parent itself *must* use the FRS 102 measurements already used in the subsidiary's financial statements, adjusted as appropriate for consolidation procedures and the effects of the business combination in which the parent acquired the subsidiary.

This does not preclude the parent from adjusting the subsidiary's assets and liabilities for a different accounting policy (e.g. cost or revaluation for accounting for property, plant and equipment) but does, however, limit the choice of exemptions (e.g. the deemed cost exemption) with respect to the financial statements of the subsidiary in the transition date consolidated financial statements.

The following example, which is adapted from an example included in IFRS 1, which has a comparable transition exemption, *[IFRS 1 Appendix D.17]*, illustrates how an entity should apply these requirements. *[IFRS 1 IG Example 9].*

Example 32.5: Subsidiary adopts FRS 102 before parent

Entity C presents its first consolidated FRS 102 financial statements for the accounting period ending 31 December 2019. Subsidiary D, wholly owned by Entity C since formation (so not acquired in a business combination), presented its first FRS 102 financial statements in 2017 (as it had been incorporated that year and chose to adopt FRS 102 early). Until 2019, Subsidiary D prepared information for internal consolidation purposes under Entity C's previous financial reporting framework.

Application of requirements

The carrying amounts of Subsidiary D's assets and liabilities at 1 January 2018 (the date of transition for Entity C) are the same in both Entity C's opening FRS 102 consolidated statement of financial position and Subsidiary D's own financial statements (except for adjustments for consolidation procedures) and are based on Subsidiary D's date of transition to FRS 102. The fact that Entity C becomes a first-time adopter in 2019 does not change those carrying amounts.

When a subsidiary adopts FRS 102 before its parent, this will limit the parent's ability to choose first-time adoption exemptions in Section 35 freely as related to that subsidiary, as illustrated in the example below.

Example 32.6: Limited ability to choose first-time adoption exemptions

Entity E presents its first consolidated FRS 102 financial statements for the accounting period ending 31 December 2019 and its date of transition is 1 January 2018. Subsidiary F adopted FRS 102 in 2015 and its date of transition was 1 December 2013:

(a) *Subsidiary F and Entity E both account for their property, plant and equipment at historical cost under Section 17.*

Upon first-time adoption, Entity E may only adjust the carrying amounts of Subsidiary F's assets and liabilities for the effects of consolidation and business combinations. Entity E can therefore not apply the exemption to use fair value as deemed cost of Subsidiary F's property, plant and equipment as at its own date of transition (1 January 2018).

(b) *Subsidiary F accounts for its property, plant and equipment at revalued amounts under Section 17, while Entity E accounts for its property, plant and equipment at historical cost under Section 17.*

Entity E would not be allowed to apply the exemption to use fair value as deemed cost of Subsidiary F's property, plant and equipment at its own date of transition because paragraph 35.10(r) would only permit adjustments for the effects of consolidation and business combinations. Although a consolidation adjustment would be necessary, this would only be to adjust Subsidiary F's revalued amounts to figures based on historical cost.

Chapter 32

5.15.3   Implementation guidance

The Implementation Guidance in IFRS 1 (which discusses the equivalent paragraphs in IFRS 1, *[IFRS 1 Appendix D.16-17]*, to paragraph 35.10(r) in FRS 102) notes the following issues, which have been adapted for the context of an FRS 102 first-time adopter.

Use of the transition exemption in paragraph 35.10(r) does not override the following requirements of Section 35: *[IFRS 1.IG 30]*

- the parent's election to use the business combinations exemption in paragraph 35.10(a) (see 5.2 above), which applies to assets and liabilities of a subsidiary acquired in a business combination that occurred *before* the parent's date of transition to FRS 102. However, the rules summarised at 5.15.2 above (parent adopting FRS 102 after subsidiary) apply only to assets and liabilities acquired and assumed by the subsidiary after the business combination and still held and owned by it at the parent's date of transition to FRS 102;

- to apply the requirements in Section 35 in measuring all assets and liabilities for which the provisions summarised in paragraph 35.10(r) regarding different parent and subsidiary adoption dates are not relevant (e.g. the use of the exemption to measure assets and liabilities at the carrying amounts in the parent's consolidated financial statements does not affect the restrictions in paragraph 35.9(c) concerning changing valuation assumptions or estimates made at the same dates under the first-time adopter's previous financial reporting framework (see 4.2 above)); and

- a first-time adopter must give all the disclosures required by Section 35 as of its own date of transition. See 6 below.

5.15.4   Adoption of FRS 102 on different dates in separate and consolidated financial statements

If a parent becomes a first-time adopter for its separate financial statements earlier or later than for its consolidated financial statements, it shall measure its assets and liabilities at the same amounts in both financial statements, except for consolidation adjustments. *[FRS 102.35.10(r)]*.

An entity may sometimes become an FRS 102 first-time adopter for its separate financial statements earlier or later than for its consolidated financial statements. Such a situation may arise for example where the parent takes advantage of an exemption from preparing consolidated financial statements. Subsequently, the parent may cease to be entitled to the exemption or may choose not to use it and, may therefore choose to apply FRS 102 in its consolidated financial statements.

As drafted, the requirement is merely that the 'same amounts', except for consolidation adjustments, be used for the measurement of the assets and liabilities in both sets of financial statements, without being explicit as to which set of financial statements should be used as the benchmark. However, it seems clear from the context that the intention is that the measurement basis used in whichever set of financial statements first comply with FRS 102 must also be used when FRS 102 is subsequently adopted in the other set.

For a UK company (or LLP) preparing statutory accounts, the Regulations (and LLP Regulations) require that any differences in accounting rules between the parent company's individual accounts and its group accounts for the financial year be disclosed in a note to the group accounts, with reasons for the difference given. *[6 Sch 4, 3 Sch 4 (LLP)].* However, application of paragraph 35.10(r) should mean that, in most cases, no differences should arise.

5.16   Hedge accounting

An FRS 102 reporter has an accounting policy choice of applying – Sections 11 and 12, IFRS 9, or IAS 39 (as adopted in the EU) – to the recognition and measurement of financial instruments. FRS 102 defines which version of IAS 39 should be applied for accounting periods beginning on or after 1 January 2018. *[FRS 102.11.2, 12.2].* See Chapter 10 at 4.

Section 12, IAS 39, and IFRS 9 all require derivatives to be recognised at fair value and all distinguish three types of hedging relationship between a hedging instrument and hedged item – cash flow hedges, fair value hedges, and hedges of a net investment in a foreign operation. The hedge accounting requirements of Section 12 are discussed in Chapter 10 at 10, while IAS 39 and IFRS 9 are discussed in Chapter 49 of EY International GAAP 2019 (with Chapter 49 at 14 addressing the main differences between IAS 39 and IFRS 9).

Section 12, IAS 39, and IFRS 9 also all require the designation and documentation of hedging relationships, but the detailed requirements for hedge accounting differ. For example, the ongoing eligibility criteria for hedge accounting in Section 12 are more relaxed compared to both IAS 39 and IFRS 9. However, in all cases, ineffectiveness must still be measured and recognised in profit or loss where appropriate, and the criteria for hedge accounting need to be assessed and continue to be met.

There are specific transition provisions regarding hedge accounting depending on whether the FRS 102 reporter applies Section 12 (see 5.16.2 below), *[FRS 102.35.10(t)(i)-(iii)],* or IAS 39 or IFRS 9 (see 5.16.3 below), *[FRS 102.35.10(t)(iv)],* to the recognition and measurement of financial instruments. The transition provisions are the same regardless of the previous financial reporting framework applied to financial instruments, although the consequences of applying the transition provisions will depend on the nature of any hedge accounting undertaken under the previous financial reporting framework. Section 35 sets out various hedge accounting exemptions for entities applying Section 12 under FRS 102, but its requirements for entities applying IAS 39 or IFRS 9 under FRS 102 (which are based on IFRS 1's requirements, with certain concessions over the timing of completing designation and documentation of hedging relationships) are mandatory.

Chapter 32

An FRS 102 first-time adopter (whatever policy choice is applied to the recognition and measurement of financial instruments) will need to:

- recognise derivatives at fair value and eliminate any deferred gains and losses arising or synthetic accounting from hedge accounting under its previous financial reporting framework (except where permitted by the transition provisions), as required by the general rules on transition to FRS 102 (see 3.5 above). *[FRS 102.12.3, 12.7-8, 35.7(a)-(b)]*. Such adjustments are reflected in retained earnings (or, if appropriate, another component of equity); *[FRS 102.35.8]*

- reflect hedging relationships in the opening statement of financial position (where required or permitted by the transitional provisions). The transition provisions, which differ depending on whether Sections 11 and 12, or IFRS 9 / IAS 39 are applied, explain the adjustments required (see 5.16.2 and 5.16.3 below respectively);

- With fair value hedges, adjustments to the carrying amounts of assets and liabilities are reflected in retained earnings (or, if appropriate, another component of equity). With cash flow hedges, adjustments are generally reflected in a cash flow hedge reserve although the situation is more complicated. For example, under Sections 11 and 12, if an entity chooses not to reflect an existing or past hedging relationship in the opening statement of financial position, the adjustments to back out the previous hedge accounting are reflected in retained earnings (or, if appropriate, another component of equity). *[FRS 102.35.8]*. See 5.16.2.C and 5.16.2.D below (for Section 12) and 5.16.3 below (for IAS 39 and IFRS 9) for discussion of the adjustments made on transition for existing and past hedging relationships. Under IFRS 9, 'costs of hedging' adjustments are reflected in a separate component of equity; *[IFRS 9.6.5.15-16]*

- designate and document hedging relationships (required where hedge accounting is to be applied, under all the standards) in accordance with the requirements of the accounting policy choice followed under FRS 102. The transition provisions however, include a relief over the timing of when such designation and documentation is completed (whatever accounting policy choice is applied to the recognition and measurement of financial instruments); *[FRS 102.35.10(t)(i), (iii)-(iv)]* and

- consider the subsequent accounting for hedging relationships reflected in the opening statement of financial position, in accordance with the accounting policy choice followed under FRS 102.

Unless FRS 105 was applied under the entity's previous financial reporting framework, derivatives should be measured already at fair value. *[IAS 39.46, 47(a), IFRS 9.4.1.4, 4.2.1(a), FRS 105.9.8(b), 10]*. However, IAS 39 and IFRS 9 (the latter in respect of financial liabilities only) may require separation of certain embedded derivatives. *[IAS 39.10-12, IFRS 9.4.3.1-7]*. Sections 11 and 12 do not permit separation of embedded derivatives. Therefore, if a previous IFRS (or FRS 101) reporter applies Sections 11 and 12 as an accounting policy choice under transition to FRS 102, financial instruments containing embedded derivatives will be measured as a hybrid instrument and it will not be possible to designate an embedded derivative as a hedging instrument (as it will no longer be separated).

Given that hedge accounting under Section 12 is simpler than under IFRS, situations may arise where an economic hedging relationship was not hedge accounted for under its financial reporting framework or failed the detailed conditions in IFRS for hedge accounting, but hedge accounting would be possible under Section 12. For a first-time adopter where Section 12 is applied, the transition provisions (see 5.16.2.A(i) below) would allow but not require such existing hedging relationships to be reflected in the opening statement of financial position on transition to FRS 102 (see 5.16.2.D below). Where IAS 39 or IFRS 9 is applied as an accounting policy choice under FRS 102, a new hedging relationship not previously identified would not be reflected in the opening statement of financial position (see 5.16.3 below). This is because retrospective designation prior to the date of transition is not permitted.

There is a relief available in respect of the timing of designation and documentation of a hedging relationship available for the first FRS 102 financial statements where Section 12, IAS 39, or IFRS 9 are followed (see 5.16.2.A(i) and (iii) and 5.16.3 below). Once an entity ceases to be a first-time adopter (i.e. in subsequent FRS 102 financial statements), the usual requirements on designation and documentation of a hedging relationship apply, regardless of which accounting policy choice is followed for the recognition and measurement of financial instruments.

Chapter 32 at 5.16 of EY UK GAAP 2017 addressed issues relevant to hedge accounting for a first-time adopter applying previous UK GAAP (withdrawn for accounting periods beginning on or after 1 January 2015) or the FRSSE (withdrawn for accounting periods beginning on or after 1 January 2016). These are not covered in this chapter as they will be relevant to few first-time adopters going forward. Most first-time adopters now will previously have applied IFRS or FRS 101 and therefore this section mainly addresses the implications for hedge accounting where IAS 39 or IFRS 9 was applied in the entity's last financial statements.

5.16.1 Reporter previously applied IAS 39 or IFRS 9

As there is no change in the hedge accounting requirements, it is not expected that transition adjustments will generally be required where an entity previously applying IAS 39 or IFRS 9 chooses to apply the same accounting policy choice to the recognition and measurement of financial instruments under FRS 102. See 3.5.5 above and 5.16.3 below.

Adjustments may arise where an entity previously applying IAS 39 or IFRS 9 makes a different accounting policy choice under FRS 102. It seems unlikely that entities already applying IFRS 9 will wish to revert to IAS 39, so this discussion focuses on a change in policy from IAS 39 to Section 12 or IFRS 9, or from IFRS 9 to Section 12. See 5.16.1.A below for some examples of areas that may give rise to adjustments to hedge accounting.

Entities will, however, need to ensure that all hedge relationships meet the qualifying conditions for hedge accounting which differ depending on the accounting policy followed. See Chapter 10 at 10 and Chapter 49 at 6 of EY International GAAP 2019.

Implementation issues, including accounting for rebalancing of hedge relationships and 'costs of hedging', when an entity moves from IAS 39 to IFRS 9 are discussed at 3.5.5.B above. See Chapter 49 at 8.2 and 7.5 of EY International GAAP 2019 for further discussion of rebalancing and 'costs of hedging'. Since IFRS 9 is mandatory for IFRS or FRS 101 reporters for accounting periods beginning on or after 1 January 2018, such implementation issues on transition to FRS 102 will generally be of short duration.

However, some IFRS or FRS 101 reporters may have continued to apply the hedge accounting requirements in IAS 39, when they adopted IFRS 9, as permitted under the transitional provisions in that standard. *[IFRS 9.7.2.1]*. This situation is discussed at 3.5.5.A above.

5.16.1.A *Key differences on hedge accounting between Section 12, IAS 39 and IFRS 9*

An entity previously applying IAS 39 or IFRS 9 that chooses to apply a different accounting policy choice to the recognition and measurement of financial instruments on transition to FRS 102 will need to consider both the different transition provisions and the ongoing requirements for hedge accounting. An appreciation of the differences between Section 12, IAS 39 and IFRS 9 would be important when determining which accounting policy choice to make and assessing what, if any, adjustments are required.

Some key differences between Section 12, IAS 39 and IFRS 9 – which may give rise to adjustments when applying a different accounting policy choice under FRS 102 include:

- more hedging relationships may be eligible under Section 12 or IFRS 9 (compared to IAS 39) so new relationships could be designated, where the specified conditions are met. An example is that Section 12 and IFRS 9 both permit the identification of a separately identifiable and reliably measurable risk component of a non-financial hedged item. *[FRS 102.12.16, 12.16C, IFRS 9.6.3.1, 6.3.7, Appendix B.6.3.8-15]*. See Chapter 10 at 10.2.2 and Chapter 49 at 2.2 of EY International GAAP 2019.

- Section 12 has simpler requirements than the hedge accounting requirements of IAS 39 or IFRS 9. For example, in determining whether the qualifying conditions for hedge accounting continue to apply, *[FRS 102.12.18-18A]*, there is no retrospective or prospective effectiveness assessment.

  However, there can be some situations for which Section 12 is more restrictive, in particular compared to IFRS 9. For example, Section 12 requires that if a group of items (including components of an item) are designated as the hedged item in a hedge relationship, those items must share the same risk and cannot contain offsetting positions. *[FRS 102.12.16, 16B]*. IFRS 9 does not have these restrictions in all circumstances, although for risk management purposes, the items in the group must be managed together on a group basis. *[IFRS 9.6.6.1]*. Therefore, more complex hedging relationships can be found under IFRS 9. IFRS 9 would permit a cash flow hedge of a net position attributable to foreign exchange risk (for example, because of forecast foreign purchases and sales) where certain conditions are met, *[IFRS 9.6.6.1(d)]*. This would not be permitted under Section 12. See Chapter 10 at 10.2.3.

- Following the Triennial review 2017, Section 12 now allows designation of the intrinsic value of an option as a hedging instrument (previously, options were required to be designated as a hedging instrument in their entirety). Similarly, an entity may separate the spot risk element of a foreign currency contract and exclude the forward element. Both IFRS 9 and IAS 39 allow designation of the intrinsic value of an option and the spot element of a forward contract. *[IAS 39.74, IFRS 9.6.2.4(a)-(b), FRS 102.12.7A(c)]*.

  Where the intrinsic value of the option or the spot risk element of a foreign currency contract is designated as the hedging instrument, the fair value movements on the time value of the option (or on the forward element of the forward contract) are recognised in profit or loss under Section 12 and IAS 39 (as these fall outside the hedging relationship). This differs from IFRS 9, which requires that the fair value movements on the time value of an option are initially recognised as 'costs of hedging' in other comprehensive income. IFRS 9 also allows (but does not require) an entity to elect on a hedge-by-hedge basis a similar accounting for the 'costs of hedging' (as applied to the time value of the option) for the forward element of a foreign currency contract. *[IFRS 9.6.5.15-6.5.16]*. This accounting will reduce profit and loss volatility compared to Section 12 and IAS 39. See Chapter 10 at 10.3 and Chapter 49 at 7.5 of EY International GAAP 2019.

- Section 12 (like IAS 39) does not allow for separation of foreign currency basis spreads when designating a hedging relationship. *[FRS 102.12.17A]*. This is permitted by IFRS 9 which also allows (but does not require) an entity to elect on a hedge-by-hedge basis to account for the 'costs of hedging' in the same way as for time value of options. *[IFRS 9.6.5.16]*. See Chapter 49 at 7.5 of EY International GAAP 2019.

- An entity applying IFRS 9 may be required to rebalance the hedge ratio on transition (and on an ongoing basis), with an adjustment in profit or loss. *[IFRS 9.6.4.1(c)(iii), 6.5.5]*. See Chapter 49 at 8.2 of EY International GAAP 2019. This is not the case if applying Section 12, as rebalancing is not a feature of Section 12. As a consequence, some hedges may show more ongoing ineffectiveness under Section 12 compared to IFRS 9, but the hedge accounting will be simpler.

- IFRS 9 does not permit an entity to voluntarily discontinue a hedge relationship whereas an entity may document an election to do so under Section 12, providing more flexibility over subsequent accounting for hedging relationships. *[FRS 102.12.25, IFRS 9.6.5.6]*. See Chapter 10 at 10.10 and Chapter 49 at 8.3 of EY International GAAP 2019.

- An entity applying Section 12 on transition to FRS 102 has a choice of whether to reflect existing or past hedging relationships meeting specified conditions in the opening statement of financial position (see 5.16.2 below). *[FRS 102.10(t)(i)-(ii)]*. This flexibility is not available when applying IAS 39 or IFRS 9 on transition to FRS 102 (see 5.16.3 below). As discussed at 5.16.2.B below, the choices made on transition will impact the future results.

It is not the intention of this discussion to provide a list of all the differences in the hedge accounting requirements of Section 12, IAS 39, and IFRS 9. See Chapter 49 at 14 of EY International GAAP 2019 for a summary of differences between hedge accounting under IAS 39 and IFRS 9. See also Chapter 10 at 2.2.3 for differences between hedge accounting in Section 12 and IFRS.

5.16.2 Transition exemptions – FRS 102 reporter applying Section 12 to the recognition and measurement of financial instruments

The transition exemptions for hedge accounting under Section 12 are set out at 5.16.2.A below. Implementation issues in applying the exemptions are discussed at 5.16.2.B to 5.16.2.E.

Chapter 32

5.16.2.A   *Optional exemption – hedge accounting*

An entity may use one or more of the following exemptions in preparing its first financial statements that conform to FRS 102: *[FRS 102.35.10(t)(i)-(iii)]*

(i) *A hedging relationship existing on the date of transition*

A first-time adopter may choose to apply hedge accounting to a hedging relationship of a type described in paragraph 12.19 (i.e. a cash flow hedge, a fair value hedge or a hedge of a net investment in a foreign operation) which exists on the date of transition between a hedging instrument and a hedged item, provided:

- the conditions for hedge accounting set out in paragraphs 12.18(a)-(c) (i.e. the existence of an economic relationship between an eligible hedging instrument and eligible hedged item, where the hedging relationship is consistent with the entity's risk management objectives for undertaking hedges) are met on the date of transition to FRS 102; and

- the conditions of paragraphs 12.18(d) and (e) (i.e. documentation of the hedge relationship and the determination of, and documentation of the causes of, hedge ineffectiveness) are met no later than the date the first financial statements that comply with FRS 102 are authorised for issue.

This choice applies to each hedging relationship existing on the date of transition.

Hedge accounting as set out in Section 12 of FRS 102 may commence from a date no earlier than the conditions of paragraphs 12.18(a) to (c) are met.

In a fair value hedge, the cumulative hedging gain or loss on the hedged item from the date hedge accounting commenced to the date of transition shall be recognised in retained earnings (or if appropriate, another category of equity).

In a cash flow hedge and net investment hedge, the lower of the following (in absolute amounts) shall be recognised in equity (in respect of cash flow hedges in the cash flow hedge reserve):

(a) the cumulative gain or loss on the hedging instrument from the date hedge accounting commenced to the date of transition; and

(b) the cumulative change in fair value (i.e. the present value of the cumulative change of expected future cash flows) on the hedged item from the date hedge accounting commenced to the date of transition.

See 5.16.2.D below for discussion of the transition provisions applicable to existing hedging relationships.

(ii) *A hedging relationship that ceased to exist before the date of transition because the hedging instrument has expired, was sold, terminated or exercised prior to the date of transition*

A first-time adopter may elect not to adjust the carrying amount of an asset or liability for previous financial reporting framework effects of a hedging relationship that has ceased to exist.

A first-time adopter may elect to account for amounts deferred in equity in a cash flow hedge under a previous financial reporting framework, as described in paragraph 12.23(d) (which sets out the subsequent accounting for amounts accumulated in the cash flow hedge reserve), from the date of transition. Any amounts deferred in equity in relation to a hedge of a net investment in a foreign operation under a previous financial reporting framework shall not be reclassified to profit or loss on disposal or partial disposal of the foreign operation.

See 5.16.2.C below for discussion of the transition provisions applicable to past hedging relationships.

(iii) *A hedging relationship that commenced after the date of transition*

A first-time adopter may elect to apply hedge accounting to a hedging relationship of a type described in paragraph 12.19 (i.e. a cash flow hedge, a fair value hedge or a hedge of a net investment in a foreign operation) that commenced after the date of transition between a hedging instrument and a hedged item, starting from the date the conditions of paragraphs 12.18(a) to (c) are met. This is provided that the conditions of paragraphs 12.18(d) and (e) (conditions on hedge documentation) are met no later than the date the first financial statements that comply with FRS 102 are authorised for issue.

The choice applies to each hedging relationship that commenced after the date of transition.

5.16.2.B   General comments

The elections described at 5.16.2.A above provide considerable flexibility for an entity applying Section 12 to begin, cease, or continue hedge accounting on transition to FRS 102. These allow entities to apply a degree of hindsight in deciding whether or not to apply hedge accounting (and to cherry pick which hedging relationships to hedge account), since they provide a relief on the timing of completing hedge documentation for both existing hedging relationships at the date of transition (see 5.16.2.D below) and those entered into after the date of transition. The FRC was mindful of this possible exploitation of the transitional arrangements, nevertheless, on balance, it believed that in the interests of the majority of entities, especially entities that have not applied hedge accounting before, flexibility should take precedence over restrictions aimed at preventing abuse. *[FRS 102.BC.B11.63].*

However, once a hedge accounting relationship has been documented in line with paragraphs 12.18(d) and (e) (conditions on hedge documentation), any subsequent election to discontinue the hedge accounting must be documented and takes effect prospectively. *[FRS 102.12.25].*

The transition provision distinguishes between the situation where a hedging relationship *exists* or *does not exist* on the date of transition. The hedging relationship *exists* where there is a cash flow hedge, fair value hedge or hedge of a net investment of a foreign operation, *and* the hedging instrument and hedged item both exist at the date of transition. A hedging relationship, therefore, *does not exist* where the hedging instrument is terminated (even if there is still a hedged item).

The transition provision permits but does not require an entity to reflect *existing* hedging relationships meeting the specified conditions in the opening statement of financial position (see 5.16.2.A(i) above and 5.16.2.D below). This choice is available on a hedge-by-hedge basis. While the transition provision is not explicit on this matter, we also consider that an entity can choose whether or not to reflect certain past hedging relationships in the opening statement of financial position on a hedge-by-hedge basis (see 5.16.2.A(ii) above and 5.16.2.C below).

Chapter 32

Where the elections are not taken, FRS 102's requirements are retrospectively applied and the hedge accounting adjustments made under an entity's previous financial reporting framework would therefore need to be eliminated to retained earnings (or other category of equity) on transition.

The way in which an entity accounts for past and existing hedging relationships on transition will, to a large extent, dictate the effect on its ongoing FRS 102 financial statements. For example, an entity's future results will for a cash flow hedge be different depending on whether the entity decides to reflect an existing hedging relationship in the opening statement of financial position (by establishing a cash flow hedge reserve) or not. Amounts accumulated in a cash flow hedge reserve at the date of transition will be reclassified from equity to profit or loss at a later date (or, for a hedge of a forecast transaction for a non-financial asset or non-financial liability adjust the initial cost or carrying amount of the asset or liability). However, if a previous IFRS reporter does not reflect a hedging relationship recognised under IFRS, it will transfer the cash flow hedge reserve previously recognised at the date of transition directly to retained earnings (and there would be no subsequent recycling from equity).

Similarly, an entity's future results would be affected depending on whether an existing fair value hedge is reflected in the opening statement of financial position or not. For short-term hedges (e.g. of anticipated sales and inventory purchases) these effects are likely to work their way out of the FRS 102 financial statements relatively quickly. However, for some hedges (e.g. hedges of long-term borrowings) an entity's results may be affected for many years. See further discussion of the choices available at 5.16.2.C and 5.16.2.D below.

5.16.2.C   Accounting for past hedging relationships

Where the conditions in the transition provision in paragraph 35.10(t)(ii) (see 5.16.2.A(ii) above) are met, the entity could choose to reflect a past hedging relationship in the opening statement of financial position. *[FRS 102.35.10(t)(ii)]*.

The transition provision sets out optional exemptions that apply to a hedging relationship that ceased to exist before the date of transition because the hedging instrument has expired, was sold, terminated or exercised prior to the date of transition. Therefore, the transition provision does not address situations where the hedging relationship still *existed* on transition, but for which hedge accounting had ceased prior to transition (e.g. the designation of the hedge was revoked, the hedge ceased to be effective, or the forecasted transaction in a cash flow hedge ceased to be highly probable but was still expected to occur). Such situations are addressed at 5.16.2.D below.

Certain implementation issues associated with the transition provision on past relationships are discussed below:

(a)   A first-time adopter may elect not to adjust the carrying amount of an asset or liability for previous financial reporting framework effects of a hedging instrument that has ceased to exist. *[FRS 102.35.10(t)(ii)]*.

Therefore, where hedging gains (losses) from a hedge of a forecast purchase or committed purchase of inventory or property, plant and equipment have been included in the carrying amount of the asset before the date of transition, there is no requirement to adjust the carrying amount of the asset to eliminate the effects of hedging gains (losses) as at the date of transition.

Also, if an entity previously applying IAS 39 or IFRS 9 had applied fair value hedge accounting for a fixed to floating interest rate swap (now terminated) hedging a fixed rate loan (that still exists), no change is needed to the hedge accounting adjustments made to the loan, as at the date of transition.

Section 35 does not spell out the subsequent accounting. In our view, this establishes a deemed carrying amount for the item and no further adjustments to the carrying amount for ongoing hedging gains and losses are made from the date of transition. However, as for a discontinuance, we consider that any adjustment to the carrying amount (arising from fair value hedge accounting) of a hedged financial instrument carried at amortised cost using the effective interest method shall be amortised to profit and loss. *[FRS 102.12.22, 25A]*. This requirement is similar to the corresponding requirements in IAS 39 and IFRS 9. *[IAS 39.91, 92, IFRS 9.6.5.6, 6.5.7, 6.5.10]*.

(b)   Not all past hedging relationships are permitted to be reflected in the opening statement of financial position, even if the hedged item still exists. For example, if a previous FRS 105 reporter had deferred a gain or loss arising on termination of a hedging instrument in the statement of financial position to be recognised as the hedged item (which still exists) affected profit or loss, the deferred balance would be eliminated against retained earnings as at the date of transition (see 5.16 above). This is because the deferred balance does not represent an asset or liability and is not covered by the transition provision (see (a) above).

(c)   A first-time adopter may elect to account for amounts deferred in equity in a cash flow hedge under a previous financial reporting framework, as described in paragraph 12.23(d) (which sets out the subsequent accounting for amounts accumulated in the cash flow hedge reserve) from the date of transition. *[FRS 102.35.10(v)(ii)]*.

This is consistent with the ongoing requirements for discontinued cash flow hedges in Section 12 (see Chapter 10 at 10.10). This situation is likely to arise where the first-time adopter previously applied IAS 39 or IFRS 9, for example:

*   Where a floating to fixed interest rate swap (now terminated) hedged a floating rate loan (that still exists), the amounts deferred in equity in the cash flow hedge would not change as at the date of transition (where this election is taken). Instead, the deferred amounts are subsequently reclassified to profit or loss, as required by paragraph 12.23(d). If the hedged future cash flows are no longer expected to occur as at the date of transition, the deferred amounts in equity need to be reclassified immediately to retained earnings as at that date. *[FRS 102.12.25A]*. This election, in effect, allows the existing treatment on discontinuation previously followed under IAS 39 or IFRS 9 to endure.

*   Where gains and losses were deferred in equity in relation to a cash flow hedge of a forecast transaction that subsequently resulted in the recognition of a non-financial asset or a non-financial liability (e.g. a purchase of a non-financial asset such as property, plant and equipment or inventory).

    The transition provision refers to paragraph 12.23(d), which requires inclusion of the associated gains and losses previously recognised through other comprehensive income in the initial cost or other carrying amount of the asset or liability (this treatment, often referred to as a 'basis adjustment', was also available by choice in IAS 39 and is required under IFRS 9). Therefore, it appears that a first-time adopter that has already recognised the non-financial asset or liability prior to the date of transition would need to retrospectively adjust its carrying amount on transition to reflect the equivalent of a basis adjustment in order to comply with paragraph 12.23(d), if this treatment had not been followed under its previous financial reporting framework.

(d)   The transition provision clarifies that amounts deferred in equity in relation to a hedge of a net investment in a foreign operation under an entity's previous financial reporting framework are not reclassified to profit or loss on disposal or partial disposal of the foreign operation (consistent with the requirements of paragraph 12.24 of FRS 102 (see Chapter 10 at 10.9), but different to the requirements of IFRS). *[FRS 102.12.24, IAS 21.48-48B].*

The transition provision does not spell out the accounting treatment where an entity does not take up the elections it permits for now ceased hedging relationships. However, entities that elect not to apply the FRS 102 hedge accounting requirements have to comply with the applicable measurement requirements for assets and liabilities set out elsewhere in FRS 102 from the date of transition. *[FRS 102.BC.B11.64].* In our view, if the first-time adopter chose not to apply these exemptions, this means that the old hedge accounting would be reversed and the previously hedged items would need to be held in the opening FRS 102 statement of financial position at the appropriate carrying amount on application of FRS 102 without regard to any previous hedge accounting (with an adjustment to retained earnings or, if appropriate, another category of equity). Similarly, the amounts relating to a cash flow hedge that were previously deferred in a cash flow hedge reserve would be reclassified to retained earnings or, if appropriate, another category of equity. *[FRS 102.35.8].*

5.16.2.D   Hedging relationships existing at the date of transition

The exemption for existing hedging relationships in paragraph 35.10(t)(i) (see 5.16.A(i) above) applies to hedging relationships of a type described in paragraph 12.19 (i.e. a cash flow hedge, fair value hedge, or hedge of a net investment in a foreign operation) (see Chapter 10 at 10.6), meeting the eligibility and documentation conditions for hedge accounting required by the transition provision. See Chapter 10 at 10.2 to 10.4.

It is clear from the context that a hedging relationship can only *exist* at the date of transition if there is both an eligible hedged item and hedging instrument at that date. If the hedging instrument has ceased to exist before the date of transition, the transition provision on past hedging relationships may apply (see 5.16.2.C above).

A first-time adopter has two possibilities for hedging relationships existing at the date of transition:

(a)   *choose not to (or is not permitted to) hedge account* – This applies if the conditions in (b) below are met (but the entity chooses not to hedge account) or if the conditions in (b) below are not met; or

(b)   *choose to apply hedge accounting* – Where one of the three permitted types of hedging relationship exists at the date of transition, the first-time adopter may choose to apply hedge accounting provided:

- the conditions in paragraphs 12.18(a) to (c) (i.e. the existence of an economic relationship between an eligible hedging instrument and eligible hedged item, where the hedging relationship is consistent with the entity's risk management objectives for undertaking hedges – see Chapter 10 at 10.4) are met on the date of transition; and

- the conditions of paragraphs 12.18(d) and (e) (i.e. documentation of the hedging relationship and the determination, and documentation of causes of ineffectiveness – see Chapter 10 at 10.4.4) are met not later than the date the first FRS 102 financial statements are authorised for issue.

This choice applies to each hedging relationship existing on the date of transition. *[FRS 102.35.10(t)(i)].*

Because Section 12 does not have the same requirements as IAS 39 for ongoing effectiveness tests, this means that even if hedge accounting under IAS 39 ceased because the hedge relationship failed the effectiveness test (but the entity continued with the hedge economically), arguably hedge accounting could be reinstated in the opening FRS 102 statement of financial position, where the above conditions are met. However, if hedge accounting ceased because a forecasted transaction in a cash flow hedge was no longer highly probable, the hedging relationship would not meet the criteria in paragraph 12.18(a) and hedge accounting could not be reinstated.

Where the entity does not re-establish hedge accounting for an existing hedging relationship or the conditions to apply hedge accounting on transition are not met, the question arises as to whether the entity can continue to reflect the hedge accounting under its previous financial reporting framework for the discontinued hedge in the statement of financial position and apply Section 12's requirements for discontinuance of hedge accounting prospectively from the date of transition (which would generally result in similar accounting to that already applied under IAS 39 or IFRS 9). Entities that elect not to apply the FRS 102 hedge accounting requirements have to comply with the applicable measurement requirements for assets and liabilities set out elsewhere in FRS 102 from the date of transition. *[FRS 102.BC.B11.64].* Where the elections to reflect the hedge accounting in the opening statement of financial position have not been taken, the FRC presumably intended that FRS 102 is applied retrospectively to the measurement of the hedged item and hedging instrument, without any regard to the hedge accounting provisions. The hedging relationship is not reflected in the opening FRS 102 statement of financial position and the hedge accounting adjustments under the previous financial reporting framework are eliminated to retained earnings (or, if appropriate, another component of equity) at the date of transition. *[FRS 102.35.8].*

Hedge accounting as set out in Section 12 may commence from a date no earlier than the conditions of paragraphs 12.18(a) to (c) are met. *[FRS 102.35.10(t)(i)].* This would appear to allow first-time adopters some flexibility over choosing when hedge accounting commences from. If hedge accounting commences at the date of transition, there will be no amounts deferred in equity for a cash flow hedge or hedge of net investment in a foreign operation, and no adjustments made to the carrying amount of the hedged item for a fair value hedge. If hedge accounting commences from the date of inception of the hedging relationship, this is likely to avoid the ineffectiveness that might result where the hedging instrument has a non-zero fair value at the commencement of hedge accounting.

Chapter 32

The choice whether or not to hedge account for existing hedging relationships meeting the above conditions is available whatever the entity's previous financial reporting framework and also whether or not the entity previously applied hedge accounting to that existing relationship. The nature of the adjustments required, however, may well depend on what previous accounting was followed. Where an entity previously applying IAS 39 or IFRS 9 chooses to continue to hedge account for a hedging relationship permitted under Section 12, there may often be no adjustment required on transition but differences may occur, for example:

- Section 12 does not allow for rebalancing a hedging relationship (as required under IFRS 9); and where this has occurred, it is possible that differences in the level of ineffectiveness may occur from the date at which the hedging relationship is established under Section 12;

- the accounting for the 'costs of hedging' where the entity designates the time value of options or the spot risk of forward currency contracts in a hedging relationship under Section 12 differs, or may differ, from that followed under IFRS 9. See 5.16.1.A above.

Where an entity chooses to apply hedge accounting to a hedging relationship existing at the date of transition, the transition provisions (see 5.16.2.A(i) above) describe how a fair value hedge, cash flow hedge or net investment hedge should be reflected at the date of transition. The intention here appears to be to reflect the same adjustments as at the date of transition, as if hedge accounting under FRS 102 had been applied from the date chosen to commence hedge accounting, using the transition exemption. Therefore, in accordance with paragraph 12.23(d), the effects of reclassifications required from the cash flow hedge reserve where the hedged item would have affected profit or loss in prior periods (had hedge accounting under FRS 102 been applied) would be reflected in retained earnings at the date of transition. See Chapter 10 at 10.7-9.

For a UK company (or an LLP) preparing statutory accounts in accordance with FRS 102, the fair value accounting rules in the Regulations (and LLP Regulations) (see Chapter 6 at 10.3) require that the cash flow hedge reserve is included in the statutory fair value reserve. *[1 Sch 40-41, 1 Sch 40-41 (LLP)].*

5.16.2.E   *Subsequent accounting for existing hedging relationships*

Where an existing hedging relationship is reflected in the opening FRS 102 statement of financial position, *[FRS 102.35.10(t)(i)],* (see 5.16.2.A(i) and 5.16.2.D above) or a hedging relationship that commences after the date of transition is hedge accounted, *[FRS 102.35.10(t)(iii)],* (see 5.16.2.A(iii) above), an entity may:

- *continue hedge accounting* – where the hedging relationship continues to comply with the conditions for hedge accounting in Section 12 (and meets the documentation requirements set out in the transition provisions); *[FRS 102.12.18]* or

- *discontinue hedge accounting prospectively* – where an entity subsequently elects to discontinue hedge accounting; the hedging instrument has expired, is sold or terminated; or the conditions for hedge accounting cease to be met. *[FRS 102.12.25].*

The entity accounts for the continuance or discontinuance of hedge accounting in accordance with Section 12 (see Chapter 10 at 10).

5.16.3 Transition provisions – FRS 102 reporter applying IAS 39 or IFRS 9 (not Sections 11 and 12) to the recognition and measurement of financial instruments

5.16.3.A Mandatory requirement – hedge accounting

The transition provisions for hedge accounting relating to a first-time adopter choosing to apply IAS 39 or IFRS 9 to the recognition and measurement of financial instruments are set out in paragraph 35.10(t)(iv). While positioned within the list of transition exemptions in Section 35, the wording of the transition provision means that it sets out mandatory requirements for hedge accounting where IAS 39 or IFRS 9 is applied. *[FRS 102.35.10(t)(iv)]*. This differs to the situation where a first-time adopter applies Section 12, where there is a choice whether or not to apply the transition exemptions for hedge accounting (see 5.16.2 above). *[FRS 102.35.10(t)(i)-(ii)]*.

Most FRS 102 reporters will have previously applied IFRS or FRS 101. As explained at 3.5.5.A, adjustments are not generally expected to be required at the date of transition where the same accounting standard (IAS 39 or IFRS 9) is applied to the recognition and measurement of financial instruments under FRS 102. Considerations where an entity previously applied IAS 39 to the accounting for hedges under its previous financial framework but chooses to apply IFRS 9 under FRS 102 are discussed at 3.5.5.B above. The transition requirements are likely to have more effect on the opening statement of financial position where the entity has not previously applied IFRS or FRS 101 – for example, entities previously reporting under FRS 105.

A first-time adopter that applies IAS 39 or IFRS 9 to the recognition and measurement of financial instruments under FRS 102 shall apply the transitional requirements applicable to hedge accounting in paragraphs B4 to B6 of IFRS 1 (see 5.16.3.B below), except that the designation and documentation of a hedging relationship may be completed after the date of transition, and no later than the date the first financial statements that comply with FRS 102 are authorised for issue, if the hedging relationship is to qualify for hedge accounting from the date of transition. *[FRS 102.35.10(t)(iv)]*.

A first-time adopter, that has entered into a hedging relationship as described in IAS 39 or IFRS 9 in the period between the date of transition and the reporting date for the first financial statements that comply with FRS 102, may elect to apply hedge accounting prospectively from the date all qualifying conditions for hedge accounting in IAS 39 or IFRS 9 are met, except that an entity shall complete the formal designation and documentation of a hedging relationship no later than the date the first financial statements that comply with FRS 102 are authorised for issue. *[FRS 102.35.10(t)(iv)]*.

The requirements under IAS 39 and IFRS 9 for designation and documentation of hedging relationships are discussed in Chapter 49 at 5.1 and 14 of EY International GAAP 2019. The ongoing requirements under IAS 39 and IFRS 9 for hedge accounting where the qualifying conditions are met (and for discontinuance of hedging relationships, where the qualifying conditions are not met) are discussed generally in Chapter 49 of EY International GAAP 2019.

The concession on timing of completion of the designation and documentation of the hedging relationship is discussed at 5.16.3.C below.

Chapter 32

5.16.3.B　Requirements of paragraphs B4 to B6 of IFRS 1

The requirements of paragraphs B4 to B6 of IFRS 1 (which are applied subject to the concession over the timing of completion of the designation and documentation of the hedging relationship) are as follows.

As required by IAS 39 or IFRS 9, at the date of transition, an entity shall: *[IFRS 1 Appendix.B4]*

- measure all derivatives at fair value; and
- eliminate all deferred losses and gains arising on derivatives that were reported in accordance with previous GAAP as if they were assets and liabilities.

An entity shall not reflect in its opening statement of financial position a hedging relationship of a type that does not qualify for hedge accounting (under the relevant IFRS that is followed). *[IFRS 1 Appendix B.5]*. Entities can only designate one of three types of hedging relationships – a fair value hedge, a cash flow hedge or a hedge of a net investment in a foreign operation. For hedges of foreign currency risk of a firm commitment, an entity may designate either a fair value hedge or a cash flow hedge. *[IAS 39.86-87, IFRS 9.6.5.2-4]*.

Paragraph B5 gives various examples of ineligible types of hedging relationships (which differ depending on whether IAS 39 or IFRS 9 is applied). The requirements on eligible types of hedging relationships for IAS 39 and IFRS 9 are discussed further in Chapter 49 at 2 to 5 and 14 of EY International GAAP 2019.

If before the date of transition, an entity had designated a hedging relationship that was of an eligible type for hedge accounting, but the hedging relationship does not meet all the conditions for hedge accounting in IAS 39 (or IFRS 9), the entity shall apply paragraphs 91 and 101 of IAS 39 (or paragraphs 6.5.6 and 6.5.7 of IFRS 9) to discontinue hedge accounting prospectively immediately after transition. Transactions entered into before the date of transition to IFRS shall not be retrospectively designated as hedges. *[IFRS 1 Appendix B.6]*.

While paragraphs B4 to B6 now refer only to IFRS 9, in the context of their application under Section 35, our view is that these should be read to include references to IAS 39 as this standard remains available for use under FRS 102.

The implementation guidance in IFRS 1 on accounting for cash flow hedges, fair value hedges and net investment hedges is not referred to by the transition provision. *[FRS 102.35.10(t)(iv)]*. However, most first-time adopters of FRS 102 will have applied IFRS or FRS 101 in their last set of financial statements. For a previous IFRS or FRS 101 reporter, paragraphs B4 to B6 of IFRS 1 should provide sufficient guidance.

Chapter 5 at 4.4 to 4.7 of EY International GAAP 2019 provides further guidance on IFRS 1's transition requirements for hedge accounting.

5.16.3.C　Concession on designation and documentation of hedging instruments

A hedging relationship *not* specifically identified under an entity's previous financial reporting framework may meet the conditions for hedge accounting under IFRS 9 or IAS 39 as at the date of transition to FRS 102 or at a later date (except that the entity completes the designation and documentation of the hedging relationship after the date of transition but before the date of approval of the financial statements). In such circumstances, we consider that the transition provisions would allow hedge accounting prospectively *from* the date of transition (or from that later date) but that the hedging relationship should not be reflected in the opening FRS 102 statement of financial position. In essence, whereas IFRS 1 would have required the designation and documentation to be in place by the date of transition in order to hedge account prospectively from the date of transition for such a relationship, the transition provision in FRS 102 extends the deadline for completing the designation and documentation to the date of authorisation of the financial statements.

As the designation and documentation of hedging relationships (which will include how effectiveness is to be assessed), *[IAS 39.88(a), IFRS 9.6.4.1(b)]*, are only required to be completed by the date of authorisation of the first FRS 102 financial statements, the first-time adopter must likewise have more time to perform the effectiveness assessments required. Under IFRS 9, the entity must continue to assess the ongoing effectiveness requirements, whereas both retrospective and prospective effectiveness tests are required under IAS 39. *[IAS 39.88(b), (e), IFRS 9.6.4.1(c)]*. Clearly, these effectiveness tests will need to be completed and satisfied at the latest by the date of authorisation of the first FRS 102 financial statements.

This concession over the timing of completion of designation and documentation is optional. Therefore, an entity may still account for a hedging relationship from the date all the requirements (including designation and documentation) for hedge accounting are met. However, this concession may still be helpful to a previous IFRS or FRS 101 reporter that applied IAS 39 in its most recent IFRS financial statements and instead applies IFRS 9 on first-time adoption of FRS 102 (particularly where the documentation needs to be improved to meet IFRS 9's requirements).

5.17 Designation of previously recognised financial instruments

An entity is permitted to designate, as at the date of transition to FRS 102, any financial asset or financial liability at fair value through profit or loss provided the asset or liability meets the criteria in paragraph 11.14(b) at that date. *[FRS 102.35.10(s)]*.

Debt instruments (that meet the conditions in paragraph 11.8(b) of FRS 102) and commitments to receive a loan and to make a loan to another entity (that meet the conditions in paragraph 11.8(c) of FRS 102) may upon their initial recognition be designated by the entity as at fair value through profit or loss, if the conditions in paragraph 11.14(b) of FRS 102 are met. *[FRS 102.11.14(b)]*. See Chapter 10 at 8.4.

The transition exemption allows a first-time adopter to make the designation as of its date of transition. This designation can be made retrospectively, providing it is made before the date of approval of the first FRS 102 financial statements.

Examples of debt instruments include accounts, notes and loans receivable and payable. *[FRS 102.11.8(b)]*. Consequently the term 'debt instruments' includes both financial assets and financial liabilities.

In the absence of this designation at fair value through profit or loss, such financial instruments would be classified as basic financial instruments under Section 11 of FRS 102. However, Section 12 requires most financial instruments that do not qualify as basic financial instruments to be carried at fair value through profit and loss in any case (although this is subject to this being permitted by the Regulations, Small Companies Regulations, LLP Regulations and Small LLP Regulations). *[FRS 102.12.8(c)]*.

Chapter 32

5.18   Compound financial instruments

FRS 102 requires an entity to split a convertible debt or similar compound financial instrument (that, from the issuer's perspective, contains both a liability and equity component) into its liability and equity components at the date of issue. A first-time adopter need not separate those two components if the liability component is not outstanding at the date of transition to FRS 102. *[FRS 102.22.13, 35.10(g), Appendix I].*

If the liability component of a compound financial instrument is no longer outstanding, a full retrospective application of Section 22 would involve identifying two components, one representing the original equity component and the other representing the cumulative interest or fair value movements on the liability component (depending on whether accounted at amortised cost or at fair value through profit or loss), both of which are accounted for in equity (see Chapter 10 at 5.6.2).

This transition exemption appears to be of limited practical effect as Section 22 merely requires that the proceeds be allocated between the liability and equity component, and that the allocation between the liability and equity component must not be revised in later periods. *[FRS 102.22.13-14].* Section 22 does not mandate that the equity component must be credited to a separate component in equity nor does it prohibit a subsequent transfer within equity. The increase in equity arising on an issue of shares is presented in the statement of financial position as determined by applicable laws. *[FRS 102.22.10].* Indeed, by final conversion or settlement of a compound instrument, the entity would generally have transferred any separately recognised component of equity to another category of equity, so that no further adjustment would be required on transition to FRS 102.

5.19   Insurance contracts

As noted in Chapter 3 at 1.2.4 and Chapter 33, FRS 103 is a transactional based standard applying to FRS 102 reporters falling within its scope.

An entity applying both FRS 102 and FRS 103 together at the first time (i.e. a first-time adopter of FRS 102) must apply both Section 35 and the transitional provisions set out in Section 6 of FRS 103. *[FRS 103.6.1-2].*

An entity applying FRS 103 for the first time need not disclose information about claims development that occurred earlier than five years before the end of the first financial year in which it applies FRS 103. Furthermore, if it is impracticable, when an entity first applies FRS 103, to prepare information about claims development that occurred before the beginning of the earliest period for which an entity presents full comparative information that complies with FRS 103, the entity shall disclose that fact. *[FRS 103.6.3, FRS 103.4.8(b)(iii)].*

If an insurer changes its accounting policies for insurance liabilities, it is permitted, but not required, to reclassify some or all of its financial assets as a financial asset at fair value through profit or loss provided those assets meet the criteria in paragraph 11.14(b) of FRS 102 (or if the entity has made the accounting policy choice to apply the recognition and measurement provisions of either IAS 39 or IFRS 9, the relevant requirements of IAS 39 or IFRS 9, as applicable) at that date. This reclassification is permitted if an insurer changes accounting polices when it first applies FRS 103 and if it makes a subsequent policy change permitted by paragraph 2.3 of FRS 103. The reclassification is a change in policy to which Section 10 of FRS 102 applies. *[FRS 103.6.4].*

These transitional provisions also apply when an entity already applying FRS 102 first applies FRS 103 and are discussed in more detail in Chapter 33. *[FRS 103.6.1]*.

6 PRESENTATION AND DISCLOSURE

Section 35 does not exempt a first-time adopter from any of the presentation and disclosure requirements in other sections of FRS 102.

6.1 Comparative information

An entity's first FRS 102 financial statements are required to be a complete set of financial statements and therefore must include at least two statements of financial position, two statements of comprehensive income, two separate income statements (if presented), two statements of cash flows (unless exempt) and two statements of changes in equity and related notes, including comparative information. *[FRS 102.3.17, 3.20, 7.1A-7.1B, 35.5]*. Where permitted by the standard, two statements of income and retained earnings may be included in place of the statements of comprehensive income and statements of changes in equity. *[FRS 102.3.18, 6.4]*. An opening statement of financial position at the date of transition is not required. *[FRS 102.35.7]*.

Small companies are not required to present a cash flow statement and small companies applying Section 1A of FRS 102 are encouraged but not mandated to present a statement of changes in equity or statement of comprehensive income. *[FRS 102.1A.8-9, 7.1B]*. See Chapter 5 at 8.

Except where FRS 102 permits or requires otherwise, comparative information in respect of the preceding period is required for all amounts presented in the financial statements, as well as for narrative and descriptive information when it is relevant to an understanding of the current period's financial statements. *[FRS 102.3.14, 35.6,]*. An entity may present comparative information for more than one preceding period.

FRS 103 provides certain disclosure reliefs for information on claims development (see 5.19 above). *[FRS 103.6.3]*.

6.2 Explanation of transition to FRS 102

A first-time adopter is required to explain how the transition from its previous financial reporting framework to FRS 102 affected its reported financial position, and financial performance. *[FRS 102.35.12]*. FRS 102 does not require an explanation of how the transition affected cash flows.

FRS 102 offers a wide range of transition exemptions that a first-time adopter may elect to apply. However, the standard does not explicitly require an entity to disclose which exemptions it has applied and how it applied them, although it does require a description of the nature of each change in accounting policy. *[FRS 102.35.13]*.

For some exemptions, it will be obvious from the reconciliations disclosed (see 6.3 below) whether or not an entity has chosen to apply the exemption. For others, users will have to rely on a first-time adopter disclosing in its summary of significant policies, those transitional accounting policies that are 'relevant to an understanding of the financial statements.' *[FRS 102.8.5]*. However, first-time adopters are expected to disclose voluntarily which transition exemptions they applied and which exceptions applied to them, as is the practice for first-time adopters transitioning to IFRS.

If a first-time adopter did not present financial statements for previous periods this fact shall be disclosed in its first financial statements that conform to FRS 102. *[FRS 102.35.15]*. For example, entities may not have prepared consolidated financial statements under their previous financial reporting framework and newly incorporated entities may never have prepared financial statements at all. In such cases, an explanation of how the transition to FRS 102 affects the entity's financial position and performance cannot be presented because relevant comparative information under the entity's previous financial reporting framework does not exist.

If it is impracticable for an entity to make one or more of the adjustments required by paragraph 35.7 at the date of transition, the entity shall apply paragraphs 35.7 to 35.10 (i.e. retrospective application of FRS 102, subject to the transition exceptions and exemptions) for such adjustments in the earliest period for which it is practicable. The entity shall identify which amounts in the financial statements have not been restated. If it is impracticable for an entity to provide any disclosures required by FRS 102 for any period before the period in which it prepares its first FRS 102 financial statements, it must disclose the omission. *[FRS 102.35.11]*. See 3.5.4 above for discussion of the meaning of 'impracticable'.

If it is not practical on first-time adoption to apply a particular requirement of paragraph 18 of IFRS 6 (impairment of exploration and evaluation assets) to previous comparative amounts an entity shall disclose that fact. *[FRS 102.34.11C]*.

6.3   Disclosure of reconciliations

A first-time adopter is required to present in its first financial statements prepared using FRS 102: *[FRS 102.35.13(b)-(c)]*

- reconciliations of its equity determined in accordance with its previous financial reporting framework to its equity determined in accordance with FRS 102 at:
  - the date of transition to FRS 102; and
  - the end of the latest period presented in the entity's most recent annual financial statements determined in accordance with its previous financial reporting framework; and
- a reconciliation of the profit or loss determined in accordance with its previous financial reporting framework for the latest period in the entity's most recent annual financial statements to its profit or loss determined in accordance with FRS 102 for the same period.

First-time adopters must also describe the nature of each change in accounting policy. *[FRS 102.35.13(a)]*.

If the entity becomes aware of errors made under its previous financial reporting framework, the reconciliations must, to the extent practicable, distinguish the correction of those errors from changes in accounting policies. *[FRS 102.35.14]*. This means that the adoption of FRS 102 should not be used to mask the error.

FRS 102 does not specify the format of the reconciliations of equity or profit or loss. In *Staff Education Note 13: Transition to FRS 102*, the FRC staff give two example layouts (in both cases, with supporting notes explaining the adjustments):

- a line-by-line reconciliation of the statement of financial position at the date of transition and at the end of the comparative period, and of the profit or loss account for the comparative period; or

- a reconciliation of total equity at the date of transition and at the end of the comparative period, and of the total profit or loss for the comparative period.

A line-by-line reconciliation may be particularly appropriate when a first-time adopter needs to make transition adjustments that affect a significant number of line items in the primary financial statements. If the adjustments are less pervasive, a straightforward reconciliation of equity and profit or loss may be able to provide an equally effective explanation.

A UK company (or LLP) will also need to comply with any requirements of the Regulations (or LLP Regulations), for example the requirements of paragraph 7(2) to disclose any adjustment made to corresponding amounts or to give particulars of the non-comparability, *[1 Sch 7(2), 1 Sch 7(2) (LLP)]*, in respect of corresponding amounts that have been adjusted or are not comparable (see Chapter 6 at 3.6.2). In most cases, the reconciliations required by Section 35 combined with an adequate explanation of the transition adjustments and how these relate to the restated figures are likely to provide sufficient information to meet these requirements. However, this statutory disclosure requirement should be borne in mind by entities when explaining the transition.

Section 35 contains no explicit requirement to disclose material presentational changes (since these do not impact total equity or profit or loss). However, the particulars of and reason for any change of formats (e.g. moving from the statutory to adapted formats on transition, say, from FRS 101 to FRS 102) would need to be explained in the notes to the financial statements. *[1 Sch 2(2), 1 Sch 2(2) (LLP)]*. See Chapter 6 at 4.3. We recommend that entities explain any material presentational changes compared to the entity's previous financial reporting framework to assist readers' understanding of the financial statements.

In our view, a first-time adopter should include all disclosures required by Section 35 within its first FRS 102 financial statements and not cross-refer to any previously reported information. Any additional voluntary information regarding the conversion to FRS 102 that was previously published but that is not specifically required by Section 35 need not be repeated in the first FRS 102 financial statements.

6.4   Repeat application of FRS 102

An entity that has applied FRS 102 in a previous reporting period but not in its most recent annual financial statements, as described in paragraph 35.2 (see 3.2.2 above), shall disclose: *[FRS 102.35.12A]*

- the reason it stopped applying FRS 102;

- the reason it is resuming the application of FRS 102;

- whether it has applied Section 35 or has applied FRS 102 retrospectively in accordance with Section 10 of FRS 102.

This disclosure is therefore only required in the accounting period in which the entity reapplies FRS 102.

6.5   Interim financial statements

FRS 102 does not address the presentation of interim financial reports; it merely requires that an entity that prepares such reports shall describe the basis for preparing and presenting the information. FRS 104 – *Interim Financial Reporting* – sets out a basis for the preparation and presentation of interim financial reports that an FRS 102 reporter may apply. *[FRS 102.3.25].*

FRS 104 is not a mandatory standard to apply. Issuers subject to the Disclosure and Transparency Rules that are not required to prepare consolidated financial statements and choose to report under FRS 102 may give a responsibility statement that the condensed set of financial statements has been prepared in accordance with FRS 104. However, we would generally expect FRS 104 to be applied where interim financial statements are prepared by a FRS 102 reporter. See Chapter 34 at 2.2 for further discussion of the scope of FRS 104.

FRS 104 (rather than Section 35) addresses the disclosures concerning transition required in interim financial reports applying FRS 102 that cover part of the first financial reporting period. *[FRS 104.16B].* See Chapter 34 at 11. Where changes to accounting policies or the use of exemptions are made between the first FRS 102 interim financial report and the first FRS 102 financial statements, neither FRS 104 nor Section 35 require disclosure of these changes (including an update to the reconciliations) in the annual financial statements. This disclosure is, however, required by an IFRS reporter. *[IFRS 1.27A].* We would encourage disclosure of such changes, where material, as relevant information in the first FRS 102 financial statements.

6.6   Non-FRS 102 comparative information and historical summaries

FRS 102 requires comparative information that is prepared on the same basis as information relating to the current reporting period. However, it does not address the presentation of historical summaries of selected data for periods before the first period for which an entity presents full comparative information under FRS 102. Such historical summaries are also often presented outside the financial statements.

Although IFRS 1 is not directly applicable, it provides the following guidance that could be helpful when an entity needs to present such summaries but cannot comply with the recognition and measurement requirements of IFRS for some of the periods presented.

If an entity presents comparative information under its previous GAAP in addition to the comparative information required by IFRS it should:

(a)   label the previous GAAP information prominently as not being prepared in accordance with IFRS; and

(b)   disclose the nature of the main adjustments that would make it comply with IFRS. An entity need not quantify those adjustments. *[IFRS 1.22].*

Such an approach may also be appropriate for first-time adopters of FRS 102. Whether the historical summaries are presented in or outside the financial statements, these explanations would clearly be of benefit to users.

7 FRS 105

It is possible that a first-time adopter may previously have applied FRS 105. The fair value accounting rules and alternative accounting rules do not apply to companies and LLPs applying the micro-entities regime. Entities applying FRS 105 are not permitted to account for investment properties or financial instruments at fair value (using the fair value accounting rules) or to account for property, plant and equipment (or other assets) at revaluation.

See 3.5.3 above for a discussion of implementation issues when restating investment property previously carried using the cost model and the use of deemed cost for property, plant and equipment (which may be of interest if the entity wishes to revalue property, plant and equipment) (see also 5.5 above).

Depending on the standard applied to the recognition and measurement of financial instruments of FRS 102, certain financial instruments (including derivatives) will be required to be carried at fair value. Where an FRS 105 reporter entered into derivatives prior to adoption of FRS 102, there will be adjustments required to reflect the derivatives at fair value, and to eliminate any deferred amounts in the balance sheet.

See 5.16 above for the transition provisions in relation to hedge accounting. In addition, Chapter 32 at 5.16 of EY UK GAAP 2017 has more detailed guidance on adjustments relevant to hedge accounting where entities applied previous UK GAAP prior to adoption of FRS 102. This discussion may be helpful for some FRS 105 reporters.

The accounting for an interest rate swap is illustrated in Example 32.7 below and the accounting for an investment in a quoted company is illustrated in Example 32.8 below.

Example 32.7: Accounting for interest rate swap

Entity A has an interest rate swap, which has a carrying amount of £nil (i.e. it is 'off balance sheet') under its previous financial reporting framework, FRS 105. The interest rate swap hedges a floating rate loan liability. The swap and loan were both taken out in 2011. In Entity A's final 2018 financial statements prepared in accordance with FRS 105, the swap was clearly identified as hedging the loan and accounted for as such. The fair value of the swap was not recognised in Entity A's statement of financial position and the periodic interest settlements on the swap were accrued and recognised as an adjustment to the loan interest expense.

Entity A's first FRS 102 financial statements are for the year ended 31 December 2019, with a date of transition of 1 January 2018. Entity A chooses to apply Sections 11 and 12 of FRS 102 to the recognition and measurement of financial instruments under FRS 102. This example ignores tax effects.

If Entity A chooses *not* to hedge account, then the derivative is recognised at its fair value of £50,000 (liability) with an adjustment to retained earnings as at the date of transition. Thereafter, it is remeasured at fair value through profit or loss.

If Entity A chooses to hedge account, then the derivative is recognised at its fair value of £50,000 (liability) and the £50,000 adjustment made to its previous carrying amount is recognised in a cash flow hedge reserve (see 5.16.2 above for discussion of the transition provisions for hedge accounting). Where Entity A is a UK company (or LLP) preparing statutory accounts, the adjustment is recognised in the statutory 'fair value reserve'. See 3.5.3 above and Chapter 6 at 10.3. The hedge accounting could commence at inception, if the specified conditions in paragraph 35.10(t)(i) are met (see 5.16.2.A(i) above). The hedge accounting could commence at inception (i.e. in 2011, if the specified conditions were met at the time). Amounts in the cash flow hedge reserve that would have been recognised in profit or loss (i.e. recycled) prior to the date of transition had hedge accounting commenced from the date chosen should be reflected in retained earnings at the date of transition. If Entity A chose to commence hedge accounting from the date of transition, there would be no cash flow hedge reserve reflected at the date of transition. However, there would likely be ineffectiveness arising in the future as a result of the non-zero starting value of the swap. Hedge accounting would be applied throughout 2018 and 2019 in the first FRS 102 financial statements.

Chapter 32

Example 32.8:   Investment in a quoted company

Entity B has a 5% trade investment in a quoted company carried at cost of £10,000 (but with a fair value of £16,000). Under FRS 102, the trade investment is measured at fair value through profit or loss. On transition, Entity B remeasures the investment to its fair value of £160,000 and recognises the £60,000 uplift in its value in retained earnings. See 3.5.3 above and Chapter 6 at 10.3.

References

1 *Charities SORP (FRS 102): Accounting and Reporting by Charities: Statement of Recommended Practice applicable to charities preparing their accounts in accordance with the Financial Reporting Standard applicable in the UK and Republic of Ireland (FRS 102)*, Charity Commission and Office of the Scottish Charity Regulator, 2014.

Chapter 33   FRS 103 – Insurance contracts

Chapter 33

Chapter 33

List of examples

Chapter 33   FRS 103 – Insurance contracts

1   INTRODUCTION

FRS 103 – *Insurance Contracts* – is relevant to entities applying FRS 102 – *The Financial Reporting Standard applicable in the UK and Republic of Ireland* – that have insurance contracts and financial instruments with a discretionary participation feature (DPF). An entity that applies FRS 102, whether or not it is an 'insurance company', should apply FRS 103 to insurance contracts (including reinsurance contracts) that it issues and reinsurance contracts that it holds, and to financial instruments that the entity issues with a DPF.

FRS 103 (and the accompanying non-mandatory Implementation Guidance) consolidates pre-existing financial reporting requirements and guidance for insurance contracts. The requirements (and the guidance in the accompanying non-mandatory Implementation Guidance) are based on the International Accounting Standards Board's (IASB) IFRS 4 – *Insurance Contracts* – extant in 2013 (except to the extent that it was amended by IFRS 13 – *Fair Value Measurement*), the requirements of FRS 27 – *Life assurance* (prior to it being withdrawn by FRS 103) and elements of the Association of British Insurers' Statement of Recommended Practice on Accounting for Insurance Business (the ABI SORP) (published in December 2005 and amended in December 2006). FRS 103 has since been updated for changes in the UK regulatory framework and as a result of *Amendments to FRS 102 Triennial review 2017 – Incremental improvements and clarifications* (Triennial review 2017).

FRS 103 allows entities, generally, to continue with their previous accounting practices for insurance contracts, but permits entities the same flexibility to make improvements (subject to legal and regulatory requirements) as entities in the UK and Republic of Ireland applying IFRS 4. This is because the FRC does not want FRS 103 to be more onerous to apply than IFRS 4.

Following the application of FRS 103, both FRS 27 and the ABI SORP were withdrawn.

1.1 Updates to FRS 103

FRS 103 was issued originally in March 2014. Revised versions have been issued in February 2017 and March 2018. This chapter reflects the March 2018 version of FRS 103. The changes made to FRS 103 since the publication of UK GAAP 2017 are as follows:

- the insertion of a paragraph to reflect a change in UK legislation relating to the computation of the long term business provision (see 8.4.4 below);
- editorial amendments reflecting legislative changes in the Republic of Ireland; and
- minor amendments as a result of the Triennial review 2017.

An entity should apply the amendments as set out in the Triennial review 2017 for accounting periods beginning on or after 1 January 2019. Early application of the Triennial review 2017 amendments was permitted provided all amendments to FRS 103 made by the triennial review were applied at the same time. *[FRS 103.1.11B]*.

This chapter incorporates all of these above amendments.

1.2 IFRS 17 – *Insurance Contracts*

IFRS 17 – *Insurance Contracts* – was issued by the IASB in May 2017 and is effective for accounting periods beginning on or after 1 January 2021. In November 2018, the IASB voted to propose a one year deferral of the effective date of IFRS 17 until 2022. The proposed deferral is subject to a public consultation which is expected in 2019. IFRS 17 establishes principles for the recognition, measurement, presentation and disclosure of insurance contracts issued, reinsurance contracts held and investment contracts with discretionary participation features issued. IFRS 17, when applied, replaces IFRS 4 (upon which FRS 103 is based).

It is stated in the Basis for Conclusions that the FRC will review the requirements of FRS 103 in the light of IFRS 17 but that the timing of this review is yet to be determined. *[FRS 103.BC57]*. An FRC press release issued in June 2017 stated that, consistent with the approach being taken to other major new IFRSs, this review is likely to take place once more IFRS implementation experience is available. At the time of writing, no target effective date for any changes to FRS 103 has been set and any detailed proposals will be consulted on in due course.[1]

1.3 Non-insurance transactions and balances

Recognition, measurement and disclosure of non-insurance transactions and balances of an insurer are accounted for in accordance with FRS 102 and are discussed in the relevant chapters of this publication.

1.4 Implementation guidance to accompany FRS 103

FRS 103 is accompanied by about 25 pages of non-mandatory implementation guidance. The Implementation Guidance is not part of, and does not carry the authority of, an accounting standard. It provides guidance on applying: *[FRS 103.1.4]*

- the requirements of FRS 103;
- the requirements or principles of FRS 102 by entities with general insurance business or long-term insurance business; and
- the requirements of Schedule 3 to the Regulations.

The Implementation Guidance has been developed from material that was previously included in either FRS 27 or the ABI SORP. Paragraphs that have been sourced from the ABI SORP, and to a lesser extent those from FRS 27, have been revised where they needed updating, for example to reflect new legislative requirements or for consistency with FRS 102. Each section of the Implementation Guidance specifies the requirements to which it relates. *[FRS 103.IG.Overview (iii)]*.

A number of the sections of FRS 102 exclude insurance contracts from their scope. However, FRS 102 requires entities developing accounting policies for transactions, other events or conditions not specifically addressed in FRS 102 (or another FRS) to consider the applicability of the requirements and guidance in FRS 102 (or another FRS) dealing with similar or related issues. Therefore, where relevant, the Implementation Guidance includes guidance on the application of certain principles of FRS 102 to insurance contracts, even though insurance contracts may not be within the scope of those sections. This is consistent with setting accounting policies in accordance with the principles of FRS 102 and FRS 103. *[FRS 103.IG.Overview (ii)]*.

2 COMPARISON BETWEEN FRS 103 AND IFRS 4

As discussed at 1 above, FRS 103 is based largely on IFRS 4. IFRS 4 provides very little guidance on accounting policies that should be used by an entity that issues insurance contracts or investment contracts with a DPF. Instead, it permits a continuation of (most) existing accounting practices under previous GAAP. Key differences between FRS 103 and IFRS 4 are detailed below.

2.1 Reporting foreign currency transactions in the functional currency

FRS 103 states that for the purposes of applying the requirements of Section 30 – *Foreign Currency Translation* – of FRS 102 an entity should treat all assets and liabilities arising from an insurance contract as monetary items. *[FRS 103.2.26]*. This means that items such as deferred acquisition costs and unearned premiums in a foreign currency will be retranslated to the entity's functional currency at prevailing rates at each reporting date.

IFRS 4 does not contain equivalent requirements and therefore deferred acquisition costs and unearned premium reserves in a foreign currency would normally be considered non-monetary items under IAS 21 – *The Effects of Changes in Foreign Exchange Rates* – and not be retranslated at the reporting date.

This means that there will be an accounting difference in respect of the retranslation of deferred acquisition costs and unearned premiums between FRS 103 and IFRS 4.

2.2 Recognition and measurement requirements for long-term insurance business

FRS 103 sets out recognition and measurement requirements for entities that are carrying out long-term insurance business. These apply unless an entity changes its accounting policies in accordance with paragraph 2.3 of FRS 103. *[FRS 103.3.1-2]*.

IFRS 4 does not set out any recognition and measurement requirements for entities that are carrying out long-term insurance business but, instead, permits an insurer to continue applying the accounting policies that it was using when it first applied IFRS 4 subject to certain exceptions. *[IFRS 4.BC83].*

2.3   Entities setting accounting policies for the first time

FRS 103 states that entities that are setting accounting policies for insurance contracts, or other financial instruments with discretionary participation features, for the first time, should for long-term insurance business either:

- first consider the requirements of Section 3 of FRS 103 – *Recognition and Measurement: Requirements for entities with long-term insurance business*, the Regulations and any relevant parts of FRS 102, as a benchmark before assessing whether to set accounting policies that differ from those benchmark policies in accordance with paragraph 2.3 of FRS 103; or

- establish accounting policies that are based on the rules under the Solvency II Directive for the recognition and measurement of technical provisions, and any relevant requirements of FRS 103, the Regulations and FRS 102. In doing so an entity should make appropriate adjustments to the Solvency II rules to ensure that the accounting policies result in information that is relevant and reliable. *[FRS 103.1.5].*

IFRS 4 contains no equivalent guidance for entities setting accounting policies in relation to long-term insurance contracts, or other financial instruments with discretionary participation features, for the first time. In practice, those entities have tended to use the accounting policies established under applicable local GAAP.

2.4   Classification of insurance contracts with discretionary participation features

FRS 103 states that an entity can only classify a discretionary participation feature (DPF) in an insurance contract as equity if permitted by the Regulations. *[FRS 103.2.30(b)].* However, the Regulations require that the fund for appropriations (FFA) is classified as a liability. In practice, therefore, there is no option to classify the DPF in UK insurance contracts as equity.

IFRS 4 permits an insurer that recognises a DPF separately from the guaranteed element to classify that feature either as a separate component of equity or as a liability. *[IFRS 4.34(b)].*

2.5   Financial instruments with discretionary participation features

Financial instruments with discretionary participation features are scoped out of Section 11 – *Basic Financial Instruments* – and Section 12 – *Other Financial Instrument Issues* – of FRS 102. However, FRS 103 requires some disclosures to be made in respect of those contracts that are set out in Section 11 of FRS 102.

Under IFRS, financial instruments with discretionary participation features are within the scope of IFRS 7 – *Financial Instruments: Disclosures*. *[IFRS 4.2(b)]*. This means that IFRS 7 requires considerably more disclosures for such contracts than FRS 103.

2.6 Equalisation and catastrophe provisions

FRS 103 allows equalisation and catastrophe provisions to be recognised as a liability but only if required by the regulatory framework that applies to the entity. *[FRS 103.2.13(a)]*.

IFRS 4 does not allow an entity to recognise as a liability any provisions for possible future claims if those claims arise under insurance contracts that are not in existence at the end of the reporting period (such as catastrophe and equalisation provisions). *[IFRS 4.14(a)]*.

Following the implementation of the Solvency II Directive, with effect from 1 January 2016, the EU regulatory framework does not permit equalisation or catastrophe provisions. Consequently this difference is unlikely to have any practical impact for UK reporting entities.

2.7 Applying IFRS 9 – *Financial Instruments* – with IFRS 4 – *Insurance Contracts*

FRS 103 does not contain the amendments to IFRS 4 issued in September 2016, *Applying IFRS 9 Financial Instruments with IFRS 4 Insurance Contracts*. These amendments permit insurers to either defer the application of IFRS 9 until accounting periods commencing during 2021 or to use an 'overlay' approach to report any additional volatility arising from adoption of IFRS 9 (compared to IAS 39 – *Financial Instruments: Recognition and Measurement*) in other comprehensive income rather than in profit or loss.

Under FRS 102, as an alternative to applying the recognition and measurement requirements of Sections 11 and 12 for financial instruments, the recognition and measurement requirements of IAS 39 or IFRS 9 are available as an accounting policy choice (see Chapter 10). In addition, as discussed at 1.2 above, the FRC have not decided whether IFRS 17 will be incorporated into UK GAAP and replace FRS 103.

2.8 Disclosure differences

Disclosures required by FRS 103 and are discussed at 11 below. These include additional disclosure requirements for with-profits business (see 11.4 below) that are not replicated in IFRS 4. In addition, insurers are required by Schedule 3 to the Regulations to make various extra disclosures in respect of insurance contracts which do not apply to IFRS reporters.

Chapter 33

3   THE OBJECTIVES, SCOPE OF AND TRANSITION TO FRS 103

3.1   The objectives of FRS 103

FRS 103 is part of a suite of accounting standards issued by the FRC that replaced almost all previously extant UK GAAP.

In developing the requirements for the future of UK GAAP, including FRS 103, the overriding objective was to enable users of accounts to receive high-quality understandable financial reporting proportionate to the size and complexity of the entity and users' information needs. *[FRS 103.BC3]*.

The FRC notes that FRS 103: *[FRS 103.BC5-9]*

- provides a financial reporting framework for entities with insurance contracts that allows them to generally continue with their existing policies whilst consolidating and modernising the relevant accounting requirements;

- is deregulatory in some areas (e.g. by permitting entities to improve their accounting policies and by including best practice guidance that allows entities some flexibility in complying with the disclosure principles);

- supplements IFRS 4 by some of the existing requirements and practice in accounting for insurance contracts in the UK and Republic of Ireland and, as a result, much of FRS 27 has been incorporated into FRS 103 or the accompanying Implementation Guidance, along with elements of the ABI SORP and company law applicable to insurance companies; and

- consolidates all relevant, existing accounting requirements and guidance applicable to entities with insurance contracts, other than company law and the requirements of the PRA handbook, which is consistent with the FRC's general approach to setting accounting standards and eliminates unnecessary duplication.

In summary, FRS 103:

- allows entities, generally, to continue with their existing accounting policies for insurance contracts including the appropriate measurement of long-term insurance business, whilst permitting limited improvements to accounting by insurers; and

- requires disclosure that:

  - identifies and explains the amounts in an insurer's financial statements arising from the insurance contracts (including reinsurance contracts) it issues and reinsurance contracts that it holds;

  - relates to the financial strength of entities carrying on long-term insurance business; and

  - helps users of those financial statements understand the amount, timing and uncertainty of future cash flows from those insurance contracts.

3.2   The scope of IFRS 103

3.2.1   *Key definitions*

The following key definitions are relevant to the application of FRS 103. *[FRS 103 Appendix I].*

Term	Definition
Cedant	The policyholder under a reinsurance contract.

Discretionary participation feature (DPF)	A contractual right to receive, as a supplement to guaranteed benefits, additional benefits:
	 (a) that are likely to be a significant portion of the total contractual benefits;
	 (b) whose amount or timing is contractually at the discretion of the issuer; and
	 (c) that are contractually based on:
	     (i) the performance of a specified pool of contracts or a specified type of contract;
	     (ii) realised and/or unrealised investment returns on a specified pool of assets held by the issuer; or
	     (iii) the profit or loss of the company, fund or other entity that issues the contract.

Financial guarantee contract	A contract that requires the issuer to make specified payments to reimburse the holder for a loss it incurs because a specified debtor fails to make payment when due in accordance with the original or modified terms of a debt instrument.
Guaranteed benefits	Payments or other benefits to which a particular policyholder or investor has an unconditional right that is not subject to the contractual discretion of the issuer.
Insurance contract	A contract under which one party (the insurer) accepts significant insurance risk from another party (the policyholder) by agreeing to compensate the policyholder if a specified uncertain future event (the insured event) adversely affects the policyholder
Insurance liability	An insurer's net contractual obligations under an insurance contract.
Insurance risk	Risk, other than financial risk, transferred from the holder of a contract to an issuer.
Insured event	An uncertain future event that is covered by an insurance contract and creates insurance risk.
Insurer	The party that has an obligation under an insurance contract to compensate a policyholder if an insured event occurs.

Chapter 33

Term	*Definition*
Policyholder	A party that has a right to compensation under an insurance contract if an insured event occurs.
Reinsurance asset	A cedant's net contractual rights under a reinsurance contract.
Reinsurance contract	An insurance contract issued by one insurer (the reinsurer) to compensate another insurer (the cedant) for losses on one or more contracts issued by the cedant. Retrocession is the reinsurance outwards of risks previously accepted by an insurer as reinsurance inwards. The recipient is known as the retrocessionaire.
Reinsurer	The party that has an obligation under a reinsurance contract to compensate a cedant if an insured event occurs.

3.2.2   Transactions within the scope of FRS 103

FRS 103 applies to financial statements prepared by an entity that applies FRS 102 and that are intended to give a true and fair view of a reporting entity's financial position and profit or loss (or income and expenditure) for a period. *[FRS 103.1.1]*.

Unless specifically excluded from its scope (see 3.2.3 below) an entity that applies FRS 102 should apply FRS 103 to: *[FRS 103.1.2]*

- insurance contracts (including reinsurance contracts) that it issues and reinsurance contracts that it holds; and

- financial instruments (other than insurance contracts) that it issues with a discretionary participation feature (see 7.2 below).

FRS 103 applies to entities with insurance contracts and financial instruments with a discretionary participation feature (DPF) within its scope as follows: *[FRS 103.1.3]*

- the sections on Scope, Accounting Policies, Recognition and Measurement, Disclosure and Transition apply to all entities;

- the sections on Recognition and Measurement: Requirements for entities with long-term insurance business and Disclosure: Additional requirements for with-profits business apply only to entities with long-term insurance business; and

- Appendix II: Definition of an insurance contract applies to all entities.

It can be seen from this that FRS 103 applies to insurance contracts and not just to entities that specialise in issuing insurance contracts. It is a transaction-based standard. Consequently, non-insurance entities will be within its scope if they issue contracts that meet the definition of an insurance contract.

FRS 103 describes any entity that issues an insurance contract as an insurer whether or not the entity is regarded as an insurer for legal or supervisory purposes. *[FRS 103.1.9]*.

Section 11 and Section 12 of FRS 102 contain scope exemptions for insurance and reinsurance contracts issued by an entity and for reinsurance contracts held by an entity and for financial instruments issued by an entity with a discretionary participation feature (DPF) (see Section 7 below). *[FRS 102.11.7(f)-(g), 12.3(d), (j)]*. Financial instruments that do not meet the definition of an insurance contract and do not contain a DPF are within the scope of either Section 11 or Section 12 of FRS 102. This will be the case even if they have the legal form of an insurance contract. *[FRS 103.1.8]*. These contracts are commonly referred to as 'investment contracts'.

The following table illustrates the standards applying.

Type of contract	Recognition and Measurement	Disclosure
Insurance contract issued (both with and without a DPF)	FRS 103	FRS 103
Reinsurance contract held and issued	FRS 103	FRS 103
Investment contract with a DPF	FRS 103	FRS 103
Investment contract without a DPF	Section 11 or Section 12 of FRS 102	Section 11 or Section 12 of FRS 102

A reinsurance contract is a type of insurance contract and therefore all references in FRS 103 to insurance contracts apply equally to reinsurance contracts. *[FRS 103.1.10]*.

Because insurance contracts and investment contracts with a DPF are scoped out of Sections 11 and 12 of FRS 102, FRS 103 applies to all the assets and liabilities arising from such contracts. These include:

- insurance and reinsurance receivables owed by the policyholder direct to the insurer;
- insurance receivables owed by an intermediary to an insurer on behalf of the policyholder where the intermediary is acting in a fiduciary capacity;
- insurance claims agreed with the policyholder and payable;
- insurance contract policy liabilities;
- claims handling cost provisions;
- the present value of acquired in-force business (discussed at 10.1 below);
- deferred or unearned premium reserves;
- reinsurance assets (i.e. expected reinsurance recoveries in respect of claims incurred);
- deferred acquisition costs; and
- liabilities related to discretionary participation features (DPF).

Receivables due from intermediaries to insurers that have a financing character and balances due from intermediaries not acting in a fiduciary capacity, for example loans to intermediaries repayable from commissions earned, are outside the scope of FRS 103 as they do not arise from insurance contracts.

3.2.3 Transactions not within the scope of FRS 103

FRS 103 applies only to accounting for insurance contracts and financial instruments with a DPF. The recognition, measurement and disclosure requirements for all other assets held and liabilities assumed by an insurer are contained in FRS 102. In particular, the recognition, measurement and disclosure requirements for financial assets held and financial liabilities assumed are contained in Sections 11, 12 and Section 34 – *Specialised Activities* – of FRS 102. *[FRS 103.1.6]*.

FRS 103 describes transactions to which FRS 103 is not applied. These primarily relate to transactions covered by sections of FRS 102 that could potentially meet the definition of an insurance contract. These transactions are discussed below.

3.2.3.A   Product warranties

Product warranties issued directly by a manufacturer, dealer or retailer are outside the scope of FRS 103. These are accounted for under Section 21 – *Provisions and Contingencies* – and Section 23 – *Revenue* – of FRS 102. *[FRS 103.1.7(a)]*. Without this exemption many product warranties would have been covered by FRS 103 as they would normally meet the definition of an insurance contract.

However, a product warranty is within the scope of FRS 103 if an entity issues it on behalf of another party i.e. the contract is issued indirectly.

Other types of warranty are not specifically excluded from the scope of FRS 103. For example, a warranty given by a vendor to the purchaser of a business, such as in respect of contingent liabilities related to unagreed tax computations of the acquired entity, is an example of a transaction that may also fall within the scope of this standard. However, since FRS 103 does not prescribe a specific accounting treatment, issuers of such warranties are likely to be able to apply their existing accounting policies although they would be subject to FRS 103's disclosure requirements.

3.2.3.B   Assets and liabilities arising from employment benefit plans

Employers' assets and liabilities under employee benefit plans and retirement benefit obligations reported by defined benefit retirement plans are excluded from the scope of FRS 103. These are accounted for under Section 26 – *Share-based Payment*, Section 28 – *Employee Benefits*, and Section 34 of FRS 102. *[FRS 103.1.7(b)]*.

Many defined benefit pension plans and similar post-employment benefits meet the definition of an insurance contract because the payments to pensioners are contingent on uncertain future events such as the continuing survival of current or retired employees. Without this exception they would have been within the scope of FRS 103.

3.2.3.C   Contingent rights and obligations related to non-financial items

Contractual rights or contractual obligations that are contingent on the future use of, or right to use, a non-financial item (for example, some licence fees, royalties, contingent lease payments and similar items) are excluded from the scope of FRS 103, as well as a lessee's residual value guarantee embedded in a finance lease. These are accounted for under Section 18 – *Intangible Assets other than Goodwill*, Section 20 – *Leases* – and Section 23 of FRS 102. *[FRS 103.1.7(c)]*.

3.2.3.D   Financial guarantee contracts

Financial guarantee contracts are excluded from the scope of FRS 103 unless the issuer has previously asserted explicitly that it regards such contracts as insurance contracts and has used accounting applicable to insurance contracts, in which case the issuer may elect to apply either Section 21 of FRS 102 or FRS 103 to them. The issuer may make that election contract by contract, but the election for each contract is irrevocable. *[FRS 103.1.7(d)]*.

When an insurer elects to use FRS 103 to account for its financial guarantee contracts, its accounting policy defaults to its previous GAAP for such contracts (subject to any limitations discussed at 9 below) unless subsequently modified as permitted by FRS 103 (see 9 below).

FRS 103 does not elaborate on the phrase 'previously asserted explicitly'. However, under the FRS 102 hierarchy in Section 10 – *Accounting Policies, Estimates and Errors*, insurers could look to the guidance in IAS 39 or IFRS 9 which states that assertions that an issuer regards contracts as insurance contracts are typically found throughout the issuer's communications with customers and regulators, contracts, business documentation and financial statements. Furthermore, insurance contracts are often subject to accounting requirements that are distinct from the requirements for other types of transaction, such as contracts issued by banks or commercial companies. In such cases, an issuer's financial statements typically include a statement that the issuer has used those accounting requirements. *[IAS 39.AG4A, IFRS 9 Appendix B.2.6.]*. Therefore, it is likely that insurers that have previously issued financial guarantee contracts and accounted for them under an insurance accounting and regulatory framework will meet these criteria. It is unlikely that an entity not subject to an insurance accounting and regulatory framework, or existing insurers that had not previously issued financial guarantee contracts would meet these criteria because they would not have previously made the necessary assertions.

3.2.3.E Contingent consideration payable or receivable in a business combination

Contingent consideration payable or receivable in a business combination is outside the scope of FRS 103. This is accounted for under Section 19 – *Business Combinations and Goodwill* – of FRS 102 – see Chapter 17 at 3.6 *[FRS 103.1.7(e)]*.

3.2.3.F Direct insurance contracts in which the entity is the policyholder

Accounting by policyholders of direct insurance contracts (i.e. those that are not reinsurance contracts) is excluded from the scope of FRS 103. However, holders of reinsurance contracts (cedants) are required to apply FRS 103. *[FRS 103.1.7(f)]*.

FRS 102 does contain some guidance on accounting for rights under insurance contracts held. In particular, Section 21 of FRS 102 addresses accounting for reimbursements from insurers of expenditure required to settle a provision and permits recognition of the reimbursement as a separate asset only when it is virtually certain that the entity will receive the reimbursement on settlement of the obligation. *[FRS 102.21.9]*. In addition, Section 17 – *Property, Plant and Equipment* – of FRS 102 addresses accounting for compensation from third parties for items of property, plant and equipment that are impaired, lost or given up and states that such compensation should be included in profit or loss only when the compensation is virtually certain. *[FRS 102.17.25]*. However, for all other aspects of accounting for insurance contracts held, a policyholder should develop its accounting policies applying Section 10 of FRS 102 which sets out a hierarchy of guidance to use (see Chapter 9 at 3.2).

Chapter 33

3.2.4   The product classification process

Insurers need to determine which transactions should be within the scope of FRS 103 and which transactions are not within its scope. Therefore, one of the main procedures required of insurers, when applying FRS 103 for the first time, is to conduct a product classification review.

The assessment of the appropriate classification for a contract will include an assessment of whether the contract contains significant insurance risk (discussed at 4 below), and whether the contract contains embedded derivatives (discussed at 5 below), deposit components (discussed at 6 below) or discretionary participation features (discussed at 7 below).

The diagram below illustrates a product classification decision tree.

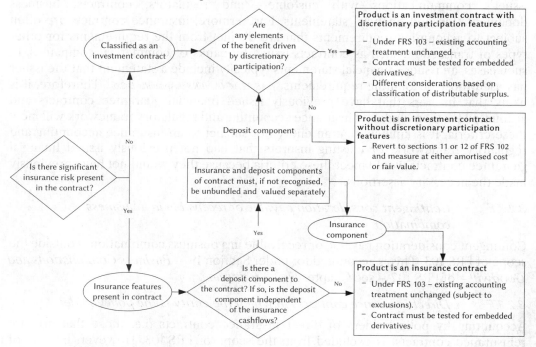

3.3   Transition to FRS 103

Section 35 – *Transition to this FRS* – of FRS 102 also applies to a first-time adopter of FRS 103. *[FRS 103.6.2]*. See Chapter 32.

FRS 103 contains no exemption or transitional relief from the basic requirement of Section 35 of FRS 102 that transition is applied retrospectively.

However, in applying paragraph 4.8(b)(iii) of FRS 103, an entity need not disclose information about claims development (see 11.3.5 below) that occurred earlier than five years before the end of the first financial year in which it applies the standard. Furthermore, if it is impracticable, when an entity first applies FRS 103, to prepare information about claims development that occurred before the beginning of the earliest period for which an entity presents full comparative information that complies with FRS 103, the entity should disclose that fact. *[FRS 103.6.3]*.

FRS 103 specifically permits an insurer to change its accounting policies for insurance contracts on adoption of FRS 103. *[FRS 103.2.3]*. Such a change should be applied retrospectively and the change must satisfy the criteria of FRS 103 for accounting policy changes (see 9 below). In addition, FRS 103 observes that one basis for changing accounting policies might be to enable them to be more consistent with the rules under the Solvency II Directive for the recognition and measurement of technical provisions. In doing so, an entity should make appropriate adjustments to the Solvency II rules to meet the requirements of paragraph 2.3. *[FRS 103.2.3A]*. If an insurer changes its accounting policies for insurance liabilities, it is permitted, but not required, to reclassify some or all of its financial assets as a financial asset at fair value through profit or loss provided those assets meet the criteria in paragraph 11.14(b) of FRS 102 (or if the entity has made the accounting policy choice under paragraphs 11.2(b) or (c) or paragraphs 12.2(b) or (c) of FRS 102 to apply the recognition and measurement provisions of either IAS 39 or IFRS 9, the relevant requirements of IAS 39 or IFRS 9, as applicable) at that date. This reclassification is permitted if an insurer changes accounting policies when it first applies FRS 103 and if it makes a subsequent policy change permitted by paragraph 2.3. The reclassification is a change in accounting policy and Section 10 of FRS 102 applies. *[FRS 103.6.4]*.

3.4 Setting accounting policies for insurance contracts for the first time

An entity may need to set accounting policies for insurance contracts or other financial instruments with a DPF for the first time when applying FRS 103. This could arise, for example, when the entity is a start-up insurer or when the entity has issued contracts that meet FRS 103's definition of an insurance contract (see 4 below) but has not previously been required to apply insurance contract accounting to those contracts (e.g. because the contracts are not regulated as insurance contracts).

Entities that are setting accounting policies for insurance contracts, or other financial instruments with discretionary participation features, for the first time, should for long-term insurance business either: *[FRS 103.1.5]*

- first consider the requirements of Section 3 of FRS 103, the Regulations and any relevant parts of FRS 102, as a benchmark before assessing whether to set accounting policies that differ from those benchmark policies in accordance with paragraph 2.3 of FRS 103; or

- establish accounting policies that are based on the rules under the Solvency II Directive for the recognition and measurement of technical provisions, and any relevant requirements of FRS 103, the Regulations and FRS 102. In doing so an entity should make appropriate adjustments to the Solvency II rules to ensure that the accounting policies result in information that is relevant and reliable This is consistent with the requirements of the Regulations for the computation of the long-term business provision to have due regard to the actuarial principles of Solvency II (see 8.4.4 below).

Entities setting accounting policies for general insurance business for the first time appear to be excluded from this guidance although these entities could still follow this guidance in the absence of any other requirements.

4   THE DEFINITION OF AN INSURANCE CONTRACT

4.1   The definition

The definition of an insurance contract in FRS 103 is:

'A contract under which one party (the insurer) accepts significant insurance risk from another party (the policyholder) by agreeing to compensate the policyholder if a specified uncertain future event (the insured event) adversely affects the policyholder'. *[FRS 103 Appendix I].*

This definition determines which contracts are within the scope of FRS 103 rather than within the scope of FRS 102.

Contracts which have the legal form of insurance contracts are not necessarily insurance contracts under FRS 103. Conversely, contracts which may not legally be insurance contracts can be insurance contracts under FRS 103.

The rest of this section discusses the definition of an insurance contract in more detail and addresses the following issues:

- the term 'uncertain future event' (see 4.2 below);
- payments in kind (see 4.3 below);
- the distinction between insurance risk and other risks (see 4.4 below);
- examples of insurance contracts (see 4.5 below);
- significant insurance risk (see 4.6 below); and
- changes in the level of insurance risk (see 4.7 below).

4.2   Uncertain future event

Uncertainty (or risk) is the essence of an insurance contract. Accordingly, FRS 103 requires at least one of the following to be uncertain at the inception of an insurance contract:

(a)   whether an insured event will occur;

(b)   when it will occur; or

(c)   how much the insurer will need to pay if it occurs. *[FRS 103 Appendix II.2].*

In some insurance contracts, the insured event is the discovery of a loss during the term of the contract, even if the loss arises from an event that occurred before the inception of the contract. In other insurance contracts, the insured event is an event that occurs during the term of the contract, even if the resulting loss is discovered after the end of the contract term. *[FRS 103 Appendix II.3].*

Some insurance contracts cover events that have already occurred but whose financial effect is still uncertain (i.e. retroactive contracts). An example is a reinsurance contract that covers a direct policyholder against adverse development of claims already reported by policyholders. In such contracts, the insured event is the discovery of the ultimate cost of those claims. *[FRS 103 Appendix II.4].*

4.3 Payments in kind

Insurance contracts that require or permit payments to be made in kind are treated the same way as contracts where payment is made directly to the policyholder. For example, some insurers replace a stolen article directly rather than compensating the policyholder. Others use their own employees, such as medical staff, to provide services covered by the contract. *[FRS 103 Appendix II.5]*.

4.3.1 Service contracts

Some fixed-fee service contracts in which the level of service depends on an uncertain event may meet the definition of an insurance contract. However, in the UK, these are not regulated as insurance contracts. For example, a service provider could enter into a maintenance contract in which it agrees to repair specified equipment after a malfunction. The fixed service fee is based on the expected number of malfunctions but it is uncertain whether a particular machine will break down. The malfunction of the equipment adversely affects the owner and the contract compensates the owner (in kind, rather than cash). Similarly, a contract for car breakdown services in which the provider agrees, for a fixed annual fee, to provide roadside assistance or tow the car to a nearby garage could meet the definition of an insurance contract even if the provider does not agree to carry out repairs or replace parts. *[FRS 103 Appendix II.6]*.

In respect of the type of service contracts described above, their inclusion seems an unintended consequence of the definition of an insurance contract. However, the FRC considers that applying FRS 103 to these contracts should be no more burdensome than applying other FRS 102 if such contracts were outside the scope of FRS 103 since:

(a) there are unlikely to be material liabilities for malfunctions and breakdowns that have already occurred;

(b) if the service provider applied accounting policies consistent with Section 23 of FRS 102, this would be acceptable either as an existing accounting policy or, possibly, an improvement of existing policies unless they involve practices prohibited by paragraph 2.3 of FRS 103 (see 9 below); and

(c) if FRS 103 did not apply to the contracts, the service provider would apply Section 21 of FRS 102 to determine whether its contracts were onerous. *[FRS 103 Appendix II.7]*.

4.4 The distinction between insurance risk and financial risk

The definition of an insurance contract refers to 'insurance risk' which is defined as 'risk, other than financial risk, transferred from the holder of a contract to the issuer'. *[FRS 103 Appendix I]*.

A contract that exposes the reporting entity to financial risk without significant insurance risk is not an insurance contract. *[FRS 103 Appendix II.8]*. 'Financial risk' is defined as 'the risk of a possible future change in one or more of a specified interest rate, financial instrument price, foreign exchange rate, index of prices or rates, credit rating or credit index or other variable, provided in the case of a non-financial variable that variable is not specific to a party to the contract'. *[FRS 103 Appendix I]*.

Chapter 33

An example of a non-financial variable that is not specific to a party to the contract is an index of earthquake losses in a particular region or an index of temperature in a particular city. An example of a non-financial variable that is specific to a party to the contract is the occurrence or non-occurrence of a fire that damages or destroys an asset of that party.

The risk of changes in the fair value of a non-financial asset is not a financial risk if the fair value reflects not only changes in the market prices for such assets (a financial variable) but also the condition of a specific non-financial asset held by a party to the contract (a non-financial variable). For example if a guarantee of the residual value of a specific car exposes the guarantor to the risk of changes in that car's condition, that risk is insurance risk. *[FRS 103 Appendix II.9]*. This is illustrated by the following example based on an example in IFRS 4.

Example 33.1:   *Residual value insurance*

Entity A issues a contract to Entity B that provides a guarantee of the fair value at the future date of an aircraft (a non-financial asset) held by B. A is not the lessee of the aircraft (residual value guarantees given by a lessee under a finance lease are within the scope of Section 20 of FRS 102).

This is an insurance contract (unless changes in the condition of the asset have an insignificant effect on its value). The risk of changes in the fair value of the aircraft is not a financial risk because the fair value reflects not only changes in market prices for similar aircraft but also the condition of the specific asset held.

However, if the contract compensated B only for changes in market prices and not for changes in the condition of B's asset, the contract would be a derivative and within the scope of Section 12 of FRS 102.

Some contracts expose the issuer to financial risk in addition to significant insurance risk. For example, many life insurance contracts both guarantee a minimum rate of return to policyholders (creating financial risk) and promise death benefits that at some times significantly exceed the policyholder's account balance (creating insurance risk in the form of mortality risk). Such contracts are insurance contracts. *[FRS 103 Appendix II.10]*.

Contracts where an insured event triggers the payment of an amount linked to a price index are insurance contracts provided the payment that is contingent on the insured event is significant. An example would be a life contingent annuity linked to a cost of living index. Such a contract transfers insurance risk because payment is triggered by an uncertain future event, the survival of the annuitant. The link to the price index is an embedded derivative but it also transfers insurance risk. If the insurance risk transferred is significant the embedded derivative meets the definition of an insurance contract (see 5 below for a discussion of derivatives embedded within insurance contracts. *[FRS 103 Appendix II.11]*.

The definition of insurance risk refers to a risk that the insurer accepts from the policyholder. In other words, insurance risk is a pre-existing risk transferred from the policyholder to the insurer. Thus, a new risk created by the contract is not insurance risk. *[FRS 103 Appendix II.12]*. Examples of new risks created by an insurance contract that are not insurance risk include:

- the loss of the ability to charge the policyholder for future investment management fees, for example if the ability to collect fees ceases if the policyholder of an investment-linked life insurance contract dies (this loss does not reflect insurance risk);

- the waiver on death of charges that would be made on cancellation or surrender of the contract (because the contract brought these charges into existence and therefore they do not compensate the policyholder for a pre-existing risk);

- a payment conditional on an event that does not cause a significant loss to the holder of the contract;

- possible reinsurance recoveries (accounted for separately); and

- the original policy premium (but not additional premiums payable in the event of claims experience).

For a contract to be an insurance contract the insured event must have an adverse effect on the policyholder. *[FRS 103 Appendix II.13]*. In other words, there must be an insurable interest. Without the notion of insurable interest the definition of an insurance contract would have encompassed gambling.

The adverse effect on the policyholder is not limited to an amount equal to the financial impact of the adverse event. So, the definition includes 'new for old' coverage that replaces a damaged or lost asset with a new asset. Similarly, the definition does not limit payment under a term life insurance contract to the financial loss suffered by a deceased's dependents nor does it preclude the payment of predetermined amounts to quantify the loss caused by a death or accident. *[FRS 103 Appendix II.13]*.

A contract that requires a payment if a specified uncertain event occurs which does not require an adverse effect on the policyholder as a precondition for payment is not an insurance contract. Such contracts are not insurance contracts even if the holder uses the contract to mitigate an underlying risk exposure. For example, if the holder uses a derivative to hedge an underlying non-financial variable that is correlated with the cash flows from an asset of the entity, the derivative is not an insurance contract because payment is not conditional on whether the holder is adversely affected by a reduction in the cash flows of the asset. Conversely, the definition of an insurance contract refers to an uncertain event for which an adverse effect on the policyholder is a contractual precondition for payment. This contractual precondition does not require the insurer to investigate whether the uncertain event actually caused an adverse effect, but permits the insurer to deny payment if it is not satisfied that the event caused an adverse effect. *[FRS 103 Appendix II.14]*.

The following example, based on an example in IFRS 4, illustrates the concept of insurable interest.

Example 33.2:   Reinsurance contract with 'original loss warranty' clause

Entity A agrees to provide reinsurance cover to airline insurer B for £5m against losses suffered. The claims are subject to an original loss warranty of £50m meaning that only losses suffered by B up to £5m from events exceeding a cost of £50m in total can be recovered under the contract. This is an insurance contract as B can only recover its own losses arising from those events.

If the contract allowed B to claim up to £5m every time there was an event with a cost exceeding £50m regardless of whether B had suffered a loss from that event then this would not be an insurance contract because there would be no insurable interest in this arrangement.

Chapter 33

4.4.1 Lapse, persistency and expense risk

Lapse or persistency risk (the risk that the policyholder will cancel the contract earlier or later than the issuer had expected in pricing the contract) is not insurance risk because, although this can have an adverse effect on the issuer, the cancellation is not contingent on an uncertain future event that adversely affects the policyholder. *[FRS 103 Appendix II.15]*.

Similarly, expense risk (the risk of unexpected increases in the administrative costs incurred by the issuer associated with the serving of a contract, rather than the costs associated with insured events) is not insurance risk because an unexpected increase in expenses does not adversely affect the policyholder. *[FRS 103 Appendix II.15]*.

Therefore, a contract that exposes the issuer to lapse risk, persistency risk or expense risk is not an insurance contract unless it also exposes the issuer to significant insurance risk. *[FRS 103 Appendix II.16]*.

4.4.2 Insurance of non-insurance risks

If the issuer of a contract which does not contain significant insurance risk mitigates the risk of that contract by using a second contract to transfer part of that first contract's risk to another party, this second contract exposes that other party to insurance risk. This is because the policyholder of the second contract (the issuer of the first contract) is subject to an uncertain event that adversely affects it and thus it meets the definition of an insurance contract. *[FRS 103 Appendix II.16]*. This is illustrated by the following example, based on an example in IFRS 4.

Example 33.3: Insurance of non-insurance risks

Entity A agrees to compensate Entity B for losses on a series of contracts issued by B that do not transfer significant insurance risk. These could be investment contracts or, for example, a contract to provide services.

The contract is an insurance contract if it transfers significant insurance risk from B to A, even if some or all of the underlying individual contracts do not transfer significant insurance risk to B. The contract is a reinsurance contract if any of the contracts issued by B are insurance contracts. Otherwise, the contract is a direct insurance contract.

4.4.3 Self insurance, pooling of insurance risk by insurance mutuals, and intragroup insurance contracts

An insurer can accept significant insurance risk from a policyholder only if the insurer is an entity separate from the policyholder. *[FRS 103 Appendix II.17]*.

Therefore, 'self insurance', such as a self-insured deductible where the insured cannot claim for losses below the excess limit of an insurance policy, is not insurance risk because there is no insurance contract. Accounting for self insurance and related provisions is covered by Section 21 of FRS 102 which requires that a provision is recognised only if there is a present obligation as a result of a past event, it is probable that an outflow of resources will occur and a reliable estimate can be determined. *[FRS 102.21.4]*.

A mutual insurer (as defined in the PRA Rulebook) accepts risk from each policyholder and pools that risk. Although policyholders bear the pooled risk collectively in their capacity as owners, the mutual has still accepted the risk that is the essence of an insurance contract and therefore FRS 103 applies to those contracts. *[FRS 103 Appendix II.17]*.

When there are insurance contracts between entities in the same group these would be eliminated in the consolidated financial statements as required by Section 9 – *Consolidated and Separate Financial Statements* – of FRS 102. *[FRS 102.9.15]*. If any intragroup insurance contract is reinsured with a third party that is not part of the group, this third party reinsurance contract should be accounted for as a direct insurance contract in the consolidated financial statements of a non-insurer because the intragroup contract will be eliminated on consolidation. This residual direct insurance contract (i.e. the policy with the third party) is outside the scope of FRS 103 from the viewpoint of the consolidated financial statements of a non-insurer because policyholder accounting is excluded from the standard as discussed at 3.2.3.F above.

4.5 Examples of insurance and non-insurance contracts

FRS 103 provides various examples of insurance and non-insurance contracts.

4.5.1 Examples of insurance contracts

The following are examples of contracts that are insurance contracts, if the transfer of insurance risk is significant: *[FRS 103 Appendix II.18]*

(a) insurance against theft or damage to property;

(b) insurance against product liability, professional liability, civil liability or legal expenses;

(c) life insurance and prepaid funeral plans (although death is certain, it is uncertain when death will occur or, for some types of life insurance, whether death will occur within the period covered by the insurance);

(d) life-contingent annuities and pensions (contracts that provide compensation for the uncertain future event – the survival of the annuitant or pensioner – to assist the annuitant or pensioner in maintaining a given standard of living, which would otherwise be adversely affected by his or her survival);

(e) disability and medical cover;

(f) surety bonds, fidelity bonds, performance bonds and bid bonds (i.e. contracts that provide compensation if another party fails to perform a contractual obligation, for example an obligation to construct a building);

(g) credit insurance that provides for specified payments to be made to reimburse the holder for a loss it incurs because a specified debtor fails to make payment when due under the original or modified terms of a debt instrument. These contracts could have various legal forms, such as that of a guarantee, some types of letter of credit, a credit derivative default contract or an insurance contract. Although these contracts meet the definition of an insurance contract they also meet the definition of a financial guarantee contract and are within the scope of Section 21 of FRS 102 and not FRS 103 unless the issuer has previously asserted explicitly that it regards such contracts as insurance contracts and has used accounting applicable to such contracts (see 3.2.3.D above);

(h) product warranties issued by another party for goods sold by a manufacturer, dealer or retailer are within the scope of FRS 103. However, as discussed at 3.2.3.A above, product warranties issued directly by a manufacturer, dealer or retailer are outside the scope of FRS 103;

(i)   title insurance (insurance against the discovery of defects in title to land that were not apparent when the contract was written). In this case, the insured event is the discovery of a defect in the title, not the title itself;

(j)   travel assistance (compensation in cash or in kind to policyholders for losses suffered while they are travelling);

(k)   catastrophe bonds that provide for reduced payments of principal, interest or both if a specified event adversely affects the issuer of the bond (unless the specified event does not create significant insurance risk, for example if the event is a change in an interest rate or a foreign exchange rate);

(l)   insurance swaps and other contracts that require a payment based on changes in climatic, geological and other physical variables that are specific to a party to the contract; and

(m)   reinsurance contracts.

These examples are not intended to be an exhaustive list.

IFRS 4 contains various illustrative examples that provide further guidance on situations which may be useful to entities applying FRS 103.

4.5.2   *Examples of transactions that are not insurance contracts*

The following are examples of transactions that are not insurance contracts: *[FRS 103 Appendix II.19]*

(a)   investment contracts that have the legal form of an insurance contract but do not expose the insurer to significant insurance risk, for example life insurance contracts in which the insurer bears no significant mortality risk;

(b)   contracts that have the legal form of insurance, but pass all significant risk back to the policyholder through non-cancellable and enforceable mechanisms that adjust future payments by the policyholder as a direct result of insured losses, for example some financial reinsurance contracts or some group contracts;

(c)   self insurance, in other words retaining a risk that could have been covered by insurance. There is no insurance contract because there is no agreement with another party (see 4.4.3 above);

(d)   contracts (such as gambling contracts) that require a payment if an unspecified uncertain future event occurs, but do not require, as a contractual precondition for payment, that the event adversely affects the policyholder. However, this does not preclude the specification of a predetermined payout to quantify the loss caused by a specified event such as a death or an accident (see 4.4 above);

(e)   derivatives that expose one party to financial risk but not insurance risk, because they require that party to make payment based solely on changes in one or more of a specified interest rate, financial instrument price, commodity price, foreign exchange rate, index of prices or rates, credit rating or credit index or other variable, provide in the case of a non-financial variable that the variable is not specific to a party to the contract;

(f)   a credit-related guarantee (or letter of credit, credit derivative default contract or credit insurance contract) that requires payments even if the holder has not incurred a loss on the failure of a debtor to make payments when due;

(g)   contracts that require a payment based on a climatic, geological or other physical variable that is not specific to a party to the contract. These are commonly described as weather derivatives and are accounted for under Sections 11 and 12 of FRS 102; and

(h)   catastrophe bonds that provide for reduced payments of principal, interest or both, based on a climatic, geological or other physical variable that is not specific to a party to the contract.

IFRS 4 contains various illustrative examples that provide further guidance on situations which may be useful to entities applying FRS 103.

If the contracts described at (a) to (h) above create financial assets or financial liabilities they are within the scope of Sections 11 and 12 of FRS 102. Among other things, this means that the parties to the contract use what is sometimes called deposit accounting, which involves the following:

- one party recognises the consideration received as a financial liability, rather than as revenue; and

- the other party recognises the consideration as a financial asset, rather than as an expense. *[FRS 103 Appendix II.20].*

If the contracts described at (a) to (h) above do not create financial assets or financial liabilities, Section 23 of FRS 102 applies. Under Section 23 of FRS 102, revenue associated with a transaction involving the rendering of services is recognised by reference to the stage of completion of the transaction if the outcome of the transaction can be estimated reliably. *[FRS 103 Appendix II.21].*

FRS 103 refers to Examples 15, 17 and 17A in the appendix to Section 23 of FRS 102 as being relevant to the recognition of revenue for the types of contract described at (a) to (h). *[FRS 103 Appendix II.22].*

Where the consideration for a contract meeting the definition of an investment contract comprises both a fee for the origination and an ongoing charge for the provision of (e.g. investment management) services, the insurance undertaking should record the origination fee as revenue on the date on which it becomes entitled to it where it can be demonstrated that the undertaking has no further obligations in respect of the fee. *[FRS 103 Appendix II.23].*

Incremental costs that are directly attributable to securing an investment management contract are recognised as an asset if they can be identified separately and measured reliably and if it is probable that they will be recovered. The asset represents the entity's contractual right to benefit from providing investment management services and is amortised as the entity recognises the related revenue. If the entity has a portfolio of investment management contracts, it may assess their recoverability on a portfolio basis. *[FRS 103 Appendix II.24].*

4.6   Significant insurance risk

A contract is an insurance contract only if it transfers 'significant insurance risk'. *[FRS 103 Appendix II.25].*

Insurance risk is 'significant' if, and only if, an insured event could cause an insurer to pay significant additional benefits in any scenario, excluding scenarios that lack commercial substance (i.e. have no discernible effect on the economics of the transaction). *[FRS 103 Appendix II.26].*

If significant additional benefits would be payable in scenarios that have commercial substance, this condition may be met even if the insured event is extremely unlikely or even if the expected (i.e. probability-weighted) present value of contingent cash flows is a small proportion of the expected present value of all the remaining contractual cash flows. *[FRS 103 Appendix II.26].* From this, we consider the intention was to make it easier, not harder, for contracts regarded as insurance contracts under previous GAAP to be insurance contracts under FRS 103.

FRS 103 does not prohibit insurance contract accounting if there are restrictions on the timing of payments or receipts, provided there is significant insurance risk, although clearly the existence of restrictions on the timing of payments may mean that the policy does not transfer significant insurance risk.

4.6.1   The meaning of 'significant'

No quantitative guidance supports the determination of 'significant' in FRS 103. This is consistent with IFRS 4. The absence of qualitative guidance was a deliberate decision made by the IASB when drafting IFRS 4 because the IASB considered that if quantitative guidance was provided it would create an arbitrary dividing line that would result in different accounting treatments for similar transactions that fall marginally on different sides of that line and would therefore create opportunities for accounting arbitrage. *[IFRS 4.BC33].*

IFRS 4 contains an example in the Implementation Guidance which states that 'significant' means that the insured benefits certainly must be greater than 101% of the benefits payable if the insured event did not occur. *[IFRS 4.IG2 E1.3].* It is, however, unclear how much greater than 101% the insured benefits must be to meet the IFRS 4 definition of 'significant'.

This practical impact of this lack of guidance is that insurers have to apply their own criteria to what constitutes significant insurance risk and there probably is inconsistency in practice as to what these dividing lines are, at least at the margins.

There is no specific requirement under FRS 103 for insurers to disclose any thresholds used in determining whether a contract has transferred significant insurance risk. However, Section 8 – *Notes to the Financial Statements* – of FRS 102 requires an entity to disclose the judgements that management has made in the process of applying the entity's accounting policies that have the most significant effect on the amounts recognised in the financial statements. *[FRS 102.8.6].*

4.6.2   The level at which significant insurance risk is assessed

Significant insurance risk must be assessed by individual contract, rather than by blocks of contracts or by reference to materiality to the financial statements. Thus, insurance risk may be significant even if there is a minimal probability of material losses for a whole book of contracts. The purpose of this is to make it easier to classify a contract as an insurance contract. *[FRS 103 Appendix II.28]*.

However, if a relatively homogeneous book of small contracts is known to consist of contracts that all transfer insurance risk, an insurer need not examine each contract within that book to identify a few non-derivative contracts that transfer insignificant insurance risk. *[FRS 103 Appendix II.28]*.

Multiple, mutually linked contracts entered into with a single counterparty (or contracts that are otherwise interdependent) should be considered a single contract for the purposes of assessing whether significant insurance risk is transferred. *[FRS 103 Appendix II.28fn]*. This requirement is intended to prevent entities entering into contracts that individually transfer significant insurance risk but collectively do not and accounting for part(s) of what is effectively a single arrangement as (an) insurance contract(s).

If an insurance contract is unbundled (see 6 below) into a deposit component and an insurance component, the significance of insurance risk transferred is assessed by reference only to the insurance component. The significance of insurance risk transferred by an embedded derivative is assessed by reference only to the embedded derivative (see 5 below). *[FRS 103 Appendix II.31]*.

4.6.3 Significant additional benefits

The 'significant additional benefits' mentioned in the definition of significant insurance risk described refer to amounts that exceed those that would be payable if no insured event occurred (see 4.6 above). These additional amounts include claims handling and claims assessment costs, but exclude: *[FRS 103 Appendix II.27]*

(a)   the loss of the ability to charge the policyholder for future services, for example where the ability to collect fees from a policyholder for performing future investment management services ceases if the policyholder of an investment-linked life insurance contract dies. This economic loss does not reflect insurance risk and the future investment management fees are not relevant in assessing how much insurance risk is transferred by a contract;

(b)   the waiver on death of charges that would be made on cancellation or surrender (i.e. to cease paying premiums such that the insurance contracts ceases to have effect) of the contract. The contract brought these charges into existence and therefore the waiver of them does not compensate the policyholder for a pre-existing risk. Hence, they are not relevant in determining how much insurance risk is transferred by a contract;

(c)   a payment conditional on an event that does not cause a significant loss to the holder of the contract, for example where the issuer must pay one million currency units if an asset suffers physical damage causing an insignificant economic loss of one currency unit to the holder. The holder in this case has transferred to the insurer the insignificant insurance risk of losing one currency unit. However, at the same time the contract creates non-insurance risk that the issuer will need to pay 999,999 additional currency units if the specified event occurs; and

(d)   possible reinsurance recoveries. The insurer will account for these separately.

It follows from this that if a contract pays a death benefit exceeding the amount payable on survival (excluding waivers under (b) above), the contract is an insurance contract unless the additional death benefit is insignificant (judged by reference to the contract rather than to an entire book of contracts). Similarly, an annuity contract that pays out regular sums for the rest of a policyholder's life is an insurance contract, unless the aggregate life-contingent payments are insignificant. *[FRS 103 Appendix II.29]*. In this case, the insurer could suffer a significant loss on an individual contract if the annuitant survives longer than expected.

Additional benefits could include a requirement to pay benefits earlier than expected if the insured event occurs earlier provided the payment is not adjusted for the time value of money. An example could be whole life insurance cover that provides a fixed death benefit whenever a policyholder dies. Whilst it is certain that the policyholder will die, the timing of death is uncertain and the insurer will suffer a loss on individual contracts when policyholders die early, even if there is no overall expected loss on the whole book of contracts. *[FRS 103 Appendix II.30]*.

4.7   Changes in the level of insurance risk

It is implicit within FRS 103 that an assessment of whether a contract transfers significant insurance risk should be made at the inception of a contract. Further, a contract that qualifies as an insurance contract at inception remains an insurance contract until all rights and obligations are extinguished or expire. *[FRS 103 Appendix II.33]*. This applies even if circumstances have changed such that insurance contingent rights and obligations have expired.

Conversely, contracts that do not transfer insurance risk at inception may become insurance contracts if they transfer insurance risk at a later time. For example, consider a contract that provides a specified investment return and includes an option for the policyholder to use the proceeds of the investment on maturity to buy a life-contingent annuity at the current annuity rates charged by the insurer to other new annuitants when the policyholder exercises the option. The contract transfers no insurance risk to the issuer until the option is exercised, because the insurer remains free to price the annuity on a basis that reflects the insurance risk transferred to the insurer at that time. However, if the contract specifies the annuity rates (or the basis for setting the annuity rates), the contract transfers insurance risk to the issuer at inception. *[FRS 103 Appendix II.32]*.

FRS 103 imposes no limitations on when contracts can be assessed for significant insurance risk. The recognition of contracts as insurance contracts occurs based on changing facts and circumstances, although there is no guidance on accounting for the recognition/derecognition.

4.7.1   *Reassessment of insurance risk of contracts acquired in a business combination*

Section 19 of FRS 102 is silent as to whether there should be a reassessment of the classification of contracts previously classified as insurance contracts under FRS 103 which are acquired as part of a business combination. In contrast, IFRS 3 – *Business Combinations* – states that there should be no reassessment of the classification of contracts previously classified as insurance contracts under IFRS 4 which are acquired as a part of a business combination. *[IFRS 3.17(b)]*.

In our view, as FRS 102 provides no specific guidance on this issue, an insurer could use the hierarchy in Section 10 of FRS 102 (see Chapter 9) in order to apply the guidance in IFRS 3 and not reassess the classification of insurance contracts acquired in a business combination.

5   EMBEDDED DERIVATIVES

FRS 103 requires an insurer to determine whether it has any separable embedded derivatives and, if the separable embedded derivative is not an insurance contract, the insurer must separate the embedded derivative from its host contract and account for it in accordance with Sections 11 and 12 of FRS 102 as if it were a financial instrument. *[FRS 103.2.20]*.

This also applies when an entity has made the accounting policy choice under paragraphs 11.2(b) or (c), or paragraphs 12.2(b) or (c) of FRS 102 to apply the recognition and measurement provisions of either IAS 39 or IFRS 9, and the disclosure requirements of Section 11 of FRS 102, as applicable. For an entity that is a financial institution (e.g. all insurers) the disclosure requirements of paragraphs 34.17 to 34.33 of FRS 102 also apply to any separable embedded derivatives. *[FRS 103.2.20]*.

Entities that apply FRS 103 will also apply FRS 102. Sections 11 and 12 of FRS 102 do not require entities to identify separable embedded derivatives but instead, as a simplification from IFRS, require a contract with certain non-typical features to be accounted for at fair value through profit or loss. It was considered whether a similar approach should be applied to insurance contracts, but the FRC decided that for insurance contracts more relevant information will be provided to users if separable embedded derivatives are recognised and measured separately from the host contract (unless the embedded derivative is itself an insurance contract). *[FRS 103.BC23]*.

A derivative is a financial instrument with all three of the following characteristics:

* its value changes in response to a change in a specified interest rate, financial instrument price, commodity price, foreign exchange rate, index of prices or rates, credit rating or credit index, or other variable, provided in the case of a non-financial variable that the variable is not specific to the underlying of the contract;

* it requires no initial net investment or an initial net investment that would be smaller than would be required for other types of contracts that would be expected to have a similar response to changes in market factors; and

* it is settled at a future date. *[FRS 103 Appendix I]*.

An embedded derivative is a component of a hybrid (combined) financial instrument that also includes a non-derivative host contract with the effect that some of the cash flows of the combined instrument vary in a way similar to a stand-alone derivative. *[FRS 103 Appendix I]*.

The following are examples of embedded derivatives that may be found in insurance contracts:

* benefits, such as death benefits, linked to equity prices or an equity index;

* options to take life-contingent annuities at guaranteed rates;

* guarantees of minimum interest rates in determining surrender or maturity values;

* guarantees of minimum annuity payments where the annuity payments are linked to investment returns or asset prices;

* a put option for the policyholder to surrender a contract. These can be specified in a schedule, based on the fair value of a pool of interest-bearing securities or based on an equity or commodity price index;

- an option to receive a persistency bonus (an enhancement to policyholder benefits for policies that remain in-force for a certain period);

- an industry loss warranty where the loss trigger is an industry loss as opposed to an entity specific loss;

- a catastrophe trigger where a trigger is defined as a financial variable such as a drop in a designated stock market;

- an inflation index affecting policy deductibles;

- contracts where the currency of claims settlement differs from the currency of loss; and

- contracts with fixed foreign currency rates.

A separable embedded derivative is one where:

- the economic characteristics and risks of the embedded derivative are not closely related to the economic characteristics and risks of the host contract;

- a separate instrument with the same terms as the embedded derivative would meet the definition of a derivative; and

- the hybrid (combined) instrument is not measured at fair value with changes in fair value recognised in profit or loss. *[FRS 103 Appendix I]*.

Somewhat unhelpfully, FRS 103 provides no further guidance but instead refers users to use 'the guidance in IAS 39 and IFRS 4' to determine whether an embedded derivative is separable. *[FRS 103 Appendix I]*. However, the embedded derivative is only separable if it is not itself an insurance contract, which means that derivatives embedded within insurance contracts do not have to be separated if the policyholder benefits from the derivative only when the insured event occurs.

As an exception to the requirements described above, an insurer need not separate, and measure at fair value, a policyholder's option to surrender an insurance contract for a fixed amount (or for an amount based on a fixed amount and an interest rate), even if the exercise price differs from the carrying amount of the host insurance liability. However, the requirements to separate embedded derivatives if the derivative is separable, described above, do apply to a put option or cash surrender option embedded in an insurance contract if the surrender value varies in response to the change in a financial variable (such as an equity or commodity price or index), or a non-financial variable that is not specific to a party to the contract. Furthermore, those requirements also apply if the holder's ability to exercise a put option or cash surrender option is triggered by a change in such a variable (for example, a put option that can be exercised if a stock market index reaches a specified level). This applies equally to options to surrender a financial instrument containing a discretionary participation feature. *[FRS 103.2.21-22]*.

5.1   Unit-linked features

Both IAS 39 and IFRS 9 state that a unit-linked feature (i.e. a contractual term that requires payments denominated in units of an internal or external investment fund) embedded in a host insurance contract (or financial instrument) is considered to be closely related to the host contract if the unit-denominated payments are measured at current unit values that reflect the fair values of the assets of the fund. *[IAS 39.AG33(g), IFRS 9 Appendix B.4.3.8(g)]*.

IAS 39 and IFRS 9 also consider that unit-linked investment liabilities should be normally regarded as puttable instruments that can be put back to the issuer at any time for cash equal to a proportionate share of the net asset value of an entity, i.e. they are not closely related. Nevertheless, the effect of separating an embedded derivative and accounting for each component is to measure the hybrid contract at the redemption amount that is payable at the end of the reporting period if the unit holders had exercised their right to put the instrument back to the issuer. *[IAS 39.AG32, IFRS 9 Appendix B.4.3.7]*. This seems somewhat to contradict the fact that the unit-linked feature is regarded as closely related (which means no separation of the feature is required) but the accounting treatment is substantially the same.

6 UNBUNDLING OF DEPOSIT COMPONENTS

Some insurance contracts contain both an insurance component and a 'deposit component'. *[FRS 103.2.23]*. Indeed, virtually all insurance contracts have an implicit or explicit deposit component, because the policyholder is generally required to pay premiums before the period of the risk and therefore the time value of money is likely to be one factor that insurers consider in pricing contracts.

A deposit component is 'a contractual component that is not accounted for as a derivative under Sections 11 and 12 of FRS 102 and would be within the scope of FRS 102 if it were a separate instrument'. *[FRS 103 Appendix I]*.

FRS 103 requires an insurer to 'unbundle' those insurance and deposit components in certain circumstances, *[FRS 103.2.23]*, i.e. to account for the components of a contract as if they were separate contracts. *[FRS 103 Appendix I]*. In other circumstances unbundling is either allowed (but not required) or is prohibited.

Unbundling has the following accounting consequences: *[FRS 103.2.25]*

(a) the insurance component is measured as an insurance contract under FRS 103; and

(b) the deposit component is measured under Sections 11 or 12 of FRS 102 (or, if the entity has made the accounting policy choice under paragraphs 11.2(b) or (c), or paragraphs 12.2(b) or (c) of FRS 102 to apply the recognition and measurement provisions of either IAS 39 or IFRS 9, the disclosure requirements of Sections 11 and 12 of FRS 102 and the recognition and measurement provisions of IAS 39 or IFRS 9 as applicable).

FRS 103 does not state what happens to the amounts received for the deposit component but they would not be recognised as revenue, but rather as changes in the deposit liability. Premiums for the insurance component are typically recognised as insurance revenue. A portion of any transaction costs incurred at inception should be allocated to the deposit component if this allocation has a material effect.

Unbundling is required only if both the following conditions are met: *[FRS 103.2.23]*

(a) the insurer can measure the deposit component (including any embedded surrender options) separately (i.e. without considering the insurance component); and

(b) the insurer's accounting policies do not otherwise require it to recognise all obligations and rights arising from the deposit component.

Chapter 33

Unbundling is permitted, but not required, if the insurer can measure the deposit component separately as in (a) above but its accounting policies require it to recognise all obligations and rights arising from the deposit component. This is regardless of the basis used to measure those rights and obligations. *[FRS 103.2.23]*.

Unbundling is prohibited when an insurer cannot measure the deposit component separately. *[FRS 103.2.23]*.

FRS 103 describes an example of a case when an insurer's accounting policies do not require it to recognise all obligations arising from a deposit component. This is where a cedant receives compensation for losses from a reinsurer, but the contract obliges the cedant to repay the compensation in future years. That obligation arises from a deposit component. If the cedant's accounting policies would otherwise permit it to recognise the compensation as income without recognising the resulting obligation, unbundling is required. *[FRS 103.2.24]*. In practice, unbundling is unlikely to apply to UK entities because previous UK GAAP required an insurer to recognise all obligations arising from an insurance contract including deposit components.

6.1   Unbundling illustration

The implementation guidance accompanying IFRS 4 provides an illustration of the unbundling of the deposit component of a reinsurance contract which is reproduced in Chapter 51 of EY International GAAP 2019.

6.2   Practical difficulties

In unbundling a contract the principal difficulty is identifying the initial fair value of any deposit component. In the IASB's illustration referred to at 6.1 above, a discount rate is provided but in practice contracts will not have a stated discount rate. The issuer and the cedant will therefore have to determine an appropriate discount rate in order to calculate the fair value of the deposit component.

However, the potential burden on insurers is reduced by the fact that the FRC has limited the requirement to unbundle to only those contracts where the rights and obligations arising from the deposit component are not recognised under insurance accounting.

Some examples of clauses within insurance contracts that might indicate the need for unbundling are:

- 'funds withheld' clauses where part or all of the premium is never paid to the reinsurer or claims are never received;
- 'no claims bonus', 'profit commission' or 'claims experience' clauses which guarantee that the cedant will receive a refund of some of the premium;
- 'experience accounts' used to measure the profitability of the contract. These are often segregated from other funds and contain interest adjustments that may accrue to the benefit of the policyholder;
- 'finite' clauses that limit maximum losses or create a 'corridor' of losses not reinsured under a contract;

- contracts that link the eventual premium to the level of claims;
- commutation clauses whose terms guarantee that either party will receive a refund of amounts paid under the contract; and
- contracts of unusual size where the economic benefits to either party are not obviously apparent.

The unbundling requirements in FRS 103 do not specifically address the issue of contracts artificially separated through the use of side letters, the separate components of which should be considered together. However, FRS 103 does state that linked contracts entered into with a single counterparty (or contracts that are otherwise interdependent) form a single contract, for the purposes of assessing whether significant insurance risk is transferred, although the standard is silent on linked transactions with different counterparties (see 4.6.2 above).

7 DISCRETIONARY PARTICIPATION FEATURES

A discretionary participation feature (DPF) is a contractual right to receive, as a supplement to guaranteed benefits, additional benefits: *[FRS 103 Appendix I]*

(a) that are likely to be a significant portion of the total contractual benefits;

(b) whose amount or timing is contractually at the discretion of the issuer; and

(c) that are contractually based on:

(i) the performance of a specified pool of contracts or a specified type of contract;

(ii) realised and/or unrealised investment returns on a specified pool of assets held by the issuer; or

(iii) the profit or loss of the company, fund or other entity that issues the contract.

Guaranteed benefits are payments or other benefits to which the policyholder or investor has an unconditional right that is not subject to the contractual discretion of the issuer. *[FRS 103 Appendix I]*. Guaranteed benefits are always accounted for as liabilities. Similarly, a guaranteed element is an obligation to pay guaranteed benefits, included in a contract that contains a DPF. *[FRS 103 Appendix I]*.

The following is an example of a contract with a DPF.

Example 33.4: Unitised with-profits policy

Premiums paid by the policyholder are used to purchase units in a 'with-profits' fund at the current unit price. The insurer guarantees that each unit added to the fund will have a minimum value which is the bid price of the unit. This is the guaranteed amount. In addition, the insurer may add two types of bonus to the with-profits units. These are a regular bonus, which may be added daily as a permanent increase to the guaranteed amount, and a final bonus that may be added on top of those guaranteed amounts when the with-profits units are cashed in. Levels of regular and final bonuses are adjusted twice per year. Both regular and final bonuses are discretionary amounts and are generally set based on expected future returns generated by the funds.

Chapter 33

DPF can appear in both insurance contracts and investment contracts. However, to qualify as a DPF, the discretionary benefits must be likely to be a 'significant' portion of the total contractual benefits. FRS 103 does not quantify what is meant by 'significant' but it could be interpreted in the same sense as in the definition of an insurance contract (see 4.6.1 above).

With contracts that have discretionary features, the issuer has discretion over the amount and/or timing of distributions to policyholders although that discretion may be subject to some contractual constraints (including related legal and regulatory constraints) and competitive constraints. Distributions are typically made to policyholders whose contracts are still in force when the distribution is made. Thus, in many cases, a change in the timing of a distribution, apart from the change in the value over time, means that a different generation of policyholders might benefit.

The main accounting question is whether the discretionary surplus or fund for future appropriations (i.e. the balance sheet item required by Schedule 3 to the Regulations to comprise all funds the allocation of which, either to policyholders and shareholders, has not been determined by the end of the reporting date), *[FRS 103 Appendix I]*, is a liability or a component of equity. The Regulations require that the fund for future appropriations (FFA) is classified as a liability and disclosed separately on the balance sheet (see 11.4 below). Once the allocation of the FFA has been determined (i.e. by a bonus declaration) then the shareholder's share of that allocation is recognised in profit or loss.

FRS 103 amends the requirements of IFRS 4 to ensure that the accounting for contracts with a DPF does not conflict with the requirements of the Regulations.

7.1   Discretionary participation features in insurance contracts

FRS 103 requires that any guaranteed element within an insurance contract with a DPF is recognised as a liability. In theory, insurers have an option as to whether to present a DPF either as a liability or as a separate component of equity. However, an insurer can classify a DPF as equity only where this is permitted by the Regulations and the Regulations do not generally permit an equity classification for unallocated funds arising from contracts with a DPF (see 7 above).

The following requirements apply: *[FRS 103.2.30(a)-(b)]*

- when the guaranteed element is not recognised separately from the DPF the whole contract must be classified as a liability;

- when the DPF is recognised separately from the guaranteed element the DPF can be classified as either a liability or as a separate component of equity (where this is permitted by the Regulations which it does not). FRS 103 does not specify how an insurer determines whether the DPF is a liability or equity. The insurer may split the DPF into liability and equity components but must use a consistent accounting policy for such a split; and

- a DPF cannot be classified as an intermediate category that is neither liability nor equity.

An insurer may recognise all premiums received from a contract with a DPF as revenue without separating any portion that relates to any equity component. *[FRS 103.2.30(c)]*. The use of the word 'may' means that an insurer can classify some of the DPF as equity but continue to record all of the contract premiums as income.

Subsequent changes in the measurement of the guaranteed element and in the portion of the DPF classified as a liability must be recognised in profit or loss. If part or all of the DPF is classified in equity, that portion of profit or loss may be attributable to that feature (in the same way that a portion may be attributable to a non-controlling interest). Where legislation permits the discretionary participation feature to be classified as a component of equity, the issuer must recognise the portion of profit or loss attributable to any equity component of a DPF as an allocation of profit or loss, not as expense or income. *[FRS 103.2.30(c)]*.

FRS 103 also requires that an issuer of a contract with a DPF:

- should, if it has made an accounting policy choice in accordance with paragraphs 11.2(b) or (c) or paragraphs 12.2(b) or (c) of FRS 102 to apply the recognition and measurement provisions of either IAS 39 or IFRS 9, and the contract contains an embedded derivative within the scope of IAS 39 or IFRS 9, apply IAS 39 and IFRS 9 to that embedded derivative; *[FRS 103.2.30(d)]* and

- continue its existing accounting policies for such contracts, unless it changes those accounting policies in a way that complies with FRS 103 (subject to the constraints noted above and those discussed at 9 below). *[FRS 103.2.30(e)]*.

7.2 Discretionary participation features in financial instruments

As discussed at 3.2.2 above, a financial instrument containing a DPF is also within the scope of FRS 103, not Sections 11 and 12 of FRS 102, and issuers of these contracts are permitted to continue applying their existing accounting policies to them rather than apply the rules in Sections 11 and 12 of FRS 102.

The requirements discussed at 7.1 above therefore apply equally to financial instruments that contain a DPF. However, in addition:

- if the issuer classifies the entire DPF as a liability, it must apply the liability adequacy test discussed at 8.8 below to the whole contract, i.e. to both the guaranteed element and the DPF. The issuer need not determine separately the amount that would result from applying IAS 39, IFRS 9 or Sections 11 and 12 of FRS 102 (depending on the accounting policy choice) to the guaranteed element; *[FRS 103.2.31(a)]*

- if the issuer classifies part or all of the DPF of that instrument as a separate component of equity, the liability recognised for the whole contract should not be less than the amount that would result from applying IAS 39, IFRS 9 or Sections 11 and 12 of FRS 102 (depending on the accounting policy choice) to the guaranteed element. That amount should include the intrinsic value of an option to surrender the contract, but need not include its time value if FRS 103 exempts that option from fair value measurement (see 5 above). The issuer need not disclose the amount that would result from applying IAS 39, IFRS 9 or Sections 11 and 12 of FRS 102 (depending on the accounting policy choice) to the guaranteed element, nor need it present the guaranteed amount separately. Furthermore, it need not determine the guaranteed amount if the total liability recognised for whole contract is clearly higher; *[FRS 103.2.31(b)]*

- although these contracts are financial instruments, the issuer may continue to recognise all premiums (including the premiums from the guaranteed element) as revenue and recognise as an expense the resulting increase in the carrying amount of the liability; *[FRS 103.2.31(c)]* and

- although these contracts are financial instruments, an issuer should disclose the total interest expense recognised in profit or loss, but need not calculate such interest expense using the effective interest method. *[FRS 103.2.31(d)]*.

7.3   Practical issues

7.3.1   Negative DPF

Cumulative unallocated realised and unrealised returns on investments backing insurance and investment contracts with a DPF may become negative and result in an unallocated amount that is negative (a cumulative unallocated loss).

When the balance on the FFA of a with-profits fund is negative, an entity should explain the nature of the negative balance, the circumstances in which it arose and why no action to eliminate it was considered necessary. *[FRS 103.5.5]*.

7.3.2   Contracts with switching features

Some contracts may contain options for the counterparty to switch between terms that would, *prima facie*, result in classification as an investment contract without DPF features (accounted for under Sections 11 and 12 of FRS 102) and terms that would result in a classification as an investment contract with DPF features (accounted for under FRS 103).

We believe that the fact that this switch option makes these contracts investment contracts with a DPF means that the issuer should continuously be able to demonstrate that the DPF feature still exists and also be able to demonstrate actual switching in order to classify these contracts as investment contracts with a DPF under FRS 103.

8   PRESENTATION, RECOGNITION AND MEASUREMENT OF INSURANCE CONTRACTS

8.1   Overall requirements for the presentation of the statement of financial position and statement of comprehensive income by insurers

Section 4 – *Statement of Financial Position* – and Section 5 – *Statement of Comprehensive Income and Income Statement* – of FRS 102 require that both the Statement of Financial Position and Statement of Comprehensive Income of an entity applying FRS 102 complies with the general rules and formats of the applicable Schedule to the Regulations. *[FRS 102.4.2, 5.5]*.

These rules apply to all entities complying with FRS 102 regardless as to whether they are required to comply with the UK Companies Act (CA 2006). Entities that do not report under the CA 2006 should comply with the Regulations (or, where applicable, the LLP Regulations) where referred to in Sections 4 and 5 of FRS 102 except to the extent that these requirements are not permitted by any statutory framework under which such entities report. *[FRS 102.4.1, 5.1]*. The Note on legal requirements to FRS 103 observes that entities preparing financial statements within other legal frameworks will need to satisfy themselves that FRS 103 does not conflict with any relevant legal obligations. *[FRS 103 Appendix III.3]*. The Regulations require that the individual accounts of an insurance company prepared under section 396 of the CA 2006 must comply with Schedule 3 to the Regulations ('Schedule 3'). A parent company of an insurance group preparing Companies Act group accounts must do so in accordance with the provisions of Part 1 of Schedule 6 as modified by Part 3 of that Schedule (which, in summary, substitutes references to Schedule 1 of the Regulations for references to Schedule 3 to the Regulations).

There is no ability for an insurance entity or group to prepare financial statements using 'adapted formats' (see Chapter 6 at 4); the statutory format must be used. In addition, an insurance entity would not qualify as a small entity eligible to apply Section 1A – *Small Entities* – of FRS 102 as insurance companies and companies that carry on insurance market activities are excluded from the small companies regime (see Chapter 5 at 4.3.3).

A company that issues insurance contracts which is not an insurance company is not required to prepare its individual accounts in accordance with Schedule 3 to the Regulations. That entity will prepare its individual accounts in accordance with another applicable Schedule (usually Schedule 1 unless it is a banking company). A UK friendly society within the scope of the Friendly Societies Act 1991 and which elects to comply with FRS 102 and FRS 103 is required to prepare financial statements in accordance with The Friendly Societies (Accounts and Related Provisions) Regulations 1994 (SI 1994/1983). These regulations requires an income and expenditure account and balance sheet account format that is virtually identical to Schedule 3.

Insurance accounting practices under previous UK GAAP had separate recognition and measurement models for general insurance and life (long-term) insurance. Similarly, Schedule 3 to the Regulations requires separate income statements for general and long-term insurance business as well as separate balance sheet line items.

Schedule 3 to the Regulations does not address the presentation of either the statement of changes in equity or the statement of cash flows. Insurers must therefore follow the requirements of FRS 102 for these primary statements (see Chapter 6 at 7 and Chapter 7).

8.1.1 Definition of an insurance company in UK law

An insurance company is defined by the CA 2006 as: *[s1165(3)]*

- an authorised insurance company; or
- any other person (whether incorporated or not) who:
  - carries on insurance market activity; or
  - may effect or carry out contracts of insurance under which the benefits provided by that person are exclusively or primarily benefits in kind in the event of accident to or breakdown of a vehicle.

An authorised insurance company means a person (whether incorporated or not) who has permission under Part 4A of the Financial Services and Markets Act (2000) (c.8) to effect or carry out contracts of insurance. *[s1165(2)]*. Insurance market activity has the meaning given in section 316(3) of the Financial Services and Markets Act 2000, *[s1165(7)]*, and refers to those engaging in insurance activity in the Lloyd's insurance market.

An insurance group is a group where the parent company is an insurance company, or where: *[s1165(5)]*

- the parent company's principal subsidiary undertakings are wholly or mainly insurance companies; and
- the parent company does not itself carry on any material business apart from the acquisition, management and disposal of interests in subsidiary undertakings.

A parent company's principal subsidiary undertakings are the subsidiary undertakings of the company whose results or financial position would principally affect the figures shown in the group accounts and the management of interests in subsidiary undertakings includes the provision of services to such undertakings. *[s1165(6)]*.

When a group contains a mixture of insurance subsidiaries and non-insurance subsidiaries, judgement may need to be exercised to determine which subsidiaries are those whose results or financial position principally affect the figures in the group financial statements and therefore whether the group is an insurance group preparing consolidated financial statements under Schedule 3 to the Regulations or a non-insurance group preparing financial statements under either Schedule 1 or Schedule 2 to the Regulations. The presentation and disclosure requirements of Schedule 1 are discussed in Chapter 6.

8.2   Statement of financial position under Schedule 3

As discussed at 8.1 above, an insurance entity is required by FRS 102 to prepare its individual balance sheet in accordance with Part 1 'General Rules and Formats' of Schedule 3 to the Regulations. An insurance group is required to prepare its consolidated balance sheet in accordance with the provisions of Part 1 of Schedule 6 to the Regulations as modified by Part 3 of that Schedule. In our view, this requirement means that an insurance entity that does not report under the UK Companies Act (e.g. a non-UK entity or a UK friendly society preparing financial statements under SI 1994/1983 – see above) must follow the formats, including the related notes to the formats, to the extent it does not conflict with its own statutory framework, but does not need to give the other disclosures in the notes to the accounts required by Schedule 3 to the Regulations. As discussed at 8.1 above, insurance entities and groups are not permitted to use 'adapted' formats; the statutory format must be used.

All applicable items denoted by a letter or a Roman number in the statutory Schedule 3 balance sheet format must be shown on the face of the statement of financial position. All applicable items denoted by an Arabic number, except for items concerning technical provisions and the reinsurers' share thereof, may be shown either on the face of the statement of financial position or in the notes thereto. The minimum line items that must be presented on the face of the statement of financial position are illustrated in Figure 33.1 below:

Figure 33.1   *Individual statement of financial position (UK insurance company)*

ASSETS

A		Called up share capital not paid
B		Intangible assets
C		Investments
	I	Land and buildings
	II	Investments in group undertakings and participating interests
	III	Other financial investments
	IV	Deposits with ceding undertakings
D		Assets held to cover linked liabilities
Da		Reinsurers' share of technical provisions
E		Debtors
	I	Debtors arising out of direct insurance operations
	II	Debtors arising out of reinsurance operations
	III	Other debtors
	IV	Called up share capital not paid
F		Other assets
	I	Tangible assets
	II	Stocks
	III	Cash at bank and in hand
	IV	Own shares
	V	Other
G		Prepayments and accrued income
	I	Accrued interest and rent
	II	Deferred acquisition costs
	III	Other prepayments and accrued income

LIABILITIES

A		Capital and reserves
	I	Called up share capital or equivalent funds
	II	Share premium account
	III	Revaluation reserve
	IV	Reserves
	V	Profit and loss account
B		Subordinated liabilities
Ba		Fund for future appropriations
C		Technical provisions
D		Technical provision for linked liabilities
E		Provisions for other risks
F		Deposits received from reinsurers
G		Creditors
	I	Creditors arising out of direct insurance operations
	II	Creditors arising out of reinsurance operations
	III	Debenture loans
	IV	Amounts owed to credit institutions
	V	Other creditors including taxation and social security
H		Accruals and deferred income

The following discussion relates to the Schedule 3 statement of financial position (or balance sheet) format only. The Schedule 3 balance sheet includes sub-headings, denoted with an Arabic number, which have not been shown in Figure 33.1 above. The main modifications required for the group balance sheet format are the identification of minority interest/non-controlling interest and the replacement of the sub-heading 'Participating interests' (see 8.2.2 below) by 'Interests in associated undertakings' and 'Other participating interests'.

The individual line items in the balance sheet format are discussed at 8.2.1 to 8.2.15 below. The rest of this section addresses the general requirements of the Schedule 3 format.

Schedule 3 requires that every balance sheet of a company must show the items listed above in the balance sheet format adopted. The items must also be shown in the order and under the headings and sub-headings given in the particular format used, but the letters or numbers assigned to that item in the format do not need to be given (and are not in practice). The items listed in the formats need to be read together with the notes to the formats, which may also permit alternative positions for any particular items. *[3 Sch 1]*. The relevant notes to the balance sheet formats are discussed for each line item at 8.2.1 to 8.2.15 below. These notes must be presented in the order in which, where relevant, the items to which they relate are presented in the balance sheet and in the profit and loss account. *[3 Sch 60(2)]*.

Where the special nature of the company's business requires it, the company's directors *must* adapt the arrangement, headings and sub-headings otherwise required in respect of items given an Arabic number in the balance sheet (or profit or loss account) format used. The directors *may* combine items to which Arabic numbers are given in the formats if their individual amounts are not material to assessing the state of affairs (or profit or loss) of the company for the financial year in question or the combination facilitates that assessment. In the latter case, the individual amounts of any items combined must be disclosed in a note to the accounts. *[3 Sch 3-4]*.

Schedule 3 allows any item to be shown in the company's balance sheet in greater detail than required by the particular format used. The balance sheet may include an item representing or covering the amount of any asset or liability not otherwise covered by any of the items listed in the format used, but preliminary expenses, the expenses of, and commission on, any issue of shares or debentures, and the costs of research may not be treated as assets in the balance sheet. *[3 Sch 3]*. FRS 102 requires additional line items, headings and subtotals to be added where relevant to an understanding of the entity's financial position. *[FRS 102.4.3]*. When additional detail is provided on the face of the balance sheet, it is usual to provide a subtotal for the heading.

For every item shown in the balance sheet, the corresponding amount for the immediately preceding financial year (i.e. the comparative) must also be shown. Where that corresponding amount is not comparable with the amount to be shown for the item in question in the current financial year, the corresponding amount may be adjusted, and particulars of the non-comparability and of any adjustment must be disclosed in a note to the accounts. *[3 Sch 5]*.

Amounts in respect of items representing assets may not be set off against amounts in respect of items representing liabilities and *vice versa* subject to the provisions of Schedule 3. *[3 Sch 6]*.

The company's directors must, in determining how amounts are presented within items in the balance sheet, have regard to the substance of the reported transaction or arrangement, in accordance with generally accepted accounting principles or practice. *[3 Sch 8]*. In addition, when an asset of liability relates to more than one item in the balance sheet, the relationship of such asset or liability to the relevant item must be disclosed either under those items or in the notes to the accounts. *[3 Sch 8A]*.

The provision of Schedule 3 which relate to long-term business apply, with necessary modifications, to business which consists of effecting or carrying out relevant contracts of general business which:

- is transacted exclusively or principally according to the technical principles of long-term business; and

- is a significant amount of the business of the company. *[3 Sch 7(1)]*.

For this purpose a contract of general insurance is a relevant contract if the risk insured against relates to accident or sickness (this must be read with certain sections and schedules of the Financial Services and Markets Act 2000). *[3 Sch 7(2)]*.

8.2.1 Intangible assets

Figure 33.2 Analysis of intangible assets

B	Intangible assets	
	1	Development costs
	2	Concessions, patents, licences, trade marks and similar rights and assets
	3	Goodwill
	4	Payments on account

Intangible assets are not defined in the CA 2006 but Note (2) to the Schedule 3 balance sheet format states that amounts are only included in the balance sheet as concessions, patents, licences, trademarks and similar rights and assets if either the assets were acquired for valuable consideration and are not required to be shown under goodwill, or the assets in question were created by the company itself. However, entities preparing FRS 102 financial statements must apply the more restrictive requirements of the standard. Note (3) to the Schedule 3 balance sheet format states that goodwill can only be included to the extent that the goodwill was acquired for valuable consideration.

Schedule 3 does not address the presentation of negative goodwill. However, FRS 102 requires that negative goodwill is disclosed immediately below positive goodwill, with a subtotal of the net amount of the positive goodwill and the negative goodwill. *[FRS 102.19.24(b)]*.

8.2.2 Investments in group undertakings and participating interests

Figure 33.3 Analysis of investments in group undertakings and participating interests

C	Investments	
II	Investments in group undertakings and participating interests	
	1	Shares in group undertakings
	2	Debt securities issued by, and loans to, group undertakings
	3	Participating interests†
	4	Debt securities issued by, and loans to, undertakings in which the company has a participating interest

† In group accounts, this line item is replaced by two items: 'Interests in associated undertakings' and 'other participating interests'

A 'participating interest' means an interest held by, or on behalf of, an undertaking in the shares of another undertaking which it holds on a long-term basis for the purpose of securing a contribution to its activities by the exercise of control or influence arising from or related to that interest. In the context of the balance sheet formats, 'participating interest' does not include an interest in a group undertaking. A holding of 20% or more of the shares of the undertaking is presumed to be a participating interest unless the contrary is shown. An interest in shares of another undertaking includes an interest which is convertible into an interest in shares and an option to acquire shares or any such interest, even if the shares are unissued until the conversion or exercise of the option. *[10 Sch 11]*.

For investments in subsidiaries, associates and jointly controlled entities in separate and individual financial statements, neither the current accounting rules, fair value accounting rules nor the alternative accounting rules of Schedule 3 permit the use of cost less impairment. Consequently, an investor can account for these only at fair value with changes in fair value recognised in other comprehensive income (except for reversals of a revaluation decrease recognised in profit or loss or a revaluation decrease which exceeds accumulated revaluation gains recognised in equity which are recognised in profit or loss) or at fair value with changes in fair value recognised in profit or loss. *[FRS 102.9.26]*.

8.2.3   Other financial investments

Figure 33.4   Analysis of other financial investments

C	Investments	
III	Other financial investments	
	1	Shares and other variable-yield securities and units in unit trusts
	2	Debt securities and other fixed-income securities
	3	Participation in investment pools
	4	Loans secured by mortgages
	5	Other loans
	6	Deposits with credit institutions
	7	Other

Note (5) to the Schedule 3 balance sheet format states that debt-securities and other fixed-income securities is to comprise transferable debt securities and any other transferable fixed-income securities issued by credit institutions, other undertakings or public bodies, in so far as they are not covered within investments in group undertakings and participating interests.

Note (6) to the Schedule 3 balance sheet format states that participation in investment pools is to comprise shares held by the company in joint investments constituted by several undertakings or pension funds, the management of which has been entrusted to one of those undertakings or to one of those pension funds.

Note (7) to the Schedule 3 balance sheet format states that loans to policyholders for which the policy is the main security are to be included in 'other loans' and their amount must be disclosed in a note to the accounts. Loans secured by mortgage are to be shown as such even where they are also secured by insurance policies. Where the amount of other loans not secured by policies is material, an appropriate breakdown must be given in the notes to the accounts.

Note (8) to the Schedule 3 balance sheet format states that deposits with credit institutions should comprise sums the withdrawal of which is subject to a time restriction. Sums deposited with no restriction must be shown under 'Cash at bank and in hand' even if they bear interest.

8.2.4 Reinsurers' share of technical provisions

Figure 33.5   Analysis of reinsurers' share of technical provisions

Da	Reinsurers' share of technical provisions
1	Provision for unearned premiums
2	Long-term business provision
3	Claims outstanding
4	Provisions for bonuses and rebates
5	Other technical provisions
6	Technical provisions for unit-linked liabilities

Note (12) to the Schedule 3 balance sheet format states that the reinsurance amounts are to comprise the actual or estimated amounts which, under contractual reinsurance arrangements, are deducted from the gross amount of technical provisions.

8.2.5 Debtors

Debtors arising out of direct insurance operations must be split between those due from policyholders and those due from intermediaries.

Note (13) to the Schedule 3 balance sheet format states that amounts owed by group undertakings and undertakings in which the company has a participating interest must be shown separately as sub-assets of the relevant asset class.

8.2.6 Other assets

Figure 33.6   Analysis of other assets

F	Other assets	
I	Tangible fixed assets	
	1	Plant and machinery
	2	Fittings, fixtures, tools and equipment
	3	Payments on account (other than deposits paid on land and buildings) and assets (other than buildings) in the course of construction
II	Stocks	
	1	Raw materials and consumables
	2	Work in progress
	3	Finished goods and goods for resale
	4	Payments on account
III	Cash at bank and in hand	
IV	Own shares	
V	Other	

Tangible fixed assets would include property, plant and equipment, as defined in FRS 102.

The items reported under stocks will generally correspond with inventories under FRS 102. *[FRS 102.13.1].*

The Regulations do not define cash at bank and in hand. This line item would include bank deposits with notice or maturity periods. Such bank deposits may or may not meet FRS 102's definition of 'cash' (i.e. cash on hand and demand deposits) or 'cash equivalents' (i.e. short-term, highly liquid investments that are readily convertible to known amounts of cash and that are subject to an insignificant risk of changes in value). *[FRS 102.7.2].* See Chapter 7 at 3.3 for the definition of cash and cash equivalents.

While 'own shares' have an asset line heading in the Schedule 3 balance sheet format, FRS 102 requires investments in own shares to be treated as treasury shares and deducted from equity. *[FRS 102.22.16].* Consequently, this line item will not be used under FRS 102.

Note (15) to the Schedule 3 balance sheet format states that 'other' is to comprise assets which are not covered by the other items and where such assets are material, they must be disclosed in a note to the accounts.

8.2.7   *Prepayments and accrued income (including deferred acquisition costs)*

Note (17) to the Schedule 3 balance sheet format states that deferred acquisition costs arising in general business must be stated separately from those arising in long-term business. In the case of general business, the amount of any deferred acquisition costs must be established on a basis consistent with that used for unearned premiums. See 8.5.7 below.

8.2.8   *Capital and reserves*

Every balance sheet of a company which carries on long-term business must show separately as an additional item the aggregate of any amounts included in capital and reserves which are not required to be treated as realised profits under section 843 of the CA 2006. *[3 Sch 11(1)].*

Called up share capital in relation to a company means so much of its share capital as equals the aggregate amounts of the calls made on its shares (whether or not those calls have been paid) together with any share capital paid up without being called, and any share capital to be paid on a specified future date under the articles, the terms of allotment of the relevant shares or any other arrangements for payment of those shares. *[s547].*

The share premium account is a statutory reserve that arises on the issue of share capital. It is beyond the scope of this publication to explain the rules governing share premium in detail but a summary explaining how the share premium arises and can be applied or reduced is contained in Chapter 6 at 5.3.12.B.

The revaluation reserve arises where an asset is carried at valuation using the alternative accounting rules in the Regulations. *[3 Sch 29].*

Figure 33.7 below shows the analysis required in respect of reserves.

Figure 33.7   Analysis of reserves

A	**Capital and reserves**	
IV	Reserves	
	1	Capital redemption reserve
	2	Reserve for own shares
	3	Reserves provided for by articles of association
	4	Other reserves

The capital redemption reserve is a statutory reserve which is established when the shares of a limited company are redeemed or purchased wholly or partly out of the company's profits, or where treasury shares are cancelled. It is beyond the scope of this chapter to explain the rules governing redemptions/purchases of shares, treasury shares and the capital redemption reserve.

The reserve for own shares is used where the company purchases its own shares to be held by an employee share ownership plan (ESOP) that is treated as an extension of the sponsoring entity or where shares are held as treasury shares. *[FRS 102.9.33-37, 22.16]*.

Where the Articles of Association specifically provide for reserves to be established, the line item 'Reserves provided for by Articles of Association' is used.

8.2.9   Subordinated liabilities

Note (18) to the Schedule 3 balance sheet format states that subordinated liabilities comprise all liabilities in respect of which there is a contractual obligation that, in the event of winding up of bankruptcy, they are to be repaid only after the claims of other creditors have been met (whether or not they are represented by certificates).

8.2.10   Fund for future appropriations (FFA)

Note (19) to the Schedule 3 balance sheet format states that the FFA is to comprise all funds the allocation of which either to policyholders or shareholders has not been determined by the end of the financial year. Transfers to and from the FFA must be shown in the profit and loss line item, 'Transfers to or from the FFA'.

The Implementation Guidance to FRS 103 states that where there is reasonable certainty over the allocation to policyholders or owners of all items recognised in the technical account for long-term business, it is inappropriate to establish an FFA. However, certain long-term business funds of:

- proprietary insurers are established in such a way that allocation between equity and policyholders' liabilities is not clear cut; and
- mutual insurers are established in such a way that allocation between disclosed surplus and policyholders' liabilities is not clear cut; and
- therefore it is appropriate to establish an FFA. *[FRS 103.IG2.50]*.

Where an FFA is established, the notes to the financial statements should indicate the reasons for its use and the nature of the funds involved (see 11.4 below). *[FRS 103.IG2.51]*.

Chapter 33

8.2.11   Technical provisions

Figure 33.8   Analysis of technical provisions

C		Technical provisions
	1	Provision for unearned premiums
	2	Long-term business provision
	3	Claims outstanding
	4	Provisions for bonuses and rebates
	5	Equalisation provision
	6	Other technical provisions

The Schedule 3 balance sheet format permits the reinsurers' share of technical provisions to be shown either separately within liabilities or under assets item Da. However, FRS 103 prohibits the offsetting of reinsurance assets against the related insurance liabilities (see 8.10 below) and therefore the reinsurers' share of technical provisions must be shown as an asset.

Note (20) to the Schedule 3 balance sheet format states that the provision for unearned premiums for long-term business may be included in the long-term business provision rather than within unearned premiums.

Note (21) to the Schedule 3 balance sheet format states that the long-term business provision is to comprise the actuarially estimated value of the company's liabilities including bonuses already declared and after deducting the actuarial value of future premiums. It should also include claims incurred but not reported plus the estimated costs of settling such claims.

Note (22) to the Schedule 3 balance sheet format states that claims outstanding is to comprise the estimated ultimate cost to the company of settling all claims arising from events which have occurred up to the end of the financial year (including, in the case of general business, claims incurred but not reported) less amounts already paid in respect of such claims.

Note (23) to the Schedule 3 balance sheet format states that provisions for bonuses and rebates is to comprise amounts intended for policyholders or contract beneficiaries by way of bonuses and rebates to the extent that such amounts have not been credited to policyholders or contract beneficiaries or included in liabilities item Ba or in liabilities item C2.

Note (24) to the Schedule 3 balance sheet format states that equalisation provisions are those required to be maintained in respect of general business by the company in accordance with the rules made by the Financial Conduct Authority or the Prudential Regulation Authority under Part 10 of the Financial Services and Markets Act 2000. They also comprise any amounts required to be set aside by a company to equalise fluctuations in loss ratios in future years or to provide for special risks in accordance with Council Directive 87/343/EEC. Since the implementation of the Solvency II Directive, effective from 1 January 2016, the UK (and EU) regulatory framework does not permit equalisation or catastrophe provisions.

Note (25) to the Schedule 3 balance sheet format states that other technical provisions are to include the provision for unexpired risks (see 8.5.5 below). Where the provision for unexpired risks is significant, it must be disclosed separately.

8.2.12 Technical provisions for linked liabilities

Note (26) to the Schedule 3 balance sheet format states that this comprises technical provisions constituted to cover liabilities relating to investment in the context of long-term policies under which the benefits payable to policyholders are wholly or partly determined by reference to the value of, or the income from, property of any description (whether or not specified in the contract), or by reference to fluctuations in, or in an index of, the value of property of any description (whether or not so specified). 'Property' in this context means any type of asset. Any additional technical provisions constituted to cover death risks, operating expenses or other risk (such as benefits payable at the maturity date or guarantee surrender values) must be included in the long-term business provision.

This item must also comprise technical provisions representing the obligations of a tontine's organiser in relation to its members.

The Implementation Guidance to FRS 103 states that the relevant provision for any contract should not be less than the element of any surrender or transfer value which is calculated by reference to the relevant fund or funds or index. *[FRS 103.IG2.47]*. The net assets held to cover linked liabilities at the reporting date may differ from the technical provisions for linked liabilities. However, the reasons for any significant mismatching should be disclosed. *[FRS 103.IG2.48]*.

Where the technical provision for linked liabilities has regard to the timing of the tax obligation, the effect of this should be excluded from the determination of deferred tax. *[FRS 103.IG2.49]*.

8.2.13 Provisions for other risks

Figure 33.9   Analysis of provisions for other risks

E	Provisions for other risks	
	1	Provisions for pensions and similar obligations
	2	Provisions for taxation
	3	Other provisions

8.2.14 Deposits received from reinsurers

Note (27) to the Schedule 3 balance sheet format states that this item is to comprise amounts deposited by or withheld from other insurance undertakings under reinsurance contracts. These amounts may not be merged with other amounts owed to or by those other undertakings. Where the company ceded insurance and has received as a deposit securities which have been transferred to its ownership, this item is to comprise the amount owned by the company by virtue of the deposit.

8.2.15   *Creditors*

Note (28) to the Schedule 3 balance sheet format states that amounts owed to group undertakings and undertakings in which the company has a participating interest must be shown separately as sub-items.

Note (29) to the Schedule 3 balance sheet format states that the amount of any convertible debenture loans must be shown separately.

8.3   Statement of comprehensive income under Schedule 3

FRS 102 requires an entity to present its total comprehensive income for a period either:
[FRS 102.5.2]

- in a single statement of comprehensive income which presents all items of income and expense (and includes a subtotal for profit or loss) (see 8.3 below); or

- in two statements – an income statement (referred to as the profit and loss account in Schedule 3 to the Regulations) and a statement of comprehensive income, in which case the income statement presents all items of income and expense recognised in the period except those that are recognised in total comprehensive income outside of profit or loss as permitted or required by FRS 102 (see 8.3 below).

These requirements apply both to consolidated and individual financial statements.

However, UK companies (and LLPs) preparing group accounts in accordance with the CA 2006 can take advantage of the exemption in section 408 of the CA 2006 (where the conditions are met) not to present the individual profit and loss account and certain related notes. *[s408, s472(2), Regulations 3(2)]*. See Chapter 1 at 6.3.2. This exemption does not extend to individual financial statements prepared under other statutory frameworks, unless permitted by these statutory frameworks.

A change from the single-statement approach to the two-statement approach, or *vice versa*, is a retrospective change in accounting policy to which Section 10 applies. *[FRS 102.5.3]*. See Chapter 9 at 3.4.

A Schedule 3 profit and loss account or income statement comprises both a technical account and a non-technical account. There are separate technical accounts for general business and long-term business. Therefore, composite insurers (i.e. those that underwrite both general and long-term business) will present a three-part profit and loss account comprising a technical account-general business, a technical account-long-term business and a non-technical account. As discussed at 8.1 above, insurance entities and groups are not permitted to use 'adapted' profit or loss formats; the statutory format must be used.

Other comprehensive income means items of income and expense (including reclassification adjustments), that are not recognised in profit or loss as required or permitted by FRS 102. *[FRS 102 Appendix I]*. Therefore, profit or loss is the default category; all comprehensive income is part of profit or loss unless FRS 102 permits or requires otherwise. Schedule 3 does not address the format or content of other comprehensive income which is discussed at 8.3.13 below.

Figure 33.10   Format of the Technical account – General business

1	Earned premiums, net of reinsurance
(a)	gross premiums written
(b)	outward reinsurance premiums
(c)	change in gross provision for unearned premiums
(d)	change in provision for unearned premiums, reinsurers' share
2	Allocated investment return transferred from the non-technical account
3	Investment income
(a)	income from participating interests, with a separate indication of that derived from group undertakings
(b)	income from other investments, with a separate indication of that derived from group undertakings
(aa)	income from land and buildings
(bb)	income from other investments
(c)	value re-adjustments on investments
(d)	gains on realisation of investments
4	Other technical income, net of reinsurance
5	Claims incurred, net of reinsurance
(a)	claims paid
(aa)	gross amount
(bb)	reinsurers' share
(b)	change in provisions for claims
(aa)	gross amount
(bb)	reinsurers' share
6	Changes in other technical provisions, net of reinsurance, not shown under other headings
7	Bonuses and rebates, net of reinsurance
8	Net operating expenses
(a)	acquisition costs
(b)	change in deferred acquisition costs
(c)	administrative expenses
(d)	reinsurance commissions and profit participation
9	Other technical charges, net of reinsurance
10	Investment expenses and charges
(a)	investment management expenses, including interest
(b)	value adjustments on investments
(c)	loss on the realisation of investments
11	Change in the equalisation provision
12	Balance on the technical account for general business

Chapter 33

Figure 33.11   *Format of the Technical account – Long-term business*

1		Earned premiums, net of reinsurance
	(a)	gross premiums written
	(b)	outward reinsurance premiums
	(c)	change in gross provision for unearned premiums
2		Investment income
	(a)	Income from participating interests, with a separate indication of that derived from group undertakings
	(b)	Income from other investments, with a separate indication of that derived from group undertakings
	(aa)	income from land and buildings
	(bb)	income from other investments
	(c)	value re-adjustments on investments
	(d)	gains on realisation of investments
3		Unrealised gains on investments
4		Other technical income, net of reinsurance
5		Claims incurred, net of reinsurance
	(a)	claims paid
	(aa)	gross amount
	(bb)	reinsurers' share
	(b)	change in provisions for claims
	(aa)	gross amount
	(bb)	reinsurers' share
6		Change in other technical provisions, net of reinsurance, not shown under other headings
	(a)	Long-term business provision, net of insurance
	(aa)	gross amount
	(bb)	reinsurers' share
	(b)	Other technical income, net of reinsurance
7		Bonuses and rebates, net of reinsurance
8		Net operating expenses
	(a)	acquisition costs
	(b)	change in deferred acquisition costs
	(c)	administrative expenses
	(d)	reinsurance commissions and profit participation
9		Investment expenses and charges
	(a)	investment management expenses, including interest
	(b)	value adjustments on investments
	(c)	loss on the realisation of investments
10		Unrealised losses on investments
11		Other technical income, net of reinsurance
11a		Tax attributable to the long-term business
12		Allocated investment return transferred to the non-technical account
12a		Transfers to or from the fund for future appropriations
13		Balance on the technical account for long-term business

Figure 33.12   *Format of the Non-technical account*

1	Balance on the general business technical account	
2	Balance on the long-term business technical account	
2a	Tax credit attributable to balance on the long-term business technical account	
3	Investment income	
	(a)	income from participating interests, with a separate indication of that derived from group undertakings
	(b)	income from other investments, with a separate indication of that derived from group undertakings
		(aa) income from land and buildings
		(bb) income from other investments
	(c)	value re-adjustments on investments
	(d)	gains on realisation of investments
3a	Unrealised gains on investments	
4	Allocated investment return transferred from the long-term business technical account	
5	Investment expenses and charges	
	(a)	investment management expenses, including interest
	(b)	value adjustments on investments
	(c)	loss on the realisation of investments
5a	Unrealised losses on investments	
6	Allocated investment return transferred to the general business technical account	
7	Other income	
8	Other charges, including value adjustments	
8a	Profit or loss on ordinary activities before tax	
9	Tax on profit or loss on ordinary activities	
10	Profit or loss on ordinary activities after tax	
11	Extraordinary income	
12	Extraordinary charges	
13	Extraordinary profit or loss	
14	Tax on extraordinary profit or loss	
15	Other taxes not shown under the preceding items	
16	Profit or loss for the financial year	

8.3.1   Gross written premiums

Note (1) to the Schedule 3 profit and loss format states that gross premiums written is to comprise all amounts during the financial year in respect of insurance contracts entered into regardless of the fact that such amounts may relate in whole or in part to a later financial year and must include:

- premiums yet to be determined, where the premium calculation can be done only at the end of the year;

- single premiums, including annuity premiums, and in long-term business, single premiums resulting from bonus and rebate provisions in so far as they must be considered as premiums under the terms of the contract;

- additional premiums in the case of half-yearly, quarterly or monthly payments and additional payments from policyholders for expenses borne by the company;

- in the case of co-insurance, the company's portion of total premiums;

- reinsurance premiums due from ceding and retroceding undertakings, including portfolio entries.

The above must be shown after deductions of cancellations and portfolio withdrawals credited to ceding and retroceding undertakings.

In addition, gross premiums written must not include the amounts of taxes or duties levied with premiums.

8.3.2   Outwards reinsurance premiums

Note (2) to the Schedule 3 profit and loss format states that outwards reinsurance premiums must comprise all premiums paid or payable in respect of outwards reinsurance contracts entered into by the company. Portfolio entries payable on the conclusion or amendment of outwards reinsurance contracts must be added; portfolio receivables must be deducted.

8.3.3   Changes in the provision for unearned premiums, net of reinsurance

Note (3) to the Schedule 3 profit and loss format states that in the case of long-term business, the change in unearned premiums may be included either in this line item or within changes in other technical provisions.

8.3.4   Claims incurred, net of reinsurance

Note (4) to the Schedule 3 profit and loss format states that this is to comprise all payments made in the financial year with the addition of the provision for claims (but after deducting the provision for claims for the preceding financial year).

The amounts must include annuities, surrenders, entries and withdrawals of loss provisions to and from ceding insurance undertakings and reinsurers and external and internal claims management costs and charges for claims incurred but not reported. Sums recoverable on the basis of salvage and subrogation must be deducted.

Where the difference between the loss provision at the beginning of the year and the payments made during the year on account of claims incurred in previous years and the loss provision shown at the end of the year for such outstanding claims is material, it must be shown in the notes to the accounts, broken down by category and amount.

8.3.5   Bonuses and rebates, net of reinsurance

Note (5) to the Schedule 3 profit and loss format states that bonuses comprise all amounts chargeable for the financial year which are paid or payable to policyholders and other insured parties or provided for their benefit, including amounts used to increase technical provisions or applied to the reduction of future premiums, to the extent that such amounts represent an allocation of surplus or profit arising on business as a whole or a section of business, after deduction of amounts provided in previous years which are no longer required. Rebates are to comprise such amounts to the extent that they represent a partial refund of premiums resulting from the experience of individual contracts.

Where material, the amount charged for bonuses and that charged for rebates must be disclosed separately in the notes to the accounts.

8.3.6   Acquisition costs

Note (6) to the Schedule 3 profit and loss format states that acquisition costs comprise costs arising from the conclusion of insurance contracts. They must cover both direct costs, such as acquisition commissions or the cost of drawing up the insurance document or including the insurance contract in the portfolio, and indirect costs, such as the advertising costs or the administrative expenses connected with the processing of proposals and the issuing of policies. In the case of long-term business, policy renewal commissions must be included within administrative expenses.

8.3.7 Administrative expenses

Note (7) to the Schedule 3 profit and loss format states that administrative expenses must include the costs arising from premium collection, portfolio administration, handling of bonuses and rebates and inward and outward reinsurance. In particular, they must include staff costs and depreciation provisions in respect of office furniture and equipment in so far as these need not be shown under acquisition costs, claims incurred or investment charges.

8.3.8 Investment income, expenses and charges

Note (8) to the Schedule 3 profit and loss format states that investment income and charges must, to the extent that they arise in the long-term technical fund, be disclosed in the long-term technical account. Other investment income, expenses and charges must either be disclosed in the non-technical account or attributed between the appropriate technical and non-technical accounts. Where the company makes such an attribution it must disclose the basis for it in the notes to the accounts. See 8.7 below.

8.3.9 Unrealised gains and losses on investments

Note (9) to the Schedule 3 profit and loss format states that in the case of investments attributed to the long-term fund, the difference between the valuation of the investments and their purchase price or, if they have previously been valued, their valuation as at the last balance sheet date, may be disclosed (in whole or in part) under either item 3 (investment income) or item 10 (investment expenses and charges), as the case may be, of the long-term technical account, and in the case of investments shown as assets held to cover linked liabilities must also be disclosed.

In the case of other investments, the difference between the valuation of investments and their purchase price or, if they have previously been valued, their valuation as at the last balance sheet date, may be disclosed (in whole or in part) under items 3a (unrealised gains on investments) or 5a (unrealised losses on investments), as the case may require, of the non-technical account.

8.3.10 Allocated investment return

Note (10) to the Schedule 3 profit and loss format states that the investment return allocated initially to one part of the profit and loss account (see 8.3.8 above) may be transferred to another part of the profit and loss account. See 8.7 below.

One reason that such a transfer might be made is so that, for example, a long-term insurer could recognise investment return in the life technical account on a longer-term rate of return basis.

Chapter 33

Where part of the investment return allocated initially to the non-technical account is transferred the general business technical account, any transfer must be deducted from item 6 in the non-technical account and added to item 2 of the technical account – general business.

Where part of the investment return allocated initially to the long-term business account is transferred to the non-technical account, the transfer to the non-technical account should be deducted from item 2 of the long-term business account and added to item 4 of the non-technical account.

The reasons for such transfers (which may consist of a reference to any relevant statutory requirement) and the basis on which they are made must be disclosed in the notes to the accounts. See 11.7 below.

8.3.11   Exchange gains or losses

Exchange differences required to be included within profit or loss under Section 30 of FRS 102 should be dealt with through the non-technical account except for long-term insurance business where exchange differences should be recognised in the technical account for long-term business. Exchange differences taken to other comprehensive income arising from translating results and financial position into a different presentational currency *[FRS 102.30.18(c)]* can, where appropriate, in the case of long-term business, be recognised in the FFA. *[FRS 103.2.32]*.

8.3.12   Employee benefits

The net interest on the net defined benefit liability during the reporting period *[FRS 102.28.23(d)]* should be recognised, as appropriate, in the technical account for long-term business or the non-technical account. *[FRS 103.2.33]*.

As an exception to the requirement in paragraph 28.23(d) of FRS 102 to remeasure the net defined benefit liability in other comprehensive income, the remeasurement of the net defined benefit liability which is not attributable to owners should be treated as an amount, the allocation of which, either to policyholders or to owners, has not been determined by the reporting date (i.e. reported within the FFA). It should be included as a separate line in the technical account for long-term insurance business immediately above the line for transfer to or from the FFA, and reflected in that transfer. The impact should be disclosed separately in the notes to the financial statements. *[FRS 103.2.34]*.

8.3.13   Other comprehensive income

As discussed at 8.3 above, Schedule 3 to the Regulations does not address the presentation of other comprehensive income. Illustrative examples of the presentation of other comprehensive income are in Chapter 6 at 6.5.2.

Other comprehensive income means items of income and expense (including reclassification adjustments), that are not recognised in profit or loss as required or permitted by FRS 102. *[FRS 102 Appendix I]*. Therefore, profit or loss is the default category; all comprehensive income is part of profit or loss unless FRS 102 permits or requires otherwise.

FRS 102 requires the following items to be included in other comprehensive income:

(a) changes in revaluation surplus relating to property, plant and equipment *[FRS 102.17.15E-F]* and intangible assets. *[FRS 102.18.18G-H]*. See Chapter 15 at 3.6.3 and Chapter 16 at 3.4.2.C;

(b) actuarial gains and losses, and the return on plan assets excluding amounts included in net interest on the net defined benefit liability (known collectively as 'remeasurements' of the net defined benefit liability) on defined benefit plans. *[FRS 102.28.23(d), 25]*. See Chapter 25 at 3.6.10.B;

(c) exchange gains and losses arising from translating the financial statements of a foreign operation (including in consolidated financial statements, exchange differences on a monetary item that forms part of the net investment in the foreign operation). However, under FRS 102, cumulative exchange differences accumulated in equity are not reclassified to profit and loss on disposal of a net investment in a foreign operation; *[FRS 102.9.18A, 30.13]*

(d) the effective portion of fair value gains and losses on hedging instruments in a cash flow hedge or a hedge of the foreign exchange risk in a net investment in a foreign operation. The amounts taken to equity in respect of the hedge of the foreign exchange risk in a net investment in a foreign operation are not reclassified to profit or loss on disposal or partial disposal of the foreign operation. *[FRS 102.12.23-24, 25A]*. See Chapter 10 at 10.8 and 10.9;

(e) fair value gains and losses through other comprehensive income for an investor that is not a parent measuring its interests in jointly controlled entities, *[FRS 102.15.9(c), 15.14-15A]*, and investments in associates in its individual financial statements. *[FRS 102.14.4(c), 14.9-10A]*. See Chapter 12 at 3.3.4 and Chapter 13 at 3.6.2;

(f) fair value gains and losses through other comprehensive income for investments in subsidiaries, associates and jointly controlled entities used by the parent in its separate financial statements or in consolidated financial statements for certain excluded subsidiaries. *[FRS 102.9.26(b), 9.26A, 9.9, 9.9A, 9.9B(b)]*. See Chapter 8 at 3.4 and 4.2; and

(g) any unrealised gain arising on an exchange of business or non-monetary assets for an interest in a subsidiary, jointly controlled entity or associate. *[FRS 102.9.31(c)]*. See Chapter 8 at 3.8.

Of the above items, only the amounts taken to other comprehensive income in relation to cash flow hedges (at (d) above) may be reclassified to profit or loss in a subsequent period under FRS 102.

Where the entity applies the recognition and measurement requirements of IAS 39 or IFRS 9 to financial instruments, further items are reported in other comprehensive income (see Chapter 10).

In addition, Schedule 3 to the Regulations restricts when unrealised profits can be reported in the profit and loss account. *[3 Sch 18(a)]*. Consequently, certain unrealised profits may be required to be reported in other comprehensive income rather than in profit or loss. Whether profits are available for distribution must be determined in accordance with applicable law. TECH 02/17BL provides guidance on the determination of the profits available for distribution (under the CA 2006). *[FRS 102 Appendix III.29]*.

8.4 Recognition and measurement requirements for long-term insurance business

Long-term insurance contracts as defined by FRS 103 are insurance contracts (including reinsurance) falling within of the classes of insurance specified in Part II of Schedule 1 to the Financial Services and Markets Act 2000 (Regulated Activities) Order 2001 (SI 2001/544). *[FRS 103 Appendix I]*.

Section 3 of FRS 103 contains recognition and measurement requirements for entities applying FRS 103 that are carrying out long-term insurance business. These requirements are set out as follows:

- paragraphs 3.3 to 3.9 and 3.16 to 3.18 apply to all long-term insurance business; and
- paragraphs 3.10 to 3.15 apply to with-profits business and with-profits funds, to which the PRA realistic capital regime (as set out in section 1.3 of INSPRU as at 31 December 2015) was being applied, either voluntarily or compulsorily, prior to 1 January 2016. *[FRS 103.3.1]*.

The requirements set out in Section 3 provide the benchmark for setting accounting policies for long-term insurance business as at 1 January 2015 (i.e. the date from which FRS 103 replaced previous UK GAAP). Entities are permitted to change their accounting policies in accordance with paragraph 2.3 of FRS 103 (see 9 below). Entities that are setting accounting policies for the first time may apply this benchmark or are permitted to set alternative policies (see 3.4 above). *[FRS 103.3.1A]*.

The requirements in Section 3 are based on those contained previously in FRS 27 and the ABI SORP. FRS 103 does not explain why the FRC felt that these requirements needed to be embedded into the standard, when no general insurance accounting requirements are embedded into the standard, but the reason seems to be to ensure that life insurers are directed towards continuing to comply with the requirements of FRS 27 in respect of with-profits business.

Notwithstanding these requirements, an entity is permitted to change its accounting policies away from the requirements if certain criteria are satisfied (see 9 below). When an entity's new accounting policies are not consistent with these requirements, those requirements that are not consistent with the entity's accounting policies need not be applied. *[FRS 103.3.2]*.

The recognition and measurement requirements are discussed below as follows:

- gross premiums written (see 8.4.1 below);
- claims recognition (see 8.4.2 below);
- deferred acquisition costs (see 8.4.3 below);
- measurement of insurance liabilities and related assets (see 8.4.4 below); and
- value of in-force life assurance business held by parents that are not insurers (see 8.4.5 below).

8.4.1 Gross premiums written and reinsurance outwards premiums

Premiums, including those for inwards reinsurance, should be recognised when due for payment. When the amount due is not known, for example with certain pensions business, estimates should be used. *[FRS 103.3.3]*. An insurer should not accrue for future premiums receivable under a contract. This is because such premiums are included within the calculation of the insurance liability (see 8.4.4 below). FRS 103 does not elaborate as to how estimates should be made when the amount due is not known.

For linked business (i.e. business where the benefits payable to policyholders are wholly or partly to be determined by reference to the value of, or the income form, property of any description or by reference to fluctuations in, or an index of, the value of property of any description), the due date for payment may be taken as the date when the liability is established. *[FRS 103.3.3]*.

Reinsurance outwards premiums should be recognised when paid or payable. *[FRS 103.3.4]*.

8.4.2 Claims recognition

Claims payable on maturity should be recognised when the claims become due for payment and claims payable on death should be recognised on notification. *[FRS 103.3.5]*.

Where a claim is payable and the policy or contract remains in force, the relevant instalments should be recognised when due for payment. There should be consistent treatment between the recognition of the claim in the technical account for long-term business and the calculation of the long-term business provision and/or the provision for linked liabilities as appropriate. *[FRS 103.3.5]*.

Surrenders should be included within claims incurred and recognised either when paid or at the earlier date on which, following notification, the policy ceases to be included within the calculation of the long-term business provision and/or the provision for linked liabilities. *[FRS 103.3.6]*.

8.4.3 Deferred acquisition costs

Acquisition costs are costs arising from the conclusion of insurance contracts including direct costs and indirect costs connected with the processing of proposals and the issuing of policies. *[FRS 103 Appendix I]*. Direct costs include acquisition commissions or the cost of drawing up the insurance document or including the insurance contract in the portfolio. Indirect costs include advertising costs or the administrative expenses connected with the processing of proposals and the issuing of policies. *[3 Sch P&L Note 1]*.

FRS 103 does not permit acquisition costs to be deferred for with-profit funds. *[FRS 103.3.10]*. This prohibition applies to with-profits business and with-profit funds to which the Prudential Regulatory Authority (PRA) realistic capital regime (as set out in section 1.3 of INSPRU as at 31 December 2015) was being applied, either voluntarily or compulsorily, prior to 1 January 2016. *[FRS 103.3.1(b)]*.

For other long-term insurance business, acquisition costs can be deferred except to the extent that: *[FRS 103.3.7]*

- the costs in question have already been recovered (for example where the design of the policy provides for the recovery of costs as incurred);

- the net present value of margins within insurance contracts is not expected to be sufficient to cover deferred acquisition costs after providing for contractual liabilities to policyholders and expenses; and

- the receipt of future premiums or the achievement of future margins is insufficiently certain based on estimates of future expected discontinuance rates or other experience.

Chapter 33

Advertising costs can only be deferred where they are directly attributable to the acquisition of new business. *[FRS 103.3.8]*.

FRS 103 does not specify a particular method for the amortisation of deferred acquisition costs. However, the costs that are carried forward should be amortised over a period no longer than the one in which, net of any related deferred tax provision, they are expected to be recoverable out of margins on related insurance contracts in force at the reporting date, and in a similar profile to those margins. *[FRS 103.3.9]*. This implies that amortisation based on profit margins arising from the business is the most appropriate methodology.

8.4.4   *Measurement of insurance liabilities and related assets*

Schedule 3 requires that technical provisions must at all times be sufficient to cover any liabilities arising out of insurance contracts as far as can reasonably be foreseen. *[3 Sch 49]*.

Schedule 3 requires that the long-term business provision must in principle be computed separately for each long-term contract, save that statistical or mathematical methods may be used where they may be expected to give approximately the same results as individual calculations. *[3 Sch 52(1)]*.

There is also a requirement that the computation of the long-term business provision must be made annually by a Fellow of the Institute or Faculty of Actuaries on the basis of recognised actuarial methods, with due regard to the actuarial principles laid down in Directive 2009/138/EC of the European Parliament and of the Council of 25 November 2009 on the taking up and pursuit of the business of Insurance and Reinsurance (Solvency II). *[3 Sch 52(3)]*. The Department for Business, Energy & Industrial Strategy (BEIS) has confirmed to the FRC that this reference should not be interpreted to mean that insurance companies are required to change their accounting basis to one consistent with Solvency II and that Solvency II should only be considered when it is relevant to the accounting basis applied in the company's accounts. *[FRS 103 Appendix III.2A]*.

8.4.4.A   *Measurement of non-profit insurance liabilities*

FRS 103 states that the established accounting treatment for long-term insurance business is to measure liabilities for policyholder benefits under the modified statutory solvency basis (MSSB). *[FRS 103.3.11]*.

The MSSB is the basis for determining insurance liabilities which is the statutory solvency basis adjusted:

- to defer new business acquisition costs incurred where the benefit of such costs will be obtained in subsequent reporting periods (see 8.4.3 above); and

- to treat investment, resilience and similar reserves, or reserves held in respect of general contingencies or the specific contingency that the fund will be closed to new business, where such items are held in respect of long-term insurance business, as reserves rather than provisions. These are included, as appropriate, within shareholders' capital and reserves or the FFA. *[FRS 103 Appendix I]*.

The statutory solvency basis is the basis of determination of insurance liabilities in accordance with rule 1 of the Prudential Sourcebook for Insurers (INSPRU) as at 31 December 2015. *[FRS 103 Appendix I]*.

The Implementation Guidance to FRS 103 provides guidance in relation to the requirement of the Regulations (see 8.4.4 above) to compute insurance liabilities. The Implementation Guidance states that the gross premium method should be used for every class of insurance business except those for which the net premium method is used in the related regulatory returns, but policyholder liabilities of overseas subsidiaries may be computed on a local basis, subject to Part 3 of Schedule 6 to the Regulations. Where the valuation is performed using a net premium method, bonuses should be included in the long-term business provision only if they have vested or have been declared as a result of the current valuation. *[FRS 103.IG2.39-40]*.

The gross premium method is a form of actuarial valuation of liabilities where the premiums brought into account are the full amounts receivable under the contract. The method includes explicit estimates of cash flows for: *[FRS 103 Appendix I]*

- premiums, adjusted for renewals and lapses;
- expected claims and for with-profits business, future regular but not occasional or terminal bonuses;
- costs of maintaining contracts; and
- future renewal expenses.

Cash flows are discounted at the valuation interest rate. The methodology may be set out in the relevant regulatory framework. The discount rate is based on the expected return on the assets deemed to back liabilities. This will be adjusted to reflect any further risks although, under this method, most of the key risks will be reflected in the modelling of the cash flows. For linked business, allowance may be made for the purchase of future units required by the contract terms and credit is taken for future charges permitted under those terms.

The net premium method is an actuarial valuation of liabilities where the premium brought into account at any valuation date is that which, on the valuation assumptions regarding interest, mortality and disability, will exactly provide for the benefits guaranteed. A variation of the net premium method involves zillmerisation. The detailed methodology for UK companies is included in the regulations contained in the PRA Rulebook as at 31 December 2015. *[FRS 103 Appendix I]*.

The Implementation Guidance to FRS 103 states that, in determining the long-term business provision, and the technical provision for linked liabilities, no policy may have an overall negative provision except as allowed by PRA rules, or a provision which is less than any guaranteed surrender or transfer value. *[FRS 103.IG2.41]*.

The Implementation Guidance also states that the long-term business provision may be calculated on a basis used for regulatory reporting subject to appropriate adjustments including the reversal of any reduction in policyholder liabilities where these liabilities already implicitly take account of a pension fund surplus through future expense assumptions which reflect lower expected contributions. *[FRS 103.IG2.42]*.

Investment reserves (realised and unrealised investment gains and exchange gains), surpluses carried forward, resilience and similar reserves, contingency and closed fund reserves which may be included in the statutory liabilities for solvency purposes under the PRA rules, should be considered to assess the extent to which they should be included in the long-term business provision. *[FRS 103.IG2.52]*.

Chapter 33

The Implementation Guidance clarifies that, where the long-term business provision has been determined on an actuarial basis that, in assessing the future net cash flows, having regard to the timing of tax relief where assumed expenses exceed attributable income, such tax relief should be excluded from the determination of deferred tax. *[FRS 103.IG2.44]*.

As stated at 8.4.4 above, BEIS has confirmed to the FRC that the reference in paragraph 52 of Schedule 3 to the Regulations that the computation of the long-term business provision must be made with due regard to the actuarial principles laid down in the Solvency II Directive should not be interpreted to mean that insurance companies are required to change their accounting basis to one consistent with Solvency II and that Solvency II should only be considered when it is relevant to the accounting basis applied in the company's accounts. *[FRS 103 Appendix III.2A]*.

8.4.4.B   *Measurement of with-profits-liabilities and related assets*

FRS 103 requires that (unless an entity has changed its accounting policies) with-profit-funds are required to use the realistic value of liabilities as the basis for the estimated value of the liabilities to be included in the financial statements. *[FRS 103.3.11]*.

The realistic values of liabilities is that element of the amount defined by rule 1.3.40 of INSPRU as at 31 December 2015, excluding current liabilities falling within the definition set out in rule 1.3.190 of INSPRU as at 31 December 2015 that are recognised separately in the statement of financial position. *[FRS 103 Appendix I]*.

For with-profits funds: *[FRS 103.3.12]*

(a)   liabilities to policyholders arising from with-profits business should be stated at the amount of the realistic value of liabilities adjusted to exclude the shareholders' share of projected future bonuses;

(b)   reinsurance recoveries that are recognised should be measured on a basis that is consistent with the value of the policyholder liabilities to which the reinsurance applies;

(c)   an amount may be recognised for the present value of future profits on non-participating business written in a with-profits fund if the determination of the realistic value of liabilities in that with-profits fund takes account, directly or indirectly, of this value;

(d)   where a with-profits life fund has an interest in a subsidiary or associate and the determination of the realistic value of liabilities to with-profits policyholders takes account of a value of that interest at an amount in excess of the net amounts included in the entity's consolidated accounts, an amount may be recognised representing this excess; and

(e)   adjustments to reflect the consequential tax effects of (a) to (d) above should be made.

Adjustments from the MSSB (see 8.4.4.A above) necessary to meet the above requirements, including the recognition of an amount in accordance with (c) and (d) above, should be included in profit or loss. An amount equal and opposite to the net amount of these adjustments should be transferred to or from the FFA and also included in profit or loss.

According to the Implementation Guidance, the shareholder's share of projected future bonuses calculated in accordance with (a) above should be calculated as the value of future transfers to shareholders using market consistent financial assumptions and assuming that transfers take place at a level consistent with those assumptions used to calculate the realistic value of liabilities. When an explicit assumption is not required in order to calculate the liabilities then continuation of the current profit-sharing arrangements should be assumed unless the entity has plans to change this approach. Non-economic assumptions should be consistent with those used in determining the realistic value of liabilities. The amount deducted for the shareholder's share of project future bonuses should be taken to the FFA. If shareholders' transfers have been included as part of the realistic value of liabilities (or otherwise included in liabilities) then the amount of such transfers should be taken out of liabilities and included in the FFA, together with any related tax liability. If shareholder transfers have not been set up as part of the realistic value of liabilities or elsewhere, no adjustment is required. *[FRS 103.IG1.2]*.

In determining the realistic value of liabilities, a with-profits fund may take account of the value of future profits expected to arise from any non-participating business that forms part of the with profits fund – sometimes referred to as the value of in-force life assurance business (VIF). An entity is permitted to recognise the VIF if that business has been taken into account in measuring the liability because excluding it whilst recognising the realistic value of liabilities in full and valuing the non-statutory participating liabilities on a statutory basis would give rise to an inconsistency in the fund's net assets. The VIF can be recognised even though there is not a direct link between the value of the assets and the amount of the liabilities. Where there is not a direct link between the value of the business and the amount of the realistic liabilities, but the value is taken into account in determining these liabilities, it is appropriate to recognise the total value of the business. Although not separately identifiable, any excess amount over the realistic liabilities will be taken to the FFA. *[FRS 103.IG1.3]*.

The amount recognised under (c) and (d) above may be regarded either as an additional asset, representing the value of future cash flows from the related insurance business or as an adjustment to the measurement of liabilities and the FFA, being the deduction from these items of the obligation to transfer an unrecognised asset or other source of value. FRS 103 requires entities to present this as an adjustment to liabilities, unless this would not be in compliance with the statutory requirements that apply to the entity, in which case the amount is permitted to be recognised as an asset. *[FRS 103.IG1.5]*.

The VIF recognised within assets as described above is determined as the discounted value of future profits expected to arise from the policies, taking into account liabilities relating to the policies measured on the statutory solvency basis. This includes adjustments made onto an MSSB for the purposes of the financial statements (for example, to adjust liabilities to exclude certain additional reserves included in the liabilities when measured on the statutory solvency basis, or where future income needed in the VIF covers deferred acquisition costs included in the statement of financial position. A corresponding adjustment to the value of in-force policies will need to be made in order to ensure a consistent valuation. *[FRS 103.IG1.6]*.

Where with-profits policyholders are entitled to a share of the profits on non-participating business it would generally be expected that the determination of the realistic liabilities would take account directly or indirectly, of the value of future profits on this business. *[FRS 103.IG1.4]*. FRS 103 permits recognition of a VIF asset when the determination of the realistic value of liabilities takes account of this value. It would not be appropriate to recognise this release of capital requirements within the VIF asset presented in the accounts because the MSSB liabilities do not include an allowance for capital. Therefore, the amount of the VIF asset should be adjusted accordingly. *[FRS 103.IG1.7]*. Some contracts written within a with-profits fund may not satisfy FRS 103's definition of an insurance contract or contain a discretionary participation feature. These contracts are therefore accounted within the appropriate section of FRS 102. The VIF recognised for such contracts should be adjusted to reflect the difference in profit recognition bases between the basis used to determine the VIF taken into account in determining the realistic value of liabilities and the profit recognition profile determined by the appropriate section of FRS 102. *[FRS 103.IG1.8]*.

In the case of a mutual, an FFA or retained surplus account is maintained that represents amounts that have not yet been allocated to specific policyholders. For such entities, the adjustments required above will be offset within profit or loss by a transfer directly to or from this FFA or retained surplus account, with the result that overall profit or loss for the year will be unchanged. *[FRS 103.3.13]*.

The realistic value of liabilities should exclude the amount which represents the shareholders' share of future bonuses. Similar adjustments should be made if other amounts due to shareholders would otherwise be included in the realistic value of liabilities. *[FRS 103.3.14]*.

An entity is permitted to recognise the excess of the market value of a subsidiary over the net amounts included in the consolidated financial statements as a deduction from the sub-total of the FFA and liabilities to policyholders in the same way as the value of in-force insurance business (VIF) described in paragraph IG1.3 of the Implementation Guidance. *[FRS 103.3.15]*. The Implementation Guidance explains that this situation could arise where the subsidiary or associate writes non-participating business and the value of the subsidiary or associate recognised incorporates the VIF of non-participating business written in the subsidiary or associate. The value of the subsidiary or associate is reduced by the subsidiary's or associate's capital requirement as noted in rule 1.3.33(3) of INSPRU as at 31 December 2015. When preparing both consolidated and non-consolidated accounts, the excess value that may be recognised should therefore be taken as the excess before the deduction of the subsidiary or associate's capital requirement. *[FRS 103.IG1.9]*.

Where the amounts on a 'realistic' basis are different from the amounts on the MSSB, a corresponding amount is transferred to or from the FFA, so that there is no effect on equity. The potential shareholders' share corresponding to additional bonuses to policyholders that have been included in the policyholders' liability should be accounted for in the FFA. Since the FFA is presented as a liability, there will generally be no change in the profit for the reporting period except where the adjustments result in a negative balance on the FFA and the entity determines that this negative balance should result in a deduction from equity through profit or loss. *[FRS 103.IG1.10]*.

Where there are options and guarantees relating to policyholders these are required to be measured either at fair value or at an amount estimated using a market-consistent stochastic model. *[FRS 103.IG1.11]*. The Implementation Guidance states that for all entities with long-term business, the best basis for measuring policyholders' options and guarantees is one that includes their time value. Any deterministic approach to valuation of a policy with a guarantee or optionality feature will generally fail to deal appropriately with the time value of an option. Therefore stochastic modelling techniques should be used to evaluate the range of potential outcomes unless a market value for the option is available. The regulatory framework includes a requirement to value options and guarantees on this basis. For liabilities of businesses not falling within the scope of paragraph 3.1(b) of FRS 103, entities are encouraged, but not required, to adopt these valuation techniques. Where options are not valued on this basis additional disclosures are required – see 11.5.2. *[FRS 103.IG1.12]*.

The Implementation Guidance further states that in determining the value of guarantees and options under the regulatory framework, the entity should take into account, under each scenario in the market-consistent stochastic modelling, management actions it anticipates would be taken in response to variations in market variables. Such actions must be realistically capable of being implemented within the timescale assumed in the scenario analysis and be consistent with the entity's published principles and practices of financial managements (PPFM). Examples of such management actions include changing the balance of the investment portfolio between debt instruments and equity, varying the amount charged to policyholders or varying its bonus policy. *[FRS 103.IG1.13]*.

As stated at 8.4.4 above, BEIS has confirmed to the FRC that the reference in paragraph 52 of Schedule 3 to the Regulations that the computation of the long-term business provision must be made with due regard to the actuarial principles laid down in the Solvency II Directive should not be interpreted to mean that insurance companies are required to change their accounting basis to one consistent with Solvency II and that Solvency II should only be considered when it is relevant to the accounting basis applied in the company's accounts. *[FRS 103 Appendix III.2A]*.

8.4.5 Value of in-force life assurance business held by parents that are not insurers

Banking and other non-insurance entities with insurance subsidiaries sometimes account for the insurance business in their consolidated financial statements on an embedded value or similar basis under which, in addition to the value of the retained surplus in the insurance subsidiary, an asset is recognised for the VIF. The continuation of such a practice is permitted only if the valuation policy is amended, if necessary, to exclude from the measurement of the value of the future profit to shareholders any value attributable to future investment margins. *[FRS 103.3.16]*.

No value should be attributed to in-force long-term insurance business other than:

- in accordance with the requirements above and at 8.4.4.B; or
- amounts recognised as an intangible asset as part of the allocation of fair values under acquisition accounting as discussed at 10 below *[FRS 103.3.17]*.

When the value attributable to a VIF asset recognised by a banking or other non-insurance entity in respect of its insurance subsidiaries in the consolidated financial statements includes an amount in relation to non-participating business written in a with-profits fund or an interest of a with-profits fund in a subsidiary or associate an adjustment should be made to eliminate any double-counting of the same VIF. *[FRS 103.3.18]*.

8.5 Recognition and measurement requirements for general insurance business

General insurance business is defined by FRS 103 as insurance contracts (including reinsurance) falling within of the classes of insurance specified in Part I of Schedule 1 to the Financial Services and Markets Act 2000 (Regulated Activities) Order 2001 (SI 2001/544). *[FRS 103 Appendix I]*.

Chapter 33

Unlike for long-term business, FRS 103 does not contain any recognition and measurement requirements for general business. However, the Implementation Guidance provides guidance on applying the principles of FRS 102 and FRS 103, as well as guidance on implementing certain requirements of Schedule 3 to the Regulations (e.g. in respect of discounting) to general insurance business as follows:

- gross written premiums (see 8.5.1 below);
- portfolio premiums and claims (see 8.5.2 below);
- claims provisions (see 8.5.3 below);
- discounting of claims provisions (see 8.5.4 below);
- unexpired risks provision (see 8.5.5 below);
- equalisation reserves (see 8.5.6 below); and
- deferred acquisition costs (see 8.5.7 below).

8.5.1   Written and earned premiums

The Implementation Guidance states that underwriting results should be determined on an annual basis, notwithstanding that this will normally require some estimation to be made at the reporting date, particularly with regard to outstanding claims. *[FRS 103.IG2.1]*.

Written premiums should comprise the total premiums receivable for the whole period of cover provided by the contracts entered into during the reporting period, regardless of whether these are wholly due for payment in the reporting period, together with any adjustments arising in the reporting period to such premiums receivable in respect of business written in prior reporting periods. *[FRS 103.IG2.2]*.

The Implementation guidance further states that regardless of the method by which commission is remitted (e.g. by an intermediary), grossing up premiums for commission should be applied, if necessary on an estimated basis, as this correctly reflects the contractual arrangements in force. This also applies where the premiums are determined by an intermediary. Where, however, policies are issued to intermediaries on a wholesale basis and they are themselves responsible for setting the final amount payable by the insured without reference to the insurer, the written premium will normally comprise the premium payable to the insurer and grossing up will be inappropriate unless it reflects the contractual position. *[FRS 103.IG2.3]*.

Written premiums should include an estimate for pipeline premiums (i.e. premiums written but not reported to the undertaking by the reporting date) relating only to those underlying contracts of insurance where the period of cover has commenced prior to the reporting date. *[FRS 103.IG2.4]*. Under some policies written premiums may be adjusted retrospectively in the light of claims experience or where the risk covered cannot be assessed accurately at the commencement of cover. Where written premiums are subject to an increase retrospectively, recognition of potential increases should be deferred until the additional amount can be ascertained with reasonable certainty. Where written premiums are subject to a reduction, a remeasurement taking account of such a reduction should be made as soon as the entity has an obligation to the policyholder. *[FRS 103.IG2.6]*.

Where an insurer has offered renewal and is therefore contractually liable to pay claims if renewal is subsequently confirmed by the policyholder, it should recognise the renewal premium in income, subject to making a provision for anticipated lapses and the necessary proportion of unearned premiums. *[FRS 103.IG2.5]*.

Additional or return premiums should be treated as a remeasurement of the initial premium. Where a claims event causes a reinstatement premium to be paid, the recognition of the reinstatement premium and the effect on the initial premium should reflect the respective incidence of risk attaching to those premiums in determining under the annual accounting basis that proportion earned and unearned at the reporting date. *[FRS 103.IG2.7]*.

Written premiums should be recognised as earned premiums over the period of the policy having regard to the incidence of risk. Time apportionment of the premium is normally appropriate if the incidence of risk is the same throughout the period of cover. If there is a marked unevenness in the incidence of risk over the period of cover, a basis which reflects the profile of risk should be used. The proportion of the written premiums relating to the unexpired period of these policies should be carried forward as an unearned premiums provision at the reporting date. *[FRS 103.IG2.8]*.

Schedule 3 requires that the provision for unearned premiums must in principle be calculated separately for each insurance contract, save that statistical methods (and in particular proportional and flat rate methods) may be used where they may be expected to give approximately the same results as individual calculations. Where the pattern of risk varies over the life of a contract, this must be taken into account in calculation methods. *[3 Sch 50]*.

8.5.2 Portfolio premiums and claims

A portfolio premium is an amount payable by one insurer to another in consideration for a contract whereby the latter agrees to assume responsibility for the claims arising on a portfolio of in-force business written by the former from a future date until the expiry of the policies. A portfolio claim is an amount payable by one insurer to another in consideration for a contract whereby the latter agrees to assume responsibility for the unpaid claims incurred by the former prior to a date specified in the contract. *[FRS 103 Appendix I]*. This is different from reinsurance where the reinsurer agrees to pay losses suffered by the reinsured rather than assuming responsibility for the losses.

The Implementation Guidance states that portfolio premiums payable should be included within premiums for reinsurance outwards in the financial statements of the transferor undertaking but deferred to subsequent reporting periods as appropriate in respect of any unexpired period of risk at the reporting date. In the financial statements of the transferee undertaking they should be included within written premiums with any amount unearned at the reporting date being carried forward in the unearned premiums provision. *[FRS 103.IG2.29]*.

Portfolio claims transfers should be recognised in the financial statements of the transferor undertaking as payments in settlement of the claims transferred in accordance with the requirements of (note 4) to the profit and loss account (see 8.3.4 above). *[FRS 103.IG2.30]*. Similarly, the consideration receivable by the transferee undertaking should be credited to claims payable in the statement of financial position. *[FRS 103.IG2.31]*. Disclosure should be made in notes to the financial statements of any claims portfolio transfers, which materially affect the transferee undertaking's exposure to risk. *[FRS 103.IG2.32]*.

8.5.3   Claims provisions

Schedule 3 requires that technical provisions must at all times be sufficient to cover any liabilities arising out of insurance contracts as far as can reasonably be foreseen. *[3 Sch 49]*.

A provision must in principle be computed separately for each claim on the basis of the costs still expected to arise, save that statistical methods may be used if they result in an adequate provision having regard to the nature of the risks. The provision must also allow for claims incurred but not reported by the balance sheet date, the amount of the allowance being determined having regard to past experience as to the number and magnitude of claims reported after previous balance sheet dates. All claims settlement costs (whether direct or indirect) must be included in the calculation of the provision. *[3 Sch 53(a)-(c), FRS 103.IG2.9]*.

Recoverable amounts arising out of salvage or subrogation must be estimated on a prudent basis and either deducted from the provision for claims outstanding (in which case if the amounts are material they must be shown in the notes to the accounts) or shown as assets. *[3 Sch 53(d)]*. Once potential recoveries qualify for recognition as separate assets (e.g. property, plant and equipment) they should be accounted for as such under the appropriate section of FRS 102.

In determining the estimate of the amount required to settle the obligation at the reporting date, the Implementation Guidance states that, in relation to an entity's existing accounting policies, the level of claims provisions should continue to be set such that no adverse run-off deviation is envisaged. In determining the estimate of the amount required to settle the obligation at the reporting date consideration should be given to the probability and magnitude of future experience being more adverse than previously assumed. An entity may not introduce this practice either if it changes its existing accounting policies or develops a new accounting policy. *[FRS 103.IG2.10]*.

The Implementation Guidance further states that provision should be made at the reporting date for all claims handling expenses to cover the anticipated future costs of negotiating and settling claims which have been incurred, whether reported or not, up to the reporting date. Separate provisions should be assessed for each category of business. *[FRS 103.IG2.11]*. In determining the provision for claims handling expenses, unless clear evidence is available to the contrary, it should be assumed that the activity of the claims handling department will remain at its current level and therefore that the contribution to its costs from future new business will remain at the same level. *[FRS 103.IG2.12]*. The provision for claims handling expenses should be included within the provision for claims outstanding but need not be separately disclosed. Claims handling expenses incurred should be included within claims incurred in the technical account for general business. *[FRS 103.IG2.13]*.

8.5.4   Discounting of claims provisions

Schedule 3 prohibits implicit discounting or deductions from general insurance claims provisions. *[3 Sch 53(7)]*.

Schedule 3 permits explicit discounting of general insurance claims subject to conditions. These conditions are: *[3 Sch 54]*

- the expected average interval between the date for settlement of the claims being discounted and the accounting date must be at least four years;
- the discounting or deductions must be effected on a recognised prudential basis;

- when calculating the total cost of settling claims, the company must take account of all factors that could cause increases in that cost;

- the company must have adequate data at its disposal to construct a reliable model of the rate of claims settlements; and

- the rate of interest used for discounting must not exceed a rate prudently estimate to be earned by assets of the company which are appropriate in magnitude and nature to cover the provisions for claims being discounted during the period necessary for the payment of such claims and must not exceed either a rate justified by the performance of such assets over the preceding five years or a rate justified by the performance of such assets during the year preceding the balance sheet date.

The Implementation Guidance to FRS 103 states that the four year test described above should be applied by reference to the end of each reporting period in respect of all claims outstanding at that date, and not just once in the accounting period in which the claims were incurred. *[FRS 103.IG2.14]*. The calculation of the average interval should be weighted on the basis of expected claims before any deduction for reinsurance. *[FRS 103.IG2.16]*.

When applied, explicit discounting should normally be adopted by reference to categories of claims (with similar characteristics but not solely by length of settlement pattern), rather than to individual claims. *[FRS 103.IG2.15]*.

In considering if there is adequate data available to construct a reliable model of the rate of claims settlement, the principal factors to be considered are the amount of future claims settlements, the timing of future cash flows and the discount rate. Procedures should be undertaken to assess the accuracy of the claims settlement pattern predicted by the model in prior periods and the current model should be adjusted, as appropriate, to reflect the out-turn and conclusions of analyses in the previous period. Cash flows should be modelled gross and net of reinsurance as reinsurance recoveries may arise later than the related claims payments. *[FRS 103.IG2.17]*.

For the purpose of determining an appropriate discount rate, justification of the rate requires consideration of the returns achieved over the period in question to the extent that this is relevant to the future. *[FRS 103.IG2.18]*.

The effect of the unwinding of discounted claims provisions during a reporting period should be disregarded in considering whether material adverse run-off deviations have arisen requiring disclosure under (Note 4) of the Notes to the Profit and Loss Account format in Schedule 3 to the Regulations (see 8.3.4 above). *[FRS 103.IG2.19]*.

Any unwinding of the discount on general insurance business claims provisions in a reporting period should be recorded under the headings for investment income or gains in the appropriate sections of the income statement (referred to as the profit and loss account in the CA 2006). Separate disclosure should then be made, where material, of the amount of the investment return which corresponds to the unwinding of the discount. *[FRS 103.IG2.20]*.

8.5.5 Unexpired risks provision

The Regulations require that the provision for unexpired risks must be computed on the basis of claims and administrative expenses likely to arise after the end of the financial year from contracts concluded before that date, in so far as their estimate value exceeds the provision for unearned premiums and any premiums receivable under those contracts. *[3 Sch 51]*.

Chapter 33

The Implementation Guidance below helps apply the requirements of paragraphs 2.14 to 2.19 of FRS 103 and the principles of Section 21 and Section 32 – *Events after the End of the Reporting Period* – to general insurance contracts.

When the estimated value of claims and expenses attributable to the unexpired periods of policies in force at the reporting date exceeds the unearned premiums provision in relation to such policies after deduction of any deferred acquisition costs, an unexpired risks provision should be established. If material, this provision should be disclosed separately either in the statement of financial position or in the notes to the financial statements. *[FRS 103.IG2.21]*.

The assessment of whether an unexpired risks provision is necessary should be made for each grouping of business which is managed together. Any unexpired risks surpluses and deficits within that grouping should be offset in that assessment. *[FRS 103.IG2.22]*. For this purpose business should only be regarded as 'managed together' where no constraints exist on the ability to use assets in relation to such business to meet any of the associated liabilities and either:

- there are significant common characteristics, which are relevant to the assessment of risk and setting of premiums for the business lines in question; or
- the lines of business are written together as separate parts of the same insurance contracts. *[FRS 103.IG2.23]*.

For delegated authorities (i.e. where the insurer is unable to influence the terms on which policies are issued) a provision should be established at the reporting date for any anticipated losses arising on policies issued in the period after the reporting date which the delegated authority entered into before that date. *[FRS 103.IG2.24]*.

The assessment of whether an unexpired risks provision is required, and if so its amount, should be based on information available at the reporting date which may include evidence of relevant previous claims experience on similar contracts adjusted for known differences, events not expected to recur and, where appropriate, the normal level of seasonal claims if the previous reporting period was not typical in this respect. The assessment should not however take into account any new claims events occurring after the reporting date, as these are non-adjusting events. In accordance with paragraph 32.10 of FRS 102 exceptional claims events occurring after the end of the reporting period but before the financial statements are authorised for issue should be disclosed in the notes to the financial statements together with an estimate of their financial effect. Where there is uncertainty concerning future events, in accordance with paragraph 2.9 of FRS 102, an insurer should include a degree of caution in the exercise of the judgements needed in making the estimates required such that liabilities are not understated. *[FRS 103.IG2.25]*.

In calculating the best estimate of the amount required to settle future claims in relation to the unexpired periods of risk on policies in force at the reporting date, the future investment return arising on investments supporting the unearned premiums provision and the unexpired risks provision may be taken into account. For the purposes of calculating this provision, the deferred acquisition costs should be deducted from the unearned premiums provision. The investment return will be that expected to be earned by the investments held until the future claims are settled. *[FRS 103.IG2.26]*.

Deferred acquisition costs should not be written off, in whole or in part, to profit or loss as being irrecoverable for the purpose of reducing or eliminating the need for an unexpired risks provision. *[FRS 103.IG2.27]*.

8.5.6 Equalisation and catastrophe provisions

An entity is allowed to recognise a liability for possible future claims only if permitted by the regulatory framework that applies to the entity. However, following the implementation of the Solvency II Directive, with effect from 1 January 2016 the UK (and EC) regulatory framework does not permit equalisation or catastrophe provisions.

Where an entity has equalisation or catastrophe provisions (e.g. in an overseas subsidiary where these are permitted by the local regulatory framework) the presentation of such liabilities must follow the requirements of the legal framework that applies to the entity. *[FRS 103.2.13(a)]*. For disclosure requirements see 11.2.1.A below.

8.5.7 Deferred acquisition costs

The Implementation Guidance for applying the requirements of Note (17) to the balance sheet – see 8.2.7 above – states that acquisition costs should be deferred commensurate with the unearned premiums provision. The proportion of acquisition costs to be deferred will be the same proportion of the total acquisition costs as the ratio of unearned premiums to gross written premiums for the class of business in question. For this purpose acquisition expenses should be allocated to classes of business. Where this is not possible for reinsurance business inwards an estimate should be made. *[FRS 103.IG2.34]*.

Advertising costs should not be deferred unless they are directly attributable to the acquisition of new business. *[FRS 103.IG2.35]*.

Related reinsurance commissions deferred should not be netted against deferred acquisition costs but should be shown as liabilities in the statement of financial position. *[FRS 103.IG2.36]*.

8.6 Insurance business in run-off

Where a decision has been made to cease underwriting the whole, or a material category, of the insurance business, that business does not constitute a discontinued operation under Section 5 of FRS 102. *[FRS 103.IG2.37]*.

Notwithstanding the above, a decision to cease underwriting the whole, or a material category, of insurance business may be a restructuring to which Section 21 of FRS 102 applies.

8.7 Allocation of investment return between technical and non-technical accounts

As required by note 10 to the profit and loss account (see 8.3.10 above) for long-term business, the investment return (which includes movements in realised and unrealised investment gains and losses) and related tax charges on assets representing reserves which are held within the long-term fund for solvency purposes under the PRA rules, should first be allocated to the long-term business technical account. *[FRS 103.IG2.53]*. General business investment return must either be disclosed in the non-technical account or allocated between the technical and non-technical account.

Chapter 33

FRS 103 permits, but does not require, a form of presentation which enables users of the financial statements to identify operating profit or loss based on the longer term rate of investment return. This return may be recorded within the general business and long-term business technical accounts and may also be disclosed separately as part of the total operating profit. *[FRS 103.IG2.64]*.

When investment return is allocated, it should be on one of the following bases:

- the longer term rate of return basis (see 8.7.1 to 8.7.3 below); or

- an allocation of the actual investment return on investments supporting the general insurance technical provisions and associated equity should be made from the non-technical account to the technical account for general business. *[FRS 103.IG2.65]*.

The allocation of investment return from the technical account for long-term business to the non-technical account should be such that the investment return remaining in the technical account for long-term business on investments directly attributable to owners reflects the longer term rate of return on these investments. *[FRS 103.IG2.67]*. The allocation may be of a negative amount which increases rather than decreases the amount of investment return included in the long-term business technical account. *[FRS 103.IG2.69]*. The allocation should be included in the long-term business technical account and the non-technical account gross of any attributable tax. The tax attributable to the allocated investment return should be deducted from the tax attributable to long-term business and added to the tax on profit or loss on ordinary activities. *[FRS 103.IG2.70]*.

The allocation from the non-technical account to the technical account for general business should be based on the longer term rate of investment return on investments supporting the general insurance technical provisions and all the relevant equity. *[FRS 103.IG2.68]*. Where it is necessary for the purpose of reflecting the longer term rate of investment return in the technical account for general business, the allocation to the technical account may exceed the actual investment return of the reporting period on the corresponding investments. *[FRS 103.IG2.69]*.

To ensure consistency of treatment in the case of an entity transacting both general and long-term insurance business:

- where the longer term rate of return basis is used, it must be applied to both the general and long-term insurance business; and

- where an allocation of the actual investment return on investments supporting the general business technical provisions and associated equity is made from the non-technical account to the technical account for general business, no allocation of investment return should be made from the technical account for long-term business to the non-technical account. *[FRS 103.IG2.66]*.

Guidance is provided on applying the requirements above as follows:

- equities and property (see 8.7.1 below);
- fixed-income securities (see 8.7.2 below);
- derivatives (see 8.7.3 below); and
- attributing tax to the transfer to the non-technical account (see 8.7.4 below).

8.7.1 The longer term rate of return for equities and properties

The longer term investment return on equities and properties should be determined using one of the following methods: *[FRS 103.IG2.72]*

- grossing-up actual income earned for each asset class by a factor representing the longer term rate of investment return divided by an assumed long-term dividend or rental yield (based on the assumption that income will reflect the mix of assets held during the reporting period). Adjustments will be required for special factors which may distort the underlying yields of the portfolio such as (in the case of equities), special or stock dividends and share buy-backs; or

- applying the longer term rate of return to investible assets held during the period (taking account of new money invested and changes in portfolio mix) by reference to the quarterly or monthly weighted average of each group of assets after excluding the effect of short-term market movements.

The longer term rate of return should be determined separately for equities and property and for each material currency in which relevant investments are held. *[FRS 103.IG2.73]*. Taking into account the investment policy followed by the entity, the longer term rate of investment return should reflect a combination of historical experience and current market expectations for each geographical area and each category of investments. The rates chosen should be best estimates based on historical market real rates of return and current inflation expectations, having regard, where appropriate, to the following factors: *[FRS 103.IG2.74]*

- comparison of the business's actual returns and market returns over the previous five years or such longer period as may be appropriate;

- longer term rates of return currently used in the business for other purposes, for example, product pricing, with-profits bonus policy, and pensions funding;

- the rate used for the purpose of achieved profits method reporting;

- consensus economic and investment market forecasts of investment returns; and

- any political and economic factors which may influence current returns.

Rates of return should be set with a view to ensuring that longer term returns credited to operating results do not consistently exceed or fall below actual returns being earned. Any downturn in expectations of longer term returns should be recognised immediately by reducing the assumed rate of return. Rates used should be reviewed at least annually although changes would be expected to be infrequent. *[FRS 103.IG2.75]*.

8.7.2 The longer term rate of return for fixed income securities

The longer term investment return on fixed income securities may be determined using one of the following methods: *[FRS 103.IG2.76]*

- a redemption yield calculated so that any excess of the purchase price over the amount repayable on maturity is recognised in profit or loss by instalments so that it is written off by the time that the security is redeemed; or

- amortised cost with realised gains and losses subject to continuing amortisation over the remaining period to the maturity date.

The Implementation Guidance explains that the longer term return may be based on interest earned where the net effect of amortisation would be immaterial. In the case of irredeemable fixed interest securities and short-term assets, the allocated longer term rate of investment return should be the interest income receivable in respect of the reporting period. *[FRS 103.IG2.76]*.

8.7.3 The longer term rate of return for derivatives

The Implementation Guidance states that where derivatives have a material effect and are used to adjust exposure to the various classes of instruments, the calculation of the longer-term rate of return for equities and properties should be adjusted to reflect the underlying economic exposure. *[FRS 103.IG2.77]*.

8.7.4 Attributing tax to the transfer to the non-technical account

The Implementation Guidance states that, in common with other types of business, taxable profits for UK entities with long-term insurance business are now derived from pre-tax profits reported in the financial statements. However, the requirement for tax expense (income) to be allocated to the same account (technical or non-technical) as the transaction or other event that resulted in the tax expense (income) means that the amount shown in the non-technical account as the transfer from (to) the long-term business technical account is net of tax. There is therefore a requirement for the tax attributable to the transfer to be brought into account in arriving at profit before tax in the non-technical account. *[FRS 103.IG2.79]*.

Entities should determine the amount to be brought into account in the non-technical account in respect of the transfer from (to) the long-term business technical account using a method which is consistent with the approach in paragraph 29.22 of FRS 102 which requires tax to be presented in the same component of total comprehensive income as the transaction or other event that resulted in the tax expense or income. This should fairly represent that part of the tax expense (income) in the long-term business technical account which is based on pre-tax accounting profits or on timing differences in the recognition of such profits for accounting and tax purposes. *[FRS 103.IG2.80]*.

The reconciliation of the tax expense included in profit or loss to the profit or loss on ordinary activities before tax multiplied by the applicable tax rate required by paragraph 29.27(b) of FRS 102 applies only to the tax expense (income) that appears in the non-technical account. *[FRS 103.IG2.81]*.

8.8 Liability adequacy testing

FRS 103 requires an insurer to assess at the end of each reporting period whether its recognised insurance liabilities are adequate, using current estimates of future cash flows under its insurance contracts. If that assessment shows that the carrying amount of its insurance liabilities (less related deferred acquisition costs and related intangible assets, such as those acquired in a business combination or portfolio transfer and discussed at 10 below) is inadequate in the light of the estimated future cash flows, the entire deficiency should be recognised in profit or loss. *[FRS 103.2.14]*.

The purpose of this requirement is to prevent material liabilities being unrecorded.

8.8.1 Using a liability adequacy test under existing accounting policies

If an insurer applies a liability adequacy test that meets specified minimum requirements, FRS 103 imposes no further requirements. The minimum requirements are the following:
[FRS 103.2.15]

(a)   the test considers current estimates of all contractual cash flows, and of related cash flows such as claims handling costs, as well as cash flows resulting from embedded options and guarantees; and

(b)   if the test shows that the liability is inadequate, the entire deficiency is recognised in profit or loss.

If the insurer's liability adequacy test meets these requirements then the test should be applied at the level of aggregation specified in that test. *[FRS 103.2.17]*.

The standard does not specify:

- what criteria in the liability adequacy test determine when existing contracts end and future contracts start;

- at what level of aggregation the test should be performed;

- whether or how the cash flows are discounted to reflect the time value of money or adjusted for risk and uncertainty;

- whether the test considers both the time value and intrinsic value of embedded options and guarantees;

- whether additional losses recognised because of the test are recognised by reducing the carrying amount of deferred acquisition costs or by increasing the carrying amount of the related insurance liabilities; or

- whether the liability adequacy test can be performed net of expected related reinsurance recoveries.

For UK general business, applying the requirements for the unexpired risks provision (see 8.5.5 above) would normally satisfy the criteria above. For UK long-term business, the measurement requirements described at 8.4.4 above would normally satisfy the criteria above.

8.8.2   Using the liability adequacy test specified in FRS 103

If an insurer's accounting policies do not require a liability adequacy test that meets the minimum criteria discussed, it should: *[FRS 103.2.16]*

(a)   determine the carrying amount of the relevant insurance liabilities less the carrying amount of:

(i)   any related deferred acquisition costs; and

(ii)   any related intangible assets such as those acquired in a business combination. However, related reinsurance assets are not considered because an insurer assesses impairment for them separately (see 8.11 below).

(b)   determine whether the amount described in (a) is less than the carrying amount that would be required if the relevant insurance liabilities were within the scope of Section 21 of FRS 102. If it is less, the entire difference should be recognised in profit or loss and the carrying amount of the related deferred acquisition costs or related intangible assets should be reduced or the carrying amount of the relevant insurance liabilities should be increased.

This test should be performed at the level of a portfolio of contracts that are subject to broadly similar risks and managed together as a single portfolio. *[FRS 103.2.17]*.

Investment margins should be reflected in the calculation if, and only if, the carrying amounts of the liabilities and any related deferred acquisition costs and intangible assets also reflect those margins. *[FRS 103.2.18]*.

Section 21 requires an amount to be recognised as a provision that is the best estimate of the expenditure required to settle the present obligation. This is the amount that an entity would rationally pay to settle the obligation at the balance sheet date or transfer it to a third party at that time. *[FRS 102.21.7]*.

Section 21's requirements are potentially more prescriptive and onerous than those applying if an insurer has an existing liability adequacy test which meets the minimum FRS 103 criteria discussed at 8.8.1 above.

8.8.3   *Interaction between the liability adequacy test and shadow accounting*

FRS 103 does not address the interaction between the liability adequacy test (LAT) and shadow accounting (discussed at 9.5 below). The liability adequacy test requires all deficiencies to be recognised in profit or loss whereas shadow accounting permits certain losses to be recognised in other comprehensive income if they are directly affected by movements in assets which were recognised in other comprehensive income.

In our view, an entity can apply shadow accounting to offset an increase in insurance liabilities to the extent that the increase is caused directly by market interest rate movements that lead to changes in the value of investments that are recognised directly in other comprehensive income. Although FRS 103 does not specify the priority of shadow accounting over the LAT, because the LAT is to be applied as a final test to the amount recognised under the insurer's accounting policies, it follows that shadow accounting has to be applied first.

8.9   Insurance liability derecognition

An insurance liability, or a part of such a liability, can be removed from the balance sheet (derecognised) when, and only when, it is extinguished i.e. when the obligation specified in the contract is discharged, cancelled or expires. *[FRS 103.2.13(c)]*. This requirement is identical to that contained in Section 11 of FRS 102 for the derecognition of financial liabilities. *[FRS 102.11.36]*.

Accordingly, insurance liabilities should not normally be derecognised as a result of entering into a reinsurance contract because this does not usually discharge the insurer's liability to the policyholder. This applies even if the insurer has delegated all claims settlement authority to the reinsurer or if a claim has been fully reinsured.

In respect of a structured settlement arrangement falling within one of the cases referred to in sections 731 to 734 of the Income Tax (Trading and Other Income) Act 2005 where either; (a) an annuity is purchased by a general insurance undertaking under which the structured settlement beneficiary is the annuitant; or (b) an annuity previously purchased by a general insurance undertaking for its own account to fund the periodic payments under a structured settlement agreement is assigned to the structured settlement beneficiary, the general insurance company will normally remain liable to the policyholder should the annuity provider fail. An annuity, paid by an annuity provider, which exactly matches the amount and timing of this liability should be recognised as an asset and measured at the same amount as the related obligation. *[FRS 103.IG2.33]*.

Derecognition should be distinguished from remeasurement. The carrying amounts of many insurance liabilities are estimates and an insurer should re-estimate its claims liabilities, and hence change their carrying amounts, if that is required by its accounting policies. However, in certain situations, the distinction between the two concepts can be blurred, for example where there is a dispute or other uncertainty over the contractual terms of an insurance policy.

FRS 103 contains no guidance on when or whether a modification of an insurance contract might cause derecognition of that contract. This will be a matter of judgement based on facts and circumstances. However, insurers could look to the guidance on circumstances when a modification of a financial liability might cause that liability to be derecognised contained in paragraph 11.37 of FRS 102.

8.10 Offsetting of insurance and related reinsurance contracts

FRS 103 prohibits offsetting of: *[FRS 103.2.13(d)]*

(a) reinsurance assets against the related insurance liabilities; or

(b) income or expense from reinsurance contracts against the expense or income from the related insurance contracts.

Offsetting of insurance and related reinsurance contracts is prohibited because a cedant normally has no legal right to offset amounts due from a reinsurer against amounts due to the related underlying policyholder. As a result, balances due from reinsurers should be shown as assets in the balance sheet, whereas the related insurance liabilities should be shown as liabilities. Because of the relationship between the two, some insurers provide linked disclosures in the notes to their financial statements.

This prohibition broadly aligns the offsetting criteria for insurance assets and liabilities with those required for financial assets and financial liabilities under FRS 102, which requires that financial assets and financial liabilities can only be offset where an entity: *[FRS 102.11.38A]*

(a) has a legally enforceable right to set-off the recognised amounts; and

(b) intends to settle on a net basis, or to realise both the asset and settle the liability simultaneously.

The FRS 103 requirements, however, appear to be less flexible than those in Section 11 of FRS 102 in that they provide no circumstances in which offsetting can be acceptable. So, for example, 'pass through' contracts that provide for reinsurers to pay claims direct to the underlying policyholder would still have to be shown gross in the balance sheet. Section 11 of FRS 102 also does not address offsetting in the income statement.

8.11 Impairment of reinsurance assets

A reinsurance asset is impaired if, and only if:

(a) there is objective evidence, as a result of an event that occurred after initial recognition of the asset, that the cedant may not receive all amounts due to it under the terms of the contract; and

(b) that event has a reliably measureable impact on the amounts that the cedant will receive from the reinsurer.

Where a reinsurance asset is impaired, its carrying amount should be reduced accordingly and the impairment loss recognised in profit or loss. *[FRS 103.2.19].*

Both Section 11 of FRS 102 and IAS 39 use an incurred loss impairment model for financial assets and both provide various indicators of impairment for financial assets, such as the significant financial difficulty of the obligor and a breach of contract, such as a default in interest or principal payments. *[FRS 102.11.22, IAS 39.59].* FRS 103 does not provide any specific indicators of impairment relating to reinsurance assets. In the absence of such indicators, it would seem appropriate for insurers to refer to those indicators as a guide to determining whether reinsurance assets are impaired.

IFRS 9 (as permitted by paragraphs 11.2(b) and 12.2(b) of FRS 102) uses an expected loss model rather than an incurred loss model. However, adoption of IFRS 9 does not result in any consequential amendments to FRS 103 in respect of impairment of reinsurance assets. Therefore, even if IFRS 9 is applied for recognition and measurement of financial assets, insurers must continue to use an incurred loss impairment model for reinsurance assets notwithstanding the fact that an expected loss model will be used for financial assets within the scope of IFRS 9.

8.12 Reporting foreign exchange transactions in the functional currency

Paragraph 30.9 of FRS 102 requires an entity, at the end of each reporting period, to translate foreign currency monetary items using the closing rate and non-monetary items using the exchange rate at the date of the transaction or the date when fair value was determined (for non-monetary items measured at fair value). For the purposes of applying the requirements of Section 30 of FRS 102 an entity should treat all assets and liabilities arising from an insurance contract as monetary items. *[FRS 103.2.26].*

The Basis for Conclusions states that the purpose of this requirement is to avoid accounting mismatches caused in the income statement. This mismatch would have arisen because some foreign currency assets and liabilities related to insurance contracts which are not monetary items (e.g. deferred acquisition costs and unearned premiums) would otherwise have been recognised at historic exchange rates whereas insurance assets and liabilities that are monetary items (e.g. claims liabilities) are retranslated at each reporting date. *[FRS 103.BC24-25].*

8.13 Accounting policy matters not specifically addressed by FRS 103

8.13.1 Derecognition of insurance and reinsurance assets

FRS 103 does not address the derecognition of insurance or reinsurance assets. Although not carried over to FRS 103, the Basis to Conclusions of IFRS 4 states that the IASB could identify no reason why the derecognition criteria for insurance assets should differ from those for financial assets accounted for under IAS 39 (IFRS 9). *[IFRS 4.BC105].*

It would seem reasonable for insurers to apply the derecognition criteria for financial assets in Section 11 of FRS 102 (or IAS 39 or IFRS 9 if applied) to insurance and reinsurance assets.

8.13.2 Impairment of insurance assets

FRS 103 does not specify the impairment model to be used for receivables arising under insurance contracts that are not reinsurance assets (discussed at 8.11 above). An example of these would be premium receivables due from policyholders. Insurers should therefore apply their existing accounting policies for determining impairment provisions for these assets, although an impairment model similar to that required by the applicable model being applied for financial assets (depending on accounting policy choice for recognition and measurement) would appear to be appropriate. As FRS 103 does not mandate an impairment model for insurance assets, there is no prohibition on an entity applying the recognition and measurement criteria of IFRS 9 (as permitted by Sections 11 and 12 of FRS 102) from using an expected loss impairment model for insurance assets.

8.13.3 Gains and losses on buying reinsurance

FRS 103 does not restrict the recognition of gains on entering into reinsurance contracts but instead requires specific disclosure of the gains and losses that arise (see 11.2.2 below).

Insurers are therefore permitted to continue applying their existing accounting policies to gains and losses on the purchase of reinsurance contracts and are also permitted to change those accounting policies according to the criteria discussed at Section 9 below.

8.13.4 Policy loans

Some insurance contracts permit the policyholder to obtain a loan from the insurer with the insurance contract acting as collateral for the loan. FRS 103 is silent on whether an insurer should treat such loans as a prepayment of the insurance liability or as a separate financial asset. Consequently, insurers can either present these loans either as separate assets or as a reduction of the related insurance liability depending on previous GAAP requirements.

8.13.5 Investments held in a fiduciary capacity

Insurers often make investments on behalf of policyholders as well as on behalf of shareholders. In some cases, this can result in the insurer holding an interest in an entity which, either on its own, or when combined with the interest of the policyholder, gives the insurer control of that entity (as defined by Section 9 – *Consolidated and Separate Financial Statements*).

9 CHANGES IN ACCOUNTING POLICIES

As discussed at 3.3 above, an entity is permitted by FRS 103 to change its existing accounting policies upon adoption of FRS 103. In addition, an insurer may change its accounting policies at any time and there is no requirement for an insurer to continue to use the recognition and measurement requirements for long-term insurance business (see 8.4 above) or the implementation guidance contained in respect of recognition and measurement of general insurance business (see 8.5 above).

However, an insurer may change its accounting policies for insurance contracts if, and only if, the change makes the financial statements more relevant to the economic decision-making needs of users and no less reliable, or more reliable and no less relevant to those needs. An insurer should judge relevance and reliability by the criteria in paragraph 10.4 of FRS 102 (see Chapter 9 at 3.4) and the qualitative characteristics of information in financial statements set out in Section 2 – *Concepts and Pervasive Principles* – of FRS 102. *[FRS 103.2.3]*.

FRS 103 observes that one basis for changing accounting policies might be to enable them to be more consistent with the rules under the Solvency II Directive for the recognition and measurement of technical provisions. In doing so an entity should make appropriate adjustments to the Solvency II rules to meet the requirements of paragraph 2.3 of FRS 103. *[FRS 103.2.3A]*. This is consistent with the requirements of the Regulations for the computation of the long-term business provision to have due regard to the actuarial principles of Solvency II (see 8.4.4 above).

These conditions for changing accounting policies described above apply both to changes made by an insurer that already applies FRS 103 and to changes made by an insurer adopting FRS 103 for the first time. *[FRS 103.2.2]*.

To justify changing its accounting policies for insurance contracts, an insurer should show that the change brings its financial statements closer to meeting the criteria in paragraph 10.4 of FRS 102, but the change need not achieve full compliance with those criteria. *[FRS 103.2.4]*. The following specific issues are discussed below:

- continuation of existing practices (see 9.1 below);
- current market interest rates (see 9.2 below);
- prudence (see 9.3 below);
- future investment margins (see 9.4 below);
- shadow accounting (see 9.5 below); and
- redesignation of financial assets (see 9.6 below).

There is often a fine line between changing an accounting policy and changing an accounting estimate and insurers should refer to the guidance in Section 10 (see Chapter 9 at 3.5) on this matter. When it is difficult to distinguish a change in accounting policy from a change in accounting estimate, the change is treated as a change in accounting estimate. *[FRS 102.10.15]*.

9.1   Continuation of existing practices

An insurer may continue the following practices but the introduction of any of them after FRS 103 has been adopted is not permitted because it does not satisfy paragraph 10.8(b) of FRS 102 (i.e. it does not provide reliable and more relevant information). *[FRS 103.2.6]*.

9.1.1   *Measuring insurance liabilities on an undiscounted basis*

An insurer is only permitted to change its accounting policies to measure insurance liabilities on an undiscounted basis if otherwise required by Schedule 3 to the Regulations (or other legal framework that applies to the entity). *[FRS 103.2.6(a)]*.

Schedule 3 to Regulations permits explicit discounting for general insurance business only subject to certain conditions (see 8.5.4 above).

9.1.2   Measuring contractual rights to future investment management fees in excess of their fair value

It is not uncommon to find insurance contracts that give the insurer an entitlement to receive a periodic investment management fee. In the FRC's opinion, these rights should not be measured at an amount that exceeds fair value as implied by a comparison with current fees charged by other market participants for similar services. The assumption is that the fair value at inception of such contractual rights will equal the origination costs paid to acquire the contract, unless future investment management fees and related costs are out of line with market comparables. *[FRS 103.2.6(b)]*.

9.1.3   Introducing non-uniform accounting policies for the insurance contracts of subsidiaries

FRS 102 requires consolidated financial statements to be prepared using uniform accounting policies for like transactions. *[FRS 102.10.17]*. However, under previous UK GAAP, some insurers consolidated subsidiaries using accounting policies for the measurement of the subsidiaries' insurance contracts (and related deferred acquisition costs and intangible assets) which were different from those of the parent and were, instead, in accordance with the relevant local GAAP applying in each jurisdiction.

The use of non-uniform accounting policies in consolidated financial statements reduces the relevance and reliability of financial statements and is not permitted by FRS 102. However, prohibiting this practice in FRS 103 would not be consistent with IFRS 4. Therefore, an insurer is permitted to continue using non-uniform accounting policies for the insurance contracts (and related deferred acquisition costs and intangible assets, if any) and change them only if the change does not make the accounting policies more diverse and also satisfied the other requirements in FRS 103. *[FRS 103.2.6(c)]*.

There is one exception to this requirement which is discussed at 9.2 below.

9.2   Current market interest rates

An insurer is permitted, but not required, to change its accounting policies so that it remeasures designated insurance liabilities (including related deferred acquisition costs and related intangible assets) to reflect current market interest rates. Any changes in these rates would need to be recognised in profit or loss. At that time, it may also introduce accounting policies that require other current estimates and assumptions for the designated liabilities. An insurer may change its accounting policies for designated liabilities without applying those policies consistently to all similar liabilities as Section 10 of FRS 102 would otherwise require. If an insurer designates liabilities for this election, it should apply current market interest rates (and, if applicable, the other current estimates and assumptions) consistently in all periods to all those liabilities until they are extinguished. *[FRS 103.2.5]*.

This concession was included in IFRS 4 to allow insurance contracts measured at locked-in interest rates to move, in whole or in part, towards the use of current interest rates. For UK life insurers, the concession is largely irrelevant because existing accounting practices already require the use of current interest rates. However, the concession may be useful if an insurer wants to changes its accounting policies for overseas contracts that may be valued using local accounting practices that do not require the use of current market interest rates (see 9.1.3 above).

Chapter 33

9.3   Prudence

'Prudence' is described as 'the inclusion of a degree of caution in the exercise of the judgements needed in making the estimates required under conditions of uncertainty, such that assets or income are not overstated and liabilities or expenses are not understated'. *[FRS 102 Appendix I]*.

Under previous UK GAAP, insurers sometimes measured insurance liabilities on what was intended to be a highly prudent basis required for regulatory purposes. However, FRS 103 does not define how much prudence is 'sufficient' and therefore does not require the elimination of 'excessive prudence'. As a result, insurers are not required under FRS 103 to change their accounting policies to eliminate excessive prudence. However, if an insurer already measures its insurance contracts with sufficient prudence, it should not introduce additional prudence. *[FRS 103.2.7]*.

The liability adequacy test requirements discussed at 8.8 above address the converse issue of understated insurance liabilities.

9.4   Future investment margins

An insurer need not change its accounting policies for insurance contracts to eliminate the recognition of future investment margins (which may occur under some forms of embedded value accounting). However, FRS 103 imposes a rebuttable presumption that an insurer's financial statements will become less relevant and reliable if it introduces an accounting policy that reflects future investment margins in the measurement of insurance contracts, unless those margins directly affect the contractual payments.

Two examples of accounting policies that reflect those margins are:

(a)   using a discount rate that reflects the estimated return on the insurer's assets; and

(b)   projecting the returns on those assets at an estimated rate of return, discounting those projected returns at a different rate and including the rate in the measurement of the liability. *[FRS 103.2.8]*.

Such accounting policies are used in US GAAP and in embedded value methodologies. The European Insurance CFO Forum European Embedded Value (EEV) Principles state that the value of future cash flows from in-force covered business should be the present value of future shareholder cash flows projected to emerge from the assets backing the liabilities of the in-force covered business reduced by the value of financial options and guarantees.[2] The EEV methodology is considered to be an indirect method of measuring the insurance liability because the measurement of the liability is derived from the related asset. In contrast, direct methods measure the liability by discounting future cash flows arising from the book of insurance contracts only. If the same assumptions are made in both direct and indirect methods, they can produce the same results.

By replicating this requirement from IFRS 4, the FRC repeats the concern of the IASB that insurers might take advantage of the lack of specific accounting guidance for insurance contracts in FRS 103 as an opportunity to change their accounting policies to an embedded value basis on the grounds that this was more relevant and no less reliable, or more reliable and no less relevant than their existing accounting policies (possibly prepared on an 'excessively prudent' regulatory basis). The IASB's view is that the cash flows arising from an asset are irrelevant for the measurement of a liability unless those cash flows affect (a) the cash flows arising from the liability or (b) the credit characteristics of the liability. *[IFRS 4.BC141-144].*

It is possible for insurers to introduce accounting policies that involve the use of asset-based discount rates for liabilities if they can overcome the rebuttable presumption described above. The rebuttable presumption can be overcome, provided it is permitted by the Regulations, if, and only if, the other components of a change in accounting policies increase the relevance and reliability of its financial statements sufficiently to outweigh the decrease in relevance and reliability caused by the inclusion of future investment margins. This is likely to be most relevant for a non-UK insurer using, for example, existing accounting policies for insurance contracts that include excessively prudent assumptions set at inception, a discount rate prescribed by a regulator without direct reference to market conditions, and which ignore some embedded options and guarantees In that situation, the insurer might make its financial statements more relevant and no less reliable by switching to a comprehensive investor-oriented basis of accounting that is widely used and involves:

- current estimates and assumptions;
- a reasonable (but not excessively prudent) adjustment to reflect risk and uncertainty;
- measurements that reflect both the intrinsic value and time value of embedded options and guarantees; and
- a current market discount rate, even if that discount rate reflects the estimated return on the insurer's assets. *[FRS 103.2.9].*

In some measurement approaches, the discount rate is used to determine the present value of a future profit margin. That profit margin is then attributed to different periods using a formula. In those approaches, the discount rate affects the measurement of the liability only indirectly. In particular, the use of a less appropriate discount rate has a limited or no effect on the measurement of the liability at inception. However, in other approaches, the discount rate determines the measurement of the liability directly. In the latter case, because the introduction of an asset-based discount rate has a more significant effect, it is considered to be highly unlikely that an insurer could overcome the rebuttable presumption described above. *[FRS 103.2.10].*

Wording in the Basis for Conclusion to IFRS 4 (not carried forward into FRS 103) states that the IASB believes that in most applications of embedded value the discount rate determines the measurement of the liability directly and therefore it is highly unlikely that an insurer could overcome the rebuttable presumption described above if it wanted to change its accounting policies for insurance contracts to an embedded value basis. *[IFRS 4.BC144].*

9.5 Shadow accounting

FRS 103 permits, but does not require, an insurer to change its accounting policies so that a recognised but unrealised gain or loss on an asset affects the related insurance liabilities in the same way that a realised gain or loss does. In other words, a measurement adjustment to an insurance liability (or deferred acquisition cost or intangible asset) arising from the remeasurement of an asset would be recognised in

Chapter 33

other comprehensive income if, and only if, the unrealised gains or losses on the asset are also recognised in other comprehensive income. This relief is known as 'shadow accounting'. Application of shadow accounting is always voluntary and in practice it is also applied selectively. *[FRS 103.2.11]*.

'Shadow accounting', ensures that all gains and losses on investments affect the measurement of the insurance assets and liabilities in the same way, regardless of whether they are realised or unrealised and regardless of whether the unrealised investment gains and losses are recognised in profit or loss or in other comprehensive income using a revaluation reserve. In particular, the relief permits certain gains or losses arising from remeasuring insurance contracts to be recognised in other comprehensive income whereas FRS 103 otherwise requires all gains and losses arising from insurance contracts to be recognised in profit or loss. Normally, this change in accounting policy would be adopted upon transition to FRS 103.

Recognition of movements in insurance liabilities (or deferred acquisition costs or intangible assets) in other comprehensive income only applies when unrealised gains on assets are recognised in other comprehensive income such as for available-for-sale investments accounted for under IAS 39 (when the IAS 39 recognition and measurement option is applied as permitted by paragraphs 11.2(b) and 12.2(b) respectively of FRS 102) or property, plant and equipment accounted for using the revaluation model under Section 17 – *Property, Plant and Equipment* – of FRS 102.

Shadow accounting is not applicable for liabilities arising from investment contracts accounted for under Sections 11 and 12 of FRS 102. Further, shadow accounting may not be used if the measurement of an insurance liability is not driven by realised gains and losses on assets held, for example if the insurance liabilities are measured using a discount rate that reflects a current market rate but that measurement does not depend directly on the carrying amount of any assets held.

The implementation guidance to IFRS 4 includes an illustrative example to show how shadow accounting through other comprehensive income might be applied. *[IFRS 4.IG10 IE4]*.

FRS 103 does not specifically address the interaction between shadow accounting and the liability adequacy test. We believe that shadow accounting is applied before the liability adequacy test and the implications of this are discussed at 8.8.3 above.

9.6   Redesignation of financial assets

When an insurer changes its accounting policies for insurance liabilities, it is permitted, but not required, to reclassify some or all of its financial assets at fair value through profit or loss provided those assets meet the criteria in paragraph 11.14(b) of FRS 102 (or if the entity has made the accounting policy choice under paragraphs 11.2(b) or (c), or paragraphs 12.2(b) or (c) of FRS 102 to apply the recognition and measurement provisions of either IAS 39 or IFRS 9, as applicable) at the reporting date. *[FRS 103.6.4]*.

This reclassification is permitted if an insurer changes its accounting policies when it first applies FRS 103 and also if it makes a subsequent policy change for accounting for insurance contracts permitted by FRS 103. This reclassification is a change in accounting policy and the requirements of Section 10 of FRS 102 apply i.e. it must be performed retrospectively unless impracticable. *[FRS 103.6.4]*.

This concession cannot be used to reclassify financial assets out of the fair value through profit or loss category.

10 INSURANCE CONTRACTS ACQUIRED IN BUSINESS COMBINATIONS AND PORTFOLIO TRANSFERS

10.1 Expanded presentation of insurance contracts

Section 19 of FRS 102 requires assets and liabilities acquired or assumed in a business combination to be measured at fair value. *[FRS 102.19.14]*. Insurance contracts are not exempt from these requirements and FRS 103 explicitly confirms that insurance liabilities assumed and insurance assets acquired in a business combination must be measured at value fair at the acquisition date. *[FRS 103.2.27]*.

However, an insurer is permitted, but not required, to use an expanded presentation that splits the fair value of acquired insurance contracts into two components:

(a)   a liability measured in accordance with the acquirer's accounting policies for insurance contracts that it issues; and

(b)   an intangible asset, representing the difference between (i) the fair value of the contractual insurance rights acquired and insurance obligations assumed and (ii) the amount described in (a). As an exception to Section 18 of FRS 102, the subsequent measurement of this asset should be consistent with the measurement of the related insurance liabilities. *[FRS 103.2.27(a)-(b)]*.

Technically, this FRS 103 intangible has no intrinsic value that can be actuarially calculated. It is no more than the balancing number between the purchase price allocated to the insurance liability and the amount recorded for the insurance liability by the purchaser under the purchaser's existing GAAP. The more prudent (higher) the basis of liability measurement, the higher the value of the intangible.

Life insurers have variously described this intangible asset as the 'present value of in-force business' (PVIF), 'present value of future profits' (PVFP or PVP) or 'value of business acquired' (VOBA). Similar principles apply in non-life insurance, for example if claims liabilities are not discounted.

An insurer acquiring a portfolio of insurance contracts (separate from a business combination) may also use the expanded presentation described above. *[FRS 103.2.28]*.

An illustration of how a business combination might be accounted for using the expanded presentation is given below.

Example 33.5:   Business combination under FRS 103

Insurance entity A purchases an insurance business owned by Entity B for £10 million. Under A's existing accounting policies for insurance contracts the carrying value of the insurance contract liabilities held by B is £8 million. Entity A estimates the fair value of the insurance contract liabilities to be £6 million. The fair value of other net assets acquired, including intangible assets, after recognising any additional deferred tax, is £13 million. The tax rate is 25%.

Chapter 33

This gives rise to the following journal entry to record the acquisition of B in A's consolidated financial statements:

	DR £m	CR £m
Cash		10.0
Present value of in-force business (PVIF) intangible (£8m less £6m)	2.0	
Carrying value of insurance liabilities (A's existing accounting policies)		8.0
Goodwill	3.5	
Other net assets acquired	13.0	
Deferred taxation on PVIF (25% × £2m)		0.5

The intangible asset described at (b) above is excluded from the scope of both Sections 18 and 27 – *Impairment of Assets* – of FRS 102. Instead, FRS 103 requires its subsequent measurement to be consistent with the measurement of the related insurance liabilities. *[FRS 103.2.27(a)-(b)]*. As a result, it is generally amortised over the estimated life of the acquired insurance contracts. This intangible asset is included within the scope of the liability adequacy test discussed at 8.8 above which acts as a quasi-impairment test on its carrying amount.

Although the VIF asset is outside the scope of Section 18 of FRS 102 for measurement purposes, an entity underwriting long-term insurance business is still required to provide the disclosures set out in paragraphs 18.27 and 18.28(a) of FRS 102 in relation to the VIF asset. *[FRS 103.IG2.54]*.

The Implementation Guidance states that, in respect of long-term business, when a group reconstruction occurs and the new group carries on substantially the same insurance business as the group which it replaces (for example where a demutualisation is effected through the establishment of a proprietary company to acquire the business of an existing mutual insurer), any VIF which would be regarded as internally-generated under the former group structure should continue to be treated as such in the new group. *[FRS 103.IG2.55]*.

Investment contracts within the scope of Sections 11 and 12 of FRS 102 are required to be measured at fair value when acquired in a business combination.

FRS 102 does not address whether there should be a reassessment of the classification of contracts previously classified as insurance contracts by the acquirer which are acquired as a part of a business combination. However, as discussed at 4.7.1 above, in our view a reporting entity could look to apply the guidance in IFRS 3 (that applies prior to adoption of IFRS 17) which states the classification of insurance contracts acquired in a business combination should not be reassessed.

10.1.1   Practical issues

10.1.1.A   The difference between a business combination and a portfolio transfer

When an entity acquires a portfolio of insurance contracts it should determine whether that acquisition meets the definition of a business. FRS 102 defines a business as 'an integrated set of activities and assets conducted and managed for the purpose of providing a return to investors or lower costs or other economic benefits directly and proportionately to policyholders or participants. A business consists of inputs, processes applied to those inputs and the resulting outputs that are, or will be, used to generate revenues'. *[FRS 102 Appendix I].* When it is considered that a business is acquired, goodwill may need to be recognised as may deferred tax liabilities in respect of any acquired intangibles. For a portfolio transfer that does not represent a business combination, neither goodwill nor deferred tax should be recognised.

The determination of whether a portfolio of contracts or a business has been acquired will be a matter of judgement based on the facts and circumstances. Acquisitions of contracts that also include the acquisition of underwriting systems and/or the related organised workforce are more likely to meet the definition of a business than merely the acquisition of individual or multiple contracts.

Rights to issue or renew contracts in the future (as opposed to existing insurance contracts) are separate intangible assets and the accounting for the acquisition of such rights is discussed at 10.2 below.

10.1.1.B   *Fair value of an insurer's liabilities*

FRS 103 does not prescribe a method for determining the fair value of insurance liabilities. However, the definition of fair value in FRS 103 is the same as that of FRS 102 and therefore any calculation of fair value must be consistent with FRS 102's valuation principles.

Deferred acquisition costs (DAC) are generally considered to have no value in a business combination and are usually subsumed into the PVIF intangible. The fair value of any unearned premium reserve will include any unearned profit element as well as the present value of the claims obligation in respect of the unexpired policy period at the acquisition date which is likely to be different from the value under existing accounting policies.

10.1.1.C   *Deferred taxation*

Section 29 – *Income Tax* – of FRS 102 requires deferred tax to be recognised in respect of timing differences arising in business combinations, for example if the amount that can be assessed for tax of the asset or liability is based on cost when the carrying amount is fair value. FRS 103 contains no exemption from these requirements. Therefore, deferred tax will often arise on timing differences created by the recognition of insurance contracts at their fair value or on the related intangible asset. The deferred tax adjusts the amount of goodwill recognised as illustrated in Example 33.5 at 10.1 above. *[FRS 102.29.11].*

10.1.1.D   *Negative intangible assets*

There are situations where the presentation described at 10.1 above may result in the creation of a negative intangible asset, at least in theory. This could arise, for example, where the acquirer's existing accounting policies are such that the contractual liabilities acquired are measured at an amount less than their fair value although this is likely to raise questions about whether the carrying value of the liabilities is adequate (see 8.8 above). FRS 102 and FRS 103 are silent on the subject of negative intangible assets but there appears to be no prohibition on their recognition.

10.2   Customer lists and relationships not connected to contractual insurance rights and obligations

The requirements discussed at 10.1 above do not apply to customer lists and customer relationships reflecting the expectation of future contracts that are not part of the contractual insurance rights and contractual insurance obligations existing at the date of the business combination or portfolio transfer. *[FRS 103.2.29]*. Sections 18 and 27 of FRS 102 apply to such assets.

11 DISCLOSURE

The disclosure principles set out in FRS 103 require entities to disclose the amounts recognised in the financial statements, and the risks and uncertainties related with those balances. These provisions are complementary to the disclosure requirements of Section 11 and the financial institutions sub-section of Section 34 of FRS 102. *[FRS 103.BC30]*.

The disclosures are set out in Sections 4 and 5 of FRS 103 with additional guidance on Companies Act and capital disclosures contained in the Implementation Guidance. Additionally, Schedule 3 to the Regulations contains other disclosures required by insurance entities that are not mentioned by FRS 103. The disclosures required by FRS 103 are in addition to the disclosure requirements of FRS 102. *[FRS 103.4.1]*. Disclosures required by FRS 102 and the Regulations in respect of non-insurance balances and transactions are discussed in the relevant chapters of this publication.

Section 4 of FRS 103 repeats the disclosure requirements of IFRS 4. These requirements are relatively high-level and contain little specific detail. For example, reconciliations of changes in insurance liabilities, reinsurance assets and, if any, related deferred acquisition costs are required but no details about the line items those reconciliations should contain are specified. By comparison, sections of FRS 102 such as Section 17, provide details of items required to be included in similar reconciliations for other balance sheet amounts.

The equivalent disclosure requirements of IFRS 4 are supplemented by sixty nine paragraphs of related implementation guidance which explains how insurers may or might apply the standard. None of this IFRS 4 implementation guidance has been included in FRS 103. However, insurers are recommended to refer to the IFRS 4 Implementation Guidance in considering how best to apply the disclosures required by Section 4 of FRS 103. According to this guidance, an insurer should decide in the light of its circumstances how much emphasis to place on different aspects of the requirements and how information should be aggregated to display the overall picture without combining information that has materially different characteristics. Insurers should strike a balance so that important information is not obscured either by the inclusion of a large amount of insignificant detail or by the aggregation of items that have materially different characteristics. To satisfy the requirements of the standard an insurer would not typically need to disclose all the information suggested in the guidance. *[IFRS 4.IG12]*.

Section 5 of FRS 103 contains additional disclosure requirements for with-profits business. These requirements are not in IFRS 4.

The Implementation Guidance to FRS 103 contains guidance explaining how to apply disclosures required by Schedule 3 to the Regulations as well as suggested disclosures for entities with long-term business necessary for providing capital disclosures in accordance with paragraph 34.31 of FRS 102. The Implementation Guidance does not carry the authority of an accounting standard and is not regarded as mandatory.

11.1   Disclosure of significant accounting policies

In accordance with paragraph 8.5 of FRS 102, an entity should disclose, in the summary of significant accounting policies, in relation to both insurance contracts and financial instruments that it issues with a discretionary participation feature: *[FRS 103.4.2]*

- the measurement basis (or bases) used; and
- the other accounting policies used that are relevant to an understanding of the financial statements.

Schedule 3 to the Regulations also requires disclosure of the accounting policies adopted in determining the amounts included in the balance sheet and profit and loss account (including such policies with respect to the depreciation and diminution in value of assets). *[3 Sch 61]*.

The IFRS 4 Implementation Guidance suggests that an insurer might need to address the treatment of some or all of the following accounting policies: *[IFRS 4.IG17]*

(a)   premiums (including the treatment of unearned premiums, renewals and lapses, premiums collected by agents and brokers but not passed on and premium taxes or other levies on premiums);

(b)   fees or other charges made to policyholders;

(c)   acquisition costs (including a description of their nature);

(d)   claims incurred (both reported and unreported), claims handling costs (including a description of their nature) and liability adequacy tests (including a description of the cash flows included in the test, whether and how the cash flows are discounted and the treatment of embedded options and guarantees in those tests. Disclosure of whether insurance liabilities are discounted might be given together with an explanation of the methodology used;

(e)   the objective of methods used to adjust insurance liabilities for risk and uncertainty (for example, in terms of a level of assurance or level of sufficiency), the nature of those models, and the source of information used in those models;

(f)   embedded options and guarantees including a description of whether:

(i)   the measurement of insurance liabilities reflects the intrinsic value and time value of these items; and

(ii)   their measurement is consistent with observed current market prices;

(g)   discretionary participation features (including an explanation of how the insurer classifies those features between liabilities and components of equity) and other features that permit policyholders to share in investment performance;

(h)   salvage, subrogation or other recoveries from third parties;

(i)   reinsurance held;

(j)   underwriting pools, coinsurance and guarantee fund arrangements;

(k)   insurance contracts acquired in business combinations and portfolio transfers, and the treatment of related intangible assets; and

(l)   the judgements, apart from those involving estimations, management has made in the process of applying the accounting policies that have the most significant effect on the amounts recognised in the financial statements. The classification of a DPF is an example of an accounting policy that might have a significant effect.

Chapter 33

If the financial statements disclose supplementary information, for example embedded value information, that is not prepared on the basis used for other measurements in the financial statements, it would be appropriate to explain the basis of preparation. Disclosures about embedded value methodology might include information similar to that described above, as well as disclosure of whether, and how, embedded values are affected by estimated returns from assets and by locked-in capital and how those effects are estimated.

If non-uniform accounting policies for the insurance liabilities of subsidiaries are adopted, it might be necessary to disaggregate the disclosures about the amounts reported to give meaningful information about amounts determined using different accounting policies.

11.2   Explanation of recognised amounts from insurance contracts

An insurer should identify and explain the amounts in its financial statements arising from insurance contracts. *[FRS 103.4.4]*.

To comply with this principle an insurer should disclose: *[FRS 103.4.5]*

(a)   the recognised assets, liabilities, income and expense (and cash flows if its statement of cash flows is presented using the direct method) arising from insurance contracts. Furthermore, if the insurer is a cedant it should disclose:

   (i)   gains or losses recognised in profit or loss on buying reinsurance; and

   (ii)   if gains and losses on buying reinsurance are deferred and amortised, the amortisation for the period and the amounts remaining unamortised at the beginning and the end of the period;

(b)   the process used to determine the assumptions that have the greatest effect on the measurement of the recognised amounts described in (a). When practicable, quantified disclosure of these assumptions should be given;

(c)   the effect of changes in assumptions used to measure insurance assets and insurance liabilities, showing separately the effect of each change that has a material effect on the financial statements; and

(d)   reconciliations of changes in insurance liabilities, reinsurance assets and, if any, related deferred acquisitions costs.

Each of these requirements is discussed in turn at 11.2.1 to 11.2.5 below.

11.2.1   *Recognised assets, liabilities, income and expense*

As discussed at 8 above, the presentation of the balance sheet and profit and loss account for insurance entities is mandated by Schedule 3 to the Regulations. Details of the presentation requirements are discussed at 8.2 and 8.3 above.

Those UK entities that underwrite insurance contracts that are not insurance entities will usually prepare financial statements under Schedule 1 to the Regulations. The Schedule 1 formats do not cater for insurance balances and therefore those entities will have to use judgement in deciding how to sub-analyse the Schedule 1 line items in order to provide separate disclosure of insurance assets, liabilities, income and expense, if material.

Schedule 3 to the Regulations requires disclosure of the total amount of commissions for direct business including acquisition, renewal, collection and portfolio management.

For this purpose, commission should exclude payments made to employees of the undertaking. *[FRS 103.4.6]*.

In respect of deferred acquisition costs, Schedule 3 to the Regulations requires disclosure of: *[3 Sch P&L Note 17(c)-(e)]*

- how the deferral of acquisition costs has been treated (unless otherwise expressly stated in the accounts); and

- where such costs are included as a deduction from the provision for unearned premiums, the amount of such deduction; or

- where the actuarial method used in the calculation of the provisions within the long-term business provision has made allowance for explicit recognition of such costs, the amount of the cost so recognised.

Section 11 of FRS 102 requires an entity to disclose the carrying amount of financial assets pledged as collateral for liabilities or contingent liabilities and any terms and conditions relating to assets pledged as collateral. *[FRS 102.11.46]*. In complying with this requirement, it might be necessary to disclose segregation requirements that are intended to protect policyholders by restricting the use of some of the insurer's assets.

11.2.1.A   Equalisation provisions

The Implementation guidance to FRS 103 states that, as guidance for applying the requirements of note 24 of the Notes to the balance sheet format in Schedule 3, disclosure should be made when an equalisation reserve has been established in accordance with the PRA Rulebook. When equalisation reserves are established, an entity should disclose the following in the notes to the financial statements: *[FRS 103.IG2.28]*

- that the amounts provided are not liabilities because they are in addition to the provisions required to meet the anticipated ultimate cost of settlement of outstanding claims at the reporting date;

- notwithstanding this, they are required by Schedule 3 to the Regulations to be included within technical provisions; and

- the impact of the equalisation reserves on equity and the effect of movements in the reserves on the profit or loss for the reporting period.

As discussed at 8.5.6 above, following the implementation of the Solvency II Directive the UK regulatory framework does not permit equalisation or catastrophe provisions.

11.2.1.B   Discounting of general insurance provisions

When general insurance provisions are discounted, the Regulations require the following disclosures: *[3 Sch 54(2)]*

- the total amount of gross provisions before discounting or deductions;

- the categories of claims which are discounted or from which deductions have been made; and

- for each category of claims, the methods used, in particular the discount rates used and the criteria adopted for estimating the period that will elapse before the claims are settled.

In addition, the Implementation Guidance suggests that separate disclosure should be made, where material, of the amount of any investment return that corresponds to the unwinding of the discount. *[FRS 103.IG2.20].*

11.2.2   Gains or losses on buying reinsurance

A cedant is required to provide specific disclosure about gains or losses on buying reinsurance as discussed at 8.13.3 and 11.2 above. In addition, if gains and losses on buying reinsurance are deferred and amortised, disclosure is required of the amortisation for the period and the amounts remaining unamortised at the beginning and end of the period. *[FRS 103.4.5(a)(i)-(ii)].*

11.2.3   Processes used to determine significant assumptions

As noted at 11.2 above, FRS 103 requires disclosure of the process used to determine the assumptions that have the greatest effect on the measurement of the recognised amounts. Where practicable, quantified disclosure of these assumptions should also be given. *[FRS 103.4.5(b)].*

FRS 103 does not prescribe specific assumptions that should be disclosed. However, the Regulations require disclosure of the principal assumptions used in making the long-term business provision. *[3 Sch 52(2)].* In order to comply with that requirement, the Implementation Guidance to FRS 103 states that an entity should disclose for each principal category of business the more significant assumptions relating to the following: *[FRS 103.IG2.43]*

- premiums;
- persistency;
- mortality and morbidity;
- interest rates;
- the discount rates used with, if relevant, an explanation of the basis of reflecting risk margins; and
- if applicable, any other significant factors.

The Implementation Guidance to IFRS 4 states that the description of the process used to describe assumptions might include a summary of the most significant of the following: *[IFRS 4.IG32]*

(a) the objective of the assumptions, for example, whether the assumptions are intended to be neutral estimates of the most likely or expected outcome ('best estimates') or to provide a given level of assurance or level of sufficiency. If they are intended to provide a quantitative or qualitative level of assurance that level could be disclosed;

(b) the source of data used as inputs for the assumptions that have the greatest effect, for example, whether the inputs are internal, external or a mixture of the two. For data derived from detailed studies that are not carried out annually, the criteria used to determine when the studies are updated and the date of the latest update could be disclosed;

(c) the extent to which the assumptions are consistent with observable market prices or other published information;

(d)   a description of how past experience, current conditions and other relevant benchmarks are taken into account in developing estimates and assumptions. If a relationship would normally be expected between past experience and future results, the reasons for using assumptions that differ from past experience and an indication of the extent of the difference could be explained;

(e)   a description of how assumptions about future trends, such as changes in mortality, healthcare costs or litigation awards were developed;

(f)   an explanation of how correlations between different assumptions are identified;

(g)   the policy in making allocations or distributions for contracts with discretionary participation features. In addition, the related assumptions that are reflected in the financial statements, the nature and extent of any significant uncertainty about the relative interests of policyholders and shareholders in the unallocated surplus associated with those contracts, and the effect on the financial statements of any changes during the period in that policy or those assumptions could be disclosed; and

(h)   the nature and extent of uncertainties affecting specific assumptions.

11.2.4   The effects of changes in assumptions

As noted at 11.2 above, FRS 103 requires disclosure of the effects of changes in assumptions used to measure insurance assets and insurance liabilities, showing separately the effect of each change that has a material impact on the financial statements. *[FRS 103.4.5(c)]*. This requirement is consistent with Section 10 of FRS 102 which requires disclosure of the nature and amount of a change in an accounting estimate. *[FRS 102.10.18]*.

Additionally, the Regulations specifically require that, where the difference between the loss provision made at the beginning of the year for outstanding claims incurred in previous years and the payments made during the year on account of claims incurred in previous years and the loss provision shown at the end of the year for outstanding claims is material, it must be shown in the notes to the accounts broken down by category and amount. *[3 Sch P&L Note 4]*. The effect of unwinding discounted claims provisions should be disregarded in considering whether material adverse run-off deviations have occurred. *[FRS 103.IG2.19]*.

Assumptions are often interdependent. When this is the case, any analysis of changes by assumption may depend on the order in which the analysis is performed and may be arbitrary to some extent. Not surprisingly, FRS 103 does not specify a rigid format or content for this analysis. This allows insurers to analyse the changes in a way that meets the objective of the disclosure requirement and is appropriate for their particular circumstances. If practicable, the impact of changes in different assumptions might be disclosed separately, particularly if changes in those assumptions have an adverse effect and others have a beneficial effect. The impact of interdependencies between assumptions and the resulting limitations of any analysis of the effect of changes in assumption might also be described.

The Implementation Guidance to IFRS 4 states that the effects of changes in assumptions both before and after reinsurance held might be disclosed, especially if a significant change in the nature or extent of an entity's reinsurance programme is expected or if an analysis before reinsurance is relevant for an analysis of the credit risk arising from reinsurance held. *[IFRS 4.IG36]*.

11.2.5   Reconciliations of changes in insurance assets and liabilities

As noted at 11.2 above, FRS 103 requires reconciliations of changes in insurance liabilities, reinsurance assets and, if any, related deferred acquisition costs, although it does not prescribe the line items that should appear in the reconciliations. *[FRS 103.4.5(d)]*.

The Implementation Guidance to IFRS 4 states that for insurance liabilities the changes might include: *[IFRS 4.IG37]*

(a)   the carrying amount at the beginning and end of the period;

(b)   additional insurance liabilities arising during the period;

(c)   cash paid;

(d)   income and expense included in profit or loss;

(e)   liabilities acquired from, or transferred to, other insurers; and

(f)   net exchange differences arising on the translation of the financial statements into a different presentation currency, and on the translation of a foreign operation into the presentation currency of the reporting entity.

A reconciliation of deferred acquisition costs might include: *[IFRS 4.IG39]*

(a)   the carrying amount at the beginning and end of the period;

(b)   the amounts incurred during the period;

(c)   the amortisation for the period;

(d)   impairment losses recognised during the period; and

(e)   other changes categorised by cause and type.

An insurer may have intangible assets related to insurance contracts acquired in a business combination or portfolio transfer. FRS 103 does not require any disclosures for intangible assets in addition to those required by Section 18 of FRS 102.

11.3   Nature and extent of risks arising from insurance contracts

FRS 103 requires that an insurer disclose information to enable the users of the financial statements to evaluate the nature and extent of risks arising from insurance contracts. *[FRS 103.4.7]*.

To comply with this principle, an insurer should disclose: *[FRS 103.4.8]*

(a)   its objectives, policies and processes for managing risks arising from insurance contracts and the methods used to manage those risks;

(b)   information about insurance risk (both before and after risk mitigation by reinsurance), including information about:

　(i)   sensitivity to insurance risk;

　(ii)   concentrations of insurance risk, including a description of how management determines concentrations and a description of the shared characteristic that identifies each concentration (e.g. type of insured event, geographical area or currency); and

(iii) actual claims compared with previous estimates (i.e. claims development). This disclosure has to go back to the period when the earliest material claim arose for which there is still uncertainty about the amount and timing of the claims payments, but need not go back more than ten years. Information about claims for which uncertainty about the amount and timing of claims payments is typically resolved within one year need not be disclosed;

(c) information about credit risk, liquidity risk and market risk that, as a financial institution, Section 34 of FRS 102 would require if insurance contracts were within the scope of Sections 11 and 12 of FRS 102. However:

(i) an insurer need not provide the maturity analyses required by paragraph 34.28 of FRS 102 if it discloses information about the estimated timing of the net cash outflows resulting from recognised insurance liabilities instead. This may take the form of an analysis, by estimated timing, of the amounts recognised in the statement of financial position rather than gross undiscounted cash flows; and

(ii) if an alternative method to manage sensitivity to market conditions, such as an embedded value analysis is used, an insurer may use that sensitivity analysis to meet the requirement in paragraph 34.39 of FRS 102. Such an insurer should also provide the disclosure required by paragraph 34.30 of FRS 102; and

(d) information about exposures to market risk arising from embedded derivatives contained in a host insurance contract if the insurer is not required to, and does not, measure the embedded derivatives at fair value.

The Implementation Guidance to IFRS 4 states that these disclosure requirements are based on two foundations: *[IFRS 4.IG41]*

(a) there should be a balance between quantitative and qualitative disclosures, enabling users to understand the nature of risk exposures and their potential impact; and

(b) disclosures should be consistent with how management perceives its activities and risks, and the objectives, policies and processes that management uses to manage those risks so that they:

(i) generate information that has more predictive value than information based on assumptions and methods that management does not use, for example, in considering the insurer's ability to react to adverse situations; and

(ii) are more effective in adapting to the continuing change in risk measurement and management techniques and developments in the external environment over time.

In developing disclosures to satisfy the requirements, the Implementation guidance to IFRS 4 states that it might be useful to group insurance contracts into broad classes appropriate for the nature of the information to be disclosed, taking into account matters such as the risks covered, the characteristics of the contracts and the measurement basis applied. These broad classes may correspond to classes established for legal or regulatory purposes, but IFRS 4 does not require this. *[IFRS 4.IG42]*.

In identifying broad classes for separate disclosure, it is useful to consider how best to indicate the level of uncertainty associated with the risks underwritten, so as to inform users whether outcomes are likely to be within a wider or a narrower range. For example, an insurer might disclose information about exposures where there are significant amounts of provisions for claims incurred but not reported (IBNR) or where outcomes and risks are unusually difficult to assess, e.g. for asbestos-related claims. *[IFRS 4.IG45]*.

The disclosures required are discussed in more detail below.

11.3.1   Objectives, policies and processes for managing insurance contract risks

As noted at 11.3 above, FRS 103 requires an insurer to disclose its objectives, policies and processes for managing risks arising from insurance contracts and the methods used to manage those risks. *[FRS 103.4.8(a)]*.

No further guidance is provided by FRS 103. However, the Implementation Guidance to IFRS 4 suggests that such disclosure provides an additional perspective that complements information about contracts outstanding at a particular time and might include information about: *[IFRS 4.IG48]*

(a)   the structure and organisation of the entity's risk management function(s), including a discussion of independence and accountability;

(b)   the scope and nature of its risk reporting or measurement systems, such as internal risk measurement models, sensitivity analyses, scenario analysis, and stress testing, and how these are integrated into the entity's operating activities. Useful disclosure might include a summary description of the approach used, associated assumptions and parameters (including confidence intervals, computation frequencies and historical observation periods) and strengths and limitations of the approach;

(c)   the processes for accepting, measuring, monitoring and controlling insurance risks and the entity's underwriting strategy to ensure that there are appropriate risk classification and premium levels;

(d)   the extent to which insurance risks are assessed and managed on an entity-wide basis;

(e)   the methods employed to limit or transfer insurance risk exposures and avoid undue concentrations of risk, such as retention limits, inclusion of options in contracts, and reinsurance;

(f)   asset and liability management (ALM) techniques; and

(g)   the processes for managing, monitoring and controlling commitments received (or given) to accept (or contribute) additional debt or equity capital when specified events occur.

It might be useful to provide disclosures both for individual types of risks insured and overall. They might include a combination of narrative descriptions and specific quantified data, as appropriate to the nature of the contracts and their relative significance to the insurer.

11.3.2   Insurance risk – general matters

As noted at 11.3 above, FRS 103 requires disclosure about insurance risk (both before and after risk mitigation by reinsurance). *[FRS 103.4.8(b)]*.

The Implementation Guidance to IFRS 4 suggests that disclosures made to satisfy this requirement might build on the following foundations: *[IFRS 4.IG51]*

(a) information about insurance risk might be consistent with (though less detailed than) the information provided internally to the entity's key management personnel so that users can assess the entity's financial position, performance and cash flows 'through the eyes of management';

(b) information about risk exposures might report exposures both gross and net of reinsurance (or other risk mitigating elements, such as catastrophe bonds issued or policyholder participation features). This is especially relevant if a significant change in the nature or extent of an entity's reinsurance programme is expected or if an analysis before reinsurance is relevant for an analysis of the credit risk arising from reinsurance held;

(c) in reporting quantitative information about insurance risk, disclosure of the strengths and limitations of those methods, the assumptions made, and the effect of reinsurance, policyholder participation and other mitigating elements might be useful;

(d) risk might be classified according to more than one dimension. For example, life insurers might classify contracts by both the level of mortality risk and the level of investment risk. It may sometimes be useful to display this information in a matrix format; and

(e) if risk exposures at the reporting date are unrepresentative of exposures during the period, it might be useful to disclose that fact.

The following disclosures required by FRS 103 might also be relevant:

- the sensitivity of profit or loss and equity to changes in variables that have a material effect on them (see 11.3.3);

- concentrations of insurance risk (see 11.3.4); and

- the development of prior year insurance liabilities (see 11.3.5).

The Implementation Guidance to IFRS 4 also suggests that disclosures about insurance risk might also include: *[IFRS 4.IG51A]*

- information about the nature of the risk covered, with a brief summary description of the class (such as annuities, pensions, other life insurance, motor, property and liability);

- information about the general nature of participation features whereby policyholders share in the performance (and related risks) of individual contracts or pools of contracts or entities. This might include the general nature of any formula for the participation and the extent of any discretion held by the insurer; and

- information about the terms of any obligation or contingent obligation for the insurer to contribute to government or other guarantee funds established by law.

11.3.3 Insurance risk – sensitivity information

As noted at 11.3 above, IFRS 4 requires disclosures about sensitivity to insurance risk. *[FRS 103.4.8(b)(i)].*

To comply with this requirement, disclosure is required of either: *[FRS 103.4.9]*

(a)   a sensitivity analysis that shows how profit or loss and equity would have been affected had changes in the relevant risk variable that were reasonably possible at the end of the reporting period occurred; the methods and assumptions used in preparing that sensitivity analysis; and any changes from the previous period in the methods and assumptions used. However, if an insurer uses an alternative method to manage sensitivity to market conditions, such as an embedded value analysis, it may meet this requirement by disclosing that alternative sensitivity analysis and the disclosures required by paragraph 34.30 of FRS 102; or

(b)   qualitative information about sensitivity, and information about those terms and conditions of insurance contracts that have a material effect on the amount, timing and uncertainty of future cash flows.

Quantitative disclosures may be provided for some insurance risks and qualitative information about sensitivity and information about terms and conditions for other insurance risks.

The Implementation Guidance to IFRS 4 states that insurers should avoid giving a misleading sensitivity analysis if there are significant non-linearities in sensitivities to variables that have a material effect. For example, if a change of 1% in a variable has a negligible effect, but a change of 1.1% has a material effect, it might be misleading to disclose the effect of a 1% change without further explanation. *[IFRS 4.IG53]*. Further, if a quantitative sensitivity analysis is disclosed and that sensitivity analysis does not reflect significant correlations between key variables, the effect of those correlations may need to be explained. *[IFRS 4.IG53A]*.

11.3.4   Insurance risk – concentrations of risk

As noted at 11.3 above, FRS 103 requires disclosure of concentrations of insurance risk, including a description of how management determines concentrations and a description of the shared characteristic that identifies each type of concentration (e.g. type of insured event, geographical area, or currency). *[FRS 103.4.8(b)(ii)]*.

The Implementation guidance to IFRS 4 states that such concentrations could arise from, for example: *[IFRS 4.IG55]*

(a)   a single insurance contract, or a small number of related contracts, for example when an insurance contract covers low-frequency, high-severity risks such as earthquakes;

(b)   single incidents that expose an insurer to risk under several different types of insurance contract. For example, a major terrorist incident could create exposure under life insurance contracts, property insurance contracts, business interruption and civil liability;

(c)   exposure to unexpected changes in trends, for example unexpected changes in human mortality or in policyholder behaviour;

(d)   exposure to possible major changes in financial market conditions that could cause options held by policyholders to come into the money. For example, when interest rates decline significantly, interest rate and annuity guarantees may result in significant losses;

(e)   significant litigation or legislative risks that could cause a large single loss, or have a pervasive effect on many contracts;

(f)   correlations and interdependencies between different risks;

(g)   significant non-linearities, such as stop-loss or excess of loss features, especially if a key variable is close to a level that triggers a material change in future cash flows; and

(h)   geographical and sectoral concentrations.

Disclosure of concentrations of insurance risk might include a description of the shared characteristic that identifies each concentration and an indication of the possible exposure, both before and after reinsurance held, associated with all insurance liabilities sharing that characteristic. *[IFRS 4.IG56].*

Disclosure about the historical performance of low-frequency, high-severity risks might be one way to help users assess cash flow uncertainty associated with those risks. For example, an insurance contract may cover an earthquake that is expected to happen, on average, once every 50 years. If the earthquake occurs during the current reporting period the insurer will report a large loss. If the earthquake does not occur during the current reporting period the insurer will report a profit. Without adequate disclosure of long-term historical performance, it could be misleading to report 49 years of large profits, followed by one large loss, because users may misinterpret the insurer's long-term ability to generate cash flows over the complete cycle of 50 years. Therefore, describing the extent of the exposure to risks of this kind and the estimated frequency of losses might be useful. If circumstances have not changed significantly, disclosure of the insurer's experience with this exposure may be one way to convey information about estimated frequencies. *[IFRS 4.IG57].* However, there is no specific requirement to disclose a probable maximum loss (PML) in the event of a catastrophe because there is no widely agreed definition of PML. *[IFRS 4.BC222].*

11.3.5   Insurance risk – claims development information

As noted at 11.3 above, FRS 103 requires disclosure of actual claims compared with previous estimates (i.e. claims development). The disclosure about claims development should go back to the period when the earliest material claim arose for which there is still uncertainty about the amount and the timing of the claims payments, but need not go back more than ten years. Disclosure need not be provided for claims for which uncertainty about claims payments is typically resolved within one year. *[FRS 103.4.8(b)(iii)].*

As discussed at 3.3 above, transitional relief is available for this disclosure requirement.

The requirement applies to all insurers, not only to property and casualty insurers. In practice, however, life insurers have not made these disclosures under IFRS. This is because the Implementation Guidance to IFRS 4 suggests that, because insurers need not disclose the information for claims for which uncertainty about the amount and timing of payments is typically resolved within a year, it is unlikely that many life insurers will need to give the disclosure. Additionally, the claims development disclosure should not normally be needed for annuity contracts because each periodic payment is regarded as a separate claim about which there is no uncertainty. *[IFRS 4.BC220, IG60]*.

The Implementation Guidance to IFRS 4 suggests that it might also be informative to reconcile the claims development information to amounts reported in the balance sheet and disclose unusual claims expenses or developments separately, allowing users to identify the underlying trends in performance. *[IFRS 4.IG59]*.

FRS 103, like IFRS 4, is silent as to whether development information should be provided on both a gross basis and a net basis. If the effect of reinsurance is significant it would seem appropriate to provide such information both gross and net of reinsurance.

FRS 103 (and IFRS 4) is also silent as to the presentation of:

- exchange differences associated with insurance liabilities arising on retranslation;
- claims liabilities acquired in a business combination or portfolio transfer; and
- claims liabilities disposed of in a business combination or portfolio transfer.

As FRS 103 is silent on these matters, a variety of treatments would appear to be permissible provided they are adequately explained to the users of the financial statements and consistently applied in each reporting period. For example, exchange rates could be fixed at the date the claims are incurred, the original reporting period dates or amounts could be retranslated at each reporting date. Claims liabilities acquired in a business combination or portfolio transfer could be reallocated to the prior reporting periods in which they were originally incurred by the acquiree or all liabilities could be allocated to the reporting period in which the acquisition/portfolio transfer occurred.

An illustrative example of one possible format for presenting claims development based on the example in IFRS 4 is reproduced below. This example presents discounted claims development information by accident year. Other formats are permitted, including for example, presenting information by underwriting year or reporting period rather than underwriting year. In the interests of brevity, this illustrative example provides only five years of data although the standard itself requires ten (subject to the transitional relief upon first-time adoption). The effect of reinsurance is ignored. Given the long tail nature of many non-life insurance claims liabilities it is likely that many non-life insurers will still have claims outstanding at the reporting date that are more than ten years old and which will need to be included in a reconciliation of the development table to the balance sheet.

Example 33.6:   *Illustrative disclosure of claims development*

This example illustrates a possible format for a claims development table for a general insurer. The top half of the table shows how the insurer's estimates of total claims for each accident year develop over time. For example, at the end of 2015, the insurer estimated that it would pay claims of CU680 for insured events relating to insurance contracts underwritten in 2015. By the end of 2016, the insurer had revised the estimate of cumulative claims (both those paid and those still to be paid) to CU673.

The lower half of the table reconciles the cumulative claims to the amount appearing in the balance sheet. First, the cumulative payments are deducted to give the cumulative unpaid claims for each year on an undiscounted basis. Second, if the claims liabilities are discounted, the effect of discounting is deducted to give the carrying amount in the balance sheet.

Accident year	2015	2016	2017	2018	2019	Total
	CU	CU	CU	CU	CU	CU
Estimate of cumulative claims:						
At end of underwriting year	680	790	823	920	968	
One year later	673	785	840	903		
Two years later	692	776	845			
Three years later	697	771				
Four years later	702					
Estimate of cumulative claims	702	771	845	903	968	
Cumulative payments	(702)	(689)	(570)	(350)	(217)	
	–	82	275	553	751	1,661
Effect of discounting	–	(14)	(68)	(175)	(285)	(542)
Present value recognised in the balance sheet	–	68	207	378	466	1,119

11.3.6 Credit risk, liquidity risk and market risk disclosures

As noted at 11.3 above, FRS 103 requires disclosure of information about credit risk, liquidity risk and market risk that, as a financial institution, Section 34 of FRS 102 would require if insurance contracts were within the scope of Sections 11 and 12 of FRS 102. *[FRS 103.4.8(c)].*

Such disclosure should include: *[FRS 102.34.24]*

- the exposures to risk and how they arise;

- the objectives, policies and processes for managing the risk and the methods used to measure the risk; and

- any changes in risk exposures, objectives, policies and processes from the previous period.

The Implementation Guidance to IFRS 4 suggests that, to be informative, the disclosure about credit risk, liquidity risk and market risk might include: *[IFRS 4.IG64]*

(a) information about the extent to which features such as policyholder participation features might mitigate or compound those risks;

(b) a summary of significant guarantees, and of the levels at which guarantees of market prices or interest rates are likely to alter cash flows; and

(c) the basis for determining investment returns credited to policyholders, such as whether the returns are fixed, based contractually on the return of specified assets or partly or wholly subject to the insurer's discretion.

11.3.6.A Credit risk disclosures

Credit risk is defined as 'the risk that one party to a financial instrument will fail to discharge an obligation and cause the other party to incur a financial loss'. *[FRS 102 Appendix I].*

For a reinsurance contract, credit risk includes the risk that the insurer incurs a financial loss because a reinsurer defaults on its obligations under the contract. Furthermore, disputes with reinsurers could lead to impairments of the cedant's reinsurance assets. The risk of such disputes may have an effect similar to credit risk. Thus, similar disclosure might be relevant. Balances due from agents or brokers may also be subject to credit risk.

The specific disclosure requirements about credit risk in Section 34 of FRS 102 are: *[FRS 102.34.25-27]*

(a)   the amount representing the maximum exposure to credit risk at the reporting date without taking account of any collateral held or other credit enhancements. Disclosure is not required for instruments whose carrying amount best represents the maximum exposure to credit risk;

(b)   in respect of the amount above, a description of the collateral held as security and other credit enhancements and the extent to which these mitigate credit risk;

(c)   the amount by which any related credit derivatives or similar instruments mitigate that maximum exposure to risk;

(d)   information about the credit quality of financial assets that are neither past due nor impaired;

(e)   for each class of financial assets:

(i)   an analysis of the age of those that are past due at the reporting date but not impaired; and

(ii)   an analysis of those that are individually determined to be impaired as at the reporting date, including the factors considered in determining that they are impaired;

(f)   when a financial institution obtains financial or non financial assets during the period by taking possession of collateral it holds as security or calling on other credit enhancements (e.g. guarantees) and such assets meet the recognition criteria in other sections of FRS 102 disclosure is required of:

(i)   the nature and carrying amount of the assets obtained; and

(ii)   when the assets are not readily convertible into cash, the entity's policies for disposing of such assets or for using them in its operations.

The disclosures in (a) to (e) above are to be given by class of financial instrument. *[FRS 102.34.25-26]*.

11.3.6.B   Liquidity risk disclosures

Liquidity risk is defined as 'the risk that an entity will encounter difficulty in meeting obligations associated with financial liabilities that are settled by delivering cash or another financial asset'. *[FRS 102 Appendix I]*.

The specific disclosure requirement about credit risk in Section 34 of FRS 102 is for a maturity analysis for financial liabilities that shows the remaining contractual maturities at undiscounted amounts separated between derivative and non-derivative liabilities. *[FRS 102.34.28]*.

Although the maturity analysis is required of undiscounted contractual maturities, an insurer need not present this analysis if, instead, it discloses information about the estimated timing of the net cash outflows resulting from recognised insurance liabilities. This may take the form of an analysis, by estimated timing, of the amounts recognised in the balance sheet. *[FRS 103.4.8(c)(i)]*.

The reason for this concession is to avoid insurers having to disclose detailed cash flow estimates for insurance liabilities that are not required for measurement purposes.

This concession is not available for investment contracts that do not contain a DPF. These contracts are within the scope of Section 34 of FRS 102 and not FRS 103. Consequently, a maturity analysis of contractual undiscounted amounts is required for these liabilities.

The Implementation Guidance to IFRS 4 suggests that an insurer might need to disclose a summary narrative description of how the cash flows in the maturity analysis (or analysis by estimated timing) could change if policyholders exercised lapse or surrender options in different ways. If lapse behaviour is likely to be sensitive to interest rates, that fact might be disclosed as well as whether the disclosures about market risk (see 11.3.6.C below) reflect that interdependence. *[IFRS 4.IG65C]*.

11.3.6.C Market risk disclosures

Market risk is defined as 'the risk that the fair value or future cash flows of a financial instrument will fluctuate because of changes in market prices'. Market risk comprises three types of risk: currency risk, interest rate risk and other price risk. *[FRS 102 Appendix I]*.

The specific disclosure requirements about credit risk in Section 34 of FRS 102 are: *[FRS 102.34.29]*

(a) a sensitivity analysis for each type of market risk (e.g. interest rate risk, currency risk, other price risk) to which there is exposure at the reporting date, showing the impact on profit or loss and equity;

(b) details of the methods and assumptions used in preparing that sensitivity analysis.

If a financial institution prepares a sensitivity analysis, such as value-at risk, that reflects interdependencies between risk variables (e.g. interest rates and exchange rates) and uses it to manage financial risks, it may use that sensitivity analysis instead. *[FRS 102.34.30]*. Similarly, if an insurer uses an alternative method to manage sensitivity to market conditions, such as an embedded value analysis, it may use that sensitivity analysis to meet the requirements of paragraph 34.29 of FRS 102. *[FRS 103.4.8(c)(ii)]*.

Because two approaches are permitted, an insurer might wish to use different approaches for different classes of business.

Where the sensitivity analysis disclosed is not representative of the risk inherent in the instrument (for example because the year-end exposure does not reflect the exposure during the year), it would be informative to disclose that fact together with the reasons the sensitivity analyses are unrepresentative.

An insurer might be able to take action to reduce the effect of changes in market conditions. For example, it may have discretion to change surrender values or maturity benefits, or to vary the amount or timing of policyholder benefits arising from discretionary participation features. There is no requirement for entities to consider the potential effect of future management actions that may offset the effect of the disclosed changes in any relevant risk variable. However, disclosure is required of the methods and assumptions used to prepare any sensitivity analysis. To comply with this requirement, disclosure of the extent of available management actions and their effect on the sensitivity analysis might be useful to readers of the financial statements.

Many life insurance contract liabilities are backed by matching assets. In these circumstances giving isolated disclosures about the variability of, say, interest rates on the valuation of the liabilities without linking this to the impact on the assets could be misleading to users of the financial statements. In these circumstances it may be useful to provide information as to the linkage of market risk sensitivities.

11.3.7   Exposures to market risk from embedded derivatives

As noted at 11.3 above, disclosure is required if there are exposures to market risk arising from embedded derivatives contained in a host insurance contract if the insurer is not required to, and does not, measure the embedded derivatives at fair value. *[FRS 103.4.8(d)].*

Fair value measurement is not required for derivatives embedded in an insurance contract if the embedded derivative is itself an insurance contract (see 5 above). Examples of these include guaranteed annuity options and guaranteed minimum death benefits as illustrated below.

Example 33.7:   Contract containing a guaranteed annuity option

An insurer issues a contract under which the policyholder pays a fixed monthly premium for thirty years. At maturity, the policyholder can elect to take either (a) a lump sum equal to the accumulated investment value or (b) a lifetime annuity at a rate guaranteed at inception (i.e. when the contract started). This is an example of a contract containing a guaranteed annuity option.

For policyholders electing to receive the annuity, the insurer could suffer a significant loss if interest rates decline substantially or if the policyholder lives much longer than the average. The insurer is exposed to both market risk and significant insurance risk (mortality risk) and the transfer of insurance risk occurs at inception of the contract because the insurer fixed the price for mortality risk at that date. Therefore, the contract is an insurance contract from inception. Moreover, the embedded guaranteed annuity option itself meets the definition of an insurance contract, and so separation is not required.

Example 33.8:   Contract containing minimum guaranteed death benefits

An insurer issues a contract under which the policyholder pays a monthly premium for 30 years. Most of the premiums are invested in a mutual fund. The rest is used to buy life cover and to cover expenses. On maturity or surrender, the insurer pays the value of the mutual fund units at that date. On death before final maturity, the insurer pays the greater of (a) the current unit value and (b) a fixed amount. This is an example of a contract containing minimum guaranteed death benefits. It is an insurance contract because the insurer is exposed to significant insurance risk as the fixed amount payable on death before maturity could be greater than the unit value.

It could be viewed as a hybrid contract comprising (a) a mutual fund investment and (b) an embedded life insurance contract that pays a death benefit equal to the fixed amount less the current unit value (but zero if the current unit value is more than the fixed amount).

Both of the examples of embedded derivatives above meet the definition of an insurance contract where the insurance risk is deemed significant. However, in both cases, market risk or interest rate risk may be much more significant than the mortality risk. So, if interest rates or equity markets fall substantially, these guarantees would have significant value. Given the long-term nature of the guarantees and the size of the exposures, an insurer might face extremely large losses in certain scenarios. Therefore, particular emphasis on disclosures about such exposures might be required.

The Implementation Guidance to IFRS 4 states that, to be informative, disclosures about such exposures may include: *[IFRS 4.IG70]*

- the sensitivity analysis discussed at 11.3.6.C above;

- information about the levels where these exposures start to have a material effect on the insurer's cash flows; and

- the fair value of the embedded derivative, although this is not a required disclosure.

11.4 Additional disclosures required by FRS 103 for with-profits business

Section 5 of FRS 103 requires additional disclosures for with-profits business written by life insurers. These replicate disclosures required under previous UK GAAP by FRS 27. However, when an entity has changed in accounting policies (see 9 above) and the new accounting policies are no longer consistent with policies on which the disclosure requirements of Section 5 are based, those requirements that are no longer consistent with the entity's accounting policies need not be applied. *[FRS 103.5.2]*.

The following presentation and disclosure requirements apply:

- the FFA must be disclosed separately in the statement of financial position and not combined with technical provisions or other liabilities. Entities that consolidate interests in an entity carrying on long-term insurance business on a basis that combines the FFA and technical provisions into a single amount of liabilities to policyholders are required to show those elements separately; *[FRS 103.5.4]* and

- where the balance on the FFA of a with-profits fund is negative, for whatever reason, disclosure is required an explaining the nature of the negative balance, the circumstances in which it arose, and why no action to eliminate it has been considered necessary. *[FRS 103.5.5]*.

In addition, amounts recognised for the present value of future profits on non-participating business written in a with-profits fund or for the excess of the realistic value of an interest in a subsidiary or associate over the net amounts included in the entity's consolidated accounts should be presented in one of the following ways: *[FRS 103.5.3]*

- where it is possible to apportion the amount recognised between an amount relating to liabilities to policyholders and amount relating to the FFA, these portions should be presented in the statement of financial position as a deduction in arriving at the amount of the liabilities to policyholders and FFA respectively; or

- where it is not possible to make a reasonably approximate apportionment of the amount recognised, the amount should be presented in the statement of financial position as a separate item deducted from a sub-total of liabilities to policyholders and the FFA; or

- where the presentation above does not comply with the statutory requirements for balance sheet presentation applying to the entity, the amount recognised should be recognised as an asset.

Chapter 33

Additionally, the Implementation Guidance to FRS 103 states that:

- where an FFA is established, the notes to the financial statements should indicate the reasons for its use and the nature of the funds involved; *[FRS 103.IG2.46]*

- for each significant class of with-profits insurance business, the insurer should disclose the extent to which the basis of preparation of the long-term business provision incorporates allowance for future bonuses. For example it should be stated (if it is the case) that explicit provision is made only for vested bonuses (including those vesting following the current valuation) and that no provision is made for future regular or terminal bonuses. If practical, insurers should disclose the amount that has been included explicitly in the long-term business provision in relation to future bonuses provided this can be done without undue cost or effort. If the valuation method makes implicit allowance for future bonuses by adjusting the discount rate used or by another methods, this fact should be stated together with a broad description of the means by which such allowance is made; *[FRS 103.IG2.45]* and

- the aggregate of the bonuses added to policies in the reporting period should be disclosed in the notes to the financial statements. *[FRS 103.IG2.46]*.

11.5 Capital disclosures for entities with long-term insurance business

As financial institutions, insurers are required to make capital disclosures in accordance with paragraphs 34.31 to 34.32 of FRS 102.

The non-mandatory Implementation Guidance to FRS 102 contains best practice guidance for providing capital disclosures for entities with long-term insurance business. The suggested disclosures are those required previously under UK GAAP by FRS 27. They go far beyond the minimum requirements of paragraphs 34.31 to 34.32 of FRS 102. It is stated in the Basis for Conclusions that the disclosures provide entities with some flexibility over how to meet the requirements of FRS 102 but does not anticipate a reduction in the usefulness of the information disclosed compared to FRS 27. *[FRS 103.BC36]*.

No best practice guidance on capital disclosures is provided for entities with general insurance business on the grounds that this was not required under previous UK GAAP and therefore its introduction would be unduly onerous in the context of an accounting standard that consolidates existing practice, pending future developments relating to the accounting and regulatory environment for insurers. *[FRS 103.BC37]*.

The non-mandatory implementation guidance is analysed as follows:

- capital statement (see 11.5.1);
- disclosures relating to liabilities and capital (see 11.5.2); and
- movements in capital (see 11.5.3).

11.5.1 Capital statement

An entity should present a statement setting out its total regulatory capital resources relating to long-term insurance business. The statement should show, for each section of that business as defined below: *[FRS 103.IG3.1]*

- equity (or in the case of a mutual, the equivalent, often described as disclosed surplus);
- adjustments to restate these amounts in accordance with regulatory requirements;

- each additional component of capital included for regulatory purposes, including capital retained within a life fund whether attributable to shareholders, policyholders or not yet allocated between shareholders and policyholders; and

- the total capital available to meet regulatory capital requirements.

Available capital will comprise a number of distinct elements, each of which will be separately disclosed, including: *[FRS 103.IG3.2]*

- equity as included in the published statement of financial position, represented by surplus held within a life fund or by assets held separately from those of the fund itself;

- amounts that are wholly attributable to owners, but held within a life fund and where the distribution out of the fund is restricted by regulatory or other considerations;

- surplus held in life funds that has yet to be attributed or allocated between owners and policyholders (in the case of a mutual all such surplus is attributable to policyholders but is not treated as a liability); and

- qualifying debt capital, whether issued by the life entity itself or by another entity within the group.

The capital statement should show as separate sections: *[FRS 103.IG3.3]*

- each UK with-profits life fund (or each Republic of Ireland with-profits fund for a Republic of Ireland entity) that is material to the group; and

- the entity's other long-term insurance business, showing the extent to which the various components of capital are subject to constraints such that they are available to meet requirements in only part of the entity's business, or are available to meet risks and regulatory capital requirements in all parts of the business.

The Implementation Guidance observes that the purpose of the capital statement is to set out the financial strength of the entity and to provide an analysis of the nature of capital, and constraints over the availability of the capital to meet risks and regulatory requirements. It is important that sources of capital are shown separately and the extent to which the capital in each section is subject to constraint in its availability to meet requirements in other parts of the entity. Such constraints can arise for any of the following reasons: *[FRS 103.IG3.4]*

- Ownership – the capital may be subject to specific ownership considerations (for example, the FFA of a UK (or Republic of Ireland) with-profits fund, for which the allocation between policyholders and shareholders has not been determined).

- Regulatory – local regulatory limitations may require the maintenance of solvency margins in particular funds or countries, or

- Financial – the availability of capital in certain cases can be restricted due to the imposition of taxes or other financial penalty in the event of the capital being required to be redeployed across the group.

The aggregate amount of regulatory capital resources included in the capital statement should be reconciled to equity, FFA and other amounts shown in the entity's statement of financial position, showing separately for each component of capital the amount relating to the entity's business other than long-term insurance business. Where such other business is significant, an explanation should be given of the extent to which this capital can be used to meet the requirements of the life assurance business. *[FRS 103.IG3.5]*.

Chapter 33

Although the detailed requirements apply to long-term insurance business, entities will need to incorporate information on other parts of the business, together with consolidation adjustments, in order to demonstrate how the aggregated capital attributed to the long-term insurance business reconciles to the total shown in the consolidated statement of financial position, and the extent to which capital outside the long-term insurance business may be made available to meet the capital requirements of the long-term insurance business. This reconciliation applies to each different type of capital shown in the capital statement. *[FRS 103.IG3.6]*.

Where the entity is a subsidiary, narrative supporting the capital statement should explain the extent to which the capital of the entity is able to be transferred to a parent or fellow subsidiaries, or the extent to which it is required to be retained within the entity. *[FRS 103.IG3.7]*.

Entities with life assurance liabilities should reconcile their regulatory capital resources to their shareholders' funds. Adjustments to reconcile the capital shown in the statement of financial position to the amount for regulatory purposes may include the following: *[FRS 103.IG3.8]*

- the difference between provisions measured on the realistic basis and the regulatory basis;

- the inclusion in capital of the FFA;

- the exclusion from capital of the shareholders' share of accrued bonus;

- the exclusion of goodwill and other intangible assets, such as an amount attributed to the acquired value of in-force life assurance business (VIF); and

- changes to the valuation of assets and the exclusion of certain non-admissible assets for regulatory purposes, for example any regulatory adjustment to a pension fund deficit that is recognised as a liability.

Disclosure of these adjustments should be sufficient to give a clear picture of the capital position from a regulatory perspective and its relationship to the equity shown in the consolidated statement of financial position.

Where the amount of a capital instrument that qualifies for inclusion as regulatory capital is restricted (for example, where a limited percentage of total regulatory capital may be in the form of debt) the full amount of the instrument should be included, with a separate deduction for the amount in excess of the restriction. *[FRS 103.IG3.9]*.

Disclosure should be made of any formal intra-group arrangements to provide capital to particular funds or business units, including intra-group loans and contingent arrangements. Where the entity is a subsidiary, disclosure should also be made of similar arrangements between the entity and a parent or fellow subsidiary. *[FRS 103.IG3.10]*.

Separate disclosure of each class of capital is important to an understanding of the funding of the business and the way any future losses would be absorbed or new business financed. Regulatory capital can include both equity and a surplus within the fund. Such surplus may be wholly attributable to owners, or remain unallocated as part of the FFA. In a mutual fund, all surplus is attributable to policyholders. Debt instruments qualifying as capital may be also be issued from the fund itself, or may form part of the owners' equity outside the life fund; a debt instrument issued by the fund to the owners may effectively transfer capital from the owners to the fund. *[FRS 103.IG3.11]*.

Intra-group arrangements should be included in the regulatory capital of a section only where they are subject to formal arrangements. *[FRS 103.IG3.12]*.

11.5.2 Disclosures relating to liabilities and capital

The capital statement should be supported by the following disclosures: *[FRS 103.IG3.13]*

- narrative or quantified information on the regulatory capital requirements applying to each section of the business shown in the capital statement, and on the capital targets set by management for that section;

- narrative disclosure of the basis of determining regulatory capital and the corresponding regulatory capital requirements, and any major inconsistencies in this basis between the different sections of the business;

- narrative disclosure showing the sensitivity of regulatory liabilities (including options and guarantees), and the components of total capital, to changes in market conditions, key assumptions and other variables, as well as future management actions in response to changes in market conditions; and

- narrative disclosure of the entity's capital management policies and objectives, and its approach to managing the risks that would affect the capital position.

The Implementation Guidance considers that these disclosures are important to the user's ability to understand the management of capital by the entity, its financial adaptability in changing circumstances, and the resources available to each group of policyholders.

In relation to liabilities arising from long-term insurance business, the entity should include the following additional information: *[FRS 103.IG3.14]*

- the process used to determine the assumptions that have the greatest effect on the measurement of liabilities including options and guarantees and, where practicable, quantified disclosure of those assumptions;

- those terms and conditions of options and guarantees relating to long-term insurance contracts that could in aggregate have a material effect on the amount, timing and uncertainty of the entity's future cash flows; and

- information about exposures to interest rate risk or market risk under options and guarantees if the entity does not measure these at fair value or at an amount estimated using a market-consistent stochastic model.

To comply with the last bullet point above, an insurer should disclose: *[FRS 103.IG3.18]*

(a) a description of the nature and extent of the options and guarantees;

(b) the basis of measurement for the amount at which these options and guarantees are stated, and the amount included, if any, for the additional payment that may arise in excess of the amounts expected to be paid if the policies did not include the option or guarantee feature;

(c) the main variables that determine the amount payable under the option or guarantee; and

(d) information on the potential effects of adverse changes in those market conditions that affect the entity's obligations under options and guarantees.

Chapter 33

The requirement of paragraph (d) above may be met by disclosing: *[FRS 103.IG3.19]*

- for options and guarantees that would result in additional payments to policyholders if current asset values and market rates continued unchanged (i.e. those that are 'in the money' for the policyholder), an indication of the change in these amounts if the variables moved adversely by a stated amount; and

- for options and guarantees that would result in additional payments to policyholders only if there was an adverse change in current asset values and market rates (i.e. those that are 'out of the money' for the policyholder):

  - an indication of the change in these variables, from current levels, which would cause material amounts to become payable under the options and guarantees; and

  - an indication of the amount that would result from a specified adverse change in these variables from the levels at which amounts first become payable under the options and guarantees.

The above disclosures may be made in aggregate for classes of options and guarantees that do not differ materially, or which are not individually material.

The Implementation Guidance states that although it is important to explain all movements in liabilities and capital during the period that are material to the group, this does not imply that the impact of each change in assumption needs to be shown separately. Where there is a common cause for the change of assumption the impacts can be grouped together. As an example, the impact of changes in investment return attributable to changing market circumstances does not need to be broken down between the various classes of investment. *[FRS 103.IG3.15]*.

The description of the process would include the objective (whether a best-estimate or a given level of assurance is intended); the sources of data; whether assumptions are consistent with observable market data or other published information; how past experience, current conditions and future trends are taken into account; correlations between different assumptions; management's policy for future bonuses; and the nature and extent of uncertainties affecting the assumptions. *[FRS 103.IG3.16]*.

Options and guarantees are features of life assurance contracts that: (a) confer potentially valuable guarantees underlying the level or nature of policyholder benefits; or (b) are options to change these benefits exercisable at the discretion of the policyholder. For the purposes of FRS 103, the term is used to refer only to those options and guarantees whose potential value is affected by the behaviour of financial variables, and not to potential changes in policyholder benefits arising solely from insurance risk (including mortality and morbidity), or from changes in the entity's creditworthiness. It includes a financial guarantee or option that applies if a policy lapses, but does not include the option to surrender or allow a policy to lapse. *[FRS 103.IG3.17]*.

The capital statement should show the amount of policyholder liabilities attributed to each section of the business shown in the statement, analysed between: *[FRS 103.IG3.20]*

- with-profits business;
- linked business;
- other long-term insurance business; and

- insurance business accounted for as financial instruments in accordance with the requirements of Sections 11 and 12 of FRS 102.

The total of these policyholder liabilities should be the amounts shown in the entity's statement of financial position.

11.5.3 Movements in capital

An entity should include a reconciliation of the movements in the total amount of available capital for long-term insurance business shown in the capital statement from the comparative amounts at the end of the previous reporting period. This disclosure should cover individually each UK (or Republic of Ireland) life fund that is separately shown in the capital statement required under 11.5.1 above, and other long-term insurance business in aggregate. *[FRS 103.IG3.21].*

This disclosure should set out in tabular form the effect of changes resulting from: *[FRS 103.IG3.22]*

- changes in assumptions used to measure liabilities from long-term insurance business, showing separately the effect of each change in an assumption that has had a material effect on the group;
- changes in management policy;
- changes in regulatory requirements and similar external developments; and new business and other factors (for example changing market prices affecting assets and liabilities, surrenders, lapses and maturities), describing any material items.

Changes in management policy above refers to significant changes in the management of the fund such as changes in investment policy or changes in the use of the inherited estate. Where management actions are clearly directly related to changes in assumptions or other factors it will be appropriate to show the net impact, but the narrative should discuss the constituent factors. An example might be the combined effect of a reduced level of bonuses assumed as a result of a reduction in the assumed level of future investment return and a reduction in investment returns earned in the period. *[FRS 103.IG3.23].*

11.6 Segmental disclosures required by Schedule 3

FRS 102 does not require segmental disclosures except for entities whose debt and equity instruments are publicly traded, or those in the process of filing financial statements with a securities commission or other regulatory organisation for the purpose of issuing any class of instruments in a public market. Those entities (as well as any entities choosing to provide segmental information voluntarily) must apply IFRS 8 – *Operating Segments. [FRS 102.1.5].*

However, UK insurance entities preparing individual financial and separate statements under Schedule 3 to the Regulations must make the segmental disclosures required by the Regulations.

Separate disclosures are required for general and long-term business as shown at 11.6.1 and 11.6.2 below. Entities preparing consolidated financial statements are not required to give the disclosures required by 11.61 to 11.62 below in respect of the group profit and loss account. *[6 Sch 40(6)].*

Chapter 33

11.6.1 *Segmental disclosures for general business required in individual and separate financial statements*

A company must disclose: *[3 Sch 85(1)]*

- gross premiums written;
- gross premiums earned;
- gross claims incurred;
- gross operating expenses; and
- the reinsurance balance.

The 'reinsurance balance' means the aggregate total of all those items included in the technical account for general business which relate to reinsurance outwards transactions including items recorded as reinsurance commissions and profit participation. *[FRS 103.IG2.62]*.

These amounts must be broken down between: *[3 Sch 85(2)]*

- direct insurance; and
- reinsurance acceptances (if reinsurance acceptances amount to 10% or more of the gross premiums written).

Where the amount of gross premiums written in direct insurance for each group exceeds €10 million, the amounts in respect of direct insurance must be further broken down into the following groups of classes: *[3 Sch 85(3)]*

- accident and health;
- motor (third party liability);
- motor (other classes);
- marine, aviation and transport;
- fire and other damage to property;
- third-party liability;
- credit and suretyship;
- legal expenses;
- assistance; and
- miscellaneous.

The entity must, in any event, disclose the amounts relating to the three largest groups of classes in its business. *[3 Sch 85(4)]*.

Total gross direct insurance premiums must also be split by the following categories if any one exceeds 5% of total gross premiums resulting from contracts concluded by the company in: *[3 Sch 87]*

- in the EU member state of the Head Office;
- in the other EU member States; and
- in other countries.

There must also be disclosed the total amount of commissions for direct insurance business accounted for in the financial year, including acquisition, renewal collection and portfolio management commissions. *[3 Sch 88]*.

11.6.2 Segmental disclosures for long-term business required in individual and separate financial statements

A company must disclose: *[3 Sch 86]*

- gross premiums written, broken down between those written by way of direct insurance and those written by reinsurance; and
- the reinsurance balance.

Gross premiums written by way of direct insurance must be further broken down, when it exceeds 10% of the gross premiums written or (as the case may be) of the gross premiums written by way of direct insurance, between:

- individual premiums and premiums under group contracts;
- periodic premiums and single premiums; and
- premiums from non-participating contracts, premiums from participating contracts and premiums from contracts where the investment risk is borne by policyholder.

The 'reinsurance balance' means the aggregate total of all those items included in the technical account for long-term which relate to reinsurance outwards transactions including items recorded as reinsurance commissions and profit participation. *[FRS 103.IG2.62]*.

Single premium contracts are those contracts under which there is no expectation of continuing premiums being paid at regular intervals. Additional single premiums paid in respect of existing individual contracts should be included. Regular premium contracts should include those contracts under which the premiums are payable at regular intervals during the policy year, including repeated or recurrent single premiums where the level of premiums is defined. *[FRS 103.IG2.56]*.

The Implementation Guidance to FRS 103 states that new annual and single premiums should be disclosed separately in the financial statements together with an explanation of the basis adopted for recognising premiums as either annual or single premiums. New annual premiums should be shown as the premiums payable in a full year (i.e. annual premium equivalent). Department for Work and Pensions rebates received on certain pensions contracts should be treated as single premiums. *[FRS 103.IG2.57]*. Internal transfers between products where open market options are available should be counted as new business. If no open market exists, the transfer should not be treated as new business. *[FRS 103.IG2.58]*.

Total gross direct insurance premiums must also be split by the following categories if any one exceeds 5% of total gross premiums resulting from contracts concluded by the company in: *[3 Sch 87]*

- in the EU member state of the Head Office;
- in the other EU member States; and
- in other countries.

There must also be disclosed the total amount of commissions for direct insurance business accounted for in the financial year, including acquisition, renewal collection and portfolio management commissions. *[3 Sch 88]*.

11.7   Disclosures in respect of the allocated investment return

Schedule 3 to the Regulations requires that, when an entity makes a transfer of investment return from one part of the profit and loss account to another (e.g. non-technical account to technical account), the reasons for such a transfer and the bases on which it is made must be disclosed in the notes to the financial statements. *[3 Sch P&L Note 8, 10]*.

The Implementation Guidance to FRS 103 recommends the following disclosures where the technical results show a longer term rate of investment return: *[FRS 103.IG2.71]*

- the methodology used to determine the longer-term rate of return for each investment category;
- for each investment category and material currency, both the longer-term rates of return and, if applicable, the long-term dividend and rental yields used to calculate the grossing-up factor for equities and property;
- a comparison over a longer-term (at least five years) of the actual return achieved with the return allocated using the longer-term rate of return analysed between returns relating to general business, long-term business and other; and
- the sensitivity of the longer-term rate of return to a 1% decrease and a 1% increase in the longer-term rate of investment return.

11.8   Disclosure of distributable profits by life insurers

Schedule 3 to the Regulations requires that every balance sheet of a company which carries on long-term business must show separately as an additional item the aggregate of any capital and reserves which are not required to be treated as realised profits under section 843 of the CA 2006. *[3 Sch 11(1)]*.

For companies authorised to carry on long-term insurance business in accordance with Article 14 of the Solvency II Directive, the realised profit or loss of the company in respect of which its relevant accounts are prepared is the amount calculated by a given formula. *[s833A]*. It is beyond the scope of this chapter to discuss the formula in detail but, in summary, it is the company's net assets as calculated by the Solvency II Directive less various deductions which include:

- any defined benefit pension surplus (net of related deferred tax);
- the value of shares in a qualifying investment subsidiary which exceeds the consideration paid (net of related deferred tax);
- excess assets held in a ring-fenced fund (net of related deferred tax);
- the excess of the value of any portfolio of assets assigned to cover the best estimate of life insurance or reinsurance obligations where the company has permission under regulation 42 of the Solvency II Regulations 2015 to apply a matching adjustment to a relevant risk-free interest rate term structure to calculate the best estimate of a portfolio of life insurance or reinsurance obligations;
- paid-in ordinary share capital together with any related share premium account;
- paid in preference shares which are not liabilities together with any related share premium account;
- any capital redemption reserve; and
- any other reserve that the company is prohibited from distributing.

For companies that are not required to comply with the Solvency II Directive, realised profits or losses are determined using the normal UK common law and statutory requirements (see Chapter 1 at 6.8).

In addition, a company which carries on long-term business must show separately, in the balance sheet or in the notes, the total amount of assets representing the long-term fund valued in accordance with the provisions of Schedule 3. *[3 Sch 11(2)]*.

References

1 *FRC defers decision on updating FRS 102 for major changes in IFRS*, FRC, June 2017.

2 *European Embedded Value Principles*, European Insurance CFO Forum, May 2004, p.3.

For companies that are not required to comply with the Solvency II Directive, reduced profit and loss are determined using the normal local minimum flow and statutory requirements (see Chapter 1 to 6.8).

In addition, a company which carries on those nondll business must show separately in the balance sheet or in the notes, the total amount of assets representing the long-term fund valued in accordance with the provisions of Schedule 3 ... view in ...

Reference

Chapter 34   FRS 104 – Interim financial reporting

Chapter 34

List of examples

Chapter 34

FRS 104 – Interim financial reporting

1 INTRODUCTION

FRS 104 – *Interim Financial Reporting* – was issued originally in March 2015. A revised version was issued in March 2018, to update the edition issued in March 2015 for the following:

- *Amendments to FRS 102 Triennial review 2017 – Incremental improvements and clarifications* (Triennial review 2017) issued in December 2017;
- The replacement of *Appendix III: Significant differences between FRS 104 and IAS 34* with a *Basis for Conclusions*; and
- Some minor typographical and presentational corrections.

This chapter reflects the March 2018 version of FRS 104.

FRS 104 does not require any entity to prepare an interim report, nor does it change the extent to which laws or regulations may require the preparation of such a report. FRS 104 is intended for use in the preparation of interim reports by entities that prepare financial statements in accordance with UK GAAP. In particular, it is intended for use by entities which apply FRS 102 – *The Financial Reporting Standard applicable in the UK and Republic of Ireland*. Most of this chapter therefore deals with the use of FRS 104 by FRS 102 preparers. However, entities which apply FRS 101 – *Reduced Disclosure Framework* – when preparing their annual financial statements may also use FRS 104 when preparing their interim financial reports.

FRS 104 is based on the equivalent international standard IAS 34 – *Interim Financial Reporting*, but with some minor adjustments and the omission of certain paragraphs which deal with presentational aspects of IAS 34 or paragraphs of IAS 34 which include disclosures not required in the annual financial statements of entities reporting under FRS 102. These amendments are summarised in the Basis for Conclusions. *[FRS 104.BC10]*.

1.1 Definitions

The standard defines an interim period as 'a financial reporting period shorter than a full financial year'. *[FRS 104 Appendix I]*.

Chapter 34

The term 'interim financial report' means a financial report for an interim period that contains either a complete set of financial statements (as described in Section 3 – *Financial Statement Presentation* – of FRS 102) or a set of condensed financial statements (see 3.2 below). *[FRS 104 Appendix I].*

2   OBJECTIVE AND SCOPE OF FRS 104

2.1   Objective

FRS 104 sets out content, recognition and measurement principles for interim financial reports. *[FRS 104.1A].* It notes that 'timely and reliable interim financial reporting can improve the ability of investors, creditors, and others to understand an entity's capacity to generate earnings and cash flows and its financial condition and liquidity'. *[FRS 104.1].*

2.2   Scope

FRS 104 is intended for use by entities that prepare annual financial statements in accordance with FRS 102. If an entity prepares its annual financial statements under FRS 101 and applies FRS 104, it should replace references to FRS 102 in FRS 104 with the equivalent requirements in EU-adopted IFRS, as amended by paragraph AG 1 of FRS 101. *[FRS 104.2A].*

This chapter is written primarily for entities that prepare their annual financial statements in accordance with FRS 102. However, a discussion on the application of FRS 104 to FRS 101 reporters is included at 5 below.

FRS 104, in itself, does not require an entity to prepare interim financial reports and does not mandate, how often, or how soon after the end of an interim period an interim financial report should be issued. Where an entity is required by laws or regulations or voluntarily chooses to prepare interim financial reports it may voluntarily choose to apply FRS 104. *[FRS 104.2].* Therefore, entities need to consider if there are any applicable laws and regulations which require them to prepare interim financial statements. For example, UK issuers not using EU-adopted IFRS that publish half-yearly reports which include a statement that a condensed set of financial statements has been prepared in accordance with FRS 104, must apply the standard. *[FRS 104.3A].* See 2.2.1 below.

In practice, we expect a limited number of entities (primarily investment trusts and venture capital trusts) will be required to apply FRS 104. However, for entities which prepare annual financial statements under FRS 101 or FRS 102, FRS 104 may be applied voluntarily for interim reporting purposes.

2.2.1   *Issuers required to comply with the Disclosure Guidance and Transparency Rules (DTR)*

Issuers of securities that are required to publish half-yearly financial reports in accordance with the Disclosure Guidance and Transparency Rules (DTR) must include a responsibility statement in the report. In accordance with paragraph 4.2.10.R of the DTR, a person making the responsibility statement will satisfy the requirement to confirm that the condensed set of financial statements gives a true and fair view of the assets, liabilities, financial position and profit or loss of the issuer (or the undertakings included in the consolidation as a whole) by including a statement that the condensed set of financial statements has been prepared in accordance with either:

- IAS 34; or
- for UK issuers not using EU-adopted IFRS, FRS 104 issued by the FRC. *[FRS 104 Appendix IV.3]*.

The application of FRS 104 is conditional upon the person making the responsibility statement having reasonable grounds to be satisfied that the condensed set of financial statements prepared under FRS 104 is not misleading. *[FRS 104 Appendix IV.4]*.

In accordance with the DTR, an issuer that is required to prepare consolidated accounts must prepare the condensed set of financial statements in accordance with IAS 34 and the requirements set out in FRS 104 do not apply to these issuers. *[FRS 104 Appendix IV.5]*. An issuer that is not required to prepare consolidated accounts must, as a minimum, apply the content and preparation requirements set out in paragraph 4.2.5.R of the DTR. The content and preparation requirements of FRS 104 are consistent with those set out in the DTR, although they are more prescriptive and detailed. *[FRS 104 Appendix IV.6]*.

2.2.2   Unlisted entities and entities not subject to the DTR

While not in the scope of the DTR, unlisted entities or entities with securities admitted to trading on an exchange not subject to the DTR may prepare and present interim financial statements. In those circumstances, there may be no requirement to follow a particular standard on interim financial reporting. However, we would expect that where annual financial statements are prepared under either FRS 101 or FRS 102 that the interim financial statements would be prepared under FRS 104.

3   FORM AND CONTENT OF AN INTERIM FINANCIAL REPORT UNDER FRS 104

FRS 104 does not prohibit or discourage an entity from:

- publishing a complete set of financial statements (as described in Section 3 of FRS 102) in its interim financial report, rather than condensed financial statements and selected explanatory notes; or
- including in condensed interim financial statements more than the components and selected explanatory notes as set out in paragraph 8 of FRS 104.

The recognition and measurement guidance in the standard, together with the note disclosures required by the standard, apply to both complete and condensed financial statements presented for an interim period. *[FRS 104.7]*.

3.1   Complete set of interim financial statements

If an entity publishes a complete set of financial statements in its interim financial report, the form and content of those statements should conform to the requirements of

Section 3 of FRS 102. *[FRS 104.9]*. A complete set of financial statements should include the following components: *[FRS 102.3.17]*

- a statement of financial position as at the reporting date;
- a statement of comprehensive income for the reporting period to be presented either as:
  - a single statement of comprehensive income for the reporting period, displaying all items of income and expense recognised during the period including those items recognised in determining profit or loss (which is a subtotal in the statement of comprehensive income) and items of other comprehensive income; or
  - a separate income statement and a separate statement of comprehensive income. In this case, the statement of comprehensive income begins with profit or loss and then displays the items of other comprehensive income;
- a statement of changes in equity for the reporting period;
- a statement of cash flows for the reporting period; and
- notes comprising significant accounting policies and other explanatory information.

The presentational requirements of Section 3 of FRS 102 are discussed in Chapter 6. In addition, the entity should make the disclosures specifically required by FRS 104 for interim financial reports (see 4 below) as well as those required by FRS 102. *[FRS 104.7]*.

An entity that will not present a statement of cash flows in its next annual financial statements is not required to include that statement in its interim financial report. *[FRS 104.9]*.

3.2   Condensed interim financial statements

In the interest of timeliness, cost, and avoiding repetition of previously reported information, an entity might be required or elect to give less information at interim dates as compared with its annual financial statements. *[FRS 104.6]*. FRS 104 defines the minimum components of an interim report, as including condensed financial statements and selected explanatory notes, as follows: *[FRS 104.6, 8]*

(a)   a condensed statement of financial position;

(b)   a single condensed statement of comprehensive income or a separate condensed income statement and a separate condensed statement of comprehensive income;

(c)   a condensed statement of changes in equity;

(d)   a condensed statement of cash flows; and

(e)   selected explanatory notes.

Other titles for the statements can be used, as long as they are not misleading. *[FRS 104.8E]*.

An entity that will not present a statement of cash flows in its next annual financial statements is not required to include that statement in its interim financial report. *[FRS 104.8F]*.

FRS 104 requires entities to confirm that the same accounting policies and methods of computation are followed in the interim financial statements as compared to their most recent annual financial statements or, if those policies or methods have changed, to describe the nature and effect of the change (see 8.1.2 below). Accordingly, an entity would only depart from the presentation applied in its most recent annual financial statements if it has determined that the format will change in its next annual financial statements. *[FRS 104.8D]*.

The condensed income statement and condensed statement of comprehensive income referred to at (b) above should be presented using the same basis as the entity's most recent annual financial statements. Accordingly, if an entity presents a separate income statement in its annual financial statements, then it should also present a separate income statement in the interim financial report. Similarly, if a single statement of comprehensive income is presented in the annual financial statements, the same format is adopted in the interim financial report. *[FRS 104.8A]*.

Where the only changes to equity arise from profit or loss, payment of dividends, corrections of prior period errors or changes in accounting policies, an entity may have presented a single statement of income and retained earnings in place of the statement of comprehensive income and statement of changes in equity in its most recent annual financial statements under FRS 102. If that continues to be the case during any of the periods for which the interim financial statements are required to be presented, the entity may continue to present a single condensed statement of income and retained earnings. *[FRS 104.8B]*.

Similarly, where an entity in its most recent annual financial statements has presented only an income statement or a statement of comprehensive income in which the bottom line is labelled profit or loss (by virtue of there being no items of other comprehensive income), that entity is permitted to use the same basis of presentation in its interim financial statements if there are no items of other comprehensive income in any of the periods for which the interim financial statements are being presented. *[FRS 104.8C]*.

As a minimum, the condensed financial statements should include each of the headings and subtotals that were included in the entity's last annual financial statements. *[FRS 104.10]*.

A strict interpretation of this minimum requirement could mean that, for example, an entity is only required to present non-current assets, current assets, etc., in an interim statement of financial position. However, one of the purposes of an interim report is to help the users of the financial statements to understand the changes in financial position and performance of the entity since the end of the last annual reporting period. *[FRS 104.15]*. To that end, FRS 104 also requires additional line items or notes to be included if their omission makes the condensed interim financial statements misleading. *[FRS 104.10]*. In addition, the overriding goal of FRS 104 is to ensure that the interim report includes all information relevant to understanding the entity's financial position and the performance during the interim period. *[FRS 104.25]*. Therefore, judgement is required to determine which line items provide useful information for decision-makers, and are presented accordingly.

Inclusion of all of the line items from the annual financial statements will often be most appropriate to help users of the interim financial statements understand the changes since the previous year-end. Nonetheless, entities may aggregate line items used in the annual financial statements, if doing so does not render the information misleading or prevent users of the interim financial statements from performing meaningful trend analysis.

The following example illustrates one possible way in which an entity might choose to combine line items presented separately in the annual financial statements when preparing a condensed set of interim financial statements for an individual set of accounts prepared under Format 1 of Schedule 1 to the Regulations. However, such presentation is at the discretion of management, based on facts and circumstances, including materiality (as discussed at 7 below), regulatory environment, and the overarching goal of FRS 104 to provide relevant information. *[FRS 104.25]*. Accordingly, other presentations may be appropriate.

Example 34.1:   *Presenting the same headings and sub-totals in condensed interim financial statements*

Statement of financial position	Annual individual financial statements ('Schedule 1 statutory format')	Condensed interim financial statements
Fixed assets		
Intangible assets	●	●
Tangible assets	●	●
Investments:		●
Investments in joint ventures	●	
Investments in associates	●	
Other investments	●	
Current assets		
Stocks	●	●
Debtors:		●
Amounts falling due within one year	●	
Amounts falling due after one year	●	
Short term deposits	●	
Cash at bank and in hand	●	●
Creditors: amounts falling due within one year	●	●
Net current assets	●	●
Total assets less current liabilities	●	●
Creditors: amounts falling due after more than one year	●	●
Provisions for liabilities	●	●
Net assets	●	●
Capital and reserves		
Called up share capital	●	●
Share premium account	●	●
Other reserves including the fair value reserve	●	●
Capital redemption reserve	●	
Reserve for own shares	●	
Equity component of convertible preference shares	●	
Merger reserve	●	●
Profit and loss account	●	●
Equity attributable to owners of the parent company	●	●
Non-controlling interests	●	●
Total capital and reserves	●	●

Income statement	Annual financial statements ('Schedule 1 statutory format')	Condensed interim financial statements
Turnover	●	●
Cost of sales	●	●
Gross profit	●	●
Operating expenses		●
Distribution costs	●	
Administrative expenses	●	
Other operating expenses	●	
Other operating income	●	●
Operating profit	●	●
Income from investments:		●
Income from shares in group undertakings	●	
Income from participating interests	●	
Profit before interest and tax	●	●
Interest payable	●	
Other finance costs	●	
Interest payable and similar expenses		●
Profit before tax	●	●
Tax on profit	●	●
Profit for the period	●	●

Statement of comprehensive income	Annual financial statements	Condensed interim financial statements
Profit for the period	●	●
Cash flow hedges	●	
Remeasurement gain/(loss) recognised on defined benefit pension schemes	●	
Movement on deferred tax relating to pension liability	●	
Total other comprehensive income	●	
Total comprehensive income for the period	●	●

A statement of changes in equity and statement of cash flows are not presented in this example.

3.3 Requirements for complete and condensed interim financial information

The general principles for preparing annual financial statements are equally applicable to interim financial statements. These principles include fair presentation, going concern, materiality and aggregation. See Chapter 6 at 9.

Furthermore, irrespective of whether an entity provides complete or condensed financial statements for an interim period, basic and diluted earnings per share should be presented for an interim period when earnings per share (EPS) information has been presented in the entity's most recent annual financial statements. *[FRS 104.11]*. Such information should be given on the face of the statement that presents components of profit or loss for an interim period. *[FRS 104.11A]*.

Chapter 34

3.4 Management commentary

A management commentary is not explicitly required by FRS 104, but we would expect one to be included by entities in their interim financial reports along with the interim financial statements.

FRS 104 allows information required under the standard to be presented outside the interim financial statements, i.e. in other parts of interim financial report. *[FRS 104.15B, 16A].* Thus, some of the required disclosures may be included in a management commentary (see 4.2.1 below). The standard itself does not establish specific requirements for the content of a management commentary beyond what should be contained in (or cross-referred from) the interim financial statements.

4 DISCLOSURES IN CONDENSED FINANCIAL STATEMENTS

FRS 104 contains a number of disclosure principles:

- Entities should provide information about events and transactions in the interim period that are significant to an understanding of the changes in financial position and performance since the end of the last annual reporting period. In this context it is not necessary to provide relatively insignificant updates to information reported in the last annual financial statements (see 4.1 below). *[FRS 104.15, 15A].*

- In addition to information to explain significant changes since the last annual reporting period, certain 'minimum' disclosures are required to be given, if not disclosed elsewhere in the interim financial report (see 4.2 below). *[FRS 104.16A].*

- The materiality assessment for disclosure is based on the interim period by itself to ensure all information is provided that is relevant to understanding of the entity's financial position and its performance during the interim period (further discussed at 7 below). *[FRS 104.25].*

Overall, applying those disclosure principles requires the exercise of judgement by the entity regarding what information is significant or relevant. The practice of interim reporting confirms that entities take advantage of that room for judgement, both for disclosures provided in the notes to the interim financial statements and outside.

4.1 Significant events and transactions

FRS 104 presumes that users of an entity's interim financial report also have access to its most recent annual financial report. *[FRS 104.15A].* On that basis, an interim financial report should explain events and transactions that are significant to an understanding of the changes in financial position and performance of the entity since the previous annual reporting period and provide an update to the relevant information included in the financial statements of the previous year. *[FRS 104.15, 15C].* The inclusion of only selected explanatory notes is consistent with the purpose of an interim financial report, to update the latest complete set of annual financial statements. Accordingly, condensed financial statements avoid repeating previously reported information and focus on new activities, events, and circumstances. *[FRS 104.6].*

Disclosure of the following events and transactions in interim financial reports, if they are significant, is required: *[FRS 104.15B]*

(a) write-down of inventories to net realisable value and the reversal of such a write-down;

(b) recognition of a loss from the impairment of financial assets, property, plant, and equipment, intangible assets, or other assets, and the reversal of such an impairment loss;

(c) reversal of any provisions for the costs of restructuring;

(d) acquisitions and disposals of items of property, plant and equipment;

(e) commitments for the purchase of property, plant and equipment;

(f) litigation settlements;

(g) corrections of prior period errors;

(h) changes in the business or economic circumstances that affect the fair value of the entity's financial assets and financial liabilities, where those assets or liabilities are measured at fair value;

(i) any loan default or breach of a loan agreement that is not remedied on or before the end of the reporting period;

(j) related party transactions, unless the transaction was entered into between two or more members of a group, provided that any subsidiary which is a party to the transaction is wholly owned by such a member; and

(k) changes in contingent liabilities or contingent assets.

FRS 104 states that the above list of events and transactions is not exhaustive and the interim financial report should explain any additional events and transactions that are significant to an understanding of changes in the entity's financial position and performance. *[FRS 104.15, 15B]*. Therefore, when information changes significantly (for example, the values of non-financial assets and liabilities that are measured at fair value), an entity should provide disclosure regarding such change, in addition to the requirements listed above; the disclosure should be sufficiently detailed to explain the nature of the change and any changes in estimates.

The disclosures in the above list can be given either in the notes to the interim financial statements or, if disclosed elsewhere in the interim financial report, cross-referred to the disclosure in the notes to the interim financial statements. *[FRS 104.15B]*.

4.1.1 Relevance of other standards in condensed financial statements

Whilst FRS 102 specifies disclosures required in a complete set of financial statements, if an entity's interim financial report includes only condensed financial statements as described in FRS 104, then the disclosures required by those other standards are not mandatory. However, if disclosure is considered to be necessary in the context of an interim report, FRS 102 provides guidance on the appropriate disclosures for many of these items. *[FRS 104.15C]*. For example, in meeting the requirements of (g) at 4.1 above to disclose the impact of corrections of prior period errors, the requirements of Section 10 would be relevant (see Chapter 9 at 3.7.3).

4.2 Other disclosures required by FRS 104

In addition to disclosing significant events and transactions as discussed at 4.1 above, FRS 104 requires an entity to include the following information either in the notes to its interim financial statements or, if disclosed elsewhere in the interim financial report, cross-referred from the notes: *[FRS 104.16A]*

(a)   a statement that the same accounting policies and methods of computation are followed in the interim financial statements as in the most recent annual financial statements or, if those policies or methods have been changed, a description of the nature and effect of the change;

(b)   explanatory comments about the seasonality or cyclicality of interim operations;

(c)   the nature and amount of items affecting assets, liabilities, equity, profit or loss, or cash flows that are unusual because of their nature, size, or incidence;

(d)   the nature and amount of changes in estimates of amounts reported in prior interim periods of the current financial year or changes in estimates of amounts reported in prior financial years;

(e)   issues, repurchases, and repayments of debt and equity securities;

(f)   dividends paid (aggregate or per share) separately for ordinary shares and other shares;

(g)   certain segment disclosures as discussed at 4.3 below; but only if the entity has presented segment information in accordance with IFRS 8 – *Operating Segments* – in its most recent annual financial statements;

(h)   events after the interim period that are not reflected in the financial statements for the interim period;

(i)   the effect of changes in the composition of the entity during the interim period, including business combinations, obtaining or losing control of subsidiaries and long-term investments, restructurings, and discontinued operations. For business combinations, the entity shall disclose the information required by paragraphs 19.25 and 19.25A of FRS 102 (see Chapter 17 at 4.1); and

(j)   for financial instruments, certain disclosures in respect of financial instruments measured at fair value and as required by paragraphs 11.43, 11.48A(e) and 34.22 of FRS 102; but only if the entity would be required to make the disclosure in the annual financial statements, as discussed at 4.4 below.

This information is normally reported on a financial year-to-date basis (see 8 below). *[FRS 104.16A]*.

For business combinations that occurred during the reporting period which, individually, are not material, FRS 102 allows the disclosure of revenue and profit or loss to date to be given in aggregate. *[FRS 102.19.25A]*. However, materiality is assessed for the interim period, which implies that FRS 104 may require more detailed disclosures on business combinations that are material to an interim period even if they could be aggregated for disclosure purposes in the annual financial statements prepared under FRS 102.

If an entity has operations that are discontinued or disposed of during an interim period, these operations should be presented separately in the condensed interim statement of comprehensive income following the principles set out in Section 5 – *Statement of Comprehensive Income and Income Statement.*

An entity contemplating a significant restructuring that will have an impact on its composition should follow the guidance in Section 21 – *Provisions and Contingencies* – for the recognition of any restructuring cost, *[FRS 102.21.11C]*, and Section 28 – *Employee Benefits* – for the recognition of any termination benefits. *[FRS 102.28.31]*. In subsequent interim periods any significant changes, including reversals, to restructuring provisions will require disclosure. *[FRS 104.15B(c)]*.

4.2.1 Location of the specified disclosures in an interim financial report

FRS 104 defines an 'interim financial report' as 'a financial report containing either a complete set of financial statements or a set of condensed financial statements for an interim period'. *[FRS 104 Appendix I]*. Therefore, since an interim financial report *contains* the interim financial statements, it is clear that these are two different concepts. Accordingly, an entity is not required to disclose the information listed at 4.1 and 4.2 above in the interim financial statements themselves, as long as a cross reference is provided from the financial statements to the location of the information included in another part of the interim financial report. *[FRS 104.15B, 16A]*.

4.3 Segment information

If an entity has presented segment information in accordance with IFRS 8 in its most recent annual financial statements, certain segment disclosures are required in its interim financial report.

An entity applying IFRS 8 in its most recent annual financial statements should include the following information in its interim financial report about its reportable segments: *[FRS 104.16A(g)]*

(a) revenues from external customers (if included in the measure of segment profit or loss reviewed by or otherwise regularly provided to the chief operating decision maker);

(b) intersegment revenues (if included in the measure of segment profit or loss reviewed by or otherwise regularly provided to the chief operating decision maker);

(c) a measure of segment profit or loss;

(d) a measure of total assets and liabilities for a particular reportable segment if such amounts are regularly provided to the chief operating decision maker and if there has been a material change from the amount disclosed in the last annual financial statements for that reportable segment;

(e) a description of differences in the basis of segmentation or in the basis of measurement of segment profit or loss from the last annual financial statements; and

(f) a reconciliation of the total profit or loss for reportable segments to the entity's profit or loss before income taxes and discontinued operations. However, if an entity allocates such items as income taxes to arrive at segment profit or loss, the reconciliation can be to the entity's profit or loss after those items. The entity should separately identify and describe all material reconciling items.

4.4 Fair value disclosures for financial instruments

If an entity would be required to make equivalent disclosures in its annual financial statements, FRS 104 requires that an entity should include the following in its interim financial report in order to help users evaluate the significance of financial instruments measured at fair value: *[FRS 104.16A(j)]*

(a)   For all financial assets and financial liabilities measured at fair value, the entity shall disclose the basis for determining fair value, e.g. quoted market price in an active market or a valuation technique. When a valuation technique is used, the entity shall disclose the assumptions applied in determining fair value for each class of financial assets or financial liabilities. For example, if applicable, an entity discloses information about the assumptions relating to prepayment rates, rates of estimated credit losses, and interest rates or discount rates. *[FRS 102.11.43]*. See Chapter 10 at 8.1.

(b)   For financial instruments at fair value through profit or loss that are not held as part of a trading portfolio and are not derivatives, any difference between the fair value at initial recognition and the amount that would be determined at that date using a valuation technique, the aggregate difference yet to be recognised in profit or loss at the beginning and end of the period, and a reconciliation of the changes in the balance of this difference. *[FRS 102.11.48A(e)]*. See Chapter 10 at 8.1.

(c)   For financial instruments held at fair value in the statement of financial position, a financial institution shall disclose for each class of financial instrument, an analysis of the level in the fair value hierarchy (as set out in paragraph 11.27) into which the fair value measurements are categorised. *[FRS 102.34.22]*. See Chapter 10 at 11.2.

The inclusion of the above disclosure requirement among the items required by the Standard to be given 'in addition to disclosing significant events and transactions', *[FRS 104.16A]*, distinguishes it from the items listed at 4.1 above, which are disclosed to update information presented in the most recent annual financial report. *[FRS 104.15]*. Therefore, disclosure of the above information is required for each interim reporting period, subject only to a materiality assessment in relation to that interim report, i.e. an entity could consider it unnecessary to disclose the above information on the grounds that it is not relevant to an understanding of its financial position and performance in that specific interim period. *[FRS 104.25]*. In making that judgement care would need to be taken to ensure any omitted information would not make the interim financial report incomplete and therefore misleading.

4.5   Disclosure of compliance with FRS 104

If an interim financial report complies with the requirements of FRS 104, this fact should be disclosed. Furthermore, an entity that makes a statement of compliance with FRS 104 shall comply with all of its provisions. FRS 104 does not need to be applied to immaterial items. *[FRS 104.3, 19]*.

5   ENTITIES REPORTING UNDER FRS 101

As noted at 2 above, FRS 104 is intended for use by entities that prepare annual financial statements in accordance with FRS 102. However it can also be used by entities that report under FRS 101, and in those circumstances references included in FRS 104 to FRS 102 should be read as references to the equivalent requirements in EU-adopted IFRS as amended by paragraph AG1 of FRS 101. *[FRS 104.2A]*.

The references to FRS 102 fall into three main categories:

- disclosure of significant events and transactions (see 5.1 below);
- business combinations (see 5.2 below); and
- financial instruments (see 5.3 below).

While there are references to FRS 102 in other paragraphs of FRS 104, we do not expect that these will give rise to any significant differences in the application of FRS 104 between FRS 101 and FRS 102 reporters. These references are in financial statement presentation, materiality, recognition and changes in accounting policy. *[FRS 104.7, 8B-8C, 9, 16B, 24, 31, 30, 33, 43-44].*

In respect of changes in accounting policies, refer to 8.1.2 below with references to FRSs being read as references to IFRSs.

5.1 Disclosure of significant events and transactions

As discussed at 4.1 above, FRS 104 requires entities to include, in their interim financial statements, an explanation of events and transactions that are significant to an understanding of changes in the financial position and performance of the entity since the end of the previous reporting period. FRS 104 sets out a non-exhaustive list of the types of transactions and events entities might include. *[FRS 104.15, 15B].*

FRS 104 refers to individual sections of FRS 102 for guidance on disclosure requirements for many of the items on the list referred to above. *[FRS 104.15C].* For entities reporting under FRS 101, this reference should be amended to the relevant standard under EU-adopted IFRS as amended by FRS 101. For example, for guidance on the disclosure requirements in respect of the acquisitions and disposals of items of property, plant and equipment, entities should refer to IAS 16 – *Property, Plant and Equipment* – rather than Section 17 – *Property, Plant and Equipment* – of FRS 102. For further discussion on any significant differences in disclosure between the relevant section of FRS 102 and the equivalent standard under EU-adopted IFRS, refer to the key differences section of the relevant chapter in this publication.

5.2 Business combinations

Paragraph 16A(i) of FRS 104 requires entities to include in their interim financial statements details of the effect of changes in the composition of the entity during the interim period including business combinations, obtaining or losing control of subsidiaries and long-term investments, restructurings and discontinued operations. In particular, entities are required to disclose the information set out in paragraphs 25 and 25A of FRS 102 Section 19 – *Business Combinations and Goodwill.* For FRS 101 reporters we believe the equivalent requirements under EU-adopted IFRS are those set out in paragraph 16A(i) of IAS 34, which cross-refer to the requirements in paragraphs 59-63 and B64-67 of IFRS 3 – *Business Combinations.*

5.3 Financial instruments

FRS 104 requires entities to include in their interim financial statements disclosures that help users to evaluate the significance of financial instruments measured at fair value. *[FRS 104.16A(i)].*

In particular, entities are required to give the disclosures set out in paragraphs 43 and 48A(e) of Section 11 – *Basic Financial Instruments* – and paragraph 22 of Section 34 – *Specialised Activities*.

For FRS 101 reporters we believe the equivalent requirements under EU-adopted IFRS are those set out in paragraphs 91-93(h), 94-96, 98 and 99 of IFRS 13 – *Fair Value Measurement* – and paragraphs 25, 26 and 28-30 of IFRS 7 – *Financial Instruments: Disclosures*.

The IFRS 13 disclosures above will only be required if an entity has financial instruments which (after initial recognition) are measured at fair value on a recurring or non-recurring basis.

FRS 101 allows qualifying entities that are not financial institutions (see Chapter 2 at 2.1 and 6.4 for the definitions of a qualifying entity and a financial institution, respectively) to take advantage of exemptions to disclose information required by IFRS 7 and paragraphs 91 to 99 of IFRS 13 in their annual financial statements, provided that equivalent disclosures are included in the consolidated financial statement of the group in which the entity is consolidated. If such disclosure exemptions are reasonably expected to be taken by the qualifying entity when preparing its annual financial statements, there is no requirement to disclose such information in the entity's interim financial report.

6.   PERIODS FOR WHICH INTERIM FINANCIAL STATEMENTS ARE REQUIRED TO BE PRESENTED

Irrespective of whether an entity presents condensed or complete interim financial statements, the components of its interim financial reports should include information for the following periods: *[FRS 104.20]*

(a)   a statement of financial position as of the end of the current interim period and a comparative statement of financial position as of the end of the immediately preceding financial year;

(b)   a statement of profit or loss and other comprehensive income for the current interim period and, if different, cumulatively for the current financial year-to-date, with comparative statements of profit or loss and other comprehensive income for the comparable interim periods (current and, if different, year-to-date) of the immediately preceding financial year;

(c)   a statement of changes in equity cumulatively for the current financial year-to-date period, with a comparative statement for the comparable year-to-date period of the immediately preceding financial year; and

(d)   a statement of cash flows cumulatively for the current financial year-to-date, with a comparative statement for the comparable year-to-date period of the immediately preceding financial year.

The requirement in paragraph (d) does not apply to entities that will not present a statement of cash flows in their next annual financial statements.

An interim financial report may present for each period either a single statement of 'profit or loss and other comprehensive income', or separate statements of 'profit or loss' and 'comprehensive income', consistent with the basis of preparation applied in its most recent annual financial statements. Accordingly, if the entity presents a separate statement for items of profit or loss in its annual financial statements, it should present a separate condensed statement of profit or loss in the interim financial report. *[FRS 104.8A].* If an entity's business is highly seasonal, then the standard encourages reporting additional financial information for the twelve months up to the end of the interim period, and comparative information for the prior twelve-month period, in addition to the financial statements for the periods set out above. *[FRS 104.21].*

An entity that presents a single condensed statement of income and retained earnings in place of the statement of comprehensive income and statement of changes in equity shall present a single condensed statement of income and retained earnings for the periods for which interim financial statements are required to be presented. *[FRS 104.20A].*

An entity that presents an income statement, or a statement of comprehensive income in which the 'bottom line' is labelled 'profit or loss' shall present an income statement or a statement of comprehensive income on that basis for the periods for which interim financial statements are required to be presented. *[FRS 104.20B].*

The examples below illustrate the periods that an entity is required and encouraged to disclose under FRS 104. *[FRS 104 Appendix II].*

Example 34.2: *Entity publishes interim financial reports half-yearly*

If an entity's financial year ends on 31 December (calendar year), it should present the following financial statements (condensed or complete) in its half-yearly interim financial report as of 30 June 2019:

Half-yearly interim report	End of the current interim period 30/6/2019	End of the comparative interim period 30/6/2018	Immediately preceding year-end 31/12/2018
Statement of financial position	●		●
Statement(s) of profit or loss and other comprehensive income			
– Current period and year-to-date (6 months) ending	●	●	
– 12 months ending	○	○	
Statement of changes in equity			
– Year-to date (6 months) ending	●	●	
– 12 months ending	○	○	
Statement of cash flows			
– Year-to-date (6 months) ending	●	●	
– 12 months ending	○	○	

● Required   ○ Disclosure encouraged if the entity's business is highly seasonal

If an entity publishes a separate interim financial report for the final interim period (i.e. second half of its financial year), it presents the following financial statements (condensed or complete) in its second half-yearly interim financial report as of 31 December 2019:

Second half-yearly interim report	End of the current interim period	End of the comparative interim period
	31/12/2019	31/12/2018
Statement of financial position	●	●
Statement(s) of profit or loss and other comprehensive income		
– Current period (6 months) ending	●	●
– Year-to-date (12 months) ending	●	●
Statement of changes in equity		
– Year-to-date (12 months) ending	●	●
Statement of cash flows		
– Year-to-date (12 months) ending	●	●

● Required

Example 34.3: Entity publishes interim financial reports quarterly

If an entity's financial year ends on 31 December (calendar year), it should present the following financial statements (condensed or complete) in its quarterly interim financial reports for 2019:

First quarter interim report	End of the current interim period	End of the comparative interim period	Immediately preceding year-end
	31/3/2019	31/3/2018	31/12/2018
Statement of financial position	●		●
Statement(s) of profit or loss and other comprehensive income			
– Current period and year-to-date (3 months) ending	●	●	
– 12 months ending	○	○	
Statement of changes in equity			
– Year-to-date (3 months) ending	●	●	
– 12 months ending	○	○	
Statement of cash flows			
– Year-to-date (3 months) ending	●	●	
– 12 months ending	○	○	

● Required   ○ Disclosure encouraged if the entity's business is highly seasonal

Second quarter interim report	End of the current interim period	End of the comparative interim period	Immediately preceding year-end
	30/6/2019	30/6/2018	31/12/2018
Statement of financial position	●		●
Statement(s) of profit or loss and other comprehensive income			
– Current period (3 months) ending	●		
– Year-to-date (6 months) ending	●	●	
– 12 months ending	○	○	
Statement of changes in equity			
– Year-to-date (6 months) ending	●	●	
– 12 months ending	○	○	
Statement of cash flows			
– Year-to-date (6 months) ending	●	●	
– 12 months ending	○	○	

● Required   ○ Disclosure encouraged if the entity's business is highly seasonal

Third quarter interim report	End of the current interim period	End of the comparative interim period	Immediately preceding year-end
	30/9/2019	30/9/2018	31/12/2018
Statement of financial position	●		●
Statement(s) of profit or loss and other comprehensive income			
– Current period (3 months) ending	●	●	
– Year-to-date (9 months) ending	●	●	
– 12 months ending	○	○	
Statement of changes in equity			
– Year-to-date (9 months) ending	●	●	
– 12 months ending	○	○	
Statement of cash flows			
– Year-to-date (9 months) ending	●	●	
– 12 months ending	○	○	

● Required   ○ Disclosure encouraged if the entity's business is highly seasonal

Chapter 34

If an entity publishes a separate interim financial report for the final interim period (i.e. fourth quarter of its financial year), it presents the following financial statements (condensed or complete) in its fourth quarter interim financial report as of 31 December 2019:

Fourth quarter interim report	End of the current interim period	End of the comparative interim period
	31/12/2019	31/12/2018
Statement of financial position	●	●
Statement(s) of profit or loss and other comprehensive income		
– Current period (3 months) ending	●	●
– Year-to-date (12 months) ending	●	●
Statement of changes in equity		
– Year-to-date (12 months) ending	●	●
Statement of cash flows		
– Year-to-date (12 months) ending	●	●

● Required

6.1 Other comparative information

For entities presenting condensed financial statements under FRS 104, there is no explicit requirement that comparative information be presented in the explanatory notes. Nevertheless, where an explanatory note is required by the standard (such as for inventory write-downs, impairment provisions, segment revenues etc.) or otherwise determined to be needed to provide useful information about changes in the financial position and performance of the entity since the end of the last annual reporting period, *[FRS 104.15]*, it would be appropriate to provide information for each period presented. However, in certain cases it would be unnecessary to provide comparative information where this repeats information that was reported in the notes to the most recent annual financial statements. *[FRS 104.15A]*. For example, it would only be necessary to provide information about business combinations in a comparative period when there is a revision of previously disclosed fair values. See Chapter 17 at 4.1.

For entities presenting complete financial statements, whilst FRS 104 sets out the periods for which components of the interim report are included, it is less clear how these rules interact with the requirement in FRS 102 to report comparative information for all amounts in the financial statements. *[FRS 102.3.14]*. In our view, a complete set of interim financial statements should include comparative disclosures for all amounts presented.

6.2 Change in financial year-end

The requirement in FRS 104 to present a comparative statement of profit or loss and other comprehensive income 'for the comparable interim periods (current and year-to-date) of the immediately preceding financial year' can give rise to diversity in practice in the case of an entity that changes its annual financial reporting date. For example, an entity changing its reporting date from 31 December to 31 March would change its half-yearly reporting date from 30 June to 30 September and therefore present its first half-yearly report after its new annual reporting date for the six month period from 1 April to 30 September. A 'comparable' comparative interim period in this scenario could be taken to mean the six months ended 30 September in the prior year, as illustrated in Example 34.4 below. *[FRS 104.20]*.

Example 34.4: Entity changes financial year-end

If an entity changes its financial year-end from 31 December (calendar year) to 31 March, and first reflects the change in its annual financial statements for the period ended 31 March 2019. It determines that the requirement for comparable comparative information in FRS 104 requires it to present the following financial statements (condensed or complete) in its half-yearly interim financial report for the six months ending 30 September 2019:

Half-yearly interim report	End of the current interim period	End of the comparative interim period	Immediately preceding year-end
	30/9/2019	30/9/2018	31/03/2019
Statement of financial position	●		●
Statement(s) of profit or loss and other comprehensive income			
– Current period and year-to-date (6 months) ending	●	●	
– 12 months ending	○	○	
Statement of changes in equity			
– Year-to date (6 months) ending	●	●	
– 12 months ending	○	○	
Statement of cash flows			
– Year-to-date (6 months) ending	●	●	
– 12 months ending	○	○	

● Required   ○ Disclosure encouraged if the entity's business is highly seasonal

The entity in the example above does not show information for the half-year ended 30 June 2018 as the comparative period, notwithstanding the fact that this period would have been the reporting date for the last published half-yearly report.

However, given the lack of clarity in FRS 104 as to the meaning of 'comparable' in the case where the current financial year runs for a period that is different to 'the immediately preceding financial year', other interpretations are possible.

7 MATERIALITY

In making judgements on recognition, measurement, classification, or disclosures in interim financial reports, the overriding goal in FRS 104 is to ensure that an interim financial report includes all information relevant to understanding an entity's financial position and performance during the interim period. *[FRS 104.25]*. The standard draws from Section 2 – *Concepts and Pervasive Principles* – of FRS 102 which defines an item as material if its omission or misstatement could influence the economic decisions of users of the financial statements, but does not contain quantitative guidance on materiality. *[FRS 102.2.6]*. FRS 104 requires materiality to be assessed based on the interim period financial data. *[FRS 104.23]*.

Therefore, decisions on the recognition and disclosure of unusual items, changes in accounting policies or estimates, and errors are based on materiality in relation to the interim period figures to determine whether non-disclosure is misleading. *[FRS 104.25]*.

Neither the previous year's financial statements nor any expectations of the financial position at the current year-end are relevant in assessing materiality for interim reporting. However, the standard adds that interim measurements may rely on estimates to a greater extent than measurements of annual financial data. *[FRS 104.23]*.

8   RECOGNITION AND MEASUREMENT

The recognition and measurement requirements in FRS 104 arise mainly from the requirement to report the entity's financial position as at the interim reporting date, but also require certain estimates and measurements to take into account the expected financial position of the entity at year-end, where those measures are determined on an annual basis (as in the case of income taxes). Many preparers misinterpret this approach as representing some form of hybrid of the discrete and integral methods to interim financial reporting. This could cause confusion in application.

In requiring the year-to-date to be treated as a discrete period, FRS 104 prohibits the recognition or deferral of revenues and costs for interim reporting purposes unless such recognition or deferral is appropriate at year-end. As with a set of annual financial statements complying with FRS 102, FRS 104 requires changes in estimates and judgements reported in previous interim periods to be revised prospectively, whereas changes in accounting policies and corrections of material prior period errors are required to be recognised by prior period adjustment. However, FRS 104 allows looking beyond the interim reporting period, for example in estimating the tax rate to be applied on earnings for the period, when a year-to-date approach does not.

The recognition and measurement requirements of FRS 104 apply regardless of whether an entity presents a complete or condensed set of financial statements for an interim period, *[FRS 104.7]*, and are discussed below.

8.1   Same accounting policies as in annual financial statements

The principles for recognising assets, liabilities, income and expenses for interim periods are the same as in the annual financial statements. *[FRS 104.29]*. Accordingly, an entity uses the same accounting policies in its interim financial statements as in its most recent annual financial statements, adjusted for accounting policy changes that will be reflected in the next annual financial statements. *[FRS 104.28]*. However, FRS 104 also states that the frequency of an entity's reporting (annual, half-yearly or quarterly) do not affect the measurement of its annual results. To achieve that objective, measurements for interim reporting purposes are on a year-to-date basis. *[FRS 104.28A]*.

8.1.1   Measurement on a year-to-date basis

Measurement on a year-to-date basis acknowledges that an interim period is a part of a full year and allows adjustments to estimates of amounts reported in prior interim periods of the current year. *[FRS 104.29]*.

The principles for recognition and the definitions of assets, liabilities, income and expenses for interim periods are the same as in the annual financial statements. *[FRS 104.29, 31]*. Therefore, for assets, the same tests of future economic benefits apply at interim dates as at year-end. Costs that, by their nature, do not qualify as assets at year-end, do not qualify for recognition at interim dates either. Similarly, a liability at the end of an interim reporting period must represent an existing obligation at that date, just as it must at the end of an annual reporting period. *[FRS 104.32]*. An essential characteristic of income and expenses is that the related inflows and outflows of assets and liabilities have already occurred. If those inflows or outflows have occurred, the related income and expense are recognised; otherwise they are not recognised. *[FRS 104.33]*.

FRS 104 lists several circumstances that illustrate these principles:

- inventory write-downs, impairments, or provisions for restructurings are recognised and measured on the same basis as at a year-end. Later changes in the original estimate are recognised in the subsequent interim period, either by recognising additional accruals or reversals of the previously recognised amount; *[FRS 104.30(a)]*

- costs that do not meet the definition of an asset at the end of an interim period are not deferred in the statement of financial position, either to await information on whether it meets the definition of an asset, or to smooth earnings over interim periods within a year. *[FRS 104.30(b)]*. For example, costs incurred in acquiring an intangible asset before the recognition criteria in FRS 102 are met are expensed under Section 18 – *Intangible Assets other than Goodwill*. Only those costs incurred after the recognition criteria are met can be recognised as an asset; there is no reinstatement as an asset in a later period of costs previously expensed because the recognition criteria were not met at that time; *[FRS 102.18.17]* and

- income tax expense is 'recognised in each interim period based on the best estimate of the weighted-average annual income tax rate expected for the full financial year, using the tax rates and laws that have been enacted or substantively enacted at the end of an interim reporting period. Amounts accrued for income tax expense in one interim period may have to be adjusted in a subsequent interim period of that financial year if the estimate of the annual income tax rate changes'. *[FRS 104.30(c)]*.

8.1.2 New accounting pronouncements and other changes in accounting policies

As noted at 8.1 above, an entity uses the same accounting policies in its interim financial statements as in its most recent annual financial statements, adjusted for accounting policy changes that will be reflected in the next annual financial statements. *[FRS 104.28]*.

FRS 104 requires that a change in accounting policy, other than where the transition rules are specified by FRS 102, should be reflected by: *[FRS 104.43]*

(a) restating the financial statements of prior interim periods of the current year and the comparable interim periods of any prior financial years that will be restated in the annual financial statements under Section 10 – *Accounting Policies, Estimates and Errors* – of FRS 102; or

(b) when it is impracticable to determine the cumulative effect at the beginning of the year of applying a new accounting policy to all prior periods, adjusting the financial statements of prior interim periods of the current year and comparable interim periods of prior years to apply the new accounting policy prospectively from the earliest date practicable.

Chapter 34

Therefore, regardless of when in a financial year an entity decides to adopt a new accounting policy, it has to be applied from the beginning of the current year. *[FRS 104.44]*. For example, if an entity that reports on a quarterly basis decides in its third quarter to change an accounting policy, it must restate the information presented in earlier quarterly financial reports to reflect the new policy as if it had been applied from the start of the annual reporting period. Disclosures regarding the restatement can be presented on the face of the financial statements or disclosed in the notes to the financial statements.

8.1.2.A   *Accounting policy changes becoming mandatory during the current year*

One objective of the year-to-date approach, described at 8.1.2 above, is to ensure that a single accounting policy is applied to a particular class of transactions throughout an entire financial year. *[FRS 104.44]*. To allow accounting policy changes to be reflected as of an interim date would mean applying different accounting policies to a particular class of transactions within a single year. This would make interim allocation difficult, obscure operating results, and complicate analysis and understandability of the interim period information. *[FRS 104.45]*.

Accordingly, when preparing interim financial information, consideration is given to which amendments to FRSs are mandatory in the next (current year) annual financial statements. The entity generally adopts these amendments in all interim periods during that year.

While FRS 104 generally prohibits an entity from reflecting the adoption of a new accounting policy as of an interim date, it makes an exception for those accounting policy changes for which FRS 102 specifically requires transition during the financial year. *[FRS 104.43]*.

The disclosure requirements with respect to amendments which are effective for the entity's next annual financial statements, but which do not contain specific disclosure requirements under FRS 104, are not clear. In some cases, it might be determined that an understanding of an amendment is material to an understanding of the entity, in which case the entity discloses this fact, as well as information relevant to assessing the possible impact of the amendment on the entity's financial statements. *[FRS 102.10.13]*. In other cases, an entity might conclude that a particular amendment is not material to an understanding of its interim financial report, and thus not disclose information about the issuance of the amendment, or its possible impact on the entity.

8.1.2.B   *Voluntary changes of accounting policy*

An entity can also elect at any time during a year to apply an amendment to an FRS before it becomes mandatory, or otherwise decide to change an accounting policy voluntarily. However, before voluntarily changing an accounting policy, consideration should be given to the interaction of the requirements of Sections 2 and 10 of FRS 102 which only permit an entity to change an accounting policy if the information results in information that is 'reliable and more relevant' to the users of the financial statements. *[FRS 102.10.8(b)]*.

When it is concluded that a voluntary change in accounting policy is permitted and appropriate, its effect is generally reflected in the first interim report the entity presents after the date on which the entity changed its policy. The entity generally restates amounts reported in earlier interim periods as far back as is practicable. *[FRS 104.44]*. One exception to this principle of retrospective adjustment of earlier interim periods is when an entity changes from the cost model to the revaluation model under Section 17 or Section 18. These are not changes in accounting policy that are covered by FRS 102 in the usual manner, but instead are required to be treated as a revaluation in the period. *[FRS 102.10.10A]*. Therefore, the general requirements of FRS 104 do not override the specific requirements of Section 10 of FRS 102 to treat such changes prospectively.

However, to avoid using two differing accounting policies for a particular class of assets in a single financial year, consideration should be given to changing from the cost model to the revaluation model at the beginning of the financial year. Otherwise, an entity will end up depreciating based on cost for some interim periods and based on the revalued amounts for later interim periods.

8.1.3 Change in going concern assumption

Another situation in which an entity applies different accounting policies in its interim financial statements as compared to its most recent annual financial statements is when the going concern assumption is no longer appropriate.

Although FRS 104 does not specifically address the issue of going concern, the general requirements of Section 3 of FRS 102 apply to both a complete set and to condensed interim financial statements. Section 3 states that when preparing financial statements, management assesses an entity's ability to continue as a going concern, and that the financial statements are prepared on a going concern basis unless management either intends to liquidate the entity or cease trading, or has no realistic alternative but to do so. *[FRS 102.3.8]*. The going concern assessment is discussed in more detail in Chapter 6 at 9.3.

Under Section 3, the going concern assessment is made based on all available information about the future, which at a minimum is twelve months from the *date when the financial statements are authorised for issue*. *[FRS 102.3.8]*. Therefore, with respect to interim reporting under FRS 104, the minimum period for management's assessment is also at least twelve months from the date when the interim report is authorised for issue; it is not limited, for example, to one year from the authorisation date of the most recent annual financial statements.

Example 34.5: Going concern assessment

An entity's financial year-end is 31 December (calendar year) and its annual financial statements as of 31 December 2018 are prepared on a going concern basis and were authorised for issue on 28 February 2019. In assessing the going concern assumption as at 31 December 2018, management considered all future available information through to 26 February 2019.

In preparing its quarterly interim financial statements (condensed or complete) as at 31 March 2019 which will be authorised for issue on 28 April 2019, management should evaluate all future available information to at least 28 April 2020.

If management becomes aware, in making its assessment, of material uncertainties related to events or conditions that may cast significant doubt upon the entity's ability to continue as a going concern, the entity should disclose those uncertainties. If the entity does not prepare financial statements on a going concern basis, it should disclose that fact, together with the basis on which it prepared the financial statements and the reason why the entity is not regarded as a going concern. *[FRS 102.3.9]*.

8.1.4　Voluntary changes in presentation

In some cases, the presentation of the interim financial statements might be changed from that used in prior interim reporting periods. However, before changing the presentation used in its interim report from that of previous periods, management should consider the interaction of the requirements of FRS 104 to include in a set of condensed financial statements the same headings and sub-totals as the most recent annual financial statements, *[FRS 104.10]*, and to apply the same accounting policies as the most recent or the next annual financial report, *[FRS 104.28]*, and the requirements of Section 3 of FRS 102 as they will relate to those next annual financial statements. Section 3 states that an entity should retain the presentation and classification of items in the financial statements, unless it is apparent following a significant change in the nature of operations or a review of the financial statements that another presentation is more appropriate, or unless the change is required by FRS 102, or another applicable FRS. *[FRS 102.3.11]*.

If a presentation is changed, the entity should also reclassify comparative amounts for both earlier interim periods of the current financial year and comparable periods in prior years. *[FRS 104.43(a)]*. In such cases, an entity should disclose the nature of the reclassifications, the amount of each item (or class of items) that is reclassified, and the reason for the reclassification. *[FRS 102.3.12]*.

8.2　Seasonal businesses

Some entities do not earn revenues or incur expenses evenly throughout the year, for example, agricultural businesses, holiday companies, domestic fuel suppliers, or retailers who experience peak demand at Christmas. The financial year-end is often chosen to fit their annual operating cycle, which means that an individual interim period would give little indication of annual performance and financial position.

An extreme application of the integral approach would suggest that they should predict their annual results and contrive to report half of that in the half-year interim financial statements. However, this approach does not portray the reality of their business in individual interim periods, and is, therefore, not permitted under the year-to-date approach adopted in FRS 104. *[FRS 104.28A]*.

8.2.1　Revenues received seasonally, cyclically or occasionally

FRS 104 prohibits the recognition or deferral of revenues that are received seasonally, cyclically or occasionally at an interim date, if recognition or deferral would not be appropriate at year-end. *[FRS 104.37]*. Examples of such revenues include dividend revenue, royalties, government grants, and seasonal revenues of retailers; such revenues are recognised when they occur. *[FRS 104.38]*.

FRS 104 also requires an entity to explain the seasonality or cyclicality of its business and the effect on interim reporting. *[FRS 104.16A(b)]*. If businesses are highly seasonal, FRS 104 encourages reporting of additional information for the twelve months up to the end of the interim period and comparatives for the prior twelve-month period (see 6 above). *[FRS 104.21]*.

8.2.2 *Costs incurred unevenly during the year*

FRS 104 prohibits the recognition or deferral of costs for interim reporting purposes if recognition or deferral of that type of cost is inappropriate at year-end, *[FRS 104.39]*, which is based on the principle that assets and liabilities are recognised and measured using the same criteria as at the year-end. *[FRS 104.29, 31]*. This principle prevents smoothing of costs in seasonal businesses. Furthermore the recognition of assets or liabilities at the interim date would not be appropriate if they would not qualify for recognition at the end of an annual reporting period.

For direct costs, this approach has limited consequences, as the timing of recognising these costs and the related revenues is usually similar. However, for indirect costs, the consequences may be greater, depending on which section of FRS 102 an entity follows.

For example, manufacturing entities that use fixed production overhead absorption rates recognise an asset in respect of attributable overheads based on the normal capacity of the production facilities in accordance with Section 13 – *Inventories*. Any variances and unallocated overheads are expensed. *[FRS 102.13.9]*.

The implications are unclear for professional service companies that recognise revenue under Section 23 – *Revenue* – using the percentage of completion method. On one hand, Section 23 includes the same guidance on the percentage of completion method for both construction contracts and service provision, *[FRS 102.23.21]*, implying that both types of entity can defer costs and the related variances at the end of an interim reporting period. On the other hand, service providers might also follow the guidance in Section 13 which gives guidance for the cost of inventories of a service provider, and which results in expensing such costs and variances at the end of the reporting period. *[FRS 102.13.14]*. However, these are issues that an entity would also face at the end of an annual reporting period. What is clear is that an entity should not diverge from these requirements just because information is being prepared for an interim period.

9 EXAMPLES OF THE RECOGNITION AND MEASUREMENT PRINCIPLES

Appendix II of FRS 104 provides several examples that illustrate the recognition and measurement principles in interim financial reports. *[FRS 104.40]*.

9.1 Property, plant and equipment and intangible assets

9.1.1 *Depreciation and amortisation*

Depreciation and amortisation for an interim period is based only on assets owned during that interim period and does not consider asset acquisitions or disposals planned for later in the year. *[FRS 104 Appendix II.26]*.

An entity applying a straight-line method of depreciation (amortisation) does not allocate the depreciation (amortisation) charge between interim periods based on the level of activity. However, under Sections 17 and 18, an entity may use a 'unit of production' method of depreciation, which results in a charge based on the expected use or output (see Chapter 15 at 3.5.6.C and Chapter 16 at 3.4.3.B). An entity can only apply this method if it most closely reflects the expected pattern of consumption of the future economic benefits embodied in the asset. The chosen method should be applied consistently from period to period unless there is a change in the expected pattern of consumption of those future economic benefits. Therefore, an entity cannot apply a straight-line method of depreciation (amortisation) in its annual financial statements, while allocating the depreciation (amortisation) charge to interim periods using a 'unit of production' based approach.

9.1.2   Impairment of assets

Section 27 – *Impairment of Assets* – of FRS 102 requires an entity to recognise an impairment loss if the recoverable amount of an asset declines below its carrying amount. *[FRS 104 Appendix II.37]*. An entity should apply the same impairment testing, recognition, and reversal criteria at an interim date as it would at year-end. *[FRS 104 Appendix II.38]*.

However, FRS 104 states that an entity is not required to perform a detailed impairment calculation at the end of each interim period. Rather, an entity should perform a review for indications of significant impairment since the most recent year-end to determine whether such a calculation is needed. *[FRS 104 Appendix II.38]*. Nevertheless, an entity is not exempt from performing impairment tests at the end of its interim periods. For example, an entity that recognised an impairment charge in the immediately preceding year, may find that it needs to update its impairment calculations at the end of subsequent interim periods because impairment indicators remain.

9.1.3   Recognition of intangible assets

An entity should apply the same definitions and recognition criteria for intangible assets, as set out in Section 18 of FRS 102, in an interim period as in an annual period. Therefore, costs incurred before the recognition criteria are met should be recognised as an expense. *[FRS 104 Appendix II.10]*. Expenditures on intangibles that are initially expensed cannot be reinstated and recognised as part of the cost of an intangible asset subsequently (e.g. in a later interim period). *[FRS 102.18.17]*. Furthermore, 'deferring' costs as assets in an interim period in the hope that the recognition criteria will be met later in the year is not permitted. Only costs incurred after the specific point in time at which the criteria are met should be recognised as part of the cost of an intangible asset. *[FRS 104 Appendix II.10]*.

9.2   Employee benefits

9.2.1   Employer payroll taxes and insurance contributions

If employer payroll taxes or contributions to government-sponsored insurance funds are assessed on an annual basis, the employer's related expense should be recognised in interim periods using an estimated average annual effective rate, even if it does not reflect the timing of payments. A common example is an employer payroll tax or insurance contribution subject to a certain maximum level of earnings per employee. Higher income employees would reach the maximum income before year-end, and the employer would make no further payments for the remainder of the year. *[FRS 104 Appendix II.3]*.

9.2.2   Year-end bonuses

The nature of year-end bonuses varies widely. Some bonus schemes only require continued employment whereas others require certain performance criteria to be attained on a monthly, quarterly, or annual basis. Payment of bonuses may be purely discretionary, contractual or based on years of historical precedent. *[FRS 104 Appendix II.7]*. A bonus is recognised for interim reporting if, and only if: *[FRS 104 Appendix II.8]*

(a) the entity has a present legal or constructive obligation to make such payments as a result of past events; and

(b) a reliable estimate of the obligation can be made.

A present obligation exists only when an entity has no realistic alternative but to make the payments. *[FRS 102.21.6]*. Section 28 of FRS 102 gives guidance on accounting for profit sharing and bonus plans (see Chapter 25 at 3.3).

In recognising a bonus at an interim reporting date, an entity should consider the facts and circumstances under which the bonus is payable, and determine an accounting policy that recognises an expense reflecting the obligation on the basis of the services received to date. Several possible accounting policies are illustrated in Example 34.6 below.

Example 34.6: *Measuring interim bonus expense*

An entity pays an annual performance bonus if earnings exceed £10 million, under which 5% of any earnings in excess over £10 million will be paid up to a maximum of £500,000. Earnings for the six months ended 30 June 2019 are £7 million, and the entity expects earnings for the full year ended 31 December 2019 to be £16 million.

The following table shows various accounting policies and the expense recognised thereunder in the interim financial statements for the six months ended 30 June 2019.

	Expense (£)
Method 1 – constructive obligation exists when earnings target is met	Nil
Method 2 – assume earnings for remainder of year will be same	200,000
Method 3 – proportionate recognition based on full-year estimate	131,250
Method 4 – one-half recognition based on full-year estimate	150,000

Method 1 is generally not appropriate, as this method attributes the entire bonus to the latter portion of the year, whereas employees provided services during the first six months to towards earning the bonus.

Likewise, Method 2 is generally not appropriate, as the expense of £200,000 [(£14 million – £10 million) × 5%] assumes that the employees will continue to provide services in the latter half of the year to achieve the bonus target, but does not attribute any services to that period.

In contrast to Methods 1 and 2, Method 3 illustrates an accounting policy whereby an estimate is made of the full-year expense and attributed to the period based on the proportion of that bonus for which employees have provided service at 30 June 2019. The amount recognised is calculated as (£7 million ÷ £16 million) × [5% × (£16 million – £10 million)].

Similar to Method 3, Method 4 also takes the approach of recognising an expense based on the full year estimate, but allocates that full-year estimate equally to each period (which is similar to the approach used for share-based payment transactions). The amount recognised is calculated as [50% × 5% × (£16 million – £10 million)].

In addition to Methods 3 and 4, which might be appropriate, depending on the facts and circumstances, an entity might determine another basis on which to recognise bonus that considers both the constructive obligation that exists as of 30 June 2019, and the services performed to date, which is also appropriate.

9.2.3   Pensions

Section 28 requires an entity to determine the present value of defined benefit obligations and the fair value of plan assets at the end of the reporting period. While Section 28 does not require an entity to involve a professionally qualified actuary in the measurement of the obligations, nor to undertake a comprehensive annual actuarial valuation, we expect that in practice most entities will do so.

Chapter 34

For interim reporting purposes, the defined benefit obligation can often be reliably measured by extrapolation of the latest actuarial valuation adjusted for changes in employee demographics such as number of employees and salary levels. *[FRS 104 Appendix II.42].*

If there are significant changes to pension arrangements during the interim period (such as changes resulting from a material business combination or from a major redundancy programme) then entities may wish to consider whether they should obtain a new actuarial valuation of scheme liabilities. Similarly, if there are significant market fluctuations, such as those arising from changes in corporate bond markets, the validity of the assumptions in the last actuarial estimate, such as the discount rate applied to scheme liabilities, should be reviewed and revised as appropriate.

Market values of plan assets as at the interim reporting date should be available without recourse to an actuary and in normal circumstances, companies will not necessarily go through the full process of measuring pension liabilities at interim reporting dates, but rather will look to establish a process to assess the impact of any changes in underlying parameters (e.g. through extrapolation). As with all estimates, the appropriateness in the circumstances should be considered.

9.2.4 Vacations, holidays and other short-term paid absences

Section 28 distinguishes between accumulating and non-accumulating paid absences. *[FRS 102.28.6-7].* Accumulating paid absences are those that are carried forward and can be used in future periods if the current period's entitlement is not used in full. Section 28 requires an entity to measure the expected cost of and obligation for accumulating paid absences at the amount the entity expects to pay as a result of the unused entitlement that has accumulated at the end of the reporting period (see Chapter 25 at 3.3). FRS 104 requires the same principle to be applied at the end of interim reporting periods. Conversely, an entity should not recognise an expense or liability for non-accumulating paid absences at the end of an interim reporting period, just as it would not recognise any at the end of an annual reporting period. *[FRS 104 Appendix II.12].*

9.3 Inventories and cost of sales

9.3.1 Inventories

The recognition and measurement principles of Section 13 are applied in the same way for interim financial reporting as for annual reporting purposes. At the end of any financial reporting period an entity would determine inventory quantities, costs and net realisable values. However, FRS 104 does comment that to save cost and time, entities often use estimates to measure inventories at interim dates to a greater extent than at annual reporting dates. *[FRS 104 Appendix II.27].*

Net realisable values are determined using selling prices and costs to complete and dispose at the end of the interim period. A write-down should be reversed in a subsequent interim period only if it would be appropriate to do so at year-end. See Chapter 11 at 3.4.2. *[FRS 104 Appendix II.28].*

9.3.2 Contractual or anticipated purchase price changes

Both the payer and the recipient of volume rebates, or discounts and other contractual changes in the prices of raw materials, labour, or other purchased goods and services should anticipate these items in interim periods if it is probable that these have been earned or will take effect. However, discretionary rebates and discounts should not be recognised because the resulting asset or liability would not meet the recognition criteria in FRS 102. *[FRS 104 Appendix II.25].*

9.3.3 Interim period manufacturing cost variances

Price, efficiency, spending and volume variances of a manufacturing entity should be recognised in profit or loss at interim reporting dates to the same extent that those variances are recognised at year-end. It is not appropriate to defer variances expected to be absorbed by year-end, which could result in reporting inventory at the interim date at more or less than its actual cost. *[FRS 104 Appendix II.30].* See 8.2.2 above for a discussion on this topic as it applies to costs incurred by service providers.

9.4 Taxation

Taxation is one of the most difficult areas of interim financial reporting, primarily because FRS 104 does not clearly distinguish between current income tax and deferred tax, referring only to 'income tax expense'. This causes tension between the approach for determining the expense and the asset or liability in the statement of financial position. In addition, the standard's provisions combine terminology, suggesting an integral approach with guidance requiring a year-to-date basis to be applied. The integral method is used in determining the effective income tax rate for the whole year, but that rate is applied to year-to-date profit in the interim financial statements. In addition, under a year-to-date basis, the estimated rate is based on tax rates and laws that are enacted or substantively enacted by the end of the interim period. Changes in legislation expected to occur before the end of the current year are not recognised in preparing the interim financial report. The assets and liabilities in the statement of financial position, at least for deferred taxes, are derived solely from a year-to-date approach, but sometimes the requirements of the standard are unclear, as discussed below.

9.4.1 Measuring interim income tax expense

FRS 104 states that income tax expense should be accrued using the tax rate applicable to expected total annual earnings, by applying the estimated weighted-average annual effective income tax rate to pre-tax income for the interim period. *[FRS 104 Appendix II.14].* However, this is not the same as estimating the total tax expense for the year and allocating a proportion of that to the interim period (even though it might sometimes appear that way), as demonstrated in the discussion below.

Because taxes are assessed on an annual basis, using the integral approach to determine the annual effective income tax rate and applying it to year-to-date actual earnings is consistent with the basic concept in FRS 104, that the same recognition and measurement principles apply in interim financial reports as in annual financial statements. *[FRS 104 Appendix II.15].*

In estimating the weighted-average annual income tax rate, an entity should consider the progressive tax rate structure expected for the full year's earnings, including changes in income tax rates scheduled to take effect later in the year that are enacted or substantively enacted as at the end of the interim period. *[FRS 104 Appendix II.15].* This situation is illustrated in Example 34.7 below which is based on the example in paragraph 17 of Appendix II to FRS 104.

Example 34.7:   Measuring interim income tax expense

An entity reporting quarterly expects to earn 10,000 pre-tax each quarter and operates in a jurisdiction with a tax rate of 20% on the first 20,000 of annual earnings and 30% on all additional earnings. Actual earnings match expectations. The following table shows the income tax expense reported each quarter:

	Pre-tax earnings	Effective tax rate	Tax expense
First quarter	10,000	25%	2,500
Second quarter	10,000	25%	2,500
Third quarter	10,000	25%	2,500
Fourth quarter	10,000	25%	2,500
Annual	40,000		10,000

10,000 of tax is expected to be payable for the full year on 40,000 of pre-tax income (20,000 @ 20% + 20,000 @ 30%), implying an average annual effective income tax rate of 25% (10,000 / 40,000).

In the above example, it might look as if the interim income tax expense is calculated by dividing the total expected tax expense for the year (10,000) by the number of interim reporting periods (4). However, this is only the case in this example because profits are earned evenly over each quarter. The expense is actually calculated by determining the effective annual income tax rate and multiplying that rate to year-to-date earnings, as illustrated in Example 34.8 below which is based on the example in paragraph 18 of Appendix II to FRS 104.

Example 34.8:   Measuring interim income tax expense – quarterly losses

An entity reports quarterly, earns 15,000 pre-tax profit in the first quarter but expects to incur losses of 5,000 in each of the three remaining quarters (thus having zero income for the year), and operates in a jurisdiction in which its estimated average annual income tax rate is 20%. The following table shows the income tax expense reported each quarter:

	Pre-tax earnings	Effective tax rate	Tax expense
First quarter	15,000	20%	3,000
Second quarter	(5,000)	20%	(1,000)
Third quarter	(5,000)	20%	(1,000)
Fourth quarter	(5,000)	20%	(1,000)
Annual	0		0

The above example shows how an expense is recognised in periods reporting a profit and a credit is recognised when a loss is incurred. This result is very different from allocating a proportion of the expected total income tax expense for the year, which in this case is zero.

If an entity operates in a number of tax jurisdictions, or where different income tax rates apply to different categories of income (such as capital gains or income earned in particular industries), the standard requires that to the extent practicable, an entity: *[FRS 104 Appendix II.16]*

- estimates the average annual effective income tax rate for each taxing jurisdiction separately and applies it individually to the interim period pre-tax income of each jurisdiction; and

- applies different income tax rates to each individual category of interim period pre-tax income.

This means that the entity should perform the analysis illustrated in Example 34.8 above for each tax jurisdiction and arrive at an interim tax charge by applying the tax rate for each jurisdiction to actual earnings from each jurisdiction in the interim period. However, the standard recognises that, whilst desirable, such a degree of precision may not be achievable in all cases and allows using a weighted-average rate across jurisdictions or across categories of income, if such rate approximates the effect of using rates that are more specific. *[FRS 104 Appendix II.16]*.

Example 34.9:   Measuring interim tax expense – many jurisdictions

An entity operates in 3 countries, each with its own tax rates and laws. In order to determine the interim tax expense, the entity determines the effective annual income tax rate for each jurisdiction and applies those rates to the actual earnings in each jurisdiction, as follows:

(All values in £)	Country A	Country B	Country C	Total
Expected annual tax rate	25%	40%	20%	
Expected annual earnings	300,000	250,000	200,000	750,000
Expected annual tax expense	75,000	100,000	40,000	215,000
Actual half-year earnings	140,000	80,000	150,000	370,000
Interim tax expense	35,000	32,000	30,000	97,000

By performing a separate analysis for each jurisdiction, the entity determines an interim tax expense of £977,000, giving an effective average tax rate of 26.2% (£97,000 ÷ £370,000). Had the entity used a weighted-average rate across jurisdictions, using the expected annual earnings, it would have determined an effective tax rate of 28.7% (£215,000 ÷ £750,000), resulting in a tax expense for the interim period of £106,190 (370,000 @ 28.7%). Whether the difference of over £9,000 lies within the range for a reasonable approximation is a matter of judgement.

9.4.2   Changes in the effective tax rate during the year

9.4.2.A   Enacted changes for the current year that apply after the interim reporting date

As noted above, the estimated income tax rate applied in the interim financial report should reflect changes that are enacted or substantively enacted as at the end of the interim reporting period, but scheduled to take effect later in the year. *[FRS 104 Appendix II.15]*. Tax rates can be regarded as substantively enacted when the remaining stages of the enactment process historically have not affected the outcome and are unlikely to do so. In particular, a UK tax rate is regarded as having been substantively enacted if it is included in: *[FRS 104 Appendix I]*

- a Bill that has been passed by the House of Commons and is awaiting only passage through the House of Lords and Royal Assent; or

- a resolution having statutory effect that has been passed under the Provisional Collection of Taxes Act 1968.

A Republic of Ireland tax rate can be regarded as having been substantively enacted if it is included in a Bill that has been passed by the Dáil.

For example, assume that the 30% tax rate (on earnings above £20,000) in Example 34.7 was substantively enacted as at the second quarter reporting date and applicable before year-end. In that case, the estimated income tax rate for interim reporting would be the same as the estimated average annual effective income tax rate computed in that example (i.e. 25%) after considering the higher rate, even though the entity's earnings are not above the required threshold at the half-year.

If legislation is enacted only after the end of the interim reporting period but before the date of authorisation for issue of the interim financial report, its effect is disclosed as a non-adjusting event. *[FRS 102.32.11(h)]*. Under Section 32 – *Events after the End of the Reporting Period* – of FRS 102 estimates of tax rates and related assets or liabilities are not revised. *[FRS 102.32.6]*.

9.4.2.B   Changes to previously reported estimated income tax rates for the current year

FRS 104 requires an entity to re-estimate at the end of each interim reporting period the estimated average annual income tax rate on a year-to-date basis. *[FRS 104 Appendix II.15]*. Accordingly, the amounts accrued for income tax expense in one interim period may have to be adjusted in a subsequent interim period if that estimate changes. *[FRS 104.30(c)]*. FRS 104 requires disclosure in interim financial statements of material changes in estimates of amounts reported in prior interim periods of the current financial year or changes in estimates of amounts reported in prior financial years. *[FRS 104.16A(d)]*.

Accordingly, just as the integral approach does not necessarily result in a constant tax charge in each interim reporting period, it also does not result in a constant effective tax rate when circumstances change.

Example 34.10:   Changes in the effective tax rate during the year

Taking the fact pattern in Example 34.7 above, an entity reporting quarterly expects to earn 10,000 pre-tax each quarter; from the start of the third quarter the higher rate of tax on earnings over 20,000 increases from 30% to 40%. Actual earnings continue to match expectations. The following table shows the income tax expense reported in each quarter:

	Period pre-tax earnings	Pre-tax earnings: year to date	Effective tax rate	Tax expense: year to date	Period tax expense
First quarter †	10,000	10,000	25%	2,500	2,500
Second quarter †	10,000	20,000	25%	5,000	2,500
Third quarter	10,000	30,000	30%	9,000	4,000
Fourth quarter	10,000	40,000	30%	12,000	3,000
Annual	40,000				12,000

† As previously reported from Example 34.7 using an effective tax rate of 25%.

The increase in the tax rate means that 12,000 of tax is expected to be payable for the full year on 40,000 of pre-tax income (20,000 @ 20% + 20,000 @ 40%), implying an average annual effective income tax rate of 30% (12,000 / 40,000). With cumulative pre-tax earnings of 30,000 as at the end of the third quarter, the estimated tax liability is 9,000, requiring a tax expense of 4,000 (9,000 – 2,500 – 2,500) to be recognised during that quarter. In the final quarter, earnings of 10,000 result in a tax charge of 3,000, using the revised effective rate of 30%.

9.4.2.C   Enacted changes applying only to subsequent years

In many cases, tax legislation is enacted that takes effect not only after the interim reporting date but also after year-end. Such circumstances are not addressed explicitly in the standard. As FRS 104 does not clearly distinguish between current income tax and deferred tax, combined with the different approaches taken in determining the expense recognised in profit or loss compared to the statement of financial position, these issues can lead to confusion in this situation.

On the one hand, the standard states that the estimated income tax rate for the interim period includes enacted or substantively enacted changes scheduled to take effect later in the year. *[FRS 104 Appendix II.15]*. This implies that the effect of changes that do not take effect in the current year is ignored in determining the appropriate rate for current tax. On the other hand, FRS 104 also requires that the principles for recognising assets, liabilities, income and expenses for interim periods are the same as in the annual financial statements. *[FRS 104.29]*. In annual financial statements, deferred tax is measured at the tax rates expected to apply to the period when the asset is realised or the liability is settled, based on tax rates (and tax laws) enacted or substantively enacted by the end of the reporting period, as required by FRS 102. *[FRS 102.29.12]*. Therefore, an entity should recognise the effect of a change applying to future periods if this change is enacted by the end of the interim reporting period.

These two requirements seem to be mutually incompatible. FRS 104 makes sense only in the context of calculating the effective *current* tax rate on income earned in the period. Once a deferred tax asset or liability is recognised, it should be measured under Section 29 – *Income Tax*. Therefore, an entity should recognise an enacted change applying to future years in measuring deferred tax assets and liabilities as at the end of the interim reporting period. One way to treat the cumulative effect to date of this remeasurement is to recognise it in full, by a credit to profit or loss or to other comprehensive income, depending on the nature of the temporary difference being remeasured, in the period during which the tax legislation is enacted, in a similar way to the treatment shown in Example 34.10 above, and as illustrated in Example 34.11 below.

Example 34.11: Enacted changes to tax rates applying after the current year

An entity reporting half-yearly operates in a jurisdiction subject to a tax rate of 30%. Legislation is enacted during the first half of the current year, which reduces the tax rate to 28% on income earned from the beginning of the entity's next financial year. Based on a gross temporary difference of 1,000, the entity reported a deferred tax liability in its most recent annual financial statements of 300 (1,000 @ 30%). Of this temporary difference, 200 is expected to reverse in the second half of the current year and 800 in the next financial year. Assuming that no new temporary differences arise in the current period, what is the deferred tax balance at the interim reporting date?

Whilst the entity uses an effective tax rate of 30% to determine the tax expense relating to income earned in the period, it should use a rate of 28% to measure those temporary differences expected to reverse in the next financial year. Accordingly, the deferred tax liability at the half-year reporting date is 284 (200 @ 30% + 800 @ 28%).

Alternatively, if the effective *current* tax rate is not distinguished from the measurement of deferred tax, it could be argued that FRS 104 allows the reduction in the deferred tax liability of 16 (300 – 284) to be included in the estimate of the effective income tax rate for the year. Approach 2 in Example 34.14 below applies this argument. In our view, because FRS 104 does not distinguish between current and deferred taxes, either approach would be acceptable provided that it is applied consistently.

9.4.3 Difference in financial year and tax year

If an entity's financial year and the income tax year differ, the income tax expense for the interim periods of that financial year should be measured using separate weighted-average estimated effective tax rates for each of the income tax years applied to the portion of pre-tax income earned in each of those income tax years. *[FRS 104 Appendix II.19]*.

Chapter 34

In other words, an entity should compute a weighted-average estimated effective tax rate for each income tax year, rather than for its financial year.

Example 34.12:   Difference in financial year and tax year

An entity's financial year ends 30 June and it reports quarterly. Its taxable year ends 31 December. For the financial year that begins 1 July 2019 and ends 30 June 2020, the entity earns 10,000 pre-tax each quarter.

The estimated average annual income tax rate is 30% in the income tax year to 31 December 2019 and 40% in the year to 31 December 2020.

Quarter ending	Pre-tax earnings	Effective tax rate	Tax expense
30 September 2019	10,000	30%	3,000
31 December 2019	10,000	30%	3,000
31 March 2020	10,000	40%	4,000
30 June 2020	10,000	40%	4,000
Annual	40,000		14,000

9.4.4   Tax loss and tax credit carrybacks and carryforwards

FRS 104 repeats the requirement in Section 29 of FRS 102 that for carryforwards of unused tax losses, a deferred tax asset should be recognised to the extent that it is probable that they will be recovered against the reversal of deferred tax liabilities or other future taxable profits. *[FRS 104 Appendix II.23]*. In assessing whether future taxable profit is available, the criteria in Section 29 are applied at the interim date. If these criteria are met as at the end of the interim period, the effect of the tax loss carryforwards is included in the estimated average annual effective income tax rate.

Example 34.13:   Tax loss carryforwards expected to be recovered in the current year

An entity that reports quarterly has unutilised operating losses of 10,000 for income tax purposes at the start of the current financial year for which a deferred tax asset has not been recognised. The entity earns 10,000 in the first quarter of the current year and expects to earn 10,000 in each of the three remaining quarters. Excluding the effect of utilising losses carried forward, the estimated average annual income tax rate is 40%. Including the carryforward, the estimated average annual income tax rate is 30%. Accordingly, tax expense is determined by applying the 30% rate to earnings each quarter as follows:

	Pre-tax earnings	Effective tax rate	Tax expense
First quarter	10,000	30%	3,000
Second quarter	10,000	30%	3,000
Third quarter	10,000	30%	3,000
Fourth quarter	10,000	30%	3,000
Annual	40,000		12,000

This result is consistent with the general approach for measuring income tax expense in the interim report, in that any entitlement for relief from current tax due to carried forward losses is determined on an annual basis. Accordingly, its effect is included in the estimate of the average annual income tax rate and not, for example, by allocating all of the unutilised losses against the earnings of the first quarter to give an income tax expense of zero in the first quarter and 4,000 thereafter.

In contrast, the year-to-date approach of FRS 104 means that the benefits of a tax loss carryback are recognised in the interim period in which the related tax loss occurs, *[FRS 104 Appendix II.22]*, and are not included in the assessment of the estimated average annual tax rate, as shown in Example 34.8 above. This approach is consistent with Section 29 of FRS 102 which requires the benefit of a tax loss that can be carried back to recover current tax already incurred in a previous period to be recognised as an asset. *[FRS 102.29.4]*. Therefore, a corresponding reduction of tax expense or increase of tax income is also recognised. *[FRS 104 Appendix II.22]*.

Where previously unrecognised tax losses are expected to be utilised in full in the current year, it seems intuitive to recognise the recovery of those carried forward losses in the estimate of the average annual tax rate, as shown in Example 34.12 above. However, where the level of previously unrecognised tax losses exceeds expected taxable profits for the current year, a deferred tax asset should be recognised for the carried forward losses that are now expected to be utilised, albeit in future years.

The examples in FRS 104 do not show how such a deferred tax asset is created in the interim financial report. In our view, two approaches are acceptable, as shown in Example 34.14 below.

Example 34.14: Tax loss carryforwards in excess of current year expected profits

An entity that reports half-yearly has unutilised operating losses of 75,000 for income tax purposes at the start of the current financial year for which no deferred tax asset has been recognised. At the end of its first interim period, the entity reports a profit before tax of 25,000 and expects to earn a profit of 20,000 before tax in the second half of the year. The entity reassesses the likelihood of generating sufficient profits to utilise its carried forward tax losses and determines that the FRS 102 recognition criteria for a deferred tax asset are satisfied for the full amount of 75,000. Excluding the effect of utilising losses carried forward, the estimated average annual income tax rate is the same as the enacted or substantially enacted rate of 40%.

As at the end of the current financial year the entity expects to have unutilised losses of 30,000 (75,000 carried forward less current year pre-tax profits of 45,000). Using the enacted rate of 40%, a deferred tax asset of 12,000 is recognised at year-end. How is this deferred tax asset recognised in the interim reporting periods?

Chapter 34

Approach 1

Under the first approach, the estimate of the average annual effective tax rate includes only those carried forward losses expected to be utilised in the current financial year and a separate deferred tax asset is recognised for those carried forward losses now expected to be utilised in future annual reporting periods.

In the fact pattern above, using 45,000 of the carried forward tax losses gives an average effective annual tax rate of nil, as follows:

Estimation of the annual effective tax rate – Approach 1

Expected annual tax expense before utilising losses carried forward (45,000 @ 40%)	18,000
Tax benefit of utilising carried forward tax losses (45,000 @ 40%)	(18,000)
Expected annual tax expense before the effect of losses carried forward to future annual periods	0
Expected annual effective tax rate	0%
Effect of tax losses carried forward to future periods (75,000 – 45,000 @ 40%)	(12,000)
Tax income to be recognised in the interim period	(12,000)

The remaining tax losses give rise to a deferred tax asset of 12,000, which is recognised in full at the half-year, to give reported profits after tax as follows:

	First half-year	Second half-year	Annual
Profit before income tax	25,000	20,000	45,000
Income tax (expense)/credit			
– at expected annual effective rate	0	0	0
– recognition of deferred tax asset	12,000	0	12,000
Net profit after tax	37,000	20,000	57,000

Approach 2

Under the second approach, the estimate of the average annual effective tax rate reflects the expected recovery of all the previously unutilised tax losses from the beginning of the period in which the assessment of recoverability changed. In the fact pattern above, recognition of the unutilised tax losses gives an average effective annual tax rate of –26.67%, as follows:

Estimation of the annual effective tax rate – Approach 2

Expected annual tax expense before utilising losses carried forward (45,000 @ 40%)	18,000
Tax benefit of recognising unutilised tax losses (75,000 @ 40%)	(30,000)
Expected annual tax credit after recognising unutilised tax losses	(12,000)
Expected annual effective tax rate (–12,000 ÷ 45,000)	–26.67%

This approach results in reported profits after tax as follows:

	First half-year	Second half-year	Annual
Profit before income tax	25,000	20,000	45,000
Income tax (expense)/credit			
– at expected annual effective rate	6,667	5,333	12,000
Net profit after tax	31,667	25,333	57,000

Approach 1 is consistent with the requirements of Section 29 as it results in recognising the full expected deferred tax asset as soon as it becomes 'probable that they will be recovered against the reversal of deferred tax liabilities or other future taxable profits'. *[FRS 102.29.7]*. However, given that FRS 104 does not specifically address this situation, and is unclear about whether the effective tax rate reflects changes in the assessment of the recoverability of carried forward tax losses, we also believe that Approach 2 is acceptable.

9.4.5 Tax credits

FRS 104 also discusses in more detail the treatment of tax credits, which may for example be based on amounts of capital expenditures, exports, or research and development expenditures. Such benefits are usually granted and calculated on an annual basis under tax laws and regulations and therefore are reflected in the estimated annual effective income tax rate used in the interim report. However, if tax benefits relate to a one-time event, they should be excluded from the estimate of the annual rate and deducted separately from income tax expense in that interim period. *[FRS 104 Appendix II.21]*.

9.5 Foreign currency translation

9.5.1 Foreign currency translation gains and losses

An entity measures foreign currency translation gains and losses for interim financial reporting using the same principles that Section 30 – *Foreign Currency Translation* – of FRS 102 requires at year-end (see Chapter 27). *[FRS 104 Appendix II.31]*. An entity should use the actual average and closing foreign exchange rates for the interim period (i.e. it may not anticipate changes in foreign exchange rates for the remainder of the current year in translating at an interim date). *[FRS 104 Appendix II.32]*. When Section 30 requires translation adjustments to be recognised as income or expense in the period in which they arise, the same approach should be used in the interim report. An entity should not defer some foreign currency translation adjustments at an interim date, even if it expects the adjustment to reverse before year-end. *[FRS 104 Appendix II.33]*.

9.5.2 Interim financial reporting in hyperinflationary economies

Interim financial reports in hyperinflationary economies are prepared using the same principles as at year-end. *[FRS 104 Appendix II.34]*. Section 31 – *Hyperinflation* – of FRS 102 requires that the financial statements of an entity that reports in the currency of a hyperinflationary economy be stated in terms of the measuring unit current at the end of the reporting period, and the gain or loss on the net monetary position be included in profit or loss. In addition, comparative financial data reported for prior periods should be restated to the current measuring unit (see Chapter 28). *[FRS 104 Appendix II.35]*. As shown in Examples 34.2 and 34.3 above, FRS 104 requires an interim report to contain many components, which are all restated to the current measuring unit at every interim reporting date.

The measuring unit used is that as of the end of the interim period, with the resulting gain or loss on the net monetary position included in that period's net income. An entity may not annualise the recognition of gains or losses, nor may it estimate an annual inflation rate in preparing an interim financial report in a hyperinflationary economy. *[FRS 104 Appendix II.36]*.

Chapter 34

While it is highly unlikely for a UK company to have the functional currency of a hyperinflationary economy, a UK based group may prepare consolidated financial statements under FRS 102 with a subsidiary that operates in, and has a functional currency of, a country subject to hyperinflation.

9.6   Provisions, contingencies and accruals for other costs

9.6.1   Provisions

FRS 104 requires an entity to apply the same criteria for recognising and measuring a provision at an interim date as it would at year-end. *[FRS 104 Appendix II.6]*. Hence, an entity should recognise a provision when it has no realistic alternative but to transfer economic benefits because of an event that has created a legal or constructive obligation. *[FRS 104 Appendix II.5]*. FRS 104 emphasises that the existence or non-existence of an obligation to transfer benefits is a question of fact, and does not depend on the length of the reporting period. *[FRS 104 Appendix II.6]*.

The obligation is adjusted upward or downward at each interim reporting date, if the entity's best estimate of the amount of the obligation changes. The standard states that any corresponding loss or gain should normally be recognised in profit or loss. *[FRS 104 Appendix II.5]*. However, an entity applying IFRIC 1 – *Changes in Existing Decommissioning, Restoration and Similar Liabilities* – under the hierarchy in Section 10 (see Chapter 15 at 3.4.3) might instead need to adjust the carrying amount of the corresponding asset rather than recognise a gain or loss.

9.6.2   Other planned but irregularly occurring costs

Many entities budget for costs that they expect to incur irregularly during the year, such as advertising campaigns, employee training and charitable contributions. Even though these costs are planned and expected to recur annually, they tend to be discretionary in nature. Therefore, it is generally not appropriate to recognise an obligation at the end of an interim financial reporting period for such costs that are not yet incurred, as they do not meet the definition of a liability. *[FRS 104 Appendix II.13]*.

As discussed at 8.2.2 above, FRS 104 prohibits the recognition or deferral of costs incurred unevenly throughout the year at the interim date if recognition or deferral would be inappropriate at year-end. *[FRS 104.39]*. Accordingly, such costs should be recognised as they are incurred and an entity should not recognise provisions or accruals in the interim report to adjust these costs to their budgeted amount.

9.6.3   Major planned periodic maintenance or overhaul

The cost of periodic maintenance, a planned major overhaul, or other seasonal expenditures expected to occur after the interim reporting date should not be recognised for interim reporting purposes unless an event before the end of the interim period causes the entity to have a legal or constructive obligation. The mere intention or necessity to incur expenditures in the future is not sufficient to recognise an obligation as at the interim reporting date. *[FRS 104 Appendix II.4]*. Similarly, an entity may not defer and amortise such costs if they are incurred early in the year, but do not satisfy the criteria for recognition as an asset as at the interim reporting date.

9.6.4 Contingent lease payments

Contingent lease payments can create legal or constructive obligations that are recognised as liabilities. If a lease includes contingent payments based on achieving a certain level of annual sales (or annual use of the asset), an obligation can arise in an interim period before the required level of annual sales (or usage) is achieved. If the entity expects to achieve the required level of annual sales (or usage), it should recognise a liability as it has no realistic alternative but to make the future lease payment. *[FRS 104 Appendix II.9]*.

9.6.5 Levies charged by public authorities

When governments or other public authorities impose levies on entities in relation to their activities, as opposed to income taxes, it is not always clear when the liability to pay a levy arises and a provision should be recognised. As there is no specific guidance on accounting for such provisions under FRS 102, entities may, under the hierarchy set out in Section 10, refer to the guidance in IFRIC 21 – *Levies* – in formulating an appropriate accounting policy for these obligations.

9.7 Earnings per share

As noted at 3.3 above, FRS 104 requires that where an entity has presented EPS information in accordance with IAS 33 – *Earnings per Share* (as adopted in the EU) in its most recent annual financial statements, then it will present basic and diluted EPS in its interim financial statements. *[FRS 104.11]*. EPS in an interim period is computed in the same way as for annual periods. However, IAS 33 does not allow diluted EPS of a prior period to be restated for subsequent changes in the assumptions used in those EPS calculations. *[IAS 33.65]*. This approach might be perceived as inconsistent to the year-to-date approach which should be followed for computing EPS for an interim period. For example, if an entity, reporting quarterly, computes diluted EPS in its first quarter financial statements, it cannot restate the reported diluted EPS subsequently for any changes in the assumptions used. However, following a year-to-date approach, the entity should consider the revised assumptions to compute the diluted EPS for the six months in its second quarter financial statements, which, in this case would not be the sum of its diluted EPS for first quarter and the second quarter.

10 USE OF ESTIMATES

FRS 104 requires that the measurement procedures followed in an interim financial report should be designed to ensure that the resulting information is reliable and that all material financial information that is relevant to an understanding of the financial position or performance of the entity is appropriately disclosed. Whilst estimation is necessary in both interim and annual financial statements, the standard recognises that preparing interim financial reports generally requires greater use of estimation methods than at year-end. *[FRS 104.41]*. Consequently, the measurement of assets and liabilities at an interim date may involve less use of outside experts in determining amounts for items such as provisions, contingencies, pensions or non-current assets revalued at fair values. Reliable measurement of such amounts may simply involve updating the previously reported year-end position. The procedures may be less rigorous than those at year-end. The example below is based on Appendix II to FRS 104. *[FRS 104 Appendix II.39-47]*.

Chapter 34

Example 34.15: Use of estimates

Inventories	Full stock-taking and valuation procedures may not be required for inventories at interim dates, although it may be done at year-end. It may be sufficient to make estimates at interim dates based on sales margins.
Classifications of current and non-current assets and liabilities	Entities may do a more thorough investigation for classifying assets and liabilities as due within one year or after more than one year (or an equivalent classification between current and non-current assets and liabilities) at annual reporting dates than at interim dates.
Provisions	Determining the appropriate provision (such as a provision for warranties, environmental costs, and site restoration costs) may be complex and often costly and time-consuming. Entities sometimes engage outside experts to assist in the annual calculations. Making similar estimates at interim dates often entails updating of the prior annual provision rather than the engaging of outside experts to do a new calculation.
Pensions	Section 28 of FRS 102 requires an entity to determine the present value of defined benefit obligations and the fair value of plan assets at the end of each reporting period. Section 28 does not require an entity to involve a professionally qualified actuary in measurement of the obligations nor does it require an annual comprehensive actuarial valuation. As discussed at 9.2.3 above, market values of plan assets as at the interim reporting date should be available without recourse to an actuary, and reliable measurement of defined benefit obligations for interim reporting purposes can often be extrapolated from the latest actuarial valuation adjusted for changes in employee demographics such as number of employees and salary levels.
Income taxes	Entities may calculate income tax expense and deferred income tax liability at annual dates by applying the tax rate for each individual jurisdiction to measures of income for each jurisdiction. Paragraph A2.16 of Appendix II (see 9.4.1 above) acknowledges that while that degree of precision is desirable at interim reporting dates as well, it may not be achievable in all cases, and a weighted-average of rates across jurisdictions or across categories of income is used if it is a reasonable approximation of the effect of using more specific rates.
Contingencies	The measurement of contingencies may involve the opinions of legal experts or other advisers. Formal reports from independent experts are sometimes obtained for contingencies. Such opinions about litigation, claims, assessments, and other contingencies and uncertainties may or may not also be needed at interim dates.
Revaluations and fair value accounting	Section 17 of FRS 102 allows an entity to choose as its accounting policy the revaluation model whereby items of property, plant and equipment are revalued to fair value. Similarly, Section 16 of FRS 102 – *Investment Property* – requires an entity to measure the fair value of investment property. For those measurements, an entity that relies on professionally qualified valuers at annual reporting dates is not required to rely on them at interim reporting dates.
Specialised industries	Because of complexity, costliness, and time, interim period measurements in specialised industries might be less precise than at year-end. An example is calculation of insurance reserves by insurance companies.

Although an entity is not required to use professionally qualified valuers at interim reporting dates, and may only update the previous year-end position, the entity is required to recognise impairments in the appropriate interim period.

11 FIRST-TIME PRESENTATION OF INTERIM REPORTS COMPLYING WITH FRS 104

FRS 104 defines 'interim period' as a financial reporting period shorter than a full financial year, *[FRS 104 Appendix I]*, and requires the format of condensed financial statements for an interim period to include each of the headings and subtotals that were included in the entity's most recent annual financial statements. *[FRS 104.10]*.

However, FRS 104 provides no guidance for an entity that chooses to issue condensed interim financial statements before it has prepared a set of FRS 102 compliant annual financial statements. This situation will arise in the entity's first year of existence. Whilst FRS 104 does not prohibit the entity from preparing a condensed set of interim financial statements, it does not specify how an entity would interpret the minimum disclosure requirements of FRS 104 when there are no annual financial statements to refer to.

The entity should consider making additional disclosures to recognise that a user of this first set of interim financial statements does not have the access otherwise assumed to the most recent annual financial report of the entity. Accordingly, the explanation of significant events and transactions and changes in financial position in the period should be more detailed than the update normally expected in FRS 104. *[FRS 104.15]*. In the absence of any specific regulatory requirements to which the entity is subject, the following are examples of additional considerations that would apply:

- since it is not possible to make a statement that the same accounting policies and methods of computation have been applied, *[FRS 104.16A(a)]*, the entity should disclose all those accounting policies and methods of computation in the same level of detail as it would in a set of annual financial statements. When the entity issues interim reports on a quarterly basis, the first quarter interim report should provide the abovementioned details; subsequent quarterly reports could refer to the details included in the first quarter report;

- similarly, the disclosure of the nature and amount of changes in estimates of amounts reported in prior periods will have to go into more detail than just the changes normally required to be disclosed; *[FRS 104.16A(d)]*

- more extensive disclosure than simply the changes since the last report date will be required for contingent liabilities and contingent assets; *[FRS 104.15B(m)]* and

- in the absence of a complete set of annual financial statements complying with FRS 102, the entity should include each of the headings and subtotals in the condensed financial statements that it would expect to include in its first financial statements prepared under FRS 102.

Chapter 34

Entities that have transitioned from another financial reporting framework to FRS 102 and have not yet published FRS 102 annual financial statements are required to make additional disclosures when presenting interim reports in accordance with FRS 104: *[FRS 104.16B]*

- a description of the nature of each change in accounting policy;

- a reconciliation of its equity determined in accordance with its previous financial reporting framework to its equity determined in accordance with the new financial reporting framework for the following dates:

  - the date of transition to the new financial reporting framework; and

  - at the end of the comparable year to date period of the immediately preceding financial year; and

- a reconciliation of profit or loss determined in accordance with its previous financial reporting framework for the comparable interim period (current and if different year-to-date) of the immediately preceding financial year.

If an entity becomes aware of errors made under its previous financial reporting framework, the reconciliations above shall, to the extent practicable, distinguish the correction of those errors from changes in accounting policies. For an entity converting to FRS 102 in their next annual financial statements, the requirements of Section 35 – *Transition to this FRS* –should be applied. Those requirements, which include the reconciliations above, are discussed in Chapter 32.

Index of standards

FRS 103

FRS 104

FRS 105

FRS 1

FRS 2

FRS 6

FRS 12

IFRS 3

IFRS 4

IFRS 10

IFRS 11

IFRS 12

IFRS 13

IFRS 15

IFRS 16

IAS 38

IAS 39

IAS 40

IAS 41

The Limited Liability Partnerships (Accounts and Audit) (Application of Companies Act 2006) Regulations (SI 2008/1911)

The Large and Medium-sized Companies and Groups (Accounts and Reports) Regulations 2008 (SI 2008/1910)

The Small Companies and Groups (Accounts and Directors' Report) Regulations 2008 (SI 2008/409)

The Large and Medium-sized Limited Liability Partnerships (Accounts) Regulations 2008 (SI 2008/1913)

The Small Limited Liability Partnerships (Accounts) Regulations 2008 (SI 2008/1912)